COMICS VALUES ANNUAL

2008 EDITION
THE COMIC BOOK PRICE GUIDE

by Alex G. Malloy

edited by Stuart W. Wells III

Preface: Robert J. Sodaro

Published by

krause publications

An Imprint of F+W Publications

700 East State Street • Iola, WI 54990-0001
715-445-2214 • 888-457-2873
www.krausebooks.com

Our toll-free number to place an order or obtain
a free catalog is (800) 258-0929.

ISSN 1062-4503

ISBN-13: 978-0-89689-605-5
ISBN-10: 89689-605-6

Designed by Stuart W. Wells III
Edited by Karen O'Brien and Stuart W. Wells III

Printed in the United States of America

About the Cover
This original painting of Iron Man was commissioned from artist
Mark Sparacio (www.marksparacio.com) for *Comics Values Annual 2008*.

Iron Man © 2008 Marvel Characters Inc.

CONTENTS

Editorial

By Alex G. Malloy with Robert J. Sodaro

The landscape of the comic book pricing market has grown a touch soft over the past 12 months. Still, before you sprint panic-stricken for your comic vaults to dispose of your favorite books before they lose their value—things aren't quite that bad. While third- and fourth-tier Golden Age titles have softened up, first-and second-tier Golden Age books are still holding their value.

Many Silver Age titles are treading water as well, with books on the lower end of the scale softening.

Silver Age Spider-Man titles are showing strong movement due to continued interest generated by the powerful showing of the films (including 2007's third outing which was released in three distinct flavors on DVD just prior to the year-end holiday shopping season). Also showing strong is Iron Man, due in part to the buzz concerning his imminent Hollywood coming-out party (due this Spring), but also to the very positive response to Marvel's release of *Ultimate Iron Man*.

As everyone knows, this Ultimate make-over was written by renowned science fiction novelist, Orson Scott Card, who has just finished putting a spit-shine on the second installment of Ultimate Iron Man's origin with *Ultimate Iron Man II*. Not only does the Golden Avenger grace our cover, we also managed to snag an interview with Mr. Card for this very issue. Seems that our own Features Editor, Robert Sodaro, has a past connection with Mr. Card from back in the mid-1980s when Bob was the managing editor and Mr. Card was a columnist for the Commodore 64 magazine entitled, *Ahoy!* Well, Mr. Card remembered Bob and consented to be interviewed—we are very grateful.

We believe that the trend in comic-to-film stories that is all the rage in Tinseltown will continue with the highly-anticipated releases of *The Dark Knight*, *Hellboy II: The Golden Army*, and even *Speed Racer*; plus the continued flow of high-end interactive video games will keep comic books as the "go to" intellectual property for the coming year. Meanwhile, we are still producing this price guide as well as our other books, while Bob is churning out more comic book stories for Guild Works Productions and the Comicbook Artists' Guild.

So stay steady, and we'll see you here again next year!

Iron Man Too: Orson Scott Card
By Bob Sodaro for CVA

Noted novelist Orson Scott Card is many things to many people, Readers of CVA *probably know him best as the creator/writer of Marvel's* **Ultimate Iron Man**, *and for his work with the Dable Brothers on* **Red Prophet** *and* **Wyrms** *(also for Marvel) while Science Fiction Fans know him as the Hugo and Nebula Award-winning author of* Ender's Game *and its sequel* Speaker for the Dead *(making him the only author to have won both of science fiction's top prizes in consecutive years). He has also contributed to other forms of contemporary fiction, including* Lost Boys and Treasure Box *as well as poetry and play writing. Personally, this writer "met" him some 25 years ago as a columnist for a fledgling Commodore 64 computer magazine (Ahoy!)*

Interestingly enough, Card is not only an active political writer, speaker and outspoken critic, but devout Mormon as well. While readers may find the dichotomy of an individual with devout religious views to be a noted science fiction writer as well (as did this writer), Card thinks nothing of the sort (and explains why).

Orson not only remembered us (fondly, even), but graciously took time out of his very busy schedule and submitted to our (intrusive) questions. I would like to personally thank Orson for doing so, and to apologize to him that, except for his Ahoy! column, and Ultimate Iron Man I never took the time to read any of his work. With this interview, that will change, I'm now making it a point to rectify that by picking up some of his other writings. We urge you to do likewise.

******

RJS: I suppose that the first question that I have to ask is a Christian Sci Fi writer? Who would have thought such an animal was even possible? Am I the only one who thinks this is odd? How do you get to be both?

OSC: There are more religiously-minded science fiction writers than you might think. It's true that science fiction has to be presented from an atheistic posture — that is, a transcendent God cannot be a character in the story. You can't have characters pray to the God of Abraham and get answers; you can't have angels show up in the story. The only exception to this is if you explain the supernatural beings in sci-fi terms — i.e.; God is a giant computer set up 10,000 years ago to monitor human progress; angels are (as in *Childhood's End*) also devils — aliens watching over us; that sort of thing.

This is actually liberating for believers who write science fiction. Why? Because we can now write seriously about religious, moral, spiritual, and cosmological issues without getting distracted by particular belief systems in today's real world.

Speaker for the Dead (sequel to Ender's Game)
© by Orson Scott Card, published by Tor books

The 1,000-Year Plan (Foundation)
© *by Isaac Asimov published by Ace Books*

We don't have God, we have a god-figure. For instance, in Isaac Asimov's original *Foundation* series, the god-figure is Hari Seldon; the people on the planet Terminus come to have deep religious faith in his prophecy of their inevitable destiny.

At the same time, Asimov also showed how religion can be faked, so on one level he was satirizing the way false religion can be used to keep an empire under control — while at the same time, he used the "real" religion — the Seldon plan — to show how faith can unite a people and give them courage and confidence in their international relations.

Then along came Asimov's "devil" — The Mule — and we had a Job-like struggle for the souls of the human race.

Now, Asimov was an atheist; I doubt he would have appreciated my typifying his fiction this way, but the impulse to have god-figures in fiction is almost irresistible — nearly everyone does it, nearly all the time. You don't have to do it on purpose. It's better if you don't, because if you plan it out, then your fiction turns into a theological essay or a religious pamphlet — so it's lousy fiction and lousy religion.

Instead, if you're a believer, you simply trust that the story that feels right and true to you will also embody, in unconscious ways, your most deeply-held beliefs. That has certainly happened with me. Whenever I openly deal with religion, I'm careful to make sure that my readers don't have to make a commitment of belief — they remain outside the faith of the characters. However unconsciously, there are elements in my stories that people have pointed out as being religious, and sometimes I have to agree they're right — but I didn't plan it. It just came up unconsciously. So that's genuine, it's part of my soul. It's not what I believe that I believe it's what I actually believe at a level so deep it doesn't occur to me it could be otherwise. So I don't have to insert it into my work deliberately, as a "message." It's just there, at the root of how I believe the universe works. In that way, everybody's faith gets into their fiction — whether they are religious or atheist.

RJS: How bad does a villain have to be to be a villain?

OSC: I'm not terribly interested in villains who are pathologically bad — serial killers, etc. They have to have volition and cleverness and a spark of human reachability to be interesting to me. Even Achilles, probably the worst villain I've ever depicted — I show the road he followed to get into the place he's in, and I still show the person he thinks he is, the self-image that allows him to live his life.

Real evil is more common than people think. Hitler, Stalin, Pol Pot — they had a spectacular scale to work their vile will. But the same degree of evil exists in many a home throughout the world, just on a smaller scale: those who torture, physically or emotionally, the most helpless people living with them. They're Hitler all over again, only without enough ambition, courage, or self-control to actually rise to power. So they rule as tyrants in their homes, or on the job, or, as criminals, on the street.

So I don't need a spectacular scale to make a villain. You can find villains in the grocery store. You can also find people who behave badly out of fear or weakness. Not villains, but still people you can't trust or rely on.

The scary thing is that I can find the full range of human emotions and desires in myself. I don't have to imagine some alien creature to discover evil. I just have to look into my own heart and see: If I didn't restrain this impulse or that one, I'd be the villain of this story. So I can see inside their heart.

That's what I do. I see villains the way they see themselves, as well as the way people outside their bodies see them. That way my readers not only have a better chance of realizing how common evil can be — they can also see it in themselves, and realize: Wow, I need to stop doing that!

RJS: Can a hero have "bad" or "villainous" traits and still be a hero?

OSC: I loathed Return of the Jedi, because after all his mass murders and individual cruelty and torture, Darth Vader was suddenly "redeemed" and depicted as the equal of Yoda and Obi-Wan — because, at the last moment, he declined to kill his own genetic offspring. Well, whoop-de-do! To me, that was not redemption, it was just his genes acting out the script all genes have: Reproduce! Protect the seed!

My heroes have doubts, fears, and even do wrong or bad things that they need to repent of or refrain from or overcome. They're human, but...the core self is, in a word, noble. It takes time to discover their nobility. But they aren't heroes unless they do something extraordinary, which is good. And it's deeply unsatisfying to read about a "hero" who did it all by accident. It makes it into a joke. A comedy of errors. Oops, I saved the world. Funny once, maybe. But not a hero. That story is only interesting if the person hates his hypocrisy or exploits it and is cynical about it but at some point later does something genuinely courageous, even if nobody knows about it. Then it's earned, and we need that, as readers.

Red Prophet #1
© *Dabel Brothers*

Look, there's a reason why fictional storytelling exists in every human culture, without exception, and is valued by most people in those societies. Fiction is where we find out what good and evil are, and what behaviors are noble, what motives are worthy, and which are base and shameful. Fiction shapes a culture and teaches children how to grow up to be civilized adults — if the culture is civilized. (Barbarian societies have stories that teach their children to be barbarians, of course.)

It's how we transmit culture. That's why elitist fiction in our society is not read by the general public — it reaffirms the self-image of the intellectual elite, while despising common people. Why should the common people embrace such stories? They read the stories that show the behavior they believe is noble and good.

Any civilization that does not promulgate the story that Wilfred Owen calls "that old lie" — "Dulce et decorum est pro patrie mori" (It's noble and sweet to die for your country) — is a civilization that has decided to die, because another group that does believe that story will come along and find no one willing to risk death to oppose them. That's when the barbarians win — when the civilized people are no longer willing to sacrifice anything but some of their money as taxes. You can't buy fierce, loyal, dependable soldiers to defend your culture against the barbarians. You can only grow them; and we grow them largely through the stories we tell them as children and young adults.

So the "bad" traits in a hero are there to make him believable, to keep him from seeming unapproachable and out of reach. But the core is the noble character that triumphs in the end — Han Solo coming back at the last minute to risk his life along with the others.

RJS: Do you perhaps like living a "bad" life vicariously through your villains, or are there types of bad behavior that you can't write about because of your beliefs? If so, why or why not?

OSC: I actually don't write much about the sins that really interest me. Why? Because I'm spending my life trying not to commit them, and the last thing I need to do is script a path into committing them. Plus, the interesting sins to me personally are not fictionally interesting. I've learned that fantasizing about doing bad things only whets your appetite for them. Much better to leave them alone.

RJS: Other than the fact that in comics you are working with illustrators who will draw the images and actions you would describe in a prose piece of fiction, are there any real differences to the way you approach storytelling when working in comics and working in prose?

OSC: Comics are like theater or film — somebody else is going to be interpreting my script. That makes it very different from writing fiction, where it's me and the reader, with no one else in between. So my scripts for comics are only plans to create a story, which someone else will perform for me. I can't control that, so I have to make the events crystal clear to the artists, and then hope they will make the story clear to the readers. But that's just what I do with plays and movie scripts as well. Comics is simply another dramatic, rather than narrative, art.

Wyrms #1
© Dabel Brothers

RJS: How did you come to write *Ultimate Iron Man* (and *Ultimate Iron Man 2*)?

OSC: Marvel asked me to write *Ultimate Iron Man*. I pointed out that I don't like superhero comics, and Iron Man was the most boring of all. Then they explained that the Ultimate series allowed me to reinvent the story from the beginning. So I got to come up with sci-fi reasons why the same guy would not only be a multimillionaire arms maker but also a workshop inventor and would then insist on wearing the suit himself! Those are three full time jobs...but I think I did a good job of making it real and compelling, at least to me. So what drew me was the challenge and the freedom Marvel gave me.

RJS: How did you approach *Ultimate Iron Man*?

OSC: As a story of my own, with only a few rules. I had a friend who loved the Iron Man comics and told me, "Any issue where he didn't actually wear the suit felt like a loser," so I made sure that in every issue, Tony Stark wears the suit — or the equivalent — or, later, at least Rhodey wears his War Machine suit.

Somebody wears a suit, and it's important to accomplishing the mini victory that marks the end of the issue.

RJS: Were you given any specific guidelines?

OSC: Really, they didn't surround me with fences. The limits were entirely practical: 20-22 pages per issue. A rational number of frames per page, with an eye to breaking them up so they weren't six, six, six, page after page. In return, I gave as much freedom as possible to the artists, so they could bring their own creativity to the page. They have way better eyes and visual imaginations than I have, so why would I want to limit them? Everybody gave everybody else all the freedom that the form allows.

RJS: Do you think that your status as a published (and award-winning) novelist (the author of *Ender's Game*) cut you any slack in what you were allowed to do?

OSC: Of course. They wouldn't have invited me to do it if it weren't for *Ender's Game*, but that was also a burden: They wanted me to justify the opportunity by producing work that was as good as my best. I tried to fulfill that expectation. I did not regard *Ultimate Iron Man* as slumming — I took it very seriously. Sometimes that caused them problems, because in my fiction I don't write something until I really believe in and care about the story. That has caused delays with *Ultimate Iron Man* that they would not tolerate from their regular writers. They've given me the patience I needed to try to get it right — or at least as right as I can get it.

Ultimate Iron Man #2
© *Marvel Entertainment Group*

RJS: I know that you are doing other comic book work with Marvel, but can we expect to see any other Marvel characters (Ultimate or other) from you? (If no, then why not?)

OSC: I don't think I'll write any more comics about existing characters after the second set of five *Ultimate Iron Man* comics is completed.

It's simply too much work for too little money. They paid me well by comic's standards, but I have a payroll to meet, and much as I have enjoyed working on this challenging project, I can't justify it, financially, for characters whose enhanced value as an intellectual property belongs to somebody else. If I write comics again, it will be for short one-shots, like the comic Shelter I did in promotion of the movie, *I Am Legend*, because it was a challenge and it was short so when it was done, it was over!

RJS: I see that you are currently working with the Dable brothers could you tell us a little about that?

OSC: The Dabel brothers approached me and we worked on *Red Prophet* and *Wyrms* as adaptations. They let me work with writers I trusted — Roland Bernard Brown on *Red Prophet* and Jake Black on *Wyrms* — and I think the results were very good, within the budgets they were working with.

RJS: If I'm reading the solicitations correctly, it appears that you are not only adapting other authors licensed concepts and characters, but creating some new material as well.

OSC: The new material I'm working on with Marvel will be in the *Ender's Game* universe.

Wyrms #5
© *Marvel Entertainment Group*

RJS: Any chance of any of your prose stories getting translated to the big screen or to comics?

OSC: We're also working on an *Ender's Game* movie; the project is in turnaround from Warner Bros. right now, but we have a good script and I know how to write an even better one, as soon as this writers' strike is over.

RJS: Which classic Marvel universe character would you enjoy working on, either for a long haul, or a limited series or story arc? Which (other) Ultimate character that hasn't been created, or had their own title would you like to write?

OSC: I'm not a comics fan. What I loved as a kid were three series: *Classics Illustrated*, *Scrooge McDuck*, and *Superboy*. Marvel doesn't do any of them, and my hunger for SuperBoy has been completely satisfied by the wonderful *Smallville* TV series. As for Scrooge McDuck, I just have to hit a few more bestseller lists to be able to get my room full of pennies to wallow in...

RJS: Is there a specific methodology or approach you take to your writing?

OSC: I think through motives of characters. That's the heart of everything. I also play around with details of the world — especially social details: customs, rituals, etc. All the rules of the world help create story possibilities — superimpose characters' motives on the societal rule set and you get strong stories.

RJS: That is to say how do you approach writing a novel? Is it different than the way you approach writing a comic book?

OSC: Novels are simply bigger. I can get farther into the world and spend more time and develop longer scenes and get inside the characters' heads a lot more. No long, talky scenes in comics — how long can comics readers stand balloons that crowd the faces out of the frames?

RJS: Does this approach change if you are writing your own material or adapting someone else's material to a new/different medium?

OSC: The goal in any medium is to create a fine work of art In That Medium. So Ender's Game: the Movie and Ender's Game: the Graphic Novel — they'll be true to the heart of the story, but many details will be left out or changed in order to make a great movie or a great graphic novel. The goal is to make it work for someone who never read the original novel. It has to work as an independent work of art.

RJS: Do you write at specific times of the day (get up early, stay up late?)

OSC: I have no routine. Whenever I accidentally get one, I inevitably (and unconsciously) subvert it. I just write in bursts until a project is finished, and then fret and get depressed until I'm ready to write the next one

RJS: As a SF author do you use a computer to write? If so, what kind and does it matter? (Yes, as your former editor on Ahoy! (a Commodore 64 magazine) I know this answer, but I'd like to hear it anyway.)

OSC: Any serious writer uses a word processor, because it makes revision instant and easy. When I wrote by hand (my plays) and on a typewriter (fiction before computers were available), there was enormous resistance to revision because it was so much work. Now it's easy to go back a few paragraphs and make changes, or globally change a name, and it all repaginates itself. Word processing, if you type quickly, as I do, allows you to approach the cadences of natural speech, which allows more music in your writing. I can create narrative and dialogue that flows in the readers' mind like speech, instead of being analyzed like Strunk-and-White-style prose.

RJS: What are your thoughts on the upcoming Iron Man movie?

OSC: The Iron Man movie draws on the original series and has nothing to do with what I wrote. Since I didn't like the original comics, I don't much care about the movie. It will either suck, like *League of Extraordinary Gentlemen* and *Fantastic Four*, or it will be good, like *X-Men* and *Spider-Man*. Maybe I'll see it and maybe I won't. I don't know yet.

RJS: Do you read comics? If so, which ones, and why?

Ultimate Iron Man II #1
© *Marvel Entertainment Group*

OSC: Do I read comics? Almost never. I used to read *Heavy Metal*. I don't like reading comics that are moody and incomprehensible — Dark Knight just infuriated me because you couldn't tell what was going on. It isn't good art if it doesn't communicate — comics are a storytelling medium, not a decorative one.

RJS: As a reader, what do you look for in a book, comic book or even in a movie?

OSC: Story, story, story. Characters I can care about, and storytelling that lets me know what happens and why. Within those rules, I then have to care about and believe in the events and the motives and causes of action. Very personal response, as with almost all people. I am never looking to be dazzled by a flashy artist — I find that annoying. So whenever someone says, "His style is so cool!" I avoid the book because it will probably be tedious showing off instead of good storytelling.

RJS: Do you read SF for pleasure? What authors?

OSC: I can't read SF for pleasure anymore. I'm like a tailor — all I can see are the stitches, not the suit.

RJS: Then what type of reading do you do for pleasure?

OSC: I read mysteries — Connelly, Mosley, Grafton, Beaton, McCrumb, and many others, and a few mainstream novels, historicals here and there, and lots of YA (Young Adult).

Mostly, though, I read history, science, biography, and current events. Have to fill up the brain in order for believable worldview to come out in my fiction.

Orson Scott Card
Bringing you cheap lies since 1951, Bargain rates for the gullible
http://www.hatrack.com/

The fearless creators of this book have also written others. Among them are:
Standard Guide to Golden Age Comics by Alex G. Malloy and Stuart W. Wells III
(KP Books, January 2006, ISBN 0-89689-181-X);
American Games by Alex G. Malloy (Krause, May 2000, ISBN 0-930615-60-9);
Kiddy Meal Collectibles by Robert J. Sodaro (Krause, ISBN 0-930625-16-1);
A Universe of Star Wars Collectibles, Identification and Price Guide, 2nd Edition,
by Stuart W. Wells III (Krause, July 2002, ISBN 0-87349-415-6);
See the copyright page for website and catalog information.

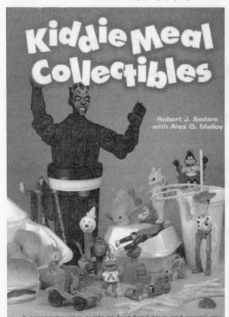

GRADING GUIDE

In David Brin's science fiction–fantasy novel, *The Practice Effect*, things improve with use. You start with a crudely made tool and keep using it until it becomes a fine instrument. If our world worked that way, you could read your Golden Age comics as often as you liked and they would just get better looking each time. Unfortunately, our world does not work that way, and reading your comics (along with just about everything else) causes comics to deteriorate.

Even if you could protect your comics from external light, heat, cold, moisture, pressure and everything else, you couldn't protect them from their own paper. Most comic books were printed on pulp paper, which has a high acid content. This means that the paper slowly turns brittle with age, no matter what you do to it, short of special museum-style preservation.

Very old, well-preserved comics are coveted collector's items. In most cases, people did not save their comic books for future generations. They read them and discarded them. Comic books were considered harmless ephemera for children. When these children outgrew their comics, their parents often threw them away. If everybody kept all of their comics, comics would not be valuable because everybody would have them scattered about the house!

The value of any comic depends on scarcity, popularity and condition. Scarcity increases with age and popularity depends on the whim of the public — only condition automatically decreases with age. Newer comics are generally available in near-mint condition, so newer comics in lesser condition have little collector potential. However, older comics are scarce, so they are still collectible in less than near-mint condition, but the value is obviously less. This is a basic tenet of all collectibles. A car is more valuable with its original paint. A baseball card is more valuable if it has not been marred by bicycle spokes. Coke bottles, stamps, coins, and toys in good condition are all more valuable than their abused counterparts. Comic books are no exception.

New comic book collectors should learn how to assess the prospective value of a comic in order to protect themselves from being fleeced by unscrupulous dealers or hucksters. Yet, a majority of dealers, especially store owners, can be considered reliable judges of comic grade. Because comic retail may be their primary source of income, certain dealers are particularly adept at noticing comic book imperfections, especially in issues they intend to purchase. As such, hobbyists and collectors must understand that dealers need to make a minimum profit on their investments. Buying collectible comics entails certain risks. Therefore, dealers must scrutinize a comic to determine if the particular book will stand a chance of resale. Well-preserved comics are invariably more desirable to dealers because they are more desirable to collectors.

There are eight standard comic grades: mint, near mint, very fine, fine, very good, good, fair, and poor. Clearly, these eight grades could be split into even finer categories when haggling over an exceptionally rare or coveted Golden Age comic. In most cases, however, comic books can be evaluated using these eight standard grades. The values listed in this book are all for comics in "Near Mint" condition. The grading/price chart given at the back of this book should be used to adjust this price for comics in different grades.

For many Golden Age comic issues, there are no known mint condition examples, but most issues have a few near mint copies in the hands of collectors. Many of these come from a few "pedigree" sources like the famous mile-high collection. There are, however, some issues where no known example is in near mint condition. To be consistent, the value listed in this price guide is still for a "near mint" copy, even if no such copy exists. The grading/price chart in the back will still yield a price for the lesser grades that actually exist. And, who knows, maybe there is another treasure trove of old comics somewhere — maybe you'll even be the one who finds it!

Mint (CGC 9.5 or above)

Finding old comics in mint condition is almost impossible because of inferior storage techniques and materials. In the early days of collecting, few people anticipated that the very boxes and bags in which they stored their comics were contributing to decay. Acid from bags, backing boards, and boxes eat away at many comics.. Mint condition comics usually fetch prices higher than price guide listings. Mint comics can sell for 120% or more of the listed price.

Mint comics are perfect comics and allow no room for imperfections. Pages and covers must be free of discoloration, wear, and wrinkles. A mint comic is one that looks like it just rolled off the press. Staples and spine must meet perfectly without cover "rollover." The cover must be crisp, bright, and trimmed perfectly. The staples must not be rusted and the cover should not have any visible creases. The interior pages of a mint comic are equally crisp and new. A mint comic must not show any signs of age or decay. Because of the paper stock used on many older comics, acid and oxygen cause interior pages to yellow and flake.

Near Mint (CGC 9.4)

A near mint comic and a mint comic are close siblings, with their differences slight, even to an experienced eye. Most of the new comics on the shelf of the local comic shop are in near mint condition. These are comics that have been handled gingerly to preserve the original luster of the book. Near mint comics are bright, clean copies with no major or minor defects. Slight stress lines near the staples and perhaps a very minor printing defect are permissible. Corners must still be sharp and devoid of creases. Interior pages of newsprint stock should show almost no discernible yellowing. Near mint comics usually trade for 100% of the listed price, with just a small discount for slightly lower grades.

Very Fine (CGC 8.0)

A very fine comic is one that is routinely found on the shelves and back issue bins of most good direct market comic shops. This grade comic has few defects, none of them major. Stress around the staples of a very fine comic are visible but not yet radical enough to create wrinkles. Both the cover and interior pages should still be crisp and sharp, devoid of flaking and creases. Interior pages may be slightly yellowed from age.

Most high-quality older comics graded as very fine can obtain 80-90% of listed prices. More, if the comic is the highest-graded comic known to exist.

Fine (CGC 6.0)

Fine comics are often issues that may have been stored carefully under a bed or on a shelf by a meticulous collector. This grade of comic is also very desirable because it shows little wear and retains much of its original sharpness. The cover may be slightly off center from rollover. The cover retains less of its original gloss and may even possess a chip or wrinkle. The comers should be sharp but may also have a slight crease. Yellowing begins to creep into the interior pages of a comic graded as fine.

Fine comics are respectable additions to collections and sell for about 40-60% of the listed price.

Very Good (CGC 4.0)

A very good comic may have been an issue passed around or read frequently. This grade is the common condition of older books. Its cover will probably have lost some luster and may have two or three creases around the staples or edges. The corners of the book may begin to show the beginnings of minor rounding and chipping, but it is by no means a damaged or defaced comic. Comics in very good condition sell for about 30-40% of listed price.

Good (CGC 2.0)

A good comic is one that has been well read and is beginning to show its age. Although both front and back covers are still attached, a good grade comic may have a number of serious wrinkles and chips. The corners and edges of this grade comic may show clear signs of rounding and flaking. There should be no major tears in a good comic nor should any pages be clipped out or missing. Interior pages may be fairly yellowed and brittle. Good comics sell for about 15-25% of the listed price.

Fair (CGC 1.0)

A fair comic is one that has definitely seen better days and has considerably limited resale value for most collectors. This comic may be soiled and damaged on the cover and interior. Fair comics should be completely intact and may only be useful as a reading copy, or a comic to lend to friends. Fair comics sell for about 10-20% of the listed price.

Poor

Comics in poor condition are generally unsuitable for collecting or reading because they range from damaged to unrecognizable. Poor comics may have been water damaged, attacked by a small child, or worse, perhaps, gnawed on by the family pet! Interior and exterior pages may be cut apart or missing entirely. A poor comic sells for about 5-15% of the listed price.

Sniffing Out Grades

Despite everything that is mentioned about comic grading, the process remains relative to the situation. A comic that seems to be in very good condition may actually be a restored copy. A restored copy is generally considered to be in between the grade it was previous to restoration and the grade it has become. Many collectors avoid restored comics entirely.

Each collector builds his collection around what he believes is important. Some want every issue of a particular series or company. Others want every issue of a favorite artist or writer. Because of this, many collectors will purchase lower-grade comics to fill out a series or to try out a new series. Mint and near mint comics are usually much more desirable to hardcore collectors. Hobbyists and readers may find the effort and cost of collecting only high-grade comics financially prohibitive.

Getting artists or writers to autograph comics has also become a source of major dispute. Some collectors enjoy signed comics and others consider those very comics defaced! The current trends indicate that most collectors do enjoy signed comics. A signature does not usually change the grade of the comic.

As mentioned, comic grading is a subjective process that must be agreed upon by the buyer and seller. Buyers will often be quick to note minor defects in order to negotiate a better price. Sellers are sometimes selectively blind to their comic's defects.

Name	Abbr.
Abel, Jack	JA
Abell, Dusty	DAb
Abnett, Dan	DAn
Abrams, Paul	PIA
Adams, Art	AAd
Adams, Neal	NA
Addeo, Stephen	StA
Adkins, Dan	DA
Adlard, Charlie	CAd
Albano, John	JAo
Albrecht, Jeff	JAl
Alcala, Alfredo	AA
Alcazar, Vincent	VAz
Alexander, Chris	CAx
Alibaster, Jo	JoA
Allred, Michael	MiA
Alstaetter, Karl	KlA
Althorp, Brian	BAp
Amaro, Gary	GyA
Amendola, Sal	Sal
Ammerman, David	DvA
Anderson, Bill	BAn
Anderson, Brent	BA
Anderson, Jeff	JAn
Anderson, Murphy	MA
Andriola, Alfred	AlA
Andru, Ross	RA
Aparo, Jim	JAp
Aragones, Sergio	SA
Arcudi, John	JAr
Artis, Tom	TAr
Ashe, Edd	EA
Asamiya	KiA
Augustyn, Brian	BAu
Austin, Terry	TA
Avison, Al	AAv
Ayers, Dick	DAy
Bachalo, Chris	CBa
Badger, Mark	MBg
Bagley, Mark	MBa
Baikie, Jim	JBa
Bailey, Bernard	BBa
Bailey, M	MBi
Bair, Michael	MlB
Baker, Kyle	KB
Baker, Matt	MB
Balent, Jim	JBa
Banks, Darryl	DBk
Barks, Carl	CB
Baron, Mike	MBn
Barr, Mike	MiB
Barras, John	DBs
Barreiro, Mike	MkB
Barreto, Ed	EB
Barry, Dan	DBa
Batista, Chris	CsB
Battlefield, D.	DB
Battlefield, Ken	KBa
Beatty, John	JhB
Beatty, Terry	TBe
Beauvais, Denis	DB
Beck, C. C.	CCB
Becker, Sam	SaB
Beeston, John	JBe
Belardinelli, M.	MBe
Bell, Bob Boze	BBB
Bell, George	GBl
Bell, Julie	JuB
Bendis, Brian Michael	BMB
Benefiel, Scott	ScB
Benes, Ed	EBe
Benitez, Joe	JBz
Benjamin, Ryan	RBn
Bennett, Joe	JoB
Bennett, Richard	RiB
Benson, Scott	StB
Berger, Charles	ChB
Bernado, Ramon	RBe
Bernstein, Robert	RbB
Bierbaum, Mary	MBm
Bierbaum, Tom	TBm
Biggs, Geoffrey	GB
Binder, Jack	JaB
Bingham, Jerry	JBi
Birch, JJ	JJB
Biro, Charles	CBi
Bisley, Simon	SBs
Bissette, Stephen	SBi
Blair, Barry	BaB
Blaisdell, Tex	TeB
Blasco, Jesus	JBl
Blevins, Bret	BBl
Blum, Alex	AB
Bode, Vaughn	VB
Bogdanove, Jon	JBg
Bolland, Brian	BB
Bolle, Frank	FBe
Boller, David	DdB
Bolton, John	JBo
Bond, Philip	PBd
Booth, Brett	BBh
Boring, Wayne	WB
Bossart, William	WmB
Boxell, Tim	TB
Bradstreet, Tim	TBd
Braithwaite, Doug	DBw
Brasfield, Craig	CrB
Braun, Russell	RsB
Breeding, Brett	BBr
Brereton, Daniel	DlB
Brewster, Ann	ABr
Breyfogle, Norm	NBy
Bridwell, E. Nelson	ENB
Briefer, Dick	DBr
Bright, Mark	MBr
Brigman, June	JBr
Broderick, Pat	PB
Brodsky, Allyn	AyB
Broom, John	JBm
Broome, Matt	MtB
Brothers, Hernandez	HB
Brown, Bob	BbB
Browne, Dick	DkB
Brunner, Frank	FB
Bryant, Rick	RkB
Buckingham, Mark	MBu
Buckler, Rich.	RB
Budget, Greg	GBu
Bulanadi, Danny	DBl
Burchett, Rick	RBr
Burgard, Tim	TmB
Burgos, Carl	CBu
Burke, Fred	FBk
Burnley, Jack	JBu
Burns, John	JBn
Burns, Robert	RBu
Burroughs, W.	WBu
Buscema, John	JB
Buscema, Sal	SB
Busiek, Kurt	KBk
Butler, Jeff	JBt
Butler, Steve	SBt
Buzz	Buzz
Byrd, Mitch	MBy
Byrne, John	JBy
Calafiore, Jim	JCf
Caldes, Charles	CCa
Callahan, Jim	JiC
Calnan, John	JCa
Cameron, Don	DCn
Cameron, Lou	LC
Campbell, Eddie	ECa
Campbell, J. Scott.	JSC
Campbell, Stan	StC
Campenella, Robert	RbC
Campos, Marc	MCa
Capullo, Greg	GCa
Cardy, Nick	NC
Carey, Mike	MCy
Cariello, Sergio	SCi
Carlin, Mike	MCr
Carpenter, Brent D.	BDC
Carralero, Ricky	RCl
Carrasco, Dario	DoC
Carter, Joe	JCt
Case, Richard	RCa
Casey, Joe	JoC
Castellaneta, Dan	DaC
Castellini, Claudio	CCt
Castrillo, Anthony	ACa
Chadwick, Paul	PC
Chan, Ernie	ECh
Chang, Bernard	BCh
Charest, Travis	TC
Chase, Bobbie	BCe
Chaykin, Howard	HC
Check, Sid	SC
Chen, Mike	MCh
Chen, Sean	SCh
Chestney, Lillian	LCh
Chiarello, Mark	MCo
Chichester, D.G.	DGC
Chiodo, Joe	JCh
Choi, Brandon	BCi
Chriscross	Ccs
Christopher, Tom	TmC
Chua, Ernie	Chu
Chun, Anthony	ACh
Churchhill, Ian	IaC
Cirocco, Frank	FC
Citron, Sam	SmC
Claremont, Chris	CCl
Clark, Mike	MCl
Clark, Scott	ScC
Cockrum, Dave	DC
Cohn, Gary	GCh
Coker, Tomm	TCk
Colan, Gene	GC
Colby, Simon	SCy
Cole, Jack	JCo
Cole, Leonard B.	LbC
Colletta, Vince	ViC
Collins, Max Allan	MCn
Collins, Mike	MC
Collins, Nancy	NyC
Colon, Ernie	EC
Conner, Amanda	ACo
Conway, Gerry	GyC
Cooper, Dave	DvC
Cooper, John	JCp
Cooper, Sam	SCp
Corben, Richard	RCo
Costanza, Peter	PrC
Cowan, Denys	DCw
Cox, Jeromy	JCx
Craig, Johnny	JCr
Crandall, Reed	RC
Crespo, Steve	SCr
Crilley, Mark	MCi
Crumb, Robert	RCr
Cruz, E. R.	ERC
Cruz, Jerry	JCz
Cruz, Roger	RCz
Cuidera, Chuck	CCu
Cullins, Paris	PCu
Currie, Andrew	ACe
Damaggio, Rodolfo	RDm
Daniel, Tony	TnD
Danner, Paul	PuD
Darrow, Geof	GfD
David, Peter	PDd
Davis, Alan	AD
Davis, Bob	BD
Davis, Dan	DDv
Davis, Guy	GyD
Davis, Jack	JDa
Davis, Malcolm.	MDa
Davison, Al	ADv
Day, Dan	Day
Day, Gene	GD
DeFalco, Tom	TDF
Deitch, Kim	KDe
Delano, Jamie	JaD
DeLaRosa, Sam.	SDR
Del Bourgo, Maurice	MDb
Delgado, Richard	RdD
Dell, John	JhD
DeMatteis, J. M.	JMD
DeMulder, Kim	KDM
Deodato, Jr., Mike	MD2
Derenick, Tom	TDr
DeZago, Todd	TDz
DeZuniga, M.	MDb
DeZuniga, Tony	TD
Diaz, Paco	PaD
Dillin, Dick	DD
Dillon, Glyn	GlD
Dillon, Steve	SDi
Dini, Paul	PDi
Disbrow, Jay	JyD
Ditko, Steve	SD
Dixon, Chuck	CDi
Dixon, John	JDx
Dobbyn, Nigel	ND
Dodson, Terry	TyD
Doherty, Peter.	PD
Dominguez, Luis	LDz
Doran, Colleen	CDo
Dorey, Mike	MDo
Dorkin, Evan	EDo
Dorman, Dave	DvD
Doucet, Julie	JDo
Dougherty, H.	HD
Drake, Stan	SDr
Dresser, Larry	LDr
Dringenberg, Mike	MDr
Drucker, Mort	MD
DuBerkr, Randy	RDB
Duffy, Jo.	JDy
Dumm, Gary	GDu
Dunn, Ben.	BDn
Duranona, Leo	LDu
Duursema, Jan	JD
Dwyer, Kieron	KD
Eastman, Kevin	KEa
Eaton, Scott	SEa
Edginton, Ian	IEd
Edlund, Ben	BEd
Egeland, Marty	MEg
Eisner, Will	WE
Elder, Bill	BE
Eldred, Tim	TEl
Elias, Lee	LEl
Elliot, D.	DE
Ellis, Warren	WEl
Ellison, Harlan	HaE
Emberlin, Randy	RyE
Englehart, Steve	SEt
Ennis, Garth	GEn
Epting, Steve	SEp
Erskine, Gary	GEr
Erwin, Steve.	StE
Esposito, Mike	ME
Estes, John	JEs
Estrada, Ric	RE
Evans, George	GE
Evans, Ray	REv
Everett, Bill	BEv
Ewins, Brett	BEw
Ezquerra, Carlos	CE
Fabry, Glenn	GF
Fago, Al	AFa

Name	Abbr	Name	Abbr	Name	Abbr	Name	Abbr
Farmer, Mark	MFm	Griffiths, Martin	MGs	Hughes, Adam	AH	Kupperberg, Paul	PuK
Fegredo, Duncan	DFg	Grindberg, Tom	TGb	Hultgren, Ken	KHu	Kurtzman, Harvey	HK
Feldstein, Al	AF	Gross, Daerick	DkG	Hund, Dave	DeH	Kwitney, Alisa	AaK
Ferry, Pascual	PFe	Gross, Peter	PrG	Hunt, Chad	CH	LaBan, Terry	TLa
Fine, Lou	LF	Grossman, R.	RGs	Immonen, Stuart	SI	Lago, Ray	RyL
Fingeroth, Danny	DFr	Gruenwald, Mark	MGu	Infantino, Carmine	CI	Laird, Peter	PLa
Finnocchiaro, Sal	SF	Grummett, Tom	TG	Infantino, Jim	JI	Lamme, Bob	BbL
Fleisher, Michael	MFl	Guardineer, Fred	FGu	Ingles, Graham	Grl	Langridge, Roger	RLg
Fleming, Robert	RFl	Guay, Rebecca	RGu	Iorio, Medio	MI	Lanning, Andy	ALa
Flemming, Homer	HFl	Guice, Jackson	JG	Isherwood, Geoff	GI	Lansdale, Joe	JLd
Flessel, Creig	CF	Guichet, Yvel	YG	Ivie, Larry	LI	Lapham, Dave	DL
Foreman, Dick	DiF	Guinan, Paul	PGn	Ivy, Chris	CIv	Lark, Michael	MLr
Forte, John	JF	Gulacy, Paul	PG	Jackson, Julius	JJn	Larkin, Bob	BLr
Forton, Gerald	GFo	Gustavson, Paul	PGv	Jaffee, Al	AJ	LaRocque, Greg	GrL
Fosco, Frank	FFo	Gustovich, Mike	MG	Janke, Dennis	DJa	Larroca, Salvador	SvL
Foster, Alan Dean	ADF	Ha, Gene	GeH	Janson, Klaus	KJ	Larsen, Erik	EL
Fox, Gardner	GaF	Haley, Matt	MHy	Javinen, Kirk	KJa	Lash, Batton	BLs
Fox, Gill	GFx	Hall, Bob	BH	Jenkins, Paul	PJe	Lashley, Ken	KeL
Fox, Matt	MF	Halsted, Ted	TeH	Jenney, Robert	RJ	Lavery, Jim	JLv
Fraga, Dan	DaF	Hama, Larry	LHa	Jensen, Dennis	DJ	Lawlis, Dan	DLw
Franchesco	Fso	Hamilton, Tim	TH	Jimenez, Leonardo	LJi	Lawrence, Terral	TLw
Frank, Gary	GFr	Hamner, Cully	CHm	Jimminiz, Phil	PJ	Lawson, Jim	JmL
Frazetta, Frank	FF	Hampton, Bo.	BHa	Johnson, Dave	DvJ	Layton, Bob	BL
Freeman, John	JFr	Hampton, Scott	SHp	Johnson, Jeff	JJ	Leach, Garry	GL
Freeman, Simon	SFr	Hanna, Scott	SHa	Johnson, Paul	PuJ	Leach, Rick	RkL
Frenz, Ron	RF	Hannigan, Ed	EH	Johnson, Todd	TJn	Lee, Elaine	ELe
Frese, George	GFs	Hanson, Neil	NHa	Johnson, Walter	WJo	Lee, Jae	JaL
Friedman, Michael Jan	MFr	Harmon, Jim	JHa	Jones, Casey	CJ	Lee, Jim	JLe
Friedrich, Mike	MkF	Harras, Bob	BHs	Jones, Gerard	GJ	Lee, Patrick	PtL
Frolechlich, August	AgF	Harris, N. Steven	NSH	Jones, J.B.	JJo	Lee, Scott	ScL
Fry III, James	JFy	Harris, Tim	THa	Jones, Jeff	JeJ	Lee, Stan	StL
Fujitani(Fuje), Bob	BF	Harris, Tony	TyH	Jones, Kelley	KJo	Leeke, Mike	MLe
Furman, Simon	SFu	Harrison, Lou	LuH	Jones, Malcolm	MJ	Leialoha, Steve	SL
Gaiman, Neil	NGa	Harrison, Simon	SHn	Jones, R.A.	RAJ	Leon, John Paul	JPL
Galan, Manny	MaG	Hart, Ernest	EhH	Jones, Robert	RJn	Leonard, Lank	LLe
Gallant, Shannon	ShG	Hartsoe, Everette.	EHr	Jurgens, Dan	DJu	Leonardi, Rick	RL
Gammill, Kerry	KGa	Hathaway, Kurt	KtH	Jusko, Joe	JJu	Levins, Rik	RLe
Garcia, Dave	DaG	Hawkins, Matt	MHw	Kaluta, Mike	MK	Lewis, Brian	BLw
Garner, Alex	AGo	Hayes, Drew	DHa	Kamen, Jack	JKa	Lieber, Larry	LLi
Garney, Ron	RG	Hayes, Rory	RHa	Kaminski, Len	LKa	Liefeld, Rob	RLd
Garzon, Carlos	CG	Haynes, Hugh.	HH	Kane & Romita	K&R	Lightle, Steve	SLi
Gascoine, Phil	PGa	Hazlewood, Douglas.	DHz	Kane, Bob	BKa	Lim, Ron	RLm
Gaudino, Stefano	SGa	Hearnes, David.	DvH	Kane, Gil.	GK	Linsner, Joseph M.	JLi
Gaughan, Jack	JGa	Hearne, Jack	JH	Kanigher, Bob	BbK	Livingstone, Rolland	RLv
Gecko, Gabe	GG	Heath, Russ	RH	Kaniuga, Trent.	TKn	Lloyd, David	DvL
Geggan	Ggn	Hebbard, Robert	RtH	Karounos, Paris T.	PaK	Lobdell, Scott	SLo
Gerard, Ruben	RGd	Heck, Don.	DH	Katz, Jack	JKz	Locke, Vince	VcL
Gerber, Steve	SvG	Heisler, Mike.	MHs	Kavanagh, Terry	TKa	Loeb, Jeph	JLb
Giacoia, Frank	FrG	Hempel, Mark.	MaH	Kaye, Stan	StK	Lopez, Jose	JL
Giarrano, Vince	VGi	Henry, Flint	FH	Kelly, Walt	WK	Lopresti, Aaron	AaL
Gibbons, Dave	DGb	Herman, Jack	JH	Kennedy, Cam	CK	Louapre, Dave	DLp
Gibson, Ian	IG	Hernandez Brothers	HB	Kennedy, Ian	IK	Lowe, John	Low
Giella, Joe	JoG	Hernandez, Gilbert	GHe	Keown, Dale	DK	Lubbers, Bob	BLb
Giffen, Keith	KG	Hernandez, Jaime	JHr	Kerschl, Karl.	KlK	Lustbader, Eric Van	ELu
Gilbert, Michael T.	MGi	Herrera,Ben.	BHr	Kesel, Babara	BKs	Luzniak, Greg	GLz
Giordano, Dick	DG	Hester, Phil	PhH	Kesel, Karl	KK	Lyle, Tom	TL
Glanzman, Sam	SG	Hewlett, Jamie	JHw	Kiefer, Henry C.	HcK	Macchio, Ralph	RMc
Goldberg, Rube	RuG	Hibbard, E.E.	EHi	Kieth, Sam	SK	Mack, David	DMk
Golden, Michael	MGo	Hicklenton, John	JHk	Kihi, H. J.	HjK	Mackie, Howard	HMe
Gonzalez, Jorge	JGz	Hicks, Arnold.	AdH	Kildale, Malcolm.	MKd	Madan, Dev	DeM
Goodman, Till	TGo	Higgins, Graham	GHi	King, Hannibal	HbK	Madureira, Joe	JMd
Goodwin, Archie	AGw	Higgins, John	JHi	Kinsler, Everett R.	EK	Maggin, Elliot S.	ESM
Gordon, Al	AG	Higgins, Michael	MHi	Kirby, Jack	JK	Maguire, Kevin	KM
Gottfredson, Floyd	FG	Hing, T. F.	TFH	Kirner	Kr	Magyar, Rick	RM
Gould, Chester	ChG	Hitch, Bryan	BHi	Kisniro, Yukito	YuK	Mahlstedt, Larry	LMa
Grandmetti, Jerry	JGr	Hobbs, Bill	BlH	Kitchen, Dennis	DKi	Mahnke, Doug	DoM
Grant, Alan	AlG	Hoberg, Rick.	RHo	Kitson, Barry.	BKi	Mandrake, Tom.	TMd
Grant, Steve	StG	Hoffer, Mike	MkH	Klein, George.	GKl	Maneely, Joe.	JMn
Grau, Peter	PGr	Hogarth, Burne	BHg	Kobasic, Kevin	KoK	Manley, Graham	GMy
Gray, Mick	MGy	Holcomb, Art.	AHo	Kolins, Scott	ScK	Manley, Mike	MM
Green, Alfonso	AGn	Holdredge, John	JHo	Krause, Peter.	PKr	Mann, Roland	RMn
Green, Dan	DGr	Hoover, Dave	DHv	Krenkel, Roy.	RKu	Mann, Roland	Man
Green, Justin	JsG	Hopgood, Kevin	KHd	Krigstein, Bernie	BK	Manning, Russ	RsM
Green, Randy	RGr	Horie, Richard	RHe	Kristiansen, Teddy H.	TKr	Marais, Raymond.	RdM
Greene, Sid	SGe	Hotz, Kyle	KHt	Kruse, Brandon	BKr	Mariotte, Jeff	JMi
Grell, Mike	MGr	Howarth, Matt.	MHo	Kubert, Adam	AKu	Maroto, Esteban	EM
Griffith, Bill	BG	Howell, Rich	RHo	Kubert, Andy.	NKu	Marrinan, Chris	ChM
Griffiths, Harley	HyG	Hudnall, James.	JHl	Kubert, Joe	JKu	Marrs, Lee	LMr

Name	Abbr.	Name	Abbr.
Martin, Gary	GyM	Morales, Rags	RgM
Martin, Joe	JMt	Moreira, Ruben	RMo
Martinbrough, Shawn	SMa	Moretti, Mark	MMo
Martinez, Henry	HMz	Morgan, Tom	TMo
Martinez, Roy Allan	RMr	Morisi, Pete	PMo
Marz, Ron	RMz	Moritz, Edward	EdM
Marzan, Jose	JMz	Morosco, Vincent	VMo
Mason, Tom	TMs	Morrison, Grant	GMo
Massengill, Nathan	NMa	Morrow, Gray	GM
Matsuda, Jeff	JMs	Mortimer, Win	WMo
Mattsson, Steve	SMt	Moskowitz, Seymour	SMz
Maus, Bill	BMs	Motter, Dean	DMt
Maxwell, Stanley	StM	Moy, Jeffrey	JMy
Mayer, Sheldon	ShM	Murray, Brian	BrM
Mayerik, Val	VMk	Musial, Joe	JoM
Mazzucchelli, David	DM	Muth, Jon J.	JMu
McCann, Gerald	GMc	Mychaels, Marat	MMy
McCarthy, Brendon	BMy	Myers	Mys
McCarthy, Jim	JMy	Naifeh, Ted	TNa
McCloud, Scott	SMI	Napolitano, Nick	NNa
McCorkindale, B	BMC	Napton, Bob	BNa
McCraw, Tom	TMw	Nauck, Todd	TNu
McCrea, John	JMC	Neary, Paul	PNe
McDaniel, Scott	SMc	Nebres, Rudy	RN
McDaniel, Walter	WMc	Nelson	Nel
McDonnell, Luke	LMc	Netzer, Mike	MN
McDuffie, Dwayne	DMD	Newton, Don	DN
McFarlane, Todd	TM	Nguyen, Hoang	HNg
McGregor, Don	DMG	Nichols, Art	ANi
McKean, Dave	DMc	Nicieza, Fabian	FaN
McKeever, Ted	TMK	Nino, Alex	AN
McKenna, Mike	MkK	Nocenti, Ann	ANo
McKie, Angus	AMK	Nocon, Cedric	CNn
McKone, Mike	MMK	Nodell, Martin	MnN
McLaughlin, Frank	FMc	Nodel, Norman	NN
McLaughlin, Sean	SML	Nolan, Graham	GN
McLeod, Bob	BMc	Nord, Cary	CNr
McMahon, M.	MMc	Norem, Earl	EN
McManus, Shawn	SwM	Nostrand, Howard	HN
McNeil, Colin	CMc	Novick, Irv	IN
McWilliams, Al	AMc	Nowlan, Kevin	KN
Meagher, Fred	FMe	Nutman, Philip	PNu
Medina, Angel	AMe	O'Barr, James	JOb
Medley, Linda	LiM	O'Neil, Denny	DON
Mercadoocasio, H.	HMo	O'Neill, Kevin	KON
Meskin, Mort	MMe	Olbrich, Dave	DO
Messmer, Otto	OM	Olivetti, Ariel	AOl
Messner-Loebs, Bill	BML	Olliffe, Patrick	PO
Micale, Albert	AIM	One, Dark	DOe
Michelinie, David	DvM	Ordway, Jerry	JOy
Miehm, Grant	GtM	Orlando, Joe	JO
Mighten, Duke	DMn	Ormston, Dean	DOr
Mignola, Michael	MMi	Ortiz, Jose	JOt
Miki, Danny	DaM	Oskner, Bob	BO
Milgrom, Al	AM	Ostrander, John	JOs
Millar, Mark	MMr	Oughton, Thomas	TO
Miller, Frank	FM	Owen, James	JOn
Miller, Mike S.	MsM	Ozkan, Tayyar	TOz
Miller, Sidney	SyM	Pace, Richard	RPc
Miller, Steve	SM	Pacella, Mark	MPa
Milligan, Peter	PrM	Pacheco, Carlos	CPa
Mills, Pat	PMs	Palais, Rudy	RP
Minor, Jason	JnM	Palais, Walter	WlP
Mitchel, Barry	BM	Palmer, Tom	TP
Moder, Lee	LMd	Palmiotti, Jimmy	JP
Moe, C. S.	CSM	Pamai, Gene	GPi
Moebius	Moe	Panalign, Noly	NPl
Moeller, Chris	CsM	Paniccia, Mark	MPc
Moench, Doug	DgM	Panosian, Dan	DPs
Moldoff, Sheldon	SMo	Parkhouse, Annie	APh
Montano, Steve	SeM	Parkhouse, Steve	SvP
Mooney, Jim	JM	Parobeck, Mike	MeP
Moore, Alan	AMo	Pascoe, James	JmP
Moore, Jeff	JMr	Pasko, Martin	MPk
Moore, Jerome	JeM	Patterson, Bruce	BrP
Moore, John Francis	JFM	Paul, Frank R.	FP
Moore, Terry	TMr	Payne, Pop	PP
Morales, Lou	LM	Pearson, Jason	JPn

Name	Abbr.	Name	Abbr.
Pekar, Harvey	HP	Roach, David	DRo
Pelletier, Paul	PaP	Robbins, Frank	FR
Peltz, George	GgP	Robbins, Trina	TrR
Pence, Eric	ErP	Roberts, Mike	MRo
Pennington, Mark	MPn	Robertson, Darrick	DaR
Pensa, Shea Anton	SAP	Robinson, Cliff	CRb
Perez, George	GP	Robinson, James	JeR
Perham, James	JPh	Robinson, Jerry	JRo
Perlin, Don	DP	Rodier, Denis	DRo
Perryman, Edmund	EP	Rodriguez, Spain	SRo
Peterson, Brandon	BPe	Roea, Doug	DgR
Peterson, Jonathan	JPe	Rogers, Boody	BRo
Petrucha, Stefan	SPr	Rogers, Marshall	MR
Peyer, Tom	TPe	Romita, John	JR
Phillips, Joe	JoP	Romita, John Jr.	JR2
Phillips, Scott	SPl	Rosenberger, J.	JRo
Phillips, Sean	SeP	Ross, Alex	AxR
Pike, Jay Scott	JsP	Ross, David	DR
Pini, Richard	RPi	Ross, John	JRs
Pini, Wendy	WP	Ross, Luke	LRs
Pino, Carlos	CPi	Roth, Werner	WR
Platt, Stephen	SPa	Royle, Jim	JRl
Pleece, Warren	WaP	Royle, John	JRe
Ploog, Mike	MP	Rozum, John	JRz
Plunkett, Kilian	KPl	Rubano, Aldo	ARu
Poch	PcH	Rubi, Melvin	MvR
Pollack, Rachel	RaP	Rubinstein, Joe	JRu
Pollard, Keith	KP	Rude, Steve	SR
Pollina, Adam	AdP	Ruffner, Sean	SRf
Polseno, Jo	JP	Russell, P. Craig	CR
Pope, Paul	PPo	Russell, Vince	VRu
Porch, David	DPo	Ryan, Matt	MRy
Portacio, Whilce	WPo	Ryan, Paul	PR
Porter, Howard	HPo	Ryder, Tom	TmR
Post, Howard	HwP	Sahle, Harry	HSa
Potts, Carl	CP	Sakakibara, Mizuki	MiS
Powell, Bob	BP	Sakai, Stan	SS
Power, Dermot	DPw	Sale, Tim	TSe
Pratt, George	GgP	Salmons, Tony	TSa
Premaini, Bruno	BPr	Saltares, Javier	JS
Prezio, Victor	VP	Sampson, Steve	SSm
Prichard, Pat	PPr	Sanders, Jim III	JS3
Priest, Christopher	CPr	Sasso, Mark	MSo
Prosser, Jerry	JeP	Saunders, Norm	NS
Pugh, Steve	StP	Saviuk, Alex	AS
Pulido, Brian	BnP	Schaffenberger, Kurt	KS
Queen, Randy	RQu	Schane, Tristan	TnS
Quesada, Joe	JQ	Schiller, Fred	FdS
Quinlan, Charles	CQ	Schmitz, Mark	MaS
Quinn, David	DQ	Schomburg, Alex	ASh
Quinones, Peter	PQ	Schrotter, Gustav	GS
Raab, Ben	BRa	Schultz, Mark	MSh
Raboy, Mac	MRa	Scoffield, Sean	SSc
Ramos, Humberto	HuR	Scott, Jeffery	JSc
Ramos, Rodney	RyR	Scott, Trevor	TvS
Ramsey, Ray	RR	Seagle, Steven T.	SSe
Randall, Ron	RoR	Sears, Bart	BS
Randon, Arthur	ARn	Sekowsky, Mike	MSy
Raney, Tom	TR	Semeiks, Val	VS
Rankin, Rich	RRa	Senior, Geoff	GSr
Rapmund, Norm	NRd	Serpe, Jerry	JyS
Rasmussen, H	HR	Severin, John	JSe
Raymond, Alex	AR	Severin, Marie	MSe
Raymond, Kim	KR	Shamray, Gerry	GSh
Redondo, J.	JRd	Shanower, Eric	EiS
Redondo, Nestor	NR	Sharp, Liam	LSh
Reed, David	DvR	Shaw, Sean	SSh
Reeves-Stevens, Judith	JRv	Shelton, Gilbert	GiS
Reinhold, Bill	BR	Sheridan, Dave	DSh
Richards, Ted	TR	Sherman, Jim	JSh
Richardson, Mike	MRi	Shoemaker, Terry	TSr
Richardson, J	JRi	Shooter, Jim	JiS
Ricketts, Mark	MRc	Shores, Syd	SSh
Rico, Don	DRi	Shum, Howard	HSm
Ridgeway, John	JRy	Shuster, Joe	JoS
Rieber, John Ney	JNR	Sibal, Jonathan	JSb
Riley, John	JnR	Siegel & Shuster	S&S
Riply	Rip	Sienkiewicz, Bill	BSz

Name	Abbr.	Name	Abbr.	Name	Abbr.	Name	Abbr.
Silvestri, Eric	EcS	Straczynski, J.Michael	MSz	Valentino, Jim	JV	Wiesenfeld, Aron	AWs
Silvestri, Mark	MS	Stradley, Randy	RSd	Vallejo, Boris	BV	Wildey, Doug	DW
Sim, Dave	DS	Strazewski, Len	LeS	Van Buren, Raeburn	RvB	Wildman, Andrew	Wld
Simon & Kirby	S&K	Streeter, Lin	LnS	Van Fleet, John	JVF	Williams, Anthony	AWi
Simon, Allen	ASm	Stroman, Larry	LSn	Vancata, Brad	BVa	Williams, David	DdW
Simon, Joe	JSm	Sturgeon, Foolbert		Vance, Steve	SVa	Williams, J.H.	JWi
Simonson, Louise	LSi	(& Frank Stack)	FSt	VanHook, Kevin	KVH	Williams, Keith	KWi
Simonson, Walt	WS	Sullivan, Lee	LS	Vargas, Vagner	VV	Williams, Kent	KW
Simpson, Don	DSs	Sutton, Tom	TS	Veitch, Rick	RV	Williams, Robert	RW
Simpson, Howard	HSn	Swan, Curt	CS	Velez, Ivan, Jr.	IV	Williams, Scott	SW
Simpson, Will	WSm	Sweetman, Dan	DSw	Velluto, Sal	SaV	Williamson, Al.	AW
Sinnott, Joe	JSt	Taggart, Tom	TTg	Vess, Charles	CV	Williamson, Skip	SWi
Siryk	Syk	Takenaga, Francis	FTa	Vey, Al	AV	Willingham, Bill	BWg
Skroce, Steve	SSr	Takezaki, Tony	ToT	Vigil, Tim	TV	Willis, Damon	DaW
Smith, Andy	ASm	Talbot, Bryan	BT	Vokes, Neil	NV	Wilshire, Mary	MW
Smith, Barry W.	BWS	Tallarico, Tony	TyT	Von Eeden, Trevor	TVE	Wilson, Colin	CWi
Smith, Beau	BSt	Tan, Billy	BTn	Vosburg, Mike	MV	Wilson, Gahan	GW
Smith, Cam	CaS	Tanaka, Masashi	MTk	Wagner, Matt	MWg	Wilson, Keith S.	KSW
Smith, Jeff	JSi	Tanghal, Romeo	RT	Wagner,Ron	RoW	Wilson, S. Clay	SCW
Smith, John	JnS	Tappin, Steve	SeT	Waid, Mark	MWa	Woch, Stan.	SnW
Smith, Kevin	KSm	Tartaglione, John	JTg	Waldinger, Morris.	MsW	Woggin, Bill	BWo
Smith, Malcolm	MSt	Taylor, David	DTy	Waldman, Ed	EW	Wojtkiewicz, Chuck	Woj
Smith, Paul	PS	Taylor, R.G.	RGT	Walker, Kevin	KeW	Wolf, Chance	CWf
Smith, Robin	RSm	Templeton, Ty	TTn	Waller, Reed	RWa	Wolfe, Joseph	JWf
Smith, Ron	RS	Teney, Tom	TmT	Walsh, William	WmW	Wolfman, Marv	MWn
Snejbjerg, Peter	PSj	Tenney, Mark	MaT	Waltrip, Jason	JWp	Wolverton, Basil.	BW
Sniegoski, Tom	TSg	Texeira, Mark	MT	Waltrip, John	JWt	Wood, Bob.	BoW
Spark	Spk	Thibert, Art	ATi	Ward, Bill	BWa	Wood, Teri Sue.	TWo
Sparling, Jack	JkS	Thomas, Dann	DTs	Warner, Chris.	CW	Wood, Wally	WW
Spector, Irving	IS	Thomas, Roy	RTs	Warren, Adam	AWa	Woodbridge, George	GWb
Spiegelman, Art.	ASp	Thomason, Derek	DeT	Warren, Jack A.	JW	Woodring, Jim.	JWo
Spiegle, Dan	DSp	Thompson, Jill.	JIT	Washington 3, Robert	3RW	Wormer, Kirk Van	KWo
Spinks, Frank	FrS	Thorne, Frank	FT	Watkiss, John	JWk	Wright, Greg	GWt
Springer, Frank	FS	Tinker, Ron	RnT	Watson, Jim	JWa	Wrightson, Berni	BWr
Sprouse, Chris	CSp	Todd, Fred	FTd	Webb, Robert.	RWb	Wyman, M.C.	MCW
St.Pierre, Joe	JPi	Torres, Angelo	AT	Weeks, Lee.	LW	Yaep, Chap	CYp
Starlin, Jim	JSn	Toth, Alex	ATh	Wein, Len	LWn	Yeates, Tom	TY
Starr, Leonard	LSt	Totleben, John	JTo	Weinstein, Howard.	HWe	Yeowell, Steve.	SY
Staton, Joe	JSon	Trapain, Sal	ST	Weiss, M.	MWs	Zabel, Joe	JZe
Steacy, Ken	KSy	Trimpe, Herb	HT	Welch, Larry	LyW	Zachary, Dean.	DZ
Steffan, Dan	DnS	Truman, Timothy	TT	Welker, Gay	GyW	Zaffino, Jorge.	JZ
Stein, Marvin	MvS	Truog, Chas	ChT	Wendel, Andrew	AdW	Zansky, Louis.	LZ
Steinberg, Irvin	ISb	Tucci, Bill	BiT	Wenzel, David	DWe	Zeck, Mike	MZ
Stelfreeze, Brian	BSf	Tucker, James	JT	Weringo, Mike	MeW	Zick, Bruce	BZ
Stephenson, Eric	ErS	Tukell, George	GTk	West, Kevin	KWe	Zulli, Michael	MZi
Steranko, Jim.	JSo	Turner, Dwayne	DT	Weston, Chris	CWn	Zyskowski, Joseph.	JZy
Stern, Roger	RSt	Turner, Ron	RTu	Wheatley, Mark	MkW	Zyskowski, Steven	SZ
Stern, Steve	SSt	Tuska, George	GT	Whedon, Joss.	JoW		
Stevens, Dave	DSt	Ulm, Chris.	CU	Whiteman, Ezra	EzW		
Stiles, Steve	SvS	Ulmer, Al	AU	Whitman, Bill	BWh		
Story, Karl	KlS	Vachss, Andrew	AVs	Whitney, Ogden	OW		
Stout, William	WiS	Vado, Dan	DVa	Wiacek, Bob	BWi		

GENERAL ABBREVIATIONS FOR COMICS LISTINGS

Adaptation	Adapt.	Giant Size	G-Size	Prestige Format	PF
Appearance of	A:	Golden Age	G.A.	Preview	Prev.
Anniversary	Anniv.	Graphic Album	GAm	Reprinted issue	rep.
Annual	Ann.#	Graphic Novel	GN or GNv	Retold	rtd.
Art & Cover	(a&c)	Hardcover	HC	Return/Revival of.	R:
Art & Plot	(a&pl)	Identity Revealed	IR:	Scripted/Written by	(s)
Art & Script	(a&s)	Inks by	(i)	Scripts & inks	(s&i)
Artist	(a)	Introduction of	I:	Silver Age	S.A.
Back-Up Story	BU:	Joins of.	J:	Softcover	SC
Beginning of	B:	King Size	K-Size	Special	Spec.
Birth of	b:	Leaving of	L:	Team-up	T.U.
Cameo Appearance	C:	New Costume	N:	Trade Paperback	TPB
Cover	(c)	No Issue Number	N#	Versus	V: or vs.
Cover and Script	(c&s)	Origin of	O:	Wedding of	W:
Crossover with	x-over	Painted Cover	P(c)	With	w/
Death/Destruction of	D:	Part	pt. or Pt.	Without	w/o
Edition	Ed.	Pencils by	(p)		
Ending of	E:	Photographic cover	Ph(c)		
Features	F:	Plotted by	(pl)		

Abbreviation	Name
3RW	Robert Washington 3
AA	Alfredo Alcala
AAd	Art Adams
AaK	Alisa Kwitney
AaL	Aaron Lopresti
AAv	Al Avison
AB	Alex Blum
ABr	Ann Brewster
ACa	Anthony Castrillo
ACe	Andrew Currie
ACh	Anthony Chun
ACo	Amanda Conner
AD	Alan Davis
ADF	Alan Dean Foster
AdH	Arnold Hicks
AdP	Adam Pollina
ADv	Al Davison
AdW	Andrew Wendel
AF	Al Feldstein
AFa	Al Fago
AG	Al Gordon
AgF	A. Frolechlich
AGn	Alfonso Green
AGo	Alex Garner
AGw	Archie Goodwin
AH	Adam Hughes
AHo	Art Holcomb
AIA	Alfred Andriola
AJ	Al Jaffee
AKu	Adam Kubert
ALa	Andy Lanning
AlG	Alan Grant
AlM	Albert Micale
AM	Al Milgrom
AMc	Al McWilliams
AMe	Angel Medina
AMK	Angus McKie
AMo	Alan Moore
AN	Alex Nino
ANi	Art Nichols
ANo	Ann Nocenti
AOl	Ariel Olivetti
APh	Annie Parkhouse
AR	Alex Raymond
ARn	Arthur Randon
ARu	Aldo Rubano
AS	Alex Saviuk
ASh	Alex Schomburg
ASm	Andy Smith
ASm	Allen Simon
ASp	Art Spiegelman
AT	Angelo Torres
ATh	Alex Toth
ATi	Art Thibert
AU	Al Ulmer
AV	Al Vey
AVs	Andrew Vachss
AW	Al Williamson
AWa	Adam Warren
AWi	Anthony Williams
AWs	Aron Wiesenfeld
AxR	Alex Ross
AyB	Allyn Brodsky
BA	Brent Anderson
BaB	Barry Blair
BAn	Bill Anderson
BAp	Brian Althorp
BAu	Brian Augustyn
BB	Brian Bolland
BBa	Bernard Bailey
BbB	Bob Brown
BBB	Bob Boze Bell
BBh	Brett Booth
BbK	Bob Kanigher
BBl	Bret Blevins
BbL	Bob Lamme
BBr	Brett Breeding
BCe	Bobbie Chase
BCh	Bernard Chang
BCi	Brandon Choi
BD	Bob Davis
BDC	Brent D Carpenter
BDn	Ben Dunn
BE	Bill Elder
BEd	Ben Edlund
BEv	Bill Everett
BEw	Brett Ewins
BF	Bob Fujitani(Fuje)
BG	Bill Griffith
BH	Bob Hall
BHa	Bo Hampton
BHg	Burne Hogarth
BHi	Bryan Hitch
BHr	Ben Herrera
BHs	Bob Harras
BiT	Bill Tucci
BK	Bernie Krigstein
BKa	Bob Kane
BKi	Barry Kitson
BKr	Brandon Kruse
BKs	Babara Kesel
BL	Bob Layton
BLb	Bob Lubbers
BlH	Bill Hobbs
BLr	Bob Larkin
BLs	Batton Lash
BLw	Brian Lewis
BM	Barry Mitchel
BMB	Brian Michael Bendis
BMc	Bob McLeod
BMC	B. McCorkindale
BML	Bill Messner-Loebs
BMs	Bill Maus
BMy	Brendon McCarthy
BNa	Bob Napton
BnP	Brian Pulido
BO	Bob Oskner
BoW	Bob Wood
BP	Bob Powell
BPe	Brandon Peterson
BPr	Bruno Premaini
BR	Bill Reinhold
BRa	Ben Raab
BrM	Brian Murray
BRo	Boody Rogers
BrP	Bruce Patterson
BS	Bart Sears
BSf	Brian Stelfreeze
BSt	Beau Smith
BSz	Bill Sienkiewicz
BT	Bryan Talbot
BTn	Billy Tan
Buzz	Buzz
BV	Boris Vallejo
BVa	Brad Vancata
BW	Basil Wolverton
BWa	Bill Ward
BWg	Bill Willingham
BWh	Bill Whitman
BWi	Bob Wiacek
BWo	Bill Woggin
BWr	Berni Wrightson
BWS	Barry Windsor-Smith
BZ	Bruce Zick
CAd	Charlie Adlard
CaS	Cam Smith
CAx	Chris Alexander
CB	Carl Barks
CBa	Chris Bachalo
CBi	Charles Biro
CBu	Carl Burgos
CCa	Charles Caldes
CCB	C. C. Beck
CCl	Chris Claremont
Ccs	Chriscross
CCt	Claudio Castellini
CCu	Chuck Cuidera
CDi	Chuck Dixon
CDo	Colleen Doran
CE	Carlos Ezquerra
CF	Creig Flessel
CG	Carlos Garzon
CH	Chad Hunt
ChB	Charles Berger
ChG	Chester Gould
ChM	Chris Marrinan
CHm	Cully Hamner
ChT	Chas Truog
Chu	Ernie Chua
CI	Carmine Infantino
CIv	Chris Ivy
CJ	Casey Jones
CK	Cam Kennedy
CMc	Colin McNeil
CNn	Cedric Nocon
CNr	Cary Nord
CP	Carl Potts
CPa	Carlos Pacheco
CPi	Carlos Pino
CPr	Christopher Priest
CQ	Charles Quinlan
CR	P. Craig Russell
CRb	Cliff Robinson
CrB	Craig Brasfield
CS	Curt Swan
CsB	Chris Batista
CSM	C. S. Moe
CsM	Chris Moeller
CSp	Chris Sprouse
CU	Chris Ulm
CV	Charles Vess
CW	Chris Warner
CWf	Chance Wolf
CWi	Colin Wilson
CWn	Chris Weston
CYp	Chap Yaep
DA	Dan Adkins
DAb	Dusty Abell
DaC	Dan Castellaneta
DaF	Dan Fraga
DaG	Dave Garcia
DaM	Danny Miki
DAn	Dan Abnett
DaR	Darrick Robertson
DaW	Damon Willis
Day	Dan Day
DAy	Dick Ayers
DB	D. Battlefield
DB	Denis Beauvais
DBa	Dan Barry
DBk	Darryl Banks
DBl	Danny Bulanadi
DBr	Dick Briefer
DBs	John Barras
DBw	Doug Braithwaite
DC	Dave Cockrum
DCn	Don Cameron
DCw	Denys Cowan
DD	Dick Dillin
DdB	David Boller
DDv	Dan Davis
DdW	David Williams
DE	D. Elliot
DeH	Dave Hund
DeM	Dev Madan
DeT	Derek Thomason
DFg	Duncan Fegredo
DFr	Danny Fingeroth
DG	Dick Giordano
DGb	Dave Gibbons
DGC	D.G. Chichester
DgM	Doug Moench
DgR	Doug Roea
DGr	Dan Green
DH	Don Heck
DHa	Drew Hayes
DHv	Dave Hoover
DHz	Douglas Hazlewood
DiF	Dick Foreman
DJ	Dennis Jensen
DJa	Dennis Janke
DJu	Dan Jurgens
DK	Dale Keown
DkB	Dick Browne
DkG	Daerick Gross
DKi	Dennis Kitchen
DL	Dave Lapham
DlB	Daniel Brereton
DLp	Dave Louapre
DLw	Dan Lawlis
DM	David Mazzucchelli
DMc	Dave McKean
DMD	Dwayne McDuffie
DMG	Don McGregor
DMk	David Mack
DMn	Duke Mighten
DMt	Dean Motter
DN	Don Newton
DnS	Dan Steffan
DO	Dave Olbrich
DoC	Dario Carrasco
DOe	Dark One
DoM	Doug Mahnke
DON	O'Neil, Denny
DOr	Dean Ormston
DP	Don Perlin
DPo	Porch, David
DPs	Dan Panosian
DPw	Power, Dermot
DQ	David Quinn
DR	Ross, David
Rd	Richard Delgado
DRi	Don Rico
DRo	Denis Rodier
DRo	David Roach
DS	Dave Sim
DSh	Dave Sheridan
DSp	Dan Spiegle
DSs	Don Simpson
DSt	Dave Stevens
DSw	Dan Sweetman
DT	Dwayne Turner
DTs	Dann Thomas
DTy	David Taylor
DvA	David Ammerman
DVa	Dan Vado
DvC	Dave Cooper
DvD	Dave Dorman
DvH	David Hearnes
DvJ	Dave Johnson
DvL	David Lloyd
DvM	David Micheline
DvR	David Reed
DW	Doug Wildey
DWe	David Wenzel
DZ	Dean Zachary
EA	Edd Ashe
EB	Ed Barreto
EBe	Ed Benes
EC	Ernie Colon
ECa	Eddie Campbell
ECh	Ernie Chan
EcS	Eric Silvestri
EdM	Edward Moritz
EDo	Evan Dorkin
EH	Ed Hannigan
EhH	Ernest Hart
EHi	E.E. Hibbard
EHr	Everette Hartsoe
EiS	Eric Shanower
EK	Everett R. Kinsler
EL	Erik Larsen

Abbr.	Name	Abbr.	Name	Abbr.	Name	Abbr.	Name
ELe	Elaine Lee	GS	Gustav Schrotter	JCt	Joe Carter	JOn	James Owen
ELu	Eric Van Lustbader	GSh	Gerry Shamray	JCx	Jeromy Cox	JoP	Joe Phillips
EM	Esteban Maroto	GSr	Geoff Senior	JCz	Jerry Cruz	JoS	Joe Shuster
EN	Earl Norem	GT	George Tuska	JD	Jan Duursema	JOs	John Ostrander
ENB	E. Nelson Bridwell	GTk	George Tukell	JDa	Jack Davis	JOt	Jose Ortiz
EP	Edmund Perryman	GtM	Grant Miehm	JDo	Julie Doucet	JoW	Joss Whedon
ERC	E.R. Cruz	GW	Gahan Wilson	JDx	John Dixon	JOy	Jerry Ordway
ErP	Eric Pence	GWb	George Woodbridge	JDy	Jo Duffy	JP	Jo Polseno
ErS	Eric Stephenson	GWt	Greg Wright	JeJ	Jeff Jones	JP	Jimmy Palmiotti
ESM	Elliot S. Maggin	GyA	Gary Amaro	JeM	Jerome Moore	JPe	Jonathan Peterson
EW	Ed Waldman	GyC	Gerry Conway	JeP	Jerry Prosser	JPh	James Perham
EzW	Ezra Whiteman	GyD	Guy Davis	JeR	James Robinson	JPi	Joe St.Pierre
FaN	Fabian Nicieza	GyM	Gary Martin	JEs	John Estes	JPL	John Paul Leon
FB	Frank Brunner	GyW	Gay Welker	JF	John Forte	JPn	Jason Pearson
FBe	Frank Bolle	HaE	Harlan Ellison	JFM	John Francis Moore	JQ	Joe Quesada
FBk	Fred Burke	HB	Hernandez Brothers	JFr	John Freeman	JR	John Romita
FC	Frank Cirocco	HbK	Hannibal King	JFy	James Fry III	JR2	John Romita, Jr.
FdS	Fred Schiller	HC	Howard Chaykin	JG	Jackson Guice	JRd	J. Redondo
FF	Frank Frazetta	HcK	Henry C. Kiefer	JGa	Jack Gaughan	JRe	John Royle
FFo	Frank Fosco	HD	H. Dougherty	JGr	Jerry Grandmetti	JRl	Jim Royle
FG	Floyd Gottfredson	HFl	Homer Flemming	JGz	Jorge Gonzalez	JRi	J Richardson
FGu	Fred Guardineer	HH	Hugh Haynes	JH	Jack Herman	JRo	J. Rosenberger
FH	Flint Henry	HjK	H. J. Kihi	JH	Jack Hearne	JRo	Jerry Robinson
FM	Frank Miller	HK	Harvey Kurtzman	JHa	Jim Harmon	JRs	John Ross
FMc	Frank McLaughlin	HMe	Howard Mackie	JhB	John Beatty	JRu	Joe Rubinstein
FMe	Fred Meagher	HMo	H. Mercadoocasio	JhD	John Dell	JRv	Judith Reeves-Stevens
FP	Frank R. Paul	HMz	Henry Martinez	JHi	John Higgins	JRy	John Ridgeway
FR	Frank Robbins	HN	Howard Nostrand	JHk	John Hicklenton	JRz	John Rozum
FrG	Frank Giacoia	HNg	Hoang Nguyen	JHl	James Hudnall	JS	Javier Saltares
FrS	Frank Spinks	HP	Harvey Pekar	JHo	John Holdredge	JS3	Jim Sanders III
FS	Frank Springer	HPo	Howard Porter	JHr	Jaime Hernandez	JSb	Jonathan Sibal
Fso	Francesco	HR	H. Rasmussen	JHw	Jamie Hewlett	JSc	Jeffery Scott
FSt	Foolbert Sturgeon	HSa	Harry Sahle	JI	Jim Infantino	JSC	J. Scott Campbell
	(& Frank Stack)	HSm	Howard Shum	JiC	Jim Callahan	JSe	John Severin
FT	Frank Thorne	HSn	Howard Simpson	JiS	Jim Shooter	JsG	Justin Green
FTa	Francis Takenaga	HT	Herb Trimpe	JJ	Jeff Johnson	JSh	Jim Sherman
FTd	Fred Todd	HuR	Humberto Ramos	JJB	JJ Birch	JSi	Jeff Smith
GaF	Gardner Fox	HWe	Howard Weinstein	JJn	Julius Jackson	JSm	Joe Simon
GB	Geoffrey Biggs	HwP	Howard Post	JJo	J.B. Jones	JSn	Jim Starlin
GBl	George Bell	HyG	Harley Griffiths	JJu	Joe Jusko	JSo	Jim Steranko
GBu	Greg Budget	IaC	Ian Churchhill	JK	Jack Kirby	JSon	Joe Staton
GC	Gene Colan	IEd	Ian Edginton	JKa	Jack Kamen	JsP	Jay Scott Pike
GCa	Greg Capullo	IG	Ian Gibson	JkS	Jack Sparling	JSt	Joe Sinnott
GCh	Gary Cohn	IK	Ian Kennedy	JKu	Joe Kubert	JT	James Tucker
GD	Gene Day	IN	Irv Novick	JKz	Jack Katz	JTg	John Tartaglione
GDu	Gary Dumm	IS	Irving Spector	JL	Jose Lopez	JTo	John Totleben
GE	George Evans	ISb	Irvin Steinberg	JLb	Jeph Loeb	JuB	Julie Bell
GeH	Gene Ha	IV	Ivan Velez, Jr.	JLd	Joe Lansdale	JV	Jim Valentino
GEn	Garth Ennis	JA	Jack Abel	JLe	Jim Lee	JVF	John Van Fleet
GEr	Gary Erskine	JaB	Jack Binder	JLi	Joseph M. Linsner	JW	Jack A Warren
GF	Glenn Fabry	JaD	Jamie Delano	JIT	Jill Thompson	JWa	Jim Watson
GfD	Geof Darrow	JaL	Jae Lee	JLv	Jim Lavery	JWf	Joseph Wolfe
GFo	Gerald Forton	JAl	Jeff Albrecht	JM	Jim Mooney	JWi	J.H. Williams
GFr	Gary Frank	JAn	Jeff Anderson	JMC	John McCrea	JWk	John Watkiss
GFs	George Frese	JAo	John Albano	JMd	Joe Madureira	JWo	Jim Woodring
GFx	Gill Fox	JAp	Jim Aparo	JMD	J.M. DeMatteis	JWp	Jason Waltrip
GG	Gabe Gecko	JAr	John Arcudi	JMi	Jeff Mariotte	JWt	John Waltrip
Ggn	Geggan	JB	John Buscema	JmL	Jim Lawson	JyD	Jay Disbrow
GgP	George Pratt	JBa	Jim Baikie	JMn	Joe Maneely	JyS	Jerry Serpe
GHe	Gilbert Hernandez	JBa	Jim Balent	JmP	James Pascoe	JZ	Jorge Zaffino
GHi	Graham Higgins	JBe	John Beeston	JMr	Jeff Moore	JZe	Joe Zabel
Gl	Geoff Isherwood	JBg	Jon Bogdanove	JMs	Jeff Matsuda	JZy	Joseph Zyskowski
GiS	Gilbert Shelton	JBi	Jerry Bingham	JMt	Joe Martin	K&R	Kane & Romita
GJ	Gerard Jones	JBl	Jesus Blasco	JMu	Jon J. Muth	KB	Kyle Baker
GK	Gil Kane	JBm	John Broom	JMy	Jeffrey Moy	KBa	Ken Battlefield
GKl	George Klein	JBn	John Burns	JMy	Jim McCarthy	KBk	Kurt Busiek
GL	Garry Leach	JBo	John Bolton	JMz	Jose Marzan	KD	Kieron Dwyer
GlD	Glyn Dillon	JBr	June Brigman	JnM	Jason Minor	KDe	Kim Deitch
GLz	Greg Luzniak	JBt	Jeff Butler	JnR	John Riley	KDM	Kim DeMulder
GM	Gray Morrow	JBu	Jack Burnley	JNR	John Ney Rieber	KEa	Kevin Eastman
GMc	Gerald McCann	JBy	John Byrne	JnS	John Smith	KeL	Ken Lashley
GMo	Grant Morrison	JBz	Joe Benitez	JO	Joe Orlando	KeW	Kevin Walker
GMy	Graham Manley	JCa	John Calnan	JoA	Jo Alibaster	KG	Keith Giffen
GN	Graham Nolan	JCf	Jim Calafiore	JoB	Joe Bennett	KGa	Kerry Gammill
GP	George Perez	JCh	Joe Chiodo	JoC	Joe Casey	KHd	Kevin Hopgood
GPi	Gene Pamai	JCo	Jack Cole	JOb	James O'Barr	KHt	Kyle Hotz
Grl	Graham Ingles	JCp	John Cooper	JoG	Joe Giella	KHu	Ken Hultgren
GrL	Greg LaRocque	JCr	Johnny Craig	JoM	Joe Musial	KiA	Kia Asamiya

Abbreviation	Name
KJ	Klaus Janson
KJa	Kirk Javinen
KJo	Kelley Jones
KK	Karl Kesel
KlA	Karl Alstaetter
KlK	Karl Kerschl
KlS	Karl Story
KM	Kevin Maguire
KN	Kevin Nowlan
KoK	Kevin Kobasic
KON	Kevin O'Neill
KP	Keith Pollard
KPl	Kilian Plunkett
KR	Kim Raymond
Kr	Kirner
KS	Kurt Schaffenberger
KSm	Kevin Smith
KSW	Keith S. Wilson
KSy	Ken Steacy
KtH	Kurt Hathaway
KVH	Kevin VanHook
KW	Kent Williams
KWe	Kevin West
KWi	Keith Williams
KWo	Kirk Van Wormer
LbC	Leonard B. Cole
LC	Lou Cameron
LCh	Lillian Chestney
LDr	Larry Dresser
LDu	Leo Duranona
LDz	Luis Dominguez
LEl	Lee Elias
LeS	Len Strazewski
LF	Lou Fine
LHa	Larry Hama
LI	Larry Ivie
LiM	Linda Medley
LJi	Leonardo Jimenez
LKa	Len Kaminski
LLe	Lank Leonard
LLi	Larry Lieber
LM	Lou Morales
LMa	Larry Mahlstedt
LMc	Luke McDonnell
LMd	Lee Moder
LMr	Lee Marrs
LnS	Lin Streeter
Low	John Lowe
LRs	Luke Ross
LS	Lee Sullivan
LSh	Liam Sharp
LSi	Louise Simonson
LSn	Larry Stroman
LSt	Leonard Starr
LuH	Lou Harrison
LW	Lee Weeks
LWn	Len Wein
LyW	Larry Welch
LZ	Louis Zansky
MA	Murphy Anderson
MaG	Manny Galan
MaH	Mark Hempel
Man	Roland Mann
MaS	Mark Schmitz
MaT	Mark Tenney
MB	Matt Baker
MBa	Mark Bagley
MBe	M. Belardinelli
MBg	Mark Badger
MBi	M. Bailey
MBm	Mary Bierbaum
MBn	Mike Baron
MBr	Mark Bright
MBu	Mark Buckingham
MBy	Mitch Byrd
MC	Mike Collins
MCa	Marc Campos
MCh	Mike Chen
MCi	Mark Crilley
MCl	Mike Clark
MCn	Max Allan Collins
MCo	Mark Chiarello
MCr	Mike Carlin
MCW	M.C. Wyman
MCy	Mike Carey
MD	Mort Drucker
MD2	Mike Deodato, Jr.
MDa	Malcolm Davis
MDb	M. DeZuniga
MDb	Maurice Del Bourgo
MDo	Mike Dorey
MDr	Mike Dringenberg
ME	Mike Esposito
MEg	Marty Egeland
MeP	Mike Parobeck
MeW	Mike Weringo
MF	Matt Fox
MFl	Michael Fleisher
MFm	Mark Farmer
MFr	Michael Jan Friedman
MG	Mike Gustovich
MGi	Michael T. Gilbert
MGo	Michael Golden
MGr	Mike Grell
MGs	Martin Griffiths
MGu	Mark Gruenwald
MGy	Mick Gray
MHi	Michael Higgins
MHo	Matt Howarth
MHs	Mike Heisler
MHw	Matt Hawkins
MHy	Matt Haley
MI	Medio Iorio
MiA	Michael Allred
MiB	Mike Barr
MiS	Mizuki Sakakibara
MJ	Malcolm Jones
MK	Mike Kaluta
MkB	Mike Barreiro
MKd	Malcolm Kildale
MkF	Mike Friedrich
MkH	Mike Hoffer
MkK	Mike McKenna
MkW	Mark Wheatley
MlB	Michael Bair
MLe	Mike Leeke
MLr	Michael Lark
MM	Mike Manley
MMc	M. McMahon
MMe	Mort Meskin
MMi	Michael Mignola
MMK	Mike McKone
MMo	Mark Moretti
MMr	Mark Millar
MMy	Marat Mychaels
MN	Mike Netzer
MnN	Martin Nodell
Moe	Moebius
MP	Mike Ploog
MPa	Mark Pacella
MPc	Mark Paniccia
MPk	Martin Pasko
MPn	Mark Pennington
MR	Marshall Rogers
MRa	Mac Raboy
MRc	Mark Ricketts
MRi	Mike Richardson
MRo	Mike Roberts
MRy	Matt Ryan
MS	Mark Silvestri
MSe	Marie Severin
MSh	Mark Schultz
MsM	Mike S. Miller
MSo	Mark Sasso
MSt	Malcolm Smith
MsW	Morris Waldinger
MSy	Mike Sekowsky
MSz	J.Michael Straczynski
MT	Mark Texeira
MtB	Matt Broome
MTk	Masashi Tanaka
MV	Mike Vosburg
MvR	Melvin Rubi
MvS	Marvin Stein
MW	Mary Wilshire
MWa	Mark Waid
MWg	Matt Wagner
MWn	Marv Wolfman
MWs	M. Weiss
Mys	Myers
MZ	Mike Zeck
MZi	Michael Zulli
NA	Neal Adams
NBy	Norm Breyfogle
NC	Nick Cardy
ND	Nigel Dobbyn
Nel	Nelson
NGa	Neil Gaiman
NHa	Neil Hanson
NKu	Andy Kubert
NMa	Nathan Massengill
NN	Norman Nodel
NNa	Nick Napolitano
NPl	Noly Panaligan
NR	Nestor Redondo
NRd	Norm Rapmund
NS	Norm Saunders
NSH	N. Steven Harris
NV	Neil Vokes
NyC	Nancy Collins
OM	Otto Messmer
OW	Ogden Whitney
PaD	Paco Diaz
PaK	Paris T. Karounos
PaP	Paul Pelletier
PB	Pat Broderick
PBd	Philip Bond
PC	Paul Chadwick
PcH	Poch
PCu	Paris Cullins
PD	Peter Doherty
PDd	Peter David
PDi	Paul Dini
PFe	Pascual Ferry
PG	Paul Gulacy
PGa	Phil Gascoine
PGn	Paul Guinan
PGr	Peter Grau
PGv	Paul Gustavson
PhH	Phil Hester
PJ	Phil Jimminiz
PJe	Paul Jenkins
PKr	Peter Krause
PlA	Paul Abrams
PLa	Peter Laird
PMo	Pete Morisi
PMs	Pat Mills
PNe	Paul Neary
PNu	Philip Nutman
PO	Patrick Olliffe
PP	Pop Payne
PPo	Paul Pope
PPr	Pat Prichard
PQ	Peter Quinones
PR	Paul Ryan
PrC	Peter Costanza
PrG	Peter Gross
PrM	Peter Milligan
PS	Paul Smith
PSj	Peter Snejbjerg
PtL	Patrick Lee
PuD	Paul Danner
PuJ	Paul Johnson
PuK	Paul Kupperberg
RA	Ross Andru
RAJ	R.A. Jones
RaP	Rachel Pollack
RB	Rich Buckler
RbB	Robert Bernstein
RbC	Robert Campenella
RBe	Ramon Bernado
RBn	Ryan Benjamin
RBr	Rick Burchett
RBu	Robert Burns
RC	Reed Crandall
RCa	Richard Case
RCl	Ricky Carralero
RCo	Richard Corben
RCr	Robert Crumb
RCz	Roger Cruz
RDB	Randy DuBerkr
RdM	Raymond Marais
RDm	Rodolfo Damaggio
RdD	Richard Delgado
RE	Ric Estrada
REv	Ray Evans
RF	Ron Frenz
RFl	Robert Fleming
RG	Ron Garney
RGd	Ruben Gerard
RgM	Rags Morales
RGr	Randy Green
RGs	R. Grossman
RGT	R.G. Taylor
RGu	Rebecca Guay
RH	Russ Heath
RHa	Rory Hayes
RHe	Richard Horie
RHo	Rick Hoberg
RHo	Rich Howell
RiB	Richard Bennett
Rip	Riply
RJ	Robert Jenney
RJn	Robert Jones
RkB	Rick Bryant
RkL	Rick Leach
RKu	Roy Krenkel
RL	Rick Leonardi
RLd	Rob Liefeld
RLe	Rik Levins
RLg	Roger Langridge
RLm	Ron Lim
RLv	R. Livingstone
RM	Rick Magyar
RMc	Ralph Macchio
RMn	Roland Mann
RMo	Ruben Moreira
RMr	Roy Allan Martinez
RMz	Ron Marz
RN	Rudy Nebres
RnT	Ron Tinker
RoR	Ron Randall
RoW	on Wagner
RP	Rudy Palais
RPc	Richard Pace
RPi	Richard Pini
RQu	Randy Queen
RR	Ray Ramsey
RRa	Rich Rankin
RS	Ron Smith
RsB	Russell Braun
RSd	Randy Stradley
RsM	Russ Manning
RSm	Robin Smith
RSt	Roger Stern
RT	Romeo Tanghal
RTH	Robert Hebbard
RTs	Roy Thomas
RTu	Ron Turner
RuG	Rube Goldberg
RV	Rick Veitch
RvB	Raeburn Van Buren

RW . . . . . Robert Williams	SLi . . . . Steve Lightle	TBd. . . . . . Tim Bradstreet	TSr . . . . Terry Shoemaker
RWa . . . . Reed Waller	SLo . . . . Scott Lobdell	TBe. . . . . Terry Beatty	TT . . . . . Timothy Truman
RWb . . . . . . Robert Webb	SM. . . . . Steve Miller	TBm . . . . . Tom Bierbaum	TTg. . . . . Tom Taggart
RyE . . . . Randy Emberlin	SMa . Shawn Martinbrough	TC. . . . . Travis Charest	TTn. . . . . . . Ty Templeton
RyL. . . . . Ray Lago	SmC. . . . . . . Sam Citron	TCk . . . . . . Tomm Coker	TV . . . . Tim Vigil
RyR. . . . . Rodney Ramos	SMc . . . . . Scott McDaniel	TD . . . . . . Tony DeZuniga	TVE. . . . Trevor Von Eeden
S&K. . . . . . Simon & Kirby	SMl . . . . . Scott McCloud	TDF . . . . . . Tom DeFalco	TvS. . . . . Trevor Scott
S&S. . . . Siegel & Shuster	SML . . . . Sean McLaughlin	TDr. . . . . . . Tom Derenick	TWo . . . . . Teri Sue Wood
SA . . . . . Sergio Aragones	SMo . . . . Sheldon Moldoff	TDz . . . . Todd DeZago	TY . . . . Tom Yeates
SaB . . . . Sam Becker	SMt . . . . . Steve Mattsson	TeB . . . . Tex Blaisdell	TyD. . . . . . . Terry Dodson
Sal . . . . Sal Amendola	SMz . . Seymour Moskowitz	TeH . . . . Ted Halsted	TyH . . . . Tony Harris
SAP . . Shea Anton Pensa	SnW . . . . Stan Woch	TEl . . . . Tim Eldred	TyT . . . . . . Tony Tallarico
SaV. . . . . Sal Velluto	SPa . . . . . Stephen Platt	TFH. . . . . T. F. Hing	VAz . . . . Vincent Alcazar
SB. . . . . Sal Buscema	Spk . . . . Spark	TG . . . . . Tom Grummett	VB . . . . . . Vaughn Bode
SBi . . . . . Stephen Bissette	SPl. . . . . . Scott Phillips	TGb . . . . Tom Grindberg	VcL . . . . . . Vince Locke
SBs . . . . Simon Bisley	SPr . . . . . Stefan Petrucha	TGo . . . . . . Till Goodman	VGi. . . . . Vince Giarrano
SBt . . . . Steve Butler	SR . . . . Steve Rude	TH. . . . . . . Tim Hamilton	ViC. . . . . Vince Colletta
SC . . . . Sid Check	SRf . . . . . . Sean Ruffner	THa . . . . Tim Harris	VMk. . . . . . . Val Mayerik
ScB . . . . . . Scott Benefiel	SRo . . . . Spain Rodriguez	TJn . . . . . . Todd Johnson	VMo. . . . Vincent Morosco
ScC . . . . Scott Clark	SS. . . . . Stan Sakai	TKa . . . Terry Kavanagh	VP . . . . Victor Prezio
SCh . . . . . Sean Chen	SSc . . . . Sean Scoffield	TKn . . . . . . Trent Kaniuga	VRu . . . . . . Vince Russell
SCi . . . . . Sergio Cariello	SSe . . . . Steven T. Seagle	TKr . . Teddy H. Kristiansen	VS . . . . Val Semeiks
ScK . . . . Scott Kolins	SSh . . . . Sean Shaw	TL . . . . Tom Lyle	VV . . . . Vagner Vargas
ScL . . . . Scott Lee	SSh . . . . Syd Shores	TLa . . . . . . Terry LaBan	WaP . . . . . Warren Pleece
SCp . . . . . . Sam Cooper	SSm . . . . Steve Sampson	TLw . . . . Terral Lawrence	WB . . . . . . Wayne Boring
SCr. . . . . . . Steve Crespo	SSr . . . . . . Steve Skroce	TM . . . . . Todd McFarlane	WBu. . . . . . W. Burroughs
SCW. . . . . S. Clay Wilson	SSt. . . . . Steve Stern	TmB . . . . . . Tim Burgard	WE . . . . Will Eisner
SCy . . . . . Simon Colby	ST . . . . Sal Trapain	TmC . . . . Tom Christopher	WEl. . . . . . . Warren Ellis
SD . . . . Steve Ditko	StA. . . . . Stephen Addeo	TMd . . . . . Tom Mandrake	WiS . . . . . William Stout
SDi . . . . Steve Dillon	StB . . . . . . Scott Benson	TMK . . . . Ted McKeever	WJo. . . . . Walter Johnson
SDr. . . . . Stan Drake	StC . . . . . Stan Campbell	TMo . . . . . Tom Morgan	WK. . . . . Walt Kelly
SDR . . . . Sam DeLaRosa	StE . . . . . . Steve Erwin	TmR . . . . Tom Ryder	Wld . . . . Andrew Wildman
SEa . . . . Scott Eaton	StG . . . . . . Steve Grant	TMr. . . . . . Terry Moore	WlP . . . . . . Walter Palais
SeM . . . . . . Steve Montano	StK. . . . . Stan Kaye	TMs . . . . . . Tom Mason	WmB . . . . William Bossart
SeP . . . . . . Sean Phillips	StL . . . . Stan Lee	TmT . . . . . . Tom Teney	WMc . . . . Walter McDaniel
SEp . . . . Steve Epting	StM . . . . Stanley Maxwell	TMw . . . . Tom McCraw	WMo. . . . . . Win Mortimer
SeT . . . . . . Steve Tappin	StP. . . . . Steve Pugh	TNa. . . . . . Ted Naifeh	WmW . . . . William Walsh
SEt . . . . . Steve Englehart	SVa . . . . . . Steve Vance	TnD. . . . . . Tony Daniel	Woj. . . . Chuck Wojtkiewicz
SF . . . . . Sal Finnocchiaro	SvG . . . . . Steve Gerber	TnS . . . . . Tristan Schane	WP . . . . Wendy Pini
SFr. . . . . Simon Freeman	SvL. . . . . Salvador Larroca	TNu. . . . . . Todd Nauck	WPo . . . . . Whilce Portacio
SFu . . . . . Simon Furman	SvP. . . . . Steve Parkhouse	TO . . . . . Thomas Oughton	WR . . . . Werner Roth
SG. . . . . . Sam Glanzman	SvS . . . . . . Steve Stiles	ToT . . . . . Tony Takezaki	WS. . . . . . Walt Simonson
SGa. . . . Stefano Gaudino	SW . . . . . Scott Williams	TOz . . . . . . Tayyar Ozkan	WSm . . . . . Will Simpson
SGe . . . . Sid Greene	SWi. . . . . Skip Williamson	TP. . . . . Tom Palmer	WW . . . . . . Wally Wood
SHa . . . . Scott Hanna	SwM. . . . Shawn McManus	TPe. . . . . . . Tom Peyer	YG . . . . Yvel Guichet
ShG. . . . Shannon Gallant	SY . . . . . . Steve Yeowell	TR . . . . Tom Raney	YuK . . . . . Yukito Kisniro
ShM . . . . . Sheldon Mayer	Syk. . . . . Siryk	TR . . . . Ted Richards	
SHn . . . . Simon Harrison	SyM. . . . . Sidney Miller	TrR. . . . . . . Trina Robbins	
SHp . . . . . Scott Hampton	SZ . . . . Steven Zyskowski	TS . . . . Tom Sutton	
SI . . . . . . Stuart Immonen	TA . . . . Terry Austin	TSa . . . . . . Tony Salmons	
SK. . . . . Sam Kieth	TAr . . . . Tom Artis	TSe . . . . Tim Sale	
SL. . . . . . . Steve Leialoha	TB . . . . Tim Boxell	TSg. . . . . Tom Sniegoski	

GENERAL ABBREVIATIONS FOR COMICS LISTINGS

A: . . . . Appearance of	GAm . . . . Graphic Album	pt. or Pt. . . . . Part
(a). . . . . Artist	GN or GNv . . . . . Graphic Novel	rep. . . . . Reprinted issue
Adapt. . . . . Adaptation	G-Size . . . . Giant Size	R:. . . . . Return/Revival of
Anniv. . . . . Anniversary	HC . . . . Hardcover	rtd. . . . . Retold
Ann.# . . . . Annual	I:. . . . . Introduction of	(s) . . . . Scripted/Written by
(a&c) . . . . Art & Cover	(i) . . . . Inks by	S.A. . . . . Silver Age
(a&pl). . . . . Art & Plot	IR: . . . . Identity Revealed	SC . . . . Softcover
(a&s). . . . . Art & Script	J: . . . . Joins of	(s&i) . . . . Scripts & inks
B: . . . . Beginning of	K-Size . . . . King Size	Spec. . . . . Special
b: . . . . Birth of	L: . . . . Leaving of	TPB . . . . . . Trade Paperback
BU: . . . . Back-Up Story	N: . . . . New Costume	T.U. . . . . Team-up
C: . . . . Cameo Appearance	N#. . . . . No Issue Number	V: or vs. . . . . Versus
(c) . . . . Cover	O: . . . . Origin of	W: . . . . Wedding of
(c&s) . . . . . Cover and Script	P(c) . . . . Painted Cover	w/ . . . . With
D: . . . . . . Death/Destruction of	(p). . . . . Pencils by	w/o . . . . Without
Ed. . . . . Edition	PF . . . . Prestige Format	x-over . . . . Crossover with
E: . . . . Ending of	Ph(c) . . . . . Photographic cover	
F: . . . . Features	(pl). . . . . Plotted by	
G.A. . . . . Golden Age	Prev. . . . . Preview	

BIBLIOGRAPHY

Daniels, Les. *Comix: A History of Comic Books in America.* New York, NY: Bonanza Books, 1971.

Gerber, Ernst. *The Photo Journal Guide to Comic Books.* Minden, NV: Gerber Publishing, 1989. Vols. 1 & 2.

Gerber, Ernst. *The Photo Journal Guide to Marvel Comics.* Minden, NV: Gerber Publishing, 1991. Vols. 3 & 4.

Goulart, Ron. *The Adventurous Decade.* New Rochelle, NY: Arlington House, 1975.

Goulart, Ron. *Comic Book Culture, An Illustrated History.* Portland, OR: Collectors Press, 2000

Goulart, Ron. *The Encyclopedia of American Comics.* New York, NY. Facts on File Publications, 1990.

Goulart, Ron. *Over 50 Years of American Comic Books.* Lincolnwood, IL: Mallard Press, 1991.

Hegenburger, John. *Collectors Guide to Comic Books.* Radnor, PA: Wallace Homestead Book Company, 1990.

Kennedy, Jay. *The Official Underground and Newave Price Guide.* Cambridge, MA: Boatner Norton Press, 1982.

Malan, Dan. *The Complete Guide to Classics Collectibles.* St. Louis, MO: Malan Classical Enterprises, 1991.

Miller, John Jackson et al. *The Standard Catalog of Comic Books.* Iola, WI: Krause Publications, 2002.

O'Neil, Dennis. *Secret Origins of DC Super Heroes.* New York, NY: Warner Books, 1976.

Overstreet, Robert. *The Overstreet Comic Book Price Guide (35th Edition).* New York, NY. Random House, 2005

Rovin, Jeff. *The Encyclopedia of Super Heroes.* New York, NY: Facts on File Publications, 1985.

Rovin, Jeff. *The Encyclopedia of Super Villians.* New York, NY: Facts on File Publications, 1987.

Thompson, Don & Maggie. *The Golden Age of Comics, Summer 1982.* Tainpa, FL: New Media Publishing, 1982.

DC COMICS

A. BIZARRO

1999

1 (of 4) SvG,MBr,F:Al Bizarro 2.50
2 SvG,MBr,A:Superman 2.50
3 SvG,MBr, ... 2.50
4 SvG,MBr, Viva Bizarro 2.50

ACCELERATE

DC/Vertigo, June, 2000

1 (of 4) Great Escape 3.00
2 Great Escape,pt.2 . . . . 3.00
3 Great Escape,pt.3 . . . . 3.00
4 Great Escape,pt.4,concl. 3.00

Action Comics #29 © DC Comics, Inc.

ACTION

June, 1938

1 JoS,I&O:Superman;Rescues Evelyn
   Curry from electric chair . 650,000.00
2 JoS,V:Emil Norvell 65,000.00
3 JoS,V:Thorton Blakely 45,000.00
4 JoS,V:Coach Randall 27,000.00
5 JoS,Emergency of
   Vallegho Dam 27,000.00
6 JoS,I:Jimmy Olsen,
   V:Nick Williams 27,000.00
7 JoS,V:Derek Niles 55,000.00
8 JoS,V:Gimpy 16,000.00
9 JoS,A:Det.Captain Reilly . . 16,000.00
10 JoS,Superman fights
   for prison reform 35,000.00
11 JoS,Disguised as
   Homer Ramsey 8,500.00
12 JoS,Crusade against
   reckless drivers 9,000.00
13 JoS,I:Ultra Humanite 17,000.00
14 JoS,BKa,V:Ultra Humanite,
   B:Clip Carson 9,000.00
15 JoS,BKa,Superman in
   Kidtown 15,000.00
16 JoS,BKa,Crusade against
   Gambling 8,000.00
17 JoS,BKa,V:Ultra Humanite. 12,000.00
18 JoS,BKa,V:Mr.Hamilton
   O:Three Aces 8,000.00
19 JoS,BKa,V:Ultra Humanite
   B:Superman (c) 10,000.00
20 JoS,BKa,V:Ultra Humanite. 10,000.00
21 JoS,BKa,V:Ultra Humanite. 10,000.00

22 JoS,BKa,War between Toran
   and Galonia 10,000.00
23 JoS,BKa,SMo,I:Lex Luthor 15,000.00
24 JoS,BKa,BBa,SMo,FGu,Meets
   Peter Carnahan 8,000.00
25 JoS,BKa,BBa,SMo,
   V:Medini 8,000.00
26 JoS,BKa,V:ClarenceCobalt . 8,000.00
27 JoS,BKa,V:Mr & Mrs.Tweed 5,000.00
28 JoS,BKa,JBu,V:Strongarm
   Bandit 5,000.00
29 JoS,BKa,V:Martin 6,000.00
30 JoS,BKa,V:Zolar 5,000.00
31 JoS,BKa,JBu,V:Baron
   Munsdorf 3,000.00
32 JoS,BKa,JBu,I:Krypto Ray Gun
   V:Mr.Preston 3,000.00
33 JoS,BKa,JBu,V:Brett Hall,
   O:Mr. America. 3,000.00
34 JoS,BKa,V:Jim Laurg. 3,000.00
35 JoS,BKa,V:Brock Walter . . . 3,000.00
36 JoS,BKa,V:StuartPemberton 3,000.00
37 JoS,BKa,V:Commissioner
   Kennedy, O:Congo Bill 3,400.00
38 JoS,BKa,V:Harold Morton . . 3,400.00
39 JoS,BKa,Meets Britt Bryson 3,400.00
40 JoS,BKa,Meets Nancy
   Thorgenson 3,400.00
41 JoS,BKa,V:Ralph Cowan,
   E:Clip Carson 2,900.00
42 V:Lex Luthor,I&O:Vigilante. . 4,000.00
43 V:Dutch O'Leary,Nazi(c) . . 2,800.00
44 V:Prof. Steffens,Nazi(c) . . . 2,800.00
45 V:Count Von Henzel,
   I:Stuff,Nazi(c) 2,800.00
46 V:The Domino 2,800.00
47 V:Lex Luthor—1st app. w/super
   powers,I:Powerstone 4,000.00
48 V:The Top. 2,500.00
49 I:Puzzler. 2,500.00
50 Meets Stan Doborak 2,500.00
51 I:Prankster. 3,000.00
52 V:Emperor of America 3,200.00
53 JBu,V:Night-Owl. 2,500.00
54 JBu,Meets Stanley
   Finchcomb 2,500.00
55 JBu,V:Cartoonist Al Hatt . . . 2,500.00
56 V:Emil Loring 2,500.00
57 V:Prankster 2,500.00
58 JBu,V:Adonis 2,500.00
59 I:Susie Thompkins,Lois
   Lane's niece 2,500.00
60 JBu,Lois Lane-Superwoman 2,500.00
61 JBu,Meets Craig Shaw 2,500.00
62 JBu,V:Admiral Von Storff . . . 2,500.00
63 JBu,V:Professor Praline. . . . 2,500.00
64 I:Toyman 2,500.00
65 JBu,V:Truman Treadwell . . . 2,500.00
66 JBu,V:Mr.Annister 2,500.00
67 JBu,Superman School for
   Officer's Training 2,500.00
68 A:Susie Thompkins 2,500.00
69 V:Prankster 2,500.00
70 JBu,V:Thinker 2,500.00
71 Superman Valentine's
   Day Special 2,000.00
72 V:Mr. Sniggle 2,000.00
73 V:Lucius Spruce. 2,000.00
74 Meets Adelbert Dribble 2,000.00
75 V:Johnny Aesop. 2,000.00
76 A Voyage with Destiny 2,000.00
77 V:Prankster 2,000.00
78 The Chef of Bohemia. 2,000.00
79 JBu,A:J. Wilbur Wolfingham 2,000.00
80 A:Mr. Mxyzptlk (2nd App.) . . 2,500.00
81 Meets John Nicholas 1,500.00
82 JBu,V:Water Sprite. 1,500.00

83 I:Hocus and Pocus. 1,500.00
84 JBu,V:Dapper Gang. 1,500.00
85 JBu,V:Toyman 1,500.00
86 JBu,V:Wizard of Wokit 1,500.00
87 V:Truck Hijackers. 1,500.00
88 A:Hocus and Pocus 1,500.00
89 V:Slippery Andy 1,500.00
90 JBu,V:Horace Rikker and the
   Amphi-Bandits 1,500.00
91 JBu,V:Davey Jones 1,200.00
92 JBu,V:Nowmie Norman 1,200.00
93 Superman Christmas story . 1,200.00
94 JBu,V:Bullwar 'Bull' Rylie . . 1,200.00
95 V:Prankster 1,200.00
96 V:Mr. Twister 1,200.00
97 A:Hocus and Pocus 1,200.00
98 V:Mr. Mxyzptlk, A:Susie
   Thompkins 1,500.00
99 V:Keith Langwell 1,200.00
100 I:InspectorErskineHawkins. 1,700.00
101 V:Specs Dour,A-Bomb(c). . 2,400.00
102 V:Mr. Mxyzptlk 1,300.00
103 V:Emperor Quexo 1,300.00
104 V:Prankster 1,300.00
105 Superman Christmas story 1,300.00
106 Clark Kent becomes Baron
   Edgestream 1,300.00
107 JBu,A:J.Wilbur Wolfingham 1,300.00
108 JBu,V:Vince Vincent 1,300.00
109 V:Prankster 1,300.00
110 A:Susie Thompkins 1,100.00
111 Cameras in the Clouds. . . . 1,100.00
112 V:Mr. Mxyzptlk 1,200.00
113 Just an Ordinary Guy 1,200.00
114 V:Mike Chesney. 1,200.00
115 Meets Arthur Parrish 1,200.00
116 A:J. Wilbur Wolfingham . . . 1,200.00
117 Superman Christmas story 1,200.00
118 Execution of Clark Kent . . . 1,200.00
119 Meets Jim Banning 1,200.00
120 V:Mike Foss 1,200.00
121 V:William Sharp 1,200.00
122 V:Charley Carson. 1,200.00
123 V:Skid Russell 1,200.00
124 Superman becomes
   radioactive 1,000.00
125 V:Lex Luthor. 1,000.00
126 V:Chameleon 1,000.00
127 JKu,Superman on Truth or
   Consequences 1,100.00
128 V:'Aces' Deucey. 1,000.00
129 Meets Gob-Gob 1,000.00

Action Comics #102 © DC Comics, Inc.

All comics prices listed are for *Near Mint* condition.

Action Comics #158 © DC Comics, Inc.

130 V:Captain Kidder 1,000.00
131 V:Lex Luthor. 1,000.00
132 Superman meets George
    Washington. 1,000.00
133 V:Emma Blotz 1,000.00
134 V:Paul Strong 1,000.00
135 V:John Morton 1,000.00
136 Superman Show-Off! 1,000.00
137 Meets Percival Winter . . . 1,000.00
138 Meets Herbert Hinkle. . . . 1,000.00
139 Clark Kent...Daredevil! . . . 1,000.00
140 Superman becomes Hermit 1,000.00
141 V:Lex Luthor. 1,000.00
142 V:Dan the Dip 1,000.00
143 Dates Nikki Larve. 1,000.00
144 O:Clark Kent reporting for
    Daily Planet 1,000.00
145 Meets Merton Gloop 1,000.00
146 V:Luthor. 1,000.00
147 V:'Cheeks' Ross. 1,000.00
148 Superman, Indian Chief. . . 1,000.00
149 The Courtship on Krypton!. 1,000.00
150 V:Morko 1,000.00
151 V:Mr.Mxyzptlk,Lex Luthor
    and Prankster 1,000.00
152 I:Metropolis Shutterbug
    Society 1,100.00
153 V:Kingpin 1,000.00
154 V:Harry Reed 1,000.00
155 V:Andrew Arvin 1,000.00
156 Lois Lane becomes Super-
    woman,V:Lex Luthor 900.00
157 V:Joe Striker 900.00
158 V:Kane Korrell
    O:Superman (retold). 2,000.00
159 Meets Oswald Whimple . . . 900.00
160 I:Minerva Kent. 900.00
161 Meets Antara. 900.00
162 V:'IT!'. 900.00
163 Meets Susan Semple 900.00
164 Meets Stefan Andriessen . . 900.00
165 V:Crime Czar 900.00
166 V:Lex Luthor 900.00
167 V:Prof. Nero 900.00
168 O:Olaf 900.00
169 Caveman Clark Kent! 900.00
170 V:Mad Artist of Metropolis. . 900.00
171 The Secrets of Superman. . . 900.00
172 Lois Lane..Witch! 900.00
173 V:Dragon Lang 900.00
174 V:Miracle Twine Gang. 900.00
175 V:John Vinden. 900.00
176 V:Billion Dollar Gang. 900.00
177 V:General 900.00
178 V:Prof. Sands 900.00
179 Superman in Mapleville 900.00
180 V:Syndicate of Five. 900.00

181 V:Diamond Dave Delaney . . 800.00
182 Return from Planet Krypton . 800.00
183 V:Lex Luthor 800.00
184 Meets Donald Whitmore . . . 800.00
185 V:Issah Pendleton. 800.00
186 The Haunted Superman . . . 800.00
187 V:Silver. 800.00
188 V:Cushions Raymond gang . 800.00
189 Meets Mr.& Mrs. Vandeveir. . 800.00
190 V:Mr. Mxyzptlk. 800.00
191 V:Vic Vordan 800.00
192 Meets Vic Vordan 800.00
193 V:Beetles Brogan 800.00
194 V:Maln. 800.00
195 V:Tiger Woman 800.00
196 Superman becomes Mental
    Man 800.00
197 V:Stanley Stark 800.00
198 The Six Lives of Lois Lane . . 800.00
199 V:Lex Luthor 800.00
200 V:Morwatha. 800.00
201 'V:Benny the Brute 800.00
202 Lois Lane's X-Ray Vision . . . 700.00
203 Meets Pietro Paresca 700.00
204 Meets Sam Spulby 700.00
205 Sergeant Superman 700.00
206 Imaginary story F:L.Lane . . . 700.00
207 Four Superman Medals!. . . . 700.00
208 V:Mr. Mxyzptlk. 700.00
209 V:'Doc' Winters 700.00
210 V:Lex,I:Superman Land 700.00
211 Superman Spectaculars . . . 700.00
212 V:Thorne Varden. 700.00
213 V:Paul Paxton 700.00
214 Superman,Sup.Destroyer! . . 700.00
215 I:Superman of 2956 . . . . . . 700.00
216 A:Jor-El 700.00
217 Meets Mr&Mrs.Roger Bliss. . 700.00
218 I:Super-Ape from Krypton. . . 700.00
219 V:Art Shaler. 700.00
220 Interplanetary Olympics 700.00
221 V:Jay Vorrell 600.00
222 The Duplicate Superman . . . 600.00
223 A:Jor-El. 600.00
224 I:Superman Island. 600.00
225 The Death of Superman 600.00
226 V:Lex Luthor 600.00
227 Man with Triple X-Ray Eyes . 600.00
228 A:Superman Museum. 600.00
229 V:Dr. John Haley. 600.00
230 V:Bart Wellins 600.00
231 Sir Jimmy Olsen, Knight of
    Metropolis 600.00
232 Meets Johnny Kirk 600.00
233 V:Torm. 600.00
234 Meets Golto 600.00
235 B:Congo Bill,
    B:Tommy Tomorrow. 600.00
236 A:Lex Luthor 600.00
237 V:Nebula Gang 600.00
238 I:King Krypton,the Gorilla . . . 600.00
239 Superman's New Face 600.00
240 V:Superman Sphinx 600.00
241 WB,A:Batman,Fortress of
    Solitude (Fort Superman) . . . 500.00
242 I&O:Braniac. 3,500.00
243 Lady and the Lion 500.00
244 CS,A:Vul-Kor,Lya-La. 500.00
245 WB,V:Kak-Kul. 500.00
246 WB,A:Krypton Island. 500.00
247 WB,Superman Lost Parents . 500.00
248 B&I:Congorilla. 500.00
249 A:Lex Luthor 500.00
250 WB,The Eye of Metropolis . . 500.00
251 E:Tommy Tomorrow 500.00
252 I&O:Supergirl 3,600.00
253 B:Supergirl 900.00
254 I:Adult Bizarro 700.00
255 I:Bizarro Lois 600.00
256 Superman of the Future 400.00
257 WB,JM,V:Lex Luthor. 400.00
258 A:Cosmic Man. 400.00

Action Comics #275 © DC Comics, Inc.

259 A:Lex Luthor,Superboy 400.00
260 A:Mighty Maid 400.00
261 I:Streaky,E:Congorilla 400.00
262 A:Bizarro. 400.00
263 O:Bizarro World 500.00
264 V:Bizarro 400.00
265 A:Hyper-Man 400.00
266 A:Streaky,Krypto 400.00
267 JM,3rd A:Legion,I:Invisible
    Kid 800.00
268 WB,A:Hercules 300.00
269 A:Jerro. 300.00
270 CS,JM,A:Batman 400.00
271 A:Lex Luthor 300.00
272 A:Aquaman 300.00
273 A:Mr.Mxyzptlk 300.00
274 A:Superwoman 300.00
275 WB,JM,V:Braimiac 300.00
276 JM,6th A:Legion,I:Brainiac 5,
    Triplicate Girl,Bouncing Boy . 500.00
277 CS,JM,V:Lex Luthor 250.00
278 CS,Perry White Becomes
    Master Man 250.00
279 JM,V:Hercules,Samson 250.00
280 CS,JM,V:Braniac,
    A:Congorilla. 250.00
281 JM,A:Krypto 250.00
282 JM,V:Mxyzptlk. 250.00
283 CS,JM,A:Legion of Super
    Outlaws 300.00
284 A:Krypto,Jerro. 250.00
285 JM,Supergirl Existence Revealed,
    C:Legion (12th app.) 300.00
286 CS,JM,V:Lex Luthor 200.00
287 JM,A:Legion 200.00
288 JM,A:Mon-El 200.00
289 JM,A:Adult Legion. 200.00
290 JM,C:Phantom Girl 200.00
291 JM,V:Mxyzptlk. 200.00
292 JM,I:Superhorse 200.00
293 JM,O:Comet-Superhorse . . . 200.00
294 JM,V:Lex Luthor 200.00
295 CS,JM,O:Lex Luthor 200.00
296 V:Super Ants. 200.00
297 CS,JM,A:Mon-El 200.00
298 CS,JM,V:Lex Luthor 200.00
299 O:Superman Robots 200.00
300 JM,A:Mxyzptlk. 250.00
301 CS(c),JM,O:Superhorse 150.00
302 CS(c),JM,O:Superhorse 150.00
303 CS(c),Red Kryptonite story . . 150.00
304 CS,JM,I&O:Black Flame 175.00
305 CS(c),O:Supergirl 150.00
306 JM,C:Mon-El,Brainiac 5 . . . . 150.00
307 CS,JM,A:Saturn Girl 150.00
308 CS(c),V:Hercules 150.00
309 CS,A:Batman,JFK,Legion. . . 175.00

310 CS,JM,I:Jewel Kryptonite ... 150.00
311 CS,JM,O:Superhorse 150.00
312 CS,JM,V:Metallo-Superman . 150.00
313 JM,A:Supergirl,Lex,Batman . 150.00
314 JM,A:Justice League 150.00
315 JM,V:Zigi,Zag........... 150.00
316 JM,A:Zigi,Zag,Zyra 150.00
317 JM,V:Lex Luthor 150.00
318 CS,JM,A:Brainiac 150.00
319 CS,JM,A:Legion,V:L.Luthor . 150.00
320 CS,JM,V:Atlas,Hercules 150.00
321 CS,JM,A:Superhorse 150.00
322 JM,Coward of Steel 150.00
323 JM,A:Superhorse 150.00
324 JM,A:Abdul 150.00
325 CS,JM,SkyscraperSuperman 150.00
326 CS,JM,V:Legion of Super
   Creatures................ 150.00
327 CS,JM,C:Brainiac 150.00
328 JM,Hands of Doom........ 150.00
329 JM,V:Drang 150.00
330 CS,JM,Krypto 150.00
331 CS,V:Dr.Supernatural 150.00
332 CS,A:Brainiac 150.00
333 CS(c),A:Lex Luthor 150.00
334 JM(c),A:Lex Luthor,80pgs... 150.00
335 CS,V:Lex Luthor 150.00
336 CS,O:Akvar............. 150.00
337 CS,V:Tiger Gang.......... 150.00
338 CS,JM,V:Muto........... 150.00
339 CS,V:Muto,Brainiac........ 150.00
340 JM,I:Parasite............ 150.00
341 CS,V:Vakox,A:Batman 125.00
342 WB,JM,V:Brainiac......... 125.00
343 WB,V:Eterno............ 125.00
344 WB,JM,A:Batman 125.00
345 CS(c),A:Allen Funt 125.00
346 WB,JM 125.00
347 CS(c),A:Supergirl, 80pgs.... 200.00
348 WB,JM,V:Acid Master..... 100.00
349 WB,JM,V:Dr.Kryptonite 100.00
350 A:JLA................. 100.00
351 WB,I:Zha-Vam............ 100.00
352 WB,V:Zha-Vam 100.00
353 WB,JM,V:Zha-Vam 100.00
354 JM,A:Captain Incredible 100.00
355 WB,JM,V:Lex Luthor...... 100.00
356 WB,JM,V:Jr. Annihilitor 100.00
357 WB,JM,V:Annihilitor 100.00
358 NA(c),CS,JM,A:Superboy ... 100.00
359 NA(c),CS,KS,C:Batman 100.00
360 CS(c),A:Supergirl, 80pgs.... 200.00
361 NA(c),A:Parasite.......... 75.00
362 RA,KS,V:Lex Luthor 75.00
363 RA,KS,V:Lex Luthor 75.00
364 RA,KS,V:Lex Luthor 75.00
365 A:Legion & J.L.A. 75.00
366 RA,KS,A:J.L.A. 75.00
367 NA(c),CS,KS,A:Supergirl 75.00
368 CS,KS,V:Mxyzptlk......... 75.00
369 CS,KS,Superman's Greatest
   Blunder 75.00
370 NA(c),CS,KS............ 75.00
371 NA(c),CS,KS............ 75.00
372 NA(c),CS,KS............ 75.00
373 A:Supergirl,(giant size) 150.00
374 NA(c),CS,KS,V:Super Thief . 50.00
375 CS,KS,The Big Forget 50.00
376 CS,KS,E:Supergirl 50.00
377 CS,KS,B:Legion 50.00
378 CS,KS,V:Marauder 50.00
379 CS,JA,MA,V:Eliminator 50.00
380 KS,Confessions of Superman. 50.00
381 CS,Dictators of Earth 50.00
382 CS,Clark Kent-Magician 40.00
383 CS,The Killer Costume...... 40.00
384 CS,The Forbidden Costume.. 40.00
385 CS,The Mortal Superman.... 40.00
386 CS,Home For Old Supermen. 40.00
387 CS,A:Legion,Even
   Supermen Die 40.00

388 CS,A:Legion,Puzzle of
   The Wild Word............ 40.00
389 A:Legion,The Kid Who
   Struck Out Superman 40.00
390 CS,Self-Destruct Superman .. 40.00
391 CS,Punishment of
   Superman's Son 40.00
392 CS,E:Legion 40.00
393 CS,MA,RA,A:Super Houdini .. 40.00
394 CS,MA................ 40.00
395 CS,MA,A:Althera.......... 40.00
396 CS,MA................ 40.00
397 CS,MA,Imaginary Story 40.00
398 NA(c),CS,MA,I:Morgan Edge . 40.00
399 NA(c),CS,MA,A:Superbaby... 40.00
400 NA(c),CS,MA,Kandor Story .. 60.00
401 CS,MA,V:Indians.......... 40.00
402 NA(c),CS,MA,V:Indians 50.00
403 CS,MA,Vigilante rep........ 50.00
404 CS,MA,Aquaman rep 50.00
405 CS,MA,Vigilante rep........ 50.00
406 CS,MA,Atom & Flash rep.... 50.00
407 CS,MA,V:Lex Luthor........ 50.00
408 CS,MA,Atom rep.......... 50.00

Action Comics #426 © DC Comics Inc.

409 CS,MA,T.Tommorrow rep..... 50.00
410 CS,MA,T.Tommorrow rep..... 50.00
411 CS,MA,O:Eclipso rep........ 50.00
412 CS,MA,Eclipso rep......... 50.00
413 CS,MA,V:Brainiac......... 50.00
414 CS,MA,B:Metamorpho 25.00
415 CS,MA,V:Metroplis Monster .. 25.00
416 CS,MA................ 25.00
417 CS,MA,V:Luthor 25.00
418 CS,MA,V:Luthor,
   E:Metamorpho............ 25.00
419 CS,MA,CI,DG,I:HumanTarget . 30.00
420 CS,MA,DG,V:Towbee 25.00
421 CS,MA,B:Green Arrow 25.00
422 CS,DG,O:Human Target 25.00
423 CS,MA,DG,A:Lex Luthor..... 25.00
424 CS,MA,Green Arrow 25.00
425 CS,DD,NA,DG,B:Atom 50.00
426 CS,MA,Green Arrow 20.00
427 CS,MA,DD,DG,Atom....... 20.00
428 CS,MA,DG,Luthor 20.00
429 CS,BO,DG,C:JLA 20.00
430 CS,MA,DG,Atom 20.00
431 CS,MA,Green Arrow 20.00
432 CS,MA,DG,Toyman 22.00
433 CS,BO,DD,DG,A:Atom 20.00
434 CS,DD,Green Arrow 20.00
435 FM(c),CS,DD,DG,Atom...... 20.00
436 CS,DD,Green Arrow 20.00
437 CS,DG,Green Arrow,100-pg .. 40.00

438 CS,BO,DD,Atom.......... 20.00
439 CS,BO,DD,Atom.......... 20.00
440 1st MGr Green Arrow 30.00
441 CS,BO,MGr,A:Green Arrow,
   Flash,R:Krypto........... 20.00
442 CS,MS,MGr,Atom 20.00
443 CS,A:JLA(100 pg.giant) 75.00
444 MGr,Green Arrow 20.00
445 MGr,Green Arrow 20.00
446 MGr,Green Arrow 20.00
447 CS,BO,RB,KJ,Atom 20.00
448 CS,BO,DD,JL,Atom 20.00
449 CS,BO,The Super-spy 30.00
450 MGr,Green Arrow 20.00
451 MGr,Green Arrow 15.00
452 CS,MGr,Green Arrow 15.00
453 CS,Atom 15.00
454 CS,E:Atom 15.00
455 CS,Green Arrow 15.00
456 CS,MGr,Green Arrow 15.00
457 CS,MGr,Green Arrow 15.00
458 CS,MGr,I:Black Rock 15.00
459 CS,BO,Blackrock 15.00
460 CS,I:Karb-Brak 15.00
461 CS,V:Karb-Brak 15.00
462 CS,V:Karb-Brak 15.00
463 CS,V:Karb-Brak 15.00
464 CS,KS,V:Pile-Driver 15.00
465 CS,FMc,Luthor 15.00
466 NA(c),CS,V:Luthor........ 15.00
467 CS,V:Mzyzptlk........... 15.00
468 NA(c),CS,FMc,V:Terra-Man .. 15.00
469 CS,TerraMan............ 15.00
470 CS,Flash Green Lantern..... 15.00
471 CS,V:Phantom Zone Female . 15.00
472 CS,V:Faora Hu-Ul......... 15.00
473 NA(c),CS,Phantom Zone
   Villians 15.00
474 KS,V:Doctor Light 15.00
475 KS,V:Karb-Brak,A:Vartox.... 15.00
476 KS,V:Vartox............ 15.00
477 CS,DD,Land Lords of Earth .. 15.00
478 CS,Earth's Last.......... 15.00
479 CS,Giant from Golden Atom .. 15.00
480 CS,A:JLA,V:Amazo........ 15.00
481 CS,A:JLA,V:Amazo........ 15.00
482 CS,Amazo............. 15.00
483 CS,Amazo,JLA 15.00
484 CS,W:Earth 2 Superman
   & Lois Lane 25.00
485 NA(c),CS,rep.Superman#233. 20.00
486 GT,KS,V:Lex Luthor 15.00
487 CS,AS,O:Atom 15.00
488 CS,AS,A:Air Wave 15.00
489 CS,AS,A:JLA,Atom........ 15.00
490 CS,Brainiac............. 15.00
491 CS,A:Hawkman.......... 15.00
492 CS,Superman's After Life 15.00
493 CS,A:UFO............. 15.00
494 CS,Secret of the Super-S.... 15.00
495 CS, Attack of Ultimate Warrior 15.00
496 CS,A:Kandor............ 15.00
497 CS,Command Performance .. 15.00
498 CS,Vartox 15.00
499 CS,Vartox 15.00
500 CS,Superman's Life Story
   A:Legion 28.00
501 KS,Mild-Mannered Superman . 7.00
502 CS,A:Supergirl,Gal.Golem 7.00
503 CS,A Save in Time 7.00
504 CS,The Power and Choice.... 7.00
505 CS,Creature that Charmed Kids 7.00
506 CS,V:Jorlan,Jor-El 7.00
507 CS,A:Jonathan Kent........ 7.00
508 CS,A:Jonathan Kent........ 7.00
509 CS,JSn,DG 7.00
510 CS,Luthor 7.00
511 CS,AS,V:Terraman,
   A:Air Wave............. 7.00
512 CS,RT,V:Luthor,A:Air Wave ... 7.00
513 CS,RT,V:Krell,A:Air Wave..... 7.00
514 CS,RT,V:Brainiac,A:Atom.... 7.00

Action Comics #496 © DC Comics, Inc.

515 CS,AS,A:Atom 7.00
516 CS,AS,V:Luthor,A:Atom 7.00
517 CS,DH,A:Aquaman. 7.00
518 CS,DH,A:Aquaman 7.00
519 CS,DH,A:Aquaman 7.00
520 CS,DH,A:Aquaman 7.00
521 CS,AS,I:Vixen,A:Atom 7.00
522 CS,AS,A:Atom 7.00
523 CS,AS,A:Atom 7.00
524 CS,AS,A:Atom 7.00
525 JSon,FMc,AS,I:Neutron
    A:Air Wave. 7.00
526 JSon,AS,V:Neutron. 7.00
527 CS,AS,I:Satanis,A:Aquaman . . 9.00
528 CS,AS,V:Brainiac,A:Aquaman . 7.00
529 GP(c),CS,DA,AS,A:Aquaman,
    V:Brainiac. 7.00
530 CS,DA,Brainiac. 7.00
531 JSon,FMc,AS,A:Atom 7.00
532 CS,C:New Teen Titans 7.00
533 CS,V:H.I.V.E.. . . . . 7.00
534 CS,AS,V:Satanis,A:Air Wave . . 7.00
535 GK(c),JSon,AS,
    A:Omega Men. 7.00
536 JSon,AS,FMc,A:Omega Men . . 7.00
537 IN,CS,AS,V:Satanis
    A:Aquaman 7.00
538 IN,AS,FMc,V:Satanis,
    A:Aquaman 7.00
539 KG(c),GK,AS,DA,A:Flash,
    Atom,Aquaman 7.00
540 GK,AS,V:Satanis. 7.00
541 GK,V:Satanis. 7.00
542 AS,V:Vandal Savage. 7.00
543 CS,V:Vandal Savage 7.00
544 CS,MA,GK,GP,45th Anniv.
    D:Ardora,Lexor 12.00
545 GK,Brainiac. 7.00
546 GK,A:JLA,New Teen Titans . . . 7.00
547 GK(c),CS,V:Planeteer. 7.00
548 GK(c),AS,Phantom Zone 7.00
549 GK(c),AS,Meets Zod Squad . . . 7.00
550 AS(c),GT,Day Earth Exploded . 7.00
551 GK,Starfire becomes
    Red Star 7.00
552 GK,Forgotten Heroes
    (inc.Animal Man) 18.00
553 GK,Forgotten Heroes(inc.
    Animal Man) 18.00
554 GK(a&c) 7.00
555 CS,A:Parasite (X-over
    Supergirl #20) 7.00
556 CS,KS,C:Batman 7.00
557 CS,Terra-man 7.00
558 KS,All-Searing Eyes 7.00

559 KS,AS,Once & Future Peril . . . 7.00
560 AS,KG,BO,A:Ambush Bug 7.00
561 KS,WB,Toyman. 7.00
562 KS,Queen Bee 7.00
563 AS,KG,BO,A:Ambush Bug 7.00
564 AS,V:Master Jailer 7.00
565 KG,KS,BO,A:Ambush Bug 7.00
566 BO(i),MR 7.00
567 KS,AS,PB 7.00
568 CS,AW,AN 7.00
569 IN,The Force of Revenge 7.00
570 KS, Jimmy Olsen's Alter-Ego . . 7.00
571 BB(c),AS,A:Thresh 222 . . . . . . 7.00
572 WB,BO 7.00
573 KS,BO,AS 7.00
574 KS 7.00
575 KS,V:Intellax 7.00
576 KS,Earth's Sister Planet 7.00
577 KG,BO,V:Caitiff 7.00
578 KS,Parasite. 7.00
579 KG,BO,Asterix Parody 7.00
580 GK(c),KS,Superman's Failure . 7.00
581 DCw(c),KS,Superman
    Requires Legal aid 7.00
582 AS,KS,Superman's Parents
    Alive. 7.00
583 CS,KS,AMo(s),Last Pre
    Crisis Superman 20.00
584 JBy,DG,A:NewTeenTitans,
    I:Modern Age Superman. . . . 10.00
585 JBy,DG,Phantom Stranger 8.00
586 JBy,DG,Legends,V:New
    Gods,Darkseid. 8.00
587 JBy,DG,Demon 8.00
588 JBy,DG,Hawkman 8.00
589 JBy,DG,Gr.Lant.Corp. 8.00
590 JBy,DG,Metal Men 8.00
591 JBy,V:Superboy,A:Legion 8.00
592 JBy,Big Barda 8.00
593 JBy,Mr. Miracle 8.00
594 JBy,A:Booster Gold. 8.00
595 JBy,A:M.Manhunter,
    I:Silver Banshee 9.00
596 JBy,A:Spectre,Millenium 9.00
597 JBy,L.Starr(i),Lois V:Lana 9.00
598 JBy,TyT,I:Checkmate. 11.00
599 RA,JBy(i),A:MetalMen,
    Bonus Book 9.00
600 JBy,GP,KS,JOy,DG,CS,MA,
    MMi,A:Wonder Woman;
    Man-Bat,V:Darkseid 15.00

Becomes:

ACTION WEEKLY
1988–89

601 GK,DSp,CS,DJu,TD, B:Superman,
    Gr.Lantern,Blackhawk,Deadman,
    Secret Six,Wilddog 3.50
602 GP(c),GK,DSp,CS,DJu,TD 3.50
603 GK,CS,DsP,DJu,TD 3.50
604 GK,DSp,CS,DJu,TD 3.50
605 NKu/AKu(c),GK,DSp,CS,
    DJu,TD 3.50
606 DSp,CS,DJu,TD 3.50
607 SLi(c),TD,DSp,CS,DJu 3.50
608 DSp,CS,DJu,TD,E:Blackhawk . 3.50
609 BB(c),DSp,DJu,TD,CS,
    E:Wild Dog,B:Black Canary. . 3.50
610 KB,DJu,CS,DSp,TD,CS
    A:Phantom Stranger 3.50
611 AN(c),DJu,DSp,CS,BKi,TD,
    BKi,B:Catwoman 3.75
612 PG(c),DSp,CS,BKi,TD,
    E:Secret Six,Deadman 3.50
613 MK(c),BKi,CS,MA,TGr,
    Nightwing,B:Phantom Stranger . 3.50
614 TG,CS,Phantom Stranger
    E:Catwoman 3.50
615 MMi(c),CS,MA,BKi,TGr,
    Blackhawk,B:Wild Dog 3.50
616 ATh(c),CS,MA,E:Bl.Canary. . . . 3.50
617 CS,MA,JO,A:Ph.Stranger 3.50

Action Comics #667 © DC Comics, Inc.

618 JBg(c),CS,MA,JKo,TD,
    B:Deadman,E:Nightwing 3.50
619 CS,MA,FS,FMc,KJo,TD,FMc,
    B:Sinister Six. 3.50
620 CS,MA,FS,FMc,KJo,TD 3.50
621 JO(c),CS,MA,FS,FMc,KJo,
    TD,MBr,E:Deadman 3.50
622 RF(c),MBr,TL,CS,MA,FS,
    FMc,A:Starman,E:Wild
    Dog,Blackhawk 3.50
623 MBr,TD,CS,MA,FS,FMc,JL,
    JKo,A:Ph.Stranger,
    B:Deadman,Shazam 3.50
624 AD(c),MBr,FS,FMc,CS,MA,
    TD,B:Black Canary 3.50
625 MBr,FS,FMc,CS,MA,
    TD,FMc 3.50
626 MBr,FS,FMc,CS,MA,JKo,TD,
    E:Shazam,Deadman 3.50
627 GK(c),MBr,RT,FS,FMc,CS,
    MA,TMd,B:Nightwing,Speedy . . 3.50
628 TY(c),MBr,RT,TMd,CS,MA,
    FS,FMc,B:Blackhawk 3.50
629 CS,MA,MBr,RT,FS,FMc,TMd . . 3.50
630 CS,MA,MBr,RT,FS,FMc,TMd,
    E:Secret Six. 3.50
631 JS(c),CS,MA,MBr,RT,TMd,
    B:Phantom Stranger 3.50
632 TGr(c),CS,MA,MBr,RT,TMd . . . 3.50
633 CS,MA,MBr,RT,TMd 3.50
634 CS,MA,MBr,RT,TMd,E:Ph.Strangr,
    Nightwing/Speedy,Bl.hawk 3.50
635 CS,MA,MBr,RT,EB,E:Black
    Canary,Green Lantern. 3.50
636 DG(c),CS,MA,NKu,MPa,FMc,
    B:Demon,Wild Dog,Ph.Lady,
    Speedy,A:Phantom Stranger . . . 3.50
637 CS,MA,KS,FMc,MPa,
    B:Hero Hotline 3.50
638 JK(c),CS,MA,KS,FMc,MPa 3.50
639 CS,MA,KS,FMc,MPa 3.50
640 CS,KS,MA,FS,FMc,MPa,
    E:Speedy,Hero Hotline 3.50
641 CS,MA,JL,DG,MPa,E:Demon,
    Phant.Lady,Superman,Wild Dog,
    A:Ph.Stranger,Hum.Target. . . . 3.50
642 GK,SD,ATi,CS,JAp,JM,CI,KN,
    Green Lantern,Superman 3.50

Becomes:

ACTION COMICS
1989–2005

643 B:RSt(s),GP,BBr,V:Intergang . . 4.50
644 GP,BBr,V:Matrix 3.50
645 GP,BBr,I:Maxima 3.50

646 KG,V:Alien Creature,
   A:Brainiac 4.00
647 GP,KGa,BBr,V:Brainiac 3.50
648 GP,KGa,BBr,V:Brainiac 3.50
649 GP,KGa,BBr,V:Brainiac 3.50
650 JOy,BBr,CS,BMc,GP,KGa,
   ATi,DJu,A:JLA,C:Lobo 5.50
651 GP,KGa,BBr,Day of Krypton
   Man #3,V:Maxima 3.50
652 GP,KGa,BBr,Day of Krypton
   Man #6,V:Eradicator 5.00
653 BMc,BBr,D:Amanda 3.50
654 BMc,BBr,A:Batman Pt.3 . . . . . . 3.50
655 BMc,BBr,V:Morrisson,Ma
   Kent's Photo Album 3.50
656 BMc,BBr,Soul Search #1,
   V:Blaze 3.50
657 KGa,BBr,V:Toyman 3.50
658 CS,Sinbad Contract #3 . . . . . . 3.50
659 BMc,BBr,K.Krimson
   Kryptonite #3 . . . . 5.00
660 BMc,BBr,D:Lex Luthor 4.50
661 BMc,BBr,A:Plastic Man 3.50
662 JOy,JM,TG,BMc,V:Silver
   Banshee,Clark tells
   Lois his identity 5.50
662a 2nd printing 5.00
663 BMc,Time & Time Again,pt.2,
   A:JSA,Legion 5.50
664 BMc,Time & Time Again,pt.5 . . 3.50
665 TG,V:Baron Sunday 3.50
666 EH,Red Glass Trilogy,pt.3. . . . . 3.50
667 JOy,JM,TG,ATi,DJu,Revenge
   of the Krypton Man,pt.4 . . . . . . 3.75
668 BMc,Luthor confirmed dead . . . 3.50
669 BMc,V:Intergang,A:Thorn 3.50
670 BMc,A:Waverider,JLA,JLE 3.50
671 KD,Blackout,pt.2 . . . . 3.50
672 BMc,Superman Meets Lex
   Luthor II 3.50
673 BMc,V:Hellgramite 3.50
674 BMc,Panic in the Sky (Prologue)
   R:Supergirl(Matrix) 6.00
675 BMc,Panic in the Sky #4,
   V:Brainiac 3.50
676 B:KK(s),JG,A:Supergirl,Lex
   Luthor II 3.50
677 JG,Supergirl V:Superman 3.50
678 JG,O:Lex Luthor II 3.50
679 JG,I:Shellshock 3.50
680 JG,Blaze/Satanus War,pt.2 . . . 3.50
681 JG,V:Hellgramite 3.50
682 DAb,TA,V:Hi-Tech 3.50
683 JG,I:Jackal,C:Doomsday 3.50
683a 2nd printing 3.00
684 JG,Doomsday Pt.4 . . . . 4.00
684a 2nd printing 3.00
685 JG,Funeral for a Friend#2. . . . . 3.50
686 JG,Funeral for a Friend#6 . . . . . 3.50
687 JG,Reign of Superman #1,Direct
   Sales,Die-Cut(c),Mini-Poster,
   F:Last Son of Krypton 3.00
687a newsstand Ed. 3.00
688 JG,V:Guy Gardner. 3.00
689 JG,V:Man of Steel,A:Superboy,
   Supergirl,R:Real Superman . . . 3.50
690 JG,Cyborg Vs. Superboy 3.00
691 JG,A:All Supermen,V:Cyborg
   Superman,Mongul 3.00
692 JG,A:Superboy,Man of Steel . . . 3.00
693 JG,A:Last Son of Krypton 3.00
694 JG,Spilled Blood#2,V:Hi-Tech . . 3.00
695 JG,Foil(c),I:Cauldron,A:Lobo . . . 3.50
695a Newsstand Ed. 3.00
696 JG,V:Alien,C:Doomsday 3.00
697 JG,Bizarro's World #3,
   V:Bizarro 3.00
698 JG,A:Lex Luthor 3.00
699 JG,A:Project Cadmus 3.00
700 JG,Fall of Metropolis#1 . . . . 4.00
700a Platinum Edition 15.00

701 JG,Fall of Metropolis#5,
   V:Luthor 3.00
702 JG,DvM,B:DyM(s),R:Bloodsport 3.00
703 JG,DvM,Zero Hour 3.00
704 JG,DvM,Eradicator 3.00
705 JG,DvM,Supes real? 3.00
706 JG,DvM,A:Supergirl. 3.00
707 JG,DvM,V:Shado Dragon 3.00
708 JG,DvM,R:Deathtrap 3.00
709 JG,DvM,A:Guy Gardner,
   Warrior. 3.00
710 JG,DvM,Death of Clark Kent,pt.3
   [new Miraweb format begins] . . 3.00
711 JG,DvM,Death of Clark
   Kent,pt.7 . . . . 3.00
712 Rescue Jimmy Olsen 3.00
713 Scarlet Salvation. 3.00
714 R:The Joker 3.00
715 DvM,DaR,V:Parasite 3.00
716 DvM,DaR,Trial of Superman. . . 3.00
717 DvM,DaR,Trial of Superman. . . 3.00
718 DvM,DRo,mystery of Demolitia . 3.00
719 DvM,DRo 3.00
720 DvM,DRo,Lois ends
   engagement. 3.50
721 DvM,DRo,lottery fever 3.00
722 DvM,DaR,Tornados in
   Smallville 3.00
723 V:Brainiac 3.00
724 V:S.T.A.R.labs monster. 3.00
725 Tolos 3.00
726 DvM(s),TMo,DRo,Krisis of the
   Krimson Kryptonite follow-up. . . 3.00
727 DvM(s),TMo,DRo,brutal weather
   in Metropolis, Final Night tie-in . 3.00
728 DvM(s),TG,DRo, Some
   Honeymoon! 3.00
729 DvM(s),TG,DRo, in Fortress of
   Solitude 3.00
730 DvM(s),TG,Ro, ... 3.00
731 DvM(s),TG,DRo, R:Cauldron . . . 3.00
732 DvM(s),TG,DRo, Atomic Skull
   rampages through Metropolis . . . 3.00
733 DvM(s),TG,DRo, V:Matallo,
   A:Ray. 3.00
734 DvM(s),TG,DRo, Superman &
   Atom in Kandor 3.00
735 DvM(s),TG,DRo, V:Savior. 3.00
736 DvM(s),TG,DRo. 3.00
737 MWa(s),TG,DRo, Luthor gets
   day in court 3.00
738 SI,JMz,Lois sent to Australia . . 3.00
739 SI,JMz,Superman imprisoned. . 3.00
740 SI,JMz,Lucy Lane disappears. . 3.00
741 SI,JMz,V:C.O.M.P.U.T.O. 3.00

742 SI,JMz 3.00
743 SI,JMz,F:Slam Bradley 3.00
744 SI,JMz,Millennium Giants
   x-over. 3.00
745 SI,JMz,The Prankster 3.00
746 SI,JMz,The Prankster,pt.2 . . . . 3.00
747 SI,JMz,The Prankster,pt.3 . . . . 3.00
748 SI,JMz,Dominus Theory 3.00
749 RMz(s),TGb,TP,City of the
   Future, pt.1 x-over 3.00
750 SI,JMz,I:Crazytop, 48-page . . . 3.50
751 SI,JMz,A:Geo-Force 3.00
752 SI,JMz,Supermen of
   America x-over 3.00
753 SI,JMz,A:JLA 3.00
754 SI,JMz,R:Dominus,
   A:Wonder Woman 3.00
755 SI&MMr(s),King of the
   World aftermath. 3.00
756 VGi,old villain is back 3.00
757 TPe(s),TGb,Hawkworld,pt.3 . . . 3.00
758 SI,JMz,V:Boss Moxie 3.00
759 RF,SB,Strange Visitor,pt.3 . . . . 3.00
760 JRu,F:Encantadora 3.00
761 JRu 3.00
762 JRu,V:Demon Etrigan 3.00
763 JRu,V:Brainiac 13 . . . . 3.00
764 JRu,marital troubles 3.00
765 JRu,V:Joker & Harley Quinn . . . 3.00
766 F:Batman 3.00
767 CriticalCondition,pt.4,x-over . . . 3.00
768 F:Marvel Family 3.00
769 Superman:Arkham,concl. 3.00
770 Superman:Emperor,48-pg. . . . 4.50
771 CDi(s),F:Nightwing 2.50
772 V:Ra's al Ghul,pt.1 . . . . 2.50
773 V:Ra's al Ghul,pt.2 . . . . 2.50
774 A:Martian Manhunter 2.50
775 48-page. 15.00
775a 2nd printing (2004) 4.50
776 Return to Krypton,pt.4. . . . . 2.50
777 Kancer. 2.50
778 MWm,Infestation x-over,pt.4 . . . 2.50
779 V:Killer,pt.1 . . . . 2.50
780 V:Killer,pt.2 . . . . 2.50
781 Our Worlds at War,All-OutWar . 2.50
782 Our Worlds at War,Casualties . 2.50
783 V:Ocean Master,Scorch 2.50
784 Joker:Last Laugh tie-in 2.50
785 R:Bizarro. 2.50
786 PFe,kidnapped by aliens 2.50
787 PFe,Byakko, Gunshin, Sakki . . 2.50
788 PFe,Jikei Ketsuki,pt.1 . . . . 2.50
789 Evil from the Gorge. 2.50
790 Krypto vs. Kancer 2.50
791 Smallville, flash-back tale 2.50
792 Superman, detective. 2.50
793 PFe,Return to KryptonII,concl. . 2.50
794 F:Quintessence. 2.50
795 Ending Battle,pt.4 . . . . 2.50
796 Ending Battle,pt.8 . . . . 2.50
797 New General Zod 2.50
798 Lost Hearts, pt.4 x-over 2.50
799 TR,SHa,F:Girl 13 . . . . 2.50
800 64-page, life re-examined 4.50
801 metahumans 2.50
802 PFe,CaS,The Harvest,pt.1 . . . . 2.50
803 PFe,CaS,The Harvest,pt.2 . . . . 2.50
804 PFe,CaS,The Harvest,pt.3 . . . . 2.50
805 PFe,CaS,The Harvest,pt.4 . . . . 2.50
806 PFe,CaS,The Harvest,pt.5 . . . . 2.50
807 PFe,CaS,Supergirls 2.50
808 PFe,CaS,Supergirls 2.50
809 PFe,CaS,murder suspect 2.50
810 PFe,CaS,New Year's 2.25
811 KlK,Strange New Visitor 3.00
812 Godfall,pt.1 . . . . 6.00
812a 2nd printing 5.00
813 Godfall,pt.4 . . . . 4.00
814 MCa,Job in jeopardy. 2.50
815 MCa,V:Gog 2.50
816 MCa,F:Teen Titans 2.50

Action Comics #745 © DC Comics Inc.

DC COMICS

817 MCa,F:W.Woman & Superboy . 2.50
818 MCa,F:W.Woman & Superboy . 2.50
819 MCa,I:Sodom & Gomorrah 2.50
820 V:Silver Banshee 2.50
821 LRs,MCa,F:Preus 2.50
822 MCa,F:Superboy 2.50
823 MCa,F:Superboy, Krypto 2.50
824 MCa,V:Preus. 2.50
825 MCa,Villains unite,40-page 3.00
826 IaC,NRd,F:Captain Marvel 3.50
827 JBy,Nel,F:Dr.Polaris,V:Repulse . 3.00
828 JBy,Nel,V:Repulse 2.50
829 JBy,Nel,Sacrifice, x-over,pt.2 . . 5.00
830 JBy,Nel,Villains United tie-in . . 2.50
831 JBy,Nel,Villains United tie-in . . 2.50
832 JBy,Nel,F:Spectre, Satanus . . . 2.50
833 JBy,Nel,F:Queen of Fables. . . . 2.50
834 JBy,Nel,F:Queen of Fables. . . . 2.50
835 JBy,Nel,I:Livewire 2.50
836 EBe,DJu,This is your life,
    Superman 2.50
837 KBk,Up,Up & Away,pt.2,x-over . 2.50
838 KBk,Up,Up & Away,pt.4,x-over . 2.50
839 KBk,Up,Up & Away,pt.6,x-over . 3.00
840 KBk,Up,Up & Away,pt.8,x-over . 3.00
841 A:Teen Titans, Nightwing 3.00
842 A:Nightwing, Firestorm 3.00
843 A:Teen Titans 3.00
844 AKu, Last Son, pt.1 . . . . 4.00
844a 2nd printing 5.00
845 AKu, Bizarro returns 3.00
846 AKu,Last Son, pt.3 . . . . 3.00
847 AKu,Last Son, pt.4 . . . . 3.00
847a part in 3-D, inc. glasses 4.00
848 FaN(s). 3.00
849 FaN(s). 3.00
850 KBk(s), F:Supergirl, 48-pgs. . . . 4.00
851 AKu,Last Son, pt.4 . . . . 3.00
851a part in 3-D inc. glasses 4.00
852 3-2-1 Action, pt.1. . . . . 3.00
853 KBk(s),Countdown tie-in 3.00
854 KBk(s),Countdown tie-in 3.00
855 Escape from Bizarro World,pt.1 3.00
856 Escape from Bizarro World,pt.2 3.00
857 Escape from Bizarro World,pt.3 3.00
858 GFr,Superman, original Legion. 3.50
Ann.#1 AAd,DG,A:Batman 8.00
Ann.#2 MMi,CS,GP,JOy,DJu,BBr,
    V:Mongul 4.00
Ann.#3 TG,Armageddon X-over. . . . 3.50
Ann.#4 Eclipso,A:Captain Marvel . . 3.50
Ann.#5 MZ(c),Bloodlines, I:Loose
    Cannon 3.50
Ann.#6 Elseworlds,JBy(a&S). 3.50
Ann.#7 Year One Annual 4.50
Ann.#8 DvM,Legends of the Dead
    Earth 3.50
Ann.#9 DvM,VGi,BBr,Pulp Heroes . 4.50
Ann. #10 . . . . 4.00
Ann. #10a variant (c) (1:10). 4.00
Gold.Ann.rep.#1. . . . . 2.50
#0 Peer Pressure,pt.4 (1994) 2.50
Spec.#1,000,000 MSh(s),RLm,JMz . 2.50

ADAM STRANGE
1990
1 NKu,A.Strange on Rann 5.00
2 NKu,Wanted:Adam Strange. 4.00
3 NKu,final issue. 4.00

2nd Series, Sept. 2004
1 (of 8) PFe,R:Adam Strange 3.00
2 PFe 3.00
3 PFe 3.00
4 PFe, F:The Omega Man 3.00
5 PFe,V:L.E.G.I.O.N 3.00
6 PFe,Planet Rann. 3.00
7 PFe,Planet Rann, Darkstars 3.00
8 PFe,concl. 3.00

Advanced Dungeons & Dragons #25
© DC Comics, Inc.

ADVANCED
DUNGEONS & DRAGONS
1988–91
1 JD,I:Onyx,Priam,Timoth,
    Cybriana,Vajra,Luna 5.00
2 JD,V:Imgig Zu,I:Conner 4.00
3 JD,V:Imgig Zu 4.00
4 JD,V:Imgig Zu,I:Kyriani 3.00
5 JD,Spirit of Myrrth I 3.00
6 JD,Spirit of Myrrth II. 3.00
7 thru 24 JD . . . . @2.50
25 thru 36 JD . . . . @2.25
Ann.#1 JD,RM,Tmd 4.00

ADVENTURE COMICS
Nov., 1938–83
[Prev: New Adventure Comics]
32 CF(c),S&S 6,000.00
33 CF(c),FGu,S&S,BKa 2,800.00
34 FGu(c),S&S,BKa 2,800.00
35 FGu(c),SMo,S&S,BKa 2,800.00
36 CF,Giant Snake(c),S&S 2,800.00
37 CF,Rampaging Elephant(c) . 2,800.00
38 CF,Tiger(c),S&S. 2,800.00
39 CF,Male Bondage(c),S&S . . 2,500.00
40 CF(c),1st app. Sandman . . 90,000.00
41 CF,Killer Shark(c),S&S 12,000.00
42 CF,Sandman(c) 20,000.00
43 CF&FGu(c),WB 7,000.00
44 CF,FGu,Sandman(c) 15,000.00
45 FGu(c),CF,BKa. 7,000.00
46 CF,Sandman(c) 12,000.00
47 CF,Sandman (c). 12,000.00
48 1st app.& B:Hourman 50,000.00
49 SMo(c),BKa,CF 5,000.00
50 BBa,Hourman(c) 5,000.00
51 BBa(c),Sandman(c) 7,000.00
52 BBa(c),Hourman(c) 5,000.00
53 BBa(c),1st app. Minuteman . 5,000.00
54 BBa(c),Hourman(c) 5,000.00
55 BBa(c),Hourman(c) 5,000.00
56 BBa(c),Hourman(c) 5,000.00
57 BBa(c),Hourman(c) 5,000.00
58 BBa(c),Hourman(c) 5,000.00
59 BBa(c),Hourman(c) 5,000.00
60 CF,Sandman(c) 7,000.00
61 CF(c),JBu,Starman(c) 25,000.00
62 JBu(c),JBu,Starman(c). 5,000.00
63 JBu(c),JBu,Starman(c). 4,000.00
64 JBu(c),JBu,Starman(c). 4,000.00
65 JBu(c),JBu,Starman(c). 4,000.00
66 JBu(c),JBu,O:Shining Knight,
    Starman(c) 5,500.00

67 JBu(c),JBu,O:Mist 4,000.00
68 JBu(c),JBu,same 4,000.00
69 JBu(c),JBu,1st app. Sandy,
    Starman(c) 4,000.00
70 JBu(c),JBu,Starman(c). 4,000.00
71 JBu(c),JBu,same 4,000.00
72 JBu(c),S&K,JBu,Sandman. 25,000.00
73 S&K(c),S&K,I:Manhunter . . 28,000.00
74 S&K(c),S&K,You Can't Escape
    Your Fate-The Sandman . 4,000.00
75 S&K(c),S&K,Sandman and
    Sandy Battle Thor. 4,000.00
76 S&K(c),Sandman(c),S&K. . . 4,000.00
77 S&K,(c),S&K,same. 4,000.00
78 S&K(c),S&K,same 4,000.00
79 S&K(c),S&K,Manhunter 7,000.00
80 S&K(c),Sandman(c),S&K. . . 4,000.00
81 S&K(c),MMe,S&K,same. . . . 2,500.00
82 S&K(c),S&K,Sandman
    X-Mas story 2,500.00
83 S&K(c),S&K,Sandman
    Boxing(c),E:Hourman 2,500.00
84 S&K(c),S&K 2,500.00
85 S&K(c),S&K,Sandman in
    The Amazing Dreams of
    Gentleman Jack 2,500.00
86 S&K(c),Sandman(c) 2,500.00
87 S&K(c),Sandman(c) 2,500.00
88 S&K(c),Sandman(c) 2,500.00
89 S&K(c),Sandman(c) 2,500.00
90 S&K(c),Sandman(c) 2,500.00
91 S&K(c),JK 2,500.00
92 S&K(c) 1,600.00
93 S&K(c),Sandman in Sleep
    for Sale 1,600.00
94 S&K(c),Sandman(c) 1,600.00
95 S&K(c),Sandman(c) 1,600.00
96 S&K(c),Sandman(c) 1,600.00
97 S&K(c),Sandman(c) 1,600.00
98 JK(c),Sandman in Hero
    of Dreams. 1,600.00
99 GK,Sandman(c) 1,600.00
100 JK(c&a) 2,000.00
101 S&K(c) 1,600.00
102 S&K(c) 1,600.00
103 B:Superboy stories,(c),BU:
    Johnny Quick,Aquaman,Shining
    Knight,Green Arrow 5,000.00
104 S&S,ToyTown USA 1,900.00
105 S&S,Palace of Fantasy . . . 1,500.00
106 S&S,Weather Hurricane . . . 1,500.00
107 S&S,The Sky is the Limit . 1,500.00
108 S&S,Proof of the Proverbs 1,500.00
109 S&S,You Can't Lose 1,500.00
110 S&S,The Farmer Takes
    it Easy. 1,500.00

Adventure Comics #62
© DC Comics, Inc.

111 S&S,The Whiz Quiz Club . .	1,500.00
112 S&S,Super Safety First . . .	1,500.00
113 S&S,The 33rd Christmas . .	1,200.00
114 S&S,Superboy Spells Danger	1,200.00
115 S&S,The Adventure of Jaguar Boy	1,200.00
116 S&S,JBu,Superboy Toy Tester	1,200.00
117 S&S,JBu,Miracle Plane . . .	1,200.00
118 S&S,JBu,The Quiz Biz Broadcast	1,200.00
119 WMo,JBu,Superboy Meets Girls	1,200.00
120 S&S,JBu,A:Perry White; I:Ringmaster . . . . :	1,300.00
121 S&S,Great Hobby Contest.	1,300.00
122 S&S,Superboy-Super-Magician	1,400.00
123 S&S,Lesson For a Bully. . .	1,300.00
124 S&S,Barbed Wire Boys Town	1,000.00
125 S&S,The Weight Before Christmas	1,000.00
126 S&S,Superboy:Crime Fighting Poet	1,000.00
127 MMe,O:Shining Knight; Super Bellboy	1,000.00
128 WMo,How Clark Kent Met Lois Lane	1,000.00
129 WMo,Pupils of the Past . . .	1,000.00
130 WMo,Superboy Super Salesman	1,000.00
131 WMo,The Million Dollar Athlete	1,000.00
132 WMo,Superboy Super Cowboy	1,000.00
133 WMo,Superboy's Report Card	1,000.00
134 WMo,Silver Gloves Sellout	1,000.00
135 WMo,The Most Amazing of All Boys	1,000.00
136 WMo,My Pal Superboy . . .	1,000.00
137 WMo,Treasure of Tondimo.	1,000.00
138 WMo,Around the World in Eighty Minutes	1,000.00
139 WMo,Telegraph Boy	1,000.00
140 Journey to the Moon	1,000.00
141 WMo,When Superboy Lost His Powers	1,000.00
142 WMo,The Man Who Walked With Trouble	1,000.00
143 WMo,Superboy Savings Bank, A:Wooden Head Jones . . .	1,000.00
144 WMo,The Way to Stop Superboy	1,000.00
145 WMo,Holiday Hijackers . . .	1,000.00
146 The Substitute Superboy . .	1,000.00
147 Clark Kent,Orphan	1,000.00
148 Superboy Meets Mummies	1,000.00
149 Fake Superboys.	1,000.00
150 FF,Superboy's Initiation . .	1,100.00
151 FF,No Hunting(c)	1,000.00
152 Superboy Hunts For a Job . .	900.00
153 FF,Clark Kent,Boy Hobo . .	1,000.00
154 The Carnival Boat Crimes . .	900.00
155 FF,Superboy-Hollywood Actor	1,000.00
156 The Flying Peril.	900.00
157 FF,The Worst Boy in Smallville	1,000.00
158 The Impossible Task.	900.00
159 FF,Superboy Millionaire? . .	1,000.00
160 Superboy's Phoney Father . .	750.00
161 FF.	1,000.00
162 Super-Coach of Smallville High!	900.00
163 FF,Superboy's Phoney Father	1,000.00
164 Discovers the Secret of a Lost Indian Tribe!	900.00

165 Superboy's School for Stunt Men!	900.00
166 Town That Stole Superboy . .	900.00
167 Lana Lang, Super-Girl! . . .	1,000.00
168 The Boy Who Out Smarted Superboy	900.00
169 Clark Kent's Private Butler . .	900.00
170 Lana Lang's Big Crush	750.00
171 Superboy's Toughest Tasks .	750.00
172 Laws that Backfired	750.00
173 Superboy's School of Hard Knocks	750.00
174 The New Lana Lang!	750.00
175 Duel of the Superboys	750.00
176 Superboy's New Parents! . . .	750.00
177 Hot-Rod Chariot Race!	750.00
178 Boy in the Lead Mask.	750.00
179 World's Whackiest Inventors	750.00
180 Grand Prize o/t Underworld .	750.00
181 Mask for a Hero	750.00
182 Super Hick from Smallville . .	650.00
183 Superboy and Cleopatra. . . .	650.00
184 Shutterbugs of Smallville . . .	650.00
185 The Mythical Monster	650.00
186 Smallville a Ghost Town	650.00
187 25th Century Superboy.	650.00
188 Bull Fighter from Smallville . .	650.00
189 Girl of Steel (Lana Lang) . . .	650.00
190 The Terrible Truant	650.00
191 The Two Clark Kents	650.00
192 Coronation of Queen Lana Lang	650.00
193 Superboy's Lost Costume. . .	650.00
194 Super-Charged Superboy. . .	650.00
195 Lana Lang's Romance on Mars!	650.00
196 Superboy vs. King Gorilla . .	650.00
197 V:Juvenile Gangs	650.00
198 Super-Carnival from Space . .	650.00
199 Superboy meets Superlad . .	650.00
200 Superboy and the Apes! . . .	900.00
201 Safari in Smallville!	600.00
202 Superboy City, U.S.A.	600.00
203 Uncle Superboy!	600.00
204 Super-Brat of Smallville . . .	600.00
205 Journey of the Second Superboy!	600.00
206 The Impossible Creatures. .	600.00
207 Smallville's Worst Athlete . . .	600.00
208 Rip Van Winkle of Smallville?	600.00
209 Superboy Week!	600.00
210 I:Krypto,The Superdog from Krypton	7,500.00

Adventure Comics #195
© DC Comics Inc.

211 Superboy's Amazing Dream!	600.00
212 Superboy's Robot Twin.	600.00
213 Junior Jury of Smallville!. . . .	600.00
214 A:Krypto	1,000.00
215 Super-Hobby of Superboy .	600.00
216 The Wizard City	600.00
217 Farewell to Smallville	600.00
218 Two World's of Superboy . . .	600.00
219 Rip Van Wrinkle of Smallville	600.00
220 Greatest Show on Earth A:Krypto.	550.00
221 The Babe of Steel	500.00
222 Superboy's Repeat Performance	500.00
223 Hercules Junior.	500.00
224 Pa Kent Superman	500.00
225 Bird with Super-Powers . . .	500.00
226 Superboy's Super Rival! . . .	500.00
227 Good Samaritan of Smallville	500.00
228 Clark Kent's Bodyguard . . .	500.00
229 End of the Kent Family	500.00
230 Secret o/t Flying Horse	450.00
231 Super-Feats of Super-Baby .	450.00
232 House where Superboy was Born	450.00
233 Joe Smith, Man of Steel . . .	450.00
234 1,001 Rides of Superboy . . .	450.00
235 Confessions of Superboy . .	450.00
236 Clark Kent's Super-Dad . . .	450.00
237 Robot War of Smallville . . .	450.00
238 Secret Past of Superboy's Father	450.00
239 Super-Tricks of the Dog of Steel.	450.00
240 Super Teacher from Krypton.	450.00
241 Super-Outlaw of Smallville .	450.00
242 The Kid From Krypton	450.00
243 Super Toys from Krypton . . .	450.00
244 Poorest Family in Smallville .	450.00
245 The Mystery of Monster X .	450.00
246 Girl Who Trapped Superboy .	450.00
247 I&O:Legion.	10,000.00
248 Green Arrow	400.00
249 CS,Green Arrow	400.00
250 JK,Green Arrow	400.00
251 JK,Green Arrow	400.00
252 JK,Green Arrow	400.00
253 JK,1st Superboy & Robin T.U.	600.00
254 JK,Green Arrow	400.00
255 JK,Green Arrow	400.00
256 JK,O:Green Arrow	1,100.00
257 CS,LEI,A:Hercules,Samson .	350.00
258 LEI,Aquaman,Superboy . . .	350.00
259 I:Crimson Archer	350.00
260 1st S.A. O:Aquaman	1,400.00
261 GA,A:Lois Lane.	300.00
262 O:Speedy	300.00
263 GA,Aquaman,Superboy . . .	300.00
264 GA,A:Robin Hood	300.00
265 GA,Aquaman,Superboy . . .	300.00
266 GA,I:Aquagirl.	300.00
267 N:Legion(2nd app.)	1,600.00
268 I:Aquaboy	300.00
269 I:Aqualad,E:Green Arrow . .	450.00
270 2nd A:Aqualad,B:Congorilla .	300.00
271 O:Lex Luthor rtd	450.00
272 I:Human Flying Fish	300.00
273 Aquaman,Superboy	300.00
274 Aquaman,Superboy	300.00
275 O:Superman/Batman T.U. rtd.	400.00
276 Superboy,3rd A:Metallo. . .	300.00
277 Aquaman,Superboy	300.00
278 Aquaman,Superboy	300.00
279 CS,Aquaman,Superboy . . .	300.00
280 CS,A:Lori Lemaris.	300.00
281 Aquaman,Superboy E:Congorilla	300.00
282 5th A:Legion,I:Starboy	400.00

All comics prices listed are for *Near Mint* condition.

Adventure Comics #303
© *DC Comics, Inc.*

283 I:Phantom Zone 400.00
284 CS,JM,Aquaman,Superboy . 250.00
285 WB,B:Bizarro World 350.00
286 I:Bizarro Mxyzptlk 350.00
287 I:Dev-Em,Bizarro Perry White,
    Jimmy Olsen 250.00
288 A:Dev-Em 250.00
289 Superboy. 250.00
290 8th A:Legion,O&J:Sunboy,
    I:Brainiac 5 . . . . 400.00
291 A:Lex Luthor 250.00
292 Superboy,I:Bizarro Lucy Lane,
    Lana Lang 250.00
293 CS,O&I:Marv-El,I:Bizarro
    Luthor 350.00
294 I:Bizarro M.Monroe,JFK 300.00
295 I:Bizarro Titano 250.00
296 A:Ben Franklin,George
    Washington 250.00
297 Lana Lang Superboy Sister . 250.00
298 The Fat Superboy 250.00
299 I:Gold Kryptonite 250.00
300 B:Legion,J:Mon-El,
    E:Bizarro World 900.00
301 CS,O:Bouncing Boy 300.00
302 CS,Legion. 250.00
303 I:Matter Eater Lad. 250.00
304 D:Lightning Lad. 250.00
305 A:Chameleon Boy 250.00
306 I:Legion of Sub.Heroes. 250.00
307 I:Element Lad 250.00
308 I:Light Lass 250.00
309 I:Legion of Super Monsters . 250.00
310 A:Mxyzptlk. 250.00
311 CS,V:Legion of Substitue
    Heroes. 250.00
312 CS&GKI(c),R:Lightning Lad . 250.00
313 CS,J:Supergirl. 250.00
314 CS&GKI(c),A:Hitler 250.00
315 A:Legion of Substitute
    Heroes. 250.00
316 CS&GKI(c),O:Legion. 200.00
317 I&J:Dreamgirl 200.00
318 Mutiny of Legionaires 200.00
319 Legion's Suicide Squad 200.00
320 CS&GKI(c),A:Dev-Em. 200.00
321 I:Time Trapper. 250.00
322 JF,A:Legion of Super Pets . . 150.00
323 JF,BU:Kypto 150.00
324 JF,I:Legion of Super Outlaws 150.00
325 JF,V:Lex Luthor. 150.00
326 BU:Superboy. 150.00
327 I&J:Timber Wolf 150.00
328 Lad who Wrecked Legion . . . 150.00
329 I:Legion of Super Bizarros . . 150.00
330 Mystery Legionnaire 150.00

331 Legion of Super-Villains 125.00
332 CS&GKI(c),Legion. 125.00
333 CS&GKI(c),Legion. 125.00
334 CS&GKI(c),Legion. 125.00
335 CS&GKI(c),Legion. 125.00
336 CS&GKI(c),Legion. 125.00
337 CS&GKI(c),Legion. 125.00
338 CS&GKI(c),Legion. 125.00
339 CS&GKI(c),Legion. 125.00
340 I:Computo 125.00
341 CS,D:Triplicate Girl (becomes
    Duo Damsel) 110.00
342 CS,Star Boy expelled 100.00
343 CS,V:Lords of Luck. 100.00
344 CS,Super Stalag,pt.1. . . . . . . 100.00
345 CS,Super Stalag,pt.2 . . . . . . 100.00
346 CS,I&J:Karate Kid,Princess
    Projectra,I:Nemesis Kid. . . . 125.00
347 CS,Legion. 100.00
348 I:Dr.Regulus 125.00
349 CS,I:Rond Vidar 100.00
350 CS,I:White Witch. 125.00
351 CS,R:Star Boy. 150.00
352 CS,I:Fatal Fire. 150.00
353 CS,D:Ferro Lad. 125.00
354 CS,Adult Legion 150.00
355 CS,J:Insect Queen 125.00
356 CS,Five Legion Orphans 125.00
357 CS,I:Controller 125.00
358 I:Hunter 125.00
359 CS,Outlawed Legion,pt.1 . . . . 125.00
360 CS,Outlawed Legion,pt.2 . . . . 125.00
361 I:Dominators (30th century) . 125.00
362 I:Dr.Mantis Morto 125.00
363 V:Dr.Mantis Morlo 125.00
364 A:Legion of Super Pets. 125.00
365 CS,I:Shadow Lass,
    V:Fatal Five 125.00
366 CS,J:Shadow Lass 125.00
367 N:Legion H.Q.,I:Dark Circle . 125.00
368 NA,Mutiny of Super-Heroines 125.00
369 CS,JAb,I:Mordru 125.00
370 CS,JAb,V:Mordru 125.00
371 CS,JAb,I:Chemical King 125.00
372 CS,JAb,J:Timber Wolf,
    Chemical King. 125.00
373 I:Tornado Twins. 65.00
374 WM,I:Black Mace 65.00
375 I:Wanderers 65.00
376 Execution of Cham.Boy 65.00
377 Heroes for Hire 65.00
378 Twelve Hours to Live 65.00
379 Burial In Space 65.00
380 The Amazing Space Odyssey
    of the Legion,E:Legion 65.00
381 The Supergirl Gang
    C:Batgirl,B:Supergirl 200.00
382 NA(c),The Superteams Split
    Up,A:Superman. 75.00
383 NA(c),Please Stop my Funeral,
    A:Superman,Comet,Streaky . . 75.00
384 KS,The Heroine Haters,
    A:Superman. 75.00
385 Supergirl's Big Sister 75.00
386 The Beast That Loved
    Supergirl 75.00
387 Wolfgirl of Stanhope;
    A:Superman;V:Lex Luthor 75.00
388 Kindergarten Criminal;
    V:Luthor,Brainiac 75.00
389 A:Supergirl's Parents,
    V:Brainiac 75.00
390 Linda Danvers Superstar
    (80 page giant) 100.00
391 The Super Cheat;A:Comet . . . 50.00
392 Supergirls Lost Costume 50.00
393 KS,Unwanted Supergirl 50.00
394 KS,Heartbreak Prison 50.00
395 Heroine in Haunted House . . . 50.00
396 Mystery o/t Super Orphan . . . 50.00
397 Now Comes Zod,N:Supergirl,
    V:Luthor. 50.00

398 Maid of Doom,A:Superman,
    Streaky,Krypto,Comet 50.00
399 CI,Johnny Dee,Hero Bum. . . . 60.00
400 MSy,35th Anniv.,Return of the
    Black Flame. 40.00
401 MSy,JAb,The Frightened
    Supergirl,V:Lex Luthor. 40.00
402 MSy,JAb,TD,I:Starfire,
    Dr.Kangle. 50.00
403 68 page giant 100.00
404 MSy,JAb,V:Starfire 35.00
405 V:Starfire,Dr.Kangle 35.00
406 MSy,JAb,Suspicion 35.00
407 MSy,JAb,Suspicion Confirmed
    N:Supergirl. 35.00
408 The Face at the Window. 35.00
409 MSy,DG,Legion rep. 50.00
410 N:Supergirl 50.00
411 CI,N:Supergirl 50.00
412 rep.Strange Adventures #180
    (I:Animal Man). 55.00
413 GM,JKu,rep.Hawkman 50.00
414 Animal Man rep. 50.00
415 BO,GM,CI,Animal Man rep. . . 50.00
416 CI,All women issue,giantsize . 50.00
417 GM,inc.rep.Adventure #161,
    Frazetta art. 45.00
418 ATh,Black Canary. 45.00
419 ATh,Black Canary. 50.00
420 Animal Man rep. 45.00
421 MSy,Supergirl 30.00
422 MSy,Supergirl 30.00
423 MSy,Supergirl 30.00
424 MSy,E:Supergirl,A:JLA 30.00
425 AN,ATh,I:Captain Fear 45.00
426 MSy,DG,JAp,Vigilante. 30.00
427 TD, The Voodoo Lizards. 38.00
428 TD,I:Black Orchid 100.00
429 TD,AN,Black Orchid 45.00
430 A:Black Orchid 45.00
431 JAp,ATh,b:Spectre 100.00
432 JAp,AN,A:Spectre,Capt.Fear . 45.00
433 JAp,AN, The Swami 45.00
434 JAp, Nightmare Dummies. . . . 45.00
435 MGr(1st work),JAp,Aquaman . 45.00
436 JAp,MGr,Aquaman 45.00
437 JAp,MGr,Aquaman 45.00
438 JAp,HC,DD,7 Soldiers 45.00
439 JAp, Voice that Doomed 45.00
440 JAp,O:New Spectre 75.00
441 JAp,B:Aquaman 20.00
442 JAp,A:Aquaman 20.00
443 JAp, The Dolphin Connection. 20.00
444 JAp, Death before Dishonor . . 20.00
445 JAp,RE,JSon,Creeper. 22.00

Adventure Comics #435
© *DC Comics, Inc.*

446 JAp,RE,JSon,Creeper 22.00
447 JAp,RE,JSon,Creeper 22.00
448 JAp,Aquaman 20.00
449 JAp,MN,TA,J'onn J'onz. 20.00
450 JAp,MN,TA,Supergirl 20.00
451 JAp,MN,TA,Hawkman 20.00
452 JAp,Aquaman 20.00
453 MA,CP,JRu,B:Superboy
   & Aqualad 20.00
454 CP,DG,A:Kryptonite Kid 20.00
455 CP,DG,A:Kryptonite Kid
   E:Aqualad 15.00
456 JSon,JA. 15.00
457 JSon,JA,JO,B:Eclipso 15.00
458 JSon,JAp,JO,BL,E:Superboy
   & Eclipso 15.00
459 IN,FMc,JAp,JSon,DN,JA,A:Wond.
   Woman,New Gods,Green Lantern,
   Flash,Deadman,(giant size) . . 25.00
460 IN,FMc,JAp,DN,DA,JSon,JA,
   D:Darkseid. 25.00
461 IN,FMc,JAp,JSon,DN,JA,
   B:JSA & Aquaman 25.00
462 IN,FMc,DH,JL,DG,JA,
   D:Earth 2,Batman 25.00
463 DH,JL,JSon,FMc. 20.00
464 DH,JAp.,JSon,DN,DA,
   Deadman. 20.00
465 DN,JSon,DG,JL. 20.00
466 MN,JL,JSon,DN,DA 20.00
467 JSon,SD,RT,I:Starman
   B:Plastic Man 25.00
468 SD,JSon 8.00
469 SD,RT,JSon,O:Starman 8.00
470 SD,JSon,Starman 8.00
471 SD,JSon,I:Brickface 8.00
472 SD,RT,JSon 8.00
473 SD,RT,JSon 8.00
474 SD,RT,JSon 8.00
475 BB(c),SD,RT,JSon,DG,
   B:Aquaman 8.00
476 SD,RT,JSon,DG 8.00
477 SD,RT,JSon,DG 8.00
478 SD,RT,JSon,DG 8.00
479 CI,DG,JSon,Dial H For Hero,
   E:Starman and Aquaman 8.00
480 CI,DJ,B:Dial H for Hero 8.00
481 CI,DJ. 8.00
482 CI,DJ,DH. 8.00
483 CI,DJ,DH. 8.00
484 GP(c),CI,DJ,DH 8.00
485 GP(c),CI,DJ. 8.00
486 GP(c),DH,RT,TVE 8.00
487 CI,DJ,DH. 8.00
488 CI,DJ,TVE 8.00
489 CI,FMc,TVE 8.00
490 GP(c),CI,E:Dial H for Hero 8.00
491 KG(c),DigestSize,DN,
   Shazam,rep.other material . . . 20.00
492 KG(c),DN,E:Shazam. 20.00
493 KG(c),GT,B:Challengers of
   the Unknown,reprints 20.00
494 KG(c),GT,Challengers,
   reprints. 20.00
495 ATh,reprints,Challengers. 20.00
496 GK(c),ATh,reprints,
   Challengers 20.00
497 ATh,DA,reps.,E:Challengers . . 20.00
498 GK(c),reprints,Rep.Legion . . . 20.00
499 GK(c),reprints,Rep 20.00
500 KG(c),Legion reprints,Rep . . . 20.00
501 reprints,Rep 20.00
502 reprints,Rep 20.00
503 reprints,final issue 20.00
Giant #1, 80 page, 7 tales (1998) . 15.00

ADVENTURE COMICS
1999
1 JeR,PSj,F:Starman & The Atom . 2.25

ADVENTURES IN THE DC UNIVERSE
1997–98
1 F:New JLA 6.00
2 F:The Flash,Catwoman 4.00
3 Wonder Woman vs. Cheetah;
   Poison Ivy vs. Batman. 4.00
4 F:Green Lantern vs. Glorious
   Godfrey; Mister Miracle. 4.00
5 F:Martian Manhunter, all alien
   issue 4.00
6 F:Ocean Master, Power Girl 4.00
7 SVa(s),F:Shazam Family 4.00
8 SVa(s),F:Blue Beetle &
   Booster Gold 4.00
9 SVa(s),F:Flash,V:Grodd,Cipher . . 4.00
10 SVa(s),Legion month 4.00
11 SVa(s),F:Gr.Lantern & W.Woman 4.00
12 SVa(s). 4.50
13 SVa(s),A:Martian Manhunter . . . 4.00
14 SVa(s),Flash races Superboy . . . 4.00
15 SVa(s),Shazam,Aquaman. 4.00
16 SVa(s),F:Green Lantern 4.00
17 SVa(s),F:Batman, Creeper 4.00
18 SVa(s),F:JLA. 4.50
19 F:Catwoman, Wonder Woman . . 4.00
Ann.#1 magic amulets,5 stories. . . . 5.00

THE ADVENTURES OF ALAN LADD
1949–51
1 Ph(c),Damascus Diamond . . 1,500.00
2 Ph(c),inc.Visit to Underworld . . 800.00
3 Ph(c),inc.Stuntman 550.00
4 Ph(c),inc.Hall of Hits 550.00
5 Ph(c),inc.Destination Danger. . 500.00
6 Ph(c),inc.Beautiful Bodyguard . 500.00
7 RMo(c&a),Hollywood Unknown 500.00
8 Grand Duchess takes over . . . 500.00
9 Deadlien in Rapula 500.00

THE ADVENTURES OF BOB HOPE
1951
1 Ph(c). 3,000.00
2 Ph(c). 1,500.00
3 Ph(c). 1,000.00
4 Ph(c). 1,000.00
5 thru 10 . . . . @750.00
11 thru 20 . . . . @600.00
21 thru 40 . . . . @400.00
41 thru 60 . . . . @300.00
61 thru 90 . . . . @150.00
91 thru 93 . . . . @125.00
94 C:Aquaman 150.00
95 1st Superhip 150.00
96 thru 105 . . . . @125.00
106 thru 109 NA. 200.00

ADVENTURES OF DEAN MARTIN AND JERRY LEWIS
1952–57
1 . . . . 2,500.00
2 . . . . 1,000.00
3 thru 5 . . . . @750.00
6 thru 10 . . . . @750.00
11 thru 20 . . . . @500.00
21 thru 40 . . . . @300.00
Becomes:

ADVENTURES OF JERRY LEWIS
1957–71
41 thru 55 . . . . @225.00
56 thru 69 . . . . @200.00
70 thru 87 . . . . @150.00
88 A:Bob Hope 150.00

Adventures of Dean Martin and Jerry Lewis #19 © DC Comics Inc.

89 thru 91 . . . . @50.00
92 C:Superman 70.00
93 Beatles 65.00
94 thru 96 . . . . @60.00
97 A:Batman & Joker. 125.00
98 thru 101. . . . . @55.00
102 NA,Beatles . . . . @125.00
103 and 104 NA. . . . . @75.00
105 A:Superman 80.00
106 thru 111 . . . . @45.00
112 A:Flash 55.00
113 thru 116 . . . . @40.00
117 A:Wonder Woman 80.00
118 thru 124 . . . . @35.00

ADVENTURES OF FORD FAIRLANE
1990
1 thru 4 DH . . . . @3.00

ADVENTURES OF THE OUTSIDERS
See: BATMAN & THE OUTSIDERS

ADVENTURES OF OZZIE AND HARRIET
1949–50
1 Ph(c). 1,500.00
2 . . . . 900.00
3 thru 5 . . . . @750.00

ADVENTURES OF REX, THE WONDER DOG
1952–59
1 ATh,Trail of Flower of Evil. . . 2,000.00
2 GK,ATh,Stunt Dog 1,000.00
3 GK,ATh,Circus Detective. 900.00
4 GK,CI,Terror Island 800.00
5 GK,Wanted, One P.O.W. 800.00
6 thru 10 . . . . @600.00
11 Atom Bomb 700.00
12 thru 20 . . . . @400.00
21 thru 46 . . . . @300.00

ADVENTURES OF SUPERBOY
See: SUPERBOY

ADVENTURES OF SUPERMAN
See: SUPERMAN

ALL-AMERICAN COMICS
1939–48

1 B:Hop Harrigan,Scribbly,Mutt&Jeff,
Red,White&Blue,Bobby Thatcher,
Skippy,Daiseybelle,Mystery Men
of Mars,Toonerville 10,000.00
2 B:Ripley's Believe It or Not . . 4,000.00
3 Hop Harrigan (c) 3,000.00
4 Flag(c). 3,000.00
5 B:The American Way 3,000.00
6 ShM(c),Fredric Marchin in
The American Way 2,500.00
7 E:Bobby Thatcher,C.H.
Claudy's A Thousand Years
in a Minute 2,500.00
8 B:Ultra Man. 5,000.00
9 A:Ultra Man. 2,500.00
10 ShM(c),E:The American Way,
Santa-X-Mas(c) 2,500.00
11 Ultra Man(c) 2,500.00
12 E:Toonerville Folks. 2,000.00
13 The Infra Red Des'Royers . . 2,000.00
14 Ultra Man 2,000.00
15 E:Tippie and Reg'lar Fellars 2,500.00
16 O&1st App:Green Lantern,
B:Lantern(c) 230,000.00
17 SMo(c). 30,000.00
18 SMo(c) 25,000.00
19 SMo(c),O&I: Atom, E:Ultra
Man. 30,000.00
20 I:Atom's Costume,Hunkle
becomes Red Tornado . . . 10,000.00
21 E:Wiley of West Point
& Skippy 6,000.00
22 SMo(c),F:Green Lantern . . . 5,800.00
23 E:Daieybelle. 6,000.00
24 E:Ripley's Believe It or Not . 7,500.00
25 O&I:Dr. Mid-Nite. 20,000.00
26 O&I:Sargon the Sorcerer . . . 7,000.00
27 I:Doiby Dickles 7,000.00
28 F:Green Lantern 3,000.00
29 ShM(c) 3,000.00
30 ShM(c) 3,000.00
31 Adventures of the Underfed
Orphans 3,000.00
32 F:Green Lantern 2,500.00
33 Green Lantern(c) 2,500.00
34 Green Lantern(c) 2,500.00
35 Doiby discovers Lantern's ID 2,500.00
36 Auto Racing (c) 2,500.00
37 Green Lantern(c) 2,500.00
38 ShM,V:A Modern Napoleon . 2,500.00
39 Green Lantern(c) 2,500.00
40 Doiby Dickles idol(c) 2,500.00
41 Gr.Lantern(c),Doiby Dickles 2,000.00
42 ShM 2,000.00
43 Gr.Lantern(c),Doiby Dickles 2,000.00
44 I Accuse the Green Lantern! 2,000.00
45 Gr.Lantern(c),Doiby Dickles 2,000.00
46 Riddle of Dickles Manor. . . . 2,000.00
47 Hop Harrigan meets the
Enemy,(c) 2,000.00
48 League of Three-Eyed Men . 2,000.00
49 Doiby Dickles Cab 2,000.00
50 E:Sargon 2,000.00
51 Murder Under the Stars 1,500.00
52 Spotlight on Crime 1,500.00
53 Green Lantern delivers
the Mail. 1,500.00
54 Crime is an Art. 1,500.00
55 The Riddle of the
Runaway Trolley. 1,500.00
56 V:Elegant Esmond 1,500.00
57 V:The Melancholy Men 1,500.00
58 Marvelous Mervyn Mystery . 1,500.00
59 The Story of the Man Who
Couldn't Tell The Truth 1,500.00
60 Desperate Dilemma 1,500.00
61 O:Soloman Grundy,Fighters
Never Quit 10,000.00
62 Da Distrik Attorney. 1,300.00
63 Garrulous Mr. Gabb 1,300.00

All-American Comics #28
© *DC Comics, Inc.*

64 A Bag of Assorted Nuts! 1,300.00
65 The Man Who Lost
Wednesday. 1,300.00
66 The Soles of Manhattan! . . . 1,300.00
67 V:King Shark 1,300.00
68 F:Napoleon & Joe Safeen . . 1,300.00
69 Backwards Man! 1,300.00
70 JKu,I:Maximillian O'Leary,
V:Colley, the Leprechaun . . 1,300.00
71 E:Red,White&Blue,The
Human Bomb 1,200.00
72 B:Black Pirate 1,200.00
73 B:Winkey,Blinky&Noddy,
Mountain Music Mayhem . . 1,200.00
74 Slap-Happy Shoes. 1,200.00
75 Man Who Heard Too Much . 1,200.00
76 Spring Time for Doiby 1,200.00
77 Hop Harrigan(c) 1,200.00
78 The Giggling Gangsters. . . . 1,200.00
79 Mutt & Jeff 1,200.00
80 Long-Eared Larceny 1,200.00
81 Two Twisted Twerps. 1,200.00
82 The Beloved Bandit 1,200.00
83 Mutt & Jeff 1,200.00
84 The Adventure of the Man
with Two Faces. 1,200.00
85 Rise & Fall of Crusher Crock 1,200.00
86 V:Crime of the Month Club . 1,200.00
87 The Strange Case of
Professor Nobody. 1,200.00
88 Canvas of Crime 1,200.00
89 O:Harlequin 1,700.00
90 O:Icicle 1,700.00
91 Wedding of the Harlequin . . 1,700.00
92 The Icicle goes South 1,700.00
93 Double Crossing Decoy 1,700.00
94 A:Harlequin 1,700.00
95 The Unmasking of the
Harlequin 1,700.00
96 ATh(c),Solve the Mystery
of the Emerald Necklaces! . 1,700.00
97 ATh(c),The Country Fair
Crimes 1,700.00
98 ATh,ATh(c),End of Sports! . . 1,700.00
99 ATh,ATh(c),E:Hop Harrigan . 1,700.00
100 ATh,I:Johnny Thunder 3,000.00
101 ATh,ATh(c),E:Mutt & Jeff . . 2,500.00
102 ATh,ATh(c),E:GrnLantern. . 7,000.00
Becomes:

ALL-AMERICAN
WESTERN
1948–52

103 A:Johnny Thunder,The City
Without Guns, All Johnny
Thunder stories 1,000.00
104 ATh(c),Unseen Allies. 700.00
105 ATh(c),Hidden Guns 600.00

106 ATh(c),Snow Mountain
Ambush 600.00
107 ATh(c),Cheyenne Justice . . . 600.00
108 ATh(c),Vengeance of
the Silver Bullet 400.00
109 ATh(c),Secret of
Crazy River 400.00
110 ATh(c),Ambush at
Scarecrow Hills 400.00
111 ATh(c),Gun-Shy Sheriff 400.00
112 ATh(c),Double Danger. 400.00
113 ATh(c),Johnny Thunder
Indian Chief 400.00
114 ATh(c),The End of
Johnny Thunder. 400.00
115 ATh(c),Cheyenne Mystery . . . 400.00
116 ATh(c),Buffalo Raiders
of the Mesa 400.00
117 ATh(c),V:Black Lightnin 300.00
118 ATh(c),Challenge of
the Aztecs 300.00
119 GK(c),The Vanishing
Gold Mine 300.00
120 GK(c),Ambush at
Painted Mountain 300.00
121 ATh(c),The Unmasking of
Johnny Thunder. 300.00
122 ATh(c),The Real
Johnny Thunder. 300.00
123 GK(c),Johnny Thunder's
Strange Rival. 300.00
124 ATh(c),The Iron Horse's
Last Run 300.00
125 ATh(c),Johnny Thunder's
Last Roundup 300.00
126 ATh(c),Phantoms of the
Desert 300.00
Becomes:

ALL-AMERICAN
MEN OF WAR
1952–66

127 (0) JGr(c),Unknown Marine 2,200.00
128 (1) IN, Bridgehead 1,200.00
2 JGr(c),Killer Bait. 900.00
3 Pied Piper of Pyong-Yang . . . 750.00
4 JGr(c),The Hills of Hate. 750.00
5 One Second to Zero 750.00
6 IN(c),Jungle Killers. 650.00
7 IN(c),Beach to Hold 650.00
8 IN(c),Sgt. Storm Cloud. 650.00
9 IN(c),Death Mist. 650.00
10 JGr(c),Operation Avalance . . 650.00
11 JGr(c),Dragon's Teeth. 650.00
12 JGr(c),Bobsled Bombadier . . 600.00
13 JGr(c),Lost Patrol 600.00
14 IN(c),Pigeon Boss. 600.00
15 JGr(c),Flying Roadblock 600.00
16 JGr(c),The Flying Jeep 600.00
17 JGr(c),Booby Trap Ridge . . . 600.00
18 JKu(c),The Ballad of
Battling Bells 600.00
19 JGr(c),IN,Torpedo Track 500.00
20 JGr(c),JKu,Lifenet to
Beach Road. 500.00
21 JGr(c),IN,RH,The
Coldest War. 500.00
22 JGr(c),IN,JKu,Snipers Nest . . 500.00
23 JGr(c),The Silent War 500.00
24 JGr(c),The Thin Line. 500.00
25 JGr(c),IN,For Rent-One
Foxhole 500.00
26 Dial W-A-R 500.00
27 JGr(c),RH,Fighting Pigeon . . 500.00
28 JGr(c),RA,JKu,Medal
for A Dog 500.00
29 IN(c),JKu,Battle Bridges 500.00
30 JGr(c),RH,Frogman Hunt . . . 500.00
31 JGr(c),Battle Seat 400.00
32 JGr(c),RH,Battle Station 400.00
33 JGr(c),IN,Sky Ambush 400.00
34 JGr(c),JKu,No Man's Alley . . 400.00

All-American Men of War #8
© DC Comics, Inc.

35 JGr(c),IN, Battle Call. 400.00
36 JGr(c),JKu,Battle Window. . . . 400.00
37 JGr(c),JKu,The Big Stretch. . . 400.00
38 JGr(c),RH,JKu,The
　　Floating Sentinel 400.00
39 JGr(c),JKu,The Four Faces
　　of Sgt. Fay. 400.00
40 JGr(c),IN,Walking Helmet 400.00
41 JKu(c),RH,JKu,The 50-50 War 300.00
42 JGr(c),JKu,Battle Arm 300.00
43 JGr(c),JKu,Command Post. . . . 300.00
44 JKu(c),The Flying Frogman . . 300.00
45 JGr(c),RH,Combat Waterboy . 300.00
46 JGr(c),IN,RH,Tank Busters . . . 300.00
47 JGr(c),JKu,MD,Battle Freight . 300.00
48 JGr(c),JKu,MD,Roadblock . . . 300.00
49 JGr(c),Walking Target 300.00
50 IN,RH,Bodyguard For A Sub. . 300.00
51 JGr(c),RH,Bomber's Moon . . . 250.00
52 JKu(c),RH,MD,Back
　　Seat Driver 250.00
53 JKu(c),JKu,Night Attack 250.00
54 JKu(c),IN,Diary of a
　　Fighter Pilot 250.00
55 JKu(c),RH,Split-Second Target 250.00
56 JKu,IN,RH,Frogman Jinx . 250.00
57 Pick-Up for Easy Co. 250.00
58 JKu(c),RH,MD,A Piece of Sky 250.00
59 JGr(c),JKu,The Hand of War . 250.00
60 JGr(c),The Time Table 250.00
61 JGr(c),IN,MD,Blind Target. . . . 250.00
62 JGr(c),RH,RA,No(c) 250.00
63 JGr(c),JKu,Frogman Carrier . . 250.00
64 JKu(c),JKu,RH,The Other
　　Man's War 250.00
65 JGr(c),JKu,MD,Same
　　Old Sarge 250.00
66 JGr(c),The Walking Fort 250.00
67 JGr(c),RH,A:Gunner&Sarge,
　　The Cover Man 800.00
68 JKu(c),Gunner&Sarge,
　　The Man & The Gun 300.00
69 JKu(c),A:Tank Killer,
　　Bazooka Hill 300.00
70 JKu(c),IN,Pigeon
　　Without Wings 250.00
71 JGr(c),A:Tank Killer,Target
　　For An Ammo Boy 200.00
72 JGr(c),A:Tank Killer,T.N.T.
　　Broom 200.00
73 JGr(c),JKu,No Detour 200.00
74 The Minute Commandos 200.00
75 JKu(c),Sink That Flattop 200.00
76 JKu(c),A:Tank Killer,
　　Just One More Tank 200.00
77 JKu(c),IN,MD,Big Fish-
　　little Fish 200.00

78 JGr(c),Tin Hat for an
　　Iron Man 200.00
79 JKu(c),RA,Showdown Soldier. 200.00
80 JGr(c),RA,The Medal Men . . . 200.00
81 JGr(c),IN,Ghost Ship of
　　Two Wars. 150.00
82 IN(c),B:Johnny Cloud,
　　The Flying Chief 300.00
83 IN(c),Fighting Blind 250.00
84 IN(c),Death Dive 150.00
85 RH(c),Battle Eagle 150.00
86 JGr(c),Top-Gun Ace 150.00
87 JGr(c),Broken Ace 150.00
88 JGr(c),The Ace of Vengeance 150.00
89 JGr(c),The Star Jockey. 150.00
90 JGr(c),Wingmate of Doom . . 125.00
91 RH(c),Two Missions To Doom 125.00
92 JGr(c),The Battle Hawk 125.00
93 RH(c),The Silent Rider 125.00
94 RH(c),Be Brave-Be Silent. . . . 125.00
95 RH(c),Second Sight
　　For a Pilot 125.00
96 RH(c),The Last Flight
　　of Lt. Moon 125.00
97 IN(c),A Target Called Johnny . 125.00
98 The Time-Bomb Ace 125.00
99 IN(c),The Empty Cockpit. 125.00
100 RH(c),Battle o/t Sky Chiefs. . 125.00
101 RH(c),Death Ship of
　　Three Wars 100.00
102 JKu(c),Blind Eagle-Hungry
　　Hawk 100.00
103 IN(c),Battle Ship-
　　Battle Heart 100.00
104 JKu(c),The Last Target 100.00
105 IN(c),Killer Horse-Ship 100.00
106 IN(c),Death Song For
　　A Battle Hawk 100.00
107 IN(c),Flame in the Sky 100.00
108 IN(c),Death-Dive of the Aces 100.00
109 IN(c),The Killer Slot. 100.00
110 RH(c),The Co-Pilot was
　　Death 100.00
111 RH(c),E:Johnny Cloud, Tag–
　　You're Dead. 100.00
112 RH(c),B:Balloon Buster,Lt.
　　Steve Savage-Balloon Buster 100.00
113 JKu(c),The Ace of
　　Sudden Death 100.00
114 JKu(c),The Ace Who
　　Died Twice 100.00
115 IN(c),A:Johnny Cloud,
　　Deliver One Enemy Ace-
　　Handle With Care 100.00
116 JKu(c),A:Baloon Buster,
　　Circle of Death. 100.00
117 Sept.–Oct., 1966 . . . . 100.00

ALL-AMERICAN COMICS
1999

1 RMz(s),F:Green Lantern &
　　Johnny Thunder. 2.25

ALL-FLASH
1941–47

1 EHi,O:Flash,I:The Monocle. 30,000.00
2 EHi,The Adventure of Roy
　　Revenge. 7,500.00
3 EHi,The Adventure of
　　Misplaced Faces 3,500.00
4 EHi,Tale of the Time Capsule 3,500.00
5 EHi,The Case of the Patsy
　　Colt! Last Quarterly 2,500.00
6 EHi,The Ray that Changed
　　Men's Souls 2,200.00
7 EHi,Adventures of a Writers
　　Fantasy, House of Horrors . 2,200.00
8 EHi,Formula to Fairyland!. . . 2,200.00
9 EHi,Adventure of the Stolen
　　Telescope 2,200.00
10 EHi,Case of the Curious Cat 2,200.00

All-Flash #14
© DC Comics Inc.

11 EHi,Troubles Come
　　in Doubles 2,000.00
12 EHi,Tumble INN to Trouble,
　　Becomes Quarterly on orders
　　from War Production Board
　　O:The Thinker. 2,000.00
13 EHi,I:The King 2,000.00
14 EHi,I:Winky, Blinky & Noddy
　　Green Lantern (c) 2,200.00
15 EHi,Secrets of a Stranger . . 2,000.00
16 EHi,A:The Sinister 2,000.00
17 Tales of the Three Wishes . . 2,000.00
18 A:Winky,Blinky&Noddy
　　B:Mutt & Jeff reprints 2,000.00
19 No Rest at the Rest Home . 2,000.00
20 A:Winky, Blinky & Noddy . . . 2,000.00
21 I:Turtle 1,500.00
22 The Money Doubler, E:Mutt
　　& Jeff reprints 1,500.00
23 The Bad Men of Bar Nothing 1,500.00
24 I:Worry Wart,3 Court
　　Clowns Get Caught 1,500.00
25 I:Slapsy Simmons,
　　Flash Jitterbugs 1,500.00
26 I:The Chef,The Boss,Shrimp
　　Coogan,A:Winky, Blinky &
　　Noddy. 1,500.00
27 A:The Thinker, Gangplank
　　Gus Story 1,500.00
28 A:Shrimp Coogan, Winky,
　　Blinky & Noddy. 1,500.00
29 The Thousand-Year Old Terror,
　　A:Winky, Blinky & Noddy . . 2,000.00
30 The Vanishing Snowman . . . 1,500.00
31 A:Black Hat,Planet of Sport . 1,500.00
32 I:Fiddler,A:Thinker 2,000.00

ALL FUNNY COMICS
1943–48

1 Genius Jones. 750.00
2 same 300.00
3 same 200.00
4 same 200.00
5 thru 10 . . . . @200.00
11 Genius Jones 200.00
12 same 200.00
13 same. 150.00
14 . . . . 150.00
15 . . . . 150.00
16 A:DC Superheroes 500.00
17 thru 23. . . . . @150.00

ALL-NEW ATOM, THE
July, 2006

1 JBy,TvS,F:Ryan Choi. 3.00

DC COMICS

2 JBy,TvS,V:M'ngalah 3.00
3 JBy,TvS,Ivytown mysteries 3.00
4 V:Giganta 3.00
5 V:Dwarfstar 3.00
6 V:Dwarfstar 3.00
7 The Time Pool, pt.1 . . . . 3.00
8 The Time Pool, pt. 2 . . . . 3.00
9 Jia, pt.1 . . . . 3.00
10 Jia, pt.2 . . . . 3.00
11 Jia, pt.3 . . . . 3.00
12 Search for Ray Palmer, pt.1 . . . 3.00
13 Search for Ray Palmer, pt.2 . . . 3.00
14 Search for Ray Palmer, pt.3 . . . 3.00
15 Search for Ray Palmer, pt.4 . . . 3.00
16 Mysteries deepen 3.00

ALL STAR BATMAN
AND ROBIN,
THE BOY WONDER
July, 2005

1 FM(s),JLe,SW 3.00
1a variant (c) 3.00
1b Special edition, 48-pg. 20.00
2 FM(s),JLe,SW 3.00
3 FM(s),JLe,SW 3.00
4 FM(s),JLe,SW, F:Black Canary . . 3.00
4a variant FM(c) 3.00
5 FM,JLe,SW 3.00
5a variant (c) (1:10) 5.00
6 FM,JLe,SW 3.00
6a variant (c) (1:10) 5.00
7 FM,JLe,SW 3.00
7a variant (c) (1:10) 3.00

ALL-STAR COMICS
1940–51

1 B:Flash,Hawkman,Hourman,
   Sandman,Spectre,Red White
   & Blue 25,000.00
2 B:Green Lantern and Johnny
   Thunder 10,000.00
3 First meeting of Justice Society
   with Flash as Chairman . . 75,000.00
4 First mission of JSA 10,000.00
5 V:Mr. X,I:Hawkgirl 8,000.00
6 Flash Leaves 5,500.00
7 Green Lantern Becomes Chairman,
   L:Hourman, C:Superman,
   Batman & Flash 6,000.00
8 I:Wonder Women;Starman and
   Dr. Mid-Nite Join,Hawkman
   Becomes Chairman 60,000.00
9 JSA in Latin America. 5,500.00

All-Star Comics #11
© *DC Comics, Inc.*

10 C:Flash & Green Lantern,
   JSA Time Travel story 5,500.00
11 Wonder Women joins;
   I:Justice Battalion 7,000.00
12 V:Black Dragon society 5,000.00
13 V:Hitler 5,000.00
14 JSA in Occupied Europe . . . 5,000.00
15 I:Brain Wave,A:JSA's
   Girl Friends 5,000.00
16 Propaganda/relevance issue 3,000.00
17 V:Brain Wave 3,000.00
18 I:King Bee 3,000.00
19 Hunt for Hawkman 3,000.00
20 I:Monster 3,000.00
21 Time Travel Story 2,500.00
22 Sandman and Dr. Fate Leave,
   I:Conscience, Good Fairy. . 2,500.00
23 I:Psycho-Pirate 2,500.00
24 Propaganda/relevance issue,
   A:Conscience&Wildcat,Mr.Terrific;
   L:Starman & Spectre; Flash
   & Green Lantern Return . . . 2,500.00
25 JSA whodunit issue 3,000.00
26 V:Metal Men from Jupiter . . . 3,500.00
27 Handicap issue,A:Wildcat . . . 3,500.00
28 Ancient curse comes to life . 3,500.00
29 I:Landor from 25th Century . 3,500.00
30 V:Brain Wave 3,500.00
31 V:Zor 3,500.00
32 V:Psycho-Pirate 2,300.00
33 V:Soloman Grundy,A:Doiby
   Dickles, Last appearance
   Thunderbolt 6,000.00
34 I:Wizard 2,000.00
35 I:Per Degaton. 2,000.00
36 A:Superman and Batman. . . 5,000.00
37 I:Injustice Society of
   the World 2,700.00
38 V:Villians of History,
   A:Black Canary. 3,500.00
39 JSA in Magic World,
   Johnny Thunder leaves . . . 2,500.00
40 A:Black Canary,Junior Justice
   Society of America 2,500.00
41 Black Canary joins,A:Harlequin,
   V:Injustice Society
   of the World 2,500.00
42 I:Alchemist 2,400.00
43 V:Interdimensional gold men 2,400.00
44 I:Evil Star 2,400.00
45 Crooks develop stellar
   JSA powers 2,400.00
46 Comedy issue 2,400.00
47 V:Billy the Kid. 2,400.00
48 Time Travel story 2,400.00
49 V:Comet-Being Invaders . . . 2,400.00
50 V:Flash's Classmate 3,000.00
51 V:Diamond Men from Center
   of the Earth. 2,400.00
52 JSA Disappears from
   Earth for Years 2,400.00
53 Time Travel issue. 2,400.00
54 Circus issue 2,400.00
55 JSA Fly to Jupiter. 2,400.00
56 V:Chameleons from
   31st Century 2,400.00
57 I:Key. 3,100.00
Becomes:

ALL STAR WESTERN
April-May, 1951

58 GK(c),Trigger Twins 800.00
59 GK(c),Trail of Double Decoys . 500.00
60 CI(c),Raiders of Rocky City . . 500.00
61 thru 64 ATh . . . . @400.00
65 CI,Green Bandanna Raiders . 400.00
66 CI,Powderkeg Town 450.00
67 GK,B:Johnny Thunder 500.00
68 thru 81 . . . . @250.00
82 thru 98 . . . . @250.00
99 FF 250.00
100 CI,Sheriff for Hire 250.00
101 thru 104 . . . . @200.00

105 O:JSA, March, 1987 . . . . 200.00
106 and 107 . . . . @200.00
108 O:Johnny Thunder 400.00
109 thru 116 . . . . @200.00
117 CI,O:Super-Chief. 250.00
118 Eyes of Johnny Thunder. . . . 200.00
119 Ghost-Town Gunfight 200.00

ALL-STAR COMICS
1976–78

58 RE,WW,R:JSA,I:Power Girl . . . 75.00
59 RE,WW,Brain Wave 40.00
60 KG,WW,I:Vulcan 40.00
61 KG,WW,V:Vulcan 40.00
62 KG,WW,A:E-2 Superman 40.00
63 KG,WW,A:E-2 Superman,
   Solomon Grundy 40.00
64 WW,Shining Knight. 40.00
65 KG,WW,E-2 Superman,
   Vandal Savage 40.00
66 JSon,BL,Injustice Society 40.00
67 JSon,BL 40.00
68 JSon,BL 40.00
69 JSon,BL,A:E-2 Superman,
   Starman,Dr.Mid-Nite 60.00
70 JSon,BL,Huntress. 40.00
71 JSon,BL 40.00
72 JSon,A:Golden.Age Huntress. . 40.00
73 JSon 40.00
74 JSon 40.00

ALL STAR COMICS
1999

1 JeR(s),F:Justice Society
   of America, V:Stalker's Seven . . 3.00
2 JeR(s) conclusion 3.00
Giant #1 80-page 5.00

ALL STAR SQUADRON
1981–87

1 RB,JOy,JSa,I:Degaton 8.00
2 RB,JOy,Robotman 5.00
3 RB,JOy,Robotman 5.00
4 RB,JOy,Robotman 5.00
5 RB/JOy,I:Firebrand(Dannette) . . . 5.00
6 JOy,Hawkgirl 5.00
7 JOy,Hawkgirl 5.00
8 DH/JOy,A:Steel 5.00
9 DH/JOy,A:Steel 5.00
10 JOy,V:Binary Brotherhood 5.00
11 JOy,V:Binary Brotherhood. 5.00
12 JOy,R:Dr.Hastor O:Hawkman . . . 5.00
13 JOy,photo(c) 5.00
14 JOy,JLA crossover 5.00
15 JOy,JLA crossover 5.00
16 I&D:Nuclear. 5.00
17 Trial of Robotman 5.00
18 V:Thor 5.00
19 V:Brainwave 5.00
20 JOy,V:Brainwave 5.00
21 JOy,I:Cyclotron (1st JOy
   Superman). 7.00
22 JOy,V:Deathbolt,Cyclotron 5.00
23 JOy,I:Amazing-Man. 5.00
24 JOy,I:Brainwave,Jr. 7.00
25 JOy,I:Infinity Inc. 7.00
26 JOy,Infinity Inc. 7.00
27 Spectre 5.00
28 JOy,Spectre. 5.00
29 JOy,retold story. 5.00
30 V:Black Dragons 5.00
31 All-Star gathering 5.00
32 O:Freedom Fighters 5.00
33 Freedom Fighters,I:Tsunami . . . 5.00
34 Freedom Fighters 5.00
35 RB,Shazam family 5.00
36 Shazam family 5.00
37 A:Shazam Family 5.00
38 V:The Real American 5.00
39 V:The Real American 5.00
40 D:The Real American 5.00

All Star Squadron #4
© *DC Comics Inc.*

41 O:Starman. 5.00
42 V:Tsunami,Kung 5.00
43 V:Tsunami,Kung 5.00
44 I:Night & Fog. 5.00
45 I:Zyklon. 5.00
46 V:Baron Blitzkrieg. 5.00
47 TM,O:Dr.Fate 10.00
48 A:Blackhawk 5.00
49 A:Dr.Occult 5.00
50 Crisis. 7.00
51 AA,Crisis 5.00
52 Crisis 5.00
53 Crisis,A:The Dummy 5.00
54 Crisis,V:The Dummy 5.00
55 Crisis,V:Anti-Monitor 5.00
56 Crisis 5.00
57 A:Dr.Occult 5.00
58 I:Mekanique 5.00
59 A:Mekanique,Spectre 5.00
60 Crisis 1942, conclusion. 5.00
61 O:Liberty Belle 5.00
62 O:The Shining Knight 5.00
63 O:Robotman 5.00
64 WB/TD,V:Funny Face. 5.00
65 DH/TD,O:Johnny Quick 5.00
66 TD,O:Tarantula 5.00
67 TD,Last Issue,O:JSA 5.00
Ann.#1 JOy,O:G.A.,Atom 5.00
Ann.#2 JOy,Infinity Inc. 5.00
Ann.#3 WB,JOy,KG,GP,DN 5.00

ALL STAR SUPERMAN
Nov., 2005
1 GMo(s). 4.00
2 GMo(s), Fortress of Solitude . . . 3.00
3 GMo(s), Lois Lane, Superwoman 3.00
4 GMo(s), F:Jimmy Olsen. 3.00
5 GMo(s),Clark Kent, convict 3.00
6 GMo(s),back to Smallville 3.00
7 GMo(s),V:Bizarro 3.00
8 GMo(s),V:Bizarro 3.00
9 GMo(s). 3.00

ALL STAR WESTERN
See: WEIRD WESTERN TALES

AMAZONS ATTACK
Apr., 2007
1 (of 6) 3.00
2 F:JLA, Teen Titans. 3.00
3 F:Supergirl and Wonder Girl 3.00
4 Target: Pres. of the US 3.00
5 Final battle begins 3.00

6 Finale. 3.00

AMBER:
THE GUNS OF AVALON
Aug., 1996
1 (of 3) adapt. of Roger Zelazny
    classic 7.00
2 and 3 conclusion . . . . @7.00

AMBUSH BUG
1985
1 KG,I:Cheeks. 3.00
2 KG thru 4 . . . . @3.00
Spec.#1 Stocking Stuffer,
    KG,R:Cheeks (1986) 3.00
Spec.#1 Nothing Special
    KG,A:Sandman,Death (1992) . . 3.50

AMERICA VS.
JUSTICE SOCIETY
Jan.–April, 1985
1 AA,R,Thomas Script 10.00
2 AA 7.00
3 AA 7.00
4 AA, ... 7.00

AMERICAN CENTURY
DC/Vertigo, March, 2001
1 HC,vet hijacks plane 5.00
2 HC,Hell hotter for Harry. 3.00
3 HC,Guatemalan Revolution. 3.00
4 HC,Bananarama 3.00
5 HC,The Protector,pt.1 . . . . 3.00
6 HC,The Protector,pt.2 . . . . 3.00
7 HC,The Protector,pt.3 . . . . 3.00
8 HC,The Protector,pt.4 . . . . 3.00
9 HC,Route 66 . . . . 3.00
10 HC,White Lightning,pt.1 . . . . . . 3.00
11 HC,White Lightning,pt.2 . . . . . . 3.00
12 HC,White Lightning,pt.3 . . . . . . 3.00
13 HC,White Lightning,pt.4 . . . . . . 3.00
14 HC,An American in Paris,pt.1 . . 3.00
15 HC,An American in Paris,pt.2 . . 3.00
16 HC,An American in Paris,pt.3 . . 3.00
17 HC,Coming Home,pt.1 . . . . 3.00
18 HC,Coming Home,pt.2 . . . . 3.00
19 HC,Coming Home,pt.3 . . . . 3.00
20 HC,Coming Home,Pt.4 . . . . 3.00
21 HC,Coming Home,pt.5 . . . . 3.00
22 HC,Tramps,pt.1 . . . . 3.00
23 HC,Tramps,pt.2. . . . . 3.00
24 HC,one-shot 3.00
25 HC,Bite the Big Apple,pt.1 . . . . 3.00
26 HC,Bite the Big Apple,pt.2 . . . . 3.00
27 HC,Bite the Big Apple,pt.3 . . . . 3.00

AMERICAN FREAK: A
TALE OF THE UN-MEN
DC/Vertigo, 1994
1 B:DLp,(s),VcL,R:Un-Men 2.25
2 VcL,A:Crassus. 2.25
3 VcL,A:Scylla. 2.25
4 VcL,A:Scylla. 2.25
5 VcL,Final Issue 2.25

AMERICAN SPLENDOR
DC/Vertigo, Sept., 2006
1 (of 4) HP 3.00
2 HP 3.00
3 HP 3.00
4 HP 3.00

AMERICAN VIRGIN
DC/Vertigo, March, 2006
1 You Always Remember Your
    First Time. 3.00
2 Head, pt. 2 . . . . 3.00

3 Head, pt. 3 . . . . 3.00
4 Head, pt. 4 . . . . 3.00
5 Going Down, pt.1 . . . . 3.00
6 Going Down, pt.2. . . . . 3.00
7 Going Down, pt.3. . . . . 3.00
8 Going Down, pt.4. . . . . 3.00
9 Going Down, epilogue 3.00
10 Adam's darkest secrets. 3.00
11 Wet 3.00
12 Caught with pants down 3.00
13 Six Good Women 3.00
14 Wet, concl. 3.00
15 Around the World, pt.1 . . . . 3.00
16 Around the World, pt.2 . . . . 3.00
17 Around the World, pt.3 . . . . 3.00
18 Around the World, pt.4 . . . . 3.00
19 Around the World, pt.5 . . . . 3.00
20 69, pt.1 . . . . 3.00

Amethyst Princess of Gemworld #1
© *DC Comics, Inc.*

AMETHYST
[Limited Series], 1983–84
[PRINCESS OF GEMWORLD]
1 Origin 2.50
2 thru 7 EC . . . . @2.50
8 EC,O:Gemworld. 2.50
9 thru 12 EC . . . . @2.50
Spec.#1 KG 2.50

[Regular Series], 1985–86
1 thru 12 EC . . . . @2.50
13 EC,Crisis,A:Dr.Fate. 2.50
14 EC. 2.50
15 EC,Castle Amethyst Destroyed . 2.50
16 EC. 2.50
Spec.#1 EM. 2.50

[Mini-Series], 1987–88
1 EM 2.00
2 EM 2.00
3 EM 2.00
4 EM,O:Mordru 2.00

ANARKY
March, 1997
1 AIG(s),NBy,JRu,Anarky vs.
    Etrigan. 4.00
2 AIG(s),NBy,JRu,V:Darkseid 2.50
3 AIG(s),NBy,JRu,A:Batman 2.50
4 AIG(s),NBy,JRu,A:Batman,concl.. 2.50

2nd Series,1999
1 AIG(s),NBy,JRu,F:JLA 2.50
2 AIG(s),NBy,JRu,F:GreenLantern . 2.50
3 AIG(s),NBy,JRu,F:GreenLantern . 2.50

4 AlG(s),NBy,JRu,V:Ra's al Ghul . . 2.50
5 AlG(s),NBy,JRu,V:Ra's
　　al Ghul,pt.2 . . . . 2.50
6 AlG(s),NBy,JRu,F:Ra's
　　al Ghul,pt.3 . . . . 2.50
7 AlG,NBy,JRu,Day of Judgment . . 2.50
8 AlG(s),NBy,JRu, final issue 2.50

ANGEL & THE APE
1991
1 Apes of Wrath,pt.1 . . . . 3.00
2 Wrath pt.2,A:G.Gardner 3.00
3 Wrath,pt.3,A:InferiorFive 3.00
4 Wrath,pt.4,A:InferiorFive 3.00

ANGEL AND THE APE
DC/Vertigo, Aug., 2001
1 (of 4) HC,F:Angel O'Day 3.00
2 thru 4 HC . . . . @3.00

ANGELTOWN
DC/Vertigo, Nov., 2004
1 (of 5) SMa 3.00
2 thru 4 SMa . . . . @3.00
5 SMa 3.00

Anima #12 © DC Comics, Inc.

ANIMA
DC/Vertigo, 1994–95
1 R:Anima 2.50
2 V:Scarecrow. 2.50
3 V:Scarecrow. 2.50
4 A:Nameless one. 2.50
5 CI,V:Arkana 2.50
6 CI,V:Arkana 2.50
7 Zero Hour. 2.50
8 Nameless One. 2.50
9 Superboy & Nameless One. 2.50
10 A:Superboy 2.50
11 V:Nameless One 2.50
12 A:Hawkman,V:Shrike 2.50
13 A:Hawkman,Shrike 2.50
14 Return to Gotham City 2.50
15 V:Psychic Vampire, final issue . . 3.00

ANIMAL ANTICS
1946–49
1 B:Racoon Kids. 600.00
2 . . . . 300.00
3 thru 10 . . . . @200.00
11 thru 23 . . . . @125.00

ANIMAL-MAN
1988–95
1 BB(c),B:GMo(s),ChT,DHz,
　　B:Animal Rights,I:Dr.Myers . . . 12.00
2 BB(c),ChT,DHz,A:Superman 6.00
3 BB(c),ChT,DHz,A:B'wana Beast . 5.00
4 BB(c),ChT,DHz,V:B'wana Beast,
　　E:Animal Rights. 5.00
5 BB(c),ChT,DHz,
　　I&D:Crafty Coyote 5.00
6 BB(c),ChT,DHz,A:Hawkman 5.00
7 BB(c),ChT,DHz,D:Red Mask 5.00
8 BB(c),ChT,DHz,V:Mirror Master . . 5.00
9 BB(c),DHz,TG,A:Martian
　　Manhunter. 5.00
10 BB(c),ChT,DHz,A:Vixen,
　　B:O:Animal Man 5.00
11 BB(c),ChT,DHz,I:Hamed Ali,
　　Tabu,A:Vixen 3.00
12 BB(c),D:Hamed Ali,A:Vixen,
　　B'wanaBeast 3.00
13 BB(c),I:Dominic Mndawe,R:B'wana
　　Beast,Apartheid 3.00
14 BB(c),TG,SeM,A:Future Animal
　　Man,I:Lennox. 3.00
15 BB(c),ChT,DHz,A:Dolphin 3.00
16 BB(c),ChT,DHz,A:JLA. 3.00
17 BB(c),ChT,DHz,A:Mirr.Master . . . 3.00
18 BB(c),ChT,DHz,A:Lennox 3.00
19 BB(c),ChT,DHz,D:Ellen,
　　Cliff,Maxine 3.00
20 BB(c),ChT,DHz,I:Bug-Man 3.00
21 BB(c),ChT,DHz,N&V:Bug-Man . . 3.00
22 BB(c),PCu,SeM,A:Rip Hunter . . . 3.00
23 BB(c),A:Phantom Stranger 3.00
24 BB(c),V:Psycho Pirate 3.00
25 BB(c),ChT,MFm,I:Comic
　　Book Limbo 3.00
26 BB(c),E:GMo(s),ChT,MFm,
　　A:Grant Morrison 3.00
27 BB(c),B:PMi(s),ChT,MFm 3.00
28 BB(c),ChT,MFm,I:Nowhere Man,
　　I&D:Front Page 3.00
29 ChT,SDi,V:National Man 3.00
30 BB(c),ChT,MFm,V:Angel Mob. . . 3.00
31 BB(c),ChT,MFm 3.00
32 BB(c),E:PMi(s),ChT,MFm 3.00
33 BB(c),B:TV(s),SDi,A:Travis
　　Cody 3.00
34 BB(c),SDi,Requiem. 3.00
35 BB(c),SDi,V:Radioactive Dogs . . 3.00
36 BB(c),SDi,A:Mr.Rainbow. 3.00
37 BB(c),SDi,Animal/Lizard Man . . 3.00
38 BB(c),SDi,A:Mr.Rainbow. 3.00
39 BB(c),TMd,SDi,Wolfpack in
　　San Diego 3.00
40 BB(c),SDi,War of the Gods
　　x-over. 3.00
41 BB(c),SDi,V:Star Labs
　　Renegades,I:Winky 3.00
42 BB(c),SDi,V:Star Labs
　　Renegades 3.00
43 BB(c),SDi,I:Tristess,A:Vixen 3.00
44 BB(c),SDi,A:Vixen. 3.00
45 BB(c),StP,SDi,I:L.Decker. 3.00
46 BB(c),SDi,I:Frank Baker 3.00
47 BB(c),SDi,I:Shining Man,
　　(B'wana Beast) 3.00
48 BB(c),SDi,V:Antagon. 3.00
49 BB(c),SDi,V:Antagon. 3.00
50 BB(c),E:TV(s),SDi,I:Metaman . . 5.00
51 BB(c),B:JaD(s),StP,B:Flesh
　　and Blood 3.00
52 BB(c),StP,Homecoming. 3.00
53 BB(c),StP,Flesh and Blood 3.00
54 BB(c),StP,Flesh and Blood 3.00
55 BB(c),StP,Flesh and Blood 3.00
56 BB(c),StP,E:Flesh and Blood,
　　Double-sized 6.00

Animal Man #60
© DC Comics, Inc.

DC/Vertigo, 1993
57 BB(c),StP,B:Recreation,
　　Ellen in NY. 3.00
58 BB(c),StP,Wild Side 3.00
59 BB(c),RsB,GHi(i),Wild Town 3.00
60 RsB,GHi(i),Wild life 3.00
61 BB(c),StP,Tooth and Claw#1 . . . 3.00
62 BB(c),StP,Tooth and Claw#2. . . . 3.00
63 BB(c),V:Leviathan. 3.00
64 DlB(c),WSm,DnS(i),
　　Breath of God 3.00
65 RDB(c),WSm,
　　Perfumed Garden 3.00
66 A:Kindred Spirit. 3.00
67 StP,Mysterious Ways #1 . . . . . . 3.00
68 StP,Mysterious Ways #2 . . . . . . 3.00
69 Animal Man's Family. 3.00
70 GgP(c),StP 3.00
71 GgP(c),StP,Maxine Alive? 3.00
72 StP 3.00
73 StP,Power Life Church 3.00
74 StP,Power Life Church 3.00
75 StP,Power Life Church 3.00
76 StP,Pilgrimage problems. 3.00
77 Cliff shot 3.00
78 StP,Animal Man poisoned. 3.00
79 New Direction 3.00
80 New Direction 3.00
81 Wild Type,pt.1 . . . . 3.00
82 Wild Type,pt.2 . . . . 3.00
83 Wild Type,pt.3 . . . . 3.00
84 F:Maxine,SupernaturalDreams. . 3.00
85 Animal Mundi,pt.1 . . . . 3.00
86 Animal Mundi,pt.2 . . . . 3.00
87 Animal Mundi,pt.3 . . . . 3.00
88 Morphogenetic Fields 3.00
89 final issue 3.00
Ann.#1 BB(c),JaD,TS(i),RIB(i),
　　Children Crusade,F:Maxine. . . . 4.25

ANIMANIACS
Warner Bros./DC May, 1995
1 F:Yakko,Wakko,Dot 8.00
2 thru 20 . . . . @4.00
21 thru 59 . . . . @3.00
Christmas Spec. 4.00

ANTHRO
1968–69
1 HwP. 150.00
2 HwP. 90.00
3 thru 5 HwP . . . . @100.00
6 HwP,WW(c&a) 100.00

AQUAMAN

[1st Regular Series], 1962–78

1 NC,I:Quisp 2,000.00
2 NC,V:Captain Sykes 1,000.00
3 NC,Aquaman from Atlantis . . . 750.00
4 NC,A:Quisp 500.00
5 NC,The Haunted Sea 500.00
6 NC,A:Quisp 400.00
7 NC,Sea Beasts of Atlantis 400.00
8 NC,Plot to Steal the Seas 400.00
9 NC,V:King Neptune 400.00
10 NC,A:Quisp 400.00
11 I: Mera 325.00
12 NC,The Cosmic Gladiators . . . 325.00
13 NC,Invasion of the Giant
Reptiles 325.00
14 NC,AquamanSecretPowers . . 325.00
15 NC,Menace of the Man-Fish . . 325.00
16 NC,Duel of the Sea Queens . . 325.00
17 NC,Man Who Vanquished
Aquaman 325.00
18 W:Aquaman & Mera 325.00
19 NC,Atlanteans for Sale 325.00
20 NC,Sea King's DoubleDoom . 325.00
21 NC,I:Fisherman 150.00
22 NC,The Trap of the Sinister
Sea Nymphs 150.00
23 NC,I:Aquababy 150.00
24 NC,O:Black Manta 150.00
25 NC,Revolt of Aquaboy 150.00
26 NC,I:O.G.R.E. 150.00
27 NC,Battle of the Rival
Aquamen 150.00
28 NC,Hail Aquababy,King of
Atlantis 150.00
29 I:Ocean Master 175.00
30 NC,C:JLA 175.00
31 NC,V:O.G.R.E. 175.00
32 NC,V:Tryton 175.00
33 NC,I:Aquagirl 200.00
34 NC,I:Aquabeast 125.00
35 I:Black Manta 125.00
36 NC,What Seeks the
Awesome Threesome? 125.00
37 I:Scavenger 125.00
38 NC,I:Liquidator 125.00
39 NC,How to Kill a Sea King . . . 125.00
40 JAp,Sorcerers from the Sea . . 125.00
41 JAp,Quest for Mera,pt.1 . . . . . 100.00
42 JAp,Quest for Mera,pt.2 . . . . . 100.00
43 JAp,Quest for Mera,pt.3 . . . . . 100.00
44 JAp,Quest for Mera,pt.4 . . . . . 100.00
45 JAp,Quest for Mera,pt.5 . . . . . 100.00
46 JAp,Quest for Mera concl. . . . 100.00
47 JAp,Revolution in Atlantis #1
rep.Adventure #268 . . . . 100.00
48 JAp,Revolution in Atlantis #2
rep.Adventure #260 . . . . 135.00
49 JAp,As the Seas Die 100.00
50 JAp,NA,A:Deadman 175.00
51 JAp,NA,A:Deadman 175.00
52 JAp,NA,A:Deadman 175.00
53 JAp,Is California Sinking? 40.00
54 JAp,Crime Wave 40.00
55 JAp,Return of the Alien 40.00
56 JAp,I&O:Crusader (1970) 40.00
57 JAp,V:Black Manta (1977) . . . 40.00
58 JAp,O:Aquaman rtd 50.00
59 JAp,V:Scavenger 40.00
60 DN,V:Scavenger 40.00
61 DN,BMc,A:Batman 40.00
62 DN,A:Ocean Master 30.00
63 DN,V:Ocean Master,
final issue 30.00

[1st Limited Series], 1986

1 V:Ocean Master 6.00
2 V:Ocean Master 4.00
3 V:Ocean Master 4.00
4 V:Ocean Master 4.00

[2nd Limited Series], 1989

1 CS,Atlantis Under Siege 3.50

2 CS,V:Invaders 3.00
3 CS,Mera turned Psychotic 3.00
4 CS,Poseidonis Under Siege 3.00
5 CS,Last Stand,final issue 3.00
Spec#1 MPa,Legend o/Aquaman . 3.00

[2nd Regular Series], 1991–92

1 Poseidonis Under Attack,
C:J'onn J'onzz,Blue Beetle 3.00
2 V:Oumland 2.50
3 I:Iqula 2.50
4 V:Iqula,A:Queequeg 2.50
5 A:Aqualad,Titans,M.Manhunter,
R:Manta 2.50
6 V: Manta 2.50
7 R:Mera 2.50
8 A:Batman,V:NKV Demon 2.50
9 Eco-Wars#1,A:Sea Devils 2.50
10 Eco-Wars#2,A:Sea Devils 2.50
11 V:Gigantic Dinosaur 2.50
12 A:Iaula 2.50
13 V:The Scavenger 2.50
14 V:The Scavenger 2.50

[3rd Regular Series], 1994–2001

0 B:PDd(s),Paternal secret 7.00
1 PDd(s),R:Aqualad,I:Charybdis . . 6.00
2 V:Charybdis 7.00
3 B:PDd(s),Superboy 4.00
4 B:PDd(s),Lobo 4.00
5 New Costume 4.00
6 V:The Deep Six 4.00
7 Kako's Metamorphosis 4.00
8 V:Corona and Naiad 4.00
9 JPi(c&a),V:Deadline,A:Koryak . . 3.00
10 A:Green Lantern,Koryak 3.00
11 R:Mera 3.00
12 F:Mera 3.00
13 V:Thanatos 3.00
14 PDd,V:Major Disaster,Underworld
Unleashed tie-in 3.00
15 PDd,V:Tiamat 3.00
16 PDd,A:Justice League 3.00
17 PDd,V:underwater gargoyles . . . 3.00
18 PDd,Biblical Sense 3.00
19 PDd,V:Ocean Master 3.00
20 PDd,V:Ocean Master 3.00
21 PDd,JCf,A:Dolphin,
V:ThiernaNaOge 3.00
22 PDd(s) 3.00
23 PDd(s),I:Deep Blue (Neptune
Perkins) 3.00
24 PDd(s),A:Neptune Perkins 3.00
25 PDd(s),MEg,HSm,Atlantis united,
Aquaman king? 3.00

Aquaman 3rd Series #38
© DC Comics Inc.

26 PDd(s),MEg,HSm,Oceans
threatened, Final Night tie-in . . . 3.00
27 PDd(s),MEg,HSm,V:Demon
Gate, dolphin killer 3.00
28 PDd(s),JCf,JP,A:J'onn J'onzz . . . 3.00
29 PDd(s),MEg,HSm, ... 3.00
30 PDd(s),MEg,HSm,The Pit 3.00
31 PDd(s),V:The Shark, mind-
controlled aquatic army 3.00
32 PDd(s),A:Swamp Thing 3.00
33 PDd(s),Aquaman's dark powers
affect him physically 3.00
34 PDd(s),V:Triton 3.00
35 PDd(s),JCf,I:Gamesman,
A:Animal Man 3.00
36 PDd(s),JCf,R:Poseidonis,
Tempest,Vulko 3.00
37 PDd,JCf,Genesis,V:Darkseid . . . 3.00
38 PDd,JCf,capitalism 3.00
39 PDd,JCf,Perkins Family Reunion 3.00
40 PDd,JCf,Dr. Polaris 3.00
41 PDd,JCf,BSf,F:Power Girl 2.50
42 PDd,JCf 2.50
43 PDd,JCf,Millennium Giants,
pt.2 x-over, A:Superman Red . . 2.50
44 PDd,JCf,F:Golden Age Flash,
Sentinel 2.50
45 PDd,JCf,V:Triton 2.50
46 PDd,JCf,news of Mera 2.50
47 DAn,Shadows on Water,pt.1 . . . . 2.50
48 DAn,Shadows on Water,pt.2 . . . . 2.50
49 DAn,ALa,JCf,V:Tempest 2.50
50 EL,NRd,New Costume 2.50
51 EL,NRd,V:King Noble 2.50
52 EL,V:Fire Trolls 2.50
53 EL,A:Superman 2.50
54 EL,A:Landlovers 2.50
55 EL,wooing Mera 2.50
56 EL,V:Piranha Man,pt.1 . . . . 2.50
57 EL,V:Piranha Man,pt.2 . . . . 2.50
58 EL,V:DemonGate & BlackManta . 2.50
59 EL,drugs in Atlantis 2.50
60 NRd,W:Tempest & Dolphin 2.50
61 NRd,Day of Judgment x-over . . . 2.50
62 EL(s),NRd 2.50
63 NRd 2.50
64 DJu,SEp,NRd 2.50
65 DJu,SEp,NRd 2.50
66 DJu,PR,NRd,F:JLA 2.50
67 DJu,SEp,NRd 2.50
68 DJu,SEp,NRd,V:Cerdia 2.50
69 DJu,SEp,NRd, ... 2.50
70 DJu,new alliance 3.00
71 DJu,SEp,NRd,A:Warlord 3.00
72 DJu,SEp,NRd,V:Ch'Rinn 3.00
73 DJu,SEp,NRd,V:Valgos 3.00
74 DJu,SEp,NRd,death of friend . . . 3.00
75 DJu,SEp,NRd,final issue 3.00
Ann.#1 Year One Annual, V:Triton,
A:Superman,Mera 4.00
Ann.#2 Legends o/t Dead Earth . . . 3.50
Ann.#3 Pulp Heroes (Hard Boiled) . 5.00
Ann.#4 PDa, Ghosts 3.50
Ann.#5 JOs(s),MBr,DG, JLApe
Gorilla Warfare 3.50
Spec.#1,000,000 DAn&ALa(s),TGb,
BAn, King of Waterworld 3.00
Secret Files #1 EL 5.00

[4th Regular Series], Dec. 2002

1 Obsidian Age aftermath 3.00
2 F:Martian Manhunter 3.00
3 New look and costume 3.00
4 F:Tempest 3.00
5 V:The Thirst 3.00
6 V:The Thirst 3.00
7 undead pirates 3.00
8 V:Black Mantra 3.00
9 V:Black Mantra 3.00
10 V:The Thirst 3.00
11 V:The Thirst 3.00
12 V:The Thirst 3.00
13 Perfect storm 2.50

14 Octo-Man 2.50
15 American Tidal,pt.1 . . . . 2.50
16 American Tidal,pt.2 . . . . 2.50
17 American Tidal,pt.3 . . . . 2.50
18 American Tidal,pt.4 . . . . 2.50
19 F:Lorena 2.50
20 American Tidal,concl. 2.50
21 With the Fishes,pt.1 . . . . 2.50
22 With the Fishes,pt.2 . . . . 2.50
23 With the Fishes,pt.3 . . . . 2.50
24 JOs(s),CsB, Sharks 2.50
25 JAr(s),in San Diego. 2.50
26 JAr(s),I:Aquagirl 2.50
27 JAr(s),V:Ocean Master 2.50
28 JAr(s),V:Malrey 2.50
29 JAr(s),Malrey vs. Conger 2.50
30 JAr(s),Black Manta returns 2.50
31 JAr(s),V:Black Manta 2.50
32 JAr(s),V:Black Manta 2.50
33 JAr(s),V:Black Manta 2.50
34 JAr(s),reunited with Mera 2.50
35 JAr(s),Omac project tie-in 2.50
36 JAr(s),Koryak returns to Atlantis . 2.50
37 JAr(s),V:Spectre 2.50
38 JAr(s),New home in Sub Diego . 2.50
39 JAr(s),V:Black Manta 2.50
Spec. Secret Files 2003. . . . . 5.00
Becomes:

AQUAMAN:
SWORD OF ATLANTIS
40 KBk,Once and Future, pt.1 . . . . 3.00
41 KBk,Once and Future, pt.2 . . . . 3.00
42 KBk,Once and Future, pt.3 . . . . 3.00
43 KBk,Once and Future, pt.4 . . . . 3.00
44 KBk,Once and Future, pt.5 . . . . 3.00
45 KBk,Once and Future, pt.6 . . . . 3.00
46 KBk,A:King Shark 3.00
47 KBk,A:Mera, Vulko 3.00
48 KBk,Way of the Fisherman 3.00
49 KBk,V:The Fisherman. 3.00
50 King of the Sea, 48-pgs. 4.00
51 Black Manta;Trident of Poseidon 3.00
52 V:Black Manta. 3.00
53 Control of Sub Diego 3.00
54 SwM,Dweller in the Depths 3.00
55 F:Arthur, Vulko 3.00
56 Aquaman's murky past 3.00
57 New Aquaman 3.00

AQUAMAN: TIME & TIDE
1993–94
1 PDd(s),O:Aquaman 3.00
2 thru 4 PDd(s),O:Aquaman . . . @3.00

ARAK
1981–85
1 EC,O:Ara 3.00
2 thru 12 EC . . . . @2.50
13 thru 23 AA . . . . @2.50
24 Double size 2.50
25 thru 50 . . . . @2.50
Ann.#1 . . . . 2.50

ARCANA: THE BOOKS
OF MAGIC
DC/Vertigo, 1994
Ann.#1 JBo(c),JNR(s),PrG,Children's
　　Crusade,R:Tim Hunter,
　　A:Free Country 4.00

ARION,
LORD OF ATLANTIS
1982–85
1 JDu,Star Spawn Sun Death 3.00
2 JDu,I:Mara 2.50
3 JDu 2.50
4 JDu,O:Arion 2.50
5 JDu 2.50

6 JDu 2.50
7 thru 12 . . . . @2.50
13 thru 15 JDu . . . . @2.50
16 thru 35 . . . . @2.50
Spec. 2.50

ARION THE IMMORTAL
1992
1 RWi,R:Arion 3.00
2 RWi,V:Garffon 2.25
3 RWi,V:Garn Daanuth 2.25
4 RWi,V:Garn Daanuth 2.25
5 RWi,Darkworlet 2.25
6 RWi,MG,A:Power Girl 2.25

ARKHAM ASYLUM:
LIVING HELL
May 2003
1 (of 6) F:Warren White 3.00
2 Food Fight 3.00
3 Humphry Dumpler 3.00
4 F:Killer Croc 3.00
5 F:Jason Blood 3.00
6 Concl. 3.00

ARMAGEDDON 2001
May, 1991
1 DJu,DG,I&O:Waverider 4.00
1a 2nd printing 2.50
1b 3rd printing (silver). 2.50
2 DJu,ATi,Monarch revealed as Hawk,
　D:Dove,L:Capt Atom(JLE) 3.00
Spec.#1 MR 3.00

Armageddon: The Alien Agenda #1
© DC Comics, Inc.

ARMAGEDDON 2001
ARMAGEDDON:
THE ALIEN AGENDA
1991–92
1 DJu,JOy,A:Monarch,Capt.Atom . . 2.50
2 V:Ancient Romans 2.50
3 JRu(i),The Old West 2.50
4 DG,GP,V:Nazi's,last issue 2.50

ARMAGEDDON:
INFERNO
1992
1 TMd,LMc,A:Creeper,Batman,
　Firestorm 2.50
2 AAd,LMc,WS,I:Abraxis,A:Lobo . . 2.50

3 AAd,WS,LMc,TMd,MN,R:Justice
　Society 2.50
4 AAd,WS,LMc,TMd,MN,DG,
　V:Abraxis,A:Justice Society 2.50

ARMY@LOVE
Vertigo, Mar., 2007
1 RV,GEr 3.00
2 RV,GEr,Hot Zone Club 3.00
3 RV,GEr,F:Switzer & Loman 3.00
4 RV,GEr,In Afbaghistan 3.00
5 RV,GEr,In Afbaghistan 3.00
6 RV,GEr, ... 3.00
7 RV,GEr,Circus Elephants 3.00
8 RV,GEr,Allie's inner bigamist 3.00

ARSENAL
Aug., 1998
1 (of 4) F:Black Canary. 2.50
2 F:Green Arrow 2.50
3 F:Vandal Savage 2.50
4 conclusion 2.50

ARTEMIS: REQUIEM
1996
1 BML(s) (of 6). 3.00
2 thru 6 BML(s),EBe, ... @3.00

ATARI FORCE
1984–85
1 JL,I:TempestDart 5.00
2 JL 3.00
3 JL 3.00
4 RA/JL/JO 3.00
5 RA/JL/JO 3.00
6 thru 12 JL . . . . @3.00
13 KG. 3.00
14 thru 21 EB . . . . @3.00

ATLANTIS CHRONICLES
1990
1 EM,Atlantis 50,000 years ago . . . 3.50
2 EM,Atlantis Sunk 3.25
3 EM,Twin Cities of Poseidonis
　& Tritons 3.25
4 EM,King Orin's Daughter
　Cora Assumes Throne. 3.25
5 EM,Orin vs. Shalako 3.25
6 EM,Contact with Surface
　Dwellers. 3.25
7 EM,Queen Atlanna gives Birth to
　son(Aquaman)48 pg.final issue. 3.25

ATOM, THE
1962–68
1 MA,GK,I:Plant Master 1,800.00
2 MA,GK,V:Plant Master. 750.00
3 MA,GK,I:Chronos. 650.00
4 MA,GK,Snapper Carr. 500.00
5 MA,GK 500.00
6 MA,GK 500.00
7 MA,GK,1st Atom & Hawkman
　team-up 600.00
8 MA,GK,A:JLA,V:Doctor Light . . 350.00
9 MA,GK 350.00
10 MA,GK 350.00
11 MA,GK. 300.00
12 MA,GK 300.00
13 MA,GK 300.00
14 MA,GK 300.00
15 MA,GK 300.00
16 MA,GK 200.00
17 MA,GK 200.00
18 MA,GK 200.00
19 MA,GK,A:Zatanna 200.00
20 MA,GK 200.00
21 MA,GK 135.00
22 MA,GK 135.00
23 MA,GK 135.00

24 MA,GK,V:Jason Woodrue.... 135.00
25 MA,GK 135.00
26 GK...................... 125.00
27 GK...................... 125.00
28 GK...................... 125.00
29 GK,A:E-2 Atom,Thinker...... 350.00
30 GK...................... 125.00
31 GK,A:Hawkman 100.00
32 GK...................... 100.00
33 GK...................... 100.00
34 GK,V:Big Head 100.00
35 GK...................... 100.00
36 GK,A:Golden Age Atom 150.00
37 GK,I:Major Mynah......... 100.00
38 Sinister stopover Earth 100.00
Becomes:

ATOM & HAWKMAN
1968–69

39 MA, V:Tekla............... 90.00
40 DD,JKu,MA................ 75.00
41 DD,JKu,MA................ 75.00
42 MA,V:Brama 75.00
43 MA,I:Gentleman Ghost....... 75.00
44 DD...................... 75.00
45 DD...................... 75.00

AVATAR
1991

1 A:Midnight & Allies........... 7.00
2 Search for Tablets 6.00
3 V:Cyric, Myrkul, final issue 6.00

AVENGERS/JLA
DC/Marvel 2003

2 (of 4) KBk,GP(c), 48-pg. 6.00
4 KBk,GP,48-pg............... 6.00

AZRAEL
1994

1 I:New Azreal,Brian Bryan....... 5.00
2 A:Batman,New Azreal 3.50
3 V:Order of St. Dumas 3.50
4 The System 3.00
5 BKi(c&a),R:Ra's al Ghul,Talia
  [new Miraweb format begins] .. 3.00
6 BKi(c&a),Ra's al Ghul,Talia 3.00
7 Sister Lily's Transformation 3.00
8 System Secret 2.50
9 Jean Paul Vanishes........... 2.50
10 DON,BKi,JmP,F:Neron,
  Underworld Unleashed tie-in... 3.00
11 DON,BKi,JmP,A:Batman....... 2.50

Azrael #20
© DC Comics Inc.

12 DON,BKi,JmP,Azrael looks
  for Shondra 2.50
13 DON,BKi,Demon Time,pt.1 .... 2.50
14 DON,BKi,Demon Time,pt.2..... 2.50
15 DON,BKi,Contagion,pt.5 .... 3.00
16 DON,BKi,Contagion,pt.10....... 2.50
17 DON,BKi,JmP,A:Dr.Orchid 2.50
18 DON,BKi,JmP,A:Dr.Orchid 2.50
19 DON(s),BKi,Save the Innocents. 2.50
20 DON(s),BKi,A Prayer of Fire.... 2.50
21 DON(s),BKi,Renunciation...... 2.50
22 DON(s),BKi,JmP,Angel in
  Hiding, pt.2 (of 3). 2.50
23 DON(s),BKi,JmP,Angel in
  Hiding, pt.3 .... 2.50
24 DON(s),BKi,JmP,The Order's
  return 2.50
25 DON(s),BKi,JmP,V:Brother
  Rollo 2.50
26 DON(s),BKi,Fall of St. Dumas .. 2.50
27 DON(s),BKi,JmP,Angel Insane,
  pt.1..................... 2.50
28 DON(s),BKi,JmP,Joker, Riddler
  & Two-Face escape from
  Arkham Asylum 2.50
29 DON(s),DBw,JmP, F:Ra's Al
  Ghul, pt.1................. 2.50
30 DON(s),DBw,JmP, F:Ra's Al
  Ghul, pt.2. .... 2.50
31 DON(s),JmP Angel and the
  Monster Maker, pt.1 (of 3)..... 2.50
32 DON(s),JmP Angel and the
  Monster Maker, pt.2. .... 2.50
33 DON(s),JmP Angel and the
  Monster Maker, pt.3 concl. 2.50
34 DON(s),JmP,Genesis,
  a parademon 2.50
35 DON(s),JmP,F:Hitman 2.50
36 DON,JmP,Return of Bane,pt.1 . 2.50
37 DON,JmP,Return of Bane,pt.2 . 2.50
38 DON,JmP,Return of Bane,pt.3 . 2.50
39 DON,JmP,Finally to Vanguish . 2.50
40 DON,JmP,Cataclysm,pt.4,x-over 4.50
41 DON,JmP,A:Devil Latour 2.50
42 DON,JmP,Madame Kalypso 2.50
43 DON,JmP,Lilhy,Brian Bryan ... 2.50
44 DON,JmP,Luc & Lilhy disappear 2.50
45 DON,JmP,V:Deathstroke,
  A:Calibax.................. 2.50
46 DON(s),JmP,V:Calibax 2.50

Becomes:

AZRAEL,
AGENT OF THE BAT
1997

47 Road to No Man's Land, flip-book
  Batman:Shadow of the Bat 5.00
48 DON(s),JmP,No Man's Land.... 2.50
49 DON(s),JmP,New Costume 2.50
50 DON(s),JmP,New Costume 2.50
51 DON(s),JmP,V:Demonic Trio ... 2.50
52 DON(s),JmP,No Man's Land. ... 2.50
53 DON(s),JmP,V:Joker........... 2.50
54 DON(s),JmP,V:Death Dancer ... 2.50
55 DON(s),JmP,V:Death Dancer ... 2.50
56 DON(s),JmP,A:Batgirl......... 2.50
57 DON(s),JmP,No Man's Land.... 2.50
58 DON(s),JmP,Day of
  Judgment x-over 2.50
59 DON(s),JmP,F:Catwoman...... 2.50
60 DON(s),JmP,Evacuation...... 2.50
61 DON(s),F:Batgirl,V:Joker 2.50
62 DON(s),JmP 2.50
63 DON(s),F:Huntress 2.50
64 DON(s),F:Huntress 2.50
65 DON(s),Nicholas Scratch 2.50
66 DON(s),F:Lilhi.............. 2.50
67 DON(s),JmP,to Africa 2.50
68 DON(s),JmP,Mirage 2.50
69 DON(s),JmP,stranded........ 2.50
70 DON(s),SCi,JmP,Prophet,pt.1... 2.50

Azrael Agent of the Bat #47
© DC Comics, Inc.

71 DON(s),SCi,JmP,Prophet,pt.2... 2.50
72 DON(s),SCi,JmP,Prophet,pt.3... 2.50
73 DON(s),SCi,JmP,Batman,pt.1 .. 2.50
74 DON(s),SCi,JmP,Batman,pt.2.. 2.50
75 DON(s),SCi,JmP,N:Azrael,
  F:Batman................. 4.50
76 DON(s),SCi,JmP,A:Batman ... 2.50
77 DON(s),SCi,V:Mr. Prymm...... 2.50
78 DON(s),SCi,Captain Death.... 2.50
79 DON(s),SCi,F:Jean Paul....... 2.50
80 DON(s),SCi,JmP,F:Jean Paul... 2.50
81 DON(s),SCi,JmP,imprisoned.... 2.50
82 DON(s),SCi,JmP,escape....... 2.50
83 DON(s),SCi,JmP,Jokerized..... 2.50
84 DON(s),SCi,JmP,madman 2.50
85 DON(s),SCi,JmP,new villain ... 2.50
86 DON(s),SCi,JmP,Spartan 2.50
87 DON(s),SCi,new foe 2.50
88 DON(s),JmP,SCi,F:Nightwing .. 2.50
89 DON(s),F:Nightwing 2.50
90 DON(s),F:Nightwing 2.50
91 Bruce Wayne:Fugitive,pt.15 ... 2.50
92 DON(s),SCi,F:Batman 2.50
93 DON(s),SCi,war on crime 3.00
94 DON(s),SCi,Demon Biis 3.00
95 DON(s),SCi,Biis,Two-face..... 3.00
96 DON(s),SCi,A:Batman,
  V:Two-Face 3.00
97 DON(s),MZ,JOy,New costume .. 3.00
98 DON(s),MZ,JOy,on the brink ... 3.00
99 DON(s),MZ,JOy, ... 3.00
100 DON(s),MZ,JOy,final issue 3.00
Ann.#1 Year One Annual 3.00
Ann.#2 Legends o/t Dead Earth ... 4.00
Ann.#3 Pulp Heroes (Hard Boiled) . 5.00
Spec.#1,000,000 DON(s),VGi,JmP
  F:Green Arrow,Robin,Hawkman 3.00
GN Azrael/Ash 5.00

AZRAEL/ASH
March, 1997

1 one-shot DON(s),JQ,V:Surtr,
  A:Batman, x-over........... 5.00

AZRAEL PLUS
Oct., 1996

1 one-shot, DON(s),VGi,F:Vic
  Sage, The Question 3.00

AZTEK:
THE ULTIMATE MAN
1996–97
1 GMo&MMr(s),NSH,I:Aztek &
Synth 6.00
2 GMo&MMr(s),NSH,A:Green
Lantern 4.00
3 GMo&MMr(s),NSH,V:Doll-Face . . 4.00
4 GMo&MMr(s),NSH,I:Lizard King,
Vanity. 4.00
5 GMo&MMr(s),NSH,O:Aztek,
V:Lizard King 4.00
6 GMo&MMr(s),NSH,V:Vanity,
A: Joker 4.00
7 GMo&MMr(s),NSH,A:Batman . . . 4.00
8 GMo&MMr(s),NSH,return to Brotherhood of Zuetzatcoatl,A:Raptor. . 4.00
9 GMo&MMr(s),NSH,V:Parasite,
A:Superman. 4.00
10 GMo&MMr(s),NSH,A:Justice
League, final issue 12.00

BABYLON 5
1995
1 From TV series 15.00
2 From TV series 8.00
3 Mysterious Assassin 8.00
4 V:Mysterious Assassin 8.00
5 Shadows of the Present,pt.1 . . . 8.00
6 Shadows of the Present,pt.2 . . . 8.00
7 Shadows of the Present,pt.3 . . . 7.00
8 Laser-Mirror Starweb,pt.1 . . . . . 7.00
9 Laser-Mirror Starweb,pt.2 . . . . . 7.00
10 Laser-Mirror-Starweb,pt.3 . . . . . 7.00
11 final issue 7.00

BABYLON 5:
IN VALEN'S NAME
Jan., 1998
1 (of 3) PDd, from TV series. 4.00
2 PDd 4.00
3 PDd 4.00

BATGIRL
Feb., 2000
1 No Man's Land follow-up 10.00
1a 2nd printing 2.50
2 saves dying man 7.00
3 A:Batman 4.00
4 A:Batman 4.00
5 V:Ezra 4.00
6 A:Batman 4.00
7 A:Batman, ... 4.00
8 V:Lady Shiva 4.00
9 Batgirl questions her motives . . . 3.50
10 Too slow to stop a killer 3.50
11 This Issue: Batman Dies! 3.50
12 Officer Down tie-in 3.50
13 Government trained killers 3.50
14 A:Batman 3.50
15 RbC,ghastly murders 3.50
16 RbC,young boy's father 3.50
17 RbC,A:Oracle,Cassandra 3.50
18 RbC,A:Robin,V:Deadeye 3.50
19 RbC,Nobody dies tonight 3.50
20 CDi,F:The Spoiler 3.50
21 CDi,Joker:Last Laugh 3.50
22 RbC,F:Cain 3.50
23 RbC,F:Lady Shiva. 3.50
24 RbC,BruceWayne:Murderer,pt.2. 3.50
25 RbC,V:Lady Shiva,40-pg. 4.00
26 VGi,Spoiler 3.00
27 RbC,Bruce Wayne:Fugitive,pt.4 . 3.00
28 RbC,I:Sensor 3.00
29 RbC,Bruce Wayne:Fugitive,pt.13 3.00
30 CDi,KJ,Roman military cult. . . . 3.00
31 CDi,F:Robin, Spoiler 3.00
32 CDi,all-star issue. 3.00
33 RbC,A:Batman,metahunt 3.00

34 RbC,A:Batman,detective skills . . 3.00
35 RbC,V:Alpha,A:Batman 3.00
36 RbC,V:Alpha 3.00
37 RbC,save the child 3.00
38 RbC,F:Spoiler 3.00
39 V:Black Wind. 3.00
40 V:Black Wind. 3.00
41 First date,A:Superboy. 3.00
42 I:New Dr. Death 3.00
43 V:Dr. Death 3.00
44 V:Dr. Death 3.00
45 RL,drug Soul 3.00
46 RL,F:Oracle. 3.00
47 RL,V:Doll Man. 2.50
48 missing girl 2.50
49 V:The Lost Girls 2.50
50 RL,V:Batman. 3.25
51 RL,V:Poison Ivy 2.50

Batgirl #30
© *DC Comics, Inc.*

52 RL,V:Poison Ivy 2.50
53 F:Girl Wonder,V:Penguin 2.50
54 RL,vs. cyborg 2.50
55 War Games,Act 1,pt.6 . . . . 2.50
56 War Games,Act 2,pt.6 . . . . 2.50
57 War Games,Act 3,pt.6 . . . . 2.50
58 Fresh Blood, x-over,pt.2 . . . . . . 2.50
59 Fresh Blood, x-over,pt.4 . . . . . . 2.50
60 Bludhaven. 2.50
61 Arms deal in Bludhaven 2.50
62 F:Spoiler 2.50
63 F:Deathstroke 2.50
64 V:Deathstroke 2.50
65 CaS,Father's Day 2.50
66 V:Verrraco, The Road Hog 2.50
67 F:Birds of Prey 2.50
68 V:Lady Shiva. 2.50
69 Frozen. 2.50
70 Destruction's Daughter 2.50
71 V:Lady Shiva & team 2.50
72 V:Mad Dog, someone dies 2.50
73 End of Cassandra Cain 2.50
Ann.#1 Planet DC,A:Batman 3.50
Spec.#1 V: Cormorant,
I:Slash (1988) 10.00
Spec. Secret Files #1, 48-pg. 5.00

BATGIRL ADVENTURES
Dec., 1997
1-shot RBr,V:Poison Ivy,A:Harley
Quinn. 4.00

BATGIRL: YEAR ONE
Dec. 2002
1 CDi(s),F:Barbara Gordon. 3.00
2 CDi(s),meets JSA 3.00
3 CDi(s),Dynamic Duo 3.00
4 CDi(s),Dynamic Duo 3.00
5 CDi(s),Killer Moth. 3.00
6 CDi(s),F:Black Canary 3.00
7 CDi(s),A:Robin. 3.00
8 CDi(s),V:Blockbuster 3.00
9 CDi(s),Origin concl. 3.00

BATMAN
Spring, 1940
1 I:Joker,Cat (Catwoman),
V:Hugo Strange 175,000.00
2 V:Joker/Catwoman team . . 30,000.00
3 V:Catwoman 20,000.00
4 V:Joker 15,000.00
5 V:Joker 9,500.00
6 V:Clock Maker 8,000.00
7 V:Joker 8,000.00
8 V:Joker 6,500.00
9 V:Joker 6,500.00
10 V:Catwoman 6,500.00
11 V:Joker,Penguin 13,000.00
12 V:Joker. 5,000.00
13 V:Joker. 5,000.00
14 V:Penguin;Propaganda sty . 5,000.00
15 V:Catwoman 5,000.00
16 I:Alfred,V:Joker 9,000.00
17 V:Penguin 4,000.00
18 V:Tweedledum &
Tweedledee 4,500.00
19 V:Joker. 5,000.00
20 V:Joker. 4,000.00
21 V:Penguin 4,000.00
22 V:Catwoman,Cavalier 4,000.00
23 V:Joker. 7,000.00
24 I:Carter Nichols, V:Tweedledum
& Tweedledee. 3,000.00
25 V:Joker/Penguin team 4,000.00
26 V:Cavalier 2,700.00
27 V:Penguin 4,500.00
28 V:Joker. 2,500.00
29 V:Scuttler 2,500.00
30 V:Penguin,I:Ally Babble 2,500.00
31 I:Punch and Judy. 2,000.00
32 O:Robin,V:Joker. 2,000.00
33 V:Penguin,Jackall 2,300.00
34 A:Ally Babble 2,000.00
35 V:Catwoman 2,000.00
36 V:Penguin,A:King Arthur . . . 1,700.00
37 V:Joker. 2,400.00
38 V:Penguin 3,500.00
39 V:Catwoman,Xmas Story . . . 1,700.00
40 V:Joker. 2,500.00
41 V:Penguin 2,300.00
42 V:Catwoman 2,000.00
43 V:Penguin 2,000.00
44 V:Joker,A:Carter Nichols,Meets
ancester Silas Wayne. 2,500.00
45 V:Catwoman 1,300.00
46 V:Joker,A:Carter Nichols,
Leonardo Da Vinci 1,300.00
47 O:Batman,V:Catwoman 5,700.00
48 V:Penguin, Bat-Cave story . . 1,700.00
49 I:Mad Hatter & Vicki Vale . . 2,700.00
50 V:Two-Face,A:Vicki Vale . . . 1,400.00
51 V:Penguin 1,300.00
52 V:Joker. 1,500.00
53 V:Joker. 1,500.00
54 V:The Treasure Hunter 1,200.00
55 V:Joker. 1,800.00
56 V:Penguin 1,400.00
57 V:Joker. 1,200.00
58 V:Penguin 1,400.00
59 I:Deadshot 1,200.00
60 V:'Shark' Marlin 1,200.00
61 V:Penguin 1,300.00

Batman #61
© DC Comics, Inc.

62 O:Catwoman,I:Knight
   & Squire 2,000.00
63 V:Joker. 1,200.00
64 V:Killer Moth. 2,000.00
65 I:Wingman,V:Catwoman . . . 1,300.00
66 V:Joker. 1,000.00
67 V:Joker. 1,000.00
68 V:Two-Face,Alfred story. . . . 1,000.00
69 I:King of the Cats,
   A:Catwoman. 1,300.00
70 V:Penguin. 850.00
71 V:Mr. Cipher 850.00
72 The Jungle Batman. 850.00
73 V:Joker,A:Vicki Vale 1,400.00
74 V:Joker 850.00
75 I:The Gorilla Boss 850.00
76 V:Penguin. 850.00
77 The Crime Predictor 850.00
78 The Manhunter from Mars . . 1,300.00
79 A:Vicki Vale 850.00
80 V:Joker. 1,200.00
81 V:Two-Face 1,100.00
82 The Flying Batman 850.00
83 V:'Fish' Frye 850.00
84 V:Catwoman 1,200.00
85 V:Joker 900.00
86 V:Joker. 900.00
87 V:Joker 900.00
88 V:Mr. Mystery 900.00
89 I:Aunt Agatha 900.00
90 I:Batboy. 900.00
91 V:Blinky Grosset 900.00
92 I:Ace, the Bat-Hound 1,000.00
93 The Caveman Batman 800.00
94 Alfred Has Amnesia 750.00
95 The Bat-Train 750.00
96 Batman's College Days 750.00
97 V:Joker. 750.00
98 A:Carter Nichols,Jules Verne . 750.00
99 V:Penguin,A:Carter Nichols,
   Bat Masterson. 750.00
100 Great Batman Contest. . . . 4,000.00
101 The Great Bat-Cape Hunt. . . 750.00
102 V:Mayne Mallok 700.00
103 A:Ace, the Bat-Hound 700.00
104 V:Devoe 700.00
105 A:Batwoman 900.00
106 V:Keene Harper Gang 800.00
107 V:Daredevils 700.00
108 Bat-Cave Story 700.00
109 1,000 Inventions of Batman . 700.00
110 V:Joker. 725.00
111 Gotham City Safari 600.00
112 I:Signalman 600.00
113 I:Fatman 600.00

114 I:Bat Ape 600.00
115 Million-Dollar Clues 600.00
116 City of Ancient Heroes 600.00
117 Mystery of Batman Bus. 600.00
118 Battle of Police Island 600.00
119 Arch-Rivals of Gotham City. . 600.00
120 Curse of the Bat-Ring. 600.00
121 I:Mr.Zero (Mr.Freeze) 750.00
122 Prisoners of Sargasso Sea . . 400.00
123 A:Joker 425.00
124 Mystery Seed from Space . . 400.00
125 Secret Life of Bat-Hound . . . 400.00
126 Mystery of the 49th Star . . . 400.00
127 A:Superman & Joker. 425.00
128 Interplanetary Batman 400.00
129 O:Robin (Retold). 450.00
130 Batman's Deadly Birthday . . 400.00
131 I:2nd Batman 375.00
132 Lair of the Sea-Fox 375.00
133 Crimes of the Kite-Man. 375.00
134 The Rainbow Creature 375.00
135 Crimes of the Wheel. 375.00
136 A:Joker, Bat-Mite. 375.00
137 V:Mr. Marvel,The Brand 375.00
138 A:Bat-Mite 375.00
139 I:Old Batgirl 375.00
140 A:Joker 375.00
141 V:Clockmaster. 375.00
142 Batman Robot Story 375.00
143 A:Bathound 375.00
144 A:Joker,Bat-Mite,Bat-Girl. . . . 375.00
145 V:Mr.50,Joker 400.00
146 A:Bat-Mite,Joker 400.00
147 Batman becomes Bat-Baby . 300.00
148 A:Joker 350.00
149 V:Maestro 300.00
150 V:Biff Warner,Jack Pine 300.00
151 V:Harris Boys 250.00
152 A:Joker 260.00
153 Other Dimension story 250.00
154 V:Dr. Dorn 200.00
155 1st S.A. Penguin 550.00
156 V:Gorilla Gang 250.00
157 V:Mirror Man 250.00
158 A:Bathound,Bat-Mite. 250.00
159 A:Joker,Clayface 250.00
160 V:Bart Cullen 225.00
161 A:Bat-Mite 225.00
162 F:Robin 225.00
163 A:Joker 225.00
164 CI,A:Mystery Analysts,new
   Batmobile. 200.00
165 V:The Mutated Man 200.00
166 Escape story 200.00
167 V:Karabi & Hydra,
   the Crime Cartel 200.00
168 V:Mr. Mammoth. 200.00
169 A:Penguin 225.00
170 V:Getaway Genius 200.00
171 CI,1st S.A. Riddler 750.00
172 V:Flower Gang 225.00
173 V:Elwood Pearson 225.00
174 V:Big Game Hunter 225.00
175 V:Eddie Repp 225.00
176 Giant rep.A:Joker,Catwom. . . 225.00
177 BK,A:Elongated Man,Atom. . . 225.00
178 CI 225.00
179 CI,2nd Riddler(Silver) 300.00
180 BK,A:Death-Man. 175.00
181 CI,I:Poison Ivy 350.00
182 A:Joker,(giant size rep). 200.00
183 CI,A:Poison Ivy 200.00
184 CI,Mystery of the Missing
   Manhunters 175.00
185 Giant rep. 175.00
186 A:Joker 175.00
187 Giant rep.A:Joker. 175.00
188 CI,A:Eraser 100.00
189 CI,A:Scarecrow 200.00
190 CI,A:Penguin. 150.00
191 CI,The Day Batman Soldout. . 100.00

192 CI,The Crystal ball that
   betrayed Batman 100.00
193 Giant rep. 150.00
194 MSy,BK,A:Blockbuster,Mystery
   Analysts of Gotham City 100.00
195 CI 100.00
196 BK,Psychic Super-Sleuth . . . 100.00
197 MSy,A:Bat Girl,Catwoman . . . 200.00
198 A:Joker,Penguin,Catwoman,
   O:Batman rtd,(G-Size rep) . . 200.00
199 CI,Peril o/t Poison Rings. . . . 100.00
200 NA(c),O:rtd,A:Joker,Pengiun,
   Scarecrow 300.00
201 A:Batman Villians 150.00
202 BU:Robin. 135.00
203 NA(c),(giant size) 200.00
204 FR(s),IN,JG. 150.00
205 FR(s),IN,JG. 150.00
206 FR(s),IN,JG. 150.00
207 FR(s),IN,JG. 150.00
208 GK,new O:Batman,
   A:Catwoman 175.00
209 FR(s),IN,JG. 175.00
210 A:Catwoman 175.00
211 FR(s),IN,JG. 150.00
212 FR(s),IN,JG. 150.00
213 RA,30th Anniv.Batman,new O:
   Robin,rep.O:Alfred,Joker. . . . 125.00
214 IN,A:Batgirl 65.00
215 IN,DG 65.00
216 IN,DG,I:DaphnePennyworth . . 65.00
217 NA(c). 65.00
218 NA(c),giant 75.00
219 NA,IN,DG,Batman Xmas. 75.00
220 NA(c),IN 50.00
221 IN,DG 50.00
222 IN,Rock'n Roll story 65.00
223 NA(c),giant 65.00
224 NA(c). 50.00
225 NA(c),IN,DG 50.00
226 IN,DG I:10-Eyed Man 50.00
227 IN,DG,A:Daphne
   Pennyworth 50.00
228 giant Deadly Traps rep. 75.00
229 IN 50.00
230 NA(c),Robin 50.00
231 F:Ten-Eyed Man 50.00
232 DON(s),NA,DG,
   I:Ras al Ghul 250.00
233 giant Bruce Wayne iss. 75.00
234 NA,DG,IN,1stS.A.Two-Face . 250.00
235 CI,V:Spook 50.00
236 NA 50.00
237 NA,I:The Reaper. 150.00
238 NA,JC,JKu,giant 150.00

Batman #186
© DC Comics Inc.

Batman #270 © DC Comics, Inc.

Batman #418 © DC Comics, Inc.

239 NA,RB 50.00	
240 NA(c),RB,giant,R-Ghul 50.00	
241 IN,DG,RB,A:Kid Flash 50.00	
242 RB,MK. 50.00	
243 NA,DG,Ras al Ghul 75.00	
244 NA,Ras al Ghul 75.00	
245 NA,IN,DG,FMc,Ras al Ghul . . 75.00	
246 Many Ways Can a Robin Die . 40.00	
247 Deadly New Year 40.00	
248 Death-Knell for a Traitor 40.00	
249 Citadel of Crime 40.00	
250 IN,DG 40.00	
251 NA,V:Joker 125.00	
252 The Spook's Master Stroke . . 40.00	
253 AN,DG,A:Shadow 40.00	
254 NA,GK,B:100 page issues . . 75.00	
255 GK,CI,NA,DG,I:CrazyQuilt . . 100.00	
256 Catwoman. 75.00	
257 IN,DG,V:Penguin 75.00	
258 IN,DG 75.00	
259 GK,IN,DG,A:Shadow. 75.00	
260 IN,DG,Joker. 100.00	
261 CI,GK,E:100 page issues . . . 75.00	
262 A:Scarecrow 50.00	
263 DG(i),A:Riddler 20.00	
264 DON(s),DG,A:Devil Dayre. . . 20.00	
265 RB,BWr. 25.00	
266 DG,Catwoman(old Costume) . 22.00	
267 DG. 20.00	
268 DON(s),IN,TeB,V:Sheikh. . . . 20.00	
269 A:Riddler 20.00	
270 B:DvR(s) 20.00	
271 IN,FMc 20.00	
272 JLUnderworld Olympics '76 . 20.00	
273 V:Underworld Olympics '76 . . 20.00	
274 Gotham City Treasure Hunt . . 20.00	
275 Ferry Blows at Midnight 20.00	
276 The Haunting of the Spook . . 20.00	
277 Man Who Walked Backwards. 20.00	
278 Stop Me Before I Kill Batman . 20.00	
279 A:Riddler 22.00	
280 The Only Crime in Town 20.00	
281 Murder Comes in Black Boxes 20.00	
282 Four Doorways to Danger . . . 20.00	
283 V:Camouflage 20.00	
284 JA,R:Dr.Tzin Tzin 20.00	
285 Mystery of Christmas Lost . . . 20.00	
286 V:Joker 30.00	
287 BWi,MGr,Penguin 25.00	
288 BWi,MGr,Penguin 25.00	
289 MGr,V:Skull 20.00	
290 MGr,V:Skull Dagger 20.00	
291 B:Underworld Olympics #1,	
A:Catwoman 30.00	
292 A:Riddler 20.00	

293 A:Superman & Luthor 20.00	
294 E:DvR(s),E:Underworld	
Olympics,A:Joker. 30.00	
295 GyC(s),MGo,JyS,V:Hamton . . 20.00	
296 B:DvR(s),V:Scarecrow 20.00	
297 RB,Mad Hatter 20.00	
298 JCA,DG,V:Baxter Bains 20.00	
299 DG. 20.00	
300 WS,DG,A:Batman E-2,	
Robin E-2 . . . . 35.00	
301 JCa,TeB 15.00	
302 JCa,DG,V:Human Dynamo . . . 15.00	
303 JCa,DG 15.00	
304 E:DvR(s),V:Spook 15.00	
305 GyC,JCa,DeH,V:Thanatos . . . 16.00	
306 JCa,DeH,DN,V:Black Spider. . 20.00	
307 B:LWn(s),JCa,DG,	
I:Limehouse Jack 20.00	
308 JCa,DG,V:Mr.Freeze 16.00	
309 E:LWn(s),JCa,FMc,	
V:Blockbuster 16.00	
310 IN,DG,A:Gentleman Ghost . . . 16.00	
311 SEt,FMc,IN,Batgirl,	
V:Dr.Phosphorus 16.00	
312 WS,DG,Calenderman 16.00	
313 IN,FMc,VTwo-Face 16.00	
314 IN,FMc,V:Two-Face 16.00	
315 IN,FMc,V:Kiteman 16.00	
316 IN,FMc,F:Robin,	
V:Crazy Quilt 16.00	
317 IN,FMc,V:Riddler. 17.00	
318 IN,I:Fire Bug 16.00	
319 JKu(c),IN,DG,A:Gentleman	
Ghost,E:Catwoman 16.00	
320 BWr(c). 17.00	
321 DG,WS,A:Joker,Catwoman . . 20.00	
322 V:Cap.Boomerang,Catwoman 16.00	
323 IN,A:Catwoman. 16.00	
324 IN,A:Catwoman. 16.00	
325 IN,Death-20 Stories High . . . 16.00	
326 A:Catwoman 16.00	
327 IN,A:Proffessor.Milo 16.00	
328 A:Two-Face. 16.00	
329 IN,A:Two-Face 16.00	
330 In,Target 16.00	
331 DN,FMc,V:Electrocutioner . . . 16.00	
332 IN,DN,Ras al Ghul.1st solo	
Catwoman story 20.00	
333 IN,DN,A:Catwoman,	
Ras al Ghul 15.00	
334 FMc,Ras al Ghul,Catwoman. . 15.00	
335 IN,FMc,Catwoman,Ras al	
Ghul 15.00	
336 JL,FMc,Loser Villains 15.00	
337 DN,V:Snow Man 15.00	
338 DN,Deathsport 15.00	
339 A:Poison Ivy 15.00	
340 GC,A:Mole 15.00	
341 A:Man Bat 15.00	
342 V:Man Bat. 15.00	
343 GC,KJ,I:The Dagger 15.00	
344 GC,KJ,Poison Ivy 15.00	
345 I:New Dr.Death,A:Catwoman . 15.00	
346 DN,V:Two Face. 15.00	
347 A:Alfred. 15.00	
348 GC,KJ,Man-Bat,A:Catwoman . 15.00	
349 GC,AA,A:Catwoman 15.00	
350 GC,TD,A:Catwoman 15.00	
351 GC,TD,A:Catwoman 15.00	
352 Col Blimp 15.00	
353 JL,DN,DA,A:Joker. 22.00	
354 DN,AA,V:HugoStrange,A:	
Catwoman 15.00	
355 DN,AA:A:Catwoman. 15.00	
356 DG,DN,Hugo Strange 15.00	
357 DN,AA,I:Jason Todd 16.00	
358 A:King Croc. 15.00	
359 DG,O:King Croc,Joker 20.00	
360 I:Savage Skull 15.00	
361 DN,Man-Bat,I:Harvey Bullock . 15.00	
362 V:Riddler 15.00	
363 V:Nocturna 15.00	

364 DN,AA,J.Todd 1st full solo	
story (cont'd Detective #531) . 15.00	
365 DN,AA,C:Joker. 15.00	
366 DN,AA,Joker,J.Todd in	
Robin Costume 20.00	
367 DN,AA,PoisonIvy 14.00	
368 DN,AA,I:2nd Robin	
(Jason Todd) 20.00	
369 DN,AA,I:Dr.Fang,V:Deadshot . 12.00	
370 DN,AA. 12.00	
371 DN,AA,V:Catman 10.00	
372 DN,AA,A:Dr.Fang 7.00	
373 DN,AA,V:Scarecrow 7.00	
374 GC,AA,V:Penguin 8.00	
375 GC,AA,V:Dr.Freeze. 7.00	
376 DN,Halloween issue 7.00	
377 DN,AA,V:Nocturna 7.00	
378 V:Mad Hatter. 7.00	
379 V:Mad Hatter. 7.00	
380 AA,V:Nocturna 7.00	
381 V:Batman 7.00	
382 A:Catwoman 8.00	
383 GC,Night in the Life of Batman. 7.00	
384 V:Calender Man 7.00	
385 V:Calender Man 7.00	
386 I:Black Mask 7.00	
387 V:Black Mask 7.00	
388 V:Capt.Boomerang & Mirror	
Master 7.00	
389 V:Nocturna,Catwoman 7.00	
390 V:Nocturna,Catwoman 7.00	
391 V:Nocturna,Catwoman 7.00	
392 A:Catwoman 7.00	
393 PG,V:Cossack. 6.00	
394 PG,V:Cossack. 6.00	
395 V:Film Freak 6.00	
396 V:Film Freak 6.00	
397 V:Two-Face,Catwoman. 7.00	
398 V:Two-Face,Catwoman. 7.00	
399 HaE(s),Two-Face 6.00	
400 BSz,AAd,GP,BB,A:Joker. . . . 30.00	
401 JBy(c),TVE,Legends,	
A:Magpie 6.00	
402 JSn,Fake Batman 6.00	
403 DCw,Batcave discovered 6.00	
404 DM,FM(s),B:Year 1,I:Modern	
Age Catwoman 25.00	
405 FM,DM,Year 1. . . . . 16.00	
406 FM,DM,Year 1 . . . . 16.00	
407 FM,DM,E:Year 1 . . . . 16.00	
408 CW,V:Joker,	
new O:Jason Todd. 15.00	
408a 2nd printing. 3.00	
409 DG,RA,V:Crime School 15.00	
409a 2nd printing. 3.00	

DC COMICS

410 DC,Jason Todd 15.00	
411 DC,DH,V:Two Face. 6.00	
412 DC,DH,I:Mime. 6.00	
413 DC,DH. 6.00	
414 JAp,Slasher. 6.00	
415 JAp,Millenium Week #2 . . . . . 6.00	
416 JAp,1st Batman/Nightwing	
T.U. 6.00	
417 JAp,B:10 Nights,I:KGBeast. . . 12.00	
418 JAp,V:KGBeast. 12.00	
419 JAp,V:KGBeast. 12.00	
420 JAp,E:10 Nights,D:KGBeast . . 12.00	
421 DG 7.00	
422 MBr,V:Dumpster Slayer 6.00	
423 TM(c),DC,Who is Batman 7.00	
424 MBr,Robin 6.00	
425 MBr,Gordon Kidnapped 6.00	
426 JAp,B:Death in the Family,	
V:Joker 22.00	
427 JAp,V:Joker. 18.00	
428 JAp,D:2nd Robin 18.00	
429 JAp,A:Superman,	
E:Death in the Family 15.00	
430 JAp,JSn,V:Madman 5.00	
431 JAp,Murder Investigation 4.00	
432 JAp 4.00	
433 JBy,JAp,Many Deaths of the	
Batman #1 . . . . 5.00	
434 JBy,Many Deaths #2 . . . . 4.50	
435 JBy,Many Deaths #3 . . . . 4.50	
436 PB,Year#3,A:Nightwing,I:Tim	
Drake as child 5.00	
436a 2ndPrint(green DC logo) 3.00	
437 PB,year#3 . . . . 4.00	
438 PB,year#3 . . . . 3.50	
439 PB,year#3 . . . . 3.50	
440 JAp,Lonely Place of Dying #1,	
A:Tim Drake (face not shown) . . 4.00	
441 JAp,Lonely Place Dying 4.00	
442 JAp,I:3rd Robin(Tim Drake) . . . 7.00	
443 JAp,I:Crimesmith 3.00	
444 JAp,V:Crimesmith 3.00	
445 JAp,I:K.G.Beast Demon 3.00	
446 JAp,V:K.G.Beast Demon 3.00	
447 JAp,D:K.G.Beast Demon 3.00	
448 JAp,A:Penguin#1 . . . . 3.50	
449 MBr,A:Penguin#3 . . . . 3.50	
450 JAp,I:Joker II 3.00	
451 JAp,V:Joker II 3.00	
452 KD,Dark Knight Dark City#1 . . . 3.00	
453 KD,Dark Knight Dark City#2 . . . 3.00	
454 KD,Dark Knight Dark City#3 . . . 3.00	
455 Identity Crisis#1, A:Scarecrow . 3.00	
456 IdentityCrisis#2 . . . . 4.00	
457 V:Scarecrow,A:Robin,	
New Costume 7.00	
457a 2nd printing 3.00	
458 R:Sarah Essen 3.00	
459 A:Sarah Essen 3.00	
460 Sisters in Arms,pt.1	
A:Catwoman 3.50	
461 Sisters in Arms,pt.2	
Catwoman V:Sarah.Essen 3.50	
462 Batman in San Francisco 3.00	
463 Death Valley 3.00	
464 V:Two-Hearts 3.00	
465 Batman/Robin T.U. 3.50	
466 Robin Trapped 3.00	
467 Shadowbox #1(sequel to	
Robin Mini-Series) 3.50	
468 Shadowbox #2 . . . . 3.00	
469 Shadowbox #3 . . . . 3.00	
470 War of the Gods x-over 3.00	
471 V:Killer Croc 3.00	
472 The Idiot Root,pt.1 . . . . 3.00	
473 The Idiot Root,pt.3 . . . . 3.00	
474 Destroyer,pt.1 (LOTDK#27) . . . 3.50	
475 R:Scarface,A:VickiVale 3.00	
476 A:Scarface 3.00	
477 Ph(c),Gotham Tale,pt.1 . . . . . . 3.00	
478 Ph(c),Gotham Tale,pt.2 . . . . . . 3.00	
479 TMd,I:Pagan 3.00	

480 JAp,To the father I never	
knew 3.00	
481 JAp,V:Maxie Zeus 3.00	
482 JAp,V:Maxie Zeus 3.00	
483 JAp,I:Crash & Burn 3.00	
484 JAp,R:Black Mask 3.00	
485 TGr,V:Black Mask 3.00	
486 JAp,I:Metalhead 3.00	
487 JAp,V:Headhunter 3.00	
488 JAp,N:Azrael 10.00	
489 JAp,Bane vs Killer Croc,	
I:Azrael as Batman 6.00	
489a 2nd Printing 3.00	
490 JAp,Bane vs.Riddler 7.00	
490a 2nd Printing 2.50	
490b 3rd Printing 2.00	
491 JAp,V:Joker,A:Bane 4.50	
491a 2nd Printing 2.00	
492 B:DgM(s),NB,Knightfall#1,	
V:Mad Hatter,A:Bane 4.00	
492a Platinum Ed. 10.00	
492b 2nd Printing 2.00	
493 NB,Knightfall,#3,Mr.Zsasz. . . . 4.00	
494 JAp,TMd,Knightfall #5,A:Bane,	
V:Cornelius,Stirk,Joker 3.50	
495 NB,Knightfall#7,V:Poison	
Ivy,A:Bane 3.50	
496 JAp,JRu,Knightfall#9,V:Joker,	
Scarecrow,A:Bane 3.50	
497 JAp,DG,Knightfall#11,V:Bane,	
Batman gets back broken 7.00	
497a 2nd Printing. 2.50	
498 JAp,JRu,Knightfall#15,A:Bane,	
Catwoman,Azrael Becomes	
Batman 3.00	
499 JAp,SHa,Knightfall#17,	
A:Bane,Catwoman. 3.00	
500 JQ(c),JAp,MM,Die Cut(c),	
Direct Market,Knightfall#19,	
V:Bane,N:Batman 6.00	
500a KJo(c),Newstand Ed. 3.50	
501 MM,I:Mekros 3.00	
502 MM,V:Mekros 3.00	
503 MM,V:Catwoman 3.00	
504 MM,V:Catwoman 3.00	
505 MM,V:Canibal 3.00	
506 KJo(c),MM,A:Ballistic 3.00	
507 KJo(c),MM,A:Ballistic 3.00	
508 KJo(c),MM,V:Abattior 3.00	
509 KJo(c),MM,KnightsEnd#1,	
A:Shiva 3.50	
510 KJo(c),MM,Knights End #7,	
V:Azrael 3.00	
511 Zero Hour, A:Batgirl 3.00	
512 Killer Croc sewer battles 3.00	
513 Two-Face and convicts 3.00	

Batman #500 © DC Comics Inc.

514 Identity Crisis 3.00	
515 KJo,Return of Bruce Wayne,	
Troika,pt.1 . . . . 3.00	
515 Collector's Edition 3.50	
516 V:The Sleeper 3.00	
517 V:The Sleeper 3.00	
518 V:The Black Spider 3.00	
519 KJo,V:The Black Spider	
[new Miraweb format begins] . . 3.00	
520 EB,A:James Gordon. 3.00	
521 R:Killer Croc 3.00	
522 R:Scarecrow 3.00	
523 V:Scarecrow 3.00	
524 DgM,KJo,V:Scarecrow 3.00	
525 DgM,KJo,Underworld	
Unleashed tie-in 3.00	
526 DgM,A:Alfred,Nightwing,Robin . 3.00	
527 DgM,V:Two-Face,I:Schism 3.00	
528 DgM,V:Two-Face,pt.2 . . . . 3.00	
529 DgM,KJo,Contagion,pt.6 . . . . 3.50	
530 DgM,KJo,The Aztec	
Connection,pt.1 . . . . 3.50	
530a collector's edition 3.50	
531 DgM,KJo,The Aztec	
Connection,pt.2 . . . . 3.00	
531a collectors edition 3.50	
532 DgM(s),KJo,The Aztec Connec-	
tion, pt.3, A:Deadman 3.00	
532a card stock cover 3.50	
533 DgM(s),KJo,Legacy prelude . . . 3.00	
534 DgM(s),KJo,Legacy,pt.5 . . . . . 3.00	
535 DgM(s),KJo,JhB,I:The Ogre,	
double size 4.00	
535a Collector's edition,	
gatefold cover 5.00	
536 DgM(s),KJo,JhB,V:Man-Bat,	
Final Night tie-in 3.00	
537 DgM(s),KJo,JhB,A:Man-Bat,	
pt.2 . . . . 3.00	
538 DgM(s),KJo,JhB,A:Man-Bat,	
pt.3 . . . . 3.00	
539 DgM(s),KJo,Boneyard Blues . . 3.00	
540 DgM(s),KJo,JhB,Spectre,pt.1 . . 3.00	
541 DgM(s),KJo,JhB,Spectre,pt.2 . . 3.00	
542 DgM(s),KJo,JhB,V:Faceless,	
pt. 1 . . . . 3.00	
543 DgM(s),KJo,JhB,pt. 2 . . . . 3.00	
544 DgM(s),KJo,JhB, F:Joker,pt.1 . . 3.00	
545 DgM(s),KJo, F:Joker, Demon,	
pt.2. . . . . 3.00	
546 DgM(s),KJo,JhB,F:Joker,	
Demon, pt.3 concl. 3.00	
547 DgM,KJo,JhB,Genesis tie-in . . 3.00	
548 DgM,KJo,JhB,V:Penguin,pt.1 . 3.00	
549 DgM,KJo,JhB,V:Penguin, pt.2 . 3.00	
550 DgM,KJo,JhB,I:Chase. 3.50	
550a deluxe, with file card inserts . 3.50	
551 DgM,KJo,JhB,F:Ragman 2.50	
552 DgM, ... 2.50	
553 DgM,KJo,SB,Cataclysm	
x-over,pt.3. . . . . 4.50	
554 DgM,KJo,SB,Cataclysm,. 3.00	
555 DGm,JhB,SB,BSf,Aftershock . . 2.50	
556 DGm,NBy,BSf,Aftershock 2.50	
557 DGm,VGi,SB,BSf,F:Ballistic . . . 2.50	
558 DGm,JAp,SB,doubts 2.50	
559 DgM(s),BH,SB,Aftershock 2.50	
560 CDi,SB,A:Nightwing & Robin . . 2.50	
561 CDi(s),JAp, No Man's Land . . . 2.50	
562 CDi(s),JAp, No Man's Land . . . 2.50	
563 No Law and A New Order, pt.3 . 6.00	
564 F:Batgirl, Mosaic,pt.1 . . . . 2.50	
565 F:Batgirl, Mosaic,pt.3 . . . . 2.50	
566 JBg,A:Superman 2.50	
567 SCi,F:Batgirl, pt.1,x-over. 2.50	
568 DJu,BSz,Fruit of the	
Earth, pt.2 . . . . 2.50	
569 F:Batgirl. 2.50	
570 MD2,No Man's Land, The	
Code, pt.1 . . . . 2.50	
571 CDi(s),MtB,Goin'Downtown,pt.1 . 2.50	
572 Jurisprudence,pt.1 . . . . 2.50	

All comics prices listed are for *Near Mint* condition.

Batman #558
© DC Comics, Inc.

573 Shellgame,pt.1,A:Lex Luthor . . 2.50
574 Endgame, pt.2 x-over 2.50
575 LHa,SMc,KIS. 2.50
576 LHa,SMc,KIS,kidnapping 2.50
577 LHa,SMc,KIS,rodents 2.50
578 LHa,SMc,MPn,serial killer. . . . 2.50
579 LHa,SMc,KIS,V:Orca,pt.1 . . . . 2.50
580 LHa,SMc,KIS,V:Orca,pt.2 . . . . 2.50
581 LHa,SMc,KIS,V:Orca,pt.3 . . . . 2.50
582 SMc,KIS,Fearless,pt.1 . . . . . . 2.50
583 SMc,KIs,Fearless,pt.2 . . . . 2.50
584 SMc,KIS,A:Penguin. 2.50
585 SMc,KIS,V:Penguin. 2.50
586 SMc,KIS,V:Penguin, This issue:
    Batman Dies!. 2.50
587 RBr,RyR,Officer Down,pt.1 . . . 2.50
588 SMc,KIS,Close Before Striking . 2.50
589 SMc,KIS,Close Before Striking . 2.50
590 SMc,KIS,Close Before Striking . 2.50
591 SMc,KIS,Shot thru the Heart . . 2.50
592 SMc,KIS,Shot thru the Heart . . 2.50
593 SMc,KIS,Worlds at War tie-in . . 2.50
594 SMc,KIS,Worlds at War tie-in . . 2.50
595 SMc,F:Lew Moxon 2.50
596 SMc,Joker:Last Laugh 2.50
597 SMc,V:Zeiss 2.50
598 SMc,Christmas in Gotham 2.50
599 Bruce Wayne:Murderer,pt.7 . . . 2.50
600 Bruce Wayne:Fugitive,pt.1 . . 6.00
600a 2nd printing 4.00
601 Bruce Wayne:Fugitive,pt.3 . . . 2.50
602 SMc,V:Nicodemus. 2.50
603 Bruce Wayne:Fugitive,pt.11 . . 2.50
604 SMc,Crime Alley 2.50
605 Bruce Wayne:Fugitive,concl. . . 3.50
606 SMc,F:Deadshot 2.50
607 SMc,F:Deadshot,pt.2 . . . . 2.50
608 JLb,JLe,SW,Hush,pt.1 . . . . 15.00
608a 2nd printing, new cover 30.00
609 JLb,JLe,SW,Hush,pt.2 . . . . . 10.00
610 JLb,JLe,SW,Hush,pt.3 . . . . . 6.00
611 JLb,JLe,SW,Hush,pt.4. . . . . . 6.00
612 JLb,JLe,SW,Hush,pt.5 . . . . . 12.00
612a 2nd printing, B&W(c). 15.00
613 JLb,JLe,SW,Hush,pt.6 . . . . . . 7.00
614 JLb,JLe,SW,Hush,pt.7 . . . . . . 5.00
615 JLb,JLe,SW,Hush,pt.8 . . . . . 18.00
616 JLb,JLe,SW,Hush,pt.9 . . . . . . 5.00
617 JLb,JLe,SW,Hush,pt.10 . . . . . 4.00
618 JLb,JLe,SW,Hush,pt.11. . . . . . 4.00
619 JLb,JLe,SW,Hush,pt.12 . . . . . 4.00
619a newsstand cover 3.00
620 Broken City, pt.1 . . . . 2.50
621 Broken City, pt.2 . . . . 2.50
622 Broken City, pt.3 . . . . 2.50

623 Broken City, pt.4 . . . . 2.50
624 Broken City, pt.5 . . . . 2.50
625 Broken City, pt.6 . . . . 2.50
626 As the Crow Flies,pt.1 . . . . 2.50
627 As the Crow Flies,pt.2. . . . . . . 2.50
628 As the Crow Flies,pt.3. . . . . . . 2.50
629 As the Crow Flies,pt.4. . . . . . . 2.50
630 As the Crow Flies,pt.5. . . . . . . 2.50
631 War Games,Act 1,pt.8 . . . . . . 2.50
632 War Games,Act 2,pt.8 . . . . . . 2.50
633 War Games,Act 3,pt.8,40-pg . . 3.00
634 War games epilogue. 2.50
635 DoM,Under the Hood,pt.1 . . . 10.00
636 DoM,Under the Hood,pt.2. . . . 6.00
637 DoM,Under the Hood,pt.3 . . . . 6.00
638 DoM,Under the Hood,pt.4 . . . . 6.00
639 DoM,Family Reunion,pt.1 . . . . 4.00
640 DoM,Family Reunion,pt.2 . . . . 4.00
641 DoM,Family Reunion,pt.3 . . . . 3.00
642 V:Killer Croc 2.50
643 War Crimes,x-over, pt.2 . . . . . 2.50
644 War Crimes,x-over, pt.4 . . . . . 2.50
645 Gotham graveyard 2.50
646 DoM,Infinite Crisis tie-in 2.50
647 DoM,Infinite Crisis tie-in 2.50
648 DoM,F:Black Mask 2.50
649 DoM,Black Mask & Red Hood . 2.50
650 DoM,Jason Todd mystery 2.50
651 Face the Face, pt.2, x-over. . . . 3.00
652 Face the Face, pt.4, x-over. . . . 2.50
653 Face the Face, pt.6, x-over. . . . 3.00
654 Face the Face, pt.8, x-over. . . . 3.00
655 GMo,NKu, Batman and Son . . 3.00
656 GMo,NKu, Batman and Son . . 3.00
657 GMo,NKu, Batman and Son . . 3.00
658 GMo,NKu, Batman and Son . . 3.00
659 GMo,NKu, Joker's revenge . . . 3.00
660 JOs,TMd,Grotesk, pt.1 . . . . . . 3.00
661 JOs,TMd,Grotesk, pt.2 . . . . . . 3.00
662 JOs,TMd,Grotesk, pt.3 . . . . . . 3.00
663 GMo,JVF,V:Joker 3.00
664 GMo,NKu,,Police corruption . . 3.00
665 GMo,NKu,3 Ghosts of Batman . 3.00
666 GMo,NKu,Numbers o/t Beast . . 3.00
667 GMo,NKu,V:Mister Mayhew . . 3.00
668 GMo,Club of Heroes 3.00
669 GMo,Club of Heroes. 3.00
670 GMo,Resurrection of
    Ra's Al Ghul. 3.00
Ann.#1 CS,O:Bat Cave. 1,600.00
Ann.#2 . . . . 900.00
Ann.#3 A:Joker. 900.00
Ann.#4 . . . . 500.00
Ann.#5 . . . . 500.00
Ann.#6 . . . . 400.00
Ann.#7 . . . . 300.00
Ann.#8 TVE,A:Ras al Ghul 10.00
Ann.#9 JOy,AN,PS. 9.00
Ann.#10 DCw,DG,V:HugoStrange . . 9.00
Ann.#11 JBy(c),AMo(s),V:Penguin. 10.00
Ann.#12 RA,V:Killer. 7.00
Ann.#13 A:Two-Face 8.00
Ann.#14 O:Two-Face 6.00
Ann.#15 Armageddon,pt.3 . . . . . . 8.00
Ann.#15a 2nd printing(silver). 4.00
Ann.#16 SK(c),Eclipso,V:Joker . . . 4.00
Ann.#17 EB,Bloodline#8,
    I:Decimator 4.00
Ann.#18 Elseworld Story 5.00
Ann.#19 Year One, O:Scarecrow. . . 6.00
Ann.#20 Legends o/t Dead Earth . . 5.00
Ann.#21 Pulp Heroes (Weird
    Mystery) DgM(s) 6.00
Ann.#22 BWr(c) Ghosts. 5.00
Ann.#23 CDi(s),GN,MPn, JLApe
    Gorilla Warfare 5.00
Ann.#24 Planet DC 5.00
Ann.#25 Jason Todd's Secrets . . . 5.00
Ann.#26 Head of the Demon. 4.00
Specials & 1-shots
Giant Ann.#1 Facsimile edition 6.00
Spec.#0 (1994) 4.00

Spec.#1 MGo,I:Wrath. 5.00
Spec.#1,000,000 DgM(s),SB,
    F:Toy Wonder 3.00
Spec.#1 Our Worlds at War (2001) . 4.00
Giant #1, 7 tales, 80-page (1998) . . 6.00
Giant #2, 80-page (1999). 6.00
Giant #3 CDi(s) 80-page (2000) . . . 7.00
Batman Allies Secret Files 2005 . . . 5.00
Batman: Arkham Asylum — Tales
    of Madness, AIG, Cataclysm
    tie-in (1998) 4.00
Batman: Batgirl, JBa,RBr,
    Girlfrenzy (1998) 3.00
Batman: Blackgate, CDi(s), JSon,
    in Blackgate prison (1996) 4.50
Batman: Blackgate — Isle of Men,
    DgM, JAp,BSf,BSz,
    Cataclysm (1998) 3.00
Batman Dark Knight Gallery (1995). 3.50
Batman: Day of Judgment 4.00
Batman: Death of Innocents, DON(s),
    JSt, BSz, Land mine victims
    (1996) 4.00
Batman Gallery,collection of past
    (c),posters,pin-ups,JQ(c) (1992) 4.00
Batman: Gotham By Gaslight,MMi,
    V:Jack the Ripper 6.00
Gotham City Secret Files #1 . . . . . 5.00
Batman: The Hill (2000). 3.00
Batman: Joker's Apprentice. 4.00
Batman: The Killing Joke,BB,AMo(s),
    O:Joker,Batgirl paralyzed
    (1988) 15.00
    2nd thru 6th printings. . . . . . . @5.00
Batman: Mitefall, V:Bane
    Mite (1995) 5.00
Batman: Penguin Triumphant
    (1992) 5.00
Batman: Plus (1997) 3.00
Batman Record Comic (1996) 2.00
Batman/Riddler: The Riddle
    Factory (1995) 5.00
Secret Files #1 SMc(c) inc.
    O:Batman (1997) 6.00
Batman: Seduction of the Gun,
    V:Illegal Gun Control (1992) . . . 3.00
Spec. The 10-Cent Adventure 2.00
3-D Batman:Scarecrow 4.00
Batman 12-cent Adventure #1,
    War Games,pt.1 . . . . 2.00
1-shot Batman/The Spirit (2006) . . . 5.00
Batman/Two-Face: Crime and
    Punishment (1995) 5.00
    2nd printing (1998) 5.00
Two-Face Strikes Twice #1 . . . . . . 5.25

Batman The 12 Cent Adventure
© DC Comics, Inc.

Two-Face Strikes Twice #2 . . . . 5.25
Batman: Vengeance of Bane,
  GN,I:Bane (1992) 30.00
  2nd Printing 5.00
Batman: Vengeance of Bane II
  (1995) 4.00
Batman Villains Secret Files,
  AIG,CDi,RMz,BB,F:Greatest Foes
  (1998) 5.00
Batman Villains Secret Files 2005. . 5.00
Elseworld 1-shots
Batman of Arkham (2000) 6.00
Batman: The Blue, The Grey, and
  The Bat, JL (1992). 6.00
Batman: Brotherhood of the Bat
  (1995) 6.00
Batman: Castle of the Bat 6.00
Batman: Dark Allegiances (1996) . . 6.00
Batman: Holy Terror (1991) 6.50
Batman: I, Joker, BH, in
  2083 (1998) 5.00
Batman: In Darkest Knight
  MiB(s),JBi (1994). 5.50
Batman Knightgallery (1995) 3.50
Batman: Masque, MGr, in turn of
  the century Gotham. 7.00
Batman: Master of the Future,EB,
  Sequel to Goth.by Gaslight
  (1991) 6.00
Batman: Master of the Future(1998) 6.00
Batman: Scar of the Bat (1996). . . . 5.00
Batman: Two Faces (1998) 5.00
Graphic Novels
The Abduction 6.00
Batman A Lonely Place of Dying
  (1990) rep. Batman #440–442
  & New Titans #60–61 . . . . . . 4.00
Batman: Blind Justice, rep. Detective
  Comics #598–#600 (1992) 7.50
Batman: Bullock's Law. 5.00
The Book of Shadows 6.00
Many Deaths of the Batman;
  rep. #433–#435 (1992). 4.00
Batman: Dreamland (2000) 6.00
Batman: Ego (2000). 7.00
Batman: Full Circle AD,
  A:Reaper (1992) 7.00
Batman/Joker: Switch 7.00
Golden Steets of Gotham 7.00
Gotham Noir, 64-page (2001) 7.00
Batman: Harley Quinn (1998) 6.00
Batman: Man Who Laughs (2005). . 7.00
Batman: Mr. Freeze 5.00
Batman/Nightwing: Bloodborne
  48-pg. (2002). 6.00
No Man's Land, 48-page No Law
  and a New Order, pt.1 . . . . 3.00
No Man's Land, lenticular (c). 4.00
No Man's Land Gallery 4.00
Nosferatu 6.00
The Order of Beasts (2004). 6.00
Batman: Poison Ivy 5.00
Batman/Poison Ivy:
  Cast Shadows (2004) 7.00
Reign of Terror 5.00
Roomful of Strangers (2004) 6.00
Batman: Scar of the Bat 5.00
Scarface—A Psychodrama (2001) . 6.00
The Scottish Connection 6.00
Batman: Ten Knights of the Beast,
  rep. #417–#420 (1994) 6.00
Batman: Two Faces 5.00
Batman: The Ultimate Evil:
  1 Novel adaptation of 2) 6.00
  2 Novel adaptation, finale 6.00
Movies
Batman, JOy, Movie adaptation 3.00
  Perfect Bound 6.00
Batman Returns, SE,JL Movie
  Adaption, ... 6.00
  Newsstand Format 4.00

Batman: Mask of the Phantasm,
  animated movie adapt. 6.00
  Newstand Ed. 3.50
Batman Forever, Movie Adaptation . 6.00
  Newsstand version 4.00
Batman and Robin, DON(s), Movie
  Adaptation (1997) 4.00
  Collector's edition, ... 6.00
Batman Begins movie adapt (2005) 7.00
GN Batman: Bane, BSz(c) movie
  tie-in (1997). 5.00
GN Batman: Batgirl, BSz(c) movie
  tie-in (1997). 5.00
GN Batman: Mr. Freeze, BSz(c)
  movie tie-in (1997). 5.00
GN Batman: Poison Ivy, BSz(c)
  movie tie-in (1997). 5.00
X-overs
Batman & Superman Adventures:
  World's Finest (1997) adaptation
  of animated adventures, 64pg. . 7.00
Batman/Captain America (DC/Marvel
  1996) Elseworlds. 6.00
Batman/Demon (1996) 5.00
Batman/Demon: A Tragedy (2000) . 6.00
Batman/Green Arrow: The Poison
  Tomorrow,MN,JRu,V:Poison
  Ivy (1992) 6.25
  GN rep. (2000) 6.00
Batman/Houdini: The Devil's
  Workshop (1993). 6.50
Batman: Huntress/Spoiler—Blunt
  Trauma, CDi,Cataclysm (1988). 3.00
Batman/Judge Dredd: Judgement on
  Gotham,SBs,V:Scarecrow, Judge
  Death (1991) 9.00
Batman/Judge Dredd: Vendetta in
  Gotham, AIG(s),V:Ventriliquist
  (1993) 5.25
Batman/Judge Dredd: The Ultimate
  Riddle (1995). 5.00
Batman/Lobo, Elseworlds (2000). . . 6.00
Batman/Phantom Stranger, AIG(s),
  Lemurian artifact (1997) 5.00
Batman/Punisher: Lake of Fire,
  DON(s),BKi,A:Punisher,V:Jigsaw
  (DC/Marvel 1994) 5.25
Batman/Spawn: War Devil, DgM,CDi,
  AIG(s), KJ,V:Croatoan (1994) . . 6.00
Batman/Spawn: War Devil (1999) . . 5.00
Batman/Spider-Man JMD,GN,KK,
  V:Kingpin&Ra's al Ghul(1997). . 5.00
Batman vs. The Incredible Hulk
  (DC/Marvel 1995) 4.00

BATMAN ADVENTURES

1992–95

(Based on cartoon series)

1 MeP,V:Penguin 5.00
2 MeP,V:Catwoman 4.00
3 MeP,V:Joker. 3.00
4 MeP,V:Scarecrow. 3.00
5 MeP,V:Scarecrow. 3.00
6 MeP,A:Robin 3.00
7 MeP,V:Killer Croc,w/card 6.00
8 MeP,Larceny my Sweet. 3.00
9 MeP,V:Two Face 3.00
10 thru 24 MeP . . . . @3.00
25 MeP,dbl.size,Superman 3.50
26 thru 32. . . . . @3.00
33 thru 36 . . . . @2.50
Ann.#1 Roxy Rocket 3.00
Ann.#2 JBa,BBl,DG,TG,SHa,BKi,MM,
  GN,JRu,V:Demon,Ra's al
  Ghul,Etrigan. 3.50
Holiday Special 3.00
Spec. Mad Love. 4.00

Batman Adventures #25
© DC Comics Inc.

BATMAN ADVENTURES: THE LOST YEARS

Nov., 1997

1 (of 5) BHa,TBe,Batgirl 2.50
2 BHa,TBe,Dick Grayson quits. . . . 2.50
3 . . . . 2.50
4 BHa,TBe,F:Tim Drake 2.50
5 BHa,TBe,Tim Drake new Robin . 2.50

BATMAN ADVENTURES: THE LOST YEARS

1999

1 (of 6) TBe. 2.50
2 thru 6 . . . . @2.50
TPB series rep. 6.00

BATMAN ADVENTURES

May 2003

1 TTn 2.25
1a newsstand edition 2.25
2 TTn,F:Riddler. 2.25
3 F:Joker & Harley 2.25
4 TTn,RBr,V:Ra's Al Ghul 2.25
5 TTn,V:Deadshot. 2.25
6 TTn,TBe,V:Black Mask 2.25
7 RBr,TBe,V:Phantasm. 2.25
8 RBr,TBe,V:Black Mask 2.25
9 death trap. 2.25
10 thru 14 RBr,TBe . . . . @2.25
15 TBe,Mr.Freeze 2.25
16 TBe,Joker & Harley wedding . . . 2.25
17 TBe,RBr 2.25

BATMAN/ALIENS II

DC/Dark Horse Dec. 2002

GN #1 (of 3) IEd(s) 6.00
GN #2 IEd(s) 6.00
GN #3 IEd(s) 6.00
TPB Batman/Aliens II. 15.00

BATMAN AND THE OUTSIDERS

Aug., 1983

1 B:MiB(s),JAp,O:Outsiders,
  O:Geo Force 4.50
2 JAp,V:Baron Bedlam 3.00
3 JAp,V:Agent Orange 2.50
4 JAp,V:Fearsome Five 2.50
5 JAp,A:New Teen Titans 3.00
6 JAp,V:Cryonic Man 2.50
7 JAp,V:Cryonic Man 2.50

Batman and the Outsiders #20
© DC Comics Inc.

8 JAp,A:Phantom Stranger 2.50
9 JAp,I:Master of Disaster 2.50
10 JAp,A:Master of Disaster 2.50
11 JAp,V:Takeo 2.50
12 JAp,DG,O:Katana 2.50
13 JAp,Day,O:Batman 2.50
14 BWg,Olympics,V:Maxi Zeus 2.50
15 TVE,Olympics,V:Maxi Zeus 2.50
16 JAp,L:Halo 2.50
17 JAp,V:Ahk-Ton 2.50
18 JAp,V:Ahk-Ton 2.50
19 JAp,A:Superman 2.50
20 JAp,V:Syonide,R:Halo 2.50
21 TVE,JeM,Solo Stories 2.50
22 AD,O:Halo,I:Aurakles 2.50
23 AD,O:Halo,V:Aurakles 2.50
24 AD,C:Kobra 2.50
25 AD,V:Kobra 2.50
26 AD 2.50
27 AD,V:Kobra 2.50
28 AD,I:Lia Briggs(Looker) 2.50
29 AD,V:Metamorpho 2.50
30 AD,C:Looker 2.50
31 AD,I&J:Looker 2.50
32 AD,L:Batman 2.50
Ann.#1 JA N:Geo-Force,
   I:Force of July 3.00
Ann.#2 V:Tremayne,W:Metamorpho
   & Sapphire Stagg 3.00
Becomes:

ADVENTURES OF
THE OUTSIDERS
May, 1986
33 AD,V:Baron Bedlam 2.25
34 AD,Masters of Disaster 2.25
35 AD,V:Adolph Hitler 2.25
36 AD,A:Masters of Disaster 2.25
37 thru 38 . . . . @2.25
39 thru 47 JAp,reprints
   Outsiders #1-#9 . . . . @2.25

BATMAN AND
THE OUTSIDERS
Oct., 2007
1 ATi,V:Metahumans 3.00
1a variant (c) (1:10) 3.00

BATMAN AND ROBIN
ADVENTURES, THE
Nov., 1995
1 TTn 3.00

2 TTn,V:Two-Face 3.00
3 TTn,V:The Riddler 3.00
4 TTn,V:The Penguin 3.00
5 TTn 3.00
6 TTn,Robin Fired? 2.50
7 TTn,V:Scarface 2.50
8 TTn(s) 2.50
9 TTn(s),F:Batgirl & Talia 2.50
10 TTn(s),F:Ra's Al Ghul 2.50
11 TTn(s),Alfred & Robin look
   for monster in Batcave 2.50
12 TTn(s),BKr,RBr, sequel to
   Bane TV episode 2.50
13 TTn(s),BKr,RBr,V:Scarecrow . . . 2.50
14 TTn(s),BKr,RBr,young criminal
   turns to Batman for help 2.50
15 TTn(s) 2.50
16 TTn(s),V:Catman,A:Catwoman . . 2.50
17 PDi&TTn(s),JSon,RBr,Mad
   Hatter dies in Arkham 2.50
18 TTn(s),BKr,TBe,A:Joker,
   Harley Quinn 2.50
19 TTn(s),BKr,TBe,The Huntress . . 2.50
20 TTn(s),BKr,TBe, office pool 2.50
21 TTn(s),JSon,Riddler kidnaps
   Commissioner Gordon 2.50
22 TTn(s),BKr,TBe,V:Two-Face 2.50
23 TTn(s),TBe,V:Killer Croc 2.50
24 TTn(c),F:Poison Ivy 2.50
25 TTn,TBe,final issue, 48pg 3.50
Ann.#1 PDi(s),TTn, sequel to
   Batman: Mask of the Phantasm 3.00
Ann.#2 JSon,TBe,V:Hypnotist 4.00
Sub-Zero one-shot, F:Mr. Freeze,
   Nora, 64pg 4.00

BATMAN & SUPERMAN:
WORLD'S FINEST
1999
1 (of 10) KK(s),DTy,RbC,48-page . . 7.00
2 KK(s),DTy,RbC 3.50
3 KK(s),DTy,RbC,Arkham Asylum . . 3.00
4 KK(s),DTy,RbC,Metropolis 3.00
5 KK(s),DTy,RbC,Batgirl 3.00
6 KK(s),DTy,RbC,trade identities . . 3.00
7 KK(s),PD,RbC 3.00
8 KK(s),PD,RbC 3.00
9 KK(s),RbC,split issue 3.00
10 concl 3.00
GN 7.00

BATMAN: THE ANKH
Nov., 2001
1 (of 2) CDi,JVF,ancient Egypt 6.00
2 CDi,JVF,V:Khatera, concl 6.00

BATMAN:
BANE OF THE DEMON
Feb., 1998
1 (of 4) CDi,GN,TP, Bane &
   Ra's al Ghul 2.50
2 CDi,GN,TP,Talia 2.50
3 CDi,GN,TP,the Lazarus Pit 2.50
4 CDi,GN,TP,Bane imprisoned 2.50

BATMAN BEYOND
Mini-series 1999
1 (of 6) RBr,TBe,Rebirth 2.50
2 RBr,TBe,Rebirth,pt.2 . . . . 2.50
3 RBr,TBe,V:Blight 2.50
4 JSon,TBe,F:Demon Etrigan 2.50
5 JSon,TBe,V:Mummy 2.50
6 JSon,TBe,V:Inque 2.50
TPB rep. mini-series 10.00

BATMAN BEYOND
1999
1 Batman: Classic vs. Future 3.00
2 V:Inque 2.50

3 . . . . 2.50
4 V:Royal Flush Gang 2.50
5 V:Shriek 2.50
6 V:Stalker 2.50
7 V:Jokerz 2.50
8 V:Vendetta 2.50
9 V:Curare 2.50
10 V:Golem 2.50
11 nanotechnology 2.50
12 F:Terminal 2.50
13 Commissioner Barbara Gordon . 2.50
14 F:Etrigan the Demon 2.50
15 thru 20 BSf(c) . . . . @2.50
21 I:Justice League Unlimited 2.50
22 In Blackest Day, concl 2.50
23 New Royal Flush Gang 2.50
24 final issue 2.50
Spec. Return of the Joker 3.00

BATMAN BLACK & WHITE
1996
1 JLe(c) numerous artists 9.00
2 thru 4 . . . . @7.00

BATMAN:
BOOK OF THE DEAD
1999
1 (of 2) DgM(s),BKi,Elseworlds . . . 5.00
2 DgM(s),BKi,Conclusion 5.00

BATMAN/CATWOMAN:
TRAIL OF THE GUN
Aug. 2004
1 & 2 48-pg. . . . . @6.00

BATMAN CHRONICLES
1995
1 CDi,LW,BSz, multiple stories 5.00
2 V:Feedback 4.00
3 All villains issue 4.00
4 F:Hitman 15.00
5 Oracle, Year One story 3.50
6 Ra's Al Ghul 3.50
7 JOy,LW, woman on death row . . . 3.50
8 Talia goes to Gotham to
   eliminate Batman 3.50
9 CDi(s),F:Batgirl, Mr. Freeze,
   Poison Ivy 3.50
10 BSn, anthology 3.50
11 CDi,JFM, Elseworlds stories 3.00
12 Cataclysm x-over 3.00

Batman Chronicles #17
© DC Comics, Inc.

13 F:GCPD 3.00
14 SB(c),F:Alfred,Huntress 3.00
15 Road to No Man's Land 3.00
16 F:Batgirl,No Man's Land tie-in . . 3.00
17 V:Penguin,No Man's Land 3.00
18 No Man's Land 3.00
19 . . . . 3.00
20 SBe(s)&IEd(s),48-pg. 3.00
21 DG,JRu,3 Elseworlds tales 3.00
22 F:Lady Shiva,48-pg. 3.00
23 BSf(c) final issue. 3.00
Gallery #1, Pin-ups 3.50
GN The Gauntlet 5.00

BATMAN: CITY OF LIGHT
Oct. 2003
1 (of 8) Gotham transformed 3.00
2 thru 8 . . . . @3.00

BATMAN: CONFIDENTIAL
Dec., 2006
1 WPo,Rules of Engagement 3.00
2 WPo,Rules of Engagement,pt.2 . 3.00
3 WPo,Rules of Engagement,pt.3 . 3.00
4 WPo,Rules of Engagement,pt.4 . 3.00
5 WPo,Rules of Engagement,pt.5 . 3.00
6 WPo,Rules of Engagement,pt.6 . 3.00
7 Who becomes a Joker? 3.00
8 Who becomes a Joker? 3.00
9 Who becomes a Joker? 3.00
10 Who becomes a Joker? 3.00

BATMAN: THE CULT
1988
1 JSn,BWr,V:Deacon Blackfire 8.00
2 thru 4 JSn,BWr. . . . . @6.00
TPB Rep.#1-#4 . . . . 15.00

BATMAN: CYBER REVOLUTION
May 2004
1 (of 5) Joker's robot army 3.00
2 thru 5 . . . . @3.00

BATMAN: DARK DETECTIVE
May, 2005
1 (of 6) TA,MR 3.00
2 TA,MR 3.00
3 TA,MR 3.00
4 TA,MR 3.00
5 TA,MR 3.00
6 TA,MR 3.00
TPB Dark Detective 15.00

BATMAN: DARK KNIGHT OF THE ROUND TABLE
1998
1 (of 2) BL,DG,Elseworlds,48pg . . 5.00
2 BL,DG, conclusion 5.00

BATMAN: THE DARK KNIGHT RETURNS
1986
1 FM,KJ,V:Two-Face 30.00
1a 2nd printing 5.00
1b 3rd printing 3.00
2 FM,KJ,V:Sons of the Batman . . 10.00
2a 2nd printing 3.00
2b 3rd printing 2.50
3 FM,KJ,D:Joker. 7.00
3a 2nd printing 3.00
4 FM,KJ,Batman vs.Superman,
  A:Green Arrow,D:Alfred 7.00
Paperback book 20.00

Warner paperback 17.00
  2nd-8th printing 13.00
TPB 10th Anniv. Spec, 224 pg. . . 15.00

BATMAN: THE DARK KNIGHT STRIKES AGAIN
Dec., 2001
1 (of 3) FM,80-pg. 8.00
2 FM, 80-pg. 8.00
3 FM, 80-pg. concl. 8.00

BATMAN: DARK VICTORY
Oct., 1999
1 (of 13) JLb,TSe,48-pg. 6.00
2 JLb,TSe 5.00
3 JLb,TSe,V:Scarecrow 4.00
4 JLb,TSe,V:Two-Face 4.00
5 JLb,TSe,F:Catwoman 4.00
6 JLb,TSe,F:Penguin 4.00
7 JLb,TSe,V:Calendar Man 4.00
8 JLb,TSe,V:Hang Man 4.00
9 JLb,TSe,F:Bruce & Dick 4.00
10 JLb,TSe,V:Two-Face 4.00
11 JLb,TSe,V:Poison Ivy 4.00
12 JLb,TSe,Revenge 4.00
13 JLb,TSe, conclusion 5.00

BATMAN: DEATH AND THE MAIDENS
Aug. 2003
1 (of 9) KJ,V:Ra's al Ghul 4.00
2 KJ,F:Nyssa 3.00
3 KJ,Ra's al Ghul, Nyssa 3.00
4 KJ,Ra's al Ghul 3.00
5 thru 8 KJ. . . . . @3.00
9 KJ 4.00

BATMAN/DEATHBLOW: AFTER THE FIRE
DC/Wildstorm March, 2002
1 (of 3)TBd,x-over,48-pg. 6.00
2 TBd, 48-pg. 6.00
3 TBd, 48-pg., concl. 6.00

BATMAN: THE DOOM THAT CAME TO GOTHAM
Sept., 2000
1 (of 3) Elseworlds 5.00
2 MMi,DJa, return from the Arctic. . 5.00
3 Elseworlds, concl. 5.00

BATMAN FAMILY
Sept.–Oct., 1975
1 MGr,NA(rep.) Batgirl &
  Robin begins,giant. 35.00
2 V:Clue Master 20.00
3 Batgirl & Robin reveal ID 20.00
4 I:Fatman. 20.00
5 I:Bat Hound 20.00
6 Joker Daughter 25.00
7 CS,A:Sportsmaster,
  G.A.Huntress 13.00
8 First solo Robin story,
  C:Joker's Daughter 13.00
9 Joker's Daughter 25.00
10 R:B'woman,1st solo Batgirl sty. 27.00
11 MR,Man-Bat begins 25.00
12 MR 25.00
13 MR,DN,BWi. 25.00
14 HC/JRu,Man-Bat. 22.00
15 MGo,Man-Bat 22.00
16 MGo,Man-Bat 22.00
17 JA,DH,MG,Batman, B:Huntress
  A:Demon,MK(c),A:Catwoman . 25.00
18 MGo,JSon,BL,Huntress,BM . . 25.00
19 MGo,JSon,BL,Huntress,BM . . 25.00

20 MGo,JSon,DH,A:Elongatedman,
  RagMan, Oct.–Nov.,1978 . . . . 25.00

BATMAN: FAMILY
Oct., 2002
1 (of 8) JFM,SFa,RHo,The Tracker 3.50
2 JFM,SFa, RHo,Athena 2.25
3 JFM,SFa,RHo,Bugg & Dr.Excess 2.25
4 JFM,SFa,RHo,Suicide King. 2.25
5 JFM,SFa,RHo,Freeway 2.25
6 JFM,RHo,The Technician 2.25
7 JFM,Mr. Fun. 2.25
8 JFM,RHo,Blackout, 48-pg.. . . . . 3.50

Batman GCPD #4
© DC Comics Inc.

BATMAN: GCPD
Mini-Series Aug., 1996
1 thru 4 CDi(s),JAp,BSz . . . . @2.50

BATMAN: GORDON'S LAW
October, 1996
1 CDi(s),KJ,Gordon looks for
  bad cops 2.50
2 CDi(s),KJ,Gordon vs. corruption . 2.50
3 CDi(s),KJ, ... 2.50
4 (of 4) CDi(s),KJ, concl. 2.50

BATMAN: GORDON OF GOTHAM
April, 1998
1 (of 4) DON,DG,KJ,F:Jim Gordon . 2.50
2 DON,DG,KJ,Cuchulain. 2.50
3 DON,DG,KJ,break-in 2.50
4 DON,DG,KJ,past revealed 2.50

BATMAN: GOTHAM ADVENTURES
April, 1998
1 TTn,RBr,TBe,F:Joker. 3.50
2 TTn,RBr,TBe,F:Two-Face 2.50
3 TTn,RBr,TBe,V:Scarecrow. 2.50
4 TTn,RBr,TBe,A:Catwoman 2.50
5 RBr,TBe,TTn,A:Mr.Freeze 2.50
6 TTn,RBr,TBe,O:Deadman 2.50
7 TTn,RBe,TBe,V:Danger Dixon. . 2.50
8 TTn,RBe,TBe,Batgirl 2.50
9 TTn,RBe,TBe,V:League
  of Assassins 2.50
10 TTn,RBe,TBe,F:Nightwing
  & Robin, A:Harley Quinn 2.50

11 TTn,RBe,TBe,V:Riddler. 2.50	18 Cavernous,F:Aquaman. 3.00
12 TTn,RBe,TBe,V:Two-Face 2.50	19 CDi,MSh,DG,F:Titus 3.00
13 RBe,TBe,V:Mastermind 2.50	20 A:Superman 3.00
14 TTn(s),TBe,V:Harley Quinn 2.50	21 TA,Retribution, pt.2 . . . . 3.00
15 V:Bane 2.50	22 TA,Chemical attack. 3.00
16 TBe,Alfred Kidnapped. 2.50	23 BB(c),F:Scarecrow 3.00
17 TBe 2.50	24 TDz,Kls,F:Bruce Wayne 3.00
18 TBe,R:Man-Bat 2.50	25 Bruce Wayne:Murderer,pt.4 . . . . 4.00
19 TBe,Eden's Own,Poison Ivy . . . 2.50	26 Bruce Wayne:Murderer,pt.10 . . . 4.00
20 TBe, ... 2.50	27 DCw,A:Man of Steel 3.00
21 TBe, ... 2.50	28 Bruce Wayne:Fugitive,pt.7 . . . . 3.00
22 TBe,F:Comm.Gordon & Batgirl. . 2.50	29 Mortician,pt.2 . . . . 3.00
23 TBe,V:Ra's al Ghul 2.50	30 Bruce Wayne:Fugitive,pt.14 . . . . 3.00
24 TBe,F:Killer Croc 2.50	31 Bruce Wayne:Fugitive,pt.17 . . . . 3.00
25 TBe,A:Flash 2.50	32 MK,lives Batman impacts 3.00
26 TBe,F:Kristov 2.50	33 SBe(s),BSz,F:Bane. 3.00
27 TBe, ... 2.50	34 SBe(s),Tabula Rasa,pt.1 . . . . . . 3.00
28 TBe,V:Riddler 2.50	35 SBe(s),Tabula Rasa,pt.2 . . . . . . 3.50
29 CDi(s),TBe,Batman poisoned. . . 2.50	36 SBe(s),F:Robin,Nightwing. 3.00
30 TBe,F:Clayface. 2.50	37 SBe(s),F:Spoiler 3.00
31 TTn,TBe,Blackout in Gotham . . . 2.50	38 SBe(s),V:Checkmate 3.00
32 TBe,V:Scarecrow 2.50	39 SBe(s),V:Checkmate 3.00
33 A:Phantom Stranger 2.50	40 SBe(s),Knight Moves 3.00
34 V:Maxie Zeus 2.50	41 SBe(s),V:Elongated Man 3.00
35 TBe,On the jury. 2.50	42 SBe(s),Alfred's illness 3.00
36 TBe,A:Superman 2.50	43 SBe(s),F:Batgirl,Robin 3.00
37 TBe,V:Joker, Penguin 2.50	44 SBe(s),death of Jason Todd 3.00
38 TBe,F:Robin, Batgirl 2.50	45 SBe(s),Knights Passed. 3.00
39 TBe,V:Clayface 2.50	46 SBe(s),F:Nightwing,Robin. 3.00
40 TBe,V:Mr. Freeze. 2.50	47 WPo,F:Bane,Nightwing. 3.00
41 TBe,The Man called Joe. 2.50	48 F:Bane,Nightwing 2.75
42 Tuesday Night. 2.50	49 F:Bane 2.75
43 TBe,F:Harley Quinn 2.50	50 V:Hush 3.00
44 TBe,F:Two-Face 2.50	51 V:Hush,Riddler,Joker 3.00
45 TBe,Running the Asylum 2.50	52 F:Tailor,Hush,40-pg. 3.00
46 TBe,Saving Face 2.50	53 F:Hush,Green Arrow,40-pg. 3.00
47 TBe,Gotham's Underworld 2.50	54 F:Joker,40-pg. 3.00
48 TBe,RBr,F:Dick Grayson 2.50	55 Hush vs. Joker, 48-pg. 4.00
49 TBe,Facade 2.50	56 War Games,Act 1,pt.4 . . . . 2.50
50 TBe,Catwoman returns. 2.50	57 War Games,Act 2,pt.4 . . . . 2.50
51 TA,Mr. Freeze 2.50	58 War Games,Act 3,pt.5 . . . . 2.50
52 TBe,Bane 2.50	59 CAd,JaL,F:Mr. Freeze 2.50
53 TBe,Poison Ivy superplant 2.50	60 JaL(c),V:Hush 2.50
54 TBe,crime spree 2.50	61 F:Hush, Ivy 2.50
55 TBe,RBr,mobsters. 2.50	62 F:Poison Ivy 2.50
56 TBe,V:Riddler? 2.50	63 F:Poison Ivy 2.50
57 TBe,V:Riddler 2.50	64 F:Poison Ivy, Hush 2.50
58 TTn,V:Ventriloquist 2.50	65 F:Poison Ivy, conc. 3.00
59 TBe,financial scandal 2.50	66 F:Kobra & Prometheus. 2.50
60 TBe,final issue 2.50	67 V:Hush,F:Poison Ivy 2.50
TPB Batman: Gotham Adventures. 10.00	68 F:Alfred 2.50
	69 F:Hush, Clayface. 2.50

BATMAN:
GOTHAM COUNTY LINE
Oct., 2005

1 (of 3) SHp, 48-page 6.00	70 F:Clayfaces. 2.50
2 SHp, 48-page. 6.00	71 Alfred arrested for Murder. 2.50
3 SHp, 48-page. 6.00	72 Dead Body, Parents Past 2.50
TPB 18.00	73 Joker returns. 2.50
	74 V:Hush, Joker 2.50
	TPB Hush Returns. 13.00

BATMAN:
GOTHAM KNIGHTS
Feb., 2000

(BATMAN:)
GOTHAM NIGHTS
[Mini-Series] 1992

1 WEi,JLe 6.00	1 Gotham City 2.50
2 JBy,BB(c),F:Batgirl. 3.00	2 thru 4 Gotham Citizens Lives. . @2.50
3 PPo,PR,BB(c),Samsara,pt.1 . . . . 3.00	
4 PR,BB(c),Samsara,pt.2 . . . . 3.00	### BATMAN:
5 BB(c)V:The Key. 3.00	### GOTHAM NIGHTS II
6 WS,PR,JPL,F:Oracle. , ... 3.00	**1995**
7 SD,PR, ... 3.00	1 Sequel to Gotham Nights 2.50
8 Transference,pt.1. . . . . 3.00	2 F:Carmine Sansone. 2.50
9 Transference,pt.2. . . . . 3.00	3 Fire. 2.50
10 Transference,pt.3, ... 3.00	4 JQ(c) Decisions 2.50
11 BB(c),Transference,pt.4,48-pg. . . 3.50	
12 This issue: Batman dies! 3.00	### BATMAN/GRENDEL
13 Officer Down,x-over,concl. 3.00	**[First Series]**
14 V:Double Dare 3.00	**DC/Comico, 1993**
15 TPe,GC,V:Poison Ivy 3.00	1 MWg,Devil's Riddle 5.25
16 Matatoa,pt.1 . . . . 3.00	2 MWg,Devil's Masque 5.25
17 Matatoa,pt.2 . . . . 3.00	

Batman/Grendel 1st Series #2
© *DC Comics, Inc.*

[Second Series]
DC/Dark Horse, 1996
1 MWg,Devil's Bones 5.00
2 MWg,Devil's Dance 5.00

BATMAN: HARLEY & IVY
April 2004
1 (of 3) PDi 2.50
2 PDi,Zombie Root 2.50
3 PDi, finale 2.50

BATMAN:
HAUNTED GOTHAM
Dec., 1999
1 (of 4) DgM,KJo,JhB,Elseworlds. . 5.00
2 thru 4 DgM,KJo,JhB. . . . . @5.00

BATMAN/HELLBOY/
STARMAN
DC/Dark Horse 1998
1 JeR(s),MMi, x-over 2.50
2 JeR(s),MMi, conclusion 2.50

BATMAN:
HOLLYWOOD KNIGHT
Feb., 2001
1 (of 3) DG,Elseworlds 2.50
2 DG,F:Byron Wyatt 2.50
3 DG, concl. 2.50

BATMAN/HUNTRESS:
CRY FOR BLOOD
April, 2000
1 (of 6) RBr,O:Huntress 2.50
2 thru 6 RBr. . . . . @2.50

BATMAN:
IT'S JOKER TIME
May, 2000
1 (of 3) BH 5.00
2 BH 5.00
3 BH, concl. 5.00

BATMAN: JAZZ
Mini-Series 1995
1 I:Blue Byrd 2.50
2 V:Brotherhood of Bop 2.50
3 F:Blue Byrd 2.50

BATMAN: JEKYLL & HYDE
Apr., 2005
1 PJe(s),JaL,SeP(c),F:Two-Face . . 3.00
2 PJe(s),JaL,SeP(c) 3.00
3 PJe(s),JaL,SeP(c) 3.00
4 PJe(s),SeP. 3.00
5 PJe(s),SeP. 3.00
6 PJe(s),SeP, finale 3.00

BATMAN: JOURNEY INTO KNIGHT
Aug., 2005
1 (12) Batman's early years 2.50
2 Plague breaks out 2.50
3 Plague 2.50
4 Plague 2.50
5 V:Carrier. 2.50
6 Double-cross 2.50
7 Crossroads 2.50
8 Mysterious fires 2.50
9 Dangerous revelations. 2.50
10 Batman's early career. 3.00
11 Enter the Joker 3.00
12 V:Joker, finale 3.00

Batman/Judge Dredd: Die Laughing #2
© DC Comics, Inc.

BATMAN/JUDGE DREDD: DIE LAUGHING
1998
1 (of 2) AIG(s),GF 48-pg. 5.00
2 AIG(s),GF conclusion. 5.00

BATMAN: LEAGUE OF BATMEN
April, 2001
1 MBr,RT,48-page, Elseworlds . . . 6.00
2 MBr,RT,48-page, concl. 6.00

BATMAN: LEGENDS OF THE DARK KNIGHT
1989
1 EH,Shaman of Gotham,pt.1,
   Yellow(c) 5.00
1a Blue,Orange or Pink(c) 4.00
2 EH,Shaman of Gotham,pt.2 . . . . 3.00
3 EH,Shaman of Gotham,pt.3 . . . . 3.00
4 EH,Shaman of Gotham,pt.4 . . . . 3.00
5 EH,Shaman of Gotham,pt.5 . . . . 3.00

6 KJ,Gothic,pt.1 . . . . 3.00
7 KJ,Gothic,pt.2 . . . . 3.00
8 KJ,Gothic,pt.3 . . . . 3.00
9 KJ,Gothic,pt.4 . . . . 3.00
10 KJ,Gothic,pt.5 . . . . 3.00
11 PG,TA,Prey,pt.1. . . . . 6.00
12 PG,TA,Prey,pt.2. . . . . 5.00
13 PG,TA,Prey,pt.3. . . . . 5.00
14 PG,TA,Prey,pt.4. . . . . 5.00
15 PG,TA,Prey,pt.5. . . . . 4.00
16 TVE,Venom,pt.1 . . . . 5.00
17 TVE,JL,Venom,pt.2 . . . . 5.00
18 TVE,JL,Venom,pt.3. . . . . 5.00
19 TVE,JL,Venom,pt.4 . . . . 5.00
20 TVE,JL,Venom,pt.5. . . . . 5.00
21 BS,Faith,pt.1. . . . . 3.00
22 BS,Faith,pt.2. . . . . 3.00
23 BS,Faith,pt.3. . . . . 3.00
24 GK,Flyer,pt.1 . . . . 3.00
25 GK,Flyer,pt.2 . . . . 3.00
26 GK,Flyer,pt.3 . . . . 3.00
27 Destroyer,pt.2 (Batman#474) . . 3.50
28 MWg,Faces,pt.1,V:Two-Face . . 4.00
29 MWg,Faces,pt.2,V:Two-Face . . 4.00
30 MWg,Faces,pt.3,V:Two-Face . . 4.00
31 BA,Family 3.00
32 Blades,pt.1 . . . . 3.00
33 Blades,pt.2 . . . . 3.00
34 Blades,pt.3 . . . . 3.00
35 BHa,Destiny Pt.1 . . . . 3.00
36 BHa,Destiny Pt.2 . . . . 3.00
37 I:Mercy,V:The Cossack 3.00
38 KON,R:Bat-Mite 3.00
39 BT,Mask#1 . . . . 3.00
40 BT,Mask#2 . . . . 3.00
41 Sunset. 3.00
42 CR,Hothouse #1 . . . . 3.00
43 CR,Hothouse #2,V:Poison Ivy . . 3.00
44 SMc,Turf #1 . . . . 3.00
45 Turf#2 . . . . 3.00
46 RH,A:Catwoman,V:Catman 3.00
47 RH,A:Catwoman,V:Catman 3.00
48 RH,A:Catwoman,V:Catman 3.00
49 RH,A:Catwoman,V:Catman 3.00
50 BBl,JLe,KN,KM,WS,MZ,BB,
   V:Joker 6.00
51 JKu,A:Ragman 3.00
52 Tao #1,V:Dragon 3.00
53 Tao #2,V:Dragon 3.00
54 MMi 3.50
55 B:Watchtower 3.00
56 CDi(s),V:Battle Guards 3.00
57 CDi(s),E:Watchtower 3.00
58 Storm. 3.00
59 DON(s),RoW,B:Qarry 3.00
60 RoW,V:Asp 3.00
61 RoW,V:Asp 3.00
62 RoW,KnightsEnd#4,A:Shiva,
   Nightwing. 4.50
63 Knights End #10,V:Azrael. 3.00
64 CBa. 3.00
65 Joker 3.00
66 Joker 3.00
67 Going Sane,pt.3 . . . . 3.00
68 Going Sane,pt.4 . . . . 3.50
69 Criminals,pt.1 . . . . 3.50
70 Criminals,pt.2 . . . . 3.50
71 Werewolf,pt.1 . . . . 3.00
72 JWk(c&a),Werewolf,pt.2
   [new Miraweb format begins] . . 3.00
73 JWk(c&a),Werewolf,pt.3 . . . . . . 3.00
74 Engins,pt.1 . . . . 3.00
75 Engins,pt.2 . . . . 3.00
76 The Sleeping,pt.1 . . . . 3.00
77 The Sleeping,pt.2 . . . . 3.00
78 The Sleeping,pt.3 . . . . 3.00
79 Favorite Things 3.00
80 Idols,pt.1 . . . . 3.00
81 Idols,pt.2 . . . . 3.00
82 Idols, climax 3.00
83 new villain 3.00
84 WEl(s). 3.00

85 JeR(s) 3.00
86 DgM,JWi,MGy,Conspiracy,pt.1 . 3.00
87 DgM,JWi,MGy,Conspiracy,pt.2 . 3.00
88 DgM,JWi,MGy,Conspiracy,pt.3 . 3.00
89 AIG(s),Clay,pt. 1 . . . . 3.00
90 AIG(s),Clay,pt. 2 . . . . 3.00
91 Freakout,pt.1 . . . . 3.50
92 GEn(s),WSm,Freakout, pt.2 . . . 3.50
93 GEn(s),WSm,Freakout, pt.3 . . . 3.50
94 MGi(s),Saul Fisher's story 3.00
95 DAn&ALa(s),AWi,ALa,Dirty
   Tricks, pt.1. . . . . 3.00
96 DAn&ALa(s),AWi,ALa,Dirty
   Tricks, pt.2. . . . . 3.00
97 DAn&ALa(s),AWi,ALa,,Dirty
   Tricks, concl. 3.00
98 PJe(s),SeP,Steps, pt.1. . . . . . . 3.00
99 PJe(s),SeP,Steps, pt.2 . . . . 3.00
100 DON ,JRo,F:Robin, 64pg. 6.00
101 CE,KN(c)100 years in future. . . 3.00
102 JRo,PuJ,Spook, pt.1 . . . . 3.00
103 JRo,PuJ,Spook, pt.2 . . . . 3.00
104 JRo,PuJ,Spook, pt.3 . . . . 3.00
105 TVE,JRu,Duty, pt.1 . . . . 3.00
106 TVE,JRu,Duty, pt.2 . . . . 3.00
107 LMr,Stalking, pt.1 . . . . 3.00
108 LMr,Stalking, pt.2 . . . . 3.00
109 SEt,DAb,Primal Riddle,pt.1. . . . 3.00
110 SEt,DAb,Primal Riddle,pt.2. . . . 3.00
111 SEt,DAb,Primal Riddle,pt.3 . . . 3.00
112 DVa,FC,V:Lord Demise,pt.1 . . . 3.00
113 DVa,FC,V:Lord Demise,pt.2 . . . 3.00
114 JeR(s),DIB,TBd 3.00
115 LMc,DIB(c) 3.00
116 IEd,Bread and Circuses,pt.1 . . 5.00
117 IEd,Bread and Circuses,pt.2 . . 2.50
118 JPn,Alfred in No Man's Land . . 2.50
119 MD2,Claim Jumping,pt.1. . . . . . 2.50
120 MD2,Assembly 5.00
121 RBr,V:Mr.Freeze 3.50
122 LHa(s),PG, Low Road to Golden
   Mountain,pt.1. . . . . 3.50
123 PR,ALa,Underground
   Railroad,pt.1 . . . . 3.50
124 CDi(s),MkK,No Man's Land . . . 3.50
125 No Man's Land 3.00
126 Endgame, pt.1 x-over 3.00
127 MRy,F:Green Arrow,pt.1 . . . . . 2.50
128 MRy,F:Green Arrow,pt.2 . . . . . 2.50
129 MRy,F:Green Arrow,pt.3 . . . . . 2.50
130 MRy,F:Green Arrow,pt.4 . . . . . 2.50
131 MRy,F:Green Arrow,pt.5 . . . . . 2.50
132 AGw,JeR,MR,BWi,Siege,pt.1 . . 2.50
133 AGw,JeR,MR,BWi,Siege,pt.2 . . 2.50

Batman Legends of the Dark
Knight #135 © DC Comics, Inc.

---

134 AGw,JeR,MR,BWi,Siege,pt.3 . . 2.50
135 AGw,JeR,MR,BWi,Siege,pt.4 . . 2.50
136 AGw,JeR,MR,BWi,Siege,pt.5 . . 2.50
137 DgM,PG,JP,Terror,pt.1 . . . . 2.50
138 DgM,PG,JP,Terror,pt.2 . . . . 2.50
139 DgM,PG,JP,Terror,pt.3 . . . . 2.50
140 DgM,PG,JP,Terror,pt.4 . . . . 2.50
141 DgM,PG,JP,Terror,pt.5 . . . . 2.50
142 CDi,JAp,Demon Laughs,pt.1 . . 2.50
143 CDi,JAp,Demon Laughs,pt.2 . . 2.50
144 CDi,JAp,Demon Laughs,pt.3 . . 2.50
145 CDi,JaP,Demon Laughs,pt.4 . . . 2.50
146 DgM,BKi,Bad,pt.1 . . . . 2.50
147 DgM,BKi,Bad,pt.2 . . . . 2.50
148 DgM,BKi,Bad,pt.3 . . . . 2.50
149 JMD,TVE, Grimm, pt.1 . . . . . . 2.50
150 JMD,TVE, Grimm, pt.2 . . . . . . 2.50
151 JMD,TVE, Grimm, pt.3 . . . . . . 2.50
152 JMD,TVE, Grimm, pt.4 . . . . . . 2.50
153 JMD,TVE, Grimm, pt.5 . . . . . . 2.50
154 MBn,BR,Colossus,pt.1 . . . . 2.50
155 MBn,BR,Colossus,pt.2 . . . . 2.50
156 DGr,Blink,pt.1 . . . . 2.50
157 DGr,Blink,pt.2 . . . . 2.50
158 DGr,Blink,pt.3 . . . . 2.50
159 JOs,DGr,Loyalties,pt.1 . . . . 2.50
160 JOs,DGr,Loyalties,pt.2 . . . . 2.50
161 JOs,DGr,Loyalties,pt.3 . . . . 2.50
162 JAr(s),Auteurism,pt.1 . . . . 2.50
163 JAr(s),Auteurism,pt.2 . . . . 2.50
164 DMD,DGr,Don't Blink,pt.1 . . . . . 2.50
165 DMD,DGr,Don't Blink,pt.2 . . . . . 2.50
166 DMD,DGr,Don't Blink,pt.3 . . . . . 2.50
167 DMD,DGr,Don't Blink,pt.4 . . . . . 2.50
168 Urban Legend 2.50
169 TyH,Irresistible,pt.1 . . . . 2.50
170 TyH,Irresistible,pt.2 . . . . 2.50
171 TyH,Irresistible,pt.3 . . . . 2.50
172 V:Rough Justice 2.50
173 V:Rough Justice 2.50
174 O:Rough Justice 2.50
175 Testament,pt.6 . . . . 2.50
176 Testament,pt.5 . . . . 2.50
177 Lost Cargo,pt.1 . . . . 2.50
178 Lost Cargo,pt.2 . . . . 2.50
179 O:Fat Man & Little Boy 2.50
180 Virtual Gotham City 2.50
181 Cyber-world 2.50
182 War Games,Act 1,pt.2 . . . . 2.50
183 War Games,Act 2,pt.2 . . . . 2.50
184 War Games,Act 3,pt.2 . . . . 2.50
185 RyR,SeP,Riddle Me That, pt.1 . 2.50
186 RyR,SeP,Riddle Me That, pt.2 . 2.50
187 RyR,SeP,Riddle Me That, pt.3 . 2.50
188 RyR,SeP,Riddle Me That, pt.4 . 2.50
189 RyR,SeP,Riddle Me That, pt.5 . 2.50
190 V:Mr. Freeze 2.50
191 V:Mr. Freeze,pt.2 . . . . 2.50
192 Snow,pt.1,O: Mr. Freeze 2.50
193 Snow,pt.2 . . . . 2.50
194 Snow,pt.3 . . . . 2.50
195 Snow,pt.4 . . . . 2.50
196 Snow,pt.5 . . . . 2.50
197 Blaze of Glory, pt.1 . . . . 2.50
198 Blaze of Glory, pt.2 . . . . 2.50
199 Blaze of Glory, pt.2 . . . . 2.50
200 ECa,F:Joker in E.R. 5.00
201 Cold Case, pt.1 . . . . 2.50
202 Cold Case, pt.2 . . . . 2.50
203 Cold Case, pt. 3 . . . . 2.50
204 Madmen of Gotham, pt.1 . . . . . 3.00
205 Madmen of Gotham, pt.2 . . . . . 3.00
206 Madmen of Gotham, pt.3 . . . . . 3.00
207 Darker Than Death, pt.1 . . . . . 3.00
208 Darker Than Death, pt.2 . . . . . 3.00
209 Darker Than Death, pt.3 . . . . . 3.00
210 Darker Than Death, pt.4 . . . . . 3.00
211 Darker Than Death, pt.5 . . . . . 3.00
212 NMa,A cheap date 3.00
213 WS(c),The Otaku 3.00
214 . . . . 3.00

*Batman: Legends of the Dark Knight
#205 © DC Comics, Inc.*

Ann.#1 JAp,KG,DSp,TL,JRu,
   MGo,JQ,`Duel',C:Joker 5.50
Ann.#2 MN,LMc,W:Gordn&Essen . . 5.00
Ann.#3 MM,I:Cardinal Sin 5.00
Ann.#4 JSon(c),Elseworlds Story . . 5.00
Ann.#5 CDi(s)Year One Annuals,
   O:Man-Bat 5.00
Ann.#6 Legends o/t Dead Earth . . . 4.00
Ann.#7 Pulp Heroes (War) 7.00
Halloween Spec.I 8.00
Halloween Spec.II 5.00
Ghosts, Halloween Special 5.00

BATMAN/LOBO:
DEADLY SERIOUS
Aug., 2007
1 (of 2) SK, 48-pgs. 6.00
2 SK 48-pgs. 6.00

BATMAN:
THE LONG HALLOWEEN
Oct., 1996
1 (of 13) JLb,TSe,Who is Holiday?
   F: usual suspects. 11.00
2 JLb(s),TSe,V:Holiday,A:Solomon
   Grundy. 8.00
3 JLb,TSe, ... 9.00
4 JLb(s),TSe,New Year's Eve 9.00
5 JLb(s),TSe,F:Poison Ivy, Search
   for Holiday 6.00
6 JLb(s),TSe,F:Poison Ivy,
   Catwoman 6.00
7 JLb(s),TSe,V:The Riddler 5.00
8 JLb(s),TSe,V:Scarecrow 5.00
9 JLb(s),TSe,A:Holiday,Scarecrow . 5.00
10 JLb(s),TSe,V:Scarecrow,Mad
   Hatter 5.00
11 JLb(s),TSe,V:Holiday 5.00
12 JLb(s),TSe,Harvey Dent 5.00
13 JLb(s),TSe,concl.,48pg. 7.00

BATMAN
AND THE MAD MONK
Aug., 2006
1 (of 6) MWg 3.50
2 MWg 3.50
3 MWg 3.50
4 MWg 3.50
5 thru 6 MWg . . . . @3.50

BATMAN: MAN-BAT
1995
1 R:Man-Bat, painted series 5.00
2 F:Marilyn Muno 5.00
3 JBo,Elseworlds story, concl. 5.00
TPB rep. mini-series 15.00

BATMAN AND
THE MONSTER MEN
Nov., 2005
1 (of 6) MWg, Dark Moon Rising . . 3.00
2 MWg,V:Super-Villains 3.00
3 MWg,V:Professor Hugo 3.00
4 MWg,Genetic mutants 3.00
5 MWg,Mobsters & Mutants 3.00
6 MWg,concl. 40-pg. 3.50
TPB Batman and the Monster Men 15.00

BATMAN: NEVERMORE
April 2003
1 (of 5) Elseworlds,BWr(c) 2.50
2 GyD,BWr(c),Raven Murders 2.50
3 GyD,BWr(c),Raven Murders 2.50
4 GyD,BWr(c),Raven Murders 2.50
5 GyD,BWr(c),concl. 2.50

BATMAN:
NO MAN'S LAND
Sept., 1999
0 F:Huntress 5.00
Secret Files #1 . . . . 5.00

BATMAN:
ORPHEUS RISING
Aug., 2001
1 (of 5) DT,DaM 2.50
2 DT,DaM,caught in cross-fire 2.50
3 DT,DaM,who's behind it 2.50
4 DT,DaM,The Deacons 2.50
5 DT,DaM,concl 2.50

BATMAN: OUTLAWS
July, 2000
1 (of 3) DgM,PG 5.00
2 DgM,PG,V:Bloodhawks 5.00
3 DgM,PG,concl. 5.00

BATMAN: RUN,
RIDDLER RUN
1992
1 MBg,Batman V:Riddler 5.50
2 MBg,Batman V:Riddler 5.25
3 MBg,V:Perfect Securities 5.25

BATMAN: SECRETS
March, 2006
1 (of 5) SK, V:The Joker 3.00
2 SK 3.00
3 SK, Toe to toe 3.00
4 SK, Mooley kidnapped. 3.00
5 SK, final battle V:Joker 3.00

BATMAN: SHADOW OF
THE BAT
1992–97
1 NB,Last Arkham Pt.1 . . . . 5.00
1a Collector set,w/posters,pop-up . 6.00
2 NB,Last Arkham Pt.2 . . . . 4.00
3 NB,Last Arkham Pt.3 . . . . 4.00
4 NB,Last Arkham Pt.4 . . . . 4.00
5 NB,A:Black Spider 3.00
6 NB,I:Chancer 3.00
7 Misfits Pt.1 . . . . 3.00
8 Misfits Pt.2 . . . . 3.00
9 Misfits Pt.3 . . . . 3.00

Batman: Shadow of the Bat #19
© DC Comics Inc.

10 MC,V:Mad Thane of Gotham . . . 3.00
11 V:Kadaver 2.50
12 V:Kadaver,A:Human Flea 2.50
13 NB,The Nobody 2.50
14 NB,Gotham Freaks#1 . . . . 2.50
15 NB,Gotham Freaks#2 . . . . 2.50
16 BBI,MM,A:Anarchy,Scarecrow . . 2.50
17 BBI,V:Scarecrow 2.50
18 BBI,A:Anarchy,Scarecrow 2.50
19 BBI,Knightquest:The Crusade,pt.2,
　　V:Gotham criminals 2.50
20 VGi,Knightquest:The Crusade,
　　V:Tally Man 2.50
21 BBI,Knightquest:The Search,
　　V:Mr.Asp 2.50
22 BBI,Knightquest:The Search,
　　In London 2.50
23 BBI,Knightquest:The Search 2.50
24 BBI,Knightquest:The Crusade . . 2.50
25 BSf(c),BBI,Knightquest: Crusade,
　　A:Joe Public,V:Corrosive Man. . 2.50
26 BSf(c),BBI,Knightquest: Crusade,
　　V:Clayface 2.50
27 BSf(c),BBI,Knightquest: Crusade,
　　I:Clayface Baby 2.50
28 BSf(c),BBI 2.50
29 BSf(c),BBI,KnightsEnd#2,
　　A:Nightwing 4.00
30 BSf(c),BBI,KnightsEnd#8,
　　V:Azrael 2.50
31 Zero Hour, V:Butler 2.50
32 Ventriloquist,Two-Face 2.50
33 Two-Face 2.50
34 V:Tally Man 2.50
35 BKi,Return of Bruce Wayne,
　　Troika,pt.2 . . . . 2.50
35a Collectors Edition 3.50
36 Black Canary 2.50
37 Joker Hunt 2.50
38 V:The Joker 2.50
39 BSf(c),R:Solomon Grundy
　　[new Miraweb format begins] . . 2.50
40 BSf(c), F:Anarky 2.50
41 Explosive Dirigible 2.50
42 BSz(c),Day the Music Died 2.50
43 Secret of the Universe,pt1 . . . . . 2.50
44 AIG,BSz(c) Secret of the
　　Universe,pt.3 . . . . 2.50
45 AIG,BSz(c) 100 year old corpse . 2.50
46 AIG,BSz(c) V:Cornelius Stirk 2.50
47 AIG,BSz(c) V:Cornelius Stirk 2.50
48 AIG 2.50
49 AIG,Contagion,pt.7 . . . . 2.50
50 AIG,Nightmare on Gotham,pt.1 . . 2.50

51 AIG,DTy, Nightmare on
　　Gotham,pt.2 (of 3) 2.50
52 AIG(s),Nightmare on Gotham,
　　pt.3 . . . . 2.50
53 AIG(s),Legacy, prelude 2.50
54 AIG(s),Legacy, pt. 4, x-over 2.50
55 AIG(s),RBr,KJ,Bruce Wayne a
　　murderer? A:Nightwing 2.50
56 AIG(s),DTy,SnW,Leaves of
　　Grass,pt.1,V:Poison Ivy 2.50
57 AIG(s),DTy,SnW,Grass,pt.2 . . . . . 2.50
58 AIG(s),DTy,SnW,Grass,pt.3 . . . . . 2.50
59 AIG(s),DTy,SnW,Killer,
　　Killer, pt.1 . . . . 2.50
60 AIG(s),DTy,SnW,Killer, pt.2 . . . . 2.50
61 AIG(s),JAp,SnW,night of
　　second chances 2.50
62 AIG(s),DTy,SnW,Two-Face,pt.1 . 2.50
63 AIG(s),DTy,SnW,Two-Face,pt.2 . 2.50
64 AIG(s),DTy,SnW,A:Jason Blood . 2.50
65 AIG(s),NBy,JRu, A:Oracle,pt.1 . . 2.50
66 AIG(s),NBy,JRu, V:Thinker,
　　Cheat, pt.2 . . . . 2.50
67 AIG(s),NBy,SnW,CsM,V:Thinker,
　　Cheat, pt.3, concl. 2.50
68 AIG(s),JAp,SnW,annual killer . . . 2.50
69 AIG(s),MBu,WF,CsM,
　　The Spirit of 2000, pt. 1 . . . . 2.50
70 AIG(s),MBu,WF,CsM, pt.2 . . . . . . 2.50
71 AIG(s),MBu,WF,CsM, detective . . 2.50
72 AIG(s),MBu,WF 2.50
73 AIG(s),MBu,WF,Cataclysm
　　x-over,pt.1 . . . . 3.50
74 AIG(s),MBu,WF,Cataclysm
　　cont. 2.50
75 AIG(s),MBu,WF,Aftershock 3.50
76 AIG(s),MBu,WF,Aftershock 2.50
77 AIG(s),MBu,WF,quake-torn 2.50
78 AIG(s),MBu,Aftershock 2.50
79 AIG(s),MBu,V:Mad Hatter,
　　Narcosis. 2.50
80 Road to No Man's Land, flip-book
　　Azrael:Agent of the Bat #47 . . 5.00
81 AIG(s),MBu,No Man's Land 2.50
82 AIG(s),MBu,No Man's Land 2.50
83 No Law and a New Order, pt.2. 14.00
84 IEd,Bread and Circuses, pt.2 . . . 5.00
85 IEd(s),Bread & Circuses,concl. . . 5.00
86 GyD,No Man's Land 3.00
87 MD2, Claim Jumping, pt.2 . . . . . 3.00
88 DJu,BSz,Fruit of
　　the Earth,pt.1 . . . . 3.00
89 IEd(s),SB,No Man's Land 3.00
90 LHa(s),PG,No Man's Land 3.00
91 PR,ALa,Underground
　　Railroad,pt.2 . . . . 3.00
92 No Man's Land,A:Superman. . . . 3.00
93 No Man's Land 3.00
94 final issue 3.00
Ann.#1 TVE,DG,Bloodlines#3,
　　I:Joe Public 4.00
Ann.#2 Elseworlds story 4.00
Ann.#3 Year One Annual 4.00
Ann.#4 Legends of the Dead
　　Earth 4.00
Ann.#5 AIG(s), Pulp Heroes. 4.00
Spec.#1,000,000 AIG(s),MBu, Origin of
　　853rd-century Dark Knight 2.00

BATMAN STRIKES, THE
Sept. 2004

1 thru 38 . . . . @2.25

BATMAN/SUPERMAN/
WONDER WOMAN:
TRINITY
June 2003

1 (of 3) MWg, first meeting 7.00
2 MWg,V:Bizarro 7.00
3 MWg,concl. 7.00

Batman Sword of Azrael #1
© DC Comics Inc.

BATMAN:
SWORD OF AZRAEL
1992–93

1 JQ,KN,I:Azrael 12.00
2 JQ,KN,A:Azrael 9.00
3 JQ,KN,V:Biis,A:Azrael 8.00
4 JQ,KN,V:Biis,A:Azrael 8.00

BATMAN: TENSES
Aug. 2003

1 JoC(s) 7.00
2 JoC(s) 7.00

BATMAN: TOYMAN
1998

1 (of 4) LHa(s),AWi,KJ 2.50
2 thru 4 LHa(s),AWi,KJ . . . . @2.50

BATMAN:
TURNING POINTS
Nov., 2000

1 (of 5) F:Gordon & Batman 2.50
2 TTn(c),Robin arrives 2.50
3 DG,JKu(c),Batgirl dead 2.50
4 CDi,BA,HC(c),Azrael 2.50
5 No Man's Land 2.50

BATMAN vs. PREDATOR
DC/Dark Horse 1991–92

1 NKu,AKu,inc.8 trading cards
　　bound in (Prestige) 5.00
1a Newsstand 4.00
2 NKu,AKu,Inc. pinups (prestige) . . 4.00
2a Newsstand 3.00
3 NKu,AKu,conclusion,inc.
　　8 trading cards (Prestige) 4.00
3a Newsstand 3.00
TPB,rep.#1-#3 . . . . 6.00

BATMAN vs. PREDATOR II
BLOODMATCH
1994–95

1 R:Predators 3.00
2 A:Huntress 3.00
3 Assassins. 3.00
4 V:Head Hunters 3.00
TPB Rep.#1-#4 . . . . 7.00

BATMAN/PREDATOR III:
BLOOD TIES
DC/Dark Horse 1997
1 (of 4) CDi,RDm,RbC, vs. pair
of Predators 2.50
2 CDi,RDm,RbC, pt.2 . . . . 2.50
3 CDi,RDm,RbC, pt.3 . . . . 2.50
4 CDi,RDm,RbC, concl. 2.50
TPB rep 8.00

BATMAN/WILDCAT
Feb., 1997
1 (of 3) CDi&BSt(s),SCi,ATi,
Batman and Robin discover
Secret Ring of combat 2.50
2 CDi&BSt(s),SCi,V:KGBeast,
Willis Danko 2.50
3 CDi&BSt(s),SCi, Batman vs.
Wildcat, concl. 2.50

BATMAN:
YEAR ONE HUNDRED
Feb., 2006
1 (of 4) PPo,48-pg. 6.00
2 thru 4 PPo, Future Gotham . . . @6.00

BEAST BOY
Nov., 1999
1 (of 4)BRa,Clv 3.00
2 BRa,Clv,A:Nightwing 3.00
3 BRa,Clv,V:Nightwing 3.00
4 BRa,Clv,F:Flamebird 3.00

BATTLE CLASSICS
Sept.–Oct., 1978
1 JKu, reprints 15.00

BEOWOLF
April-May, 1975
1 . . . . 25.00
2 thru 3 . . . . @10.00
4 Dracula 15.00
5 . . . . 10.00
6 Flying Saucer,Feb.–Mar.1976 . . 12.00

BEST OF THE
BRAVE & THE BOLD
1988
1 JL(c),NA,rep.B&B #85. . . . . 5.00
2 thru 6 JL(c),NA,rep.B&B . . . . . @5.00

BEWARE THE CREEPER
1968–69
1 SD,Where Lurks the Menace . 175.00
2 thru 6 SD . . . . @80.00

BEWARE THE CREEPER
DC/Vertigo, April 2003
1 thru 5 . . . . @3.00

BIG ALL-AMERICAN
COMIC BOOK
Dec., 1944
1 JKu,132-pages 20,000.00

BIG BOOK OF FUN
COMICS
Spring, 1936
1 . . . . 30,000.00

BIG TOWN
1951–58
1 TV, radio tie-in 1,100.00

Big Town #11
© DC Comics, Inc.

2 . . . . 500.00
3 thru 10 . . . . @350.00
11 thru 20 . . . . @300.00
21 thru 30 . . . . @250.00
31 thru 40 . . . . @150.00
41 thru 50 . . . . @125.00

BIRDS OF PREY:
MANHUNT
1996
1 CDi(s),MHy,F:Black Canary,
Oracle 10.00
2 CDi(s),MHy,V:Archer Braun,
A:Catwoman 7.00
3 CDi(s),MHy,V:Catwoman,
Huntress 7.00
4 CDi(s),MHy,V:Lady Shiva 7.00
1-shot Birds of Prey: Batgirl CDi,
Batgirl & Black Canary (1997) . . 3.00
1-shot Birds of Prey: Revolution
CDi(s),BMc 3.00
1-shot Birds of Prey: The Ravens,
CDi, Girlfrenzy (1998) 3.00
1-shot Birds of Prey: Wolves
CDi,DG (1997) 3.00

BIRDS OF PREY
1998
1 CDi(s),Black Canary & Oracle . . 12.00
2 CDi(s),V:Jackie Pajamas 7.00
3 CDi(s),V:Hellbound 7.00
4 CDi(s),V:Ravens 7.00
5 CDi(s),V:Ravens,pt.2 . . . . 3.00
6 CDi(s),V:Ravens,pt.3 . . . . 3.00
7 CDi(s),PKr 3.00
8 CDi(s),F:Nightwing 40.00
9 CDi(s),V:Iron Brigade 3.00
10 CDi(s),DG,V:Dr.Pop 3.00
11 CDi(s),DG 3.00
12 CDi(s),DG,F:Catwoman 3.00
13 CDi(s),DG 3.00
14 CDi(s),DG,V:Lashina 3.00
15 CDi(s),JG 3.00
16 CDi(s),JG,V:maniac 2.50
17 CDi(s),JG,V:Joker 2.50
18 CDi(s),JG,Transbelvia 2.50
19 CDi(s),JG,A:Nightwing,Robin . . . 2.50
20 CDi(s),Hunt for Oracle,pt.2 . . . . 2.50
21 CDi(s),Hunt for Oracle,concl. . . . 2.50
22 CDi(s),Gorilla City 2.50
23 CDi(s),Gorilla City 2.50
24 CDi,search for heart donor 3.00
25 CDi,Deathstroke,Blue Beetle . . 2.50

26 CDi,This issue Batman dies! . . . 2.50
27 Officer Down x-over,pt.3 . . . . . . 2.50
28 CDi,History Lession,pt.1 . . . . . . 2.50
29 CDi,History Lession,pt.2 . . . . . . 2.50
30 CDi,History Lession,pt.3 . . . . . . 2.50
31 CDi,star-crossed love 2.50
32 CDi,love, and marriage? 2.50
33 CDi,Black Canary,Ra's Al Ghul . . 2.50
34 CDi,A:Power Girl,Blue Beetle . . . 2.50
35 CDi,rescue Black Canary 2.50
36 CDi,Joker: Last Laugh 2.50
37 CDi,Last Laugh aftermath 2.50
38 CDi,F:Dinah 2.50
39 CDi,BruceWayne:Murderer,pt.5 . 6.00
40 CDi,BruceWayne:Murderer,pt.12 6.50
41 CDi,BruceWayne:Fugitive,pt.2 . . 6.50
42 CDi,GF,F:Power Girl 5.00
43 CDi,BruceWayne:Fugitive,pt.10 . 5.00
44 CDi,Deathstroke 2.50
45 CDi,Deathstroke, dinosaurs 2.50
46 CDi,Deathstroke 2.50
47 TMr(s),JP,Heartache,pt.1 . . . . . 2.50
48 TMr(s),JP,Heartache,pt.2 . . . . . 2.50
49 TMr(s),JP,Heartache,pt.3 . . . . . 2.50
50 GHe,CJ 2.50
51 GHe,CJ 2.50
52 GHe,CJ 2.50
53 GHe,CJ 2.50
54 GHe,CJ 2.50
55 GHe,CJ 2.50
56 EBe,V:Savant 6.00
57 EBe,V:Savant 5.00
58 EBe,V:Savant 5.00
59 EBe,V:Savant 4.00
60 EBe,R:Huntress 4.00
61 EBe,consequences 3.00
62 EBe,F:Lady Shiva 3.00
63 EBe,F:Lady Shiva 3.00
64 EBe,V:Cheshire 2.50
65 EBe,F:Cheshire 2.50
66 MGo,MM,ATh(c) 2.50
67 EBe,Sensei and Student 2.50
68 Date for Huntress 2.50
69 Between Dark and Dawn,pt.1 . . . 2.50
70 Between Dark and Dawn,pt.2 . . . 2.50
71 Between Dark and Dawn,pt.3 . . . 2.50
72 Between Dark and Dawn,pt.4 . . . 2.50
73 Between Dark and Dawn,pt.5 . . . 2.50
74 Between Dark and Dawn,pt.6 . . . 2.50
75 EBe,40-pg. BU: EB 3.00
76 EBe,Hero Hunters,pt.1 . . . . 5.00
77 EBe,Hero Hunters,pt.2 . . . . 2.50
78 Hero Hunters,pt.3 . . . . 2.50
79 EBe,Hero Hunters,pt.4 . . . . 2.50
80 EBe,Hero Hunters,pt.5, concl. . . 2.50
81 JoB,The Battle Within 2.50
82 JoB,F:Wildcat 2.50
83 JoB,Omac tie-in 2.50
84 JoB,mission to Singapore 2.50
85 JoB,The Battle Within, concl. . . . 2.50
86 Moving day-to Metropolis 2.50
87 JoB,Oracle, Calculator 2.50
88 JoB,V:Calculator 2.50
89 JoB,V:Calculator 2.50
90 V:Deathstroke 2.50
91 JP,Organ Donar 2.50
92 One Year Later 2.50
93 Vengeance 2.50
94 V:Prometheus 3.00
95 Progeny 3.00
96 Headhunting,pt.1 . . . . 3.00
97 Headhunting,pt.2 . . . . 3.00
98 A:Batgirl 3.00
99 New outfits 3.00
100 DHz,New Team, 48-pg 4.00
101 DHz,F:Oracle, Manhunter 3.00
102 DHz,F:Oracle 3.00
103 DHz,Blood & Circuits finale . . . 3.00
104 DHz,F:Secret Six 3.00
105 DHz,V:Secret Six 3.00
106 DHz,V:Secret Six 3.00
107 DHz,V:Secret Six 3.00

DC COMICS

108 V:Spy Smasher 3.00
109 DHz,Death of a New God 3.00
110 DHz,F:Oracle 3.00
111 Oracle & Calculator 3.00
Spec. Secret Files 2003 . . . . 5.00

BIRDS OF PREY:
Feb. 2003
Catwoman/Batgirl
1 JFM,JP,DaR 6.00
Catwoman/Oracle
2 JFM,JP,DaR 6.00

BITE CLUB
DC/Vertigo, April 2004
1 (of 6) HC(s),vampire,mafia 5.00
2 HC(s),Bikinis 4.00
3 HC(s),Leto Del Toro 3.00
4 HC(s),plot for revenge 3.00
5 HC(s),Leto learns truth 3.00
6 HC(s),concl. 3.00
TPB 10.00

BITE CLUB:
VAMPIRE CRIME UNIT
DC/Vertigo, April, 2006
1 (of 5) HC, Breathe in, Bleed Out . 3.00
2 thru 5 HC . . . . @3.00

BLACK ADAM:
THE DARK AGE
Aug., 2007
1 (of 8) NRd,DoM 3.00
1a variant AxR (c) (1:10) 3.00
2 DoM,F:Superman,Batman,JSA . . 3.00
3 DoM,V:Hawkman 3.00

BLACK CANARY
[Limited Series], 1991–92
1 TVE/DG,New Wings,pt.1 . . . . 2.50
2 TVE/DG,New Wings,pt.2 . . . . 2.50
3 TVE/DG,New Wings,pt.3 . . . . 2.50
4 TVE/DG,New Wings,pt.4,Conc . . 2.50

[Regular Series], 1993
1 TVE,Hero Worship,pt.1 . . . . 3.00
2 TVE,Hero Worship,pt.2 . . . . 3.00
3 TVE,Hero Worship,pt.3 . . . . 3.00
4 TVE,V:Whorrsman 3.00
5 TVE,Blynde Woman's Bluff 3.00
6 TVE,Caged Canary 3.00

Black Canary #7
© DC Comics Inc.

7 TVE,V:Maniacal Killer 3.00
8 TVE,The Fish 3.00
9 TVE,A:Huntress 3.00
10 TVE,A:Nightwing,Huntress 3.00
11 TVE,A:Nightwing 3.00
12 Canary's Grave, final issue 3.00

BLACK CANARY
July, 2007
1 (of 4) League of Assassins 3.00
2 thru 4 . . . . @3.00
Spec. Black Canary Wedding
   Planer 3.00

BLACK CANARY/ORACLE:
BIRDS OF PREY
1996
1-shot DDi, double size 10.00

BLACK CONDOR
1992–93
1 I&O:Black Condor 3.00
2 thru 11 . . . . @3.00

BLACKHAWK
Prev: Golden Age
1957–1984
108 DD,CCu,DD&CCu(c),The Threat
   from the Abyss A:Blaisie 800.00
109 DD,CCu,DD&CCu(c),The
   Avalance Kid 275.00
110 DD,CCu,DD&CCu(c),Mystery
   of Tigress Island 275.00
111 DD,CCu,DD&CCu(c),Menace
   of the Machines 275.00
112 DD,CCu,DD(c),The Doomed
   Dog Fight 275.00
113 DD,CCu,CCu(c),Volunteers
   of Doom 275.00
114 DD,CCu,DD&CCu(c),Gladiators
   of Blackhawk Island 275.00
115 DD,CCu,DD&CCu(c),The
   Tyrant's Return 275.00
116 DD,CCu,DD&CCu(c),Prisoners
   of the Black Island 275.00
117 DD,CCu,DD&CCu(c),Menace
   of the Dragon Boat 275.00
118 DD,CCu,DD&SMo(c),FF,The
   Bandit With 1,000 Nets 300.00
119 DD,CCu,DD&SMo(c),
   V:Chief Blackhawk 200.00
120 DD,CCu,DD&SMo(c),The
   Challenge of the Wizard 200.00
121 DD,CCu,DD&CCu(c),Secret
   Weapon of the Archer 200.00
122 DD,CCu,DD&CCu(c),The
   Movie That Backfired 200.00
123 DD,CCu,DD&CCu(c),The
   Underseas Gold Fort 200.00
124 DD,CCu,DD&CCu(c),Thieves
   With A Thousand Faces 200.00
125 DD,CCu,DD&CCu(c),Secrets
   o/t Blackhawk Time Capsule . 200.00
126 DD,CCu,DD&CCu(c),Secret
   of the Glass Fort 200.00
127 DD,CCu,DD&CCu(c),Blackie-
   The Winged Sky Fighter 200.00
128 DD,CCu,DD&CCu(c),The
   Vengeful Bowman 200.00
129 DD,CCu,DD&CCu(c),The
   Cavemen From 3,000 B.C. . . 200.00
130 DD,CCu,DD&SMo(c),The
   Mystery Missle From Space . 200.00
131 DD,CCu,DD&CCu(c),The
   Return of the Rocketeers . . . 175.00
132 DD,CCu,DD&CCu(c),Raid
   of the Rocketeers 175.00
133 DD,CCu,DD&CCu(c),Human
   Dynamo 175.00

134 DD,CC,DD&CC(c),The
   Sinister Snowman 175.00
135 DD,CCu,DD&CCu(c),The
   Underworld Supermarket . . . 175.00
136 DD,CCu,DD&CCu(c),The
   Menace of the Smoke-Master 175.00
137 DD,CCu,DD&CCu(c),The
   Weapons That Backfired 175.00
138 DD,CCu,DD&SMo(c),The
   Menace of the Blob 175.00
139 DD,CCu,DD&CCu(c),The
   Secret Blackhawk 175.00
140 DD,CCu,DD&CCu(c),The
   Space Age Marauders 175.00
141 DD,CCu,DD&CCu(c),Crimes
   of the Captive Masterminds . 125.00
142 DD,CCu,DD&CCu(c),Alien
   Blackhawk Chief 125.00
143 DD,SMo,DD&CCu(c),Lady
   Blackhawk's Rival 125.00
144 DD,CCu,DD&CCu(c),The
   Underworld Sportsmen 125.00
145 DD,CCu,DD&CCu(c),The
   Deadly Lensman 125.00
146 DD,CCu,DD&CCu(c),Black-
   hawk's Fantastic Fables 125.00
147 DD,SMo,DD&CCu(c),The
   Blackhawk Movie Queen 125.00
148 DD,CCu,DD&CCu(c),Four
   Dooms For The Blackhawks . 125.00
149 DD,CCu,DD&CCu(c),Masks
   of Doom 125.00
150 DD,CCu,DD&SMo(c), Black-
   hawk Mascot from Space . . . 125.00
151 DD,CCu,Lost City 135.00
152 DD,CCu,DD&SMo(c),Noah's
   Ark From Space 125.00
153 DD,CCu,DD&SMo(c),
   Boomerang Master 125.00
154 DD,CCu,DD&SMo(c),The
   Beast Time Forgot 125.00
155 DD,CCu,DD&CCu(c),Killer
   Shark's Land Armada 125.00
156 DD,CCu,DD&SMo(c),Peril of
   the Plutonian Raider 125.00
157 DD,CCu,DD&SMo(c),Secret
   of the Blackhawk Sphinx 125.00
158 DD,CCu,DD&SMo(c),Bandit
   Birds From Space 125.00
159 DD,CCu,DD&SMo(c),Master
   of the Puppet Men 125.00
160 DD,CCu,DD&CCu(c),The
   Phantom Spy 125.00
161 DD,SMo,DD&SMo(c),Lady
   Blackhawk's Crime Chief 125.00

Blackhawk #145
© DC Comics, Inc.

162 DD,CCu,DD&CCu(c),The
   Invisible Blackhawk 125.00
163 DD,CCu,DD&SMo(c),
   Fisherman of Crime 125.00
164 DD,O:Blackhawk retold 135.00
165 DD,V:League of Anti
   Blackhawks 125.00
166 DD,A:Lady Blackhawk 125.00
167 DD,The Blackhawk Bandits . . 90.00
168 DD,Blackhawk Time
   Travelers 80.00
169 DD,Sinister Hunts of Mr.
   Safari 80.00
170 DD,A:Lady Blackhawk,V:Killer
   Shark 80.00
171 DD,Secret of Alien Island 80.00
172 DD,Challenge of the
   GasMaster 80.00
173 DD,The Super Jungle Man . . . 80.00
174 DD,Andre's Impossible
   World 80.00
175 DD,The Creature with
   Blackhawk's Brain 80.00
176 DD,Stone Age Blackhawks . . . 75.00
177 DD,Town that time Forgot 75.00
178 DD,Return of the Scorpions . . 75.00
179 DD,Invisible Dr.Dunbar 75.00
180 DD,Son of Blackhawk 75.00
181 DD,I:Tom Thumb Blackhawk . 80.00
182 DD,A:Lady Blackhawk 100.00
183 DD,V:Killer Shark 100.00
184 DD,Island of Super
   Monkeys 100.00
185 DD,Last 7 days of the
   Blackhawks 100.00
186 DD,A:Lady Blackhawk 100.00
187 DD,V:Porcupine 100.00
188 DD,A:Lady Blackhawk 100.00
189 DD:O:rtd 100.00
190 DD,FantasticHumanStarfish . 100.00
191 DD,A:Lady Blackhawk 100.00
192 DD,V:King Condor 50.00
193 DD,The Jailer's Revenge 50.00
194 DD,The Outlaw Blackhawk . . . 50.00
195 DD,A:Tom Thumb Blackhawk . 50.00
196 DD,Blackhawk WWII Combat
   Diary story 50.00
197 DD:new look 50.00
198 DD:O:rtd 70.00
199 DD,Attack with the Mummy
   Insects 70.00
200 DD,A:Lady Blackhawk,
   I:Queen Killer Shark 90.00
201 DD,Blackhawk Detached Diary
   Story,F:Hendrickson 70.00

Blackhawk #225
© DC Comics, Inc.

202 DD,Combat Diary,F:Andre . . . 70.00
203 DD:O:Chop-Chop 70.00
204 DD,A:Queen Killer Shark 70.00
205 DD,Combat Diary story 70.00
206 DD,Combat Diary, F:Olaf 70.00
207 DD,Blackhawk Devil Dolls . . . 70.00
208 DD,Detached service diary
   F:Chuck 70.00
209 DD,V:King Condor 70.00
210 DD,Danger..Blackhawk Bait
   rep.Blackhawk #139 . . . . 50.00
211 DD,GC,Detached service
   diary 40.00
212 DD,Combat Diary,
   F:Chop-Chop 40.00
213 DD,Blackhawk goes
   Hollywood 40.00
214 DD,Team of Traitors 40.00
215 DD,Detached service diary
   F:Olaf 40.00
216 DD,A:Queen Killer Shark 40.00
217 DD,Detached service diary
   F:Stanislaus 40.00
218 DD,7 against Planet Peril 40.00
219 DD,El Blackhawk Peligroso . . 40.00
220 DD,The Revolt of the
   Assembled Man 40.00
221 DD,Detach service diary
   F:Hendrickson 40.00
222 DD,The Man from E=MC2 . . . 40.00
223 DD,V:Mr.Quick CHange 40.00
224 DD,Combat Diary,
   F:Stanislaus 40.00
225 DD,A:Queen Killer Shark 40.00
226 DD,Secret Monster of
   Blackhawk Island 40.00
227 DD,Detached Service diary
   F:Chop-Chop 40.00
228 DD (1st art on JLA characters)
   Blackhawks become super-heroes,
   Junk-Heap heroes #1(C:JLA) . 50.00
229 DD,Junk-Heap Heroes #2
   (C:JLA) 40.00
230 DD,Junk-Heap Heroes concl.
   (C:JLA) 40.00
231 DD,A:Lady Blackhawk 40.00
232 DD,A:Lady Blackhawk 40.00
233 DD,Too Late,The Leaper 40.00
234 DD,The Terrible Twins 40.00
235 DD,A Coffin for
   a Blackhawk 40.00
236 DD,Melt,Mutant, Melt 40.00
237 DD,Magnificent 7 Assassins . . 40.00
238 DD,Walking Booby-Traps 40.00
239 DD,The Killer That Time
   Forgot 40.00
240 DD,He Who Must Die 40.00
241 DD,A Blackhawk a Day 40.00
242 Blackhawks back in blue &
   black costumes 40.00
243 Mission Incredible (1968) 40.00

[Series Pause:] 1969–75
244 GE,new costumes,Blackhawks
   become mercenaries (1976) . . . 25.00
245 GE,Death's Double Deal 25.00
246 RE,GE,Death's Deadly Dawn . 25.00
247 RE,AM,Operation:Over Kill . . . 25.00
248 JSh,Vengeance is Mine!..
   Sayeth the Cyborg 25.00
249 RE,GE,V:Sky-Skull 25.00
250 RE,GE,FS,D:Chuck (1977) . . . 25.00

[Series Pause:] 1978–81
251 DSp,Back to WWII (1982) 20.00
252 thru 258 DSp . . . . @20.00
259 HC(c),DSp 20.00
260 HC,ATh 20.00
261 thru 271 DSp . . . . @20.00
272 DSp 20.00
273 DSp 20.00
274 DSp 20.00

[2nd Series], 1988
1 HC Mini-series,Blackhawk accused
   of communism 5.00
2 HC,visits Soviet Union 4.00
3 HC,Atom Bomb threat to N.Y. . . 4.00

[3rd Series], 1989
1 All in color for a Crime,pt.1
   I:The Real Lady Blackhawk 4.00
2 All in color for a Crime,pt.2 . . . . 2.50
3 Agent Rescue Attempt in Rome . . 2.50
4 Blackhawk's girlfriend murdered . 2.50
5 I:Circus Organization 2.50
6 Blackhawks on false mission 2.50
7 V:Circus,A:Suicide Squad, rep.
   1st Blackhawk story 3.00
8 Project: Assimilation. 2.50
9 V:Grundfest 2.50
10 Blackhawks Attacked 2.50
11 Master plan revealed 2.50
12 Raid on BlackhawkAirwaysHQ . . 2.50
13 Team Member Accused of 2.50
14 Blackhawk test pilots 2.50
15 Plans for independence 2.50
16 Independence, final issue 2.50
Ann.#1 Hawks in Albania 3.00
Spec.#1 Assassination of JFK
   to Saigon,1975 . . . . 3.50

Black Hood Ann. #1
© DC Comics, Inc.

BLACK HOOD
Impact, 1991–92
1 O:Black Hood 4.00
2 thru 12 . . . . @3.00
Ann#1 Earthquest,w/trading card . 3.00

BLACK LAMB, THE
DC/Helix, Sept., 1996
1 TT,Vampire saga 2.50
2 thru 6 TT . . . . @2.50

BLACK LIGHTNING
1977–78
1 TVE/FS,I&O:Black Lightning . . . 15.00
2 TVE/FS,A:Talia 7.00
3 TVE,I:Tobias Whale 7.00
4 TVE,A:Jimmy Olsen 8.00
5 TVE,A:Superman 8.00
6 TVE,I:Syonide 7.00
7 TVE,V:Syonide 7.00
8 TVE,V:Tobias Whale 7.00
9 TVE,V:Annihilist 7.00
10 TVE,V:Trickster 7.00
11 TVE,BU:The Ray 10.00

[2nd Series], 1995–96

1 He's Back.	3.00
2 V:Painkiller.	3.00
3 V:Painkiller.	3.00
4 V:Painkiller,Royal Family	3.00
5 Flashbacks of Past	3.00
6 V:Gangbuster.	3.00
7 V:Gangbuster.	3.00
8 V:Tobias Whale	3.00
9 I&V:Demolition	3.00
10 Jefferson Pierce becomes Black Lightning full time	3.00
11 Hunt for Sick Nick	3.00
12 V:Sick Nick's death squad	3.00
13 final issue	3.00

BLACK MASK
1993–94

1 I:Black Mask	5.00
2 V:Underworld	5.00
3 V:Valentine	5.00

BLACK ORCHID
1993–95

1 DMc,O:Black Orchid, A:Batman,Luthor,Poison Ivy	6.00
2 DMc,O:cont,Arkham Asylum	7.00
3 DMc,A:SwampThing,conc.	6.00
TPB rep. #1 thru #3	20.00

DC/Vertigo

1 DMc(c),B:DiF(s),JIT,SnW,I:Sherilyn Somers,I:Logos,F:Walt Brody	2.50
1a Platinum Ed.	12.00
2 JIT,SnW,Uprooting,V:Logos	2.50
3 JIT,SnW,Tainted Zone, V:Fungus	2.50
4 JIT,SnW,I:Nick & Orthia	2.50
5 DMc(c),JIT,SnW, A:Swamp Thing	2.50
6 JIT,BMc(i),God in the Cage	2.50
7 JIT,RGu,SnW, Upon the Threshold.	2.50
8 DMc(c),RGu,A:Silent People	2.50
9 DMc(c),RGu.	2.50
10 DMc(c),RGu	2.50
11 DMc(c),RGu,In Tennessee	2.50
12 DMc(c),RGu	2.50
13 DMc(c),RGu,F:Walt Brody	2.50
14 DMc(c),RGu,Black Annis	2.50
15 DMc(c),RGu,Kobolds	2.50
16 DMc(c),RGu,Suzy,Junkin	2.50
17 Twisted Season,pt.1	2.50
18 Twisted Season,pt.2	2.50
19 Twisted Season,pt.3	2.50
20 Twisted Season,pt.4	2.50
21 Twisted Season,pt.5	2.50
22 Twisted Season,pt.6, final iss.	2.50
Ann.#1 DMc(c),DiF(s),GyA,JnM,F:Suzy, Childrens Crusade,BU:retells Adventure Comics#430	4.25

BLOOD: A TALE
DC/Vertigo, Sept., 1996
[Mini-series, re-release of Marvel Epic]

1 JMD(s),KW, quest for truth begins	3.00
2 JMD(s),KW, Blood falls in love	3.00
3 JMD(s),KW, companion dies	3.00
4 JMD(s),KW, finale	3.00
TPB (2004).	20.00

BLOOD & SHADOWS
DC/Vertigo, 1996

1	6.00
2 Journal of Justice Jones	6.00
3 Chet Daley flung into 21st century.	6.00
4 V:God of the Razor, finale	6.00

BLOOD AND WATER
DC/Vertigo March 2003

1 (of 5) F:Adam Heller	3.00
2 vampire	3.00
3 sex for Adam	3.00
4 past, present, future.	3.00
5 concl.	3.00

BLOODBATH
1993

1 A:Superman.	4.00
2 A:New Heroes, Hitman	8.00

BLOODHOUND
July 2004

1 F:Travis Clevenger	3.00
2 thru 4 Concl.	@3.00
5 Firestorm x-over.	3.00
6 Return from prison.	3.00
7 Psychic assault	3.00
8 V:Zeiss	3.00
9 V:Zeiss	3.00
10 V:Zeiss	3.00

BLOODPACK
[Mini-Series], 1995

1 I:Blood Pack, V:Demolition	2.25
2 A:Superboy	2.25
3 Loira's Corpse	2.25
4 Real Heroes Final Issue	2.25

BLOOD OF THE DEMON
March, 2005

1 JBy,F:Jason Blood	2.50
2 JBy,V:Etrigan.	2.50
3 JBy,F:Batman & Zatanna.	2.50
4 JBy,F:Morgain Le Fey	2.50
5 JBy,Jason Blood	2.50
6 JBy,F:Batman, Superman	2.50
7 JBy,Day of Vengeance tie-in	2.50
8 JBy,DGr	2.50
9 JBy,DGr	2.50
10 JBy,DGr.	2.50
11 JBy, DGr, Joshua	2.50
12 JBy,DGr.	2.50
13 JBy,DGr, One Year Later	2.50
14 JBy,DGr,Breaking of Etrigan.	2.50
15 JBy,V:Lord of the Damned	3.00
16 JBy,DGr, V:Lord of the Damned	3.00
17 JBy,DGr,final issue	3.00

BLOOD SYNDICATE
DC/Milestone, 1993–96

1 I:Blood Syndicate,Rob Chaplick, Dir.Mark.Ed.,w/B puzzle piece, Skybox card,Poster	3.50
1a Newstand Ed.	2.50
2 thru 9	@2.50
10 WS(c),Ccs,Shadow War,I:Iota, Sideshow,Rainsaw,Slag,Ash, Bad Betty,Oro	2.75
11 thru 34	@2.50
35 final issue	3.50

BLOODY MARY
DC/Helix, Aug., 1996

1 (of 4) GEn(s),CE, near-future war	3.00
2 thru 4 GEn(s),CE, near-future war, concl.	@3.00
TPB	20.00

BLOODY MARY: LADY LIBERTY
DC/Helix, July, 1996

1 (of 4) GEn(s),CE,	4.00
2 GEn(s),CE,V:Achilles Seagal	4.00

3 GEn(s),CE,V:Vatman	4.00
4 GEn(s),CE,V:Vatman, concl.	4.00

Blue Beetle #14
© DC Comics Inc.

BLUE BEETLE
1986–88

1 O:Blue Beetle.	5.00
2 V:Fire Fist	2.50
3 V:Madmen	2.50
4 V:Doctor Alchemy	2.50
5 A:Question	2.50
6 V:Question	2.50
7 A:Question	2.50
8 A:Chronos	2.50
9 A:Chronos	2.50
10 Legends, V:Chronos	2.50
11 A:New Teen Titans	2.50
12 A:New Teen Titans	2.50
13 A:New Teen Titans	2.50
14 Pago Island,I:Catalyst.	2.50
15 RA:V:Carapax.	2.50
16 RA,Chicago Murders	2.50
17 R:Dan Garrett/Blue Beetle	2.50
18 D:Dan Garrett	2.50
19 RA,R:Dr. Cyber.	2.50
20 RA,Millennium,A:JLI	3.00
21 RA,A:Mr.Miracle, Millennium tie in.	2.25
22 RA,Prehistoric Chicago.	2.25
23 DH,V:The Madmen	2.25
24 DH,final issue	2.25

BLUE BEETLE
March, 2006

1 CHm,Who's Under the Mask?	4.00
2 CHm,Totally changed world.	3.00
3 Trouble at 100 m.p.h.	3.00
4	3.00
5 Phantom Stranger	3.00
6 Secret of Beetle's armor	3.00
7 CHm,	3.00
8 Hits the road	3.00
9 Back in El Paso	3.00
10 CHm,F:Brenda & a Mother Box	3.00
11 Lost in Space, again	3.00
12 Reach	3.00
13 Alien Scarab owners.	3.00
14 Call for Guy Gardner	3.00
15 Meet Little Blue.	3.00
16 Countdown tie-in	3.00
17 V:Typhoon.	3.00
18 F:Titans, x-over.	3.00
19 Truce with La Dama	3.00
20 Sinestro Corps War tie-in	3.00

BLUE DEVIL
1984–86
1 O:Blue Devil. 4.00
2 . . . . 2.50
3 . . . . 2.50
4 . . . . 2.50
5 . . . . 2.50
6 thru 16 . . . . @2.50
17 Crisis 3.00
18 Crisis 3.00
19 thru 31 . . . . @2.50
Ann.#1 . . . . 2.50

BOB, THE GALACTIC BUM
[Mini-Series], 1995
1 A:Lobo 2.50
2 Planet Gnulp,A:Lobo 2.50
3 V:Khunds 2.50
4 Rando's Coronation 2.50

BODY DOUBLES
Aug., 1999
1 (of 4) DAn,ALa,JoP 2.50
2 DAn,ALa,JoP 2.50
3 DAn,ALa,JoP 2.50

BOMBA,
THE JUNGLE BOY
1967–68
1 CI,MA,I:Bomba 200.00
2 The Phantom City of Death . . . 150.00
3 My Enemy...The Jungle 150.00
4 Deadly Sting of Ana Conda 150.00
5 Tampu Lives–Bombs Dies 150.00
6 Krag 150.00
7 Nightmare 150.00

BOOK OF FATE, THE
1997–98
1 KG(s),RoW,BR, ... 3.00
2 KG(s),RoW,BR,The Chaos-
   Order War, pt.1 (of 4) 3.00
3 KG(s),RoW,BR,The Chaos-
   Order War, pt.2 . . . . 3.00
4 KG(s),RoW,BR,The Chaos-
   Order War, pt.3, A:Two-Face . . . 3.00
5 KG(s),RoW,BR,The Chaos-
   Order War, pt.4 . . . . 3.00
6 KG(s),RoW,BR,Convergence,
   pt.1 x-over 3.00
7 KG(s),RoW,BR, Signs, pt.1 . . . . 3.00
8 KG(s),RoW,BR, Signs, pt.2 . . . . 3.00
9 KG,AIG,BR,Signs, pt.3 . . . . 3.00
10 KG,AIG,BR,Signs,pt.4 . . . . 3.00
11 KG,AIG, in a Swiss Jail 3.00
12 AIG,KG,F:Lobo, final issue 3.00

BOOKS OF FAERIE, THE
DC/Vertigo, Jan., 1997
1 PrG,F:Titania and Auberon 3.00
2 thru 3 PrG, ... @3.00
TPB 15.00

BOOKS OF FAERIE, THE:
AUBERON'S TALE
DC/Vertigo, June, 1998
1 (of 3) PrG,VcL,F:Early life of
   King Auberon 3.00
2 thru 3 PrG,VcL, early life . . . . . @3.00
TPB Books of Faerie 15.00

BOOKS OF FAERIE, THE:
MOLLY'S STORY
DC/Vertigo, 1999
1 (of 4) JNR(s) 3.00
2 thru 4 CV(c) . . . . @3.00

Books of Magic #54
© DC Comics, Inc.

BOOKS OF MAGIC
[Limited Series], 1990–91
1 B:NGa(s),JBo,F:Phantom Stranger,
   A:J.Constantine,Tim Hunter,
   Doctor Occult,Mister E 11.00
2 SHp,F:J.Constantine,A:Spectre,
   Dr.Fate,Demon,Zatanna 11.00
3 CV,F:Doctor Occult,
   A:Sandman 8.00
4 E:NGa(s),PuJ,F:Mr.E,A:Death . . 9.00
TPB rep.#1–#4 . . . . 20.00

[Regular Series]
DC/Vertigo, 1994–97
1 MkB,B:Bindings,R:Tim Hunter . . 13.00
1a Platinum Edition 25.00
2 CV(c),MkB,V:Manticore 8.00
3 CV(c),MkB,E:Bindings 8.00
4 CV(c),MkB,A:Death 8.00
5 CV(c),I:Khara 4.00
6 Sacrifices,pt.I 4.00
7 Sacrifices,pt.II 4.00
8 Tim vs. evil Tim 4.00
9 Artificial Heart,pt.1 . . . . 4.00
10 Artificial Heart,pt.2 . . . . 4.00
11 Artificial Heart,pt.3 . . . . 4.00
12 Small Glass Worlds,pt.1 . . . . . . 4.00
13 Small Glass Worlds,pt.2 . . . . . . 4.00
14 CV(c),A:The Wobbly 4.00
15 Hell and Back,pt.1 . . . . 4.00
16 Hall and Back,pt.2 . . . . 3.50
17 Playgrounds,pt.1 . . . . 3.50
18 JNR,PrG,Playgrounds,cont. 3.50
19 JNR,PrG,Playgrounds,concl. . . . 3.50
20 Barabatos gives the orders 3.50
21 JNR,PrG,Molly seeks Mayra . . . 3.50
22 . . . . 3.50
23 JNR,V:Margraves Strafenkinder . 3.50
24 JNR,PrG,F:Molly vs. Amadan . . 3.50
25 JNR,PrG,Death and the Endless . 3.50
26 JNR,PrG,Rites of Passage, pt.1 . 3.00
27 JNR,PrG,Rites of Passage, pt.2 . 3.00
28 JNR,PrG,Rites of Passage, pt.3,
   Cupid & Psyche 3.00
29 JNR,PrG,Rite of Passage 3.00
30 JNR,PrG,Rite of Passage 3.00
31 JNR,PrG,Rite of Passage 3.00
32 JNR(s),PSj,Rites of Passage . . . 3.00
33 JNR(s),PSj,Rites of Passage . . . 3.00
34 JNR(s),PSj,Rites of Passage . . . 3.00
35 JNR(s),PrG,Rites of Passage . . . 3.00
36 JNR,Rites of Passage, cont 3.00
37 JNR,Rites of Passage, cont. . . . 3.00
38 JNR,Rites of Passage, concl. . . . 3.00

39 PrG, at Sphinx casino 3.00
40 JNR(s),F:Tim & Molly 3.00
41 JNR(s),V:Gargoyles 3.00
42 JNR(s),JIT,magical havok 3.00
43 JNR(s),PrG,F:The Wobbly 3.00
44 JNR(s),goodbye to Zatanna 3.00
45 JNR(s) Slave of Heavens, pt.1 . . 3.00
46 JNR(s) Slave of Heavens, pt.2 . . 3.00
47 JNR(s) Slave of Heavens, pt.3 . . 3.00
48 JNR(s) Slave of Heavens, pt.4 . . 3.00
49 JNR(s) Slave of Heavens, pt.5 . . 3.00
50 JNR(s) Slave of Heavens, pt.6 . . 3.00
51 PrG,MK,an Opener 2.50
52 PrG,MK,Homecoming 2.50
54 PrG,MK,V:Thomas 2.50
55 PrG,MK,Coming of the Other . . . 2.50
56 PrG,MK,Last Molly Story 2.50
57 PrG,MK,after car crash 2.50
58 PrG,MK,The Other 2.50
59 PrG,MK,The Other 2.50
60 PrG,MK,The Other 2.50
61 PrG,MK(c),The Other, concl. . . . 2.50
62 PrG,MK(c),crossroads. 2.50
63 GyA,MK(c), ... 2.50
64 PrG,MK(c),Wild Hunt. 2.50
65 PrG,MK,new life cont. 2.50
66 PrG,A Day,A Night &
   A Dream,pt.1 . . . . 2.50
67 PrG,A Day, A Night &
   A Dream,concl. 2.50
68 PrG 2.50
69 PrG 2.50
70 PrG 2.50
71 PrG,MK(c) 2.50
72 PrG,MK(c),F:Timothy Hunter. . . . 2.50
73 PrG,MK(c),V:Other self 2.50
74 PrG,MK(c),V:Other self 2.50
75 PrG,MK(c), final issue 2.50
Ann.#2 JNR(s) Minotaur 4.00
Ann.#3 PrG 4.00

BOOKS OF MAGICK, THE:
LIFE DURING WARTIME
DC/Vertigo, July 2004
1 NGa(s),F:Timothy Hunter 3.00
2 thru 4 NGa(s) . . . . @3.00
5 DOr 3.00
6 DFg 3.00
7 SeP, pt.1 . . . . 3.00
8 DOr 3.00
9 Tumbling Dice,pt.1,DOr 3.00
10 Tumbling Dice,pt.2,DOr 3.00
11 DOr 3.00
12 DOr 3.00
13 Losing My Religion,pt.1,DOr. . . . 3.00
14 Losing My Religion,pt.2,DOr. . . . 3.00
15 series finale. 3.00
TPB Vol. 1 . . . . 10.00

BOOSTER GOLD
1986–88
1 DJ,V:Blackguard 4.00
2 DJ,V:Minddancer 3.00
3 thru 25 DJ . . . . @3.00

BOOSTER GOLD
Aug., 2007
1 DJu,NRd 3.00
2 DJu,NRd,F:Sinestro. 3.00
3 DJu,NRd,A:Jonah Hex. 3.00

BOY COMMANDOS
Winter, 1942–43
1 S&K,O:Liberty Belle;Sandman
   & Newsboy Legion 10,000.00
2 S&K,Hitler(c). 3,500.00
3 S&K,WWII(c). 2,000.00
4 WWII(c). 1,200.00
5 WWII(c). 1,200.00
6 S&K,WWII(c). 1,200.00

7 S&K,WWII(c)	750.00
8 S&K,WWII(c)	750.00
9 WWII(c)	900.00
10 S&K,WWII(c)	750.00
11 WWII(c)	750.00
12 WWII(c)	750.00
13 WWII(c)	750.00
14	750.00
15 1st Crazy Quilt	700.00
16	600.00
17 Science Fiction(c)	700.00
18 S&K	500.00
19 S&K	500.00
20 Science Fiction (c)	700.00
21	400.00
22 Judy Canova	400.00
23 S&K,S&K,(c)	500.00
24 Superhero	500.00
25 superhero(c)	450.00
26 Science Fiction(c)	450.00
27	500.00
28	550.00
29 S&K story	500.00
30 Baseball Story	550.00
31	500.00
32 A:Dale Evans(c)	550.00
33	400.00
34 I:Wolf	400.00
35	400.00
36 Sci-Fi(c),Nov.–Dec., 1949	500.00

BRAINBANX
DC/Helix, Jan., 1997

1 ELe(s),Down Upon the Darkness	2.50
2 ELe(s),Anna flees to the Sheol	2.50
3 Ele(s),Anna stranded	2.50
4 ELe(s),Anna & Logan	2.50
5 ELe(s),To Enter the Kingdom	2.50
6 (of 6)	2.50

BRAVE AND THE BOLD
Aug.–Sept., 1955

1 JKu,RH,IN,I:VikingPrince,Golden Gladiator,Silent Knight	7,000.00
2 F:Viking Prince	2,500.00
3 F:Viking Prince	1,500.00
4 F:Viking Prince	1,500.00
5 B:Robin Hood	1,300.00
6 JKu,F:Robin Hood,E:Golden Gladiator	900.00
7 JKu,F:Robin Hood	900.00
8 JKu,F:Robin Hood	900.00
9 JKu,F:Robin Hood	900.00

The Brave and the Bold #3
© *DC Comics, Inc.*

10 JKu,F:Robin Hood	900.00
11 JKu,F:Viking Prince	700.00
12 JKu,F:Viking Prince	700.00
13 JKu,F:Viking Prince	700.00
14 JKu,F:Viking Prince	650.00
15 JKu,F:Viking Prince	650.00
16 JKu,F:Viking Prince	650.00
17 JKu,F:Viking Prince	650.00
18 JKu,F:Viking Prince	650.00
19 JKu,F:Viking Prince	650.00
20 JKu,F:Viking Prince	650.00
21 JKu,F:Viking Prince	650.00
22 JKu,F:Viking Prince	650.00
23 JKu,O:Viking Prince	950.00
24 JKu,E:Viking Prince,Silent Knight	700.00
25 RA,I&B:Suicide Squad	900.00
26 F:Suicide Squad	600.00
27 Creature of Ghost Lake	600.00
28 I:Justice League of America,O:Snapper Carr	11,000.00
29 F:Justice League	4,200.00
30 F:Justice League	3,300.00
31 F:Cave Carson	800.00
32 F:Cave Carson	500.00
33 F:Cave Carson	500.00
34 JKu,I&O:S.A. Hawkman	4,500.00
35 JKu:F:Hawkman	1,000.00
36 JKu:F:Hawkman	1,000.00
37 F:Suicide Squad	500.00
38 F:Suicide Squad	400.00
39 F:Suicide Squad	400.00
40 JKu,F:Cave Carson	300.00
41 F:Cave Carson	300.00
42 JKu,F:Hawkman	600.00
43 JKu,O:Hawkman	700.00
44 JKu,F:Hawkman	600.00
45 CI,F:Strange Sports	200.00
46 CI,F:Strange Sports	200.00
47 CI,F:Strange Sports	200.00
48 CI,F:Strange Sports	200.00
49 CI,F:Strange Sports	200.00
50 F:GreenArrow & J'onnJ'onzz	400.00
51 F:Aquaman & Hawkman	500.00
52 JKu,F:Sgt.Rock	350.00
53 ATh,F:Atom & Flash	275.00
54 I&O:Teen Titans	600.00
55 F:Metal Man & Atom	200.00
56 F:Flash & J'onn J'onzz	200.00
57 I&O:Metamorpho	400.00
58 F:Metamorpho	225.00
59 F:Batman & Green Lantern	250.00
60 A:Teen Titans,I:Wonder Girl	250.00
61 MA,O:Starman,BlackCanary	300.00
62 MA,O:Starman,BlackCanary	300.00
63 F:Supergirl&WonderWoman	150.00
64 F:Batman,V:Eclipso	200.00
65 DG,FMc,F:Flash & Doom Patrol	150.00
66 F:Metamorpho & Metal Men	175.00
67 CI,F:Batman & Flash	150.00
68 F:Batman,Metamorpho,Joker, Riddler,Penguin	200.00
69 F:Batman & Green Lantern	150.00
70 F:Batman & Hawkman	150.00
71 F:Batman & Green Arrow	150.00
72 CI,F:Spectre & Flash	150.00
73 F:Aquaman & Atom	150.00
74 B:Batman T.U.,A:Metal Men	150.00
75 F:Spectre	150.00
76 F:Plastic Man	150.00
77 F:Atom	150.00
78 F:Wonder Woman	150.00
79 NA,F:Deadman	200.00
80 NA,DG,F:Creeper	150.00
81 NA,F:Flash	150.00
82 NA,F:Aquaman,O:Ocean Master	150.00
83 NA,F:Teen Titans	150.00
84 NA,F:Sgt.Rock	150.00
85 NA,F:Green Arrow	150.00
86 NA,F:Deadman	150.00

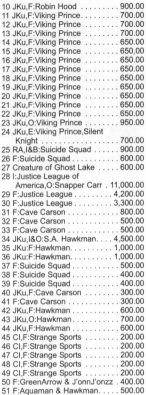

The Brave and the Bold #106
© *DC Comics Inc.*

87 F:Wonder Woman	75.00
88 F:Wildcat	75.00
89 RA,F:Phantom Stranger	75.00
90 F:Adam Strange	75.00
91 F:Black Canary	75.00
92 F:Bat Squad	75.00
93 NA,House of Mystery	100.00
94 NC,F:Teen Titans	90.00
95 F:Plastic Man	90.00
96 F:Sgt.Rock	75.00
97 NC(i),F:Wildcat	75.00
98 JAp,F:Phantom Stranger	75.00
99 NC,F:Flash	75.00
100 NA,F:Green Arrow	100.00
101 JA,F:Metamorpho	50.00
102 NA,JA,F:Teen Titans	50.00
103 FMc,F:Metal Men	35.00
104 JAp,F:Deadman	35.00
105 JAp,F:Wonder Woman	35.00
106 JAp,F:Green Arrow	35.00
107 JAp,F:Black Canary	35.00
108 JAp,F:Sgt.Rock	35.00
109 JAp,F:Demon	35.00
110 JAp,F:Wildcat	35.00
111 JAp,F:Joker	40.00
112 JAp,F:Mr.Miracle	75.00
113 JAp,F:Metal Men	75.00
114 JAp,F:Aquaman	75.00
115 JAp,O:Viking Prince	75.00
116 JAp,F:Spectre	75.00
117 JAp,F:Sgt.Rock	75.00
118 JAp,F:Wildcat,V:Joker	75.00
119 JAp,F:Man-Bat	20.00
120 JAp,F:Kamandi	20.00
121 JAp,F:Metal Men	20.00
122 JAp,F:Swamp Thing	20.00
123 JAp,F:Plastic Man	20.00
124 JAp,F:Sgt.Rock	20.00
125 JAp,F:Flash	20.00
126 JAp,F:Aquaman	20.00
127 JAp,F:Wildcat	20.00
128 JAp,F:Mr.Miracle	20.00
129 F:Green Arrow,V:Joker	25.00
130 F:Green Arrow,V:Joker	25.00
131 JAp,F:WonderWoman, A:Catwoman	22.00
132 JAp,F:King Fu Foom	20.00
133 JAp,F:Deadman	20.00
134 JAp,F:Green Lantern	20.00
135 JAp,F:Metal Men	20.00
136 JAp,F:Metal Men,Green Arr.	20.00
137 F:Demon	20.00
138 JAp,F:Mr.Miracle	20.00
139 JAp,F:Hawkman	20.00

DC COMICS

140 JAp,F:Wonder Woman 20.00
141 JAp,F:Bl.Canary,A:Joker 30.00
142 JAp,F:Aquaman 15.00
143 O:Human Target 15.00
144 JAp,F:Green Arrow 15.00
145 JAp,F:Phantom Stranger 15.00
146 JAp,F:E-2 Batman 15.00
147 JAp,A:Supergirl 15.00
148 JSon,JAp,F:Plastic Man 15.00
149 JAp,F:Teen Titans 18.00
150 JAp,F:Superman 15.00
151 JAp,F:Flash 18.00
152 JAp,F:Atom 15.00
153 DN,F:Red Tornado 15.00
154 JAp,F:Metamorpho 15.00
155 JAp,F:Green Lantern 15.00
156 DN,F:Dr.Fate 15.00
157 JAp,F:Kamandi 15.00
158 JAp,F:Wonder Woman 15.00
159 JAp,A:Ras al Ghul 15.00
160 JAp,F:Supergirl 15.00
161 JAp,F:Adam Strange 15.00
162 JAp,F:Sgt.Rock 15.00
163 DG,F:Black Lightning 15.00
164 JL,F:Hawkman 15.00
165 DN,F:Man-bat 15.00
166 DG,TA,DSp,F:Black Canary
    A:Penguin,I:Nemesis 15.00
167 DC,DA,F:Blackhawk 15.00
168 JAp,DSp,F:Green Arrow 9.00
169 JAp,DSp,F:Zatanna 9.00
170 JA,F:Nemesis 9.00
171 JL,DSp,V:Scalphunter 9.00
172 CI,F:Firestorm 9.00
173 JAp,F:Guardians 9.00
174 JAp,F:Green Lantern 9.00
175 JAp,A:Lois Lane 9.00
176 JAp,F:Swamp Thing 9.00
177 JAp,F:Elongated Man 9.00
178 JAp,F:Creeper 9.00
179 EC,F:Legion o/Superheroes . . . 9.00
180 JAp,F:Spectre,Nemesis 9.00
181 JAp,F:Hawk & Dove 9.00
182 JAp,F:E-2 Robin 9.00
183 CI,V:Riddler 10.00
184 JAp,A:Catwoman 10.00
185 F:Green Arrow 9.00
186 JAp,F:Hawkman 9.00
187 JAp,F:Metal Men 9.00
188 JAp,F:Rose & Thorn 9.00
189 JAp,A:Thorn 9.00
190 JAp,F:Adam Strange 9.00
191 JAp,V:Joker,Penguin 15.00
192 JAp,F:Superboy 9.00
193 JAp,D:Nemesis 9.00
194 CI,F:Flash 9.00
195 JA,I:Vampire 9.00
196 JAp,F:Ragman 9.00
197 JSon,W:Earth II Batman &
    Catwoman 9.00
198 F:Karate Kid 9.00
199 RA,F:Spectre 9.00
200 DGb,JAp,A:Earth-2 Batman,I:
    Outsiders (GeoForce,Katana,Halo),
    E:Batman T.U.,final issue 15.00
Ann. #1-1969 80-page giant (2001)10.00

[Limited Series]
1 SAP,Green Arrow/Butcher T.U. . . 2.50
2 SAP,A:Black Canary,Question . . . 2.50
3 SAP,Green Arrow/Butcher 2.50
4 SAP,GA on Trial;A:Black
    Canary 2.50
5 SAP,V:Native Canadians,I.R.A. . . 2.50

BRAVE AND THE
BOLD, THE
Feb., 2007
1 MWa,BWi,GP, Batman (c) 3.00
1 variant Green Lantern (c) 3.00
2 MWa,GP,BWi,F:Supergirl 3.00
3 MWa,GP,BWi,V:Fatal Five 3.00

The Brave and the Bold #189
© DC Comics, Inc.

4 MWa,GP,BWi,F:Lobo 3.00
5 MWa,GP,BWi,Book of Destiny . . . 3.00
6 MWa,GP,BWi,Book of Destiny . . . 3.00
7 MWa,GP,BWi,F:Power Girl 3.00

BRAVE OLD WORLD
DC/Vertigo, Dec., 1999
1 (of 4) BML,GyD,PhH,Y2K story . . 2.50
2 thru 4 BML,GyD,PhH . . . . @2.50

BREACH
Jan., 2005
1 F:Major Tim Porter,40-page 3.00
2 Long in the future, in Africa 2.50
3 South Africa 2.50
4 F:JLA 2.50
5 JLA fallout 2.50
6 Fallout continues 2.50
7 Rifter fallout 2.50
8 V:Talia's Kobra forces 2.50
9 F:Heardsman 2.50
10 F:Talia al Ghul 2.50
11 V:The Smoking Lady 2.50

BREATHTAKER
1990
1 I:Breathtaker(Chase Darrow) . . . 6.00
2 Chase Darrow captured 6.00
3 O:Breathtaker 6.00
4 V:The Man, final issue 5.00
TPB Breathtaker 15.00

BROTHER POWER,
THE GEEK
Sept.–Oct., 1968
1 . . . . 85.00
2 Nov.–Dec., 1968 . . . . 50.00

BUGS BUNNY
1990
1 Search for Fudd Statues 3.50
2 V:WitchHazel 3.50
3 Bugs&Co.in outer space, final . . . 3.50
TPB Bugs & Friends Celebration
    Celebration (2000) 15.00

BUTCHER, THE
[Limited Series], 1990
1 MB,I:John Butcher 3.50
2 MB,in San Francisco 3.00
3 MB,V:Corporation 3.00

4 MB,A:Green Arrow 2.50
5 MB,A:Corvus,final issue 2.25

BUZZY
1944–58
1 . . . . 500.00
2 . . . . 300.00
3 thru 5 . . . . @250.00
6 thru 10 . . . . @150.00
11 thru 15 . . . . @150.00
16 thru 25 . . . . @150.00
26 thru 35 . . . . @125.00
36 thru 45 . . . . @100.00
46 thru 77 . . . . @75.00

CAMELOT 3000
Dec., 1982
1 BB,O:Arthur,Merlin 3.50
2 BB,A:Morgan LeFay 3.00
3 BB,J:New Knights 3.00
4 BB,V:McAllister 3.00
5 BB,O:Morgan Le Fay 3.00
6 BB,TA,W:Arthur 3.00
7 BB,TA,R:Isolde 3.00
8 BB,TA,D:Sir Kay 3.00
9 BB,TA,L:Sir Percival 3.00
10 BB,TA,V:Morgan Le Fay 3.00
11 BB,TA,V:Morgan Le Fay 3.00
12 BB,TA,D:Arthur 3.00

CAPER
Oct. 2003
1 (of 12) organized crime 3.00
2 . . . . 3.00
3 Jewish Mafia hitmen 3.00
4 Jacob & Isadore Weiss 3.00
5 thru 8 JSe . . . . @3.00
9 thru 12 . . . . @3.00

CAPTAIN ACTION
[Based on toy] Oct.–Nov., 1968
1 WW,I:Captain Action,Action
    Boy,A:Superman 150.00
2 GK,WW, V:Krellik 125.00
3 GK,I:Dr.Evil 125.00
4 GK,A:Dr.Evil 125.00
5 GK,WW,A:Matthew Blackwell . . 75.00

CAPTAIN ATOM
March, 1987
1 PB,O:Captain Atom 4.50
2 PB,C:Batman 2.50
3 PB,O:Captain Atom 2.50
4 PB,A:Firestorm 2.50
5 PB,A:Firestorm 2.50
6 PB,Dr.Spectro 2.50
7 R:Plastique 2.50
8 PB,Capt.Atom/Plastique 2.50
9 V:Bolt 2.50
10 PB,A:JLI 2.50
11 PB,A:Firestorm 2.50
12 PB,I:Major Force 2.50
13 PB,Christmas issue 2.50
14 PB,A:Nightshade 2.50
15 PB,Dr.Spectro, Major Force 2.50
16 PB,A:JLI,V:Red Tornado 2.50
17 V:Red Tornado;A:Swamp
    Thing,JLI 2.50
18 PB,A:Major Force 2.50
19 PB,Drug War 2.50
20 FMc,BlueBeetle 2.50
21 PB,A:Plastique,Nightshade 2.50
22 PB,A:MaxLord,Nightshade,
    Plastique 2.50
23 PB,V:The Ghost 2.50
24 PB,Invasion X-over 2.50
25 PB,Invvasion X-over 2.50
26 A:JLA,Top Secret,pt.1 . . . . 2.50
27 A:JLA,Top Secret,pt.2 . . . . 2.50
28 V:Ghost, Top Secret,pt.3 . . . . . . 2.50

Captain Atom #43
© DC Comics Inc.

29 RT,Captain Atom cleared
  (new direction). 2.50
30 Janus Directive #11,V:Black
  Manta. 2.50
31 RT,Capt.Atom's Powers,
  A:Rocket Red 2.50
32 Loses Powers 2.50
33 A:Batman 3.00
34 C:JLE 2.50
35 RT,Secret o/t Silver Shield,
  A:Major Force 2.50
36 RT,Las Vegas Battle,A:Major
  Force 2.50
37 I:New Atomic Skull 2.50
38 RT,A:Red Tornado,
  Black Racer. 2.50
39 RT,A:Red Tornado. 2.50
40 RT,V:Kobra 2.50
41 RT,A:Black Racer,
  Red Tornado 2.50
42 RT,A:Phantom Stranger,Red
  Tornado,Black Racer,
  Death from Sandman 2.50
43 RT,V:Nekron 2.50
44 RT,V:Plastique. 2.50
45 RT,A:The Ghost,I:Ironfire 2.50
46 RT,A:Superman. 2.50
47 RT,A:SupermanV:Ghost 2.50
48 RT,R:Red Tornado 2.50
49 RT,Plastique on trial 2.50
50 RT,V:The Ghost,DoubleSize . . . 3.00
51 RT 2.50
52 RT,Terror on RTE.91 . . . . 2.50
53 RT,A:Aquaman 2.50
54 RT,A:Rasputin,Shadowstorm . . . 2.50
55 RT,Inside Quantum Field 2.50
56 RT,Quantum Field cont. 2.50
57 RT,V:ShadowStorm,
  Quantum.Field. 2.50
Ann.#1 I:Maj.Force. 3.50
Ann.#2 A:RocketRed,Maj.Force. . . . 3.50

CAPTAIN CARROT
1982–83
1 RA,A:Superman,Starro 3.00
2 AA 3.00
3 thru 20 . . . . @3.00

CAPTAIN CARROT AND
THE FINAL ARK
Oct., 2007
1 (of 3) BMo, Countdown tie-in. . . . 3.00

CAPTAIN STORM
May-June, 1964
1 IN(c),Killer Hunt 150.00
2 IN(c),First Shot-Last Shot 100.00
3 JKu,Death of a PT Boat. 100.00
4 IN(c),First Command-Last
  Command 100.00
5 IN(c), Killer Torpedo. 100.00
6 JKu,IN(c),Medals for an Ocean 100.00
7 IN(c),A Bullet For The General 100.00
8 IN(c),Death of A Sub 125.00
9 IN(c),Sink That Flattop. 100.00
10 IN(c),Only The Last Man Lives 100.00
11 IN(c),Ride a Hot Torpedo 100.00
12 JKu(c),T.N.T. Tea Party Abroad
  PT 47. . . . . 100.00
13 JKu,Yankee Banzai. 100.00
14 RH(c),Sink Capt. Storm 100.00
15 IN(c),My Enemy-My Friend. . . 100.00
16 IN(c),Battle of the Stinging
  Mosquito 100.00
17 IN(c),First Shot for a
  Dead Man 100.00
18 March-April, 1967 . . . . 100.00

CARTOON CARTOONS
Jan., 2001
1 thru 33 From TV shows . . . . . @2.25

CARTOON NETWORK
ACTION PACK
May, 2006
1 . . . . 2.25
2 thru 18 . . . . @2.25

CARTOON NETWORK
BLOCK PARTY
Sept. 2004
1 thru 2 . . . . @2.25
3 thru 38 . . . . @2.25
Spec. Jam-Packed Action 8.00
TPB Vol. 1 thru 4 . . . . @7.00

CARTOON NETWORK
PRESENTS
Warner Bros./DC June, 1997
1 Dexter's Laboratory 4.50
2 thru 24 from TV shows. . . . . . @2.50

CARTOON NETWORK
STARRING
Warner Bros./DC, 1999
1 F:Powerpuff Girls. 4.00
2 thru 18 From TV shows . . . . . @2.50

CATWOMAN
[Limited Series], 1989
1 O:Catwoman 11.00
2 Catwoman'sSister kidnapped . . 10.00
3 Battle 9.00
4 Final,V:Batman 9.00

[Regular Series], 1993
0 JBa,O:Catwoman. 3.50
1 B:JDy(s),JBa,DG,A:Bane. 5.00
2 JBa,DG,A:Bane 3.50
3 JBa,DG,at Santa Prisca 3.50
4 JBa,DG,Bane's Secret 3.00
5 JBa,V:Ninjas 3.00
6 JBa,A:Batman 3.00
7 JBa,A:Batman 3.00
8 JBa,V:Zephyr 3.00
9 JBa,V:Zephyr 3.00
10 JBa,V:Arms Dealer 3.00
11 JBa 3.00
12 JBa,Knights End #6,A:Batman . 5.00
13 JBa,Knights End,Aftermath#2. . . 3.00

14 JBa,Zero Hour 3.00
15 JBa,new path 3.00
16 JBa,Island forterss 3.00
17 JBa,Thief of Paris 3.00
18 JBa,Here Comes the Bride. 3.00
19 Amazonia 3.00
20 Hollywood 3.00
21 JBa(c&a)V:Movie Monster
  [new Miraweb format begins] . . 2.50
22 JBa(c&a) Family Ties,pt.1. . . . . . 2.50
23 Family Ties,pt.2. . . . . 2.50
24 JBa,Family Ties,pt.3 . . . . 2.50
25 A:Robin,Psyba-Rats 3.00
26 AIG,JBa,The Secret of the
  Universe,pt.2 (of 3) 2.50
27 CDi,Underworld Unleashed tie-in 2.50
28 CDi,Catwoman enlists help. 2.50
29 CDi,A:Penguin 2.50
30 CDi,JBa,Great Plane Robbery . 2.50
31 CDi,JBa,Flesh and Fire. 3.00
32 CDi,JBa,Contagion,pt.9 . . . . . . 3.00
33 CDi,JBa,Hellhound,pt.1. . . . . . . 2.50
34 CDi,JBa,Hellbound,pt.2 (of 3). . . 2.50
35 CDi,JBa. 3.00
36 CDi,JBa, Legacy, pt.2 x-over . . . 3.00
37 CDi,JBa, Panara, the Leopard
  Woman 2.50
38 DgM(s),JBa,MPn,Catwoman,
  Year One, pt.1 (of 3) 2.50
39 DgM(s),JBa,MPn,Catwoman,
  Year One, pt. 2 . . . . 2.50
40 DgM(s),JBa,MPn,Catwoman,
  Year One, pt. 3 . . . . 2.50
41 DgM(s),JBa,I:MorelandMcShane 2.50
42 DgM(s),JBa,RedFangClaw,pt.1 . 2.50
43 DgM(s),JBa,RedFangClaw,pt.2 . 2.50
44 DgM(s),JBa,Red FangClaw,pt.3 . 2.50
45 DgM(s),JBa,Nine Deaths of
  the Cat. 2.50
46 DgM(s),JBa,F:Two Face,pt.1 . . . 2.50
47 DgM(s),JBa,F:Two Face,pt.2 . . . 2.50
48 DgM(s),JBa,V:Morella,pt.1 . . . . 2.50
49 DgM(s),JBa,V:Morella,pt. 2. . . . 2.50
50 DgM(s),JBa,V:Cybercat 2.50
50a metallic cover, collectors ed. . . 3.00
51 DgM(s),JBa,F:Huntress,pt.1 . . . 2.50
52 DgM(s),JBa,F:Huntress,pt.2 . . . 2.50
53 DgM(s),JBa,F:identity learned . . 2.50
54 JBa,improving security 2.50
55 JBa,Shared Mentality 2.50
56 JBa,Cataclysm x-over,pt.6 . . . . 4.00
57 JBa,Cataclysm,V:Poison Ivy . . . 3.00
58 JBa,F:Scarecrow, pt.1. . . . . 2.50
59 JBa,F:Scarecrow, pt.2. . . . . 2.50
60 JBa,F:Scarecrow, pt.3. . . . . 2.50
61 JBa,Bank robbery 2.50
62 JBa,A:Nemesis 2.50
63 JBa,A:Batman & Joker, pt.1 . . . 2.50
64 JBa,A:Batman & Joker, pt.2 . . . 2.50
65 JBa,A:Batman & Joker, pt.3 . . . 2.50
66 JBa,I'll Take Manhattan,pt.1 . . . 2.50
67 JBa,I'll Take Manhattan,pt.2 . . . 2.50
68 JBa,I'll Take Manhattan,pt.3 . . . 2.50
69 JBa,I'll Take Manhattan,pt.4 . . . 2.50
70 JBa,I'll Take Manhattan,pt.5 . . . 2.50
71 JBa,I'll Take Manhattan,pt.6 . . . 2.50
72 JOs(s),JBa,A:Batman 2.50
73 JOs(s),JBa,No Man's Land. 2.50
74 JOs(s),JBa,No Man's Land. 2.50
75 JOs(s),JBa,No Man's Land. 2.50
76 JOs(s),JBa,No Man's Land. 2.50
77 JOs(s),JBa,No Man's Land. 2.50
78 Plus Ca Change 2.50
79 A:Batman 2.50
80 going to jail 2.50
81 solitary confinement 2.50
82 payback time. 2.50
83 A:Batman,CommissionerGordon 2.25
84 F:Harley Quinn 2.25
85 anger & revenge 2.25
86 V:Banner. 2.25
87 NSH, from Catwoman's past . . . 2.25

DC COMICS

88 V:Banner 2.25
89 This issue: Batman dies! 2.25
90 Officer Down x-over,pt.4 . . . . . . 2.25
91 Second Catwoman 2.25
92 JFM(s), V:Scarecrow,pt.1 . . . . . . 2.25
93 JFM(s), V:Scarecrow,pt.2 . . . . . 2.25
94 JFM(s), final issue. 2.25
Ann.#1 Elseworlds Story,A:Ra's Al
    Ghul 3.50
Ann.#2 JBa(c&a) Year One Annuals,
    Young Selina Kyle 4.50
Ann.#3 Legends of the Dead Earth . 4.00
Ann.#4 Pulp Heroes (Macabre) 4.50
Spec. Catwoman Defiant,TGr,DG,
    V:Mr.Handsome. 6.00
Spec. Catwoman Plus, LKa,AWi,
    ALa, F:Screamqueen (1997) . . . 3.00
Spec.#1,000,000 JBa, on prison
    planet of Pluto 2.00
TPB The Catfile, rep.#15–#19 . . . . 10.00

CATWOMAN
Nov., 2001
1 MiA,R:Selina Kyle 7.00
2 MiA,serial murders. 4.00
3 MiA,Selina undercover. 3.00
4 MiA,V:Serial killer. 3.00
5 Selina & Holly 2.50
6 F:Holly 2.50
7 Holly in danger. 2.50
8 RBr,East End's Crooked Cops . . 2.50
9 RBr,Disguises 2.50
10 RBr,Death's Row killer 2.50
11 F:Slam Bradley 2.50
12 F:Slam Bradley, Bruce Wayne . . 2.50
13 F:Slam Bradley, Holly 2.50
14 Holly 2.50
15 V:Black Mask 2.50
16 V:Black Mask 2.50
17 No Easy Way Down,pt.1 . . . . 2.50
18 No Easy Way Down,pt.2 . . . . 2.50
19 No Easy Way Down,pt.3 . . . . 2.50
20 A: Wildcat 2.50
21 V:Captain Cold 2.50
22 V:Captain Cold 2.50
23 Opal City 2.50
24 Wild Ride, concl. 2.50
25 JP,PG,back to Gotham 2.50
26 JP,PG,kidnapping 2.50
27 JP,PG,F:Batman 2.50
28 JP,PG,V:Penguin 2.50
29 JP,PG 2.50
30 JP,PG,V:Zeiss 2.50
31 JP,PG,Selina Kyle missing 2.50
32 SeP,East End 2.50
33 PG,JP,V:Galante 2.50
34 War Games,Act 1,pt.7,PG,JP . . . 2.50
35 War Games,Act 2,pt.7,PG,JP . . . 2.50
36 War Games,Act 3,pt.7,PG,JP . . . 2.50
37 JP,PG 2.50
38 JP,PG,I:Wooden Nickel 2.50
39 JP,PG,Wooden Nickel,pt.2 . . . . . 2.50
40 JP,PG,Wooden Nickel,pt.3 . . . . . 2.50
41 JP,PG,Immigrants from Brazil . . 2.50
42 JP,PG,Dog fights 2.50
43 RBr,V:Killer Croc 2.50
44 V:Hush 2.50
45 Selina's new apartment 2.50
46 Deal with Hush 2.50
47 V:Hammer and Sickle 2.50
48 Heart of danger. 2.50
49 V:Black Mask 2.50
50 A:Zatanna 2.50
51 F:Batman 3.50
52 V:Black Mask 3.50
53 Selina Kyle not Catwoman 3.50
54 Holly 2.50
55 New Catwoman in training 3.00
56 A:Wildcat, Angle Man 3.00
57 The Replacements, concl. 3.00
58 F:Zatanna 3.00
59 Baby's Dad, V:Film Freak, ... 3.00

60 Black Mask dead, Holly in Jail . . 3.00
61 V:Film Freak 3.00
62 AH(c),Catwoman's baby 3.00
63 AH(c),in Metropolis 3.00
64 AH(c),at LexCorp 3.00
65 AH(c),Escape from LexCorp. . . . 3.00
66 AH(c),Hammer and Sickle 3.00
67 AH(c), Body count 3.00
68 AH(c),Countdown tie-in 3.00
69 AH(c),Catwoman dies, concl. . . . 3.00
70 AH(c),Amazons Attack tie-in . . . 3.00
71 AH(c),Amazons Attack tie-in . . . 3.00
72 AH(c),No more Selina Kyle 3.00
GN Catwoman: The Movie 5.00
Spec. Secret Files #1. . . . . 5.00

CATWOMAN:
GUARDIAN OF GOTHAM
1999
1 (of 2) Elseworlds,V:Bat-Man 6.00
2 DgM,JBa 6.00

CATWOMAN:
WHEN IN ROME
Sept. 2004
1 (of 6) JLb(s),TSe 3.50
2 JLb(s),TSe 3.50
3 JLb,TSe 3.50
4 JLb,TSe,V:Cheetah 3.50
5 JLb,TSe 3.50
6 JLb,TSe,concl. 3.50

CATWOMAN/WILDCAT
June, 1998
1 (of 4) CDi,TP,SCi,BSf,
    V:Claw Hammer 3.00
2 CDi,BSt,TP,SCi,BSf, ... 3.00
3 CDi,BSt,TP,SCi,BSf, ... 3.00
4 CDi,BSt,TP,SCi,BSf 3.00

CENTURIONS
June, 1987
1 DH,V:Doc Terror. 2.50
2 DH,O:Centurions 2.50
3 DH,V:Doc Terror. 2.50
4 DH,Sept., 1987 . . . . 2.50

CHAIN GANG WAR
1993–94
1 I:Chain Gang 3.00
2 V:8-Ball 2.50
3 C:Deathstroke 2.50
4 C:Deathstroke 2.50
5 Embossed(c),A:Deathstroke 3.00
6 A:Deathstroke,Batman 2.50
7 V:Crooked Man 2.50
8 B:Crooked Man 2.50
9 V:Crooked Man 2.50
10 A:Deathstroke,C:Batman 2.50
11 A:Batman. 2.50
12 E:Crooked Man,D:Chain Gang,
    Final Issue 2.50

CHALLENGERS OF
THE UNKNOWN
1958
1 JK&JK(c),The Man Who
    Tampered With Infinity 5,000.00
2 JK&JK(c),The Monster
    Maker 1,600.00
3 JK&JK(c),The Secret of the
    Sorcerer's Mirror. 1,500.00
4 JK,WW,JK(c),The Wizard of
    Time. 1,000.00
5 JK,WW&JK(c),The Riddle of
    the Star-Stone. 1,000.00
6 JK,WW,JK(c),Captives of
    the Space Circus 1,000.00

Challengers of the Unknown #9
© DC Comics, Inc.

7 JK,WW,JK(c),The Isle of
    No Return 1,000.00
8 JK,WW,JK&WW(c),The
    Prisoners o/t Robot Planet . 1,000.00
9 The Plot To Destroy Earth 600.00
10 The Four Faces of Doom 600.00
11 The Creatures From The
    Forbidden World 500.00
12 The Three Clues To Sorcery . . 500.00
13 The Prisoner of the
    Tiny Space Ball 500.00
14 O: Multi Man 500.00
15 Lady Giant and the Beast 500.00
16 Prisoners of the Mirage World 350.00
17 The Secret of the
    Space Capsules. 350.00
18 Menace of Mystery Island. . . . 350.00
19 The Alien Who Stole a Planet. 350.00
20 Multi-Man Strikes Back 350.00
21 Weird World That Didn't Exist. 350.00
22 The Thing In
    Challenger Mountain 350.00
23 The Island In The Sky. 150.00
24 The Challengers Die At Dawn 150.00
25 Captives of the Alien Hunter . . 150.00
26 Death Crowns The
    Challenge King 150.00
27 Master of the Volcano Men . . . 150.00
28 The Riddle of the
    Faceless Man 150.00
29 Four Roads to Doomsday 150.00
30 Multi-Man...Villain Turned
    Hero. 150.00
31 O:Challengers. 200.00
32 One Challenger Must Die 100.00
33 Challengers Meet
    Their Master 100.00
34 Beachhead, USA 100.00
35 War Against The Moon Beast. 100.00
36 Giant In Challenger Mountain. 100.00
37 Triple Terror of Mr. Dimension 100.00
38 Menace the Challengers Made 100.00
39 Phantom of the Fair 100.00
40 Super-Powers of the
    Challengers 100.00
41 The Challenger Who Quit 75.00
42 The League of
    Challenger-Haters 75.00
43 New look begins 75.00
44 The Curse of the Evil Eye 75.00
45 Queen of the
    Challenger-Haters 75.00
46 Strange Schemes of the
    Gargoyle 75.00
47 The Sinister Sponge 75.00

All comics prices listed are for *Near Mint* condition.

Challengers of the Unknown #27
© *DC Comics Inc.*

48 A:Doom Patrol. 75.00
49 Tyrant Who Owned the World . 75.00
50 Final Hours for the
   Challengers. 75.00
51 A:Sea Devil. 75.00
52 Two Are Dead - Two To Go. . . . 75.00
53 Who is the Traitor Among Us? . 75.00
54 War of the Sub-Humans. 75.00
55 D:Red Ryan 75.00
56 License To Kill. 75.00
57 Kook And The Kilowatt Killer . . 75.00
58 Live Till Tomorrow. 75.00
59 Seekeenakee - The Petrified
   Giant 75.00
60 R:Red Ryan 75.00
61 Robot Hounds of Chang. 75.00
62 Legion of the Weird 75.00
63 None Shall Escape the
   Walking Evil. 75.00
64 JKu(c),Invitation to a Hanging . 75.00
65 The Devil's Circus. 50.00
66 JKu(c),Rendezvous With
   Revenge 50.00
67 NA(c),The Dream Killers. 50.00
68 NA(c),One of Us is a Madman . 50.00
69 JKu(c),I:Corinna 50.00
70 NA(c),Scream of Yesterdays. . . 50.00
71 NC(c),When Evil Calls 50.00
72 NA(c),A Plague of Darkness. . . 50.00
73 NC(c),Curse of the Killer
   Time Forgot. 50.00
74 GT&NA(c),A:Deadman 125.00
75 JK(c),Ultivac Is Loose. 40.00
76 JKu(c),The Traitorous
   Challenger 40.00
77 JK(c),Menace of the
   Ancient Vials 40.00
78 JK(c),The Island of No Return . 40.00
79 JKu(c),The Monster Maker. . . . 40.00
80 NC(c),The Day The Earth
   Blew Up. 40.00
81 MN&NA(c),Multi-Man's
   Master Plan 20.00
82 MN&NA(c),Swamp Thing 20.00
83 Seven Doorways to Destiny . . . 20.00
84 To Save A Monster 20.00
85 The Creature From The End
   Of Time 20.00
86 The War At Time's End. 20.00
87 final issue, July, 1978 . . . . 20.00

CHALLENGERS OF
THE UNKNOWN
[Mini-Series], 1991
1 BB(c) In The Spotlight 3.00

2 thru 8 . . . . @2.50

CHALLENGERS OF
THE UNKNOWN
1997
1 StG(s),JPL 3.00
2 StG(s),LKa,JPL,SMa,Zombies. . . 2.50
3 StG(s),JPL,death of Challenger. . 2.50
4 StG&LKa(s),JPL,SMa,
   O:Challengers 2.50
5 StG&LKa(s)JPL,SMa, V:The
   Fearslayer 2.50
6 StG(s),JPL,SMa,Convergence
   pt. 3 x-over 2.50
7 StG(s),JPL,PastPerfect,pt.1 . . . . 2.50
8 StG(s),JPL,PastPerfect,pt.2 . . . . 2.50
9 StG(s),JPL,PastPerfect,pt.3 . . . . 2.50
10 StG(s),JIT,F:Brenda Ruskin . . . 2.50
11 StG(s),JPL,in Gothan, pt.1 . . . . 2.50
12 StG(s),JPL,in Gothan, pt.2 . . . . 2.50
13 StG(s),F:Marlon Corbett 2.50
14 StG(s),Dark Waters. 2.50
15 StG(s),JPL,Millennium Giants
   pt. 3, x-over 2.75
16 StG(s),JPL,MZ, original Chalis . . 2.75
17 StG(s),JPL,disappearances . . . 2.75
18 StG(s),DRo,MZ, final issue 2.75

CHALLENGERS OF
THE UNKNOWN
June 2004
1 (of 6) HC 3.00
2 thru 5 HC . . . . @3.00
6 HC, concl. 3.00

CHASE
Dec., 1997
1 JWi,MGy,from Batman #550 . . . . 2.50
2 JWi,MGy 2.50
3 JWi,MGy,Rocket Reds. 2.50
4 JWi,MGy,F:Teen Titans 2.50
5 JWi,MGy,flashback story 2.50
6 JWi,MGy,Chase's past. 2.50
7 JWi,Shadowing the Bat,pt.1 . . . . 2.50
8 JWi,Shadowing the Bat,pt.2 . . . . 2.50
9 JWi,MBr,MGy,A:Green Lantern . . 2.50
Spec.#1,000,000 Final Issue 2.50

CHECKMATE
April, 1988
1 From Vigilante & Action Comics . 4.00
2 Chicago Bombings cont. 2.50
3 V:Terrorist Right. 2.50
4 V:Crime Lords Abroad,B.U.Story
   `Training of a Knight' begins . . . 2.50
5 Renegade nation of Quarac 2.50
6 Secret Arms Deal. 2.50
7 Checkmate Invades Quarac 2.50
8 Consequences-Quarac Invasion . 2.50
9 Checkmate's security in doubt. . . 2.50
10 V:Counterfeiting Ring 2.50
11 Invasion X-over. 2.50
12 Invasion Aftermath extra. 2.50
13 CommanderH.Stein's vacation . 2.50
14 R:Blackthorn 2.50
15 Janus Directive #1 . . . . 2.50
16 Janus Directive #3 . . . . 2.50
17 Janus Directive #6 . . . . 2.50
18 Janus Directive #9 . . . . 2.50
19 Reorganization of Group. 2.50
20 Shadow of Bishop
   A:Peacemaker,pt.1 . . . . 2.50
21 Peacemaker behind Iron
   Curtain,pt.2 . . . . 2.50
22 Mystery of Bishop Cont.,pt.3 . . . 2.50
23 European Scientists
   Suicides,pt.4 . . . . 2.50
24 Bishop Mystery cont.,pt.5 . . . . . 2.50
25 Bishop's Identity Revealed 2.50

26 Mazarin kidnaps H.Stein's kids. . 2.50
27 Stein rescue attempt,I:Cypher . . 2.50
28 A:Cypher, Bishop-Robots 2.50
29 A:Cypher,Blackthorn 2.50
30 Irish Knight W.O'Donnell/British
   Knight L.Hawkins team-up 2.50
31 Patriotic Knights,pt.1 . . . . 2.50
32 Patriotic Knights,pt.2 . . . . 2.50
33 Patriotic Knights,pt.3 . . . . 2.50

CHECKMATE
April, 2006
1 Balance of power. 3.00
2 Super-powered nations 3.00
3 F:White Bishop 3.00
4 The Game of Kings 3.00
5 Selection 3.00
6 Suicide Squad returns 3.00
7 Original Suicide Squad member . 3.00
8 Rival agency 3.00
9 Keep the mission alive. 3.00
10 Pawn 502, conclusion. 3.00
11 Corvalho, pt.1 . . . . 3.00
12 Corvalho, pt.2 . . . . 3.00
13 Checkout, pt.1 Outsiders x-over. 3.00
14 Checkout, pt.3 Outsiders x-over. 3.00
15 Checkout, pt.5 Outsiders x-over. 3.00
16 Black Queen vs. White Queen . . 3.00
17 Alpine headquarters 3.00
18 Fall of the Wall, pt.1 . . . . 3.00
19 Fall of the Wall, pt.2 . . . . 3.00

CHILDREN'S CRUSADE
DC/Vertigo, 1993–94
1 NGa(s),CBa,MkB(i),F:Rowland,
   Payne (From Sandman) 4.75
2 NGa(s),AaK(s),JaD(s),PSj,A:Tim
   Hunter,Suzy,Maxine,final issue . 4.50

CHRISTMAS WITH
THE SUPER-HEROES
1988–89
1 JBy(c). 5.00
2 PC,GM,JBy,NKu,DG A:Batman
   Superman,Deadman,(last
   Supergirl appearance). 4.00

CHRONOS
Jan., 1998
1 JFM,PGn,SL,Time Travel 2.50
2 JFM,PGn,SL 2.50
3 JFM,PGn,SL, in 1873 . . . . 2.50

Chronos #1
© *DC Comics Inc.*

4 JFM,PGn,SL,in Chronopolis 2.50
5 JFM,PGn,DHz,SL,WalkerGabriel. 2.50
6 JFM,PGn,Tattooed man 2.50
7 JFM,PGn,DRo,SL,Star City 2.50
8 JFM,PGn,DRo,SL,
   V:Metrognomes 2.50
9 JFM(s),PGn,SL, The Man
   Who Chose Not to Exist 2.50
10 JFM(s),PGn,SL,Forever Engin . . 2.50
11 JFM(s),PGn,SL final issue 2.50
Spec.#1,000,000 JFM(s) Steals
   time gauntlets 2.50

CINDER & ASHE
March, 1988
1 JL,I:Cinder & Ashe 2.50
2 JL,Viet Nam Flashbacks 2.50
3 JL,Truth About Lacey revealed . . 2.50
4 JL,final issue, June, 1988 . . . . . . 2.50

Cinnamon: El Cicclo #2
© DC Comics, Inc.

CINNAMON: EL CICLO
Aug. 2003
1 (of 5) RbC, New West 2.50
2 thru 5 RbC,HC(c) . . . . @2.50

CLASH
1991
1 AKu,I:Joe McLash(b/w) 5.00
2 AKu,Panja-Rise to Power 5.00
3 AKu,V:Archons,conclusion 5.00

CLAW THE
UNCONQUERED
May-June, 1975
1 ECh,I&O:Claw 15.00
2 ECh 8.00
3 ECh,Bloodspear, nudity panel . . 10.00
4 thru 7 ECh . . . . @8.00
8 KG,Master of the Seventh Void . . 8.00
9 KG/BL,Origin 8.00
10 JKu(c),KG,Eater of Souls 8.00
11 JKu(c),KG,Death at Darkmorn . . 8.00
12 KG/BL,Aug.–Sept., 1978 . . . . . . 8.00

CODENAME: KNOCKOUT
DC/Vertigo, April, 2001
0 sexy spy thriller satire 3.00
1 MFm,JCh,Devil You Say,pt.1 . . . . 3.00
1a variant JCh(c) (1:2) 3.00
2 MFm,JCh,Devil You Say,pt.2 . . . . 2.50
3 MFm,Little Orphan Angela 2.50
4 MFm,St. Grace Under Fire 2.50

5 MFm,Arms & Legs for Hostages . 2.50
6 MFm,Arms & Legs for Hostages . 2.50
7 MFm,Go-Go-A-Go-Go 2.50
8 MFm,A is for Anarchy 2.50
9 JP,ACo,Enigma Variations 2.50
10 Undressed to Kill,pt.1 . . . . 2.50
11 Undressed to Kill,pt.2 . . . . 2.50
12 Undressed to Kill,pt.3 . . . . 2.50
13 Fleshback 1932:Roma 2.50
14a JP,JLe(c) 2.50
14b variant JSC(c) 2.50
15 EBe,F:Whole cast 2.50
16 EBe,Amok in America,pt.1 . . . . . 2.75
17 EBe,Amok in America,pt.2 . . . . . 2.75
18 EBe,Amok in America,pt.3 . . . . . 2.75
19 Fleshback '69 . . . . 2.75
20 Rebel Yell 2.75
21 Secrets & Thighs,pt.1 . . . . 2.75
22 Secrets & Thighs,pt.2 . . . . 2.75
23 final issue 2.75

COMET, THE
Impact, 1991–92
1 TL,I&O:Comet 3.00
2 thru 9 TL . . . . @2.50
10 thru 18 . . . . @2.50
Ann.#1 Earthquest,w/trading card . . 2.50

COMIC CAVALCADE
1942–43
1 Green Lantern, Flash,
   Wildcat, Wonder Woman,
   Black Pirate 17,000.00
2 ShM,B:Mutt & Jeff. 4,000.00
3 ShM,B:HotHarrigan,Sorcerer 2,700.00
4 Gay Ghost, A:Scribby,
   A:Red Tornado 2,500.00
5 Gr.Lantern,Flash,W.Woman . 2,400.00
6 Flash,W.Woman,Gr.Lantern . 2,000.00
7 A:Red Tornado, E:Scribby . . 2,000.00
8 Flash,W.Woman,Gr.Lantern . 2,000.00
9 Flash,W.Woman,Gr.Lantern . 2,000.00
10 Flash,W.Woman,Gr.Lantern . 2,000.00
11 Flash,W.Woman,Gr.Lantern . 1,500.00
12 E:Red, White & Blue 1,500.00
13 A:Solomon Grundy 2,500.00
14 Flash,W.Woman,Gr.Lantern . 1,500.00
15 B:Johnny Peril 1,500.00
16 Flash,W.Woman,Gr.Lantern . 1,800.00
17 Flash,W.Woman,Gr.Lantern . 1,500.00
18 Flash,W.Woman,Gr.Lantern . 1,500.00
19 Flash,W.Woman,Gr.Lantern . 1,500.00
20 Flash,W.Woman,Gr.Lantern . 1,500.00
21 Flash,W.Woman,Gr.Lantern . 1,500.00
22 A:Atom 1,500.00

Comic Cavalcade #4
© DC Comics, Inc.

23 A:Atom 1,500.00
24 A:Solomon Grundy 2,200.00
25 A:Black Canary 2,000.00
26 ATh, E:Mutt & Jeff 2,000.00
27 ATh,ATh(c) 2,000.00
28 ATh E:Flash, Wonder Woman
   Green Lantern 2,000.00
29 E:Johnny Peril 1,500.00
30 RG,B:Fox & Crow 700.00
31 thru 39 RG . . . . @500.00
40 RG,ShM 300.00
41 thru 49 RG,ShM . . . . @275.00
50 thru 62 RG,ShM . . . . @350.00
63 RG,ShM, July, 1954 . . . . 500.00

CONGO BILL
1954–56
1 NC(c&a),Chota the Chimp . . 2,500.00
2 NC(c&a),Elephants' Grave . . 2,000.00
3 thru 6 NC(c&a) . . . . @1,500.00
7 NC(c&a) . . . . @2,000.00

CONGO BILL
DC/Vertigo, 1999
1 (of 4) RCo(c) 3.00
2 thru 4 . . . . @3.00

CONGORILLA
1992–93
1 R:Congo Bill 2.50
2 thru 4 BB(c),V:Congo Bill . . . . . @2.50

CONJURORS
1999
1 (of 3) CDi(s),EB, Elseworlds 3.00
2 CDi(s),EB 3.00
3 CDi(s),EB 3.00

CONNOR HAWKE:
DRAGON'S BLOOD
Nov., 2006
1 (of 6) CDi 3.00
2 thru 6 CDi . . . . @3.00

CONQUEROR OF
THE BARREN EARTH
1985
1 RoR,The Ravager 3.00
2 thru 4 RoR . . . . @3.00

COOL WORLD
1992
1 Prequel to Movie 2.25
2 Movie characters 2.25
3 Movie characters 2.25
4 Movie characters 2.25
1-shot Movie Adaptation 3.50

COPS
1988–89
1 PB,O:Cops,double-size 3.50
2 PB,V:Big Boss 2.50
3 PB,RT,V:Dr.Bad Vibes 2.50
4 BS,A:Sheriff Sundown 2.50
5 PB,Blitz the Robo-Dog. 2.50
6 PB,A:Ms.Demeaner 2.50
7 PB,A:Tramplor 2.50
8 PB,V:BigBoss & Ally 2.50
9 PB,Cops Trapped 2.50
10 PB,Dr.Bad Vibes becomes
   Dr.Goodvibes. 2.50
11 PB,V:Big Boss. 2.50
12 PB,V:Dr.Badvibe's T.H.U.G.S . . 2.50
13 Berserko/Ms.Demeanor
   marriage proposal 2.50
14 A:Buttons McBoom-Boom. 2.50
15 Cops vs. Crooks, final issue 2.50

COSMIC BOY
Dec., 1986
1 KG,EC,Legends tie-in 2.50
2 KG,EC,Is History Destiny 2.50
3 KG,EC,Past,Present,Future 2.50
4 KG,EC,Legends 2.50

COSMIC ODYSSEY
1988
1 MMi,A:Superman,Batman,John
  Stewart,Starfire,J'onn J'onzz,
  NewGods,Demon,JSn story . . . 6.00
2 MMi,Disaster'(low dist) 6.00
3 MMi,Return to New Genesis 6.00
4 MMi,A:Dr.Fate, final 6.00
TPB Cosmic Odyssey (2003) 20.00

COUNTDOWN
May, 2007
51 PDi(s),NKu(c) 3.00
50 JP(s),JCf,NKu(c) 3.00
49 NKu(c) 3.00
48 . . . . 3.00
47 . . . . 3.00
46 JP(s) 3.00
45 . . . . 3.00
44 . . . . 3.00
43 JP(s) 3.00
42 . . . . 3.00
41 . . . . 3.00
40 . . . . 3.00
39 JCf. 3.00
38 . . . . 3.00
37 . . . . 3.00
36 . . . . 3.00
35 . . . . 3.00
34 . . . . 3.00
33 . . . . 3.00
32 . . . . 3.00
31 . . . . 3.00
30 . . . . 3.00
29 . . . . 3.00
28 thru 26 . . . . @3.00

COUNTDOWN PRESENTS: LORD HAVOK AND THE EXTREMISTS
Oct., 2007
1 (of 6) F:Lord Havok 3.00

COUNTDOWN PRESENTS: THE SEARCH FOR RAY PALMER
Sept., 2007
Spec. #1 RMz(s),AAd(c), Wildstorm 3.00
Spec. #1 Crime Syndicate 3.00

COUNTDOWN TO ADVENTURE
Aug., 2007
1 (of 8) F:Adam Strange, Starfire . . 4.00
2 F:Champ Hazard, 48-pgs. 4.00
3 F:Starfire, 48-pgs. 4.00

COUNTDOWN TO MYSTERY
Sept., 2007
1 (of 8) F:Kent Nelson, 48-pgs. . . . 4.00
2 F:Doctor Fate, 48-pgs. 4.00

CREATURE COMMANDOS
March, 2000
1 (of 8) TT,SEa, ... 2.50
2 TT,SEa,V:Saturna 2.50
3 TT,SEa, ... 2.50

Creature Commandos #1
© DC Comics Inc.

4 TT,SEa, ... 2.50
5 TT,SEa,F:Claw 2.50
6 TT,SEa,V:Saturna 2.50
7 TT,SEa,V:Claw. 2.50
8 TT,SEa,War Movie, concl. 2.50

CREEPER, THE
Oct., 1997
1 LKa,SMa,SB,R:Creeper. 3.00
2 LKa,SMa,SB,A:Dr. Skolos 3.00
3 LKa,SMa,SB,V:Proteus 3.00
4 LKa,SMa,SB 3.00
5 LKa,SMa,SB, new job 3.00
6 LKa,SMa,SB, strange meals 3.00
7 LKa,SMa,SB,F:Joker, pt.1 . . . . . . 3.00
8 LKa,SMa,SB,F:Joker, pt.2 . . . . . . 3.00
9 DAn,ALa,All-star issue 3.00
10 LKa,SB,Jack Ryder. 3.00
11 LKa,SB,SMa,Creeper splits
  again 3.00
Spec.#1,000,000 LKa,SB,final issue 3.00

CREEPER, THE
Aug., 2006
1 (of 6) F:Jack Ryder 3.00
2 Axeman 3.00
3 Dr. Katz's serum 3.00
4 A:Batman 3.00
5 V:The Joker 3.00
6 A:Batman 3.00

CRIME BIBLE: THE FIVE LESSONS OF BLOOD
Oct., 2007
1 (of 5) TMd,Monk o/t Dark Faith . . 3.00

CRIMSON AVENGER
1988
1 Mini-series 2.50
2 V:Black Cross 2.50
3 V:Killers of the Dark Cross 2.50
4 V:Dark Cross,final issue 2.50

CRISIS AFTERMATH: THE BATTLE FOR BLUDHAVEN
April, 2006
1 (of 6) JP,DJu 3.00
2 thru 6 JP,DJu . . . . @3.00

CRISIS AFTERMATH: THE SPECTRE
May, 2006
1 (of 3) Spectre has new host 3.00
2 F:Crispus Allen 3.00
3 Crispus Allen becomes Spectre. . 3.00

CRISIS ON INFINITE EARTHS
April, 1985
1 B:MWn(s),GP,DG,I:Pariah,I&O:Alex
  Luthor,D:Crime Syndicate 18.00
2 GP,DG,V:Psycho Pirate,
  A:Joker,Batman 12.00
3 GP,DG,D:Losers 10.00
4 GP,D:Monitor,I:2nd Dr.Light 10.00
5 GP,JOy,I:Anti-Monitor. 10.00
6 GP,JOy,I:2nd Wildcat,A:Fawcett,
  Quality & Charlton heroes 10.00
7 GP,JOy,DG,D:Supergirl 25.00
8 GP,JOy,D:1st Flash 22.00
9 GP,JOy,D:Aquagirl 10.00
10 GP,JOy,D:Psimon,A:Spectre . . . 10.00
11 GP,JOy,D:Angle Man 12.00
12 E:MWn(s),GP,JOy,D:Huntress,Kole,
  Kid Flash becomes 2nd Flash,
  D:Earth 2 . . . . 15.00
TPB MWn,GP,DG,JOy,(2001) 30.00

CROSSING MIDNIGHT
DC/Vertigo, Nov., 2006
1 . . . . 3.00
2 MCy(s),MPn. 3.00
3 MCy(s),MPn. 3.00
4 Cut Here, pt.1 . . . . 3.00
5 Cut Here, pt.2 . . . . 3.00
6 A Map of Midnight, pt.1 . . . . 3.00
7 A Map of Midnight, pt.2 . . . . 3.00
8 A Map of Midnight, pt.3 . . . . 3.00
9 A Map of Midnight, pt.4 . . . . 3.00
10 MCy(s),Supernatural slasher . . . 3.00
11 MCy(s),Supernatural slasher . . . 3.00
12 Comb, Mirror, High-heeled shoe. 3.00

CRUCIBLE
Impact, 1993
1 JQ,F:The Comet 2.50
2 thru 6 JQ . . . . @2.50

CRUEL AND UNUSUAL
DC/Vertigo, 1999
1 (of 4) JaD&TPe(s),JMC,satire . . . 3.00
2 thru 4 JaD&TPe(s),JMC. . . . . . . @3.00

CRUSADERS
Impact, May, 1992
1 DJu(c),I:Crusaders,inc Trading
  cards 2.50
2 thru 8 . . . . @2.50

CRUSADES, THE
DC/Vertigo, March, 2001
1 KJo,F:Venus 5.00
2 KJo,V:Dark Ages Knight 3.50
3 KJo,MBu,in San Francisco 3.50
4 KJo,MBu,Anton Marx. 3.00
5 KJo,Marx eats crow. 3.00
6 KJo,second Crusade 3.00
7 KJo,V:The Knight. 3.00
8 KJo,Knight's lair. 3.00
9 KJo,Godfrey. 3.00
10 KJo,sex, sin, subjugation 3.00
11 KJo,origin of the Knight?. 3.00
12 KJo,Knight's hidden enclave. . . . 3.00
13 KJo,Third Crusade begins 3.00
14 KJo,Ash Wednesday Killer 3.00
15 KJo,Ash Wednesday Killer 3.00

16 KJo,Ash Wednesday Killings . . . 3.00
17 KJo,Venus Kostopikas 3.00
18 KJo,Shockjock Anton 3.00
19 KJo,back to Medieval times 3.00
20 KJo,final issue. 3.00
Spec. Urban Decree, KJo,48-page . 4.00

CYBERELLA
DC/Helix, Sept., 1996
1 HC(s),DCn, ... 2.25
2 thru 12 HC(s),DCn, ... @2.25

DALE EVANS COMICS
1948–52
1 Ph(c),ATh,B:Sierra Smith . . . 1,700.00
2 Ph(c),ATh. 800.00
3 ATh. 700.00
4 . . . . 425.00
5 . . . . 425.00
6 thru 11 . . . . @425.00
12 thru 20 . . . . @325.00
21 thru 24 . . . . @300.00

DAMAGE
1994–96
1 I:Damage,V:Metallo 4.00
2 Afterschool Special 3.00
3 The Damage Done 3.00
4 Troll's Day,A:Wyldheart 3.00
5 thru 20 . . . . @3.00
Spec. 0 Back Again 3.50

DANGER TRAIL
July-Aug., 1950
1 CI,ATh,I:King For A Day 2,000.00
2 ATh, King Faraday 1,400.00
3 ATh, King Faraday 2,000.00
4 ATh, King Faraday 1,200.00
5 March-April, 1951, John
    Pearl 1,200.00

DANGER TRAIL
[Mini-Series], 1993
1 thru 4 CI,FMc,F:King Faraday
    V:Cobra 2.25

DARK MANSION OF
FORBIDDEN LOVE, THE
Sept.–Oct., 1971
1 . . . . 300.00
2 NA(c) 150.00
3 and 4 March-April, 1972 . . . @125.00

DARKSEID VS.
GALACTUS THE HUNGER
1995
1-shot Orion vs. Silver Surfer 5.00
GN JBy,in Apokolips. 6.00

DARKSTARS
1992–96
0 History 2.00
1 TC(c),LSn,I:Darkstars 3.50
2 TC(c),LSn,F:Ferin Colos 2.50
3 LSn,J:Mo,Flint,V:Evil Star 2.50
4 TC,V:Evilstar 3.00
5 TC,A:Hawkman,Hawkwoman . . . 3.00
6 TC,A:Hawkman 2.50
7 TC,V:K'llash 2.50
8 F:Ferris Colos 2.50
9 Colos vs K'lassh 2.50
10 V:Con Artists 2.50
11 TC,Trinity#4,A:Green Lantern,
    L.E.G.I.O.N. 2.50
12 TC(c),Trinity#7,A:Green Lantern,
    L.E.G.I.O.N. 2.50
13 thru 38 . . . . @2.50

A Date With Judy #9
© DC Comics Inc.

A DATE WITH JUDY
1947
1 Teen-age 500.00
2 . . . . 350.00
3 . . . . 300.00
4 . . . . 300.00
5 . . . . 300.00
6 thru 10 . . . . @300.00
11 thru 20 . . . . @250.00
21 thru 30 . . . . @150.00
31 thru 50 . . . . @125.00
51 thru 78 . . . . @125.00
79 MD 150.00

DAY OF JUDGMENT
Sept., 1999
1 (of 5) Spectre x-over 6.00
2 F:Wonder Woman, Supergirl 5.00
3 F:Superman & Green Lantern . . . 5.00
4 F:Superman's team 5.00
5 conclusion 5.00
Spec. Secret Files #1 . . . . 6.00

DAY OF VENGEANCE
Apr., 2005
1 (of 6) F:Spectre, Enchantress . . . 8.00
1a 2nd printing 5.00
2 WS(c) Shadowpact 3.00
3 WS(c). 2.50
4 WS(c). 2.50
5 WS(c). 2.50
6 WS(c), The Death of Magic. 2.50
TPB 13.00
Spec. Infinite Crisis, 48-pg. 4.00

DC CHALLENGE
Nov., 1985
1 GC,Batman 3.00
2 Superman 2.50
3 CI,Adam Strange 2.50
4 GK/KJ,Aquaman 2.50
5 DGb,Dr.Fate,Capt.Marvel 2.50
6 Dr. 13 . . . . 2.50
7 Gorilla Grodd 2.50
8 DG,Outsiders, New Gods 2.50
9 New Teen Titans,JLA 2.50
10 CS,New Teen Titans,JLA 2.50
11 KG,Outsiders 2.50
12 DCw,TMd,DSp,New Teen Titans,
    Oct., 1986 . . . . 2.50

DC COMICS PRESENTS
July-Aug., 1978
[all have Superman]
1 JL,DA,F:Flash 30.00
2 JL,DA,F:Flash 20.00
3 JL,F:Adam Strange 20.00
4 JL,F:Metal Men,A:Mr.IQ 20.00
5 MA,F:Aquaman 8.00
6 CS,F:Green Lantern 8.00
7 DD,F:Red Tornado. 8.00
8 MA,F:Swamp Thing 8.00
9 JSon,JA,RH,F:Wonder Woman . . 8.00
10 JSon,JA,F:Sgt.Rock 8.00
11 JSon,F:Hawkman 7.00
12 RB,DG,F:Mr.Miracle 7.00
13 DD,DG,F:Legion 8.00
14 DD,DG,F:Superboy 7.00
15 JSon,F:Atom,C:Batman 7.00
16 JSon,F:Black Lightning 7.00
17 JL,F:Firestorm. 7.00
18 DD,F:Zatanna 7.00
19 JSon,F:Batgirl 7.00
20 JL,F:Green Arrow 6.00
21 JSon,JSa,F:Elongated Man 6.00
22 DD,FMc,F:Captain Comet 6.00
23 JSon,F:Dr.Fate 6.00
24 JL,F:Deadman 6.00
25 DD,FMc,F:Phantom Stranger . . . 6.00
26 GP,DG,JSn,I:New Teen Titans,
    Cyborg,Raven,Starfire
    A:Green Lantern 45.00
27 JSn,RT,I:Mongul 7.00
28 JSn,RT,GK,F:Mongul 6.00
29 JSn,RT,AS,F:Spectre 6.00
30 CS,AS,F:Black Canary 6.00
31 JL,DG,AS,F:Robin. 6.00
32 KS,AS,F:Wonder Woman 6.00
33 RB,DG,AS,F:Captain Marvel . . . 6.00
34 RB,DG,F:Marvel Family 6.00
35 CS,GK,F:Man-bat 6.00
36 JSn,F:Starman 7.00
37 JSn,AS,F:Hawkgirl 6.00
38 GP(c),DH,AS,DG,D:Crimson
    Avenger,F:Flash 6.00
39 JSon,AS,F:PlasticMan,Toyman. . 6.00
40 IN,FMc,AS,F:Metamorpho 6.00
41 JL,FMc,GC,RT,I:New Wonder
    Woman,A:Joker. 8.00
42 IN,FMc,F:Unknown Soldier. 6.00
43 BB(c),CS,F:Legion 6.00
44 IN,FMc,F:Dial H for Hero 7.00
45 RB,F:Firestorm 6.00
46 AS,I:Global Guardians 6.00
47 CS,I:Masters of Universe. 20.00
48 GK(c),AA,IN,FMc,F:Aquaman. . . 5.00
49 RB,F:Shazam!,V:Black Adam . . . 5.00
50 KS,CS,F:Clark Kent 5.00
51 AS,FMc,CS,F:Atom,Masters
    of the Universe 7.00
52 KG,F:Doom Patrol,
    I:Ambush Bug 5.00
53 CS,TD,RA,DG,I:Atari Force 5.00
54 DN,DA,F:Gr.Arrow,Bl.Canary . . . 5.00
55 AS,F:Air Wave,A:Superboy 5.00
56 GK(c),F:Power Girl 5.00
57 AS,FMc,F:Atomic Knights 5.00
58 GK(c),AS,F:Robin,Elongated
    Man 5.00
59 GK,KS,F:Ambush Bug 5.00
60 GK(c),IN,TD,F:Guardians 5.00
61 GP,F:Omac 5.00
62 GK(c),IN,F:Freedom Fighters . . . 5.00
63 AS,EC,F:Amethyst 5.00
64 GK(c),AS,FMc,F:Kamandi 5.00
65 GM,F:Madame Xanadu 5.00
66 JKu,F:Demon 5.00
67 CS,MA,F:Santa Claus. 5.00
68 GK(c),CS,MA,F:Vixen 5.00
69 IN,DJ,F:Blackhawk 5.00
70 AS,TD,F:Metal Men 5.00
71 CS,F:Bizarro 5.00

DC Comics Presents #35
© DC Comics, Inc.

72 AS,DG,F:Phant.Stranger,Joker . . 6.00
73 CI,F:Flash 5.00
74 AS,RT,F:Hawkman 5.00
75 TMd,F:Arion 5.00
76 EB,F:Wonder Woman 5.00
77 CS,F:Forgotten Heroes 5.00
78 CS,F:Forgotten Villains 6.00
79 CS,AW,F:Legion 6.00
80 CS,F:Clark Kent 5.00
81 KG,BO,F:Ambush Bug 5.00
82 KJ,F:Adam Strange. 5.00
83 IN,F:Batman/Outsiders. 5.00
84 JK,ATh,MA,F:Challengers. 7.00
85 RV,AW,AMo(s),
    F:Swamp Thing 7.00
86 Crisis,F:Supergirl 5.00
87 CS,AW,Crisis,I:Earth Prime
    Superboy. 5.00
88 KG,Crisis,F:Creeper 5.00
89 MMi(c),AS,F:Omega Men 5.00
90 DCw,F:Firestorm,Capt.Atom 5.00
91 CS,F:Captain Comet. 5.00
92 CS,F:Vigilante 5.00
93 JSn(c),AS,KS,F:Elastic Four. 5.00
94 GP(c),TMd,DH,Crisis,F:Lady
    Quark,Pariah,Harbinger. 5.00
95 MA(i),F:Hawkman 5.00
96 JSon,KS,F:Blue Devil 5.00
97 RV,F:Phantom Zone Villians,
    final issue,double-sized 5.00
Ann.#1,RB,F:Earth 2 Superman . . . 5.00
Ann.#2 GK(c),KP,I:Superwoman . . . 5.00
Ann.#3 GK,F:Captain Marvel. 5.00
Ann.#4 EB,JOy,F:Superwoman 5.00

DC COMICS PRESENTS
July 2004
The Atom #1 . . . . 2.50
Batman #1 . . . . 2.50
The Flash #1 . . . . 2.50
Green Lantern #1. . . . . 2.50
Hawkman #1 . . . . 2.50
Justice League of America #1 . . . . 2.50
Mystery in Space #1 . . . . 2.50
Superman #1 . . . . 2.50

DC COUNTDOWN
March, 2005
1 80-page 3.00

DC/MARVEL: ALL ACCESS
October 1996
sequel to DC Versus Marvel
1 (of 4) RMz(s),JG,JRu, crossover
    crisis again, 48pg 4.00
2 RMz(s),JG,JRu,F:Jubilee,Robin,
    Daredevil,Two-Face. 3.00
3 RMz(s),JG,JRu,F:Doctor
    Strange, X-Men 3.00
4 RMz(s),JG,JRu,48pg 3.50

DC FIRST
May, 2002
Superman/Lobo, 48-pg. 3.50
The Flash/Superman, 48-pg. 3.50
Batgirl/The Joker, 48-pg. 3.50
Green Lantern/Green Lantern 3.50

DC GRAPHIC NOVEL
Nov., 1983
1 JL,Star Raiders 16.00
2 Warlords. 16.00
3 EC,Medusa Chain 16.00
4 JK,Hunger Dogs 60.00
5 Me and Joe Priest 16.00
6 Space Clusters. 16.00

DC INFINITE HALLOWEEN SPECIAL
Oct., 2007
1 13 stories 6.00

DC MILLENNIUM EDITIONS
Dec., 1999–2000
Action Comics #1. . . . . 4.00
Action Comics #252. . . . . 2.50
Adventure Comics #247 . . . . 2.50
Adventure Comics #761 . . . . 4.00
All-Star Comics #3 . . . . 4.00
All-Star Comics #3, chromium 5.00
All Star Comics #8 . . . . 4.00
All-Star Western #10 . . . . 3.00
Batman #1 . . . . 4.00
Batman #1 chromium. 5.00
Batman: Dark Knight Returns #1. . . 6.00
The Brave and the Bold #28 . . . . . 2.50
The Brave and the Bold #85 . . . . . 2.50
Crisis on Infinte Earths #1 . . . . . . 2.50
Detective Comics #27 . . . . 4.00
Detective Comics #38 . . . . 2.50
Detective Comics #327. . . . . 2.50
Detective Comics #359 . . . . 2.50
Detective Comics #395. . . . . 2.50
Flash Comics #1 . . . . 4.00
Flash #123 . . . . 2.50
Gen 13 #1 . . . . 2.50
Green Lantern/Green Arrow #76 . . . 2.50
Hellblazer #1 . . . . 3.00
House of Mystery #1 . . . . 2.50
House of Secrets #92 . . . . 2.50
JLA #1 . . . . 2.50
Justice League #1 . . . . 2.50
Justice League #1, chromium 5.00
Kingdom Come #1 . . . . 6.00
The Man of Steel #1 . . . . 2.50
Military Comics #1 . . . . 4.00
More Fun Comics #101 . . . . 3.00
Mysterious Suspense #1 . . . . 2.50
New Gods #1 . . . . 2.50
New Teen Titans #1 . . . . 2.50
Our Army at War #81 . . . . 2.50
Plop! #1 . . . . 2.50
Police Comics #1. . . . . 4.00
Preacher #1 . . . . 3.00
Saga of the Swamp Thing #21 . . . . 2.50
Sandman #1. . . . . 3.00

Sensation Comics #1 . . . . 4.00
The Shadow #1 . . . . 2.50
Showcase #22 . . . . 2.50
Showcase #4 . . . . 2.50
Spirit #1 . . . . 4.00
Superboy #1. . . . . 3.00
Superman #1 . . . . 4.00
Superman #1 Chromium edition . . . 5.00
Superman #76 . . . . 3.00
Superman #75 Death of Superman . 2.50
Superman's Pal Jimmy Olsen #1 . . 2.50
Watchmen #1. . . . . 2.50
Whiz Comics #2. . . . . 4.00
WildC.A.T.S #1. . . . . 2.50
Wonder Woman 1st.Series #1 . . . . . 4.00
Wonder Woman #1 . . . . 2.50
World's Finest Comics #71 . . . . . . 2.50
Young Romance #1, JK, JSm 3.00

DC: THE NEW FRONTIER
Jan. 2004
1 (of 6) Silver age universe 8.00
2 thru 6 . . . . @7.00

DC 100-PAGE SUPERSPECTACULAR
May 2004
Spec. Facsimile edition (2004) 7.00

DC ONE MILLION
1998
1 GMo(s),VS,in 853rd-century 3.00
2 GMo(s),VS,V:Hourman Virus. . . . 2.50
3 GMo(s),VS,V:Solaris 2.50
4 GMo(s),VS,finale 2.50
TPB series rep. 15.00

DC REPLICA EDITIONS
1999–2000
DC 100-Page Super-Spectacular:
    Love Stories 7.00
Justice Society of America
    100-page Super Spectacular #1 7.00
Teen Titans Annual #1 (1967) 5.00
Sgt. Rock's Prize Battle Tales
    80-pg. Giant. 6.00

DC SCIENCE FICTION GRAPHIC NOVEL
1985–87
1 KG,Hell on Earth 15.00
2 Nightwings 15.00
3 Frost and Fire 15.00
4 Merchants of Venus. 15.00
5 Metalzoic 15.00
6 MR,Demon-Glass Hand. 15.00
7 Sandkings 15.00

DC SPECIAL
Oct.–Dec., 1968
[All reprint]
1 CI,F:Flash,Batman,Adam Strange,
    (#1 thru #21 reps) 125.00
2 F:Teen Titans 175.00
3 GA,F:Black Canary 125.00
4 Mystery 65.00
5 JKu,F:Viking Prince/Sgt.Rock . . 65.00
6 Wild Frontier 65.00
7 F:Strangest Sports Stories 65.00
8 Joker-Luthor, Incorporated. 65.00
9 F:Strangest Sports Stories 65.00
10 Stop, You Can't Beat the Law. . 65.00
11 NA,BWr,F:Monsters 65.00
12 JKu,F:Viking Prince 65.00
13 F:Strangest Sports Stories 65.00
14 Wanted,F:Penguin/Joker 60.00
15 GA,F:Plastic Man (1971) 60.00
16 F:Super Heroes & Gorillas 30.00

17 F:Green Lantern 30.00
18 Earth Shaking Stories 30.00
19 F:War Against Gianta 30.00
20 Green Lantern. 30.00
21 F:War Against Monsters 30.00
22 Three Musketeers, Robin Hood 30.00
23 Three Musketeers, Robin Hood 30.00
24 Three Musketeers, Robin Hood 30.00
25 Three Musketeers, Robin Hood 30.00
26 F:Enemy Ace 30.00
27 RB,JR,F:Captain Comet 30.00
28 DN,DA,Earth disasters 30.00
29 JSon,BL,O:JSA 50.00

DC SPECIAL SERIES
Sept., 1977
1 MN,DD,IN,FMc,JSon,JA,BMc,
  JRu,F:Batman,Flash,Green
  Lantern,Atom,Aquaman. 30.00
2 BWr(c),BWr,F:Swamp
  Thing rep. 15.00
3 JKu(c),F:Sgt.Rock 18.00
4 AN,RT,Unexpected Annual 18.00
5 CS,F:Superman 24.00
6 BMc(i),Secret Society Vs.JLA . . 18.00
7 AN,F:Ghosts 18.00
8 RE,DG,F:Brave&Bold,Deadman 18.00
9 SD,RH,DAy,F:Wonder Woman . 25.00
10 JSon,MN,DN,TA,Secret Origins,
  O:Dr.Fate. 18.00
11 JL,KS,MA,IN,WW,AS,F:Flash . . 18.00
12 MK(c),RT,RH,TS,Secrets of
  Haunted House 20.00
13 JKu(c),RT,SBi,RE,F:Sgt.Rock . . 20.00
14 BWr(c),F:Swamp Thing rep. . . . 18.00
15 MN,JRu,MR,DG,MGo,
  F:Batman. 25.00
16 RH,D:Jonah Hex. 75.00
17 F:Swamp Thing rep. 12.00
18 JK(c),digest,F:Sgt.Rock rep. . . . 18.00
19 digest,Secret Origins
  O:Wonder Woman 18.00
20 BWr(c),F:Swamp Thing rep. . . . 12.00
21 FM,JL,DG,RT,DA,F:Batman,
  Legion 35.00
22 JKu(c),F:G.I.Combat 18.00
23 digest size,F:Flash 18.00
24 F:Worlds Finest. 18.00
25 F:Superman II,Photo Album . . . 18.00
26 RA,F:Superman's Fortress 22.00
27 JL,DG,F:Batman vs.Hulk. 35.00

DC SPECIAL: THE
RETURN OF DONNA TROY
June, 2005
1 (of 4) GP,PJ 3.00
2 thru 4 GP,PJ . . . . @3.00

DC SUPER-STARS
1976–78
1 F:Teen Titans rep. 35.00
2 F:DC Super-Stars of Space 12.00
3 CS,F:Superman,Legion 12.00
4 DC,MA,F:Super-Stars of Space. 12.00
5 CI,F:Flash rep. 12.00
6 MA,F:Super-Stars of Space 12.00
7 F:Aquaman rep. 12.00
8 CI,MA,F:Adam Strange 15.00
9 F:Superman rep. 12.00
10 DD,FMc,F:Superhero Baseball
  Special,A:Joker 15.00
11 GM,Super-Stars of Magic 12.00
12 CS,MA,F:Superboy. 12.00
13 SA 25.00
14 RB,BL,JA,JRu,Secret Origins . . 12.00
15 JKu(c),RB,RT(i),War Heroes . . 12.00
16 DN,BL,I:Star Hunters 12.00
17 JSon,MGr,BL,I&O:Huntress,O:Gr.
  Arrow,D:EarthII Catwoman . . . 65.00

DC Super-Star #2
© DC Comics Inc.

18 RT,DG,BL,F:Deadman,Phantom
  Stranger. 20.00

DC TWO THOUSAND
July, 2000
1 (of 2) TPe,VS. 7.00
2 TPe,VS,JLA & Golden age JSA . 7.00

DC UNIVERSE
1997–2003
Heroes, Secret Files #1 . . . . 5.00
Villains, Secret Files #1 . . . . 5.00
GN Holiday Bash #1 (1997). 4.00
GN Holiday Bash #2 (1998). 4.00
GN Holiday Bash #3 (1999). 5.00
Spec. Infinite X-mas special (2006). 5.00

DCU:
BRAVE NEW WORLD
June, 2006
1-shot new projects preview, 80-pg. 3.00

DC UNIVERSE: TRINITY
1993
1 TC,GeH,BKi,F:Darkstars,Green
  Lantern,L.E.G.I.O.N.,V:Triarch. . 4.00
2 BKi,SHa,F:Darkstars,Green Lantern,
  L.E.G.I.O.N.,V:Triarch 4.00

DC VS. MARVEL
1996
1 RMz 5.50
1 2nd printing 4.00
2 & 3 see Marvel
4 PDa 5.00

DEAD CORPS(E)
DC/Helix, July, 1998
1 StP, C.J.Rataan 2.50
2 StP, CJ becomes an expired . . . 2.50
3 StP,Death is not the end 2.50
4 StP, conclusion. 2.50

DEADENDERS
DC/Vertigo, Jan., 2000
1 WaP,Stealing the Sun,pt.1 . . . . . 2.50
2 WaP,Stealing the Sun,pt.2 . . . . . 2.50
3 WaP,Stealing the Sun,pt.3 . . . . . 2.50
4 WaP,Stealing the Sun,pt.4 . . . . . 2.50
5 WaP,Now and Then,pt.1 . . . . . . 2.50
6 WaP,Now and Then,pt.2 . . . . . . 2.50

7 WaP,Now and Then,pt.3 . . . . . . 2.50
8 WaP,scooter races. 2.50
9 More Fun in New World,pt.1 . . . 2.50
10 More Fun in New World,pt.2. . . . 2.50
11 Sector 9. . . . . 2.50
12 V:Science Corp. 2.50
13 Scooter race 2.50
14 Behind the Wheel, pt.1 . . . . 2.50
15 Behind the Wheel, pt.2 . . . . 2.50
16 Behind the Wheel, pt.3 . . . . 2.50
TPB Stealing the Sun 10.00

DEADMAN
May, 1985
1 CI,NA,rep. 4.00
2 thru 7 NA,rep. . . . . @3.00
[Mini-Series], 1986
1 JL,A:Batman 3.00
2 JL,V:Sensei,A:Batman. 3.00
3 JL,D:Sensei 3.00
4 JL,V:Jonah, final issue. 3.00

DEADMAN
Dec., 2001
1 SVa(s) F:Boston Brand 2.50
2 SVa(s),Sirna. 2.50
3 SVa(s),F:Duroc, drugs 2.50
4 SVa(s),nuclear submarine 2.50
5 SVa(s),Death & the Maiden,pt.1 . 2.50
6 SVa(s),Death & the Maiden,pt.2 . 2.50
7 SVa(s),children of Nanda Parbat. 2.50
8 SVa(s),Nanda Parbat,Onyx 2.50
9 SVa(s),final issue. 2.50

DEADMAN
DC/Vertigo, Aug., 2006
1 JWk, F:Brandon Caycs 3.00
2 thru 4 JWk . . . . @3.00
5 JWk 3.00
6 JWk, Homecoming, pt.1 . . . . . . 3.00
7 JWk, Homecoming, pt.2 . . . . . . 3.00
8 thru 13 JWk . . . . @3.00

DEADMAN: DEAD AGAIN
Aug., 2001
1 SVa,RBr,A:Flash 2.50
2 SVa,RBr,JAp,A:Robin 2.50
3 SVa,RBr,A:Superman,Doomsday 2.50
4 SVa,RBr,MBr,A:Green Lantern . . 2.50
5 SVa,RBr,concl. 2.50

DEADMAN: EXORCISM
[Limited-Series], 1992
1 KJo,A:Phantom Stranger. 5.25
2 KJo,A:Phantom Stranger. 5.25

DEADMAN: LOVE
AFTER DEATH
1989–90
1 KJo,Circus of Monsters 4.25
2 KJo,Circus of Monsters 4.25

DEADSHOT
1988–89
1 LMc,From Suicide Squad 2.50
2 LMc,Search for Son 2.50
3 LMc,V:Pantha 2.50
4 LMc,final issue. 2.50

DEADSHOT
Dec., 2004
1 (of 5) JP,MZ&JOy(c) 3.00
2 JP,A:Green Arrow 3.00
3 JP,V:Green Arrow. 3.00
4 JP,Star City criminals 3.00
5 JP,conclusion 3.00

DEATH GALLERY
DC/Vertigo
1 DMc(c),NGa Death Sketch
Various Pinups.............3.50

DEATH: THE HIGH COST OF LIVING
DC/Vertigo, 1993
1 B:NGa(s),CBa,MBu(i),Death
becomes Human,A:Hettie.....6.00
1a Platinum Ed. 50.00
2 CBa,MBu(i),V:Eremite,A:Hettie ..6.00
3 E:NGa(s),CBa,MBu(i),V:Eremite,
A:Hettie...................6.00
3a Error Copy................7.00
TPB w/Tori Amos Intro.........20.00

DEATH OF THE NEW GODS
Oct., 2007
1 (of 8) JSn................3.50
1a variant (c) (1:10) 3.50
2 JSn......................3.50

DEATH: THE TIME OF YOUR LIFE
DC/Vertigo, 1995
1 NGa,MBu,four-issue miniseries..3.00
2 NGa,MBu,F:Foxglove 3.00
3 NGa,MBu,conclusion...........3.00
TPB NGa(s),rep. 13.00

DEATHSTROKE: THE TERMINATOR
1991–94
1 MZ(c),(from New Teen Titans)
SE,I:2nd Ravager 4.00
1a Second Printing,Gold.........3.00
2 MZ(c),SE,Quraci Agents 4.00
3 SE,V:Ravager 4.00
4 SE,D:2ndRavager(Jackel) 3.00
5 Winter Green Rescue Attempt...3.00
6 MZ(c),SE,B:City of Assassins,
A:Batman.................3.00
7 MZ(c),SE,A:Batman...........2.50
8 MZ(c),SE,A:Batman...........2.50
9 MZ(c),SE,E:City of Assassins,
A:Batman;I:2nd Vigilante......2.50
10 MZ(c),ANi,GP,A:2nd Vigilante...2.50

Deathstroke: The Terminator #17
© DC Comics, Inc.

11 MZ(c),ANi,GP,A:2nd Vigilante...2.50
12 MGo,Short Stories re:Slade 2.50
13 SE,V:Gr.Lant.,Flash,Aquaman ..2.50
14 ANi,Total Chaos#1,A:New Titans,
Team Titans,V:Nightwing......2.50
15 ANi,Total Chaos#4,A:New Titans,
Team Titans,I:Sweet Lili.......2.50
16 ANi,Total Chaos#7 ....2.50
17 SE,Titans Sell-Out #2
A:Brotherhood of Evil 2.50
18 SE,V:Cheshire,R:Speedy 2.50
19 SE,V:Broth.of Evil,A:Speedy....2.50
20 SE,MZ(c),V:Checkmate 2.50
21 SE,MZ(c),A:Checkmate 2.50
22 MZ(c),Quality of Mercy#1 .....2.50
23 MZ(c),Quality of Mercy#2 .....2.50
24 MZ(c),V:The Black Dome 2.50
25 MZ(c),V:The Black Dome 2.50
26 MZ(c),SE,in Kenya 2.50
27 MZ(c),SE,B:World Tour,
in Germany 2.50
28 MZ(c),SE,in France...........2.50
29 KM(c),SE,in Hong Kong 2.50
30 SE,A:Vigilante..............2.50
31 SE,in Milwaukie.............2.50
32 SE,in Africa 2.50
33 SE,I:Fleur de Lis 2.50
34 SE,E:World Tour............2.50
35 V:Mercenaries..............2.50
36 V:British General............2.50
37 V:Assassin 2.50
38 A:Vigilante.................2.50
39 A:Vigilante.................2.50
40 Wedding in Red 2.50
Ann.#1 Eclipso,A:Vigilante........4.00
Ann.#2 SE,I:Gunfire............4.00
Ann.#3 Elseworlds Story 4.25
TPB Full Circle rep#1-#4,
New Titans#70............13.00
Becomes:

DEATHSTROKE: THE HUNTED
1994–95
0 Slade 2.50
41 Bronze Tiger 2.50
42 Wounded.................2.50
43 ....2.50
44 ....2.50
45 A:New Titans..............2.50
Becomes:

DEATHSTROKE
1995–96
46 Checkmate,Wintergreen.......2.50
47 I:New Vigilante 2.50
48 Crimelord/Syndicate War,pt.1 ...2.50
49 Crimelord/Syndicate War,pt.4
A:Supergirl, New Titans,
Hawkman, Blood Pack 2.50
50 A:Titans,Outsiders,Steel 3.50
51 No Fate or Future,pt.1 ....2.50
52 No Fate or Future,pt.2 ....2.50
53 The Borgia Plague,pt.1 ....2.50
54 The Borgia Plague,pt.2 ....2.50
55 MWn,Rebirth?..............2.50
56 MWn,Night of the Karrion,pt.2 ..2.50
57 ....2.50
58 MWn,V:The Joker...........2.50
59 MWn,F:Hellriders............2.50
60 MWn,final issue 2.50

DEATHWISH
1994–95
1 New mini-series 2.50
2 F:Rahme 2.50
3 ....2.50
4 V:Boots 2.50

DEMOLITION MAN
1993–94
1 thru 4 Movie Adapt............2.50

The Demon #18
© DC Comics, Inc.

DEMON
[1st Regular Series], 1972–74
1 JK,I:Demon 90.00
2 JK......................45.00
3 JK......................30.00
4 JK......................30.00
5 JK......................30.00
6 thru 16 JK.............@25.00

[Limited Series], 1987
1 MWg,B:Jason Blood's Case 3.00
2 MWg,Fight to Save Gotham 3.00
3 MWg,Fight to Save Gotham 3.00
4 MWg,final issue 3.00

[2nd Regular Series], 1990–95
0 Relationships...............2.50
1 VS,A:Etrigan (32 pages) 4.00
2 VS,V:TheCrone..............3.00
3 VS,A:Batman...............3.00
4 VS,A:Batman...............3.00
5 VS,ThePit..................3.00
6 VS,In Hell..................3.00
7 VS,Etrigan-King of Hell 3.00
8 VS,Klarion the Witch Boy 3.00
9 VS,Jason Leaves Gotham......3.00
10 VS,A:PhantomStranger........3.00
11 VS,A:Klarion,C:Lobo..........3.00
12 VS,Etrigan Vs. Lobo 3.00
13 VS,Etrigan Vs. Lobo 3.00
14 VS,V:Odd Squad,A:Lobo 3.00
15 VS,Etrigan Vs.Lobo 3.00
16 VS,Etrigan & Jason Blood
switch bodies...............3.00
17 VS, War of the Gods x-over 3.00
18 VS,V:Wotan,A:Scape Goat.....3.00
19 VS,O:Demon,Demon/Lobo
pin-up.....................3.50
20 VS,V:Golden Knight 2.50
21 VS,Etrigan/Jason,
A:Lobo,Glenda.............2.50
22 MWg,V:Mojo & Hayden 2.50
23 VS,A:Robin.................2.50
24 VS,A:Robin.................2.50
25 VS,V:Gideon Ryme..........2.50
26 VS,B:America Rules 2.50
27 VS,A:Superman 2.50
28 VS,A:Superman 2.50
29 VS,E:America Rules 2.50
30 R:Asteroth.................2.50
31 VS(c),A:Lobo...............2.50

32 VS(c),A:Lobo,W.Woman 2.50
33 VS(c),A:Lobo,V:Asteroth 2.50
34 A:Lobo 2.50
35 A:Lobo,V:Belial 2.50
36 A:Lobo,V:Belial 2.50
37 A:Lobo,Morax 2.50
38 A:Lobo,Morax 2.50
39 A:Lobo 2.50
40 New Direction,B:GEn(s) 3.50
41 V:Mad Bishop 3.00
42 V:Demons 3.00
43 A:Hitman 10.00
44 V:Gotho-Demon,A:Hitman . . . 15.00
45 V:Gotho-Demon,A:Hitman . . . 15.00
46 R:Haunted Tank 5.00
47 V:Zombie Nazis 5.00
48 A:Haunted Tank,V:Zombie
    Nazis 5.00
49 b:Demon's Son,A:Joe Gun 2.50
50 GEn(s) 3.00
51 GEn(s),Son & Lovers 2.50
52 Etrigan & son–Hitman 4.00
53 Glenda & child–Hitman 4.00
54 Suffer the Children 4.00
55 Rebellion 2.50
56 F:Etrigan 2.50
57 Last Stand 2.50
58 Last issue 2.50
Ann.#1 Eclipso,V:Klarion 3.25
Ann.#2 I:Hitman 15.00

DEMON, THE:
DRIVEN OUT
Sept. 2003

1 (of 6) ATi,F:Etrigan 2.50
2 . . . . 2.50
3 . . . . 2.50
4 thru 6 ATi . . . . @2.50

DESPERADOES:
QUIET OF THE GRAVE
Homage/DC May, 2001

1 (of 5) JMi,JSe 3.00
2 JMi,JSe 3.00
3 JMi,JSe 3.00
4 JMi,JSe 3.00
5 JMi,JSe, concl. 3.00
TPB JMi,JSe series rep. 15.00

DESTINY: A CHRONICLE
OF DEATHS FORETOLD
DC/Vertigo, Sept., 1997

1 (of 3) F:Destiny of the Endless . . 6.00
2 Destiny of the Endless, pt.2 . . . . . 6.00
3 Destiny of the Endless, pt.3 . . . . . 6.00
TPB series rep. 15.00

DETECTIVE COMICS
March, 1937

1 I:Slam Bradley 100,000.00
2 JoS, Skyscraper Death 35,000.00
3 JoS,A Stowaway in Need . . 25,000.00
4 JoS,The Rajah's Ruby 12,000.00
5 JoS,Slam Bradley 10,000.00
6 JoS,Speed Saunders 8,000.00
7 JoS,In Atlantic City 7,500.00
8 JoS,Mr. Chang(c) 12,000.00
9 JoS,Case of the Hobo Hero . 9,000.00
10 CF,Mystery at Oak Gables . 7,500.00
11 CF,Anarchist Sub Plot 6,000.00
12 CF,Indian Oil Well Mystery . 6,000.00
13 CF,Little Tomm Murder Case 6,000.00
14 CF,Mystery of Hondoku Isle . 6,000.00
15 CF,Mystery of Darby Pearls . 6,000.00
16 CF,Case of Missing Corpse . 6,000.00
17 CF,I:Fu Manchu 6,000.00
18 S&S,Fu Manchu(c) 10,000.00
19 FGu,The Grogan Case 6,000.00
20 I:Crimson Avenger 9,000.00

21 FGu,The Glass of Poison . . 5,000.00
22 S&S,Return of Fui Onyui . . 6,500.00
23 FGu,The Ski Murder 5,000.00
24 FGu,Persian Jewel Mystery . 5,000.00
25 FGu,The Death Sled 5,000.00
26 FGu,Artists of Death 5,000.00
27 BK,I:Batman 500,000.00
28 BK,V:Frenchy Blake 45,000.00
29 BK,I:Doctor Death 65,000.00
30 BK,V:Dr. Death 15,000.00
31 BK,I:Monk 65,000.00
32 BK,V:Monk 13,000.00
33 O:Batman,V:Scarlet Horde 80,000.00
34 V:Due D'Orterre 9,500.00
35 V:Sheldon Lenox 22,000.00
36 I:Hugo Strange 16,000.00
37 V:Count Grutt, last
    Batman solo 15,000.00
38 I:Robin, the Boy Wonder . 100,000.00
39 V:Green Dragon 14,000.00
40 I:Clayface (Basil Karlo) . . 15,000.00
41 V:Graves 7,500.00
42 V:Pierre Antal 5,000.00
43 V:Harliss Greer 5,000.00
44 Robin Dream Story 5,000.00
45 V:Joker 7,500.00
46 V:Hugo Strange 5,000.00
47 Meets Harvey Midas 5,000.00
48 Meets Henry Lewis 5,000.00
49 V:Clayface 5,000.00
50 V:Three Devils 5,000.00
51 V:Mindy Gang 4,000.00
52 V:Loo Chung 4,000.00
53 V:Toothy Hare Gang 4,000.00
54 V:Hook Morgan 4,000.00
55 V:Dr. Death 4,000.00
56 V:Mad Mack 4,000.00
57 Meet Richard Sneed 4,000.00
58 I:Penguin 9,000.00
59 V:Penguin 3,500.00
60 V:Joker,I:Air Wave 3,000.00
61 The Three Racketeers 2,700.00
62 V:Joker 4,000.00
63 I:Mr. Baffle 2,700.00
64 I:Boy Commandos,V:Joker . 8,000.00
65 Meet Tom Bolton 5,000.00
66 I:Two-Face 8,000.00
67 V:Penguin 4,500.00
68 V:Two-Face 3,200.00
69 V:Joker 3,200.00
70 Meet the Amazing Carlo . . 2,200.00
71 V:Joker 2,600.00
72 V:Larry the Judge 1,900.00
73 V:Scarecrow 2,300.00
74 I:Tweedledum&Tweedledee . 2,200.00
75 V:Robber Baron 2,200.00
76 V:Joker 2,800.00

Detective Comics #6
© DC Comics, Inc.

77 V:Dr. Matthew Thorne 2,200.00
78 V:Baron Von Luger 2,200.00
79 Destiny's Auction 2,200.00
80 V:Two-Face 2,500.00
81 I:Cavalier 1,500.00
82 V:Blackee Blondeen 1,500.00
83 V:Dr. Goodwin 1,600.00
84 V:Ivan Krafft 1,500.00
85 V:Joker 2,000.00
86 V:Gentleman Jim Jewell . . . 1,500.00
87 V:Penguin 1,600.00
88 V:Big Hearted John 1,500.00
89 V:Cavalier 1,500.00
90 V:Capt. Ben 1,500.00
91 V:Joker 2,400.00
92 V:Braing Bulow 1,400.00
93 V:Tiger Ragland 1,400.00
94 V:Lefty Goran 1,400.00
95 V:The Blaze 1,400.00
96 F:Alfred 1,400.00
97 V:Nick Petri 1,400.00
98 Meets Casper Thurbridge . . 1,400.00
99 V:Penguin 1,400.00
100 V:Digger 1,400.00
101 V:Joe Bart 1,400.00
102 V:Joker 1,400.00
103 Meet Dean Gray 1,400.00
104 V:Fat Frank Gang 1,400.00
105 V:Simon Gurlan 1,400.00
106 V:Todd Torrey 1,400.00
107 V:Bugs Scarpis 1,400.00
108 Meet Ed Gregory 1,400.00
109 V:Joker 2,500.00
110 V:Prof. Moriarty 1,500.00
111 Coaltown, USA 1,500.00
112 Case Without A Crime . . . 1,500.00
113 V:Blackhand 1,500.00
114 V:Joker 1,500.00
115 V:Basil Grimes 1,500.00
116 A:Carter Nichols,
     Robin Hood 1,500.00
117 Steeplejack's Slowdown . . . 1,500.00
118 V:Joker 2,000.00
119 V:Wiley Derek 1,200.00
120 V:Penguin 2,700.00
121 F:Commissioner Gordon . . 1,200.00
122 V:Catwoman 2,500.00
123 V:Shiner 1,100.00
124 V:Joker 1,600.00
125 V:Thinker 1,000.00
126 V:Penguin 1,000.00
127 V:Dr. Agar 1,000.00
128 V:Joker 1,600.00
129 V:Diamond Dan Mob 1,200.00
130 BK,V:Briggs Carson 1,200.00
131 V:Trigger Joe 1,200.00
132 V:Human Key 1,200.00
133 Meets Arthur Loom 1,200.00
134 V:Penguin 1,200.00
135 A:Baron Frankenstein,
     Carter Nichols 1,200.00
136 A:Carter Nichols 1,200.00
137 V:Joker 1,400.00
138 V:Joker,O:Robotman 1,800.00
139 V:Nick Bailey 1,200.00
140 I:Riddler 8,000.00
141 V:Blackie Nason 1,200.00
142 V:Riddler 2,000.00
143 V:Pied Piper 1,000.00
144 A:Kay Kyser (radio
     personality) 1,000.00
145 V:Yellow Mask Mob 1,000.00
146 V:J.J. Jason 1,000.00
147 V:Tiger Shark 1,000.00
148 V:Prof. Zero 1,000.00
149 V:Joker 1,500.00
150 V:Dr. Paul Visio 1,000.00
151 I&O:Pow Wow Smith 1,200.00
152 V:Goblin 1,000.00
153 V:Slits Danton 1,200.00
154 V:Hatch Marlin 1,000.00
155 A:Vicki Vale 1,000.00

Detective Comics #162
© *DC Comics, Inc.*

156 The Batmobile of 1950 ... 1,000.00
157 V:Bart Gillis 1,000.00
158 V:Dr. Doom 1,000.00
159 V:T. Worthington Chubb... 1,000.00
160 V:Globe-Trotter 1,000.00
161 V:Bill Waters 1,000.00
162 Batman on Railroad...... 1,000.00
163 V:Slippery Jim Elgin...... 1,000.00
164 Bat-signal story 1,000.00
165 The Strange Costumes
    of Batman............. 1,000.00
166 Meets John Gillen 1,000.00
167 A:Carter Nichols, Cleopatra 1,000.00
168 O:Joker 6,500.00
169 V:Squint Tolmar 1,000.00
170 Batman Teams with Navy
    and Coast Guard 1,000.00
171 V:Penguin 1,200.00
172 V:Paul Gregorian 950.00
173 V:Killer Moth 950.00
174 V:Dagger............... 950.00
175 V:Kangaroo Kiley 950.00
176 V:Mr. Velvet............. 950.00
177 Bat-Cave Story 900.00
178 V:Baron Swane 900.00
179 Mayor Bruce Wayne....... 900.00
180 V:Joker 900.00
181 V:Human Magnet 900.00
182 V:Maestro Dorn........... 900.00
183 V:John Cook............. 900.00
184 I:Firefly(Garfield Lynns)..... 900.00
185 Secrets of Batman's
    Utility Belt 900.00
186 The Flying Bat-Cave....... 900.00
187 V:Two-Face.............. 900.00
188 V:William Milden 900.00
189 V:Styx 900.00
190 Meets Dr. Sampson,
    O:Batman 1,100.00
191 V:Executioner 900.00
192 V: Nails Riley 900.00
193 V:Joker 900.00
194 V:Sammy Sabre 900.00
195 Meets Hugo Marmon 900.00
196 V:Frank Lumardi 900.00
197 V:Wrecker 900.00
198 Batman in Scotland........ 900.00
199 V:Jack Baker............. 900.00
200 V:Brand Keldon........... 900.00
201 Meet Human Target 900.00
202 V:Jolly Roger 900.00
203 V:Catwoman 900.00
204 V:Odo Neral 900.00
205 O:Bat-Cave............. 900.00
206 V:Trapper 900.00
207 Meets Merko the Great..... 900.00

208 V:Groff................. 900.00
209 V:Inventor 900.00
210 V:Brain Hobson.......... 900.00
211 V:Catwoman 900.00
212 Meets Jonathan Bard 900.00
213 O:Mirror-Man............ 900.00
214 The Batman Encyclopedia .. 900.00
215 I:Ranger, Legionairy, Gaucho &
    Musketeer,A:Knight & Squire
    (See: World's Finest 89) 750.00
216 A:Brane Taylor 750.00
217 Meets Barney Barrows 750.00
218 V:Dr. Richard Marston 750.00
219 V:Marty Mantee.......... 750.00
220 A:Roger Bacon, historical
    scientist/philosopher 750.00
221 V:Paul King.............. 750.00
222 V:'Big Jim' Jarrell 750.00
223 V:'Blast' Varner 750.00
224 The Batman Machine 750.00
225 I&O:Martian Manhunter
    (J'onn J'onzz) 10,000.00
226 O:Robin's costume,
    A:J'onn J'onzz 2,500.00
227 A:Roy Raymond, J'onn
    J'onzz 1,000.00
228 A:Roy Raymond, J'onn
    J'onzz 1,000.00
229 A:Roy Raymond, J'onn
    J'onzz 1,000.00
230 A:Martian Manhunter,
    I:Mad Hatter 1,100.00
231 A:Batman,Jr.,Roy Raymond
    J'onn J'onzz............. 700.00
232 A:J'onn J'onzz........... 700.00
233 SMo(c),I&O:Batwoman ... 2,400.00
234 SMo(c),V:Jay Caird........ 700.00
235 SMo(c),O:Batman's
    Costume............. 1,100.00
236 SMo(c),V:Wallace Walby .. 1,000.00
237 SMo(c),F:Robin.......... 700.00
238 SMo(c),V:Checkmate(villain) 700.00
239 SMo(c),Batman robot story.. 700.00
240 SMo(c),V:Burt Weaver 700.00
241 SMo(c),The Rainbow Batman 700.00
242 SMo(c),Batcave story 500.00
243 SMo(c),V:Jay Vanney 500.00
244 SMo(c),O:Batarang........ 500.00
245 SMo(c),F:Comm.Gordon.... 500.00
246 SMo(c),.................. 500.00
247 SMo(c),I:Professor Milo 500.00
248 Around the World in 8 Days . 500.00
249 V:Collector 500.00
250 V:John Stannor.......... 500.00
251 V:Brand Ballard........... 500.00
252 Batman in a movie 500.00
253 I:Terrible Trio 500.00
254 SMo(c),A:Bathound........ 500.00
255 V:Fingers Nolan 500.00
256 Batman outer-space story... 500.00
257 Batman sci-fi story 500.00
258 Batman robot story 500.00
259 SMo,I:Calendar Man....... 500.00
260 Batman outer space story.. 500.00
261 I:Dr. Double X............ 400.00
262 V:Jackal-Head........... 400.00
263 V:The Professor 400.00
264 Peril at Playland Isle....... 400.00
265 O:Batman retold 500.00
266 SMo,V:Astro 400.00
267 SMo,I&O:Bat-Mite........ 500.00
268 V:'Big Joe' Foster 400.00
269 V:Director 400.00
270 Batman sci-fi story 400.00
271 V:Crimson Knight,O:Martian
    Manhunter(retold) 400.00
272 V:Crystal Creature 400.00
273 A:Dragon Society 300.00
274 V:Nails Lewin 300.00
275 SMo,A:Zebra-Man......... 300.00
276 A:Batmite............... 300.00
277 Batman Monster story..... 300.00

278 A:Professor Simms 300.00
279 Batman robot story 300.00
280 A:Atomic Man 300.00
281 Batman robot story 250.00
282 Batman sci-fi story 250.00
283 V:Phantom of Gotham City . 250.00
284 V:Hal Durgan 250.00
285 V:Harbin................ 250.00
286 A:Batwoman 250.00
287 SMo,A:Bathound......... 250.00
288 V:Multicreature 250.00
289 SMo,A:Bat-Mite.......... 250.00
290 SMo,Batman's robot story .. 250.00
291 Batman sci-fi story 250.00
292 Last Roy Raymond........ 250.00
293 A:Aquaman,J'onn J'onzz ... 250.00
294 V:Elemental Men,
    A:Aquaman 250.00
295 A:Aquaman 250.00
296 A:Aquaman 250.00
297 SMo,A:Aquaman......... 250.00
298 I:Clayface(Matt Hagen)..... 500.00
299 Batman sci-fi stories 250.00
300 SMo,I:Mr.Polka-dot,
    E:Aquaman 250.00
301 A:J'onn J'onzz............ 200.00
302 A:J'onn J'onzz............ 150.00
303 A:J'onn J'onzz............ 150.00
304 A:Clayface,J'onnJ'onz...... 150.00
305 Batman sci-fi story 150.00
306 A:J'onn J'onzz............ 150.00
307 A:J'onn J'onzz............ 150.00
308 A:J'onn J'onzz............ 150.00
309 A:J'onn J'onzz............ 150.00
310 A:Bat-Mite,J'onn J'onzz ... 150.00
311 I:Cat-Man,Zook 175.00
312 A:Clayface,J'onn J'onzz ... 150.00
313 A:J'onn J'onzz............ 150.00
314 A:J'onn J'onzz............ 150.00
315 I:Jungle Man 150.00
316 A:Dr.Double X,J'onn J'onzz . 150.00
317 A:J'onn J'onzz............ 150.00
318 A:Cat-Man,J'onn J'onzz.... 150.00
319 A:J'onn J'onzz............ 150.00
320 A:Vicki Vale............. 150.00
321 I:Terrible Trio 150.00
322 A:J'onn J'onzz............ 150.00
323 I:Zodiac Master,
    A:J'onn J'onzz 150.00
324 A:Mad Hatter,J'onn J'onzz . 150.00
325 A:Cat-Man,J'onn J'onzz ... 150.00
326 Batman sci-fi story 150.00
327 CI,25th ann,symbol change . 250.00
328 D:Alfred,I:WayneFoundation. 250.00

Detective Comics #299
© *DC Comics Inc.*

DC COMICS

329 A:Elongated Man 150.00
330 "Fallen Idol of Gotham". 150.00
331 A:Elongated Man 150.00
332 A:Joker 125.00
333 CK(c),A:Gorla 125.00
334 Man Who Stole from Batman 125.00
335 CI,Trail of the Talking Mask . 125.00
336 CI,V:Outsider. 125.00
337 CI,Deep Freeze Menace. . . . 125.00
338 CI,Power-Packed Punch. . . . 125.00
339 CI,V:Living Beast-Bomb 125.00
340 CI,Outsider Strikes Again . . . 125.00
341 A:Joker 125.00
342 CI,Raid of the Robin Gang . . 125.00
343 BK,CI,Elongated Man 125.00
344 CI,I&V:Johnny Witts 125.00
345 CI,I:Blockbuster. 125.00
346 Inescapable Doom-Trap 125.00
347 CI,Elongated Man 125.00
348 Elongated Man 125.00
349 BK(c),CI,Blockbuster. 125.00
350 Elongated Man 125.00
351 CI,A:Elongated Man,
     I:Cluemaster 125.00
352 BK,Elongated Man 125.00
353 V:Weather Wizard 125.00
354 BK,Elongated Man,I:Dr.
     Tzin-Tzin 125.00
355 CI,Elongated Man 125.00
356 BK,Outsider,Alfred 125.00
357 CI,Wayne Unmasks Batman. 125.00
358 BK,Elongated Man 125.00
359 CI,I:new Batgirl 275.00
360 Case of Abbreviated Batman 125.00
361 CI,Double-Deathtrap 125.00
362 CI,Elongated Man 125.00
363 CI,Elongated Man 125.00
364 CI,BK,Elongated Man 125.00
365 CI,A:Joker 125.00
366 CI,Elongated Man 125.00
367 CI,Elongated Man 125.00
368 CI,BK,Elongated Man 125.00
369 CA,Elongated Man,
     Catwoman 175.00
370 NA,BK,Elongated Man 150.00
371 CI,BK,Elongated Man 175.00
372 NA,BK,Elongated Man 100.00
373 BK,Elongated Man 100.00
374 BK,Elongated Man 100.00
375 CI,Elongated Man 100.00
376 Batman–Hunted or Haunted. 100.00
377 MA,Elongated Man,
     V:Riddler 100.00
378 Elongated Man 100.00
379 CI,Elongated Man 100.00
380 Elongated Man 100.00
381 GaF,Marital Bliss Miss 100.00
382 FR(s),BbB,JoG,GaF(s),SGe . 100.00
383 FR(s),BbB,JoG,GaF(s),SGe . 100.00
384 FR(s),BbB,JoG,GaF(s),SGe,
     BU:Batgirl 100.00
385 E:FR(s),BbB,JoG,NA(c&a),GK,
     MA,MkF,BU:Batgirl 100.00
386 BbK,MkF,BbB,JoG,
     BU:Batgirl 100.00
387 RA,rep.Detective #27 . . . . . . 150.00
388 JBr(s),BbB,JoG,
     GK,MA,FR(s). 150.00
389 NA,FR(s),BbB,JoG,GK,MA . . 100.00
390 FR(s),BbB,JoG,GK,MA,
     A:Masquerader 100.00
391 FR(s),NA(c),BbB,
     JoG,GK,MA 75.00
392 FR(s),BbB,JoG,I:Jason Bard . 75.00
393 FR(s),BbB,JoG,GK,MA 75.00
394 FR(s),BbB,JoG,GK,MA 75.00
395 FR(s),NA,DG,GK,MA 100.00
396 FR(s),BbB,JoG,GK,MA 75.00
397 DON(s),NA,DG,GK,MA 100.00
398 FR(s),BbB,JoG,GK,ViC. 75.00
399 NA(c),DON(s),BbB,JoG,
     GK,ViC,Robin 100.00

400 FR(s),NA,DG,GK,I:Man-Bat . 250.00
401 NA(c),FR(s),JoG,
     BbB,JoG,GK,ViC 60.00
402 FR(s),NA,DG,V:Man-Bat . . . 100.00
403 FR(s),BbB,JoG,NA(c),GK,ViC,
     BU:Robin 100.00
404 NA,GC,GK,A:Enemy Ace . . . 110.00
405 IN,GK,I:League of Assassins 100.00
406 DON(s),BbB,FrG 100.00
407 FR(s),NA,DG,V:Man-bat 110.00
408 MWn(s),LWn(s),NA,DG,
     V:DrTzin Tzin 110.00
409 B:FR(s),BbB,FrG,DH,DG 80.00
410 DON(s),FR(s),NA,DG,DH 80.00
411 NA(c),DON(s),BbB,DG,DH . . . 70.00
412 NA(c),BbB,DG,DH. 70.00
413 NA(c),BbB,DG,DH. 70.00

Detective Comics #417
© *DC Comics, Inc.*

414 DON(s),IN,DG,DH. 75.00
415 BbB,DG,DH. 75.00
416 DH. 75.00
417 BbB,DG,DH,BU:Batgirl 75.00
418 DON(s),DH,IN,DG,A:Creeper . 75.00
419 DON(s),DH 75.00
420 DH 75.00
421 DON(s),BbB,DG,DH,A:Batgirl . 70.00
422 BbB,DG,DH,Batgirl 70.00
423 BbB,DG,DH. 70.00
424 BbB,DG,DH,Batgirl 70.00
425 BWr(s),DON(s),IN,DG,DH. . . . 70.00
426 LWn(s),DG,A:Elongated Man . 50.00
427 IN,DG,DH,BU:Batgirl 50.00
428 BbB,DG,ENB(s),DD,JoG,
     BU:Hawkman. 50.00
429 DG,JoG,V:Man-Bat 50.00
430 BbB,NC,ENS(s),DG,
     A:Elongated Man 50.00
431 DON(s),IN,MA. 50.00
432 MA,A:Atom 50.00
433 DD,DG,MA 50.00
434 IN,DG,ENB(s),RB,DG 50.00
435 E:FR(s),DG,IN 50.00
436 MA,(i),DG,A:Elongated Man . . 50.00
437 JA,WS,I:Manhunter 85.00
438 JA,WS,Manhunter. 100.00
439 DG,WS,O:Manhunter,Kid
     Eternity rep. 100.00
440 JAp,WS 100.00
441 HC,WS 100.00
442 ATh,WS 100.00
443 WS,D:Manhunter 100.00
444 JAp,B:Bat-Murderer,
     A:Ra's Al Ghul 100.00
445 JAp,MGr,A:Talia 100.00
446 JAp,last giant 30.00

447 DG(i),A:Creeper 30.00
448 DG(i),E:Bat-Murderer,
     A:Creeper,Ra's Al Ghul 30.00
449 Midnight Rustler in Gotham . . 30.00
450 TA,WS 30.00
451 TA 30.00
452 ECh,V:The Crime Exchange. . 30.00
453 ECh,V:The Crime Exchange. . 30.00
454 ECh,The Set-Up Caper. 30.00
455 MGr,A:Hawkman,V:Vampire . . 30.00
456 V:Ulysses Vulcan 30.00
457 O:Batman rtd 30.00
458 A:Man Bat 30.00
459 A:Man Bat 30.00
460 I:Capt.Stingaree 30.00
461 V:Capt.Stingaree 25.00
462 V:Capt.Stingaree,A:Flash . . . 25.00
463 TA,MGr,Atom,I:Calc.,Bl.Spider 25.00
464 MGr,BlackCanary 25.00
465 TA,Elongated Man 25.00
466 MR,TA,V:Signalman 35.00
467 MR,TA,RB 35.00
468 MR,TA,A:JLA 35.00
469 WS,I:Dr.Phosphorus 25.00
470 WS,AM,V:Dr.Phosphorus . . . 25.00
471 MR,TA,A:Hugo Strange 35.00
472 MR,TA,A:Hugo Strange 35.00
473 MR,TA,R:Deadshot 35.00
474 MR,TA,A:Penguin,
     N:Deadshot 35.00
475 MR,TA,A:Joker 75.00
476 MR,TA,A:Joker 75.00
477 MR,DG,rep.NA 35.00
478 MR,DG,TA,I:3rd Clayface 35.00
479 MR,DG,A:3rd Clayface 35.00
480 DN,MA 25.00
481 JSt,CR,DN,DA,MR,
     A:ManBat. 30.00
482 HC,MGo,DG,A:Demon 27.00
483 DN,DA,SD,A:Demon,
     40 Anniv. 25.00
484 DN,DA,Demon,O:1st Robin . . 25.00
485 DN,DA,D:Batwoman,A:Demon
     A:Ras al Ghul 25.00
486 DN,DA,DG,I:Odd Man,
     V:Scarecrow 25.00
487 DN,DA,A:Ras Al Ghul 25.00
488 DN,V:Spook,Catwoman 25.00
489 IN,DH,DN,DA,Ras Al Ghul . . . 25.00
490 DN,DA,PB,FMc,A:Black
     Lightning;A:Ras Al Ghul 25.00
491 DN,DA,PB,FMc,A:Black
     Lightning;V:Maxie Zeus 25.00
492 DN,DA,A:Penguin 25.00
493 DN,DA,A:Riddler. 25.00
494 DN,DA,V:Crime Doctor 25.00
495 DN,DA,V:Crime Doctor 25.00
496 DN,DA,A:Clayface I 15.00
497 DN,DA. 15.00
498 DN,DA,V:Blockbuster 15.00
499 DN,DA,V:Blockbuster 15.00
500 DG,CI,WS,TY,JKu,Deadman,
     Hawkman,Robin 25.00
501 DN,DA. 15.00
502 DN,DA. 15.00
503 DN,DA,Batgirl,Robin,
     V:Scarecrow 15.00
504 DN,DA,Joker. 20.00
505 DN,DA,RB. 15.00
506 DN,DA,RB. 15.00
507 DN,DA,RB. 15.00
508 DN,DA,V:Catwoman 17.00
509 DN,DA,V:Catman,Catwoman . 17.00
510 DN,DA,V:Madhatter 15.00
511 DN,DA,RB,I:Mirage 15.00
512 GC,45th Anniv. 15.00
513 RB,V:Two-Face 17.00
514 RB 15.00
515 RB 15.00
516 RB 15.00
517 The Monster in the Mirror . . . 15.00
518 RB,V:Deadshot 15.00

Detective Comics #500
© DC Comics, Inc.

519 Dreadnought in the Sky 15.00
520 A:Hugo Strange,
    Catwoman 17.00
521 IN,TVE,A:Catwoman,B:
    BU:Green Arrow 20.00
522 D:Snowman 15.00
523 V:Solomon Grundy 15.00
524 2nd A:J.Todd 17.00
525 J.Todd 15.00
526 DN,AA,A:Joker,Catwoman
    500th A:Batman 30.00
527 V:Man Bat 7.00
528 Green Arrow,Ozone 7.00
529 I:Night Slayer,Nocturna 7.00
530 V:Nocturna 7.00
531 GC,AA,Chimera,J.Todd (see
    Batman #364) 7.00
532 GC,Joker. 9.00
533 Look to the Mountaintop 7.00
534 GC,A:Gr.Arrow,V:PoisonIvy . . . 7.00
535 GC,A:Gr.Arrow,V:Crazy Quitt
    2nd A:New Robin 9.00
536 GC,A:Gr.Arrow,V:Deadshot . . 7.00
537 GC,A:Gr.Arrow 7.00
538 GC,A:Gr.Arrow,V:Catman 7.00
539 GC,A:Gr.Arrow 7.00
540 GC,A:Gr.Arrow,V:Scarecrow . . 7.00
541 GC,A:Gr.Arrow,V:Penguin 7.00
542 GC,A:Gr.Arrow 9.00
543 GC,A:Gr.Arrow,V:Nightslayer . . 7.00
544 GC,A:Gr.Arrow,V:Nightslayer . . 7.00
545 By Darkness Masked 7.00
546 Hill's Descent 7.00
547 PB,KJ 7.00
548 PB,Beasts A-Prowl 7.00
549 PB,KJ,AMo(s),Gr.Arrow 9.00
550 KJ,AMo(s),Gr.Arrow 9.00
551 PB,V:Calendar Man 7.00
552 V:Black Mask 7.00
553 V:Black Mask 7.00
554 KJ,N:Black Canary 7.00
555 GC,DD,GreenArrow 7.00
556 GC,Gr.Arrow,V:Nightslayer . . . 7.00
557 V:Nightslayer 7.00
558 GC,Green Arrow 7.00
559 GC,Green Arrow 7.00
560 GC,A:Green Arrow 7.00
561 GC,Flying Hi 7.00
562 GC,V:Film Freak 7.00
563 V:Two Face 7.00
564 V:Two Face 7.00
565 GC,A:Catwoman 9.00
566 GC,Joker. 10.00
567 GC,HarlanEllison 7.00

568 KJ,Legends tie-in,A:Penguin . . 9.00
569 AD,V:Joker 9.00
570 AD,EvilCatwoman,A:Joker 9.00
571 AD,V:Scarecrow 7.00
572 AD,CI,A:Elongated Man,Sherlock
    Holmes,SlamBradley,50thAnn. 10.00
573 AD,V:Mad Hatter. 7.00
574 AD,End old J.Todd/Robin sty . . 7.00
575 AD,Year 2,pt.1,I:Reaper 25.00
576 TM,AA,Year 2,pt.2,
    R:Joe Chill. 25.00
577 TM,AA,Year 2,pt.3,V:Reaper. . 25.00
578 TM,AA,Year 2,pt.4,
    D:Joe Chill. 25.00
579 I:NewCrimeDoctor. 6.00
580 V:Two Face 6.00
581 V:Two Face 6.00
582 Millennium X-over 6.00
583 I:Ventriloquist 6.00
584 V:Ventriloquist 6.00
585 I:Rat Catcher 6.00
586 V:Rat Catcher 6.00
587 NB,V:Corrosive Man 6.00
588 NB,V:Corrosive Man 6.00
589 Bonus Book #5 . . . . 6.00
590 NB,V:Hassan 6.00
591 NB,V:Rollo 6.00
592 V:Psychic Vampire 6.00
593 NB,V:Stirh 6.00
594 NB,A:Mr.Potato 6.00
595 IN,bonus book #11 . . . . 6.00
596 V:Sladek 6.00
597 V:Sladek 6.00
598 DCw,BSz,Blind Justice #1 . . . . 7.00
599 DCw,BSz,Blind Justice #2 . . . . 7.00
600 DCw,BSz,Blind Justice #3,
    50th Anniv.(double size) 7.00
601 NB,I:Tulpa 4.00
602 NB,A:Jason Blood. 3.00
603 NB,A:Demon. 3.00
604 NB,MudPack #1,V:Clayface,
    poster insert. 3.00
605 NB,MudPack #2,V:Clayface . . 3.00
606 NB,MudPack #3,V:Clayface . . 3.00
607 NB,MudPack #4,V:Clayface,
    poster insert. 3.00
608 NB,I:Anarky. 3.00
609 NB,V:Anarky 3.00
610 NB,V:Penguin 4.00
611 NB,V:Catwoman,Catman 4.00
612 NB,A:Vicki Vale 3.00
613 Search for Poisoner 3.00
614 V:Street Demons. 3.00
615 NB,Return Penguin #2 (see
    Batman #448-#449). 3.50
616 NB 3.00
617 A:Joker 3.00
618 NB,DGA:Tim Drake 3.00
619 NB,V:Moneyspider 3.00
620 NB,V:Obeah,Man 3.00
621 NB,SM,Obeah,Man. 3.00
622 Demon Within,pt.1 . . . . 3.00
623 Demon Within,pt.2 . . . . 3.00
624 Demon Within,pt.3 . . . . 3.00
625 JAp,I:Abattior 3.00
626 JAp,A:Electrocutioner 3.00
627 600th issue w/Batman,rep.
    Detective #27 . . . . 5.00
628 JAp,A:Abattoir. 3.00
629 JAp,The Hungry Grass 3.00
630 JAp,I:Stiletto 3.00
631 JAp,V:Neo-Nazi Gangs. 3.00
632 JAp,V:Creature 3.00
633 TMd,Fake Batman? 3.00
634 The Third Man 3.00
635 Video Game,pt.1. . . . . 3.00
636 Video Game,pt.2. . . . . 3.00
637 Video Game,pt.3. . . . . 3.00
638 JAp,Walking Time Bomb. 3.00
639 JAp,The Idiot Root,pt.2 . . . . 3.00
640 JAp,The Idiot Root,pt.4 . . . . 3.00

Detective Comics #636
© DC Comics, Inc.

641 JAp,Destroyer,pt.3
    (see LOTDK#27) 3.00
642 JAp,Faces,pt.2 . . . . 3.00
643 JAp,Librarian of Souls. 3.00
644 TL,Electric City,pt.1
    A:Electrocutioner. 3.00
645 TL,Electric City,pt.2. . . . . 3.00
646 TL,Electric City,pt.3 . . . . 3.00
647 TL,V:Cluemaster,I:Spoiler 15.00
648 MWg(c),TL,V:Cluemaster 10.00
649 MWg(c),TL,V:Cluemaster 10.00
650 TL,A:Harold,Ace 3.00
651 TL,A Bullet for Bullock 3.00
652 GN,R:Huntress 3.00
653 GN,A:Huntress 3.00
654 MN,The General,pt.1 . . . . 3.00
655 MN,The General,pt.2 . . . . 3.00
656 MN,The General,pt.3,C:Bane . . 4.00
657 MN,A:Azrael,I:Cypher 5.00
658 MN,A:Azrael 3.50
659 MN,Knightfall#2,
    V:Ventriloquist,A:Bane. 3.50
660 Knightfall#4,Bane Vs.
    Killer Croc 3.00
661 GN,Knightfall#6,V:Firefly,
    Joker,A:Bane 3.00
662 GN,Knightfall#8,V:Firefly,
    Joker,A:Huntress,Bane 3.00
663 GN,Knightfall#10,V:Trogg,
    Zombie,Bird,A:Bane 3.00
664 GN,Knightfall#12,A:Azrael 3.00
665 GN,Knightfall#16,A:Azrael 3.00
666 GN,SHa,A:Azrael,Trogg,
    Zombie,Bird 3.00
667 GN,SHa,Knightquest:Crusade,
    V:Trigger Twins 3.00
668 GN,SHa,Knightquest:Crusade,
    Robin locked out of Batcave . . . 3.00
669 GN,SHa,Knightquest:Crusade,
    V:Trigger Twins 3.00
670 GN,SHa,Knightquest:Crusade,
    F:Rene Montoya 3.00
671 GN,SHa,V:Joker 3.00
672 KJ(c),GN,SHa,Knightquest:
    Crusade,V:Joker 3.00
673 KJ(c),GN,SHa,Knightquest:
    Crusade,V:Joker 3.00
674 KJ(c),GN,SHa,Knightquest:
    Crusade. 3.00
675 Foil(c),KJ(c),GN,SHa,Knightquest:
    Crusade,V:Gunhawk,foil(c) 4.00
675a Newsstand ed. 3.00
675b Platinum edition 5.00

All comics prices listed are for *Near Mint* condition.

676 KJ(c),GN,SHa,Knights End #3,
  A:Nightwing 4.00
677 KJ(c),GN,SHa,Knights End #9
  V:Azrael 3.00
678 GN,SHa,Zero Hour 3.00
679 Ratcatcher 3.00
680 Batman,Two-Face 3.00
681 CDi,GN,KJ,Jean-Paul Valley . . 3.00
682 CDi,GN,SHa,Return of Bruce
  Wayne,Troika,pt.3 . . . . 3.00
682a Collector's Edition 3.50
683 R:Penguin,I:Actuary 3.00
684 Daylight Heist 3.00
685 Chinatown War 3.00
686 V:King Snake,Lynx 3.00
687 CDi,SHa,V:River Pirate 3.00
688 V:Captian Fear 3.00
689 F:Black Mask,Firefly 3.00
690 F:Black Mask,Firefly 3.00
691 V:Spellbinder 3.00
692 CDi,SHa,Underworld
  Unleashed tie-in 3.00
693 CDi,SHa,V:Poison Ivy
  & Agent Orange 3.00
694 CDi,find plant-killer 3.00
695 CDi 3.00
696 CDi,GN,SHa,Contagion,pt.8 . . . 3.00
697 CDi,GN,SHa,pt.1 (of 3)
  V:Lock-up 3.00
698 CDi(s),A:Two-Face 3.00
699 CDi(s), ... 3.00
700 double size, Legacy, pt.1
  x-over, R:Bane. 3.50
700a cardstock cover. 6.00
701 Legacy, pt. 6 x-over, V:Bane. . . 3.00
702 CDi(s),GN,SHa,Legacy
  aftermath 3.00
703 CDi(s),GN,SHa, riots in Gotham
  City, Final Night tie-in 3.00
704 CDi(s),GN,TP,V:Al Gabone . . . 3.00
705 CDi(s),GN,Riddler & Cluemaster
  clash 3.00
706 CDi(s),GN 3.00
707 CDi(s),GN,Riddler/Cluemaster
  concl. 3.00
708 CDi(s),GN,BSz,F:Deathstroke,
  R:Gunhawk,pt.1 (of 3) 3.00
709 CDi(s),GN,BSz,F:Deathstroke,
  Gunhawk,pt.2 . . . . 3.00
710 CDi(s),GN,BSz,F:Deathstroke,
  Gunhawk,pt.3 . . . . 3.00
711 CDi(s),GN,CaS,Bruce Wayne
  fights crime 3.00
712 CDi(s),GN,I:Gearhead 3.00
713 CDi(s),GN,V:Gearhead,pt.2 . . . 3.00
714 CDi(s),GN,F:MartianManhunter 3.00
715 CDi(s),GN,F:MartianManhunter 3.00
716 CDi,JAp,SNw,BSf 3.00
717 CDi,GN,BSf,V:Gearhead,pt.1 . . 3.00
718 CDi,GN,BSf,V:Gearhead,pt.2 . . 3.00
719 CDi,JAp,BSz,Sound & Fury . . . 3.00
720 CDi,GN,KJ,Cataclysm
  x-over,pt.5 . . . . 4.00
721 CDi,GN,KJ,Cataclysm. 3.00
722 CDi,JAp,BSf,Aftershock 3.00
723 CDi,BSz,Brotherhood of
  the Fist x-over,pt.2 . . . . 3.00
724 CDi,JAp,BSf,F:Nightwing 3.00
725 CDi,TP,BSf,Aftershock 3.00
726 CDi(s),BSf,V:Joker 3.00
727 CDi,SB,Road to No Man's Land 3.00
728 CDi(s),BSf,SB,No Man's Land . 3.00
729 CDi(s),SB,No Man's Land. 3.00
730 No Law and a New Order,
  concl. 5.00
731 F:Batgirl, Mosaic, pt.2. . . . . 3.00
732 F:Batgirl, Mosaic, pt.4. . . . . 3.00
733 SB,Alfreds advice 3.00
734 F:Batgirl,pt.2 x-over 3.00
735 DJu,BSz,Fruit of
  the Earth,pt.3. . . . . 3.00
736 LHa(s),MD2,V:Bane 3.00

Detective #810
© DC Comics Inc.

737 TMo, No Man's Land,
  The Code, concl. 3.00
738 CDi,MtB,Goin'Downtown,pt.2 . . 3.00
739 Jurisprudence,concl. 3.00
740 Shellgame,pt.2 . . . . 3.00
741 Endgame, pt.3,40-pg.x-over . . . 3.00
742 SMa,40-pg. 3.00
743 SMa,40-pg,new logo 3.00
744 SMa,40-pg. 3.00
745 SMa,V:Whisperer 3.00
746 SMa,B.U.:The Jacobian 3.00
747 JJ,F:Renee Montoya. 3.00
748 JJ,Urban Renewal,pt.1 . . . . 3.00
749 JJ,PhH,Urban Renewal,pt.2 . . . 3.00
750 V:Ra's Al Ghul,64-pg. 6.00
751 SMa,JJ,DPS,F:Poison Ivy 4.00
752 SMa,JJ,DPs,F:Poison Ivy 3.00
753 SMa,JJ,DPs,This issue:
  Batman dies! 3.00
754 Officer Down x-over,pt.6 . . . . . . 3.00
755 SMa,DPs,V:Two-Face. 3.00
756 Lord of the Ring x-over pt.2 . . . 3.00
757 RBr,RyR,DPs,Air Time 3.00
758 SMa,Crooked Cops in Gotham. 3.00
759 SMa,BU:Catwoman,pt.1 . . . . . . 3.00
760 SMa,V:Mad Hatter,BU:pt.2 . . . . 3.00
761 SMa,BU:Catwoman,pt.3 . . . . . . 3.00
762 RBr,BU:Catwoman,concl. 3.00
763 SMa,F:Sasha,V:Cucilla 3.00
764 SMa,F:Vesper 3.00
765 RBr,James Gordon. 3.00
766 Bruce Wayne:Murderer,pt.1 . . . 3.00
767 Bruce Wayne:Murderer,pt.8 . . . 5.00
768 MGy,shipment of heroin 3.00
769 Bruce Wayne:Fugitive,pt.5 . . . . 3.00
770 Bruce Wayne:Fugitive,pt.8 . . . . 3.00
771 BruceWayne:Fugitive,pt.12. . . . 2.75
772 BruceWayne:Fugitive,pt.16. . . . 2.75
773 F:Sasha Bordeaux in prison . . . 2.75
774 BSz(c),Checkmate 2.75
775 BSz(c),V:Checkmate 48-pg. . . . 3.50
776 BWi,A cop's vendetta 3.00
777 Dead Reckoning,pt.1 . . . . 3.00
778 Dead Reckoning,pt.2 . . . . 3.00
779 Dead Reckoning,pt.3 . . . . 3.00
780 Dead Reckoning,pt.4 . . . . 3.00
781 Dead Reckoning,pt.5 . . . . 3.00
782 Dead Reckoning,pt.6 . . . . 3.00
783 SMa,KJ,More Perfect 3.00
784 Made of Wood,pt.1 . . . . 3.00
785 Made of Wood,pt.2 . . . . 3.00
786 Made of Wood,pt.3 . . . . 3.00
787 RBr,Low,Mad Hatter,Man-Bat . . 3.00
788 Randori Stone, pt.1. . . . . 3.00
789 Randori Stone,pt.2. . . . . 3.00

790 CaS,Scarification 3.00
791 CaS,The Surrogate,pt.1 . . . . . . 3.00
792 CaS,The Surrogate,pt.2 . . . . . . 3.00
793 CaS,The Surrogate,pt.3 . . . . . . 3.00
794 CaS,The Rotting,pt.1 . . . . 3.00
795 CaS,The Rotting,pt.2 . . . . 3.00
796 CaS,Mr.Zsasz 3.00
797 War Games,Act 1,pt.1,40-pg. . . 3.00
798 War Games,Act 2,pt.1,40-pg. . . 3.00
799 War Games,Act 3,pt.1,40-pg. . . 3.00
800 DL,CaS,48-page 3.50
801 DL,NMa,City of Crime,pt.1 . . . . 3.00
802 DL,NMa,City of Crime,pt.2 . . . . 3.00
803 DL,NMa,City of Crime,pt.3 . . . . 3.00
804 DL,NMa,City of Crime,pt.4 . . . . 3.00
805 DL,NMa,City of Crime,pt.5. . . . .3.00
806 DL,NMa,City of Crime,pt.6 . . . . 3.00
807 DL,NMa,City of Crime,pt.7 . . . . 3.00
808 DL,NMa,City of Crime,pt.8 . . . . 3.00
809 War Crimes, x-over, pt.1 . . . . . . 3.00
810 War Crimes, x-over, pt.3 . . . . . . 3.00
811 DL,NMa,City of Crime,pt.9 . . . . 3.00
812 DL,NMa,City of Crime,pt.10 . . . 3.00
813 DL,NMa,City of Crime,pt. 11. . . 3.00
814 DL,NMa,City of Crime,pt. 12. . . 3.00
815 Victims,pt.1 . . . . 3.00
816 Victims,pt.2 . . . . 3.00
817 Face the Face, pt.1, x-over. . . . 3.00
818 Face the Face, pt.3, x-over. . . . 3.00
819 Face the Face, pt.5, x-over. . . . 3.00
820 Face the Face, pt.7, x-over. . . . 3.00
821 PDi,JWi, V:Facade 3.00
822 PDi,JWi,F:The Riddler 3.00
823 PDi,F:Poison Ivy 3.00
824 PDi,Night of the Penguin 3.00
825 F:Doctor Phosphorous 3.00
826 PDi,V:Joker,A:Robin 3.00
827 PDi,V:New Ventriloquist 3.00
828 PDi,V:Sea monster. 3.00
829 The Siege, pt.1 . . . . 3.00
830 The Siege, pt.2 . . . . 3.00
831 PDi,F:Harley Quinn. 3.00
832 V:Terrible Trio 3.00
833 PDi,F:Zatanna, pt.1. . . . . 3.00
834 PDi,F:Zatanna, pt.2. . . . . 3.00
835 TMd,Scarecrow is Back, pt.1 . . 3.00
836 TMd,Scarecrow is Back, pt.2 . . 3.00
837 PDi,F:Harley Quinn & Riddler. . 3.00
Ann.#1 KJ,TD,A:Question,Talia,
  V:Penguin 6.00
Ann.#2 VS,A:Harvey Harris 6.00
Ann.#3 DJu,DG,Batman in Japan . . 3.00
Ann.#4 Armageddon,pt.10 . . . . 3.00
Ann.#5 SK(c),TMd,Eclipso,V:The
  Ventriloquist,Joker 3.00
Ann.#6 JBa,I:Geist. 3.00
Ann.#7 CDi,Elseworlds Story. 3.25
Ann.#8 CDi,KD(c) Year One Annual
  O:The Riddler 4.00
Ann.#9 Legends o/t Dead Earth . . . 3.00
Ann.#10 Pulp Heroes (War) CDi(s),
  SB,KJ. 4.00
Spec.#1,000,000 CDi(s). 3.00

DETENTION COMICS

Aug., 1996

one-shot DON(s) 64pg, 3 stories. . . 3.50

DEXTER'S LABORATORY

Warner Bros./DC, 1999

1 Kirbytron 6000 . . . . 5.00
2 Let's Save the World, You Jerk . 4.00
3 thru 10 . . . . @3.00
11 thru 24 . . . . @2.50
25 thru 34 . . . . @2.25

DISAVOWED

Homage/DC Jan., 2000

1 BCi. 2.50
2 thru 6 BCi(s). . . . . @2.50

DMZ
DC/Vertigo, Nov., 2005
1 by Brian Wood 3.00
2 Through War-torn Manhattan . . . 3.00
3 Matty captured by Gov. Army . . . 3.00
4 In Central Park 3.00
5 Interview with tribal boss 3.00
6 Body of a Journalist, pt.1 . . . . . . 3.00
7 Body of a Journalist, pt.2 . . . . . . 3.00
8 Body of a Journalist, pt.3 . . . . . . 3.00
9 Body of a Journalist, pt.4 . . . . . . 3.00
10 Body of a Journalist, pt.5 . . . . . . 3.00
11 Origin of Zee 3.00
12 A Guide to the DMZ 3.00
13 Public Works, pt.1 . . . . 3.00
14 Public Works, pt.2 . . . . 3.00
15 Public Works, pt.3 . . . . 3.00
16 Public Works, pt.4 . . . . 3.00
17 Public Works, pt.5 . . . . 3.00
18 Friendly Fire, pt.1 . . . . 3.00
19 Friendly Fire, pt.2 . . . . 3.00
20 Friendly Fire, pt.3 . . . . 3.00
21 Friendly Fire, pt.4 . . . . 3.00
22 Friendly Fire, pt.5 . . . . 3.00
23 The Hidden War 3.00
24 The Hidden War 3.00

Doc Savage #3 © DC Comics Inc.

DOC SAVAGE
1987–88
1 AKu/NKu,D:Orig. Doc Savage . . . 3.00
2 AKu/NKu,V:Nazi's 3.00
3 AKu/NKu,V:Nazi's 3.00
4 AKu/NKu,V:Heinz 3.00

[2nd Series], 1988–90
1 Five in the Sky'(painted cov.) 3.00
2 Chip Lost in Himalayas 3.00
3 Doc declares war on USSR 3.00
4 Doc Savage/Russian team-up . . . 3.00
5 V:The Erisians 3.00
6 U.S.,USSR,China Alliance
    vs. Erisians 3.00
7 Mind Molder,pt.1, I:Pat Savage . . 3.00
8 . . . . 3.00
9 In Hidalgo 3.00
10 V:Forces of the Golden God 3.00
11 Sunlight Rising,pt.1 . . . . 3.00
12 Sunlight Rising,pt.2 . . . . 3.00
13 Sunlight Rising,pt.3 . . . . 3.00
14 Sunlight Rising,pt.4 . . . . 3.00
15 SeaBaron #1 . . . . 3.00
16 EB,Shadow & Doc Savage 3.50
17 EB,Shadow & Doc Savage 3.00
18 EB,Shadow/Doc Savage conc . . . 4.00
19 All new 1930's story 3.00

20 V:Airlord & his Black Zepplin . . . 3.00
21 Airlord (30's story conc.) 3.00
22 Doc Savages Past,pt.1 . . . . 3.00
23 Doc Savages Past,pt.2 . . . . 3.00
24 Doc Savages Past,pt.3 (final) . . . 3.00
Ann.#1 1956 Olympic Games 4.50

DOCTOR FATE
July, 1987
1 KG,V:Lords of Chaos 3.00
2 KG,New Dr. Fate 3.00
3 KG,A:JLI 3.00
4 KG,V:Lords of Chaos Champion . 3.00

[2nd Series], 1988–92
1 New Dr.Fate,V:Demons 4.00
2 A:Andrew Bennett(I,Vampire) . . . 3.00
3 A:Andrew Bennett(I,Vampire) . . . 3.00
4 V:I,Vampire 3.00
5 Dr.Fate & I,Vampire in Europe . . . 3.00
6 A:Petey 3.00
7 Petey returns home dimension . . 3.00
8 Linda become Dr.Fate again 3.00
9 Eric's Mother's Ghost,
    A:Deadman 3.00
10 Death of Innocence,pt.1 . . . . 3.00
11 Return of Darkseid, Death of
    Innocence,pt.2 . . . . 3.00
12 Two Dr.Fates Vs.Darkseid,
    Death of Innocence,pt.3 . . . . . . 3.00
13 Linda in the Astral Realm,
    Death of Innocence,pt.4 . . . . . . 3.00
14 Kent & Petey vs. Wotan 3.00
15 V:Wotan,A:JLI 3.50
16 Flashback-novice Dr.Fate 2.50
17 Eric's Journey thru afterlife 2.50
18 Search for Eric 2.50
19 A:Dr.Benjamine Stoner, Lords of
    Chaos, Phantom Stranger,
    Search for Eric continued 2.50
20 V:Lords of Chaos,Dr.Stoner,
    A:Phantom Stranger 2.50
21 V:Chaos,A:PhantomStranger . . . 2.50
22 A:Chaos and Order 2.50
23 Spirits of Kent & Inza Nelson . . . 2.50
24 L:Dr.Fate Characters 2.50
25 I:New Dr. Fate 2.50
26 Dr.Fate vs. Orig.Dr.Fate 2.50
27 New York Crime 2.50
28 Diabolism 2.50
29 Kent Nelson 2.50
30 Resurrection 2.50
31 Resurrection' contd. 2.50
32 War of the Gods x-over 2.50
33 War of the Gods x-over 2.50
34 A:T'Gilian. 2.50
35 Kent Nelson in N.Y. 2.50
36 Search For Inza,A:Shat-Ru 2.50
37 Fate Helmet Powers revealed . . . 2.50
38 The Spirit Motor,'Flashback 2.50
39 U.S.Senate Hearing 2.50
40 A:Wonder Woman 2.50
41 O:Chaos and Order,last issue . . . 2.50
Ann.#1 TS,R:Eric's dead mother . . . 3.00

DR. FATE
Aug. 2003
1 (of 5) Hector Hall 2.50
2 Salem mystics 2.50
3 Nabu disappeared 2.50
4 The Curse 2.50
5 Concl. 2.50

DOCTOR FATE
Apr., 2007
1 PG, Helmet of Fate 3.00
1a variant (c) (1:10) 3.00
2 The Accidental Sorcerer 3.00

DOCTOR MID-NITE
1999
1 (of 3) MWg,F:Dr. Piter Cross 6.00
2 MWg 6.00
3 MWg, conclusion 6.00
TPB 20.00

DOOM FORCE
1992
Spec.#1 MMi(c),RCa,WS,PCu,KSy,
    I:Doom Force 3.00

DOOM PATROL
[1st series]
See: MY GREATEST
ADVENTURE

DOOM PATROL
[2nd Regular Series], 1987
1 SLi,R:Doom Patrol,plus Who's Who
    background of team, I:Kalki 5.00
2 SLi,V:Kalki 3.50
3 SLi,I:Lodestone 3.50
4 SLi,I:Karma 3.50
5 SLi,R:Chief 3.50
6 B:PuK(s),EL,GyM(i),
    I:Scott Fischer 4.50
7 EL,GyM(i),V:Shrapnel 3.50
8 EL,GyM(i),V:Shrapnel 3.50
9 E:PuK(s),EL,GyM(i),V:Garguax,
    & Bonus Book 3.50
10 EL,A:Superman 3.50
11 EL,R:Garguax 3.00
12 EL,A:Garguax 3.00
13 EL,A:Power Girl 3.00
14 EL,A:Power Girl 3.00
15 EL,Animal-Veg-.Mineral Man . . . 3.00
16 V:GenImmotus,Animal-Veg.-
    Mineral Man 3.00
17 D:Celsius,A:Aquaman & Sea
    Devils, Invasion tie-in 4.00
18 Invasion 3.00
19 B:GMo(s),New Direction,
    I:Crazy Jane 18.00
20 I:Rebis(new Negative-Being),
    A:CrazyJane,Scissormen 10.00
21 V:Scissormen 10.00
22 City of Bone,V:Scissormen 10.00
23 A:RedJack,Lodestone kidnap . . . 5.00
24 V:Red Jack 5.00
25 Secrets of New Doom Patrol . . . 5.00
26 I:Brotherhood of Dada 4.00
27 V:Brotherhood of Dada 4.00

Doom Patrol #9 © DC Comics, Inc.

28 Trapped in nightmare,V:Dada. . . 4.00
29 Trapped in painting,
   A:Superman. 4.00
30 SBs(c),V:Brotherhood of Dada . . 4.00
31 SBs(c),A:The Pale Police 4.00
32 SBs(c),V:Cult of
   Unwritten Book 4.00
33 SBs(c),V:Cult,A:Anti-God
   the DeCreator 4.00
34 SBs(c),Robotman vs. his brain,
   R:The Brain & Mr.Mallah 4.00
35 SBs(c),A:Men from
   N.O.W.H.E.R.E. 15.00
36 SBs(c),V:Men from
   N.O.W.H.E.R.E. 22.00
37 SBs(c),Rhea Jones Story 4.00
38 SBs(c),V:Aliens 4.00
39 SBs(c),V:Aliens 4.00
40 SBs(c),Aliens 4.00
41 SBs(c),Aliens 4.00
42 O:Flex Mentallo. 25.00
43 SBs(c),V:N.O.W.H.E.R.E. 12.00
44 SBs(c),V:N.O.W.H.E.R.E. 12.00
45 SBs(c),The Beard Hunter 7.00
46 SBs(c),RCa,MkK,A:Crazy Jane,
   Dr.Silence 5.00
47 Scarlet Harlot (Crazy Jane) 4.00
48 V:Mr.Evans 4.00
49 TTg(c),RCa,MGb,I:Mr.Nobody . . 4.00
50 SBs(c),V:Brotherhood of Dada
   & bonus artists portfolio. 4.00
51 SBs(c),Mr.Nobody Runs for
   President 4.00
52 SBs(c),Mr.Nobody saga conc . . 4.00
53 SBs(c),Parody Issue,A:Phantom
   Stranger,Hellblazer,Mr.E 4.00
54 Rebis Transformation 4.00
55 SBs(c),V:Crazy Jane,
   Candle Maker 4.00
56 SBs(c),RCa,V:Candle Maker . . . 4.00
57 SBs(c),RCa,V:Candle Maker,
   O:Team,Double-sized 4.00
58 SBs(c),V:Candle Maker 4.00
59 TTg(c),RCa,SnW(i),A:Candlemaker
   D:Larry Trainor 4.00
60 JHw(c),RCa,SnW(i),
   V:Candlemaker,A:Magnus. 4.00
61 TTg(c),RCa,SnW(i),A:Magnus
   D:Candlemaker 4.00
62 DFg(c),RCa,SnW(i),
   V:Nanomachines 4.00
63 E:GMo(s),RCa,R:Crazy Jane,
   V:Keysmiths,BU:Sliding from the
   Wreckage 4.00

DC/Vertigo, 1993
64 BB(c),B:RaP(s),RCa,SnW(i),
   B:Sliding from the Wreckage,
   R:Niles Caulder. 3.00
65 TTg(c),RCa,SnW(i),Nannos 3.00
66 RCa,E:Sliding from the
   Wreckage 3.00
67 TTg(c),LiM,GHi(i),New HQ,I:Charlie,
   George,Marion,V:Wild Girl. 3.00
68 TTg(c),LiM,GHi(i),I:Indentity
   Addict. 3.00
69 TTg(c),LiM,GHi(i),V:Identity
   Addict. 3.00
70 TTg(c),SEa,TS(i),I:Coagula,
   V:Codpiece 3.00
71 TTg(c),LiM,TS(i),Fox & Crow . . . 3.00
72 TTg(c),LiM,TS(i),Fox vs Crow. . . 3.00
73 LiM,GPi(i),Head's Nightmare . . . 3.00
74 LiM,TS(i),Bootleg Steele. 3.00
75 BB(c),TMK,Teiresias Wars#1,
   Double size 3.00
76 Teiresias Wars#2 . . . . 3.00
77 BB(c),TMK,N:Cliff 3.00
78 BB(c),V:Tower of Babel. 3.00
79 BB(c),E:Teiresias Wars 3.00
80 V:Yapping Dogs 3.00
81 B:Masquerade. 3.00
82 E:Masquerade. 3.00

83 False Memory 3.00
84 The Healers 3.00
85 Charlie the Doll 3.00
86 Imagine Ari's Friends 3.00
87 KB(c),final issue 3.00
Ann.#1 A:Lex Luthor 3.00
Ann.#2 RaP(s),MkW,Children's
   Crusade,F:Dorothy,A:Maxine . . 4.25
Doom Patrol/Suicide Squad #1 EL,
   D:Mr.104,Thinker,Psi,Weasel . . 3.00
TPB SBs(c),rep.#19-#25 . . . . 20.00

DOOM PATROL
Oct., 2001
1 JAr,R:Doom Patrol. 3.00
2 JAr,F:Robotman, Thayer 3.75
3 JAr,V:Gomz 2.50
4 JAr,new Doom Patrol? 2.50
5 JAr,Doom Force. 2.50
6 JAr,Robotman gone 2.50
7 JAr,search for Robotman 2.50
8 JAr,new Robotman 2.50
9 JAr,Cliff Steele, Robotman. 2.50
10 JAr,Black Vulture,Amazo 2.50
11 JAr,in Hell 2.50
12 JAr,V:Demon Raum 2.50
13 JAr(s),Monsters,pt.1 . . . . 2.50
14 JAr(s),Monsters,pt.2 . . . . 2.50
15 JAr(s),F:Robotman 2.50
16 JAr(s),V:Purple Purposeless . . . 2.50
17 JAr(s),R:Tycho 2.50
18 JAr(s),ancient China 2.50
19 JAr(s),R:Tycho 2.50
20 television studios 2.50
21 O:Tycho. 2.50
22 final issue 2.50

DOOM PATROL
July 2004
1 JBy,DHz,V:Crucifer 2.50
2 JBy,DHz,escaped specimens . . . 2.50
3 JBy,DHz,Cold Night's Death 2.50
4 JBy,DHz, Waters Under World . . . 2.50
5 JBy,DHz 2.50
6 JBy,DHz,Robot Wars,pt.2 . . . . . . 2.50
7 JBy,DHz,V:Devolutionists,pt.1 . . . 2.50
8 JBy,DHz,V:Devolutionists,pt.2 . . . 2.50
9 JBy,DHz,V:Negative Man. 2.50
10 JBy,DHz,F:Metamorpho 2.50
11 JBy,DHz,F:Metamorpho 2.50
12 JBy,DHz,F:Metamorpho 2.50
13 JBy,DHz,time travel technology . 2.50
14 JBy,TA,alternate realities 2.50
15 JBy,DHz,hospital patients dead . 2.50
16 JBy,DHz,F:Nudge 2.50
17 JBy,DHz,Negative Man. 2.50
18 JBy,DHz,final issue 2.50

DOOMSDAY
1995
Ann.#1 Year One annuals 4.00

DOORWAY TO
NIGHTMARE
1978
1 I:Madame Xanadu 20.00
2 thru 5 . . . . @15.00

DOUBLE ACTION
COMICS
Jan., 1940
2 Pre-Hero DC. 27,000.00

DRAGONLANCE
1988–91
1 Krynn's Companion's advent. . . . 4.00
2 thru 7 . . . . @3.50
8 thru 34 . . . . @3.00

Dragonlance #28
© DC Comics, Inc.

Ann.#1 Myrella of the Robed
   Wizards 3.00

DREAMING, THE
DC/Vertigo, June, 1996
1 TLa(s),PSj,GoldieFactor,pt.1 . . . 4.50
2 TLa(s),PSj,GoldieFactor,pt.2 . . . 4.00
3 TLa(s),PSj,GoldieFactor,pt.3 . . . 4.00
4 SvP,The Lost Boy,pt.1 . . . . 3.50
5 SvP,The Lost Boy,pt.2 . . . . 2.50
6 SvP,The Lost Boy,pt.3 . . . . 2.50
7 SvP,The Lost Boy,pt.4 . . . . 2.50
8 AaK(s),MZi,visitor from past 2.50
9 BT(s),PD,TOz,Weird Romance,
   pt.1. 2.50
10 BT(s),PD,TOz,Romance,pt.2 . . . 2.50
11 BT(s),PD,TOz,Romance,pt.3 . . . 2.50
12 BT(s),PD,TOz,Romance,pt.4 . . . 2.50
13 TLa,JIT,Coyote's Kiss,pt.1. . . . . 2.50
14 TLa,JIT,Coyote's Kiss,pt.2 . . . . 2.50
15 . . . . 2.50
16 GyA,F:Nuala 2.50
17 PD,DMc,Souvenirs,pt.1 . . . . . . 2.50
18 PD,DMc,Souvenirs, pt.2 . . . . . . 2.50
19 PD,DMc,Souvenirs,pt.3 . . . . . . 2.50
20 ADv, The Dark Rose, pt.1 . . . . . 2.50
21 ADv, The Dark Rose, pt.2 . . . . . 2.50
22 The Unkindness of One, pt.1 . . . 2.50
23 The Unkindness of One, pt.2 . . . 2.50
24 The Unkindness of One, pt.3 . . . 2.50
25 My Life as a Man 2.50
26 Restitution. 2.50
27 Caretaker Cain 2.50
28 Victims of famous fires 2.50
29 PSj,DMc,Abel'sHouse ofSecrets. 2.50
30 DMc(c),Lucien's mysteries 2.50
31 House of Secrets, 48-pg. 4.00
32 DG,SvP 2.50
33 The Little Mermaid 2.50
34 MaH, Cave of Nightmares 2.50
35 DMc(c),Kaleidoscope 2.50
36 DMc(c),The Gyres,pt.1 . . . . . . 2.50
37 DMc(c),The Gyres, pt.2 . . . . . . 2.50
38 DMc(c),The Gyres, pt.3 . . . . . . 2.50
39 DMc(c),Lost Language
   of Flowers 2.50
40 DMc(c),Foxes & Hounds,pt.1 . . 2.50
41 DMc(c),Foxes & Hounds,pt.2 . . 2.50
42 DMc(c),Foxes & Hounds,pt.3 . . 2.50
43 DMc(c),Foxes & Hounds,pt.4 . . 2.50
44 Trinket,pt.1 . . . . 2.50
45 Trinket,pt.2 . . . . 2.50
46 Trinket,pt.3 . . . . 2.50
47 CV,RoR 2.50

48 DMc(c),Scary Monsters 2.50
49 DMc(c),The Dawn Stone 2.50
50 DMc(c),rebuilding 2.50
51 DMc(c),in Manhattan 2.50
52 Exiles,pt.1 . . . . 2.50
53 Exiles,pt.2 . . . . 2.50
54 Exiles,pt.3 . . . . 2.50
55 F:Danny Nod. 2.50
56 1stAdventure of CatterinaPoe. . . 2.50
57 Rise,pt.1 . . . . 2.50
58 Rise,pt.2 . . . . 2.50
59 Rise,pt.3 . . . . 2.50
60 Rise,pt.4 . . . . 2.50

DYNAMIC CLASSICS
Sept-Oct., 1978
1 NA,WS,rep.Detective 395&438 . 15.00

ECLIPSO
1992–94
1 BS,MPn,V:South American
 Drug Dealers 2.50
2 BS,MPn,A:Bruce Gordon. 2.25
3 BS,MPn,R:Amanda Waller 2.25
4 BS,A:Creeper,Cave Carson. 2.25
5 A:Creeper,Cave Carson. 2.25
6 LMc,V:Bruce Gordon 2.25
7 London,1891 . . . . 2.25
8 A:Sherlock Holmes 2.25
9 I:Johnny Peril. 2.25
10 CDo,V:Darkseid 2.25
11 A:Creeper,Peacemaker,Steel . . . 2.25
12 V:Shadow Fighters 2.25
13 D:Manhunter,Commander Steel,
 Major Victory,Peacemaker,
 Wildcat,Dr.Midnight,Creeper . . . 2.25
14 A:JLA. 2.25
15 A:Amanda Waller 2.25
16 V:US Army 2.25
17 A:Amanda Waller,Martian
 Manhunter,Wonder Woman,Flash,
 Bloodwynd,Booster Gold. 2.25
18 A:Spectre,JLA,final issue 2.25
Ann.#1 I:Prism 2.50

ECLIPSO: THE DARKNESS WITHIN
1992
1 BS,Direct w/purple diamond,
 A:Superman,Creeper. 4.00
1a BS,Newstand w/out diamond . . 3.00
2 BS,MPn,DC heroes V:Eclipso,
 D:Starman 3.00

EGYPT
1995–96
1 College Experiments 3.50
2 thru 7 . . . . @3.00

80 PAGE GIANTS
Aug., 1964
1 Superman 750.00
2 Jimmy Olsen 400.00
3 Lois Lane. 325.00
4 Golden Age-Flash 325.00
5 Batman 325.00
6 Superman 400.00
7 JKu&JKu(c),Sgt. Rock's Prize
 Battle Tales 400.00
8 Secret Origins,O:JLA,Aquaman,
 Robin,Atom, Superman 650.00
9 Flash 300.00
10 Superboy. 600.00
11 Superman,A:Lex Luthor 400.00
12 Batman 350.00
13 Jimmy Olsen. 250.00
14 Lois Lane 250.00
15 Superman & Batman 250.00
16 thru 89 in regular series runs

El Diablo #6 © DC Comics, Inc.

EL DIABLO
1989–91
1 I:El Diablo, double-size 3.00
2 thru 16 . . . . @2.50
DC/Vertigo, Jan., 2001
1 (of 4) Weird Western Tales 2.50
2 thru 4 . . . . @2.50

ELECTRIC WARRIOR
1986–87
1 SF series,I:Electric Warriors 2.50
2 thru 18 . . . . @2.25

ELFQUEST: THE DISCOVERY
Jan., 2006
1 (of 4) RPi,WP, F:Sunbeam 4.00
2 RPi,WP 4.00
3 RPi,WP 4.00
4 RPi,WP, concl. 4.00
TPB 15.00

ELFQUEST: 25th ANNIVERSARY EDITION
DC 2003
Spec. WP,RPi, rep. Elfquest #1 . . . . 3.00

ELONGATED MAN
1992
1 A:Copperhead 2.25
2 Modora,A:Flash,I:Sonar. 2.25
3 A:Flash,V:Wurst Gang 2.25

ELRIC: THE MAKING OF A SORCERER
Sept. 2004
1 (of 4) WS, from M.Moorcock 6.00
2 thru 4 WS. . . . . @6.00

ELSEWORLD'S FINEST
DC/Elseworlds 1998
1 (of 2) JFM,KD,F:Bruce Wayne
 and Clark Kent, ... 5.00
2 JFM,KD,concl. 5.00
GN Supergirl & Batgirl 6.00

ELVIRA
1986–87
1 DSp,BB(c) 5.00

2 thru 10 . . . . @4.00
11 DSt(c)Find Cain. 5.00

EMPIRE
June 2003
0 JmP,from Gorilla Comics 5.00
1 thru 6 BKi,JmP. . . . . @2.50
TPB 15.00

ENEMY ACE: WAR IN HEAVEN
March, 2001
1 (of 2) GEn, 48-page 6.00
2 GEn,48-page 6.00
TPB Enemy Ace:War in Heaven . . 15.00

ENGINEHEAD
April 2004
1 (of 8) TMK,six heroes in one 2.50
2 TMK,why am I here? 2.50
3 TMK,cosmic mechanic. 2.50
4 TMK,V:Metallo 2.50
5 TMk,band of terrorists 2.50
6 TMk,Metal Men 2.50

ENIGMA
DC/Vertigo, 1993
1 B:PrM(s),DFg,I:Enigma,Michael
 Smith,V:The Head 3.00
2 DFg,I:The Truth 3.00
3 DFg,V:The Truth,I:Envelope Girl,
 Titus Bird 3.00
4 DFg,D:The Truth,I:Interior
 League. 3.00
5 DFg,I:Enigma's Mother 3.00
6 DFg,V:Envelope Girl 3.00
7 DFg,V:Enigma's Mother,D:Envelope
 Girl,O:Enigma 3.00
8 E:PrM(s),DFg,final issue 3.00
TPB Rep. #1–#8. . . . . 20.00

ERADICATOR
1996
1 IV,Low, ... 2.50
2 IV,Low, ... 2.50
3 IV,Low,Reign of the Superman
 concl.,A:Superboy 2.50

ESSENTIAL VERTIGO: SWAMP THING
DC/Vertigo, Sept., 1996
B&W reprints
1 AMo(s), rep. Saga of
 the Swamp Thing #21. . . . . 3.00
2 thru 11 AMo(s), rep. Saga of
 the Swamp Thing #22–#31. . @3.00
12 AMo(s) rep. Saga Ann. #2 . . . . 3.00
13 AMo(s) rep. Saga #32–#42. . . @3.00
24 AMo,Windfall, final issue. 3.00

ESSENTIAL VERTIGO: THE SANDMAN
DC/Vertigo, 1996
3 NGa(s),SK,MDr,rep. 3.00
4 NGa(s),SK,MDr,rep. F:Etrigan . . 3.00
5 NGa(s),SK,MJ,F:Morpheus,
 John Dee. 3.00
6 NGa(s),SK,MJ,V:Dr. Destiny 3.00
7 . . . . 3.00
8 NGa(s),MDr,MJ,The Sound
 of Her Wings 3.00
9 NGa(s),MDr,MJ,The Doll's
 House, F:Nada 3.00
10 NGa(s),MDr,Doll's House . . . 3.00
11 NGa(s),MDr,RT 3.00
12 NGa(s),CBa,MJ,Doll'sHouse . . . 3.00
13 NGa,rep.Doll's House,pt.4 . . . . 3.00

DC

14 NGa,rep.Doll's House,pt.5 . . . . . 3.50
15 NGa,rep.Doll's House,pt.6 . . . . . 3.00
16 NGa,rep.Lost Hearts 3.00
17 NGa,rep.Dream Country 3.00
18 NGa,Dream of Thousand Cats . . 3.00
19 NGa,rep.Sandman #19 . . . . 3.00
20 NGa,rep.Sandman #20 . . . . 3.00
21 NGa,rep.Sandman #21 . . . . 3.00
22 NGa,rep.Season of Mists pt.1 . . 3.00
23 NGa,rep.Season of Mists pt.2 . . 3.00
24 NGa,rep.Season of Mists pt.3 . . 3.00
25 NGa,rep.Season of Mists pt.4 . . 3.00
26 NGa,rep.Season of Mists pt.5 . . 3.00
27 NGa,rep.Season of Mists,pt.6. . . 3.00
28 NGa,rep.Season of Mists,epilog. 3.00
29 NGa,rep.Thermidor 3.00
30 NGa,rep.August 3.00
31 NGa,rep.Three Septembers
   and a January 3.00
32 NGa,rep. Sandman Special #1
   final issue 4.50

EVERYTHING HAPPENS
TO HARVEY
1953–54

1 Teen-age humor 325.00
2 . . . . 175.00
3 thru 7 . . . . @125.00

EXTERMINATORS, THE
DC/Vertigo, Jan., 2006

1 F:Henry James 3.00
2 Bug Brothers, pt.2 . . . . 3.00
3 Bug Brothers, pt.3 . . . . 3.00
4 Bug Brothers, pt.4 . . . . 3.00
5 Bug Brothers, pt.5 . . . . 3.00
6 Insurgency, pt.1 . . . . 3.00
7 Insurgency,pt.2 . . . . 3.00
8 Two Girlfriends 3.00
9 Insurgency,pt.3 . . . . 3.00
10 Insurgency,pt.4 . . . . 3.00
11 Brother #38, pt.1 . . . . 3.00
12 Brother #38, pt.2 . . . . 3.00
13 Lies of our Fathers, pt.1 . . . . . . 3.00
14 Lies of our Fathers, pt.2 . . . . . . 3.00
15 Lies of our Fathers, pt.3 . . . . . . 3.00
16 Lies of our Fathers, pt.4 . . . . . . 3.00
17 Showdown at Scatshot, pt.1 . . . 3.00
18 Showdown at Scatshot, pt.2 . . . 3.00
19 Crossfire and Collateral, pt.1 . . 3.00
20 Crossfire and Collateral, pt.2 . . 3.00
21 Crossfire and Collateral, pt.3 . . 3.00
22 Crossfire and Collateral, pt.4 . . 3.00

EXTREME JUSTICE
1995–96

O New Group 3.50
1 V:Captain Atom 3.00
2 V:War Cyborgs 3.00
3 V:Synge 3.00
4 R:Firestorm the Nuclear Man . . . 3.00
5 Firestorm & Elementals 3.00
6 Monarch,Captain Atom, Booster
   Gold, Maxima 3.00
7 F:Monarch,Captain Atom 3.00
8 Look Before You Quantum Leap . 3.00
9 F:Firestorm 3.00
10 Underworld Unleashed tie-in . . . 3.00
11 Underworld Unleashed tie-in . . . 3.00
12 Monarch's scheme revealed 3.00
13 Monarch vs. Captain Atom 3.00
14 . . . . 3.00
15 TMo,V:The Slavemaster from
   the Stars 3.00
16 TMo,V:Legion of Doom 3.00
17 TMo,V:Legion of Doom 3.00

EXTREMIST
DC/Vertigo, 1993

1 B:PrM(s),TMK,I:The Order,
   Extremist(Judy Tanner) 2.50
1a Platinum Ed. 5.00
2 TMK,D:Extremist(Jack Tanner) . 2.25
3 TMK,V:Patrick 2.25
4 E:PrM(s),TMK,D:Tony Murphy . . 2.25

FABLES
DC/Vertigo, May, 2002

1 SL, Legends in Exile,pt.1 . . . . . 20.00
1a variant (c) 20.00
2 SL, Legends in Exile,pt.2 . . . . . 15.00
3 SL, Legends in Exile,pt.3 . . . . . . 8.00
4 BWg,Legends in Exile,pt.4 . . . . 7.00
5 SL, Legends in Exile,pt.5 . . . . . . 7.00
6 MBu,SL,Animal Farm,pt.1 . . . . . 7.00
7 MBu,SL,Animal Farm,pt.2 . . . . . 4.00
8 MBu,SL,Animal Farm,pt.3 . . . . . 4.00
9 MBu,SL,Animal Farm,pt.4 . . . . . 4.00
10 MBu,SL,Animal Farm,pt.5 . . . . 4.00
11 Jack of the Tales 4.00
12 Fables caper,pt.1 . . . . 4.00
13 Fables caper,pt.2 . . . . 3.00
14 Storybook Love,pt.1 . . . . 3.00
15 Storybook Love,pt.2 . . . . 3.00
16 Storybook Love,pt.3 . . . . 3.00
17 Storybook Love,pt.4 . . . . 3.00
18 The Barley Corn Brides 2.50
19 MBu,SL 2.50
20 MBu,SL 2.50
21 MBu,SL 2.50
22 JP,Ex-wives Club 2.50
23 MBu,SL 2.50
24 MBu,SL,Boy Blue missing 2.50
25 MBu,SL,Wooden Soldiers 2.50
26 MBu,SL,Wooden Soldiers 2.50
27 MBu,SL,Wooden Soldiers 2.50
28 JP,War Stories,pt.1 . . . . 2.50
29 JP,War Stories,pt.2 . . . . 2.50
30 MBu,SL,The Year After,pt.1 . . . 2.50
31 MBu,SL,The Year After,pt.2 . . . 2.50
32 MBu,SL,The Year After 2.50
33 MBu,SL,The Year After,concl. . . 2.50
34 Jack be Nimble, pt.1 . . . . 2.50
35 Jack be Nimble, pt.2 . . . . 2.50
36 Return to the Homelands,pt.1 . . 2.50
37 Return to the Homelands,pt.2 . . 2.50
38 Return to the Homelands,pt.3 . . 2.50
39 Fabletown 2.50
40 Return to the Homelands,pt.4 . . 3.00
41 Return to the Homelands,pt.5 . . 2.75
42 Arabian Nights & Days 2.75
43 Arabian Nights & Days 2.75
44 Arabian Nights & Days 2.75
45 Arabian Nights & Days 2.75
46 Ballad of Rodney and June 2.75
47 Ballad of Rodney and June 2.75
48 Wolves, pt.1 . . . . 2.75
49 Wolves, pt.2 . . . . 3.00
50 64-pg. 4.00
51 in Smalltown 3.00
52 Sons of the Empire,pt.1 . . . . . . 3.00
53 Sons of the Empire,pt.2 . . . . . . 3.00
54 Sons of the Empire,pt.3 . . . . . . 3.00
55 Sons of the Empire,pt.4 . . . . . . 3.00
56 MBu,X-mas special 3.50
57 MiA,Father and Son, pt.1 . . . . . 3.00
58 MiA,Father and Son, pt.2 . . . . . 3.00
59 Burning questions answered . . . 3.00
60 The Good Prince, pt.1 . . . . 3.00
61 The Good Prince, pt.2 . . . . 3.00
62 The Good Prince, pt.3 . . . . 3.00
63 The Good Prince, pt.4 . . . . 3.00
64 The Farm 3.00
65 The Magic Mirror 3.00
66 Homecoming 3.00
Spec. The Last Castle 6.00
Spec. Reprint of #1 (2006) 0.25

FAKER
Vertigo, July, 2007

1 (of 6) MCy 3.00
2 thru 4 MCy . . . . @3.00

FALLEN ANGEL
July 2003

1 PDd(s),Bete Noire 2.50
2 PDd(s),Asia Minor 2.50
3 PDd(s),Little Better,pt.1 . . . . . . 2.50
4 PDd(s),Little Better,pt.2 . . . . . . 2.50
5 PDd(s),Little Better,pt.3 . . . . . . 2.50
6 PDd(s),Little Better,pt.4 . . . . . . 2.50
7 PDd(s),F:Black Mariah 2.50
8 PDd(s),F:Black Mariah 2.50
9 PDd(s),F:Black Mariah 2.50
10 PDd(s),F:Black Mariah 3.00
11 PDd(s),F:Black Marian 2.50
12 PDd(s),Doctor Juris 2.50
13 PDd(s),V:Asia Minor 2.50
14 PDd(s),Bete Noire 2.50
15 PDd(s) 2.50
16 PDd(s) 2.50
17 PDd(s),MK(c) 3.00
18 PDd(s),V:Hierachy 3.00
19 PDd(s),GP(c),A:Sachs & Violens 3.00
20 PDd(s),Sacred Cows, concl. . . 3.00
TPB 13.00

FAMILY MAN
Paradox 1995

1 I:Family Man 5.50
2 V:Brother Charles 5.50
3 Escape 5.50

FANBOY
1999

1 (of 6) SA, various artists 2.50
2 A:Hal Jordan 2.50
3 A:JLA 2.50
4 SA, A:Sgt. Rock 2.50
5 SA, A:Batman 2.50
6 SA, A:Wonder Woman, concl. . . 2.50
TPB F:Finster, 144-page(2001) . . 13.00

FATE
1994–96

0 . . . . 3.00
1 Dr. Fate 2.50
2 Nabu,Astral plane 2.25
3 Bloodstain 2.25
4 Decisions 2.25

Fate #4
© DC Comics, Inc.

All comics prices listed are for *Near Mint* condition.

5 Judged by Enclave 2.25
6 V:Grimoire 2.25
7 V:Dark Agent 2.25
8 V:Dark Agent 2.25
9 Tries to change his destiny 2.25
10 A:Zatanna 2.25
11 . . . . 2.25
12 A:Sentinel 2.25
13 V:Blaze 2.25
14 LKa,ALa,AWi,Underworld
Unleashed tie-in 2.25
15 LKa,ALa,AWi,V:Charnelle 2.25
16 LKa,ALa,AWi,canibal drug-cult . . 2.25
17 LKa,ALa,AWi. 2.25
18 LKa,ALa,AWi,V:Charnelle 2.25
19 LKa,ALa,AWi,V:men in black . . . 2.25

FAULT LINES
DC/Vertigo, March, 1997
Mini-series

1 LMr(s),F:Tracey Farrand 2.50
2 LMr(s) 2.50
3 LMr(s) 2.50
4 LMr(s) 2.50
5 (of 6) LMr(s) 2.50
6 LMrs(s) concl. 2.50

Feature Films #2 © DC Comics Inc.

FEATURE FILMS
1950

1 Captain China 1,200.00
2 Riding High, Bing Crosby . . 1,200.00
3 The Eagle and the Hawk . . . 1,100.00
4 Fancy Pants, Bob Hope 1,400.00

52
May, 2006

1 52 Weeks without Superman,
  Batman & Wonder Woman 2.50
2 Looking Back at Tomorrow 2.50
3 New World Order. 2.50
4 Dances with Monsters 2.50
5 Stars in Their Courses. 2.50
6 F:China's super-hero team 2.50
7 F:Booster Gold. 2.50
8 F:John Henry Irons 2.50
9 New JLA 2.50
10 I:Supernova. 2.50
11 New protector of Gotham 2.50
12 F:Black Adam 2.50
13 F:Sue Dibny 2.50
14 F:Steel and Montoya. 2.50
15 O:Metamorpho 2.50
16 F:Black Adam and Isis 2.50
17 Lobo 2.50
18 Croatoans 2.50

19 Your own superhero identity 2.50
20 O:Adam Strange 2.50
21 Raven 2.50
22 Kon-El didn't die in Crisis 2.50
23 Isis. 2.50
24 Join New Justice League 2.50
25 Black Marvel Family 2.50
26 LexCorp 2.50
27 O:Power Girl 2.50
28 Red Tornado 2.50
29 O:Joker 2.50
30 Batman no more 2.50
31 Origin of the Metal Man 2.50
32 Origin of Blue Beetle. 2.50
33 Origin of Two-Face 2.50
34 Cliffhanger. 2.50
35 Origin of Black Canary 2.50
35a variant (c) 2.50
36 Origin of Green Arrow 2.50
37 Origin of Firestorm 2.50
38 Origin of Red Tornado 2.50
39 Origin of Mr. Terrific 2.50
40 . . . . 2.50
41 . . . . 2.50
42 . . . . 2.50
43 . . . . 2.50
44 . . . . 2.50
45 PO. 2.50
46 CsB 2.50
47 JoB 2.50
48 . . . . 2.50
49 . . . . 2.50
50 . . . . 2.50
51 . . . . 2.50
52 World War III 2.50

52 AFTERMATH:
THE FOUR HORSEMEN
Aug., 2007

1 (of 6) KG,PO 3.00
2 KG,PO,The dead walk 3.00
3 KG,PO 3.00

FIGHT FOR TOMORROW
DC/Vertigo, Sept., 2002

1 (of 6) DCw,JLe(c) kung-fu 2.50
2 DCw,KW, more kung-fu 2.50
3 thru 6 DCw . . . . @2.50

FIGHTING AMERICAN
1994

1 GrL,R:Fighting American 2.50
2 GrL,Media Circus 2.50

Flighting American #6
© DC Comics, Inc.

3 GrL,I&V:Gross Nation Product,
  Def Iffit 2.50
4 GrL,V:Gross Nation Product,
  Def Iffit 2.50
5 GrL,PhorOptor 2.50
6 Final Issue 2.50

FILTH, THE
DC/Vertigo, June, 2002

1 (of 13) GMo 3.00
2 GMo, Perfect Victim. 3.00
3 GMo, unexpected guest 3.00
4 GMo, Otto Von Vermun 3.00
5 GMo, Pornomancer 3.00
6 GMo,World of Anders Klimaaks. . 3.00
7 GMo,Libertania 3.00
8 GMo,Libertania 3.00
9 GMo,Answers 3.00
10 GMo,Mother Dirt 3.00
11 GMo,Greg Feely 3.00
12 GMo,Mother Dirt 3.00
13 GMo,concl. 3.00
TPB 20.00

FINAL NIGHT, THE
Sept., 1996
[Cross-Over Series]

1 KK(s),SI,JMz, Alien crash lands
  on Earth. 7.00
2 KK(s),SI,JMz, Earth's sun
  extinguished 5.00
3 KK(s),SI,JMz, Attempts to stave
  off inevitable 5.00
4 KK(s),SI,JMz, Can they save the
  world, and at what price? 10.00
TPB rep. 13.00

FIREBRAND
1995

1 SaV,Alex Sanchez becomes
  Firebrand 2.25
2 SaV 2.25
3 SaV,Generation Prime case
  climax 2.25
4 SaV,Young gang member 2.25
5 SaV,V;serial killer(s). 2.25
6 thru 9 . . . . @2.25

FIRESTORM
March, 1978

1 AM,JRu,I&O:Firestorm. 15.00
2 AM,BMc,A:Superman 7.00
3 AM,I:Killer Froat. 7.00
4 AM,BMc,I:Hyena 7.00
5 AM,BMc,Hyena 7.00

FIRESTORM
May 2004

1 Ccs,F:Jason Rusch 2.50
2 Ccs,Eye Contact,pt.2 . . . . 2.50
3 Ccs,power's price 2.50
4 Ccs,Everybody Wants You 2.50
5 Ccs,Everybody Wants You 2.50
6 CsB,DGr,x-over 2.50
7 ALa,LSh,Bloodhound x-over 2.50
8 Heroes 2.50
9 Old foe 2.50
10 Return of Ronnie Raymond? . . . 2.50
11 V:Multiplex & Typhoon 2.50
12 V:Multiplex & Typhoon 2.50
13 Ronnie Raymond, concl. 2.50
14 Both Jason and Firestorm 2.50
15 Secret Origins, pt.1. . . . . 2.50
16 Secret Origins, pt.2. . . . . 2.50
17 Villains United tie-in 2.50
18 Omac project tie-in 2.50
19 Infinite Crisis 2.50
20 Infinite Crisis, A:Animal Man . . . 2.50
21 Building a Better Firestorm 2.50

22 Building a Better Firestorm 2.50
Becomes:

FIRESTORM THE NUCLEAR MAN

23 One Year Later 2.50
24 Firehawk vs. Killer Frost 2.50
25 V:Killer Frost & Mr. Freeze 3.00
26 F:The Pupil 3.00
27 Firehawk vs. Pupil 3.00
28 In My Father's House,pt.1 . . . . . 3.00
29 In My Father's House,pt.2 . . . . . 3.00
30 In My Father's House,pt.3 . . . . . 3.00
31 In My Father's House,pt.4 . . . . . 3.00
32 In My Father's House, pt.5 . . . . . 3.00
33 DMD,DJu,KeL,F:Mr. Miracle 3.00
34 DMD,F:Mr. Miracle 3.00
35 DMD,V:Kalibak, final issue 3.00

FIRESTORM, THE NUCLEAR MAN See: FURY OF FIRESTORM

First Issue Special #12
© DC Comics, Inc.

FIRST ISSUE SPECIAL
April, 1975

1 JK,Atlas 20.00
2 Green Team 15.00
3 Metamorpho 15.00
4 Lady Cop 10.00
5 JK,Manhunter 20.00
6 JK,Dingbats 20.00
7 SD,Creeper 20.00
8 MGr,Warlord 30.00
9 WS,Dr.Fate 15.00
10 Outsiders(not Batman team). . . 12.00
11 NR,AM Code:Assassin 12.00
12 new Starman 12.00
13 return of New Gods 30.00

FLASH COMICS
Jan., 1940

1 SMo,SMo(c),O:Flash,Hawkman,The
   Whip & Johnny Thunder,B:Cliff
   Cornwall,Minute Movies . 150,000.00
2 B:Rod Rain 25,000.00
3 SMo,SMo(c),B:The King . . . 15,000.00
4 SMo,SMo(c),F:The Whip . . 12,000.00
5 SMo,SMo(c),F:The King . . 10,000.00
6 F:Flash 15,000.00
7 Hawkman(c) 12,000.00
8 Male bondage(c). 6,500.00
9 Hawkman(c) 7,000.00
10 SMo,SMo(c),Flash(c). 7,000.00
11 SMo,SMo(c) 5,000.00
12 SMo,SMo(c),B:Les Watts. . 5,000.00

13 SMo,SMo(c). 5,000.00
14 SMo,SMo(c). 5,500.00
15 SMo,SMo(c). 5,500.00
16 SMo,SMo(c). 5,500.00
17 SMo,SMo(c),E:CliffCornwall 5,500.00
18 SMo,SMo(c). 5,500.00
19 SMo,SMo(c). 5,500.00
20 SMo,SMo(c). 5,500.00
21 SMo(c) 6,000.00
22 SMo,SMo(c). 5,000.00
23 SMo,SMo(c). 5,000.00
24 SMo,SMo(c),Flash V:Spider-
   Men of Mars,A:Hawkgirl . . . 5,500.00
25 SMo,SMo(c). 2,700.00
26 SMo,SMo(c). 2,700.00
27 SMo,SMo(c). 2,700.00
28 SMo,SMo(c),Flash goes
   to Hollywood. 2,700.00
29 SMo,SMo(c),Flash inAdventure
   of the Curiosity Ray!. 2,700.00
30 SMo,SMo(c),Flash inAdventure
   of the Curiosity Ray!. 2,700.00
31 SMo,SMo(c),Hawkman(c) . . 2,700.00
32 SMo,SM(c),Flash inAdventure
   of the Fictious Villians. 2,700.00
33 SMo,SMo(c). 2,700.00
34 SMo,SMo(c),Flash in The Robbers
   of the Round Table 2,700.00
35 SMo,SMo(c). 2,700.00
36 SMo,SMo(c),F:Flash,Mystery of
   Doll Who Walks Like a Man 2,700.00
37 SMo,SMo(c). 2,200.00
38 SMo,SMo(c). 2,200.00
39 SMo,SMo(c). 2,200.00
40 SMo,SMo(c),F:Flash, Man Who
   Could Read Man's Souls!. . 2,000.00
41 SMo,SMo(c). 2,000.00
42 SMo,SMo(c),Flash V:The
   Gangsters Baby!. 2,000.00
43 SMo,SMo(c). 2,000.00
44 SMo,SMo(c),Flash V:The
   Liars Club 2,000.00
45 SMo,SMo(c),F:Hawkman,Big
   Butch Makes Hall of Fame . 2,000.00
46 SMo,SMo(c). 2,000.00
47 SMo,SMo(c),Hawkman in Crime
   Canned for the Duration. . . 1,800.00
48 SMo,SMo(c). 1,800.00
49 SMo,SMo(c). 1,800.00
50 SMo,SMo(c),Hawkman, Tale
   of the 1,000 Dollar Bill 1,800.00
51 SMo,SMo(c). 1,800.00
52 SMo,SMo(c),Flash, Machine
   that Thinks Like a Man 1,800.00
53 SMo,SMo(c),Hawkman, Simple
   Simon Met the Hawkman . . 1,800.00
54 SMo,SMo(c),Flash, Mysterious
   Bottle from the Sea 1,800.00
55 SMo,SMo(c),Hawkman, Riddle of
   the Stolen Statuette! 1,800.00
56 SMo,SMo(c). 1,800.00
57 SMo,SMo(c),Hawkman,
   Adventure of the Gangster
   & the Ghost 1,800.00
58 SMo,SMo(c),Merman meets
   the Flash. 1,800.00
59 SMo,SMo(c),Hawkman
   V:Pied Piper 1,800.00
60 SMo,SMo(c),Flash
   V:The Wind Master. 1,800.00
61 SMo,SMo(c),Hawkman
   V:The Beanstalk 1,800.00
62 JKu,Flash in High Jinks
   on the Rinks 2,000.00
63 JKu(c),Hawkman in The
   Tale of the Mystic Urn. 1,500.00
64 The Fire Bandits 1,500.00
65 JKu(c),Hawkman in Return
   of the Simple Simon 1,500.00
66 Flash and the Black Widow . 1,500.00
67 JKu(c). 1,500.00
68 Flash in The Radio that
   Ran Wild. 1,500.00

Flash Comics #72
© DC Comics, Inc.

69 Adventure o/t Violent Violin . 1,500.00
70 JKu(c). 1,500.00
71 JKu(c),Hawkman in Battle
   of the Birdmen 1,500.00
72 JKu,Wizard o/t Wax Works . 1,500.00
73 JKu(c). 1,500.00
74 JKu(c). 1,500.00
75 JKu(c),Hawkman in Magic
   at the Mardi Gras 1,500.00
76 A:Worry Wart 1,500.00
77 Hawkman in The Case of
   the Curious Casket. 1,500.00
78 Haunted Halloween 1,500.00
79 Hawkman in The Battle
   of the Birds. 1,500.00
80 Flash in The Story of
   the Boy Genius. 1,500.00
81 JKu(c),Hawkman's Voyage
   to Venus 1,500.00
82 A:Walter Jordan 1,500.00
83 JKu,JKu(c),Hawkman in
   Destined for Disaster 1,600.00
84 Flash V:The Changeling . . . 1,600.00
85 JKu,JKu(c),Hawkman in
   Hollywood. 1,600.00
86 JKu,1st Black Canary,Flash
   V:Stone Age Menace 7,000.00
87 Hawkman meets the Foil . . . 2,200.00
88 JKu,Flash in The Case
   of the Vanished Year! 2,200.00
89 I:The Thorn 3,500.00
90 Flash in Nine Empty
   Uniforms 2,200.00
91 Hawkman V:The Phantom
   Menace 2,500.00
92 1st full-length Black
   Canary story. 7,000.00
93 Flash V:Violin of Villainy . . . 2,500.00
94 JKu(c). 2,500.00
95 CI(c),The Golden Flash 2,500.00
96 JKu,Return of the Centaurs . 2,500.00
97 Flash in The Dream
   that Didn't Vanish 2,500.00
98 JKu(c),Hawkman in
   Crime Costume! 2,500.00
99 Flash in The Star Prize
   of the Year 2,500.00
100 Hawkman in The Human
   -Fly Bandits! 5,500.00
101 CI,A Switch in Time 4,500.00
102 Hawkman in The Flying
   Darkness 4,500.00
103 CI,The Sword of Time 4,500.00
104 JKu,Hawkman in Flaming
   Darkness' Feb., 1949 . . . . 18,000.00
Revived as:

FLASH, THE
Feb.–March, 1959

105 CI,O:Flash,I:Mirror
   Master. 15,000.00
106 CI,I&O:Gorilla Grodd,
   O:Pied Piper 5,000.00
107 CI,A:Grodd 2,500.00
108 CI,A:Grodd 2,000.00
109 CI,A:Mirror Master 1,500.00
110 CI,MA,I:Kid Flash,
   Weather Wizard 4,500.00
111 CI,A:Kid Flash,The Invasion
   Of the Cloud Creatures . . . 1,500.00
112 CI,I&O:Elongated Man,
   A:Kid Flash. 1,500.00
113 CI,I&O:Trickster 1,100.00
114 CI,A:Captain Cold 1,000.00
115 CI,A:Grodd 750.00
116 CI,A:Kid Flash,The Man
   Who Stole Central City 750.00
117 CI,MA,I:Capt.Boomerang . . 800.00
118 CI,MA 650.00
119 CI,W:Elongated Man 650.00
120 CI,A:Kid Flash,Land of
   Golden Giants 650.00
121 CI,A:Trickster 550.00
122 CI,I&O:The Top 550.00
123 I:Earth 2,R:G.A.Flash 3,000.00
124 CI,A:Capt.Boomerang 500.00
125 CI,A:Kid Flash,The
   Conquerors of Time 500.00
126 CI,A:Mirror Master 500.00
127 CI,A:Grodd 500.00
128 CI,O:Abra Kadabra 500.00
129 CI,A:Capt.Cold,Trickster,A:Gold.
   Age Flash,C:JLA (flashback) . 600.00
130 CI,A:Mirror Master,
   Weather Wizard 450.00
131 CI,A:Green Lantern 300.00
132 CI,A:Daphne Dean 300.00
133 CI,A:Abra Kadabra 300.00
134 CI,A:Captain Cold 300.00
135 CI,N:Kid Flash 300.00
136 CI,A:Mirror Master 300.00
137 CI,Vandal Savage,R:JSA,
   A:G.A.Flash 900.00
138 CI,A:Pied Piper 350.00
139 CI,I&O:Prof.Zoom(Reverse
   Flash) 350.00
140 CI,O:Heat Wave 350.00
141 CI,A:Top 250.00
142 CI,A:Trickster 250.00
143 CI,A:Green Lantern 250.00
144 CI,A:Man Missile,Kid Flash . 250.00
145 CI,A:Weather Wizard 250.00
146 CI,A:Mirror Master 250.00
147 CI,A:Mr.Element,A:Reverse
   Flash 250.00
148 CI,A:Capt.Boomerang. 250.00
149 CI,A:Abra Kadabra 250.00
150 CI,A:Captain Cold 250.00
151 CI,A:Earth II Flash,
   The Shade. 275.00
152 CI,V:Trickster 300.00
153 CI,A:Mr.Element,Rev.Flash . . 300.00
154 CI,The Day Flash Ran Away
   with Himself. 300.00
155 CI,A:MirrorMaster,Capt.Cold,Top
   Capt. Boomerang,Grodd 300.00
156 CI,A:Kid Flash,The Super Hero
   who Betrayed the World 300.00
157 CI,A:Doralla Kon,The Top . . . 300.00
158 CI,V:The Breakaway Bandit
   A:The Justice League 250.00
159 CI,A:Kid Flash 200.00
160 CI,giant 250.00
161 CI,A:Mirror Master 200.00
162 CI,Who Haunts the Corridor
   of Chills 200.00
163 CI,A:Abra kadabra 200.00
164 CI,V:Pied Piper,A:Kid Flash . 200.00
165 CI,W:Flash,Iris West 200.00

Flash #192
© DC Comics Inc.

166 CI,A:Captain Cold 200.00
167 CI,O:Flash,I:Mopee 200.00
168 CI,A:Green Lantern 200.00
169 CI,O:Flash rtd,giant 210.00
170 CI,A:Abra Kadabra,
   G.A.Flash 200.00
171 CI,A:Dexter Myles,Justice
   League,Atom;V:Dr Light 200.00
172 CI,A:Grodd 200.00
173 CI,A:Kid Flash,EarthII Flash
   V:Golden Man 250.00
174 CI,A:Mirror Master,Top
   Captain Cold 200.00
175 2nd Superman/Flash race,
   C:Justice League o/America . 225.00
176 giant-size. 200.00
177 RA,V:The Trickster 200.00
178 CI,(giant size) 225.00
179 RA,Fact or Fiction 200.00
180 RA,V:Baron Katana. 175.00
181 RA,V;Baron Katana. 150.00
182 A:Abra Kadabra 150.00
183 RA,V:The Frog 150.00
184 RA,V:Dr Yom. 150.00
185 RA,Threat of the High Rise
   Buildings 150.00
186 RA,A:Sargon. 150.00
187 CI,AbraKadabra,giant 125.00
188 A:Mirror Master 100.00
189 JKu(c),RA,A:Kid Flash 100.00
190 JKu(c),RA,A:Dexter Myles . . 100.00
191 JKu(c),RA,A:Green Lantern . 100.00
192 RA;V:Captain Vulcan 100.00
193 A:Captain Cold 100.00
194 NA(c). 100.00
195 GK,MA,NA 100.00
196 CI,giant 125.00
197 GK. 100.00
198 GK. 100.00
199 GK. 100.00
200 IN,MA 100.00
201 IN,MA,A:G.A. Flash 60.00
202 IN,MA,A:Kid Flash 60.00
203 IN 60.00
204 NA. 60.00
205 giant 100.00
206 NA,A:Mirror Master 60.00
207 NA. 60.00
208 NA. 60.00
209 A:Capt.Boomerang,Grodd
   Trickster. 60.00
210 CI 60.00
211 NA,O:Flash 60.00
212 A:Abra Kadabra 60.00

213 CI,NA 60.00
214 CI,rep.Showcase #37
   (O:Metal Men),giant size. 70.00
215 IN,FMc,NA,rep.Showcase#14. 70.00
216 A:Mr.Element. 70.00
217 NA,A:Gr.Lant,Gr.Arrow 70.00
218 NA,A:Gr.Lant,Gr.Arrow 70.00
219 NA,L:Green Arrow. 70.00
220 IN,DG,A:KidFlash,Gr.Lantern . 60.00
221 IN 30.00
222 IN 30.00
223 DG,Green Lantern. 30.00
224 IN,DG,A:Green Lantern. 30.00
225 IN,DG,A:Gr.Lant,Rev.Flash. . 30.00
226 NA,A:Capt. Cold 35.00
227 IN,FMc,DG,Capt.Boomerang,
   Green Lantern. 25.00
228 IN 25.00
229 IN,FMc,A:Green Arrow,
   V:Rag Doll (giant size). 75.00
230 A:VandalSavage,Dr.Alchemy . 25.00
231 FMc. 25.00
232 giant 75.00
233 giant 75.00
234 V:Reverse Flash 20.00
235 DG(c),V:Vandal Savage 18.00
236 MGr. 18.00
237 IN,FMc,MGr,A:Prof Zoom,
   Green Lantern 20.00
238 MGr. 18.00
239 Tailor Made Crimes. 18.00
240 MGr. 18.00
241 A:Mirror Master 18.00
242 MGr,D:Top. 18.00
243 IN,FMc,MGr,TA,O:Top,
   A:Green Lantern 18.00
244 IN,FMc,A:Rogue's Gallery . . . 18.00
245 FMc,IN,DD,TA,I:PlantMaster.. 18.00
246 IN,FMc,DD,TA,I:PlantMaster.. 18.00
247. . . . . 18.00
248 FMc,IN,I:Master 18.00
249 FMc,IN,V:Master 18.00
250 IN,FMc,I:Golden Glider 18.00
251 FMc,IN,V:Golden Glider 15.00
252 FMc,IN,I:Molder 15.00
253 FMc,IN,V:Molder 15.00
254 FMc. 15.00
255 FMc,A:MirrorMaster 15.00
256 FMc,V:Top. 15.00
257 FMc,A:Green Glider 15.00
258 FMc,A:Black Hand 15.00
259 FMc,IN 15.00
260 FMc,IN 15.00
261 FMc,IN,V:Golden Glider 15.00
262 FMc,IN,V:Golden Glider 15.00
263 FMc,IN,V:Golden Glider 15.00
264 FMc,IN,V:Golden Glider 15.00
265 FMc,IN 15.00
266 FMc,IN,V:Heat Wave 15.00
267 FMc,IN,V:Heat Wave 15.00
268 FMc,IN,A:E2 Flash 15.00
269 FMc,IN,A:Kid Flash. 15.00
270 FMc,IN,V:Clown 15.00
271 RB,V:Clown. 15.00
272 RB,V:Clown. 15.00
273 RB. 15.00
274 RB. 15.00
275 AS,D:Iris West,PCP story 20.00
276 AS,A:JLA. 15.00
277 AS,FMc,A:JLA,
   V:MirrorMaster. 15.00
278 A:Captain Boomerang
   & Heatwave. 15.00
279 A:Captain Boomerang
   & Heatwave 15.00
280 DH. 15.00
281 DH,V:Reverse Flash 20.00
282 DH,V:Reverse Flash 20.00
283 DH,V:Reverse Flash 20.00
284 DH,Flash's life story
   I:Limbo Lord 15.00
285 DH,V:Trickster 15.00

Flash #344
© DC Comics Inc.

286 DH,I:Rainbow Raider 15.00
287 DH,V:Dr.Alchemy 15.00
288 DH,V:Dr.Alchemy 15.00
289 DH,GP,1st GP DC art; V:Dr.
   Alchemy;B.B.U.Firestorm 20.00
290 GP 10.00
291 GP,DH,V:Sabretooth 10.00
292 GP,DH,V:Mirror Master 10.00
293 GP,DH,V:Pied Piper 10.00
294 GP,DH,V:Grodd 10.00
295 CI,JSn,V:Grodd 10.00
296 JSn,A:Elongated Man 10.00
297 CI,A:Captain Cold 10.00
298 CI,V:Shade,Rainbowraider . . . 10.00
299 CI,V:Shade,Rainbowraider . . . 10.00
300 A:New Teen Titans 12.00
301 CI,A:Firestorm 10.00
302 CI,V:Golden Glider 10.00
303 CI,V:Golden Glider 10.00
304 CI,PB,I:Col.Computron;E:B.U.
   Firestorm 10.00
305 KG,CI,A:G.A.Flash,B:Dr.Fate . 10.00
306 CI,KG,V:Mirror Master 10.00
307 CI,KG,V:Pied Piper 10.00
308 CI,KG 10.00
309 CI,KG 10.00
310 CI,KG,V:Capt.Boomerang 6.00
311 CI,KG,V:Capt.Boomerang 6.00
312 CI,A:Heatwave 6.00
313 KG,A:Psylon,E:Dr.Fate 6.00
314 CI,I:Eradicator 6.00
315 CI,V:Gold Face 6.00
316 CI,V:Gold Face 6.00
317 CI,V:Gold Face 6.00
318 CI,DGb,V:Eradicator;B:
   B.U.Creeper 6.00
319 CI,DGb,V:Eradicator 6.00
320 CI,V:Eradicator 6.00
321 CI,D:Eradicator 5.00
322 CI,V:Reverse Flash 5.00
323 CI,V:Reverse Flash;E:
   B.U.Creeper 5.00
324 CI,D:Reverse Flash 5.50
325 CI,A:Rogues Gallery 5.00
326 CI,A:Weather Wizard 5.00
327 CI,A:JLA,G.Grodd 5.00
328 CI 5.00
329 CI,A:J.L.A.,G.Grodd 5.00
330 CI,FMc,V:G.Grodd 5.00
331 CI,FMc,V:G.Grodd 5.00
332 CI,FMc,V:Rainbow Raider 5.00
333 CI,FMc,V:Pied Piper 5.00
334 CI,FMc,V:Pied Piper 5.00
335 CI,FMc,V:Pied Piper 5.00
336 CI,FMc,V:Pied Piper 5.00

337 CI,FMc,V:Pied Piper 5.00
338 CI,FMc,I:Big Sir 5.00
339 CI,FMc,A:Big Sir 5.00
340 CI,FMc,Trial,A:Big Sir 5.00
341 CI,FMc,Trial,A:Big Sir 5.00
342 CI,FMc,Trial,V:RogueGallery . . 5.00
343 CI,FMc,Trial,A:GoldFace 5.00
344 CI,O:Kid Flash,Trial 5.00
345 CI,A:Kid Flash,Trial 5.00
346 CI,FMc,Trial,V:AbraKadabra . . 5.00
347 CI,FMc,Trial,V:AbraKadabra . . 5.00
348 CI,FMc,Trial,V:AbraKadabra . . 5.00
349 CI,FMc,Trial,V:AbraKadabra . . 5.00
350 CI,FMc,Trial,V:AbraKadabra . . 7.00
Ann.#1 O:ElongatedMan,
   G.Grodd 800.00

[2nd Series] June, 1987
1 JG,Legends,C:Vandal Savage . . 12.00
2 JG,V:Vandal Savage 5.00
3 JG,I:Kilgore 5.00
4 JG,A:Cyborg 4.00
5 JG,V:Speed Demon 4.00
6 JG,V:Speed Demon 4.00
7 JG,V:Red Trinity 4.00
8 JG,V:BlueTrinity,Millennium 4.00
9 JG,I:Chunk,Millennium 4.00
10 V:Chunk,Chunks World 3.00
11 Return to Earth 3.00
12 Velocity 9 . . . . 3.00
13 Vandal Savage,V:Velocity 9
   Adicts 3.00
14 V:Vandal Savage 3.00
15 A:Velocity 9 Junkies 3.00
16 C:V.Savage,SpeedMcGeePt.1 . 3.00
17 GLa,Speed McGee,pt.2 . . . . . . 3.00
18 GLa,SpeedMcGeePt.3,
   V:V.Savage 3.00
19 JM:+bonus book,R:Rogue
   Gallery,O:Blue/Red Trinity 3.00
20 A:Durlan 3.00
21 A:Manhunter,Invasion x-over . . 3.00
22 A:Manhunter,Invasion x-over . . 3.00
23 V:Abrakadabra 3.00
24 GLa,FlashRegainsSpeed,
   A:L.Lane 3.00
25 GLa,Search for Flash 3.00
26 GLa,I:Porcupine Man 3.00
27 GLa,Porcupine Man as Flash . . 3.00
28 GLa,A:Golden Glider,
   Capt.Cold 3.00
29 A:New Phantom Lady 3.00
30 GLa,Turtle Saga,pt.1 . . . . 3.00
31 GLa,Turtle Saga,pt.2 . . . . 3.00
32 GLa,Turtle Saga,pt.3,
   R:G.A.Turtle 3.00
33 GLa,Turtle Saga,pt.4 . . . . 3.00
34 GLa,Turtle Saga,pt.5 . . . . 3.00
35 GLa,Turtle Saga,pt.6,
   D:G.A.Turtle 3.00
36 GLa,V:Cult 3.00
37 GLa,V:Cult 3.00
38 GLa,V:Cult 3.00
39 GLa,V:Cult 3.00
40 GLa,A:Dr.Alchemy 3.00
41 GLa,A:Dr.Alchemy 3.00
42 GLa,MechanicalTroubles 3.00
43 GLa,V:Kilgore 3.00
44 GLa,V:Velocity 3.00
45 V:Gorilla Grod 3.00
46 V:Gorilla Grod 3.00
47 V:Gorilla Grod 3.00
48 Persistence of Vision 3.00
49 A:Vandal Savage 3.00
50 N:Flash (double sz)V:Savage . . 5.00
51 I:Proletariat 3.00
52 I.R.S. Mission 3.00
53 A:Superman,Race to Save
   Jimmy Olsen 3.00
54 Terrorist Airline Attack 3.00
55 War of the Gods x-over 3.00
56 The Way of a Will,pt.1 . . . . 3.00
57 The Way of a Will,pt.2 . . . . 3.00

Flash 2nd Series #12
© DC Comics, Inc.

58 Meta Gene-activated Homeless . 3.00
59 The Last Resort 3.00
60 Love Song of the Chunk 3.00
61 Wally's Mother's Wedding Day . . 3.00
62 GLa,Year 1,pt.1 . . . . 5.00
63 GLa,Year 1,pt.2 . . . . 4.00
64 GLa,Year 1,pt.3 . . . . 4.00
65 GLa,Year 1,pt.4 . . . . 4.00
66 A:Aq'man,V:Marine Marauder . . 4.00
67 GLa,V:Abra Kadabra 4.00
68 GLa,V:Abra Kadabra 4.00
69 GLa,Gorilla Warfare#2 . . . . 4.00
70 Gorilla Warfare#4 . . . . 4.00
71 GLa,V:Dr.Alchemy 4.00
72 GLa,V:Dr.Alchemy,C:Barry
   Allen 4.00
73 GLa,Xmas Issue,R:Barry Allen . . 6.00
74 GLa,A:Barry Allen? 5.00
75 GLa,A:Reverse Flash,V:Mob
   Violence 5.00
76 GLa,A:Reverse Flash 5.00
77 GLa,G.A.Flash vs
   Reverse Flash 5.00
78 GLa,V:Reverse Flash 5.00
79 GLa,V:Reverse Flash,48 pgs . . . 5.00
80 AD(c),V:Frances Kane 5.00
80a Newstand Ed 3.00
81 AD(c) 4.00
82 AD(c),A:Nightwing 4.00
83 AD(c),A:Nightwing,Starfire 4.00
84 AD(c),I:Razer 4.00
85 AD(c),V:Razer 4.00
86 AD(c),A:Argus 4.00
86 V:Santa Claus 4.00
87 Chrismas issue 4.00
88 Mean Streak 4.00
89 On Trial 4.00
90 On Trial#2 . . . . 4.00
91 Out of Time 5.00
92 I:3rd Flash 20.00
93 A:Impulse 5.00
94 Zero Hour 5.00
95 Terminal Velocity,pt.1 . . . . 4.00
96 Terminal Velocity,pt.2 . . . . 5.00
97 Terminal Velocity,pt.3 . . . . 4.00
98 Terminal Velocity,pt.4 . . . . 4.00
99 Terminal Velocity,pt.5 . . . . 4.00
100 I:New Flash 5.00
100a Collector's Edition 4.00
101 Velocity Aftermath 4.00
102 V:Mongul 3.00
103 Supernatural threat from
   Linda's Past Secret 3.00
104 Exorcise Demons 3.00

105 Through a Glass Darkly 3.00
106 R:Magenta 3.00
107 MWa,Underworld Unleashed
   tie-in. 3.00
108 MWa,Dead Heat,pt.1 . . . . 3.00
109 MWa,Dead Heat,pt.2 . . . . 3.00
110 MWa,Dead Heat,pt.4 . . . . 3.00
111 MWa,Dead Heat,pt.6 . . . . 3.00
112 MWa,New Flash in town 3.00
113 MWa,F:Linda 3.00
114 MWa,V:Chillblaine 3.00
115 thru 117 . . . . @3.00
118 MWa&BAu(s),Flash returns
   from the future 3.00
119 MWa&BAu(s),PR,Final Night
   tie-in. 3.00
120 MWa&BAu(s),PR,Presidential
   Race,pt.1 . . . . 3.00
121 MWa&BAu(s),PR,Presidential
   Race,pt.2 . . . . 3.00
122 MWa&BAu(s),PR, ... 3.00
123 MWa&BAu(s),PR,Flash moves
   to Santa Marta 3.00
124 MWa&BAu(s),PR,Wally doesn't
   know reality from illusion 3.00
125 MWa&BAu(s),PR,California,
   V:Major Disaster 3.00
126 MWa&BAu(s),PR,V:Major
   Disaster 3.00
127 MWa&BAu(s),PR,Hell to Pay,
   pt.1 . . . . 3.00
128 MWa&BAu(s),PR,Hell to Pay
   pt.2, A:JLA 3.00
129 MWa&BAu(s),PR,HellPay,pt.3 . 3.00
130 GMo&MMr(s),PR,new menace. 3.00
131 GMo&MMr(s),PR,V:The Suit. . 3.50
132 GMo&MMr(s),PR,V:The Suit. . 3.50
133 GMo&MMr(s),PR,V:Mirror
   Master 3.00
134 GMo&MMr(s),PR,V:Weather
   Wizard & Captain Cold 3.00
135 GMo&MMr(s), ... 3.00
136 GMo&MMr(s),PR,Human
   Race,pt.1 . . . . 3.00
137 GMo&MMr(s),PR,Human
   Race,pt.2 . . . . 3.00
138 GMo&MMr(s),PR,Human
   Race,pt.3 . . . . 3.00
139 MMr(s),Clv,Black Flash,pt.1 . . 3.00
140 MMr(s),Clv,Black Flash,pt.2 . . 3.00
141 MMr(s),Clv,Black Flash,pt.3 . . 3.00
142 MWa&BAu(s),Clv,SLi,wedding of
   Wally West & Linda Park 3.00
143 MWa&BAu(s),Clv,V:CobaltBlue 3.00
144 MWa&BAu(s),Clv,O:CobaltBlue 3.00
145 MWa&BAu(s),PaP,VRu,
   Chain Lightning, pt.1 . . . . 3.00
146 MWa&BAu(s),PaP,VRu,
   Chain Lightning, pt.2 . . . . 3.00
147 MWa&BAu(s),PaP,VRu,
   Chain Lightning, pt.3 . . . . 3.00
148 MWa&BAu(s),PaP,VRu,
   Chain Lightning, pt.5 . . . . 3.00
149 MWa&BAu(s),PaP,VRu,
   Chain Lightning, pt.5 . . . . 3.00
150 MWa&BAu(s),PaP,VRu, Chain
   Lightning, pt.6, 48-page. 4.00
151 MWa&BAu(s),PaP,A:Robin
   & Aqualad, flashback issue 2.50
152 MWa&BAu(s),PaP,VRu,
   new costume 2.50
153 MWa&BAu(s),PaP,JMz,
   V:Folded Man 2.50
154 MWa&BAu(s),PaP,JMz, ... 2.50
155 MWa&BAu(s),PaP,JMz,
   V:Replicant 2.50
156 MWa&BAu(s),PaP,JMz 2.50
157 MWa&BAu(s),PaP,JMz,fate of
   Linda Park 2.50
158 MWa&BAu(s),PaP,DHz 2.50
159 MWa&BAu(s),PaP,Dark Flash . 3.00
160 BAu(s),Honeymoon on the Run 2.50

Flash 2nd Series #80
© DC Comics, Inc.

161 PaP,DHz,F:Original JSA 2.50
162 PaP,DHz,R:Felix Faust 2.50
163 RLm,DHz,A:JLA 2.50
164 DHz,BBo(c),Wonderland,pt.1 . 11.00
165 DHz,Wonderland,pt.2 . . . . 2.50
166 DHz,Wonderland,pt.3 . . . . 2.50
167 DHz,Wonderland,pt.4 . . . . 2.50
168 DHz,Wonderland,pt.5 . . . . 2.50
169 DHz,Wonderland,pt.6 . . . . 2.50
170 DHz,Blood Will Run,pt.1 . . . . . 2.50
171 DHz,Blood Will Run,pt.2 . . . . . 2.50
172 DHz,Blood Will Run,pt.3 . . . . . 2.50
173 DHz,Blood Will Run,pt.4 . . . . . 2.50
174 DHz,Moving Right Along. 2.50
175 DHz,Deadly storm. 2.50
176 DHz,The Rainmaker 2.50
177 DHz,interdimensional menace . 2.50
178 DHz,Caged,V:Gorilla Grodd . . 2.50
179 DHz,Joker:Last Laugh 2.50
180 DHz,V:Peekaboo 2.50
181 DHz,BB(c),V:Fallout 2.50
182 DPs,Absolute Zero 2.50
183 DHz,BB(c),new Trickster. 2.50
184 DHz,BB(c),Crossfire,pt.1 . . . . . 2.50
185 DHz,BB(c),Crossfire,pt.2 . . . . . 2.50
186 DHz,BB(c),Crossfire,pt.3 . . . . . 2.50
187 DHz,BB(c),Crossfire,pt.4 . . . . . 2.50
188 DHz,BB(c),Crossfire,pt.5 . . . . . 3.00
189 RBr,DPs,F:Cyborg, ... 2.50
190 Rogues spotlight,Pied Piper . . 2.50
191 ScK,DHz,F:Hawkman 2.50
192 ScK,DHz,Run Riot,pt.1 . . . . . . 2.50
193 ScK,DHz,Run Riot,pt.2 . . . . . . 2.50
194 ScK,DHz,Run Riot,pt.3 . . . . . . 2.50
195 ScK,DHz,The Top 2.50
196 V:Peek-a-Boo 2.50
197 ScK,Blitz,pt.1. . . . . 10.00
198 ScK,Blitz,pt.2. . . . . 5.00
199 ScK,Blitz,pt.3. . . . . 3.00
200 ScK,DHz,Blitz,concl.48-pg. . . . 4.00
201 Ignition,pt.1 . . . . 2.25
202 Ignition,pt.2 . . . . 2.25
203 Ignition,pt.3 . . . . 2.25
204 Ignition,pt.4 . . . . 2.25
205 Ignition,pt.5 . . . . 2.25
206 Ignition,pt.6,concl. 2.25
207 Kid Flash & Jay Garrick 7.00
208 Kid Flash & Jay Garrick 4.00
209 Fastest Hero Alive. 3.00
210 F:New Teen Titans 3.00
211 F:Nightwing 3.00
212 F:Mirror Master 3.00
213 Sins of the Father,pro. 3.00
214 Sins of the Father,pt.1 . . . . 3.00
215 Sins of the Father,pt.2 . . . . 3.00

216 Sins of the Father, pt.3 . . . . 3.00
217 Identity Crisis aftermath 3.00
218 F:Heat Wave 3.00
219 Truth or Dare, x-over, pt.1. . . . . 9.00
220 Rogue War,pt.1 . . . . 4.00
221 Rogue War,pt.2 . . . . 2.50
222 Rogue War,pt.3 . . . . 2.50
223 Rogue War,pt.4 . . . . 2.50
224 Rogue War,pt.5 . . . . 2.50
225 Rogue War,pt.6 . . . . 2.50
226 Wally climbs a mountain 2.50
227 ATi(c),Infinite Crisis approaches 2.50
228 ATi(c),Finish Line 2.50
229 ATi(c),Finish Line, pt.3 . . . . 2.50
230 ATi(c),V:Vandal Savage 2.50
231 . . . . 3.00
232 MWa,Menace beneath home . . 3.00
233 MWa,F:JLA 3.00
Ann.#1 JG,The Deathtouch 4.00
Ann.#2 A:Wally's Father. 3.00
Ann.#3 Roots 3.00
Ann.#4 Armageddon,pt7 . . . . 3.00
Ann.#5 TC(1st Full Work),Eclipso,
   V:Rogue's Gallery 8.00
Ann.#6 Bloodlines#4,I:Argus 3.00
Ann.#7 Elseworlds story 3.50
Ann.#8 Year One story. 4.00
Ann.#9 Legends o/t Dead Earth . . . 3.50
Ann.#10 Pulp Heroes (Romance) . . 4.50
Ann.#11 BAu,BWr, Ghosts. 3.50
Ann.#12 DBw,AAd(c),JLApe: Gorilla
   Warfare 3.50
Ann.#13 Planet DC 4.00
Ann.#1 (1963) replica ed.(2001) . . . 7.50
Spec #1,IN,DG,CI,50th Anniv.,
   Three Flash's. 5.00
Spec.#1,000,000 MWa(s),JMz,
   A:Capt.Marvel of 853rd-cent. . . . 2.50
Spec.#1 Our Worlds at War,48-pg . . 3.50
T.V. Spec.#1,JS,w/episode guide. . . 4.25
GN Iron Heights, 48-page 6.00
GN Time Flies, 48-pg. (2002) 6.00
Secret Files #1 MWa,BAu,PRy,
   O:Flash family 6.00
Secret Files #2 (1999) 6.00
Secret Files #3, 48-page (2001) 6.00
Giant #1 MWa,80-page (1998) 5.00
Giant #2 80-page 5.00

FLASH, THE:
FASTEST MAN ALIVE
June, 2006

1 KeL 3.00
1a variant NKu & JKu (c) 3.00
2 Betrayed by his family? 3.00
3 KIK, new hero of Keystone 3.00
4 Secret of the Speed Force 3.00
5 After the Speed Force 3.00
6 Lightning in a Bottle 3.00
7 Speedquest 3.00
8 Smackdown on the Strip 3.00
9 Team player, but which team? . . . 3.00
10 Good cop, bad cop 3.00
11 Full Throttle, V:Rogues 3.00
12 Full Throttle 3.00
13 ATi,Full Throttle 3.00
13a variant (c) 3.00
14 ATi,What happens to the Flash?. 3.00
15 ATi 3.00
15a variant (c) 3.00
Spec. 80-page Giant, Countdown . . 5.00

FLASH & GREEN
LANTERN: THE BRAVE
& THE BOLD
1999

1 (of 6) MWa&TPe(s),BKi 2.50
2 MWa&TPe(s),BKi. 2.50
3 MWa&TPe(s),BKi. 2.50
4 MWa&TPe(s),BKi. 2.50

5 MWa&TPe(s),BKi. 2.50
6 MWa&TPe(s),BKi,concl. 2.50
TPB Flash & Green Lantern,
 Brave and the Bold, 144-page 13.00

THE FLASH PLUS
Nov., 1996
1 MWa(s),F:Wally West, Dick
 Grayson 3.50

FLASH GORDON
1988
1 DJu,I:New Flash Gordon 3.00
2 DJu,A:Lion-Men,Shark-Men 3.00
3 DJu,V:Shark-Men 3.00
4 DJu,Dale Kidnapped by Voltan . . 3.00
5 DJu,Alliance Against Ming. 3.00
6 DJu,Arctic City 3.00
7 DJu,Alliance vs. Ming 3.00
8 DJu,Alliance vs. Ming 3.00
9 DJu,V:Ming, final issue 3.00

FLASHPOINT
Oct., 1999
1 (of 3) NBy,Elseworlds 3.00
2 NBy,Flash in wheelchair 3.00
3 NBy 3.00

FLINCH
DC/Vertigo, 1999
1 JLe,RCo,horror anthology 2.50
2 BSz,RCo(c),3 horror tales 2.50
3 KJo,3 horror tales 2.50
4 TTn,PGu,3 horror tales 2.50
5 JLd(s),RBr,3 horror tales 2.50
6 WML(s) 2.50
7 WML(s) 2.50
8 . . . . 2.50
9 3 Tales of horror. 2.50
10 . . . . 2.50
11 JLd(s) 2.50
12 . . . . 2.50
13 Hubris & dark whimsy. 2.50
14 . . . . 2.50
15 3 grim tales 2.50
16 RCo(c) final issue 2.50

FLINTSTONES AND THE JETSONS, THE
Warner Bros./DC, 1997
1 Ancestors & Descendents meet . 3.00
2 thru 21 . . . . @3.00

FLIPPITY & FLOP
1952
1 Funny animal. 325.00
2 . . . . 175.00
3 thru 5 . . . . @150.00
6 thru 10 . . . . @100.00
11 thru 20 . . . . @125.00
21 thru 47 . . . . @100.00

FLY, THE
Impact, 1991–92
1 I&O:Fly I:Arachnus,Chromium. . . 3.00
2 thru 17 . . . . @2.50
Ann.#1 Earthquest,pt.4,w/card. . . . 3.00

FORBIDDEN TALES OF DARK MANSION
May-June, 1972
5 DH 75.00
6 JK 30.00
7 MK(c&a 25.00
8 MK(c&a) 25.00
9 NA(c),MK,AA 30.00
10 thru 15 Feb.–March, 1974 . . . 25.00

FOREVER MAELSTROM
Nov., 2002
1 (of 6) HC,EB,time-jumping. 3.00
2 HC,EB,time past 3.00
3 HC,EB,V:Praetor 3.00
4 HC,EB,V:Ragnarok 3.00
5 HC,EB,robots. 3.00
6 HC,EB,concl. 3.00

FOREVER PEOPLE, THE
1971–72
1 JK,I:Forever People,A:Superman,
 A:Darkseid 125.00
2 JK,A:Darkseid 75.00
3 JK,A:Darkseid 75.00
4 JK,A:Darkseid 75.00
5 JK. 50.00
6 thru 11 JK . . . . @40.00

FOREVER PEOPLE
1988
1 Return of Forever People 3.00
2 Return of Earth of Yesterday 3.00
3 A:Mark Moonrider 3.00
4 The Dark controlls M.Moonrider . 3.00
5 R:MotherBox,Infinity Man 3.00
6 Donny's Fate, final issue 3.00

FORGOTTEN REALMS
1989–91
1 A:RealmsMaster, PriamAgrivar . . 4.00
2 Mystic Hand of Vaprak. 3.00
3 thru 5 . . . . @2.75
6 thru 13 . . . . @2.50
14 thru 25. . . . . @2.25
Ann.#1 V:Advanced D&D crew . . . 3.50

FORMERLY KNOWN AS THE JUSTICE LEAGUE
July 2003
1 (of 6) F:Maxwell Lord. 2.50
2 JRu,KM. 2.50
3 JRu,KM,V:Roulette 2.50
4 JRu,KM,F:Mary Marvel 2.50
5 JRu,R:G'nort 2.50
6 JRu,concl. 2.50
TPB 12.50

FOUR HORSEMEN
DC/Vertigo, Dec., 1999
1 (of 4) F:Famine 2.50
2 F:War. 2.50
3 F:Pestilence 2.50
4 F:Death, concl.. . . . . 2.50

FOUR STAR BATTLE TALES
1973
1 MD 40.00
2 RH 25.00
3 MD 25.00
4 MD,JKo 25.00
5 MD,RH,BK. 25.00

FOUR STAR SPECTACULAR
March-April, 1976
1 . . . . 25.00
2 thru 6 . . . . @12.00

FOUR WOMEN
Homage/DC Oct., 2001
1 (of 5) SK 3.00
2 SK 3.00
3 thru 5 SK . . . . @3.00
TPB SK rep. #1-#5. . . . . 18.00

Fox and the Crow #91
© DC Comics, Inc.

FOX AND THE CROW
Dec.–Jan., 1951
1 . . . . 1,700.00
2 . . . . 800.00
3 . . . . 500.00
4 . . . . 500.00
5 . . . . 500.00
6 thru 10 . . . . @350.00
11 thru 20 . . . . @250.00
21 thru 40 . . . . @175.00
41 thru 60 . . . . @150.00
61 thru 80 . . . . @125.00
81 thru 94 . . . . @125.00
95 . . . . 125.00
96 thru 99. . . . . @75.00
100 . . . . 75.00
101 thru 108 . . . . @75.00
Becomes:

STANLEY & HIS MONSTER
109 thru 112 Oct.Nov.,1968 . . . . @50.00

FREEDOM FIGHTERS
March-April, 1976
1 Freedom Fighters go to Earth-1 50.00
2 . . . . 20.00
3 . . . . 20.00
4 . . . . 20.00
5 A:Wonder Woman 25.00
6 . . . . 20.00
7 . . . . 20.00
8 . . . . 20.00
9 . . . . 20.00
10 O:Doll Man 20.00
11 O:Ray 20.00
12 O:Firebrand. 25.00
13 O:Black Condor 25.00
14 A:Batgirl. 25.00
15 O:Phantom Lady. 25.00

FROM BEYOND THE UNKNOWN
Oct.–Nov., 1969
1 JKu,CI 100.00
2 MA(c),CI,ATh 60.00
3 NA(c),CI. 50.00
4 MA(c),CI. 50.00
5 MA(c),CI. 50.00
6 NA(c),I:Glen Merrit. 60.00
7 CI,JKu(c) 60.00
8 NA(c),CI. 60.00
9 NA(c),CI. 60.00

10 MA(c),CI	60.00
11 MA(c),CI	60.00
12 JKu(c),CI	60.00
13 JKu(c),CI,WW	60.00
14 MA(c),CI	60.00
15 MA(c),CI	60.00
16 MA(c),CI	60.00
17 MA(c),CI	60.00
18 MK(c),CI,Star Rovers	50.00
19 MK(c),CI,Star Rovers	50.00
20	50.00
21	50.00
22 MA(c)	55.00
23 CI,Space Museum	50.00
24 CI	50.00

Frontier Fighters #8
© DC Comics Inc.

FRONTIER FIGHTERS
1955–56

1 JKu,Davy Crocket, Buffalo Bill.	900.00
2 JKu.	500.00
3 thru 8 JKu.	@475.00

FUNNY FOLKS
1946–1950

1 Nutsy Squirrel	500.00
2	250.00
3	175.00
4 1st Nutsy Squirrel(c)	175.00
5 HK	175.00
6	125.00
7	125.00
8	125.00
9	125.00
10	125.00
11 thru 20	@125.00
21 thru 26	@125.00

Becomes:

HOLLYWOOD
FUNNY FOLKES
1950–54

27	150.00
28 thru 40	@125.00
41 thru 60	@100.00

FUNNY STOCKING
STUFFER
March, 1985

1	5.00

FUNNY STUFF
Summer, 1944

1 B:3 Mouseketeers Terrific Whatzit	1,500.00
2	750.00
3	400.00
4	400.00
5	400.00
6 thru 10	@300.00
11 thru 20	@250.00
21	175.00
22 C:Superman	600.00
23 thru 30	@200.00
31 thru 78	@150.00
79 July-Aug., 1954.	150.00

Becomes:

DODO AND THE FROG
1954

80 F:Doodles Duck	250.00
81 thru 91	@150.00
92 scarce	200.00

FURY OF FIRESTORM
June, 1982

1 PB,I:Black Bison	7.00
2 PB,V:Black Bison	3.00
3 PB,V:Pied Piper, Killer Frost	2.50
4 PB,A:JLA,Killer Frost	2.50
5 PB,V:Pied Piper	2.50
6 V:Pied Piper	2.50
7 I:Plastique	2.50
8 V:Typhoon	2.50
9 V:Typhoon	2.50
10 V:Hyena	2.50
11 V:Hyena.	2.50
12 PB,V:Hyena	2.50
13 PB,Split	2.50
14 PB,I:Enforcer,A:Multiplex	2.50
15 V:Multiplex	2.50
16 V:Multiplex	2.50
17 I:2000 Committee,Firehawk	2.50
18 I:Tokamak,A:Multiplex	2.50
19 GC,V:Goldenrod	2.50
20 A:Killer Frost	2.50
21 D:Killer Frost	3.00
22 O:Firestorm	3.00
23 I:Bug & Byte	2.50
24 I:Blue Devil,Bug & Byte	2.75
25 I:Silver Deer	2.50
26 V:Black Bison	2.50
27 V:Black Bison	2.50
28 I:Slipknot	2.50
29 I:2000 C'tee,I:Breathtaker	2.50
30 V:2000 Committee	2.50
31 V:2000 Committee	2.50
32 Phantom Stranger	2.50
33 A:Plastique	2.50
34 I:Killer Frost 2	2.50
35 V:K.Frost/Plastique,I:Weasel	2.50
36 V:Killer Frost & Plastique	2.50
37 Not in our Stars but in Ourselves	2.50
38 V:Weasel	2.50
39 V:Weasel	2.50
40 Graduation Day	2.50
41 Crisis	2.50
42 Crisis,A:Firehawk	2.50
43 V:Typhoon	2.50
44 V:Typhoon	2.50
45 V:Multiplex	2.50
46 A:Blue Devil	2.50
47 A:Blue Devil	2.50
48 I:Moonbow	2.50
49 V:Moonbow	2.50
50 W:Ed Raymond	2.50
51 A:King Crusher	2.50
52 A:King Crusher	2.50
53 V:Steel Shadow	2.50
54 I:Lava	2.50
55 Legends,V:World's Luckiest Man	2.50

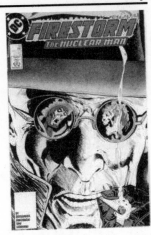

Fury of Firestorm #62
© DC Comics Inc.

56 Legends,A:Hawk.	2.50
57 Due Monday	2.50
58 I:Parasite II	2.50
59 Glasshouse, V:Parasite	2.50
60 Secret behind Hugo's accident.	2.50
61 V:Typhoon	2.50
61a Superman Logo	40.00
62 A:Russian Firestorm	2.50
63 A:Capt.Atom	2.50
64 A:Suicide Squad	2.50
Ann.#1 EC,A:Firehawk, V:Tokamak.	2.50
Ann.#2 An Illustrated Novella.	2.50
Ann.#3 Spark.	2.50
Ann.#4 KG,CS,GC,DG.	2.50

Becomes:

FIRESTORM, THE
NUCLEAR MAN
Nov., 1987

65 A:New Firestorm	2.50
66 A:Green Lantern	2.50
67 Millenium, Week 1	2.50
68 Millenium.	2.50
69 V:Zuggernaut,Stalnivolk USA	2.50
70 V:Flying Dutchman	2.50
71 Trapped in the Timestream.	2.50
72 V:Zuggernaut	2.50
73 V:Stalnivolk & Zuggernaut	2.50
74 Quest for Martin Stein	2.50
75 Return of Martin Stein.	2.50
76 Firestorm & Firehawk vs Brimstone	2.50
77 Firestorm & Firehawk in Africa	2.50
78 Exile From Eden,pt.1	2.50
79 Exile From Eden,pt.2	2.50
80 A:Power Girl,Starman,Invasion x-over.	2.50
81 A:Soyuz,Invasion aftermath	2.50
82 Invasion Aftermath	2.50
83 V:Svarozhich	2.50
84 Souls of Fire	2.50
85 Soul of Fire,N:Firestorm	2.50
86 TMd,Janus Directive #7	2.50
87 TMd.	2.50
88 TMd,E:Air Wave B:Maser	2.50
89 TMd,V:Firehawk,Vandermeer Steel.	2.50
90 TMd,Elemental War #1	2.50
91 TMd,Elemental War #2	2.50
92 TMd,Elemental War #3	2.50
93 TMd,Elemental War concl.	2.50
94 TMd,A:Killer Frost	2.50
95 TMd,V:Captains of Industry	2.50

DC

96 TMd,A:Shango,African God &
   Obatala,Lord o/t White Cloth . . . 2.50
97 TMd,A:Obatala,V:Shango 2.50
98 TMd,A:Masar 2.50
99 TMd,A:Brimstone,PlasmaGiant. . 2.50
100 TMd,AM,V:Brimstone (Firestorm
   back-up story) final issue 3.00
Ann.#5 JLI,Suicide Squad
   I:New Firestorm 2.50

GAMMARAUDERS
1989

1 I:Animal-Warrior Bioborgs 2.25
2 thru 10 . . . . @2.25

Gang Busters #35 © DC Comics, Inc.

GANG BUSTERS
1947–58

1 DBa,Crime Agency 1,400.00
2 DBa 600.00
3 DBa,Fall Guy 400.00
4 DBa,Jailbreak 400.00
5 DBa 400.00
6 DBa 400.00
7 DBa 400.00
8 DBa 400.00
9 DBa,Ph(c) 300.00
10 DBa,Ph(c) 300.00
11 CS,Ph(c) 250.00
12 DBa,CS,Ph(c) 250.00
13 CS,Ph(c) 250.00
14 FF,Ph(c) 500.00
15 CS 200.00
16 CS, Death on Wheels 200.00
17 Dead Man's Beat 500.00
18 CS, Black Ace Gang 175.00
19 DBa,CS,Broadway Squad . . . 175.00
20 CS 175.00
21 thru 25 . . . . @150.00
26 JK 150.00
27 thru 40 . . . . @150.00
41 thru 44 . . . . @125.00
45 Comics Code 125.00
46 thru 50 . . . . @125.00
51 MD 125.00
52 thru 67 . . . . @125.00

GANGLAND
April, 1998

1 (of 4) crime anthology 3.00
2 Platinum Nights 3.00
3 Gang Buff 3.00
4 conclusion 3.00
TPB series rep. 13.00

GEMINI BLOOD
DC/Helix, 1996–97

1 Species: Paratwa, pt.1 . . . . 2.25
2 Species: Paratwa, pt.2 . . . . 2.25
3 Species: Paratwa, pt.3 . . . . 2.50
4 Species: Paratwa, pt.4 . . . . 2.25
5 WSi(c),Species: Paratwa,pt.5 . . . 2.25
6 Species: Paratwa, pt.6 . . . . 2.50
7 BSz, Gillian's secret revealed . . . 2.50
8 Loothka BI-Modal,pt.1 . . . . 2.50
9 Loothka BI-Modal,pt.2 . . . . 2.50

GENESIS
Aug., 1997

1 (of 4) JBy,RoW,JRu,AD,MFm,
   Marvel x-over. 3.00
2 JBy,RoW,JRu,AD,MFm,x-over. . . 3.00
3 JBy,RoW,JRu,AD,MFm,x-over. . . 3.00
4 JBy,RoW,JRu,AD,MFm,concl. . . . 3.00

GHOSTDANCING
DC/Vertigo, 1995
[Mini-Series]

1 I:Snake,Ghost Dancing 2.50
2 Secrets. 2.50
3 I:Father Craft 2.50
4 Coyote prisoner 2.50
5 F:Snot Boy 2.50

GHOSTS
Sept.–Oct., 1971

1 JAp,NC(c),Death's Bride-
   groom! 250.00
2 WW,NC(c),Mission
   Supernatural 125.00
3 TD,NC(c),Death is my Mother . . 90.00
4 GT,NC(c),The Crimson Claw . . . 90.00
5 NC(c),Death, The Pale
   Horseman 90.00
6 NC(c),A Specter Poured
   The Potion 40.00
7 MK(c),Death's Finger Points . . . 40.00
8 NC(c),The Cadaver In
   The Clock 40.00
9 AA,NC(c),The Last Ride
   Of Rosie The Wrecker. 40.00
10 NC(c),A Specter Stalks Saigon. 40.00
11 NC(c),The Devils Lake 25.00
12 NC(c),The Macabre Mummy
   Of Takhem-Ahtem 25.00
13 NC(c),Hell Is One Mile High . . 25.00
14 NC(c),The Bride Wore
   A Shroud 25.00
15 AA,NC(c),The Ghost That
   Wouldn't Die 25.00
16 NC(c),Death's Grinning Face . . 25.00
17 NC(c),Death Held the
   Lantern High 25.00
18 AA,NC(c),Graveyard of
   Vengeance. 25.00
19 AA,NC(c),The Dead Live On . . 25.00
20 NC(c),The Haunting Hussar
   Of West Point 25.00
21 NC(c),The Ghost In The
   Devil's Chair 15.00
22 NC(c),The Haunted Horns
   Of Death 15.00
23 NC(c),Dead Is My Darling! 15.00
24 AA,NC(c),You Too, Will Die. . . . 15.00
25 AA,NC(c),Three Skulls On
   The Zambezi 15.00
26 DP,NC(c),The Freaky Phantom
   Of Watkins Glen 15.00
27 NC(c),Conversation With
   A Corpse 15.00
28 DP,NC(c),Flight Of The
   Lost Phantom 15.00
29 NC(c),The Haunted Lady
   Of Death 15.00

30 NC(c),The Fangs of
   the Phantom 15.00
31 NC(c),Blood On The Moon 15.00
32 NC(c),Phantom Laughed Last . 15.00
33 NC(c),The Hangman of
   Haunted Island 15.00
34 NC(c),Wrath of the Ghost Apes 15.00
35 NC(c),Feud with a Phantom . . . 15.00
36 NC(c),The Boy Who Returned
   From The Gave 15.00
37 LD(c),Fear On Ice 15.00
38 LD(c),Specter In The Surf. 15.00
39 LD(c),The Haunting Hitchhiker 15.00
40 LD(c),The Nightmare That
   Haunted The World 30.00
41 LD(c),Ship of Specters 20.00
42 LD(c),The Spectral Sentries . . . 20.00
43 LD(c),3 Corpses On A Rope . . . 20.00
44 LD(c),The Case of the
   Murdering Specters 20.00
45 LD(c),Bray of the
   Phantom Beast 20.00
46 LD(c),The World's Most
   Famous Phantom 20.00
47 LD(c),Wrath of the
   Restless Specters 20.00
48 DP,LD(c),The Phantom Head . . 20.00
49 The Ghost in the Cellar. 20.00
50 Home Is Where The Grave Is. . 20.00
51 The Ghost Who Would Not Die . 20.00
52 LD(c),Thunderhead Phantom . . 20.00
53 LD(c),Whose Spirit Invades Me 20.00
54 LD(c),The Deadly Dreams
   Of Ernie Caruso. 20.00
55 LD(c),The House That Was
   Built For Haunting 20.00
56 LD(c),The Triumph Of The
   Teen-Age Phantom 20.00
57 LD(c),The Flaming Phantoms
   of Oradour. 20.00
58 LD(c),The Corpse in the Closet 20.00
59 LD(c),That Demon Within Me. . 20.00
60 LD(c),The Spectral Smile
   of Death 10.00
61 LD(c),When Will I Die Again . . . 10.00
62 LD(c),The Phantom Hoaxer!. . . 10.00
63 LD(c),The Burning Bride. 10.00
64 LD(c),Dead Men Do Tell Tales . 10.00
65 LD(c),The Imprisoned Phantom 10.00
66 LD(c),Conversation With A
   Corpse. 10.00
67 LD(c),The Spectral Sword 10.00
68 LD(c),The Phantom of the
   Class of '76 . . . . 9.00
69 LD(c),The Haunted Gondola 9.00
70 LD(c),Haunted Honeymoon 9.00
71 LD(c),The Ghost Nobody Knew . 9.00
72 LD(c),The Ghost of
   Washington Monument 9.00
73 LD(c),The Specter Of The
   Haunted Highway 9.00
74 LD(c),The Gem That Haunted
   the World! 9.00
75 LD(c),The Legend Of The
   Lottie Lowry 9.00
76 LD(c),Two Ghosts of
   Death Row. 9.00
77 LD(c),Ghost, Where Do
   You Hide? 9.00
78 LD(c),The World's Most
   Famous Phantom 9.00
79 LD(c),Lure of the Specter 9.00
80 JO(c),The Winged Specter 9.00
81 LD(c),Unburied Phantom 9.00
82 LD(c),The Ghost Who
   Wouldn't Die 9.00
83 LD(c),Escape From the Haunt
   of the Amazon Specter 9.00
84 LD(c),Torment of the
   Phantom Face 9.00
85 LD(c),The Fiery Phantom
   of Faracutin 9.00

All comics prices listed are for *Near Mint* condition.

86 LD(c),The Ghostly Garden 9.00
87 LD(c),The Phantom Freak 9.00
88 LD(c),Harem In Hell 9.00
89 JKu(c),Came The Specter
   Shrouded In Seaweed. 9.00
90 The Ghost Galleon 9.00
91 LD(c),The Haunted Wheelchair . . 9.00
92 DH(c),Double Vision 9.00
93 MK(c),The Flaming Phantoms
   of Nightmare Alley 9.00
94 LD(c),Great Caesar's Ghost 9.00
95 All The Stage Is A Haunt. 9.00
96 DH(c),Dread of the
   Deadly Domestic 9.00
97 JAp(c),A Very Special Spirit
   A:Spectre. 15.00
98 JAp(c),The Death of a Ghost
   A:Spectre. 15.00
99 EC(c),Till Death Do Us Join
   A:Spectre. 15.00
100 EC&DG(c),The Phantom's
   Final Debt 12.00
101 MK(c),The Haunted Hospital . . 5.00
102 RB&DG(c),The Fine Art
   Of Haunting 10.00
103 RB&DG(c),Visions and
   Vengeance. 10.00
104 LD(c),The First Ghost 10.00
105 JKu(c) 10.00
106 JKu(c) 10.00
107 JKu(c) 10.00
108 JKu(c) 10.00
109 EC(c). 10.00
110 EC&DG(c). 10.00
111 JKu(c) 10.00
112 May, 1982 . . . . 10.00

GIANTKILLER
1999

1 (of 6) 2.50
2 DIB 2.50
3 DIB 2.50
4 DIB,O:Jill 2.50
5 DIB,V:Nox 2.50
6 . . . . 2.50

G.I. COMBAT
Jan., 1957
Prev: Golden Age

44 RH,JKu,The Eagle and
   the Wolves 1,100.00
45 RH,JKu,Fireworks Hill. 500.00
46 JKu,The Long Walk
   To Wansan. 400.00
47 RH, The Walking Weapon . . . 400.00
48 No Fence For A Jet. 400.00
49 Frying Pan Seat 400.00
50 Foxhole Pilot. 400.00
51 RH,The Walking Grenade. . . . 400.00
52 JKu,JKu(c),Call For A Tank . . . 300.00
53 JKu,The Paper Trap 300.00
54 RH,JKu,Sky Tank 300.00
55 Call For A Gunner. 300.00
56 JKu,JKu(c),The D.I.-And the
   Sand Fleas 400.00
57 RH,Live Wire For Easy. 350.00
58 JKu(c),Flying Saddle. 350.00
59 JKu,Hot Corner. 300.00
60 RH,Bazooka Crossroads 300.00
61 JKu(c),The Big Run 275.00
62 RH,JKu,Drop An Inch 275.00
63 MD,JKu(c),Last Stand. 275.00
64 MD,RH,JKu,JKu(c),The
   Silent Jet 275.00
65 JKu,Battle Parade. 275.00
66 MD,The Eagle of Easy
   Company 375.00
67 JKu,I:Tank Killer 375.00
68 JKu,RH,The Rock 1,200.00
69 JKu,RH,The Steel Ribbon. . . 250.00
70 JKu,Bull's-Eye Bridge 250.00

G.I. Combat #56
© DC Comics, Inc.

71 MD,JKu(c),Last Stand. 250.00
72 MD,JKu(c),Ground Fire. 250.00
73 RH,JKu(c),Window War 250.00
74 RH,A Flag For Joey 250.00
75 RH,Dogtag Hill 300.00
76 MD,RH,JKu,Bazooka For
   A Mouse 300.00
77 RH,JKu,H-Hour For A Gunner 300.00
78 MD,RH,JKu(c),Who Cares
   About The Infantry. 300.00
79 JKu,RH,Big Gun-Little Gun. . . 300.00
80 JKu,RH(c),Flying Horsemen . . 300.00
81 Jump For Glory. 250.00
82 IN,Get Off My Back. 250.00
83 Too Tired To Fight 250.00
84 JKu(c),Dog Company
   Is Holding 250.00
85 IN,JKu(c),The T.N.T. Trio 250.00
86 JKu,RH(c),Not Return. 250.00
87 JKu(c),I:Haunted Tank 1,200.00
88 RH,JKu(c),Haunted Tank Vs.
   Ghost Tank 400.00
89 JA,RH,IN,Tank With Wings. . . 250.00
90 JA,IN,RH,Tank Raiders 250.00
91 IN,RH,Tank and the Turtle . . . 250.00
92 JA,IN,The Tank of Doom 250.00
93 RH(c),JA,No-Return Mission . 250.00
94 IN,RH(c),Haunted Tank Vs.
   The Killer Tank. 250.00
95 JA,RH(c),The Ghost of
   the Haunted Tank 250.00
96 JA,RH(c),The Lonesome Tank 250.00
97 IN,RH(c),The Decoy Tank. . . . 250.00
98 JA,RH(c),Trap of Dragon's
   Teeth 250.00
99 JA,JKu,RH(c),Battle of the
   Thirsty Tanks 250.00
100 JA,JKu,Return of the
   Ghost Tank 250.00
101 JA,The Haunted Tank Vs.
   Attila's Battle Tiger. 175.00
102 JKu(c),Haunted Tank
   Battle Window 175.00
103 JKu,JA,RH(c),Rabbit Punch
   For A Tiger. 175.00
104 JA,JKu,RH(c),Blind
   Man's Radar 175.00
105 JA,JKu(c),Time Bomb Tank . 175.00
106 JA,JKu(c),Two-Sided War. . . 175.00
107 JKu(c),The Ghost Pipers . . . 175.00
108 JKu(c),The Wounded
   Won't Wait,I:Sgt.Rock 175.00
109 JKu(c),Battle of the Tank
   Graveyard 175.00

110 IN,JKu(c),Choose Your War . 175.00
111 JA,JKu(c),Death Trap 175.00
112 JA,JKu(c),Ghost Ace. 160.00
113 JKu,RH(c),Tank Fight In
   Death Town 160.00
114 JA,RH(c),O:Haunted Tank. . . 200.00
115 JA,RH(c),MedalsForMayhem 160.00
116 IN,JA,JKu(c),Battle Cry
   For A Dead Man 160.00
117 JA,RH,JKu(c),Tank In
   The Ice Box 250.00
118 IN,JA,RH(c),My Buddy-
   My Enemy 160.00
119 IN,RH(c),Target For
   A Firing Squad. 160.00
120 IN,JA,RH(c),Pull a Tiger'sTail 160.00
121 RH(c),Battle of Two Wars . . 125.00
122 JA,JKu(c),Who Dies Next? . . 125.00
123 IN,RH(c),The Target of Terro 125.00
124 IN,RH(c),Scratch That Tank . 125.00
125 RH(c),Stay Alive-Until Dark. . 125.00
126 JA,RH(c),Tank Umbrella 125.00
127 JA,JKu(c),Mission-Sudden
   Death. 125.00
128 RH(c),The Ghost of
   the Haunted Tank 125.00
129 JA,RH(c),Hold That Town
   For A Dead Man 125.00
130 RH(c),Battle of the Generals 125.00
131 JKu&RH(c),Devil For Dinner. 125.00
132 JA,JKu(c),The Executioner. . 125.00
133 JKu(c),Operation:Death Trap 125.00
134 MD,JKu(c),Desert Holocaust 125.00
135 GE,JKu(c),Death is the Joker 125.00
136 JKu(c),Kill Now-Pay Later. . . 125.00
137 JKu(c),We Can't See 125.00
138 JKu(c),I:The Losers 200.00
139 JKu(c),Corner of Hell 100.00
140 RH,MD,JKu(c),The LastTank 100.00
141 MD,JKu(c),Let Me Live..
   Let Me Die. 50.00
142 RH,JKu(c),Checkpoint-Death . 50.00
143 RH,JKu(c),Iron Horseman . . . 50.00
144 RH,MD,JKu(c),Every
   Man A Fort. 60.00
145 MD,JKu(c),Sand,Sun
   and Death 60.00
146 JKu(c),Move the World 60.00
147 JKu(c),Rebel Tank 60.00
148 IN,JA,JKu(c),The Gold-Plated
   General 60.00
149 JKu(c),Leave The
   Fighting To Us 50.00
150 JKu(c),The Death of the
   Haunted Tank 50.00
151 JKu(c),A Strong Right Arm . . . 50.00
152 JKu(c),Decoy Tank 50.00
153 JKu(c),The Armored Ark 50.00
154 JKu(c),Battle Prize 50.00
155 JKu(c),The Long Journey 25.00
156 JKu(c),Beyond Hell 25.00
157 JKu(c),The Fountain 25.00
158 What Price War. 25.00
159 JKu(c),Mission Dead End 25.00
160 JKu(c),Battle Ghost. 25.00
161 JKu(c),The Day of the Goth . . 25.00
162 JKu(c),The Final Victor 25.00
163 A Crew Divided 25.00
164 Siren Song 25.00
165 JKu(c),Truce,Pathfinder 25.00
166 Enemy From Yesterday 25.00
167 JKu(c),The Finish Line 25.00
168 NA(c),The Breaking Point. . . . 35.00
169 WS(c),The Death of the
   Haunted Tank 25.00
170 Chain of Vengeance 25.00
171 JKu(c),The Man Who
   Killed Jeb Stuart 25.00
172 RH(c),At The Mercy of
   My Foes. 25.00
173 JKu(c),The Final Crash. 25.00
174 JKu(c),Vow To A Dead Foe. . . 25.00

G.I. Combat #164
© DC Comics, Inc.

175 JKu(c),The Captive Tank 25.00
176 JKu(c),A Star Can Cry 25.00
177 JKu(c),The Tank That
Missed D-Day 25.00
178 JKu(c),A Tank Is Born 25.00
179 JKu(c),One Last Charge 25.00
180 JKu(c),The Saints Go
Riding On 25.00
181 JKu(c),The Kidnapped Tank . . 25.00
182 JKu(c),Combat Clock 25.00
183 JKu(c),6 Stallions To
Hell- And Back 25.00
184 JKu(c),Battlefield Bundle . . . 25.00
185 JKu(c),No Taps For A Tank . . . 25.00
186 JKu(c),Souvenir
From A Headhunter 25.00
187 JKu(c),The General
Died Twice 25.00
188 The Devil's Pipers 25.00
189 The Gunner is a Gorilla 25.00
190 The Tiger and The Terrier 25.00
191 Decoy For Death 25.00
192 The General Has Two Faces . 25.00
193 JKu(c),The War That
Had To Wait 25.00
194 GE(c),Blitzkrieg Brain 25.00
195 JKu(c),The War That
Time Forgot 25.00
196 JKu(c),Dead Men Patrol 25.00
197 JKu(c),Battle Ark 25.00
198 JKu(c),The Devil
Rides A Panzer 25.00
199 JKu(c),A Medal From A Ghost 25.00
200 JKu(c),The Tank That Died . . 25.00
201 NA&RH(c),The Rocking
Chair Soldiers 35.00
202 NA&RH(c),Walking Wounded
Don't Cry 35.00
203 JKu(c),To Trap A Tiger 25.00
204 JKu(c),A Winter In Hell 25.00
205 JKu(c),A Gift From
The Emperor 25.00
206 JKu(c),A Tomb For A Tank . . . 25.00
207 JKu(c),Foxhole for a Sherman 25.00
208 JKu(c),Sink That Tank 25.00
209 JKu(c),Ring Of Blood 25.00
210 JKu(c),Tankers Also Bleed . . . 25.00
211 JKu(c),A Nice Day For Killing . 20.00
212 JKu(c),Clay Pigeon Crew 20.00
213 JKu(c),Back Door To War . . . 20.00
214 JKu(c),The Tanker Who
Couldn't Die 20.00
215 JKu(c),Last Stand For Losers . 20.00
216 JKu(c),Ghost Squadron 20.00
217 JKu(c), The Pigeon Spies 20.00

218 JKu(c), 48 Hours to Die 20.00
219 thru 230 . . . . @20.00
231 thru 288 . . . . @20.00

GILGAMESH II
1989
1 JSn,O:Gilgamesh 5.00
2 JSn,V:Nightshadow 4.50
3 JSn,V:Robotic Ninja 4.50
4 JSn,final issue 4.00

GIRLS' LOVE STORIES
1949
1 ATh,EK,Romance 800.00
2 EK 400.00
3 thru 10 . . . . @275.00
11 thru 20 . . . . @200.00
21 EK 150.00
22 thru 83 . . . . @100.00

Girls Romances #8
© DC Comics, Inc.

GIRLS' ROMANCES
1950
1 Ph(c) 800.00
2 ATh,Ph(c) 400.00
3 Ph(c) 275.00
4 thru 6 Ph(c) . . . . @250.00
7 thru 10 . . . . @250.00
11 . . . . 175.00
12 . . . . 175.00
13 ATh(c) 200.00
14 thru 20 . . . . @175.00
21 thru 31 . . . . @150.00
32 thru 50 . . . . @125.00
51 thru 80 . . . . @100.00

GIRL WHO WOULD
BE DEATH, THE
DC/Vertigo, 1998
1 thru 4 F:Plath . . . . @2.50

GODDESS
DC/Vertigo, 1995–96
[Mini-Series]
1 I:Rosie Nolan 4.00
2 Rosie arrested 4.00
3 I:Jenny 4.00
4 CIA Chase 4.00
5 V:Agent Hooks 4.00
6 V:Harry Hooks 4.00
7 Mudhawks Past 4.00
8 finale 4.00
TPB Goddess, GEn, 256-page . . . 20.00

GOLDEN AGE
Elseworld 1993–94
1 PS,F:JSA,All-Star Squadron 8.00
2 PS,I:Dynaman 7.00
3 PS,IR:Mr. Terrific is
Ultra-Humanite 7.00
4 PS,D:Dynaman,Mr. Terrific 6.00
1 Secret Files,48-page(2000) 5.00

GOTHAM CENTRAL
Dec. 2002
1 MLr,F:Gotham Detectives 3.50
2 MLr,cop murdered 3.00
3 MLr,V:Firebug 3.00
4 MLr,V:Firebug 2.50
5 MLr,two cases 2.50
6 MLr,Half a Life,pt.1 . . . . 2.50
7 MLr,Half a Life,pt.2 . . . . 2.50
8 MLr,Half a Life,pt.3 . . . . 2.50
9 MLr,Half a Life,pt.4 . . . . 2.50
10 MLr,Half a Life,pt.5 . . . . 2.50
11 F:Stacy 2.50
12 A sniper strikes 2.50
13 shadow of the Joker 2.50
14 Joker's reign of terror 2.50
15 Joker sniper spree 2.50
16 Sarge and Crowe 2.50
17 Murder of businesswoman 2.50
18 Hot homicide case 2.50
19 Harvey Bullock 2.50
20 Mad Hatter, Penguin 2.50
21 Mad Hatter, Penguin, Harvey . . 2.50
22 High School BB Massacre 2.50
23 War Games tie-in 2.50
24 War Games tie-in 2.50
25 MLr,SGa 2.50
26 MLr(c),F:Catwoman 2.50
27 MLr(c),F:Catwoman 2.50
28 MLr(c) 2.50
29 MLr(c),Keystone Ci ty 2.50
30 MLr(c) 2.50
31 Dr. Alchemy 2.50
32 Robin's body 2.50
33 Robin's body 2.50
34 F:Teen Titans 2.50
35 Batman's not talking 2.50
36 Dead Robin, concl. 2.50
37 A:Captain Marvel 2.50
38 The Spectre? 2.50
39 A Hero fallen 2.50
40 Another officer gone 2.50

GOTHAM GIRLS
Aug., 2002
1 (of 5) F:Catwoman 2.25
2 Catwoman,Batgirl,P.Ivy,H.Quinn . 2.25
3 Poison Ivy, Harley Quinn 2.25
4 Batgirl 2.25
5 Renee Montoya, concl. 2.25

GOTHAM UNDERGROUND
Oct., 2007
1 (of 8) Countdown tie-in 3.00

GREEN ARROW
[Limited Series], 1983
1 TVE,DG,O:Green Arrow 5.00
2 TVE,DG,A:Vertigo 4.00
3 TVE,DG,A:Vertigo 4.00
4 TVE,DG,A:Black Canary 4.00
[Regular Series], 1988–97
1 EH,DG,V:Muncie 5.00
2 EH,DG,V:Muncie 4.00
3 EH,DG,FMc,V:Fyres 4.00
4 EH,DG,FMc,V:Fyres 4.00
5 EH,DG,FMc,Gauntlet 4.00
6 EH,DG,FMc,Gauntlet 4.00
7 EB,DG,A:Black Canary 4.00
8 DG,Alaska 3.50

9 EH,DG,FMc,R:Shado	3.50
10 EH,DG,FMc,A:Shado	3.50
11 EH,DG,FMc,A:Shado	3.50
12 EH,DG,FMc,A:Shado	3.00
13 DJu,DG,FMc,Moving Target	3.00
14 EH,DG,FMc	3.00
15 EH,DG,FMc,Seattle And Die	3.00
16 EH,DG,FMc,Seattle And Die	3.00
17 DJu,DG,FMc,The Horse Man	3.00
18 DJu,DG,FMc,The Horse Man	3.00
19 EH,DG,FMc,A:Hal Jordan	3.00
20 EH,DG,FMc,A:Hal Jordan	3.00
21 DJu,DG,B:Blood of Dragon, A:Shado	4.00
22 DJu,DG,A:Shado	3.00
23 DJu,DG,A:Shado	3.00
24 DJu,DG,E:Blood of Dragon	3.00
25 TVE,Witch Hunt #1	3.00
26 Witch Hunt #2	3.00
27 DJu,DG,FMc,R:Warlord	3.00
28 DJu,DG,FMc,A:Warlord	3.00
29 DJu,DG,FMc,Coyote Tears	3.00
30 DJu,DG,FMc,Coyote Tears	2.50
31 FMc,V:Drug Dealers	2.50
32 FMc,V:Drug Dealers	2.50
33 DJu,FMc,Psychology Issue	2.50
34 DJu,DG,A:Fryes,Arrested	2.50
35 B:Black Arrow Saga,A:Shade	2.50
36 Black Arrow Saga,A:Shade	2.50
37 Black Arrow Saga,A:Shade	2.50
38 E:Black Arrow Saga,A:Shade	2.50
39 DCw,Leaves Seattle	2.50
40 MGr,Spirit Quest,A: Indian Shaman	2.50
41 DCw,I.R.A.	2.50
42 DCw,I.R.A.	2.50
43 DCw,I.R.A.	2.50
44 DCw,Rock'n'Runes,pt.1	2.50
45 Rock'n'Runes,pt.2	2.50
46 DCw,Africa	2.50
47 DCw,V:Trappers	2.50
48 DCw,V:Trappers	2.50
49 V:Trappers	2.50
50 MGr(c),50th Anniv.,R:Seattle	3.00
51 Tanetti's Murder,pt.1	2.50
52 Tanetti's Murder,pt.2	2.50
53 The List,pt.1,A:Fyres	2.50
54 The List,pt.2,A:Fyres	2.50
55 Longbow Hunters tie-in	2.50
56 A:Lt. Cameron	2.50
57 And Not A Drop to Drink,pt.1	2.50
58 And Not A Drop to Drink,pt.2	2.50
59 Predator,pt.1	2.50
60 Predator,pt.2	2.50
61 FS,F:Draft Dodgers	2.50
62 FS	2.50
63 FS,B:Hunt for Red Dragon	2.50
64 FS,Hunt for Red Dragon	2.50
65 MGr(c),Hunt for Red Dragon	2.50
66 MGr(c),E:Hunt for Red Dragon	2.50
67 MGr(c),FS,V:Rockband Killer	2.50
68 MGr(c),FS,BumRap	2.50
69 MGr(c),Reunion Tour #1	2.50
70 Reunion Tour #2	2.50
71 Wild in the Streets #1	2.50
72 MGr(c),Wild in the Streets#2	2.50
73 MGr(c),F:Vietnam Vet	2.50
74 SAP,MGr(c),V:Sniper	2.50
75 MGr(c),A:Speedy Shado, Black Canary	3.00
76 MGr(c),R:Eddie Fyers	2.50
77 MGr(c),A:Eddie Fyers	2.50
78 MGr(c),V:CIA	2.50
79 MGr(c),V:CIA	2.50
80 MGr(c),E:MGr(s),V:CIA	2.50
81 B:CDi(s),JAp,V:Shrapnel, Nuklon	2.50
82 JAp,I:Rival	2.50
83 JAp,V:Yakuza	2.50
84 E:CDi(s),JAp,In Las Vegas	2.50
85 AlG(s),JAp,A:Deathstroke	2.50
86 DgM(s),JAp,A:Catwoman	2.50

Green Arrow #77
© DC Comics Inc.

87 JAp,V:Factory Owner	2.50
88 JAp,A:M.Manhunter,Bl.Beetle	2.50
89 JAp,A:Anarky	2.50
90 Zero Hour	2.50
91 Hitman	2.50
92 Partner attacked	2.50
93 Secrets of Red File	2.50
94 I:Camo Rouge	2.50
95 V:Camo Rouge	2.50
96 I:Slyfox,A:Hal Jordan	3.00
97 Where Angels Fear to Tread	2.50
98 Where Angels Fear to Tread,pt.3, A:Arsenal	2.50
99 Where Angels Fear to Tread	2.50
100 JAp,Angels Fear to Tread	12.00
101 A:Superman,Black Canary	35.00
102 CDi,RbC,Underworld Unleashed tie-in	3.00
103 CDi,RbC,Underworld Unleashed tie-in	3.00
104 CDi,RbC,A:Green Lantern	3.00
105 CDi,RbC,A:Robin	3.00
106 CDi,RbC	2.50
107 CDi,RbC,protects child-king	2.50
108 CDi,A:Thorn	2.50
109 CDi,JAp,BSz in Metropolis	2.50
110 CDi(s),RbC,I:Hatchet, Green Lantern x-over	3.50
111 CDi(s),RbC,I:Hatchet, Green Lantern x-over	3.50
112 CDi(s),RbC	2.50
113 CDi(s),RbC,In the Mongolian wastes	2.50
114 CDi(s) RbC,airplane downed, Final Night tie-in	2.50
115 CDi(s),RbC,IronDeath,pt.1	2.50
116 CDi(s),RbC,IronDeath,pt.2	2.50
117 CDi(s),RbC,IronDeath,pt.3	2.50
118 CDi(s),DBw,RbC,Endangered Species, pt.1	2.50
119 CDi(s),DBw,RbC,Endangered Species, pt.2	2.50
120 CDi(s),RbC,at grandfather's ranch	2.50
121 CDi(s),RbC,V:The Silver Monkey	2.50
122 CDi(s),RbC, at Idaho ranch	2.50
123 CDi(s),JAp,KJ,The Stormbringers, concl.	2.50
124 CDi(s),RbC,V:Milo Armitage	2.50
125 CDi(s),DBw,Green Lantern x-over,pt.1, 48pg	3.50
126 CDi(s),DBw,x-over, pt.3	3.00
127 CDi(s),DBw,to San Francisco	3.00

128 CDi(s),DWb,Russian Mob	3.00
129 CDi,DBw,Jansen prisoner,pt.2	3.00
130 CDi,DBw,	3.00
131 CDi,DBw,F:Crackshot	3.00
132 CDi,DBw,Eddie Fyers returns	3.00
133 CDi,DBw,Eddie Fyers pt.2	3.00
134 CDi,DBw,Brotherhood of the Fist x-over,pt.1	3.00
135 CDi,DBw,Brotherhood of the Fist x-over, concl.	3.00
136 CDi,DBw,Green Pastures,pt.1	3.00
137 CDi(s),A:Superman	15.00
Ann.#1 A:Question,FablesII	4.00
Ann.#2 EH,DG,FMc,A:Question	3.50
Ann.#3 A:Question	3.50
Ann.#4 The Black Alchemist	3.50
Ann.#5 TVE,FS,Eclipso,Batman	3.50
Ann.#6 JBa(c),I:Hook	3.50
Ann.#7 CDi, Year One	4.25
Spec. #0 Return	2.50
Spec.#1,000,000 CDi(s), A:Superman final issue	2.50

GREEN ARROW
Feb., 2001

1 PhH,Quiver,pt.1	15.00
1a 2nd printing	3.00
2 PhH,Quiver,pt.2	8.00
3 PhH,Quiver,pt.3	6.00
4 PhH,Quiver,pt.4,A:JLA	6.00
5 PhH,Quiver,pt.5,A:Batman	6.00
6 PhH,Quiver,pt.6,F:Arsenal	4.00
7 PhH,Quiver,pt.7	4.00
8 PhH,Quiver,pt.8	4.00
9 PhH,Quiver,pt.9	4.00
10 PhH,Quiver,concl.	4.00
11 KSm(s),PhH,rediscovery	3.50
12 KSm(s),PhH,Ollie,Connor	4.00
13 KSm(s),PhH,Oliver & Connor	4.00
14 KSm(s),PhH,Onomatopoeia	4.00
15 KSm(s),PhH,last Smith issue	4.00
16 PhH,Archers Quest,pt.1	5.00
17 PhH,Archers Quest,pt.2	3.50
18 PhH,Archers Quest,pt.3	3.50
19 PhH,Archers Quest,pt.4,F:JLA	3.50
20 PhH,Archers Quest,pt.5	3.50
21 PhH,Archers Quest,pt.6	3.50
22 PhH,V:Count Vertigo	3.00
23 CAd,Urban Knights,pt.1 x-over	3.00
24 CAd,Urban Knights,pt.3 x-over	3.00
25 CAd,Urban Knights,pt.5 x-over	3.00
26 PhH,Straight Shooter,pt.1	2.50
27 PhH,Straight Shooter,pt.2	2.50
28 PhH,Straight Shooter,pt.3	2.50
29 PhH,Straight Shooter,pt.4	2.50
30 PhH,Straight Shooter,pt.5	2.50
31 PhH,Straight Shooter,pt.6	2.50
32 F:Arsenal,Green Arrow II	2.50
33 SMa,F:Superman,Plastic Man	2.50
34 PhH,City Walls,pt.1	2.50
35 PhH,City Walls,pt.2	2.50
36 PhH,City Walls,pt.3	2.50
37 PhH,City Walls,pt.4	2.50
38 PhH,City Walls,pt.5	2.50
39 PhH,City Walls,pt.6	2.50
40 PhH,New Blood,pt.1	2.50
41 PhH,New Blood,pt.2	2.50
42 PhH,New Blood,pt.3	2.50
43 PhH,New Blood, pt.4	5.00
44 PhH,New Blood, pt.5	3.00
45 PhH,New Blood, pt.6	2.50
46 RyR,Team Green road trip	2.50
47 RyR,V:Brick, El Pasan Assassin	2.50
48 RyR,V:Duke of Oil	2.50
49 RyR,V:Drakon	2.50
50 RyR,F:Batman, 40-page	3.50
51 Anarky returns	2.50
52 Heading into the Light	2.50
53 Heading into the Light	2.50
54 Heading into the Light	2.50
55 Heading Into the Light	2.50
56 Heading Into the Light, pt.3	2.50

57 Heading into the Light, concl. . . . 2.50
58 Star City Under Attack 2.50
59 V:Merlyn 2.50
60 SMc,One Year Later 2.50
61 SMc,V:Deathstroke 3.00
62 SMc,V:Deathstroke 3.00
63 SMc,Flesh-eating monsters 3.00
64 SMc,Zombies attack 3.00
65 SMc,Away Game,pt.1 . . . . 3.00
66 SMc,Away Game,pt.2 . . . . 3.00
67 SMc,Deadly mercenaries 3.00
68 SMc,End of Ollie's training 3.00
69 SMc,A:Batman 3.00
70 SMc,A:Batman 3.00
71 SMc,V:Red Hood, A:Batman . . . 3.00
72 SMc,Seeing Red. 3.00
73 SMc,Mayor of Star City 3.00
74 SMc,Secrets revealed. 3.00
75 SMc,Gr. Arrow proposes, 40-pgs.3.50
Spec. Secret Files #1,64-pg. 5.00
GN Green Arrow by Jack Kirby 6.00

GREEN ARROW/ BLACK CANARY
Oct., 2007
1 New team, 40-pgs. 3.50
1a variant (c) (1:10) 3.50
Spec. Wedding Special 4.00

GREEN ARROW LONGBOW HUNTERS
Aug., 1987
1 MGr,N:GreenArrow,I:Shado. 7.00
1a 2nd printing 3.00
2 MGr,Shadow Revealed 5.00
2a 2nd printing 3.00
3 MGr,Tracking Snow 5.00

GREEN ARROW: THE WONDER YEARS
1993
1 MGr,GM,B:New O:Green Arrow . 2.50
2 MGr,GM,I:Brianna Stone 2.50
3 MGr,GM,A:Brianna Stone 2.50
4 MGr,GM,Conclusion 2.50

GREEN ARROW: YEAR ONE
July, 2007
1 (of 6) O:Green Arrow 3.00
2 thru 6 . . . . @3.00

GREEN CANDLES
1995
1 Paradox Mystery,F:John Halting. 6.00
2 F:John Halting 6.00
3 finale 6.00
TPB B&W rep. #1–#3 . . . . 10.00

GREEN LANTERN
[Original Series], Autumn, 1941
1 O:Green Lantern, V:Master of
  Light, Arson in the Slums . 65,000.00
2 V:Baldy,Tycoon's Legacy . 12,000.00
3 War cover 8,500.00
4 Doiby and Green Lantern
  join the Army. 6,500.00
5 V:Nazis and Black
  Prophet,A:General Prophet 4,400.00
6 V:Nordo & Hordes of War Hungry
  Henchmen,Exhile of Exiles,
  A:Shiloh 3,500.00
7 The Wizard of Odds 3,500.00
8 The Lady and Her Jewels,
  A:Hop Harrigan. 3,500.00
9 V:The Whistler, The School
  for Vandals 3,000.00

Green Lantern, Original Series #13
© DC Comics, Inc.

10 V:Vandal Savage,The Man Who
  Wanted the World,O:Vandal
  Savage 3,000.00
11 The Distardly Designs of
  Doiby Dickles' Pals. 2,400.00
12 O:The Gambler 2,400.00
13 A:Angela Van Enters 2,400.00
14 Case of the Crooked Cook . 2,400.00
15 V:Albert Zero, One...Two...
  Three...Stop Thinking 2,400.00
16 V:The Lizard. 2,400.00
17 V:Kid Triangle, Reward for
  Green Lantern 2,400.00
18 V:The Dandy,The Connoisseur
  of Crime, X-mas(c) 2,700.00
19 V:Harpies, Sing a Song of
  Disaster A:Fate. 2,100.00
20 A:Gambler 2,100.00
21 V:The Woodman, The Good
  Humor Man. 1,800.00
22 A:Dapper Dan Crocker. 1,800.00
23 Doiby Dickles Movie
  Ajax Pictures 1,800.00
24 A:Mike Mattson,OnceA Cop. 1,800.00
25 The Diamond Magnet 1,800.00
26 The Scourge of the Sea. . . . 1,800.00
27 V:Sky Pirate 1,800.00
28 The Tricks of the
  Sports Master 1,800.00
29 Meets the Challenge of
  the Harlequin 1,800.00
30 I:Streak the Wonder Dog . . . 1,800.00
31 The Terror of the Talismans . 1,600.00
32 The Case of the
  Astonishing Juggler 1,600.00
33 Crime Goes West 1,600.00
34 Streak meets the Princess. . 1,600.00
35 V:Three-in-One Criminal . . . 1,600.00
36 The Mystery of the
  Missing Messenger 1,900.00
37 A:Sargon 1,900.00
38 DoublePlay,May-June,1949. 1,900.00

GREEN LANTERN
[1st Regular Series], 1960–72, 1976–86
1 GK,O:Green Lantern. 8,700.00
2 GK,I:Qward,Pieface 1,700.00
3 GK,V:Qward 1,000.00
4 GK,Secret of GL Mask. 900.00
5 GK,I:Hector Hammond 900.00
6 GK,I:Tomar-Re. 900.00
7 GK,I&O:Sinestro 700.00
8 GK,1st Story in 5700 A.D. 600.00
9 GK,A:Sinestro 600.00

10 GK,O:Green Lantern's Oath 2,000.00
11 GK,V:Sinestro 550.00
12 GK,Sinestro,I:Dr.Polaris 550.00
13 GK,A:Flash,Sinestro 750.00
14 GK,I&O:Sonar,1st Jordan
  Brothers story 500.00
15 GK,Zero Hour story. 500.00
16 GK,MA,I:Star Saphire,
  O:Abin Sur. 500.00
17 GK,V:Sinestro 500.00
18 GK. 500.00
19 GK,A:Sonar. 500.00
20 GK,A:Flash 500.00
21 GK,O:Dr.Polaris 350.00
22 GK,A:Hector Hammond,Jordan
  Brothers story 350.00
23 GK,I:Tattooed Man 350.00
24 GK,O:Shark. 350.00
25 GK,V:Sonar,HectorHammond. 350.00
26 GK,A:Star Sapphire 350.00
27 GK. 350.00
28 GK,I:Goldface 350.00
29 GK,I:Black Hand 350.00
30 GK,I:Katma Tui 350.00
31 GK,Jordan brothers story 300.00
32 GK. 300.00
33 GK,V:Dr. Light. 300.00
34 GK,V:Hector Hammond 300.00
35 GK,I:Aerialist. 300.00
36 GK. 300.00
37 GK,I:Evil Star 300.00
38 GK,A:Tomar-Re. 300.00
39 GK,V:Black Hand 300.00
40 GK,O:Guardians,A:Golden
  Age Green Lantern. 1,000.00
41 GK,A:Star Sapphire 200.00
42 GK,A:Zatanna 200.00
43 GK,A:Major Disaster 200.00
44 GK,A:Evil Star 200.00
45 GK,I:Prince Peril,A:Golden
  Age Green Lantern 350.00
46 GK,V:Dr.Polaris 200.00
47 GK,5700 A.D. V:Dr.Polaris . . . 200.00
48 GK,I:Goldface 200.00
49 GK,I:Dazzler 200.00
50 GK,V:Thraxon the Powerful . . 200.00
51 GK,Green Lantern's Evil
  Alter-ego 150.00
52 GK,A:Golden Age Green
  Lantern Sinestro 150.00
53 GK,CI,Jordon brothers story . . 150.00
54 GK,Menace in the Iron Lung. . 150.00
55 GK,Cosmic Enemy #1 . . . . . . 150.00
56 GK. 150.00
57 GK,V:Major Disaster 150.00
58 GK,Perils of the Powerless
  Green Lantern 150.00
59 GK,I:Guy Gardner(imaginary
  story) 375.00
60 GK,I:Lamplighter. 125.00
61 GK,A:Gold.Age Gr.Lantern . . 125.00
62 Steel Small,Rob Big 125.00
63 NA(c),This is the Way the
  World Ends 125.00
64 MSy,We Vow Death to Green
  Lantern 125.00
65 MSy,Dry up and Die 125.00
66 MSy,5700 AD story 125.00
67 DD,The First Green Lantern . . 125.00
68 GK,I Wonder Where The
  Yellow Went?. 125.00
69 GK,WW,If Earth Fails the
  Test.. It Means War 125.00
70 GK,A Funny Thing Happened
  on the way to Earth 125.00
71 GK,DD,MA,Jordan brothers . . 100.00
72 GK,Phantom o/t SpaceOpera. 100.00
73 GK,MA,A:Star Sapphire,
  Sinestro 100.00
74 GK,MA,A:Star Sapphire,
  Sinestro 100.00
75 GK,Qward. 100.00

Green Lantern, 1st Series #12
© DC Comics, Inc.

76 NA,Gr.Lantern & Gr.Arrow
  team-up begins 600.00
77 NA,Journey to Desolation 150.00
78 NA,A:Black Canary,A Kind of
  Loving..A Way to Death. 125.00
79 NA,DA,A:Black Canary,Ulysses
  Star is Still Alive. 125.00
80 NA,DG,Even an Immortal
  can die. 125.00
81 NA,DG,A:Black Canary,Death
  be my Destiny 125.00
82 NA,DG,A:Black Canary,
  V:Sinestro,(BWr 1 page) 125.00
83 NA,DG,A:BlackCanary,Gr.Lantern
  reveals I.D. to Carol Ferris . . 125.00
84 NA,BWr,V:Black Hand 125.00
85 NA,Speedy on Drugs,pt.1,
  rep.Green Lantern #1 . . . . . . 150.00
86 NA,DG,Speedy on Drugs,pt.2,
  ATh(rep)Golden Age G.L. . . . 150.00
87 NA,DG,I:John Stewart,
  2nd Guy Gardner app. 125.00
88 all reprints. 75.00
89 NA,And Through Him Save
  the World 125.00
90 MGr,New Gr.Lantern rings 50.00
91 MGr,V:Sinestro 25.00
92 MGr,V:Sinestro 25.00
93 MGr,TA,War Against the
  World Builders. 25.00
94 MGr,TA,DG,Green Arrow
  Assassin,pt.1 . . . . 25.00
95 MGr,Gr.Arrow Assassin,pt.2 . . . 25.00
96 MGr,A:Katma Tui 25.00
97 MGr,V:Mocker. 25.00
98 MGr,V:Mocker 25.00
99 MGr,V:Mocker 25.00
100 MGr,AS,I:Air Wave 45.00
101 MGr,A:Green Arrow. 30.00
102 AS,A:Green Arrow. 15.00
103 AS,Earth-Asylum for an Alien . . 15.00
104 AS,A:Air Wave 15.00
105 AS,Thunder Doom 15.00
106 MGr,Panic..In High Places
  & Low 15.00
107 AS,Green Lantern Corp.story . . 15.00
108 MGr,BU:G.A.Green Lantern,
  V:Replikon 20.00
109 MGr,Replicon#2,GA.GL.#2 . . . 15.00
110 MGr,GA.GL.#3 . . . . 15.00
111 AS,O:Green Lantern,
  A:G.A.Green Lantern. 20.00
112 AS,O&A:G.A. Green Lantern. . 30.00
113 AS,Christmas story 15.00
114 AS,I:Crumbler 15.00

115 AS,V:Crumbler. 15.00
116 Guy Gardner as Gr.Lantern . . 50.00
117 JSon,I:KariLimbo,V:Prof.Ojo . . 12.00
118 AS,V:Prof.Ojo 12.00
119 AS,G.L.& G.A.solo storys. . . . 12.00
120 DH,A:Kari,V:El Espectro. 6.00
121 DH,V:El Espectro 6.00
122 DH,A:Guy Gardner,Superman 10.00
123 JSon,DG,E:Green Lantern/Green
  Arrow T.U.,A:G.Gardner,
  V:Sinestro 12.00
124 JSon,V:Sinestro 6.00
125 JSon,FMc,V:Sinestro 6.00
126 JSon,FMc,V:Shark 6.00
127 JSon,FMc,V:Goldface 6.00
128 JSon,V:Goldface 6.00
129 JSon,V:Star Sapphire 6.00
130 JSon,FMc,A:Sonar,B:Tales of the
  Green Lantern Corps. 6.00
131 JSon,AS,V:Evil Star 6.00
132 JSon,AS,E:Tales of GL Corps
  B:B.U.Adam Strange 6.00
133 JSon,V:Dr.Polaris 5.00
134 JSon,V:Dr.Polaris 5.00
135 JSon,V:Dr.Polaris 5.00
136 JSon,A:Space Ranger,
  Adam Strange 5.00
137 JSon,CI,MA,I:Citadel,A:Space
  Ranger,A.Strange 5.00
138 JSon,A&O:Eclipso. 6.00
139 JSon,V:Eclipso 5.00
140 JSon,I:Congressman Block
  Adam Strange 5.00
141 JSon,I:OmegaMen. 7.00
142 JSon,A:OmegaMen. 6.00
143 JSon,A:OmegaMen. 6.00
144 JSon,D:Tattooed Man,Adam
  Strange 5.00
145 JSon,V:Goldface 5.00
146 JSon,CI,V:Goldface
  E:B.U.Adam Strange 5.00
147 JSon,CI,V:Goldface 5.00
148 JSon,DN,DA,V:Quardians. 5.00
149 JSon,A:GL.Corps 5.00
150 JSon,anniversary 6.00
151 JSon,GL.Exiled in space. 5.00
152 JSon,CI,GL Exile #2 . . . . 5.00
153 JSon,CI,Gr.Lantern Exile #3 . . 5.00
154 JSon,Gr.Lantern Exile #4 . . . . . 5.00
155 JSon,Gr.Lantern Exile #5 . . . . . 5.00
156 GK,Gr.Lantern Exile #6 . . . . . . 5.00
157 KP,IN,Gr.Lantern Exile #7 . . . . 5.00
158 KP,IN,Gr.Lantern Exile #8 . . . . 5.00
159 KP,Gr.Lantern Exile #9 . . . . . . 5.00
160 KP,Gr.Lantern Exile #10 . . . . . 5.00
161 KP,A:Omega Men,Exile #11 . . . 5.00
162 KP,Gr.Lantern Exile #12 . . . . . 6.00
163 KP,Gr.Lantern Exile #13 . . . . . 6.00
164 KP,A:Myrwhidden,Exile #14 . . . 5.00
165 KP,A:John Stewart & Gr.Arrow
  Green Lantern Exile #15 . . . . . 5.00
166 GT,FMc,DGi,Exile #16 . . . . 5.00
167 GT,FMc,G.L.Exile #17 . . . . 5.00
168 GT,FMc,G.L. Exile #18 . . . . . . 5.00
169 Green Lantern Exile #19. . . . . . 5.00
170 GT,MSy,GreenLanternCorps. . . 5.00
171 ATh,TA,DGb,Green Lantern
  Exile #20 . . . . 5.00
172 DGb,E:Gr.Lant.Exile. 5.00
173 DGb,I:Javelin,A:Congressman
  Bloch 5.00
174 DGb,V:Javelin. 4.50
175 DGb,A:Flash 4.50
176 DGb,V:The Shark 4.50
177 DGb,rep. Gr.Lant #128 . . . . . . 4.50
178 DGb,A:Monitor,V:Demolition
  Team 4.50
179 DGb,I:Predator 4.50
180 DGb,A:JLA 4.50
181 DGi,Hal Jordan quits as Green
  Lantern 5.00

182 DGi,John Stewart takes over
  V:Major Disaster 10.00
183 DGi,V:Major Disaster 3.50
184 DGb,Rep. Gr.Lant. #59. . . . . . 4.00
185 DGi,DH,V:Eclipso 5.00
186 DGi,V:Eclipso 4.00
187 BWi,John Stewart meets
  Katma Tui 3.50
188 JSon,C:GrArrow,V:Sonar,John
  Stewart reveals I.D. to world . . . 7.00
189 JSon,V:Sonar 3.50
190 JSon,A:Green Arrow/Black
  Canary,Guy Gardner 3.50
191 JSon,IR:Predator is Star
  Sapphire 3.50
192 JSon,O:Star Sapphire. 3.50
193 JSon,V:Replikon,A:G.Gardner . 3.50
194 JSon,Crisis,R:G.Gardner. 6.00
195 JSon,Guy Gardner as Green
  Lantern,develops attitude 12.00
196 JSon,V:Shark,Hal Jordan
  regains ring 4.00
197 JSon,V:Shark,Sonar,
  Goldface 4.00
198 JSon,D:Tomar-Re,Hal returns as
  Green Lantern,(double size) . . . 6.00
199 JSon,V:Star Sapphire 3.50
200 JSon,final Gr.Lantern issue. . . . 5.00
Becomes:

GREEN LANTERN
CORPS
1986–88

201 JSon,I:NewGr.LantCorps,V:Star
  Sapphire, Sonar, Dr.Polaris. . . . 3.50
202 JSon,set up headquarters. 3.50
203 JSon,tribute to Disney. 3.50
204 JSon,Arisia reaches puberty. . . 3.50
205 JSon,V:Black Hand. 3.50
206 JSon,V:Black Hand. 3.00
207 JSon, Legends crossover 3.00
208 JSon,I:Rocket Red Brigade,
  Green Lanterns in Russia#1 . . . 3.00
209 JSon,In Russia #2. . . . . 3.00
210 JSon,In Russia #3. . . . . 3.00
211 JSon,John Stewart proposes
  to Katma Tui 3.00
212 JSon,W:J.Stewart&KatmaTui . . 3.00
213 JSon,For Want of a Male 3.00
214 IG,5700 A.D. Story 3.00
215 IG,Salaak and Chip quit 3.00
216 IG,V:Carl 3.00
217 JSon,V:Sinestro 3.00

Green Lantern Corps #220
© DC Comics, Inc.

218 BWg,V:Sinestro. 3.00
219 BWg,V:Sinestro. 3.00
220 JSon,Millennium,pt.3. . . . . 3.00
221 JSon,Millennium 3.00
222 JSon,V:Sinestro. 3.00
223 GK,V:Sinestro. 3.00
224 GK,V:Sinestro. 3.00
Ann.#1 GK 3.00
Ann.#2 JSa,BWg,S:AnM 3.50
Ann.#3 JBy,JL,JR. 3.00
Spec.#1 A:Superman. 3.00
Spec.#2 MBr,RT,V:Seeker 3.00
TPB rep.#84-#87,#89,Flash
  #217-#219 . . . . 13.00
TPB rep. reprints of #1-#7 . . . . . . 9.00

Green Lantern 2nd Series #3
© DC Comics, Inc.

GREEN LANTERN

[2nd Regular Series], 1990
1 PB,A:Hal Jordan,John Stuart,
  Guy Gardner 5.00
2 PB,A:Tattooed Man 4.50
3 PB,Jordan vs.Gardner. 4.00
4 PB,Vanishing Cities 4.00
5 PB Return to OA 4.00
6 PB 3GL'sCaptive 4.00
7 PB R:Guardians. 4.00
8 PB R:Guardians. 4.00
9 JSon,G.Gardner,pt.1 . . . . 4.00
10 JSon,G.Gardner,pt.2 . . . . 4.00
11 JSon,G.Gardner,pt.3 . . . . 4.00
12 JSon,G.Gardner,pt.4 . . . . 4.00
13 Jordan,Gardner,Stuart(giant) . . . 4.00
14 PB,Mosaic,pt.1 . . . . 4.00
15 RT,Mosaic,pt.2 . . . . 4.00
16 MBr,RT,Mosaic,pt.3 . . . . 4.00
17 MBr,RT,Mosaic,pt.4 . . . . 4.00
18 JSon,JRu,G.Gardner,
  A:Goldface. 4.00
19 MBr,PB,JSon,A:All Four G.L.'s,
  O:Alan Scott,A:Doiby Dickles
  (D.Size-50th Ann.Iss.) 5.00
20 PB,RT,Hal Jordan G.L. Corp
  story begins, A:Flicker 3.00
21 PB,RT,G.L. Corp.,pt.2,
  V:Flicker. 3.00
22 PB,RT,G.L. Corp.,pt.3,
  R:Star Sapphire 3.00
23 PB,RT,V:Star Sapphire,
  A:John Stuart. 3.00
24 PB,RT,V:Star Sapphire 3.00
25 MBr,JSon,RT,Hal Vs.Guy,
  A:JLA. 3.00
26 MBr,V:Evil Star,Starlings 3.00

27 MBr,V:Evil Star,Starlings 3.00
28 MBr,V:Evil Star,Starlings 3.00
29 MBr,RT,R:Olivia Reynolds 3.00
30 MBr,RT,Gorilla Warfare#1 . . . . . 3.00
31 MBr,RT,Gorilla Warfare#3 . . . . . 3.00
32 RT(i),A:Floro,Arisia 3.00
33 MBr,RT,Third Law#1,
  A;New Guardians 3.00
34 MBr,RT,Third Law#2,I:Entropy . . 3.00
35 MBr,RT,Third Law#3,V:Entropy. . 3.00
36 V:Dr.Light 3.00
37 MBg,RT,A:Guy Gardner 3.00
38 MBr,RT,A:Adam Strange. 3.00
39 MBr,RT,A:Adam Strange. 3.00
40 RT(i),A:Darkstar,
  V:Reverse Flash 3.00
41 MBr,RT,V:Predator,
  C:Deathstroke 3.00
42 MBr,RT,V:Predator,
  Deathstroke. 3.00
43 RT(i),A:Itty. 3.00
44 RT(i),Trinity#2,A:L.E.G.I.O.N. . . 3.00
45 GeH,Trinity#5,A:L.E.G.I.O.N.,
  Darkstars 3.00
46 MBr,A:All Supermen,
  V:Mongul 8.00
47 A:Green Arrow 6.00
48 KM(c),B:Emerald Twilight,I:Kyle
  Rayner (Last Green Lantern) . 10.00
49 KM(c),GJ(s),A:Sinestro. 9.00
50 KM(c),GJ(s),D:Sinestro,Kiliwog,
  Guardians,I:Last Green
  Lantern (in Costume). 10.00
51 V:Ohm,A:Mongul. 6.00
52 V:Mongul 4.00
53 A:Superman,V:Mongul 4.00
54 D:Alex,V:Major Force 4.00
55 Zero Hour,A:Alan Scott,
  V:Major Force 4.00
56 Green Lantern and ring 3.50
57 Psimon 3.50
58 Donna Troy,Felix Faust. 3.50
59 V:Dr. Polaris 3.50
60 Capital Punishment,pt.3 . . . . . . 3.50
61 V:Kalibak,A:Darkstar. 3.50
62 V:Duality,R:Ganthet 3.50
63 Parallax View: The Resurrection
  of Hal Jordan,pt.1 . . . . 3.00
64 Parallax View,pt.2,A:Superman,
  Flash,V:Parallax 3.00
65 Siege of ZiCharan,pt.2 . . . . 3.00
66 V:Sonar 3.00
67 A:Flash,V:Sonar 3.00
68 RMz,RT,Underworld
  Unleashed tie-in 3.00
69 RMz,RT,Underworld
  Unleashed tie-in 3.00
70 RMz,RT,A:Supergirl 3.00
71 RMz,RT,Hero Quest,pt.1. . . . . . 3.00
72 RMz,RT,Hero Quest,pt.2. . . . . . 3.00
73 RMz,RT,Hero Quest,pt.3. . . . . . 3.00
74 RMz,RT,A:Adam Strange,
  V:Grayven. 3.00
75 A:Adam Strange 3.00
76 Green Arrow x-over. 3.00
77 Green Arrow x-over. 3.00
78 RMz(s),A Beginning 3.00
79 V:Sonar 3.00
80 RMz(s),JWi,MGy,V:Dr. Light,
  Final Night tie-in 3.00
81 RMz(s),DBk,RT,Memorial for
  Hal Jordan 6.00
81a deluxe edition + extra stories,
  foil cover on cardstock 9.00
82 RMz(s),TGb,RT,F:Kyle Rayner,
  Alan Scott, Guy Gardner &
  John Stewart 3.00
83 RMz,Retribution,pt.1 . . . . 3.00
84 Retribution, pt.2 . . . . 3.00
85 Retribution, concl. 3.00
86 RMz,JJ,RT,A:Jade, V:Obsidian . . 3.00

87 RMz,TGb,RT,A:Martian
  Manhunter, vs. Alien Invasion . . 3.00
88 RMz(s),DBk,TA,A:Donna Troy,
  Visit Kyle's Mom 3.00
89 RM(s),TA,V:Machine Messiah . . 3.00
90 RM(s),Why did Kyle Rayner
  become Green Lantern 3.00
91 RMz(s),DBk,TA,V:Desaad. 3.00
92 RMz(s),DBk,TA,A:Green Arrow,
  x-over. 3.00
93 RMz(s),DBk,TA,F:Deadman . . . 3.00
94 RMz(s),PaP,TA,F:Superboy . . . 3.00
95 RMz(s),JSn,TA, deep space . . . 3.00
96 RMz(s) 3.00
97 RMz(s),MMK,TA,V:Grayven . . . 3.00
98 RMz,DBk,TA,Future Shock,pt.1 . 3.00
99 RMz,DBk,TA,Future Shock,pt.2 . 4.50
100 RMz,DBk,AT,Kyle Rayner and
  Hal Jordan,V:Sinestro, 48pg . . 6.00
100a deluxe edition 4.00
101 RMz(s),JJ,BWi,Emerald
  Knights,pt.1, bi-weekly 4.00
102 RMz(s),PaP,TA,Emerald
  Knights,pt.2, bi-weekly 4.00
103 RMz(s),JJ,BWi,Emerald
  Knights,pt.3, bi-weekly 4.00
104 RMz(s),JJ,BWi,Greener Pastures
  x-over, concl., Emerald
  Knights,pt.4, bi-weekly 4.00
105 RMz(s),JJ,SEa,BWi,Emerald
  Knights,pt.5, bi-weekly 4.00
106 RMz(s),PaP,TA,Emerald
  Knights,concl. 4.00
107 RMz(s),TA,Emerald Knights
  aftermath 2.50
108 DBk,TA,A:Wonder Woman 2.50
109 RMz(s),PaP,TA 2.50
110 RMz(s),TA,A:Green Arrow. 2.50
111 RMz(s),TA,DBk,V:Fatality 2.50
112 RMz(s),TA,DBk,back to Earth . . 2.50
113 RMz(s),TA,DBk,Burning
  in Effigy,pt.1 . . . . 2.50
114 RMz(s),TA,DBk,Burning
  in Effigy,pt.2 . . . . 2.50
115 DJu(s),A:Plastic Man &
  Booster Gold, pt.1 . . . . 2.50
116 DJu(s),A:Plastic Man &
  Booster Gold, pt.1 . . . . 2.50
117 RMz(s),DBk,TA,R:Donna Troy . 2.50
118 RMz(s),DBk,TA,Day of
  Judgment x-over 2.50
119 RMz,DBk,CaS,Day of
  Judgment aftermath 9.00
120 RMz,DBk,CaS. 2.50

Green Lantern 2nd Series #57
© DC Comics, Inc.

121 RMz,DBk,CaS. 2.50	
122 RMz,DBk,CaS. 2.50	
123 RMz,DBk,V:Controllers 2.50	
124 RMz,DBk,V:Controllers 2.50	
125 RMz,Unmooning secrets 2.50	
126 Goes undercover 2.50	
127 F:Effigy & Killer Frost 2.50	
128 F:Arsenal. 2.50	
129 DBk,ASm,V:Manhuters 2.50	
130 DBk,ASm,V:Manhunters 2.50	
131 DBk,ASm,V:Manhunters 2.50	
132 DBk,While Rome Burned,pt.1 . . 2.50	
133 DBk,MBr,Rome Burned,pt.2 . . . 2.50	
134 DBk,While Rome Burned,pt.3 . . 2.50	
135 DBk,While Rome Burned,pt.4 . . 2.50	
136 DBk,While Rome Burned,pt.5 . . 2.50	
137 DBk,Friends & Lovers 2.50	
138 DBk,Away From Home,pt.1 . . . 2.50	
139 DBk,Away From Home,pt.2 . . . 2.50	
140 DBk,A:Alan Scott 2.50	
141 DBk,A:Jade,V:arsonist 2.50	
142 V:Inferno 2.50	
143 JLe(c),Joker:Last Laugh,tie-in . . . 2.50	
144 Battle to control his powers . . . 2.50	
145 V:Nero. 7.00	
146 incredible metamorphosis 6.00	
147 F:John Stewart 2.50	
148 A:Superman,R:Jade 2.50	
149 F:JLA. 2.50	
150 End of Ion,48-pg. 5.00	
151 JLe(c),Hand of God,aftermath . 2.50	
152 RbC,uncontrollable madness . . . 2.50	
153 JLe(c),high school reunion . . . 2.50	
154 JLe&SW(c),attacked 2.50	
155 JLe&SW(c),A:Flash,JLA 2.50	
156 John Stewart back,A:Sentinel. . 2.50	
157 Girl Talk 2.50	
158 industrialist nomads 2.50	
159 Boar Beasts 2.50	
160 Child Guardians 2.50	
161 V:Amazon 2.50	
162 CAd,Urban Knights,pt.2 x-over. 2.50	
163 CAd,Urban Knights,pt.4 x-over. 2.50	
164 CAd,Urban Knights,pt.6 x-over. 2.50	
165 RBr,A Tiny Spark. 2.50	
166 RBr,The Blind,pt.1. . . . . 2.50	
167 RBr,The Blind,pt.2. . . . . 2.50	
168 RBr 2.50	
169 RBr,Kilowog's soul 2.50	
170 RBr 2.50	
171 Wanted, pt.1 . . . . 2.50	
172 kidnappers 2.50	
173 V:Weapons of Qward. 2.50	
174 V:Black Circle 2.50	
175 Qwardians,48-pg. 3.50	
176 LRs,RyR,Homecoming,pt.1 . . 4.00	
177 LRs,RyR,Homecoming,pt.2 . . 4.00	
178 LRs,RyR,Homecoming,pt.3 . . 4.00	
179 LRs,RyR,Homecoming,pt.4 . . 4.00	
180 LRs,RyR,Homecoming,pt.5 . . 4.00	
181 LRs,RyR,Homecoming,pt.6 . . 4.00	
Ann.#1 Eclipso,V:Star Sapphire . . 4.00	
Ann.#1 80pg, rep. 5.00	
Ann.#2 Bloodlines#7,I:Nightblade . 4.00	
Ann.#3 Elseworlds Story 3.50	
Ann.#4 Year One story. 4.00	
Ann.#5 Legends o/t Dead Earth . . 3.50	
Ann.#6 RMz(s),JJ,Low,Pulp	
Heroes, 64pg. 4.50	
Ann.#7 SV,RLm,Clv,BWr,Ghosts . . 3.50	
Ann.#8 MCa,AAd(c),JLApe:Gorilla	
Warfare 3.50	
Ann.#9 Planet DC 4.00	
Spec.#1,000,000 RMz(s),BHi,PNe . 2.50	
Spec. 3-D #1 V:Dr. Light 4.00	
Spec.#1 Our Worlds at War(2001) . 3.00	
Secret Files #1. . . . . 5.00	
Secret Files Spec.#2 . . . . 5.00	
Secret Files #3, 48-pg.. . . . . 5.00	
Green Lantern Plus, 1-shot RMz(s),	
F:The Ray,V:Dr. Polaris 3.00	

Green Lantern/Silver Surfer, 1-shot
DC/Marvel RMz,TA A:Thanos
   vs. Parallax 5.00
Green Lantern Gallery, 1 one-shot . 3.50
Green Lantern: Ganthet's Tale,
   1-shot, JBy,O:Guardians 7.00
Giant #1 80-page 5.50
Giant #2 80-page 5.50
Giant #3 80-page 6.00
GN Ganthet's Tale, JBy 6.00
GN Green Lantern/Superman:
   Legends of the Green Flame . . 6.00
GN 1001 Emerald Nights(2001) . . . 7.00
GN Brightest Day/Blackest Night. . . 6.00

GREEN LANTERN
May, 2005

1 F:Hal Jordan, No Fear,40-page. . 3.50
2 No Fear, pt.2 . . . . 3.00
3 No Fear, pt.3 . . . . 3.00
4 F:Gilowog. 3.00
5 V:Shark 3.00
6 V:Black Hand 3.00
7 A:Green Arrow 3.00
8 A Perfect Life, pt.1 . . . . 3.00
9 A Perfect Life, pt.2, A:Batman . . . 3.00
10 One Year Later 3.00
11 Revenge of the Green Lanterns . 3.00
12 Revenge of the Green Lanterns . 3.00
13 Wanted: Hal Jordan, pt.1 . . . . . 3.00
14 Wanted: Hal Jordan, pt.2 . . . . . 3.00
15 Wanted: Hal Jordan, pt.3 . . . . . 3.00
16 Wanted: Hal Jordan, pt.4 . . . . . 3.00
17 Wanted: Hal Jordan, concl.. . . . 3.00
18 Mystery of Star Sapphire 3.00
19 Mystery of Star Sapphire 3.00
20 Mystery of Star Sapphire 3.00
21 Sinestro Corps, pt.1 . . . . 3.00
21a variant (c) (1:10) 3.00
22 Sinestro Corps, pt.2 . . . . 3.00
23 Sinestro Corps War. 3.00
24 Sinestro Corps War. 3.00
Spec. Sinestro Corps Special #1 . . 5.00
Secret Files 2005, 48-page 5.00

GREEN LANTERN & SENTINEL: HEART OF DARKNESS
Feb., 1998

1 (of 3) RMz(s),PaP,DDv 3.00
2 RMz(s),PaP,DDv 3.00
3 RMz(s),PaP,DDv 3.00

GREEN LANTERN: CIRCLE OF FIRE
Aug., 2000

1 (of 2) NBy,64-pg. x-over 5.00
2 48-pg.x-over concl. 5.00
Spec.Gr.Lant.: Adam Strange #1 . . 2.50
Spec.Gr.Lant.: The Atom #1. . . . . 2.50
Spec.Gr.Lant.: Firestorm #1. . . . . 2.50
Spec.Gr.Lant.: Green Lantern #1. . 2.50
Spec.Gr.Lant.: Power Girl #1 . . . . 2.50

GREEN LANTERN CORPS
June, 2006

1 DGb 3.00
2 thru 6 DGb . . . . @3.00
7 Dark Side of the Green, pt.1 . . . 3.00
8 Dark Side of the Green, pt.2 . . . 3.00
9 Dark Side of the Green, pt.3 . . . 3.00
10 Lantern vs. Lantern. 3.00
11 Children of the White Lobe . . . 3.00
12 Refuge on Mogo. 3.00
13 Mogo's forests. 3.00
14 Mogo under fire. 3.00
15 The Battle of Mogo 3.00
16 Sinestro Corps War. 3.00
17 Sinestro Corps War. 3.00

Green Lantern Corps Quarterly #5
© DC Comics Inc.

GREEN LANTERN CORPS QUARTERLY
1992–94

1 DAb,JSon,FH,PG,MBr,F:Alan
   Scott G'nort 3.00
2 DAb,JSon,PG,AG,Alan Scott 2.75
3 DAb,RT,F:Alan Scott,G'Nort 2.75
4 TA,AG(i),F:H.Jordan, G'Nort 2.75
5 F:Alan Scott,I:Adam. 2.75
6 JBa,TC,F:Alan Scott 3.25
7 Halloween Issue 3.25
8 GeH,SHa,final issue 3.25

GREEN LANTERN CORPS: RECHARGE
Sept., 2005

1 (of 5) 40-page 3.50
2 thru 5 . . . . @3.00
TPB Recharge 13.00

GREEN LANTERN: DRAGON LORD
April, 2001

1 (of 3) PG, 48-page 5.00
2 PG, 48-page. 5.00
3 PG, 48-page. 5.00

GREEN LANTERN: EMERALD DAWN
[1st Limited Series], 1989–90

1 MBr,RT,I:Mod.Age.Gr.Lantern . . . 5.00
2 MBr,RT,I:Legion (not group) 4.00
3 MBr,RT,V:Legion 3.00
4 MBr,RT,A:Green Lantern Corps.. 3.00
5 MBr,RT,V:Legion 3.00
6 MBr,RT,V:Legion 3.00
TPB rep#1–#6. . . . . 5.50

[2nd Limited Series], 1991

1 MBr,A:Sinestro,Guy Gardner. . . . 2.00
2 MBr,RT,V:Alien Aliance 2.00
3 MBr,RT,Sinestro's Home Planet . 2.00
4 MBr,RT,Korugar Revolt 2.00
5 MBr,RT,A:G.Gardner 2.00
6 MBr,RT, Trial of Sinestro. 2.00

GREEN LANTERN: EVIL'S MIGHT
Aug., 2002

1 (of 3) HC, Elseworlds, 48-pg. . . . 6.00

2 HC,F:Kyle Rayner 6.00
3 HC,concl. 6.00

GREEN LANTERN/ GREEN ARROW
1983–84

1 NA rep. 5.00
2 thru 7 NA,DG rep. . . . . @4.00
TPB Roadback. 9.00
TPB Traveling Heroes,Vol.1 . . . . . 13.00
TPB Traveling Heroes, Vol.2 . . . 13.00

GREEN LANTERN: MOSAIC
1992–93

1 F:John Stewart. 2.25
2 thru 18 . . . . @2.25

GREEN LANTERN: THE NEW CORPS
1999

1 (of 2) CDi(s),SEa 5.00
2 CDi(s),SEa, concl. 5.00

GREEN LANTERN: REBIRTH
Oct. 2004

1 (of 6) 40-pg. 3.00
2 F:JLA 3.50
3 V:Spectre 3.50
4 A:JLA,JSA,&Teen Titans 3.00
5 To restore Hal Jordan 3.00
6 Hal Jordan's return 3.00

GREGORY
DC/Piranha

1 MaH , b&w 8.00
2 MaH 5.00
3 MaH Bookshelf Ed. 5.00
3a Platinum Ed. 8.00
4 MaH, b&w 5.00
TPB #1 Gregory Treasury,MaH . . . 10.00
TPB #2 Gregory Treasury,MaH . . . 10.00

GRIFFIN
1991–92

1 I:Matt Williams as Griffin 5.50
2 V:Carson 5.25
3 A:Mary Wayne 5.25
4 A:Mary Wayne 5.25
5 Face to Face with Himself 5.25
6 Final Issue 5.25

GRIP: THE STRANGE WORLD OF MEN
DC/Vertigo, Nov., 2001

1 (of 5) GHe 2.50
2 GHe 2.50
3 thru 5 GHe . . . . @2.50

GROSS POINT
July, 1997

1 MWa&BAu(s) parody 2.50
2 thru 14 . . . . @2.50

GUARDIANS OF METROPOLIS
Nov., 1994

1 Kirby characters. 2.25
2 Donovan's creations 2.25
3 . . . . 2.25
4 Female Furies 2.25

Guardians of Metropolis #1
© DC Comics, Inc.

GUNFIRE
1994–95

1 B:LWn(s),StE,I:Ricochet 2.25
2 thru 13 . . . . @2.25

GUNS OF THE DRAGON
Aug., 1998

1 (of 4) TT, set in 1920s 2.50
2 TT. 2.50
3 TT. 2.50
4 TT conclusion 2.50

GUY GARDNER
1992–94

1 JSon,A:JLA,JLE 2.50
2 JSon,A:Kilowog 2.50
3 JSon,V:Big,Ugly Alien 2.50
4 JSon,G.Gardner vs Ice 2.50
5 JSon,A:Hal Jordan,V:Goldface . . 2.50
6 JSon,A:Hal Jordan,V:Goldface . . 2.50
7 JSon,V:Goldface 2.50
8 JSon,V:Lobo 2.50
9 JSon,Boodikka 2.50
10 JSon,V:Boodikka 2.50
11 JSon,B:Year One 2.50
12 JSon,V:Batman,Flash,Green
    Lantern 2.50
13 JSon,Year One#3 . . . . 2.50
14 JSon,E:Year One 2.50
15 V:Bad Guy Gardner 2.50
16 B:CDi(s),MaT,V:Guy's Brother . 2.50
Becomes:

GUY GARDNER: WARRIOR
1994–96

17 V:Militia 2.50
18 B:Emerald Fallout,N:Guy Gardner,
    V:Militia 4.00
19 A:G.A.Green Lantern,V:Militia . . 4.00
20 A:JLA,Darkstars 2.50
21 E:Emerald Fallout,V:H.Jordan . . 2.50
22 I:Dementor 2.50
23 A:Buck Wargo 2.50
24 Zero Hour 2.50
25 A:Buck Wargo 3.00
26 Zero Hour 2.50
27 Capital Punishment. 2.50
28 Capital Punishment,pt.2 . . . . . . 2.50
29 I:Warriors Bar 2.50
29a Collector's Edition 3.25
30 V:Superman,Supergirl. 2.50

31 A:Sentinel,Supergirl,
    V:Dementor 2.50
32 Way of the Warrior,pt.1,A:JLA . 2.50
33 Way of the Warrior,pt.4 . . . . . . 2.50
34 . . . . 2.50
35 Return of an Old Foe 2.50
36 Underworld Unleashed tie-in . . 2.50
37 Underworld Unleashed tie-in . . 2.50
38 A new woman 2.50
39 Guest stars galore 2.50
40 . . . . 2.50
41 V:Dungeon 2.50
42 Martika revealed as Seductress . 2.50
43 V:5 Foes 2.50
Ann.#1 Year One Annual, Leechun
    vs. Vuldarians 4.00
Ann.#2 Dead Earth 3.50

GUY GARDNER: COLLATERAL DAMAGE
Nov., 2006

1 (of 2) HC 6.00
2 HC. 6.00

GUY GARDNER: REBORN
1992

1 JSon,JRu,V:Goldface,C:Lobo . . . 6.00
2 JSon,JRu,A:Lobo,V:Weaponers
    of Qward 5.50
3 JSon,JRu,A:Lobo,N:G.Gardner
    V:Qwardians 5.50

HACKER FILES
1992–93

1 TS,Soft Wars#1,I:Jack Marshall . 2.25
2 TS,Soft Wars#2 . . . . 2.25
3 TS,Soft Wars#3 . . . . 2.25
4 TS,Soft Wars#4 . . . . 2.25
5 TS,A:Oracle(Batgirl) 2.25
6 TS,A:Oracle,Green Lantern 2.25
7 TS,V:Digitronix 2.25
8 TS,V:Digitronix 2.25
9 TS,V:Digitronix 2.25
10 V:Digitronix 2.25
11 TS,A:JLE 2.25
12 TS,V:Digitronix,final issue 2.25

HAMMER LOCKE
1992–93

1 I:Hammerlocke. 3.00
2 thru 8 . . . . @2.25

HARDCORE STATION
May, 1998

1 (of 6) JSn,JRu,F:Maximillian . . . 2.50
2 JSn,JRu,V:Synnar 2.50
3 JSn,JRu,F:Kyle Rayner 2.50
4 JSn,JRu,V:Synnar 2.50
5 JSn,JRu,F:JLA 2.50
6 JSn,JRu,conclusion 2.50

HARD TIME
DC Focus Feb. 2004

1 F:Ethan Harrow 2.50
2 thru 12 . . . . @2.50
TPB rep, #1-#6 . . . . 10.00
TPB 50 to Life 10.00

HARD TIME SEASON TWO
Dec., 2005

1 . . . . 2.50
2 . . . . 2.50
3 F:Cutter 2.50
4 F:Cindy 2.50
5 . . . . 2.50
6 . . . . 3.00
7 Finale 3.00

Hardware #1
© DC Comics, Inc.

HARDWARE
DC/Milestone, 1993–96
1 DCw,I:Hardware,Edwin Alva,Reprise,
   Dir.Mark.Ed.,w/A puzzle piece,
   Skybox Card,Poster 4.00
1a NewsstandEd. 2.50
1b Platinum Ed. 6.00
2 thru 15 . . . . @2.50
16 Die-Cut(c),JBy(c),DCw,
   N:Hardware 4.25
16a Newsstand ED. 2.50
17 thru 24 . . . . @2.50
25 V:Death Row, Sanction. 3.00
26 thru 49 . . . . @2.50
50 DGC(s), 48pg. anniversary issue 4.00
51 DMc(s) final issue 2.50

HARLEY QUINN
October, 2000
1 KK,TyD,A:Batman,48 pg. 3.00
2 KK,TyD,A:Two-Face,Poison Ivy . . 2.50
3 KK,TyD,A:Catwoman 2.50
4 KK,TyD,I:Quinntettes 2.50
5 KK,TyD,F:Quinntettes 2.50
6 KK,TyD,A:Oracle 2.50
7 KK,TyD,F:Big Barda 2.50
8 KK,TyD,Harley's Past 2.50
9 KK,TyD,V:Quinntettes 2.50
10 KK,TyD,F:Barbara Gordon 2.50
11 KK,TyD,F:Nightwing 2.50
12 KK,TyD,40-page 3.50
13 KK,Joker:Last Laugh 2.50
14 KK,TyD,to Metropolis 2.50
15 KK,TyD,Lovers advice 2.50
16 KK,TyD,City of Tomorrow 2.50
17 KK,TyD,F:Bizarro 2.50
18 KK,TyD,F:Bizarro 2.50
19 KK,TyD,A:Superman. 2.50
20 KK,Harley pays price for evil . . . 2.50
21 KK,ultimate prison. 2.50
22 KK,TyD,Highwater. 2.50
23 KK,TyD,World Without Harley. . . 2.50
24 KK,DDv,back from Hell 2.50
25 KK,DDv,F:Batman,A:Joker 2.50
26 wanted for murder. 2.50
27 Harley a psychiatrist 2.50
28 new patient 2.50
29 a stalker 2.50
30 Who framed Harley?. 2.50
31 Harley and Doc. 2.50
32 A:Joker 2.50
33 Behind Blue Eyes,pt.1 . . . . 2.50
34 Behind Blue Eyes,pt.2 . . . . 2.50

35 Behind Blue Eyes,pt.3 . . . . 2.50
36 Behind Blue Eyes,pt.4 . . . . 2.50
37 Behind Blue Eyes,pt.5 . . . . 2.50
38 CAd,final issue 2.50
Spec.#1 Our Worlds at War,48-pg. . 3.25
GN Harley & Ivy, Love on the Lam . 6.50

HAVEN:
THE BROKEN CITY
Dec., 2001
1 (of 9) AOI,F:JLA. 2.50
2 AOI,A:JLA 2.50
3 AOI,A:Superman,I:HankVelveeda 2.50
4 AOI,F:Nia 2.50
5 AOI,Eater of Filth 2.50
6 AOI,search for crash survivors. . . 2.50
7 AOI,V:Ivas the ultra-powerful . . . 2.50
8 AOI,Anathema 2.50
9 AOI,Valadin 2.50

HAWK & DOVE
[1st Regular Series], 1968–69
1 SD 150.00
2 SD 100.00
3 GK 75.00
4 GK 75.00
5 GK,C:Teen Titans. 75.00
6 GK 75.00

[Limited Series], 1988–89
1 RLd,I:New Dove. 4.00
2 RLd,V:Kestrel 3.50
3 RLd,V:Kestrel 3.50
4 RLd,V:Kestrel 3.50
5 RLd,V:Kestrel,O:New Dove 3.50
TPB rep. #1-#5 . . . . 10.50

[2nd Regular Series], 1989–91
1 A:Superman,Green Lantern
   Hawkman. 2.50
2 V:Aztec Goddess 2.50
3 V:Aztec Goddess 2.50
4 I:The Untouchables 2.50
5 I:Sudden Death, A:1st Dove's
   Ghost. 2.50
6 A:Barter,Secrets o/Hawk&Dove . 2.50
7 A:Barter,V:Count St.Germain. . . . 2.50
8 V:Count St.Germain. 2.50
9 A:Copperhead 2.50
10 V:Gauntlet & Andromeda 2.50
11 A:New Titans,V:M.A.C.,
   Andromeda Gauntlet 2.50
12 A:New Titans,V:Scarab 2.50
13 1960's,I:Shellshock 2.50
14 Prelue to O:Hawk & Dove,
   V:Kestrel 2.50
15 O:Hawk & Dove begins 2.50
16 HawkV:Dove,V:Lord of Chaos . . 2.50
17 V:Lords-Order & Chaos 2.50
18 The Creeper #1. . . . . 2.50
19 The Creeper #2. . . . . 2.50
20 KM,DG,Christmas Story 2.50
21 Dove 2.50
22 V:Sudden Death 2.50
23 A:Velv.Tiger,SuddenDeath 2.50
24 A:Velv.Tiger,SuddenDeath 2.50
25 Recap 1st 2 yrs.(48 pg) 2.50
26 Dove's past 2.50
27 The Hunt for Hawk 2.50
28 War of the Gods,A:Wildebeest
   A:Uncle Sam,final issue,
   double size 3.00
Ann.#1 In Hell 3.00
Ann.#2 CS,KGa,ArmageddonPt.5 . . 3.00
TPB RLd 10.00

HAWK & DOVE
Sept., 1997
1 (of 5) MBn,DZ,DG,Sasha Martens
   & Wiley Wolverman. 2.50
2 MBn,DZ,DG,Vixen & Vigilante . . 2.50

3 MBn,DZ,DG,grave desecrations . 2.50
4 MBn,DZ,DG,V:Suicide Squad . . . 2.50

HAWKMAN
[1st Regular Series], 1964–68
1 MA,V:Chac 1,400.00
2 MA,V:Tralls 500.00
3 MA,V:Sky Raiders 500.00
4 MA,I&O:Zatanna 450.00
5 MA 300.00
6 MA 300.00
7 MA,V:I.Q. 300.00
8 MA 300.00
9 MA,V:Matter Master 300.00
10 MA,V:Caw 300.00
11 MA 250.00
12 MA. 200.00
13 MA. 200.00
14 GaF,MA,V:Caw 200.00
15 GaF,MA,V:Makkar. 200.00
16 GaF,MA,V:Ruthvol 200.00
17 GaF,MA,V:Raven 200.00
18 GaF,MA,A:Adam Strange 150.00
19 GaF,MA,A:Adam Strange 150.00
20 GaF,MA,V:Lionmane. 100.00
21 GaF,MA,V:Lionmane. 100.00
22 V:Falcon 100.00
23 V:Dr.Malevolo 100.00
24 Robot Raiders from
   Planet Midnight 100.00
25 DD,V:Medusa,G.A.Hawkman . 100.00
26 RdM,CCu,DD 100.00
27 DD,JKu(c),V:Yeti 100.00

[2nd Regular Series], 1986–87
1 DH,A:Shadow Thief 3.00
2 DH,V:Shadow Thief 2.50
3 DH,V:Shadow Thief 2.50
4 DH A:Zatanna 2.50
5 DH,V:Lionmane. 2.50
6 DH,V:Gentleman Ghost,
   Lionmane. 2.50
7 DH,Honor Wings 2.50
8 DH,Shadow War contd. 2.50
9 DH,Shadow War contd. 2.50
10 JBy(c),D:Hyatis Corp 2.50
11 End of Shadow War 2.50
12 Hawks on Thanagar 2.50
13 DH,Murder Case. 2.50
14 DH,Mystery o/Haunted Masks . 2.50
15 DH,Murderer Revealed. 2.50
16 DH,Hawkwoman lost 2.50
17 EH,DH,final issue 2.50
TPB rep.Brave & Bold apps. 20.00

[3rd Regular Series], 1993–96
1 B:JOs(s),JD,R:Hawkman,
   V:Deadline 5.00
2 JD,A:Gr.Lantern,V:Meta-Tech . . . 3.00
3 JD,I:Airstryke 2.75
4 JD,RM 2.50
5 JD(c),V:Count Viper. 2.50
6 JD(c),A:Eradicator 2.50
7 JD(c),PuK(s),LMc,B:King of the
   Netherworld 2.50
8 LMc,E:King of the Netherworld . . 2.50
9 BML(s) 2.50
10 I:Badblood 2.50
11 V:Badblood 2.50
12 V:Hawkgod 2.75
13 V:Hawkgod 2.75
14 New abilities,pt.1. . . . . 2.50
15 New abilities,pt.2. . . . . 2.50
16 Eyes of the Hawk,pt.3. . . . . 2.50
17 Eyes of the Hawk,pt.4. . . . . 2.50
18 Seagle,Ellis, Pepoy. 2.50
19 F:Hawkman 2.50
21 RLm,V:Shadow Thief,
   Gentleman Ghost 2.75
22 Way of the Warrior,pt.3
   A:Warrior,JLA 2.75
23 Way of the Warrior,pt.6 . . . . 2.75
24 . . . . 2.75

Hawkman 3rd Series #10
© DC Comics, Inc.

25 V:Lionmane,painted(c) 2.75
26 WML,Underworld
     Unleashed tie-in 2.75
27 WML,Underworld
     Unleashed tie-in 2.75
28 WML,V:Doctor Polaris. 2.75
29 HC(c),V:Vandal Savage 2.75
30 . . . . 2.75
31 serial killer has Tangarian
     technology. 2.75
32 MC,Search for serial killer 2.75
Ann.#1 JD,I:Mongrel 4.00
Ann.#2 Year One Annual 4.00

[4th Regular Series], 2002
1 RgM,MiB,Hawkman & Hawkgirl. . 2.50
2 RgM,MiB,F:Hawkgirl 2.50
3 RgM,MiB,inter-dimensional portal 2.50
4 RgM,MiB,trapped in Battlelands . 2.50
5 RgM,MiB,Slings and Arrows,pt.1 . 2.50
6 RgM,MiB,Slings and Arrows,pt.2. 2.50
7 RgM,TT,Lives past 2.50
8 RgM,MiB,F:Atom 2.50
9 RgM,F:Dr.Fate 2.50
10 RgM,find Speed Saunders 2.50
11 RgM,V:Hath-Set 2.50
12 RgM,V:Darkraven 2.50
13 Hawk vs. Hawk 2.50
14 Hawkgirl's parents' murderer . . . 2.50
15 Shayera Thai 2.50
16 RgM,The Thanagarian,pt.1. . . . . 2.50
17 RgM,The Thanagarian,pt.2. . . . . 2.50
18 RgM,The Thanagarian,pt.3. . . . . 2.50
19 F:Black Adam 2.50
20 RgM,MIB,V:Headhunter,pt.1 . . . 2.50
21 RgM,MIB,V:Headhunter,pt.2 . . . 2.50
22 RgM,MIB,V:Headhunter,pt.3 . . . 2.50
23 Black Reign,pt.2,x-over. 2.50
24 Black Reign,pt.4,x-over. 2.50
25 Black Reign,pt.6,x-over. 2.50
26 Rabid vampires. 2.50
27 SeP,Past Lives 2.50
28 Fate's Warning,pt.1 . . . . 2.50
29 Fate's Warning,pt.2 . . . . 2.50
30 Fate's Warning,pt.3 . . . . 2.50
31 Fate's Warning,pt.4 . . . . 2.50
32 JoB,F:The Atom 2.50
33 ASm,MGy,F:Monolith 2.50
34 V:Manticore. 2.50
35 JoB,V:Zombies 2.50
36 JoB,V:Zombies,A:Deadman 2.50
37 JoB,V:Fadeaway Man. 2.50
38 previous incarnations visit. 4.00
39 JoB,Hawkman missing 3.00
40 JoB,F:Dr. Fate. 3.00

41 JoB,new Hawkman. 5.00
42 JP(s),JoB,V:Pilgrim 2.50
43 JoB,Golden Eagle. 2.50
44 JoB,Golden Eagle. 2.50
45 JoB,F:JSA. 2.50
46 ATi,AKu(c),Rann/Thanagar War . 2.50
47 CsB,CaS,Coalition in Crisis 2.50
48 CsB,CaS,Coalition in Crisis 2.50
49 CsB,CaS,Coalition in Crisis 2.50
Spec. Secret Files #1, 48-pg. 5.00
TPB Endless Flight 13.00
TPB Enemies & Allies 15.00
TPB Wings of Fury. 18.00
TPB Golden Age Hawkman 50.00
TPB Golden Eagle. 18.00
Becomes:

HAWKGIRL
March, 2006
50 WS,HC, One Year Later 2.50
51 WS,HC,St. Roch Museum 2.50
52 WS,HC,Lizard Kings voodoo . . . 2.50
53 WS,HC,V:Khimaera 3.00
54 WS,HC,Friend from the pst 3.00
55 WS,HC,Hawkman returns. 3.00
56 WS,HC,Truths and Evils. 3.00
57 WS,JoB,HC(c). 3.00
58 WS,JoB,HC(c). 3.00
59 WS,JSA Classified x-over, pt.1 . . 3.00
60 WS,JSA Classified x-over,pt.4 . . 3.00
61 WS,HC(c),Search for Hath-Set. . 3.00
62 WS,HC(c),Search for Hath-Set. . 3.00
63 WS,HC(c),Search for Hath-Set. . 3.00
64 WS,HC(c),A:Superman,Oracle . . 3.00
65 WS,HC(c),Fate of the Hawks . . . 3.00
66 WS,V:Hath-Set, final issue 3.00

HAWKWORLD
1989
1 TT,Hawkman, Origin retold 5.00
2 TT,Katar tried for treason. 4.00
3 TT,Hawkgirl's debut 4.00

[1st Regular Series], 1990–93
1 GN,Byth on Earth,R:Kanjar Ro . . 3.00
2 GN,Katar & Shayera in Chicago . 2.50
3 GN,V:Chicago Crime 2.50
4 GN,Byth's Control Tightens 2.50
5 GN,Return of Shadow Thief 2.50
6 GN,Stolen Thanagarian Ship. . . . 2.50
7 GN,V:Byth. 2.50
8 GN,Hawkman vs. Hawkwoman . . 2.50
9 GN,Hawkwoman in Prison. 2.50
10 Shayera returns to Thanagar . . . 2.50
11 GN,Blackhawk,Express. 2.50
12 GN,Princess Treska 2.50
13 TMd,A:Firehawk,V:Marauder . . . 2.50
14 GN,Shayera's Father 2.50
15 GN,War of the Gods X-over 2.50
16 GN War of the Gods X-over 2.50
17 GN,Train Terrorists 2.50
18 GN,V:Atilla 2.50
19 GN,V:Atilla 2.50
20 V:Smir'Beau 2.50
21 GN,Thanagar Pt.1,
     A:J.S.A. Hawkman 2.50
22 GN,Thanagar Pt.2. . . . . 2.50
23 GN,Thanagar Pt.3. . . . . 2.50
24 GN,Thanagar Pt.4. . . . . 2.50
25 GN,Thanagar Pt.5. . . . . 2.50
26 GN,V:Attilla battle armor. 2.50
27 JD,B:Flight's End 2.50
28 JD,Flight's End #2. . . . . 2.50
29 TT(c),JDu,Flight's End #3 . . . . . 2.50
30 TT,Flight's End #4 . . . . 2.50
31 TT,Flight's End #5 . . . . 2.50
32 TT,V:Count Viper,final issue 3.00
Ann.#1 A:Flash. 4.50
Ann.#2 Armageddon,pt.6 . . . . 4.00
Ann.#2a reprint (Silver) 3.50
Ann.#3 Eclipso tie-in 3.25

HEAVY LIQUID
DC/Vertigo, 1999
1 PPo,pt 1 of 5 . . . . 6.00
2 thru 5 PPo,pt.2 thru pt.5. . . . . @6.00
TPB PPo, 240-page. 30.00

HECKLER, THE
1992–93
1 KG,MJ,I:The Heckler 2.25
2 KG,MJ,V:The Generic Man 2.25
3 KG,MJ,V:Cosmic Clown. 2.25
4 KG,V:Bushwacker 2.25
5 KG,Theater Date 2.25
6 KG,I:Lex Concord. 2.25
7 KG,V:Cuttin'Edge 2.25

HELLBLAZER
Jan., 1988
1 B:JaD(s),JRy,F:John
     Constantine 20.00
2 JRy,I:Papa Midnight. 10.00
3 JRy,I:Blathoxi 8.00
4 JRy,I:Resurrection Crusade,
     Gemma 8.00
5 JRy,F:Pyramid of Fear. 8.00
6 JRy,V:Resurrection Crusade,
     I:Nergal 6.00
7 JRy,V:Resurrection Crusade,
     I:Richie Simpson 6.00
8 JRy,AA,Constantine receives
     demon blood,V:Nergal. 6.00
9 JRy,A:Swamp Thing 7.00
10 JRy,V:Nergal. 6.00
11 MBu,Newcastle Incident,pt.1 . . . 5.00
12 JRy,D:Nergal. 5.00
13 JRy,John has a Nightmare 5.00
14 JRy,B:The Fear Machine,
     I:Mercury,Marj,Eddie 5.00
15 JRy,Shepard's Warning. 5.00
16 JRy,Rough Justice 5.00
17 MkH,I:Mr. Wester 5.00
18 JRy,R:Zed 5.00
19 JRy,I:Simon Hughes,Sandman . 10.00
20 JRy,F:Mr.Webster 6.00
21 JRy,I:Jallakuntilliokan 6.00
22 JRy,E:The Fear Machine. 6.00
23 I&D:Jerry O'Flynn 5.00
24 E:JaD(s),I:Sammy Morris 5.00
25 GMo(s),DvL,Early Warning. 5.00
26 GMo(s) 5.00
27 NGa(s),DMc,Hold Me 22.00
28 B:JaD(s),RnT,KeW,F:S.Morris . . 5.00
29 RnT,KeW,V:Sammy Morris 5.00
30 RnT,KeW,D:Sammy Morris 5.00
31 E:JaD(s),SeP,Constantine's
     Father's Funeral 5.00
32 DiF(s),StP,I&D:Drummond 4.50
33 B:JaD(s),MPn,I:Pat McDonell . . . 4.50
34 SeP,R:Mercury,Marj 4.50
35 SeP,Constantine's Past. 4.50
36 Future Death,(preview of
     World Without End). 4.50
37 Journey to England's Secret
     Mystics. 4.50
38 Constantine's Journey contd. . . . 4.50
39 Journey to Discovery 4.50
40 DMc,I:2nd Kid Eternity 5.00
41 B:GEn(s),WSm,MPn,Dangerous
     Habits 10.00
42 Dangerous Habits 4.50
43 I:Chantinelle 4.50
44 Dangerous Habits 4.50
45 Dangerous Habits 4.50
46 Dangerous Habits epilogue,
     I:Kit(John's girlfriend). 4.50
47 SnW(i),Pub Where I Was Born . . 4.00
48 Love Kills 4.00
49 X-mas issue,Lord o/t Dance 4.00
50 WSm,Remarkable Lives,A:Lord
     of Vampires (48pgs) 6.00

Hellblazer #4
© DC Comics, Inc.

51 JnS,SeP,Laundromat-
   Possession 5.00
52 GF(c),WSm, Royal Blood 5.00
53 GF(c),WSm, Royal Blood 5.00
54 GF(c),WSm, Royal Blood 5.00
55 GF(c),WSm, Royal Blood 5.00
56 GF(c),B:GEn(s),DvL,
   V:Danny Drake 5.00
57 GF(c),SDi,Mortal Clay#1,
   V:Dr. Amis 5.00
58 GF(c),SDi,Mortal Clay#2,
   V:Dr. Amis 5.00
59 GF(c),WSm,MkB(i),KDM,B:Guys
   & Dolls 5.00
60 GF(c),WSm,MkB(i),F:Tali,
   Chantinelle. 5.00
61 GF(c),WSm,MkB(i),E:Guys &
   Dolls, V:First of the Fallen 5.00
62 GF(c),SDi,End of the Line,I:Gemma,
   AIDS storyline insert w/Death . . 6.00

DC/Vertigo, 1993

63 GF(c),SDi,C:Swamp Thing,Zatanna
   Phantom Stranger 5.00
64 GF(c),SDi,B:Fear & Loathing,
   A:Gabriel (Racism) 4.00
65 GF(c),SDi,D:Dez 4.00
66 GF(c),SDi,E:Fear and Loathing . 4.00
67 GF(c),SDi,Kit leaves John 4.00
68 GF(c),SDi,F:Lord of Vampires,
   Darius,Mary 4.00
69 GF(c),SDi,D:Lord of Vampires . . 4.00
70 GF(c),SDi,Kit in Ireland. 4.00
71 GF(c),SDi,A:WWII Fighter Pilot . 4.00
72 GF(c),SDi,B:Damnation's
   Flame,A:Papa Midnight 4.00
73 GF(c),SDi,Nightmare NY,
   A:JFK. 4.00
74 GF(c),SDi,I:Cedella,A:JFK 4.00
75 GF(c),SDi,E:Damnation'sFlame . 4.00
76 GF(c),SDi,R:Brendan 4.00
77 Returns to England. 4.00
78 GF(c),SDi,B:Rake at the
   Gates of Hell 4.00
79 GF(c),SDi,In Hell. 4.00
80 GF(c),SDi,In London. 4.00
81 GF(c),SDi 4.00
82 Kit 4.00
83 Rake,Gates of Hell 4.00
84 John's past 4.00
85 Warped Notions,pt.1 . . . . 4.00
86 Warped Notions,pt.2 . . . . 4.00
87 Warped Notions,pt.3 . . . . 4.00
88 Warped Notions,pt.4 . . . . 4.00
89 Dreamtime 4.00

90 Dreamtime,pt.2 . . . . 4.00
91 Visits Battlefield. 4.00
92 Critical Mass,pt.1 . . . . 4.00
93 Critical Mass,pt.2 . . . . 4.00
94 Critical Mass,pt.3 . . . . 4.00
95 SeP,Critical Mass,pt.4 . . . . 4.00
96 SeP,Critical Mass,pt.5 . . . . 4.00
97 SeP,Critical Mass epilogue 4.00
98 SeP, helps neighbor 4.00
99 SeP 4.00
100 SeP, In a coma 5.00
101 SeP,deal with a demon 3.50
102 SeP,DifficultBeginnings,pt.1 . . . 3.50
103 SeP,DifficultBeginnings,pt.2 . . . 3.50
104 SeP,DifficultBeginnings,pt.3 . . . 3.50
105 . . . . 3.50
106 PJe(s),SEp,In the Line of
   Fire, pt.1 (of 2). 3.50
107 PJe(s),SEp,Line of Fire,pt.2 . . . 3.50
108 PJe(s),SeP,a Bacchic
   celebration 3.50
109 PJe(s),SeP,cattle mutilations
   in Northern England 3.50
110 PJe(s),SeP,Last Man
   Standing,pt.1 . . . . 3.50
111 PJe(s),SeP,Last Man,pt.2 . . . . . 3.50
112 PJe(s),SeP,Last Man,pt.3 . . . . . 3.50
113 PJe(s),SeP,Last Man,pt.4 . . . . . 3.50
114 PJe(s),SeP,Last Man,pt.5 . . . . . 3.50
115 PJe(s),SeP(s),Dani's ex-
   boyfriend 3.50
116 SeP,Widdershins,pt.1 (of 2) . . . 3.50
117 SeP,Widdershins,pt.2 . . . . 3.50
118 PJe(s),SeP,John's a Godfather . 4.00
119 PJe(s),SeP,disasters 3.50
120 PJe(s),SeP,10th anniv. 48pg . . . 3.00
121 PJe(s),SeP, Up the Down
   Staircase pt.1. . . . . 3.00
122 PJe(s),SeP, Up the Down
   Staircase pt.2. . . . . 3.00
123 PJe(s),SeP, Up the Down
   Staircase pt.3. . . . . 3.00
124 PJe(s),SeP, Up the Down
   Staircase pt.4. . . . . 3.00
125 PJe(s),SeP, How to Play
   with Fire, pt.1. . . . . 3.00
126 PJe(s),SeP,Play/Fire,pt.2 . . . . . 3.00
127 PJe(s),SeP,Play/Fire,pt.3 . . . . . 3.00
128 PJe(s),SeP,Play/Fire,pt.4 . . . . . 3.00
129 . . . . 3.00
130 GEn,JHi,GF,Son of Man,pt.2 . . . 3.00
131 GEn,JHi,GF,Son of Man,pt.3 . . . 3.00
132 GEn,JHi,GF,Son of Man,pt.4 . . . 3.00
133 GEn,JHi,GF,Son of Man,pt.5 . . . 3.00
134 WEI(s),JHi,Haunted,pt.1 . . . . . . 3.00
135 WEI(s),JHi,Haunted,pt.2 . . . . . . 3.00
136 WEI(s),JHi,Haunted,pt.3 . . . . . . 3.00
137 WEI(s),JHi,Haunted,pt.4 . . . . . . 3.00
138 WEI(s),JHi,Haunted,pt.5 . . . . . . 3.00
139 WEI(s),JHi,Haunted,pt.6 . . . . . . 3.00
140 WEI(s),Locked. 3.00
141 WEI(s),ALa 3.00
142 WEI,TBd,Setting Sun 3.00
143 WEI,TBd,Telling Tales 3.00
144 GEr,ALa,Ashes & Honey,pt.1 . . 3.00
145 GEr,ALa,Ashes & Honey,pt.2 . . 3.00
146 RC,Hard Time 3.00
147 RC,Hard Time,pt.2 . . . . 3.00
148 RC,Hard Time,pt.3 . . . . 3.00
149 RC,Hard Time,pt.4 . . . . 3.00
150 RC,Hard Time,concl. 3.00
151 Good Intentions,pt.1 . . . . 3.00
152 Good Intentions,pt.2 . . . . 3.00
153 Good Intentions,pt.3 . . . . 3.00
154 Good Intentions,pt.4 . . . . 3.00
155 Good Intentions,pt.5 . . . . 3.00
156 Good Intentions,pt.6 . . . . 3.00
157 SDi,"...and buried?". 3.00
158 Freezes Over,pt.1 . . . . 3.00
159 Freezes Over,pt.2 . . . . 3.00
160 Freezes Over,pt.3 . . . . 3.00
161 Freezes Over,pt.4 . . . . 3.00

162 Lapdogs and Englishmen 3.00
163 Lapdogs and Englishmen 3.00
164 Highwater, pt.1 . . . . 3.00
165 Highwater, pt.2 . . . . 3.00
166 Highwater, pt.3 . . . . 3.00
167 Highwater, pt.4 . . . . 3.00
168 A Fresh Coat of Red Paint 3.00
169 Constantine in LA 3.00
170 Ashes and Dust,pt.1 . . . . 3.00
171 Ashes and Dust,pt.2 . . . . 3.00
172 Ashes and Dust,pt.3 . . . . 3.00
173 Ashes and Dust,pt.4 . . . . 3.00
174 Ashes and Dust,pt.5 . . . . 3.00
175 SDi,JP,High on Life,pt.1 . . . . . . 3.00
176 SDi,JP,High on Life, pt.2 . . . . . 3.00
177 Red Sepulchre,pt.1 . . . . 3.00
178 Red Sepulchre,pt.2 . . . . 3.00
179 Red Sepulchre,pt.3 . . . . 3.00
180 Red Sepulchre,pt.4 . . . . 3.00
181 Red Sepulchre,concl. 3.00
182 MCy(s),Black Flowers,pt.1 . . . . 3.00
183 MCy(s),Black Flowers,pt.2 . . . . 3.00
184 MCy(s),Wild Card 3.00
185 MCy(s),Ordeal. 3.00
186 MCy(s),The Pit 3.00
187 MCy(s),Bred in Bone,pt.1 . . . . 3.00
188 MCy(s),Bred in Bone,pt.2 . . . . 3.00
189 MCy(s),Staring at Wall,pt.1 . . . . 3.00
190 MCy(s),Staring at Wall,pt.2 . . . . 3.00
191 MCy(s),Staring at Wall,pt.3 . . . . 3.00
192 MCy(s),Staring at Wall,pt.4 . . . . 3.00
193 MCy(s),Staring at Wall,pt.5 . . . . 3.00
194 MCy(s) 3.00
195 MCy(s),Out of Season,pt.1 . . . . 3.00
196 MCy(s),Out of Season,pt.2 . . . . 3.00
197 Stations of the Cross,pt.1 . . . . . 3.00
198 Stations of the Cross,pt.2 . . . . . 3.00
199 Stations of the Cross,pt.3 . . . . . 3.00
200 Married life 4.50
201 Thieves 3.00
202 Reasons to be Cheerful,pt.1. . . 3.00
203 Reasons to be Cheerful,pt.2. . . 3.00
204 Reasons to be Cheerful,pt.3. . . 3.00
205 Reasons to be Cheerful,pt.4. . . 3.00
206 Chas' rampage 3.00
207 Down in the Ground,pt.1. . . . . . 3.00
208 Down in the Ground,pt.2. . . . . . 3.00
209 Down in the Ground,pt.3. . . . . . 3.00
210 Down in the Ground,pt.4. . . . . . 3.00
211 Down in the Ground,pt.5. . . . . . 3.00
212 Down in the Ground,pt.6. . . . . . 3.00
213 Back from Hell 3.00
214 MCy(s),R.S.V.P., pt.1 . . . . 3.00
215 MCy(s) 3.00
216 Empathy is the Enemy, pt.1 . . . 3.00
217 Empathy is the Enemy, pt.2 . . . 3.00
218 Empathy is the Enemy, pt.3 . . . 3.00
219 Empathy is the Enemy, pt.4 . . . 3.00
220 Empathy is the Enemy, pt.5 . . . 3.00
221 Empathy is the Enemy, pt.6 . . . 3.00
222 Empathy is the Enemy, pt.7 . . . 3.00
223 Empathy is the Enemy, concl . . 3.00
224 The Red Right Hand, pt.1 . . . . . 3.00
225 The Red Right Hand, pt.2. . . . . 3.00
226 The Red Right Hand, pt.3 . . . . . 3.00
227 The Red Right Hand, pt.4. . . . . 3.00
228 The Red Right Hand, pt.5. . . . . 3.00
229 MCy,JPL 3.00
230 In at the Deep End, pt.1 . . . . . . 3.00
231 In at the Deep End, pt.2 . . . . . . 3.00
232 Wheels of Chance,pt.1 . . . . 3.00
233 Wheels of Chance, pt.2 . . . . . . 3.00
234 Joyride, pt.1 . . . . 3.00
235 Joyride, pt. 2 . . . . 3.00
236 Joyride, pt. 3 . . . . 3.00
237 Joyride, pt. 4 . . . . 3.00
Ann.#1 JaD(s),BT,Raven Scar 7.00
Spec.#1 GF(c),GEn(s),SDi,John
   Constantine's teenage years . . . 4.50
Secret Files #1 . . . . 5.00

HELLBLAZER/ THE BOOKS OF MAGIC
Oct., 1997
1 (of 2) PJe,JNR 2.50
2 PJe,JNR 2.50

HELLBLAZER SPECIAL: BAD BLOOD
DC/Vertigo, July, 2000
1 (of 4) JaD,PBd 3.50
2 JaD,PBd 3.50
3 JaD,PBd 3.50
4 JaD,PBd,concl. 3.50

HELLBLAZER SPECIAL: LADY CONSTANTINE
DC/Vertigo, Dec. 2002
1 (of 4) F:Johanna Constantine . . . 3.00
2 thru 4 . . . . @3.00

HELMET OF FATE, THE
Jan., 2007
Spec. #1 Ibis the Invincible 3.00
Spec. #1 Detective Chimp 3.00
Spec. #1 Sargon the Sorcerer 3.00
Spec. #1 Zauriel 3.00
Spec. #1 Black Alice 3.00

HERCULES UNBOUND
Oct.–Nov., 1975
1 WW 20.00
2 thru 8 . . . . @12.00
9 thru 12 WS,Aug.–Sept.,1977 . . . 10.00

HERE'S HOWIE COMICS
1952–54
1 Teen-age humor 350.00
2 . . . . 200.00
3 & 4 . . . . @150.00
5 Military humor 150.00
6 thru 10 . . . . @125.00
11 thru 18 . . . . @100.00

H-E-R-O
Feb. 2003
1 Jerry Feldon 9.00
2 life-saving mission 5.00
3 F:Molly 5.00
4 Powers and Abilities 5.00
5 F:Matt Allen 3.00
6 F:Andrea Allen 3.00
7 Chaos, Inc. 3.00
8 Chaos, Inc.,pt.2 . . . . 3.00
9 World Made of Glass,pt.1 . . . . . 3.00
10 World Made of Glass,pt.2 . . . . . 2.50
11 Prehistoric superhero? 2.50
12 Ch-Ch-Ch-Changes,pt.1 . . . . . . 2.50
13 Ch-Ch-Ch-Changes,pt.2 . . . . . . 2.50
14 Ch-Ch-Ch-Changes,pt.3 . . . . . . 2.50
15 Good Guys & Bad Guys,pt.1 . . . 2.50
16 Good Guys & Bad Guys,pt.2 . . . 2.50
17 Good Guys & Bad Guys,pt.3 . . . 2.50
18 Good Guys & Bad Guys,pt.4 . . . 2.50
19 Picking Up the Pieces,pt.1 . . . . 2.50
20 Picking Up the Pieces,pt.2 . . . . 2.50
21 Picking Up the Pieces,pt.3 . . . . 2.50
22 final battle over H-E-R-O device . 2.50
Spec. Double Feature,rep.#1&#2 . . 5.00
TPB Powers and Abilities. 10.00

HEROES
DC/Milestone, 1996
1 Six heroes join 3.50
2 thru 6 . . . . @2.50

HEROES AGAINST HUNGER
1986
1 NA,DG,JBy,CS,AA,BWr,BS,
  Superman,Batman. 4.00

HERO HOTLINE
1989
1 thru 6, Mini-series . . . . @2.00

HEX
Sept., 1985
1 MT,I:Hex 7.00
2 MT 5.00
3 MT,V:Conglomerate 5.00
4 MT,V:Conglomerate 5.00
5 MT,A:Chainsaw Killer 5.00
6 MT,V:Conglomerate 5.00
7 MT,Tries to Return to own era . . . 5.00
8 MT,The Future 6.00
9 MT,Future Killer Cyborgs 5.00
10 MT,V:Death Cult 5.00
11 MT,V:The Batman 6.00
12 MT,A:Batman,V:Terminators 6.00
13 MT,I:New Supergroup 5.00
14 MT,A:The Dogs of War 5.00
15 KG,V:Chainsaw Killer 5.00
16 KG,V:Dogs of War. 5.00
17 KG,Hex/Dogs of War T.U.
  V:XXGG 5.00
18 KGr,Confronting the Past,
  final issue 5.00

HI HI PUFFY AMIYUMI
Jan., 2006
Spec. Photo (c) 2.25
1 thru 3 . . . . @2.25

HISTORY OF DC UNIVERSE
Sept., 1986
1 GP, From start to WWII 5.00
2 GP, From WWII to present 5.00
TPB MWn(s),GP,KK,AxR(c)(2002) 10.00

HITCHHIKER'S GUIDE TO THE GALAXY
1993
1 Based on Douglas Adams book . 7.00
2 Based on the book 6.50
3 Based on the book 6.50
GN from Douglas Adams book . . . 15.00

HITMAN
1996–2001
1 GEn, F:Tommy Monaghan 10.00
2 GEn, Attempt to kill Joker 7.00
3 GEn(s),JMC, Mawzin & The
  Arkanonne 5.00
4 GEn(s),JMC, ... 4.00
5 GEn(s),JMC, ... 4.00
6 GEn(s),JMC,A:Johnny Navarone,
  Natt the Hatt 3.00
7 GEn(s),JMC, Pat's dead, Hitman
  wants revenge 3.00
8 GEn(s),JMC,barricaded in
  Noonan's Bar, Final Night tie-in. 3.00
9 GEn(s),JMC,A:Six-Pack 3.00
10 GEn(s),JMC,A:Green Lantern . . 3.00
11 . . . . 3.00
12 GEn(s),JMC,Local Heroes,
  A:Green Lantern 3.00
13 . . . . 3.00
14 GEn(s),JMC, Zombie Night at
  the Aquarium, concl. 3.00
15 GEn(s),JMC, Ace of
  Killers, pt.1, V:Mawzir 3.00

Hitman #2
© DC Comics, Inc.

16 GEn(s),JMC,Ace of Killers,pt.2 . . 3.00
17 GEn(s),JMC,Ace of Killers,pt.3,
  A:Catwoman, Demon Etrigan . . 3.00
18 GEn(s),JMC,Ace of Killers,pt.4,
  A:Demon Etrigan, Baytor 3.00
19 GEn(s),JMC,Ace/Killers,pt.5, . . . 3.00
20 GEn(s),JMC,Ace/Killers,concl. . . 3.00
21 GEn(s),JMC,Romeo & Juliet . . . 2.50
22 GEn(s),JMC,holiday special 2.50
23 GEn(s),JMc,Who Dares
  Wins,pt.1 . . . . 2.50
24 GEn(s),JMc,Dares/Wins,pt.2 . . . 2.50
25 GEn(s),JMc,Dares/Wins,pt.3 . . . 2.50
26 GEn(s),JMc,Dares/Wins,pt.4 . . . 2.50
27 GEn(s),JMc,Dares/Wins,pt.5 . . . 2.50
28 GEn(s),JMC,aftermath 2.50
29 GEn(s),JMC,Tommy's
  Heroes,pt.1 . . . . 2.50
30 GEn(s),JMC,Heroes, pt.2 . . . . . 2.50
31 GEn(s),JMC,Heroes, pt.3 . . . . . 2.50
32 GEn(s),JMC,Heroes, pt.4 . . . . . 2.50
33 GEn(s),JMC,Heroes, pt.5 . . . . . 2.50
34 GEn(s),A:Superman 2.50
35 GEn(s),Frances Monaghan 2.50
36 GEn(s), ... 2.50
37 GEn(s). 2.50
38 GEn(s),Dead Man's Land, concl. 2.50
39 GEn(s),JMC,A:RingoChen,pt.1. . 2.50
40 GEn(s),JMC,A:RingoChen,pt.2. . 2.50
41 GEn(s),JMC,A:RingoChen,pt.3. . 2.50
42 GEn(s),JMC,A:RingoChen,pt.4. . 2.50
43 GEn(s),JMC, ... 2.50
44 GEn(s),JMC 2.50
45 GEn(s),JMC 2.50
46 GEn(s),JMC 2.50
47 GEn(s),JMC,Old Dog 2.50
48 GEn(s),JMC,Old Dog,pt.2 . . . . . 2.50
49 GEn(s),JMC,Old Dog,pt.3 . . . . . 2.50
50 GEn(s),JMC,Hitman's future 2.50
51 GEn(s),JMC,Superguy,pt.1 . . . . 2.50
52 GEn(s),JMc,Superguy,pt.2 . . . . 2.50
53 GEn(s),JMc,ClosingTime,pt.1 . . . 2.50
54 GEn(s),JMc,ClosingTime,pt.2 . . . 2.50
55 GEn(s),JMc,ClosingTime,pt.3 . . . 2.50
56 GEn,JMC,GL,O:Tommy
  Monaghan 2.50
57 GEn,JMC,GL,O:Natt 2.50
58 GEn,JMC,GL,Closing 2.50
59 GEn,JMC,GL,Closing time 2.50
60 GEn,JMC,GL,Closing time,final . 2.50
Ann.#1 Pulp Heroes (Western) 4.00
Spec.#1,000,000 GEn(s),JMC 2.50
Spec. Hitman/Lobo: That
  Stupid Bastich! 4.00

Hopalong Cassidy #86
© DC Comics, Inc.

HOPALONG CASSIDY
Feb., 1954

86 GC,Ph(c):William Boyd & Topper,
   Secret o/t Tattooed Burro . . . 500.00
87 GC,Ph(c),Tenderfoot Outlaw. . 300.00
88 Ph(c),GC,15 Robbers of Rimfire
   Ridge 175.00
89 GC,Ph(c),One-Day Boom
   Town 175.00
90 GC,Ph(c),Cowboy Clown
   Robberies 175.00
91 GC,Ph(c),The Riddle of
   the Roaring R Ranch. 175.00
92 GC,Ph(c),Sky-RidingOutlaws . 150.00
93 GC,Ph(c),Silver Badge
   of Courage. 150.00
94 GC,Ph(c),Mystery of the
   Masquerading Lion 150.00
95 GC,Ph(c),Showdown at the
   Post-Hole Valley 150.00
96 GC,Ph(c),Knights of
   the Range 150.00
97 GC,Ph(c),The Mystery of
   the Three-Eyed Cowboy 150.00
98 GC,Ph(c),Hopalong's
   Unlucky Day 150.00
99 GC,Ph(c),Partners in Peril . . . 150.00
100 GC,Ph(c),The Secrets
   of a Sheriff. 175.00
101 GC,Ph(c),Way Out West
   Where The East Begins 125.00
102 GC,Ph(c),Secret of the
   Buffalo Hat. 125.00
103 GC,Ph(c),The Train-Rustlers
   of Avalance Valley 125.00
104 GC,Ph(c),Secret of the
   Surrendering Outlaws 125.00
105 GC,Ph(c),Three Signs
   to Danger. 125.00
106 GC,Ph(c),The Secret of
   the Stolen Signature 125.00
107 GC,Ph(c),The Mystery Trail
   to Stagecoach Town 125.00
108 GC,Ph(c),The Mystery
   Stage From Burro Bend 125.00
109 GC,The Big Gun on Saddletop
   Mountain 125.00
110 GC,The Dangerous Stunts
   of Hopalong Cassidy 100.00
111 GC,Sheriff Cassidy's
   Mystery Clue 100.00
112 GC,Treasure Trail to
   Thunderbolt Ridge. 100.00

113 GC,The Shadow of the
   Toy Soldier. 100.00
114 GC,Ambush at Natural
   Bridge 100.00
115 GC,The Empty-Handed
   Robberies 100.00
116 GC,Mystery of the
   Vanishing Cabin. 100.00
117 GC,School for Sheriffs 100.00
118 GC,The Hero of
   Comanche Ridge. 100.00
119 GC,The Dream Sheriff of
   Twin Rivers 100.00
120 GC,Salute to a Star-Wearer . 100.00
121 GC,The Secret of the
   Golden Caravan 100.00
122 GC,The Rocking
   Horse Bandits 100.00
123 GK,Mystery of the
   One-Dollar Bank Robbery . . . 100.00
124 GK,Mystery of the
   Double-X Brand. 100.00
125 GK,Hopalong Cassidy's
   Secret Brother 100.00
126 GK,Trail of the
   Telltale Clues 100.00
127 GK,Hopalong Cassidy's
   Golden Riddle 100.00
128 GK,The House That
   Hated Outlaws 100.00
129 GK,Hopalong Cassidy's
   Indian Sign 100.00
130 GK,The Return of the
   Canine Sheriff 100.00
131 GK&GK(c),The Amazing
   Sheriff of Double Creek. 100.00
132 GK,Track of the
   Invisible Indians. 100.00
133 GK,Golden Trail to Danger . . 100.00
134 GK,Case of the
   Three Crack-Shots 100.00
135 GK,May-June, 1959 . . . . 100.00

HORRORIST
DC/Vertigo, 1995

1 I:Horrorist 6.50
2 conclusion 6.50

HOT WHEELS
March-April, 1970

1 ATh 200.00
2 ATh 100.00
3 NA,ATh 125.00
4 ATh 100.00
5 ATh 100.00
6 NA(c) 125.00

HOURMAN
1999

1 TPe,RgM,A:JLA 2.50
2 TPe(s),RgM,F:Tomorrow Woman 2.50
3 TPe(s),RgM,Timepoint,pt.1 . . . . . 2.50
4 TPe(s),RgM,Timepoint,pt.2 . . . . . 2.50
5 TPe(s),RgM,Rex Tyler's life 2.50
6 TPe,RgM,JLAndroids,pt.1 . . . . . 2.50
7 TPe,RgM,JLAndroids,pt.2 . . . . . 2.50
8 TPe,RgM,Day of Judgment
   x-over. 2.50
9 TPe,RgM,F:Rick Tyler 2.50
10 TPe,RgM. 2.50
11 TPe,RgM,One Million,pt.1 . . . . . 2.50
12 TPe,RgM,One Million,pt.2 . . . . . 2.50
13 TPe,RgM,One Million,pt.3 . . . . . 2.50
14 TPe,RgM,V:Undersoul 2.50
15 TPe,RgM,human secrets 2.50
16 TPe,RgM,F:Snapper 2.50
17 TPe,100 Years of Solitude 2.50
18 TPe,RgM,High Society,pt.1 . . . . 2.50
19 TPe,RgM,High Society,pt.2 . . . . 2.50
20 TPe,RgM,F:Snapper. 2.50
21 TPe,RgM,reduced to nothing . . 2.50

22 TPe,TyH 2.50
23 TPe,RgM,Unbelievable
   Truth,pt.1 . . . . 2.50
24 TPe,RgM,Unbel.Truth,pt.2 . . . . 2.50
25 TPE,RgM,final issue 2.50

HOUSE OF MYSTERY
Dec.–Jan., 1952

1 I Fell In Love With
   a Monster 3,800.00
2 The Mark of X 1,700.00
3 The Dummy of Death 1,200.00
4 The Man With the Evil Eye . . . 900.00
5 The Man With the Strangler
   Hands! 900.00
6 The Monster in Clay! 750.00
7 Nine Lives of Alger Denham! . . 750.00
8 Tattoos of Doom 750.00
9 Secret of the Little Black Bag . 750.00
10 The Wishes of Doom 750.00
11 Deadly Game of G-H-O-S-T . . 600.00
12 The Devil's Chessboard 600.00
13 The Theater Of A
   Thousand Thrills! 600.00
14 The Deadly Dolls 600.00
15 The Man Who Could Change
   the World 600.00
16 Dead Men Tell No Tales! 500.00
17 Man With the X-Ray Eyes . . . 400.00
18 Dance of Doom. 400.00
19 The Strange Faces of Death. . 400.00
20 The Beast Of Bristol 400.00
21 Man Who Could See Death . . 400.00
22 The Phantom's Return 400.00
23 Stamps of Doom 400.00
24 Kill The Black Cat 400.00
25 The Man With Three Eyes! . . . 400.00
26 The Man with Magic Ears 350.00
27 Fate Held Four Aces! 350.00
28 The Wings Of Mr. Milo! 350.00
29 CS,Hangman's House 350.00
30 The Demon Gun 350.00
31 The Incredible Illusions! 350.00
32 Pied Piper of the Sea 350.00
33 Mr. Misfortune! 350.00
34 The Hundred Year Duel 350.00
35 The Fatal Superstition. 350.00
36 The Treasure of Montezuma! . 300.00
37 MD,The Statue That
   Came to Life 300.00
38 The Voyage Of No Return . . . 300.00
39 Professor Smith's Magic Lamp 300.00
40 The Coins That Came To Life. 300.00
41 The Impossible Tricks! 300.00
42 The Stranger From Out There 300.00

House of Mystery #30
© DC Comics Inc.

House of Mystery #86
© DC Comics, Inc.

43 Imp on the Flying Trapeze . . . 300.00
44 The Secret Of Hill 14 . . . . 300.00
45 The Magic Kite 300.00
46 The Bird of Fate 300.00
47 The Robot Named Think. 300.00
48 The Man Marooned On Earth. 300.00
49 The Mysterious Mr. Omen . . . 300.00
50 The Amazing Swami. 325.00
51 Man Who Stole Teardrops . . . 275.00
52 The Man With The Golden
    Shoes 275.00
53 The Man Who Hated Mirrors . 275.00
54 The Woman Who Lived Twice 275.00
55 I Turned Back Time. 275.00
56 The Thing In The Black Box . . 275.00
57 The Untamed 275.00
58 Haunted Melody 275.00
59 The Tomb Of Ramfis. 275.00
60 The Prisoner On Canvas 275.00
61 JK,Superstition Day 275.00
62 The Haunting Scarecrow 250.00
63 JK,The Lady & The Creature . 275.00
64 The Golden Doom 250.00
65 JK,The Magic Lantern. 350.00
66 JK,Sinister Shadow. 350.00
67 The Wizard of Water. 250.00
68 The Book That Bewitched. . . . 250.00
69 The Miniature Disasters 250.00
70 JK,The Man With Nine Lives . 250.00
71 Menace of the Mole Man 250.00
72 JK,Dark Journey 250.00
73 Museum That Came to Life . . 250.00
74 Museum That Came To Life . . 250.00
75 Assignment Unknown! 250.00
76 JK,Prisoners Of The Tiny
    Universe 250.00
77 The Eyes That Went Berserk . 200.00
78 JK(c),The 13th Hour 250.00
79 JK(c),The Fantastic Sky
    Puzzle 250.00
80 Man With Countless Faces! . . 200.00
81 The Man Who Made Utopia . . 200.00
82 The Riddle of the Earth's
    Second Moon 200.00
83 The Mystery of the
    Martian Eye 200.00
84 JK,BK,100-Century Doom . . . 275.00
85 JK(c),Earth's Strangest
    Salesman. 265.00
86 The Baffling Bargains 250.00
87 The Human Diamond 250.00
88 Return of the Animal Man. . . 250.00
89 The Cosmic Plant! 250.00
90 The Invasion Of the Energy
    Creatures! 250.00

91 DD&SMo(c),The Riddle of the
    Alien Satellite. 250.00
92 DD(c),Menace of the
    Golden Globule 250.00
93 NC(c),I Fought The
    Molten Monster 250.00
94 DD&SMo(c),The Creature
    In Echo Lake 250.00
95 The Wizard's Gift 250.00
96 The Amazing 70-Ton Man. . . . 250.00
97 The Alien Who Change
    History 250.00
98 DD&SMo(c),The Midnight
    Creature. 250.00
99 The Secret of the
    Leopard God 250.00
100 The Beast Beneath Earth . . . 275.00
101 The Magnificent Monster . . . 200.00
102 Cellmate to a Monster 200.00
103 Hail the Conquering Aliens . . 200.00
104 I was the Seeing-Eye Man . . 200.00
105 Case of the Creature X-14 . . 200.00
106 Invaders from the Doomed
    Dimension 200.00
107 Captives of the Alien
    Fisherman 200.00
108 RMo,Four Faces of Frank
    Forbes 200.00
109 ATh,JKu,Secret of the Hybrid
    Creatures. 200.00
110 Beast Who Stalked Through
    Time. 200.00
111 Operation Beast Slayer 200.00
112 Menace of Craven's
    Creatures. 200.00
113 RMo,Prisoners of Beast
    Asteroid 200.00
114 The Movies from Nowhere . . 200.00
115 Prisoner o/t Golden Mask . . 200.00
116 RMo,Return of the
    Barsfo Beast 200.00
117 Menace of the Fire Furies. . . 150.00
118 RMo,Secret o/SuperGorillas . 150.00
119 Deadly Gift from the Stars . . 150.00
120 ATh,Catman of KarynPeale . 150.00
121 RMo,Beam that Transformed
    Men 150.00
122 Menace fo the Alien Hero . . . 150.00
123 RMo,Lure o/t Decoy
    Creature. 150.00
124 Secret of Mr. Doom. 150.00
125 Fantastic Camera Creature . 150.00
126 The Human Totem Poles . . . 150.00
127 RMo,Cosmic Game o/Doom. 150.00
128 NC,The Sorcerer's Snares . . 150.00
129 Man in the Nuclear Trap . . . 150.00
130 The Alien Creature Hunt . . . 150.00
131 Vengeance o/t GeyserGod . . 125.00
132 MMe,Beware My Invisible
    Master 125.00
133 MMe,Captive Queen of
    Beast Island. 125.00
134 MMe,Secret Prisoner of
    Darkmore Dungeon 125.00
135 MMe,Alien Body Thief. 125.00
136 MMe,Secret o/t StolenFace . 125.00
137 MMe,Tunnel to Disaster 125.00
138 MMe,Creature Must Die 125.00
139 MMe,Creatures of
    Vengeful Eye 125.00
140 I&Only app.:Astro 125.00
141 MMe,The Alien Gladiator . . . 125.00
142 MMe,The Wax Demons 125.00
143 J'onn J'onzz begins 400.00
144 J'onn J'onzz on Weird
    World of Gilgana 150.00
145 J'onn J'onzz app. 125.00
146 BP,J'onn J'onzz. 125.00
147 J'onn J'onzz 125.00
148 J'onn J'onzz 125.00
149 ATh,J'onn J'onzz. 125.00
150 MMe,J'onn J'onzz. 125.00

151 J'onn J'onzz 125.00
152 MMe,J'onn J'onzz. 125.00
153 J'onn J'onzz 125.00
154 J'onn J'onzz 125.00
155 J'onn J'onzz 125.00
156 JM,I:Dial H for Hero (Giantboy
    Cometeer,Mole)J.J'onzz sty . 125.00
157 JM,Dial H for Hero (Human
    Bullet,Super Charge,Radar
    Sonar Man) J.J'onzz sty . 125.00
158 JM,Dial H for Hero (Quake
    MasterSquid)J'onn J'onzz sty 100.00
159 JM,Dial H for Hero (Human
    Starfish,Hypno Man,Mighty
    Moppet) J'onn J'onzz sty. . . . 100.00
160 JM,Dial H for Hero (King Kandy
    A:Plastic Man,I:Marco Xavier (J'onn
    J'onzz new secret I.D.) 125.00
161 JM,Dial H for Hero (Magneto,
    Hornet Man,Shadow Man) . . . 75.00
162 JM,Dial H for Hero (Mr.Echo,
    Future Man) J'onnJ'onzz sty . 75.00
163 JM,Dial H for Hero(Castor&Pollux,
    King Coil) J'onnJ'onzz sty . . . 75.00
164 JM,Dial H for Hero (Super Nova
    Zip Tide) J'onnJ'onzz sty. . . . 75.00
165 JM,Dial H for Hero (Whoozis,
    Whatsis,Howzis) J'onn J'onzz
    story. 75.00
166 JM,Dial H for Hero (Yankee
    Doodle Kid,Chief Mighty Arrow)
    J'onn J'onzz sty. 75.00
167 JM,Dial H for Hero (Balloon Boy,
    Muscle Man,Radar Sonar Man)
    J'onn J'onzz sty. 75.00
168 JM,Dial H for Hero (Thunderbolt,
    Mole,Cometeer,Hoopster)
    J'onn J'onzz sty. 75.00
169 JM,I:Gem Girl in Dial H for
    Hero,J'onn J'onzz sty 75.00
170 JM,Dial H for Hero (Baron
    BuzzSaw,Don Juan,Sphinx
    Man) J'onn J'onzz sty 75.00
171 JM,Dial H for Hero (King Viking
    Whirl-I-Gig)J'onn J'onzz sty. . . 70.00
172 JM,Dial H for Hero 70.00
173 E:Dial H for Hero,F:J'onn
    J'onzz 70.00
174 New direction,SA pg.13 . . . . 350.00
175 I:Cain. 250.00
176 SA,Cain's Game Room. 200.00
177 Curse of the Car 200.00
178 NA,The Game. 200.00
179 BWr,NA,JO,Widow'sWalk . . . 250.00
180 GK,WW,BWr,SA,Room 13 . . 200.00
181 BWr,The Siren of Satan 200.00
182 ATh,The Devil's Doorway 60.00
183 BWr,WW(i),DeadCanKill. . . . 150.00
184 ATh,GK,WW,Eye o/Basilisk . . 60.00
185 AW,The Beautiful Beast 60.00
186 BWr,NA,Nightmare 60.00
187 ATh,Mask of the Red Fox 50.00
188 TD,BWr,NA(c),House of
    Madness 70.00
189 WW(i),NA(c),Eyes of the Cat . 50.00
190 ATh,Fright 50.00
191 BWr,TD,NA(c),Christmas
    Story 75.00
192 JAp,GM,DH,NA(c),Garnener
    of Eden 50.00
193 BWr(c), Voodoo Vengeance . . 50.00
194 ATh,NR,RH(rep),JK(rep)
    Born Loser. 75.00
195 NR,BWr,ThingsOld..Things
    Forgotten. 90.00
196 GM,GK,ATh(rep)A Girl &
    Her Dog. 60.00
197 DD,NR,NA(c),House of
    Horrors. 65.00
198 MSy,NC,Day of the Demon . . 75.00
199 WW,RB,NA(c),Sno'Fun. 85.00
200 MK,TD,The Beast's Revenge . 85.00

House of Mystery #321
© DC Comics, Inc.

201 JAp,The Demon Within 60.00
202 MSy,GC(rep),SA,The Poster
    Plague,John Prentice? 60.00
203 NR,Tower of Prey 60.00
204 BWr,AN,All in the Family 75.00
205 The Coffin Creature 35.00
206 MSy,TP,The Burning 35.00
207 JSn,The Spell 40.00
208 Creator of Evil 35.00
209 AA,JAp,Tomorrow I Hang . . . 40.00
210 The Immortal 35.00
211 NR,Deliver Us From Evil 40.00
212 MA,AN,Ever After 35.00
213 AN,Back from the Realm of
    the Damned 40.00
214 NR,The Shaggy Dog 40.00
215 The Man Who Wanted Power
    over Women 35.00
216 TD,Look into My Eyes & Kill . . 35.00
217 NR,AA,Swamp God 40.00
218 FT,An Ice Place to Visit. 35.00
219 AA,NR,BWr(c),Pledge to
    Satan 45.00
220 AA,AN,They Hunt Butterflies
    Don't They? 35.00
221 FT,BWr,MK,He Who Laughs
    Last 45.00
222 AA,Night of the Teddy Bear . . 30.00
223 Demon From the Deep 30.00
224 FR,AA,SheerFear,B:100pg . . . 80.00
225 AA,FT,AN,See No Evil 80.00
226 AA,FR,NR,SA,Monster in House
    Tour of House of Mystery 80.00
227 NR,AA,The Carriage Man. . . . 80.00
228 FR,NA(i),The Rebel 80.00
229 NR,Nightmare Castle,
    last 100 pages 80.00
230 Experiment In Fear 25.00
231 Cold,Cold Heart 25.00
232 Last Tango in Hell 25.00
233 FR,Cake! 25.00
234 AM,Lafferty's Luck. 25.00
235 NR,Wings of Black Death . . . 25.00
236 SD,NA(i),BWr(c),Death
    Played a Sideshow 35.00
237 FT,Night of the Chameleon . . . 25.00
238 A Touch of Evil 25.00
239 Day of the Witch 25.00
240 The Murderer 25.00
241 FR,NR,Death Pulls theStrings 25.00
242 FR,The Balloon Vendor 25.00
243 Brother Bear 25.00
244 FT,Kronos..Zagros-Eborak . . . 25.00

245 AN,Check the J.C.Demon
    Catalogue Under...Death 25.00
246 DeathVault of Eskimo Kings . . 25.00
247 SD,Death Rides the Waves . . 25.00
248 NightJamieGaveUp theGhost. 25.00
249 Hit Parade of Death 25.00
250 AN,Voyage to Hell. 25.00
251 WW,AA,NA(c),The Collector,
    68-pages 35.00
252 DP,RT,AA,FR,AN,NA(c),
    ManKillers 35.00
253 TD,AN,GK,KJ,NA(c),Beware
    the Demon Child 35.00
254 SD,AN,MR,NA(c),The
    Devil's Place 35.00
255 RE,GM,BWr(c),Sometimes
    Leopards 35.00
256 DAy,AN,BWr(c),Museum of
    Murders 35.00
257 RE,MGo,TD(i),MBr,Xmas iss. . 35.00
258 SD,RB,BMc,DG(i),The Demon
    and His Boy 35.00
259 RE,RT,MGo,DN,BL,Hair Today,
    Gone Tomorrow, last giant. . . . 35.00
260 Go to Hades 15.00
261 The Husker 15.00
262 FreedFrom Infernos of Hell. . . 15.00
263 JCr,Is There Vengeance
    After Death? 15.00
264 Halloween Issue 15.00
265 The Perfect Host. 15.00
266 The Demon Blade. 15.00
267 A Strange Way to Die 15.00
269 Blood on the Grooves. 15.00
270 JSh,JRu,JBi,Black Moss. 15.00
271 TS,HellHound of
    Brackenmoor 15.00
272 DN,DA,theSorcerer's Castle. . 15.00
273 The Rites of Inheritance 15.00
274 MR,JBi,Hell Park. 15.00
275 JCr,Final Installment 15.00
276 SD,MN,Epode. 15.00
277 HC,AMi,Limited Engagement . 15.00
278 TV or Not TV. 15.00
279 AS,Trial by Fury 15.00
280 VMK,DAy,Hungry Jaws
    of Death. 15.00
281 Now Dying in this Corner 15.00
282 JSw,DG,Superman/Radio
    Shack ins. 15.00
283 RT,AN,Kill Me Gently 15.00
284 KG,King and the Dragon 15.00
285 Cold Storage 15.00
286 Long Arm of the Law. 15.00
287 NR,AS,BL,Legend o/t Lost . . . 15.00
288 DSp,Piper at Gates of Hell . . . 15.00
289 Brother Bobby's Home for
    Wayward Girls & Boys. 15.00
290 TS,I:I..Vampire 27.00
291 TS,DAy,I..Vampire #2 . . . . 15.00
292 TS,MS,TD,RE,DSp,Wendigo . 15.00
293 GT,TS,A:I..Vampire #3 . . . . . . 15.00
294 CI,TY,GT,TD,The Darkness . . 15.00
295 TS,TVE,JCr,I..Vampire #4 . . . . 15.00
296 CI,BH,Night Women 15.00
297 TS,DCw,TD,I..Vampire #5 . . . . 15.00
298 TS,Stalker on a StarlessNight. . 15.00
299 TS,DSp,I..Vampire #6 . . . . . . 15.00
300 GK,DA,JSon,JCr,DSp,Anniv.. 20.00
301 JDu,TVE,KG,TY `...Virginia' . 15.00
302 TS,NR,DSp,I..Vampire #7 . . . 17.00
303 TS,DSp,I..Vampire #8 . . . . . . 17.00
304 EC,RE,I..Vampire #9 . . . . 17.00
305 TVE,EC,I..Vampire #10 . . . . . 17.00
306 TS,TD,I..Vampire #11,
    A:Jack the Ripper 17.00
307 TS,I..Vampire #12 . . . . 17.00
308 TS,MT,NR,I..Vampire #13 . . . . 17.00
309 TS,I..Vampire #14 . . . . 17.00
310 TS(i),I..Vampire #15 . . . . 17.00
311 I..Vampire #16 . . . . 17.00
312 TS(i),I..Vampire #17 . . . . 17.00

313 TS(i),CI,I..Vampire #18 . . . . . . 17.00
314 TS,I..Vampire #19 . . . . 17.00
315 TS(i),TY,I..Vampire #20. . . . . 17.00
316 TS(i),GT,TVE,I..Vampire #21 . 17.00
317 TS(i),I..Vampire #22 . . . . 17.00
318 TS(i),I..Vampire #23 . . . . 17.00
319 TS,JOy,I..Vampire conc. 25.00
320 GM,Project: Inferior. 25.00
321 final issue 25.00
Welcome Back to the House of Mystery
    GN BWr(c) horror stories rep. . 25.00

HOUSE OF SECRETS
Nov.–Dec., 1956

1 MD,JM,The Hand of Doom. . . 2,600.00
2 MMe,RMo,NC,Mask of Fear . . 900.00
3 JM,JK,MMe,The Three
    Prophecies. 750.00
4 JM,JK,MMe,Master of
    Unknown 600.00
5 MMe,The Man Who
    Hated Fear 400.00
6 NC,MMe,Experiment 1000 . . . 400.00
7 RMo,Island o/t Enchantress . . 400.00
8 JK,RMo,The Electrified Man . . 450.00
9 JM,JSt,The Jigsaw Creatures . 375.00
10 JSt,NC,I was a Prisoner
    of the Sea 375.00
11 KJ(c),NC,The Man who
    Couldn't Stop Growing. 375.00
12 JK,The Hole in the Sky. 400.00
13 The Face in the Mist. 300.00
14 MMe,The Man who Stole Air . 300.00
15 The Creature in the Camera. . 300.00
16 NC,We Matched Wits with a
    Gorilla Genius 250.00
17 DW,Lady in the Moon 250.00
18 MMe,The Fantastic
    Typewriter 250.00
19 MMe,NC,Lair of the
    Dragonfly. 250.00
20 Incredible Fireball Creatures. . 250.00
21 Girl from 50,000 Fathoms. . . . 250.00
22 MMe,Thing from Beyond 250.00
23 MMe,I&O:Mark Merlin 275.00
24 NC,Mark Merlin story 250.00
25 MMe,Mark Merlin story 225.00
26 NC,MMe, Mark Merlin story . . 225.00
27 MMe,Mark Merlin 225.00
28 MMe,Mark Merlin 225.00
29 NC,MMe,Mark Merlin 225.00
30 JKu,MMe,Mark Merlin. 225.00
31 DD,MMe,RH,Mark Merlin 200.00
32 MMe,Mark Merlin 200.00

House of Secrets #37
© DC Comics Inc.

33 MMe,Mark Merlin	200.00
34 MMe,Mark Merlin	200.00
35 MMe,Mark Merlin	200.00
36 MMe,Mark Merlin	200.00
37 MMe,Mark Merlin	200.00
38 MMe,Mark Merlin	200.00
39 JKu,MMe,Mark Merlin	200.00
40 NC,MMe,Mark Merlin	200.00
41 MMe,Mark Merlin	200.00
42 MMe,Mark Merlin	200.00
43 RMo,MMe,CI,Mark Merlin	200.00
44 MMe,Mark Merlin	200.00
45 MMe,Mark Merlin	200.00
46 MMe,Mark Merlin	200.00
47 MMe,Mark Merlin	200.00
48 ATh,MMe,Mark Merlin	200.00
49 MMe,Mark Merlin	200.00
50 MMe,Mark Merlin	200.00
51 MMe,Mark Merlin	200.00
52 MMe,Mark Merlin	200.00
53 CI,Mark Merlin	200.00
54 RMo,MMe,Mark Merlin	200.00
55 MMe,Mark Merlin	200.00
56 MMe,Mark Merlin	200.00
57 MMe,Mark Merlin	200.00
58 MMe,O:Mark Merlin	200.00
59 MMe,Mark Merlin	200.00
60 MMe,Mark Merlin	200.00
61 I:Eclipso,A:Mark Merlin	225.00
62 MMe,Eclipso,Mark Merlin	200.00
63 GC,ATh,Eclipso,Mark Merlin	150.00
64 MMe,ATh,M Merlin,Eclipso	150.00
65 MMe,ATh,M Merlin,Eclipso	150.00
66 MMe,ATh,M Merlin,Eclipso	150.00
67 MMe,ATh,M Merlin,Eclipso	150.00
68 MMe,Mark Merlin,Eclipso	150.00
69 MMe,Mark Merlin,Eclipso	150.00
70 MMe,Mark Merlin,Eclipso	150.00
71 MMe,Mark Merlin,Eclipso	150.00
72 MMe,Mark Merlin,Eclipso	150.00
73 MMe,D:Mark Merlin,I:Prince Ra-Man; Eclipso	150.00
74 MMe,Prince Ra-Man,Eclipso	150.00
75 MMe,Prince Ra-Man,Eclipso	150.00
76 MMe,Prince Ra-Man,Eclipso	150.00
77 MMe,Prince Ra-Man,Eclipso	150.00
78 MMe,Prince Ra-Man,Eclipso	150.00
79 MMe,Prince Ra-Man,Eclipso	150.00
80 MMe,Prince Ra-Man,Eclipso	150.00
81 I:Abel, new mystery format Don't Move It	300.00
82 DD,NA,One & only, fully guaran- teed super-permanent 100%	100.00
83 ATh,The Stuff that Dreams are Made of	100.00
84 DD,If I had but world enough and time	100.00
85 DH,GK,NA,Second Chance	125.00
86 GT,GM,Strain	125.00
87 DD,DG,RA,MK,BWr,The Coming of Ghaglan	135.00
88 DD,The Morning Ghost	125.00
89 GM,DH,Where Dead Men Walk	125.00
90 GT,RB,NA,GM,The Symbionts	135.00
91 WW,MA,The Eagle's Talon	125.00
92 BWr,TD(i),I:Swamp Thing (Alex Olson)	1,000.00
93 JAp,TD,ATh(rep.)Lonely in Death	100.00
94 TD,ATh(rep.)Hyde and go Seek	100.00
95 DH,NR,The Bride of Death	100.00
96 DD,JAb,WW,BWr,the Monster	100.00
97 JAp,Divide and Murder	100.00
98 MK,ATh(rep),Born Losers	100.00
99 NR,TD(i),BWr,Beyond His Imagination	75.00
100 TP,TD,AA,BWr,Rest in Peace	100.00
101 AN,MK,Small Invasion	40.00
102 NR,MK,A Lonely Monstrosity	40.00
103 AN,BWr,Village on Edge of Forever	40.00

House of Secrets #75
© DC Comics, Inc.

104 NR,AA,GT,Ghosts Don't Bother Me...But...	40.00
105 JAp,AA,MK,An Axe to Grind	40.00
106 AN,AA,BWr,This Will Kill You	40.00
107 AA,BWr(c),The Night of the Nebbish	40.00
108 A New Kid on the Block	40.00
109 AA,AN...And in Death, there is no Escape	40.00
110 Safes Have Secrets, Too	40.00
111 TD,Hair-I-Kari	40.00
112 Case of the Demon Spawn	40.00
113 MSy,NC,NR,Spawns of Satan	40.00
114 FBe,Night Game	40.00
115 AA,AN,Nobody Hurts My Brother	40.00
116 NR,Like Father,Like Son	40.00
117 AA,AN,Revenge for the Deadly Dummy	40.00
118 GE,Very Last Picture Show	40.00
119 A Carnival of Dwarves	40.00
120 TD,AA,The Lion's Share	40.00
121 Ms.Vampire Killer	40.00
122 AA,Requiem for Igor	25.00
123 ATh,A Connecticut Ice Cream Man in King Arthur's Court	25.00
124 Last of the Frankensteins	25.00
125 AA,FR,Instant Re-Kill	25.00
126 AN,On Borrowed Time	25.00
127 MSy,A Test of Innocence	25.00
128 AN,Freak Out!	25.00
129 Almost Human	25.00
130 All Dolled Up!	25.00
131 AN,Point of No Return	25.00
132 Killer Instinct	25.00
133 Portraits of Death	25.00
134 NR,Inheritance of Blood	25.00
135 BWr,The Vegitable Garden	25.00
136 BWr,NR,Last Voyage of Lady Luck	25.00
137 BWr,The Harder They Fall	25.00
138 Where Dreams are Born	30.00
139 SD,NR,A Real Crazy Kid	30.00
140 NR,O:Patchwork Man	40.00
141 You Can't Beat the Devil	20.00
142 Playmate	20.00
143 The Evil Side	20.00
144 The Vampire of Broadway	20.00
145 Operation was Successful,But	20.00
146 GM,Snake's Alive	20.00
147 AN,GM,See-Through Thief	20.00
148 GM,SD,Sorcerer's Apprentice	20.00
149 MK,The Evil One	20.00

150 JSN(c),A:Phantom Stranger and Dr.13	20.00
151 MGo,MK,Nightmare	20.00
152 Sister Witch	20.00
153 VM,AN,Don't Look Now	20.00
154 TS,MK,JL,Last issue	20.00

HOUSE OF SECRETS
DC/Vertigo, Aug., 1996

1 SSe(s),TKr, judgments on your darkest secrets	4.00
2 SSe(s),TKr, F:Rain	3.00
3 SSe(s),TKr,Seattle's citizens secrets	3.00
4 SSe(s),TKr,Eric's secrets exposed	3.00
5 SSe(s),TKr,Foundation Epilogue	3.00
6 SSe(s),DFg,Other rooms: Meeting	3.00
7 SSe(s),TKr,Blueprint: Elevation A	3.00
8 SSe(s),TKr,Road to You,pt.1	3.00
9 SSe(s),TKr,Road to You,pt.2	3.00
10 SSe(s),TKr,Road to You,pt.3	3.00
11 The Book of Law, pt.1 (of 5)	3.00
12 The Book of Law, pt.2	3.00
13 SSe,The Book of Law, pt.3	3.00
14 SSe,The Book of Law, pt.4	3.00
15 SSe,The Book of Law, pt.5	3.00
16 SSe,Book of Law, epilogue	3.00
17 SSe,The Road to You, pt.1	3.00
18 SSe,The Road to You, pt.2	3.00
19 SSe,The Road to You, pt.3	3.00
20 SSe,Other Rooms story	3.00
21 SSe,Basement, pt.1	3.00
22 SSe,Basement, pt.2	3.00
23 SSe,Basement, pt.3	3.00
24 SSe,TKr,Attic	3.00
25 SSe,TKr, final issue	3.00
TPB Foundation, rep.#1–#5	15.00

HOUSE OF SECRETS: FACADE
DC/Vertigo, March, 2001

1 (of 2) TKr, 48-page	6.00
2 TKr,48-page	6.00

HUMAN DEFENSE CORPS
May 2003

1 (of 6) TTn	2.50
2 TTn,Parasitic aliens	2.50
3 TTn,What dreams may come	2.50
4 TTn,Seance	2.50
5 TTn,War is Hell	2.50
6 TTn,concl.	2.50

HUMAN RACE, THE
March, 2005

1 (of 7) F:Delta Chi Delta	3.00
2 F:Ulysses	3.00
3 V:Paracelsus	3.00
4 Extraterrestrial parasite	3.00
5 Ulysses, Nymph	3.00
6 Ulysses, Nymph	3.00
7 finale	3.00

HUMAN TARGET SPECIAL
1991

1 DG(i),Prequel to T.V. Series	3.00

HUMAN TARGET
DC/Vertigo, 1999

1 (of 4) PrM(s)	3.50
2 PrM(s)	3.00
3 PrM(s)	3.00
4 PrM(s), concl.	3.00
TPB	13.00

HUMAN TARGET
DC/Vertigo, Aug. 2003
1 PrM(s),40-pg.	3.00
2 PrM(s),Unshredded Man,pt.1	3.00
3 PrM(s),Unshredded Man,pt.2	3.00
4 PrM(s),Ball Game, pt.1	3.00
5 PrM(s),Ball Game, pt.2	3.00
6 PrM(s),For I Have Sinned	3.00
7 PrM(s),Wind Blows,pt.1	3.00
8 PrM(s),Wind Blows,pt.2	3.00
9 PrM(s),Wind Blows,pt.3	3.00
10 PrM(s),Five Days Grace	3.00
11 PrM(s),F:Mary	3.00
12 PrM(s),Crossing the Border	3.00
13 PrM(s),Crossing the Border	3.00
14 PrM(s),Second Coming,pt.1	3.00
15 The Second Coming,pt.2	3.00
16 The Second Coming	3.00
17 You Made Me Love You	3.00
18 Letter From the Front Line	3.00
19 The Stealer, pt.1	3.00
20 The Stealer, pt.2	3.00
21 The Stealer, pt.3	3.00
TPB Human Target: Final Cut	20.00
TPB Strike Zones	10.00
TPB Living in Amerika (2005)	15.00

HUNTER: THE AGE OF MAGIC
DC/Vertigo, July, 2001
1 R:The Hunter	3.50
10 thru 25	@3.00

HUNTER'S HEART
1995
1 Cops vs. Serial Killer	5.00
2 thru 3	@5.00

HUNTRESS, THE
1989–90
1 JSon/DG	2.50
2 JSon,Search for Family's Murderer	2.50
3 JSon,A:La Bruja	2.50
4 JSon,Little Italy/Chinatown Gangs	2.50
5 JSon,V:Doctor Mandragora	2.50
6 JSon,Huntress'secrets revealed	2.50
7 JSon,V:Serial Killer	2.50
8 JSon,V:Serial Killer	2.50
9 JSon,V:Serial Killer	2.50
10 JSon,Nuclear Terrorists in NY.	2.50
11 JSon,V:Wyvern,Nuclear Terrorists contd.	2.50
12 JSon,V:Nuclear Terrorists cont	2.50
13 JSon,Violence in NY	2.50
14 JSon,Violence contd.,New Mob boss	2.50
15 JSon,I:Waterfront Warrior	2.50
16 JSon,Secret of Waterfront Warrior revealed	2.50
17 JSon,Batman+Huntress#1	2.50
18 JSon,Batman+Huntress#2	2.50
19 JSon,Batman+Huntress#3,final issue	2.50

HUNTRESS
[Limited Series], 1994
1 CDi(s),MN,V:Redzone	2.25
2 MN,V:Redzone	2.25
3 MN,V:Redzone	2.25
4 MN,V:Spano,Redzone	2.25

iCANDY
Sept. 2003
1 DAn&ALa(s)	2.50
2 DAn&ALa(s) thru 6	@2.50

Icon #7
© *DC Comics, Inc.*

ICON
DC/Milestone, 1993–96
1 Direct Market Ed.,MBr,MG,I:Icon, Rocket,S.H.R.E.D.,w/poster, card,C puzzle piece	3.50
1a Newsstand Ed.	2.00
2 thru 24	@2.50
25 V:Oblivion	3.00
26 thru 45	@2.50

IDENTITY CRISIS
June 2004
1 (of 7) RgM,MIB,48-pg.	7.50
2 thru 5 RgM,MIB,40-pg.	@6.00
6 RgM,MIB,40-page	4.00
7 RgM,MIB,concl.	4.00
1a thru 7a reps.	@4.00
TPB	15.00

IMPULSE
1995–2002
1 Young Flash Adventures	6.00
2 V:Terrorists	3.50
3 thru 12	@3.00
13 thru 25	@2.50
26 thru 89	@2.50
Ann.#2 Pulp Heroes (Western)	4.00
Spec.#1,000,000 BML(s)	2.25
GN Bart Saves the Universe	6.00
Spec. Impulse/Atom Double-Shot DJu, x-over concl. (1997)	3.00
Spec. Impulse Plus 48pg. with Grossout (1997)	3.00

INDUSTRIAL GOTHIC
DC/Vertigo, 1995
1 Jail Break Plans	2.50
2 thru 5 Jail Break Plans	@2.50

INFERIOR FIVE
March-April, 1967
1 MSy,Super-hero Satire	100.00
2 MSy,A:Plastic Man	45.00
3 MSy,Darwin of the Apes	40.00
4 MSy,Valhallaballoo	40.00
5 MSy,I was a Guillotine-age Hero	40.00
6 MSy,DC Stars and office	25.00
7 WMo,Drainy Day	25.00
8 WMo,V:Dr. Gruesome	25.00
9 WMo,Mummy's the Word	25.00
10 WMo,A:Superman (1968)	35.00

11 JO(c&a) (1972)	25.00
12 JO(c&a)	25.00

INFERNO
Aug., 1997
1 (of 4) SI, from Legion	4.00
2 SI,mall grrls	3.00
3 SI,Legion Month tie-in	3.00
4 SI, concl.	3.00

INFINITE CRISIS
Oct., 2005
1 (of 7) PJ,ALa	5.00
1a variant (c).	6.00
2 (of 7) PJ,ALa	4.00
2a variant (c).	4.00
3 PJ,ALa	4.00
3a variant GP (c)	4.00
4 PJ,ALa, Batman vs. Nightwing	4.00
4a variant GP (c)	4.00
5 PJ,ALa,Superman vs. Superman	4.00
5a variant (c).	4.00
6 PJ,ALa,One Year Later	4.00
6a variant (c).	4.00
7 Conclusion.	4.00
7a variant (c).	4.00
Spec. Secret Files 64-pg. (2006).	6.00
Spec. Villains United	5.00
TPB Infinite Crisis Companion	15.00

INFINITY, INC.
March, 1984
1 JOy,O:Infinity Inc.	5.00
2 JOy,End of Origin	4.00
3 JOy,O:Jade	3.00
4 JOy,V:JSA	3.00
5 JOy,V:JSA	3.00
6 JOy,V:JSA	3.00
7 JOy,V:JSA	3.00
8 JOy,V:Ultra Humanite	3.00
9 JOy,V:Ultra Humanite	3.00
10 JOy,V:Ultra Humanite	3.00
11 DN,GT,O:Infinity Inc.	3.00
12 Infinity Unmasks,I:Yolanda Montez (New Wildcat)	3.00
13 DN,V:Rose & Thorn	3.00
14 1st TM DC art,V:Chroma	10.00
15 TM,V:Chroma	4.00
16 TM,I:Helix (Mr. Bones)	4.00
17 TM,V:Helix.	4.00
18 TM,V:Crisis	4.00
19 TM,JSA,JLA x-over, I:Mekanique	4.00
20 TM,Crisis	4.00
21 TM,Crisis,I:Hourman II, Dr.Midnight	4.00
22 TM,Crisis	4.00
23 TM,Crisis	4.00
24 TM,Crisis	4.00
25 TM,Crisis,JSA	4.00
26 TM,V:Carcharo	4.00
27 TM,V:Carcharo	4.00
28 TM,V:Carcharo	4.00
29 TM,V:Helix.	4.00
30 TM,Mourning of JSA	4.00
31 TM,V:Psycho Pirate	4.00
32 TM,V:Psycho Pirate	4.00
33 TM,O:Obsidian	4.00
34 TM,A: Global Guardians	4.00
35 TM,V:Infinitors	4.00
36 TM,V:Injustice Unl.	4.00
37 TM,TD,O:Northwind	4.00
38 Helix on Trial	3.00
39 O:Solomon Grundy	3.00
40 V:Thunderbolt	3.00
41 Jonni Thunder	3.00
42 TD,V:Hastor,Fury	3.00
43 TD,V:Hastor,Silver Scarab	3.00
44 TD,D:Silver Scarab	3.00
45 MGu,A:New Teen Titans, V:Ultra-Humanite	3.00

Infinity Inc. #47 © DC Comics, Inc.

46 TD,Millennium,V:Floronic Man . . 3.00
47 TD,Millennium,V:Harlequin 3.00
48 TD,O:Nuklon 3.00
49 Silver Scarab becomes
   Sandman 3.00
50 TD,V:The Wizard,O:Sandman . . 3.50
51 W:Fury & Sandman,D:Skyman . . 3.00
52 V:Helix. 3.00
53 V:Justice Unlimited,last issue . . . 3.00
Ann.#1 TM,V:Thorn 4.00
Ann.#2 V:Degaton,x-over Young
   All-Stars Annual #1 . . . . 3.00
Spec.#1 TD,A:Outsiders,V:Psycho
   Pirate 3.00

INFINITY INC.
Sept., 2007
1 PrM(s),A:John Henry Irons 3.00
2 PrM(s),A:Superman 3.00

INVASION!
1988–89
1 TM,I:Vril Dox,Dominators
   (20th century) 4.00
2 TM,KG,DG,I:L.E.G.I.O.N. 3.00
3 BS,DG,I:Blasters 3.00
Daily Planet-Invasion! 16p 2.00

INVISIBLES
DC/Vertigo, 1994–96
1 GMo(s). 7.00
2 GMo(s),Down & Out,pt.1 . . . . 4.00
3 GMo(s),Down & Out,pt.2 . . . . 4.00
4 GMo(s),Down & Out,pt.3 . . . . 4.00
5 Arcadia,pt.1 . . . . 4.00
6 Arcadia,pt.2 . . . . 4.00
7 Arcadia,pt.3 . . . . 4.00
8 Arcadia,pt.4 . . . . 4.00
9 SeP(c),L:Dane 3.00
10 SeP(c),CWn,Jim Crow v. 3
    Zombies. 3.00
11 V:New Breed of Hunter 3.00
12 GMo,Best Man Fall. 3.00
13 GMo,Sheman,pt.1. . . . . 3.00
14 GMo,SeP,Sheman,pt.2 . . . . 3.00
15 GMo,Sheman,pt.3. . . . . 3.00
16 GMo,An offer from Sir Miles . . . 3.00
17 GMo,Entropy in the U.K.,pt.1 . . . 3.00
18 GMo,Entropy in the U.K.,pt.2 . . . 3.00
19 GMo,Entropy in the U.K.,pt.3 . . . 3.00
20 GMo,F:RaggedRobin,Dane,Boy . 4.00
21 GMo,PuJ,F:Dane 4.00
22 GMo(s),MBu,MPn 4.00
23 GMo(s),MBu,MPn 4.00

24 GMo(s),MBu,MPn 4.00
25 GMo(s),MBu,MPn,final issue
   Aug., 1996. . . . . 5.00
[Volume 2] DC/Vertigo, 1996
1 GMo(s),PJ,Black Science,pt.1 . . . 4.00
2 GMo(s),PJ,Black Science,pt.2 . . . 3.00
3 GMo(s),PJ,Black Science,pt.3 . . . 3.00
4 GMo(s),PJ,Black Science,pt.4 . . . 3.00
5 GMo(s),PJ,In SanFrancisco,pt.1 . 3.00
6 GMo(s),PJ,In SanFrancisco,pt.2 . 3.00
7 GMo(s),PJ,BB(c),Time Machine
   Go, concl. 3.00
8 GMo(s),PJ,BB(c),Sensitive
   Criminals,pt.1. . . . . 3.00
9 GMo(s),PJ,BB(c),Criminals,pt.2. . 3.00
10 GMo(s),PJ,Criminals,pt.3, ... 3.00
11 GMo(s),PJ,BB(c),Hand of Glory
   pt.1 . . . . 3.00
12 GMo(s),PJ,BB(c),Glory,pt.2 . . . . 3.00
13 GMo(s),PJ,BB(c),Glory,concl. . . . 3.00
14 GMo(s),BB(c),Archons aftermath 3.00
15 GMo(s),BB(c), The Philadelphia
   Experiment, pt.1 . . . . 3.00
16 GMo(s),BB(c),Experiment,pt.2 . . 3.00
17 GMo,CWn,BB,Black Science II
   pt.1. . . . . 3.00
18 GMo,CWn,BB,Science,pt.2. . . . . 3.00
19 GMo,CWn,BB,Science,pt.3. . . . . 3.00
20 GMo,CWn,BB(c),Science,pt.4 . . . 2.50
21 GMo,CWn,BB(c),King Mob 2.50
22 GMo,CWn,BB(c) The Tower 2.50
[Volume 3] DC/Vertigo, 1999
12 GMo,Satanstorm,pt.1 . . . . 3.00
11 GMo,Satanstorm,pt.2 . . . . 3.00
10 GMo,Satanstorm,pt.3 . . . . 3.00
9 GMo,Satanstorm,pt.4. . . . . 3.00
8 GMo,Karmageddon,pt.1 . . . . 3.00
7 GMo,Karmageddon,pt.2 . . . . 3.00
6 GMo,Karmageddon,pt.3 . . . . 3.00
5 GMo. 3.00
4 GMo,Invisible Kingdom,pt.1 . . . . . 3.00
3 GMo,Invisible Kingdom,pt.2 . . . . . 3.00
2 GMo,Invisible Kingdom,pt.3 . . . . . 3.00
1 GMo,conclusion. 3.00
GN The Mystery Play 10.00

ION
April, 2006
1 RMz, Kyle Rayner returns 3.00
2 RMz, Is Kyle going mad? 3.00
3 RMz, F:Mogo 3.00
4 RMz,F:Green Lantern 3.00
5 RMz,F:Green Lantern 3.00
6 RMz,Guardians of the Universe . 3.00
7 RMz,Return to earth 3.00
8 RMz,A remote world 3.00
9 RMz 3.00
10 RMz,Twilight of Ion 3.00
11 RMz,Kyle Raner & Donna Troy . . 3.00
12 RMz,finale. 3.00

IRONWOLF
1986
1 HC,rep. 2.25

ISIS
Oct.–Nov., 1976
1 RE/WW 25.00
2 thru 6 . . . . @15.00
7 O:Isis 18.00
8 Dec.–Jan., 1977–78. . . . . 15.00

IT'S GAMETIME
Sept.–Oct., 1955
1 . . . . 1,100.00
2 Dodo and the Frog. 900.00
3 . . . . 900.00
4 March-April, 1956 . . . . 950.00

JACK CROSS
Aug., 2005
1 (of 4) WEI,GEr 2.50
2 WEI,GEr. 2.50
3 WEI,GEr. 2.50
4 WEI,GEr, conclusion 2.50

JACKIE GLEASON AND THE HONEYMOONERS
June-July, 1956
1 Based on TV show 1,300.00
2 . . . . 750.00
3 thru 11 . . . . @600.00
12 April-May, 1958 . . . . 850.00

JACK KIRBY'S FOURTH WORLD
Jan., 1997
1 JBy,Worlds of New Genesis &
   Apokolips become one 2.25
2 JBy,F:Big Barda vs. Thor 2.25
3 JBy,at Wall of the Source 2.25
4 JBy,Can Highfather save his son 2.25
5 JBy,conflict between the gods . . . 2.25
6 JBy,Cause of Orion's
   transformation 2.25
7 JBy,Orion taught lesson. 2.25
8 JBy,WS,Genesis tie-in 2.25
9 JBy,WS(c),Genesis aftermath . . 2.25
10 JBy,WS, ... 2.25
11 JBy,WS,F:Orion. 2.25
12 JBy,WS,F:Mister Miracle. 2.25
13 JBy,WS 2.25
14 JBy,WS,Promethean Giant 2.25
15 JBy,WS,Armaghetto 2.25
16 JBy,WS,Kalibak vs. Darkseid . . . 2.25
17 JBy,WS,Darkseid 2.25
18 JBy,WS,Darkseid freed 2.25
19 JBy,WS,two stories 2.25
20 JBy,WS,A:Superman,final issue . 2.25
TPB JK. 13.00

JACK OF FABLES
DC/Vertigo, July, 2006
1 BWg 3.00
2 BWg,Mr. Revise 3.00
3 BWg,Mr. Revise's prisoner 3.00
4 Great Escape is on 3.00
5 . . . . 3.00
6 Jack Frost, pt.1 . . . . 3.00
7 Jack Frost, pt.2 . . . . 3.00
8 Jack of Hearts, pt.1 . . . . 3.00
9 in Las Vegas 3.00
10 V:Mister Revise. 3.00
11 Jack Frost, pt.2 . . . . 3.00
12 The Bad Prince, pt.1. . . . . 3.00
13 The Bad Prince, pt.2. . . . . 3.00
14 The Bad Prince, pt.3. . . . . 3.00
15 The Bad Prince, pt.4. . . . . 3.00
16 Halloween Issue 3.00

JAGUAR
Impact, 1991
1 I&O:Jaguar 2.25
2 thru 14 . . . . @2.25
Ann.#1 Earthquest,w/trading card . . 2.50

JEMM, SON OF SATURN
Sept., 1984
1 GC/KJ mini-series 2.50
2 GC 2.50
3 GC,Origin 2.50
4 A:Superman 2.50
5 Kin 2.50
6 thru 12 GC, Aug., 1985 . . . . . @2.50

JIMMY WAKELY
Sept.–Oct., 1949
1 Ph(c),ATh,The Cowboy
   Swordsman 1,700.00
2 Ph(c),ATh,The Prize Pony 700.00
3 Ph(c),ATh,The Return of
   Tulsa Tom 650.00
4 Ph(c),ATh,FF,HK,Where There's
   Smoke There's Gunfire 625.00
5 ATh,The Return of the
   Conquistadores 500.00
6 ATh,Two Lives of
   Jimmy Wakely 500.00
7 The Secret of Hairpin Canyon . 500.00
8 ATh,The Lost City of
   Blue Valley 500.00
9 ATh,The Return of the
   Western Firebrands 350.00
10 ATh,Secret of Lantikin'sLight . 350.00
11 ATh,Trail o/a Thousand Hoofs. 350.00
12 ATh,JKU,The King of Sierra
   Valley 350.00
13 ATh,The Raiders of Treasure
   Mountain 350.00
14 ATh(c),JKu,The Badmen
   of Roaring Flame Valley 350.00
15 GK(c),Tommyguns on the
   Range 350.00
16 GK(c),The Bad Luck Boots . . . 300.00
17 GK(c),Terror atThunderBasin . 300.00
18 July-Aug., 1952 . . . . 350.00

JLA
Nov., 1996
1 GMo(s),HPo,JhD,V:Hyperclan . . 16.00
2 GMo(s),HPo,JhD,V:Hyperclan . . 12.00
3 GMo(s),HPo,JhD,War of the
   Worlds 10.00
4 GMo(s),HPo,JhD,battle of the
   super-heroes, conc 10.00
5 GMo(s),HPo,JhD Woman of
   Tomorrow 7.00
6 GMo(s),HPo,JhD,Fire in theSky . 6.00
7 GMo(s),HPo,JhD,Heaven on
   Earth 6.00
8 GMo(s),HPo,JhD,Imaginary
   Stories, F:Green Arrow 6.00
9 GMo(s),V:The Key 6.00
10 GMo(s),HPo,JhD,R:Injustice
   Gang, pt.1 (of 6) 6.00
11 GMo(s),HPo,JhD,Rock of Ages,
   pt.2 . . . . 6.00
12 GMo(s),HPo,JhD,Rock of Ages,
   pt.3, A:Hourman 6.00
13 GMo(s),HPo,JhD,Rock of Ages,
   pt.4 . . . . 6.00
14 GMo(s),HPo,JhD,Rock of Ages,
   pt.5 . . . . 6.00
15 GMo(s),HPo,JhD,Rock of Ages
   pt.6, concl, 48 pg. 6.00
16 GMo(s),HPo,JhD, new member . 6.00
17 GMo(s),HPo,JhD,V:Prometheus. 6.00
18 MWa,Engine of Chance, pt.1 . . 6.00
19 MWa,Engine of Chance, pt.2 . . . 6.00
20 MWa,F:Adam Strange,pt.1 . . . . 6.00
21 MWa,F:Adam Strange,pt.2 . . . . 6.00
22 GMo(s),The Star Conqueror 2.50
23 GMo,V:Star Conqueror,
   A:Sandman 2.50
24 GMo,HPo,Ultra-Marines,pt.1. . . . 2.50
25 GMo,HPo,Ultra-Marines,pt.2. . . . 2.50
26 GMo,HPo,Ultra-Marines,pt.3. . . . 2.50
27 GMo,HPo,CrisisTimesFive,pt.1. . 2.50
28 GMo,HPo,CrisisTimesFive,pt.2. . 2.50
29 GMo,HPo,CrisisTimesFive,pt.3. . 2.50
30 GMo,HPo,CrisisTimesFive,pt.4. . 2.50
31 GMo,HPo,CrisisTimes
   Five,concl. 2.50
32 MWa(s),No Man's Land 2.50
33 MWa(s),No Man's Land 2.50
34 GMo,Super-villains riot 2.50

JLA A#20 © DC Comics Inc.

35 JMD(s),F:New Spectre 2.50
36 GMo,HPo,World War 3,pt.1 . . . . 2.50
37 GMo,HPo,World War 3,pt.2 . . . . 2.50
38 GMo,HPo,World War 3,pt.3 . . . . 2.50
39 GMo,HPo,World War 3,pt.4 . . . . 2.50
40 GMo,HPo,World War 3,pt.5 . . . . 2.50
41 GMo,HPo,World War 3,
   concl.48-pg. 4.00
42 Miniscule civilization 2.50
43 MWa(s),HPo,V:Ra's al Ghul 2.50
44 HPo,Tower of Babel,pt.2 . . . . . . 2.50
45 HPo,Tower of Babel,pt.3. . . . . . 2.50
46 HPo,Tower of Babel,concl. 2.50
47 MWa,BHi,PNe,Queen ofFables . 2.50
48 MWa,BHi,PNe,Queen ofFables . 2.50
49 MWa,BHi,PNe,Queen ofFables . 2.50
50 MWa,BHi,PNe,48-page. 5.00
51 MWa,MsM,Man and Superman . 2.50
52 MWa,BHi,PNe. 2.50
53 MWa,BHi,PNe. 2.50
54 MWa,BHi,PNe,Man & Superman 2.50
55 MWa,Terror Incongita,pt.1 . . . . . 2.50
56 MWa,Terror Incongita,pt.2 . . . . . 2.50
57 MWa,Terror Incongita,pt.3. . . . . 2.50
58 MWa,Terror Incongita,pt.4. . . . . 2.50
59 CDi,DBk,Joker:Last Laugh 2.50
60 MWa,F:Santa Claus 2.50
61 DoM,TG,+16-pg.PowerCompany 2.50
62 DoM,Golden Perfect,pt.1 . . . . . . 2.50
63 DoM,Golden Perfect,pt.2 . . . . . . 2.50
64 DoM,Golden Perfect,pt.3 . . . . . . 2.50
65 DoM,Batman & Plastic Man 2.50
66 DoM,warrior priests 2.50
67 DoM,human sacrifice 2.50
68 DoM,Obsidian Age prologue. . . . 2.50
69 Hunt for Aquaman,pt.1 . . . . 2.50
70 DoM,Hunt for Aquaman,pt.2 . . . 2.50
71 DoM,Hunt for Aquaman,pt.3 . . . . 2.50
72 DoM,Hunt for Aquaman,pt.4 . . . 2.50
73 DoM,Hunt for Aquaman,pt.5 . . . 2.50
74 DoM,Hunt for Aquaman,pt.6 . . . 2.50
75 DoM,Hunt for Aquaman,64-pg. . . 5.00
76 DoM,after Obsidian Age 2.25
77 RV(s),memories stolen 2.25
78 DoM, ... 2.25
79 DoM,F:Faith 2.25
80 White Rage,pt.1 . . . . 2.25
81 White Rage,pt.2 . . . . 2.25
82 White Rage,pt.3 . . . . 2.25
83 Qurac 2.25
84 Trial by Fire,pt.1 . . . . 2.25
85 Trial by Fire,pt.2 . . . . 2.25
86 Trial by Fire,pt.3 . . . . 2.25
87 Trial by Fire,pt.4 . . . . 2.25
88 Trial by Fire,pt.5 . . . . 2.25

89 Trial by Fire,pt.6 . . . . 2.25
90 F:Batman,Wonder Woman 2.25
91 DON(s),Extinction,pt.1 . . . . 2.25
92 DON(s),Extinction,pt.2 . . . . 2.25
93 DON(s),Extinction,pt.3 . . . . 2.25
94 JBy,JOy,10th Circle,pt.1 . . . . . . 2.25
95 JBy,JOy,10th Circle,pt.2 . . . . . . 2.25
96 JBy,JOy,10th Circle,pt.3 . . . . . . 2.25
97 JBy,JOy,10th Circle,pt.4 . . . . . . 2.25
98 JBy,JOy,10th Circle,pt.5 . . . . . . 2.25
99 JBy,JOy,10th Circle,pt.6 . . . . . . 2.25
100 R:The Elite,48-pg. 3.50
101 RG,Pain of the Gods,pt.1 . . . . 2.25
102 RG,Pain of the Gods,pt.2 . . . . 2.25
103 RG,Pain of the Gods,pt.3 . . . . 2.25
104 RG,Pain of the Gods,pt.4 . . . . 2.25
105 RG,Pain of the Gods,pt.5 . . . . 2.25
106 RG,Pain of the Gods,pt.6 . . . . 2.25
107 KBk(s),RG,DGr,space egg 5.00
108 KBk,Syndicate Rules,pt.2 . . . . 4.00
109 KBk,Syndicate Rules,pt.3 . . . . 2.25
110 KBk,Syndicate Rules,pt.4 . . . . 2.25
111 KBk,Syndicate Rules,pt.5 . . . . 2.25
112 KBk,Syndicate Rules,pt.6 . . . . 2.25
113 KBk,Syndicate Rules,pt.7 . . . . 2.25
114 KBk,Syndicate Rules,pt.8 . . . . 2.25
115 MFm,Crisis of Conscience,pt.1 . 5.00
116 MFm,Crisis of Conscience,pt.2 . 3.00
117 MFm,Crisis of Conscience,pt.3 . 2.50
118 MFm,Crisis of Conscience,pt.4 . 2.50
119 MFm,Crisis of Conscience,pt.5 . 2.50
120 World Without Justice League . 2.50
121 World Without Justice League . 2.50
122 World Without Justice League . 2.50
123 World Without Justice League . 2.50
124 World Without Justice League . 2.50
125 World Without Justice League . 2.50
Ann.#1 Pulp Heroes (Hard Boiled) . 4.50
Ann.#2 TTn,BWr,Ghosts 3.50
Ann.#3 JLApe Gorilla Warfare 3.50
Ann.#4 Planet DC 4.00
Spec.#1,000,000 GMo(s),HPo,
   V:Justice Legion A 2.50
SuperSpec.#1 Justice League
   of America 6.00
Spec.#1 Our Worlds at War,48-pg . 3.00
Giant #1, 7 new stories, 80-pg. 5.00
Giant #2, 80-page. 5.00
Giant #3, 80-page. 6.00
SC Secret Origins, oversize. 8.00
JLA: Tomorrow Woman, 1-shot
   TPe,Girlfrenzy (1998) 2.00
GN New World Order GMo(s),HPo,
   JhD, rep. #1–#4. . . . . 6.00
GN American Dreams rep.#5–#9. . . 8.00
GN Secret Files 4.00
GN Secret Files deluxe 5.00
GN Secret Files #2 . . . . 4.00
GN Secret Files #3 How Talia stole
   Batman's Secret Files 5.00
GN Foreign Bodies 6.00
GN JLA/WildC.A.T.S, GMo(s),
   VS,x-over. 6.00
GN JLA/Haven: Arrival (2001) 6.00
GN Gods and Monsters 7.00
GN Seven Caskets,DIB, 48-page . 6.00
GN JLA: Superpower. 6.00
GN JLA Primeval 6.00
GN Shogun of Steel,Elseworlds . . 7.00
GN JLA/Haven:Anathema (2002) . . 6.00
GN The Island of Dr. Moreau,GP
   Elseworlds (2002) 7.00
GN JLA: Liberty and Justice 10.00
JLA/Witchblade, x-over 6.00
JLA Showcase 80-pg Giant #1 . . . . 5.00
Spec. JLA: Workprevel 7.00
Spec. Secret Files 2004. . . . . 5.00
Spec. JLA/Cyberforce (2005). 6.00
Spec. Amazing Adventures of JLA. . 4.00

JLA: ACT OF GOD
Nov., 2000
1 (of 3) Elseworlds,48-page 5.00
2 powers gone,48-page 5.00
3 concl.,48-page 5.00

JLA: AGE OF WONDER
April 2003
1 (of 2) Elseworlds 6.00
2 concl. 6.00

JLA: BLACK BAPTISM
March, 2001
1 (of 4) F:Faust 2.50
2 F:Faust 2.50
3 V:Daiblos 2.50
4 concl. 2.50

JLA: CLASSIFIED
Nov., 2004
1 GMo(s),V:Gorilla Grodd 3.00
2 GMo(s),V:Gorilla Grodd 3.00
3 GMo(s),V:Gorilla Grodd,concl. . . . 3.00
4 KG&JMD(s),KM&JRu, I Can't Believe
   it's Not the Justice League,pt.1 . 3.00
5 KG&JMD(s),KM&JRu, pt.2 . . . . . 3.00
6 KG&JMD(s),KM&JRu, pt.3 . . . . . 3.00
7 KG&JMD(s),KM&JRu, pt.4 . . . . . 3.00
8 KG&JMD(s),KM&JRu, pt.5 . . . . . 3.00
9 KG&JMD(s),KM&JRu, pt.6 . . . . . 3.00
10 WEl(s),New Maps of Hell,pt.1 . . 3.00
11 WEl(s),New Maps of Hell,pt.2 . . 3.00
12 WEl(s),New Maps of Hell,pt.3 . . 3.00
13 WEl(s),New Maps of Hell,pt.4 . . 3.00
14 WEl(s),New Maps of Helll,pt.5 . . 3.00
15 WEl(s),New Maps of Hell,concl. . 3.00
16 KJ,Hypothetical Woman,pt.1 . . . 3.00
17 KJ,Hypothetical Woman,pt.2 . . . 3.00
18 KJ,Hypothetical Woman,pt.3 . . . 3.00
19 KJ,Hypothetical Woman,pt.4 . . . 3.00
20 KJ,Hypothetical Woman,pt.5 . . . 3.00
21 KJ,Hypothetical Woman,pt.6 . . . 3.00
22 MFm, A Game of Chance,pt.1 . . 3.00
23 MFm, A Game of Chance,pt.2 . . 3.00
24 MFm, A Game of Chance,pt.3 . . 3.00
25 MFm, A Game of Chance,pt.4 . . 3.00
26 HC,KPl,Secret Trust, pt.1 . . . . . 3.00
27 HC,KPl,Secret Trust, pt.2 . . . . . 3.00
28 HC,KPl,Secret Trust, pt.3 . . . . . 3.00
29 HC,KPl,Secret Trust, pt.4 . . . . . 3.00
30 HC,KPl,Sacred Trust, pt.5 . . . . . 3.00
31 HC,KPl,Sacred Trust, pt.6 . . . . . 3.00
32 DJu,4th Parallel, pt.1, 48-pgs. . . 4.00
33 DJu,4th Parallel, pt.2 . . . . 3.00
34 DJu,4th Parallel, pt.3 . . . . 3.00
35 DJu,4th Parallel, pt.4 . . . . 3.00
36 DJu,4th Parallel, pt.5 . . . . 3.00
37 Kid Amazo, pt.1 . . . . 3.00
38 Kid Amazo, pt.2 . . . . 3.00
39 Kid Amazo, pt.3 . . . . 3.00
40 Kid Amazo, pt.4 . . . . 3.00
41 Kid Amazo, pt.5 . . . . 3.00
42 The Ghosts of Mars, pt.1 . . . . . . 3.00
43 The Ghosts of Mars, pt.2 . . . . . . 3.00
44 The Ghosts of Mars, pt.3 . . . . . . 3.00
45 The Ghosts of Mars, pt.4 . . . . . . 3.00

JLA CLASSIFIED: COLD STEEL
Dec., 2005
1 (0f 2) 48-pg. 6.00
2 48-pg. 6.00

JLA: CREATED EQUAL
Feb., 2000
1 FaN,KM,JRu,Elseworlds 6.00
2 FaN,KM,JRu 6.00

JLA: DESTINY
June, 2002
1 (of 4) TMd,48-pg 6.00
2 JAr(s),TMd, Elseworlds 6.00
3 JAr(s),TMd,Luthor,Mongul 6.00
4 JAr(s),TMc,concl. 6.00

JLA: GATEKEEPER
Oct., 2001
1 (of 3) TT, 48-page 5.00
2 TT, 48-page 5.00
3 TT,48-page, concl. 5.00

JLA/HITMAN
Sept., 2007
1 (of 2) GEn,Hitman is back 4.00
2 finale 4.00

JLA Incarnations #4 © DC Comics, Inc.

JLA: INCARNATIONS
May, 2001
1 (of 7) JOs,VS,V:Wotan 3.50
2 JOs,VS,Batman joins 3.50
3 JOs,VS,V:Lex Luthor, Kobra 3.50
4 JOs,VS,F:Aquaman 3.50
5 JOs,VS,F:Aquaman 3.50
6 JOs,VS,two tales 3.50
7 JOs,VS,concl. 3.50

JLA/JSA
Nov., 2002
1 Secret files, Team-up,
   prelude,64-pg. 5.00
TPB Virtue and Vice 18.00

JLA: PARADISE LOST
Nov., 1997
1 (of 3) MMr,AOl,F:Zauriel 2.25
2 MMr,AOl,F:Zauriel,Martian
   Manhunter 2.25

JLA: SCARY MONSTERS
Mar. 2003
1 (of 6) CCl,V:Ancient spirits 2.50
2 CCl 2.50
3 CCl,ancient evil 2.50
4 CCl,Kishana secret 2.50
5 CCl,Kishana's origin 2.50
6 CCl,concl. 2.50

JLA/THE SPECTRE: SOUL WAR
Jan. 2003
1 (of 2) DBk,PNe 6.00
2 DBk,PNe 6.00

JLA/TITANS
1998
1 (of 3) JLA vs. Teen Titans 3.00
2 . . . . 3.00
3 conclusion, New Titans 3.00
TPB The Technis Imperative 13.00

JLA WEDDING SPECIAL
Sept., 2007
1 ALa,MMK,EBe(c),48-pgs. 4.00

JLA: WORLD WITHOUT GROWN-UPS
June, 1998
1 (of 2) I:Young Justice 48pg 5.00
2 Young Justice, concl. 5.00
TPB World Without Grown-Ups . . . 10.00

JLA: YEAR ONE
Nov., 1997
1 (of 12) MWa,BAu,BKi,48pg. 6.00
2 MWa,BAu,BKi,V:Vandal Savage . 4.00
3 MWa,BAu,BKi 4.00
4 MWa,BAu,BKi,V:Locus 4.00
5 MWa,BAu,BKi,F:Doom Patrol . . . 4.00
6 MWa,BAu,BKi,V:Doom Patrol . . . 4.00
7 MWa,BAu,BKi,V:Weapon Master 4.00
8 MWa,BAu,BKi,MIB,V:Locus 4.00
9 MWa,BAu,BKi,MIB,V:Locus 3.00
10 MWa,BAu,BKi,MIB,V:Locus . . . 3.00
11 MWa,BAu,BKi,MIB 3.00
12 MWa,BAu,BKi,MIB, concl. 3.50
TPB Year One 20.00

JLA-Z
Sept. 2003
1 (of 3) handbook 2.50
2 thru 3 . . . . @2.50

JOHN CONSTANTINE— HELLBLAZER SPECIAL: PAPA MIDNITE
DC/Vertigo, Feb., 2005
1 (of 5) 3.00
2 thru 5 . . . . @3.00

JOHNNY THUNDER
Feb.–March, 1973
1 ATh 30.00
2 GK,MD 15.00
3 ATh,GK,MD,July-Aug., 1973 . . . 15.00

JOKER, THE
1975–76
1 IN,DG,A:TwoFace 90.00
2 IN,JL WillieTheWeeper 40.00
3 JL,A:Creeper 40.00
4 JL,A:GreenArrow 30.00
5 IN,Joker Goes "Wilde" 30.00
6 IN,V:Sherlock Holmes 30.00
7 IN,A:Luthor. 30.00
8 IN,A:Scarecrow 30.00
9 IN,A:Catwoman 40.00
The Devil's Advocate HC GN 30.00
GN 13.00

JOKER, THE: LAST LAUGH
Oct., 2001
1 (of 6) CDi,Oracle vs. villains 3.00
2 CDi,Batman,Riot in the Slab 3.00
3 CDi,F:JLA vs. Joker army 3.00
4 CDi,F:Mr. Mind, Lex Luthor 3.00
5 CDi,Harley Quinn is last hope . . . 3.00
6 CDi,Joker's final stand 3.00
Secret Files #1 64-page. 6.00

JONAH HEX
1977–85
1 Vengeance For A Fallen
  Gladiator 200.00
2 The Lair of the Parrot 100.00
3 The Fugitive 75.00
4 The Day of Chameleon 75.00
5 Welcome to Paradise 75.00
6 The Lawman 60.00
7 Son of the Apache 75.00
8 O:Jonah Hex 75.00
9 BWr(c) 50.00
10 GM(c),Violence at Vera Cruz . . 50.00
11 The Holdout. 40.00
12 JS(c),Search for 'Gator Hawes . . 40.00
13 The Railroad Blaster 40.00
14 The Sin Killer 40.00
15 Saw Dust and Slow Death 40.00
16 The Wyandott Verdict! 35.00
17 Voyage to Oblivion 35.00
18 Amazon Treasure, and Death. . 35.00
19 The Duke of Zarkania! 35.00
20 Phantom Stage to William
   Bend 35.00
21 The Buryin'!. 35.00
22 Requiem For A Pack Rat 35.00
23 Massacre of the Celestials 35.00
24 Minister of the Lord 35.00
25 The Widow Maker. 35.00
26 Death Race to Cholera Bend!. . 20.00
27 The Wooden Six Gun! 20.00
28 Night of the Savage 20.00
29 The Innocent. 20.00
30 O:Jonah Hex. 20.00
31 A:Arbee Stoneham 20.00
32 A:Arbee Stoneham 20.00
33 The Crusader 20.00
34 Christmas in an Outlaw Town . . 20.00
35 The Fort Charlotte Brigade 20.00
36 Return to Fort Charlotte 20.00
37 DAy,A:Stonewall Jackson 20.00
38 DSp,Iron Dog's Gold. 20.00
39 The Vow of a Samurai! 20.00
40 DAy,The Rainmaker 20.00
41 DAy,Two for the Hangman!. . . . 20.00
42 Wanted for Murder 20.00
43 JKu(c),Death by Fire. 20.00
44 JKu(c),DAy 20.00
45 DAy,Jonah gets married 20.00
46 JKu(c),DAy,Showdown 20.00
47 DAy,Doom Rides the Sundown
   Town 20.00
48 DAy,A:El Diablo. 20.00
49 DAy,Reap the Grim Harvest . . . 20.00
50 DAy,The Hunter 20.00
51 DAy,The Comforter 8.00
52 DAy,Rescue! 8.00
53 DAy,The Haunting. 8.00
54 TD,Trapped in the Parrot's Lair . 8.00
55 Trail of Blood. 8.00
56 DAy,The Asylum 8.00
57 B:El Diablo backup story 8.00
58 DAy,The Treasure of Catfish
   Pond 8.00
59 DAy,Night of the White Lotus . . . 8.00
60 DAy,Domain of the Warlord 8.00
61 DAy,In the Lair of
   the Manchus 8.00
62 DAy,Belly of the Malay Tiger. . . . 8.00
63 DAy,Ship of Doom 8.00

64 DAy,The Pearl! 8.00
65 DAy,The Vendetta! 8.00
66 DAy,Requiem for a Coward 8.00
67 DAy,Deadman's Hand! 8.00
68 DAy,Gunfight at Gravesboro! . . . 8.00
69 DAy,The Gauntlet!. 8.00
70 DAy,Mountain of the Manitou . . 8.00
71 DAy,The Masquerades 8.00
72 DAy,Tarantula 8.00
73 DAy,Jonah in a wheel chair 8.00
74 DAy,A:Railroad Bill 8.00
75 DAy,JAp,A:Railroad Bill. 8.00
76 DAy,Jonah goes to Jail 7.00
77 DAy,Over the Wall. 7.00
78 DAy,Me Ling returns 7.00
79 DAy,Duel in the Sand 7.00
80 DAy,TD,A:Turnbull 7.00
81 thru 89 DAy . . . . @8.00
90 thru 91 GM . . . . @8.00
92 GM,A Blaze of Glory 25.00

JONAH HEX
Nov., 2005
1 LRs,Cemetery Without Crosses . 2.50
2 LRs,Cross of solid gold 2.50
3 LRs,F:Bat Lash 2.50
4 LRs,JP 2.50
5 LRs,Nuns with Guns 2.50
6 LRs,V:Nuns with Guns. 3.00
7 LRs,Oil Baron 3.00
8 JP,An old acquaintance 3.00
9 JP,TD,Flowers on a grave 3.00
10 JP,Louisiana swamplands. 3.00
11 JP,return of El Diablo 3.00
12 JP,Snowstorm 3.00
13 JP,Origin, pt.1 . . . . 3.00
14 JP,Legend of Jonah Hex, pt.2. . 3.00
15 JP,Legend of Jonah Hex, pt.3. . 3.00
16 JP,I:Tallulah Black 3.00
17 JP,Tallulah Black's vengeance . . 3.00
18 JP,Hex heads to Texas 3.00
19 JP,Friends reunited 3.00
20 JP,Friends reunited 3.00
21 JP,Greatest Inventor 3.00
22 JP,Wizards of Electricity 3.00
23 JP,Two armies out for blood 3.00
24 JP,El Diablo & Bat Lash return . . 3.00

JONAH HEX AND OTHER WESTERN TALES
Sept.–Oct., 1979
1 TD,The Hundred Dollar Deal . . . 20.00
2 NA,ATh,SA,GK 25.00
3 Jan.–Feb., 1980. . . . . 20.00

JONAH HEX: RIDERS OF THE WORM AND SUCH
[Mini-Series] DC/Vertigo, 1995
1 R:Ronah Hex. 4.00
2 At Wildes West Ranch. 4.00
3 History Lesson. 4.00
4 I:Autumn Brothers 4.00
5 V:Big worm, final issue 4.00

JONAH HEX: SHADOWS WEST
DC/Vertigo, 1998
1 (of 3) JLd(s),TTn 4.00
2 JLd(s),TTn 4.00
3 JLd(s),TTn concl. 4.00

JONAH HEX: TWO-GUN MOJO
DC/Vertigo, 1993
1 B:JLd(s),TT,SG(i),R:Jonah Hex,
   I:Slow Go Smith. 7.00
1a Platinum Ed. 17.00

2 TT,SG(i),D:Slow Go Smith,I:Doc
   Williams,Wild Bill Hickok 4.00
3 TT,SG(i),Jonah captured 4.00
4 TT,SG(i),O:Doc Williams 4.00
5 TT,SG(i),V::Doc Williams 4.00

JONNI THUNDER
Feb., 1985
1 DG,origin issue. 2.25
2 DG 2.25
3 DG 2.25

JONNY DOUBLE
DC/Vertigo, July, 1998
1 . . . . 3.00
2 MCo(c) detective 3.00
3 . . . . 3.00
4 . . . . 3.00
TPB series rep. 13.00

JSA #10
© *DC Comics, Inc.*

JSA
1999
1 JeR,V:Dark Lord 10.00
2 JeR,AD&Mfm(c),A:Hawkgirl. 6.00
3 JeR,AD&Mfm(c),V:Dark Lord . . . 5.00
4 JeR,AD&Mfm(c),V:Mordru 5.00
5 JeR,AD&Mfm(c),. 5.00
6 AD&MFm,Justice Like Lightning . 4.00
7 Darkness Falls, pt.1. . . . . 4.00
8 Darkness Falls, pt.2. . . . . 4.00
9 Darkness Falls, pt.3. . . . . 4.00
10 V:Injustice Society. 4.00
11 V:Kobra 4.00
12 V:Kobra,Whitehorse project 4.00
13 Hunt for Extant,pt.1. . . . . 4.00
14 Hunt for Extant,pt.2. . . . . 4.00
15 Hunt for Extant,concl. 4.00
16 Injustice be Done, pt.1 . . . . 4.00
17 Injustice be Done, pt.2 . . . . 4.00
18 Injustice be Done, pt.3 . . . . 4.00
19 Injustice be Done, pt.4 . . . . 4.00
20 Injustice be Done, pt.5 . . . . 4.00
21 Hawkman prologue. 4.00
22 Hawkman prologue. 7.00
23 Return of Hawkman,pt.1 . . . . 8.00
24 Return of Hawkman,pt.2. . . . . . . 6.00
25 Return of Hawkman,pt.3,48-pg. . 6.50
26 Return of Hawkman,pt.4. . . . . . . 4.00
27 F:Captain Marvel,V:Black Adam . 3.00
28 V:Roulette 3.00
29 PSj,Joker:Last Laugh,tie-in. 3.00
30 V:Roulette 3.00

31 RgM(c),MakingWaves,A:Batman	3.00
32 RgM(c),Stealing Thunder,prev.	3.00
33 RgM(c),Stealing Thunder,pt.1	3.00
34 RgM(c),Stealing Thunder,pt.2	3.00
35 RgM(c),Stealing Thunder,pt.3	3.00
36 RgM(c),Stealing Thunder,pt.4	3.00
37 RgM(c),Thunder,pt.5,40-pg.	4.00
38 RgM(c),F:Rick Tyler	3.00
39 RgM(c),F:Power Girl	3.00
40 RgM(c),Shadower's grandson	3.00
41 RgM(c),V:Black Barax.	3.00
42 V:Black Barax	3.00
43 F:JSA B.C.	3.00
44 F:Vandal Savage	3.00
45 F:Doctor Fate	3.00
46 Princes of Darkness,pt.1	3.00
47 Princes of Darkness,pt.2	3.00
48 Princes of Darkness,pt.3	3.00
49 Princes of Darkness,pt.4	3.00
50 Princes of Darkness,concl.	4.50
51 Dr. Fate	3.00
52 F:Black Adam	3.00
53 V:Crimson Avenger	3.00

JSA #58
© *DC Comics, Inc.*

54 F:Superman,Batman	3.00
55 F:Original members	2.50
56 Black Reign,pt.1,x-over.	3.00
57 Black Reign,pt.3,x-over.	3.00
58 Black Reign,pt.5,x-over.	3.00
59 SeP,F:Degaton	2.50
60 Redemption Lost,pt.1	2.50
61 TMd,Redemption Lost,pt.2	2.50
62 TMc,Redemption Lost,pt.3	2.50
63 JOy,Wake of Sandman,pt.1	2.50
64 JOy,Wake of Sandman,pt.2	2.50
65 Out of Time,pt.1	2.50
66 Out of Time,pt.2	2.50
67 DGb,Identity Crisis, tie-in	3.00
68 AxR(c),JSA/JSA	2.50
69 AxR(c),JSA/JSA,pt.2.	2.50
70 JSA/JSa,pt.3.	2.50
71 JSA/JSA,pt.4.	2.50
72 JSA/JSA,pt.5.	2.50
73 Black Vengeance,pt.1	5.00
74 Black Vengeance,pt.2	4.00
75 Black Vengeance,pt.3, 40-page	3.50
76 F:Mr. Terrific, Roulette.	2.50
77 Alan Scott and Hal Jordan	2.50
78 A Day of Vengeance, tie-in	2.50
79 A Day of Vengeance, tie-in	2.50
80 Mordru vs. Dr. Fate.	2.50
81 Stargirl's Past	2.50
82 GP,BWi,Infinite Crisis	2.50
83 RgM,LRs,One Year Later	2.50
84 RGm,LRs	2.50

85 RGm,LRs,O:Gentleman Ghost	3.00
86 RGm,JOy,LRs, A trap	3.00
87 RGm,JOy,LRs,final issue	3.00
Ann.#1 Planet DC	4.00
Spec.#1 Our Worlds at War,48-pg.	3.50
Secret Files #1.	7.00
Secret Files #2, 64-page	7.00

JSA: ALL-STARS
May 2003

1 (of 8) SaV,past and present	2.50
2 JLb,TSe,F:Hawkgirl	2.50
3 Salem Mass.	2.50
4 F:Stargirl	2.50
5 F:Hourman	2.50
6 F:Dr. Mid-Nite.	2.50
7 40 pg.,BU: Mr. Terrific	3.50
8 F:Spectre	2.50
TPB	15.00

JSA CLASSIFIED
July, 2005

1 JP,ACo,O:Power Girl	5.00
2 JP,ACo,O:Power Girl	3.00
3 JP,ACo,O:Power Girl	3.00
4 JP,ACo,O:Power Girl, concl.	3.00
5 PO,Honor Among Thieves	2.50
6 PO,Honor Among Thieves,pt.2	2.50
7 PO,Honor Among Thieves,pt.3	2.50
8 F:Wildcat & Flash	2.50
9 F:Wildcat & Flash	2.50
10 PG,JP, One Year Later	2.50
11 Fall & Rise of Vandal Savage	2.50
12 Fall & Rise of Vandal Savage	3.00
13 Fall & Rise of Vandal Savage	3.00
14 Double Trouble,pt.1	3.00
15 Double Trouble,pt.2	3.00
16 Double Trouble,pt.3	3.00
17 SMc,The Venom Connection	3.00
18 SMc,Hourman & Bane	3.00
19 RgM,Skin Game, pt.1	3.00
20 RgM,Skin Trade, pt.2	3.00
21 WS,Hawkgirl x-over, pt.2	3.00
22 WS,Hawkgirl x-over, pt.3	3.00
23 Unleashed, pt.1	3.00
24 Unleashed, pt.2.	3.00
25 Reformed villain	3.00
26 F:Wildcat, pt.1.	3.00
27 F:Wildcat, pt.2.	3.00
28 FaN,F:Jakeem Thunder	3.00
29 Mr. Horrific, pt. 1	3.00
30 Mr. Horrific, pt. 2	3.00
31 Mr. Horrific, pt. 3	3.00

JSA: THE LIBERTY FILES
Dec., 1999

1 (of 2) Elseworlds	7.00
2 TyH, concl.	7.00

JSA: STRANGE
ADVENTURES #3
Aug. 2004

1 (of 6) BKi,GEr,V:Dynamo	3.50
2 thru 6 BKi,GEr	@3.50

JSA: THE UNHOLY THREE
Feb. 2003

1 (of 2) Elseworlds	7.00
2 concl.	7.00

JUDGE DREDD
1994–96

1 R:Judge Dredd.	3.00
2 Silicon Dreams.	2.50
3 Terrorists	2.75
4 Mega-City One crisis	2.50
5 Solitary Dredd	2.50
6 V:Richard Magg	2.50
7 48 Hours,Heaven is Hell	2.50

8 V:Ministry of Fear.	2.50
9 V:Mister Synn	2.50
10 D:Judge Dredd	2.50
11 Mega-City One Chaos	2.50
12 V:Wally Squad	2.50
13 Block Wars,pt.1.	2.50
14 Block Wars,pt.2.	2.50
15 Block Wars,pt.3.	2.50
16 R:Judge with a Grudge.	2.50
17 F:Judge Cadet Lewis, Nova Scotia.	2.50
18 final issue	2.50
Movie Adaptation	6.00

JUDGE DREDD: LEGENDS OF THE LAW
1994–95

1 Organ Donor,pt.1	3.00
2 Organ Donor,pt.2.	2.50
3 Organ Donor,pt.3.	2.50
4 Organ Donor,pt.4.	2.50
5 Trial By Gunfire,pt.1.	2.50
6 Trial By Gunfire,pt.2.	2.50
7 JHi(c),Trial By Gunfire,pt.3	2.50
8 JBy(s),Fall From Grace,pt.1	2.50
9 Fall From Grace,pt.2	2.50
10 Fall From Grace,pt.3.	2.50
11 Dredd of Night,pt.1	2.50
12 Dredd of Night,pt.2	2.50
13 Dredd of Night,pt.3,final issue	2.50

JUSTICE
2005

1 (of 12) DBw,AxR,JLA,40-page.	5.00
2 DBw,AxR,Batman, Riddler.	4.00
3 DBw,AxR,Martian Manhunter	4.00
4 DBw,AxR,	4.00
5 DBw,AxR,Superman	4.00
6 DBw,AxR,	4.00
7 DBw,AxR,A:Metamorpho	4.00
8 DBw,AxR,	4.00
9 DBw,AxR,Black Adam	4.00
10 DBw,AxR,F:Green Arrow	4.00
11 DBw,AxR,V:Sinestro	4.00
12 DBw,AxR, finale	4.00

JUSTICE, INC.
May-June, 1975

1 AMc,JKu(c),O:Avenger	25.00
2 JK,The Skywalker	20.00
3 JK,The Monster Bug	20.00
4 JK,JKu(c),Slay Ride in the Sky Nov.–Dec., 1975	20.00

[Mini-Series], 1989

1 PerfectBound 'Trust & Betrayal'	4.00
2 PerfectBound	4.00

JUSTICE LEAGUE ADVENTURES
Nov., 2001

1 TTn,based on Cartoon show	3.00
2	2.25
3	2.25
4	2.25
5	2.25
6 thru 10	@2.25
11 thru 34	@2.25

JUSTICE LEAGUE AMERICA
See: JUSTICE LEAGUE INTERNATIONAL)

JUSTICE LEAGUE ELITE
July 2004

1 (of 12) DoM	2.50
2 thru 4 DoM	@2.50
5 DoM,I:Aftermath.	2.50

6 DoM,F:JSA	2.50
7 DoM,V:Drug cartel	2.50
8 DoM,V:Drug cartel	2.50
9 DoM,V:Eve	2.50
10 DoM,V:Aftermath	2.50
11 DoM,F:Manchester Black	2.50
12 DoM, finale	2.50

JUSTICE LEAGUE
EUROPE
1989–93

1 BS,A:Wonder Woman	4.00
2 BS,Search for Nazi-Killer	3.00
3 BS,A:Jack O'Lantern, Queen Bee	2.50
4 BS,V:Queen Bee	2.50
5 JRu,BS,Metamorpho's Baby, A:Sapphire Starr	2.50
6 BS,V:Injustice League	2.50
7 BS,Teasdale Imperative#2, A:JLA	2.50
8 BS,Teasdale Imperative#4, A:JLA	2.50
9 BS,ANi,A:Superman	2.50
10 BS,V:Crimson Fox	2.50
11 BS,C:DocMagnus&Metal Men	2.50
12 BS,A:Metal Men	2.50
13 BS,V:One-Eyed Cat, contd from JLA #37	2.50
14 I:VCR	2.50
15 BS,B:Extremists Vector saga, V:One-Eyed Cat,A:BlueJay	2.50
16 BS,A:Rocket Reds, Blue Jay	2.50
17 BS,JLI in Another Dimension	2.50
18 BS,Extremists Homeworld	2.50
19 BS,E:Extremist Vector Saga	2.50
20 MR,I:Beefeater,V:Kilowog	2.50
21 MR,JRu,New JLE embassy in London,A:Kilowog	2.50
22 MR,JLE's Cat stolen	2.50
23 BS,O:Crimson Fox	2.50
24 BS,Worms in London	2.50
25 BS,V:Worms	2.50
26 BS,V:Starro	2.50
27 BS,JLE V:JLE,A:JLA,V:Starro	2.50
28 BS, JLE V:JLE,A:J'onn J'onzz, V:Starro	2.50
29 BS,Breakdowns #2,V:Global Guardians	2.50
30 Breakdowns#4,V:J.O'Lantern	2.50
31 Breakdowns #6,War of the Gods tie-in	2.50
32 Breakdowns #8,A:Chief(Doom Patrol)	2.50

Justice League Europe #11
© DC Comics, Inc.

33 Breakdowns #10,Lobo vs. Despero	2.50
34 Breakdowns #12,Lobo vs.Despero	2.50
35 Breakdowns #14,V:Extremists, D:Silver Sorceress	2.50
36 Breakdowns #16,All Quit	2.50
37 B:New JLE,I:Deconstructo	2.50
38 V:Deconstructo,A:Batman	2.50
39 V:Deconstructo,A:Batman	2.50
40 J:Hal Jordan,A:Metamorpho	2.50
41 A:Metamorpho,Wond.Woman	2.50
42 A:Wonder Woman,V:Echidna	2.50
43 V:Amos Fortune	2.50
44 V:Amos Fortune	2.50
45 Red Winter#1,V:Rocket Reds	2.50
46 Red Winter#2	2.50
47 Red Winter#3,V:Sonar	2.50
48 Red Winter#4,V:Sonar	2.50
49 Red Winter #5,V:Sonar	2.50
50 Red Winter#6,Double-sized, V:Sonar,J:Metamorpho	3.50
Ann.#1 A:Global Guardians	2.50
Ann.#2 MR,CS,ArmageddonPt.7	3.00
Ann.#3 RT(i),Eclipso tie-in	2.75
Justice League Spectacular JLE(c) New Direction	2.50

Becomes:

JUSTICE LEAGUE
INTERNATIONAL
[2nd Series]

JUSTICE LEAGUE
[INTERNATIONAL]
[1st Series], 1987

1 KM,TA,New Team,I:Max. Lord	10.00
2 KM,AG,A:BlueJay & Silver Sorceress	6.00
3 KM,AG,J:Booster Gold, V:Rocket Lords	5.00
3a Superman Logo	60.00
4 KM,AG,V:Royal Flush	5.00
5 KM,AG,A:The Creeper	5.00
6 KM,AG,A:The Creeper	5.00

Becomes:

JUSTICE LEAGUE
INTERNATIONAL
1988–89

7 KM,AG,L:Dr.Fate,Capt.Marvel, J:Rocket Red,Capt.Atom (Double size)	4.00
8 KM,AG,KG,Move to Paris Embassy, I:C.Cobert,B.U.Glob.Guardians	3.50
9 KM,AG,KG,Millennium,Rocket Red-Traitor	3.50
10 KG,KM,AG,A:G.L.Corps, Superman,I:G'Nort	3.50
11 KM,AG,V:Construct,C:Metron	3.50
12 KG,KM,AG,O:Max Lord	3.50
13 KG,AG,A:Suicide Squad	3.50
14 SL,AG,J:Fire&Ice,L:Ron, I:Manga Kahn	3.50
15 SL,AG,V:Magna Kahn	3.50
16 KM,AG,I:Queen Bee	3.50
17 KM,AG,V:Queen Bee	3.50
18 KM,AG,MPn,A:Lobo,Guy Gardner (bonus book)	3.50
19 KM,JRu,A:Lobo vs.Guy Gardner, J:Hawkman & Hawkwoman	3.50
20 KM,JRu(i),A:Lobo,G.Gardner	3.50
21 KM,JRu(i),A:Lobo vs.Guy Gardner	3.50
22 KM,JRu,Imskian Soldiers	3.50
23 KM,JRu,I:Injustice League	3.50
24 KM,JRu,DoubleSize + Bonus Bk#13,I:JusticeLeagueEurope	4.00
25 KM(c),JRu(i),Vampire story	2.50
Ann.#1 BWg,DG,CR	2.50
Ann.#2 BWg,JRu,A:Joker	3.00

Justice League International #11
© DC Comics Inc.

Ann.#3 KM(c),JRu,JLI Embassies	2.50
Spec.#1 Mr.Miracle	2.00
Spec.#2,The Huntress	3.00
TPB new beginning,rep.#1-#7	13.00
TPB The Secret Gospel of Maxwell Lord Rep. #8-#12, Ann.#1	13.00

Becomes:

JUSTICE LEAGUE
AMERICA
1989–96

26 KM(c),JRu(i),Possessed Blue Beetle	3.00
27 KM(c),JRu,DG(i),'Exorcist', (c)tribute	2.50
28 KM(c),JRu(i), A:Black Hand	2.50
29 KM(c),JRu(i),V:Mega-Death	2.50
30 KM(c),BWg,JRu,J:Huntress, D:Mega-Death	2.50
31 ANi,AH,JRu,Teasdale Imperative #1,N:Fire,Ice,A:JLE	3.00
32 ANi,AH,Teasdale Imperative #3, A:JLE	3.00
33 ANi,AH,GuyGardner vs.Kilowog	2.50
34 ANi,AH,`Club JLI,'A:Aquaman	2.50
35 ANi,JRu,AH,A:Aquaman	2.50
36 Gnort vs. Scarlet Skier	2.50
37 ANi,AH,I:Booster Gold	2.50
38 JRu,AH,R:Desparo,D:Steel	2.50
39 JRu,AH,V:Desparo,D:Mr.Miracle, Robot	2.50
40 AH,Mr.Miracle Funeral	2.50
41 MMc,MaxForce	2.50
42 MMc,J:L:Booster Gold	2.50
43 AH,KG,The Man Who Knew Too Much #1	2.50
44 AH,Man Who Knew Too Much #2	2.50
45 AH,MJ,JRu,Guy & Ice's 2nd date	2.50
46 Glory Bound #1,I:Gen.Glory	2.50
47 Glory Bound #2,J:Gen.Glory	2.50
48 Glory Bound #3,V:DosUberbot	2.50
49 Glory Bound #4	2.50
50 Glory Bound #5 (double size)	3.00
51 JRu,AH,V:BlackHand, R:Booster Gold	2.50
52 TVE,Blue Beetle Vs. Guy Gardner A:Batman	2.50
53 Breakdowns #1, A:JLE	2.50
54 Breakdowns #3, A:JLE	2.50
55 Breakdowns #5,V:Global Guardians	2.50
56 Breakdowns #7, U.N. revokes JLA charter	2.50

57 Breakdowns #9,A:Lobo,
    V:Despero, ... 2.50
58 BS,Breakdowns #11,Lobo
    Vs.Despero 2.50
59 BS,Breakdowns #13,
    V:Extremists. 2.50
60 KM,TA,Breakdowns #15,
    End of J.L.A. 2.50
61 DJu,I:Weapons Master,B:New
    JLA Line-up,I:Bloodwynd 3.00
62 DJu,V:Weapons Master 2.50
63 DJu,V:Starbreaker. 2.50
64 DJu,V:Starbreaker. 2.50
65 DJu,V:Starbreaker. 2.50
66 DJu,Superman V:Guy Gardner. . 2.50
67 DJu,Bloodwynd mystery 2.50
68 DJu,V:Alien Land Baron 2.50
69 DJu, Doomsday Pt.1-A 10.00
69a 2nd printing 2.50
70 DJu,Funeral for a Friend#1 . . . . 6.00
70a 2nd printing 2.50
71 DJu,J:Agent Liberty,Black Condor,
    The Ray,Wonder Woman 5.00
71a Newsstand ed. 2.50
71b 2nd Printing 2.50
72 DJu,A:Green Arrow,Black
    Canary,Atom,B:Destiny's Hand . 4.00
73 DJu,Destiny's Hand #2 . . . . 3.00
74 DJu,Destiny's Hand #3 . . . . 2.50
75 DJu,E:Destiny's Hand #4,Martian
    Manhunter as Bloodwynd 2.50
76 DJu,Blood Secrets#1,
    V:Weaponmaster 2.50
77 DJu,Blood Secrets#2,
    V:Weaponmaster 2.50
78 MC,V:The Extremists 2.50
79 MC,V:The Extremists 2.50
80 KWe,N:Booster Gold 2.50
81 KWe,A:Captain Atom 2.50
82 KWe,A:Captain Atom 2.50
83 KWe,V:Guy Gardner. 2.50
84 KWe,A:Ice. 2.50
85 KWe,V:Frost Giants 2.50
86 B:Cults of the Machine 2.50
87 N:Booster Gold 2.50
88 E:Cults of the Machine 2.50
89 Judgement Day#1,
    V:Overmaster 2.50
90 Judgement Day#4. . . . . 2.50
91 Aftershocks #1 . . . . 2.50
92 Zero Hour,I:Triumph 2.50
93 Power Girl and child 2.50
94 Scarabus. 2.50
95 Where the Wild Things Are. . . . 2.50
96 Funeral 2.50
97 I:Judgment 2.50
98 J:Blue Devil, Ice Maiden 2.50
99 V:New Metahumes 2.50
100 GJ,Woj,V:Lord Havok,dbl.size . 4.50
100a Collector's Edition 4.50
101 GJ,Woj,Way of the
    Warrior,pt.2 . . . . 2.50
102 Way of the Warrior,pt.5 . . . . . . 2.50
103 Oh, To Be Nobody 2.50
104 F:Metamorpho. 2.50
105 GJ,Woj,Underworld
    Unleashed tie-in 2.50
106 GJ,Woj,Underworld
    Unleashed tie-in 2.50
107 GJ,Woj,secret of Power
    Girl's son 2.50
108 GJ,Woj,The Arcana revealed . . 2.50
109 DJu,Woj,All That Yazz 2.50
110 GJ,Woj,V:El Diablo 2.50
111 GJ,Woj,The Purge,pt.1 (of 3) . . 2.50
112 GJ,Woj,The Purge,pt.2 (of 3) . . 2.50
113 GJ,Woj,The Purge,pt.3 (of 3) . . 2.50
Ann.#4 GM(c),I:JL Antartica 3.50
Ann.#5 MR,KM,DJu,Armageddon . 3.50
Ann.#5a 2nd Printing,silver 2.50
Ann.#6 DC,Eclipso. 3.00
Ann.#7 I:Terrorsmith. 3.00

Ann.#8 Elseworlds Story 3.50
Ann.#9 Year One Annual 4.00
Ann.#10 CPr(s),SCi,NNa,Legends
    of the Dead Earth 3.50
Justice League Spectacular DJu,
    JLA(c) New Direction. 2.50
Archives Vol. 4 . . . . 50.00

Justice League International #55
© DC Comics, Inc.

JUSTICE LEAGUE
INTERNATIONAL
[2nd Regular Series], 1993–94
Prev: Justice League Europe

51 Aztec Cult 2.25
52 V:Aztec Cult 2.25
53 R:Fox's Husband 2.25
54 RoR,I:Creator 2.25
55 RoR,A:Creator 2.25
56 RoR,V:Terrorists 2.25
57 RoR,V:Terrorists 2.25
58 RoR,V:Aliens. 2.25
59 RoR,A:Guy Gardner 2.25
60 GJ(s),RoR. 2.25
61 GJ(s),V:Godfrey 2.25
62 GJ(s),N:Metamorpho,V:Godfrey . 2.25
63 GJ(s),In Africa 2.25
64 GJ(s),V:Cadre 2.25
65 JudgmentDay#3,V:Overmaster. . 2.25
66 JudgmentDay#6,V:Overmaster . . 2.25
67 Aftershock #3 . . . . 2.25
68 Zero Hour, Final Issue 2.25
Ann.#4 Bloodlines#9,I:Lionheart . . 2.75
Ann.#5 . . . . 3.25
Ann.#6 Elseworlds Story 3.00

JUSTICE LEAGUE
[INTERNATIONAL]
QUARTERLY
1990–94

1 I:Conglomerate 4.00
2 MJ(i),R:Mr.Nebula 3.50
3 V:Extremists,C:Original JLA. . . . 3.50
4 KM(c),MR,CR,A:Injustice
    League. 3.00
5 KM(c),Superhero Attacks. 3.00
6 EB,Elongated Man,B.U.Global
    Guardians,Powergirl,B.Beetle . . 3.00
7 EB,DH,MR.Global Guardians . . . 3.00
8 . . . . 3.00
9 DC,F:Power Girl,Booster Gold . . 3.50
10 F:Flash,Fire & Ice 3.50
11 F:JL Women 3.50

12 F:Conglomerate 3.50
13 V:Ultraa 7.00
14 MMi(c),PuK(s),F:Captain Atom,Blue
    Beetle,Nightshade,Thunderbolt . 3.75
15 F:Praxis. 3.50
16 F:Gen Glory 3.50
17 Final Issue 3.50

JUSTICE LEAGUE:
A MIDSUMMER'S
NIGHTMARE
1996

1 (of 3) MWa(s),FaN,JJ,DaR, ... 5.00
2 MWa(s),FaN,JJ,DaR,Batman &
    Superman attempt to free
    other heroes 4.00
3 MWa&FaN(s), Know-Man's plot
    revealed, finale 4.00
TPB Rep. 3 issues. 9.00

JUSTICE LEAGUE
OF AMERICA
Oct.–Nov., 1960

1 MSy,I&O:Despero 12,000.00
2 MSy,A:Merlin. 2,500.00
3 MSy,I&O:Kanjar Ro. 1,700.00
4 MSy,J:Green Arrow. 1,000.00
5 MSy,I&O:Dr.Destiny 900.00
6 MSy,Prof. Fortune 700.00
7 MSy,Cosmic Fun-House 700.00
8 MSy,For Sale-Justice League . 700.00
9 MSy,O:JLA 1,100.00
10 MSy,I:Felix Faust 700.00
11 MSy,A:Felix Faust 500.00
12 MSy,I&O:Dr Light 500.00
13 MSy,A:Speedy. 500.00
14 MSy,J:Atom. 500.00
15 MSy,V:Untouchable Aliens . . 500.00
16 MSy,I:Maestro. 400.00
17 MSy,A:Tornado Tyrant. 400.00
18 MSy,V:Terrane,Ocana 400.00
19 MSy,A:Dr.Destiny 400.00
20 MSy,V:Metal Being 400.00
21 MSy,R:JSA,1st S.A Hourman,
    Dr.Fate. 700.00
22 MSy,R:JSA 650.00
23 MSy,I:Queen Bee 350.00
24 MSy,A:Adam Strange 350.00
25 MSy,I:Draad,the Conqueror . 350.00
26 MSy,A:Despero 350.00
27 MSy,V:I,A:Amazo 350.00
28 MSy,I:Headmaster Mind,
    A:Robin 350.00
29 MSy,I:Crime Syndicate,A:JSA,
    1st S.A. Starman 400.00
30 MSy,V:Crime Syndicate,
    A:JSA. 350.00
31 MSy,J:Hawkman 300.00
32 MSy,I&O:Brain Storm 250.00
33 MSy,I:Endless One 200.00
34 MSy,A:Dr.Destiny,Joker 225.00
35 MSy,A:Three Demons 200.00
36 MSy,A:Brain Storm,
    Handicap story 200.00
37 MSy,J:JSA,x-over,
    1st S.A.Mr.Terrific 275.00
38 MSy,A:JSA,Mr.Terrific 275.00
39 Giant. 275.00
40 MSy,A:Shark,Penguin 225.00
41 MSy,I:Key 225.00
42 MSy,A:Metamorpho 150.00
43 MSy,I:Royal Flush Gang 150.00
44 MSy,A:Unimaginable. 150.00
45 MSy,I:Shaggy Man 150.00
46 MSy,A:JSA,Blockbuster,Solomon
    Grundy,1st S.A.Sandman . . . 175.00
47 MSy,A:JSA,Blockbuster,
    Solomon Grundy 150.00
48 Giant 160.00
49 MSy,A:Felix Faust 150.00

Justice League of America #35
© DC Comics Inc.

50 MSy,A:Robin 150.00
51 MSy,A:Zatanna,Elong.Man . . . 150.00
52 MSy,A:Robin,Lord of Time . . . 150.00
53 MSy,A:Hawkgirl. 150.00
54 MSy,A:Royal Flush Gang 150.00
55 MSy,A:JSA,E-2 Robin 165.00
56 MSy,A:JSA,E-2 Robin 150.00
57 MSy,Brotherhood 150.00
58 Reprint(giant size). 150.00
59 MSy,V:Impossibles 150.00
60 MSy,A:Queen Bee,Batgirl 150.00
61 MSy,A:Lex Luthor,Penguin . . . 100.00
62 MSy,V:Bulleters. 100.00
63 MSy,A:Key 100.00
64 DD,I:Red Tornado,A:JSA 110.00
65 DD,A:JSA 110.00
66 DD,A:Demmy Gog 100.00
67 MSy,Giant reprints. 110.00
68 DD,V:Choas Maker. 100.00
69 DD,L:Wonder Woman. 100.00
70 DD,A:Creeper. 100.00
71 DD,L:J'onn J'onzz. 100.00
72 DD,A:Hawkgirl. 100.00
73 DD,A:JSA 100.00
74 DD,D:Larry Lance,A:JSA 100.00
75 DD,J:Black Canary. 100.00
76 Giant,MA,two page pin-up . . . 100.00
77 DD,A:Joker,L:Snapper Carr . . . 75.00
78 DD,R:Vigilante 75.00
79 DD,A:Vigilante. 75.00
80 DD,A:Tomar-Re,Guardians. . . . 75.00
81 DD,V:Jest-Master 75.00
82 DD,A:JSA 70.00
83 DD,A:JSA,Spectre 90.00
84 DD,Devil in Paradise. 60.00
85 Giant reprint 90.00
86 DD,V:Zapper. 60.00
87 DD,A:Zatanna,I:Silver
    Sorceress,Blue Jay 75.00
88 DD,A:Mera 75.00
89 DD,A:Harlequin Ellis,
    (i.e. Harlan Ellison) 75.00
90 CI(c),MA(ci),DD,V:Pale People. 75.00
91 DD,A:JSA,V:Solomon Grundy . 75.00
92 DD,A:JSA,V:Solomon Grundy . 75.00
93 DD:A:JSA,(giant size) 75.00
94 DD,NA,O:Sandman,rep.
    Adventure #40 . . . . 175.00
95 DD,rep.More Fun Comics #67,
    All American Comics #25 . . . 90.00
96 DD,I:Starbreaker. 80.00
97 DD,MS,O:JLA 75.00
98 DD,A:Sargon,Gold.Age reps. . . 75.00
99 DD,G.A. reps. 75.00

100 DD,A:JSA,Metamorpho,
     R:7 Soldiers of Victory. 90.00
101 DD,A:JSA,7 Soldiers. 50.00
102 DD,DG,A:JSA,7 Soldiers
     D:Red Tornado 50.00
103 DD,DG,Halloween issue,
     A:Phantom Stranger 30.00
104 DD,DG,A:Shaggy Man,
     Hector Hammond 30.00
105 DD,DG,J:ElongatedMan 30.00
106 DD,DG,J:RedTornado 30.00
107 DD,DG,I:Freedom Fighters,
     A:JSA. 35.00
108 DD,DG,A:JSA,
     Freedom Fighters 35.00
109 DD,DG,L:Hawkman. 35.00
110 DD,DG,A:John Stewart,
     Phantom Stranger 75.00
111 DD,DG,I:Injustice Gang 75.00
112 DD,DG,A:Amazo 75.00
113 DD,DG,A:JSA 75.00
114 DD,DG,A:SnapperCarr 75.00
115 DD,FMc,A:J'onn J'onzz. 75.00
116 DD,FMc,I:Golden Eagle 75.00
117 DD,FMc,R:Hawkman 30.00
118 DD,FMc. 30.00
119 DD,FMc,A:Hawkgirl. 30.00
120 DD,FMc,A:Adam Strange 30.00
121 DD,FMc,W:Adam Strange 30.00
122 DD,FMc,JLA casebook story
     V:Dr.Light. 30.00
123 DD,FMc,A:JSA 35.00
124 DD,FMc,A: JSA. 35.00
125 DD,FMc,A:Two-Face. 30.00
126 DD,FMc,A:Two-Face. 30.00
127 DD,FMc,V:Anarchist 30.00
128 DD,FMc,J:W.Woman 30.00
129 DD,FMC,D:RedTornado 30.00
130 DD,FMc,O:JLASatellite 30.00
131 DD,FMc,V:Queen Bee,Sonar . 30.00
132 DD,FMc,A:Supergirl 30.00
133 DD,FMc,A:Supergirl 30.00
134 DD,FMc,A:Supergirl 30.00
135 DD,FMc,A:Squad.of Justice . . 30.00
136 DD,FMc,A:E-2Joker 35.00
137 DD,FMc,Superman vs.
     Capt. Marvel 35.00
138 NA(c),DD,FMc,A:Adam
     Strange 30.00
139 NA(c),DD,FMc,A:AdamStrange,
     Phantom Stranger,doub.size . 25.00
140 DD,FMc,Manhunters. 25.00
141 DD,FMc,Manhunters. 25.00
142 DD,FMc,F:Aquaman,Atom,
     Elongated Man 25.00
143 DD,FMc,V:Injustice Gang 25.00
144 DD,FMc,O:JLA 25.00
145 DD,FMc,A:Phant.Stranger . . . 25.00
146 J:Red Tornado,Hawkgirl 25.00
147 DD,FMc,A:Legion 25.00
148 DD,FMc,A:Legion 25.00
149 DD,FMc,A:Dr.Light 25.00
150 DD,FMc,A:Dr.Light 25.00
151 DD,FMc,A:Amos Fortune 20.00
152 DD,FMc. 20.00
153 GT,FMc,I:Ultraa 20.00
154 MK(c),DD,FMc 20.00
155 DD,FMc. 20.00
156 DD,FMc. 20.00
157 DD,FMc,W:Atom 20.00
158 DD,FMc,A:Ultraa. 20.00
159 DD,FMc,A:JSA,Jonah Hex,
     Enemy Ace 18.00
160 DD,FMc,A:JSA,Jonah Hex,
     Enemy Ace 18.00
161 DD,FMc,J:Zatanna 18.00
162 DD,FMc. 18.00
163 DD,FMc,V:Mad Maestro 18.00
164 DD,FMc,V:Mad Maestro 18.00
165 DD,FMc. 18.00
166 DD,FMc,V:Secret Society . . . 18.00
167 DD,FMc,V:Secret Society 18.00

168 DD,FMc,V:Secret Society 18.00
169 DD,FMc,A:Ultraa. 18.00
170 DD,FMc,A:Ultraa. 18.00
171 DD,FMc,A:JSA,D:Mr.Terrific . . 18.00
172 DD,FMc,A:JSA,D:Mr.Terrific . . 18.00
173 DD,FMc,A:Black Lightning . . . 18.00
174 DD,FMc,A:Black Lightning . . . 18.00
175 DD,FMc,V:Dr.Destiny 18.00
176 DD,FMc,V:Dr.Destiny 15.00
177 DD,FMc,V:Desparo 10.00
178 JSn(c),DD,FMc,V:Desparo . . . 10.00
179 JSn(c),DD,FMc,J:Firestorm . . 10.00
180 JSn(c),DD,FMc,V:Satin Satan 10.00
181 DD,FMc,L:Gr.Arrow,V:Star . . . 11.00
182 DD,FMc,A:Green Arrow,
     V:Felix Faust 11.00
183 JSn(c),DD,FMc,A:JSA,
     NewGods. 11.00
184 GP,FMc,A:JSA,NewGods 11.00
185 JSn(c),GP,FMc,A:JSA,
     New Gods 10.00
186 FMc,GP,V:Shaggy Man. 7.50
187 DH,FMc,N:Zatanna. 7.50
188 DH,FMc,V:Proteus. 7.50
189 BB(c),RB,FMc,V:Starro. 7.50
190 BB(c),RB,LMa,V:Starro. 7.50
191 RB,V:Amazo 7.50
192 GP,O:Red Tornado 7.50
193 GP,RB,JOy,I:AllStarSquad 7.50
194 GP,V:Amos Fortune 7.50
195 GP,A:JSA,V:Secret Society. . . . 7.50
196 GP,RT,A:JSA,V:Secret Soc. . . . 7.50
197 GP,RT,KP,A:JSA,V:Secret
     Society. 7.50
198 DH,BBr,A:J.Hex,BatLash 7.50
199 GP(c),DH,BBr,A:Jonah Hex,
     BatLash 7.50
200 GP,DG,BB (1st Batman),PB,TA,
     BBr,GK,CI,JAp,JKu,Anniv.,A:Adam
     Strange,Phantom Stranger,
     J:Green Arrow 10.00
201 GP(c),DH,A:Ultraa 5.00
202 GP(c),DH,BBr,JLA in Space . . 5.00
203 GP(c),DH,RT,V:Royal
     Flush Gang 5.00
204 GP(c),DH,RT,V:R.FlushGang . . 5.00
205 GP(c),DH,RT,V:R.FlushGang . . 5.00
206 DH,RT,A:Demons 3 . . . . 5.00
207 GP(c),DH,RT,A:All Star
     Squadron,JSA 6.00
208 GP(c),DH,RT,A:All Star
     Squadron,JSA 6.00
209 GP(c),DH,RT,A:All Star
     Squadron,JSA 5.00
210 RB,RT,JLA casebook #1 . . . . . 5.00
211 RB,RT,JLA casebook #2 . . . . . 5.00
212 GP(c),RB,PCu,RT,c.book #3 . . 5.00
213 GP(c),DH,RT. 5.00
214 GP(c),DH,RT,I:Siren Sist.h'd. . 5.00
215 GP(c),DH,RT. 5.00
216 DH. 5.00
217 GP(c),RT(i) 5.00
218 RT(i),A:Prof.Ivo 5.00
219 GP(c),RT(i),A:JSA. 5.00
220 GP(c),RT,O:Bl.Canary,A:JSA . 4.00
221 Beasts #1 . . . . 3.00
222 RT(i),Beasts #2 . . . . 3.00
223 RT(i),Beasts #3 . . . . 3.00
224 DG(i),V:Paragon 3.00
225 V:Hellrazor 3.00
226 FMc(i),V:Hellrazor 3.00
227 V:Hellrazor,I:Lord Claw 3.00
228 GT,AN,R:J'onn J'onzz,War of
     the Worlds,pt.1 . . . . 3.00
229 War of the Worlds,pt.2 . . . . . . 3.00
230 War of the Worlds conc. 3.00
231 RB(i),A:JSA,Supergirl 3.00
232 A:JSA Supergirl 3.00
233 New JLA takes over book,
     B:Rebirth,F:Vibe 3.00
234 F:Vixen 3.00
235 F:Steel 3.00

236 E:Rebirth,F:Gypsy 3.00
237 A:Superman,Flash,WWoman . . 3.00
238 A:Superman,Flash,WWoman . . 3.00
239 V:Ox 3.00
240 MSy,TMd. 3.00
241 GT,V:Amazo 3.00
242 GT,V:Amazo,Mask(Toy tie-in)
     insert 3.00
243 GT,L:Aquaman,V:Amazo 3.00
244 JSon,Crisis,A:InfinityInc,JSA. . 4.00
245 LMc,Crisis,N:Steel. 4.00
246 LMc,JLA leaves Detroit. 3.00
247 LMc,JLA returns to old HQ . . . 3.00
248 LMc,F:J'onn J'onzz. 3.00
249 LMc,Lead-in to Anniv. 3.00
250 LMc,Anniv.,A:Superman,
     Green Lantern,Green Arrow,
     Black Canary,R:Batman 3.00
251 LMc,V:Despero 3.00
252 LMc,V:Despero,N:Elongated
     Man 3.00
253 LMc,V:Despero 3.00
254 LMc,V:Despero 3.00
255 LMc,O:Gypsy 3.00
256 LMc,Gypsy 3.00
257 LMc,A:Adam,L:Zatanna 3.00
258 LMc,Legends x-over,D:Vibe . . 3.00
259 LMc,Legends x-over 3.00
260 LMc,Legends x-over,D:Steel. . 6.00
261 LMc,Legends,final issue 8.00
Ann.#1 DG(i),A:Sandman 3.50
Ann.#2 I:NewJLA. 3.00
Ann.#3 MG(i),Crisis 3.00

JUSTICE LEAGUE
OF AMERICA
July, 2006

0 Batman, Superman, W.Woman. . 3.00
0a variant JSC (c). 3.00
1 EBe,The Tornado's Path 3.00
2 EBe, ... 3.00
3 EBe, V:Dr. Impossible 3.00
4 EBe 3.00
1a thru 4a variant (c). . . . . @3.00
5 EBe,The Tornado's Path, pt.5 . . 3.00
5a variant (c). 3.00
6 EBe, 40-pgs. 3.50
6a variant AH (c) (1:10) 3.50
7 EBe, New team, new HQ 3.50
7a variant (c) (1:10) 3.50
8 EBe,Lightning Saga, pt.1 x-over . 3.00
8a variant (c) (1:10) 3.00
9 EBe,Lightning Saga, pt.3 x-over . 3.00
9a variant (c) (1:10) 3.00
10 EBe,Lightning Saga,pt.5 x-over . 3.00
10a variant (c) (1:10) 3.00
11 Two burried alive. 3.00
11a variant (c) (1:10) 3.00
12 EBe, Monitor Duty. 3.50
12a variant AxR (c) (1:1) 3.50
12b variant (c) (1:10) 3.50
13 JBz,Injustice League Unlimited. 3.00
13a variant (c) (1:1) 3.00
14 Injustice League 3.00

JUSTICE LEAGUE OF
AMERICA: ANOTHER NAIL
May 2004

1 AD,MFm,F:Superman 6.00
2 AD,MFm,Darkseid's secrets . . . 6.00
3 AD,MFm,concl. 6.00

JUSTICE LEAGUE OF
AMERICA: THE NAIL
June, 1998
Elseworlds

1 World without a Superman 5.00
2 AID,MFm,Robin & Batgirl dead . 5.00
3 AID,MFm,concl. 5.00

JUSTICE LEAGUES
Jan., 2001

Pt.1 Justice Leagues #1,GP(c) 2.50
Pt.2 Just.League of Amazons #1. . . 2.50
Pt.3 Just.League of Atlantis #1 . . . . 2.50
Pt.4 Just.League of Arkham #1 . . . . 2.50
Pt.5 Just.League of Aliens #1 . . . . . 2.50
Pt.6 Just.League of America #1. . . . 2.50

Justice League Task Force #5
© DC Comics, Inc.

JUSTICE LEAGUE
TASK FORCE
1993–96

1 F:Mart.Manhunter,Nightwing,
   Aquaman,Flash,Gr.Lantern 2.25
2 V:Count Glass,Blitz 2.25
3 V:Blitz,Count Glass 2.25
4 DG,F:Gypsy,A:Lady Shiva 2.25
5 JAl,Knightquest:Crusade,F:Bronze
   Tiger,Green Arrow,Gypsy 2.25
6 JAl,Knightquest:Search,F:Bronze
   Tiger,Green Arrow,Gypsy 2.25
7 PDd(s),F:Maxima,Wonder Woman,
   Dolphin,Gypsy,Vixen,V:Luta . . 2.25
8 PDd(s),SaV,V:Amazons. 2.25
9 GrL,V:Wildman. 2.25
10 Purification Plague #1. . . . . 2.25
11 Purification Plague #2. . . . . 2.25
12 Purification Plague #3. . . . . 2.25
13 Judgement Day #2, ... 2.25
14 Judgement Day#5,
   V:Overmaster 2.25
15 Aftershocks #2 . . . . 2.25
16 Zero Hour,A:Triumph 2.25
17 Savage 2.25
18 Savage 2.25
19 Martian Manhunter 2.25
20 thru 35 . . . . @2.25

JUSTICE LEAGUE
UNLIMITED
Sept. 2004

1 From animated series 2.25
2 thru 38 . . . . @2.25

JUSTICE RIDERS
1999

1-shot, Elseworlds 7.00

JUSTICE SOCIETY
OF AMERICA
[Limited Series]
April–Nov., 1991

1 B:Veng.From Stars,A:Flash 3.00
2 A:BlackCanary,V:Solomon Grundy,
   C:G.A.Green Lantern. 2.50
3 A:G.A.Green Lantern,Black Canary,
   V:Sol.Grundy 2.50
4 A:G.A.Hawkman,C:G.A.Flash. . . 2.50
5 A:G.A.Hawkman,Flash 2.50
6 FMc(i),A:Bl.Canary,G.A.Gr.Lantern,
   V:Sol.Grundy,V.Savage 2.50
7 JSA united,V:Vandal Savage . . . 2.50
8 E:Veng.FromStar,V:V.Savage,
   Solomon Grundy 2.50
Spec.#1 DR,MG,End of JSA 2.50

[Regular Series], 1992–93

1 V:The New Order. 2.50
2 V:Ultra Gen 2.50
3 R:Ultra-Humanite 2.50
4 V:Ultra-Humanite 2.50
5 V:Ultra-Humanite 2.50
6 F:Johnny Thunderbolt 2.50
7 ..Or give me Liberty 2.50
8 Pyramid Scheme 2.50
9 V:Kulak. 2.50
10 V:Kulak,final issue. 2.50
TPB Justice Society
   Returns (2003) 20.00

JUSTICE SOCIETY
OF AMERICA
Dec., 2006

1 ATi,AxR(c),The Next Age, pt.1 . . . 4.00
1a variant (c) (1:10) 4.00
2 ATi,AxR(c),The Next Age, pt.2 . . . 3.00
2a variant (c) (1:10) 3.00
3 ATi,AxR(c),The Next Age, pt.3 . . . 3.00
3a variant (c) (1:10) 3.00
4 ATi,AxR(c),The Next Age, pt.4 . . . 3.00
4a variant (c) (1:10) 3.00
5 ATi,Lightning Saga, pt.2 x-over . . 3.00
6 Lightning Saga, pt.4 x-over 3.00
6a variant (c) (1:10) 3.00
7 F:Citizen Steel 3.00
7a variant (c) (1:10) 3.00
8 F:Liberty Belle 3.00
8a variant (c) (1:10) 3.00
9 Wildcat vs. Wildcat 3.00
9a variant (c) (1:10) 3.00
10 AxR(c) Thy Kingdom Come 3.00
10a variant (c) (1:10) 3.00

KAMANDI, THE LAST
BOY ON EARTH
Oct.–Nov., 1972

1 JK,O:Kamandi 125.00
2 JK,Year of the Rat 75.00
3 JK,Thing tht Grew on the Moon. 75.00
4 JK,I:Prince Tuftan 60.00
5 JK,The One-Armed Bandit 60.00
6 JK,Flower. 50.00
7 JK,The Monster Fetish 50.00
8 JK,Beyond Reason 50.00
9 JK,Traking Site 50.00
10 JK,Killer Germ. 50.00
11 JK,The Devil 30.00
12 JK,Devil and Mister Sacker . . . 30.00
13 thru 24 JK . . . . @30.00
25 thru 28 JK . . . . @25.00
29 JK,A:Superman. 30.00
30 JK,U.F.O. Wildest Trip Ever . . . 25.00
31 JK,The Gulliver Effect. 25.00
32 JK,Double size 25.00
33 thru 57 . . . . @25.00
58 DAy,A:Karate Kid 30.00
59 JSn,A:Omac, Sept.–Oct,1978. . 30.00

Kamandi at Earth's End #2
© DC Comics, Inc.

KAMANDI: AT EARTH'S END
[Mini-Series], 1993
1 R:Kamandi	2.50
2 V:Kingpin,Big Q	2.50
3 A:Sleeper Zom,Saphira	2.50
4 A:Superman	2.50
5 A:Superman,V:Ben Boxer	2.50
6 final issue	2.50

KARATE KID
March-April, 1976
1 I:Iris Jacobs,A:Legion	20.00
2 A:Major Disaster	12.00
3 thru 10	@12.00
11 A:Superboy/Legion	12.00
12 A:Superboy/Legion	12.00
13 A:Superboy/Legion	12.00
14 A:Robin	12.00
15 July-Aug., 1978	12.00

KENTS, THE
1997
1 (of 12) JOs(s),TT,MiB	3.00
2 JOs(s),TT,MiB, tragedy strikes	3.00
3 JOs,TT,MiB,Jed & Nate Kent	3.00
4 JOs,TT,MiB,Bleeding Kansas, concl.	3.00
5 JOs,TT,Brother vs.Brother pt.1	3.00
6 JOs,TT,Brother vs.Brother pt.2	3.00
7 JOs,TT,MiB,Quantrill, Wild Bill Hickcock	3.00
8 JOs,	3.00
9 JOs,TMd,To the Stars by Hard Ways,pt.1	3.00
10 JOs,TMd,To the Stars,pt.2	3.00
11 JOs,TMd,To the Stars,pt.3	3.00
12 JOs,TMd,To the Stars,pt.4	3.00
TPB The Kents, rep.	20.00

KID ETERNITY
1991
1 GMo(s),DFg,O:Kid Eternity	5.50
2 GMo(s),DFg,A:Mr.Keeper	5.50
3 GMo(s),DFg,True Origin revealed, final issue	5.50

KID ETERNITY
DC/Vertigo, 1993–94
1 B:ANo(s),SeP,R:Kid Eternity, A:Mdm.Blavatsky,Hemlock	2.75

2 SeP,A:Sigmund Freud,Carl Jung, A:Malocchio	2.50
3 SeP,A:Malocchio,I:Dr.Pathos	2.25
4 SeP,A:Neal Cassady	2.25
5 SeP,In Cyberspace	2.25
6 SeP,A:Dr.Pathos,Marilyn Monroe	2.25
7 SeP,I:Infinity	2.25
8 SeP,In Insane Asylum	2.25
9 SeP,Asylum,A:Dr.Pathos	2.25
10 SeP,Small Wages	2.25
11 ANi(s),I:Slap	2.25
12 SeP,A:Slap	2.25
13 SeP,Date in Hell,pt.1	2.25
14 SeP,Date in Hell,pt.2	2.25
15 SeP,Date in Hell,pt.3	2.25
16 SeP,The Zone	2.25
TPB GMo,DFg (2006)	15.00

KILL YOUR BOYFRIEND
DC/Vertigo, 1995, 1999
GNv PBd(c) (1995)	5.00
1-shot GMo (1999)	6.00

KINETIC
DC Focus, March 2004
1 WaP,F:Tom Morell	2.50
2 WaP,newfound super-powers	2.50
3 thru 9 WaP	@2.50
TPB rep.	10.00

KINGDOM, THE
1998
1 (of 2) MWa,AOl	5.00
2 MWa,MZ,JhB,V:Gog	4.00
Spec.#1 Kid Flash	2.25
Spec.#1 Offspring	2.25
Spec.#1 Nightstar	2.25
Spec.#1 Planet Krypton	2.25
Spec.#1 Son of the Bat	2.25
DirectCurrents Spec.	free
TPB	15.00

KINGDOM COME
Elseworlds 1996
1 MWa,AxR	9.00
2 MWa,AxR,R:JLA	9.00
3 MWa,AxR,A:Capt. Marvel	8.00
4 MWa,AxR, final issue	8.00
TPB MWa,AxR, rep.	15.00

KOBALT
DC/Milestone, 1994–95
1 JBy(c),I:Kobalt,Richard Page	3.00
2 thru 13	@2.50
14 Long Hot Summer, V:Harvester	3.00
15 Long Hot Summer	3.00

KOBRA
1976–77
1 JK,I:Kobra & Jason Burr	15.00
2 I:Solaris	7.50
3 KG/DG,TA,V:Solaris	7.50
4 V:Servitor	7.50
5 RB/FMc,A:Jonny Double	7.50
6 MN/JRu,A:Jonny Double	7.50
7 MN/JRu,A:Jonny Double last iss.	7.50

KONG THE UNTAMED
June-July, 1975
1 AA,BWr(c)	20.00
2 AA,BWr(c)	12.00
3 AA	10.00
4	10.00
5 Feb.–March, 1976	10.00

Korak, Son of Tarzan #46
© DC Comics Inc.

KORAK, SON OF TARZAN
1975
(Prev. published by Gold Key)
46 JKu(c),B:Carson of Venus	20.00
47 JKu(c)	10.00
48 JKu(c)	10.00
49 JKu(c),Origin of Korak	15.00
50 thru 59 JKu(c),1975	10.00
Becomes:

TARZAN FAMILY

KRYPTON CHRONICLES
1981
1 CS,A:Superman	5.00
2 CS,A:Black Flame	4.00
3 CS,O:Name of Kal-El	4.00

KRYPTO THE SUPERDOG
Aug., 2006
1 From TV cartoon	2.25
2 thru 6	@2.25

LAB RATS
April, 2002
1 by the one and only JBy	7.00
1a 2nd printing	4.50
2 JBy, amusement park	6.00
2a 2nd printing	4.50
3 JBy,	2.50
4 JBy,time travel,pt.1	2.50
5 JBy,time travel,pt.2	2.50
6 JBy,time travel,pt.3,A:Superman	2.50
7 JBy,interplanetary adventure	2.50
8 JBy, final issue	2.50

LAND OF THE BLINDFOLDED
2005
Vol. 2 thru Vol. 9	@10.00

LAST DAYS OF THE JUSTICE SOCIETY
1986
1	5.00

LAST ONE
DC/Vertigo, 1993
1 B:JMD(s),DSw,I:Myrwann,Patrick Maguire's Story	3.25
2 DSw,Pat's Addiction to Drugs	3.00
3 DSw,Pat goes into Coma	3.00

4 DSw,In Victorian age 3.00
5 DSw,Myrwann Memories 3.00
6 E:JMD(s),DSw,final Issue 3.00

L.A.W.
1999
1 (of 6) BL,DG,Living Assault
Weapons 2.50
2 thru 6 BL,DG . . . . @2.50

LAZARUS FIVE
May, 2000
1 (of 5) THy,F:Inquisitors 2.50
2 thru 5 THy . . . . @2.50

Leading Comics #12
© DC Comics, Inc.

LEADING COMICS
Winter, 1941–42
1 O:Seven Soldiers of Victory,
B:Crimson Avenger,Green Arrow
& Speedy,Shining Knight,
A:The Dummy 8,500.00
2 MMe,V:Black Star 3,500.00
3 V:Dr. Doome 2,500.00
4 Seven Steps to Conquest,
V:The Sixth Sense 2,000.00
5 The Miracles that Money
Couldn't Buy 2,000.00
6 Treasure that Time Forgot . . 1,500.00
7 The Wizard of Wisstark 1,500.00
8 Seven Soldiers Go back
through the Centuries. 1,500.00
9 V:Mr. X,Chameleon of Crime 1,500.00
10 King of the Hundred Isles . . 1,500.00
11 The Hard Luck Hat! 1,100.00
12 The Million Dollar
Challenge! 1,100.00
13 The Trophies of Crime 1,100.00
14 Bandits from the Book 1,100.00
15 (fa) King Oscar's Court 350.00
16 thru 22 (fa) . . . . @150.00
23 (fa),I:Peter Porkchops 300.00
24 thru 30 (fa) . . . . @125.00
31 (fa) 100.00
32 (fa) 100.00
33 (fa) 100.00
34 thru 40 (fa) . . . . @100.00
41 (fa),Feb.–March, 1950 . . . . . 100.00
Becomes:

LEADING
SCREEN COMICS
1950
42 thru 50 Funny Animal . . . . . @125.00
51 thru 60 . . . . @100.00
61 thru 70 . . . . @100.00

---

71 thru 77 . . . . @100.00

LEAGUE OF JUSTICE
1996
1 (of 2) Elseworlds 6.00
2 (of 2) Elseworlds 6.00

LEAVE IT TO BINKY
1948
1ShM, teen-age 450.00
2 ShM 225.00
3 . . . . 135.00
4 . . . . 135.00
5 A:Superman 200.00
6 . . . . 125.00
7 . . . . 125.00
8 . . . . 125.00
9 . . . . 125.00
10 . . . . 125.00
11 thru 13 . . . . @100.00
14 ShM 125.00
15 thru 20 . . . . @90.00
21 thru 27 . . . . @100.00
28 MD 125.00
29 . . . . 100.00
30 thru 60 . . . . @100.00
61 thru 71 . . . . @35.00

LEGEND OF
THE HAWKMAN
July, 2000
1 BRa,Hawkman & Hawkgirl 5.00
2 BRa,V:Thanagarian zealots 5.00
3 BRa,concl. 5.00

LEGEND OF
THE SHIELD
DC/Impact, 1991–92
1 I:Shield, ... 2.50
2 thru 16 . . . . @2.50
Ann.#1 Earthquest,w/trading card. . 2.25

LEGEND OF
WONDER WOMAN
1986
1 Return of Atomia 4.00
2 A:Queens Solalia & Leila 3.50
3 Escape from Atomia 3.50
4 conclusion 3.50

LEGENDS
1986–87
1 JBy,V:Darkseid 5.00
2 JBy,A:Superman 4.00
3 JBy,I:Suicide Squad 4.00
4 JBy,V:Darkseid 4.00
5 JBy,A:Dr. Fate 4.00
6 JBy,I:Justice League 5.00
TPB rep.#1–#6 JBy(c) 10.00

LEGENDS OF
DANIEL BOONE, THE
Oct., 1955–Jan., 1957
1 . . . . 900.00
2 . . . . 600.00
3 thru 8 . . . . 500.00

LEGENDS OF
THE DARK KNIGHT
See: BATMAN

LEGENDS OF
THE DC UNIVERSE
Dec., 1997
1 JeR,VS,PNe,A:Superman, pt.1 . . 3.50

Legends of Daniel Boon #1
© DC Comics, Inc.

2 JeR,VS,PNe,A:Superman, pt.2 . . 4.00
3 JeR,VS,PNe,A:Superman, pt.3 . . 2.50
4 BML,MD2,VRu,Moments, pt.1 . . . 2.50
5 BML,MD2,VRu,Moments, pt.2 . . . 2.50
6 DTy,KN,Robin meets Superman . 2.50
7 DON,DG,Peacemakers, pt.1 . . . . 2.50
8 DON,DG,Peacemakers, pt.2 . . . . 2.50
9 DON,DG,Peacemakers, pt.3 . . . . 2.50
10 TyD,KN,F:Batman & Batgirl,pt.1 . 2.50
11 KN,TyD,F:Batman & Batgirl,pt.2 . 2.50
12 CPr(s),Critical Mass,pt.1 . . . . . . 2.50
13 CPr(s),Critical Mass,pt.2 . . . . . . 2.50
14 JK,BR,SR,64-page 5.00
15 RCa,Dark Matters, pt.1 . . . . 2.50
16 RCa,Dark Matters, pt.2 . . . . 2.50
17 RCa,Dark Matters, pt.3 . . . . 2.50
18 MWn(s),JG,F:New Teen Titans . 2.50
19 RT,F:Impulse 2.50
20 StG(s),MZ,KJ,Trail of the
Traitor, pt.1 . . . . 2.50
21 StG(s),MZ,KJ,Trail of the
Traitor, pt.2 . . . . 2.50
22 Transilvane,pt.1 . . . . 2.50
23 Transilvane,pt.2 . . . . 2.50
24 StP,The Jump,pt.1 . . . . 2.50
25 StP,The Jump,pt.2 . . . . 2.50
26 TVE,JRu,Aquaman&Joker,pt.1 . . 2.50
27 TVE,JRu,Aquaman&Joker,pt.2 . . 2.50
28 GK,KJ,pt.1 . . . . 2.50
29 GK,KJ,pt.2,F:Traitor 2.50
30 CPr(s),Wonder Woman,pt.1 . . . . 2.50
31 CPr(s),Wonder Woman,pt.2 . . . . 2.50
32 CPr(s),Wonder Woman,pt.3 . . . . 2.50
33 JMD,MZi,VcL,F:Spectre,pt.1 . . . 2.50
34 JMD,MZi,VcL,F:Spectre,pt.2 . . . 2.50
35 JMD,MZi,VcL,F:Spectre,pt.3 . . . 2.50
36 JMD,MZi,VcL,F:Spectre,pt.4 . . . 2.50
37 ScK,KJ,Traitor Trilogy,pt.1 . . . . 2.50
38 ScK,KJ,V:Traitor,pt.2 . . . . 2.50
39 RGr,Sole Survivor of Earth 2.50
40 RGr,Lessons in Time,pt.1 . . . . . 2.50
41 RGr,Lessons in Time,pt.2 . . . . . 2.50
Giant #1 JKu(c), 80 pg. 5.00
Spec 3-D Gallery #1 . . . . 3.00
GN Crisis on Infinite Earths 5.00

LEGENDS OF
THE LEGION
Dec., 1997
1 (of 4) BKi,TPe,TNu,O:Ultra Boy. . 2.75
2 thru 4 BKi,TPe . . . . @2.50

LEGENDS OF THE WORLD FINEST
1994

1 WS(s),DIB,V:Silver Banshee,
  Blaze,Tullus,Foil(c) 6.00
2 WS(s),DIB,V:Silver Banshee,
  Blaze,Tullus,Foil(c) 6.00
3 WS(s),DIB,V:Silver Banshee,
  Blaze,Tullus,Foil(c) 6.00
TPB 15.00

L.E.G.I.O.N. '89-94
1989–94

1 BKi,V:Computer Tyrants 6.00
2 BKi,V:Computer Tyrants 3.50
3 BKi,V:Computer Tyrants,
  A:Lobo 3.50
4 BKi,V: Lobo 3.50
5 BKi,J:Lobo(in the rest of the
  series),V:Konis-Biz 3.50
6 BKi,V:Konis-Biz 3.50
7 BKi,Stealth vs. Dox 3.50
8 BKi,R:Dox 3.50
9 BKi,J:Phase (Phantom Girl) 3.00
10 BKi,Stealth vs Lobo 3.00
11 BKi,V:Mr.Stoorr 3.00
12 BKi,V:Emerald Eye 3.00
13 BKi,V:Emerald Eye 3.00
14 BKi,V:Pirates 3.00
15 BKi,V:Emerald Eye 3.00
16 BKi,J:LarGand 3.00
17 BKi,V:Dragon-Ro 3.00
18 BKi,V:Dragon-Ro 3.00
19 V:Lydea,L:Stealth 3.00
20 Aftermath 3.00
21 D:Lyrissa Mallor,V:Mr.Starr . . . 3.00
22 V:Mr.Starr 3.00
23 O:R.J.Brande(double sized) 3.50
24 BKi,V:Khunds 3.00
25 BKi,V:Khunds 3.00
26 BKi,V:Khunds 3.00
27 BKi,J:Lydea Mallor 3.00
28 KG,Birth of Stealth's Babies . . . 3.00
29 BKi,J:Capt.Comet,Marij'n Bek . . 3.00
30 BKi,R:Stealth 3.00
31 Lobo vs.Capt.Marvel 4.00
32 V:Space Biker Gang 3.00
33 A:Ice-Man 3.00
34 MPn,V:Ice Man 3.00
35 Legion Disbanded 3.00
36 Dox proposes to Ignea 3.00
37 V:Intergalactic Ninjas 3.00
38 BKi,Lobo V:Ice Man 3.00

L.E.G.I.O.N. '92 #39
© DC Comics Inc.

---

39 BKi,D:G'odd,V:G'oddSquad 3.00
40 BKi,V:Kyaltic Space Station 3.00
41 BKi,A:Stealth'sBaby 3.00
42 BKi,V:Yeltsin-Beta 3.00
43 BKi,V:Yeltsin-Beta 3.00
44 V:Yeltsin-Beta,C:Gr.Lantern . . . 3.00
45 BKi,New Perspectives 3.00
46 BKi,A:Hal Jordan 3.00
47 BKi,Lobo vs Hal Jordan 3.00
48 BKi,R:Ig'nea 3.00
49 BKi,V:Ig'nea 3.00
50 BKi,V:Ig'nea,A:Legion'67 . . . . . 4.00
51 F:Lobo,Telepath 3.00
52 BKi,V:Cyborg Skull of Darius . . . 3.00
53 BKi,V:Shadow Creature 3.00
54 BKi,V:Shadow Creature 3.00
55 BKi,V:Shadow Beast 3.00
56 BKi,A:Masked Avenger 3.00
57 BKi,Trinity,V:Green Lantern 3.00
58 BKi,Trinity#6,A:Green Lantern,
  Darkstar 3.00
59 F:Phase 3.00
60 V:Phantom Riders 3.00
61 Little Party 3.00
62 A:R.E.C.R.U.I.T.S. 3.00
63 A:Superman 3.00
64 BKi(c),V:Mr.B 3.00
65 BKi(c),V:Brain Bandit 3.00
66 Stealth and Dox name child 3.00
67 F:Telepath 3.00
68 Our Porduct is Peace 3.00
69 F:Phase & Jo; Minutes to Go . . . 3.00
70 Zero Hour, last issue 3.50
Ann.#1 A:Superman,V:Brainiac 5.50
Ann.#2 Armageddon 2001 . . . . 3.50
Ann.#3 Eclipso tie-in 3.25
Ann.#4 SHa(i),I:Pax 3.75
Ann.#5 Elseworlds story 3.50

LEGION, THE
Oct., 2001

1 DAn,ALa, New era dawns 5.00
2 DAn,ALa,F:Oversight Watch 4.00
3 DAn,ALa,new headquarters 4.00
4 DAn,ALa,Footstep Drive Tech. . . 3.50
5 DAn,ALa,Return to Lost Galaxy . 3.00
6 DAn,ALa,Moon & Inhabitants . . . 3.00
7 DAn,ALa,V:Ra's Al Ghul 3.00
8 DAn,ALa,V:Ra's Al Ghul 3.00
9 DAn,ALa,Apparition,Ultra-Boy . . 3.00
10 DAn,ALa,Robotica to Earth 3.00
11 DAn,ALa,F:Robotica 2.75
12 DAn,ALa,F:JLA 2.75
13 DAn,ALa,V:Robotica 2.75
14 DAn,ALa,V:Robotica 2.75
15 DAn,ALa,F:Timber Wolf 2.75
16 DAn,ALa,F:Lone Wolf 2.75
17 DAn,ALa,The Fittest,pt.1 . . . . . 2.75
18 DAn,ALa,The Fittest,pt.2 . . . . . 2.50
19 DAn,MFm,Dream Crime,pt.1 . . . 2.50
20 DAn,MFm,Dream Crime,pt.2 . . . 2.50
21 DAn,MFm,Dream Crime,pt.3 . . . 2.50
22 DAn,MFm,Dream Crime,pt.4 . . . 2.50
23 DAn,MFm,Dream Crime,pt.5 . . . 2.50
24 DAn,ALa,F:Umbra 2.50
25 Foundations,pt.1,48-pg. 4.00
26 DAn,ALa,Foundations,pt.2 . . . . 2.50
27 DAn,ALa,Foundations,pt.3 . . . . 2.50
28 DAn,ALa,Foundations,pt.4 . . . . 2.50
29 DAn,ALa,Foundations,pt.5 . . . . 2.50
30 DAn,ALa,Foundations,pt.6 . . . . 2.50
31 KG,AM,deadly virus 2.50
32 DAn,ALa,V:Credo 2.50
33 DAn,ALa,F:Livewire 2.50
34 SLi,Wildfire,Qward 2.50
35 DJu,ASm,No Better Reason 2.50
36 DJu,ASm,No Better Reason 2.50
37 DJu,ASm,No Better Reason 2.50
38 DJu,ASm,No Better Reason 2.50
GN Legion Secret Files 3003 . . . . 5.00
TPB The Legion: Foundations 20.00

LEGION LOST
March, 2000

1 (of 12) DAn,ALa 8.00
2 DAn,ALa,V:Progeny 4.00
3 DAn,ALa,V:Progeny 4.00
4 DAn,ALa, ... 4.00
5 DAn,ALa,Brainiac 5.1 . . . . 4.00
6 DAn,ALa,F:Umbra 3.00
7 DAn,ALa,F:Ultra Boy 3.00
8 DAn,ALa, ... 3.00
9 DAn,ALa 3.00
10 DAn,ALa 3.00
11 DAn,ALA 3.00
12 DAn,ALA conclusion 3.00

LEGIONNAIRES
1992

1 CSp,V:Mano and the Hand,Bagged
  w/SkyBox promo card 4.00
1a w/out card 3.00
2 CSp,V:Mano 3.00
3 CSp,I:2nd Emerald Empress 3.00
4 CSp,R:Fatal Five 3.00
5 CSp,V:Fatal Five 3.00
6 thru 17 . . . . @3.00
18 Zero Hour, LSH 3.00
19 thru 49 . . . . @2.50
50 RSt&TMw(s),JMy,The Bride of
  Mordru, 48pg, with poster 5.00
51 thru 81 . . . . @2.50
Ann.#1 Elseworlds Story 3.50
Ann.#2 Year One Story 3.50
Ann.#3 RSt&TMw(s) 4.00
Spec.#1,000,000 TPe(s),SeP, Justice
  Legion L 2.50

LEGIONNAIRES THREE
1986

1 EC,Saturn Girl,Cosmic Boy 4.00
2 EC,V:Time Trapper,pt.1 . . . . 3.00
3 EC,V:Time Trapper,pt.2 . . . . 3.00
4 EC,V:Time Trapper,pt.3 . . . . 3.00

LEGION OF SUBSTITUTE HEROES
1985

Spec.#1 KG 3.00

LEGION OF SUPER-HEROES
[Reprint Series], 1973

1 rep. Tommy Tomorrow 50.00
2 rep. Tommy Tomorrow 30.00
3 rep. Tommy Tomorrow 30.00
4 rep. Tommy Tomorrow 30.00

[1st Regular Series], 1980–84
Prev: SUPERBOY (& LEGION)

259 JSon,L:Superboy 20.00
260 RE,I:Circus of Death 10.00
261 RE,V:Circus of Death 10.00
262 JSh,V:Engineer 10.00
263 V:Dagon the Avenger 10.00
264 V:Dagon the Avenger 10.00
265 JSn,DG,Superman/Radio Shack
  insert 10.00
266 R:Bouncing Boy,Duo Damsel . 10.00
267 SD,V:Kantuu 10.00
268 SD,BWi,V:Dr.Mayavale 10.00
269 V:Fatal Five 10.00
270 V:Fatal Five 10.00
271 V:Tharok (Dark Man) 6.00
272 CI,SD,O:J:Blok, I:New
  Dial 'H' for Hero 6.00
273 V:Stargrave 6.00
274 SD,V:Captain Frake 6.00
275 V:Captain Frake 6.00
276 SD,V:Mordru 6.00
277 A:Reflecto(Superboy) 6.00

Legion of Super-Heroes #282
© DC Comics, Inc.

278 A:Reflecto(Superboy) 6.00
279 A:Reflecto(Superboy) 6.00
280 R:Superboy 6.00
281 SD,V:Time Trapper 6.00
282 V:Time Trapper 6.00
283 O:Wildfire 6.00
284 PB,V:Organleggor 6.00
285 PB,KG(1st Legion)V:Khunds . . . 8.00
286 PB,KG,V:Khunds 8.00
287 KG,V:Kharlak 8.00
288 KG,V:Kharlak 8.00
289 KG,Stranded 8.00
290 KG,B:Great Darkness Saga,
    J:Invisible Kid II 8.00
291 KG,V:Darkseid's Minions 6.00
292 KG,V:Darkseid's Minions 6.00
293 KG,Daxam destroyed 6.00
294 KG,E:Great Darkness Saga,
    V:Darkseid,A:Auron,Superboy . . 8.00
295 KG,A:Green Lantern Corps 3.50
296 KG,D:Cosmic Boys family 3.50
297 KG,O:Legion,A:Cosmic Boy 3.50
298 KG,EC,I:Amethyst 3.50
299 KG,R:Invisible Kid I 3.50
300 KG,CS,JSon,DC,KS,DG 6.00
301 KG,R:Chameleon Boy 3.50
302 KG,A:Chameleon Boy 3.50
303 KG,V:Fatal Five 3.50
304 KG,V:Fatal Five 3.50
305 KG,V:Micro Lad 3.50
306 KG,CS,RT,O:Star Boy 3.50
307 KG,GT,Omen 3.50
308 KG,V:Omen 3.50
309 KG,V:Omen 3.50
310 KG,V:Omen 3.50
311 KG,GC,New Headquarters 3.50
312 KG,V:Khunds 3.50
313 KG,V:Khunds 3.50
Ann.#1 IT,KG,I:Invisible Kid 4.00
Ann.#2 DGb,W:Karate Kid and
    Princess Projectra 3.00
Ann.#3 CS,RT,A:Darkseid 3.00
Ann.#4 thru Ann.# 5 reprints . . . . @3.00
Becomes:

TALES OF LEGION OF
SUPER HEROES

LEGION OF
SUPER-HEROES
[3rd Regular Series], 1984–89
1 KG,V:Legion of Super-Villains . . . 5.00
2 KG,V:Legion of Super-Villains . . . 4.00

3 KG,V:Legion of Super-Villians . . . 4.00
4 KG,D:Karate Kid 4.00
5 KG,D:Nemesis Kid 4.00
6 JO,F:Lightning Lass 3.00
7 SLi,A:Controller 3.00
8 SLi,V:Controller 3.00
9 Sli,V:Sklarians 3.00
10 V:Khunds 3.00
11 EC,KG,L:Orig 3 members 3.00
12 SLi,EC,A:Superboy 3.00
13 SLi,V:Lythyls,F:TimberWolf 3.00
14 SLi,J:Sensor Girl (Princess
    Projectra),Quislet,Tellus,Polar
    Boy,Magnetic Kid 3.00
15 GLa,V:Dr. Regulus 3.00
16 SLi,Crisis tie-in,F:Braniac5 . . . . 3.00
17 GLa,O:Legion 3.00
18 GLa,Crisis tie-in,V:InfiniteMan . . 3.00
19 GLa,V:Controller 3.00
20 GLa,V:Tyr 3.00
21 GLa,V:Emerald Empress 4.00
22 GLa,V:Restorer,A:Universo 4.00
23 SLi,GLa,A:Superboy,
    Jonah Hex 4.00
24 GLa,NBi,A:Fatal Five 4.00
25 GLa,V:FatalFive 4.00
26 GLa,V:FatalFive,O:SensorGirl . . . 3.00
27 GLa,GC,A:Mordru 3.00
28 GLa,L:StarBoy 3.00
29 GLa,V:Starfinger 3.00
30 GLa,A:Universo 3.00
31 GLa,A:Ferro Lad,Karate Kid 3.00
32 GLa,V:Universo,I:Atmos 3.00
33 GLa,V:Universo 3.00
34 GLa,V:Universo 3.00
35 GLa,V:Universo,R:Saturn Girl . . . 3.00
36 GLa,R:Cosmic Boy 3.00
37 GLa,V:Universo,I:Superboy
    (Earth Prime) 15.00
38 GLa,V:TimeTrapper,
    D:Superboy 14.00
39 CS,RT,O:Colossal Boy 3.00
40 GLa,I:New Starfinger 3.00
41 GLa,V:Starfinger 3.00
42 GLa,Millennium,V:Laurel Kent . . 3.00
43 GLa,Millennium,V:Laurel Kent . . 3.00
44 GLa,O:Quislet 3.00
45 GLa,CS,MGr,DC,30th Ann. 4.00
46 GLa,Conspiracy 3.00
47 GLa,PB,V:Starfinger 3.00
48 GLa,Conspiracy,A:Starfinger . . . 3.00
49 PB,Conspiracy,A:Starfinger 3.00
50 KG,V:Time Trapper,A:Infinite
    Man,E:Conspiracy 4.00
51 KG,V:Gorak,L:Brainiac5 . . . . 3.00
52 KG,V:Gil'Dishpan 3.00
53 KG,V:Gil'Dishpan 3.00
54 KG,V:Gorak 3.00
55 KG,EC,JL,EL,N:Legion 3.00
56 EB,V:Inquisitor 3.00
57 KG,V:Emerald Empress 3.00
58 KG,V:Emerald Empress 3.00
59 KG,MBr,F:Invisible Kid 3.00
60 KG,B:Magic Wars 3.00
61 KG,Magic Wars 3.00
62 KG,D:Magnetic Lad 3.00
63 KG,E:Magic Wars #4,final iss. . . 3.50
Ann.#1 KG,Murder Mystery 3.00
Ann.#2 KG,CS,O:Validus,
    A:Darkseid 3.50
Ann.#3 GLa,I:2nd Karate Kid 3.00
Ann.#4 BKi,V:Starfinger 3.00
Ann #5 I:2nd Legion Sub.Heroes . . 3.00

[4th Regular Series], 1989–97
1 KG,R:Cosmic Boy, Chameleon . . 5.00
2 KG,R:Ultra Boy,I:Kono 4.00
3 KG,D:Block,V:Roxxas 4.00
4 KG,V:Time Trapper 4.00
5 KG,V:Mordru,A:Glorith 4.00
6 KG,I:Laurel Gand 4.00
7 KG,V:Mordru 3.00
8 KG,O:Legion 3.00

Legion of Super-Heroes 4th Series #11
© DC Comics, Inc.

9 KG,O:Laurel Gand 3.00
10 KG,V:Roxxas 3.00
11 KG,V:Roxxas 3.00
12 KG,I:Kent Shakespeare 3.00
13 KG,V:Dominators,posters 3.00
14 KG,J:Tenzil Kem 3.00
15 KG,Khund Invasion 3.00
16 KG,V:Khunds 3.00
17 KG,V:Khunds 3.00
18 KG,V:Khunds 3.00
19 KG,cont.from Adv.of Superman
    #478,A:Original Dr. Fate 3.00
20 KG,V:Dominators 3.00
21 KG,B:Quiet Darkness,
    A:Lobo,Darkseid 3.50
22 KG,A:Lobo,Darkseid 3.00
23 KG,A:Lobo,Darkseid 3.00
24 KG,E:Quiet Darkness,A:Lobo,
    Darkseid,C:Legionairres 4.00
25 DAb,I:Legionairres 3.50
26 JPn,B:Terra Mosaic,V:B.I.O.N. . . 2.50
27 JPn,V:B.I.O.N. 2.50
28 JPn,O:Sun Boy 2.50
29 JPn,I:Monica Sade 2.50
30 JPn,V:Dominators 2.50
31 CS,AG,F:Shvaughn as man 2.50
32 JPn,D:Karate Kid,Prin.Projectra,
    Chameleon Boy(Legionaires) . . 2.50
33 R:Kid Quantum 2.50
34 R:Sun Boy 2.50
35 JPN,V:Dominators 2.50
36 JPn,E:Terra Mosaic. 2.50
37 JBr,R:Star Boy,Dream Girl 2.50
38 JPn,Earth is destroyed 5.00
39 SI,A:Legionnaires 2.50
40 SI,Legion meets Legionnaires . . 2.50
41 SI,F:The Legionnaires 2.50
42 SI,V:Glorith 2.50
43 SI,B:Mordru Arises 2.50
44 SI,R:Karate Kid 2.50
45 SI,R:Roxxas 2.50
46 SI,Battle with the Dead 2.50
47 SI,Last Rites 2.50
48 SI,E:Mordru Arises 2.50
49 F:Matter Eater Lad 2.50
50 W:Tenzil & Saturn Queen,
    R:Wildfire,V:B.I.O.N. 4.00
51 R:Kent,Celeste,Ivy,V:Grimbor . . 2.50
52 F:Timber Wolf 2.50
53 SI,V:Glorith 2.50
54 SI,Foil,Die-Cut(c),
    N:L.E.G.I.O.N. 5.00
55 SI,On Rimbor 2.50
56 SI,R:Espionage Squad 2.50

57 SI,R:Khund Legionnaires	2.50
58 SI,D:Laurel Gand	2.50
59 SI,R:Valor,Dawnstar	2.50
60 SI,End of an Era#3	2.50
61 SI,End of an Era#6	2.50
62 I:New Team	2.50
63 Alien Attack	2.50
64 Sibling Rivalry	2.50
65 Breakout	2.50
66 I:New Team Members	2.50
67 F:Leviathan	2.50
68 F:Leviathan	2.50
69 V:Durlan	2.50
70 A:Andromeda, Brainiac 5	2.50
71 Planet Trom	2.50
72 Absent Friends	2.50
73 Sibling Rivalry,pt.1	2.50
74 Future Tense,pt2	2.50
75 Two Timer,pt.1 (of 2)	2.50
76 F:Valor & Triad	2.50
77 F:Brainiac 5	2.50
78 The Gathering Doom	2.50
79 Fatal Five attacks	2.50
80 V:Fatal Five	2.50
81 R:Dirk Morgna	2.50
82 Lifestyles of the Dead	2.50
83 TPe&TMw(s),Big Tears	2.50
84 TPe&TMw(s),Emerald Legion	2.50
85 TPe&TMw(s),LMd,A:Superman, back in 20th century	2.50
86 TPe&TMw(s),LMd,Final Night tie-in	2.50
87 TPe&TMw(s),LMd,F:Deadman	2.50
88 TPe&TMw(s),LMd,A:Impulse	2.50
89 TPe&TMw(s),LMd,	2.50
90 TPe&TMw(s),LMd,V:Dr. Psycho	2.50
91 TPe&TMw(s),LMd,Legion back together, but trapped in timestream	2.50
92 TPe&TMs(s),LMd,Displaced in Time	2.50
93 TPe&TMw(s),MC, All-tragedy issue	2.50
94 TPe&TMw(s),LMd,22 short pages about the Legion of Super-Heroes	2.50
95 MFm,F:Brainiac 5	2.50
96 MFm,wedding	2.50
97 TPe,LMd,Genesis tie-in	2.50
98 TPe&TMC,LMd,C.O.M.P.U.T.O. the Conqueror, pt.1	2.50
99 TPe&TMw,LMd,Computo, pt.2	2.50
100 TPe&TMw,LMd,Computo, pt.3	7.50
101 TPe&TMw(s),AD&MFm(c), F:Sparks	2.50
102 TPe&TMw(s),	2.50
103 TPe&TMw,AD&MFm(c),Star Boy	2.50
104 TPe&TMw,AD&MFm(c), changes	2.50
105 TPe&TMw,AD&MFm(c), Adventures in Action x-over	2.50
106 TPe&TMw,AD&MFm(c),Dark Circle Rising, x-over pt.2	2.50
107 TPe&TMw,AD&MFm(c),Dark Circle Rising, x-over pt.4	2.50
108 TPe&TMw,AD&MFm(c),Dark Circle Rising, x-over pt.6	2.50
109 DDv,AD,MFm,F:Violet	2.50
110 TPe,V:Thunder	2.50
111 TPe&TMw(s),V:Daxamite	2.50
112 TPe&TMw(s),In Space	2.50
113 TPe&TMw(s),Kinetix	2.50
114 TPe&TMw(s),Bizarro Legion,pt.1	2.50
115 TPe&TMw(s),Bizarro Legion, pt.2	2.50
116 TPe&TMw(s),V:Pernisius,pt.1	2.50
117 TPe&TMw(s),V:Pernisius,pt.2	2.50
118 TPe&TMw(s),V:Pernisius,pt.3	2.50
119 TPe&TMw(s),A:Valor & Phase	2.50
120 TPe,TMw,V:Fatal Four,pt.1	2.50

121 TPe,TMw,V:Fatal Five,pt.2	2.50
122 DAn,ALa,Legion of the Damned,pt.1	2.50
123 DAn,ALa,Legion of the Damned,pt.3	2.50
124 DAn,ALa,Legion of the Damned, aftermath	10.00
125 DAn,ALa,final issue	2.50
Ann.#1 O:Ultra Boy,V:Glorith	3.50
Ann.#2 O:Valor	3.50
Ann.#3 N:Timberwolf	4.00
Ann.#4 I:Jamm	3.50
Ann.#5 SI(c),CDo,MFm,TMc, Elseworlds Story	3.75
Ann.#6 Year One Annual + pin-up	4.00
Ann.#7 TPe(s),MC,MFm,Legends of the Dead Earth	3.50
Spec.#1,000,000 TPe(s),KG,AG	2.50
GN Secret Files, inc.O:Legion	5.00
GN Secret Files #2	5.00

LEGION OF SUPER-HEROES
Dec., 2004

1 MWa(s),BKi,40-page	3.00
2 MWa(s),BKi,work with the law?	3.00
3 MWa(s),BKi,F:Triplicate Girl	3.00
4 MWa(s),DGb,F:Invisible Kid	3.00
5 MWa(s),BKi,ATi,Lightning Lad & Saturn Girl	3.00
6 MWa(s),BKi,ATi	3.00
7 MWa(s),BKi,ATi	3.00
8 MWa(s),BKi,ATi, team split	3.00
9 MWa(s),ATi,split widens	3.00
10 MWa(s),BKi,ATi,V:Terror Firma	3.00
11 MWa(s),BKi,V:Terror Firma	3.00
12 MWa(s),BKi,Team in shambles	3.00
13 MWa(s),BKi,Fifth Dimension	3.00
14 MWa(s),BKi,I:Atom Girl	3.00
15 MWa(s),BKi,31st century heroes	3.00

Becomes:

SUPERGIRL AND THE LEGION OF SUPERHEROES
March, 2006

16 MWa,BKi, newest member	3.00
17 MWa,BKi, newest member	3.00
18 MWa,BKi,Mysteries Unfold	3.00
19 MWa,BKi,F:Chameleon	3.00
20 MWa,BKi,Brainiac & Dream Girl	3.00
21 MWa,BKi,Colossal Boy's home	3.00
22 MWa,BKi,Supergirl's Boyfriend	3.00
23 MWa,BKi,Supergirl on Krypton	3.00
23a variant (c)	3.00
24 MWa,BKi,Super-powered Villains	3.00
25 MWa,BKi	3.00
26 MWa,BKi,V:Dominators	3.00
27 MWa,BKi,F:L.Lad & Mekt Ranzz	3.00
28 MWa,BKi,V:Dominators	3.00
29 MWa,BKi,V:Dominator Empire	3.00
30 MWa,BKi,V:Dominators	3.00
31 BKi,Dominators, concl	3.00
32 Quest for Cosmic Boy	3.00
33 Quest for Cosmic Boy	3.00
34 Quest for Cosmic Boy	3.00
35 Quest for Cosmic Boy	3.00

LEGION OF SUPER-HEROES IN THE 31ST CENTURY, THE
Apr., 2007

1 V:Fatal Five	2.25
2 F:Timber Wolf	2.25
3 Auditions	2.25
4 F:Brainy	2.25
5 F:Lightning Lad	2.25
6 F:Teen Lantern	2.25
7 New Themyscira	2.25

LEGION: SCIENCE POLICE
June, 1998

1 (of 4) DvM,PR,JRu,set in 30th century	2.50
2 DvM,PR,JRu,Jarik Shadder	2.50
3 DvM,PR,JRu,	2.50
4 DvM,PR,JRu	2.25

LEGION WORLDS
April, 2001

1 (of 6) DAn,ALa	4.00
2 DAn,ALa	4.00
3 DAn,ALa, On Braal	4.00
4 DAn,ALa, heading for Xanthu	4.00
5 DAn,ALa, SDi, on Steele	4.00
6 DAn,ALa, concl	4.00

LEX LUTHOR: MAN OF STEEL
March, 2005

1 (of 5) Superman, alien villain	3.00
2	3.00
3 F:Batman	3.00
4 and 5	@3.00
TPB Lex Luthor: Man of Steel	13.00

Life, The Universe and Everything #2 © DC Comics Inc.

LIFE, THE UNIVERSE AND EVERYTHING
1996

1 thru 3 Doug Adams adapt	@7.00

LIGHT BRIGADE, THE
Feb. 2004

1 thru 4 PSj	@6.00
TPB The Light Brigade (2005)	20.00

LIMITED COLLECTORS EDITION
Summer, 1973

21 Shazam	40.00
22 Tarzan	35.00
23 House of Mystery	45.00
24 Rudolph, the Red-nosed Reindeer	125.00
25 NA,NA(c),Batman	60.00
27 Shazam	35.00
29 Tarzan	35.00

DC COMICS

31 NA,O:Superman	35.00
32 Ghosts	50.00
33 Rudolph	100.00
34 X-Mas with Superheroes	35.00
35 Shazam	30.00
36 The Bible	30.00
37 Batman	40.00
38 Superman	30.00
39 Secret Origins	30.00
40 Dick Tracy	30.00
41 ATh,Super Friends	30.00
42 Rudolph	65.00
43 X-mas with Super-Heroes	30.00
44 NA,Batman	30.00
45 Secret Origins-Super Villians	30.00
46 ATh,JLA	30.00
47 Superman	30.00
48 Superman-Flash Race	30.00
49 Superboy & Legion of Super-Heroes	30.00
50 Rudolph	60.00
51 NA,NA(c),Batman	35.00
52 NA,NA(c),The Best of DC	30.00
57 Welcome Back Kotter	30.00
59 NA,BWr,Batman,1978	35.00

LITTLE SHOP OF HORRORS
Feb., 1987

1 GC 2.50

LOBO
[1st Limited Series], 1990–91

1 SBs,Last Czarnian #1	4.00
1a 2nd Printing	2.00
2 SBs,Last Czarnian #2	3.00
3 SBs,Last Czarnian #3	3.00
4 SBs,Last Czarnian #4	3.00
Ann.#1 Bloodlines#1,I:Layla	3.75
Lobo Paramilitary X-Mas SBs	5.50
Lobo:Blazing Chain of Love,DCw	2.00

[Regular Series], 1993–97

0 O:Lobo (1994, between #9&#10)	3.00
1 VS,Foil(c),V:Dead Boys	3.25
2 VS,Quigly Affair	3.00
3 VS,Quigly Affair	2.75
4 VS,Quigly Affair	2.75
5 V:Bludhound	2.50
6 I:Bim Simms	2.50
7 A:Losers	2.50
8 A:Losers	2.50
9 V:Lobo	2.50
10 Preacher	2.50
11 Goldstar vs. Rev.Bo	2.50

Lobo #4 © DC Comics, Inc.

12 AIG	2.50
13 AIG	2.50
14 Lobo, P.I.	2.50
15 Lobo, P.I.,pt.2	2.50
16 Lobo, P.I.,pt.3	2.50
17 Lobo, P.I.,pt.4	2.50
18 Lobo, P.I.,pt.5	2.50
19 AIG	2.50
20 Toilot Fight	2.50
21 AIG,KON,R:Space Cabby	2.50
22 AIG,UnderworldUnleashed tie-in.	2.50
23 AIG,Stargaze Rally,pt.1	2.50
24 AIG,Stargaze Rally,pt.2	2.50
25 AIG	2.50
26 AIG,V:Erik the Khund	2.50
27 AIG,V:Billy Krono	2.50
28 AIG,The Heiress,pt.1	2.50
29 AIG,The Heiress,pt.2	2.50
30 AIG,The Heiress,pt.3	2.50
31 AIG,The Heiress,pt.4	2.50
32 AIG(s),Lobo attends a seance, frags himself	2.50
33 AIG(s),Lobo returns from spirit world	2.50
34 AIG(s),vs. Japan, whaling,	2.50
35 AIG(s), Deathtrek	2.50
36 AIG(s)	2.50
37 AIG(s),BKi,Lobo's Guide to Girls	2.50
38 AIG(s),Bomandi The Last Boy on Earth	2.50
39 AIG(s),In the Belly of the Behemoth,pt. 1	2.50
40 AIG(s),Belly of Behemoth,pt.2.	2.50
41 AIG(s),roommates	2.50
42 AIG(s),A:Perfidia	2.50
43 AIG(s),A:Jonas	2.50
44 AIG(s),Genesis tie-in	2.50
45 AIG(s),battle royale	2.50
46 AIG(s),Jackie Chin	2.50
47 AIG(s),V:Kiljoy Riggs	2.50
48 AIG(s),F:the penguins	2.50
49 AIG(s)	2.50
50 AIG(s),war on DC universe	2.50
51 AIG(s),Slater and Candy	2.50
52 AIG(s),Goldstar funeral	2.50
53 AIG(s),disrupted ceremony	2.50
54 AIG(s),Good Vibes machine	2.50
55 AIG(s),Sheepworld	2.50
56 AIG(s),MPn,GLz,the wedding	2.50
57 AIG(s),MPn,GLz, Intergalactic Police convention	2.50
58 KG&AIG(s)	2.50
59 AIG(s),V:Bad Wee Bastards	2.50
60 AIG(s),All-New, Nonviolent Adventures of Superbo, pt.1	2.50
61 AIG(s),Superbo, pt.2	2.50
62 AIG(s),Superbo, pt.3	2.50
63 AIG(s),Soul Brothers,pt.1	2.50
64 AIG(s),Soul Brothers,pt.2	2.50
Ann.#1 Bloodlines	4.00
Ann.#2 Elseworlds Story	3.50
Ann.#3 AIG Year One.	5.00
Spec.#1,000,000 AIG(s),GLz	2.50
Spec. Lobo's Big Babe Spring Break, Miss Voluptuous Contest.	2.50
Spec. Blazing Chains of Love	2.00
Spec. Bounty Hunting for Fun and Profit, F:Fanboy	5.00
Spec. Lobo: Chained AIG(s), Lobo in prison	2.50
Spec. Lobo/Demon: Hellowe'en, AIG(s),VGi	2.25
Spec. Lobo In the Chair, AIG(s)	2.25
Spec. Lobo:I Quit,AIG, nicotine withdrawal	2.25
Spec. Lobo/Judge Dredd: Psycho Bikers vs. Mutants From Hell	5.00
Spec. Lobo: Portrait of a Victim VS,I:John Doe	2.25
GN Fragtastic Voyage AGr, miniaturized	6.00
Convention Special, comic con	2.00

LOBO: A CONTRACT ON GAWD
1994

1 AIG(s),KD	2.50
2 AIG(s),KD,A:Dave	2.50
3 AIG(s),KD	2.50
4 AIG(s),KD,Final Issue	2.50

Lobo's Back #4 © DC Comics, Inc.

LOBO'S BACK
1992

1 SBs,w/3(c) inside,V:Loo	2.50
1a 2nd printing	2.00
2 SBs,Lobo becomes a woman	2.50
3 SBs,V:Heaven	2.50
4 SBs,V:Heaven	2.50
TPB GF(c),rep.#1–#4	10.00

LOBO: DEATH & TAXES
[Mini-Series], Aug., 1996

1 (of 4) KG&AIG(s)	2.25
2 KG&AIG(s),Interstellar Revenue learns Lobo doesn't pay taxes	2.25
3 KG&AIG(s),Lobo walks into IRS trap	2.25
4 KG&AIG(s),Lobo destroys IRS	2.25

LOBO: INFANTICIDE
1992–93

1 KG,V:Su,Lobo Bastards	2.50
2 Lobo at Boot Camp	2.50
3 KG,Lobo Vs.his offspring	2.50
4 KG,V:Lobo Bastards	2.50

LOBO/MASK

1 AIG&JAr(s),DoM,Kwi, humorous x-over.	6.00
2 AIG&JAr(s),DoM,Kwi, concl.	6.00

LOBO: UNAMERICAN GLADIATORS
1993

1 CK,V:Satan's Brothers	2.50
2 CK,V:Jonny Caesar	2.50
3 CK,MMi(c),V:Satan Brothers	2.50
4 CK,MMi(c),V:Jonny Caeser	2.50

LOBO UNBOUND
June 2003

1 (of 6) mass-murder	3.00
2 thru 6	@3.00

LOBOCOP
1 StG(s)................ 2.25

LOIS LANE
Aug., 1986
1 and 2 GM............. @3.00

LONG HOT SUMMER, THE
Milestone, 1995
1 Blood Syndicate v. G.R.I.N.D. 3.00
2 A:Icon,Xombi,Hardware....... 2.50

LOONEY TUNES
1994
1 thru 6 Warner Bros. cartoons.. @3.00
7 thru 11 Warner Bros........ @3.00
12 thru 25................. @2.50
26 thru 155................ @2.25
Spec. Back in Action: Movie 4.00

LOSERS
DC/Vertigo, June 2003
1 crime espionage 4.00
2 thru 6 Goliath,pt.1–pt.5 .... @3.50
7 SMa,Downtime,pt.1 .... 3.00
8 SMa,Downtime,pt.2 .... 3.00
9 Island Life,pt.1 .... 3.00
10 Island Life,pt.2 .... 3.00
11 Island Life,pt.3............ 3.00
12 Island Life,pt.4 .... 3.00
13 Sheikdown,pt.1 .... 3.00
14 Sheikdown,pt.2 .... 3.00
15 F:Aisha 3.00
16 The Pass,pt.1 .... 3.00
17 The Pass,pt.2 .... 3.00
18 The Pass, pt.3............. 3.00
19 The Pass, pt.4............. 3.00
20 London Calling, pt.1 .... 3.00
21 London Calling, pt.2 .... 3.00
22 London Calling, pt.3 .... 3.00
23 Anti-Heist, pt.1 .... 3.00
24 Anti-Heist, pt.2 .... 3.00
25 Anti-Heist, pt.3 .... 3.00
26 CWi,Unamerica,pt.1 .... 3.00
27 CWi,Unamerica,pt.2 .... 3.00
28 CWi,Unamerica,pt.3 .... 3.00
29 Endgame, pt.1 .... 3.00
30 Endgame, pt.2 .... 3.00
31 Endgame, pt.3 .... 3.00
32 final issue 3.00

LOSERS SPECIAL
1985
1 Crisis,D:Losers 4.00

LOVELESS
DC/Vertigo, Oct. 2005
1 Western, A Kin of Homecoming.. 3.00
2 A Kin of Homecoming,pt.2..... 3.00
3 A Kin of Homecoming,pt.3...... 3.00
4 A Kin of Homecoming,pt.4...... 3.00
5 A Kin of Homecoming 3.00
6 A Peace of Iron 3.00
7 F:Ruth Cutter............... 3.00
8 Born bad? 3.00
9 Thicker Than Blackwater,pt.1 ... 3.00
10 Thicker Than Blackwater,pt.2 ... 3.00
11 Thicker Than Blackwater,pt.3 ... 3.00
12 Thicker Than Blackwater,pt.4 ... 3.00
13 F:Colonel Silas Redd 3.00
14 .... 3.00
15 F:Boyd Johnson 3.00
16 Blackwater Falls, pt.1 .... 3.00
17 Blackwater Falls, pt.2 .... 3.00
18 Blackwater Falls, pt.3 .... 3.00
19 Blackwater Falls, pt.4 .... 3.00
20 Blackwater Falls, pt.5 .... 3.00

LUCIFER
DC/Vertigo, Apr., 2000
1 Lucifer strugles to regain power . 7.50
2 Living Tarot Deck............. 4.50
3 V:Jill Presto 4.50
4 WaP,F:Elaine Belloc.......... 4.00
5 PrG,House of Windowless
   Rooms,pt.1 .... 3.50
6 PrG,Windowless Rooms,pt.2.... 3.50
7 PrG,Windowless Rooms,pt.3.... 3.50
8 PrG,Windowless Rooms,pt.4.... 3.50
9 Immortality 3.50
10 Children & Monsters,pt.1 ..... 3.50
11 Children & Monsters,pt.2 ..... 3.00
12 Children & Monsters,pt.3 ..... 3.00
13 Children & Monsters,pt.4 ..... 3.00
14 Triptych 3.00
15 Triptych,Two Edge Sword..... 3.00
16 Triptych,Ancestral Deed 3.00
17 Dalliance with the Dead,pt.1.... 3.00
18 Dalliance with the Dead,pt.2.... 3.00
19 Dalliance with the Dead,pt.3.... 3.00
20 The Thunder Sermon 3.00
21 Paradiso,pt.1............... 3.00
22 Paradiso,pt.2............... 3.00
23 Paradiso,pt.3............... 3.00
24 The Writing on the Wall 3.00
25 Purgatorio,pt.1 .... 3.00
26 Purgatorio,pt.2 .... 3.00
27 Purgatorio,pt.3 .... 3.00
28 F:Gaudium 3.00
29 MCy,Inferno,pt.1 .... 3.00
30 MCy,Inferno,pt.2 .... 3.00
31 MCy,Inferno,pt.3 .... 3.00
32 MCy,Inferno,pt.4 .... 3.00
33 MCy,robbery 3.00
34 MCy,Come to Judgment,pt.1 ... 3.00
35 MCy,Come to Judgment,pt.2 ... 3.00
36 MCy,Naglfar,pt.1 .... 3.00
37 MCy,Naglfar,pt.2 .... 3.00
38 MCy,Naglfar,pt.3 .... 3.00
39 MCy,Naglfar,pt.4 .... 3.00
40 MCy,Naglfar,pt.5 .... 3.00
41 MCy,Sisters of Mercy 3.00
42 MCy,Brothers in Arms,pt.1 .... 3.00
43 MCy,Brothers in Arms,pt.2 .... 3.00
44 MCy,Brothers in Arms,pt.3 .... 3.00
45 MCy(s)F:John Sewell 3.00
46 Stitchglass Slide,pt.1........ 3.00
47 Stitchglass Slide,pt.2........ 3.00
48 Stitchglass Slide,pt.3........ 3.00
49 Stitchflass Slide,pt.4........ 3.00
50 CR,48-pg. 4.00
51 Wolf Beneath the Tree,pt.1 .... 3.00
52 Wolf Beneath the Tree,pt.2.... 3.00
53 Wolf Beneath the Tree,pt.3.... 3.00
54 Wolf Beneath the Tree,pt.4.... 3.00
55 MCy,MaH,new religion 3.00
56 PrG,Lilith, Elaine,pt.1 .... 3.00
57 PrG,Lilith, Elaine,pt.2 .... 3.00
58 Escape to new universe 3.00
59 Breach, pt.1 .... 3.00
60 Breach, pt.2 .... 3.00
61 Breach, pt.3 .... 3.00
62 MCy,CDo................... 3.00
63 Moringstar,pt.1 .... 3.00
64 Moringstar,pt.2 .... 3.00
65 Moringstar,pt.3 .... 3.00
66 MK,Creation crumbles 3.00
67 Moringstar,pt.4 .... 3.00
68 Morningstar,pt.5 .... 3.00
69 Morningstar,pt.6 .... 3.00
70 MCy....................... 3.00
71 Evensong, pt.1 .... 3.00
72 Evensong, pt.2 .... 3.00
73 Someone expendable........ 3.00
74 Elaine Belloc picks up Godhood. 3.50
75 finale, 48-pg. 4.50
GN Nirvana, 48-pg. 6.00

MADAME XANADU
1981
1 MR/BB................... 5.00

MAJESTIC
Aug. 2004
1 (of 4) KIK,F:Mr.Majestic........ 3.00
2 KIK 3.00
3 KIK 3.00
4 KK,finale 3.00
TPB Strange New Visitor 15.00

MAJOR BUMMER
June, 1997
1 JAr(s),DoM,I:Major Bummer ... 2.50
2 thru 15 .... @2.50

Man-Bat #1
© DC Comics Inc.

MAN-BAT
1975–76
1 SD,AM,A:Batman............ 40.00
2 V:The Ten-Eyed Man........ 30.00
Reprint NA(c)................ 20.00

MAN-BAT
1996
1 CDi,terrorizes city 2.25
2 thru 3 .... @2.25

MAN-BAT
April, 2006
1 (of 5) R:Man-Bat............ 2.50
2 Kirk Langstrom must flee....... 3.00
3 Only Man-Bat remains......... 3.00
4 Batman vs. Man-Bat 3.00
5 finale 3.00

MAN-BAT vs. BATMAN
1 NA,DG,reprint............... 4.00

A MAN CALLED AX
Aug., 1997
1 MWn(s),SwM, part rep......... 2.50
2 thru 8 MWn(s),SwM, ... @2.50

MANHUNTER
1988–90
1 from Millennium-Suicide Squad.. 2.50
2 in Tokyo,A:Dumas 2.25
3 The Yakuza,V:Dumas 2.25

4 Secrets Revealed-Manhunter,
  Dumas & Olivia 2.25
5 A:Silvia Kandery. 2.25
6 A:Argent,contd.Suicide Squad
  Annual #1 . . . . 2.25
7 Vlatavia, V:Count Vertigo. 2.25
8 FS,A:Flash, Invasion x-over 2.25
9 FS,Invasion Aftermath extra
  (contd from Flash #22) 2.25
10 Finders Keepers 2.25
11 Losers Weepers 2.25
12 Losers Weepers 2.25
13 V:Catman 2.25
14 Janus Directive #5 . . . . 2.25
15 I:Mirage 2.25
16 V:Outlaw 2.25
17 In Gotham, A:Batman 2.25
18 Saints & Sinners,pt.1,R:Dumas . 2.25
19 Saints & Sinners,pt.2,V:Dumas. . 2.25
20 Saints & Sinners,pt.3,V:Dumas. . 2.25
21 Saints & Sinners,pt.4,
   A:Manhunter Grandmaster 2.25
22 Saints & Sinners,pt.5,
   A:Manhunter Grandmaster 2.25
23 Saints & Sinners,pt.6,V:Dumas. . 2.25
24 DG,Showdown, final issue 2.25

[2nd Series], 1994–95

0 Here Comes the Night. 2.50
1 True Fiction 2.50
2 N:Wild Huntsman 2.50
3 V:Malig 2.50
4 Necrodyne 2.50
5 V:Skin Walker 2.50
6 V:Barbarian,Incarnate 2.50
7 V:Incarnate,A:White Lotus
  & Capt. Atom 2.25
8 V:Butcher Boys 2.25
9 V:Butcher Boys 2.25
10 V:Necrodyne 2.25
11 Return of Old Enemy 2.25
12 Underworld Unleashed, finale. . 2.25

[3rd Series],Aug. 2004

1 JP,JLe(c),Identity Crisis 3.00
2 thru 3 JP,JLe(c) . . . . @4.00
4 JP. 4.00
5 JP,A:JLA 6.00
6 JP,Supervillain Trial 3.00
7 JP,Supervillain Trial 3.00
8 JP,V:Shadow Thief 3.00
9 JP,V:Phobia 3.00
10 Manhunted 3.00
11 JP,Two ex-manhunters 3.00
12 Masks Upon Masks 3.00
13 Kate Spencer & Cameron Chase 3.00
14 Secret of Project Manhunter. . . 3.00
15 Suit's secret history. 3.00
16 Manhunted aftermath 2.50
17 About to be Unmasked 2.50
18 An Old Foe 2.50
19 V:Her father. 2.50
20 Psychobabble 2.50
21 JSA family connection. 2.50
22 Trial of Dr. Psycho 3.00
23 New villain. 3.00
24 V:Dr. Psycho 3.00
25 F:Kate Spencer, final issue. . . . 3.00
26 AAd(c),Unleashed, pt.1 . . . . . . 3.00
26a variant PJ (c). 3.00
27 HC(c), Unleashed, pt.2 . . . . . . 3.00
28 KN(c), Unleashed, pt.3 . . . . . . 3.00
29 SeP(c),Unleashed, pt.4. . . . . . 3.00
30 Final issue 3.00

MAN OF STEEL
1986

1 JBy,DG,I:Modern Superman . . 7.00
1a 2nd edition 7.00
2 JBy,DG,R:Lois Lane. 5.00
3 JBy,DG,A:Batman 5.00
4 JBy,DG,V:Lex Luther 5.00
5 JBy,DG,I:Modern Bizarro 5.00

Man of Steel #6
© DC Comics, Inc.

6 JBy,DG,A:Lana Lang 5.00
TPB rep. Man of Steel #1–#6 . . . . 20.00
TPBa 2nd printing 8.00

MANY LOVES OF DOBIE GILLIS
May-June, 1960

1 From TV show 500.00
2 . . . . 250.00
3 . . . . 150.00
4 . . . . 150.00
5 thru 9 . . . . @125.00
10 thru 25 . . . . @125.00
26 Oct., 1964 . . . . 125.00

MARTIAN MANHUNTER
1988

1 A:JLI. 3.00
2 A:JLI,V:Death God 2.50
3 V:Death God,A:Dr.Erdel 2.50
4 A:JLI,final issue 2.50

[Mini-Series]

1 EB,American Secrets #1 . . . . . . 5.25
2 EB,American Secrets #2 . . . . . . 5.25
3 EB,American Secrets #3 . . . . . . 5.25

MARTIAN MANHUNTER
Aug., 1998

0 JOs,TMd,A:Batman,Superman . . 3.00
1 JOs,TMd,V:Headman 2.50
2 JOs,TMd,V:Antares 2.50
3 JOs,TMd,V:Bette Noir 2.50
4 JOs,TMd,J'emm, Son of Saturn . 2.50
5 JAr,JD,A:Chase 2.50
6 JOs,TMd,A:JLA,pt.1 . . . . 2.50
7 JOs(s),TMd,A:JLA,pt.2 . . . . 2.50
8 JOs(s),TMd,A:JLA,pt.3 . . . . 2.50
9 JOs(s),TMd,A:JLA,pt.4 . . . . 2.50
10 JOs(s),A:Fire. 2.50
11 JOs,PNe,BHi, ... 2.50
12 JOs,TMd,Day of Judgment
   x-over. 2.50
13 JOs,TMd,Rings of Saturn,pt.1 . 2.50
14 JOs,TMd,Rings of Saturn,pt.2 . 2.50
15 JOs,TMd,Rings of Saturn,pt.3 . 2.50
16 JOs,TMd,Rings of Saturn,pt.4 . 2.50
17 JOs,TMd,Rings of Saturn,pt.5 . 2.50
18 JOs,TMd,V:Kanto 2.50
19 JOs,TMd,defeated, captured . . 2.50
20 JOs,TMd,year one on earth . . 2.50
21 JOs,TT,A:Abin Sur 2.50
22 JOs,TMd,A:Batman. 2.50

23 JOs,TMd,F:Spectre 2.50
24 JOs,TMd,F:Just.Leag.Int. 2.50
25 JOs,TMd,F:Gypsy 2.50
26 JOs,TMd,Renegades of Mars . . 2.50
27 JOs,TMd,Renegades of Mars . . 2.50
28 JOs,TMd,at Stonehenge 2.50
29 JOs,TMd,telepath 2.50
30 JOs,TMd,Altered Egos,pt.1 . . . 2.50
31 JOs,TMd,Altered Egos,pt.2. . . 2.50
32 TMd,V:Bloodworms of Mars . . 2.50
33 TMd,J'onn J'onzz hidden life . . 2.50
34 JOs,V:Darkseid. 2.50
35 JOs,V:Malefic 2.50
36 JOs,final issue 2.50
Ann.#1 TT,AOI,BWr,Ghosts x-over . 3.00
Ann.#2 AAd(c),JLApe:Gorilla
  Warfare 3.00
Spec.#1,000,000 JOs,TMd 2.00

MARTIAN MANHUNTER
Aug., 2006

1 Martian Manhunter's past 3.00
2 Martian artifact 3.00
3 Truth behind the Lies. 3.00
4 Under attack 3.00
5 . . . . 3.00
6 HC(c),F:Superman, Batman . . . 3.00
7 Betrayal 3.00
8 finale 3.00

MASK
Dec., 1985

1 HC(c),TV tie-in,I:Mask Team . . . 2.50
2 HC(c),In Egypt,V:Venom 2.50
3 HC(c),Anarchy in the U.K. 2.50
4 HC(c),V:Venom, final issue,
  March, 1986 . . . . 2.50

[2nd Series], Feb.–Oct., 1987

1 CS/KS,reg.series 2.50
2 CS/KS,V:Venom. 2.50
3 CS/KS,V:Venom. 2.50
4 CS/KS,V:Venom. 2.50
5 CS/KS,Mask operatives hostage 2.50
6 CS/KS,I:Jacana 2.50
7 CS/KS,Mask gone bad? 2.50
8 CS/KS,Matt Trakker,V:Venom . . 2.50
9 CS/KS,V:Venom, last issue 2.50

MASTERS OF THE UNIVERSE
May, 1986

1 GT,AA,O:He-Man. 6.00
2 GT,AA,V:Skeletor 5.00
3 GT,V:Skeletor 5.00

'MAZING MAN
Jan., 1986

1 I:Maze 3.00
2 Easy Money 2.50
3 Doing What Married People Do . 2.50
4 The Male Machine 2.50
5 Writer's Block. 2.50
6 Shea Stadium 2.50
7 Shea Stadium 2.50
8 Cat-Sitting 2.50
9 Bank Hold-up. 2.50
10 Big Brother's Watching 2.50
11 Jones Beach 2.50
12 FM(c),last issue, Dec., 1986. . . 3.00
Spec.#1 . . . . 2.25
Spec.#2 . . . . 2.25
Spec.#3 KB/TM 2.25

MEN OF WAR
Aug., 1977

1 I:Gravedigger,Code Name:
  Gravedigger,I:Enemy Ace 35.00
2 JKu(c),The Five-Walled War . . . 20.00
3 JKu(c),The Suicide Strategem. . 20.00

Men of War #13
© DC Comics, Inc.

4 JKu(c),Trail by Fire 20.00
5 JKu(c),Valley of the Shadow . . . 20.00
6 JKu(c),A Choice of Deaths 20.00
7 JKu(c),Milkrun 20.00
8 JKu(c),Death-Stroke 20.00
9 JKu(c),Gravedigger-R.I.P. 20.00
10 JKu(c),Crossroads 20.00
11 JKu(c),Berkstaten 15.00
12 JKu(c),Where Is Gravedigger? . 15.00
13 JKu(c),Project Gravedigger -
    Plus One 15.00
14 JKu(c),The Swirling
    Sands of Death 15.00
15 JKu(c),The Man With the
    Opened Eye 15.00
16 JKu(c),Hide and Seek The Spy 15.00
17 JKu(c),The River of Death 15.00
18 JKu(c),The Amiens Assault. . . . 15.00
19 JKu(c),An Angel Named Marie . 15.00
20 JKu(c),Cry:Jerico 15.00
21 JKu(c),Home-Is Where
    The Hell Is 15.00
22 JKu(c),The Swirling
    The Boardwalk 15.00
23 JKu(c),Mission: Six Feet Under 15.00
24 JKu(c)&DG(c),The Presidential
    Peril 15.00
25 GE(c),Save the President. 15.00
26 March, 1980 . . . . 15.00

METAL MEN
1965–78
[1st Regular Series]
1 RA,I:Missile Men. 1,100.00
2 RA,Robot of Terror. 400.00
3 RA,Moon's Invisible Army 250.00
4 RA,Bracelet of Doomed Hero . 250.00
5 RA,Menace of the Mammoth
    Robots 250.00
6 RA,I:Gas Gang 175.00
7 RA,V:Solar Brain 150.00
8 RA,Playground of Terror 150.00
9 RA,A:Billy. 150.00
10 RA,A:Gas Gang 150.00
11 RA,The Floating Furies. 150.00
12 RA,A:Missle Men 125.00
13 RA,I:Nameless 125.00
14 RA,A:Chemo. 125.00
15 RA,V:B.O.L.T.S. 125.00
16 RA,Robots for Sale 125.00
17 JKu(c),RA,V:Bl.Widow Robot . 125.00
18 JKu(c),RA 125.00
19 RA,V:Man-Horse of Hades . . 125.00

20 RA,V:Dr.Yes 125.00
21 RA,C:Batman & Robin,Flash
    Wonder Woman. 100.00
22 RA,A:Chemo. 100.00
23 RA,A:Sizzler 100.00
24 RA,V:Balloonman 100.00
25 RA,V:Chemo. 100.00
26 RA,V:Metal Mods 100.00
27 RA,O:Metal Men,rtd 125.00
28 RA,You Can't Trust a Robot . . 100.00
29 RA,V:Robot Eater 100.00
30 RA,GK,in the Forbidden Zone 100.00
31 RA,GK,School for Robots 75.00
32 RA,Robot Amazon Blues 75.00
33 MS,The Hunted Metal Men . . . 75.00
34 MS,Death Comes Calling 75.00
35 MS,Danger–Doom Dummies . . 75.00
36 MS,The Cruel Clowns. 75.00
37 MS,To walk among Men 75.00
38 MS,Witch Hunt–1979 . . . . 75.00
39 MS,Beauty of the Beast 75.00
40 MS,Destroy Doc Magnus 75.00
41 MS,Requiem for a Robot(1970) 75.00

1973–78
42 RA,reprint 25.00
43 RA,reprint 25.00
44 RA,reprint,V:Missile Men 25.00
45 WS 25.00
46 WS,V:Chemo 25.00
47 WS,V:Plutonium Man 25.00
48 WS,A:Eclipso 30.00
49 WS,A:Eclipso 30.00
50 WS,JSa 20.00
51 JSn,V:Vox 20.00
52 JSn,V:Brain Children. 20.00
53 JA(c),V:Brain Children 20.00
54 JSn,A:Green Lantern 20.00
55 JSn,A:Green Lantern 20.00
56 JSn,V:Inheritor 20.00

[Limited Series], 1993–94
1 DJu,BBr,Foil(c). 5.00
2 DJu,BBr,O:Metal Men 3.00
3 DJu,BBr,V:Missile Men 3.00
4 DJu,BBr,final issue. 3.00

METAL MEN
Aug., 2007
1 (of 8) Le Cabinet Noir 3.00
2 Magnus attemps a rescue 3.00
3 Magnus & Robot Renegades . . . 3.00

METAMORPHO
July-Aug., 1965
[Regular Series]
1 A:Kurt Vornok. 300.00
2 Terror from the Telstar 150.00
3 Who stole the USA 150.00
4 V:Cha-Cha Chaves 100.00
5 V:Bulark 100.00
6 JO,SMo 100.00
7 thru 9 . . . . @75.00
10 I:Element Girl 100.00
11 thru 17 March-April, 1968 . . . @75.00

[Mini-Series], 1993
1 GN,V:The Orb of Ra 2.50
2 GN,A:Metamorpho's Son. 2.50
3 GN,V:Elemental Man 2.50
4 GN,final Issue 2.50

METAMORPHO YEAR ONE
Oct., 2007
1 (of 6) DJu, O:Metamorpho. 3.00
2 DJu 3.00

METROPOLIS S.C.U.
Nov., 1994
1 Special Police unit 2.25
2 Eco-terror in Metropolis 2.25
3 Superman 2.25

Michael Moorcock's Multiverse #11
© DC Comics Inc.

4 final issue. 2.25

MICHAEL MOORCOCK'S
MULTIVERSE
DC/Helix, Sept., 1997
1 WS,three stories, inc. Eternal
    Champion adapt. 2.50
2 WS,Existential Price of Fish 2.50
3 WS,Being and Nothingness. 2.50
4 WS,Loser Wins 2.50
5 WS,Longitude of Meaning 2.50
6 WS,Duke Elric 2.50
7 WS,Metatemporal Detective 2.50
8 WS,Castle Silverskin 2.50
9 WS,Duke Elric 2.50
10 WS,Eternal Champion 2.50
11 WS,Silverskin 2.50
12 WS,Harmonies of Chaos 2.50
TPB rep. #1–#12 . . . . 20.00

MIDNIGHT, MASS
DC/Vertigo, April, 2002
1 JRz,F:Adam & Julia 2.50
2 JRz,a lone farmhouse 2.50
3 JRz,JP. 2.50
4 JRz,JP,The Four Sisters,pt.1 . . . 2.50
5 JRz,JP,The Four Sisters,pt.2 . . . 2.50
6 JRz,JP,The Four Sisters,pt.3 . . . 2.50
7 JRz,JP,3 uninvited visitors 2.50
8 JRz,Secrets 2.50

MIDNIGHT, MASS:
HERE THERE BE
MONSTERS
DC/Vertigo, Jan. 2004
1 (of 6) 3.00
2 thru 6 . . . . @3.00

MILLENNIUM
Jan., 1988
1 JSa,SEt, The Plan 3.00
2 JSa,SEt, The Chosen 2.50
3 JSa,SEt, Reagen/Manhunters . . . 2.50
4 JSa,SEt, Mark Shaw/Batman . . . 2.50
5 JSa,SEt, The Chosen 2.50
6 JSa,SEt, Superman 2.50
7 JSa,SEt, Boster Gold. 2.50
8 JSa,SEt,I:New Guardians 2.50

MILLENNIUM FEVER
1995–96
1 Young Love 2.50
2 Nightmares Worsen 2.50
3 Worst Nightmare 2.50
4 . . . . 2.50

MINX, THE
DC/Vertigo, Aug., 1998
1 PrM,SeP,The Chosen, pt.1 . . . . . 3.00
2 PrM,SeP,The Chosen, pt.2 . . . . . 2.50
3 PrM,SeP,The Chosen, pt.3 . . . . . 2.50
4 PrM,SeP,Monkey Quartet,pt.1 . . . 2.50
5 PrM,SeP,Monkey Quartet,pt.2 . . . 2.50
6 PrM,SeP,Monkey Quartet,pt.3 . . . 2.50
7 PrM,SeP,Monkey Quartet,pt.4 . . . 2.50
8 PrM,SeP,final issue 2.50

MISS BEVERLY HILLS
OF HOLLYWOOD
1949–50
1 Alan Ladd 900.00
2 William Holdon 600.00
3 . . . . 500.00
4 Betty Hutton 500.00
5 Bob Hope 500.00
6 Lucile Ball 425.00
7 . . . . 425.00
8 Ronald Reagan 550.00
9 Wendell Corey 425.00

MISS MELODY LANE
OF BROADWAY
1950
1 . . . . 900.00
2 Sid Caesar 500.00
3 Ed Sullivan 500.00

MISTER E
1991
1 (From Books of Magic) 2.50
2 A:The Shadower 2.50
3 A:The Shadower 2.50
4 A:Tim Hunter, Dr. Fate, Phantom
  Stranger, final issue 2.50

MISTER MIRACLE
1971–78
1 JK,I:Mr.Miracle 150.00
2 JK,I:Granny Goodness 75.00
3 JK,Paranoid Pill 75.00
4 JK,I:Barda, 52-page 80.00
5 JK,I:Vermin Vundabar, 52-page . 80.00
6 JK,I:Female Furies, 52-page . . . 80.00
7 JK,V:Kanto, 52-page 80.00
8 JK,V:Lump, 52-page 80.00
9 JK,O:Mr.Miracle,C:Darkseid . . . 30.00
10 JK,A:Female Furies 30.00
11 JK,V:Doctor Bedlum 30.00
12 JK,Mystivac 30.00
13 JK,The Dictator's Dungeon . . . 30.00
14 JK,I:Madame Evil Eye 30.00
15 JK,O:Shilo Norman 30.00
16 JK,F:Shilo Norman 30.00
17 JK,Murder Lodge 30.00
18 JK,W:Mr.Miracle & Barda 30.00
19 MR,NA,DG,TA,JRu,AM 30.00
20 MR,Eclipse 15.00
21 MR,Command Performance . . . 15.00
22 MR, Midnight of the Gods 15.00
23 MG, As Ethos is my Judge . . . 15.00
24 MG,RH,Double-Bind 15.00
25 MG,RH,Doom Unto Others . . . 15.00
Spec.#1 SR (1987) 3.50

[2nd Series], 1989–91
1 IG,O:Mister Miracle 3.00
2 IG 2.50
3 IG,A:Highfather, Forever People . 2.50

---

4 IG,A:The Dark,Forever People . . 2.50
5 IG,V:TheDark,A:Forever People . 2.50
6 A:G.L. Gnort 2.50
7 A:Blue Beetle,Booster Gold . . . 2.50
8 RM,A:Blue Beetle,Booster Gold . 2.50
9 I:Maxi-Man 2.50
10 V:Maxi-Man 2.50
11 What? And Give up Show Biz? . . 2.50
12 Head of the Clash 2.50
13 Manga Khan Saga begins,
  A:L-Ron,A:Lobo 2.50
14 A:Lobo 3.00
15 Manga Khan cont. 2.50
16 MangaKhan cont.,JLA#39tie-in. . 2.50
17 On Apokolips,A:Darkseid 2.50
18 On Apokolips 2.50
19 Return to Earth, contd
  from JLA#42 . . . . 2.50
20 IG,Oberon 2.50
21 Return of Shilo 2.50
22 New Mr.Miracle revealed 2.50
23 Secrets of the 2 Mr. Miracles
  revealed, A:Mother Box 2.50
24 Nightmare 2.50
25 Big Barda and Friends 2.50
26 Monster Party,pt.1 . . . . 2.50
27 Monster Party,pt.2,
  A:Justice League 2.50
28 final issue 2.50

[3rd Series], 1996
1 JK, new mythology 2.25
2 V:Justice League 2.25
2 How can Scott Free save
  Big Barda 2.25
3 accepts his powers 2.25
4 corruption throughout
  the cosmos 2.25
5 SCr. 2.25
6 SCr. 2.25
7 SCr,final issue 2.25
TPB Jack Kirby's Mister Miracle . 13.00

MR. DISTRICT
ATTORNEY
Jan.–Feb., 1948
1 The Innocent Forger 1,500.00
2 The Richest Man In Prison . . . 700.00
3 The Honest Convicts 500.00
4 The Merchant of Death 500.00
5 The Booby-Trap Killer 500.00
6 The D.A. Meets Scotland Yard 350.00
7 The People vs. Killer Kane . . . 350.00
8 The Rise and Fall of 'Lucky'
  Lynn 350.00

Mr. District Attorney #42
© DC Comics, Inc.

---

9 The Case of the Living
  Counterfeit 350.00
10 The D.A. Takes a Vacation . . . 250.00
11 The Game That Has
  No Winners 250.00
12 Fake Accident Racket 250.00
13 The Execution of Caesar
  Larsen 250.00
14 The Innocent Man In
  Murderers' Row 250.00
15 Prison Train 250.00
16 The Wire Tap Crimes 250.00
17 The Bachelor of Crime 250.00
18 The Case of the Twelve
  O'Clock Killer 250.00
19 The Four King's Of Crime . . . 250.00
20 You Catch a Killer 250.00
21 I Was A Killer's Bodyguard . . . 175.00
22 The Marksman of Crime 175.00
23 Diary of a Criminal 175.00
24 The Killer In The Iron Mask . . 175.00
25 I Hired My Killer 175.00
26 The Case of the Wanted
  Criminals 175.00
27 The Case of the Secret Six . . 175.00
28 Beware the Bogus Beggars . . 175.00
29 The Crimes of Mr. Jumbo . . . 175.00
30 Man of a Thousand Faces . . . 175.00
31 The Hot Money Gang 175.00
32 The Case o/t Bad Luck Clues. 175.00
33 A Crime Is Born 175.00
34 The Amazing Crimes of Mr. X. 175.00
35 This Crime For Hire 175.00
36 The Chameleon of Crime . . . 175.00
37 Miss Miller's Big Case 175.00
38 The Puzzle Shop For Crime . . 175.00
39 Man Who Killed Daredevils . . 175.00
40 The Human Vultures 175.00
41 The Great Token Take 175.00
42 Super-Market Sleuth 175.00
43 Hotel Detective 175.00
44 S.S. Justice,B:Comics Code . . 150.00
45 Miss Miller, Widow 150.00
46 Mr. District Attorney,
  Public Defender 150.00
47 The Missing Persons Racket . 150.00
48 Manhunt With the Mounties . . 150.00
49 The TV Dragnet 150.00
50 The Case of Frank Bragan,
  Little Shot 150.00
51 The Big Heist 150.00
52 Crooked Wheels of Fortune . . 150.00
53 The Courtroom Patrol 150.00
54 The Underworld Spy Squad . . 150.00
55 The Flying Saucer Mystery . . 150.00
56 The Underworld Oracle 150.00
57 The Underworld Employment
  Agency 150.00
58 The Great Bomb Scare 150.00
59 Great Underworld Spy Plot . . 150.00
60 The D.A.'s TV Rival 150.00
61 SMo(c),Architect of Crime . . . 150.00
62 A-Bombs For Sale 150.00
63 The Flying Prison 150.00
64 SMo(c),The Underworld
  Treasure Hunt 150.00
65 SMo(c),World Wide Dragnet . . 150.00
66 SMo(c),The Secret of the
  D.A.'s Diary 150.00
67 Jan.–Feb., 1959 . . . . 150.00

MNEMOVORE
DC/Vertigo, Apr., 2005
1 (of 6) 3.00
2 thru 5 . . . . @3.00

MOBFIRE
1994–95
1 WaP,Gangsters in London 2.50
2 WaP, ... 2.50
3 WaP,The Bocor 2.50

All comics prices listed are for *Near Mint* condition.

4 WaP,V:Bocor	2.50
5 WaP,Voice in My Head	2.50
6 WaP,Genetic Babies, final issue	2.50

MODESTY BLAISE

1 DG,V:Gabriel	5.00
2 DG,V:Gabriel	5.00
GN Spy Thriller	20.00

MONOLITH, THE
Feb. 2004

1 JP(s),56-pg.	3.50
2 JP(s)	3.00
3 JP(s),Heart of Stone	3.00
4 JP(s),Last Rites,pt.1	3.00
5 JP(s),Last Rites,pt.2	3.00
6 JP(s),Friendly Fire,pt.1	3.00
7 JP(s),Friendly Fire,pt.2	3.00
8 JP(s),Friendly Fire,pt.3	3.00
9 JP(s),gangsters retaliate	3.00
10 JP(s)	3.00
11 JP(s),Slavers	3.00
12 JP(s),finale	3.00

MOONSHADOW
DC/Vertigo, 1994–95

1 JMD(s),JMu,rep.	2.50
2 thru 4 JMD	@2.50
5 fully painted	2.50
6	2.50
7 F:Shady Lady	2.50
8 Rep. Search for Ira	2.50
9 JMD,JMu,A:Tittletat Twins	2.50
10 JMD,JMu,Interplanetary Prostitutes	2.50
11 JMu,Ira's life story	2.50
12 Rep. w/6pg new material	3.50

MORE FUN COMICS
See: NEW FUN COMICS

MOVIE COMICS
1939

1 Gunga Din.	5,500.00
2 Stagecoach	3,500.00
3 East Side of Heaven.	2,500.00
4 Captain Fury,B:Oregon Trail.	2,000.00
5 Man in the Iron Mask	2,200.00
6 Phantom Creeps.	3,000.00

MS. TREE QUARTERLY
1990

1 MGr,A:Batman	5.00
2 A:Butcher	4.00
3 A:Butcher	4.00
4 Paper Midnight.	4.00
5 Murder/Rape Investigation.	4.50
6 Gothic House.	4.50
7 The Family Way.	4.50
8 CI,FMc,Ms Tree Pregnant(c), B.U. King Faraday.	4.50
9 Child Kidnapped	4.50
10 V:International Mob.	4.00

MUCHA LUCHA
April 2003

1 (of 3)	2.25
2 It's All Buena	2.25
3 Flea loses match	2.25

MUKTUK WOLFSBREATH: HARD-BOILED SHAMAN
DC/Vertigo, June, 1998

1 (of 3) TLa,SvP,Lady Shaman.	2.50
2	2.50
3 TLa,SvP, concl.	2.50

Mutt and Jeff #6
© DC Comics, Inc.

MUTT AND JEFF
1939

1	2,000.00
2	1,000.00
3 Bucking Broncos	700.00
4 and 5	@600.00
6 thru 10	@350.00
11 thru 20	@250.00
21 thru 30	@225.00
31 thru 50	@200.00
51 thru 70	@150.00
71 thru 80	@125.00
81 thru 99	@100.00
100	125.00
101 thru 103	@100.00
104 thru 148	@100.00

MY GREATEST ADVENTURE
Jan.–Feb., 1955

1 LSt,I Was King Of Danger Island.	2,500.00
2 My Million Dollar Dive	1,200.00
3 I Found Captain Kidd's Treasure	900.00
4 I Had A Date With Doom	900.00
5 I Escaped From Castle Morte	800.00
6 I Had To Spend A Million	800.00
7 I Was A Prisoner On Island X	600.00
8 The Day They Stole My Face	600.00
9 I Walked Through The Doors of Destiny	600.00
10 We Found A World Of Tiny Cavemen	600.00
11 LSt(c),My Friend, Madcap Manning.	500.00
12 MMe(c),I Hunted Big Game in Outer Space.	500.00
13 LSt(c),I Hunted Goliath The Robot	500.00
14 LSt,I Had the Midas Touch of Gold	500.00
15 JK, I Hunted the Worlds Wildest Animals	500.00
16 JK,I Died a Thousand Times	500.00
17 JK,I Doomed the World	500.00
18 JK(c),We Discovered The Edge of the World	700.00
19 I Caught Earth's Strangest Criminal	400.00
20 JK,I Was Big-Game on Neptune	400.00

21 JK,We Were Doomed By The Metal-Eating Monster	400.00
22 I Was Trapped In The Magic Mountains	375.00
23 I Was A Captive In Space Prison	375.00
24 NC(c),I Was The Robinson Crusoe of Space	375.00
25 I Led Earth's Strangest Safari!	375.00
26 NC(c),We Battled The Sand Creature	375.00
27 I Was the Earth's First Exile	375.00
28 I Stalked the Camouflage Creatures.	375.00
29 I Tracked the Forbidden Powers	300.00
30 We Cruised Into the Supernatural!	300.00
31 I Was A Modern Hercules	250.00
32 We Were Trapped In A Freak Valley!	250.00
33 I Was Pursued by the Elements	250.00
34 DD,We Unleashed The Cloud Creatures.	250.00
35 I Solved the Mystery of Volcano Valley.	250.00
36 I Was Bewitched By Lady Doom.	250.00
37 DD&SMo(c),I Hunted the Legendary Creatures!	250.00
38 DD&SMo(c),I Was the Slave of the Dream-Master	250.00
39 DD&SMo(c),We were Trapped in the Valley of no Return	250.00
40 We Battled the StormCreature	250.00
41 DD&SMo(c),I Was Tried by a Robot Court.	200.00
42 DD&SMo(c),My Brother Was a Robot.	200.00
43 DD&SMo(c),I Fought the Sonar Creatures	200.00
44 DD&SMo(c),We Fought the Beasts of Petrified Island	200.00
45 DD&SMo(c),We Battled the Black Narwahl.	200.00
46 DD&SMo(c),We Were Prisoners of the Sundial of Doom	200.00
47 We Became Partners of the Beast Brigade	200.00
48 DD&SMo(c),I Was Marooned On Earth	200.00

My Greatest Adventure #40
© DC Comics Inc.

All comics prices listed are for *Near Mint* condition.

49 DD&SMo(c),I Was An Ally
  Of A Criminal Creature 200.00
50 DD&SMo(c),I Fought the
  Idol King 200.00
51 DD&SMo(c),We Unleashed
  the Demon of the Dungeon . . 175.00
52 DD&SMo(c),I Was A
  Stand-In for an Alien 175.00
53 DD&SMo(c),I, Creature Slayer 175.00
54 I Was Cursed With
  an Alien Pal 175.00
55 DD&SMo(c),I Became The
  Wonder-Man of Space 175.00
56 DD&SMo(c),My Brother-The
  Alien. 175.00
57 DD&SMo(c),Don't Touch Me
  Or You'll Die. 175.00
58 DD&SMo(c),ATh, I was Trapped
  in the Land of L'Oz 200.00
59 DD&SMo(c),Listen Earth-I
  Am Still Alive 200.00
60 DD&SMo(c),ATh,I Lived in
  Two Worlds 200.00
61 DD&SMo(c),ATh,I Battled For
  the Doom-Stone 200.00
62 DD&SMo(c),I Fought For
  An Alien Enemy 150.00
63 DD&SMo(c),We Braved the
  Trail of the Ancient Warrior . . 150.00
64 DD&SMo(c),They Crowned My
  Fiance Their King! 150.00
65 DD&SMo(c),I Lost the Life
  or Death Secret 150.00
66 DD&SMo(c),I Dueled with
  the Super Spirits 150.00
67 I Protected the Idols
  of Idoro! 150.00
68 DD&SMo(c),My Deadly Island
  of Space 150.00
69 DD&SMo(c),I Was A Courier
  From the Past 150.00
70 DD&SMo(c),We Tracked the
  Fabled Fish-Man! 150.00
71 We Dared to open the Door
  of Danger Dungeon 150.00
72 The Haunted Beach 150.00
73 I Defeiller Mountain. 150.00
74 GC(c),We Were Challenged
  By The River Spirit 150.00
75 GC(c),Castaway Cave-Men
  of 1950 . . . . 150.00
76 MMe(c),We Battled the
  Micro-Monster 150.00
77 ATh,We Found the Super-
  Tribes of Tomorrow 150.00
78 Destination-'Dead Man's Alley' 150.00
79 Countdown in Dinosaur Valley 125.00
80 BP,I:Doom Patrol 1,000.00
81 BP,ATh,I:Dr. Janus 350.00
82 BP,F:Doom Patrol 300.00
83 BP,F:Doom Patrol 300.00
84 BP,V:General Immortus 300.00
85 BP,ATh,F:Doom Patrol 300.00
Becomes:

DOOM PATROL
March, 1964
86 BP,I:Brogherhood of Evil 200.00
87 BP,O:Negative Man 125.00
88 BP,O:Chief 125.00
89 BP,I:Animal-Veg.-MineralMan . 125.00
90 BP,A:Brotherhood of Evil . . . 125.00
91 BP,I:Manto, Gargvax 125.00
92 BP,I:Dr.Tyme, A:Mento 125.00
93 BP,A:Brotherhood of Evil . . . 125.00
94 BP,I:Dr.Radich, The Claw . . . 125.00
95 BP,A:Animal-Vegetable
  -Mineral Man 125.00
96 BP,A:General Immortus,
  Brotherhood of Evil 125.00
97 BP,A:General Immortus,
  Brotherhood of Evil 125.00
98 BP,I:Mr.103 . . . . 125.00

Doom Patrol #89
© DC Comics, Inc.

99 I:Beast Boy 120.00
100 BP,O:Beast Boy,Robotman . . 130.00
101 BP,A:Beast Boy 75.00
102 BP,A:Beast Boy,Challengers
  of the Unknown 70.00
103 BP,A:Beast Boy. 70.00
104 BP,W:Elasti-Girl,Mento,
  C:JLA,Teen Titans 70.00
105 BP,A:Beast Boy. 70.00
106 BP,O:Negative Man 70.00
107 BP,A:Beast Boy, I:Dr.Death. . . 70.00
108 BP,A:Brotherhood of Evil . . . 70.00
109 BP,I:Mandred 70.00
110 BP,A:Garguax,Mandred,
  Brotherhood of Evil 50.00
111 BP,I:Zarox-13,A:Brotherhood
  of Evil. 50.00
112 BP,O:Beast Boy,Madame
  Rouge 50.00
113 BP,A:Beast Boy,Mento 50.00
114 BP,A:Beast Boy 50.00
115 BP,A:Beast Boy 50.00
116 BP,A:Madame Rouge 50.00
117 BP,I:Black Vulture 50.00
118 BP,A:Beast Boy 50.00
119 BP,A:Madam Rouge 50.00
120 I:Wrecker. 50.00
121 JO,D:Doom Patrol 150.00
122 rep.Doom Patrol #89. . . . . . . 15.00
123 rep.Doom Patrol #95. . . . . . . 15.00
124 rep.Doom Patrol #90. . . . . . . 15.00

[2nd Series]
See: DOOM PATROL

MY NAME IS CHAOS
1992
1 JRy,Song Laid Waste to Earth. . 5.00
2 JRy,Colonization of Mars. 5.00
3 JRy,Search for Eternal Beings. . . 5.00
4 JRy,final issue 5.00

MY NAME IS HOLOCAUST
DC/Milestone, 1995
[Mini-Series]
1 F:Holocaust (Blood Syndicate) . . 2.50
2 V:Cantano 2.50
3 A:Blood Syndicate 2.50

MYSTERY IN SPACE
April-May, 1951
1 CI&FrG(c),FF,B:Knights of the
  Galaxy,Nine Worlds to
  Conquer 6,000.00

2 CI(c),MA,A:Knights of the
  Galaxy, Jesse James-
  Highwayman of Space 2,500.00
3 CI(c),A:Knights of the
  Galaxy, Duel of the Planets 2,000.00
4 CI(c),S&K,MA,A:Knights of the
  Galaxy, Master of Doom. . . 1,700.00
5 CI(c),A:Knights of the Galaxy,
  Outcast of the Lost World. . 1,700.00
6 CI(c),A:Knights of the Galaxy,
  The Day the World Melted . 1,200.00
7 GK(c),ATh,A:Knights of the Galaxy,
  Challenge o/t Robot Knight 1,200.00
8 MA,It's a Women's World . . . 1,200.00
9 MA(c),The Seven Wonders
  of Space 1,000.00
10 MA(c),The Last Time I
  Saw Earth. 1,000.00
11 GK(c),Unknown Spaceman . . . 800.00
12 MA,The Sword in the Sky. . . . 800.00
13 MA(c),MD,Signboard
  in Space. 800.00
14 MA,GK(c),Hollywood
  in Space. 800.00
15 MA(c),Doom from Station X . . 800.00
16 MA(c),Honeymoon in Space . . 800.00
17 MA(c),The Last Mile of
  Space. 800.00
18 MA(c),GK,Chain Gang
  of Space 800.00
19 MA(c),The Great
  Space-Train Robbery. 800.00
20 MA(c),The Man in the
  Martian Mask. 750.00
21 MA(c),Interplanetary
  Merry- Go-Round 750.00
22 MA(c),The Square Earth. 750.00
23 MA(c),Monkey-Rocket
  to Mars 750.00
24 MA(c),A:Space Cabby,
  Hitchhiker of Space 750.00
25 MA(c),Station Mars on the Air. 700.00
26 GK(c),Earth is the Target 700.00
27 The Human Fishbowl 700.00
28 The Radio Planet 700.00
29 GK(c),Space-Enemy
  Number One 700.00
30 GK(c),The Impossible
  World Named Earth. 700.00
31 GK(c),The Day the Earth
  Split in Two 500.00
32 GK(c),Riddle of the
  Vanishing Earthmen 500.00
33 The Wooden World War 500.00
34 GK(c),The Man Who
  Moved the World 500.00
35 The Counterfeit Earth 500.00
36 GK(c),Secret of the
  Moon Sphinx 500.00
37 GK(c),Secret of the
  Masked Martians. 500.00
38 GK(c),The Canals of Earth . . . 500.00
39 GK(c),Sorcerers of Space 500.00
40 GK(c),Riddle of the
  Runaway Earth 500.00
41 GK(c),The Miser of Space . . . 450.00
42 GK(c),The Secret of the
  Skyscraper Spaceship. 450.00
43 GK(c),Invaders From the
  Space Satellites. 450.00
44 GK(c),Amazing Space Flight
  of North America 450.00
45 GK(c),MA,Flying Saucers
  Over Mars 450.00
46 GK(c),MA,Mystery of the
  Moon Sniper 450.00
47 GK(c),MA,Interplanetary Tug
  of War 450.00
48 GK(c),MA,Secret of the
  Scarecrow World 450.00
49 GK(c),The Sky-High Man 450.00

Mystery in Space #48
© DC Comics, Inc.

50 GK(c),The Runaway
Space-Train 450.00
51 GK(c),MA,Battle of the
Moon Monsters 450.00
52 GK(c),MSy,Mirror Menace
of Mars 450.00
53 GK(c),B:Adam Strange stories,
Menace o/t Robot Raiders . 4,000.00
54 GK(c),Invaders of the
Underground World 1,000.00
55 GK(c),The Beast From
the Runaway World 800.00
56 GK(c),The Menace of
the Super-Atom 500.00
57 GK(c),Mystery of the
Giant Footsteps 500.00
58 GK(c),Chariot in the Sky . . . 500.00
59 GK(c),The Duel of the
Two Adam Stranges 500.00
60 GK(c),The Attack of the
Tentacle World. 500.00
61 CI&MA(c),Threat of the
Tornado Tyrant. 400.00
62 CI&MA(c),The Beast with
the Sizzling Blue Eyes. 400.00
63 The Weapon that
Swallowed Men 400.00
64 The Radioactive Menace 400.00
65 Mechanical Masters of
Rann 400.00
66 Space-Island of Peril. 400.00
67 Challenge of the
Giant Fireflies 400.00
68 CI&MA(c),Fadeaway Doom . . 400.00
69 CI&MA(c),Menace of the
Aqua-Ray Weapon 400.00
70 CI&MA(c),Vengeance of
the Dust Devil 400.00
71 CI&MA(c),The Challenge of
the Crystal Conquerors 400.00
72 The Multiple Menace Weapon 300.00
73 CI&MA(c),The Invisible
Invaders of Rann. 300.00
74 CI&MA(c),The Spaceman
Who Fought Himself 300.00
75 CI&MA(c),The Planet That
Came to a Standstill 300.00
76 CI&MA(c),Challenge of
the Rival Starman 300.00
77 CI&MA(c),Ray-Gun in the Sky 300.00
78 CI&MA(c),Shadow People
of the Eclipse. 300.00
79 CI&MA(c),The Metal
Conqueror of Rann 300.00

80 CI&MA(c),The Deadly
Shadows of Adam Strange . . 300.00
81 CI&MA(c),The Cloud-Creature
That Menaced Two Worlds . . 200.00
82 CI&MA(c),World War on
Earth and Rann 200.00
83 CI&MA(c),The Emotion-Master
of Space 200.00
84 CI&MA(c),The Powerless
Weapons of Adam Strange . . 200.00
85 CI&MA(c),Riddle of the
Runaway Rockets 200.00
86 CI&MA(c),Attack of the
Underworld Giants. 200.00
87 MA(c),The Super-Brain of
Adam Strange,B:Hawkman . . 500.00
88 CI&MA(c),The Robot Wraith
of Rann 450.00
89 MA(c),Siren o/t Space Ark . . . 400.00
90 CI&MA(c),Planets and
Peril, E:Hawkman 400.00
91 CI&MA(c),Puzzle of
the Perilous Prisons 150.00
92 DD&SMo(c),The Alien Invasion
From Earth,B:Space Ranger . 150.00
93 DD&SMo(c),The Convict
Twins of Space 150.00
94 DD&SMo(c),The Adam
Strange Story 150.00
95 The Hydra-Head From
Outer Space 150.00
96 The Coins That Doomed
Two Planets. 150.00
97 The Day Adam Strange
Vanished 150.00
98 The Wizard of the Cosmos . . . 150.00
99 DD&SMo(c),The World-
Destroyer From Space 150.00
100 DD&SMo(c),GK,The Death
of Alanna 150.00
101 GK(c),The Valley of
1,000 Dooms 150.00
102 GK,The Robot World of Rann 150.00
103 The Billion-Dollar Time-
Capsule(Space Ranger),I:Ultra
the Multi-Agent 150.00
104 thru 109 . . . . @100.00
110 Series ends, Sept., 1966 . . . 100.00
[Series Revived], Sept., 1980
111 JAp,SD,MR,DSp, ... 10.00
112 JAp,TS,JKu(c). 10.00
113 JKu(c),MGo 10.00
114 JKu(c),JCr,SD,DSp 10.00
115 JKu(c),SD,GT,BB 10.00
116 JSn(c),JCr,SD 10.00
117 DN,GT,March, 1981 . . . . 10.00

MYSTERY IN SPACE
Sept., 2006
1 JSn, 48-pg. 4.00
1a variant NA (c). 4.00
2 JSn, Captain Comet 3.00
3 JSn, Hardcore Station 4.00
4 JSn,V:Lady Styx. 4.00
5 JSn,The Weird. 4.00
6 JSn,League of Insect Assassins . 4.00
7 JSn,Captain Comet must die. . . . 4.00
8 JSn,RLm,finale 4.00

MYTHOS:
THE FINAL TOUR
DC/Vertigo, Oct., 1996
1 JNR(s),GyA,PrG,F:Rock Star
Adam Case 6.00
2 JNR(s),PSj,F:Rock Star Adam
Case 6.00
3 JNR(s), finale. 6.00

NAMES OF MAGIC, THE
DC/Vertigo, Dec., 2000
1 (of 5) JBo(c),F:Tim Hunter. 10.00
2 thru 5 JBo(c) . . . . @10.00
TPB rep. 15.00

NATHANIEL DUSK
Feb., 1984
1 GC(p). 2.25
2 thru 4 GC(p). . . . . @2.25

NATHANIEL DUSK II
Oct., 1985
1 thru 4 GC,Jan., 1986 . . . . @2.25

NATIONAL COMICS
1999
1 MWa(s),AAl,F:Flash &
Mr. Terrific 2.25

Nazz #2
© DC Comics Inc.

NAZZ, THE
1990–91
1 Michael's Book. 5.50
2 Johnny's Book 5.00
3 Search for Michael Nazareth. . . . 5.00
4 V:Retaliators,final issue 5.00

NEIL GAIMAN'S
NEVERWHERE
DC/Vertigo, June, 2005
1 (of 9) GF 3.00
2 thru 4 novel adaptation . . . . . . @3.00
5 novel adaptation 3.00
6 thru 9 GF . . . . @3.00
TPB 20.00

NEVADA
DC/Vertigo, March, 1998
1 (of 6) SvG,SL,show girl 2.50
2 thru 6 SvG,SL. . . . . @2.50
TPB Nevada, rep. 15.00

NEW ADVENTURES
OF CHARLIE CHAN
1958
1 GK,SGe,Secret of the Phantom
Bells 1,000.00
2 SGe,Riddle of the Runaway
Mummy 700.00

3 SGe,Two Lives of Charlie
  Chan 550.00
4 SGe,Case o/t Vanishing Man . 550.00
5 SGe,Monarch of Menace. . . . 550.00
6 SGe,Trail Across the Sky. 550.00

NEW ADVENTURES
OF SUPERBOY
See: SUPERBOY

NEW BOOK OF COMICS
1937
1 Dr.Occult. 30,000.00
2 Dr.Occult. 15,000.00

NEW COMICS
1935
1 . . . . 35,000.00
2 . . . . 14,000.00
3 thru 6 . . . . @9,000.00
7 thru 11 . . . . @8,000.00
Becomes:

NEW ADVENTURE
COMICS
Jan., 1937
12 S&S 7,500.00
13 thru 20 . . . . @6,000.00
21 . . . . 5,000.00
22 thru 31 . . . . @4,000.00
Becomes:

ADVENTURE COMICS

NEW FUN COMICS
Feb., 1935
1 B:Oswald the Rabbit,
  Jack Woods 70,000.00
2 . . . . 35,000.00
3 . . . . 20,000.00
4 . . . . 20,000.00
5 . . . . 20,000.00
6 S&S,B:Dr.Occult,
  Henri Duval. 35,000.00
Becomes:

MORE FUN COMICS
Jan., 1936
7 S&S,WK 17,000.00
8 S&S,WK 15,000.00
9 S&S,E:Henri Duval 18,000.00
10 S&S 10,000.00
11 S&S,B:Calling all Girls 10,000.00
12 S&S 10,000.00
13 S&S 10,000.00
14 S&S,Color,Dr.Occult. 19,000.00
15 S&S 10,000.00
16 S&S,Christmas(c) 10,000.00
17 S&S,CF 9,000.00
18 S&S,CF 3,500.00
19 S&S,CF 3,500.00
20 HcK,S&S 3,500.00
21 S&S,CF 3,800.00
22 S&S,CF 3,800.00
23 S&S,CF 3,800.00
24 S&S,CF 3,800.00
25 S&S,CF 3,500.00
26 S&S,CF 3,200.00
27 S&S,CF 3,200.00
28 S&S,CF 3,000.00
29 S&S,CF 3,000.00
30 S&S 3,000.00
31 S&S,CF 3,200.00
32 S&S,E:Dr. Occult 3,000.00
33 S&S,BKa 3,000.00
34 S&S,BKa 3,000.00
35 S&S,BKa,CF(c) 3,000.00
36 B:Masked Ranger 3,000.00
37 thru 40 . . . . @3,500.00
41 E:Masked Ranger 4,200.00

More Fun #44 © DC Comics, Inc.

42 thru 50 . . . . @3,000.00
51 I:The Spectre 8,000.00
52 O:The Spectre,pt.1,
  E:Wing Brady 120,000.00
53 O:The Spectre,pt.2,
  B:Capt.Desmo 65,000.00
54 E:King Carter,Spectre(c) . . 25,000.00
55 I:Dr.Fate,E:Bulldog Martin,
  Spectre(c). 27,000.00
56 B:Congo Bill,Dr.Fate(c) . . . 12,000.00
57 Spectre(c) 8,000.00
58 Spectre(c) 8,000.00
59 A:Spectre 8,000.00
60 Spectre(c) 8,000.00
61 Spectre(c) 8,000.00
62 Spectre(c) 6,000.00
63 Spectre(c),E:St.Bob Neal . . 6,000.00
64 Spectre(c),B:Lance Larkin . . 6,000.00
65 Spectre(c) 6,000.00
66 Spectre(c) 6,000.00
67 Spectre(c),O:Dr. Fate,
  E:Congo Bill,Biff Bronson. 12,000.00
68 Dr.Fate(c),B:Clip Carson . . 5,000.00
69 Dr.Fate(c). 5,000.00
70 Dr.Fate(c),E:Lance Larkin . . 5,000.00
71 Dr.Fate(c),I:Johnny Quick . 10,000.00
72 Dr. Fate has Smaller Helmet,
  E:Sgt. Carey,Sgt.O'Malley . 5,000.00
73 Dr.Fate(c),I:Aquaman,Green
  Arrow,Speedy 27,000.00
74 Dr.Fate(c),A:Aquaman . . . 5,500.00
75 Dr.Fate(c). 5,000.00
76 Dr.Fate(c),MMe,E:Clip Carson,
  B:Johnny Quick 5,000.00
77 MMe,Green Arrow(c) 5,000.00
78 MMe,Green Arrow(c) 5,000.00
79 MMe,Green Arrow(c) 5,000.00
80 MMe,Green Arrow(c) 3,500.00
81 MMe,Green Arrow(c) 4,000.00
82 MMe,Green Arrow(c) 4,000.00
83 MMe,Green Arrow(c) 4,000.00
84 MMe,Green Arrow(c) 5,000.00
85 MMe,Green Arrow(c) 2,500.00
86 MMe 2,500.00
87 MMe,E:Radio Squad 2,500.00
88 MMe,Green Arrow(c) 2,500.00
89 MMe,O:Gr.Arrow&Speedy . . 2,600.00
90 MMe,Green Arrow(c) 3,500.00
91 MMe,Green Arrow(c) 2,000.00
92 MMe,Green Arrow(c) 2,000.00
93 MMe,B:Dover & Clover 3,000.00
94 MMe,Green Arrow(c) 1,500.00
95 MMe,Green Arrow(c) 1,500.00
96 MMe,Green Arrow(c) 1,500.00
97 MMe,JKu,E:Johnny Quick . . 1,700.00
98 E:Dr. Fate. 2,000.00
99 Green Arrow(c) 1,800.00

100 Anniversary Issue 1,800.00
101 O&I:Superboy,
  E:The Spectre 16,000.00
102 A:Superboy 2,500.00
103 A:Superboy 1,800.00
104 Superboy(c) 1,500.00
105 Superboy(c) 1,500.00
106 Superboy(c) 1,500.00
107 E:Superboy 1,500.00
108 A:Genius Jones,Genius
  Meets Genius 500.00
109 A:Genius Jones, The
  Disappearing Deposits 500.00
110 A:Genius Jones, Birds,
  Brains and Burglary. 500.00
111 A:Genius Jones, Jeepers
  Creepers 500.00
112 A:Genius Jones, The
  Tell-Tale Tornado 500.00
113 A:Genius Jones, Clocks
  and Shocks 500.00
114 A:Genius Jones, The
  Milky Way 500.00
115 A:Genius Jones,Foolish
  Questions 500.00
116 A:Genius Jones,Palette
  For Plunder 500.00
117 A:Genius Jones,Battle of
  the Pretzel Benders. 500.00
118 A:Genius Jones,The
  Sinister Siren 500.00
119 A:Genius Jones,A
  Perpetual Jackpot 500.00
120 A:Genius Jones,The Man
  in the Moon 500.00
121 A:Genius Jones,The
  Mayor Goes Haywire. 500.00
122 A:Genius Jones,When Thug-
  Hood Was In Floor 500.00
123 A:Genius Jones,Hi Diddle Diddle,
  the Cat and the Fiddle. 500.00
124 A:Genius Jones,
  The Zany Zoo 500.00
125 Genius Jones,
  Impossible But True 1,500.00
126 A:Genius Jones,The Case
  of the Gravy Spots. 350.00
127 Nov.–Dec., 1947. . . . . 750.00

NEW GODS, THE
Feb.–March, 1971
1 JK,I:Orion 150.00
2 JK,O'Deadly Darkseid. 100.00
3 JK,Death is the Black Racer . . . 50.00
4 JK,O:Manhunter, rep.. . . . . . 40.00
5 JK,I:Fastbak & Black Racer. . . . 40.00
6 JK,The Glory Boat 40.00
7 JK,O:Orion. 40.00
8 JK,Death Wish of Terrible Turpin 40.00
9 JK,I:Forager 40.00
10 JK,Earth–The Domed Dominion 40.00
11 JK,Darkseid and Sons (1972) . . 40.00
12 DN,DA,R:New Gods (1977) . . 10.00
13 DN,DA,AM(c) 10.00
14 DN,DA,RB&AM(c). 10.00
15 RB,BMc,Apocalypse Child . . 10.00
16 DN,DA,Titan and the Hunter . . 10.00
17 DN,DA, The Memory Machine . 10.00
18 DN,DA,Song of the Source. . . 10.00
19 DN,DA,The Secret Within Us . . 10.00

NEW GODS
(Reprints) 1984
1 JK reprint. 4.00
2 thru 5 JK reprint. . . . . @3.50
6 JK rep.+New Material 3.50

NEW GODS
[2nd Series], 1989
1 From Cosmic Odyssey 3.00
2 A:Orion of New Genesis 2.50

3 A:Orion 2.50
4 Renegade Apokolyptian Insect
  Colony 2.50
5 Orion vs. Forager. 2.50
6 A:Eve Donner, Darkseid. 2.50
7 Bloodline #1. . . . . 2.50
8 Bloodline #2 . . . . 2.50
9 Bloodline #3. . . . . 2.50
10 Bloodline #4 . . . . 2.50
11 Bloodline #5 . . . . 2.50
12 Bloodlines #6 . . . . 2.50
13 Back on Earth 2.50
14 I:Reflektor 2.50
15 V:Serial Killer 2.50
16 A:Fastbak & Metron 2.50
17 A:Darkseid, Metron 2.50
18 A:YugaKhan,Darkseid,
  Moniters. 2.50
19 V:Yuga Khan. 2.50
20 Darkseid Dethroned,
  V:Yuga Khan 2.50
21 A:Orion 2.50
22 A:Metron 2.50
23 A:Forever People 2.50
24 A:Forever People 2.50
25 The Pact #1,R:Infinity Man . . . 2.50
26 The Pact #2 . . . . 2.50
27 Asault on Apokolips,Pact#3 . . . 2.50
28 Pact #4, final issue 2.50

[3rd Series], 1995–97

1 F:Orion vs. Darkseid 2.50
2 RaP,UnderworldUnleashed tie-in. . 2.50
3 RaP,Darkseid destroyed 2.50
4 RaP,F:Lightray 2.50
5 RaP,F:Orion 2.50
6 RaP,Destruction of the Beast. . . 2.50
7 RaP,R:Darkseid 2.50
8 RaP,DZ,F:Highfather,Darkseid. . . 2.50
9 thru 11 . . . . @2.50
12 JBy,BWi,F:Metron 2.50
13 JBy,BWi,Orion reappears
  on Earth. 2.50
14 JBy,BWi,A:Forever People,
  Lightray 2.50
TPB rep. #1–#11,b&w 12.00
Secret Files #1 KK,JBy 5.00

NEW GUARDIANS
1988–89

1 JSon,from Millennium series 3.00
2 JSon,Colombian Drug Cartel. . . 2.25
3 JSon,in South Africa,
  V:Janwillem's Army 2.25

New Guardians #8
© DC Comics Inc.

4 JSon,V:Neo-Nazi Skinheads
  in California 2.25
5 JSon,Tegra Kidnapped 2.25
6 JSon, In China, Invasion x-over . . 2.25
7 JSon, Guardians Return Home . . 2.25
8 JSon, V:Janwillem 2.25
9 JSon, A:Tome Kalmaku,
  V:Janwillem 2.25
10 JSon, A:Tome Kalmaku. 2.25
11 PB,Janwillem's secret 2.25
12 PB,New Guardians Future
  revealed, final issue. 2.25

NEW TEEN TITANS
Nov., 1980

1 GP,RT,V:Gordanians (see DC
  Comics Presents #26 . . . . . . 12.00
2 GP,RT,I:Deathstroke the
  Terminator, I&D:Ravager. 35.00
3 GP,I:Fearsome Five. 7.00
4 GP,RT,A:JLA,O:Starfire 6.00
5 CS,RT,O:Raven,I:Trigon 6.00
6 GP,V:Trigon,O:Raven. 6.00
7 GP,RT,O:Cyborg 6.00
8 GP,RT,A Day in the Life 6.00
9 GP,RT,A:Terminator,
  V:Puppeteer. 6.00
10 GP,RT,A:Terminator 9.00
11 GP,RT,V:Hyperion 4.00
12 GP,RT,V:Titans of Myth 4.00
13 GP,RT,R:Robotman. 4.00
14 GP,RT,I:New Brotherhood of
  Evil,V:Zahl and Rouge. 4.00
15 GP,RT,D:Madame Rouge 4.00
16 GP,RT,I:Captain Carrot 4.00
17 GP,RT,I:Frances Kane 3.50
18 GP,RT,A:Orig.Starfire 3.50
19 GP,RT,A:Hawkman 3.50
20 GP,RT,V:Disruptor. 3.50
21 GP,RT,GC,I:Brother Blood,
  Night Force 3.50
22 GP,RT,V:Brother Blood 3.50
23 GP,RT,I:Blackfire 3.50
24 GP,RT,A:Omega Men,I:X-hal . . . 3.50
25 GP,RT,A:Omega Men 3.50
26 GP,RT,I:Terra,Runaway #1 . . . . 5.00
27 GP,RT,A:Speedy,Runaway #2. . . 3.00
28 GP,RT,V:Terra 4.00
29 GP,RT,V:Broth.of Evil 3.00
30 GP,RT,V:Broth.of Evil,J:Terra . . . 3.00
31 GP,RT,V:Broth.of Evil 3.00
32 GP,RT,I:Thunder & Lightning . . . 3.00
33 GP,I:Trident 3.00
34 GP,RT,V:The Terminator. 3.00
35 KP,RT,V:Mark Wright. 3.00
36 KP,RT,A:Thunder & Lightning . . . 3.00
37 GP,RT,A:Batman/Outsiders(x-over
  BATO#5),V:Fearsome Five . . . 3.00
38 GP,O:Wonder Girl 3.00
39 GP,Grayson quits as Robin. 5.00
40 GP,A:Brother Blood 3.00
Ann.#1 GP,RT,Blackfire 3.50
Ann.#2 GP,I:Vigilante 3.00
Ann.#3 GP,DG,D:Terra,A:Deathstroke
  V:The H.I.V.E. 3.50
Ann.#4 rep.Direct Ann.#1. . . . . . 2.50

[Special Issues]

Keebler:GP,DG,Drugs 2.50
Beverage:Drugs,RA. 2.50
IBM:Drugs 3.00
Becomes:

TALES OF THE
TEEN TITANS
1984–88

41 GP,A:Brother Blood 3.00
42 GP,DG,V:Deathstroke 5.00
43 GP,DG,V:Deathstroke 5.00
44 GP,DG,I:Nightwing,O:Deathstroke
  Joe Wilson becomes Jericho . . 8.00
45 GP,A:Aqualad,V:The H.I.V.E. . . . 3.00

46 GP,A:Aqualad,V:The H.I.V.E. . . . 3.00
47 GP,A:Aqualad,V:The H.I.V.E. . . . 3.00
48 SR,V:The Recombatants 3.00
49 GP,CI,V:Dr.Light,A:Flash. 3.00
50 GP/DG W:Wonder Girl &
  Terry Long,C:Batman,
  Wonder Woman. 4.00
51 RB,A:Cheshire 2.50
52 RB,A:Cheshire 2.50
53 RB,I:Ariel,A:Terminator 2.50
54 RB,A:Terminator 2.50
55 A:Terminator 2.50
56 A:Fearsome Five. 2.50
57 A:Fearsome Five. 2.50
58 thru 91 rep. . . . . @2.50

NEW TEEN TITANS
[Direct sales series]
Aug., 1984

1 B:MWn(s),GP,L:Raven. 6.00
2 GP,D:Azareth,A:Trigon. 4.00
3 GP,V:Raven 4.00
4 GP,V:Trigon,Raven 4.00
5 GP,D:Trigon,Raven disappears . . 4.00
6 GP,A:Superman,Batman. 3.00
7 JL,V:Titans of Myth 3.00
8 JL,V:Titans of Myth 3.00
9 JL,V:Titans of Myth,I:Kole 3.00
10 JL,O:Kole 3.00
11 JL,O:Kole 2.50
12 JL,Ghost story. 2.50
13 EB,Crisis 2.50
14 EB,Crisis 2.50
15 EB,A:Raven 2.50
16 EB,A:OmegaMen 2.50
17 EB,V:Blackfire 2.50
18 E:MWn(s),EB,V:Blackfire 2.50
19 EB,V:Mento 2.50
20 GP(c),EB,V:Cheshire,J.Todd . . . 2.50
21 GP(c),EB,V:Cheshire,J.Todd . . . 2.50
22 GP(c),EB,V:Blackfire,Mento,
  Brother Blood 2.50
23 GP(c),V:Blackfire 2.50
24 CB,V:Hybrid 2.50
25 EB,RT,V:Hybrid,Mento,A:Flash. . 2.50
26 KGa,V:Mento 2.50
27 KGa,Church of Br.Blood. 2.50
28 EB,RT,V:BrotherBlood,A:Flash . . 2.50
29 EB,RT,V:Brother Blood,
  A:Flash,Robin 2.50
30 EB,Batman,Superman 2.50
31 EB,RT,V:Brother Blood,A:Flash
  Batman,Robin,Gr.Lantern Corps
  Superman 2.50

New Teen Titans #28
© DC Comics, Inc.

DC COMICS

32 EB,RT,Murder Weekend	2.50
33 EB,V:Terrorists	2.50
34 EB,RT,V:Mento,Hybrid	2.50
35 PB,RT,V:Arthur & Eve	2.50
36 EB,RT,I:Wildebeest	2.50
37 EB,RT,V:Wildebeest	2.50
38 EB,RT,A:Infinity	2.50
39 EB,RT,F:Raven	2.50
40 EB,RT,V:Gentleman Ghost	2.50
41 EB,V:Wildebeest,A:Puppeteer, Trident,Wildebeest	2.50
42 EB,RT,V:Puppeteer,Gizmo, Trident,Wildebeest	2.50
43 CS,RT,V:Phobia	2.50
44 RT,V:Godiva	2.50
45 EB,RT,A:Dial H for Hero	2.50
46 EB,RT,A:Dial H for Hero	2.50
47 O:Titans,C:Wildebeest	2.50
48 EB,RT,A:Red Star	2.50
49 EB,RT,A:Red Star	2.50
Ann.#1 A:Superman,V:Brainiac	2.50
Ann.#2 JBy,JL,O:Brother Blood	3.00
Ann.#3 I:Danny Chase	2.50
Ann.#4 V:Godiva	2.50

Becomes:

NEW TITANS
1988–96

50 B:MWn(s),GP,BMc,B:Who is Wonder Girl?	7.00
51 GP,BMc	3.00
52 GP,BMc	3.00
53 GP,RT	3.00
54 GP,RT,E:Who is Wonder Girl?	3.00
55 GP,RT,I:Troia	3.00
56 MBr,RT,Tale of Middle Titans	3.00
57 GP,BMc,V:Wildebeast	3.00
58 GP,TG,BMc,V:Wildebeast	3.00
59 GP,TG,BMc,V:Wildebeast	3.00
60 GP,TG,BMc,3rd A:Tim Drake (Face Revealed),Batman	5.00
61 GP,TG,BMc,A:Tim Drake, Batman	5.00
62 TG,AV,A:Deathstroke	3.00
63 TG,AV,A:Deathstroke	3.00
64 TG,AV,A:Deathstroke	3.00
65 TG,AV,A:Deathstroke,Tim Drake, Batman	3.00
66 TG,AV,V:Eric Forrester	2.50
67 TG,AV,V:Eric Forrester	2.50
68 SE,V:Royal Flush Gang	2.50
69 SE,V:Royal Flush Gang	2.50
70 SE,A:Deathstroke	3.00
71 TG,AV,B:Deathstroke, B:Titans Hunt	5.00
72 TG,AV,D:Golden Eagle	4.00
73 TG,AV,I:Phantasm	4.00
74 TG,AV,I:Pantha	3.00
75 TG,AV,IR:Jericho/Wildebeest	3.00
76 TG,AV,V:Wildebeests	2.50
77 TG,AV,A:Red Star,N:Cyborg	2.50
78 TG,AV,V:Cyborg	2.50
79 TG,AV,I:Team Titans	3.00
80 KGa,PC,A:Team Titans	2.50
81 CS,AV,War of the Gods	2.50
82 TG,AV,V:Wildebeests	2.50
83 TG,AV,D:Jericho	3.00
84 TG,AV,E:Titans Hunt	2.50
85 TG,AV,I:Baby Wildebeest	2.50
86 CS,AV,E:Deathstroke	2.50
87 TG,AV,A:Team Titans	2.50
88 TG,AV,CS,V:Team Titans	2.50
89 JBr,I:Lord Chaos	2.50
90 TG,AV,Total Chaos#2,A:Team Titans,D'stroke,V:Lord Chaos	2.50
91 TG,AV,Total Chaos#5,A:Team Titans,D'stroke,V:Lord Chaos	2.50
92 E:MWn(s),TG,AV,Total Chaos#8, A:Team Titans,V:Lord Chaos	2.50
93 TG,AV,Titans Sell-Out#3	2.50
94 PJ,F:Red Star & Cyborg	2.50
95 PJ,Red Star gains new powers.	2.50

New Titans #97 © DC Comics, Inc.

96 PJ,I:Solar Flare, V:Konstantine	2.50
97 TG,AV,B:The Darkening,R:Speedy V:Brotherhood of Evil	2.50
98 TG,AV,V:Brotherhood of Evil	2.50
99 TG,AV,I:Arsenal (Speedy)	2.50
100 TG,AV,W:Nightwing&Starfire, V:Deathwing,Raven,A:Flash,Team Titans,Hologram(c)	4.00
101 AV(i),L:Nightwing	2.50
102 AV(i),A:Prester John	2.50
103 AV(i),V:Bro. of Evil	2.50
104 Terminus #1	2.50
105 Terminus #2	2.50
106 Terminus #3	2.50
107 Terminus #4	2.50
108 A:Supergirl,Flash	2.50
109 F:Starfire	2.50
110 A:Flash,Serg.Steele	2.50
111 A:Checkmate	2.50
112 A:Checkmate	2.50
113 F:Nightwing	2.75
114 L:Starfire, Nightwing,Panthra, Wildebeest	2.50
115 A:Trigon	2.50
116 Changling	2.50
117 V:Psimon	2.50
118 V:Raven + Brotherhood	2.50
119 Suffer the Children,pt.1	2.50
120 Forever Evil,pt.2	2.50
121 Forever Evil,pt.3	2.50
122 Crimelord/Syndicate War,pt.2 J:Supergirl	2.50
123 MWn(s),RRa,O:Minion	2.50
124 The Siege of Zi Charan	2.50
125 The Siege of Zi Charan	3.00
126 Meltdown,pt.1	2.50
127 MWn,Meltdown, cont.	2.50
128 MWn,Meltdown, cont.	2.50
129 MWn,Meltdown, cont.	2.50
130 MWn,Meltdown, final issue	2.50
Ann.#5 V:Children of the Sun	3.00
Ann.#6 CS,F:Starfire	3.00
Ann.#7 Armageddon 2001,I:Future Teen Titans	4.00
Ann.#8 PJ,Eclipso,V:Deathstroke	3.75
Ann.#9 Bloodlines#5,I:Anima	3.75
Ann.#10 Elseworlds story	3.75
Ann.#11 Year One Annual	4.00
#0 Spec. Zero Hour,new team	2.50
TPB Terra Incognito (2006)	20.00

NEW T.H.U.N.D.E.R. AGENTS, THE
July, 2003

1 JP	3.00

NEW YEAR'S EVIL:
Dec., 1997

Body Doubles #1 DAn,ALa,JoP, JPn(c)	2.00
Dark Nemesis #1 DJu,Ccs,JPn(c)	2.00
Darkseid #1 JBy,SB,JPn(c)	2.00
Gog #1 MWa,JOy,DJa,JPn(c)	2.00
Mr. Mxyzptlk #1 AlG,TMo,JPn(c)	2.00
Prometheus #1 GMo,JPn(c)	2.00
Scarecrow #1 PrM,DFg,JPn(c)	2.00
The Rogues #1 BAu,RoW,JPn(c)	2.00

NEW YORK WORLD'S FAIR
1939–40

1 1939	45,000.00
2 1940	30,000.00

NEXT, THE
July, 2006

1 Cross-over from other dimension	3.00
2 A:Superman	3.00
3 Trapped in a time anomaly	3.00
4 The Fist of the Iron Ring	3.00
5 Showdown	3.00
6 Finale	3.00

NIGHTFALL: THE BLACK CHRONICLES
Homage/DC, Oct., 1999

1 monsters living among us	3.00
2	3.00
3	3.00

NIGHT FORCE
Aug., 1982

1 GC,1:Night Force	5.00
2 thru 13 GC	@3.00
14 GC,Sept.,1983	3.00

NIGHT FORCE
Oct., 1996

1 MWn(s),BA,Baron Winters leads.	2.50
2 MWn(s)	2.25
3 MWn(s)	2.25
4 MWn(s),EB,HellSeemsHeaven	2.25
5 MWn(s),Low,SMa,Dreamers of Dreams,pt.1	2.25
6 MWn(s),Low,SMa,Dreamers,pt.2.	2.25
7 MWn(s),Low,SMa,Dreamers,pt.3.	2.25
8 MWn(s),Convergence, x-over	2.25
9 MWn(s),Low,Sma,The Eleventh Man pt.1 (of 3).	2.25
10 MWn(s),Eleventh Man, pt.2	2.50
11 MWn(s),Eleventh Man, pt.3	2.50
12 MWn(s),Lady of the Leopard final issue,Sept., 1997	2.50

NIGHTWING
1995

1 R:Nightwing	5.00
2 N:Nightwing	4.00
3 visit to Kravia	4.00
4 conclusion	4.00
1-shot Alfred's Return, DG	5.00

NIGHTWING
Aug., 1996

1 CDi(s),SMc,KIS,Nightwing goes to Bluhaven	15.00
2 CDi(s),SMc,KIS,V:smugglers	8.00

3 CDi(s),SMc,KIS,run-down bank
iheld up 8.00
4 CDi(s),SMc,KIS,V:Lady Vick 6.00
5 CDi(s),SMc,KIS, ... 6.00
6 CDi(s),SMc,KIS,A:Tim Drake 125.00
7 CDi(s),SMc,KIS,Rough Justice . . . 6.00
8 CDi(s),SMc,KIS,V: the kingpin
of Bluhaven 6.00
9 CDi(s),SMc,KIS,kidnapping,pt.1 . 6.00
10 CDi(s),SMc,KIS,nightmare
or dream? 6.00
11 CDi(s),SMc,V:Soames,
Blockbuster 6.00
12 CDi(s),SMc,Mutt 4.00
13 CDi(s),SMc,KIS,A:Batman 4.00
14 CDi(s),SMc,KIS,A:Batman,pt.2 . . 4.00
15 CDi(s),SMc,KIS,A:Batman,pt.3 . . 3.00
16 CDi(s),SMc,KIS,Nightwingmobile 3.00
17 CDi(s),SMc,KIS,V:Man-Bat 3.00
18 CDi(s),SMc,KIS 3.00
19 CDi(s),SMc,KIS,Cataclysm
x-over,pt.2 . . . . 4.00
20 CDi(s),SMc,KIS,Cataclysm 3.00
21 CDi(s),SMc,KIS,post Cataclysm 3.00
22 CDi(s),SMc,KIS,V:Lady Vic 3.00
23 Brotherhood of
the Fist x-over, pt.4 . . . . 3.00
24 CDi(s),SMc,KIS,cop story 3.00
25 CDi(s),SMc,KIS,A:Robin 3.00
26 CDi(s),SMc,KIS,A;Huntress 3.00
27 CDi(s),SMc,KIS,V:Torque 3.00
28 CDi(s),SMc,KIS,V:Torque 3.00
29 CDi(s),SMc,KIS,A:Huntress 3.00
30 CDi(s),SMc,KIS,A:Superman . . . 3.00
31 CDi(s),SMc,KIS,A:Nite-Wing. . . . 3.00
32 CDi(s),SMc,KIS,V:DoubleDare . . 3.00
33 CDi(s),SMc,KIS,
V:Electrocutioner 3.00
34 CDi(s),SMc,KIS,x-over 3.00
35 CDi(s),SMc,KIS,No
Man's Land,pt.1 . . . . 3.00
36 CDi(s),SMc,No
Man's Land,pt.2 . . . . 3.00
37 CDi(s),SMc,KIS,No Man's
Land, concl. 3.00
38 CDi(s),SMc,KIS,F:Oracle 3.00
39 CDi(s),SMc,KIS. 3.00
40 CDi(s),SMc,KIS,R:Tarantula 3.00
41 CDi(s),Police Academy grad. . . . 2.50
42 CDi(s),V:Nite-wing 2.50
43 CDi(s),V:Torque 2.50
44 CDi(s),F:Nite-wing. 2.50
45 CDi(s),Hunt for Oracle,pt.1 . . . . . 2.50
46 CDi(s),Hunt for Oracle,pt.3 . . . . . 2.50
47 CDi(s),showdown 2.50
48 CDi(s),JMz,F:Slyph. 2.50
49 CDi(s),JMz,F:Torque. 2.50
50 CDi,JMz,at crossroads,48-pg. . . 4.00
51 CDi,KD,O:Nite-wing 2.50
52 CDi,This issue: Batman dies! . . . 2.50
53 Officer Down x-over,pt.5 . . . . 2.50
54 CDi,life-threatening accident. . . . 2.50
55 CDi,A:Blockbuster,Shrike 2.50
56 CDi,V:Blockbuster,Shrike 2.50
57 CDi,RL,MFm,V:Shrike. 2.50
58 CDi,V:Shrike 2.50
59 CDi,RL,Where's Freddy Minh . . . 2.50
60 CDi,Low,V:Transbelvan mob . . . 2.50
61 CDi,V:Bank Robbers 2.50
62 CDi,Joker:Last Laugh 2.50
63 CDi,Last Laugh, aftermath 2.50
64 CDi,On a Christmas Evening . . . 2.50
65 CDi,BruceWayne:Murderer,pt.3 . 2.50
66 CDi,BruceWayne:Murderer,pt.9 . 2.50
67 CDi,V:Amygdala 2.50
68 CDi,BruceWayne:Fugitive,pt.6 . . 2.50
69 CDi,BruceWayne:Fugitive,pt.9 . . 2.50
70 CDi,in Arizona 2.50
71 RL,Something About Mary,pt.1 . . 2.50
72 RL,Something About Mary,pt.2. . 2.50
73 RL,Something About Mary,pt.3. . 2.50
74 RL,Something About Mary,pt.4. . 2.50

75 RL,MGo,40-pg 3.50
76 MGo(c) 2.50
77 cops go bad 2.50
78 V:new Tarantula 2.50
79 Source of madness. 2.50
80 Venn Diagram,pt.1 . . . . 2.50
81 Venn Diagram,pt.2 . . . . 4.00
82 Venn Diagram,pt.3 . . . . 2.50
83 Murder of Chief Redhorn 2.50
84 RL,Chief Redhorn case 2.50
85 Tarantula or Nite-Wing 2.50
86 Cyber-punks 2.50
87 V:Blockbuster 2.50
88 V:Blockbuster 2.50
89 V:Blockbuster 2.50
90 V:Blockbuster 2.50
91 V:Shrike 2.50
92 V:Blockbuster 2.50
93 V:Blockbuster showdown 2.50
94 F:Tarantula 2.50
95 Tarantula vs. Copperhead. 2.50
96 War Games,Act 1,pt.3 . . . . 2.50
97 War Games,Act 2,pt.3 . . . . 2.50
98 War Games,Act 3,pt.3 . . . . 2.50
99 SMc,Back to the Life. 2.50
100 V:Trantula, 40-pg 3.00
101 SMc,Nightwing,Year One,pt.1. . 8.00
102 SMc,Nightwing,Year One,pt.2. . 5.00
103 SMc,Nightwing,Year One,pt.3. . 6.00
104 SMc,Nightwing,Year One,pt.4. . 5.00
105 SMc,Nightwing,Year One,pt.5. . 3.00
106 SMc,Nightwing,Year One,pt.6. . 3.00
107 PhH,Bludhaven left. 3.00
108 PhH,in New York. 3.00
109 PhH,V:Black Mask 3.00
110 PhH,F:Robin 3.00
111 Dick Grayson undercover 2.50
112 V:Deathstroke 2.50
113 Villains united 2.50
114 PHe,Nightwing gone 2.50
115 PHe,V:Deathstroke 2.50
116 PHe,V:Deathstroke 2.50
117 PHe,V:Deathstroke 2.50
118 Hiding in New York 2.50
119 Twin Nightwings 2.50
120 V:Pierce Bros.. . . . . 3.00
121 Dick Grayson to the rescue . . . 3.00
122 Only one Nightwing remaining . 3.00
123 Fire-throwing killer 3.00
124 Heads of the unferworld 3.00
125 MWn,DJu,NRd,V:Raptor. 3.00
126 MWn,DJu,NRd 3.00
127 MWn,DJu,NRd,new villain 3.00
128 MWn,DJu,NRd,Raptor 3.00
129 MWn,Bride and Groom. 3.00
130 MWn,Bride and Groom. 3.00
131 MWn,Bride and Groom. 3.00
132 MWn,Bride and Groom, concl. . 3.00
133 MWn,Grayson's lost year 3.00
134 MWn,The Missing Year. 3.00
135 MWn,O:Vigilante 3.00
136 MWn,It's a Set-up. 3.00
137 MWn,Vigilante, Metal Eddie . . . 3.00
Ann.#1 Pulp Heroes (Romance) . . 4.50
Ann. #2 Nightwing's lost year 4.50
Spec.#1,000,000 CDi(s),SMc,KIS . 2.50
Secret Files #1 64-page. 5.50
Spec.#1 Our Worlds at War,48-pg. 3.50
Giant #1 80-pg.CDi,I:Hella. 6.00
GN The Target,CDi,SMc,48-page . . 6.00

NIGHTWING
AND HUNTRESS
March, 1998

1 (of 4) BSz,conflict 2.50
2 BSz,good cop, bad cop 2.50
3 BSz,Malfatti 2.50
4 BSz,concl. 2.50

NUTSY SQUIRREL
Sept.–Oct., 1954

61 SM. 150.00
62 thru 71. . . . . @125.00
72 Nov., 1957. . . . . 125.00

OMAC
Sept.–Oct., 1974

1 JK,I&O:Omac. 75.00
2 JK,I:Mr.Big 30.00
3 JK,100,000 foes. 30.00
4 JK,V:Kafka 30.00
5 JK,New Bodies for Old 30.00
6 JK,The Body Bank. 30.00
7 JK,The Ocean Stealers 30.00
8 JK,Last issue 30.00

[2nd Series], 1991
1 JBy,B&W prestige 5.00
2 JBy,The Great Depression era . . 4.50
3 JBy,To Kill Adolf Hitler 4.50
4 JBy,D:Mr.Big 4.50

OMAC
July, 2006

1 (of 8) Dawn of a new Omac 3.00
2 In Las Vegas 3.00
3 Brother Eye 3.00
4 Mike Costner 3.00
5 Return of Brother Eye 3.00
6 Total Control. 3.00
7 New Omac. 3.00
8 finale 3.00

OMAC PROJECT, THE
Apr., 2005

1 (of 6) Checkmate 2.50
2 Brother Eye satellite 2.50
3 F:Sasha Bordeaux. 2.50
4 Brother Eye breaks free. 2.50
5 Pawn No More. 2.50
6 concl. 2.50
Spec. Infinite Crisis Special 5.00
TPB 15.00

OMEGA MEN
Dec., 1982

1 KG,V:Citadel. 3.50
2 KG,O:Broot. 3.00
3 KG,I:Lobo. 9.00
4 KG,D:Demonia,I:Felicity. 3.00
5 KG,V:Lobo 3.00

Omega Men #9 © DC Comics Inc.

DC COMICS

6 KG,V:Citadel,D:Gepsen	2.50
7 O:Citadel,L:Auron	2.50
8 R:Nimbus,I:H.Hokum	2.50
9 V:HarryHokum,A:Lobo	2.50
10 A:Lobo (First Full Story)	6.00
11 V:Blackfire	2.50
12 R:Broots Wife	2.50
13 A:Broots Wife	2.50
14 Karna	2.50
15 Primus Goes Mad	2.50
16 Spotlight Issue	2.50
17 V:Psions	2.50
18 V:Psions	2.50
19 V:Psions,C:Lobo	2.50
20 V:Psions,A:Lobo	2.50
21 Spotlight Issue	2.50
22 Nimbus	2.50
23 Nimbus	2.50
24 Okaara	2.50
25 Kalista	2.50
26 V:Spiderguild	4.00
27 V:Psions	4.00
28 V:Psions	2.50
29 V:Psions	2.50
30 R:Primus,I:Artin.	2.50
31 Crisis tie-in	2.50
32 Felicity	2.50
33 Regufe World	2.50
34 A:New Teen Titans	2.50
35 A:New Teen Titans	2.50
36 Last Days of Broot	2.50
37 V:Spiderguild,A:Lobo	5.00
38 A:Tweener Network.	2.50
Ann.#1 KG,R:Harpis.	2.50
Ann.#2 KG,O:Primus	2.50

OMEGA MEN, THE
Oct., 2006

1 (of 6) Crimes Agains the Galaxy	3.00
2	3.00
3 A:Superman.	3.00
4 F:Lady Styx	3.00
5 F:Omega Women	3.00
6 finale	3.00

100 BULLETS
DC/Vertigo, 1999

1 F:Dizzy Cordova & AgentGraves.	9.00
2 Dizzy,pt.2	6.00
3 F:Mr.Shepard.	4.00
4 Shot, Water Back,pt.1	4.00
5 Shot, Water Back,pt.2	4.00
6 Short Con, Long Odds,pt.1	3.50
7 Short Con, Long Odds,pt.2	3.50
8 F:Agent Graves	3.50
9 Right Ear,Left in the Cold,pt.1	3.50
10 Right Ear,Left in the Cold,pt.2.	3.50
11 F:Lilly Roach	3.50
12 Parlez Kung Vous,pt.1	3.50
13 Parlez Kung Vous,pt.2	3.50
14 Parlez Kung Vous,concl.	3.50
15 Hang Up on Hang Low,pt.1	3.50
16 Hang Up on Hang Low,pt.2	3.50
17 Hang Up on Hang Low,pt.3	3.00
18 Hang Up on Hang Low,pt.4	3.00
19 Hang Up on Hang Low,pt.5	3.00
20 Hot House.	3.00
21 Sell Fish & Out to Sea,pt.1	3.00
22 Sell Fish & Out to Sea,pt.2	3.00
23 Red Prince Blues,pt.1.	3.00
24 Red Prince Blues,pt.2.	3.50
25 Red Prince Blues,pt.3.	3.00
26 Mr. Branch & the Family Tree.	2.50
27 Idol Chatter	2.50
28 Contrabandolero,pt.1	2.50
29 Contrabandolero,pt.2	2.50
30 Contrabandolero,pt.3	2.50
31 Counterfeit Detective,pt.1	2.50
32 Counterfeit Detective,pt.2	2.50
33 Counterfeit Detective,pt.3	2.50
34 Counterfeit Detective,pt.4	2.50

35 Counterfeit Detective,pt.5	2.50
36 Counterfeit Detective,pt.6	2.50
37 On Accidental Purpose.	2.50
38 Cole Burns Slow Hand	2.50
39 Ambition's Audition	2.50
40 Night of the Payday	2.50
41 A Crash	2.50
42 V:Wylie Times	2.50
43 Chill in the Oven,pt.1	2.50
44 Chill in the Oven,pt.2	2.50
45 Chill in the Oven,pt.3	2.50
46 Chill in the Oven,pt.4	2.50
47 In Stinked,pt.1	2.50
48 In Stinked,pt.2	2.50
49 In Stinked,pt.3	2.50
50 Agent Graves,40-pg.	3.50
51 Wylie Runs the Voodoo Down	2.50
52 Wylie Runs the Voodoo Down	2.50
53 Wylie Runs the Voodoo Down	2.50
54 Wylie Runs the Voodoo Down	2.50
55 Wylie Runs the Voodoo Down	2.50
56 Wylie Runs the Voodoo Down	2.50
57 Wylie Runs the Voodoo Down	2.50
58 Lono & Loop Hughes	2.50
59 F:Victor "The Saint".	2.50
60 Staring at the Son,pt.1	2.50
61 Staring at the Son,pt.2	2.50
62 Staring at the Son,pt.3	2.50
63 The Trust.	2.75
64 Jack heads to Atlantic City	2.75
65 Loop, Lono & Victor	2.75
66 Loop, Lono & Victor	2.75
67 Dizzy & Wylie	2.75
68 More dead Trust members	2.75
69 F:Augustus Medici	2.75
70 Gambling with their lives.	2.75
71 A Wake, pt.1	2.75
72 A Wake, pt.2	3.00
73 A Wake, pt.3	3.00
74 A Wake, pt.4	3.00
75 The Briefcase	3.00
76 Secret Armies of the Trust	3.00
77 On to Mexico.	3.00
78 In Mexico	3.00
79 Punch Line, pt.4	3.00
80	3.00
81	3.00
82	3.00
83 in Rome	3.00
84 Lake Tahoe	3.00
85 The Other woman	3.00

100%
DC/Vertigo, June, 2002

1 (of 5) PPo, 48-pg. b&w	6.00
2 thru 5 PPo, Sci-fi, 48-pg. b&w	@6.00
TPB PPo	25.00

ORION
April, 2000

1 WS,Darkseid	2.50
2 WS,V:Darkseid.	2.50
3 WS,FM,V:Suicide Jockeys.	2.50
4 WS,DGb,V:Darkseid	2.50
5 WS,V:Darkseid.	2.50
6 WS,EL,AG,F:Mortalla.	2.50
7 WS,HC,V:Kalibak.	2.50
8 WS,RLe,JLb,V:Kalibak.	2.50
9 WS,V:Desaad	2.50
10 WS,AAd,V:Desaad.	2.50
11 WS,New Genesis,Anti-Life	2.50
12 WS,JLe,return to Apokolips	2.50
13 WS,TA,JBy,F:Captain Marvel.	2.50
14 WS,TA,JBy,F:Captain Marvel .	2.50
15 WS,JPL,48-page.	4.50
16 WS,Abysmal Plane,V:Clockwerx	2.50
17 WS,Abysmal Plane,V:Clockwerx	2.50
18 WS,AM,F:Rakar.	2.50
19 WS,ECa,Joker-crazed Deep Six.	2.50
20 WS,fall from Grace.	2.50
21 WS,V:Arnicus Wolfram	2.50

22 WS,young teen	2.50
23 WS,BWi,young teen	2.50
24 WS,BWi, Tactical nuke.	2.50
25 WS,BWi,48-pg.final issue	4.25
TPB The Gates of Apokolips	13.00

OTHER SIDE, THE
DC/Vertigo, Oct., 2006

1 (of 5) Vietnam	3.00
2	3.00
3	3.00
4	3.00
5 finale	3.00

OTHERWORLD
DC/Vertigo, March, 2005

1 (of 12) PJ,ALa	3.00
2 thru 7 PJ,ALa	@3.00
TPB Book One.	20.00

*Our Army at War #4 ©
DC Comics, Inc.*

OUR ARMY AT WAR
Aug., 1952

1 CI(c),Dig Your FoxholeDeep.	3,500.00
2 CI(c),Champ	1,500.00
3 GK(c),No Exit	1,000.00
4 IN(c),Last Man.	900.00
5 IN(c),T.N.T. Bouquet	750.00
6 IN(c),Battle Flag.	750.00
7 IN(c),Dive Bomber	750.00
8 IN(c),One Man Army	750.00
9 GC(c),Undersea Raider	750.00
10 IN(c),Soldiers on the High Wire.	750.00
11 IN(c),Scratch One Meatball.	750.00
12 IN(c),The Big Drop	750.00
13 BK(c),Ghost Ace	750.00
14 BK(c),Drummer of Waterloo.	750.00
15 IN(c),Thunder in the Skies	650.00
16 IN(c),A Million To One Shot	650.00
17 IN(c),The White Death	650.00
18 IN(c),Frontier Fighter	650.00
19 IN(c),The Big Ditch	650.00
20 IN(c),Abandon Ship	650.00
21 IN(c),Dairy of a Flattop	500.00
22 JGr(c),Ranger Raid.	500.00
23 IN(c),Jungle Navy	500.00
24 IN(c),Suprise Landing.	500.00
25 JGr(c),Take 'Er Down	500.00
26 JGr(c),Sky Duel	500.00
27 IN(c),MD,Diary of a Frogman.	500.00
28 JGr(c),Detour-War.	500.00
29 IN(c),Grounded Fighter.	500.00
30 JGr(c),Torpedo Raft	500.00
31 IN(c),Howitzer Hill.	500.00

    All comics prices listed are for *Near Mint* condition.

Our Army at War #29
© DC Comics Inc.

32 JGr(c),Battle Mirror 500.00
33 JGr(c),Fighting Gunner 500.00
34 JGr(c),Point-Blank War 500.00
35 JGr(c),Frontline Tackle 500.00
36 JGr(c),Foxhole Mascot 500.00
37 JGr(c),Walking Battle Pin . . . 500.00
38 JGr(c),Floating Pillbox 500.00
39 JGr(c),Trench Trap 500.00
40 RH(c),Tank Hunter 500.00
41 JGr(c),Jungle Target 500.00
42 IN(c),Shadow Targets 400.00
43 JGr(c),A Bridge For Billy 400.00
44 JGr(c),Thunder In The Desert . 400.00
45 JGr(c),Diary of a Fighter Pilot. 400.00
46 JGr(c),Prize Package 400.00
47 JGr(c),Flying Jeep 400.00
48 JGr(c),Front Seat 400.00
49 JKu(c),Landing Postponed . . . 400.00
50 JGr(c),RH,Mop-Up Squad . . . 400.00
51 JGr(c),Battle Tag 400.00
52 JGr(c),Pony Express Pilot. . . . 400.00
53 JGr(c),One Ringside-For War. 400.00
54 JKu(c),No-Man Secret 400.00
55 JGr(c),No Rest For A Raider. . 400.00
56 JKu(c),You're Next 400.00
57 JGr(c),Ten-Minute Break. 400.00
58 JKu(c),The Fighting SnowBird 400.00
59 JGr(c),The Mustang Had
    My Number 400.00
60 JGr(c),Ranger Raid. 400.00
61 JGr(c),A Pigeon For Easy Co. 300.00
62 JKu(c),Trigger Man 300.00
63 JGr(c),The Big Toss 300.00
64 JKu(c),Tank Rider 300.00
65 JGr(c),Scramble-War Upstairs 300.00
66 RH(c),Gunner Wanted 300.00
67 JKu(c),MD,Boiling Point 300.00
68 JGr(c),MD,End of the Line . . . 300.00
69 JGr(c),Combat Cage. 300.00
70 JGr(c),Torpedo Tank 300.00
71 JGr(c),Flying Mosquitoes . . . 300.00
72 JGr(c),No. 1 Pigeon 300.00
73 JKu(c),Shooting Gallery 300.00
74 JGr(c),Ace Without Guns 300.00
75 JGr(c),Blind Night Fighter 300.00
76 JKu(c),Clipped Hellcat 300.00
77 JGr(c),Jets Don't Dream. 300.00
78 IN(c),Battle Nurse 300.00
79 JGr(c),MD,What's the Price
    of a B-17? 300.00
80 JGr(c),The Sparrow And
    The...Hawk 300.00
81 JGr(c),Sgt. Rock in The
    Rock of Easy Co. 5,000.00
82 JGr(c),MD,Gun Jockey 1,200.00

83 JGr(c),MD,B:Sgt.Rock Stories,
    The Rock and the Wall. . . . 3,800.00
84 JKu(c),Laughter On
    Snakehead Hill 650.00
85 JGr(c),Ice Cream Soldier 800.00
86 RH(c),Tank 711. . . . . 600.00
87 RH(c),Calling Easy Co. 600.00
88 JKu(c),The Hard Way 600.00
89 RH(c),No Shoot From Easy . . 600.00
90 JKu(c),3 Stripes Hill 600.00
91 JGr(c),No Answer from
    Sarge 1,500.00
92 JGr(c),Luck of Easy 500.00
93 JGr(c),Deliver One Airfield . . . 500.00
94 JGr(c),Target-Easy Company. 500.00
95 JKu(c),Battle of the Stripes. . . 500.00
96 JGr(c),MD,Last Stand
    For Easy 500.00
97 JKu(c),What Makes A
    Sergeant Run? 500.00
98 JKu(c),Soldiers Never Die . . . 500.00
99 JKu(c),Easy's Hardest Battle . 500.00
100 JKu(c),No Exit For Easy 500.00
101 JKu(c),End Of Easy 400.00
102 JKu(c),The Big Star. 400.00
103 RH(c),Easy's Had It 400.00
104 JKu(c),A New Kind Of War . . 400.00
105 JKu(c),T.N.T. Birthday. 400.00
106 JKu(c),Meet Lt. Rock 400.00
107 JKu(c),Doom Over Easy 400.00
108 JGr(c),Unknown Sergeant . . 400.00
109 JKu(c),Roll Call For Heroes . 400.00
110 JKu(c),That's An Order 400.00
111 JKu(c),What's The Price
    Of A Dog Tag 400.00
112 JKu(c),Battle Shadow 400.00
113 JKu(c),Eyes Of A
    Blind Gunner 400.00
114 JKu(c),Killer Sergeant 400.00
115 JKu(c),Rock's Battle Family . 400.00
116 JKu(c),S.O.S. Sgt. Rock 400.00
117 JKu(c),Snafu Squad 400.00
118 RH(c),The Tank Vs. The
    Tin Soldier 400.00
119 JKu(c),A Bazooka For
    Babyface 400.00
120 JGr(c),Battle Tags
    For Easy Co. 250.00
121 JKu(c),New Boy In Easy. . . . 200.00
122 JKu(c),Battle of the
    Pajama Commandoes 200.00
123 JKu(c),Battle Brass Ring . . . 200.00
124 JKu(c),Target-Sgt. Rock 200.00
125 JKu(c),Hold-At All Costs 200.00
126 RH(c),The End Of
    Easy Company 200.00
127 JKu(c),4 Faces of Sgt. Rock. 200.00
128 JKu(c),O:Sgt. Rock. 450.00
129 JKu(c),Heroes Need
    Cowards 200.00
130 JKu(c),No Hill For Easy 200.00
131 JKu(c),One Pair of
    Dogtags For Sale 200.00
132 JKu(c),Young Soldiers
    Never Cry 200.00
133 JKu(c),Yesterday's Hero 200.00
134 JKu(c),The T.N.T. Book. 200.00
135 JKu(c),Battlefield Double . . . 200.00
136 JKu(c),Make Me A Hero 200.00
137 JKu(c),Too Many Sergeants . 200.00
138 JKu(c),Easy's Lost Sparrow . 200.00
139 JKu(c),A Firing Squad
    For Easy 200.00
140 JKu(c),Brass Sergeant 200.00
141 JKu(c),Dead Man's Trigger. . 200.00
142 JKu(c),Easy's New Topkick. . 200.00
143 JKu(c),Easy's T.N.T. Crop. . . 200.00
144 JKu(c),The Sparrow And
    The Tiger 200.00
145 JKu(c),A Feather For
    Little Sure Shot 200.00

146 JKu(c),The Fighting Guns
    For Easy 200.00
147 JKu(c),Book One:Generals
    Don't Die 200.00
148 JKu(c),Book Two:Generals
    Don't Die:Generals Are
    Sergeants With Stars. 200.00
149 JKu(c),Surrender Ticket 200.00
150 JKu(c),Flytrap Hill 200.00
151 JKu(c),War Party,
    I:Enemy Ace 750.00
152 Jku(c),Last Man-Last Shot . . 200.00
153 JKu(c),Easy's Last Stand . . . 400.00
154 JKu(c),Boobytrap Mascot . . . 150.00
155 JKu(c),No Stripes For Me . . . 400.00
156 JKu(c),The Human Tank Trap 150.00
157 JKu(c),Nothin's Ever
    Lost In War 150.00
158 JKu(c),Iron Major-Rock
    Sergeant 150.00
159 JKu(c),The Blind Gun 150.00
160 JKu(c),What's The Color
    Of Your Blood 150.00
161 JKu(c),Dead End
    For A Dogface 150.00
162 JKu(c),The Price and
    The Sergeant. 150.00
163 JKu(c),MD,RE,Kill Me-Kill Me 150.00
164 JKu(c),CE,No Exit For Easy,
    reprint from #100. . . . . 350.00
165 GE,JKu(c),The Return of the
    Iron Major 150.00
166 GE,JKu(c),Half A Sergeant . . 150.00
167 GE,JKu(c),Kill One-
    Save One 150.00
168 GE,JKu(c),I Knew The
    Unknown Soldier 300.00
169 GE,JKu(c),Nazi On My Back 125.00
170 GE,JKu(c),Buzzard Bait Hill . 125.00
171 GE,JKu(c),The Sergeant
    Must Die 125.00
172 GE,JKu(c),A Slug for a
    Sergeant 125.00
173 GE,JKu(c),Easy's Hardest
    Battle, reprint from #99 . . . . 125.00
174 GE,JKu(c),One Kill Too
    Many 125.00
175 JKu(c),T.N.T. Letter. 125.00
176 MD,JKu(c),Give Me Your
    Stripes 125.00
177 RH,JKu(c),Target-Easy Company,
    reprint from #94, giant-size . . 200.00
178 RH,JKu(c),Only One Medal
    For Easy 100.00

Our Army at War #203
© DC Comics Inc.

DC COMICS

179 RH,JKu(c),A Penny Jackie
    Johnson.............. 100.00
180 RH,JKu(c),You Can't
    Kill A General......... 100.00
181 RH,Monday's Coward-
    Tuesday's Hero........ 100.00
182 NA,RH,The Desert Rats
    of Easy 125.00
183 RH,NA,JKu(c),Sergeants
    Don't Stay Dead....... 150.00
184 RH,JKu(c),Candidate For A
    Firing Squad.......... 100.00
185 RH,JKu(c),Battle Flag For
    A G.I................. 100.00
186 RH,NA,JKu(c),3 Stripes Hill
    reprint from #90, Origin..... 100.00
187 RH,JKu(c),Shadow of a
    Sergeant 90.00
188 RH,JKu(c),Death Comes for
    Easy.................. 90.00
189 RH,JKu(c),The Mission Was
    Murder................ 90.00
190 RH,JKu(c),What Make's A
    Sergeant Run?, reprint
    from #97, giant-size..... 150.00
191 RH,JKu(c),Death Flies High,
    A:Johnny Cloud........ 175.00
192 RH,JKu(c),A Firing Squad
    For A Sergeant........ 150.00
193 RH,JKu(c),Blood In
    the Desert............ 150.00
194 RH,JKu(c),Time For
    Vengeance............. 150.00
195 RH,JKu(c),Dead Town ... 150.00
196 RH,JKu(c),Stop The War-
    I Want To Get Off........ 150.00
197 RH,JKu(c),Last Exit For Easy 150.00
198 RH,JKu(c),Plugged Nickel .. 150.00
199 RH,JKu(c),Nazi Ghost Wolf . 150.00
200 RH,GE,JKu(c),The
    Troubadour 100.00
201 RH,JKu(c),The Graffiti Writer . 75.00
202 RH,JKu(c),Sarge Is Dead.... 75.00
203 RH,MD,JKu(c),Easy's Had It,
    reprint from # 103, giant-size 125.00
204 RH,JKu(c)................. 75.00
205 RH,JKu(c)................. 60.00
206 RH,JKu(c),There's A War On . 60.00
207 RH,JKu(c),A Sparrow's
    Prayer 60.00
208 RH,JKu(c),A Piece of Rag...
    And A Hank of Hair........ 60.00
209 RH,JKu(c),I'm Still Alive 60.00
210 RH,JKu(c),I'm Kilroy....... 60.00
211 RH,JKu(c),The Treasure of
    St. Daniel.............. 60.00
212 RH,MD,JKu(c),The Quiet War 60.00
213 RH,JKu(c),A Letter For
    Bulldozer 60.00
214 RH,JKu(c),Where Are You? .. 60.00
215 RH,JKu(c),Pied Piper of Peril . 60.00
216 RH,JKu(c),Doom Over Easy,
    reprint from # 107, Giant-size 100.00
217 RH,JKu(c),Surprise Party 50.00
218 RH,JKu(c),Medic!......... 50.00
219 RH,JKu(c),Yesterday's Hero . . 50.00
220 RH,JKu(c),Stone-Age War ... 50.00
221 RH,JKu(c),Hang-Up 50.00
222 RH,JKu(c),Dig In, Easy...... 50.00
223 RH,JKu(c),On Time......... 50.00
224 RH,JKu(c),One For The
    Money 50.00
225 RH,JKu(c),Face Front....... 50.00
226 RH,JKu(c),Death Stop 50.00
227 RH,JKu(c),Traitor's Blood.... 50.00
228 RH,JKu(c),It's A Dirty War... 50.00
229 RH,JKu(c),The Battle of the
    Sergeants, reprint #128,
    Giant-size............. 75.00
230 RH,JKu(c),Home Is The
    Hunter................ 30.00

Our Army at War #219
© *DC Comics, Inc.*

231 RH,JKu(c),My Brother's
    Keeper................ 30.00
232 RH,JKu(c),3 Men In A Tub .. 30.00
233 RH,JKu(c),Head Count...... 30.00
234 RH,JKu(c),Summer In Salerno 30.00
235 RH,ATh,JKu(c),Pressure
    Point, giant-size.......... 45.00
236 RH,JKu(c),Face The Devil,
    giant-size.............. 45.00
237 RH,JKu(c),Nobody Cares,
    giant-size.............. 45.00
238 RH,JKu(c),I Kid You Not,
    giant-size.............. 45.00
239 RH,JKu(c),The Soldier,
    giant-size.............. 45.00
240 RH,JKu(c),NA, giant-size 75.00
241 RH,ATh,JKu(c),War Story,
    giant-size.............. 45.00
242 RH,JKu(c),Infantry........ 45.00
243 RH,MD,JKu(c),24 Hour Pass . 40.00
244 RH,MD,JKu(c),Easy's First
    Tiger 40.00
245 RH,JKu(c),The Prisoner 40.00
246 RH,JKu(c),Naked Combat ... 40.00
247 RH,JKu(c),The Vision...... 25.00
248 RH,JKu(c),The Firing Squad. . 25.00
249 RH,JKu(c),The Luck of
    Easy,WW 30.00
250 RH,JKu(c),90 Day Wonder ... 25.00
251 RH,JKu(c),The Iron Major.... 25.00
252 RH,JKu(c),The Iron Hand 25.00
253 RH,JKu(c),Rock and Iron 25.00
254 RH,ATh,JKu(c),The Town 25.00
255 RH,JKu(c),What's It Like..... 25.00
256 RH,JKu(c),School For
    Sergeants.............. 25.00
257 RH,JKu(c),The Castaway 25.00
258 RH,JKu(c),The Survivors 25.00
259 RH,JKu(c),Lost Paradise 25.00
260 RH,JKu(c),Hell's Island..... 25.00
261 RH,JKu(c),The Medal That
    Nobody Wanted......... 25.00
262 RH,JKu(c),The Return 25.00
263 RH,JKu(c),The Cage 25.00
264 RH,JKu(c),The Hunt 25.00
265 RH,JKu(c),The Brother 25.00
266 RH,GE,JKu(c),The Evacuees . 25.00
267 RH,JKu(c),A Bakers Dozen . 25.00
268 RH,JKu(c),The Elite 25.00
269 RH,MD,GE,JKu(c), giant-size . 75.00
270 RH,JKu(c),Spawn of the
    Devil................. 25.00
271 RH,JKu(c),Brittle Harvest ... 20.00
272 RH,JKu(c),The Bloody Flag .. 20.00
273 RH,JKu(c),The Arena 20.00

274 RH,GE,JKu(c),Home Is The
    Hero.................. 20.00
275 RH,MD,JKu(c),Graveyard
    Battlefield, giant-size........ 75.00
276 RH,GE,JKu(c),A Bullet For
    Rock.................. 22.00
277 RH,JKu(c),Gashouse Gang .. 22.00
278 RH,GE,JKu(c),Rearguard
    Action................. 22.00
279 RH,JKu(c),Mined City 22.00
280 RH,GE,MD,JKu(c),Mercy
    Mission 25.00
281 RH,JKu(c),Dead Man's Eyes . 18.00
282 JKu(c),Pieces of Time...... 18.00
283 JKu(c),Dropouts 18.00
284 JKu(c),Linkup........... 18.00
285 JKu(c),Bring Him Back 18.00
286 JKu(c),Firebird 15.00
287 MGr,JKu(c),The Fifth
    Dimension............. 15.00
288 JKu(c),Defend-Or Destroy . 15.00
289 JKu(c),The Line 15.00
290 JKu(c),Super-Soldiers...... 15.00
291 JKu(c),Death Squad 15.00
292 JKu(c),A Lesson In Blood 15.00
293 JKu(c),It Figures 15.00
294 JKu(c),Coffin For Easy 15.00
295 JKu(c),The Devil in Paradise . 15.00
296 JKu(c),Combat Soldier 15.00
297 JKu(c),Percentages 15.00
298 JKu(c),Return to Chartres.... 15.00
299 JKu(c),Three Soldiers 15.00
300 JKu(c),300th Hill 18.00
301 JKu(c),The Farm 15.00
Becomes:

SGT. ROCK
1977–88

302 JKu(c),Anzio-The Bloodbath,
    part I 40.00
303 JKu(c),Anzio, part II 20.00
304 JKu(c),Anzio, part III 20.00
305 JKu(c),Dead Man's Trigger,
    reprint from #141......... 20.00
306 JKu(c),The Last Soldier 20.00
307 JKu(c),I'm Easy........... 20.00
308 JKu(c),One Short Step 20.00
309 JKu(c),Battle Clowns 20.00
310 JKu(c),Hitler's Wolf Children.. 20.00
311 JKu(c),The Sergeant and
    the Lady............... 15.00
312 JKu(c),No Name Hill 15.00
313 JKu(c),A Jeep For Joey 15.00
314 JKu(c),Gimme Sky 15.00
315 JKu(c),Combat Antenna ... 15.00
316 JKu(c),Another Hill...... ... 15.00
317 JKu(c),Hell's Oven 15.00
318 JKu(c),Stone-Age War 15.00
319 JKu(c),To Kill a Sergeant 15.00
320 JKu(c),Never Salute a
    Sergeant 15.00
321 JKu(c),It's Murder Out Here .. 10.00
322 JKu(c),The Killer......... 10.00
323 JKu(c),Monday's Hero 10.00
324 JKu(c),Ghost of a Tank..... 10.00
325 JKu(c),Future Kill, part I 10.00
326 JKu(c),Future Kill, part II..... 10.00
327 JKu(c),Death Express...... 10.00
328 JKu(c),Waiting For Rock 10.00
329 JKu(c),Dead Heat 10.00
330 JKu(c),G.I. Trophy........ 10.00
331 JKu(c),The Sons of War 10.00
332 JKu(c),Pyramid of Death. ... 10.00
333 JKu(c),Ask The Dead 10.00
334 JKu(c),What's Holding Up
    The War............... 10.00
335 JKu(c),Killer Compass 10.00
336 JKu(c),The Red Maple Leaf .. 10.00
337 JKu(c),A Bridge Called Charlie 10.00
338 JKu(c),No Escape From
    the Front 10.00
339 JKu(c),I Was Here Before.... 10.00
340 JKu(c),How To Win A War.... 10.00

341 JKu(c),High-Flyer 10.00
342 JKu(c),The 6 sides of
    Sgt. Rock 10.00
343 thru 350 . . . . @10.00
351 thru 422 . . . . @7.00

OUR FIGHTING FORCES
Oct.–Nov., 1954

1 IN,JGr(c),Human Booby Trap 2,000.00
2 RH,IN,IN(c),Mile-Long Step . . . 800.00
3 RA,JKu(c),Winter Ambush 600.00
4 RA,JGr(c),The Hot Seat 500.00
5 IN,RA,JGr(c),The Iron Punch . 500.00
6 IN,RA,JGr(c),The Sitting Tank . 425.00
7 RA,JKu,JGr(c),Battle Fist 425.00
8 IN,RA,JGr(c),No War
    For A Gunner 425.00
9 JKu,RH,JGr(c),Crash-
    Landing At Dawn 425.00
10 WW,RA,JGr(c),Grenade
    Pitcher 425.00
11 JKu,JGr(c),Diary of a Sub . . . 350.00
12 IN,JKu,JGr(c),Jump Seat 350.00
13 RA,JGr(c),Beach Party 350.00
14 JA,RA,IN,JGr(c),Unseen War . 350.00
15 RH,JKu,JGr(c),Target For
    A Lame Duck 350.00
16 RH,JGr(c),Night Fighter 350.00
17 RA,JGr(c),Anchored Frogman 350.00
18 RH,JKu,JGr(c),Cockpit Seat . . 350.00
19 RA,JKu(c),StraightenThatLine 350.00
20 RA,MD,JGr(c),The
    Floating Pilot 400.00
21 RA,JKu(c),The Bouncing
    Baby of Company B 250.00
22 JKu,RA,JGr(c),3 Doorways
    To War 250.00
23 RA,IN,JA,JGr(c),Tin Fish Pilot 250.00
24 RA,RH,JGr(c),Frogman Duel . 250.00
25 RA,JKu(c),Dead End 250.00
26 IN,RH,JKu(c),Tag Day 250.00
27 MD,RA,JKu(c),TNT Escort . . . 250.00
28 RH,MD,JKu(c),AllQuiet atC.P. . 250.00
29 JKu,JKu(c),Listen To A Jet . . . 250.00
30 IN,RA,JKu(c),Fort
    For A Gunner 250.00
31 MD,RA,JKu(c),Silent Sub 250.00
32 RH,MD,RH(c),PaperWorkWar 250.00
33 RH,JKu,JKu(c),Frogman
    In A Net 250.00
34 JA,JGr,JKu(c),Calling U-217 . . 250.00
35 JA,JGr,JKu(c),Mask of
    a Frogman 250.00
36 MD,JA,JKu(c),Steel Soldier . . 250.00

Our Fighting Forces #29
© DC Comics, Inc.

37 JA,JGr,JGr(c),Frogman
    In A Bottle 250.00
38 RH,RA,JA,JGr(c),Sub Sinker . 250.00
39 JA,RH,RH(c),Last Torpedo . . . 250.00
40 JGr,JA,JKu,JKu(c),The
    Silent Ones 250.00
41 JGr,RH,JA,JKu(c),Battle
    Mustang 300.00
42 RH,MD,JGr(c),Sorry-
    Wrong Hill 225.00
43 MD,JKu,JGr(c),Inside Battle . . 225.00
44 MD,RH,RA,JGr(c),Big Job
    For Baker. 225.00
45 RH,RA,JGr(c),B:Gunner and
    Sarge, Mop-Up Squad. 700.00
46 RH,RA,JGr(c),Gunner's
    Squad 300.00
47 RH,JKu(c),TNT Birthday 225.00
48 JA,RH,JGr(c),A Statue
    For Sarge 225.00
49 RH,MD,JGr(c),Blind Gunner . . 275.00
50 JA,RH,JGr(c),I:Pooch,My
    Pal, The Pooch 225.00
51 RA,JA,RH(c),Underwater
    Gunner. 200.00
52 RA,JKu,JKu(c),The Biggest
    Target in the World 150.00
53 MD,JKu,JKu(c),The Gunner
    and the Nurse 150.00
54 JA,RA,An Egg for Sarge 150.00
55 MD,RH,JGr(c),The Last Patrol 150.00
56 RH,RA,JGr(c),Bridge of
    Bullets 150.00
57 JA,IN,JGr(c),A Tank For Sarge 150.00
58 JA,JGr(c),Return of the Pooch 150.00
59 RH,JA,JGr(c),Pooch-Patrol
    Leader 150.00
60 RH,JA,JGr(c),Tank Target 150.00
61 JA,JGr(c),Pass to Peril 150.00
62 JA,JGr(c),The Flying Pooch . . 150.00
63 JA,RH,JGr(c),Pooch-Tank
    Hunter 150.00
64 JK,RH,JGr(c),A Lifeline
    For Sarge 150.00
65 IN,JA,JGr(c),Dogtag Patrol . . . 150.00
66 JKu,JA,JGr(c),Trail of the
    Ghost Bomber 150.00
67 IN,JA,JGr(c),Purple Heart
    For Pooch 150.00
68 JA,JGr(c),Col. Hakawa's
    Birthday Party 150.00
69 JA,JKu,JGr(c),
    Destination Doom 150.00
70 JA,JKu(c),The Last Holdout . . 150.00
71 JA,JGr(c),End of the Marines . 125.00
72 JA,JGr(c),Four-Footed Spy . . . 125.00
73 IN,JGr(c),The Hero Maker . . . 125.00
74 IN,JGr(c),Three On A T.N.T.
    Bull's-Eye. 125.00
75 JKu(c),Purple Heart Patrol . . . 125.00
76 JKu(c),The T.N.T. Seat 125.00
77 JKu(c),No Foxhole-No Home . 125.00
78 JGr(c),The Last Medal 125.00
79 JA,JGr(c),Backs to the Sea . . . 125.00
80 JA,JGr(c),Don't Come Back . . 125.00
81 JA,JGr(c),Battle of
    the Mud Marines 125.00
82 JA,JGr(c),Battle of the
    Empty Helmets 125.00
83 RA,JKu(c),Any Marine
    Can Do It. 125.00
84 JA,JKu(c),The Gun of Shame. 125.00
85 Ja,JKu(c),The TNT Pin-Points 125.00
86 JKu(c),3 Faces of Combat . . . 125.00
87 JKu(c),Battle of the
    Boobytraps 125.00
88 GC,JKu(c),Devil Dog Patrol . . 125.00
89 JKu(c),TNT Toothache 125.00
90 JKu(c),Stop the War 125.00
91 JKu(c),The Human Shooting
    Gallery 75.00

Our Fighting Forces #77
© DC Comics, Inc.

92 JA,JKu(c),The Bomb That
    Stopped The War. 75.00
93 IN,JKu(c),The Human Sharks. . 75.00
94 RH(c),E:Gunner,Sarge & Pooch,
    The Human Blockbusters 75.00
95 GC,RH(c),B:The Fighting Devil
    Dog, Lt. Rock, The
    Fighting Devil Dog. 75.00
96 JA,RH(c),Battle of Fire 75.00
97 IN(c),Invitation To A
    Firing Squad 75.00
98 IN(c),E:The Fighting Devil
    Dog, Death Wore A Grin 75.00
99 JA,JKu(c),B:Capt. Hunter,
    No Mercy in Vietnam. 75.00
100 GC,IN(c),Death Also
    Stalks the Hunter. 75.00
101 JA,RH(c),Killer of Vietnam . . . 50.00
102 RH,JKu(c),Cold Steel
    For A Hot War 50.00
103 JKu(c),The Tunnels of Death . 50.00
104 JKu(c),Night Raid In Vietnam . 50.00
105 JKu(c),Blood Loyality 50.00
106 IN(c),Trail By Fury. 50.00
107 IN(c),Raid Of The Hellcats . . . 50.00
108 IN(c),Kill The Wolf Pack 50.00
109 IN(c),Burn, Raiders, Burn 50.00
110 IN(c),Mountains Full of Death . 50.00
111 IN(c),Train of Terror. 50.00
112 IN(c),What's In It For
    The Hellcats? 50.00
113 IN(c),Operation-Survival 50.00
114 JKu(c),No Loot For The
    Hellcats 50.00
115 JKu(c),Death In The Desert . . 50.00
116 JKu(c),Peril From the Casbah 50.00
117 JKu(c),Colder Than Death . . . 50.00
118 JKu(c),Hell Underwater. 50.00
119 JKu(c),Bedlam In Berlin 50.00
120 JKu(c),Devil In The Dark 50.00
121 JKu(c),Take My Place. 50.00
122 JKu(c),24 Hours To Die 50.00
123 JKu(c),B:Born Losers,No
    Medals No Graves. 100.00
124 JKu(c),Losers Take All 35.00
125 Daughters of Death. 35.00
126 JKu(c),Lost Town 35.00
127 JKu(c),Angels Over Hell's
    Corner 35.00
128 JKu(c),7 11 War 35.00
129 JKu(c),Ride The Nightmare . . 35.00
130 JKu(c),Nameless Target 35.00
131 JKu(c),Half A Man. 35.00
132 JKu(c),Pooch, The Winner . . . 35.00
133 JKu(c),Heads or Tails,
    giant-size 50.00

134 JKu(c),The Real Losers,
   giant-size 50.00
135 JKu(c),Death Picks A Loser,
   giant-size 50.00
136 JKu(c),Decoy For Death,
   giant-size 50.00
137 JKu(c),God Of The Losers,
   giant-size 50.00
138 JKu(c),The Targets 30.00
139 JKu(c),The Pirate 30.00
140 JKu(c),Lost...One Loser 30.00
141 JKu(c),Bad Penny, The 30.00
142 JKu(c), 1/2 A Man 30.00
143 JKu(c),Diamonds Are
   For Never 30.00
144 JKu(c),The Lost Mission 30.00
145 JKu(c),A Flag For Losers 30.00
146 JKu(c),The Forever Walk 30.00
147 NA(c),The Glory Road 40.00
148 JKu(c),The Last Charge 30.00
149 FT(c),A Bullet For
   A Traitor 30.00
150 JKu(c),Mark Our Graves 30.00
151 JKu(c),Kill Me With Wagner . . 32.00
152 JK(c),A Small Place In Hell . . . 32.00
153 JK(c),Big Max 32.00
154 JK(c),Bushido,Live By The
   Code, Die By The Code 32.00
155 JK(c),The Partisans 32.00
156 JK(c),Good-Bye Broadway . . . 32.00
157 JK(c),Panama Fattie 32.00
158 JK(c),Bombing Out On
   The Panama Canal 32.00
159 JK(c),Mile-A-Minute Jones . . . 32.00
160 JKu(c),Ivan 32.00
161 JKu(c),The Major's Dream . . . 32.00
162 Gung-Ho 32.00
163 JKu(c),The Unmarked Graves 25.00
164 JKu(c),A Town Full Of Losers . 25.00
165 LD(c),The Rowboat Fleet 25.00
166 LD(c),Sword of Flame. 25.00
167 LD(c),A Front Seat In Hell. . . . 25.00
168 LD(c),A Cold Day To Die. 25.00
169 JKu(c),Welcome Home-And
   Die. 25.00
170 JKu(c),A Bullet For
   The General 25.00
171 JKu(c),A Long Day...
   A Long War 25.00
172 JKu(c),The Two-Headed Spy . 25.00
173 JKu(c),An Appointment
   With A Direct Hit 25.00
174 JKu(c),Winner Takes-Death . . 25.00
175 JKu(c),Death Warrant 25.00
176 JKu(c),The Loser Is A
   Teen-Ager 25.00
177 JKu(c),This Loser Must Die . . 25.00
178 JKu(c),Last Drop For Losers . 25.00
179 JKu(c),The Last Loser 25.00
180 JKu(c),Hot Seat In A
   Cold War 25.00
181 JKu(c),Sept.–Oct., 1978 . . . . . 30.00

OUTCASTS
Oct., 1987
1 thru 11 . . . . @2.25

OUTLAW NATION
DC/Vertigo, Aug., 2000
1 JaD(s),F:pulp-fiction writer 2.50
2 JaD(s),Southern bayou 2.50
3 JaD,F:Devil Kid 2.50
4 JaD,F:Kid Gloves 2.50
5 JaD,F:Kid Gloves 2.50
6 JaD, ... 2.50
7 JaD, ... 2.50
8 JaD,Women,tequila & guns 2.50
9 JaD,Hell Holes 2.50
10 JaD,V:Gloves 2.50
11 JaD,Hate, Murder and Revenge. 2.50
12 JaD,Temptation 2.50

13 JaD,Desperado 2.50
14 JaD,The Devil Kid 2.50
15 JaD,The Devil Kid 2.50
16 JaD,Under siege 2.50
17 JaD,Quicksand 2.50
18 JaD,Old Asa 2.50
19 JaD,final issue 2.50

Outlaws #5
© DC Comics, Inc.

OUTLAWS
1991
1 LMc,I:Hood 2.25
2 thru 7 LMc . . . . @2.25

OUTSIDERS, THE
Nov., 1985
[1st Regular Series]
1 JAp,I:Looker. 3.00
2 JAp,V:Nuclear Family 2.50
3 JAp,V:Force of July 2.50
4 JAp,V:Force of July 2.50
5 JAp,Christmas Issue 2.50
6 JAp,V:Duke of Oil 2.50
7 JAp,V:Duke of Oil 2.50
8 JAp,Japan 2.50
9 JAp/SD/JOp,Bik Lightning 2.50
10 JAp,I:Peoples Heroes 2.50
11 JAp,Imprisoned in death camp . 2.50
12 JAp,Imprisoned in death camp . 2.50
13 JAp,Desert island 2.50
14 JAp,Looker/murder story 2.50
15 DJu,V:Bio-hazard 2.50
16 Halo vs.Firefly. 2.50
17 JAp,J:Batman 2.50
18 JAp,BB,V:Eclipso 2.50
19 JAp,V:Windfall. 2.50
20 JAp,Masters of Disaster 2.50
21 JAp,V:Kobra,I:Clayface IV 2.50
22 JAp,V:Strike Force Kobra 2.50
23 Return of People's Heroes 2.50
24 TVE,JAp,V:Skull,A:Duke of Oil . 2.50
25 JAp,V:Skull 2.50
26 JAp,in Markovia 2.50
27 EL,Millennium 2.50
28 EL,Millennium,final issue 2.50
Ann.#1,KN,V:Skull,A:Batman 2.50
Spec.#1,A:Infinity,Inc 2.50

[2nd Regular Series], 1993–95
1 Alpha,TC(c),B:MiB(s),PaP,
   I:Technocrat,Faust,Wylde 3.00
1a Omega,TC(c),PaP,V:Vampires . 3.00
2 PaP,V:Sanction 2.25
3 PaP,V:Eradicator 2.25
4 PaP,A:Eradicator 2.25

5 PaP,V:Atomic Knight,A:Jihad 2.25
6 PaP,V:Jihad 2.25
7 PaP,C:Batman 2.25
8 PaP,V:Batman,I:Halo 2.25
9 PaP,V:Batman 2.25
10 PaP,B:Final Blood, R:Looker . . . 2.50
11 PaP,Zero Hour,E:Final Blood . . . 2.25
12 PaP 2.25
13 New base 2.25
14 Martial Arts Spectacular 2.25
15 V:New Year's Evil 2.25
16 R:Windfall 2.25
17 A:Green Lantern 2.25
18 Sins of the Father 2.25
19 Sins of the Father, pt.2 . . . . 2.25
20 DvA,V:Metamorpho. 2.25
21 A:Apokolips 2.25
22 Alien Assassin 2.25
23 V:Defilers 2.25
24 finale 2.25

OUTSIDERS
June 2003
1 TR,SHa 10.00
1a 2nd printing 4.00
2 TR,SHa,F:Jade 5.00
3 TR,SHa,Gorilla Grodd 3.00
4 Ccs,V:Brother Blood 3.00
5 CCs,V:Brother Blood 3.00
6 CCs,V:Brother Blood 2.50
7 TR,SHa,two Metamorphos 2.50
8 TR,F:Huntress 2.50
9 TR,F:Black Lightning 2.50
10 TR,F:Captain Marvel Jr. 2.50
11 F:Arsenal 2.50
12 V:Psimon. 2.50
13 TR,Five by Five,pt.1 . . . . 2.50
14 TR,Five by Five,pt.2 . . . . 2.50
15 TR,Five by Five,pt.3 . . . . 2.50
16 V:Arsenal 2.50
17 TR,Most Wanted 2.50
18 Most Wanted, pt.2. . . . . 2.50
19 Most Wanted, pt.3. . . . . 2.50
20 Shift & Indy on a date 2.50
21 F:Batman 2.50
22 Arsenal vs. Batman. 2.50
23 Lockdown 2.50
24 The Insiders, x-over, pt.2 . . . . . 2.50
25 The Insdiers, x-over, pt.4 . . . . . 3.50
26 Tick Tock, pt.1, A:Batman 2.50
27 Tick Tock, pt.2,A:Batman,Katana 2.50
28 ATi,Insider aftermath 2.50
29 ATi,Day of Vengeance tie-in . . . 2.50
30 ATi,Day of Vengeance tie-in . . . 2.50
31 ATi,Infinite Crisis tie-in. 2.50
32 ATi,Infinite Crisis tie-in. 2.50
33 ATi,Infinite Crisis tie-in. 2.50
34 ATi,One Year Later 2.50
35 ATi,Vs brutal regime 3.00
36 ATi,Nightwing's African Mission . 3.00
37 ATi,Monsieur Mallah & Brain. . . . 3.00
38 ATi,Mallah & Brain. 3.00
39 ATi 3.00
40 ATi 3.00
41 ATi, Old foe 3.00
42 ATi 3.00
43 ATi 3.00
44 ATi,Pay as You Go, pt.1 . . . . . . 3.00
45 Pay as you Go, pt.2 . . . . 3.00
46 Pay as you Go, pt.3 . . . . 3.00
47 Checkout,pt.2;Checkmate x-over 3.00
48 Checkout,pt.4;Checkmate x-over 3.00
49 Checkout,finale:x-over 3.00
50 A:Batman, final issue 3.00
Ann. #1 Filling in the Gaps 4.00

OUTSIDERS:
FIVE OF A KIND
Aug., 2007
1 Nightwing/Boomerang 3.00
2 Katana/Shazam 3.00

3 Thunder/Martian Manhunter 3.00
4 Metamorpho/Aquaman 3.00
5 Grace/Wonder Woman 3.00

PARALLAX: EMERALD NIGHT
Nov., 1996
1 RMz(s),MMK,MkK, pivotal tie-in
  to Final Night.............. 4.50

PAT BOONE
1959
1 Ph(c),Jimmy Rodgers 750.00
2 Edd "Kookie" Byrnes 500.00
3 Fabian, Connie Francis 500.00
4 Bobby Darin, Johnny Mathis .. 500.00
5 Dick Clark, Frankie Avalon ... 500.00

PEACEMAKER
Jan., 1988
1 A:Dr.Tzin-Tzin 2.50
2 The Wages of Tzin........... 2.50
3 and 4 .... @2.50

PENGUIN TRIUMPHANT
1 JSon,A:Batman,Wall Street 6.00

Peter Cannon: Thunderbolt #2
© DC Comics Inc.

PETER CANNON: THUNDERBOLT
1992–93
1 thru 6 MC .... @2.25
7 MC,Battleground 2.25
8 MC,Cairo Kidnapped 2.25
9 MC...................... 2.25
10 MC,A:JLA 2.25
11 MC,V:Havoc,A:Checkmate 2.25
12 MC,final Issue 2.25

PETER PANDA
Aug.–Sept., 1953
1 The Magic Rainbow......... 600.00
2 The Stolen Wand 300.00
3 thru 30 .... @200.00
31 Aug.–Sept., 1958 .... 200.00

PETER PORKCHOPS
Nov.–Dec., 1949
1 .... 400.00

2 .... 200.00
3 thru 10 .... @150.00
11 thru 30 .... @100.00
31 thru 61 .... @100.00
62 Oct.–Dec., 1960 .... 100.00

PHANTOM, THE
Oct., 1987
1 JO,A:Modern Phantom,13th
  Phantom 3.00
2 JO,Murder Trial in Manhattan ... 3.00
3 JO,A:Chessman............. 3.00
4 JO,V:Chessman,final issue 3.00

PHANTOM, THE
1989–90
1 LMc,V:Gun Runners 3.00
2 LMc,V:Gun Runners 2.50
3 LMc,V:Drug Smugglers 2.50
4 LMc,In America,A:Diana Palner.. 2.50
5 LMc,Racial Riots 2.50
6 LMc,in Africa,Toxic Waste
  Problem 2.50
7 LMc,Gold Rush 2.50
8 LMc,Train Surfing 2.50
9 LMc,The Slave Trade 2.50
10 LMc,Famine in Khagana....... 2.50
11 LMc,Phantom/Diana Wedding
   proposal................. 2.50
12 LMc,Phantom framed for
   murder................. 2.50
13 W:Phantom & Diana Palner
   C:Mandrake last issue....... 2.50

PHANTOM STRANGER
Aug.–Sept., 1952
1 .... 3,000.00
2 .... 1,700.00
3 thru 5.............. @1,500.00
6, June-July, 1953 .... 1,500.00

PHANTOM STRANGER
May-June, 1969
1 CI rep.&new material 300.00
2 CI rep.&new material 125.00
3 CI rep.&new material 125.00
4 NA,I:Tala,1st All-new issue ... 150.00
5 MSy,MA,A:Dr.13........... 100.00
6 MSy,A:Dr.13.............. 100.00
7 JAp,V:Tala 100.00
8 JAp,A:Dr.13 .... 100.00
9 JAp,A:Dr.13 .... 100.00
10 JAp,I:Tannarak 100.00
11 JAp,V:Tannarak............ 50.00
12 JAp,TD,Dr.13 solo story 50.00
13 JAp,TD,Dr.13 solo.......... 50.00
14 JAp,TD,Dr.13 solo.......... 50.00
15 JAp,ATh(rep),TD,Iron Messiah,
   giant-size.............. 60.00
16 JAp,TD,MMes(rep)Dr.13 solo
   giant-size.............. 60.00
17 JAp,I:Cassandra Craft,
   giant-size.............. 60.00
18 TD,Dr.13 solo, giant-size 60.00
19 JAp,TD,Dr.13 solo, giant-size .. 60.00
20 JAp,Child Shall Lead Them ... 50.00
21 JAp,TD,Dr.13 solo.......... 30.00
22 JAp,TD,I:Dark Circle........ 30.00
23 JAp,MK,I:Spawn-Frankenstein . 30.00
24 JAp,MA,Spawn Frankenstein .. 50.00
25 JAp,MA,Spawn Frankenstein .. 50.00
26 JAp,A:Frankenstein.......... 60.00
27 V:Dr. Zorn 50.00
28 BU:Spawn of Frankenstein 50.00
29 V:Dr.Zorn,BU:Frankenstein 50.00
30 E:Spawn of Frankenstein 50.00
31 B:BU:Black Orchid 55.00
32 NR,BU:Black Orchid 30.00
33 MGr,A:Deadman 40.00
34 BU:Black Orchid 30.00

35 BU:Black Orchid 30.00
36 BU:Black Orchid 30.00
37 Crimson Gold,BU:BlackOrchid . 30.00
38 Images of the Dead 30.00
39 A:Deadman............... 40.00
40 A:Deadman............... 40.00
41 A:Deadman............... 40.00

PHANTOM STRANGER
Oct., 1987–Jan., 1988
1 MMi,CR,V:Eclipso 3.00
2 and 4 MMi,CR,V:Eclipso ..... @3.00

PHANTOM ZONE, THE
Jan., 1982
1 GD/TD,A:Jax-Ur............. 2.50
2 GC/TD,A:JLA............... 2.50
3 GC/TD,A:Mon-El............ 2.50
4 GC/TD 2.50

PICTURE STORIES FROM THE BIBLE
Autumn, 1942–43
1 thru 4 Old Testament ...... @300.00
1 thru 3 New Testament ..... @400.00

PINKY AND THE BRAIN
Warner Bros./DC, 1996
1 from animated TV series 3.00
2 thru 27 .... @3.00

PLASTIC MAN
[1st Series]
Nov.–Dec., 1966
1 GK,I:Dr.Drome (1966 series
  begins).................. 150.00
2 V:The Spider 75.00
3 V:Whed 75.00
4 V:Dr.Dome 75.00
5 1,001 Plassassins 75.00
6 V:Dr.Dome 60.00
7 O:Plastic Man Jr.,A:Original
  Plastic Man,Woozy Winks.... 60.00
8 V:The Weasel 60.00
9 V:Joe the Killer Pro 60.00
10 V:Doll Maker(series ends) 60.00
11 (1976 series begins) 15.00
12 I:Carrot-Man 15.00
13 A:Robby Reed............. 15.00
14 V:Meat By-Product & Sludge .. 15.00
15 I:Snuffer,V:Carrot-Man....... 15.00
16 V:Kolonel Kool 15.00
17 O:Plastic Man 15.00
18 V:Professor Klean.......... 15.00
19 I&Only App.Marty Meeker..... 15.00
20 V:Snooping Sneetches
   Oct.–Nov., 1977........... 15.00

PLASTIC MAN
1988–89
1 Mini-series,Origin retold....... 2.25
2 V:The Ooze Brothers.......... 2.25
3 In Los Angeles.............. 2.25
4 End-series,A:Superman....... 2.25

PLASTIC MAN
1999
Spec.#1 TTn(s),ALo,RBr,48-page .. 4.00

PLASTIC MAN
DC Dec. 2003
1 KB,O:Plastic Man............. 2.50
2 KB,Eel O'Brien on the Lam 3.00
3 KB,Eel O'Brien on the Lam 3.00
4 KB,Eel O'Brien on the Lam 3.00
5 KB,ghosts of his past......... 3.00
6 KB,Eel O'Brien,concl. 3.00

DC COMICS

7 Love Makes a Fella Woozy 3.00
8 Continuity Bandit,pt.1. . . . . 3.00
9 Continuity Bandit,pt.2. . . . . 3.00
10 Halloween issue 3.00
11 Homeland Security 3.00
12 KB. 3.00
13 KB. 3.00
14 KB. 3.00
15 thru 18 KB . . . . @3.00
19 Edwina Crisis, pt.2 . . . . 3.00
20 final issue 3.00
GN The Lost Annual, rep. 7.00

PLOP!
Sept.–Oct., 1973
1 SA-AA,GE,ShM 50.00
2 AA,SA 25.00
3 AA,SA 25.00
4 BW,SA 30.00
5 MA,MSy,SA,BWr 22.00
6 MSy,SA 20.00
7 SA 20.00
8 SA 20.00
9 SA 20.00
10 SA 20.00
11 ATh,SA 20.00
12 SA 20.00
13 WW(c),SA 22.00
14 WW,SA 22.00
15 WW(c),SA 22.00
16 SD,WW,SA 22.00
17 SA 22.00
18 SD,WW,SA 22.00
19 WW,SA 22.00
20 SA,WW 22.00
21 JO,WW 25.00
22 JO,WW,BW 25.00
23 BW,WW 25.00
24 SA,WW,Nov.–Dec., 1976 . . . . . 25.00

POWER COMPANY, THE
Jan., 2002
1 KBk,TG,V:Doctor Cyber 2.50
2 thru 6 KBk . . . . @2.50
7 thru 18 KBk 2.75

POWER OF SHAZAM!
1995–98
1 R:Captain Marvel 4.00
2 V:Arson Fiend 3.00
3 V:Ibac 3.00
4 JOy,R:Mary Marvel,Tawky,
    Tawny 3.00

Power of Shazam #22
© DC Comics, Inc.

5 JOy(c&a),F:Mary Marvel,
    V:Black Adam 3.00
6 R:Captain Marvel 3.00
7 V:Captain Nazi 3.00
8 R:Captain Marvel,Jr. 3.00
9 JOy,MM,V:Black Adam 3.00
10 JOy,MM,V:Seven Deadly
    Enemies of Man 3.00
11 JOy,MM,R:Ibis as Capt.Marvel . . 3.00
12 JOy,MM,How Billy Batson's
    father met Shazam 3.00
13 JOy,MM 3.00
14 JOy,GK,MM,F:CaptainMarvelJr . 3.00
15 JOy,MM,V:Mr.Mind 3.00
16 thru 18 . . . . @3.00
19 JOy(s),GK,MM,Captain Marvel
    Jr. V:Captain Nazi 3.00
20 JOy(s),PKr,MM,A:Superman . . . 3.00
21 JOy(s),PKr,MM,V:Liquidator . . . 2.50
22 JOy(s),PKr,MM,A:Batman 2.50
23 JOy(s),PKr,MM, ... 2.50
24 JOy(s),PKr,MM,V:Baron Blitz-
    krieg, prelude to new family . . . 2.50
25 JOy(s),PKr,MM,The Marvel
    Family '97 . . . . 2.50
26 JOy(s),PKr,MM,new Capt.
    Marvel framed for murder 2.50
27 JOy(s),PKr,MM,D:Captain
    Marvel 2.50
28 JOy(s),DG, V:Patty Patty
    Bang Bang 2.50
29 JOy(c),DG,F:Hoppy 2.50
30 JOy(c),PKr,DG,V:Mr. Finish. . . . 2.50
31 JOy,PKr,DG,Genesis x-over . . . 2.50
32 JOy,PKr,DG,Genesis aftermath. . 2.50
33 JOy,PKr,DG,Madam M, Sin. . . . 2.50
34 JOy,PKr,DG,F:Gangbuster 2.50
35 JOy,PKr,DG,Lightning &
    Stars, pt.2 x-over 2.50
36 JOy 2.50
37 JOy,MM,DG,F:Capt.Marvel Jr. . 2.50
38 JOy,PKr,DG,Monster Society
    of Evil, pt.1 . . . . 2.50
39 JOy,PKr,DG,Monster, pt.2 . . . . 2.50
40 JOy,PKr,DG,Monster, pt.3. . . . . 2.50
41 JOy,PKr,DG,Monster, pt.4 . . . . . 2.50
42 JOy,DG,new logo & design . . . 2.50
43 JOy,DG,I:Bulletgirl 2.50
44 JOy,DG,V:Chain Lightning 2.50
45 JOy,DG,A:JLA 2.50
46 JOy,DG,A:Superman 2.50
47 JOy,V:Black Adam, final issue . 2.50
Ann.#1 JOy(s),MM,Legends of
    the Dead Earth 3.00
Spec.#1,000,000 JOy,DG 2.50
GN Power of Shazam 7.50
GNv JOy(a&s),O:Captain Marvel. . 10.00
TPB JOy, reoffer 7.50

POWER OF THE ATOM
1988–89
1 1st Issue, Origin retold. 2.25
2 Return of Powers. 2.25
3 I:Strobe 2.25
4 A:Hawkman+bonus book #8 . . . . 2.25
5 DT,A:Elongated Man 2.25
6 JBy,V:Chronos 2.25
7 GN,Invasion,V:Khunds,Chronos . 2.25
8 GN,Invasion,V:Chronos 2.25
9 GN,A:Justice League. 2.25
10 GN,I:Humbug 2.25
11 GN,V:Paul Hoben 2.25
12 GN,V:Edg the Destroyer 2.25
13 GN,Blood Stream Journey 2.25
14 GN,V:Humbug 2.25
15 GN,V:Humbug. 2.25
16 GN,V:The CIA 2.25
17 GN,V:The Sting 2.25
18 GN,V:The CIA, last issue 2.25

POWERPUFF GIRLS
Warner Bros./DC March, 2000
1 . . . . 3.50
2 thru 70 . . . . @2.25
Double Whammy, rep. #1 & #2 . . . 4.00
Spec.Powerpuff Girls movie comic . 3.00

PREACHER
DC/Vertigo, 1995
1 I:Jesse Custer, Genesis. 22.00
2 Saint of Killers 18.00
3 GF(c),I:Angels 15.00
4 GF(c),V:Saint of Killers 10.00
5 Naked City,pt.1 . . . . 10.00
6 Naked City,pt.2 . . . . 10.00
7 Naked City,pt.3 . . . . 8.00
8 GEn,SDi,All in the Family,pt.1 . . 5.00
9 GEn,SDi,All in the Family,pt.2 . . 5.00
10 GEn,SDi,All in the Family,pt.3 . 5.00
11 GEn,SDi,All in the Family,pt.4 . . 5.00
12 GEn,SDi,All in the Family,pt.5 . 6.00
13 GEn,SDi,Hunters,pt.1 . . . . 5.00
14 GEn,SDi,Hunters,pt.2 (of 4) . . . 4.00
15 and 16. . . . . @4.00
17 Star captures Cassidy. 3.00
18 GEn(s),SDi,secret of Jesse
    Custer's cigarette lighter 3.00
19 GEn(s),SDi,Crusaders, pt.1 . . . 3.00
20 GEn(s),SDi,Crusaders, pt.2 . . . 3.00
21 GEn(s),SDi,Crusaders, pt.3 . . . 3.00
22 GEn(s),SDi,Crusaders, pt.4 . . . 3.00
23 GEn(s),SDi,Crusaders, pt.5 . . . 3.00
24 GEn(s),SDi,Crusaders, concl. . . 3.00
25 GEn(s),SDi,Cry Blood, Cry
    Erin 3.00
26 GEn(s),SDi,To the Streets of
    Manhattan I Wandered Away . . 2.50
27 GEn(s),SDi, Jessie & Tulip in
    New York, pt.1 . . . . 2.50
28 GEn(s),SDi, Jessie & Tulip in
    New York, pt.2 . . . . 2.50
29 GEn(s),SDi, south to New
    Orleans 2.50
30 GEn,SDi,in New Orleans 2.50
31 GEn,SDi,in New Orleans 2.50
32 GEn,SDi,in New Orleans 2.50
33 GEn,SDi,in New Orleans,concl. . 2.50
34 GEn,SDi,War in the Sun,pt.1 . . 2.50
35 GEn,SDi,War in the Sun,pt.2 . . 2.50
36 GEn,SDi,War in the Sun,pt.3 . . 2.50
37 GEn,SDi,War in the Sun,pt.4 . . 2.50
38 GEn,SDi,GF,Utah radioactive . . 2.50
39 GEn,SDi,GF,out of the desert. . . 2.50
40 GEn,SDi,GF,Arsefaced World. . . 2.50
41 . . . . 2.50
42 GEn(s),SDi,GF,V:Meatman. 2.50
43 GEn(s),SDi,GF,V:Meat Man . . . 2.50
44 GEn(s),SDi,GF,Gunther Hahn . . 2.50
45 GEn(s),SDi,GF,V:Meat Man . . . 2.50
46 GEn(s),SDi,GF,Miss Oatlash . . 2.50
47 GEn(s),SDi,GF,Salvation 2.50
48 GEn(s),SDi,GF,Salvation 2.50
49 GEn(s),SDi,GF,First Contact. . . 2.50
50 GEn(s),SDi,GF,48-page
    I:100 Bullets. 4.00
51 GEn(s),SDi,GF,Tulip's past,pt.1 4.00
52 GEn(s),SDi,GF,Tulip's past,pt.2 . 2.50
53 GEn(s),SDi,GF,road trip story. . . 2.50
54 GEn(s),SDi,GF,Jesse & Tulip . . 2.50
55 GEn(s),SKi,GF 2.50
56 GEn(s),GF. 2.50
57 GEn(s), ... 2.50
58 GEn(s),SDi, ... 2.50
59 thru 64 GEn(s),SDi,
    Alamo,pt.1 thru pt.6 . . . . @2.50
65 GEn(s),SDi,Alamo,pt.7 . . . . 5.00
66 GEn(s),SDi,Alamo,pt.8,
    final issue 5.00
GN Preacher Spec. Cassidy: Blood
    and Whisky, GEn(s) (1997) 6.00
GN Tall in the Saddle. 6.00

Spec. The Good Old Boys, parody . 5.50
Spec. The Story of You-Know-Who
    GEn(s),RCa,O:Arseface (1996) 5.00
Spec. One Man's War 5.00

PREACHER SPECIAL: SAINT OF KILLERS
DC/Vertigo, 1996
1 GEn(s),StP 5.00
2 GEn(s),StP 4.50
3 GEn(s),StP 3.50
4 GEn(s),StP 3.00

PREZ
Aug.–Sept., 1973
1 I:Prez (from Sandman #54) 40.00
2 thru 4 F:Prez 20.00

PRIDE & JOY
DC/Vertigo, May, 1997
[Mini-series]
1 (of 4) GEn(s),JHi, ... 2.50
2 GEn(s),JHi 2.50
3 GEn(s),JHi 2.50
4 GEn(s),JHi,concl 2.50
TPB (2004) 15.00

PRIMAL FORCE
1994–95
O New Team 2.25
1 Claw 2.25
2 thru 14 . . . . @2.25

PRINCE
DC/Piranha Press 1991
1 DCw,KW,based on rock star 7.00
1a Second printing 2.50
1b 3rd printing 2.00

PRINCESS NATASHA
June, 2006
1 (0f 4) 2.25
2 Undercover cheerleader 2.25
3 Robot Hamsters 2.25
4 concl 2.25

PRISONER, THE
1988–89
1 Based on TV series 4.00
2 By Hook or by Crook 4.00
3 Confrontation 4.00
4 Departure, final issue 4.00

PROPOSITION PLAYER
DC/Vertigo, Oct., 2000
1 (of 6) PGn,BWg, ... 2.50
2 thru 6 PGn,BWg, ... @2.50
TPB 15.00

PSYBA-RATS, THE
[Mini-Series], 1995
1 CDi,A:Robin 2.50
2 CDi,A:Robin 2.00
3 CDi,F:Razorsharp,final issue 2.00

PSYCHO, THE
1991
1 I:Psycho 9.00
2 Sonya Rescue 8.00
3 Psycho against the World 7.00

PULP FANTASTIC
DC/Vertigo, Dec., 1999
1 (of 3) HC,RBr,detective 2.50
2 HC,RBr 2.50

3 HC,RBr,conclusion 2.50

QUEST FOR CAMELOT
June, 1998
1-shot movie adaptation 5.00

QUESTION, THE
Feb., 1987
1 DCw,R:Question,I:Myra,A:Shiva . 3.00
2 thru 10 . . . . @2.50
11 thru 20 . . . . @2.50
21 thru 36 . . . . @2.50
Ann.#1 DCw,A:Batman,G.A. 3.00
Ann.#2 A:Green Arrow 4.00

QUESTION, THE
Nov., 2004
1 (of 6) F:Vic Sage 3.00
2 in Metropolis 3.00
3 Luthor's Science Spire 3.00
4 F:Superman 3.00
5 Sceince Spire 3.00
6 finale 3.00

QUESTION QUARTERLY
1990–92
1 DCw 4.50
2 DCw 4.00
3 DCw(c) Film 3.00
4 DCw,MM,Waiting for Phil 3.00
5 DCw,MMi,MM,last issue 3.00

RAGMAN
[1st Limited Series], 1976–77
1 I&O:Ragman 25.00
2 I:Opal 15.00
3 V:Mr. Big 10.00
4 JKu(1st interior on character) . . . 10.00
5 JKu,O:Ragman,final issue 10.00
[2nd Limited Series], 1991–92
1 PB,O:Ragman 3.00
2 PB,O:Ragman Powers 3.00
3 PB,Original Ragman 3.00
4 PB,Gang War 3.00
5 PB,V:Golem 3.00
6 PB,V:Golem,A:Batman 3.00
7 PB,V:Golem,A:Batman 3.00
8 PB,V:Golem,A:Batman 3.00

RAGMAN: CRY OF THE DEAD
1993–94
1 JKu(c),R:Ragman 3.50
2 JKu(c),A:Marinette 3.00
3 JKu(c),V:Marinette 3.00
4 JKu(c),Exorcism 3.00
5 JKu(c),V:Marinette 3.00
6 JKu(c),final issue 3.00

RANN/THANAGAR WAR, THE
May, 2005
1 MCa,F:Adam Strange 6.00
1a 2nd printing 4.00
2 MCa,V:Khund hordes 3.50
3 MCa 3.00
4 MCa 3.00
5 MCa 3.00
6 MCa, Infinite Crisis lead-in 3.00
TPB 13.00
Spec. Infinite Crisis 5.00

THE RAY
[Limited Series], 1992
1 JQ,ANi,I&O:Ray(Ray Torril) 5.00
2 JQ,ANi,I:G.A. Ray 3.00
3 JQ,ANi,A:G.A. Ray 3.00

The Ray #13 © DC Comics Inc.

4 JQ,ANi,V:Dr.Polaris 4.00
5 JQ,ANi,V:Dr.Polaris 3.00
6 JQ,ANi,C:Lobo,final issue 3.00
TPB In A Blaze of Power 10.00
[Regular Series], 1994–96
1 JQ(c),RPr,V:Brinestone,
    A:Superboy 3.00
1a Newsstand Ed. 2.25
2 RPr,V:Brinestone,A:Superboy . . 2.25
3 RPr,I:Death Masque 2.25
4 JQ(c),RPr,I:Death Masque,
    Dr. Polarus 2.25
5 JQ(c),RPr,V:G.A.Ray 2.25
6 thru 28 . . . . @2.25
Ann.#1 Year One Annual 4.00

REAL FACT COMICS
March-April, 1946
1 S&K,Harry Houdini story 1,000.00
2 S&K, Rin-Tin-Tin story 650.00
3 H.G. Wells story 500.00
4 Jimmy Stewart story,B:Just
    Imagine 550.00
5 Batman & Robin(c) 3,000.00
6 O:Tommy Tomorrow 2,000.00
7 The Flying White House 300.00
8 VF,A:Tommy Tomorrow 1,000.00
9 S&K,Glen Miller story 500.00
10 MMe(s),The Vigilante 500.00
11 EK,How the G-Men Capture
    Public Enemies! 250.00
12 How G-Men are Trained 250.00
13 Dale Evans story 700.00
14 Will Rogers Story,Diary of
    Death 300.00
15 A:The Master Magician-
    Thurston,A-Bomb 300.00
16 A:Four Reno Brothers,
    T.Tommorrow 800.00
17 I Guard an Armored Car 250.00
18 The Mystery Man of
    Tombstone 250.00
19 Weapon that Won the West . . 250.00
20 JKu,Daniel Boone 275.00
21 JKu,KitCarson,July-Aug.,1949 250.00

REAL SCREEN COMICS
Spring, 1945
1 B:Fox & the Crow,Flippity
    & Flop 1,400.00
2 inc. Tito and His Burrito 650.00
3 (fa) 400.00
4 thru 7 (fa) . . . . @250.00
8 thru 11 (fa) . . . . @200.00
12 thru 20 (fa) . . . . @175.00

Real Screen Comics #38
© DC Comics, Inc.

21 thru 30 (fa) . . . . @150.00
31 thru 40 (fa) . . . . @125.00
41 thru 128 (fa) . . . . @100.00
Becomes:

TV SCREEN CARTOONS
129 thru 137. . . . . @100.00
138 Jan.–Feb., 1961 . . . . 100.00

REALWORLDS
March, 2000
GN Batman, 48-pg. 6.00
GN Wonder Woman, 48-pg. 6.00
GN JLA, 48-pg. 6.00
GN Superman 6.00

R.E.B.E.L.S '94–'96
0 New team. 2.50
1 L.E.G.I.O.N.,Green Lantern 2.50
2 Dissent. 2.50
3 Brains. 2.50
4 Ship goes Insane. 2.50
5 F:Dox. 2.25
6 Dox Defeated. 2.25
7 John Sin. 2.25
8 V:Galactic Bank. 2.25
9 F:Dox,Ignea,Garv,Strata 2.25
10 V:World Bank. 2.25
11 Comet's Tail. 2.25
12 F:Iceman Assassin 2.25
13 Underworld Unleashed tie-in . . . 2.25
14 F:Lyrl Dox 2.25
15 V:Lyrl Dox 2.25
16 V:Lyrl Dox's satellite 2.25

RED TORNADO
1985
1 CI/FMc. 3.00
2 CI/FMc,A:Superman 3.00
3 & 4 CI/FMc. . . . . @3.00

REIGN OF THE ZODIAC
Aug. 2003
1 thru 8 BWi,CDo . . . . @2.75

REMARKABLE WORLDS
OF PHINEAS B. FUDDLE
DC/Paradox, 1999
1 (of 4) F:Angus & McKee 6.00
2 . . . . 6.00
3 ancient India 6.00
4 concl. 6.00
TPB 192-page 20.00

RESTAURANT AT THE
END OF THE UNIVERSE
1994
1 Adapt. 2nd book in Hitchhikers'
  Guide to the Galaxy,
  I:The Restaurant 7.00
2 V:The Meal 7.00
3 Final issue 7.00

RESURRECTION MAN
March, 1997
1 DAn(s),JG,lenticular death's
  head cover. 6.00
2 DAn(s),JG,V:Amazo. 5.00
3 DAn(s),JG,Scorpion Memories
  pt.1 (of 3) 4.00
4 DAn(s),JG,Scorpion,pt.2 . . . . . 4.00
5 DAn(s),JG,Scorpion,pt.3, ... 4.00
6 DAn&ALa(s),JoP,Genesis tie-in . . 3.00
7 DAn&ALa(s),TGb,BG,A:Batman . 3.00
8 DAn&ALa(s),BG,Big Howler. . . . 3.00
9 DAn&ALa(s),F:Hitman, pt.1 . . . 3.00
10 DAn&ALa(s),F:Hitman, pt.2 . . . 3.00
11 DAn&ALa(s), Origin of the
  Species,pt.1 . . . . 2.50
12 DAn&ALa(s), Origin of the
  Species,pt.2 . . . . 2.50
13 DAn&ALa(s),Candy Man 2.50
14 DAn&ALa(s),really dead? 2.50
15 DAn&ALa(s),JG,V:Rider 2.50
16 DAn&ALa(s),BG,Avenging
  Angels x-over pt.1 . . . . 2.50
17 DAn&ALa(s),BG,Avenging
  Angels x-over pt.3 . . . . 2.50
18 DAn&ALa(s),A:Phantom Stranger,
  Deadman 2.50
19 DAn&ALa(s),Cape Fear, pt.1 . . 2.50
20 DAn&ALa(s),Cape Fear, pt.2 . . 2.50
21 DAn&ALa(s),Cape Fear, pt.3 . . 2.50
22 DAn&ALa(s) 2.50
23 DAn&ALa(s),Resurrection
  Woman 2.50
24 DAn&ALa(s) 2.50
25 DAn&ALa(s)Millennium
  Meteor,pt.1 . . . . 2.50
26 DAn&ALa(s)Millennium Meteor,
  pt.2,A:Superman, Titans 2.50
27 DAn&ALa(s)Millennium Meteor,
  pt.3,final issue 2.50
Spec.#1,000,000 DAn&ALa(s). . . . 2.50

RICHARD DRAGON,
KUNG FU FIGHTER
April-May, 1975
1 O:Richard Dragon 15.00
2 JSn/AM 13.00
3 JK. 11.00
4 thru 8 RE/WW . . . . @10.00
9 thru 17 RE . . . . @8.00
18 Nov.–Dec., 1977 . . . . 8.00

RICHARD DRAGON
May 2004
1 thru 12 CDi(s),SMc . . . . @2.50

RIMA,
THE JUNGLE GIRL
April-May, 1974
1 NR,I:Rima,O:Pt. 1 . . . . 25.00
2 NR,O:Pt.2 . . . . 15.00
3 NR,O:Pt.3 . . . . 15.00
4 NR,O:Pt.4 . . . . 15.00
5 NR 15.00
6 NR 15.00
7 April-May, 1975 . . . . 15.00

RING, THE
[OF THE NIEBLUNG]
1989
1 GK,Opera Adaption 12.00
2 GK,Sigfried's Father's Sword . . . 7.00
3 GK,to save Brunhilde. 6.00
4 GK, final issue 6.00
TPB rep.#1 thru #4 . . . . 20.00

RIP HUNTER,
TIME MASTER
March-April, 1961
1 . . . . 1,100.00
2 . . . . 500.00
3 thru 5 . . . . @350.00
6 and 7 Ath . . . . @250.00
8 thru 15 . . . . @200.00
16 thru 20 . . . . @200.00
21 thru 28 . . . . @150.00
29 Nov.–Dec., 1965 . . . . 150.00

ROBIN
[1st Limited Series], 1991
1 TL,BB(c),Trial,pt.1(&Poster). . . . 5.00
1a 2nd printing 2.50
1b 3rd printing 2.25
2 TL,BB(c) Trial,pt.2 . . . . 3.00
2a 2nd printing 2.25
3 TL,BB(c) Trial,pt.3 . . . . 3.00
4 TL,Trial,pt.4 . . . . 3.00
5 TL,Final issue,A:Batman 3.00
TPB BB(c),rep 8.00

[2nd Limited Series], 1991
[ROBIN II: THE JOKER'S WILD]
1 Direct,Hologram(c)Joker face . . 3.00
1a (c)Joker straightjacket 2.25
1b (c)Joker standing 2.25
1c (c)Batman 2.25
1d Newsstand(no hologram). 2.25
1e collectors set,extra holo. 10.00
2 Direct,Hologram(c) Robin/Joker
  Knife 2.50
2a (c)Joker/Robin-Dartboard 2.25
2b (c)Robin/Joker-Hammer 2.25
2c Newsstand (no hologram). 2.25
2d collectors set,extra holo. 9.00
3 Direct,Holo(c)Robin standing . . . 2.50
3a (c)Robin swinging 2.25
3b Newsstand(no hologram). 2.25
3c collectors set,extra holo. 7.00
4 Direct,Hologram 2.50
4a Newsstand (no hologram) 2.25
4b collectors set,extra holo. 2.25
Collectors set (#1 thru #4). 30.00

[3rd Limited Series], 1992–93
[ROBIN III: CRY OF THE
HUNTRESS]
1 TL,A:Huntress,Collector's Ed.
  movable(c),poster 3.00
1a MZ(c),Newsstand Ed. 2.25
2 TL,V:KGBeast,A:Huntress 2.75
2a MZ(c),Newsstand Ed. 2.25
3 TL,V:KGBeast,A:Huntress 2.75
3a MZ(c),newsstand Ed. 2.25
4 TL,V:KGBeast,A:Huntress 2.75
4a MZ(c),newsstand Ed. 2.25
5 TL,V:KGBeast,A:Huntress 2.75
5a MZ(c),newsstand Ed. 2.25
6 TL,V:KGBeast,King Snake,
  A:Huntress. 2.75
6a MZ(c),newsstand Ed. 2.25

[Regular Series], 1993–2002
1 B:CDi(s),TG,SHa,V:Speedboyz . . 4.00
1a Newstand Ed. 2.25
2 TG,V:Speedboyz 2.50
3 TG,V:Cluemaster,
  Electrocutioner. 2.50

Robin, Regular Series #12
© DC Comics Inc.

4 TG,V:Cluemaster,Czknown,
   Electrocutioner. 2.50
5 TG,V:Cluemaster,Czknown,
   Electrocutioner. 2.50
6 TG,A:Huntress 2.50
7 TG,R:Robin's Father 2.50
8 TG,KnightsEnd#5,A:Shiva 3.00
9 TG,Knights End:Aftermath 2.50
10 TG,Zero Hour,V:Weasel 2.50
11 New Batman 2.50
12 Robin vs. thugs 2.50
13 V:Steeljacket 2.50
14 CDi(s),TG,Return of Bruce
   Wayne,Troika,pt.4 . . . . 3.00
14a Collector's edition 3.00
15 Cluemaster Mystery 2.50
16 F:Spoiler 2.50
17 I:Silver Monkey,V:King Snake,Lynx
   [New Miraweb format begins] . . 2.50
18 Gotham City sabotaged 2.50
19 V:The General. 2.50
20 F:Robin. 2.50
21 Ninja Camp,pt.1 . . . . 2.50
22 CDi,TG,Ninja Camp,pt.2 . . . . 2.50
23 CDi,Underworld Unleashed tie-in 2.50
24 CDi,V:Charaxes 2.50
25 CDi,F:Green Arrow 2.50
26 CDi,The Hard Lessons 2.50
27 CDi,Contagion. 2.50
28 CDi,Contagion: conclusion 2.50
29 CDi,FFo,SnW,A:Maxie Zeus 2.50
30 CDi,FFo,SnW,A:Maxie Zeus 2.50
31 CDi(s),A:Wildcat 2.50
32 CDi(s),Legacy, pt. 3 x-over. 2.50
33 CDi(s),Legacy, pt.7 x-over 2.50
34 CDi(s),JhD,action at a
   Shakespear play 2.50
35 CDi(s),Robin & Spoiler, Final
   Night tie-in 2.50
36 CDi(s),V:Toyman, The General. . 2.50
37 CDi(s),V:The General, Toyman . . 2.50
38 CDi(s),. 2.50
39 CDi(s), pt.2 . . . . 2.50
40 CDi(s), ... 2.50
41 CDi(s),F:Tim and Ariana 2.50
42 CDi(s),F:Crocky the Crocodile . . 2.50
43 CDi(s),A:Spoiler 2.50
44 CDi(s) Pt.2 (of 2). 2.50
45 CDi(s) Tim Drake grounded 2.50
46 CDi(s) Genesis tie-in. 2.50
47 CDi,V:General, pt.1 . . . . 2.50
48 CDi,V:General, pt.2. . . . . 2.50
49 CDi,to Paris. 2.50

50 CDi(s),F:Lady Shiva & King
   Snake, 48pg 3.50
51 CDi(s) 2.50
52 CDi(s) Cataclysm x-over,pt.7 . . . 3.00
53 CDi(s),SnW,Cataclysm concl. . . . 3.00
54 CDi(s),SnW,Aftershock 2.50
55 CDi(s),SnW, Brotherhood of
   the Fist x-over, pt.3 . . . . 2.50
56 CDi(s),SnW,tearful turning point. 2.50
57 CDi(s),SnW,A:Spoiler 2.50
58 CDi(s),SnW,A:Spoiler 2.50
59 CDi(s),SnW,V:Steeljacket 2.50
60 CDi(s),SnW,Alvin Draper 2.50
61 CDi(s),SnW,V:Phil Delinger 2.50
62 CDi(s),SnW,A:Flash, pt.1 . . . . . . 2.50
63 CDi(s),SnW,A:Flash, pt.2 . . . . . . 2.50
64 CDi(s),SnW,A:Flash, pt.3 . . . . . . 2.50
65 CDi(s),SnW,A:Spoiler 2.50
66 CDi(s),SnW,V:demons 2.50
67 CDi(s),SnW,No Man's Land . . . 2.50
68 CDi(s),No Man's Land 2.50
69 CDi(s),No Man's Land 2.50
70 CDi(s),No Man's Land 2.50
71 CDi(s),V:Killer Croc. 2.50
72 CDi(s) 2.50
73 CDi(s),F:Batgirl 2.50
74 CDi(s),F:Batman & Nightwing. . . 2.50
75 CDi(s),48-pg. 3.50
76 CDi(s),R:Man-Bat 2.50
77 CDi(s),I:Jaeger 2.50
78 CDi(s),V:Arrakhat 2.50
79 CDi(s),F:Green Arrow 2.50
80 CDi(s),A:Star. 2.50
81 CDi(s),MPn,. 2.50
82 CDi(s),Spoiler,Star. 2.50
83 CDi,Vacation time 2.50
84 CDi,A:Lagoon Boy 2.50
85 CDi,This issue: Batman dies! . . . 2.50
86 Officer Down x-over,pt.2 . . . . 5.00
87 CDi,A:Spoiler 2.50
88 CDi,Road trip 2.50
89 CDi,to Himalayas 2.50
90 CDi,V:mini-yeti 2.50
91 CDi,F:Danny Temple. 2.50
92 CDi,SBe,A:Batman,Spoiler 2.50
93 CDi,F:Spoiler. 2.50
94 CDi,F:Spoiler,Wesley 2.50
95 CDi,Joker:Last Laugh tie-in 2.50
96 CDi,Last Laugh aftermath. 2.50
97 CDi,F:Normandy. 2.50
98 Bruce Wayne:Murderer,pt.8 . . . . 5.00
99 Bruce Wayne:Murderer,pt.11 . . . 5.00
100 CDi,Spoiler,48-pg. 2.50
101 WorldWithoutYoungJustice,pt.3 2.50
102 Spoiler. 2.50
103 Nocturna's secret 2.50
104 Astrology Lady 2.50
105 riddle of Natalia 2.50
106 A:Batman 2.50
107 F:Charaxis. 2.50
108 F:Charaxis. 2.50
109 V:Charaxis 2.50
110 F:Nightwing 2.50
111 F:Spoiler 2.50
112 to Pennsylvania 2.50
113 V:The Riddler 2.50
114 The Wrong Town 2.50
115 The Wrong Town 2.50
116 Identity compromised 2.50
117 Identity compromised 2.50
118 Traitor's identity 2.50
119 Traitor's identity 2.50
120 Hell in a handbasket. 2.50
121 BWg(s),Johnny Got His Gun . . 4.00
122 BWg(s),Bad to the Bone. 3.00
123 BWg(s),Nemesis. 3.00
124 F:Spoiler 3.00
125 BWg(s),secret identity 3.00
126 BWg(s),search for new Robin. . 4.00
127 BWg(s),Girl Wonder,Batman . . 3.00
128 BWg(s),V:Scarab 2.50
129 War Games,Act 1,pt.5 . . . . 2.50

130 War Games,Act 2,pt.5 . . . . 2.50
131 War Games,Act 3,pt.4 . . . . 2.50
132 Fresh Blood, x-over, pt.1 . . . . . 2.50
133 Fresh Blood, x-over, pt.3 . . . . . 2.50
134 Bludhaven. 2.50
135 Rising Sun Archer & Dark Rider 2.50
136 V:Dark Rider 2.50
137 Rising Sun Archer & Dark Rider 2.50
138 V:Penguin 2.50
139 SMc,V:Junkyard Dog 2.50
140 SMc,F:The Veteran. 2.50
141 Black Ops opportunity. 2.50
142 Old Flame 2.50
143 Omac tie-in 2.50
144 Omac tie-in 2.50
145 A:Shadowpact. 2.50
146 F:Teen Titans 2.50
147 F:Teen Titans 2.50
148 Wanted for Murder 2.50
149 Robin: Boy Wanted. 2.50
150 Who Framed Robin?. 3.00
151 League of Assassins job offer. . 3.00
152 V:Captain Boomerang. 3.00
153 V:Captain Boomerang. 3.00
154 Kidnappings 3.00
155 Superhero wannabe 3.00
156 A Life to save 3.00
157 F:Klarion the Witch Boy 3.00
158 F:Klarion the Witch Boy 3.00
159 A first date. 3.00
160 New drug epidemic. 3.00
161 V:Lords of the Avenues. 3.00
162 Save the Lords of the Avenues 3.00
163 V:The Jury. 3.00
164 V:Dodge 3.00
165 Hospital ward hostage 3.00
166 F:Zatara & Ravager 3.00
167 Boy Wonder 3.00
Ann.#1 TL,Eclipso tie-in,V:Anarky . . 3.00
Ann.#2 KD,JL,Bloodlines#10,
   I:Razorsharp 2.75
Ann.#3 Elseworlds Story 3.25
Ann.#4 Year One Annual 3.00
Ann.#5 CDi,Legends of the Dead
   Earth 3.00
Ann.#5 Legends o/t Dead Earth . . . 3.00
Ann.#6 Pulp Heroes (Western),
   CDi(s) 4.00
Ann. #7 F:Ra's Al Ghul 4.00
Spec.#1,000,000 CDi(s),SnW 2.00
Spec. Robin/Argent Double Shot
   DJu,CDi,V:Spoiler x-over (1997) 2.00
80-page Giant #1 CDi 6.00

ROBIN PLUS
1996
1 MWa&BAu(s), F:Bart Allen, skiing
   rips, V:Mystral 3.00
2 LKa,CDi,AWi,ALa,F:Fang 3.00

ROBIN 3000
1992
1 CR,Elseworlds,V:Skulpt. 5.25
2 CR,Elseworlds,V:Skulpt. 5.25

ROBIN: YEAR ONE
October, 2000
1 CDi,SBe,F:Dick Grayson 5.00
2 CDi,SBe,F:Dick Grayson 5.00
3 CDi,SBe,RbC,F:Dick Grayson . . . 5.00
4 CDi,SBe,concl. 5.00
TPB series rep. 15.00

ROBIN HOOD TALES
1957–58
7 . . . . 500.00
8 thru 14 . . . . @400.00

All comics prices listed are for *Near Mint* condition.

ROBOTECH DEFENDERS
1985
1 MA,mini-series 3.50
2 MA 3.00

ROGAN GOSH
DC/Vertigo, 1994
1 PF PrM(s) (From Revolver) 7.25

Romance Trail #1
© DC Comics Inc.

ROMANCE TRAIL
1949–50
1 EK,ATh 900.00
2 EK 400.00
3 EK,ATh 425.00
4 ATh 350.00
5 . . . . 300.00
6 EK 300.00

RONIN
July, 1983
1 FM,1:Billy 6.00
2 FM,I:Casey 5.00
3 FM,V:Agat 5.00
4 FM,V:Agat 5.00
5 FM,V:Agat 6.00
6 FM,D:Billy 8.00
Paperback, FM inc. Gatefold 12.00

ROOTS OF THE SWAMP THING
July, 1986
1 BWr,rep.SwampThing#1&#2 . . . 3.50
2 BWr,rep.SwampThing#3&#4 . . . 3.50
3 BWr,rep.SwampThing#5&#6 . . . 3.50
4 BWr,rep.SwampThing#7&#8 . . . 3.50
5 BWr,rep.SwampThing#9&#10,
   H.O.S. #92, final issue 3.50

ROSE & THORN
Dec. 2003
1 thru 6 DGr . . . . @3.00

RUDOLPH THE RED– NOSED REINDEER
Dec., 1950
1950 . . . . 275.00
1951 thru 1954 . . . . @150.00
1955 thru 1962 Winter . . . . . @125.00

RUSH CITY
Nov., 2006
1 CDi, Racing thru New York City . . 3.00
2 CDi, Under the streets 3.00
3 CDi, A:Black Canary 3.00
4 CDi, Missing twin doubles 3.00
5 CDi, Death race with the mob . . . 3.00
6 CDi,finale 3.00

SAGA OF RAS AL GHUL
1988
1 NA,DG,reprints 6.00
2 rep. 5.00
3 rep.Batman #242&#243 . . . . 5.00
4 rep.Batman #244&#245 . . . . 5.00
TPB reps 18.00

SAGA OF THE SWAMP THING
1982–85
1 JmP(s),TY,DSp,O:Swamp Thing,
   BU:PhantomStranger 7.00
2 Ph(c),TY,DSp,I:Grasp 4.00
3 TY,DSp, V:Vampires 4.00
4 TY,TD,V:Demon 4.00
5 TY,Scream of Hungry Flesh 4.00
6 TY,I:General Sunderland 4.00
7 TYmHaunting of Amanda Dove . . 4.00
8 TY,Here's Lookin' at You, Kid 4.00
9 TY,Prelude to Holocaust 4.00
10 TY,Number of the Beast 4.00
11 TY,I:Golem 4.00
12 LWn(s),TY 4.00
13 TY,D:Grasp 4.00
14 A:Phantom Stranger 4.00
15 TY,BHa,Empires Made of Sand . 4.00
16 SBi,JTo,TY,Secret Truths 5.00
17 I:Matthew Cable 5.00
18 JmP(s),LWn(s),SBi,JTo,BWr,
   R:Arcane 5.00
19 JmP(s),SBi,JTo,V:Arcane 5.00
20 B:AMo(s),Day,JTo(i),D:Arcane
   (Original incarnation) 22.00
21 SBi,JTo,O:Swamp Thing,I:Floronic
   Man,D:General Sunderland . . . 20.00
22 SBi,JTo,O:Floronic Man 15.00
23 SBi,JTo,V:Floronic Man 15.00
24 SBi,JTo,V:Floronic Man,A:JLA,
   In Arkham 15.00
25 SBi,A:Jason Blood,I:Kamara . . 16.00
26 SBi,A:Demon,
   D:Matthew Cable 10.00
27 SBi,D:Kamara,A:Demon 10.00
28 SwM,Burial of Alec Holland 10.00
29 SBi,JTo,R:Arcane 10.00
30 SBi,AA,D:Abby,C:Joker,
   V:Arcane 9.00
31 RV,JTo,D:Arcane 9.00
32 SwM,Tribute to WK Pogo strip . . 9.00
33 rep.H.O.S.#92,A:Cain & Abel . . . 9.00
34 SBi,JTo,Swamp Thing & Abby
   Fall in Love 9.00
35 SBi,JTo,Nukeface,pt.1 . . . . 9.00
36 SBi,JTo,Nukeface,pt.2 . . . . 9.00
37 RV,JTo,I:John Constantine,
   American Gothic,pt.1 . . . . 40.00
38 SnW,JTo,V:Water-Vampires
   (Pt.1) A:J.Constantine 9.00
39 SBi,JTo,V:Water-Vampires
   (Pt.2) A:J.Constantine 9.00
40 SBi,JTo,C:J.Constantine,
   The Curse 9.00
41 SBi,AA,Voodoo Zombies #1 . . . . 4.00
42 SBi,JTo,RoR,
   Voodoo Zombies #2 . . . . 4.00
43 SnW,RoR,Windfall,
   I:Chester Williams 4.00
44 SBi,JTo,RoR,V:Serial Killer,
   C:Batman,Constantine,Mento . . 5.00

45 SnW,AA,Ghost Dance 4.00
Ann.#1 MT,TD,Movie Adaption . . . 4.00
Ann.#2 AMo(s),E:Arcane,A:Deadman,
   Phantom Stranger,Spectre,
   Demon,Resurrection of Abby . . 8.00
Becomes:

SWAMP THING

SAMURAI JACK
Warner Bros./DC July, 2002
Spec. #1 64-pg. 4.00

SANDMAN
[1st Regular Series], 1974–75
1 JK,I&O:Sandman,I:General
   Electric 100.00
2 V:Dr.Spider 50.00
3 Brain that Blanked
   out the Bronx 50.00
4 JK,Panic in the Dream Stream . 50.00
5 JK,Invasion of the Frog Men . . . 50.00
6 JK,WW,V:Dr.Spider 55.00

[2nd Regular Series], 1989–93
1 B:NGa(s),SK,I:2nd Sandman . . . 45.00
2 SK,A:Cain,Abel 20.00
3 SK,A:John Constantine 15.00
4 SK,A:Demon 15.00
5 SK,A:Mr.Miracle,J'onn J'onzz . . 15.00
6 V:Doctor Destiny 10.00
7 V:Doctor Destiny 10.00
8 Sound of her wings,F:Death . . . 25.00
8a Guest Ed.Pin-Up Cover 65.00
9 Tales in the Sand,Doll's House
   prologue 10.00
10 B:Doll's House,A:Desire
   & Despair,I:Brut & Glob 10.00
11 MovingIn,A:2ndS-man 10.00
12 Play House,D;2ndS'man 10.00
13 Men of Good Fortune,A:Death,
   Lady Constantine 10.00
14 Collectors,D:Corinthian 10.00
15 Into' Night,DreamVortex 10.00
16 E:Doll's House,Lost Hearts 10.00
17 Calliope 10.00
18 Dream of a 1000 Cats 10.00
18a error pg.1 . . . . 25.00
19 Midsummer Nights Dream 6.00
19a error copy 22.00
20 Strange Death Element Girl,
   A:Death 7.00
21 Family Reunion,B:Season
   of Mists 8.00
22 Season of Mists,I:Daniel Hall . . 13.00
23 Season of Mists 7.00
24 Season of Mists 7.00
25 Season of Mists 7.00
26 Season of Mists 6.00
27 E:Season of Mists 6.00
28 Ownership of Hell 6.00
29 A:Lady J.Constantine 5.00
30 Ancient Rome;A:Death,Desire . . 5.00
31 Ancient Rome,pt.2 . . . . 5.00
32 B:The Game of You 5.00
33 The Game of You 5.00
34 The Game of You 4.00
35 The Game of You 4.00
36 The Game of You,48pgs 5.00
37 The Game of You,Epilogue 4.00
38 Convergence 4.00
39 Convergence,A:Marco Polo 4.00
40 Convergence,A:Cain,Abel,Eve,
   Matthew the Raven 4.00
41 JIT,VcL,(i),B:Brief Lives,
   F:Endless 4.00
42 JIT,VcL,(i),F:Delirium,Dream . . . 4.00
43 JIT,VcL,(i),A:Death,Etain 4.00
44 JIT,VcL,(i),R:Corinthian,
   Destruction 4.00
45 JIT,VcL,(i),F:Tiffany,
   Ishtar(Belli) 4.00

Sandman #1
© *DC Comics, Inc.*

46 JIT,VcL,(i),F:Morpheus/Bast,
A:Aids insert story,F:Death 4.00
DC/Vertigo, 1994–96
47 JIT,VcL,(i),A:Endless 4.00
48 JIT,VcL,(i),L:Destruction 4.00
49 JIT,VcL,(i),E:Brief Lives,
F:Orpheus 4.00
50 DMc(c),CR,Tales of Baghdad,
pin-upsby TM,DMc,MK 5.00
50a Gold Ed. 22.00
51 BT,MBu(i),B:Inn at the end of
the World,Gaheris' tale 4.00
52 BT,MBu(i),JWk,Cluracan's
Story 4.00
53 BT,DG,MBu(i),MZi,Hob's
Leviathan 4.00
54 BT,MiA,MBu(i),R:Prez 4.00
55 SAp,VcL,BT,MBu(i),F:Klaproth
Cerements's Story 4.00
56 BT,MBu(i),DG(i),SLi(i),GyA,TyH(i),
E:Inn at the end of the World,
C:Endless 4.00
57 MaH,B:Kindly Ones,Inc.American
Freak Preview 5.00
58 MaH,Kindly Ones,pt.2,
A:Lucifer 5.00
59 MaH,Kindly Ones,pt.3,R:Fury . . . 5.00
60 MaH,Kindly Ones,pt.4 . . . . 5.00
61 MaH,Kindly Ones,pt.5 . . . . 5.00
62 Kindly Ones,pt.6,Murder 5.00
63 MaH,Kindly Ones,pt.7,
A:Rose Walker. 5.00
64 Kindly Ones,pt.8 . . . . 5.00
65 MaH,Kindly Ones,pt.9,Dream
Kingdom 5.00
66 MaH,Kindly Ones,pt.10 . . . . 5.00
67 MaH,Kindly Ones,pt.11 . . . . 5.00
68 MaH,Kindly Ones,pt.12 . . . . 5.00
69 MaH,Kindly Ones finale 6.00
70 The Wake,pt.1 . . . . 4.00
71 The Wake,pt.2 . . . . 4.00
72 NGa,DMc,The Wake,pt.3 . . . . . . 4.00
73 NGa,Sunday Mourning 4.00
74 NGa,V:Lord of Dreams 4.00
75 NGa,last issue 5.00
Sandman Covers, 1989–96 . . . . . . 40.00
Spec.BT,Glow in the Dark(c),The
Legend of Orpheus,
(inc. Portrait Gallery) 6.00
1 special edition, 48-pg.(2006) 0.50

SANDMAN MYSTERY THEATRE
DC/Vertigo, 1993–99
1 B:MWg(s),GyD,R:G.A.Sandman,
B:Tarantula,I:Mr.Belmont,
Dian Belmont. 5.00
2 GyD,V:Tarantula. 3.00
3 GyD,V:Tarantula. 3.00
4 GyD,E:Tarantula 3.00
5 JWk,B:The Face 3.00
6 JWk,The Face #2 . . . . 3.00
7 JWk,The Face #3 . . . . 3.00
8 JWk,E:The Face 3.00
9 RGT,B:The Brute,I:Rocket
Ramsey. 3.00
10 RGT,The Brute#2 . . . . 3.00
11 RGT,The Brute#3 . . . . 3.00
12 RGT,E:The Brute 3.00
13 GyD,B:The Vamp 3.00
14 GyD,The Vamp#2 . . . . 3.00
15 GyD,The Vamp#3 . . . . 3.00
16 GyD,E:The Vamp 3.00
17 GyD,B:The Scorpion. 3.00
18 GyD,The Scorpion,pt.2 . . . . 3.00
19 GyD,The Scorpion,pt.3 . . . . 3.00
20 GyD,The Scorpion,pt.4 . . . . 3.00
21 Dr. Death. 3.00
22 Dr. Death,pt.2 . . . . 3.00
23 Dr. Death,pt.3 . . . . 3.00
24 Dr. Death,pt.4 . . . . 3.00
25 The Butcher,pt.1 . . . . 3.00
26 The Butcher,pt.2 . . . . 3.00
27 The Butcher,pt.3 . . . . 3.00
28 The Butcher,pt.4 . . . . 3.00
29 The Hourman,pt.1 . . . . 3.00
30 The Hourman,pt.2 . . . . 3.00
31 The Hourman,pt.3 . . . . 3.00
32 The Hourman,pt.4 . . . . 3.00
33 The Python,pt.1 . . . . 3.00
34 The Python,pt.2 . . . . 3.00
35 The Python,pt.3 . . . . 3.00
36 The Python,pt.4 . . . . 3.00
37 The Mist,pt.1 . . . . 3.00
38 The Mist,pt.2 . . . . 3.00
39 The Mist,pt.3 . . . . 3.00
40 The Mist,pt.4 . . . . 3.00
41 MWg&SSe(s),GyD,Phantom of
the Fair,pt.1 . . . . 2.50
42 MWg&SSe(s),GyD,Phantom of
the Fair,pt.2 . . . . 2.50
43 MWg&SSe(s),GyD,Phantom of
the Fair pt. 3 . . . . 2.50
44 MWg&SSe(s),GyD,Phantom of
the Fair pt. 4 . . . . 2.50
45 MWg&SSe(s),Blackhawk,pt.1 . . 2.50
46 MWg&SSe(s),Blackhawk,pt.2 . . 2.50
47 MWg&SSe(s),Blackhawk,pt.3 . . 2.50
48 MWg&SSe(s),RCa,Blackhawk . . 2.50
49 MWg&SSe(s),ScarletGhost,pt.1 . 2.50
50 MWg&SSe(s),The Scarlet
Ghost, pt.2, 48pg. 4.50
51 MWg&SSe(s),ScarletGhost,pt.3 . 2.50
52 MWg&SSe(s),ScarletGhost,pt.4 . 2.50
53 MWg&SSe(s),The Crone,pt.1 . . . 2.50
53 MWg&SSe(s),The Crone,pt.2 . . . 2.50
54 SSe&MWg(s),The Crone,pt.3 . . . 2.50
55 SSe&MWg(s),The Crone,pt.4 . . . 2.50
56 SSe&MWg(s),The Crone, concl. . . 2.50
57 SSe&MWg(s),The Cannon,pt.1 . 2.50
58 SSe&MWg(s),The Cannon,pt.2 . 2.50
59 SSe&MWg(s),The Cannon,pt.3 . 2.50
60 SSe&MWg(s),The Cannon,pt.4 . 2.50
61 SSe(s),GyD,The City, pt.1 . . . . 2.50
62 SSe(s),GyD,The City, pt.2 . . . . 2.50
63 SSe(s),GyD,The City, pt.3 . . . . 2.50
64 SSe(s),GyD,The City, pt.4 . . . . 2.50
65 SSe,GyD,The Goblin, pt.1 . . . . 2.50
66 SSe,GyD,The Goblin, pt.2 . . . . 2.50
67 SSe,GyD,The Goblin, pt.3 . . . . 2.50
68 SSe,GyD,The Goblin, pt.4 . . . . 2.50
69 SSe,GyD 2.50

70 SSe,GyD,final issue 2.50
Ann.#1 . . . . 4.00

SANDMAN PRESENTS:
LOVE STREET
DC/Vertigo, 1999
1 (of 3) MZi,VcL, ... 3.00
2 MZi,VcL,F:John Constantine 3.00
3 MZi,VcL,Concl. 3.00

LUCIFER
DC/Vertigo, 1999
1 (of 3) SHp, Morningstar Option . . 3.00
2 SHp 3.00
3 SHp, conclusion. 3.00

PETREFAX
DC/Vertigo, 2000
1 (of 4) SL. 3.00
2 thru 4 SL . . . . @3.00

DEAD BOY DETECTIVES
DC/Vertigo, 2001
1 (of 4) 2.50
2 thru 4 SL . . . . @2.50

CORINTHIAN, THE
DC/Vertigo, 2001
1 (of 3) 2.50
2 thru 3 . . . . @2.50

THESSALIAD, THE
DC/Vertigo, 2002
1 (of 4) 2.50
2 thru 4 DMc(c). . . . . @2.50

BAST
DC/Vertigo, 2003
1 (of 3) F:Lady Bast 3.00
2 thru 3 . . . . @3.00
Spec.1-Shot, Merv Pumpkinhead
Agent of Dream,MBu. 6.00
Spec. Everything You've Ever
Wanted to Know About Dreams
But Were Afraid to Ask 4.50
TPB The Furies (2003) 18.00
TPB Taller Tales (2003) 20.00

THESSALY
DC Vertigo, Feb. 2004
1 (of 4) Witch for Hire 3.00
2 thru 4 . . . . @3.00

SANDMAN MYSTERY THEATRE: SLEEP OF REASON
Vertigo, Dec., 2006
1 (of 5) 3.00
2 thru 5 . . . . @3.00

SCALPED
Vertigo, Jan., 2007
1 F:Dashiell Bad Horse. 3.00
2 Life on the Rez 3.00
3 Indian Country 3.00
4 Hoka Hey, pt.1 . . . . 3.00
5 Hoka Hey, pt.2 . . . . 3.00
6 Casino Boogie, pt.1 . . . . 3.00
7 Casino Boogie, pt.2 . . . . 3.00
8 Casino Boogie, pt.3 . . . . 3.00
9 Casino Boogie, pt.4 . . . . 3.00
10 Casino Boogie, pt.5 . . . . 3.00

SCARAB
DC/Vertigo, 1993–94
1 GF(c),B:JnS(s),SEa,MkB(i),
R&O:Scarab,V:Halaku-umid . . . 2.25
2 thru 8 GF(c),SEa,MkB(i) . . . . . @2.25

SCARE TACTICS
Oct., 1996
1 LKa(s),AWi,ALa, ... 2.25
2 thru 11 . . . . @2.25

SCARLETT
1993–94
1 I:Scarlett,Blood of the Innocent . . 3.50
2 Blood of the Innocent cont. 2.25
3 Blood of the Innocent cont. 2.25
4 thru 14 . . . . @2.25

SCENE OF THE CRIME
DC/Vertigo, 1999
1 (of 4) 2.50
2 thru 4 . . . . @2.50
TPB A Little Piece of Goodnight . . 13.00

S.C.I.-SPY
DC/Vertigo, Feb., 2002
1 (of 6) DgM,PG,JP,F:Sebastian
　　Starchild secret agent 2.50
2 thru 6 DgM,PG,JP . . . . @2.50

SCOOBY-DOO
Warner Bros./DC June, 1997
1 . . . . 5.00
2 thru 50 . . . . @2.50
51 thru 125 . . . . @2.25
Spooky Spectacular 2000 . . . . 4.00
Spooky Summer Special #1 . . . . . . 4.00
Spec. Super Scarefest #1 . . . . 4.00
Spec. Dollar Comic, rep.#1 . . . . . . 1.00

SCRATCH
June 2004
1 (of 5) SK,werewolf v.Batman 2.50
2 thru 5 SK . . . . @2.50

SCRIBBLY
Aug., 1948–Dec.–Jan., 1951–52
1 SM 1,400.00
2 . . . . 900.00
3 thru 5 . . . . @750.00
6 thru 10 . . . . @500.00
11 thru 15 . . . . @450.00

SEA DEVILS
Sept.–Oct., 1961
1 RH 1,000.00
2 RH 550.00
3 RH 400.00
4 RH 350.00
5 RH 350.00
6 thru 10 RH . . . . @275.00
11 . . . . 250.00
12 . . . . 250.00
13 JKu,GC,RA 250.00
14 thru 20 . . . . @250.00
21 I:Capt X,Man Fish 150.00
22 thru 35, May-June, 1967 . . . @150.00

SEAGUY
DC/Vertigo, May 2004
1 (of 3) GMo(s) 3.00
2 thru 3 GMo(s) . . . . @3.00
TPB GMo(s) 10.00

SEBASTIAN O
DC/Vertigo, 1993
1 GMo(s),SY,I:Sebastian O,A:Lord
　　Lavender,Roaring Boys 2.50
2 GMo(s),SY,V:Roaring Boys,
　　Assassins,A:Abbe 2.50
3 GMo(s),SY,D:Lord Lavender 2.50

SECRET FILES & ORIGINS
2000
TPB DAn,ALa,guide to DCU 7.00
GN Secret Files Guide to DCU
2001-2002 . . . . 5.00

Secret Hearts #7
© DC Comics, Inc.

SECRET HEARTS
Sept.–Oct., 1949–July, 1971
1 Make Believe Sweetheart 800.00
2 ATh,Love Is Not A Dream 400.00
3 Sing Me A Love Song 300.00
4 ATh 300.00
5 ATh 300.00
6 . . . . 300.00
7 scarce 600.00
8 thru 20 . . . . @225.00
21 thru 26 . . . . @175.00
27 B:Comics Code 150.00
28 thru 30 . . . . @150.00
31 thru 70 . . . . @100.00
71 thru 110 . . . . @50.00
111 thru 120 . . . . @40.00
121 thru 150 . . . . @30.00
151 thru 153 . . . . @25.00

SECRET ORIGINS
Feb., 1973–Oct., 1974
1 O:Superman,Batman,Ghost,
　　Flash 65.00
2 O:Green Lantern,Atom,
　　Supergirl 35.00
3 O:Wonder Woman,Wildcat 35.00
4 O:Vigilante by MMe 35.00
5 O:The Spectre 35.00
6 O:Blackhawk,Legion of Super
　　Heroes 35.00
7 O:Robin, Aquaman 35.00

SECRET ORIGINS
April, 1986
1 JOy,WB,F:Superman 7.00
2 GK,F:Blue Beetle 4.00
3 JBi,F:Captain Marvel 4.00
4 GT,F:Firestorm 4.00
5 GC,F:Crimson Avenger 4.00
6 DG,MR,F:Batman 5.00
7 F:Sandman,Guy Gardner 3.50
8 MA,F:Shadow Lass,Dollman . . . 2.50
9 GT,F:Skyman,Flash 2.50
10 JL,JO,JA,F:Phantom Stranger . . 2.50
11 LMc,TD,F:Hawkman,Powergirl . 2.50
12 F:Challengers of the Unknown
　　I:G.A. Fury 2.50

13 EL,F:Nightwing 3.00
14 F:Suicide Squad 2.50
15 KMo,DG,F:Deadman,Spectre . . 2.50
16 AKu,F:Hourman,Warlord 2.50
17 KGi,F:Green Lantern 2.75
18 KGi,F:Green Lantern, Creeper . 2.50
19 JM(c),MA,Uncle Sam, Guardian . 2.50
20 RL,DG,F:Batgirl 3.00
21 GM,MA,F:Jonah Hex 2.50
22 F:Manhunter,Millennium tie-in . 2.50
23 F:Manhunter,Millennium tie-in . . 2.50
24 F:Dr.Fate,Blue Devil 2.50
25 F:The Legion 2.50
26 F:Black Lightning 2.50
27 F:Zatanna, Zatara 2.50
28 RLd,GK,F:Nightshade,Midnight . 2.50
29 F:Atom,Red Tornado 2.50
30 F:Elongated Man 2.50
31 F:Justice Society of America . . . 2.50
32 F:Justice League America 3.00
33 F:Justice League Inter. 2.50
34 F:Justice League Inter. 2.50
35 KSu,F:Justice League Inter. . . . 2.50
36 F:Green Lantern 3.00
37 F:Legion of Subst. Heroes 2.50
38 F:Green Arrow,Speedy 2.50
39 F:Batman,Animal Man 3.50
40 F:Gorilla City 2.50
41 F:Flash Villains 2.75
42 DC,F:Phantom Girl 2.50
43 TVE,TT,F:Hawk & Dove 2.50
44 F:Batman,Clayface tie-in 3.00
45 F:Blackhawk,El Diablo 2.50
46 CS,F:All Headquarters 2.50
47 CS,F:The Legion 2.50
48 KG,F:Ambush Bug 2.50
49 F: The Cadmus Project 2.50
50 GP,CI,DG,F:Batman,Robin,
　　Flash,Black Canary 4.00
Ann.#1 JBy,F:Doom Patrol 3.00
Ann.#2 CI,MA,F:Flash 2.50
Ann.#3 F:The Teen Titans 3.00
Spec.#1 SK,PB,DG,F:Batman's worst
　　Villians,A:Penguin 4.00
TPB DG,New Origin Batman 4.50
GN rep of 1961 Annual 5.00
Replica Edition 80-page 5.00
Vol.3 Even More Secret Origins . . . 7.00

SECRET ORIGINS OF SUPER-VILLAINS
2000
1 80-pg. Giant 5.00

SECRET SIX
May, 2006
1 (of 6) JP 3.00
2 thru 6 JP . . . . @3.00

SECRET SOCIETY OF SUPER-HEROES
Aug., 2000
1 (of 2) HC,MMK,JP,Elseworlds . . . 6.00
2 HC,MMK,JP,concl. 6.00

SECRET SOCIETY OF SUPER-VILLAINS
May-June, 1976
1 A:Capt.Boomerang, Grodd,
　　Sinestro 30.00
2 R:Capt.Comet,A:Green Lantern 15.00
3 A:Mantis, Darkseid 12.00
4 A:Kalibak,Darkseid,Gr.Lantern. . 12.00
5 RB,D:Manhunter,A:JLA 12.00
6 RB/BL,A:Black Canary 12.00
7 RB/BL,A:Hawkgirl,Lex Luthor . . 12.00
8 RB/BL,A:Kid Flash 12.00
9 RB/BMc,A:Kid Flash, Creeper . . 12.00
10 DAy/JAb,A:Creeper 12.00

11 JO,N:Wizard 12.00
12 BMc,A:Blockbuster 12.00
13 A:Crime Syndicate of America . 12.00
14 A:Crime Syndicate of America . 12.00
15 A:G.A.Atom, Dr. Mid Nite 12.00

SECRETS OF HAUNTED HOUSE
April-May, 1975

1 LD(c),Dead Heat 75.00
2 ECh(c),A Dead Man. 30.00
3 ECh(c),Pathway To Purgatory . . 30.00
4 LD(c),The Face of Death. 30.00
5 BWr(c),Gunslinger! 35.00
6 JAp(c),Deadly Allegiance. 25.00
7 JAp(c),It'll Grow On You 25.00
8 MK(c),Raising The Devil 25.00
9 LD(c),The Man Who Didn't
  Believe in Ghosts 25.00
10 MK(c),Ask Me No Questions . . 25.00
11 MK(c),Picasso Fever! 25.00
12 JO&DG(c),Yorick's Skull 25.00
13 JO&DG(c),The Cry of the
  Warewolf 25.00
14 MK(c),Selina 25.00
15 LD(c),Over Your Own Dead
  Body 20.00

Secrets of Haunted House #46
© DC Comics Inc.

16 MK(c),Water, Water Every Fear 20.00
17 LD(c),Papa Don 20.00
18 LD(c),No Sleep For The Dying . 20.00
19 LD(c),The Manner of Execution 20.00
20 JO(c),The Talisman of the
  Serpent 20.00
21 LD(c),The Death's Head
  Scorpion 20.00
22 LD(c),See How They Die 20.00
23 LD(c),The Creeping Red Death 20.00
24 LD(c),Second Chance To Die . . 20.00
25 LD(c),The Man Who Cheated
  Destiny. 20.00
26 MR(c),Elevator to Eternity. 20.00
27 DH(c),Souls For the Master . . . 20.00
28 DH(c),Demon Rum 20.00
29 MK(c),Duel of Darkness 20.00
30 JO(c),For the Love of Arlo 20.00
31 I:Mister E. 25.00
32 The Legend of the Tiger's Paw. 15.00
33 In The Attic Dwells Dark Seth. . 15.00
34 Double Your Pleasure 15.00
35 Deathwing, Lord of Darkness . . 15.00
36 RB&DG(c),Sister Sinister 15.00
37 RB&DG(c),The Third Wish Is
  Death. 15.00

38 RB&DG(c),Slaves of Satan. . . . 15.00
39 RB&DG(c),The Witch-Hounds
  of Salem 15.00
40 RB&DG(c),The Were-Witch
  of Boston 15.00
41 JKu(c),House at Devil's Tail . . . 15.00
42 JKu(c),Mystic Murder 15.00
43 JO(c),Mother of Invention 15.00
44 BWr(c),Halloween God 15.00
45 EC&JO(c),Star-Trakker. 15.00
46 March, 1982 . . . . 15.00

SINISTER HOUSE OF SECRET LOVE
Oct.–Nov., 1971–April–May, 1972

1 Curse of the MacIntyres 300.00
2 TD,To Wed the Devil 125.00
3 ATh,Bride of the Falcon 140.00
4 TD,Kiss of the Serpent 125.00
Becomes:

SECRETS OF SINISTER HOUSE
June-July, 1972

5 NC(c),Death at Castle Dunbar. . 65.00
6 MK,JO,Brief Reunion 40.00
7 NR,MK,Panic 40.00
8 NC,Man Who Cried Werewolf . . 40.00
9 JkS(c),Dance of the Damned . . 40.00
10 JkS(c),Castle Curse 50.00
11 thru 16 . . . . @25.00
17 DBa,NC,HC,WMo 25.00
18 NC,GK,June-July, 1974 . . . . . . 25.00

SECRETS OF THE LEGION OF SUPER-HEROES
Jan., 1981

1 O:Legion 3.50
2 O:Brainiac 5. . . . . 3.50
3 March, 1981,O:Karate Kid 3.50

SEEKERS INTO THE MYSTERY
1996

1 Pilgrimage of Lucas Hart,pt.1 . . 2.50
2 Pilgrimage of Lucas Hart,pt.2 . . 2.50
3 Pilgrimage of Lucas Hart,pt.3 . . 2.50
4 Pilgrimage of Lucas Hart,pt.4 . . 2.50
5 Pilgrimage of Lucas Hart,pt.5 . . 2.50
6 Falling Down to Heaven,pt.1 . . . 2.50
7 Falling Down to Heaven,pt.2 . . . 2.50
8 Falling Down to Heaven,pt.3 . . . 2.50
9 JMD(s),MZi,Falling Down from
  Heaven,pt.4 concl. 2.50
10 JMD(s),JMu,F:Charlie Limbo . . 2.50
11 JMD(s),JIT,God's Shadow,pt.1 . . 2.50
12 JMD(s),JIT,God's Shadow,pt.2 . . 2.50
13 JMD(s),JIT,God's Shadow,pt.3 . . 2.50
14 JMD(s),JIT,God's Shadow,pt.4 . . 2.50
15 JMD(s),JMu,Hart meets
  Magician, final issue 3.00

SENSATION COMICS
1942–52

1 I:Wonder Woman,Wildcat. . 60,000.00
2 I:Etta Candy & the Holiday
  Girls, Dr. Poison 10,000.00
3 Diana Price joins Military
  Intelligence 5,000.00
4 I:Baroness PaulaVonGunther 4,000.00
5 V:Axis Spies 3,000.00
6 Wonder Woman receives magic
  lasso,V:Baroness Gunther . 3,000.00
7 V:Baroness Gunther 2,200.00
8 Meets Gloria Bullfinch. 2,200.00
9 A:The Real Diana Price . . . 2,200.00

10 V:Ishti. 2,200.00
11 I:Queen Desira. 2,200.00
12 V:Baroness Gunther 1,700.00
13 V:Olga,Hitler(c) 2,200.00
14 The Fir Tree's Story 1,700.00
15 V:Simon Slikery 1,700.00
16 V:Karl Schultz 1,700.00
17 V:Princess Yasmini 1,700.00
18 V:Quito 1,700.00
19 Wonder Woman Goes
  Berserk 1,700.00
20 V:Stoffer 1,700.00
21 V:American Adolf 1,500.00
22 V:Cheetah 1,500.00
23 'War Laugh Mania'. 1,500.00
24 I:Wonder Woman's
  Mental Radio 1,500.00
25 Kidnapper o/t Astral Spirits . 1,500.00
26 A:Queen Hippolyte. 1,500.00
27 V:Ely Close 1,500.00
28 V:Mayor Prude. 1,500.00
29 V:Mimi Mendez 1,500.00
30 V:Anton Unreal. 1,500.00
31 Grow Down Land. 1,100.00
32 V:Crime Chief. 1,100.00
33 Meets Percy Pringle. 1,100.00
34 I:Sargon 1,200.00
35 V:Sontag Henya in Atlantis . 1,000.00
36 V:Bedwin Footh 1,000.00
37 A:Mala((1st app. All-Star #8) 1,000.00
38 V:The Gyp 1,000.00
39 V:Nero 1,000.00
40 I:Countess Draska Nishki . . 1,000.00
41 V:Creeper Jackson 900.00
42 V:Countess Nishki. 900.00
43 Meets Joel Heyday 900.00
44 V:Lt. Sturm 900.00
45 V:Jose Perez. 900.00
46 V:Lawbreakers Protective
  League. 900.00
47 V:Unknown 900.00
48 V:Topso and Teena 900.00
49 V:Zavia 900.00
50 V:'Ears' Fellock 900.00
51 V:Boss Brekel 800.00
52 Meets Prof. Toxino 800.00
53 V:Wanta Wynn 800.00
54 V:Dr. Fiendo 800.00
55 V:Bughumans 800.00
56 V:Dr. Novel 800.00
57 V:Syonide 800.00
58 Meets Olive Norton 800.00
59 V:Snow Man 700.00
60 V:Bifton Jones. 700.00
61 V:Bluff Robust. 700.00
62 V:Black Robert of Dogwood . 700.00
63 V:Prof. Vibrate. 700.00

Sensation #12
© DC Comics Inc.

DC COMICS

64 V:Cloudmen	700.00
65 V:Lim Slait	750.00
66 V:Slick Skeener	750.00
67 V:Daredevil Dix	750.00
68 Secret of the Menacing Octopus	750.00
69 V:Darcy Wells	800.00
70 Unconquerable Woman of Cocha Bamba	800.00
71 V:Queen Flaming	800.00
72 V:Blue Seal Gang	800.00
73 Wonder Woman time travel story	800.00
74 V:Spug Spangle	800.00
75 V:Shark	800.00
76 V:King Diamond	800.00
77 V:Boss Brekel	800.00
78 V:Furiosa	800.00
79 Meets Leila and Solala	800.00
80 V:Don Enrago	800.00
81 V:Dr. Frenzi	700.00
82 V:King Lunar	600.00
83 V:Prowd	600.00
84 V:Duke Daxo	600.00
85 Meets Leslie M. Gresham	600.00
86 Secret of the Amazing Bracelets	600.00
87 In Twin Peaks(in Old West)	600.00
88 Wonder Woman in Holywood	600.00
89 V:Abacus Rackeett Gang	600.00
90 The Secret of the Modern Sphinx	600.00
91 Survivors of the Stone Age	600.00
92 V:Duke of Deceptions	600.00
93 V:Talbot	600.00
94 Girl Issue	750.00
95 CI,Dr. Pat's First Love	750.00
96 CI,W.Woman's RomanticRival	750.00
97 W.Woman Romance Editor	750.00
98 Strange Mission	750.00
99 I:Astra	750.00
100 W.Woman Hollywood Star	800.00
101 Battle for the Atom World	750.00
102 Queen of the South Seas	750.00
103 V:Robot Archers	750.00
104 The End of Paradise Island	750.00
105 Secret of the Giant Forest	750.00
106 E:Wonder Woman	750.00
107 ATh,Mystery issue	1,200.00
108 ATh,GK,I:Johnny Peril	1,000.00
109 Ath,GK,A:Johnny Peril	1,500.00

Becomes:

Sensation Mystery #111
© DC Comics, Inc.

SENSATION MYSTERY
1952–53

110 MA(c),B:Johnny Peril	700.00
111 GK,Spectre in the Flame	650.00
112 GK,Death Has 5 Guesses	650.00
113 CI,The End of Death	650.00
114 GK,GC,The Haunted Diamond	650.00
115 GK,The Phantom Castle	650.00
116 The Toy Assassins	650.00

SENSATION COMICS
1999

1 JeR(s),ScB, F:Wonder Woman & Hawkgirl	2.25

SERGEANT BILKO
May-June, 1957

1 Based on TV show	1,000.00
2	500.00
3	400.00
4	350.00
5	350.00
6 thru 17	@300.00
18 March-April, 1960	300.00

SERGEANT BILKO'S PVT. DOBERMAN
June-July, 1958

1	600.00
2	300.00
3 and 4	@225.00
5 photo (c)	225.00
6 thru 10	@150.00
11 Feb.–March, 1960	150.00

SGT. ROCK
See: OUR ARMY AT WAR

SGT. ROCK SPECIAL
Oct., 1988

#1 rep.Our Army at War#162-#63	11.00
#2 rep.Brave & Bold #52	7.00
#3 rep.Showcase #45	7.00
#4 rep.Our Army at War#147-#48	7.00
#5 rep.Our Army at War#81&#103	7.00
#6 rep.Our Army at War #160	7.00
#7 rep.Our Army at War #85	7.00
#8 thru #20 reprints	@7.00
Spec. #1 TT,MGo,JKu,CR,(new stories)	5.00

SGT. ROCK'S PRIZE BATTLE TALES
Winter, 1964

1	550.00

SGT. ROCK: THE PROPHECY
Jan., 2006

1 (of 6) JKu	3.00
1a & b variant (c)s	@3.00
2 JKu	3.00
3 JKu	3.00
4 JKu, Road to Riga	3.00
5 JKu, Farmer's Barn	3.00
6 JKu,concl	3.00

SEVEN SOLDIERS
Feb., 2005

0 GMo(s),JWi,48-page	3.00
1 48-pg	4.00
1 GMo(s),JWi,culmination	3.00

SEVEN SOLDIERS: THE BULLETEER
Nov., 2005

1 (of 4) GMo(s)	3.00
2 thru 4 GMo(s)	@3.00

SEVEN SOLDIERS: FRANKENSTEIN
Nov., 2005

1 (of 4) GMo(s),DoM	3.00
2 GMo(s),DoM, on Mars	3.00
3 GMo(s),DoM,A:The Bride	3.00
4 GMo(s),DoM,V:Death Fairies	3.00

SEVEN SOLDIERS: GUARDIAN
March, 2005

1 (of 4) GMo(s),masthead	3.00
2 GMo(s)	3.00
3 GMo(s)	3.00
4 GMo(s)	3.00

SEVEN SOLDIERS: KLARION THE WITCH BOY
Apr., 2005

1 GMo(s),F:Klarion and Teek	3.00
2 GMo(s)	3.00
3 GMo(s)	3.00
4 GMo(s)	3.00

SEVEN SOLDIERS: MISTER MIRACLE
Sept., 2005

1 (of 4) GMo(s),PFe	3.00
2 GMo(s),PFe(c)	3.00
3 GMo(s),I:Baron Bedlam	3.00
4 GMo(s),Forever-Flavored Man	3.00

SEVEN SOLDIERS: SHINING KNIGHT
March, 2005

1 (of 4) GMo(s),fantasy epic	3.00
2 GMo(s)	3.00
3 GMo(s)	3.00
4 GMo(s)	3.00

SEVEN SOLDIERS: ZATANNA
Apr., 2005

1 GMo(s),F:Zatanna	3.00
2 GMo(s)	3.00
3 & 4 GMo(s)	@3.00

SHADE
June-July, 1977
[1st Regular Series]

1 SD,I&O: Shade	25.00
2 SD,V:Form	20.00
3 SD,V:The Cloak	15.00
4 SD,Return to Meta-Zone	15.00
5 SD,V:Supreme Decider	15.00
6 SD,V:Khaos	15.00
7 SD,V:Dr.Z.Z.	15.00
8 SD,last issue	15.00

SHADE, THE
Feb., 1997

1 (of 4) JeR(s),GeH,A:Ludlows	3.00
2 JeR(s),JWi,MGy,poisoned by love of his life	3.00
3 JeR(s),BBl,Golden Age Flash Jay Garrick retiring	3.00
4 JeR(s),MZi,V:last of the Ludlows	3.00

SHADE, THE CHANGING MAN
July, 1990
1 B:PrM(s),CBa,MPn,I:Kathy George, I&D:Troy Grezer 5.00
2 CBa,MPn,Who Shot JFK#1 . . . . 4.00
3 CBa,MPn,Who Shot JFK#2 . . . . 3.00
4 CBa,MPn,V:American Scream . . 3.00
5 CBa,MPn,V:Hollywood
Monsters 3.00
6 CBa,MPn,V:Ed Loot. 3.00
7 CBa,MPn,I:Arnold Major 3.00
8 CBa,Mpn,I:Lenny 3.00
9 CBa,MPn,V:Arnold Major 3.00
10 CBa,MPn,Paranoia 2.75
11 CBa,MPn,R:Troy Grezer 2.50
12 CBa,MPn,V:Troy Grezer 2.50
13 CBa,MPn,I:Fish Priest 2.50
14 CBa,MPn,V:Godfather of Guilt . . 2.50
15 CBa,MPn,I:Spirit 2.50
16 CBa,MPn,V:American Scream . . 2.50
17 RkB(i),V:Rohug 2.50
18 MPn,E:American Scream 2.50
19 MPn,V:Dave Messiah Seeker . . . 2.50
20 JD,CBa,MPn,RkB,R:Roger 2.50
21 MPn,The Road,A:Stringer 2.25
22 The Road,Childhood 2.25
23 The Road 2.25
24 The Road 2.25
25 The Road 2.25
26 MPn(i),F:Lenny 2.25
27 MPn(i),Shade becomes female . 2.25
28 MPn(i),Changing Woman #2 . . . 2.25
29 MPn(i),Changing Woman #3 . . . 2.25
30 Another Life. 2.25
31 Ernest & Jim #1 . . . . 2.25
32 Ernest & Jim #2 . . . . 2.25
DC/Vertigo, 1993
33 CBa,B:Birth Pains 2.25
34 CBa,RkB(i),GID(i),A:Brian Juno, Garden of Pain 2.25
35 CBa,RkB(i),E:Birth Pains,
V:Juno 2.25
36 CBa,PrG(i),RkB(i),B:Passion child, I:Miles Laimling 2.25
37 CBa,RkB(i),Shade/Kathy 2.25
38 CBa,RkB(i),Great American Novel 2.25
39 CBa,SEa,RkB(i),Pond Life 2.25
40 PBd,at Hotel Shade 2.25
41 GID,Pandora's Story,Kathy is pregnant 2.25

Shade the Changing Man #35
© DC Comics Inc.

42 CBa,RkB(i),SY,B:History Lesson, A:John Constantine 2.50
43 CBa,RkB(i),PBd,Trial of William Matthieson,A:J.Constantine. . . 2.50
44 CBa,RkB(i),E:History Lesson, D:William Matthieson,A:John Constantine 2.50
45 CBa,B:A Season in Hell 2.25
46 CBa(c),GID,Season in Hell#2 . . 2.25
47 CBa(c),GID,A:Lenny 2.25
48 CBa(c),GID 2.25
49 CBa(c),GID,Kathy's Past 2.25
50 GID,BBI,MiA,pin-up gallery 3.25
51 GID,BBI,MiA,Masks,pt.1 . . . . . 2.00
52 GID,BBI,MiA,Masks,pt.2 . . . . . 2.00
53 GID,BBI,MiA,Masks,pt.3 . . . . . 2.00
54 MBu,RkB,Perpetual Motion 2.00
55 MBu,RkB,Life is Short,pt.1 . . . . 2.00
56 MBu,RkB,Life is Short,pt.2 . . . . . 2.00
57 MBu,PrM,RkB,Life is Short,pt.3 . 2.00
58 PrM,Michael Lark 2.00
59 MBu,PrM,Nasty Infections,pt.1 . . 2.25
60 MBu,PrM,Nasty Infections,pt.2 . . 2.25
61 MBu,PrM,Nasty Infections,pt.3 . . 2.25
62 Nasty Infections,pt.4 . . . . 2.25
63 Nasty Infections,finale. 2.25
64 The Madness 2.25
65 The Roots of Madness,pt.1 . . . . 2.25
66 The Roots of Madness,pt.2 . . . . 2.25
67 The Roots of Madness,pt.3 . . . . 2.25
68 After Kathy,pt.1 . . . . 2.25
69 After Kathy,pt.2 . . . . 2.25
70 After Kathy,pt.3, final issue 2.25

SHADO, SONG OF THE DRAGON
1992
1 GM(i),From G.A. Longbow Hunters 5.50
2 GM(i),V:Yakuza 5.00
3 GM(i),V:Yakuza 5.00
4 GM(i),V:Yakuza 5.00

SHADOW, THE
[1st Regular Series], 1973–75
1 MK,The Doom Puzzle 75.00
2 MK,V:Freak Show Killer 35.00
3 MK,BWr 40.00
4 MK,HC,BWr,Ninja Story 35.00
5 FR 30.00
6 MK 32.00
7 FR 15.00
8 FR 15.00
9 FR 15.00
10 JCr 20.00
11 A:Avenger 15.00
12. . . . . 15.00
[Limited Series], 1986
1 HC,R:Shadow 5.00
2 HC,O:Shadow 4.00
3 HC,V:Preston Mayrock 3.00
4 HC,V:Preston Mayrock 3.00
TPB rep. #1 thru #4 . . . . 13.00
[2nd Regular Series], 1987–89
1 BSz,Shadows & Light,pt.1 . . . . . 3.50
2 BSz,Shadows & Light,pt.2 . . . . . 3.50
3 BSz,Shadows & Light,pt.3 . . . . . 3.50
4 BSz,Shadows & Light,pt.4 . . . . . 3.50
5 BSz,Shadows & Light,pt.5 . . . . . 3.50
6 BSz,Shadows & Light,pt.6 . . . . . 3.50
7 MR,KB,Harold Goes to Washington 3.00
8 KB,Seven Deadly Finns,pt.1 . . . 3.00
9 KB,Seven Deadly Finns,pt.2 . . . 3.00
10 KB,Seven Deadly Finns,pt.3 . . . 3.00
11 KB,Seven Deadly Finns,pt.4 . . . 3.00
12 KB,Seven Deadly Finns,pt.5 . . . 3.00
13 KB,Seven Deadly Finns,pt.6 . . . 3.00
14 KB,Body And Soul,pt.1 . . . . 3.00
15 KB,Body And Soul,pt.2 . . . . 3.00

16 KB,Body And Soul,pt.3 . . . . 3.00
17 KB,Body And Soul,pt.4 . . . . 3.00
18 KB,Body And Soul,pt.5 . . . . 3.00
19 KB,Body And Soul,pt.6 . . . . 3.00
Ann.#1 JO,AA,Shadows & Light prologue. 4.00
Ann.#2 KB,Agents 3.50

SHADOW CABINET
Milestone, 1994–95
0 WS(c),3RL,Shadow War,Foil(c),A:All Milestone characters 3.00
1 JBy(c),3RW,I&D:Corpsicle 2.50
2 thru 17 . . . . @2.50

SHADOWDRAGON
1995
Ann.#1 Year One Annual 3.50

SHADOW OF BATMAN
1 reprints of Detective Comics . . . 10.00
2 thru 4 . . . . @7.50

SHADOW OF THE BATMAN
1985–86
1 WS,AM,MR,rep. 7.00
2 MR,TA,rep.A:Hugo Strange 5.00
3 MR,TA,rep.A:Penguin 5.00
4 MR,TA,rep.A:Joker 6.00
5 MR,DG,rep. 5.00

SHADOWPACT
2006
1 BWg,A:Superman 3.00
2 BWg. 3.00
3 BWg,V:Pentacle 3.00
4 BWg,F:Blue Devil. 3.00
5 BWg,Killers assemble 3.00
6 Goodbye Ragman & Enchantress 3.00
7 BWg,V:The Congregation 3.00
8 BWg,V:The Congregation 3.00
9 BWg,to Budapest. 3.00
10 BWg,Demon Triptych 3.00
11 BWg,Demon Triptych 3.00
12 BWg, Die by the Sword 3.00
13 BWg,F:Zauriel 3.00
14 BWg,Blue Devil tries to quit 3.00
15 BWg,Zauriel joins Shadowpact. . 3.00
16 V:Doctor Gotham 3.00
17 DBw,V:Horde of Zombies 3.00
18 Detective Chimp & Enchantress . 3.00

SHADOW'S FALL
1994–95
1 JVF,Voyage of self-discovery 3.00
2 JVF,More of tale 3.00
3 JVF,Shen confronts shadow 3.00
4 JVF,Gale wounded 3.00
5 JVF,Shadow goes Berserk 3.00
6 JVF,F:Warren Gale,final issue . . . 3.00

SHADOW STRIKES!, THE
1989–92
1 EB,Death's Head 3.00
2 EB,EB,PoliticalKiller,V:Rasputin . . 2.50
3 EB,V:Mad Monk,V:Rasputin 2.50
4 EB,D:Mad Monk,V:Rasputin 4.00
5 EB,Shadow & Doc Savage#1 . . . 4.00
6 Shadow & Doc Savage #3 . . . . . 2.50
7 RM,A:Wunderkind,O:Shadow's
    Radio Show 2.50
8 EB,A:Shiwan Khan 2.50
9 Fireworks#2 . . . . 2.50
10 EB,Fireworks#3 . . . . 2.50
11 EB,O:Margo Lane 2.50
12 EB,V:Chicago Mob 2.50
13 EB,V:Chicago Mob 2.50
14 EB,V:Chicago Mob 2.50
15 EB,V:Chicago Mob 2.50
16 Assassins,pt.1 . . . . 2.50
17 Assassins,pt.2 . . . . 2.50
18 Shrevvie 2.50
19 NY,NJ Tunnel 2.50
20 Shadow+Margo Vs.Nazis 2.50
21 V:Shiwan Khan 2.50
22 V:Shiwan Khan 2.50
23 V:Shiwan Khan 2.50
24 Search for Margo Lane 2.50
25 In China 2.50
26 V:Shiwan Khan 2.50
27 V:Shiwan Khan,Margo
    Rescued 2.50
28 SL,In Hawaii 2.50
29 DSp,Valhalla,V:Nazis 2.50
30 The Shadow Year One,pt.1 . . . . 2.50
31 The Shadow Year One,pt.2 . . . . 2.50
Ann.#1 DSp, Crimson Dreams 4.00

SHADOW WAR
OF HAWKMAN
May, 1985
1 AA,V:Thangarians 2.50
2 AA,V:Thangarians 2.50

The Shadow Strikes! #12
© *DC Comics, Inc.*

3 AA,V:Thangarians,A:Aquaman,
    Elong.Man 2.50
4 AA,V:Thangarians 2.50
Spec.#1 V:Thangarians 2.50

SHAZAM!
1973–78
[1st Regular Series]
1 B:DON(s),CCB,O:Capt.Marvel . 75.00
2 CCB,A:Mr.Mind 25.00
3 CCB,V:Shagg Naste 25.00
4 E:DON(s),CCB,V:Ibac 25.00
5 B:ESM(s),CCB,A:Leprechaun . . 25.00
6 B:DON(s),CCB,Dr,Sivana 20.00
7 CCB,A:Capt Marvel Jr. 20.00
8 CCB,O:Marvel Family 90.00
9 E:DON(S)DC,CCB,A:Mr.Mind,
    Captain Marvel Jr. 20.00
10 ESM(s)CCB,BO 20.00
11 ViCKS,BO,rep. 20.00
12 BO,DG 75.00
13 BO,KS,A:Luther 75.00
14 KS,A:Monster Society 75.00
15 KS,BO,Luther 75.00
16 KS,BO 75.00
17 KS,BO 75.00
18 KS,BO 15.00
19 KS,BO,Mary Marvel 15.00
20 KS,A:Marvel Family 15.00
21 reprint 15.00
22 reprint 15.00
23 reprint 15.00
24 reprint 15.00
25 KS,DG,I&O:Isis 22.00
26 KS 15.00
27 KS,A:Kid Eternity 22.00
28 KS 15.00
29 KS 15.00
30 KS 15.00
31 KS,A:Minute Man 15.00
32 KS 15.00
33 KS 15.00
34 O:Capt.Marvel Jr. 15.00
35 DN,KS,A:Marvel Family 15.00
GN Power of Hope,64-page 15.00

SHAZAM! FAMILY
July, 2002
Annual #1 (1953, rep.) 80-pg. 6.00

SHAZAM: THE MONSTER
SOCIETY OF EVIL
Feb., 2007
1 (of 4) JSi,48-pgs. 6.00
2 thru 4 JSi, 48-pgs. . . . . @6.00

SHAZAM, THE
NEW BEGINNING
April, 1987
1 O:Shazam & Capt.Marvel 2.50
2 V:Black Adam 2.50
3 V:Black Adam 2.50
4 V:Black Adam 2.50

SHAZAM/SUPERMAN:
FIRST THUNDER
Sept., 2005
1 (of 4) V:Cult, Giant Robots 3.50
2 A:Lex Luthor & Dr.Sivana 3.50
3 F:Eclipso 3.50
4 V:Dr. Sivana 3.50

SHERLOCK HOLMES
Sept.–Oct., 1975
1 ERc,WS 35.00

SHOWCASE
1956–70
1 F:Fire Fighters 6,500.00
2 JKu,F:Kings of Wild 1,800.00
3 F:Frogmen 1,700.00
4 CI,JKu,I&O:S.A. Flash
    (Barry Allen) 50,000.00
5 F:Manhunters 1,800.00
6 JK,I&O:Challengers of the
    Unknown 7,000.00
7 JK,F:Challengers 3,500.00
8 CI,F:Flash,I:Capt.Cold 19,000.00
9 F:Lois Lane 12,000.00
10 F:Lois Lane 5,500.00
11 JK(c),F:Challengers 3,000.00
12 JK(c),F:Challengers 3,000.00
13 CI,F:Flash,Mr.Element . . . 8,000.00
14 CI,F:Flash,Mr.Element . . . 8,500.00
15 I:Space Ranger 3,500.00
16 F:Space Ranger 2,000.00
17 GK(c),I:Adam Strange . . . 4,500.00
18 GK(c),F:Adam Strange . . . 2,500.00
19 GK(c),F:Adam Strange . . . 2,700.00
20 I:Rip Hunter 1,800.00
21 F:Rip Hunter 1,000.00
22 GK,I&O:S.A. Green Lantern
    (Hal Jordan) 9,000.00
23 GK,F:Green Lantern 3,000.00
24 GK,F:Green Lantern 3,000.00
25 JKu,F:Rip Hunter 750.00
26 JKu,F:Rip Hunter 750.00
27 RH,I:Sea Devils 1,600.00
28 RH,F:Sea Devils 900.00
29 RH,F:Sea Devils 900.00
30 O:Aquaman 1,500.00
31 GK(c),F:Aquaman 1,000.00
32 F:Aquaman 1,000.00
33 F:Aquaman 1,100.00
34 GK,MA,I&O:S.A. Atom . . . 2,700.00
35 GK,MA,F:Atom 1,500.00
36 GK,MA,F:Atom 1,000.00
37 RA,I:Metal Man 1,300.00
38 RA,F:Metal Man 800.00
39 RA,F:Metal Man 650.00
40 RA,F:Metal Man 600.00
41 F:Tommy Tomorrow 400.00
42 F:Tommy TOmorrow 400.00
43 F:Dr.No(James Bond 007) . . . 600.00
44 F:Tommy Tomorrow 300.00
45 JKu,O:Sgt.Rock 300.00
46 F:Tommy Tomorrow 250.00
47 F:Tommy Tomorrow 250.00
48 F:Cave Carson 300.00
49 F:Cave Carson 275.00

Showcase #55
© *DC Comics Inc.*

50 MA,CI,F:I Spy	225.00
51 MA,CI,F:I Spy	225.00
52 F:Cave Carson	225.00
53 JKu(c),RH,F:G.I.Joe	250.00
54 JKu(c),RH,F:G.I.Joe	250.00
55 MA,F:Dr.Fate,Spectre,1st S.A.	
Gr. Lantern,Solomon Grundy	500.00
56 MA,F:Dr.Fate.	300.00
57 JKu,F:Enemy Ace	700.00
58 JKu,F:Enemy Ace	500.00
59 F:Teen Titans	300.00
60 MA,F:Spectre	600.00
61 MA,F:Spectre	300.00
62 JO,I:Inferior 5	200.00
63 JO,F:Inferior 5.	125.00
64 MA,F:Spectre	300.00
65 F:Inferior 5	125.00
66 I:B'wana Beast	100.00
67 F:B'wana Beast.	100.00
68 I:Maniaks.	125.00
69 F:Maniaks.	125.00
70 I:Binky	100.00
71 F:Maniaks	90.00
72 JKu,ATh,F:Top Gun	90.00
73 SD,I&O:Creeper	200.00
74 I:Anthro	90.00
75 SD,I:Hawk & Dove	125.00
76 NC,I:Bat Lash	200.00
77 BO,I:Angel & Ape	75.00
78 I:Jonny Double	65.00
79 I:Dolphin	90.00
80 NA(c),F:Phantom Stranger	150.00
81 I:Windy & Willy	75.00
82 I:Nightmaster.	300.00
83 BWr,MK,F:Nightmaster	200.00
84 BWr,MK,F:Nightmaster	200.00
85 JKu,F:Firehair	50.00
86 JKu,F:Firehair	50.00
87 JKu,F:Firehair	50.00
88 F:Jason's Quest	30.00
89 F:Jason's Quest	30.00
90 F:Manhunter	30.00
91 F:Manhunter	30.00
92 F:Manhunter	30.00
93 F:Manhunter (1970)	30.00

[Series Resumes], 1977

94 JA,JSon,I&O:2nd	
Doom Patrol	30.00
95 JA,JSon,F:2nd Doom Patrol	20.00
96 JA,JSon,F:2nd Doom Patrol	20.00
97 JO,JSon,O:Power Girl	12.00
98 JSon,DG,Power Girl	12.00
99 JSon,DG,Power Girl	12.00
100 JSon,all star issue.	20.00
101 JKu(c),AM,MA,Hawkman	12.00
102 JKu(c),AM,MA,Hawkman	12.00
103 JKu(c),AM,MA,Hawkman	12.00
104 RE,OSS Spies	12.00
TPB Rep.1956–59	20.00

SHOWCASE '93

1 AAd(c),EH,AV,F:Catwoman,	
Blue Devil,Cyborg	4.00
2 KM(c),EH,AV,F:Catwoman,	
Blue Devil,Cyborg	3.50
3 KM(c),EH,TC,F:Catwoman,	
Blue Devil,Flash	3.00
4 F:Catwoman,Blue Devil,	
Geo-Force	3.00
5 F:KD,DG,BHi,F:Robin,Blue	
Devil,Geo-Force	3.00
6 MZ(c),KD,DG,F:Robin,Blue	
Devil,Deathstroke	3.00
7 BSz(c),KJ,Knightfall#13,F:Two-	
Face,Jade&Obsidian	5.00
8 KJ,Knightfall#14,F:Two-Face,	
Peacemaker,Fire and Ice	4.00
9 F:Huntress,Peacemaker,Shining	
Knight	3.00
10 BWg,SI,F:Huntress,Batman,	
Dr.Light,Peacemaker,Deathstroke,	
Katana,M.Manhunter	3.00

Showcase '93 #12
© DC Comics Inc.

11 GP(c),F:Robin,Nightwing,	
Peacemaker,Deathstroke,Deadshot,	
Katana,Dr.Light,Won.Woman	3.00
12 AD(c),BMc,F:Robin,Nightwing,	
Green Lantern,Creeper	3.00

SHOWCASE '94

1 KN,F:Joker,Gunfire,Orion,Metro	3.00
2 KON(c),E:Joker,B:Blue Beetle	3.00
3 MMi(c),B:Razorsharpe.	3.00
4 AIG(s),DG,F:Arkham Asylum inmates	
E:Razorsharpe,Blue Bettle	3.00
5 WS(c),CDi(s),PJ,B:Robin&Huntress,	
F:Bloodwynd,Loose Cannon	3.00
6 PJ,KK(s),F:Robin & Huntress	3.00
7 JaL(c),PDd(s),F:Comm. Gordon	3.00
8 AIG(s),O:Scarface,Ventriloquist,	
F:Monarch,1st Wildcat.	3.25
9 AIG(s),DJ,O:Scarface,Ventriloquist,	
F:Monarch,Waverider	3.00
10 JQ(c),AIG(s),F:Azrael,Zero Hour,	
B:Black Condor	3.25
11 Black Condor, Man-Bat.	3.00
12 Barbara Gordon	3.00

SHOWCASE '95

1 Supergirl	3.00
2	3.00
3 F:Eradicator,Claw	3.00
4 A:Catwoman,Hawke	3.00
5 F:Thorne,Firehawk.	3.00
6 thru 12	@3.00

SHOWCASE '96

1 F:Steel & Warrior	3.00
2 F:Steel and Warrior	3.00
3 thru 7	@3.00
8 F:Superman, Superboy &	
Supergirl	5.00
9 F:Lady Shiva & Shadowdragon,	
Martian Manhunter	3.00
10 F:Ultra Boy, Captain Comet	3.00
11 Legion of Super-Heroes	3.00
12 10,000 Brainiacs	3.00

SILVER AGE DC CLASSICS

Action #252(rep)	3.00
Adventure #247(rep)	3.00
Brave and Bold #28 (rep)	3.00
Detective #225 (rep)	3.00
Detective #327 (rep)	3.00
Green Lantern #76 (rep)	3.00

House of Secrets #92 (rep)	3.00
Showcase #4 (rep).	3.00
Showcase #22 (rep).	3.00
Sugar & Spike #99(1st printing).	3.00

SILVER AGE
May, 2000

Secret Files #1	5.00
Justice League of America #1	2.50
Challengers of the Unknown #1	2.50
Teen Titans #1	2.50
Doom Patrol #1	2.50
Dial "H" For Hero #1	2.50
The Flash #1	2.50
Green Lantern #1.	2.50
The Brave and the Bold #1	2.50
Showcase #1	2.50
80-Page Giant #1, 80-pg	6.50
Silver Age #1, 48-pg	4.00

SILVERBLADE
Sept., 1987

1 KJ,GC,maxi-series.	2.25
2 thru 12 GC	@2.25

SIMON DARK
Oct., 2007

1 SHp,Gotham's Newest Defender	3.00

SINS OF YOUTH
March, 2000

Aquaboy/Lagoon Man #1 x-over	2.50
Batboy & Robin #1 x-over	2.50
JLA/Jr. #1 x-over	2.50
Kid Flash/Impulse #1 x-over	2.50
Secret/Deadboy #1 x-over	2.50
Starwoman & JSA #1 x-over	2.50
Superman,Jr./Superboy,Sr.#1	
x-over.	2.50
Wonder Girls #1 x-over	2.50

SKIN GRAFT
DC/Vertigo, 1993

1 B:JeP(s),WaP,I:John Oakes,	
A:Tattooed Man(Tarrant)	3.25
2 WaP,V:Assassins	3.00
3 WaP,In Kyoto,I:Mizoguchi Kenji	3.00
4 E:JeP(s),WaP,V:Tarrant,Kenji	3.25

SKREEMER
May, 1989

1 thru 6	@2.25
TPB (2002).	20.00

SKULL AND BONES
1992

1 EH,I&O:Skull & Bones	5.00
2 EH,V:KGB	5.00
3 EH,V:KGB	5.00

SLASH MARAUD
Nov., 1987

1 PG	2.25
2 PG	2.25
3 thru 10 PG	@2.25

SMALLVILLE
Sept., 2002

Spec. TV series	4.00

SMALLVILLE
March 2003

1 Camping trip, from TV show	5.00
2 Miss Smallville Pageant.	4.00
3 F:Lex Luthor.	4.00
4 F:Lex Luthor.	4.00
5 Untold Tales.	4.00

DC COMICS

6 Lex & Clark,48-pg. 4.00
7 TG,Television x-over,pt.1 . . . . . . 4.00
8 TG,Television x-over,pt.2 . . . . . . 4.00
9 Mysterious men 4.00
10 Who shot Lionel Luthor. 4.00
11 48-page 4.00
TPB Rep. 10.00

SMASH COMICS
1999
1 TPe(s),F:Doctor Mid-Nite
   & Hourman 2.25

SMAX
DC/Vertigo, 2003
1 (of 5) AMo(s) 3.00
2 thru 4 AMo(s) 3.00

SOLO
2004
1 TSe,48-pg. 4.00
2 RCo, 5 stories 5.00
3 PPo 5.00
4 HC 5.00
5 Darwyn Cooke 5.00
6 . . . . 5.00
7 MiA 5.00
8 NGa(s) 5.00
9 SHp 5.00
10 Five stories 5.00
11 SA 5.00
12 BMc,final issue 5.00

SONIC DISRUPTORS
1987–88
1 thru 10 . . . . @3.00

SON OF AMBUSH BUG
July, 1986
1 thru 6 KG . . . . @2.25

SON OF VULCAN
June, 2005
1 (of 6) Mikey Devante 3.00
2 . . . . 3.00
3 F:Green Lantern & JLA 3.00
4 Vulcan's superpowers 3.00
5 Coalition of Crime 3.00
6 Coalition of Crime, concl.. . . . . . 3.00

Sovereign Seven #18
© DC Comics, Inc.

SOVEREIGN SEVEN
1995–98
1 CCI(s),DT,I:Sovereign Seven,
   V:Female Furies,A:Darkseid . . . 3.00
2 thru 11 CCI(s). . . . . @2.50
12 thru 36 CCI(s) . . . . @2.25
Ann.#1 CCI, Year One Annual 4.00
Ann.#2 CCI(s),RL,KJ,Legends of
   the Dead Earth 3.00
1-shot Sovereign Seven Plus
   (1977) 3.00
TPB CCI(s),DT, rep.#1–#5 . . . . . 13.00

SPACE GHOST
Nov., 2004
1 AOI,O:Space Ghost 15.00
2 AOI 6.00
3 thru 6 AOI,V:Zorak . . . . @3.00
TPB 15.00

SPANNER'S GALAXY
Dec., 1984
1 mini-series 2.25
2 thru 6 . . . . @2.25

SPECIAL EDITION
1944–45
(Reprint giveaways for U.S. Navy)
1 Action Comics #80,WB 750.00
2 Action Comics#81,WB 750.00
3 Superman #33 . . . . 750.00
4 Detective Comics#97 . . . . 750.00
5 Superman #34 . . . . 750.00
6 Action Comics #84,WB 750.00

SPECTRE, THE
1967–69
1 MA,V:Captain Skull 300.00
2 NA,V:Dirk Rawley 175.00
3 NA,A:Wildcat 175.00
4 NA 175.00
5 NA 175.00
6 MA 125.00
7 MA,BU:Hourman 125.00
8 MA,Parchment of Power
   Perilous 125.00
9 BWr(2nd BWr Art) 200.00
10 MA. 150.00

[2nd Regular Series], 1987–89
1 GC,O:Spectre 5.00
2 GC,Cult of BRM 4.00
3 GC,Fashion Model Murders 3.00
4 GC 3.00
5 GC,Spectre's Murderer 3.00
6 GC,Spectre/Corrigan separated . 3.00
7 A:Zatanna,Wotan 3.00
8 A:Zatanna,Wotan 3.00
9 GM,Spectre's Revenge 3.00
10 GM,A:Batman,Millennium 3.00
11 GM,Millennium 3.00
12 GM,The Talisman,pt.1 . . . . 3.00
13 GM,The Talisman,pt.2 . . . . 3.00
14 GM,The Talisman,pt.3 . . . . 3.00
15 GM,The Talisman,pt.4 . . . . 3.00
16 Jim Corrigan Accused 3.00
17 New Direction,Final Destiny . . . 3.00
18 Search for Host Body 3.00
19 Dead Again 3.00
20 Corrigan Detective Agency 3.00
21 A:Zoran 3.00
22 BS,Sea of Darkness,A:Zoran . . . 3.00
23 A:Lords of Order,
   Invasion x-over 3.00
24 BWg,Ghosts i/t Machine#1 . . . . 3.00
25 Ghosts in the Machine #2 . . . . . 3.00
26 Ghosts in the Machine #3 . . . . . 3.00
27 Ghosts in the Machine #4 . . . . . 3.00
28 Ghosts in the Machine #5 . . . . . 3.00

Spectre 2nd Series #28
© DC Comics, Inc.

29 Ghosts in the Machine #6 . . . . . 3.00
30 Possession 3.00
31 Spectre possessed, final issue . 3.00
Ann.#1, A:Deadman 3.00

[3rd Regular Series], 1992–97
1 B:JOs(s),TMd,R:Spectre,
   Glow in the dark(c) 7.00
2 TMd,Murder Mystery 6.00
3 TMd,O:Spectre. 4.00
4 TMd,O:Spectre. 4.00
5 TMd,BB(c),V:Kidnappers 3.50
6 TMd,Spectre prevents evil 3.50
7 TMd 3.50
8 TMd,Glow in the dark(c) 5.00
9 TMd,MWg(c),V:The Reaver. 3.00
10 TMd,V:Michael 3.00
11 TMd,V:Azmodeus 3.00
12 V:Reaver 3.00
13 TMd,V:Count Vertigo,
   Glow in the Dark(c) 4.00
14 JoP,A:Phantom Stranger 2.50
15 TMd,A:Phantom Stranger,Demon,
   Doctor Fate,John Constantine. . 2.50
16 JAp,V:I.R.A. 2.50
17 TT(c),TMd,V:Eclipso 2.50
18 TMd,D:Eclipso. 2.50
19 TMd,V:Hate 2.50
20 A:Lucien 2.50
21 V:Naiad,C:Superman 3.00
22 A:Superman 2.50
23 Book of Judgment, pt.1 . . . . 2.50
24 Book of Judgment, pt.2 . . . . 2.50
25 Book of Judgment, pt.3 . . . . 2.50
26 The Door of the Solstice 2.50
27 R:Azmodus 2.50
28 V:Azmodus 2.50
29 V:Azmodus 2.50
30 V:Azmodus 2.50
31 Descent into Pandemonium . . . 2.50
32 V:Killo 2.50
33 JOs 2.50
34 Power of the Undead 2.50
35 JOs,TMd,Underworld
   Unleashed tie-in 2.50
36 JOs,TMd,Underworld
   Unleashed tie-in 2.50
37 JOs,TMd,The Haunting of
   America,pt.1 . . . . 2.50
38 JOs,TMd,The Haunting of
   America,pt.2 . . . . 2.50
39 JOs,TMd,The Haunting of
   America,pt.3 . . . . 2.50
40 JOs,TMd,The Haunting of
   America,pt.4 . . . . 2.50
41 JOs,TMd,The Haunting of
   America,pt.5 . . . . 2.50

42 JOs,TMd,The Haunting of
   America,pt.6 . . . . 2.50
43 Witchcraft 2.50
44 Madame Xanadu 2.50
45 JOs(s),Acts of God 2.50
46 JOs(s),TMd,discovery of the
   Spear of Destiny 2.50
47 JOs(s),TMd,The Haunting of
   America, Final Night tie-in 2.50
48 JOs(s),TMd,The Haunting of
   America 2.50
49 JOs(s),TMd,The Haunting of
   America 2.50
50 JOs(s),TMd, ... 2.50
51 JOs(s),TMd,A:Batman,Joker. . . 2.50
52 JOs(s),TMd,Nate Kane discovers
   murder evidence 2.50
53 JOs(s),TMd,Haunting of Jim
   Corrigan, cont. 2.50
54 JOs(s),TMd,hunt for murderer of
   Mister Terrific. 2.50
55 JOs(s),TMd,Corrigan implicated
   in murder 2.50
56 JOs(s),TMd,JTo, Haunting of Jim
   Corrigan. 2.50
57 JOs(s),TMd,Spectre & Jim
   Corrigan in Heaven 2.50
58 JOs,TMd,Genesis tie-in 2.50
59 JOs,TMd,BWr(c), alien pod . . . 2.50
60 JOs,TMd,Quest for God, cont. . . 2.50
61 JOs,TMd,Quest for God, concl. . 2.50
62 JOs,TMd,final issue 2.50
Ann.#1 JOs,TMd,Year One 4.00

SPECTRE, THE
Jan., 2001
1 JMD,F:Hal Jordan 3.00
2 JMD,Redeeming the Demon,pt.1 2.50
3 JMD,Redeeming the Demon,pt.2 2.50
4 JMD,Redeeming the Demon,pt.3 2.50
5 JMD,F:Two-Face/Harvey Dent . . 2.50
6 JMD,The Redeemer,pt.1 . . . . . . 2.50
7 JMD,The Redeemer,pt.2 . . . . . . 2.50
8 JMD,The Redeemer,pt.3 . . . . . . 2.50
9 JMD,stolen soul 2.50
10 JMD,Joker:Last Laugh 2.50
11 JMD,F:Phantom Stranger 2.50
12 JMD,Spectre of Christmas 2.50
13 JMD,Eternity in an Hour 2.50
14 JMD,vampire-lord 2.50
15 JMD,NBy,Mystery in Space,pt.1 2.50
16 JMD,NBy,Mystery in Space,pt.2 2.50
17 JMD,NBy,Mystery in Space,pt.3 2.50
18 JMD,NBy,Abin Sur, Materna. . . . 2.50
19 NBy,DJa,V:Darkseid. 2.50
20 NBy,DJa,magazine publisher . . 2.75
21 NBy,DJa,Stigmonus,C.Ferris . . 2.75
22 NBy,DJa:G.Arrow,
   M.Manhunter 2.75
23 JMD,NBy,DJa,Return of
   Sinestro,pt.3 . . . . 2.75
24 JMD,DJa,F:DCU characters 2.75
25 JMD,DJa,F:Rabid 2.75
26 JMD,DJa,terrorist 2.75
27 JMD,DJa,final issue 2.75

SPEED FORCE
Sept., 1997
1 MWa,BAu,JBy,BML,JAp,BSn,
   Flash stories, 64pg. 4.00

SPELLJAMMER
Sept., 1990
1 RogueShip#1 . . . . 3.00
2 RogueShip#2 . . . . 2.50
3 thru 15 . . . . @2.25

SPIRIT, THE
Dec., 2006
1 F:Denny Colt 3.00

2 F:P'Gell 3.00
3 A dead gunman 3.00
4 Mexican bordertown 3.00
5 Spirit Pork & Beans Spread 3.00
6 A fallen meteor. 3.00
7 Three tales. 3.00
8 Time Bomb. 3.00
9 V:El Morte 3.00
10 Murder case 3.00
11 F:El Morte, Central City gangs . . 3.00

STALKER
1975–1976
1 SD,WW,O&I:Stalker 20.00
2 thru 4 SD,WW . . . . @15.00

STANLEY & HIS MONSTER
See: FOX AND THE CROW

STANLEY & HIS MONSTER
1993
1 R:Stanley 2.25
2 I:Demon Hunter 2.25
3 A:Ambrose Bierce 2.25
4 final issue 2.25

S.T.A.R. CORPS
1993
1 A:Superman 2.25
2 I:Fusion,A:Rampage 2.25
3 thru 6 . . . . @2.25

STAR CROSSED
DC/Helix, April, 1997
1 (of 3) MHo,Dyltah's romance
   with Saa. 2.50
2 MHo,Love During Wartime 2.50
3 concl. 2.50

[NEIL GAIMAN & CHARLES VESS']
STARDUST
DC/Vertigo, Oct., 1997
1 (of 4) NGa(s),CV 6.00
2 NGa(s),CV adult faerie tale 6.00
3 NGa(s),CV. 6.00
4 NGa(s),CV. 6.00

STARFIRE
1976–77
1 . . . . 20.00
2 . . . . 12.00
3 thru 8 . . . . @12.00

STAR HUNTERS
Oct.–Nov., 1977
1 DN&BL. 15.00
2 LH&BL 12.00
3 MN&BL,D:Donovan Flint 12.00
4 thru 7 . . . . @12.00

STARMAN
1988–92
1 TL,I&O:New Starman 4.00
2 TL,V:Serial Killer,C:Bolt 3.00
3 TL,V:Bolt 3.00
4 TL,V:Power Elite 2.50
5 TL,Invasion,A:PowerGirl,
   Firestorm 2.50
6 TL,Invasion,A:G.L.,Atom 2.50
7 TL,Soul Searching Issue 2.50
8 TL,V:LadyQuark. 2.50
9 TL,A:Batman,V:Blockbuster. . . . 2.50
10 TL,A:Batman,V:Blockbuster . . . 2.50
11 TL,V:Power Elite 2.50

12 TL,V:Power Elite,A:Superman . . 2.50
13 TL,V:Rampage 2.50
14 TL,A:Superman,V:Parasite . . . 2.50
15 TL,V:Deadline 2.50
16 TL,O:Starman 2.50
17 TL,V:Dr.Polaris,A:PowerGirl . . . 2.50
18 TL,V:Dr.Polaris,A:PowerGirl . . . 2.50
19 TL,V:Artillery 2.50
20 TL,FireFighting 2.50
21 TL,Starman Quits 2.50
22 TL,V:Khunds 2.50
23 TL,A:Deadline 2.50
24 TL,A:Deadline 2.50
25 TL,V:Deadline 2.50
26 V:The Mist. 6.00
27 V:The Mist. 5.00
28 A:Superman 7.00
29 V:Plasmax. 2.50
30 Seduction of Starman #1 . . . . . 2.50
31 Seduction of Starman #2 . . . . . 2.50
32 Seduction of Starman #3 . . . . . 2.50
33 Seduction of Starman #4 . . . . . 2.50
34 A:Batman 2.50
35 A:Valor,Mr.Nebula,ScarletSkier . . 2.50
36 A:Les Mille Yeux 2.50
37 A:Les Mille Yeux 2.50
38 War of the Gods X-over 2.50
39 V:Plasmax. 2.50
40 V:Las Vegas 2.50
41 V:Maaldor 2.50
42 Star Shadows,pt.1,A:Eclipso. . . . 3.00
43 Star Shadows,pt.2,A:Lobo,
   Eclipso. 2.50
44 Star Shadows,pt.3,A:Eclipso
   V:Lobo 2.50
45 Star Shadows,pt.4, V:Eclipso . . . 2.50

[2nd Series], 1994
0 New Starman 8.00
1 Sins of the Father,pt.2 . . . . 8.00
2 Sins of the Father,pt.3 . . . . 7.00
3 Sins of the Father,pt.4 . . . . 6.00
4 A Day in the Opal. 6.00
5 V:Starman 6.00
6 Times Past Features 6.00
7 Sinister Circus 6.00
8 TyH(c),Sinister Circus 5.00
9 TyH(c),Mist's daughter breaks
   out of prison. 5.00
10 Sins of the Chile,prelude 5.00
11 JeR,TyH,13 Years Ago:5 Friends 5.00
12 JeR,TyH,Sins of the Child,pt.1 . . 5.00
13 JeR,TyH,Sins of the Child,pt.2 . . 5.00
14 JeR,TyH,Sins of the Child,pt.3 . . 5.00
15 JeR,TyH,Sins of the Child,pt.4 . . 5.00
16 JeR,TyH,Sins of the Child,pt.5 . . 5.00
17 JeR,TyH 5.00

Starman 2nd Series #0
© DC Comics Inc.

All comics prices listed are for *Near Mint* condition.

18 JeR,TyH,Orig.Starman
   vs.The Mist 4.00
19 JeR,TyH,Talking with David 2 . . . 4.00
20 JeR(s),TyH,GyD,Sand and
   Stars,pt.1 . . . . 4.00
21 JeR,TyH,GyD,Sand/Stars,pt.2 . . 3.00
22 JeR,TyH,GyD,Sand/Stars,pt.3 . . 3.00
23 JeR,TyH,GyD,Sand/Stars,pt.4 . . 3.00
24 JeR(s),TyH,Hell & Back,pt.1 . . . 3.00
25 JeR(s),TyH,Hell & Back,pt.2 . . . 3.00
26 JeR(s),TyH,Hell & Back,pt.3 . . . 3.00
27 JeR(s),Christmas Knight 3.00
28 JeR(s)Superfreaks and
   Backstabbers 3.00
29 JeR(s),TyH,GyD,V:The Shade,
   Starman history 3.00
30 JeR(s),TyH,Infernal Devices
   pt.1 (of 6) 3.00
31 JeR(s),TyH,Devices,pt.2 . . . . . . 3.00
32 JeR(s),TyH,Devices,pt.3 . . . . . . 3.00
33 JeR(s),TyH,Infernal Devices
   pt.4,A:Batman, Sentinel 3.00
34 JeR(s),TyH,A:Batman, Sentinel,
   Floronic Man 3.00
35 JeR(s),TyH,A:Batman, Floronic
   Man, Sentinel 3.00
36 JeR(s),TyH,F:Will Payton 3.00
37 JeR(s),TyH,F:GoldenAgeHeroes 3.00
38 JeR(s),TyH,new JLE 2.50
39 JeR(s),TyH,Lightning &
   Stars, pt.1 x-over 2.50
40 JeR(s),TyH 2.50
41 JeR(s),GEr,TyH 2.50
42 JeR(s),MS,Nazis,Demon 2.50
43 JeR(s),TyH,help from JLA 2.50
44 JeR(s),times past story 2.50
45 JeR(s),search for Will Payton . . 2.50
46 JeR(s),TyH,Bobo. 2.50
47 JeR,SY,TyH 2.50
48 JeR,SY,A:Swamp Thing 2.50
49 JeR,SY,Talking with David 2.50
50 JeR(s),PSj,48-page. 5.00
51 JeR(s),PSj,to Krypton 2.50
52 JeR(s),PSj,A:Adam Strange 2.50
53 JeR(s),PSj,A:Adam Strange 2.50
54 JeR(s),Times Past tale 2.50
55 JeR(s),PSj,A:Space Cabby 2.50
56 JeR(s),PSj,A:ElongatedMan 2.50
57 JeR(s),PSj,TyH,AxR,A:Tigorr
   & Fastbak, pt.1 . . . . 2.50
58 JeR,TyH,AxR, pt.2 . . . . 2.50
59 JeR,TyH,AxR, pt.3 . . . . 2.50
60 JeR,TyH,AxR, concl. 2.50
61 JeR,TyH,AxR 2.50
62 JeR,PSj,Grand Guignol,pt.1 . . . . 2.50
63 JeR,PSj,Grand Guignol,pt.2 . . . . 2.50
64 JeR,PSj,Grand Guignol,pt.3 . . . . 2.50
65 JeR,PSj,Grand Guignol,pt.4 . . . . 2.50
66 JeR,PSj,Grand Guignol,pt.5 . . . . 2.50
67 JeR,PSj,Grand Guignol,pt.6 . . . . 2.50
68 JeR,PSj,Grand Guignol,pt.7 . . . . 2.50
69 JeR,PSj,flashback. 2.50
70 JeR,PSj,Grand Guignol,pt.8 . . . . 2.50
71 JeR,PSj,Grand Guignol,pt.9 . . . . 2.50
72 JeR,PSj,Grand Guignol, concl. . . 2.50
73 JeR,PSj,Grand Guignol,Eulogy . 2.50
74 JeR,RH,Times Past 2.50
75 JeR,A:Superman. 2.50
76 JeR,Talking With David:2001 . . . 2.50
77 JeR,1951,pt.1 . . . . 2.50
78 JeR,1951,pt.2 . . . . 2.50
79 JeR,1951,pt.3 . . . . 2.50
80 JeR,48-page final issue 4.50
Ann.#1 Legends o/t Dead Earth . . . 4.00
Ann.#2 Pulp Heroes (Romance) . . . 4.50
Spec.#1,000,000 JeR(s),PSj 2.50
Secret Files #1,O:Starmen 5.00
Giant #1 80-page 5.00
Spec. Starman: The Mist, F:Mary
   Marvel, Girlfrenzy (1998) 2.50

STARS AND S.T.R.I.P.E.
1999
0 LMd,DDv,I:Courtney Whitman . . . 3.00
1 LMd,DDv,O:Star-Spangled Kid . . 2.50
2 LMd,DDv,V:Paintball 2.50
3 LMd,DDv,V:Skeeter 2.50
4 LMd,DDv,Day of Judgment
   x-over. 2.50
5 LMd,DDv,F:Young Justice,pt.1. . . 2.50
6 . . . . 2.50
7 LMd,DDv,F:Mike Dugan. 2.50
8 LMd,DDv 2.50
9 LMd,DDv,R:Nebula Man 2.50
10 LMd,DDv,cheating. 2.50
11 DDv,V:Dr. Graft 2.50
12 DDv,V:Dragon King 2.50
13 DDv,V:Dragon King 2.50
14 LMd,DDv,final issue 2.50

STAR SPANGLED COMICS
Oct., 1941
1 O:Tarantula,B:Captain X of the
   R.A.F.,Star Spangled Kid,
   Armstrong of the Army 9,000.00
2 Star Spang.Kid V:Dr.Weerd . 2,700.00
3 Star Spang.Kid V:Dr.Weerd . 2,000.00
4 V:The Needle 2,000.00
5 V:Dr. Weerd, V:The Needle . 2,000.00
6 E:Armstrong 1,200.00
7 S&K,O&1st app:The Guardian,
   B:Robotman,The Newsboy
   Legion, TNT 11,000.00
8 O:TNT & Dan the Dyna-Mite 3,500.00
9 S&K(c&a),Newsboy Legion . 2,700.00
10 S&K(c&a),Newsboy Legion . 2,700.00
11 S&K(c&a),Newsboy Legion . 2,000.00
12 S&K(c&a),Newsboy Legion,
   Prevue of Peril!. 2,000.00
13 S&K(c&a),Suicide Slum 2,000.00
14 S&K,Meanest Man on Earth . 2,000.00
15 S&K(c&a),Playmates ofPeril 2,000.00
16 S&K(c&a),Newsboy Legion . 2,000.00
17 S&K(c&a),V:Rafferty Mob . . 2,000.00
18 S&K,O:Star Spangled Kid . . 2,500.00
19 S&K(c&a),E:Tarantula 2,000.00
20 S&K(c&a),B:Liberty Belle . . . 2,000.00
21 S&K,Newsboy Legion 1,800.00
22 S&K,Brains for Sale. 1,800.00
23 S&K,Art for Scrapper'sSake 1,800.00
24 S&K,Death Strikes Bargain . 1,800.00
25 S&K,Victuals for Victory 1,800.00
26 S&K,Newsboy Legion 1,800.00
27 S&K,Turn on the Heat 1,800.00
28 S&K,Poor Man's Rich Man . . 1,800.00

Star Spangled Comics #6
© DC Comics, Inc.

29 JK,Cabbages and Comics . . 1,800.00
30 JK,Lady of Linden Lake 1,200.00
31 S&K,Questions Please! 1,200.00
32 The Good Samaritan 1,200.00
33 Case of the Baleful Bride. . . 1,200.00
34 From Rags to Ruin 1,200.00
35 The Proud Poppa. 1,200.00
36 Cowboy of Suicide Slum . . . 1,200.00
37 Diamonds in the Rough 1,200.00
38 Roll Out the Barrels 1,200.00
39 Two Guardians are a Crowd 1,200.00
40 Farewell to Crime. 1,000.00
41 Time Out for the Guardian . . . 900.00
42 JK,(c),Power of the Press 900.00
43 CS(c),Trials of a Tenor 900.00
44 Etiquette in Suicide Slum 900.00
45 Crime Gets Clipped 900.00
46 Clothes Make the Criminal . . . 900.00
47 Triumph of Tommy 900.00
48 CS(c),Booty & the Blizzard . . . 900.00
49 CS(c),One Ounce to Victory . . 900.00
50 JKu,Guardian(c). 900.00
51 A:Robot Robber 900.00
52 Rehearsal for Crime 900.00
53 The Poet of Suicide Slum 900.00
54 Dead-Shot Dade's Revenge . . 900.00
55 Gabby Strikes a Gusher 900.00
56 The Treasurer of Araby 900.00
57 Recruit for the Legion 900.00
58 Matadors of Suicide Slum. . . . 900.00
59 JK,Answers Inc. 750.00
60 CS(c),Steve Brodie Da 2nd . . 750.00
61 CS,Great Ballroom Race 750.00
62 Prevue of Tomorrow 750.00
63 CS,Code of the Newsstand . . . 750.00
64 Criminal Cruise 750.00
65 B:Robin,(c) & stories 2,400.00
66 V:No Face 1,300.00
67 The Castle of Doom. 1,100.00
68 WMo(c&a),Octopus (c) 1,100.00
69 The Stolen Atom Bomb 2,000.00
70 V:The Clock 1,100.00
71 Perils of the Stone Age 1,100.00
72 Robin Crusoe 1,100.00
73 V:The Black Magician 1,100.00
74 V:The Clock 1,100.00
75 The State vs. Robin 1,100.00
76 V:The Fence 1,100.00
77 The Boy who Wanted Robin
   for Christmas 1,100.00
78 Rajah Robin 1,100.00
79 V:The Clock,The Tick-Tock
   Crimes 1,100.00
80 The Boy Disc Jockey. 1,000.00
81 The Seeing-Eye Dog Crimes . 900.00
82 The Boy who Hated Robin . . . 900.00
83 Who is Mr. Mystery,B:Captain
   Compass backup story 900.00
84 How can we Fight Juvenile
   Delinquency? 1,000.00
85 Peril at the Pole 850.00
86 The Barton Brothers 850.00
87 V:Sinister Knight 1,200.00
88 Robin Declares War on
   Batman, B:Batman app. . . . 1,000.00
89 Batman's Utility Belt? 1,000.00
90 Rancho Fear! 1,000.00
91 Cops 'n' Robbers? 1,000.00
92 Movie Hero No. 1? 1,000.00
93 Riddle of the Sphinx 1,000.00
94 Underworld Playhouse 1,100.00
95 The Man with the Midas Touch,
   E:Robin(c),Batman story . 1,100.00
96 B:Tomahawk(c) & stories 750.00
97 The 4 Bold Warriors 600.00
98 Robin's Rival 600.00
99 The Second Pocahontas 600.00
100 The Frontier Phantom. 750.00
101 Peril on the High Seas 600.00
102 Riddle of Mohawk Valley . . . 600.00
103 Tomahawk's Death Duel! . . . 600.00
104 Race with Death! 600.00

Star Spangled Comics #91
© DC Comics, Inc.

105 The Unhappy Hunting
Grounds. 600.00
106 Traitor in the War Paint. 600.00
107 The Brave who Hunted
Tomahawk 600.00
108 'The Ghost called Moccasin
Foot!' 600.00
109 The Land Pirates of
Jolly Roger Hill! 600.00
110 Sally Raines Frontier Girl . . . 600.00
111 The Death Map of Thunder
Hill 600.00
112 Coin of Courage 600.00
113 FF,V:The Black Cougar. 750.00
114 Return of the Black Cougar . 750.00
115 Journey of a Thousand
Deaths. 600.00
116 The Battle of Junction Fort . . 600.00
117 Siege?. 600.00
118 V:Outlaw Indians. 500.00
119 The Doomed Stockade? 500.00
120 Revenge of Raven Heart!. . . . 550.00
121 Adventure in New York! 500.00
122 I:Ghost Breaker,(c)& stories . 700.00
123 The Dolls of Doom 450.00
124 Suicide Tower 450.00
125 The Hermit's Ghost Dog! 450.00
126 The Phantom of Paris! 450.00
127 The Supernatural Alibi! 450.00
128 C:Batman,The Girl who
lived 5,000 Years! 450.00
129 The Human Orchids 500.00
130 The Haunted Town,
July, 1952 . . . . 600.00
Becomes:

STAR SPANGLED
WAR STORIES
Aug., 1952
131 CS&StK(c),I Was A Jap
Prisoner of War 1,600.00
132 CS&StK(c),The G.I. With
The Million-Dollar Arm 1,100.00
133 CS&StK(c),Mission-San
Marino. 1,000.00
3 CS&StK(c),Hundred-Mission
Mitchell 750.00
4 CS&StK(c),The Hot Rod Tank . 750.00
5 LSt(c),Jet Pilot 750.00
6 CS(c),Operation Davy Jones . 750.00
7 CS(c),Rookie Ranger,The 700.00
8 CS(c),I Was A
Hollywood Soldier 700.00
9 CS&StK(c),Sad Sack Squad . . 700.00
10 CS,The G.I. & The Gambler . . 700.00
11 LSt(c),The Lucky Squad 700.00

12 CS(c),The Four Horseman of
Barricade Hill. 700.00
13 No Escape 700.00
14 LSt(c),Pitchfork Army 700.00
15 The Big Fish 700.00
16 The Yellow Ribbon 700.00
17 IN(c),Prize Target 700.00
18 IN(c),The Gladiator 700.00
19 IN(c),The Big Lift. 700.00
20 JGr(c),The Battle of
the Frogmen 700.00
21 JGr(c),Dead Man's Bridge . . . 400.00
22 JGr(c),Death Hurdle 400.00
23 JGr(c),The Silent Frogman . . . 400.00
24 JGr(c),Death Slide 400.00
25 JGr(c),S.S. Liferaft 400.00
26 JGr(c),Bazooka Man. 400.00
27 JGr(c),Taps for a Tail Gunner . 400.00
28 JGr(c),Tank Duel. 500.00
29 JGr(c),A Gun Called Slugger . 400.00
30 JGr(c),The Thunderbolt Tank . 400.00
31 IN(c),Tank Block 300.00
32 JGr(c),Bridge to Battle 300.00
33 JGr(c),Pocket War 300.00
34 JGr(c),Fighting...Snowbirds . . 300.00
35 JGr(c),Zero Hour. 300.00
36 JGr(c),A G.I. Passed Here . . . 300.00
37 JGr(c),A Handful of T.N.T. . . . 300.00
38 RH(c),One-Man Army 300.00
39 JGr(c),Flying Cowboy 300.00
40 JGr(c),Desert Duel 300.00
41 IN(c),A Gunner's Hands 250.00
42 JGr(c),Sniper Alley 250.00
43 JGr(c),Top Kick Brother 250.00
44 JGr(c),Tank 711
Doesn't Answer 250.00
45 JGr(c),Flying Heels 250.00
46 JGr(c),Gunner's Seat 250.00
47 JGr(c),Sidekick 250.00
48 JGr(c),Battle Hills 250.00
49 JGr(c),Payload 250.00
50 JGr(c),Combat Dust 250.00
51 JGr(c),Battle Pigeon 200.00
52 JGr(c),Cannon-Man 200.00
53 JGr(c),Combat Close-Ups . . . 200.00
54 JGr(c),Flying Exit 200.00
55 JKu(c),The Burning Desert . . . 200.00
56 JKu(c),The Walking Sub 200.00
57 JGr(c),Call For a Frogman . . . 200.00
58 JGr(c),MD,Waist Punch 200.00
59 JGr(c),Kick In The Door 200.00
60 JGr(c),Hotbox 200.00
61 JGr(c),MD,Tow Pilot 200.00
62 JGr(c),The Three GIs 200.00
63 JGr(c),Flying Range Rider . . . 200.00
64 JGr(c),MD,Frogman Ambush . 200.00
65 JGr(c),JSe,Frogman Block . . . 200.00
66 JGr(c),Flattop Pigeon 200.00
67 RH(c),MD,Ashcan Alley 200.00
68 JGr(c),The Long Step 200.00
69 JKu(c),Floating Tank, The. . . . 200.00
70 JKu(c),No Medal For
Frogman 200.00
71 JKu(c),Shooting Star. 200.00
72 JGr(c),Silent Fish 200.00
73 JGr(c),MD,The Mouse &
the Tiger 200.00
74 JGr(c),MD,Frogman Bait. 200.00
75 JGr(c),MD,Paratroop
Mousketeers 200.00
76 MD,JKu(c),Odd Man 200.00
77 MD,JKu(c),Room to Fight 200.00
78 MD,JGr(c),Fighting Wingman . 200.00
79 MD,JKu(c),Zero Box 200.00
80 MD,JGr(c),Top Gunner 200.00
81 MD,RH(c),Khaki Mosquito . . . 200.00
82 MD,JKu(c),Ground Flier 200.00
83 MD,JGr(c),Jet On
My Shoulder 200.00
84 MD,IN(c),O:Mademoiselle
Marie 350.00
85 IN(c),A Medal For Marie 250.00

Star Spangled War Stories #98
© DC Comics, Inc.

86 JGr(c),A Medal For Marie 250.00
87 JGr(c),T.N.T. Spotlight. 250.00
88 JGr(c),The Steel Trap 250.00
89 IN(c),Trail of the Terror 250.00
90 RA(c),Island of
Armored Giants 800.00
91 JGr(c),The Train of Terror 200.00
92 Last Battle of the
Dinosaur Age. 250.00
93 Goliath of the Western Front . 200.00
94 JKu(c),The Frogman and
the Dinosaur 500.00
95 Guinea Pig Patrol,Dinosaurs . 300.00
96 Mission X,Dinosaur. 300.00
97 The Sub-Crusher, Dinosaur . . 300.00
98 Island of Thunder, Dinosaur . . 300.00
99 The Circus of Monsters,
Dinosaur 300.00
100 The Volcano of Monsters,
Dinosaur 350.00
101 The Robot and the Dinosaur 250.00
102 Punchboard War,Dinosaur . . 250.00
103 Doom at Dinosaur Island,
Dinosaur 250.00
104 The Tree of Terror,
Dinosaurs 250.00
105 The War of Dinosaur Island . 250.00
106 The Nightmare War,
Dinosaurs 250.00
107 Battle of the Dinosaur
Aquarium 250.00
108 Dinosaur D-Day 250.00
109 The Last Soldiers 250.00
110 thru 133 . . . . @250.00
134 NA. 250.00
135 . . . . 250.00
136 . . . . 250.00
137 Dinosaur 250.00
138 Enemy Ace 275.00
139 O:Enemy Ace 200.00
140 . . . . 150.00
141 . . . . 150.00
142 . . . . 150.00
143 . . . . 150.00
144 NA,JKu 200.00
145 . . . . 150.00
146 Enemy Ace(c) 100.00
147 New Enemy Ace 100.00
148 New Enemy Ace 100.00
149 . . . . 100.00
150 JKu,Viking Prince 100.00
151 I:Unknown Soldier 250.00
152 Rep. New Enemy Ace. 100.00
153 . . . . 100.00
154 O:Unknown Soldier 200.00

155 Rep. New Enemy Ace 75.00
156 I:Battle Album 75.00
157 thru 160 . . . . 50.00
161 E:Enemy Ace 50.00
162 thru 170 . . . . @40.00
171 thru 200 . . . . @25.00
201 thru 204 . . . . @20.00

Unknown Soldier #224
© DC Comics, Inc.

Becomes:

UNKNOWN SOLDIER

April-May, 1977

205 thru 247 . . . . @17.00
248 and 249 O:Unknown Soldier @12.00
250 . . . . 12.00
251 B:Enemy Ace 12.00
252 thru 268 . . . . @12.00

STAR SPANGLED COMICS

1999

1 CWn, F:Sandman & Star
  Spangled Kid 2.25

STAR TREK

1984–88

[1st Regular Series]

1 TS,The Wormhole Connection . 15.00
2 TS,The Only Good Klingon 8.00
3 TS,Errand of War 7.00
4 TS,Deadly Allies 7.00
5 TS,Mortal Gods 7.00
6 TS,Who is Enigma? 6.00
7 EB,O:Saavik 6.00
8 TS,Blood Fever 6.00
9 TS,Mirror Universe Saga #1 . . . 6.00
10 TS,Mirror Universe Saga #2 . . . 6.00
11 TS,Mirror Universe Saga #3 . . . 6.00
12 TS,Mirror Universe Saga #4 . . . 6.00
13 TS,Mirror Universe Saga #5 . . . 5.00
14 TS,Mirror Universe Saga #6 . . . 5.00
15 TS,Mirror Universe Saga #7 . . . 5.00
16 TS,Mirror Universe Saga end . . 5.00
17 TS,The D'Artagnan Three 5.00
18 TS,Rest & Recreation 5.00
19 DSp,W.Koenig story 5.00
20 TS,Girl 5.00
21 TS,Dreamworld 5.00
22 TS,The Wolf #1 . . . . 5.00
23 TS,The Wolf #2 . . . . 4.00
24 TS,Double Blind #1 . . . . 4.00
25 TS,Double Blind #2 . . . . 4.00
26 TSV:Romulans 4.00
27 TS,Day in the Life 4.00
28 GM,The Last Word 4.00
29 Trouble with Bearclaw 4.00

30 Cl,F:Uhura 4.00
31 TS,Maggie's World 4.00
32 TS,Judgment Day 4.00
33 TS,20th Anniv. 5.00
34 V:Romulans 3.00
35 GM,Excelsior 3.00
36 GM,StarTrek IV tie-in 3.00
37 StarTrek IV tie-in 3.00
38 AKu,The Argon Affair 3.00
39 TS,A:Harry Mudd 3.00
40 TS,A:Harry Mudd 3.00
41 TS,V:Orions 3.00
42 TS,The Corbomite Effect 3.00
43 TS,Paradise Lost #1 . . . . 3.00
44 TS,Paradise Lost #2 . . . . 3.00
45 TS,Paradise Lost #3 . . . . 3.00
46 TS,Getaway 3.00
47 TS,Idol Threats 3.00
48 TS,The Stars in Secret
    Influence 3.00
49 TS,Aspiring to be Angels 3.00
50 TS,Anniv. 4.00
51 TS,Haunted Honeymoon 3.00
52 TS,'Hell in a Hand Basket 3.00
53 You're Dead,Jim 3.00
54 Old Loyalties 3.00
55 TS,Finnegan's Wake 3.00
56 GM,Took place during 5 year
    Mission 3.00
Ann.#1 All Those Years Ago 4.00
Ann.#2 DJw,The Final Voyage . . . 3.00
Ann.#3 CS,F:Scotty 3.00
Star Trek III Adapt.TS 2.50
Star Trek IV Adapt. TS 2.50
StarTrek V Adapt. 2.50

[2nd Regular Series], 1989–96

1 The Return 9.00
2 The Sentence 5.00
3 Death Before Dishonor 4.00
4 Reprocussions 4.00
5 Fast Friends 4.00
6 Cure All 4.00
7 Not Sweeney! 4.00
8 Going,Going. 3.50
9 ...Gone. 3.50
10 Trial of James Kirk #1 . . . . 3.50
11 Trial of James Kirk #2 . . . . 3.50
12 Trial of James Kirk #3 . . . . 3.50
13 Return of Worthy #1 . . . . 3.50
14 Return of Worthy #2 . . . . 3.50
15 Return of Worthy #3 . . . . 3.50
16 Worldsinger 3.00
17 Partners? #1 . . . . 3.00
18 Partners? #2 . . . . 3.00
19 Once A Hero 3.00
20 . . . . 3.00
21 Kirk Trapped 3.00
22 A:Harry Mudd 3.00
23 The Nasgul,A:Harry Mudd 3.00
24 25th Anniv.,A:Harry Mudd 4.00
25 Starfleet Officers Reunion 3.00
26 Pilkor 3 . . . . 3.00
27 Kirk Betrayed 3.00
28 V:Romulans 3.00
29 Mediators 3.00
30 Veritas #1 . . . . 3.00
31 Veritas #2 . . . . 3.00
32 Veritas #3 . . . . 3.00
33 Veritas #4 . . . . 3.00
34 JD,F:Kirk,Spock,McCoy 3.00
35 Tabukan Syndrome#1 . . . . 3.00
36 Tabukan Syndrome#2 . . . . 3.00
37 Tabukan Syndrome#3 . . . . 3.00
38 Tabukan Syndrome#4 . . . . 3.00
39 Tabukan Syndrome#5 . . . . 3.00
40 Tabukan Syndrome#6 . . . . 3.00
41 Runaway 3.00
42 Helping Hand 3.00
43 V:Binzalans 3.00
44 Acceptable Risk 3.00
45 V:Trelane 3.00
46 V:Captain Klaa 3.00

47 F:Spock & Saavik 3.00
48 The Neutral Zone 3.00
49 Weapon from Genesis 3.00
50 "The Peacemaker" 4.00
51 "The Price" 3.00
52 V:Klingons 3.00
53 Timecrime #1 . . . . 3.00
54 Timecrime #2 . . . . 3.00
55 Timecrime #3 . . . . 3.00
56 Timecrime #4 . . . . 3.00
57 Timecrime #5 . . . . 3.00
58 F:Chekov. 3.00
59 Uprising 3.00
60 Hostages 3.00
61 On Talos IV 3.00
62 Alone,pt.1, V:aliens 3.00
63 Alone,pt.2 . . . . 3.00
64 Kirk 3.00
65 Kirk in Space 3.00
66 Spock 3.00
67 Ambassador Stonn 3.00
68 . . . . 3.00
69 Wolf in Cheap Clothing,pt.1 . . . 3.00
70 Wolf in Cheap Clothing,pt.2 . . . 3.00
71 Wolf in Cheap Clothing,pt.3 . . . 2.75
72 Wolf in Cheap Clothing,pt.4 . . . 2.75
73 Star-crossed,pt.1 . . . . 2.75
74 Star-crossed,pt.2 . . . . 2.50
75 Star-crossed,pt.3 . . . . 4.50
76 Tendar 2.50
77 to the Romulan Neutral Zone . . 2.50
78 The Chosen,pt.1 (of 3) 2.50
79 The Chosen,pt.2 . . . . 2.50
80 The Chosen,pt.3 . . . . 2.50
Ann.#1 GM,sty by G.Takei(Sulu) . . . 4.00
Ann.#2 Kirks 1st Yr At Star
    Fleet Academy. 4.00
Ann.#3 KD,F:Ambassador Sarek . . . 4.00
Ann.#4 F:Spock on Pike's ship . . . 4.00
Ann.#6 Convergence,pt.1 . . . . 4.50
Spec.#1 PDd(s),BSz 4.00
Spec.#2 The Defiant 4.50
Spec.#3 V:Orion pirates 4.50
Spec. 25th Anniv. 7.00
Star Trek VI,movie adapt(direct) . . . 6.00
Star Trek VI,movie(newsstand) . . . 3.00

STAR TREK: THE MODALA IMPERATIVE

1991

1 Planet Modula 6.00
2 Modula's Rebels 4.50
3 Spock/McCoy rescue Attempt . . . 4.00
4 Rebel Victory 4.00
TPB reprints both minis 20.00

STAR TREK: THE NEXT GENERATION

Feb., 1988

[1st Regular Series]

1 based on TV series,Where No
    Man Has Gone Before 10.00
2 Spirit in the Sky 8.00
3 Factor Q. 5.00
4 Q's Day 5.00
5 Q's Effects 5.00
6 Here Today 5.00

[2nd Regular Series], 1989–95

1 Return to Raimon 15.00
2 Murder Most Foul 9.00
3 Derelict. 7.50
4 The Hero Factor 7.50
5 Serafin's Survivors 6.00
6 Shadows in the Garden 6.00
7 The Pilot. 5.00
8 The Battle Within 5.00
9 The Pay Off 5.00
10 The Noise of Justice 5.00
11 The Imposter 4.00

12 Whoever Fights Monsters...... 4.00
13 The Hand of the Assassin...... 4.00
14 Holiday on Ice............... 4.00
15 Prisoners of the Ferengi....... 3.50
16 I Have Heard the Mermaids
   Singing.................... 3.50
17 The Weapon................. 3.50
18 MM,Forbidden Fruit........... 3.50
19 The Lesson................. 3.50
20 Lost Shuttle................ 3.50
21 Lost Shuttle cont............ 3.50
22 Lost Shuttle cont............ 3.50
23 Lost Shuttle cont............ 3.50
24 Lost Shuttle conc............ 3.50
25 Okona S.O.S................ 3.50
26 Search for Okona 3.50
27 Worf,Data,Troi,Okona trapped
   on world.................. 3.50
28 Worf/K'Ehleyr story........... 3.50
29 Rift,pt.1................... 3.50
30 Rift,pt.2................... 3.50
31 Rift conclusion 3.50
32 .... 3.50
33 R:Mischievous Q............. 3.50
34 V:Aliens,F:Mischievous Q...... 3.50
35 Way of the Warrior 3.50
36 Shore Leave in Shanzibar#1 ... 3.25
37 Shore Leave in Shanzibar#2 ... 3.25
38 Shore Leave in Shanzibar#3 ... 3.25
39 Divergence #1.............. 3.25
40 Divergence #2.............. 3.25
41 V:Strazzan Warships.......... 3.25
42 V:Strazzans................ 3.25
43 V:Strazzans................ 3.25
44 Disrupted Lives............. 3.25
45 F:Enterprise Surgical Team ... 3.25
46 Deadly Labyrinth............ 3.25
47 Worst of Both World's#1...... 3.00
48 Worst of Both World's#2...... 3.00
49 Worst of Both World's#3...... 3.00
50 Double Sized,V:Borg......... 4.00
51 V:Energy Beings............. 3.00
52 in the 1940's............... 3.00
53 F:Picard................... 3.00
54 F:Picard................... 3.00
55 Data on Trial............... 3.00
56 Abduction 3.00
57 Body Switch................ 3.00
58 Body Switch................ 3.00
59 B:Children in Chaos.......... 3.00
60 Children in Chaos#2.......... 3.00
61 E:Children in Chaos 3.00
62 V:Stalker.................. 3.00
63 A:Romulans................ 3.00
64 Geordie................... 3.00
65 Geordie................... 3.00
66 .... 3.00
67 Friends/Strangers........... 3.00
68 Friends/Strangers,pt.2 .... 3.00
69 Friends/Strangers,pt.3 .... 3.00
70 Friends/Strangers,pt.4 .... 3.00
71 War of Madness,pt.1.......... 3.00
72 War of Madness,pt.2.......... 3.00
73 War of Madness,pt.3.......... 3.00
74 War of Madness,pt.4.......... 3.00
75 War of Madness,pt.5.......... 4.50
76 F:Geordi 3.00
77 Gateway, pt.1 .... 3.00
78 Gateway, pt.2 .... 3.00
79 Crew transformed into androids 3.00
80 Mysterious illness 3.00
Ann.#1 A:Mischievous Q 4.00
Ann.#2 BP,V:Parasitic Creatures ... 4.00
Ann.#3 .... 4.00
Ann.#4 MiB(s),F:Dr.Crusher..... 4.00
Ann.#6 Convergence,pt.2 ...... 4.50
Series Finale 4.25
Spec.#1 .... 3.75
Spec.#2 CCl(s)............... 4.00
Star Trek N.G.:Sparticus....... 5.00
TPB Beginnings, BSz(c) rep...... 20.00

STAR TREK:
THE NEXT GENERATION
DEEP SPACE NINE
1994–95
1 Crossover with Malibu 2.50
2 .... 2.50

STAR TREK:
THE NEXT GENERATION
ILL WIND
1995–96
1 Solar-sailing race............ 2.50
2 Explosion Investigated........ 2.50
3 A bomb aboard ship.......... 2.50
4 finale 2.50

STAR TREK
THE NEXT GENERATION
MODALA IMPERATIVE
1991
1 A:Spock,McCoy 6.00
2 Modula Overrun by Ferengi..... 5.00
3 Picard,Spock,McCoy & Troi
   trapped................... 4.00
4 final issue.................. 4.00

STAR TREK
THE NEXT GENERATION
SHADOWHEART
1994–95
1 thru 3 .... @2.50
4 Worf Confront Nikolai 2.50

STATIC
Milestone, 1993–96
1 JPL,I:Static,Hotstreak,Frieda Goren,
   w/poster,card,D puzzle piece .. 4.00
1a Newstand Ed............... 2.50
1b Platinum Ed. 8.00
2 thru 13 .... @2.50
14 Worlds Collide,V:Rift......... 3.00
15 thru 24 .... @2.50
25 V:Dusk, 48pgs............. 4.00
26 thru 47 .... @2.50

STATIC SHOCK!:
REBIRTH OF THE COOL
DC/Milestone, Nov., 2001
1 (of 4) DMD................. 2.50
2 DMD,F:Hardware............ 2.50
3 DMD,A:Hardware,Iron Butterfly .. 2.50
4 DMD,V:Power Junkie.......... 2.50

STEEL
1994–98
1 JBg(c),B:LSi(s),CsB,N:Steel 3.00
2 JBg(c),CsB,V:Toastmaster..... 2.50
3 JBg(c),CsB,V:Amertek........ 2.50
4 JBg(c),CsB................ 2.50
5 JBg(c),CsB,V:Sister's Attacker . 2.50
6 JBg(c),CsB,Worlds Collide,pt.5 . 2.50
7 Worlds Collide,pt.6........... 2.50
8 Zero Hour,I:Hazard 2.50
9 F:Steel 2.50
10 F:Steel................... 2.50
11 .... 2.50
12 .... 2.50
13 A:Maxima 2.50
14 A:Superman 2.50
15 R:White Rabbit 2.50
16 V:White Rabbit
   [new Miraweb format begins] .. 2.50
17 Steel controls armor powers.... 2.50
18 Abduction 2.50

Steel #14
© DC Comics Inc.

19 .... 2.50
20 Body Rejects Armor 2.50
21 LSi,Underworld Unleashed tie-in 2.50
22 Steel separated from Superboy . 2.50
23 Steel attacked.............. 2.50
24 V:Hazard's................. 2.50
25 .... 2.50
26 Natasha gains superpowers.... 2.50
27 LSi,V:Hazard............... 2.50
28 .... 2.50
29 .... 2.50
30 .... 2.50
31 LSi(s),V:Armorbeast 2.50
32 V:Blockbuster.............. 2.50
33 JAp,DG,Natasha's drug abuse .. 2.50
34 CPr(s),DCw,TP,A:Natasha, in
   Jersey City................ 2.50
35 CPr(s),DCw,TP,............. 2.50
36 CPr(s),DCw,TP,Combing the
   sewers of Jersey City 2.50
37 CPr(s),DCw,TP,John Irons,
   Amanda Quick & Skorpio a
   romantic triangle 2.50
38 CPr(s),DCw,TP,A:The Question . 2.50
39 CPr(s),DCw,TP,V:Crash 2.50
40 CPr(s),VGi,Steel tries out
   new hammer 2.50
41 CPr(s),DCw,TMo, John Irons
   guilty of murder?............ 2.50
42 CPr(s),DCw,TP,Irons and
   Amanda assaulted.......... 2.50
43 CPr(s),DCw,TP,to Metropolis ... 2.50
44 CPr(s),DCw,TP,Genesis tie-in.... 2.50
45 CPr(s),DCw,TP,seek policeman . 2.50
46 CPr(s),DCw,TP,F:Superboy 2.50
47 CPr(s),DCw,TP,F:Amanda 2.50
48 .... 2.50
49 CPr(s),DCw,TP,V:Deadline 2.50
50 CPr(s),DCw,TP,Millennium
   Giants 2.50
51 CPr(s),DCw,TP,bounty hunter... 2.50
52 CPr(s),final issue............ 2.50
1-shot, movie adaptation 5.00
Ann.#1 Elseworlds story 3.00
TPB The Forging of a Hero LSi(s). 20.00

STEEL, THE
INDESTRUCTIBLE MAN
March, 1978
1 DH,I:Steel................. 12.00
2 thru 4 DH .... @8.00
5 Oct.–Nov., 1978............ 12.00

Strange Adventures #9
© DC Comics, Inc.

STRANGE ADVENTURES
1950–74

1 The Menace of the Green
  Nebula 6,000.00
2 S&K,JM(c),Doom From
  Planet X 2,700.00
3 The Metal World 1,800.00
4 BP,The Invaders From the
  Nth Dimension 1,800.00
5 The World Inside the Atom . . 1,800.00
6 Confessions of a Martian . . . 1,800.00
7 The World of Giant Ants 1,800.00
8 MA,ATh,Evolution Plus 1,800.00
9 MA,B:Captain Comet,The
  Origin of Captain Comet. . . 3,500.00
10 MA,CI,The Air Bandits
  From Space 1,500.00
11 MA,CI,Day the Past
  Came Back. 1,000.00
12 MA,CI,GK(c),The Girl From
  the Diamond Planet 1,000.00
13 MA,CI,GK(c),When the Earth
  was Kidnapped. 1,000.00
14 MA,CI,GK(c),Destination
  Doom 1,000.00
15 MA,CI,GK(c),Captain Comet-
  Enemy of Earth. 1,000.00
16 MA,CI,GK(c),The Ghost of
  Captain Comet. 1,000.00
17 MA,CI,GK(c),Beware the
  Synthetic Men. 1,000.00
18 CI,MA(c),World of Flying
  Men. 1,000.00
19 CI,MA(c),Secret of the
  Twelve Eternals 1,200.00
20 CI,Slaves of the Sea Master 1,200.00
21 CI,MA(c),Eyes of the
  Other Worlds 800.00
22 CI,The Guardians of the
  Clockwork Universe. 800.00
23 CI,MA(c),The Brain Pirates
  of Planet X. 800.00
24 CI,MA(c),Doomsday on Earth. 800.00
25 CI,GK(c),The Day
  That Vanished 800.00
26 CI,Captain Vs. Miss Universe. 800.00
27 CI,MA(c),The Counterfeit
  Captain Comet. 800.00
28 CI,Devil's Island in Space . . . 800.00
29 CI,The Time Capsule From
  1,000,000 B.C. 800.00
30 CI,MA(c),Menace From the
  World of Make-Believe 750.00
31 CI,Lights Camera Action 750.00

32 CI,MA(c),The Challenge of
  Man-Ape the Mighty 750.00
33 CI,MA(c),The Human Beehive 750.00
34 CI,MA(c) 750.00
35 CI,MA(c),Cosmic Chessboard 750.00
36 CI,MA(c),The Grab-Bag
  Planet 750.00
37 CI,MA(c),The Invaders From
  the Golden Atom 750.00
38 CI,MA(c),Seeing-Eye Humans 750.00
39 CI,MA(c),The Guilty Gorilla. . 750.00
40 CI,MA(c),The Mind Monster . 750.00
41 CI,MA(c),The Beast From Out
  of Time. 750.00
42 CI,MD,MA(c),The Planet of
  Ancient Children 750.00
43 CI,MD,MA(c),The Phantom
  Prize Fighter 750.00
44 CI,MA(c),The Planet That
  Plotted Murder. 750.00
45 CI,MD,MA(c),Gorilla World . . 750.00
46 CI,MA(c),E:Captain Comet
  Interplanetary War Base 750.00
47 CI,MA(c),The Man Who Sold
  the Earth 750.00
48 CI,MA(c),Human Phantom . . . 750.00
49 CI,MA(c),The Invasion
  from Indiana 750.00
50 CI,MA(c),The World Wrecker . 600.00
51 CI,MA(c),The Man Who
  Stole Air 600.00
52 CI,MA(c),Prisoner of the
  Parakeets 600.00
53 CI,MA(c),The Human Icicle. . 600.00
54 CI,MA(c),The Electric Man . . 400.00
55 CI,MA(c),The Gorilla Who
  Challanged the World,pt.I . . . 400.00
56 CI,The Jungle Emperor,pt.II . . 400.00
57 CI,The Spy from Saturn 400.00
58 CI,I Hunted the Radium Man . 400.00
59 CI,The Ark From Planet X. . . 400.00
60 CI,Across the Ages 400.00
61 CI,The Mirages From Space . 400.00
62 CI,The Fireproof Man 400.00
63 CI,I Was the Man in the Moon 400.00
64 CI,GK(c),Gorillas In Space . . 400.00
65 CI,GK(c),Prisoner From Pluto. 400.00
66 CI,GK(c),The Human Battery . 400.00
67 CI,GK(c),Martian Masquerader 400.00
68 CI,The Man Who Couldn't
  Drown 400.00
69 CI,Gorilla Conquest of Earth. . 400.00
70 CI,Triple Life of Dr. Pluto . . . 400.00
71 CI,MSy,Zero Hour For Earth. . 300.00
72 CI,The Skyscraper That Came
  to Life. 300.00
73 CI,Amazing Rain of Gems . . . 300.00
74 CI,The Invisible Invader
  From Dimension X. 300.00
75 CI,Secret of the Man-Ape. . . . 300.00
76 CI,B:Darwin Jones,The Robot
  From Atlantis 300.00
77 CI,A:Darwin Jones,The World
  That Slipped Out of Space . . 300.00
78 CI,The Secret of the Tom
  Thumb Spaceman 300.00
79 CI,A:Darwin Jones,Invaders
  from the Ice World 300.00
80 CI,Mind Robbers of Venus . . . 300.00
81 CI,The Secret of the
  Shrinking Twins 300.00
82 CI,Giants of the Cosmic Ray . 250.00
83 CI,Assignment in Eternity 250.00
84 CI,Prisoners of the Atom
  Universe 250.00
85 CI,The Amazing Human Race 250.00
86 CI,The Dog That Saved the
  Earth 250.00
87 CI,New Faces For Old 250.00
88 CI,A:Darwin Jones,The Gorilla
  War Against Earth 250.00
89 CI,Earth For Sale 250.00

90 CI,The Day I Became a
  Martian 250.00
91 CI,Midget Earthmen of Jupiter 250.00
92 CI,GK(c),The Amazing Ray
  of Knowledge. 250.00
93 CI,GK(c),A:Darwin Jones,
  Space-Rescue By Proxy 250.00
94 MA,CI,GK(c),Fisherman of
  Space. 250.00
95 CI,The World at my Doorstep. 250.00
96 CI,MA(c),The Menace of
  Saturn's Rings 250.00
97 CI,MA(c),MSy,Secret of the
  Space-Giant 250.00
98 CI,GK(c),MSy,Attack on Fort
  Satellite 250.00
99 CI,MSy,GK(c),Big Jump Into
  Space. 250.00
100 CI,MSy,The Amazing Trial
  of John (Gorilla) Doe 300.00
101 CI,MSy,GK(c),Giant From
  Beyond 200.00
102 MSy,GK(c),The Three Faces
  of Barry Morrell 200.00
103 GK(c),The Man Who
  Harpooned Worlds. 200.00
104 MSy,GK(c),World of Doomed
  Spacemen 200.00
105 MSy,GK(c),Fisherman From
  the Sea 200.00
106 MSy,CI,GK(c),Genie in the
  Flying Saucer 200.00
107 MSy,CI,GK(c),War of the
  Jovian Bubble-Men 200.00
108 MSy,CI,GK(c),The Human
  Pet of Gorilla Land 200.00
109 MSy,CI,GK(c),The Man Who
  Weighed 100 Tons. 200.00
110 MSy,CI,GK(c),Hand From
  Beyond 200.00
111 MSy,CI,GK(c),Secret of
  the Last Earth-Man 200.00
112 MSy,CI,GK(c),Menace of
  the Size-Changing Spaceman 200.00
113 MSy,CI,GK(c),Deluge From
  Space. 200.00
114 MSy,CI,GK(c),Secret of the
  Flying Buzz Saw 200.00
115 MSy,CI,GK(c),The Great
  Space-Tiger Hunt. 200.00
116 MSy,CI,RH,GK(c),Invasion
  of the Water Warriors 200.00
117 MSy,CI,GK(c),I:Atomic
  Knights 1,000.00
118 MSy,CI,The Turtle-Men of
  Space. 225.00

Strange Adventures #105
© DC Comics Inc.

119 MSy,CI,MA(c),Raiders
From the Giant World 200.00
120 MSy,CI,MA,Attack of the Oil
Demons 500.00
121 MSy,CI,MA(c),Invasion of the
Flying Reptiles 175.00
122 MSy,CI,MA(c),David and the
Space-Goliath 175.00
123 MSy,CI,MA(c),Secret of the
Rocket-Destroyer. 300.00
124 MSy,CI,MA(c),The Face-Hunter
From Saturn 200.00
125 MSy,CI,The Flying Gorilla
Menace 175.00
126 MSy,CI,MA(c),Return of the
Neanderthal Man. 300.00
127 MSy,CI,MA(c),Menace
From the Earth-Globe 175.00
128 MSy,CI,MA(c),The Man
With the Electronic Brain. . . . 175.00
129 MSy,CI,MA(c),The Giant
Who Stole Mountains 200.00
130 MSy,CI,MA.War With the
Giant Frogs 175.00
131 MSy,CI,MA(c),Emperor
of the Earth 175.00
132 MSy,CI,MA(c),The Dreams
of Doom. 200.00
133 MSy,CI,MA(c),The Invisible
Dinosaur 175.00
134 MSy,CI,MA(c), The Aliens
Who Raided New York 200.00
135 MSy,CI,MA(c),Fishing Hole
in the Sky. 200.00
136 MSy,CI,MA(c),The Robot
Who Lost Its Head. 150.00
137 MSy,CI,MA(c),Parade of the
Space-Toys 150.00
138 MSy,CI,MA(c),Secret of the
Dinosaur Skeleton. 200.00
139 MSy,CI,MA(c),Space-Roots
of Evil. 150.00
140 MSy,CI,MA(c),Prisoner of
the Space-Patch 150.00
141 MSy,CI,MA(c),Battle Between
the Two Earths 200.00
142 MSy,CI,MA(c),The Return of
the Faceless Creature. 150.00
143 MSy,CI,MA(c),The Face in
the Atom-Bomb Cloud 150.00
144 MSy,CI,MA(c),A:Atomic
Knights, When the Earth
Blacked Out. 200.00
145 MSy,CI,MA,The Man Who
Lived Forever 150.00
146 MSy,CI,MA(c),Perilous Pet
of Space 150.00
147 MSy,CI,MA(c),The Dawn-
World Menace 200.00
148 MSy,CI,MA(c),Earth Hero,
Number One 150.00
149 MSy,CI,MA(c),Raid of
the Rogue Star 150.00
150 MSy,CI,MA(c),When Earth
Turned into a Comet 200.00
151 MSy,CI,MA(c),Invasion Via
Radio-Telescope 150.00
152 MSy,MA(c),The Martian
Emperor of Earth. 150.00
153 MSy,MA(c),Threat of the
Faceless Creature 150.00
154 CI,MSy,MA,GK(c),Earth's
Friendly Invaders. 150.00
155 MSy,MA,GK(c),Prisoner
of the Undersea World 150.00
156 MSy,CI,MA(c),The Man
With the Head of Saturn 150.00
157 MSy,CI,MA(c),Plight of
the Human Cocoons 150.00
158 MSy,CI,MA(c),The Mind
Masters of Space. 150.00

159 MSy,CI,MA(c),The Maze
of Time. 150.00
160 MSy,CI,MA(c),A:Atomic
Knights, Here Comes the
Wild Ones 150.00
161 MSy,CI,MA(c),Earth's Frozen
Heat Wave,E:Space Museum 100.00
162 CI,MA(c),Mystery of the
12 O'Clock Man. 100.00
163 MA(c),The Creature in
the Black Light. 100.00
164 DD&SMo(c),I Became
a Robot 100.00
165 DD&SMo(c),I Broke the
Supernatural Barrier 100.00
166 DD&SMo(c),I Lived in
Two Bodies 100.00
167 JkS(c),The Team That
Conqured Time 100.00
168 JkS(c),I Hunted Toki
the Terrible. 100.00
169 DD&SMo(c),The Prisoner
of the Hour Glass 100.00
170 DD&SMo(c),The Creature
From Strange Adventures . . . 100.00
171 The Diary of the
9-Planet Man? 100.00
172 DD&SMo(c),I Became
the Juggernaut Man 100.00
173 The Secret of the
Fantasy Films 100.00
174 JkS(c),The Ten Ton Man. . . . 100.00
175 Danger: This Town is
Shrinking 100.00
176 DD&SMo(c),The Case of
the Cosmonik Quartet. 100.00
177 I Lived a Hundred Lives,
O:Immortal Man. 100.00
178 JkS(c),The Runaway Comet. 100.00
179 JkS(c),I Buried Myself Alive . 100.00
180 CI,I:Animal Man,I Was the
Man With Animal Powers . . . 300.00
181 The Man of Two Worlds 100.00
182 JkS(c),The Case of the
Blonde Bombshell 100.00
183 JM(c),The Plot to Destroy
the Earth 100.00
184 GK(c),A:Animal Man,The
Return of the Man With
Animal Powers 300.00
185 JkS(c),Ilda-Gangsters Inc. . . 100.00
186 Beware the Gorilla Witch . . . 100.00
187 JkS(c),O:The Enchantress . . 120.00
188 SD,JkS(c),I Was the
Four Seasons 100.00
189 SD,JkS(c),The Way-Out
Worlds of Bertram Tilley 100.00
190 CI,A:Animal Man,A-Man-the
Hero with Animal Powers . . . 350.00
191 JkS(c),Beauty vs. the Beast . 100.00
192 Freak Island 100.00
193 The Villian Maker 100.00
194 JkS(c),The Menace of the
Super- Gloves 100.00
195 JkS(c),Secret of the Three
Earth Dooms,A:Animal Man . 150.00
196 JkS(c),Mystery of the
Orbit Creatures 100.00
197 The Hostile Hamlet 75.00
198 JkS(c),Danger! Earth
is Doomed 75.00
199 Robots of the Round Table. . . 75.00
200 The Guardian Eye. 75.00
201 JkS,Animal Man 100.00
202 Robinson Crusoe of the Sky. . 75.00
203 The Split Man 75.00
204 GK,Crazy Quilt Man 75.00
205 CI,I&O:Deadman. 250.00
206 NA,MSy,F:Deadman 200.00
207 NA,F:Deadman. 150.00
208 NA,F:Deadman. 150.00
209 NA,F:Deadman 150.00

210 NA,F:Deadman 150.00
211 thru 216 NA,F:Deadman . . @150.00
217 MA,MSy,A:Adam Strange 25.00
218 MA,CI,MSy 50.00
219 CI,JKu. 50.00
220 CI,JKu. 50.00
221 CI,Two Adam Stranges 50.00
222 MA,New Adam Strange 75.00
223 MA,CI 50.00
224 MA,CI 50.00
225 MA,JKu. 50.00
226 MA,JKu,New Adam Strange . . 75.00

Strange Adventures #231
© DC Comics, Inc.

227 JKu 50.00
228 NA(c). 70.00
229 MA,The Last Mile of Space. . . 60.00
230 GM(c) 50.00
231 E:Atomic Knights 50.00
232 JKu 50.00
233 JKu 50.00
234 JKu 50.00
235 NA(c). 60.00
236 CI,Human Fishbowl 40.00
237 Ray-Gun in the SKy 25.00
238 MK(c) 25.00
239 Metal Conqueror of Rann 25.00
240 MK(c) 25.00
241 F:Adam Strange 25.00
242 MA. 25.00
243 F:Adam Strange 25.00
244 Oct.–Nov., 1974 . . . . 25.00

STRANGE ADVENTURES
DC/Vertigo, Sept., 1999

1 (of 4) BB,DGb 2.50
2 KJ,Expiration Date. 2.50
3 & 4 . . . . @2.50

STRANGE SPORTS
STORIES
Sept.–Oct., 1973

1 CS,DG 40.00
2 thru 6 . . . . @25.00

STREETS
1993

1 Tenderloin 5.00
2 Procurement 5.00
3 . . . . 5.00

SUGAR & SPIKE
April-May, 1956

1 SM 4,500.00

DC COMICS

2 SM	1,500.00
3 SM	1,000.00
4 SM	1,000.00
5 SM	1,000.00
6 thru 10 SM	@600.00
11 thru 20 SM	@500.00
21 thru 29 SM	@350.00
30 SM,A:Scribbly	350.00
31 thru 50 SM	@300.00
51 thru 70 SM	@225.00
71 thru 79 SM	@200.00
80 SM,I:Bernie the Brain	200.00
81 thru 97 SM	@150.00
98 SM,Oct.–Nov., 1971	150.00
1 Facsimile Edition,rep.(2002)	3.00

Suicide Squad #41
© DC Comics, Inc.

SUICIDE SQUAD
1987–91

1 LMc,Legends,I:Jihad	4.00
2 LMc,V:The Jihad	2.50
3 LMc,V:Female Furies	2.50
4 LMc,V:William Hell	2.50
5 LM,A:Penguin	3.00
6 LM,A:Penguin	3.00
7 thru 12 LMc	@2.50
13 LMc,X-over,JLI#13	4.00
14 thru 22	@2.50
23 LMc,Invasion	4.00
24 thru 47	@2.25
48 GI,New Thinker	4.00
49 thru 63	@2.25
64 GI,A:Task Force X	4.00
65 GI,Bronze Tiger	2.25
66 GI,Final Iss.E:Suicide Squad	2.25
Ann.#1 GN,V:Argent,A:Manhunter	2.25

[2nd Series] Sept., 2001

1 KG,R:Suicide Squad	2.50
2 thru 12	@2.50

SUICIDE SQUAD:
RAISE THE FLAG
Sept., 2007

1 (of 8) F:Rick Flag, Jr.	3.00
2	3.00

SUPERBOY
1949–76

1 WB&StK,Superman(c)	16,000.00
2 The Stunts of Superboy	4,000.00
3 Buperboy's Hall of Fame	2,900.00
4 The Oracle of Smallville	2,700.00

5 Superboy meets Supergirl, Pre-Adventure #252	2,700.00
6 I:Humpty Dumpty,the Hobby Robber	2,000.00
7 WB,V:Humpty Dumpty	2,000.00
8 CS,I:Superbaby,V:Humpty Dumpty	1,900.00
9 V:Humpty Dumpty	1,900.00
10 CS,I:Lana Lang	1,900.00
11 CS,2nd Lang,V:Humpty Dumpty	1,500.00
12 CS,The Heroes Club	1,400.00
13 CS,Scout of Smallville	1,400.00
14 CS,I:Marsboy	1,400.00
15 CS,A:Superman	1,500.00
16 CS,A:Marsboy	1,400.00
17 CS,Superboy's Double	1,400.00
18 CS,Lana Lang-Hollywood Star	1,400.00
19 CS,The Death of Young Clark Kent	1,400.00
20 CS,The Ghost that Haunted Smallville	1,400.00
21 CS,Lana Lang-Magician	750.00
22 CS,The New Clark Kent	750.00
23 CS,The Super Superboy	750.00
24 CS,The Super Fat Boy of Steel	750.00
25 CS,Cinderella of Smallville	750.00
26 CS,A:Superbaby	750.00
27 CS,Clark Kent-Runaway	750.00
28 CS,The Man Who Defeated Superboy	750.00
29 CS,The Puppet Superboy	750.00
30 CS,I:Tommy Tuttle	700.00
31 CS,The Amazing Elephant Boy From Smallville	700.00
32 CS,His Majesty King Superboy	700.00
33 CS,The Crazy Costumes of the Boy of Steel	700.00
34 CS,Hep Cats o/Smallville	700.00
35 CS,The Five Superboys	700.00
36 CS,The Superboy Souvenirs	700.00
37 CS,I:Thaddeus Lang	700.00
38 CS,Public Chimp #1	700.00
39 CS,Boy w/Superboy Powers	700.00
40 CS,The Magic Necklace	500.00
41 CS,Superboy Meets Superbrave	500.00
42 CS,Gaucho of Smallville	500.00
43 CS,Super-Farmer of Smallville	500.00
44 The Amazing Adventure of Superboy's Costume	500.00
45 A Trap For Superboy	500.00
46 The Battle of Fort Smallville	500.00
47 CS,A:Superman	500.00
48 CS,Boy Without Super-Suit	500.00
49 I:Metalo (Jor-El's Robot)	500.00
50 The Super-Giant of Smallville	500.00
51 I:Krypto	400.00
52 CS,The Powerboy from Earth	400.00
53 CS,A:Superman	400.00
54 CS,The Silent Superboy	400.00
55 CS,A:Jimmy Olson	400.00
56 CS,A:Krypto	400.00
57 CS,One-Man Baseball Team	400.00
58 CS,The Great Kryptonite Mystery	400.00
59 CS,A:Superbaby	400.00
60 The 100,000 Cowboy	400.00
61 The School For Superboys	300.00
62 I:Gloria Kent	300.00
63 CS,The Two Boys of Steel	300.00
64 CS,A:Krypto	300.00
65 Superboy's Moonlight Spell	300.00
66 The Family with X-Ray Eyes	300.00
67 I:Klax-Ar	300.00
68 O&I:Bizarro	1,000.00

Superboy #83
© DC Comics, Inc.

69 How Superboy Learned To Fly	250.00
70 O:Superboy's Glasses	250.00
71 A:Superbaby	250.00
72 The Flying Girl of Smallville	250.00
73 CS,A:Superbaby	250.00
74 A:Jor-El & Lara	250.00
75 A:Superbaby	250.00
76 I:Super Monkey	250.00
77 Superboy's Best Friend	250.00
78 O:Mr.Mzyzptlk	350.00
79 A:Jar-El & Lara	250.00
80 Superboy meets Supergirl	300.00
81 The Weakling From Earth	200.00
82 A:Bizarro Krypto	200.00
83 I:Kryptonite Kid	200.00
84 A:William Tell	200.00
85 Secret of Mighty Boy	200.00
86 I:PeteRoss,A:Legion	300.00
87 I:Scarlet Jungle of Krypton	200.00
88 The Invader from Earth	200.00
89 I:Mon-El	200.00
90 A:Pete Ross	200.00
91 CS,Superboy in Civil War	200.00
92 CS,I:Destructo,A:Lex Luthor	200.00
93 A:Legion	225.00
94 I:Superboy Revenge Squad, A:Pete Ross	175.00
95 Imaginary Story,The Super Family From Krypton	175.00
96 A:Pete Ross,Lex Luther	175.00
97 Krypto Story	175.00
98 Legion,I&O:Ultraboy	200.00
99 O: The Kryptonite Kid	350.00
100 I:Phantom Zone	150.00
101 The Handsome Hound of Steel	150.00
102 O:Scarlet Jungle of Krypton	150.00
103 CS,A:King Arthur,Jesse James Red Kryptonite	150.00
104 O:Phantom Zone	150.00
105 CS,The Simpleton of Steel	150.00
106 CS,A:Brainiac	150.00
107 CS,I:Superboy Club of Smallville	175.00
108 The Kent's First Super Son	150.00
109 The Super Youth of Bronze	150.00
110 A:Jor-El	150.00
111 Red Kryptonite Story	125.00
112 CS,A:Superbaby	125.00
113 The Boyhood of Dad Kent	125.00
114 A:Phantom Zone, Mr.Mxyzptlk	125.00
115 A:Phantom Zone,Lex Luthor	125.00
116 The Wolfboy of Smallville	125.00

117 A:Legion 125.00
118 CS,The War Between
   Superboy and Krypto. 125.00
119 V:Android Double 125.00
120 A:Mr.Mxyzptlk 125.00
121 CS,A:Jor-El,Lex Luthor 125.00
122 Red Kryptonite Story 125.00
123 CS,The Curse of the
   Superboy Mummy 125.00
124 I:Insect Queen 125.00
125 O:Kid Psycho 125.00
126 O:Krypto 125.00
127 A:Insect Queen 100.00
128 A:Phantom Zone,Kryptonite
   Kid,Dev En 100.00
129 rep.A:Mon-El,SuperBaby . . . 150.00
130 CS,Search for a Pet 100.00
131 A;Lex Luthor,Mr.Mxyzptlk,I:
   Space Canine Patrol Agents . 100.00
132, CS,A:Space Canine
   Patrol Agents 100.00
133 A:Robin, repr. 100.00
134 The Scoundrel of Steel 100.00
135 A:Lex Luthor 100.00
136 A:Space Canine Agents 100.00
137 Mysterious Mighty Mites 100.00
138 giant, Superboy's Most
   Terrific Battles 125.00
139 The Samson of Smallville . . . 100.00
140 V:The Gambler 75.00
141 No Mercy for a Hero 75.00
142 A:Super Monkey 75.00
143 NA(c),The Big Fall 75.00
144 Superboy's Stolen Identity . . 75.00
145 NA(c)Kents become young. . 75.00
146 NA(c),CS,The Runaway 75.00
147 giant O:Legion 100.00
148 NA(c),CS,C:PolarBoy 75.00
149 NA(c),A:Bonnie & Clyde 75.00
150 JAb,V:Mr.Cipher 75.00
151 NA(c),A:Kryptonite Kid 75.00
152 NA(c),WW 75.00
153 NA(c),WW,A;Prof Mesmer . . 75.00
154 WW(i),A:Jor-El & Lara
   Blackout For Superboy 75.00
155 NA(c),WW,Revolt of the
   Teenage Robots 75.00
156 Farewell to Smallville,giant . . 75.00
157 WW,NA(c),Get Lost Superboy 75.00
158 WW,A:Jor-El & Lara 50.00
159 WW(i),A:Lex Luthor 50.00
160 WW,I Chose Eternal Exile . . . 50.00
161 WW,The Strange Death of
   Superboy 50.00
162 A:Phantom Zone 50.00
163 NA(c),Reform School Rebel . . 50.00
164 NA(c),Your Death Will
   Destroy Me 50.00
165 CS,Superdog,giant-size 50.00
166 NA(c),A:Lex Luthor 30.00
167 NA(c),MA,A:Superbaby. 30.00
168 NA(c),MA,Hitler. 30.00
169 MA,A:Lex Luthor 30.00
170 MA,A:Genghis Khan 30.00
171 MA,A:Aquaboy 30.00
172 MA(i),GT,A:Legion,
   O:Lightning Lad,Yango 35.00
173 NA(c),GT,DG,O:CosmicBoy . . 30.00
174 CS,Colossal Superdog,giant. . 50.00
175 NA(c),MA,Rejuvenation of
   Ma & Pa Kent 30.00
176 NA(c),MA,GT,WW,A:Legion . . 30.00
177 MA,A:Lex Luthor 40.00
178 NA(c),MA,Legion Reprint 40.00
179 MA,A:Lex Luthor 40.00
180 MA,O:Bouncing Boy 40.00
181 MA,CS,Insect Queen 40.00
182 MA,A:Bruce Wayne. 40.00
183 MA,GT,CS(rep),A:Legion 40.00
184 MA,WW,O:Dial H rep. 40.00
185 A:Legion 20.00
186 MA,Mutiny of the Damned . . . 20.00

Superboy #168
© DC Comics Inc.

187 MA,Iron Cage for a Hero 20.00
188 MA,DC,O:Karkan,A:Legn 20.00
189 MA,Runaway Superbaby 20.00
190 MA,WW,Murder the Leader . . 20.00
191 MA,DC,O:SunBoy retold. 20.00
192 MA,The Deadly Dawn. 20.00
193 MA,WW,N:Chameleon Boy,
   Shrinking Violet 20.00
194 MA,Super-Merman of the Sea 20.00
195 MA,WW,I:Wildfire,
   N:Phantom Girl 20.00
196 last Superboy solo 30.00
197 DC,Legion begins, New
   Costumes,I:Tyr 30.00
198 DC,N:Element Lad,
   Princess Projects. 20.00
199 DC,A:Tyr, Otto Orion. 20.00
200 DC,M:Bouncing Boy
   & Duo Damsel 30.00
201 DC,Wildfire returns 18.00
202 N:Light Lass 75.00
203 MGr,D:Invisible Kid 25.00
204 MGr,A:Supergirl 15.00
205 MGr,CG,100 pages 50.00
206 MGr,A:Ferro Lad 25.00
207 MGr,O:Lightning Lad. 25.00
208 MGr,CS,68pp,Legion of
   Super Villains. 28.00
209 MGr,N:Karate Kid 20.00
210 MGr,O:Karate Kid 25.00
211 MGr,The Ultimate Revenge . . 18.00
212 MGr,L:Matter Eater Lad 18.00
213 MGr,V:Benn Pares 18.00
214 MGr,V:Overseer 18.00
215 MGr,A:Emerald Empress 18.00
216 MGr,I:Tyroc 18.00
217 MGr,I:Laurel Kent 18.00
218 J:Tyroc,A:Fatal Five 18.00
219 MGr,A:Fatal Five. 18.00
220 MGi,BWi 18.00
221 MGr,BWi,I:Grimbor 15.00
222 MGr,BWi,MN,BL,A:Tyroc 15.00
223 MGr,BWi 15.00
224 MGr,BWi,V:Pulsar Stargrave. . 15.00
225 MGr(c),BWi,JSh,MN 15.00
226 MGr(c),MN,JSh,JA,
   I:Dawnstar 15.00
227 MGr(c),JSon,JA,V:Stargrave . . 15.00
228 MGr(c),JSh,JA,
   D:Chemical King 15.00
229 MGr(c),JSh,JA,V:Deregon . . . 15.00
230 MGr(c),JSh,V:Sden 15.00
Spec. #147 facsimile (2003) 10.00
Becomes:

SUPERBOY & THE LEGION OF SUPER-HEROES
1976-79
231 MGr(c),JSh,MN,JA,doub.size
   begins,V:Fatal Five 18.00
232 MGr(c),JSh,RE,JA,V:
   Dr.Regulus. 18.00
233 MGr(c),JSh,BWi,MN,BL,
   I:Infinite Man 18.00
234 MGr(c),RE,JA,V:Composite
   Creature. 18.00
235 MGr,GT. 18.00
236 MGr(c),BMc,JSh,MN,JRu,
   V:Khunds 18.00
237 MGr(c),WS,JA. 18.00
238 JSn(c),reprint 18.00
239 MGR(c),JSn,JRu,Ultra Boy
   accused 18.00
240 MGr(c),HC,BWi,JSh,BMc,
   O:Dawnstar;V:Grimbor 18.00
241 JSh,BMc,A:Ontir 18.00
242 JSh,BMc,E:Double Size 18.00
243 MGr(c),JA,JSon 18.00
244 JSon,V:Dark Circle 18.00
245 MA,JSon,V:Mordu 18.00
246 MGr(c),JSon,DG,MA,
   V:Fatal Five 15.00
247 JSon,JA,anniv.issue. 15.00
248 JSon 15.00
249 JSon,JA. 15.00
250 JSn,V:Omega 15.00
251 JSn,Brainiac 5 goes insane . . 15.00
252 JSon,V:Starburst bandits 12.00
253 JSon,I:Blok,League of
   Super Assassins 12.00
254 JSon,V:League of Super
   Assassins 12.00
255 JSon,A:Jor-El 12.00
256 JSon 12.00
257 SD,JSon,DA,V:Psycho
   Warrior 12.00
258 JSon,V:Psycho Warrior 12.00
Becomes:

LEGION OF SUPER HEROES
[2nd Series]

[NEW ADVENTURES OF] SUPERBOY
Jan., 1980
1 KS 6.00
2 KS 3.00
3 KS 3.00
4 KS 3.00
5 KS 3.00
6 KS 3.00
7 KS,JSa. 3.00
8 thru 33 KS . . . . @3.00
34 KS,I:Yellow Peri 3.00
35 thru 44 KS. . . . . @3.00
45 KS,I:Sunburst 3.00
46 KS,A:Sunburst 3.00
47 KS,A:Sunburst 3.00
48 KS 3.00
49 KS,A:Zatara 3.00
50 KS,KG,A:Legion 3.00
51 KS,FM(c)In Between Years. 3.00
52 KS 3.00
53 KS 3.00
54 KS 3.00

SUPERBOY
1990-91
1 TV Tie-in,JM,photo(c) 5.00
2 JM,T.J.White Abducted 3.00
3 JM,Fountain of Youth. 3.00
4 JM,Big Man on Campus 3.00

DC COMICS

Superboy #6
© DC Comics Inc.

5 JM,Legion Homage 3.00
6 JM,Luthor 3.00
7 JM,Super Boy Arrested 3.00
8 JM,AAd(i),Bizarro. 3.00
9 JM/CS,PhantomZone#1 . . . . . . 3.00
10 JM/CS,PhantomZone#2 . . . . . . 3.00
11 CS 3.00
12 CS,X-Mas in Smallville 3.00
Becomes:

ADVENTURES OF
SUPERBOY
1991
13 A:Mr.Mxyzptlk 3.50
14 CS,A:Brimstone 3.00
15 CS,Legion Homage 3.00
16 CS,Into the Future 3.00
17 CS,A:Luthor 3.00
18 JM,At the Movies 3.00
19 JM,Blood Transfusion 3.00
20 JM,O:Nicknack,(G.Gottfried
    script) 3.00
21 V:Frost Monster 3.00
22 . . . . 3.00
Spec.#1 CS,A:Ma Kent 2.50

SUPERBOY
[2nd Series], 1994
1 B:KK(s),TG,DHz,V:Sidearm 4.00
2 TG,DHz,I:Knockout 2.50
3 TG,DHz,I:Scavenger 2.50
4 TG,DHz,MeP,I:Lock n' Load . . . 2.50
5 TG,DHz,I:Silver Sword 2.50
6 TG,DHz,Worlds Collide,pt.3
    C:Rocket 2.50
7 Worlds Collide, pt.8,V:Rift 2.50
8 Zero Hour,A:Superboy 2.50
9 Silican Dragon 2.50
10 Monster 2.50
11 Techno. 2.50
12 Copperhead 2.50
13 Watery Grave,pt.1. . . . . 2.50
14 Watery Grave,pt.2. . . . . 2.50
15 Watery Grave,pt.3. . . . . 2.50
16 TG,DHz,KK,V:Loose Cannon
    [New Miraweb format begins] . . 2.50
17 TG,DHz,KK Looking for
    Roxy Leech 2.50
18 V:Valor. 2.50
19 TG,KK,DHz, T-K-O 2.50
20 R:Scavenger 2.50
21 KK,TG,DHz,Future Tense,Pt.1 . 2.50

22 KK,TG,DHz,Underworld
    Unleashed x-over 2.50
23 KK,TG,DHz,V:Technician 2.50
24 KK,TG,DHz,V:Silversword. 2.50
25 New Gods. 3.00
26 KK,DHz,Losin'it,pt.2 . . . . 2.50
27 KK,DHz,Losin'it,pt.3 . . . . 2.50
28 KK,DHz,Losin'it,pt.4 . . . . 2.50
29 KK,DHz,Losin'it,pt.5 . . . . 2.50
30 KK,DHz,Losin'it,pt.6 . . . . 2.50
31 KK,Summer Fun,V:Morpheriste . 2.50
32 RMz(s),RBe,DHz,V:King Shark . 2.50
33 RMz(s),RBe,DHz, survivors flee
    to Hawaii, Final Night tie-in . . . 2.50
34 RMz(s),RBe,DHz, V:Dubbilex . . 2.50
35 RMz(s),RBe,DHz, Superboy
    abducted 2.50
36 RMz(s),RBe,DHz,V:King SHark . 2.50
37 RMz(s),SB,V:Sledge 2.50
38 RMz,RBe,DHz,Meltdown,pt.1 . . 2.50
39 RMz,RBe,DHz,Meltdown,pt.2 . . 2.50
40 RMz,RBe,DHz,Meltdown,pt.2,
    x-over. 2.50
41 RMz,RBe,DHz,Meltdown,pt.3 . . 2.50
42 SB,Ashes to Ashes 2.50
43 SB,Lanie & Ken 2.50
44 SB,island of teenagers 2.50
45 RMz,DHz,TGu,A:Legion 2.50
46 RMz,DHz,TGu,V:Silver Sword . 2.50
47 RMz,DHz,TGu,F:Green Lantern . 2.50
48 BKs,DHz,TGu,theme park 2.50
49 DHz,Searching 2.50
50 KK,TGu,Last Boy on Earth pt.1 . 2.50
51 KK,TGu,Last Boy on Earth pt.2 . 2.50
52 KK,TGu,Last Boy on Earth pt.3 . 2.50
53 KK,TGu,Last Boy on Earth pt.4 . 2.50
54 KK,TGu,A:Wild Men 2.50
55 KK,TGu,V:Grokk, Hex. 2.50
56 KK,TGu,Project Cadmus 2.50
57 KK,TGu,Demolition Run,pt.1 . . . 2.50
58 KK,TGu,Demolition Run,pt.2 . . . 2.50
59 KK,DAb,A:Superman 2.50
60 KK,TGu,A:JLA,Hyper-Tension . . 2.50
61 KK,TGu,Hyper-Tension,pt.2 . . . 2.50
62 KK,TGu,Hyper-Tension,pt.3 . . . 2.50
63 KK,TGu,Hyper-Tension,pt.4 . . . 2.50
64 KK,TGu,Hyper-Tension,pt.5 . . . 2.50
65 KK,TGu,guest-star packed 2.50
66 KK,TGu,Wild Lands 2.50
67 KK,AaL, in Wild Lands 2.50
68 KK,TG,MM,Day of Judgment
    x-over,F:Demon 2.50
69 KK,TG,return to Hawaii 2.50
70 KK,TG,Evil Factory,pt.1 . . . . 2.50
71 KK,TG,Evil Factory,pt.2 . . . . 2.50
72 KK,TG,Evil Factory,pt.3 . . . . 2.50
73 KK,TG,Evil Factory,pt.4 . . . . 2.50
74 KK,TG,Sins of Youth 2.50
75 KK,TG,as normal teenager 2.50
76 KK,TG,still Superboy. 2.50
77 KK,TG,MBa,V:Kossak 2.50
78 KK,TG,prisoners 2.50
79 KK,TG,V:Kossak the Slaver . . . 2.50
80 BHr,F:The Titans,pt.1 . . . . 2.50
81 BHr,F:The Titans,pt.2 . . . . 2.50
82 JMz,V:Negative G. 2.50
83 PFe,F:Young Justice. 2.50
84 PFe,off to L.A. 2.50
85 PFe,A:Batman,Batgirl 2.50
86 PFe,shotgun wedding 2.50
87 V:Shrapnel,Deadman 2.50
88 PFe,V:DNAngels. 2.50
89 PFe,Our Worlds at War, tie-in . . 2.50
90 PFe,Our Worlds at War, tie-in . . 2.50
91 PFe,Our Worlds at War, tie-in . . 2.50
92 PFe,R:Doctor Sin 2.50
93 PFe,Joker:Last Laugh, tie-in. . . 2.50
94 JMC,finding an apartment. 2.50
95 JP,JMC,Slaughterhouse Six . . . 2.50
96 JP,Trixie & Wipeout. 2.50
97 JP,JMC,F:Wipeout. 2.50
98 JP,JMC,F:Jimmy Olsen. 2.50

Super 2nd Series #10
© DC Comics, Inc.

99 WorldWithoutYoungJustice,pt.4 . 2.50
100 JP,KK,TG,48-pg. 3.50
Ann.#1 Elseworlds Story 3.50
Ann.#2 KK, BKs, Year One 4.50
Ann.#3 Legends o/t Dead Earth . . . 3.50
Ann.#4 Pulp Heroes (High-
    Adventure). 4.50
Spec.#1,000,000 KK,TGu 2.50

SUPERBOY
& THE RAVERS
1996–98
1 KK&SMt(s),PaP,DDv, ... 2.50
2 KK&SMt(s),PaP,DDv,InterC.E.P.T.
    pursues Superboy and Kaliber . 2.50
3 KK&SMT(s),PaP,DDv,teleported
    to Rann,V:Half-Life 2.50
4 KK&SMt(s),PaP,DDv,A:Adam
    Strange 2.50
5 KK&SMt(s),PaP,DDv,O:Hero . . . 2.50
6 KK&SMt(s),PaP,DDv, ... 2.50
7 KK&SMt(s),PaP,DDv, Road Trip,
    pt.1,A:Impulse 2.50
8 KK&SMt(s),PaP,DDv, Road Trip,
    pt.2,A:Guy Gardner 2.50
9 KK&SMt(s),PaP,DDv, Road Trip,
    pt.3,A:Aura. 2.50
10 KK&SMt(s),DDv,Meltdown,pt.4 . 2.50
11 KK&SMt(s),PaP,DDv, Superboy
    presumed dead 2.50
12 KK(s),AaL. 2.50
13 KK(s),SMt,F:Hero,Sparx 2.50
14 KK&SMt(s),Genesis tie-in 2.50
15 KK&SMt(s),new Rave 2.50
16 KK&SMt(s),Half-Life 2.50
17 KK&SMt(s),Kaliber 2.50
18 KK&SMt(s),V:Qward 2.50
19 . . . . 2.50

SUPERBOY PLUS
Nov., 1996
1 RMz(s),ASm,F:Captain
    Marvel Jr. 3.50
2 LKa,AWi,ALa,F:Slither 3.00

SUPERBOY/RISK
DOUBLE-SHOT
Dec., 1997
1 DJu,JoP,x-over. 2.50

SUPERBOY'S LEGION
Feb., 2001
1 (of 2) Elseworlds, 48-page......6.00
2 MFm,AD, concl..............6.00

SUPER DC GIANT
1970–71, 1976
S-13 Binky.................200.00
S-14 JKu,GK,Top Guns of
   the West.................75.00
S-15 JKu,GK,Western Comics...65.00
S-16 JKu,Best of the Brave
   & the Bold...............50.00
S-17 Love 1970.............450.00
S-18 Three Mouseketeers......150.00
S-19 NA,Jerry Lewis.........175.00
S-20 NA,JK,House of Mystery...100.00
S-21 Love 1971.............600.00
S-22 JKu,Top Guns of the West..50.00
S-23 The Unexpected.........50.00
S-24 Supergirl.............50.00
S-25 Challengers of the Unknown.50.00
S-26 Aquaman..............40.00
S-27 GK,Strange Flying Saucer
   Adventures (1976).........40.00

SUPER FRIENDS
Nov., 1976
1 ECh(c),JO,RE,Fury of the
   Superfoes,A:Penguin.......60.00
2 RE,A:Penguin.............30.00
3 RF(c),RF,A:JLA...........25.00
4 RF,V:Riddler,I:Skyrocket.....25.00
5 RF(c),RF,V:Greenback.......25.00
6 RF(c),RF,A:Atom...........20.00
7 RF(c),RF,I:Zan & Jana,
   A:Seraph................20.00
8 RF(c),RF,A:JLA............20.00
9 RF(c),RF,A:JLA,I:Iron Maiden..20.00
10 RF(c),RFTheMonkeyMenace...20.00
11 RF(c),RF...............15.00
12 RF(c),RF,A:TNT..........15.00
13 RF(c),RF...............15.00
14 RF(c),RF...............15.00
15 RF(c),RF, A:The Elementals..15.00
16 RF(c),RF,V:The Cvags......15.00
17 RF(c),RF,A:Queen Hippolyte..15.00
18 KS(c),V:Tuantra,Time Trapper.15.00
19 RF(c),RF,V:Menagerie Man...15.00
20 KS(c),KS,V:Frownin' Fritz.....15.00
21 RF(c),RF,V:Evil Superfriends
   Doubles................15.00
22 RF(c),RF,V:Matador Mob.....15.00
23 FR(c),RF,V:Mirror Master.....15.00
24 RF(c),RF,V:Exorians.......15.00
25 RF(c),V:Overlord,
   A:Green Lantern, Mera....15.00
26 RF(c),RF,A:Johnny Jones.....15.00
27 RF(c),RF,The Spaceman Who
   Stole the Stars...........15.00
28 RF(c),RF,A:Felix Faust.......15.00
29 RF(c),RF,B.U.KS,Scholar From
   the Stars...............15.00
30 RF(c),RF,V:Grodd & Giganta...15.00
31 RF(c),RF,A:Black Orchid......18.00
32 KS(c),KS,A:Scarecrow.......12.00
33 RF(c),RF,V:Menagerie Man...12.00
34 RF(c)oRF,The Creature That
   Slept a Million Years........12.00
35 RT,Circus o/t Super Stars.....12.00
36 RF(c),RF,A:Plastic Man
   & Woozy................12.00
37 RF(c),RF,A:Supergirl;
   B.U. A:Jack O'Lantern.......12.00
38 RF(c),RF,V:Grax;
   B.U. A:Serpah.............12.00
39 RF(c),RF,A:Overlord;
   B.U. A:Wonder Twins.......12.00
40 RF(c),RF,V:The Monacle;
   B.U. Jack O'Lantern.......12.00

41 RF(c),RF,V:Toyman;
   B.U. A:Seraph............12.00
42 RT,A:Flora,V:Flame; B.U.Wonder
   Twins' Christmas Special....12.00
43 KS(c),RT,V:Futuro; B.U.JSon
   A:Plastic Man............12.00
44 KS(c),RT,Peril o/t Forgotten
   Identities'; B.U:Jack O'Lantern 12.00
45 KS(c),RT,A:Bushmaster,
   Godiva, Rising Sun, Olympian,
   Little Mermaid, Wild Huntsman;
   B.U. Plastic Man,V: Sinestro..12.00
46 RT,V:The Conqueror;
   B.U. BO,Seraph...........12.00
47 KS(c),RT,A:Green Fury
   Aug., 1981..............12.00

SUPERGIRL
[1st Regular Series]
Nov., 1972—Sept., 1974
1 Trail of the Madman';
   Superfashions From Fans;
   B:B.U. DG,Zatanna........90.00
2 BO(c)A:Prof.Allan,Bottle
   City of Kandor...........40.00
3 BO(c),The Garden of Death...35.00
4 V:Super Scavanger.........40.00
5 BO(c),A:Superman,V:Dax; B.U.
   MA:Rep.Hawkman #4......50.00
6 BO(c),Love & War.........40.00
7 BO(c),A:Zatanna..........40.00
8 BO(c),A:Superman,Green
   Lantern, Hawkman.......50.00
9 BO(c),V:Sharkman.........40.00
10 A:Prey,V:Master Killer.......40.00

[DARING NEW ADVENTURES OF] SUPERGIRL
[2nd Regular Series]
Nov., 1982
1 CI,BO,I:Psi; B:B.U.Lois Lane....3.00
2 CI,BO,C:Decay.............3.00
3 CI,BO,V:Decay,Decay Day.....3.00
4 CI,BO,V:The Gang..........3.00
5 CI,BO,V:The Gang..........3.00
6 CI,BO,V:The Gang..........3.00
7 CI,BO,V:The Gang..........3.00
8 CI,BO,A:Doom Patrol........3.00
9 CI,BO,V:Reactron
   A:Doom Patrol...........3.00
10 CI,BO,Radiation Fever.......3.00
11 CI,BO,V:Chairman..........3.00
12 CI,BO,V:Chairman..........3.00
13 CI,BO,N:Supergirl,A:Superman
   V:Blackstarr..............3.00
Becomes:

SUPERGIRL
Dec., 1983–Sept., 1984
14 GK(c),CI,BO,V:Blackstarr
   A:Rabbi Nathan Zuber.......3.00
15 CI,BO,V:Blackstarr,
   A:Blackstarr's Mom.........3.00
16 KG/BO(c),CI,BO,
   A:Ambush Bug...........3.00
17 CI/DG(c),CI,BO,V:Matrix
   Prime..................3.00
18 DG(c),CI,BO, V:Kraken......3.00
19 EB/BO(c),CI,BO,Who Stole
   Supergirl's Life............3.00
20 CI,BO,C:JLA,Teen Titans:
   Teh Parasite.............3.00
21 EB/BO(c),EB,Kryptonite Man...3.00
22 EB(c),CI,BO,I Have Seen the
   Future & it is Me..........3.00
23 EB(c),CI,BO,The Future
   Begins Today............3.00
Spec.#1 JL/DG(c),GM,MovieAdapt.3.00
Spec.#1 AT,Honda give-away.....3.00

[Limited Series], 1994
1 KGa(c),B:RSt(s),JBr,O:Supergirl.5.00
2 KGa(c),JBr.................4.00
3 KGa(c),JBr,D:Clones.........3.00
4 KGa(c),RSt(s),JBr,final Issue....3.00

SUPERGIRL
Sept., 1996
1 PDd(s),GFr,CaS,............11.00
1a 2nd printing.............3.00
2 PDd(s),GFr,CaS,V:Chakat......5.00
3 PDd(s),GFr,CaS,V:Grodd, Final
   Night tie-in..............5.00
4 PDd(s),GFr,CaS,transformed into
   savage.................4.00
5 PDd(s),GFr,CaS,Supergirl visits
   the Kents,V:Chemo.........4.00
6 PDd(s),GFr,CaS,...........4.00
7 PDd(s),GFr,CaS,Supergirl learns
   about Linda Danvers........4.00
8 PDd(s),GFr,CaS,Buzz gets date
   with Supergirl.............4.00
9 PDd(s),GFr,CaS,V:Tempus.....4.00
10 PDd(s),Linda tries to relax.....4.00
11 PDd(s),CaS,V:Silver Banshee..4.00
12 PDd(s),Mattie possessed by
   Silver Banshee............4.00
13 CaS, 3 girls dreams invaded by
   incubus.................3.00
14 PDa,CaS,Genesis tie-in.......3.00
15 PDa,CaS,V:Extremists........3.00
16 PDa,CaS,F:Power Girl........3.00
17 PDa,CaS,L-Ron, Despero.....3.00
18 PDa,CaS,V:Despero.........3.00
19....................3.00
20 PDa,CaS,Millennium Giants....3.00
21 PDa,CaS,Comet...........3.00
22 PDa,...................3.00
23 PDa,A:Steel.............3.00
24 PDa,Avenging Angels x-over...3.00
25 PDa,truth about Comet........3.00
26 PDd,truth discovered........3.00
27 PDd(s),V:Female Furies,pt.1...3.00
28 PDd(s),V:Female Furies,pt.2...3.00
29 PDd(s),V:Female Furies,pt.3...3.00
30 PDd(s),V:Matrix...........3.00
31 PDd(s),A:Superman.........3.00
32 PDd(s),SeP,V:Mr.Carnivean...3.00
33 PDd(s),V:Mr.Carnivean.......3.00
34 PDd(s),V:Parasite..........3.00
35 PDd(s),V:Parasite, concl.......3.00
36 PDd(s),Hell's Angel's,pt.2.....2.50
37 PDd(s),Hell's Angels,pt.4......2.50

Supergirl #17
© DC Comics, Inc.

Supergirl Ann. #2
© DC Comics, Inc.

38 PDd(s),Day of Judgment x-over . 2.50
39 PDd(s),F:Comet 2.50
40 PDd(s). 2.50
41 PDd(s),F:Ember,V:Satan Girl . . . 2.50
42 PDd(s),dates Dick Malverne. . . . 2.50
43 PDd(s),date become nightmare . 2.50
44 PDd(s),F:Dick Malverne,dying . . 2.50
45 PDd(s),F:Comet,V:Carnivore . . . 2.50
46 PDd(s),V:Comet,Carnivore 2.50
47 PDd(s),V:Carnivore. 2.50
48 PDd(s),. 2.50
49 PDd(s),V:Carnivore. 2.50
50 PDd(s),48-pg. 4.00
51 PDd(s),to Metropolis, minus
   powers. 2.50
52 PDd(s),V:Riot & Prankster 2.50
53 PDd(s),F:Green Lantern 2.50
54 PDd(s),F:Green Lantern 2.50
55 PDd(s),A:Lex Luthor 2.50
56 PDd(s),Buzz's daughter 2.50
57 PDd(s),Daddy's Little Girl 2.50
58 PDd(s),Buzz close to death 2.50
59 PDd(s),Our Worlds at War,tie-in . 2.50
60 PDd(s),Our Worlds at War,tie-in . 2.50
61 PDd(s),Our Worlds at War,tie-in . 2.50
62 PDd(s),A:Two-Face. 2.50
63 PDd(s),Joker:Last Laugh,tie-in . 5.00
64 PDd(s),A:Lagoon Boy. 2.50
65 PDd(s),hearing-impaired kids . . . 2.50
66 PDd(s),F:Demon Etrigan 2.50
67 PDd(s),F:Demon Etrigan 2.50
68 PDd(s),F:Mary Marvel. 4.00
69 PDd(s),F:Capt.Marvel,Jr. 5.00
70 PDd(s),F:Mary Marvel. 2.50
71 PDd(s),V:Tara 2.50
72 PDd(s),V:Quetzlcoatl 2.50
73 PDd(s),Garden of Eden 2.50
74 PDd(s),Linda,Supergirl re-merge 2.50
75 PDd(s),EBe,spacecraft crashes . 8.00
76 PDd(s),F:Superboy,Kara Zor-El 12.00
77 PDd(s),V:Fatalist. 6.00
78 PDd(s),V:Fatalist. 5.00
79 PDd(s),S.A.Supergirl. 5.00
80 PDd(s),V:Kara & Xenon 5.00
Ann.#1 Legends o/t Dead Earth . . 3.00
Ann.#2 TPe,CDi,ACa, Pulp Heroes 4.00
Spec.#1,000,000 PDd(s),DAb 2.00
GN Wings, Elseworlds, 48-page . . 6.00
Spec. Supergirl/Lex Luthor JBr,
   F:Lex Luthor (1993). 4.00
Spec. Supergirl/Prysm Double-Shot
   DJu,TGb,CIv, x-over (1997) . . . 2.00

SUPERGIRL
Aug., 2005

0 JLb(s),IaC,NRd,F:Kara Zor-el . . . 4.00
1 JLb(s),IaC,NRd,V:Power Girl. . . . 5.00
1a variant (c). 5.00
2 JLb(s),IaC,NRd,V:Superboy 4.00
3 JLb(s),IaC,NRd,Spying on Kara . 4.00
4 JLb(s),IaC,NRd,F:JLA 4.00
4a variant (c). 3.00
5 JLb(s),IaC,NRd,Mistress of Might 5.00
5a 2nd printing 3.00
6 JLb(s),IaC,NRd,A:Batman, Wonder
   Woman, F:Superman 5.00
7 IaC,New Flamebird & Nightwing . 3.00
8 EBe,V:Power Girl. 3.00
9 IaC,Supergirl's boyfriend 3.00
10 IaC,New secret identity. 3.00
11 IaC,NRd,A:Outsiders. 3.00
12 IaC,NRd,A:Batgirl, League of
   Assassins 3.00
13 IaC,NRd,F:Power Boy 3.00
14 IaC,NRd,V:Batgirl, to the death . 3.00
15 IaC,NRd,F:Powerboy 3.00
16 Sent to kill Superman 3.00
17 F:JLA,Wonder Girl 3.00
18 A:Superman 3.00
19 V:Superman 3.00
20 Amazons Attack tie-in 3.00
21 Countdown tie-in. 3.00
22 V:Karate Kid 3.00

SUPER HEROES BATTLE SUPER GORILLA
Winter, 1976

1 Superman Flash rep. 20.00

SUPERMAN
1939–86

1 JoS,O:Superman,reprints Action
   Comics #1-#4 . . . . 375,000.00
2 JoS,I:George Taylor 25,000.00
3 JoS,V:Superintendent
   Lyman 14,000.00
4 JoS,V:Lex Luthor 14,000.00
5 JoS,V:Lex Luthor 10,000.00
6 JoS,V:Brute' Bashby 5,500.00
7 JoS,I:Perry White 5,000.00
8 JoS,V:Jackal 5,000.00
9 JoS,V:Joe Gatson. 5,000.00
10 JoS,V:Lex Luthor 4,000.00
11 JoS,V:Rolf Zimba 3,800.00
12 JoS,V:Lex Luthor 3,800.00
13 JoS,I:Jimmy Olsen,V:Lex
   Luthor,The Archer. 3,800.00
14 JoS,I:Lightning Master. 6,000.00
15 JoS,V:The Evolution King . . . 3,800.00
16 JoS,V:Mr. Sinus. 3,000.00
17 JoS,V:Lex Luthor,Lois Lane
   first suspects Clark
   is Superman 3,000.00
18 JoS,V:Lex Luthor 3,000.00
19 JoS,V:Funnyface,
   1st Imaginary story. 3,000.00
20 JoS,V:Puzzler,Leopard 3,000.00
21 JoS,V:Sir Gauntlet 2,400.00
22 JoS,V:Prankster. 2,400.00
23 JoS,Propaganda story 2,400.00
24 V:Cobra King 3,500.00
25 Propaganda story 3,500.00
26 I:J.Wilbur Wolfingham,
   A:Mercury 3,500.00
27 V:Toyman 3,500.00
28 V:J.Wilbur Wolfingham,
   A:Hercules 3,500.00
29 V:Prankster 3,500.00
30 I&O:Mr. Mxyztplk 4,000.00
31 V:Lex Luthor. 1,700.00
32 V:Toyman. 1,700.00
33 V:Mr. Mxyzptlk. 1,700.00
34 V:Lex Luthor. 1,700.00

35 V:J.Wilbur Wolfingham. 1,700.00
36 V:Mr. Mxyztplk. 1,700.00
37 V:Prankster,A:Sinbad. 1,700.00
38 V:Lex Luthor. 1,700.00
39 V:J.Wilbur Wolfingham. 1,700.00
40 V:Mr. Mxyzptlk,A:Susie
   Thompkins 1,700.00
41 V:Prankster 1,500.00
42 V:J.Wilbur Wolfingham. 1,500.00
43 V:Lex Luthor. 1,500.00
44 V:Toyman,A:Shakespeare . . 1,500.00
45 A:Hocus & Pocus,Lois Lane
   as Superwoman 1,500.00
46 V:Mr. Mxyzptlk,Lex Luthor,
   Superboy flashback 1,500.00
47 V:Toyman 1,500.00
48 V:Lex Luthor. 1,500.00
49 V:Toyman 1,500.00
50 V:Prankster 1,500.00
51 V:Mr. Mxyzptlk 1,200.00
52 V:Prankster 1,200.00
53 WB,O:Superman 4,500.00
54 V:Wrecker 1,200.00
55 V:Prankster. 1,200.00
56 V:Prankster 1,200.00
57 V:Lex Luthor. 1,200.00
58 V:Tiny Trix 1,200.00
59 V:Mr.Mxyzptlk. 1,200.00
60 V:Toyman 1,200.00
61 I:Kryptonite,V:Prankster 2,400.00
62 V:Mr.Mxyzptlk,A:Orson
   Welles. 1,200.00
63 V:Toyman 1,200.00
64 V:Prankster 1,200.00
65 V:Mala,Kizo and U-Ban 1,200.00
66 V:Prankster 1,200.00
67 A:Perry Como,I:Brane
   Taylor 1,200.00
68 V:Lex Luthor. 1,200.00
69 V:Prankster,A:Inspector
   Erskine Hawkins 1,200.00
70 V:Prankster 1,200.00
71 V:Lex Luthor. 1,100.00
72 V:Prankster 1,100.00
72a giveaway 1,200.00
73 Flashback story 1,100.00
74 V:Lex Luthor. 1,100.00
75 V:Prankster. 1,100.00
76 A:Batman, Superman &
   Batman reveal each other's
   identities 3,000.00
77 A:Pocahontas. 1,100.00
78 V:Kryptonian snagriff,
   A:Lana Lang 1,100.00
79 V:Lex Luthor,A:Inspector
   Erskine Hawkins 1,100.00
80 A:Halk Kar 1,100.00

Superman #76 © DC Comics, Inc.

81 V:Lex Luthor	1,100.00
82 V:Mr. Mxyzptlk	900.00
83 V:The Brain	900.00
84 Time-travel story	900.00
85 V:Lex Luthor	900.00
86 V:Mr.Mxyzptlk	900.00
87 WB,V:The Thing from 40,000 AD	900.00
88 WB,V:Lex Luthor,Toyman, Prankster team	1,000.00
89 V:Lex Luthor	900.00
90 V:Lex Luthor	1,000.00
91 The Superman Stamp	900.00
92 Goes back to 12th Century England	900.00
93 V:The Thinker	900.00
94 Clark Kent's Hillbilly Bride	900.00
95 A:Susie Thompkins	900.00
96 V:Mr. Mxyzptlk	700.00
97 Superboy's Last Day In Smallville	700.00
98 Clark Kent, Outlaw!	700.00
99 V:Midnite gang	700.00
100 F:Superman-Substitute Schoolteacher	3,500.00
101 A:Lex Luthor	600.00
102 I:Superman Stock Company	600.00
103 A:Mr.Mxyzptlk	600.00
104 F:Clark Kent,Jailbird	600.00
105 A:Mr.Mxyzptlk	600.00
106 A:Lex Luthor	650.00
107 F:Superman In 30th century (pre-Legion)	600.00
108 I:Perry White Jr.	600.00
109 I:Abner Hokum	600.00
110 A:Lex Luthor	600.00
111 Becomes Mysto the Great	600.00
112 A:Lex Luthor	600.00
113 A:Jor-El	600.00
114 V:The Great Mento	600.00
115 V:The Organizer	600.00
116 Return to Smallville	600.00
117 A:Lex Luthor	600.00
118 F:Jimmy Olsen	600.00
119 A:Zoll Orr	600.00
120 V:Gadget Grim	600.00
121 I:XL-49 (Futureman)	450.00
122 In the White House	450.00
123 CS,pre-Supergirl tryout A:Jor-El & Lara	500.00
124 F:Lois Lane	450.00
125 F:Superman College Story	450.00
126 F:Lois Lane	450.00
127 WB,I&O:Titano	500.00
128 V:Vard & Boka	450.00
129 WB,I&O:Lori Lemaris	500.00
130 A:Krypto,the Superdog	450.00
131 A:Mr. Mxyzptlk	450.00
132 A:Batman & Robin	450.00
133 F:Superman Joins Army	450.00
134 A:Supergirl & Krypto	450.00
135 A:Lori Lemaris,Mr.Mxyzptlk	450.00
136 O:Discovery Kryptonite	450.00
137 CS,I:Super-Menace	450.00
138 A:Titano,Lori Lemaris	450.00
139 CS,O:Red Kryptonite	450.00
140 WB,I:Bizarro Jr,Bizarro Supergirl,Blue Kryptonite	450.00
141 I:Lyla Lerrol,A:Jor-EL & Lara	350.00
142 WB,CS,A:Al Capone	350.00
143 WB,F:Bizarro meets Frankenstein	350.00
144 O:Superboy's 1st Public Appearance	350.00
145 F:April Fool's Issue	350.00
146 F:Superman's life story	400.00
147 CS,I:Adult Legion	350.00
148 CS,V:Mxyzptlk	300.00
149 CS:A:Luthor,C:JLA	300.00
150 CS,KS,V:Mxyzptlk	250.00

150 CS,KS,V:Mxyzptlk	250.00
151 CS	250.00
152 A:Legion	250.00
153 CS	250.00
154 CS,V:Mzyzptlk	250.00
155 WB,CS,V:Cosmic Man	250.00
156 CS,A:Legion,Batman	250.00
157 CS,I:Gold kryptonite	250.00
158 CS,I:Nightwing&Flamebird	250.00
159 CS,Imaginary Tale F:Lois Lane	250.00
160 CS,F:Perry White	250.00
161 D:Ma & Pa Kent	250.00
162 A:Legion	250.00
163 CS	250.00
164 CS,Luthor,I:Lexor	250.00
165 CS,A:Saturn Woman	250.00
166 CS	250.00
167 CS,I:Ardora,Brainiac	275.00
168 CS	200.00
169 Great DC Contest	200.00
170 CS,A:J.F.Kennedy,Luthor	200.00
171 CS,Mxyzptlk	200.00
172 CS,Luthor,Brainiac	200.00
173 CS,A:Batman	200.00
174 Mxyzptlk	200.00
175 CS,Luthor	200.00
176 CS,Green Kryptonite	200.00
177 Fortress of Solitude	200.00
178 CS, Red Kryptonite	200.00
179 CS,Clark Kent in Marines	200.00
180 CS	200.00
181 Superman 2965	200.00
182 CS,Toyman	200.00
183 giant	200.00
184 Secrets of the Fortress	150.00
185 JM,Superman's Achilles Heel	150.00
186 CS,The Two Ghosts of Superman	150.00
187 giant	150.00
188 V:Zunial,The Murder Man	150.00
189 WB,The Mystery of Krypton's Second Doom	150.00
190 WB,I:Amalak	150.00
191 The Prisoner of Demon	150.00
192 CS,Imaginary Story, I:Superman Jr.	150.00
193 giant	150.00
194 CS,Imaginary,A:Supes Jr.	150.00
195 CS,V:Amalak	150.00
196 WB,reprint	150.00
197 giant	150.00
198 CS,F:The Real Clark Kent	150.00
199 CS,F:Superman/Flash race, A:JLA	500.00

Superman #143 © DC Comics Inc.

200 WB,A:Brainiac	125.00
201 CS,F:Clark Kent Abandons Superman	100.00
202 A:Bizarro, (giant size)	125.00
203 F:When Superman Killed His Friends	100.00
204 NA(c),RA,A:Lori Lemaris	100.00
205 NA(c),I:Black Zero	100.00
206 NA(c),F:The Day Superman Became An Assistant	100.00
207 CS,F:The Case Of the Collared Crimefighter	125.00
208 NA(c),CS	100.00
209 CS,F:The Clark Kent Monster	100.00
210 CS,F:Clark Kent's Last Rites	100.00
211 CS,RA	100.00
212 giant	150.00
213 CS,JA,V:Luthor,C:Brainiac 5.	100.00
214 NA(c),CS,JA,F:The Ghosts That Haunted Superman	100.00
215 NA(c),CS,JA,V:Luthor, Imaginary Story	100.00
216 JKu(c),RA,Superman in Nam	100.00
217 CS,A:Mr.Mxyzptlk	100.00
218 CS,JA,A:Mr.Mxyzptlk	100.00
219 CS,F:Clark Kent-Hero, Superman Public Enemy	100.00
220 CS,A:Flash	100.00
221 CS,F:The Two Ton Superman	100.00
222 giant	150.00
223 CS,A:Supergirl	75.00
224 CS,Imaginary Story	75.00
225 CS,F:The Secret of the Super Imposter	75.00
226 CS,F:When Superman Became King Kong	75.00
227 Krypton,(giant)	100.00
228 CS,DA	75.00
229 WB,CS	75.00
230 CS,DA,Luthor	75.00
231 CS,DA,Luthor	75.00
232 F:Krypton,(giant)	100.00
233 CS,MA,I:Quarrum	75.00
234 NA(c),CS,MA	75.00
235 CS,MA	75.00
236 CS,MA,DG,A:Green Arrow	75.00
237 NA(c),CS,MA	75.00
238 CS,MA,GM	75.00
239 giant	100.00
240 CS,DG,MK,A:I-Ching	50.00
241 CS,MA,A:Wonder Woman	50.00
242 CS,MA,A:Wonder Woman	50.00
243 CS,MA	50.00
244 CS,MA	50.00
245 100 pg reprints	50.00
246 CS,MA,RB,I:S.T.A.R. Labs	50.00
247 CS,MA,Guardians o/Universe	50.00
248 CS,MA,A:Luthor,I:Galactic Golem	50.00
249 CS,MA,DD,NA,I:Terra-Man	75.00
250 CS,MA,Terraman	50.00
251 CS,MA,RB	50.00
252 NA(c),rep.100pgs	50.00
253 CS,MA	50.00
254 CS,MA,NA	75.00
255 CS,MA,DG	30.00
256 CS,MA	30.00
257 CS,MA,DD,DG,A:Tomar-Re	30.00
258 CS,MA,DC	30.00
259 CS,MA,A:Terra-Man	30.00
260 CS,DC,I:Valdemar	30.00
261 CS,MA,V:Star Sapphire	30.00
262 CS,MA	30.00
263 CS,MA,DD,FMc	30.00
264 DC,CS,I:Steve Lombard	30.00
265 CS,MA	30.00
266 CS,MA,DD,V:Snowman	30.00
267 CS,MA,BO	30.00
268 CS,BO,DD,MA,A:Batgirl	30.00
269 CS,MA	30.00

All comics prices listed are for *Near Mint* condition.

DC COMICS

270 CS,MA,V:Valdemar 30.00	324 CS,A:Atomic Skull. 12.00	404 CI,BO,V:Luthor 5.00
271 CS,BO,DG,V:Brainiac 30.00	325 CS 12.00	405 KS,KK,AS,F:Super-Batman . . . 5.00
272 100pg.reprints 50.00	326 CS,V:Blackrock 12.00	406 IN,AS,KK. 5.00
273 CS,DG 30.00	327 CS,KS,V:Kobra,C:JLA 12.00	407 IN,V:Mxyzptlk 5.00
274 CS 30.00	328 CS,KS,V:Kobra 12.00	408 CS,AW,JRu,F:Nuclear
275 CS,DG,FMc 30.00	329 KS,CS 12.00	Holocaust. 5.00
276 CS,BO,I&O:Captain Thunder . 30.00	330 CS,F:glasses explained 12.00	409 CS,AW,KS. 5.00
277 CS 30.00	331 CS,I:Master Jailer 12.00	410 CS,AW,V:Luthor 5.00
278 CS,BO,Terraman,100page . . 75.00	332 CS,V:Master Jailer 12.00	411 CS,MA,F:End Earth-Prime . . . 5.00
279 CS,Batgirl,Batman 25.00	333 CS,V:Bizarro 12.00	412 CS,AW,V:Luthor 5.00
280 CS,BO. 25.00	334 CS 7.00	413 CS,AW,V:Luthor 5.00
281 CS,BO,I:Vartox 25.00	335 CS,W:Mxyzptlk 7.00	414 CS,AW,Crisis tie-in 6.00
282 CS,KS,N:Luthor 25.00	336 CS,V:Rose And Thorn. 7.00	415 CS,AW,Crisis,W:Super Girl. . . 6.00
283 CS,BO,Mxyzptlk 25.00	337 CS,A:Brainiac,Bizarro 7.00	416 CS,AW,Luthor 5.00
284 CS,BO,100p reprint 50.00	338 CS,F:Kandor enlarged 7.00	417 CS,V:Martians 5.00
285 CS,BO. 25.00	339 CS,I:N.R.G.X. 7.00	418 CS,V:Metallo 5.00
286 CS,BO. 25.00	340 CS,V:N.R.G.X 7.00	419 CS,V:Iago 5.00
287 CS,BO,R:Krypto 25.00	341 CS,F:Major Disaster 7.00	420 CS,F:Nightmares 5.00
288 CS,BO. 25.00	342 CS,V:Chemo 7.00	421 CS,V:Mxyzptlk 5.00
289 CS,BO,JL 25.00	343 CS 7.00	422 BB(c),CS,TY,LMa,V:Werewolf. . 5.00
290 CS,V:Mxyzptlk. 25.00	344 CS,A:Phantom Stranger 7.00	423 AMo(s),CS,GP,F:Last
291 CS,BO. 25.00	345 CS,When time ran backward . . 7.00	Superman 12.00
292 CS,BO,AM,O:Luthor 25.00	346 CS,Streak of Bad Luck 7.00	Ann.#1 I:Supergirl Rep 2,000.00
293 CS,BO. 25.00	347 JL 7.00	Ann.#2 I&O:Titano 750.00
294 CS,JL,A:Brain Storm 25.00	348 CS 7.00	Ann.#3 I:Legion 500.00
295 CS,BO. 25.00	349 CS,V:Mxyzptlk 7.00	Ann.#4 O:Legion 450.00
296 CS,BO,Identity Crisis #1 . . . 25.00	350 CS,Clark Kent's Vanishing	Ann.#5 A:Krypton 350.00
297 CS,BO,Identity Crisis #2 . . . 25.00	Classmate 6.00	Ann.#6 A:Legion. 350.00
298 CS,BO,Identity Crisis #3 . . . 25.00	351 CS,JL,A:Mxyzptlk 6.00	Ann.#7 O:Superman,Silver Anniv. 250.00
299 CS,BO,Identity Crisis #4	352 CS,RB. 6.00	Ann.#8 F:Secret origins 200.00
A:Luthor,Brainiac,Bizarro. . . . 25.00	353 CS,origin 6.00	Ann.#9 GK(c),ATh,TA,CS,
300 CS,BO,2001,anniversary . . . 40.00	354 CS,JSon,I:Superman 2020 . . 6.00	A:Batman. 7.00
301 BO,JL,V:Solomon Grundy . . . 15.00	355 CS,JSon,F:Superman 2020 . . 6.00	Ann.#10 CS,MA,F:Sword of
302 JL,BO,V:Luthor,A:Atom. 15.00	356 CS,V:Vartox. 6.00	Superman 5.00
303 CS,BO,I:Thunder&Lightning . . 15.00	357 CS,DCw,F:Superman 2020 . . 6.00	Ann.#11 AMo(s),DGb,A:Batman,
304 CS,BO,V:Parasite 15.00	358 CS,DG,DCw 6.00	Robin,Wonder Woman 6.00
305 CS,BO,V:Toyman 15.00	359 CS. 6.00	Ann.#12 BB(c),AS,A:Lex Luthor,
306 CS,BO,V:Bizarro. 15.00	360 CS,AS,F:World of Krypton . . . 6.00	Last War Suit. 4.00
307 NA(c),JL,FS,A:Supergirl 15.00	361 CS,AS 6.00	Game Give-away. 10.00
308 NA(c),JL,FS,A:Supergirl 15.00	362 CS,KS,DA 6.00	Giveaway CS,AT 2.25
309 JL,FS,A:Supergirl 15.00	363 CS,RB,C:Luthor 6.00	Pizza Hut 1977 . . . . 6.00
310 CS,V:Metallo 15.00	364 GP(c),RB,AS. 6.00	Radio Shack 1980 JSw,DG 5.00
311 CS,FS,A:Flash 15.00	365 CS,KS 6.00	Radio Shack 1981 CS 5.00
312 CS,FS,A:Supergirl 15.00	366 CS,KS 6.00	Radio Shack 1982 CS 5.00
313 NA(c),CS,DA,A:Supergirl . . . 15.00	367 CS,GK,F:World of Krypton . . . 6.00	Spec.#1 GK 3.50
314 NA(c),CS,DA,A:Gr.Lantern . . 15.00	368 CS,AS 6.00	Spec.#2 GK,V:Brainiac 3.50
315 CS,DA,V:Blackrock 12.00	369 RB,FMc,V:Parasite 6.00	Spec.#3 IN,V:Amazo 3.50
316 CS,DA,V:Metallo 12.00	370 CS,KS,FMc,A:Chemo 6.00	Superman III Movie,CS 2.50
317 NA(c),CS,DA,V:Metallo 12.00	371 CS 6.00	Superman IV Movie,DH,DG,FMc. . 2.50
318 CS 12.00	372 CS,GK,F:Superman 2021 . . . 6.00	**Becomes:**
319 CS,V:Solomon Grundy 12.00	373 CS,V:Vartox. 6.00	
320 CS,V:Solomon Grundy 12.00	374 GK(c),CS,DA,KS,V:Vartox . . . 6.00	
321 CS,V:Parasite 20.00	375 CS,DA,GK,V:Vartox 6.00	
322 CS,V:Solomon Grundy 20.00	376 CS,DA,CI,BO,SupergirlPrev. . . 5.00	
323 CS,DA,I:Atomic Skull 15.00	377 GK(c),CS,V:Terra-Man 5.00	

Superman #289
© DC Comics, Inc.

378 CS 5.00	
379 CS,V:Bizarro. 5.00	
380 CS 5.00	
381 GK(c),CS. 5.00	
382 GK(c),CS. 5.00	
383 CS 5.00	
384 GK(c),CS. 5.00	
385 GK(c),CS,V:Luthor 5.00	
386 GK(c),CS,V:Luthor 5.00	
387 GK(c),CS. 5.00	
388 GK(c),CS. 5.00	
389 GK(c),CS. 5.00	
390 GK(c),CS,V:Vartox 5.00	
391 GK(c),CS,V:Vartox 5.00	
392 GK(c),CS,V:Vartox 5.00	
393 IN,DG,V:Master Jailer 5.00	
394 CS,V:Valdemar 5.00	
395 CS,V:Valdemar 5.00	
396 CS 5.00	
397 EB,V:Kryptonite Man. 5.00	
398 CS,AS,DJ 5.00	
399 CS,BO,EB. 5.00	
400 HC(c),FM,AW,JO,JSo,MR,	
TA,WP,MK,KJ,giant 8.00	
401 CS,BO,V:Luthor 5.00	
402 CS,BO,WB 5.00	
403 CS,BO,AS. 5.00	

ADVENTURES OF SUPERMAN
1987

424 JOy,I:Man O'War. 6.00
425 JOy,Man O'War. 3.00
426 JOy,Legends,V:Apokolips 3.00
427 JOy,V:Qurac 3.00
428 JOy,V:Qurac,I:JerryWhite . . . 3.00
429 JOy,V:Concussion. 3.00
430 JOy,V:Fearsome Five 3.00
431 JOy,A:Combattor. 3.00
432 JOy,I:Jose Delgado. 3.00
433 JOy,V:Lex Luthor 3.00
434 JOy,I:Gang Buster 3.00
435 JOy,A:Charger 3.00
436 JOy,Millennium x-over 5.00
437 JOy,Millennium X-over 3.50
438 JOy,N:Brainiac 3.00
439 JOy,R:Superman Robot 3.00
440 JOy,A:Batman,Wond.Woman . . 3.00
441 JOy,V:Mr.Mxyzptlk. 3.00
442 JOy,V:Dreadnaught,A:JLI 3.00
443 JOy,DHz,I:Husque 3.00
444 JOy,Supergirl SagaPt.2 . . . . . 3.00
445 JOy,V:Brainiac. 3.00
446 JOy,A:Gangbuster,
A:Luthor's Old Costume 3.00
447 JOy,A:Gangbuster. 3.00
448 JOy,I:Dubbilex,A:Gangbuster . . 3.00
449 JOy,Invasion X-over 3.00
450 JOy,Invasion X-over 3.00

The Adventures of Superman #501
© DC Comics, Inc.

451 JOy,Superman in Space 3.00
452 DJu,V:Wordbringer 3.00
453 JOy,DJu,A:Gangbuster 3.00
454 JOy,DJu,I:New Mongul 4.00
455 DJu,ATb,A:Eradicator 3.50
456 DJu,ATb,V:Turmoil 3.50
457 DJu,V:Intergang 3.50
458 DJu,KJ,R:Elastic Lad
(Jimmy Olsen) 3.50
459 DJu,V:Eradicator 3.50
460 DJu,NKu,V:Eradicator 3.50
461 DJu,GP,V:Eradicator 3.50
462 DJu,ATb,Homeless
Christmas Story 3.50
463 DJu,ATb,Superman Races
Flash 3.50
464 DJu,ATb,Day of Krypton
Man #2,A:Lobo 6.00
465 DJu,ATb,Day of Krypton
Man #5,V:Draaga 3.00
466 DJu,DG,V:Team Excalibur
Astronauts,I:Hank Henshaw
(becomes Cyborg Superman) . . 4.50
467 DJu,ATb,A:Batman 3.00
468 DJu,ATb,Man Of Steel's
Journal,V:Hank Henshaw 3.00
469 DJu,ATb,V:Dreadnaught 3.00
470 DJu,ATb,Soul Search #3,
D:Jerry White 3.00
471 CS,Sinbad Contract #2 . . . . 3.00
472 DJu,Krisis of Krimson
Kryptonite #2 . . . . 3.00
473 DJu,ATb,A:Green Lantern,
Guy Gardner 3.00
474 DJu,ATb,Drunk Driving issue . . 3.00
475 DJu,ATb,V:Kilgrave,Sleez 3.00
476 DJu,BBr,Time & Time Again,pt.1,
A:Booster Gold,Legion 3.00
477 DJu,BBr,T & T Again,pt.4,
A:Legion 3.00
478 DJu,BBr,T & T Again,pt.7,
A:Legion,Linear Man 3.00
479 EH,Red Glass Trilogy#2 . . . . . . 3.00
480 JOy,DJu,BMc,TG,BBr,CS,
Revenge of the Krypton
Man,pt.3. . . . . 3.00
481 1st TG Supes,DHz,V:Parasite . . 3.00
482 TG,DHz,V:Parasite 3.00
483 TG,DHz,V:Blindspot 3.00
484 TG,Blackout #1,V:Mr.Z 3.00
485 TG,DHz,Blackout #5,A:Mr.Z . . . 3.00
486 TG,V:Purge 3.00
487 TG,DHz,X-mas,A:Agent
Liberty 3.00

488 TG,Panic in the Sky,pt.3,
V:Brainiac 4.00
489 TG,Panic in the Sky,Epiloge . . 4.00
490 TG,A:Agent Liberty,Husque. . . . 3.00
491 TG,DHz,V:Cerberus,Metallo . . . 3.00
492 WS(c),V:Sons of Liberty,
A:Agent Liberty 3.00
493 TG,Blaze/Satanus War,pt.1 . . 3.00
494 TG,DHz,I:Kismet 3.00
495 TG,DHz,A:Forever People,
Darkseid 3.00
496 V:Mr.Mxyzptlk,C:Doomsday . . . 5.00
496a 2nd printing 2.50
497 TG,Doomsday Pt.3,A:Maxima,
Bloodwynd 5.00
497a 2nd printing 2.50
498 TG,Funeral for a Friend#1 . . . . 4.00
498a 2nd Printing 2.50
499 TG,DHz,Funeral for a
Friend#5 . . . . 3.50
500 JOy(c),B:KK(s),TG,DJu,JBg,JG,
BBr,Bagged,Superman in limbo,
I:Four Supermen,Direct Sales . . 3.50
500a Newsstand Ed. 3.00
500b Platinum Ed. 20.00
501 TG,Reign of Supermen#2,Direct
Sales,Die-Cut(c),Mini-poster
F:Superboy 3.00
501a Newstand Ed. 2.25
502 TG,A:Supergirl,V:Stinger 2.25
503 TG,Cyborg Superman Vs.
Superboy 2.50
504 TG,DHz,A:All Supermen,
V:Mongul 2.50
505 TG,DHz,Superman returns to
Metropolis,Holografx(c) 3.00
505a Newstand Ed. 2.25
506 TG,DHz,A:Guardian 2.50
507 Spilled Blood#1,V:Bloodsport . . 2.50
508 BKi,A:Challengers of the
Unknown 2.50
509 BKi,A:Auron 2.50
510 BKi,Bizarro's World #2,
V:Bizarro 2.50
511 BKi,A:Guardian 2.50
512 BKi,V:Parasite 2.50
513 BKi,Battle for Metropolis #4 . . . 2.50
514 BKi,Fall of Metropolis #4 . . . . . 2.50
515 BKi,Massacre in Metropolis . . . 2.50
516 BKi,Zero Hour,I:Alpha
Centurion 2.50
517 BKi,deathtrap 2.50
518 BKi 2.50
519 KK,BKi,Secret of Superman's
Tomb 2.50
520 SI,KK,JMz,100 crimes at
midnight 2.50
521 SI,KK,R:Thorn. 2.50
522 SI,KKIdentity known 2.50
523 SI,KK,Death of C.Kent,pt.2 . . . . 2.50
524 SI,KK,Death of C.Kent,pt.6
[New Miraweb format begins] . . 2.50
525 SI,KK. 2.50
526 Bloodsport vs. Bloodsport. 2.50
527 KK,SI,JMz,The Return 2.50
528 Trial of Superman,prelude 2.50
529 Trial of Superman 2.50
530 KK,SI,JMz,Trial of Superman . . 2.50
531 KK,SI,JMz,Trial of Superman,
concl. 2.50
532 KK,SI,JMz, return of Lori
Lemaris 2.50
533 KK,SI,JMz. 2.50
534 KK,SI,JMz,V:Lord Satannus . . . 2.50
535 KK,SI,JMz,Lois & LoriLemaris . 2.50
536 Identity Crisis,pt.1:Cages 2.50
537 KK,SI,JMz. 2.50
538 KK,SI,JMz,Fatal Obsession . . . 2.50
539 F:Guardian and the Newsboy
Legion 2.50
540 KK(s),TyD,KIS,A:Ferro, Final
Night tie-in 2.50

Adventures of Superman #516
© DC Comics Inc.

541 KK(s),SI,JMz,on Honeymoon,
A:Superboy,Tana Moon,Kekona 2.50
542 KK&JOy(s),PR,JMz,V:Misa. . . . 2.50
543 KK,SI,JMz,Honeymoon's Over . 2.50
544 KK(s),SI,JMz,Who Killed Clark
Kent in broad daylight? 2.50
545 KK(s),SEa,JMz,Return of the
Atomic Skull,new blue costume 2.50
546 KK(s),SI,JMz,V:Metallo, uses
new powers 2.50
547 KK(s),SI,JMz,Superman goes
to Kandor,A:The Atom 2.50
548 KK(s),SI,JMz,V:Lex Luthor 2.50
549 KK(s),SI,JMz,F:Jimmy Olsen . . 2.50
550 KK(s),SI,TGu,JMz,DRo, 48pg. . 3.50
551 DJu,TGu,DRo,Genesis,
V:Cyborg 2.50
552 KK,TGu,DRo,V:Parasite 2.50
553 KK,TGu,DRo,disappearances. . 2.50
554 KK,TGu,DRo,disappearances. . 2.50
555 KK,TRu,DRo,Red/Blue x-over . 2.50
556 KK,TRu,DRo,Red & Blue 2.50
557 KK,VS,DRo,Millennium Giants
x-over. 2.50
558 KK,JOy,DRo,silver age?,pt.1 . . 2.50
559 KK,JOy,DRo,silver age?,pt.2 . . 2.50
560 KK,JOy,DRo,silver age?,pt.3 . . 2.50
561 KK,JOy,TGu,DRo,Waverider. . . 2.50
562 KK(s),JOy,TGu,DRo,Lexcom . . 2.50
563 RMz,TGb,City of the
Future, pt.4 x-over. 2.50
564 KK&JOy(s),TGu,DRo,
A:Geo-Force 2.50
565 KK&JOy(s),TGu,DRo,A:JLA . . . 2.50
566 KK&JOy(s),TGu,DRo,V:Lex
Luthor 2.50
567 KK&JOy(s),DRo,PR, ... 2.50
568 LSi(s),TMo,DRo,V:Metallo 2.50
569 LSi(s),TMo,DRo,V:S.C.U 2.50
570 RMz&TPe(s),TGb,TP,
A:JLA,pt.2 x-over. 2.50
571 LSi(s),DRo,V:Atomic Skull 2.50
572 RF,SB,Strange Visitor,pt.2 . . . . 2.50
573 SI,SEp,DRo,flashbacks. 2.50
574 SI,F:Obsession 2.50
575 SI,F:Lex Luthor 2.50
576 SI,V:Brainiac 13 . . . . 2.50
577 SI,JMz,A:Luthor 2.50
578 JMD(s),JMz,alien utopia. 2.50
579 JMD(s),Lois has vanished 2.50
580 JMD(s),CriticalCondition,pt.2 . . 2.50
581 JMD(s),V:Adversary,Lex Luthor 2.50
582 JMD,JMz,Arkham,pt.2 . . . . 4.00
583 JMD,JMz,Superman:Emperor . . 2.50

All comics prices listed are for *Near Mint* condition.

584 JMD(s),JMz,V:Devouris 2.50
585 JMD,JMz,V:LexLuthor,Satanus . 2.50
586 JMD,JMz,V:Satanus 2.50
587 JMD,JMz,V:Satanus 2.50
588 JoC,JMz,V:Satanus 2.50
589 JoC,JMz,Return toKrypton,pt.2 . 2.50
590 JoC,JMz,Luthor's Lackey? 2.50
591 MWm,Infestation x-over,pt.2 . . . 2.50
592 JoC,JMz,F:Jimmy Olson 2.50
593 JoC,JMz,V:Manchester Black . . 2.50
594 JoC,MeW,All-Out War,x-over . . . 2.50
595 JoC,MeW,Casualties of War . . . 2.50
596 JoC,MeW,No Superman's Job . 6.00
597 JoC,Joker:Last Laugh tie-in . . . 2.50
598 JoC,JMz,F:Perry White 2.50
599 JoC,JMz,Russian submarine . . . 2.50
600 JoC,Lex Luthor, 64-pg. 5.00
601 JoC,Cult of Persuasion,pt.1 . . . 2.25
602 JoC,Cult of Persuasion,pt.2 . . . 2.25
603 JoC,F:Superbaby 2.25
604 JoC,V:Ultra-Man 2.25
605 JoC,F:Superbaby, concl. 2.25
606 JoC,Return to KryptonII,pt.2 . . . 2.25
607 F:Argent 2.25
608 JoC,Ending Battle,pt.2 . . . . 2.25
609 JoC,Ending Battle,pt.6 . . . . 2.25
610 JoC,in Guatemala 2.25
611 Lost Hearts,pt.2 x-over 2.25
612 JoC,Hollow Man 2.25
613 JoC,Captain Cold 2.25
614 JoC,Hollow Men 2.25
615 JoC,Hollow Men 2.25
616 JoC,Hollow Men 2.25
617 JoC,V:two Mr.Mxyzptlks 2.25
618 JoC,CAd,Mxy Twins 2.25
619 JoC,Lois and Clark 2.25
620 JoC,the Candidate 2.25
621 JoC,Minuteman 2.25
622 prophecy of the Minuteman . . . 2.25
623 Superman & Lois 2.50
624 KlK,Strange New Visitor 2.50
625 Godfall,pt.2 . . . . 3.00
626 Godfall,pt.5 . . . . 2.50
627 Special Crimes Unit 2.50
628 F:Wond.Woman & Gr.Lantern . 2.50
629 Lois,Replikon 2.50
630 Hostage situation 2.50
631 Lois behind enemy lines 2.50
632 V:Propaganda 2.50
633 ALa, New Parasites 2.50
634 ALa,V:Parasites 2.50
635 ALa,V:Parasites,pt.2 . . . . 2.50
636 Identity Crisis aftermath 2.50
637 Ruin hunts down Lois 2.50
638 Mr.Mxyzptik returns. 2.50
639 IaC,NRn,Lightning Strikes,pt.2 . 2.50
640 Unmasking of Ruin 2.50
641 Betrayal. 2.50
642 Sacrifice,x-over, pt.3 . . . . 2.50
643 Where to go from here 2.50
644 V:Zatanna 2.50
645 Omac assault 2.50
646 Myx is back. 2.50
647 V:Ruin 2.50
648 KlK,Infinite Crisis tie-in 2.50
649 KlK,This is your life, Superman 3.00
Becomes:

SUPERMAN
650 KBk,Up,Up & Away,pt.1,x-over 2.50
651 KBk,Up,Up & Away,pt.3,x-over . 2.50
652 KBk,Up,Up & Away,pt.5,x-over . 3.00
653 KBk,Up,Up & Away,pt.7,x-over . 3.00
654 KBk,CPa,V:Intergang 3.00
655 KBk,CPa,Time-traveling magic . 3.00
656 KBk,CPa,V:Subjekt-17 . . . . 3.00
657 KBk,CPa, End of Civilization . . 3.00
658 KBk,CPa, End of Civilization . . 3.00
659 KBk,RL,CPa,F:Krypto 3.00
660 KBk,CPa,Camelot Falls, pt.1 . . 3.00
661 KBk,CPa,Camelot Falls, pt.2 . . 3.00
662 KBk,CPa,Young Gods. 3.00
663 KBk,CPa,Young Gods. 3.00

The Adventures of Superman Ann. #2
© *DC Comics, Inc.*

664 KBk,CPa,Camelot Falls 3.00
665 KBk,RL,F:Jimmy Olson. 3.00
666 KBk,WS,Goes to Hell, 48-pgs. . 4.00
667 KBk,Camelot Falls, pt.1 . . . . . . 3.00
668 KBk,Camelot Falls, pt.2 . . . . . . 3.00
669 KBk,Third Kryptonian 3.00
Ann.#1 JSn(c),DJu,I:Word Bringer . 3.00
Ann.#2 CS/JBy,KGa/DG,BMc,
  A:L.E.G.I.O.N.'90 (Lobo) 4.00
Ann.#3 BHi,JRu,DG,
  Armageddon 2001. . . . . 3.00
Ann.#4 BMc,A:Lobo,Guy Gardner,
  Eclipso tie-in 3.00
Ann.#5 TGI,Sparx 2.75
Ann.#6 MMi(c),Elseworlds Story . . 3.00
Ann.#7 Year One Story 4.00
Ann.#8 Legends o/t Dead Earth . . 3.00
Ann.#9 Pulp Heroes (Western) . . . 4.00
Spec.#1,000,000 ALa&DAn(s)LMa,
  A:Teen Titans, V:Solaris 3.00
GN Vol. 1 Up, Up and Away 7.00
GN Vol. 2 Never-Ending Battle 7.00
Spec. Superman Through the Ages. 4.00

SUPERMAN'S BUDDY
1954
1 w/costume, giveaway 2,000.00
1 w/out costume, giveaway . . . 1,000.00

SUPERMAN'S
CHRISTMAS ADVENTURE
1 (1940) giveaway 6,500.00
2 (1944) giveaway 1,700.00

SUPERMAN AND THE
GREAT CLEVELAND FIRE
1948
1 for Hospital Fund, giveaway . . 900.00

SUPERMAN (miniature)
1942
1 Py-Co-Pay Tooth Powder
  Give- Away 1,000.00
2 CS,Superman Time Capsule . . 600.00
3 CS,Duel in Space 500.00
4 CS,Super Show in Metropolis . 500.00

SUPERMAN RECORD
COMIC
1966
1 w/record. 300.00
1 w/out record. 150.00

SUPERMAN
SPECTACULAR
1982
1 A:Luthor & Terra-Man 2.50

SUPERMAN-TIM
STORE PAMPHLETS
1942
Superman-Tim store Monthly Membership Pamphlets, stories, games
  (1942), each 2,000.00
  (1943), each 600.00
  (1944), each 550.00
  (1945), each 450.00
  (1946), color(c) each 550.00
  (1947), color(c) each 400.00
  (1948), color(c) each 350.00
  (1949), color(c) each 350.00
  (1950), color(c) each 400.00
Superman-Tim stamp albums,
  (1946) 400.00
  (1947) Superman story 600.00
  (1948) 400.00

SUPERMAN WORKBOOK
1945
1 rep. Superman #14. . . . . . . 1,300.00

SUPERMAN
[2nd Regular Series], 1987
1 JBy,TA,I:Metallo 6.00
2 JBy,TA,V:Luthor. 3.00
3 JBy,TA,Legends tie-in 3.00
4 JBy,KK,V:Bloodsport 3.00
5 JBy,KK,V:Host 3.00
6 JBy,KK,V:Host 3.00
7 JBy,KK,V:Rampage 3.00
8 JBy,KK,A:Superboy,Legion . . . 3.00
9 JBy,KK,V:Joker 5.00
10 JBy,KK,V:Rampage. 3.00
11 JBy,KK,V:Mr.Mxyzptlk 3.00
12 JBy,KK,Millennium 3.00
13 JBy,KK,A:Lori Lemerias 3.00
14 JBy,KK,A:Green Lantern 3.00
15 JBy,KK,I:New Prankster 3.00
16 JBy,KK,A:Prankster. 4.00
17 JBy,KK,O:Silver Banshee 3.00
18 MMi,KK,A:Hawkman 3.00
19 JBy,V:Skyhook 3.00
20 JBy,KK,A:Doom Patrol 3.00
21 JBy,A:Supergirl 4.00
22 JBy,A:Supergirl 4.00
23 MMi,CR,O:Silver Banshee 3.00
24 KGa,V:Rampage 3.00
25 KGa,V:Brainiac 3.00
26 KGa,BBr,V:Baron Sunday 3.00
27 KGa,BBr,V:Guardian 3.00
28 KGa,BBr,Supes Leaves Earth . 3.00
29 DJu,BBr,V:Word Bringer 3.00
30 KGa,DJu,A:Lex Luthor 3.00
31 DJu,PCu,V:Mxyzptlk 3.00
32 KGa,V:Mongul. 3.00
33 KGa,A:Cleric 3.00
34 KGa,V:Skyhook. 3.00
35 CS,KGa,A:Brainiac 3.00
36 JOy,V:Prankster 3.00
37 JOy,A:Guardian 3.00
38 JOy,Jimmy Olsen Vanished . . . 3.00
39 JOy,KGa,V:Husque. 3.00
40 JOy,V:Four Armed Terror 3.00
41 JOy,Day of Krypton Man #1,
  A:Lobo. 3.50

Superman, 2nd Series #46
© DC Comics Inc.

42 JOy,Day of Krypton Man #4,
  V:Draaga 3.50
43 JOy,V:Krypton Man 2.50
44 JOy,A:Batman 2.50
45 JOy,F:Jimmy Olsen's Dairy 2.50
46 DJu,JOy,A:Jade,Obsidian,
  I:New Terra-Man 2.50
47 JOy,Soul Search #2,V:Blaze 2.50
48 CS,Sinbad Contract #1 . . . . 2.50
49 JOy,Krisis of K.Kryptonite #1 . . . 3.00
50 JBy,KGa,DJu,JOy,BBr,CS,Krisis
  of Krimson Kryptonite #4,
  Clark Proposes To Lois 6.00
50a 2nd printing 2.50
51 JOy,I:Mr.Z 2.50
52 KGa,V:Terra-Man 2.50
53 JOy,Superman reveals i.d. 3.50
53a 2nd Printing 2.50
54 JOy,KK,Time & Time Again#3 . . . 2.50
55 JOy,KK,Time & Time Again#6 . . . 2.50
56 EH,KK,Red Glass Trilogy#1 . . . . 2.50
57 JOy,DJu,BBr,ATi,JBg,BMc,TG,
  Revenge o/t Krypton Man #2 . 3.50
58 DJu,BBr,I:Bloodhounds 2.50
59 DJu,BBr,A:Linear Men 2.50
60 DJu,EB,I:Agent Liberty,
  V:Intergang 2.50
61 DJu,BBr,A:Waverider,
  V:Linear Men 2.50
62 DJu,BBr,Blackout #4,A:Mr.Z . . . 2.50
63 DJu,A:Aquaman 2.50
64 JG,Christmas issue 2.50
65 DJu,Panic in the Sky#2,
  I:New Justice League 3.50
66 DJu,Panic in the Sky#6,
  V:Brainiac 8.00
67 DJu,Aftermath 2.50
68 DJu,V:Deathstroke 2.50
69 WS(c),DJu,A:Agent Liberty 2.50
70 DJu,BBr,A:Robin,V:Vampires . . . 2.50
71 DJu,Blaze/Satanus War 2.50
72 DJu,Crisis at Hand#2 . . . . 2.50
73 DJu,A:Waverider,V:Linear
  Men,C:Doomsday 5.00
73a 2nd printing 2.50
74 DJu,V:Doomsday,A:JLA 8.00
74a 2nd printing 2.00
75 DJu,V:Doomsday,D:Superman,
  Collectors Ed. 20.00
75a newstand Ed. 9.00
75b 2nd printing 4.00
75c 3rd printing 2.50
75d 4th Printing 2.50
75e Platinum Ed. 65.00

76 DJu,BBr,Funeral for Friend#4 . . . 3.00
77 DJu,BBr,Funeral for Friend#8 . . . 3.00
78 DJu,BBr,Reign of Supermen#3,
  Die-Cut(c),Mini poster,F:Cyborg
  Supes,A:Doomsday 3.00
78a Newsstand Ed. 2.50
79 DJu,BBr,Memorial Service for
  Clark 3.00
80 DJu,BBr,Coast City Blows up,
  V:Mongul 4.00
81 DJu,O:Cyborg Superman 3.50
82 DJu,Chromium(c),A:All Supermen,
  V:Cyborg Superman 15.00
82a Newstand Ed. 5.00
83 DJu,A:Batman 3.00
84 DJu,V:Toyman 3.00
85 DJu,V:Toyman 3.00
86 DJu,A:Sun Devils 3.00
87 DJu(c&s),Sl,JRu,Bizzaro's
  World#1, R:Bizarro 3.00
88 DJu(c&s),Sl,JRu,Bizzaro's
  World#5, D:Bizarro 3.00
89 DJu(c&s),V:Cadmus Project 3.00
90 DJu(c&s),Battle for
  Metropolis#3 . . . . 3.00
91 DJu(c&s),Fall of Metropolis#3. . . 3.00
92 Massacre in Metropolis 3.00
93 Zero Hour,A:Batman 3.00
94 Conduit 3.00
95 Brainiac 3.00
96 Virtual Reality 3.00
97 Shadow Dragon 3.00
98 R:Shadow Strike 3.00
99 R:Agent Liberty 3.00
100 BBr,DJu,Death of C.Kent,pt.1 . . 4.00
100a Collectors Edition 4.00
101 Death of Clark Kent,pt.5
  [New Miraweb format begins] . . 3.00
102 DJu,A:Captain Marvel 3.00
103 O:Arclight 3.00
104 Revenge of Apokolips 3.00
105 A:Green Lantern 3.00
106 DJu,RF,The Trial of Superman . 3.00
107 DJu,RF,The Trial of Superman . 3.00
108 DJu,RF,The Trial of Superman . 3.00
109 DJu,RF,V:Kill Fee 3.00
110 F:Plastic Man 3.00
111 DJu,RF,Cat Grant in charge . . . 3.00
112 DJu,RF,Lois & Clark 3.00
113 DJu(s),RF,JRu, ... 3.00
114 DJu(s),RF,JRu,A:Brainiac 3.00
115 DJu(s),RF,JRu,Lois leaves
  Metropolis 3.00
116 DJu(s),RF,JRu,battle city siga
  concl., V:Daxamite,B.U. Teen
  Titans preview 3.00
117 DJu(s),RF,JRu,V: his own
  robots, Final Night tie-in 3.00
118 DJu(s),RF,JRu,F:time-lost
  Legion of Super Heroes 3.00
119 DJu(s),RF,JRu,A:Legion of
  Super Heroes 3.00
120 DJu(s),RF,JRu, ... 3.00
121 DJu(s),RF,JRu,They Call it
  Suicide Slum 3.00
122 DJu(s),RF,JRu,Lois visits
  Fortress of Solitude 3.00
123 DJu(s),RF,Jru,Superman gets
  New Costume 4.00
123a DJu collector's edition, glow-in-
  the-dark cover, ... 6.00
124 DJu(s),RF,JRu,A:Scorn, prince
  of Kandor 2.50
125 DJu(s),RF,JRu,Kandor and
  Metropolis,A:Atom 2.50
126 DJu(s),RF,JRu,A:Batman 2.50
127 DJu(s),RF,JRu,F:Jimmy Olsen . 2.50
128 DJu(s),RF,JRu, Genesis tie-in . . 2.50
129 DJu(s),PR,JRu,A:Scorn 2.50
130 DJu(s),RF,JRu,dragon's tooth . . 2.50
131 DJu(s),RF,JRu,Luthor &
  Contessa's kid 2.50

132 DJu,RF,JRu,Red/Blue x-over . . 2.50
133 DJu,RF,JRu,Millennium Guard . 2.50
134 DJu,RF,JRu,Millennium Giants . 2.50
135 DJu,RF,JRu,aftermath 3.50
136 DJu,PR,JRu,The Superman
  of 2999 A.D., pt.1 . . . . 2.50
137 DJu,PR,JRu,2999 AD,pt.2 . . . . 2.50
138 DJu,PR,JRu,2999 AD,pt.3 . . . . 2.50
139 DJu(s),JSn,JRu,V:Dominus . . . 2.50
140 RMz(s),TGb,TP,City of the
  Future, pt.3 x-over 2.50
141 DJu(s),SEa,JRu,I:Outburst 2.50
142 DJu(s),JRu,F:Outburst 2.50
143 DJu(s),SEp,JRu, ... 2.50
144 DJu(s),SEp,JRu,V:Lex Luthor . . 2.50
145 DJu(s),SEp,JRu,hate mail 2.50
146 DJu(s),SEp,JRu,V:Toyman 2.50
147 RMz(s),TGb,BAn,A:JLA,pt.1 . . 2.50
148 DJu(s),SEp,JRu, ... 2.50
149 RF,SB,Strange Visitor,pt.1 . . . . 2.50
150 DJu(s),SEp,JRu,48-pg. 3.50
150a foil cover 4.50
151 JLb,MMK,Faster than a
  speeding bullet 3.00
152 JLb,MMK. 2.50
153 JLb,MMK,V:Imperiex. 3.00
154 JLb,CaS,V:Brainiac 13 . . . . . . 17.00
155 JLb,CaS,F:Superboy. 7.00
156 JLb,CaS,V:Parasite. 5.00
157 JLb,CaS,Lois vs. Superman? . . 5.00
158 JLb,CaS,CriticalCondition,pt.1 . 3.00
159 JLb,CaS,F:Green Lantern. 3.00
160 JLb,CaS,Arkham,pt.1 . . . . 10.00
161 JLb,CaS,Superman:Emperor? . 3.50
162 JLb,CaS,A:Aquaman,pt.1 . . . . 3.00
163 JLb,PaP,CaS,F:Aquaman,pt.2 . 2.50
164 JLb,CaS,V:Bizarro 2.50
165 JLb,AAd,A:Linear Man 2.50
166 JLb,CaS,O:Superman(new) . . 12.00
166a holofoil(c) 7.00
167 JLb,CaS,Return toKrypton,pt.1. 2.50
168 JLb,CaS,Lord of the Ring,pt.1 . 6.00
169 MWm,Infestation x-over,pt.1 . . 2.50
170 JLb,CaS,DK,V:Mogul 2.50
171 JLb,OurWorlds atWar,prelude . 2.50
172 JLb,All-Out War. 2.50
173 JLb,Casualties of War. 2.50
174 JLb,CaS,War aftermath 2.50
175 JLb,CaS,Last Laugh,48-pg . . . 3.50
176 JLb,IaC,NRd,F:Dr. Foster 2.25
177 JLb,CaS,F:Toyman,Metallo. . . . 2.25
178 JLb,CaS,F:Uncle Sam 2.25
179 JLb,African-American hero 2.25
180 JLb,IaC,NRd,V:Dracula. 3.50
181 JLb,CaS,F:Bizarro. 3.50

Superman 2nd Series #139
© DC Comics Inc.

All comics prices listed are for *Near Mint* condition.

182 JLb,CaS,F:Suicide Squad. 2.25
183 JLb,CaS,Clarke fired from job . 2.25
184 PFe,CaS,Return to Krypton II. . 2.25
185 BA,PFe(c),baseball game. 2.25
186 PFe,CaS,Ending Battle,pt.1 . . . 2.25
187 PFe,CaS,Ending Battle,pt.5 . . . 2.25
188 F:Lois Lane. 2.25
189 PFe,Lost Hearts,pt.1 x-over . . . 2.25
190 SSe(c),SMc,rogue robot 2.25
190a spec.newsstand ed.,56-pg. . . 4.50
191 F:The Flash. 2.25
192 Supergirl vs. Radion 4.00
193 Supergirl vs. Radion 2.25
194 SMc,I:Ed 2.25
195 SMc,Futuresmiths. 2.25
196 SMc,new adversary 2.25
197 SMc,deaf Superman,Krypto . . . 2.25
198 SMc,V:Bizarro. 2.25
199 SMc,Supergirl origins 2.25
200 SMc,Futuresmiths, 48-pg. 5.00
201 KIK,Strange New Visitor 5.00
202 Godfall,pt.3 . . . . 5.00
203 Godfall,pt.6 . . . . 4.00
204 JLe,SW,I:FatherLeone,40-pg. . . 3.00
205 JLe,SW,For Tomorrow,pt.2 . . . . 3.50
206 JLe,SW,For Tomorrow,pt.3 . . . . 3.00
207 JLe,SW,For Tomorrow,pt.4 . . . . 3.00
208 JLe,SW,For Tomorrow,pt.5 . . . . 3.00
209 JLe,SW,For Tomorrow,pt.6 . . . . 2.50
210 JLe,SW,For Tomorrow,pt.7 . . . . 2.50
211 JLe,SW,For Tomorrow 2.50
212 JLe,SW,Superman vanishes. . . 2.50
213 JLe,SW,For Tomorrow 2.50
214 JLe,SW,For Tomorrow 2.50
215 JLe,SW,For Tomorrow 3.50
216 IaC,NRd,Lightning Strikes. 3.50
217 EBe,new Fortress of Solitude . . 5.00
218 EBe,I:Blackrock. 5.00
219 EBe,Sacrifice, x-over, pt.1 . . . . 5.00
220 EBe(c),Return of the Supermen 2.50
221 EBe,V:Bizarro 2.50
222 EBe,Crisis Begins 2.50
223 EBe,Infinite Crisis tie-in. 2.50
224 EBe,Infinite Crisis tie-in. 2.50
225 Infinite Crisis tie-in 2.50
226 This is Your Life, Superman . . . 2.50
Ann.#1 RF,BBr,A:Titano 4.00
Ann.#2 RF,BBr,R:Newsboy Legion
　& Guardian 4.00
Ann.#3 DAb(1st Work),TA,DG,
　Armageddon 2001. . . . . 9.00
Ann.#3a 2nd printing(silver). 3.00
Ann.#4 Eclipso. 3.00
Ann.#5 Bloodlines#6,DL,I:Myriad. . 3.00
Ann.#6 Elseworlds Story 3.50
Ann.#7 WS(s),Year One Annual
　A:Dr. Occult 4.50
Ann.#8 Legends o/t Dead Earth . . . 3.00
Ann.#9 Pulp Heroes (High-
　Adventure) DJu 4.50
Ann.#10 DJu(s),PR,CIv,BWr,
　Ghosts 3.00
Ann.#11 JoP,AAd(c),JLApe:Gorilla
　Warfare 3.50
Ann.#12 Planet DC 3.50
Spec.#1,000,000 DAn&ALa(s),NBy . 2.50
Giant Ann.#1 Replica edition 5.00
Giant #1 80-page 5.00
Giant #2 80-page 5.00
Giant #3 80-page 6.00
Spec.#0 PeerPressure,pt.3 (1994) . 2.00
Spec.King of the World, foil 5.00
Spec.King of the World, reg. 4.00
Spec. Superman: Lois Lane,
　Girlfrenzy (1998) 2.00
Spec.#1 WS,V:L.Luthor,
　Sandman (1992) 6.00
Spec. Superman Plus One (1997) . . 3.00
Spec.#1 Superman: The Earth
　Stealers, JBy,CS,JOy (1988). . . 3.50
　2nd printing 3.00
Spec. Superman:Emperor?(2000) . . 3.50

Spec. Superman Forever, KK,DJu,LSi,
　JBy,SI,DG, Luthor's kidnapped
　daughter (1998). 5.00
　Deluxe ed.,AxR(c), lenticular. . . 6.00
Spec.#1 Superman: The Legacy of
　Superman,WS,JG,F:Guardian,
　Waverider,Sinbad (1993). 4.00
Spec. Superman & Savage Dragon:
　Metropolis, KK,JBg,x-over. 5.00
Spec. Superman/Toyman (1996) . . 2.00
Spec. Team Superman, MMr(s),
　DHz,48-page,F:Superboy,
　Supergirl & Steel 3.00
Spec. 3-D #1 LSi,V:Mainframe 4.00
Spec. Whatever Happened to the
　Man of Tomorrow. 6.00
Spec. Superman Y2K,JBg (1999) . . 5.00
Newstime-The Life and Death of
　the Man of Steel-Magazine,
　DJu,BBr,JOy,JG,JBg 3.25
Spec.#1 Superman Gallery (1993) . 3.00
Superman Secret Files, DJu,JOy,
　etc.,inc. O:Superman (1997). . . 10.00
Secret Files #1 Superman Villains. 10.00
Secret Files #2. . . . . 10.00
Secret Files #1 Our Worlds at War 10.00
Secret Files #1 President Luthor . 10.00
Secret Files 2004. . . . . 10.00
Secret Files 2005. . . . . 5.00
Spec. Metropolis Secret Files #1. . . 5.00
Spec. Team Superman Secret Files 5.00
Spec. 1-shot,Superman:Lex 2000,
　JLb,TyH,DoM,Vote for Lex 3.50
Spec. 10-Cent Adventure,SMc. . . . 0.10
Spec. Superman vs. Darkseid:
　Apokolips Now, MSh(s),48-pg. . 3.00
Spec. Blood of my Ancestors 7.00
GN Death of Superman rep.(1993) . 6.00
　Later printings 6.00
　Platinum Edition 15.00
GN Superman At Earth's End
　(Elseworlds 1995) 5.00
GN Superman: Distant Fires, HC,GK,
　nuclear winter (1997). 6.00
GN Superman: Earth Day 1991, KGa
　Metropolis Clean-Up 5.50
GN Superman For Earth (1991) . . . 5.00
GN Superman: Kal, Medieval
　Superman (Elseworlds 1995) . . 6.00
GN Superman: Last God of Krypton 5.00
GN Last Stand on Krypton (2003) . . 7.00
GN Superman's Metropolis, RLo &
　RTs(s),TMK, in Fritz Lang's
　Metropolis (Elseworlds 1996) . . 6.00
GN The Superman Monster. 7.00
GN A Nation Divided 5.00
GN Superman: The Odyssey. 5.00
GN Peace on Earth, oversized . . . 10.00
GN Superman Red/Superman Blue,
　V:Toyman, Cyborg, Superman
　split into two entities (1997). . . . 4.00
　Deluxe, 3-D cover 5.00
GN Superman: Silver Banshee, 48pg,
　prestige format (1998). 5.00
GN Superman: Speeding Bullets,
　EB (Elseworlds 1993) 6.00
GN Superman, Under a Yellow Sun
　by Clark Kent,KGa,EB (1994). . 6.00
GN Superman: The Wedding Album,
　collector's edition, 96 pg.,
　cardstock cover 5.00
GN War of the Worlds,Elseworlds . . 6.00
GN Superman, Inc. 7.00
GN Superman: Mann & Superman . 6.00
GN Superman:Where is thy Sting? . 7.00
GN Superman & Savage Dragon:
　Chicago, x-over, EL (2002) 6.00
　Metropolis, x-over,KK,JBg. 5.00

SUPERMAN
ADVENTURES
Sept., 1996

1 PDi(s),RBr,TA, from animated
　TV show 3.00
2 thru 20 . . . . @2.50
21 Supergirl Adventures, 64pg. . . . 5.50
22 thru 66 (c) . . . . @2.50
Ann.#1 JoS,DDv,V:Akamin 4.50
TPB rep.#1–#6. . . . . 8.00
Spec. #1 Superman vs. Lobo –
　Misery in Space, DvM,MM,
　A:Man of Tomorrow. 4.00
Vol. 3 Last Son of Krypton (2006) . . 7.00
Vol. 4 The Man of Steel (2006) 7.00

Superman/Batman #1
© DC Comics, Inc.

SUPERMAN/BATMAN
Aug., 2003

1 JLb,V:Metallo 30.00
2 JLb,both injured 10.00
3 JLb,V:Gorilla Grodd 10.00
4 F:Captain Atom,Luthor. 6.00
5 JLb(s),V:Luthor 6.00
6 JLb(s),V:Luthor 13.00
7 JLb(s),F:Robin,Superboy 8.00
8 Supergirl from Krypton,pt.1 . . . . . 6.00
9 Supergirl from Krypton,pt.2 . . . . . 4.00
10 Supergirl from Krypton,pt.3. . . . . 4.00
11 Supergirl from Krypton,pt.4. . . . . 3.50
12 Supergirl from Krypton,pt.5. . . . . 3.50
13 JLb(s) V:Darkseid 4.00
14 JLb(s),Absolute Power,pt.1 . . . . . 3.50
15 JLb(s),Absolute Power,pt.2 . . . . . 3.25
16 JLb(s),Absolute Power,pt.3 . . . . . 3.25
17 JLb(s),Absolute Power,pt.4 . . . . . 3.25
18 JLb(s),Absolute Power,pt.5 . . . . . 3.25
19 JLb(s),IaC,NRd,F:Supergirl. 3.00
20 JLb(s),With a Vengeance,pt.1 . . . 6.00
21 JLb(s),With a Vengeance,pt.2 . . . 3.00
22 JLb(s),With a Vengeance,pt.3. . . 3.00
23 JLb(s),With a Vengeance,pt.4. . . 3.00
24 JLb(s),With a Vengeance,pt.5. . . 3.00
25 JLb(s),With a Vengeance,concl . 3.00
25a variant (c) 3.00
26 40-pg. 4.00
27 F:Power Girl & The Huntress . . . 3.00
28 The Enemies Among Us,pt.1 . . . 3.00
29 The Enemies Among Us,pt.2 . . . 3.00
30 The Enemies Among Us,pt.3 . . . 3.00
31 V:Lex Luthor 3.00
32 ALa,F:Lex Luthor 3.00
33 ALa,V:Aliens 3.00

34 PtL,V:Metal Men 3.00
35 PtL,V:Metal Men 3.00
36 PtL,V:Metal Men, concl. 3.00
37 Torment, pt.1 . . . . 3.00
37a variant (c) (1:10) 3.00
38 Torment, pt.2 . . . . 3.00
39 Torment, pt.3 . . . . 3.00
40 Torment, pt.4 . . . . 3.00
41 Torment, pt.5 . . . . 3.00
Ann. #1 (2006) 4.00
Spec. Secret Files (2003) 10.00

SUPERMAN & BATMAN: GENERATIONS — AN IMAGINARY TALE
1998
1 (of 4) JBy, Elseworlds 5.00
2 JBy,V:Bat-Mite 5.00
3 JBy 5.00
4 JBy, conclusion 5.00
TPB, rep. 15.00

SUPERMAN & BATMAN: GENERATIONS II
Aug., 2001
1 (of 4) JBy,Elseworlds,48-page . . . 6.00
2 JBy,48-page 6.00
3 JBy,48-page 6.00
4 JBy,48-page, concl. 6.00
TPB JBy 20.00

SUPERMAN & BATMAN: GENERATIONS III
Jan., 2003
1 (of 12) JBy,Elseworlds 3.00
2 JBy,Super Twins 3.00
3 JBy,22nd Century 3.00
4 JBy,23rd Century 3.00
5 JBy,24th Century 3.00
6 JBy,25th Century 3.00
7 JBy,26th Century 3.00
8 JBy,26th Century 3.00
9 JBy,27th Century 3.00
10 JBy,28th Century 3.00
11 JBy,29th century Superboy 3.00
12 JBy,earth destroyed 3.00

SUPERMAN & BATMAN VS ALIENS & PREDATORS
Jan., 2007
1 MSh(s),AOI 6.00
2 MSh(s),AOI, conclusion 6.00
TPB 13.00

SUPERMAN & BATMAN: WORLD'S FUNNEST
Nov., 2000
1-shot, Elseworlds, ... 7.00

SUPERMAN & BUGS BUNNY
1999
1 (of 4) JSon,TP 2.50
2 thru 4 TP,JSon . . . . @2.50

SUPERMAN: BIRTHRIGHT
July 2003
1 (of 12) F:Jor-El,40-pg. 4.00
2 South Africa,40-pg. 3.50
3 O:retold 3.50
4 Job interview 3.50
5 anti-terrorism weapons 3.50
6 Lex & Clark 3.00

7 Inhuman alien 3.00
8 Lex Luthor 3.00
9 Lex's Plans; Krypton 3.00
10 Threat to Krypton 3.00
11 Krypton Invades Earth 3.00
12 conclusion 3.00

SUPERMAN CONFIDENTIAL
Nov., 2006
1 TSe,Kryptonite 3.00
2 TSe,Superman vs. a Volcano . . . 3.00
3 TSe,Origin of Kryptonite, pt.1 . . 3.00
4 TSe,Origin of Kryptonite, pt.2 . . 3.00
5 TSe,Origin of Kryptonite, pt.3 . . 3.00
6 TSe,Origin of Kryptonite,concl. . . 3.00
7 JP,F:Lori Lemaris 3.00
8 JP,F:Lex,Lori, & Lois 3.00

SUPERMAN: THE DARK SIDE
Elseworlds, Aug., 1998
1 JFM,KD,First Son of Apokolips . . 5.00
2 . . . . 5.00
3 KD, conclusion 5.00
TPB Superman: The Dark Side . . . 13.00

SUPERMAN: DAY OF DOOM
Nov., 2002
1 (of 4) DJu,BSz,F:Ty Duffy 3.00
2 DJu,BSz 3.00
3 DJu,BSz 3.00
4 DJu,BSz,concl. 3.00

SUPERMAN/DOOMSDAY: HUNTER/PREY
1994
1 DJu(a&s),BBr,R:Doomsday,R:Cyborg
  Superman,A:Darkseid 5.50
2 DJu(a&s),BBr,V:Doomsday,Cyborg
  Superman,A:Darkseid 5.25
3 DJu(a&s),BBr,V:Doomsday 5.25
TPB Rep. #1-#3 . . . . 15.00

SUPERMAN: THE DOOMSDAY WARS
1998
1 DJu,BBr,R:Doomsday 5.00
2 DJu,BBr,R:Doomsday 5.00
3 DJu,BBr,R:Doomsday 5.00

SUPERMAN FOR ALL SEASONS
June, 1998
1 (of 4) JLb,TSe, from farmboy
  to superhero 7.00
2 JLb,TSe,V:Lex Luthor 5.00
3 JLb,TSe,V:Lex Luthor 5.00
4 JLb,TSe, conclusion 5.00

SUPERMAN/GEN13
DC/Wildstorm April, 2000
1 (of 3) AH, x-over 2.50
1a variant cover (1:4) 2.50
2 AH,x-over 2.50
2a variant cover (1:4) 2.50
3 AH, 40-pg. 3.50

SUPERMAN: LAST SON OF EARTH
July, 2000
1 (of 2) Elseworlds 6.00
2 Green Lantern's powers 6.00

SUPERMAN: METROPOLIS
Feb. 2003
1 (of 12) F:Jimmy Olsen 3.00
2 Mystery of the Tech 3.00
3 Rebecca 3.00
4 The Tech or the Devil 3.00
5 Jimmy and Lena 3.00
6 Jimmy and Lena 3.00
7 thru 12 . . . . @3.00

Superman The Man of Steel #22
© DC Comics, Inc.

SUPERMAN: THE MAN OF STEEL
1991–2003
1 B:LSi(s),DJu,BMc,JOy,BBr,TG,
  Revenge o/t Krypton Man#1 . . . 5.00
2 JBg,V:Cerberus 4.00
3 JBg,War of the Gods X-over 3.00
4 JBg,V:Angstrom 3.00
5 JBg,CS,V:Atomic Skull 3.00
6 JBg,Blackout#3,A:Mr.Z 3.00
7 JBg,V:Cerberus 3.00
8 KD,V:Jolt,Blockhouse 3.00
9 JBg,Panic in the Sky#1,
  V:Brainiac 3.50
10 JBg,Panic in the Sky#5,
  D:Draaga 3.00
11 JBg,V:Flashpoint 3.00
12 JBg,V:Warwolves 3.00
13 JBg,V:Cerberus 3.00
14 JBg,A:Robin,V:Vampires 3.00
15 KG,KGa,Blaze/Satanus War . . . 3.00
16 JBg,Crisis at Hand#1 . . . . 3.00
17 JBg,V:Underworld,
  C:Doomsday 8.00
17a 2nd printing 2.50
18 JBg,I:Doomsday,V:Underworld . 10.00
18a 2nd printing 4.00
18b 3rd printing 2.50
19 JBg,Doomsday,pt.5 . . . . 7.00
19a 2nd printing 2.50
20 JBg,Funeral for a Friend#3 . . . . 3.00
21 JBg,Funeral for a Friend#7 . . . . 3.00
22 JBg,Reign of Supermen#4,Direct
  Sales,Die-Cut(c),mini-poster,
  F:Man of Steel 2.50
22a Newsstand Ed. 2.50
23 JBg,V:Superboy 2.50
24 JBg,V:White Rabbit,A:Mongul . . 2.50
25 JBg,A:Real Superman 3.00
26 JBg,A:All Supermen,V:Mongul,
  Cyborg Superman 2.75

27 JBg,A:Superboy,Lex Luthor 2.50
28 JBg(c),A:Steel 2.50
29 LSi(s),JBg,Spilled Blood#3,
    V:Hi-Tech,Blood Thirst 2.50
30 LSi(s),JBg,V:Lobo,Vinyl(c) 3.50
30a Newstand Ed. 2.50
31 MBr,A:Guardian 2.50
32 MBr,Bizarro's World#4,
    V:Bizarro 2.50
33 MBr,V:Parasite 2.50
34 JBg,A:Lex Men,Dubbile Men . . . 2.50
35 JBg,Worlds Collide#1,
    I:Fred Bentson 2.50
36 JBf,Worlds Collide,pt.10,V:Rift
    A:Icon 2.50
37 JBg,Zero Hour,A:Batman 2.50
38 Mystery 2.50
39 JBg,Luthor. 2.50
40 JBg,Mind Games 2.50
41 Locke 2.50
42 F:Locke 2.50
43 V:Deathtrap 2.50
44 Prologue to Death. 2.50
45 JGb,DJa,Death of Clark Kent,pt.4
    [New Miraweb format begins] . . 2.50
46 JBg,DJa,A:Shadowdragon 2.50
47 O:Bloodsport. 2.50
48 JBg,Here be Monsters 2.50
49 Skyhook 2.50
50 JBg,DJa,The Trial of
    Superman, 48pg 4.00
51 JBg,The Trial of Superman . 2.50
52 JBg,The Trial of Superman 2.50
53 JBg,DRo,A:Lex Luthor,Contessa 2.50
54 JBg 2.50
55 JBg,DJa, Clark dates Lori
    Lemaris 2.50
56 JBg,DJa, manipulator revealed. . 2.50
57 RSt,JBg,DJa, more twisters 2.50
58 LSi(s),JBg,DJa,A:Supergirl 2.50
59 LSi(s),JBg,DJa,Parasite, Steel . . . 2.50
60 LSi(s),JBg,DJa,R:Bottled City
    of Kandor. 2.50
61 LSi(s),JBg,DJa,V:Riot 2.50
62 LSi(s),JBg,DJa, Superman
    looses powers, Final Night tie-in 2.50
63 LSi(s),JBg,DJa,Clark is
    kidnapped & revealed identity. . 2.50
64 LSi(s),JBg,DJa,Superman tries to
    restore his powers. 2.50
65 LSi(s),SB,DJa,V:Superman
    Revenge Squad. 2.50
66 LSi(s),JBg,DJa,V:Rajiv 2.50
67 LSi(s),JBg,DJa,New powers
    prequel. 3.00
68 LSi(s),JBg,DJa,V:Metallo 3.00
69 KK&LSi(s),SEa,DJa,A:Atom,
    in Kandor. 2.50
70 LSi(s),SEa,DJa,V:Saviour. 2.50
71 LSi(s),SEa,DJa,V:Mainframe,
    Superman Revenge Squad. . . . 2.50
72 LSi(s),SEa,JP,DJa,JBg,Genesis
    V:Mainframe 2.50
73 LSi&MWa(s),SEa,DJa,V:Revenge
    Squad 2.50
74 LSi(s),SEa,DJa,dragon's tooth . . 2.50
75 LSi(s),DJa,JBg,Mr.Mxyzptlk dies
    parody of Superman #75. . . . . . 2.50
76 LSi(s),JBb,DJa,V:Mokkari. 2.50
77 JBg,Triangles 2.50
78 JBg, Millennium Giants, pt.1
    x-over. 2.50
79 JBg, Millennium Giants. 2.50
80 LSi,JBg,DJa,golden age?,pt.1 . . 2.50
81 LSi,JBg,DJa,golden age?,pt.2 . . 2.50
82 LSi,JBg,DJa,golden age?,pt.3 . . 2.50
83 LSi,SEa,DJa,Dominus 2.50
84 RMz(s),TGb,TP,City of the
    Future, x-over. 2.50
85 JBg,DJa,V:Simyan & Mokkari. . 2.50
86 LSi(s),SEa,DJa,dreams
    of disasters 2.50

87 MSh(s),DoM,DJa,A:Steel,
    Superboy, Supergirl. 2.50
88 MSh(s),DoM,DJa 2.50
89 MSh(s),DoM,V:Dominus 2.50
90 MSh(s),V:Superman's Robot . . . 2.50
91 MSh(s),DoM,paranoia. 2.50
92 TPe(s),TGb,TP,Secret
    origins,concl. 2.50
93 MSh,DoM 2.50
94 RF,SB,Strange Visitor,concl. 2.50
95 MSh,DoM,Fortress of Solitude . 2.50
96 MSh,DoM, ... 2.50
97 MSh,DoM,F:Eradicator 2.50
98 MSh,DoM,V:Brainiac 13 . . . . 2.50
99 MSh,DoM,new armor 2.50
100 MSh,DoM,new Fortress of
    Solitude, 48-pg. 4.00
100a Collectors edition 4.25
101 MSh,DoM,growing sicker 2.50
102 MSh,DoM,Crit.Condition,pt.3 . . 2.50
103 MSh,DoM,A:Supergirl 2.50
104 MSh,DoM,Arkham,pt.3 . . . . 2.50
105 MSh,DoM,Superman:Emperor . 2.50
106 MSh,HuR,V:Kosnor,Netkon . . . 2.50
107 MSh,DoM, to Phantom Zone . . 2.50
108 MSh,DoM, from Phantom Zone 2.50
109 MSh,A:Linear Man 2.50
110 MSh,DoM,A:Star-SpangledKid . 2.50
111 MSh,DoM,Return-Krypton,pt.3 . 2.50
112 MSh,A:Superdog. 2.50
113 MWm,Infestation x-over,pt.3 . . . 2.50
114 MSh,DoM,R:Eradicator 2.50
115 MSh,DoM,Metropolis abducted. 2.50
116 MSh,DoM,JMz,All-out War 2.50
117 MSh,DoM,Casualties of War. . . 2.50
118 MSh,DoM,F:Spectre 2.50
119 MSh,Joker:Last Laugh,tie-in . . . 8.00
120 MSh,V:LexCorp. 2.25
121 TNu,Royal Flush Gang 2.25
122 MSh(s),Entropy Aegis Armor . . 2.25
123 MSh(s),Metropolis Gangs,pt.1 . 2.25
124 MSh(s),Metropolis Gangs,pt.2 . 2.25
125 MSh(s),Metropolis Gangs,pt.3 . 2.25
126 MSh(s),The Pantheon,pt.1 . . . . 2.25
127 MSh(s),The Pantheon,pt.2 . . . . 2.25
128 MSh(s),ReturntoKryptonII,pt.3 . 2.25
129 Bloodsport. 2.25
130 MSh(s),Ending Battle,pt.3. . . . . 2.25
131 MSh(s),Ending Battle,pt.7. . . . . 2.25
132 MSh,Parade, A:Mr.Mxyzptlk . . . 2.25
133 Lost Hearts,pt.3 x-over 2.25
134 MSh,40-pg.,final issue 3.00
Ann.#1 Eclipso tie-in,A:Starman . . 3.00
Ann.#2 Bloodlines#2,I:Edge. 3.00
Ann.#3 MBr,Elseworlds Story 3.50
Ann.#4 Year One Annual 3.50
Ann.#5 Legends o/t Dead Earth . . 3.50
Ann.#6 Pulp Heroes (Hard Boiled)
    LSi(s),DJa 4.50
Spec.#1,000,000 KK&JOy(s),
    AWi,DJa. 3.00
Gallery 1. . . . . 3.50

SUPERMAN: THE MAN OF TOMORROW
1995–96

1 TGu,BBr,RSt(s),V:Lex Luthor. . . . 2.50
2 V:Parasite 2.50
3 TG,BBr, The Trial of Superman . 2.50
4 RSt(s),PR,BBr,A:Shazam 2.50
5 RSt(s),PR,BBr,Wedding of Lex
    Luthor 2.50
6 RSt(s),PR,BBr,Superman V:
    Jackal again 2.50
7 RSt(s),PR,BBr,. 2.50
8 RSt(s),PR,BBr,V:Carbide 2.50
9 RSt(s),PR,BBr,Ma and Pa Kent
    open their album 2.50
10 . . . . 2.50
11 LSi(s),PR,DJa,BBr 2.50
12 LSi(s),PR,DJa, ... 2.50

Superman: The Man of Tomorrow #7
© DC Comics, Inc.

13 LSi(s),PR,DJa,A:JLA. 2.50
14 LSi(s),PR,DJa,V:Riot 2.50
15 Day of Judgment x-over,48-pg. . 3.00
Spec.#1,000,000 MSh(s),DRo 2.50

SUPERMAN: RED SON
April 2003

1 (of 3) Elseworlds,MMr(s) 6.00
2 MMr(s) 6.00
3 MMr(s),concl. 6.00
TPB series rep. 18.00

SUPERMAN RETURNS
July, 2006

GN The Movie Adaptation, 72-pg. . . 7.00
TPB Movie & Other Tales, 168-pg. 13.00
Spec: Krypton to Earth, JBy. 4.00
Spec: Ma Kent, KIK 4.00
Spec: Lois Lane 4.00
Spec: Lex Luthor, RL 4.00
TPB The Prequels 13.00

SUPERMAN: SECRET IDENTITY
Jan. 2004

1 (of 4) SI 6.00
2 SI Clark Kent gains powers. 6.00
3 SI 6.00
4 SI concl. 6.00
TPB Series rep. 20.00

SUPERMAN'S GIRL FRIEND, LOIS LANE
1958–74

1 CS,KS,Witch of Metropolis . 8,000.00
2 CS,KS,Secret Sweetheart . . 2,000.00
3 CS,KS,spanking panel 1,400.00
4 CS,KS,Super-Courtship 1,000.00
5 CS,KS,Greatest Sacrifice . . . 1,000.00
6 CS,KS,Superman Junior 750.00
7 CS,KS,Kiss of Death 750.00
8 CS,KS,Superwoman 650.00
9 CS,KS, A:Pat Boone 650.00
10 CS,KS,Cry-Baby of Metropolis 650.00
11 CS,KS,Leopard Girl of Jungle. 400.00
12 CS,KS,Mermaid of Metropolis 400.00
13 CS,KS,Lois Lane's Parents . 400.00
14 KS,Three Nights in the
    Fortress of Solitude. 400.00
15 KS,I:Van-Zee. 400.00
16 KS, Lois' Signal-Watch 400.00

17 KS,CS,A:Brainiac 400.00
18 KS,A:Astounding Man 400.00
19 KS,Superman of the Past 400.00
20 KS,A:Superman 450.00
21 KS,A:Van-Zee 300.00
22 KS,A:Robin Hood 300.00
23 KS,A:Elastic Lass, Supergirl . . 300.00
24 KS,A:Van-Zee, Bizarro 300.00
25 KS,Lois' Darkest Secret 300.00
26 KS,A:Jor-El 300.00
27 KS,CS,A:Bizarro 300.00
28 KS,A:Luthor 300.00
29 CS,A:Aquaman,Batman,Green
  Arrow 300.00
30 KS,A:Krypto,Aquaman 200.00
31 KS,A:Lori Lemaris 200.00
32 KS,CS,A:Bizarro 200.00
33 KS,CS,A:Phantom Zone,Lori
  Lemaris, Mon-El 200.00
34 KS,A:Luthor,Supergirl 200.00
35 KS,CS,A:Supergirl 200.00
36 KS,CS,Red Kryptonite Story . . 200.00
37 KS,CS,The Forbidden Box . . . 200.00
38 KS,CS,A:Prof.Potter,
  Supergirl 200.00
39 KS,CS,A:Supergirl,Jor-El,
  Krypto, Lori Lemaris 200.00
40 KS,Lois Lane, Hag! 200.00
41 KS,CS,The Devil and
  Lois Lane 200.00
42 KS,A:Lori Lemaris 200.00
43 KS,A:Luthor 200.00
44 KS,A:Lori Lemaris,Braniac,
  Prof. Potter 200.00
45 KS,CS,The Superman-Lois
  Hit Record 200.00
46 KS,A:Luthor 200.00
47 KS,The Incredible Delusion . . 200.00
48 KS,A:Mr. Mxyzptlk 200.00
49 KS,The Unknown Superman . 200.00
50 KS,A:Legion 225.00
51 KS,A:Van-Zee & Lori Lemaris . 150.00
52 KS,Truce Between Lois
  Lane and Lana Lang 150.00
53 KS,A:Lydia Lawrence 150.00
54 KS,CS,The Monster That
  Loved Lois Lane 150.00
55 KS,A:Supergirl 150.00
56 KS,Lois Lane's
  Super-Gamble! 150.00
57 KS,The Camera From
  Outer Space 150.00
58 KS,The Captive Princess 150.00
59 KS,CS,A:Jor-El & Batman . . . 150.00
60 KS,Get Lost,Superman! 150.00

61 KS,A:Mxyzptlk 150.00
62 KS,A:Mxyzptlk 150.00
63 KS,The Satanic Schemes
  of S.K.U.L. 150.00
64 KS,A:Luthor 150.00
65 KS,A:Luthor 150.00
66 KS,They Call Me the Cat! 150.00
67 KS,The Bombshell of
  the Boulevards 150.00
68 giant size 200.00
69 KS,Lois Lane's Last Chance . 150.00
70 KS,I:Silver Age Catwoman,
  A:Batman,Robin,Penguin . . . 500.00
71 KS,A:Catwoman,Batman,
  Robin,Penguin 300.00
72 KS,CS,A:Ina Lemaris 100.00
73 KS,The Dummy and
  the Damsel! 100.00
74 KS,A:Justice League & Bizarro
  World,I:Bizarro Flash 125.00
75 KS,The Lady Dictator 100.00
76 KS,A:Hap-El 100.00
77 giant size 150.00
78 KS,Courtship,Kryptonian Style 100.00
79 KS,B:NA(c) 100.00
80 KS,Get Out of My Life,
  Superman 100.00
81 KS,No Witnesses in
  Outerspace 100.00
82 GT,A:Brainiac&Justice League . 60.00
83 GT,Witch on Wheels 60.00
84 GT,KS,Who is Lois Lane? 60.00
85 GT,KS,A:Kandorians 60.00
86 giant size 75.00
87 GT,KS,A:Cor-Lar 60.00
88 GT,KS,Through a Murderer's
  Eyes 60.00
89 CS,A:Batman & Batman Jr. . . . 75.00
90 GT,A:Dahr-nel 60.00
91 GT,A:Superlass 60.00
92 GT,A:Superhorse 60.00
93 GT,A:Wonder Woman 60.00
94 GT,KS,A:Jor 60.00
95 giant size 100.00
96 GT,A:Jor 50.00
97 GT,KS,A:Lori Lemaris,
  Luma Lynai,Lyla Lerrol 50.00
98 GT,A:Phantom Zone 50.00
99 GT,KS,A:Batman 50.00
100 GT,A:Batman 50.00
101 GT,KS,The Super-Reckless
  Lois Lane 50.00
102 GT,KS,When You're Dead,
  You're Dead 50.00
103 GT,KS,A:Supergirl 50.00
104 giant size 75.00
105 RA,I&O:Rose & Thorn 75.00
106 WR,I am Curious Black! 60.00
107 WR,The Snow-Woman Wept . 50.00
108 WR,The Spectre Suitor 50.00
109 WR,I'll Never Fall
  in Love Again 50.00
110 WR,Indian Death Charge! . . . 50.00
111 WR,A:Justice League 50.00
112 WR,KS,A:Lori Lemaris 60.00
113 giant size 75.00
114 WR,KS,A:Rose & Thorn 50.00
115 WR,A:The Black Racer 50.00
116 WR,A:Darkseid & Desaad . . . 50.00
117 WR,S.O.S From Tomorrow! . . 50.00
118 WR,A:Darkseid & Desaad . . . 50.00
119 WR,A:Darkseid & Lucy Lane . 50.00
120 WR,Who Killed Lucy Lane? . . 50.00
121 WR,A:The Thorn 50.00
122 WR,A:The Thorn 50.00
123 JRo,Ten Deadly Division
  of the 100 . . . . 50.00
124 JRo,The Hunters 30.00
125 JRo,Death Rides Wheels! . . . 30.00
126 JRo,The Brain Busters 30.00
127 JRo,Curse of the Flame 30.00
128 JRo,A:Batman & Aquaman . . 30.00

129 JRo,Serpent in Paradise 30.00
130 JRo,The Mental Murster 30.00
131 JRo,Superman–Marry Me! . . 30.00
132 JRo,Zatanna B.U. 30.00
133 JRo,The Lady is a Bomb 30.00
134 JRo,A:Kandor 30.00
135 JRo,Amazing After-Life
  of Lois Lane 30.00
136 JRo,A:Wonder Woman 30.00
137 JRo,The Stolen Subway 40.00
Ann.#1 . . . . 500.00
Ann.#2 . . . . 300.00

SUPERMAN:
SILVER BANSHEE
1998
1 (of 2) DIB(s),ALa 2.25
2 DIB(s),ALa, conclusion 2.25

SUPERMAN'S NEMESIS,
LEX LUTHOR
1999
1 (of 4) VS,DJa, ... 2.50
2 VS,DJa 2.50
3 VS,DJa 2.50
4 VS,DJa, conclusion 2.50

SUPERMAN'S PAL,
JIMMY OLSEN
1954–74
1 CS,The Boy of 100 Faces! . 11,000.00
2 CS,The Flying Jimmy Olsen . 3,000.00
3 CS,The Man Who Collected
  Excitement 1,700.00
4 CS,King For A Day! 1,200.00
5 CS,The Story of Superman's
  Souvenirs 1,200.00
6 CS,Kryptonite story 800.00
7 CS,The King of Marbles 800.00
8 CS,Jimmy Olsen, Crooner . . . 800.00
9 CS,The Missile of Steel 800.00
10 CS,Jungle Jimmy Olsen 800.00
11 CS,TNT.Olsen,The Champ . . 550.00
12 CS,Invisible Jimmy Olsen . . . 550.00
13 CS,Jimmy Olsen's
  Super Issue 550.00
14 CS,The Boy Superman 550.00
15 CS,Jimmy Olsen,Speed
  Demon 550.00
16 CS,The Boy Superman 550.00
17 CS,J.Olsen as cartoonist . . . 550.00
18 CS,A:Superboy 550.00

Superman's Pal Jimmy Olsen #16
© DC Comics Inc.

Superman's Girl Friend Lois Lane #70
© DC Comics, Inc.

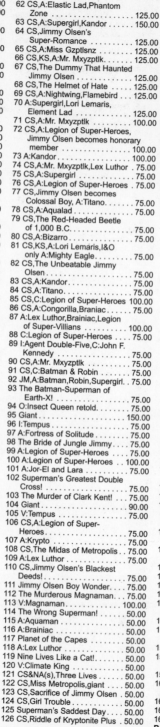

Superman's Pal Jimmy Olsen #66
© DC Comics, Inc.

Superman's Pal Jimmy Olsen #122
© DC Comics Inc.

19 CS,Supermam's Kid Brother. . 550.00
20 CS,Merman of Metropolis 550.00
21 CS,The Wedding of Jimmy
   Olsen 375.00
22 CS,The Super Brain of
   Jimmy Olsen 375.00
23 CS,The Adventure of
   Private Olsen 375.00
24 CS,The Gorilla Reporter 375.00
25 CS,The Day There Was
   No Jimmy Olsen 375.00
26 CS,Bird Boy of Metropolis . . . 375.00
27 CS,The Outlaw Jimmy Olsen . 375.00
28 CS,The Boy Who Killed
   Superman 375.00
29 CS,A:Krypto 375.00
30 CS,The Son of Superman . . . 375.00
31 CS,I:Elastic Lad 300.00
32 CS,A:Prof.Potter 300.00
33 CS,Human Flame Thrower . . . 300.00
34 CS,Superman's Pal of Steel . . 300.00
35 CS,Superman's Enemy 300.00
36 CS,I:Lois Lane,O:Jimmy Olsen
   as Superman's Pal 300.00
37 CS,O:Jimmy Olsen's SignalWatch,
   A:Elastic Lad(Jimmy Olsen) . 300.00
38 CS,Olsen's Super-Supper . . . 300.00
39 CS,The Super-Lad of Space . . 300.00
40 CS,A:Supergirl,Hank White
   (Perry White's son) 300.00
41 CS,The Human Octopus. 200.00
42 CS,Jimmy The Genie 200.00
43 WB,CS,Jimmy Olsen's Private
   Monster 200.00
44 CS,Miss Jimmy Olsen. 200.00
45 CS,A:Kandor. 200.00
46 CS,A:Supergirl,Elastic Lad . . 200.00
47 CS,Monsters From Earth! . . . 200.00
48 CS,I:Superman Emergency
   Squad 200.00
49 CS,A:Congorilla & Congo Bill . 200.00
50 CS,A:Supergirl,Krypto,Bizarro 200.00
51 CS,A:Supergirl 175.00
52 CS,A:Mr. Mxyzptlk,
   Miss Gzptlsnz 175.00
53 CS,A:Kandor,Lori Lemaris,
   Mr.Mxyztlk 175.00
54 CS,A:Elastic Lad 175.00
55 CS,A:Aquaman,Thor. 175.00
56 KS,Imaginary story 175.00
57 KS,A:Supergirl,Imaginary story 125.00
58 CS,C:Batman 125.00
59 CS,A:Titano. 125.00
60 CS,The Fantastic Army of
   General Olsen 125.00
61 CS,Prof. Potter 125.00

62 CS,A:Elastic Lad,Phantom
   Zone 125.00
63 CS,A:Supergirl,Kandor 150.00
64 CS,Jimmy Olsen's
   Super-Romance 125.00
65 CS,A:Miss Gzptlsnz 125.00
66 CS,KS,A:Mr. Mxyzptlk. 125.00
67 CS,The Dummy That Haunted
   Jimmy Olsen 125.00
68 CS,The Helmet of Hate 125.00
69 CS,A:Nightwing,Flamebird . . . 125.00
70 A:Supergirl,Lori Lemaris,
   Element Lad 125.00
71 CS,A:Mr. Mxyzptlk 100.00
72 CS,A:Legion of Super-Heroes,
   Jimmy Olsen becomes honorary
   member 100.00
73 A:Kandor. 100.00
74 CS,A:Mr. Mxyzptlk,Lex Luthor . 75.00
75 CS,A:Supergirl 75.00
76 CS,A:Legion of Super-Heroes . 75.00
77 CS,Jimmy Olsen becomes
   Colossal Boy, A:Titano. 75.00
78 CS,A:Aqualad 75.00
79 CS,The Red-Headed Beetle
   of 1,000 B.C. 75.00
80 CS,A:Bizarro. 75.00
81 CS,KS,A:Lori Lemaris,I&O
   only A:Mighty Eagle 75.00
82 CS,The Unbeatable Jimmy
   Olsen 75.00
83 CS,A:Kandor. 75.00
84 CS,A:Titano. 75.00
85 CS,C:Legion of Super-Heroes 100.00
86 CS,A:Congorilla,Braniac. 75.00
87 A:Lex Luthor,Brainiac,Legion
   of Super-Villains 100.00
88 C:Legion of Super-Heroes . . . 75.00
89 I:Agent Double-Five,C:John F.
   Kennedy 75.00
90 CS,A:Mr. Mxyzptlk 75.00
91 CS,C:Batman & Robin 75.00
92 JM,A:Batman,Robin,Supergirl . 75.00
93 The Batman-Superman of
   Earth-X! 75.00
94 O:Insect Queen retold. 75.00
95 Giant 150.00
96 I:Tempus 75.00
97 A:Fortress of Solitude 75.00
98 The Bride of Jungle Jimmy . . 75.00
99 A:Legion of Super-Heroes . . . 75.00
100 A:Legion of Super-Heroes . . 100.00
101 A:Jor-El and Lara 75.00
102 Superman's Greatest Double
   Cross! 75.00
103 The Murder of Clark Kent! . . 75.00
104 Giant 90.00
105 V:Tempus 75.00
106 CS,A:Legion of Super-
   Heroes. 75.00
107 A:Krypto 75.00
108 CS,The Midas of Metropolis . . 75.00
109 A:Lex Luthor 75.00
110 CS,Jimmy Olsen's Blackest
   Deeds! 75.00
111 Jimmy Olsen Boy Wonder. . . 75.00
112 The Murderous Magnaman. . 75.00
113 V:Magnaman. 100.00
114 The Wrong Superman! 50.00
115 A:Aquaman 50.00
116 A:Brainiac. 50.00
117 Planet of the Capes 50.00
118 A:Lex Luthor 50.00
119 Nine Lives Like a Cat!. 50.00
120 V:Climate King 50.00
121 CS&NA(s),Three Lives 50.00
122 CS,Miss Metropolis,giant . . . 50.00
123 CS,Sacrifice of Jimmy Olsen . 50.00
124 CS,Girl Trouble 50.00
125 Superman's Saddest Day . . . 50.00
126 CS,Riddle of Kryptonite Plus . 50.00

127 CS,Jimmy in Revolutionary
   War. 50.00
128 I:Mark Olsen(Jimmy'sFather) . 50.00
129 MA,A:Mark Olsen. 50.00
130 MA,A:Robin,Brainiac. 50.00
131 CS,Birdboy of Metropolis . . . 75.00
132 MA,When Olsen Sold out
   Superman 50.00
133 JK,B:New Newsboy Legion,
   I:Morgan Edge 100.00
134 JK,I:Darkseid. 125.00
135 JK,I:New Guardian 75.00
136 JK,O:New Guardian,
   I:Dubbilex. 65.00
137 JK,I:Four Armed Terror 50.00
138 JK,V:Four Armed Terror 50.00
139 JK,A:Don Rickles,I:Ugly
   Mannheim 50.00
140 Rep. Jimmy Olsen #69, #72
   and Superman #158 . . . . . . 50.00
141 JK,A:Don Rickles,Lightray
   B:Newsboy Legion rep 50.00
142 JK,I:Count Dragorian 50.00
143 JK,V:Count Dragorian. 50.00
144 JK,A Big Thing in a Deep
   Scottish Lake. 50.00
145 JK,Brigadoon 50.00
146 JK,Homo Disastrous. 50.00
147 JK,Superman on New
   Genesis,A:High Father,
   I:Victor Volcanium 50.00
148 JK,V:Victor Volcanium,
   E:Newsboy Legion rep 50.00
149 BO(i),The Unseen Enemy,
   B:Plastic Man rep. 50.00
150 BO(i) A Bad Act to Follow . . . 50.00
151 BO(i),A:Green Lantern 30.00
152 MSy,BO,I:Real Morgan Edge . 30.00
153 MSy,Murder in Metropolis. . . 30.00
154 KS,The Girl Who Was Made
   of Money 30.00
155 KS,Downfall of Judas Olsen . . 30.00
156 KS,Last Jump for
   a Skyjacker 30.00
157 KS,Jimmy as Marco Polo . . . 30.00
158 KS,A:Lena Lawrence
   (Lucy Lane) 30.00
159 KS,Jimmy as Spartacus 30.00
160 KS,A:Lena Lawrence
   (Lucy Lane) 30.00
161 KS,V:Lucy Lane 30.00
162 KS,A:Lex Luthor 30.00
163 KS,Jimmy as Marco Polo . . . 30.00
Becomes:

DC COMICS

SUPERMAN FAMILY
1974–82
164 KS,NC(c),Jimmy Olsen:Death
Bites with Fangs of Stone 75.00
165 KS,NC(c),Supergirl:Princess
of the Golden Sun 50.00
166 KS,NC(c),Lois Lane:The
Murdering Arm of Metropolis . . 35.00
167 KS,NC(c),Jimmy Olsen:A
Deep Death for Mr. Action 35.00
168 NC(c),Supergirl:The Girl
with the See-Through Mind . . . 35.00
169 NC(c),Lois Lane:Target of
the Tarantula 35.00
170 KS(c),Jimmy Olsen:The Kid
Who Adopted Jimmy Olsen. . . . 25.00
171 ECh(c),Supergirl:Cleopatra-
Queen of America 25.00
172 KS(c),Lois Lane:The Cheat
the Whole World Cheered. . . . 25.00
173 KS(c),Jimmy Olsen:Menace
of the Micro-Monster 25.00
174 KS(c),Supergirl:Eyes of
the Serpent 25.00
175 KS(c),Lois Lane:Fadeout
For Lois 25.00
176 KS(c),Jimmy
Olsen:Nashville, Super-Star . . 25.00
177 KS(c),Supergirl:Bride
of the Stars 20.00
178 KS(c),Lois Lane:The Girl
With the Heart of Steel 20.00
179 KS(c),Jimmy Olsen:I Scared
Superman to Death 20.00
180 KS,Supergirl:The Secret of
the Spell-Bound Supergirl 20.00
181 ECh(c),Lois Lane:The Secret
Lois Lane Could Never Tell . . . 20.00
182 CS&NA(c),Jimmy Olsen:
Death on Ice 20.00
183 NA(c),Supergirl:Shadows
of Phantoms 20.00
184 NA(c),Supergirl:The
Visitors From The Void 20.00
185 NA(c),Jimmy Olsen: The
Fantastic Fists and Fury
Feet of Jimmy Olsen 20.00
186 JL&DG(c),Jimmy Olsen:
The Bug Lady 20.00
187 JL(c),Jimmy Olsen:The
Dealers of Death 20.00
188 JL&DG(c),Jimmy Olsen:
Crisis in Kandor. 20.00
189 JL(c),Jimmy Olsen:The
Night of the Looter 20.00
190 Jimmy Olsen:Somebody
Stole My Town 20.00
191 Superboy:The Incredible
Shrinking Town 20.00
192 RA&DG(c),Superboy:This
Town For Plunder 20.00
193 RA&DG(c),Superboy:Menace
of the Mechanical Monster . . . 20.00
194 MR,Superboy:When
the Sorcerer Strikes. 20.00
195 RA&DG(c),Superboy:The Curse
of the Un-Secret Identity 20.00
196 JL&DG(c),Superboy:The
Shadow of Jor-El 20.00
197 JL(c),Superboy:Superboy's
Split Personality 20.00
198 JL(c),Superboy:Challenge
of the Green K-Tastrophe 20.00
199 RA&DG(c),Supergirl:The
Case of Cape Caper 20.00
200 RA&DG(c),Lois Lane:
Unhappy Anniversary 22.00
201 RA&DG(c),Supergirl:The
Face on Cloud 9 . . . . 8.00
202 RA&DG(c),Supergirl:The
Dynamic Duel 8.00
203 RA&DG(c),Supergirl:The
Supergirl From Planet Earth . . . 8.00
204 RA&DG(c),Supergirl:The
Earth-quake Enchantment. 8.00
205 RA&DG(c),Supergirl:Magic
Over Miami 8.00
206 RA&DG(c),Supergirl:Strangers
at the Heart's Core 8.00
207 RA&DG(c),Supergirl:Look
Homeward, Argonian. 8.00
208 RA&DG(c),Supergirl:The
Super-Switch to New York. 8.00
209 Supergirl:Strike Three-
You're Out 8.00
210 Supergirl:The Spoil Sport
of New York 8.00
211 RA&DG(c),Supergirl:The Man
With the Explosive Mind 8.00
212 RA&DG(c):Supergirl:Payment
on Demand 8.00
213 thru 222 . . . . @8.00

SUPERMAN:
SAVE THE PLANET
Aug., 1998
1 LSi,SEa,DRo,JP,KN, last
front page 3.00
1 collector's edition 4.00

SUPERMAN: STRENGTH
Jan., 2005
1 (of 3) TA,48-page 6.00
2 TA. 6.00
3 TA,ARo(c) 6.00

SUPERMAN,
THE KANSAS SIGHTING
Nov. 2003
GN #1 F:Jor-El. 7.00
GN #2 F:Jor-El. 7.00

SUPERMAN,
THE SECRET YEARS
Feb., 1985
1 CS,KS,FM(c) 3.00
2 CS,KS,FM(c) 2.50
3 CS,KS,FM(c) 2.50
4 CS,KS,FM(c), May, 1985 . . . . . . 2.50

Superman, The Secret Years #4
© DC Comics Inc.

SUPERMAN VS.
AMAZING SPIDER-MAN
DC/Marvel April, 1976
1 RA/DG,oversized 125.00
1a 2nd printing, signed 225.00

SUPERMAN
VS. PREDATOR
DC/Dark Horse May, 2000
1 (of 3) weakened by virus 5.00
2 . . . . 5.00
3 conclusion 5.00

SUPERMAN/
WONDER WOMAN:
WHOM GODS DESTROY
Elseworlds Oct., 1996
1 CCl(s),DAb, Lois becomes the
immortal Wonder Woman 5.00
2 CCl(s),DAb, search for Lana
Lang. 5.00
3 . . . . 5.00
4 CCl(s),DAb, romance of the
century, concl. 5.00

SUPERMEN OF AMERICA
1999
GN with membership kit. 5.00
GN standard edition. 4.00
1 (of 6) FaN,DBw, ... 2.50
2 FaN,DBw,V:Lex Luthor 2.50
3 FaN,DBw,F:Brahma. 2.50
4 FaN,DBw,F:White Lotus 2.50
5 FaN,F:The Loser 2.50
6 FaN,A:Superman,concl.. . . . . . . 2.50

SUPER POWERS
1984
[Kenner Action Figures]
1 A:Batman & Joker 5.50
2 A:Batman & Joker 5.50
3 A:Batman & Joker 5.50
4 A:Batman & Joker 5.50
5 JK(c),JK,A:Batman & Joker 5.50
[2nd Series], 1985–86
1 JK,Seeds of Doom. 4.00
2 JK,When Past & Present Meet . . 4.00
3 JK,Time Upon Time 4.00
4 JK,There's No Place Like Rome . 4.00
5 JK,Once Upon a Tomorrow 4.00
6 JK,Darkkseid o/t Moon 4.00
[3rd Series], 1986
1 CI,Threshold 3.50
2 CI,Escape 3.50
3 CI,Machinations. 3.50
4 CI,A World Divided 3.50

SUPER-TEAM FAMILY
1975–78
1 Reprints, giant-size 35.00
2 Creeper/Wildcat. 18.00
3 RE/WW,Flash & Hawkman 18.00
4 Revenge of Solomon Grundy . . . 20.00
5 Batman vs. Eclipso 20.00
6 Return of Composite Superman 20.00
7 To Order is to Destroy 20.00
8 JSh,Challengers 22.00
9 JSh,Challengers 22.00
10 JSh,Challengers 22.00
11 Supergirl,Flash,Atom. 22.00
12 Green Lantern,Hawkman 22.00
13 Aquaman, Capt. Comet 22.00
14 Wonder Woman,Atom. 22.00
15 Flash & New Gods 25.00

Swamp Thing #1 © DC Comics, Inc.

SWAMP THING
[1st Regular Series]
Oct.–Nov., 1972

1 B:LWn(s),BWr,O:Swamp Thing	250.00
2 BWr,I:Arcane	100.00
3 BWr,I:Patchwork Man	75.00
4 BWr	65.00
5 BWr	65.00
6 BWr	65.00
7 BWr,A:Batman	75.00
8 BWr,Lurker in Tunnel 13	60.00
9 BWr	60.00
10 E:BWr,A;Arcane	60.00
11 thru 24 NR	@25.00

TPB rep.#1–#10,House of Secrets
#92, Dark Genesis Saga 25.00

SWAMP THING
1986–96
Previously:
SAGA OF THE SWAMP THING

46 B:AMo(s) cont'd,SBi,JTo,Crisis, A:John Constantine,Phantom Stranger	5.00
47 SBi,Parliment of Trees,Full origin,A:Constantine	5.00
48 SBi,JTo,V:Brujeria, A:Constantine	4.00
49 SBi,AA,A:Constantine,Demon,Ph. Stranger,Spectre,Deadman	4.00
50 SBi,AA,AA:Floor American Gothic,D:Zatara&Sargon, Double Size	6.00
51 RV,AA,L:Constantine	4.00
52 RV,AA,Arkham Asylum,A:Flor. Man,Lex Luthor,C:Joker, 2-Face,Batman	4.00
53 JTo,V:Batman,Swamp Thing Banished to Space	5.00
54 JTo script,RV,AA,C:Batman	4.00
55 RV,AA,JTo,A:Batman	4.00
56 RV,AA,My Blue Heaven	4.00
57 RV,AA,A:Adam Strange	4.00
58 RV,AA,A:Adam Strange,GC, Spectre preview	4.00
59 JTo,RV,AA,D:Patchwork Man	4.00

Direct Sales Only

60 JTo,Loving the Alien	4.00
61 RV,AA,All Flesh is Grass G.L.Corps X-over	4.00
62 RV(&script),AA,Wavelength, A:Metron,Darkseid	4.00
63 RV,AA,Loose Ends(reprise)	4.00

64 E:AMo(s),SBi,TY,RV,AA, Return of the Good Gumbo	4.00
65 RV,JTo,A:Constantine	3.50
66 RV,Elemental Energy	3.00
67 RV,V:Solomon Grundy, Hellblazer preview	4.00
68 RV,O:Swamp Thing	3.00
69 RV,O:Swamp Thing	3.00
70 RV,AA,Quest for SwampThing	3.00
71 RV,AA,Fear of Flying	3.00
72 RV,AA,Creation	3.00
73 RV,AA,A:John Constantine	3.50
74 RV,AA,Abbys Secret	3.00
75 RV,AA,Plant Elementals	3.00
76 RV,AA,A:John Constantine	3.50
77 TMd,AA,A:John Constantine	3.50
78 TMd,AA,Phantom Pregnancy	3.00
79 RV,AA,A:Superman,Luthor	3.00
80 RV,AA,V:Aliens	3.00
81 RV,AA,Invasion x-over	3.00
82 RV,AA,A:Sgt.Rock & Easy Co.	3.00
83 RV,AA,A:Enemy Ace	3.00
84 RV,AA,A:Sandman	8.00
85 RV,TY,Time Travel contd	3.00
86 RV,TY,A:Tomahawk	3.00
87 RV,TY,Camelot,A:Demon	3.00
88 RV,TY,A:Demon,Golden Gladiator	3.00
89 MM,AA,The Dinosaur Age	3.00
90 BP,AA,Birth of Abbys Child (Tefe)	3.25
91 PB,AA,Abbys Child (New Elemental)	3.00
92 PB,AA,Ghosts of the Bayou	3.00
93 PB,AA,New Power	3.00
94 PB,AA,Ax-Murderer	3.00
95 PB,AA,Toxic Waste Dumpers	3.00
96 PB,AA,Tefes Powers	3.00
97 PB,AA,Tefe,V:Nergal, A:Arcane	3.00
98 PB,AA,Tefe,in Hell	3.00
99 PB,AA,Tefe,A:Mantago, John Constantine	3.50
100 PB,AA,V:Angels of Eden, (48 pages)	4.00
101 AA,A:Tefe	3.00
102 V:Mantagos Zombies,inc. prev. of Worlds Without End.	3.00
103 Green vs. Grey	3.00
104 Quest for Elementals,pt.1	3.00
105 Quest for Elementals,pt.2	3.00
106 Quest for Elementals,pt.3	3.00
107 Quest for Elementals,pt.4	3.00
108 Quest for Elementals,pt.5	3.00
109 Quest for Elementals,pt.6	3.00
110 TMd,A:Father Tocsin	3.00
111 V:Ghostly Zydeco Musician	3.00
112 TMd,B:Swamp Thing for Governor	3.00
113 E:Swamp Thing for Governor	3.00
114 TMd,Hellblazer	3.25
115 TMd,A:Hellblazer,V:Dark Conrad	3.25
116 From Body of Swamp Thing	3.00
117 JD,The Lord of Misrule, Mardi Gras	3.00
118 A Childs Garden,A:Matthew the Raven	3.00
119 A:Les Perdu	3.00
120 F:Lady Jane	3.00
121 V:Sunderland Corporation	3.00
122 I:The Needleman	3.00
123 V:The Needleman	3.00
124 In Central America	3.00
125 V:Anton Arcane,20th Anniv.	4.00
126 Mescalito	3.00
127 Project Proteus #1	3.00
128 Project proteus #2.	3.00

DC/Vertigo, 1993

129 CV(c),B:NyC(s),SEa,KDM(i), Sw.Thing's Deterioration	3.00

130 CV(c),SEa,KDM(i),A:John Constantine,V:Doctor Polygon	3.00
131 CV(c),SEa,KDM(i),I:Swamp Thing's,Doppleganger, F:The Folk	3.50
132 CV(c),SEa,KDM(i), V:Doppleganger	3.50
133 CV(c),SEa,KDM(i),R:General Sunderland,V:Thunder Petal	3.50
134 CV(c),SEa,KDM(i),Abby Leaves, C:John Constantine	3.50
135 CV(c),SEa,KDM(i),A:J.Constantine, Swamp Thing Lady Jane meld	3.50
136 CV(c),RsB,KDM(i),A:Lady Jane, Dr.Polygon,John Constantine	3.50
137 CV(c),E:NyC(s),RsB,KDM(i), IR:Sunderland is Anton Arcane, A:J.Constantine	3.50
138 CV(c),DiF(s),RGu,KDM,B:Mind Fields	3.50
139 CV(c),DiF(s),RGu,KDM,A:Black Orchid,In Swamp Thing's mind, cont'd fr.Black Orchid #5	3.50
140 B:Bad Gumbo	4.00
140a Platinum Ed.	12.00
141 A:Abigail Arcane	3.00
142 Bad Gumbo#3	3.00
143 E:Bad Gumbo	3.00
144 In New York City	3.00
145 In Amsterdam	3.00
146 V:Nelson Strong	3.00
147 Hunter	3.00
148 Sargon	3.00
149 Sargon	3.00
150 V:Sargon	3.50
151	3.00
152 River Run,pt.1	3.00
153 River Run	3.00
154 River Run	3.00
155 River Run	3.00
156 PJ,River Run.	3.00
157	3.00
158	3.00
159 Swamp Dog	3.00
160 PhH,KDM,Atmospheres	3.00
161 Atmospheres	2.50
162 Atmospheres	2.50
163 Atmospheres	2.50
164	2.50
165 CS,KDM,F:Chester Williams	2.50
166 PhH,KDM,Trial by Fire,pt.1	2.50
167 PhH,KDM,Trial by Fire,pt.2	2.50
168 MMr(s),PhH,KDM,Trial,pt.3	2.50
169 MMr(s),PhH,KDM,Trial,pt.4	2.50
170 MMr(s),PhH,KDM,Trial,pt.5	2.50
171 MMr(s),PhH,KDM,Trial by Fire, pt.6, last issue	2.50
Ann.#3 AMo(s),Ape issue	4.00
Ann.#4 PB/AA,A:Batman	4.00
Ann.#5 A:BrotherPower Geek	4.00
Ann.#6 Houma	4.00
Ann.#7 CV(c),NyC(s),MBu(i),Childrens Crusade,F:Tefe,A:Maxine,BU: Beautyand the Beast	7.00

SWAMP THING
DC/Vertigo, March, 2000

1 JRu,F:Tefe Holland	4.00
2 JRu,new secrets	3.00
3 JRu,	3.00
4 Killing Time,pt.1	3.00
5 Killing Time,pt.2	3.00
6 Killing Time,pt.3	3.00
7 RM	3.00
8 RM	3.00
9 RM	3.00
10 RM	3.00
11 RM,Red Harvest, pt.1	3.00
12 RM,Red Harvest, pt.2	3.00
13 RM,Red Harvest, pt.3	3.00
14 RM,Red Harvest, pt.4	3.00
15 RM,Red Harvest, pt.5	3.00

DC COMICS

16 RM,Red Harvest, pt.6 . . . . 3.00
17 Red Harvest, pt.7 . . . . 3.00
18 R:Original Swamp Thing 3.00
19 The Tree of Knowledge 3.00
20 final issue 3.00
Secret Files #1, 64-pg. 5.00

SWAMP THING
DC/Vertigo, March 2004
1 classic Swamp Thing 3.00
2 Bad Seed,pt.2 . . . . 3.00
3 Bad Seed,pt.3 . . . . 3.00
4 Bad Seed,pt.4 . . . . 3.00
5 Bad Seed,pt.5,40-pg. 3.00
6 Bad Seed,pt.6 . . . . 3.00
7 RCo,Missing Links,pt.1 . . . . 3.00
8 RCo,Missing Links,pt.2 . . . . 3.00
9 Love in Vain, pt.1 . . . . 3.00
10 Love in Vain, pt.2 . . . . 3.00
11 Love in Vain, pt.3 . . . . 3.00
12 Love in Vain, pt.4 . . . . 3.00
13 Measure of Faith, pt.1 . . . . 3.00
14 Measure of Faith, pt.2 . . . . 3.00
15 Healing the Breach,pt.1 . . . . . . 3.00
16 Healing the Breach,pt.2 . . . . . . 3.00
17 Healing the Breach,pt.3 . . . . . . 3.00
18 Healing the Breach,pt.4 . . . . . . 3.00
19 Alec's bizarre mentor 3.00
20 RCo, sub-atomic size 3.00
21 The Bleeding Raconteur 3.00
22 The Bleeding Raconteur 3.00
23 The Bleeding Raconteur 3.00
24 The Bleeding Raconteur 3.00
25 F:Abby. 3.00
26 Unforgivable actions 3.00
27 The Prison Tree, pt.1 . . . . 3.00
28 Floronic Man. 3.00
29 final issue 3.00

Sword of Sorcery #1
© DC Comics, Inc.

SWORD OF SORCERY
Feb.–March, 1973
1 MK(c),HC 25.00
2 BWv,NA,Hc 30.00
3 BWv,HC,MK,WS 25.00
4 HC,WS 10.00
5 Nov.–Dec., 1973 . . . . 10.50

SWORD OF THE ATOM
Sept., 1983
1 GK 3.00
2 GK 3.00
3 GK 3.00
4 GK 3.00
Spec.#1 GK 2.50

Spec.#2 GK 2.50
Spec.#3 PB 2.50

TAILGUNNER JO
Sept., 1988
1 . . . . 2.50
2 thru 6 . . . . @2.50

TAKION
1996
1 PuK,AaL,Josh Sanders
  becomes Takion. 2.50
2 thru 4 . . . . @2.50
5 PuK,AaL,Adventures of Source
  Elemental, cont. 2.50
6 PuK,AaL,Final Night tie-in 2.50
7 PuK,AaL,Arzaz trains Takion,
  final issue 2.50

TALES OF THE GREEN LANTERN CORPS
May, 1981
1 JSon,FMc,O:Green Lantern. 2.50
2 JSon,FMc. 2.50
3 JSon,FMc. 2.50

TALES OF THE LEGION OF SUPER HEROES
Aug., 1984
Prev: Legion of Super Heroes)
314 KG,V:Ontiir 2.50
315 KG(i),V:Dark Circle 2.50
316 KG(i),O:White Witch 2.50
317 KG(i),V:Dream Demon 2.50
318 KG(i),V:Persuader. 2.50
319 KG(i),V:Persuader,
  A:Superboy 2.50
320 DJu,V:Magpie 2.50
321 DJu,Exile,V:Kol 2.50
322 DJu,Exile,V:Kol 2.50
323 DJu,Exile,V:Kol 2.50
324 DJu,EC,V:Dev-Em 2.50
325 DJu,V:Dark Circle 2.50
326 thru 354 rep. of Legion of Super
  Heroes, 3rd Series #1–#29 . . . . 2.50
Ann.#4 rep. Baxter Ann.#1. . . . . . 2.50
Ann.#5 rep. Baxter Ann.#2. . . . . . 2.50

TALES OF THE NEW TEEN TITANS
June, 1982
1 GP, O:Cyborg. 3.50
2 GP, O:Raven 3.50
3 GD, O:Changling 3.50
4 GP/EC,O:Starfire 3.50

TALES OF THE SINESTRO CORPS PRESENTS
Sept., 2007
Spec #1 RMz,Parallax 3.00
Spec. #1 The Anti-Monitor 3.00
Spec. #1 Superman. 3.00

TALES OF THE TEEN TITANS
See: NEW TEEN TITANS

TALES OF THE UNEXPECTED
1956–68
1 The Out-Of-The-World Club . 2,400.00
2 Gorilla Who Saved the World 1,200.00
3 LSt,Man With 100 Wigs 800.00
4 Seven Steps to the Unknown . 800.00
5 2nd Life of Geoffrey Hawkes . 800.00
6 The Girl in the Bottle 600.00

Tales of the Unexpected #9
© DC Comics Inc.

7 NC(c),Pen That Never Lied . . . 600.00
8 LSt,Camera that Could Rob . . 600.00
9 LSt(c),The Amazing Cube 600.00
10 MMe(c),The Strangest Show
  On Earth 600.00
11 LSt(c),Who Am I? 400.00
12 JK,Four Threads of Doom . . . 500.00
13 JK(c),Weapons of Destiny . . . 500.00
14 SMo(c),The Forbidden Game . 400.00
15 JK,MMe,Three Wishes
  to Doom 600.00
16 JK,The Magic Hammer. 600.00
17 JK,Who Is Mr. Ashtar? 600.00
18 JK(c),MMe,A Man Without A
  World 600.00
19 NC,Man From Two Worlds . . . 550.00
20 NC(c),The Earth Gladiator . . . 550.00
21 JK,The Living Phantoms. 550.00
22 JK(c),The Man From Robot
  Island. 550.00
23 JK,The Invitation From Mars! . 550.00
24 LC,The Secret Of Planetoid
  Zero! 550.00
25 The Sorcerer's Asteroid! 300.00
26 MMe,The Frozem City 300.00
27 MMe,The Prison In Space . . . 300.00
28 The Melting Planet 300.00
29 The Phantom Raider. 300.00
30 The Jinxed Planet. 300.00
31 RH,Keep Off Our Planet 250.00
32 Great Space Cruise Mystery. . 250.00
33 The Man Of 1,000 Planets . . . 250.00
34 Ambush In Outer Space 250.00
35 MMe,I was a Space Refugee . 250.00
36 The Curse Of The
  Galactic Goodess 250.00
37 The Secret Prisoners
  Of Planet 13 . . . . 250.00
38 The Stunt Man Of Space 250.00
39 The Creatures From The
  Space Globe 250.00
40 B:Space Ranger,The Last
  Days Of Planet Mars! 2,400.00
41 SMo(c),The Destroyers From
  The Stars! 800.00
42 The Secret Of The
  Martian Helmet 800.00
43 The Riddle Of The Burning
  Treasures,I:Space Ranger . 1,700.00
44 DD&SMo(c),The Menace Of
  The Indian Aliens. 600.00
45 DD&SMo(c),The Sheriff
  From Jupiter 600.00
46 DD&SMo(c),The
  Duplicate Doom! 600.00

Tales of the Unexpected #53
© DC Comics, Inc.

47 DD(c),The Man Who Stole
    The Solar System 450.00
48 Bring 'Em Back Alive-
    From Earth 450.00
49 RH,The Fantastic Lunar-Land 450.00
50 MA,King Barney The Ape 450.00
51 Planet Earth For Sale 450.00
52 Prisoner On Pluto 450.00
53 InterplanetaryTroubleShooter . 450.00
54 The Ugly Sleeper Of Klanth,
    Dinosaur 450.00
55 The Interplanetary
    Creature Trainer 450.00
56 B:Spaceman At Work,Invaders
    From Earth 450.00
57 The Jungle Beasts Of Jupiter . 450.00
58 The Boss Of The
    Saturnian Legion 450.00
59 The Man Who Won A World . . 450.00
60 School For Space Sleuths . . 450.00
61 The Mystery Of The
    Mythical Monsters 300.00
62 The Menace Of The Red
    Snow Crystals 300.00
63 Death To Planet Earth 300.00
64 Boy Usurper Of Planet Zonn . 300.00
65 The Creature That
    Couldn't Exist 300.00
66 MMe,Trap Of The Space
    Convict. 300.00
67 The Giant That
    Devoured A Village 300.00
68 Braggart From Planet Brax . . 200.00
69 Doom On Holiday Asteroid . . 200.00
70 The Hermit Of Planetoid X . . 200.00
71 Manhunt In Galaxy G-2! 200.00
72 The Creature Of 1,000 Dooms 200.00
73 The Convict Defenders
    Of Space!. 200.00
74 Prison Camp On Asteroid X-3! 200.00
75 The Hobo Jungle Of Space . . 200.00
76 The Warrior Of Two Worlds! . . 200.00
77 Dateline-Outer Space 200.00
78 The Siren Of Space 200.00
79 Big Show On Planet Earth!. . . 200.00
80 The Creature Tamer!. 200.00
81 His Alien Master!. 200.00
82 Give Us Back Our Earth!,
    E:Space Ranger 200.00
83 DD&SMo(c),The Anti-Hex
    Merchant!. 125.00
84 DD&SMo(c),The Menace Of
    The 50-Fathom Men 125.00
85 JkS(c),The Man Who Stole My
    Powers,B:Green Glob 125.00

86 DD&SMo(c),They'll Never
    Take Me Alive! 100.00
87 JkS(c),The Manhunt Through
    Two Worlds 100.00
88 DD&SMo(c),GK,The Fear
    Master 100.00
89 DD,SMo(c),Nightmare on
    Mars. 100.00
90 JkS(c),The Hero Of 5,000 BC. 100.00
91 JkS(c),The Prophetic Mirages,
    I:Automan 125.00
92 The Man Who Dared To Die! . 100.00
93 JkS(c),Prisoners Of Hate
    Island. 100.00
94 The Monster Mayor - USA . . . 100.00
95 The Secret Of Chameleo-Man 100.00
96 Wanted For Murder...1966...
    6966. . . . . 100.00
97 One Month To Die. 100.00
98 Half-Man/Half Machine 100.00
99 JkS(c),Nuclear Super-Hero! . . 100.00
100 Judy Blonde, Secret Agent! . 125.00
101 The Man In The Liquid Mask!. 75.00
102 Bang!Bang! You're Dead 75.00
103 JA,ABC To Disaster 75.00
104 NA(c),Master Of The
     Voodoo Machine 75.00

Becomes:

UNEXPECTED, THE
1968–82

105 The Night I Watched
     Myself Die 100.00
106 B:Johnny Peril,The Doorway
     Into Time 75.00
107 MD,JkS(c),The Whip Of
     Fear! 75.00
108 JkS(c),Journey To
     A Nightmare. 75.00
109 JkS(c),Baptism By Starfire!. . . 75.00
110 NA(c),Death Town, U.S.A.! . . . 75.00
111 NC(c),Mission Into Eternity . . . 75.00
112 NA(c),The Brain Robbers!. . . . 75.00
113 NA(c),The Shriek Of
     Vengeance. 75.00
114 NA(c),My Self-My Enemy!. . . . 60.00
115 BWr,NA(c),Diary Of
     A Madman 60.00
116 NC(c),Express Train
     To Nowhere! 55.00
117 NC(c),Midnight Summons
     The Executioner! 50.00
118 NA(c),A:Judge Gallows,Play
     A Tune For Treachery 50.00
119 BWr,NC(c),Mirror,Mirror
     On The Wall. 75.00
120 NC(c),Rambeau's Revenge . . 50.00
121 BWr,NA(c),Daddy's
     Gone-A-Hunting. 50.00
122 WW,DG(c),The Phantom
     Of The Woodstock Festival . . . 50.00
123 NC(c),Death Watch! 40.00
124 NA(c),These Walls Shall
     Be Your Grave. 40.00
125 NC(c),Screech Of Guilt! 40.00
126 ATh,NC(c),You Are Cordially
     Invited To Die! 40.00
127 GT,JK,ATh,NC(c),Follow The
     Piper To Your Grave 40.00
128 DW,BWr,NC(c),Where Only
     The Dead Are Free!. 40.00
129 NC(c),Farewell To A
     Fading Star 40.00
130 NC(c),One False Step 40.00
131 NC(c),Run For Your Death! . . 40.00
132 MD,GT,NC(c),The Edge Of
     Madness 40.00
133 WW,JkS(c),A:Judge Gallows,
     Agnes Doesn't Haunt Here
     Anymore!. 40.00
134 GT,NC(c),The Restless Dead . 40.00
135 NC(c),Death, Come
     Walk With Me! 40.00

136 SMo,GT,NC(c),An Incident
     of Violence 40.00
137 WW,NC(c),Dark Vengeance! . 25.00
138 WW,NC(c),Strange Secret of
     the Huan Shan Idol 30.00
139 GT,NC(c),The 2 Brains of
     Beast Bracken! 25.00
140 JkS(c),The Anatomy of Hate. . 25.00
141 NC(c),Just What Did Eric
     See? 25.00
142 NC(c),Let The Dead Sleep! . . 25.00
143 NC(c),Fear is a Nameless
     Voice 25.00
144 NC(c),The Dark Pit of
     Dr. Hanley 25.00
145 NC(c),Grave of Glass 25.00
146 NC(c),The Monstrosity! 25.00
147 NC(c),The Daughter of
     Dr. Jekyll 25.00
148 NC(c),Baby Wants Me Dead! . 25.00
149 NC(c),To Wake the Dead 25.00
150 NC(c),No One Escapes From
     Gallows Island 25.00
151 NC(c),Sorry, I'm Not Ready
     To Die! 25.00
152 GT,NC(c),Death Wears Many
     Faces. 25.00
153 NC(c),Who's That Sleeping
     In My Grave?. 25.00
154 NC(c),Murder By Madness . . . 25.00
155 NC(c),Non-Stop Journey
     Into Fear 25.00
156 NC(c),A Lunatic Is Loose
     Among Us!. 25.00
157 NC(c),The House of
     the Executioner 60.00
158 NC(c),Reserved for Madmen
     Only 60.00
159 NC(c),A Cry in the Night 60.00
160 NC(c),Death of an Exorcist . . 60.00
161 BWr,NC(c),Has Anyone
     Seen My Killer 60.00
162 JK,NC(c),I'll Bug You
     To Your Grave 60.00
163 DD,LD(c),Room For Dying . . . 20.00
164 House of the Sinister Sands . . 20.00
165 LD(c),Slayride in July 20.00
166 LD(c),The Evil Eyes of Night . 20.00
167 LD(c),Scared Stiff 20.00
168 LD(c),Freak Accident 20.00
169 LD(c),What Can Be Worse
     Than Dying? 20.00
170 LD(c),Flee To Your Grave 20.00
171 LD(c),I.O.U. One Corpse 20.00
172 LD(c),Strangler in Paradise . . 20.00
173 LD(c),What Scared Sally? . . . 20.00
174 LD(c),Gauntlet of Fear 20.00
175 LD(c),The Haunted Mountain . 20.00
176 JkS(c),Having A
     Wonderful Crime 20.00
177 ECh(c),Reward for the Wicked 20.00
178 LD(c),Fit To Kill! 20.00
179 LD(c),My Son, The Mortician . 20.00
180 GT,LD(c),The Loathsome
     Lodger of Nightmare Inn 22.00
181 LD(c),Hum of the Haunted . . . 20.00
182 LD(c),Sorry, This Coffin
     is Occupied 20.00
183 LD(c),The Dead Don't
     Always Die. 20.00
184 LD(c),Wheel of Misfortune! . . . 20.00
185 LD(c),Monsters from a
     Thousand Fathoms 20.00
186 LD(c),To Catch a Corpse 20.00
187 LD(c),Mangled in Madness . . . 20.00
188 LD(c),Verdict From The Grave 20.00
189 SD,LD(c),Escape From The
     Grave 20.00
190 LD(c),The Jigsaw Corpse . . . 20.00
191 MR,JO(c),Night of the Voodoo
     Curse. 22.00
192 LD(c),A Killer Cold & Clammy. 18.00

193 DW,LD(c),Don't Monkey the
  Murder 18.00
194 LD(c),Have I Got a Ghoul
  For You 18.00
195 JCr,LD(c),Whose Face is at
  My Window 18.00
196 LD(c),The Fear of Number 13 15.00
197 LD(c),Last Laugh of a Corpse 15.00
198 JSn(c),Rage of the
  Phantom Brain. 15.00
199 LD(c),Dracula's Daughter 15.00
200 GT,RA&DG(c),A:Johnny Peril,
  House on the Edge of Eternity 15.00
201 Do Unto Others. 15.00
202 JO,LD(c),Death Trap. 15.00
203 MK(c),Hang Down Your
  Head, Joe Mundy 15.00
204 DN,JKu(c),Twinkle, Twinkle
  Little Star 15.00
205 JkS,A:Johnny Peril,The Second
  Possession of Angela Lake . . 15.00
206 JkS,A:Johnny Peril,The
  Ultimate Assassin 15.00
207 JkS,A:Johnny Peril,Secret of
  the Second Star. 15.00
208 JkS,A:Johnny Peril,Factory
  of Fear 15.00
209 JkS,Game for the Ghastly . . . 15.00
210 Vampire of the Apes,Time
  Warp 15.00
211 A:Johnny Peril,The Temple
  of the 7 Stars 15.00
212 JkS,MK(c),A:Johnny Peril,The
  Adventure of the Angel's Smile 15.00
213 A:Johnny Peril,The Woman
  Who Died Forever. 15.00
214 JKu(c),Slaughterhouse Arena. 15.00
215 JKu(c),Is Someone
  Stalking Sandra 15.00
216 GP,JKu(c),Samurai Nightmare 15.00
217 ShM,DSp,EC(c),Dear Senator 15.00
218 KG,ECh&DG(c),I'll Remember
  You Yesterday 15.00
219 JKu(c),A Wild Tale. 15.00
220 ShM,JKu(c),The Strange
  Guide 15.00
221 SD,ShM,JKu(c),Em the
  Energy Monster. 15.00
222 KG,SD(c). 15.00

TALES OF THE UNEXPECTED
Oct., 2006
1 F:Spectre 4.00
2 . . . . 4.00
3 . . . . 4.00
4 . . . . 4.00
5 Malpractice 4.00
6 The Spectre 4.00
7 The Reality Breaker. 4.00
8 Finale. 4.00

TANGENT COMICS
(All Oct., 1997)
The Atom #1 DJu,PR,V:Fatal Five. . 3.00
The Flash #1, TDz,GFr,CaS 3.00
Doom Patrol #1 DJu,SCh, ... 3.00
Green Lantern #1 JeR,JWi,MGy . . 3.00
The Joker #1 KK,MHy, ... 3.00
Metal Men #1 MRz,MkK 3.00
Nightwing #1 JOs,JD 3.00
Sea Devils #1 KBk,VGi,TP 3.00
The Secret Six #1 CDi,TG, ... 3.00

TANGENT '98
(All June, 1998)
The Batman #1 DJu,KJ 2.25
JLA #1 DJu,DBk,V:UltraHumanites . 2.25
Joker's Wild #1 KK 2.25
Nightwing: Night Force #1 JOs 2.25

Tangent Nightwing #1
© DC Comics, Inc.

Powergirl #1 RMz 2.25
The Superman #1 Harvey Dent. . . . 2.25
Tales of the Green Lantern #1 . . . . 2.25
The Trials of the Flash #1,
  V:Plastic Man. 2.25
Wonder Woman #1 PDa,. 2.25

TANK GIRL
1995
1 Movie Adaptation 6.00

TANK GIRL: APOCALYPSE
1995–96
1 AIG,BBo(c) 3.00
2 AIG,BBo(c)Tank Girl Pregnant . . . 3.00
3 AIG,BBo(c) 3.00
4 AIG, finale. 3.00

TANK GIRL: THE ODYSSEY
DC/Vertigo, 1995
1 New Limited Series 3.00
2 BBo(c),Land of Milk & Honey . . . 3.00
3 I:The Sirens 3.00

TARZAN
April, 1972
(Prev. published by Gold Key)
207 JKu,O:Tarzan,pt.1 . . . . 100.00
208 thru 210 JKu,O:Tarzan,pt.2–4. 40.00
211 thru 229 . . . . @30.00
230 RH. 50.00
231 thru 235 . . . . @45.00
236 and 237 . . . . @20.00
238 giant-size. 30.00
239 thru 258 Feb., 1977. . . . . . . @20.00

TARZAN FAMILY
Nov.–Dec., 1975
(Prev.: Korak, Son of Tarzan)
60 B:Korak. 20.00
61 thru 66 Nov.–Dec.,1976 . . . . @15.00

TATTERED BANNERS
1998
1 (of 4) AIG(s),MMc 3.00
2 AIG&KG(s),MMc 3.00
3 AIG(s),MMc 3.00
4 AIG(s),MMc, conclusion. 3.00

TEAM TITANS
1992–94
1 KM,Total Chaos#3,A:New Titans,
  Deathstroke,V:Lord Chaos,
  BU:KGa,Killowat 4.00
1a thru 1d variant (c)s. . . . . @2.50
2 thru 24 . . . . @2.50
Ann.#1 I:Chimera. 3.50
Ann.#2 PJ,Elseworlds Story. 3.75

TEEN BEAT
Nov.–Dec., 1967
1 Monkees photo 175.00
Becomes:

TEEN BEAM
2 Monkees 150.00

TEEN TITANS
[1st Series]
Jan., 1966
1 NC,Titans join Peace Corps . . 500.00
2 NC,I:Garn Akaru 225.00
3 NC,I:Ding Dong Daddy 150.00
4 NC,A:Speedy 150.00
5 NC,I:Ant 150.00
6 NC,A:Beast Boy. 125.00
7 NC,I:Mad Mod 125.00
8 IN/JAb,I:Titans Copter 125.00
9 NC,A:Teen Titan Sweatshirts. . 125.00
10 NC,I:Bat-Bike 125.00
11 IN/NC A:Speedy 100.00
12 NC,in Spaceville 125.00
13 NC,Christmas story. 100.00
14 NC,I:Gargoyle. 100.00
15 NC,I:Capt. Rumble 100.00
16 NC,I:Dimension X 100.00
17 NC,A:Mad Mod 100.00
18 NC,1:Starfire (Russian). 100.00
19 GK,WW,J:Speedy 100.00
20 NA,NC J:Joshua 125.00
21 NA,NC,A:Hawk,Dove 125.00
22 NA,NC,O:Wondergirl. 125.00
23 GK,NC,N:Wondergirl. 75.00
24 GK,NC. 75.00
25 NC,I:Lilith,A:J.L.A 75.00
26 NC,I:Mal 75.00
27 NC,Nightmare in Space 75.00
28 NC,A:Ocean Master 75.00
29 NC,A:Ocean Master 75.00
30 NC,A:Aquagirl 75.00
31 NC,GT,A:Hawk,Dove 75.00
32 NC,I:Gnarrk. 40.00
33 GT,NS,A:Gnarrk 40.00
34 GT,NC. 40.00

Teen Titans #28 © DC Comics, Inc.

35 GT,NC,O:Mal.	40.00
36 GT,NC,JAp,V:Hunchback	40.00
37 GT,NC.	40.00
38 GT,NC.	40.00
39 GT,NC,Rep.Hawk & Dove.	40.00
40 NC,A:Aqualad.	40.00
41 NC,DC,Lilith Mystery	40.00
42 NC,Slaves o/t Emperor Bug	40.00
43 NC,Inherit the Howling Night	40.00
44 C:Flash (1976)	40.00
45 IN,V:Fiddler.	40.00
46 IN,A:Fiddler.	40.00
47 C:Two-Face.	20.00
48 I:Bumblebee,Harlequin, A:Two-Face.	40.00
49 R:Mal As Guardian	20.00
50 DH,I:Teen Titans West	35.00
51 DH,A:Teen Titans West.	20.00
52 DH,A:Teen Titans West.	20.00
53 O:Teen Titans, A:JLA	20.00

TEEN TITANS, THE
Aug., 1996

1 DJu(s),GP,Titan's Children, pt.1 (of 3).	5.00
2 DJu(s),GP,Titan's Children, pt.2,V:Prysm.	4.00
3 DJu(s),GP,Titan's Children, pt.3.	4.00
4 DJu(s),GP,Coming Out,pt.1, A:Robin.	3.00
5 DJu(s),GP,Coming Out,pt.2	3.00
6 DJu(s),DJu,GP,F:Risk	3.00
7 DJu(s),DJu,GP,The Atom quits team.	3.00
8 DJu(s),DJu,GP,J:Atom,V:Dark Nemesis.	3.00
9 DJu(s),DJu,GP,Lost World of Skartaris, pt.1	3.00
10 DJu(s),DJu,GP,Lost World of Skartaris, pt.2	3.00
11 DJu(s),DJu,GP,Lost World of Skartaris, concl.,A:Warlord.	3.00
12 DJu(s),DJu,GP,Original Titans, pt.1 (of 4) 48pg	4.00
13 DJu,GP,Original Titans, pt.2 Genesis tie-in	3.00
14 DJu,GP,Original Titans, pt.3	3.00
15 DJu,GP,Original Titans, pt.4	3.00
16 DJu,GP,aftermath	3.00
17 DJu,PJ,team reunites	3.00
18 DJu,PR	3.00
19 DJu,PJ,Millennium Giants, A:Superman Red.	3.00
20 DJu, night with the Titans	3.00
21 DJu,Titans Hunt,pt.1	3.00
22 DJu,Titans Hunt,pt.2	3.00
23 DJu,Titans Hunt,pt.3	3.00
24 DJu,Titans Hunt,pt.4	3.00
Ann.#1 Pulp Heroes (High-Adventure).	4.50
Ann.#1 (1967) 80-page, rep.	5.00

TEEN TITANS
July 2003

1 MMK	8.00
1a 2nd printing	3.50
2 MMK,Cyborg	4.00
3 MMK,	7.00
4 MMK,disobey order	4.00
5 MMk,Infighting	4.00
6 MMk,	2.50
7 MMk,F:Superman	2.50
8 TG,F:Raven	2.50
9 Raven Rising,pt.1	2.50
10 Raven Rising,pt.2	2.50
11 Raven Rising,pt.3	2.50
12 Raven Rising,pt.4	2.50
13 Raven Rising,pt.5	2.50
14 Beast Boys and Girls,pt.1	2.50
15 Beast Boys and Girls,pt.2	2.50

16 MMk,Lost to the Legion,pt.1	5.00
17 MMk,Titans Tomorrow,pt.1	5.00
18 MMk,Titans Tomorrow, pt.2	10.00
19 MMk,Titans Tomorrow, pt.3	5.00
20 TG,Nel,V:Warp,Electrocutioner	4.00
21 MMk,Lights Out,pt.1	8.00
22 MMK,Lights Out,pt. 2	5.00
23 MMK,Lights Out,pt. 3	5.00
24 MFm,The Insiders,x-over,pt.1	4.00
25 MFm,The Insiders,x-over,pt.3	3.50
26 TnD,F:Superboy,Raven	2.50
27 RLd,Cosmic chaos	2.50
28 RLd,Cosmic chaos, pt.2	2.50
29 V:Red Hood	2.50
30 Brother Blood Returns,pt.1	2.50
31 V:Brother Blood.	2.50
32 Infinite Crisis tie-in	2.50
33 MWm(s),Infinite Crisis tie-in	2.50
34 One Year Later, New Teen Titans,pt.1.	2.50
34a variant (c)	2.50
35 New Teen Titans, pt.2	2.50
36 New Teen Titans, pt.3	3.00
37 New Teen Titans, pt.4	3.00
38 Titans Around the World,pt.1	3.00
39 Titans Around the World,pt.2	3.00
40 Titans Around the World,pt.3	3.00
41 Titans Around the World, concl.	3.00
42 F:Kid Devil V:BLue Devil.	3.00
43 Titans East, pt.1	3.00
44 Titans East, pt.2	3.00
45 Titans East, pt.3	3.00
46 Titans East, pt.4	3.00
47 Countdown begins	3.00
48 Amazon's Attack tie-in.	3.00
49 Amazon's Attack x-over	3.00
50 48-pgs.	4.00
50a variant (c) (1:10)	4.00
51 Titans of Tomorrow	3.00
52 V:Starro.	3.00
Ann. #1 MWm(s), 48-pg.(2006)	5.00
Spec. Swingin' Elseworlds Spec.	6.00
Spec. Teen Titans/Legion.	4.00
Spec. Teen Titans Outsiders, Secret Files	6.00
Spec. Teen Titans/Secret Files 2005	5.00

TEEN TITANS GO!
Nov. 2003

1 F:Robin,Cyborg,Beast Boy	2.50
2 thru 48	@2.25

TEEN TITANS SPOTLIGHT
Aug., 1986

1 DCw,DG,Starfire Apartheid.	4.00
2 DCw,DG,Starfire Apartheid#2.	3.00
3 RA,Jericho.	3.00
4 RA,Jericho	3.00
5 RA,Jericho	3.00
6 RA,Jericho	3.00
7 JG,Hawk.	4.00
8 JG,Hawk.	3.00
9 Changeling.	3.00
10 EL,Aqualad And Mento.	3.00
11 JO,Brotherhood of Evil	3.00
12 EC,Wondergirl.	3.00
13 Cyborg	3.00
14 1st Nightwing/BatmanTeam-up	4.00
15 EL,Omega Men.	3.00
16 Thunder And Lightning	3.00
17 DH,Magennta	3.00
18 ATi,Aqualad,A:Aquaman	3.00
19 Starfire,A:Harbinger,Millennium X-over	3.00
20 RT(i),Cyborg	3.00
21 DSp,Flashback sty w/orig.Teen Titans.	3.00

Teen Titans Spotlight #9 ©
DC Comics, Inc.

TEMPEST
Mini-series Sept., 1996

1 (of 4) from Aquaman	2.25
2 new costume	2.25
3 O:Tempest	2.25
4 finale	2.25

TEMPUS FUGITIVE
1990

1 KSy,Time Travel,I:Ray 27	6.00
2 KSy,Viet Nam.	6.00
3 KSy,World War I.	6.00
4 KSy,final issue	6.00

TERMINAL CITY
DC/Vertigo, 1996–97

1 thru 3 DMt(s),MLr,	@2.50
4 DMt(s),MLr,I:Kid Gloves.	2.50
5 DMt(s),MLr,Missing link on the loose	2.50
6 DMt(s),MLr,	2.50
7 DMt(s),MLr,A:Lady in Red	2.50
8 DMt(s),MLr,	2.50
9 (of 9) DMt(s),MLr,finale	2.50
TPB rep. mini-series	20.00

TERMINAL CITY:
AERIAL GRAFFITI
DC/Vertigo, Sept., 1997

1 (of 5) DMt,MLr,MCo(c).	2.50
2 DMt,MLr,MCo(c),F:Cosmo Quinn	2.50
3 DMt,MLr,MCo(c),	2.50
4 DMt,MLr,MCo(c)	2.50

TESTAMENT
DC/Vertigo, Dec., 2005

1 LSh	3.00
2 LSh, Rain of Fire	3.00
3 LSh, Reprogramming.	3.00
4 LSh,Gargantuan war machines.	3.00
5 LSh,V:Demolition robots	3.00
6 LSh(c),West of Eden, pt.1	3.00
7 West of Eden, pt.2.	3.00
8 Down to Egypt, pt.1	3.00
9 Down to Egypt, pt.2	3.00
10 Down to Egypt, pt.3	3.00
11 F:Tyrone	3.00
12	3.00
13 Babel, pt.1.	3.00
14 Babel, pt.2.	3.00
15 Babel, pt.3.	3.00

3-D Batman Adventures #1a (1966)
© DC Comics Inc.

16 Babel, pt.4 . . . . 3.00
17 Blood Brothers, pt.1 . . . . 3.00
18 Blood Brothers, pt.2 . . . . 3.00
19 Exodus, pt.1 . . . . 3.00
20 Exodus, pt.2 . . . . 3.00

3-D ADVENTURES OF SUPERMAN
1953
N# O:Superman 1,600.00

3-D BATMAN ADVENTURES
1953, 1966
1 with Bat-glasses 1,600.00
1a A:Tommy Tomorrow (1966) . . 500.00

THE THREE MOUSEKETEERS
1956–60
1 . . . . 300.00
2 . . . . 150.00
3 . . . . 125.00
4 . . . . 125.00
5 . . . . 125.00
6 thru 10 . . . . @125.00
11 thru 20 . . . . @100.00
21 thru 26 . . . . @100.00

THRILLER
Nov., 1983
1 TVE 2.25
2 TVE,O:Thriller 2.25
3 TVE 2.25
4 TVE 2.25
5 TVE,DG,Elvis satire 2.25
6 TVE,Elvis satire 2.25
7 thru 10 TVE . . . . @2.25
11 & 12 AN . . . . @2.25

THRILLING COMICS
1999
1 CDi(s),RH,F:Hawkman &
 Wildcat 2.25

THRILLKILLER
Elseworlds 1997
1 HC(s),DIB,F:Robin and Batgirl . . 3.50
2 HC(s),DIB 3.00
3 HC(s),DIB,conl. 3.00

THRILLKILLERS '62
Feb., 1998
GN HC,DIB 5.00

TIMBER WOLF
1992–93
1 AG(i),V:Thrust 2.25
2 V:Captain Flag 2.25
3 AG(i),V:Creeper 2.25
4 AG(i),V:Captain Flag 2.25
5 AG(i),V:Dominators,Capt.Flag . . 2.25

TIME BREAKERS
DC/Helix, 1997
1 (of 5) RaP(s),CWn,time
 paradoxes created 2.50
2 RaP(s),CWn, ... 2.50
3 RaP(s),CWn,expedition to 20th
 century England 2.50
4 RaP(s),CWn,Angela travels back
 in time 2.50
5 RaP(s),CWn,final issue 2.50

TIME MASTERS
Feb., 1990
1 ATi,O:Rip Hunter,A:JLA 2.50
2 ATi,A:Superman 2.25
3 ATi,A:Jonah Hex, Cave Carson . . 2.25
4 thru 8 ATi, ... @2.25

TIME WARP
Oct.–Nov., 1979
1 JAp,RB,SD,MK(c),DN,TS 20.00
2 DN,JO,TS,HC,SD,MK(c),GK . . . 15.00
3 DN,SD,MK(c),TS 15.00
4 MN,SD,MK(c),DN 15.00
5 DN,MK(c),July, 1980 . . . . 12.00

TITANS
1999
1 MBu, new team, two covers 3.50
2 MBu,A:Superman 3.00
3 MBu 3.00
4 MBu,V:Goth 3.00
5 MBu,A:Siren 3.00
6 MBu,A:Green Lantern 3.00
7 MBu,Velocity 10, pt.1 . . . . 3.00
8 MBu,Velocity 10, pt.2 . . . . 3.00
9 Day of Judgment x-over 3.00
10 MBu,F:Changeling
 & Deathstroke 3.00
11 MBu. 3.00
12 MBu,This Immortal Coil,pt.3 . . . 3.50
13 internal fight 3.00
14 to Scotland 3.00
15 MBu,pt.1 . . . . 3.00
16 MBu,V:Gargoyle 3.00
17 ALa,into space 3.00
18 ALa,into space,pt.2 . . . . 3.00
19 ALa,into space,pt.3 . . . . 3.00
20 ALa,end of Cyborg 3.00
21 PaP,Hangmen 3.00
22 PaP,Arsenal vs. Deathstroke . . . 3.00
23 PaP,Who's Troia?,pt.1 . . . . 3.00
24 PaP,Who's Troia?,pt.2 . . . . 3.00
25 MWn,GP,48-page 4.00
26 PaP,V:Shockwave 3.00
27 PaP,F:Cheshire,Epsilon 3.00
28 PaP,The All-Nighter 3.00
29 PaP,tower of troublemakers 3.00
30 JP,Sins of the Past 3.00
31 JP,V:Theta 3.00
32 V:Dakota Jameson 3.00
33 V:Theta 3.00
34 Cheshire Smile,Last Laugh 3.00
35 F:Beast Boy & Flamebird 3.00
36 V:Wildebeests 3.00
37 BKi,in the Orphanage 3.00
38 BKi,V:Epsilon,final stand 3.00

39 BKi,V:Dark Nemesis 3.00
40 BKi,F:The Favored 3.00
41 PGr,F:Nikki 3.00
42 BKi,Chemical World,pt.1 . . . . . . 3.00
43 BKi,Chemical World,pt.2 . . . . . . 3.00
44 BKi,JmP,Chemical World,pt.3 . . . 3.00
45 BKi,JmP,F:Damage 3.00
46 BKi,JmP,F:Damag,Jesse 3.00
47 TPe,BKi,PGr,JmP 3.00
48 TPe,BKi,JmP,Murder,pt.1 . . . . . 3.00
49 TPe,BKi,JmP,Murder,pt.2 . . . . . 3.00
50 TPe,JmP,final issue 3.00
Ann.#1 Planet DC 4.00
Spec. Secret Files #1 . . . . 5.50
Spec. Secret Files #2 . . . . 5.50
GN Scissors, Paper, Stone, manga
 style (1997) 5.50

TITANS SELL-OUT SPECIAL
1 SE,AV,I:Teeny Titans,
 w/Nightwing poster 3.75

TITANS, THE/LEGION OF SUPER-HEROES: UNIVERSE ABLAZE
Jan., 2000
1 (of 4) DJu,PJ 5.00
2 thru 4 DJu,PJ . . . . @5.00

TITANS, THE/ YOUNG JUSTICE: GRADUATION DAY
May 2003
1 (of 3) 20.00
2 Indigo 11.00
3 Concl. 13.00

TOE TAGS FEATURING GEORGE ROMERO
2004
1 . . . . 3.00
2 thru 6 . . . . @3.00

TOMAHAWK
1950
1 Prisoner Called Tomahawk . . 2,500.00
2 FF(4pgs),Four Boys
 Against the Frontier 1,000.00
3 Warpath 750.00
4 Tomahawk Wanted: Dead
 or Alive 750.00

Tomahawk #2
© DC Comics Inc.

5 The Girl Who Was Chief 750.00
6 Tomahawk-King of the Aztecs . 600.00
7 Punishment of Tomahawk 600.00
8 The King's Messenger 600.00
9 The Five Doomed Men 600.00
10 Frontied Sabotage 600.00
11 Girl Who Hated Tomahawk . . . 400.00
12 Man From Magic Mountain . . . 400.00
13 Dan Hunter's Rival 400.00
14 The Frontier Tinker 400.00
15 The Wild Men of
  Wigwam Mountain 400.00
16 Treasure of the Angelique. . . . 400.00
17 Short-Cut to Danger 400.00
18 Bring In M'Sieur Pierre 400.00
19 The Lafayette Volunteers 400.00
20 NC(c),The Retreat of
  Tomahawk 400.00
21 NC(c),The Terror of the
  Wrathful Spirit 300.00
22 CS(c),Admiral Tomahawk 300.00
23 CS(c),The Indian Chief
  from Oxford 300.00
24 NC(c),Adventure In the
  Everglades. 300.00
25 NC(c),The Star-Gazer of
  Freemont 300.00
26 NC(c),Ten Wagons For
  Tomahawk 300.00
27 NC(c),Frontier Outcast 300.00
28 I:Lord Shilling 325.00
29 Conspiracy of Wounded Bear. 350.00
30 The King of the Thieves 300.00
31 NC(c),The Buffalo Brave
  From Misty Mountain. 300.00
32 NC(c),The Clocks That
  Went to War. 300.00
33 The Paleface Tribe 300.00
34 The Capture of General
  Washington 300.00
35 Frontier Feud 300.00
36 NC(c),A Cannon for Fort
  Reckless 300.00
37 NC(c),Feathered Warriors. . . . 300.00
38 The Frontier Zoo. 300.00
39 The Redcoat Trickster. 300.00
40 Fearless Fettle-Daredevil 300.00
41 The Captured Chieftain. 300.00
42 The Prisoner Tribe 300.00
43 Tomahawk's Little Brother. . . . 300.00
44 The Brave Named Tomahawk 300.00
45 The Last Days of Chief Tory . . 300.00
46 The Chief With 1,000 Faces . . 200.00
47 The Frontier Rain-Maker. 200.00
48 Indian Twin Trouble. 200.00
49 The Unknown Warrior 200.00
50 The Brave Who Was Jinxed . . 200.00
51 General Tomahawk. 200.00
52 Tom Thumb of the Frontier . . . 200.00
53 The Four-Footed Renegade . . 200.00
54 Mystery of the 13th Arrows . . 200.00
55 Prisoners of the Choctaw 200.00
56 The Riddle of the
  Five Little Indians 200.00
57 The Strange Fight
  at Fort Bravo 250.00
58 Track of the Mask 150.00
59 The Mystery Prisoner of
  Lost Island 150.00
60 The Amazing Walking Fort . . . 150.00
61 Tomahawk's Secret Weapons. 125.00
62 Strongest Man in the World . . 125.00
63 The Frontier Super Men 125.00
64 The Outcast Brave 125.00
65 Boy Who Wouldn't Be Chief . . 125.00
66 DD&SMo(c),A Trap For
  Tomahawk 125.00
67 DD&SMo(c),Frontier Sorcerer 125.00
68 DD&SMo(c),Tomahawk's
  Strange Ally 125.00
69 DD&SMo(c),Tracker-King
  of the Wolves. 125.00

Tomahawk #55
© DC Comics, Inc.

70 DD&SMo(c),Three Tasks
  for Tomahawk 125.00
71 DD&SMo(c),The Boy Who
  Betrayed His Country 125.00
72 DD&SMo(c),The Frontier Pupil 125.00
73 DD&SMo(c),The Secret of
  the Indian Sorceress 125.00
74 DD&SMo(c),The Great
  Paleface Masquerade 125.00
75 DD&SMo(c),The Ghost of
  Lord Shilling. 125.00
76 DD&SMo(c),The Totem-Pole
  Trail 125.00
77 DD&SMo(c),The Raids of
  the One-Man Tribe 125.00
78 DD&SMo(c),The Menace
  of the Mask 100.00
79 DD&SMo(c),Eagle Eye's
  Debt of Honor 100.00
80 DD&SMo(c),The Adventures
  of Tracker 75.00
81 The Strange Omens of
  the Indian Seer 75.00
82 The Son of the Tracker. 75.00
83 B:Tomahawk Rangers,
  Against the Tribe 75.00
84 There's a Coward Among
  the Rangers 75.00
85 The Wispering War. 75.00
86 Rangers vs. King Colossus . . 65.00
87 The Secrets of Sgt.
  Witch Doctor 65.00
88 The Rangers Who Held
  Back the Earth. 65.00
89 The Terrible Tree-Man 65.00
90 The Prisoner In The Pit. 65.00
91 The Tribe Below the Earth . . . 65.00
92 The Petrified Sentry of
  Peaceful Valley 65.00
93 The Return of King Colosso . . 65.00
94 Rip Van Ranger 65.00
95 The Tribe Beneath the Sea. . . 65.00
96 The Ranger Killers 65.00
97 The Prisoner Behind the
  Bull's-Eye. 65.00
98 The Pied Piper Rangers 65.00
99 The Rangers vs.ChiefCobweb . 65.00
100 The Weird Water-Tomahawk . 75.00
101 Tomahawk, Enemy Spy 50.00
102 The Dragon Killers 50.00
103 The Frontier Frankenstein . . 50.00
104 The Fearful Freak of
  Dunham's Dungeon. 50.00
105 The Attack of the Gator God. . 50.00
106 The Ghost of Tomahawk. . . . 50.00

107 Double-Cross of the
  Gorilla Ranger. 50.00
108 New Boss For the Rangers . . 50.00
109 The Caveman Ranger 50.00
110 Tomahawk Must Die 50.00
111 Vengeance of the Devil-Dogs . 50.00
112 The Rangers vs. Tomahawk . . 50.00
113 The Mad Miser of
  Carlisle Castle 50.00
114 The Terrible Power of
  Chief Iron Hands 50.00
115 The Deadly Flaming Ranger. . 50.00
116 NA(c),The Last Mile of
  Massacre Trail 50.00
117 NA(c),Rangers'Last Stand. . . . 50.00
118 NA(c),Tomahawk, Guilty
  of Murder. 50.00
119 NA(c),Bait For a Buzzard 50.00
120 NC(c),The Coward Who
  Lived Forever 50.00
121 NA(c),To Kill a Ranger 50.00
122 IN(c),Must the Brave Die 50.00
123 NA(c),The Stallions of Death . 50.00
124 NA(c),The Valley of
  No Return 50.00
125 NA(c),A Chief's Feather
  For Little Bear 50.00
126 NA(c),The Baron of
  Gallows Hill 50.00
127 NA(c),The Devil is Waiting . . . 50.00
128 NA(c),Rangers-Your 9
  Lives For Mine. 50.00
129 NA(c),Treachery at
  Thunder Ridge. 50.00
130 NA(c),Deathwatch at
  Desolation Valley. 50.00
131 JKu(c),B:Son of Tomahawk,
  Hang Him High 50.00
132 JKu(c),Small Eagle...Brother
  Hawk 30.00
133 JKu(c),Scalp Hunter 30.00
134 JKu(c),The Rusty Ranger 30.00
135 JKu(c),Death on Ghost
  Mountain 30.00
136 JKu(c),A Piece of Sky 40.00
137 JKu(c),Night of the Knife. . . . 40.00
138 JKu(c),A Different Kind
  of Christmas 40.00
139 JKu(c),Death Council 50.00
140 Jku(c),The Rescue 40.00

TOR
May-June, 1975

1 JKu,O:Tor. 20.00
2 thru 6, Tor reprints . . . . @12.00

TOTAL JUSTICE
Sept., 1996

1 thru 3 CPr(s),RBe,DG, toy
  line tie-in . . . . @2.25

TOTAL RECALL
1990

1 Movie Adaption 3.00

TOUCH
DC Focus Apr. 2004

1 Rory Goodman, Las Vegas 2.50
2 thru 6 . . . . @2.50

TRANSMETROPOLITAN
DC/Helix, July, 1997

1 WEI,DaR,JeM, gonzo journalism
  in 21st century. 15.00
2 WEI,DaR,Angels 8 district 8.00
3 WEI,DaR, riot in Angels 8 . . . . . 7.00
4 WEI,DaR, Vs President of US . . . 4.00
5 WEI,DaR, Watches TV 4.00
6 WEI,DaR,evangelicals 4.00
7 WEI,DaR 4.00

8 WEI,DaR,AnotherColdMorning . . 4.00
9 WEI,DaR,Wild in the Country . . . 3.00
10 WEI,DaR,Freeze Me with
   Your Kiss, pt.1 . . . . 3.00
11 WEI,DaR,Freeze Me, pt.2 . . . . . 3.00
12 WEI,DaR,Freeze Me, pt.3 . . . . . 3.00
13 WEI,DaR,JaL(c),Year of the
   Bastard, pt.1 . . . . 3.00
14 WEI,DaR,JaL(c),Bastard,pt.2 . . 3.00
15 WEI,DaR,JaL(c),Bastard,pt.3 . . 3.00
16 WEI,DaR,Bastard,pt.4 . . . . 3.00
17 WEI,DaR,Bastard,pt.5 . . . . 3.00
18 WEI,DaR,Bastard, concl. 3.00
19 WEI,DaR,New Scum,pt.1 . . . . . . 3.00
20 WEI,DaR,New Scum,pt.2 . . . . . . 3.00
21 WEI,DaR,New Scum,pt.3 . . . . . . 2.50
22 WEI,DaR,New Scum,pt.4 . . . . . . 2.50
23 WEI,DaR,New Scum,pt.5 . . . . . . 2.50
24 WEI,DaR,New Scum,pt.6 . . . . . . 2.50
25 WEI,DaR,JLe(c),Days in
   the City #1 . . . . 2.50
26 WEI,DaR,RyR,JLe(c),Days in
   the City #2 . . . . 2.50
27 WEI,DaR,RyR,JLe(c) 2.50
28 WEI,DaR,RyR,LonelyCity,pt.1. . . 2.50
29 WEI,DaR,RyR,LonelyCity,pt.2. . . 2.50
30 WEI,DaR,RyR,LonelyCity,pt.3. . . 2.50
31 WEI,DaR,RyR,F:Spider. 2.50
32 WEI,DaR,RyR, ... 2.50
33 WEI,DaR,RyR. 2.50
34 WEI,DaR,RyR,Gouge Away,pt.1. 2.50
35 WEI,DaR,RyR,Gouge Away,pt.2. 2.50
36 WEI,DaR,RyR,Gouge Away,pt.3. 2.50
37 WEI,DaR,Back to Basics,pt.1 . . . 2.50
38 WEI,DaR,Back to Basics,pt.2 . . . 2.50
39 WEI,DaR,Back to Basics,pt.3 . . . 2.50
40 WEI,DaR,Streets atNight,pt.1 . . . 2.50
41 WEI,DaR,Streets atNight,pt.2 . . . 2.50
42 WEI,DaR,Streets atNight,pt.3 . . . 2.50
43 WEI,DaR,Dirge,pt.1 . . . . 2.50
44 WEI,DaR,Dirge,pt.2. . . . . 2.50
45 WEI,DaR,Dirge,pt.3. . . . . 2.50
46 WEI,DaR,Dirge aftermath 2.50
47 WEI,DaR,A Disaster Zone 2.50
48 WEI,DaR,Year Four begins. 2.50
49 WEI,DaR,rebuild Spider's case. . 2.50
50 WEI,DaR,Filthy Assistants 2.50
51 WEI,DaR,F:Mitchell Royce 2.50
52 WEI,DaR,The Cure,pt.1 . . . . 2.50
53 WEI,DaR,The Cure,pt.2 . . . . 2.50
54 WEI,DaR,The Cure,pt.3 . . . . 2.50
55 WEI,DaR,Vita Severn Zone 2.50
56 WEI,DaR,Martial law. 2.50
57 WEI,DaR,White House siege . . . 2.50
58 WEI,DaR,martial law. 2.50
59 WEI,DaR,final meeting 2.50
60 WEI,DaR,final issue 2.50
GN I Hate it Here. 6.00
GN Filth of the City 6.00

TRENCHCOAT BRIGADE
DC/Vertigo, 1999
1 (of 4) JNR(s),F:John Constantine,
   Mister E, Dr.Occult, Phantom
   Stranger 2.50
2 JNR 2.50
3 JNR 2.50
4 JNR, conclusion. 2.50

TRIALS OF SHAZAM
Aug., 2006
1 (of 12) HPo, The Boy & The Man 3.00
2 thru 4 HPo 3.00
5 thru 9 HPo . . . . @3.00

TRIGGER
DC/Vertigo, Dec., 2004
1 JWk,F:Deirdre Myers. 3.00
2 JWk 3.00
3 JWk 3.00
4 JWk 3.00

5 JWk 3.00
6 JWk, concl. 3.00
7 JWk, I:Leonard. 3.00
8 JWk 3.00

TRIUMPH
[Mini-Series], 1995
1 From Zero Hour. 2.25
2 Teamates Peril. 2.25
3 V:Mind Readers. 2.25

TROUBLE MAGNET
Dec., 1999
1 (of 4) KPI, F:robot whose mind
   has been stolen. 2.50
2 KPI 2.50
3 KPI 2.50
4 KPI,concl. 2.50

TV SCREEN CARTOONS
See: REAL SCREEN COMICS

2020 VISIONS
DC/Vertigo, April, 1997
1 (of 12) the Disunited States
   of America 2.25
2 JaD(s), ... 2.25
3 JaD(s), ... 2.25
4 JaD(s),WaP,La Tormenta,pt.1 . . . 2.25
5 JaD(s),WaP,La Tormenta,pt.2 . . . 2.25
6 JaD(s),WaP,La Tormenta,pt.3 . . . 2.25
7 JaD(s),Renegade,pt.1 . . . . 2.25
8 JaD(s),Renegade,pt.2 . . . . 2.25
9 JaD(s),Renegade,pt.3 . . . . 2.25
10 JaD(s),Repro-Man,pt.1 . . . . 2.25
11 JaD(s),Repro-Man,pt.2 . . . . 2.25
12 JaD(s),Repro-Man,pt.3 . . . . 2.25

Twilight #2
© DC Comics Inc.

TWILIGHT
1990–91
1 JL,Last Frontier 5.50
2 JL,K.SorensenVs.T.Tomorrow . . . 5.00
3 JL,K.SorensenVs.T.Tomorrow . . . 5.00

UNAUTHORIZED BIO OF LEX LUTHOR
1989
1 EB 4.00

UNCLE SAM
DC/Vertigo, Nov, 1997
GN 1 (of 2) AxR. 5.00
GN 2 AxR. 5.00
TPB 10.00

UNCLE SAM AND THE FREEDOM FIGHTERS
July, 2006
1 (of 8) JP, Shade task force 3.00
2 JP, Wanted: Uncle Sam. 3.00
3 JP, Arizona Desert 3.00
4 JP. 3.00
5 JP. 3.00
6 thru 8JP . . . . @3.00
Vol. 2, 2007
1 (of 8) JP. 3.00
2 JP. 3.00

UNDERWORLD
Dec., 1987
1 EC,New Yorks Finest. 2.50
2 EC,A:Black Racer 2.50
3 EC,V:Black Racer 2.50
4 EC,final issue. 2.50

UNDERWORLD UNLEASHED
1995–96
1 PWa,F:Neron. 5.00
2 PWa,Neron Vs.Green Lantern. . . 4.00
3 PWa,conclusion 4.00
Abyss—Hell's Sentinel 1-shot 3.00
Apokolips-Dark Uprising 1-shot . . . 3.00
Batman—Devil's Asylum 1-shot
   AIG,BSz 3.00
Patterns of Fear 1-shot 3.00

UNEXPECTED, THE
See: TALES OF THE UNEXPECTED

UNKNOWN SOLDIER
See: STAR SPANGLED

UNKNOWN SOLDIER
April, 1988
1 True Origin revealed,Viet
   Nam 1970 . . . . 4.00
2 Origin contd.,Iran 1977 . . . . 3.00
3 Origin contd.Afghanistan1982 . . . 3.00
4 Nicaragua 3.00
5 Nicaragua contd. 3.00
6 . . . . 3.00
7 Libia 3.00
8 Siberia, U.S.S.R. 3.00
9 North Korea 1952 . . . . 3.00
10 C.I.A. 3.00
11 C.I.A., Army Intelligence 3.00
12 final issue,1989. . . . . 3.00

UNKNOWN SOLDIER
DC/Vertigo, Feb., 1997
1 (of 4) GEn(s),KPI,F:maverick
   CIA agent. 7.00
2 GEn(s),KPI,search for Unknown
   Soldier continues. 5.00
3 GEn(s),KPI,search for Unknown
   Soldier continues. 5.00
4 GEn(s),KPI,intrigue, finale 5.00
TPB series rep. 13.00

UN-MEN, THE
Vertigo, Aug., 2007
1 Get Your Freak On, pt.1 . . . . 3.00
2 Get Your Freak On, pt.2 . . . . 3.00
3 Get Your Freak On, pt.3 . . . . 3.00

Untold Legend of Batman #1
© DC Comics, Inc.

UNTOLD LEGEND
OF BATMAN
July, 1980

1 JA,JBy,(1st DC work)O:Batman . 6.00
2 JA,O:Joker&Robin 4.50
3 JA,O:Batgirl 4.50

USER
DC/Vertigo, Jan., 2001

1 (of 3) 48-page 6.00
2 JBo,SeP,48-page 6.00
3 JBo,SeP,48-page 6.00

V
(TV Adaptation)
Feb., 1985

1 CI/TD 3.00
2 thru 5 CI/TD . . . . @2.25
6 thru 16 CI/TD . . . . @2.25
17 & 18 DG . . . . @2.25

VALOR
1992–94

1 N:Valor,A:Lex Luthor Jr 3.00
2 MBr,AG,V:Supergirl 2.50
3 MBr,AG,V:Lobo 2.50
4 MBr,AG,V:Lobo 2.50
5 MBr,A:Blasters 2.50
6 A:Blasters,V:Kanjar Ru 2.50
7 A:Blasters 2.50
8 AH(c),V:The Unimaginable 2.50
9 AH(c),PCu,A:Darkstar 2.50
10 AH(c),V:Unimaginable 2.50
11 A:Legionnaires 2.50
12 AH(c),B:D.O.A. 3.00
13 AH(c),D:Valor's Mom 3.00
14 AH(c),A:JLA,Legionnaires 2.50
15 SI(c),D.O.A #4. . . . . 2.50
16 CDo,D.O.A #5. . . . . 2.50
17 CDo,LMc,D:Valor 2.50
18 A:Legionnaires 2.50
19 CDo,A:Legionnaires,V:Glorith . . 2.50
20 CDo,A:Wave Rider 2.50
21 . . . . 2.50
22 End of an Era,pt.2 . . . . 2.50
23 Zero Hour 2.50

VAMPS
DC/Vertigo, 1994–95

1 BB(c) 3.00

2 thru 6 BB(c) . . . . @3.00
TPB 10.00

VAMPS:
HOLLYWOOD & VEIN
DC/Vertigo, 1996

1 F:Mink 2.50
2 . . . . 2.50
3 I:Maggot 2.50
4 F:Mink,Screech 2.50
5 off to rescue Hugh Evans (of 6) . 2.50
6 . . . . 2.50

VAMPS: PUMPKIN TIME
DC/Vertigo, 1998

1 (of 3) Halloween mini-series 2.50
2 thru 3 . . . . @2.50

VERMILLION
DC/Helix, Aug., 1996

1 ADv,MKu(c) Lucius Shepard
  story. 2.50
2 ADv,MKu(c) Jonathan Cave's
  cover blown 2.50
3 ADv,riot aboard space ship,
  Ildiko's tale. 2.50
4 ADv,Starship's engines run wild . . 2.50
5 ADv 2.50
6 ADv,Creation of Vermillion 2.50
7 ADv,Jonathan Cave discovers
  hiding place of enemy 2.50
8 ADv,Joyland 2.50
9 GEr, the library in Kaia Mortai . . . 2.50
10 GEr, Lord Iron and Lady
  Manganese, pt.2 . . . . 2.50
11 GEr,Lord Iron and Lady
  Manganese, concl. 2.50
12 final issue 2.50

VERTICAL
DC/Vertigo, Dec. 2003

Spec. MiA,64-pg. 5.00

VERTIGO GALLERY:
DREAMS AND
NIGHTMARES
1995

1 Various artists 3.50

VERTIGO JAM
1993

1 GF(c),NGa(s),ANo(s),PrM(s),GEn(s),
  JaD(s),KN,SDi,SEa,NyC(s),EiS,PhH,
  KDM(i),SeP,MiA,RaP(s),MPn(i),
  Vertigo Short Stories 4.50

VERTIGO POP!
TOKYO
DC/Vertigo, July, 2002

1 (of 4) by Seth Fisher 3.00
2 thru 4 . . . . @3.00

LONDON
DC/Vertigo, Nov., 2002

1 (of 4) PrM,PBd 3.00
2 thru 4 PrM,PBd . . . . @3.00

BANGKOK
DC/Vertigo, May 2003

1 (of 4) 3.00
2 thru 4 . . . . @3.00

VERTIGO PREVIEW
1992

Preview of new Vertigo titles,
  new Sandman story. 2.25

VERTIGO SECRET FILES:
HELLBLAZER
Jan., 2005

1 rep. 5.00

VERTIGO VERITE:
HELL ETERNAL
Feb., 1998

1-shot JaD,SeP 7.00

THE SYSTEM

1 thru 3 . . . . @3.00
GN Seven Miles a Second 8.00

THE UNSEEN HAND
DC/Vertigo, 1996

1 thru 3 TLa . . . . @2.50
4 TLa, final issue 2.50

DR. OCCULT

1 F:Dr. Occult 4.00

DR. THIRTEEN
DC/Vertigo, July, 1998

GN evil artificial intelligence. 6.00

VERTIGO VISIONS:
THE GEEK
1993

1 RaP(s),MiA,V:Dr.Abuse 4.25

PHANTOM STRANGER
1993

1 AaK(s),GyD,The Infernal House . 3.75

THE EATERS
1995

1 I:The Quills. 5.00

TOMAHAWK
DC/Vertigo, May, 1998

GN RaP,TY 5.00

VEXT
1999

1 KG,MMK,MkM 2.50
2 th`ru 6 KG,MMK,MkM. . . . . @2.50

V FOR VENDETTA
Sept., 1988

1 Reps.Warrior Mag(U.K.),I:V,
  A:M.Storm (Moore scripts). 6.00
2 Murder Spree. 5.00
3 Govt. Investigators close in 4.00
4 T.V. Broadcast take-over 4.00
5 Govt.Corruption Expose 4.00
6 Evey in Prison 4.00
7 Evey released 4.00
8 Search for V,A:Finch 4.00
9 V:Finch 4.00
10 D:V 4.00
TPB 1990 . . . . 25.00

VIGILANTE
Oct., 1983

1 KP,DG,F:Adrian Chase 3.50
2 KP 3.00
3 KP,Cyborg 2.50
4 DN,V:Exterminator 2.50
5 KP 2.50
6 O:Vigilante 3.00
7 O:Vigilante 3.00
8 thru 16 . . . . @2.50
17 Moore 4.00
18 Moore 4.00
19 thru 49 . . . . @2.50
50 KSy(c)D:Vigilante 3.00
Ann.#1 . . . . 3.00
Ann.#2 V:Cannon. 2.50

Vigilante #1 © DC Comics, Inc.

VIGILANTE
Sept., 2005
1 (of 6) 3.00
2 thru 6 . . . . @3.00

VIGILANTE: CITY LIGHTS, PRAIRIE JUSTICE
1995–96
1 JeR,MCo,(of 4) 2.50
2 JeR,V:Bugsy Siegel. 2.50
3 JeR 2.50
4 finale 2.50

VILLAINS UNITED
May, 2005
1 (of 6) F:Mockingbird. 10.00
1a 2nd printing 4.00
2 . . . . 3.50
2a 2nd printing 3.00
3 The Six. 3.00
4 . . . . 3.00
5 Catman vs. Deadshot 3.00
6 F:Mockingbird, concl. 3.00
TPB Villains United 13.00

VIMANARAMA!
DC/Vertigo, Feb., 2005
1 (of 3) GMo(s),PBd 3.00
2 GMo(s),PBd 3.00
3 GMo(s),PBd 3.00
TPB Vimanarama, GMo(s),PBd. . . 13.00

VINYL UNDERGROUND, THE
Vertigo, Oct., 2007
1 Snogging for England 3.00

VIPER
1994
1 Based on the TV Show 2.25
2 . . . . 2.25
3 . . . . 2.25
4 final issue. 2.25

WANDERERS
June, 1988
1 I:New Team 3.00
2 thru 13 . . . . @3.00

WANTED: THE WORLD'S MOST DANGEROUS VILLIANS
July-Aug., 1972
1 GK,rep. Batman,Green Lantern. 50.00
2 CI,Batman/Joker/Penguin 40.00
3 JK,MMe,Dr. Fate 30.00
4 Green Lantern 30.00
5 GK,Dollman/Green Lantern . . . 30.00
6 JK,Starman 30.00
7 JK,MMe,Hawkman/Flash. 30.00
8 Dr. Fate/Flash 30.00
9 Sandman/Superman 30.00

WARLORD
Jan., 1976
1 MGr,O:Warlord. 40.00
2 MGr,I:Machiste. 20.00
3 MGr,War Gods of Skartaris 15.00
4 MGr,Duel of the Titans. 15.00
5 MGr,The Secret of Skartaris . . . 15.00
6 MGr,I:Mariah,Stryker 9.00
7 MGr,O:Machiste. 9.00
8 MGr,A:Skyra 9.00
9 MGr,N:Warlord 9.00
10 MGr,I:Ashiya 9.00
11 MGr,rep.1st Issue special #8 . . . 6.00
12 MGr,I:Aton. 6.00
13 MGr,D:Stryker 6.00
14 MGr,V:Death 6.00
15 MGr,I:Joshua. 6.00
16 MGr,I:Saaba 6.00
17 MGr,Citadel of Death 6.00
18 MGr,I:Shadow 6.00
19 MGr,Wolves of the Steppes . . . 6.00
20 MGr,I:Joshua clone. 7.00
21 MGr,D:Joshua clone,Shadow . . . 5.00
22 MGr,Beast in the Tower 10.00
23 MGr,Children of Ba'al 5.00
24 MGr,I:Iigia 5.00
25 MGr,I:Ahir 5.00
26 MGr,The Challenge 5.00
27 MGr,Atlantis Dying 5.00
28 MGr,I:Wizard World. 5.00
29 MGr,I:Mongo Ironhand 5.00
30 MGr,C:Joshua. 5.00
31 MGr,Wing over Shamballah 5.00
32 MGr,I:Shakira 5.00
33 MGr,Birds of Prey,A:Shakira . . . 5.00
34 MGr,Sword of the Sorceror,
   I:Hellfire 5.00
35 MGr,C:Mike Grell 5.00
36 MGr,Interlude 5.00
37 MGr,JSn,I:Firewing,B:Omac 6.00
38 MGr,I:Jennifer,A:Omac 5.00
39 MGr,JSn,Feast of Agravar 5.00
40 MGr,N:Warlord 5.00
41 MGr,A:Askir. 5.00
42 MGr,JSn,A:Tara,Omac 5.00
43 MGr,JSn,Berserk'A:Omac. 5.00
44 MGr,The Gamble 5.00
45 MGr,Nightmare in Vista
   Vision,A:Omac 5.00
46 MGr,D:Shakira 5.00
47 MGr,I:Mikola,E:Omac 5.00
48 MGr,EC,TY,I:Arak,Claw(B) 5.00
49 MGr,TY,A:Shakira,E:Claw 3.00
50 MGr,By Fire and Ice 3.00
51 MGr,TY,rep.#1,
   I(B):Dragonsword 3.00
52 MGr,TY,Back in the U.S.S.R. . . . 3.00
53 MT,TY,Sorcerer's Apprentice . . . 3.00
54 MT,Sorceress Supreme,
   E:Dragonsword 3.00
55 MT,Have a Nice Day 3.00
56 MT,JD,I:Gregmore,(B):Arion . . . 3.00
57 MT,The Two Faces of
   Travis Morgan 3.00
58 MT,O:Greamore 3.00
59 MGr,A:Joshua. 3.00

60 JD,Death Dual 3.00
61 JD,A:Greamore. 3.00
62 JD,TMd,A:Mikola,E:Arion 3.00
63 JD,RR,I(B):Barren Earth. 4.00
64 DJu,RREIsewhere. 3.00
65 DJu,RR,A:Wizard World,
   No Barren Earth 3.00
66 DJuWizard World,
   No Barren Earth 3.00
67 DJu,RR,The Mark. 3.00
68 DJu,RR 3.00
69 DJu,RR 3.00
70 DJu,Outback 3.00
71 DJu/DA,The Journey Back
   No Barren Earth 3.00
72 DJu,DA,I:Scarhart,No Barren
   Earth 3.00
73 DJ,DA,Cry Plague. 3.00
74 DJu,No Barren Earth 3.00
75 DJu,All Dreams Must Pass
   No Barren Earth 3.00
76 DJu,DA,RR,A:Sarga 3.00
77 DJu,RR,Let My People Go . . 3.00
78 DJu,RR,Doom's Mouth. 3.00
79 PB,RM,Paradox,No Barren
   Earth 3.00
80 DJu,DA,RR,Future Trek 3.00
81 DJu,DA,RR,Thief's Magic 3.00
82 DJu,DA,RR,Revolution 3.00
83 DJu,RR,All the President's
   Men 3.00
84 DJu,DA,RR,Hail to the Chief . . . 3.00
85 DJu,RR,The Price of Change . . . 3.00
86 DJ,DA,No Barren Earth 3.00
87 DJu,RB,RR,I:Hawk 3.00
88 DJu,RB,RR,I:Patch,E:Barren
   Earth 3.00
89 RB,I:Sabertooth 3.00
90 RB,Demon's of the Past 3.00
91 DJu,DA,I:Maddox,O:Warlord
   O:Jennifer 3.00
92 NKu,Evil in Ebony. 3.00
93 RR,A:Sabertooth. 3.00
94 Assassin's Prey 3.00
95 AKu,Dragon's Doom 3.00
96 Nightmare Prelude 3.00
97 RB,A:Saaba,D:Scarhart 3.00
98 NKu,Crisis tie-in 3.00
99 NKuFire and Sword 3.00
100 AKu,D:Greamore,Sabertooth . . 4.00
101 MGr,Temple of Demi-god 3.00
102 I:Zuppara,Error-Machiste
   with two hands. 3.00
103 JBi,Moon Beast. 3.00
104 RR,Dragon Skinner. 3.00

Warlord #72 © DC Comics Inc.

105 RR,Staliters of Skinner 3.00
106 RR,I:Daimon 3.00
107 RR,Bride of Yano 3.00
108 RR,I:Mortella 3.00
109 RR,A:Mortella 3.00
110 RR,A:Skyra III 3.00
111 RR,Tearing o/t Island Sea 3.00
112 RR,Obsession 3.00
113 RR,Through Fiends
  Destroy Me 3.00
114 RR,Phenalegeno Dies 3.00
115 RR,Citadel of Fear 3.00
116 RR,Revenge of the Warlord . . . 3.00
117 RR,A:Power Girl 3.00
118 RR,A:Power Girl 3.00
119 RR,A:Power Girl 3.00
120 ATb,A:Power Girl 3.00
121 ATb,A:Power Girl 3.00
122 ATb,A:Power Girl 3.00
123 JD,TMd,N:Warlord 3.00
124 JD,TMd,I:Scavenger 3.00
125 JD,TMd,D:Tara 3.00
126 JD,TMd,A:Machiste 3.00
127 JD,The Last Dragon 3.00
128 JD,I:Agife 3.00
129 JD,Vision of Quest 3.00
130 JD,A:Maddox 3.00
131 JD,RLd,Vengeful Legacies 5.00
132 A New Beginning 3.00
133 JD,final issue (44pg) 4.00
Ann.#1 MGr,A:Shakira 4.00
Ann.#2 I:Krystovar 3.00
Ann.#3 DJu,Full Circle 3.00
Ann.#4 A:New Gods,
  Legends tie-in 3.00
Ann.#5 AKu,Hellfire 3.00
Ann.#6 F:New Gods 3.00
TPB Warlord:Savage Empire,
  Rep.#1–#10,#12,Special #8 . . 20.00

[Limited Series], 1992
1 Travis Morgan retrospective 2.25
2 Fate of T. Morgan revealed 2.25
3 Return of Deimos 2.25
4 V:Deimos 2.25
5 MGr(c),Skartaros at War 2.25
6 finale 2.25

WARLORD, THE
Feb., 2006
1 BS, F:Travis Morgan 3.00
2 BS, Return of the Warlord 3.00
3 BS, Travis Morgan 3.00
4 BS, In Skartaris 3.00
5 BS, Sword of Truth 3.00
6 BS,Somewhere in Skartaris 3.00
7 BS,F:Brovis 3.00
8 BS, Someone dies 3.00
9 BS, Revenge 3.00
10 Final Issue 3.00

WAR OF THE GODS
1991
1 GP,A:Lobo,Misc.Heroes,Circe . . . 2.25
2 GP,A:Misc.Heroes,V:Circe,
  w/poster 2.25
2a (Newsstand) 2.25
3 GP,A:Misc.Heroes,V:Circe,
  w/poster 2.25
3a Newsstand 2.25
4 GP,A:Misc.Heroes,V:Circe,
  w/poster 2.25
4a Newsstand 2.25

WAR STORY
DC/Vertigo, Sept., 2001
Spec. Johann's Tiger,GEn 5.00
Spec. D-Day Dodgers,GEn 5.00
Spec. Screaming Eagles,GEn 5.00
Spec. The Reivers 5.00
Spec. Nightingale,GEn 5.00

Spec. J for Jenny 5.00
Spec. Condors 5.00
Spec. Archangel 5.00
Spec. Johann's Tiger 5.00

WASTELAND
Dec., 1987
1 Selection of Horror stories 2.25
2 thru 10 . . . . @2.25
11 thru 18 . . . . @2.25

WATCHMEN
Sept., 1986
1 B:AMo,DGb,D:Comedian 10.00
2 DGb,Funeral for Comedian 6.00
3 DGb,F:Dr.Manhattan 5.00
4 DGb,O:Dr.Manhattan 5.00
5 DGb,F:Rorschach 5.00
6 DGb,O:Rorschach 5.00
7 DGb,F:Nite Owl 5.00
8 DGb,F:Silk Spectre 5.00
9 DGb,O:Silk Spectre 5.00
10 DGb,A:Rorschach 5.00
11 DGb,O:Ozymandius 5.00
12 DGb,D:Rorsharch 5.00
TPB rep.#1–#12 . . . . 15.00
TPB 20.00

WEB, THE
DC/Impact, 1991–92
1 I:Gunny, Bill Grady, Templar . . . 2.25
Ann.#1 Earthquest,w/trading card . . 2.50

Weird #2
© *DC Comics, Inc.*

WEIRD, THE
April, 1988
1 BWr,A:JLI 4.00
2 BWr,A:JLI 3.00
3 BWr,V:Jason 3.00
4 final issue 3.00

WEIRD
DC/Paradox Press, 1997
1 B&W magazine 3.00
2 . . . . 3.00
3 . . . . 3.00

WEIRD SECRET ORIGINS
Aug. 2004
Spec. 80-page giant 6.00

WEIRD WAR TALES
Sept.–Oct., 1971
1 JKu(c),JKu,RH,Fort which
  Did Not Return 400.00
2 JKu,MD,Military Madness 150.00
3 JKu(c),RA,The Pool 150.00
4 JKu(c),Ghost of Two Wars . . . 125.00
5 JKu(c),RH,Slave 125.00
6 JKu(c),Pawns, The Sounds
  of War 75.00
7 JKu(c),JKu,RH,Flying Blind . . . 75.00
8 NA(c),The Avenging Grave . . . 100.00
9 NC(c),The Promise 75.00
10 NC(c),Who is Haunting
  the Haunted Chateau 75.00
11 NC(c),ShM,Oct. 30, 1918:
  The German Trenches, WWI . 50.00
12 MK(c),God of Vengeance 50.00
13 LD(c),The Die-Hards 50.00
14 LD(c),ShM,The Ghost of
  McBride's Woman 50.00
15 LD(c),Ace King Just Flew
  In From Hell 50.00
16 LD(c),More Dead Than Alive . . 50.00
17 GE(c),Dead Man's Hands 50.00
18 GE(c),Captain Dracula 50.00
19 LD(c),The Platoon That
  Wouldn't Die 50.00
20 LD(c),Operation Voodoo 50.00
21 LD(c),One Hour To Kill 30.00
22 LD(c),Wings of Death 30.00
23 LD(c),The Bird of Death 30.00
24 LD(c),The Invisible Enemy 30.00
25 LD(c),Black Magic...White
  Death 30.00
26 LD(c),Jump Into Hell 30.00
27 LD(c),Survival of the
  Fittest 30.00
28 LD(c),Isle of Forgotten
  Warriors 30.00
29 LD(c),Breaking Point 30.00
30 LD(c),The Elements of Death . . 30.00
31 LD(c),Death Waits Twice 30.00
32 LD(c),The Enemy, The Stars . . 30.00
33 LD(c),Pride of the Master
  Race 30.00
34 LD(c),The Common Enemy . . . 30.00
35 LD(c),The Invaders 30.00
36 JKu(c),Escape 35.00
37 LD(c),The Three Wars of
  Don Q 15.00
38 JKu(c),Born To Die 15.00
39 JKu(c),The Spoils of War 15.00
40 ECh(c),Back From The Dead . . 15.00
41 JL(c), The Dead Draftees of
  Regiment Six 15.00
42 JKu(c),Old Soldiers Never
  Die 15.00
43 ECh(c),Bulletproof 15.00
44 JKu(c),ShM,The Emperor
  Weehawken 15.00
45 JKu(c),The Battle of Bloody
  Valley 15.00
46 Kill Or Be Killed 15.00
47 JKu(c),Bloodbath of the Toy
  Soldiers 15.00
48 JL(c),Ultimate Destiny 15.00
49 The Face Of The Enemy 15.00
50 ECh(c),-An Appointment With
  Destiny 15.00
51 JKu(c),Secret Weapon 15.00
52 JKu(c),The Devil Is A
  Souvenir Hunter 15.00
53 JAp(c), Deadly Dominoes 15.00
54 GM(c),Soldier of Satan 15.00
55 JKu(c),A Rebel Shall Rise
  From The Grave 15.00
56 AM(c),The Headless Courier . . 15.00
57 RT(c),Trial By Combat 15.00
58 JKu(c),Death Has A Hundred
  Eyes 15.00
59 The Old One 15.00

60 JKu(c),Night Flight 15.00
61 HC(c),Mind War 12.00
62 JKu(c),The Grubbers 12.00
63 JKu(c),Battleground 12.00
64 JKu(c),FM(1st DC),D-Day. 40.00
65 JKu(c),The Last Cavalry
   Charge 12.00
66 JKu(c),The Iron War 12.00
67 JKu(c),The Attack of the
   Undead 12.00
68 FM,JKu(c),The Life and Death of
   Charlie Golem 30.00
69 JKu(c),The Day After Doomsday 9.00
70 LD(c),The Blood Boat 9.00
71 LD(c),False Prophet 9.00
72 JKu(c),Death Camp 9.00
73 GE(c),The Curse of Zopyrus . . . 9.00
74 GE(c),March of the Mammoth . . 9.00
75 JKu(c),The Forgery 9.00
76 JKu(c),The Fire Bug 9.00
77 JKu(c),Triad 9.00
78 JKu(c),Indian War In Space 9.00
79 JKu(c),The Gods Themselves . . 9.00
80 JKu(c),An Old Man's Profession. 9.00

Weird War Tales #117
© DC Comics, Inc.

81 JKu(c),It Takes Brains To
   Be A Killer 9.00
82 GE(c),Funeral Fire 9.00
83 GE(c),Prison of the Mind 9.00
84 JKu(c),Devil's Due 9.00
85 thru 124 June, 1983 . . . . @9.00

WEIRD WAR TALES
DC/Vertigo, April, 1997
1 (of 4) anthology 3.00
2 MK(c) 3.00
3 . . . . 3.00
4 final issue. 3.00
Spec.#1 GEn (2000) 5.00

ALL-STAR WESTERN
Aug.–Sept., 1970
1 NA(c),CI 75.00
2 NA(c),GM,B:Outlaw 60.00
3 NA(c),GK,O:El Diablo 60.00
4 NA(c),GK,JKu,GM 60.00
5 NA(c),JAp,E:Outlaw. 60.00
6 GK,B:Billy the Kid 60.00
7 JKu 50.00
8 E:Billy the Kid 50.00
9 FF 50.00
10 GM,I:Jonah Hex 750.00
11 GM,A:Jonah Hex. 350.00

Becomes:

WEIRD WESTERN TALES
June-July, 1972
12 NA,BWr,JKu 250.00
13 . . . . 150.00
14 ATh 100.00
15 NA(c),GK. 75.00
16 thru 17. . . . . @60.00
18 Jonah Hex 100.00
19 thru 28. . . . . @60.00
29 O:Jonah Hex. 75.00
30 thru 38. . . . . @35.00
39 I&O:Scalphunter 35.00
40 thru 70. . . . . @20.00

WEIRD WESTERN TALES
DC/Vertigo, Feb., 2001
1 (of 4) 2.50
2 thru 4 . . . . @2.50

WEIRD WORLDS
Aug.–Sept., 1971
1 JO,MA,John Carter 50.00
2 NA,JO(c),MA,BWr 40.00
3 MA,NA 25.00
4 MK(c),MK. 20.00
5 MK(c),MK. 20.00
6 MK(c),MK. 20.00
7 John Carter ends. 20.00
8 HC,I:Iron Wolf 20.00
9 and 10 HC . . . . @20.00

WESTERN COMICS
Jan.–Feb., 1948
1 MMe,B:Vigilante,Rodeo Rick,
   Wyoming Kid, Cowboy
   Marshal. 1,500.00
2 MMe,Vigilante vs. Dirk Bigger . 600.00
3 MMe,Vigilante vs. Pecos Kid . . 700.00
4 MMe,Vigilante as Pecos Kid . . 700.00
5 I:Nighthawk 500.00
6 Wyoming Kid vs. The
   Murder Mustang 300.00
7 Wyoming Kid in The Town
   That Was Never Robbed. . . . 300.00
8 O:Wyoming Kid 500.00
9 Wyoming Kid vs. Jack
   Slaughter. 300.00
10 Nighthawk in Tunnel of Terror . 300.00
11 Wyoming Kid vs. Mayor Brock 275.00
12 Wyoming Kid vs. Baldy Ryan . 275.00
13 I:Running Eagle 275.00
14 Wyoming Kid in The Siege
   of Prairie City. 275.00
15 Nighthawk in Silver, Salt
   and Pepper 275.00
16 Wyoming Kid vs. Smilin' Jim. . 275.00
17 BP,Wyoming Kid vs. Prof.
   Penny 275.00
18 LSt on Nighthawk,Wyoming Kid
   in Challenge of the Chiefs. . . 275.00
19 LSt,Nighthawk in The
   Invisible Rustlers 275.00
20 LSt,Nighthawk in The Mystery
   Mail From Defender Dip 225.00
21 LSt,Nighthawk in Rattlesnake
   Hollow 225.00
22 LSt,I:Jim Pegton 225.00
23 LSt,Nighthawk reveals
   ID to Jim 225.00
24 The $100,000 Impersonation . 225.00
25 V:Sioux Invaders. 225.00
26 The Storming of the Sante
   Fe Trail 225.00
27 The Looters of Lost Valley . . . 225.00
28 The Thunder Creek Rebellion . 225.00
29 Six Guns of the Wyoming Kid. 225.00
30 V:Green Haired Killer 225.00
31 The Sky Riding Lawman. 225.00
32 Death Rides the Stage Coach 225.00

Western Comics #26
© DC Comics Inc.

33 Wyoming Kid's Magic Finger . 225.00
34 Prescription For Killers 225.00
35 The River of Rogues. 225.00
36 Nighthawk(c),Duel in the Dark 200.00
37 The Death Dancer 200.00
38 Warpath in the Sky 200.00
39 Death to Fort Danger 200.00
40 Blind Man's Bluff. 200.00
41 thru 60. . . . . @175.00
61 thru 85. . . . . @150.00

WE3
DC/Vertigo, Aug. 2004
1 (of 3) GMo,Animal assassins. . . . 3.00
2 GMo. 3.00
3 concl. 3.00
TPB 13.00

WHO'S WHO
1985–87
1 . . . . 5.00
2 thru 26 . . . . @4.00

WHO'S WHO IN
THE DC UNIVERSE
1990–92
1 inc. Superman 6.00
1a 2nd printing 5.50
2 inc. Flash 5.00
2a 2nd printing 5.50
3 inc. Green Lantern. 5.50
4 inc. Wonder Woman 5.50
5 inc. Batman. 5.50
6 inc. Hawkman 5.50
7 inc. Shade 5.50
8 inc. Lobo 6.00
9 inc. Legion of Super-Heroes 5.50
10 inc. Robin 5.50
11 inc. L.E.G.I.O.N. '91 . . . . 5.50
12 inc. Aquaman 5.50
13 Villains issue, inc. Joker 6.00
14 inc. New Titans 5.50
15 inc. Doom Patrol 5.50
16 inc. Catwoman,final issue. 5.00

WHO'S WHO
IN IMPACT
1991
1 Shield. 5.00
2 Black Hood 5.00

DC

WHO'S WHO IN THE LEGION
1987–88
1 History/Bio of Legionnaires 3.50
2 inc. Dream Girl. 3.50
3 inc. Karate Kid 3.50
4 inc. Lightning Lad 3.50
5 inc. Phantom Girl. 3.50
6 inc. Timber Wolf. 3.50
7 wraparound(c) 3.50

WHO'S WHO IN STAR TREK
1987
1 HC(c) 6.00
2 HC(c) 6.00

WHO'S WHO UPDATE '87
1 inc. Blue Beetle 3.00
2 inc. Catwoman. 3.00
3 inc. Justice League 3.00
4 . . . . 3.00
5 inc. Superboy. 3.00

WHO'S WHO UPDATE '88
1 inc. Brainiac. 3.00
2 inc. JusticeLeagueInternational . . 3.00
3 inc. Shado 3.00
4 inc. Zatanna 3.00

WHO'S WHO UPDATE '93
1 F:Eclipso,Azrael. 5.25

WILD DOG
Sept., 1987
1 mini series DG(i),I:Wild Dog 3.00
2 DG(i),V:Terrorists 2.50
3 DG(i) 2.50
4 DG(i),O:Wild Dog, final issue. . . . 2.50
Spec.#1 . . . . 2.50

WILD WILD WEST
1999
1-shot movie adaptation 5.00

WINDY & WILLY
May-June, 1969
1 . . . . 65.00
2 thru 4 . . . . @40.00

WISE SON: THE WHITE WOLF
DC/Milestone, Sept., 1996
1 by Ho Che Anderson 2.50
2 thru 4 . . . . @2.50

WITCHCRAFT
DC/Vertigo, 1994
1 CV(c),Three Witches from
 Sandman 4.00
2 F:Mildred 3.50
3 Final issue 3.25
TPB rep. mini-series 15.00

WITCHCRAFT: LA TERREUR
Feb., 1998
1 (of 3) JeR, sequel 2.50
2 & 3 JeR . . . . @2.50

WITCHING, THE
DC/Vertigo, June 2004
1 Triple Goddess. 3.00

2 thru 4 . . . . @3.00
5 MBu 3.00
6 thru 9 . . . . @3.00
10 final issue 3.00

WITCHING HOUR
1969–78
1 NA,ATh,Let the Judge Be You. 200.00
2 ATh, The Trip of Fools 100.00
3 ATh,BWr. 100.00
4 ATh,A Matter of Conscience . . 65.00
5 ATh,BWr. 100.00

Witching Hour #33
© DC Comics, Inc.

6 ATh,A Face in the Crowd. 100.00
7 ATh. 60.00
8 NA,ATh,3 Day Free Home Trial. 60.00
9 ATh,The Lonely Road Home . . . 60.00
10 ATh,Hold Softly, Hand of Death 60.00
11 ATh,The Mark of the Witch . . . 60.00
12 ATh,Double Edge 60.00
13 NA 75.00
14 AW,CG,NA(c) 90.00
15 thru 20 . . . . @30.00
21 thru 30 . . . . @25.00
31 thru 37 . . . . @25.00
38 100-pg. 90.00
39 thru 60 . . . . @20.00
61 thru 85 . . . . @15.00

THE WITCHING HOUR
DC/Vertigo, Dec., 1999
1 (of 3) JLb,CBa,ATi 6.00
2 JLb,CBa,ATi. 6.00
3 JLb,CBa,ATi, concl. 6.00
TPB 20.00

WONDER GIRL
Sept., 2007
1 (of 6) 3.00
2 F:Hercules 3.00

WONDER WOMAN
1942–86
1 O:Wonder Woman,A:Paula
 Von Gunther. 46,000.00
2 I:Earl of Greed,Duke of Deception
 and Lord Conquest. 7,500.00
3 Paula Von Gunther reforms . 3,500.00
4 A:Paula Von Gunther 2,800.00
5 I:Dr. Psycho,A:Mars 2,800.00
6 I:Cheetah 2,400.00
7 Adventure of the Life Vitamin 2,400.00

8 I:Queen Clea. 2,400.00
9 I:Giganto 2,400.00
10 I:Duke Mephisto Saturno . . 2,500.00
11 I:Hypnoto 1,700.00
12 I:Queen Desira. 1,700.00
13 V:King Rigor & the Seal Men 1,700.00
14 I:Gentleman Killer 1,700.00
15 I:Solo 1,700.00
16 I:King Pluto 1,700.00
17 Wonder Woman goes to
 Ancient Rome. 1,700.00
18 V:Dr. Psycho 1,700.00
19 V:Blitz. 1,700.00
20 V:Nifty and the Air Pirates . . 1,700.00
21 I:Queen Atomia 1,500.00
22 V:Saturno. 1,500.00
23 V:Odin and the Valkyries . . . 1,500.00
24 I:Mask 1,500.00
25 V:Purple Priestess 1,500.00
26 I:Queen Celerita. 1,500.00
27 V:Pik Socket. 1,500.00
28 V:Cheetah,Clea,Dr. Poison,
 Giganta,Hypnata,Snowman,
 Zara (Villainy,Inc.). 2,000.00
29 V:Paddy Gypso 2,000.00
30 The Secret of the
 Limestone Caves 2,000.00
31 V:Solo 1,000.00
32 V:Uvo. 1,000.00
33 V:Inventa 1,000.00
34 V:Duke of Deception 1,000.00
35 Jaxo,Master of Thoughts . . . 1,000.00
36 V:Lord Cruello 1,000.00
37 A:Circe 1,000.00
38 V:Brutex. 1,000.00
39 The Unmasking of Wonder
 Woman 1,000.00
40 Hollywood Goes To Paradise
 Island 1,000.00
41 Wonder Woman,Romance
 Editor. 900.00
42 V:General Vertigo 900.00
43 The Amazing Spy Ring
 Mystery 900.00
44 V:Master Destroyer. 900.00
45 The Amazon and the
 Leprachaun. 1,600.00
46 V:Prof. Turgo. 800.00
47 V:Duke of Deception 800.00
48 V:Robot Woman 800.00
49 V:Boss. 800.00
50 V:Gen. Voro 800.00
51 V:Garo. 800.00
52 V:Stroggo 600.00
53 V:Crime Master of Time 600.00
54 A:Merlin. 600.00
55 The Chessmen of Doom 600.00
56 V:Plotter Gang 600.00
57 V:Mole Men. 600.00
58 V:Brain 600.00
59 V:Duke Dozan. 600.00
60 A:Paula Von Gunther 600.00
61 Earth's Last Hour 550.00
62 V:Angles Andrews. 550.00
63 V:Duke of Deception 550.00
64 V:Thought Master 550.00
65 V:Duke of Deception 550.00
66 V:Duke of Deception 550.00
67 Confessions of a Spy 550.00
68 Landing of the Flying
 Saucers 550.00
69 A:Johann Gutenberg,Chris.
 Columbus, Paul Revere
 and the Wright Brothers 550.00
70 I:Angle Man. 550.00
71 One-Woman Circus 550.00
72 V:Mole Goldings 550.00
73 V:Prairie Pirates 550.00
74 The Carnival of Peril. 500.00
75 V:Angler 500.00
76 Bird Reveals Secret Identity . . 500.00
77 V:Smokescreen gang 500.00

Wonder Woman #66
© DC Comics, Inc.

Wonder Woman #215
© DC Comics Inc.

130 A:Angle Man	200.00
131 Proving of Wonder Woman	250.00
132 V:Flying Saucer	250.00
133 A:Miss X	275.00
134 V:Image-Maker	250.00
135 V:Multiple Man	250.00
136 V:Machine Men	300.00
137 V:Robot Wonder Woman	275.00
138 V:Multiple Man	275.00
139 Amnesia revels Identity	275.00
140 A:Morpheus,Mr.Genie	300.00
141 A:Angle Man	250.00
142 A:Mirage Giants	275.00
143 A:Queen Hippolyte	250.00
144 I:Bird Boy	250.00
145 V:Phantom Sea Beast	250.00
146 $1,000 Dollar Stories	250.00
147 Wonder Girl becomes Bird Girl and Fish Girl	225.00
148 A:Duke of Deception	250.00
149 Last Day of the Amazons	275.00
150 V:Phantome Fish Bird	250.00
151 F:1st Full Wonder Girl story	200.00
152 F:Wonder Girl	200.00
153 V:Duke of Deception	200.00
154 V:Boiling Man	200.00
155 I married a monster	200.00
156 V:Brain Pirate	225.00
157 A:Egg Fu,the First	225.00
158 A:Egg Fu,the First	225.00
159 Origin	250.00
160 A:Cheetah,Dr. Psycho	150.00
161 A:Angle Man	150.00
162 O:Diana Prince	150.00
163 A:Giganta	150.00
164 A:Angle Man	150.00
165 A:Paper Man,Dr.Psycho	125.00
166 A:Egg Fu,The Fifth	125.00
167 A:Crimson Centipede	125.00
168 RA,ME,V:Giganta	125.00
169 RA,ME,Crimson Centipede	125.00
170 RA,ME,V:Dr.Pyscho	125.00
171 A:Mouse Man	125.00
172 IN,A:Android Wonder Woman	125.00
173 A:Tonia	125.00
174 A:Angle Man	125.00
175 V:Evil Twin	125.00
176 A:Star Brothers	125.00
177 A:Super Girl	150.00
178 MSy,DG,I:New Wonder Woman	150.00
179 D:Steve Trevor,I:Ching	100.00
180 MSy,DG,wears no costume I:Tim Trench	100.00
181 MSy,DG,A:Dr.Cyber	100.00
182 MSy,DG	100.00
183 MSy,DG,V:War	100.00
184 MSy,DG,A:Queen Hippolyte	75.00
185 MSy,DG,V:Them	75.00
186 MSy,DG,I:Morgana	75.00
187 MSy,DG,A:Dr.Cyber	75.00
188 MSy,DG,A:Dr.Cyber	75.00
189 MSy,DG	75.00
190 MSy,DG	75.00
191 MSy,DG	75.00
192 MSy,DG	75.00
193 MSy,DG	75.00
194 MSy,DG	75.00
195 MSy,WW	75.00
196 MSy,DG,giant,Origin rep.	80.00
197 MSy,DG	80.00
198 MSy,DG	80.00
199 JJ(c),DG	100.00
200 JJ(c),DG	125.00
201 DG,A:Catwoman	50.00
202 DG,A:Catwoman,I:Fafhrd & the Gray Mouser	50.00
203 DG,Womens lib	35.00
204 DH,BO,rewears costume	60.00
205 DH,BO,Target WonderWoman	35.00
206 DH,O:Wonder Woman	35.00

78 V:Angle Man	500.00
79 V:Spider	500.00
80 V:Machino	500.00
81 V:Duke of Deception, Angle Man	500.00
82 A:Robin Hood	500.00
83 The Boy From Nowhere	500.00
84 V:Duke of Deception, Angle Man	500.00
85 V:Capt. Virago	500.00
86 V:Snatcher	500.00
87 The Day the Clocks Stopped	500.00
88 V:Duke of Deception	500.00
89 The Triple Heroine	500.00
90 Wonder Woman on Jupiter	500.00
91 The Interplanetary Olympics	400.00
92 V:Angle Man	400.00
93 V:Duke of Deception	400.00
94 V:Duke of Deception, A:Robin Hood	400.00
95 O:Wonder Woman's Tiara	400.00
96 V:Angle Man	400.00
97 The Runaway Time Express	400.00
98 The Million Dollar Penny	400.00
99 V:Silicons	400.00
100 Anniversary Issue	450.00
101 V:Time Master	350.00
102 F:Steve Trevor	350.00
103 V:Gadget-Maker	350.00
104 A:Duke of Deception	350.00
105 O,I:Wonder Woman	1,700.00
106 W.Woman space adventure	350.00
107 Battles space cowboys	500.00
108 Honored by U.S. Post Off.	350.00
109 V:Slicker	350.00
110 I:Princess 1003	350.00
111 I:Prof. Menace	350.00
112 V:Chest of Monsters	300.00
113 A:Queen Mikra	300.00
114 V:Flying Saucers	300.00
115 A:Angle Man	300.00
116 A:Professor Andro	300.00
117 A:Etta Candy	300.00
118 A:Merman	300.00
119 A:Mer Boy	300.00
120 A:Hot & Cold Alien	300.00
121 A:Wonder Woman Family	250.00
122 I:Wonder Tot	250.00
123 A:Wonder Girl,Wonder Tot	250.00
124 A:Wonder Girl,Wonder Tot	250.00
125 WW-Battle Prize	250.00
126 I:Mr.Genie	250.00
127 Suprise Honeymoon	200.00
128 O:InvisiblePlane	200.00
129 A:WonderGirl,WonderTot	200.00

207 RE,The Four Dooms	35.00
208 RE,The Titanic Trials	35.00
209 RE,Planet of Plunder	35.00
210 RE,The Shrinking Formula	35.00
211 RE,giant	100.00
212 CS,A:Superman,tries to rejoin JLA	30.00
213 IN,A:Flash	30.00
214 CS,giant,A:Green Lantern	100.00
215 A:Aquaman	25.00
216 A:Black Canary	25.00
217 DD,A:Green Arrow,giant	40.00
218 KS,Red Tornado	25.00
219 CS,A:Elongated Man	25.00
220 DG,NA,A:Atom	25.00
221 CS,A:Hawkman	25.00
222 A:Batman	25.00
223 R:Steve Trevor	25.00
224 Wonder Woman vs. USA	25.00
225 Maximus, Emperor	25.00
226 A Life in Flames	25.00
227 My World in Ashes	25.00
228 B:War stories	25.00
229 Tomorrow Belongs to Me	25.00
230 V:Cheetah	25.00
231 This War has Been Cancelled	25.00
232 MN,A:JSA	25.00
233 GM,Seadeath	25.00
234 And Death my Destiny	25.00
235 The Biology Bomb	25.00
236 Armageddon Day	25.00
237 RB(c),A:Wonder Woman	30.00
238 RB(c),Assassin	20.00
239 RB(c),Duke named Deception	20.00
240 Wanted Dead or Alive	20.00
241 JSon,DG,A:Spectre	22.00
242 Tomorrow's Gods & Demons	15.00
243 The Five-Sided Square	15.00
244 The Terrorist Dooms	15.00
245 Vengeance From Ice to Fire	15.00
246 Darkness Everywhere	15.00
247 The Inside-Out Man	15.00
248 D:Steve Trevor	20.00
249 A:Hawkgirl	15.00
250 I:Orana	15.00
251 O:Orana	15.00
252 Empress of the Silver Snake	20.00
253 Spirit of Silver Spirit of Gold	15.00
254 The Angle in the Stars	15.00
255 V:Bushmaster	15.00
256 V:Royal Flush Gang	15.00
257 Case o/t Impossible Crimes	15.00
258 Long Grey Line of Death	15.00
259 A Power Gone Mad	15.00

Wonder Woman #278
© DC Comics, Inc.

260 A Warrior in Chains 15.00
261 Palace at the Edge of Time . . 15.00
262 RE,A:Bushmaster 15.00
263 Power and the Pampas 15.00
264 A Bomb in the Bird 15.00
265 Land of the Scaled Gods 15.00
266 The Uninvited 15.00
267 R:Animal Man 20.00
268 A:Animal Man 20.00
269 WW(i),Rebirth of Wonder
     Woman,pt.1 . . . . 12.00
270 Rebirth,pt.2 . . . . 12.00
271 JSon,B:Huntress,Rebirth,pt.3 . 12.00
272 JSon 12.00
273 JSon,A:Angle Man 12.00
274 JSon,I:Cheetah II 12.00
275 JSon,V:Cheetah II. 12.00
276 JSon,V:Kobra 12.00
277 JSon,V:Kobra 12.00
278 JSon,V:Kobra 12.00
279 JSon,A:Demon,Catwoman . . . 12.00
280 JSon,A:Demon,Catwoman . . . 12.00
281 JSon,Earth 2 Joker 10.00
282 JSon,Earth 2 Joker 10.00
283 Earth 2 Joker 10.00
284 Shadow of the Dragon 7.00
285 JSon,V:Red Dragon 7.00
286 Be Wonder Woman and Die . . . 7.00
287 DH,RT,JSon,Teen Titans 8.00
288 GC,RT,New Wonder Woman . . 8.00
289 GC,RT,JSon,New W.Woman . . 7.00
290 GC,RT,JSon,New W.Woman . . 7.00
291 GC,FMc,A:Zatanna 8.00
292 GC,FMc,RT,Supergirl 8.00
293 GC,FMc,Starfire,Raven 8.00
294 GC,FMc,JSon,V:Blockbuster . . 7.00
295 GC,FMc,JSon,Huntress 7.00
296 GC,Fmc,JSon 7.00
297 MK(c),GC,FMc,JSon. 7.00
298 GC,FMc,JSon 7.00
299 GC,FMc,JSon 7.00
300 GC,FMc,RA,DG,KP,RB,KG
     C:New Teen Titans 9.00
301 GC,FMc. 7.00
302 GC,FMc,V:Artemis 7.00
303 GC,FMc,Huntress 7.00
304 GC,FMc,Huntress 7.00
305 GC,Huntress,I:Circe 8.00
306 DH,Huntress 7.00
307 DH,Huntress,Black Canary . . . 7.00
308 DH,Huntress,Black Canary . . . 7.00
309 DH,Huntress 7.00
310 DH,Huntress 7.00
311 DH,Huntress 7.00
312 DH,DSp,A:Gremlins 7.00

313 DH,V:Circe 7.00
314 DH,Huntress 7.00
315 DH,Huntress 7.00
316 DH,Huntress 7.00
317 DH,V:Cereberus 7.00
318 DH,V:Space Aliens 7.00
319 DH,V:Dr.Cyber 7.00
320 DH,Launch on Warning 7.00
321 DH,Huntress 7.00
322 IN,Bid Time Return 7.00
323 DH,A:Cheetah, Angle Man . . . 7.00
324 DH,The Cassandra Complex . . 7.00
325 DH,Gremlin from the Kremlin . 7.00
326 DH,Tropidor Heat 7.00
327 DH,Crisis 7.00
328 DH,Crisis 7.00
329 DH,Crisis, giant 15.00

WONDER WOMAN
[2nd Regular Series], 1987

1 GP,O:Amazons,Wonder Woman . 8.00
2 GP,I:Steve Trevor. 6.00
3 GP,I:Julia Vanessa. 6.00
4 GP,V:Decay 6.00
5 GP,V:Deimos, Phobos 6.00
6 GP,V:Ares 5.00
7 GP,I:Myndi Mayer 5.00
8 GP,O:Legends,A:JLA,Flash . . . 5.00
9 GP,I:New Cheetah 5.00
10 GP,V:Seven Headed Hydra,
     Challenge of the Gods,pt.1,
     gatefold(c). 4.00
10a regular(c). 3.00
11 GP,V:Echidna,Challenge
     of the Gods,pt.3. . . . . 4.00
12 GP,Millennium,V:Pan, Challenge
     of the Gods,pt.3,
     Millennium x-over. 4.00
13 GP,Millennium,A:Ares,Challenge
     of the Gods,pt.4. . . . . 4.00
14 GP,A:Hercules. 4.00
15 GP,I:New Silver Swan. 4.00
16 GP,V:Silver Swan 4.00
17 GP,DG,V:Circe. 4.00
18 GP,DG,V:Circe,+Bonus bk#4 . . 4.00
19 GP,FMc,V:Circe. 4.00
20 GP,BMc,D:Myndi Mayer 4.00
21 GP,BMc,L:Greek Gods,
     Destruction of Olympus 3.00
22 GP,BMc,F:Julia, Vanessa 3.00
23 GP,R:Hermes,V:Phobos,
     Prelude to New Titans #50 . . . 3.00
24 GP,V:Ixion, Phobos. 3.00
25 CMa,Invasion,A:JLA 3.00
26 CMa,Invasion,V:Capt.Atom. . . . 3.00
27 CMa,V:Khunds,A:Cheetah 3.00
28 CMa,V:Cheetah. 3.00
29 CMa,V:Cheetah. 3.00
30 CMa,V:Cheetah. 3.00
31 CMa,V:Cheetah. 3.00
32 TG,V:Amazons,A:Hermes 3.00
33 CMa,V:Amazons,Cheetah. 3.00
34 CMa,I:Shim'Tar 3.00
35 CMa,V:Shim'Tar 3.00
36 CMa,A:Hermes 3.00
37 CMa,V:Discord,A:Superman. . . . 3.00
38 CMa,V:Eris 3.00
39 CMa,V:Eris,A:Lois Lane 3.00
40 CMa,V:Eris,A:Lois Lane 3.00
41 CMa,RT,F:Julia,Ties that Bind . 3.00
42 CMa,RT,V:Silver Swan 3.00
43 CMA,RT,V:Silver Swan 3.00
44 CMa,RT,V:SilverSwan 3.00
45 CM,RT,Pandora's Box. 3.00
46 RT,Suicide Issue,D:Lucy. 3.00
47 RT,A:Troia 3.00
48 RTP,A:Troia 3.00
49 recap of 1st four years 3.00
50 RT,SA,BB,AH,CM,KN,PCR,MW
     A:JLA,Superman 4.00
51 RT,V:Mercury 3.00
52 CM,KN,Shards,V:Dr.Psycho . . . 3.00

Wonder Woman 2nd Series #57
© DC Comics, Inc.

53 RT,A:Pariah. 3.00
54 RT,V:Dr.Psycho. 3.00
55 RT,V:Dr.Psycho. 3.00
56 RT,A:Comm.Gordon 3.00
57 RT,A:Clark Kent,Bruce Wayne . . 3.00
58 RT,War of the Gods,V:Atlas 3.50
59 RT,War of the Gods,
     A:Batman Robin 3.50
60 RT,War of the Gods,
     A:Batman, Lobo. 3.50
61 RT,War of the Gods,V:Circe . . . 3.50
62 War o/t Gods,Epilogue. 3.00
63 BB(c)A:Deathstroke,Cheetah . . 5.00
64 BB(c),Kidnapped Child 2.50
65 BB(c),PCu,V:Dr.Psycho 2.50
66 BB(c),PCu,Exodus In Space#1. . 2.50
67 BB(c),PCu,Exodus In Space#2. . 2.50
68 BB(c),PCu,Exodus In Space#3. . 2.50
69 PCu, Exodus In Space#4 . . . . . 2.50
70 PCu,Exodus In Space#5. . . . . . 2.50
71 BB(c),DC,RT,Return fr.space . . 2.50
72 BB(c),O:retold 16.00
73 BB(c),Diana gets a job 3.00
74 BB(c),V:White Magician 2.50
75 BB(c),A:The White Magician. . . 2.50
76 BB(c),A:Doctor Fate 2.50
77 BB(c). 2.50
78 BB(c),A:Flash 2.50
79 BB(c),V:Mayfly,A:Flash 2.50
80 BB(c),V:Ares Buchanan 2.50
81 BB(c),V:Ares Buchanan 2.50
82 BB(c),V:Ares Buchanan 2.50
83 BB(c),V:Ares Buchanan 2.50
84 BB(c),V:Ares Buchanan 2.50
85 BB(c). 13.00
86 BB(c),Turning Point. 6.00
87 BB(c),No Quarter,NoSanctuary . 6.00
88 BB(c),A:Superman 10.00
89 BB(c),A:Circle 10.00
90 New Direction 7.00
91 Choosing Wonder Woman 4.00
92 New Wonder Woman 4.00
93 New Wonder Woman 4.00
94 . . . . 5.00
95 V:Cheetah. 5.00
96 V:The Joker. 5.00
97 V:The Joker. 5.00
98 BB(c),F:Artemis 3.00
99 BB(c),A:White Magician 3.00
100 BB(c) White Magician defeats
     Artemis 6.00
100a Collector's ed., holo(c) 6.00
101 V:White Magician 3.00
102 V:Metron,Darkseid 2.50

103 JBy,A:Darkseid 2.50
104 JBy,Diana takes crown? 2.50
105 JBy,Grecian artifact comes
    to life 2.50
106 JBy,A:The Demon,Phantom
    Stranger 2.50
107 . . . . 2.50
108 JBy,F:The Demon,Arion,The
    Phantom Stranger 2.50
109 JBy,V:The Flash,I:Champion . . 2.50
110 JBy,V:Sinestro 2.50
111 JBy,I:New Wonder Girl,
    V:Doomsday 2.50
112 JBy,V:Doomsday,A:Superman . 3.00
113 JBy,Wonder Girl vs. Decay . . . 2.50
114 JBy,V:Doctor Psycho. 2.50
115 JBy,beneath the Arctic ice. . . . 2.50
116 JBy,beneath the Arctic ice. . . . 2.50
117 JBy,V:Earth Moovers. 2.50
118 JBy 2.50
119 JBy,fight to regain Cheetah's
    humanity, cont. 2.50
120 JBy,48pg., pin-ups 4.00
121 JBy,Wonder Woman reverting
    to clay 2.50
122 JBy,Gods of Olympus are back 2.50
123 JBy,R:Artemis 2.50
124 JBy,A:Demon 2.50
125 JBy,A:Donna Troy & JLA 2.50
126 JBy,JL,Genesis tie-in 2.50
127 JBy,JL(c),new era 2.50
128 JBy,JL,V:Egg Fu 2.50
129 JBy,JL,Hippolyta debuts as
    replacement Wonder Woman . . 2.50
130 JBy,JL,pt.1,A:Golden-age
    Flash 2.50
131 JBy,pt.2 . . . . 2.50
132 JBy,pt.3,A:Justice Society. . . . 2.50
133 . . . . 2.50
134 JBy,Who is Donna Troy? 2.50
135 JBy,secret revealed 2.50
136 JBy,back to Earth 2.50
137 CPr,V:Circe, pt.1 . . . . 2.50
138 MBr,F:Hippolyta,V:Circe,pt.2. . 2.50
139 MBr, ... 2.50
140 BMc,A:Superman & Batman. . . 2.50
141 BMc,A:Superman & Batman. . . 2.50
142 BMc,The Wonder Dome 2.50
143 BMc,Devastation,pt.1 . . . . 2.50
144 BMc,Devastation,pt.2 . . . . 2.50
145 BMc,Devastation,pt.3 . . . . 2.50
146 BMc,Devastation,pt.4 . . . . 2.50
147 BMc,GodWar begins. 2.50
148 BMc,GodWar, pt.2. . . . . 2.50
149 RBr,BMc,GodWar,pt.3. . . . . . . 2.50
150 GodWar, 48-pg 4.00
151 AH(c),V:Dr. Poison 2.50
152 . . . . 2.50
153 MMr,F:Wonder Girl 2.50
154 Three Hearts,pt.1 . . . . 2.50
155 Three Hearts,pt.2 . . . . 2.50
156 Devastation Returns,pt.1 . . . . . 2.50
157 Devastation Returns,pt.2 . . . . . 2.50
158 Devastation Returns,concl. 2.50
159 WonderDome comes to Earth . 2.50
160 A Piece of You,pt.1 . . . . 3.00
161 A Piece of You,pt.2 . . . . 3.00
162 GodComplex,pt.1,A:Aquaman . 2.50
163 GodComplex,pt.2,A:Aquaman . 2.50
164 Gods of Gotham,pt.1 . . . . 6.00
165 Gods of Gotham,pt.2 . . . . 3.00
166 Gods of Gotham,pt.3 . . . . 3.00
167 Gods of Gotham,pt.4 . . . . 3.00
168 GP,Paradise Island Lost,pt.1 . . 2.50
169 GP,Paradise Island Lost,pt.2 . . 2.50
170 PJ,ALa,Lois & Diana. 2.50
171 Our Worlds at War, tie-in 2.50
172 Our Worlds at War, tie-in 3.00
173 Our Worlds at War, tie-in 2.50
174 PJ,ALa,Witch & Warrior,pt.1 . . 2.50
175 PJ,ALa,Witch & Warrior,pt.2 . . 8.00
176 PJ,ALa,Witch & Warrior,pt.3 . . 2.50

Wonder Woman 2nd Series #139
© DC Comics Inc.

177 PJ,ALa,Our Worlds at War 2.50
178 PJ,ALa,date with Trevor 2.50
179 PJ,ALa,V:Villainy,Inc. 2.50
180 PJ,ALa,O:new Villainy, Inc. . . . 2.50
181 PJ,ALa,prisoners of Skartaris . . 2.50
182 PJ,ALa,Shamballa 2.50
183 PJ,ALa,Skartaris mastermind . . 2.50
184 PJ,ALa,Diana,pt.1 . . . . 2.50
185 PJ,ALa,Diana in '40s,pt.2 . . . . 2.50
186 PJ,ALa,V:Barbara Minerva . . . 2.50
187 PJ,ALa,Cat fight 2.50
188 PJ,ALa,Day in the Life 2.50
189 WS,JOy,CR,Game Gods,pt.1 . . 2.50
190 WS,JOy,CR,Game Gods,pt.2 . . 4.00
191 WS,JOy,CR,Game Gods,pt.3 . . 2.50
192 WS,JOy,CR,Game Gods,pt.4 . . 2.50
193 WS,JOy,CR,Game Gods,pt.5 . . 2.50
194 WS,JOy,CR,Game Gods,pt.6 . . 2.50
195 AH 3.00
196 Down to Earth,pt.1 . . . . 2.50
197 Down to Earth,pt.2 . . . . 2.50
198 Down to Earth,pt.3 . . . . 2.50
199 Down to Earth,pt.4 . . . . 2.50
200 Down to Earth, 64-pg. 4.00
201 Themyscira 2.50
202 V:Veronica Cale 2.50
203 Bitter Pills,pt.1. . . . . 2.50
204 Bitter Pills,pt.2. . . . . 2.50
205 Bitter Pills,pt.3. . . . . 2.50
206 Stoned,pt.1 . . . . 2.50
207 Stoned,pt.2 . . . . 2.50
208 Stoned,pt.3 . . . . 2.50
209 Stoned,pt.4 . . . . 2.50
210 Stoned, concl. 2.50
211 SeP 2.50
212 F:JLA 2.50
213 War on Olympus 2.50
214 Truth or Dare, F:Flash, x-over 15.00
215 RgM,MIB,Tartarus,pt.1 . . . . . . 2.50
216 RgM,MIB,The Bronze Doors. . . 2.50
217 RgM,MIB,The Bronze Doors. . . 2.50
218 RgM,MIB, ... 2.50
219 Sacrifice,Superman,x-over,pt.4 10.00
220 A:Checkmate. 2.50
221 RgM,Power of Omac 2.50
222 RgM,F:Donna Troy, Cheetah . . 2.50
223 RgM,V:Omacs. 2.50
224 RgM,Omacs attack 2.50
225 Uncertain Future 2.50
226 Final issue 2.50
Ann.#1,GP,AAd,RA,BB,JBo,JL,CS
    Tales of Paradise Island 4.00
Ann.#2 CM,F:Mayer Agency 4.00
Ann.#3 Eclipso tie-in 3.00
Ann.#4 Year One Annual 4.00

Ann.#5 JBy,DC,NBy,Legends of the
    Dead Earth 3.50
Ann.#6 Pulp Heroes (Macabre). . . . 4.50
Ann.#7 Ghosts 3.50
Ann.#8 JLApe Gorilla Warfare 3.50
Annual #1 (1967) (rep.2003) 5.00
Spec.#1,000,000 CPr(s),MC,BMc . . 3.00
Spec #1 A:Deathstroke,Cheetah . . 2.50
Spec.#0 History of Amazons 7.00
Spec.#1 Our Worlds at War,48-pg . . 3.00
GN Amazonia, BML 8.00
GN The Once and Future Story. . . . 5.00
GN Amazonia, Elseworlds 8.00
GN The Gods of Gotham, rep. 6.00
Secret Files #2. . . . . 5.00
Secret Files #3, 48-pg 5.00
Spec. Wonder Woman: Donna Troy
    Girlfrenzy (1998) 2.50
Spec. Wonder Woman Plus CPr(s),
    MC, TP,Jesse Quick & Wonder
    Woman (1996). 3.00
Spec. The Blue Amazon (2003). . . . 7.00

WONDER WOMAN
June, 2006

1 TyD, Who is Wonder Woman . . . 3.00
1a variant (c). 3.00
2 TyD,F:Wonder Girl 3.00
3 TyD,Who is Wonder Woman 3.00
4 TyD,Cheetah, Giganta 3.00
5 TyD,Who is Wonder Woman,pt.5 3.00
6 TyD(c),F:The Amazons 3.00
7 TyD(c),F:The Amazons 3.00
8 TyD,Amazon's Attack prequel . . . 3.00
9 TyD,Amazon's Attack tie-in 3.00
10 TyD,Crossing the line 3.00
11 TyD,Sarge Steel missing. 3.00
12 TyD,Amazons Attack tie-in 3.00
13 TyD,The Circle 3.00
Ann. #1 Who is W.Woman,48-pgs. . 4.00

WORLD OF KRYPTON
July, 1979

1 HC/MA,O:Jor-El 10.00
2 HC/MA,A:Superman 6.00
3 HC 6.00

[2nd Series], 1987–88

1 MMi,John Byrne script. 3.00
2 MMi,John Byrne script. 3.00
3 MMi,John Byrne script. 3.00
4 MMi,A:Superman 3.00

WORLD OF METROPOLIS
1988

1 DG(i),O:Perry White. 2.50
2 DG(i),O:Lois Lane 2.50
3 DG(i),O:Clark Kent 2.50
4 DG(i),O:Jimmy Olsen. 2.50

WORLD OF SMALLVILLE
1988

1 KS/AA,Secrets of Ma&Pa Kent . . 3.00
2 KS/AA,Stolen Moments 3.00
3 KS/AA,Lana Lang/Manhunter . . . 3.00
4 KS/AA,final issue 3.00

WORLDS COLLIDE
1994

1 MBr(c),3RW,CsB,Ccs,DCw,
    TG,A:Blood Syndicate,Icon,
    Hardware,Static,Superboy,
    Superman,Steel,Vinyl Cling(c). . 4.25
1a Newsstand Ed. 2.75

WORLD'S BEST COMICS
Oct. 2003

Spec. G.A. DC Archives Sampler. . . 1.00
Spec. S.A. DC Archives Sampler. . . 1.00

World's Best Comics #1
© DC Comics, Inc.

WORLD'S BEST COMICS
Spring, 1941
1 Superman vs. the Rainmaker,
  Batman vs. Wright 27,000.00
Becomes:

WORLD'S FINEST
COMICS
1941–86
2 Superman V:The Unknown X,
  Batman V:Ambrose Taylor 12,000.00
3 I&O:Scarecrow 7,000.00
4 Superman V:Dan Brandon,
  Batman V:Ghost Gang 5,000.00
5 Superman V:Lemuel P.Potts,
  Batman V:Brains Kelly 4,500.00
6 Superman V:Metalo,Batman
  meets Scoop Scanlon 3,500.00
7 Superman V:Jenkins,Batman
  V:Snow Man Bandits 3,500.00
8 Superman:Talent Unlimited
  Batman V:Little Nap Boyd,
  B:Boy Commandos 3,000.00
9 Superman:One Second to
  Live,Batman V:Bramwell B.
  Bramwell 3,500.00
10 Superman V:The Insect Master,
  Batman reforms OliverHunt 3,000.00
11 Superman V:Charlie Frost,
  Batman V:Rob Calendar . . 2,500.00
12 Superman V:Lynx,Batman:
  Alfred Gets His Man 2,500.00
13 Superman V:Dice Dimant,
  Batman,V:Swami Pravhoz . 2,500.00
14 Superman V:Al Bandar,Batman
  V:Jib Buckler. 2,500.00
15 Superman V:Derby Bowser,
  Batman V:Mennekin 2,500.00
16 Superman:Music for the Masses,
  Batman V:Nocky Johnson . 2,500.00
17 Superman:The Great Godini,
  Batman V:Dr.Dreemo 2,500.00
18 Superman:The Junior Reporters,
  Batman V:Prof.Brane 2,200.00
19 A:The Joker 2,200.00
20 A:Toyman 2,200.00
21 Superman:Swindle in
  Sweethearts!. 1,800.00
22 Batman V:Nails Finney 1,800.00
23 Superman:The Colossus
  of Metropolis. 1,800.00
24 . . . . 1,800.00
25 Superman V:Ed Rook,Batman:
  The Famous First Crimes. . 1,800.00
26 Confessions of Superman . . 1,800.00

27 The Man Who Out-Supered
  Superman. 1,800.00
28 A:Lex Luther, Batman V:Glass
  Man. 1,800.00
29 Superman:The Books that
  Couldn't be Bound 1,800.00
30 Superman:Sheriff Clark Kent,
  Batman V:Joe Coyne 1,800.00
31 Superman's Super-Rival,Batman:
  Man with the X-Ray Eyes . . 1,500.00
32 Superman Visits
  Ancient Egypt 1,500.00
33 Superman Press, Inc.,
  Batman V:James Harmon . 1,500.00
34 The Un-Super Superman . . 1,500.00
35 Daddy Superman,A:Penguin 1,500.00
36 Lois Lane,Sleeping Beauty 1,500.00
37 The Superman Story,Batman
  V:T-Gun Jones 1,500.00
38 If There were No Superman 1,500.00
39 Superman V:Big Jim Martin,
  Batman V:J.J.Jason 1,500.00
40 Superman V:Check,Batman:
  Four Killers Against Fate!. . 1,100.00
41 I:Supermanium,
  E:Boy Commandos 1,100.00
42 Superman goes to Uranus,
  A:Marco Polo & Kubla Khan1,100.00
43 A:J.Wilbur Wolfingham. 1,100.00
44 Superman:The Revolt of the
  Thought Machine 1,100.00
45 Superman:Lois Lane and Clark
  Kent,Private Detectives . . . 1,100.00
46 Superman V:Mr. 7 . . . . 1,100.00
47 Superman:The Girl Who
  Hated Reporters 1,100.00
48 A:Joker. 1,100.00
49 Superman Meets the
  Metropolis Shutterbug
  Society, A:Penguin 1,100.00
50 Superman Super Wrecker . 1,100.00
51 Superman:The Amazing
  Talents of Lois Lane 1,100.00
52 A:J.Wilbur Wolfingham. 1,100.00
53 Superman V:Elias Toomey. . 1,100.00
54 The Superman Who Avoided
  Danger!. 1,100.00
55 A:Penguin 1,100.00
56 Superman V:Dr.Vallin,Batman
  V:Big Dan Hooker. 1,100.00
57 The Artificial Superman 1,100.00
58 Superman V:Mr.Fenton 1,100.00
59 A:Lex Luthor,Joker. 1,100.00
60 A:J.Wilbur Wolfingham. 1,100.00
61 A:Joker,Superman's
  Blackout. 900.00
62 A:Lex Luthor 900.00
63 Superman:Clark Kent,
  Gangster 900.00
64 Superman:The Death of Lois
  Lane,Batman:Bruce Wayne...
  Amateur Detective. 900.00
65 The Confessions of Superman,
  Batman V:The Blaster 1,300.00
66 Superman,Ex-Crimebuster;
  Batman V:Brass Haley 900.00
67 Superman:Metropolis-Crime
  Center!. 900.00
68 Batman V:The Crimesmith . . 900.00
69 A:Jor-El,Batman
  V:Tom Becket 900.00
70 The Two Faces of Superman,
  Batman:Crime Consultant . . 900.00
71 B:Superman/Batman
  team-ups 2,200.00
72 V:Heavy Weapon gang 1,400.00
73 V:Fang 1,400.00
74 The Contest of Heroes 1,100.00
75 V:The Purple Mask Mob . . 1,000.00
76 When Gotham City
  Challenged Metropolis. 800.00
77 V:Prof.Pender 800.00

World's Finest Comics #88
© DC Comics, Inc.

78 V:Varrel mob 800.00
79 A:Aladdin. 800.00
80 V:Mole. 800.00
81 Meet Ka Thar from future . . . 600.00
82 A:Three Musketeers 600.00
83 The Case of the Mother
  Goose Mystery 600.00
84 V:Thad Linnis Gang 600.00
85 Meet Princess Varina 600.00
86 V:Henry Bartle. 600.00
87 V:Elton Craig. 600.00
88 1st team-up Luthor & Joker . . 650.00
89 I:Club of Heroes 600.00
90 A:Batwoman 600.00
91 V:Rohtul,Descendent of Lex
  Luthor 400.00
92 1st & only A:Skyboy. 400.00
93 V:Victor Danning. 400.00
94 O:Superman/Batman team,
  A:Lex Luthor 1,200.00
95 Battle o/t Super Heroes 400.00
96 Super-Foes from Planet X . . 400.00
97 V:Condor Gang. 400.00
98 I:Moonman 400.00
99 JK,V:Carl Verril 400.00
100 A:Kandor, Lex Luthor. 1,000.00
101 A:Atom Master 300.00
102 V:Jo-Jo Groff gang,
  B:Tommy Tomorrow. 300.00
103 The Secrets of the
  Sorcerer's Treasure. 300.00
104 A:Lex Luthor 300.00
105 V:Khalex 300.00
106 V:Duplicate Man 300.00
107 The Secret of the Time
  Creature. 300.00
108 The Star Creatures 300.00
109 V:Fangan 300.00
110 The Alien Who Doomed
  Robin! 300.00
111 V:Floyd Frisby 300.00
112 Menace of Superman's Pet. . 300.00
113 1st Bat-Mite/Mr.Mxyzptlk
  team-up 300.00
114 Captives o/t Space Globes . . 300.00
115 The Curse That Doomed
  Superman 250.00
116 V:Vance Collins 250.00
117 A:Batwoman,Lex Luthor 250.00
118 V:Vath-Gar. 250.00
119 V:General Grambly 250.00
120 V:Faceless Creature 250.00
121 I:Miss Arrowette 250.00
122 V:Klor. 175.00
123 A:Bat-Mite & Mr. Mxyzptlk. . . 175.00

All comics prices listed are for *Near Mint* condition.

124 V:Hroguth,E:Tommy
Tomorrow............... 175.00
125 V:Jundy,B:Aquaman 175.00
126 A:Lex Luthor 175.00
127 V:Zerno................. 175.00
128 V:Moose Morans.......... 175.00
129 Joker/Luthor T.U. 175.00
130 Riddle of the Four Planets . . 175.00
131 V:Octopus 175.00
132 V:Denny Kale,Shorty Biggs . 175.00
133 Beasts of the Supernatural . . 175.00
134 V:Band of Super-Villians.... 175.00
135 V:The Future Man......... 175.00
136 The Batman Nobody
Remembered............. 175.00
137 A:Lex Luthor 175.00
138 V:General Grote 175.00
139 V:Sphinx Gang,E:Aquaman . 175.00
140 CS,V:Clayface............ 175.00
141 CS,A:Jimmy Olsen 175.00
142 CS,O:Composite Man...... 175.00
143 CS,A:Kandor,I:Mailbag 125.00
144 CS,A:Clayface,Brainiac..... 125.00
145 CS,Prison for Heroes 125.00
146 CS,Batman,Son of Krypton. . 125.00
147 CS,A:Jimmy Olsen 125.00
148 CS,A:Lex Luthor,Clayface... 125.00
149 CS,The Game of the
Secret Identities........... 125.00
150 CS,V:Rokk and Sorban..... 125.00
151 CS,A:Krypto,BU:Congorilla. . 125.00
152 CS,A:The Colossal Kids,Bat-
mite,V:Mr.Mxyzptlk 125.00
153 CS,V:Lex Luthor 125.00
154 CS,The Sons of Batman &
Superman(Imaginary) 125.00
155 CS,The 1000th Exploit of
Batman & Superman....... 125.00
156 CS,I:BizarroBatman,V:Joker. 125.00
157 CS,The Abominable Brats
(Imaginary story) 110.00
158 CS,V:Brainiac 110.00
159 CS,A:Many Major villians,I:Jim
Gordon as Anti-Batman & Perry
White as Anti-Superman. 110.00
160 V:Dr Zodiac. 110.00
161 CS,80 page giant 125.00
162 V:The Jousting Master 75.00
163 CS,The Court of No Hope ... 75.00
164 CS,I:Genia,V:Brainiac....... 75.00
165 CS,The Crown of Crime 75.00
166 CS,V:Muto & Joker 100.00
167 CS,The New Superman &
Batman(Imaginary) V:Luthor . . 75.00
168 CS,R:Composite Superman .. 75.00
169 The Supergirl/Batgirl Plot;
V:Batmite,Mr.Mxyzptlk...... 75.00
170 80 page giant,reprint....... 125.00
171 CS,V:The Executioners...... 75.00
172 CS,Superman & Batman
Brothers (Imaginary) 75.00
173 CS,The Jekyll-Hyde
Heroes................. 150.00
174 CS,Secrets of the Double
Death Wish 100.00
175 NA(1st Batman),C:Flash.... 100.00
176 NA,A:Supergirl & Batgirl 100.00
177 V:Joker & Luthor.......... 100.00
178 CS,The Has-Been Superman . 75.00
179 CS,giant 125.00
180 RA,ME,Supermans Perfect
Crime.................. 75.00
181 RA,ME................. 75.00
182 RA,ME,The Mad Manhunter . . 75.00
183 RA,ME,Superman's Crimes
of the Ages.............. 75.00
184 RA,ME,A:JLA,Robin 75.00
185 CS,The Galactic Gamblers ... 75.00
186 RA,ME,The Bat Witch....... 75.00
187 RA,ME,Demon Superman .. 75.00
188 giant,reprint. 100.00
189 RA,ME,V:Lex Luthor 50.00

World's Finest Comics #181
© DC Comics Inc.

190 RA,V:Lex Luthor 40.00
191 RA,A:Jor-El,Lara........... 40.00
192 RA,The Prison of No Escape . 40.00
193 The Breaking of Batman
and Superman........... 40.00
194 RA,ME,Inside the Mafia 40.00
195 RA,ME,Dig Now-Die Later ... 40.00
196 CS,The Kryptonite Express,
E:Batman............... 40.00
197 giant 100.00
198 DD,B:Superman T.U.,
A:Flash 125.00
199 DD,Superman & Flash race . 125.00
200 NA(c),DD,Prisoners of the
Immortal World; A:Robin 50.00
201 NA(c),DD,A Prize of Peril,
A:Green Lantern,Dr. Fate..... 35.00
202 NA(c),DD,Vengeance of the
Tomb Thing,A:Batman...... 35.00
203 NA(c),DD,Who's Minding the
Earth,A:Quamar............ 35.00
204 NA(c),DD,Journey to the End
of Hope,A:Wonder Woman ... 35.00
205 NA(c),DD,The Computer that
Captured a Town,Frazetta Ad,
A:Teen Titans.............. 40.00
206 DD,giant reprint............ 75.00
207 DD,Superman,A:Batman,
V:Dr.Light................ 40.00
208 NA(c),DD,A:Dr Fate 40.00
209 NA(c),DD,A:Green Arrow,
Hawkman,I&V:The Temper... 40.00
210 NA(c),DD,A:Batman 40.00
211 NA(c),DD,A:Batman 40.00
212 CS(c),And So My World
Begins,A:Martian Manhunter.. 40.00
213 DD,Peril in a Very Small
Place,A:The Atom 40.00
214 DD,A:Vigilante............. 40.00
215 DD,Saga of the Super Sons
(Imaginary story) 60.00
216 DD,R:Super Sons,Little Town
with a Big Secret 20.00
217 DD,MA,Heroes with
Dirty Hands 20.00
218 DD,DC,A:Batman,
BU:Metamorpho 20.00
219 DD,Prisoner of Rogues Rock;
A:Batman............... 20.00
220 DD,MA,Let No Man Write My
Epitaph,BU:Metamorpho 20.00
221 DD,Cry Not For My Forsaken
Son; R:Super Sons 20.00
222 DD,Evil In Paradise........ 20.00

223 DD,giant,A:Deadman,Aquaman
Robotman 60.00
224 DD,giant,A:Super Sons,
Metamorpho,Johnny Quick ... 60.00
225 giant,A:Rip Hunter,Vigilante,
Black Canary,Robin 60.00
226 A:Sandman,Metamorpho,
Deadman,Martian Manhunter . 60.00
227 MGr,BWi,A:The Demonic Duo,
Vigilante,Rip Hunter,Deadman,
I:Stargrave 60.00
228 ATh,A:Super Sons,Aquaman,
Robin,Vigilante 60.00
229 I:Powerman,A:Metamorpho .. 30.00
230 A:Super-Sons,Deadman,
Aquaman, giant-size 50.00
231 A:Green Arrow,Flash....... 18.00
232 DD,The Dream Bomb 18.00
233 A:Super-Sons 18.00
234 CS,Family That Fled Earth .. 18.00
235 DD,V:Sagitaurus 18.00
236 DD,A:The Atom........... 18.00
237 Intruder from a Dead World .. 18.00
238 DD,V:Luthor,A:Super-Sons... 18.00
239 CS,A:Gold(from Metal Men) . 18.00
240 DD,A:Kandor............. 15.00
241 Make Way For a new World.. 15.00
242 EC,A:Super-Sons 15.00
243 CS,AM,A:Robin............ 15.00
244 NA(c),JL,MA,MN,TA,giant
B:Green Arrow............ 25.00
245 NA(C),CS,MA,MN,TA,
GM,JSh,BWi,giant.......... 25.00
246 NA(c),KS,MA,MN,TA,GM,
DH,A:JLA............... 25.00
247 KS,GM,giant 25.00
248 KS,GM,DG,TVE,A:Sgt.Rock . 20.00
249 KS,SD,TVE,A:Phantom
Stranger,B:Creeper 20.00
250 GT,SD,Superman,Batman,
Wonder Woman,Green Arrow,
Black Canary,team-up....... 22.00
251 GT,SD,JBi,BL,TVE,RE,
JA,A:Poison Ivy,Speedy,
I:CountVertigo 22.00
252 GT,TVE,SD,JA,giant 22.00
253 KS,DN,TVE,SD,B:Shazam .. 15.00
254 GT,DN,TVE,SD,giant 15.00
255 JL,DA,TVE,SD,DN,KS,
E:Creeper 15.00
256 MA,DN,KS,DD,Hawkman,Black
Lightning,giant 15.00
257 DD,FMc,DN,KS,GT,RB,
RT,giant................ 15.00
258 NA(c),RB,JL,DG,DN,KS,RT,
giant.................. 17.00
259 RB,DG,MR,MN,DN,KS 15.00
260 RB,DG,MN,DN 15.00
261 RB,DG,AS,RT,EB,DN,
A:Penguin, Terra Man 15.00
262 DG,DN,DA,JSon,RT,
Aquaman............... 15.00
263 RB,DG,DN,TVE,JSh,Aquaman,
Adam Strange 15.00
264 RB,DG,TVE,DN,Aquaman... 15.00
265 RB,DN,RE,TVE............ 15.00
266 RB,TVE,DN.............. 15.00
267 RB,DG,TVE,AS,DN,
A:Challengers of the Unknown 15.00
268 DN,TVE,BBr,RT,AS......... 15.00
269 RB,FMc,TVE,BBr,AS,DN,DA . 15.00
270 RB,RT,TVE,AS,
DN,LMa 15.00
271 GP(c),RB,FMc,O:Superman/
Batman T.U.............. 15.00
272 RB,DN,TVE,BBr,AS 14.00
273 TVE,LMa,JSon,AS,DN,DA,
A:Plastic Man 14.00
274 TVE,LMa,BBr,GC,AS,DN,
Green Arrow 14.00
275 RB,FMc,TVE,LMa,DSp,AS,
DN,DA,A:Mr.Freeze........ 14.00

All comics prices listed are for *Near Mint* condition.

DC COMICS

World's Finest Comics #291
© *DC Comics, Inc.*

276 GP(c),RB,TVE,LMa,DSp,CI,
   DN,DA 14.00
277 GP(c),RT,TVE,DSp,AS,DN,
   DH,V:Dr.Double X 14.00
278 GP(c),RB,TVE,LMa,DSp,DN . 14.00
279 KP,TVE,LMa,AS,DN,
   B:Kid Eternity 14.00
280 RB,TVE,LMa,AS,DN 14.00
281 GK(c),IN,TVE,LMa,AS,DN . . 14.00
282 IN,FMc,GK,CI,last giant
   E:Kid Eternity 14.00
283 GT,FMc,GK 14.00
284 GT,DSp,A:Legion;E:G.Arrow . 14.00
285 FM(c),RB,A:Zatanna 14.00
286 RB,A:Flash 14.00
287 TVE,A:Flash 14.00
288 A:JLA 14.00
289 GK(c),Kryll way of Dying. . . . 14.00
290 TD(i),I:Stalagron 14.00
291 WS(c),TD(i),V:Stalagron 14.00
292 . . . . 14.00
293 . . . . 14.00
294 . . . . 14.00
295 FMc(i) 14.00
296 RA 14.00
297 GC,V:Pantheon. 14.00
298 V:Pantheon 14.00
299 GC,V:Pantheon. 14.00
300 RA,GP,KJ,MT,FMc,A:JLA . . . 14.00
301 Rampage 7.00
302 DM,NA(rep). 7.00
303 Plague. 7.00
304 SLi,O:Null&Void 7.00
305 TVE,V:Null&Void 7.00
306 SLi,I:Swordfish & Barracuda. . 7.00
307 TVE,V:Null&Void 7.00
308 GT,Night and Day 7.00
309 MT,AA,V:Quantum 7.00
310 I:Sonik. 7.00
311 A:Monitor. 7.00
312 AA,I:Network 7.00
313 AA(i),V:Network 7.00
314 AA(i),V:Executrix 7.00
315 V:Cathode 7.00
316 LSn,I:Cheapjack 7.00
317 LSn,V:Cheapjack 7.00
318 AA(i),A:Sonik 7.00
319 AA(i),I:REM 7.00
320 AA(i),V:REM 7.00
321 AA,V:Chronos 7.00
322 KG,The Search 7.00
323 AA(i),final issue 7.00
Spec.#1 Our Worlds at War,48-pg . . 6.00

WORLD'S FINEST
[Limited Series], 1990
1 SR,KK,Worlds Apart 8.00
2 SR,KK,Worlds Collide 6.00
3 SR,KK,Worlds At War 6.00
TPB rep.#1-#3 . . . . 20.00

WORLD'S FINEST: SUPERBOY/ROBIN
Oct., 1996
1 (of 2) CDi&KK(s),TG,SHa,
   V:Poison Ivy, Metallo 5.00
2 CDi&KK(s),TG,SHa, V:Poison
   Ivy, Metallo. 5.00

WORLD'S GREATEST SUPER-HEROES
1977
1 A:Batman,Robin. 35.00

WORLD WAR III
Apr., 2007
Pt. 1 A Call to Arms 2.50
Pt. 2 The Valiant 2.50
Pt. 3 Hell is For Heroes 2.50
Pt. 4 United We Stand 2.50

WORLD WITHOUT END
1990
1 The Host, I:Brother Bones. 5.00
2 A:Brother Bones. 3.50
3 . . . . 3.50
4 House of Fams 2.50
5 Female Fury. 2.50
6 conclusion 2.50

WRATH OF THE SPECTRE
May, 1988
1 JAp,rep.Adventure #431-#433. . . 4.00
2 JAp,rep.Adventure #434-#436. . . 4.00
3 JAp,rep.Adventure #437-#440. . . 4.00
4 JAp,reps.,final issue. 5.00
TPB (2005). 20.00

XENOBROOD
1994–95
0 New team. 2.25
1 Battles 2.25
2 Bestiary 2.25
3 A:Superman. 2.25
4 V:Bestiary. 2.25
5 V:Vimian. 2.25
6 final issue. 2.25

XERO
March, 1997
1 Cpr(s),Ccs,Trane Walker/Xero . . 3.00
2 Cpr(s),Ccs,The Rookie 2.50
3 Cpr(s),Ccs,The Beast 2.50
4 CPr(s) 2.50
6 CPr, Genesis tie-in. 2.50
7 CPr(s),O:Zero, pt.1 . . . . 2.50
8 CPr,O:Zero. 2.25
9 CPr(s), ... 2.25
10 CPr,a matter of ethics 2.25
11 . . . . 2.25
12 CPr, final issue, Xero dead. . . . 2.25

XOMBI
Milestone, 1994–96
0 WS(c),DCw,Shadow War,Foil(c),
   I:Xombi,Twilight 2.50
1 JBy(c),B:Silent Cathedrals 2.00
1a Platinum ed. 7.00

2 I:Rabbi Simmowitz,Golms,Liam
   Knight of the Spoken Fire 2.50
3 A:Liam 2.00
4 Silent Cathedrals 2.00
5 thru 20 . . . . @2.50
21 final issue 3.50

Y: THE LAST MAN
DC/Vertigo, July, 2002
1 JMz,UnManned,pt.1,40-pg. . . . 30.00
2 JMz,UnManned,pt.2. . . . . 25.00
3 JMz,UnManned,pt.3. . . . . 20.00
4 JMz,UnManned,pt.4. . . . . 12.00
5 JMz,UnManned,pt.5. . . . . 10.00
6 JMz,Cycles,pt.1 . . . . 7.00
7 JMz,Cycles,pt.2 . . . . 6.00
8 JMz,Cycles,pt.3 . . . . 6.00
9 JMz,Cycles,pt.4 . . . . 6.00
10 JMz,Cycles,pt.5 . . . . 4.00
11 JMz,One Small Step,pt.1 . . . . . 4.00
12 JMz,One Small Step,pt.2 . . . . . 4.00
13 JMz,One Small Step,pt.3 . . . . . 4.00
14 JMz,One Small Step,pt.4 . . . . . 3.50
15 JMz,One Small Step,pt.5 . . . . . 3.50
16 JMz,Comedy&Tragedy,pt.1. . . . 3.50
17 JMz,Comedy&Tragedy,pt.2. . . . 3.00
18 JMz,Safeword,pt.1 . . . . 3.00
19 JMz,Safeword,pt.2 . . . . 3.00
20 JMz,Safeword,pt.3 . . . . 3.00
21 JMz,Widow's Pass,pt.1. . . . . . . 3.00
22 JMz,Widow's Pass,pt.2. . . . . . . 3.00
23 JMz,Widow's Pass,pt.3. . . . . . . 3.00
24 JMz,Tongues of Flame,pt.1. . . . 3.00
25 JMz,Tongues of Flame,pt.2. . . . 3.00
26 JMz,Hero's Journey 3.00
27 JMz,Ring of Truth,pt.1. . . . . . . 3.00
28 Ring of Truth, pt.2. . . . . 3.00
29 Ring of Truth, pt.3. . . . . 3.00
30 Ring of Truth, pt.4. . . . . 3.00
31 Ring of Truth, pt.5. . . . . 3.00
32 thru 35 Girl on Girl, pt.1–pt.4 . @3.00
36 F:Beth Deville 3.00
37 Paper Dolls, pt.1 . . . . 3.00
38 Paper Dolls, pt.2. . . . . 3.00
39 Paper Dolls, pt.3 . . . . 3.00
40 The Women Left Behind 3.00
41 O:Agent 355 . . . . 3.00
42 F:Ampersand 3.00
43 A trip to Japan. 3.00
44 Kimono Dragons 3.00
45 Kimono Dragons 3.00
46 Kimono Dragons, concl. 3.00
47 Secret origin of Dr. Allison Mann 3.00
48 O:Alter Tse'elon 3.00
49 Motherland, pt.1 . . . . 3.00
50 Motherland, pt.2 . . . . 3.00
51 Motherland, pt.3 . . . . 3.00
52 Motherland, pt.4 . . . . 3.00
53 . . . . 3.00
54 Fish & Bicycle Theatre Troupe . . 3.00
55 Whys and Wherefores, pt.1 . . . . 3.00
56 Whys and Wherefores, pt.2 . . . . 3.00
57 Whys and Wherefores, pt.3 . . . . 3.00
58 Whys and Wherefores, pt.4 . . . . 3.00
59 Whys and Wherefores, pt.5 . . . . 3.00

YEAR ONE: BATMAN/RA'S AL GHUL
June, 2005
1 (of 2) PG,JP48-page 6.00
2 PG,JP. 6.00
TPB 10.00

YEAR ONE: BATMAN/SCARECROW
May, 2005
1 (of 2) 48-page 6.00
2 . . . . 6.00

YEAH!
Homage/DC, 1999
1 GHe	3.00
2 GHe	3.00
3 GHe	3.00
4 GHe,Origins of Yeah,pt.1	3.00
5 GHe,Origins of Yeah,pt.2	3.00
6 GHe,	3.00
7 GHe,	3.00
8 GHe,	3.00
9 GHe,final issue	3.00

YOUNG ALL STARS
June, 1987
1 I:IronMunro&FlyingFox,D:TNT	4.50
2 V:Axis Amerika	2.50
3 V:Axis Amerika	2.25
4 I:The Tigress	2.25
5 I:Dyna-mite,O:Iron Munro	2.25
6	2.25
7 Baseball Game,A:Tigress	2.25
8 Millennium	2.25
9 Millennium	2.25
10 Hugo Danner	2.25
11 Birth of Iron Munro	2.25
12 Secret of Hugo Danner	2.25
13 V:Deathbolt,Ultra-Humanite	2.25
14 Fury+Ultra Humanite	2.25
15 IronMunro At high school	2.25
16 Ozyan Inheritance	2.25
17 Ozyan Inheritance	2.25
18 Ozyan Inheritance	2.25
19 Ozyan	2.25
20 O:Flying Fox	2.25
21 Atom & Evil#1	2.25
22 Atom & Evil#2	2.25
23 Atom & Evil#3	2.25
24 Atom & Evil#4	2.25
25	2.25
26 End of the All Stars?	2.25
27 Sons of Dawn' begins	2.25
28 Search for Hugo Danner	2.25
29 A:Hugo Danner	2.25
30 V:Sons of Dawn	2.25
31 V:Sons of Dawn,last issue	2.25
Ann.#1 MG,V:Mekanique	2.50

YOUNG HEROES IN LOVE
April, 1997
1 DeM,F:Hard Drive	3.00
2 DeM,sex, lies and superheroics	2.50
3 A:Superman	2.50
4 F:Hard Drive	2.50
5 Genesis tie-in	2.50
6 The Rat Pack	2.50
7 Secret Identity Issue	2.50
8 V:Scarecrow	2.50
9 F:Frostbite & Bonfire	2.50
10 V:Grundo'mu	2.50
11 V:Grundo'mu	2.50
12 Hard Drive dead?	2.50
13 New leader picked	2.50
14 Man of Inches vs. Man of Candles	2.50
15 Junior vs. Birthday Boy	2.50
16 DeM,Zip-Kid	2.50
17 DeM,Monstergirl's Uncle	2.50
Spec.#1,000,000 DeM final issue	3.00

YOUNG JUSTICE
July, 1998
1 PDd,TNu,Robin,Superboy, Impulse	4.50
2 PDd,TNu,V:Super-Cycle	3.00
3 PDd(s),TNu,V:Mr.Mxyzptlk	3.00

4 PDd(s),TNu,Girls join team	3.00
5 PDd(s),TNu,V:Harm.	3.00
6 PDd(s),TNu,F:JLA	3.00
7 PDd(s),TNu,A:Nightwing	3.00
8 CDi(s),TNu,A:Razorsharp	3.00
9 PDd(s),V:Huggathugees	3.00
10 PDd(s),V:The Acolyte	3.00
11 PDd(s),Rescue Red Tornado	3.00
12 PDd(s),TNu,Supergirl x-over Hell's Angels,pt.1	3.00
13 PDd(s), Hell's Angels,pt.3	3.00
14 PDd(s),Day of Judgment x-over	3.00
15 PDd(s),F:Arrowette	3.00
16 PDd(s).	3.00
17 PDd(s),A:A.P.E.S.	3.00
18 PDd(s),Young Injustice	3.00
19 PDd(s),I:Empress	3.00
20 PDd(s),new team	3.00
21 PDd(s),all new?	2.75
22 Day in the life	2.75
23 PDd,TNu,AustraliaGames,pt.1	2.75
24 PDd,TNu,AustraliaGames,pt.2	2.75
25 PDd,TNu,Into space,pt.1	2.75
26 PDd,TNu,Into space,pt.2	2.75
27 PDd,TNu,Into space,pt.3	2.75
28 PDd,TNu,New Genesis	2.75
29 PDd,TNu,F:Forever People	2.75
30 PDd,TNu,Secret vs. Spoiler	2.75
31 PDd,TNu,F:Empress	2.75
32 PDd,TNu,F:Empress.	2.75
33 PDd,TNu,WendyWerewolfHunter	2.75
34 PDd,TNu,wolf bites	2.75
35 PDd,TNu,Worlds at War,tie-in	2.75
36 PDd,TNu,Worlds at War,tie-in.	2.75
37 PDd,TNu,stuck in Hell	2.75
38 PDd,TNu,jokerized Match.	2.75
39 PDd,TNu,F:New Genesis	2.75
40 PDd(s),TNu,Christmas Past	2.75
41 PDd(s),TNu,F:Ray	2.75
42 PDd(s),TNu,F:Hal Jordan	2.75
43 PDd(s),TNu,F:Traya	2.75
44 PDd(s),TNu,WorldWithoutYJ,pt.1	2.75
45 PDd(s),TNu,WorldWithoutYJ,pt.5	2.75
46 PDd(s),TNu,election day at HQ	2.75
47 PDd(s),TNu,Fighting MAAD,pt.1	2.75
48 PDd(s),TNu,Fighting MAAD,pt.2.	2.75
49 PDd(s),TNu,Fighting MAAD,pt.3.	2.75
50 PDd(s),TNu,F.MAAD,pg.4,48-pg.	4.00
51 PDd(s),TNu, on Zandia.	2.75
52 PDd(s),TNu,Real World	2.75
53 PDd(s),TNu,V:Secret	2.75
54 PDd(s),TNu,V:Secret	2.75
55 PDd(s),TNu,final issue	2.75
Spec.#1,000,000 PDd(s),TNu	3.00
Giant#1 Secret Origins, 80-page	5.00
Giant#1 80-page	5.00
Secret Files #1	5.00
Spec.#1 Young Justice in No Man's Land, CDi(s)	4.00
Spec.#1 Young Justice: The Secret Impulse,Superboy,Robin (1998)	2.50
Spec.#1 Our Worlds at War	3.00
TPB A League of Their Own	15.00

YOUNG JUSTICE: SINS OF YOUTH
March, 2000
1 (of 2) PDd,x-over	4.00
2 PDd,x-over	4.00
Secret Files #1	5.00
TPB Sins of Youth	20.00

YOUNG LOVE
Sept.–Oct., 1963
39	75.00
40 thru 50	@50.00

Young Love #125
© DC Comics Inc.

51 thru 60	@40.00
61 thru 68	@40.00
69 giant size	90.00
70 thru 80	@40.00
81 thru 99 giants, 52-page	@35.00
100	45.00
101 thru 106	@30.00
107 GC, Giant, 100-page	125.00
108 thru 114 Giant, 100-page	@100.00
115 thru 126 52-page	@50.00

ZATANNA
1987
1 R:Zatanna	2.25
2 N:Zatanna	2.25
3 Come Together	2.25
4 V:Xaos	2.25

ZERO GIRL
DC/Homage Dec., 2000
1 (of 5) SK,F:Amy Snooster	3.00
2 SK,	3.00
3 SK,Vice Principal Hooly	3.00
4 SK,Mr. Foster.	3.00
5 SK, concl..	3.00
TPB series rep. 144-page	13.00

ZERO GIRL: FULL CIRCLE
DC/Vertigo, Nov., 2002
1 (of 5) SK	3.00

ZERO HOUR: CRISIS IN TIME
1994
4 DJu(a&s),JOy,A:All DC Heroes, D;2nd Flash	4.50
3 DJu(a&s),JOy,D:G.A.Sandman, G:A.Atom,Dr.Fate,1st Wildcat IR:Time Trapper is Rokk Krinn, Hawkmen merged	2.50
2 DJu(a&s),Joy	2.50
1 DJu(a&s),JOy,b:Power Gir's Child	2.50
0 DJu(A&s),JOy,Gatefold(c),Extant vs. Spectre.	2.50

All comics prices listed are for *Near Mint* condition.

AMALGAM

Amazon #1
© DC/Marvel

Coctor Strangefate #1
© DC/Marvel

Magnetic Men Featuring Magneto #1
© DC/Marvel

AMAZON
DC, 1996–97

1 JBy,TA 3.00
1 one-shot JBy,Princess Ororo
   is Wonder Woman 2.25

ASSASSINS
DC, 1996–97

1 DGC,SMc 3.00
1 one-shot DGC(s),SMc,F:Dare
   and Catsai 2.25

BAT-THING
DC, 1997

1 one-shot LHa(s),RDm,BSz,
   V:motorcycle gang 2.25

BRUCE WAYNE:
AGENT OF S.H.I.E.L.D.
Marvel, 1996

1 CDi, ... 3.00

BULLETS & BRACELETS
Marvel, 1996

1 JOs,GFr,CaS 3.00

CHALLENGERS OF
THE FANTASTIC
Marvel, 1997

1 KK,TGu,AV 2.25

DARK CLAW
ADVENTURES, THE
DC, 1997

1 one-shot TTy,RBr,V:Ladia Talia . . 2.25

DC VERSUS MARVEL
MARVEL VERSUS DC

1 (DC)DJu 6.00
1a 2nd printing 4.00
2 (Marvel)PDd,DJu 5.00
2a 2nd printing 4.00
3 (Marvel)DJu 4.00
4 (DC)PDd,DJu 4.00
TPB rep. mini series #1–#4 . . . . . . 13.00

DOCTOR STRANGEFATE
DC, 1996–97

1 RMz,KN 3.00
1 one-shot RMz(s),JL,KN,Supreme
   Lord of Order 2.25

EXCITING X-PATROL
Marvel, 1997

1 BKs,BHi 2.25

GENERATION HEX
DC, 1997

1 one-shot,PrM(s),AdP,F:Jono Hex,
   Madam Banshee 2.25

IRON LANTERN
Marvel, 1997

1 KB,PSm,AW 2.25

JLX
DC 1996–97

1 MWa,GJ, ... 3.00
1 one-shot,MWa(s),GJ,HPo,JhD . . 2.25

JLX UNLEASHED
DC, 1997

1 one-shot, CPr,The Inextinguish-
   able Flame 2.25

LEGENDS OF
THE DARK CLAW
DC, 1996–97

1 LHa,JBa, ... 3.00
1 one-shot LHa(s),JBa, ... 2.25
1 2nd printing 2.25

LOBO THE DUCK
DC, 1997

1 one-shot, AlG,VS, ... 2.25

MAGNETO &
THE MAGNETIC MEN
Marvel, 1996

1 MWa,GJ,JMs,ATi 3.00

MAGNETIC MEN
FEATURING MAGNETO
Marvel, 1997

1 TPe,BKi,DPs 2.25

SPEED DEMON
Marvel, 1996

1 HMe,SvL,AM 3.00

SPIDER-BOY
Marvel, 1996

1 KK,MeW 3.00

SPIDER-BOY TEAM-UP
Marvel, 1997

1 KK,RSt 2.25

SUPER-SOLDIER
DC, 1996–97

1 MWa,DGb 3.00
1-shot MWa(s),DGb,V:Ultra-
   Metallo, Green Skull, Hydra . . . 2.25

SUPER SOLDIER:
MAN OF WAR
DC, 1997

1 one-shot MWa(s),DGb,JP,
   V:Nazis 2.25

THORION OF
THE NEW ASGODS
Marvel, 1997

1 KG,JR2 . . . . 2.25

X-PATROL
Marvel, 1996

1 KK,BKs, ... 3.00
The Amalgam Age of Comics: The DC
Comics Collection TPBs 13.00
The Amalgam Age of Comics: The
Marvel Comics Collection TPBs . . 13.00
Return to the Amalgam Age of Comics:
The DC Comics Collection TPB . . 13.00

      All comics prices listed are for *Near Mint* condition.

MARVEL

ABOMINATIONS
1996
1 (of 3) IV,AMe, Future Imperfect
  spin-off 2.25
2 IV,AMe 2.25
3 IV,AMe 2.25

ABRAHAM STONE
1995
1 JKu, Early 20th century 7.00
2 Wandering Man in the 20s. 7.00

ACTION FORCE
March, 1987
1 U.K. G.I. Joe Series 2.25
2 thru 40 . . . . @2.25

ACTUAL CONFESSIONS
See: LOVE ADVENTURES

ACTUAL ROMANCES
Oct., 1949
1 . . . . 150.00
2 Photo Cover. 100.00

ADVENTURE INTO FEAR
See: FEAR

ADVENTURE INTO MYSTERY
Marvel Atlas, 1956–57
1 BP,BEv(c),Future Tense 500.00
2 Man on the 13th Floor 300.00
3 Next Stop Eternity 300.00
4 BP,AW, The Hex 300.00
5 JO,BEv,The People Who
  Weren't 300.00
6 The Wax Man 300.00
7 AT,BEv(c). 300.00
8 AT,JWo,TSe 300.00

ADVENTURES INTO TERROR
See: JOKER COMICS

ADVENTURES INTO WEIRD WORLDS
Jan., 1952–June, 1954
1 RH,GT,The Walking Death . . 1,200.00
2 GT,JMn,Thing in the Bottle . . . 600.00
3 JMn,The Thing That Waited . . 450.00
4 BEv,RH,TheVillageGraveyard . 450.00
5 BEv,I Crawl Thru Graves 450.00
6 The Ghost Still Walks 450.00
7 OW,Monsters In Disguise 450.00
8 DAy,Nightmares. 450.00
9 Do Not Feed 450.00
10 BEv,Down In The Cellar 450.00
11 JMn,Phantom 400.00
12 GT,Lost In the Graveyard 400.00
13 JeR,DRi,Where Dead Men
  Walk. 400.00
14 A Shriek In the Night. 400.00
15 GT,Terror In Our Town 400.00
16 The Kiss of Death 400.00
17 RH,He Walks With A Ghost . . 400.00
18 Ivan & Petroff 400.00
19 It Happened One Night. 400.00
20 JMn,The Doubting Thomas . . 400.00
21 JF,What Happened In
  the Cave,Hitler. 450.00

Adventures into Weird Worlds #6
© Marvel Entertainment Group

22 JMn,RH,Vampire's Partner . . . 400.00
23 JMn,The Kiss of Death 300.00
24 JF,Halfway Home 300.00
25 BEv,JSt,The Mad Mamba 300.00
26 DAy,Good-Bye Earth. 300.00
27 The Dwarf of Horror Moor. . . . 600.00
28 DW,Monsters From the Grave 400.00
29 Bone Dry. 250.00
30 JSt,The Impatient Ghost. 250.00

ADVENTURES OF CAPTAIN AMERICA
Sept., 1991
1 KM,JRu,O:Capt. America. 6.00
2 KM,KWe,TA,O:Capt.America. . . . 5.50
3 KM,KWe,JRu,D:Lt.Col.Fletcher . 5.50
4 KWe,JRu,V:Red Skull 5.50

ADVENTURES OF CYCLOPS & PHOENIX
1994
1 SLo(s),GeH,AV,O:Cable 5.00
2 thru 4 SLo(s),GeH,AV,O:Cable @4.00

ADVENTURES OF HOMER GHOST
Atlas, June–Aug., 1957
1 . . . . 150.00
2 . . . . 150.00

ADVENTURES OF PINKY LEE
Marvel Atlas, July, 1955
1 . . . . 400.00
2 . . . . 300.00
3 thru 5 . . . . @250.00

ADVENTURES OF SNAKE PLISSKIN
1997
1-shot LKa, *Escape From L.A.*
  movie adapt. 3.00

ADVENTURES OF SPIDER-MAN
1996
1 from animated TV show. 3.00
2 V:Hammerhead 3.00
3 thru 8 . . . . 3.00
8 AS,V:Kingpin 3.00
9 MHi,A:Dr. Strange,. 3.00
10 AS,V:The Beetle 3.00
11 AS,V:Doctor Octopus, Venom. . . 3.00
12 AS,V:Doctor Octopus, Venom. . . 3.00

THE ADVENTURES OF BIG BOY
Marvel Timely Comics, 1956
1 . . . . 1,500.00
2 . . . . 750.00
3 . . . . 300.00
Becomes:

ADVENTURES OF THE BIG BOY
Marvel Timely Comics, 1956
4 . . . . 250.00
5 . . . . 250.00
6 . . . . 200.00
7 . . . . 200.00
8 thru 10 . . . . @200.00
11 thru 20 . . . . @150.00
21 thru 30 . . . . @100.00
31 thru 40 . . . . @50.00
41 thru 50 . . . . @35.00
51 thru 60 . . . . @25.00
61 thru 70 . . . . @25.00

ADVENTURES OF THE THING
April–July, 1992
1 rep. Marvel 2 in 1 #50 . . . . 2.50
2 rep. Marvel 2 in 1 #80 . . . . 2.25
3 rep. Marvel 2 in 1 #51 . . . . 2.25
4 rep. Marvel 2 in 1 #77 . . . . 2.25

ADVENTURES OF THE UNCANNY X-MEN
1995
1 Rep. 2.50

ADVENTURES OF THE X-MEN
1996–97
1 from animated TV show. 3.00
2 X-Factor vs. X-Men 3.00
3 thru 12 . . . . @3.00

ADVENTURES ON THE PLANET OF THE APES
Oct., 1975
1 GT,Planet of the Apes Movie
  Adaptation 50.00
2 GT,Humans Captured 20.00
3 GT,Man Hunt 20.00
4 GT,Trial By Fear. 20.00
5 GT, Fury in the Forbidden Zone 20.00
6 GT,The Forbidden Zone,Cont'd. 35.00
7 AA,Man Hunt Cont'd 35.00
8 AA,Brent & Nova Enslaved 20.00
9 AA,Mankind's Demise 15.00
10 AA,When Falls the Lawgiver. . . 20.00
11 AA,Final Chapter,Dec.,1976 . . . 25.00

AGENT X
July, 2002–Oct., 2003
1 Taskmaster trainee,40-pg. 3.50
2 thru 4 . . . . @3.00
5 thru 9 . . . . @2.50
10 thru 15 . . . . @2.50

AGENTS OF ATLAS
Aug., 2006
1 F:The Spaceman, The Goddess,
   The Robot, The Gorilla, The Spy 3.00
2 A:Venus 3.00
3 A:Marvel Boy 3.00
4 A:Namora. 3.00
5 The Temple of Atlas 3.00
6 finale, The Temple of Atlas 3.00

AGE OF INNOCENCE
1995
1-shot Timeslid aftermath 2.50

Airtight Garage #4
© Marvel Entertainment Group

AIRTIGHT GARAGE
Epic, July–Oct., 1993
1 thru 4 rep.Moebius GNv. . . . . . @3.50

AKIRA
Epic, Sept., 1988
1 The Highway,I:Kaneda,Tetsuo,
   Koy,Ryu,Colonel,Takaski 35.00
1a 2nd printing 4.00
2 Pursuit,I:Number27,(Masaru) . . 17.00
2a 2nd printing 3.50
3 Number 41,V:Clown Gang. 12.00
4 King of Clowns,V:Colonel 12.00
5 Cycle Wars,V:Clown Gang 12.00
6 D:Yamagota 10.00
7 Prisoners and Players,I:Miyo. . . 10.00
8 Weapon of Vengeance 10.00
9 Stalkers 10.00
10 The Awakening 10.00
11 Akira Rising 7.00
12 Enter Sakaki 7.00
13 Desperation. 7.00
14 Caught in the Middle. 7.00
15 Psychic Duel 7.00
16 Akira Unleashed 7.00
17 Emperor of Chaos. 7.00
18 Amid the Ruins 6.00
19 To Save the Children 6.00
20 Revelations 6.00
21 . . . . 6.00
22 . . . . 6.00

23 . . . . 6.00
24 Clown Gang 6.00
25 Search For Kay. 6.00
26 Juvenile A Project 6.00
27 Kay and Kaneda. 6.00
28 Tetsuo 6.00
29 Tetsuo 6.00
30 Tetsuo,Kay,Kaneda 6.00
31 D:Kaori,Kaneda,Vs.Tetsuo . . . 6.00
32 Tetsuo'sForces vs.U.S.Forces . 6.00
33 Tetsuo V:Kaneda. 6.00
34 64pt. R:Otomo. 14.00
35 Leads toward final battle. . . . 14.00
36 Lady Miyako 14.00
37 ghost of Tetsuo 14.00
38 conclusion 14.00

ALF
Star, March, 1988
1 Photo Cover. 4.00
1a 2nd printing 2.50
2 thru 19 . . . . @2.50
20 thru 22 . . . . @3.00
23 thru 30 . . . . @2.50
31 thru 43 . . . . @3.00
44 thru 45. . . . . @4.00
46 thru 49 . . . . @3.00
50 giant size. 4.00
Ann.#1 Evol.War 3.00
Ann.#2 . . . . 3.00
Spring Spec.#1. . . . . 3.00
Holiday Spec.#2 . . . . 3.00

ALIAS
Marvel Max, Sept., 2001
1 BMB(s). 10.00
2 BMB(s), F:Jessica Jones. 6.00
3 BMB(s). 6.00
4 BMB(s),DMk(c) 6.00
5 BMB(s),DMk(c) 4.00
6 BMB(s),DMk(c), ... 4.00
7 BMB(s),BSz, ... 4.00
8 BMB(s),BSz 4.00
9 BMB(s),2nd story, concl. 4.00
10 BMB(s),J.J.Jameson,Jessica . . 3.50
11 BMB(s),to small town 3.50
12 BMB(s),in small town 3.50
13 BMB(s) 3.50
14 BMB(s),DMk(c),case concludes . 3.50
15 BMB(s),DMk(c),Cage again . . . 3.50
16 BMB(s),DMk(c),Underneath . . . 3.50
17 BMB(s),DMk(c),Underneath . . . 3.50
18 BMB(s),DMk(c),Underneath . . . 3.50
19 BMB(s),DMk(c),Underneath . . . 3.50
20 BMB(s),DMk(c),Underneath . . . 3.50
21 BMB(s),DMk(c),Underneath . . . 3.50
22 BMB(s),DMk(c),Jessica Jones . 3.25
23 BMB(s),DMk(c),Jessica Jones . 3.25
24 BMB(s),DMk(c),Purple,pt.1 . . . 3.25
25 BMB(s),DMk(c),Purple,pt.2 . . . 3.25
26 BMB(s),DMk(c),Purple,pt.3 . . . 3.25
27 BMB(s),DMk(c),Purple,pt.4 . . . 3.25
28 BMB(s),DMk(c),Purple,pt.5 . . . 4.00

ALIEN LEGION
Epic, April, 1984
1 FC,TA,I:Sarigar,Montroc 4.00
2 FC,TA,CP,V:Harkilons 3.50
3 thru 20 . . . . @3.00

[2nd Series], Aug., 1987
1 LSn,I:Guy Montroc. 3.00
2 thru 18 . . . . @2.50
GN Grimrod 6.00
1-shot Alien Legion: Binary Deep
   with trading card (1993) 3.50

ALIEN LEGION:
JUGGER GRIMROD
Epic, Aug., 1992
Book One 6.00

ALIEN LEGION: ONE
PLANET AT A TIME
Epic, Heavy Hitters May, 1993
1 HNg,CDi,One Planet at a Time . . 5.00
2 HNg,CDi. 5.00
3 HNg,CDi. 5.00

ALIEN LEGION:
ON THE EDGE
Epic, Nov., 1990
1 LSn,V:B'Be No N'ngth 5.00
2 LSn,V:B'Be No N'ngth 5.00
3 LSn,V:B'Be No N'ngth 5.00
4 LSn,V:B'Be No N'ngth 5.00

ALIEN LEGION:
TENANTS OF HELL
Epic, 1991
1 LSn,Nomad Squad On
   Combine IV 5.00
2 LSn,L:Torie Montroc,I:Stagg . . . 5.00

ALL-NEW OFFICIAL
HANDBOOK OF THE
MARVEL UNIVERSE
A to Z
Jan., 2006
1 . . . . 4.00
2 thru 11 . . . . @4.00
12 . . . . 4.00
Update #1 thru #4 . . . . @4.00

ALL SELECT COMICS
Marvel Timely, (Daring Comics)
Fall, 1943
1 ASh(c),B:Capt.America,Sub-Mariner,
   Human Torch;WWII 25,000.00
2 ASh(c),A:Red Skull, V:Axis
   Powers 8,000.00
3 ASh(c),B:Whizzer,V:Axis. . . 5,000.00
4 ASh(c),V: Axis 3,500.00
5 ASh(c),E:Sub-Mariner,V:Axis 3,500.00
6 ASh,A:The Destroyer,V:Axis . 2,500.00
7 ASh,MSu,E:Whizzer,V:Axis. . 2,500.00
8 ASh(c),MSu,V:Axis Powers . 2,500.00
9 ASh(c),V:Axis Powers. 2,500.00
10 ASh(c),E:Capt.America,Human
   Torch;A:The Destroyer 2,500.00
11 SSh, I:Blonde Phantom,
   A:Miss America. 4,200.00
Becomes:

BLONDE PHANTOM
1946
12 SSh, B:Miss America;
   The Devil's Playground . . . 2,500.00
13 SSh,B:Sub-Mariner;Horror
   In Hollywood. 1,600.00
14 SSh,E:Miss America;Horror
   At Haunted Castle 1,500.00
15 SSh,The Man Who Deserved
   To Die 1,500.00
16 SSh,A:Capt.America,Bucky;
   Modeled For Murder. 2,000.00
17 Torture & Rescue. 1,400.00
18 SSh,Jealously,Hate&Cruelty 1,400.00
19 SSh(c),Killer In the Hospital. 1,400.00
20 Blonde Phantom's Big Fall . 1,400.00
21 SSh,Murder At the Carnival. 1,400.00
22 V: Crime Bosses 1,400.00

Blonde Phantom #22
© Marvel Entertainment Group

Becomes:

LOVERS
1949

23 Love Stories	300.00
24 My Dearly Beloved	150.00
25 The Man I Love.	150.00
26 thru 29.	@125.00
30 MK.	150.00
31 thru 36	@125.00
37	200.00
38 BK.	200.00
39	125.00
40	125.00
41 BEv.	150.00
42 thru 65	@125.00
66	100.00
67 ATh	125.00
68 thru 86 Aug., 1957.	@100.00

ALL SURPRISE
Marvel Timely, Fall, 1943

1 (fa),F:Super Rabbit,Gandy, Sourpuss	450.00
2	200.00
3	150.00
4 thru 10	@150.00
11 HK	165.00
12 Winter, 1946	150.00

ALL-TRUE CRIME
See: OFFICIAL TRUE
CRIME CASES

ALL WINNERS COMICS
Marvel Timely, Summer, 1941

1 S&K,BEv,B:Capt.America & Bucky, Human Torch & Toro,Sub-Mariner A:The Angel,Black Marvel	42,000.00
2 S&K,SSh, B:Destroyer, Whizzer.	10,000.00
3 BEv,Bucky & Toro Captured .	6,000.00
4 BEv,AAv,Battle For Victory For America	6,500.00
5 AAv,V:Nazi Invasion Fleet. . .	4,500.00
6 SSh,AAv,V:Axis Powers, A:Black Avenger	5,000.00
7 V:Axis Powers.	3,600.00
8 V:Axis Powers.	3,500.00
9 V:Nazi Submarine Fleet	3,500.00
10 V:Nazi Submarine Fleet. . . .	3,600.00
11 V: Nazis	2,500.00
12 ASh(c),A:Red Skull,E:Destroyer; Jap P.O.W. Camp.	3,500.00

13 ASh(c),V:Japanese Fleet. . .	2,500.00
14 ASh(c),V:Japanese Fleet. . .	2,500.00
15 ASh(c),Jap Supply Train . . .	2,500.00
16 ASh(c),In Alaska V:Gangsters	2,500.00
17 V:Gangsters;Atomic Research Department	2,500.00
18 ASh(c),V:Robbers;Internal Revenue Department	2,600.00
19 ASh(c),SSh,I:All Winners Squad, Fall, 1946	10,000.00
21 SSh,AAv,A:All-Winners Squad; Riddle of Demented Dwarf .	7,500.00

Becomes:

ALL TEEN COMICS
1947

20 F:Georgie,Willie, Mitzi,Patsy Walker	200.00

Becomes:

TEEN COMICS
1947

21 HK,A:George,Willie,Mitzi, Patsy Walker, Hey Look	200.00
22 A:George,Willie,Margie, Patsy Walker	125.00
23 SSh,A:P.Walker,Cindy,George	125.00
24	150.00
25 thru 27	@125.00
28	150.00
29	125.00
30 HK,Hey Look.	150.00
31 thru 34	@125.00
35 May, 1950	125.00

Becomes:

JOURNEY INTO
UNKNOWN WORLDS
Marvel Atlas, Sept., 1950

36(1) RH,End of the Earth. . . .	4,000.00
37(2) BEv,GC,When Worlds Collide.	1,700.00
38(3) GT,Land of Missing Men	1,500.00
4 MSy,RH,Train to Nowhere. . .	900.00
5 MSy,Trapped in Space.	900.00
6 GC,RH,World Below the Atlantic.	900.00
7 BW,RH,JMn,House That Wasn't.	1,500.00
8 RH,JMn,The Stone Thing . . .	1,000.00
9 MSy,JSt,The People Who Couldn't Exist	1,000.00
10 The Undertaker	1,000.00
11 BEv,Frankie Was Afraid	700.00
12 BK,Last Voice You Hear	700.00

Journey Into Unknown Worlds #37
© Marvel Entertainment Group

13 The Witch Woman	600.00
14 BW,BEv,CondemnedBuilding	1,200.00
15 JMn,They Crawl By Night . .	1,200.00
16 JMn,Scared to Death	600.00
17 BEv,GC,RH,The Ice Monster Cometh	700.00
18 The Broth Needs Somebody .	700.00
19 MF,GC,The Long Wait	700.00
20 GC,RH,The Race That Vanished	600.00
21 MF,JMn,JSt,Decapitation . . .	400.00
22 thru 32	@400.00
33 SD,The Man in the Box	400.00
34 MK,AT,DAy	350.00
35 AT,MD	350.00
36 thru 44	@300.00
45 AW,SD.	300.00
46 & 47.	@300.00
48 GW,GM.	300.00
49 JF,JMn.	300.00
50 JDa,RC	300.00
51 WW,SD,JSe	300.00
52	300.00
53 RC,BP	300.00
54 AT,BP	300.00
55 AW,RC,BEv.	300.00
56 BEv	300.00
57 JO	250.00
58 MD,JMn.	250.00
59 AW,Aug., 1957	350.00

ALL WINNERS COMICS
[2nd Series], Aug., 1948

1 SSh,F:Blonde Phantom,A:Capt.Am. Sub-Mariner,Human Torch	5,000.00

Becomes:

ALL WESTERN
WINNERS
1948–49

2 SSh,B,I&O:Black Rider, B:Two-Gun Kid, Kid-Colt . .	1,200.00
3 Black Rider V: Satan	600.00
4 Black Rider Unmasked	600.00

Becomes:

WESTERN WINNERS
1949

5 I Challenge the Army	500.00
6 The Mountain Mystery	450.00
7 Ph(c) Randolph Scott	450.00

Becomes:

BLACK RIDER
1950–55

8 Ph(c) of Stan Lee,B:Black Rider; Valley of Giants	750.00
9 SSh,JMn,Wrath of the Redskin	400.00
10 O:Black Rider	425.00
11 Redmen on the Warpath. . . .	300.00
12 GT,The Town That Vanished.	300.00
13 SSh,The Terrified Tribe	300.00
14 The Tyrant of Texas	300.00
15 Revolt of the Redskins	250.00
16	250.00
17	250.00
18.	250.00
19 SSh,GT,A:Two-Gun Kid	250.00
20 GT.	300.00
21 SSh,GT,A:Two-Gun Kid	250.00
22 SSh,DAy(c),A:Two-Gun Kid . .	250.00
23 SSh,A:Two-Gun Kid	250.00
24 SSh,JSt.	250.00
25 SSh,JSt,A:Arrowhead.	250.00
26 SSh,A:Kid-Colt	250.00
27 SSh,JMn(c),A:Kid-Colt	300.00

Becomes:

WESTERN TALES OF
BLACK RIDER
1955

28 JSe,D:Spider	300.00

MARVEL

MARVEL

29	200.00
30	200.00
31	200.00

Becomes:

GUNSMOKE WESTERN
1955–63

32 MD,MB,F:Kid Colt,Billy Buckskin	300.00
33 MD	200.00
34 MB	175.00
35 GC	200.00
36 AW,GC	200.00
37 JDa	175.00
38	150.00
39 GC	150.00
40 AW	175.00
41 thru 43	@125.00
44 AT	125.00
45 & 46	@125.00
47 JK	150.00
48 & 49	@125.00
50 JK,RC	200.00
51 JK	150.00
52 thru 54	@125.00
55 & 56 MB	@125.00
57 Two Gun Kid	100.00
58 & 59	@100.00
60 Sam Hawk (Kid Colt)	125.00
61 RC	150.00
62 thru 67 JK	@100.00
68	100.00
69 JK	100.00
70	100.00
71 JK	125.00
72 O:Kid Colt	125.00
73 JK	135.00
74 thru 76	@100.00
77 JK,July, 1963	150.00

(TIMELY PRESENTS:) ALL-WINNERS
Oct., 1999

Spec. 48-pg.	4.00

ALPHA FLIGHT
Aug., 1983

1 JBy,I:Puck,Marrina,Tundra	4.00
2 JBy,I:Master,Vindicator Becomes Guardian,B:O:Marrina	2.50
3 JBy,O:Master,A:Namor,Invisible Girl	2.50
4 JBy,A:Namor,Invisible Girl, E:O:Marrina,A:Master	2.50

Alpha Flight #1
© Marvel Entertainment Group

5 JBy,B:O:Shaman,F:Puck	2.50
6 JBy,E:O:Shaman,I:Kolomag	2.50
7 JBy,B:O:Snowbird,I:Delphine Courtney & Deadly Ernest	2.50
8 JBy,E:O:Snowbird,O:Deadly Ernest,I:Nemesis	2.50
9 JBy,O:Aurora,A:Wolverine, Super Skrull	2.50
10 JBy,O:Northstar,V:SuperSkrull	2.50
11 JBy,I:Omega Flight,Wild Child O:Sasquatch	2.50
12 JBy,D:Guardian,V:Omega Flight	2.50
13 JBy,C:Wolverine,Nightmare	3.00
14 JBy,V:Genocide	2.50
15 JBy,R:Master	2.50
16 JBy,BWi,V:Master,C:Wolverine I:Madison Jeffries	2.75
17 JBy,BWi,A:Wolverine,X-Men	3.00
18 JBy,BWi,J:Heather,I:Ranaq	2.50
19 JBy,I:Talisman,V:Ranaq	2.50
20 JBy,I:Gilded Lily,N:Aurora	2.50
21 JBy,BWi,O:Gilded Lily,Diablo	2.50
22 JBy,BWi,I:Pink Pearl	2.50
23 JBy,BWi,D:Sasquatch, I:Tanaraq	2.50
24 JBy,BWi,V:Great Beasts,J:Box	2.50
25 JBy,BWi,V:Omega Flight I:Dark Guardian	2.50
26 JBy,BWi,A:Omega Flight,Dark Guardian	2.50
27 JBy,V:Omega Flight	2.50
28 JBy,Secret Wars II,V:Omega Flight,D:Dark Guardian	2.50
29 MMi,V:Hulk,A:Box	2.50
30 MMi,I&O:Scramble,R:Deadly Ernest	2.50
31 MMi,D:Deadly Ernest, O:Nemesis	2.50
32 MMi(c),JBg,O:Puck,I:2nd Vindicator	2.50
33 MMi(c),SB,X-Men,I:Deathstrike	4.00
34 MMi(c),SB,Wolverine,V: Deathstrike	3.00
35 DR,R:Shaman	2.50
36 MMi(c),DR,A:Dr.Strange	2.50
37 DR,O:Pestilence,N:Aurora	2.50
38 DR,A:Namor,V:Pestilence	2.50
39 MMi(c),DR,WPo,A:Avengers	2.75
40 DR,WPo,W:Namor & Marrina	2.75
41 DR,WPo,I:Purple Girl, J:Madison Jeffries	2.75
42 DR,WPo,I:Auctioneer,J:Purple Girl,A: Beta Flight	2.75
43 DR,WPo,V:Mesmero,Sentinels	2.75
44 DR,WPo,D:Snowbird, A:Pestilence	2.75
45 JBr,WPo,R:Sasquatch, L:Shaman	2.75
46 JBr,WPo,I:2nd Box	2.75
47 MMi,WPo,TA,Vindicator solo	2.75
48 SL(i),I:Omega	2.75
49 JBr,WPo,I:Manikin,D:Omega	2.75
50 WS(c),JBr,WPo,L:Northstar,Puck, Aurora,A:Loki,Double size	3.00
51 JLe(1st Marv),WPo(i),V:Cody	7.00
52 JBr,WPo(i),I:Bedlam, A:Wolverine	3.00
53 JLe,WPo(i),I:Derangers,Goblyn D&V:Bedlam,A:Wolverine	4.00
54 WPo(i),O&J:Goblyn	3.50
55 JLe,TD,V:Tundra	3.50
56 JLe,TD,V:Bedlamites	3.50
57 JLe,TD,V:Crystals, C:Dreamqueen	3.50
58 JLe,AM,V:Dreamqueen	3.50
59 JLe,AM,I:Jade Dragon,R:Puck	3.50
60 JLe,AM,V:J.Dragon,D.Queen	3.50
61 JLe,AM,on Trial (1st JLe X-Men)	3.50
62 JLe,AM,V:Purple Man	3.50
63 MG,V:U.S.Air Force	2.50

Alpha Flight #48
© Marvel Entertainment Group

64 JLe,AM,V:Great Beasts	3.50
65 JLe(c),AM(i),Dream Issue	3.00
66 JLe(c),I:China Force	3.00
67 JLe(c),O:Dream Queen	3.00
68 JLe(c),V:Dream Queen	3.00
69 JLe(c),V:Dream Queen	3.00
70 MM(i),V:Dream Queen	2.50
71 MM(i),I:Sorcerer	2.50
72 V:Sorcerer	2.50
73 MM(i),V:Sorcerer	2.50
74 MM(i),Alternate Earth	2.50
75 JLe(c),MMi(i),Double Size	3.00
76 MM(i),V:Sorcerer	2.25
77 MM(i),V:Kingpin	2.25
78 MM(i),A:Dr.Strange,Master	2.25
79 MM(i),AofV,V:Scorpion,Nekra	2.25
80 MM(i),AofV,V:Scorpion,Nekra	2.25
81 JBy(c),MM(i),B:R:Northstar	2.25
82 JBy(c),MM(i),E:R:Northstar	2.25
83 JSh	2.25
84 MM(i),Northstar	2.25
85 MM(i)	2.25
86 MBa,MM,V:Sorcerer	2.25
87 JLe(c),MM(i),A:Wolverine	3.00
88 JLe(c),MM(i),A:Wolverine	3.00
89 JLe(c),MM(i),R:Guardian,A: Wolverine	3.00
90 JLe(c),MM(i),A:Wolverine	3.00
91 MM(i),V:Dr.Doom	2.25
92 Guardian vs.Vindicator	2.25
93 MM(i),A:Fant.Four,I:Headlok	2.25
94 MM(i),V:Fant.Four,Headlok	2.25
95 MM(i),Lifelines	2.25
96 MM(i),A:Master	2.25
97 B:Final Option,A:Her.	2.25
98 A:Avengers	2.25
99 A:Avengers	2.25
100 JBr,TMo,DR,LMa,E:Final Option A:Galactus,Avengers,D: Guardian,G-Size	2.50
101 TMo,Final Option Epilogue, A:Dr.Strange,Avengers	2.25
102 TMo,I:Weapon Omega,	2.25
103 TMo,V:Diablo,U.S.Agent	2.25
104 TMo,N:Alpha Flight,Weapon Omega is Wild Child	2.25
105 TMo,V:Pink Pearl	2.25
106 MPa,Aids issue,Northstar acknowledges homosexuality	3.00
106a 2nd printing	2.50
107 A:X-Factor,V:Autopsy	2.25
108 A:Soviet Super Soldiers	2.25
109 V:Peoples Protectorate	2.25
110 PB,Infinity War,I:2nd Omega Flight,A:Wolverine	2.25

111 PB,Infinity War,V:Omega
Flight,A:Wolverine 2.25
112 PB,Infinity War,V:Master 2.25
113 V:Mauler 2.25
114 A:Weapon X 2.25
115 PB,I:Wyre,A:Weapon X. 2.25
116 PB,I:Rok,V:Wyre 2.25
117 PB,V:Wyre. 2.25
118 PB,V:Thunderball 2.25
119 PB,V:Wrecking Crew. 2.25
120 PB,10th Anniv.,V:Hardliners,
w/poster. 3.00
121 PCu,V:Brass Bishop,A:Spider-
Man,Wolverine,C:X-Men 2.50
122 PB,BKi,Inf.Crusade 2.50
123 PB,BKi,Infinity Crusade 2.50
124 PB,BKi,Infinity Crusade 2.50
125 PB,V:Carcass 2.50
126 V:Carcass 2.50
127 SFu(s),Infinity Crusade. 2.50
128 B:No Future 2.50
129 C:Omega Flight. 2.50
130 E:No Future,last issue,
Double Sized 3.00
Ann.#1 LSn,V:Diablo,Gilded Lily . . . 3.00
Ann.#2 JBr,BMc. 2.50
Spec.#1 PB,A:Wolverine,
O:First Team,V:Egghead 3.75
Spec.#1–#3 Newsstand versions
of #97–#99. . . . . @2.50
Spec.#4 Newsstand ver.of #100 . . . 2.50

[2nd Series] 1997
1 SSe,ScC, former team kidnapped,
I:Murmur, Radius,Flex,Guardian 5.00
2 SSe,ScC 4.00
2 variant cover 3.50
3 SSe,ScC, ... 3.50
4 SSe,ScC,V:Mesmero 3.00
5 SSe,ScC,A:Mesmero 3.00
6 SSe,What's up with Sasquatch? . 3.00
7 SSe,Evils explode 3.00
8 SSe,ScC,North & South prelude . 3.00
9 SSe,ScC,North & South pt.1,
X-Men x-over. 3.00
10 SSe,Flung into Prometheus Pit . 3.00
11 SSe,race to save 2 worlds 3.00
12 SSe,Alphan dies,48pg. 3.50
13 SSe,F:Basil Killbrew 2.50
14 SSe,I:Brass Bishop 2.50
15 SSe 2.50
16 SSe,V:Brass Bishop 2.50
17 SSe,V:X the Unknown 2.50
18 SSe,Alpha:Omega,pt.1 . . . . 2.50
19 SSe,Alpha:Omega,pt.2. . . . . 2.50
20 SSe,Alpha:Omega,pt.3 . . . . 2.50
Spec. #1 SSe,In the Beginning,
Flashback, A:Wolverine. 2.50
Ann.1998 Alpha Flight/Inhumans. . 3.50

[3rd Series] March, 2004
1 SLo,You Gotta Be Kiddin,pt.1 . . 3.00
2 SLo,You Gotta Be Kiddin,pt.2 . . 3.00
3 SLo,You Gotta Be Kiddin,pt.3 . . 3.00
4 SLo,You Gotta Be Kiddin,pt.4 . . 3.00
5 SLo,You Gotta Be Kiddin,pt.5 . . 3.00
6 SLo,You Gotta Be Kiddin,pt.6 . . 3.00
7 Waxing Poetic,pt.1 . . . . 3.00
8 Waxing Poetic,pt.2 . . . . 3.00
9 Days of Future Present,pt.1 . . . . 3.00
10 Days of Future Present,pt.2 . . . 3.00
11 Days of Future Present,pt.3 . . . 3.00
12 Days of Future Present,pt.4 . . . 3.00

AMAZING ADVENTURES
June, 1961
1 JK,SD,O&B:Dr.Droom;Torr . 2,500.00
2 JK,SD,This is Manoo 1,000.00
3 JK,SD,Trapped in the
Twilight World 850.00
4 JK,SD, I Am X 800.00
5 JK,SD, Monsteroso 800.00
6 JK,SD,E:Dr.Droom; Sserpo . . 800.00

Becomes:
AMAZING ADULT FANTASY
Dec., 1961
7 SD,Last Man on Earth 1,000.00
8 SD,The Coming of the Krills . . 900.00
9 SD,The Terror of Tim Boo Ba . 700.00
10 SD,Those Who Change 700.00
11 SD,In Human Form. 700.00
12 SD,Living Statues 700.00
13 SD,At the Stroke of Midnight . 700.00
14 SD,Beware of the Giants 750.00
Becomes:
AMAZING FANTASY
Aug., 1962
15 JK(c),SD,I&O:Spider-Man,I:Aunt
May, Flash Thompson, Burglar,
I&D:Uncle Ben 50,000.00
Marvel Milestone rep.#15 (1992). . . 4.00

[Second Series], 1995
15a gold Rep. (1995). 25.00
16 KBk, O:Spider-Man,painted . . . 4.00
17 KBk, More early adventures . . . 4.00
18 KBk,conclusion 4.00

AMAZING ADVENTURES
Aug., 1970
[1st Regular Series]
1 JK,JB,B:Inhumans,Bl.Widow . . . 90.00
2 JK,JB,A:Fantastic Four 45.00
3 JK,GC,BEv,V:Mandarin 45.00
4 JK,GC,BEv,V:Mandarin 45.00
5 NA,TP,DH,BEv,V:Astrologer . . . 60.00
6 NA,DH,SB,V:Maximus 60.00
7 NA,DH,BEv 60.00
8 NA,DH,BEv,E:Black Widow,
A:Thor,(see Avengers #95) . . . 60.00
9 MSy,BEv,V:Magneto 40.00
10 GK(c),MSy,V:Magneto,
E:Inhumans 40.00
11 GK(c),TS,B:O:New Beast,
A:X-Men. 250.00
12 GK(c),TS,MP,A:Iron Man 75.00
13 JR(c),TS,V:New Br'hood
Evil Mutants,I:Buzz Baxter
(Mad Dog) 75.00
14 GK(c),TS,JM,V:Quasimodo . . . 75.00
15 JSn(c),TS,A:X-Men,V:Griffin . . . 75.00
16 JSn(c),FMc(i),V:Juggernaut . . . 75.00
17 JSn,A:X-Men,E:Beast 75.00
18 HC,NA,B:Killraven. 75.00
19 HC,Sirens on 7th Avenues . . . 12.00
20 Coming of the Warlords 12.00
21 Cry Killraven 12.00
22 Killraven 12.00
23 Killraven 12.00
24 New Year Nightmare-2019AD. . 12.00
25 RB,V:Skar 12.00
26 GC,V:Ptson-Rage Vigilante . . . 12.00
27 CR,JSn,V:Death Breeders 12.00
28 JSn,CR,V:Death Breeders 12.00
29 CR,Killraven 12.00
30 CR,Killraven 12.00
31 CR,Killraven 12.00
32 CR,Killraven 12.00
33 CR,Killraven 12.00
34 CR,D:Hawk 12.00
35 KG,Killraven Continued. 12.00
36 CR,Killraven Continued 12.00
37 CR,O:Old Skull 12.00
38 CR,Killraven Continued. 12.00
39 CR,E:Killraven. 12.00

[2nd Regular Series], 1979
1 rep.X-Men#1,38,Professor X . . . 10.00
2 thru 14 reps. . . . . @8.00

AMAZING COMICS
Marvel Timely, 1944
1 ASh(c),F:Young Allies,Destroyer,
Whizzer, Sergeant Dix 4,000.00
Becomes:
COMPLETE COMICS
2 ASh(c),F:Young Allies,Destroyer,
Whizzer Sergeant Dix; 3,000.00

AMAZING DETECTIVE CASES
Marvel Atlas, Nov., 1950
3 Detective/Horror Stories 400.00
4 Death of a Big Shot 250.00
5 . . . . 250.00
6 Danger in the City 250.00
7 . . . . 200.00
8 . . . . 200.00
9 GC, The Man Who Wasn't 200.00
10 GT. 200.00
11 The Black Shadow 450.00
12 MSy,BK, Harrigan's Wake. . . . 450.00
13 BEv,JSt,. 500.00
14 Hands Off; Sept., 1952. . . . . . 400.00

AMAZING FANTASY
June, 2004
1 (of 6) 4.00
2 thru 5 . . . . @4.00
6 . . . . 3.00
7 F:Scorpion,pt.1 . . . . 3.00
8 Motherless Country 3.00
9 Identity Politics. 3.00
10 F:all-new Scorpion 3.00
11 The New Pollution 3.00
12 Poison Tomorrow 3.00
13 KK,I:Vegas 3.00
14 KK,F:Vegas 3.00
15 48-pg. 4.00
16 Unnatural Selection,pt.1 . . . . . . 3.00
17 Unnatural Selection,pt.2 . . . . . . 3.00
18 Unnatural Selection,pt.3 . . . . . . 3.00
19 Unnatural Selection,pt.4 . . . . . . 3.00
20 Unnatural Selection,pt.5 . . . . . . 3.00
Digest Scorpion: Poison Tomorrow . 8.00

AMAZING HIGH ADVENTURE
Aug., 1984
1 BSz,JSo,JS. 4.00
2 PS,AW,BSz,TA,MMi,BBl,CP,CW . 3.00

Amazing High Adventure #1
© *Marvel Entertainment Group*

3 MMi,VM,JS 3.00
4 JBo,JS,SBi 3.00
5 JBo; Oct., 1986 . . . . 3.00

AMAZING MYSTERIES
Marvel-Comics, 1949–50
32 The Isle of No Return 1,400.00
33 The Thing in the Vault 700.00
34 Photo(c) 300.00
35 Photo(c) 300.00

AMAZING
SCARLET SPIDER
1995
1 MBa,LMa,VirtualMortality,pt.2 . . . 2.50
2 TDF,MBa,CyberWar,pt.2 . . . . . . 2.50

AMAZING SPIDER-GIRL
Oct., 2006
0 RF,TDF,Spec., F:Mayday Parker . 2.00
1 RF,TDF, V:Black Tarantula 3.00
2 RF,TDF, V:Hobgoblin 3.00
3 RF,TDF,V:Hobgoblin 3.00
4 RF,TDF,V:Mad Dog 3.00
5 RF,TDF,V:Black Tarantula 3.00
6 RF,TDF,V:Mad Dog, Hobgoblin . . 3.00
7 RF,TDF,Obsession 3.00
8 RF,TDF,Midtown High 3.00
9 RF,TDF,V:Carnage, pt.1 . . . . 3.00
10 RF,TDF,V:Carnage, pt.2 . . . . . . 3.00
11 RF,TDF,V:Carnage, pt.3 . . . . . . 3.00
12 RF,TDF,V:Carnage, pt.4 . . . . . . 3.00
13 RF,TDF,I, Hobgoblin 3.00
14 RF,TDF,Know Thy Enemy 3.00

AMAZING SPIDER-MAN
March, 1963
1 JK(c),SED,I:Chameleon,J.Jonah &
  John Jameson,A:F.Four . . 40,000.00
2 SD,I:Vulture,Tinkerer
  C:Mysterio(disguised) 10,000.00
3 SD,I&O:Dr.Octopus 7,500.00
4 SD,I&O:Sandman,I:Betty
  Brant,Liz Allen 7,000.00
5 SD,V:Dr.Doom,C:Fant.Four . 7,000.00
6 SD,I&O:Lizard,The Connors . 4,000.00
7 SD,V:Vulture 3,000.00
8 SD,JK,I:Big Brain,V:Human
  Torch,A:Fantastic Four 2,500.00
9 SD,I&O:Electro 3,000.00
10 SD,I:Enforcers,Big Man . . . 2,600.00
11 SD,V:Dr.Octopus,
  D:Bennett Brant 2,000.00
12 SD,V:Dr.Octopus 2,000.00
13 SD,I:Mysterio 2,500.00
14 SD,I:Green Goblin,
  V:Enforcers, Hulk 4,700.00
15 SD,I:Kraven,A:Chameleon . . 2,400.00
16 SD,A:Daredevil,
  V:Ringmaster 1,700.00
17 SD,2nd A:Green Goblin,
  A:Human Torch 2,200.00
18 SD,V:Sandman,Enforcers,
  C:Avengers,F.F.,Daredevil . 1,200.00
19 SD,V:Sandman,I:Ned Leeds
  A:Human Torch 1,000.00
20 SD,I&O:Scorpion 1,800.00
21 SD,A:Beetle,Human Torch . 1,100.00
22 SD,V:The Clown,Masters of
  Menace 900.00
23 SD,V:GreenGoblin(3rd App.) 1,500.00
24 SD,V:Mysterio 800.00
25 SD,I:Spider Slayer,Spencer
  Smythe,C:Mary Jane 850.00
26 SD,I:CrimeMaster,V:Green
  Goblin 1,000.00
27 SD,V:CrimeMaster,
  Green Goblin 1,000.00
28 SD,I:Molten Man,Peter Parker
  Graduates High School . . . 2,000.00

Amazing Spider-Man #23
© *Marvel Entertainment Group*

29 SD,V:Scorpion 750.00
30 SD,I:Cat Burglar 750.00
31 SD,I:Gwen Stacy,Harry Osborn
  Prof.Warren,V:Dr.Octopus . . . 750.00
32 SD,V:Dr.Octopus 450.00
33 SD,V:Dr.Octopus 450.00
34 SD,V:Kraven 450.00
35 SD,V:Molten Man 450.00
36 SD,I:The Looter 450.00
37 SD,V:Professor Stromm,
  I:Norman Osborn 450.00
38 SD,V:Joe Smith(Boxer) 450.00
39 JR,IR:Green Goblin is Norman
  Osborn 1,000.00
40 JR,O:Green Goblin 1,200.00
41 JR,I:Rhino,C:Mary Jane 750.00
42 JR,V:John Jameson,I:Mary
  Jane (Face Revealed) 450.00
43 JR,O:Rhino 400.00
44 JR,V:Lizard(2nd App.) 400.00
45 JR,V:Lizard 400.00
46 JR,I&O:Shocker 425.00
47 JR,V:Kraven 400.00
48 JR,I:Fake Vulture,A:Vulture . . 400.00
49 JR,V:Fake Vulture,Kraven . . 400.00
50 JR,I:Kingpin,Spidey Quits,
  C:Johnny Carson 1,700.00
51 JR,V:Kingpin 750.00
52 JR,V:Kingpin,I:Robbie
  Robertson,D:Fred Foswell . . 300.00
53 JR,V:Dr.Octopus 350.00
54 JR,V:Dr.Octopus 350.00
55 JR,V:Dr.Octopus 350.00
56 JR,V:Dr.Octopus,I:Capt.Stacy . 350.00
57 JR,DH,A:Ka-Zar 350.00
58 JR,DH,V:Spencer Smythe,
  Spider Slayer 350.00
59 JR,DH,V:Kingpin 350.00
60 JR,DH,V:Kingpin 350.00
61 JR,DH,V:Kingpin 350.00
62 JR,DH,V:Medusa 200.00
63 JR,DH,V:1st & 2nd
  Vulture 200.00
64 JR,DH,V:Vulture 200.00
65 JR,JM,V:Prisoners 200.00
66 JR,DH,V:Mysterio 200.00
67 JR,JM,V:Mysterio,I:Randy
  Robertson 200.00
68 JR,JM,V:Kingpin 225.00
69 JR,JM,V:Kingpin 225.00
70 JR,JM,V:Kingpin 225.00
71 JR,JM,V:Quicksilver,C:Scarlet
  Witch,Toad,A:Kingpin 200.00
72 JR,JB,JM,V:Shocker 200.00

73 JR,JB,JM,I:Man Mountain Marko,
  Silvermane 200.00
74 JR,JM,V:Silvermane 160.00
75 JR,JM,V:Silvermane,A:Lizard . 150.00
76 JR,JM,V:Lizard,A:H.Torch . . . 150.00
77 JR,JM,V:Lizard,A:H.Torch . . . 150.00
78 JR,JM,I&O:Prowler 135.00
79 JR,JM,V:Prowler 135.00
80 JR,JB,JM,V:Chameleon 135.00
81 JR,JB,JM,I:Kangaroo 135.00
82 JR,JM,V:Electro 135.00
83 JR,I:Richard Fisk(as Schemer),
  Vanessa(Kingpin's wife) 135.00
84 JR,JB,JM,V:Schemer,Kingpin . 135.00
85 JR,JB,JM,V:Schemer,Kingpin . 135.00
86 JR,JM,V:Black Widow, C:Iron
  Man, Hawkeye 135.00
87 JR,JM,Reveals ID to his
  friends,changes mind 135.00
88 JR,JM,V:Dr.Octopus 135.00
89 GK,JR,V:Dr.Octopus 135.00
90 GK,JR,V:Dr.Octopus
  D:Capt.Stacy 150.00
91 GK,JR,I:Bullit 135.00
92 GK,JR,V:Bullit,A:Iceman 135.00
93 JR,V:Prowler 135.00
94 JR,SB,V:Beetle,O:Spider-Man 150.00
95 JR,SB,London,V:Terrorists . . 135.00
96 GK,JR,A:Green Goblin,Drug
  Mention,No Comic Code 150.00
97 GK,V:Green Goblin,Drugs . . . 150.00
98 GK,V:Green Goblin,Drugs . . . 150.00
99 GK,Prison Riot,A:Carson . . . 135.00
100 JR(c),GK,Spidey gets four
  arms from serum 350.00
101 JR(c),GK,I:Morbius,the
  Living Vampire,A:Lizard 325.00
101a Reprint,Metallic ink 5.00
102 JR(c),GK,O:Morbius,
  V:Lizard 135.00
103 GK,V:Kraven,A:Ka-Zar 100.00
104 GK,V:Kraven,A:Ka-Zar 100.00
105 GK,V:Spenser Smythe,
  Spider Slayer 100.00
106 JR,V:Spenser Smythe,
  Spider Slayer 100.00
107 JR,V:Spenser Smythe,
  Spider Slayer 100.00
108 JR,R:Flash Thompson,
  I:Sha-Shan,V:Vietnamese . . . 100.00
109 JR,A:Dr.Strange,
  V:Vietnamese 100.00
110 JR,I:The Gibbon 100.00
111 JR,V:The Gibbon,Kraven . . . 100.00
112 JR,Spidey gets an Ulcer 100.00
113 JSn,JR,I:Hammerhead
  V:Dr.Octopus 100.00
114 JSn,JR,V:Hammerhead,Dr.
  Octopus,I:Jonas Harrow . . . 100.00
115 JR,V:Hammerhead,
  Dr.Octopus 100.00
116 JR,JM,V:The Smasher 100.00
117 JR,JM,V:Smasher,Disruptor . 100.00
118 JR,JM,V:Smasher,Disruptor . 100.00
119 JR,A:Hulk 125.00
120 GK,JR,V:Hulk 125.00
121 GK,JR,V:Green Goblin
  D:Gwen Stacy,Drugs 375.00
122 GK,JR,D:Green Goblin 400.00
123 GK,JR,A:Powerman 100.00
124 GK,JR,I:Man-Wolf 110.00
125 RA,JR,O:Man-Wolf 100.00
126 JM(c),RA,JM,V:Kangaroo,
  A: Human Torch 100.00
127 JR(c),RA,V:3rd Vulture,
  A:Human Torch 100.00
128 JR(c),RA,V:3rd Vulture 100.00
129 K&R(c),RA,I:Punisher,Jackal 750.00
130 JR(c),RA,V:Hammerhead,
  Dr.Octopus,I:Spider-Mobile . . 75.00
131 GK(c),RA,V:Hammerhead,
  Dr.Octopus 75.00

All comics prices listed are for *Near Mint* condition.

Amazing Spider-Man #105
© Marvel Entertainment Group

132 GK(c),JR,V:Molten Man 75.00
133 JR(c),RA,V:Molten Man 75.00
134 JR(c),RA,I:Tarantula,C:
    Punisher(2nd App.) 80.00
135 JR(c),RA,V:Tarantula,
    A:Punisher 150.00
136 JR(c),RA,I:2nd GreenGoblin . 150.00
137 GK(c),RA,V:Green Goblin . . . 110.00
138 K&R(c),RA,I:Mindworm 50.00
139 K&R(c),RA,I:Grizzly,V:Jackal . 50.00
140 GK(c),RA,I:Gloria Grant,
    V:Grizzly,Jackal 50.00
141 JR(c),RA,V:Mysterio 50.00
142 JR(c),RA,V:Mysterio 50.00
143 K&R(c),RA,I:Cyclone 50.00
144 K&R(c),RA,V:Cyclone 50.00
145 K&R(c),RA,V:Scorpion 50.00
146 RA,JR,V:Scorpion 50.00
147 JR(c),RA,V:Tarantula 50.00
148 GK(c),RA,V:Tarantula,IR:Jackal
    is Prof.Warren 60.00
149 K&R(c),RA,D:Jackal 100.00
150 GK(c),RA,V:Spenser Smythe . 70.00
151 RA,JR,V:Shocker 60.00
152 K&R(c),RA,V:Shocker 40.00
153 K&R(c),RA,V:Paine 40.00
154 JR(c),SB,V:Sandman 40.00
155 JR(c),SB,V:Computer 40.00
156 JR(c),RA,I:Mirage,W:Ned
    Leeds & Betty Brant 40.00
157 JR(c),RA,V:Dr.Octopus 40.00
158 JR(c),RA,V:Dr.Octopus 40.00
159 JR(c),RA,V:Dr.Octopus 40.00
160 K&R(c),RA,V:Tinkerer 40.00
161 K&R(c),RA,A:Nightcrawler,
    C:Punisher 50.00
162 JR(c),RA,Nightcrawler,
    Punisher,I:Jigsaw. 50.00
163 JR(c),RA,Kingpin 35.00
164 JR(c),RA,Kingpin 35.00
165 JR(c),RA,Lizard. 35.00
166 JR(c),RA,Lizard. 35.00
167 JR(c),RA,V:Spiderslayer,
    I:Will-o-the Wisp 35.00
168 JR(c),KP,V:Will-o-the Wisp . . . 40.00
169 RA,V:Dr.Faustas 35.00
170 RA,V:Dr.Faustas 35.00
171 RA,A:Nova 40.00
172 RA,V:Molten Man 35.00
173 JR(c),RA,JM,V:Molten Man . . 35.00
174 RA,TD,JM,A:Punisher 40.00
175 RA,JM,A:Punisher,D:Hitman . 40.00
176 RA,TD,V:Green Goblin 40.00
177 RA,V:Green Goblin 40.00

178 RA,JM,V:Green Goblin 40.00
179 RA,V:Green Goblin 40.00
180 RA,IR&V:Green Goblin is Bart
    Hamilton). 40.00
181 GK(c),SB,O:Spider-Man. 35.00
182 RA,A:Rocket Racer. 35.00
183 RA,BMc,V:Rocket Racer. 35.00
184 RA,V:White Tiger 35.00
185 RA,V:White Tiger 35.00
186 KP,A:Chameleon,Spidey
    cleared by police of charges . . 35.00
187 JSn,BMc,A:Captain
    America,V:Electro 35.00
188 KP,A:Jigsaw 35.00
189 JBy,JM,A:Man-Wolf. 35.00
190 JBy,JM,A:Man-Wolf. 35.00
191 KP,V:Spiderslayer 35.00
192 KP,JM,V:The Fly 35.00
193 KP,JM,V:The Fly 35.00
194 KP,I:Black Cat 65.00
195 KP,AM,JM,O:Black Cat 35.00
196 AM,JM,D:Aunt May,A:Kingpin . 25.00
197 KP,JM,V:Kingpin 25.00
198 SB,JM,V:Mysterio 25.00
199 SB,JM,V:Mysterio 25.00
200 JR(c),KP,JM,D:Burglar,Aunt May
    alive,O:Spider-Man 55.00
201 KP,JM,A:Punisher 25.00
202 KP,JM,A:Punisher 25.00
203 FM(c),KP,A:Dazzler. 15.00
204 JR2(c),KP,V:Black Cat 15.00
205 KP,JM,V:Black Cat 15.00
206 JBy,GD,V:Jonas Harrow 15.00
207 JM,V:Mesmero 15.00
208 JR2,AM,BBr,V:Fusion(1stJR2
    SpM art),I:Lance Bannon. 15.00
209 KJ,BMc,JRu,BWi,AM,
    I:Calypso, V:Kraven. 25.00
210 JR2,JSt,I:Madame Web 15.00
211 JR2,JM,A:Sub-mariner 15.00
212 JR2,JM,I:Hydro-Man 15.00
213 JR2,JM,V:Wizard 15.00
214 JR2,JM,V:Frightful Four,
    A: Namor,Llyra. 15.00
215 JR2,JM,V:Frightful Four,
    A: Namor,Llyra. 15.00
216 JR2,JM,A:Madame Web 15.00
217 JR2,JM,V:Sandman,
    Hydro-Man. 15.00
218 FM(c),JR2,JM,AM,V:Sandman
    Hydro-Man. 15.00
219 FM(c),LMc,JM,V:Grey
    Gargoyle,A:Matt Murdock 15.00
220 BMc,A:Moon Knight 12.00
221 JM(i),A:Ramrod. 12.00
222 WS(c),BH,JM,I:SpeedDemon . 12.00
223 JR2,AM,A:Red Ghost 12.00
224 JR2,V:Vulture 12.00
225 JR2,BWi,V:Foolkiller 12.00
226 JR2,JM,A:Black Cat 12.00
227 JR2,JM,A:Black Cat 12.00
228 RL,Murder Mystery 12.00
229 JR2,JM,V:Juggernaut 12.00
230 JR2,JM,V:Juggernaut 12.00
231 JR2,AM,V:Cobra 12.00
232 JR2,JM,V:Mr.Hyde 12.00
233 JR2,JM,V:Tarantula 12.00
234 JR2,DGr,V:Tarantula 12.00
235 JR2,V:Tarantula,C:Deathlok
    O:Will-o-the Wisp 12.00
236 JR2,D:Tarantula 12.00
237 BH,A:Stilt Man. 12.00
238 JR2,JR,I:Hobgoblin (inc.
    Tattoo transfer) 100.00
238a w/out Tattoo 12.00
239 JR2,V:Hobgoblin 60.00
240 JR2,BL,Vulture 12.00
241 JR2,O:Vulture 12.00
242 JR2,Mad Thinker 12.00
243 JR2,Peter Quits School 12.00
244 JR2,KJ,V:Hobgoblin 18.00
245 JR2,V:Hobgoblin 20.00

Amazing Spider-Man #228
© Marvel Entertainment Group

246 JR2,DGr,Daydreams issue . . . 12.00
247 JR2,JR,V:Thunderball 12.00
248 JR2,BBr,RF,TA,V:Thunderball,
    Kid who Collects Spider-Man . 12.00
249 JR2,DGr,V:Hobgoblin,
    A:Kingpin 20.00
250 JR2,KJ,V:Hobgoblin 20.00
251 RF,KJ,V:Hobgoblin,Spidey
    Leaves for Secret Wars 20.00
252 RF,BBr,returns from Secret
    Wars,N:Spider-Man 50.00
253 RL,I:Rose 12.00
254 RL,JRu,V:Jack O'Lantern 10.00
255 RF,JRu,Red Ghost 10.00
256 RF,JRu,I:Puma,A:Black Cat . . 10.00
257 RF,JRu,V:Puma,
    A:Hobgoblin 10.00
258 RF,JRu,A:Black Cat,Fant.Four,
    Hobgoblin,V:Black Costume . . 15.00
259 RF,JRu,A:Hobgoblin,O:
    Mary Jane 15.00
260 RF,JRu,BBr,V:Hobgoblin. 12.00
261 CV(c),RF,JRu,V:Hobgoblin . . . 12.00
262 Ph(c),BL,Spidey Unmasked . . 13.00
263 RF,BBr,I:Spider-Kid 10.00
264 Paty,V:Red Nine 10.00
265 RF,JRu,V:Black Fox,
    I:Silver Sable 18.00
265a 2nd printing. 3.00
266 RF,JRu,I:Misfits,Toad 10.00
267 BMc,PDd(s),A:Human Torch. . 10.00
268 JBy(c),RF,JRu,Secret WarsII . 10.00
269 RF,JRu,V:Firelord 10.00
270 RF,BMc,V:Firelord,
    A:Avengers,I:Kate Cushing . . . 10.00
271 RF,JRu,A:Crusher Hogan,
    V:Manslaughter 10.00
272 SB,KB,I&O:Slyde 10.00
273 RF,JRu,Secret Wars II,
    A:Puma 10.00
274 TMo,JR,Secret Wars II,
    Beyonder V:Mephisto,A:1st
    Ghost Rider 10.00
275 RF,JRu,V:Amaz.Fantasy#15 Spidey
    (From Amaz.Fantasy#15) 25.00
276 RF,BBr,V:Hobgoblin 15.00
277 RF,BL,CV,A:Daredevil,Kingpin 10.00
278 A:Hobgoblin,V:Scourge,
    D:Wraith. 10.00
279 RL,A:Jack O'Lantern,
    2nd A:Silver Sable 10.00
280 RF,BBr,V:Sinister Syndicate,
    A:Silver Sable,Hobgoblin,
    Jack O'Lantern 10.00

Amazing Spider-Man #266
© Marvel Entertainment Group

281 RF,BBr,V:Sinister Syndicate,
A:Silver Sable,Hobgoblin,
Jack O'Lantern 15.00
282 RL,BL,A:X-Factor 10.00
283 RF,BL,V:Titania,Absorbing
Man,C:Mongoose 10.00
284 RF,BBr,JRu,B:Gang War,
A: Punisher,Hobgoblin 15.00
285 MZ(c),A:Punisher,Hobgoblin . . 15.00
286 ANi(I),V:Hobgoblin,A:Rose . . . 15.00
287 EL,ANi,A:Daredevl,Hobgoblin. 15.00
288 E:Gang War,A:Punisher,
Falcon,Hobgoblin,Daredevil,
Black Cat,Kingpin. 15.00
289 TMo,IR:Hobgoblin is Ned Leeds,
I:2nd Hobgoblin (Jack O'
Lantern) 30.00
290 JR2,Peter Proposes 10.00
291 JR2,V:Spiderslayer 10.00
292 AS,V:Spiderslayer,Mary
Jane Accepts proposal 10.00
293 MZ,BMc,V:Kraven. 12.00
294 MZ,BMc,D:Kraven. 12.00
295 BSz(c),KB(i),Mad Dog,pt.#2 . . 10.00
296 JBy(c),AS,V:Dr.Octopus 10.00
297 AS,V:Dr.Octopus 10.00
298 TM,BMc,V:Chance,C:Venom
(not in costume). 75.00
299 TM,BMc,V:Chance,I:Venom . . 40.00
300 TM,O:Venom 125.00
301 TM,A:Silver Sable 20.00
302 TM,V:Nero,A:Silver Sable . . . 20.00
303 TM,A:Silver Sable,Sandman. . 20.00
304 TM,JRu,V:Black Fox,Prowler
I:Jonathan Caesar. 18.00
305 TM,JRu,V:BlackFox,Prowler. . 18.00
306 TM,V:Humbug,Chameleon . . . 15.00
307 TM,O:Chameleon 15.00
308 TM,V:Taskmaster,J.Caesar. . . 15.00
309 TM,I:Styx & Stone 15.00
310 TM,V:Killershrike. 15.00
311 TM,Inferno,V:Mysterio 15.00
312 TM,Inferno,Hobgoblin V:
Green Goblin 22.00
313 TM,Inferno,V:Lizard. 15.00
314 TM,X-mas issue,V:J.Caesar. . 15.00
315 TM,V:Venom,Hydro-Man. 22.00
316 TM,V:Venom 22.00
317 TM,V:Venom,A:Thing 22.00
318 TM,V:Scorpion 22.00
319 TM,V:Scorpion,Rhino 15.00
320 TM,B:Assassin Nation Plot
A:Paladin,Silver Sable 15.00
321 TM,A:Paladin,Silver Sable . . . 12.00

322 TM,A:Silver Sable,Paladin . . . 12.00
323 TM,A:Silver Sable,Paladin,
Captain America. 12.00
324 TM(c),EL,AG,V:Sabretooth,A:
Capt.America,Silver Sable . . . 12.00
325 TM,E:Assassin Nation Plot,
V:Red Skull,Captain America,
Silver Sable 12.00
326 V:Graviton,A of V. 7.00
327 EL,AG,V:Magneto,A of V. 7.00
328 TM,V:Hulk,A of V. 12.00
329 EL,V:Tri-Sentinel 7.00
330 EL,A:Punisher,Black Cat. 7.00
331 EL,A:Punisher,C:Venom 6.00
332 EL,V:Venom,Styx & Stone 7.00
333 EL,V:Venom,Styx & Stone 7.00
334 EL,B:Sinister Six,A:Iron Man . . . 5.00
335 EL,TA,A:Captain America 5.00
336 EL,D:Nathan Lubensky,
A:Dr.Strange,Chance. 5.00
337 WS(c),EL,TA,A:Nova 5.00
338 EL,A:Jonathan Caesar 5.00
339 EL,JR,E:Sinister Six,A:Thor
D:Jonathan Caesar. 5.00
340 EL,V:Femme Fatales 5.00
341 EL,V:Tarantula,Powers Lost . . . 5.00
342 EL,A:Blackcat,V:Scorpion 5.00
343 EL,Powers Restored,
C:Cardiac,V:Chameleon 5.00
344 EL,V:Rhino,I:Cardiac,Cletus
Kassady(Carnage),A:Venom . . 15.00
345 MBa,V:Boomerang,C:Venom,
A:Cletus Kassady(infected
with Venom-Spawn). 15.00
346 EL,V:Venom 12.00
347 EL,V:Venom 10.00
348 EL,A:Avengers 4.00
349 EL,A:Black Fox 4.00
350 EL,V:Doctor Doom,Black Fox . . 6.00
351 MBa,A:Nova,V:Tri-Sentinal . . . 6.00
352 MBa,A:Nova,V:Tri-Sentinal . . . 4.00
353 MBa,B:Round Robin:The Side
Kick's Revenge,A:Punisher,
Nova,Moon Knight,Darkhawk . . 4.00
354 MBa,A:Nova,Punisher,
Darkhawk,Moon Knight. 4.00
355 MBa,A:Nova,Punisher,
Darkhawk,Moon Knight 4.00
356 MBa,A:Moon Knight,
Punisher,Nova 4.00
357 MBa,A:Moon Knight,
Punisher,Darkhawk,Nova 4.00
358 MBa,E:Round Robin:The Side
Kick's Revenge,A:Darkhawk,
Moon Knight,Punisher,Nova,
Gatefold(c). 4.00
359 CMa,A:Cardiac,C:Cletus
Kasady (Carnage) 5.00
360 CMa,V:Cardiac,C:Carnage . . . 6.00
361a MBa,I:Carnage 9.00
361a 2nd printing 3.00
362 MBa,V:Carnage,Venom 6.00
362a 2nd printing 3.00
363 MBa,V:Carnage,Venom. 6.00
364 MBa,V:Shocker. 3.00
365 MBa,JR,V:Lizard,30th Anniv.,
Hologram(c),w/poster,Prev.of
Spider-Man 2099 by RL 6.00
366 JBi,A:Red Skull,Taskmaster . . . 3.00
367 JBi,A:Red Skull,Taskmaster . . . 3.00
368 MBa,B:Invasion of the Spider
Slayers #1,BU:Jonah Jameson. 3.00
369 MBa,V:Electro,BU:Green
Goblin 3.00
370 MBa,V:Scorpion,BU:A.May. . . . 3.00
371 MBa,V:Spider-Slayer,
BU:Black Cat. 3.00
372 MBa,V:Spider-Slayer. 3.00
373 MBa,V:Sp.-Slayer,BU:Venom . 4.00
374 MBa,V:Venom 5.00
375 MBa,V:Venom,30th Anniv.,Holo
graphx(c) 6.00

376 V:Styx&Stone,A:Cardiac 3.00
377 V:Cardiac,O:Styx&Stone 3.00
378 MBa,Total Carnage#3,V:Shriek,
Carnage,A:Venom,Cloak. 3.00
379 MBa,Total Carnage#7,
V:Carnage,A:Venom 3.00
380 MBa,Maximum Carnage#11 . . . 3.00
381 MBa,V:Dr.Samson,A:Hulk. 3.00
382 MBa,V:Hulk,A:Dr.Samson. 3.00
383 MBa,V:Jury 3.00
384 MBa,AM,V:Jury. 3.00
385 B:DvM(s),MBa,RyE,V:Jury 3.00
386 MBa,RyE,B:Lifetheft,V:Vulture . 3.00
387 MBa,RyE,V:Vulture 3.00
388 Blue Foil(c),MBa,RyE,RLm,TP,
E:Lifetheft,D:Peter's Synthetic
Parents,BU:Venom,Cardiac,
Chance, ... 5.00
388a Newsstand Ed. 3.00
389 MBa,RyE,E:Pursuit,
V:Chameleon. 3.00
390 MBa,RyE,B:Shrieking,
A:Shriek,w/cel 4.00
390a Newsstand Ed. 3.00
391 MBa,RyE,V:Shriek,Carrion 3.00
392 MBa,RyE,V:Shriek,Carrion 3.00
393 MBa,RyE,E:Shrieking,
V:Shriek,Carrion 3.00
394 MBa,RyE,Power & Responsibility,
pt.2,V:Judas Traveller,. 4.00
394a w/flip book,2 covers 3.00
395 MBa,RyE,R:Puma. 3.00
396 MBa,RyE,A:Daredevil,
V:Vulture, Owl 3.00
397 MBa,Web of Death,pt.1,
V:Stunner,Doc Ock 3.50
398 MBa,Web of Death,pt.3 . . . . . . 4.00
399 MBa,Smoke and Mirrors,pt.2 . . 2.50
400 MBa,Death of a Parker. 6.00
400a die-cut cover 10.00
401 MBa,The Mark of Kaine,pt.2. . . . 3.00
402 MBa,R:Judas Travellor 3.00
403 MBa,JMD,LMa The Trial of
Peter Parker, pt.2 . . . . 3.00
404 Maximum Clonage. 3.00
405 JMD,DaR,LMa,Exiled,pt.2,. . . . 3.00
406 I:New Doc Ock 3.00
407 TDF,MBa,LMa,Return of
Spider-Man,pt.2 . . . . 3.00
408 TDF,MBa,LMa,Media
Blizzard,pt.2. . . . . 3.00
409 . . . . 3.00
410 . . . . 3.00
411 TDF,MBa,LMa,Blood
Brothers,pt.2 . . . . 3.00
412 . . . . 3.00
413 . . . . 3.00
414 A:The Rose 3.00
415 Onslaught saga,V:Sentinels . . . 3.00
416 Onslaught epilogue. 3.00
417 TDF,RG,secrets of Scrier &
Judas Traveler. 3.00
418 Revelations,pt.3, R:Norman
Osborn. 3.00
419 TDF,SSr,V:Black Tarantula 3.00
420 TDF,SSr,X-Man x-over,pt.1 . . . . 3.00
421 TDF,SSr,I:Dragonfly; Electro
Kidnapped 3.00
422 TDF,SSr,V:Electro,Tarantula . . . 3.00
423 TDF,V:Electro 3.00
424 TDF,JoB,V:Black Tarantula, The
Hand, Dragonfly, Delilah,
The Rose, Elektra 3.00
425 TDF,SSr, V:Electro,double size. 4.00
426 TDF,SSr,V:Doctor Octopus 3.00
427 TDF,SSr,JR gatefold cover,
V:Doctor Octopus 4.00
428 TDF,SSr,V:Doctor Octopus 3.00
429 TDF,A:Daredevil, X-Man,
Absorbing Man, Titania 3.00
430 TDF,SSr,V:Carnage,A:Silver
Surfer. 3.00

MARVEL

Amazing Spider-Man #406
© Marvel Entertainment Group

431 TDF,SSr,V:Carnage (with Silver
    Surfer's powers) 3.00
432 SSr,JR2,Spider-Hunt,pt.2
    x-over. 4.00
432a variant cover 4.00
433 TDF,TL,Identity Crisis prelude,
    good-bye to Joe Robertson. . . . 3.00
434 TDF,JoB,Identity Crisis, as
    Ricochet vs. Black Tarantula . . . 3.00
435 TDF,MD2,Ricochet,A:Delilah . . 3.00
436 TDF,JoB,V:Black Tarantula 3.00
437 TDF,JoB,V:Plant Man 3.00
Bi-weekly
438 TDF,V:Daredevil 3.00
439 TDF,future history chronicle . . . 3.00
440 JBy,The Gathering of the Five,
    Pt.2 (of 5) x-over 3.00
441 JBy,V:Green Goblin, The
    Final Chapter, pt.1 . . . . 5.00
Minus 1 Spec., TDF,JBe, flashback,
    early Kingpin 2.50
Ann.#1 SD,I:Sinister Six 2,000.00
Ann.#2 SD,A:Dr.Strange 700.00
Ann.#3 JR,DH,A:Avengers 300.00
Ann.#4 A:H.Torch,V:Mysterio,
    Wizard 250.00
Ann.#5 JR(c),A:Red Skull,I:Peter
    Parker's Parents 250.00
Ann.#6 JR(c),Rep.Ann.#1,Fant.
    Four Ann.#1 . . . . 75.00
Ann.#7 JR(c),Rep.#1,#2,#38 . . . . 75.00
Ann.#8 Rep.#46,#50 . . . . 75.00
Ann.#9 JR(c),Rep.Spec.SpM #2 . . 75.00
Ann.#10 JR(c),GK,V:Human Fly . . 30.00
Ann.#11 GK(c),DP,JM,JR2,AM, . . 20.00
Ann.#12 JBy(c),KP,Rep.#119,
    #120. . . . . 25.00
Ann.#13 JBy,TA,V:Dr.Octopus . . . 25.00
Ann.#14 FM,TP,A:Dr.Strange,
    V:Dr.Doom,Dormammu 25.00
Ann.#15 FM,KJ,BL,Punisher 25.00
Ann.#16 JR2,JR,I:New Captain
    Marvel,A:Thing 10.00
Ann.#17 EH,JM,V:Kingpin 10.00
Ann.#18 RF,BL,JG,V:Scorpion 10.00
Ann.#19 JR(c),MW,V:Spiderslayer. 10.00
Ann.#20 BW(i),V:Iron Man 2020 . . 10.00
Ann.#21 JR(c),PR,W:SpM,direct . . 20.00
Ann.#21a W:SpM,news stand 15.00
Ann.#22 JR(c),MBa(1stSpM),SD,
    JG,RLm,TD,Evolutionary War,
    I:Speedball,New Men 8.00
Ann.#23 JBy(c),RLd,MBa,RF,
    AtlantisAttacks#4,A:She-Hulk . . 7.00

Ann.#24 GK,SD,MZ,DGr,
    A:Ant Man 4.00
Ann.#25 EL(c),SB,PCu,SD,
    Vibranium Vendetta#1,Venom . . 6.00
Ann.#26 Hero Killers#1,A:New
    Warriors,BU:Venom,Solo. 6.00
Ann.#27 TL,I:Annex,w/card 4.00
Ann.#28 SBt(s),V:Carnage,BU:Cloak
    & Dagger,Rhino 4.00
Ann. '96 two new stories, 48pg,. . . 3.50
Ann. '97 RSt,TL,RJn, 48pg, ... 3.50
Ann. '98 TL,TDF,F:Spider-Man &
    Devil Dinosaur, 48pg 3.00
G-Size Superheroes #1 GK,
    A:Morbius,Man-Wolf 75.00
G-Size #1 JR(c),RA,DH,
    A:Dracula. 40.00
G-Size #2 K&R(c),RA,AM,
    A:Master of Kung Fu 40.00
G-Size #3 GK(c),RA,DocSavage. . 40.00
G-Size #4 GK(c),RA,Punisher 75.00
G-Size #5 GK(c),RA,V:Magnum . . 30.00
G-Size #6 Rep.Ann.#4. . . . . 30.00
G-Size Spec.#1 O:Symbiotes 5.00
Marvel Milestone rep. #1 (1993) . . 3.00
Marvel Milestone rep. #3 (1995) . . 3.00
Marvel Milestone rep. #129 (1992) . 3.00
Marvel Milestone rep. #149 (1994) . 3.00
Nothing Can Stop the Juggernaut . . 4.00
Sensational Spider-Man,reps. 5.00
Skating on Thin Ice(Canadian) . . . 15.00
Skating on Thin Ice(US). 2.00
Soul of the Hunter MZ,BMc,
    R:Kraven 7.00
Unicef:Trial of Venom,
    A:Daredevil,V:Venom 50.00
See Also:
PETER PARKER;
SPECTACULAR SPIDER-MAN;
WEB OF SPIDER-MAN

AMAZING SPIDER-MAN
Jan., 1999
1 HMe,JBy,DHz,V:Scorpion,48-page
    prismatic etched (c). 7.00
1a Dynamic Forces JR2 . . . . 12.00
2 HMe,JBy,DHz,I:Shadrac 5.00
2a variant BiT cover 6.00
3 HMe,JBy,DHz,V:Shadrac,
    A:Iceman 3.00
4 HMe,JBy,SHa,A:Fantastic Four . . 3.00
5 HMe,JBy,SHa,I:new
    Spider-Woman. 3.00
6 JBy,HMe,SHa,F:Spider-Woman . 3.00
7 JBy,HMe,SHa,Reality Bent 3.00
8 JMy,HMe,SHa,JR2(c),
    Reality Bent x-over 3.00
9 JMy,HMe,SHa,JR2(c),V:Scorpion 3.00
10 JMy,HMe,SHa,JR2(c),MaryJane. 3.00
11 HMe,SHa,JBy,marital problems . 3.00
12 HMe,SHa,JBy,48-pg. 4.00
13 HMe,JBy 3.00
14 HMe,JBy,A:Sp.-Woman,x-over . . 3.00
15 HMe,JBy,DGr,x-over 3.00
16 HMe,JBy,DGr,Mary Jane gone . . 3.00
17 HMe,JBy,DGr,A:Sandman 3.00
18 HMe,JBy,JR,V:Green Goblin . . . 3.00
19 HMe,EL,DGr,Eddie Brock 3.00
20 HMe,EL,JBy,100-pg 3.50
21 HMe,EL,JhB,AlistairSmythe 3.00
22 HMe,JR2,SHa,Senator Ward . . . 3.00
23 HMe,JR2,SHa,Ranger 3.00
24 HMe,JR2,SHa,Max.Security. . . . 3.00
25 HMe,JR2,SHa,A:Green Goblin . . 3.00
25a holographic foil(c) 7.00
26 HMe,JR2,SHa,F:Spidey's dad . . 3.00
27 HMe,JR2,SHa,V:A.I.M. 3.00
28 HMe,JR2,SHa,Enforcers. 7.00
29 HMe,JR2,SHa,x-over 10.00
30 B:MSz(s),JR2,JSC(c) 12.00
31 MSz(s),JR2,JSC(c) 8.00
32 MSz(s),JR2,SHa,Ezekiel. 8.00

Amazing Spider-Man Vol. 2 #1
© Marvel Entertainment Group

33 MSz(s),JR2,SHa,Morlun 8.00
34 MSz(s),JR2,SHa,V:Morlun 8.00
35 MSz(s),JR2,SHa,pt.1 . . . . 8.00
36 MSz(s),JR2,SHa 15.00
37 MSz(s),JR2,SHa 5.00
38 MSz(s),JR2,SHa,'Nuff Said 3.00
39 MSz(s),JR2,SHa,Aunt May 3.00
40 MSz(s),JR2,SHa,Aunt May 3.00
41 MSz(s),JR2,SHa 3.00
42 MSz(s),JR2,SHa 3.00
43 MSz(s),JR2,SHa 3.00
44 MSz(s),JR2,SHa 3.00
45 MSz(s),JR2,SHa 3.00
46 MSz(s),JR2,SHa 3.00
47 MSz(s),JR2,SHa 3.00
48 MSz(s),JR2,SHa 3.00
49 MSz(s),JR2,SHa 3.00
50 MSz(s),JR2,SHa,F:Mary Jane . . 4.50
51 MSz(s),JR2,SHa,F:Mary Jane . . 2.50
52 MSz(s),JR2,SHa,F:Mary Jane . . 2.50
53 MSz(s),JR2,SHa,F:Mary Jane . . 2.50
54 MSz(s),JR2,Digger 2.50
55 MSz(s),JR2,Consequences,pt.1 . 2.50
56 MSz(s),JR2,Consequences,pt.2 . 2.50
57 MSz(s),JR2,pt.1 . . . . 2.50
58 MSz(s),JR2,pt.2 . . . . 2.50
500 MSz(s),JR2,48-pg. 4.00
501 MSz(s),JR2 . . . . 2.50
502 MSz(s),JR2 . . . . 2.50
503 JR2,A Dark Shadow,pt.1 . . . . . 2.50
504 JR2,A Dark Shadow,pt.2 . . . . . 2.50
505 MSz(s),JR2,Ezekiel,pt.1 . . . . . 2.50
506 MSz(s),JR2,Ezekiel,pt.2 . . . . . 2.50
507 MSz(s),JR2,Ezekiel,pt.3 . . . . . 2.50
508 MSz(s),JR2,Ezekiel,pt.4 . . . . . 2.50
509 MSz(s),MD2,Sins Past,pt.1. . . . 2.50
510 MSz(s),MD2,Sins Past,pt.2. . . . 2.50
511 MSz(s),MD2,Sins Past,pt.3. . . . 2.50
512 MSz(s),MD2,Sins Past,pt.4. . . . 2.50
513 MSz(s),MD2,Sins Past,pt.5. . . . 2.50
514 MSz(s),MD2. . . . . 2.50
515 MSz(s),MD2,Skin Deep 2.50
516 MSz(s),MD2,Skin Deep 2.50
517 MSz(s),MD2,Skin Deep 2.50
518 MSz(s),MD2,JJu(c),Skin Deep . 2.50
519 MSz(s),MD2,NewAvengers,pt.1 2.50
520 MSz(s),MD2,NewAvengers,pt.2 2.50
521 MSz(s),MD2,Moving Up 2.50
522 MSz(s),MD2,V:Hydra 2.50
523 MSz(s),MD2,Moving Up 2.50
524 MSz(s),MD2,Acts of Aggression 2.50
525 PDd(s),The Other,x-over,pt. 3. . 4.00
526 MD2,The Other,x-over,pt.6 . . . . 4.00
526a 2nd printing. 5.00

527 MSz(s),The Other,x-over,pt.9 . . 2.50
527a 2nd printing 5.00
528 MSz(s),The Other,x-over,pt.12 . 2.50
528a 2nd printing 5.00
529 MSz(s),RG, new outfit 12.00
529a 2nd printing 7.00
530 MSz(s),RG 2.50
531 Mr. Parker Goes to Washington 4.00
532 MSz(s),RG,War at Home,pt.1 . . 4.00
533 MSz(s),RG,War at Home,pt.2 . . 5.00
534 MSz(s),RG,War at Home,pt.3 . . 4.00
535 MSz(s),RG,War at Home,pt.4 . . 3.00
536 MSz(s),RG,War at Home,pt.5 . . 3.00
537 MSz(s),RG,War at Home,pt.6 . . 3.00
538 MSz,RG,The War at Home . . . 3.00
539 MSz,RG,Back in Black,pt.1 . . 3.00
540 MSz,RG,Back in Black, pt.2 . . 3.00
541 MSz,RG,Back in Black, pt.3 . . 3.00
542 MSz,RG,Back in Black, pt.4 . . 3.00
543 MSz,RG,V:Kingpin 3.00
544 MSz,JQ,One More Day, pt.1 . . 4.00
544a variant (c) 4.00
545 MSz,JQ,One More Day,pt.4 . . 4.00
545a variant (c) 4.00
Spec. Must Have,Rep. #30–#32 . . 4.00
Ann.1999 JB,HMe, 48-page 4.00
Ann.2000 HMe,48-pg. 4.00
Ann.2001 48-page 4.00
Giant Sized 80-pg. 4.50
Spec.Spider-Man/Sentry,PJe,RL,TA 3.00
Spec.Spider-Man/Marrow,SLo . . . 3.00
Spec.Coll. ed.,rep #30–#32 . . . . . 4.00
Coll.Classics rep. #300 . . . . 2.50
Coll.Classics rep. Sp-M #1. . . . . . 2.50

AMAZING SPIDER-MAN INDEX
See: OFFICIAL MARVEL INDEX TO THE AMAZING SPIDER-MAN

AMAZING SPIDER-MAN COLLECTION
1 Mark Bagley card set. 3.00
2 and 3 MBa, from card set . . . . @3.00

AMAZING X-MEN, THE
March–June, 1995
1 X-Men after Xavier. 4.00
2 Exodus,Dazzler,V:Abyss 3.00
3 F:Bishop. 3.00
4 V:Apocalypse. 2.50

A-NEXT
Aug., 1998
1 TDF,RF,BBr,Next Generation of
Avengers 3.00
2 thru 12 . . . . @2.25

ANIMATED MOVIE-TUNES
Marvel-Margood Publ., 1945
1 Super Rabbit 350.00
2 Super Rabbit 350.00
Becomes:

MOVIE TUNES
Marvel-Margood Publ., 1946
3 . . . . 150.00
Becomes:

FRANKIE
Marvel-Margood, 1946–48
4 . . . . 200.00
5 thru 9 . . . . @125.00
10 . . . . 100.00
11 . . . . 100.00
Becomes:

FRANKIE & LANA
Marvel-Margood, 1949
12 . . . . 100.00

13 . . . . 100.00
14 . . . . 100.00
15 . . . . 100.00
Becomes:

FRANKIE FUDDLE
Marvel-Margood, 1949
16 . . . . 100.00
17 . . . . 100.00

ANIMAX
Star, 1986–87
1 Based on Toy Line 3.00
2 thru 4 . . . . @3.00

ANNEX
Aug.–Nov., 1994
1 WMc,I:Brace, Crucible of Power . 2.25
2 WMc, V:Brace, Crucible, pt.2 . . . 2.25
3 Crucible of Power, pt.3 . . . . 2.25
4 Crucible of Power, pt.4 . . . . 2.25

ANNIE
(Treasury Edition)
Oct., 1982
1 Movie Adaptation 3.00
2 Nov., 1982 . . . . 3.00

Annie Oakley #4
© Marvel Entertainment Group

ANNIE OAKLEY
Marvel Timely, Spring, 1948
1 A:Hedy Devine 700.00
2 CCB,I:Lana,A:Hedy Devine . 450.00
3 . . . . 300.00
4 . . . . 300.00
5 JMn(c) 250.00
6 . . . . 250.00
7 . . . . 250.00
8 GWb. 250.00
9 AW. 250.00
10 GWb 200.00
11 JSe(c), June, 1956 . . . . 200.00

ANNIHILATION
Sept., 2006
1 Silver Surfer, Super-Skrull, Ronan
& Nova, V:Annihilus. 3.00
2 F:Nova Ronan & Drax 3.00
3 F:Nova, Ronan. 3.00
4 F:Drax, Thanos, Nova 3.50
5 . . . . 3.00
6 finale 3.00
Spec. Annihilation Saga. 2.00
Spec. Conquest Prologue 4.00

ANNIHILATION: CONQUEST
Nov., 2007
1 (of 6) Phalanx vs. Kree Empire . . 3.00

ANNIHILATION: CONQUEST – QUASAR
July, 2007
1 (of 4) F:Phyla-Vell 3.00
2 thru 4 . . . . @3.00

ANNIHILATION: CONQUEST – STAR-LORD
July, 2007
1 (of 4) F:Peter Quill. 3.00
2 thru 4 KG(s) . . . . @3.00

ANNIHILATION: CONQUEST – WRAITH
July, 2007
1 (of 4) 3.00
2 thru 4 . . . . @3.00

ANNIHILATION: HERALDS OF GALACTUS
Feb., 2007
1 Terrax & Stardust. 4.00
2 Tenebrous & Aegis. 4.00
(3) Silver Surfer/Firelord 4.00

ANNIHILATION: NOVA
April, 2006
1 V:Annihilation Wave. 3.00
2 thru 4 . . . . @3.00

ANNIHILATION: THE NOVA CORPS
Aug., 2006
1 Nova Corps files 4.00

ANNIHILATION: PROLOGUE
March, 2006
1 KG,V:Annihilation Wave. 4.00

ANNIHILATION: RONAN
April, 2006
1 V:Annihilation Wave. 3.00
2 thru 4 . . . . @3.00

ANNIHILATION: SILVER SURFER
April, 2006
1 V:Annihilation Wave. 7.00
2 thru 3 . . . . @5.00
4 . . . . @7.00

ANNIHILATION: SUPER-SKRULL
April, 2006
1 V:Annihilation Wave. 3.00
2 thru 4 . . . . @3.00

ANT-MAN
Dec., 2003
1 (of 5) Size does matter 3.00
2 thru 5 . . . . @3.00

ANT-MAN
Oct., 2006
1 & 2 PhH . . . . @3.00
3 thru 12 PhH . . . . @3.00

ANT-MAN'S BIG CHRISTMAS
Dec., 1999
GN 48-pg. 6.00

A-1
1993
1 The Edge 8.00
2 Cheeky,Wee Budgie Boy 8.00
3 King Leon. 8.00
4 King Leon. 8.00

APACHE KID
Marvel-Comics, 1950–52
1 (53) 500.00
2 . . . . 275.00
3 . . . . 200.00
4 . . . . 200.00
5 . . . . 200.00
6 . . . . 150.00
7 RH 200.00
8 thru 10 . . . . @150.00
11 RH 100.00
12 JMn 100.00
13 RH 100.00
14 thru 19 . . . . @100.00
Becomes:

WESTERN GUNFIGHTERS
Marvel Atlas, 1956–57
20 GC,JSe 150.00
21 RC 150.00
22 WW,BP 250.00
23 AW 200.00
24 ATh 200.00
25 GM 100.00
26 GC 100.00
27 GC,JSe 100.00

APACHE SKIES
July, 2002
1 (of 4) JOs,Apache Kid,wild west . 3.00
2 thru 4 JOs . . . . @3.00

APOCALYPSE STRIKEFILES
1 After Xavier special 2.50

ARANA: THE HEART OF THE SPIDER
Jan., 2005
1 Freshman Flu. 3.00
1a variant JQ(c) 3.00
2 A Tangled Web. 3.00
3 Ultimatum. 3.00
4 Between Life and Death,
    A:Spider-Man. 3.00
5 Heart of the Spider 3.00
6 Heart of the Spider,concl. 3.00
7 Unexpected Pasts,pt.1. . . . . 3.00
8 Unexpected Pasts,pt.2. . . . . 3.00
9 Unexpected Pasts,pt.3. . . . . 3.00
10 Unexpected Pasts,pt.4,V:Jade . 3.00
11 V:Jade 3.00
12 V:Wasps 3.00

ARCHANGEL
1996
1-shot B&W 2.50

ARES
Jan., 2006
1 F:Ares, God of War 3.00
2 thru 5 . . . . @3.00

ARIZONA KID
Atlas, March, 1951
1 RH,Coming of the Arizons Kid. 300.00
2 RH,Code of the Gunman 150.00
3 RH(c) 125.00
4 PMo 125.00
5 PMo 125.00

6 PMo,JSt,Jan., 1952 . . . . 125.00

ARRGH!
Dec., 1974
Satire
1 MSy,TS,Vampire Rats 35.00
2 AA,TS. 25.00
3 TS,AA(c),Beauty and the
    Big Foot 25.00
4 The Night Gawker 25.00
5 Sept., 1975 . . . . 25.00

ARROWHEAD
April, 1954
1 JSt,Indian Warrior Stories 200.00
2 JSt, JMn(c). 125.00
3 JSt, RH(c) 125.00
4 JSt, Nov., 1954 . . . . 125.00

MARVEL BOY
Dec., 1950
1 RH,O:Marvel Boy,Lost World 1,700.00
2 BEv,The Zero Hour 1,200.00
Becomes:

ASTONISHING
1951
3 BEv,Marvel Boy,V:Mr Death . 1,500.00
4 BEv,Stan Lee,The
    Screaming Tomb 1,100.00
5 BEv,Horror in the Caves of
    Doom 1,100.00
6 BEv,My Coffin is Waiting
    E:Marvel Boy 1,100.00
7 JR,JMn,Nightmare 500.00
8 RH,Behind the Wall 500.00
9 RH(c),The Little Black Box . . . 500.00
10 BEv,Walking Dead 500.00
11 BF,JSt.Mr Mordeau 350.00
12 GC,BEv,Horror Show 350.00
13 BK,MSy,Ghouls Gold 500.00
14 BK,The Long Jump Down. . . . 500.00
15 BEv(c),Grounds for Death . . . 375.00
16 BEv(c),DAy,SSh,Don't Make
    a Ghoul of Yourself 375.00
17 Who Was the Wilmach
    Werewolf? 375.00
18 BEv(c),JR,Vampire at My
    Window 375.00
19 BK,Back From the Grave 375.00
20 GC,Mystery at Midnight 375.00
21 Manhunter. 325.00
22 RH(c),Man Against Werewolf. 325.00
23 The Woman in Black. 350.00
24 JR,The Stone Face 350.00

Astonishing #6
© Marvel Entertainment Group

25 RC,I Married a Zombie 350.00
26 RH(c),I Died Too Often 275.00
27 . . . . 275.00
28 TLw,No Evidence 275.00
29 BEv(c),GC,Decapitation(c) . . . 275.00
30 Tentacled eyeball story 450.00
31 JMn 250.00
32 A Vampire Takes a Wife 250.00
33 SMo,JMn. 250.00
34 JMn,Transformation 250.00
35 . . . . 250.00
36 Pithecanthrope Giant 250.00
37 BEv,TLw,Poor Pierre. 250.00
38 The Man Who Didn't Belong. . 175.00
39 . . . . 175.00
40 . . . . 175.00
41 MD 175.00
42 TLw 175.00
43 BP,JR 175.00
44 RC,BP 200.00
45 BK 200.00
46 . . . . 200.00
47 BK,JO,BEv 200.00
48 BP 175.00
49 BEv 175.00
50 DCn 175.00
51 . . . . 175.00
52 GM 175.00
53 SD,JF,BEv 200.00
54 BEv 200.00
55 BEv 225.00
56 JMn,JK 175.00
57 JR 225.00
58 JF,JO 175.00
59 TSe,BEv 175.00
60 JF,BEv. 175.00
61 GM,JO,JR,BEv 175.00
62 MD,BEv. 225.00
63 BEv,August, 1957 . . . . 225.00

ASTONISHING TALES
Aug., 1970
1 BEv(c),JK,WW,Ka-Zar,Dr.Doom 90.00
2 JK,WW,Ka-Zar,Dr.Doom 40.00
3 BWS,WW,Ka-Zar,Dr.Doom . . . 50.00
4 BWS,WW,Ka-Zar,Dr.Doom . . . 50.00
5 BWS,GT,Ka-Zar,Dr.Doom 50.00
6 BWS,BEv,GT,I:Bobbi Morse . . 50.00
7 HT,GC,Ka-Zar,Dr.Doom 25.00
8 HT,TS,GT,GC,Ka-Zar 25.00
9 GK(c),JB,Ka-Zar,Dr.Doom . . . 20.00
10 GK(c),BWS,SB,Ka-Zar 25.00
11 GK,O:Ka-Zar 25.00
12 JB,DA,NA,V:Man Thing 50.00
13 JB,RB,DA,V:Man Thing 35.00
14 GK(c),rep. Ka-Zar 15.00
15 GK,TS,Ka-Zar 15.00
16 RB,AM,A:Ka-Zar 15.00
17 DA,V:Gemini 15.00
18 JR(c),DA,A:Ka-Zar 15.00
19 JR(c),DA,JSn,JA,I:Victorious . . 15.00
20 JR(c),A:Ka-Zar 15.00
21 RTs(s),DAy,B:It 40.00
22 RTs(s),DAy,V:Granitor. 30.00
23 RTs(s),DAy,A:Fin Fang Foom . . 30.00
24 RTs(s),DAy,E:It 30.00
25 RB(a&s),B:I&O:Deathlok,
    GP(1st art). 75.00
26 RB(a&s),I:Warwolf 20.00
27 RB(a&s),V:Warwolf 20.00
28 RB(a&s),V:Warwolf 20.00
29 rep.Marv.Super Heroes #18 . . . 15.00
30 RB(a&s),KP, ... 15.00
31 RB(a&s),BW,KP,V:Ryker. . . . 18.00
32 RB(a&s),KP,V:Ryker 18.00
33 RB(a&s),KJ,I:Hellinger 18.00
34 RB(a&s),KJ,V:Ryker. 18.00
35 RB(a&s),KJ,I:Doomsday-Mech. 18.00
36 RB(a&s),KP,E:Deathlok,
    I:Godwulf 25.00

MARVEL

ASTONISHING X-MEN
March–June, 1995
1 Uncanny X-Men. 5.00
2 V:Holocaust 3.50
3 V:Abyss 3.00
4 V:Beast,Infinities 3.00

ASTONISHING X-MEN
July, 1999
1 (of 3) BPe,HMe,new X-Men team 2.50
2 BPe,HMe,The Shattering x-over . 2.50
3 BPe,HMe,Shattering,concl. 2.50

ASTONISHING X-MEN
May, 2004
1 Gifted,pt.1 . . . . 6.00
1a variant (c). 6.00
1b Director's Cut. 10.00
2 thru 6 Gifted,pt.2 thru pt.6 . . . . @6.00
7 thru 12 JoW(s),Dangerous,pt.1
    thru pt. 6 . . . . @4.00
13 thru 18 JoW(s), Torn, pt.1
    thru pt. 6 . . . . @4.00
19 JoW(s) Unstoppable, pt.1 . . . . 3.00
19a variant (c) 3.00
20 JoW(s),Unstoppable, pt.2 . . . . 3.00
21 JoW(s),Unstoppable, pt.3 . . . . 3.00
22 JoW(s),Unstoppable, pt.4 . . . . 3.00
23 JoW(s),Unstoppable, pt.5 . . . . 3.00
20a thru 23a variant (c)s . . . . . . @3.00
1-shot Astonishing X-Men Saga
    48-pg. 4.00

A-Team #3
© Marvel Entertainment Group

A-TEAM
March, 1984
1 thru 3 . . . . @5.00

ATOMIC AGE
Epic, Nov., 1990
1 AW. 4.50
2 AW 4.50
3 AW,Feb., 1991 . . . . 4.50

AVATAARS: COVENANT
OF THE SHIELD
July, 2000
1 (of 3) LKa,Capt.Avalon 3.00
2 LKa,Dreadlord 3.00

AVENGERS
Sept., 1963
1 JK,O:Avengers,V:Loki 7,000.00
2 JK,V:Space Phantom 2,000.00
3 JK,V:Hulk,Sub-Mariner 900.00
4 JK,R&J:Captain America 3,500.00
5 JK,L:Hulk,V:Lava Men 850.00
6 JK,I:Masters of Evil 850.00
7 JK,V:BaronZemo,Enchantress. 850.00
8 JK,I:Kang 750.00
9 JK(c),DH,I&D:Wonder Man . . 750.00
10 JK(c),DH,I:Immortus 450.00
11 JK(c),DH,A:Spider-Man,
    V:Kang. 750.00
12 JK(c),DH,V:Moleman,
    Red Ghost 350.00
13 JK(c),DH,I:Count Nefaria . . . 350.00
14 JK,DH,V:Count Nefaria 350.00
15 JK,DH,D:Baron Zemo 300.00
16 JK,J:Hawkeye,Scarlet Witch,
    Quicksilver 300.00
17 JK(c),DH,V:Mole Man,A:Hulk . 250.00
18 JK(c),DH,V:The Commisar . . . 250.00
19 JK(c),DH,I&O:Swordsman,
    O:Hawkeye 250.00
20 JK(c),DH,WW,V:Swordsman,
    Mandarin 200.00
21 JK(c),DH,WW,V:Power Man
    (not L.Cage),Enchantress . . . 200.00
22 JK(c),DH,WW,V:Power Man . . 200.00
23 JK(c),DH,JR,V:Kang 150.00
24 JK(c),DH,JR,V:Kang 150.00
25 JK(c),DH,V:Dr.Doom 150.00
26 DH,V:Attuma 150.00
27 DH,V:Attuma,Beetle 150.00
28 JK(c),DH,I:1st Goliath,
    I:Collector 150.00
29 DH,V:Power Man,Swordsman 150.00
30 JK(c),DH,V:Swordsman 150.00
31 DH,V:Keeper of the Flame . . . 125.00
32 DH,I:Bill Foster 100.00
33 DH,V:Sons of the Serpent
    A:Bill Foster 100.00
34 DH,V:Living Laser 100.00
35 DH,V:Mandarin 100.00
36 DH,V:The Ultroids 100.00
37 GK(c),DH,V:Ultroids 150.00
38 GK(c),DH,V:Enchantress,
    Ares,J:Hercules 100.00
39 DH,V:Mad Thinker 100.00
40 DH,V:Sub-Mariner 100.00
41 JB,V:Dragon Man,Diablo 80.00
42 JB,V:Dragon Man,Diablo 80.00
43 JB,V:Red Guardian 80.00
44 JB,V:Red Guardian,
    O:Black.Widow 80.00
45 JB,V:Super Adoptoid. 80.00
46 JB,V:Whirlwind 80.00
47 JB,GT,V:Magneto 150.00
48 GT,I&O:New Black Knight. . . . 150.00
49 JB,V:Magneto 125.00
50 JB,V:Typhon 125.00
51 JB,GT,R:Iron Man,Thor,
    V:Collector. 125.00
52 JB,J:Black Panther,
    I:Grim Reaper 125.00
53 JB,GT,A:X-Men; x-over
    X-Men #45 . . . . 180.00
54 JB,GT,V:Masters of Evil
    I:Crimson Cowl(Ultron) 150.00
55 JB,I:Ultron,V:Masters of Evil . 150.00
56 JB,D:Bucky retold,
    V:Baron Zemo 150.00
57 JB,I:Vision,V:Ultron 300.00
58 JB,O&J:Vision 125.00
59 JB,I:Yellowjacket 125.00
60 JB,W:Yellowjacket & Wasp . . . 125.00
61 JB,A:Dr.Strange,x-over
    Dr. Strange #178 . . . . 125.00
62 JB,I:Man-Ape,A:Dr.Strange. . . 125.00
63 GC,I&O:2nd Goliath(Hawkeye)
    V:Egghead. 125.00

Avengers #58
© Marvel Entertainment Group

64 GC,V:Egghead,O:Hawkeye . . 125.00
65 GC,V:Swordsman,Egghead . . 125.00
66 BWS,I:Ultron 6,Adamantium . . 135.00
67 BWS,V:Ultron 6. . . . . 135.00
68 SB,V:Ultron 120.00
69 SB,I:Nighthawk,Grandmaster,
    Squadron Supreme, V:Kang . 120.00
70 SB,O:Squadron Supreme
    V:Kang 120.00
71 SB,I:Invaders,V:Kang 150.00
72 SB,V:Captain Marvel,
    I:Zodiac 75.00
73 HT(i),V:Sons of Serpent 75.00
74 JB,TP,V:Sons of Serpent,
    IR:Black Panther on TV 75.00
75 JB,TP,I:Arkon 75.00
76 JB,TP,V:Arkon 75.00
77 JB,TP,V:Split-Second Squad. . . 75.00
78 SB,TP,V:Lethal Legion 75.00
79 JB,TP,V:Lethal Legion 75.00
80 JB,TP,I&O:Red Wolf 75.00
81 JB,TP,A:Red Wolf 75.00
82 JB,TP,V:Ares,A:Daredevil 75.00
83 JB,TP,I:Valkyrie,
    V:Masters of Evil 75.00
84 JB,TP,V:Enchantress,Arkon . . . 75.00
85 JB,V:Squadron Supreme 75.00
86 JB,JM,A:Squad Supreme 75.00
87 SB(i),O:Black Panther,
    V:.A.I.M. 100.00
88 JB,JM,V:Psyklop,A:Hulk,
    Professor.X 95.00
88a 2nd Printing 10.00
89 SB,B:Kree/Skrull War 65.00
90 SB,V:Sentry #459,Ronan,
    Skrulls 65.00
91 SB,V:Sentry #459,Ronan,
    Skrulls 65.00
92 SB,V:Super Skrull,Ronan, ... 75.00
93 NA,TP,V:Super-Skrull,G-Size . 200.00
94 NA,JB,TP,V:Super-Skrull,
    I:Mandroids 125.00
95 NA,TP,V:Maximus,Skrulls,
    A:Inhumans,O:Black Bolt . . . 100.00
96 NA,TP,V:Skrulls,Ronan 100.00
97 GK&BEv(c),JB,TP,E:Kree-Skrull
    War,V:Annihilus,Ronan,Skrulls,
    A:Golden Age Heroes 75.00
98 BWS,SB,V:Ares,R:Hercules,
    R&N:Hawkeye 75.00
99 BWS,TS,V:Ares 75.00
100 BWS,JSr,V:Ares & Kratos . . . 150.00
101 RB,DA,A:Watcher 40.00

102 RB,JSt,V:Grim Reaper,
    Sentinels 40.00
103 RB,JSt,V:Sentinels 40.00
104 RB,JSt,V:Sentinels 40.00
105 JB,JM,V:Savage Land
    Mutates; A:Black Panther 40.00
106 GT,DC,RB,V:Space Phantom . 40.00
107 GT,DC,JSn,V:Space
    Phantom,Grim Reaper 40.00
108 DH,DC,JSt,V:Space
    Phantom,Grim Reaper 40.00
109 DH,FMc,V:Champion,
    L:Hawkeye. 40.00
110 DH,V:Magneto,A:X-Men 65.00
111 DH,J:Bl.Widow,A:Daredevil,
    X-Men,V:Magneto 65.00
112 DH,I:Mantis,V:Lion-God,
    L:Black Widow. 50.00
113 FBe(i),V:The Living Bombs . . . 30.00
114 JR(c),V:Lion-God,J:Mantis,
    Swordsman 30.00
115 JR(c),A:Defenders,V:Loki,
    Dormammu. 30.00
116 JR(c),A:Defenders,S.Surfer
    V:Loki,Dormammu. 30.00
117 JR(c),FMc(i),A:Defenders,Silv.
    Surfer,V:Loki,Dormammu . . . 30.00
118 JR(c),A:Defenders,S.Surfer
    V:Loki,Dormammu. 30.00
119 JR(c),DH(i),V:Collector 30.00
120 JSn(c),DH(i),V:Zodiac 30.00
121 JR&JSn(c),JB,DH,V:Zodiac . . 30.00
122 K&R(c),V:Zodiac 30.00
123 JR(c),DH(i),O:Mantis. 30.00
124 JR(c),JB,DC,V:Kree,O:Mantis. 30.00
125 JR(c),JB,DC,V:Thanos 40.00
126 DC(i),V:Klaw,Solarr 30.00
127 GK(c),SB,JSon,A:Inhumans,
    V:Ultron,Maximus 30.00
128 K&R(c),SB,JSon,V:Kang. 30.00
129 SB,JSon,V:Kang 30.00
130 GK(c),SB,JSon,V:Slasher,
    Titanic Three 30.00
131 GK(c),SB,JSon,V:Kang,
    Legion of the Unliving 30.00
132 SB,JSon,Kang,Legion
    of the Unliving 30.00
133 GK(c),SB,JSon,O:Vision 30.00
134 K&R(c),SB,JSon,O:Vision 30.00
135 JSn&JR(c),GT,O:Mantis,
    Vision,C:Thanos 40.00
136 K&R(c),rep Amazing Adv#12 . 20.00
137 JR(c),GT,J:Beast,
    Moondragon 20.00
138 GK(c),GT,V:Toad. 20.00
139 K&R(c),GT,V:Whirlwind 18.00
140 K&R(c),GT,V:Whirlwind 18.00
141 GK(c),GP,V:Squad.Sinister . . . 12.00
142 K&R(c),GP,V:Squadron
    Sinister,Kang 12.00
143 GK(c),GP,V:Squadron
    Sinister,Kang 12.00
144 GP,GK(c),V:Squad.Sinister,
    O&J:Hellcat,O:Guy Baxter . . . 30.00
145 GK(c),DH,V:Assassin 12.00
146 GK(c),DH,KP,V:Assassin 12.00
147 GP,V:Squadron Supreme 12.00
148 JK(c),GP,V:Squad.Supreme . . 12.00
149 GP,V:Orka 15.00
150 GP,JK,rep.Avengers #16. . . . . 15.00
151 GP,new line-up,
    R:Wonder Man 15.00
152 JB,JSt,I:New Black Talon 15.00
153 JB,JSt,V:L.Laser,Whizzer . . . 12.00
154 GP,V:Attuma 12.00
155 SB,V:Dr.Doom,Attuma 12.00
156 SB,I:Tyrak,V:Attuma 12.00
157 DH,V:Stone Black Knight 12.00
158 JK(c),SB,I&O:Graviton 12.00
159 JK(c),SB,V:Graviton, ... 12.00
160 GP,V:Grim Reaper 60.00
161 GP,V:Ultron,A:Ant-Man 14.00

162 GP,V:Ultron,I:Jocasta 14.00
163 GT,A:Champions,V:Typhon. . . 15.00
164 JBy,V:Lethal Legion 15.00
165 JBy,V:Count Nefario 14.00
166 JBy,V:Count Nefario 14.00
167 GP,A:Guardians,A:Nighthawk,
    Korvac,V:Porcupine. 8.00
168 GP,A:Guardians,V:Korvac,
    I:Gyrich 8.00
169 SB,I:Eternity Man 8.00
170 GP,R:Jocasta,C:Ultron,
    A:Guardians. 8.00
171 GP,V:Ultron,A:Guardians,
    Ms Marvel 8.00
172 SB,KJ,V:Tyrak 8.00
173 SB,V:Collector. 8.00
174 GP(c),V:Collector 8.00
175 V&O:Korvac,A:Guardians 8.00
176 V:Korvac,A:Guardians 8.00
177 DC(c),D:Korvac,A:Guardians . . 8.00
178 CI,V:Manipulator 8.00
179 JM,AG,V:Stinger,Bloodhawk . . 8.00
180 JM,V:Monolith,Stinger,
    D:Bloodhawk 8.00
181 JBy,GD,I:Scott Lang 10.00
182 JBy,KJ,V:Maximoff 10.00
183 JBy,KJ,J:Ms.Marvel 10.00
184 JBy,KJ,J:Falcon,
    V:Absorbing Man 10.00
185 JBy,DGr,O:Quicksilver & Scarlet
    Witch,I:Bova,V:Modred 10.00
186 JBy,DGr,V:Modred,Chthon . . . 10.00
187 JBy,DGr,V:Chthon,Modred . . 10.00
188 JBy,DGr,V:The Elements 10.00
189 JBy,DGr,V:Deathbird 10.00
190 JBy,DGr,V:Grey Gargoyle,
    A:Daredevil 10.00
191 JBy,DGr,V:Grey Gargoyle,
    A:Daredevil 10.00
192 I:Inferno. 8.00
193 FM(c),SB,DGr,O:Inferno 10.00
194 GP,JRu,J:Wonder Man 10.00
195 GP,JRu,A:Antman,
    I&C:Taskmaster 12.00
196 GP,JA,A:Antman,
    V:Taskmaster, ... 12.00
197 CI,JAb,V:Red Ronin 10.00
198 GP,DGr,V:Red Ronan 10.00
199 GP,DGr,V:Red Ronan 10.00
200 GP,DGr,V:Marcus,
    L:Ms.Marvel 12.00
201 GP,DGr,F:Jarvis 5.00
202 GP,V:Ultron 5.00
203 CI,V:Crawlers,F:Wonderman . . 5.00
204 DN,DGr,V:Yellow Claw 5.00
205 DGr,V:Yellow Claw 5.00
206 GC,DGr,V:Pyron 5.00
207 GC,DGr,V:Shadowlord 5.00
208 GC,DGr,V:Berserker 5.00
209 DGr,A:Mr.Fantastic,V:Skrull . . 5.00
210 GC,DGr,V:Weathermen 5.00
211 GC,DGr,Moon Knight,J:Tigra . . 5.00
212 DGr,V:Elfqueen 5.00
213 BH,DGr,L:Yellowjacket 5.00
214 BH,DGr,V:Gh.Rider,A:Angel . . 7.00
215 DGr,A:Silver Surfer,
    V:Molecule Man. 5.00
216 DGr,A:Silver Surfer,
    V:Molecule Man. 5.00
217 BH,DGr,V:Egghead,
    R:Yellowjacket,Wasp3 . . . . . . 5.00
218 DP,V:M.Hardy 5.00
219 BH,A:Moondragon,Drax 5.00
220 BH,DGr,D:Drax,V:MnDragon . . 5.00
221 JI:She Hulk 5.00
222 V:Masters of Evil. 5.00
223 A:Antman 5.00
224 AM,A:Antman 5.00
225 A:Black Knight. 5.00
226 A:Black Knight. 5.00
227 J:2nd Captain Marvel,
    O:Avengers 5.00

228 V:Masters of Evil 5.00
229 JSt,V:Masters of Evil 5.00
230 A:Cap.Marvel,L:Yellowjacke . . . 5.00
231 AM,JSi,J:2nd Captain Marvel,
    Starfox 5.00
232 AM,JSi. 5.00
233 JBy,V:Annihilus 5.00
234 AM,JSi,O:ScarletWitch 5.00
235 AM,JSi,V:Wizard 5.00
236 AM,JSi,A:SpM,V:Lava Men . . . 4.50
237 AM,JSi,A:SpM,V:Lava Men. . . . 4.50
238 AM,JSi,V:Moonstone,
    O:Blackout. 4.00
239 AM,JSi,A:David Letterman . . . 4.00
240 AM,JSi,A:Dr.Strange 4.00
241 AM,JSi,V:Morgan LeFey 4.00
242 AM,JSi,Secret Wars 4.00
243 AM,JSi,Secret Wars 4.00
244 AM,JSi,V:Dire Wraiths. 4.00
245 AM,JSi,V:Dire Wraiths 4.00
246 AM,JSi,V:Eternals 4.00
247 AM,JSi,A:Eternals,V:Deviants. . 4.00
248 AM,JSi,A:Eternals,V:Deviants. . 4.00
249 AM,JSi,A:Maelstrom 4.00
250 AM,JSi,A:W.C.A.
    V:Maelstrom 5.00
251 BH,JSi,A:Paladin 4.00
252 BH,JSi,J:Hercules
    V:Blood Brothers 4.00
253 BH,JSi,J:Black Knight 4.00
254 BH,JSi,A:W.C.A. 4.00
255 TP,p(c),JB,Legacy of
    Thanos/Sanctuary II 4.00
256 JB,TP,A:Ka-Zar. 4.00
257 JB,TP,D:Savage Land,
    I:Nebula 4.00
258 JB,TP,A:SpM,Firelord,Nebula . . 4.00
259 JB,TP,V:Nebula 4.00
260 JB,TP,SecretWarsII, IR:Nebula
    is Thanos' Granddaughter 4.00
261 JB,TP,Secret War II. 4.00
262 JB,TP,J:Submariner 4.00
263 JB,TP,X-Factor tie-in,
    Rebirth,Marvel Girl,pt.1 . . . . . 7.00
264 JB,TP,I:2nd Yellow Jacket. . . . 4.00
265 JB,TP,Secret Wars II 3.50
266 JB,TP,Secret Wars II,A:
    Silver Surfer. 3.50
267 JB,TP,V:Kang 3.50
268 JB,TP,V:Kang 3.50
269 JB,TP,V:Kang,A:Immortus. . . . 3.50
270 JB,TP,V:Moonstone 3.50
271 JB,TP,V:Masters of Evil. 3.50
272 JB,TP,A:Alpha Flight 3.50

MARVEL

273 JB,TP,V:Masters of Evil. 3.50
274 JB,TP,V:Masters of Evil. 3.50
275 JB,TP,V:Masters of Evil. 3.50
276 JB,TP,V:Masters of Evil. 3.50
277 JB,TP,V:Masters of Evil. 3.50
278 JB,TP,V:Tyrok,J:Dr.Druid. 3.50
279 JB,TP,new leader 3.50
280 BH,KB,O:Jarvis. 3.50
281 JB,TP,V:Olympian Gods 3.50
282 JB,TP,V:Cerberus 3.50
283 JB,TP,V:Olympian Gods 3.50
284 JB,TP,V:Olympian Gods 3.50
285 JB,TP,V:Zeus 3.50
286 JB,TP,V:Fixer 3.50
287 JB,TP,V:Fixer 3.50
288 JB,TP,V:Sentry 459. . . . . 3.50
289 JB,TP,J:Marrina. 3.50
290 JB,TP,V:Adaptoid. 3.50
291 JB,TP,V:Marrina. 3.50
292 JB,TP,V:Leviathon. 3.50
293 JB,TP,V:Leviathon. 3.50
294 JB,TP,V:Nebula. 3.50
295 JB,TP,V:Nebula. 3.50
296 JB,TP,V:Nebula. 3.50
297 JB,TP,V:Nebula. 3.50
298 JB,TP,Inferno,Edwin Jarvis . . . 3.50
299 JB,TP,Inferno,V:Orphan
    Maker,R:Gilgemesh. 3.50
300 JB,TP,WS,Inferno,V:Kang,
    O:Avengers,J:Gilgemesh,
    Mr.Fantastic,Invis.Woman 5.00
301 BH,DH,A:SuperNova 3.50
302 RB,TP,V:SuperNova,
    A:Quasar. 3.50
303 RB,TP,V:SuperNova,A:FF. . . . 3.50
304 RB,TP,V:U-Foes,Puma 3.50
305 PR,TP,V:Lava Men 5.00
306 PR,TP,O:Lava Men 3.50
307 PR,TP,V:Lava Men 3.50
308 PR,TP,A:Eternals,J:Sersi. 3.50
309 PR,TP,V:Blastaar 3.50
310 PR,TP,V:Blastaar 3.50
311 PR,TP,Acts of Veng.,V:Loki. . . 3.50
312 PR,TP,Acts of Vengeance,
    V:Freedom Force. 3.50
313 PR,TP,Acts of Vengeance,
    V:Mandarin,Wizard 3.50
314 PR,TP,J:Sersi,A:Spider-Man,
    V:Nebula 4.00
315 PR,TP,A:SpM,V:Nebula 4.00
316 PR,TP,J:Spider-Man 4.00
317 PR,TP,A:SpM,V:Nebula 4.00
318 PR,TP,A:SpM,V:Nebula 4.00
319 PR,B:Crossing Line 3.00
320 PR,TP,A:Alpha Flight 3.00
321 PR,Crossing Line#3 . . . . 3.00
322 PR,TP,Crossing Line#4. . . . . . 3.00
323 PR,TP,Crossing Line#5. . . . . . 3.00
324 PR,TP,E:Crossing Line 3.00
325 V:MotherSuperior,3
    Machinesmith 3.00
326 TP,I:Rage 5.00
327 TP,V:Monsters 3.00
328 TP,O:Rage 4.00
329 TP,J:Sandman,Rage 3.00
330 TP,V:Tetrarch of Entropy 3.00
331 TP,J:Rage,Sandman 3.00
332 TP,V:Dr.Doom 3.00
333 HT,V:Dr.Doom 3.00
334 NKu,TP,B:Collector,
    A:Inhumans 3.00
335 RLm(c),SEp,TP,V:Thane
    Ector,A:Collector. 3.00
336 RLm(c),SEp,TP. 3.00
337 RLm(c),SEp,TP,V:ThaneEctor . 3.00
338 RLm(c),SEp,TP,A:Beast,. 3.00
339 RLm(c),SEp,TP,E:Collector. . . 3.00
340 RLm(c),F:Capt.Amer.,Wasp . . 3.00
341 SEp,TP,A:New Warriors,V:Sons
    of Serpents 3.00
342 SEP,TP,A:New Warriors,
    V:Hatemonger 3.00

Avengers #393
© Marvel Entertainment Group

343 SEp,TP,J:Crystal,C&I:2nd
    Swordsman,Magdalene. 3.00
344 SEp,TP,I:Proctor. 3.00
345 SEp,TP,Oper. Galactic Storm
    Pt.5,V:Kree,Shiar. 3.00
346 SEp,TP,Oper. Galactic Storm
    Pt.12,I:Star Force 3.00
347 SEp,TP,Oper. Galactic Storm
    Pt.19,D:Kree Race,Conclusion . 3.00
348 SEp,TP,F:Vision 3.00
349 SEp,TP,V:Ares 3.00
350 SEp,TP,rep.Avengers#53,A:Prof.
    X,Cyclops,V:StarJammers. 4.00
351 KWe,V:Star Jammers 3.00
352 V:Grim Reaper 3.00
353 V:Grim Reaper 3.00
354 V:Grim Reaper 3.00
355 BHs(s),SEp,I:Gatherers,
    Coal Tiger 3.00
356 B:BHs(s),SEp,A:Bl.Panther
    D:Coal Tiger 3.00
357 SEp,TP,A:Watcher 3.00
358 SEp,TP,V:Arkon 3.00
359 SEp,TP,A:Arkon 3.00
360 SEp,TP,V:Proctor,double-size,
    bronze foil(c). 4.50
361 SEp,I:Alternate Vision. 2.50
362 SEp,TP,V:Proctor 3.00
363 SEp,TP,V:Proctor,D:Alternate
    Vision,C:Deathcry,Silver Foil(c),
    30th Anniv. 4.00
364 SEp,TP,I:Deathcry,V:Kree. 3.00
365 SEp,TP,V:Kree 3.00
366 SEp,TP,V:Kree,N:Dr.Pym,Gold
    Foil(c). 5.00
367 F:Vision 3.00
368 SEp,TP,Bloodties#1,
    A:X-Men. 4.00
369 SEp,TP,E:BHs(s),Bloodties#5,
    D:Cortez,V:Exodus,Platinum
    Foil(c). 4.00
370 SEp(c),TP(c),GI,V:Deviants,
    A:Kro,I:Delta Force 3.00
371 GM,TP,V:Deviants,A:Kro. 3.00
372 B:BHs(s),SEp,TP,I:2nd
    Gatherers,A:Proctor. 3.00
373 SEp,TP,I:Alternate Jocasta,
    V:Sersi 3.00
374 SEp,TP,O&I:Proctor is Alternate
    Black Knight 3.00
375 SEp,TP,Double Sized,D:Proctor,
    L:Sersi,Black Knight 3.50
376 F:Crystal,I:Terrigen 3.00
377 F:Quicksilver. 3.00

378 TP,I:Butcher 3.00
379 TP,Hercules,V:Hera. 3.00
379a Avengers Double Feature #1
    flip-book with Giant-Man #1 . . . 3.50
380 Hera 6.00
380a Avengers Double Feature #2
    flip-book with Giant Man #2. . . . 5.00
381 Quicksilvr, Scarlet Witch. 4.00
381a Avengers Double Feature #3
    flip-book with Giant Man #3. . . . 3.00
382 Wundagore 2.50
382a Avenders Double Feature #4
    flip-book with Giant Man #4. . . . 3.00
383 A:Fantastic Force,V:Arides 3.00
384 Hercules Vs. Stepmom. 4.00
385 V:Red Skull 3.00
386 F:Black Widow 3.00
387 Taking A.I.M.,pt.2 . . . . 3.00
388 Taking A.I.M.,pt.4 . . . . 3.00
389 B:Mike Deodato 3.00
390 BHs,TP,The Crossing, prelude . 3.00
391 BHs,Cont. From Avg. Crossing. 3.00
392 BHs,TP,The Crossing 3.00
393 BHs,TP,The Crossing 3.00
394 BHs,TP,The Crossing 3.00
395 BHs,TP,Timeslide concludes . . 3.00
396 . . . . 3.00
397 TP,Incred.Hulk #440 x-over . . . 3.00
398 TP,V:Unknown foe 3.00
399 . . . . 3.00
400 MeW,MWa,double size 4.50
401 MeW,MWa,Onslaught saga . . . 3.00
402 MWa,MD2,Onslaught, finale. . . 3.00
Ann.#1 DH,V:Mandarin,
    Masters of Evil. 250.00
Ann.#2 DH,JB,V:Scar.Centurion . 150.00
Ann.#3 rep.#4,T.ofSusp.#66-68 . . 100.00
Ann.#4 rep.#5,#6 . . . . 50.00
Ann.#5 JK(c),rep.#8,#11 . . . . 25.00
Ann.#6 GP,HT,V:Laser,Nuklo,
    Whirlwind. 20.00
Ann.#7 JSn,JRu,V:Thanos,A:Captain
    Marvel,D:Warlock(2nd) 65.00
Ann.#8 GP,V:Dr.Spectrum 15.00
Ann.#9 DN,V:Arsenal 10.00
Ann.#10 MGo,A:X-Men,Spid.Woman,
    I:Rogue,V:Br.o/Evil Mutants. . . 40.00
Ann.#11 DP,V:Defenders 6.00
Ann.#12 JG,V:Inhumans,Maximus. . 5.00
Ann.#13 JBy,V:Armin Zola 5.00
Ann.#14 JBy,KB,V:Skrulls 5.00
Ann.#15 SD,KJ,V:Freedom Force . . 5.00
Ann.#16 RF,BH,TP,JR2,BSz,KP,AW,
    MR,BL,BWi,JG,KN,A:Silver
    Surfer,Rebirth Grandmaster . . . 5.00
Ann.#17 MBr,MG,Evol.Wars,J:2nd
    Yellow Jacket. 5.00
Ann.#18 MBa,MG,Atlan.Attack#8,
    J:Quasar 4.00
Ann.#19 HT,Terminus Factor 4.00
Ann.#20 Subterran.Odyssey#1 . . . . 4.00
Ann.#21 Citizen Kang#4 . . . . 4.00
Ann.#22 I:Bloodwraith,w/card 4.00
Ann.#23 JB 4.00
G-Size#1 JR(c),RB,DA,I:Nuklo . . 35.00
G-Size#2 JR(c),DC,O:Kang,
    D:Swordsman,O:Rama-Tut . . . 20.00
G-Size#3 GK(c),DC,V:Kang,Legion
    of the Unliving 20.00
G-Size#4 K&R(c),DH,W:Scarlet Witch
    &Vision,O:Mantis,Moondragon 25.00
G-Size#5 rep,Annual #1. . . . . 15.00
GNv Death Trap:The Vault RLm,
    A:Venom 20.00
Marvel Milestone rep. #1 (1993) . . 3.00
Marvel Milestone rep. #4 (1995) . . 3.00
Marvel Milestone rep. #16 (1993) . . 3.00
Spec. Avengers Log,GP(c), History
    of the Avengers (1994) 2.25
Spec. Avengers Strikefile, BHa(s),
    Avengers pin-ups (1994). 2.25

Spec. Avengers: The Crossing,BHs,
   Death of an Avenger (1995) 6.00
Spec. Avengers/Ultraforce x-over
   V:Malibu's Ultraforce (1995) . . . 4.00

[2nd Series] Nov., 1996
1 RLd,JV,CYp,JSb,Heroes Reborn,
   F:Thor, Captain America,
   V:Loki. 6.00
1A Variant cover 8.00
1 gold signature edition, bagged . 20.00
2 RLd,JV,CYp,JSb,V:Kang 4.00
3 RLd,JV,CYp,JSb,V:Kang,A:Nick
   Fury 4.00
4 RLd,JLb,CYp,JSb, ... 4.00
4A variant cover 4.00
5 RLd,CYp,JSb,V:Hulk,concl. 5.00

Avengers 2nd Series #4
© Marvel Entertainment Group

6 RLd,JLb,CYp,JSb,Industrial
   Revolution, pt.1 x-over 5.00
7 RLd,JLb,IaC,JSb,. 4.00
8 RLd,JLb,IaC,JSb,F:Simon
   Williams (Wonder Man),V:Ultron,
   Lethal Legion. 4.00
9 JLb,RLd,IaC,F:Vision, Wonder
   Man 5.00
10 WS,. 4.00
11 . . . . 4.00
12 WS,Galactus Saga, x-over 4.00
13 JeR, Wildstorm x-over 4.00
Minus 1 Spec., JLb,RLd,IaC,JSb,
   flashback. 2.50

[3rd Series] Dec., 1997
1 GP,KBk,AV,F:Everyone,48 pg. . . . 5.00
1a Variant (c) 10.00
2 KBk,GP,AV,A:Scarlet Witch 5.00
3 KBk,GP,AV,trapped in midieval
   present. 4.00
4 KBk,GP,AV,who makes the
   team?. 5.00
5 KBk,GP,AV,Squadron Supreme. . 5.00
6 KBk,GP,AV,SquadronSupreme. . 5.00
7 KBk,GP,AV,Live Kree or Die,pt.4 . 2.50
8 KBk,GP,AV,I:Triathlon 2.50
9 KBk,GP,AV,Moses Magnum 2.50
10 KBk,GP,AV,V:Grim Reaper 2.50
11 KBk,GP,AV,V:Grim Reaper 2.50
12 KBk,GP,AV,V:Thunderbolts,
   48-page 40.00
12a Variant, white background 3.00
13 KBk,GP,AV,R:New Warriors 2.50
14 KBk,GP,AV,R:Beast. 2.50
15 KBk,GP,AV,A:Iron Man 2.50
16 JOy,AG,R:Photon 5.00
16a variant JOy,GP cover 2.50

17 JOy,AG,A:Warbird &
   Black Knight 2.50
18 JOy,AG,V:Wrecking Crew 2.50
19 KBk,GP,AV,Ultron,pt.1. . . . . 2.50
19a signed. 30.00
20 KBk,GP,AV,Ultron,pt.2. . . . . 2.50
21 KBk,GP,AV,Ultron,pt.3. . . . . 2.50
22 KBk,GP,AV,Ultron,pt.4. . . . . 2.50
23 KBk,GP,AV,V:Wonder Man 2.50
24 KBk,GP,AV 2.50
25 KBk,GP,AV, 48-pg. 3.50
26 KBk,GP,AV,SI,V:Triune 2.50
27 KBk,GP,AV,100-pg. 3.50
28 KBk,GP,AV,Kulan Gath,pt.1 . . . . 2.50
29 KBk,GP,AV,Kulan Gath,pt.2 . . . . 2.50
30 KBk,GP,AV,Kulan Gath,pt.3 . . . . 2.50
31 KBk,GP,AV,F:Vision 2.50
32 KBk,GP,AV,F:Black Widow 2.50
33 KBk,GP,AV,Thunderbolts 2.50
34 KBk,GP,AV,Thunderbolts 3.50
35 KBk,JR2,AV,MaximumSecurity . 2.50
36 KBk,SEp,AV,A:Capt.Am.+poster. 2.50
37 KBk,SEp,AV,F:Capt.Am. 2.50
38 KBk,AD,MFm 2.50
39 KBk,AD,MFm,F:Silverclaw 2.50
40 KBk,AD,MFm,F:Hulk,Silverclaw . 2.50
41 KBk,AD,MFm,A:Kang 2.50
42 KBk,AD,MFm,A:Kang 2.50
43 KBk,AD,MFm,V:Kang 2.50
44 KBk,KK,V:Kang,Thor berserk . . . 2.50
45 KBk,KK,V:Conqueror 2.50
46 KBk,Kang Dynasty 2.50
47 KBk,Kang Dynasty 2.50
48 KBk,KD,100-page 4.00
49 KBk,KD,F:Kang,'Nuff Said 2.50
50 KBk,KD,V:Kang, 48-pg. 4.00
51 KBk,KD,F:Wonder Man,
   Scarlet Witch 2.25
52 KBk,KD,Kang War 2.25
53 KBk,KD,Avengers Avenge 2.25
54 KBk,KD,Kang War,concl. 2.25
55 KBk,KD,Kang War,aftermath . . . 2.25
56 KBk,F:Beast, She-Hulk,USAgent. 2.25
57 KD,World Trust, pt.1 . . . . 2.75
58 KD,World Trust, pt.2 . . . . 2.25
59 KD,World Trust, pt.3 . . . . 2.25
60 KD,World Trust, concl.,40-pg . . . 4.00
61 GFr,. 2.25
62 GFr 2.25
63 AD,MFm,Standoff,pt.3,x-over . . . 3.00
64 F:Falcon 2.25
65 ALa,Red Zone,pt.1 . . . . 2.25
66 ALa,Red Zone,pt.2 . . . . 2.25
67 ALa,Red Zone,pt.3 . . . . 2.25
68 ALa,Red Zone,pt.4 . . . . 2.25
69 ALa,Red Zone,pt.5 . . . . 2.25
70 ALa,Red Zone,pt.6 . . . . 2.25
71 V:Wasp, Yellowjacket 2.25
72 ScK,Search for She-Hulk,pt.1. . . 2.25
73 ScK,Search for She-Hulk,pt.2. . . 2.25
74 ScK,Search for She-Hulk,pt.3. . . 2.25
75 ScK,Search for She-Hulk,pt.4. . . 2.25
76 JaL(c),an Avenger falls 2.25
77 Lionheart of Avalon,pt.1 . . . . . . 2.25
78 Lionheart of Avalon,pt.2 . . . . . . 2.25
79 Lionheart of Avalon,pt.3 . . . . . . 2.25
80 Lionheart of Avalon,pt.4 . . . . . . 2.25
81 Lionheart of Avalon, concl. 2.25
82 Once an Invader,pt.1 . . . . 2.25
83 Once an Invader,pt.2 . . . . 2.25
84 Once an Invader,pt.3 . . . . 2.25
500 BMB,Disassembled,pt.1,48-pg. 5.00
500a Director's Cut,64-pg. 8.00
501 BMB,Disassembled,pt.2,48-pg. 5.00
502 BMB,Disassembled,pt.3,48-pg. 5.00
503 BMB,Disassembled,pt.4,48-pg. 4.00
Ann. '98 Avengers/Squadron Supreme
   KBk,CPa,GP, 48pg 2.50
Ann.1999 KBk,JFM, Why Avengers
   disbanded, 48-page. 3.50
Ann.2000 KBk,NBy,48-pg 3.50
Ann.2001 KBk,IaC,NRd 3.00

Rough Cut Edition KBk,GP, 48pg,
   original pencils of #1, b&w . . . 3.00
Spec. 1-1/2, 32-pg.RSt. 2.50
Spec. Avengers: Year in Review . . . 3.00
Spec. Avengers Finale (2004) 3.00

AVENGERS AND POWER PACK ASSEMBLE
Apr., 2006
1 thru 4 . . . . @3.00

AVENGERS: CELESTIAL QUEST
Sept., 2001
1 (of 8) SEt,SHa 2.50
2 SEt,SHa,F:Mantis 3.00
3 SEt,SHa,F:Quoi,Mantis 3.00
4 SEt,SHa,F:Quoi,Mantis 2.50
5 SEt,SHa,F:Thanos 2.50
6 SEt,SHa,F:Mantis & Vision 2.50
7 SEt,SHa,F:Mantis,Quoi,Vision. . . 2.50
8 SEt,SHa,finale,48-pg. 3.50

AVENGERS CLASSIC
June, 2007
1 reps 4.00
2 thru 6 . . . . @3.00

AVENGERS: EARTH'S MIGHTIEST HEROES
Nov., 2004
1 JoC,ScK, Avengers early days . . 3.50
2 thru 8 JoC,ScK. . . . . @3.50

AVENGERS: EARTH'S MIGHTIEST HEROES II
Nov., 2006
1 JoC, Avengers early days 4.00
2 JoC 4.00
3 thru 8 JoC . . . . @4.00

AVENGERS FOREVER
Oct., 1998
1 (of 12) GP,KBk,CPa,Rick Jones
   radiation poisoning 4.00
2 GP,KBk,CPa,new Avengers 3.00
3 GP,KBk,CPa,Kang/Immortus. . . . 3.00
4 KBk,different eras 3.00
4a, b & c variant covers . . . . @3.00
5 KBk,RSt,A:1950s Avengers 3.00
6 KBk,RSt,V:Immortus 3.00
7 KBk,RSt,reunited 3.00
8 KBk,Immortus' plan 3.00
9 KBk,RSt,Kang the Conqueror . . . 3.00
10 KBk,RSt,V:Immortus 3.00
11 KBk,RSt,V:Avengers Battalion . . 3.00
12 KBk,RSt,concl. 3.00

AVENGERS HANDBOOK
June, 2007
Spec. F:Mighty Avengers 4.00

AVENGERS ICONS: TIGRA
March, 2002
1 (of 4) MD2,. 3.00
2 MD2,Brethren of the Blue Fist. . . 3.00
3 MD2,Brethren of the Blue Fist. . . 3.00
4 MD2,concl. 3.00

AVENGERS ICONS: THE VISION
Aug., 2002
1 (of 4) 3.00
2 thru 4 . . . . @3.00

AVENGERS INDEX
See: OFFICIAL MARVEL
INDEX TO THE
AVENGERS

AVENGERS INFINITY
July, 2000
1 (of 4) RSt,SCh,SHa		3.00
2 RSt,SCh,SHa,Servitors		3.00
3 RSt,SCh,SHa,Infinites		3.00
4 RSt,SCh,SHa,concl		3.00

AVENGERS NEXT
Nov. 2006
1 RLm,V:Zombie Avengers,A:Nova		3.00
2 RLm		3.00
3 RLm		3.00
4 RLm		3.00
5 RLm, finale		3.00

AVENGERS SPOTLIGHT
Aug., 1989
Formerly: Solo Avengers
21 AM,DH,TMo,JRu,Hawkeye, Starfox	3.00
22 AM,DH,Hawkeye,O:Swordsman	2.50
23 AM,DH,KD,Hawkeye,Vision	2.50
24 AM,DH,Hawkeye,O:Espirita	2.50
25 AM,TMo,Hawkeye,Rick Jones	2.50
26 A of V,Hawkeye,Iron Man	2.50
27 A of V,AM,DH,DT,Hawkeye Avengers	2.50
28 A of V,AM,DH,DT,Hawkeye, Wonder Man,Wasp	2.50
29 A of V,DT,Hawkeye,Iron Man	2.50
30 AM,DH,Hawkeye,New Costume	2.50
31 AM,DH,KW,Hawkeye,U.S.Agent	2.50
32 AM,KW,Hawkeye,U.S.Agent	2.50
33 AM,DH,KW,Hawkeye,U.S.Agent	2.50
34 AM,DH,KW,SLi(c),Hawkeye U.S.Agent	2.50
35 JV,Gilgamesh	2.50
36 AM,DH,Hawkeye	2.50
37 BH,Dr.Druid	2.50
38 JBr,Tigra	2.50
39 GCo,Black Knight	2.50
40 Vision,Last Issue	2.50

AVENGERS: THE INITIATIVE
April, 2007
1 Classified	3.00
1a variant (c)	3.00
2 Hero Moment	3.00
3 Bug Hunt	3.00
4 Green Zone	3.00
5 Green Zone	3.00
6 The Gauntlet	3.00
7 Triple Threat	3.00
Ann. #1	4.00

AVENGERS: THE TERMINATRIX OBJECTIVE
1993
1 B:MGu(s),MG,Holografx(c), V:Terminatrix	2.75
2 MG,V:Terminatrix,A:Kangs	2.25
3 MG,V:Terminatrix,A:Kangs	2.25
4 MG,Last issue	2.25

AVENGERS/ THUNDERBOLTS
March, 2004
1 (of 6) FaN&KBk(s),BKi	3.00
2 FaN&KBk(s),BKi	3.00
3 thru 6 FaN&KBk(s),TG	@3.00

AVENGERS: TIMESLIDE
1996
1 BHs,TKa,End of the Crossing Megallic chrome cover	5.00

AVENGERS TWO: WONDER MAN & THE BEAST
Mar., 2000
1 (of 3) RSt,MBa,		3.00
2 RSt,MBa,		3.00
3 RSt,MBa,concl.		3.00

AVENGERS: UNITED THEY STAND
Sept., 1999
1 TTn,RCa, Cartoon tie-in	3.00
2 TTn,	2.25
3 TTn,	2.25
4 TTn,	2.25
5 TTn,Hawkeye&Black Widow	2.25
6 TTn,A:Capt.America	2.25
7 TTn,F:Devil Dinosaur,Moonboy	3.25

AVENGERS UNIVERSE
June, 2000
1 rep. 3 stories, 80-pg.	5.00
2 rep. 3 stories, 80-pg.	5.00
3 rep. 3 stories, 80-pg.	5.00
4 rep. 3 stories, 80-pg.	4.25
5 rep. 3 stories, 80-pg.	4.25

AVENGERS UNLEASHED
1995
1 V:Count Nefarious	2.25

Avengers Unplugged #6
© Marvel Entertainment Group

Becomes:

AVENGERS UNPLUGGED
1996
2 Crushed by Graviton	2.25
3 x-over with FF Unplugged	2.25
4 The Old Ball and Chain	2.25
5 A:Captain Marvel	2.25
6 final issue	2.25

AVENGERS WEST COAST
Sept., 1989
Prev: West Coast Avengers
47 JBy,V:J.Random	3.00

48 JBy,V:J.Random	3.00
49 JBy,V:J.Random,W.Man	3.00
50 JBy,R:G.A.Human Torch	4.00
51 JBy,R:Iron Man	2.50
52 JBy,V:MasterPandmonum.	2.50
53 JBy,Acts ofVeng.,V:U-Foes	2.50
54 JBy,Acts ofVeng.,V:MoleMan	2.50
55 JBy,Acts ofVeng.finale,V:Loki Magneto kidnaps Sc.Witch	4.00
56 JBy,V:Magneto	11.00
57 JBy,V:Magneto	5.00
58 V:Vibro.	2.50
59 TMo,V:Hydro-Man,A:Immortus	2.50
60 PR,V:Immortus,	2.50
61 PR,V:Immortus	2.50
62 V:Immortus	2.50
63 PR,I:Living Lightning	2.50
64 F:G.A.Human Torch	2.50
65 PR,V:Ultron,Grim Reaper	2.50
66 PR,V:Ultron,Grim Reaper	2.50
67 PR,V:Ultron,Grim Reaper	2.50
68 PR,V:Ultron	2.50
69 PR,USAgent vs Hawkeye, I:Pacific Overlords	2.50
70 DR,V:Pacific Overlords	3.00
71 DR,V:Pacific Overlords	3.00
72 DR,V:Pacific Overlords	3.00
73 DR,V:Pacific Overlords	3.00
74 DR,J:Living Lightning,Spider Woman,V:Pacific Overlords.	3.00
75 HT,A:F.F,V:Arkon,double	3.00
76 DR,Night Shift,I:Man-Demon	2.50
77 DR,A:Satannish & Nightshift.	2.50
78 DR,V:Satannish & Nightshift.	2.50
79 DR,A:Dr.Strange,V:Satannish	2.50
80 DR,Galactic Storm,pt.2	2.50
81 DR,Galactic Storm,pt.9	2.50
82 DR,Galactic Storm,pt.16 A:Lilandra	2.50
83 V:Hyena	2.50
84 DR,I:Deathweb,A:SpM, O:Spider-Woman	3.00
85 DR,A:SpM,V:Death Web	2.50
86 DR,A:SpM,V:Death Web	2.50
87 DR,A:Wolverine,V:Bogatyri	3.00
88 DR,A:Wolverine,V:Bogatyri	2.50
89 DR,V:Ultron	2.50
90 DR,A:Vision,V:Ultron.	2.50
91 DR,V:Ultron,I:War Toy	2.50
92 DR,V:Goliath(Power Man)	2.50
93 DR,V:Doctor Demonicus	2.50
94 DR,J:War Machine	2.50
95 DR,A:Darkhawk,V:Doctor Demonicus.	2.50
96 DR,Inf.Crusade x-over	2.50
97 ACe,Inf.Crusade,V:Power Platoon	2.50
98 DR,I:4th Lethal Legion	2.50
99 DR,V:4th Lethal Legion.	2.50
100 DR,D:Mockingbird,V:4th Lethal Legion,Red Foil(c)	4.50
101 DR,Bloodties#3,V:Exodus.	4.00
102 DR,L:Iron Man,Spider-Woman, US Agent,Scarlet Witch,War Machine,last issue	4.00
Ann.#4 JBy,TA,MBa,Atlan.Attacks #12,V:Seven Brides of Set	4.00
Ann.#5 Terminus Factor	3.50
Ann.#6 Subterranean Odyssey#5	2.50
Ann.#7 Assault on Armor City#4	2.25
Ann.#8 DR,I:Raptor w/card	3.25

BALDER THE BRAVE
Nov., 1985
1 WS,SB,V:Frost Giants	3.00
2 WS,SB,V:Frost Giants	3.00
3 WS,SB,V:Frost Giants	3.00
4 WS,SB,V:Frost Giants;Feb,1986	3.00

BANNER

Startling Stories, July, 2001
1 (of 4) RCo, F:Hulk	3.00
2 RCo,	3.00
3 RCo,	3.00
4 RCo, concl.	3.00

BARBIE

Jan., 1991
1 polybagged with Credit Card	16.00
2	10.00
3 thru 49	@8.00
50 Anniv. issue, Disney World(c)	12.00
51 thru 66	@7.00

BARBIE FASHION

Jan., 1991
1 bagged with doorknob hanger	15.00
2 thru 63	@10.00

Battle #11
© Marvel Entertainment Group

BATTLE

Marvel Atlas, March, 1951
1 They called Him a Coward	400.00
2 The War Department Secrets	200.00
3 The Beast of the Bataan	150.00
4 JMn,I:Buck Private O'Toole	150.00
5 Death Trap Of Gen. Wu.	150.00
6 RH, JMn.	150.00
7 Enemy Sniper	150.00
8 A Time to Die	150.00
9 RH	100.00
10	100.00
11 SC	100.00
12 thru 21	@110.00
22	100.00
23 BK	100.00
24	100.00
25	100.00
26 JR	100.00
27	100.00
28 JSe	100.00
29	100.00
30	100.00
31 RH,JMn.	100.00
32 JSe,GT	100.00
33 GC,JSe,JSt	100.00
34 JSe	100.00
35	100.00
36 BEv	100.00
37 RA,JSt.	125.00
38 thru 46	@100.00
47 JO	100.00
48	100.00
49 JDa	100.00

50 BEv	100.00
51	100.00
52 GWb	100.00
53 BP	100.00
54	100.00
55 GC,AS,BP,AW,GWb	125.00
56	100.00
57	100.00
58	100.00
59 AT	100.00
60 A:Combat Kelly	100.00
61 JMn,A:Combat Kelly	100.00
62 A:Combat Kelly	100.00
63 SD	150.00
64 JK	150.00
65 JK	150.00
66 JSe,JK,JDa	150.00
67 JSe,JK,AS,JDa	150.00
68 JSe,JK,AW,SD	150.00
69 RH,JSe,JK,SW	175.00
70 BEv,SD; June, 1960	175.00

BATTLE ACTION

Marvel Atlas, Feb., 1952
1	350.00
2	200.00
3 JSt,RH	100.00
4	100.00
5	100.00
6 JeR	100.00
7 JeR	100.00
8 RH	125.00
9 thru 15	@100.00
16 thru 27	@100.00
28 GWb	100.00
29	100.00
30 GWb,Aug., 1957	100.00

BATTLEBOOKS

Nov., 1998
Captain America, BiT(c)	4.00
Citizen V, BiT(c)	4.00
Colossus, BiT(c)	4.00
Elektra, BiT(c)	4.00
Gambit, BiT(c)	4.00
Iron Man, BiT(c)	4.00
Rogue, BiT(c)	4.00
Spider-Girl, BiT(c)	4.00
Spider-Man, BiT(c)	4.00
Storm, BiT(c)	4.00
Thor, BiT(c)	4.00
Wolverine, BiT(c)	4.00

BATTLE BRADY

See: MEN IN ACTION

BATTLEFIELD

Marvel Atlas, April, 1952
1 RH, Slaughter on Suicide Ridge	275.00
2 RH	150.00
3 Ambush Patrol	150.00
4	150.00
5 Into the Jaws of Death	150.00
6 thru 10	@100.00
11 GC,May, 1953	100.00

BATTLEFRONT

Marvel Atlas, June, 1952
1 JeR,RH(c),Operation Killer	375.00
2 JeR	200.00
3 JeR,Spearhead	150.00
4 JeR,Death Trap of General Chun	150.00
5 JeR,Terror of the Tank Men	150.00
6 A:Combat Kelly	150.00
7 A:Combat Kelly	150.00
8 A:Combat Kelly	150.00
9 A:Combat Kelly	150.00
10 A:Combat Kelly	150.00

Battlefront #34
© Marvel Entertainment Group

11 thru 20	@125.00
21 thru 39	@125.00
40 AW	125.00
41	125.00
42 AW	125.00
43 thru 48 Aug.,1957	@135.00

BATTLEGROUND

Marvel Atlas, Sept., 1954
1	275.00
2 JKz	150.00
3 thru 8	@100.00
9 BK	100.00
10	100.00
11 AW,GC,GT	125.00
12 MD,JSe	100.00
13 AW	100.00
14 JD	125.00
15 thru 17	@100.00
18 AS	125.00
19 JMn,JSe	100.00
20 Aug., 1957	100.00

BATTLESTAR GALACTICA

March, 1979
1 EC,B:TV Adaptation; Annihalation	12.00
2 EC,Exodus	9.00
3 EC,Deathtrap	9.00
4 WS,Dogfight	9.00
5 WS,E:TV Adaptation;Ambush	9.00
6 Nightmare	8.00
7 Commander Adama Trapped	8.00
8 Last Stand	8.00
9 Space Mimic	8.00
10 This Planet Hungers	8.00
11 WS,Starbuck's Dilemma	8.00
12 WS,Memory Ends	8.00
13 WS,All Out Attack	8.00
14 Radiation Threat	8.00
15 Ship of Crawling Death	8.00
16	8.00
17 Animal on the Loose	8.00
18 Battle For the Forbidden Fruit	8.00
19 Starbuck's Back	8.00
20 Duel to the Death	8.00
21 To Slay a Monster..To Destroy a World	8.00
22 WS,A Love Story?	8.00
23 Dec., 1981	8.00

MARVEL

MARVEL (side tab)

BATTLETIDE
1990
1 thru 4 F: Death's Head II and
  Killpower . . . . @2.25

BATTLETIDE II
1993
1 Foil embossed cover 3.25
2 thru 8 F: Death's Head II and
  Killpower . . . . @2.25

Beast #1
© Marvel Entertainment Group

BEAST
March, 1997
1 (of 3) KG,CNn,F:Karma, Cannonball, V:Viper & Spiral 3.00
2 KG,CNn,V:Spiral. 3.00
3 KG,CNn, concl. 3.00

BEAUTY AND THE BEAST
Jan., 1985
1 DP,Beast & Dazzler,direct 3.00
1a DP,Beast & Dazzler,UPC. 3.00
2 thru 4 DP,Beast & Dazzler . . . . @3.00

BEAVIS & BUTT-HEAD
March, 1994
1 Based on the MTV Show. 5.00
1a 2nd Printing 2.50
2 Dead from the Neck up 3.50
3 Break out at Burger World. 3.00
4 thru 28 . . . . @2.50

BEFORE THE
FANTASTIC 4:
GRIMM AND LOGAN
May, 2000
1 (of 3) LHa,Wolverine&Thing . . . 3.25
2 LHa,A:Carol Danvers. 3.25
3 LHa,concl. 3.25

REED RICHARDS
July, 2000
1 (of 3) PDa,DFg,V:Dr.Doom 3.25
2 PDa,DFg,. 3.25
3 PDa,DFg,concl. 3.25

THE STORMS
Oct., 2000
1 (of 3) TKa,CAd,F:Sue & J. Storm 3.25

---

2 V:St. Germaine 3.25
3 TKa,CaD,concl. 3.25

BEST LOVE
Marvel-Manvis Publ., 1949
(Formerly: Sub-Mariner #32)
33 JKu 150.00
34 . . . . 100.00
35 BEv 125.00
36 BEv 125.00

BEST WESTERN
June, 1949
58 A:KidColt,BlackRider,Two-Gun
  Kid; Million Dollar Train
  Robbery. 325.00
59 A:BlackRider,KidColt,Two-Gun
  Kid;The Black Rider Strikes. . 300.00
Becomes:

WESTERN OUTLAWS
& SHERIFFS
1949
60 PH(c),Hawk Gaither 300.00
61 Ph(c),Pepper Lawson 250.00
62 Murder at Roaring
  House Bridge. 250.00
63 thru 65. . . . . @250.00
66 Hanging. 250.00
67 Cannibalism 250.00
68 thru 72. . . . . @225.00
73 June, 1952. . . . . 225.00

BEWARE
March, 1973
1 Reprints 25.00
2 thru 8 . . . . @20.00
Becomes:

TOMB OF DARKNESS
1974
9 Reprints 30.00
10 thru 22 . . . . @20.00
23 November, 1976 . . . . 25.00

BEYOND!
July, 2006
1 DMD,ScK, Nine heroes vs. Space
  Phantom 3.00
2 thru 6 . . . . @3.00

BIBLE TALES FOR
YOUNG FOLK
Marvel/Atlas, 1953
1 . . . . 350.00
2 BEv,BK. 250.00
3 . . . . 200.00
4 JeR 225.00
5 . . . . 200.00

BILL & TED'S
EXCELLENT COMICS
Dec., 1991
1 From Movie; Wedding Reception 2.25
2 thru 12 . . . . @2.25
1-shot Bill & Ted's Bogus Journey
  Movie Adaption (1991) 3.25

BILLY BUCKSKIN
WESTERN
Marvel Atlas, Nov., 1955
1 MD,Tales of the Wild Frontier . 250.00
2 MD,Ambush 150.00
3 MD,AW, Thieves in the Night . 200.00
Becomes:

2-GUN KID
1956
4 SD,A: Apache Kid 200.00
Becomes:

TWO-GUN WESTERN
1956
5 B:Apache Kid,Doc Holiday,
  Kid Colt Outlaw 250.00
6 . . . . 225.00
7 . . . . 225.00
8 RC 200.00
9 AW 200.00
10 . . . . 200.00
11 AW. 225.00
12 Sept., 1957,RC 200.00

BISHOP
1994
1 Mountjoy, foil cover 4.00
2 foil stamped cover 4.00
3 JOs 3.50
4 V:Mountjoy. 3.50

BISHOP:
THE LAST X-MAN
Aug., 1999
1 R:Bishop, 48-page debut. 6.00
2A I:Nom,Link,Jinx & Scorch 2.50
2B variant (c) 2.50
3 thru 15 . . . . @2.50
16 NMa,Dream'sEnd,pt.3,x-over . . 8.00

BISHOP: XAVIER'S
SECURITY ENFORCER
Nov., 1997
1 (of 3) JOs,SEp. 3.00
2 JOs,SEp,hunted by X.S.E. 3.00
3 JOs,SEp,Bishop v. Rook, concl. . 3.00

BIZARRE ADVENTURES
See: MARVEL PREVIEW

BLACK AXE
1993
1 JR2(c),A:Death's Head II. 3.00
2 JR2(2),A:Sunfire,V:The Hand . . . 3.00
3 A:Death's Head II,V:Mesphisto . . 3.00
4 in ancient Egypt. 3.00
5 KJ(c),In Wakanda 3.00
6 KJ(c),A:Black Panther 3.00
7 KJ(c),A:Black Panther 3.00
8 thru 13 . . . . @3.00

BLACK CAT
[Limited Series]
1 Wld,A:Spider-Man,V:Cardiac,
  I:Faze. 2.25
2 Wld,V:Faze 2.25
3 Wld,Cardiac. 2.25
4 Wld,V:Scar 2.25

BLACK DRAGON
Epic, May, 1985
1 JBo. 4.00
2 thru 6 JBo. . . . . @3.00

BLACK GOLIATH
Feb., 1976—Nov., 1976
1 GT,O:Black Goliath,Cont's
  From Powerman #24 . . . . 30.00
2 GT,V:Warhawk 15.00
3 GT,D:Atom-Smasher 15.00
4 KP,V:Stilt-Man 15.00
5 D:Mortag 15.00

Black Goliath #5
© Marvel Entertainment Group

BLACK KNIGHT, THE
Marvel Atlas, 1955–56
1 JMn,O: Crusader;The Black
   Knight Rides 1,500.00
2 JMn,Siege on Camelot 900.00
3 JMn,Black Knight Unmasked . 750.00
4 JMn,Betrayed 750.00
5 JMn,SSh,The Invincible Tartar. 750.00

BLACK KNIGHT
June, 1990—Sept., 1990
1 TD,R:Original Black Knight 2.00
2 TD,A:Dreadknight 2.00
3 RB,A:Dr.Strange 2.00
4 RB,TD,A:Dr Strange, Valkyrie . . . 2.00

BLACK KNIGHT: EXODUS
1996
1-shot R:Black Knight,A:Sersi,
   O:Exodus. 2.50

BLACK PANTHER
[1st Series]
Jan., 1977—May, 1979
1 JK,V:Collectors 40.00
2 JK,V:Six Million Year Man 20.00
3 JK,V:Ogar 20.00
4 JK,V:Collectors 20.00
5 JK,V:Yeti 20.00
6 JK,V:Ronin. 20.00
7 JK,V:Mister Little 20.00
8 JK,D:Black Panther 20.00
9 JK,V:Jakarra 20.00
10 JK,V:Jakarra 20.00
11 JK,V:Kilber the Cruel. 20.00
12 JK,V:Kilber the Cruel 20.00
13 JK,V:Kilber the Cruel 20.00
14 JK,A:Avengers,V:Klaw 25.00
15 JK,A:Avengers,V:Klaw 25.00

BLACK PANTHER
July, 1988—Oct., 1988
[1st Mini-Series]
1 I:Panther Spirit 4.00
2 V:Supremacists 4.00
3 A:Malaika 4.00
4 V:Panther Spirit 4.00
[2nd Mini-Series]
PANTHER'S PREY
May, 1991
1 thru 4 DT,V:Solomon Prey . . . . @5.00

BLACK PANTHER
[2nd Series] Sept., 1998
1 CPr,MT,A:T'Challa 7.00
2 CPr,MT,A:Mephisto 3.00
2a variant cover 3.00
3 CPr,MT,JQ,I:Achebe 3.00
4 CPr,MT,JQ,V:Mephisto. 3.00
5 CPr,V:Mephisto 3.00
6 thru 35 CPr. . . . . @2.50
36 CPr,SaV,100-page 4.00
37 thru 56 . . . . @2.50
57 thru 63. . . . . @3.00
[3rd Series] Feb., 2005
1 JR2 . . . . 5.00
2 thru 6 JR2 . . . . @3.00
7 thru 17 . . . . @3.00
18 SEa,Bride of the Panther, 48-pg. 6.00
18a variant (c) 8.00
19 thru 20 . . . . @3.00
21 Civil War 10.00
22 Civil War 4.50
23 Foreign Affairs, pt.1, Civil War . . 4.00
24 Foreign Affairs, pt.2, Civil War . . 4.00
25 Foreign Affairs, pt.3, Civil War . . 9.00
26 Two Plus Two 3.00
27 Classified 3.00
28 Good Eatin', pt. 1 . . . . 3.00
29 Good Eatin', pt. 2 . . . . 3.00
30 Good Eatin', pt. 3 . . . . 3.00
31 Size Matters 3.00
32 Little Green Men 3.00

BLACK RIDER
See: ALL WINNERS COMICS

BLACK RIDER RIDES AGAIN
Marvel Atlas, Sept., 1957
1 JK,Treachery at Hangman's
   Ridge 350.00

BLACKSTONE, THE MAGICIAN
May, 1948—Sept., 1948
2 B:Blonde Phantom 1,000.00
3 BO(c),bondage (c) 650.00
4 Bondage(c) 650.00

BLACK WIDOW
Apr. 1999
1 (of 3) Black Widow replaced? . . . 6.00
1a variant cover (1:4) 7.00
2 A:Daredevil 4.00
3 conclusion 4.00

BLACK WIDOW
Nov., 2000
1 (of 3) SHp,Natasha vs.Yelena . . . 3.00
2 SHp,. 3.00
3 SHp,concl. 3.00

BLACK WIDOW
Sept., 2004
1 (of 6) BSz,F:Natasha Romanova. 3.00
2 BSz 3.00
3 thru 6 BSz . . . . @3.00

BLACK WIDOW: PALE LITTLE SPIDER
Marvel Max, April, 2002
1 (of 3) F:Belova 3.25
2 . . . . 3.25
3 concl. 3.25

BLACK WIDOW 2
Sept., 2005
1 (of 6) BSz,Things They Say 3.00
2 thru 6 BSz,Things They Say
   About Her. . . . . @3.00

Blackwulf #8
© Marvel Entertainment Group

BLACKWULF
1994–95
1 AMe,Embossied(c),I:Mammoth,
   Touchstone,Toxin,D:Pelops,
   V:Tantalus, ... 3.00
2 AMe,I:Sparrow,Wildwind 2.25
3 AMe,I:Scratch 2.25
4 AMe,I:Giant-man 2.25
5 AMe 2.25
6 AMe,Tantalus 2.25
7 AMe,V:Tantalus 2.25
8 AMe 2.25
9 Seven Worlds of Tantalus,pt.1
   A:Daredevil 2.25
10 Seven Worlds of Tantalus,pt.2,
   last issue 2.25

BLADE, THE VAMPIRE HUNTER
1994–95
1 Foil(c),Clv(i),R:Dracula 3.50
2 Clv(i),V:Dracula 2.50
3 Clv(i) 2.50
4 Clv(i) 2.50
5 Clv(i) 2.50
6 Clv(i) 2.50
7 Clv(i) 2.50
8 Bible John, Morbius 2.50
9 . . . . 2.50
10 R:Dracula 2.50
11 Dracula Untombed,pt.2 . . . . 2.50

BLADE
Sept., 1998
1 (of 6) DMG,40-page, photo(c) . . . 3.50
1a variant cover (1:4) 3.50
2 DMG,A:Morbius,Dominique 3.00
2a variant cover 3.00
3 DMG, ... 3.00
4 DMG,F:Morbius 3.00
1-shot Blade: Crescent City Blues,
   MPe,V:Deacon Frost (1998) . . . 3.50
1-shot DMG, movie tie-in (1998) . . . 3.00
1-shot movie adaptation,48 pg 6.00

BLADE: VAMPIRE HUNTER
Oct., 1999
1 (of 6) BS, 48-pg.	4.00
2 BS	3.00
3 BS,V:Reaper	3.00
4 BS,V:Hrolf	3.00
5 BS,V:Reaper	3.00
6 BS,V:Reaper, concl.	3.00

BLADE
Marvel Max, March, 2002
1 StP,V:Tryks.	3.25
2 StP,F:Tryks,Seven	3.25
3 StP,date with Susan.	3.25
4 StP,Fofo's missing fingers	3.25
5 StP,V:Rowks.	3.25
6 horror hits home	3.25
GN Bloodhunt, movie adapt.	6.00

BLADE
Sept., 2006
1 HC, A:Spider-Man	3.00
2 HC, V:Dr. Doom	3.00
3 HC	3.00
4 HC,Night before X-mas	3.00
5 HC,Casualties of War, Civil War	3.00
6 HC,Blade's Father	3.00
7 HC,Blade dies	3.00
8 HC,F:Hannibal King	3.00
9 HC,F:Union Jack	3.00
10 HC,V:Spider-Man	3.00
11 HC,V:father	3.00
12 HC finale issue	3.00

BLADE RUNNER
Oct., 1982
1 AW, Movie Adaption.	4.00
2 AW,.	4.00

BLAZE
[Limited Series], 1993–94
1 HMe(s),RoW,A:Clara Menninger.	2.50
2 HMe(s),RoW,I:Initiate.	2.50
3 HMe(s),RoW,.	2.50
4 HMe(s),RoW,D:Initiate.	2.50

[Regular Series], Aug., 1994
1 HMz,LHa,foil (c).	3.50
2 thru 5 HMz,LHa	@2.50
6 thru 12	@2.50

BLAZE CARSON
Sept., 1948
1 SSh(c),Fight,Lawman or Crawl	350.00
2 Guns Roar on Boot Hill	250.00
3 A:Tex Morgan	250.00
4 SSh,A:Two-Gun Kid	250.00
5 A:Tex Taylor	275.00
Becomes:

REX HART
1949
6 CCB,Ph(c),B:Rex Hart, A:Black Rider	350.00
7 Ph(c),Mystery at Bar-2 Ranch	250.00
8 Ph(c),The Hombre Who Killed His Friends	250.00
Becomes:

WHIP WILSON
1950
9 Ph(c),B:Whip Wilson,O:Bullet; Duel to the Death	800.00
10 Ph(c),Wanted for Murder	400.00
11 Ph(c)	400.00
Becomes:

Gunhawk #12
© *Marvel Entertainment Group*

GUNHAWK, THE
1950
12 The Redskin's Revenge	350.00
13 GT,The Man Who Murdered Gunhawk	300.00
14	250.00
15	250.00
16 EC	250.00
17	250.00
18 JMn,Dec., 1951.	250.00

BLAZE OF GLORY
Dec., 1999
1 (of 4) JOs,F:John Woo	3.00
2 JOs,	3.00
3 JOs,	3.00
4 JOs,concl.	3.00

BLAZE, THE WONDER COLLIE
Oct., 1949
2 Ph(c),Blaze-Son of Fury	300.00
3 Ph(c), Lonely Boy;Feb.,1950.	300.00

BLINK
Dec., 2000
1 (of 4) SLo,AKu(c).	3.25
2 SLo,Age of Apocalypse story.	3.25
3 SLo,AKu(c),in love.	3.25
4 SLo,AKu(c),V:Blastaar.	3.25

BLONDE PHANTOM
See: ALL-SELECT COMICS

BLOOD
Feb., 1988—April, 1988
1	6.00
2 thru 4	@5.00

BLOOD & GLORY
1993
1 KJ Cap & the Punisher	6.00
2 KJ Cap & the Punisher	6.00
3 KJ Cap & the Punisher	6.00

BLOODLINES
Epic, 1992
1 F:Kathy Grant-Peace Corps	6.00

BLOODSEED
1993
1 LSh,I:Bloodseed	2.25
2 LSh,V:Female Bloodseed	2.25

BLOODSTONE
Oct., 2001
1 DAn,ALa,SHa,F:Elsa Bloodstone	3.25
2 DAn,ALa,SHa,F:Dracula	3.25
3 DAn,ALa,SHa,Living Mummy	3.25
4 DAn,ALa,SHa, concl.	3.25

BOOK OF LOST SOULS
Icon, Oct., 2005
1 thru 3 MSz,CDo,Dragons in the Dishwater.	@3.00
4 thru 6 MSz,CDo	@3.00

BOOK OF THE DEAD
1993–94
1 thru 5 Horror rep	@4.00

BOOKS OF DOOM
Nov., 2005
1 F:Victor von Doom, early years	3.00
2 thru 6	@3.00

BORN
June, 2003
1 (of 4) GEn(s),O:Punisher.	6.00
2 GEn(s),Capt. Frank Castle	4.00
3 GEn(s),attacked.	4.00
4 GEn(s),concl.	4.00

BOZZ CHRONICLES, THE
Epic, Dec., 1985
1 thru 5	@3.00
6 May, 1986	3.00

BRATS BIZARRE
Epic, *Heavy Hitters* 1994
1 with trading card	3.25
2 thru 4 with trading card	@2.75

BREAK THE CHAIN
1 KB,KRS-One,w/audio tape	7.00

BROTHERHOOD, THE
May, 2001
1 BSz(c),F:Magneto	2.75
2A BSz(c),	2.50
2B variant cover	2.50
3 BSz(c)	2.50
4 JP,BWS(c)	2.50
5 JP,GF(c).	2.50
6 JP,GF(c) message to daddy	2.50
7 SeP,KW, X speaks out.	2.50
8 SeP,KW,	2.50
9 SeP,KW, final issue	2.50

BRUTE FORCE
Aug., 1990
1 JD/JSt	2.50
2 thru 3	@2.50
4 November, 1990	2.50

B-SIDES
Sept., 2002
1 SK, super-team from New Jersey	3.00
2 SK, F:Fantastic Four	3.00
3 SK, F:Fantastic Four	3.00

BUCK DUCK
Marvel Atlas, June, 1953
1 (fa) stories	200.00
2 thru 4 Dec., 1953	@100.00

Buckaroo Banzai #2
© Marvel Entertainment Group

BUCKAROO BANZAI
Dec., 1984
1 Movie Adaption 3.00
2 Conclusion, Feb., 1985 . . . . 2.50

BUG
1997
1-shot 48pg. 3.25

BULLET POINTS
Nov., 2006
1 . . . . 3.00
2 thru 5 MSz(s) . . . . @3.00

BULLSEYE: GREATEST HITS
Sept., 2004
1 (of 5) SDi,O:Bullseye 3.00
2 thru 5 SDi,F:Punisher. . . . . . . @3.00

BULLWINKLE & ROCKY
Star, Nov., 1987
1 EC&AM,Based on 1960's TV . . . 4.00
2 thru 9 EC&AM . . . . @3.00

CABLE
[Limited Series], 1992
1 JR2,DGr,V:Mutant Liberation
  Front,A:Weapon X 4.00
2 JR2,DGr,V:Stryfe,O:Weapon X . . 3.00

[Regular Series], 1993
1 B:FaN(s),ATi,O:Cable,V:New
  Canaanites,A:Stryfe,foil(c) 5.00
2 ATi,V:Stryfe. 4.00
3 ATi,A:Six Pack 4.00
4 ATi,A:Six Pack 4.00
5 DaR,V:Sinsear. 4.00
6 DT,A:Tyler,Zero,Askani,
  Mr.Sinister,C:X-Men. 4.00
7 V:Tyler,A:Askani,X-Men,Domino . 4.00
8 O:Cable,V:Tyler,A:X-Men,Cable is
  Nathan Summers 4.00
9 MCW,B:Killing Field,A:Excalibur,
  V:Omega Red 4.00
10 MCW,A:Acolytes,Omega Red. . . 4.00
11 MCW,E:Killing Field,D:Katu . . . 4.00
12 SLo(s),B:Fear & Loathing,
  V:Senyaka 4.00
13 V:D'Spayre 4.00
14 V:S'yM. 4.00

15 A:Thorn 4.00
16 Foil(c),Dbl-size,A:Jean,Scott
  Logan,V:Phalanx 9.00
16a Newsstand ed. 3.00
17 Deluxe ed. 3.00
17a Newsstand ed. 2.25
18 Deluxe ed. 3.00
18a Newsstand ed. 2.25
19 Deluxe ed. 3.00
19a Newsstand ed. 2.25
20 V:Legion, Deluxe ed. w/card. . . 5.00
20a Newsstand ed. 2.25
21 Cable makes tough decisions,
  A:Domino. 3.00
22 V:Fortress 3.00
23 IaC,A:Domino 3.00
24 F:Blaquesmith 3.00
25 IaC,SHa,F:Cable's Wife,foil(c) . 5.00
26 Tries to return to X-Mansion . . . 3.00
27 IaC, A:Domino. 3.00
28 IaC,SHa,concl. war in Genosha . 3.00
29 . . . . 3.00
30 . . . . 3.00
31 IaC, cont.X-Men/Cable war. . . . 3.00
32 Onslaught saga. 3.50
33 Onslaught saga. 3.00
34 Onslaught saga. 3.00
35 Onslaught saga. 3.00
36 . . . . 3.00
37 JLb,IaC,SHa,V:Askani'son,Kane. 3.00
38 JLb,IaC,SHa,V:PSycho-Man,
  A:Kane. 3.00
39 JLb,IaC,SHa,V:Psycho-Man . . . 3.00
40 TDz,IaC,SHa,A:Renee Majcomb . 3.00
41 TDz,SHa,F:Bishop 3.00
42 TDz,RGr,SHa,The Prophecy
  of the Twelve 3.00
43 TDz,RGr,Images of Nathan's
  past 3.00
44 TDz,RGr,SHa,A:Madelyne Pryor
  (Cable's mom) 3.00
45 JeR,RGr,Zero Tolerance,
  No Escape,pt.2 . . . . 3.00
46 JeR,RGr,SHa,Zero Tolerance,
  No Escape, pt.2 (of 3) 3.00
47 JeR,RGr,SHa, Operation Zero
  Tolerance, V:Batsion 3.00
48 JeR,SHa,V:Hellfire Club 3.00
49 JeR,SHa,V:Hellfire Club 3.00
50 JeR,SHa,A:Cyclops, Phoenix,
  Union Jack, 48pg. 4.00
51 JeR,Hellfire Hunt. 2.50
52 JeR,Hellfire Hunt, pt.5. . . . . 2.50
53 JoC,Hellfire Hunt, concl. 2.50
54 JoC,A:Black Panther,V:Klaw. . . . 2.50
55 JoC,A:Irene Merryweather,
  Domino 2.50
56 JoC,V:Stilt-Man & Hydro-Man. . 2.50
57 JoC,Cable powers altered by
  EMP wave 2.50
58 JoC,Persecution, pt.1 . . . . 2.50
59 JoC,I:Agent 18,V:Zzaxx 2.50
60 JoC,Nemesis Contract,pt.2 . . . . 2.50
61 JoC,Nemesis Contract,pt.3 . . . . 2.50
62 JoC,Nemesis Contract,pt.4 . . . . 2.50
63 JoC,Blood Brothers,pt.2,x-over. . 2.50
64 JoC,O:Cable. 2.50
65 JoC,Millennium countdown 2.50
66 JoC,Sign of the End Times,pt.1 . 2.50
67 JoC,Sign of the End Times,pt.2 . 2.50
68 JoC,Sign of the End Times,pt.3 . 2.50
69 JoC,A:Blaquesmith,Archangel . . 2.50
70 JoC,A:Archangel 2.50
71 RLd,abandons his destiny,
  with RLd poster 2.50
72 RLd,reunited with X-force 2.50
73 RLd,reunited 2.50
74 V:Caliban 2.50
75 RLd,Apocalypse 11.00
76 Apocalypse The 12:pt.6 . . . . . . 8.00
77 Ages of Apocalypse,pt.2 . . . . . 15.00
78 mutant no more. 3.00

Cable #100
© Marvel Entertainment Group

79 X-Men: Revolution 3.00
79a variant (c) 3.50
80 Apocalypse gone 2.50
81 The Undying 2.50
82 Nathan Summers, murderer?. . . 2.50
83 R:Domino 2.50
84 Phoenix & Beast 2.50
85 Mother Askani, Gaunt. 2.50
86 Gaunt 2.50
87 Dream'sEnd,pt.2,x-over 8.00
88 F:Nightcrawler. 2.50
89 in Washington DC. 2.50
90 Dark Sisterhood 2.50
91 Dark Sisterhood 2.50
92 Cable quits X-Men? 2.50
93 V:Dark Sisterhood. 2.50
94 V:Dark Sisterhood 2.50
95 V:Dark Sisterhood,concl. 2.50
96 Old Man Coll. 2.50
97 Path of Most Resistance. 2.50
98 Shining Path 2.50
99 V:Shining Path 2.50
100 V:Techno-OrganicVirus,64-pg. . 4.50
101 Macedonian Plot. 2.50
102 Albanians' deadly plan 2.50
103 shot in the head 2.50
104 on the wrong side? 2.50
105 in Rio. 2.50
106 In Kazakhstan. 2.50
107 final issue 2.50
Ann. '98 AOI(c) F:Cable vs. Machine
  Man, O:Bastion 3.00
Ann.1999 48-page 2.50
Minus 1 Spec., TDz,JeR, flashback. 2.00
GN Cable/Wolverine Guts 'N' Glory. 6.00
Cable: Second Genesis 4.00

CABLE & DEADPOOL
Nov., 2003
1 RLd(c),Looks Could Kill,pt.1 . . . 3.50
2 RLd(c),Looks Could Kill,pt.2 . . . 3.50
3 RLd(c),Looks Could Kill,pt.3 . . . 3.00
4 RLd(c),Looks Could Kill,pt.4 . . . 3.00
5 RLd(c),Looks Could Kill,pt.5 . . . 3.00
6 Looks Could Kill,pt.6 . . . . 3.00
7 Passion of the Cable,pt.1 . . . . . 3.00
8 Passion of the Cable,pt.2 . . . . . 3.00
9 Passion of the Cable,pt.3 . . . . . 3.00
10 Passion of the Cable,pt.4 . . . . . 3.00
11 FaN,Thirty Pieces,pt.1 . . . . 3.00
12 FaN,Thirty Pieces,pt.2 . . . . 3.00
13 A Murder in Paradise,pt.1 . . . . . 3.00
14 A Murder in Paradise,pt.2 . . . . . 3.00

MARVEL

15 Enema of the State,pt.1 . . . . . . 3.00	
16 Enema of the State,pt.2 . . . . . . 3.00	
17 Enema of the State,pt.3 . . . . . . 3.00	
18 Enema of the State,pt.4 . . . . . . 3.00	
19 FaN,Why, When I Was Your Age 3.00	
20 FaN, Bosom Buddies 3.00	
21 FaN, Bosom Buddies 3.00	
22 FaN, Bosom Buddier 3.00	
23 FaN,Bosom Buddies 3.00	
24 FaN,V:Spider-Man 3.00	
25 FaN,Living Legends 3.00	
26 FaN,Born Again, pt.1 . . . . 3.00	
27 FaN,Born Again, pt.2 . . . . 3.00	
28 FaN, ... 3.00	
29 FaN, ... 3.00	
30 FaN,The Hero Hunter 3.00	
31 FaN,For King and Country 3.00	
32 FaN, ... 3.00	
33 FaN,RLd(c) Domino Principle . . . 3.00	
34 FaN,RLd(c) 3.00	
35 FaN 3.00	
36 FaN,Unfinished Business,pt.1 . 3.00	
37 FaN,Unfinished Business,pt.2 . 3.00	
38 FaN,Unfinished Business,pt.3 . 3.00	
39 FaN,Unifinished Business,pt.4 . 3.00	
40 FaN,Unifinished Business,pt.5 . 3.00	
41 FaN,Fractured, pt.1. . . . . 3.00	
42 FaN,Fractured, pt.2. . . . . 3.00	
43 FaN,Deadpool & Wolverine . . . 3.00	
44 FaN,Deadpool & Wolverine . . . 3.00	
45 FaN,F:Capt. America 3.00	
46 . . . . 3.00	
47 FaN. 3.00	

CABLE & X-FORCE
1995–97
Cable & X-Force '95 Spec. 4.00
Cable & X-Force '96 Spec.48pg. . . . 3.50
Cable & X-Force '97 Spec.#1
  JFM,CJ,V:Malekith,48pg. 3.50

CADILLACS & DINOSAURS
Epic, Nov., 1990
1 Rep.Xenozoic Tales 5.00
2 thru 6 Rep.Xenozoic Tales . . . . @3.00

CAGE
1992–93
1 DT,R:Luke Cage,I:Hardcore, ... 3.00
2 thru 20 . . . . @2.50

Cage #5
© *Marvel Entertainment Group*

CAGE
Marvel Max, Feb., 2002
1 (of 5) RCo,Justice isn't cheap . . . 5.00
2 RCo,teen-age girl murdered 4.00
3 RCo, ... 4.00
4 RCo,secret shame. 4.00
5 RCo,Hammerhead. 4.00

CALL, THE
April, 2003
1 PO, everyday heroes. 2.25
2 thru 4 PO . . . . @2.25

CALL OF DUTY, THE: THE BROTHER HOOD
June, 2002
1 (of 6) ATi,F:FDNY,48-pg. 4.00
2 thru 6 ATi,F:FDNY . . . . @2.50
The Call of Duty, Must Have ed. . . . 3.00

THE CALL OF DUTY: THE PRECINCT
July, 2002
1 (of 5) TMd,F:NYPD 3.00
2 thru 5 TMd . . . . @2.50

THE CALL OF DUTY: THE WAGON
Marvel Aug., 2002
1 (of 4) F:NYC EMS 2.50
2 thru 4 . . . . @2.50

CAMP CANDY
May, 1990
1 thru 6, Oct., 1990 . . . . @4.00

CAPTAIN AMERICA COMICS
Timely/Atlas, 1941–54
1 S&K,SSh,JK(c),Hitler(c),I&O:Capt.
  America & Bucky,A:Red Skull,
  B:Hurricane, Tuk 175,000.00
2 S&K,RC,AAv,Hitler(c),
  I:Circular Shield;Trapped
  in the Nazi Stronghold . . . 30,000.00
3 ASh(c),S&K,RC,AAv,Stan Lee's
  1st Text,A:Red Skull,
  Bondage(c) 25,000.00
4 ASh(c),S&K,AAv,Horror
  Hospital 14,000.00
5 S&K,AAv,SSh,Ringmaster's
  Wheel of Death 13,000.00
6 S&K,AAv,SSh,O:Father Time,
  E:Tuk 13,000.00
7 S&K,SSh,A: Red Skull 14,000.00
8 S&K, The Tomb 9,000.00
9 S&K,RC,V:Black Talon 9,000.00
10 S&K,RC,Chamber
  of Horrors 9,000.00
11 AAv,SSh,E:Hurricane;Feuding
  Mountaneers. 7,000.00
12 AAv,SSh,B:Imp,E:Father Time;
  Pygmie's Terror. 6,500.00
13 AAv,O:Secret Stamp;All Out
  For America 7,000.00
14 AAv,V:Japs;Pearl Harbor
  Symbol cover 7,000.00
15 AAv,Den of Doom 7,000.00
16 AAv,A:R.Skull;Captain America
  Unmasked 9,000.00
17 AAv,I:Fighting Fool;
  Graveyard. 5,500.00
18 AAv,SSh,V:Japanese 5,500.00
19 AAv,V:Ghouls,
  B:Human Torch. 5,000.00
20 AAv,A:Sub-Mariner,V:Nazis . 5,000.00

Captain America #35
© *Marvel Entertainment Group*

21 SSh(c),Bucky Captured 4,500.00
22 SSh(c),V:Japanese 4,500.00
23 SSh(c),V:Nazis. 4,500.00
24 SSh(c),V:Black
  Dragon Society. 4,500.00
25 SSh(c),V:Japs;Drug Story . . 4,500.00
26 ASh(c),SSh,V:Nazi Fleet . . . 4,300.00
27 ASh(c),SSh,AAv,CapAm&Russians
  V:Nazis, E:Secret Stamp . . 4,300.00
28 ASh(c),SSh,Nazi Torture
  Chamber. 4,300.00
29 ASh(c),SSh,V:Nazis;French
  Underground. 4,300.00
30 SSh(c),Bucky Captured 4,300.00
31 ASh(c),Bondage(c). 4,000.00
32 SSh(c),V: Japanese Airforce 4,000.00
33 ASh(c),V:Nazis;BrennerPass 4,000.00
34 SSh(c),Bondage(c) 4,000.00
35 SSh(c),CapA in Japan 4,000.00
36 SSh(c),V:Nazis;Hitler(c). . . . 5,500.00
37 ASh(c),SSh,Captain America
  in Berlin, A:Red Skull 5,000.00
38 ASh(c),V:Japs;Bondage(c). . 4,200.00
39 ASh(c),SSh,V:Japs;Boulder
  Dam 4,200.00
40 SSh(c),V:Japs;Ammo Depot 4,200.00
41 ASh(c),FinalJapaneseWar(c) 4,000.00
42 ASh(c),SSh,V:BankRobbers 4,000.00
43 ASh(c),V:Gangsters 4,000.00
44 ASh(c),V:Gangsters 4,000.00
45 ASh(c),V:Bank Robbers 4,000.00
46 ASh(c),Holocaust(c). 4,500.00
47 ASh(c),Final Nazi War(c) . . . 4,500.00
48 ASh(c),V:Robbers 3,500.00
49 ASh(c),V:Saboteurs 3,500.00
50 ASh(c),V:Gorilla Gang 3,600.00
51 ASh(c),V:Gangsters 3,500.00
52 ASh(c),V:AtomBombThieves 3,500.00
53 ASh(c),V:Burglars 3,500.00
54 ASh(c),TV Studio,
  V:Gangsters 3,500.00
55 SSh,V:Counterfeiters 3,500.00
56 SSh(c),V:Art Theives 3,500.00
57 SSh,AAv,Symbolic CapA(c). 3,500.00
58 ASh(c),V:Bank Robbers. . . . 2,600.00
59 SSh(c)O:CapA Retold;Private
  Life of Captain America . . . 5,000.00
60 SSh,V:The Human Fly 2,600.00
61 SSh(c),V:Red Skull;
  Bondage(c). 5,000.00
62 SSh(c),Kingdom of Terror . . 2,600.00
63 SSh(c),AAv,I&O:Asbestos Lady;
  The Parrot Strikes. 3,100.00
64 SSh,Diamonds Spell Doom . 3,200.00
65 SSh,AAv,Friends Turn Foes 3,200.00

66 SSh,O:Golden Girl;Bucky
Shot 3,300.00
67 SSh,E:Toro(in Human Torch);
Golden Girl Team-Up 3,200.00
68 A:Golden Girl;Riddle of
the Living Dolls 3,200.00
69 Weird Tales of the Wee
Males, A:Sun Girl 3,200.00
70 A:Golden Girl,Sub-Mariner,
Namora;Worlds at War 3,200.00
71 A:Golden Girl; Trapped 3,200.00
72 AAv,Murder in the Mind 3,200.00
73 The Outcast of Time 3,200.00
74 A:Red Skull;Capt.America's
Weird Tales 11,000.00
75 Thing in the Chest 3,200.00
76 JR(c),Capt.America,Commie
Smasher 3,200.00
77 Capt.A,Commie Smasher . . 2,000.00
78 JR(c),V:Communists 2,000.00

CAPTAIN AMERICA
Prev: Tales of Suspense
April, 1968

100 JK,A:Avengers 500.00
101 JK,I:4th Sleeper 150.00
102 JK,V:Red Skull,4th Sleeper . 150.00
103 JK,V:Red Skull 150.00
104 JK,DA,JSo,V:Red Skull 150.00
105 JK,DA,A:Batroc 150.00
106 JK,Cap.Goes Wild 150.00
107 JK,Red Skull 150.00
108 JK,Trapster 150.00
109 JK,O:Captain America 200.00
110 JSo,JSt,A:Hulk,Rick Jones
in Bucky Costume 175.00
111 JSo,JSt,I:Man Killer 175.00
112 JK,GT,Album 125.00
113 JSo,TP,Avengers,
D:Madame Hydra 150.00
114 JR,SB,C:Avengers 60.00
115 JR,SB,A:Red Skull 60.00
116 GC,JSt,A:Avengers 60.00
117 JR(c),GC,JSt,I:Falcon 100.00
118 JR(c),GC,JSt,A:Falcon 50.00
119 GC,JSt,O:Falcon 50.00
120 GC,JSt,A:Falcon 50.00
121 GC,JSt,V:Man Brute 35.00
122 GC,JSt,Scorpion 35.00
123 GC,JSt,A:NickFury,
V:Suprema. 35.00
124 GC,JSt,I:Cyborg 35.00
125 GC,Mandarin. 35.00
126 JK&BEv(c),GC,A:Falcon. . . . 35.00
127 GC,WW,A:Nick Fury 35.00
128 GC,V:Satan's Angels 35.00
129 GC,Red Skull 35.00
130 GC,I:Batroc 35.00
131 GC,V:Hood 35.00
132 GC,A:Bucky Barnes 35.00
133 GC,O:Modok,B:Capt.America/
Falcon Partnership 35.00
134 GC,V:Stone Face 35.00
135 JR(c),GC,TP,A:Nick Fury 35.00
136 GC,BEv,V:Tyrannus 35.00
137 GC,BEv,A:Spider-Man 40.00
138 JR,A:Spider-Man. 40.00
139 JR,Falcon solo 35.00
140 JR,O:Grey Gargoyle 35.00
141 JR,JSt,V:Grey Gargoyle 25.00
142 JR,JSt,Nick Fury 25.00
143 JR,Red Skull 25.00
144 GM,JR,N:Falcon,V:Hydra . . . 25.00
145 GK,JR,V:Hydra 25.00
146 JR(c),SB,V:Hydra 22.00
147 GK(c),SB,V:Hydra. 22.00
148 SB,JR,Red Skull 22.00
149 GK(c),SB,JM,V:Batroc 22.00
150 K&R(c),SB,V:The Stranger . . 22.00
151 SB,V:Mr.Hyde 22.00
152 SB,V:Scorpion,Mr.Hyde 22.00

153 SB,JM,V:'50's Cap. 22.00
154 SB,V:'50's Cap. 22.00
155 SB,FMc,O:'50's Cap 22.00
156 SB,FMc,V:'50's Cap. 22.00
157 SB,I:The Viper 22.00
158 SB,V:The Viper 22.00
159 SB,V:PlantMan,Porcupine . . 22.00
160 SB,FMc,V:Solarr. 22.00
161 SB,V:Dr.Faustus 22.00
162 JSn(c),SB,V:Dr.Faustus 22.00
163 SB,I:Serpent Squad 22.00
164 JR(c),I:Nightshade 22.00
165 SB,FMc,V:Yellow Claw 22.00
166 SB,FMc,V:Yellow Claw 22.00
167 SB,V:Yellow Claw 22.00
168 SB,I&O:Phoenix
(2nd Baron Zemo) 22.00
169 SB,FMc,C:Black Panther . . . 22.00
170 K&R(c),SB,C:Black Panther . . 22.00
171 JR(c),SB,A:Black Panther. . . 22.00
172 GK(c),SB,C:X-Men 25.00
173 GK(c),SB,A:X-Men 28.00
174 GK(c),SB,A:X-Men 28.00
175 SB,A:X-Men 28.00
176 JR(c),SB,O:Capt.America. . . . 18.00
177 JR(c),SB,A:Lucifer,Beast 15.00
178 SB,A:Lucifer 15.00
179 SB,A:Hawkeye 15.00
180 GK(c),SB,I:1st Nomad(Cap) . . 25.00
181 GK(c),SB,I&O:New Cap 20.00
182 FR,Madam Hydra 10.00
183 GK(c),FR,R:Cap,D:New Cap . 15.00
184 K&R(c),HT,A:Red Skull 10.00
185 GK(c),SB,FR,V:Red Skull . . . 10.00
186 GK(c),FR,O:Falcon 15.00
187 K&R(c),FR,V:Druid 10.00
188 GK(c),SB,V:Druid 10.00
189 GK(c),FR,V:Nightshade 10.00
190 GK(c),FR,A:Nightshade 10.00
191 FR,A:Stilt Man,N.Fury 10.00
192 JR(c),FR,A:Dr.Faustus 10.00
193 JR(c),JK,`Mad Bomb' 20.00
194 JK,I:Gen.Heshin 22.00
195 JK,1984. . . . . 22.00
196 JK,Madbomb. 22.00
197 JK,Madbomb. 22.00
198 JK,Madbomb. 22.00
199 JK,Madbomb. 22.00
200 JK,Madbomb. 20.00
201 JK,Epilogue. 15.00
202 JK,Night People 15.00
203 JK,Night People 15.00
204 JK,I:Argon. 15.00
205 JK,V:Argon 15.00
206 JK,I:Swine 15.00
207 JK,V:Swine 15.00
208 JK,I:Arnim Zola,D:Swine. . . . 15.00
209 JK,O:Arnim Zola,I:Primus . . . 15.00
210 JK,A:Red Skull 15.00
211 JK,A:Red Skull 15.00
212 JK,A:Red Skull 15.00
213 JK,I:Night Flyer 15.00
214 JK,D:Night Flyer 15.00
215 GT,Redwing 10.00
216 Reprint,JK 10.00
217 JB, I:Quasar(Marvel Boy)
I:Vamp 10.00
218 SB,A:Iron Man 6.00
219 SB,JSt,V:TheCorporation 6.00
220 SB,D:L.Dekker 6.00
221 SB,Ameridroid. 6.00
222 SB,I:Animus(Vamp). 6.00
223 SB,Animus 6.00
224 MZ,V:Animus 6.00
225 SB,A:Nick Fury 6.00
226 SB,A:Nick Fury 6.00
227 SB,A:Nick Fury 6.00
228 SB,Constrictor. 6.00
229 SB,R:SuperAgents of Shield. . . 8.00
230 SB,A:Hulk 8.00
231 SB,DP,A:Grand Director 6.00
232 SB,DP,V:Grand Director 6.00

Captain America #237
© Marvel Entertainment Group

233 SB,DP,D:Sharon Carter 6.00
234 SB,DP,A:Daredevil 6.00
235 SB,FM,A:Daredevil 8.00
236 SB,V:Dr.Faustus 6.00
237 SB,`From the Ashes'. 6.00
238 SB,V:Hawk Riders 6.00
239 JBy(c),SB,V:Hawk Riders 6.00
240 SB,V:A Guy Named Joe 6.00
241 A:Punisher. 30.00
242 JSt,A:Avengers 6.00
243 GP(c),RB,V:Adonis 6.00
244 TS,`A Monster Berserk'. 6.00
245 CI,JRn,Nazi Hunter 6.00
246 GP(c),JBi,V:Joe 6.00
247 JBy,V:BaronStrucker 10.00
248 JBy,JRu,Dragon Man 10.00
249 JBy,O:Machinesmith,
A:Air-Walker 10.00
250 JBy,Cap for Pres. 10.00
251 JBy,V:Mr.Hyde. 10.00
252 JBy,V:Batrok 10.00
253 JBy,V:Baron Blood 10.00
254 JBy,D:B.Blood,UnionJack,I:3rd
Union Jack. 10.00
255 JBy,40th Anniv.,O:Cap 10.00
256 GC,V:Demon Druid. 3.50
257 A:Hulk 3.50
258 MZ,V:Blockbuster 3.50
259 MZ,V:Dr. Octopus 3.50
260 AM,In Jail 3.50
261 MZ,A:Nomad. 4.00
262 MZ,V:Ameridroid 3.50
263 MZ,V:Red Skull. 3.50
264 MZ,X-Men. 4.00
265 MZ,A:Spider-Man,N.Fury 3.50
266 MZ,A:Spider-Man 3.50
267 MZ,V:Everyman 3.00
268 MZ,A:Defenders(x-over from
Def.#106). 3.00
269 MZ,A:Team America 3.00
270 MZ,V:Tess-One 3.00
271 MZ,V:Mr.X 3.00
272 MZ,I:Vermin. 3.50
273 MZ,A:Nick Fury 3.00
274 MZ,D:SamSawyer. 3.00
275 MZ,V:Neo-Nazis 3.00
276 MZ,V:Baron Zemo. 3.00
277 MZ,V:Baron Zemo. 3.00
278 MZ,V:Baron Zemo. 3.00
279 MZ,V:Primus. 3.00
280 MZ,V:Scarecrow 3.00
281 MZ,A:Spider Woman,
R:'50's Bucky 3.00
282 MZ,I:2nd Nomad 6.00

All comics prices listed are for *Near Mint* condition.

282a (second printing) 2.50	354 KD,AM,I:USAgent,	399 Operation Galactic Storm
283 MZ,A:Viper 4.00	V:Machinesmith 3.50	Pt.8,V:Kree Empire 2.50
284 SB,Nomad. 3.00	355 RB,AM,A:Falcon,Battlestar 3.00	400 Operation Galactic Storm
285 MZ,V:Porcupine 3.00	356 AM,V:Sisters of Sin 3.00	Pt.15,BU:rep.Avengers #4 . . . . . 4.00
286 MZ,V:Deathlok 5.00	357 KD,AM,V:Sisters of Sin	401 R:D-Man,A:Avengers 2.50
287 MZ,V:Deathlok 5.00	Baron Zemo,Batroc 3.00	402 RLe,B:Man & Wolf,
288 MZ,V:Deathlok,D:Hellinger 5.00	358 KD,B:Blood Stone Hunt 3.00	A:Wolverine 2.50
289 MZ,A:Red Skull 3.00	359 KD,V:Zemo,C:Crossbones 3.00	403 RLe,A:Wolverine 2.50
290 JBy(c),RF,A:Falcon 3.00	360 KD,I:Crossbones 3.00	404 RLe,A:Wolverine 2.50
291 JBy(c),HT,V:Tumbler 3.00	361 KD,V:Zemo,Batroc 3.00	405 RLe,A:Wolverine 2.50
292 I&O:Black Crow 3.00	362 KD,V:Zemo,Crossbones 3.00	406 RLe,A:Wolverine 2.50
293 V:Mother Superior. 3.00	363 KD,E:Blood Stone Hunt,	407 RLe,A:Wolverine,Cable. 2.50
294 R:Nomad. 3.00	V:Crossbones,C:Wolverine 3.00	408 RLe,E:Man & Wolf 2.50
295 V:Sisters of Sin 3.00	364 KD,V:Crossbones 3.00	409 RLe,V:Skeleton Crew 2.50
296 V:Baron Zemo. 4.00	365 KD,Acts of Vengeance,	410 RLe,V:Crossbones,Skel.Crew . 2.50
297 O:Red Skull 4.00	V:SubMariner,Red Skull 3.00	411 RLe,V:Snapdragon 2.50
298 V:Red Skull 3.00	366 1st RLm Capt.Amer.,Acts of	412 RLe,V:Batroc,A:Shang-Chi 2.50
299 V:Red Skull 3.00	Vengeance,V:Controller. 3.00	413 A:Shang-Chi,V:Superia 2.50
300 D:Red Skull. 4.00	367 KD,Acts of Vengeance,	414 RLe,A:Ka-Zar,Black Panther . . . 2.50
301 PNe,A:Avengers 3.00	Magneto Vs. Red Skull 3.00	415 Rle,A:Black Panther,Ka-Zar . . . 2.50
302 PNe,I:Machete,V:Batroc 3.00	368 RLm,V:Machinesmith 3.00	416 RLe,Savage Land Mutates,
303 PNe,V:Batroc 3.00	369 RLm,I:Skeleton Crew 3.00	A:Black.Panther,Ka-Zar. 2.50
304 PNe,V:Stane Armor. 3.00	370 RLm,V:Skeleton Crew. 3.00	417 RLe,A:Black Panther,Ka-Zar,
305 PNe,A:Capt.Britain,V:Modred . . 3.00	371 RLm,V:Trump,Poundcakes 3.00	V:AIM 2.50
306 PNe,A:Capt.Britain,V:Modred . . 3.00	372 RLm,B:Streets of Poison,	418 RLe,V:Night People 2.50
307 PNe,I:Madcap 3.00	Cap on Drugs,C:Bullseye 3.00	419 RLe,V:Viper. 2.50
308 PNe,I:Armadillo,	373 RLm,V:Bullseye,A:Bl.Widow . . . 3.00	420 RLe,I:2nd Blazing Skull,
Secret WarsII 3.00	374 RLm,V:Bullseye,A:Daredevil . . . 3.00	A:Nightshift 3.00
309 PNe,V:Madcap 3.00	375 RLm,V:Daredevil 3.00	421 RLe,V:Nomad 2.50
310 PNe,V:Serpent Society,I:Cotton	376 RLm,A:Daredevil. 3.00	422 RLe,I:Blistik 2.50
Mouth,Diamondback 3.00	377 RLm,V:Crossbones,Bullseye . . 3.00	423 RTs(s),MCW,V:Namor. 2.50
311 PNe,V:Awesome Android 3.00	378 RLm,E:Streets of Poison,Red	424 MGv(s),A:Sidewinder 2.50
312 PNe,I:Flag Smasher 3.00	Skull vs Kingpin,V:Crossbones . 3.00	425 B:MGu(s),DHv,Embossed(c),
313 PNe,D:Modok 3.00	379 RLm(c),V:Serpent Society 3.00	I:2nd SuperPatriot,DeadRinger . 4.00
314 PNe,A:Nighthawk 3.00	380 RLm,V:Serpent Society. 3.00	426 DHv,A:Super Patriot,Dead
315 PNe,V:Serpent Society 3.00	381 RLm,V:Serpent Society. 3.00	Ringer,V:Resistants 2.50
316 PNe,A:Hawkeye 3.00	382 RLm,V:Serpent Society. 3.00	427 DHv,V:Super Patriot,Dead
317 PNe,I:Death-Throws 3.00	383 RLm(c),RLm,50th Anniv.	Ringer 2.50
318 PNe,V&D:Blue Streak 3.00	64Pages 5.00	428 DHv,I:Americop 2.50
319 PNe,V:Scourge,D:Vamp 3.00	384 RLm,A:Jack Frost 2.50	429 DHv,V:Kono. 2.50
320 PNe,V:Scourge 3.00	385 RLm,A:USAgent 2.50	430 Daemon Dran, Americop 2.50
321 PNe,V:Flagsmasher,	386 RLm,Cap./USAgent T.U. 2.50	431 DHv,I:Free Spirit 2.50
I:Ultimatum 3.00	387 B:Superia Strategem 2.50	432 DHv,Fighting Chance 2.50
322 PNe,V:Flagsmasher 3.00	388 A:Paladin 2.50	433 DHv,Baron Zemo 2.50
323 PNe,I:Super Patriot	389 Superia Strategem #3 . . . . 2.50	434 DHv,A:Fighting Spirit,
(US Agent) 5.00	390 Superia Strategem #4. . . . . 2.50	V:King Cobra. 2.50
324 PNe,V:Whirlwind,Trapster 3.00	391 Superia Strategem #5. . . . . 2.50	435 DHv,Fighting Chance 2.50
325 I:Slug,A:Nomad. 3.00	392 E:Superia Strategem 2.50	436 V:King Cobra, Mister Hyde,
326 V:Dr.Faustus. 3.00	393 V:Captain Germany 2.50	Fighting Chance conclusion . . . 2.50
327 MZ(c)V:SuperPatriot 4.00	394 A:Red Skull,Diamondback 2.50	437 Cap in a Coma 2.50
328 MZ(c),I:Demolition Man 3.00	395 A:Red Skull,Crossbones 2.50	438 I:New Body Armor. 2.50
329 MZ(c),A:Demolition Man 3.00	396 I:2nd Jack O'Lantern. 2.50	439 Dawn's Early Light,pt.2 . . . . . . 2.50
330 A:Night Shift,Shroud 3.00	397 V:Red Skull,X-Bones,Viper. . . . 2.50	440 Taking A.I.M.,pt.1 . . . . 2.50
331 A:Night Shift,Shroud 3.00	398 Operation:Galactic Storm	441 Taking A.I.M.,pt.3 . . . . 2.50
332 BMc,Rogers resigns 7.00	Pt.1,V:Warstar 2.50	442 Batroc, Cap,V:Zeitgeist 2.50
333 B:John Walker Becomes		443 MGu,24 hours to live 2.50
6th Captain America 5.00		444 MWa,RG,President Kidnapped . 6.00
334 I:4th Bucky 5.00		445 MWa,RG,R:Captain America. . . 4.00
335 V:Watchdogs. 4.00		446 MWa,RG,Operation
336 A:Falcon 3.00		Rebirth,pt.2 . . . . 4.00
337 TMo,I:The Captain 3.00		447 MWa,RG,Op.Rebirth,pt.3 . . . . . 4.00
338 KD,AM,V:Professor Power 3.00		448 MWa,RG,Operation
339 KD,TD,Fall of Mutants,		Rebirth,pt.4,double size. 6.00
V:Famine 3.00		449 MWa,RG,A:Thor 4.00
340 KD,AM,A:Iron Man,. 3.00		450 MWa,RG,Man Without a
341 KD,AM,I:Battlestar,A:Viper 3.00		Country, pt,1 . . . . 4.00
342 KD,AM,A:D-Man,Falcon,		450a alternate cover 4.00
Nomad,Viper 3.00		451 MWa,RG,DRo,Man Without
343 KD,AM,A:D-Man,Falcon,		A Country,pt.2,new costume . . . 3.50
Nomad. 3.00		452 MWa,RG,Man Without a
344 KD,AM,A:D-Man,Nomad. 4.00		Country, pt.3 . . . . 3.50
345 KD,AM,V:Watchdogs 4.00		453 MWa,RG Man Without a
346 KD,AM,V:Resistants 4.00		Country, concl.,old costume . . . 3.50
347 KD,AM,V:RWinger&LWinger. . . 4.00		454 MWa,RG,A:Avengers 3.50
348 KD,AM,V:Flag Smasher 4.00		Ann.#1 rep. 50.00
349 KD,AM,V:Flag Smasher 4.00		Ann.#2 rep. 35.00
350 KD,AM,doub-size,Rogers Ret.		Ann.#3 JK, ... 25.00
as Captain Am,V:Red Skull,		Ann.#4 JK,V:Magneto,I:Mutant
E:6th Cap 5.00	*Captain America #403*	Force 25.00
351 KD,AM,A:Nick Fury. 3.00	© *Marvel Entertainment Group*	Ann.#5 `Deathwatcher' 6.00
352 KD,AM,I:Supreme Soviets 3.00		Ann.#6 A:Contemplator 6.00
353 KD,AM,V:Supreme Soviets. . . . 3.00		Ann.#7 O:Shaper of Worlds. 6.00

Ann.#8 MZ,A:Wolverine 35.00
Ann.#9 MBa,SD,Terminus Factor
  #1,N:Nomad 4.50
Ann.#10 MM,Baron Strucker,pt.3
  (see Punisher Ann.#4). 4.00
Ann.#11 Citizen Kang#1 . . . . 4.00
Ann.#12 I:Bantam,w/card. 4.00
Ann.#13 RTs(s),MCW 4.00
Drug Wars PDd(s),SaV,A:New
  Warriors 3.00
G-Size#1 GK(c),rep.O:Cap.Amer. . 7.00
Medusa Effect RTs(s),MCW,RB,
  V:Master Man 3.50
Movie Adapt 3.00
Spec.#1 Rep.Cap.A #110,#111 . . 2.00
Spec.#2 Rep.Cap.A #113
  & Strange Tales #169 . . . . 2.00
Collector's Preview 2.00
Ashcan. 75

Captain America, 2nd Series, #5
© Marvel Entertainment Group

[2nd Series], Nov., 1996
1 RLd,CDi,JSb, Heroes Reborn,
  I:Nick Fury,48pg. 7.00
1A Stars and stripes background
  variant cover 7.50
1b gold signature edition,
  cardstock cover 18.00
1c San Diego Con edition 25.00
2 RLd,JLb,JSb,Falcon & Red Skull 3.00
3 RLd,JLb,JSb,A:Hulk,V:Red Skull
  & Master Man 3.00
4 RLd,JLb,JSb,F:Prince Namor,. . . 3.00
5 RLd,JLb,JSb,V:Crossbones. 3.00
6 RLd,JLb,JSb,Industrial
  Revolution, epilogue,A:Cable . . 3.00
7 RLd,JLb,DaF,. 3.00
8 RLd,JLb,SPa,A:Nick Fury,
  WWII story. 3.00
9 JLb,RLd,SPa,WWII story. 3.00
10 JLb,RLd,SPa,WWII story, concl.. 3.00
11 JeR,JoB,Odyssey across
  America, pt.4, concl. 3.00
12 JeR,JoB,Heroes Reborn, Galactus
  concl. 4.00
13 JeR,RLm,Wildstorm x-over 3.00
Ashcan, ComicCon 5.00

[3rd Series], Nov., 1997
1 MWa,RG,BWi,A:Lady Deathstrike,
  Red Skull, Sharon Carter, 48pg 4.00
1a variant cover 10.00
2 MWa,RG,BWi,A devastating loss. 5.00
2a variant cover 4.00
3 MWa,RG,BWi,V:Hydra 4.00
4 MWa,RG,BWi,F:Batroc 3.00

5 MWa,RG,BWi,V:Hordes of Hydra 3.00
6 MWa,RG,V:Skrulls 3.00
7 MWa,NKu,Power & Glory concl. . 3.00
8 MWa,Nku,Live Kree or Die, pt.2
  x-over. 3.50
9 MWa,NKu,American Nightmare,
  pt.1. 3.00
10 MWa,NKu,American Nightmare,
  pt.2. 3.00
11 MWa,NKu,American
  Nightmare, pt.3 . . . . 3.00
12 MWa,NKu,American Night-
  mare, pt.4, 48-page. 4.00
13 MWa,MFm,R:Red Skull 2.50
14 MWa,MFm,R:Red Skull 2.50
15 MWa,NKu,V:Red Skull 2.50
16 MWa,NKu,V:Red Skull 2.50
17 MWa,NKu,V:Red Skull 2.50
18 MWa,LW,RbC,V:Cosmic Cube
  double-size 3.50
19 MWa,NKu,V:2 foes 2.50
20 MWa,NKu,Shield secrets 2.50
21 MWa,NKu,A:Black Panther. . . . 2.50
22 MWa,NKu,A:Black Panther. . . . 2.50
23 MWa,Capt.America convict?. . . 2.50
24 TDF,RF,V:Hydra 2.50
25 DJu,NKu,DGr,Twisted
  Tomorrows,pt.1 . . . . 4.00
26 DJu,NKu,DGr,Twisted,pt.2 . . . . 2.50
27 DJu,NKu,DGr,Twisted,pt.3 . . . . 2.50
28 DJu,NKu,DGr,V:CountNefaria. . 2.50
29 DJu,DGr,A:Ka-Zar. 2.50
30 DJu,DGr,NKu,Savage Land . . . 2.50
31 DJu,NKu,DGr,F:Sharon Carter . 2.50
32 DJu,JO,kidnapped 2.50
33 DJu,ATi,Protocide 2.50
34 DJu,ATi,Cache 2.50
35 DJu,ATi,Protocide 2.50
36 DJu,ATi,Maximum Security. . . . 2.50
37 DJu,ATi,V:Protocide 2.50
38 DJu,ATi,Capt.Am. unleashed . . 2.50
39 DJu,V:A.I.M. 2.50
40 DJu,V:A.I.M. 2.50
41 DJu,Batroc the Leaper 2.50
42 DJu,BL,V:Crimson Dynamo . . . 2.50
43 DJu,DR,BL,A:David Ferrari. . . . 2.50
44 DJu,BL,A:Taskmaster 2.50
45 DJu,BL,America Lost,pt.1 . . . . . 2.50
46 DJu,BL,America Lost,pt.2 . . . . . 2.50
47 DJu,BL,America Lost,pt.3 . . . . . 2.50
48 DJu,BL,America Lost,pt.4 . . . . . 2.50
49 DJu,BL,F:Sam Wilson. 2.50
50 96-page, last issue 6.50

Captain America, 3rd Series #9
© Marvel Entertainment Group

Ann.1998 Captain America/
  Citizen V,KBk,KK, 48-page 4.00
Ann. 1999 JoC,V:Flag Smasher . . . 4.00
Ann.2000 DJu,DGr,48-pg. 4.00
Ann.2001 DJu,48-page 3.50
Spec.#1 Captain America (2000). . . 2.50
Spec.Cap: A Universe X Special . . . 4.00
GN Captain America/Nick Fury:
  The Otherworld War (2001). . . . 7.00

CAPTAIN AMERICA
April, 2002
1 JNR(s), terrorism, 48-pg. 4.00
2 JNR(s), terrorism,pt.2 . . . . 3.50
3 JNR(s), terrorism,pt.3 . . . . 3.50
4 JNR(s), terrorism,pt.4 . . . . 3.50
5 JNR(s), terrorism,pt.5 . . . . 3.50
6 JNR(s), terrorism,concl. 3.50
7 JNR(s) 3.50
8 JNR(s),Extremists,pt.2 . . . . 3.50
9 JNR(s),Extremists,pt.3 . . . . 3.50
10 JNR(s),Extremists,pt.4 . . . . 3.50
11 JNR(s),Extremists,pt.5 . . . . 3.50
12 JNR(s),JaL,Ice,pt.1 . . . . 3.50
13 JNR(s),JaL,Ice,pt.2 . . . . 3.50
14 JNR(s),JaL,Ice,pt.3 . . . . 3.50
15 JNR(s),JaL,Ice,pt.4 . . . . 3.50
16 JNR(s),JaL,Ice,pt.5 . . . . 3.50
17 LW,Cap.Am Lives Again,pt.1 . . . 3.50
18 LW,Cap.Am Lives Again,pt.2 . . . 3.50
19 LW,Cap.Am Lives Again,pt.3 . . . 3.50
20 LW,Cap.Am Lives Again,pt.4 . . . 3.50
21 CBa,Homeland,pt.1. . . . . 3.00
22 CBa,Homeland,pt.2. . . . . 3.00
23 CBa,Homeland,pt.3. . . . . 3.00
24 CBa,Homeland,pt.4. . . . . 3.00
25 CBa,Homeland,pt.5. . . . . 3.00
26 CBa,F:Bucky Barnes 3.00
27 ECa. 3.00
28 ECa. 3.00
29 Avengers Disassembled tie-in . . 3.00
30 Avengers Disassembled,pt.2 . . . 3.00
31 Avengers Disassembled,pt.3 . . . 3.00
32 SEa,Disassembled,tie-in,pt.4 . . . 3.00

CAPTAIN AMERICA
Nov., 2004
1 SEp,V:Red Skull 6.00
2 SEp, ... 5.00
3 SEp,F:Sharon Carter 4.00
4 SEp,home from Europe 4.00
5 SEp,flash-backs. 4.00
6 SEp,Out of Time, finale 4.00
7 SEp,Winter Soldier,pt.1 . . . . 4.00
7a variant (c). 3.00
8 SEp,Winter Soldier,pt.1 . . . . 3.00
8a variant (c). 3.00
9 SEp,Winter Soldier,pt.2 . . . . 3.00
10 SEp,Winter Soldier,pt.3 . . . . 3.00
11 SEp,Winter Soldier,pt.4 . . . . 3.00
12 SEp,Winter Soldier,pt.5. . . . . . . 3.00
13 SEp,Winter Soldier,pt. 3.00
14 SEp,Winter Soldier,pt. 3.00
15 A:Crossbones, Sin 3.00
16 F:Crossbones, Sin 3.00
17 F:Corssbones, Sin 3.00
18 SEp,Twenty-First Century Blitz . . 3.00
19 SEp,Twenty-First Century Blitz . . 3.00
20 SEp,Twenty-First Century Blitz . . 3.00
21 SEp,Twenty-First Century Blitz . . 3.00
22 Civil War tie-in. 3.00
23 Civil War tie-in. 3.00
24 Civil War tie-in. 3.00
25 SEp, Death of a Dream, pt.1 . . . 4.00
25a variant (c) 4.00
25b director's cut 4.00
26 SEp, Death of a Dream, pt.2 . . . 3.00
27 SEp, Death of a Dream, pt.3 . . . 3.00
28 SEp, New Serpent Squad. 3.00
29 SEp, Winter Soldier 3.00
30 SEp, Winter Soldier 3.00

MARVEL

31 SEp,Prisoner of Red Skull 3.00
32 SEp,Death of Capt. America. . . . 3.00
Spec. 65th Anniversary #1, 48-pg.. . 5.00

CAPTAIN AMERICA & THE FALCON
March, 2004

1 BS,Two Americas,pt.1 . . . . 3.00
2 BS,Two Americas,pt.2 . . . . 3.00
3 BS,Two Americas,pt.3 . . . . 3.00
4 BS,Two Americas,pt.4 . . . . 3.00
5 Avengers Disassembled tie-in . . . 3.00
6 Avengers Disassembled,pt.2 . . . . 3.00
7 Avengers Disassembled,pt.3 . . . . 3.00
8 JoB,Brothers & Keepers,pt.1 . . . . 3.00
9 . . . . 3.00
10 . . . . 3.00
11 CPr(s),JoB,Brothers & Keepers . 3.00
12 CPr(s),JoB,Brothers & Keepers . 3.00
13 CPr(s),DJu,American Psycho . . . 3.00
14 CPr(s),DJu,finale. 3.00

CAPTAIN AMERICA: DEAD MAN RUNNING
Jan., 2002

1 (of 3) distress call 3.25
2 . . . . 3.25
3 concl. 3.25

CAPTAIN AMERICA: SENTINEL OF LIBERTY
July, 1998

1 MWa,RG,new foe, in future 2.50
1 signed by MWa & RG 5.00
2A MWa,RG(c&a) F:Invaders,
   V:Nazis 2.25
2B variant JSm(c) 2.25
3 MWa,RG,DGr,A:Sub-Mariner. . . . 2.25
4 MWa,RG,DGr,A:Human Torch . . . 2.25
5 MWa,RG,MFm,Tales of
   Suspense pt.1 . . . . 2.25
6 MWa,RG,MFm,Tales of
   Suspense pt.2 . . . . 3.50
7 RSt,RF,civil war tale concl. 2.25
8 MWa,R:Falcon 2.25
9 MWa,A:Falcon 2.25
10 psychedelic look back. 2.25
11 MWa,A:Human Torch 2.25
12 MWa,DGr,F:Bucky,48-page 3.50
Spec.RoughCut #1,MWa,RG,48-pg . 3.00

CAPTAIN AMERICA: THE CHOSEN
Sept., 2007

1 (of 6) 4.00
1a thru 4a variant (c) . . . . @4.00
2 thru 4 . . . . @4.00

CAPTAIN AMERICA: WHAT PRICE GLORY
March, 2003

1 (of 4) SR 3.25
2 thru 4 SR . . . . @3.25

CAPTAIN BRITAIN CLASSICS

1 AD rep. 2.50

CAPTAIN CONFEDERACY
Epic, Nov., 1991

1 I:Capt.Confederacy,Kid Dixie. . . . 2.25
2 Meeting of Superhero Reps. 2.25
3 Framed for Murder. 2.25
4 Superhero conference,final iss. . . 2.25

CAPTAIN JUSTICE
March, 1988

1 Based on TV Series 2.25
2 April, 1988 . . . . 2.25

Captain Marvel #24
© Marvel Entertainment Group

CAPTAIN MARVEL
May, 1968

1 GC,O:retold,V:Sentry#459. . . . 225.00
2 GC,V:Super Skrull 100.00
3 GC,V:Super Skrull 60.00
4 GC,Sub-Mariner. 60.00
5 DH,I:Metazoid 60.00
6 DH,I:Solam 40.00
7 JR(c),DH,V:Quasimodo 40.00
8 DH,I:Cuberex 40.00
9 DH,D:Cuberex 40.00
10 DH,V:Number 1. . . . . 40.00
11 BWS(c),I:Z0. . . . . 40.00
12 K&R(c),I:Man-Slayer. 25.00
13 FS,V:Man-Slayer. 25.00
14 FS,Iron Man 25.00
15 TS,DA,Z0 . . . . 22.00
16 DH,Ronan 22.00
17 GK,DA,O:R.Jones ret,N:Capt.
   Marvel 25.00
18 GK,JB,DA,I:Mandroid 22.00
19 GK,DA,Master.of.MM 22.00
20 GK,DA,I:Rat Pack 22.00
21 GK,DA,Hulk. 22.00
22 GK(c),WB,V:Megaton 22.00
23 GK(c),WB,FMc,V:Megaton 22.00
24 GK(c),WB,ECh,I:L.Mynde. 22.00
25 1st JSn,Cap.Marvel,Cosmic
   Cube Saga Begins 35.00
26 JSn,DC,Thanos(2ndApp.)
   A:Thing 40.00
27 JSn,V:Thanos,A:Mentor,
   Starfox, I:Death 35.00
28 JSn,DGr,Thanos Vs.Drax,
   A:Avengers 35.00
29 JSn,AM,O:Zeus,C:Thanos
   I:Eon,O:Mentor 25.00
30 JSn,AM,Controller,C:Thanos . . 25.00
31 JSn,AM,Avengers,
   Thanos,Drax,Mentor 28.00
32 JSn,AM,DGr,O:Drax,
   Moondragon,A:Thanos 28.00
33 JSn,KJ,E:Cosmic Cube Saga
   1st D:Thanos 40.00
34 JSn,JA,V:Nitro(leads to
   his Death) 25.00
35 GK(c),AA,Ant Man 10.00
36 AM,Watcher,Rep.CM#1 . . . . . . 10.00
37 AM,KJ,Nimrod 10.00

38 AM,KJ,Watcher 10.00
39 AM,KJ,Watcher 10.00
40 AM,AMc,Watcher 10.00
41 AM,BWr,CR,BMc,TA,Kree. 12.00
42 AM,V:Stranger,C:Drax. 8.00
43 AM,V:Drax. 8.00
44 GK(c),AM,V:Drax 12.00
45 AM,I:Rambu 12.00
46 AM,TA,D:Fawn 8.00
47 AM,TA,A:Human Torch 8.00
48 AM,TA,I:Chetah. 8.00
49 AM,V:Ronan,A:Cheetah. 8.00
50 AM,TA,Avengers,
   V:Super Adaptiod. 9.00
51 AM,TA,V:Mercurio,4-D Man . . . 12.00
52 AM,TA,V:Phae-dor 12.00
53 AM,TA,A:Inhumans 8.00
54 PB,V:Nitro 8.00
55 PB,V:Death-grip 8.00
56 PB,V:Death-grip 8.00
57 PB,V:Thor,A;Thanos 12.00
58 PB,Drax/Titan 8.00
59 PB,Drax/Titan,I:Stellarax 8.00
60 PB,Drax/Titan 8.00
61 PB,V:Chaos 8.00
62 PB,V:Stellarax. 8.00
G-Size #1 reprints 10.00

CAPTAIN MARVEL
1989

1 MBr,I:Powerkeg,V:Moonstone . . . 3.00
1 DyM(s),MBr,V:Skinhead(1993) . . 2.50
PF Death of Captain Marvel 8.00

CAPTAIN MARVEL
1995

1 FaN,R:Captain Marvel(son of). . . 4.00
2 FaN,V:X-Treme,Erik the Red. . . . 3.00
3 FaN,V:X-treme. 3.00
4 thru 6 FaN . . . . @3.00

CAPTAIN MARVEL
Jan., 2000

1A PDd,Ccs,A:Rick Jones 5.00
1B variant JOy (c). 5.50
2 PDd,Ccs. 7.00
3 PDd,Ccs,V:Wendigo 3.00
4 PDd,Ccs,A:Moondragon 3.00
5 PDd,Ccs,V:Drax. 3.00
6 PDd,Ccs,V:Marlo 3.00
7 PDd,Ccs,A:Comet Man 3.00
8 PDd,Ccs,V:Super-Skrull. 3.00
9 PDd,Ccs,V:Hyssta 3.00
10 PDd,Ccs,V:Genis 3.00
11 PDd,JSn 3.00
12 PDd,Ccs,Maximum Security 3.00
13 PDd,Ccs,V:kids of Yon-Rogg . . . 3.00
14 PDd,Ccs,F:Psycho-Man 3.00
15 PDd,Ccs,F:Psycho-Man 3.00
16 PDd,Ccs,V:Psycho-Man 3.00
17 PDd,JSn,AM,V:Thanos 3.00
18 PDd,JSn,AM,A:Thor,Thanos. . . . 3.00
19 PDd,Ccs,A:Thor,Thanos 3.00
20 PDd,Ccs,. 3.00
21 PDd,Ccs,. 3.00
22 PDd,Ccs,Supreme Intelligence . . 3.00
23 PDd,Ccs,. 3.00
24 PDd,Ccs,Negative Zone 3.00
25 PDd,Ccs,V:Quasar. 3.00
26 PDd,F:Rick Jones,'Nuff Said 3.00
27 PDd,CCs,Time Flies,pt.1 . . . . 3.00
28 PDd,Time Flies, pt.2 . . . . 3.00
29 PDd,Time Flies, pt.3 . . . . 3.00
30 PDd,Time Flies, pt.4 . . . . 3.00
31 PDd,Ccs,F:Marlo,V:Mephisto . . . 3.00
32 PDd,Ccs,F:Moondragon 3.00
33 PDd,Ccs,V:Magus. 3.50
34 PDd,Ccs,V:Magus,Rick Jones . . 3.00
35 PDd, last issue 3.00

CAPTAIN MARVEL
Sept., 2002
1 PDd,Ccs, U-Decide 3.00
1b Variant JJu(c) 2.25
1c Variant AxR(c) 2.25
2 PDd,Ccs,F:Punisher 2.25
3 PDd,Ccs,AxR 2.25
3a Director's Cut, AxR, 40-pg. . . . 3.50
4 PDd,CCs 2.25
5 PDd,CCs 2.25
6 PDd,CCs 2.25
7 PDd,A:Thor,pt.1 . . . . 2.25
8 PDd,A:Thor,pt.2 . . . . 3.00
9 PDd,Coven,pt.1 . . . . 3.00
10 PDd,Coven,pt.2 . . . . 3.00
11 PDd,Coven,pt.3 . . . . 3.00
12 PDd,Coven,pt.4 . . . . 3.00
13 PDd,Pop,V:Badoon 3.00
14 PDd,accidents do happen. 3.00
15 PDd,NA(c),V:Kree 3.00
16 PDd,Crazy Like a Fox,pt.2 . . . . 3.00
17 PDd,Crazy Like a Fox,pt.3 . . . . 3.00
18 PDd,Crazy Like a Fox,pt.4 . . . . 3.00
19 PDd,Odyssey,pt.1 . . . . 3.00
20 PDd,Odyssey,pt.2 . . . . 3.00
21 PDd,Odyssey,pt.3 . . . . 3.00
22 PDd,AsL,Odyssey,pt.4 . . . . 3.00
23 PDd,AsL,Odyssey,pt.5 . . . . 3.00
24 PDd,Odyssey,pt.6 . . . . 3.00
25 PDd,Exit Strategy 3.00

CAPTAIN MARVEL
Nov., 2007
1 (of 5) 3.00

CAPTAIN PLANET
Oct., 1991
1 I&O:Captain Planet 5.00
2 thru 12 . . . . @3.00

CAPT. SAVAGE & HIS
LEATHERNECK RAIDERS
Jan., 1968
1 SSh(c),C:Sgt Fury;The Last
  Bansai 75.00
2 SSh(c),O:Hydra;Return of Baron
  Strucker 35.00
3 SSh,Two Against Hydra 35.00
4 SSh,V:Hydra;The Fateful Finale 35.00
5 SSh,The Invincible Enemy 35.00
6 Mission;Save a Howler 35.00
7 SSh,Objective:Ben Grimm 35.00

Capt. Savage #1
© Marvel Entertainment Group

8 Mission:Foul Ball 35.00
Becomes:

CAPT. SAVAGE & HIS
BATTLEFIELD RAIDERS
1968
9 . . . . 35.00
10 To the Last Man 35.00
11 A:Sergeant Fury 35.00
12 V:The Japanese 35.00
13 The Junk Heap Juggernauts. . . 35.00
14 Savage's First Mission 35.00
15 Within the Temple Waits Death. 30.00
16 V:The Axis Powers 30.00
17 V:The Axis Powers 30.00
18 V:The Axis Powers 30.00
19 March, 1970 . . . . 30.00

CAPTAIN UNIVERSE
Nov., 2005
1 F:Hulk 3.00
2 F:Daredevil 3.00
3 F:X-23 . . . . 3.00
4 F:Invisible Woman 3.00
5 F:Silver Surfer 3.00

CARE BEARS
Star, Nov., 1985
1 . . . . 3.00
2 thru 14 . . . . @3.00
Marvel 1988
15 thru 20 . . . . @3.00

CARNAGE
1-shot Carnage: Its a Wonderful
  Life (1996) 3.00
1-shot Carnage: Mindbomb
  foil cover (1996) 3.50

CARTOON KIDS
Marvel Atlas, 1957
1 JMn,A:Dexter the Demon, Little
  Zelda,Willie,Wise Guy 150.00

CAR WARRIORS
Epic, 1990
1 Based on Roll Playing Game . . . 2.50
2 Big Race Preparations 2.50
3 Ft.Delorean-Lansing Race begin. 2.50
4 Race End, Final issue 2.50

CASEY–CRIME
PHOTOGRAPHER
Aug., 1949
1 Ph(c),Girl on the Docks 325.00
2 Ph(c),Staats Cotsworth 250.00
3 Ph(c),He Walked With Danger 250.00
4 Ph(c),Lend Me Your Life 250.00
Becomes:

TWO GUN WESTERN
[1st Series], 1950
5 JB,B,I&O:Apache Kid 300.00
6 JMn,The Outcast 225.00
7 Human Sacrifice 225.00
8 JR,DW,A:Kid Colt,Texas Kid,
  Doc Holiday 225.00
9 JMn,GM,A:Kid Colt,Marshall
  'Frosty' Bennet Texas Kid . . . 225.00
10 . . . . 225.00
11 thru 14 JMn,June, 1952 . . . @150.00

CAT, THE
Nov., 1972—June, 1973
1 JM,I&O:The Cat 50.00
2 JM,V:The Owl 25.00
3 BEv,V:Kraken 25.00
4 JSn,V:Man-Bull 30.00

CAUGHT
Marvel-Vista Publications, 1956
1 JSe,Crime 350.00
2 MD,JSe 200.00
3 MMe,Al,JSe 200.00
4 MMe,JSe 200.00
5 RC,JSe,BK. 200.00

CENTURY:
DISTANT SONS
1996
1-shot DAn,48pg. 3.25

CHAMBER OF CHILLS
Nov., 1972
1 SSh,A Dragon Stalks By
  Night,(H.Ellison Adapt.) 40.00
2 FB,BEv,SD,Monster From the
  Mound,(RE Howard Adapt.) . . 20.00
3 FB,BEv,SD, Thing on the Roof . 20.00
4 FB,BEv,SD, Opener of the
  Crypt,(J.Jakes,E.A.Poe Adapt) 20.00
5 FB,BEv,SD, Devils Dowry 20.00
6 FB,BEv,SD, Mud Monster 20.00
7 thru 24 FB,BEv,SD . . . . @20.00
25 FB,BEv,SD Nov., 1976 . . . . . 20.00

Chamber of Darkness #5
© Marvel Entertainment Group

CHAMBER OF DARKNESS
Oct., 1969
1 JB, Tales of Maddening Magic 125.00
2 NA(script),Enter the Red Death. 75.00
3 JK,BWS,JB, Something Lurks
  on Shadow Mountain. 60.00
4 JK Monster Man Came Walking,
  BU:BWS 75.00
5 JCr,JK,SD, And Fear Shall
  Follow, plus Lovecraft adapt... 50.00
6 SD 50.00
7 SD,JK,BWr, Night of the
  Gargoyle 75.00
8 BWr(c),DA,BEv, Beast that Walks
  Like a Man Special, 5 Tales of
  Maddening Magic, Jan.,1972 125.00
Becomes:

MONSTERS ON
THE PROWL
1971
9 SAD,BWS,Monster Stories
  Inc,Gorgilla 45.00
10 JK,Roc 25.00
11 JK,A Titan Walks the Land . . . 25.00

All comics prices listed are for *Near Mint* condition.

12 HT,JK,Gomdulla The Living
    Pharoah 25.00
13 HT,JK,Tragg 30.00
14 JK,SD,Return of the Titan 30.00
15 FrG,JK,The Thing Called It 25.00
16 JSe,SD,JK, Serpent God of
    Lost Swamp,A:King Kull 25.00
17 JK,SD,Coming of Colossus 25.00
18 JK,SD,Bruttu 25.00
19 JK,SD,Creature From the
    Black Bog 25.00
20 JK,SD,Oog Lives Again 25.00
21 JK,SD,A Martian Stalks
    the City 25.00
22 JK,SD,Monster Runs Amok . . . 18.00
23 JK,The Return of Grogg 18.00
24 JK,SD, Magnetor 18.00
25 JK,Colossus Lives Again 18.00
26 JK,SD,The Two Headed Thing . 18.00
27 JK,Sserpo 18.00
28 JK,The Coming of Monsteroso . 18.00
29 JK,SD Monster at my Window . . 18.00
30 JK,Diablo Demon from the 5th
    Dimension, Oct., 1974 . . . . . . 18.00

Champions #15
© Marvel Entertainment Group

CHAMPIONS
Oct., 1975
1 GK(c),DH,I&O:Champions 50.00
2 DH,O:Champions 20.00
3 GT,Assault on Olympus 20.00
4 GT,`Murder at Malibu' 20.00
5 DH,I:Rampage 20.00
6 JK(c),GT,V:Rampage 20.00
7 GT,O:Black Widow,I:Darkstar . . 20.00
8 BH,O:Black Widow 18.00
9 BH,BL,V:Crimson Dynamo 18.00
10 BH,BL,V:Crimson Dynamo . . . 18.00
11 JBy,A:Black Goliath,Hawkeye . . 25.00
12 JBy,BL,V:Stranger 25.00
13 JBy,BL,V:Kamo Tharn 25.00
14 JBy,I:Swarm 25.00
15 JBy,V:Swarm 25.00
16 BH,A:Magneto,Dr.Doom,
    Beast 18.00
17 GT,JBy,V:Sentinels,last issue . . 20.00

CHAMPIONS, THE
Sept., 2007
1 . . . . 3.00

CHILI
May, 1969
1 Millie's Rival 125.00
2 . . . . 75.00
3 . . . . 75.00
4 . . . . 75.00
5 . . . . 75.00
6 thru 15 . . . . @50.00
16 thru 20 . . . . @40.00
21 thru 25 . . . . @35.00
26 Dec., 1973 . . . . 35.00
Spec.#1, 1971 . . . . 45.00

CHUCK NORRIS
Star, Jan.–Sept., 1987
1 SD 4.00
2 thru 5 . . . . @5.00

CINDY COMICS
See: KRAZY COMICS

CITIZEN V
April, 2001
1 (of 3) FaN,F:V-Battalion 3.25
2 FaN, ... 3.25
3 FaN,F:Iron Cross 3.25

CITIZEN V
& THE V BATTALION:
THE EVERLASTING
Feb., 2002
1 (of 4) FaN, ... 3.25
2 FaN,Marduk 3.25
3 FaN, ... 3.25
4 FaN, concl. 3.25

CIVIL WAR
May, 2006
1 F: everybody, x-over-48-pg 5.00
1a variant (c) 22.00
1b director's cut, 64-pg. 6.00
2 . . . . 7.00
2a variant (c) 6.00
2b 2nd printing 6.00
3 . . . . 5.00
3a variant (c) 15.00
4 . . . . 3.50
4a variant (c) 8.00
5 . . . . 3.50
6 . . . . 3.00
7 . . . . 3.00
3a to 7a variant (c)s 5.00
Spec. Civil War Files #1 . . . . 4.00
Spec. Daily Bugle Civil War issue . 0.50
Spec. Battle Damage Report 4.00
Spec. The Initiative, BMB,WEI,MS . 5.00
Spec. The Return, PJe (2007) 3.00
Spec. War Crimes (2006) 4.00

CIVIL WAR CHRONICLES
July, 2007
1 PJe 5.00
2 MSz(s),RG 5.00
3 MSz(s),RG 5.00
4 PJe 5.00
5 MSz(s),RG 5.00

CIVIL WAR: FRONT LINE
June, 2006
1 Embeded 5.00
2 thru 11 . . . . @4.00

CIVIL WAR: X-MEN
July, 2006
1 . . . . 4.00
1a variant (c) 10.00
2 thru 4 . . . . @3.50

CIVIL WAR: YOUNG
AVENGERS & RUNAWAYS
July, 2006
1 . . . . 4.00
2 thru 4 . . . . @3.50

CLANDESTINE
Oct., 1994–Sept., 1995
Preview issue, Intro (1994) 2.00
1 MFm,AD,foil(c). 3.25
2 Wraparound (c),A:Silver Surfer . . 2.75
3 I:Argent,Kimera,A:SilverSurfer. . . 2.75
4 R:Adam 2.75
5 MFm,AD,O:Adam Destine 2.75
6 A:Spider-Man 2.75
7 A:Spider-Man 2.75
8 A:Dr.Strange. 2.75
9 thru 14 . . . . @2.75

CLASSIC CONAN
See: CONAN SAGA

CLASSIC X-MEN
See: X-MEN

CLAWS
Aug., 2006
1 JP,F:Wolverine & Black Cat 4.00
2 JP 4.00
3 JP 4.00

CLIVE BARKER'S
BOOK OF THE DAMNED
Epic, Nov., 1991
1 JBo,Hellraiser companion 5.00
2 MPa,Hellraiser Companion 5.00

CLIVE BARKER'S
HELLRAISER
Epic, 1989–93
1 BWr,DSp 7.00
2 . . . . 6.00
3 . . . . 6.50
4 . . . . 6.00
5 . . . . 6.00
6 . . . . 7.00
7 The Devil's Brigade #1 . . . . 7.00
8 The Devil's Brigade #2&3 . . . . . 7.00
9 The Devil's Brigade #4&5 . . . . . 7.00
10 The Devil's Brigade #6&7
    foil Cover 7.00
11 The Devil's Brigade #8&9 . . . . . 6.00
12 The Devil's Brigade #10-12 . . . . 6.00
13 MMi,RH,Devil's Brigade #13 . . . . 6.00
14 The Devil's Brigade #14 . . . . . . 6.00
15 The Devil's Brigade #15 . . . . . . 6.00
16 E:Devil's Brigade 6.00
17 BHa,DR,The Harrowing 10.00
18 O:Harrowers 6.00
19 A:Harrowers 6.00
20 NGa(s),DMc,Last Laugh. 9.00
Dark Holiday Spec.#1 (1992) 6.00
Spring Slaughter Spec.#1 (1994). . . 7.00
Summer Spec.#1 (1992) 6.00

CLOAK & DAGGER
(Limited Series) Oct., 1983
1 RL,TA,I:Det.O'Reilly,
    Father Delgado 3.00
2 RL,TA,V:Duane Hellman 3.00
3 RL,TA,V:Street Gang 3.00
4 RL,TA,O:Cloak & Dagger, ... 3.00

CLOAK & DAGGER
[1st Regular Series], July, 1985
1 RL,Pornography. 3.00
2 RL,Dagger's mother 2.50

3 RL,A:Spider-Man 2.50
4 RL,Secret Wars II 2.50
5 RL,I:Mayhem 2.50
6 RL,A:Mayhem 2.50
7 RL,A:Mayhem 2.50
8 TA, Drugs. 2.50
9 AAd,TA,A:Mayhem. 2.75
10 BBI,TA,V:Dr. Doom 2.50
11 BBI,TA,Last Issue 2.50

[Mutant Misadventures of]
CLOAK & DAGGER
[2nd Regular Series]
Oct., 1988

1 CR(i),A:X-Factor 3.00
2 CR(i),C:X-Factor,V:Gromitz 2.50
3 SW(i),JLe(c),A:Gromitz 2.50
4 TA(i),Inferno,R:Mayhem 2.50
5 TA(i),R:Mayhem 2.50
6 TA(i),A:Mayhem. 2.50
7 A:Crimson Daffodil,V:Ecstacy . . . 2.50
8 Acts of Vengeance prelude 2.50
9 Acts of Vengeance. 2.50
10 Acts of Vengeance,X-Force
 name used,Dr.Doom 2.50
11 . . . . 2.50
12 A:Dr.Doom. 2.50
13 A:Dr.Doom. 2.50
14 & 15 RL . . . . @2.50
16 RL,A:Spider-Man 2.50
17 A:Spider-Man, ... 2.50
18 Inf.Gauntlet X-over,
 A:Spider-Man, Ghost Rider 2.50
19 O:Cloak & Dagger,final issue . . . 2.50
GN Predator and Prey 15.00

A CLUELESS VALENTINE
1 characters from movie, 48pg. . . . 2.50

CODENAME: GENETIX
1993
1 PGa,A:Wolverine 3.00
2 PGa,V:Prime EvilA:Wolverine . . . 3.00
3 . . . . 3.00
4 A:Wolverine,Ka-Zar 3.00

CODE OF HONOR
1996
1 (of 4) CDi,TnS,I:Jeff Piper,
 fully painted 6.00
2 thru 4 CDi, ... @6.00

CODE NAME: SPITFIRE
See: SPITFIRE AND
THE TROUBLESHOOTERS

COLOSSUS
Aug., 1997
1-shot BRa,Colossus & Meggan
 V:Arcade, 48pg 3.50

COLOSSUS:
GOD'S COUNTRY
PF V:Cold Warriors 7.00

COMBAT
Marvel Atlas, June, 1952
1 JMn,War Stories, Bare
 Bayonets 350.00
2 RH, Break Thru,(Dedicated to
 US Infantry) 200.00
3 JMn(c) 150.00
4 BK 160.00
5 thru 10 . . . . @150.00
11 April, 1953. . . . . 200.00

COMBAT CASEY
See: WAR COMBAT

Combat Kelly #12
© Marvel Entertainment Group

COMBAT KELLY AND
THE DEADLY DOZEN
Marvel Atlas, Nov., 1951
1 RH,Korean War Stories 375.00
2 Big Push 200.00
3 The Volunteer 175.00
4 JMn,V:Communists 175.00
5 JMn,OW,V:Communists 175.00
6 V:Communists 175.00
7 JMn,V:Communists 175.00
8 JMn,Death to the Reds 175.00
9 . . . . 175.00
10 JMn(c). 175.00
11 . . . . 150.00
12 thru 16. . . . . @150.00
17 A:Combat Casey. 175.00
18 A:Battle Brady 125.00
19 V:Communists 125.00
20 V:Communists 125.00
21 Transvestite Cover 75.00
22 thru 40 . . . . @100.00
41 thru 44 Aug., 1957 . . . . @100.00

COMBAT KELLY
June, 1972
1 JM, Stop the Luftwaffe 40.00
2 The Big Breakout. 20.00
3 O:Combat Kelly 25.00
4 Mutiny,A:Sgt.Fury and the
 Howling Commandoes 25.00
5 Escape or Die 20.00
6 The Fortress of Doom 20.00
7 Nun Hostage,V:Nazis 20.00
8 V:Nazis. 20.00
9 Oct., 1973 . . . . 20.00

COMBAT ZONE
Jan., 2005
1 (of 5) DJu,G.I.s in Iraq 3.00
2 DJu 3.00
3 DJu,Hellfires to Avoid Damnation 3.00
4 and 5 . . . . @3.00

COMEDY COMICS
Marvel Timely, 1942
9 . . . . 4,400.00
10 . . . . 3,500.00
11 . . . . 750.00
12 . . . . 250.00
13 Funny animal 250.00
14 Super Rabbit. 750.00
15 . . . . 200.00
16 . . . . 200.00

17 . . . . 200.00
18 . . . . 200.00
19 . . . . 200.00
20 . . . . 200.00
21 thru 32 . . . . @150.00
33 HK 200.00
34 BW 300.00
Becomes:

MARGIE COMICS
Marvel Comics, 1946
35 thru 39 Glamour Girl . . . . . . @250.00
40 . . . . 200.00
41 thru 49 . . . . @225.00
Becomes:

RENO BROWNE
Marvel Comics, 1950
50 Photo(c); Western babe 400.00
51 Photo(c); 350.00
52 Photo(c); 350.00

COMEDY COMICS
Marvel Animirth 1948–49
1 HK, Romance,F:Hedy, Millie,
 Tessie 425.00
2 . . . . 200.00
3 . . . . 200.00
4 HK, 'Hey Look'. 225.00
5 . . . . 125.00
6 . . . . 125.00
7 . . . . 125.00
8 . . . . 125.00
9 . . . . 125.00
10 . . . . 125.00

COMET MAN
Feb., 1987
1 BSz(c),I:Comet Man 2.50
2 BSz(c),A:Mr.Fantastic 2.50
3 BSz(c),A:Hulk 2.50
4 BSz(c),A:Fantistic Four 2.50
5 BSz(c),A:Fantastic Four. 2.50
6 BSz(c),Last issue, July,1987 . . . . 2.50

COMIC CAPERS
Marvel Comics, 1944
1 Funny animal, Super Rabbit . . 350.00
2 . . . . 200.00
3 . . . . 150.00
4 . . . . 150.00
5 . . . . 150.00
6 . . . . 150.00

COMICS FOR KIDS
Marvel Timely, 1945
1 Funny animal. 300.00
2 . . . . 300.00

COMIX BOOK
(black & white magazine) 1974
1 BW. 40.00
2 BW 30.00
3 . . . . 25.00
4 & 5 . . . . @30.00

COMIX ZONE
1 video game tie-in 2.50
2 video game tie-in 2.50

COMMANDO
ADVENTURES
Marvel Atlas, June, 1957
1 Seek, Find and Destroy 200.00
2 MD, Hit 'em and Hit 'em
 Hard, Aug.,1957 . . . . 125.00

COMPLETE COMICS
See: AMAZING COMICS

MARVEL

Complete Mystery #4
© *Marvel Entertainment Group*

COMPLETE MYSTERY
Aug., 1948
1 Seven Dead Men 650.00
2 Jigsaw of Doom. 500.00
3 Fear in the Night 500.00
4 A Squealer Dies Fast. 500.00
Becomes:

TRUE COMPLETE MYSTERY
1949
5 Rice Mancini,
  The Deadly Dude 325.00
6 Ph(c),Frame-up that Failed . . . 250.00
7 Ph(c),Caught 250.00
8 Ph(c),The Downfall of Mr.
  Anderson, Oct., 1949 . . . . . 250.00

CONAN
1995–96
1 Pit Fighter 3.00
2 LHa,Hyborean tortue factory . . . 3.00
3 V:Cannibals 3.00
4 LHa,JP,Rune Conan Prelude. . . 3.00
5 LHa,V:yeti 3.00
6 LHa, the plague 3.00
7 LHa,BBI,V:The Iron Man 3.00
8 thru 11 . . . . @3.00

CONAN: DEATH COVERED IN GOLD
July, 1999
1 (of 3) RTs 3.00
2 RTs. 3.00
3 RTs,JB,concl. 3.00

CONAN THE ADVENTURER
1994–95
1 RT(s),RK,Red Foil(c) 3.00
2 RT(s),RK 2.50
3 RT(s),RK 2.50
4 thru 14 . . . . @2.50

CONAN THE BARBARIAN
Oct., 1970
1 BWS/DA,O:Conan,A:Kull. 350.00
2 BWS/SB,Lair o/t Beast-Men . . 125.00
3 BWS,SB,Grey God Passes . . . 225.00
4 BWS,SB,Tower o/t Elephant . . 100.00
5 BWS,Zukala's Daughter 100.00

6 BWS,SB,Devil Wings Over
  Shadizar 75.00
7 BWS,SB,DA,C:Thoth-Amon,
  I:Set 75.00
8 BWS,TS,TP,Keepers o/t Crypt. . 75.00
9 BWS,SB,Garden of Fear 75.00
10 BWS,SB,JSe,Beware Wrath of
  Anu;BU:Kull. 100.00
11 BWS,SB,Talons of Thak 100.00
12 BWS,GK,Dweller in the Dark,
  Blood of the Dragon B.U. . . . 75.00
13 BWS,SB,Web o/t Spider-God . . 75.00
14 BWS,SB,Green Empress of
  Melnibone 75.00
15 BWS,SB 75.00
16 BWS,Frost Giant's Daughter . . 60.00
17 GK,Gods of Bal-Sagoth,
  A:Fafnir 35.00
18 GK,DA,Thing in the Temple,
  A:Fafnir 35.00
19 BWS,DA,Hawks from
  the Sea 60.00
20 BWS,DA,Black Hound of
  Vengeance,A:Fafnir 60.00
21 BWS,CR,VM,DA,SB, Monster
  of the Monoliths. 45.00
22 BWS,DA,rep.Conan #1. . . . . . 50.00
23 BWS,DA,Shadow of the
  Vulture,I:Red Sonja 75.00
24 BWS,Song of Red Sonja 75.00
25 JB,SB,JSe,Mirrors of Kharam
  Akkad,A:Kull 25.00
26 JB,Hour of the Griffin 20.00
27 JB,Blood of Bel-Hissar 20.00
28 JB,Moon of Zembabwei 20.00
29 JB,Two Against Turan 20.00
30 JB,The Hand of Nergal 20.00
31 JB,Shadow in the Tomb 15.00
32 JB,Flame Winds of Lost Khitai . 15.00
33 JB,Death & 7 Wizards 15.00
34 JB,Temptress in the Tower
  of Flame 15.00
35 JB,Hell-Spawn of Kara-Shehr . 15.00
36 JB,Beware of Hyrkanians
  bearing Gifts 15.00
37 NA,Curse of the Golden Skull. . 30.00
38 JB,Warrior & Were-Woman . . . 12.00
39 JB,Dragon from the
  Inland Sea 12.00
40 RB,Fiend from Forgotten City. . 12.00
41 JB,Garden of Death & Life . . . 15.00
42 JB,Night of the Gargoyle 15.00
43 JB,Tower o/Blood,A:RedSonja . 15.00
44 JB,Flame&Fiend,A:RedSonja . . 15.00
45 JB,NA,Last Ballad of
  Laza-Lanti 12.00
46 JB,NA,JSt,Curse of the
  Conjurer. 12.00
47 JB,DA,Goblins in the
  Moonlight 12.00
48 JB,DG,DA,Rats Dance at Raven
  gard,BU:Red Sonja 12.00
49 JB,DG,Wolf-Woman 12.00
50 JB,DG,Dweller in the Pool . . . 12.00
51 JB,DG,Man Born of Demon . . . 8.00
52 JB,TP,Altar and the Scorpion . . 8.00
53 JB,FS,Brothers of the Blade . . . 8.00
54 JB,TP,Oracle of Ophir 8.00
55 JB,TP,Shadow on the Land . . . 8.00
56 JB,High Tower in the Mist 8.00
57 MP,Incident in Argos 8.00
58 JB,Queen o/tBlackCoast,
  2nd A:Belit. 10.00
59 JB,Ballad of Belit,O:Belit. 7.00
60 JB,Riders o/t River Dragons . . . 7.00
61 JB,She-Pirate,I:Amra 7.00
62 JB,Lord of the Lions,O:Amra . . 7.00
63 JB,Death Among Ruins,
  V&D:Amra 7.00
64 JSon,AM,rep.Savage Tales#5 . 7.00
65 JB,Fiend o/tFeatheredSerpent . 7.00

Conan The Barbarian #11
© *Marvel Entertainment Group*

66 JB,Daggers & Death Gods,
  C:Red Sonja 6.00
67 JB,Talons of the Man-Tiger,
  A:Red Sonja 6.00
68 JB,Of Once & Future Kings,
  V:KingKull,A:Belit,Red Sonja. . . 6.00
69 VM,Demon Out of the Deep . . . 6.00
70 JB,City in the Storm 6.00
71 JB,Secret of Ashtoreth 6.00
72 JB,Vengeance in Asgalun 6.00
73 JB,..In the Well of Skelos 6.00
74 JB,Battle at the Black Walls
  C:Thoth-Amon 6.00
75 JB,Hawk-Riders of Harakht . . . 7.00
76 JB,Swordless in Stygia 7.00
77 JB,When Giants Walk
  the Earth 7.00
78 JB,rep.Savage Sword #1,
  A:Red Sonja 7.00
79 HC,Lost Valley of Iskander 7.00
80 HC,Trial By Combat 6.00
81 HC,The Eye of the Serpent 5.00
82 HC,The Sorceress o/t Swamp . . 5.00
83 HC,The Dance of the Skull 5.00
84 JB,Two Against the Hawk-City,
  I:Zula 5.00
85 JB,Of Swordsmen & Sorcerers,
  O:Zulu 5.00
86 JB,Devourer of the Dead 5.00
87 TD, rep. Savage Sword #3. . . . 5.00
88 JB,Queen and the Corsairs . . . 5.00
89 JB,Sword & the Serpent,
  A:Thoth-Amon 5.00
90 JB,Diadem of the Giant-Kings . 5.00
91 JB,Savage Doings in Shem . . . 5.00
92 JB,The Thing in the Crypt. 5.00
93 JB,Of Rage & Revenge 5.00
94 JB,BeastKing ofAbombi,L:Zulu . 5.00
95 JB,The Return of Amra 5.00
96 JB,Long Night of Fang
  & Talon,pt.1 . . . . 5.00
97 JB,Long Night of Fang
  & Talon,pt.2 . . . . 5.00
98 JB,Sea-Woman 5.00
99 JB,Devil Crabs o/t Dark Cliffs . . 5.00
100 JB,Death on the Black Coast,
  D:Belit (double size) 7.00
101 JB,The Devil has many Legs . . 3.00
102 JB,The Men Who
  Drink Blood. 3.00
103 JB,Bride of the Vampire 3.00
104 JB,The Vale of Lost Women . . 3.00
105 JB,Whispering Shadows 3.00
106 JB,Chaos in Kush 3.00

107 JB,Demon of the Night 3.00
108 JB,Moon-Eaters of Darfar 3.00
109 JB,Sons of the Bear God 3.00
110 JB,Beward the Bear of Heaven 3.00
111 JB,Cimmerian Against a City. . . 3.00
112 JB,Buryat Besieged 3.00
113 JB,A Devil in the Family 3.00
114 JB,The Shadow of the Beast . . 3.00
115 JB,A War of Wizards, A:Red
    Sonja Double size 10th Anniv.
    (L:Roy Thomas script) 4.00
116 JB,NA,Crawler in the Mist. 5.00
117 JB,Corridor of Mullah-Kajar. . . . 3.00
118 JB,Valley of Forever Night 3.00
119 JB,Voice of One Long Gone . . . 3.00
120 JB,The Hand of Erlik. 3.00
121 JB,BMc,Price of Perfection. . . . 3.00
122 JB,BMc,The City Where Time
    Stood Still. 3.00
123 JB,BMc,Horror Beneath the
    Hills 3.00
124 JB,BMc,the Eternity War. 3.00
125 JB,BMc,the Witches ofNexxx . 3.00
126 JB,BMc,Blood Red Eye
    of Truth 3.00
127 GK,Snow Haired Woman
    of the Wastes 3.00
128 GK,And Life Sprang Forth
    From These 3.00
129 GK,The Creation Quest 3.00
130 GK,The Quest Ends 3.00
131 GK,The Ring of Rhax 3.00
132 GK,Games of Gharn. 3.00
133 GK,The Witch of Windsor. 3.00
134 GK,A Hitch in Time 3.00
135 MS,JRu,Forest of the Night . . . 3.00
136 JB,The River of Death 3.00
137 AA,Titans Gambit 3.00
138 VM,Isle of the Dead 3.00
139 VM,In the Lair of
    the Damned. 3.00
140 JB,Spider Isle 3.00
141 JB,The Web Tightens 3.00
142 JB,The Maze,the Man,
    the Monster 3.00
143 JB,Life Among the Dead. 3.00
144 JB,The Blade & the Beast 3.00
145 Son of Cimmeria. 3.00
146 JB,Night o/t Three Sisters. 3.00
147 JB,Tower of Mitra 3.00
148 JB,The Plague of Forlek. 3.00
149 JB,Deathmark. 3.00
150 JB,Tower of Flame 3.00
151 JB,Vale of Death 3.00
152 JB,Dark Blade of
    Jergal Zadh 3.00
153 JB,Bird Men of Akah Ma'at. . . . 3.00
154 JB,the Man-Bats of
    Ur-Xanarrh. 3.00
155 JB,SL,The Anger of Conan. . . . 3.00
156 JB,The Curse 3.00
157 JB,The Wizard 3.00
158 JB,Night of the Wolf 3.00
159 JB,Cauldron of the Doomed . . . 3.00
160 Veil of Darkness 3.00
161 JB,House of Skulls,A:Fafnir . . . 3.00
162 JB,Destroyer in the Flame,
    A:Fafnir 3.00
163 JB,Cavern of the Vines of
    Doom,A:Fafnir 3.00
164 The Jeweled Sword of Tem . . . 3.00
165 JB,V:Nadine 3.00
166 JB,Gl,Blood o/t Titan,A:Fafnir . . 3.00
167 JB,Creature From Time's
    Dawn,A:Fafnir 3.00
168 JB,Bird Woman & the Beast. . . 3.00
169 JB,Tomb of the Scarlet Mage . . 3.00
170 JB,Dominion of the Dead,
    A&D:Fafnir 3.00
171 JB,Barbarian Death Song. 3.00
172 JB,Reavers in Borderland. 3.00
173 JB,Honor Among Thieves. 3.00

174 JB,V:Tetra 3.00
175 JB,V:Spectre ofDeath 3.00
176 JB,Argos Rain. 2.50
177 JB,Nostume 2.50
178 JB,A:Tetra,Well of Souls 2.50
179 JB,End of all there is,A:Kiev . . . 2.50
180 JBV:AnitRenrut 2.50
181 JB,V:KingMaddoc II 2.50
182 JB,V:King of Shem 2.50
183 JB,V:Imhotep 2.50
184 JB,V:Madoc. 2.50
185 JB,R:Tetra. 2.50
186 JB,The Crimson Brotherhood. . 2.50
187 JB,V:Council of Seven 2.50
188 JB,V:Devourer-Souls 2.50
189 JB,V:Devourer-Souls 2.50
190 JB,Devourer-Souls 2.50
191 Deliverance. 2.50
192 JB,V:TheKeeper 2.50
193 Devourer-Souls. 2.50
194 V:Devourer-Souls 2.50
195 Blood of Ages 2.50
196 V:Beast 2.50
197 A:Red Sonja 2.50
198 A:Red Sonja 2.50
199 O:Kaleb. 2.50
200 JB,D.sizeV:Dev-Souls. 5.00
201 NKu,Gl,Thulsa Doom 2.50
202 . . . . 2.50
203 V:Thulsa Doom 2.50
204 VS,Gl,A:Red Sonja,I:Strakkus . 2.50
205 A:Red Sonja 2.50
206 VS,Gl,Heku trilogy,pt.1 . . . . . . 2.50
207 VS,Gl,Heku,pt.2,O:Kote 2.50
208 VS,Gl,Heku,pt.3 . . . . 2.50
209 VS,Gl,Heku epilogue 2.50
210 VS,Gl,V:Sevante 2.50
211 VS,Gl,V:Sevante 2.50
212 EC,Gl 2.50
213 V:Ghamud Assassins 2.50
214 AA 2.50
215 VS,AA,Conan Enslaved 2.50
216 V:Blade of Zed 2.50
217 JLe(c),V:Blade of Zed 2.50
218 JLe(c),V:Picts 2.50
219 JLe(c),V:Forgotten Beasts 2.50
220 Conan the Pirate. 2.50
221 Conan the Pirate. 2.50
222 AA,DP,Revenge 2.50
223 AA,Religious Cult 2.50
224 AA,Cannibalism. 2.50
225 AA,Conan Blinded. 2.50
226 AA,Quest for Mystic Jewel . . . 2.50
227 AA,Mystic Jewel,pt.2 . . . . 2.50
228 AA,Cannibalism,pt.1 . . . . 2.50

Conan The Barbarian #154
© Marvel Entertainment Group

229 AA,Cannibalism,pt.2 . . . . 2.50
230 FS,SDr,Citadel,pt.1 . . . . 2.50
231 FS,DP,Citadel,pt.2. . . . . 2.50
232 RLm,Birth of Conan 3.00
233 RLm,DA,B:Conan as youth . . 2.50
234 RLm,DA 2.50
235 RLm,DA 2.50
236 RLm,DA 2.50
237 DA,V:Jormma. 2.50
238 DA,D:Conan 2.50
239 Conan Possessed 2.50
240 Conan Possessed. 2.50
241 TM(c),R:RoyThomasScript . . . 3.50
242 JLe(c),A:Red Sonja. 2.50
243 WPo(c),V:Zukala, ... 2.50
244 A:Red Sonja,Zula 2.50
245 A:Red Sonja,V:King
    of Vampires 2.50
246 A:Red Sonja,V:MistMonster . . 2.50
247 A:Red Sonja,Zula 2.50
248 V:Zulu 2.50
249 A:Red Sonja,Zula 2.50
250 A:RedSonja,Zula,V:Zug
    double size. 5.00
251 Cimmeria,V:Shumu Gorath. . . 3.00
252 ECh. 3.00
253 ECh,V:Kulan-Goth(X-Men
    Villain) 3.00
254 ECh,V:Shuma-Gorath (Dr.
    Strange Villain) 3.00
255 ECh,V:Shuma-Gorath 3.00
256 ECh,D:Nemedia's King 3.00
257 ECh,V:Queen Vammator 3.00
258 AA(i),A:Kulan Gath 3.00
259 V:Shuma-Gorath 3.00
260 AA(i),V:Queen Vammatar 3.00
261 V:Cult of the Death Goddess . . 3.00
262 V:The Panther. 3.00
263 V:Malaq 3.00
264 V:Kralic 3.00
265 V:Karlik 3.00
266 Conan the Renegade (adapt.) . 3.00
267 adapt.,pt.2 . . . . 3.00
268 adapt.,pt.3 . . . . 3.00
269 V:Agohoth,Prince Borin. 3.00
270 Devourer of the Dead 3.00
271 V:Devourer of Souls 3.00
272 V:Devourer 3.00
273 V:Purple Lotus 3.00
274 V:She-Bat 3.00
275 RTs(s),Last Issue cont. in
    Savage Sword of Conan 5.00
G-Size#1 GK,TS,Hour of the
    Dragon, inc.rep.Conan#3,
    I:Belit 25.00
G-Size#2 GK,TS,Conan Bound,
    inc. rep Conan #5 . . . . 12.00
G-Size#3 GK,TS,To Tarantia
    & the Tower,inc.rep.Conan#6 . . 8.00
G-Size#4,GK,FS, Swords of the
    South,inc.rep.Conan #7. . . . . . . 8.00
G-Size#5 rep.Conan #14,#15
    & Back-up story #12 . . . . 8.00
KingSz.#1 rep.Conan #2,#4. . . . . 13.00
Ann.#2 BWS,Phoenix on the Sword
    A:Thoth-Amon 10.00
Ann.#3 JB,HC,Mountain of
    the Moon God, B.U.Kull story . . 8.00
Ann.#4 JB,Return of the
    Conqueror,A:Zenobia 8.00
Ann.#5 JB,W:Conan/Zenobia 5.00
Ann.#6 GK,King of the
    Forgotten People. 5.00
Ann.#7 JB,Red Shadows
    & Black Kraken 4.00
Ann.#8 VM,Dark Night of the
    White Queen 4.00
Ann.#9 . . . . 4.00
Ann.#10 Scorched Earth
    (Conan #176 x-over) 4.00
Ann.#11 . . . . 4.00
Conan-Barbarian Movie Spec.#1. . . 3.00

MARVEL

MARVEL

Conan-Barbarian Movie Spec.#2 . . . 3.00
Conan-Destroyer Movie Spec.#1 . . . 3.00
Conan-Destroyer Movie Spec.#2 . . . 3.00
Red Nails Special Ed.BWS 4.00

CONAN: THE FLAME AND THE FIEND
June, 2000
1 (of 3) RTs,GI,V:Kulan Gath 3.00
2 RTs,GI,Bone Dragon 3.00
3 RTs,GI,concl. 3.00

CLASSIC CONAN
June, 1987
1 BWS,rep. 7.00
2 BWS,rep. 5.00
3 BWS,rep. 5.00
Becomes:

CONAN SAGA
1987
4 thru 10 rep. . . . . @3.50
11 thru 98 rep. . . . . @3.00

Conan Classics #10
© Marvel Entertainment Group

CONAN CLASSICS
1994–95
1 rep. Conan #1 . . . . 2.25
2 rep. Conan #2 . . . . 2.25
3 rep. Conan #3 . . . . 2.25
2 thru 11 rep. . . . . @2.25

CONAN/RUNE
1995
1 BWS,Conan Vs. Rune 3.50

CONAN
1997
1 CCt, ... 2.00
2 CCt,V:Sorcerer. 2.00
3 (of 3) CCt, ... 2.00

CONAN: RIVER OF BLOOD
April, 1998
1 (of 3) Valeria, vs. giant crocs 2.50
2 Caught in the middle of a war . . . 2.50
3 Lord of the Crocodiles, concl. . . . 2.50

CONAN THE BARBARIAN VS. THE LORD OF THE SPIDERS
Jan., 1998
1 (of 3) RTs,V:Harpagus 2.50
2 RTs, ... 2.50
3 RTs,V:Harpagus. 2.50

CONAN: THE RETURN OF STYRM
July, 1998
1 (of 3) V:Mecora 2.50
2 (of 3) V:Mecora 3.00
3 conclusion 3.00

CONAN: THE SCARLET SWORD
Oct., 1998
1 (of 3) RTs,V:Thun'da 3.00
2 RTs,A:Helliana 3.00
3 RTs,conclusion. 3.00

CONAN: THE USURPER
Oct., 1997
1 (of 3) CDi,KJ,Conan attacks
   Cimmeria? 2.50
2 CDi,KJ, ... 2.50
3 CDi,KJ, concl. 2.50

KING CONAN
March, 1980
1 JB,ECh,I:Conn,V:Thoth-Amon . . . 7.00
2 thru 19 . . . . @4.00
Becomes:

CONAN THE KING
1984
20 MS,The Prince is Dead. 4.00
21 thru 55 . . . . @3.00

CONAN THE SAVAGE
(B&W Magazine), 1995–96
1 New Series 3.00
2 thru 10 . . . . @3.00

CONEHEADS
1994
1 Based Saturday Night Live 2.25
2 There Goes the Neighborhood . . 2.25
3 In Paris. 2.25

CONSPIRACY
Dec., 1997
1 (of 2) DAn,Were the origins of
   Marvel's superheroes really a
   conspiracy, not an accident? . . . 3.00
2 DAn,concl. 3.00

CONTEST OF CHAMPIONS
June, 1982
1 JR2,Grandmaster vs. Mistress
   Death, A:Alpha Flight. 8.00
2 JR2,Grandmaster vs. Mistress
   Death, A:X-Men 7.00
3 JR2,D:Grandmaster, Rebirth
   Collector, A:X-Men 7.00

CONTEST OF CHAMPIONS II
July, 1999
1 (of 5) CCI,Marvel vs. Marvel 3.00
2 CCI,Atlas vs. Storm 3.00
3 CCI,super hero slugfest 3.00
4 CCI 3.00

5 CCI, conclusion 3.00

COPS: THE JOB
1992
1 MGo(c),V:Serial killer. 2.25
2 MGo(c). 2.25
3 MGo(c),V:Eviscerator. 2.25
4 MGo(c),D:Eviscerator,Nick 2.25

COSMIC POWERS
1994
1 RMz(s),RLm,JP,F:Thanos 2.75
2 RMz(s),JMr,F:Terrax 2.75
3 RMz(s),F:Jack of Hearts 2.75
4 RMz(s),RLm,F:Legacy 2.75
5 RMz(s),F&O:Morg 2.75
6 RMz(s),F&O:Tyrant 2.75

COSMIC POWERS UNLIMITED
1995–96
1 Surfer vs. Thanos 4.25
2 Jack of Hearts vs. Jakar 4.25
3 GWt,JB,F:Lunatik,64pg. 4.25
4 GWt,SEa,cont.StarMasters#3 . . 4.25
5 GWt,SEa,R:Captain Universe . . 4.25

COUNT DUCKULA
Star, Nov., 1988
1 O:CountDuckula,B:DangerMouse 4.00
2 A:Danger Mouse 3.00
3 thru 15 . . . . @3.00

COWBOY ACTION
See: WESTERN THRILLERS

COWBOY ROMANCES
Oct., 1949
1 Ph(c),Outlaw and the Lady . . . 300.00
2 Ph(c),William Holden/Mona
   Freeman,Streets of Laredo . . 250.00
3 Phc,Romance in
   Roaring Valley 175.00
Becomes:

YOUNG MEN
1950
4 A Kid Names Shorty. 250.00
5 Jaws of Death 200.00
6 Man-Size 200.00
7 The Last Laugh 200.00
8 Adventure stories continued . . 200.00
9 Draft Dodging story 200.00
10 JMn,US Draft Story 200.00
11 Adventure stories continued . . 200.00
12 JMn,B:On the Battlefield,
   inc.Spearhead 200.00
13 RH,Break-through 200.00
14 GC,RH,Fox Hole 200.00
15 GC,JMn,Battlefield stories
   cont 200.00
16 Sniper Patrol 200.00
17 Battlefield stories cont, ... 200.00
18 BEv,Warlord 200.00
19 BEv 200.00
20 BEv,E:On the Battlefield 200.00
21 B:Flash Foster and his High
   Gear Hot Shots 200.00
22 Screaming Tires 200.00
23 E:Flash Foster and his High
   Gear Hot Shots 200.00
24 BEv,B:Capt. America,Human
   Torch,Sub-Mariner,O:Capt.
   America,Red Skull 4,000.00
25 BEv,JR, Human Torch,Capt.
   America,Sub-Mariner 1,800.00
26 BEv,Human Torch, Capt.
   America,Sub Mariner 1,800.00

All comics prices listed are for *Near Mint* condition.

Young Men #28
© *Marvel Entertainment Group*

27 Bev, Human Torch/Toro
  V:Hypnotist 1,600.00
28 E:Human Torch, Capt.America,
  Sub Mariner,June, 1954 . . . 1,600.00

COWGIRL ROMANCES
See: DARING MYSTERY

COYOTE
Epic, June, 1983
1 SL, ... 3.00
2 SL 2.50
3 BG 2.50
4 thru 6 SL . . . . @2.50
7 SL,SD 2.50
8 SL 2.50
9 SL,SD 2.50
10 SL 2.50
11 FS,1st TM art,O:Slash 7.00
12 TM. 4.00
13 TM. 4.00
14 FS,TM,A:Badger 4.00
15 SL 3.00
16 SL,A:Reagan,Gorbachev 3.00

CRASH RYAN
Epic, Oct., 1984
1 War Story 2.25
2 thru 4 . . . . @2.25

CRAZY
Marvel Atlas, Dec., 1953
1 JMn,BEv,satire, Frank N.
  Steins Castle 450.00
2 JMn,BEv,Beast from 1000
  Fathoms. 300.00
3 JMn,BEv,RH,Madame Knock-
  wurst's Whacks Museum. . . . 250.00
4 JMn,BEv,DAv,I Love Lucy
  satire 250.00
5 JMn,BEv,Censorship satire . . 250.00
6 JMn,BEv,MD,satire 300.00
7 JMn,BEv,RH,satire,July, 1954 250.00

CRAZY
Feb., 1973–June, 1973
1 Not Brand Echh reps,
  Forbushman 35.00
2 Big,Batty Love & Hisses issue . 25.00
3 Stupor-Man,A:FantasticalFour. . 25.00

CREATURES ON
THE LOOSE
See: TOWER OF
SHADOWS

CREW
May, 2003
1 JoB,DaM,Big Trouble,pt.1 . . . . . . 2.50
2 thru 7 JoB,Big Trouble,pt.2–7 . @2.50

CRIME CAN'T WIN
See: KRAZY COMICS

CRIME CASES COMICS
Marvel Atlas, 1950–52
(Formerly: WILLIE COMICS)
(See: IDEAL)
1 (24) Police 250.00
2 (25) 200.00
3 (26) 150.00
4 (27) 150.00
5 . . . . 150.00
6 . . . . 150.00
7 . . . . 150.00
8 . . . . 150.00
9 . . . . 150.00
10 . . . . 150.00
11 . . . . 150.00
12 . . . . 150.00

CRIME EXPOSED
Marvel Atlas Comics, 1948–52
1 . . . . 450.00
2 . . . . 250.00
3 GT 150.00
4 GT 150.00
5 thru 7 . . . . @150.00
8 MMe(c). 175.00
9 . . . . 150.00
10 . . . . 150.00
11 JeR 175.00
12 BK,JeR 200.00
13 BK 200.00
14 . . . . 125.00

CRIMEFIGHTERS
April, 1948–Nov., 1949
1 Police Stories 350.00
2 Jewelry Robbery 200.00
3 The Nine Who Were Doomed,
  addiction 225.00
4 Human Beast at Bay 150.00

Crimefighters #1
© *Marvel Entertainment Group*

5 V:Gangsters 150.00
6 Pickpockets 150.00
7 True Cases, Crime Can't Win . 150.00
8 True Cases, Crime Can't Win . 150.00
9 Ph(c),It Happened at Night . . . 150.00
10 Ph(c),Killer at Large 150.00
Becomes:

CRIME FIGHTERS
ALWAYS WIN
Marvel Atlas, 1954–1955
11 JMn,V:Gangsters. 175.00
12 V:Gangsters 150.00
13 Clay Pidgeon 150.00

CRIME MUST LOSE!
Marvel Atlas, 1950
4 . . . . 250.00
5 . . . . 175.00
6 . . . . 175.00
7 . . . . 175.00
8 . . . . 175.00
9 JeR 200.00
10 . . . . 175.00
11 . . . . 175.00
12 . . . . 175.00

CRIMINAL
Icon, Oct., 2006
1 SeP 3.00
2 SeP 3.00
3 thru 10 . . . . @3.00

CRIMSON DYNAMO
Marvel Epic, June, 2003
1 high tech weapon 3.00
2 thru 6 . . . . @2.50

CRITICAL MASS
Epic, Jan.–July, 1990
1 KS,GM,BSzF:ShadowlineSaga . . 5.00
2 thru 7 . . . . @5.00

CRYPT OF SHADOWS
Jan., 1973
1 BW,RH,GK,Midnight on Black
  Mountain 40.00
2 GT,BEv,JMn,Monster at
  the Door. 30.00
3 Dead Man's Hand 25.00
4 CI,Secret in the Vault. 25.00
5 JM,The Graveyard Ghoul 25.00
6 BEv,GK,Don't Bury Me Deep. . . 30.00
7 JSt,The Haunting of Bluebeard . 30.00
8 How Deep my Grave 25.00
9 Beyond Death 25.00
10 A Scream in the Dark 25.00
11 The Ghouls in my Grave. 20.00
12 BP,Behind the Locked Door . . . 25.00
13 BEv,SD,Back From the Dead . . 25.00
14 The Thing that Creeps 20.00
15 My Coffin is Crowded 20.00
16 . . . . 20.00
17 In the Hands of Shandu 20.00
18 SD,Face of Fear 25.00
19 SD,Colossus that Challenged
  the World. 25.00
20 A Monster walks Among Us . . . 20.00
21 SD,Death Will Be Mine,
  Nov., 1975 . . . . 25.00

CUPID
Dec., 1949–March, 1950
1 Ph(c),Cora Dod's Amazing
  Decision. 250.00
2 Ph(c),BP,Bettie Page 500.00

MARVEL

CURSE OF THE WEIRD
1993–94
1 thru 4 SD,rep. 50's Sci-Fi 2.25

CUTTING EDGE
1995
1 WML,F:Hulk,Ghosts of the
    Future tie-in 3.25

CYBERSPACE 3000
1993
1 A:Dark Angel,Galactus,V:Badoon,
    Glow in the dark(c) 3.25
2 thru 11 . . . . @2.25

CYCLOPS
Aug., 2001
1 (of 4) MT,JP 2.75
2 MT,JP,I:Ulysses 2.75
3 MT,JP,in a savage land 2.75
4 MT,JP,V:Ulysses 2.75

DAILY BUGLE
B&W 1996
1 (of 3) KIK,GA 2.75
2 thru 3 KIK,GA . . . . @2.75

Dakota North #1
© Marvel Entertainment Group

DAKOTA NORTH
1986–87
1 (Now in Cage) 2.25
2 thru 5 . . . . @2.25

DAMAGE CONTROL
May, 1989
1 EC/BWi;A:Spider-Man 3.00
2 EC/BWi;A:Fant.Four 2.50
3 EC/BWi;A:Iron Man 2.50
4 EC/BWi;A:X-Men 2.50
[2nd Series], 1989–90
1 EC,A:Capt.America&Thor 3.00
2 EC,A:Punisher 2.50
3 EC 2.50
4 EC,Punisher 2.50
[3rd Series], 1991
1 Clean-up Crew Returns 2.50
2 A:Hulk,New Warriors 2.50
3 A:Avengers W.C.,Wonder Man,
    Silver Surfer 2.50
4 A:SilverSurfer & others 2.50

DANCES WITH DEMONS
Frontier 1993
1 CAd 3.50
2 CAd,V:Manitou 2.50
3 CAd,V:Manitou 2.50
4 CAd,last issue 2.50
5 Okay, there's more! 2.50
6 . . . . 2.50

DAREDEVIL
April, 1964
1 B:StL(s),JK(c),BEv,I&O:Daredevil,
    I:Karen Page,Foggy Nelson 6,000.00
2 JK(c),JO,V:Electro 1,500.00
3 JK(c),JO,I&O:The Owl 1,200.00
4 JK(c),JO,I&O:Killgrave 1,000.00
5 JK(c),WW,V:Masked Matador . . 800.00
6 WW,I&O Original Mr. Fear 500.00
7 WW,I:Red Costume,V:Namor 1,500.00
8 WW,I&O:Stiltman 350.00
9 WW(i),Killers Castle 350.00
10 WW(i),V:Catman 350.00
11 WW(i),R:Cat 250.00
12 JK,JR,2nd A:Ka-Zar 250.00
13 JK,JR,O:Ka-Zar 250.00
14 JR,If This Be Justice 250.00
15 JR,A:Ox 250.00
16 JR,A:Spider-Man,
    I:Masked Marauder 300.00
17 JR,A:Spider-Man 300.00
18 DON(s),JR,I:Gladiator 225.00
19 JR,V:Gladiator 150.00
20 JR(c),GC,V:Owl 150.00
21 GC,BEv,V:Owl 150.00
22 GC,V:Tri-man 150.00
23 GC,V:Tri-man 125.00
24 GC,A:Ka-Zar 160.00
25 GC,V:Leapfrog 150.00
26 GC,V:Stiltman 150.00
27 GC,Spider-Man 150.00
28 GC,V:Aliens 150.00
29 GC,V:The Boss 150.00
30 BEv(c),GC,A:Thor 150.00
31 GC,V:Cobra 100.00
32 GC,V:Cobra 100.00
33 GC,V:Beetle 100.00
34 BEv(c),GC,O:Beetle 100.00
35 BEv(c),GC,A:Susan Richards. 100.00
36 GC,A:FF 100.00
37 GC,V:Dr.Doom 100.00
38 GC,A:FF 100.00
39 GC,GT,V:Unholy Three 100.00
40 GC,V:Unholy Three 100.00
41 GC,D:Mike Murdock 85.00
42 GC,DA,I:Jester 85.00
43 JK(c),GC,A:Capt.America 85.00
44 JSo(c),GC,V:Jester 75.00
45 GC,V:Jester 75.00
46 GC,V:Jester 75.00
47 GC,'Brother Take My Hand' . . . 75.00
48 GC,V:Stiltman 75.00
49 GC,V:Robot,I:Starr Saxon 75.00
50 JR(c),BWS,JCr,V:Robot 85.00
51 B:RTs(s),BWS,V:Robot 85.00
52 BWS,JCr,A:Black Panther 85.00
53 GC,O:Daredevil 75.00
54 GC,V:Mr.Fear,A:Spidey 75.00
55 GC,V:Mr.Fear 50.00
56 GC,V:Death Head 50.00
57 GC,V:Death Head 50.00
58 GC,V:Stunt Master 50.00
59 GC,V:Torpedo 50.00
60 GC,V:Crime Wave 50.00
61 GC,V:Cobra 50.00
62 GC,O:Night Hawk 40.00
63 GC,V:Gladiator 40.00
64 GC,A:Stuntmaster 40.00
65 GC,V:BrotherBrimstone 40.00
66 GC,V:BrotherBrimstone 40.00
67 BEv(c),GC,Stiltman 40.00

Daredevil #20
© Marvel Entertainment Group

68 AC,V:Kragg Blackmailer,
    a:Bl.Panther,DD'sID Rev. 40.00
69 E:RTs(s),GC,V:Thunderbolts,
    A:Bl.Panther(DD's ID Rev) . . . 40.00
70 GC,V:Terrorists 40.00
71 RTs(s),GC,V:Terrorists 40.00
72 GyC(s),BEv,Tagak,V:Quother . . 40.00
73 GC,V:Zodiac 40.00
74 B:GyC(s),GC,I:Smasher 40.00
75 GC,V:El Condor 40.00
76 GC,TP,V:El Condor 40.00
77 GC,TP,V:Manbull 40.00
78 GC,TP,V:Manbull 40.00
79 GC,TP,V:Manbull 40.00
80 GK(c),GC,TP,V:Owl 40.00
81 GK(c),GC,JA,A:Black Widow . . 60.00
82 GK(c),GC,JA,V:Scorpion 30.00
83 JR(c),BWS,BEv,V:Mr.Hyde 35.00
84 GK(c),GC,Assassin 30.00
85 GK(c),GC,A:Black Widow 30.00
86 GC,TP,V:Ox 30.00
87 GC,TP,V:Electro 30.00
88 GK(c),GC,TP,O:Black Widow . . 30.00
89 GC,TP,A:Black Widow 30.00
90 E:StL(s),GK(c),GC,TP,V:Ox 30.00
91 GK(c),GC,TP,I:Mr. Fear III 30.00
92 GK(c),GC,TP,A:BlackPanther . . 30.00
93 GK(c),GC,TP,A:Black Widow . . 30.00
94 GK(c),GC,TP,V:Damon Dran . . 30.00
95 GK(c),GC,TP,V:Manbull 30.00
96 GK(c),GC,ECh,V:Manbull 30.00
97 GK(c),V:Dark Messiah 30.00
98 E:GyC(s),GC,ECh,V:Dark
    Messiah 30.00
99 B:SvG(s),JR(c),V:Hawkeye. . . . 30.00
100 GC,V:Angar the Screamer . . . 45.00
101 RB,A:Angar the Screamer . . . 20.00
102 A:Black Widow 20.00
103 JR(c),DH,A:Spider-Man 20.00
104 GK(c),DH,V:Kraven 20.00
105 DH,JSn,DP,C:Thanos 25.00
106 JR(c),DH,A:Black Widow 18.00
107 JSn(c),JB(i),A:Capt.Marvel . . . 18.00
108 K&R(c),PG(i),V:Beetle 18.00
109 GK(c),DH(i),V:Beetle 18.00
110 JR(c),GC,A:Thing,O:Nekra . . . 18.00
111 JM(i),I:Silver Samurai 20.00
112 GK(c),GC,V:Mandrill 18.00
113 JR(c),V:Gladiator 18.00
114 GK(c),I:Death Stalker 18.00
115 V:Death Stalker 18.00
116 GK(c),GC,V:Owl 18.00
117 E:SvG(s),K&R(c),V:Owl 18.00
118 JR(c),DH,I:Blackwing 18.00

119 GK(c),DH(i),V:Crusher 18.00
120 GK(c),V:Hydra,I:El Jaguar . . . 18.00
121 GK(c),A:Shield 15.00
122 GK(c),V:Blackwing 15.00
123 V:Silvermane,I:Jackhammer . . 15.00
124 B:MWn(s),GK(c),GC,KJ,
    I:Copperhead. 15.00
125 GK(c),KJ(i),V:Copperhead . . . 15.00
126 GK(c),KJ(i),D: 2nd Torpedo . . 15.00
127 GK(c),KJ(i),V:3rd Torpedo. . . . 15.00
128 GK(c),KJ(i),V:Death Stalker . . 15.00
129 KJ(i),V:Man Bull 15.00
130 KJ(i),V:Brother Zed 15.00
131 KJ(i),I&O:2nd Bullseye 100.00
132 KJ(i),V:Bullseye. 60.00
133 JM(i),GK(c),V:Jester 15.00
134 JM(i),V:Chameleon 15.00
135 JM(i),V:Jester 15.00
136 JB,JM,V:Jester 15.00
137 JB,V:Jester 15.00
138 JBy,A:Ghost Rider 20.00
139 SB,V:A Bomber. 15.00
140 SB,V:Gladiator 15.00
141 GC,Bullseye 35.00
142 GC,V:Cobra 15.00
143 E:MWn(s),GC,V:Cobra 15.00
144 GT,V:Manbull 15.00
145 GT,V:Owl. 15.00
146 GC,V:Bullseye. 40.00
147 GC,V:Killgrave 15.00
148 GC,V:Deathstalker 15.00
149 KI,V:Smasher 15.00
150 GC,KJ,I:Paladin 15.00
151 GC,Daredevil Unmasked 15.00
152 KJ,V:Paladin 15.00
153 GC,V:Cobra 15.00
154 GC,V:Mr. Hyde 15.00
155 V:Avengers 15.00
156 GC,V:Death Stalker. 15.00
157 GC,V:Death Stalker. 15.00
158 FM,V:Death Stalker. 125.00
159 FM,V:Bullseye 60.00
160 FM,Bullseye 50.00
161 FM,V:Bullseye 50.00
162 SD,JRu,`Requiem' 15.00
163 FM,V:Hulk,I:Ben Urich 30.00
164 FM,KJ,A:Avengers 30.00
165 FM,KJ,V:Dr.Octopus 25.00
166 FM,KJ,V:Gladiator. 25.00
167 FM,KJ,V:Mauler 25.00
168 FM,KJ,I&O:Elektra 150.00
169 FM,KJ,V:Bullseye 60.00
170 FM,KJ,V:Bullseye 25.00
171 FM,KJ,V:Bullseye 22.00
172 FM,KJ,V:Bullseye 22.00
173 FM,KJ,V:Gladiator. 22.00
174 FM,KJ,A:Gladiator 26.00
175 FM,KJ,A:Elektra,V:Hand 30.00
176 FM,KJ,A:Elektra 25.00
177 FM,KJ,A:Stick 30.00
178 FM,KJ,A:PowerMan&I.Fist . . 25.00
179 FM,KJ,V:Elektra 25.00
180 FM,KJ,V:Kingpin 25.00
181 FM,KJ,V:Bullseye,D:Elektra,
    A:Punisher. 42.00
182 FM,KJ,A:Punisher. 18.00
183 FM,KJ,V:PunisherDrug 18.00
184 FM,KJ,V:PunisherDrug 18.00
185 FM,KJ,V:King Pin 12.00
186 FM,KJ,V:Stiltman 12.00
187 FM,KJ,A:Stick 12.00
188 FM,KJ,A:Black Widow 12.00
189 FM,KJ,A:Stick,A:BlackWidow . 12.00
190 FM,KJ,R:Elektra 12.00
191 FM,TA,A:Bullseye 12.00
192 KJ,V:Kingpin 5.00
193 KJ,Betsy 5.00
194 KJ,V:Kingpin 5.00
195 KJ,Tarkington Brown. 5.00
196 KJ,A:Wolverine. 16.00
197 V:Bullseye. 5.00
198 V:Dark Wind 5.00

Daredevil #182
© Marvel Entertainment Group

199 V:Dark Wind 5.00
200 JBy(c),V:Bullseye 7.00
201 JBy(c),A:Black Widow 5.00
202 I:Micah Synn 5.00
203 JBy(c),I:Trump 5.00
204 BSz(c),V:Micah Synn 5.00
205 I:Gael 5.00
206 V:Micah Synn 5.00
207 BSz(c),A:Black Widow 5.00
208 Harlan Ellison 6.00
209 Harlan Ellison 6.00
210 DM,V:Micah Synn 5.00
211 DM,V:Micah Synn 5.00
212 DM,V:Micah Synn 5.00
213 DM,V:Micah Synn 5.00
214 DM,V:Micah Synn 5.00
215 DM,A:Two-Gun Kid 5.00
216 DM,V:Gael 5.00
217 BS(c),V:Gael 5.00
218 KP,V:Jester 5.00
219 FM,JB 6.00
220 DM,D:Heather Glenn 5.00
221 DM,Venice. 5.00
222 DM,A:Black Widow 5.00
223 DM,Secret Wars II 5.00
224 DM,V:Sunturion. 5.00
225 DM,V:Vulture. 5.00
226 FM(plot),V:Gladiator 5.00
227 FM,Kingpin,Kar.Page 10.00
228 FM,DM,V:Kingpin 8.00
229 FM,Kingpin,Turk 8.00
230 R:Matt's Mother 8.00
231 FM,DM,V:Kingpin 8.00
232 FM,V:Kingpin,Nuke 8.00
233 FM,Kingpin,Nuke,Capt.Am. . . 8.00
234 SD,KJ,V:Madcap. 5.00
235 SD,KJ,V:Mr. Hyde 5.00
236 BWS,A:Black Widow. 6.00
237 AW(i),V:Klaw 5.00
238 SB,SL,AAd(c)V:Sabretooth. . . 7.00
239 AAd(c),AW,GI(i),V:Rotgut . . . 5.00
240 AW,V:Rotgut 5.00
241 MZ(c),TM,V:Trixter 6.00
242 KP,V:Caviar Killer 5.00
243 AW,V:Nameless One 5.00
244 TD(i),V:Nameless One 5.00
245 TD(i),A:Black Panther 5.00
246 TD(i),V:Chance 5.00
247 KG,A:Black Widow 5.00
248 RL,AW,A:Wolverine,
    V:Bushwhacker. 7.00
249 RL,AW,V:Wolverine,
    Bushwhacker. 7.00
250 JR2,AW,I:Bullet 5.00

251 JR2,AW,V:Bullet 5.00
252 JR2,AW,Fall o/Mutants 6.00
253 JR2,AW,V:Kingpin. 5.00
254 JR2,AW,I:Typhoid Mary 13.00
255 JR2,AW,A:Kingpin,TMary 6.00
256 JR2,AW,A:Kingpin,TMary 6.00
257 JR2,AW,A:Punisher 10.00
258 RLm,V:Bengal. 6.00
259 JR2,AW,V:TyphoidMary 5.00
260 JR2,AW,V:T.Mary,K.pin 5.00
261 JR2,AW,HumanTorch 5.00
262 JR2,AW,Inferno. 5.00
263 JR2,AW,Inferno. 5.00
264 SD,AW,MM,V:The Owl 5.00
265 JR2,AW,Inferno. 5.00
266 JR2,AW,V:Mephisto. 5.00
267 JR2,AW,V:Bullet 5.00
268 JR2,AW,V:TheMob 5.00
269 JR2,AW,V:Pyro&Blob 5.00
270 JR2,AW,A:Spider-Man,
    I:Blackheart. 5.00
271 JR2,AW,I:Number9 . . . . 5.00
272 JR2,AW,I:Shotgun. 5.50
273 JR2,AW,V:Shotgun. 5.00
274 JR2,AW,V:Inhumans 5.00
275 JR2,AW,ActsOfVen.,V:Ultron . . 5.00
276 JR2,AW,ActsOfVen.,V:Ultorn . . 5.00
277 RL,AW,Vivian's Story 5.00
278 JR2,AW,V:Blackheart,
    A:Inhumans 5.00
279 JR2,AW,V:Mephisto,
    A:Inhumans 5.00
280 JR2,AW,V:Mephisto,
    A:Inhumans 5.00
281 JR2,AW,V:Mephisto,
    A:Inhumans 5.00
282 JR2,AW,V:Mephisto,
    A:Silver Surfer, Inhumans 5.00
283 MBa,AW,A:Captain America . . . 5.00
284 LW,AW,R:Bullseye 5.00
285 LW,AW,B:Bullseye
    become DD#1 . . . . 5.00
286 LW,AW,GCa,Fake
    Daredevil #2 . . . . 5.00
287 LW,AW,Fake Daredevil #3 . . . 5.00
288 LW,AW,A:Kingpin 5.00
289 LW,AW,A:Kingpin 5.00
290 LW,AW,E:Fake Daredevil 5.00
291 LW,AW,V:Bullet 5.00
292 LW,A:Punisher,V:Tombstone. . . 5.00
293 LW,A:Punisher,V:Tombstone. . . 5.00
294 LW,V:The Hand. 5.00
295 LW,V:The Hand,A:GhostRider. . 5.00
296 LW,AW,V:The Hand 5.00
297 B:DGC(s),LW,AW,B:Last Rites,
    V:Typhoid Mary,A:Kingpin 5.00
298 LW,AW,A:Nick Fury,Kingpin . . 5.00
299 LW,AW,A:Nick Fury,Kingpin . . . 5.00
300 LW,AW,E:Last Rites, ... 8.00
301 V:The Owl 5.00
302 V:The Owl. 5.00
303 V:The Owl. 5.00
304 AW,Non-action issue. 5.00
305 AW,A:Spider-Man 5.00
306 AW,A:Spider-Man 5.00
307 1st SMc DD,Dead Man's
    Hand #1,A:Nomad. 6.00
308 SMc,Dead Man's Hand #5,
    A:Punisher,V:Silvermane. 5.00
309 SMc,Dead Man's Hand#7,
    A:Nomad,Punisher 5.00
310 SMc,Inf.War,V:Calipso 5.00
311 SMc,V:Calypso 5.00
312 Firefighting issue. 5.00
313 SMc,V:Pyromaniac 5.00
314 SMc,V:Mr.Fear,I:Shock 5.00
315 SMc,V:Mr.Fear. 5.00
316 Goes Underground 5.00
317 SMc,Comedy Issue. 5.00
318 SMc,V:Taskmaster 5.00
319 SMc,Fall from Grace Prologue,
    A:Silver Sable,Garrett,Hand . . . 7.00

MARVEL

319a 2nd Printing 3.00
320 SMc,B:Fall from Grace,
   V:Crippler,S.Sable,A:Stone 7.00
321 SMc,N:Daredevil,A:Venom,
   Garret, V:Hellspawn,Glow
   in the Dark(c). 6.00
321a Newsstand Ed. 5.00
322 SMc,A:Venom,Garret,Siege . . . 4.00
323 SMc,V:Venom,A:Siege,Garret,
   I:Erynys 4.00
324 SMc,A:Garret,R:Elektra,
   A:Stone, Morbius 4.00
325 SMc,E:Fall from Grace, A:Garret,
   Siege,Elektra,Morbius,V:Hand,
   D:Hellspawn,Double size 4.00
326 SMc,B:Tree of Knowledge,
   I:Killobyte,A:Capt.America 3.00
327 E:DGC(s),SMc,A:Capt.Amer. . . 3.00
328 GtW(s),V:Wirehead,A:Captain
   America,S.Sable,Wild Pack. . . . 3.00
329 B:DGC(s),SMc,A:Captain
   America,S.Sable,Iron Fist. 3.00
330 SMc,A:Gambit. 3.00
331 SMc,A:Captain America,
   VLHydra. 3.00
332 A:Captain America,Gambit . . . 3.00
333 TGb,GWt. 3.00
334 TGb,GWt. 3.00
335 . . . . 3.00
336 . . . . 3.00
337 V:Kingpin,A:Blackwulf 3.00
338 Wages of Sin,pt.1 . . . . 3.00
339 Wages of Sin,pt.2 . . . . 3.00
340 R:Kingpin 3.00
341 Kingpin 3.00
342 DGc,KP,V:Kingpin 3.00
343 Without Costume 3.00
344 Identity Crisis,pt.1 . . . . 3.00
345 Identity Crisis,pt.2 . . . . 3.00
346 V:Sir 3.00
347 V:mystery man 3.00
348 In NY City 3.50
349 Retreats to the Chaste 3.50
350 Double size 4.00
351 . . . . 3.00
352 Return of Matt Murdock 3.00
353 KK,CNr,A:Mr. Hyde 3.00
354 KK,CNr,A:Spider-Man 3.00
355 KK,CNr,A:Pyro 3.00
356 KK,CNr, ... 3.00
357 KK,CNr, ... 3.00
358 KK,CNr,MRy,A:Mysterio 3.00
359 KK,CNr,A:Absorbing Man 3.00
360 KK,CNr,MRy,V:Onslaught 3.00
361 KK,CNr,MRy,A:Black Widow . . 3.00
362 KK,CNr,Romance 3.00
363 KK,GC,CaS,V:Insomnia 3.00
364 KK,CNr,MRy,V:Insomnia 3.00
365 CNr,MRy,V:Mr. Fear,
   A:Molten Man 3.00
366 GC,V:Gladiator 3.00
367 GC,V:Gladiator, concl. 3.00
368 GC,A:Black Widow and Omega
   Red 3.00
369 AOI,V:Soviet Super Soldiers . . . 3.00
370 GC,Black Widow, concl. 3.00
371 AOI,Matt Murdock & Karen
   Page's relationship 3.00
372 AOI,Killers after Karen Page. . . 3.00
373 AOI,V:The 3. . . . . 3.00
374 AOI,V:Mr. Fear 3.00
375 AOI,RL,V:Mr. Fear,double size . 4.00
376 SLo,CHm,Daredevil deep
   undercover. 3.00
377 SLo,TMo,SHa,Flying Blind,pt.2 3.00
378 SLo,TMo,SHa,Flying Blind,pt.3 . 3.00
379 SLo,CHm,Flying Blind,concl. . . 3.00
380 DGC,LW,RbC, V:Bullseye,Bush-
   wacker,Kingpin, double size . . . 5.00
Minus 1 Spec., GC, flashback 5.00
Ann.#1 GC 275.00
Ann.#2 reprints. 200.00

Ann.#3 reprints. 150.00
Ann.#4 (1976)GT,A:Black
   Panther,Namor 7.00
Ann.#5 (1989)MBa,JLe,JR2,KJ,
   WPo,AM,Atlantis Attacks,
   A:Spider-Man. 5.00
Ann.#6 TS,Lifeform#2,A:Typhoid
   Mary. 5.00
Ann.#7 JG,JBr,Von Strucker
   Gambit,pt.1,A:Nick Fury 5.00
Ann.#8 Sys.Bytes#2,A:Deathlok . . 5.00
Ann.#9 MPa,I:Devourer,w/card,tie-in
   to Fall From Grace 5.00
Ann.#10 I:Ghostmaker,A:Shang
   Chi, Elektra 4.00
G-Size #1 GK(c),reprints 12.00

Daredevil Vol. 2 #6
© Marvel Entertainment Group

DAREDEVIL
Sept., 1998

1 JP,JQ,F:Matt Murdock 14.00
1a Deluxe edition 10.00
2 JP,JQ,blind faith dilemma 10.00
2a variant JSC cover 10.00
3 JP,JQ,Guardian Devil,pt.3 . . . . . 6.00
4 JP,JQ,Guardian Devil,pt.4 . . . . . 6.00
5 JP,JQ,Guardian Devil,pt.5 . . . . . 6.00
5a Variant (c) 7.00
6 JP,JQ,Guardian Devil,pt.6 . . . . . 4.00
7 JP,JQ,Guardian Devil,pt.7 . . . . . 4.00
8 JP,JQ,Guardian Devil,concl. 4.00
8a signed 20.00
9 JP,JQ,DMk,V:Kingpin 4.00
9a signed 15.00
10 JP,JQ,DMk,I:Echo 4.00
11 JP,JQ,DMk,A:Kingpin 4.00
12 JP,JQ,DMk,V:Kingpin 4.00
13 JP,JQ,DMk,V:Kingpin 4.00
14 JQ,DMk,V:Kingpin. 5.00
15 JQ,DMk,V:Echo 4.00
16 BMB,DMk, ... 5.00
17 BMB,DMk,F:Ben Urich 5.00
18 BMB,DMk,F:Ben, Timmy 4.00
19 BMB,DMk,F:Ben, Timmy 5.00
20 40-page,BU:F:Spider-Man 5.00
21 A:Jester. 4.00
22 Matt Murdock vs. Daredevil . . . 4.00
23 Matt Murdock vs. Daredevil . . . 4.00
24 MPn,the trial begins 4.00
25 Playing to the Camera 4.00
26 BMB,V:Nitro 10.00
27 BMB,V:Silke,Kingpin 5.00
28 BMB,Elektra x-over,'Nuff Said . 5.00
29 BMB,Kingpin's Empire 5.00
30 BMB,Kingpin's Secrets 5.00
31 BMB,plot twist 5.00

32 BMB,Kingpin's Empire 7.00
33 BMB,F:Matt Murdock 4.00
34 BMB, anger's terms 3.00
35 BMB,V:Mr. Hyde 3.00
36 BMB,F:Luke Cage 3.00
37 BMB,F:Elektra. 3.00
38 BMB,Trial of White Tiger,pt.1 . . 3.00
39 BMB,Trial of White Tiger,pt.2 . . 3.00
40 BMB,Trial of the Century 4.00
41 BMB,Lowlife,pt.1 . . . . 4.00
42 BMB,Lowlife,pt.2. . . . . 3.00
43 BMB,Lowlife,pt.3 . . . . 3.00
44 BMB,Lowlife,pt.4. . . . . 3.00
45 BMB,Lowlife,concl. 3.00
46 BMB,Hardcore,pt.1 . . . . 3.00
47 BMB,Hardcore,pt.2 . . . . 3.00
48 BMB,Hardcore,pt.3 . . . . 3.00
49 BMB,Hardcore,pt.4 . . . . 3.00
50 BMB,Hardcore,pt.5 . . . . 5.00
51 DMk,R:Echo,pt.1 . . . . 3.00
52 DMk,V:Echo,pt.2. . . . . 3.00
53 DMk,V:Echo,pt.3 . . . . 3.00
54 DMk,V:Echo,pt.4,F:Wolverine . . . 3.00
55 DMk,Echo's vision quest. 3.00
56 BMB,New Kingpin 3.00
57 BMB,A:Spider-Man 3.00
58 BMB,King of Hell's Kitchen,pt.3 . 3.00
59 BMB,King of Hell's Kitchen,pt.4 . 3.00
60 BMB,King of Hell's Kitchen,pt.5 . 3.00
61 BMB,The Widow,pt.1 . . . . 3.00
62 BMB,The Widow,pt.2 . . . . 3.00
63 BMB,The Widow,pt.3 . . . . 3.00
64 BMB,The Widow,pt.4 . . . . 3.00
65 BMB,Anniversary Spec.,48-pg . . 4.00
66 BMB,Golden Age,pt.1 . . . . 3.00
67 BMB,Golden Age,pt.2 . . . . 3.00
68 BMB,Golden Age,pt.3 . . . . 3.00
69 BMB,Golden Age,pt.4 . . . . 3.00
70 BMB,Golden Age,pt.5 . . . . 3.00
71 BMB,Decalogue,pt.1 . . . . 3.00
72 BMB,Decalogue,pt.2. . . . . 3.00
73 BMB,Decalogue,pt.3 . . . . 3.00
74 BMB,Decalogue,pt.4 . . . . 3.00
75 BMB,Decalogue,pt.5, 48-pg. . . . 4.00
76 BMB,The Murdock Papers,pt.1 . 3.00
77 BMB,The Murdock Papers,pt.2 . . 3.00
78 BMB,The Murdock Papers,pt.3. . 3.00
79 BMB,The Murdock Papers,pt.4 . . 3.00
80 BMB, The Murdock Papers,pt.5 . 3.00
81 BMB 3.00
82 MLr,Devil in Cell Block D,36-pg . 3.50
83 MLr,Devil in Cell Block D 3.00
84 MLr,Devil in Cell Block D 3.00
85 MLr,Devil in Cell Block D 3.00
86 MLr,Devil in Cell Block D 3.00
87 MLr,Devil in Cell Block D 3.00
88 MLr,Secret Life of Foggy Nelson 3.00
89 MLr,Devil Takes A Ride, pt.1 . . . . 3.00
90 MLr,Devil Takes A Ride, pt.2 . . . 3.00
91 MLr,Devil Takes A Ride, pt.3 . . . 3.00
92 MLr 3.00
93 MLr,Devil Takes A Ride 3.00
94 JR(c), Blind Love 3.00
95 MLr,To the Devil, His Due 3.00
96 MLr,To the Devil, His Due 3.00
97 MLr,To the Devil, His Due 3.00
98 MLr,To the Devil, His Due 3.00
99 MLr,To the Devil, His Due 3.00
100 MLr,Without Fear, 104-pgs. . . . 4.00
100a variant (c) 4.00
100b variant wraparound (c) 4.00
101 MLr,Without Fear, pt.2 . . . . 3.00
102 MLr,V:Mr. Fear 3.00
Ann. #1 . . . . 4.00
Spec.Daredevil vs. Punisher 3.50
Spec. Daredevil/Deadpool, BCh, JHo,
   Two annuals in one,48pg.(1997)5.00
Spec. Daredevil/Batman, DGC,
   SMc, 48pg. (1997) 6.00
Spec.#1 Daredevil (2000) 2.25
Spec. Daredevil Movie adapt. 3.50

MARVEL

DAREDEVIL: BATTLIN' JACK MURDOCK
June, 2007
1 . . . . 4.00
2 thru 4 . . . . @4.00

DAREDEVIL: FATHER
April, 2004
1 (of 5) JQ,DaM 3.50
#1 Director's Cut. 3.00
2 thru 6 JQ . . . . @3.00

DAREDEVIL: THE MAN WITHOUT FEAR
1993–94
1 B:FM(s),JR2,AW,O:Daredevil,
  A:Stick,D:Daredevil's Father . . . 7.00
2 JR2,AW,A:Stick,Stone,Elektra . . 6.00
3 JR2,AW,A:Elektra,Kingpin 6.00
4 JR2,AW,A:Kingpin,I:Mickey 6.00
5 JR2,AW,A:Mickey,Last Issue . . . 6.00

DAREDEVIL: NINJA
Oct., 2000
1 (of 3) BMB,Stick. 5.00
2 BMB,V:Hand 5.00
3 BMB,concl. 5.00

DAREDEVIL: REDEMPTION
Feb., 2005
1 (of 6) Redemption Valley murder. 3.00
2 thru 6 BSz(c) . . . . @3.00

DAREDEVIL/SHI SHI/DAREDEVIL
Marvel/Crusade 1996
1 (Daredevil/Shi) TSg,AW,
  x-over,pt.1 . . . . 5.00
1 (Shi/Daredevil) x-over, pt.2 . . . . . 5.00

DAREDEVIL/SPIDER-MAN
Nov., 2000
1 (of 4) AxR,PJe, ... 4.00
2 AxR,PJe,Gladiator,Stilt-Man. 4.00
3 AxR,PJe,Owl,Copperhead 4.00
4 AxR,PJe,TP,concl. 4.00

DAREDEVIL: THE TARGET
Nov., 2002
1 (of 4) KSm,GF,V:Bullseye 3.50

DAREDEVIL VS. PUNISHER
July, 2005
1(of 6) DL,Means and Ends 3.00
2 DL,Means and End 3.00
3 DL 3.00
4 DL 3.00
5 DL 3.00
6 DL 3.00

DAREDEVIL: YELLOW
March, 2001
1 (of 6) JLb,TSe,O:Daredevil 10.00
2 JLb,TSe,Vengeance 7.00
3 JLb,TSe,F:Fantastic Four 7.00
4 JLb,TSe,V:Electro 7.00
5 JLb,TSe,V:Owl 7.00
6 JLb,TSe,last yellow costume . . . 7.00

Daring Mystery Comics #2
© Marvel Entertainment Group

DARING MYSTERY COMICS
Marvel Timely, Jan., 1940
1 ASh(c),JSm,O:Fiery Mask,
  A:Monako John Steele,Doc Doyle,
  Flash FosterBarney Mullen,
  Sea Rover, Bondage (c). . 40,000.00
2 ASh(c),JSm,O:Phantom Bullet
  A:Zephyr Jones & K4,Laughing
  Mask Mr.E,B:Trojak 25,000.00
3 ASh(c),JSm,A:Phantom
  Reporter,Marvex,Breeze
  Barton, B:Purple Mask . . 10,000.00
4 ASh(c),A:G-Man Ace,K4,
  Monako,Marvex,E:Purple
  Mask,B:Whirlwind Carter . . 6,000.00
5 ASh(c),JSm,B:Falcon,A:Fiery
  Mask,K4, Little Hercules,
  Bondage(c) 6,000.00
6 S&K,O:Marvel Boy,A:Fiery
  Mask, Flying Fame,Dynaman,
  Stuporman,E:Trojak 9,000.00
7 ASh(c),S&K,O:Blue Diamond,
  A:The Fin, Challenger,Captain
  Daring, Silver Scorpion,
  Thunderer. 6,000.00
8 S&K,O:Citizen V,A:Thunderer,
  Fin Silver Scorpion,Captain
  Daring Blue Diamond 5,000.00
Becomes:

DARING COMICS
1944
9 ASh(c),B:Human Torch,Toro,
  Sub Mariner 2,500.00
10 ASh(c),A;The Angel 2,000.00
11 ASh(c),A:The Destroyer 2,000.00
12 E:Human Torch,Toro,Sub-
  Mariner, Fall, 1945 . . . . . . 2,000.00
Becomes:

JEANIE COMICS
1947
13 B:Jeanie,Queen of the
  Teens Mitzi,Willie. 300.00
14 Baseball(c) 200.00
15 Schoolbus(c). 200.00
16 Swimsuit(c) 225.00
17 HK,Fancy Dress Party(c),
  Hey Look 175.00
18 HK,Jeanie's Date(c), Hey
  Look. 150.00
19 Ice-Boat(c),Hey Look 175.00
20 Jukebox(c) 150.00
21 . . . . 150.00
22 HK,Hey Look. 175.00

23 thru 25. . . . . @150.00
26 . . . . 150.00
27 E:Jeanie,Queen of Teens 150.00
Becomes:

COWGIRL ROMANCES
1950
28 Ph(c),Mona Freeman/MacDonald
  Carey,Copper Canyon. 300.00

DARK ANGEL
See: HELL'S ANGEL

DARK CRYSTAL
April, 1983
1 movie adaption 3.00
2 movie adaption,May, 1983. . . . . . 3.00

DARK GUARD
1993–94
1 A:All UK Heroes. 3.00
2 A:All UK Heroes. 2.25
3 V:Leader,MyS-Tech 2.25
4 V:MyS-Tech 2.25
5 . . . . 2.25
6 and 7 . . . . @2.25

DARKHAWK
March, 1991
1 MM,I&O:Darkhawk,
  A:Hobgoblin. 5.00
2 MM,A:Spider-Man,V:Hobgoblin . . 3.00
3 MM,A:Spider-Man,V:Hobgoblin . . 3.00
4 MM,I:Savage Steel 3.00
5 MM,I:Portal 3.00
6 MM,A:Cap.Am,D.D.,Portal,
  V:U-Foes 3.00
7 MM,I:Lodestone 2.50
8 MM,V:Lodestone 2.50
9 MM,A:Punisher,V:Savage Steel. . 2.50
10 MM,A&N:Tombstone 2.50
11 MM,V:Tombstone 2.50
12 MM,V:Tombstone,R:Dark
  Hawks'Father. 2.50
13 MM,V:Venom 3.00
14 MM,V:Venom,D:Dark
  Hawks Father 3.00
15 thru 24 . . . . @2.25
25 MM,O:Darkhawk,V:Evilhawk,
  Holo-graphx(c). 3.50
26 thru 49 . . . . @2.25
50 V:Overhawk 3.00

Darkhawk #20
© Marvel Entertainment Group

Ann.#1 MM,Assault on ArmorCity . . 3.00
Ann.#2 GC,AW,I:Dreamkiller,
   w/Trading card. 3.00
Ann.#3 I:Damek. 3.00

DARKHOLD
1992–94
1 RCa,I:Redeemers,Polybagged
   w/poster,A:Gh.Rider,Blaze. 3.00
2 RCa,R:Modred. 2.50
3 thru 16 . . . . @2.25

DARK MAN
MOVIE ADAPTION
Sept., 1990
1 BH/MT/TD 3.00
2 BH/TD 2.50
3 BH/TD,final issue 2.50

DARKMAN
Sept., 1990
1 JS,R:Darkman 4.50
2 JS,V:Witchfinder 3.00
3 JS,Witchfinder 3.00
4 JS,V:Dr.West 3.00
5 JS,Durant. 3.00
6 JS,V:Durant 3.00

DARK TOWER:
THE GUNSLINGER BORN
Feb., 2007
1 (of 7) PDd(s),JaL. 5.00
1a JaL variant sketch (c) 75.00
1b JQ variant (c) 10.00
1c 2nd printing 4.00
2 PDd(s),JaL. 7.00
2a variant (c). 10.00
3 PDd(s),JaL. 4.00
3a variant (c) 10.00
4 PDd(s),JaL. 4.00
4a variant JaL sketch (c) 35.00
4b variant (c). 15.00
5 PDd(s),JaL. 4.00
5a variant JaL sketch (c) 30.00
5b variant (c). 15.00
6 . . . . 4.00
6a variant (c) 10.00
7 PDd(s),JaL. 4.00
7a variant JaL sketch (c) 20.00
7b variant (c). 10.00
Spec. Gunslinger's Guidebook 4.00
Spec. Sketchbook (2006) freebee . . 1.00

A DATE WITH MILLIE
Marvel Atlas, Oct., 1956
[1st Series]
1 . . . . 350.00
2 . . . . 200.00
3 thru 7 . . . . @150.00
[2nd Series], Oct., 1959
1 . . . . 200.00
2 thru 7 . . . . @150.00
Becomes:

LIFE WITH MILLIE
1960
8 . . . . 100.00
9 & 10 . . . . @60.00
11 thru 20 . . . . @50.00
Becomes:

MODELING WITH MILLIE
1963
21 . . . . 100.00
22 thru 54 June, 1967 . . . . @50.00

A DATE WITH PATSY
Sept., 1957
1 A:Patsy Walker. 150.00

DAUGHTERS
OF THE DRAGON
Jan., 2006
1 JP. 3.00
2 thru 6 JP. . . . . @3.00
Spec. #1 Deadly Hands, 80-pg.. . . 4.00

DAYDREAMERS
Aug., 1997
1 (of 3) JMD,MEg,HSm 2.75
2 JMD,MEg,HSm, ... 2.75
3 JMD,TDz,MEg,HSm,concl. 2.75

DAZZLER
March, 1981
1 AA,JR2,A:X-Men,Spm,
   O:Dazzler. 5.00
2 WS,JR2,AA,X-Men,A:SpM. 3.00
3 JR2,Dr.Doom 3.00
4 FS,Dr.Doom 3.00
5 FS,I:Blue Shield 3.00
6 FS,Hulk 3.00
7 FS,Hulk 3.00
8 FS,Quasar 3.00
9 FS,D:Klaw 3.00
10 FS,Galactus 3.00
11 FS,Galactus 3.00
12 FS,The Light That Failed 3.00
13 FS,V:Grapplers 3.00
14 FS,She Hulk 3.00
15 FS,BSz,Spider Women 3.00
16 FS,BSz,Enchantress. 3.00
17 FS,Angel,V:Doc Octopus 3.00
18 FS,BSz,A:Fantastic Four,Angel,
   V:Absorbing Man 3.00
19 FS,Blue Bolt,V:Absorbing Man . . 3.00
20 FS,V:Jazz and Horn 3.00
21 FS,A:Avengers,F.F.,C:X-Men,
   (double size) 3.00
22 FS,V:Rogue,Mystique 4.00
23 FS,V:Rogue,A:Powerman,
   Iron Fist 3.00
24 FS,V:Rogue,A:Powerman,
   Iron Fist 4.00
25 FS,`The Jagged Edge' 3.00
26 FS,Lois London 3.00
27 FS,Fugitive 3.50
28 FS,V:Rogue 4.00
29 FS,Roman Nekoboh 3.00
30 FS,Moves to California 3.00

Dazzler #42
© Marvel Entertainment Group

31 FS,The Last Wave 3.00
32 FS,A:Inhumans. 3.00
33 Chiller 3.50
34 FS,Disappearance 3.00
35 FS,V:Racine Ramjets 3.00
36 JBy(c),FS,V:Tatterdemalion 3.00
37 JBy(c),FS 3.00
38 PC,JG,X-Men 5.00
39 PC,JG,Caught in the grip of
   death 3.00
40 PC,JG,Secret Wars II 3.50
41 PC,JG,A:Beast 3.50
42 PC,JG,A:Beast,last issue 3.50

DEADLIEST HEROES
OF KUNG FU
Summer, 1975
1 Magazine size 30.00

DEADLINE
April, 2002
1 (of 4) GyD, F:Katherine Farrell
   Daily Bugle reporter. 3.25
2 thru 3 GyD,The Judge . . . . @3.25
4 GyD,finale 3.25

DEADLY FOES
OF SPIDER-MAN
May, 1991
1 AM,KGa,V:Sinister Syndicate . . . 4.00
2 AM,Boomerang on Trial. 3.00
3 AM,Deadly Foes Split 3.00
4 AM,Conclusion. 3.00

DEADLY HANDS
OF KUNG FU
April, 1974
1 NA(c),JSa,JSon,O:Sons of
   the Tiger, B:Shang-Chi,
   Bruce Lee Pin-up 75.00
2 NA(c),JSa 50.00
3 NA(c),JSon,A:Sons of the Tiger. 40.00
4 NA(Bruce Lee)(c),JSon,Bruce
   Lee biography 40.00
5 BWS,PG 35.00
6 GP,JSon,A:Sons of the Tiger . . 35.00
7 GP,JSon,A:Sons of the Tiger . . 40.00
8 GP,JSon,A:Sons of the Tiger . . 30.00
9 GP,JSon,A:Sons of the Tiger . . 30.00
10 GP,JSon,A:Sons of the Tiger . . 35.00
11 NA(c),GP,JSon,A:Sons
   of the Tiger 30.00
12 NA(c),GP,JSon,A:Sons
   of the Tiger 30.00
13 GP,JSon,A:Sons of the Tiger . . 30.00
14 NA(c),GP,HC,JSon,A:Sons
   of the Tiger 90.00
15 JS,PG,JSn,,Annual #1 . . . . . . 30.00
16 JSn,A:Sons of the Tiger 30.00
17 NA(c),JSn,KG,A:Sons
   of the Tiger 30.00
18 JSn,A:Sons of the Tiger 30.00
19 JSn,I:White Tiger 35.00
20 GP,O:White Tiger 30.00
21 . . . . 30.00
22 KG,C:Jack of Hearts 30.00
23 GK,Jack of Hearts. 35.00
24 KG,Ironfist 35.00
25 I:Shimaru 35.00
26 . . . . 35.00
27 . . . . 30.00
28 Bruce Lee Special 100.00
29 Ironfist vs. Shang Chi 35.00
30 Swordquest 30.00
31 JSon, Jack of Hearts 30.00
32 MR,JSon,Daughters of the
   Dragon. 30.00
33 MR,Feb., 1977 . . . . 32.00
Spec. Album Ed.,NA, Sum.,1974. . 35.00

MARVEL

DEAD OF NIGHT
Dec., 1973–Aug., 1975
1 JSt,Horror reprints,A Haunted
  House is not a Home. 35.00
2 BEv(c),House that Fear Built . . 20.00
3 They Lurk Below. 20.00
4 Warewolf Beware. 20.00
5 Deep Down 20.00
6 Jack the Ripper 20.00
7 SD,The Thirteenth Floor 20.00
8 Midnight Brings Dark Madness 20.00
9 Deathride 20.00
10 SD,I Dream of Doom 20.00
11 GK/BWr(c),I:Scarecrow, Fires
  of Rebirth,Fires of Death 40.00

DEADPOOL
1993
1 B:FaN(s),JMd,MFm(i),
  V:Slayback,Nyko 7.00
2 JMd,MFm(i),V:Black Tom
  Cassidy,Juggernaut. 5.00
3 JMd,MFm(i),A:Slayback,
  Makeshift,Rive,A:Slayback 5.00
4 E:FaN(s),JMd,MFm(i),
  A:Slayback,Kane 5.00
[2nd Limited Series], 1994
1 A:Banshee,Syrin,Juggernaut
  Black Tom 4.00
2 A:Banshee,Syrin,V:Juggernaut . . 4.00
3 A:Syrin,Juggernaut 4.00
4 Final issue 4.00

DEADPOOL
1996
1 NMa,V:Sasquatch,48pg, ... 12.00
2 NMa,A:Copycat. 7.00
3 NMa,A:Siryn. 6.00
4 NMa,Will Hulk cure him?. 6.00
5 NMa,A:Siryn,T-Ray 6.00
6 NMa,I: 6.00
7 AaL,A:Typhoid Mary. 6.00
8 NMa, cont. from Daredevil/
  Deadpool '97,A:Gerry 6.00
9 NMa, new villain 6.00
10 NMa,A:Great Lake Avengers . . . 5.00
11 NMa,Fall through time, A:Alfred . 7.00
12 NMa,Typhoid Mary, Zoe
  Cullodon & Siryn return. 6.00
13 NMa,V:T-Ray 5.00
14 WMc,Deal of a Lifetime 5.00

Deadpool #5
© Marvel Entertainment Group

15 WMc,A:Landau, Luckman
  & Lake. 5.00
16 WMc, in middle east 5.00
17 WMc, Landau, Luckman
  & Lake's plan. 5.00
18 WMc,V:Ajax 5.00
19 WMc,more secrets of blind Al. . . 5.00
20 Cosmic Messiah 5.00
21 . . . . 6.00
22 WMc,A:Cable 6.00
23 WMc,Dead Reckoning,pt.1
  48-page 6.00
24 WMc,Dead Reckoning,pt.2 . . . . 6.00
25 WMc,Dead Reckoning,pt.3 . . . . 6.00
26 Dead Reckoning,aftermath 6.00
27 V:A.I.M. concl. 6.00
28 R:Weasel 4.00
29 V:Bullseye. 4.00
30 A:Mercedes,T-Ray 4.00
31 V:T-Ray. 5.00
32 V:T-Ray,A:Mercedes 5.00
33 V:T-Ray 7.00
34 CPr,Chapter Pt.1. . . . . 3.00
35 CPr 3.00
36 CPr 3.00
37 CPr,Chapter X,Addendum 3.00
38 CPr,F:Taskmaster 3.00
39 CPr,F:Taskmaster 3.00
40 CPr,space station 3.00
41 CPr,V:Dirty Wolf 3.00
42 V:Humbug 3.00
43 CPr,JCf,V:Rasputin. 3.00
44 CPr,JCf,CatTrap,pt.1,x-over . . . 3.00
45 CPr,JCf,Constrictor 3.00
46 JJu,JP,PC,CruelSummer,pt.1 . . 3.00
47 JP,PC,CruelSummer,pt.2 . . . . . 3.00
48 JP,PC,CruelSummer,pt.3 . . . . . 3.00
49 JP,dating? 3.00
50 AAd,JP,DaR,I:Kid Deadpool . . 3.00
51 JP,DaR,F:Kid Deadpool 3.00
52 JP,AWi,ALa,V:Mercy Sisters . . . 3.00
53 JP,AWi,ALa,V:Mercy Sisters . . . 3.00
54 JP,V:Punisher 12.00
55 JP,V:Punisher, round two 10.00
56 F:Siryn. 3.00
57 JHo,BWS(c),Agent of Weapon X 3.00
58 JHo,BWS(c),Agent of Weapon X 3.00
59 JHo,BWS(c),Agent of Weapon X 3.00
60 JHo,BWS(c),Agent of Weapon X 3.00
61 Funeral For a Freak 1. . . . . 2.50
62 Funeral For a Freak 2. . . . . 2.50
63 Funeral For a Freak 3. . . . . 2.50
64 Funeral For a Freak 4. . . . . 2.50
65 Did Deadpool survive 3.50
66 steal from Rhino? 3.50
67 R:Dazzler 3.50
68 V:Black Swan, insanity 3.50
69 V:Black Swan 3.50
Ann. '98 BCh(c) F:Deadpool & Death,
  48pg. 3.00
Minus 1 Spec., ALo, flashback,
  O:Deadpool 2.50
Spec. Deadpool Team-Up,2
  Deadpools,F:Widdle Wade . . . 3.00
Spec. Baby's First Deadpool Book . 3.00
Spec. Encyclopedia Deadpoolica . . 3.00

DEADPOOL/GLI
July, 2007
Summer Fun Spectacular 4.00

DEATH3
1993
1 I:Death Metal,Death Wreck 3.00
2 V:Ghost Rider 2.50
3 A:Hulk,Cable,Storm,Thing 2.50
4 Last issue. 2.50

DEATHLOK
[Limited Series], July, 1990
1 JC,SW,I:Michael Colins
  (2nd Deathlok). 5.00
2 JC,SW,V:Wajler. 4.00
3 DCw,SW,V:Cyberants 4.00
4 DCw,SW,V:Sunfire,final issue . . 4.00
[Regular Series], 1991–94
1 DCw,MM,V:Warwolf. 3.00
2 DCw,MM,A:Dr.Doom,Machine
  Man,Forge. 2.50
3 DCw,MM,V:Dr.Doom,
  A:Mr.Fantastic 2.50
4 DCw,MM,A:X-Men,F.F.,Vision,
  O:Mechadoom. 2.50
5 DCw,MM,V:Mechadoom,
  A:X-Men,Fantastic Four. 2.50
6 DCw,MM,A:Punisher,
  V:Silvermane 2.50
7 DCw,MM,A:Punisher,
  V:Silvermane 2.50
8 A:Main Frame,Ben Jacobs 2.00
9 DCw,MM,A:Ghost Rider,
  V:Nightmare. 2.50
10 DCw,MM,A:GhR,V:Nightmare. . . 2.50
11 DCw,MM,V:Moses Magnum . . . 2.50
12 DCw,MM,Biohazard Agenda . . . 2.50
13 DCw,MM,Biohazard Agenda . . . 2.50
14 DCw,MM,Biohazard Agenda . . . 2.50
15 DCw,MM,Biohazard Agenda . . . 2.50
16 DCw,MM,Inf.War,V:Evilok 2.50
17 WMc,MM,B:Cyberwar. 2.50
18 WMc,A:Silver Sable 2.50
18a Newstand Ed. 2.50
19 SMc,Cyberwar#3 . . . . 3.50
20 SMc,Cyberwar#4 . . . . 2.50
21 E:Cyberwar,A:Cold Blood
  Nick Fury. 2.50
22 V:MosesMagnum,A:Bl.Panther. . 2.50
23 A:Bl.Panther,V:Phreak,Stroke . . 2.50
24 V:MosesMagnum,A:Bl.Panther. . 2.50
25 WMc,V:MosesMagnum,A:Black
  Panther,holo-grafx(c). 3.50
26 V:Hobogoblin. 2.50
27 R:Siege 2.50
28 Infinty Crusade 2.50
29 Inner Fears 2.50
30 KHd,V:Hydra 2.50
31 GWt(s),KoK,B:Cyberstrike,
  R:1st Deathlok. 2.50
32 GWt(s),KoK,A:Siege 2.50
33 GWt(s),KoK,V:Justice Peace . . . 2.50
34 GWt(s),KoK,E:Cyberstrike,V:Justice
  Peace,final issue 2.50

Deathlok #30
© Marvel Entertainment Group

MARVEL

MARVEL

Ann.#1 JG,I:Timestream 3.00
Ann.#2 I:Tracer,w/card 3.25

DEATHLOK
July, 1999
1 JoC,JQ&JaL(c),Marvel Tech 2.50
2 JoC,A:Nick Fury 2.50
2a variant cover 2.50
3 JoC,I:Billy Bailey 2.50
4 JoC,R:Clown 2.50
5 JoC,I:Jack Truman 2.50
6 JoC, ... 2.50
7 JoC,V:Serpent Society 2.50
8 JoC,Nick Fury 2.50
9 JoC,V:Ringmaster 2.50
10 JoC,V:Clown 2.50
11 JoC,V:Clown 2.50

DEATHLOK: DETOUR
Jan., 2004
1 (of 4) DaR 3.00
2 thru 4 DaR . . . . @3.00

DEATHLOK SPECIAL
1991
1 Rep.Mini Series 2.50
2 Rep.Mini Series 2.50
3 Rep.Mini Series 2.50
4 Rep.Mini Series, final issue 2.50

DEATH METAL
Marvel UK, 1994
1 JRe,I:Argon,C:Alpha Flight 2.50
2 JRe,V:Alpha Flight 2.50
3 JRe,I:Soulslug 2.50
4 Re,Last Issue 2.50

DEATH METAL
VS. GENETIX
Marvel UK, 1993–94
1 PaD,w/card 3.00
2 PaD,w/card 3.00

DEATH'S HEAD
Marvel UK, Dec., 1988
1 V:Backbreaker 5.00
2 A:Dragons Claws 4.00
3 . . . . 4.00
4 V:Plague Dog 3.00
5 V:Big Shot 3.00

Death's Head #1
© Marvel Entertainment Group

---

6 V:Big Shot 3.00
7 & 8 . . . . @3.00
9 A:Fantastic Four 3.50
10 A:Iron Man 3.50

DEATH'S HEAD
[Limited Series]
1 A:`Old' Death's Head 2.50

DEATH'S HEAD II
Marvel UK, March, 1992
[Limited Series]
1 LSh,I:2nd Death's Head,
  D:1st Death's Head 4.00
1a 2nd printing,Silver 2.50
2 LSh,A:Fantastic Four 3.00
2a 2nd printing,Silver 3.00
3 LSh,I:Tuck 3.50
4 LSh,A:Wolverine,Spider-Man,
  Punisher 3.50

[Regular Series], 1992
1 LSh,A:X-Men,I:Wraithchilde 3.00
2 LSh,A:X-Men 2.50
3 LSh,A:X-Men,V:Raptors 2.50
4 LSh,A:X-Men,V:Wraithchilde 2.50
5 V:UnDeath's Head II,
  A:Warheads 2.50
6 R:Tuck,V:Major Oak 2.50
7 V:Major Oak 2.50
8 V:Wizard Methinx 2.50
9 BHi,V:Cybernetic Centaurs 2.50
10 DBw,A:Necker 2.50
11 SCy,R:Charnel 2.50
12 DAn(s),SvL,V:Charnel 2.50
13 SvL,A:Liger 2.50
14 SvL,Brain Dead Cold,Blue
  Foil(c). 3.25
15 SvL,V:Duplicates 2.50
16 SvL,DAn 2.50
17 SvL,DAn 2.50
18 SvL,DAn 2.50
Spec. Gold Ed. LSh(a&s) 4.00

DEATH'S HEAD II/DIE CUT
Marvel UK, 1993
1 I:Die Cut 3.25
2 O:Die Cut 2.50

DEATH'S HEAD II/
KILLPOWER: BATTLETIDE
[1st Limited Series]
1 GSr,A:Wolverine 2.50
2 thru 4 GSr,A:Wolverine . . . . . @2.50

[2nd Limited Series]
1 A:Hulk 3.25
2 V:Hulk 2.50
3 A:Hulk 2.50
4 last issue 2.50

DEATH-WRECK
Marvel UK, 1994
1 A:Death's Head II 2.50
2 V:Gangsters 2.50
3 A:Dr.Necker 2.50
4 last issue 2.50

DECIMATION:
HOUSE OF M
Nov., 2005
Spec. The Day After 4.00

DEEP, THE
Nov., 1977
1 CI,Movie Adaption 15.00

Defenders #65
© Marvel Entertainment Group

DEFENDERS
Aug., 1972
1 SB,I&D:Necrodames 200.00
2 SB,V:Calizuma 100.00
3 GK(c),SB,JM,V:UndyingOne . . 65.00
4 SB,FMc,Bl.Knight,V:Valkyrie . . 65.00
5 SB,FMc,D:Omegatron 65.00
6 SB,FMc,V:Cyrus Black 40.00
7 SB,FBe,A:Hawkeye 35.00
8 SB,FBe,Avengers,SilverSurfer . 45.00
9 SB,FMc,Avengers 45.00
10 SB,FBe,Thor vs. Hulk 125.00
11 SB,FBe,A:Avengers 40.00
12 SB,JA,Xemnu 20.00
13 GK(c),SB,KJ,J:Night Hawk . . . 20.00
14 SB,DGr,O:Hyperion 20.00
15 SB,KJ,A:Professor X,V:Magneto,
  Savage Land Mutates 25.00
16 GK(c),SB,Professor X,V:Magneto,
  Savage Land Mutates 25.00
17 SB,DGr,Power Man 12.00
18 GK(c),SB,DGr,A:Power Man . . 12.00
19 GK(c),SB,KJ,A:Power Man . . . 12.00
20 K&R(c),SB,A:Thing 12.00
21 GK(c),SB,O:Valkyrie 8.00
22 GK(c),SB,V:Sons o/t Serpent . 8.00
23 GK(c),SB,A:Yellow Jacket 8.00
24 GK(c),SB,BMc,A:Daredevil . . . 8.00
25 GK(c),SB,JA,A:Daredevil 8.00
26 K&R(c),SB,A:Guardians 10.00
27 K&R(c),SB,A:Guardians
  C:Starhawk 10.00
28 K&R(c),SB,A:Guardians
  I:Starhawk 10.00
29 K&R(c),SB,A:Guardians 10.00
30 JA(i),A:Wong 6.00
31 GK(c),SB,JM,Nighthawk 6.00
32 GK(c),SB,JM,O:Nighthawk 6.00
33 GK(c),SB,JM,V:Headmen 6.00
34 SB,JM,V:Nebulon 6.00
35 GK(c),SB,KJ,I:Red Guardian . . . 6.00
36 GK(c),SB,KJ,A:Red Guardian . . 12.00
37 GK(c),SB,KJ,J:Luke Cage 7.00
38 SB,KJ,V:Nebulon 12.00
39 SB,KJ,V:Felicia 5.00
40 SB,KJ,V:Assassin 5.00
41 KG,KJ,Nighthawk 5.00
42 KG,KJ,V:Rhino 5.00
43 KG,KJ,Cobalt Man,Egghead . . . 5.00
44 KG,KJ,I:Hellcat,V:Red Rajah . . . 5.00
45 KG,KJ,Valkyrie V:Hulk 5.00
46 KG,KJ,L:DrStrange,LukeCage . . 5.00
47 KG,KJ,Moon Knight 5.00
48 KG,A:Wonder Man 5.00

---

49 KG,O:Scorpio 5.00
50 KG,Zodiac,D:Scorpio. 5.00
51 KG,Moon Knight 5.00
52 KG,Hulk,V:Sub Mariner. 5.00
53 KG,DC,MG,TA,C&I:Lunatik 4.00
54 MG,Nigh Fury 4.00
55 CI,O:Red Guardian. 4.00
56 CI,KJ,Hellcat,V:Lunatik 4.00
57 DC,Ms.Marvel. 4.00
58 Return of Dr.Strange. 4.00
59 I:Belathauzer. 4.00
60 V:Vera Gemini. 4.00
61 Spider-Man,A:Lunatik 5.00
62 Hercules,C:Polaris 3.00
63 Mutli Heroes 3.00
64 Mutli Heroes 3.00
65 Red Guardian 3.00
66 JB,Valkyrie I 3.00
67 Valkryie II 3.00
68 HT,When Falls the Mountain . . . 3.00
69 HT,A:The Anything Man 3.00
70 HT,A:Lunatik 3.00
71 HT,O:Lunatik. 3.00
72 HT,V:Lunatik. 3.00
73 HT,Foolkiller,V:WizardKing 5.00
74 HT,Foolkiller,L:Nighthawk 5.00
75 HT,Foolkiller 4.00
76 HT,O:Omega. 3.00
77 HT,Moon Dragon. 3.00
78 HT,Yellow Jacket. 3.00
79 HT,Tunnel World 3.00
80 HT,DGr,Nighthawk 3.00
81 HT,Tunnel World 3.00
82 DP,JSt,Tunnel World. 3.00
83 DP,JSt,Tunnel World 3.00
84 DP,JSt,Black Panther 3.00
85 DP,JSt,Black Panther 3.00
86 DP,JSt,Black Panther 3.00
87 DP,JSt,V:Mutant Force 3.00
88 DP,JSt,Matt Mardock 3.00
89 DP,JSt,D:Hellcat's
 Mother, O:Mad-Dog. 3.00
90 DP,JSt,Daredevil 3.00
91 DP,JSt,Daredevil 3.00
92 DP,JSt,A:Eternity,
 Son of Satan 3.00
93 DP,JSt,Son of Satan 3.00
94 DP,JSt,I:Gargoyle 4.00
95 DP,JSt,V:Dracula,O:Gargoyle . . . 2.50
96 DP,JSt,Ghost Rider. 4.00
97 DP,JSt,False Messiah 2.50
98 DP,JSt,A:Man Thing 2.50
99 DP,JSt,Conflict 2.50
100 DP,JSt,DoubleSize,V:Satan . . 6.00
101 DP,JSt,Silver Surfer 4.00
102 DP,JSt,Nighthawk 2.50
103 DP,JSt,I:Null 2.50
104 DP,JSt,Devilslayer,J:Beast . . . 2.50
105 DP,JSt,V:Satan 2.50
106 DP,Daredevil,D:Nighthawk . . . 2.50
107 DP,JSt,Enchantress,A:D.D. . . . 2.50
108 DP,A:Enchantress. 2.50
109 DP,A:Spider-Man. 3.00
110 DP,A:Devilslayer. 2.50
111 DP,A:Hellcat. 2.50
112 DP,A:SquadronSupreme 2.50
113 DP,A:SquadronSupreme 2.50
114 DP,A:SquadronSupreme 2.50
115 DP,A:Submariner. 2.50
116 DP,Gargoyle 2.50
117 DP,Valkyrie 2.50
118 DP,V:Miracleman. 2.50
119 DP,V:Miracleman. 2.50
120 DP,V:Miracleman. 4.00
121 DP,V:Miracleman. 4.00
122 DP,A:Iceman 4.00
123 DP,I:Cloud,V:Secret Empire . . . 2.50
124 DP,V:Elf. 2.50
125 DP,New Line-up:Gargoyle,Moon
 dragon,Valkyrie,Iceman,Beast,
 Angel,W:Son of Satan & Hellcat
 I:Mad Dog 5.00

126 DP,A:Nick Fury 2.50
127 DP,V:Professor Power 2.50
128 DP,V:Professor Power 2.50
129 DP,V:Professor Power,New
 Mutants X-over 2.50
130 DP,V:Professor Power 2.50
131 DP,V:Walrus,A:Frogman. 2.50
132 DP,V:Spore Monster 2.50
133 DP,V:Spore Monster 2.50
134 DP,I:Manslaughter. 2.50
135 DP,V:Blowtorch Brand. 2.50
136 DP,V:Gargoyle. 2.50
137 DP,V:Gargoyle. 2.50
138 DP,O:Moondragon. 2.50
139 DP,A:Red Wolf,V:Trolls 2.50
140 DP,V:Asgardian Trolls 2.50
141 DP,All Flesh is Grass 2.50
142 DP,V:M.O.N.S.T.E.R. 2.50
143 DP,I:Andromeda,Runner 2.50
144 DP,V:Moondragon 2.50
145 DP,V:Moondragon 2.50
146 DP,Cloud. 2.50
147 DP,A:Andromeda,I:Interloper . . 2.50
148 DP,A:Nick Fury 2.50
149 DP,V:Manslaughter,O:Cloud . . . 2.50
150 DP,O:Cloud,double-size 5.00
151 DP,A:Interloper 2.50
152 DP,Secret Wars II,D:Moon-
 dragon,Valkyrie,Gargoyle 5.00
G-Size#1 GK(c),JSn,AM,O:Hulk . . 22.00
G-Size#2 GK,KJ,Son of Satan . . . 15.00
G-Size#3 JSn,DA,JM,DN,A:D.D. . . 10.00
G-Size#4 GK(c),DH,A:YellowJack . 20.00
G-Size#5 K&R(c),DH,A:Guardians 25.00
Ann.#1 SB,KJ. 30.00

DEFENDERS
Jan., 2001
1 EL,KBk,KJ,48-page 6.00
2A EL,KBk,KJ, ... 3.00
2B variant AAd(c) 3.50
3 EL,KBk,KJ,V:Pluto 2.50
4 EL,KBk,KJ,V:Pluto 2.50
5 EL,KBk,KJ,A:Dr.Strange 2.50
6 EL,KBk,KJ,A:Red Raven 2.50
7 EL,KBk,KJ,A:Red Raven 2.50
8 EL,KBk,AG,V:Headmen 2.50
9 EL,KBk,RF,V:Headmen 2.50
10 EL,KBk,SB,V:Headmen 2.50
11 EL,KBk,SB,V:Attuma,DeepSix . . 2.50
12 EL,KBk,'Nuff Said,48-pg. 3.50
Spec.Day of the Defenders, mag. . . 3.50

DEFENDERS
July, 2005
1(of 5) KG,JMD 3.00
2 KG,Hulk vs. Mindless Ones. 3.00
3 KG,JMD 3.00
4 KG,JMD 3.00
5 KG 3.00

DEFENDERS OF
DYNATRON CITY
1992
1 FC,I:Defenders of Dynatron City
 (from video game & TV ser.) . . . 3.00
2 FC,O:Defender of D.City 3.00
3 FC,A:Dr Mayhem. 3.00
4 FC 3.00
5 FC,V:Intelligent Fleas 3.00
6 FC,V:Dr.Mayhem 3.00

DEFENDERS OF
THE EARTH
Jan., 1987—Sept., 1984
1 AS,Flash Gordon & Mandrake. . . 5.00
2 AS,Flash Gordon & Mandrake. . . 4.00
3 AS,O:Phantom 4.00
4 AS,O:Mandrake 4.00

DELLA VISION
Marvel Atlas, April, 1955
1 The Television Queen 250.00
2 . . . . 200.00
3 . . . . 200.00
Becomes:

PATTY POWERS
1955
4 . . . . 200.00
5 & 6 . . . . @125.00
7 Oct., 1956 . . . . 100.00

Dennis the Menace #7
© Marvel Entertainment Group

DENNIS THE MENACE
Nov., 1981–Nov., 1982
1 . . . . 12.00
2 thru 13 . . . . @7.00

DESTROYER, THE
1989–90
1 Black & White Mag. 3.50
2 thru 10 . . . . @2.50

THE DESTROYER:
TERROR
Dec., 1991
1 V:Nuihc 2.50
2 V:Nuihc 2.25
3 GM,V:Nuihc 2.25
4 DC,`The Last Dinosaur'. 2.25

DEVIL DINOSAUR
April, 1978—Dec., 1978
1 JK,I:Devil Dinosaur,Moon Boy . 25.00
2 JK,War With the Spider God . . . 15.00
3 JK,Giant 15.00
4 JK,Objects From the Sky 15.00
5 JK,The Kingdom of the Ants . . . 15.00
6 JK,The Fall 15.00
7 JK,Prisoner of the Demon Tree 15.00
8 JK,V:Dino Riders 15.00
9 JK,Lizards That Stand 15.00

DEVIL DINOSAUR
SPRING FLING
1997
Spec. F:Devil Dinosaur,Moon-Boy. . 3.00

MARVEL

DEVIL-DOG DUGAN
Marvel Atlas, July, 1956
1 War Stories 200.00
2 JSe(c) 150.00
3 . . . . 100.00
Becomes:

TALES OF THE MARINES
4 BP,War Stories 100.00
Becomes:

MARINES AT WAR
5 War Stories 125.00
6 . . . . 125.00
7 The Big Push, Aug., 1957 . . . 125.00

DEXTER THE DEMON
See: MELVIN THE MONSTER

DIE-CUT
Marvel UK, 1993–94
1 A:Beast 2.50
2 V:X-Beast. 2.25
3 A:Beast,Prof.X 2.25
4 V:Red Skull 2.25

DIE-CUT VS. G-FORCE
Marvel UK, 1993
1 SFr(s),LSh(c),I:G-Force 3.00
2 SFr(s),LSh(c),Last issue 3.00

Digitek #1
© Marvel Entertainment Group

DIGITEK
Marvel UK, 1992–93
1 DPw,I:Digitek,C:Deathlok. 2.25
2 DPw,A:Deathlok,V:Bacillicons . . . 2.25
3 DPw,A:Deathlok,V:Bacillicons . . . 2.25
4 DPw,V:Bacillicons 2.25

DINOSAURS: A CELEBRATION
Epic, 1992
Horns and Heavy Armor 5.00
Bone-Heads and Duck-Bills. 5.00
Terrible Claws and Tyrants 5.00
Egg Stealers and Earth Shakers . . 5.00

DIPPY DUCK
Marvel Atlas, 1957
1 Funny animal 100.00

DISNEY AFTERNOON
1994–95
1 DarkwingDuck vs.FearsomeFive . 3.50
2 thru 10 . . . . @3.00

DISNEY COMIC HITS
1995
1 . . . . 5.00
2 thru 9 . . . . @4.00
10 Hunchback of Notre Dame 5.00
11 thru 17 . . . . @4.00

DISNEY PRESENTS
1 F:Aladdin 2.50
2 F:Timon & Pumbaa 2.50
3 . . . . 2.50

DISTRICT X
May, 2004
1 Mr.M,pt.1,F:Bishop,Ismael 3.00
2 thru 6 Mr.M,pt.2 thru pt.6 . . . @3.00
7 Underground,pt.1 . . . . 3.00
8 Underground,pt.2 . . . . 3.00
9 Underground,pt.3 . . . . 3.00
10 Underground,pt.4 . . . . 3.00
11 Underground,pt.5 . . . . 3.00
12 Underground, concl. 3.00
13 One of Us,pt.1. . . . . 3.00
14 One of Us,pt.2. . . . . 3.00

DOC SAMSON
1996
1 From The Incredible Hulk 2.25
2 A:She-Hulk. 2.25
3 . . . . 2.25
4 . . . . 2.25

DOC SAMSON
Jan., 2006
1 . . . . 3.00
2 . . . . 3.00
3 A: New Scorpion 3.00
4 . . . . 3.00
5 . . . . 3.00

DOC SAVAGE
Oct., 1972
1 JM,Pulp Adapts,Death Eighty
Stories High 30.00
2 JSo(c),The Feathered Serpent
Strikes 20.00
3 JSo(c),Silver Death's Head . . . 20.00
4 JSo(c),The Hell Diver 15.00
5 GK(c),Night of the Monsters . . 15.00
6 JSo(c),Where Giants Walk 15.00
7 JSo(c),Brand of the Werewolfs . 15.00
8 In the Lair of the Werewolf
Jan., 1974 . . . . 15.00
G-Size#1 thru #2 Reprints 12.00

DOC SAVAGE
Aug., 1975
(black & white magazine)
1 JB,Ph(c),Ron Ely 20.00
2 JB 15.00
3 JB 15.00
4 thru 7 . . . . @15.00
8 Spring 1977 . . . . 15.00

DOCTOR OCTOPUS: NEGATIVE EXPOSURE
Oct., 2003
1 (of 5) 2.50
2 V:Vulture 2.50
3 thru 5 . . . . @3.00

DOCTOR SPECTRUM
Aug., 2004
1 (of 6) F:Corporal Joe Ledger 3.00
2 thru 6 . . . . @3.00

DR. STRANGE
[1st Series], June, 1968
Prev: Strange Tales
169 DA,O:Dr.Strange 225.00
170 DA,A:Ancient One. 75.00
171 TP,DA,V:Dormammu. 65.00
172 GC,TP,V:Dormammu 65.00
173 GC,TP,V:Dormammu 65.00
174 GC,TP,I:Satannish 65.00
175 GC,TP,I:Asmodeus 65.00
176 GC,TP,V:Asmodeus 65.00
177 GC,TP,D:Asmodeus,
N:Dr.Strange 65.00
178 GC,TP,A:Black Knight. 65.00
179 BWS(c),rep.Amazing Spider-
Man Ann.#2 . . . . 65.00
180 GC,TP,V:Nightmare. 65.00
181 FB(c),GC,TP,I:Demons of
Despair 65.00
182 GC,TP,V:Juggernaut 60.00
183 BEv(c),GC,TP,
I:Undying Ones 60.00

[2nd Regular Series], 1974–87
1 FB,DG,I:Silver Dagger 100.00
2 FB,DG,I:Soul Eater 50.00
3 FB,A:Dormammu 30.00
4 FB,DG,V:Death 30.00
5 FB,DG,A:Silver Dagger 30.00
6 FB(c),GC,KJ,A:Umar,I:Gaea . . . 15.00
7 GC,JR,A:Dormammu 15.00
8 GK(c),GC,TP,O:Clea 15.00
9 GK(c),GC,A:Dormammu,O:Clea 15.00
10 B:MWn(s),GK(c),GC,A:Eternity. 15.00
11 JR(c),GC,TP,A:Eternity 9.00
12 GC,TP,A:Eternity. 9.00
13 GC,TP,A:Eternity. 9.00
14 GC,TP,A:Dracula 9.00
15 GC,TP,A:Devil 9.00
16 GC,TP,A:Devil. 9.00
17 GC,TP,A:Styggro 9.00
18 GC,A:Styggro 9.00
19 GC,AA,I:Xander 9.00
20 A:Xander 9.00
21 DA,O:Dr.Strange. 8.00
22 I:Apalla 8.00
23 E:MWn(s),JSn,A:Wormworld . . 8.00
24 JSn,A:Apalla,I:Visamajoris . . . 8.00
25 AM,V:Dr.Strange Yet 8.00
26 JSn,A:The Ancient One 8.00
27 TS,A:Stygyro,Sphinx 8.00
28 TS,A:Ghost Rider,
V:In-Betweener 6.00
29 TS,A:Nighthawk 5.00
30 I:Dweller 5.00
31 TS,A:Sub Mariner 5.00
32 A:Sub Mariner 5.00
33 TS,A:The Dreamweaver 5.00
34 TS,A:Nightmare,D:CyrusBlack . 5.00
35 TS,V:Dweller,I:Ludi 5.00
36 Thunder of the Soul 5.00
37 Fear,the Final Victor 5.00
38 GC,DG,A:Baron Mordo 5.00
39 GC,DG,A:Baron Mordo 5.00
40 GC,A:Asrael 5.00
41 GC,A:Man Thing 4.00
42 GC,A:Black Mirror 4.00
43 V:Shadow Queen 4.00
44 GC,A:Princess Shialmar. 4.00
45 GC,A:Demon in the Dark 4.00
46 FM,A:Sibylis 4.00
47 MR,TA,I:Ikonn 4.00
48 MR,TA,Brother Voodoo 4.00
49 MR,TA,A:Baron Mordo 4.00
50 MR,TA,A:Baron Mordo 4.00

Doc Strange #76
© *Marvel Entertainment Group*

51 MR,TA,A:Sgt. Fury,
   V:Baron Mordo 4.00
52 MR,TA,A:Nightmare 5.00
53 MR,TA,A:Nightmare,Fantastic
   Four,V:Rama-Tut 5.00
54 PS,V:Tiboro 5.00
55 MGo,TA,V:Madness 5.00
56 PS,TA,O:Dr.Strange 6.00
57 KN,TA,A:Dr.Doom 5.00
58 DGr,TA,V:Dracula 5.00
59 DGr,TA,V:Dracula 6.00
60 DGr,TA,Scarlet Witch 6.00
61 DGr,TA,V:Dracula 6.00
62 SL,V:Dracula 6.00
63 CP,V:Topaz 5.00
64 TSa,`Art Rage' 5.00
65 PS,Charlatan. 5.00
66 PS, `The Cosen One'. 5.00
67 SL,A:Jessica Drew,Shroud 5.00
68 PS,A:Black Knight. 5.00
69 PS,A:Black Knight. 5.00
70 BBI,V:Umar 5.00
71 DGr,O:Dormammu 4.00
72 PS,V:Umar 4.00
73 PS,V:Umar 4.00
74 MBg,Secret Wars II. 4.00
75 A:Fantastic Four 4.00
76 A:Fantastic Four 4.00
77 A:Topaz. 4.00
78 A:Cloak,I:Ecstacy 3.50
79 A:Morganna. 3.00
80 A:Morganna,C:Rintah 3.00
81 V:Urthona,I:Rintah. 3.00
Ann.#1 CR,`Doomworld' 20.00
GN Dr.Strange: What is it that
   Distrubs you, Stephen?, CR,
   revised from Dr.Strange Ann.#1,
   48pg bookshelf (Aug., 1997). . 10.00
G-Size#1 K&R(c),reps Strange
   Tales#164-#168. . . . . 10.00

[3rd Regular Series], 1988–96
1 V:Dorammu 4.00
2 V:Dorammu 3.00
3 I:Dragon Force. 3.00
4 EL(c),A:Dragon Force 3.00
5 JG,V:Baron Mordo 3.50
6 JG,I:Mephista 3.00
7 JG,V:Agamotto,Mephisto 3.00
8 JG,V:Mephisto & Satanish 3.00
9 JG,O:Dr.Strange. 3.00
10 JG,V:Morbius. 3.50
11 JG,A of V,V:Hobgoblin,
   C:Morbius. 4.00
12 JG,A of V,V:Enchantress 2.75
13 JG,A of V,V:Arkon 2.75

14 JG,B:Vampiric Verses,
   A:Morbius 3.50
15 JG,A:Morbius,Amy Grant(C) 5.00
16 JG,A:Morbius,Brother Voodoo . . 3.50
17 JV,TD,A:Morbius,Br.Voodoo 3.50
18 JG,E:Vampiric Verses,A:Morbius,
   Brother Voodoo,R:Varnae 3.50
19 GC,A:Azrael 2.50
20 JG,TD,A:Morbius,V:Zom 3.50
21 JG,TD,B:Dark Wars,
   R:Dormammu 2.50
22 JG,TD,LW,V:Dormammu. 2.50
23 JG,LW,V:Dormammu. 2.50
24 JG,E:Dark Wars,V:Dormammu . . 2.50
25 RLm,A:Red Wolf, Black Crow . . . 2.50
26 GI,V:Werewolf By Night 2.50
27 GI,V:Werewolf By Night 2.50
28 X-over Ghost Rider #12,
   V:Zodiac 3.00
29 A:Baron Blood. 2.50
30 Topaz' Fate 2.50
31 TD,Inf.Gauntlet,A:Silver Surfer . . 3.00
32 Inf.Gauntlet,A:Warlock,Silver
   Surfer,V:Silver Dagger. 2.50
33 Inf.Gauntlet,V:Thanos,
   Zota,A:Pip 2.50
34 Inf.Gauntlet,V:Dr.Doom,
   A:Pip,Scarlet Witch. 2.50
35 Inf.Gauntlet,A:Thor,Pip,
   Scarlet Witch 2.50
36 Inf.Gauntlet,A:Warlock(leads
   into Warlock&Inf.Watch#1) 3.00
37 GI,V:Frankensurfer 2.50
38 GI,Great Fear #1. . . . . 2.50
39 GI,Great Fear #2. . . . . 2.50
40 GI,Great Fear #3,A:Daredevil . . . 2.50
41 GI,A:Wolverine 3.00
42 GI,Infinity War,V:Galactus,A:
   Silver Surfer. 2.50
43 GI,Infinity War,Galactus Vs.
   Agamotto,A:Silver Surfer. 2.50
44 GI,Infinity War,V:Juggernaut 2.50
45 GI,Inf.War,O:Doctor Strange. . . . 2.50
46 GI,Inf.War,R:old costume 2.50
47 GI,Inf.War,V:doppleganger 2.50
48 GI,V:The Vishanti 2.50
49 GI,R:Dormammu. 2.50
50 GI,A:Hulk,Ghost Rider,Silver
   Surfer,V:Dormammu(leads into
   Secret Defenders)holo-grafx(c) . 3.50
51 GI,V:Religious Cult 2.50
52 GI,A:Morbius. 2.50
53 GI,Closes Mansion,L:Wong 2.50
54 GI,Infinity Crusade 2.50
55 GI,Inf.Crusade. 2.50
56 GI,Inf.Crusade. 2.50
57 A:Kyllian,Urthona 2.50
58 V:Urthona 2.50
59 GI,V:Iskelior 2.50
60 B:DQ(s),Siege of
   Darkness,pt.#7 . . . . 4.00
61 Siege of Darkness,pt.#15 . . . . . . 3.25
62 V:Dr.Doom 2.50
63 JJ(c),V:Morbius. 2.50
64 MvR,V:Namor. 2.50
65 MvR,V:Namor,Vengeance. 2.75
66 A:Wong 2.75
67 R:Clea. 2.75
68 MvR 2.50
69 MvR. 2.50
70 A:Hulk 2.50
71 V:Hulk 2.50
72 Metallic(c),Last Rites,pt.1 . . . . . 2.50
73 Last Rites,pt.2. . . . . 2.50
74 SY,DQ,Last Rites,pt.3 . . . . 2.50
75 Prismatic cover 4.00
76 I:New Costume 2.50
77 Mob Clean-up 2.50
78 R:Chton 2.50
79 Doc's new Asylum. 2.50
80 Missing for four months? 2.50
81 A:Nick Fury 2.50

82 A:Hellstorm 2.50
83 V:Tempo Mob,Dormammu 2.50
84 The Homecoming,pt.1 . . . . 2.50
85 The Homecoming,pt.2 . . . . 2.50
86 The Homecoming,pt.3 . . . . 2.50
87 The Homecoming,pt.4 . . . . 2.50
88 The Fall of the Tempo,pt.1 . . . . . 2.50
89 The Fall of the Tempo,pt.2 . . . . . 2.50
90 final issue 2.50
Ann #2 Return of Defenders,Pt4 . . . 5.00
Ann #3 GI,I:Killiam,w/card 3.50
Ann.#4 V:Salome 3.50
Spec. Dr. Strange/Ghost Rider#1
   Newsstand vers. of Dr.
   Strange #28 (1991) 6.00
Spec.#1 Dr. Strange vs. Dracula
   rep. MWn(s),GC (1994). 2.50
Ashcan. .75

DOCTOR STRANGE
Dec., 1998
1 (of 4) TyH,killer pursued 3.00
2 TyH,secrets in Topaz 3.00
3 TyH,magic in Manhattan 3.00
4 TyH,PC,conclusion 3.00

DR. STRANGE CLASSICS
March, 1984
1 SD,Reprints 3.50
2 thru 4 . . . . @3.50

DOCTOR STRANGE:
THE OATH
Oct., 2006
1 . . . . 3.00
2 thru 5 . . . . @3.00

DOCTOR WHO
1984–86
1 BBC TV Series,UK reprints,
   Return of the Daleks 7.00
2 Star Beast 6.00
3 Transformation 5.00
4 A:K-9,Daleks 5.00
5 V:Time Witch,Colin Baker
   interview 5.00
6 B:Ancient Claw saga 5.00
7 . . . . 5.00
8 The Collector 5.00
9 The Life Bringer 5.00
10 This is your Life 5.00
11 The Deal 5.00

Doctor Who #5
© *Marvel Entertainment Group*

MARVEL

12 End of the Line 5.00
13 V:The Cybermen 5.00
14 Clash of the Neutron Knight 5.00
15 B:Peter Davison-Dr. Who 5.00
16 Into the Realm of Satan, ... 5.00
17 Peter Davison Interview 5.00
18 A:Four Dr.Who's 5.00
19 A:The Sontarans 5.00
20 The Stockbridge Horror. 5.00
21 The Stockbridge Horror. 5.00
22 The Stockbridge Horror. 5.00
23 The Unearthly Child 5.00

DR. ZERO
Epic, April, 1988
1 BSz,DCw,I:Dr.Zero. . . . . @2.50
2 thru 8 . . . . @2.25

DOLLY DILL
1945
1 Newsstand 250.00

DOMINATION FACTOR
Sept., 1999
1.1 Fantastic Four (of 4) DJu,
   JOy,BMc,x-over 2.50
1.2 Avengers, DJu,JO,
   DJa, x-over 2.50
2.3 Fantastic Four, DJu,BMc 2.50
2.4 Avengers, DJu,JOy,DJa 2.50
3.5 Fantastic Four, DJu,BMc 2.50
3.6 Avengers, JOy,DJa 2.50
4.7 Fantastic Four, DJu,BMc 2.50
4.8 Avengers, DJa,JOy,concl. 2.50

DOMINO
1996
1 thru 3 . . . . @2.25

DOMINO
May, 2003
1 (of 4) BSf 2.50
2 thru 4 BSf. . . . . @2.50

DOOM 2099
1993—96
1 PB,I:Doom 2099,V:Tiger Wylde,
   foil(c) 3.00
2 I:Rook Seven 2.50
3 PB,V:Tiger Wylde. 2.50
4 PB,V:Tiger Wylde. 2.50
5 PB,I:Fever 2.50
6 I:Duke Stratosphear. 2.50

Doom 2099 #2
© Marvel Entertainment Group

7 PB,I:Paloma,V:Duke,Fever Haze 2.50
8 PB,C:Ravage 2.50
9 EC,V:Jack the Ripper 2.50
10 PB,w/Poster 2.50
11 PB,I:Thandaza 2.50
12 PB,V:Thandaza. 2.50
13 PB(c),JFm(s),V:Necrotek 2.50
14 RLm(c),PB,Fall o/t Hammer#4 . . 2.50
15 PB,I:Radian. 2.50
16 EC(a&s), ... 2.50
17 PB,V:Radian,w/card 2.50
18 PB, ... 2.50
19 PB,C:Bloodhawk. 2.50
20 PB,A:Bloodhawk. 2.50
21 PB,Shadow King. 2.50
22 PB,R:Duke Stratosphere. 2.50
23 PB,R:Tyger Wylde 2.50
24 PB 2.50
25 PB 3.50
25a foil cover 4.00
26 . . . . 2.50
27 Revolution 2.50
28 Prologue to D-Day 2.50
Becomes:

DOOM 2099 A.D.
1995
29 Doom Invades America. 4.00
29a Chromium Cover. 4.00
30 D:Corporate Head. 2.50
31 PB,One Nation Under Doom . . . 2.50
32 Ravage Aftermath 2.50
33 . . . . 2.50
34 I:Anthony Herod 2.50
35 E:One Nation Under Doom. 2.50
36 thru 39. . . . . @2.50
40 Rage Against Time,pt.1. . . . . . . 2.50
41 Rage Against Time,pt.2. . . . . . . 2.50

DOOM
Aug., 2000
1 (of 3) CDi,F:Dr.Doom. 3.00
2 CDi,Al Khalad 3.00
3 CDi,concl. 3.00

DOOM:
THE EMPEROR RETURNS
Nov., 2001
1 CDi,F:Dr. Doom 2.50
2 CDi,center of Counter-Earth 2.50
3 CDi, ... 2.50

DOPEY DUCK COMICS
Marvel Timely, Fall, 1945
1 A:Casper Cat,Krazy Krow . . . 250.00
2 A:Casper Cat,Krazy Krow . . . 225.00
Becomes:

WACKY DUCK
1946
3 Paperchase(c) 225.00
4 Wacky Duck(c) 200.00
5 Duck & Devil(c) 175.00
6 Cliffhanger(c) 175.00
1 Basketball(c) 125.00
2 Traffic Light(c) 125.00
Becomes:

JUSTICE COMICS

DOUBLE DRAGON
July, 1991
1 I:Billy&Jimmy Lee 2.50
2 Dragon Statue Stolen,V:Stelth . . 2.50
3 Billy Vs. Jimmy 2.50
4 Dragon Force out of control. 2.50
5 V:Stealth. 2.50
6 V:Nightfall, final issue 2.50

DOUBLE EDGE
1995
Alpha Punisher vs. Nick Fury 5.00
Omega D:Major Character. 5.00

D.P. 7
Nov., 1986
1 O:DP7 . . . . 2.50
2 thru 20 V:Headhunter. . . . . . . @2.50
21 thru 32. . . . . @3.00
Ann.#1,I:Witness 3.00

DRACULA LIVES
B&W Magazine, 1973—75
1 GC 100.00
2 NA,GC,JSn,O:Dracula. 65.00
3 NA,JB, ... 60.00
4 MP 35.00
5 GC 35.00
6 JB,GC 35.00
7 GE 35.00
8 GC 35.00
9 AA,RG 35.00
10 . . . . 45.00
11 thru 13 . . . . @40.00

DRACULA:
LORD OF THE UNDEAD
Oct., 1998
1 (of 3) PO,TP,R:Dracula 3.00
2 PO,TP,V:Seward 3.00
3 PO,TP,conclusion 3.00

DRAFT, THE
1988
1 Sequel to The Pit. 3.75

DRAGON LINES
Epic, *Heavy Hitters* 1993
[1st Limited Series]
1 RLm,V:Terrorist on Moon,
   Embossed(c) 3.00
2 RLm,V:Kuei Emperor. 2.25
3 RLm,V:Spirit Boxer 2.25
4 RLm,K:Kuei Emperor. 2.25
[Regular Series]
1 B:PQ(s),RLm,I:Tao. 2.50
2 RLm, ... 2.50

DRAGONSLAYER
Oct.–Nov., 1981
1 Movie adapt. 3.00
2 Movie adapt. 3.00

DRAGON STRIKE
1994
1 Based on TSR Game 2.25

DRAGON'S TEETH/
DRAGON'S CLAWS
July, 1988
1 GSr,I:Mercy Dragon,
   Scavenger,Digit Steel 2.25
2 GSr,V:Evil Dead 2.25
3 GSr,Go Home 2.25
4 GSr 2.25
5 GSr,I:Death's Head 18.00
6 thru 10 GSr . . . . @2.00

DRAX THE DESTROYER
Sept., 2005
1 (of 4) KG(s) 4.00
2 thru 4 KG(s). . . . . @3.00

All comics prices listed are for *Near Mint* condition.

DREADLANDS
Epic, 1992
1 Post-Apocalyptic Mini-series	4.00
2 Trapped in Prehistoric Past	4.00
3 V:Alien Time Travelers	4.00
4 Final Issue	4.00

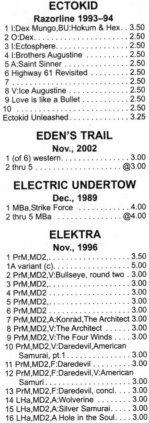

Dreadstar #23
© *Marvel Entertainment Group*

DREADSTAR
Epic, Nov., 1982
1 JSn,I:Lord Papal	5.00
2 thru 5	@3.50
6 thru 7	@4.00
8 thru 26	@3.00
Ann.#1 JSn,The Price	3.00

See COLOR COMICS section

DREADSTAR & COMPANY
July, 1985
1 JSo,reprint	2.25
2 thru 5 JSo,rep.	@2.25

DREAM POLICE
June, 2005
1 MD2, 48-pg.	4.00

DROIDS
Star, April, 1986
1 JR	25.00
2 AW	15.00
3 JR/AW	15.00
4 AW	15.00
5 AW	15.00
6 EC/AW,A:Luke Skywalker	15.00
7 EC/AW,A:Luke Skywalker	15.00
8 EC/AW,A:Luke Skywalker	15.00

DRUID
1995
1 R:Dr. Druid Surprise!!!	3.50
2 F:Nekra	3.00
3 deranged canibal wisemen	3.00
4 Why Must He Die?.	3.00

DUNE
April–June, 1985
1 Movie Adapt,Rep. Marvel Super Spec,BSz	3.50
2 Movie Adapt,BSz	3.50
3 Movie Adapt,BSz,	3.50

DYNOMUTT
Nov., 1977
1 Based on TV series	50.00
2 thru 5	@30.00
6 Sept., 1978	30.00

EARTHWORM JIM
1995–96
1 I:Earthworm Jim.	3.00
2 Cow tipping	3.00
3 V:Lawyers,conclusion	3.00

EARTH X
Jan., 1999
0 (of 14) AxR,JPL,Machine Man & Watcher	6.00
0a signed	25.00
1 AxR,JPL,V:Inhumans,32-page	8.00
1a signed	30.00
2 AxR,JPL,fate of Fant.Four	4.00
3 AxR,JPL,World Super Powers	4.00
4 JPL,AxR(c),A:new Hulk	4.00
5 JPL,AxR(c),V:Doombots	4.00
6 JPL,AxR(c),different X-Men	4.00
7 JPL,AxR(c),A:Hulk	4.00
8 JPL,AxR(c),A:Venom	4.00
9 JPL,AxR(c),Revelations	4.00
10 JPL,AxR(c)	4.00
11 JPL,AxR(c),V:Skull	4.00
12 JPL,AxR(c),concl	4.00
Spec.X AxR(c) concl.,48-pg	6.00
Sketchbook	6.00

ECTOKID
Razorline 1993–94
1 I:Dex Mungo,BU:Hokum & Hex	3.50
2 O:Dex.	2.50
3 I:Ectosphere.	2.50
4 I:Brothers Augustine	2.50
5 A:Saint Sinner	2.50
6 Highway 61 Revisited	2.50
7	2.50
8 V:Ice Augustine	2.50
9 Love is like a Bullet	2.50
10	2.50
Ectokid Unleashed	3.25

EDEN'S TRAIL
Nov., 2002
1 (of 6) western.	3.00
2 thru 5	@3.00

ELECTRIC UNDERTOW
Dec., 1989
1 MBa,Strike Force	4.00
2 thru 5 MBa	@4.00

ELEKTRA
Nov., 1996
1 PrM,MD2,	3.50
1A variant (c).	5.00
2 PrM,MD2,V:Bullseye, round two	3.00
3 PrM,MD2,	3.00
4 PrM,MD2	3.00
5 PrM,MD2,	3.00
6 PrM,MD2	3.00
7 PrM,MD2,A:Konrad,The Architect	3.00
8 PrM,MD2,V:The Architect	3.00
9 PrM,MD2,V:The Four Winds	3.00
10 PrM,MD2,V:Daredevil,American Samurai, pt.1	3.00
11 PrM,MD2,F:Daredevil	3.00
12 PrM,MD2,F:Daredevil,V:American Samuri	3.00
13 PrM,MD2,F:Daredevil, concl.	3.00
14 LHa,MD2,A:Wolverine	3.00
15 LHa,MD2,A:Silver Samurai.	3.00
16 LHa,MD2,A Hole in the Soul.	3.00

Elektra #12
© *Marvel Entertainment Group*

17 LHa,MD2,V:The Hand.	3.00
18 LHa,MD2,A:Shang-Chi&Kingpin.	3.00
19 LHa,MD2,last issue.	3.00
Minus 1 Spec.,PMg,MD2,flashback.	3.00

ELEKTRA
July, 2001
1 BMB,non-comics code series	5.00
2A BMB,A:S.H.I.E.L.D.	3.00
2B variant BSz(c)	3.00
3 BMB,A:Hydra	3.50
3a nude	20.00
4 BMB,A:Nick Fury	3.50
5 BMB,concl	3.50
6 BMB,F:Daredevil,'Nuff Said	3.50
7 Hubris, pt.1	3.50
8 Hubris, pt.2	3.50
9 Hubris, pt.3	3.50
10 Hubris, concl.	3.00
11 Elektra between jobs.	3.00
12 F:Mr. Locke.	3.00
13 DaM	3.00
14 DaM,Elektra fights back	3.00
15 DaM	3.00
16 DaM	3.00
17 DaM	3.00
18 DaM	3.00
19 DaM	3.00
20 DaM,V:The Hand	3.00
21 V:The Hand.	3.00
22 V:The Hand, concl.	3.00
23 BSz(c),pt.1	3.00
24 BSz(c),pt.2	3.00
25 BSz(c),How to,pt.1	3.00
26 How to,pt.2	3.00
27 How to,pt.3,concl.	3.00
28 Tables turned	3.00
29 Assassination	3.00
30 Prophet & Loss,pt.2	3.00
31 Prophet & Loss,pt.3	3.00
32 Fever,pt.1	3.00
33 Fever,pt.2	3.00
34 Fever,pt.3	3.00
35 Visits grave	3.00
36 JoB,pt.1	3.00
Spec., Elektra: The Movie	3.00

ELEKTRA: ASSASSIN
Aug., 1986
1 FM,BSz,V:Shield	8.00
2 FM,BSz,I:Garrett	5.00
3 FM,BSz,V:Shield,A:Garrett	5.00
4 FM,BSz,V:Shield,A:Garrett	5.00

5 FM,BSz,I:Chastity,A:Garrett. 5.00
6 FM,BSz,A:Nick Fury,Garrett 5.00
7 FM,BSz,V:Ken Wind,A:Garrett . . . 5.00
8 FM,BSz,V:Ken Wind,A:Garrett . . . 6.00

ELEKTRA: GLIMPSE & ECHO
July, 2002
1 (of 4) F:The Hand 3.50
2 thru 4 . . . . @3.50

ELEKTRA: THE HAND
Sept., 2004
1 (of 5) The First Impression 3.00
2 thru 5 . . . . @3.00

ELEKTRA: ROOT OF EVIL
1 V:Snakeroot. 3.00
2 V:Snakeroot. 3.00
3 Elektra's Brother 3.00
4 V:The Hand 3.00

ELEKTRA: SAGA
Feb., 1984
1 FM,rep.Daredevil. 7.00
2 FM,rep.Daredevil. 7.00
3 FM,rep.Daredevil. 7.00
4 FM,rep.Daredevil. 7.00
GN Book One FM,KJ, rep. from
  Daredevil, 96pg 4.00
GN Book Two FM,KJ, rep. from
  Daredevil, 96pg 4.00

ELEKTRA & WOLVERINE: THE REDEEMER
Nov., 2001
GN#1 painted, 48-page 6.50
GN#2 48-page 6.50
GN#3 concl., 48-page 6.50

ELEKTRA/WITCHBLADE
1-shot Devil's Reign,
  pt.6, x-over 3.00

ELFQUEST
Star, Aug., 1985
1 WP,reprints. 4.00
2 thru 31 WP. . . . . @2.50
32 WP,Conclusion, March, 1988 . . . 2.50

ELSEWHERE PRINCE
Epic, May–Oct., 1990
1 thru 6 . . . . @3.00

ELVIRA
Oct., 1988
Spec.B&W, Movie Adapt. 3.00

EMMA FROST
July, 2003
1 RGr,Higher Learning,pt.1. . . . . . 7.00
2 RGr,Higher Learning,pt.2. . . . . . 4.00
3 RGr,Higher Learning,pt.3. . . . . . 4.00
4 RGr,Higher Learning,pt.4. . . . . . 4.00
5 RGr,Higher Learning,pt.5. . . . . . 4.00
6 RGr,White Queen 4.00
7 Mind Games,pt.1 . . . . 3.50
8 Mind Games,pt.2 . . . . 3.50
9 Mind Games,pt.3 . . . . 3.50
10 Mind Games,pt.4 . . . . 3.50
11 Mind Games,pt.5 . . . . 3.50
12 Mind Games,pt.6 . . . . 3.50
13 Bloom,pt.1 . . . . 3.50
14 Bloom,pt.2 . . . . 3.50
15 Bloom,pt.3 . . . . 3.50
16 Bloom,pt.4 . . . . 3.50
17 Bloom,pt.5 . . . . 3.50

18 Bloom,pt.6 . . . . 3.50
Digest Vol. 1: Higher Learning. . . . 8.00
Digest Vol. 2: Mind Games 8.00
Digest Vol. 3: Bloom 8.00

EPIC
1992
1 Wildcards,Hellraiser. 6.00
2 Nightbreed,Wildcards 6.00
3 DBw,MFm,Alien Legion. 6.00
4 Stalkers,Metropol,Wildcards . . . 6.00

EPIC ANTHOLOGY
April, 2004
1 . . . . 6.00

Epic Illustrated #19
© *Marvel Entertainment Group*

EPIC, ILLUSTRATED
Spring, 1980
1 Black and White/Color Mag. . . . 14.00
2 thru 10 . . . . @8.00
11 thru 20 . . . . @10.00
21 thru 25 . . . . @12.00
26 thru 34, March, 1986. . . . . @14.00

EPIC, LITE
Epic, Nov., 1991
One-shot short stories 4.00

ETERNAL
Marvel Max, June, 2003
1 Gift of the Gods,pt.1 . . . . 3.00
2 thru 6 Gift of the Gods,pt.2–6 . @3.00

ETERNALS
[1st Series], July, 1976
1 JK,I:Ikaris,25 cent edition 25.00
2 JK,I:Ajak,25 cent edition 15.00
3 JK,I:Sersi. 10.00
4 JK,Night of the Demons. 10.00
5 JK,I:Makarri,Zuras Thena,Domo 10.00
6 JK,Gods & Men at City College . 10.00
7 JK,V:Celestials. 10.00
8 JK,I:Karkas, Reject 10.00
9 JK,I:Sprite,Reject vs. Karkas . . 10.00
10 JK,V:Celestials. 10.00
11 JK,I:Kingo Sunen 10.00
12 JK,I:Uni-Mind 15.00
13 JK,I:ForgottenOne(Gilgamesh). 15.00
14 JK,V:Hulk 15.00
15 JK,V:Hulk 15.00
16 JK,I:Dromedan 15.00
17 JK,I:Sigmar 10.00
18 JK,I:Nerve Beast. 10.00

19 JK,Secret o/t Pyramid. 10.00
Ann.#1 JK,V:Timekillers. 12.00
[2nd Series], Oct., 1985
1 SB,I:Cybele 3.00
2 thru 7 SB,V:Deviants . . . . @2.50
8 thru 10 WS,SB,V:Deviants. . . . @2.50
11 &12 WS,KP,V:Deviants . . . . . @2.50

ETERNALS
June, 2006
1 NGa,JR2 . . . . 4.00
2 thru 7 NGa,JR2 . . . . @4.00
2a variant (c) 8.00
7a variant JR2(c) 4.00

ETERNALS: HEROD FACTOR
Nov., 1991
1 MT/BMc,A:Sersi (giant size) . . . 2.50

EVERYMAN
Epic, 1991
1-shot Supernatural Story 8.00

EWOKS
Star, June, 1985—Sept., 1987
1 Based on TV Series. 18.00
2 . . . . 15.00
3 . . . . 15.00
4 A:Foonars 15.00
5 Wicket vs. Ice Demon. 15.00
6 Mount Sorrow, A:Teebo 15.00
7 A:Logray,V:Morag 15.00
8 . . . . 15.00
9 Lost in Time 15.00
10 AW,Lost in Time 18.00
11 thru 15 . . . . @15.00

EXCALIBUR
April, 1988
1 AD,Special,O:Excalibur,
  V:Technet. 5.00
1a 2nd Printing 2.50
1b 3rd Printing 2.00
2 AAd,Mojo Mayhem,A:X-Babies . . 4.00
3 Air Apparent Spec.RLm,KJ,JG,TP,
  RL,EL,JRu,A:Coldblood. 4.00
[Regular Series]
1 B:CCl(s),AD,V:Warwolves,
  I:Widget. 6.00
2 AD,V:Warwolves,I:Kylun 5.00
3 AD,V:Juggernaut. 4.00
4 AD,V:Arcade,Crazy Gang 4.00
5 AD,V:Arcade. 3.00
6 AD,Inferno,I:Alistaire Stuart . . . 3.00
7 AD,Inferno. 3.00
8 RLm,JRu,A:New Mutants 3.00
9 AD,I:Nazi-Excalibur. 3.00
10 MR,V:Nazi-Excalibur 3.00
11 MR,V:Nazi-Excalibur 3.00
12 AD,Fairy Tale Dimension 3.00
13 AD,The Prince,N:Capt.Britian . 3.00
14 AD,Too Many Heroes 2.50
15 AD,I:US James Braddock 2.50
16 AD,V:Anjulie 2.50
17 AD,C:Prof.X,Starjammers. . . . 2.50
18 DJ,DA,V:Jamie Braddock 2.50
19 RL,TA,AM,V:Jamie Braddock . 2.50
20 RLm,JRu,V:Demon Druid 2.50
21 I:Crusader X 2.50
22 V:Crusader X 2.50
23 AD,V:Magik 2.50
24 AD,Return Home,C:Galactus . . 2.50
25 E:CCl(s),AM,A:Galactus,Death,
  Watcher 2.50
26 RLm,JRu,V:Mastermind 2.50
27 BWS,BSz,A:Nth Man 3.00
28 BBI,Night at Bar 2.50

Excalibur #17
© *Marvel Entertainment Group*

29 JRu,V:Nightmare,A:PowerPack . 2.50
30 DR,AM,A:Doctor Strange 2.50
31 DR,AM,V:Son of Krakoa 2.50
32 V:Mesmero 2.50
33 V:Mesmero 2.50
34 V:Mesmero 2.50
35 AM,Missing Child 2.50
36 AM,V:Silv.Sable,Sandman 2.50
37 A:Avengers W.C.,Dr.Doom 2.50
38 A:Avengers W.C.,Dr.Doom 2.50
39 A:Avengers W.C.,Dr.Doom 2.50
40 O:Excalibur,Trial-Lockheed 2.50
41 V:Warwolves,C:Cable 3.00
42 AD,Team Broken Up 3.50
43 AD,Nightcrawler,V:Capt.Brit 3.00
44 AD,Capt.Britain On Trial 3.00
45 AD,I:N-Men 3.00
46 AD,Return of Kylun,C:Cerise . . . 3.00
47 AD,I:Cerise 3.00
48 AD,A:Anti-Phoenix 3.00
49 AD,MFm,V:Necrom,R:Merlyn . . . 3.00
50 AD,Phoenix,V:Necrom,Merlyn . . 5.00
51 V:Giant Dinosaurs 2.50
52 O:Phoenix,A:Prof X,MarvGirl . . . 2.50
53 A:Spider-Man,V:The Litter 2.50
54 AD,MFm,V:Crazy Gang 2.50
55 AD,MFm,A:Psylocke 2.50
56 AD,MFm,A:Psylocke,
   V:Saturyne,Jamie Braddock . . . 2.50
57 A:X-Men,Alchemy,V:Trolls 2.75
58 A:X-Men,Alchemy,V:Trolls 2.75
59 A:Avengers 2.50
60 A:Avengers 2.50
61 AD,MFm,Phoenix Vs.Galactus . . 2.50
62 AD,MFm,A:Galactus 2.50
63 AD,MFm,V:Warpies 2.50
64 AD,MFm,V:RCX,R:Rachel 2.50
65 AD,MFm,R:Dark Phoenix 2.50
66 AD,MFm,V:Ahab,Sentinels,
   O:Widget 2.50
67 AD,MFm,V:Ahab,Sentinels 2.50
68 V:Starjammers 2.50
69 A:Starjammers 2.50
70 A:Starjammers 2.50
71 DaR,Hologram(c),N:Excalibur . . 5.00
72 KeL,V:Siena Blaze 2.50
73 TSr,V:Siena Blaze 2.50
74 InC,A:Mr.Sinster,Siena Blaze . . . 2.50
75 SLo(s),KeL,I:Daytripper(Amanda
   Sefton),Britannic(Capt.Britain),
   BU:Nightcrawler 4.00
75a Newstand Ed. 2.25
76 KeL,V:D'spayre 2.50

77 KeL,R:Doug Ramsey 2.50
78 A:Zero,Doug Ramsey 2.50
79 A:Zero,Doug Ramsey 2.50
80 A:Zero,Doug Ramsey 2.50
81 Doug Ramsey 2.50
82 . . . . 3.00
82a foil(c) 4.00
83 regular ed. 2.25
83a Deluxe ed. Kitty,Nightcrawler . . 2.50
84 regular ed. 2.25
84a Deluxe ed. 2.50
85 regular ed. 2.25
85a Deluxe ed. 2.50
86 regular ed. 2.25
86a Deluxe ed. 2.50
87 KeL,Secrets of the Genoshan
   Mutate Technology 2.50
88 Dream Nails,pt.1 . . . . 2.50
89 Dream Nails,pt.2 . . . . 2.50
90 Between Uncreated,Phalanx . . . 4.00
91 F:Colossus 2.50
92 F:Colossus 2.50
93 F:Wolfsbane 2.50
94 A:Karma & Psylocke 2.50
95 . . . . 2.50
96 . . . . 2.50
97 BWi,B.Braddock's secrets told . . 2.50
98 . . . . 2.50
99 European Hellfire Club,
   Onslaught 2.50
100 Onslaught saga, double size . . . 4.00
101 . . . . 2.50
102 . . . . 2.50
103 WEl,F:Colossus,Kitty &
   Nichtcrawler. 2.50
104 JAr,BHi,PNe,Douglock's
   dark side 2.50
105 JAr,BHi,PNe,V:Moonstar, ... 2.50
106 . . . . 2.50
107 SvL,New direction 2.50
108 Dragons of the Crimson Dawn . 2.50
109 V:Spiral,A:Captain Britain 2.50
110 V:The Dragons of the
   Crimson Dawn 2.50
111 F:Shadowcat,R:Rory Cambell
   (Ahab?) 2.50
112 Quicksilver tie-in 2.50
113 BRa,Colossus & Meggan 2.50
114 BRa,Vanisher 2.50
115 BRa,Quarantine,F:GenerationX 2.50
116 BRa,Legacy Virus, cont. 2.50
117 BRa,F:Kitty Pryde, Colossus &
   Nightcrawler. 2.50
118 BRa,V:Creatures from the
   Shadows 2.50

Excalibur #99
© *Marvel Entertainment Group*

119 BRa,V:Nightmare 2.50
120 BRa,F:Kitty Pryde & Pete
   Wisdom 2.50
121 BRa,to Egypt. 2.50
122 BRa,V:Original X-Men? 2.50
123 BRa,V:Mimic 2.50
124 BBr,Captain Britain's bachelor
   party 2.50
125 TvS,SHa, W:Captain Britain &
   Meggan, final issue 4.00
Minus 1 Spec., flashback,
   F:Nightcrawler 2.50
Ann.#1 I:Khaos,w/card 3.25
Spec #1 The Possession 4.00
Spec #2 RLm,DT,JG,RL,
   A:Original X-Men 3.00
PF Cold Blood 5.00
GN Weird War III 10.00
GN Wild, Wild Life 6.00

EXCALIBUR
May, 2004

1 CCl,Forging the Sword,pt.1 . . . . 3.00
2 CCl,Forging the Sword,pt.2 . . . . 3.00
3 CCl,Forging the Sword,pt.3 . . . . 3.00
4 CCl,Forging the Sword,pt.4 . . . . 3.00
5 CCl,Food Fight,pt.1 . . . . 3.00
6 CCl,Food Fight,pt.2 . . . . 3.00
7 CCl,Food Fight,pt.3 . . . . 3.00
8 ALo,Saturday Night Fever,pt.1. . 3.00
9 ALo,Saturday Night Fever,pt.2. . 7.00
10 CCl,ALo,Saturday Night Fever . . 3.00
11 CCl,ALo,Save My Child,pt.1 . . . 3.00
12 CCl,ALo,Save My Child,pt.2 . . . 3.00
13 CCl,ALo,House of M, prelude . . 5.00
14 CCl,ALo,A:Dr. Strange 4.00

EXCALIBUR:
SWORD OF POWER
Dec., 2000

1 (of 4) IaC,BRa,F:Capt.Britain . . . 3.00
2 BRa, ... 3.00
3 BRa,V:Roma 3.00
4 BRa, concl 3.00

EXILES
June, 2001

1 MkK,F:Blink, 48-page 10.00
2A MkK, ... 7.00
2B variant JWi(c) 6.00
3 MkK,trial of Phoenix. 4.00
4 MkK,trial of Phoenix. 4.00
5 MkK,JCf,F:Hulk 4.00
6 MkK,JCf,F:Alpha Flight 4.00
7 MkK,'Nuff Said (no words) 4.00
8 MkK,A World Apart,pt.1 . . . . 4.00
9 MkK,A World Apart,pt.2 . . . . 4.00
10 MkK,A World Apart,pt.3 . . . . 4.00
11 MkK,F:Morph. 3.50
12 MkK,New team 3.50
13 MkK,team must kill 3.50
14 MkK,V:Dr. Doom 3.50
15 MkK,Mimic vs. Namor. 3.50
16 MkK, ... 3.50
17 world gone reptile 3.50
18 MkK,F:Morph 3.50
19 MkK,JHa 3.50
20 JCf,V:Legacy Virus,pt.1 . . . . . . 3.00
21 JCf,V:Legacy Virus,pt.2 . . . . . . 3.00
22 JCf,One gone down 3.00
23 With an Iron Fist,pt.1 . . . . 3.00
24 With an Iron Fist,pt.2 . . . . 3.00
25 With an Iron Fist,pt.3 . . . . 3.50
26 Hard Choices,pt.1 . . . . 3.00
27 Hard Choices,pt.2 . . . . 3.00
28 Unnatural Selection,pt.1 . . . . . . 3.00
29 Unnatural Selection,pt.2 . . . . . . 3.00
30 Unnatural Selection,pt.3 . . . . . . 3.00
31 Avengers Forever,pt.1 . . . . 3.00
32 Avengers Forever,pt.2 . . . . 3.00

MARVEL

33 A Second Farewell,pt.1 . . . . 3.00
34 A Second Farewell,pt.2 . . . . 3.00
35 Fantastic Voyage,pt.1 . . . . 3.00
36 Fantastic Voyage,pt.2 . . . . 3.00
37 Fantastic Voyage,pt.3 . . . . 4.00
38 King Hyperion,pt.1 . . . . 4.00
39 King Hyperion,pt.2 . . . . 4.00
40 King Hyperion,pt.3 . . . . 4.00
41 A Nocturne's Tale,pt.1 . . . . 3.00
42 A Nocturne's Tale,pt.2 . . . . 3.00
43 Blink in Time,pt.1 . . . . 3.00
44 Blink in Time,pt.2 . . . . 3.00
45 Blink in Time,pt.3 . . . . 3.00
46 Earn Your Wings,pt.1 . . . . 3.00
47 Earn Your Wings,pt.2 . . . . 3.00
48 Earn Your Wings,pt.3 . . . . 3.00
49 Capitol dome dump. 3.00
50 The Big M,pt.1 . . . . 3.00
51 The Big M,pt.2 . . . . 3.00
52 Living Planet,pt.1 . . . . 3.00
53 Living Planet,pt.2 . . . . 3.00
54 Chain Lightning. 3.00
55 Bump in the Night, pt.1. . . . . . . 3.00
56 Bump in the Night, pt.2. . . . . . . 3.00
57 Bump in the Night, pt.3 . . . . 3.00
58 F:Sasquatch, Tanaraq. 3.00
59 F:Blink. 3.00
60 Son of Apocalypse,pt.1 . . . . 4.00
61 Son of Apocalypse,pt.2 . . . . 4.00
62 Timebreakers,pt.1 . . . . 4.00
63 Timebreakers,pt.2 . . . . 3.00
64 Timebreakers,pt.3 . . . . 3.00
65 Timebreakers,pt.4 . . . . 3.00
66 Destroy All Monsters,pt.1 . . . . . 3.00
67 Destroy All Monsters,pt.2 . . . . . 3.00
68 Destroy All Monsters,pt.3 . . . . . 3.00
69 PaP,World Tour: Earth 616 . . . . 3.00
70 PaP,World Tour: Earth 616 . . . . 3.00
71 World Tour: House of M 3.00
72 World Tour: New Universe, pt. 1. 3.00
73 World Tour: New Universe, pt. 2. 3.00
74 World Tour: New Universe, pt. 3. 3.00
75 World Tour: 2099, pt. 1 . . . . . . 3.00
76 World Tour: 2099, pt. 2 . . . . . . 3.00
77 World Tour: Squadron Supreme. 3.00
78 World Tour: Squadron Supreme. 3.00
79 World Tour: Future Imperfect . . . 3.00
80 World Tour: Future Imperfect . . . 3.00
81 World Tour: Heroes Reborn 3.00
82 World Tour: Heroes Reborn 3.00
83 It's Your Funeral 3.00
84 Back in the Saddle 3.00
85 The New Exiles. 3.00
86 Countdown to Infinite Wolverines 3.00
87 Superguardians, pt.1 . . . . 3.00
88 Superguardians, pt.2 . . . . 3.00
89 JCf, Wallflower 3.00
90 CCI,PaP,J:Psylocke 3.00
91 CCI,PaP,F:Blink. 3.00
92 CCI,PaP,V:Hand 3.00
93 . . . . 3.00
94 CCI,PaP,Enemy of the Stars. . . . 3.00
95 CCI 3.00
96 CCI, Dream of Two Good Men . . . 3.00
97 CCI 3.00
98 CCI 3.00
99 Dream of Two Good Men 3.00
Ann. #1 JCf 4.00

FACTOR X
1995
1 After Xavier 4.00
2 Scott vs. Alex Summers. 3.00
3 Cyclops vs. Havok. 3.00
4 Jean & Scott 3.00

FAFHRD AND THE
GRAY MOUSER
Epic, Oct., 1990
1 MMi,Fritz Leiber adapt. 5.00
2 thru 4 MMi, Feb., 1991. . . . . . @5.00

FAITHFUL
Nov., 1949
1 Ph(c),I Take This Man 150.00
2 Ph(c),Love Thief,Feb.,1950 . . 150.00

Falcon #1
© *Marvel Entertainment Group*

FALCON
Nov., 1983
1 PS,V:Nemesis 3.00
2 V:Sentinels. 3.00
3 V:Electro 3.00
4 A:Capt.America, Feb., 1984 . . . . 3.00

FALLEN ANGELS
April, 1987
1 KGa,TP,A:Sunspot,Warlock. 3.00
2 KGa,TP,I:Gomi,Fallen Angels . . 2.50
3 KGa,TP,A:X-Factor 2.50
4 KGa,TP,A:Moon Boy, Devil
  Dinosaur 2.50
5 JSon,D:Angel,Don 2.50
6 JSon,Coconut Grove 2.50
7 KGa,Captured in CoconutGrove . 2.50
8 KGa,L:Sunspot,Warlock. 2.50

FALLEN SON: THE DEATH
OF CAPTAIN AMERICA
May, 2007
1-shot Capt. America, JLb,JR2 . . . . 3.00
1-shot-a variant (c). 3.00
1-shot JLb, Spider-Man 3.00
1-shot-a variant (c) 3.00
1-shot JLb, Iron Man 3.00
1-shot-a variant (c) 3.00

FANTASTIC FIVE
Aug., 1999
1 TDF,PR,AM,New Team:Human Torch
  Thing,Ms.Fantastic,Psilord
  & Big Brain 2.25
2A TDF,PR,AM,Bloody
  Reunions x-over 2.25
2B variant MSh(c). 2.25
3 TDF,PR,AM,A:Spider-Girl 2.25
4 TDF,PR,AM 2.25
5 TDF,PR,AM,A:Kristoff 2.25
Digest In Search of Doom 8.00

July, 2007
1 RLm, The Final Doom 3.00
2 RLm, The Final Doom 3.00
3 RLm, The Final Doom 3.00

4 RLm, The Final Doom 3.00
5 RLm, The Final Doom 3.00

FANTASTIC FORCE
1994–96
1 Foil stamped cover 3.00
2 thru 18 . . . . @2.25

FANTASTIC FOUR
Nov., 1961
1 JK,I&O:Mr.Fantastic,Thing
  Invisible Girl,Human Torch
  Mole Man 38,000.00
2 JK,I:Skrulls 9,000.00
3 JK,I:Miracleman 6,000.00
4 JK,R:Submariner 7,500.00
5 JK,JSt,I&O:Doctor Doom . . . 9,000.00
6 JK,V:Doctor Doom 5,000.00
7 JK,I:Kurrgo 3,000.00
8 JK,I:Alicia Masters,I&O:
  Puppet Master 3,000.00
9 JK,V:Submariner. 3,000.00
10 JK,V:Doctor Doom,I:Ovoids . 3,000.00
11 JK,I:Impossible Man. 2,500.00
12 JK,V:Hulk 5,000.00
13 JK,SD,I&O:Red Ghost,
   I:Watcher 1,500.00
14 JK,SD,V:Submariner 1,200.00
15 JK,I:Mad Thinker 1,200.00
16 JK,V:Doctor Doom 1,200.00
17 JK,V:Doctor Doom 1,200.00
18 JK,I:Super Skrull 1,200.00
19 JK,I&O:Rama Tut. 1,200.00
20 JK,I:Molecule Man 1,000.00
21 JK,I:Hate Monger 800.00
22 JK,V:Mole Man 500.00
23 JK,V:Doctor Doom 500.00
24 JK,I:Infant Terrible. 500.00
25 JK,Thing vs.Hulk 1,200.00
26 JK,V:Hulk,A:Avengers 1,200.00
27 JK,A:Doctor Strange 750.00
28 JK,1st X-Men x-over 1,000.00
29 JK,V:Red Ghost 500.00
30 JK,I&O:Diablo 500.00
31 JK,V:Mole Man 400.00
32 JK,V:Superskrull 400.00
33 JK,I:Attuma 400.00
34 JK,I:Gideon 400.00
35 JK,I:Dragon Man,A:Diablo . . 400.00
36 JK,I:Medusa,Frightful Four . . 400.00
37 JK,V:Skrulls. 375.00
38 JK,V:Frightful Four,I:Trapster . 375.00
39 JK,WW,A:Daredevil. 375.00
40 JK,A:Daredevil,Dr.Doom. . . . 375.00
41 JK,V:Fright.Four,A:Medusa . . 250.00
42 JK,V:Frightful Four 250.00
43 JK,V:Frightful Four 250.00
44 JK,JSt,I:Gorgon,
   V:Dragon Man 250.00
45 JK,JSt,I:Inhumans(Black Bolt,
   Triton,Lockjaw,Crystal,
   Karnak) 500.00
46 JK,JSt,V:Seeker 275.00
47 JK,JSt,I:Maximus,Attilan,
   Alpha Primitives. 275.00
48 JK,JSt,I:Silver Surfer,
   C:Galactus 1,500.00
49 JK,JSt,A:Silver Surfer,
   V:Galactus 750.00
50 JK,JSt,V:Galactus,Silver
   Surfer,I:Wyatt Wingfoot 900.00
51 JK,JSt,I:Negative Zone 500.00
52 JK,JSt,I:Black Panther 750.00
53 JK,JSt,I:Klaw,Vibranium. . . . 325.00
54 JK,JSt,I:Prester John 200.00
55 JK,JSt,A:Silver Surfer 400.00
56 JK,JSt,O:Klaw,A:Inhumans,
   C:Silver Surfer. 200.00
57 JK,JSt,V:DocDoom,A:S.Surfer. 200.00
58 JK,JSt,V:DocDoom,A:S.Surfer. 200.00
59 JK,JSt,V:DocDoom,A:S.Surfer. 200.00

60 JK,JSt,V:DocDoom,A:S.Surfer. 200.00
61 JK,JSt,V:Sandman,A:S.Surfer 200.00
62 JK,JSt,I:Blastaar 150.00
63 JK,JSt,V:Blastaar 150.00
64 JK,JSt,I:The Kree,Sentry 150.00
65 JK,JSt,I:Ronan,Supreme
   Intelligence 150.00
66 JK,JSt,O:Him,A:Crystal 225.00
67 JK,JSt,I:Him 225.00
68 JK,JSt,V:Mad Thinker 150.00
69 JK,JSt,V:Mad Thinker 150.00
70 JK,JSt,V:Mad Thinker 150.00
71 JK,JSt,V:Mad Thinker 150.00
72 JK,JSt,V:Watcher,S.Surfer . . . 200.00
73 JK,JSt,A:SpM,DD,Thor 200.00
74 JK,JSt,A:Silver Surfer 150.00
75 JK,JSt,A:Silver Surfer 150.00
76 JK,JSt,V:Psycho Man,S.Surf. . 150.00
77 JK,JSt,V:Galactus,S.Surfer . . 100.00
78 JK,JSt,V:Wizard 100.00
79 JK,JSt,A:Crystall,V:Mad
   Thinker. 100.00
80 JK,JSt,A:Crystal 100.00
81 JK,JSt,J:Crystal,V:Wizard . . . 100.00
82 JK,JSt,V:Maximus 100.00
83 JK,JSt,V:Maximus 100.00
84 JK,JSt,V:Doctor Doom 100.00
85 JK,JSt,V:Doctor Doom 75.00
86 JK,JSt,V:Doctor Doom 75.00
87 JK,JSt,V:Doctor Doom 75.00
88 JK,JSt,V:Mole Man 75.00
89 JK,JSt,V:Mole Man 75.00
90 JK,JSt,V:Skrulls 75.00
91 JK,JSt,V:Skrulls,I:Torgo. 75.00
92 JK,JSt,V:Torgo,Skrulls. 75.00
93 JK,V:Torgo,Skrulls. 75.00
94 JK,JSt,I:Agatha Harkness. . . . 75.00
95 JK,JSt,I:Monocle 75.00
96 JK,JSt,V:Mad Thinker 75.00
97 JK,JSt,V:Monster from
   Lost Lagoon. 75.00
98 JK,JSt,V:Kree Sentry 75.00
99 JK,JSt,A:Inhumans. 75.00
100 JK,JSt,V:Puppetmaster 200.00
101 JK,JSt,V:Maggia 75.00
102 JK,JSt,V:Magneto 75.00
103 JR,V:Magneto 75.00
104 JR,V:Magneto 75.00
105 JR,L:Crystal 75.00
106 JR,JSt,`Monster's Secret'. . . 75.00
107 JK,JSt,V:Annihilus. 75.00
108 JK,JB,JR,JSt, V:Annihilus. . . 75.00
109 JB,JSt,V:Annihilus. 75.00
110 JB,JSt,V:Annihilus. 75.00

Fantastic Four #88
© Marvel Entertainment Group

111 JB,JSt,A:Hulk. 75.00
112 JB,JSt,Thing vs. Hulk 250.00
113 JB,JSt,I:Overmind 60.00
114 JR(c),JB,V:Overmind. 60.00
115 JR(c),JB,JSt,I:Eternals 60.00
116 JB,JSt,O:Stranger 75.00
117 JB,JSt,V:Diablo 50.00
118 JR(c),JB,JM,V:Diablo 50.00
119 JB,JSt,V:Klaw 50.00
120 JB,JSt,I:Gabriel(Airwalker)
   (Robot). 50.00
121 JB,JSt,V:Silver Surfer,D:
   Gabriel Destroyer 75.00
122 JR(c),JB,JSt,V:Galactus,
   A:Silver Surfer 75.00
123 JB,JSt,V:Galactus,
   A:Silver Surfer 75.00
124 JB,JSt,V:Monster 50.00
125 E:StL(s),JB,JSt,V:Monster. . . 50.00
126 B:RTs(s),JB,JSt,
   O:FF,MoleMan. 50.00
127 JB,JSt,V:Mole Man 50.00
128 JB,JSt,V:Mole Man 50.00
129 JB,JSt,I:Thundra,
   V:Frightful Four 50.00
130 JSo(c),JB,JSt,V:Frightful Four. 50.00
131 JSo(c),JB,JSt,V:QuickSilver . . 50.00
132 JB,JSt,J:Medusa 50.00
133 JSt(i),V:Thundra 50.00
134 JB,JSt,V:Dragon Man 50.00
135 JB,JSt,V:Gideon 50.00
136 JB,JSt,A:Shaper 50.00
137 JB,JSt,A:Shaper 50.00
138 JB,JSt,O:Miracle Man 50.00
139 JB,V:Miracle Man 50.00
140 JB,JSt,O:Annihilus 50.00
141 JR(c),JB,JSt,V:Annihilus. . . . 50.00
142 RB,JSt,A:Doc Doom 50.00
143 GK(c),RB,V:Doc Doom 50.00
144 RB,JSt,V:Doc Doom 50.00
145 JSt&GK(c),RA,I:Ternak 50.00
146 RA,JSt,V:Ternak 50.00
147 RB,JSt,V:Subby 50.00
148 RB,JSt,V:Frightful Four. 50.00
149 RB,JSt,V:Sub-Mariner. 50.00
150 GK(c),RB,JSt,W:Crystal &
   Quicksilver,V:Ultron 60.00
151 RB,JSt,O:Thundra. 25.00
152 JR(c),RB,JM,A:Thundra 25.00
153 GK(c),RB,JSt,A:Thundra. . . . 25.00
154 GK(c),rep.Str.Tales #127. . . . 25.00
155 RB,JSt,A:Surfer. 30.00
156 RB,JSt,A:Surfer,V:Doom 30.00
157 RB,JSt,A:Surfer. 30.00
158 RB,JSt,V:Xemu 25.00
159 RB,JSt,V:Xemu 25.00
160 K&R(c),JB,V:Arkon 25.00
161 RB,JSt,V:Arkon 15.00
162 RB,DA,JSt,V:Arkon 15.00
163 RB,JSt,V:Arkon 15.00
164 JK(c),GP,JSt,V:Crusader,R:
   Marvel Boy,I:Frankie Raye . . . 15.00
165 GP,JSt,O:Crusader,
   O&D:Marvel Boy 15.00
166 GP,V:Hulk 30.00
167 JK(c),GP,JSt,V:Hulk 30.00
168 RB,JSt,J:Luke Cage 15.00
169 RB,JSt,V:Puppetmaster 15.00
170 GP,JSt,L:Luke Cage 15.00
171 JK(c),RB,GP,JSt,I:Gor. 15.00
172 JK(c),GP,JSt,V:Destroyer . . . 15.00
173 JB,JSt,V:Galactus,O:Heralds . 15.00
174 JB,V:Galactus 15.00
175 JB,A:High Evolutionary. 15.00
176 GP,JSt,V:Impossible Man . . . 15.00
177 JP,JS,A:Frightful Four
   I:Texas Twister,Capt.Ultra . . . 15.00
178 GP,V:Frightful Four,Brute . . . 15.00
179 JSt,V:Annihilus 15.00
180 reprint #101. . . . . 15.00
181 E:RTs(s),JSt,V:Brute,
   Annihilus 15.00

Fantastic Four #180
© Marvel Entertainment Group

182 SB,JSt,V:Brute,Annihilus. . . . 15.00
183 SB,JSt,V:Brute,Annihilus. . . . 15.00
184 GP,JSt,V:Eliminator. 15.00
185 GP,JSt,V:Nich.Scratch 15.00
186 GP,JSi,I:Salem's Seven 15.00
187 GP,JSt,V:Klaw,Molecule Man . 15.00
188 GP,JSt,V:Molecule Man 15.00
189 reprint FF Annual #4. . . . . . . 15.00
190 SB,O:Fantastic Four 15.00
191 GP,JSt,V:Plunderer,
   Team Breaks Up 15.00
192 GP,JSt,V:Texas Twister. 15.00
193 KP,JSt,V:Darkoth,Diablo 15.00
194 KP,V:Darkoth,Diablo 15.00
195 KP,A:Sub-Mariner 15.00
196 KP,V:Invincible Man (Reed),
   A:Dr.Doom,Team Reunited . . . 15.00
197 KP,JSt,Red Ghost 15.00
198 KP,JSt,V:Doc Doom 15.00
199 KP,JSt,V:Doc Doom 15.00
200 KP,JSt,V:Doc Doom 25.00
201 KP,JSt,FF's Machinery 8.00
202 KP,JSt,V:Quasimodo. 8.00
203 KP,JSt,V:Mutant 8.00
204 KP,JSt,V:Skrulls 8.00
205 KP,JSt,V:Skrulls 8.00
206 KP,JSt,V:Skrulls,A:Nova 8.00
207 SB,JSt,V:Monocle,A:SpM 8.00
208 SB,V:Sphinx,A:Nova 8.00
209 JBy,JSt,I:Herbie,A:Nova 10.00
210 JBy,JS,A:Galactus 8.00
211 JBy,JS,I:Terrax,A:Galactus . . 10.00
212 JBy,JSt,V:Galactus,Sphinx . . . 8.00
213 JBy,JSt,V:Terrax,Galactus
   Sphinx 8.00
214 JBy,JSt,V:Skrull 8.00
215 JBy,JSt,V:Blastaar. 8.00
216 JBy,V:Blastaar. 8.00
217 JBy,JSt,A:Dazzler 8.00
218 JBy,JSt,V:FrightfulFour,
   A:Spider-Man. 8.00
219 BSz,JSt,A:Sub-Mariner 7.00
220 JBy,JSt,A:Vindicator 7.00
221 JBy,JSt,V:Vindicator 7.00
222 BSz,JSt,V:Nicholas Scratch . . . 7.00
223 BSz,JSt,V:Salem's Seven 7.00
224 BSz,A:Thor 7.00
225 BSz,A:Thor 7.00
226 BSz,A:Shogun. 7.00
227 BSz,JSt,V:Ego-Spawn. 7.00
228 BSz,JSt,V:Ego-Spawn. 7.00
229 BSz,JSt,I:Firefrost,Ebon
   Seeker 7.00
230 BSz,JSt,A:Avengers,
   O:Firefrost & Ebon Seeker 7.00

All comics prices listed are for *Near Mint* condition.

MARVEL

Fantastic Four #249
© Marvel Entertainment Group

231 BSz,JSt,V:Stygorr 7.00
232 JBy,New Direction,V:Diablo . . . 8.00
233 JBy,V:Hammerhead 7.00
234 JBy,V:Ego 7.00
235 JBy,O:Ego 7.00
236 JBy,V:Dr.Doom,A:Puppet
    Master, 20th Anniv. 7.00
237 JBy,V:Solons 6.00
238 JBy,O:Frankie Raye,
    new Torch 6.00
239 JBy,I:Aunt Petunia,
    Uncle Jake. 6.00
240 JBy,A:Inhumans,b:Luna 6.00
241 JBy,A:Black Panther 6.00
242 JBy,A:Daredevil,Thor,Iron Man
    Spider-Man,V:Terrax 6.00
243 JBy,A:Daredevil,Dr.Strange,
    Spider-Man,Avengers,V:Galactus,
    Terrax. 6.00
244 JBy,A:Avengers,Dr.Strange,
    Galactus, Becomes Nova 6.00
245 JBy,V:Franklin Richards 6.00
246 JBy,V:Dr.Doom,
    A:Puppet Master 6.00
247 JBy,A:Dr.Doom,I:Kristoff,
    D:Zorba 6.00
248 JBy,A:Inhumans 6.00
249 JBy,V:Gladiator 6.00
250 JBy,A:Capt.Am.,SpM,
    V:Gladiator. 6.00
251 JBy,A:Annihilus 6.00
252 JBy,1st sideways issue,V:
    Ootah,A:Annihilus,w/tattoo . . 6.00
252a w/o tattoo 6.00
253 JBy,V:Kestorans,A:Annihilus. . . 6.00
254 JBy,V:Mantracora,
    A:She-Hulk,Wasp 6.00
255 JBy,A:Daredevil,Annihilus,
    V:Mantracora 6.00
256 JBy,A:Avengers,Galactus,
    V:Annihilus,New Costumes . . . 6.00
257 JBy,A:Galactus,Death,Nova,
    Scarlet Witch 5.00
258 JBy,A:Dr.Doom,D:Hauptmann . 5.00
259 JBy,V:Terrax,Dr.Doom,
    C:Silver Silver 5.00
260 JBy,V:Terrax, Dr.Doom,
    A:Silver Surfer,Sub-Mariner. . . 6.00
261 JBy,A:Sub-Mariner,Marrina,
    Silver Surfer,Sc.Witch,Lilandra . 6.00
262 JBy,O:Galactus,A:Odin,
    (J.Byrne in story) 5.00
263 JBy,V:Messiah,A:Mole Man . . . 5.00
264 JBy,V:Messiah,A:Mole Man . . . 5.00

265 JBy,A:Trapster,Avengers,
    J:She-Hulk,Secret Wars 5.00
266 KGa,JBy,A:Hulk,Sasquatch,
    V:Karisma 5.00
267 JBy,A:Hulk,Sasquatch,Morbius,
    V:Dr.Octopus,Sue miscarries . . 5.00
268 JBy,V:Doom's Mask 5.00
269 JBy,R:Wyatt Wingfoot,
    I:Terminus 5.00
270 JBy,V:Terminus 5.00
271 JBy,V:Gormuu 5.00
272 JBy,I:Warlord (Nathaniel
    Richards) 5.00
273 JBy,V:Warlord 5.00
274 JBy,AG,cont.from Thing#19,
    A:Spider-Man's Black Costume. 5.00
275 JBy,AG,V:T.J.Vance. 5.00
276 JBy,JOy,V:Mephisto,
    A:Dr.Strange 5.00
277 JBy,JOy,V:Mephisto,
    A:Dr.Strange,R:Thing 5.00
278 JBy,JOy,O:Dr.Doom,A:Kristoff
    (as Doom) 5.00
279 JBy,JOy,V:Dr.Doom(Kristoff),
    I:New Hate-Monger 5.00
280 JBy,JOy,I:Malice,
    V:Hate-Monger 5.00
281 JBy,JOy,A:Daredevil,V:Hate
    Monger,Malice 5.00
282 JBy,JOy,A:Power Pack,Psycho
    Man,Secret Wars II 5.00
283 JBy,JOy,V:Psycho-Man. 5.00
284 JBy,JOy,V:Psycho-Man. 5.00
285 JBy,JOy,Secret Wars II
    A:Beyonder 5.00
286 JBy,TA,R:Jean Grey,
    A:Hercules Capt.America 6.00
287 JBy,JSt,A:Wasp,V:Dr.Doom . . . 5.00
288 JBy,JSt,V:Dr.Doom,Secret
    Wars II 6.00
289 JBy,AG,D:Basilisk,V:Blastaar,
    R:Annihilus 5.00
290 JBy,AG,V:Annihilus 5.00
291 JBy,CR,A:Nick Fury 5.00
292 JBy,AG,A:Nick Fury,V:Hitler . . . 5.00
293 JBy,AG,A:Avengers.W.C. 5.00
294 JOy,AG,V:FutureCentralCity . . . 3.00
295 JOy,AG,V:Fut.Central City. 3.00
296 BWS,KGa,RF,BWi,AM,KJ,JB,
    SL,MS,JRu,JOy,JSt,25th
    Anniv.,V:MoleMan 5.00
297 JB,SB,V:Umbra-Sprite 3.00
298 JB,SB,V:Umbra-Sprite 3.00
299 JB,SB,She-Hulk,V:Thing,
    A:Spider-Man,L:She-Hulk 3.00
300 JB,SB,W:Torch & Fake Alicia
    (Lyja),A:Puppet-Master,Wizard,
    Mad Thinker,Dr.Doom 4.00
301 JB,SB,V:Wizard,MadThinker . . 3.00
302 JB,SB,V:Project Survival. 3.00
303 JB,RT,A:Thundra,V:Machus . . . 3.00
304 JB,JSt,V:Quicksilver. 3.00
305 JB,JSt,V:Quicksilver,
    J:Crystal,A:Dr.Doom 3.00
306 JB,JSt,A:Capt.America,
    J:Ms.Marvel,V:Diablo 3.00
307 JB,JSt,L:Reed&Sue,V:Diablo . . 3.00
308 JB,JSt,I:Fasaud 3.00
309 JB,JSt,V:Fasaud 3.00
310 KP,JSt,V:Fasaud,N:Thing
    & Ms.Marvel 3.00
311 KP,JSt,A:Black Panther,
    Dr.Doom,V:THRob. 3.00
312 KP,JSt,A:Black Panther,
    Dr.Doom,X-Factor 3.00
313 SB,JSt,V:Lava Men,
    A:Moleman 3.00
314 KP,JSt,V:Belasco 3.00
315 KP,JSt,V:Mast.Pandem. 3.00
316 KP,JSt,A:CometMan 3.00
317 KP,JSt,L:Crystal 3.00

318 KP,JSt,V:Dr.Doom 3.00
319 KP,JSt,G-Size,O:Beyonder 3.00
320 KP,JSt,Hulk vs Thing 3.00
321 RLm,RT,A:She-Hulk 3.00
322 KP,JSt,Inferno,V:Graviton 3.00
323 KP,JSt,RT,Inferno A:Mantis 3.00
324 KP,JSt,RT,A:Mantis 3.00
325 RB,RT,A:Silver Surfer,
    D:Mantis 3.00
326 KP,RT,I:New Frightful Four 3.00
327 KP,RT,V:Frightful Four. 3.00
328 KP,RT,V:Frightful Four. 3.00
329 RB,RT,V:Mole Man 3.00
330 RB,RT,V:Dr.Doom 3.00
331 RB,RT,V:Ultron 3.00
332 RB,RT,V:Aron 3.00
333 RB,RT,V:Aron,Frightful Four . . . 3.00
334 RB,Acts of Vengeance 3.00
335 RB,RT,Acts of Vengeance 3.00
336 RLm,Acts of Vengeance, ... 3.00
337 WS,A:Thor,Iron Man,
    B:Timestream saga 4.00
338 WS,V:Deathshead,A:Thor,
    Iron Man 3.00
339 WS,V:Gladiator 3.00
340 WS,V:Black Celestial 3.00
341 WS,A:Thor,Iron Man 3.00
342 A:Rusty,C:Spider-Man 3.00
343 WS,V:Stalin 3.00
344 WS,V:Stalin 3.00
345 WS,V:Dinosaurs 3.00
346 WS,V:Dinosaurs 3.00
347 AAd,ATi(i)A:Spider-Man,
    GhostRider,Wolverine,Hulk . . 4.00
347a 2nd printing 3.00
348 AAd,ATi(i)A:Spider-Man,
    GhostRider,Wolverine,Hulk . . 4.00
348a 2nd printing 3.00
349 AAd,ATi(i),AM(i)A:Spider-Man,
    Wolverine,GhostRider,Hulk,
    C:Punisher 3.50
350 WS,AM(i),R:Ben Grimm as
    Thing,(48p) 3.50
351 MBa,Kubic. 3.00
352 WS,Reed Vs.Dr.Doom 3.00
353 WS,E:Timestream Saga,
    A:Avengers. 3.00
354 WS,Secrets of the Time
    Variance Authority 3.00
355 AM,V:Wrecking Crew 3.00
356 B:TDF(s),PR,A:New Warriors,
    V:Puppet Master 3.00
357 PR,V:Mad Thinker,
    Puppetmaster, ... 3.00
358 PR,AAd,30th Anniv.,1st Marv.
    Die Cut(c),D:Lyja,V:Paibok,
    BU:Doom 3.50
359 PR,I:Devos the Devastator 3.00
360 PR,V:Dreadface 3.00
361 PR,V:Dr.Doom,X-masIssue . . . 3.00
362 PR,A:Spider-Man,
    I:WildBlood 3.00
363 PR,I:Occulus,A:Devos 3.00
364 PR,V:Occulus 3.00
365 PR,V:Occulus 3.00
366 PR,Infinity War,R:Lyja 3.00
367 PR,Inf.War,A:Wolverine 3.00
368 PR,V:Infinity War X-Men 3.00
369 PR,Inf.War,R:Malice,
    A:Thanos 3.00
370 PR,Inf.War,V:Mr.Fantastic
    Doppleganger 3.00
371 PR,V:Lyja,foil(c) 4.00
371a 2nd Printing 3.00
372 PR,A:Spider-Man,Silver
    Sable 3.00
373 PR,V:Aron,Silver sable 3.00
374 PR,V:Secret Defenders 3.00
375 V:Dr.Doom,A:Inhumans,Lyja,
    Holo-Grafix(c) 3.50
376 PR,A:Nathan Richards,V:Paibok,
    Devos,w/Dirt Magazine 3.50

376a w/out Dirt Magazine 2.50
377 PR,V:Paibok,Devos,Klaw,
   I:Huntara 2.50
378 PR,A:Sandman,SpM,DD. 2.50
379 PR,V:Ms.Marvel 2.50
380 PR,A:Dr.Doom,V:Hunger 2.50
381 PR,D:Dr.Doom,Mr.Fantastic,
   V:Hunger 5.00
382 PR,V:Paibok,Devos,Huntara. . 3.00
383 PR,V:Paibok,Devos,Huntara . 2.50
384 PR,A:Ant-Man,V:Franklin
   Richards 2.50
385 PR,A:Triton,Tiger Shark,
   Starblast#7. . . . . 2.50
386 PR,Starblast#11,A:Namor,Triton,
   b:Johnny & Lyja child 2.50
387 Die-Cut & Foil (c),PR,N:Invisible
   Woman,J:Ant-Man,A:Namor . . . 4.00
387a Newsstand Ed. 2.50
388 PR,I:Dark Raider,V:FF,
   Avengers,w/cards 2.50
389 PR,I:Raphael Suarez,A:Watcher,
   V:Collector. 2.50
390 PR,A:Galactus. 2.50
391 PR,I:Vibraxas. 2.50
392 Dark Raider. 2.50
393 . . . . 2.50
394 Neon(c) w/insert print 3.00
394a Newsstand ed.,no bag/inserts 2.50
395 Thing V:Wolverine. 2.50
396 . . . . 2.50
397 Resurrection,pt.1. . . . . 2.50
398 regular edition. 2.50
398a Enhanced cover 3.00
399 Watcher's Lie 3.00
399a Foil stamped cover 3.00
400 Watcher's Lie,pt.3 . . . . 5.00
401 V:Tantalus. 2.50
402 Atlantis Rising,Namor
   vs. Black Bolt. 2.50
403 TDF,PR,DBi,F:Thing,Medusa . 2.50
404 R:Namor,I:New Villian. 2.50
405 J:Namor 2.50
406 TDF,PR,DBI,R:Dr. Doom,
   I:Hyperstorm 2.50
407 TDF,PR,DBi,Return of
   Reed Richards. 2.50
408 TDF,PR,DBi,Original FF unite. . 2.50
409 TDF,PR,DBi,All new line-up . . 2.50
410 . . . . 2.50
411 . . . . 2.50
412 TDF,PR,DBi,Mr.Fantastic
   vs. Sub-Mariner. 2.50
413 . . . . 2.50

Fantastic Four #404
© *Marvel Entertainment Group*

414 Galactus vs. Hyperstorm 2.50
415 Onslaught saga, A:X-Men. 4.00
416 Onslaught saga, A:Dr. Doom,
   double size, finale 5.00
Ann.#1 JK,SD,I:Atlantis,Dorma,
   Krang,V:Namor,O:FF 1,700.00
Ann.#2 JK,JSt,O:Dr.Doom . . . 1,000.00
Ann.#3 JK,W:Reed and Sue 400.00
Ann.#4 JK,JSt,I:Quasimodo. . . . 250.00
Ann.#5 JK,JSt,A:Inhumans,Silver
   Surfer,Black Panther,
   I:Psycho Man. 250.00
Ann.#6 JK,JSt,I:Annihilus,
   Franklin Richards 250.00
Ann.#7 JK(c),reprints 100.00
Ann.#8 JR(c),reprints 50.00
Ann.#9 JK(c),reprints. 50.00
Ann.#10 reprints Ann.#3 . . . . 50.00
Ann.#11 JK(c),JB,A:The Invaders . 12.00
Ann.#12 A:The Invaders 12.00
Ann.#13 V:The Mole Man 12.00
Ann.#14 GP,V:Salem's Seven 12.00
Ann.#15 GP,V:Dr.Doom,Skrulls . . 10.00
Ann.#16 V:Dragonlord 10.00
Ann.#17 JBy,V:Skrulls 10.00
Ann.#18 KGa,V:Skrulls,W:Black
   Bolt and Medusa,A:Inhumans . 10.00
Ann.#19 JBy,V:Skrulls 10.00
Ann.#20 TD(i),V:Dr.Doom 4.00
Ann.#21 JG,JSt,Evol.Wars 4.00
Ann.#22 RB,Atlantis Attacks,
   A:Avengers 4.00
Ann.#23 JG,GCa,Days of Future
   Present #1 . . . . 5.00
Ann.#24 JG,AM,Korvac Quest #1,
   A:Guardians of the Galaxy 3.00
Ann.#25 Citizen Kang #3. . . . . 3.00
Ann.#26 HT,I:Wildstreak,
   V:Dreadface,w/card 3.50
Ann.#27 MGu,V:Justice Peace . . . 3.50
G-Size#1 RB,Thing/Hulk 17.00
G-Size#2 K&R(c),JB,Time to Kill . 15.00
G-Size#3 RB,JSt,Four Horseman . 15.00
G-Size#4 JB,JSt,I:Madrox 15.00
G-Size#5 JK(c),V:Psycho Man,
   Molecule Man 12.00
G-Size#6 V:Annihilus. 12.00
Spec.#1 Rep.Ann.#1 JBy(c). 2.50
Marvel Milestone rep. #1 (1991) . . 3.00
Marvel Milestone rep. #5 (1992) . . 3.00
Ashcan 75
Spec. The Origin of Galactus. 2.50
Spec. Marvel's Greatest Comic:
   rep. #52: I:Black Panther (2006) 3.00

[2nd Series], Nov., 1996

1 JLe,BCi,SW, 48pg 5.00
1A Mole Man cover. 12.00
1B Gold signature, bagged,
   limited 25.00
2 JLe,BCi,V:Namor. 5.00
3 JLe,BCi,SW,A:Avengers 4.00
4 JLe,BCi,SW,I:Black Panther . . . 4.00
4A x-mas cover. 5.00
5 JLe,BCi,SW,V:Dr. Doom 4.00
6 JLe,BCi,SW,Industrial Revolution
   prologue. 3.00
7 JLe,BCi,BBh,V:Blastaar. 3.00
8 JLe,BCi,BBh,V:Inhumans 3.00
9 JLe,BCi,BBh,V:Inhumans 3.00
10 JLe,BCi,BBh,A:Silver Surfer,
   Tyrax 3.00
11 JLe,BCi,BBh,A:Silver Surfer,
   Firelord, Terrax 3.00
12 JLe,BCi,BBh,GalactusSaga,pt.1,
   reunited 5.00
13 JeR,Wildstorm x-over 3.00
Ashcan, signed, numbered 10.00

[3rd Series], Nov., 1997

1 SLo,AD,MFm, The Ruined, 48pg
   debut 5.00
2 SLo,AD,MFm,A:Iconoclast. 4.00
3 SLo,AD,MFm,V:Red Ghost 4.00

Fantastic Four 3rd Series #1
© *Marvel Entertainment Group*

4 SLo,SvL,ATi,A:Silver Surfer,
   double size 4.00
4 signed by SLo, (500 copies) . . . 20.00
5 SLo,SvL,ATi,V:The Crucible 3.00
6 CCI,SvL, new villains. 3.00
7 CCI,SvL,ATi,V:Technet. 3.00
8 CCI,SvL,ATi,V:Captain Britain corp. . . 3.00
9 CCI,SvL,A:Spider-Man. 3.00
10 CCI,SvL,ATi. 3.00
11 CCI,SvL,ATi,Crucible—unleashed
   in Genosha 3.00
12 CCI,SvL,ATi,V:Fantastic Four
   double-size 4.50
13 CCI,SvL,A:Ronan the Accuser . 2.50
14 CCI,SvL,V:Ronan 2.50
15 CCI,SvL,ATi,Iron Man x-over . . 2.50
16 CCI,SvL,ATi,V:Kree Avengers . . 2.50
17 CCI,SvL,ATi,I:Lockdown 2.50
18 CCI,SvL,ATi,Jail Break 2.50
19 CCI,SvL,ATi,V:Annihilus 2.50
20 CCI,SvL,ATi,V:Ruined 2.50
21 CCI,SvL,ATi,V:Hades 2.50
22 CCI,SvL,ATi,V:Valeria
   Von Doom 2.50
23 CCI,SvL,ATi,A:She-Hulk 2.50
24 CCI,SvL,ATi,F:FranklinRichards . 2.50
25 CCI,SvL,ATi,V:Dr.Doom 3.50
26 CCI,SvL,ATi,F:ValeriaVonDoom . 3.00
27 CCI,SvL,F:Invisible Woman . . . 3.00
28 CCI,SvL,ATi,Planet Doom. 3.00
29 CCI,SvL,ATi,Frightful Four 2.50
30 CCI,SvL,ATi,Castle Doom. 2.50
31 CCI,SvL,ATi,InvisibleWoman . . . 2.50
32 CCI,SvL,ATi,InvisibleWoman . . . 2.50
33 JFM,SvL,ATi,Kid Colt 2.50
34 JFM,SvL,ATi,aliens 2.50
35A CPa,Diablo,foil (c). 5.00
35B painted (c) 2.50
36 CPa,Diablo triumphant 2.50
37 CPa,F:Johnny Storm. 2.50
38 CPa,JLb,V:Grey Gargoyle 2.50
39 CPa,JLb,V:Grey Gargoyle 2.50
40 CPa,JLb,Negative Zone 2.50
41 CPa,JLb,Hellscout 2.50
42 CPa,JLb,SI,V:Namor. 2.50
43 CPa,JLb,JoB,new Fant.Four. . . . 2.50
44 CPa,JLb,Negative Zone,concl. . . 2.50
45 CPa,JLb,one new costume. . . . 2.50
46 CPa,JLb,Abraxas Saga 2.50
47 CPa,JLb,Abraxas,pt.3. . . . . 2.50
48 CPa,JLb,Abraxas,pt.4 . . . . 2.50
49 CPa,JLb,Abraxas,pt.5. . . . . 2.50
50 Four new stories,BWS(c),64-pg. . 5.00
51 MBa,KK,F:Inhumans. 3.50

52 MBa,KK,F:Dr. Doom 2.25
53 MBa,KK,Inhumans 2.25
54 MBa,KK,Inhumans, 100-pg. 4.00
55 KK,SI,Thing,Human Torch 2.25
56 F:Thing 2.25
57 AWa,F:Thing,pt.1 . . . . 2.25
58 AWa,F:Thing,pt.2 . . . . 2.25
59 AWa,F:Thing,pt.3 . . . . 2.25
60 MWa,KK 2.25
61 MWa,KK 3.00
62 MWa,KK,Sentient,pt.1, 48-pg . . 3.00
63 MWa,KK,Sentient,pt.2 . . . . 3.00
64 MWa,KK,Sentient,pt.3 . . . . 3.00
65 MWa,MBu,Small Stuff/Big Stuff. . 3.00
66 MWa,MBu,Small Stuff/Big Stuff. . 3.00
67 MWa,KK,Unthinkable 5.00
68 MWa,KK,Unthinkable 3.50
69 MWa,KK,Unthinkable 3.50
70 MWa,Unthinkable 3.50
500 MWa,Unthinkable,48-pg. 5.00
500a Director's Cut, foil 6.00
501 MWa,CJ,Fifth Wheel,pt.1 . . . . . 2.25
502 MWa,CJ,Fifth Wheel,pt.2 . . . . . 2.25
503 MWa,Authoritative Action,pt.1. . 2.25
504 MWa,Authoritative Action,pt.2. . 2.25
505 MWa,Authoritative Action,pt.3. . 2.25
506 MWa,Authoritative Action,pt.4. . 2.25
507 MWa,Authoritative Action,pt.5. . 2.25
508 MWa,Authoritative Action,pt.6. . 2.25
509 MWa,Hereafter,pt.1 . . . . 2.25
510 MWa,Hereafter,pt.2 . . . . 2.25
511 MWa,Hereafter,pt.3 . . . . 2.25
512 MWa,Spider Sense,pt.1 . . . . . . 2.25
513 MWa,Spider Sense,pt.2 . . . . . . 2.25
514 MWa&KK(s),Dysfunctional,pt.1. 2.25
515 MWa&KK(s),Dysfunctional,pt.2. 2.25
516 MWa,KK(s),Dysfunctional,pt.3 . 2.25
517 MWa(s),Fourtitude,pt.1 . . . . . . 3.00
518 Fourtitude,pt.2 . . . . 3.00
519 Fourtitude,pt.3 . . . . 3.00
520 . . . . 3.00
521 . . . . 3.00
522 MWa,MeW,Galactus 3.00
523 MWa,MeW,Rising Storm, concl. 3.00
524 MWa,MeW, ... 3.00
525 KK,TGu,Dream Fever,pt.1 . . . . 3.00
526 KK,TGu,Dream Fever,pt.2 . . . . 3.00
527 MMK,Distant Music, Entity 5.00
528 MMK,Random Factors, Entity . . 3.00
529 MMK,Appointment Overdue . . . 3.00
530 MMK,Reunion with destiny 3.00
531 MSz(s),MMK,V:The Entity,pt.5 . 3.00
532 MSz(s),MMK,V:The Entity,pt.6 . 3.00
533 MSz(s),MMK,A:Hulk 3.00

534 MSz(s),MMK,A:Hulk 3.00
535 MSz(s),MMK,A:Hulk 3.00
536 MSz(s),MMK,Road to Civil War 7.00
537 MSz(s),MMK,Road to Civil War 7.00
538 MSz(s),MMK,Civil War tie-in. . 3.50
539 MSz(s),MMK,Civil War tie-in. . 3.50
540 MSz(s),MMK,Civil War tie-in. . 3.50
541 MSz(s),MMK,Civil War tie-in. . 3.50
542 MSz(s),MMK,Civil War tie-in. . 3.50
543 MSz(s),MMK,Civil War tie-in. . 3.50
544 DMD(s),PaP 3.00
545 DMD(s),PaP 3.00
546 DMD(s),PaP,V:Epoch 3.00
547 DMD(s),PaP,V:The Wizard . . . 3.00
548 . . . . 3.00
549 DMD(s),PaP 3.00
550 DMD(s),PaP 3.00
551 . . . . 3.00
552 DMD(s),PaP,V:Dr. Doom 3.00
Ann.1998 Fant.Four & Fant.Four. . 4.00
Ann.1999 CCl,I:Mechamage 4.00
Ann.2000 LSi,SvL,48-pg. 4.00
Ann.2001 Galactus,48-page 3.50
Spec.#1 KIK FantasticFour (2000). 2.25
Spec. Fantastic Four/Sentry 3.00
Spec. Fantastic Fourth Voyage
  of Sinbad, 48-page (2001) 6.00
Spec. The Movie,DJu (2005) 5.00
Spec. Franklin Richards, Son
  Of a Genius, Rep. Power Pack . 3.00
Spec. The Wedding (2006) 5.00

FANTASTIC FOUR: ATLANTIS RISING
1995
1 B:Atlantis Rising 5.00
2 TDF,MCW,finale, acetate(c). 5.00

FANTASTIC FOUR: A DEATH IN THE
May, 2006
1 64-pg. 4.00

FANTASTIC FOUR INDEX
See: OFFICIAL MARVEL
INDEX TO THE
FANTASTIC FOUR

FANTASTIC FOUR: FIRST FAMILY
Mar., 2006
1 CWn 3.00
2 thru 6 CWn . . . . @3.00

FANTASTIC FOUR: FOES
Jan., 2005
1 (of 6) Puppet Master & Mad
  Thinker. 3.00
2 Annihilus 3.00
3 Green Goblin 3.00
4 Mole Man 3.00
5 Red Ghost 3.00
6 conclusion 3.00

FANTASTIC FOUR: HOUSE OF M
July, 2005
1 (of 3) SEa, A:Magneto, Doom . . . 3.00
2 Sea 3.00
3 SEa, concl.. . . . . 3.00

FANTASTIC FOUR/ IRON MAN: BIG IN JAPAN
Oct., 2005
1 . . . . 3.50
2 All-out Monster Riot 3.50

Fantastic Four Ann. #24
© *Marvel Entertainment Group*

3 Do you know kung fu 3.50
4 Chock Full'O Monsters 3.50

FANTASTIC FOUR: 1 2 3 4
June, 2001
1 (of 4) GMo,JaL,F:Thing 3.00
2 GMo,JaL,F:Invisible Woman . . . 3.00
3 GMo,JaL,F:Human Torch. 3.00
4 GMo,JaL,F:Mr. Fantastic 3.00

FANTASTIC FOUR AND POWER PACK
July, 2007
1 Attack of the Super-Bullies 3.00
2 . . . . 3.00
3 . . . . 3.00
4 . . . . 3.00

FANTASTIC FOUR ROAST
May, 1982
1 FH/MG/FM/JB/MA/TA 5.00

FANTASTIC FOUR'S BIG TOWN
Nov., 2000
1 (of 4) SEt,MMK,MkK,48-page . . . 3.50
2 SEt,MMK,MkK 3.00
3 SEt,MMK,MkK 3.00
4 SEt,MMK,MkK,48-page 3.50

FANTASTIC FOUR: THE END
Nov., 2006
1 AD 4.00
1a 3.00
2 AD 3.00
3 thru 6 AD . . . . @3.00

FANTASTIC FOUR 2099
1996
1 Cont. from 2099 Genesis. 4.00
2 thru 5 . . . . @2.25

FANTASTIC FOUR UNLIMITED
1993–96
1 HT,A:Bl.Panther,V:Klaw 4.50
2 HT,JQ(c),A:Inhumans 4.25
3 HT,V:Blastaar,Annihilus 4.25
4 RTs(s),HT,V:Mole Man,A:Hulk . . 4.25
5 RTs(s),HT,V:Frightful Four 4.25
6 RTs(s),HT,V:Namor 4.00
7 HT,V:Monsters 4.00
8 . . . . 4.00
9 A:Antman 4.00
10 RTs,HT,V:Maelstrom,A:Eternals . 4.00
11 RTs,HT,Atlantis Rising fallout . . . 4.00
12 RTs,TDF,V:Hyperstorm 4.00
13 . . . . 4.00

FANTASTIC FOUR UNPLUGGED
1995–96
1 comic for a buck 2.50
2 Reed Richard's Will 2.50
3 F:Mr. Fantastic 2.50
4 . . . . 2.50
5 Back in NY,V:Blastaar 2.50

FANTASTIC FOUR: UNSTABLE MOLECULES
Jan., 2003
1 (of 4) GyD 3.00
2 GyD 3.00

3 GyD 3.00

FANTASTIC FOUR VS. X-MEN
Feb., 1987
1 JBg,TA,V:Dr.Doom. 5.00
2 JBg,TA,V:Dr.Doom. 4.00
3 JBg,TA,V:Dr.Doom. 4.00
4 JBg,TA,V:Dr.Doom, June, 1987. . 4.00

FANTASTIC FOUR THE WORLD'S GREATEST COMIC MAGAZINE
Dec., 2000
1 (of 12) EL,ErS,V:Dr.Doom 3.00
2 F:Dr.Doom,Crystal 3.00
3 A:X-Men,Spider-Man 3.00
4 A:X-Men,Capt.America 3.00
5 EL(c),Hulk vs. Thing 3.00
6 MGo(c),A:Silver Surfer. 3.00
7 KG(c),A:Dr.Doom,Inhumans 3.00
8 KG(c),F:Avengers 3.00
9 EL,KG,A:Dr.Doom 3.00
10 EL,KG,Cosmic Cube 3.00
11 RF,Planet Doom 3.00
12 StL,EL,JSt, concl. 3.00

FANTASTIC WORLD OF HANNA-BARBERA
Dec., 1977
1 . . . . 30.00
2 . . . . 20.00
3 June, 1978 . . . . 20.00

![Fantasy Masterpieces #12]

Fantasy Masterpieces #12
© Marvel Entertainment Group

FANTASY MASTERPIECES
Feb., 1966
1 JK/DH/SD,reprints 250.00
2 JK,SD,DH,Fin Fang Foom. . . . 100.00
3 GC,DH,JK,SD,Capt.A rep. 100.00
4 JK,Capt.America rep. 100.00
5 JK,Capt.America rep. 100.00
6 JK,Capt.America rep. 100.00
7 SD,Sub Mariner rep. 100.00
8 H.Torch & Sub M.rep. 100.00
9 SD,MF,O:Human Torch Rep . . 100.00
10 rep.All Winners #19 . . . . 100.00
11 JK,(rep),O:Toro 100.00
Becomes:

MARVEL SUPER-HEROES

FANTASY MASTERPIECES
[Volume 2], Dec., 1979
1 JB,JSt,Silver Surfer rep. 5.00
2 thru 7 JB,JSt,Silver Surfer rep. @5.00
8 thru 11 JB/JSn,.Strange Tales . @4.00
12 thru 14 JB,JSn,rep.Warlock . . @4.00

FAREWELL TO WEAPONS
1 DirtBag,W/Nirvana Tape 3.50

FEAR
Nov., 1970
1 JK,1950's Monster rep.B:I
   Found Monstrum,The Dweller
   in the Black Swamp. 75.00
2 JK,X The Thing That Lived 40.00
3 JK,Zzutak, The Thing That
   Shouldn't Exist. 40.00
4 JK,I Turned Into a Martian. 40.00
5 JK,I Am the Gorilla Man. 40.00
6 JK,SD,The Midnight Monster. . . 40.00
7 JK,SD,I Dream of Doom 25.00
8 JK,SD,It Crawls By Night! 25.00
9 JK,Dead Man's Escape 25.00
Becomes:

ADVENTURE INTO FEAR
1972
10 HC,GM,B:Man-Thing 55.00
11 RB,I:Jennifer Kale,Thog 25.00
12 JSn,RB 25.00
13 VM,Where World's Collide 18.00
14 VM,Plague o/t Demon Cult. . . . 18.00
15 VM,Lord o/t Dark Domain 18.00
16 VM,ManThing in Everglades. . . 18.00
17 VM,I:Wundarr(Aquarian) 18.00
18 VM. 18.00
19 VM,FMc,I:Howard the Duck,
   E:Man-Thing 55.00
20 PG,GK,B:Morbius 55.00
21 GK,V:Uncanny Caretaker 20.00
22 RB,V:Cat-Demond 20.00
23 GC,GK,1st CR art,A World He
   Never Made. 20.00
24 CR,SMn,V:Blade, The Vampire
   Slayer 35.00
25 FR,GK,You Always Kill the
   One You Love 15.00
26 FR,GK,V:Uncanny Caretaker . . 15.00
27 FR,GK,V:Simon Stroud. 15.00
28 GK,Doorway Down into Hell. . . 15.00
29 Death has a Thousand Eyes . . 15.00
30 Bloody Sacrifice 15.00
31 FR,GK,last issue,Dec., 1975 . . 15.00

FEUD
Epic, 1993
1 I:Skids,Stokes,Kite 3.00
2 thru 4 . . . . @2.25

FIGHT MAN
1993
1 I:Fight Man. 2.25

FILM FUNNIES
Marvel Chipiden Publ., 1949–50
1 Funny animal 250.00
2 . . . . 175.00

FIRESTAR
March, 1986
1 MW,SL,O:Firestar,A:X-Men,
   New Mutants 5.00
2 MW,BWI,A:New Mutants 4.00
3 AAd&BSz(c),MW,SL,
   A:White Queen 4.00
4 MW,SL,V:White Queen 4.00
Digest X-Men: Firestar (2006) 8.00

FISH POLICE
1992–93
1 V:S.Q.U.I.D,Hook. 2.50
2 thru 6 . . . . @2.50

FLASH GORDON
1995
1 R:Flash Gordon 3.00
2 AW,V:Ming, final issue 3.00

FLINTSTONE KIDS
Star, Aug., 1987
1 thru 10 . . . . @5.00
11 April, 1989. . . . . 5.00

FLINTSTONES
Oct., 1977–Feb., 1979
1 From TV Series 75.00
2 . . . . 50.00
3 . . . . 30.00
4 A:Jetsons 30.00
5 thru 7 . . . . @35.00

FLYING HERO BARBIE
1 Super Hero Barbie. 2.25

FOOFUR
Star, Aug., 1987
1 thru 6 . . . . @3.00

FOOLKILLER
Oct., 1990
1 I:Kurt Gerhardt
   (Foolkiller III) 3.50
2 O:Foolkiller I & II 3.00
3 Old Costume 3.00
4 N:Foolkiller. 2.50
5 Body Count 2.50
6 thru 10 . . . . @2.25
Oct., 2007
1 (of 5) Fool's Paradise 4.00
2 Fool's Paradise, pt.2 . . . . 4.00

FORCE WORKS
1994–96
1 TmT,Pop-up(c),I:Century,V:Kree,
   N:US Agent 4.00
2 thru 11 . . . . @2.25
12 V:Recorder 3.00
13 thru 20 . . . . @2.25

![Force Works #3]

Force Works #3
© Marvel Entertainment Group

MARVEL

411
April, 2003
1 thru 3 . . . . @3.50

FOR YOUR EYES ONLY
1 HC,James Bond rep. 3.00
2 HC,James Bond rep. 3.00

Fraggle Rock #4
© Marvel Entertainment Group

FRAGGLE ROCK
1985
1 thru 8 . . . . @5.00
[Volume 2], April, 1988
1 thru 5 rep.. . . . . @2.50
6 Sept., 1988 . . . . 2.50

FRANCIS, BROTHER
OF THE UNIVERSE
1980
1-shot SB. 5.00

FRANKLIN RICHARDS
Mar, 2007
Spec. March Madness! 3.00
Spec. World Be Warned 3.00
Spec. Monster Mash 3.00
Spec. Fall Football Fiasco! 3.00

FRANKENSTEIN
See: MONSTER OF
FRANKENSTEIN

FRED HEMBECK
1-shot Destroys the Marvel
  Universe, parody (1989) 2.25
1-shot Sells the Marvel Universe
  parody (1990) 2.25

FRIENDLY NEIGHBOR-
HOOD SPIDER-MAN
Oct., 2005
1 PDd(s),The Other, x-over,pt.1 . . 6.00
1a 2nd printing 5.00
2 PDd(s),The Other, x-over,pt.4 . . 3.00
2a 2nd printing 6.00
3 PDd(s),The Other, x-over,pt.7 . . 3.00
3a 2nd printing 6.00
4 PDd(s),The Other, x-over,pt.10 . . 3.00
5 PDd(s),Weblog 3.00
6 PDd(s),Wrestling 3.00

7 PDd(s),Wrestling 3.00
8 PDd(s),MeW 3.00
9 PDd(s),Jumping the Tracks 3.00
10 PDd(s),Jumping the Tracks . . . 3.00
11 PDd(s),I Hate a Mystery,pt.1 . . . 3.00
12 PDd(s),I Hate a Mystery,pt.2 . . . 3.00
13 PDd(s),I Hate a Mystery,pt.3 . . . 3.00
14 PDd(s),A:Deb Whitman,V:Vulture 3.00
15 PDd(s),SEa,V:Vulture 3.00
16 PDd(s),SEa,V:Vulture 3.00
17 PDd(s),TNu,Back in Black 3.00
17a variant (c) 5.00
18 PDd(s),TNu,Back in Black 3.00
19 PDd(s),TNu,Back in Black 3.00
20 PDd(s),TNu,Back in Black 3.00
21 PDd(s),TNu,Back in Black 3.00
22 PDd(s),TNu,Back in Black 3.00
23 PDd(s),TNu,Back in Black 3.00
24 MSz,JQ,One More Day, pt.2 . . . 4.00
24a variant (c) 4.00
Ann. #1 PDd(s) 4.00

FRIGHT
June, 1975
1 Son of Dracula 15.00

FRONTIER WESTERN
Feb., 1956
1 RH,. 275.00
2 AW,GT,GC,JMn 200.00
3 MD 200.00
4 MD,Ringo Kid 150.00
5 RC,DW,JDa 200.00
6 AW,GC 175.00
7 JR,JMn. 150.00
8 RC,DW. 150.00
9 JMn 150.00
10 SC,Aug., 1957 . . . . 150.00

FUNNY FROLICS
Summer, 1945
1 Shardy Fox,KrazyKroid,(fa) . . . 300.00
2 . . . . 150.00
3 . . . . 100.00
4 . . . . 100.00
5 HK 125.00

FUNNY TUNES
Marvel Timely, 1944–46
(KRAZY KOMICS spinoff)
16 Animated Funny
  Comic-Tunes 250.00
17 . . . . 200.00
18 . . . . 200.00
19 . . . . 200.00
20 . . . . 200.00
21 . . . . 200.00
22 . . . . 200.00
23 HK 200.00
Becomes:

OSCAR

FURTHER ADVENTURES
OF CYCLOPS
AND PHOENIX
1996
1 thru 4 . . . . @3.00

FURY
1994
1 MCW,O:Fury,A:S.A. Heroes 3.25

FURY
Marvel Max, Sept., 2001
1 (of 6) GEn,DaR,JP,F:Nick Fury . . 6.00
2 GEn,DaR,JP,F:Rudi Gagarin 4.00

3 GEn,DaR,JP 4.00
4 GEn,DaR,JP 4.00
5 GEn,DaR,JP 4.00
6 GEn,DaR,JP 4.00

FURY/AGENT 13
March, 1998
1 (of 2) TKa,is Nick Fury alive? . . . 3.00
2 TKa,MZ(c),Sharon Carter's searches
  for Nick 3.00

FURY OF S.H.I.E.L.D.
1995
1 Foil etched cover 3.00
2 A:Iron Man 2.50
3 J:Hydra 2.50
4 w/decoder card 3.00

FURY: PEACEMAKER
Feb., 2006
1 GEn,DaR,JP, Kasserine Pass . . . 3.50
2 GEn,DaR,JP, War Without Army . 3.50
3 thru 6 GEn,DaR,JP . . . . @3.50

GALACTIC GUARDIANS
1994
1 KWe,C:Woden 2.50
2 KWe,I:Hazmat,Savant,Ganglia . . 2.50
3 KWe 2.50
4 KWe,final issue 2.50

GALACTUS
THE DEVOURER
April, 1999
1 (of 6) JMu,LSi,A:Silver Surfer,
  Fant.Four & Avengers,48-page . 4.00
2 LSi,JB,BSz. 3.00
3 LSi,JB,BSz. 3.00
4 LSi,JB,BSz,A:Silver Surfer. 3.00
5 LSi,JB,BSz. 3.00
6 LSi,JB,BSz,concl. 3.50

GAMBIT
1997
1 HMe(c),LW,KJ,V:Assassin'sGuild,
  D:Henri LeBeau,Embossed(c). . 5.00
1a Gold Ed.. . . . . 15.00
2 LW,KJ,C:Gideon,A:Rogue 3.00
3 LW,KJ,A:Candra,Rogue,
  D:Gambit's Father 3.00
4 LW,KJ,A:Candra,Rogue,D:Tithe
  Collector 3.00

GAMBIT
1997
1 (of 4) HMe,KJ,In Miami 3.50
2 HMe,KJ, ... 3.00
3 HMe,KJ,in the Vatican 3.00
4 HMe V:Stoker, concl. 3.00

GAMBIT
Dec., 1998
1 FaN,SSr,O:Gambit,48-page. 4.00
1a signed 25.00
2 FaN,SSr,V:Storm 3.00
2a variant cover 3.00
3 FaN,SSr,V:Mengo Brothers 2.50
4 FaN,SSr,A:Blade 2.50
5 FaN,SSr,R:Rogue 2.50
6 FaN,SSr,I:The Pig 2.50
7 FaN,SSr, ... 2.50
8 FaN,A:Sinister,Sabretooth 2.50
9 FaN,The Shattering,x-over 2.50
10 FaN,V:Candra & Fenris 2.50
11 FaN,A:Daredevil 2.50
12 FaN 2.50
13 FaN,Black Womb 2.50

14 FaN,ALa,A:Mr. Sinister	2.50
15 FaN,F:Rogue	2.50
16 FaN,X-Men: Revolution	2.50
16a variant (c)	2.50
17 FaN,AssassinationGame,pt.1	2.25
18 FaN,AssassinationGame,pt.2	2.25
19 FaN,AssassinationGame,pt.3	2.25
20 FaN,Fontanelle	2.25
21 FaN,Remy LeBeau	2.25
22 FaN,Neo,Remy LeBeau,Rax	2.25
23 FaN,X-Cutioner	2.25
24 FaN,V:New Son	2.25
25 SLo, 48-page	3.50
Ann.1999 48-page	3.50
Ann.2000 FaN,F:X-Men	3.50
Giant Sized Gambit, 96-page, rep.	4.00

GAMBIT
Sept., 2004

1 House of Cards,pt.1	3.00
2 House of Cards,pt.2	3.00
3 House of Cards,pt.3	3.00
4 House of Cards,pt.4	3.00
5 House of Cards,pt.5	3.00
6 House of Cards, Concl.	3.00
7 Voodoo Economics,pt.1	3.00
8 Voodoo Economics,pt.2	3.00
9 Voodoo Economics,pt.3	3.00
10 Hath No Fury,pt.1	3.00
11 Hath No Fury,pt.2	3.00
12 Hath No Fury,pt.3	3.00

GAMBIT & BISHOP:
SONS OF THE ATOM
Jan., 2001

1 SLo,Bishop captured	2.25
2 SLo,on the run	2.25
3 SLo,common enemy	2.25
4 SLo,	2.25
5 SLo,Ultimate sacrifice	2.25
6 SLo,finale	2.25
Spec. Alpha, SLo,CNr	2.25
Spec. Genesis,CCI	3.50

GAMBIT AND
THE X-TERNALS
1995

1 X-Force after Xavier	3.50
2 V:Deathbird,Starjammers	2.50
3 V:Imperial Guard	2.50
4 Charles Kidnapped	2.50

Gargoyle #3
© Marvel Entertainment Group

GARGOYLE
June, 1985

1 BWr(c),from `Defenders'	4.00
2 thru 4	@3.00

GARGOYLES
1995–96

1 TV Series	4.00
2 TV Series	3.00
3 F:Broadway	3.00
4 V:Statues	3.00
5 Humanoid Gargoyles	3.00
6 Medusa Project concl.	3.00
7 Demona & Triad	3.00
8 I:The Pack	3.00
9 V:Demonia,Triad	3.00
10 Demonia gains magical powers	3.00
11 Elisa turns to Xanatos	3.00
12 Sorceress traps Gargoyles	3.00
13 Behind Enemy Lines	3.00
14 thru 16	@3.00

GAY COMICS
Marvel Timely, 1944

1 BW,Guys and gals humor	750.00
18 BW	450.00
19 BW	400.00
20 BW	400.00
21 BW	400.00
22 BW	400.00
23 BW	400.00
24 BW,HK,Hey Look	400.00
25 BW	400.00
26 BW	400.00
27 BW	400.00
28 BW	400.00
29 BW,HK,Hey Look	400.00
30 HK,Hey Look	200.00
31 HK,Hey Look	200.00
32	125.00
33 HK,Hey Look	200.00
34 HK,Hey Look	200.00
35 thru 40	@125.00

Becomes:

HONEYMOON
Marvel Comics, 1950

41 Photo(c)	125.00

GENE DOGS
Marvel UK, 1993–94

1 I:Gene DOGS,w/cards	3.00
2 V:Genetix	2.25
3 V:Hurricane	2.25
4 last issue	2.25

GENERATION M
Nov., 2005

1 Decimation	3.00
2 thru 5	@3.00

GENERATION NEXT
1995

1 Generation X AX	3.50
2 Genetic Slave Pens	2.50
3 V:Sugar Man	2.50
4 V:Sugar Man	2.50

GENERATION X
Oct., 1994

1 CBa,Banshee & White Queen	7.00
2 CBa,SLo	4.00
2a Deluxe edition	4.00
3 CBa	3.00
3a Deluxe edition	4.00
4 CBa,V:Nanny,Orphanmaker	3.00
4a Deluxe edition	4.00
5 SLo,CBa,MBu,two new young mutants at the Academy	3.50

Generation X #45
© Marvel Entertainment Group

6 A:Wolverine	3.50
7 SLo,F:Banshee,A:White Queen	3.50
8 F:Banshee	3.50
9 SLo,TG,Chamber in a kilt	3.50
10 SLo,TG,MBu,Banshee vs. OmegaRed	3.50
11 SLo,TG,V:Omega Red	3.00
12 SLo,TG,V:Emplate	3.00
13	3.00
14	3.00
15 SLo,MBu,Synch goes psycho	3.00
16	3.00
17 SLo,CBa,Onslaught saga, X-Cutioner vs. Skin	3.00
18 SLo,CBa,Onslaught saga	3.00
19 SLo,CBa,	3.00
20 SLo,CBa,	3.00
21 SLo,CBa,MBu,F:Skin & Chamber, A:Beverly Switzer, Howard the Duck	3.00
22 SLo,CBa,	3.00
23 SLo,CBa,V:Black Tom Cassidy	3.00
24 SLo,MBy,F:Monet,Emplate	3.00
25 SLo,CBa,double size	4.00
26 SLo,CBa,Shot down over the Atlantic	3.00
27 SLo,CBa,on nuclear sub	3.00
28 SLo,CBa,No Exit prelude	3.00
29 JeR,CBa, V:Sentinels	3.00
30 JeR,CBa, V:Zero Tolerance	3.00
31 JeR,CBa,	3.00
32 TDF,MBu,F:Banshee, Moira McTaggert	3.00
33 LHa,MBu,new direction	3.00
34 LHa,Truth behind M	3.00
35 LHa,Jubilee,V:Emplate	3.00
36 LHa,Final Fate of M	3.00
37 LHa,Final Fate of M	3.00
38 LHa,TyD,kids save universe	2.50
39 LHa,TyD, multi-dimensional trip	2.50
40 LHa,TyD,Penance mystery revealed	2.50
41 LHa,TyD,Jubilee,V:Bastion, Omega Red, Sabretooth	2.50
42 LHa,TyD,results of EMP wave	2.50
43 LHa,TyD,V:Bianca LaNiege	2.50
44 LHa,TyD,V:White Queen	2.50
45 LHa,TyD,F:Banshee	2.50
46 LHa,TyD,F:Forge	2.50
47 LHa,TyD,Danger Room	2.50
48 TyD,Jubilee vs. M	2.50
49 TyD,V:Maggott	2.50
50 TyD,War of the Mutants,pt.1	3.50
50a signed	20.00
51 V:Hunter Brawn	2.50

52 TyD,blackmail 2.50	
53 TyD,V:Rising Sons,A:Paladin . . 2.50	
54 TyD,A:Paladin 2.50	
55 TyD,in bodies of Hellions 2.50	
56 TyD,A:X-Men of past. 2.50	
57 TyD, double sized 3.50	
58 TyD, new Penance 2.50	
59 TyD,. 2.50	
60 TyD,F:Siryn. 2.50	
61 TyD,ATi,R:Mondo 2.50	
62 TyD,F:Monet St. Croix. 2.50	
63 WEI,X-Men Revolution 2.50	
63a variant (c) 2.50	
64 WEI,Correction,pt.2. . . . . 2.25	
65 WEI,Correction,pt.3. . . . . 2.25	
66 WEI,Correction,pt.4. . . . . 2.25	
67 WEI,Come On Die Young,pt.1 . . 2.25	
68 WEI,Come On Die Young,pt.2 . . 2.25	
69 WEI,Come On Die Young,pt.3 . . 2.25	
70 WEI,Come On Die Young,pt.4 . . 2.25	
71 WEI,Four Days,pt.1. . . . . 2.25	
72 AAd(c),StP,Four Days,pt.2 . . . 2.25	
73 AAd(c),StP,Four Days,pt.3 . . . 2.25	
74 AAd(c),StP,Four Days,pt.4 . . . 2.25	
75 AAd(c),StP,final issue 3.50	

Minus 1 Spec., JeR,CBa, flashback,
 F:Banshee 2.50
Ann. '95 SLo,J:Mondo,
 V:Hellfire Club 4.50
Ann. '96 GN MGo,JJ,DPs,V:Fenris . 3.50
Ann. '97, Haunted by Ghosts
 of Hellions 3.50
Ann.1998 Generation X/Dracula . . . 4.00
Ann.1999 48-pg. 4.00
Holliday Spec. 48-page 1-shot. 4.00

GENERATION X/GEN 13
Dec., 1997
1-shot JeR,SvL,V:Mr. Pretorious . . . 4.00
1a variant cover CBa (1:4). 4.00

GENERATION X:
UNDERGROUND
March, 1998
1-shot by Jim Mahfood, b&w 2.50

GENERIC COMIC
1 . . . . 2.25

GENETIX
Marvel UK, 1993–94
1 B:ALa(s),w/cards 3.00

Genetix #1
© *Marvel Entertainment Group*

2 I:Tektos 2.25
3 V:Tektos 2.25
4 PGa,V:MyS-Tech 2.25
5 PGa,V:MyS-Tech 2.25
6 V:Tektos 2.25

GEORGIE COMICS
Spring, 1945
1 Georgie stories begin 350.00
2 Pet Shop (c) 175.00
3 Georgie/Judy(c) 135.00
4 Wedding Dress(c) 135.00
5 Monty/Policeman(c) 135.00
6 Classroom(c) 150.00
7 Fishing(c) 135.00
8 Soda Jerk(c) 135.00
9 Georgie/Judy(c),HK,Hey Look 135.00
10 Georgie/Girls(c),HK,Hey Look 135.00
11 Table Tennis(c),A:Margie,Millie 100.00
12 Camping(c). 100.00
13 Life Guard(c),HK,Hey Look. . . 150.00
14 Classroom(c),HK,Hey Look . 150.00
15 Winter Sports(c) 100.00
16 . . . . 100.00
17 HK,Hey Look. 150.00
18 . . . . 100.00
19 Baseball(c) 100.00
Becomes:

GEORGIE & JUDY COMICS
20 . . . . 125.00
21 . . . . 100.00
Becomes:

GEORGIE COMICS
22 Georgie comics 100.00
23 & 24. . . . . @100.00
25 Driben painted (c) 125.00
26 thru 28 . . . . @100.00
29 . . . . 125.00
30 thru 38 . . . . @100.00
39 Oct., 1952 . . . . 100.00

GETALONG GANG
May, 1985—March, 1986
1 thru 6 . . . . @3.50

GHOST RIDER
1967
1 O&I:Ghost Rider (western) . . . 150.00
2 V:Tarantula. 75.00
3 Cougar's Circus of Fear 50.00
4 Sting Ray 50.00
5 Tarantula Strikes Back 50.00
6 Behold a Falling Star 50.00
7 Mystery of Massacre Mountain . 50.00

GHOST RIDER
[1st Regular Series],
Sept., 1973
1 GK,JSt,C:Son of Satan 175.00
2 GK,I:Son of Satan,A:Witch
 Woman 75.00
3 JR,D:Big Daddy Dawson,
 new Cycle 50.00
4 GK,A:Dude Jensen 50.00
5 GK,JR,I:Roulette 50.00
6 JR,O:Ghost Rider 35.00
7 JR,A:Stunt Master 35.00
8 GK,A:Satan,I:Inferno 35.00
9 GK,TP,O:Johnny Blaze 35.00
10 JSt,A:Hulk 35.00
11 GK,KJ,SB,A:Hulk 35.00
12 GK,KJ,FR,A:Phantom Eagle . . 20.00
13 GK,JS,GT,A:Trapster 20.00
14 GT,A:The Orb 20.00
15 SB,O:The Orb. 20.00
16 DC,GT,Blood in the Water . . . 20.00
17 RB,FR,I:Challenger. 20.00
18 RB,FR,A:Challenger,
 Spider-Man 20.00

Ghost Rider #68
© *Marvel Entertainment Group*

19 GK,FR,A:Challenger. 20.00
20 GK,KJ,JBy,A:Daredevil 22.00
21 A:Gladiator,D:Eel. 11.00
22 AM,DH,KP,JR,A:Enforcer 11.00
23 JK,DH,DN,I:Water Wiz. 11.00
24 GK,DC,DH,A:Enforcer. 11.00
25 GK,DH,A:Stunt Master 11.00
26 GK,DP,A:Dr. Druid. 11.00
27 SB,DP,A:Hawkeye. 11.00
28 DP,A:The Orb 11.00
29 RB,DP,A:Dormammu 11.00
30 DP,A:Dr.Strange 11.00
31 FR,DP,BL,A:Bounty Hunt. 11.00
32 KP,BL,DP,A:Bounty Hunt. 11.00
33 DP,I:Dark Riders 11.00
34 DP,C:Cyclops 11.00
35 JSn,AM,A:Death 16.00
36 DP,Drug Mention. 11.00
37 DP,I:Dick Varden 11.00
38 DP,A:Death Cult 11.00
39 DP,A:Death Cult 11.00
40 DP,I:Nuclear Man 11.00
41 DP,A:Jackal Gang 11.00
42 DP,A:Jackal Gang 11.00
43 CI:Crimson Mage 11.00
44 JAb,CI,A:Crimson Mage 11.00
45 DP,I:Flagg Fargo 11.00
46 DP,A:Flagg Fargo 11.00
47 AM,DP. 11.00
48 BMc,DP. 11.00
49 DP,I:The Manitou. 11.00
50 DP,A:Night Rider 15.00
51 AM,PD,A:Cycle Gang 7.00
52 AM,DP. 7.00
53 DP,I:Lord Asmodeus 7.00
54 DP,A:The Orb 7.00
55 DP,A:Werewolf By Night 7.00
56 DP,A:Moondark,I:Night Rider . . . 7.00
57 AM,DP,I:The Apparition. 7.00
58 DP,FM,A:Water Wizard 7.00
59 V:Water Wizard,Moon Dark 7.00
60 DP,HT,A:Black Juju. 7.00
61 A:Arabian Knight 7.00
62 KJ,A:Arabian Knight 7.00
63 LMc,A:The Orb 7.00
64 BA,V:Azmodeus 7.00
65 A:Fowler 7.00
66 BL,A:Clothilde. 7.00
67 DP,A:Sally Stantop 7.00
68 O:Ghost Rider. 7.00
69 . . . . 7.00
70 I:Jeremy 7.00
71 DP,I:Adam Henderson 7.00
72 A:Circus of Crime 7.00

73 A:Circus of Crime 7.00
74 A:Centurions 7.00
75 I:Steel Wind 7.00
76 DP,A:Mephisto,I:Saturnine 7.00
77 O:Ghost Rider's Dream 7.00
78 A:Nightmare 7.00
79 A:Man Cycles 7.00
80 A:Centurions 7.00
81 D:Ghost Rider 15.00

[2nd Regular Series], 1990–98
1 JS,MT,I:2nd Ghost Rider,
   Deathwatch 6.00
1a 2nd printing 3.00
2 JS,MT,I:Blackout 3.00
3 JS,MT,A:Kingpin,V:Blackout,
   Deathwatch 3.00
4 JS,MT,V:Mr.Hyde 3.00
5 JLe(c),JS,MT,A:Punisher 3.00
5a rep.Gold 2.50
6 JS,MT,A:Punisher 3.00
7 MT,V:Scarecrow 3.00
8 JS,MT,V:H.E.A.R.T 3.00
9 JS,MT,A:Morlocks,X-Factor 2.50
10 JS,MT,V:Zodiac 2.50
11 LSn,MT,V:Nightmare,
   A:Dr.Strange 2.50
12 JS,MT,A:Dr.Strange 2.50
13 MT,V:Snow Blind,R:J.Blaze . . . 2.50
14 MT,Blaze Vs.Ghost Rider 2.50
15 MT,A:Blaze,V:Blackout
   Glow in Dark(c) 3.00
15a 2nd printing (gold) 2.50
16 MT,A:Blaze,Spider-Man,
   V:Hobgoblin 2.50
17 MT,A:Spider-Man,Blaze,
   V:Hobgoblin 2.50
18 MT,V:Reverend Styge 2.50
19 MT,A:Mephisto 2.50
20 MT(i),O:Zodiac 2.50
21 MT(i),V:Snowblind,
   A:Deathwatch 2.50
22 MT,A:Deathwatch,Ninjas 2.50
23 MT,I:Hag & Troll,A:Deathwatch . . 2.50
24 MT,V:Deathwatch,D:Snowblind,
   C:Johnny Blaze 2.50
25 V:Blackout (w/Center spread
   pop-up) 3.00
26 A:X-Men,V:The Brood 3.00
27 A:X-Men,V:The Brood 3.00
28 NKu,JKu,Rise of the Midnight
   Sons#1,V:Lilith,w/poster 3.00
29 NKu,JKu,A:Wolverine,Beast 2.50
30 NKu,JKu,V:Nightmare 2.50
31 NKu,JKu,Rise o/t Midnight
   Sons#6, A:Dr.Strange,Morbius,
   Nightstalkers,Redeemers,
   V:Lilith,w/poster 3.00
32 BBi,A:Dr.Strange 2.50
33 BBI,AW,V:Madcap (inc.Superman
   tribute on letters page) 2.50
34 BBI,V:Deathwatchs' ninja 2.50
35 BBI,AW,A:Heart Attack 2.50
36 BBI,V:Mr.Hyde,A:Daredevil 2.50
37 BBI,A:Archangel,V:HeartAttack . . 2.50
38 MM,V:Scarecrow 2.50
39 V:Vengeance 2.50
40 Midnight Massacre#2,
   D:Demogblin 3.00
41 Road to Vengeance#1 . . . . 2.50
42 Road to Vengeance#2 . . . . 2.50
43 Road to Vengeance#3 . . . . 2.50
44 Siege of Darkness,pt.#2 . . . . . . 2.50
45 Siege of Darkness,pt.#10 . . . . . 2.50
46 HMe(s),New Beginning 2.50
47 HMe(s),RG, ... 2.50
48 HMe(s),RG,A:Spider-Man 2.50
49 HMe(s),RG,A:Hulk,w/card 2.50
50 Red Foil(c),AKu,SMc,A:Blaze,
   R:2nd Ghost Rider 3.25
50a Newsstand Ed. 2.75
51 SvL 2.50
52 SvL 2.50

53 SvL,V:Blackout 2.50
54 SvL,V:Blackout 2.50
55 V:Mr. Hyde 2.50
56 The Next Wave 2.50
57 A:Wolverine 2.50
58 HMe,SvL,Betrayal,pt.1 . . . . 2.50
59 Betrayal,pt.2 . . . . 2.50
60 Betrayal,pt.3 . . . . 2.50
61 Betrayal,pt.4 . . . . 3.00
62 EventInChains,pt.1,A:Fury 2.50
63 EventInChains,pt.2 . . . . 2.50
64 EventInChains,pt.3 . . . . 2.50
65 EventInChains,pt.4,R:Blackout . . . 2.50
66 V:Blackout 2.50
67 A:Gambit,V:Brood 2.50
68 A:Gambit,Wolverine,V:Brood . . . 2.50
69 Domestic Violence 2.50
70 New Home in Bronx 2.50
71 . . . . 2.50
72 . . . . 2.50
73 John Blaze is back 2.50
74 A:Blaze, Vengeance 2.50
75 . . . . 2.50
76 V:Vengeance 2.50
77 A:Dr. Strange 2.50
78 new costume, A:Dr. Strange 2.50
79 IV,New costume, A:Valkyrie, . . . 2.50
80 IV,V:Furies,Valkyrie
   A:Black Rose 2.50
81 IV,A:Howard the Duck,
   Devil Dinosaur 2.25
82 IV,A:Devil Dinosaur 2.25
83 IV,A:Scarecrow,Lilith 2.25
84 IV,A:Scarecrow, Lilith 2.25
85 IV,V:Lilith, Scarecrow 2.25
86 IV,rampage through the Bronx . . 2.25
87 IV,KIK,AM, ... 2.25
88 IV, V:Pao Fu,Blackheart 2.25
89 IV,JS, ... 2.25
90 IV,JS,Last Temptation, pt.1 . . . . 5.00
91 IV,JS,A:Blackheart 5.00
92 IV,JS,Journey into the past 5.00
93 IV,JS,MT,Last Temptation concl.,
   double sized 10.00
94 IV,JS,MT,Becomes Lord of the
   Underworld, last issue 2.00
Ann.#1 I:Night Terror,w/card 3.25
Ann.#2 F:Scarecrow 3.00
GN Ghost Rider/Captain America:
   Fear, AW, V:Scarecrow (1992) . 6.25
GN Ghost Rider/Wolverine/Punisher:
   Dark Design (1994) 6.00
GN Ghost Rider/Wolverine/Punisher:
   Hearts of Darkness, JR2/KJ,V:
   Blackheart, gatefold(c) (1991) . . 5.50
Poster Book 5.00
Spec. Crossroads 4.00
Minus 1 Spec., IV,JS, flashback . . . 2.00

GHOST RIDER
1 Director's Cut, GEn(s),48-pg. . . . 4.00

GHOST RIDER
Sept., 2005
1 (of 6) GEn(s),Road to Damnation 3.00
2 thru 6 Gen(s),Road to
   Damnation . . . . @3.00

GHOST RIDER
July., 2006
1 (of 6) MT,JS,Vicious Cycle 3.00
1a variant (c) 3.00
2 thru 5 MT, JS,Vicious Cycle . . . @3.00
6 RCo,Hell to Pay, pt.1 . . . . 3.00
7 RCo,Hell to Pay, pt.2 . . . . 3.00
8 MT,JS,Sleepy Hollow Illinois . . . 3.00
9 MT,JS,Sleepy Hollow Illinois . . . 3.00
10 MT,JS, Sleepy Hollow Illinois . . . 3.00
11 MT,JS,Sleepy Hollow Illinois . . . 3.00
12 JS,Apocalypse Soon,pt.1 . . . . . 3.00
12a 2nd printing 3.00

13 JS,Apocalypse Soon, pt.2 . . . . . 3.00
14 JS,MT,Revelations, pt.1 . . . . . . 3.00
15 JS,MT,Revelations, pt.2 . . . . . . 3.00
16 JS,MT,Revelations, pt.3 . . . . . . 3.00
17 JS,MT,Revelations, pt.4 . . . . . . 3.00
Ann. #1 I:Mr. Eleven 4.00

GHOST RIDER/
BALLISTIC/CYBLADE
Marvel/Top Cow 1996
1-shot IV,ACh,Devil's Reign,
   pt.2, x-over 3.25
1-shot WEI,BTn,Devil's
   Reign, pt.3, x-over 3.00

Ghost Rider Spirits of Vengeance #2
© Marvel Entertainment Group

GHOST RIDER/BLAZE
SPIRITS OF VENGEANCE
1992–94
1 AKu,polybagged w/poster,V:Lilith,
   Rise of the Midnight Sons#2 . . . 3.50
2 AKu,V:Steel Wind 3.00
3 AKu,CW,V:The Lilin 3.00
4 AKu,V:Hag & Troll,C:Venom 3.00
5 AKu,BR,Spirits of Venom#2,
   A:Venom,Spidey,Hobgoblin 5.00
6 AKu,Spirits of Venom#4,A:Venom,
   Spider-Man,Hobgoblin 3.50
7 AKu,V:Steel Vengeance 2.25
8 V:Mephisto 2.25
9 I:Brimstone 2.25
10 AKu,V:Vengeance 2.25
11 V:Human Spider Creature 2.25
12 AKu,BR,Vengeance,glow in the
   dark(c) 3.25
13 AKu,Midnight Massacre#5 . . . . . 2.50
14 Missing Link#2 . . . . 2.25
15 Missing Link#3 . . . . 2.25
16 V:Zarathos,Lilith 2.25
17 HMe(s),Siege/Darkness,pt.8 . . . . 2.25
18 HMe(s),Siege/Darkness,pt.13 . . . 2.25
19 HMe(s),HMz,V;Vampire 2.25
20 HMe(s),A:Steel Wind 2.25
21 HMe(s),HMz,V:Werewolves 2.25
22 HMe(s),HMz,V:Cardiac 2.25
23 HMe(s),HMz,A:Steel Wind 2.25

GHOST RIDER FINALE
Jan., 2007
Inc. Ghost Rider #93 reprint 4.00

All comics prices listed are for *Near Mint* condition.

GHOST RIDER:
THE HAMMER LANE
June, 2001

1 (of 6) TKn	3.00
2 TKn,DaM	3.00
3 TKn,DaM,Gunmetal Gray	3.00
4 TKn,DaM,Gunmetal Gray	3.00
5 TKn,DaM,Gunmetal Gray	3.00
6 TKn,DaM,Gunmetal Gray	3.00

GHOST RIDER:
HIGHWAY TO HELL
June, 2001

Spec. 64-pages	3.50

GHOST RIDER:
TRAIL OF TEARS
Feb., 2007

1 (of 6) GEn, Trail of Tears, pt.1	3.00
2 thru 5 GEn	@3.00

GHOST RIDER 2099
1994–96

1 Holografx(c),LKa,CBa,MBu,I:Ghost Rider 2099,w/card	3.00
1a Newsstand Ed.	2.25
2 LKa,CBa,MBu	2.25
3 LKa,CBa,MBu,I:Warewolf	2.25
4 LKa,CBa,MBu,V:Warewolf	2.25
5 LKa,CBa,MBu	2.25
6 LKa,CBa,MBu	2.25
7 LKa,CBa,MBu	2.25
8 LKa,CBa,MBu	2.25
9	2.25
10	2.25
11 V:Bloodsport Society	2.25
12 I:Coda	2.25
Becomes:	

GHOST RIDER 2099 A.D.
1995

13 F:Doom	2.25
14 Deputized by Doom	2.25
15 One Nation Under Doom	2.25
16 V:Max Synergy	2.25
17	2.25
18 V:L-Cipher	2.25
19 V:L-Cipher	2.25
20	2.25
21 V:Vengeance 2099	2.25
22 V:Vengeance 2099	2.25
23	2.25
24	2.25
25 Double size final issue	3.50

GIANT-SIZE CHILLERS
1975

1 AA	75.00
2	35.00
3 BWr,Night of the Gargoyle	50.00

GIANT-SIZE CHILLERS
1974

1 I&O:Lilith,F:Curse of Dracula	75.00
Becomes:	

GIANT-SIZE DRACULA

2 Vengeance of the Elder Gods	40.00
3 rep. Uncanny Tales #6	25.00
4 SD,Demon of Devil's Lake	25.00
5 JBy, 1st Marvel art	60.00

GIANT-SIZE
MINI-MARVELS:
STARRING SPIDEY
Dec., 2001

1 F:Hawkeye, 48-pg.	3.50

G.I. Joe: A Real American Hero #16
© Marvel Entertainment Group

G.I. JOE:
A REAL AMERICAN HERO
June, 1982

1 HT,BMc,Baxter paper	35.00
2 DP,JAb,North Pole	25.00
3 HT,JAb,Trojan Robot	15.00
4 HT,JAb,Wingfield	15.00
5 DP,Central Park	15.00
6 HT,V:Cobra	15.00
7 HT,Walls of Death	15.00
8 HT,Sea Strike	15.00
9 The Diplomat	15.00
10 Springfield	15.00
11 thru 20	@12.00
21 SL(i),Silent Interlude	30.00
22 V:Destro	7.00
23 I:Duke	7.00
24 RH,I:Storm Shadow	7.00
25 FS,I:Zartan	7.00
26 SL(i),O:Snake Eyes	9.00
27 FS,O:Snake Eyes	9.00
28 Swampfire	7.00
29 FS,V:Destro	7.00
30 JBy(c),FS,V:Dreddnoks	7.00
31 thru 60	@3.00
2a to 36a 2nd printings	@2.00
60 TM,I:Zanzibar	6.00
61 thru 90	@3.00
91 TSa,V:Red Ninjas,D:Blind Masters	4.00
92 MBr,V:Cobra Condor	4.00
93 MBr,V:Baroness	12.00
94 MBr,A:Snake Eyes	6.00
95 MBr,A:Snake Eyes	6.00
96 MBr,A:Snake Eyes	6.00
97 thru 109	@4.00
110 Mid-East Crisis	5.00
111 thru 119	@4.00
120 V:Red Ninjas,Slice & Dice	6.00
121 thru 134	@4.00
135 thru 143	@5.00
144 O: Snake Eyes	8.00
145 thru 147	@5.00
148 F:Star Brigade	8.00
149	5.00
150 Cobra Commander vs. Snake Eyes	20.00
151 V:Cobra	25.00
152 First G.I. Joe	23.00
153 V:Cobra	28.00
154	38.00
155 final issue	60.00
SC GI Joe and the Transformers	5.00

Spec. TM rep.#61	4.00
Ann.#1	4.00
Ann.#2	4.00
Ann.#3	4.00
Ann.#4	4.00
Ann.#5	4.00
Yearbook #1 (1985)	4.00
Yearbook #2 (1986)	4.00
Yearbook #3 (1987)	4.00
Yearbook #4 (1988)	4.00

G.I. JOE
EUROPEAN MISSIONS
June, 1988

1 British rep.	7.00
2	5.00
3	7.00
4 thru 15	@5.00

G.I. JOE
SPECIAL MISSIONS
Oct., 1986

1 HT,New G.I. Joe	4.00
2 thru 9 HT	@4.00
10 thru 20 HT	@4.00
21 thru 28	@5.00

G.I. JOE AND
THE TRANSFORMERS
1987

1 thru 4 HT,mini-series	@3.00

G.I. JOE UNIVERSE

1 Biographies rep.#1	3.50
2 thru 4	@2.50

G.I. TALES
See: SERGEANT BARNEY BARKER

GIRL COMICS
Marvel Atlas, Nov., 1949

1 Ph(c),True love stories,I Could Escape From Love	275.00
2 Ph(c),JKu,Blind Date	150.00
3 BEv,Ph(c),Liz Taylor	350.00
4 PH(c),Borrowed Love	125.00
5 Love stories	125.00
6 same	125.00
7 same	125.00
8 same	125.00
9 same	125.00
10 The Deadly Double-Cross	125.00
11 Love stories	125.00
12 BK,The Dark Hallway	150.00
Becomes:	

GIRL CONFESSIONS
1952

13	150.00
14	125.00
15	125.00
16 BEv	150.00
17 BEv	150.00
18 BEv	150.00
19	110.00
20	110.00
21 thru 34	@100.00
35 Aug., 1954	100.00

GIRLS' LIFE
Marvel Atlas, Jan., 1954

1	150.00
2	125.00
3	100.00
4	100.00
5	100.00
6 November, 1954	100.00

G.L.A.
April, 2005
1 (of 4) F:Great Lakes Avengers . . 3.00
2 Dis-membership Drive 3.00
3 . . . . 3.00
4 Countdown to a Miscount 3.00

GLADIATOR/SUPREME
1997
1 KG,ASm,x-over 5.00

GLX-MAS
Dec., 2005
1-shot X-mas special 4.00

Godzilla #17
© Marvel Entertainment Group

GODZILLA
Aug., 1977
1 HT,JM,Based on Movie Series . 30.00
2 HT,FrG,GT,Seattle Under Seige 12.00
3 HT,TD,A;Champions 20.00
4 TS,TD,V;Batragon 10.00
5 TS,KJ,Isle of the Living
    Demons 10.00
6 HT,A Monster Enslaved 10.00
7 V:Red Ronin 10.00
8 V:Red Ronin 10.00
9 Las Gamble in Las Vegas 10.00
10 V:Yetrigar 10.00
11 V;Red Ronin,Yetrigar. 8.00
12 Star Sinister 8.00
13 V:Mega-Monster 8.00
14 V:Super-Beasts 8.00
15 Stampede 8.00
16 Jaws of Fear. 8.00
17 Godzilla Shrunk 8.00
18 Battle Beneath Eighth Avenue . 8.00
19 Panic on the Pier 8.00
20 A;Fantastic Four 10.00
21 V;Devil Dinosaur 8.00
22 V:Devil Dinosaur 8.00
23 A;Avengers 10.00
24 July, 1979 . . . . 8.00

GRAVITY
June, 2005
1(of 5) F:Greg Willis 3.00
2 . . . . 3.00
3 V:Black Death 3.00
4 . . . . 3.00
5 Finale 3.00

GREEN GOBLIN
1995–96
1 I:New Green Goblin 4.00
2 thru 13 . . . . @2.25

GROO CHRONICLES
Epic, 1989
1 SA 5.00
2 thru 6 SA . . . . @4.00

[SERGIO ARAGONE'S]
GROO, THE WANDERER
(see Pacific, Eclipse)
Epic, 1985–95
1 SA,I:Minstrel 15.00
2 SA,A:Minstrel 8.00
3 SA,Medallions 8.00
4 SA,Airship 8.00
5 SA,Slavers 8.00
6 SA,The Eye of the Kabala 8.00
7 SA,A:Sage 8.00
8 SA,A:Taranto 8.00
9 SA,A:Sage 8.00
10 SA,I:Arcadio 8.00
11 thru 18 SA . . . . @6.00
19 thru 29 SA . . . . @4.00
30 thru 49 . . . . @4.00
50 SA,double size 4.00
51 thru 87 SA . . . . @3.00
88 SA,V:Cattlemen,B.U. Sage 4.00
89 thru 99 SA . . . . @3.00
100 SA,Groo gets extra IQ points . . 8.00
101 thru 120 SA . . . . @4.00

GROOVY
March, 1968—July, 1968
1 Monkeys,Ringo Starr,Photos . . 140.00
2 Cartoons,Gags,Jokes 100.00
3 . . . . 100.00

GUARDIANS
2004
1 (of 5) Reach for the Stars 3.00
2 thru 5 Reach for the Stars . . . . @3.00

GUARDIANS OF
THE GALAXY
June, 1990
1 B:JV(a&s),I:Taserface,R:Aleta . . . 4.00
2 MZ(c),JV,V:Stark,C:Firelord 3.00
3 JV,V:Stark,I:Force,C:Firelord 3.00
4 JV,V:Stark,A:Force,Firelord 3.00
5 JV,TM(c),V:Force,I:Mainframe
    (Vision) 3.00
6 JV,V:Force,Vance Possesses
    Capt.America Shield 3.00
7 GP(c),JV,I:Malevolence,
    O:Starhawk 3.00
8 SLi(c),JV,V:Yondu,C:Rancor 3.00
9 RLd(c),JV,I:Replica,Rancor 3.00
10 JLe(c),JV,V:Rancor,The Nine
    I&C:Overkill(Taserface) 3.00
11 BWi(c),JV,V:Rancor,I:Phoenix . . 3.00
12 ATb(c),JV,V:Overkill
    A:Firelord 3.00
13 JV,A:Ghost Rider,Force,
    Malevolence 3.00
14 JS(c),JV,A:Ghost Rider,Force,
    Malevolence 3.00
15 JSn(c),JV,I:Protege,V:Force 3.00
16 JV,V:Force,A:Protege,
    Malevolence,L:Vance Astro 3.00
17 JV,V:Punishers(Street Army),
    L:Martinex,N:Charlie-27. . . . . . 2.50
18 JV,V:Punishers,I&C:Talon,A:
    Crazy Nate 3.00
19 JV,V:Punishers,A:Talon. 2.50

Guardians of the Galaxy #20
© Marvel Entertainment Group

20 JV,I:Major Victory (Vance Astro)
    J:Talon & Krugarr. 2.50
21 JV,V:Rancor 2.50
22 JV,V:Rancor 2.50
23 MT,V:Rancor,C:Silver Surfer. . . . 2.50
24 JV,A:Silver Surfer 3.00
25 JV, Prismatic Foil(c)
    V:Galactus,A:SilverSurfer 3.50
25a 2nd printing,Silver 2.50
26 JV,O:Guardians(retold) 2.25
27 JV,Infinity War,O:Talon,
    A:Inhumans 2.25
28 JV,Inf.War,V:Various Villians . . . 2.25
29 HT,Inf.War,V:Various Villians. . . . 2.25
30 KWe,A:Captain America 2.25
31 KWe,V:Badoon,A:Capt.A. 2.25
32 KWe,V:Badoon Gladiator 2.25
33 KWe,A:Dr.Strange,R:Aleta 2.25
34 KWe,J:Yellowjacket II 2.25
35 KWe,A:Galatic Guardians,
    V:Bubonicus 2.25
36 KWe,A:Galatic Guardians,
    V:Dormammu 2.25
37 KWe,V:Dormammu,A:Galatic
    Guardians 2.25
38 KWe,N:Y.jacket,A:Beyonder . . . 2.25
39 KWe,Rancor Vs. Dr.Doom,Holo-
    grafx(c) 3.25
40 KWe,V:Loki,Composite. 2.25
41 KWe,V:Loki,A:Thor 2.25
42 KWe,I:Woden 2.25
43 KWe,A:Woden,V:Loki 2.25
44 KWe,R:Yondu 2.25
45 KWe,O:Starhawk. 2.25
46 KWe,N:Major Victory. 2.25
47 KWe,A:Beyonder,Protege,
    Overkill. 2.25
48 KWe,V:Overkill 2.25
49 KWe,A:Celestial 2.25
50 Foil(c),R:Yondu,Starhawk sep-
    arated,BU:O:Guardians 3.25
51 KWe,A:Irish Wolfhound. 2.25
52 KWe,A:Drax 2.25
53 KWe,V:Drax 2.25
54 KWe,V:Sentinels 2.25
55 KWe,Ripjack 2.25
56 Ripjack 2.25
57 R:Keeper 2.25
58 . . . . 2.25
59 A:Keeper 2.25
60 F:Starhawk 2.25
61 F:Starhawk 2.25
62 Guardians Stop War of the Worlds
    last issue 2.25

MARVEL

Ann.#1 Korvac Quest #4,I:Krugarr.. 3.25
Ann.#2 HT,I:Galactic Guardians,
  System Bytes #4 . . . . 3.25
Ann.#3 CDo,I:Irish Wolfhound,
  w/Trading card 3.25
Ann.#4 V:Nine 3.25

GUNHAWK, THE
See: BLAZE CARSON

Gunhawks #1
© Marvel Entertainment Group

GUNHAWKS
Oct., 1972
1 SSh,B:Reno Jones & Kid
  Cassidy Two Rode Together . . 35.00
2 Ride out for Revenge. 30.00
3 Indian Massacre 30.00
4 Trial by Ordeal 30.00
5 The Reverend Mr. Graves 30.00
6 E:Reno Jones & Kid Cassidy
  D:Kid Cassidy 30.00
7 A Gunhawks Last Stand
  A;Reno Jones, Oct., 1973 . . . 30.00

GUNRUNNER
Marvel UK, 1993–94
1 I:Gunrunner,w/trading cards 3.00
2 A:Ghost Rider 2.25
3 V:Cynodd 2.25
4 . . . . 2.25
5 A:Enhanced 2.25
6 final issue. 2.25

GUNSLINGERS
Dec., 1999
1-shot 64-pg. 3.00

GUNSLINGER
See: TEX DAWSON,
GUNSLINGER

GUNSMOKE WESTERN
See: ALL WINNERS
COMICS

GUN THEORY
Marvel Epic, Aug., 2003
1 (of 4) 2.50
2 thru 4 . . . . @2.50

HALO: UPRISING
July, 2007
1 BMB(s). 4.00
2 thru 4 BMB(s), finale . . . . @4.00

HARROWERS
1993–94
1 MSt(s),GC,F:Pinhead. 3.50
2 GC,AW(i),. 3.00
3 GC,AW(i),. 3.00
4 GC,AW(i),. 3.00
5 GC,AW(i),Devil's Pawn#1 . . . . . 3.00
6 GC,AW(i),Devil's Pawn#2 . . . . . 3.00

HARVEY
Oct., 1970–Dec., 1972
1 . . . . 150.00
2 thru 6 . . . . @100.00

HARVEY PRESENTS:
CASPER
1 . . . . 2.25

HAUNT OF HORRORS:
EDGAR ALLAN POE
May, 2006
1 RCo, b&w, inc. The Raven 4.00
2 RCo, b&w, inc. Tell-Tale Heart . . . 4.00
3 RCo, b&w, three stories. 4.00

HAVOK & WOLVERINE
Epic, March, 1988
1 JMu,KW,V:KGB,Dr.Neutron 5.00
2 JMu,KW,V:KGB,Dr.Neutron 4.00
3 JMu,KW,V:Meltdown 4.00
4 JMu,KW,V:Meltdown,Oct.1989 . . 4.00

HAWKEYE
[1st Limited Series], Sept., 1983
1 A:Mockingbird 3.00
2 I:Silencer 3.00
3 I:Bombshell,Oddball. 3.00
4 V:Crossfire,W:Hawkeye &
  Mockingbird, Dec., 1983 . . . . 3.00
[2nd Limited Series], 1994
1 B:CDi(s),ScK,V:Trickshot,
  I:Javelynn,Rover 2.25
2 ScK,V:Viper 2.25
3 ScK,A:War Machine,N:Hawkeye,
  V:Secret Empire 2.25
4 E:CDi(s),ScK,V:Trickshot,Viper,
  Javelynn 2.25

HAWKEYE
Oct., 2003
1 FaN(s),High,Hard Shaft,pt.1 . . . . 3.00
2 FaN(s),High,Hard Shaft,pt.2 . . . . 3.00
3 FaN(s),High,Hard Shaft,pt.3 . . . . 3.00
4 FaN(s),High,Hard Shaft,pt.4 . . . . 3.00
5 FaN(s),High,Hard Shaft,pt.5 . . . . 3.00
6 FaN(s),High,Hard Shaft,pt.6 . . . . 3.00
7 FaN(s),A Little Murder,pt.1 . . . . . 3.00
8 FaN(s),A Little Murder,pt.2 . . . . . 3.00

HAWKEYE: EARTH'S
MIGHTIEST MARKSMAN
Aug., 1998
1-shot TDF,MBa,JJ,DR,AM 48pg. . . 3.00

HEADMASTERS
Star, July, 1987
1 FS,Transformers 2.25
2 and 3 . . . . @2.25
4 Jan., 1988 . . . . 2.25

HEATHCLIFF
Star, April, 1985
1 . . . . 7.00
2 thru 10 . . . . @4.00
11 thru 16 . . . . @3.00
17 Masked Moocher 5.00
18 thru 49 . . . . @3.00
50 Double-size. 3.00
51 thru 55 . . . . @3.00

HEATHCLIFF'S
FUNHOUSE
Star, May, 1987
1 thru 9 . . . . @3.00
10 1988 . . . . 3.00

HEAVY HITTERS
Ann.#1 (1993) 4.00

HEDGE KNIGHT II:
SWORN SWORD
Apr., 2007
1 (of 6) 3.00
2 thru 6 . . . . @3.00

HEDY DEVINE COMICS
Aug., 1947—Sept., 1952
22 I:Hedy Devine 350.00
23 BW,Beauty and the Beach,
  HK,Hey Look 225.00
24 High Jinx in Hollywood,
  HK, Hey Look 225.00
25 Hedy/Bull(c),HK,Hey Look . . . 225.00
26 Skating(c),HK,Giggles&Grins . . 250.00
27 Hedy at Show(c),HK,HeyLook 225.00
28 Hedy/Charlie(c),HK,HeyLook . 225.00
29 Tennis(c),HK,Hey Look 225.00
30 . . . . 175.00
31 thru 35. . . . . @175.00
Becomes:

HEDY HOLLYWOOD
36 thru 50 . . . . @175.00

HEDY WOLFE
Marvel Atlas, Aug., 1957
1 Patsy Walker's Rival 125.00

HELLCAT
July, 2000
1 (of 3) SEt,NBy,F:PatsyWalker . . . 3.00
2 SEt,NBy, ... 3.00
3 SEt,NBy,Concl. 3.00

HELLHOUND
1993–94
1 Hellhound on my Trial 3.00
2 Love in Vain 3.00
3 Last Fair Deal Gone Down 3.00

HELLRAISER
See: CLIVE BARKER'S
HELLRAISER

HELLRAISER III
HELL ON EARTH
1 Movie Adaptation,(prestige) 5.00
1a Movie Adapt.(magazine) 3.00

HELLSTORM,
PRINCE OF LIES
1993
1 R:Daimon Hellstrom,
  Parchment(c). 3.50
2 A:Dr.Strange,Gargoyle 3.00
3 O:Hellstorm. 2.75

All comics prices listed are for *Near Mint* condition.

4 V:Ghost Rider 2.75
5 MB, ... 2.50
6 MB,V:Dead Daughter. 2.50
7 A:Armaziel 2.50
8 Hell is where the heart is. 2.50
9 LKa(s),Highway to Heaven 2.50
10 LKa(s),Heaven's Gate 2.50
11 LKa(s),PrG,Life in Hell. 2.50
12 Red Miracles. 2.50
13 Red Miracles Sidewalking. 2.50
14 Red Miracles Murder is Easy . . . 2.50
15 Cigarette Dawn. 3.00
16 Down Here 2.50
17 The Saint of the Pit. 2.50
18 thru 21. . . . . @2.50

HELLSTORM: SON OF SATAN
Oct., 2006

1 Equinox, pt.1 . . . . 4.00
2 Equinox, pt.2 . . . . 4.00
3 Equinox, pt.3 . . . . 4.00
4 Equinox, pt.4 . . . . 4.00
5 Equinox, pt.5 . . . . 4.00

HELL'S ANGEL
1992

1 GSr,A:X-Men,O:Hell's Angel 3.00
2 GSr,A:X-Men,V:Psycho Warriors . 2.50
3 GSr,A:X-Men,V:MyS-Tech 2.25
4 GSr,A:X-Men,V:MyS-Tech 2.25
5 GSr,A:X-Men,V:MyS-Tech 2.25
6 Gfr,A:X-Men,V:MyS-Tech. 2.25
Becomes:

DARK ANGEL
1992

7 DMn,A:Psylocke,V:MyS-Tech . . . 2.25
8 DMn,A:Psylocke 2.25
9 A:Punisher 2.25
10 MyS-Tech Wars tie-in 2.25
11 A:X-Men,MyS-Tech wars tie-in . . 2.25
12 A:X-Men 2.25
13 A:X-Men,Death's Head II 2.25
14 Aftermath#2. . . . . 2.25
15 Aftermath#3. . . . . 2.25
16 SvL,E:Aftermath,last issue 2.25

HERCULES
April, 2005

1 (of 5) MT 3.00
2 MT,v:king Eurytheses. 3.00
3 MT,12 Labors for Reality TV 3.00

Dark Angel #7
© Marvel Entertainment Group

4 MT,Final four labors. 3.00
5 MT,final Four Labors 3.00

HERCULES AND THE HEART OF CHAOS
Limited Series Aug., 1997

1 (of 3) TDF,RF,PO, ... 2.50
2 TDF,RF,PO, ... 2.50
3 TDF,RF,PO,V:Ares, concl. 2.50

HERCULES PRINCE OF POWER
Sept., 1982

1 BL,I:Recorder. 5.00
2 BL,I:Layana Sweetwater 3.00
3 BL,V:The Brothers,C:Galactus . 3.00
4 BL,A:Galactus 3.00

[2nd Series], March, 1984

1 BL,I:Skyypi. 3.00
2 BL,A:Red Wolf 2.50
3 BL,A:Starfox. 2.50
4 BL,D:Zeus, June, 1984 . . . . 2.50

HERO
May, 1990

1 . . . . 2.50
2 thru 6 . . . . @2.25

HERO FOR HIRE
June, 1972

1 GT,JR,I&O:Power Man 100.00
2 GT,A:Diamond Back 50.00
3 GT,I:Mace 40.00
4 V:Phantom of 42nd St. 40.00
5 GT,A:Black Mariah. 40.00
6 V:Assassin 25.00
7 GT,Nuclear Bomb issue. 25.00
8 GT,A:Dr.Doom 25.00
9 GT,A:Dr.Doom,Fant.Four. 25.00
10 GT,A:Dr.Death,Fant.Four 25.00
11 GT,A:Dr.Death. 15.00
12 GT,C:Spider-Man 15.00
13 A:Lion Fang. 15.00
14 V:Big Ben 15.00
15 Cage Goes Wild 15.00
16 O:Stilletto,D:Rackham. 15.00
Becomes:

POWER MAN

HEROES FOR HIRE
July, 1997

1 JOs,PFe,F:Iron Fist 5.00
2 JOs,PFe,V:Nitro. 3.00
2A Variant PFe cover 3.00
3 JOs,PFe,V:Nitro. 3.00
4 JOs,Power Man vs. Iron Fist 3.00
5 JOs,V:Sersi, Diabolical Deviants . 3.00
6 JOs,PFe, Deviants. 3.00
7 JOs V:Thunderbolts 3.00
8 JOs,Iron Fist's agenda revealed . 3.00
9 JOs,Search for Punisher 3.00
10 JOs,Deadpool hired 3.00
11 JOs,PFe,A:Deadpool, V:Silver
     Sable and Wild Pack. 3.00
12 JOs,PFe,Traitor revealed, 48pg . 3.50
13 JOs,PFe,V:Master. 3.00
14 JOs,F:Black Knight 3.00
15 JOs,PFe,Siege of Wundagore,
     pt.1 (of 5) 3.00
16 JOs,PFe,Siege of Wundagore,
     pt.3. . . . . 3.00
17 JOs,DBw,F:Luke Cage
     & She-Hulk 3.00
18 JOs,PFe,A:Wolverine 3.00
19 JOs,PFe,F:Wolverine 3.00

Ann.'98 JOs,BWi,PFe,Heroes For
   Hire/Quicksilver, The Siege of
   Wundagore, pt.5 (of 5) 48pg . . . 3.00

HEROES FOR HIRE
Aug., 2006

1 JP,BiT,Civil War tie-in 3.00
2 thru 4 JP,BiT. . . . . @3.00
5 JP,BiT. 3.00
6 JP,BiT(c). 3.00
7 JP,BiT(s). 3.00
8 TP 3.00
9 . . . . 3.00
10 . . . . 3.00
11 World War Hulk. 3.00
11a 2nd printing. 3.00
12 World War Hulk. 3.00
13 World War Hulk. 3.00
14 World War Hulk. 3.00
15 World War Hulk. 3.00

HEROES FOR HOPE
1985

1 TA/JBy/HC/RCo/BWr,A:XMen . . . 7.00

HEROES REBORN: THE RETURN
Oct., 1997

? Heroes Reborn prequel, (Marvel/
   Wizard 1996) 7.50
1 (of 4) PDd,ATi,SvL,F:Franklin
   Richards 4.00
2 PDd,ATi,SvL, F:Spider-Man,
   Thunderbolts & Doctor Strange . 4.00
3 PDd,SvL,ATi,A UniverseMayDie . 4.00
4 PDd,SvL,ATi, crossover to Marvel
   Universe? 4.00

HOKUM & HEX
Razorline 1993–94

1 BU:Saint Sinner 3.00
2 thru 9 . . . . @2.25

HOLIDAY COMICS
Marvel Star, Jan., 1951

1 LbC(c),Christmas(c). 500.00
2 LbC(c),Easter Parade(c) 525.00
3 LbC(c),4th of July(c) 325.00
4 LbC(c),Summer Vacation. 300.00
5 LbC(c),Christmas(c). 300.00
6 LbC(c),Birthday(c) 300.00
7 LbC(c),Rodeo (c). 300.00
8 LbC(c),Xmas(c) Oct., 1952 . . . 300.00

Holiday Comics #7
© Marvel Entertainment Group

Becomes:

FUN COMICS
Marvel Star, 1953

9 LbC	300.00
10 LbC	250.00
11 LbC	250.00
12 LbC	250.00

Becomes:

MIGHTY BEAR
Marvel Star, 1954

13 LbC	100.00
14 LbC	100.00

Becomes:

UNSANE
Marvel Star, 1954

15	475.00

HOLLYWOOD SUPERSTARS
Epic, Nov., 1990

1 DSp	3.00
2 thru 5 DSp, March, 1991	@2.50

Homer, The Happy Ghost #1
© Marvel Entertainment Group

HOMER, THE HAPPY GHOST
March, 1955

1	300.00
2	200.00
3	175.00
4 thru 15	@175.00
16 thru 22	@150.00

[2nd Series], Nov., 1969

1	200.00
2 thru 5	@125.00

HOMER HOOPER
Marvel Atlas, 1953

1 Teen-age romance humor	125.00
2	100.00
3	100.00
4	100.00

HONEYMOON
See: GAY COMICS

HOOD, THE
Marvel Max, May, 2002

1 (of 6) F:Parker Robbins,40-pg.	6.00
2 FBI attention	6.00
3 diamond heist	5.00
4	5.00

5	5.00
6 concl.	6.00

HOOK
1992

1 JRy,GM,movie adaption.	2.25
2 JRy,Return to Never Land	2.25
3 Peter Pans Magic	2.25
4 conclusion	2.25
Hook Super Spec.#1	3.00

HORRORS, THE
Marvel Star Publications, Jan., 1953–April, 1954

11 LbC(c),JyD,Horrors of War	400.00
12 LbC(c),Horrors of War	375.00
13 LbC(c),Horrors of Mystery	350.00
14 LbC(c),Horrors of the Underworld	375.00
15 LbC(c),Horrors of the Underworld	375.00

HOT SHOTS
AVENGERS

1 Painted Pin-ups (1995)	3.00

SPIDER-MAN

1 Painted pin-ups	3.00

X-MEN

1 Painted pin-ups	3.00

HOUSE II

1 1987, Movie Adapt.	2.00

HOUSE OF M
June, 2005

1 (of 8) F:X-Men, New Avengers	3.00
2 BMB,V:the Scarlet Witch	3.00
3 BMB,F:Wolverine	3.00
4 BMB,F:Layla Miller.	3.00
5 BMB,F:Spider-man	3.00
6 BMB	3.00
7 BMB	3.00
8 BMB	3.00
1a thru 8a variant (c).	@3.00
Spec. Secrets of the House of M.	4.00

HOUSE OF M: AVENGERS
Nov., 2007

1 (of 5)	3.00

HOWARD THE DUCK
Jan., 1976

1 FB,SL,A:Spider-Man,I:Beverly	35.00
2 FB,V:TurnipMan&Kidney Lady.	15.00
3 JB,Learns Quack Fu	12.00
4 GC,V:Winky Man	12.00
5 GC,Becomes Wrestler	10.00
6 GC,V:Gingerbread Man	7.00
7 GC,V:Gingerbread Man	7.00
8 GC,A:Dr.Strange,ran for Pres.	7.00
9 GC,V:Le Beaver.	7.00
10 GC,A:Spider-Man	7.00
11 GC,V:Kidney Lady.	7.00
12 GC,I:Kiss.	35.00
13 GC,A:Kiss	40.00
14 thru 32 GC	@4.00
33 BB(c),The Material Duck.	6.00
Ann.#1, V:Caliph of Bagmom	3.00
Holiday Spec. LHa,ATi,PFe (1996)	3.50

HOWARD THE DUCK
Marvel Max, Jan., 2002

1 (of 6) SvG,Making the Band	4.00
2 SvG,Beverly's ex	3.00
3 SvG,GF,The former Duck.	3.00

Howard the Duck #27
© Marvel Entertainment Group

4 SvG,GF,House of Mystery	3.00
5 SvG,GF,House of Mystery,pt.2.	3.00
6 SvG,GF,Duck or Mouse	3.00

HOWARD THE DUCK
Oct., 2006

1 (of 4) TTn.	3.00
2	3.00

[NICK FURY'S] HOWLING COMMANDOS
Oct., 2005

1 KG,F:horror characters	3.00

HUGGA BUNCH
Star, Oct., 1986—Aug., 1987

1	4.00
2 thru 6	@3.00

HULK, THE
Feb., 1999

1 JBy,RG,DGr,48-page	4.00
1a signed	20.00
1b gold foil cover	10.00
2 JBy,RG,DGr,Hulk unleashed	3.00
2a variant AdP cover	3.00
3 JBy,RG,DGr,Hulk berserk	3.00
4 JBy,RG,DGr,old foe	3.00
5 JBy,RG,DGr,V:Man-Thing	3.00
6 JBy,RG,DGr,V:Man-Thing	3.00
7 JBy,RG,DGr,A:Avengers	3.00
8 JBy,RG,DGr,V:Wolverine	17.00
9 RG,V:Thing.	3.00
10 RG.	3.00
11 PJe,RG,SB,A:DocSamson	3.00

Becomes:

INCREDIBLE HULK
2000

12 PJe,RG,SB,48-pg	3.00
13 PJe,RG,SB,new Hulk	2.50
14 PJe,RG,SB,V:Ryker	2.50
15 PJe,RG,SB,Dogs of War,pt.2	2.50
16 PJe,RG,SB,Dogs of War,pt.3	2.50
17 PJe,RG,SB,Dogs of War,pt.4	2.50
18 PJe,RG,SB,Dogs of War,pt.5	2.50
19 PJe,RG,SB,Dogs of War,pt.6	2.50
20 PJe,RG,SB,Dogs of War,pt.7	2.50
21 PJe,Maximum Security	2.50
22 PJe,Joe Fixit's Money.	2.50
23 PJe,Nobby Stiles.	2.50
24 PJe,JR2,V:Abomination	2.50

25 PJe,JR2,V:Abomination 3.50
26 Psyche of child-like Hulk. 2.50
27 PJe,JR2,TP. 2.50
28 PJe,JR2,TP,V:Devil Hulk. 2.50
29 FaN,A:Angela,Doc Samson 2.50
30 PJe,JoB,TP, ... 2.50
31 PJe,JoB,TP,Banner gone 2.50
32 PJe,JoB,TP,Ant-Man inside 2.50
33 CPr,JBg,100-page. 4.00
34 JR2,TP,The beast within 5.00
35 JR2,TP,crosses the line? 3.00
36 JR2,TP,Gangs All Here,pt.1 . . . . 3.00
37 JR2,TP,Remember This,pt.2. . . . 3.00
38 JR2,TP, ... 3.00
39 JR2,TP,Tag-You're Dead. 3.00
40 LW,TP,madman with gun 3.00
41 LW,TP,madman with gun. 3.00
42 LW,TP,hostage crisis. 3.00
43 JR2,TP,hostage crisis,concl. 3.00
44 SI. 3.00
45 SI,dream lover 3.00
46 SI. 3.00
47 SI. 3.00
48 SI. 3.00
49 SI. 3.00
50 MD2,R:Abomination,pt.1. . . . . . . 4.00
51 MD2,R:Abomination,pt.2. . . . . . . 3.00
52 MD2,R:Abomination,pt.3. . . . . . . 3.00
53 MD2,R:Abomination,pt.4. . . . . . . 3.00
54 MD2,R:Abomination,pt.5. . . . . . . 3.00
55 Hide in Plain Sight,pt.1 . . . . 3.00
56 Hide in Plain Sight,pt.2 . . . . 3.00
57 Hide in Plain Sight,pt.3 . . . . 3.00
58 Hide in Plain Sight,pt.4 . . . . 3.00
59 Hide in Plain Sight,pt.5 . . . . 3.00
60 MD2,Split Decisions,pt.1. . . . . . . 3.00
61 MD2,Split Decisions,pt.2. . . . . . . 3.00
62 MD2,Split Decisions,pt.3. . . . . . . 3.00
63 MD2,Split Decisions,pt.4. . . . . . . 3.00
64 MD2,Split Decisions,pt.5. . . . . . . 3.00
65 MD2,Split Decisions,concl. 3.00
66 MD2,Bury Me Not,pt.1 . . . . 3.00
67 DBw,MD2(c),Bury Me Not,pt.2 . . 3.00
68 DBw,MD2(c),Bury Me Not,pt.3 . . 3.00
69 DBw,MD2(c),Bury Me Not,pt.4 . . 3.00
70 MD2, Marvel Knights Hulk 3.00
71 MD2,Big Things,pt.1 . . . . 3.00
72 MD2,Big Things,pt.2 . . . . 3.00
73 MD2,Big Things,pt.3 . . . . 3.00
74 DBw,Big Things,pt.4 . . . . 3.00
75 DaR,Wake to Nightmare,48-pg. . 3.50
76 DBw,Shattered,48-pg. 3.50
77 PDd(s),LW,Tempest Fugit,pt.1 . . 4.00
78 PDd(s),LW,Tempest Fugit,pt.2 . . 3.00
79 PDd(s),LW,Tempest Fugit,pt.3 . . 3.00
80 PDd(s),LW,Tempest Fugit,pt.4 . . 3.00
81 PDd(s),LW,Tempest Fugit,pt.5 . . 3.00
82 PDd(s),JaL,vengeance 3.00
83 PDd(s),The Last Refuge,pt.1 . . . 3.00
84 PDd(s),The Last Refuge,pt.2 . . . 3.00
85 PDd(s),The Last Refuge,pt.3 . . . 3.00
86 PDd(s),The Last Refuge,pt.4 . . . 3.00
87 PDd(s),AKu,F:New Scorpion . . . 3.00
88 Peace in Our Time, pt.1 . . . . 3.50
89 Peace in Our Time, pt.2 . . . . 3.50
90 Peace in Our Time, pt.3 . . . . 3.50
91 Peace in Our Time, pt.4 . . . . 3.50
92 Planet Hulk: Exile, pt.1 . . . . 6.00
93 Planet Hulk: Exile, pt.2 . . . . 3.00
94 Planet Hulk: Exile, pt.3 . . . . 3.00
95 Planet Hulk: Exile, pt.4 . . . . 3.00
96 AaL,Planet Hulk: Anarchy, pt.1 . . 3.00
97 AaL,Planet Hulk: Anarchy, pt.2 . . 3.00
98 AaL,Planet Hulk: Anarchy, pt.3 . . 3.00
99 AaL,Planet Hulk: Anarchy, pt.4 . . 3.00
100 Hulk sized 104-pg. 4.00
100a variant (c) 3.00
101 AaL,Allegiance,pt.2 . . . . 3.00
102 AaL,Allegiance,pt.3 . . . . 3.00
103 AaL,Allegiance,pt.4 . . . . 3.00
104 Planet Hulk 3.00
105 . . . . 3.00

106 Warbound, pt.1 . . . . 3.00
106a later printing 3.00
107 GFr,F:Amadeus Cho. 3.00
107a 2nd printing. 3.00
108 F:Amadeus Cho 3.00
109 F:Amadeus Cho 3.00
110 F:Amadeus Cho 3.00
111 . . . . 3.00
112 . . . . 3.00
Ann. 1999 JBy,DGr,48-page 4.00
Ann. 2001 EL,V:Thor 3.50
Spec. Hulk/Sentry 3.50
GN The End, DK, ... 6.00
Spec. Must Have, rep. #34–#36 . . . 4.00
Spec. Planet Hulk: Gladiator
  Guidebook (2006) 4.00

HULK AND POWER PACK
Mar., 2007

1 (of 4) 3.00
2 thru 4 . . . . 3.00

HULK: DESTRUCTION
July, 2005

1 (of 4) PDd 3.00
2 PDd,v:Abomination 3.00
3 PDd 3.00
4 PDd 3.00

HULK: GRAY
Oct., 2003

1 JLb,TSe 3.50
2 thru 6 JLb,TSe . . . . @3.50

HULK: THE MOVIE
June, 2003

Spec. Movie adaptation, 48-pg. 3.50

HULK: NIGHTMERICA
June, 2003

1 (of 6) 3.00
2 thru 6 . . . . @3.00

HULK SMASH
Jan., 2001

1 (of 2) GEn,JMC 3.00
2 GEn,JMC 3.00

HULK & THING:
HARD KNOCKS
Sept., 2004

1 (of 4) JaL 3.50
2 JaL 3.50
3 . . . . 3.00
4 . . . . 3.00

HULK 2099
1994–95

1 GJ,Foil(c),V:Draco 3.00
2 GJ,V:Draco 2.25
3 I:Golden Boy 2.25
4 . . . . 2.25
5 Ultra Hulk. 2.25
Becomes:

HULK 2099 A.D.
1995

6 Gamma Ray Scientist 2.25
7 A:Doom,Dr.Apollo 2.25
8 One Nation Under Doom. 2.25
9 California Quake 2.25

HULK/WOLVERINE:
6 HOURS
Jan., 2003

1 (of 4) ScK,SBs(c),rescue 3.00
2 ScK,SBs(c) 3.00

3 ScK,SBs(c) 3.00
4 ScK,SBs(c),concl. 3.00

HUMAN FLY
July, 1987

1 I&O:Human Fly,A:Spider-Man . 10.00
2 A:Ghost Rider 12.00
3 DC,JSt(c),DP,Fortress of Fear . . . 5.00
4 JB/TA(c),David Drier 5.00
5 V:Makik 5.00
6 Fear in Funland 5.00
7 ME,Fury in the Wind 5.00
8 V:White Tiger 5.00
9 JB/TA(c),ME,V:Copperhead,A:
  White Tiger,Daredevil 7.00
10 ME,Dark as a Dungeon 5.00
11 ME,A:Daredevil 5.00
12 ME,Suicide Sky-Dive 5.00
13 BLb/BMc(c),FS,V:Carl Braden . . 5.00
14 BLb/BMc(c),SL,Fear Over
  Fifth Avenue. 5.00
15 BLb/BMc(c),War in the
  Washington Monument 5.00
16 BLb/BMc(c),V:Blaze Kendall. . . . 5.00
17 BLb,DP,Murder on the Midway . . 5.00
18 V:Harmony Whyte. 5.00
19 BL(c),V:Jacopo Belbo
  March, 1979 . . . . 10.00

RED RAVEN COMICS
Marvel Timely Comics Aug., 1940

1 JK,O:Red Raven,I:Magar,A:Comet
  Pierce & Mercury,Human Top,
  Eternal Brain 25,000.00
Becomes:

HUMAN TORCH
Marvel Comcis, 1940–49

2 (#1)ASh(c),BEv,B:Sub-Mariner
  A:Fiery Mask,Falcon,Mantor,
  Microman 60,000.00
3 (#2)Ash(c),BEv,V:Sub-
  Mariner,Bondage(c) 10,000.00
4 (#3)ASh(c),BEv,O:Patriot . . 7,500.00
5 (#4)V:Nazis,A:Patriot,Angel
  crossover 6,000.00
5a(#5)ASh(c),V:Sub-Mariner . 9,500.00
6 ASh(c),Doom Dungeon. 4,500.00
7 ASh(c),V:Japanese 4,700.00
8 ASh(c),BW,V:Sub-Mariner . . 6,000.00
9 ASh(c),V:General Rommel . . 5,000.00
10 ASh(c),BW,V:Sub-Mariner . . 5,000.00

Human Torch #2
© *Marvel Entertainment Group*

11 ASh(c),Nazi Oil Refinery . . . 3,000.00
12 ASh(c),V:Japanese,
   Bondage(c). 5,500.00
13 ASh(c),V:Japanese,
   Bondage(c). 3,000.00
14 ASh(c),V:Nazis. 3,000.00
15 ASh(c),Toro Trapped 3,000.00
16 ASh(c),V:Japanese 2,500.00
17 ASh(c),V:Japanese 2,500.00
18 ASh(c),V:Japanese,
   MacArthurs HQ. 2,500.00
19 ASh(c),Bondage(c). 2,700.00
20 ASh(c),Last War Issue 2,500.00
21 ASh(c),V:Organized Crime. . 2,200.00
22 ASh(c),V:Smugglers. 2,200.00
23 ASh(c),V:Giant Robot. 2,800.00
24 SSh(c),V:Mobsters. 2,700.00
25 The Masked Monster 2,500.00
26 SSh(c),Her Diary of Terror. . 2,500.00
27 SSh(c),BEv,V:The Asbestos
   Lady. 2,500.00
28 BEv,The Twins Who Weren't 2,500.00
29 SSh(c),You'll Die Laughing . 2,500.00
30 SSh(c),BEv,The Stranger,
   A:Namora 2,500.00
31 A:Namora 2,000.00
32 SSh(c),A:Sungirl,Namora. . . 2,000.00
33 Capt.America crossover . . . 2,000.00
34 The Flat of the Land 2,000.00
35 A;Captain America,Sungirl . . 2,200.00
Becomes:

LOVE TALES
Revived As:

HUMAN TORCH
Marvel Comics, 1954
36 A:Submariner. 2,000.00
37 BEv,A:Submariner 1,800.00
38 BEv,A:Submariner 1,800.00

HUMAN TORCH
Sept., 1974
1 JK,rep.StrangeTales #101 . . . . 30.00
2 rep.Strange Tales #102 . . . . 25.00
3 rep.Strange Tales #103 . . . . 25.00
4 rep.Strange Tales #104 . . . . 25.00
5 rep.Strange Tales #105 . . . . 25.00
6 rep.Strange Tales #106 . . . . 25.00
7 rep.Strange Tales #107 . . . . 25.00
8 rep.Strange Tales #108 . . . . 25.00
Becomes:

HUMAN TORCH
April, 2003
1 KK(s),Burn,pt.1 . . . . 2.50
2 KK(s),Burn,pt.2 . . . . 2.50
3 KK(s),Burn,pt.3 . . . . 2.50
4 KK(s),Burn,pt.4 . . . . 2.50
5 KK(s),Burn,pt.5 . . . . 2.50
6 KK(s),Burn,concl. 2.50
7 KK(s),Plague of Locusts,pt.1 . . . 2.50
8 KK(s),Plague of Locusts,pt.2 . . . 3.00
9 KK(s),Plague of Locusts,pt.3 . . . 3.00
10 KK(s),Plague of Locusts,pt.4 . . . 3.00
11 KK(s),F:Namorita 3.00
12 KK(s),series finale. 3.00

HUMAN TORCH COMICS
Feb., 1999
1-shot V:Sub-Mariner, 48-page 4.00

HYPERKIND
Marvel/Razorline 1993
1 I:Hyperkind,BU:EctoKid 3.00
2 thru 9 . . . . @2.25

HYPERKIND UNLEASHED
1994
1 BU,V:Thermakk 3.25

Iceman #3
© Marvel Entertainment Group

ICEMAN
Dec., 1984
1 DP,mini-series 3.00
2 DP,V:Kali 3.00
3 DP,A;Original X-Men,Defenders
   Champions 3.00
4 DP,Oblivion,June, 1985 . . . . 4.00

ICEMAN
Oct., 2001
1 (of 4) DAn,ALa,KIK 3.00
2 DAn,ALa,KIK,A:Augmen 3.00
3 DAn,ALa,KIK,F:Foe-Dog,Augmen 3.00
4 DAn,ALa, concl. 3.00

IDEAL
Marvel Timely, July, 1948
1 Antony and Cleopatra 450.00
2 The Corpses of Dr.Sacotti . . . 375.00
3 Joan of Arc 350.00
4 Richard the Lionhearted
   A:The Witness 550.00
5 Phc,Love and Romance 250.00
Becomes:

LOVE ROMANCES
6 Ph(c),I Loved a Scoundrel . . . 250.00
7 Ph(c) 175.00
8 Ph(c) 200.00
9 thru 12 Ph(c) . . . . @150.00
13 thru 20 . . . . @150.00
21 BK 125.00
22 . . . . 125.00
23 . . . . 125.00
24 BK 125.00
25 . . . . 125.00
26 thru 35 . . . . @125.00
36 BK 125.00
37 . . . . 125.00
38 BK 150.00
39 thru 44 . . . . @125.00
45 MB. 150.00
46 . . . . 150.00
47 . . . . 150.00
48 . . . . 125.00
49 ATh 150.00
50 . . . . 125.00
51 . . . . 125.00
52 . . . . 125.00
53 ATh 140.00
54 . . . . 125.00
55 . . . . 125.00
56 . . . . 125.00

57 MB. 135.00
58 thru 74 . . . . @135.00
75 MB. 135.00
76 . . . . 125.00
77 MB. 135.00
78 . . . . 125.00
79 . . . . 125.00
80 RH(c). 125.00
81 . . . . 125.00
82 MB,JK(c). 150.00
83 JSe,JK(c) 150.00
84 JK 150.00
85 JK 150.00
86 thru 95 . . . . @100.00
96 JK 150.00
97 . . . . 150.00
98 JK 160.00
99 JK 160.00
100 thru 104 . . . . @160.00
105 JK 160.00
106 JK,July, 1963 . . . . 160.00

IDEAL COMICS
Marvel Timely, Fall, 1944
1 B:Super Rabbit,Giant Super
   Rabbit V:Axis(c) 300.00
2 Super Rabbit at Fair(c) 200.00
3 Beach Party(c). 200.00
4 How to Catch Robbers 200.00
Becomes:

WILLIE COMICS
1946
5 B:Willie,George,Margie,Nellie
   Football(c) 250.00
6 Record Player(c) 175.00
7 Soda Fountain(c),HK 175.00
8 Fancy Dress(c) 150.00
9 . . . . 150.00
10 HK,Hey Look. 175.00
11 HK,Hey Look. 175.00
12 . . . . 150.00
13 . . . . 150.00
14 . . . . 150.00
15 . . . . 150.00
16 thru 18 . . . . @150.00
19 . . . . 175.00
20 Li'L Willie Comics 150.00
21 Li'L Willie Comics 150.00
22 . . . . 150.00
23 May, 1950 . . . . 150.00
Becomes:

CRIME CASES

IDENTITY DISK
June, 2004
1 (of 5) JP 3.00
2 thru 5 . . . . @3.00

IDOL
Epic, 1992
1 I:Idol. 3.25
2 Phantom of the Set 3.25
3 Conclusion 3.25

I ♥ MARVEL
Feb., 2006
Marvel AI 3.00
Masked Intentions #1 . . . . 3.00
My Mutant Heart 3.00
Outlaw Love #1 . . . . 3.00
Web of Romance #1 . . . . 3.00

ILLUMINATOR
1993
1 . . . . 5.50
2 . . . . 5.50
3 . . . . 3.25
4 . . . . 3.25

Illuminator #2
© *Marvel Entertainment Group*

IMMORTAL IRON FIST
Nov., 2006

1	3.00
1a Director's Cut	4.00
2	3.00
3	3.00
4	3.00
5	3.00
6	3.00
7 F:Wu Ao-Shi	3.00
8 Seven Capital Cities of Heaven	3.00
9 Seven Capital Cities of Heaven	3.00
10	3.00
11 Seven Capital Cities of Heaven	3.00
Ann. #1	4.00

IMMORTALIS

1 A:Dr.Strange	2.25
2 A:Dr.Strange	2.25
3 A:Dr.Strange,V:Vampires	2.25
4 Mephisto, final issue	2.25

IMPERIAL GUARD
[Limited Series], 1997

1 (of 3) BAu,Woj,	2.25
2 and 3 BAu,Woj	@2.25

IMPOSSIBLE MAN SUMMER VACATION
1990–91

1 GCa,DP	2.50
2	2.50
Summer Fun Spec. TPe, Vacation on Earth	2.50

INCAL, THE
Epic, Nov., 1988

1 Moebius,Adult	12.00
2 Moebius,Adult	12.00
3 Moebius,Adult, Jan., 1989	12.00

INCOMPLETE DEATH'S HEAD
1993

1	3.50
2 thru 11 rep.Death's Head #1 thru #11	@2.25

INCREDIBLE HULK
May, 1962

1 JK,I:Hulk(Grey Skin),Rick Jones, Thunderbolt Ross,Betty Ross, Gremlin,Gamma Base	27,000.00
2 JK,SD,O:Hulk,(Green skin).	5,500.00
3 JK,O:rtd.,I:Ring Master, Circus of Crime.	3,200.00
4 JK,V:Mongu	3,000.00
5 JK,I:General Fang.	3,000.00
6 SD,I:Metal Master.	3,800.00

See: Tales to Astonish #59-#101

April, 1968

102 MSe,GT,O:Retold	700.00
103 MSe,I:Space Parasite	250.00
104 MSe,O&N:Rhino	200.00
105 MSe,GT,I:Missing Link	150.00
106 MSe,HT,GT	150.00
107 HT,V:Mandarin	150.00
108 HT,JMe,A:Nick Fury	150.00
109 HT,JMe,A:Ka-Zar	125.00
110 HT,JMe,A:Ka-Zar.	125.00
111 HT,DA,I:Galaxy Master	100.00
112 HT,DA,O:Galaxy Master	80.00
113 HT,DA,V:Sandman	80.00
114 HT,DA	80.00
115 HT,DA,A:Leader	80.00
116 HT,DA,V:Super Humanoid	80.00
117 HT,DA,A:Leader	80.00
118 HT,V:Sub-Mariner	80.00
119 HT,V:Maximus	75.00
120 HT,V:Maximus	75.00
121 HT,I:The Glob	75.00
122 HT,V:Thing	100.00
123 HT,V:Leader	75.00
124 HT,SB,V:Rhino,Leader	75.00
125 HT,V:Absorbing Man	75.00
126 HT,A:Dr.Strange	75.00
127 HT,Moleman vs.Tyrannus I:Mogol.	50.00
128 HT,A:Avengers	50.00
129 HT,V:Glob	50.00
130 HT,Banner vs. Hulk.	50.00
131 HT,A:Iron Man.	50.00
132 HT,JSe,V:Hydra	50.00
133 HT,JSe,I:Draxon	50.00
134 HT,SB,I:Golem	50.00
135 HT,SB,V:Kang.	50.00
136 HT,SB,I:Xeron.	50.00
137 HT,V:Abomination	50.00
138 HT,V:Sandman	50.00
139 HT,V:Leader	50.00
140 HT,V:Psyklop	50.00
141 HT,JSe,I&O:Doc.Samson	125.00
142 HT,JSe,V:Valkyrie,A:Doc Samson	60.00
143 DA,JSe,V:Dr.Doom	60.00
144 DA,JSe,V:Dr.Doom	60.00
145 HT,JSe,O:Retold	65.00
146 HT,JSe,Leader	30.00
147 HT,JSe,Doc.Samson loses Powers.	30.00
148 HT,JSe,I:Fialan	30.00
149 HT,JSe,I:Inheritor	30.00
150 HT,JSe,I:Viking,A:Havoc	30.00
151 HT,JSe,C:Ant Man	30.00
152 HT,DA,Many Cameos	30.00
153 HT,JSe,C:Capt.America	30.00
154 HT,JSe,A:Ant Man, V:Chameleon.	30.00
155 HT,JSe,I:Shaper of Worlds	30.00
156 HT,V:Hulk	30.00
157 HT,I:Omnivac,Rhino	30.00
158 HT,C:Warlock,V:Rhino	30.00
159 HT,V:Abomination,Rhino	30.00
160 HT,V:Tiger Shark.	30.00
161 HT,V:Beast	40.00
162 HT,I:Wendigo I	90.00
163 HT,I:Gremlin	25.00
164 HT,I:Capt.Omen	25.00
165 HT,I:Aquon	25.00

Incredible Hulk #129
© *Marvel Entertainment Group*

166 HT,I:Zzzax.	25.00
167 HT,JAb,V:Modok.	25.00
168 HT,JAb,I:Harpy	25.00
169 HT,JAb,I:Bi-Beast	25.00
170 HT,JAb,V:Volcano	25.00
171 HT,JAb,A:Abomination,Rhino	25.00
172 HT,JAb,X:X-Men	50.00
173 HT,V:Cobolt Man	22.00
174 HT,V:Cobolt Man.	22.00
175 JAb,V:Inhumans	22.00
176 HT,JAb,A:Man-Beast,C:Warlock Crisis on Counter-Earth.	25.00
177 HT,JAb,D:Warlock.	25.00
178 HT,JAb,Warlock Lives.	25.00
179 HT,JAb	22.00
180 HT,JAb,I:Wolverine V:Wendigo I.	400.00
181 HT,JAb,A:Wolverine (1st Full Story),V:Wendigo II	1,500.00
182 HT,JAb,I&D:Crackajack Jackson,C:Wolverine.	175.00
183 HT,V:Zzzax	18.00
184 HT,V:Living Shadow	18.00
185 HT,V:General Ross	18.00
186 HT,I:Devastator	18.00
187 HT,JSt,V:Gremlin.	18.00
188 HT,JSt,I:Droog.	18.00
189 HT,JSt,I:Datrine.	18.00
190 HT,MSe,Toadman	18.00
191 HT,JSt,Toadman,I:Glorian	18.00
192 HT,V:The Lurker	18.00
193 HT,JSt,Doc.Samson regains Powers.	18.00
194 SB,JSt,V:Locust	18.00
195 SB,JSt,V:Abomination.	18.00
196 SB,JSt,V:Army	18.00
197 BWr(c),SB,JSt,A:Man-Thing	18.00
198 SB,JSt,A:Man-Thing	18.00
199 SB,JSt,V:Shield,Doc.Samson	18.00
200 SB,JSt,Multi,Hulk in Glenn Talbots Brain	40.00
201 SB,JSt,V:Fake Conan	7.00
202 SB,JSt,A:Jarella	7.00
203 SB,JSt,A:Jarella	7.00
204 SB,JStI:Kronus	7.00
205 SB,JSt,D:Jarella	7.00
206 SB,JSt,C:Dr.Strange	7.00
207 SB,JSt,A:Dr.Strange	7.00
208 SB,JSt,V:Absorbing Man.	7.00
209 SB,JSt,V:Absorbing Man.	7.00
210 SB,A:Dr.Druid,O:Merlin II	7.00
211 SB,A:Dr.Druid	7.00
212 SB,I:Constrictor.	8.00
213 SB,TP,I:Quintronic Man	7.00
214 SB,Jack of Hearts.	7.00
215 SB,V:Bi-Beast.	6.00

MARVEL

216 SB,Gen.Ross 6.00	290 SB,JSt,V:Modok 5.00	338 TM,I:Mercy,V:Shield 12.00
217 SB,I:Stilts,A:Ringmaster 6.00	291 SB,JSt,V:Thunderbolt Ross . . 5.00	339 TM,A:RickJones 12.00
218 SB,KP,Doc.Samson versus	292 SB,JSt,V:Dragon Man 5.00	340 TM,Hulk vs Wolverine 50.00
Rhino 6.00	293 SB,V:Nightmare 5.00	341 TM,V:Man Bull 9.00
219 SB,V:Capt.Barracuda 6.00	294 SB,V:Boomerang 5.00	342 TM,V:Leader 9.00
220 SB,Robinson Crusoe 6.00	295 SB,V:Boomerang 5.00	343 TM,V:Leader 9.00
221 SB,AA,A:Sting Ray 6.00	296 SB,A:Rom 5.00	344 TM,V:Leader 9.00
222 JSn,AA,Cavern of Bones 6.00	297 SB,V:Nightmare 5.00	345 TM,V:Leader,Double-Size 10.00
223 SB,V:Leader 6.00	298 KN(c),SB,V:Nightmare 5.00	346 TM,EL,L:Rick Jones 9.00
224 SB,V:The Leader 6.00	299 SB,A:Shield 5.00	347 In Las Vegas,I:Marlo Chandler,
225 SB,V:Leader,A:Doc.Samson . . 6.00	300 SB,A:Spider-Man,Avengers	V:Absorbing Man 5.00
226 SB,JSt,A:Doc.Samson 6.00	Doctor Strange 8.00	348 V:Absorbing Man 4.00
227 SB,JK,A:Doc.Samson 6.00	301 SB,Crossroads 4.00	349 A:Spider-Man 4.00
228 SB,BMc,I:Moonstone,V:Doc	302 SB,Crossroads 4.00	350 Hulk vs Thing,A:Beast
Samson 8.00	303 SB,V:The Knights 4.00	V:Dr.Doom 5.00
229 SB,O:Moonstone,V:Doc	304 SB,V:U-Foes 4.00	351 R:Jarella's World 3.00
Samson 6.00	305 SB,V:U-Foes 4.00	352 V:Inquisitor 3.00
230 JM,BL,A:Bug Thing 6.00	306 SB,V:Klaatu 4.00	353 R:Bruce Banner 3.00
231 SB,I:Fred Sloan 6.00	307 SB,V:Klaatu 4.00	354 V:Maggia 3.00
232 SB,A:Capt.America 6.00	308 SB,V:Puffball Collective 4.00	355 V:Glorian 3.00
233 SB,A:Marvel Man 6.00	309 SB,V:Goblin & Glow 4.00	356 V:Glorian,Cloot 3.00
234 SB,Marvel Man Changes name	310 Crossroads 4.00	357 V:Glorian,Cloot 3.00
to Quasar 6.00		358 V:Glorian,Cloot 3.00
235 SB,A:Machine Man 6.00		359 JBy(c),C:Wolverine(illusion) . . . 4.00
236 SB,A:Machine Man 6.00		360 V:Nightmare & Dyspare 3.00
237 SB,A:Machine Man 6.00		361 A:Iron Man,V:Maggia 3.00
238 SB,JAb,Jimmy Carter 6.00		362 V:Werewolf By Night 3.00
239 SB,I:Gold Bug 6.00		363 Acts of Vengeance 3.00
240 SB,Eldorado 6.00		364 A:Abomination,B:Countdown . . 3.00
241 SB,A:Tyrannus 6.00		365 A:Fantastic Four 3.00
242 SB,Eldorado 6.00		366 A:Leader,I:Riot Squad 3.00
243 SB,A:Gammemon 6.00		367 1st DK Hulk,I:Madman(Leader's
244 SB,A:It. 6.00		brother),E:Countdown 13.00
245 SB,A:Super Mandroid 6.00		368 SK,V:Mr.Hyde 5.00
246 SB,V:Capt.Marvel 6.00		369 DK,V:Freedom Force 3.00
247 SB,A:Bat Dragon 6.00		370 DK,R:Original Defenders 3.00
248 SB,V:Gardener 6.00		371 DK,BMc,A:Orig.Defenders 3.00
249 SD,R:Jack Frost 6.00		372 DK,R:Green Hulk 10.00
250 SB,A:Silver Surfer 15.00		373 DK,Green Hulk & Grey Hulk . . . 4.00
251 MG,A:3-D Man 5.00		374 DK,BMc,Skrulls,
252 SB,A:Woodgod 5.00		R:Rick Jones 4.00
253 SB,A:Woodgod 5.00		375 DK,BMc,V:Super Skrull 4.00
254 SB,I:U-Foes 5.00		376 DK,BMc,Green Hulk,Grey
255 SB,V:Thor 5.00		Hulk & Banner fight 5.00
256 SB,I&O:Sabra 5.00		377 DK,BMc,New Green Hulk,
257 SB,I&O:Arabian Knight 5.00		combination of green, grey, and
258 I:Soviet Super Soldiers 5.00		Bruce Banner,A:Ringmaster . . 11.00
259 SB,A:Soviet Super-Soldiers,	*Incredible Hulk #278*	377a 2nd printing (gold) 5.00
O:Darkstar 5.00	*© Marvel Entertainment Group*	378 V:Rhino,Christmas Issue 3.00
260 SB,Sugata 5.00		379 DK,MFm,I:Pantheon 4.00
261 SB,V:Absorbing Man 5.00	311 Crossroads 4.00	380 A:Nick Fury,D:Crazy-8 . . . . . . 3.00
262 SB,I:Glazer 5.00	312 Secret Wars II,O:Bruce 4.50	381 DK,MFm,Hulk,J:Pantheon 4.00
263 SB,Avalanche 5.00	313 A:Alpha Flight 4.00	382 DK,MFm,A:Pantheon 4.00
264 SB,A:Corruptor 5.00	314 JBy,V:Doc.Samson 6.00	383 DK,MFm,Infinity Gauntlet 4.00
265 SB,I:Rangers 5.00	315 JBy,A:Doc.Samson,Banner	384 DK,MFm,Infinity Gauntlet 4.00
266 SB,V:High Evolutionary 5.00	& Hulk Separated 4.00	385 DK,MFm,Infinity Gauntlet 4.00
267 SB,V:Rainbow,O:Glorian 5.00	316 JBy,A:Avengers,N:Doc	386 DK,MFm,V:Sabra,A:Achilles . . 4.00
268 SB,I:Pariah 5.00	Samson 4.00	387 DK,MFm,V:Sabra,A:Achilles . . 4.00
269 SB,I:Bereet 5.00	317 JBy,I:Hulkbusters,A:Doc	388 DK,MFm,I:Speed Freak,Jim
270 SB,A:Abomination 5.00	Samson 4.00	Wilson,revealed to have AIDS . 5.00
271 SB,I:Rocket Raccoon,	318 JBy,A:Doc.Samson 5.00	389 1st Comic art By Gary Barker
20th Anniv. 5.00	319 JBy,W:Bruce & Betty 6.00	(Garfield),A:Man-Thing,Glob . . . 3.00
272 SB,C:X-Men,I:Wendigo III. 6.00	320 AM,A:Doc.Samson 3.00	390 DK,MFm,B:War & Pieces,
273 SB,A:Alpha Flight 5.00	321 AM,A:Avengers 3.00	C:X-Factor 4.00
274 SB,Beroct 5.00	322 AM,A:Avengers 3.00	391 DK,MFm,V:X-Factor 4.00
275 SB,JSt,I:Megalith 5.00	323 AM,A:Avengers 3.00	392 DK,MFm,E:War & Pieces,
276 SB,JSt,V:U-Foes 5.00	324 AM,R:Grey Hulk(1st since #1),	A:X-Factor 4.00
277 SB,JSt,U-Foes 5.00	A:Doc.Samson. 15.00	393 DK,MFm,R:Igor,A:Soviet Super
278 SB,JSt,C:X-Men,	325 AM,Rick Jones as Hulk 6.00	Soldiers,30th Ann.,Green foil(c) 6.00
Avengers,Fantastic Four 6.00	326 A:Rick Jones,New Hulk 7.00	393a 2nd printing,Silver. 2.50
279 SB,JSt,C:X-Men,	327 AM,F:General Ross 3.00	394 MFm(i),F:Atalanta,I:Trauma . . . 3.00
Avengers,Fantastic Four 6.00	328 AM,1st PDd(s),Outcasts 8.00	395 DK,MFm,A:Punisher,
280 SB,JSt,Jack Daw 5.00	329 AM,V:Enigma 5.00	I:Mr.Frost 3.00
281 SB,JSt,Trapped in Space 5.00	330 1st TM Hulk,D:T-bolt Ross . . . 22.00	396 DK,MFm,A:Punisher,
282 SB,JSt,A:She Hulk 5.00	331 TM,V:Leader 22.00	V:Mr.Frost 3.00
283 SB,JSt,A:Avengers 5.00	332 TM,V:Leader 12.00	397 DK,MFm,B:Ghost of the
284 SB,JSt,A:Avengers 5.00	333 TM,V:Leader 12.00	Past,V:U-Foes,A:Leader 3.00
285 SB,JSt,Northwind,V:Zzzax 5.00	334 TM,I:Half-life 12.00	398 DK,MFm,D:Marlo,V:Leader. . . . 3.00
286 SB,JSt,V:Soldier 5.00	335 Horror Issue 6.00	399 JD,A:FF,Dr.Strange 3.00
287 SB,JSt,V:Soldier 5.00	336 TM,A:X-Factor 12.00	400 JD,MFm,E:Ghost of the Past,
288 SB,JSt,V:Abomination 5.00	337 TM,A:X-Factor, A:DocSamson 12.00	V:Leader,1st Holo-grafx(c),1st
289 SB,JSt,V:Modok 5.00		GFr Hulk(pin-up) 3.50

400a 2nd Printing. 4.00
401 JDu,O:Agememnon 3.00
402 JDu,V:Juggernaut 3.00
403 GFr,V:Red Skull,A:Avengers . . . 3.00
404 GFr,V:Red Skull,Juggernaut,
   A:Avengers 3.50
405 GFr,Ajax vs. Achilles 3.00
406 GFr,V:Captain America 3.00
407 GFr,I:Piecemeal,A:Madman,
   B:O:Ulysses 3.00
408 GFr,V:Madman,Piecemeal,
   D:Perseus,A:Motormouth,
   Killpower 3.00
409 GFr,A:Motormouth,Killpower,
   V:Madman 3.00
410 GFr,A:Nick Fury,S.H.I.E.L.D.,
   Margo agrees to marry Rick . . . 3.00
411 GFr,V:Nick Fury,S.H.I.E.L.D. . . 3.00
412 PaP,V:Bi-Beast,A:She-Hulk . . . 3.00
413 GFr,CaS,B:Troyjan War,
   I:Cassiopea,Armageddon,
   V:Trauma 3.00
414 GFr,CaS,V:Trauma,C:S.Surfer . 3.00
415 GFr,CaS,V:Trauma,A:Silver
   Surfer,Starjammers 3.00
416 GFr,CaS,E:Troyjan War,D:Trauma,
   A:S.Surfer,Starjammers 3.00
417 GFr,CaS,Rick's/Marlo's Bachelor/
   Bachelorette Party. 5.00
418 GFr,CaS,W:Rick & Marlo,
   A:Various Marvel persons,
   Die Cut(c) 5.00
418a Newsstand ed. 4.00
419 CaS,V:Talos 3.00
420 GFr,CaS,AIDS Story,
   D:Jim Wilson 3.50
421 CaS,B:Myth Conceptions 3.00
422 GFr,Myth Conceptions,pt.2 . . . 3.00
423 GFr,CaS,Myth Concept.,pt.3 . . 3.00
424 B:Fall of the Hammer 3.00
425 Regular edition 3.00
425a Enhanced cover 4.00
426 PDa,LSh,R:Mercy 3.00
426a Deluxe edition. 3.00
427 A:Man-Thing 4.00
427a Deluxe edition 8.00
428 Suffer The Children. 3.00
429 Abortion Issue 3.00
430 A:Speed Freak 3.00
431 PDa,LSh R:Abomination. 3.00
432 V:Abomination. 3.00
433 PDd,V:Abomination. 3.00
434 Funeral of the Year 3.00
435 Hulk vs. Rhino baseball 4.00

Incredible Hulk #425
© *Marvel Entertainment Group*

436 PDd,AMe,Ghosts of the
   Future,pt.1 . . . . 3.00
437 PDd,AMe,Ghosts of the
   Future,pt.2 . . . . 3.00
438 PDd,AMe,Ghosts of the
   Future,pt.3 . . . . 3.00
439 PDd,AMe,Ghosts of the
   Future,pt.4 . . . . 3.00
440 PDd,AMe. 3.00
441 PDd,AMe,A:She-Hulk 3.00
442 A:Molecule Man, She-Hulk . . . 3.00
443 Janis 3.00
444 Onslaught saga, V:Cable 4.50
445 Onslaught saga. 4.00
446 Blamed for loss of Fantastic
   Four and Avengers 3.50
447 PDd,MD2,F:Unleashed Hulk. . . 4.00
447a Variant Tank Smashing cover . 7.50
448 PDd,MD2,V:The Pantheon 3.00
449 PDd,MD2,I:Thunderbolts 9.00
450 PDd,MD2,F:Doctor Strange,
   56pg. 6.00
451 PDd,MD2, ... 3.00
452 PDd,MD2, ... 3.00
453 PDd,MD2,V:Future Hulk 3.00
454 PDd,AKu,MFm,A God,
   In Savage Land 3.00
455 PDd,AKu,MFm,in X-Mansion . . 3.00
456 PDd,AKu,MFm,A:Apocalypse . . 3.00
457 PDd,Hulk vs. Juggernaut 3.00
458 PDd,AKu,MFm,V:Mercy 3.00
459 PDd,AKu,MFm,V:Abomination . 3.00
460 PDa,AKu,MFm, Return of Bruce
   Banner. 4.00
461 PDa,V:Thunderbolt Ross 3.00
462 PDa,AKu,MFm,V:Thunderbolt
   Ross 3.00
463 PDa,AKu,MFm,V:Thunderbolt
   Ross 3.00
464 PDa,AKu,MFm,V:Troygens &
   Silver Surfer. 3.00
465 PDa,MFm,Poker game 3.00
466 PDa,AKu,MFm,tragic loss. 5.00
467 PDa,AKu,MFm,Hulk attempts
   suicide 5.00
468 JoC,new direction 2.50
469 JoC,LMa,F:Super-Adaptoid . . . 3.00
470 JoC,NMa,V:Ringmaster
   & Circus of Crime 2.50
471 JoC,NMa,Circus of
   Crime,concl.. . . . . 2.50
472 JoC,Great Astonishment,pt.1 . . 2.50
473 JoC,Great Astonishment,pt.2 . . 2.50
474 JoC,Great Astonishment,pt.3 . . 4.00
Spec.#1 A:Inhumans (1968) 175.00
Spec.#2 rep.O:Hulk,A:Leader
   (1969) 90.00
Spec.#3 rep.A:Leader (1971). . . . 35.00
Spec.#4 IR:Hulk/Banner (1972). . . 35.00
Ann.#5 V:Xemnu,Diablo (1976) . . . 18.00
Ann.#6 HT,A:Dr.Strange,I:Paragon
   (Her) (1977). 12.00
Ann.#7 JBy,BL,A:Angel,Iceman
   A:Doc.Samson (1978) 12.00
Ann.#8 Alpha Flight (1979) 12.00
Ann.#9 Checkmate (1980). 6.00
Ann.#10 A:Captain Universe (1981) 6.00
Ann.#11 RB,JSt,A:Spider-Man,
   Avengers,V:Unis (1982) 5.00
Ann.#12 (1983) 4.00
Ann.#13 (1984) 4.00
Ann.#14 JBy,SB (1985) 4.00
Ann.#15 V:Abomitation (1986). . . . 4.00
Ann.#16 HT,Life Form #3,
   A:Mercy (1990) 4.00
Ann.#17 Subterran.Odyssey #2
   (1991) 4.00
Ann #18 KM,TA,TC(1st Work),Return
   of the Defenders,Pt.1 (1992). . . 7.00
Ann.#19 I:Lazarus,w/card (1993). . . 4.00
Ann.#20 SvL,SI (1994) 4.00
Ann.'98 F:Hulk&Sub-Mariner, 48pg . 3.00

Ann. Hulk 1999 . . . . 3.50
Marvel Milestone rep. #1 (1991) . . . 3.00
G-Size#1 rep. Greatest Foes. 10.00
Minus 1 Spec., PDd,AKu,MFm,
   flashback 3.00
Spec. '97 Onslaught aftermath 3.00
Spec. Incredible Hulk
   vs. Superman, 48-pg. 6.00
Spec. Hulk vs. Superman, signed . 20.00
Milestone #181, F:Wolverine 3.00
Hulk vs. Thing, rep. 4.00

INCREDIBLE HULK: FUTURE IMPERFECT
1993
1 GP,V:Maestro 10.00
2 GP,V:Maestro 8.00

INCREDIBLE HULK/PITT
1997
Spec. PDd,DK,x-over. 6.00

INCREDIBLE HULK VS. WOLVERINE
Oct., 1986
1 HT,rep. #181 B:,V:Wolverine. . . 12.00
1a 2nd printing 4.00

INDEPENDENCE DAY
1996
0 . . . . 5.00
1 and 2 . . . . @2.50

[Further Adventures of] INDIANA JONES
Jan., 1983–Mar., 1986
1 JBy/TA 3.00
2 JBy/TA 2.50
3 . . . . 2.50
4 KGa 2.50
5 KGa 2.50
6 HC/TA 2.50
7 thru 24 KGa . . . . @2.50
25 thru 34 SD . . . . @2.50

INDIANA JONES AND THE LAST CRUSADE
1 B&W,Mag.,movie adapt, 1989. . . 3.00
[Mini-Series], 1989
1 Rep., Movie adapt., 1989. . . . . . . 3.50

Indiana Jones #11
© *Marvel Entertainment Group*

All comics prices listed are for *Near Mint* condition.

MARVEL

2 Rep., Movie adapt. 3.50
3 Rep., Movie adapt. 3.50
4 Rep., Movie adapt. 3.50

INDIANA JONES AND THE TEMPLE OF DOOM
1984
1 Movie adapt. 3.00
2 Movie adapt. 3.00
3 Movie adapt. 3.00

INFINITY ABYSS
June, 2002
1 (of 6) JSn,AM,V:Thanos 3.00
2 JSn,AM,F:Adam Warlock 3.00
3 JSn,AM,Spider-Man,Capt.Marvel 3.00
4 JSn,AM,Eternity & Infinity 3.00
5 JSn,AM 3.00
6 48-pg. 3.50

Infinity Crusade #3
© Marvel Entertainment Group

INFINITY CRUSADE
1993
1 RLm,AM,I:Goddess,A:Marvel
Heroes,foil(c) 4.00
2 RLm,AM,V:Goddess 3.00
3 RLm,AM,V:Goddess,Mephisto. . . 3.00
4 RLm,AM,V:Goddess,A:Magnus . . 3.00
5 RLm,AM,V:Goddess 3.00
6 RLm,AM,V:Goddess 3.00

INFINITY GAUNTLET
July, 1991
1 GP,O:Infinity Gauntlet 5.00
2 GP,JRu,2nd Rebirth:Warlock 4.00
3 GP,JRu,I:Terraxia 4.00
4 GP,JRu,RLm,V:Thanos 4.00
5 JRu,RLm,V:Thanos,D:Terraxia . . 4.00
6 RLm,JRu,V:Nebula 4.00

INFINITY WAR
1992
1 RLm,AM,R:Magus,Thanos 5.00
2 RLm,AM,V:Magus,A:Everyone . . 3.00
3 RLm,AM,V:Magus,A:Everyone . . 2.50
4 RLm,AM,Magus gets Gauntlet . . 2.50
5 RLm,AM,V:Magus 2.50
6 RLm,AM,V:Magus 2.50

INHUMANOIDS
Star, Jan.–July, 1987
1 Hasbro Toy. 3.00
2 O:Inhumanoids 3.00
3 V:D'Compose. 3.00
4 A:Sandra Shore 3.00

INHUMANS
Oct., 1975
1 GP,V:Blastaar. 28.00
2 GP,V:Blastaar. 15.00
3 GP,I:Kree S 20.00
4 GK,Maximus 20.00
5 GK,V:Maximus 20.00
6 GK,Maximus 20.00
7 GK,DP,I:Skorn 20.00
8 GP,DP,Skorn 20.00
9 rep., V:Mor-Tog 20.00
10 KP,D:Warkon. 20.00
11 KP,JM,I:Pursuer 20.00
12 KP,Hulk 20.00
Spec.#1(The Untold Saga),
O:Inhumans 4.00
Spec. Atlantis Rising story 3.00

INHUMANS
Sept., 1998
1 (of 12) PJe,JaL,F:Black Bolt,
Medusa, Karnak, Triton, Gorgon,
Crystal, Lockjaw 9.00
2 PJe,JaL,F:Tonaje 4.00
2a Variant cover 3.00
3 PJe,JaL,Attilan's dark side 3.00
4 PJe,JaL,War against Attilan 3.00
5 PJe,JaL,Earth vs. Attilan 3.00
6 PJe,JaL,V:Maximus 3.00
7 PJe,JaL,F:Black Bolt 3.00
8 PJe,JaL,F:Lockjaw. 3.00
9 PJe,JaL,F:Triton. 3.00
10 PJe,JaL,F:Woz & Medusa 3.00
11 PJe,JaL,F:Black Bolt 3.00
12 PJe,JaL,concl. 3.00

INHUMANS
Apr. 2000
1 (of 4) V:Ronan the Accuser 3.00
2 A:Kree 3.00
3 Maximus the Mad 3.00
4 concl. 3.00

INHUMANS
May, 2003
1 Lunar,pt.1. . . . . 2.50
2 Lunar,pt.2. . . . . 2.50
3 Lunar,pt.3. . . . . 2.50
4 Culture Shock,pt.1 . . . . 2.50
5 Culture Shock,pt.2 . . . . 2.50
6 Culture Shock,pt.3 . . . . 2.50
7 San finds love 3.00
8 Alaris 3.00
9 No Matter the Cost,pt.1 . . . . 3.00
10 No Matter the Cost,pt.2 . . . . . . 3.00
11 No Matter the Cost,pt.3. . . . . . . 3.00
12 No Matter the Cost,pt.4 . . . . . . 3.00

INTERFACE
Epic, Dec., 1989
1 ESP 2.50
2 thru 8 . . . . @2.25

INVADERS
Aug., 1975
1 FR,JR(c),A:Invaders,
A:Mastermind 75.00
2 FR,JR(c),I:Brain Drain 25.00
3 FR,JR(c),I:U-Man 25.00
4 FR,O&V:U-Man 25.00
5 RB,JM,V:Red Skull 25.00

6 FR,V:Liberty Legion. 25.00
7 FR,I:Baron Blood,
1st Union Jack. 25.00
8 FR,FS,J:Union Jack. 15.00
9 FR,FS,O:Baron Blood 15.00
10 FR,FS,rep.Captain
America Comics #22 . . . . 15.00
11 FR,FS,I:Blue Bullet 10.00
12 FR,FS,I:Spitfire 10.00
13 FR,FS,GK(c),I:Golem,
Half Face. 10.00
14 FR,FS,JK(c),I:Crusaders. 10.00
15 FR,FS,JK(c),V:Crusaders. 10.00
16 FR,JK(c),V:Master Man 10.00
17 FR,FS,GK(c),I:Warrior Woman . 10.00
18 FR,FS,GK(c),R:1st Destroyer . 10.00
19 FR,FS,V:Adolph Hitler. 10.00
20 FR,FS,GK(c),I&J:2nd Union Jack,
BU:rep.Marvel Comics #1 . . . . 15.00
21 FR,FS,GK(c),BU:rep.Marvel
Mystery #10. . . . . 10.00
22 FR,FS,GK(c),O:Toro 8.00
23 FR,FS,GK(c),I:Scarlet Scarab . . 8.00
24 FR,FS,GK(c),rep.Marvel
Mystery #17. . . . . 10.00
25 FR,FS,GK(c),V:Scarlet Scarab . . 8.00
26 FR,FS,GK(c),V:Axis Agent 8.00
27 FR,FS,GK(c),V:Axis Agent 8.00
28 FR,FS,I:2nd Human Top,
Golden Girl,Kid Commandos. . . 8.00
29 FR,FS,I:Teutonic Knight 8.00
30 FR,FS,V:Teutonic Knight. 8.00
31 FR,FS,V:Frankenstein 8.00
32 FR,FS,JK(c),A:Thor 10.00
33 FR,FS,JK(c),A:Thor 10.00
34 FR,FS,V:Master Man 8.00
35 FR,FS,I:Iron Cross 8.00
36 FR,FS,O:Iron Cross 8.00
37 FR,FS,V:Iron Cross. 8.00
38 FR,FS,V:Lady Lotus 8.00
39 FR,FS,O:Lady Lotus 8.00
40 FR,FS,V:Baron Blood 8.00
41 E:RTs(s)FR,FS,V:Super Axis,
double-size 18.00
Ann.#1 A:Avengers,R:Shark 65.00
G-Size#1 FR,rep.Submariner #1 . . 25.00

[Limited Series], 1993
1 R:Invaders. 2.50
2 V:Battle Axis. 2.50
3 R:Original Vison (1950's). 2.50
4 V:The Axis 2.50

INVADERS
June, 2004
0 Once an Invader,pt.4 . . . . 3.00
1 To End All Wars,pt.1 . . . . 3.00
2 To End All Wars,pt.2 . . . . 3.00
3 To End All Wars,pt.3 . . . . 3.00
4 To End All Wars,pt.4 . . . . 3.00
5 To End All Wars,pt.5 . . . . 3.00
Becomes:

NEW INVADERS
6 Oil & Water,pt.1,A:Wolverine 3.00
7 Cruel and Unusual,pt.1 . . . . 3.00
8 Cruel and Unusual,pt.2 . . . . 3.00
9 Cruel and unusual, concl. 3.00

IRON FIST
Nov., 1975
1 JBy,A:Iron Man 90.00
2 JBy,V:H'rythl. 50.00
3 JBy,KP,KJ,V:Ravager. 30.00
4 JBy,V:Radion 30.00
5 JBy,V:Scimitar 30.00
6 JBy,O:Misty Knight. 30.00
7 JBy,V:Khimbala Bey. 30.00
8 JBy,V:Chaka 30.00
9 JBy,V:Chaka 30.00
10 JBy,DGr,A:Chaka 30.00
11 JBy,V:Wrecking Crew 30.00

All comics prices listed are for *Near Mint* condition.

Iron Fist #5
© Marvel Entertainment Group

12 JBy,DGr,V:Captain America . . . 30.00
13 JBy,A:Boomerang 25.00
14 JBy,I:Sabretooth 200.00
15 JBy,A&N:Wolverine,A:X-Men
    Sept., 1977 . . . . 90.00
Marvel Milestone rep. #14 (1992) . . 4.00

IRON FIST
May, 1998
1 (of 3) DJu,JG, from Heroes For
    Hire 3.00
2 DJu,JG,search for Scorpio Key,
    V:S.H.I.E.L.D. 3.00
3 DJu,JG,concl. 3.00

IRON FIST
March, 2004
1 Breathless,pt.1 . . . . 3.00
2 thru 6 Breathless,pt.2–pt.6 . . . . @3.00

IRON FIST/WOLVERINE
Sept., 2000
1 (of 4) F:DannyRand,Junzo Moto . 3.00
2 K'un L'un 3.00
3 A:Capt.America,Dragon Kings . . . 3.00
4 concl. 3.00

IRON MAN
May, 1968
1 B:StL,AGw(s),JCr,GC,
    I:Mordius 750.00
2 JCr,I:Demolisher 250.00
3 JCr,V:The Freak. 200.00
4 JCr,A:Unicorn. 150.00
5 JCr,GT,I:Cerebos 150.00
6 JCr,GT,V:Crusher. 125.00
7 JCr,GT,V:Gladiator. 125.00
8 JCr,GT,O:Whitney Frost. 125.00
9 JCr,GT,A:Mandarin 125.00
10 JCr,GT,V:Mandarin 125.00
11 JCr,GT,V:Mandarin 100.00
12 JCr,GT,I:Controller 100.00
13 JCr,GT,A:Nick Fury 100.00
14 JCr,V:Night Phantom 100.00
15 JCr,GT,A:Red Ghost 100.00
16 JCr,GT,V:Unicorn 75.00
17 JCr,GT,I:Madam Masque,
    Midas. 75.00
18 JCr,GT,V:Madame Masque. . . . 75.00
19 JCr,GT,V:Madame Masque. . . . 75.00
20 JCr,I:Charlie Gray 75.00
21 JCr,I:Eddie 35.00

22 JCr,D:Janice Cord 35.00
23 JCr,I:Mercenary. 38.00
24 JCr,GT,V:Madame Masque. . . . 35.00
25 JCr,A:Sub-Mariner 45.00
26 JCr,DH,J:Val-Larr. 35.00
27 JCr,DH,I:Firebrand 35.00
28 E:AGw(s),JCr,DH,
    V:Controller 35.00
29 B:StL,AyB(s),DH,V:Myrmidon . . 35.00
30 DH,I:Monster Master. 35.00
31 DH,I:Mastermind. 35.00
32 GT,I:Mechanoid. 35.00
33 DH,I:Spy Master 35.00
34 DH,A:Spy Master 35.00
35 DH,A:Daredevil,Spy Master . . . 35.00
36 E:AyB(s),DH,I:Ramrod 35.00
37 DH,A:Ramrod 35.00
38 GT,Jonah. 35.00
39 HT,I:White Dragon 30.00
40 GT,A:White Dragon 30.00
41 GT,JM,I:Slasher 30.00
42 GT,I:Mikas. 30.00
43 GT,JM,A:Mikas,I:Guardsmen . . 50.00
44 GT,A:Capt.America 30.00
45 GT,A:Guardsman 30.00
46 GT,D:Guardsman 30.00
47 BS,JM,O:Iron Man 35.00
48 GT,V:Firebrand 22.00
49 GT,V:Adaptoid. 22.00
50 B:RTs(s),GT,V:Prin.Python . . . 22.00
51 GT,C:Capt.America 22.00
52 GT,I:Raga 22.00
53 GT,JSn,I:Black Lama 22.00
54 GT,BEv,Sub-Mariner,I:Madame
    MacEvil (Moondragon) 50.00
55 JSn,I:Destroyer,Thanos,Mentor
    Starfox(Eros),Blood Bros. . . . 225.00
56 JSn,I:Fangor. 45.00
57 GT,R:Mandarin 20.00
58 GT,V:Mandarin 20.00
59 GT,A:Firebrand 20.00
60 GT,C:Daredevil 20.00
61 GT,Marauder 20.00
62 whiplash 20.00
63 GT,A:Dr.Spectrum 20.00
64 GT,I:Rokk 20.00
65 GT,O:Dr.Spectrum 20.00
66 GT,V:Thor. 30.00
67 GT,V:Freak. 20.00
68 GT,O:Iron Man 16.00
69 GT,V:Mandarin 15.00
70 GT,A:Sunfire 15.00
71 GT,V:Yellow Claw 15.00
72 E:RTs(s),GT,V:Black Lama . . . 15.00
73 B:LWn(s),KP,JM,V:Titanic
    Three 15.00
74 KP,V:Modok. 15.00
75 V:Black Lama 15.00
76 Rep., A:Hulk 15.00
77 V:Thinker. 15.00
78 GT,V:Viet Cong 15.00
79 GT,I:Quasar(not Current one) . . 15.00
80 JK(c),O:Black Lama 15.00
81 A:Black Lama 15.00
82 MSe,A:Red Ghost. 15.00
83 E:LWn(s),HT,MSe,Red Ghost . . 15.00
84 HT,A:Dr.Ritter 15.00
85 HT,MSe,A:Freak 15.00
86 B:MWn(s),GT,I:Blizzard. 15.00
87 GT,V:Blizzard 15.00
88 E:MWn(s),GT,
    V:Blood Brothers 15.00
89 GT,A:D.D.,Blood Bros. 15.00
90 JK(c),GT,Controller,A:Thanos . . 14.00
91 GT,BL,A:Controller 12.00
92 JK(c),GT,V:Melter 12.00
93 JK(c),HT,V:Kraken 12.00
94 JK(c),HT,V:Kraken 12.00
95 JK(c),GT,PP,V:Ultimo 12.00
96 GT,DP,V:Ultimo 12.00
97 GT,DP,I:Guardsman II 12.00
98 GT,DP,A:Sunfire 12.00

99 GT,V:Mandarin 12.00
100 JSn(c),GT,V:Mandarin. 35.00
101 GT,I:Dread Knight 14.00
102 GT,O:Dread Knight 14.00
103 GT,V:Jack of Hearts 14.00
104 GT,V:Midas 9.00
105 GT,V:Midas 9.00
106 GT,V:Midas 9.00
107 KP,V:Midas 9.00
108 CI,A:Growing Man 9.00
109 JBy(c),CI,V:Van Guard 9.00
110 KP,I:C.Arcturus 9.00
111 KP,O:Rigellians 9.00
112 AA,KP,V:Punisher from
    Beyond 9.00
113 KP,HT,V:Unicorn,Spy Master. . 10.00
114 KG,I:Arsenal 9.00
115 JR2,O:Unicorn,V:Ani-men. . . . 9.00
116 JR2,BL,V:Madame Masque . . 9.00
117 BL,JR2,1st Romita Jr 11.00
118 JBy,BL,A:Nick Fury 12.00
119 BL,JR2,Alcoholic Plot 11.00
120 JR2,BL,A:Sub-Mariner,I:Rhodey
    (becomes War Machine),
    Justin Hammer. 11.00
121 BL,JR2,A:Submariner 10.00
122 DC,CI,BL,O:Iron Man 10.00
123 BL,JR2,V:Blizzard 10.00
124 BL,JR2,A:Capt.America 8.00
125 BL,JR2,A:Ant-Man 8.00
126 BL,JR2,V:Hammer 8.00
127 BL,JR2,Battlefield 8.00
128 BL,JR2,Alcohol 20.00
129 SB,A:Dread Night 7.00
130 BL,V:Digital Devil 7.00
131 BL,V:Hulk 10.00
132 BL,V:Hulk 10.00
133 BL,A:Hulk,Ant-Man 7.00
134 BL,V:Titanium Man 7.00
135 BL,V:Titanium Man 7.00
136 V:Endotherm. 7.00
137 BL,Fights oil rig fire. 7.00
138 BL,Dreadnought,Spymaster . . 7.00
139 BL,Dreadnought,Spymaster . . 7.00
140 BL,V:Force 7.00
141 BL,JR2,V:Force. 7.00
142 BL,JR2,Space Armor 7.00
143 BL,JR2,V:Sunturion 7.00
144 BL,JR2,Sunturion,O:Rhodey. . 7.00
145 BL,JR2,A:Raiders 7.00
146 BL,JR2,I:Black Lash 7.00
147 BL,JR2,V:Black Lash 7.00
148 BL,JR2,V:Terrorists 7.00
149 BL,JR2,V:Dr.Doom 7.00

Invaders #126
© Marvel Entertainment Group

150 BL,JR2,V:Dr.Doom,Dble 10.00	
151 TA,BL,A:Ant-Man 5.00	
152 BL,JR2,New Armor 5.00	
153 BL,JR2,V:Living Laser 5.00	
154 BL,JR2,V:Unicorn 5.00	
155 JR2,V:Back-Getters 5.00	
156 JR2,I:Mauler 5.00	
157 V:Spores 5.00	
158 CI,AM,Iron Man Drowning 5.00	
159 PS,V:Diablo 5.00	
160 SD,V:Serpent'sSquad 5.00	
161 A:Moon Knight 5.00	
162 V:Space Ships 5.00	
163 V:Chessmen 5.00	
164 LMc,A:Bishop 5.00	
165 LMc,Meltdown 5.00	
166 LMc,V:Melter 5.00	
167 LMc,Alcoholic Issue 5.00	
168 LMc,A:Machine Man 5.00	
169 LMc,B:Rhodey as 2nd	
Iron Man 10.00	
170 LMc,2nd Iron Man 8.00	
171 LMc,2nd Iron Man 5.00	
172 LMc,V:Firebrand 3.00	
173 LMc,Stane International 3.00	
174 LMc,Alcoholism 3.50	
175 LMc,Alcoholism 3.50	
176 LMc,Alcoholism 3.50	
177 LMc,Alcoholism 3.00	
178 LMc,V:Wizard 3.00	
179 LMc,V:Mandarin 3.00	
180 LMc,V:Mandarin 3.00	
181 LMc,V:Mandarin 3.00	
182 LMc,Secret Wars 3.00	
183 LMc,Turning Point 3.00	
184 LMc,Moves to California 3.00	
185 LMc,V:Zodiac Field 3.00	
186 LMc,I:Vibro 3.00	
187 LMc,V:Vibro 3.00	
188 LMc,I:New Brother's Grimm . . . 3.00	
189 LMc,I:Termite 3.00	
190 LMc,O:Termite,A:Scar.Witch . . . 3.00	
191 LMc,New Grey Armor 3.00	
192 LMc,V:Iron Man(Tony Stark) . . . 5.00	
193 LMc,V:Dr.Demonicus 3.00	
194 LMc,I:Scourge,A:West Coast	
Avengers 3.00	
195 LMc,A:Shaman 3.00	
196 LMc,V:Dr.Demonicus 3.00	
197 LMc,Secret Wars II 3.00	
198 SB,V:Circuit Breaker 3.00	
199 LMc,E:Rhodey as 2nd Iron Man,	
V:Obadiah Stone 3.00	
200 MBr,D:Obadiah Stone 6.00	
201 MBr,V:Madam Masque 3.00	
202 A:Ka-Zar 3.00	
203 MBr,A:Hank Pym 3.00	
204 MBr,V:Madame Masque 3.00	
205 MBr,V:A.I.M. 3.00	
206 MBr,V:Goliath 3.00	
207 MBr,When the Sky Rains Fire . 3.00	
208 MBr,V:A.I.M. 3.00	
209 V:Living Laser 3.00	
210 MBr,V:Morgan LeFey 3.00	
211 AS,V:Living Laser 3.00	
212 DT,V:Iron Monger 3.00	
213 A:Dominic Fortune 3.00	
214 A:Spider-Woman 4.00	
215 BL,A.I.M. 4.00	
216 BL,MBr,D:Clymenstra 3.00	
217 BL,MRr,V:Hammer 3.00	
218 BL,MBr,Titanic 3.00	
219 BL,V:The Ghost 3.00	
220 BL,MBr,V:The Ghost,	
D:Spymaster 3.00	
221 BL,MBr,V:The Ghost 3.00	
222 BL,MBr,R:Abrogast 3.00	
223 BL,MBr,V:Blizzard,Beetle 3.00	
224 BL,V:Justin Hammer,Force . . . 3.00	
225 BL,MBr,B:Armor Wars 5.00	
226 BL,MBr,V:Stingray 4.50	
227 BL,MBr,V:Mandroids, ... 4.00	

Iron Man #218
© Marvel Entertainment Group

228 BL,MBr,V:Guardsmen 4.00	
229 BL,D:Titanium Man 4.00	
230 V:Firepower, ... 4.00	
231 V:Firepower,N:Iron Man 4.00	
232 BWS,Nightmares,E:Armor	
Wars 4.50	
233 JG,BL,A:Ant-Man 2.50	
234 JG,BL,A:Spider-Man 4.00	
235 JG,BL,V:Grey Gargoyle 3.00	
236 JG,BL,V:Grey Gargoyle 3.00	
237 JG,BL,V:SDI Monster 3.00	
238 JG,BL,V:Rhino,D:M.Masque . . . 2.50	
239 JG,BL,R:Ghost 2.50	
240 JG,BL,V:Ghost 2.50	
241 BL,V:Mandarin 2.50	
242 BL,BWS,V:Mandarin 3.00	
243 BL,BWS,Stark Paralyzed 3.00	
244 BL,V:Fixer,A:Force,double-size 5.00	
245 BL(c),V:Dreadnaughts 2.50	
246 BL,HT,V:A.I.M.,Maggia 2.50	
247 BL,A:Hulk 4.00	
248 BL,Tony Stark Cured 2.50	
249 BL,V:Dr.Doom 2.50	
250 BL,V:Dr.Doom,A of V 3.00	
251 HT,AM,V:Wrecker,A of V 2.50	
252 HT,AM,V:Chemistro,A of V . . . 2.50	
253 BL,V:Slagmire 2.50	
254 BL,V:Spymaster 2.50	
255 HT,V:Devestator	
I:2nd Spymaster 2.50	
256 JR2,V:Space Station 2.50	
257 V:Samurai Steel 2.50	
258 JR2,BWi,B:Armor Wars II,V:	
Titanium Man. 2.50	
259 JR2,BWi,V:Titanium Man 2.50	
260 JR2,BWi,V:Living Laser 2.50	
261 JR2,BWi,A:Mandarin 2.50	
262 JR2,BWi,A:Mandarin 2.50	
263 JR2,BWi,A:Wonderman,	
V:Living Laser 2.50	
264 JR2,BWi,A:Mandarin 2.50	
265 JR2,BWi,V:Dewitt 2.50	
266 JR2,BWi,E:Armor Wars II 2.50	
267 PR,BWi,B:New O:Iron Man,	
Mandarin,V:Vibro 2.50	
268 PR,BWi,E:New O:Iron Man. . . . 2.50	
269 PR,BWi,A:Black Widow 2.50	
270 PR,BWi,V:Fin Fang Foom 2.50	
271 PR,BWi,V:Fin Fang Foom 2.50	
272 PR,BWi,O:Mandarin 2.50	
273 PR,BWi,V:Mandarin 2.50	
274 MBr,BWi,V:Mandarin 2.50	
275 PR,BWi,A:Mandarin,Fin Fang	
Foom, double-size. 4.00	

276 PR,BWi,A:Black Widow 2.50	
277 PR,BWi,A:Black Widow 2.50	
278 BWi,Galactic Storm,pt.6	
A:Capt.America,V:Shatterax . . . 2.50	
279 BWi,Galactic Storm,pt.13,	
V:Ronan,A:Avengers 2.50	
280 KHd,V:The Stark 2.50	
281 KHd,I&V:Masters of Silence,	
C:War Machine Armor 5.00	
282 KHd,I:War Machine Armor,	
V:Masters of Silence 4.00	
283 KHd,V:Masters of Silence 2.50	
284 KHd,Stark put under Cryogenic	
Freeze,B:Rhodey as Iron Man . 3.50	
285 KHd,BWi(i),Tony's Funeral 2.50	
286 KHd,V:Avengers West Coast . . 2.50	
287 KHd,I:New Atom Smasher 2.50	
288 KHd,30th Anniv.,V:Atom	
Smasher,foil(c). 4.50	
289 KHd,V:Living Laser,	
R:Tony Stark 2.50	
290 KHd,30th Anniv.,N:Iron Man,	
Gold foil(c) 5.00	
291 KHd,E:Rhodey as Iron Man,	
Becomes War Machine 2.50	
292 KHd,Tony reveals he is alive . . 2.50	
293 KHd,V:Controller 2.50	
294 KHd,Infinity Crusade 2.50	
295 KHd,Infinity Crusade 2.50	
296 KHd,V:Modam,A:Omega Red . . 2.50	
297 KHd,V:Modam,Omega Red . . . 2.50	
298 KHd(c),I:Earth Mover 2.50	
299 KHd(c),R:Ultimo 2.50	
300 KHd,TMo,N:Iron Man,I:Iron	
Legion,A:War Machine,V:Ultimo	
Foil(c). 5.00	
300a Newsstand ed. 2.75	
301 KHd,B:Crash and Burn,	
A:Deathlok,C:Venom 2.50	
302 KHd,V:Venom 2.50	
303 KHd,V:New Warriors,	
C:Thundrstrike 2.50	
304 KHd,C:Hulk,V:New Warriors,	
Thundrstrike,N:Iron Man 2.50	
305 KHd,V:Hulk, ... 2.50	
306 KHd,E:Stark Enterprise. 2.50	
307 TMo,I:Vor/Tex,R:Mandarin . . . 2.50	
308 TMo,Vor/Tex 2.50	
309 TMo,Vor/Tex 2.50	
310 regular. 3.00	
310a Neon(c),with insert print 3.50	
311 V:Mandarin 2.50	
312 double-size 3.00	
313 LKa,TMo,AA Meeting 2.50	
314 LKa,TMo,new villain 2.50	
315 A:Black Widow 2.50	
316 I:Slag,A:Crimson Dynamo 2.50	
317 In Dynamos Armor 3.00	
318 LKa,TMo,V:Slag 2.50	
319 LKa,TMo,New Space Armor . . . 2.50	
320 F:Hawkeye 2.50	
321 Cont. From Avg. Crossing 2.50	
322 TKa,TheCrossing,V:JackFrost . 2.50	
323 TKa,V:Avengers 2.50	
324 TKa,The Crossing 2.50	
325 TKa,Avengers:Timeslide after. . 3.50	
326 First Sign,pt.3 . . . . 2.50	
327 Frostbite 2.50	
328 TKa,Tony Stark at ColumbiaU. . 2.50	
329 Stark Enterprises taken over . . 2.50	
330 & 331 . . . . @2.50	
332 final issue 4.00	
Ann.#1 rep.Iron Man #25. . . . . 45.00	
Ann.#2 rep.Iron Man #6 . . . . 25.00	
Ann.#3 SB,Manthing 15.00	
Ann.#4 DP,GT,V:Modok,	
A:Champions 10.00	
Ann.#5 JBr,A:Black Panther 6.00	
Ann.#6 A:Eternals,V:Brother	
Tode. 6.00	
Ann.#7 LMc,A:West Coast	
Avengers, I:New Goliath 6.00	

Iron Man Ann. #12
© Marvel Entertainment Group

Ann.#8 A:X-Factor 6.00
Ann.#9 V:Stratosfire,A:Sunturion . . . 5.00
Ann.#10 PS,BL,Atlantis Attacks #2
   A:Sub-Mariner 4.00
Ann.#11 SD,Terminus Factor #2 . . . . 4.00
Ann.#12 Subterran.Odyssey #4. . . . . 4.00
Ann.#13 GC,AW,Assault on Armor
   City,A:Darkhawk 4.00
Ann.#14 TMo,I:Face Theif,w/card,
   BU:War Machine 4.00
Ann.#15 GC,V:Controller 4.00
Spec.#1 rep.Sub-Mariner x-over . . 40.00
Spec.#2 rep.(1971) 20.00
Marvel Milestone rep. #55 (1992) . . 15.00
G-Size#1 Reprints 15.00
1-shot Iron Manual, BSz(c),Guide
   to Iron Man's technology 2.50
1-shot Iron Man/Force Works Collec-
   tors' Preview, Neon wrap-around
   cover, double size, X-over 2.50
GN Iron Man 2020 . . . . 6.00

[2nd Series], Nov., 1996
1 JLe,SLo,WPo,SW,A:Bruce
   Banner, New O:Hulk,48pg. 4.00
1A variant Hulk showing cover 5.00
1 gold signature ed., bagged 18.00
2 JLe,SLo,WPo,SW 4.00
3 JLe,SLo,WPo,SW,Heroes brawl . 3.00
4 JLe,SLo,WPo,SW,V:Laser 3.00
4A X-mas cover 5.00
5 JLe,SLo,WPo,SW, Whirlwind. . . . 3.00
6 JLe,SLo,WPo,SW,Industrial
   Revolution, pt.2 x-over 3.00
7 JLe,SLo,WPo,SW,A:Pepper
   Potts,Villain revealed. 3.00
8 JLe,SLo,RBn,fate of Rebel 3.00
9 JLe,SLo,RBn,V:Mandarin 3.00
10 JLe,SLo,RBn,F:The Hulk 3.00
11 JLb,RBn,V:Dr. Doom,A:Hydra . . 3.00
12 WPo,JLe,JLb,F:Dr. Doom,
   Galactus 3.00
13 JeR,LSn,Wildstorm x-over 3.00

[3rd Series], 1997
1 SCh,KBk,V:Mastermind,48pg. . . 5.00
2 KBk,SCh,in Switzerland. 3.50
3 KBk,SCh,V:Hydra Dreadnought
   Robot. 3.00
4 KBk,SCh,R:Firebrand 3.00
5 KBk,SCh,V:Firebrand. 3.00
6 KBk,F:Black Widow 3.00
7 KBk,SCh,Live Kree or Die,pt.1
   x-over. 3.00
8 KBk,SCh,secret identity out. . . . 3.00
9 KBk,SCh,A:Black Widow 3.00

10 KBk,SCh,A:Avengers 3.00
11 KBk,SCh,A:Warbird &
   War Machine 3.00
12 KBk,V:War Machine 3.00
13 KBk,SCh,V:Controller,48-pg. . . 4.00
13a signed 20.00
14 KBk,SCh,Fant.Four x-over 3.00
15 KBk,SCh,V:Nitro 3.00
16 KBk,RSt,V:Dragon Lord 3.00
17 KBk,RSt,SCh,V:Fin Fang Foom . 3.00
18 KBk,RSt,SCh,V:War Machine . . 3.00
19 KBk,RSt,SCh,V:War Machine . . 3.00
20 KBk,RSt,SCh,V:War Machine . . 3.00
21 KBk,RSt,TGu,MBa,
   Eighth Day prologue 3.00
22 KBk,RSt,Eighth Day,pt.2,
   I:Carnivore 3.00
23 KBk,RSt,UltimateDanger,pt.1 . . 3.00
24 KBk,RSt,UltimateDanger,pt.2 . . 3.25
25 KBk,RSt,Ultimate
   Danger,pt.3, 48-pg. 3.50
26 JQ,Mask of Iron Man,pt.1 . . . . 2.50
27 JQ,Mask of Iron Man,pt.2 . . . . 2.50
28 JQ,Mask of Iron Man,pt.3 . . . . 2.50
29 JQ,Mask of Iron Man,pt.4 . . . . 2.50
30 JQ,Mask of Iron Man,pt.5 . . . . 2.50
31 JQ,Sons of Yinsen,pt.1 . . . . . . 2.50
32 JQ,Sons of Yinsen,pt.2 . . . . . . 2.50
33 JQ,Sons of Yinsen,pt.3 . . . . . . 2.50
34 JQ,Dr. Power 2.50
35 JQ,Maximum Security 2.50
36 CDi,PR 2.50
37 JQ,F:Tyberius Stone 2.50
38 R:classic foe 2.50
39 MPn,Remote Control 2.50
40 MPn,Remote Control 2.50
41 new art team 2.50
42 Big Bang Theory,pt.1 . . . . 2.50
43 Big Bang Theory,pt.2 . . . . 2.50
44 Big Bang,pt.3,new armor 2.50
45 Big Bang Theory,pt.4 . . . . 2.50
46 Frankenstein Syndrome,pt.1
   100-pages 4.00
47 IaC,Frankenstein Syndrome . . . 2.50
48 IaC,Frankenstein Syndrome . . . 2.50
49 CsB,V:Titanium Man 2.50
50 MGr,48-pg. 4.00
51 MGr,Jane Doe,pt.1 . . . . 2.50
52 MGr,Jane Doe,pt.2 . . . . 2.50
53 MGr,Book of Ten Rings 2.50
54 MGr,Temugin. 2.50
55 MGr,would be #400 issue,54-pg. 4.00
56 MGr,fall-out begins 2.50
57 MGr,fight on, fight on 2.50
58 MGr 2.50
59 MGr,In Shining Armor 2.50
60 MGr,In Shining Armor,pt.2. . . . . 2.50
61 MGr,In Shining Armor,pt.3. . . . . 2.50
62 MGr,You Can't Always Get,pt.1 2.50
63 MGr,You Can't Always Get,pt.2 2.50
64 AD,MFm,MGr,Standoff,pt.1 . . . 2.50
65 MGr,Manhunt,pt.1 . . . . 2.50
66 MGr,Manhunt,pt.2 . . . . 2.50
67 MGr,Manhunt,pt.3 . . . . 3.00
68 MGr,Manhunt,pt.4 . . . . 3.00
69 MGr,Manhunt,pt.5 . . . . 3.00
70 Vegal Bleeds Neon,pt.1 . . . . . . 3.00
71 Vegas Bleeds Neon,pt.2 . . . . . . 3.00
72 Vegas Bleeds Neon,pt.3 . . . . . . 3.00
73 The Best Defense,pt.1 . . . . 3.00
74 The Best Defense,pt.2 . . . . 3.00
75 Secretary of Defense? 3.00
76 The Best Defense,pt.4 . . . . 3.00
77 The Best Defense,pt.5 . . . . 3.00
78 The Best Defense,pt.6 . . . . 3.00
79 The Deep End,pt.1 . . . . 3.00
80 The Deep End,pt.2 . . . . 3.00
81 The Deep End,pt.3 . . . . 3.00
82 The Deep End,pt.4 . . . . 3.00
83 F:Titanium Man 3.00
84 Top-secret materials 5.00
85 Top-secret materials 5.00

86 Singularity,pt.1 . . . . 3.00
87 Singularity,pt.2 . . . . 3.00
88 Singularity,pt.3 . . . . 3.00
89 Singularity,pt.4 . . . . 3.00
Ann.1998 Iron Man/Captain
   America, KBk,MWa, 48-pg. 3.50
Ann.1999 KBk,JoC,48-pg. 3.50
Ann.2000 Sons of Yin-Sen,pt.3 . . 3.50
Ann.2001 CCl,48-pg. 3.00
Spec.#1 Age of Innocence, Avengers:
   Timeslide 2.50

IRON MAN
Nov., 2004
1 WEI,Extremis 3.00
2 WEI,Extremis 3.00
3 WEI,Extremis 3.00
4 WEI,Extremis 3.00
5 WEI,Extremis 3.00
6 WEI,Extremis 3.00
7 The List 3.00
7a variant (c) 7.00
8 The List 3.00
9 SHa,Execute Program. 3.00
10 SHa,Execute Program 3.00
11 SHa,Execute Program 3.00
12 SHa,Execute Program 3.00
13 SHa,Civil War tie-in. 3.00
14 SHa,Civil War tie-in. 3.00
15 Civil War The Initiative 3.00
15 variant (c) 3.00
16 Civil War: The Initiative 3.00
17 Civil War: The Initiative 3.00
18 Civil War: The Initiative 3.00
19 World War Hulk tie-in 3.00
19a 2nd printing. 3.00
20 World War Hulk tie-in 3.00
21 . . . . 3.00
22 . . . . 3.00
23 . . . . 3.00

IRON MAN AND POWER PACK
Nov., 2007
1 (of 4) 3.00

IRON MAN & SUBMARINER
April, 1968
1 GC, 2 stories 300.00

Iron Man & SUbmariner #1
© Marvel Entertainment Group

MARVEL

IRON MAN: BAD BLOOD
July, 2000
1 (of 4) BL,DvM,V:JustinHammer . . 3.00
2 BL,DvM,Spymaster 3.00
3 BL,DvM,James Rhodes. 3.00
4 BL,DvM,Justin Hammer. 3.00

IRON MAN/ CAPTAIN AMERICA: CASUALTIES OF WAR
Dec., 2006
1-shot Civil War 4.00
1-shot-a variant (c) 4.00

IRON MAN: DIRECTOR OF S.H.I.E.L.D.
Nov., 2007
Ann. #1 V: Madame Hydra 4.00

IRON MAN: ENTER THE MANDARIN
Aug., 2007
1 JoC 3.00
2 thru 3 . . . . @3.00

IRON MAN: HOUSE OF M
July, 2005
1 (of 3) 3.00
2 . . . . 3.00
3 finale 3.00

IRON MAN: HYPERVELOCITY
Jan., 2007
1 (of 6) AWa(s&c) 3.00
2 thru 6 AWa(s) . . . . @3.00

IRON MAN: INEVITABLE
Dec., 2005
1 JoC 3.00
2 thru 6 . . . . @3.00

IRON MAN: THE IRON AGE
June, 1998
1 (of 2) KBk,48pg bookshelf 6.00
2 KBk,48pg bookshelf, concl. 6.00

ISLAND OF DR. MOREAU
Oct., 1977
1 GK(c),movie adapt. 8.00

IT'S A DUCK'S LIFE
Feb., 1950
1 F;Buck Duck,Super Rabbit . . . 150.00
2 . . . . 100.00
3 thru 11 . . . . @100.00

JACK KIRBY'S GALACTIC BOUNTY HUNTERS
Icon, July, 2006
1 JK, 56-pg. 4.00
2 thru 6 JK. . . . . @3.00

JACK OF HEARTS
Jan., 1984
1 thru 4 . . . . @2.50

JAMES BOND JR.
1992
1 I&O:JamesBondJr.(TVseries) . . . 3.00
2 thru 12 . . . . @2.25

JANN OF THE JUNGLE
See: JUNGLE TALES

JEANIE COMICS
See: DARING MYSTERY

JIHAD
Epic
1 Cenobites vs. Nightbreed 4.50
2 E:Cenobites vs. Nightbreed. 4.50

JLA/AVENGERS
Marvel/DC, Sept., 2003
1 KBk,GP(c),x-over,48-pg. 6.00
3 KBk,GP,x-over,48-pg. 6.00

John Carter, Warlord of Mars #1
© Marvel Entertainment Group

JOHN CARTER, WARLORD OF MARS
June, 1977
1 GK,DC,O:John Carter,Created
by Edgar Rice Burroughs 15.00
2 GK/DC(c),GK,RN, White Apes
of Mars 7.00
3 GK,RN,Requiem for a Warlord . . 7.00
4 GK,RN, Raiding Party 7.00
5 GK,RN,Giant Battle Issue 7.00
6 GK/DC(c),GK,Alone Against a
World 7.00
7 GK,TS,Showdown 7.00
8 GK,RN,Beast With Touch of
Stone 7.00
9 GK,RN,Giant Battle Issue 7.00
10 GK,The Death of Barsoom? . . . 7.00
11 RN,O:Dejah Thoris 7.00
12 RN,City of the Dead 7.00
13 RN,March of the Dead 7.00
14 RN,The Day Helium Died 7.00
15 RN,GK,Prince of Helium
Returns 7.00
16 RN,John Carters Dilemna. 7.00
17 BL,What Price Victory. 10.00
18 FM,Tars Tarkas Battles Alone . . 7.00
19 RN(c),War With the Wing Men . . 7.00
20 RN(c),Battle at the Bottom
of the World 7.00
21 RN(c),The Claws of the Banth . . 7.00

22 RN(c),The Canyon of Death 7.00
23 Murder on Mars 7.00
24 GP/TA(c),Betrayal. 7.00
25 Inferno. 7.00
26 Death Cries the Guild of
Assassins 7.00
27 Death Marathon 7.00
28 Guardians of the Lost
City Oct., 1979 . . . . 7.00
Ann.#1 RN(c),GK,Battle story 7.00
Ann.#2 RN(c),GK,Outnumbered . . 7.00
Ann.#3 RN(c),GK,Battle story 7.00

JOHN ROMITA JR 30TH ANNIVERSARY SPECIAL
Dec., 2006
Spec. 4.00

JOKER COMICS
Marvel Timely, April, 1942
1 BW,I&B:Powerhouse Pepper,
A:Stuporman 4,700.00
2 BW,I:Tessie the Typist 1,600.00
3 BW,A:Tessie the Typist,
Squat Car Squad 1,000.00
4 BW,Squat Car (c) 900.00
5 BW,same 900.00
6 BW 750.00
7 BW 750.00
8 BW 750.00
9 BW 750.00
10 BW,Shooting Gallery (c) 750.00
11 BW 750.00
12 BW 750.00
13 BW 750.00
14 BW 750.00
15 BW 750.00
16 BW 750.00
17 BW 750.00
18 BW 750.00
19 BW 750.00
20 BW 750.00
21 BW 750.00
22 BW 750.00
23 BW,HK,Hey Look 750.00
24 BW,HK,Laff Favorites 800.00
25 BW,HK,same. 800.00
26 BW,HK,same. 800.00
27 BW 800.00
28 . . . . 250.00
29 BW 500.00
30 BW 500.00
31 BW 500.00
32 B:Millie,Hedy 200.00
33 HK 225.00
34 . . . . 200.00
35 HK 225.00
36 HK 200.00
37 . . . . 200.00
38 . . . . 200.00
39 . . . . 200.00
40 . . . . 200.00
41 A:Nellie the Nurse 200.00
42 I:Patty Pin-up 225.00
Becomes:

ADVENTURES INTO TERROR
1950
43(1)AH,B:Horror Stories 1,000.00
44(2)AH,Won't You Step Into
My Palor 600.00
3 GC,I Stalk By Night 400.00
4 DR,The Torture Room 400.00
5 GC,DR,The Hitchhiker 450.00
6 RH,The Dark Room 350.00
7 GT(c),BW,JMn,Where Monsters
Dwell 900.00
8 JSt,Enter... the Lizard 400.00

Adventures Into Terror #20
© Marvel Entertainment Group

9 RH(c),JSt,The Dark
    Dungeon 375.00
10 JMn,When the Vampire Calls . 375.00
11 JMn,JSt,Dead Man's Escape . 325.00
12 BK,Man Who Cried Ghost . . . 350.00
13 BEv(c),The Hands of Death . . 350.00
14 GC,GT,The Hands 300.00
15 Trapped by the Tarantula . . . 300.00
16 RH(c),Her Name Is Death . . . 300.00
17 I Die Too Often,Bondage(c) . . 350.00
18 He's Trying To Kill Me 300.00
19 The Girl Who Couldn't Die . . . 275.00
20 . . . . 275.00
21 GC,JMn 250.00
22 JMn 250.00
23 . . . . 250.00
24 MF,GC 250.00
25 MF 300.00
26 GC. 250.00
27 . . . . 250.00
28 GC. 250.00
29 GC,JMn. 250.00
30 . . . . 250.00
31 May, 1954 . . . . 250.00

JOURNEY INTO MYSTERY
June, 1952

1 RH(c),B:Mystery/Horror
    stories 5,500.00
2 Don't Look 2,000.00
3 I Didn't See Anything 1,500.00
4 RH,BEv(c),I'm Drowning,
    Severed Hand (c) 1,500.00
5 RH,BEv(c),Fright 1,000.00
6 BEv(c),Till Death Do
    Us Part 1,000.00
7 BEv(c),Ghost Guard 1,000.00
8 He Who Hesitates 1,000.00
9 BEv(c),I Made A Monster . . . 1,000.00
10 The Assassin of Paris 1,000.00
11 RH,GT,Meet the Dead. 900.00
12 A Night At Dragmoor Castle . . 750.00
13 The Living and the Dead 750.00
14 DAy,RH,The Man Who
    Owned A World 750.00
15 RH(c),Till Death Do Us Part . . 750.00
16 DW,Vampire Tale 750.00
17 SC,Midnight On Black
    Mountain 750.00
18 He Wouldn't Stay Dead. 750.00
19 JF,The Little Things. 750.00
20 BEv,BP,After Man, What. . . . 750.00
21 JKu,The Man With No Past . . 750.00
22 Haunted House. 750.00

23 GC,Gone, But Not Forgotten . 500.00
24 The Locked Drawer 500.00
25 The Man Who Lost Himself . . 500.00
26 The Man From Out There. . . . 500.00
27 BP,JSe,Masterpiece 500.00
28 The Survivor 500.00
29 Three Frightened People 500.00
30 JO,The Lady Who Vanished. . . 500.00
31 The Man Who Had No Fear . . 500.00
32 Elevator In The Sky 500.00
33 SD,AW,There'll Be Some
    Changes Made 600.00
34 BP,BK,The Of The
    Mystic Ring 500.00
35 LC,JF,Turn Back The Clock . . 500.00
36 I, The Pharaoh 500.00
37 BEv(c),The Volcano 500.00
38 SD,Those Who Vanish 500.00
39 BEv(c),DAy,WW,The
    Forbidden Room 500.00
40 BEv(c),JF,The Strange
    Secret Of Henry Hill 500.00
41 BEv(c),GM,RC,I Switched
    Bodies 450.00
42 BEv(c),GM,What Was
    Farley's Other Face. 450.00
43 AW,Ghost Ship 450.00
44 SD,JK,BEv 450.00
45 BEv,JO 400.00
46 . . . . 400.00
47 BEv 400.00
48 . . . . 400.00
49 . . . . 400.00
50 SD 400.00
51 SD,JK 450.00
52 JK 400.00
53 DH 400.00
54 AW 450.00
55 . . . . 450.00
56 thru 61 SD,JK . . . . @350.00
62 SD,JK,I:Xemnu 450.00
63 SD,JK 450.00
64 SD,JK 450.00
65 SD,JK 450.00
66 Hulk Type 500.00
67 SD,JK 325.00
68 SD,JK 325.00
69 SD,JK 325.00
70 Sandman Type 450.00
71 JK,SD 325.00
72 JK,SD 325.00
73 JK,DH,Spider-Man type 700.00
74 . . . . 325.00
75 JK,DH 325.00
76 JK,DH 300.00
77 DH,SD,JK 300.00
78 DH,Dr.Strange Type 450.00
79 JK,DH,SD 400.00
80 JK,DH,SD 300.00
81 JK,DH,SD 300.00
82 JK,DH,SD 300.00
83 JK,SD,I&O:Thor 13,000.00
84 JK,SD,DH,I:Executioner. . . . 4,000.00
85 JK,SD,I:Loki,Heimdall,Balder,
    Tyr,Odin,Asgard 2,500.00
86 JK,SD,DH,V:Tomorrow Man 1,300.00
87 JK,SD,V:Communists. 1,000.00
88 JK,SD,V:Loki 1,000.00
89 JK,SD,O:Thor(rep). 1,000.00
90 SD,I:Carbon Copy. 700.00
91 JSt,SD,I:Sandu 700.00
92 JSt,SD,V:Loki,I:Frigga. 700.00
93 DAy,JK,SD,I:Radioactive Man 800.00
94 JSt,SD,V:Loki 625.00
95 JSt,SD,I:Duplicator 625.00
96 JSt,SD,I:Merlin II 625.00
97 JK,I:Lava Man,O:Odin 750.00
98 DH,JK,I&O:Cobra 600.00
99 DH,JK,I:Mr.Hyde,Surtur 600.00
100 DH,JK,V:Mr.Hyde 600.00
101 JK,V:Tomorrow Man 400.00
102 JK,I:Sif,Hela 400.00

103 JK,I:Enchantress,
    Executioner 400.00
104 JK,Giants 400.00
105 JK,V:Hyde,Cobra 400.00
106 JK,O:Balder. 400.00
107 JK,I:Grey Gargoyle,Karnilla . 400.00
108 JK,A:Dr.Strange 400.00
109 JK,V:Magneto 750.00
110 JK,V:Hyde,Cobra,Loki 400.00
111 JK,V:Hyde,Cobra,Loki 400.00
112 JK,V:Hulk,O:Loki 850.00
113 JK,V:Grey Gargoyle 350.00
114 JK,I&O:Absorbing Man 350.00
115 JK,O:Loki,V:Absorbing Man . 400.00
116 JK,V:Loki,C:Daredevil 350.00
117 JK,V:Loki. 350.00
118 JK,I:Destroyer. 350.00
119 JK,V:Destroyer,I:Hogun,
    Fandrall,Volstagg. 350.00
120 JK,A:Avengers,Absorbing
    Man 350.00
121 JK,V:Absorbing Man 350.00
122 JK,V:Absorbing Man 350.00
123 JK,V:Absorbing Man 350.00
124 JK,A:Hercules 375.00
125 JK,A;Hercules 375.00
Annual #1, JK,I:Hercules 450.00
Becomes:

THOR

Journey Into Mystery, 2nd Series #2
© Marvel Entertainment Group

JOURNEY INTO MYSTERY
[2nd series], Oct., 1972

1 GK,TP,MP,Dig Me No Grave . . 45.00
2 GK,Jack the Ripper 30.00
3 JSn,TP,Shambler From
    the Stars 30.00
4 GC,DA,Haunter of the Dark,
    H.P. Lovecraft adaptation 30.00
5 RB,FrG,Shadow From the
    Steeple,R. Bloch adaptation . . 30.00
6 thru 19 Mystery Stories . . . . @25.00

JOURNEY INTO
UNKNOWN WORLDS
See: ALL WINNERS COMICS

JUBILEE
Sept., 2004

1 In Los Angeles. 3.00
2 F:Meg Devereaux 3.00
3 thru 6 . . . . @3.00

J-2
Aug., 1998
1 TDF,RLm,AM,F:J2 with the powers
of Juggernaut 2.25
2 thru 12 TDF,RLm,AM . . . . @2.25

JUGGERNAUT
1997
1-shot 48pg. 3.00

JUGGERNAUT:
THE EIGHTH DAY
Sept., 1999
1-shot JoC,TSr,AKu(c),x-over,pt.4 . . 3.00

JUNGLE ACTION
Marvel Atlas, Oct., 1954
1 JMn,JMn(c),B:Leopard Girl . . . 450.00
2 JMn,JMn(c) 475.00
3 thru 6 JMn,JMn(c) . . . . @300.00

JUNGLE ACTION
Oct., 1972—Nov., 1976
1 JB(c),Lorna,Tharn,Jann
reprints 25.00
2 GK(c),same 15.00
3 JSn(c),same 15.00
4 GK(c),same 15.00
5 JR(c),JB,B:Black Panther,
V:Man-Ape 30.00
6 RB/FrG(c),RB,V:Kill-Monger . . 25.00
7 RB/KJ(c),RB,V:Venomn 15.00
8 RB/KJ(c),RB,GK,
O:Black Panther 20.00
9 GK/KJ(c),RB,V:Baron Macabre 15.00
10 GK/FrG(c),V:King Cadaver . . . 15.00
11 GK(c),V:Baron Macabre,Lord
Karnaj 15.00
12 RB/KJ(c),V:Kill Monger 10.00
13 GK(c)/JK(c),V:White Gorilla,
Sombre 10.00
14 GK(c),V:Prehistoric Monsters . 10.00
15 GK(c),V:Prehistoric Monsters . 10.00
16 GK(c),V:Venomm 10.00
17 GK(c),V:Kill Monger 10.00
18 JKu(c),V:Madame Slay 10.00
19 GK(c),KK,Sacrifice of Blood 10.00
20 V:KKK,Slaughter In The
Streets 10.00
21 V:KKK,Cross Of Fire, Cross
Of Death 9.00
22 JB(c),V:KKK,Soul Stranger 9.00
23 JBy(c),V:KKK 9.00

Jungle Action #19
© Marvel Entertainment Group

---

24 GK(c),I:Wind Eagle 9.00

JUNGLE TALES
Marvel Atlas, Sept., 1954
1 B:Jann of the Jungle,Cliff
Mason,Waku 500.00
2 GT,Jann Stories cont. 350.00
3 Cliff Mason,White Hunter,
Waku Unknown Jungle 350.00
4 Cliff Mason,Waku,Unknown
Jungle 350.00
5 RH(c),SSh,Cliff Mason,Waku,
Unknown Jungle 350.00
6 DH,SSh,Cliff Mason,Waku,
Unknown Jungle 350.00
7 DH,SSh,Cliff Mason,Waku,
Unknown Jungle 350.00
Becomes:

JANN OF THE
JUNGLE
1955
8 SH,SSh,The Jungle Outlaw . . . 450.00
9 With Fang and Talons 250.00
10 AW,The Jackal's Lair. 250.00
11 Bottomless Pit 250.00
12 The Lost Safari 250.00
13 When the Trap Closed 250.00
14 V:Hunters 250.00
15 BEv(c),DH,V:Hunters 250.00
16 BEv(c),AW,JungleVengeance . 275.00
17 BEv(c),DH,AW,June, 1957 . . . 275.00

JUSTICE
Nov., 1986
1 I:Justice 2.25
2 . . . . 2.25
3 Yakuza Assassin 2.25
4 thru 31 . . . . @2.25
32 Last issue,A:Joker 2.25

JUSTICE COMICS
Marvel Atlas, Fall, 1947
7(1) B:FBI in Action,Mystery of
White Death. 400.00
8(2),HK,Crime is For Suckers . . 250.00
9(3),FBI Raid 225.00
4 Bank Robbery 225.00
5 Subway(c) 200.00
6 E:FBI In Action 200.00
7 Symbolic(c) 200.00
8 Funeral(c) 200.00
9 B:True Cases Proving Crime
Can't Win 200.00
10 Ph(c),Bank Hold Up 200.00
11 Ph(c),Behind Bars 200.00
12 Ph(c),The Crime of
Martin Blaine 135.00
13 Ph(c),The Cautious Crook . . . 135.00
14 Ph(c) 135.00
15 Ph(c) 135.00
16 F:"Ears"Karpik-Mobster. 125.00
17 The Ragged Stranger 125.00
18 Criss-Cross 125.00
19 Death Of A Spy 125.00
20 Miami Mob 125.00
21 Trap. 125.00
22 The Big Break 125.00
23 thru 40 . . . . @100.00
41 Electrocution cover 200.00
42 thru 51 . . . . @100.00
52 Flare Up 100.00
Becomes:

TALES OF JUSTICE
May, 1955—Aug., 1957
53 BEv,Keeper Of The Keys 200.00
54 thru 57. . . . . @175.00
58 BK. 150.00
59 BK. 150.00
60 thru 63. . . . . @100.00

---

64 RC,DW,JSe. 125.00
65 RC. 125.00
66 JO,AT 125.00
67 DW 125.00

JUSTICE:
FOUR BALANCE
1994
1 A:Thing, Yancy Street Gang . . 2.25
2 V:Hate Monger 2.25
3 the story continues... . . . . 2.25
4 ...to its conclusion 2.25

KABUKI
Icon, July, 2004
1 DMk,The Alchemy,pt.1 . . . . . . 3.00
2 thru 6 DMk,The Alchemy,pt.2–6@3.00
7 DMk. 3.00
8 DMk. 3.00
GN Kabuki Reflections. 5.00

KATHY
**Marvel Atlas,
Oct., 1959—Feb., 1964**
1 Teenage Tornado 160.00
2 . . . . 125.00
3 thru 15 . . . . @75.00
16 thru 27 . . . . @60.00

KA-ZAR
[Reprint Series], Aug., 1970
1 X-Men ID 50.00
2 Daredevil 12, 13 . . . . 35.00
3 DDH,Spider-Man,March, 1971 . 35.00

[1st Series], Jan., 1974
1 O:Savage Land 20.00
2 DH,JA,A:Shanna The She-Devil 10.00
3 DH,V:Man-God,A:El Tigre 10.00
4 DH,V:Man-God 10.00
5 DH,D:El-Tigre. 8.00
6 JB/AA,V:Bahemoth 8.00
7 JB/BMcRevenge of the
River-Gods 8.00
8 JB/AA,Volcano of
Molten Death 8.00
9 JB,Man Who Hunted Dinosaur . 8.00
10 JB,Dark City of Death. 8.00
11 DH/FS,Devil-God of Sylitha . . . 7.00
12 RH,Wizard of Forgotten
Death. 7.00
13 V:Lizard Men. 7.00
14 JAb,V:Klaw 7.00
15 VM,V:Klaw,Hellbird 7.00
16 VM,V:Klaw 7.00
17 VM,V:Klaw 7.00
18 VM,V:Klaw,Makrum. 7.00
19 VM,V:Klaw,Raknor the Slayer . 7.00
20 VM,V:Klaw,Fortress of Fear . . . 7.00

[2nd Series], Apr. 1981
1 BA,O:Ka-Zar 4.00
2 thru 7 BA . . . . @3.00
8 BA,Ka-Zar Father. 2.50
9 BA 2.50
10 BA,Direct D. 2.50
11 BA/GK,Zabu 2.50
12 BA,Panel Missing 2.50
12a Scarce Reprint 2.50
13 BA 2.50
14 BA/GK,Zabu 2.50
15 BA 2.50
16 . . . . 2.50
17 Detective 2.50
18 & 19. . . . . @2.50
20 A:Spider-Man 3.00
21 . . . . 3.00
22 A:Spider-Manna 3.00
23 A:Spider-Man 3.00
24 A:Spider-Man 3.00
25 A:Spider-Man 3.00

26 A:Spider-Man 3.00
27 A:Buth 3.00
28 Pangea 3.00
29 W:Ka-Zar & Shanna, Doub.Size . . 3.00
30 V:Pterons 3.00
31 PangeaWarII 3.00
32 V:Plunderer 3.00
33 V:Plunderer 3.00
34 Last Issue Doub.Size 3.00

[3rd Series], 1997

1 MWa,NKU,Ka-Zar, Shanna, Zabu,
  V:Gregor, 40pg 5.00
1a 2nd printing 2.50
2 MWa,NKU,V:Gregor 4.00
2A NKu variant cover 3.00
3 MWa,NKu,Ka-Zar's son dead? . . 3.00
4 MWa,NKu,in New York City 3.00
5 MWa,NKu, ... 2.50
6 MWa,V:Rampaging Rhino 2.25
7 MWa,NKu,F:Shanna the
  She-Devil 2.25
8 MWa,NKu, Urban Jungle, pt.1 . . 2.25
9 MWa,NKu, Urban Jungle, pt.2 . . 2.25
10 MWa,NKu, Urban Jungle, pt.3 . . 2.25
11 MWa,NKu, Urban Jungle, pt.4,
  concl. 2.25
12 MWa,A:High Evolutionary 2.25
13 MWa,A:High Evolutionary 2.25
14 MWa,NKu,end old & begin new
  storyline, double size 3.50
15 A:Punisher. 3.00
16 A:Punisher. 2.25
17 Ka-Zar clears his name,
  A:Jameka. 2.25
18 People of the Savage Land
  revolt 2.25
19 V:Gregor 2.25
20 A:Gregor,Zira, final issue 2.25
Ann. '97 V:Garrok, Petrified Man . . 2.50
Ann. '98 Ka-Zar/Daredevil heroes
  unite. 3.00
1-shot Ka-Zar of the Savage Land,
  CDi,V:Sauron, 48-pg., prelude to
  3rd series (1996) 3.00
1-shot Ka-Zar: Sibling Rivalry,
  MWa,TDz,Flashback (1997) . . . 2.00

KELLYS, THE
See: KID KOMICS

KENT BLAKE OF THE
SECRET SERVICE

May, 1951—July, 1953

1 U.S. Govt. Secret Agent
  stories,Bondage cover 250.00
2 JSt,Drug issue,Man with
  out A Face 175.00
3 JMn,Trapped By The Chinese
  Reds 125.00
4 Secret Service Stories 125.00
5 RH(c),Condemned To Death . . 125.00
6 Cases from Kent Blake files . . 125.00
7 RH(c),Behind Enemy Lines . . . 125.00
8 GT,V:Communists 125.00
9 thru 14 . . . . @125.00

KICKERS INC.

Nov., 1986

1 SB,O:Kickers 2.50
2 SB 2.50
3 RF,Witches. 2.50
4 RF,FIST 2.50
5 RF,A:D.P.7 . . . . 2.50
6 thru 12 . . . . @2.50

KID & PLAY

1 Based on Rap Group. 2.25
2 thru 9 . . . . @2.25

Kid Colt Outlaw #4
© *Marvel Entertainment Group*

KID COLT OUTLAW

Marvel Atlas, Aug., 1948

1 B:Kid Colt,A:Two-Gun Kid . . 1,600.00
2 Gun-Fighter and the Girl 750.00
3 SSh,Colt-Quick Killers
  For Hire 600.00
4 Wanted,A:Tex Taylor 600.00
5 Mystery of the Misssing
  Mine,A:Blaze Carson. 600.00
6 A:Tex Taylor,Valley of
  the Werewolf 400.00
7 B:Nimo the Lion 400.00
8 . . . . 400.00
9 . . . . 400.00
10 The Whip Strikes,E:Nimo
  the Lion. 400.00
11 O:Kid Colt 500.00
12 . . . . 250.00
13 DRi 250.00
14 . . . . 250.00
15 Gun Whipped in ShotgunCity . 250.00
16 . . . . 250.00
17 . . . . 250.00
18 DRi 250.00
19 . . . . 225.00
20 The Outlaw 225.00
21 thru 30 . . . . @225.00
31 . . . . 225.00
32 . . . . 225.00
33 thru 45 A:Black Rider . . . . @200.00
46 RH(c). 200.00
47 DW 200.00
48 RH(c),JKu 200.00
49 . . . . 200.00
50 . . . . 200.00
51 thru 56 . . . . @125.00
57 AW 125.00
58 AW 125.00
59 AW 125.00
60 AW 125.00
61 . . . . 100.00
62 . . . . 100.00
63 . . . . 100.00
64 RC 110.00
65 RC 110.00
66 AW 150.00
67 thru 78. . . . . @100.00
79 Origin Retold 110.00
80 thru 86 . . . . @100.00
87 JDa(reprint) 110.00
88 AW 120.00
89 AW,Matt Slade 120.00
90 thru 99 . . . . @100.00
100 JK 120.00

101 JK 75.00
102 JK 75.00
103 JK,The Great Train Robbery . . 75.00
104 JKu(c),DH,Trail of
  Kid Colt. 75.00
105 DH,V:Dakota Dixon 75.00
106 JKu(c),The Circus
  of Crime. 75.00
107 JK,SciFi(c). 100.00
108 BEv 75.00
109 DAy,V:The Barracuda 75.00
110 GC,V:Iron Mask 100.00
111 JKu(c),V:Sam Hawk, The
  Man Hunter 65.00
112 JKu(c),V:Mr. Brown 65.00
113 JKu(c),GC,V:Bull Barton 65.00
114 JKu(c),Return of Iron Mask. . . 65.00
115 JKu(c),V:The Scorpion 65.00
116 JKu(c),GC,V:Dr. Danger &
  Invisible Gunman. 65.00
117 JKu(c),GC,V:The Fatman &
  His Boomerang 65.00
118 V:Scorpion,Bull Barton,
  Dr. Danger. 65.00
119 DAy(c),JK,V:Bassett The
  Badman 65.00
120 Cragsons Ride Again 65.00
121 A:Rawhide Kid,Iron Mask 50.00
122 V:Rattler Ruxton 50.00
123 V:Ringo Barker 50.00
124 A:Phantom Raider 50.00
125 A:Two-Gun Kid 50.00
126 V:Wes Hardin 50.00
127 thru 129 . . . . @50.00
130 O:Kid Colt 65.00
131 thru 150 . . . . @30.00
151 thru 200 reprints . . . . . . @25.00
201 thru 228 reprints . . . . . . @20.00
229 April, 1979. . . . . 20.00

KID FROM DODGE CITY

Marvel Atlas, July, 1957—Sept.,
1957

1 . . . . 150.00
2 . . . . 100.00

KID FROM TEXAS

Marvel Atlas, June, 1957—Aug.,
1957

1 . . . . 125.00
2 . . . . 100.00

KID KOMICS

Marvel Timely, Feb., 1943

1 SSh(c),BW,O:Captain Wonder
  & Tim Mulrooney I:Whitewash,
  Knuckles,Trixie Trouble,
  Pinto Pete Subbie. 7,500.00
2 AsH(c),F:Captain Wonder
  Subbie, B:Young Allies,
  B:Red Hawk,Tommy Tyme 3,500.00
3 ASh(c),AAv,SSh,A:The Vision
  & Daredevils 3,000.00
4 ASh(c),B:Destroyer,A:Sub-Mariner,
  E:Red Hawk, Tommy Tyme 2,200.00
5 ASh(c),V:Nazis 1,800.00
6 ASh(c),V:Japanese 1,800.00
7 ASh(c),B;Whizzer 1,600.00
8 ASh(c),V:Train Robbers 1,600.00
9 ASh(c),V:Elves 1,600.00
10 ASh(c),E:Young Allies,
  The Destoyer,The Whizzer 1,600.00
Becomes:

KID MOVIE KOMICS

1946

11 F:Silly Seal,Ziggy Pig
  HK,Hey Look 300.00
Becomes:

RUSTY COMICS
1947

12 F:Rusty,A:Mitzi 225.00
13 Do not Disturb(c). 125.00
14 Beach(c),BW,HK,Hey Look . . 250.00
15 Picnic(c),HK,Hey Look 175.00
16 Juniors Grades,HK,HeyLook . 175.00
17 John in Trouble,HK,HeyLook . 175.00
18 John Fired. 125.00
19 Fridge raid(c),HK 125.00
20 And Her Family,HK 200.00
21 And Her Family,HK 250.00
22 HK. 250.00
Becomes:

KELLYS, THE
1950

23 F:The Kelly Family(Pop,
　Mom,Mike,Pat & Goliath) . . 125.00
24 Mike's Date,A;Margie 75.00
25 Wrestling(c). 75.00
Becomes:

SPY CASES
1950

26(#1) Spy stories. 350.00
27(#2) BEv,Bondage(c) 300.00
28(#3) Sabotage,A:Douglas
　Grant Secret Agent. 175.00
4 The Secret Invasion 150.00
5 The Vengeance of Comrade
　de Casto 150.00
6 A:Secret Agent Doug Grant . . 150.00
7 GT,A:Doug Grant 150.00
8 Atom Bomb(c),Frozen
　Horror 250.00
9 Undeclared War 125.00
10 Battlefield Adventures. 125.00
11 Battlefield Adventures. 125.00
12 Battlefield Adventures. 125.00
13 Battlefield Adventures. 125.00
14 Battlefield Adventures. 125.00
15 Doug Grant. 125.00
16 Doug Grant. 125.00
17 Doug Grant. 125.00
18 Contact in Ankara 125.00
19 Final Issue,Oct., 1953. . . . . . 125.00

KID SLADE GUNFIGHTER
See: MATT SLADE

KILLFRENZY
1 . . . . 2.25
2 Castle Madspike 2.25

KILLPOWER:
THE EARLY YEARS
1993

1 B:MiB,Goes on Rampage 3.25
2 thru 3 O:Killpower . . . . @2.25
4 E:MiB,last issue. 2.25

KILLRAVEN
Dec., 2000

Spec. JLi,R:Killraven 3.00

KILLRAVEN
Oct., 2002

1 (of 6) AD,MFm,V:Martians. 3.00
2 AD,MFm. 3.00
3 AD,MFm. 3.00
4 AD,MFm. 3.00
5 AD,MFm. 3.00
6 AD,MFm. 3.00

KING ARTHUR & THE
KNIGHTS OF JUSTICE
1993–94

1 Based on Cartoon 2.25

Killpower: The Early Years #4
© Marvel Entertainment Group

2 Based on Cartoon 2.25
3 Based on Cartoon 2.25

KING CONAN:
See: CONAN THE KING

KINGPIN
Nov., 1997

1-shot StL,JR, bookshelf 48pg. . . . 6.00

KINGPIN
June, 2003

1 SeP,KJ,Wilson Fixk 2.50
2 thru 7 SeP,KJ. . . . . @2.50

KISSNATION
1997

1 Rock & Roll, A:X-Men 10.00

KITTY PRYDE:
AGENT OF S.H.I.E.L.D.
Oct., 1997

1 (of 3) LHa,V:Ogun 2.50
2 LHa,V:Ogun. 2.50
3 LHa,Ogun's Slave? 2.50

KITTY PRYDE
& WOLVERINE
Nov., 1984

1 AM,V:Ogun. 6.00
2 AM,V:Ogun. 5.00
3 thru 5 AM,V:Ogun. . . . . @5.00
6 AM,D:Ogun, April, 1985. . . . . . . 5.00

KNIGHTS OF
PENDRAGON
[1st Regular Series], July, 1990

1 GEr 2.75
2 thru 18 . . . . @2.25

[2nd Regular Series], 1992

1 GEr,A:Iron Man,R:Knights of
　Pendragon 2.25
2 thru 15 . . . . @2.25

KOMIC KARTOONS
Marvel Timely, 1945

1 Funny Animal. 225.00
2 . . . . 225.00

KRAZY KOMICS
Marvel Timely, July, 1942

1 B:Ziggy Pig,Silly Seal 750.00
2 Toughy Tomcat(c) 325.00
3 Toughy Tomcat/Bunny(c) 250.00
4 Toughy Tomcat/Ziggy(c) 250.00
5 Ziggy/Buzz Saw(c) 250.00
6 Toughy/Cannon(c) 250.00
7 Cigar Store Indian(c) 250.00
8 Toughy/Hammock(c) 250.00
9 Hitler(c) 275.00
10 Newspaper(c) 225.00
11 Canoe(c) 225.00
12 Circus(c) 300.00
13 Pirate Treasure(c). 200.00
14 Fishing(c) 200.00
15 Ski-Jump(c). 175.00
16 Airplane(c). 125.00
17 Street corner(c). 125.00
18 Mallet/Bell(c) 125.00
19 Bicycle(c) 125.00
20 Ziggy(c) 125.00
21 Toughy's date(c) 125.00
22 Crystal Ball(c) 125.00
23 Sharks in bathtub(c) 150.00
24 Baseball(c) 125.00
25 HK,Krazy Krow(c). 150.00
26 Super Rabbit(c). 125.00
Becomes:

CINDY COMICS
1947

27 HK,B:Margie,Oscar. 250.00
28 HK,Snow sled(c). 150.00
29 . . . . 150.00
30 . . . . 150.00
31 HK. 150.00
32 . . . . 100.00
33 A;Georgie 100.00
34 thru 40. . . . . @100.00
Becomes:

CRIME CAN'T WIN
1950

41 Crime stories. 350.00
42 . . . . 200.00
43 GT,Horror story. 250.00
4 thru 11 . . . . @150.00
12 Sept., 1953 . . . . 125.00

KRAZY KOMICS
Marvel Timely
[2nd Series], 1948

1 BW,HK,B:Eustice Hayseed . . . 600.00
2 BW,O:Powerhouse Pepper . . . 400.00

KRAZY KROW
Summer, 1945

1 B:Krazy Krow 250.00
2 . . . . 150.00
3 Winter, 1945-46 . . . . 150.00

KREE-SKRULL WAR
Sept.–Oct., 1983

1 & 2 JB,NA,reprints . . . . @5.00

KRULL
Nov.–Dec., 1983

1 Ph(c),BBI,movie adapt. 2.50
2 BBI,rep.,Marvel Super Spec. . . . 2.50

KULL THE CONQUEROR
[1st Series], June, 1971

1 MSe,RA,WW,A King Comes
　Riding,O:Kull 75.00
2 MSe,JSe,Shadow Kingdom. . . . 30.00
3 MSe,JSe,Death Dance of
　Thulsa Doom. 30.00
4 MSe,JSe,Night o/t Red Slayers. 30.00

Kull The Conqueror #1
© Marvel Entertainment Group

5 MSe,JSe,Kingdom By the Sea . 30.00
6 MSe,JSe,Lurker Beneath
   the Sea 15.00
7 MSe,JSe,Delcardes'Cat,
   A:Thulsa Doom 15.00
8 MSe,JSe,Wolfshead 15.00
9 MSe,JSe,The Scorpion God . . . 15.00
10 MSe,Swords o/t White Queen . 15.00
11 MP,King Kull Must Die, O:Kull
   cont.,A:Thulsa Doom. 10.00
12 MP,SB,Moon of Blood,V:Thulsa
   Doom,B:SD,B.U.stories 10.00
13 MP,AM,Torches From Hell,
   V:Thulsa Doom 10.00
14 MP,JA,The Black Belfry,
   A:Thulsa Doom 10.00
15 MP,Wings o/t Night-Beast,
   E:SD,B.U.stories 10.00
16 EH,Tiger in the Moon,
   A:Thulsa Doom 12.00
17 AA,EH,Thing from Emerald
   Darkness 6.00
18 EH,AA,Keeper of Flame
   & Frost. 6.00
19 EH,AA,The Crystal Menace . . 6.00
20 EH,AA,Hell Beneath Atlantis. . . 6.00
21 City of the Crawling Dead. . . . 10.00
22 Talons of the Devil-Birds. 10.00
23 Demon Shade. 10.00
24 Screams in the Dark. 9.00
25 A Lizard's Throne 9.00
26 Into Death's Dimension. 9.00
27 The World Within 9.00
28 Creature and the Crown,
   A:Thulsa Doom 9.00
29 So Sit the Topaz Throne,
   V:Thulsa Doom, final issue . . . 9.00

[2nd Series], 1982
1 JB,Brule 4.00
2 Misareenia 3.00

[3rd Series], 1983–85
1 JB,BWi,DG,Iraina 3.50
2 JB,Battle to the Death 3.00
3 JB. 3.00
4 JB. 3.00
5 JB 3.00
6 JB 3.00
7 JB,Masquerade Death 3.00
8 JB 3.00
9 JB 3.00
10 JB 3.00

KULL AND THE BARBARIANS
May, 1975
1 NA,GK,reprint Kull #1 . . . . 30.00
2 BBI,reprint,Dec., 1983 . . . . 25.00
3 NA,HC,O:Red Sonja 25.00

LABRYNTH
1986–87
1 Movie adapt. 3.00
2 and 3 . . . . @3.00

LAFF-A-LYMPICS
1978–79
1 F;Hanna Barbera 45.00
2 thru 5 . . . . @30.00
6 thru 13 . . . . @35.00

LANA
Aug., 1948
1 F:Lana Lane The Show Girl,
   A:Rusty,B:Millie 275.00
2 HK,Hey Look,A:Rusty 200.00
3 Show(c),B:Nellie 100.00
4 Ship(c) 100.00
5 Audition(c) 100.00
6 Stop sign(c) 100.00
7 Beach(c) 100.00
Becomes:

LITTLE LANA
1949
8 Little Lana(c) 100.00
9 Final Issue,March, 1950 . . . . 100.00

LANCE BARNES: POST NUKE DICK
Epic, 1993
1 I:Lance Barnes. 2.50
2 Cigarettes 2.50
3 Warring Mall Tribe 2.50
4 V:Ex-bankers,last issue 2.50

LAST AMERICAN
Epic, 1990–91
1 . . . . 3.50
2 . . . . 3.00
3 . . . . 2.50
4 Final issue.. . . . . 2.25

THE LAST AVENGERS STORY
1995
1 PDd, Alterverse,Future world. . . . 6.00
2 PDd, Final fate,fully painted. 6.00

LAST FANTASTIC FOUR STORY, THE
Aug., 2007
Spec. StL(s),JR2 . . . . 5.00

LAST HERO STANDING
June, 2005
1 (of 5) PO 3.00
2 thru 5 Po . . . . @3.00

LAST PLANET STANDING
May, 2006
1 (of 5) PO 3.00
2 thru 5 Po . . . . @3.00

LAST STARFIGHTER, THE
Oct.–Dec., 1984
1 JG(c),BBI,Movie adapt. 2.25

Lawbreakers Always Lose #2
© Marvel Entertainment Group

2 Movie adapt. 2.25
3 BBI 2.25

LAWBREAKERS ALWAYS LOSE
Marvel Crime Bureau Stories, 1948–49
1 HK; FBI Reward Poster Photo
   Adam and Eve, HK,Giggles
   and Grins. 500.00
2 FBI V:Fur Theives 250.00
3 . . . . 200.00
4 AyB(c),Vampire 200.00
5 AyB(c) 200.00
6 Anti Wertham Edition 225.00
7 Crime at Midnight 350.00
8 Prison Break 150.00
9 Ph(c),He Prowled at Night . . . 150.00
10 Phc(c),I Met My Murderer. . . . 150.00

LAWDOG
1993
1 B:CDi(s),FH,I:Lawdog 2.50
2 thru 10 FH . . . . @2.25
1-shot Lawdog & Grimrod: Terror
   at the Crossroads 3.50

LEGION OF MONSTERS
Sept., 1975
(black & white magazine)
1 NA(c),GM,I&O:Legion of
   Monsters,O:Manphibian 40.00

LEGION OF MONSTERS
2007
Spec.#1 Werewolf by Night (2-2007)3.00
Spec.#1 Man-Thing (3-2007). 3.00
Spec.#1 Morbius (5-2007). 3.00
Spec.#1 Satana (6-2007). 3.00

LEGION OF NIGHT
Oct., 1991
1 WPo/SW,A:Fin Fang Foom 5.50
2 WPo,V:Fin Fang Foom 5.50

LETHAL FOES OF SPIDER-MAN
1993
1 B:DFr(s),SMc,R:Stegron 3.00
2 SMc,A:Stegron. 3.00

MARVEL

3 SMc,V:Spider-Man 3.00
4 E:DFr(s),SMc,Last Issue 3.00

LIFE OF CAPTAIN MARVEL
Aug., 1985
1 rep.Iron Man #55,
  Capt.Marvel #25,26 . . . . 7.00
2 rep.Capt.Marvel#26-28 . . . . 5.00
3 rep.Capt.Marvel#28-30
  Marvel Feature #12 . . . . 5.00
4 rep.Marvel Feature #12,Capt.
  Marvel #31,32,Daredevil#105 . . 5.00
5 rep.Capt.Marvel #32-#34 . . . . . . 5.00

LIFE OF CHRIST
1993
1 Birth of Christ 5.00
2 MW,The Easter Story 5.00

LIFE OF POPE JOHN-PAUL II
1983
1 JSt, Jan., 1983 . . . . 6.00
1a Special reprint 4.00

LIFE WITH MILLIE
See: DATE WITH MILLIE

LIGHT AND DARKNESS WAR
Epic, Oct., 1988
1 . . . . 4.00
2 . . . . 3.00
3 thru 6 Dec., 1989 . . . . @2.50

LINDA CARTER, STUDENT NURSE
Atlas, Sept., 1961
1 . . . . 90.00
2 thru 9, Jan., 1963 . . . . @60.00

LION KING
1 based on Movie 2.75

LI'L KIDS
Aug., 1970–June, 1973
1 . . . . 125.00
2 thru 12 . . . . @60.00

Li'l Kinds #1
© Marvel Entertainment Group

LI'L PALS
Sept., 1972
1 . . . . 90.00
2 thru 5, May, 1973 . . . . @50.00

LITTLE ASPIRIN
Marvel Comics, 1949
1 HK 200.00
2 HK 125.00
3 . . . . 100.00

LITTLE LANA
See: LANA

LITTLE LENNY
Marvel Classic Detective, 1949
1 . . . . 135.00
2 . . . . 100.00
3 . . . . 100.00

LITTLE LIZZIE
June, 1949
1 Roller Skating(c) 150.00
2 Soda(c) 100.00
3 Movies(c) 100.00
4 Lizzie(c) 100.00
5 Lizzie/Swing(c) April,1950 . . . 100.00
[2nd Series] Sept., 1953
1 . . . . 100.00
2 . . . . 75.00
3 Jan., 1954 . . . . 75.00

LITTLE MERMAID, THE
1993
1 . . . . 3.50
2 thru 13 . . . . @2.50

LIVEWIRES
Feb., 2005
1 (of 6) AWa(s), ... 3.00
2 Awa(s&c) 3.00
3 AWa(s&c) 3.00
4 AWa(s&c) 3.00
5 Awa(s&c) 3.00
6 AWa(s&c), finale 3.00
Digest Vol. 1: Clockwork Thugs, Yo. 8.00

LOGAN
1-shot HMe,48pg 6.00
1-shot Logan: Path of the
  Warrior (1996) 5.00
1-shot Logan: Shadow Society,
  HMe,TCk Early life of
  Wolverine (1996) 5.00

LOGAN'S RUN
Jan., 1977
1 GP,From Movie 16.00
2 GP,Cathedral Kill 10.00
3 GP,Lair of Laser Death 10.00
4 GP,Dread Sanctuary 10.00
5 GP,End Run 10.00
6 MZ,B.U.Thanos/Drax 25.00
7 TS,Cathedral Prime 10.00

LOKI
July, 2004
1 (of 4) 7.50
2 thru 4 . . . . @7.50

LONERS, THE
Apr., 2007
1 . . . . 3.00
2 thru 6 . . . . @3.00

LONGSHOT
Sept., 1985
1 AAd,WPo(i),BA,I:Longshot 8.00
2 AAd,WPo(i),I:RicoshetRita 6.00
3 AAd,WPo(i),I:Mojo,Spiral 6.00
4 AAd,WPo(i),A:Spider-Man 6.00
5 AAd,WPo(i),A:Dr. Strange 6.00
6 AAd,WPo(i),A:Dr. Strange 6.00
1-shot, JMD,MZi,AW (1997) 4.00

LOOSE CANNONS
1 and 2 DAn . . . . @2.50
3 DAn 2.75

Lorna, The Jungle Girl #20
© Marvel Entertainment Group

LORNA, THE JUNGLE GIRL
Marvel Atlas, 1953–57
1 Terrors of the Jungle,O:Lorna . 500.00
2 Headhunter's Strike
  I:Greg Knight 250.00
3 . . . . 200.00
4 . . . . 200.00
5 . . . . 200.00
6 RH(c),GT 175.00
7 RH(c) 175.00
8 Jungle Queen Strikes Again . . 175.00
9 . . . . 175.00
10 White Fang 175.00
11 Death From the Skies 175.00
12 Day of Doom 125.00
13 thru 17 . . . . @125.00
18 AW(c) 150.00
19 thru 26 . . . . @125.00

LOVE ADVENTURES
Marvel Atlas, Oct., 1949
1 Ph(c) 250.00
2 BP,Ph(c),Tyrone Power/
  Gene Tierney 225.00
3 thru 12 . . . . @150.00
Becomes:

ACTUAL CONFESSIONS
1952
13 . . . . 100.00
14 Dec., 1952 . . . . 100.00

LOVE CLASSICS
Marvel Classic Detective, 1949
1 . . . . 200.00
2 . . . . 200.00

LOVE DRAMAS
Oct., 1949
1 Ph(c),JKa 225.00
2 Jan., 1950 . . . . 150.00

LOVELAND
1949
1 Ph(c) 150.00
2 Ph(c) 150.00

LOVE ROMANCES See: IDEAL

LOVERS
See: ALL-SELECT COMICS

LOVE SECRETS
Oct., 1949
1 . . . . 200.00
2 Jan., 1950 . . . . 150.00

LOVE TALES
Marvel Atlas, 1949–56
(Formerly: The Human Torch)
36 Ph(c) 250.00
37 . . . . 175.00
38 . . . . 150.00
39 thru 41 . . . . @150.00
42 thru 44 . . . . @125.00
45 BP 150.00
46 thru 51 . . . . @125.00
52 BK 150.00
53 thru 68 . . . . @125.00
69 BEv 150.00
70 thru 75 . . . . @100.00

LOVE TRAILS
Marvel Current Detective, 1949
1 western romance 200.00
2 . . . . 200.00

LUNATIK
1995
1 KG 2.25
2 V:The Avengers 2.25
3 conclusion 2.25

MACHINE MAN
April, 1978
1 JK,From 2001 . . . . 20.00
2 JK 12.00
3 JK,V:Ten-For,The Mean
  Machine 12.00
4 JK,V;Ten-For,Battle on A
  Busy Street 12.00
5 JK,V;Ten-For,Day of the
  Non-Hero 12.00
6 JK,V;Ten-For 12.00
7 JK,With A Nation Against Him . . 12.00
8 JK,Escape:Impossible 12.00
9 JK,In Final Battle 12.00
10 SD,Birth of A Super-Hero 7.00
11 SD,V;Binary Bug 7.00
12 SD,Where walk the Gods 7.00
13 SD,Xanadu 7.00
14 SD,V:Machine Man 7.00
15 SD,A:Thing,Human Torch 7.00
16 SD,I:Baron Brimstone And the
  Satan Squad 7.00
17 SD,Madam Menace 7.00
18 A:Alpha Flight 25.00
19 I:Jack o'Lantern 25.00

MACHINE MAN
[Limited-Series]
Oct., 1984
1 HT,BWS,V:Baintronics 4.00
2 HT,BWS,C:Iron Man of 2020 . . . 4.00
3 HT,BWS,I:Iron Man of 2020 . . . . 4.00
4 HT,BWS,V:Iron Man of 2020 . . . 4.00

MACHINE MAN 2020
1994
1 rep. limited series #1–#2 . . . . . 2.25
2 rep. limited series #3–#4 . . . . . 2.25

MACHINE TEEN
May, 2005
1 (of 5) F:Adam Aaronson 3.00
2 History 101001 . . . . 3.00
3 History 101001 . . . . 3.00
4 Trust no one 3.00
5 Finale 3.00

MAD ABOUT MILLIE
April, 1969
1 . . . . 125.00
2 thru 3 . . . . @100.00
4 thru 10 . . . . @50.00
11 thru 16 . . . . @45.00
17 Dec., 1970 . . . . 45.00
Ann.#1 . . . . 50.00

MADBALLS
Star, Sept., 1986
1 Based on Toys 4.00
2 thru 9 . . . . @4.00
10 June, 1988 . . . . 4.00

MAD DOG
1 from Bob TV Show 2.50
2 V:Trans World Trust Corp 2.50
3 V:Cigarette Criminals 2.50
4 V:Dogs of War 2.50
5 thru 6 . . . . @2.50

MADE MEN
May, 1998
1-shot HMe gangster epic 6.00

MADROX
Sept., 2004
1 (of 5) PDd(s),F:Jamie Madrox . . 3.00
2 PDd(s) 3.00
3 . . . . 3.00
4 . . . . 3.00
5 PDd(c),V:Clay,concl. 3.00

MAGIK
Dec., 1983
1 JB,TP,F:Storm and Illyana 4.00
2 JB,TP,A:Belasco,Sym 3.00
3 TP,A:New Mutants,Belasco 3.00
4 TP,V:Belasco,A:Sym 3.00

MAGNETO
1993
0 JD,JBo,rep. origin stories 6.00
0a Gold ed. 8.00
0b Platinum ed. 10.00

MAGNETO
1996
1 (of 4) PrM,KJo,JhB, Joseph 2.50
2 PrM,KJo,JhB, Joseph's search
  for his past life 2.50
3 PrM,KJo,JhB 2.50
4 PrM,KJo,JhB, concl. 2.50

MAGNETO:
DARK SEDUCTION
April, 2000
1 (of 4) FaN,X-Men: Revolution . . . 3.00
2 FaN,Scarlet Witch 3.00

3 FaN,RCz,V:Scarlet Witch 3.00
4 FaN,RCz,concl. 3.00

MAGNETO REX
March, 1999
1 (of 3) BPe,takes over Genosha . . 2.50
1a signed 20.00
2 BPe,V:Rogue 2.50
3 BPe,A:Rogue,Quicksilver 2.50
GN Magneto Ascendant,
  96-page rep. 4.00

MAN COMICS
Marvel Atlas, 1949–53
1 GT 350.00
2 GT 250.00
3 . . . . 200.00

Man Comics #12
© Marvel Entertainment Group

4 . . . . 200.00
5 . . . . 200.00
6 . . . . 200.00
7 JeR 200.00
8 BEv 200.00
9 EC,TSe,War format begins . . . 150.00
10 JeR,MMe(c) 150.00
11 RH,TSe,MMe 150.00
12 . . . . 150.00
13 . . . . 150.00
14 GT,JeR 175.00
15 . . . . 150.00
16 . . . . 150.00
17 RH 175.00
18 . . . . 150.00
19 . . . . 150.00
20 . . . . 150.00
21 EC-RH. 175.00
22 BEv(c),BK 175.00
23 GT,JSt 175.00
24 . . . . 150.00
25 BEv(c) 175.00
26 . . . . 150.00
27 . . . . 150.00
28 Where Mummies Prowl 150.00

MANDRAKE
1995
1 fully painted series 3.25
2 V:Octon 3.25
3 final issue 3.25

MAN FROM ATLANTIS
Feb., 1978–Aug., 1978
1 TS,From TV Series,O:Mark
  Harris 20.00

2 FR,FS,The Bermuda Triangle
Trap 12.00
3 FR,FS,Undersea Shadow 12.00
4 FR,FS,Beware the Killer
Spores 12.00
5 FR,FS,The Ray of the
Red Death 12.00
6 FR,FS,Bait for the Behemoth . . 12.00
7 FR,FS,Behold the Land
Forgotten. 12.00

Man-Thing #19
© Marvel Entertainment Group

MAN-THING
[1st Series] Jan., 1974
1 FB,JM,A:Howard the Duck 75.00
2 VM,ST,Hell Hath No Fury 30.00
3 VM,JA,I:Original Foolkiller 25.00
4 VM,JA,O&D:Foolkiller 20.00
5 MP,Night o/t Laughing Dead . . 20.00
6 MP,V:Soul-Slayers,Drug Issue. . 20.00
7 MP,A Monster Stalks Swamp. . . 20.00
8 MP,Man Into Monster. 20.00
9 MP,Deathwatch 20.00
10 MP,Nobody Dies Forever 20.00
11 MP,Dance to the Murder 20.00
12 KJ,Death-Cry of a Dead Man . . 12.00
13 TS,V:Captain Fate 12.00
14 AA,V:Captain Fate 12.00
15 A Candle for Saint Cloud 12.00
16 JB,TP,Death of a Legend 12.00
17 JM,Book Burns in Citrusville. . . 12.00
18 JM,Chaos on the Campus 12.00
19 JM,FS,I:Scavenger 12.00
20 JM,A:Spider-Man,Daredevil,
Shang-Chi,Thing 14.00
21 JM,O:Scavenger,Man Thing . . . 12.00
22 JM,C:Howard the Duck. 12.00
G-Size #1 MP,SD,JK,rep.TheGlob. 10.00
G-Size #2 JB,KJ,The
Monster Runs Wild 10.00
G-Size #3 AA,A World He
Never Made 10.00
G-Size #4 FS,EH,inc.Howard the
Duck vs.Gorko. 10.00
G-Size #5 DA,EH,inc.Howard the
Duck vs.Vampire 12.00
[2nd Series] 1979–1981
1 JM,BWi. 11.00
2 BWi,JM,Himalayan Nightmare. . 10.00
3 BWi,JM,V:Snowman 10.00
4 BWi,DP,V:Mordo,A:Dr Strange . 10.00
5 DP,BWi,This Girl is Terrified. . . 10.00
6 DP,BWi,Fraternity Rites 10.00
7 BWi,DP Return of Captain Fate. 10.00

8 BWi,DP,V:Captain Fate 10.00
9 BWi(c),Save the Life of My
Own Child 10.00
10 BWi,DP,Swampfire 10.00
11 Final issue. 10.00
[3rd Series] Oct., 1997
1 JMD,LSh, non-code. 3.00
2 JMD,LSh, reunion with ex-wife,
A:Dr. Strange. 3.00
3 JMD,LSh, visit to Devil Slayer. . . 3.00
4 JMD,LSh, V:Devil-Slayer 3.00
5 JMD,LSh, new abilities revealed . 3.00
6 JMD,LSh, V:Cult of Entropy. . . . 3.00
7 JMD,LSh, Muck Monster, Namor. 3.00
8 JMD,LSh, Muck Monster turned
back into Ted Sallis 3.00
Storyline continues in Strange Tales

MAN-THING
July, 2004
1 (of 3) movie prequel. 3.00
2 movie prequel,pt.2 . . . . 3.00
3 movie prequel,pt.3 . . . . 3.00

MARINES AT WAR
See: DEVIL-DOG DUGAN

MARINES IN ACTION
Marvel Atlas, June, 1955
1 B:Rock Murdock,Boot Camp
Brady 125.00
2 thru 13 . . . . @100.00
14 Sept., 1957 . . . . 100.00

MARINES IN BATTLE
Marvel Atlas, Aug., 1954
1 RH,B:Iron Mike McGraw 250.00
2 . . . . 150.00
3 thru 6 . . . . @125.00
7 thru 17 . . . . @125.00
18 thru 22 . . . . @100.00
23 . . . . 125.00
24 . . . . 100.00
25 Sept., 1958 . . . . 125.00

MARK HAZZARD: MERC
Nov., 1986–Oct., 1987
1 GM,O:Mark Hazard 2.25
2 GM. 2.25
3 M,Arab Terrorists 2.25
4 thru 8 GM . . . . @2.25
9 NKu/AKu 2.25
10 thru 12 . . . . @2.25
Ann.#1 D:Merc. 2.25

MARSHALL LAW
Epic, 1987–89
1 . . . . 4.50
2 . . . . 3.00
3 thru 6 . . . . @2.50

MARVEL ACTION HOUR:
FANTASTIC FOUR
1994–95
1 regular 2.25
1a bagged with insert print from
animated series. 3.00
2 thru 8 . . . . @2.25

MARVEL ACTION HOUR:
IRON MAN
1994–95
1 regular 2.25
1a bagged with insert print from
animated series. 3.25
2 thru 8 . . . . @2.25

Marvel Action Hour: Iron Man #5
© Marvel Entertainment Group

MARVEL ACTION
UNIVERSE
TV Tie-in, Jan., 1989
1 Rep.Spider-Man & Friends 4.00

MARVEL ADVENTURES
Feb., 1997
1 RMc,F:The Hulk. 2.25
2 thru 20 RMc . . . . @2.25

MARVEL ADVENTURES
Flipbook, June, 2005
1 Marvel Adventures Spider-Man #1
& Fantastic Four #1. . . . . 4.00
2 thru 13 . . . . @4.00
14 thru 17 . . . . @5.00

MARVEL ADVENTURES
FANTASTIC FOUR
May, 2005
0 SEa,Dr. Doom 2.00
1 . . . . 2.50
2 thru 10 . . . . @2.50
11 thru 18 . . . . @3.00
19 thru 30 . . . . @3.00

MARVEL ADVENTURES
HULK
July, 2007
1 . . . . 3.00
2 thru 5 . . . . 3.00

MARVEL ADVENTURES
IRON MAN
May, 2007
1 . . . . 3.00
2 thru 7 . . . . @3.00

MARVEL ADVENTURES
SPIDER-MAN
March, 2005
1 Birth of Spider-Man 2.25
2 thru 13 . . . . @2.50
14 thru 21 . . . . @3.00
22 thru 33 . . . . @3.00

MARVEL ADVENTURES STARRING DAREDEVIL
Dec., 1975–Oct., 1976
1 Rep,Daredevil #22 . . . . 15.00
2 thru 6, Rep.,Daredevil . . . . . @10.00

MARVEL ADVENTURES THE AVENGERS
May, 2006
1 . . . . 3.00
2 thru 7 . . . . @3.00
8 thru 18 . . . . @3.00
Giant Sz #1 . . . . 5.00
Digest Vol. 1 Heroes Assembled . . 7.00

MARVEL ADVENTURES THE THING
March, 2005
1 (of 4) Destiny's Song 2.25
2 Thing Vs. Hulk 2.25
3 Invisible Things 2.50

MARVEL ADVENTURES TWO-IN-ONE
July, 2007
1 . . . . 5.00
2 thru 5 . . . . @5.00

MARVEL AGE: FANTASTIC FOUR
April, 2004
1 V:Mole Man 2.25
2 thru 12 . . . . @2.25
Digest #1 All for One 6.00
Digest #2 Doom 6.00
Digest #3 Return of Doctor Doom . . 6.00

MARVEL AGE: FANTASTIC FOUR TALES
Feb., 2005
1 V:Black Panther 2.25
Digest Vol. 1: Fantastic Four Tales . 8.00

MARVEL AGE: HULK
Sept., 2004
1 . . . . 2.50
2 . . . . 2.50
3 . . . . 3.00
4 . . . . 3.00
Digest, rep. #1–#4 . . . . 6.00

MARVEL AGE RUNAWAYS
Digest #3 The Good Die Young 8.00

MARVEL AGE: SENTINEL
2004
1 Salvage, digest 8.00
2 No Hero, digest 8.00

MARVEL AGE: SPIDER-MAN
March, 2004
1 V:Vulture 2.25
2 thru 20 . . . . @2.25
Digest #1 thru #4 . . . . @6.00
Digest, rep. #17–#20 . . . . 6.00

MARVEL AGE SPIDER-MAN TALES
Feb., 2005
1 O:Spider-Man 2.25

MARVEL AGE: SPIDER-MAN TEAM-UP
Sept., 2004
1 F:Fantastic Four 2.50
2 F:Captain America 2.50
3 . . . . 2.25
4 . . . . 2.25
5 F:storm 2.25
Digest, rep. #1–4 . . . . 6.00
Digest Vol. 1: A Little Helf From
My Friends 8.00

MARVEL & DC PRESENTS
Nov., 1982
1 WS,TA,X-Men & Titans,A:Darkseid,
Deathstroke(3rd App.), ... 25.00

MARVEL BOY
See: ASTONISHING

MARVEL ATLAS
Nov., 2007
1 (of 2) 4.00

MARVEL BOY
June, 2000
1 (of 6) GMo,F:Noh-Varr 4.00
2 GMo,V:Human Race 3.50
3 GMo,Hexus 3.50
4 GMo,Exterminatrix 3.50
5 GMo,Oubliette 3.50
6 GMo,V:Dr. Midas,concl. 3.50

MARVEL CHILLERS
Oct., 1975
1 GK(c),I:Mordred the Mystic 20.00
2 E:Mordred 12.00
3 HC/BWr(c),B:Tigra,The Were
Woman 22.00
4 V:Kraven The Hunter 12.00
5 V:Rat Pack,A:Red Wolf 12.00
6 RB(c),JBy,V:Red Wolf 12.00
7 JK(c),GT,V:Super Skrull
E:Tigra,Oct., 1976 . . . . 12.00
GN MGu(s),LSh,F:The Hulk 10.00
GN LHa(s) F:Wolverine 10.00

MARVEL CHRISTMAS SPECIAL
1 DC/AAd/KJ/SB/RLm,A:Ghost Rider
X-Men,Spider-Man. 2.25

MARVEL CLASSICS COMICS
1976–78
1 GK/DA(c),B:Reprints from
Pendulum Illustrated Comics
Dr.Jekyll & Mr. Hyde 30.00
2 GK(c),AN,Time Machine 20.00
3 GK/KJ(c) The Hunchback of
Notre Dame 20.00
4 GK/DA(c),20,000 Leagues-
Beneath the Sea by Verne . . 20.00
5 GK(c),RN,Black Beauty 20.00
6 GK(c),Gulliver Travels 20.00
7 GK(c),Tom Sawyer 20.00
8 GK(c),AN,Moby Dick 20.00
9 GK(c),NR,Dracula 20.00
10 GK(c),Red Badge of Courage . 20.00
11 GK(c),Mysterious Island 15.00
12 GK/DA(c),AN,3 Musketeers . . 15.00
13 GK(c),Last of the Mohicans . . . 15.00
14 GK(c),War of the Worlds. 15.00
15 GK(c),Treasure Island 15.00
16 GK(c),Ivanhoe 12.00

17 JB/ECh(c),The Count of
Monte Cristo 12.00
18 ECh(c),The Odyssey 12.00
19 JB(c),Robinson Crusoe 12.00
20 Frankenstein 12.00
21 GK(c),Master of the World . . . 12.00
22 GK(c),Food of the Gods 12.00
23 Moonstone by Wilkie Collins . . 12.00
24 GK/RN(c),She 12.00
25 The Invisible Man by H.G.Wells 12.00
26 JB(c),The Illiad by Homer 12.00
27 Kidnapped 12.00
28 MGo(1st art) The Pit and
the Pendulum 15.00
29 The Prisoner of Zenda 12.00
30 The Arabian Nights 12.00
31 The First Men in the Moon 12.00
32 GK(c),White Fang 12.00
33 The Prince and the Pauper. . . . 12.00
34 AA,Robin Hood 12.00
35 FBe,Alice in Wonderland 12.00
36 A Christmas Carol 12.00

Marvel Collectors Item Classics#11
© Marvel Entertainment Group

MARVEL COLLECTORS ITEM CLASSICS
Feb., 1965
1 SD,JK,reprint FF #2 . . . . 200.00
2 SD,JK,reprint FF #3 . . . . 100.00
3 SD,JK,reprint FF #4 . . . . 135.00
4 SD,JK,reprint FF #7 . . . . 135.00
5 thru 10 SD,JK,rep.F.Four . . @100.00
11 thru 22 SD,JK,rep.F.Four . . . @75.00
Becomes:

MARVEL'S GREATEST COMICS
1969–81
23 thru 34 SD,JK,rep.F.Four . . . @30.00
35 thru 37 JK,rep.F.Four . . . . . @20.00
38 thru 50 JK,rep.F.Four . . . . . @15.00
51 thru 75 JK,rep.F.Four . . . . . @10.00
76 thru 96 rep.F.Four . . . . @9.00

MARVEL COMICS
Oct.-Nov., 1939
1 FP(c),BEv,CBu,O:Sub-Mariner
I&B:The Angel,A:Human Torch,
Ka-Zar,Jungle Terror,
B:The Masked Raider . . 430,000.00
Becomes:

Marvel Mystry Comics #2
© Marvel Entertainment Group

MARVEL MYSTERY COMICS

2 CSM(c),BEv,CBu,PGv,
B:American, Ace,Human
Torch,Sub-Mariner,Ka-Zar 55,000.00
3 ASh(c),BEv,CBu,PGv,
E:American Ace 29,000.00
4 ASh(c),BEv,CBu,PGv,
I&B:Electro,The Ferret,
Mystery Detective 25,000.00
5 ASh(c),BEv,CBu,PGv,
Human Torch(c) 45,000.00
6 ASh(c),BEv,CBu,PGv,
Anglel(c) 15,000.00
7 ASh(c),BEv,CBu,PGv,
Bondage(c) 15,000.00
8 ASh(c),BEv,CBu,PGv,Human
TorchV:Sub-Mariner 20,000.00
9 ASh(c),BEv,CBu,PGv,Human
Torch V:Sub-Mariner(c) . . 50,000.00
10 ASh(c),BEv,CBu,PGv,B:Terry
Vance Boy Detective 16,000.00
11 ASh(c),BEv,CBu,PGv,
Human Torch V:Nazis(c). . . 6,500.00
12 ASh(c),BEv,CBu,
PGv,Angel(c) 7,000.00
13 ASh(c),BEv,CBu,PGv,S&K,
I&B:The Vision 9,000.00
14 ASh(c),BEv,CBu,PGv,S&K,
Sub-Mariner V:Nazis 4,800.00
15 ASh(c),BEv,CBu,PGv,S&K,
Sub-Mariner(c) 4,800.00
16 ASh(c),BEv,CBu,PGv,S&K,
HumanTorch/NaziAirbase . . 4,800.00
17 ASh(c),BEv,CBu,PGv,S&K
Human Torch/Sub-Mariner 5,000.00
18 ASh(c),BEv,CBu,PGv,S&K,
Human Torch & Toro(c) . . . 4,500.00
19 ASh(c),BEv,CBu,PGv,S&K,
O:Toro,E:Electro 4,500.00
20 ASh(c),BEv,CBu,PGv,S&K,
O:The Angel 4,500.00
21 ASh(c),BEv,CBu,PGv,S&K,
I&B:The Patriot 4,500.00
22 ASh(c),BEv,CBu,PGv,S&K,
AAv,Toro/Bomb(c) 4,000.00
23 ASh(c),BEv,CBu,PGv,S&K,
O:Vision,E:The Angel 4,000.00
24 ASh(c),BEv,CBu,S&K,
AAv,Human Torch(c) 4,000.00
25 BEv,CBu,S&K,ASh Nazi(c) . 4,000.00
26 ASh(c),BEv,CBu,S&K,
Sub-Mariner(c) 3,500.00
27 ASh(c),BEv,CBu,
S&K,E:Ka-Zar 3,500.00

28 ASh(c),BEv,CBu,S&K,Bondage
(c),B:Jimmy Jupiter 3,500.00
29 ASh(c),BEv,CBu,SSh,
Bondage(c). 3,500.00
30 BEv,CBu,SSh,Pearl
Harbor(c) 3,500.00
31 BEv,CBu,Human Torch(c) . . 4,200.00
32 CBu,I:The Boboes 3,200.00
33 ASh(c),CBu,SSh,Jap(c) 3,000.00
34 ASh(c),CBu,SSh,V:Hitler . . . 3,500.00
35 ASh(c),SSh,BeachAssault(c) 3,000.00
36 ASh(c),Nazi Invasion of NY . 3,000.00
37 SSh(c),Nazi(c) 3,000.00
38 ASh(c),Battlefield(c). 3,000.00
39 ASh(c),Nazis/U.S(c) 3,000.00
40 ASh(c),SSh,Zeppelin(c) . . . 3,000.00
41 ASh(c),Jap. Command(c) . . 2,500.00
42 ASh(c),Japanese Sub(c) . . . 2,500.00
43 ASh(c),SSh,Destroyed
Bridge(c) 2,500.00
44 ASh(c),Nazi Super Plane(c). 2,500.00
45 ASh(c),SSh,Nazi(c) 2,500.00
46 ASh(c),Hitler Bondage(c) . . . 2,500.00
47 ASh(c),Ruhr Valley Dam(c) . 2,500.00
48 ASh(c),E:Jimmy Jupiter,
Vision,Allied Invasion(c) . . . 2,500.00
49 SSh(c),O:Miss America,
Bondage(c) 3,000.00
50 ASh(c),Bondage(c),Miss
Patriot 2,700.00
51 ASh(c),Nazi Torture(c) 2,400.00
52 ASh(c),Bondage(c). 2,400.00
53 ASh(c),Bondage(c). 2,400.00
54 ASh(c),Bondage(c). 2,400.00
55 ASh(c),Bondage(c). 2,400.00
56 ASh(c),Bondage(c). 2,400.00
57 ASh(c),Torture/Bondage(c) . 2,400.00
58 ASh(c),Torture(c). 2,400.00
59 ASh(c),Testing Room(c). . . . 2,400.00
60 ASh(c),Japanese Gun(c) . . . 2,400.00
61 ASh(c),Torturer Chamber(c). 2,400.00
62 ASh(c),Violent(c) 2,400.00
63 ASh(c),Nazi High
Command(c). 2,400.00
64 ASh(c),Last Nazi(c) 2,400.00
65 ASh(c),Bondage(c). 2,400.00
66 ASh(c),Last Japanese(c) . . . 2,400.00
67 ASh(c),Treasury raid(c) 2,400.00
68 ASh(c),Torture Chamber(c) . 3,000.00
69 ASh(c),Torture Chamber(c) . 2,200.00
70 Cops & Robbers(c) 2,200.00
71 ASh(c),Egyptian(c). 2,200.00
72 Police(c) 2,200.00
73 Werewolf Headlines(c). 2,200.00
74 ASh(c),Robbery(c),E:The
Patriot 2,200.00
75 SSh,Tavern(c),B:YoungAllies 2,200.00
76 ASh(c),Shoot-out(c),B:Miss
America 2,200.00
77 SSh,Human Torch/Sub-
Mariner(c) 2,200.00
78 SSh,Safe Robbery(c). 2,200.00
79 SSh,Super Villians(c),E:The
Angel 2,200.00
80 SSh,I:Capt.America
(in Marvel) 2,500.00
81 SSh,Mystery o/t Crimson
Terror 2,000.00
82 SSh,I:Sub-Mariner/Namora
Team-up, O:Namora,A:Capt.
America 4,500.00
83 SSh,The Photo Phantom,
E;Young Allies. 1,700.00
84 SSh,BEv,B:Blonde Phantom 2,500.00
85 SSh,BEv,A:Blonde Phantom,
E;Miss America. 1,800.00
86 BEv,Blonde Phantom ID
Revealed,E:Bucky 1,700.00
87 SSh,BEv,I:Capt.America/Golden
Girl Team-up 2,500.00
88 SSh,BEv,E:Toro 1,700.00

89 SSh,BEv,AAv,I:Human Torch/
Sun Girl Team-up 1,700.00
90 BEv,Giant of the Mountains 1,700.00
91 BEv,I:Venus,E:Blonde
Phantom,Sub-Mariner 1,700.00
92 BEv,How the Human Torch was
Born,D:Professor Horton,I:The
Witness,A:Capt.America. . . 5,500.00
92a Marvel #33(c)rare,reps. . . 40,000.00
Becomes:

MARVEL TALES
Aug., 1949

93 The Ghoul Strikes 2,200.00
94 BEv,The Haunted Love 1,400.00
95 The Living Death. 950.00
96 MSy,SSh(c),Monster Returns . 950.00
97 DRi,MSy,The Wooden
Horror 1,200.00
98 BEv,BK,MSy,The Curse of
the Black Cat 1,000.00
99 DRi,The Secret of the Wax
Museum. 900.00
100 The Eyes of Doom. 1,000.00
101 The Man Who Died Twice . . 900.00
102 BW,A Witch Among Us . . . 1,300.00
103 RA,A Touch of Death 1,000.00
104 RH(c),BW,BEv,The Thing
in the Mirror 1,300.00
105 RH(c),GC,JSt,The Spider. . 1,000.00
106 RH(c),BK,BEv,In The Dead of
the Night 750.00
107 GC,OW,BK,The Thing in the
Sewer 750.00
108 RH(c),BEv,JR,Horror in the
Moonlight 500.00
109 BEv(c),Sight for Sore Eyes. . 500.00
110 RH,SSh,A Coffin for Carlos . 500.00
111 BEv,Horror Under the Earth . 500.00
112 The House That Death Built . 500.00
113 RH,Terror Tale. 500.00
114 BEv(c),GT,JM,2 for Zombie. . 500.00
115 The Man With No Face. 500.00
116 JSt. 500.00
117 BEv(c),GK,Terror in the
North. 500.00
118 RH,DBr,GC,A World
Goes Mad 500.00
119 RH,They Gave Him A Grave. 500.00
120 GC,Graveyard(c) 500.00
121 GC,Graveyard(c) 400.00
122 JKu,Missing One Body 400.00
123 No Way Out 400.00
124 He Waits at the Tombstone. . 400.00
125 JF,Horror House 400.00
126 DW,It Came From Nowhere . 375.00

Marvel Tales #96
© Marvel Entertainment Group

127 BEv(c),GC,MD,Gone is the
   Gargoyle 375.00
128 Emily,Flying Saucer(c) 375.00
129 You Can't Touch Bottom . . . 375.00
130 RH(c),JF,The Giant Killer . . . 375.00
131 GC,BEv,Five Fingers 375.00
132 . . . . 250.00
133 . . . . 250.00
134 BK,JKu,Flying Saucer(c). . . . 250.00
135 thru 143 . . . . @250.00
144 AW 265.00
145 . . . . 250.00
146 MD 200.00
147 BEv 250.00
148 thru 151 BEv . . . . @225.00
152 JMn 225.00
153 BEv 250.00
154 thru 158 . . . . @200.00
159 Aug., 1957 . . . . 225.00

MARVEL COMICS
PRESENTS
Sept., 1988

1 WS(c),B:Wolverine(JB,KJ),Master
  of Kung Fu(TS),Man-Thing(TGr,DC)
  F:Silver Surfer(AM) 10.00
2 F:The Captain(AM) 5.00
3 JR2(c),F:The Thing(AM) 5.00
4 F:Thor(AM) 5.00
5 F:Daredevil(DT,MG) 5.00
6 F:Hulk 4.00
7 F:Submariner(SD) 4.00
8 CV(c),E:Master of Kung Fu,F:
  Iron Man(JS) 4.00
9 F:Cloak,El Aquila 4.00
10 E:Wolverine,B:Colossus(RL,CR),
  F:Machine Man(SD,DC) 4.00
11 F:Ant-Man(BL),Slag(RWi) 3.00
12 E:Man-Thing,F:Hercules(DH),
  Namorita(FS) 3.00
13 B:Black Panther(GC,TP),F:
  Shanna,Mr.Fantastic &
  Invisible Woman 3.00
14 F:Nomad(CP),Speedball(SD) . . . 3.00
15 F:Marvel Girl(DT,MG),Red
  Wolf(JS). 3.00
16 F:Ka-Zar(JM),Longshot(AA) 3.00
17 E:Colossus,B:Cyclops(RLm),
  F:Watcher(TS) 4.00
18 F:She-Hulk(JB,BWi),Willie
  Lumpkin(JSt) 3.00
19 RLd(c)B:Dr.Strange(MBg),
  I:Damage Control(EC,AW) 3.00
20 E:Dr.Strange,F:Clea(RLm) 3.00
21 F:Thing,Paladin(RWi,DA) 3.00
22 F:Starfox(DC),Wolfsbane &
  Mirage 3.00
23 F:Falcon(DC),Wheels(RWi) 3.00
24 E:Cyclops,B:Havok(RB,JRu),
  F:Shamrock(DJ,DA) 3.00
25 F:Ursa Major,I:Nth Man. 4.00
26 B&I:Coldblood(PG),F:Hulk 2.50
27 F:American Eagle(RWi) 2.50
28 F:Triton(JS) 2.50
29 F:Quasar(PR) 2.50
30 F:Leir(TMo) 2.50
31 EL,E:Havok,B:Excalibur
  (EL,TA) 4.00
32 TM(c),F:Sunfire(DH,DC) 3.00
33 F:Namor(JLe) 4.00
34 F:Captain America(JsP) 3.00
35 E:Coldblood,F:Her(EL,AG) 4.00
36 BSz(c),F:Hellcat(JBr) 4.00
37 E:Bl.Panther,F:Devil-Slayer 3.00
38 E:Excalibur,B:Wonderman(JS),
  Wolverine(JB),F:Hulk(MR,DA). . 4.00
39 F:Hercules(BL),Spider-Man 3.50
40 F:Hercules(BL),Overmind(DH) . . 3.50
41 F:Daughters of the Dragon(DA),
  Union Jack(KD) 3.50
42 F:Iron Man(MBa),Siryn(LSn). . . . 3.50

43 F:Iron Man(MBa),Siryn(LSn). . . . 3.50
44 F:Puma(BWi),Dr.Strange 3.50
45 E:Wonderman,F:Hulk(HT),
  Shooting Star. 3.50
46 RLd(c),B:Devil-Slayer,F:Namor,
  Aquarian 3.50
47 JBy(c),E:Wolverine,F:Captain
  America,Arabian Knight(DP) . . . 3.50
48 B:Wolverine&Spider-Man(EL),
  F:Wasp,Storm&Dr.Doom 5.00
49 E:Devil-Slayer,F:Daredevil(RWi),
  Gladiator(DH) 4.50
50 E:Wolverine&Spider-Man,B:Comet
  Man(KJo),F:Captain Ultra(DJ),
  Silver Surfer(JkS) 4.50
51 B:Wolverine(RLd),F:Iron Man
  (MBr,DH),Le Peregrine 4.00
52 F:Rick Jones,Hulk(RWi,TMo) . . . 4.00
53 E:Wolverine,Comet Man,F:
  Silver Sable&Black Widow
  (RLd,BWi),B:Stingray. 4.00
54 B:Wolverine&Hulk(DR),
  Werewolf,F:Shroud(SD,BWi). . . 6.00
55 F:Collective Man(GLa) 6.00
56 E:Stingray,F:Speedball(SD) 6.00
57 DK(c),B:Submariner(MC,MFm),
  Black Cat(JRu) 6.00
58 F:Iron Man(SD) 6.00
59 E:Submariner,Werewolf,
  F:Punisher 6.00
60 B:Poison,Scarlet Witch,
  F:Captain America(TL) 6.00
61 E:Wolverine&Hulk,
  F:Dr.Strange 6.00
62 F:Wolverine(PR),Deathlok(JG) . . 6.00
63 F:Wolverine(PR),E:Scarlet
  Witch,Thor(DH) 4.00
64 B:Wolverine&Ghost Rider(MT),
  Fantastic Four(TMo),F:Blade. . . 4.00
65 F:Starfox(ECh) 3.50
66 F:Volstagg 3.50
67 E:Poison,F:Spider-Man(MG). . . . 3.50
68 B:Shanna(PG),E:Fantastic Four
  F:Lockjaw(JA,AM) 3.50
69 B:Daredevil(DT),F:Silver Surfer . 3.50
70 F:BlackWidow&Darkstar(AM) . . . 3.50
71 E:Wolverine&Ghost Rider,F:
  Warlock(New Mutants)(SMc). . . 3.50
72 B:Weapon X(BWS),E:Daredevil,
  F:Red Wolf(JS) 7.00
73 F:Black Knight(DC),
  Namor(JM). 5.00
74 F:Constrictor(SMc),Iceman &
  Human Torch(JSon,DA). 5.00
75 F:Meggan & Shadowcat,
  Dr.Doom(DC). 5.00
76 F:Death's Head(BHi,MFm),
  A:Woodgod(DC) 5.00
77 F:Shanna,B:Sgt.Fury&Dracula
  (TL,JRu),F:Namor 4.50
78 F:Iron Man(KSy),Hulk&Selene . . 4.50
79 F:Sgt.Fury&Dracula,F:Dr.Strange,
  Sunspot(JBy). 4.50
80 F:Daughters of the Dragon,Mister
  Fantastic(DJ),Captain America
  (SD,TA) 4.50
81 F:Captain America(SD,TA),
  Daredevil(MR,AW),Ant-Man . . . 4.00
82 B:Firestar(DT),F:Iron Man(SL),
  Power Man 4.00
83 F:Hawkeye,Hum.Torch(SD,EL) . 4.00
84 E:Weapon X 4.00
85 B:Wolverine(SK),Beast(RLd,JaL-
  1st Work),F:Speedball(RWi),
  I:Cyber 7.00
86 F:PaladinE:RLd on Beast 5.00
87 E:Firestar,F:Shroud(RWi) 5.00
88 F:Solo,Volcana(BWi). 5.00
89 F:Spitfire(JSn),Mojo(JMa) 5.00
90 B:Ghost Rider & Cable,F:
  Nightmare 4.50
91 F:Impossible Man 3.50

Marvel Comics Presents #47
© Marvel Entertainment Group

92 E:Wolverine,Beast,
  F:Northstar(JMa) 3.50
93 SK(c),B:Wolverine,Nova,
  F:Daredevil 3.00
94 F:Gabriel 3.00
95 SK(c),E:Wolverine,F:Hulk 3.00
96 B:Wolverine(TT),E:Nova,
  F:Speedball 3.00
97 F:Chameleon,Two-Gun Kid,
  E:Ghost Rider/Cable 3.00
98 E:Wolverine,F:Ghost Rider,
  Werewolf by Night 2.50
99 F:Wolverine,Ghost Rider,
  Mary Jane,Captain America. . . . 2.50
100 SK,F:Ghost Rider,Wolverine,
  Dr.Doom,Nightmare 3.00
101 SK(c),B:Ghost Rider&Doctor
  Strange,Young Gods,Wolverine
  &Nightcrawler,F:Bar With
  No Name 2.50
102 RL,GC,AW,F:Speedball 2.50
103 RL,GC,AW,F:Puck 2.50
104 RL,GC,AW,F:Lockheed. 2.50
105 RL,GC,AW,F:Nightmare 2.50
106 RL,GC,AW,F:Gabriel,E:Ghost
  Rider&Dr.Strange. 2.50
107 GC,AW,TS,B:Ghost Rider&
  Werewolf 2.50
108 GC,AW,TS,SMc,E:Wolverine&
  Nightcrawler,B:Thanos 2.50
109 SLi,TS,SMc,B:Wolverine&
  Typhoid Mary,E:Young Gods . . . 2.50
110 SLi,SMc,F:Nightcrawler. 2.50
111 SK(c),SLi,RWi,F:Dr.Strange,
  E:Thanos 2.50
112 SK(c),SLi,F:Pip,Wonder Man,
  E:Ghost Rider&Werewolf. 2.50
113 SK(c),SLi,B:Giant Man,
  Ghost Rider&Iron Fist 2.50
114 SK(c),SLi,F:Arabian Knight 2.50
115 SK(c),SLi,F:Cloak&Dagger 2.50
116 SK(c),SLi,E:Wolverine &
  Typhoid Mary 2.50
117 SK,PR,B:Wolverine&Venom,
  I:Ravage 2099 . . . . 4.00
118 SK,PB,RWi,E:Giant Man,
  I:Doom 2099 . . . . 3.00
119 SK,GC,B:Constrictor,E:Ghost
  Rider&Iron Fist,F:Wonder Man . 3.00
120 SK,GC,E:Constrictor,B:Ghost
  Rider/Cloak & Dagger,
  F:Spider-Man 2.50
121 SK,GC,F:Mirage,Andromeda . . 2.50

122 SK(c),GK,E:Wolverine&Venom,
   Ghost Rider&Cloak&Dagger,F:
   Speedball&Rage,Two-Gun Kid . 2.50
123 SK(c),DJ,SLi,B:Wolverine&Lynx,
   Ghost Rider&Typhoid Mary,
   She-Hulk,F:Master Man 2.50
124 SK(c),DJ,MBa,SLi,F:Solo 2.50
125 SLi,SMc,DJ,B:Iron Fist 2.50
126 SLi,DJ,E:She-Hulk 2.50
127 SLi,DJ,DP,F:Speedball 2.50
128 SLi,DJ,RWi,F:American Eagle . 2.50
129 SLi,DJ,F:Ant Man 2.50
130 DJ,SLi,RWi,E:Wolverine&Lynx,
   Ghost Rider&Typhoid Mary,Iron
   Fist,F:American Eagle 2.50
131 MFm,B:Wolverine,Ghost Rider&
   Cage,Iron Fist&Sabretooth,
   F:Shadowcat 2.50
132 KM(c),F:Iron Man 2.50
133 F:Cloak & Dagger 2.50
134 SLi,F:Vance Astro 2.50
135 SLi,F:Daredevil 2.50
136 B:Gh.Rider&Masters of Silence,
   F:Iron Fist,Daredevil 2.50
137 F:Ant Man 2.50
138 B:Wolverine,Spellbound 2.50
139 F:Foreigner 2.50
140 F:Captain Universe 2.50
141 BCe(s),F:Iron Fist 2.50
142 E:Gh.Rider&Masters of Silence,
   F:Mr.Fantastic 2.50
143 Siege of Darkness,pt.#3,
   B:Werewolf,Scarlet Witch,
   E:Spellbound 2.50
144 Siege of Darkness,pt.#6,
   B:Morbius 2.50
145 Siege of Darkness,pt.#11 . . . . . 2.50
146 Siege of Darkness,pt.#14 . . . . . 2.50
147 B:Vengeance,F:Falcon,Masters of
   Silence,American Eagle 2.50
148 E:Vengeance,F:Capt.Universe,
   Black Panther 2.50
149 F:Daughter o/t Dragon,Namor,
   Vengeance,Starjammers 2.50
150 ANo(s),SLi,F:Typhoid Mary,DD,
   Vengeance,Wolverine 2.50
151 ANo(s),F:Typhoid Mary,DD,
   Vengeance 2.50
152 CDi(s),PR,B:Vengeance,Wolverine,
   War Machine,Moon Knight 2.50
153 CDi(s),A:Vengeance,Wolverine,
   War Machine,Moon Knight 2.50
154 CDi(s),E:Vengeance,Wolverine,
   War Machine,Moon Knight 2.50

Marvel Comics Presents #163
© Marvel Entertainment Group

155 CDi(s),B:Vengeance,Wolverine,
   War Machine,Kymaera 2.50
156 B:Shang Chi,F:Destroyer 2.50
157 F:Nick Fury 2.50
158 AD,I:Clan Destine,E:Kymaera,
   Shang Chi,Vengeance 2.50
159 B:Hawkeye, New Warriors,
   F:Fun,E:Vengeance 2.50
160 B:Vengeance,Mace 2.50
161 E:Hawkeye 2.50
162 B:Tigra,E:Mace 2.50
163 E:New Warriors 2.50
164 Tigra, Vengeance 2.50
165 Tigra, Vengeance 2.50
166 Turbo, Vengeance 2.50
167 Turbo, Vengeance 2.50
168 Thing, Vengeance 2.50
169 Mandarin, Vengeance 2.50
170 Force, Vengeance 2.50
171 Nick Fury 2.50
172 Lunatik 2.50
173 . . . . 2.50
174 . . . . 2.50
175 . . . . 2.50

MARVEL COMICS PRESENTS
Sept., 2007

1 F:Hellcat 4.00
2 F:Hellcat 4.00
3 F:Magneto 4.00

MARVEL COMICS SUPER SPECIAL
[Magazine, 1977]

1 JB,WS,Kiss,Features &Photos 200.00
2 JB,Conan(1978) 25.00
3 WS,Close Encounters 15.00
4 GP,KJ,Beatles story 65.00
Becomes:

MARVEL SUPER SPECIAL

5 Kiss 1978 . . . . 200.00
6 GC,Jaws II 15.00
7 Does Not Exist
8 Battlestar Galactica(Tabloid) . . . 20.00
9 Conan 15.00
10 GC,Starlord 11.00
11 JB,RN,Weirdworld 11.00
12 JB,Weirdworld, ... 11.00
13 JB,Weirdworld, ... 11.00
14 GC,Meteor,adapt. 11.00
15 Star Trek 11.00
15a Star Trek 12.00
16 AW,B:Movie Adapts,Empire
   Strikes Back. 12.00
17 Xanadu 7.00
18 HC(c),JB,Raiders of the Lost
   Ark 7.00
19 HC,For Your Eyes Only 9.00
20 Dragonslayer 7.00
21 JB,Conan 7.00
22 JSo(c),AW,Bladerunner 9.00
23 Annie 9.00
24 Dark Crystal 9.00
25 Rock and Rule 9.00
26 Octopussy 8.00
27 AW,Return of the Jedi 9.00
28 PH(c),Krull. 8.00
29 DSp,Tarzan of the Apes 8.00
30 Indiana Jones and the Temple
   of Doom 9.00
31 The Last Star Fighter 9.00
32 Muppets Take Manhattan 9.00
33 Buckaroo Banzai. 11.00
34 GM,Sheena. 9.00
35 JB,Conan The Destroyer 9.00
36 Dune 9.00
37 2010 . . . . 9.00
38 Red Sonja. 9.00
39 Santa Claus 9.00

40 JB,Labrynth 9.00
41 Howard the Duck,Nov.,1986. . . . 9.00

MARVEL DOUBLE FEATURE
Dec., 1973

1 JK,GC,B:Tales of Suspense
   Reprints,Capt.America,
   Iron-Man 20.00
2 JK,GC ,A:Nick Fury 15.00
3 JK,GC 15.00
4 JK,GC,Cosmic Cube 15.00
5 JK,GC,V:Red Skull 15.00
6 JK,GC,V:Adaptoid 15.00
7 JK,GC,V:Tumbler 15.00
8 JK,GC,V:Super Adaptoid 15.00
9 GC,V:Batroc 15.00
10 GC. 15.00
11 GC,Capt.America Wanted. 10.00
12 GC,V:Powerman,Swordsman . . 10.00
13 GC,A:Bucky 10.00
14 GC,V:Red Skull 10.00
15 GK,GC,V:Red Skull. 10.00
16 GC,V;Assassin 10.00
17 JK,GC,V:Aim,Iron Man &
   Sub-Mariner #1 . . . . 10.00
18 JK,GC,V:Modok,Iron Man #1 . . 10.00
19 JK,GC,E:Capt.America 10.00
20 JK(c) 9.00
21 Capt.America,Black Panther
   March, 1977 . . . . 9.00

MARVEL DOUBLE-SHOT
Nov., 2002

1 JJu(c),Hulk, Thor 3.00
2 JJu(c),Doom & Avengers. 3.00
3 JJu(c),F:Mr. Fantastic 3.00
4 JJu(c),F:Iron Man. 3.00

MARVEL FANFARE
March, 1972

1 MG,TA,PS,F:Spider-Man,
   Daredevil,Angel 15.00
2 MG,SM,FF,TVe,F:SpM,Ka-Zar. . 10.00
3 DC,F:X-Men. 10.00
4 PS,TA,MG,F:X-Men,Deathlok . . 10.00
5 MR,F:Dr.Strange 8.00
6 F:Spider-Man,Scarlet Witch. . . . 9.00
7 F:Hulk/Daredevil 6.00
8 CI,TA,GK,F:Dr.Strange 6.00
9 GM,F:Man Thing 6.00
10 GP,B:Black Widow 7.00
11 GP,D:M.Corcoran 7.00
12 GP,V:Snapdragon 7.00
13 GP,E:B.Widow,V:Snapdragon . . 7.00
14 F:Fantastic Four,Vision 3.00
15 BWS,F:Thing,Human Torch 3.00
16 DC,JSt,F:Skywolf 2.50
17 DC,JSt,F:Skywolf 2.50
18 FM,JRu,F:Captain America. 3.00
19 RL,F:Cloak and Dagger 2.50
20 JSn,F:Thing&Dr.Strange 3.00
21 JSn,F:Thing And Hulk 3.00
22 KSy,F:Iron Man 2.50
23 KSy,F:Iron Man 2.50
24 F:Weird World 3.00
25 F:Weird World 2.50
26 F:Weird World 2.50
27 F:Daredevil 2.50
28 KSy,F:Alpha Flight 2.50
29 JBy,F:Hulk. 3.00
30 BA,AW,F:Moon Knight 2.50
31 KGa,F:Capt.America,
   Yellow Claw 2.50
32 KGa,PS,F:Capt.America,
   Yellow Claw 2.50
33 JBr,F:X-Men 5.00
34 CV,F:Warriors Three 2.50
35 CV,F:Warriors Three 2.50
36 CV,F:Warriors Three 2.50

37 CV,F:Warriors Three 2.50
38 F:Captain America 2.50
39 JSon,F:Hawkeye,Moon Knight . . 2.50
40 DM,F:Angel,Storm,Mystique 3.00
41 DGb,F:Dr.Strange 2.50
42 F:Spider-Man 3.00
43 F:Sub-Mariner,Human Torch. . . 2.50
44 KSy,F:Iron Man vs.Dr.Doom 2.50
45 All Pin-up Issue,WS,AAd,MZ,
    JOy,BSz,KJ,HC,PS,JBy. 3.00
46 F:Fantastic Four 2.50
47 MG,F:Spider-Man,Hulk 3.00
48 KGa,F:She-Hulk 2.50
49 F:Dr.Strange 2.50
50 JSon,JRu,F:Angel. 3.00
51 JB,JA,GC,AW,F:Silver Surfer . . 4.00
52 F:Fantastic Four 2.50
53 GC,AW,F:Bl.Knight,Dr.Strange . . 2.50
54 F:Black Knight,Wolverine 3.50
55 F:Powerpack,Wolverine 3.50
56 CI,DH,F:Shanna t/She-Devil. . . . 2.50
57 BBl,AM,F:Shanna,Cap.Marvel . . 2.50
58 BBl,F:Shanna,Vision/Sc.Witch . . 2.50
59 BBl,F:Shanna,Hellcat 2.50
60 PS,F:Daredevil,Capt.Marvel 2.50

MARVEL FANFARE
Second Series 1996
1 Captain America, Falcon 2.25
2 New Fantastic Four 2.25
3 BbB,F:Spider-Man, Ghost Rider,. 2.25
4 F:Longshot. 2.25
5 F:Longshot. 2.25
6 F:Power Man & Iron Fist V:
    Sabretooth. 2.25

MARVEL FEATURE
[1st Regular Series]
Dec., 1971
1 RA,BE,NA,I&O:Defenders &
    Omegatron. 250.00
2 BEv,F:The Defenders 125.00
3 BEv,F:The Defenders 100.00
4 F:Ant-Man 45.00
5 F:Ant-Man 25.00
6 F:Ant-Man 20.00
7 CR,F:Ant-Man 20.00
8 JSc,CR,F:Ant-Man,O:Wasp . . . 20.00
9 CR,F:Ant-Man 20.00
10 CR,F:Ant-Man. 20.00
11 JSn,JSt,F:Thing & Hulk 90.00
12 JSn,JSt,F:Thing,Iron Man,
    Thanos,Blood Brothers 50.00

[2nd Regular Series]
(All issues feature Red Sonja)
1 DG,The Temple of Abomination. 12.00
2 FT,Blood of the Hunter. 7.00
3 FT,Balek Lives 7.00
4 FT,Eyes of the Gorgon. 8.00
5 FT,The Bear God Walks 8.00
6 FT,C:Conan,Belit 8.00
7 FT,V:Conan,A:Belit,Conan#68. . 12.00

MARVEL FRONTIER
COMICS SPECIAL
1 All Frontier Characters. 3.25
1994 . . . . 3.00

MARVEL GRAPHIC NOVEL
1982
1 JSn,D:Captain Marvel,A:Most
    Marvel Characters. 30.00
1a 2nd printing 10.00
1b 3rd-5th printing. 8.00
2 F:Elric,Dreaming City. 12.00
2a 2nd printing 7.00
3 JSn,F:Dreadstar. 15.00
3a 2nd-3rd printing 7.00

Marvel Graphic Novel #10
© *Marvel Entertainment Group*

4 BMc,I:New Mutants,Cannonball
    Sunspot,Psyche,Wolfsbane. . . 22.00
4a 2nd printing 10.00
4b 3rd-4th printing. 8.00
5 BA,F:X-Men. 22.00
5a 2nd printing 9.00
5b 3rd-5th printing. 7.00
6 WS,F:Starslammers. 10.00
6a 2nd printing 7.00
7 CR,F:Killraven 10.00
8 RWi,AG,F:Super Boxers 10.00
8a 2nd printing 7.00
9 DC,F:Futurians 12.00
9a 2nd printing 7.00
10 RV,F:Heartburst 10.00
10a 2nd printing. 6.00
11 VM,F:Void Indigo. 12.00
12 F:Dazzler the Movie 10.00
12a 2nd printing. 6.00
13 MK,F:Starstruck 10.00
14 JG,F:SwordsofSwashbucklers . 10.00
15 CV,F:Raven Banner 10.00
16 GLa,F:Alladin Effect 10.00
17 MS,F:Living Monolith 10.00
18 JBy,F:She-Hulk 15.00
18 later printings 14.00
19 F:Conan 15.00
20 F:Greenberg the Vampire 10.00
21 JBo,F:Marada the She-wolf . . . 10.00
22 BWr,Hooky,F:Spider-Man 16.00
23 DGr,F:Dr.Strange 10.00
24 FM,BSz,F:Daredevil 15.00
25 F:Dracula 10.00
26 FC,TA,F:Alien Legion 15.00
27 BH,F:Avengers 15.00
28 JSe,F:Conan the Reaver 16.00
29 BWr,F:Thing & Hulk 10.00
30 F:A Sailor's Story 10.00
31 F:Wolf Pack 10.00
32 SA,F:Death of Groo 17.00
33 F:Thor. 10.00
34 AW,F:Cloak & Dagger. 10.00
35 MK/RH,F:The Shadow 18.00
36 F:Willow movie adaption. 10.00
37 BL,F:Hercules. 15.00
38 JB,F:Silver Surfer 20.00
39 F:Iron Man,Crash 14.50
40 JZ,F:The Punisher 12.00
41 F:Roger Rabbit 10.00
42 F:Conan of the Isles 15.00
43 EC,F:Ax. 12.00
44 BJ,F:Arena 10.00
45 JRy,F:Dr.Who 12.00
46 TD,F:Kull. 10.00
47 GM,F:Dreamwalker. 10.00
48 F:Sailor's Storm II 10.00
49 MBd,F:Dr.Strange&Dr.Doom. . . 25.00

50 F:Spider-Man,Parallel Lives . . . 12.00
51 F:Punisher,Intruder 14.00
52 DSp,F:Roger Rabbit 12.00
53 PG,F:Conan 12.00
54 HC,F:Wolverine & Nick Fury. . . 20.00

MARVEL HALLOWEEN: THE SUPERNATURALS TOUR BOOK
Sept., 1999
1-shot, 16-page, cardstock cov 3.00

MARVEL HEROES
1 StL,FaN,Mega-Jam,48-pg.. . . . . 3.00

MARVEL HEROES
Flipbook, June, 2005
1 New Avengers #1
    & Captain America #1 . . . . 4.00
2 New Aveng.#2 & Cap.Am.#2. . . . 4.00
3 New Aveng.#3 & Cap.Am.#3 . . . 4.00
4 New Aveng.#4 & Cap.am.#4 . . . 4.00
5 New Aveng.#5 & Cap.Am.#5 . . . 4.00
6 thru 13 . . . . @4.00
14 thru 17 . . . . @5.00

MARVEL: HEROES AND LEGENDS 1997
Aug., 1997
1-shot, Stan Lee, JR(c) 6.00

MARVEL HOLIDAY SPECIAL
1991–2006
1 AAd (1991). 4.00
n/n RLm,JSn,TA (1993) 3.50
n/n StG(s),PDd(s),RLm,PB (1994). . 3.25
1-shot MWa,KK (1996) 3.00
1-shot Marvel Holiday Special 2004 3.00
1-shot Marvel Holiday (2006). 8.00
1-shot Marvel Holiday (2007). 4.00

MARVEL ILLUSTRATED
July, 2007
1 Man in the Iron Mask. 3.00
2 thru 4 Man in the Iron Mask. . . @3.00

MARVEL ILLUSTRATED
June, 2007
1 Treasure Island 3.00
2 thru 5 Treasure Island . . . . @3.00

MARVEL ILLUSTRATED
May, 2007
1 Last of the Mohicans 3.00
2 thru 6 Last of the Mohicans . . . @3.00

MARVEL ILLUSTRATED
Nov., 2007
1 Picture of Dorian Gray. 3.00
2 thru 5 Man in the Iron Mask. . . @3.00
2 thru 6 Treasure Island . . . . @3.00

MARVEL KIDS
1999
Fantastic Four: Franklin's
    Adventures 3.50
Incredible Hulk: Project Hide 3.50
Spider-Man Mysteries 3.50
X-Men: Mutant Search R.U.1. . . . . 3.50

MARVEL KNIGHTS
May, 2000
1 JQ,JP,KJ 3.50
2A JQ,KJ,CDi,EB,V:Ulik 3.00

MARVEL

2B variant EB(c) 3.00
3 JQ,KJ,CDi,EB,V:Ulik 3.00
4 JQ,KJ,CDi,EB,Zaran 3.00
5 JQ,KJ,CDi,EB,DaddyWronglegs . 3.00
6 JQ,KJ,CDi,EB,MaximumSecurity. 3.00
7 JQ,KJ,CDi,EB,F:Dr.Strange 3.00
8 JQ,CDi,EB,V:Cloak 3.00
9 JQ,CDi,EB,Dagger vs. Cloak. . . . 3.00
10 JQ,CDi,EB,Punisher 3.00
11 CDi,EB,Luke Cage,Power Man. . 3.00
12 CDi,EB,A:Cloak. 3.00
13 CDi,EB,A:Black Widow,Dagger . 3.00
14 CDi,EB,one quits 3.00
15 CDi,EB,V:S.H.I.E.L.D. 3.00
GN Millennial Visions,TyH,48-pg. . . 4.00

MARVEL KNIGHTS
March, 2002
1 Punisher,Daredevil,Black Widow. 3.00
2 thru 6 . . . . @3.00

MARVEL KNIGHTS:
DOUBLE-SHOT
Oct., 2001
1 GEn,JQ,Daredevil & Punisher . . . 3.00
2 GEn,Nick Fury & Man-Thing 3.00
3 GF(c),Elektra & Cloak&Daggar . . 3.00
4 GeH,GF(c),Iron Fist 3.00
5 GeH,GF(c),Daredevil 3.00

MARVEL KNIGHTS 4
Feb., 2004
1 Wolf at the Door,pt.1 . . . . 3.00
2 thru 4 Wolf at the Door. . . . . . . @3.00
5 thru 7 The Pine Barrens. . . . . . @3.00
8 Frozen,pt.1. . . . . 3.00
9 Frozen,pt.2. . . . . 3.00
10 Stuff of Dreams,pt.1 . . . . 3.00
11 Stuff of Dreams,pt.2 . . . . 3.00
12 Stuff of Dreams,pt.3 . . . . 3.00
13 Eyes Without a Face 3.00
14 Eyes Without a Face 3.00
15 Divine Time, prologue 3.00
16 Divine Time. 3.00
17 Divine Time. 3.00
18 Divine Time. 3.00
19 Inhumane,pt.1. . . . . 3.00
20 Inhumane,pt.2. . . . . 3.00
21 Desperate Housewife. 3.00
22 The Yancy Street Golem. 3.00
23 F:Impossible Man 3.00
24 F:Impossible Man 3.00
25 Resurrection of Nicholas Scratch 3.00
26 Resurrection of Nicholas Scratch 3.00
27 Resurrection of Nicholas Scratch 3.00
28 Private Lives/Public Faces 3.00
29 Super Hero's Apprentice, pt.1. . . 3.00
30 Super Hero's Apprentice, pt.2. . . 3.00

MARVEL KNIGHTS
SPIDER-MAN
April, 2004
1 TyD,Down Among the Dead,pt.1 . 3.00
2 TyD,Down Among the Dead,pt.2 . 3.00
3 TyD,Down Among the Dead,pt.3 . 3.00
4 TyD,Down Among the Dead,pt.4 . 3.00
5 Venomous,pt.1. . . . . 3.00
6 TyD,Venomous,pt.2 . . . . 3.00
7 TyD,Venomous,pt.3 . . . . 3.00
8 TyD,Venomous,pt.4 . . . . 3.00
9 TyD,The Last Stand,pt.1 . . . . 3.00
10 MMr,TyD,The Last Stand 3.00
11 MMr,TyD,V:Sinister Twelve 3.00
12 MMr,TyD,The Last Stand 3.00
13 BTn,Wild Blue Yonder 3.00
14 BTn,Wild Blue Yonder 3.00
15 BTn,Wild Blue Yonder 3.00
16 BTn,Wild Blue Yonder 3.00
17 BTn,Wild Blue Yonder 3.00

18 BTn,Wild Blue Yonder. 3.00
19 PDd(s), The Other,x-over,pt.2. . 3.00
20 PDd(s), The Other,x-over,pt.5. . 3.00
21 PDd(s), The Other,x-over,pt.8. . 3.00
22 PDd(s), The Other,x-over,pt.11 . 3.00
Digest Marvel Age, Vol. 1 . . . . 8.00
Becomes:

SENSATIONAL
SPIDER-MAN
Feb., 2006
23 AMe, Feral, pt.1 . . . . 3.00
24 AMe, Feral, pt.2 . . . . 3.00
25 AMe, Feral, pt.3 . . . . 3.00
26 AMe, Feral, pt.4 . . . . 3.00
27 AMe, Feral, pt.5 . . . . 3.00
28 AMe,War at Home tie-in 3.00
29 AMe,Deadly Foes of Spider-Man 3.00
30 AMe,Deadly Foes of Spider-Man 3.00
31 AMe,Deadly Foes of Spider-Man 3.00
32 The Husband or the Spider?. . . . 3.00
33 Wounds. 3.00
34 V:Black Cat 3.00
35 Strange Case of, pt.1 . . . . 4.00
36 Strange Case of, pt.2 . . . . 4.00
37 . . . . 4.00
38 Last Temptation, pt.1 . . . . 4.00
39 Last Temptation, pt.2 . . . . 4.00
40 The Book of Peter. 4.00
41 One More Day, pt.3 . . . . 4.00
Ann. #1 SvL, Till Death Do Us Part . 4.00

MARVEL KNIGHTS
TOUR BOOK
Aug., 1998
1-shot, cardstock cover 3.00

MARVEL KNIGHTS 2009
Sept., 2004
Spec. Daredevil #1. . . . . 3.00
Spec. Black Panther #1 . . . . 3.00
Spec. Inhumans #1 . . . . 3.00
Spec. Punisher #1 . . . . 3.00
Spec. Mutant #1. . . . . 3.00

MARVEL LEGACY
Feb., 2006
1 The 1960s Handbook 5.00
2 The 1970s Handbook 5.00
3 The 1980s Handbook 5.00
4 The 1990s Handbook 5.00

MARVEL:
THE LOST GENERATION
Jan., 2000
12 (of 12) JBy,AM,Fireball, Flatiron,
   Cassandra, Oxbow, etx. 3.00
11 JBy,AM,F:Justice. 3.00
10 JBy,AM,O:Walkabout 3.00
9 JBy,AM,Effigy,Black Fox 3.00
8 JBy,AM,Nocturne 3.00
7 JBy,AM,Knight Templar 3.00
6 JBy,AM,First Line 3.00
5 JBy,AM,F:Thor. 3.00
4 JBy,AM,Yankee Clipper 3.00
3 JBy,AM,Liberty Girl 3.00
2 JBy,AM,V:Yankee Clipper 3.00
1 JBy,AM,concl. 3.00

MARVEL MAGIC
HANDBOOK
May, 2007
Spec. 64-pgs. 4.00

MARVEL MANGAVERSE
Jan., 2002
New Dawn #1 BDn 3.00

Marvel Mangaverse Spider-Man #1
© Marvel Entertainment Group

Avengers #1 . . . . 2.25
Fantastic Four #1 AWa 2.25
Ghost Rider #1 . . . . 2.25
Punisher #1 PDd(s) 2.25
Spider-Man #1 . . . . 2.25
X-Men #1 JMs 2.25
Eternal Twilight #1 BDn 3.00

MARVEL MANGAVERSE
April, 2002
1 BDn, F:Marvin Elwood. 3.00
2 BDn, Inhumans 2.25
3 BDn, V:Galactus 2.25
4 BDn, UN held hostage. 2.25
5 BDn 2.25
6 BDd, only Doom knows 2.25

MARVEL MASTERPIECES
COLLECTION
1993
1 Joe Jusko Masterpiece Cards . . . 3.25
2 F:Wolverine,Thanos,Apocalypse . 3.00
3 F:Gambit,Venom,Hulk 3.00
4 F:Wolverine Vs. Sabretooth. 3.00

MARVEL MASTERPIECES
II COLLECTION
1994
1 thru 3 w/cards . . . . @3.00

MARVEL MILESTONES
March, 2005
1 Iron Man, silver-age reps. 4.00
2 Venom & Hercules, reps. 4.00
3 Wolverine, X-Men, Tuk
   The Cave Boy, Silver Age Reps. 4.00
4 Dr. Doom, Sub-Mariner
   & Red Skull, silver-age reps. . . . 4.00
5 Dr. Strange, Silver Surfer
   Sub-mariner & Hulk, Reps. 4.00
6 Captain Britain, Psylocke
   Golden Age Sub-Mariner, reps. 4.00
7 Ghost Rider, Black Widow
   Iceman, Silver-age Reps. 4.00
8 Blade, Man-Thing, and
   Satanna, silver-age reps. 4.00
9 Ultimate Spider-Man, Ultimate
   X-Men, Microman 4.00
10 Bloodstone, X-51 & Captain
   Marvel II. 4.00
11 Dragon Lord, Speedball

and The Man in the Sky 4.00
12 Star Brand & Quasar 4.00
13 Beast & Kitty 4.00
14 Black Panther & Storm 4.00
15 Rawhid Kid & Two-Gun 4.00
16 Millie the Model & Patsy
　Walker 4.00
17 X-Men & The Starjammers 4.00
18 X-Men & The Starjammers 4.00
19 Legion of Monsters, Spider-
　Man and Brother Voodoo 4.00
20 Onslaught 4.00

MARVEL MINI-BOOKS
1966
(black & white)
1 F:Capt.America,Spider-Man,Hulk
　Thor,Sgt.Fury 75.00
2 F:Capt.America,Spider-Man,Hulk
　Thor,Sgt.Fury 75.00
3 F:Capt.America,Spider-Man,Hulk
　Thor,Sgt.Fury 75.00
4 thru 6 F:Capt.America,Spider-Man,
　Hulk,Thor,Sgt.Fury . . . . . . @75.00

MARVEL MONSTERS
Oct., 2005
1-shot Devil Dinosaur,rep. 4.00
1-shot Where Monsters Dwell, rep . 4.00
1-shot Fin Fang Four, rep. 4.00
1-shot Monsters on the Prowl, rep. . 4.00
1-shot Marvel Monsters 4.00

MARVEL MOVIE PREMIERE
B&W Magazine, 1975
1 Land That Time Forgot 20.00

MARVEL MOVIE SHOWCASE FEATURING STAR WARS
Nov., 1982
1 Rep,Stars Wars #1-6 . . . . 5.00
2 Dec., 1982 . . . . 5.00

MARVEL MOVIE SPOTLIGHT FEATURING RAIDERS OF THE LOST ARK
Nov., 1982
1 Rep,Raiders of Lost Ark#1-3 . . . 3.00

MARVEL MYSTERY COMICS
See: MARVEL COMICS

MARVEL MYSTERY COMICS
Oct., 1999
Spec. 80-pg. 4.00

MARVEL NEMESIS: THE IMPERFECTS
May, 2005
1 (of 6) Rise of the Imperfects . . . 3.00
2 Rise of the Imperfects 3.00
3 Birth of the Imperfects 3.00
4 JaL(c) 3.00
5 Jal(c) 3.00
6 Rise of the Imperfects, finale. . . 3.00

MARVEL NO-PRIZE BOOK
Jan., 1983
1 MGo(c),Stan Lee as
　Dr.Doom(c) 7.00

Marvel Portraits of a Universe #1
© Marvel Entertainment Group

MARVEL: PORTRAITS OF A UNIVERSE
1 Fully painted moments 3.00
2 Fully painted moments 3.00
3 F:Death of Elektra 3.00
4 final issue. 3.00

MARVEL POSTER BOOK
June, 2001
Summer 2001, 64-page 3.50
Winter 2001, 64-page 3.50

MARVEL PREMIERE
April, 1972
1 GK,O:Warlock,Receives Soul Gem,
　Creation of Counter Earth . . . 100.00
2 GK,JK,F:Warlock 50.00
3 BWS,F:Dr.Strange 90.00
4 FB,BWS,F:Dr.Strange 35.00
5 MP,CR,F:Dr.Strange,I:Sligguth . 30.00
6 MP,FB,F:Dr.Strange 25.00
7 MP,CR,F:Dr.Strange,I:Dagoth . . 25.00
8 JSn,F:Dr.Strange 25.00
9 NA,FB,F:Dr.Strange 25.00
10 FB,F:Dr.Strange,
　D:Ancient One 30.00
11 NA,FB,F:Dr.Strange,I:Shuma . . 15.00
12 NA,FB,F:Dr.Strange 15.00
13 NA,FB,F:Dr.Strange 15.00
14 NA,FB,F:Dr.Strange 15.00
15 GK,DG,I&O:Iron Fist,pt.1 . . . 125.00
16 DG,O:Iron Fist,pt.2,V:Scythe. . 50.00
17 DG,Citadel on the
　Edge of Vengeance 30.00
18 DG,V:Triple Irons 30.00
19 DG,A:Ninja 30.00
20 I:Misty Knight 30.00
21 V:Living Goddess 30.00
22 V:Ninja 30.00
23 PB,V:Warhawk 30.00
24 PB,V:Monstroid 30.00
25 1st JBy,AMc,E:Iron Fist. 35.00
26 JK,GT,F:Hercules 10.00
27 F:Satana 15.00
28 F:Legion Of Monsters,A:Ghost
　Rider,Morbius,Werewolf. 25.00
29 JK,I:Liberty Legion,
　O:Red Raven. 6.00
30 JK,F:Liberty Legion. 6.00

31 JK,I:Woodgod 6.00
32 HC,F:Monark. 5.00
33 HC,F:Solomon Kane. 5.00
34 HC,F:Solomon Kane. 5.00
35 I&O:Silver Age 3-D Man 5.00
36 F:3-D Man. 5.00
37 F:3-D Man. 5.00
38 AN,MP,I:Weird World 5.00
39 AM,I:Torpedo(1st solo) 5.00
40 AM,F:Torpedo 5.00
41 TS,F:Seeker 3000 . . . . 5.00
42 F:Tigra. 5.00
43 F:Paladin. 5.00
44 KG,F:Jack of Hearts(1stSolo) . . 5.00
45 GP,F:Manwolf 5.00
46 GP,F:Manwolf 5.00
47 JBy,I:2nd Antman(Scott Lang) . 10.00
48 JBy,F:2nd Antman. 10.00
49 F:The Falcon. 5.00
50 TS,TA,F:Alice Cooper 20.00
51 JBi,F:Black Panther,V:Klan. . . . 5.00
52 JBi,F:B.Panther,V:Klan 5.00
53 JBi,F:B.Panther,V:Klan 5.00
54 GD,TD,I:Hammer 5.00
55 JSt,F:Wonderman(1st solo) . . . 6.00
56 HC,TA,F:Dominic Fortune. 5.00
57 WS(c),I:Dr.Who. 7.00
58 TA(c),FM,F:Dr.Who 5.00
59 F:Dr.Who. 5.00
60 WS(c),DGb,F:Dr.Who 5.00
61 TS,F:Starlord. 5.00

MARVEL PRESENTS
Oct., 1975
1 BMc,F:Bloodstone. 15.00
2 BMc,O:Bloodstone. 9.00
3 AM,B:Guardians/Galaxy 20.00
4 AM,I:Nikki 12.00
5 AM,Planet o/t Absurd 12.00
6 AM,V:Karanada 12.00
7 AM,Embrace the Void 12.00
8 AM,JB,JSt,reprint.S.Surfer#2 . . 15.00
9 AM,O:Starhawk 12.00
10 AM,O:Starhawk 12.00
11 AM,D:Starhawk's Children . . . 12.00
12 AM,E:Guardians o/t Galaxy . . 12.00

MARVEL PREVIEW
Feb., 1975
(black & white magazine)
1 NA,AN,Man Gods From
　Beyond the Stars 25.00
2 GM(c),O:Punisher 150.00
3 GM(c),Blade the VampireSlayer 30.00
4 GM(c),I&O:Starlord 20.00
5 Sherlock Holmes 20.00
6 Sherlock Holmes 20.00
7 KG,Satana,A:Sword in the Star . 20.00
8 GM,MP,Legion of Monsters 30.00
9 Man-God,O:Starhawk 15.00
10 JSn,Thor the Mighty 30.00
11 JBy,I:Starlord 15.00
12 MK,Haunt of Horror. 10.00
13 JSn(c),Starhawk 10.00
14 JSn(c),Starhawk 10.00
15 MK(c),Starhawk. 10.00
16 GC,Detectives. 10.00
17 GK,Black Mask 6.00
18 GC,Starlord 6.00
19 Kull 6.00
20 HC,NA,GP,Bizarre Adventures . . 7.00
21 SD,Moonlight 7.00
22 JB,King Arthur. 6.00
23 JB,GC,FM,Bizarre Adventures . . 7.00
24 Debut Paradox 6.00
Becomes:

BIZARRE ADVENTURES
1981
25 MG,TA,MR,Lethal Ladies 12.00
26 JB(c),King Kull 12.00

MARVEL

27 JB,AA,GP,Phoenix,A:Ice-Man . 15.00
28 MG,TA,FM,NA,The Unlikely
   Heroes,Elektra. 15.00
29 JB,WS,Horror 10.00
30 JB,Tomorrow 10.00
31 JBy,After the Violence Stops. . . 12.00
32 Gods 12.00
33 Ph(c),Horror 12.00
34 PS,Christmas Spec,Son of Santa
   Howard the Duck,Feb.,1983 . . 10.00

MARVEL PREVIEW
1993
Preview of 1993 . . . . 4.00

MARVEL REMIX
Nov., 1998
1 (of 3) Fantastic Four 3.00
1a signed 20.00
2 Fantastic Four:Fireworks 3.00
3 Fantastic Four:Fireworks 3.00

MARVEL ROMANCE REDUX
March., 2006
1 . . . . 3.00
2 Guys & Dolls 3.00
3 Restraining Orders for Other Girls 3.00
4 I Should Have Been A 3.00
5 Love is a Four Letter Word 3.00

MARVELS
1994
1 B:KBk(s),AxR,I:Phil Sheldon,
   A:G.A.Heroes,Human Torch Vs
   Namor. 10.00
2 AxR,A:S.A.Avengers,FF,X-Men . . 8.00
3 AxR,FF vs Galactus. 8.00
4 AxR,Final issue 8.00

Marvel Saga #10
© Marvel Entertainment Group

MARVEL SAGA
Dec., 1985
1 JBy,Fantastic Four,Wolv. 3.00
2 Hulk 2.50
3 Spider-Man 3.00
4 X-Men 3.00
5 thru 24 . . . . @2.50
25 O:Silver Surfer,Dec.,1987 . . . . . 2.75

MARVEL SELECT
Flipbook, June, 2005
1 Astonishing X-Men #1
   & New X-men: Academy X #1 . . 4.00
2 Aston.X-Men#2 & Acad.X#2 . . . . 4.00
3 Aston.X-Men#3 & Acad.X#3 . . . . 4.00
4 Aston.x-men#4 & Acad.x#4 . . . . 4.00
5 Aston.X-Men#5 & Acad.X#5 . . . . 4.00
6 thru 18 . . . . @4.00

MARVEL SELECTS: FANTASTIC FOUR
Nov., 1999
1 (of 12) 2.75
2 rep. Vol. 1, #108, AD(c) 2.75
3 rep. Vol. 1, #109, AD(c) 2.75
4 rep. Vol. 1, #110, AD(c) 2.75
5 rep. Vol. 1, #111, AD(c) 2.75
6 rep. Vol. 1, #112, AD(c) 2.75

MARVEL SELECTS: SPIDER-MAN
Nov., 1999
1 (of 12) 2.75
2 rep. Amaz.Sp-M #101 . . . . 2.75
3 rep. Amaz.Sp-M #102 . . . . 2.75
4 rep. Amaz.Sp-M #103 . . . . 2.75
5 rep. Amaz.Sp-M #104 . . . . 2.75
6 rep. Amaz.Sp-M #105 . . . . 2.75

MARVEL: SHADOWS & LIGHT
B&W 1996
1-shot MGo,JPL,KJ,48-pg. 3.00

MARVEL 1602
Aug., 2003–March, 2004
1 thru 7 NGa(s),NKu . . . . @3.50
8 NGa(s),NKu,48-pg. 4.00

MARVEL 1602: FANTASTICK FOUR
Sept., 2006
1 V:Count Otto von Doom 3.50
2 thru 3 . . . . @3.50
4 PDd(s) 3.50
5 PDd(s) 3.50

MARVEL 1602: NEW WORLD
Aug., 2005
1 (of 5) Bruce David Banner. 3.50
2 Peter Parquagh 3.50
3 Superpowers outlawed 3.50
4 Lord Iron vs. Hulk 3.50
5 War in Roanoke. 3.50

MARVEL 65th ANNIVERSARY
Sept., 2004
Spec. F:Sub-Mariner,Human
   Torch,48-pg.. . . . . 5.00

MARVEL SPECTACULAR
Aug., 1973–Nov., 1975
1 JK,rep Thor #128 . . . . 15.00
2 thru 10 rep.Thor#129–#139 . . . @7.00
11 thru 19 rep Thor #140–#148 . . @6.00

MARVEL SPOTLIGHT
[1st Regular Series] Nov., 1971
1 NA(c)WW,F:Red Wolf 65.00
2 MP,BEv,NA,I&O:Werewolf 300.00
3 MP,F:Werewolf. 90.00

4 SD,MP,F:Werewolf. 90.00
5 SD,MP,I&O:Ghost Rider 300.00
6 MP,TS,F:Ghost Rider. 65.00
7 MP,TS,F:Ghost Rider. 65.00
8 JM,MB,F:Ghost Rider 65.00
9 TA,F:Ghost Rider. 50.00
10 SD,JM,F:Ghost Rider 50.00
11 SD,F:Ghost Rider 50.00
12 SD,2nd A:Son of Satan 50.00
13 F:Son of Satan 18.00
14 JM,F:Son of Satan,I:Ikthalon . . 18.00
15 JM, F:Son of Satan,
   I:Baphomet 15.00
16 JM,F:Son of Satan 15.00
17 JM,F:Son of Satan 15.00
18 F:Son of Satan, I:Allatou 15.00
19 F:Son of Satan 15.00
20 F:Son of Satan 15.00
21 F:Son of Satan 15.00
22 F:Son of Satan, Ghost Rider . . 18.00
23 F:Son of Satan 15.00
24 JM,F:Son of Satan 15.00
25 GT,F:Sinbad 15.00
26 F:The Scarecrow 12.00
27 F:The Sub-Mariner 22.00
28 F:Moon Knight (1st full solo). . 50.00
29 F:Moon Knight 40.00
30 JSt,JB,F:Warriors Three 22.00
31 HC,JSn,F:Nick Fury 22.00
32 I:Spiderwoman, Jessica Drew . 22.00
33 F:Deathlok, I:Devilslayer. 10.00

[2nd Regular Series] 1979
1 PB,F:Captain Marvel 4.00
1a No'1' on Cover. 12.00
2 FM(c),F:Captain Marvel,A:Eon . 3.00
3 PB,F:Captain Marvel 3.00
4 PB,F:Captain Marvel 3.00
5 FM(c),SD,F:Dragon Lord 3.00
6 F:Star Lord 3.00
7 FM(c),F:StarLord 3.00
8 FM,F:Captain Marvel 7.00
9 FM(c),SD,F:Captain Universe . . 3.00
10 SD,F:Captain Universe 3.00
11 SD,F:Captain Universe 3.00

MARVEL SPOTLIGHT
Dec., 2005
1 John Cassady & Saen McKeever 3.00
2 Warren Ellis, Jim Cheung 3.00
3 Joss Whedon & Michael Lark . . . 3.00
4 David Finch & Roberto
   Aquirre-Sacasa 3.00
5 Daniel Way & Olivier Coipel 3.00
6 Mark Millar & Steve McNiven . . . 3.00
7 Neil Gaiman & Salvador Laroca . 3.00
8 Robert Kirkman & Greg Land . . . 3.00
9 Ed Brubaker & Billy Tan. 3.00
10 Stan Lee & Jack Kirby 3.00
11 Brian Michael Bendis &
   Mark Bagley 3.00

MARVEL SPOTLIGHT: CIVIL WAR
May, 2007
1-shot Civil War Remembered. 3.00
1-shot, Aftermath, 48-pgs. 3.00

MARVEL SPOTLIGHT
Dec., 2006
Spec. Ghost Rider (2006) 3.00
Spec. Dark Tower (2007) 3.00
Spec. Spider-Man, Back in Black. . 3.00
Spec. Fantastic Four (2007) 3.00
Spec. Halo (2007) 3.00
Spec. World War Hulk (2007) 3.00
Spec. Thor (2007) JR2. . . . . 3.00
Spec. Marvel Zombies (2007) 3.00
Spec. Spider-Man One More Day/
   Brand New Day. 3.00

MARVEL SPOTLIGHT ON CAPTAIN AMERICA
1 thru 4, Captain America rep. . . @3.00

MARVEL SPOTLIGHT ON DR. STRANGE
1 thru 4, Dr. Strange, rep. . . . . . @3.00

MARVEL SPOTLIGHT ON SILVER SURFER
1 thru 4, Silver Surfer, rep. . . . . @3.00

MARVEL SUPER ACTION
Jan., 1976
1-shot TD,GE,FS,MP,HC,F:Punisher,
  Weirdworld,Dominic Fortune,
  I:Huntress(Mockingbird) 100.00

MARVEL SUPER ACTION
May, 1977–Nov., 1981
1 JK,reprint,Capt.America #100 . . 15.00
2 JK,reprint,Capt.America #101 . . 10.00
3 JK,reprint,Capt.America #102 . . 10.00
4 BEv,RH,reprint,Marvel Boy #1. . 10.00
5 JK,reprint,Capt.America #103 . . 10.00
6 JK,reprint,Capt.America #104 . . . 8.00
7 JK,reprint,Capt.America #105 . . . 8.00
8 JK,reprint,Capt.America #106 . . . 8.00
9 JK,reprint,Capt.America #107 . . . 8.00
10 JK,reprint,Capt.America #108. . . 8.00
11 JK,reprint,Capt.America #109. . . 8.00
12 JSo,reprint,Capt.America #110. . 8.00
13 JSo,reprint,Capt.America #111 . . 8.00
14 JB,reprint,Avengers #55 . . . . . . 8.00
15 JB,reprint,Avengers #56 . . . . . . 8.00
16 Reprint,Avengers,annual #2 . . . 5.00
17 Reprint,Avengers # 5.00
18 JB(c),reprint,Avengers #57. . . . . 5.00
19 JB(c),reprint,Avengers #58. . . . . 5.00
20 JB(c),reprint,Avengers #59 . . . . 5.00
21 Reprint,Avengers #60. . . . . 4.00
22 JB(c),reprint,Avengers #61. . . . . 4.00
23 Reprint,Avengers #63. . . . . 4.00
24 Reprint,Avengers #64. . . . . 4.00
25 Reprint,Avengers #65. . . . . 4.00
26 Reprint,Avengers #66. . . . . 4.00
27 BWS,Reprint,Avengers #67 . . . . 4.00
28 BWS,Reprint,Avengers #68 . . . . 4.00
29 Reprint,Avengers #69. . . . . 4.00
30 Reprint,Avengers #70. . . . . 4.00
31 Reprint,Avengers #71. . . . . 4.00

Marvel Super Action #11
© Marvel Entertainment Group

32 Reprint,Avengers #72. . . . . 4.00
33 Reprint,Avengers #73. . . . . 4.00
34 Reprint,Avengers #74. . . . . 4.00
35 JB(c),Reprint,Avengers #75 . . . . 4.00
36 JB(c),Reprint,Avengers #75 . . . . 4.00
37 JB(c),Reprint,Avengers #76 . . . . 4.00

MARVEL SUPERHEROES
Oct., 1966
1-shot Rep. D.D. #1, Avengers #2,
  Marvel Mystery #8. . . . . 200.00

MARVEL SUPER-HEROES
[1st Regular Series] 1967–71
(Prev.: Fantasy Masterpieces)
12 GC,I&O:Captain Marvel 225.00
13 GC,2nd A:Captain Marvel. . . . 125.00
14 F:Spider-Man 150.00
15 GC,F:Medusa 75.00
16 I:Phantom Eagle 75.00
17 O:Black Knight 75.00
18 GC,I:Guardians o/t Galaxy 90.00
19 F:Ka-Zar 45.00
20 F:Dr.Doom,Diablo 50.00
21 thru 31 reprints . . . . @25.00
32 thru 55 rep. Hulk/Submariner
  from Tales to Astonish . . . . . @10.00
56 reprints Hulk #102. . . . . 7.00
57 thru 105 reps.Hulk issues . . . . . @7.00

MARVEL SUPERHEROES
[2nd Regular Series] May, 1990
1 RLm,F:Hercules,Moon Knight,
  Magik,Bl.Panther,Speedball. . . . 7.00
2 . . . . 3.50
3 F:Captain America,Hulk,Wasp. . . 4.00
4 AD,F:SpM,N.Fury,D.D.,Speedball
  Wond.Man,Spitfire,Bl.Knight . . . 3.50
5 F:Thor,Thing,Speedball,
  Dr.Strange. 3.50
6 RB,SD,F:X-Men,Power Pack,
  Speedball,Sabra 3.00
7 RB,F:X-Men,Cloak & Dagger . . . 2.75
8 F:X-Men,Iron Man,Namor 2.75
9 F:Avengers W.C,Thor,Iron Man . . 3.00
10 DH,F:Namor,Fantastic Four,
  Ms.Marvel#24 . . . . 3.50
11 F:Namor,Ms.Marvel#25. . . . . . . 3.00
12 F:Dr.Strange,Falcon,Iron Man. . . 3.00
13 F:Iron Man 3.00
14 BMc,RWi,F:Iron Man,
  Speedball, Dr.Strange 3.00
15 KP,DH,F:Thor,Iron Man,Hulk . . . 3.00
Holiday Spec.#1 AAd,DC,JRu,F:FF,
  X-Men,Spider-Man,Punisher. . . 3.25
Holiday Spec.#2 AAd(c),SK,MGo,
  RLm,SLi,F:Hulk,Wolverine,
  Thanos,Spider-Man. 3.25
Fall Spec.RB,A:X-Men,Shroud,
  Marvel Boy,Cloak & Dagger . . . 3.00

MARVEL SUPERHEROES MEGAZINE
1 thru 6 rep. . . . . @3.00

MARVEL SUPER SPECIAL
See: MARVEL COMICS

MARVEL SWIMSUIT
1992
1 Schwing Break. 10.00

MARVEL TAILS
Nov., 1983
1 ST,Peter Porker 5.00

Marvel Tales #37
© Marvel Entertainment Group

MARVEL TALES
1964
1 All reprints,O:Spider-Man. . . . 550.00
2 rep.Avengers #1,X-Men #1,
  Hulk #3 . . . . 300.00
3 rep.Amaz.SpM.#6 . . . . 150.00
4 rep.Amaz.SpM.#7 . . . . 100.00
5 rep.Amaz.SpM.#8 . . . . 100.00
6 rep.Amaz.SpM.#9 . . . . 100.00
7 rep.Amaz.SpM.#10 . . . . 100.00
8 rep.Amaz.SpM.#13 . . . . 75.00
9 rep.Amaz.SpM.#14 . . . . 75.00
10 rep.Amaz.SpM.#15 . . . . 75.00
11 rep.Amaz.SpM.#16 . . . . 75.00
12 rep.Amaz.SpM.#17 . . . . 75.00
13 rep.Amaz.SpM.#18
  rep.1950's Marvel Boy. 75.00
14 rep.Amaz.SpM.#19,
  reps.Marvel Boy. 50.00
15 rep.Amaz.SpM.#20,
  reps.Marvel Boy. 50.00
16 rep.Amaz.SpM.#21,
  reps.Marvel Boy. 50.00
17 thru 22 rep.Amaz.SpM.
  #22-#27 . . . . @50.00
23 thru 27 rep.Amaz.SpM.
  #30-#34 . . . . @50.00
28 rep.Amaz.SpM.#35&36. . . . . . . 50.00
29 rep.Amaz.SpM.#39&40. . . . . . . 50.00
30 rep.Amaz.SpM.#58&41. . . . . . . 50.00
31 rep.Amaz.SpM.#42 . . . . 50.00
32 rep.Amaz.SpM.#43&44. . . . . . . 50.00
33 rep.Amaz.SpM.#45&47. . . . . . . 50.00
34 rep.Amaz.SpM.#48 . . . . 15.00
35 rep.Amaz.SpM.#49 . . . . 15.00
36 thru 41 rep.
  Amaz.SpM#51-#56 . . . . . . @15.00
42 thru 53 rep.
  Amaz.SpM#59-#70 . . . . . . @15.00
54 thru 80 rep.
  Amaz.SpM#73-#99 . . . . . . @15.00
81 rep.Amaz.SpM.#103. . . . . 15.00
82 rep.Amaz.SpM.#103-4 . . . . 15.00
83 thru 97 rep.
  Amaz.SpM#104-#118. . . . . @15.00
98 rep.Amaz.SpM.#121. . . . . 15.00
99 rep.Amaz.SpM.#122 . . . . 15.00
100 rep.Amaz.SpM.#123,BU:Two
  Gun Kid,Giant-Size 4.00
101 thru 105 rep.Amaz.
  SpM.#124-#128 . . . . @4.00
106 rep.Amaz.SpM.#129,
  (I:Punisher) 4.00
107 thur 110 rep.Amaz.
  SpM.#130-133 . . . . @4.00
111 Amaz.SpM.#134,A:Punisher. . . . 4.00

112 Amaz.SpM#135,A:Punisher . . 4.00
113 thru 125 rep.Amaz.Spider
   Man #136-#148 . . . . @4.00
126 rep.Amaz.Spider-Man#149 . . . . 4.00
127 rep.Amaz.Spider-Man#150 . . . . 4.00
128 rep.Amaz.Spider-Man#151 . . . . 4.00
129 thru 136 rep.Amaz.Spider
   Man #152-#159 . . . . @4.00
137 rep.Amaz.Fantasy#15. . . . . . . 7.00
138 rep.Amaz.SpM.#1 . . . . 7.00
139 thru 149 rep.
   AmazSpM#2-#12 . . . . @4.00
150 rep.AmazSpM Ann#1 . . . . 4.00
151 rep.AmazSpM#13 . . . . 4.00
152 rep.AmazSpM#14 . . . . 4.00
153 thru 190
   rep.AmazSpM#15-52 . . . . . @2.50
191 rep. #96-98 . . . . 2.50
192 rep. #121-122 . . . . 2.50
193 thru 198 rep.Marv.Team
   Up#59-64 . . . . @2.50
199 . . . . 2.50
200 rep. SpM Annual 14 . . . . 2.50
201 thru 206 rep.Marv.
   Team Up#65-70 . . . . @2.50
207 thru 208 . . . . 2.50
209 MZ(c),rep.SpM#129,Punisher . . 3.00
210 MZ(c),rep.SpM#134 . . . . 4.00
211 MZ(c),rep.SpM#135 . . . . 4.00
212 MZ(c),rep.Giant-Size#4. . . . . . 4.00
213 MZ(c),rep.Giant-Size#4. . . . . . 4.00
214 MZ(c),rep.SpM#161 . . . . 4.00
215 MZ(c),rep.SpM#162 . . . . 3.00
216 MZ(c),rep.SpM#174 . . . . 3.00
217 MZ(c),rep.SpM#175 . . . . 3.00
218 MZ(c),rep.SpM#201 . . . . 3.00
219 MZ(c),rep.SpM#202 . . . . 3.00
220 MZ(c),rep.Spec.SpM #81 . . . . 3.00
221 MZ(c),rep.Spec.SpM #82 . . . . 3.00
222 MZ(c),rep.Spec.SpM #83 . . . . 2.25
223 thru 227 TM(c),rep.
   SpM #88-92 . . . . @2.50
228 TM(c),rep.Spec.SpM.#17 . . . . 2.25
229 TM(c),rep.Spec.SpM.#18 . . . . 2.25
230 TM(c),rep.SpM #203 . . . . 2.25
231 TM(c),rep.Team-Up#108 . . . . . 2.25
232 TM(c),rep. 2.25
233 thru 236 TM(c),rep. X-Men . . @2.25
237 TM(c),rep. 2.25
238 TM(c),rep. 2.25
239 TM(c),rep.SpM,Beast 2.25
240 rep.SpM,Beast,MTU#90 . . . . . 2.25
241 rep.MTU#124 . . . . 2.25
242 rep.MTU#89,Nightcrawler 2.25
243 rep.MTU#117,SpM,Wolverine . . 2.25
244 MR(c),rep. 2.25
245 MR(c),rep. 2.25
246 MR(c),rep. 2.25
247 MR(c),rep.MTU Annual #6 . . . 2.25
248 MR(c),rep. 2.25
249 MR(c),rep.MTU #14 . . . . 2.25
250 MR(c),rep.MTU #100 . . . . 2.25
251 rep.Amaz.SpM.#100 . . . . 2.25
252 rep.Amaz.SpM.#101 . . . . 3.50
253 rep.Amaz.SpM.#102 . . . . 3.00
254 rep.MTU #15,inc.2 Ghost
   Rider pin-ups by JaL 3.00
255 SK(c),rep.MTU #58,
   BU:Ghost Rider 2.25
256 rep. MTU 2.25
257 rep.Amaz.SpM.#238 . . . . 2.25
258 rep.Amaz.SpM.#239 . . . . 2.25
259 thru 261 rep.Amaz.SpM.#249
   thru #251 . . . . @2.25
262 rep Marvel Team-Up #53 . . . . 2.25
263 rep Marvel Team-Up #54 . . . . 2.25
264 rep.B.Amaz.SpM.Ann.#5 . . . . 2.25
265 rep.E.Amaz.SpM.Ann.#5 . . . . 2.25
266 thru 275 rep.AmazSpM#252
   thru #261 . . . . @2.25
276 rep.Amaz.SpM#263 . . . . 2.25
277 rep.Amaz.SpM#265 . . . . 2.25

278 thru 282 rep.Amaz.SpM#268
   thru #272 . . . . @2.25
283 rep.Amaz.SpM#273 . . . . 2.25
284 thru 287 rep.AmazSpM#275
   thru #278 . . . . @2.25
288 rep.Amaz.SpM#280 . . . . 2.25
289 rep.Amaz.SpM#281 . . . . 2.25
290 & 291 rep.Amaz.SpM 2.25

MARVEL TALES
Flipbook, June, 2005
1 Amazing Spider-Man #34
   & Amazing Fantasy #1 . . . . . . 4.00
2 Amaz.Sp-M#35 & Amaz.Fant.#2 . 4.00
3 Amaz.Sp-M#33 & Amaz.Fant.#3 . 4.00
4 Amaz.sp-m#33 & Amaz.fant.#4 . . 4.00
5 thru 16 . . . . @4.00

MARVEL TALES
See: MARVEL COMICS

MARVEL TEAM-UP
March, 1972
(Spider-Man in all,unless *)
1 RA,F:Hum.Torch,V:Sandman . . 225.00
2 RA,F:Hum.Torch,V:Sandman . . 75.00
3 F:Human Torch,V:Morbius . . . 100.00
4 GK,F:X-Men,A:Morbius 100.00
5 GK,F:Vision 40.00
6 GK,F:Thing,O:Puppet Master,
   V:Mad Thinker 40.00
7 RA,F:Thor 40.00
8 JM,F:The Cat. 40.00
9 RA,F:Iron Man 40.00
10 JM,F:Human Torch 40.00
11 JM,F:The Inhumans 20.00
12 RA,F:Werewolf 35.00
13 GK,F:Captain America 30.00
14 GK,F:Sub-Mariner. 20.00
15 RA,F:Ghostrider 35.00
16 GK,JM,F:Captain Marvel 20.00
17 GK,F:Mr.Fantastic,
   A:Capt.Marvel 20.00
18 *F:Hulk,Human Torch 20.00
19 SB,F:Ka-Zar 20.00
20 SB,F:Black Panther 17.00
21 SB,F:Dr.Strange 11.00
22 SB,F:Hawkeye 12.00
23 *F:Human Torch,Iceman,
   C:Spider-Man,X-Men 12.00
24 JM,F:Brother Voodoo 12.00
25 JM,F:Daredevil 12.00

Marvel Team-Up #1
© *Marvel Entertainment Group*

26 *F:H.Torch,Thor,V:Lavamen . . . 12.00
27 JM,F:The Hulk 12.00
28 JM,F:Hercules. 12.00
29 *F:Human Torch,Iron Man. 12.00
30 JM,F:The Falcon 12.00
31 JM,F:Iron Fist 12.00
32 *F:Hum.Torch,Son of Satan . . . 12.00
33 SB,F:Nighthawk 12.00
34 SB,F:Valkyrie 12.00
35 SB,*F:H.Torch,Dr.Strange 12.00
36 SB,F:Frankenstein 10.00
37 SB,F:Man-Wolf 10.00
38 SB,F:Beast 10.00
39 SB,F:H.Torch,I:Jean Dewolff. . . 10.00
40 SB,F:Sons of the Tiger 10.00
41 SB,F:Scarlet Witch 10.00
42 SB,F:Scarlet Witch,Vision 10.00
43 SB,F:Dr.Doom. 10.00
44 SB,F:Moon Dragon 10.00
45 SB,F:Killraven 10.00
46 SB,F:Deathlok. 8.00
47 F:The Thing 7.00
48 SB,F:Iron Man,I:Wraith 7.00
49 SB,F:Iron Man. 7.00
50 SB,F:Dr.Strange 7.00
51 SB,F:Iron Man 7.00
52 SB,F:Captain America 7.00
53 1st JBy New X-Men,F:Hulk. . . . 35.00
54 JBy,F:Hulk,V:Woodgod 8.00
55 JBy,F:Warlock,I:Gardener 9.00
56 SB,F:Daredevil 8.00
57 SB,F:Black Widow 8.00
58 SB,F:Ghost Rider,V:Trapster . . . 8.00
59 JBy,F:Yellowjacket,V:Equinox . . . 8.00
60 JBy,F:Wasp,V:Equinox 8.00
61 JBy,F:Human Torch. 8.00
62 JBy,F:Ms.Marvel 8.00
63 JBy,F:Iron Fist. 8.00
64 JBy,F:Daughters o/t Dragon . . . 8.00
65 JBy,I:Captain Britain(U.S.)
   I:Arcade 7.50
66 JBy,F:Captain Britain 7.00
67 JBy,F:Tigra,V:Kraven 7.00
68 JBy,F:Man-Thing,I:D'Spayre . . . 7.00
69 JBy,F:Havok 7.00
70 JBy,F:Thor. 7.00
71 F:The Falcon,V:Plantman 6.00
72 F:Iron Man 6.00
73 F:Daredevil 6.00
74 BH,F:Not ready for prime time
   players(Saturday Night Live). . . 6.00
75 JBy,F:Power Man 7.00
76 HC,F:Dr.Strange 6.00
77 HC,F:Ms.Marvel 6.00
78 DP,F:Wonderman 6.00
79 JBy,TA,F:Red Sonja 6.00
80 SpM,F:Dr.Strange,Clea. 5.00
81 F:Satana 5.00
82 SB,F:Black Widow 6.00
83 SB,F:Nick Fury 5.00
84 SB,F:Master of Kung Fu 5.00
85 SB,F:Bl.Widow,Nick Fury 5.00
86 BMc,F:Guardians o/t Galaxy. . . . 4.00
87 GC,F:Black Panther 4.00
88 SB,F:Invisible Girl 4.00
89 RB,F:Nightcrawler 4.50
90 BMc,F:The Beast 4.00
91 F:Ghost Rider 4.00
92 CI,F:Hawkeye,I:Mr.Fear IV 3.50
93 CI,F:Werewolf
   I:Tatterdemalion (named) 4.00
94 MZ,F:Shroud 3.50
95 I:Mockingbird(Huntress) 4.00
96 F:Howard the Duck 3.50
97 *F:Hulk,Spider-Woman 3.50
98 F:Black Widow 3.50
99 F:Machine Man 3.50
100 FM,JBy,F:F.F.,I:Karma,
   BU:Storm & Bl.Panther 8.00
101 F:Nighthawk 3.00
102 F:Doc Samson,Rhino 3.00
103 F:Antman 3.00

Marvel Team-Up #113
Universe #10 © Marvel Ent. Group

104 *F:Hulk,Ka-zar 3.00
105 *F:Powerman,Iron Fist,Hulk . . . 3.00
106 HT,F:Captain America 3.00
107 HT,F:She-Hulk 3.00
108 HT,F:Paladin 3.00
109 HT,F:Dazzler 3.00
110 HT,F:Iron Man 3.00
111 HT,F:Devil Slayer 3.00
112 HT,F:King Kull 3.00
113 HT,F:Quasar,V:Lightmaster 3.00
114 HT,F:Falcon 3.00
115 HT,F:Thor 3.00
116 HT,F:Valkyrie 3.00
117 HT,F:Wolv,V:Prof Power 12.00
118 HT,F:Professor X 4.00
119 KGa,F:Gargoyle 3.00
120 KGa,F:Dominic Fortune 3.00
121 KGa,F:Human Torch,I:Leap
    Frog(Frog Man) 3.00
122 KGa,F:Man-Thing 3.00
123 KGa,F:Daredevil 3.00
124 KGa,F:Beast 3.50
125 KGa,F:Tigra 3.00
126 BH,F:Hulk 3.00
127 KGa,F:Watcher,X-mass issue . . 3.00
128 Ph(c)KGa,F:Capt.America 3.00
129 KGa,F:The Vision 3.00
130 KGa,F:The Scarlet Witch 3.00
131 KGa,F:Leap Frog 3.00
132 KGa,F:Mr.Fantastic 3.00
133 KGa,F:Fantastic Four 3.00
134 F:Jack of Hearts 3.00
135 F:Kitty Pryde 3.00
136 F:Wonder Man 3.00
137 *F:Aunt May & F.Richards 3.00
138 F:Sandman,I:New Enforcers . . . 3.00
139 F:Sandman,Nick Fury 3.00
140 F:Black Widow 3.00
141 SpM(2nd App Black Costume)
    F:Daredevil 12.00
142 F:Captain Marvel(2nd one) 3.00
143 F:Starfox 3.00
144 F:M.Knight,V:WhiteDragon 3.00
145 F:Iron Man 3.00
146 F:Nomad 3.50
147 F:Human Torch 3.00
148 F:Thor 3.00
149 F:Cannonball 3.50
150 F:X-Men,V:Juggernaut 5.50
Ann.#1 SB,F:New X-Men 30.00
Ann.#2 F:The Hulk 10.00
Ann.#3 F:Hulk,PowerMan 6.00
Ann.#4 F:Daredevil,Moon Knight . . . 5.00

Ann.#5 F:Thing,Scarlet Witch,
    Quasar,Dr.Strange 5.00
Ann.#6 F:New Mutants,Cloak &
    Dagger(cont.New Mutants#22) . 5.00
Ann.#7 F:Alpha Flight 3.00

MARVEL TEAM-UP INDEX
**See: OFFICIAL MARVEL
INDEX TO
MARVEL TEAM-UP**

MARVEL TEAM-UP
1997
1 TPe,PO,AW, F:Spider-Man,
    Generation X 2.25
2 TPe,PO,AW, F:Spider-Man &
    Hercules 2.25
3 TPe,DaR,AW, F:Spider-Man &
    Sandman 2.25
4 TPe,DaR,F:Spider-Man &
    Man-Thing 2.25
5 TPe,DaR,F:Spider-Man &
    Mystery guest 2.25
6 TPe,F:Spider-Man & Sub-Mariner 2.25
7 MWn,TPe,F:Spider-Man & Blade 2.25
8 TPe,F:Sub-Mariner & Doctor
    Strange 2.25
9 TPe,F:Sub-Mariner & Captain
    America 2.25
10 TPe,AW,F:Sub Mariner & Thing . 2.25
11 TPe,AW,PO,F:Sub-Mariner & Iron
    Man, final issue 2.25

MARVEL TEAM-UP
Nov., 2004
1 ScK, Golden Child, pt.1 . . . . 2.25
2 ScK, Golden Child, pt.2 . . . . 2.25
3 ScK, Fant. Four & Dr. Strange . . . 2.25
4 ScK, Iron Man, Hulk 2.25
5 Sck, Spider-man, X-23 . . . . 2.25
6 ScK,The Golden Child 2.25
7 ScK,Ring of the Master 2.25
8 Sck,Master of the Ring,pt.2 . . . . 3.00
9 ScK,Master of the Ring,pt.3 . . . . 3.00
10 ScK,Master of the Ring,pt.4 . . . 3.00
11 Titannus War,pt.1 . . . . 3.00
12 Titannus War,pt.2 . . . . 3.00
13 Titannus War,pt.3 . . . . 3.00
14 F:Spider-Man 3.00
15 League of Losers, pt.1 . . . . 3.00
16 League of Losers, pt.2 . . . . 3.00
17 League of Losers, pt.3 . . . . 3.00
18 League of Losers, pt.4 . . . . 3.00
19 Wolv. & Cable vs. Ringmaster . . 3.00
20 Freedom Ring 3.00
21 Freedom Ring 3.00
22 Freedom Ring 3.00
23 Freedom Ring 3.00
24 Freedom Ring 3.00
25 Final Issue 3.00

MARVEL
Treasury Edition
Sept., 1974
1 SD,Spider-Man,I:Contemplator . 75.00
2 JK,F:Fant.Four,Silver Surfer . . . 30.00
3 F:Thor 25.00
4 BWS,F:Conan 25.00
5 O:Hulk 25.00
6 GC,FB,SD,F:Dr.Strange 25.00
7 JB,JK,F:The Avengers 25.00
8 F:X-Mass stories 25.00
9 F:Super-Hero Team-Up 25.00
10 F:Thor 25.00
11 F:Fantastic Four 20.00
12 F:Howard the Duck 20.00
13 F:X-Mas stories 20.00
14 F:Spider-Man 22.00
15 BWS,F:Conan,Red Sonja 22.00
16 F:Defenders 20.00

17 F:The Hulk 20.00
18 F:Spider Man,X-Men 25.00
19 F:Conan 22.00
20 F:Hulk 22.00
21 F:Fantastic Four 22.00
22 F:Spider-Man 25.00
23 F:Conan 22.00
24 F:The Hulk 22.00
25 F:Spider-Man,Hulk 22.00
26 GP,F:Hulk,Wolverine,Hercules . 25.00
27 HT,F:Hulk,Spider-Man 22.00
28 JB,JSt,F:SpM/Superman 50.00

MARVEL TREASURY
OF OZ
(oversized) 1975
1 JB,movie adapt. 30.00

MARVEL TREASURY
SPECIAL
Vol. I Spider-Man, 1974 . . . . 30.00
Vol. II Capt. America, 1976 . . . . . . 35.00

MARVEL TRIPLE ACTION
Feb., 1972
1 Rep. 30.00
2 thru 5 rep. . . . . @20.00
6 thru 10 rep. . . . . @15.00
11 thru 47 rep. . . . . @8.00
G-Size#1 F:Avengers 10.00
G-Size#2 F:Avengers 10.00

MARVEL TWO-IN-ONE
Jan., 1974
(Thing in all, unless *)
1 GK,F:Man-Thing 100.00
2 GK,JSt,F:Namor,Namorita 35.00
3 F:Daredevil 35.00
4 F:Capt.America,Namorita 25.00
5 F:Guardians of the Galaxy 25.00
6 F:Dr.Strange 25.00
7 F:Valkyrie 14.00
8 F:Ghost Rider 25.00
9 F:Thor 14.00
10 KJ,F:Black Widow 14.00
11 F:Golem 10.00
12 F:Iron Man 10.00
13 F:Power Man 10.00
14 F:Son of Satan 11.00
15 F:Morbius 11.00
16 F:Ka-Zar 10.00

Marvel Two-In-One #1
© Marvel Entertainment Group

17 F:Spider-Man	10.00
18 F:Spider-Man	10.00
19 F:Tigra	10.00
20 F:The Liberty Legion	10.00
21 F:Doc Savage	7.00
22 F:Thor,Human Torch	7.00
23 F:Thor,Human Torch	7.00
24 SB,F:Black Goliath	7.00
25 F:Iron Fist	7.00
26 F:Nick Fury	7.00
27 F:Deathlok	7.00
28 F:Sub-Mariner	8.00
29 F:Master of Kung Fu	7.00
30 JB,F:Spiderwoman	15.00
31 F:Spiderwoman	7.00
32 F:Invisible girl	7.00
33 F:Modred the Mystic	7.00
34 F:Nighthawk,C:Deathlok	7.00
35 F:Skull the Slayer	7.00
36 F:Mr.Fantastic	7.00
37 F:Matt Murdock	7.00
38 F:Daredevil	7.00
39 F:The Vision	7.00
40 F:Black Panther	7.00
41 F:Brother Voodoo	5.00
42 F:Captain America	5.00
43 JBy,F:Man-Thing	6.00
44 GD,F:Hercules	4.00
45 GD,F:Captain Marvel	5.00
46 F:The Hulk	12.00
47 GD,F:Yancy Street Gang,	
I:Machinesmith	4.00
48 F:Jack of Hearts	4.00
49 GD,F:Dr.Strange	4.00
50 JBy,JS,F:Thing & Thing	4.00
51 FM,BMc,F:Wonderman,Nick	
Fury, Ms.Marvel	8.00
52 F:Moon Knight,I:Crossfire	4.00
53 JBy,JS,F:Quasar,C:Deathlok	4.00
54 JBy,JS,D:Deathlok,	
I:Grapplers	11.00
55 JBy,JS,I:New Giant Man	4.00
56 GP,GD,F:Thundra	3.00
57 GP,GD,F:Wundarr	3.00
58 GP,GD,I:Aquarian,A:Quasar	3.00
59 F:Human Torch	3.00
60 GP,GD,F:Impossible Man,	
I:Impossible Woman	3.00
61 GD,F:Starhawk,I&O:Her	4.00
62 GD,F:Moondragon	4.00
63 GD,F:Warlock	4.00
64 DP,GD,F:Stingray,	
I:Serpent Squad	3.00
65 GP,GD,F:Triton	3.00
66 GD,F:Scarlet Witch,	
V:Arcade	3.00
67 F:Hyperion,Thundra	3.00
68 F:Angel,V:Arcade	3.00
69 GD,F:Guardians o/t Galaxy	3.00
70 F:The Inhumans	3.00
71 F:Mr.Fantastic,I:Deathurge,	
Maelstrom	3.00
72 F:Stingray	3.00
73 F:Quasar	3.00
74 F:Puppet Master,Modred	3.00
75 F:The Avengers,O:Blastaar	4.00
76 F:Iceman,O:Ringmaster	3.00
77 F:Man-Thing	3.00
78 F:Wonder Man	3.00
79 F:Blue Diamond,I:Star Dancer	3.00
80 F:Ghost Rider	3.50
81 F:Sub-Mariner	2.50
82 F:Captain America	2.50
83 F:Sasquatch	3.50
84 F:Alpha Flight	3.50
85 F:Giant-Man	3.00
86 O:Sandman	3.00
87 F:Ant-Man	3.00
88 F:She-Hulk	3.00
89 F:Human Torch	3.00
90 F:Spider-Man	4.00
91 V:Sphinx	3.00

92 F:Jocasta,V:Ultron	3.00
93 F:Machine Man,D:Jocasta	3.00
94 F:Power Man,Iron Fist	3.00
95 F:Living Mummy	3.00
96 F:Sandman,C:Marvel Heroes	3.00
97 F:Iron Man	3.00
98 F:Franklin Richards	3.00
99 JBy(c),F:Rom	3.00
100 F:Ben Grimm	5.00
Ann.#1 SB,F:Liberty Legion	15.00
Ann.#2 JSn,2nd D:Thanos,A:Spider	
Man,Avengers,Capt.Marvel,	
I:Lord Chaos,Master Order	50.00
Ann.#3 F:Nova	7.00
Ann.#4 F:Black Bolt	7.00
Ann.#5 F:Hulk,V:Pluto	4.00
Ann.#6 I:American Eagle	4.00
Ann.#7 I:Champion,A:Hulk,Thor,	
DocSamson,Colossus,Sasquatch,	
Wonder Man	4.00

MARVEL TWO-IN-ONE
July, 2007

1	5.00
2 thru 5 64-pg.	@5.00

MARVEL UNIVERSE:
OFFICIAL HANDBOOK TO
Jan., 1983

1 Abomination-Avengers'	
Quintet	7.50
2 BaronMordo-Collect.Man	6.00
3 Collector-Dracula	5.00
4 Dragon Man-Gypsy Moth	5.00
5 Hangman-Juggernaut	5.00
6 K-L	4.00
7 Mandarin-Mystique	4.00
8 Na,oria-Pyro	4.00
9 Quasar to She-Hulk	4.00
10 Shiar-Sub-Mariner	4.00
11 Subteraneans-Ursa Major	4.00
12 Valkyrie-Zzzax	4.00
13 Book of the Dead	4.00
14 Book of the Dead	4.00
15 Weaponry	4.00

[2nd Series] 1985

1 Abomination-Batroc	5.00
2 Beast-Clea	4.00
3 Cloak & D.-Dr.Strange	4.00
4 Dr.Strange-Galactus	4.00
5 Gardener-Hulk	4.00
6 Human Torch-Ka-Zar	3.25
7 Kraven-Magneto	3.25
8 Magneto-Moleman	3.25
9 Moleman-Owl	3.25
10	3.25
11	3.00
12 S-T	3.00
13	3.00
14 V-Z	3.00
15	3.00
16 Book of the Dead	3.00
17 Handbook of the Dead,inc.	
JLe illus.	3.00
18	3.00
19	3.00
20 Inc.RLd illus.	3.00

Marvel Universe Update

1 thru 8	@3.00

Marvel Universe Packet

1 inc. Spider-Man	5.50
2 inc. Captain America	4.50
3 inc. Ghost Rider	5.00
4 inc. Wolverine	4.50
5 inc. Punisher	4.25
6 inc. She-Hulk	4.00
7 inc. Daredevil	4.00
8 inc. Hulk	4.00
9 inc. Moon Knight	4.00
10 inc. Captain Britain	4.00

11 inc. Storm	4.00
12 inc. Silver Surfer	4.00
13 inc. Ice Man	4.50
14 inc. Thor	4.50
15 thru 22	@4.50
23 inc. Cage	4.50
24 inc. Iron Fist	4.50
25 inc.Deadpool,Night Thrasher	4.50
26 inc. Wonder Man	5.00
27 inc.Beta Ray Bill,Pip	5.00
28 inc.X-Men	5.00
29 inc.Carnage	5.00
30 thru 36	@5.00

MARVEL UNIVERSE
1996

1 Post Onslaught	3.25

MARVEL UNIVERSE
April, 1998

1 CPa(c),RSt,SEp,AW,F:Human	
Torch,Capt.Am.,Namor,48-pg.	3.00
2A JBy(c),RSt,SEp,AW,V:Hydra,	
Baron Strucker	2.25
2B DGb(c)	2.25
3 RSt,SEp,AW,V:Hydra	2.25
4 RSt,MM, all-star jam cover,	
F:Monster Hunters	2.25
5 MM,RSt,F:The Monster Hunters	2.25
6 MM,RSt,F:Monster Hunters,pt.3	2.25
7 MM,RSt,F:Monster Hunters,pt.4	2.25

MARVEL UNIVERSE:
MILLENNIAL VISIONS
Dec., 2001

Spec.2001 48-page	4.00

MARVEL UNIVERSE:
THE END
March, 2003

1 (of 6) JSn,AM	2.25
2 JSn,AM	2.25
3 JSn,AM	3.00
4 thru 6 JSn,AM	@3.00

MARVEL
VALENTINE'S SPECIAL
1997

1-shot MWa,TDF, 48-pg.	3.00

Marvel Valentine's Special #1
© *Marvel Entertainment Group*

MARVEL WESTERNS
July., 2006
1 Three new tales 4.00
2 Kid Colt & Arizona Annie 4.00
3 Two-Gun Kid 4.00
4 The Black 4.00
Spec. Outlaw Files #1 . . . . 4.00

MARVEL X-MEN COLLECTION
1994
1 thru 3 JL from the 1st series
X-Men Cards . . . . @3.25

MARVEL YOUNG GUNS SKETCH BOOK
Dec., 2004
2004 . . . . 3.00

MARVEL ZOMBIES
Dec., 2005
1 . . . . 2.50
2 thru 5 . . . . 3.00

MARVEL ZOMBIES
Mar., 2007
1 Army of Darkness x-over 4.00
2 Army of Darkness x-over 4.00
3 Army of Darkness x-over 3.00
4 Army of Darkness x-over 3.00
5 Army of Darkness x-over 3.00
Spec. Dead Days 4.00
Spec. Book of Angels, Demons 4.00

MARVEL ZOMBIES 2
Oct., 2007
1 (of 5) Marvel Zombies Civil War . 3.00
2 . . . . 3.00

MARVELOUS ADVENTURES OF GUS BEEZER
April, 2003
Spec. F:Spider-Man 3.00
Spec. F:X-Men 3.00
Spec. F:The Hulk 3.00

MARVILLE
Sept., 2002
1 U-Decide 3.00
1b foil (c) 40-pg. 4.00
1c variant foil (c) 4.00
2 thru 6 . . . . @2.25
5a thru 6a MBr,variant (c) . . . . . @2.25
7 . . . . 3.00

MARVIN MOUSE
Marvel Atlas, Sept., 1957
1 BEv,F:Marvin Mouse 150.00

MARY JANE
June, 2004
1 thru 4 . . . . 2.25
Digest Vol. 1 Circle of Friends 6.00

MARY JANE: HOMECOMING
March, 2005
1 (of 4) The Cheating Thing 3.00
2 the Friendship Thing 3.00
3 The Regret Thing 3.00
4 The Homecoming Thing 3.00
Digest Vol. 2 Homecoming 7.00

MASTER OF KUNG FU, SPECIAL MARVEL ED.
April, 1974
Prev: Special Marvel Edition
17 JSn,I:Black Jack Tarr 40.00
18 PG,1st Gulacy Art 20.00
19 PG,A:Man-Thing 22.00
20 GK(c),PG,AM,V:Samurai. 15.00
21 AM,Season of Vengeance..
Moment of Death. 10.00
22 PG,DA,Death. 10.00
23 AM,KJ,River of Death 10.00
24 JSn,WS,AM,ST,Night of the
Assassin 12.00
25 JSt(c),PG,ST,Fists Fury...
Rites of Death 10.00
26 KP,ST,A:Daughter of
Fu Manchu 10.00
27 SB,FS,A:Fu Manchu. 10.00
28 EH,ST,Death of a Spirit. 10.00
29 PG,V:Razor-Fist 10.00
30 PG,DA,Pit of Lions 10.00
31 GK&DA(c),PG,DA,Snowbuster . 10.00
32 GK&ME(c),SB,ME,Assault on an
Angry Sea 10.00
33 PG,Messenger of Madness,
I:Leiko Wu 10.00
34 PG,Captive in A Madman's
Crown 10.00
35 PG,V:Death Hand 10.00
36 The Night of the Ninja's 10.00
37 V:Darkstrider & Warlords of
the Web. 5.00
38 GK(c),PG,A:The Cat 5.00
39 GK(c),PG,A:The Cat 5.00
40 PG,The Murder Agency. 5.00
41 . . . . 5.00
42 GK(c),PG,TS,V:Shockwave . . . 5.00
43 PG,V:Shockwave 5.00
44 SB(c),PG,V:Fu Manchu. 5.00
45 GK(c),PG,Death Seed. 5.00
46 PG,V:Sumo 5.00
47 PG,The Cold White
Mantle of Death. 5.00
48 PG,Bridge of a 1,000 Dooms . . 5.00
49 PG,V:Shaka Kharn,The
Demon Warrior 5.00
50 PG,V:Fu Manchu. 5.00
51 PG(c),To End...To Begin 5.00
52 Mayhem in Morocco 5.00
53 . . . . 5.00
54 JSn(c),Death Wears Three
Faces. 5.00
55 PG(c),The Ages of Death 5.00
56 V:The Black Ninja 5.00
57 V:Red Baron 5.00
58 Behold the Final Mask 5.00
59 GK(c),B:Phoenix Gambit,
Behold the Angel of Doom 5.00
60 A:Dr.Doom,Doom Came 5.00
61 V:Skull Crusher 4.50
62 Coast of Death 4.50
63 GK&TA(c),Doom Wears
Three Faces 4.50
64 PG(c),To Challenge a Dragon . . 4.50
65 V:Pavane 4.50
66 V:Kogar. 4.50
67 PG(c),Dark Encounters 4.50
68 Final Combats,V:The Cat 4.50
69 . . . . 4.50
70 A:Black Jack Tarr,Murder
Mansion 4.50
71 PG(c),Ying & Yang (c) 4.50
72 V:Shockwave 4.50
73 RN(c),V:Behemoths 4.50
74 TA(c),A:Shockwave. 4.50
75 Where Monsters Dwell 4.50
76 GD,Battle on the Waterfront 4.00
77 GD,I:Zaran 4.00
78 GD,Moving Targets 4.00
79 GD,This Side of Death 4.00

80 GD,V:Leopard Men 4.00
81 GD,V:Leopard Men 4.00
82 GD,Flight into Fear 4.00
83 GD, ... 4.00
84 GD,V:Fu Manchu 4.00
85 GD,V:Fu Manchu 4.00
86 GD,V:Fu Manchu 4.00
87 GD,V:Zaran. 4.00
88 GD,V:Fu Manchu 4.00
89 GD,D:Fu Manchu 4.00
90 MZ,Death in Chinatown 4.00
91 GD,Gang War,drugs 5.00
92 GD,Shadows of the Past 4.00
93 GD,Cult of Death 4.00
94 GD,V:Agent Synergon 4.00
95 GD,Raid 4.00
96 GD,I:Rufus Carter 4.00
97 GD,V:Kung Fu's Dark Side 4.00
98 GD,Fight to the Finish. 4.00
99 GD,Death Boat 4.00
100 GD,Doublesize 6.00
101 GD,Not Smoke,Nor Beads,
Nor Blood 3.75
102 GD,Assassins,1st GD(p). 4.00
103 GD,V:Assassins 3.75
104 GD,Fight without Reason,
C:Cerberus 3.75
105 GD,I:Razor Fist 3.75
106 GD,C:Velcro 3.75
107 GD,A:Sata. 3.75
108 GD. 3.75
109 GD,Death is a Dark Agent 3.75
110 GD,Perilous Reign 3.75
111 GD. 3.75
112 GD(c),Commit and Destroy. . . . 3.75
113 GD(c),V:Panthers 3.75
114 Fantasy o/t Autumn Moon 3.75
115 GD. 3.75
116 GD. 3.75
117 GD,Devil Deeds Done
in Darkness 3.75
118 GD,D:Fu Manchu,double 4.50
119 GD. 3.75
120 GD,Dweller o/t Dark Stream . . . 3.75
121 Death in the City of Lights 3.00
122 . . . . 3.00
123 V:Ninjas. 3.00
124 . . . . 3.00
125 double-size 6.00
G-Size#1,CR,PG 20.00
G-Size#2 PG,V:Yellow Claw 3.00
G-Size#3 . . . . 3.00
G-Size#4 JK,V:Yellow Claw 3.00
Spec.#1 Bleeding Black 3.00

Master of Kung Fu #47
© Marvel Entertainment Group

MASTER OF KUNG FU: BLEEDING BLACK
1 V:ShadowHand, 1991 . . . . 3.00

MASTERS OF TERROR
July–Sept., 1975
1 GM(c),FB,BWS,JSn,NA . . . 30.00
2 JSn(c),GK,VM, ... 25.00

MASTERS OF THE UNIVERSE
Star, May, 1986—March, 1988
1 I:Hordak 7.00
2 thru 11 . . . . @4.00
12 D:Skeletor 8.00
Movie #1 GT 2.00

Matt Slade, Gunfighter #1
© Marvel Entertainment Group

MATT SLADE, GUNFIGHTER
Atlas, May, 1956
1 AW,AT,F:Matt Slade,Crimson
  Avenger 250.00
2 AW,A:Crimson Avenger 175.00
3 A:Crimson Avenger 150.00
4 A:Crimson Avenger 125.00
Becomes:

KID SLADE GUNFIGHTER
5 F:Kid Slade 125.00
6 . . . . 100.00
7 AW,Duel in the Night 110.00
8 July, 1957 . . . . 100.00

MAVERICK
1997
1 JGz,F:Christopher Nord/David
  North/Maverick, 48-pg. 3.50
2 JGz,A:Victor Creed and Logan . . 3.00
2a variant cover 3.00
3 JGz,V:Puck & Vindicator 3.00
4 JGz,A:Wolverine 3.00
5 JGz,A:The Blob 3.00
6 JGz,V:Sabretooth. 3.00
7 JGz,V:Sabretooth. 3.00
8 JGz,V:The Confessor 3.00
9 JGz,Maverick's secrets 3.00
10 JGz,V:Ivan the Terrible, Chris
  Bradley becomes Bolt 3.00
11 JGz,A:Darkstar,Vanguard,
  Ursa Major. 3.00

12 JGz, double sized last issue 3.50
1-shot LHa, V:Sabretooth,48-pg. . . . 3.00

MAXIMUM SECURITY
Oct., 2000
1 (of 3) KBk,JOy,x-over 3.00
2 KBk,JOy,x-over 3.00
3 KBk,JOy,x-over,concl. 3.00
Spec. Thor vs. Ego, 64-pg.,SL,JK . . 3.00
Spec. Dangerous Planet 3.00

MEET MISS BLISS
Marvel Atlas, 1955
1 . . . . 150.00
2 thru 4 . . . . @100.00

MEGA MORPHS
Aug., 2005
1 (of 4) Toy tie-in 3.00
2 . . . . 3.00
3 Red Rampage 3.00
4 The Pawns and the Power 3.00

MEKANIX
Oct., 2002
1 (of 6) CCI,F:Kitty Pryde 3.00
2 CCI,back in school. 3.00
3 thru 6 CCI. . . . . @3.00

MELVIN THE MONSTER
Marvel Atlas, July, 1956
1 JMn 175.00
2 thru 6 . . . . @125.00
Becomes:

DEXTER THE DEMON
Sept., 1957
7 . . . . 100.00

MEMORIES
Epic
1 Space Adventures 2.50

MENACE
Marvel Atlas, May, 1953
1 RH,BEv,GT,One Head Too
  Many 1,000.00
2 RH,BEv,GT,JSt,Burton'sBlood . 650.00
3 BEv,RH,JR,The Werewolf 500.00
4 BEv,RH,The Four Armed Man . 500.00
5 BEv,RH,GC,GT,I&O:Zombie . . 750.00
6 BEv,RH,JR,The Graymoor
  Ghost 450.00
7 JSt,RH,Fresh out of Flesh 400.00
8 RH,The Lizard Man 400.00
9 BEv,The Walking Dead 425.00
10 RH(c),Half Man,Half.... . . . . 400.00
11 JKz,JR,Locked In,May, 1954 . 400.00

MEN IN ACTION
Marvel Atlas, April, 1952
1 Sweating it Out 200.00
2 US Infantry stories 150.00
3 RH 100.00
4 War stories 100.00
5 JMn,Squad Charge 100.00
6 War stories 100.00
7 RH(c),BK,No Risk Too Great . 150.00
8 JRo(c),They Strike By Night . 100.00
9 SSh(c),Rangers Strike Back . . 100.00
Becomes:

BATTLE BRADY
10 SSh(c),F:Battle Brady 150.00
11 SSh(c) 100.00
12 SSh(c),Death to the Reds. . . 100.00
13 . . . . 100.00
14 Final Issue,June, 1953 . . . . . 100.00

MEN IN BLACK
1 ANi, prequel to movie (1997) 4.00
Spec. Movie Adaptation (1997) 4.00

MEN IN BLACK: RETRIBUTION
Aug., 1997
1 continuation from movie 4.00

MEN'S ADVENTURES
See: TRUE WESTERN

MEPHISTO vs. FOUR HEROES
April–July, 1987
1 JB,BWi,A:Fantastic Four 3.50
2 JB,BWi,A:X-Factor 3.00
3 JB,AM,A:X-Men 3.00
4 JB,BWi,A:Avengers 3.00

METEOR MAN
1993–94
1 R:Meteor Man 2.25
2 V:GhostStrike,Malefactor,Simon . 2.25
3 A:Spider-Man 2.25
4 A:Night Thrasher 2.25
5 Exocet 2.25
6 final issue 2.25

[TED McKEEVER'S} METROPOL
Epic, 1991–92
1 Ted McKeever 3.00
2 thru 12 . . . . @3.00

METROPOL A.D.
Epic, 1992
1 R:The Angels 3.50
2 V:Demons 3.50
3 V:Nuclear Arsenal 3.50

MICRONAUTS
[1st Series] Jan., 1979
1 MGo,JRu,O:Micronauts 5.00
2 thru 36 MGo,JRu,Earth . . . . . @3.00
37 KG,Nightcrawler 4.00
38 thru 59 GK,1st direct. . . . . . @2.50
Ann.#1,SD 2.50
#2 SD 2.50
[2nd Series] 1984
1 V:The Makers 2.50
2 thru 20 . . . . @2.50

MICRONAUTS
(Special Edition) Dec., 1983
1 MGo/JRu,rep. 3.00
2 MGo/JRu,rep. 3.00
3 & 4 Rep.MG/JRu . . . . @3.00
5 Rep.MG/JRu,April, 1984 . . . . 3.00

MIDNIGHT MEN
Epic Heavy Hitters, 1993
1 HC,I:Midnight Men 3.00
2 HC,J:Barnett 2.25
3 HC,Pasternak is Midnight Man . 2.25
4 HC,Last issue 2.25

MIDNIGHT SONS UNLIMITED
1993–95
1 JQ,JBi,MT(c),A:Midnight Sons. . 4.25
2 BSz(c),F:Midnight Sons. 4.25
3 JR2(c),JS,A:Spider-Man 4.25
4 Siege of Darkness #17,
  D:2nd Ghost Rider. 4.25

Midnight Sons Unlimited #3
© Marvel Entertainment Group

5 DQ(s),F:Mordred,Vengeance,
  Morbius,Werewolf,Blaze,
  I:Wildpride 4.25
6 DQ(s),F:Dr.Strange 4.00
7 DQ(s),F:Man-Thing 4.00
8 . . . . 4.00
9 J:Mighty Destroyer 4.00

MIGHTY AVENGERS
Mar., 2007
1 BMB(s). 4.00
2 thru 7 BMB(s) 3.00

MIGHTY HEROES
Nov., 1997
1-shot SLo, Diaper Man, Rope Man,
  Cuckoo Man, Tornado Man, Strong
  Man, etc. 3.00

MIGHTY MARVEL WESTERN
Oct., 1968
1 JK,All reprints,B:Rawhide Kid
  Kid Colt,Two-Gun Kids 100.00
2 JK,DAy,Beware of the Barker
  Brothers 75.00
3 HT(c),JK,DAy,Walking Death . . . 75.00
4 HT(c),DAy 75.00
5 HT(c),DAy,Ambush 75.00
6 HT(c),DAy Doom in the Desert . 75.00
7 DAy,V:MurderousMasquerader . 75.00
8 HT(c),DAy,Rustler's on the
  Range 75.00
9 JSe(c),JK,DAy,V:Dr Danger . . . 75.00
10 OW,DH,Cougar. 75.00
11 V:The Enforcers 50.00
12 JK,V:Blackjack Bordon 55.00
13 V:Grizzly 55.00
14 JK.V:The Enforcers. 55.00
15 Massacre at Medicine Bend. . . 55.00
16 JK,Mine of Death 55.00
17 Ambush at Blacksnake Mesa . . 35.00
18 Six-Gun Thunderer 35.00
19 Reprints cont. 35.00
20 same 35.00
21 same. 25.00
22 . . . . 25.00
23 same 25.00
24 JDa,E:Kid Colt 25.00
25 B:Matt Slade 25.00
26 thru 31 Reprints . . . . @25.00
32 JK,AW,Ringo Kid #23 . . . . 20.00
33 thru 36 Reprints . . . . @20.00

37 JK,AW Two-Gun #51 . . . . 20.00
38 thru 45 Reprints . . . . @20.00
46 same,Sept., 1976 . . . . 20.00

[SABAN'S] MIGHTY MORPHIN POWER RANGERS
1 SLo,FaN,New ongoing series . . . 2.25
2 thru 7 . . . . @2.25
Photo Adaptation 3.00

[SABAN'S] MIGHTY MORPHIN POWER RANGERS: NINJA RANGERS/ VR TROOPERS
1 FaN,RLm,JP,flip book 2.25
2 JP,flip book. 2.25
3 thru 6 . . . . @2.25

MIGHTY MOUSE
[1st Series] Fall, 1946
1 Terrytoons Presents 2,200.00
2 . . . . 900.00
3 . . . . 600.00
4 Summer, 1947 . . . . 600.00

MIGHTY MOUSE
Oct., 1990
1 EC,Dark Mite Returns 3.00
2 EC,V:The Glove. 2.25
3 EC/JBr(c)Prince Say More 2.25
4 EC/GP(c)Alt.Universe #1 . . . . . . 2.25
5 EC,Alt.Universe #2 . . . . 2.25
6 Ferment',A:MacFurline 2.25
7 EC,V:Viral Worm 2.25
8 EC,BAT-BAT:Year One,
  O:Bug Wonder. 2.25
9 EC,BAT-BAT:Year One,
  V:Smoker. 2.25
10 Night o/t Rating Lunatics 2.25

MILLIE THE MODEL
Winter, 1945
1 O:Millie the Model,
  Bowling(c) 1,500.00
2 Totem Pole(c) 750.00
3 Anti-Noise(c) 500.00
4 Bathing Suit(c) 500.00
5 Blame it on Fame 500.00
6 Beauty and the Beast 500.00
7 Bathing Suit(c) 500.00
8 Fancy Dress(c),HK,Hey Look . 500.00
9 Paris(c),BW 600.00
10 Jewelry(c),HK,Hey Look 500.00
11 HK,Giggles and Grins 350.00
12 A:Rusty,Hedy Devine 250.00
13 A:Hedy Devine,HK,Hey Look . 275.00
14 HK,Hey Look. 275.00
15 HK,Hey Look. 250.00
16 HK,Hey Look. 250.00
17 thru 20 . . . . @275.00
21 thru 75 . . . . @225.00
76 thru 99 . . . . @150.00
100 . . . . 200.00
101 thru 126 . . . . @150.00
127 Millie/Clicker 165.00
128 A:Scarlet Mayfair. 125.00
129 The Truth about Agnes 125.00
130 thru 153 . . . . @125.00
154 B:New Millie 125.00
155 thru 206 . . . . @125.00
207 Dec., 1973 . . . . 125.00
Ann.#1 How Millie Became
  a Model 450.00
Ann.#2 Millies Guide to
  the World of Modeling 300.00

Ann.#3 Many Lives of Millie. 200.00
Ann.#4 Many Lives of Millie. 175.00

MISS AMERICA COMICS
1944
1 Miss America(c),pin-ups . . . 2,700.00

MISS AMERICA MAGAZINE
Nov., 1944—Nov., 1958
2 Ph(c),Miss America costume
  I;Patsy Walker,Buzz Baxter,
  Hedy Wolfe 2,000.00
3 Ph(c),A:Patsy Walker,Miss
  America 750.00
4 Ph(c),Betty Page,A:Patsy
  Walker,Miss America 750.00
5 Ph(c),A:Patsy Walker,Miss
  America 750.00
6 Ph(c),A:Patsy Walker. 200.00
7 Patsy Walker stories 175.00
8 same 175.00
9 same 175.00
10 same 175.00
11 same 175.00
12 same 175.00
13 thru 18 . . . . @175.00
21 . . . . 200.00
22 thru 93 . . . . @125.00

Miss Fury Comics #1
© Marvel Entertainment Group

MISS FURY COMICS
Marvel Timely, Winter, 1942-43
1 Newspaper strip reprints,
  ASh(c):O:Miss Fury 6,500.00
2 V:Nazis(c) 3,000.00
3 Hitler/Nazi Flag(c) 2,500.00
4 ASh(c),Japanese(c) 2,000.00
5 ASh(c),Gangster(c) 1,500.00
6 ASh(c),Gangster(c). 1,500.00
7 Gangster(c) 1,200.00
8 Atom-Bomb Secrets(c)
  Winter, 1946 . . . . 1,200.00

MISSION: IMPOSSIBLE
May, 1996
1 RLd,MWn(s),Movie adapt. 3.00

MISTY
Star, Dec., 1985
1 F:Millie the Models Niece 3.50
2 thru 5 . . . . @3.50
6 May, 1986 . . . . 3.50

MARVEL

MITZI COMICS
Marvel Timely, Spring, 1948
1 HK:Hey Look,Giggles
and Grins 350.00
Becomes:

MITZI'S BOYFRIEND
2 F:Chip,Mitzi/Chip(c) 200.00
3 Chips adventures 125.00
4 thru 7 same . . . . @125.00
Becomes:

MITZI'S ROMANCES
8 Mitzi/Chip(c) 125.00
9 . . . . 100.00
10 Dec., 1949 . . . . 100.00

MODELING WITH MILLIE
See: DATE WITH MILLIE

MOEBIUS
Epic, Oct., 1987
1 . . . . 12.00
2 . . . . 12.00
3 . . . . 15.00
4 . . . . 12.00
5 . . . . 12.00
6 1988 . . . . 12.00

MOEBIUS: FUSION
1 128-pg. Sketchbook 20.00

MOLLY MANTON'S ROMANCES
Sept., 1949
1 Ph(c),Dare Not Marry 200.00
2 Ph(c),Romances of 150.00
Becomes:

ROMANTIC AFFAIRS
3 Ph(c) 125.00

MOMENT OF SILENCE
Dec., 2001
Spec. 9-11-01 tribute issue 3.50

THE MONKEY AND THE BEAR
Marvel Atlas, 1953
1 . . . . 100.00
2 . . . . 65.00

MONSTER MENACE
1 thru 4 SD,rep. . . . . @3.00

MONSTER OF FRANKENSTEIN
Jan., 1973
1 MP,Frankenstein's Monster . . . 75.00
2 MP,Bride of the Monster 50.00
3 MP,Revenge 50.00
4 MP,Monster's Death. 50.00
5 MP,The Monster Walks
Among Us. 50.00
Becomes:

FRANKENSTEIN
1973–75
6 MP,Last of the Frankensteins . . 30.00
7 JB,The Fiend and the Fury 30.00
8 JB,A:Dracula 45.00
9 JB,A:Dracula 45.00
10 JB,Death Strikes Frankenstein 25.00
11 Carnage at CastleFrankenstein 20.00
12 Frankenstein's Monster today. . 20.00
13 Undying Fiend. 20.00
14 Fury of the Night Creature 20.00
15 Trapped in a Nightmare 20.00
16 The Brute and the Berserker . . 20.00

Frankenstein #13
© Marvel Entertainment Group

17 Phoenix Aflame. 20.00
18 Children of the Damned 20.00

MONSTERS ON THE PROWL
See: CHAMBER OF DARKNESS

MONSTERS UNLEASHED
July, 1973
1 GM(c),GC,DW,B&W Mag 65.00
2 JB,FB,BEv,B:Frankenstein 50.00
3 NA(c),GK,GM,GT,B:Man-Thing 50.00
4 JB,GC,BK,I:Satana 50.00
5 JB 35.00
6 MP 25.00
7 AW 35.00
8 GP,NA 40.00
9 A:Wendigo 40.00
10 O:Tigra 40.00
11 FB(C),April, 1975 . . . . 40.00
Ann.#1 GK 40.00

MOON KNIGHT
[1st Regular Series] Nov., 1980
1 BSz,O:Moon Knight 7.00
2 BSz,V:Slasher 3.50
3 BSz,V:Midnight Man 3.50
4 BSz,V:Committee of 5 . . . . 3.50
5 BSz,V:Red Hunter 3.50
6 BSz,V:White Angels 3.50
7 BSz,V:Moon Kings. 3.50
8 BSz,V:Moon Kings, Drug 3.00
9 BSz,V:Midnight Man 3.00
10 BSz,V:Midnight Man 3.00
11 BSz,V:Creed (Angel Dust) 3.00
12 BSz,V:Morpheus 3.00
13 BSz,A:Daredevil & Jester 3.00
14 BSz,V:Stained Glass Scarlet . . 3.00
15 FM(c),BSz,1st Direct. 4.00
16 V:Blacksmith 3.00
17 BSz,V:Master Sniper. 3.00
18 BSz,V:Slayers Elite 3.00
19 BSz,V:Arsenal 3.00
20 BSz,V:Arsenal 3.00
21 A:Bother Voodoo 2.50
22 BSz,V:Morpheus 2.50
23 BSz,V:Morpheus 2.50
24 BSz,V:Stained Glass Scarlet . . 2.50
25 BSz,Black Specter 2.50
26 KP,V:Cabbie Killer 2.50
27 A:Kingpin. 2.50
28 BSz,Spirits in the Sands 2.50
29 BSz,V:Werewolf 2.50

30 BSz,V:Werewolf 2.50
31 TA,V:Savage Studs 2.50
32 KN,Druid Walsh 2.50
33 KN,V:Druid Walsh 2.50
34 KN,Marc Spector. 2.50
35 KN,X-Men,FF,V:The Fly
DoubleSized 3.00
36 A:Dr.Strange 2.50
37 V:Zohar 2.50
38 V:Zohar 2.50

[2nd Regular Series] 1985
1 O:Moon Knight,DoubleSize 2.50
2 Yucatan 2.50
3 V:Morpheus 2.50
4 A:Countess 2.50
5 V:Lt.Flint. 2.50
6 GI,LastIssue. 2.50

[3rd Regular Series] 1989–94
1 V:Bushmaster 4.00
2 A:Spider-Man 3.00
3 V:Bushmaster 2.50
4 RH,A:Midnight,Black Cat 2.50
5 V:Midnight,BlackCat. 2.50
6 A:BrotherVoodoo 2.50
7 A:BrotherVoodoo 2.50
8 TP,A:Punisher,A of V 3.00
9 TP,A:Punisher,A of V 3.00
10 V:Killer Shrike,A of V. 2.00
11 TP,V:Arsenal 2.00
12 TP,V:Bushman,A:Arsenal 2.50
13 TP,V:Bushman 2.50
14 TP,V:Bushman 2.50
15 TP,Trial o/Marc Spector #1,A:
Silv.Sable,Sandman,Paladin . . 3.00
16 TP,Trial o/Marc Spector #2,A:
Silv.Sable,Sandman,Paladin . . 3.00
17 TP,Trial o/Marc Spector #3 . . . . 3.00
18 TP,Trial o/Marc Spector #4 . . . . 3.00
19 RLd(c),TP,SpM,Punisher. 3.00
20 TP,A:Spider-Man,Punisher 3.00
21 TP,Spider-Man,Punisher 3.00
22 I:Harbinger 2.50
23 Confrontation 2.50
24 A:Midnight 2.50
25 MBa,TP,A:Ghost Rider 3.00
26 BSz(c),TP,B:Scarlet Redemption
V:Stained Glass Scarlet 2.50
27 TP,V:Stained Glass Scarlet 2.50
28 TP,V:Stained Glass Scarlet 2.50
29 TP,V:Stained Glass Scarlet 2.50
30 TP,V:Stained Glass Scarlet 2.50
31 TP,E:Scarlet Redemption,
A:Hobgoblin 2.75
32 TP,V:Hobgoblin,SpM(in Black) . 3.00
33 TP,V:Hobgoblin,A:Spider-Man. . 3.00
34 V:Killer Shrike 2.50
35 TP,Return of Randall Spector
Pt.1,A:Punisher 2.50
36 TP,A:Punisher,Randall 2.50
37 TP,A:Punisher,Randall 2.50
38 TP,A:Punisher,Randall 2.50
39 TP,N:Moon Knight,A:Dr.Doom . 2.50
40 TP,V:Dr.Doom 2.50
41 TP,Infinity War,I:Moonshade . . . 2.50
42 TP,Infinity War,V:Moonshade . . 2.50
43 TP(i),Infinity War 2.50
44 Inf.War,A:Dr.Strange.FF 2.50
45 V:Demogoblin 2.50
46 V:Demogoblin 2.50
47 Legacy Quest Scenario 2.50
48 I:Deadzone 2.50
49 V:Deadzone 2.50
50 A:Avengers,I:Hellbent,
Die-cut(c) 3.50
51 A:Gambit,V:Hellbent 2.50
52 A:Gambit,Werewolf 2.50
53 Pang 2.50
54 . . . . 2.50
55 SPa,V:Sunstreak 6.00
56 SPa,V:Seth 6.00
57 SPa,Inf.Crusade 4.00
58 SPa(c),A:Hellbent 3.00

MARVEL

59 SPa(c), ... 3.50
60 E:TKa(s),SPa,D:Moonknight. . . . 5.00
Spec.#1 ANi,A:Shang-Chi 2.50
1-shot Moon Knight: Divided We Fall
  DCw,V:Bushman (1992) 5.00

MOON KNIGHT
(Special Edition) Nov., 1983
1 BSz,reprints 2.50
2 BSz,reprints 2.50
3 BSz,reprints,Jan., 1984 . . . . 2.50

MOON KNIGHT
Nov., 1997–Feb., 1998
1 (of 4) DgM, Moon Knight returns . 2.50
1A signed by Tommy Lee Edwards
  (250 copies). 20.00
2 DgM,A:Scarlet 2.50
3 DgM,Resurrection War,V:Black
  Spectre 2.50
4 DgM,Resurrecton War, concl. . . . 2.50

MOON KNIGHT
Dec., 1998
1 (of 4) DgM,MT,A:Marlene 3.00
2 DgM,MT. 3.00
3 DgM,MT. 3.00
4 DgM,MT,concl. 3.00

MOON KNIGHT
April, 2006
1 The Bottom, pt.1 . . . . 3.00
2 thru 6 The Bottom, pt.2 – pt.6 . @3.00
7 Midnight Sun, pt.1 . . . . 3.00
8 Mignight Sun, pt.2, Civil War . . . 3.00
9 Midnight Sun, pt.3, Civil War . . . 3.00
10 Midnight Sun, pt.4, Civil War . . . 3.00
11 Midnight Sun, pt.5, Civil War . . . 3.00
12 Midnight Sun, concl. 3.00
13 48-pgs. 4.00
Ann. #1 . . . . 4.00

MOONSHADOW
Epic, May, 1985
1 JMu,O:Moonshadow 6.00
2 thru 12 . . . . @4.00

MORBIUS
1992–95
1 V:Lilith,Lilin,A:Blaze,Gh.Rider,
  Rise o/t Midnight Sons #3,
  polybagged w/poster 3.00
2 V:Simon Stroud 2.50

Morbius #11
© Marvel Entertainment Group

3 A:Spider-Man 2.25
4 I:Dr.Paine,C:Spider-Man 2.25
5 V:Basilisk,(inc Superman tribute
  on letters page) 2.25
6 V:Basilisk 2.25
7 V:Vic Slaughter 2.25
8 V:Nightmare 2.25
9 V:Nightmare. 2.25
10 Two Tales 2.25
11 A:Nightstalkers 2.25
12 Midnight Massacre#4 . . . . 2.50
13 R:Martine,A:Lilith. 2.25
14 RoW,V:Nightmare,A:Werewolf . . 2.25
15 A:Ghost Rider,Werewolf 2.25
16 GWt(s),Siege of Darkness#5 . . . 2.25
17 GWt(s),Siege of Darkness#17 . . 2.25
18 GWt(s),A:Deathlok 2.25
19 GWt(s),A:Deathlok 2.25
20 GWt(s),I:Bloodthirst. 2.25
21 B:Dance of the Hunter,A:SpM. . . 2.25
22 A:Spider-Man 2.25
23 E:Dance of the Hunter,A:SpM. . . 2.25
24 Return of the Dragon 2.25
25 RoW 2.50
26 . . . . 2.00
27 . . . . 2.00
28 A:Werewolf 2.00
29 . . . . 2.00
30 New Morbius 2.00
31 A:Mortine. 2.00
32 Another Kill 2.00

MORBIUS REVISITED
1993
1 WMc,rep.Fear #20 . . . . 2.25
2 WMc,rep.Fear #28. . . . . 2.25
3 WMc,rep.Fear #29. . . . . 2.25
4 WMc,rep.Fear #30. . . . . 2.25
5 WMc,rep.Fear #31. . . . . 2.25

MORLOCKS
April, 2002
1 (of 4) SMa, outsiders 2.50
2 SMa,mutants stay hidden 2.50
3 SMa,where lurk the Morlocks . . . 2.50
4 SMa,concl 2.50

MORT THE DEAD
TEENAGER
1993–94
1 LHa(s),I:Mort 2.25
2 thru 4 LHa(s), ... @2.25

MOTHER TERESA
1984
1 Mother Teresa Story 5.00

MOTOR MOUTH
& KILLPOWER
Marvel UK, 1992–93
1 GFr,A:Nick Fury,I:Motor
  Mouth,Killpower 2.50
2 GFr,A:Nick Fury, ... 2.25
3 GFr,V:Killpower,A:Punisher 2.25
4 GFr,A:Nick Fury,Warheads,
  Hell's Angel,O:Killpower 2.25
5 GFr,A:Excalibur,Archangel. 2.25
6 GFr,A:Cable,Punisher 2.25
7 EP,A:Cable,Nick Fury 2.25
8 JFr,A:Cable,Nick Fury 2.25
9 JFr,A:Cable,N.Fury,V:Harpies . . . 2.25
10 V:Red Sonja 2.25
11 V:Zachary Sorrow 2.25
12 A:Death's Head II 2.25
13 A:Death's Head II 2.25

MS. MARVEL
Jan., 1977
1 JB,O:Ms Marvel 15.00
2 JB,JSt,V:Scorpion 8.00
3 JB,JSt,V:Doomsday Man 8.00
4 JM,JSt,V:Destructor 8.00
5 JM,JSt,A:V:Vision 8.00
6 JM,JSt,V:Grotesk 8.00
7 JM,JSt,V:Modok 8.00
8 JM,JSt,GF(c),V:Grotesk. 8.00
9 KP,JSt,I:Deathbird 9.00
10 JB,TP,V:Deathbird,Modok. 7.00
11 V:Elementals 6.00
12 JSn(c),V:Hecate 6.00
13 Bedlam in Boston 6.00
14 CI,TA(c),V:Steeplejack 6.00
15 V:Tigershark 6.00
16 TA,V:Tigershark,A:Beast. 15.00
17 TA,C:Mystique. 12.00
18 I:Mystique,A:Avengers 22.00
19 A:Captain Marvel 6.00
20 V:Lethal Lizards,N:Ms.Marvel . . 6.00
21 V:Lethal Lizards 6.00
22 TA,V:Deathbirds 6.00
23 The Woman who Fell to Earth
  April, 1979 . . . . 6.00

Ms. Marvel #22
© Marvel Entertainment Group

MS. MARVEL
Mar., 2006
1 . . . . 3.00
2 thru 9 . . . . @3.00
10 A:Rogue, Beast. 3.00
11 V:Doomsday Man 3.00
12 V:Doomsday Man 3.00
13 AaL,The Deal,pt.1 . . . . 3.00
14 AaL,The Deal,pt.1 . . . . 3.00
15 AaL,Ready, A.I.M., Fire, pt.1 . . . 3.00
16 AaL,Ready, A.I.M., Fire, pt.2 . . . 3.00
17 AaL,Ready, A.I.M., Fire, pt.3 . . . 3.00
18 Puppets,pt.1 . . . . 3.00
19 AaL,Puppets,pt.2. . . . . 3.00
20 Puppets,pt.3 . . . . 3.00
21 Monster Island 3.00
Spec.F:Wonder Man 3.00

MUPPET BABIES
Star, Aug., 1984
1 thru 10 . . . . @2.25
11 thru 25 July, 1989 . . . . @2.25

MARVEL

MUPPETS TAKE MANHATTAN
1 movie adapt,November, 1984 . . . 3.00
2 movie adapt 3.00
3 movie adapt,Jan., 1985 . . . . 3.00

MUTANTS: THE AMAZING X-MEN
1 X-Men After Xavier 3.50
2 Exodus, Dazzler,V:Abyss 2.25
3 F:Bishop 2.25
4 V:Apocalypse 2.25

MUTANTS: THE ASTONISHING X-MEN
1 Uncanny X-Men 3.50
2 V:Holocaust 2.25
3 V:Abyss 2.25
4 V:Beast,Infinities 2.25

MUTANTS: GENERATION NEXT
1 Generation X Ax 3.50
2 Genetic Slave Pens 2.25
3 V:Sugar Man 2.25
4 V:Sugar Man 2.25

MUTANT 2099
Sept., 2004
1 . . . . 3.00

MUTANT X
Aug., 1998
1 HMe,TR,F:Havok, 48-pg 3.00
2 HMe,TR,F:Havok 2.50
2a variant cover 2.50
3 HMe,TR,V:Pack 2.50
4 HMe,TR,V:Goblin Queen 2.50
5 HMe,F:Brute, Fallen 2.50
6 HMe,A:Mutant-X Spider-Man . . . 2.50
7 HMe,Trial of the Brute 2.50
8 HMe,V:Goblin Queen 2.50
9 HMe,V:Sentinels 2.50
10 HMe,V:The Six 2.50
11 HMe,Bloodstorm vs. Havok . . . 2.50
12 HMe,O:Goblin Queen,Havok,
    48-page 3.50
13 O:Bloodstorm 2.50
14 HMe,CNr,I:Cyclops 2.50
15 HMe,F:Havok 2.50
16 HMe 2.50
17 HMe,CNr,V:Cyclops 2.50
18 HMe,CNr,A:Punisher 2.50
19 HMe,A:Professor X 2.50
20 HMe,A:Havok 2.50
21 HMe,BS,Prof.X & Apocalypse . . 2.50
22 HMe,BS,Galactus 2.50
23 HMe,TL,Apocalypse 2.50
24 HMe,TL,Master Planner 2.50
25 HMe,TL,The Six,48-pg 3.50
26 HMe,TL,The Six,Bloodstorm . . . 2.50
27 HMe,TL,Dagger,Outcasts 2.50
28 HMe,TL,F:Wolverine 2.50
29 HMe,TL,F:Wolverine 2.50
30 HMe,RLm,F:Capt.America 2.50
31 HMe,RLm,F:Capt.America 2.50
32 HMe,RLm,48-page, final 3.00
GN Mutant X, rep.#1 & #2 . . . . . . 6.00
Ann.1999, 48-page 3.50
Ann.2000 HMe,secrets 3.50
Ann.2001 HMe,48-page 3.00

MUTANT X
Oct., 2001
1 HC,JHo, TV show tie-in 3.00
2 HC,JHo, ... 2.50
Spec.#1 48-pg.,photo(c) (2002) . . 3.50
Spec.Dangerous Discoveries (2002) 3.50

MUTANT X: FUTURE SHOCK
May, 2002
1 CCI,F:Shalimar,54-pg. 3.50

MUTATIS
Epic
1 I:Mutatis 2.50
2 O:Mutatis 2.50
3 A:Mutatis 2.50

MUTIES
Feb., 2002
1 (of 6) F:Jared 2.50
2 in Japan, I:Seiji 2.50
3 F:Riek Bukenya 2.50
4 . . . . 2.50
5 . . . . 2.50
6 concl 2.50

MUTOPIA X
July, 2005
1 (of 5) House of M tie-in 3.00
2 House of M Tie-in 3.00
3 thru 5 . . . . @3.00

MY DIARY
Dec., 1949–March, 1950
1 Ph(c),The Man I Love 175.00
2 Ph(c),I Was Anybody's Girl . . . 150.00

WESTERN LIFE ROMANCES
Marvel Comics, 1949
1 . . . . 225.00
2 . . . . 200.00
Becomes:

MY FRIEND IRMA
Marvel Atlas, 1950
3 . . . . 225.00
4 HK 250.00
5 HK 175.00
6 . . . . 125.00
7 HK 125.00
8 . . . . 125.00
9 Paper dolls 150.00
10 . . . . 125.00
11 . . . . 100.00
12 thru 22 . . . . @100.00
23 FF(one page) 125.00
24 thru 48 . . . . @100.00

My Friend Irma #10
© Marvel Entertainment Group

MY GIRL PEARL
Marvel Atlas, 1955–61
1 . . . . 175.00
2 . . . . 150.00
3 . . . . 125.00
4 . . . . 125.00
5 . . . . 125.00
6 . . . . 125.00
7 . . . . 100.00
8 . . . . 100.00
9 . . . . 100.00
10 . . . . 100.00
11 . . . . 100.00

MY LOVE
July, 1949
1 Ph(c),One Heart to Give 175.00
2 Ph(c),Hate in My Heart 125.00
3 Ph(c), ... 125.00
4 Ph(c),Betty Page, April,1950 . . 500.00

MY LOVE
Sept., 1969
1 Love story reprints 100.00
2 thru 9 . . . . @40.00
10 . . . . 50.00
11 thru 38 . . . . @30.00
39 March, 1976 . . . . 30.00

MY ROMANCE
Sept., 1948
1 Romance Stories 175.00
2 . . . . 125.00
3 . . . . 125.00
Becomes:

MY OWN ROMANCE
4 Romance Stories Continue . . . 250.00
5 thru 10 . . . . @150.00
11 thru 20 . . . . @150.00
21 thru 50 . . . . @125.00
51 thru 54 . . . . @100.00
55 ATh 125.00
56 thru 60 . . . . @100.00
61 thru 70 . . . . @100.00
71 AW 125.00
72 thru 76 . . . . @100.00
Becomes:

TEENAGE ROMANCE
77 Romance Stories Continue . . . 100.00
78 thru 85 . . . . @100.00
86 March, 1962 . . . . 100.00

MYS-TECH WARS
Marvel UK, 1993
1 BHi,A:FF,X-Men,Avengers 2.25
2 A:FF,X-Men,X-Force 2.25
3 BHi,A:X-Men,X-Force 2.25
4 A:Death's Head II 2.25

MYSTERY TALES
Marvel Atlas, March, 1952
1 GC,Horror Strikes at
    Midnight 1,400.00
2 BK,BEv,OW,The Corpse
    is Mine 700.00
3 RH,GC,JM, Vampire Strikes . . 550.00
4 Funeral of Horror 550.00
5 Blackout at Midnight 550.00
6 A-Bomb Picture 550.00
7 JRo,The Ghost Hunter 550.00
8 BEv 550.00
9 BEv(c),the Man in the Morgue 550.00
10 BEV(c),GT,What Happened
    to Harry 550.00
11 BEv(c) 450.00
12 GT,MF 475.00
13 . . . . 400.00
14 BEv(c),GT 400.00

15 RH(c),EK. 400.00
16 . . . . 400.00
17 RH(c). 400.00
18 AW,DAy,GC. 475.00
19 . . . . 400.00
20 Electric Chair 400.00
21 JF,MF,BP,Decapitation 400.00
22 JF,MF 400.00
23 thru 27. . . . . @350.00
28 . . . . 300.00
29 thru 32. . . . . @325.00
33 BEv. 300.00
34 . . . . 300.00
35 BEv,GC. 300.00
36 . . . . 325.00
37 DW,BP,JR. 300.00
38 BP,BEv. 300.00
39 BK,BEv 325.00
40 JM 325.00
41 MD,BEv. 300.00
42 JeR 300.00
41 GC. 300.00
44 AW 300.00
45 SD 275.00
46 RC,SD,JP 275.00
47 DAy,BP 275.00
48 BEv 300.00
49 GM,AT,DAy 300.00
50 JO,AW,GM 275.00
51 DAy,JO 275.00
52 DAy 275.00
53 BEv 275.00
54 RC,Aug., 1957 . . . . 300.00

MYSTICAL TALES
Marvel Atlas, June, 1956
1 BEv,BP,JO,Say the Magical
   Words 750.00
2 BEv(c),JO,Black Blob 500.00
3 BEv(c),RC,Four Doors To 550.00
4 BEv(c).The Condemned 550.00
5 AW,Meeting at Midnight 550.00
6 BK,AT,He Hides in the Tower . 400.00
7 BEv,JF,JO,AT,FBe,The
   Haunted Tower 400.00
8 BK,SC, Stone Walls Can't
   Stop Him,Aug., 1957 . . . . . . 400.00

MYSTIC ARCANA
June 2007
Spec. Magik. 3.00
Spec. Black Knight. 3.00
Spec. Scarlet Witch 3.00
Spec. Sister Grimm 3.00

MYSTIC COMICS
Marvel Timely, March, 1940
[1st Series]
1 ASh(c),SSh,O;Blue Blaze,Dynamic,
   Man,Flexo,B:Dakor the Magician,
   A:Zephyr Jones,3X's, Deep Sea,
   Demon,bondage(c). 25,000.00
2 ASh(c),B:The Invisible Man
   Mastermind,Blue Blaze . . . 8,000.00
3 ASh(c),O:Hercules 5,500.00
4 ASh(c),O:Thin Man,Black Widow
   E:Hercules,Blue Blazes,Dynamic
   Man,Flexo,Invisible Man. . . 6,000.00
5 ASh(c)O:The Black Marvel,
   Blazing Skull,Super Slave
   Terror,Sub-Earth Man . . . 5,500.00
6 ASh(c),O:The Challenger,
   B:The Destroyer 6,500.00
7 S&K(c),B:The Witness,O:Davey
   and the Demon,E;The Black
   Widow,Hitler(c) 7,000.00
8 Bondage(c). 3,500.00
9 MSy,DRi,Hitler/Bondage(c) . 3,700.00
10 E:Challenger,Terror 3,600.00

[2nd Series] Oct., 1944
1 SSh,B:The Angel,Human Torch,
   Destroyer,Terry Vance,
   Tommy Tyme,Bondage(c) . 4,000.00
2 E:Human Torch,Terry
   Vance,Bondage(c) 2,000.00
3 E:The Angel,Tommy Tyme
   Bondage(c) 1,800.00
4 ASh(c),A:Young Allies
   Winter, 1944-45 . . . . 1,800.00

MYSTIC
[3rd Series] March, 1951
1 MSy,Strange Tree 1,700.00
2 MSy,Dark Dungeon 800.00
3 GC,Jaws of Creeping Death . . 700.00
4 BW,MSy,The Den of the
   Devil Bird 1,500.00
5 MSy,Face 600.00
6 BW,She Wouldn't Stay Dead 1,600.00
7 GC,Untold Horror waits
   in the Tomb 500.00
8 DAy(c),BEv,GK,A Monster
   Among Us 500.00
9 BEv 500.00
10 GC. 500.00
11 JR,The Black Gloves 400.00
12 GC. 400.00
13 In the Dark 400.00
14 The Corpse and I 400.00
15 GT,JR,House of Horror 350.00
16 A Scream in the Dark 350.00
17 BEv,Behold the Vampire 350.00
18 BEv(c),The Russian Devil. . . . 350.00
19 Swamp Girl 350.00
20 RH(c). 350.00
21 BEv(c),GC. 325.00
22 RH(c). 325.00
23 RH(c),RA,RMn,Chilling Tales . 325.00
24 GK,RMn,How Many Times Can
   You Die 325.00
25 RH(c),RA,E.C.Swipe. 325.00
26 Severed Head(c). 325.00
27 Who Walks with a Zombie . . . 300.00
28 DW,RMn(c),Not Enough Dead 300.00
29 SMo,RMn(c),The Unseen 300.00
30 RH(c),DW 300.00
31 SC,JKz,RMn(c). 300.00
32 The Survivor 300.00
33 thru 36. . . . . @300.00
37 thru 51. . . . . @275.00
52 WW,RC 300.00
53 thru 57. . . . . @275.00
58 thru 60. . . . . @300.00
61 . . . . 250.00

Mystic #58
© *Marvel Entertainment Group*

MYTHOS
2007
Spec. Ghost Rider, PJe (1-2007 . . . 4.00
Spec. Spider-Man, PJe (6-2007) . . . 4.00
Spec. Hulk, PJe (8-2007). 4.00
Spec. Fantastic Four,PJe (10-2007) 4.00

MYSTIQUE
April, 2003
1 JLi(c),Drop Dead Gorgeous,pt.1 . 3.00
2 JLi(c),Drop Dead Gorgeous,pt.2 . 3.00
3 JLi(c),Drop Dead Gorgeous,pt.3 . 3.00
4 JLi(c),Drop Dead Gorgeous,pt.4 . 3.00
5 JLi(c),Drop Dead Gorgeous,pt.5 . 3.00
6 JLi(c),Drop Dead Gorgeous,pt.6 . 3.00
7 Tinker,Tailor,Mutant,Spy,pt.1 . . . 3.00
8 Tinker,Tailor,Mutant,Spy,pt.2 . . . 3.00
9 Tinker,Tailor,Mutant,Spy,pt.3 . . . 3.00
10 Tinker,Tailor,Mutant,Spy,pt.4 . . . 3.00
11 Maker's Mark,pt.1 . . . . 3.00
12 Maker's Mark,pt.2 . . . . 3.00
13 F:Shortpack. 3.00
14 Unnatural,pt.1 . . . . 3.00
15 Unnatural,pt.2 . . . . 3.00
16 Unnatural,pt.3 . . . . 3.00
17 Unnatural,pt.4 . . . . 3.00
18 Unnatural,pt.5 . . . . 3.00
19 Assassin's bullet 3.00
20 Quiet,pt.1 . . . . 3.00
21 Quiet,pt.2 . . . . 3.00
22 Quiet,pt.3 . . . . 3.00
23 Quiet,pt.4 . . . . 3.00
24 Quiet, concl. 3.00

MYTHOS
Jan., 2006
1 PJe,X-Men. 4.00
2 PJe,Hulk 4.00

'NAM, THE
Dec., 1986
1 MGo,Vietnam War 3.00
1a 2nd printing 2.50
2 MGo,Dust Off. 2.50
3 thru 8 MGo. . . . . @2.25
9 MGo,Action Issue,Tunnel Rat . . . 3.50
10 thru 49 MGo . . . . @2.25
52 Frank Castle(Punisher)#1. . . . . 3.00
52a 2nd printing 2.25
53 Punisher #2. . . . . 2.50
54 thru 84. . . . . @2.25

'NAM MAGAZINE, THE
(B&W) Aug., 1988–May, 1989
1 Reprints 3.00
2 thru 10 . . . . @2.50

NAMOR
April, 2003
1 MiS,manga. 2.25
2 MiS. 2.25
3 SvL. 2.25
4 SvL,F:Sandy 2.25
5 SvL,F:Sandy 2.25
6 SvL,Namor's choice. 2.25
7 PO, In Deep, pt.1. . . . . 2.25
8 PO, In Deep, pt.2. . . . . 2.25
9 PO, In Deep, pt.3. . . . . 3.00
10 PO,In Deep, pt.4. . . . . 3.00
11 JoB,In Deep,pt.5 . . . . 3.00
12 JoB,finale 3.00

NAMORA
Fall, 1948–Dec., 1948
1 BEv,DR 4,000.00
2 BEv,A:Sub-Mariner,Blonde
   Phantom 2,000.00
3 BEv,A:Sub-Mariner 2,300.00

MARVEL

MARVEL (vertical side tab)

NAMOR THE SUB-MARINER
April, 1990

1 JBy,BWi,I:Desmond
  & Phoebe Marrs 5.00
2 JBy,BWi,V:Griffin 3.00
3 JBy,BWi,V:Griffin 3.00
4 JBy,A:Reed & Sue Richards,
  Tony Stark 3.00
5 JBy,A:FF,IronMan,C:Speedball . . 3.00
6 JBy,V:Sluj 3.00
7 JBy,V:Sluj 3.00
8 JBy,V:Headhunter,R:D.Rand . . . 3.00
9 JBy,V:Headhunter 3.00
10 JBy,V:Master Man,Warrior
  Woman 2.50
11 JBy,V:Mast.Man,War.Woman . . 2.50
12 JBy,R:Invaders,Spitfire 2.50
13 JBy,Namor on Trial,A:Fantastic
  Four,Captain America,Thor . . . 2.50
14 JBy,R:Lady Dorma,A:Ka-Zar
  Griffin 2.50
15 JBy,A:Iron Fist. 2.50
16 JBy,A:Punisher,V:Iron Fist 2.50
17 JBy,V:Super Skrull(Iron Fist). . . 2.50
18 JBy,V:SuperSkrull,A:Punisher. . 2.50
19 JBy,V:Super Skrull,D:D.Marrs. . 2.50
20 JBy,Search for Iron Fist,
  O:Namorita 2.50
21 JBy,Visit to K'un Lun. 2.50
22 JBy,Fate of Iron Fist,
  C:Wolverine. 2.50
23 JBy,BWi,Iron Fist Contd.,
  C:Wolverine. 2.50
24 JBy,BWi,V:Wolverine 3.00
25 JBy,BWi,V:Master Khan 2.50
26 JaL,BWi,Search For Namor 5.00
27 JaL,BWi,V:Namorita 4.00
28 JaL,BWi,A:Iron Fist 3.00
29 JaL,BWi,After explosion 3.00
30 JaL,A:Doctor Doom 3.00
31 JaL,V:Doctor Doom 3.00
32 JaL,V:Doctor Doom,
  Namor regains memory. 3.00
33 JaL,V:Master Khan 2.50
34 JaL,R:Atlantis 2.50
35 JaL,V:Tiger Shark 2.50
36 JaL,I:Suma-Ket,A:Tiger Shark . 2.50
37 JaL,Blue Holo-Grafix,Altantean
  Civil War,N:Namor 2.75
38 JaL,O:Suma-Ket. 2.50
39 A:Tigershark,V:Suma-Ket 2.50
40 V:Suma-Ket. 2.50

Namor the Sub-Mariner #57
© Marvel Entertainment Group

41 V:War Machine 2.50
42 MCW,A:Stingray,V:Dorcas 2.50
43 MCW,V:Orka,Dorcas. 2.50
44 I:Albatross. 2.50
45 GI,A:Sunfire,V:Attuma. 2.50
46 GI, ... 2.50
47 GI,Starblast #2 . . . . 2.50
48 GI,Starblast #9,A:FF 2.50
49 GI,A:Ms. Marrs 2.50
50 GI,Holo-grafx(c),A:FF 4.00
50a Newsstand Ed. 2.50
51 AaL, ... 2.50
52 GI,I:Sea Leopard 2.50
53 GI,V:Sea Leopard 2.50
54 GI,I:Llyron. 2.50
55 GI,V:Llyron. 2.50
56 GI,V:Llyron. 2.50
57 A:Capt. America, V:Llyron. 2.50
58 . . . . 2.50
59 GI,V:Abomination 2.50
60 A:Morgan Le Fay 2.50
61 Atlantis Rising 2.50
62 V:Triton 2.50
Ann.#1 Subterran.Odyssey #3. . . . 3.00
Ann.#2 Return o/Defenders,pt.3 . . 4.00
Ann.#3 I:Assassin,A:Iron Fist,
  w/Trading card. 3.25
Ann.#4 V:Hydra 3.25

NAVY ACTION
Aug., 1954

1 BP,US Navy War Stories 225.00
2 TLn,Navy(c). 125.00
3 BEv 100.00
4 and 5 . . . . @100.00
6 JH(c) 100.00
7 MD,JMn 100.00
8 JMn,GC. 100.00
9 thru 15 . . . . @100.00
16 BEv(c). 100.00
17 MD,BEv(c). 100.00
18 Aug., 1957. . . . . 100.00

NAVY COMBAT
Marvel Atlas, June, 1955

1 DH,JMn(c),B:Torpedo Taylor . . 225.00
2 DH 125.00
3 DH,BEv. 100.00
4 DH 100.00
5 DH 100.00
6 JMn,A:Battleship Burke 100.00
7 thru 10 . . . . @100.00
11 MD,GC,JMn 100.00
12 RC. 125.00
13 GT 100.00
14 AT,GT 100.00
15 GT 100.00
16 . . . . 100.00
17 AW,AT,JMn 110.00
18 . . . . 100.00
19 . . . . 100.00
20 BEv,BP,AW,Oct., 1958 . . . . . 110.00

NAVY TALES
Marvel Atlas, Jan., 1957

1 BEv(c),BP,Torpedoes 200.00
2 AW,RC,JMn(c),One Hour
  to Live 175.00
3 JSe(c) 150.00
4 JSe(c),GC,JSt,RC,July, 1957 . 150.00

NELLIE THE NURSE
Marvel Atlas, 1945

1 Beach(c) 550.00
2 Nellie's Date(c) 250.00
3 Swimming Pool(c) 200.00
4 Roller Coaster(c) 200.00
5 Hospital(c),HK,Hey Look 200.00
6 Bedside Manner(c) 200.00
7 Comic book(c)A:Georgie . . . 200.00

8 Hospital(c),A:Georgie 200.00
9 BW,Nellie/Swing(c)A:Millie . . . 200.00
10 Bathing Suit(c),A:Millie 200.00
11 HK,Hey Look. 225.00
12 HK,Giggles 'n' Grins 200.00
13 HK 125.00
14 HK 150.00
15 HK 150.00
16 HK 150.00
17 HK,A:Annie Oakley 150.00
18 HK 150.00
19 . . . . 125.00
20 . . . . 125.00
21 . . . . 100.00
22 . . . . 100.00
23 . . . . 100.00
24 . . . . 100.00
25 . . . . 100.00
26 . . . . 100.00
27 . . . . 100.00
28 HK,Rusty Reprint 100.00
29 thru 35. . . . . @100.00
36 Oct., 1952 . . . . 100.00

NEW ADVENTURES OF CHOLLY & FLYTRAP
Epic

1 . . . . 5.00
2 . . . . 4.00
3 . . . . 4.00

NEW AVENGERS
Nov., 2004

1 BMB, The Breakout. 4.00
1a variant (c). 6.00
2 BMB, The Breakout 3.00
2a variant (c). 4.00
3 BMB,The Breakout,pt.3 . . . . 3.00
3a variant (c). 15.00
4 BMB,The Breakout,pt.4 . . . . 3.00
5 BMB,The Breakout,pt.5 . . . . 2.25
6 BMB,F:Captain America 2.25
7 BMB,the Sentry,pt.1. . . . . 2.25
8 BMB,SB, The Sentry,pt.2. . . . . . 2.50
9 BMB,The Sentry,pt.3 . . . . 2.50
5a thru 9a Variant(c) . . . . @2.50
10 BMB,The Sentry,pt.4. . . . . 2.50
11 BMB,Ronin,pt.1 . . . . 2.50
12 BMB,Ronin,pt.2. . . . . 2.50
13 BMB,Ronin,pt.3. . . . . 2.50
14 BMB,F:Spider-Woman 2.50
15 BMB,V:J. Jonah Jameson 2.50
16 BMB,The Collective, prologue . 2.50
17 BMB,The Collective 3.50
18 BMB,The Collective 3.00
19 BMB,The Collective 3.00
20 BMB,The Collective 3.00
21 BMB,Civil War tie-in 4.00
22 BMB,Civil War tie-in 4.00
23 BMB,Civil War tie-in 4.00
24 BMB,Civil War tie-in 4.00
25 BMB,Civil War tie-in 4.00
26 BMB,A:Dr. Strange 3.00
27 BMB(s) 3.00
28 BMB(s),Team is formed 5.00
29 BMB(s) 3.00
30 BMB(s),V:The Hand 3.00
31 BMB(s) 3.00
32 BMB(s) 3.00
33 BMB(s) 3.00
34 BMB(s),Wolverine vs. The Hood 3.00
35 BMB(s) The Hood 3.00
36 BMB(s), Symbiote. 3.00
Ann. #1 BMB 4.00
Spec.#1 Director's Cut (2004) 3.00
Spec. Handbook bios. 4.00
Spec. Illuminati. 4.00
New Avengers: Must-Haves 4.00

NEW AVENGERS: ILLUMINATI
Dec., 2006
1 (of 5) BMB(s) 3.00
2 thru 5 BMB(s) . . . . @3.00

NEW AVENGERS/ TRANSFORMERS
July, 2007
1 . . . . 3.00
2 thru 4 . . . . @3.00

NEW ETERNALS: APOCALYPSE NOW
Dec., 1999
1-shot JoB,SHa,64-pg.. . . . . 4.00

NEW EXCALIBUR
Nov., 2005
1 CCl 3.00
2 CCl,Defenders of the Realm 3.00
3 CCl,V: Original X-Men 3.00
4 CCl,Choose Your Destiny 3.00
5 CCl,Choose Your Destiny 3.00
6 CCl,Black Monday 3.00
7 CCl,Black Monday 3.00
8 CCl,So Why is it I'm Not Dead . . 3.00
9 Chest Pains 3.00
10 The Last Days of Camelot 3.00
11 The Last Days of Camelot 3.00
12 The Last Days of Camelot 3.00
13 Unredeemed, pt.1 . . . . 3.00
14 JCf,Unredeemable 3.00
15 JCf,Unredeemable 3.00
16 CCl,SEa,Fallen Friend, pt.1 . . . 3.00
17 CCl,SEa,Fallen Friend, pt.2 . . . 3.00
18 CCl,SEa,Battle for Eternity,pt.1. . 3.00
19 CCl,SEa,Battle for Eternity,pt.2. . 3.00
20 CCl,SEa,Battle for Eternity,pt.3. . 3.00
21 CCl,Battle for Eternity,pt.4 . . . . 3.00
22 CCl,Battle for Eternity,pt.5 . . . . 3.00
23 CCl,Battle for Eternity,pt.6 . . . . 3.00
24 CCl,Battle for Eternity,pt.7 . . . . 3.00

NEW MANGAVERSE
Jan., 2006
1 Rings of Fate 3.00
2 thru 5 . . . . @5.00

NEW MUTANTS, THE
March, 1983
1 BMc,MG,O:New Mutants 5.00
2 BMc,MG,V:Sentinels 4.00
3 BMc,MG,V:Brood Alien 3.50
4 SB,BMc,A:Peter Bristow 3.50
5 SB,BMc,A:Dark Rider 3.50
6 SB,AG,V:Viper 3.50
7 SB,BMc,V:Axe 3.50
8 SB,BMc,I:Amara Aquilla. 3.50
9 SB,TMd,I:Selene 3.50
10 SB,BMc,C:Magma 3.50
11 SB,TMd,I:Magma 3.50
12 SB,TMd,J:Magma 3.50
13 SB,TMd,I:Cypher(Doug Ramsey)
A:Kitty Pryde,Lilandra 3.00
14 SB,TMd,J:Magik,A:X-Men. 3.00
15 SB,TMd,Mass.Academy 3.00
16 SB,TMd,V:Hellions,I:Warpath
I:Jetstream. 20.00
17 SB,TMd,V:Hellions,A:Warpath . . 4.00
18 BSz,V:Demon Bear,I:New
Warlock,Magus 5.00
19 BSz,V:Demon Bear. 3.00
20 BSz,V:Demon Bear. 3.00
21 BSz,O&J:Warlock,doub.sz 5.00
22 BSz,A:X-Men 3.50
23 BSz,Sunspot,Cloak & Dagger. . 3.00

24 BSz,A:Cloak & Dagger 3.00
25 BSz,A:Cloak & Dagger 6.00
26 BSz,I:Legion(Prof.X's son) 7.00
27 BSz,V:Legion 4.00
28 BSz,O:Legion 4.00
29 BSz,V:Gladiators,I:Guido
(Strong Guy) 3.00
30 BSz,A:Dazzler. 3.00
31 BSz,A:Shadowcat 3.00
32 SL,V:Karma. 3.00
33 SL,V:Karma. 3.00
34 SL,V:Amahl Farouk. 3.00
35 BSz,J:Magneto 3.00
36 BSz,A:Beyonder 3.00
37 BSz,D:New Mutants 3.00
38 BSz,A:Hellions 3.00
39 BSz,A:White Queen 3.00
40 JG,KB,V:Avengers. 3.00
41 JG,TA,Mirage 3.00
42 JG,KB,A:Dazzler 3.00
43 SP,V:Empath,A:Warpath 3.00
44 JG,V:Legion. 5.00
45 JG,A:Larry Bodine. 3.00
46 JG,KB,Mutant Massacre 3.50
47 JG,KB,V:Magnus 3.00
48 JG,CR,Future 3.00
49 VM,Future. 3.00
50 JG,V:Magus,R:Prof.X 4.00
51 KN,A:Star Jammers 3.00
52 RL,DGr,Limbo 3.00
53 RL,TA,V:Hellions 3.00
54 SB,TA,N:New Mutants 3.00
55 BBl,TA,V:Aliens. 3.00
56 JBr,TA,V:Hellions,A:Warpath. . . 3.00
57 BBl,TA,I&J:Bird-Boy. 3.00
58 BBl,TA,Bird-Boy 3.00
59 BBl,TA,Fall of Mutants,
V:Dr.Animus. 3.00
60 BBl,TA,F.of M.,D:Cypher 2.50
61 BBl,TA,Fall of Mutants 2.50
62 JMu,A:Magma,Hellions 2.50
63 BHa,JRu,Magik 2.50
64 BBl,TA,R:Cypher 2.50
65 BBl,TA,V:FreedomForce 2.50
66 BBl,TA,V:Forge 2.50
67 BBl,I:Gosamyr. 2.50
68 BBl,V:Gosamyr. 2.50
69 BBl,AW,I:Spyder 2.50
70 TSh,AM,V:Spyder 2.50
71 BBl,AW,V:N'Astirh 2.50
72 BBl,A,Inferno. 2.50
73 BBl,W,A:Colossus. 3.00
74 BBl,W,A:X-Terminators 2.50
75 JBy,Mc,Black King,V:Magneto . 3.50
76 RB,TP,J:X-Terminators 2.50
77 RB,V:Mirage. 2.50
78 RL,AW,V:FreedomForce 2.50
79 BBl,AW,V:Hela 2.50
80 BBl,AW,Asgard 2.50
81 LW,TSh,JRu,A:Hercules 2.50
82 BBl,AW,Asgard 2.50
83 BBl,Asgard 2.50
84 TSh,AM,A:QueenUla 2.50
85 RLd&TMc(c),BBl,V:Mirage 5.00
86 RLd,BWi,V:Vulture,C:Cable . . . 6.00
87 RLd,BWi,I:Mutant Liberation
Front,Cable 25.00
87a 2nd Printing. 3.00
88 RLd,2nd Cable,V:Freedom
Force 7.50
89 RLd,V:Freedom Force 6.00
90 RLd,A:Caliban,V:Sabretooth. . . 6.00
91 RLd,A:Caliban,Masque,
V:Sabretooth. 6.00
92 RLd(c),BH,V:Skrulls 4.00
93 RLd,A:Wolverine,Sunfire,
V:Mutant Liberation Front 6.00
94 RLd,A:Wolverine,Sunfire,
V:Mutant Liberation Front 5.00
95 RLd,Extinction Agenda,V:Hodge
A:X-Men,X-Factor,D:Warlock . . 5.00
95a 2nd printing(gold) 5.00

New Mutants #43
© *Marvel Entertainment Group*

96 RLd,ATb,JRu,Extinction Agenda
V:Hodge,A:X-Men,X-Factor. . . . 5.00
97 E:LSi(s),RLd(c),JRu,Extinction
Agenda,V:Hodge 5.00
98 FaN(s),RLd,I:Deadpool,Domino,
Gideon,L:Rictor 25.00
99 FaN(s),RLd,I:Feral,Shatterstar,
L:Sunspot,J:Warpath 5.00
100 FaN(s),RLd,J:Feral,Shatterstar,
I:X-Force,V:Masque,Imperial
Protectorate,A:MLF 6.00
100a 2nd Printing(Gold). 4.00
100b 3rd Printing(Silver) 3.50
Ann.#1 BMc,TP,L.Cheney 7.00
Ann.#2 AD,V:Mojo,I:Psylocke,Meggan
(American App.). 10.00
Ann.#3 AD,PN,V:Impossible Man . . 4.00
Ann.#4 JBr,BMc,Evol.Wars 6.00
Ann.#5 RLd,JBg,MBa,KWi,Atlantis
Attacks,A:Namorita,I:Surf 8.00
Ann.#6 RLd(c),Days o/Future Present
V:FranklinRichards,(Pin-ups). . . 6.00
Ann.#7 JRu,RLd,Kings of Pain,
I:Piecemeal & Harness,
Pin-ups X-Force. 5.00
Spec #1,AAd,TA,Asgard War. 6.00
Summer Spec.#1 BBl,Megapolis . . . 3.50

NEW MUTANTS
Sept., 1997
1 (of 3) BRa,BCh,F:Cannonball,
Moonstar, Wolfsbane,Karma &
Sunspot 2.50
2 BRa,BCh,meeting with mutants
of the past 2.50
3 BRa,BCh, will Magik return
for good? 2.50

NEW MUTANTS
May, 2003
1 R:Original New Mutants. 2.50
2 F:Dani Moonstar 2.50
3 new student 2.50
4 F:Karma. 2.50
5 mutant teens 2.50
6 V:Reavers 2.50
7 CBa(c),Ties That Bind,pt.1 . . . . 2.50
8 CBa(c),Ties That Bind,pt.2 . . . . 2.50
9 CBa(c),Ties That Bind,pt.3 . . . . 2.50
10 CBa(c),Ties That Bind,pt.4 . . . . 3.00
11 CBa(c),Ties That Bind,pt.5 . . . . 3.00
12 CBa(c),Ties That Bind,pt.6 . . . . 3.00
13 The More Things Change. 3.00

NEW THUNDERBOLTS
See: THUNDERBOLTS

NEW UNIVERSAL
Dec., 2006
1 WEI,SvL	3.00
2 WEI,SvL,Trauma	3.00
3 WEI,SvL,Mathematics	3.00
4 WEI,SvL,The White Event	3.00
5 WEI,SvL	3.00
6 WEI,SvL	3.00

NEW WARRIORS
July, 1990
1 B:FaN(s),MBa,AW,V:Terrax, O:New Warriors	5.00
1a Gold rep.	2.50
2 thru 10	@3.50
11 thru 49	@2.50
50 reg. (c)	2.25
50a Glow-in-the-dark(c),V:Sphinx	3.25
51 thru 59	@2.25
60 Nova Omega,pt.2	2.50
61 thru 71	@2.25
Ann.#1 MBa,A:X-Force,V:Harness, Piecemeal,Kings of Pain #2	4.00
Ann.#2 Hero Killers #4,V:Sphinx	2.75
Ann.#3 LMa(i),E:Forces of Light, Forces of Darkness,I:Darkling w/card	3.25
Ann.#4 DaR(s),V:Psionex	3.25

NEW WARRIORS
Aug., 1999
1 F:Speedball,48-page	3.00
2 thru 10	@2.50

June, 2005
1 (of 6)	3.00
2 thru 6	@3.00

June, 2007
1	3.00
2 thru 6	@3.00

NEW X-MEN
See: X-MEN

NEW X-MEN
May, 2004
1 Choosing Sides,pt.1	3.00
2 Choosing Sides,pt.2	3.00
3 Choosing Sides,pt.3	3.00
4 Choosing Sides,pt.4	3.00
5 Choosing Sides,pt.5	3.00
6 Choosing Sides,pt.6	3.00
7 Haunted	3.00
8 Haunted	3.00
9 Haunted, Concl.	3.00
10 Too Much Information,pt.1	3.00
11 Too Much Information	3.00
12 X-Posed	3.00
13 Campfire	3.00
14 Year's End,pt.1	3.00
15 Year's End,pt.2	3.00
16 AaL,House Divided,pt.1	3.00
17 AaL,House Divided,pt.2	3.00
18 AaL,House Divided,pt.3	3.00
19 AaL,House Divided,pt.4	3.00
20 Childhood's End,pt.1	3.00
21 Childhood's End,pt.2	3.00
22 Childhood's End,pt.3	3.00
23 Childhood's End,pt.4	3.00
24 Crusade,pt.1	3.00
25 Crusade,pt.2	3.00
26 Crusade,pt.3	3.00
27 Crusade,pt.4	3.00
28 Nimrod,pt.1	3.00
29 Nimrod,pt.2	3.00
30 Nimrod,pt.3	3.00
31 Nimrod,pt.4	3.00

32 Whatever Happened to Wither	3.00
33 Mercury Falling, pt.1	3.00
34 Mercury Rising	3.00
35 Mercury Falling	3.00
36 Mercury Rising, concl.	3.00
37 Quest For Magik, prelude	3.00
38 Quest For Magik, pt.1	3.00
39 Quest For Magik, pt.2	3.00
40 Quest For Magik, pt.3	3.00
41 Quest For Magik, pt.4	3.00
42 Children of X-Men	3.00
43 Children of X-Men	3.00
44 Messiah Complex, pt.4 x-over	3.00
Spec. Academy X Yearbook,AaL	4.00

NEW X-MEN: HELLIONS
May, 2005
1 (of 4)	3.00
2	3.00
3 Fortune and Glory	3.00
4 Fortune and Glory	3.00

NEXTWAVE
Jan., 2006
1 WEI,SI	3.00
2 thru 5 WEI,SI	@3.00
Becomes:	

NEXTWAVE: AGENTS OF H.A.T.E.
6 thru 10 Agents of H.A.T.E.	@3.00
11 WEI,SI,Not a Civil War tie-in	3.00
12 WEI,SI	3.00

NFL SUPERPRO
1	7.00
Spec.#1 reprints	2.50

[Regular Series] Oct., 1991
1 A:Spider-Man,I:Sanzionaire	2.50
2 V:Quickkick	2.50
3 I:Instant Replay	2.50
4 V:Sanction	2.50
5 A:Real NFL Player	2.50
6 Racism Iss.,recalled by Marvel	6.00
7 thru 11	@2.50
12 V:Nefarious forces of evil	2.50

NICK FURY, AGENT OF S.H.I.E.L.D.
[1st Regular Series] June, 1968
1 JSo/JSt,I:Scorpio	200.00
2 JSo,A:Centaurius	125.00

Nick Fury, Agent of S.H.I.E.L.D. #1
© Marvel Entertainment Group

3 JSo,DA,V:Hell Hounds	125.00
4 FS,O:Nick Fury	125.00
5 JSo,V:Scorpio	150.00
6 FS,Doom must Fall	100.00
7 FS,V:S.H.I.E.L.D.	100.00
8 FS,Hate Monger	60.00
9 FS,Hate Monger	60.00
10 FS,JCr,Hate Monger	60.00
11 BS(c),FS,Hate Monger	60.00
12 BS	65.00
13	65.00
14	65.00
15 I:Bullseye	125.00
16 JK,rep.	40.00
17 JK,rep.	40.00
18 JK,rep.	40.00

[Limited Series] 1983–94
1 JSo,rep.	4.00
2 JSo,rep.	3.50

[2nd Regular Series] 1989–93
1 BH,I:New Shield,V:Death's Head(not British hero)	3.00
2 KP,V:Death's Head	2.25
3 KP,V:Death's Head	2.25
4 KP,V:Death's Head	2.25
5 KP,V:Death's Head	2.25
6 KP,V:Death's Head	2.25
7 KP,Chaos Serpent #1	2.25
8 KP,Chaos Serpent #2	2.25
9 KP,Chaos Serpent #3	2.25
10 KP,Chaos Serpent ends, A:Capt.America	2.25
11 D:Murdo MacKay	2.25
12 Hydra Affair #1	2.25
13 Hydra Affair #2	2.25
14 Hydra Affair #3	2.25
15 Apogee of Disaster #1	2.25
16 Apogee of Disaster #2	2.25
17 Apogee of Disaster #3	2.25
18 Apogee of Disaster #4	2.25
19 Apogee of Disaster #5	2.25
20 JG,A:Red Skull	2.50
21 JG,R:Baron Strucker	2.25
22 JG,A:Baron Strucker,R:Hydra	2.25
23 JG,V:Hydra	2.25
24 JG,A:Capt.Am,Thing,V:Mandarin	2.25
25 JG,Shield Vs. Hydra	2.25
26 JG,A:Baron Strucker, C:Wolverine	2.50
27 JG,V:Hydra,A:Wolverine	2.50
28 V:Hydra,A:Wolverine	2.50
29 V:Hydra,A:Wolverine	2.50
30 R:Leviathan,A:Deathlok	2.50
31 A:Deathlok,V:Leviathan	2.25
32 V:Leviathan	2.25
33 Super-Powered Agents	2.25
34 A:Bridge(X-Force),V:Balance of Terror	2.25
35 A:Cage,V:Constrictor	2.25
36	2.25
37	2.25
38 Cold War of Nick Fury #1	2.25
39 Cold War of Nick Fury #2	2.25
40 Cold War of Nick Fury #3	2.25
41 Cold War of Nick Fury #4	2.25
42 I:Strike Force Shield	2.25
43 R:Clay Quatermain	2.25
44 A:Captain America	2.25
45 A:Bridge	2.25
46 V:Gideon,Hydra	2.25
47 V:Baron Strucker,last issue	2.25

NICK FURY, VERSUS S.H.I.E.L.D.
June, 1988
1 JSo(c),D:Quartermail	6.00
2 BSz(c),Into The Depths	5.00
3 Uneasy Allies	4.00
4 V:Hydra	4.00
5 V:Hydra	4.00
6 V:Hydra, Dec., 1988	4.00

NICK FURY'S HOWLING COMMANDOS
Oct., 2005
1 KG 3.00
1a expanded edition 4.00
2 thru 6 KG . . . . @3.00

NIGHTBREED
Epic, April, 1990
1 . . . . 4.00
2 . . . . 3.00
3 thru 10 . . . . @2.50
11 thru 20 . . . . @2.25
21 thru 25 . . . . @2.50
Nightbreed:Genesis, Rep.#1-#4 . . 10.00

NIGHTCAT
1 DCw,I&O:Night Cat 4.50

NIGHTCRAWLER
Nov., 1985
1 DC,A;Bamfs 4.00
2 DC 3.50
3 DC,A:Other Dimensional X-Men . 3.50
4 DC,A:Lockheed,V:Dark Bamf . . . 3.50

Nightcrawler #1
© *Marvel Entertainment Group*

NIGHTCRAWLER
Nov., 2001
1 (of 4) Passion Play 2.50
2 thru 4 . . . . @2.50

NIGHTCRAWLER
Sept., 2004
1 DaR,Diabolique,pt.1 . . . . 3.00
2 DaR,Diabolique,pt.2 . . . . 3.00
3 DaR,The Devil Inside 3.00
4 DaR,The Devil Inside 3.00
5 DaR,Ghosts on the Rails,pt.1 . . . 3.00
6 DaR,Ghosts on the Rails 3.00
7 DaR,The Winding Way, pt.1 . . . . 3.00
8 DaR,The Winding Way, Pt.2 . . . . 3.00
9 DaR,The Winding Way, pt.3 . . . . 3.00
10 DaR,The Winding Way, pt.4 . . . 3.00
11 DaR,The Winding Way, pt.5 . . . 3.00
12 DaR,Loose Ends 3.00

NIGHTHAWK
July, 1998
1 (of 3) RCa,BWi,Nighthawk shake
off coma 3.00

2 (of 3) RCa,BWi,V:Mephisto 3.00
3 RCa,BWi,conclusion 3.00

NIGHTMARE
1994
1 ANo 2.25
2 & 3 ANo . . . . @2.25

NIGHTMARE CIRCUS
1 video-game tie-in 2.50
2 video-game tie-in 2.50

NIGHTMARE ON ELM STREET
Oct., 1989
1 RB/TD/AA.,Movie adapt. 3.00
2 AA,Movie adapt,Dec., 1989 . . . . 2.25

NIGHTMASK
Nov., 1986
1 O:Night Mask 2.50
2 thru 12 . . . . @2.50

NIGHT NURSE
Nov., 1972
1 The Making of a Nurse 175.00
2 Moment of Truth 125.00
3 . . . . 125.00
4 Final Issue,May, 1973 . . . . 125.00

NIGHT RIDER
Oct., 1974–Aug., 1975
1 Reprint Ghost Rider #1 . . . . 20.00
2 Reprint Ghost Rider #2 . . . . 15.00
3 Reprint Ghost Rider #3 . . . . 15.00
4 Reprint Ghost Rider #4 . . . . 15.00
5 Reprint Ghost Rider #5 . . . . 15.00
6 Reprint Ghost Rider #6 . . . . 15.00

NIGHTSIDE
Oct., 2001
1 (of 4) TDr,The OThers 3.00
2 TDr,The Others 3.00
3 TDr,Sydney Taine 3.00
4 TDr,Black Dragons. 3.00

NIGHTSTALKERS
1992–94
1 TP(i),Rise o/t Midnight Sons#5
A:GR,J.Blaze,I:Meatmarket,
polybagged w/poster 3.00
2 thru 18 . . . . @2.50

NIGHT THRASHER
[Limited Series] 1992–93
1 B:FaN(s),DHv,N:Night Thrasher,
V:Bengal 2.50
2 thru 4 . . . . @2.25
[Regular Series] 1993–95
1 B:FaN(s),MBa,JS,V:Poison
Memories. 3.50
2 thru 21 . . . . @2.25

NIGHTWATCH
1994–95
1 RLm,I:Salvo,Warforce Holo(c) . . . 3.00
1a Newsstand ed. 2.25
2 thru 12 . . . . @2.25

NOCTURNE
1995
1 DAn, in London 2.25
2 DAn,O:Nocturne 2.25
3 Interview with Amy 2.25
4 V:Dragon 2.25

NO ESCAPE
1994
1 & 2 Movie adaptation . . . . @2.25

NOMAD
[Limited Series] Nov., 1990
1 B:FaN(s),A:Capt.America 3.00
2 thru 4 . . . . @2.50

Nightwatch #2
© *Marvel Entertainment Group*

[Regular Series] 1992–94
1 B:FaN(s),R:Nomad,[Gatetfold(c),
map]. 3.00
2 V:Road Kill Club. 2.50
3 thru 25 . . . . @2.25

NORTHSTAR
1994
1 SFr,DoC,V:Weapon:P.R.I.M.E. . . 2.25
2 SFr,DoC,V:Arcade 2.25
3 SFr,DoC,V:Arcade 2.25
4 SFr,DoC,final issue 2.25
N Presents James O'Barr 2.50

NOT BRAND ECHH
Aug., 1967
1 JK(c),BEv,Forbush Man(c) . . . 150.00
2 MSe,FrG,Spidey-Man,Gnat-Man
& Rotten 75.00
3 MSe(C),TS,JK,FrG,O:Charlie
America 75.00
4 GC,JTg,TS,Scaredevil,
ECHHs-Men 75.00
5 JK,TS,GC,I&O:Forbush Man . . 75.00
6 MSe(c),GC,TS,W:Human
Torch 75.00
7 MSe(c),JK,GC,TS,O:Fantastical
Four,Stupor Man 75.00
8 MSe(c),GC,TS,C:Beatles 75.00
9 MSe,GC,TS,Bulk
V:Sunk-Mariner 75.00
10 JK,TS,MSe,The Worst of.... . . 100.00
11 King Konk 100.00
12 MSe,Frankenstein,
A:Revengers 100.00
13 GC,MSe,Stamp Out Trading
Cards(c). 100.00

NOTHING CAN STOP THE JUGGERNAUT
1989
1 JR2,rep.SpM#229&#230 . . . . . . 4.00

NOVA

[1st Regular Series] Sept., 1976

1 B:MWn(s),JB,JSt,I&O:Nova 20.00
2 JB,JSt,I:Condor,Powerhouse . . . 12.00
3 JB,JSt,I:Diamondhead 12.00
4 SB,TP,A:Thor,I:Corruptor 12.00
5 SB,V:Earthshaker 10.00
6 SB,V:Condor,Powerhouse,
    Diamondhead,I:Sphinx 10.00
7 SB,War in Space,O:Sphinx 10.00
8 V:Megaman 10.00
9 V:Megaman 10.00
10 V:Condor,Powerhouse,
    Diamond-head Sphinx 10.00
11 V:Sphinx 11.00
12 A:Spider-Man 12.00
13 I:Crimebuster,A:Sandman 7.00
14 A:Sandman 7.00
15 CI,C:Spider-Man, Hulk 7.00
16 CI,A:Yellow Claw 7.00
17 A:Yellow Claw 7.00
18 A:Yellow Claw, Nick Fury 7.00
19 CI,TP,I:Blackout 7.00
20 What is Project X? 7.00
21 JB,BMc,JRu 7.00
22 CI,I:Comet. 7.00
23 CI,V:Dr.Sun 7.00
24 CI,I:New Champions,V:Sphinx . . 7.00
25 E:MWn(s),CI,A:Champions,
    V:Sphinx 7.00

[2nd Regular Series] 1994–95

1 B:FaN(s),ChM,V:Gladiator,Foil
    Embossed(c) 3.50
2 ChM,V:Tail Hook Rape 2.25
3 ChM,A:Spider-Man,Corruptor . . . 2.25
4 ChM,I:NovaO:O 2.25
5 ChM,R:Condor,w/card 2.25
6 ChM,Time & Time Again,pt.3 . . . 2.25
7 ChM,Time & Time Again,pt.6 . . . 2.25
8 ChM,I:Shatterforce 2.25
9 ChM,V:Shatterforce 2.25
10 ChM,V:Diamondhead 2.25
11 ChM,V:Diamondhead 2.25
12 ChM,A:Inhumans 2.25
13 ChM,A:Inhumans 2.25
14 A:Condor 2.25
15 V:Brethern of Zorr 2.25
16 Countdown Conclusion 2.25
17 Nova Loses Powers 2.25
18 Nova Omega,pt.1 . . . . 2.25

NOVA

March, 1999

1 EL,JoB,F:Rich Rider,48-page . . . 3.00
2 EL,JoB,A:Capt.America. 2.25
2a variant JoB cover 2.25
3 EL,JoB,A:Capt.America & Hulk . . 2.25
4 EL,JoB,A:Mr.Fantastic 2.25
5 EL,JoB,A:Spider-Man 2.25
6 EL,JoB,V:Sphinx 2.25
7 EL,JoB, final issue 2.25

NOVA

Apr., 2007

1 DAn 3.00
2 DAn,ALa,A:Iron Man 3.00
3 DAn,ALa,A:Thunderbolts 3.00
4 DAn,ALa,Annihilation: Conquest . 3.00
5 DAn,ALa,Annihilation: Conquest . 3.00
6 DAn,ALa,Annihilation: Conquest . 3.00
7 DAn,ALa 3.00
8 DAn,ALa 3.00

Nth MAN

Aug., 1989

1 . . . . 2.25
2 thru 7 . . . . @2.25
8 DK 2.25
9 thru 16, finale, Sept., 1990. . @2.25

NYX

Oct., 2003

1 JQ,gutterpunks 7.00
2 JQ,self-preservation's price 6.00
3 JQ,Y-23 . . . . 35.00
4 JQ,F:Tatiana 6.00
5 JQ 4.00
6 JQ 3.00
7 JQ,finale. 3.00
NYX Must Have, rep.#1–#3 . . . . . . 5.00
NYX Must Have, rep.#4 & #5 . . . . . 4.00

OBNOXIO THE CLOWN

April, 1983

1 X-Men 3.50

OFFCASTES

Epic Heavy Hitters, 1993

1 MV,I:Offcastes 2.50
2 MV,V:Kaoro 2.25
3 MV,Last Issue 2.25

OFFICIAL HANDBOOK OF THE MARVEL UNIVERSE

Avengers 2004 . . . . 4.00
Daredevil 2004 . . . . 4.00
Hulk 2004 . . . . 4.00
Spider-Man 2004 . . . . 4.00
Wolverine 2004 . . . . 4.00
X-Men 2004 . . . . 4.00
Book of the Dear 2004 . . . . 4.00
Golden Age Marvel 2004 . . . . 4.00
Horror 2005 . . . . 4.00
Women of Marvel 2005 . . . . 4.00
Marvel Knights 2005 . . . . 4.00
Age of Apocalypse 2005 . . . . 4.00
Spider-Man 2005 . . . . 4.00
Teams 2005 . . . . 4.00
Fantastic Four 2005 . . . . 4.00
Avengers 2005 . . . . 4.00
Spider-Man & Fantastic Four (2005) 4.00
Alternate Universes (2005) 4.00
X-Men (2005) 4.00
Squadron Supreme (2005) 4.00
Ultimate Marvel Universe #2 . . . . . . 4.00

OFFICIAL MARVEL INDEX:

1985–88

TO THE AMAZING SPIDER-MAN

Index 1 . . . . 3.00
Index 2 thru 9 . . . . @2.50

TO THE AVENGERS

Index 1 thru 7 . . . . @2.50

TO THE FANTASTIC FOUR

Index 1 thru 12 . . . . @2.25

TO MARVEL TEAM-UP

Index 1 thru 6 . . . . @2.25

TO THE X-MEN

Index 1 thru 7 . . . . @3.00

[Vol. 2] 1994

Index 1 thru 5 . . . . @2.25

OFFICIAL MARVEL TIMELINE

1-shot, 48-pg. 6.00

OFFICIAL TRUE CRIME CASES

Fall, 1947

24 (1)SSh(c),The Grinning Killer . 300.00
25 (2)She Made Me a Killer,HK . . 225.00
Becomes:

ALL-TRUE CRIME

1948

26 SSh(c),The True Story of Wilbur
    Underhill 450.00
27 Electric Chair(c),Robert Mais . 350.00
28 Cops V:Gangsters(c) 150.00
29 Cops V:Gangsters(c) 150.00
30 He Picked a Murderous Mind . 150.00
31 Hitchiking Thugs(c) 150.00
32 Jewel Thieves(c). 150.00
33 The True Story of Dinton
    Phillips 150.00
34 Case of the Killers Revenge . . 150.00
35 Ph(c),Date with Danger 150.00
36 Ph(c). 150.00
37 Ph(c),Story of Robert Marone . 150.00
38 Murder Weapon,Nick Maxim . 150.00
39 Story of Vince Vanderee 150.00
40 . . . . 150.00
41 Lou 'Lucky' Raven 150.00
42 BK,Baby Face Nelson. 150.00
43 Doc Channing Paulson 125.00
44 Murder in the Big House 125.00
45 While the City Sleeps 125.00
46 . . . . 125.00
47 Gangster Terry Craig 125.00
48 GT,They Vanish By Night 125.00
49 BK,Squeeze Play 150.00
50 Shoot to Kill. 125.00
51 Panic in the Big House 125.00
52 Prison Break, Sept., 1952. . . . 125.00

OLYMPIANS

Epic, July, 1991

1 Spoof Series 4.00
2 Conclusion. 4.00

OMEGA FLIGHT

April, 2007

1 ScK 3.00
2 thru 5 ScK . . . . @3.00

OMEGA THE UNKNOWN

March, 1976

1 JM,I:Omega 15.00
2 JM,A:Hulk 10.00
3 JM,A:Electro 10.00
4 JM,V:Yellow Claw 9.00
5 JM,V:The Wrench 9.00
6 JM,V:Blockbuster. 9.00
7 JM,V:Blockbuster. 9.00
8 JM,C:New Foolkiller,V:Nitro 10.00

Omega the Unknown #3
© Marvel Entertainment Group

9 JM,A:New Foolkiller,
  D:Blockbuster 14.00
10 JM,D:Omega the Unknown. 8.00

OMEGA: THE UNKNOWN
Oct., 2007
1 (of 10) 3.00
2 . . . . 3.00

ONE, THE
Epic, July, 1985
1 thru 5 . . . . @2.50
6 Feb., 1986 . . . . 2.50

100 GREATEST MARVELS
Sept., 2001
1 (of 5) weekly, 112-pages 8.00
2 thru 5 112-pages . . . . @8.00
5 Top 5 #5, 32-pages 4.00
4 Top 5 #4, 32-pages 4.00
3 Top 5 #3, 48-pages 4.00
2 Top 5 #2, 48-pages 4.00
1 Top 5 #1, 48-pages 4.00

101 WAYS TO END
THE CLONE SAGA
1-shot (1997) 2.50

ONSLAUGHT
1996–97
Marvel Universe: AKu,SLo,MWd,
  Marvel Heroes vs. Onslaught . . 8.00
Marvel Universe: Gold edition . . . 100.00
X-Men: AKu,SLo,MWd (1996) 7.00
X-Men: Gold editon 75.00
Onslaught: Epilogue (1997). 9.00

ONSLAUGHT REBORN
Nov., 2006
1 RLd 3.00
1a variant (c). 3.00
2 JLb,RLd 3.00
3 JLb,RLd 3.00
4 JLb,RLd 3.00
5 JLb,RLd 3.00
2a thru 5a variant (c). . . . . @3.00

ONYX OVERLORD
Epic, 1992–93
1 JBi,Sequel to Airtight Garage . . . 3.00
2 JBi,The Joule. 3.00
3 JBi,V:Overlord 3.00
4 V:Starbilliard. 3.00

OPEN SPACE
Dec., 1989–Aug., 1990
1 . . . . 6.00
2 thru 4 . . . . @5.25

ORDER, THE
Feb., 2002
1 (of 6) KBk,JDy,MHy,F:Hulk, Namor,
  Dr. Strange, & Silver Surfer. . . . 2.25
2 KBk,JDy,MHy,A:Avengers 2.25
3 KBk,JDy,MHy,DPs,V:Avengers . . 2.25
4 KBk,JDy,DPs,Hulk,Nighthawk . . . 2.25
5 KBk,JDy,DPs,F:Nighthawk 2.25
6 KBk,JDy,DPs,V:everybody. 2.25

ORDER, THE
July, 2007
1 BKi. 3.00
2 thru 5 BKi. . . . . @3.00

ORIGIN
Aug., 2001
1 (of 6) PJe,NKu,F:Wolverine 3.50
2 PJe,NKu,JQ(c). 3.50
3 PJe,NKu,JQ(c). 3.50
4 PJe,NKu,JQ(c). 3.50
5 PJe,NKu,JQ(c), ... 3.50
6 PJe,NKu,final part 3.50

ORIGINAL GHOST RIDER
1992–94
1 MT(c),rep. 2.25
2 thru 23 rep.. . . . . @2.25

ORIGINAL GHOST
RIDER RIDES AGAIN
July, 1991
1 rep.GR#68+#69(O:JohnnyBlaze) 3.00
2 thru 7 rep.Ghost Rider. . . . . . . @2.25

ORORO:
BEFORE THE STORM
June, 2005
1 (of 4) Ororo Monroe in Cairo 3.00
2 thru 4 . . . . @3.00

OSBORN JOURNALS, THE
1997
1-shot KHt,F:Norman Osborn 3.00

OSCAR COMICS
Marvel USA Comics, 1947–49
(FUNNY TUNES spin-off)
1 (24) 225.00
2 (25) BW,HK,Hey Look 250.00
3 . . . . 135.00
4 . . . . 135.00
5 . . . . 135.00
6 thru 9 . . . . @135.00
10 HK 175.00
Becomes:

AWFUL OSCAR
Marvel USA Comics, 1949
11 . . . . 125.00
12 . . . . 125.00
Becomes:

OSCAR
13 . . . . 135.00

Our Love Story #5
© *Marvel Entertainment Group*

OUR LOVE
Sept., 1949
1 Ph(c),Guilt of Nancy Crane . . 175.00
2 Ph(c),My Kisses Were Cheap 125.00

OUR LOVE STORY
Oct., 1969
1 JB. 100.00
2 JB. 40.00
3 JB. 40.00
4 . . . . 40.00
5 JSo,JB 125.00
6 thru 13 . . . . @50.00
14 Gary Friedrich &Tarpe Mills . . . 55.00
15 thru 37 . . . . @30.00
38 Feb., 1976. . . . . 30.00

OUTLAW FIGHTERS
Marvel Atlas, Aug., 1954
1 GT,Western Tales 150.00
2 GT ,JMn(c). 100.00
3 . . . . 100.00
4 A;Patch Hawk 100.00
5 RH, Final Issue,April, 1955 . . . 100.00

OUTLAW KID
Atlas, Sept., 1954
1 SSh,DW,JMn(c),B&O:Outlaw Kid,
  A;Black Rider 350.00
2 DW,JMn(c),A:Black Rider 175.00
3 DW,AW,GWb,JMN(c) 175.00
4 DW(c),Death Rattle 150.00
5 JMn 150.00
6 JMn 150.00
7 JMn 150.00
8 AW,DW,JMn 150.00
9 . . . . 125.00
10 JSe 125.00
11 thru 17 . . . . @100.00
18 AW,JMn. 100.00
19 JSe,Sept., 1957 . . . . 100.00
[2nd series] Aug., 1970
1 JSe(c),DW,Jo,Showdown,rep . . 40.00
2 DW,One Kid Too Many 25.00
3 HT(c),DW,Six Gun Double
  Cross 25.00
4 DW 20.00
5 DW 20.00
6 DW 20.00
7 HT(c),DW,Treachery on
  the Trail 20.00
8 HT(c),DW,RC,Six Gun Pay Off . 30.00
9 JSe(c),DW,GWb,The Kids
  Last Stand 20.00
10 GK(c),DAy,NewO:Outlaw Kid . . 40.00
11 GK(c),Thunder Along the
  Big Iron 20.00
12 The Man Called Bounty Hawk . 20.00
13 The Last Rebel 20.00
14 The Kid Gunslingers of
  Calibre City 20.00
15 GK(c),V:Madman of Monster
  Mountain 20.00
16 The End of the Trail 20.00
17 thru 29. . . . . @20.00
30 Oct., 1975 . . . . 20.00

OVER THE EDGE
AND UNDER A BUCK
1995–96
1 F:Daredevil vs. Mr. Fear 2.25
2 F:Doctor Strange 2.25
3 F:Hulk 2.25
4 in Cypress Hills 2.25
5 . . . . 2.25
6 F:Daredevil 2.25
7 Doc & Nightmare 2.25

All comics prices listed are for *Near Mint* condition.

PARADISE X: THE HERALDS
Oct., 2001
1 (of 3) AxR, Earth X trilogy 3.50
2 AxR, ... 3.50
3 AxR,StP,concl. 3.50

PARADISE X
Feb., 2002
1 (of 13) AxR,Earth X trilogy 3.50
2 AxR,DBw,F:Captain Mar-Vell 3.50
3 AxR,DBw,King Britain,Medusa . . . 3.00
4 AxR,DBw,nature of new Paradise 3.00
5 AxR,DBw 3.00
6 AxR,DBw,the new Death 3.00
7 AxR,DBw 3.00
8 AxR,DBw 3.00
9 AxR,DBw,O:Ghost Rider 3.00
10 AxR,DBw,F:Matt Murcock 3.00
11 AxR,DBw,F:Harry Pym 3.00
12 AxR,DBw,concl. 3.00
Spec.#0, AxR, prologue to series . 3.50
Special A DBw 3.00
Special 1-shot, Earth X 3.00
GN Paradise X:Xen, 56-pg. 4.50
GN Devils AxR, 48-pg. 4.50

PARADISE X/RAGNAROK
Jan., 2003
1 (of 2) AxR. 3.00
2 AxR 3.00

PARAGON
1 I:Paragon,Nightfire. 5.00

PATSY & HEDY
Marvel Atlas, Feb., 1952
1 AJ(c),B:Patsy Walker &
   Hedy Wolfe 300.00
2 Skating(c) 175.00
3 Boyfriend Trouble 150.00
4 Swimsuit(c) 150.00
5 Patsy's Date(c) 150.00
6 Swimsuit/Picnic(c) 150.00
7 Double-Date(c) 150.00
8 AJ(c),The Dance 150.00
9 . . . . 150.00
10 . . . . 150.00
11 thru 25 . . . . @125.00
26 thru 50 . . . . @100.00
51 thru 60 . . . . @100.00
61 thru 109 . . . . @100.00
110 Feb., 1967 . . . . 100.00

PATSY & HER PALS
May, 1953
1 MWs(c),F:Patsy Walker 225.00
2 MWs(c),Swimsuit(c) 125.00
3 MWs(c),Classroom(c) 100.00
4 MWs(c),Golfcourse(c) 100.00
5 MWs(c).Patsy/Buzz(c) 100.00
6 thru 10 . . . . @100.00
11 thru 28 . . . . @100.00
29 Aug., 1957. . . . . 100.00

PATSY WALKER
1945
1 F:Patsy Walker Adventures . . 750.00
2 Patsy/Car(c) 350.00
3 Skating(c) 300.00
4 Perfume(c) 300.00
5 Archery Lesson, Eye Injury(c) 325.00
6 Bus(c) 300.00
7 Charity Drive(c) 300.00
8 Organ Driver Monkey(c) 300.00
9 Date(c) 300.00
10 Skating(c),Wedding Bells,
   A:Millie. 300.00

Patsy Walker #16
© *Marvel Entertainment Group*

11 Date with a Dream,A:Mitzi . . . 175.00
12 Love in Bloom,Artist(c),
   A:Rusty 175.00
13 Swimsuit(c),There Goes My
   Heart;HK,Hey Look 175.00
14 An Affair of the Heart,
   HK,Hey Look 175.00
15 Dance(c) 175.00
16 Skating(c) 175.00
17 Patsy's Diary(c),HK,Hey Look 225.00
18 Autograph(c) 200.00
19 HK,Hey Look. 200.00
20 HK,Hey Look 200.00
21 HK,Hey Look. 200.00
22 HK,Hey Look. 200.00
23 . . . . 150.00
24 . . . . 150.00
25 HK,Rusty. 200.00
26 . . . . 125.00
27 . . . . 125.00
28 . . . . 125.00
29 . . . . 125.00
30 HK,Egghead Double 125.00
31 . . . . 125.00
32 thru 56 . . . . @100.00
57 thru 58 AJ(c) . . . . @125.00
59 thru 99 . . . . @100.00
100 . . . . 100.00
Fashion Parade #1 . . . . 150.00

PENANCE: RELENTLESS
Sept., 2007
1 (of 5)PJe,PG 3.00
2 thru 3 . . . . @3.00

PETER PARKER, THE SPECTACULAR SPIDER-MAN
Dec., 1976
1 SB,V:Tarantula 75.00
2 SB,V:Kraven,Tarantula. 25.00
3 SB,I:Lightmaster 20.00
4 SB,V:Vulture,Hitman 20.00
5 SB,V:Hitman,Vulture 20.00
6 SB,V:Morbius,rep.M.T.U.#3 . . . 22.00
7 SB,V:Morbius,A:Human Torch . 23.00
8 SB,V:Morbius. 23.00
9 SB,I:White Tiger 20.00
10 SB,A:White Tiger 15.00
11 JM,V:Medusa 15.00
12 SB,V:Brother Power 15.00

13 SB,V:Brother Power 15.00
14 SB,V:Brother Power 15.00
15 SB,V:Brother Power 15.00
16 SB,V:The Beetle 15.00
17 SB,A:Angel & Iceman
   Champions disbanded 15.00
18 SB,A:Angel & Iceman 15.00
19 SB,V:The Enforcers 12.00
20 SB,V:Lightmaster 12.00
21 JM,V:Scorpion. 10.00
22 MZ,A:Moon Knight,V:Cyclone . . 12.00
23 A:Moon Knight,V:Cyclone 12.00
24 FS,A:Hypno-Hustler 10.00
25 JM,FS,I:Carrion 11.00
26 JM,A:Daredevil,V:Carrion 10.00
27 DC,FM,I:Miller Daredevil,
   V:Carrion 50.00
28 FM,A:Daredevil,V:Carrion 40.00
29 JM,FS,V:Carrion 7.00
30 JM,FS,V:Carrion 7.00
31 JM,FS,D:Carrion 7.00
32 BL,JM,FS,V:Iguana 7.00
33 JM,FS,O:Iguana 7.00
34 JM,FS,V:Iguana,Lizard 7.00
35 V:Mutant Mindworm 7.00
36 JM,V:Swarm 7.00
37 DC,MN,V:Swarm. 7.00
38 SB,V:Morbius 7.00
39 JM,JR2,V:Schizoid Man 8.00
40 FS,V:Schizoid Man 8.00
41 JM,V:Meteor Man,A:GiantMan . . 7.00
42 JM,A:Fant.Four,V:Frightful 4 . . . 7.00
43 JBy(c),MZ,V:The Ringer,
   V:Belladonna 7.00
44 JM,V:The Vulture 7.00
45 MSe,V:The Vulture 7.00
46 FM(c),MZ,V:Cobra 7.00
47 MSe,A:Prowler II 7.00
48 MSe,A:Prowler II 7.00
49 MSe,I:Smuggler 7.00
50 JR2,JM,V:Mysterio 7.00
51 MSe&FM(c),V:Mysterio. 7.00
52 FM(c),D:White Tiger 7.00
53 JM,FS,V:Terrible Tinkerer 7.00
54 FM,WS,MSe,V:Silver Samurai . . 7.00
55 LMc,JM,V:Nitro 7.00
56 FM,JM,V:Jack-o-lantern 12.00
57 JM,V:Will-o-the Wisp. 6.00
58 JBy,V:Ringer,A:Beetle. 7.00
59 JM,V:Beetle 6.00
60 JM&FM(c),O:Spider-Man,
   V:Beetle 7.00
61 JM,V:Moonstone. 5.00
62 JM,V:Goldbug 5.00
63 JM,V:Molten Man 5.00

*Peter Parker The Spectacular
Spider-Man #20* © *Marvel Ent.Group*

64 JM,I:Cloak & Dagger........ 15.00	
65 BH,JM,V:Kraven,Calypso 5.00	
66 JM,V:Electro 5.00	
67 AMb,V:Boomerang 5.00	
68 LMc,JM,V:Robot of Mendell	
Stromm 5.00	
69 AM,A:Cloak & Dagger........ 10.00	
70 A:Cloak & Dagger........... 10.00	
71 JM,Gun Control issue 5.00	
72 AM,V:Dr.Octopus 5.00	
73 AM,JM,V:Dr.Octopus,A:Owl ... 5.00	
74 AM,JM,V:Dr.Octopus,R:Bl.Cat .. 5.00	
75 AM,JM,V:Owl,Dr.Octopus 6.00	
76 AM,Black Cat on deathbed 5.00	
77 AM,V:Gladiator,Dr.Octopus..... 5.00	
78 AM,V:Dr.Octopus,C:Punisher ... 5.00	
79 AM,V:Dr.Octopus,A:Punisher ... 5.00	
80 AM,F:J.Jonah Jameson 5.00	
81 A:Punisher................ 6.00	
82 A:Punisher................ 6.00	
83 A:Punisher................ 8.00	
84 AM,F:Black Cat 4.00	
85 AM,O:Hobgoblin powers	
(Ned Leeds)............... 11.00	
86 FH,V:Fly.................. 4.00	
87 AM,Reveals I.D.to Black Cat ... 4.00	
88 AM,V:Cobra,Mr.Hyde 4.00	
89 AM,Secret Wars,A:Kingpin 5.00	
90 AM,Secret Wars 6.00	
91 AM,V:Blob 4.00	
92 AM,I:Answer............... 4.00	
93 AM,V:Answer 4.00	
94 AM,A:Cloak & Dagger,V:	
Silver Mane............... 4.00	
95 AM,A:Cloak & Dagger,V:	
Silvermane............... 4.00	
96 AM,A:Cloak & Dagger,V:	
Silvermane............... 4.00	
97 HT,JM,A:Black Cat 4.00	
98 HT,JM,I:Spot 4.00	
99 HT,JM,V:Spot 4.00	
100 AM,V:Kingpin,C:Bl.Costume ... 6.00	
101 JBy(c),AM,V:Killer Shrike 3.00	
102 JBy(c),AM,V:Backlash 3.00	
103 AM,V:Blaze;Not John Blaze ... 3.00	
104 JBy(c),AM,V:Rocket Racer 3.00	
105 AM,A:Wasp............... 3.00	
106 AM,A:Wasp............... 3.00	
107 RB,D:Jean DeWolf,I:SinEater.. 4.00	
108 RB,A:Daredevil,V:Sin-Eater ... 3.00	
109 RB,A:Daredevil,V:Sin-Eater ... 3.00	
110 RB,A:Daredevil,V:Sin-Eater ... 3.00	
111 RB,Secret Wars II 3.00	
112 RB,A:Santa Claus,Black Cat... 3.00	
113 RB,Burglars,A:Black Cat...... 3.00	
114 BMc,V:Lock Picker.......... 3.00	
115 BMc,A:Black Cat,Dr.Strange,	
I:Foreigner................ 4.00	
116 A:Dr.Strange, Foreigner,	
Black Cat, Sabretooth 10.00	
117 DT,C:Sabretooth,A:Foreigner,	
Black Cat,Dr.Strange........ 4.00	
118 MZ,D:Alexander,V:SHIELD.... 3.00	
119 RB,BMc,V:Sabretooth,	
A:Foreigner,Black Cat 10.00	
120 KG.................... 3.00	
121 RB,BMc,V:Mauler 3.00	
122 V:Mauler 3.00	
123 V:Foreigner,Black Cat....... 3.00	
124 V:Dr.Octopus............. 3.00	
125 V:Wr.Crew,A:Spiderwoman.... 3.00	
126 JM,A:Sp.woman,V:Wrecker ... 3.00	
127 AM,V:Lizard............... 3.00	
128 C:DDevil,A:Bl.Cat,Foreigner... 3.50	
129 A:Black Cat,V:Foreigner...... 3.00	
130 A:Hobgoblin............... 6.00	
131 MZ,BMc,V:Kraven........... 7.00	
132 MZ,BMc,V:Kraven........... 7.00	
133 BSz(c),Mad Dog,pt.3 .... 5.00	
Ann.#1 RB,JM,V:Dr.Octopus 10.00	
Ann.#2 JM,I&O:Rapier 7.00	
Ann.#3 JM,V:Manwolf 5.00	

Ann.#4 AM,O:Aunt May,A:Bl.Cat ... 5.00	
Ann.#5 I:Ace,Joy Mercado........ 5.00	
Ann.#6 V:Ace................. 4.50	
Ann.#7 Honeymoon iss,A:Puma ... 4.50	
Becomes:	

SPECTACULAR
SPIDER-MAN

PETER PARKER:
SPIDER-MAN
Nov., 1998

1 JR2,HMe,SHa,A:new Spider-Man,	
V:Ranger,48-page 3.00	
1a signed 15.00	
2 JR2,HMe,SHa,A:Thor 4.00	
2a variant cover 4.00	
3 HMe,JR2,SHa,A:Iceman,	
V:Shadrac 3.00	
4 HMe,JR2,SHa,V:Marrow 3.00	
5 HMe,SHa,BS,JBy(c),F:Spider-	
Woman,Aunt May, Black Cat... 3.00	
6 HMe,SHa,RJ2,JBy(c),V:Kingpin . 3.00	
7 JR2,HMe,SHa,Reality Bent..... 3.00	
8 JR2,HMe,SHa,V:Bullseye 3.00	
9 JR2,HMe,SHa,R:Venom 3.00	
10 JR2,HMe,SHa,R:Carnage...... 3.00	
11 JR2,HMe,SHa,Eighth Day,pt.3	
x-over................... 3.00	
12 JR2,HMe,SHa, 48-pg......... 3.50	
13 JR2,HMe................. 3.00	
14 JR2,HMe,A:Hulk 3.50	
15 JR2,HMe,x-over............. 3.50	
16 JR2,HMe,V:Sinister Six....... 3.00	
17 JR2,HMe,SHa,V:Kraven....... 2.50	
18 HMe,JR2,SHa,V:Green Goblin . 2.50	
19 HMe,JR2,SHa,Mary Jane dies .. 2.50	
20 PJe,MBu,DGr,Mary Jane dead.. 3.00	
21 PJe,MBu,DGr,HumanTorch..... 2.50	
22 PJe,MBu,DGr,FlintMarko 2.50	
23 PJe,MBu,DGr,Type Face 2.50	
24 PJe,MBu,DGr,Max.Security 2.50	
25 PJe,MBu,DGr,V:Green Goblin .. 3.50	
26 PJe,JoB,DGr,F:NYPD......... 2.50	
27 PJe,MBu,DGr,F:NYPD 2.50	
28 PJe,MBu,DGr,............. 2.50	
29 PJe,CAd,DGr,x-over.......... 7.00	
30 PJe,MBu,HuR(c),I:Terminal ... 7.00	
31 PJe,MBu,HuR(c),I:Fusion...... 3.50	
32 PJe,MBu,HuR(c),V:Fusion 2.50	
33 PJe,MBu,HuR(c),ballpark 2.50	
34 PJe,MBu,cleanse the city 2.50	
35 PJe,MBu,Jamal............. 2.50	
36 PJe,MBu,private-eye.......... 2.50	
37 PJe,slice-of-life 2.50	
38 PJe,MBu,V:Mimes,'Nuff Said ... 2.50	
39 PJe,MBu,return of Dr. Octopus.. 2.50	
40 PJe,MBu,Doc Octopus,pt.2 .... 2.50	
41 PJe,MBu,Doc Octopus,pt.3 .... 2.50	
42 Spring Break,pt.1 .... 2.50	
43 Spring Break,pt.2 .... 2.50	
44 PJe,HuR,R:Green Goblin 6.00	
45 PJe,HuR,R:Green Goblin,pt.2 ... 4.00	
46 PJe,HuR,R:Green Goblin,pt.3 ... 2.50	
47 PJe,HuR,R:Green Goblin,pt.4 ... 2.50	
48 PJe,MBu 2.50	
49 PJe,MBu 2.50	
50 PJe,MBu 4.00	
51 pt.1 .... 2.50	
52 pt.2 .... 2.50	
53 pt.1 .... 2.50	
54 pt.2 .... 2.50	
55 pt.3 .... 2.50	
56 SK,Reborn,pt.1,F:Sandman 2.50	
57 SK,Reborn,pt.2,F:Sandman 2.50	
Ann.1999,CCs, 48-pg........... 4.00	
Ann.2000 CCl,JoB,80-pg......... 4.00	
Ann.2001 South America, 28-pg.... 3.50	
Spec. Peter Parker, Spider-	
Man 2000 .... 4.00	

PETER PORKER
Star, May, 1985

1 Parody................... 4.50	
2 thru 17 .... @3.00	

PETER, THE LITTLE PEST
Nov., 1969–May, 1970

1 F:Peter.................. 85.00	
2 Rep,Dexter & Melvin 60.00	
3 Rep,Dexter & Melvin 60.00	
4 Rep,Dexter & Melvin 60.00	

The Phantom #3
© Marvel Ent.Group

PHANTOM
1995

1 Lee Falk's Phantom 4.00	
2 V:General Babalar............ 4.00	
3 final issue................. 4.00	

PHANTOM 2040
1995

1 Based on cartoon 2.50	
2 V:Alloy 2.50	
3 MPa,V:Crime Syndicate........ 2.50	
4 Vision Quest 2.50	

PHOENIX
(UNTOLD STORY)
April, 1984

1 JBy,O:Phoenix (R.Summers)... 15.00

PILGRIM'S PROGRESS
1 adapts John Bunyans novel ... 10.00

PINHEAD
1993–94

1 Red Foil(c),from Hellraiser...... 3.00	
2 DGC(s),V:Cenobites 2.50	
3 DGC(s),V:Cenobites 2.50	
4 DGC(s),V:Cenobites 2.50	
5 DGC(s),Devil in Disguise....... 2.50	
6 DGC(s),.................. 2.50	

PINHEAD VS.
MARSHALL LAW
1993

1 KON,In Hell 3.00	
2 KON.................... 3.00	

PINOCCHIO & THE EMPEROR OF THE NIGHT
March, 1988
1 Movie adapt. 3.00

PINT-SIZED X-BABIES: MURDERAMA
June, 1998
1-shot, Mojo, Arcade, 48-pg. 3.00

PIRATES OF DARK WATERS
Nov., 1991
1 based on T.V. series 3.00
2 Search for 13 Treasures 3.00
3 V:Albino Warriors,Konk 3.00
4 A:Monkey Birds 3.00
5 Tula Steals 1st Treasuer 3.00
6 thru 9 . . . . @3.00

PITT, THE
March, 1988
1 SB,SDr,A:Spitfire 4.00

PLANET OF THE APES
Aug., 1974–Feb., 1977
(black & white magazine)
1 MP 45.00
2 MP 30.00
3 thru 10 . . . . @25.00
11 thru 20 . . . . @30.00
21 thru 29 . . . . @65.00

Planet Terry #12
© Marvel Entertainment Group

PLANET TERRY
Star, April, 1985
1 thru 11 . . . . @3.00
12 March, 1986 . . . . 3.00

PLASMER
Marvel UK, 1993–94
1 A:Captain America 3.50
2 A:Captain Britain,Black Knight . . . 2.25
3 A:Captain Britain 2.25
4 A:Captain Britain 2.25
5 thru 7 . . . . @2.00

PLASTIC FORKS
Epic, 1990
1 . . . . 6.00
2 thru 5 . . . . @5.50

POLICE ACADEMY
Nov., 1989
1 Based on TV Cartoon 2.25
2 thru 5 . . . . @2.25
6 Feb., 1990 . . . . 2.25

POLICE ACTION
Jan., 1954
1 JF,GC,JMn(c),Riot Squad 250.00
2 JF,Over the Wall 150.00
3 JMn 125.00
4 DAy 125.00
5 DAy,JMn. 125.00
6 . . . . 125.00
7 BPNov., 1954 . . . . 125.00

POLICE BADGE #479
Marvel Atlas, 1955
5 . . . . 125.00

POLICE BADGE
See: SPY THRILLERS

POPPLES
Star, Dec., 1986
1 Based on Toys 3.00
2 thru 5 . . . . @3.00

POWDERED TOAST-MAN
Spec. F:Powder Toast-Man. 3.25

POWERHOUSE PEPPER COMICS
1943—Nov., 1948
1 BW,Movie Auditions(c) 3,000.00
2 BW,Dinner(c) 1,300.00
3 BW,Boxing Ring(c) 1,200.00
4 BW,Subway(c) 1,200.00
5 BW,Bankrobbers(c) 1,400.00

POWERLESS
June, 2004
1 (of 6) 3.00
2 thru 6 . . . . @3.00

POWER LINE
Epic, May, 1988
1 BMc(i) 2.25
2 Aw(i) 2.25
3 A:Dr Zero 2.25
4 . . . . 2.25
5 GM 2.25
6 GM 2.25
7 GM 2.25
8 GM Sept., 1989 . . . . 2.25

POWER MAN
Prev: Hero for Hire
Feb., 1974
17 GT,A:Iron Man. 25.00
18 GT,V:Steeplejack. 15.00
19 GT,V:Cottonmouth 15.00
20 GT,Heroin Story 15.00
21 V:Original Power Man. 10.00
22 V:Stiletto & Discus 10.00
23 V:Security City 10.00
24 GT,I:BlackGoliath(BillFoster). . 10.00
25 A:Circus of Crime 10.00
26 GT,V:Night Shocker 10.00
27 GP,AMc,V:Man Called X 10.00
28 V:Cockroach 10.00

Power Man #34
© Marvel Entertainment Group

29 V:Mr.Fish. 10.00
30 RB,KJ,KP,I:Piranha. 10.00
31 SB,NA(i),V:Piranha. 10.00
32 JSt,FR,A:Wildfire. 8.00
33 FR,A:Spear 8.00
34 FR,A:Spear,Mangler 8.00
35 DA,A:Spear,Mangler 8.00
36 V:Chemistro 8.00
37 V:Chemistro 8.00
38 V:Chemistro 8.00
39 KJ,V:Chemistro,Baron 8.00
40 V:Baron. 8.00
41 TP,V:Thunderbolt,Goldbug 8.00
42 V:Thunderbolt,Goldbug. 8.00
43 AN,V:Mace 8.00
44 TP,A:Mace. 8.00
45 JSn,A:Mace. 8.00
46 GT,I:Zzzax(recreated). 8.00
47 BS,A:Zzzax 10.00
48 JBy,A:Iron Fist 15.00
49 JBy,A:Iron Fist. 15.00
Becomes:

POWER MAN & IRON FIST
1978
50 JBy,I:Team-up with Iron Fist . . . 15.00
51 MZ,Night on the Town. 4.00
52 MZ,V:Death Machines 4.00
53 SB,O:Nightshade 4.00
54 TR,O:Iron Fist. 4.00
55 Chaos at the Coliseum 4.00
56 Mayhem in the Museum 4.00
57 X-Men,V:Living Monolith. 35.00
58 1st El Aguila(Drug) 4.00
59 BL(c),TVE,V:Big Apple
    Bomber. 4.00
60 BL(c),V:Terrorists 4.00
61 BL(c),V:The Maggia 4.00
62 BL(c),KGa,V:Man Mountain
    D:Thunerbolt 4.00
63 BL(c),Cage Fights Fire 4.00
64 DGr&BL(c),V:Suetre,Muertre . . . 4.00
65 BL(c),A:El Aquila, ... 4.00
66 FM(c),Sabretooth(2nd App.) . . . 50.00
67 V:Bushmaster 4.00
68 FM(c),V:Athur Nagan 4.00
69 V:Soldier 4.00
70 FM(c)V:El Supremo 4.00
71 FM(c),I:Montenegro 4.00
72 FM(c),V:Chako 4.00
73 FM(c),V:Rom. 4.00
74 FM(c),V:Ninja 4.00
75 KGa,O:IronFist 4.00
76 KGa,V:Warhawk 4.00
77 KGa,A:Daredevil 4.00

Power Man (continued)

78 KGa,A:El Aguila,Sabretooth
  (Slasher)(3rd App.) 32.00
79 V:Dredlox 3.00
80 KJ(c),V:Montenegro 3.00
81 V:Black Tiger 3.00
82 V:Black Tiger 3.00
83 V:Warhawk 3.00
84 V:Constrictor,A:Sabertooth
  (4th App.) 32.00
85 KP,V:Mole Man 3.00
86 A:Moon Knight 3.00
87 A:Moon Knight 3.00
88 V:Scimtar 3.00
89 V:Terrorists 3.00
90 V:Unus BS(c) 3.00
91 Paths and Angles 3.00
92 V:Hammeread,I:New Eel 3.00
93 A:Chemistro 3.00
94 V:Chemistro 3.00
95 Danny Rand 3.00
96 V:Chemistro 3.00
97 K'unlun,A:Fera 3.00
98 V:Shades & Commanche 3.00
99 R:Daught.of Dragon 3.00
100 O:K'unlun,DoubleSize 5.00
101 A:Karnak 3.00
102 V:Doombringer 3.00
103 O:Doombringer 3.00
104 V:Dr.Octopus,Lizard 3.00
105 F:Crime Buster 3.00
106 Luke Gets Shot 3.00
107 JBy(c),Terror issue 3.00
108 V:Inhuman Monster 3.00
109 V:The Reaper 3.00
110 V:Nightshade,Eel 3.00
111 I:Captain Hero 3.00
112 JBy(c),V:Control7 . . . . 3.00
113 JBy(c),A:Capt.Hero 3.00
114 JBy(c),V:Control7 . . . . 3.00
115 JBy(c),V:Stanley 3.00
116 JBy(c),V:Stanley 3.00
117 R:K'unlun 3.00
118 A:Colleen Wing 3.00
119 A:Daught.of Dragon 3.00
120 V:Chiantang 3.00
121 Secret Wars II 3.00
122 V:Dragonkin 3.00
123 V:Race Killer 3.00
124 V:Yellowclaw 3.00
125 MBr,LastIssue;D:Iron Fist 5.00
G-Size#1 reprints 4.00
Ann.#1 Earth Shock 20.00

POWER PACHYDERMS
Sept., 1989
1 Elephant Superheroes 2.50

POWER PACK
Aug., 1984
1 JBr,BWi,I&O:Power Pack,
  I:Snarks 2.50
2 JBr,BWi,V:Snarks 2.25
3 JBr,BWi,V:Snarks 2.25
4 JBr,BWi,V:Snarks 2.25
5 JBr,BWi,V:Bogeyman 2.25
6 JBr,BWi,A:Spider-Man 2.25
7 JBr,BWi,A:Cloak & Dagger 2.25
8 JBr,BWi,A:Cloak & Dagger 2.25
9 BA,BWi,A:Marrina 2.25
10 BA,BWi,A:Marrina 2.25
11 JBr,BWi,V:Morlocks 2.25
12 JBr,BWi,A:X-Men,V:Morlocks . . 3.00
13 BA,BWi,Baseball issue 2.25
14 JBr,BWi,V:Bogeyman 2.25
15 JBr,BWi,A:Beta Ray Bill 2.25
16 JBr,BWi,I&O:Kofi,J:Tattletale
  (Franklin Richards) 2.25
17 JBr,BWi,V:Snarks 2.25
18 BA,SW,Secret Wars II,V:Kurse . 2.25
19 BA,SW,Doub.size,Wolverine . . . 4.00
20 BMc,A:NewMutants 2.25

21 BA,TA,C:Spider-Man 2.25
22 JBg,BWi,V:Snarks 2.25
23 JBg,BWi,V:Snarks,C:FF 2.25
24 JBg,BWi,V:Snarks,C:Cloak 2.25
25 JBg,BWi,A:FF,V:Snarks 2.25
26 JBg,BWi,A:Cloak & Dagger 2.25
27 JBg,AG,A:Wolverine,X-Factor,
  V:Sabretooth 5.00
28 A:Fantastic Four,Hercules 2.25
29 JBg,DGr,A:SpM,V:Hobgoblin . . 2.50
30 VM,Crack 2.25
31 JBg,I:Trash 2.25
32 JBg,V:Trash 2.25
33 JBg,A:Sunspot,Warlock,
  C:Spider-Man 2.25
34 TD,V:Madcap 2.25
35 JBg,A:X-Factor,D:Plague 2.25
36 JBg,V:Master Mold 2.25
37 SDr(i),I:Light-Tracker 2.25
38 SDr(i),V:Molecula 2.25
39 V:Bogeyman 2.25
40 A:New Mutants,V:Bogeyman . . 2.25
41 SDr(i),V:The Gunrunners 2.25
42 JBg,SDr,Inferno,V:Bogeyman . . 2.25
43 JBg,SDr,AW,Inferno,
  V:Bogeyman 2.25
44 JBr,Inferno,A:New Mutants 2.25
45 JBr,End battle w/Bogeyman 2.25
46 WPo,A:Punisher,Dakota North . . 2.50
47 JBg,I:Bossko 2.25
48 JBg,Toxic Waste #1 . . . . 2.25
49 JBg,JSh,Toxic Waste #2 . . . . . . 2.25
50 AW(i),V:Snarks 2.25
51 GM,I:Numinus 2.25
52 AW(i),V:Snarks,A:Numinus 2.25
53 EC,A of V,A:Typhoid Mary 2.25
54 JBg,V:Mad Thinker 2.25
55 DSp,V:Mysterio 2.25
56 TMo,A:Fant.Four,Nova 2.25
57 TMo,A:Nova,V:Star Stalker 2.25
58 TMo,A:Galactus,Mr.Fantastic . . 2.25
59 TMo,V:Ringmaster 2.25
60 TMo,V:Puppetmaster 2.25
61 TMo,V:Red Ghost & Apes 2.25
62 V:Red Ghost & Apes
  (last issue) 2.25
Holiday Spec.JBr,Small Changes . . 2.25

POWER PACK
April, 2005
1 (of 4) I know what we did
  That Summer 3.00
2 Misadventures in Babysitting 3.00
3 F:Fantastic Four 3.00
4 End of the Rainbow 3.00
Digest Vol. 1 . . . . 7.00

POWER PACK:
PEER PRESSURE
June, 2000
1 (of 4) TA,CDo 3.00
2 TA,CDo,V:Snarks 3.00
3 TA,CDo, ... 3.00
4 Ta,CDo,concl 3.00

POWERS
Marvel Icon, July, 2004
1 BMB,F:Deena Pilgrim 3.00
2 thru 5 BMB . . . . @3.00
6 thru 12 . . . . @3.00
13 thru 18 Cosmic . . . . @3.00
19 thru 24 Secret Identity . . . . . . @3.00
25 25 Coolest Dead Super Heroes . 2.95
25a variant (c) 2.95
26 25 Coolest Dead Superheroes . . 2.95
27 25 Coolest Dead Superheroes . . 3.95
28 25 Coolest Dead Superheroes . . 3.95
Spec. Encyclopedia, Vol. 1 . . . .

PRINCE NAMOR,
THE SUB-MARINER
Sept., 1984
1 I:Dragonrider, Dara 3.00
2 I:Proteus 2.50
3 . . . . 2.50
4 Dec., 1984 . . . . 2.50

PRINCE VALIANT
1994–95
1 JRy,CV,Thule, Camelot
  and the Misty Isles 4.00
2 JRy,CV 4.00
3 JRy,CV 4.00
4 JRy,CV, final issue 4.00

PRIVATE EYE
Marvel Atlas, Jan., 1951
1 . . . . 275.00
2 . . . . 175.00
3 GT 175.00
4 . . . . 125.00
5 . . . . 125.00
6 JSt 125.00
7 . . . . 125.00
8 March, 1952 . . . . 125.00

PROFESSOR XAVIER
AND THE X-MEN
1995
1 1st Year Together 3.00
2 V:The Vanisher 2.50
3 FaN,F:The Blob 2.50
4 V:Magneto & Brotherhood 2.50
5 & 6 . . . . @2.50
7 FdS,Sub-Mariner 2.50
8 thru 12 . . . . @2.50
13 AHo,F:Juggernaut 2.50
14 JGz,V:Juggernaut, ... 2.50
15 JGz,F:Quicksilver & Scarlet
  Witch 2.50
16 . . . . 2.50
17 JGz,V:Sentinels,F:Beast 2.50
18 JGz,X-Men vs. Sentinels,
  final issue 2.50

PROWLER, THE
1994
1 Creatures of the Night, pt.1 . . . . 2.25
2 V:Nightcreeper, Creatures, pt.2 . . 2.25

Prowler #3
© Marvel Entertainment Group

MARVEL

Psi Force #9
© Marvel Entertainment Group

3 Creatures of the Night, pt.3 . . . . . 2.25
4 V:Vulture, Creatures, pt.4 . . . . . . 2.25

PSI FORCE
Nov., 1986
1 MT,O:PSI Force 2.50
2 thru 9 MT . . . . @2.50
10 thru 32 . . . . @2.50
Ann.#1 . . . . 3.00

PSYCHONAUTS
Epic, 1993–94
1 thru 4 War in the Future . . . . . @5.50

PSYLOCKE & ANGEL: CRIMSON DAWN
1997
1 SvL,ATi,V:Obsideon 3.00
2 SvL,ATi 3.00
3 BRa,SvL,ATi 3.00
4 (of 4) BRa,SvL,ATi 3.00

PULSE, THE
Feb., 2004
1 BMB,MBa,Thin Air,pt.1 . . . . 5.00
2 BMB,MBa,Thin Air,pt.2,F:Vulture . 3.50
3 BMB,MBa,Thin Air,pt.3 . . . . 3.00
4 BMB,MBa,Thin Air,pt.4 . . . . 3.00
5 BMB,MBa,Thin Air,pt.5 . . . . 3.00
6 BMB,BA,Secret War,pt.1 . . . . . . 3.00
7 BMB,BA,Secret War,pt.2 . . . . . . 3.00
8 BMB,Secret War,pt.3 . . . . 3.00
9 BMB,Secret War,pt.4, concl. 3.00
10 BMB,House of M tie-in 4.00
11 BMB,Birth of Jessica Jones & Luke Cage's Baby 3.00
12 BMB, A:D-Man 3.00
13 BMB,F:Jessica Jones, baby 3.00
14 BMB,F:Luke Cage 3.00
Spec. BMB,House of M 0.50

PUNISHER
[Limited Series] Jan., 1986
1 MZ,Circle of Blood,double size . 25.00
2 MZ,Back to the War 15.00
3 MZ,V:The Right 12.00
4 MZ,V:The Right 12.00
5 V:Jigsaw,end Mini-Series. 12.00
[Regular Series] 1987–95
1 KJ,V:Wilfred Sobel,Drugs 12.00
2 KJ,V:General Trahn,Bolivia 6.00

---

3 KJ,V:Colonel Fryer 5.00
4 KJ,I:The Rev,Microchip Jr 5.00
5 KJ,V:The Rev 5.00
6 DR,KN,V:The Rosettis 5.00
7 DR,V:Ahmad,D:Rose 5.00
8 WPo,SW(1st Punisher), V:Sigo & Roky 4.00
9 WPo,SW,D:MicrochipJr,V:Sigo . . 4.00
10 WPo,SW,A:Daredevil (x-over w/Daredevil #257) 7.00
11 WPo,SW,O:Punisher 3.00
12 WPo,SW,V:Gary Saunders 3.00
13 WPo,SW,V:Lydia Spoto 3.00
14 WPo,SW,I:McDowell,Brooks 3.00
15 WPo,SW,V:Kingpin 3.00
16 WPo,SW,V:Kingpin 3.00
17 WPo,SW,V:Kingpin 3.00
18 WPo,SW,V:Kingpin,C:X-Men . . . 3.00
19 LSn,In Australia 3.00
20 WPo(c),In Las Vegas 3.00
21 EL,SW,Boxing Issue 3.00
22 EL,SW,I:Saracen 3.00
23 EL,SW,V:Scully 3.00
24 EL,SW,A:Shadowmasters 3.00
25 EL,AW,A:Shadowmasters 3.00
26 RH,Oper.Whistle Blower#1 . . . . 3.00
27 RH,Oper.Whistle Blower#2 . . . . 3.00
28 BR,A:Dr.Doom,A of Veng 3.00
29 BR,A:Dr.Doom,A of Veng 3.00
30 BR,V:Geltrate 3.00
31 BR,V:Bikers #1 . . . . 2.50
32 BR,V:Bikers #2 . . . . 2.50
33 BR,V:The Reavers 2.50
34 BR,V:The Reavers 2.50
35 BR,MF,Jigsaw Puzzle #1 . . . . . . 2.50
36 MT,MF,Jigsaw Puzzle #2 . . . . . . 2.50
37 MT,Jigsaw Puzzle #3 . . . . 2.50
38 BR,MF,Jigsaw Puzzle #4 . . . . . . 2.50
39 JSh,Jigsaw Puzzle #5. . . . . 2.50
40 BR,JSh,Jigsaw Puzzle #6 . . . . . . 2.50
41 BR,TD,V:Terrorists 2.50
42 MT,V:Corrupt Mili. School 2.50
43 BR,Border Run 2.50
44 Flag Burner 2.50
45 One Way Fare 2.50
46 HH,Cold Cache 2.50
47 HH,Middle East #1 . . . . 2.50
48 HH,Mid.East #2,V:Saracen 2.50
49 HH,Punisher Hunted 2.50
50 HH,MGo(c),I:Yo Yo Ng 2.50
51 Chinese Mafia 2.50
52 Baby Snatchers 2.50
53 HH,in Prison 2.50
54 HH,in Prison 2.50
55 HH,in Prison 2.50
56 HH,in Prison 2.50
57 HH,in Prison 2.50
58 V:Kingpin's Gang,A:Micro 2.50
59 MT(c),V:Kingpin 2.50
60 VM,AW,Black Punisher, A:Luke Cage 2.50
61 VM,A:Luke Cage 2.50
62 VM,AW,A:Luke Cage 2.50
63 MT(c),VM,V:Thieves 2.50
64 Eurohit #1 . . . . 2.50
65 thru 70 Eurohit . . . . @2.50
71 AW(i) 2.50
72 AW(i) 2.50
73 AW(i),Police Action #1 . . . . 2.50
74 AW(i),Police Action #2 . . . . 2.50
75 AW(i),Police Action #3,foil(c), double size 3.00
76 LSn,in Hawaii 2.50
77 VM,Survive#1 . . . . 2.50
78 VM,Survive#2 . . . . 2.50
79 VM,Survive#3 . . . . 2.50
80 Goes to Church 2.50
81 V:Crooked Cops 2.50
82 B:Firefight 2.50
83 Firefight#2 . . . . 2.50
84 E:Firefight 2.50
85 Suicide Run 2.25

Punisher #99
© Marvel Entertainment Group

86 Suicide Run#3,Foil(c), ... 3.00
87 Suicide Run#6 . . . . 2.25
88 LSh(c),Suicide Run#9 . . . . 2.25
89 . . . . 2.25
90 Hammered 2.25
91 Silk Noose 2.25
92 Razor's Edge 2.25
93 Killing Streets 2.25
94 B:No Rules 2.25
95 No Rules 2.25
96 . . . . 2.25
97 CDi 2.25
98 . . . . 2.25
99 . . . . 2.25
100 New Punisher 4.00
100a Enhanced ed. 5.00
101 CC,Raid's Franks Tomb 3.00
102 A:Bullseye 3.00
103 Countdown 4 . . . . 3.00
104 CDi,Countdown 1, V:Kingpin, final issue 4.00
Ann.#1 MT,A:Eliminators, Evolutionary War 4.00
Ann.#2 JLe,Atlantis Attacks #5, A:Moon Knight 3.50
Ann.#3 LS,MT,Lifeform #1 . . . . . . 3.50
Ann.#4 Baron Strucker,pt.2 (see D.D.Annual #7) 3.50
Ann.#5 System Bytes #1 . . . . 3.50
Ann.#6 I:Eradikator,w/card 3.50
GNv 5.00
Summer Spec.#1 VM,MT 3.50
Summer Spec.#2 SBs(c) 2.50
Summer Spec.#3 V:Carjackers . . . 2.50
Summer Spec.#4 . . . . 3.25
Spec. Punisher/Batman,CDi,JR2, 48-pg. (1994) 5.00
Spec.#1 Punisher/Daredevil, rep. Daredevil 6.00
Punisher:No Escape A:USAgent, Paladin (1990) 5.50
Punisher Movie Spec.BA (1989) . . . 6.00
GNv Punisher: The Prize (1990) . . . 5.50
Punisher:Bloodlines DC 6.25
Punisher:Blood on the Moors 17.00
Punisher:G-Force 5.25
Punisher:Origin of Mirco Chip #1, O:Mirco Chip 2.50
Punisher:Origin of Mirco Chip #2 V:The Professor 2.50
Punisher:Back To School Spec. #1 JRy,short stories 3.25
#2 BSz 3.00

All comics prices listed are for *Near Mint* condition.

Punisher Ann. #1
© Marvel Entertainment Group

Classic Punisher rep early
B&W magazines 7.00
Punisher:Die Hard in the Big
Easy Mardi Gras 5.25
Holiday Spec.#1 V:Young
Mob Capo 3.25
Holiday Spec #2 . . . . 3.00
Punisher:Ghosts of the Innocent#1
TGr, V:Kingpin's Dead Men 6.00
Punisher:Ghosts of the Innocent#2
TGr, V:Kingpin,Snake 6.00

[2nd Regular Series] 1995
1 JOs,TL,Clv,Punisher sent to
the Electric Chair, foil(c) 3.00
2 JOs,TL,Clv,Crime family boss . . . 2.50
3 JOs,TL,Clv,V:Hatchetman 2.50
4 JOs,TL,Clv,A:Daredevil,Jigsaw . . 2.50
5 . . . . 2.50
6 . . . . 2.50
7 JOs,TL,Clv,V:Son of Nick Fury . . 2.50
8 . . . . 2.50
9 . . . . 2.50
10 . . . . 2.50
11 Onslaught saga. 2.50
12 A:X-Cutioner 3.00
13 JOs,TL, Working for S.H.I.E.L.D.?,
A:X-Cutioner 2.50
14 . . . . 2.50
15 JOs,TL, X-Cutioner 2.50
16 JOs,TL, concl.? 2.50
17 JOS,TL,A:Daredevil,Doc Samson,
Spider-Man 2.50
18 JOS,TL,Frank Castle amnesia? . 2.50
19 JOS,TL,V:Taskmaster. 2.50
20 JOS,TL, fugitive Punisher. 2.50

PUNISHER
Sept., 1998
1 (of 4) BWr,JP,TSg,F:Frank
Castle 3.00
2 BWr,JJu,JP,A:Hellstrom 3.00
3 BWr,JJu,TSg,JP,A:Gabriel 7.00
4 BWr,JJu,TSg,JP,Hell on Earth . . . 3.00

PUNISHER
Jan., 2000
1 (of 12) JP,GEn,SDi,R:Punisher . . 3.00
2A JP,GEn,SDi,V:Ma Gnucci 3.00
2B variant SDi(c). 3.00
3 GEn,JP,SDi,polybaged 8.00
4 GEn,JP,SDi,Gnuccis 3.00
5 GEn,JP,SDi,Mr.Payback 3.00
6 GEn,JP,SDi,Elite 3.00

7 GEn,JP,SDi,Mr.Payback 3.00
8 GEn,JP,SDi,Gnuccis 3.00
9 GEn,JP,SDi,Russian 3.00
10 GEn,JP,SDi,Russian 3.00
11 GEn,JP,SDi,Russian 3.00
12 GEn,JP,SDi,concl. 3.00
Spec. Punisher/Painkiller Jane 3.50
GN Punisher Kills the Marvel
Universe, 48-pg. GEn,DBw. . . . 6.00

PUNISHER
June, 2001
1 GEn,JP,SDi,pt.1 . . . . 5.00
2A GEn,JP,SDi,pt.2. . . . . 3.00
2B variant SDi(c). 3.00
3 GEn,JP,SDi,Grand Nixon Island . 3.00
4 GEn,JP,SDi,Survivor 3.00
5 GEn,JP,SDi,V:Kriegkopf. 3.00
6 GEn,JP,Viet Nam. 3.00
7 SDi,JP,'Nuff Said 3.00
8 TPe,Taxi Wars 3.00
9 TPe,Taxi Wars 3.00
10 TPe,Taxi Wars. 3.00
11 TPe,Taxi Wars, Medallion 3.00
12 TPE,Taxi Wars, concl. 3.00
13 GeN,SDi, to South America 3.00
14 GeN,SDi, in Columbia. 3.00
15 GeN,SDi,F:Wolverine 3.00
16 GeN,SDi,F:Wolverine 3.00
17 GeN,DaR,F:Wolverine 3.00
18 GeN,SDi,Northern Ireland. 3.00
19 GeN,SDi,. 3.00
20 GEn,SDi,Brotherhood,pt.1 . . . . . 3.00
21 GEn,SDi,Brotherhood,pt.2 . . . . . 3.00
22 GEn,SDi 3.00
23 GEn,SDi,Giant Squid 3.00
24 GEn,TMd,Hidden,pt.1 . . . . 3.00
25 GEn,TMd,Hidden,pt.2 . . . . 3.00
26 GEn,TMd,Hidden,pt.3 . . . . 3.00
27 GEn,SDi,F:Elektra. 3.00
28 GEn,CK,Streets of Loredo,pt.1 . . 3.00
29 GEn,CK,Streets of Loredo,pt.2 . . 3.00
30 GEn,CK,Streets of Loredo,pt.3 . . 3.00
31 GEn,CK,Streets of Loredo,pt.4 . . 3.00
32 GEn,CK,Streets of Loredo,pt.5 . . 3.00
33 GEn,JMC,Dunces,pt.1 . . . . 3.00
34 GEn,JMC,Dunces,pt.2 . . . . 3.00
35 GEn,JMC,Dunces,pt.3 . . . . 3.00
36 GEn,JMC,Dunces,pt.4 . . . . 3.00
37 GEn,JMC,Dunces,pt.5 . . . . 4.00

PUNISHER
Max, 2004
1 GEn,In the Beginning,pt.1 . . . . . . 9.00
2 GEn,In the Beginning,pt.2 . . . . . . 5.00
3 GEn,In the Beginning,pt.3 . . . . . . 5.00
4 GEn,In the Beginning,pt.4 . . . . . . 3.00
5 GEn,In the Beginning,pt.5 . . . . . . 3.00
6 GEn,In the Beginning,pt.6 . . . . . . 3.00
7 GEn,Kitchen Irish,pt.1 . . . . 3.00
8 GEn,Kitchen Irish,pt.2 . . . . 3.00
9 GEn,Kitchen Irish,pt.3 . . . . 3.00
10 GEn,Kitchen Irish,pt.4 . . . . 3.00
11 GEn,Kitchen Irish,pt.5 . . . . 3.00
12 GEn,Kitchen Irish,pt.6 . . . . 3.00
13 GEn,DBw,Mother Russia, pt.1 . . 3.00
14 GEn,DBw,Mother Russia, pt.2 . . 3.00
15 GEn,DBw,Mother Russia, pt. 3 . . 3.00
16 GEn,DBw,Mother Russia, pt.4 . . 3.00
17 GEn,DBw,Mother Russia 3.00
18 GEn,DBw,Mother Russia 3.00
19 GEn,DBw,Up is Down and
Black Is White,pt.1. . . . . 3.00
20 GEn,Up is Down, Black is White 3.00
21 GEn,Up is Down, Black is White 3.00
22 GEn,Up is Down, Black is White 3.00
23 GEn,Up is Down, Black is White 3.00
24 GEn,Up is Down, Black is White 3.00
25 GEn,The Slavers,pt.1 . . . . 3.00
26 GEn,The Slavers,pt.2 . . . . 3.00
27 GEn,The Slavers,pt.3 . . . . 3.00

28 GEn,The Slavers,pt.4 . . . . 3.00
29 GEn,The Slavers,pt.5 . . . . 3.00
30 GEn,The Slavers,pt.6 . . . . 3.00
31 GEn,Barracuda,pt.1 . . . . 3.00
32 GEn,Barracuda,pt.2 . . . . 3.00
33 GEn,Barracuda,pt.3 . . . . 3.00
34 GEn,Barracuda,pt.4 . . . . 3.00
35 GEn,Barracuda,pt.5 . . . . 3.00
36 GEn,Barracuda,pt.6 . . . . 3.00
37 GEn,Man of Stone, pt.1 . . . . 3.00
38 GEn,Man of Stone, pt.2 . . . . 3.00
39 GEn,Man of Stone, pt.3 . . . . 3.00
40 GEn,Man of Stone, pt.4 . . . . 3.00
41 GEn. 3.00
42 GEn,Man of Stone 3.00
43 GEn,Widowmaker, pt.1 . . . . 3.00
44 GEn,Widowmaker, pt.2 . . . . 3.00
45 GEn,Widowmaker, pt.3 . . . . 3.00
46 GEn,Widowmaker, pt.4 . . . . 3.00
47 GEn,Widowmaker, pt.5 . . . . 3.00
48 GEn,Widowmaker, pt 6 . . . . 3.00
49 GEn,Widowmaker, pt.7 . . . . 3.00
50 GEn,Long Cold Dark, pt.1 . . . . . 4.00
51 GEn,Long Cold Dark, pt.2 . . . . . 3.00
52 GEn,Long Cold Dark, pt.3 . . . . . 3.00
Ann. #1 The Hunted 4.00
Spec. Punisher: Red X-Mas (2004). 3.00
Spec. Punisher: The End,RCo. 5.00
Spec. X-Mas Special, The List. . . . 4.00
1-shot The Cell, GEn,56-pg. 5.00
1-shot Punisher Valentine's One . . . 4.00
1-shot Punisher Silent Night (2005). 4.00
1-shot Punisher: The Tyger (2006) . 5.00

PUNISHER ARMORY
July, 1990
1 JLe(c). 3.00
2 JLe(c). 2.50
3 . . . . 2.50
4 thru 6 . . . . @2.50
7 thru 10 . . . . @2.50

PUNISHER/
CAPTAIN AMERICA:
BLOOD AND GLORY
1 thru 3 KJ,V:Drug Dealers. . . . . @6.25

CLASSIC PUNISHER
1 TDz 5.00

PUNISHER KILLS
THE MARVEL UNIVERSE
1995
1-shot Alterniverse 20.00

PUNISHER MAGAZINE
Oct., 1989
1 MZ,rep.,Punisher #1 . . . . 3.00
2 MZ,rep 2.50
3 thru 13 KJ,rep. . . . . @2.50
14 rep. PWJ #18&#2 . . . . 2.50
15 rep. PWJ. 2.50
16 rep.,1990. . . . . 2.50

PUNISHER
MEETS ARCHIE
1994
1 JB. 4.25
1a newsstand ed. 3.25

PUNISHER MOVIE COMIC
Nov., 1989
1 Movie adapt. 2.25
2 Movie adapt 2.25
3 Movie adapt,Dec., 1989 . . . . 2.25

MARVEL

PUNISHER: THE MOVIE
March, 2004
1 (of 3) PO 3.00
2 and 3 PO . . . . @3.00

PUNISHER PRESENTS:
BARRACUDA MAX
Feb., 2007
1 (of 5) GEn(s) 4.00
2 thru 5 GEn(s) . . . . @4.00

PUNISHER P.O.V.
July, 1991
1 BWr,Punisher/Nick Fury. 5.50
2 BWr,A:Nick Fury,Kingpin 5.50
3 BWr,V:Mutant Monster,
   A:Vampire Slayer. 5.50
4 BWr,A:Nick Fury 5.25

PUNISHER 2099
1993–95
1 TMo,Jake Gallows family
   Killed, foil(c). 2.50
2 TMo,I:Fearmaster,Kron,Multi
   Factor 2.25
3 TMo,V:Frightening Cult 2.25
4 TMo,V:Cyber Nostra 2.25
5 TMo,V:Cyber Nostra,Fearmaster. 2.25
6 TMo,V:Multi-Factor 2.25
7 TMo,Love and Bullets#1 . . . . 2.25
8 TMo,Love and Bullets#2 . . . . 2.25
9 TMo,Love and Bullets#3 . . . . 2.25
10 TMo,I:Jigsaw. 2.25
11 TMo,V:Jigsaw 2.25
12 TMo,A:Spider-Man 2099 . . . . . . 2.25
13 TMo,Fall of the Hammer#5 . . . . . 2.25
14 WSm, ... 2.25
15 TMo,V:Fearmaster,
   I:Public Enemy 2.25
16 TMo,V:Fearmaster,
   Public Enemy 2.25
17 TMo,V:Public Enemy 2.25
18 TMo,I:Goldheart 2.25
19 TMo,I:Vendetta 2.25
20 . . . . 2.25
21 . . . . 2.25
22 V:Hotwire 2.25
23 I:Synchron,V:Hotwire 2.25
24 V:Synchron 2.25
25 Enhanced cover 3.50
25a newsstand ed. 2.25
26 V:Techno-Shaman 2.25
27 R:Blue Max 2.25
Becomes:
PUNISHER 2099 A.D.
28 Minister of Punishment 2.25
29 Minister of Punishment 2.25
30 One Nation Under Doom 2.25
31 . . . . 2.25
32 Out of Ammo. 2.25
33 Counddown to final issue 2.25
34 final issue 2.25

PUNISHER VS. BULLSEYE
Nov., 2005
1 The Man's Got Style 3.00
2 The Drop 3.00
3 Massacre on 34th Street 3.00
4 Two of a Kind. 3.00
5 Profit and Loss. 3.00

PUNISHER
WAR JOURNAL
Nov., 1988
1 CP,JLe,O:Punisher 5.00
2 CP,JLe,A:Daredevil 4.00
3 CP,JLe,A:Daredevil 4.00
4 CP,JLeV:The Sniper. 4.00

Punisher War Journal #2
© Marvel Entertainment Group

5 CP,JLe,V:The Sniper 4.00
6 CP,JLe,A:Wolverine 4.00
7 CP,JLe,A:Wolverine 4.00
8 JLe,I:Shadowmasters 4.00
9 JLe,A:Black Widow 4.00
10 JLe,V:Sniper 4.00
11 JLe,Shock Treatment 3.50
12 JLe,AM,V:Bushwacker 3.50
13 JLe(c),V:Bushwacker 3.50
14 JLe(c),DR,RH,A:Spider-Man. . . 3.50
15 JLe(c),DR,RH,A:Spider-Man. . . 3.50
16 MT(i),Texas Massacre 3.50
17 JLe,AM,Hawaii 3.00
18 JLe,AM,Kahuna,Hawaii. 3.00
19 JLe,AM,Traume in Paradise . . . 3.00
20 AM. 3.00
21 TSm,AM 3.00
22 TSm,AM,Ruins #1. . . . . 3.00
23 TSm,AM,Ruins #2. . . . . 3.00
24 . . . . 3.00
25 MT. 3.00
26 MT,A:Saracen 3.00
27 MT,A:Saracen 3.00
28 MT. 3.00
29 MT,A:Ghostrider 3.00
30 MT,A:Ghostrider 3.00
31 NKu,Kamchatkan
   Konspiracy#1. . . . . 3.00
32 Kamchatkan Konspiracy #2 . . . 3.00
33 Kamchatkan Konspiracy #3 . . . . 3.00
34 V:Psycho. 3.00
35 Movie Stuntman 3.00
36 Radio Talk Show #1 . . . . 3.00
37 Radio Talk Show #2 . . . . 3.00
38 . . . . 3.00
39 DGr,V:Serial Killer. 3.00
40 MWg 3.00
41 Armageddon Express 3.00
42 Mob run-out 3.00
43 JR2(c). 3.00
44 Organ Donor Crimes. 3.00
45 Dead Man's Hand #3,V:Viper . . . 3.00
46 Dead Man's Hand #6,V:Chainsaw
   and the Praetorians. 3.00
47 Dead Man's Hand #7,A:Nomad,
   D.D,V:Hydra,Secret Empire. . . . 3.00
48 B:Payback. 3.00
49 JR2(c),V:Corrupt Cop 3.00
50 MT,V:Highjackers,I:Punisher
   2099. . . . . 3.00
51 E:Payback. 3.00
52 A:Ice(from The'Nam) 3.00
53 A:Ice(from the Nam) 3.00
54 Hyper#1 . . . . 3.00

55 Hyper#2 . . . . 3.00
56 Hyper#3 . . . . 3.00
57 A:Ghost Rider,Daredevil 3.00
58 A:Ghost Rider,Daredevil 3.00
59 F:Max the Dog 3.00
60 CDi(s),F:Max the Dog. 3.00
61 CDi(s),Suicide Run#1,Foil(c) . . 3.00
62 CDi(s),Suicide Run#4 . . . . 2.50
63 CDi(s),Suicide Run#7 . . . . 2.50
64 CDi(s),Suicide Run#10 . . . . 3.00
64a Newsstand Ed. 2.50
65 B:Pariah 2.50
66 A:Captain America 2.50
67 Pariah#3 . . . . 2.50
68 A:Spider-Man 2.50
69 E:Pariah 2.50
70 . . . . 2.50
71 . . . . 2.50
72 V:Fake Punisher 2.50
73 E:Frank Castle 2.50
74 . . . . 2.50
75 MT(c). 3.00
76 First Entry 2.50
77 R:Stone COld 2.50
78 V:Payback,Heathen 2.50
79 Countdown 3. . . . . 2.50
80 Countdown 0, A:Nick Fury,
   V:Bullseye, final issue 2.50

PUNISHER WAR JOURNAL
Nov., 2006
1 . . . . 5.00
2 Civil War 4.00
3 Civil War tie-in 4.00
4 MD2,Small Wake for a Tall Man . 3.00
5 AOI, ... 3.00
6 AOI, Blood and Sand, pt.1 . . . . . 3.00
7 AOI, Blood and Sand, pt.2 . . . . . 3.00
7a variant AOI (c) 3.00
8 AOI, Blood and Sand, pt.3. . . . . 3.00
9 AOI, Blood and Sand, pt.4. . . . . 3.00
10 AOI 3.00
11 . . . . 3.00
12 World War Hulk 4.00
13 Hunter/Hunted, pt.1 . . . . 4.00

PUNISHER WAR ZONE
1992
1 JR2,KJ,Punisher As Johnny Tower
   Die-Cut Bullet Hole(c) 3.00
2 JR2,KJ,Mafia Career. 2.25
3 JR2,KJ,Punisher/Mafia,contd . . . 2.25
4 JR2,KJ,Cover gets Blown 2.25
5 JR2,KJ,A:Shotgun 2.25
6 JR2,KJ,A:Shotgun 2.25
7 JR2,V:Rapist in Central Park. . . . 2.25
8 JR2,V:Rapist in Central Park. . . . 2.25
9 JR2,V:Magnificent Seven 2.25
10 JR2,V:Magnificent Seven 2.25
11 JR2,MM,V:Magnificent Seven. . . 2.25
12 Punisher Married 2.25
13 Self-Realization. 2.25
14 Psychoville#3 . . . . 2.25
15 Psychoville#4 . . . . 2.25
16 Psychoville#5 . . . . 2.25
17 Industrial Esponiage 2.25
18 Jerico Syndrome#2 . . . . 2.25
19 Jerico Syndrome#3. . . . . 2.25
20 B:2 Mean 2 Die. 2.25
21 2 Mean 2 Die#2 . . . . 2.25
22 A:Tyger Tyger 2.25
23 Suicide Run#2,Foil(c) 3.25
24 Suicide Run#5, ... 2.25
25 Suicide Run#8, ... 2.50
26 CDi(s),JB,Pirates 2.25
27 CDi(s),JB, ... 2.25
28 CDi(s),JB,Sweet Revenge 2.25
29 CDi(s),JB,The Swine 2.25
30 CDi(s),JB. 2.25
31 CDi(s),JB,River of Blood,pt.1 . . . 2.25
32 CDi(s),JB,River of Blood,pt.2 . . . 2.25

MARVEL

Punisher War Zone #37
© Marvel Entertainment Group

33 CDi(s),JB,River of Blood,pt.3 . . . 2.25
34 CDi(s),JB,River of Blood,pt.4 . . . 2.25
35 River of Blood,pt.5 . . . . 2.25
36 River of Blood,pt.6 . . . . 2.25
37 O:Max 2.25
38 Dark Judgment,pt.1 . . . . 2.25
39 Dark Judgment,pt.2 . . . . 2.25
40 In Court 2.25
41 CDi,Countdown 2, final issue . . . 2.25
Ann.#1 Jb,MGo,(c),I:Phalanx,
    w/Trading card 3.25
Ann.#2 CDi(s),DR 3.00

PUNISHER: YEAR ONE
1994
1 O:Punisher 2.50
2 thru 4 . . . . @2.50

PUSSYCAT
(B&W Magazine) Oct., 1968
1 BEv,BWa,WW 300.00

QUASAR
Oct., 1989
1 O:Quasar 3.00
2 V:Deathurge,A:Eon 2.50
3 A:Human Torch,V:The Angler . . . 2.50
4 Acts of Vengeance,A:Aquarian . . 2.50
5 A of Veng,V:Absorbing Man 2.50
6 V:Klaw,Living Laser,Venom,
    Red Ghost 3.00
7 MM,A:Cosmic SpM,V:Terminus . . 2.50
8 MM,A:New Mutants,BlueShield . . 2.25
9 MM,A:Modam 2.25
10 MM,A:Dr.Minerva 2.25
11 MM,A:Excalibur,A:Modred 2.25
12 MM,A:Makhari,Blood Bros. 2.25
13 JLe(c)MM,J.into Mystery #1 . . . . 2.25
14 TM(c)MM,J.into Mystery #2 . . . . 2.25
15 MM,Journey into Mystery #3 . . . . 2.25
16 MM,Double sized 2.25
17 MM,Race,A:Makkari,Whizzer,
    Quicksilver,Capt.Marv,Super
    Sabre,Barry Allen Spoof 2.25
18 GCa,N:Quasar 2.25
19 GCa,B:Cosmos in Collision,
    C:Thanos 2.25
20 GCa,A:Fantastic Four 2.25
21 GCa,V:Jack of Hearts 2.25
22 GCa,D:Quasar,A:Ghost Rider . . . 2.25
23 GCa,A:Ghost Rider 2.25
24 GCa,A:Thanos,Galactus,
    D:Maelstrom 2.25

25 GCa,A:Eternity & Infinity,N:Quasar,
    E:Cosmos Collision 2.25
26 GCa,Inf.Gauntlet,A:Thanos. 2.50
27 GCa,Infinity Gauntlet,I:Epoch . . . 2.25
28 GCa,A:Moondragon,Her,
    X-Men 2.25
29 GCa,A:Moondragon,Her 2.25
30 GCa,What If? tie-in 2.25
31 GCa,R:New Universe 2.25
32 GCa,Op.GalacticStorm,pt.3 . . . . 2.25
33 GCa,Op.GalacticStorm,pt.10 . . 2.25
34 GCa,Op.GalacticStorm,pt.17 . . 2.25
35 GCa,Binary V:Her 2.25
36 GCa,V:Soul Eater 2.25
37 GCa,V:Soul Eater 2.25
38 GCa,Inf.War,V:Warlock 2.25
39 SLi,Inf.War,V:Deathurge 2.25
40 SLi,Inf.War,V:Deathurge 2.25
41 R:Marvel Boy 2.25
42 V:Blue Marvel 2.25
43 V:Blue Marvel 2.25
44 V:Quagmire 2.25
45 V:Quagmire,Antibody 2.25
46 Neutron,Presence 2.25
47 1st Full Thunderstrike Story 2.25
48 A:Thunderstrike. 2.25
49 Kalya Vs. Kismet. 2.25
50 A:Man-Thing,Prism(c) 3.50
51 V:Angler,A:S.Supreme 2.25
52 V:Geometer. 2.25
53 . . . . 2.25
54 MGu(s),Starblast #2 . . . . 2.25
55 MGu(s),A:Stranger 2.25
56 MGu(s),Starblast #10 . . . . 2.25
57 MGu(s),A:Kismet. 2.25
58 . . . . 2.25
59 A:Thanos,Starfox. 2.25
60 final issue 2.25

QUEST
June, 2003
1 (of 6) Manga,F:Katherine West . . 2.50
2 Quest & Kaori 2.50

QUESTPROBE
Aug., 1984
1 JR,A:Hulk,I:Chief Examiner 3.00
2 AM,JM,A:Spider-Man 3.00
3 JSt,A:Thing & Torch 3.00

QUICKSILVER
Sept., 1997
1 CJ,TPe, V:Exodus, cont. from
    Excalibur #113 . . . . 3.00
2 TPe,CJ,A:Knights of Wundagore. 2.25
3 TPe,CJ,V:Arkon 2.25
4 TPe, Crystal returns. 2.25
5 TPe,V:Inhumans 2.25
6 TPe,Inhumands trilogy concl. 2.25
7 JOs,F:The Black Knight 2.25
8 JOs,F:Pietro,V:Pyro 2.25
9 JOs,Savage Land concl.,A:High
    Evolutionary. 2.25
10 JOS,Live Kree or Die, pt.3,
    x-over. 2.25
11 JOs,The Seige of Wundagore,
    pt.2 (of 5). 2.25
12 JOs,The Seige of Wundagore,
    pt.4 (of 5) 48-pg. 3.00
13 JOs,Seige of Wundagore,pt.5,
    final issue 2.25

QUICK-TRIGGER
WESTERN
See: WESTERN
THRILLERS

RAIDERS OF
THE LOST ARK
Sept., 1981
1 JB/KJ,movie adaption 3.00
2 JB/KJ. 3.00
3 JB/KJ,Nov.,1981 . . . . 3.00

RAMPAGING HULK, THE
May, 1998
1 RL,double size, savage Hulk era. 3.00
2A RL,DGr,I:Ravage 2.25
2B JQ,JP,variant cover 2.25
3 RL,DGr,V:Ravage, concl. 2.25
4 DR,Trapped by an Avalanche . . . 2.25
5 RL,F:Fantastic Four 2.25
6 RL,DGr,V:Puma 2.25

RANGELAND LOVE
Marvel Comics, 1949
1 Robert Taylor 200.00
2 . . . . 150.00

RAVAGE 2099
1992–95
1 PR,I:Ravage 3.00
2 PR,V:Deathstryk 2.25
3 PR,V:Mutroids 2.25
4 PR,V:Mutroids 2.25
5 PR,Hellrock 2.25
6 PR,N:Ravage. 2.25
7 PR,New powers 2.25
8 V:Deathstryke 2.25
9 PR,N:Ravage. 2.25
10 V:Alchemax 2.25
11 A:Avatarr 2.25
12 Ravage Transforms 2.25
13 V:Fearmaster 2.25
14 V:Punisher 2099 . . . . 2.25
15 Fall of the Hammer #2 . . . . 2.25
16 I:Throwback 2.25
17 GtM,V:Throwback,O:X-11 . . . . . . 2.25
18 GtM,w/card 2.25
19 GtM, ... 2.25
20 GtM,V:Hunter 2.25
21 Savage on the Loose 2.25
22 Exodus 2.25
23 Blind Justice 2.25
24 Unleashed. 2.25
25 Flame Bearer 2.25
25a Deluxe ed. 3.00
26 V:Megastruck 2.25

Ravage 2099 #20
© Marvel Entertainment Group

27 V:Deathstryke 2.25
28 R:Hela 2.25
29 V:Deathstryke 2.25
30 King Ravage 2.25
Becomes:

RAVAGE 2099 A.D.

31 V:Doom 2.25
32 One Nation Under Doom 2.25
33 Final issue 2.25

RAWHIDE KID

Atlas, March, 1955—May, 1979
1 JMn,B:Rawhide Kid & Randy,
  A:Wyatt Earp 1,400.00
2 JMn,Shoot-out(c) 600.00
3 V:Hustler 400.00
4 Rh(c) 400.00
5 GC,JMn 400.00
6 JMn,Six-Gun Lesson 350.00
7 AW 350.00
8 . . . . 350.00
9 . . . . 350.00
10 thru 16 Sept. 1957 . . . . . . @300.00
17 JK,O:Rawhide Kid; Aug. 1960 300.00
18 thru 20 . . . . @300.00
21 . . . . 300.00
22 . . . . 300.00
23 JK,O:Rawhide Kid Retold . . . 350.00
24 thru 30 . . . . @250.00
31 JK,DAy,No Law in Mesa 250.00
32 JK,DAy,Beware of the
  Parker Brothers 250.00
33 JK(c),JDa,V:Jesse James . . . 250.00
34 JDa,JK,V:Mister Lightning . . . 250.00
35 JK(c),GC,JDa,
  I&D:The Raven 250.00
36 DAy,A Prisoner in
  Outlaw Town 150.00
37 JK(c),DAy,GC,V:The Rattler . 150.00
38 DAy.V:The Red Raven 200.00
39 DAy 150.00
40 JK(c),DAy,A:Two Gun Kid . . 150.00
41 JK(c),The Tyrant of
  Tombstone Valley 150.00
42 JK 150.00
43 JK 200.00
44 JK(c),V:The Masked Maverick 150.00
45 JK(c),O:Rawhide Kid Retold . . 175.00
46 JK(c),ATh 150.00
47 JK(c),The Riverboat Raiders . 110.00
48 GC,V:Marko the Manhunter . . 100.00
49 The Masquerader 100.00
50 A;Kid Colt,V:Masquerader . . . 100.00
51 DAy,Trapped in the
  Valley of Doom 100.00
52 DAy,Revenge at
  Rustler's Roost 100.00
53 Guns of the Wild North 100.00
54 DH,BEv,The Last Showdown . 100.00
55 . . . . 100.00
56 DH,JTgV:The Peacemaker . . 100.00
57 V:The Scorpion 100.00
58 DAy 100.00
59 V:Drako 100.00
60 DAy,HT,Massacre at Medicine
  Bend 100.00
61 DAy,TS,A:Wild Bill Hickok 75.00
62 Gun Town,V:Drako 75.00
63 Shootout at Mesa City 75.00
64 HT,Duel of the Desparadoes . . 75.00
65 JTg,HT,BE 75.00
66 JTg,BEv,Death of a Gunfighter 75.00
67 Hostage of Hungry Hills 75.00
68 JB,V:The Cougar 75.00
69 JTg,The Executioner 75.00
70 JTg,The Night of the Betrayers 50.00
71 JTg,The Last Warrior 50.00
72 JTg,The Menace of Mystery
  Valley 50.00
73 JTg,The Manhunt 50.00
74 JTg,The Apaches Attack 50.00

Rawhide Kid #21
© Marvel Entertainment Group

75 JTg,The Man Who Killed
  The Kid 50.00
76 JTg,V:The Lynx 50.00
77 JTg,The Reckoning 50.00
78 JTg 50.00
79 JTg,AW,The Legion of the Lost 50.00
80 Fall of a Hero 50.00
81 thru 85 . . . . @50.00
86 JK,O:Rawhide Kid retold 55.00
87 thru 89 . . . . @75.00
90 Kid Colt 80.00
91 . . . . 30.00
92 & 93 giants . . . . @35.00
94 thru 99 . . . . @40.00
100 O:Rawhide Kid retold 30.00
101 thru 124 . . . . @25.00
125 JDa 28.00
126 thru 151 . . . . @25.00

RAWHIDE KID

Aug., 1985
1 JSe,mini-series 6.00
2 thru 4 . . . . @5.00

RAWHIDE KID

Marvel Max, Feb., 2003
1 (of 5) JSe 3.00
2 thru 5 JSe . . . . @3.00
3 JSe 3.00
4 JSe 3.00
5 JSe,concl 3.00

RAZORLINE FIRST CUT

1993
1 Intro Razorline 2.25

REAL EXPERIENCES
See: TESSIE THE TYPIST

RED RAVEN
See: HUMAN TORCH

RED SONJA

[1st Series] Jan., 1977
1 FT,O:Red Sonja,Blood of the
  Unicorn 20.00
2 FT,Demon of the Maze 10.00
3 FT,The Games of Gita 10.00
4 FT,The Lake of the Unknown . . 10.00
5 FT,Master of the Bells 10.00
6 FT,The Singing Tower 10.00
7 FT,Throne of Blood 10.00

8 FT,Vengeance o/t Golden Circle 10.00
9 FT,Chariot o/t Fire-Stallions 10.00
10 FT,Red Lace,pt.1 . . . . 10.00
11 FT,Red Lace,pt.2 . . . . 9.00
12 JB/JRu,Ashes & Emblems . . . 9.00
13 JB/AM,Shall Skranos Fall 9.00
14 SB/AM,Evening on the Border . . 9.00
15 JB/TD,Tomb of 3 Dead Kings
  May, 1979 . . . . 9.00
[2nd Series] Feb., 1983
1 TD,GC, The Blood That Binds . . 4.00
2 GC, March,1983 . . . . 4.00
[3rd Series] Aug., 1983
1 . . . . 3.00
2 thru 13 . . . . @3.00
1 movie adaption, 1985 . . . . 2.50
2 movie adaption, 1985 . . . . 2.50

RED SONJA
1-shot Bros.Hildebrandt(c),48-pg. . . 3.00

RED WARRIOR

Atlas, Jan.–Dec., 1951
1 GT,Indian Tales 200.00
2 GT(c),The Trail of the Outcast 125.00
3 The Great Spirit Speaks 100.00
4 O:White Wing 100.00
5 . . . . 100.00
6 JMn(c) final issue 100.00

RED WOLF

May, 1972–Sept., 1973
1 SSh(c),GK,JSe,F:Red Wolf
  & Lobo 35.00
2 GK(c),SSh,Day of the Dynamite
  Doom 20.00
3 SSh,War of the Wolf Brothers . 20.00
4 SSh,V:Man-Bear 20.00
5 GK(c),SSh 20.00
6 SSh,JA,V;Devil Rider 20.00
7 SSh,JA,Echoes from a Golden
  Grave 20.00
8 SSh,Hell on Wheels 20.00
9 DAy,To Die Again,O:Lobo 20.00

REN AND STIMPY SHOW

1992–96
1 Polybagged w/Air Fowlers,
  Ren(c) 5.00
1a Stimpy(c) 4.00
1b 2nd Printing 3.00
1c 3rd Printing 2.00
2 Frankenstimpy 3.00
2a 2nd Printing 2.00
3 Christmas issue 3.00
3a 2nd Printing 2.00
4 thru 12 . . . . @3.00
13 Halloween issue 2.50
14 Mars needs Vecro 2.50
15 thru 24 . . . . @2.25
25 regular (c) 2.25
25a die-cut(c),A new addition 3.00
26 thru 42 . . . . @2.25
Spec.#1 . . . . 3.25
Spec.#2 . . . . 3.25
Spec.#3 Powder Toast Man 3.25
Spec.#4 . . . . 3.25
Spec.#5 Virtual Stupidity 3.25
Spec.#6 History of Music 3.25
Holiday Special 3.00
Spec. Radio Dazed & Confused . . 2.50
Spec. Around the World in a Daze . 3.00

RETURN OF THE JEDI

1 AW,movie adapt 3.00
2 AW,movie adapt 3.00
3 AW,movie adapt 3.00
4 AW,movie adapt 3.00

MARVEL

REX HART
See: BLAZE CARSON

RICHIE RICH
1 Movie Adaptation 3.00

RINGO KID
[2nd Series] Jan., 1970
1 AW,Reprints 35.00
2 JSe,Man Trap 20.00
3 JR,Man from the Panhandle . . 20.00
4 HT(c),The Golden Spur 20.00
5 JMn,Ambush 20.00
6 Capture or Death 20.00
7 HT(c),JSe,JA,Terrible Treasure
 of Vista Del Oro 20.00
8 The End of the Trail 20.00
9 JSe,Mystery of the Black
 Sunset 20.00
10 Bad day at Black Creek 20.00
11 Bullet for a Bandit 20.00
12 A Badge to Die For 30.00
13 DW,Hostage at Fort Cheyenne. 15.00
14 Showdown in the Silver
 Cartwheel 15.00
15 Fang,Claw, and Six-Gun. 15.00
16 Battle of Cattleman's Bank 15.00
17 Gundown at the Hacienda 15.00
18 . . . . 15.00
19 Thunder From the West 15.00
20 AW 15.00
21 thru 29. . . . . @15.00
30 Nov., 1973. . . . . 15.00

RINGO KID WESTERN
Atlas, Aug., 1954
1 JMn,JSt,O:Ringo Kid,
 B:Ringo Kid 400.00
2 JMn,I&O:Arab,A:Black Rider . 200.00
3 JMn 125.00
4 JMn 125.00
5 JMn 125.00
6 & 7 . . . . @125.00
8 JSe. 125.00
9 . . . . 100.00
10 JSe(c),AW 125.00
11 JSe(c) 100.00
12 JO 100.00
13 AW 125.00
14 thru 20. . . . . @100.00
21 Sept., 1957 . . . . 100.00

RIOT
Marvel Atlas, 1954–56
1 RH,MMe,GC,BEv. 400.00
2 MMe,Li'l Abner. 275.00
3 MMe(c). 250.00
4 JSe,MMe,BEv,Marilyn Monroe 300.00
5 JSe,MMe,BEv,Marilyn Monroe 325.00
6 MMe,JSe 250.00

ROBOCOP
March, 1990
1 LS,I:Nixcops. 6.00
2 LS,V:Nixcops 4.00
3 LS 3.00
4 LS 3.00
5 LS,WarzonePt1 . . . . 3.00
6 LS,WarzonePt2 . . . . 3.00
7 thru 10 LS . . . . @2.50
11 HT 2.50
12 thru 23. . . . . @2.50
Robocop Movie Adapt 5.00
Robocop II Movie Adapt. 5.00

ROBOCOP II
Aug., 1990
1 MBa,rep.Movie Adapt 2.50
2 and 3 MBa,rep.Movie adapt. . . @2.50

ROBOTIX
Feb., 1986
1 Based on toys 3.00

ROCKET RACCOON
May, 1985—Aug., 1985
1 thru 4 MM. . . . . @3.00

Rocko's Modern Life #1
© *Marvel Entertainment Group*

ROCKO'S MODERN LIFE
1994
1 and 2 . . . . @2.25
3 and 4 . . . . @2.25

ROGUE
1995
1 Enhanced cover. 4.50
2 A:Gambit 4.00
3 Gamtit or Rogue? 3.00
4 final issue. 3.00

ROGUE
Aug., 2001
1 (of 4) AaL,RyE, ... 2.50
2 AaL,RyE 2.50
3 AaL,RyE, leaves school. 2.50
4 AaL,RyE,JuB(c) 2.50

ROGUE
July, 2004
1 Going Rogue,pt.1. . . . . 3.00
2 Going Rogue,pt.2. . . . . 3.00
3 Going Rogue,pt.3. . . . . 3.00
4 Going Rogue,pt.4. . . . . 3.00
5 Going Rogue,pt.5. . . . . 3.00
6 Going Rogue,pt.6. . . . . 3.00
7 Forget-Me-Not 3.00
8 Forget-Me-Not,A:Sunfire 3.00
9 Forget-Me-Not 3.00
10 Forget-Me-Not,V:Lady
 Deathstrike 3.00
11 Forget-Me-Not. 3.00
12 Forget-Me-Not, concl. 3.00

ROM
Dec., 1979
1 SB,I&O:Rom 15.00
2 thru 16 . . . . @5.00
17 SB,A:X-Men 10.00
18 SB,A:X-Men 10.00
19 thru 23 . . . . @5.00
24 thru 27 . . . . @7.00

28 thru 30 . . . . @4.00
31 thru 49. . . . . @3.00
50 SB,D:Torpedo,V:Skrulls 4.00
51 thru 55 . . . . @3.00
56 A:Alpha Flight 3.00
57 A:Alpha Flight 3.00
58 JG(c),A:Antman 3.00
59 SD,BL,V:Microbe Menace. 3.00
60 SD,TP,V:Dire Wraiths 5.00
61thru 74 . . . . @2.50
75 SD,CR,Doublesize,last issue . . . 7.00
Ann.#1 PB,A:Stardust 3.00
Ann.#2 I:Knights of Galador. 3.00
Ann.#3 A:New Mutants 3.00
Ann.#4 V:Gladiator. 3.00

ROMANCE DIARY
Dec., 1949
1 . . . . 175.00
2 March, 1950 . . . . 150.00

THE ROMANCES OF NURSE HELEN GRANT
Marvel Atlas, 1957
1 . . . . 100.00

ROMANCES OF THE WEST
Nov., 1949
1 Ph(c),Calamity Jane,
 Sam Bass 300.00
2 March, 1950 . . . . 175.00

ROMANCE TALES
Oct., 1949
(no #1 thru 6)
7 . . . . 150.00
8 . . . . 100.00
9 March, 1950 . . . . 100.00

ROMANTIC AFFAIRS
See: MOLLY MANTON'S ROMANCES

ROYAL ROY
Star, May, 1985
1 thru 5 . . . . @3.00
6 March, 1986 . . . . 3.00

RUGGED ACTION
Atlas, Dec., 1954
1 AyB,Man-Eater 150.00
2 JSe,DAy,JMn(c),Manta-Ray . . 100.00
3 DAy,JMn(c) 100.00
4 . . . . 100.00
Becomes:

STRANGE STORIES OF SUSPENSE
5 RH,JMn(c),Little Black Box . . . 500.00
6 BEv,The Illusion 300.00
7 JSe(c),BEv,Old John's House . 325.00
8 AW,BP,TYhumbs Down 325.00
9 BEv(c),Nightmare 350.00
10 RC,MME,AT 350.00
11 BEv(c) 225.00
12 AT 225.00
13 BEv,GM. 225.00
14 AW 250.00
15 BK 250.00
16 MF,BP, Aug., 1957 . . . . 250.00

RUINS
1995
1 Marvel's Alterverse 5.00
2 Fully painted, 32-pg. 5.00

MARVEL

RUNAWAYS
April, 2003
1 Pride & Joy, pt.1 . . . . 11.00
2 Pride & Joy, pt.2 . . . . 7.00
3 Pride & Joy, pt.3 . . . . 7.00
4 Pride & Joy, pt.4 . . . . 7.00
5 Pride & Joy, pt.5 . . . . 3.50
6 Pride & Joy, pt.6 . . . . 3.50
7 Teenage Wasteland,pt.1 . . . . . . 3.00
8 Teenage Wasteland,pt.2 . . . . . . 3.00
9 Teenage Wasteland,pt.3 . . . . . . 3.00
10 Teenage Wasteland,pt.4 . . . . . . 3.00
11 Lost & Found,pt.1 . . . . 3.00
12 Lost & Found,pt.2 . . . . 3.00
13 thru 17 The Good Die Young . @3.50
18 Season Finale. 3.00
Spec Runaways/Sentinel flip book . 4.00

RUNAWAYS
Feb., 2005
1 True Believers, pt.1 . . . . 6.00
2 True Believers, Pt.2 . . . . 5.00
3 True Believers, pt.3 . . . . 4.00
4 True Believers, pt.4 . . . . 4.00
5 True Believers, Pt.5 . . . . 4.00
6 True Believers, pt.6 . . . . 4.00
7 Sinister plan, Part 1 . . . . 4.00
8 Sinister Plan, Part 2. . . . . 4.00
9 East Coast/West Coast 3.00
10 East Coast/West Coast. 3.00
11 East Coast/West Coast. 3.00
12 East Coast/West Coast. 3.00
13 Molly Hayes alone 3.00
14 Parental Guidance,pt.1 . . . . 3.00
15 Parental Guidance,pt.2 . . . . 3.00
16 Parental Guidance,pt.3 . . . . 3.00
17 Parental Guidance,pt.4 . . . . 3.00
18 Parental Guidance,pt.5 . . . . 3.00
19 Dead Means Dead,pt.1 . . . . 3.00
20 Dead Means Dead,pt.2 . . . . 3.00
21 Dead Means Dead,pt.3 . . . . 3.00
22 Live Fast, pt.1 . . . . 3.00
23 Live Fast, pt.2 . . . . 3.00
24 Live Fast, pt.3 . . . . 3.00
25 . . . . 3.00
26 JoW,Dead End Kids 3.00
27 JoW,Dead End Kids 3.00
28 JoW,Dead End Kids 3.00
Spec. Runaways Saga . . . . @4.00

RUSTY COMICS
See: KID KOMICS

SABLE & FORTUNE
Jan., 2006
1 F:Silver Sable & Dominic Fortune 3.00
2 thru 4 . . . . @3.00

SABRETOOTH
[Limited Series] 1993
1 B:LHa(s),MT,A:Wolverine 5.00
2 MT,A:Mystique,C:Wolverine. 4.00
3 MT,A:Mystique,Wolverine 4.00
4 E:LHa(s),MT,D:Birdy 4.00

SABRETOOTH
Oct., 2004
1 (of 5) BS,F:Sasquatch. 3.00
2 thru 4 BS,F:Sasquatch. . . . . . @3.00

SABRETOOTH CLASSICS
1994–95
1 rep. Power Man/Iron Fist #66 . . . 4.00
2 rep. Power Man/Iron Fist #78 . . . 3.00
3 rep. Power Man/Iron Fist #84 . . . 3.00
4 rep. Spider-Man #116 . . . . 3.00
5 rep. Spider-Man #119 . . . . 3.00
6 reprints. 3.00
7 reprints. 3.00

Sabretooth, Limited Series #4
© *Marvel Entertainment Group*

8 reprints 3.00
9 reprints 3.00
10 Morlock Massacre. 3.00
11 rep. Daredevil #238. . . . . 3.00
12 rep. V:Wolverine 3.00
13 rep. 3.00
14 A:Mauraders 3.00
15 Mutant Massacre, rep.
    Uncanny X-Men #221 . . . . 3.00

SABRETOOTH
Spec.#1 FaN, cont.from X-Men#48 . 5.00

SABRETOOTH
Oct., 1997
1-shot,F:Wildchild 2.50

SABRETOOTH
& MYSTIQUE
1 JGz,AOl, ... 2.50
2 thru 4 JGz,AOl . . . . @2.50

SABRETOOTH: MARY
SHELLEY OVERDRIVE
June, 2002
1 (of 4) F:Creed 3.00
2 TyH 3.00
3 . . . . 3.00
4 TyH 3.00

SACHS & VIOLENS
Epic, 1993–94
1 GP,PDd(s) 3.00
2 GP,PDd(s),V:Killer 2.50
3 GP,PDd(s),V:White Slavers 2.50
4 GP,PDd(s),D:Moloch 2.50

SAGA OF CRYSTAR
May, 1983
1 O:Crystar 5.00
2 A:Ika 4.00
3 A:Dr.Strange. 4.00
4 . . . . 4.00
5 . . . . 4.00
6 A:Nightcrawler 4.00
7 I:Malachon 4.00
8 . . . . 4.00
9 . . . . 4.00
10 Chaos 4.00
11 Alpha Flight,Feb., 1985. . . . . . . 4.00

SAGA OF ORIGINAL
HUMAN TORCH
1 RB,O:Original Human Torch 3.00
2 RB,A:Toro 2.50
3 RB,V:Adolph Hitler. 2.50
4 RB,Torch vs. Toro 2.50

ST. GEORGE
Epic, June, 1988
1 KJ,Shadow Line. 2.25
2 thru 8 . . . . @2.25

SAINT SINNER
Razorline 1993–94
1 I:Phillip Fetter. 2.75
2 thru 8 . . . . @2.25

SAM & MAX
GO TO THE MOON
1 Dirtbag Special,w/Nirvana Tape. . 4.00
[Regular Series]
1 MMi,AAd,F:Skull Boy 3.25
2 AAd,MMi 3.25
3 . . . . 3.25

SAMURAI CAT
Epic, 1991
1 I:MiaowaraTomokato 2.25
2 I:Con-Ed,V:Thpaghetti-Thoth 2.25
3 EmpireStateStrikesBack 2.25

SATANA
Nov., 1997
1 JaL,WEI,AOl,V:Doctor Strange,
    non-code series. 3.00
2 WEI,AOl,to the gates of Hell 3.00

SAVAGE SWORD
OF CONAN
Aug., 1974
(black & white magazine)
1 BWS,JB,NA,GK,O:Blackmark,
    3rdA:Red Sonja,Boris(c) 165.00
2 NA(c),HC,GK,Black Colossus,
    B.U.King Kull;B.U.Blackmark . 75.00
3 JB,BWS,GK,At The Mountain
    of the Moon God;B.U.s:
    Kull;Blackmark. 50.00
4 JB,RCo,GK,Iron Shadows in the
    Moon B.U.Blackmark,Boris(c). 40.00
5 JB,Witch Shall be Born,Boris(c) 30.00
6 AN,Sleeper'Neath the Sands . 30.00
7 JB,Citadel at the Center
    of Time Boris(c) 30.00
8 inc.GK,Corsairs against Stygia . 30.00
9 Curse of the Cat-Goddess,
    Boris(c),B.U.King Kull 30.00
10 JB,Sacred Serpent of Set
    Boris(c) 30.00
11 JB,The Abode of the Damned. . 22.00
12 JB,Haunters of Castle Crimson
    Boris(c) 22.00
13 GK,The Thing in the Temple,
    B.U. Solomon Kane. 22.00
14 NA,Shadow of Zamboula,
    B.U.Solomon Kane. 22.00
15 JB,Boris(c),Devil in Iron 22.00
16 JB,BWS,People of the Black
    Circle,B.U.Bran Mak Morn. . . 22.00
17 JB,On to Yimsha!,
    B.U.Bran Mak Morn. 22.00
18 JB,The Battle of the Towers
    B.U. Solomon Kane. 22.00
19 JB,Vengeance in Vendhya
    B.U. Solomon Kane. 22.00
20 JB,The Slithering Shadow
    B.U. Solomon Kane. 18.00

Savage Sword of Conan #2
© Marvel Entertainment Group

21 JB,Horror in the Red Tower . . . 18.00
22 JB,Pool o/t Black One
    B.U. Solomon Kane 18.00
23 JB,FT,Torrent of Doom
    B.U. Solomon Kane 18.00
24 JB,BWS,Tower of the
    Elephant,B.U.Cimmeria 18.00
25 DG,SG,Jewels of Gwahlur,
    B.U.Solomon Kane 18.00
26 JB/TD,Beyond the Black River,
    B.U.Solomon Kane 18.00
27 JB/TD,Children of Jhebbal Sag 18.00
28 JB/AA,Blood of the Gods 18.00
29 ECh,FT,Child of Sorcery,
    B.U. Red Sonja 18.00
30 FB,The Scarlet Citadel 18.00
31 JB/TD,The Flaming Knife,pt.1 . . 15.00
32 JB/TD,Ghouls of Yanaldar,pt.2 . 15.00
33 GC,Curse of the Monolith,
    B.U.Solomon Kane 15.00
34 CI/AA,MP,Lair o/t Ice Worm;B.U.
    Solomon Kane,B.U.King Kull . . 15.00
35 ECh,Black Tears 15.00
36 JB,AA,Hawks over Shem 15.00
37 SB,Sons of the White Wolf
    B.U. Solomon Kane 15.00
38 JB/TD,The Road of the Eagles. 15.00
39 SB/TD,The Legions of the Dead,
    B.U.Solomon Kane concl. 15.00
40 JB/TD,A Dream of Blood 15.00
41 JB/TD,Quest for the Cobra Crown
    A:Thoth-Amon,B.U.Sol.Kane. . 15.00
42 JB/TD,Devil-Tree of Gamburu,
    A:Thoth-Amon,B.U.Sol.Kane. . 15.00
43 JB/TD,King Thoth-Amon,
    B.U.King Kull 15.00
44 SB/TD,The Star of Khorala 15.00
45 JB/TD,The Gem in the Tower,
    B.U. Red Sonja 15.00
46 EC/TD,Moon of Blood,
    B.U. Hyborian Tale 15.00
47 GK/JB/JRu,Treasure of Tranicos
    C:Thoth-Amon 15.00
48 JB/KJ,A Wind Blows from Stygia
    C:Thoth-Amon 15.00
49 JB/TD,When Madness Wears the
    Crown, B.U.Hyborian Tale 15.00
50 JB/TD,Swords Across the
    Alimane 18.00
51 JB/TD,Satyrs' Blood 10.00
52 JB/TD,Conan the Liberator 10.00
53 JB,The Sorcerer and the Soul,
    B.U. Solomon Kane 10.00
54 JB,The Stalker Amid the Sands,
    B.U. Solomon Kane 10.00

55 JB,Black Lotus & Yellow Death
    B.U. King Kull 10.00
56 JB/TD,The Sword of Skelos . . . 10.00
57 JB/TD,Zamboula 10.00
58 JB/TD,KGa,For the Throne of
    Zamboula,B.U.OlgerdVladislav 10.00
59 AA,ECh,City ofSkulls,B.U.Gault 10.00
60 JB,The Ivory Goddess 10.00
61 JB,Wizard Fiend of Zingara . . . 10.00
62 JB/ECh,Temple of the Tiger,
    B.U. Solomon Kane 10.00
63 JB/ECh,TP/BMc,Moat of Blood
    I:Chane of the Elder Earth. . . . 10.00
64 JB/ECh,GK,Children of Rhan,
    B.U. Chane 10.00
65 GK,JB,Fangs of the Serpent,
    B.U. Bront 10.00
66 thru 80 . . . . @10.00
81 JB/ECh,Palace of Pleasure,
    B.U. Bront 10.00
82 AA,BWS,Devil in the Dark.Pt.1
    B.U.repConan#24,Swamp Gas 10.00
83 AA,MW,NA,ECh,Devil in the Dark
    Pt.2,B.U. Red Sonja,Sol.Kane. 10.00
84 VM,Darksome Demon of
    Rabba Than. 10.00
85 GK,Daughter of the God King. . 10.00
86 GK,Revenge of the Sorcerer . . 10.00
87 . . . . 10.00
88 JB,Isle of the Hunter 10.00
89 AA,MW,Gamesman of Asgalun,
    B.U. Rite of Blood 10.00
90 JB,Devourer of Souls 10.00
91 JB,VM,Forest of Friends,
    B.U. The Beast,The Chain . . . 10.00
92 JB,The Jeweled Bird 10.00
93 JB/ECh,WorldBeyond the Mists 10.00
94 thru 101. . . . . @10.00
102 thru 161. . . . . @8.00
162 thru 175. . . . . @7.00
176 thru 235. . . . . @5.00
Ann.#1 SB,BWS,inc.Beware the
    Wrath of Anu,B.U. King
    Kull Vs.Thulsa Doom. 5.00

SAVAGE TALES
May, 1971
(black & white magazine)
1 GM,BWS,JR,I&O:Man-Thing,
    B:Conan,Femizons,A:Ka-Zar 300.00
2 GM,FB,BWS,AW,BWr,A:King
    Kull rep,Creatures on
    the Loose #10 . . . . 90.00
3 FB,BWS,AW,JSo 60.00
4 NA(c),E:Conan 50.00
5 JSn,JB,B:Brak the Barbarian . . 50.00
6 NA(c),JB,AW,B:Ka-Zar 35.00
7 GM,NA 30.00
8 JB,A:Shanna,E:Brak 30.00
9 MK,A:Shanna 30.00
10 RH,NA,AW,A:Shanna 30.00
11 RH 30.00
12 Summer, 1975 . . . . 30.00
Ann.#1 GM,GK,BWS,O:Ka-Zar . . 30.00

SAVAGE TALES
Nov., 1985–March, 1987
(black & white magazine)
1 MGo,I:The `Nam 6.00
2 thru 9 MGo . . . . @4.00

SCARLET SPIDER
1995–96
1 HMe,GK,TP,VirtualMortality,pt.3 . 2.25
2 HMe,JR2,AW,CyberWar,pt.3 . . . . 2.25
3 and 4 HMe . . . . @2.25

SCARLET SPIDER UNLIMITED
1995
1 True Origin,64-pg. 4.50

SCARLET WITCH
1994
1 ALa(s),DAn(s),JH,I:Gargan,
    C:Master Pandemonium 2.25
2 C:Avengers West Coast 2.25
3 A:Avengers West Coast. 2.25
4 V:Lore,last issue 2.25

SCOOBY-DOO
Oct., 1977
1 B:DynoMutt 40.00
2 thru 9 Feb., 1979 . . . . @30.00

SECRET DEFENDERS
1993–95
1 F:Dr.Strange(in all),Spider
    Woman,Nomad,Darkhawk,
    Wolverine,V:Macabre 3.25
2 F:Spider Woman,Nomad,Darkhawk,
    Wolverine,V:Macabre 2.50
3 F:Spider Woman,Nomad,Darkhawk,
    Wolverine,V:Macabre 2.25
4 F:Namorita,Punisher,
    Sleepwalker,V:Roadkill 2.25
5 F:Naromita,Punisher,
    Sleepwalker, V:Roadkill. 2.25
6 F:Spider-Man,Scarlet Witch,Captain
    America,V:Suicide Pack 2.25
7 F:Captain America,Scarlet Witch,
    Spider-Man 2.25
8 F:Captain America,Scarlet Witch,
    Spider-Man 2.25
9 F:War Machine,Thunderstrike,
    Silver Surfer. 2.25
10 F:War Machine,Thunderstrike,
    Silver Surfer. 2.25
11 TGb,F:Hulk,Nova,Northstar. . . . 2.25
12 RMz(s),TGb,F:Thanos 2.75
13 RMz(s),TGb,F:Thanos,Super Skrull,
    Rhino,Nitro,Titanium Man 2.25
14 RMz(s),TGb,F:Thanos,Super Skrull,
    Rhino,Nitro,Titanium Man,
    A:Silver Surfer. 2.25
15 thru 17 F:Dr.Druid,Cage,
    Deadpool 2.25
18 F:Iron Fist,Giant Man 2.25
19 F:Dr.Druid,Cadaver,
    Shadowoman. 2.25
20 V:Venom 2.25

Secret Defenders #6
© Marvel Entertainment Group

MARVEL

21 V:Slaymaker 2.25
22 thru 24 Final Defense,pt.1–pt.2@2.25
25 V:Dr.Druid 2.25

SECRET STORY ROMANCES
Marvel Atlas, 1953
1 BEv 175.00
2 . . . . 125.00
3 thru 9 . . . . @100.00
10 thru 21 ViC (in many) . . . . . @100.00

SECRET WAR
Feb., 2004
Book One BMB 8.00
Book One, Commemorative ed. . . 6.00
Book Two BMB 5.00
Book Three BMB 4.00

SECRET WAR
2005
1 (of 5) BMB, 48-pg. 4.00
2 thru 5 BMB, 48-pg. 4.00
Spec. From the Files of Nick Fury . . 4.00

SECRET WARS
May, 1984
1 MZ,A:X-Men,Fant.Four,Avengers,
  Hulk,SpM in All,I:Beyonder 7.00
2 MZ,V:Magneto 6.00
3 MZ,I:Titania & Volcana. 6.00
4 BL,V:Molecule Man 6.00
5 BL,F:X-Men 6.00
6 MZ,V:Doctor Doom 6.00
7 MZ,I:New Spiderwoman. 7.00
8 MZ,I:Alien Black Costume
  (for Spider-Man) 25.00
9 MZ,V:Galactus 5.00
10 MZ,V:Dr.Doom 5.00
11 MZ,V:Dr.Doom. 5.00
12 MZ,Beyonder Vs. Dr.Doom. . . . 7.00

Secret Wars II #6
© Marvel Entertainment Group

SECRET WARS II
July, 1985
1 AM,SL,A:X-Men,New Mutants . . . 5.00
2 AM,SL,A:Fantastic Four. 3.00
3 AM,SL,A:Daredevil. 3.00
4 AM,I:Kurse 3.00
5 AM,SL,I:Boom Boom 3.50
6 AM,SL,A:Mephisto 3.00
7 AM,SL,A:Thing. 3.00
8 AM,SL,A:Hulk. 3.00
9 AM,SL,A:Everyone,double-size . . 5.00

SECTAURS
June, 1985
1 Based on toys 3.00
2 . . . . 3.00
3 . . . . 3.00
4 . . . . 3.00
5 thru 10 1986. . . . . @3.00

SEEKER 3000
April, 1998
1 (of 4) DAn,IEd,sci-fi adventure,
  48-pg. 3.00
2 DAn,IEd,encounter with aliens . . 3.00
3 DAn,IEd,V:Hkkkt,. 3.00
4 DAn,IEd,V:Hkkkt, concl. 3.00

SEMPER FI
Dec., 1988
1 JSe. 2.50
2 JSe. 2.50
3 JSe. 2.50
4 JSe. 2.50
5 JSe. 2.50
6 and 8 . . . . @2.50
9 Aug., 1989,final issue 2.50

SENSATIONAL SPIDER-MAN
1 KM/TP/KJ,rep. (1989) 6.00

SENSATIONAL SPIDER-MAN
Jan., 1996
0 DJu,KJ,Return of Spider-Man,pt.1
  Lenticular cover. 6.00
1 DJu,KJ,Media Blizzard,pt.1,
  V:New Mysterio 4.00
2 DJu,KJ,Return of Kaine,pt.2 . . . . 4.00
3 DJu,KJ,Web of Carnage,pt.1 . . . 4.00
4 DJu,KJ,Blood Brothers,pt.1 . . . . 4.00
5 DJu 4.00
6 DJu 3.00
7 TDz,A:Onslaught 3.00
8 TDz,The Looter 3.00
9 TDz,Onslaught tie-in 3.00
10 TDz,RCa,V:Swarm 3.00
11 TDz,Revelations, pt.2 . . . . 3.00
11A bagged with card, etc. 5.00
12 TDz,SwM, V:Trapster 3.00
13 TDz,RCa,A:Ka-Zar, Shanna 3.00
14 TDz,RCa,Savage Land saga . . . 3.00
15 TDz,RCa,Savage Land saga . . . 3.00
16 TDz,RCa,R:Black Cat,
  V:Prowler,Vulture 3.00
17 TDz,RCa,V:Black Cat,
  Prowler,Vulture 3.00
18 TDz,RCa,V:Vulture 3.00
19 TDz,RCa,R:Living Monolith 2.50
20 TDz,RCa,Living Pharoah, concl. . 2.50
21 TDz,RCa,Techomancers. 2.50
22 TDz,RCa,A:Doctor Strange. 2.50
23 TDz,RCa,A:Doctor Strange. 2.50
24 TDz,RCa,A:S.H.I.E.L.D., Looter . 3.00
25 TDz,RCa,Spider-Hunt,pt1 x-over 4.00
26 TDz,RCa,JoB,Identity Crisis
  prelude. 2.50
27 TDz,RCa,MeW,Identity Crisis,
  as Hornet V:Phaeton. 2.50
28 TDz,RCa,as Hornet, V:Vulture . . 2.50
29 TDz,RCa,V:Arcade, Black Cat . . 2.50
30 TDz,A:Black Cat,V:Arcade 2.50
31 TDz,MeW,RCa,V:Rhino 2.50
32 TDz,JoB,The Gathering of the
  Five, pt.1 (of 5) 2.50
33 TDz,JoB,Gathering of
  the Five,pt.5. . . . . 2.50
Minus 1 Spec.,TDz,RCa, flashback. 3.00

SENSATIONAL SPIDER-MAN
See: MARVEL KNIGHTS SPIDER-MAN

SENTINEL
April, 2003
1 Salvage,pt.1. . . . . 3.00
2 Salvage,pt.2. . . . . 3.00
3 Salvage,pt.3. . . . . 3.00
4 Salvage,pt.4. . . . . 3.00
5 Salvage,pt.5. . . . . 2.50
6 Salvage,pt.6. . . . . 2.50
7 No Hero,pt.1 . . . . 2.50
8 No Hero,pt.2 . . . . 2.50
9 No Hero,pt.3 . . . . 2.50
10 Awakening,pt.1 . . . . 3.00
11 Awakening,pt.2 . . . . 3.00
12 Awakening,pt.3 . . . . 3.00

SENTINEL
Nov., 2005
1 V:Stealth Sentinel 3.00
2 thru 5 . . . . @3.00
Digest Past Imperfect 8.00

SENTINEL SQUAD O*N*E
Jan., 2006
1 Decimation tie-in 3.00
2 thru 5 . . . . @3.00

SENTRY
July, 2000
1 (of 5) PJe,JaL 15.00
2 PJe,JaL,Unicorn 10.00
3 PJe,JaL,Hulk,Spider-Man 10.00
4 PJe,JaL,Prof.X. 10.00
5 PJe,JaL, ... 10.00
Spec.#1 Sentry vs. The Void,
  JaL,PJe (2001) 20.00

SENTRY, THE
Sept., 2005
1 JR2,V:Hords of Attuma 3.00
1a Rough Cut, Jr2 . . . . 4.00
2 thru 8 JR2 . . . . @3.00

SERGEANT BARNEY BARKER
Aug., 1956
1 JSe,Comedy 250.00
2 JSe,Army Inspection(c) 150.00
3 JSe,Tank(c) 150.00
Becomes:

G.I. TALES
4 JSe,At Grips with the Enemy . 125.00
5 . . . . 100.00
6 JO,BP,GWb, July, 1957 . . . . . 100.00

SGT. FURY & HIS HOWLING COMMANDOS
May, 1963–Dec., 1981
1 Seven Against the Nazis . . . 3,200.00
2 JK,Seven Doomed Men 750.00
3 JK,Midnight on Massacre
  Mountain 400.00
4 JK,V:Lord Ha-Ha,D:Junior
  Juniper 400.00
5 JK,V:Baron Strucker 400.00
6 JK,The Fangs of the Fox 250.00
7 JK,Fury Court Martial 250.00
8 JK,V:Dr Zemo,I:Percival
  Pinkerton 250.00
9 DAy,V:Hitler 250.00
10 DAy,On to Okinwawa,I:Capt.
  Savage 250.00
11 DAy,V:Capt.Flint 125.00

Sgt. Fury and His Howling Commandos #18 © Marvel EntertainmEnt Group

12 DAy,Howler deserts 125.00
13 DAy,JK,A;Capt.America 650.00
14 DAy,V:Baron Strucker 125.00
15 DAy,SD,Too Small to Fight
    Too Young to Die 125.00
16 DAy,In The Desert a Fortress
    Stands 125.00
17 DAy,While the Jungle Sleeps . 125.00
18 DAy,Killed in Action 125.00
19 DAy,An Eye for an Eye 125.00
20 DAy,V:the Blitz Squad 125.00
21 DAy,To Free a Hostage. 100.00
22 DAy,V:Bull McGiveney 100.00
23 DAy,The Man who Failed 100.00
24 DAy,When the Howlers Hit
    the Home Front 100.00
25 DAy,Every Man my Enemy . . . 100.00
26 DAy,Dum Dum Does it the
    Hard Way 100.00
27 DAy,O:Fury's Eyepatch 100.00
28 DAy,Not a Man Shall Remain
    Alive 100.00
29 DAy,V:Baron Strucker 100.00
30 DAy,Incident in Italy 100.00
31 DAy,Into the Jaws of Death . . . 75.00
32 DAy,A Traitor in Our Midst 75.00
33 DAy,The Grandeur That was
    Greece 75.00
34 DAy,O:Howling Commandos . 60.00
35 DAy,Berlin Breakout,J:Eric
    Koenig 60.00
36 DAy,My Brother My Enemy . . . 60.00
37 DAy,In the Desert to Die 60.00
38 This Ones For Dino 60.00
39 Into the Fortress of Fear 60.00
40 That France Might be Free . . . 60.00
41 V:The Blitzers 60.00
42 Three Were AWOL 60.00
43 Scourge of the Sahara,A:Bob
    Hope,Glen Miller 60.00
44 JSe,The Howlers First Mission . 60.00
45 JSe,I:The War Lover 60.00
46 JSe,They Also Serve 60.00
47 Tea and Sabotage 60.00
48 A:Blitz Squad 60.00
49 On to Tarawa 60.00
50 The Invasion Begins 60.00
51 The Assassin 60.00
52 Triumph at Treblinka 60.00
53 To the Bastions of Bavaria . . . 60.00
54 Izzy Shoots the Works 60.00
55 Cry of Battle, Kiss of Death . . . 50.00
56 Gabriel Blow Your Horn 50.00
57 TS,The Informer 50.00
58 Second Front 50.00
59 D-Day for Dum Dum 50.00

60 Authorised Personnel Only . . . 50.00
61 The Big Breakout 50.00
62 The Basic Training of Fury 50.00
63 V:Nazi Tanks 50.00
64 The Peacemonger,A:Capt
    Savage 50.00
65 Eric Koenig,Traitor 50.00
66 Liberty Rides the Underground . 50.00
67 With a Little Help From My
    Friends 75.00
68 Welcome Home Soldier 50.00
69 While the City Sleeps 50.00
70 The Missouri Marauders 50.00
71 Burn,Bridge,Burn 50.00
72 Battle in the Sahara 50.00
73 Rampage on the
    Russian Front 50.00
74 Each Man Alone 50.00
75 The Deserter 30.00
76 He Fought the Red Baron 30.00
77 A Traitor's Trap,A:Eric Koenig . . 30.00
78 Escape or Die 30.00
79 Death in the High Castle 30.00
80 To Free a Hostage 30.00
81 The All American 30.00
82 Howlers Hit The
    Home Front,rep 25.00
83 Dum DumV:Man-Mountain
    McCoy 25.00
84 The Devil's Disciple 25.00
85 Fury V:The Howlers 25.00
86 Germ Warfare 25.00
87 Dum Dum does it...rep 25.00
88 Save General Patton 25.00
89 O:Fury's eyepatch,rep 25.00
90 The Chain That Binds 25.00
91 Not A Man...rep 25.00
92 Some Die Slowly, giant-sz 28.00
93 A Traitor...rep 20.00
94 GK(c),Who'll Stop the Bombs . 20.00
95 7 Doomed Men, rep 20.00
96 GK(c),Dum-Dum Sees it
    Through 20.00
97 Till the Last Man Shall Fail . . . 20.00
98 A:Deadly Dozen 20.00
99 Guerillas in Greece 20.00
100 When a Howler Falls 25.00
101 Pearl Harbor 18.00
102 Death For A Dollar 18.00
103 Berlin Breakout 18.00
104 The Tanks Are Coming 18.00
105 My Brother,My Enemy 18.00
106 Death on the Rhine 18.00
107 Death-Duel in the Desert 18.00

Sgt. Fury and His Howling Commandos #136 © Marvel EntertainmEnt Group

108 Slaughter From the Skies 18.00
109 This Ones For Dino,rep 18.00
110 JSe(c),The Reserve 18.00
111 V:Colonel Klaw 18.00
112 V:Baron Strucker 18.00
113 That France Might
    Be Free,rep 18.00
114 Jungle Bust Out 18.00
115 V:Baron Strucker 18.00
116 End of the Road 18.00
117 Blitz Over Britain 18.00
118 War Machine 18.00
118 War Machine 18.00
119 They Strike by Machine 18.00
120 Trapped in the Compound of
    Death 18.00
121 An Eye for an Eye 12.00
122 A;The Blitz Squad 12.00
123 To Free a Hostage 12.00
124 A:Bull McGiveney 12.00
125 The Man Who Failed 12.00
126 When the Howlers Hit Home . . 12.00
127 Everyman My Enemy,rep 12.00
128 Dum Dum does it...rep 12.00
129 O:Fury's Eyepatch 12.00
130 A:Baron Strucker 12.00
131 Armageddon 12.00
132 Incident in Italy 12.00
133 thru 140 . . . . @12.00
141 thru 150 . . . . @12.00
151 thru 167 . . . . @12.00
Ann.#1 Korea #4,#5 . . . . 250.00
Ann.#2 This was D-Day 100.00
Ann.#3 Vietnam 60.00
Ann.#4 Battle of the Bulge 40.00
Ann.#5 Desert Fox 30.00
Ann.#6 Blaze of Battle 30.00
Ann.#7 Armageddon 30.00

SERGIO ARAGONES MASSACRES MARVEL
1996
1-shot Parody 5.00

SEVEN BLOCK
Epic, 1990
1 . . . . 2.50

SHADOWMASTERS
Oct., 1989–Jan., 1990
1 RH 7.00
2 . . . . 5.00
3 . . . . 4.00
4 . . . . 4.00

SHADOWRIDERS
1993
1 I:Shadowriders,A:Cable,
    Ghost Rider 3.00
2 A:Ghost Rider 2.50
3 A:Cable 2.50
4 A:Cable 2.50

SHADOWS & LIGHT
Dec., 1997
1 BSf,RMz,LWn,BWr,GeH,SD,B&W
    anthology series 3.00
2 JSn,LW,LSh,GK 3.00
3 BL,JSn 3.00
4 three new tales 3.00

SHANG-CHI: MASTER OF KUNG FU
Marvel Max, Sept., 2002
1 (of 6) DgM,PG 3.00
2 DgM,PG,JP 3.00
3 thru 6 PG,JP . . . . @3.00

MARVEL

SHANNA, THE SHE-DEVIL
Dec., 1972–Aug., 1973
1 GT,F:Shanna 40.00
2 RA,The Dungeon of Doom . . . 30.00
3 RA,The Hour of the Bull 20.00
4 RA,Mandrill 20.00
5 JR(c),RA,V:Nekra 20.00

SHANNA, THE SHE-DEVIL
Feb., 2005
1 (of 7) by Frank Cho 3.50
2 thru 7 . . . . @3.50

SHANNA THE SHE DEVIL: SURVIVAL OF THE FITTEST
Aug., 2007
1 (of 4) JP 3.00
2 thru 4 JP . . . . @3.00

SHEENA
Dec., 1984–Feb., 1985
1 and 2 Movie adapt . . . . @3.00

She-Hulk #18
© Marvel Entertainment Group

SHE-HULK
[1st Regular Series] Feb., 1980
1 JB,BWi,I&O:She-Hulk 10.00
2 BWi,D:She-Hulk's best friend . . . 7.00
3 BWi,Wanted for Murder 7.00
4 BWi,V:Her Father 7.00
5 BWi,V:Silver Serpent 7.00
6 A:Iron Man 5.00
7 BWi,A:Manthing 5.00
8 BWi,A:Manthing 5.00
9 BWi,Identity Crisis 5.00
10 V:The Word 5.00
11 BWi,V:Dr.Morbius 5.00
12 V:Gemini 5.00
13 V:Man-Wolf 5.00
14 V:Hellcat 5.00
15 V:Lady Kills 5.00
16 She Hulk Goes Berserk 5.00
17 V:Man-Elephant 5.00
18 V:Grappler 5.00
19 V:Her Father 5.00
20 A:Zapper 5.00
21 V:Seeker 5.00
22 V:Radius 5.00
23 V:Radius 5.00
24 V:Zapper 5.00

25 Double-sized,last issue 5.00

[2nd Regular Series] 1989–94
1 JBy,V:Ringmaster 4.00
2 JBy 2.50
3 JBy,A:Spider-Man 2.50
4 JBy,I:Blond Phantom 3.00
5 JBy 2.50
6 JBy,A:U.S.1,Razorback 2.50
7 JBy,A:U.S.1,Razarback 2.50
8 JBy,A:Saint Nicholas 2.50
9 AM(i) 2.50
10 AM(i) 2.50
11 . . . . 2.50
12 . . . . 2.50
13 SK(c) 2.50
14 MT(c),A:Howard the Duck 3.00
15 SK(c) 3.00
16 SK(c) 3.00
17 SK(c),V:Dr.Angst 3.00
18 SK(c) 2.50
19 SK(c),V:Nosferata 2.50
20 SK(c),Darkham Asylum 2.50
21 SK(c),V:Blonde Phantom 3.00
22 SK(c),V:Blonde Phantom,A:All
   Winners Squad 3.00
23 V:Blonde Phantom 3.00
24 V:Deaths'Head 4.00
25 A:Hercules,Thor 2.50
26 A:Excalibur 2.50
27 Cartoons in N.Y. 2.50
28 Game Hunter Stalks She-Hulk . . 2.50
29 A:Wolv.,Hulk,SpM,Venom 2.50
30 MZ(c),A:Silver Surfer,Thor
   Human Torch 2.25
31 JBy,V:Spragg the Living Hill 2.50
32 JBy,A:Moleman,V:Spragg 2.50
33 JBy,A:Moleman,V:Spragg 2.50
34 JBy,Returns to New York 2.50
35 JBy,V:X-Humed Men 2.50
36 JBy,X-mas issue (#8 tie-in) 2.50
37 JBy,V:Living Eraser 2.50
38 JBy,V:Mahkizmo 2.50
39 JBy,V:Mahkizmo 2.50
40 JBy,V:Spraggs,Xemnu 2.50
41 JBy,V:Xemnu 2.50
42 JBy,V:USArcher 2.50
43 JBy,V:Xemnu 2.50
44 JBy,R:Rocket Raccoon 2.50
45 JBy,A:Razorback 2.50
46 JBy,A:Rocket Raccoon 2.50
47 V:D'Bari 2.50
48 JBy,A:Rocket Raccoon 2.50
49 V:Skrulls,D'Bari 2.50
50 JBy,WS,TA,DGb,AH,HC,
   D:She-Hulk 4.00
51 TMo,V:Savage She-Hulk 2.50
52 D:She-Hulk,A:Thing,Mr.Fantastic,
   I:Rumbler,V:Titania 2.50
53 AH(c),A:Zapper 2.50
54 MGo(c),A:Wonder Man 2.50
55 V:Rumbler 2.50
56 A:War Zone 2.50
57 A:Hulk 2.50
58 V:Electro 2.50
59 V:Various Villains 2.50
60 last issue 2.50

SHE-HULK
March, 2004
1 F:Avengers 3.00
2 Class Action Comics 3.00
3 Dead Certain,F:The Thing 3.00
4 Web of Lies 3.00
5 The Big Picture,pt.1 . . . . 3.00
6 The Big Picture,pt.2 . . . . 3.00
7 Space Cases,pt.1 . . . . 3.00
8 Engagement Ring,pt.2 . . . . 3.00
9 A:Hercules 3.00
10 Titania 3.00
11 Balance of Power 3.00
12 Acceptable Losses 3.00

SHE-HULK 2
Nov., 2005
1 A:New Avengers,Titan 3.00
2 Cause & Effect 3.00
3 104-pg. special 4.00
Becomes:

SHE-HULK
4 Return to Bone 3.00
5 New Kid in Town 3.00
6 I'm With Cupid 3.00
7 Beaus & Eros. 3.00
8 Civil War tie-in 12.00
8a 2nd printing 6.00
9 My Spoiler with Spoiler 3.00
10 V:Man-Wolf 3.00
11 Creature Comforts. 3.00
12 F:Starfox, A:Thanos 3.00
13 Remember the Titans 3.00
14 RBr,Awesome Andy 3.00
15 RBr,Planet Without a Hulk,pt.1 . . 3.00
16 RBr,Planet Without a Hulk,pt.2 . . 3.00
17 RBr,Planet Without a Hulk,pt.3 . . 3.00
18 RBr,Planet Without a Hulk,pt.4 . . 3.00
19 RBr,The Gamma Defense 3.00
20 RBr,What the @#*%?!! 3.00
21 . . . . 3.00
22 PDd(s), Jaded, pt.1 . . . . 3.00
23 PDd(s), Jaded, pt.2 . . . . 3.00

SHE HULK: CEREMONY
1989
1 JBr/SDr 4.00
2 JBr/FS 4.00

SHERRY THE SHOWGIRL
Marvel Atlas, 1956
1 . . . . 200.00
2 . . . . 135.00
3 . . . . 125.00
4 . . . . 125.00
5 thru 7 . . . . @125.00

SHIELD
Feb., 1973
1 JSo. 25.00
2 JSo. 20.00
3 JB,JSo,JK 20.00
4 JSo. 20.00
5 JSo,Oct., 1973 . . . . 20.00

SHOGUN WARRIORS
Feb., 1979
1 HT,DGr,F:Raydeen, Combatra,
   Dangard Ace 15.00
2 HT,DGr,V:Elementals of Evil . . . 10.00
3 AM(c),HT,DGr,V:Elementals
   of Evil 10.00
4 HT,DGr,Menace of the
   Mech Monsters. 10.00
5 HT,DGr,Into The Lair
   of Demons 10.00
6 HT,ME 10.00
7 HT,ME 10.00
8 HT,ME 10.00
9 War Beneath The Waves. 10.00
10 Five Heads of Doom. 10.00
11 TA(c) 8.00
12 WS(c) 8.00
13 Demons on the Moon 8.00
14 V:Dr. Demonicus 8.00
15 . . . . 8.00
16 . . . . 8.00
17 . . . . 8.00
18 . . . . 8.00
19 A:Fantastic Four 8.00
20 Sept., 1980 . . . . 8.00

MARVEL

SHOWGIRLS
Marvel Atlas, 1957
1 . . . . 150.00
2 . . . . 125.00

SHROUD
Limited Series 1994
1 B:MiB(s),MCW,A:Spider-Man,
   V:Scorpion 2.25
2 MCW . . . . @2.25

SILENT WAR
Jan., 2007
1 (of 6) Fant.Four V:Gorgon 3.00
2 thru 4 . . . . @3.00
5 Sentry vs. Black Bolt . . . . @3.00
6 F:Black Bolt 3.00

SILLY TUNES
Marvel Timely, 1945–47
1 Ziggy Pig 275.00
2 . . . . 150.00
3 . . . . 110.00
4 . . . . 110.00
5 . . . . 110.00
6 . . . . 110.00
7 . . . . 110.00

SILVERHAWKS
Aug., 1987
1 thru 5 . . . . @3.00
6 June, 1988 . . . . 3.00

Silver Sable #3
© *Marvel Entertainment Group*

SILVER SABLE
1992–95
1 Foil stamped(c),A:Sandman,
   Spider-Man 3.00
2 I:Gattling 2.50
3 V:Gattling,Foreigner 2.50
4 Infinity War,V:Doctor Doom 2.50
5 Infinity War,V:Doctor Doom 2.50
6 A:Deathlok 2.50
7 A:Deathlok 2.50
8 V:Hydra 2.50
9 O:Silver Sable 2.50
10 A:Punisher,Leviathan 2.50
11 Cyber Warriors,Hydra 2.25
12 V:Cyberwarriorss,R:Sandman . 2.25
13 For Love Nor Money#3,
    A:Cage,Terror 2.25
14 For Love Nor Money#6,
    A:Cage,Terror 2.25

15 V:Viper,A:Captain America 2.25
16 SBt,Infnty Crusade 2.25
17 Infinity Crusade 2.25
18 A:Venom 2.25
19 Siege of Darkness x-over 2.25
20 GWt(s),StB,BU:Sandman,Fin . . 2.25
21 Gang War 2.25
22 . . . . 2.25
23 GWt(s),A:Deadpool,Daredevil,
    BU:Sandman 2.25
24 GWt(s),BU:Crippler,w/card 2.25
25 V:Hydra 2.50
26 F:Sandman 2.25
27 A:Code Blue 2.25
28 F:Chen 2.25
29 A:Wild Pack 2.25
30 problems with law 2.25
31 V:terrorists 2.25
32 A:The Foreigner 2.25
33 V:Hammerhead 2.25
34 . . . . 2.25
35 Li'l Silvie Tale 2.25

SILVER SURFER
[1st Series] Aug., 1968
1 B:StL(s),JB,JSr,GC,O:Silver Surfer,
   O:Watcher,I:Shala Bal 800.00
2 JB,JSr,GC,A:Watcher 500.00
3 JB,JSr,GC,I:Mephisto 400.00
4 JB,A:Thor,low distribution
   scarce 800.00
5 JB,A:Fant.Four,V:Stranger 250.00
6 JB,FB,A:Watcher 300.00
7 JB,A:Watcher,I:Frankenstein's
   Monster 275.00
8 JB,DA,A:Mephisto,I:Ghost . . . 250.00
9 JB,DA,A:Mephisto,A:Ghost . . . 250.00
10 JB,DA,South America 300.00
11 JB,DA 300.00
12 JB,DA,V:The Abomination . . . 250.00
13 JB,DA,V:Doomsday Man . . . 250.00
14 JB,DA,A:Spider-Man 275.00
15 JB,DA,A:Human Torch 150.00
16 JB,V:Mephisto 150.00
17 JB,V:Mephisto 150.00
18 E:StL(s),JK,V:Inhumans 150.00

[2nd Regular Series] 1982
1 JBy,TP,Direct Only,V:Mephisto . 12.00

[3rd Regular Series] July, 1987
1 MR,JRu,A:Fantastic Four,
   Galactus,V:Champion 12.00
2 MR,A:Shalla Bal,V:Skrulls 6.00
3 MR,V:Collector & Runner 5.00
4 MR,JRu,A:Elders,I:Obliterator . . . 5.00
5 MR,JRu,V:Obliterator 5.00
6 MR,JRu,O:Obliterator,A:Kree,
   Skrulls 5.00
7 MR,JRu,V:Supremor,Elders/
   Soul Gems 5.00
8 MR,JRu,V:Supremor 5.00
9 MR,Elders Vs.Galactus 5.00
10 MR,A:Galactus,Eternity 5.00
11 JSon,JRu,V:Reptyl 4.50
12 MR,JRu,V:Reptyl,A:Nova 4.50
13 JSon,DC,V:Ronan 4.50
14 JSon,JRu,V:Skrull Surfer 4.50
15 RLm,JRu,A:Fantastic Four . . . 6.00
16 RLm,Inbetweener possesses
   Soul Gem,A:Fantastic Four 4.00
17 RLm,A:Inbetweener,Galactus,
   Fantastic Four,D:Trader,
   Possessor,Astronomer 4.00
18 RLm,Galactus V:Inbetweener . . . 4.00
19 RLm,MR,V:Firelord 4.00
20 RLm,A:Superskrull,Galactus . . . 4.00
21 MR,DC,V:Obliterator 4.00
22 RLm,V:Ego 4.00
23 RLm,V:Dragon 4.00
24 RLm,V:G.I.G.O. 4.00
25 RLm,V:Ronan,Kree Skrull War . . 4.00
26 RLm,V:Nenora 4.00

Silver Surfer, 1st Series #13
© *Marvel Entertainment Group*

27 RLm,V:Stranger 4.00
28 RLm,D:Super Skrull,V:Reptyl . . . 4.00
29 RLm,V:Midnight Sun 4.00
30 RLm,V:Midnight Sun 4.00
31 RLm,O:Living Tribunal &
   Stranger (double size) 4.50
32 RF,JSt,A:Mephisto 4.00
33 Rlm,V:Impossible Man 4.00
34 RLm,(1stJSn),2nd R:Thanos . . . 5.00
35 RLm,A:Thanos,R:Drax 4.00
36 RLm,V:Impossible Man,A:Warlock
   Capt.Marvel,C:Thanos 4.00
37 RLm,V:Drax,A:Mentor 4.00
38 RLm,V:Thanos(continued in
   Thanos Quest) 4.00
39 JSh,V:Algol 3.00
40 RLm,V:Dynamo City 4.00
41 RLm,V:Dynamo City,A:Thanos . . 4.00
42 RLm,V:Dynamo City,A:Drax . . . 3.00
43 RLm,V:DynamoCity 3.00
44 RLm,R:Thanos,Drax,
   O:Inf.Gems 4.00
45 RLm,Thanos vs. Mephisto 4.00
46 RLm,R:Warlock,A:Thanos 4.00
47 RLm,Warlock V:Drax,
   A:Thanos 4.00
48 RLm,A:Galactus,Thanos 4.00
49 RLm,V:Thanos Monster 4.00
50 RLm,Silver Stamp(D.size),
   V:Thanos Monster 8.00
50a 2nd printing 3.00
50b 3rd printing 3.00
51 RLm,Infinity Gauntlet x-over . . . 3.00
52 RLm,Infinity Gauntlet x-over . . . 3.00
53 RLm,Infinity Gauntlet x-over . . . 3.00
54 RLm,I.Gauntlet x-over,V:Rhino . 3.00
55 RLm,I.Gauntlet x-over,Universe
   According to Thanos,pt.1 . . . . . 3.00
56 RLm,I.Gauntlet x-over,Universe
   According to Thanos,pt.2 . . . . . 3.00
57 RLm,Infinity Gauntlet x-over . . . 3.00
58 RLm(c),Infinity Gauntlet x-over,
   A:Hulk,Namor,Dr.Strange 3.00
59 RLm(c),TR,Infinity Gauntlet,
   Thanos V:Silver Surfer 3.00
60 RLm,V:Midnight Sun,
   A:Inhumans 2.50
61 RLm,I:Collection.Agency 2.50
62 RLm,O:Collection Agency 2.50
63 RLm,A:Captain Marvel 2.50
64 RLm,V:Dark Silver Surfer 2.50
65 RLm,R:Reptyl,I:Princess
   Alaisa 2.50
66 RLm,I:Avatar,Love & Hate 2.50

MARVEL

Silver Surfer 3rd Series #140
© Marvel Entertainment Group

67 RLm(c),KWe,Inf.War,V:Galactus
  A:DrStrange 2.50
68 RLm(c),KWe,Inf.War,O:Nova . . . 2.50
69 RLm(c),KWe,Infinity War,
  A:Galactus 2.50
70 RLm(c),Herald War#1,I:Morg . . 2.50
71 RLm(c),Herald War#2,V:Morg . . 2.50
72 RLm(c),Herald War#3,R:Nova . . 2.50
73 RLm,R:Airwalker 2.50
74 RLm,V:Terrax 2.50
75 RLm,E:Herald Ordeal,V:Morg,
  D:Nova 3.00
76 RLm,A:Jack of Hearts 2.50
77 RLm,A:Jack of Hearts 2.50
78 RLm,R:Morg,V:Nebula 2.50
79 RLm,V:Captain Atlas 2.50
80 RLm,I:Ganymede,Terrax
  Vs.Morg 2.50
81 RLm,O:Ganymedel:Tyrant 2.50
82 RLm,V:Tyrant,double sized. 2.50
83 Infinity Crusade 2.50
84 RLm(c),Infinity Crusade 2.50
85 RLm(c),Infinity Crusade 2.50
86 RLm(c), Blood & Thunder,pt.2
  V:Thor,A:Beta Ray Bill 2.50
87 RLm(c),Blood & Thunder,pt.7 . . . 2.50
88 RLm(c),Blood & Thunder,pt.10 . . 2.50
89 RLm(c),CDo,C:Legacy 2.50
90 RLm(c),A:Legacy,C:Avatar 2.50
91 RLm 2.50
92 RLm,V:Avatar 2.50
93 V:Human Torch 2.50
94 A:Fantastic Four, Warlock 2.50
95 SEa,A:Fantastic Four 2.50
96 A:Fantastic Four,Hulk 2.50
97 A:Fantastic Four,R:Nova 2.50
98 R:Champion 2.50
99 A:Nova 2.50
100 V:Mephisto 2.50
100a enhanced ed. 5.00
101 RMz,JoP,A:Shalla Bal 2.50
102 V:Galactus 2.50
103 I:Death quad 2.50
104 Surfer Rampage 2.50
105 V:Super Skrull 2.50
106 A:Legacy,Morg 2.50
107 TGb,BAn,A:Galactus,Morg,
  Tyrant. 2.50
108 Galactus Vs. Tyrant 2.50
109 Morg has Ultimate Nulifier 2.50
110 JB,F:Nebula 2.50
111 GP,TGb,BAn,to Other Side
  of Galaxy 2.50
112 GP,TGb,BAn,. 2.50

113 GP,TGb,BAn,V:Blackbody 2.50
114 . . . . 2.50
115 GP,TGb,BAn,Surfer in pieces . . 2.50
116 GP,TGb,BAn,Pieces cause
  trouble 2.50
117 thru 119 . . . . @2.50
120 . . . . 2.50
121 A:Quasar, Beta Ray Bill 2.50
122 GP,SEa, returns to Marvel
  Universe 2.50
123 GP,RG. 2.50
124 GP,RG. 2.50
125 RG,V:Hulk, double size 3.50
126 JMD,RG,BWi,A:Dr. Strange . . . 2.50
127 JMD,RG,BWi,A:Alicia Masters . 2.50
128 JMD,RG,BWi,V:Puppet Master . 2.50
129 JMD,RG,BWi,back in time,
  late 1940s 2.50
130 JMD,CNr,BWi, trapped in past . 2.50
131 JMD,RG,BWi, ... 2.50
132 JMD,PaP,Puppet Master
  missing 2.50
133 JMD,MRy,PaP,V:PuppetMaster 2.50
134 JMD,TGm,MRy,Regains his
  memories, pt.1 (of 4) 2.50
135 JMD,TGm,MRy,Alicia summons
  Scrier 2.50
136 JMD,TGm,MRy, ... 2.50
137 JMD,TGm,MRy,Mephisto v.
  Scrier. 2.50
138 JMD,RCz,MRy,A:The Thing,
  tie-in 2.50
139 JMD,RCz,MRy,V:Gargoyle 2.50
140 JMD,JMu,on Zenn-La untouched
  by Galactus 2.50
141 JMD,JMu,A:Sama-D,Alicia
  Masters 2.50
142 JMD,JMu,Tenebrae,The Union,
  Cipher 2.50
143 JMD,DCw,Tenebrae,V:Psycho
  Man 2.50
Bi-Weekly Issues
144 JMD,JMu,V:Psycho-Man,
  A:Tenebrae 2.50
145 JMD,JMu,A:Psycho-Man,
  Tenebrae,Cypphyrr 2.50
146 TDF,DCw,V:Firelord 2.50
Minus 1 Spec., JMD,RG,BWi,
  flashback, first human contact. . 2.50
Spec. Silver Surfer: Dangerous Arti-
  facts,RMz, Galactus,Thanos
  (1996) 4.00
Spec. Silver Surfer: Inner Demons,
  rep. JMD,RGa,BWi (1998) . . . 3.00
Ann.#1 RLm,JSon,Evolution War . 7.00
Ann.#2 RLm,Atlantis Attacks 5.00
Ann.#3 RLm,Lifeform #4 . . . . 4.00
Ann.#4 RLm,Korvac Quest #3,A:
  Guardians of Galaxy 3.00
Ann.#5 RLm,Ret.o/Defenders #3. . 3.00
Ann.#6 RLm(c),I:Legacy,w/card. . . 3.75
Ann.'97 1 JMD,VS,KJ,V:Scrier,
  48-pg. 3.00
Ann.'98 MPe,RBe,TDF,F:Thor. . . . 3.00

SILVER SURFER
Epic, Dec., 1988
1 Moebius,V:Galactus. 5.00
2 Moebius,V:Galactus. 5.00
Graphic Novel 15.00

SILVER SURFER
July, 2003
1 JJu(c),children disappear. 2.50
2 JaL(c),Denise Waters 2.50
3 Denise Waters 2.50
4 Communion,pt.4 . . . . 2.50
5 Communion,pt.5 . . . . 2.50
6 Communion,pt.6 . . . . 2.50
7 Revelation,pt.1 . . . . 3.00
8 Revelation,pt.2 . . . . 3.00

9 Revelation,pt.3 . . . . 3.00
10 Revelation,pt.4 . . . . 3.00
11 Revelation,pt.5 . . . . 3.00
12 Revelation,pt.6 . . . . 3.00
13 Revelation,pt.7 . . . . 3.00
14 Revelation,pt.8 . . . . 3.00

SILVER SURFER:
IN THY NAME
Nov., 2007
1 (of 4) 3.00

SILVER SURFER:
LOFTIER THAN MORTALS
Aug., 1999
1 MFr,V:Dr. Doom 2.50
2 MFr,V:Dr. Doom, concl. 2.50

SILVER SURFER:
REQUIEM
May, 2007
1 (of 4) MSz(s) 4.00
2 MSz(s), Kyrie 4.00
3 MSz(s),Sanctus 4.00
4 MSz(s),Agnus Dei 4.00

SILVER SURFER/
SUPERMAN
Marvel/DC 1996
Spec. GP,RLm,TA, x-over 6.00

SILVER SURFER VS.
DRACULA
1994
1 rep,MWn(s),GC,TP 2.50

SILVER SURFER/
WARLOCK:
RESURRECTION
1993
1 JSn,V:Mephisto,Death 3.50
2 JSn,TA,V:Death 3.00
3 & 4 JSn,TA,V:Mephisto . . . . . . @3.00

SILVER SURFER/
WEAPON ZERO
Marvel/Top Cow 1997
1-shot Devil's Reign, pt.8 . . . . 4.00

SISTERHOOD OF STEEL
Epic, Dec., 1984
1 I:Sisterhood 4.00
2 thru 8 . . . . @3.00

SIX FROM SIRIUS
Epic, July, 1984
1 PG,limited series 3.00
2 thru 4 PG . . . . @2.25

SIX FROM SIRIUS II
Epic, Feb., 1986
1 PG 2.25

SIX-GUN WESTERN
Marvel Atlas, Jan., 1957
1 JSe(c),RC,JR,Kid Yukon
  Gunslinger 250.00
2 SSh,AW,DAy,JO,His Guns
  Hang Low 175.00
3 AW,BP,DAy 175.00
4 JSe(c),JR,GWb 125.00

SKELETON WARRIORS
1995
1 based on cartoon	2.25
2 Legion of Light	2.25
3 V:Grimstar	2.25
4 Grimskull abandons Legion of Light	2.25

SKRULL KILL CREW
1995
1 I:Kill Crew	3.00
2 V:Hydra	3.00
3 V:Captain America	3.00
4 V:Fantastic Four	3.00
5 Conclusion	3.00

Skull, The Slayer #6
© Marvel Entertainment Group

SKULL, THE SLAYER
Aug., 1975
1 GK(c),O:Skull the Slayer	15.00
2 GK(c),Man Against Gods	10.00
3 Trapped in the Tower of Time	10.00
4 Peril of the Pyramids, A:Black Knight	10.00
5 A:Black Knight	10.00
6 The Savage Sea	10.00
7 Dungeon of Blood	10.00
8 JK(c),Nov., 1976	10.00

SLAPSTICK
1992–93
1 TA(i),I:Slapstick	2.25
2 TA(i),A:Spider-Man,V:Overkill	2.25
3 V:Dr.Denton	2.25
4 A:GR,DD,FF,Cap.America	2.25

SLEDGE HAMMER
Feb., 1988
1	5.00
2 March, 1988	3.00

SLEEPWALKER
June, 1991
1 BBI,I:Rick Sheridan,C:8-Ball	3.00
2 BBI,V:8-Ball	2.25
3 BBI,A:Avengers,X-Men,X-Factor, FF,I:Cobweb,O:Sleepwalker	2.25
4 RL,I:Bookworm	2.25
5 BBI,A:SpM,K.Pin,V:Ringleader	2.25
6 BBI,A:SpM,Inf.Gauntlet x-over	2.25

7 BBI,Infinity Gauntlet x-over, V:Chain Gang	2.25
8 BBI,A:Deathlok	2.25
9 BBI,I:Lullaby	2.25
10 BBI,MM,I:Dream-Team	2.25
11 BBI,V:Ghost Rider	2.25
12 JQ,A:Nightmare	3.00
13 BBI,MM,I:Spectra	2.25
14 BBI,MM,V:Spectra	2.25
15 BBI,MM,I:Thought Police	2.25
16 BBI,MM,A:Mr.Fantastic,Thing	2.25
17 BBI,A:Spider-Man,Darkhawk, V:Brotherhood o/Evil Mutants	2.25
18 JQ(c),Inf.War,A:Prof.X	2.25
19 V:Cobweb,w/pop out Halloween Mask	2.50
20 V:Chain Gang,Cobweb	2.25
21 V:Hobgoblin	2.25
22 V:Hobgoblin,8-Ball	2.25
23 V:Cobweb,Chain Gang	2.25
24 Mindfield#6	2.25
25 O:Sleepwalker,Holo-grafx(c)	3.50
26 V:Mindspawn	2.25
27 A:Avengers	2.25
28 I:Psyko	2.25
29 DG,V:Psyko	2.25
30 V:Psyko	2.25
31 DG(ci),A:Spectra	2.25
32 V:Psyko	2.25
33 V:Mindspawn,Last issue	2.25
Holiday Spec.#1 JQ(c)	2.50

SLEEZE BROTHERS
Aug., 1989
1 Private Eyes	2.25
2	2.25
3	2.25
4 thru 6	@2.25

SLINGERS
Oct., 1998
1 Ccs,F:Ricochet, Hornet, Prodigy & Dusk, 48-page:	
1a Ricochet edition	3.00
1b Hornet edition	3.00
1c Prodigy edition	3.00
1d Dusk edition	3.00
2 CCs,V:Maggia	2.50
2a variant cover	2.25
3 CCs,F:Prodigy	2.25
4 CCs,F:Prodigy	2.25
5 CCs,F:Black Marvel	2.25
6 CCs,Truth or Dare	2.25
7 CCs,V:The Griz	2.25
8 CCs,V:The Griz	2.25
9 CCs,A:Ricochet	2.25
10 CCs,Raising Hell'sChildren,pt.1	2.25
11 CCs,Raising Hell'sChildren,pt.2	2.25
12 CCs,Hell's Children,pt.3 final	2.25

SMURFS
Dec., 1982
1	9.00
2	6.00
3	6.00
Treasury Edition	30.00

SOLARMAN
Jan., 1989
1 JM	3.00
2 MZ/NR,A:Dr.Doom, May, 1990	3.00

SOLDIER X
July, 2002
1 Cable's future, 40-pg.	3.00
2	2.25
3 to Russia without love	2.25
4 Geo debuts	2.25
5	2.25
6	2.25

7	2.25
8 Askani religion	2.25
9 V:Racist militia group	2.25
10 V:Racism	3.00
11 SEa,Dead Ends,pt.1	3.00
12 SEa,Dead Ends,pt.2	3.00

SOLO
[Limited Series] 1994
1 RoR,I:Cygnus	2.25
2 RoR,V:A.R.E.S.	2.25
3 RoR,V:Spidey	2.25
4 final issue	2.25

Solo Avengers #15
© Marvel Entertainment Group

SOLO AVENGERS
Dec., 1987
1 MBr,JRu,JLe,AW,Hawkeye; Mockingbird	4.00
2 MBr,JRu,KD,BMc,Hawkeye; Capt.Marvel	2.50
3 MBr,JRu,BH,SDr,Hawkeye; Moon Knight	2.50
4 RLm,JRu,PR,BL,Hawkeye; Black Knight	2.50
5 MBr,JRu,JRy,Hawkeye; Scarlet Witch	2.50
6 MBr,JRu,TGr,Hawkeye;Falcon	2.50
7 MBr,JG,BL,Hawkeye;Bl.Widow	2.50
8 MBr,Hawkeye;Dr.Pym	2.50
9 MBr,JBr,SDr,Hawkeye;Hellcat	2.50
10 MBr,LW,Hawkeye;Dr.Druid	2.50
11 MBr,JG,BL,Hawkeye;Hercules	2.50
12 RLm,SDr,Hawkeye; New Yellow Jacket	2.50
13 RLm,JG,Hawkeye;WonderMan	2.50
14 AM,AD,JRu,Hawkeye;She-Hulk	2.50
15 AM,Hawkeye;Wasp	2.50
16 AM,DP,JA,Hawkeye; Moondragon	2.50
17 AM,DH,DC,Hawkeye; Sub-Mariner	2.50
18 RW,DH,Hawkeye;Moondragon	2.50
19 RW,DH,Hawkeye,BlackPanther	2.50
20 RW,DH,Hawkeye;Moondragon	2.50
Becomes:

AVENGERS SPOTLIGHT

SOLOMON KANE
Sept., 1985
1 F:Solomon Kane	3.00
2	3.00

3 BBI,Blades of the Brotherhood . . 3.00
4 MMi 3.00
5 Hills of the Dead 3.00
6 . . . . 3.00

SON OF M
Dec., 2005
1 F:Quicksilver 3.00
2 thru 5 . . . . @3.00

SON OF SATAN
Dec., 1975–Feb., 1977
1 GK(c),JM,F:Daimon Hellstrom. . 32.00
2 Demon War,O:Possessor 20.00
3 . . . . 20.00
4 The Faces of Fear 15.00
5 V:Mind Star 15.00
6 A World Gone Mad 15.00
7 Mirror of Judgement 15.00
8 RH,To End in Nightmare 15.00

SOVIET SUPER SOLDIERS
1 AMe,JS,I:Redmont 4 . . . . 2.25

SPACEKNIGHTS
Aug., 2000
1 (of 5) JSn,R:Spaceknights 3.00
2 JSn,Terminator. 3.00
3 JSn,Deathwings. 3.00
4 JSn,Wraith Knights 3.00
5 JSn,concl. 3.00

Spaceman #1
© Marvel Entertainment Group

SPACEMAN
Marvel Atlas, Sept., 1953
1 BEv(c),F:Speed Carter and
  the Space Sentinals 1,000.00
2 JMn,Trapped in Space. 600.00
3 BEv(c),JMn,V:Ice Monster . . . 475.00
4 JMn, A-Bomb 500.00
5 GT 475.00
6 JMn,Thing From Outer Space 475.00

SPACE SQUADRON
Atlas, June, 1951
1 AyB,F:Capt. Jet Dixon,Blast,
  Dawn,Revere,Rusty Blake 1,000.00
2 GT(c), ... 800.00
3 Planet of Madness,GT. 700.00
4 . . . . 700.00
5 AyB 700.00
Becomes:

SPACE WORLDS
April, 1952
6 Midnight Horror 650.00

SPECIAL COLLECTOR'S EDITION
Dec., 1975
1 Kung-Fu,Iron Fist 10.00

SPECIAL MARVEL EDITION
Jan., 1971
1 JK,B:Thor,B:Reprints 40.00
2 JK,V:Absorbing Man 25.00
3 JK,While a Universe
  Trembles 25.00
4 JK,Hammer and the Holocaust,
  E:Thor 25.00
5 JSe(c),JK,DAy,B:Sgt. Fury . . . 25.00
6 HT(c),DAy,Death Ray of
  Dr. Zemo 12.00
7 DAy,V:Baron Strucker 12.00
8 JSe(c),DAy,On To Okinawa . . 12.00
9 DAy,Crackdown-CaptainFlint . . 12.00
10 DAy 12.00
11 JK,DAy,A:Captain
   America & Bucky 12.00
12 DAy,V:Baron Strucker 12.00
13 JK/DAy(c),DAy,SD,Too Small
   to Fight, Too Young To Die . . 12.00
14 DAy,E:Reprints,Sgt. Fury . . . 12.00
15 JSn,AM,I:Shang-Chi & Master of
   Kung Fu,I&O:Nayland Smith,
   Dr. Petrie 175.00
16 JSn,AM,I&O:Midnight 75.00
KingSz.Ann.#1 A:Iron Fist 18.00
Becomes:

MASTER OF KUNG FU

SPECTACULAR SCARLET SPIDER
1995
1 SB,BSz,Virtual Morality,pt.4 . . . 2.25
2 SB,BSz,CyberWar,pt.4. . . . . . . 2.25

SPECTACULAR SPIDER-MAN
(Magazine) July, 1968
1 JR,JM. 200.00
2 JR,JM,V:Green Goblin. 175.00

SPECTACULAR SPIDER-MAN
Dec., 1976
Prev: Peter Parker
134 SB,A:Sin-Eater,V:Electro 4.00
135 SB,A:Sin-Eater,V:Electro . . . 3.00
136 SB,D:Sin-Eater,V:Electro . . . 3.00
137 SB,I:Tarantula II 3.00
138 SB,A:Capt.A.,V:Tarantula II . . 3.00
139 SB,O:Tombstone. 4.00
140 SB,A:Punisher,V:Tombstone . 3.50
141 SB,A:Punisher,V:Tombstone. . 5.00
142 SB,A:Punisher,V:Tombstone. . 5.00
143 SB,A:Punisher,D:Persuader,
    I:Lobo Brothers. 5.00
144 SB,V:Boomerang 3.00
145 SB,A:Boomerang 3.00
146 SB,R:Green Goblin 5.00
147 SB,V:Hobgoblin (Demonic
    Power) 14.00
148 SB,Inferno. 3.00
149 SB,V:Carrion II 5.00
150 SB,A:Tombstone,Trial
    J.Robertson 3.00

151 SB,V:Tombstone 3.00
152 SB,O:Lobo Bros.,A:Punisher,
    Tombstone. 4.00
153 SB,V:Hammerhead,A:
    Tombstone. 3.00
154 SB,V:Lobo Bros.,Puma 3.00
155 SB,V,Tombstone 3.00
156 SB,V:Banjo,A:Tombstone 3.00
157 SB,V:Shocker,Electro,
    A:Tombstone 3.00
158 SB,Super Spider Spec.,
    I:Cosmic Spider-Man 9.00
159 Cosmic Powers,V:Brothers
    Grimm 5.00
160 SB,A:Hydro Man,Shocker,
    Rhino,Dr.Doom 4.00
161 SB,V:Hobgoblin,Hammerhead,
    Tombstone 3.00
162 SB,V:Hobgoblin,Carrion II. . . . 3.00
163 SB,V:Hobgoblin,D:Carrion II . . 3.00
164 SB,V:Beetle. 3.00
165 SB,SDr,D:Arranger,I:Knight
    & Fogg. 3.00
166 SB,O:Knight & Fogg 3.00
167 SB,D:Knight & Fogg 3.00
168 SB,A:Kingpin,Puma,
    Avengers 3.00
169 SB,I:Outlaws,A:R.Racer,
    Prowler,Puma,Sandman 3.00
170 SB,A:Avengers,Outlaws 3.00
171 SB,V:Puma 2.50
172 SB,V:Puma 2.50
173 SB,V:Puma 2.50
174 SB,A:Dr.Octopus. 2.50
175 SB,A:Dr.Octopus. 2.50
176 SB,I:Karona. 2.50
177 SB,V:Karona,A:Mr.Fantastic . . 2.50
178 SB,B:Child Within,V:Green
    Goblin, A:Vermin 2.50
179 SB,V:Green Goblin,Vermin . . . 2.50
180 SB,V:Green Goblin,Vermin . . . 2.50
181 SB,V:Green Goblin 2.50
182 SB,V:Green Goblin 2.50
183 SB,V:Green Goblin 2.50
184 SB,E:Child Within,V:Green
    Goblin 2.50
185 SB,A:Frogman,White Rabbit. . . 2.50
186 SB,B:FuneralArrangements
    V:Vulture 2.50
187 SB,V:Vulture 2.50
188 SB,E:Funeral Arrangements
    V:Vulture 2.50
189 SB,30th Ann.,Hologram(c),
    V:Green Goblin 6.00

Spectacular Spider-Man #138
© Marvel Entertainment Group

189a Gold 2nd printing 3.00
190 SB,V:Rhino,Harry Osborn. 2.50
191 SB,Eye of the Puma 2.50
192 SB,Eye of the Puma 2.50
193 SB,Eye of the Puma 2.50
194 SB,Death of Vermin#1 . . . . . . 2.50
195 SB,Death of Vermin#2 . . . . . . 4.00
195a Dirtbag Spec,w/Dirt#2 tape . . 2.50
196 SB,Death of Vermin#3 . . . . . . 2.50
197 SB,A:X-Men,V:Prof.Power 2.50
198 SB,A:X-Men,V:Prof.Power 2.50
199 SB,A:X-Men,Green Goblin 2.50
200 SB,V:Green Goblin,D:Harry
      Osborn,Holografx(c) 5.00
201 SB,Total Carnage,V:Carnage,
      Shriek,A:Black Cat,Venom 4.00
202 SB,Total Carnage#9,A:Venom,
      V:Carnage 4.00
203 SB,Maximum Carnage#13 . . . . 4.00
204 SB,A:Tombstone 2.50
205 StG(s),SB,V:Tombstone,
      A:Black Cat 2.50
206 SB,V:Tombstone 2.50
207 SB,A:The Shroud 2.50
208 SB,A:The Shroud 2.50
209 StB,SB,I:Dead Aim,
      BU:Black Cat 2.50
210 StB,SB,V:Dead Aim,
      BU:Black Cat 2.50
211 Pursuit#2,V:Tracer 2.50
212 . . . . 2.50
213 ANo(s),V:Typhiod Mary,w/cel . . 3.50
213a Newsstand Ed. 2.50
214 V:Bloody Mary. 2.50
215 V:Scorpion 2.50
216 V:Scorpion 2.50
217 V:Judas Traveller,clone. 3.00
217a Foil(c),bonus stuff 5.00
218 V:Puma 2.50
219 Back from the Edge,pt.2 . . . . . 3.00
220 Web of Death,pt.3 . . . . 3.00
221 Web of Death,finale 3.00
222 The Price of Truth 2.50
223 Aftershocks,pt.4 . . . . 3.00
223a enhanced cover 3.00
224 The Mark of Kaine,pt.4 . . . . . . 2.50
225 SB,TDF,BSz,I:New Green
      Goblin, 48-pg. 3.00
225a 3-D HoloDisk Cover 5.00
226 SB,BSz,The Trial of Peter
      Parker,pt.4, identity revealed. . . 3.00
227 TDF,SB,BSz,Maximum
      Clonage,pt.5 . . . . 2.50
228 Timebomb,pt.1 . . . . 2.50
229 Greatest Responsibility,pt.3 . . 3.00
229a Special cover 2.50
230 SB,Return of Spider-Man,pt.4. . 2.50
231 SB,Return of Kaine,pt.1 . . . . . 2.50
232 . . . . 2.50
233 SB,JP,Web of Carnage,pt.4 . . 2.50
234 SB,Blood Brothers,pt.4 . . . . . . 2.50
235 . . . . 2.50
236 . . . . 2.50
237 V:Lizard 2.50
238 V:Lizard 2.50
239 V:Lizard 2.50
240 TDz,LRs,Book of Revelations,
      pt.1 (of 4) 3.00
241 Revelations epilogue 2.50
242 JMD,LRs,R:Chameleon,
      A:Kangaroo 2.50
243 JMD,LRs,R:Chameleon 2.50
244 JMD,LRs,V:Chameleon 2.50
245 JMD,LRs,V:Chameleon,
      A:Kangaroo 2.50
246 JMD,LRs,V:Kangaroo,Grizzly . . 2.50
247 JMD,LRs,F:JackO'Lantern,pt.1. 2.50
248 JMD,LRs,DGr,F:Jack O'
      Lantern, pt.2 . . . . 2.50
249 JMD,LRs,DGr, Last Temptation
      of Flash Thompson 2.50

250 JR, V:Original Green Goblin,
      double gatefold cover 3.50
251 JMD,LRs,DGr,V:Kraven the
      Hunter 2.50
252 JMD,LRs,DGr,V:Norman
      Osborn. 2.50
253 JMD,LRs,DGr,V:Norman Osborn,
      Gibbon, Grizzly 2.50
254 JMD,LRs,DGr,V:Prof.Angst. . . . 2.50
255 JMD,LRs,DGr,Spider-Hunt,pt.4
      x-over, double size 3.00
256 JMD,LRs,DGr,Identity Crisis
      prelude, A:Prodigy 2.50
257 JMD,LRs,DGr,Identity Crisis,
      as Prodigy, V:Conundrum 2.50
258 JMD,LRs,DGa,as Prodigy. 2.50
259 RSt,LRs,DGa,V:Hobgoblin 2.50
260 JR,RSt,LRs,DGa,Green Goblin
      vs. Hobgoblin. 2.50
261 RSt,LRs,AM,Goblins at the
      Gate,pt.3 . . . . 2.50
262 JBy, AM, LRs, The Gathering of
      the Five, pt.4 (of 5) x-over. . . . 2.50
263 JBy,AM,LRs,The Final
      Chapter,pt.3 x-over 4.00
Ann.#8 MBa,RLm,TD,Evolutionary
      Wars,O:Gwen Stacy Clone . . . 7.00
Ann.#9 DR,MG,DJu,MBa,Atlantis
      Attacks. 4.00
Ann.#10 SLi(c),RB,MM,TM,RA 6.00
Ann.#11 EL(c),RWi,Vib.Vendetta . . . 3.00
Ann.#12 Hero Killers#2,A:New
      Warriors,BU:Venom 4.50
Ann.#13 I:Noctune,w/Card. 3.25
Ann.#14 V:Green Goblin 3.00
Super-Size Spec.#1 Planet of the
      Symbiotes,pt.4,64-pg.flip-book . 4.00
Minus 1 Spec., JMD,LRs,DGr,
      flashback, F:Flash Thompson . . 2.00

SPECTACULAR SPIDER-MAN
June, 2003

1 HuR,V:Venom,pt.1 . . . . 3.00
2 HuR,V:Venom,pt.2 . . . . 2.50
3 HuR,V:Venom,pt.3 . . . . 2.50
4 HuR,V:Venom,pt.4 . . . . 2.50
5 HuR,V:Venom,pt.5 . . . . 2.50
6 HuR,Countdown,pt.1,V:Doc Ock . 2.50
7 HuR,Countdown,pt.2 . . . . 2.50
8 HuR,Countdown,pt.3 . . . . 2.50
9 HuR,Countdown,pt.4 . . . . 2.50
10 HuR,Countdown,concl. 2.50
11 The Lizard's Tale,pt.1 . . . . 2.25
12 The Lizard's Tale,pt.2 . . . . 2.25
13 The Lizard's Tale,pt.3 . . . . 2.25
14 F:Morbius 2.25
15 F:Captain America 2.25
16 F:Captain America 2.25
17 Changes,pt.1. . . . . 2.25
18 Changes,pt.2. . . . . 2.25
19 Changes,pt.3. . . . . 2.25
20 Disassembled, tie-in,pt.4 . . . . . 2.25
21 . . . . 2.25
22 . . . . 2.25
23 SEa,Sins Remembered,pt.1 . . . 2.25
24 SEa,Sins Remembered,pt.2 . . . 2.25
25 SEa,Sins Remembered,pt.3 . . . 2.25
26 SEa,Sins Remembered,pt.4 . . . 2.25
27 PJe,MBu,finale 3.00

SPEEDBALL
Sept., 1988

1 SD,JG,O:Speedball 2.50
2 SD,JG,V:Sticker,GraffitiGorillas . . 2.50
3 SD,V:Leaper Logan 2.50
4 SD,DA,Ghost Springdale High. . . 2.50
5 SD,V:Basher 2.50
6 SD,V:Bug-Eyed Voice 2.50
7 SD,V:Harlequin Hit Man. 2.50
8 SD,V:Bonehead Gang 2.50

9 SD,V:Nathan Boder 2.50
10 SD,V:Mutated Pigs,Killer
      Chickens, last issue. 2.50

SPELLBINDERS
March, 2005

1 (of 6) F:Witches of Salem 3.00
2 Salem Ghosts 3.00
3 Pillar of Smoke 3.00
4 Pillar of Smoke 3.00
5 The Halls of the Dead 3.00
6 World of the Dead, finale. 3.00
Digest Vol. 1: Signs and Wonders. . 8.00

Spellbound #11
© *Marvel Entertainment Group*

SPELLBOUND
Marvel Atlas, March, 1952

1 AyB(c),Step into my Coffin . . 1,200.00
2 BEv,RH,Horror Story,
      A:Edgar A. Poe 600.00
3 RH(c),OW 500.00
4 RH,Decapitation story 500.00
5 AyB,BEv,JM,Its in the Bag 500.00
6 AyB,BK,The Man Who Couldn't
      be Killed. 500.00
7 AyB,BEv,JMn,Don't Close
      the Door. 400.00
8 BEv(c),RH,JSt,DAy,
      The Operation 400.00
9 BEv(c),RH,The Death of
      Agatha Slurl. 400.00
10 AyB,BEv,RH,JMn(c),The Living
      Mummy 400.00
11 The Empty Coffin 350.00
12 RH,My Friend the Ghost. 350.00
13 JM,AyB,The Dead Men 350.00
14 BEv(c),RH,JMn,Close Shave . 350.00
15 AyB,CI,Get Out of my
      Graveyard 350.00
16 RH,BEv,JF,JSt,Behind
      the Door. 350.00
17 BEv(c),GC,BK,Goodbye
      Forever 350.00
18 BEv(c),JM 325.00
19 BEv(c),BP,Witch Doctor 325.00
20 RH(c),BP 325.00
21 RH(c). 400.00
22 . . . . 400.00
23 . . . . 400.00
24 JMn(c),JR 375.00
25 JO,AyB,Look Into My Eyes. . . 375.00
26 JR,AyB,Things in the Box. . . . 375.00
27 JMn,JR,AyB,Trap in the
      Mirage 375.00

28 BEv 375.00
29 JSe(c),SD 400.00
30 BEv(c) 375.00
31 JMn 375.00
32 BP,AyB,Almost Human 375.00
33 AT 375.00
34 June, 1957 . . . . 375.00

SPELLBOUND
Jan., 1988

1 thru 5 . . . . 2.50
6 double-size 3.00

SPIDER-GIRL
Aug., 1998

0 TDF,RF,BSz, cont. from What-If?
  #105, Peter & Mary Jane's
  daughter 5.00
1 TDF,PO,AW, F:Mayday Parker,
  V:Mr. Nobody 7.00
2 TDF,PO,AW,V:Crazy Eight
  & Darkdevil 4.00
2a variant cover 4.00
3 TDF,PO,AW,A:Fantastic Five . . . 2.50
4 TDF,PO,AW,turning points 2.50
5 TDF,PO,AW,Ghosts of the Past. . 2.50
6 TDF,PO,AW,Majority Rules 2.50
7 TDF,PO,AW,Last Days of
  Spider-Man 2.50
8 TDF,PO,AW,A:Spider-Man,
  Uneasy Allies 2.50
8a autographed. 20.00
9 TDF,PO,AW,Critical Choices . . . 2.50
10 TDF,PO,AW,Incredible Journeys 2.50
11 TDF,PO.AW,V:Spider-Man 2.50
12 TDF,PO,AW,A:Darkdevil 2.50
13 TDF,Po,AW,Joins A-Next 2.50
14 TDF,PO,AW,Bloody Reunions
  x-over. 2.50
15 TDF,PO,AW,A:Speedball 2.50
16 TDF,PO,AW. 2.50
17 TDF,PO,AW,48-pg. 3.00
18 TDF,SB,RF,A:Buzz 2.50
19 TDF,AW,PO,V:A-Next foes 2.50
20 TDF,AW,PO,R:Green Goblin . . . 2.50
21 TDF,AW,PO,V:Earthshaker. 2.50
22 TDF,AW,PO,Darkdevil 2.50
23 TDF,AW,PO,Basketball 2.50
24 TDF,AW,PO,Dragonfist 2.50
25 TDF,AW,PO,Savage Six 3.50
26 TDF,AW,PO,Phil Urich 2.50
27 TDF,AW,PO,Parker/Osborn
  war concl. 2.50
28 TDF,AW,PO,V:Raptor 2.50
29 TDF,AW,PO,A:Nova 2.50
30 TDF,AW,PO,V:Avengers 2.50
31 TDF,AW,PO,V:Avengers 2.50
32 TDF,PO,Steel Spider 2.50
33 TDF,AW,PO,A:Spider-Man 2.50
34 TDF,AW,PO,A:Fant.Five 2.50
35 TDF,AW,PO,V:Canis 2.50
36 TDF,AW,PO,V:Canis 2.50
37 TDF,AW,PO,V:Green Goblin . . . 2.50
38 TDF,AW,PO,V:Green Goblin . . . 2.50
39 TDF,AW,PO,Green Goblin 2.50
40 TDF,AW,PO,Death in the family . 2.50
41 TDF,AW,PO,V:Canis,'Nuff Said. . 2.50
42 TDF,RF,mothers 2.50
43 TDF,AW,PO,original Spider-Man. 2.50
44 TDF,AW,PO,F:Ben Reilly 2.50
45 TDF,AW,PO,A:Big Brain,H.Torch 2.50
46 TDF,AW,PO,F:Fantastic Five . . . 2.50
47 TDF,RF,V:Apox,+ Chapter 1 . . . 2.50
48 TDF,AW,PO,Spider-Man,Kaine . . 2.50
49 TDF,AW,PO,V:Green Goblin . . . 2.50
50 TDF,AW,PO,48-pg. 4.00
51 CJ, ... 2.50
52 TDF,AW,RF 2.50
53 TDF,AW,PO. 2.50
54 TDF,AW,PO,Serpent,pt.1 . . . . . 2.50
55 TDF,AW,PO,Serpent,pt.2 . . . . . 2.50

Spider-Girl #68
© Marvel Entertainment Group

56 TDF,AW,PO,Serpent,pt.3 . . . . . 2.50
57 TDF,AW,PO,Serpent,pt.4 . . . . . 2.50
58 TDF,AW,PO,Serpent,pt.5 . . . . . 2.50
59 TDF,RF,Serpent,pt.6 . . . . 3.00
60 TDF,RF,finale 3.00
61 TDF,RF,Marked for Death,pt.1 . . 3.00
62 TDF,RF,Marked for Death,pt.2 . . 3.00
63 TDF,RF,Marked for Death,pt.3 . . 3.00
64 TDF,RF,Marked for Death,pt.4 . . 3.00
65 TDF,RF,Marked for Death,pt.5 . . 3.00
66 TDF,RF,Marked for Death,pt.6 . . 3.00
67 TDF,RF,Monsters 3.00
68 TDF,RF,The Rules 3.00
69 TDF,RF,Truth,pt.1 . . . . 3.00
70 TDF,RF,Truth,pt.2 . . . . 3.00
71 TDF,RF,F:Doc Magus 3.00
72 TDF,RF,Whispers in the Night . . 3.00
73 TDF,RF,PO,F:Claw,the Cat 3.00
74 TDF,RF,PO,F:Claw,the Cat 3.00
75 TDF,RF,Team Spider 3.00
76 TDF,RF,Spider-Man Must Die. . . 3.00
77 TDF,RF,Betrayed. 3.00
78 TDF,RF,People Played
  by Games 3.00
79 RF,If this be my destiny 3.00
80 TDF(s),PO,V:Dragon King 3.00
81 TDF(s),PO F:Electro. 3.00
82 TDF(s),RF,V:Venom 3.00
83 TDF(s),RF,Back in Black. 3.00
84 TDF(s),RF,V:New Venom 3.00
85 TDF(s),RF,V:Funny Face 3.00
86 TDF(s),RF,Family Business,pt.1 . 3.00
87 TDF(s),RF,Family Business,pt.2 . 3.00
88 TDF(s),RF,Family Business,pt.3 . 3.00
89 TDF(s),RF, ... 3.00
90 TDF(s),RF, spider-creature 3.00
91 TDF(s),RF,The Sinister Secret
  Of the Spider Shoppe 3.00
92 TDF(s),RF,In the Shadow of Evil 3.00
93 TDF(s),RF,Something Osborn This
  Way Comes 3.00
94 TDF(s),RF,V:Avengers 3.00
95 TDF(s),RF,A:Green Goblin 3.00
96 TDF(s),RF,A:Kaine 3.00
97 TDF(s),RF,Here Comes
  Hobgoblin 3.00
98 TDF(s),RF,In black costume . . . 3.00
99 TDF(s),RF,A:Tarantula 3.00
100 TDF(s),RF,A:Spider-man,
  104-pg. 4.00
Ann.#1 TDF,PO,AW,A:Green Goblin 6.00
Digest Marvel Age, Vol. 1 . . . . 8.00
Digest Vol. 1: Legacy 8.00

Digest Vol. 2: Like Father, Like
  Daughter 8.00
Digest Vol. 3: Avenging Allies 8.00
Digest Vol. 4: Turning Point 8.00
Digest Vol. 5: Endgame 8.00
Digest Vol. 6: Too Many Spiders . . . 8.00
Digest Vol. 7: Betrayed 8.00

SPIDER-GIRL PRESENTS:
THE BUZZ
May, 2000

1 (of 3) TDF,RF,SB 3.00
2 TDF,RF,SB,A:Spider-Girl 3.00
3 TDF,RF,SB,Dr.Jade 3.00

SPIDER-GIRL PRESENTS:
DARKDEVIL
Sept., 2000

1 (of 3) TDF,RF,AM,Kingpin 3.00
2 TDF,RF,AM,O:Darkdevil 3.00
3 TDF,RF,AM, concl 3.00

SPIDER-MAN
Aug., 1990

1 TM Purple Web(c),V:Lizard,
  A:Calypso,B:Torment. 5.00
1a Silver Web(c) 6.00
1b Bag,Purple Web. 12.00
1c Bag,Silver Web 15.00
1d 2nd print,Gold(c) 5.00
1e 2nd print Gold UPC(rare). . . . 150.00
1f Platinum Ed. 125.00
2 TM,V:Lizard,A:Calypso 6.00
3 TM,V:Lizard,A:Calypso 6.00
4 TM,V:Lizard,A:Calypso 6.00
5 TM,V:Lizard,A:Calypso,
  E:Torment 6.00
6 TM,A:Ghost Rider,V:Hobgoblin . . 6.00
7 TM,A:Ghost Rider,V:Hobgoblin . . 6.00
8 TM,B:Perceptions,A:Wolverine
  I:Wendigo IV 8.00
9 TM,A:Wolverine,Wendigo 8.00
10 TM,RLd,SW,JLe(i),A:Wolv. 8.00
11 TM,A:Wolverine,Wendigo. 8.00
12 TM,E:Perceptions,A:Wolv. 8.00
13 TM,V:Morbius,R:Black Cost. . . . 6.00
14 TM,V:Morbius,A:Black Cost. 6.00
15 EL,A:Beast 6.00
16 TM,RLd,A:X-Force,V:Juggernaut,
  Black Tom,cont.in X-Force#4 . 6.00
17 RL,AW,A:Thanos,Death 4.00
18 EL,B:Return of the Sinister Six,
  A:Hulk 4.00
19 EL,A:Hulk,Deathlok 4.00
20 EL,A:Nova. 4.00
21 EL,A:Hulk,Deathlok,Solo. 4.00
22 EL,A:Ghost Rider,Hulk 4.00
23 EL,E:Return of the Sinister Six,
  A:Hulk,G.Rider,Deathlok,FF . . . 4.00
24 Infinity War,V:Hobgoblin,
  Demogoblin 4.00
25 CMa,A:Excalibur,V:Arcade 4.00
26 RF,MBa,Hologram(c),30th Anniv.
  I:New Burglar. 5.00
27 MR,Handgun issue 3.00
28 MR,Handgun issue 3.00
29 CMa,Ret.to Mad Dog Ward#1 . . 3.00
30 CMa,Ret.to Mad Dog Ward#2 . . 3.00
31 CMa,Ret.to Mad Dog Ward#3 . . 3.00
32 BMc,A:Punisher,V:Master of
  Vengeance. 3.00
33 BMc,A:Punisher,V:Master of
  Vengeance. 3.00
34 BMc,A:Punisher,V:Master of
  Vengeance. 3.00
35 TL,Total Carnage#4,V:Carnage,
  Shriek,A:Venom,Black Cat 4.00
36 TL,Total Carnage#8,V:Carnage,
  A:Venom,Morbius. 4.00

Spider-Man #57
© Marvel Entertainment Group

37 TL,Total Carnage#12,
    V:Carnage 4.00
38 thru 40 KJ,V:Electro 3.00
41 TKa(s),JaL,I:Platoon,
    A:Iron Fist 3.00
42 TKa(s),JaL,V:Platoon,
    A:Iron Fist 3.00
43 TKa(s),JaL,V:Platoon,
    A:Iron Fist 3.00
44 HMe(s),TL,V:Hobgoblin 3.00
45 HMe(s),TL,SHa,Pursuit#1,
    V:Chameleon 2.50
46 HMe(s),TL,V:Hobgoblin,w/cel . . 3.25
46a Newsstand Ed. 2.25
47 TL,SHa,V:Demogoblin 2.50
48 TL,SHa,V:Hobgoblin,
    D:Demogoblin 2.50
49 TL,SHa,I:Coldheart 2.50
50 TL,SHa,I:Grim Hunter,foil(c) . . . 5.00
50a newsstand ed. 2.50
51 TL,SHa,Power,pt.3,foil(c) 4.00
51a newsstand ed. 2.50
52 TL,SHa,Spide-clone,V:Venom . . 2.50
53 TL,SHa,Clone,V:Venom 2.50
54 Web of Life,pt.3 . . . . 3.00
55 Web of Life,finale 2.50
56 Smoke and Mirrors 2.50
57 Aftershocks,pt.1 . . . . 2.50
57a enhanced cover 3.00
58 The Mark of Kaine,pt.3 . . . . 2.50
59 F:Travellor,Host. 2.50
60 TL,SHa,HMa,The Trial of
    Peter Parker,pt.3 . . . . 2.50
61 TL,Maximum Clonage,pt.4 . . . . . 2.50
62 HMe,TL,Exiled,pt.3 . . . . 2.50
63 HMe,TL,Greatest
    Responsibility,pt.2 . . . . 2.50
64 HMe,JR2,Return of
    Spider-Man,pt.3 . . . . 2.50
65 HMe,JR2,AW,Media
    Blizzard,pt.3 . . . . 2.50
66 HMe,JR2,Return of Kaine,pt.4 . . 2.50
67 HMe,JR2,Web of Carnage,pt.3. . 3.00
68 HMe,JR2,AW,Blood
    Brothers,pt.3 . . . . 2.50
69 HMe,JR2,Blood Brothers
    aftermath 2.50
70 HMe,JR2,A:Onslaught 3.00
71 HMe,JR2, ... 3.00
72 HMe,JR2,Onslaught saga. 3.00
73 HMe,JR2. . . . . 3.00
74 HMe,JR2,AW,A:Daredevil,
    V:Fortunato 3.00
75 HMe,JR2,Revelations, pt.4 . . . . . 3.50

76 HMe,JR2,SHa,Post-Onslaught
    world,I:Shoc. 2.50
77 HMe,JR2,SHa,V:Morbius 2.50
Becomes:

PETER PARKER, SPIDER-MAN

78 HMe,JR2,SHa,F:Mary Jane
    Parker 2.50
79 HMe,JR2,SHa,V:Hydra,A:Captain
    Arthur Stacy 2.50
80 HMe,JR2,SHa,V:S.H.O.C. 2.50
81 HMe,JR2,SHa,V:Shang-Chi,pt.1 . 2.50
82 HMe,JR2,SHa,Anti-Mutant
    Movement 2.50
83 HMe,JR2,SHa,V:Morbius 2.50
85 HMe,JR2,SHa,V:Friends of
    Humanity 2.50
86 HMe,JR2,SHa,F:Jimmy Six,
    Hammerhead. 2.50
87 HMe,JR2,SHa,A:Trapster &
    Shocker 2.50
88 HMe,JR2,SHa,Spider-Man is
    Public Enemy #1 . . . . 2.50
89 HMe,JR2,SHa,Spider-Hunt,pt.3
    x-over. 3.00
90 HMe,JR2,SHa,Identity Crisis
    prelude. 2.50
91 HMe,JR2,SHa,Identity Crisis,
    as Dusk 2.50
92 HMe,JR2,as Dusk, V:Trapster . . 2.50
93 HMe,JS,R:Ghost Rider 2.50
94 HMe,JR2,SHa,Who wasJoeyZ? . 2.50
95 HMe,JR2,SHa,Trapped in
    elevator shaft. 2.50
96 HMe,JR2,SHa,The Gathering of
    the Five (pt. 3 (of 5)x-over. 2.50
97 HMe,JR2,SHa,JBy(c),The Final
    Chapter,pt.2 x-over 2.50
98 HMe,JR2,SHa,JBy(c),The Final
    Chapter,pt.4 x-over 2.50
98a alternate JBy(c) (1:2) 2.50
Minus 1 Spec., HMe,JR2,SHa,
    flashback, A:Stacys 2.50
Ann.'97 Simon Garth—Zombie . . . 3.50
Ann.'98 HMe, Spider-Man/Elektra,
    V:The Silencer, 48-pg. 3.00
Spec. Chaos in Calgary 2.50
Spec. Double Trouble 2.50
Spec. Hit and Run, Canadian 2.50
Spec. Skating on Thin Ice 2.50
Spec. Trial of Venom,UNICEF 15.00
Spec.#1 Spider-Man (2000). 2.50
Spec. Spider-Man vs. Punisher . . . 3.00
Spec. Year in Review(1999)48-pg. . 3.00
Holiday Spec.'95 . . . . 3.00
Sup.Sz.Spec#1 Planet of the
    Symbiotes, pt.2;
    flipbook F:Scarlet Spider 4.00
Giant-Sized CCI,JBy 4.00
1-shot Spider-Man Startling Stories:
    Megalomaniacal Spider-Man . . . 3.00
Spec.#1 Spider-Man/Daredevil . . . 3.00
GN Fear Itself 13.00
GN Nothing Stops Juggernaut. 4.00
GN Parallel Lives. 9.00
GN JMD,MZ,Soul of the Hunter. . . . 6.00
GN Spider-Man: Made Men
    HMe,gangster epic (1998). 6.00
GN Spider-Man ParallelLives(2002) 6.00
GN Sweet Charity,Scorpion,64-pg. . 5.00

SPIDER-MAN ADVENTURES
1994–96

1 From animated series 2.25
1a foil (c). 3.00
2 Animated Adventures. 2.25
3 V:Spider-Slayer 2.25
4 Animated Adventures. 2.25
5 V:Mysterio 2.25

6 V:Kraven 2.25
7 V:Doctor Octopus 2.25
8 O:Venom,pt.1 . . . . 2.25
9 O:Venom,pt.2 . . . . 2.25
10 V:Venom 2.25
11 V:Hobgoblin 2.25
12 V:Hobgoblin 2.25
13 V:Chameleon 2.25
14 V:Doc Octopus 2.25
15 Doc Conners. 2.25

SPIDER-MAN & AMAZING FRIENDS
Dec., 1981
1 DSp,A:Iceman,I:Firestar. 10.00

SPIDER-MAN AND POWER PACK
Nov., 2006
1 V: Sandman & Vulture 3.00
2 thru 4 . . . . @3.00

SPIDER-MAN & WOLVERINE
June, 2003
1 (of 4) Stuff of Legends 3.00
2 . . . . 3.00
3 . . . . 3.00
4 concl. 3.00

SPIDER-MAN: BACK IN BLACK HANDBOOK
Mar., 2007
Spec. 4.00

SPIDER-MAN/BADROCK
Marvel/Maximum Press 1997
1 x-over, pt.1 . . . . 3.00
2 x-over, pt. 2 . . . . 3.00

SPIDER-MAN/BATMAN
1995
1 JMD,MBa,MFm,V:Carnage,Joker 6.00

SPIDER-MAN/BLACK CAT: THE EVIL THAT MEN DO
June, 2002
1 (of 5) KSm,TyD 3.00
2 KSm,TyD 3.00
3 KSm,TyD 3.00

Spider-Man/Black Cat #1
© Marvel Entertainment Group

MARVEL

4 KSm,TyD,concl.(2005 . . . . 3.00
5 KSm,TyD,concl.,pt.2 (2005). 3.00
6 KSm,TyD, concl., pt.3 (2006) 3.00

SPIDER-MAN: BLUE
May, 2002
1 (of 6) JLb,TSe,Green Goblin . . . 5.00
2 JLb,TSe,Gwen Stacy,Rhino 4.00
3 JLb,TSe,Gwen & Mary Jane 4.00
4 JLb,TSe,college years 4.00
5 thru 6 JLb,TSe, ... @4.00

SPIDER-MAN: BREAKOUT
April, 2005
1 (of 5) MD2(c) 3.00
2 MD2(c) 3.00
3 MD2(c) 3.00
4 . . . . 3.00
5 Finale 3.00

SPIDER-MAN, CHAPTER 1
Oct., 1998
1 (of 13) JBy,formative years . . . 2.50
1a signed 20.00
2 JBy,A:Fantastic Four 2.50
2a variant JBy cover 5.00
2b signed, both covers 30.00
3 JBy,V:J.Jonah Jameson 2.50
4 JBy,V:Dr.Octopus & Dr.Doom . . . 2.50
5 JBy,V:Lizard 2.50
6 JBy,V:Electro 2.50
7 JBy,V:Mysterio 2.50
8 JBy,V:Green Goblin 2.50
9 JBy,V:Circus of Crime 2.50
10 JBy,V:Green Goblin 2.50
11 JBy,V:Giant-Man 2.50
12 JBy,V:Sandman, double size
    final issue 4.00
Spec.#0 JBy,O:Sandman,Vulture
    & Lizard 2.50

SPIDER-MAN CLASSICS
1993–94
1 rep.Amazing Fantasy#15 . . . . . . 2.50
2 thru 14 rep.Amaz.SpM . . . . @2.50
15 rep.Amaz.SpM#14,w/cel 3.25
15a Newsstand Ed. 2.50

SPIDER-MAN COMICS MAGAZINE
Jan., 1987
1 . . . . 7.00
2 thru 13 . . . . @6.00

SPIDER-MAN: DEAD MAN'S HAND
1997
1-shot, RSt,DaR,JeM,V:Carrion . . . 3.00

SPIDER-MAN: DEATH & DESTINY
June, 2000
1 (of 3) LW,RCa,F:Gwen Stacy 3.00
2 LW,RCa,Doctor Octopus 3.00
3 LW,RCa,concl. 3.00
Spec.Death of Gwen Stacy,64-pg.
    rep. of Amaz.Sp-M #88–#90 . . . 3.50

SPIDER-MAN/ DOCTOR OCTOPUS: OUT OF REACH
2004
1 (of 5) 3.00
2 thru 5 concl. . . . . @3.00
Digest 8.00

SPIDER-MAN/DOCTOR OCTOPUS: YEAR ONE
June, 2004
1 (of 5) First battle 3.00
2 thru 5 concl. . . . . @3.00

SPIDER-MAN FAIRY TALES
May, 2007
1 (of 4) 3.00
2 thru 4 . . . . @3.00

SPIDER-MAN FAMILY
Oct., 2005
1-shot,TDF(s),RLm, Spider-Man
    Family 5.00
1-shot Featuring Spider-Clan 5.00
1-shot Featuring Amazing Friends . . 5.00
Feb., 2007
1 104-pgs. 5.00
2 thru 5 F:Dr. Strange, 104 pgs. . . @5.00

SPIDER-MAN/ FANTASTIC FOUR
April, 2007
1 (of 4) 3.00
2 thru 3 . . . . 3.00

SPIDER-MAN: THE FINAL ADVENTURE
1995–96
1 FaN,DaR,Clv,I:Tendril 3.00
2 FaN,DaR,JAl,V:Tendril 3.00
3 FaN,DaR,JAl,V:Tendril 3.00
4 FaN,DaR,JAl,V:Tendril,concl. 3.00

SPIDER-MAN: FRIENDS AND ENEMIES
1995
1 V:Metahumes 2.00
2 A:Nova,Darkhawk,Speedball 2.00
3 V:Metahumes 2.00
4 F:Metahumes 2.00

SPIDER-MEN: FUNERAL FOR AN OCTOPUS
1995
1 Doc Oc Dead 2.50
2 A:Sinister Six 2.00
3 Final Issue 2.00

SPIDER-MAN/GEN13
Marvel/Wildstorm 1996
1-shot PDd,SI,CaS x-over 5.00

SPIDER-MAN: GET KRAVEN
June, 2002
1 (of 7) F:Alyosha Kravinoff 3.00
2 wants to make a movie 2.25
3 thru 6 JQ(c) . . . . @2.25

SPIDER-MAN: HOBGOBLIN LIVES
1997
1 (of 3) RSt,RF,GP 2.50
2 RSt,RF,GP,Who was the original
    Hobgoblin? 2.50
3 RSt,RF,GP,Original identity
    revealed 2.50

SPIDER-MAN: HOUSE OF M
June, 2005
1 (of 5) MWa&TPe(s),SvL 3.00
2 MWa&tpe(s),Svl 3.00
3 MWa&TPe(s),Svl 3.00
4 MWa&TPe(s),SvL 3.00
5 MWa&TPe(s),Svl 3.00

SPIDER-MAN/ HUMAN TORCH
Jan., 2005
1 (of 5) TTn 3.00
2 TTn,catch You on the Flip-side . . 3.00
3 TTn 3.00
4 TTn,A:Black Cat 3.00
5 TTn,together Again 3.00
Digest I'm With Stupid 8.00

SPIDER-MAN & THE INCREDIBLE HULK
A.C.T.O.R./Marvel Epic, 2003
1-shot benefit issue 2.50

SPIDER-MAN: INDIA
Nov., 2004
1 (of 5) F:Pavitr Prabhakar 3.00
2 . . . . 3.00
3 V:Doc Ock 3.00
4 V:Green Goblin 3.00
5 . . . . 3.00

SPIDER-MAN: LEGEND OF THE SPIDER-CLAN
Marvel Mangaverse Oct., 2002
1 (of 3) 2.25
2 F:Manga Daredevil 2.25
3 F:Manga Green Govlin 2.25
4 . . . . 2.25
5 concl. 2.25

SPIDER-MAN: LIFELINE
Feb., 2001
1 (of 3) FaN,SR,BWi, ... 3.00
2 FaN,SR,BWi,V:Hammerhead . . . 3.00
3 FaN,SR,BWi,concl. 3.00

Spider-Man: Lifeline #1
© *Marvel Entertainment Group*

All comics prices listed are for *Near Mint* condition.

SPIDER-MAN LOVES MARY JANE
Dec., 2005
1 The Boyfriend Thing 3.00
2 thru 12 . . . . @3.00
13 thru 19 . . . . @3.00
Digest Vol. 1: Super Crush 8.00

SPIDER-MAN: THE MANGA
Black & White, Oct., 1997
Bi-weekly
1 imported, translated 4.00
2 thru 14 . . . . @3.00
15 V:Mysterio, double size 4.00
16 thru 37 . . . . @3.00

SPIDER-MAN: MAXIMUM CLONAGE
1995
Alpha Maximum Clonage,pt.1 . . . . . 5.50
Omega TL,Maximum Clonage,pt.6 . 5.00

SPIDER-MAN MEGAZINE
1994–95
1 thru 4 rep . . . . @3.00
5 Vision rep 3.00
6 V:Thing & Torch, rep 3.00

SPIDER-MAN: THE MOVIE
April, 2002
GN StL,AD,photo(c), 48-pg 6.00

SPIDER-MAN 2: THE MOVIE
June, 2004
1-shot 48-pg. 3.50

SPIDER-MAN: MUTANT AGENDA
0 thru 2 Paste in Book . . . . @2.25
3 Paste in Book 2.25

SPIDER-MAN: THE MYSTERIO MANIFESTO
Nov., 2000
1 (of 3) TDF,BMc,LW 3.00

Spider-Man: Mutant Agenda #1
© Marvel Entertainment Group

2 TDF,BMc,LW 3.00
3 TDF,BMc,LW,concl. 3.00

SPIDER-MAN: ONE MORE DAY
Aug., 2007
Sketchbook JQ. 3.00

SPIDER-MAN: POWER OF TERROR
1995
1 R:Silvermane,A:Deathlok 2.25
2 V:Silvermane 2.25
3 New Scorpion 2.25
4 V:Silvermane 2.25

SPIDER-MAN/PUNISHER
Part 1 TL,A:Tombstone 3.00
Part 2 TL,A:Tombstone 3.00

SPIDER-MAN/PUNISHER/ SABERTOOTH: DESIGNER GENES
1 SMc,Foil(c). 9.50

SPIDER-MAN: QUALITY OF LIFE
May, 2002
1 (of 4) V:The Lizard, 40-pg 3.00
2 the Yith 3.00
3 V:The Lizard 3.00
4 concl 3.00

SPIDER-MAN: REDEMPTION
1996
1 thru 4 JMD,MZ,BMc, Mary Jane
    arrested for Murder . . . . @2.25

SPIDER-MAN/RED SONJA
Aug., 2007
1 Kulan Gath 3.00
2 Kulan Gath 3.00
3 Kulan Gath vs. Venom 3.00
4 Kulan Gath & Venom combined . 3.00

SPIDER-MAN: REIGN
Dec., 2006
1 (of 4) 4.00
1a variant (c) 4.00
2 thru 4 . . . . @4.00

SPIDER-MAN: REVENGE OF THE GREEN GOBLIN
Aug., 2000
1 (of 3) RCa,LW,RSt,R:Norman
    Osborn. 3.00
2 LW,RSt,F:Norman Osborn 3.00
3 RSt,RF,PO, concl. 3.00

SPIDER-MAN SAGA
Nov., 1991
1 SLi(c),History from Amazing
    Fantasy #15-Amaz.SpM #100 . . 3.25
2 SLi(c),Amaz.SpM #101-#175 . . . . 3.25
3 Amaz.SpM #176-#238 . . . . 3.25
4 Amaz.SpM #239-#300 . . . . 3.25

SPIDER-MAN SPECIAL
Sept., 2006
1-shot Black and Blue and Read All 4.00

SPIDER-MAN SUPER SIZE SPECIAL
1 Planet of the Symbiotes,pt.2 . . . . 4.00

SPIDER-MAN TEAM-UP
1995–96
1 MWa,KeL,V:Hellfire Club 3.00
2 thru 4 . . . . @3.00
5 SvG,DaR,JFr,F:Gambit,
    Howard the Duck. 3.00
6 JMD,LHa,F:Hulk & Doctor
    Strange 3.00
7 KBk,SB,F:Thunderbolts 3.00

SPIDER-MAN TEAM-UP
March, 2005
1-shot Spider-Man & Fantastic Four
    Vs. Mole Man 3.00

Spider-Man: The Arachnis Project #1
© Marvel Entertainment Group

SPIDER-MAN: THE ARACHNIS PROJECT
1984–95
1 Wld, beginnings 2.25
2 Wld,V:Diggers 2.25
3 Wld,V:Jury 2.25
4 Wld,V:Life Foundation 2.25
5 Wld,V:Jury 2.25

SPIDER-MAN: THE CLONE JOURNALS
1-shot (1995) 2.25

SPIDER-MAN: THE JACKAL FILES
1 Files of the Jackal (1995) 2.25

SPIDER-MAN: THE LOST YEARS
1995
0 JMD,JR2,LSh,64-pg.,rep. 4.00
1 History of Kaine,Ben 3.00
2 JMD,JR2,KJ,Kaine & Ben 3.00
3 Ben vs. Kaine 3.00

SPIDER-MAN: THE OTHER
Oct., 2005
Spec. Sketchbook 3.00

SPIDER-MAN:
THE PARKER YEARS
1995
1 JR2,JPi,F:The Real Clone 2.50

SPIDER-MAN 2099
1992–96
1 RL,AW,I:Spider-Man 2099 . . . . . . 4.00
2 RL,AW,O:Spider-Man 2099 . . . . . 3.00
3 RL,AW,V:Venture 2.50
4 RL,AW,I:Specialist,
  A:Doom 2099 . . . . 2.50
5 RL,AW,V:Specialist 2.50
6 RL,AW,I:New Vulture 2.50
7 RL,AW,Vulture of 2099 . . . . 2.50
8 RL,AW,V:New Vulture 2.50
9 KJo,V:Alchemax 2.50
10 RL,AW,O:Wellvale Home 2.50
11 RL,AW,V:S.I.E.G.E. 2.25
12 RL,AW,w/poster 2.25
13 RL,AW,V:Thanatos 2.25
14 PDd(s),RL(c),TGb,Downtown . . 2.25
15 PDd(s),RL,I:Thor 2099,
  Heimdall 2099 . . . . 2.25
16 PDd(s),RL,Fall of the
  Hammer #1 . . . . 2.25
17 PDd(s),RL,V:Bloodsword 2.25
18 PDd(s),RLm,V:Lyla 2.25
19 PDd(s),RL,w/card 2.25
20 PDd(s),RL,Crash & Burn 2.25
21 V:Gangs 2.25
22 V:Gangs 2.25
23 RL,I:Risque 3.00
24 Kasey 2.25
25 A:Hulk 2099, dbl-size,foil(c) . . . 4.00
25a Newsstand ed. 2.50
26 V:Headhunter, Travesty 2.25
27 V:Travesty 2.25
28 V:Travesty 2.25
29 V:Foragers 2.25
30 V:Flipside 2.25
31 I:Dash 2.25
Becomes:

SPIDER-MAN 2099 A.D.
32 I:Morgue 2.25
33 One Nation Under Doom 2.25
34 V:Alchemex 2.25
35 . . . . 2.25
36a Spider-Man 2099(c) 2.25
36b Venom 2099(c) 2.25
37a Venom 2099 . . . . 2.25
37b variant cover 2.25

Spiderman 2099 #25
© *Marvel Entertainment Group*

38 . . . . 2.25
39 A:Venom 2099 . . . . 2.25
40 V:Goblin 2099 . . . . 2.25
41 and 42 . . . . @2.25
43 V:Sub-Mariner 2099 . . . . 2.25
Ann.#1 PDd(s),RL 3.00
Spec.#1 I:3 new villains 4.00

SPIDER-MAN UNLIMITED
1993
1 RLm,Maximun Carnage #1,
  I:Shriek,R:Carnage 6.00
2 RLm,Maximum Carnage #14 . . . 4.50
3 RLm,O:Doctor Octopus 4.50
4 RLm,V:Mystrerio,Rhino 4.25
5 RLm,A:Human Torch,
  I:Steel Spider 4.25
6 RLm,A:Thunderstrike 4.25
7 RLm,A:Clone 4.25
8 Tom Lyle 4.25
9 The Mark of Kaine,pt.5 . . . . 4.25
10 SwM,Exiled,pt.4 . . . . 4.25
11 FaN,V:Black Cat 4.25
12 Blood Brother,tie-in 4.25
13 . . . . 3.25
14 JoB, an ally dies 3.25
15 TDF,JoB,F:Puma 3.25
16 cont. from X-Force #64 . . . . . . 3.25
17 JoB, Revelations, sequel 3.25
18 TDF,JoB,F:Doctor Octopus . . . 3.25
19 JoB,F:Lizard 3.25
20 JoB,A:Hannibal King, V:Lilith . . 3.25
21 MD2,Frankenstein Monster Lives 3.25
22 MD2,V:The Scorpion 3.25

SPIDER-MAN UNLIMITED
Nov., 1999
1 cartoon, tie-in 3.50
2 thru 4 . . . . @2.25

SPIDER-MAN UNLIMITED
Jan., 2004
1 V:Slyde 3.00
2 F:Mary Jane 3.00
3 thru 10 . . . . @3.00
11 thru 15 . . . . @3.00

SPIDER-MAN UNIVERSE
Jan., 2000
1 rep. 3 stories, 80-pg. 5.00
2 thru 6 rep. 3 stories, 80-pg. . @5.00
7 thru 9 rep. 3 stories, 80-pg . . @4.00

SPIDER-MAN UNMASKED
1996
1-shot 64-pg. information source . . 6.00

SPIDER-MAN VS.
DRACULA
1994
1 rep. 2.25

SPIDER-MAN VS. VENOM
1990
1 TM(c) 9.00

SPIDER-MAN:
THE VENOM AGENDA
Nov., 1997
1-shot LHa,TL, J. Jonah Jameson,
  V:Venom 3.00

SPIDER-MAN VS.
WOLVERINE
1990
1 MBr,AW,D:Ned Leeds(the original
  Hobgoblin),V:Charlie 25.00
1a reprint. 5.00

SPIDER-MAN:
WEB OF DOOM
1994
1 3-part series. 2.25
2 Spidey falsely accused 2.25
3 conclusion 2.25

SPIDER-MAN &
X-FACTOR:
SHADOW GAMES
1 PB,I:Shadowforce 2.25
2 PB,V:Shadowforce 2.25
3 PB,V:Shadowforce, final issue. . . 2.25

SPIDER-WOMAN
April, 1978
1 CI,TD,O:Spider-Woman 22.00
2 CI,TD,I:Morgan LeFey 6.00
3 CI,TD,I:Brothers Grimm 6.00
4 CI,TD,V:Hangman 6.00
5 CI,TD,Nightmares 6.00
6 CI,A:Werewolf By Night 7.00
7 CI,SL,AG,V:Magnus 6.00
8 CI,AG,Man Who Would Not Die . 6.00
9 CI,AG,A:Needle,Magnus 6.00
10 CI,AG,I:Gypsy Moth 6.00
11 CI,AG,V:Brothers Grimm 6.00
12 CI,AG,V:Brothers Grimm 6.00
13 CI,AG,A:Shroud. 6.00
14 BSz(c),CI,AG,A:Shroud. 6.00
15 BSz(c),CI,AG,A:Shroud. 6.00
16 BSz(c),CI,AG,V:Nekra. 6.00
17 CI,Death Plunge 6.00
18 CI,A:Flesh 6.00
19 CI,A:Werewolf By Night,
  V:Enforcer 7.00
20 FS,A:Spider-Man 7.00
21 FS,A:Bounty Hunter 6.00
22 FS,A:Killer Clown 6.00
23 TVE,V:The Gamesmen. 6.00
24 TVE,V:The Gamesmen. 6.00
25 SL,Two Spider-Women 6.00
26 JBy(c),SL,V:White Gardenia . . 6.00
27 BSz(c),JBi,A:Enforcer 6.00
28 BSz(c),SL,A:Enforcer,Spidey . . 7.00
29 JR2(c),ECh,FS,A:Enforcer,
  Spider-Man 7.00
30 FM(c),SL,JM,I:Dr.Karl Malus. . . 6.00
31 FM(c),SL,JM,A:Hornet 6.00
32 FM(c),SL,JM,A:Werewolf 6.00
33 SL,V:Yesterday's Villain 6.00
34 SL,AM,V:Hammer and Anvil . . . 6.00
35 SL,AG,V:Angar the Screamer . . . 6.00
36 SL,Spider-Woman Shot 6.00
37 SL,TA,BWi,AM,FS,A:X-Men,I:
  Siryn,V:Black Tom 10.00
38 SL,BWi,A:X-Men,Siryn 10.00
39 SL,BWi,Shadows 5.00
40 SL,BWi,V:The Flying Tiger 5.00
41 SL,BWi,V:Morgan LeFay 5.00
42 SL,BWi,V:Silver Samurai 5.00
43 SL,V:Silver Samurai 5.00
44 SL,V:Morgan LeFay 5.00
45 SL,Spider-Man Thief cover 5.00
46 SL,V:Mandroids,A:Kingpin 5.00
47 V:Daddy Longlegs. 5.00
48 O:Gypsy Moth 5.00
49 A:Tigra. 5.00
50 PH(c),D:Spider-Woman 15.00

[Limited Series] 1993–94
1 V:Therak 2.25

MARVEL

2 O:Spider-Woman 2.25
3 V:Deathweb 2.25
4 V:Deathweb, last issue 2.25

SPIDER-WOMAN
May, 1999
1 JBy,BS,48-pg. 3.00
1a signed 20.00
2 BS,JBy,A:Dr. Octopus 2.25
2a variant JR2 cover. 2.25
3 BS,JBy,V:Flesh & Bones 2.25
4 BS,JBy,V:Flesh & Bones 2.25
5 BS,JBy,I:Shadowcaster 2.25
6 BS,JBy,V:Shadowcaster 2.25
7 BS,JBy 2.25
8 BS,JBy,A:Cluster,x-over. 2.25
9 BS,JBy,A:Mattie 2.25
10 BS,JBy,A:Rhino. 2.25
11 BS,JBy,V:Exomorph 2.25
12 BS,JBy,F:J.Jonah Jameson . . . 2.25
13 BS,JBy,V:Werewolf. 2.25
14 JBy,GN,BS(c),V:Nighteyes . . . 2.25
15 JBy,BS,Itch & Scratch. 2.25
16 JBy,BS,Flesh. 2.25
17 JBy,BS,Flesh & Bones 2.25
18 JBy,BS,final issue 2.25

SPIDER-WOMAN
July, 2005
Giant Size #1 classic reprints 5.00

SPIDER-WOMAN: ORIGIN
Dec., 2005
1 BMB(s). 3.00
2 thru 5 BMB(s) 3.00

SPIDEY AND
THE MINI MARVELS
April, 2003
Spec. Bullpen bits, 40-pg. 3.50

SPIDEY SUPER
STORIES
Oct., 1974
1 Younger reader's series in
   association with the Electric
   Company,O:Spider-Man 65.00
2 A:Kraven 35.00
3 A:Ringleader 25.00
4 A:Medusa 25.00
5 A:Shocker 25.00
6 A:Iceman 25.00
7 A:Lizard, Vanisher 25.00
8 A:Dr. Octopus 25.00
9 A:Dr. Doom 25.00
10 A:Green Goblin 25.00
11 A:Dr. Octopus 20.00
12 A:The Cat,V:The Owl 20.00
13 A:Falcon 20.00
14 A:Shanna 20.00
15 A:Storm 22.00
16 . . . . 20.00
17 A:Captain America 20.00
18 A:Kingpin. 20.00
19 A:Silver Surfer,Dr. Doom. 20.00
20 A:Human Torch,Invisible Girl . . 20.00
21 A:Dr. Octopus 20.00
22 A:Ms. Marvel,The Beetle. 20.00
23 A:Green Goblin 20.00
24 A:Thundra 20.00
25 A:Dr. Doom 20.00
26 A:Sandman 20.00
27 A:Thor,Loki 20.00
28 A:Medusa 20.00
29 A:Kingpin. 20.00
30 A:Kang 20.00
31 A:Moondragon,Dr. Doom 18.00
32 A:Spider-Woman,Dr. Octopus. . 18.00
33 . . . . 18.00

Spidey Super Stories #38
© *Marvel Entertainment Group*

34 A:Sub-Mariner. 18.00
35 . . . . 18.00
36 A:Lizard. 18.00
37 A:White Tiger 18.00
38 A:Fantastic Four 18.00
39 A:Hellcat,Thanos. 20.00
40 A:Hawkeye 18.00
41 A:Nova,Dr. Octopus 18.00
42 A:Kingpin. 18.00
43 A:Daredevil,Ringmaster 18.00
44 A:Vision. 18.00
45 A:Silver Surfer,Dr. Doom. 18.00
46 A:Mysterio. 18.00
47 A:Spider-Woman,Stilt-Man 18.00
48 A:Green Goblin 18.00
49 Spidey for President 18.00
50 A:She-Hulk 18.00
51 and 52. . . . . @18.00
53 A:Dr. Doom 18.00
54 Attack of the Bird-Man 18.00
55 A:Kingpin. 18.00
56 A:Captain Britain,
   Jack O'Lantern 18.00
57 March, 1982 . . . . 18.00

SPITFIRE AND THE
TROUBLESHOOTERS
Oct., 1986
1 HT/JSt 2.50
2 HT 2.50
3 HT,Macs Armor 2.50
4 TM/BMc(Early TM work) 3.50
5 HT/TD,A:Star Brand. 2.50
6 HT,Trial. 2.50
7 HT 2.50
8 HT,New Armor 2.50
9 . . . . 2.50
Becomes:

CODE NAME: SPITFIRE
10 MR/TD. 2.25
11 thru 13 . . . . @2.25

SPOOF
Oct., 1970
1 MSe 25.00
2 MSe,Brawl in the Family 15.00
3 MSe,Richard Nixon cover 15.00
4 MSe,Blechhula. 15.00
5 MSe,May, 1973 . . . . 20.00

SPORT STARS
Nov., 1949
1 The Life of Knute Rockne 650.00
Becomes:

SPORTS ACTION
2 BP(c),Life of George Gipp 650.00
3 BEv,Hack Wilson 350.00
4 Art Houtteman 300.00
5 Nile Kinnick 300.00
6 Warren Gun 300.00
7 Jim Konstanty 300.00
8 Ralph Kiner 325.00
9 Ed 'Strangler' Lewis 300.00
10 JMn,The Yella-Belly 300.00
11 The Killers 300.00
12 BEv,Man Behind the Mask . . . 300.00
13 BEv,Lew Andrews 310.00
14 MWs,Ken Roper,Sept.,1952 . . 310.00

SPOTLIGHT
Sept., 1978
1 F:Huckleberry Hound,Yogi Bear 50.00
2 Quick Draw McGraw 35.00
3 The Jetsons 35.00
4 Magilla Gorilla, March, 1979 . . . 30.00

SPUMCO COMIC BOOK
1 I:Jimmy the Hapless Boy. 7.00
2 . . . . 7.00
3 64-pgs. of sick humor 7.00
4 More sick humor 7.00

SPY CASES
See: KID KOMICS

SPY FIGHTERS
March, 1951
1 GT 350.00
2 GT 150.00
3 . . . . 125.00
4 thru 13 . . . . @125.00
14 thru 15 July, 1953 . . . . @135.00

SPYKE
Epic *Heavy Hitters*, 1993
1 MBn,BR,I:Spyke. 2.75
2 MBn,BR,V:Conita. 2.75
3 thru 4 MBn,BR . . . . @2.00

SPY THRILLERS
Atlas, Nov., 1954
1 AyB(c),The Tickling Death 300.00
2 V:Communists 150.00
3 . . . . 100.00
4 . . . . 100.00
Becomes:

POLICE BADGE
5 Sept., 1955 . . . . 125.00

SQUADRON SUPREME
Sept., 1985
1 BH,L:Nighthawk 5.00
2 BH,F:Nuke,A:Scarlet Centurion. . 4.00
3 BH,D:Nuke. 4.00
4 BH,L:Archer 4.00
5 BH,L:Amphibian. 4.00
6 PR,I:Institute of Evil 4.00
7 JB,JG,V:Hyperion 4.00
8 BH,V:Hyperion 4.00
9 BSz(c),PR,D:Tom Thumb 4.00
10 PR,V:Quagmire. 4.00
11 PR,V:Redeemers 4.00
12 PR,D:Nighthawk,Foxfire,
   Black Archer 4.00
GN Death of a Universe 12.00

MARVEL

SQUADRON SUPREME
March, 2006
1 MSz(s) 3.00
2 thru 7 MSz(s) . . . . @3.00
8 MSz(s),MD2 . . . . 3.00
9 MSz(s),MD2 . . . . 3.00
Spec.#1 Saga of the Squadron
    Supreme (Feb., 2006) 4.00

SQUADRON SUPREME: HYPERION VS. NIGHTHAWK
1 (of 4) PG 3.00
2 thru 4 PG . . . . @3.00

STALKERS
Epic, 1990–91
1 MT 2.25
2 thru 12 MT . . . . @2.25

STAN LEE MEETS...
Sept., 2006
Spider-Man #1 . . . . 4.00
Dr. Strange #1 . . . . 4.00
The Thing #1 . . . . 4.00
Silver Surfer #1 . . . . 4.00
Dr. Doom #1 . . . . 4.00

STARBLAST
1994
1 MGu(s),HT,After the Starbrand . . 2.25
2 MGu(s),HT,After the Starbrand . . 2.25
3 MGu(s),HT,After the Starbrand . . 2.25
4 MGu(s),HT,final issue 2.25

STARBRAND
Oct., 1986
1 JR2,O:Starbrand 2.50
2 thru 8 JR2/AW . . . . @2.50
9 thru 15 . . . . @2.50
16 thru 19 . . . . @3.00
Ann.#1 . . . . 3.00

STAR COMICS MAGAZINE
Dec., 1986 (digest size)
1 F:Heathcliff,Muppet Babies,
    Ewoks 2.25
2 thru 13 1988 . . . . @2.25

STARJAMMERS
1995–96
1 I:The Uncreated 3.00
2 thru 4 . . . . @3.00

STARJAMMERS
July, 2004
1 (of 6) Cadet & Corsairs,pt.1 . . . . 3.00
2 thru 6 Cadet and the Corsairs,
    pt.2 thru pt.6 . . . . @3.00

STAR-LORD, SPECIAL EDITION
Feb., 1982
1 JBy reprints 6.00

STARLORD
Mini-Series 1996
1 (of 3) DLw 2.50
2 DLw 2.50
3 DLw,V:Damyish 2.50

STAR MASTER
1 MGu,Cosmic Avengers assemble 2.25

2 MGu,World Engine saga 2.25
3 MGu,Cauldron of Conversion . . . 2.25

STARRIORS
Aug., 1984
1 . . . . 4.00
2 . . . . 3.00
3 . . . . 3.00
4 . . . . 3.00

STARSTRUCK
March, 1985
1 MK 3.00
2 thru 8 MK, Feb., 1986 . . . . @3.00

STARTLING STORIES: THE THING–NIGHT FALLS ON YANCY ST.
May, 2003
1 (of 4) EDo(s),40-pg 3.50
2 EDo(s),40-pg. 3.50
3 EDo(s),40-pg. 3.50
4 EDo(s),concl. 3.50
Spec. Last Line of Defense 3.50

STARTLING STORIES: THE INCORRIGIBLE HULK
Jan., 2004
1-shot 3.00

STAR TREK
April, 1980
1 DC,KJ,rep.1st movie adapt. 17.00
2 DC,KJ,rep.1st movie adapt. 9.00
3 DC,KJ,rep.1st movie adapt. 9.00
4 thru 16 . . . . @9.00
17 EH,TP,The Long Nights Dawn . 15.00
18 A Thousand Deaths,last issue . 20.00

STAR TREK: DEEP SPACE NINE
1996
1 HWe(s),TGb,AM,DS9 in the
    Gamma Quadrant,pt.1 (of 2) . . . 3.00
2 thru 15 . . . . @2.50

Star Trek Early Voyages #6
© *Marvel Entertainment Group*

STAR TREK: EARLY VOYAGES
Dec., 1996
1 DAn,IEd,Captain Pike's crew,
    double size premier 4.00
2 thru 17 . . . . @2.50

STAR TREK
GN Star Trek, First Contact
    Movie adapt. 6.00
1-shot Mirror, Mirror (1996) 4.00
1-shot Operation Assimilation 3.00
1-shot Telepathy War, pt.4
    x-over, 48-pg.(1997) 3.00

STAR TREK: THE NEXT GENERATION RIKER SPECIAL
May, 1998
1-shot, DAn,IEd,Riker photo cover . 3.50

STAR TREK: THE NEXT GENERATION/X-MEN: SECOND CONTACT
March, 1998
1-shot, DAn,IEd,64-pg. 5.00
1-shot, variant CNr cover (1:5) 5.00

STAR TREK: STARFLEET ACADEMY
1996
1 Cadets vs. Gorns 2.50
2 thru 19 . . . . @2.50

STAR TREK: UNLIMITED
1996
1 DAn,IEd,MBu,JeM,AW, Classic
    series & TNG 5.00
2 thru 10 . . . . @4.00

STAR TREK: THE UNTOLD VOYAGES
Jan., 1998
1 . . . . 3.00
2 . . . . 3.00
3 . . . . 3.00
4 . . . . 3.00
5 48-pg. finale 3.50

STAR TREK: VOYAGER
1996
1 . . . . 3.00
2 thru 15 . . . . @3.00

STAR TREK: VOYAGER: SPLASHDOWN
Jan., 1998
1 thru 4 AM . . . . @3.00

STAR TREK/X-MEN
1-shot SLo,MS, 64-pg. 5.00
1a rep. of STAR TREK/X-MEN 5.00

STAR WARS
July, 1977
1 HC,30 Cent,movie adaption 65.00
1a HC,35 Cent(square Box). . . . 725.00
1b "Reprint" 7.50
2 HC,movie adaptation 30.00
2b "Reprint" 4.00
3 HC,movie adaptation 25.00
3b "Reprint" 4.00
4 HC,SL,movie adapt.(low dist.) . . 22.00

Star Wars #17
© Marvel Entertainment Group

4b "Reprint". 4.00
5 HC,SL,movie adaptation 22.00
5b "Reprint". 3.00
6 HC,DSt,E:movie adaption 22.00
6b "Reprint". 3.00
7 HC,FS,F:Luke & Chewbacca. . 20.00
8 HC,TD,Eight against a World . . 20.00
9 HC,TP,V:Cloud Riders 20.00
7b thru 9b "Reprint". . . . . @2.50
10 HC,TP,Behemoth From Below . 22.00
11 CI,TP,Fate of Luke Skywalker . 20.00
12 TA,CI,Doomworld 20.00
13 TA,JBy,CI,Deadly Reunion . . . 20.00
14 TA,CI 20.00
15 CI,V:Crimson Jack 20.00
16 WS,V:The Hunter 20.00
17 Crucible, low dist. 20.00
18 CI,Empire Strikes,low dist. . . . 20.00
19 CI,Ultimate Gamble,low dist . . 20.00
20 CI,Death Game, scarce 20.00
21 TA,CI,Shadow of a Dark
    Lord(Scarce) 20.00
22 CI,Han Solo vs.Chewbacca . . 15.00
23 CI,Flight Into Fury 15.00
24 CI,Ben Kenobi Story 15.00
25 CI,Siege at Yavin 15.00
26 CI,Doom Mission 15.00
27 CI,V:The Hunter 15.00
28 CI,Cavern o/t Crawling Death . 15.00
29 CI,Dark Encounter 15.00
30 CI,A Princess Alone 15.00
31 CI,Return to Tatooine 15.00
32 CI,The Jawa Express 15.00
33 CI,GD,V:Baron Tagge 15.00
34 CI,Thunder in the Stars. 15.00
35 CI,V:Darth Vader. 15.00
36 CI,V:Darth Vader. 15.00
37 CI,V:Darth Vader. 15.00
38 TA,MG,Riders in the Void 15.00
39 AW,B:Empire Strikes Back . . . 25.00
40 AW,Battleground Hoth. 25.00
41 AW,Imperial Pursuit. 25.00
42 AW,Bounty Hunters. 25.00
43 AW,Betrayal at Bespin 25.00
44 AW,E:Empire Strikes Back . . . 25.00
45 CI,GD,Death Probe. 15.00
46 DI,TP,V:Dreamnaut Devourer . 15.00
47 CI,GD,Droid World 15.00
48 CI,Leia vs.Darth Vader 15.00
49 SW,TP,The Last Jedi 15.00
50 WS,AW,TP,G-Size issue. 15.00
51 WS,TP,Resurrection of Evil. . . 12.00
52 WS,TP,D:Death Star II 12.00
53 CI,WS,Gift of Alderaan 12.00

54 CI,WS,Starfire Rising 12.00
55 thru 66 WS,TP . . . . @12.00
67 TP, The Darker 12.00
68 GD,TP,O:Boba Fett. 20.00
69 GD,TP,Death in City of Bone . . 20.00
70 A:Han Solo 20.00
71 A:Han Solo 20.00
72 Fool's Boontu 20.00
73 Secret of Planet Lansbane . . . 20.00
74 thru 91 . . . . @20.00
92 BSz(c),The Dream 22.00
93 thru 97. . . . . @20.00
98 AW,Supply & Demand 20.00
99 Touch of Goddess. 20.00
100 Painted(c),double-size 22.00
101 BSz, Far,Far Away 22.00
102 KRo's Back 15.00
103 thru 106. . . . . @15.00
107 WPo(i),last issue. 90.00
Ann.#1 WS(c),V:Winged Warlords 100.00
Ann.#2 RN 15.00
Ann.#3 RN,Darth Vader(c) 15.00

STEELGRIP STARKEY
Epic, July, 1986
1 . . . . 2.50
2 thru 5 . . . . @2.50
6 June, 1987 . . . . 2.50

STEELTOWN ROCKERS
April, 1990—Sept., 1990
1 SL 2.25
2 thru 6 SL . . . . @2.25

STOKER'S DRACULA
Oct., 2004
1 (of 4) RTs,DG 4.00
2 . . . . 4.00
3 RTs(s),DG 4.00
4 Rts(s),Dg 4.00

STORIES OF ROMANCE
Marvel Atlas, 1956
5 MB,ViC(c) 150.00
6 . . . . 100.00
7 . . . . 100.00
8 . . . . 100.00
9 ViC 125.00
10 . . . . 100.00
11 MB,ViC,JR. 150.00
12 . . . . 120.00
13 ABr 150.00

STORM
1 TyD,KIS,V:Candra 4.00
2 . . . . 4.00
3 . . . . 4.00
4 TyD,KIS, conclusion,foil cover . . . 4.00

STORM
Feb., 2006
1 Storm & Black Panther 3.00
2 thru 6 . . . . @3.00

STORMBREAKER: THE
SAGA OF BETA RAY BILL
Jan., 2005
1 (of 6) 3.00
2 I:stardust 3.00
3 V:Stardust 3.00
4 . . . . 3.00
5 Return to Asgard 3.00
6 Vs. Spider-Man 3.00

STRANGE
Sept., 2004
1 MSz,BPe,O:Dr.Strange 3.50
2 MSz,BPe,. 3.50

3 . . . . 3.50
4 MSz(s),BPe 3.50
5 MSz(s),Bpe,new Costume. 3.50
6 MSz(s),BPe, finale. 3.50

STRANGE COMBAT
TALES
1 and 2 . . . . @2.75
3 Tiger by the Tail 2.50
4 Midnight Crusade. 2.50

STRANGE STORIES OF SUS-
PENSE See: RUGGED ACTION

STRANGE TALES
[1st Regular Series] June, 1951
1 The Room. 4,800.00
2 Trapped In A Tomb 1,500.00
3 JMn,Man Who Never Was . . 1,200.00
4 BEv,Terror in the Morgue . . 1,300.00
5 A Room Without A Door . . . 1,200.00
6 RH(c),The Ugly Man 800.00
7 Who Stands Alone 800.00
8 BEv,Something in the Fog. . . 800.00
9 Drink Deep Vampire 800.00
10 BK,Hidden Head. 900.00
11 BEv(c),GC,'O'Malley's Friend . 600.00
12 Graveyard At Midnight 600.00
13 BEv(c),Death Makes A Deal . . 600.00
14 GT,Horrible Herman 600.00
15 BK,Don't Look Down. 600.00
16 Decapitation cover 600.00
17 DBr,JRo,Death Feud. 600.00
18 Witch Hunt 600.00
19 RH(c),The Rag Doll 600.00
20 RH(c),GC,SMo,Lost World . . 600.00
21 BEv 500.00
22 BK,JF 500.00
23 Strangest Tale in the World. . 500.00
24 The Thing in the Coffin 500.00
25 . . . . 500.00
26 . . . . 500.00
27 JF,The Garden of Death 500.00
28 Come into my Coffin 500.00
29 Witch-Craft 500.00
30 The Thing in the Box 500.00
31 Man Who Played with Blocks . 500.00
32 . . . . 500.00
33 JMn(c),Step Lively Please . . . 500.00
34 Flesh and Blood 475.00
35 The Man in the Bottle 400.00
36 . . . . 400.00
37 Out of the Storm 400.00
38 . . . . 400.00

Strange Tales #33
© Marvel Entertainment Group

39 Karnoff's Plan	400.00
40 BEv,Man Who Caught a Mermaid	400.00
41 BEv,Riddle of the Skull	425.00
42 DW,BEv,JMn,Faceless One	425.00
43 JF,The Mysterious Machine	400.00
44	400.00
45 JKa,Land of Vanishing Men	425.00
46 thru 57	@425.00
58 AW	400.00
59 BK	400.00
60	375.00
61 BK	400.00
62	375.00
63	400.00
64 AW	400.00
65	375.00
66	375.00
67 thru 78	@450.00
79 SD,JK,Dr.Strange Prototype	450.00
80 thru 83 SD,JK	@350.00
84 SD,JK,Magneto Prototype	350.00
85 SD,JK	350.00
86 SD,JK,I Created Mechano	350.00
87 SD,JK,Return of Grogg	350.00
88 SD,JK,Zzutak	350.00
89 SD,JK,Fin Fang Foom	900.00
90 SD,JK,Orrgo Unconquerable	350.00
91 SD,JK,The Sacrifice	350.00
92 SD,JK,Thing That Waits	350.00
93 SD,JK,The Wax People	350.00
94 SD,JK,Pildorr the Plunderer	350.00
95 SD,JK,Two-Headed Thing	350.00
96 SD,JK,I Dream of Doom	350.00
97 SD,JK,When A Planet Dies	700.00
98 SD,JK,No Human Can Beat Me	350.00
99 SD,JK,Mister Morgan's Monster	350.00
100 SD,JK,I Was Trapped in the Crazy Maze	350.00
101 B:StL(s),SD,JK, B:Human Torch	2,500.00
102 SD,JK,I:Wizard	900.00
103 SD,JK,I:Zemu	700.00
104 SD,JK,I:The Trapster	700.00
105 SD,JK,V:Wizard	700.00
106 SD,A:Fantastic Four	600.00
107 SD,V:Sub-Mariner	750.00
108 SD,JK,A:FF,I:The Painter	600.00
109 SD,JK,I:Sorcerer	600.00
110 SD,I&B:Dr.Strange, Nightmare	3,000.00
111 SD,I:Asbestos,Baron Mordo	900.00
112 SD,I:The Eel	325.00

Strange Tales #99
© Marvel Entertainment Group

113 SD,I:Plant Man	325.00
114 SD,JK,A:Captain America	1,000.00
115 SD,O:Dr.Strange	1,000.00
116 SD,V:Thing	400.00
117 SD,V:The Eel	300.00
118 SD,V:The Wizard	400.00
119 SD,C:Spider-Man	400.00
120 SD,1st Iceman/Torch T.U.	450.00
121 SD,V:Plant Man	200.00
122 SD,V:Dr.Doom	175.00
123 SD,A:Thor,I:Beetle	200.00
124 SD,I:Zota	175.00
125 SD,V:Sub-Mariner	200.00
126 SD,I:Dormammu,Clea	175.00
127 SD,V:Dormammu	175.00
128 SD,I:Demon	175.00
129 SD,I:Tiboro	175.00
130 SD,C:Beatles	175.00
131 SD,I:Dr.Vega	175.00
132 SD,I:Orini	175.00
133 SD,I:Shazana	175.00
134 SD,E:Torch,I:Merlin	175.00
135 SD,JK:I:Shield & Hydra B:Nick Fury	300.00
136 SD,JK,V:Dormammu	135.00
137 SD,JK,A:Ancient One	150.00
138 SD,JK,I:Eternity	150.00
139 SD,JK,V:Dormammu	150.00
140 SD,JK,V:Dormammu	150.00
141 SD,JK,I:Fixer,Mentallo	100.00
142 SD,JK,I:THEM,V:Hydra	100.00
143 SD,JK,V:Hydra	100.00
144 SD,JK,V:Druid,I:Jasper Sitwell	100.00
145 SD,JK,I:Mr.Rasputin	100.00
146 SD,JK,V:Dormammu,I:A.I.M.	100.00
147 BEv,JK,F:Wong	100.00
148 BEv,JK,O:Ancient One	90.00
149 BEv,JK,V:Kaluu	100.00
150 BEv,JK,JB(1st Marvel Art) I:Baron Strucker,Umar	100.00
151 JK,JSo(1st Marvel Art), I:Umar	150.00
152 BEv,JK,JSo,V:Umar	100.00
153 JK,JSo,MSe,V:Hydra	100.00
154 JSo,MSe,I:Dreadnought	100.00
155 JSo,MSe,A:L.B.Johnson	100.00
156 JSo,MSe,I:Zom	100.00
157 JSo,MSe,A:Zom,C:Living Tribunal	100.00
158 JSo,MSe,A:Zom,I:Living Tribunal(full story)	100.00
159 JSo,MSe,O:Nick Fury,A:Capt. America,I:Val Fontaine	125.00
160 JSo,MSe,A:Captain America, I:Jimmy Woo	100.00
161 JSo,I:Yellow Claw	100.00
162 JSo,DA,A:Captain America	100.00
163 JSo,DA,V:Yellow Claw	90.00
164 JSo,DA,V:Yellow Claw	90.00
165 JSo,DA,V:Yellow Claw	90.00
166 DA,GT,JSo,A:AncientOne	90.00
167 JSo,DA,V:Doctor Doom	125.00
168 JSo,DA,E:Doctor Strange,Nick Fury,V:Yandroth	100.00
169 JSo,I&O:Brother Voodoo	30.00
170 JSo,O:Brother Voodoo	25.00
171 GC,V:Baron Samed	25.00
172 GC,DG,V:Dark Lord	25.00
173 GC,DG,I:Black Talon	25.00
174 JB,JM,O:Golem	20.00
175 SD,R:Torr	20.00
176 F:Golem	20.00
177 FB,F:Golem	20.00
178 JSn,B&O:Warlock,I:Magus	60.00
179 JSn,I:Pip,I&D:Capt.Autolycus	55.00
180 JSn,I:Gamora,Kray-tor	55.00
181 JSn,E:Warlock	55.00
182 SD,GK,rep. Str.Tales #123,124	20.00
183 SD,rep.Str.Tales #130,131	20.00
184 SD,rep.Str.Tales #132,133	20.00

185 SD,rep.Str.Tales #134,135	20.00
186 SD,rep.Str.Tales #136,137	20.00
187 SD,rep.Str.Tales #138,139	20.00
188 SD,rep.Str.Tales #140,141	20.00
Ann.#1 V:Grottu,Diablo	1,000.00
Ann.#2 A:Spider-Man	1,500.00
Marvel Milestone rep. stories from #110–#111, #114–#115 (1995)	3.00

[2nd Regular Series] 1987–88

1 BBl,CW,B:Cloak&Dagger,Dr. Strange,V:Lord of Light	3.00
2 BBl,CW,V:Lord of Light,Demon	2.50
3 BBl,AW,CW,A:Nightmare,Khat.	2.50
4 BBl,CW,V:Nightmare	2.50
5 BBl,V:Rodent,A:Defenders	2.50
6 BBl,BWi,V:Erlik Khan, A:Defenders	2.50
7 V:Nightmare,A:Defenders	2.50
8 BBl,BWi,V:Kaluu	2.50
9 BBl,BWi,A:Dazzler,I:Mr.Jip, V:Kaluu	2.50
10 BBl,BWi,RCa,A:Black Cat, V:Mr.Jip,Kaluu	2.50
11 RCa,BWi,V:Mr.Jip,Kaluu	2.50
12 WPo,BWi,A:Punisher,V:Mr.Jip	2.50
13 JBr,BWi,RCa,Punisher, Power Pack	2.50
14 JBr,BWi,RCa,Punisher,P.Pack	2.50
15 RCa,BMc,A:Mayhem	2.50
16 RCa,BWi,V:Mr.Jip	2.50
17 RCa,BWi,V:Night	2.50
18 RCa,KN,A:X-Factor,V:Night	2.50
19 MMi(c),EL,TA,RCa,A:Thing	2.50

STRANGE TALES
June, 1998

1 JMD,PJe,LSh,Man-Thing, 64-pg.	5.00
2A JMD,PJe,LSh,Man-Thing, Werewolf, 64-pg.	5.00
2B variant cover	5.00
3 JMD,PJe,NA(c),Man-Thing, Werewolf, 64-pg.	5.00
4 JMD,PJe,LSh,F:Man-Thing final issue	5.00

STRANGE TALES: DARK CORNERS
March, 1998

1-shot JEs, three stories, 48-pg. 4.00

STRANGE TALES OF THE UNUSUAL
Dec., 1955—Aug., 1957

1 JMn(c),BP,DH,JR,Man Lost	650.00
2 BEv,Man Afraid	400.00
3 AW,The Invaders	400.00
4 The Long Wait	250.00
5 RC,SD,The Threat	300.00
6 BEv	250.00
7 JK,JO	250.00
8	250.00
9 BEv(c),BK	275.00
10 GM,AT	250.00
11 BEv(c),Aug., 1957	250.00

STRANGE WORLDS
Dec., 1958

1 JK,SD,Flying Saucer	1,300.00
2 SD	750.00
3 JK	600.00
4 AW	550.00
5 SD	450.00

STRAWBERRY SHORTCAKE
Star, June, 1985—April, 1986

1	
2 thru 7	@3.00

STRAY TOASTERS
Epic, Jan., 1988

1 BSz 5.00
2 BSz 4.50
3 and 4 BSz . . . . @4.00

STRIKEFORCE MORITURI
Dec., 1986

1 BA,SW,WPo(1st pencils-
   3 pages),I:Blackwatch 3.00
2 BA,SW,V:The Horde 2.50
3 BA,SW,V:The Horde 2.50
4 BA,SW,WPo,V:The Horde 2.50
5 BA,SW,V:The Horde 2.50
6 BA,SW,V:The Horde 2.50
7 BA,SW,V:The Horde 2.50
8 BA,SW,V:The Horde 2.50
9 BA,SW,V:THe Horde 2.50
10 WPo(1st pencils-full story),
   SW,R:Black Watch,O:Horde . . 3.00
11 BA,SW,V:The Horde 2.50
12 BA,SW,D:Jelene 2.50
13 BA,SW,Old vs. NewTeam 2.50
14 BA,AW,V:The Horde 2.50
15 BA,AW,V:The Horde 2.50
16 WPo,SW,V:The Horde 2.50
17 WPo(c),SW,V:The Horde 2.50
18 BA,SW,V:Hammersmith 2.50
19 BA,SW,V:THe Horde,D:Pilar. . . 2.50
20 BA,SW,V:The Horde 2.50
21 MMi(c),TD(i),V:The Horde. 2.50
22 TD(i),V:The Horde. 2.50
23 MBa,VM,V:The Horde. 2.50
24 VM(i),I:Vax,V:The Horde. 2.50
25 TD(i),V:The Horde. 3.00
26 MBa,VM,V:The Horde. 3.00
27 MBa,VM,O:Morituri Master 3.00
28 MBa,V:The Tiger 3.00
29 MBa,V:Zakir Shastri 3.00
30 MBa,V:Andre Lamont,The Wind . 3.00
31 MBa(c),V:The Wind,last issue . . 3.00

STRONG GUY REBORN
Spec. TDz,ASm,ATi (1997) 3.00

STRYFE'S STRIKE FILE
1 LSn,NKu,GCa,BP,C:Siena
   Blaze,Holocaust (1993). 4.00
1a 2nd printing 2.25

SUB-MARINER
May, 1968

1 JB,O:Sub-Mariner 400.00
2 JB,A:Triton 150.00
3 JB,A:Triton 100.00
4 JB,V:Attuma 100.00
5 JB,I&O:Tiger Shark 100.00
6 JB,DA,V:Tiger Shark 125.00
7 JB,I:Ikthon 100.00
8 JB,V:Thing 100.00
9 MSe,DA,A:Lady Dorma 100.00
10 GC,DA,O:Lemuria. 100.00
11 GC,V:Capt.Barracuda 60.00
12 MSe,I:Lyna 60.00
13 MSe,JS,A:Lady Dorma 60.00
14 MSe,V:Fake Human Torch . . . 65.00
15 MSe,V:Dragon Man 60.00
16 MSe,I:Nekaret,Thakos 65.00
17 MSe,I:Stalker,Kormok 60.00
18 MSe,A:Triton 35.00
19 MSe,I:Stingray 35.00
20 JB,V:Dr.Doom 35.00
21 MSe,D:Lord Seth 35.00
22 MSe,A:Dr.Strange 35.00
23 MSe,I:Orka 35.00
24 JB,JM,V:Tiger Shark 35.00
25 SB,JM,O:Atlantis. 30.00
26 SB,A:Red Raven. 30.00
27 SB,I:Commander Kraken 30.00
28 SB,V:Brutivae 30.00

Sub-Mariner #67
© *Marvel Entertainment Group*

29 SB,V:Hercules. 25.00
30 SB,A:Captain Marvel 28.00
31 SB,A:Triton 25.00
32 SB,JM,I&O:Llyra 28.00
33 SB,JM,I:Namora 30.00
34 SB,JM,AK,1st Defenders 100.00
35 SB,JM,A:Silver Surfer. 100.00
36 BWr,SB,W:Lady Dorma 35.00
37 RA,D:Lady Dorma. 35.00
38 RA,JSe,O:Rec,I:Thakorr,Fen . 35.00
39 RA,JM,V:Llyra. 35.00
40 GC,I:Turalla,A:Spidey 25.00
41 GT,V:Rock. 22.00
42 GT,JM,V:House Named Death . 22.00
43 GC,V:Tunal,king-sz. 30.00
44 MSe,JM,V:Human Torch 25.00
45 MSe,JM,V:Tiger Shark 25.00
46 GC,D:Namor's Father. 20.00
47 GC,A:Stingray,V:Dr.Doom . . . 20.00
48 GC,V:Dr.Doom 20.00
49 GC,V:Dr.Doom 20.00
50 BEv,I:Namorita 22.00
51 BEv,O:Namorita,C:Namora . . . 20.00
52 GK,V:Sunfire 20.00
53 BEv,V:Sunfire 18.00
54 BEv,AW,V:Sunfire,I:Lorvex . . . 18.00
55 BEv,V:Torg 18.00
56 DA,I:Coral 18.00
57 BEv,I:Venus. 18.00
58 BEv,I:Tamara. 18.00
59 BEv,V:Tamara,A:Thor 25.00
60 BEv,V:Tamara 15.00
61 BEv,JM,V:Dr.Hydro 15.00
62 HC,JSt,I:Tales of Atlantis. 15.00
63 HC,JSt,V:Dr.Hydro,I:Arkus . . . 15.00
64 HC,JSe,I:Maddox 15.00
65 DH,DP,V:She-Devil,inc.BEv
   Eulogy pin-up 15.00
66 DH,V:Orka,I:Raman 15.00
67 DH,A:FF,V:Triton,N:Namor
   I&O:Force 15.00
68 DH,O:Force 15.00
69 GT,V:Spider-Man. 18.00
70 GT,I:Piranha 15.00
71 GT,V:Piranha 15.00
72 DA,V:Slime/Thing 15.00
Spec.#1 rep. Tales to Astonish
   #70-#73 . . . . 30.00
Spec.#2 rep. Tales to Astonish
   #74-#76 . . . . 25.00

[Limited Series]
1 RB,BMc,Namor's Birth. 2.50
2 RB,BMc,Namor Kills Humans . . 2.25
3 RB,BMc,V:Surface Dwellers . . . 2.25

4 RB,BMc,V:Human Torch 2.25
5 RB,BMc,A:Invaders 2.25
6 RB,BMc,V:Destiny 2.25
7 RB,BMc,A:Fantastic Four 2.25
8 RB,BMc,V:Hulk,Avengers 2.25
9 RB,BMc,A:X-Men,Magneto 2.25
10 RB,BMc,V:Thing. 2.25
11 RB,BMc,A:Namorita,Defenders . 2.25
12 RB,BMc,A:Dr.Doom,
   Alpha Flight 2.25

(SAGA OF THE) SUB-MARINER
[Mini-Series] Nov., 1988

1 RB,BMc,Namor's Birth. 3.00
2 RB,BMc,Namor Kills Humans . . . 3.00
3 RB,BMc,V:Surface Dwellers 3.00
4 RB,BMc,V:Human Torch 3.00
5 RB,BMc,A:Invaders 3.00
6 RB,BMc,V:Destiny 3.00
7 RB,BMc,A:Fantastic Four 3.00
8 RB,BMc,V:Hulk,Avengers 3.00
9 RB,BMc,A:X-Men,Magneto 3.50
10 RB,BMc,V:Thing 3.00
11 RB,BMc,A:Namorita,Defenders . 3.00
12 RB,BMc,A:Dr.Doom,Alp.Flight . . 3.00

SUB-MARINER COMICS
Marvel Timely, Spring, 1941

1 ASh(c),BEv,PGv,B:Sub-
   Mariner, The Angel 65,000.00
2 ASh(c),BEv,Nazi
   Submarine (c) 10,000.00
3 ASh(c),BEv,Churchill. 9,500.00
4 ASh(c),BEv,BW 6,000.00
5 V:Axis Powers. 5,000.00
6 ASh(c),Panama Canal 4,500.00
7 ASm&FrG(c). 4,500.00
8 ASh(c),PGv 4,500.00
9 ASh(c),BW,Flag(c) 4,500.00
10 ASh(c),GS 4,500.00
11 ASh(c),Dragon(c) 4,500.00
12 ASh(c) 3,500.00
13 ASh(c),Bondage(c). 3,500.00
14 ASh(c) 3,500.00
15 ASh(c),V:Japs 3,500.00
16 ASh(c),CI,ASm,GS. 2,500.00
17 ASh(c),V:Japs 2,500.00
18 ASh(c),ASm 2,500.00
19 . . . . 2,500.00
20 ASh(c),V:Crooks 2,500.00
21 SSh(c),BEv,Last Angel. . . . 2,200.00
22 SSh(c),BEv,A:Young Allies . . 2,200.00
23 SSh(c),BEv,Human Torch . . 2,200.00

Sub-Mariner Comics #11
© *Marvel Entertainment Group*

MARVEL

MARVEL

24 MSy(c),BEv,A:Namora,
bondage cover 2,200.00
25 MSy(c),HK,B:The Blonde
Phantom, A:Namora,
bondage(c) 2,400.00
26 BEv,SSh,A:Namora 2,000.00
27 DRi(c),BEv,A:Namora 2,000.00
28 DRi(c),BEv,A:Namora 2,000.00
29 BEv,SSh,A:Namora,Human
Torch 2,000.00
30 DRi(c),BEv,Slaves Under
the Sea 2,000.00
31 BEv,The Man Who Grew,
A:Capt. America,E:Blonde
Phantom 2,000.00
32 BEv,O:Sub-Mariner 2,500.00
33 BEv,O:Sub-Mariner,A:Human
Torch,B:Namora 2,200.00
34 BEv,A:Human Torch,bondage
cover 2,000.00
35 BEv,A:Human Torch 2,000.00
36 BEv,Hidden World 2,000.00
37 JMn(c),BEv 2,000.00
38 SSh(c),BEv,JMn,
O:Sub-Mariner 2,300.00
39 JMn(c),BEv,Commie
Frogman 2,000.00
40 JMn(c),BEv,Secret Tunnel . . 2,000.00
41 JMn(c),BEv,A:Namora 2,000.00
42 BEv,Oct., 1955 . . . . 2,400.00

SUB-MARINER
June, 2007
1 (of 6) Revolution 3.00
2 thru 6 . . . . @3.00

SUBURBAN JERSEY
NINJA SHE-DEVILS
1 I:Ninja She-Devils 2.25

SUNFIRE & BIG HERO 6
July, 1998
1 (of 3) SLo,from Alpha Flight. 2.50
2 SLo,V:Everwraith 2.50
3 SLO,conclusion 2.50

SUN GIRL
Marvel Comics, 1948
1 Miss America 2,400.00
2 Blonde Phantom 1,700.00
3 . . . . 1,700.00

SUPERNATURALS
Oct., 1998
1 (of 4) BnP,JBa(c),F:Brother Voodoo,
V:Jack O'Lantern, with mask. . . 30.00
1a signed 30.00
2 BnP,JBa(c), with mask. 4.00
3 BnP,JBa(c), with mask. 4.00
4 BnP,JBa(c), with mask, concl. . . 4.00

SUPERNATURAL
THRILLERS
Dec., 1972
1 JSo(c),JSe,FrG,IT! 50.00
2 VM,DA,The Invisible Man 30.00
3 GK,The Valley of the Worm 30.00
4 Dr. Jekyll and Mr. Hyde 30.00
5 RB,The Living Mummy 75.00
6 GT,JA,The Headless Horseman 40.00
7 VM,B:The Living Mummy,
Back From The Tomb 40.00
8 VM,He Stalks Two Worlds 40.00
9 GK/AM(c),VM,DA,Pyramid of
the Watery Doom 40.00
10 VM,A Choice of Dooms 40.00
11 VM,When Strikes the ASP 40.00

Supernatural Thrillers #9
© Marvel Entertainment Group

12 VM,KJ,The War That Shook
the World 40.00
13 VM,DGr,The Tomb of the
Stalking Dead 40.00
14 VM,AMc,All These Deadly
Pawns 40.00
15 TS, E:The Living Mummy,Night
of Armageddon, Oct.,1975 . . . 40.00

SUPER RABBIT
Marvel Timely, 1943
1 Hitler 1,200.00
2 . . . . 500.00
3 . . . . 350.00
4 . . . . 350.00
5 . . . . 350.00
6 Origin of Super Rabbit 325.00
7 . . . . 225.00
8 . . . . 225.00
9 . . . . 225.00
10 . . . . 225.00
11 HK,Hey Look 250.00
12 . . . . 250.00
13 . . . . 250.00
14 . . . . 250.00

SUPER SOLDIERS
Marvel UK, 1993
1 I:Super Soldier,A:USAgent 2.75
2 A:USAgent 2.25
3 A:USAgent 2.25
4 A:USAgent,Avengers 2.25
5 A:Captain America,AWC 2.25
6 O:Super Soldiers 2.25
7 in Savage Land 2.25

SUPER-VILLAIN
CLASSICS
May, 1983
1 O:Galactus 6.00

SUPER-VILLAIN
TEAM-UP
Aug., 1975
1 GT/BEv(c),B:Dr.Doom/Sub-
Mariner,A:Attuma,Tiger Shark 50.00
2 SB,A:Tiger Shark, Attuma 20.00
3 EH(c),JA,V:Attuma 20.00
4 HT,JM,Dr.Doom vs. Namor 20.00
5 RB/JSt(c),HT,DP,A:Fantastic
Four,I:Shroud 20.00
6 HT,JA,A:Shroud,Fantastic Four . 18.00

7 RB/KJ(c),HT,O:Shroud 18.00
8 KG,V:Ringmaster 18.00
9 ST,A:Avengers,Iron Man 18.00
10 BH,DP,A:Capt.America,
V:Attuma,Red Skull 18.00
11 DC/JSt(c),BH,DP,B:Dr. Doom,
Red Skull,A:Capt. America . . . 18.00
12 DC/AM(c),BH,DP,Dr.Doom vs.
Red Skull 18.00
13 KG,DP,Namor vs. Krang 18.00
14 JBy/TA(c),BH,DP,V:Magneto,
x-over with Champions #15. . . 18.00
15 GT,ME,A:Red Skull 18.00
16 CI,A:Dr. Doom. 18.00
17 KP(c),Red Skull Vs.Hatemonger
June, 1976. . . . . 18.00
G-Size#1 F:Namor, Dr.Doom. . . . 18.00
G-Size#2 F:Namor, Dr.Doom. . . . 18.00

SUPER-VILLAIN TEAM-
UP/M.O.D.O.K.'S 11
July, 2007
1 (of 5) 3.00
2 thru 5 . . . . @3.00

SUPREME POWER
Marvel Max, July, 2003
1 MSz(s),GFr 7.00
1a special edition, JQ(c) 10.00
2 MSz(s),GFr 4.00
3 MSz(s),GFr 4.00
4 thru 10 MSz(s),GFr . . . . @3.00
11 thru 18 MSz(s),GFr . . . . @3.00

SUPREME POWER:
HYPERION
Sept., 2005
1 (of 5) MSz(s),DJu 3.00
2 DJu,MD2,Hunting the Alien 3.00
3 thru 5 . . . . @3.00

SUPREME POWER:
NIGHTHAWK
Sept., 2005
1 SDi,F:Kyle Richmond. 3.00
2 SDi,put on a Happy Face 3.00
3 thru 6 . . . . @3.00

SUSPENSE
Marvel Atlas, Dec., 1949
1 BP,Ph(c),Sidney Greenstreet/
Peter Lorne (Maltese Falcon) 900.00
2 Ph(c),Dennis O'Keefe/Gale
Storm (Abandoned) 450.00
3 B:Horror stories,The Black
Pit 550.00
4 Thing In Black 350.00
5 BEv,GT,RH,BK,DBr,
Hangman's House 400.00
6 BEv,GT,PMo,RH,Madness
of Scott Mannion 400.00
7 DBr,GT,DR,Murder. 350.00
8 GC,DRi,RH,Don't Open
the Door. 350.00
9 GC,DRi,Back From The Dead. 350.00
10 JMn(c),WIP,RH,Trapped
In Time. 350.00
11 MSy,The Suitcase 300.00
12 GT,Dark Road 300.00
13 JMn(c),Strange Man,
bondage cover. 300.00
14 RH,Death And Doctor Parker . 450.00
15 JMn(c),OW,The Machine 300.00
16 OW,Horror Backstage. 300.00
17 Night Of Terror 300.00
18 BK,The Cozy Coffin 350.00
19 BEv,RH 300.00
20 . . . . 300.00

Suspense #6
© Marvel Entertainment Group

21 BEv(c) 300.00
22 BEv(c),BK,OW 300.00
23 BEv 300.00
24 RH,GT 350.00
25 I Died At Midnight 400.00
26 BEv(c) 250.00
27 DBr 275.00
28 BEv 275.00
29 JMn,BF,JRo,April, 1953 . . . . . 275.00

SWORDS OF THE SWASHBUCKLERS
Epic, 1985–87
1 JG,Adult theme 3.00
2 thru 7 JG . . . . @2.50
8 thru 12, June, 1987 . . . . @2.50

TALE OF THE MARINES
See: DEVIL-DOG DUGAN

TALES OF ASGARD
Oct., 1968
1 . . . . 75.00
Vol.2 #1 Feb,1984 . . . . 6.00

TALES OF G.I. JOE
Jan., 1988
1 reprints,#1 . . . . 3.00
2 thru 7 reprints . . . . @2.50

TALES OF JUSTICE
See: JUSTICE COMICS

TALES OF THE AGE OF APOCALYPSE
1996
1-shot SLo,JoB,Age of Apocalypse
stories 5.00
GN, rep. 6.00

TALES OF THE AGE OF APOCALYPSE: SINISTER BLOODLINE
Dec., 1997
GN JFM,SEp, 48-pg. bookshelf 6.00

TALES OF THE MARVELS: BLOCKBUSTER
Fully painted (1995) 6.00

TALES OF THE MARVELS: INNER DEMONS
Fully painted, 48-pg. (1996) 6.00

TALES OF THE MARVELS: WONDER YEARS
1 & 2 DAb (1995) . . . . @5.00

TALES OF SUSPENSE
Jan., 1959
1 AW,DH,JB,SD,JK 3,300.00
2 SD,JK,RH,Robot 1,100.00
3 SD,JK,JB(c),Flying Saucer . . 1,100.00
4 AW,JK,BEv,SD 900.00
5 JK,SD,JF 650.00
6 SD,JK. 650.00
7 SD,JK, ... 700.00
8 SD,BEv,JK,Lava Man 650.00
9 SD,JK,TF,Iron man type 700.00
10 SD,RH,JK 600.00
11 SD,JK 500.00
12 RC,SD,JK 500.00
13 SK,JK,Elektro 500.00
14 SD,JK,Colossus (1) 650.00
15 SD,JK 500.00
16 JK,Metallo (1) 600.00
17 JK 500.00
18 JK 500.00
19 JK 500.00
20 JK,Colossus (2) 500.00
21 JK/DAy(c),SD,This Is Klagg . . 400.00
22 JK/DAy(c),SD,Beware
Of Bruttu 400.00
23 JK,DAy,SD,The Creature
in the Black Bog 400.00
24 JK,DAy,SD,Insect Man 400.00
25 JK,DAy,SD,The Death of
Monstrollo 400.00
26 JK,DAy,SD,The Thing That
Crawled By Night 350.00
27 JK,DAy,SD,When Oog Lives
Again 350.00
28 JK,DAy,SD,Back From
the Dead 350.00
29 JK,DAy,SD,DH,The Martian
Who Stole A City 300.00
30 JK,DAy,SD,DH,The Haunted
Roller Coaster 350.00
31 JK,DAy,SD,DH,The Monster
in the Iron Mask. 375.00
32 JK,DAy,SD,DH,The Man in
the Bee-Hive 550.00
33 JK,DAy,SD,DH,Chamber of
Fear 300.00
34 JK,DAy,SD,DH,Inside The
Blue Glass Bottle 300.00
35 JK,DAy,SD,DH,The Challenge
of Zarkorr 400.00
36 SD,Meet Mr. Meek 300.00
37 DH,SD,Hagg 300.00
38 JDa,The Teenager Who Ruled
the World 300.00
39 JK,O&I:Iron Man 11,000.00
40 JK,C:Iron Man 3,500.00
41 JK,A:Iron Man,V:Dr.Strange. 2,000.00
42 DH,SD,I:Red Pharoah 1,000.00
43 JK,DH,I:Kala,A:Iron Man . . . 1,000.00
44 DH,SD,V:Mad Pharoah 1,000.00
45 DH,V:Jack Frost. 1,000.00
46 DH,CR,I:Crimson Dynamo . . . 700.00
47 SD,V:Melter. 700.00
48 SD,N:Iron Man 800.00
49 SD,A:Angel 1,200.00
50 DH,I:Mandarin. 450.00
51 DH,I:Scarecrow. 375.00
52 DH,I:Black Widow 550.00
53 DH,O:Watcher. 350.00
54 DH,V:Mandarin 300.00
55 DH,V:Mandarin 300.00
56 DH,I:Unicorn 300.00

Tales of Suspense #57
© Marvel Entertainment Group

57 DH,I&O:Hawkeye 550.00
58 DH,GT,B:Captain America . . . 650.00
59 DH,1st S.A. Solo Iron
America,I:Jarvis 650.00
60 DH,JK,V:Assassins 325.00
61 DH,JK,V:Mandarin 200.00
62 DH,JK,O:Mandarin 200.00
63 JK,O:Captain America 450.00
64 DH,JK,A:Black Widow,
Hawkeye 200.00
65 DH,JK,I:Red Skull 350.00
66 DH,JK,O:Red Skull 350.00
67 DH,JK,V:Adolph Hitler. 150.00
68 DH,JK,V:Red Skull 150.00
69 DH,JK,I:Titanium Man. 150.00
70 DH,JK,GT,V:Titanium Man . . . 150.00
71 DH,JK,WW,GT,V:TitaniumMan 125.00
72 DH,JK,GT,V:The Sleeper 125.00
73 JA,JK,GT,A:Black Knight 125.00
74 JA,JK,GT,V:The Sleeper. 125.00
75 JA,JK,I:Batroc,Sharon Carter . 125.00
76 JA,JR,V:Mandarin 125.00
77 JA,JK,JR,V:Ultimo,I:Peggy
Carter. 125.00
78 JA,GC,JK,V:Ultimo 125.00
79 JA,GC,JK,V:Red Skull,
I:Cosmic Cube. 150.00
80 JA,GC,JK,V:Red Skull 160.00
81 JA,GC,JK,V:Red Skull 125.00
82 GC,JK,V:The Adaptoid 125.00
83 GC,JK,V:The Adaptoid 125.00
84 GC,JK,V:Mandarin 125.00
85 GC,JK,V:Batroc. 125.00
86 GC,JK,V:Mandarin 125.00
87 GC,V:Mole Man 125.00
88 GK,JK,GC,V:Power Man. 125.00
89 GK,JK,GC,V:Red Skull 125.00
90 GK,JK,GC,V:Red Skull 125.00
91 GK,GC,JK,V:Crusher 125.00
92 GC,JK,A:Nick Fury 125.00
93 GC,JK,V:Titanium Man 125.00
94 GC,JK,I:Modok 125.00
95 GC,JK,V:Grey Gargoyle,
IR:Captain America 125.00
96 GC,JK,V:Grey Gargoyle 125.00
97 GC,JK,I:Whiplash,
A:Black Panther. 125.00
98 GC,JK,I:Whitney Frost
A:Black Panther. 175.00
99 DH,JK,A:Black Panther 200.00
Marvel Milestone rep. #39 (1993) . . 3.00
Becomes:

CAPTAIN AMERICA

MARVEL

TALES OF SUSPENSE: CAPTAIN AMERICA/ IRON MAN

Dec., 2004

1 Commemorative Edition 3.00

TALES OF THE ZOMBIE

Aug., 1973

(Black & White Magazine)

1 Reprint Menace #5,O:Zombie . 60.00
2 GC,GT 50.00
3 . . . . 50.00
4 Live and Let Die. 50.00
5 BH 50.00
6 . . . . 50.00
7 thru 9 AA . . . . @50.00
10 March, 1975 . . . . 50.00

TALES TO ASTONISH

Marvel Atlas, Jan., 1959

1 JDa,Ninth Wonder of the
  World 3,500.00
2 SD,Capture A Martian. 1,300.00
3 SD,JK,The Giant From
  Outer Space 900.00
4 SD,JK,The Day The
  Martians Struck 900.00
5 SD,AW,The Things on
  Easter Island 900.00
6 SD,JK,Invasion of the
  Stone Men 700.00
7 SD,JK,The Thing on Bald
  Mountain 700.00
8 DAy,SD,JK,Mmmex, King of
  the Mummies 700.00
9 DAy,JK(c),SD,Droom, the
  Living Lizard 700.00
10 DAy,JK,SD,Titano. 700.00
11 DAy,JK,SD,Monstrom, the Dweller
  in the Black Swamp. 500.00
12 JK/DAy(c),SD,Gorgilla 500.00
13 JK,SD,Groot, the Monster
  From Planet X 500.00
14 JK,SD,Krang. 500.00
15 JK/DAy,The Blip 650.00
16 DAy,JK,SD,Thorr. 550.00
17 JK,SD,Vandoom 500.00
18 DAy,JK,SD,Gorgilla Strikes
  Again 500.00
19 DAy,JK,SD,Rommbu. 500.00

Tales to Astonish #19
© *Marvel Entertainment Group*

20 JK,SD,X, The Thing
  That Lived 500.00
21 JK,SD,Trull the Inhuman. . . . 500.00
22 JK,SD,The Crawling
  Creature. 400.00
23 JK,SD,Moomba is Here!. . . . 400.00
24 JK,SD,The Abominable
  Snowman. 400.00
25 JK,SD,The Creature From
  Krogarr. 400.00
26 JK,SD,Four-Armed Things . . . 400.00
27 StL(s),SD,JK,I:Ant-Man 8,500.00
28 JK,SD,I Am the Gorilla Man . . 350.00
29 JK,SD,When the Space
  Beasts Attack. 350.00
30 JK,SD,Thing From the
  Hidden Swamp 350.00
31 JK,SD,The Mummy's Secret. . 350.00
32 JK,SD,Quicksand 350.00
33 JK,SD,Dead Storage. 350.00
34 JK,SD,Monster at Window . . . 350.00
35 StL(s),JK,SD, B:Ant-Man
  (2nd App.). 3,500.00
36 JK,SD,V:Comrade X 1,500.00
37 JK,SD,V:The Protector 800.00
38 JK,SD,Betrayed By the Ants. . 800.00
39 JK,DH,V:Scarlet Beetle. 800.00
40 JK,SD,DH,The Day Ant-Man
  Failed. 800.00
41 DH,St,SD,V:Kulla 600.00
42 DH,JSe,SD,Voice of Doom. . . 600.00
43 DH,SD,Master of Time 600.00
44 JK,SD,I&O:Wasp 800.00
45 DH,SD,V:Egghead 350.00
46 DH,SD,I:Cyclops(robot) 350.00
47 DH,SD,V:Trago. 350.00
48 DH,SD,I:Porcupine 350.00
49 JK,DH,AM,Ant-Man Becomes
  Giant-Man 425.00
50 JK,SD,I&O:Human Top 250.00
51 JK,V:Human Top 250.00
52 I&O:Black Knight. 250.00
53 DH,V:Porcupine 250.00
54 DH,I:El Toro 225.00
55 V:Human Top 225.00
56 V:The Magician 225.00
57 A:Spider-Man 500.00
58 V:Colossus(not X-Men one) . . 225.00
59 V:Hulk,Black Knight 550.00
60 SD,B:Hulk,Giant Man 550.00
61 SD,I:Glenn Talbot,
  V:Egghead 250.00
62 I:Leader,N:Wasp 250.00
63 SD,O:Leader(1st full story) . . . 250.00
64 SD,V:Leader 300.00
65 BP,DH,SD,N:Giant-Man,. 250.00
66 BP,JK,SD,V:Leader,
  Chameleon 250.00
67 BP,JK,SD,I:Kanga Khan 250.00
68 BP,JK,N:Human Top,V:Leader 250.00
69 BP,JK,V:Human Top,Leader,
  E:Giant-Man 250.00
70 GC,JK,B:Sub-Mariner/Hulk,I:
  Neptune. 275.00
71 GC,JK,V:Leader,I:Vashti 100.00
72 GC,JK,V:Leader 100.00
73 GC,JK,V:Leader,A:Watcher . . 100.00
74 GC,JK,V:Leader,A:Watcher . . 100.00
75 GC,JK,A:Watcher 100.00
76 GC,JK,JK,Atlantis 100.00
77 JK,V:Executioner 100.00
78 BEv,GC,JK,Prince and
  the Puppet. 100.00
79 BEv,GC,JK,Hulk vs.Hercules . 100.00
80 BEv,GC,JK,Moleman vs.
  Tyrannus 100.00
81 BEv,GC,JK,I:Boomerang,Secret
  Empire,Moleman vs.Tyrannus 100.00
82 BEv,GC,JK,V:Iron Man 110.00
83 BEv,JK,V:Boomerang 100.00
84 BEv,GC,JK,Like a Beast
  at Bay 100.00

85 BEv,GC,JB,Missile &
  the Monster 100.00
86 BEv,JB,V:Warlord Krang. . . . 100.00
87 BEv,JB,IR:Hulk 100.00
88 BEv,GK,V:Boomerang. 100.00
89 BEv,GK,V:Stranger 100.00
90 JK,GK,BEv,I:Abomination . . . 100.00
91 GK,BEv,DA,V:Abomination . . 100.00
92 MSe,C:Silver Surfer x-over . . 110.00
93 MSe,Silver Surfer x-over. . . . 150.00
94 BEv,MSe,V:Dragorr,High
  Evolutionary. 100.00
95 BEv,MSe,V:High Evolutionary. 100.00
96 MSe,Skull Island,High Evol. . . 100.00
97 MSe,C:Ka-Zar,X-Men 110.00
98 DA,MSe,I:Legion of the Living
  Lightning,I:Seth 100.00
99 DA,MSe,V:Legion of the Living
  Lighting 100.00
100 MSe,DA,Hulk vs.Sub-Mariner 125.00
101 MSe,GC,V:Loki 125.00
Becomes:

INCREDIBLE HULK

TALES TO ASTONISH

[2nd Series] Dec., 1979

1 JB,rep.Sub-Mariner#1 . . . . 5.00
2 thru 14 JB,rep.Sub-Mariner . . . @3.00

TANGLED WEB

April, 2001

1 GEn,JMC,The Thousand. 3.00
2 GEn,JMC,The Thousand 3.00
3 GEn,JMC,V:The Thousand 3.00
4 Severance Package. 3.00
5 PrM,DFg,Flowers for Rhino 3.00
6 PrM,DFg,Flowers/Rhino,pt.2 . . . 3.00
7 Gentlemen's Agreement 3.00
8 Gentlemen's Agreement 3.00
9 LW,Gentlemen's Agreement,pt.3 . 3.00
10 Impact on Kids 3.00
11 Open All Night, 48-pg. 3.50
12 I Was A Teenaged Frog-Man . . 3.00
13 SeP,Double Shots. 3.00
14 The Last Shoot 3.00
15 The Collaborator. 3.00
16 F:Tombstone, Kangaroo 3.00
17 Tombstone in jail. 3.00
18 TMK 3.00
19 F:Grizzly & Rhino 3.00
20 J.Jonah Jameson 3.00
21 . . . . 3.00
22 The System. 3.00

TARZAN

June, 1977

1 JB,Edgar Rice Burroughs Adapt.20.00
2 JB,O:Tarzan 15.00
3 JB,The Alter of the Flaming
  God,I:LA 15.00
4 JB,TD,V:Leopards 15.00
5 JB,TD,Vengeance,A:LA 10.00
6 JB,TD,Rage of Tantor,A:LA . . . 10.00
7 JB,TD,Tarzan Rescues The
  Moon 10.00
8 JB,Battle For The Jewel Of
  Opar. 10.00
9 JB,Histah, the Serpent. 10.00
10 JB,The Deadly Peril of
  Jane Clayton 10.00
11 JB 10.00
12 JB,Fangs of Death 10.00
13 JB,Lion-God 10.00
14 JB,The Fury of Fang and Claw. 10.00
15 JB,Sword of the Slaver. 10.00
16 JB,Death Rides the Jungle
  Winds. 10.00
17 JB,The Entrance to the
  Earths Core 10.00
18 JB,Corsairs of the Earth's Core 10.00

19 Pursuit. 10.00
20 Blood Bond 10.00
21 Dark and Bloody Sky 8.00
22 JM,RN,War In Pellucidar 8.00
23 To the Death 8.00
24 The Jungle Lord Returns 8.00
25 RB(c),V:Poachers 8.00
26 RB(c),Caged 8.00
27 RB(c),Chaos in the Caberet 8.00
28 A Savage Against A City 8.00
29 Oct., 1979 . . . . 8.00
Ann.#1 JB 7.00
Ann.#2 Drums of the
  Death-Dancers 7.00
Ann.#3 Ant-Men and the
  She-Devils 7.00

TARZAN OF THE APES
July, 1984
1 (movie adapt.) 4.00
2 . . . . 4.00

TASKMASTER
Feb., 2002
1 (of 4) F:Iron Man 3.00
2 crime syndicates 3.00
3 syndicates catch on 3.00
4 concl. 3.00

TEAM AMERICA
June, 1982
1 O:Team America 2.50
2 V:Marauder 2.50
3 LMc,V:Mr.Mayhem 2.50
4 LMc,V:Arcade Assassins 2.50
5 A:Marauder 2.50
6 A.R.U. Ready 2.50
7 LMc,V:Emperor of Texas 2.50
8 DP,V:Hydra 2.50
9 A:Iron Man 2.50
10 V:Minister Ashe 2.50
11 A:Marauder,V:Ghost Rider 3.00
12 DP,Marauder unmasked,
  May, 1983 . . . . 2.50

TEAM HELIX
1993
1 A:Wolverine 2.25
2 A:Wolverine 2.25

TEAM X/TEAM 7
1996
1-shot LHa,SEp,MRy 5.00

TEAM X 2000
Dec., 1998
1-shot, 48-page 3.50

TEEN COMICS
See: ALL WINNERS COMICS

TEENAGE ROMANCE
See: MY ROMANCE

TEK WORLD
See: WILLIAM SHATNER'S TEK
WORLD

TERMINATOR 2
Sept., 1991
1 KJ,movie adaption 3.00
2 KJ,movie adaption 3.00
3 KJ,movie adaption 3.00
Terminator II (bookshelf format). . . . 5.00
Terminator II (B&W mag. size). 2.25

TERRARISTS
Epic, 1993–94
1 thru 4 w/card . . . . @2.50
5 thru 7 . . . . @2.50

TERROR INC.
1992–93
1 JZ,I:Hellfire. 3.00
2 JZ,I:Bezeel,Hellfire. 2.50
3 JZ,A:Hellfire 2.25
4 JZ,A:Hellfire,V:Barbados 2.25
5 JZ,V:Hellfire,A:Dr. Strange 2.25
6 JZ,MT,A:Punisher 2.25
7 JZ,V:Punisher 2.25
8 Christmas issue 2.25
9 JZ,V:Wolverine 2.25
10 V:Wolverine 2.25
11 A:Silver Sable,Cage 2.25
12 For Love Nor Money#4,A:Cage,
  Silver Sable 2.25
13 Inf.Crusade,A:Gh.Rider. 2.25

TERROR, INC.
Aug., 2007
1 . . . . 4.00
2 Mr. Terror. 4.00
3 Mr. Terror Smash 4.00
4 . . . . 4.00

TESSIE THE TYPIST
Marvel Timely, Summer, 1944
1 BW,Doc Rockblock 1,000.00
2 BW,Powerhouse Pepper 500.00
3 Football cover 200.00
4 BW 350.00
5 BW 350.00
6 BW,HK,Hey Look 350.00
7 BW 350.00
8 BW 350.00
9 BW,HK,Powerhouse Pepper . . 375.00
10 BW,A:Rusty. 375.00
11 BW,A:Rusty. 375.00
12 BW,HK 375.00
13 BW,A:Millie The Model,Rusty . 375.00
14 BW 375.00
15 HK,A:Millie,Rusty 375.00
16 HK 225.00
17 HK,A:Millie, Rusty. 225.00
18 HK 225.00
19 Annie Oakley story 150.00
20 . . . . 150.00
21 A:Lana, Millie 150.00
22 . . . . 150.00
23 . . . . 150.00
Becomes:

TINY TESSIE
24 . . . . 100.00
Becomes:

REAL EXPERIENCES
25 Ph(c),Jan., 1950 . . . . 100.00

TEXAS KID
Marvel Atlas, Jan., 1951
1 GT,JMn,O:Texas Kid 300.00
2 JMn 200.00
3 JMn,Man Who Didn't Exist . . . 150.00
4 thru 9 JMn . . . . @150.00
10 JMn,July, 1952 . . . . 150.00

TEX DAWSON, GUN-SLINGER
Jan., 1973
1 JSo(c) 35.00
Becomes:

GUNSLINGER
2 . . . . 25.00
3 June, 1973 . . . . 25.00

WESTERN ACTION AND THRILLS!

Tex Morgan #4
© Marvel Entertainment Group

TEX MORGAN
Aug., 1948
1 Tex Morgan & Lobo 350.00
2 Boot Hill Welcome For A
  Bad Man 225.00
3 A:Arizona Annie 150.00
4 SSh,Trapped in the Outlaw's
  Den, A:Arizona Annie 125.00
5 Valley of Missing Cowboys . . . 125.00
6 Never Say Murder,
  A:Tex Taylor 150.00
7 CCB,Ph(c),Captain Tootsie,
  A:Tex Taylor 225.00
8 Ph(c),Terror Of Rimrock
  Valley, A:Diablo 225.00
9 Ph(c),Death to Tex Taylor,
  Feb., 1950 . . . . 225.00

TEX TAYLOR
Sept., 1948
1 SSh,Boot Hill Showdown 400.00
2 When Two-Gun Terror Rides
  the Range 200.00
3 SSh,Thundering Hooves and
  Blazing Guns 150.00
4 Ph(c),Draw or Die Cowpoke . . 200.00
5 Ph(c),The Juggler of Yellow
  Valley,A:Blaze Carson 200.00
6 Ph(c),Mystery of Howling Gap. 200.00
7 Ph(c),Trapped in Time's Lost
  Land,A:Diablo 225.00
8 Ph(c),The Mystery of Devil-
  Tree Plateau,A:Diablo 225.00
9 Ph(c),Guns Along the Border,
  A:Nimo,March, 1950 . . . . . . 225.00

THANOS
Oct., 2003
1 JSn. 3.00
2 JSn,Galactus,Adam Warlock . . . 3.00
3 JSn,F:Moondragon 3.00
4 JSn,Epiphany,pt.4 . . . . 3.00
5 JSn,Epiphany,pt.5 . . . . 3.00
6 JSn,concl. 3.00
7 KG,RLm 3.00
8 KG,RLm 3.00
9 KG,RLm 3.00
10 KG,RLm,V:The Maker 3.00
11 KG,RLm. 3.00
12 KG,RLm. 3.00

THANOS QUEST
1990
1 JSn,RLm,V:Elders,
for Soul Gems 8.00
2 JSn,RLm,O:SoulGems,I: Infinity
Gauntlet (story cont.in Silver
Surfer #44) 8.00
1a & 2a 2nd printings . . . . @4.00

THANOS QUEST
Jan., 2000
GN JSn,RLm,96-pg... . . . . 4.00

THING, THE
July, 1983
1 JBy,O:Thing 3.50
2 JBy,Woman from past 2.50
3 JBy,A:Inhumans 2.50
4 JBy,A:Lockjaw 2.50
5 JBy,A:Spider-Man,She-Hulk . . . 2.50
6 JBy,V:Puppet Master 2.50
7 JBy,V:Goody Two Shoes 2.50
8 JBy,V:Egyptian Curse 2.50
9 JBy,F:Alicia Masters 2.50
10 JBy,Secret Wars 2.50
11 JBy,B:Rocky Grimm 2.50
12 JBy,F:Rocky Grimm 2.50
13 JBy,F:Rocky Grimm 2.50
14 F:Rocky Grimm 2.50
15 F:Rocky Grimm 2.50
16 F:Rocky Grimm 2.50
17 F:Rocky Grimm 2.50
18 F:Rocky Grimm 2.50
19 F:Rocky Grimm 2.50
20 F:Rocky Grimm 2.50
21 V:Ultron 2.50
22 V:Ultron 2.50
23 R:Thing to Earth,A:Fant. Four . 2.50
24 V:Rhino,A:Miracle Man 2.50
25 V:Shamrock 2.50
26 A:Vance Astro 2.50
27 I:Sharon Ventura 2.50
28 A:Vance Astro 2.50
29 A:Vance Astro 2.50
30 Secret Wars II,A:Vance Astro . . 2.50
31 A:Vance Astro 2.50
32 A:Vance Astro 2.50
33 A:Vance Astro,I:New Grapplers . 2.50
34 V:Titania,Sphinx 2.50
35 I:New Ms.Marvel,Power Broker . 2.50
36 Last Issue,A:She-Hulk 2.50

[Mini-Series]
1 rep.Marvel Two-in-One #50 . . . . . 2.50
2 rep Marvel Two-in-One,V:GR 2.50
3 rep Marvel Two-in-One #51 . . . . . 2.00
4 rep Marvel Two-in-One #43 . . . . . 2.00

THING, THE
Nov., 2005
1 Money Changes Every Thing . . . 3.00
2 Fun 'N Games 3.00
3 Fun 'N Games 3.00
4 Paws ...and Fast Forward 3.00
5 Give Till It Hurts 3.00
6 Friendly Neighborhood Brouhaha 3.00
7 On the Way to the Forum 3.00
8 Poker game 3.00

THING/SHE-HULK
March, 1998
1-shot TDz,V:Dragon Man, 48-pg . 3.00
1-shot The Long Night, 48-pg 3.00

THING, THE: FREAKSHOW
June, 2002
1 (of 4) ALa,grumpiest super-hero . 3.00
2 ALa,people are enthralled 3.00
3 ALa,ScK 3.00
4 ALa,ScK,concl... . . . . 3.00

THOR, THE MIGHTY
Prev: Journey Into Mystery
March, 1966
126 JK,V:Hercules 400.00
127 JK,I:Pluto,Volla 200.00
128 JK,V:Pluto,A:Hercules. 200.00
129 JK,V:Pluto,I:Ares. 200.00
130 JK,V:Pluto,A:Hercules. 200.00
131 JK,I:Colonizers 200.00
132 JK,A:Colonizers,I:Ego 200.00
133 JK,A:Colonizers,A:Ego 200.00
134 JK,I:High Evolutionary,
Man-Beast 225.00
135 JK,O:High Evolutionary 150.00
136 JK,F:Odin 150.00
137 JK,I:Ulik 150.00
138 JK,V:Ulik,A:Sif 150.00
139 JK,V:Ulik 150.00
140 JK,V:Growing Man 150.00
141 JK,V:Replicus 100.00
142 JK,V:Super Skrull 100.00
143 JK,BEv,V:Talisman 100.00
144 JK,V:Talisman 100.00
145 JK,V:Ringmaster 100.00
146 JK,O:Inhumans Part 1 . . . . . 150.00
147 JK,O:Inhumans Part 2 . . . . . 150.00
148 JK,I:Wrecker,O:Black Bolt . . 150.00
149 JK,O:Black Bolt,Medusa . . . 150.00
150 JK,A:Triton 150.00
151 JK,V:Destroyer 125.00
152 JK,V:Destroyer 125.00
153 JK,F:Dr.Blake 125.00
154 JK,I:Mangog 125.00
155 JK,V:Mangog 125.00
156 JK,V:Mangog 125.00
157 JK,D:Mangog 125.00
158 JK,O:Don Blake Part 1 . . . . . 160.00
159 JK,O:Don Blake Part 2 . . . . . 125.00
160 JK,I:Travrians 100.00
161 JK,Shall a God Prevail 100.00
162 JK,O:Galactus 110.00
163 JK,I:Mutates,A:Pluto 75.00
164 JK,A:Pluto,V:Greek Gods 75.00
165 JK,V:Him/Warlock 150.00
166 JK,V:Him/Warlock 125.00
167 JK,F:Sif 70.00
168 JK,O:Galactus. 100.00
169 JK,O:Galactus. 100.00
170 JK,BEv,V:Thermal Man 75.00
171 JK,BEv,V:Wrecker. 75.00
172 JK,BEv,V:Ulik 75.00
173 JK,BEv,V:Ulik,Ringmaster. . . . 75.00
174 JK,BEv,V:Crypto-Man 75.00
175 JK,Fall of Asgard,V:Surtur . . . 75.00

Thor, The Mighty #195
© Marvel Entertainment Group

176 JK,V:Surtur 75.00
177 JK,I:Igon,V:Surtur 75.00
178 JK,C:Silver Surfer 90.00
179 JK,MSe,C:Galactus. 75.00
180 NA,JSi,V:Loki 90.00
181 NA,JSi,V:Loki 90.00
182 JB,V:Dr.Doom 50.00
183 JB,V:Dr.Doom 50.00
184 JB,I:The Guardian. 50.00
185 JB,JSt,V:Silent One. 50.00
186 JB,JSt,V:Hela 50.00
187 JB,JSt,V:Odin 50.00
188 JB,JM,F:Odin 50.00
189 JB,JSt,V:Hela 50.00
190 JB,I:Durok 50.00
191 JB,JSt,V:Loki 50.00
192 JB 50.00
193 JB,SB,V:Silver Surfer 100.00
194 JB,SB,V:Loki 50.00
195 JB,JR,V:Mangog 50.00
196 JB,NR,V:Kartag. 50.00
197 JB,V:Mangog 50.00
198 JB,V:Pluto 50.00
199 JB,V:Pluto,Hela 50.00
200 JB,Ragnarok. 75.00
201 JB,JM,Odin resurrected. 40.00
202 JB,V:Ego-Prime 40.00
203 JB,V:Ego-Prime 40.00
204 JB,JM,Demon from t/Depths. . 40.00
205 JB,V:Mephisto. 40.00
206 JB,V:Absorbing Man 30.00
207 JB,V:Absorbing Man 30.00
208 JB,V:Mercurio 30.00
209 JB,I:Druid 30.00
210 JB,DP,I:Ulla,V:Ulik. 30.00
211 JB,DP,V:Ulik 30.00
212 JB,JSt,V:Sssthgar 30.00
213 JB,DP,I:Gregor 30.00
214 SB,JM,V:Dark Nebula 30.00
215 JB,JM,J:Xorr 30.00
216 JB,JM,V:4D-Man. 30.00
217 JB,SB,I:Krista,V:Odin 30.00
218 JB,JM,A:Colonizers. 30.00
219 JB,I:Protector 30.00
220 JB,V:Avalon. 30.00
221 JB,V:Olympus 30.00
222 JB,JSe,A:Hercules,V:Pluto . . . 30.00
223 JB,A:Hercules,V:Pluto. 30.00
224 JB,V:Destroyer 30.00
225 JB,JSi,I:Fire Lord 35.00
226 JB,A:Watcher,Galactus 25.00
227 JB,JSi,V:Ego 25.00
228 JB,JSi,A:Galactus,D:Ego 25.00
229 JB,JSi,A:Hercules,I:Dweller . . 25.00
230 JB,A:Hercules 25.00
231 JB,DG,V:Armak 25.00
232 JB,JSi,A:Firelord 25.00
233 JB,Asgard Invades Earth 25.00
234 JB,V:Loki 25.00
235 JB,JSi,I:Possessor
(Kamo Tharnn) 25.00
236 JB,JSi,V:Absorbing Man 25.00
237 JB,JSi,V:Ulik. 25.00
238 JB,JSi,V:Ulik 25.00
239 JB,JSi,V:Ulik 25.00
240 SB,KJ,V:Seth 25.00
241 JB,JGi,I:Geb 25.00
242 JB,JSi,V:Servitor 25.00
243 JB,JSt,V:Servitor 25.00
244 JB,JSt,V:Servitor 25.00
245 JB,JSt,V:Servitor 25.00
246 JB,JSt,A:Firelord 25.00
247 JB,JSt,A:Firelord 25.00
248 JB,V:Storm Giant 25.00
249 JB,V:Odin 25.00
250 JB,D:Igron,V:Mangog 25.00
251 JB,A:Sif 15.00
252 JB,V:Ulik 15.00
253 JB,I:Trogg 15.00
254 JK,O:Dr.Blake rep. 15.00
255 Stone Men of Saturn rep. 15.00
256 JB,I:Sporr 15.00

Thor, The Mighty #292
© Marvel Entertainment Group

257 JK,JB,I:Fee-Lon 15.00
258 JK,JB,V:Grey Gargoyle 15.00
259 JB,A:Spider-Man 15.00
260 WS,I:Doomsday Star 15.00
261 WS,I:Soul Survivors 15.00
262 WS,Odin Found,I:Odin Force . 15.00
263 WS,V:Loki 15.00
264 WS,V:Loki 15.00
265 WS,V:Destroyer 15.00
266 WS,Odin Quest 15.00
267 WS,F:Odin 15.00
268 WS,V:Damocles 15.00
269 WS,V:Stilt-Man 15.00
270 WS,V:Blastaar 15.00
271 Avengers,Iron Man x-over. . . . 15.00
272 JB,Day the Thunder Failed . . 15.00
273 JB,V:Midgard Serpent 15.00
274 JB,D:Balder,I:Hermod,Hoder . 15.00
275 JB,V:Loki,I:Sigyn 15.00
276 JB,Trial of Loki 15.00
277 JB,V:Fake Thor 15.00
278 JB,V:Fake Thor 15.00
279 A:Pluto,V:Ulik 15.00
280 V:Hyperion 15.00
281 O:Space Phantom 10.00
282 V:Immortus,I:Tempus 10.00
283 JB,V:Celestials 10.00
284 JB,V:Gammenon 10.00
285 JB,R:Karkas 10.00
286 KP,KRo,D:Kro,I:Dragona. . . . 10.00
287 KP,2nd App. & O:Forgotten
    One(Hero) 10.00
288 KP,I:Forgotten One 10.00
289 KP,V:Destroyer 10.00
290 I:Red Bull(Toro Rojo) 10.00
291 KP,A:Eternals,Zeus. 10.00
292 KP,V:Odin 10.00
293 KP,Door to Mind's Eye 10.00
294 KP,O:Odin & Asgard,I:Frey . . 10.00
295 KP,I:Fafnir,V:Storm Giants . . . 10.00
296 KP,D:Siegmund. 10.00
297 KP,V:Sword of Siegfried 10.00
298 KP,V:Dragon(Fafnir) 10.00
299 KP,A:Valkyrie,I:Hagen 10.00
300 KP,giant,O:Odin & Destroyer,
    Rindgold Ring Quest ends,D:
    Uni-Mind,I:Mother Earth . . 20.00
301 KP,O:Mother Earth,V:Apollo . . 10.00
302 KP,V:Locus 10.00
303 Whatever Gods There Be. . . . 10.00
304 KP,V:Wrecker 10.00
305 KP,R:Gabriel(Air Walker) 10.00
306 KP,O&V:Firelord,O:Air Walker. 10.00
307 KP,I:Dream Demon 10.00
308 KP,V:Snow Giants. 10.00

309 V:Bomnardiers 10.00
310 KP,V:Mephisto. 10.00
311 KP,GD,A:Valkyrie. 10.00
312 KP,V:Tyr 10.00
313 KP,Thor Trial 7.00
314 KP,A:Drax,Moondragon 7.00
315 KP,O:Bi-Beast 7.00
316 KP,A:Iron Man,Man Thing,
    V:Man-Beast 7.00
317 KP,V:Man-Beast 7.00
318 GK,V:Fafnir 7.00
319 KP,I&D:Zaniac 7.00
320 KP,V:Rimthursar 7.00
321 I:Menagerie 7.00
322 V:Heimdall. 7.00
323 V:Death 7.00
324 V:Graviton 7.00
325 JM,O:Darkoth,V:Mephisto . . . 7.00
326 I:New Scarlet Scarab 7.00
327 V:Loki & Tyr. 7.00
328 I:Megatak 7.00
329 HT,V:Hrungnir 7.00
330 BH,I:Crusader 7.00
331 Threshold of Death 7.00
332 V:Dracula 7.00
333 BH,V:Dracula 7.00
334 Quest For Rune Staff 7.00
335 V:Possessor 7.00
336 A:Captain Ultra 7.00
337 WS,I:Beta Ray Bill,A:Surtur . . 10.00
338 WS,O:Beta Ray Bill,I:Lorelei. . 9.00
339 WS,V:Beta Ray Bill 6.00
340 WS,A:Beta Ray Bill 6.00
341 WS,V:Fafnir 6.00
342 WS,V:Fafnir,I:Eilif 6.00
343 WS,V:Fafnir 6.00
344 WS,Balder vs. Loki,I:Malekith . 6.00
345 WS,V:Malekith 6.00
346 WS,V:Malekith 6.00
347 WS,V:Malekith,I:Algrim
    (Kurse). 6.00
348 WS,V:Malekith 6.00
349 WS,R:Beta Ray Bill,O:Odin,
    I&O:Vili & Ve(Odin's brothers). . 6.00
350 WS,V:Surtur 6.00
351 WS,V:Surtur 6.00
352 WS,V:Surtur 6.00
353 WS,V:Surtur,D:Odin 5.00
354 WS,V:Hela 5.00
355 WS,SB,A:Thor's Great
    Grandfather 5.00
356 BL,BG,V:Hercules 5.00
357 WS,A:Beta Ray Bill 5.00
358 WS,A:Beta Ray Bill 5.00
359 WS,V:Loki 5.00
360 WS,V:Hela 5.00
361 WS,V:Hela 5.00
362 WS,V:Hela 5.00
363 WS,Secret Wars II,V:Kurse. . . 5.00
364 WS,I:Thunder Frog 5.00
365 WS,A:Thunder Frog 5.00
366 WS,A:Thunder Frog 5.00
367 WS,D:Malekith,A:Kurse 5.00
368 WS,F:Balder t/Brave,Kurse. . . 5.00
369 WS,F:Balder the Brave 5.00
370 JB,V:Loki 5.00
371 SB,I:Justice Peace,V:Zaniac. . 5.00
372 SB,V:Justice Peace 5.00
373 SB,A:X-Factor,(Mut.Mass) . . . 5.00
374 WS,SB,A:X-Factor,(Mut.Mass)
    A:Sabretooth 6.00
375 WS,SB,N:Thor(Exoskeleton) . . 4.00
376 WS,SB,V:Absorbing Man 4.00
377 WS,SB,N:Thor,A:Ice Man 4.00
378 WS,SB,V:Frost Giants 4.00
379 WS,V:Midgard Serpent 4.00
380 WS,V:Midgard Serpent 4.00
381 WE,SB,A:Avengers. 4.00
382 WS,SB,V:Frost Giants,Loki. . . 5.00
383 BBr,Secret Wars story 4.00
384 RF,BBr,I:Future Thor(Dargo). . 6.00
385 EL,V:Hulk 4.00

Thor, The Mighty #391
© Marvel Entertainment Group

386 RF,BBr,I:Leir 4.00
387 RF,BBr,V:Celestials. 4.00
388 RF,BBr,V:Celestials. 4.00
389 RF,BBr,V:Celestials. 4.00
390 RF,BBr,A:Avengers,V:Seth . . . 4.00
391 RF,BBr,I:Mongoose,Eric
    Masterson,A:Spider-Man. . . . 6.00
392 RF,I:Quicksand 5.00
393 RF,BBr,V:Quicksand,A:DD . . . 5.00
394 RF,BBr,V:Earth Force 5.00
395 RF,V:Earth Force 5.00
396 RF,A:Black Knight 5.00
397 RF,A:Loki. 5.00
398 RF,DH,R:Odin,V:Seth 5.00
399 RF,RT,R:Surtur,V:Seth 5.00
400 RF,JSt,CV,V:Surtur,Seth 6.00
401 V:Loki 4.00
402 RF,JSt,V:Quicksand 5.00
403 RF,JSt,V:Executioner 4.00
404 RF,JSt,TD,V:Annihilus. 4.00
405 RF,JSt,TD,V:Annihilus. 4.00
406 RF,JSt,TD,V:Wundagore. 4.00
407 RF,JSt,R:Hercules,High Evol. . 4.00
408 RF,JSt,I:Eric Masterson/Thor,
    V:Mongoose 4.50
409 RF,JSt,V:Dr.Doom. 4.00
410 RF,JSt,V:Dr.Doom,She-Hulk . . 4.00
411 RF,JSt,C:New Warriors
    V:Juggernaut,A of V 3.00
412 RF,JSt,I:New Warriors
    V:Juggernaut,A of V 3.50
413 RF,JSt,A:Dr.Strange 3.00
414 RF,JSt,V:Ulik 3.00
415 HT,O:Thor 3.00
416 RF,JSt,A:Hercules 3.00
417 RF,JSt,A:High Evolutionary. . . . 3.00
418 RF,JSt,V:Wrecking Crew. 3.00
419 RF,JSt,B:Black Galaxy
    Saga,I:Stellaris. 3.00
420 RF,JSt,A:Avengers,V:Stellaris . . 3.00
421 RF,JSt,V:Stellaris. 3.00
422 RF,JSt,V:High Evol.,Nobilus . . . 3.00
423 RF,JSt,A:High Evol.,Celestials
    Count Tagar. 3.00
424 RF,JSt,V:Celestials,E:Black
    Galaxy Saga 3.00
425 RF,AM,V:Surtur,Ymir. 3.00
426 RF,JSt,HT,O:Earth Force 3.00
427 RF,JSt,A:Excalibur 3.00
428 RF,JSt,A:Excalibur 3.00
429 RF,JSt,A:Ghost Rider 3.00
430 RF,AM,A:Mephisto,Gh.Rider. . . 3.00
431 HT,AM,V:Ulik,Loki 3.00

Thor, The Mighty #501
© Marvel Entertainment Group

432 RF,D:Loki,Thor Banished,Eric
    Masterson becomes 2nd Thor. . 3.50
433 RF,V:Ulik 4.00
434 RF,AM,V:Warriors Three 3.00
435 RF,AM,V:Annihilus 3.00
436 RF,AM,V:Titania,Absorbing
    Man,A:Hercules 3.00
437 RF,AM,V:Quasar 3.00
438 RF,JSt,A:Future Thor(Drago) . . 3.00
439 RF,JSt,A:Drago 3.00
440 RF,AM,I:Thor Corps 4.00
441 RF,AM,Celestials vs.Ego 4.00
442 RF,AM,Don Blake,Beta Ray
    Bill,Mephisto 3.00
443 RF,AM,A:Dr.Strange,Silver
    Surfer,V:Mephisto 3.00
444 RF,AM,Special X-mas tale 3.00
445 AM,Galactic Storm,pt.7,
    V:Gladiator. 3.00
446 AM,Galactic Storm,pt.14,
    A:Avengers 3.00
447 RF,AM,V:Absorbing Man,
    A:Spider-Man. 3.00
448 RF,AM,V:Titania,A:SpM 3.00
449 RF,AM,V:Ulik 3.00
450 RF,AM,V:Heimdall,A:Code Blue
    Double-Sized,Gatefold(c),rep.
    Journey Into Mystery#87 . . . . . . 3.00
451 RF,AM,I:Bloodaxe 3.00
452 RF,AM,V:Bloodaxe 3.00
453 RF,AM,V:Mephisto 3.00
454 RF,AM,V:Mephisto,Loki,
    Karnilla. 3.00
455 AM(i),V:Loki,Karnilla,R:Odin,
    A:Dr.Strange 3.00
456 RF,AM,V:Bloodaxe 3.00
457 RF,AM,R:1st Thor 3.00
458 RF,AM,Thor vs. Eric 3.00
459 RF,AM,C&I:Thunderstrike(Eric
    Masterson) 3.00
460 I:New Valkyrie 3.00
461 V:Beta Ray Bill 3.00
462 A:New Valkyrie 3.00
463 Infinity Crusade. 3.00
464 Infinity Crusade,V:Loki 3.00
465 Infinity Crusade. 3.00
466 Infinity Crusade. 3.00
467 Infinity Crusade. 3.00
468 RMz(s),Blood & Thunder#1 . . . 3.00
469 RMz(s),Blood & Thunder#5 . . . 3.00
470 MCW,Blood & Thunder#9 . . . . 3.00
471 MCW,E:Blood & Thunder 3.00
472 B:RTs(s),MCW,I:Godling,C:High
    Evolutionary. 3.00

473 MCW,V:Godling,High Evolutionary,
    I&C:Karnivore(Man-Beast) 3.00
474 MCW,C:High Evolutionary 3.00
475 MCW,Foil(c),A:Donald Blake,
    N:Thor 3.50
475a Newsstand ed. 3.00
476 V:Destroyer. 3.00
477 V:Destroyer,A:Thunderstrike . . 3.00
478 V:Norvell Thor 3.00
479 V:Norvell Thor 3.00
480 V:High Evolutionary 3.00
481 V:Grotesk 3.00
482 Don Blake construct 3.00
483 RTs,MCW,V:Loki 3.00
484 Badoy and Soul 3.00
485 V:The Thing 3.00
486 High Evolutionary,Godpack. . . . 3.00
487 V:Kurse 3.00
488 RTs,MCW,Kurse Saga concl. . . 3.00
489 RTs,V:Kurse,A:Hulk. 3.00
490 TDF,after Thunderstrike 3.00
491 N:Thor. 7.50
492 Worldengine's Secrets 5.00
493 Worldengine trigers Ragnarok . 3.00
494 Worldengine saga conclusion. . 3.00
495 BML,Avengers:Timeslide 3.00
496 MD2,BML,A:Capt.America 3.00
497 MD2,BML,Thor Must Die 3.00
498 BML,V:Absorbing Man 3.00
499 MD2,BML 3.00
500 MD2,BML,double size,A:Dr.
    Strange 3.50
501 MD2,BML,I:Red Norvell 3.00
502 MD2,BML,Onslaught tie-in, A:Red
    Norvell, Jane Foster, Hela 3.00
Becomes:

JOURNEY INTO MYSTERY

[Third Series] Nov., 1996
503 TDF,MD2, The Lost Gods, New
    Norse gods? 2.50
504 TDF,Golden Realm in ruins,
    V:Ulik the Troll 2.50
505 TDF,MD2, V:Wrecker,
    A:Spider-Man. 2.50
506 TDF,MD2, R:Heimdall 2.50
507 TDF,Odin kidnapped 2.50
508 TDF 2.50
509 TDF,Battle for the Future
    of Asgard 2.50
510 TDF,Return of Loki,A:Seth 2.50
511 TDF,EBe,Lost Gods reunited
    with Odin 2.50
512 EBe, Odin vs. Seth 2.50
513 TDF,SB,AM, Odin vs.
    Seth, concl. 2.50
514 BRa,VRu,F:Shang Chi, Master
    of Kung Fu. 2.50
515 BRa,VRu,F:Shang Chi, Master
    of Kung Fu, pt.2. . . . . 2.50
516 BRa,VRu,F:Shang Chi, Master
    of Kung Fu, pt.3. . . . . 2.50
517 SLo,RGr,F:Black Widow 2.50
518 SLo,RGr,F:Black Widow 2.50
519 SLo,RGr,F:Black Widow, concl. 2.50
520 MWn,F:Hannibal King, pt.1 . . . 2.50
521 MWn,F:Hannibal King, pt.2 . . . 2.50
Ann.#2 JK,V:Destroyer 125.00
Ann.#3 JK,rep,Grey Gargoyle 50.00
Ann.#4 JK,rep,TheLivingPlanet. . . . 30.00
Ann.#5 JK,JB,Hercules,O:Odin . . . 30.00
Ann.#6 JK,JB,A:Guardians of the
    Galaxy,V:Korvac 30.00
Ann.#7 WS,Eternals. 25.00
Ann.#8 JB,V:Zeus 25.00
Ann.#9 LMc,Dormammu 25.00
Ann.#10 O:Chthon,Gaea,A:Pluto. . 15.00
Ann.#11 O:Odin 15.00
Ann.#12 BH,I:Vidar(Odin's son). . . 15.00
Ann.#13 JB,V:Mephisto 15.00
Ann.#14 AM,DH,Atlantis Attacks . . 7.00
Ann.#15 HT,Terminus Factor #3 . . 5.00

Journey Into Mystery #503
© Marvel Entertainment Group

Ann.#16 Korvac Quest,pt.2,
    Guardians of Galaxy 3.00
Ann.#17 Citizen Kang#2 . . . . 3.00
Ann.#18 TGr,I:The Flame,w/card. . . 3.50
Ann.#19 V:Flame 3.50
G-Size.#1 Battles,A:Hercules 14.00
Minus 1 Spec., TDF,EBe,flashback . 2.00
1-shot, Rough Cut, DJu,JR,original
    pencils, b&w 48-pg. 3.00

THOR

May, 1998
1 JR2,KJ,DJu,The hero returns,
    48-pg. 6.00
2A JR2,KJ,DJu,V:Destroyer,A:Hela,
    Marnot. 3.50
2B JR2,KJ variant cover 3.50
3 DJu,JR2,KJ,A:Marnot,V:Sedna . . 3.00
4 DJu,JR2,KJ,A:Namor,Sedna 3.00
5 DJu,JR2,KJ,V:Charles Diamond . 3.00
6 DJu,JR2,KJ,V:Hercules 3.00
7 DJu,JR2,KJ,V:Zeus 3.00
8 DJu,JR2,KJ,PeterParker x-over. . 3.00
9 DJu,JB,JOy,War on
    Asgard,prelude 3.00
10 DJu,JR2,KJ,War on Asgard,pt.1 . 3.00
11 DJu,JR2,KJ,War on Asgard,pt.2 . 3.00
12 DJu,JR2,KJ,War on
    Asgard,concl. 48-page 3.50
12a signed 20.00
13 DJu,JR2,KJ,A:Marnot 2.50
14 DJu,Hammer secret 2.50
15 DJu,KJ,JR2(c),A:Warriors 3 . . . . 2.50
16 DJu,KJ,JR2,A:Warriors 3 . . . . . . 2.50
17 DJu,KJ,JR2,Eighth
    Day,pt.1, x-over 2.50
18 DJu,KJ,JR2,V:Enrakt 2.50
19 DJu 2.50
20 DJu,V:Loki. 2.50
21 DJu,JR2,KJ,R:Thanos 2.50
22 DJu,JR2,KJ,V:Thanos 2.50
23 DJu,JR2,DG,V:Thanos 2.50
24 DJu,JR2,DG,V:Thanos 2.50
25A DJu,JR2,DG,48-pg.,foil(c) 6.00
25B variant (c) 3.00
26 DJu,EL,KJ,V:AbsorbingMan . . . 2.25
27 DJu,EL,KJ,Dr.Jane Foster 2.25
28 DJu,EL,KJ,WarriorsThree 2.25
29 DJu,NKu,SHa,Jagrfelm. 2.25
30 DJu,NKu,SHa,MaxSecurity. . . . 2.25
31 DJu,NKu,SHa,V:Malekith 2.25
32 DJu,NKu,SHa,100-page 4.00
33 DJu,SI,I:new 2.25
34 DJu,NKu,SHa 2.25

35 DJu,NKu,SHa,V:Gladiator,
    48-page 3.50
36 DJu,R:Loki,A:Destroyer 2.25
37 DJu,JSn,AM,A:Watcher 2.25
38 DJu,SI,BWS(c),V:Destroyer 2.25
39 DJu,SI,BWS(c),V:Surtur 2.25
40 DJu,SI,V:Surtur 3.00
41 DJu,SI,V:Surtur,concl 2.25
42 DJu,SI,Asgard,Midgard 2.25
43 DJu,JoB,Thor:King of Asgard . . . 2.25
44 DJu,SI,Odin funeral,'Nuff Said . . 2.25
45 TR,new King in Asgard 2.25
46 DJu,SHa,TR,F:Thor-Girl 2.25
47 DJu,SHa,TR,Enchantress 2.25
48 DJu,JoB,TP,V:Desak 2.25
49 DJu,TR,SHa,V:Desak 2.25
50 DJu,TR,SHa,64-pg 6.00
51 DJu,TR,SHa,F:Spider-Man 2.25
52 DJu,TP 2.25
53 DJu 2.25
54 DJu,TR,SHa 2.25
55 DJu,TR,SHa 2.25
56 DJu,TR, ... 2.25
57 DJu,JoB 2.25
58 DJu,AD,Standoff,pt.1,x-over 2.50
59 CPr(s) 2.50
60 DJu,JoB,Spiral,pt.1 . . . . 2.25
61 DJu,Spiral,pt.2 . . . . 2.25
62 DJu,Spiral,pt.3 . . . . 3.00
63 DJu,Spiral,pt.4 . . . . 3.00
64 DJu,Spiral,pt.5 . . . . 3.00
65 DJu,Spiral,pt.6 . . . . 3.00
66 DJu,Spiral,pt.7 . . . . 3.00
67 DJu,Spiral,concl 3.00
68 DJu,SEa,The Reigning,prologue 3.00
69 DJu,SEa,The Reigning,pt.1 . . . . 3.00
70 DJu,SEa,The Reigning,pt.2 . . . . 3.00
71 DKi,SEa,The Reigning,pt.3 . . . . . 3.00
72 DJu,SEa,The Reigning,pt.4 . . . . 3.00
73 DJu,SEa,The Reigning,pt.5 . . . . 3.00
74 DJu,SEa,The Reigning,concl 3.00
75 DJu,SEa,Gods & Men,pt.1 . . . . . 3.00
76 DJu,SEa,Gods & Men,pt.2 . . . . . 3.00
77 DJu,SEa,Gods & Men,pt.3 . . . . . 3.00
78 DJu,SEa,Gods & Men,pt.4 . . . . . 3.00
79 DJu,SEa,Gods & Men,pt.5 . . . . . 3.00
80 F:The Avengers 15.00
81 F:The Avengers 10.00
82 Avengers Disassembled tie-in . . 7.00
83 Ragnarok,pt.3 . . . . 7.00
84 Ragnarok,pt.4 . . . . 6.00
85 Ragnarok,pt.5 . . . . 9.00
Ann.1999 DJu,KJ, 48-page 3.50
Ann.1999 signed 20.00
Ann.2000, 48-pg. 3.50
Ann.2001 TG,DJu,48-page 3.50
Spec.#1 Thor (2000) 2.25
Spec. rep.#1 & #2 . . . . 6.00

THOR
July, 2007

1 MSz(s) 3.00
2 thru 5 MSz(s) . . . . @3.00
2a thru 5a variant (c) . . . . @3.00

THOR: BLOOD OATH
Sept., 2005

1 (of 6) Classic Thor 3.00
2 Thor & Warriors 3.00
3 V:Hercules 3.00
4 thru 6 . . . . @3.00

THOR CORPS
[Limited Series]

1 TDF(s),PO,V:Demonstaff 2.25
2 TDF(s),PO,A:Invaders 2.25
3 TDF(s),PO,A:Spider-Man 2099 . . 2.25
4 TDF(s),PO,last issue 2.25

THOR: GODSTORM
Sept., 2001

1 (of 3) KBk,SR. 3.50
2 KBk,SR,V:Loki 3.50
3 KBk,SR,V:Loki,concl. 3.50

THOR: SON OF ASGARD
March, 2004

1 (of 6) The Warriors Teen,pt.1 . . . . 3.00
2 The Warriors Teen,pt.2 . . . . 3.00
3 The Warriors Teen,pt.3 . . . . 3.00
4 The Warriors Teen,pt.4 . . . . 3.00
5 The Warriors Teen,pt.5 . . . . 3.00
6 The Warriors Teen,pt.6 . . . . 3.00
7 Enchanted,pt.1. . . . . 3.00
8 Enchanted,pt.2. . . . . 3.00
9 Enchanted,pt.3. . . . . 3.00
10 . . . . 3.00
11 . . . . 3.00
12 Worthy, finale 3.00
Digest,Vol. 1 Warriors Teen 8.00
Digest,Vol. 2 Worthy 8.00

THOR: VIKINGS
Marvel Max, July, 2003

1 GEn(s),GF,Zombie Vikings 5.00
2 GEn(s),GF,F:Doctor Strange 4.00
3 GEn(s),GF 4.00
4 GEn(s),GF,back in time 4.00
5 GEn(s),GF,Zombie Vikings 4.00

3-D ACTION
Marvel Atlas 1954

1 Battle Brady. 500.00

3-D TALES OF THE WEST
Marvel Atlas, 1954

1 . . . . 500.00

THREE MUSKETEERS
1 thru 2 movie adapt. 2.25

THUNDERBOLTS
Feb., 1997

1 KBk,MBa,VRu,Post-onslaught new
    team:Citizen V, Meteorite, Techno,
    Songbird, Atlas & Mach-1 . . . . 10.00
1 rep. 3.00
2 KBk,MBa,VRu,V:Mad Thinker . . . 6.00
2a variant cover by MBa&VRu 6.00
2 rep. 4.50
3 KBk,MBa,VRu,Freedom's Plaza . 4.50
4 KBk,MBa,VRu,I:Jolt 4.50
5 KBk,MBa,VRu,V:Elements-Doom 4.50
6 KBk,MBa,VRu,V:Elements-Doom 4.50
7 KBk,MBa,VRu,F:Citizen V 4.00
8 KBk,MBa,VRu,Songbird alone. . . 4.00
9 KBk,MBa,VRu,Black Widow 4.00
10 KBk,MBa,VRu,Identy discovered 4.00
11 KBk,MBa,VRu,V:Citizen V 4.00
12 KBk,MBa,VRu,A:FF,Avengers . 10.00
13 KBk,MBa,SHa,on trial 3.00
14 KBk,MBa,VRu,V:Citizen V 3.00
15 KBk,MBa,VRu,V:S.H.I.E.L.D. . . . 3.00
16 KBk,MBa,SHa,V:Lightningrods . . 3.00
17 KBk,MBa,SHa,V:Graviton 3.00
18 KBk,MBa,SHa,villains again? . . . 3.00
19 KBk,MBa,SHa 3.00
20 KBk,MBa,SHa,V:Masters-Evil . . . 3.00
21 KBk,MBa,SHa,F:Songbird 3.00
22 KBk,MBa,SHa,A:Hercules 3.00
23 KBk,MBa,SHa,V:U.S.Agent 3.00
24 KBk,MBa,SHa,R:Citizen V 3.00
25 KBk,MBa,SHa,48-page. 3.50
25a signed 20.00
26 KBk,MBa,SHa,JoC,A:Mach-1 . . . 2.50
27 KBk,MBa,SHa,A:Archangel 2.50
28 KBk,MBa,SHa,V:Graviton 2.50
29 KBk,MBa,SHa,V:Graviton 2.50

Thunderbolts #1
© Marvel Entertainment Group

30 KBk,MBa,SHa,V:Graviton 2.50
31 KBk,MBa,SHa,R:Citizen V 2.50
32 KBk,MBa,SHa,V:Citizen V 2.50
33 KBk,MBa,SHa,F:Jolt 2.50
34 MBa,SHa. 2.50
35 FaN,MBa,SHa. 2.50
36 FaN,MBa,SHa,V:Beetle 2.50
37 FaN,MBa,SHa,A:Hawkeye 2.50
38 FaN,MBa,SHa,V:Citizen V 2.50
39 FaN,MBa,SHa,100-pg. 3.00
40 FaN,MBa,SHa,V:Citizen V 2.25
41 FaN,MBa,Sandman 2.25
42 FaN,MBa,Avengers x-over 2.25
43 FaN,MBa,Avengers x-over 2.25
44 FaN,MBa,Avengers x-over 2.25
45 FaN,MBa,Maximum Security . . . 2.25
46 FaN,MBa,V:Scourge. 2.25
47 FaN,MBa,A:Songbird 2.25
48 FaN,MBa,V:Scourge,pt.1 . . . . . . 2.25
49 FaN,V:Scourge,face shown 2.25
50 FaN,MBa,48-page. 4.00
51 FaN,AV,rescue mission. 2.25
52 FaN,AV,V:Dr.Doom 2.25
53 FaN,AV,F:Charcoal 2.25
54 FaN,AV,F:Fixer 2.25
55 FaN,AV,V:Redeemers 2.25
56 FaN,AV,V:Graviton 2.25
57 FaN,AV,V:Graviton 2.25
58 FaN,AV,V:Graviton 2.25
59 FaN,MBa,AV,Songbird,'NuffSaid. 2.25
60 FaN,MBa,AV,Chain Gang 2.25
61 FaN,Heroes Return,pt.2 . . . . 2.25
62 FaN,Heroes Return,pt.3 . . . . 2.25
63 FaN,Hawkeye,Screaming Mimi . 2.25
64 FaN,F:Zemo 2.25
65 FaN,V:Masters of Evil 2.25
66 FaN,F:Baron Zemo,Jolt 2.25
67 FaN,F:Harrier, Hawkeye 2.25
68 FaN,F:Moonstone,PhantomEagle2.25
69 FaN,AV 2.25
70 FaN, ... 2.25
71 FaN 2.25
72 FaN 2.25
73 FaN,AV 2.25
74 FaN 2.25
75 FaN,48-pg. 3.50
76 Fight club 2.25
77 JAr(s) 2.25
78 JAr(s) 3.00
79 JAr(s) 3.00
80 JAr(s),F:Spider-Man,pt.1 . . . . . . 2.25
81 JAr(s),F:Spider-Man,pt.2 . . . . . . 2.25
Continued As:

All comics prices listed are for *Near Mint* condition.

NEW THUNDERBOLTS
Nov., 2004
1 FaN,TG,Zeroes to Heroes,pt.1 . . 3.00
2 FaN,TG,Zeroes to Heroes,pt.2 . . 3.00
3 FaN,TG,Zeroes to Heroes,pt.3 . . 3.00
4 FaN,TG,Enemy of the State,
   Wolverine X-over 3.00
5 FaN,TG,V:Fathom 5 . . . . 3.00
6 FaN,TG,V:Hydra 3.00
7 Fan,TG,modern Marvels 3.00
8 FaN,TG,F:Speed Demon,Blizzard 3.00
9 FaN,TG,F:Photon 3.00
10 FaN,TG,Purple Reign,pt.1 . . . . . 3.00
11 FaN,TG,Purple Reign,pt.2 . . . . . 3.00
12 FaN,TG,Purple Reign,pt.3 . . . . . 3.00
13 FaN,TG,A:New Avengers 3.00
14 FaN,TG,A:New Avengers 3.00
15 FaN,TG,F:Songbird 3.00
16 FaN,TG,New Squadron Sinister . 3.00
17 FaN,TG,V:Baron Zemo 3.00
18 FaN,TG,R:Moonstone 3.00
Becomes:

THUNDERBOLTS
March, 2006
100 FaN,TG, V:Photon, 104-pg. . . . 4.00
101 FaN,TG, Zemo & Songbird 3.00
102 FaN,TG, V:Speed Demon 3.00
103 FaN,TG, Civil War tie-in 6.00
103a 2nd printing 3.50
104 FaN,TG, Civil War tie-in 4.00
105 FaN,TG, Civil War tie-in 3.00
106 FaN,TG, Supervillain Army 3.00
107 FaN,TG, Supervillain Army 3.00
108 FaN,TG, V:Grandmaster 3.00
109 FaN,TG, Weight of the World . . 3.00
110 MD2,Faith in Monsters, pt.1 . . . 3.00
111 MD2,Faith in Monsters, pt.2 . . . 3.00
112 MD2,Faith in Monsters, pt.3 . . . 3.00
112a variant PFe (c) 3.00
113 MD2,Faith in Monsters, pt.4 . . . 3.00
114 MD2,Faith in Monsters, pt.5 . . . 3.00
115 MD2,Faith in Monsters, pt.6 . . . 3.00
115a variant (c) 3.00
116 WEI,MD2,Caged Angels 3.00
117 WEI,MD2,Caged Angels 3.00
118 . . . . 3.00
Ann. '97 KBk,MBa,TGu,GP,
   O:Thunderbolts, 48-pg. 3.00
Ann.2000 FaN,NBy, 48-pg. 3.50
Spec.#0 Wizard Nov., 1998 . . . . . . 5.00
Spec.First Strikes, rep.#1 & #2 . . . . 5.00
Spec #1 Distant Rumblings KBk,
   SEp,Flashback,F:Citizen V 2.50
Spec.Life Sentences (2001) 3.50
Spec. Desperate Measures 3.00
Spec. Breaking Point (2007) 3.00

THUNDERBOLTS
PRESENTS: ZEMO –
BORN BETTER
1 (of 4) FaN,TG 3.00
2 thru 4 FaN,TG . . . . @3.00

THUNDERCATS
Star, Dec., 1985
1 JM,TV tie-in 10.00
1a 2nd printing 7.00
2 thru 10 . . . . @7.00
11 thru 24 . . . . @7.00

THUNDERSTRIKE
1993–95
1 B:TDF(s),RF,Holografx(c),
   V:Bloodaxe,I:Car Jack 3.25
2 RF,V:Juggernaut 2.25
3 RF,I:Sangre 2.25
4 RF,A:Spider-Man,I:Pandora 2.25
5 RF,A:Spider-Man,V:Pandora 2.25

6 RF,I:Blackwulf,Bristle,Schizo,Lord
   Lucian,A:SpM,Code:Blue,Stellaris,
   V:SHIELD,Pandora,C:Tantalus . 2.25
7 KP,V:Tantalus,D:Jackson 2.25
8 RF,I&V:Officer ZERO 2.25
9 RF,V:Bloodaxe 2.25
10 RF,A:Thor 2.25
11 RF,A:Wildstreak 2.25
12 RF,A:Whyte Out 2.25
13 RF,Inferno 42 . . . . 2.25
13a Double Feature flip book
   with Code Blue #1 . . . . 2.50
14 RF, Inferno 42 . . . . 2.25
14a Double Feature flip book 2.50
15 RF,V:Methisto 2.25
15a Double Feature flip book
   with Code Blue #3 . . . . 2.50
16 . . . . 2.25
17 V:Bloodaxe 2.25
18 V:New Villain 2.25
19 Shopping Network 2.25
20 A:Black Panther 2.25
21 A:War Machine,V:Loki 2.25
22 TDF,AM,RF,Mystery of Bloodaxe
   blows open 2.25
23 TDF,A:Avengers 2.25
24 TDF,V:Bloodaxe, final issue 2.25

TIMELY PRESENTS:
HUMAN TORCH COMICS
Aug., 1998
1-shot GN 6.00

TIMESLIP COLLECTION
Sept., 1998
1-shot, 48-page 3.00

TIMESLIP: THE COMING
OF THE AVENGERS
Aug., 1998
1-shot GN 6.00

TIMESPIRITS
Epic, Jan., 1985
1 TY 3.00
2 thru 8 . . . . @2.25

TIMESTRYKE
1 . . . . 2.25
2 . . . . 2.25

TINY TESSIE
See: TESSIE THE TYPIST

TOMB OF DARKNESS
See: BEWARE

TOMB OF DRACULA
April, 1972
1 GC,Night of the Vampire 300.00
2 GC,Who Stole My Coffin? 125.00
3 GC,TP,I:Rachel Van Helsing . . 100.00
4 GC,TP,Bride of Dracula! 100.00
5 GC,TP,To Slay A Vampire 100.00
6 GC,TP,Monster of the Moors . . . 75.00
7 GC,TP,Child is Slayer of
   the Man 75.00
8 GC(p),The Hell-Crawlers 75.00
9 The Fire Cross 75.00
10 GC,I:Blade Vampire Slayer . . . 250.00
11 GC,TP,Master of the Undead
   Strikes Again! 50.00
12 GC,TP,House that Screams 75.00
13 GC,TP,O:Blade 100.00
14 GC,TP,Vampire has Risen
   from the Grave 50.00
15 GC,TP,Stay Dead 50.00
16 GC,TP,Back from the Grave . . . 50.00

Tomb of Dracula #19
© Marvel Entertainment Group

17 GC,TP,A Vampire Rides This
   Train! 50.00
18 GC,TP,A:Werewolf By Night . . . 60.00
19 GC,TP,Snowbound in Hell 50.00
20 GC,TP,Manhunt For A Vampire 50.00
21 GC,TP,A:Blade 40.00
22 GC,TP,V:Gorna 30.00
23 GC,TP,Shadow over Haunted
   Castle 30.00
24 GC,TP,I am your Death 35.00
25 GC,TP,Blood Stalkers of Count
   Dracula 35.00
26 GC,TP,A Vampire Stalks the
   Night 30.00
27 GC,TP,...And the Moon Spews
   Death! 30.00
28 GC,TP,Five came to Kill a
   Vampire 35.00
29 GC,TP,Vampire goes Mad? . . . 30.00
30 GC,TP,A:Blade 30.00
31 GC,TP,Child of Blood 30.00
32 GC,TP,The Vampire Walks
   Among Us 30.00
33 GC,TP,Blood on My Hands 30.00
34 GC,TP,Bloody Showdown 30.00
35 GC,TP,A:Brother Voodoo 30.00
36 GC,TP,Dracula in America 30.00
37 GC,TP,The Vampire Walks
   Among Us 30.00
38 GC,TP,Bloodlust for a Dying
   Vampire 30.00
39 GC,TP,Final Death of Dracula . 30.00
40 GC,TP,Triumph of Dr.Sun 30.00
41 GC,TP,A:Blade 30.00
42 GC,TP,V:Dr.Sun 30.00
43 GC,TP,A:NewYear'sNightmare . 30.00
44 GC,TP,A:Dr.Strange 30.00
45 GC,TP,A:Hannibal King 30.00
46 GC,TP,W:Dracula & Domini . . . 20.00
47 GC,TP,Death-Bites 20.00
48 GC,TP,A:Hannibal King 20.00
49 GC,TP,A:Robin Hood,
   Frankenstein's Monster 20.00
50 GC,TP,A:Silver Surfer 30.00
51 GC,TP,A:Blade 15.00
52 GC,TP,V:Demon 15.00
53 GC,TP,A:Hannibal King,Blade . 15.00
54 GC,TP,Twas the Night Before
   Christmas 15.00
55 GC,TP,Requiem for a Vampire . 15.00
56 GC,TP,A:Harold H. Harold 15.00
57 GC,TP,The Forever Man 15.00
58 GC,TP,A:Blade 35.00
59 GC,TP,The Last Traitor 15.00
60 GC,TP,The Wrath of Dracula . . 15.00
61 GC,TP,Resurrection 15.00

62 GC,TP,What Lurks Beneath . . . 15.00
63 GC,TP,A:Janus 15.00
64 GC,TP,A:Satan 15.00
65 GC,TP,Where No Vampire
    Has Gone Before. 15.00
66 GC,TP,Marked for Death 15.00
67 GC,TP,A:Lilith 15.00
68 GC,TP,Dracula Turns Human . . 15.00
69 GC,TP,Cross of Fire 15.00
70 GC,TP,double size,last issue . . 30.00
Savage Return of Dracula. rep.
    Tomb of Dracula #1,#2 . . . . . . 2.50
Wedding of Dracula. rep.Tomb
    of Dracula #30,#45,#46 . . . . . . 2.50
Requiem for Dracula. rep.Tomb
    of Dracula #69,#70 . . . . 2.50

TOMB OF DRACULA
(B&W Mag.) Nov., 1979
1 . . . . 25.00
2 SD 18.00
3 FM 18.00
4 . . . . 15.00
5 . . . . 15.00
6 Sept., 1980 . . . . 15.00

TOMB OF DRACULA
[Mini-Series] Nov., 1991
1 GC,AW,Day of Blood 6.00
2 GC,AW,Dracula in D.C. 5.50
3 GC,AW,A:Blade 5.50
4 GC,AW,D:Dracula 5.50

TOMB OF DRACULA
2004
1 BSz(c) F:Blade. 3.00
2 . . . . 3.00
3 . . . . 3.00
4 Bsz(c). 3.00

TOMORROW KNIGHTS
Epic, June, 1990
1 . . . . 2.25
2 thru 6 . . . . @2.25

TOP DOG
Star, April, 1985
1 . . . . 3.00
2 thru 14, June, 1987 . . . . @3.00

Top Dog #9
© Marvel Entertainment Group

TOR
Epic *Heavy Hitters,* 1993
1 JKu,R:Tor,magazine format 6.25
2 JKu. 6.25
3 JKu,V:The Iduard Ring 6.25

TOUGH KID SQUAD COMICS
Marvel Timely, March, 1942
1 AAv,SSh,O:The Human Top,
   Tough Kid Squad,A:The Flying
   Flame, V:Doctor Klutch . . 18,000.00

TOWER OF SHADOWS
Sept., 1969
1 JR(c),JSo,JCr,At The Stroke
   of Midnight. 150.00
2 JR(c),DH,DA,NA,The Hungry
   One 100.00
3 GC,BWs,GT,Midnight in the
   Wax Museum. 100.00
4 DH,Within The Witching Circle . 75.00
5 DA,BWS,WW,Demon That
   Stalks Hollywood 75.00
6 WW,SD,Pray For the Man in
   the Rat-Hole 75.00
7 BWS,WW,Titano 75.00
8 WW,SD,Demons of
   Dragon-Henge. 75.00
9 BWr(c),TP,Lovecraft story 75.00
Becomes:

Creatures on the Loose #16
© Marvel Entertainment Group

CREATURES ON THE LOOSE
March, 1971
10 BWr,A:King Kull 75.00
11 DAy,rep. Moomba is Here. 30.00
12 JK,I Was Captured By Korilla . . 30.00
13 RC,The Creature
    From Krogarr. 30.00
14 MSe,Dead Storage 30.00
15 SD,Spragg the Living Mountain 30.00
16 GK,BEv,GK,B&O:Gullivar Jones,
    Warrior of Mars. 25.00
17 GK,Slaves o/t Spider Swarm . . 25.00
18 RA,The Fury of Phra. 25.00
19 WB,JM,GK,Red Barbarian
    of Mars 25.00
20 GK(c),GM,SD,The Monster...
    And the Maiden 25.00
21 JSo(c),GM,Two Worlds To
    Win,E:Guilliver. 25.00

22 JSo(c),SD,VM,B:Thongor,
    Warrior of Lost Lemuria. 28.00
23 VM,The Man-Monster Strikes . . 12.00
24 VM,Attack of the Lizard-Hawks 12.00
25 VM,GK(c),Wizard of Lemuria . . 12.00
26 VM,Doom of the Serpent Gods 12.00
27 VM,SD,Demons Dwell in the
    Crypts of Yamath. 12.00
28 SD,The Hordes of Hell 12.00
29 GK(c),Day of the Dragon Wings,
    E:Thongor,Warrior of Lemuria . 12.00
30 B:Man-Wolf,Full Moon, Dark
    Fear. 30.00
31 GT,The Beast Within. 15.00
32 GT,V:Kraven the Hunter 15.00
33 GK(c),GP,The Name of the
    Game is Death 15.00
34 GP,Nightflight to Fear 12.00
35 GK(c),GP 12.00
36 GK(c),GP,Murder by Moonlight. 12.00
37 GP,Sept., 1975 . . . . 12.00

TOXIC AVENGER
March, 1991
1 VM(i),I&O:Toxic Avenger 2.25
2 VM(i) 2.25
3 VM(i),Night of Living H.bodies. . . 2.25
4 Legend of Sludgeface 2.25
5 I:Biohazard. 2.25
6 V:Biohazard 2.25
7 Sewer of Souviaki 2.25
8 Sewer of Souviaki' conc. 2.25
9 Abducted by Aliens 2.25
10 Die,Yuppie Scum,pt.1 . . . . 2.25

TOXIC CRUSADERS
1992
1 F:Toxic Avengers & Crusaders . . 2.25
2 SK(c),V:Custard-Thing 2.25
3 SK(c),V:Custard-Thing. 2.25
4 V:Giant Mutant Rats 2.25
5 V:Dr.Killemoff 2.25
6 V:Dr.Killemoff 2.25
7 F:Yvonne 2.25
8 V:Psycho 2.25
[2nd Series]
1 . . . . 2.25
2 . . . . 2.25

TOXIN
April, 2005
1 (of 6) DaR 3.00
2 Dar,cut to the Chase 3.00
3 The Answer, My Friend 3.00
4 Zero Hour. 3.00
5 Razor Fist 3.00
6 DaR,V:Razor-Fist,concl. 3.00

TRANSFORMERS
[1st Regular Series] Sept., 1984
1 FS,Toy Comic 22.00
2 FS,OptimusPrime V:Megatron. . 13.00
3 FS.A:Spider-Man 11.00
4 MT(c),FS 10.00
5 Transformers Dead? 10.00
6 Autobots vs.Decepticons 10.00
7 KB,V:Megatron. 10.00
8 KB,A:Dinobots 10.00
9 MM,A:Circuit Breaker. 10.00
10 Dawn of the Devastator 10.00
11 HT 9.00
12 HT,V:Shockwave. 9.00
13 DP,Return of Megatron 9.00
14 DP,V:Decepticons 9.00
15 DP 9.00
16 KN,A:Bumblebee 9.00
17 DP,I:New Transformers,pt.1 . . . 9.00
18 DP,I:New Transformers,pt.2 . . . 9.00
19 DP,I:Omega Supreme. 9.00
20 HT,Skid vs.Ravage 9.00

MARVEL

21 DP,I:Aerialbots	9.00
22 DP,I:Stuntacons(Menasor)	9.00
23 DP,Return of Circuit Breaker	9.00
24 DP,D:Optimus Prime	9.00
25 DP,Decpticons (full story)	9.00
26 DP	9.00
27 DP,V:Head Hunter	9.00
28 DP	9.00
29 DP,I:Scraplets, Triplechangers	9.00
30 DP,V:Scraplets	9.00
31 DP,Humans vs. Decepticons	9.00
32 DP,Autobots for Sale	9.00
33 DP,Autobots vs.Decepticons	9.00
34 V:Sky Lynx	9.00
35 JRy,I:U.K.version Transformers	9.00
36	9.00
37	9.00
38	9.00
39	9.00
40 Autobots' New Leader	9.00
41	9.00
42 Return of Optimus Prime	9.00
43 Optimus Prime,Goldbug	9.00
44 FF,Return of Circuit Breaker	9.00
45 V:The Jammers	9.00
46 I:New Transformers	9.00
47 B:Underbase saga,I:Seacons	9.00
48 Optimus Prime/Megatron (past story)	9.00
49 Underbase saga cont.	9.00
50 E:Underbase saga,I:new characters	10.00
51 I:Pretender Decepticon Beasts.	10.00
52 I:Mecannibles,pt.1	10.00
53 Mecannibles,pt.2	10.00
54 I:Micromasters	10.00
55 MG	10.00
56 Return of Megatron	10.00
57 Optimus Prime vs.Scraponok	10.00
58 V:Megatron	10.00
59 A:Megatron,D:Ratchet	10.00
60 Battle on Cybertron	11.00
61 O:Transformers	11.00
62 B:Matrix Quest,pt.1	11.00
63	11.00
64 I:The Klud	11.00
65 GSr	15.00
66 E:Matrix Quest,pt.5	15.00
67 V:Unicorn,also Alternative World	15.00
68 I:Neoknights	15.00
69 Fate of Ratchet & Megatron revealed	15.00
70 Megatron/Ratchet fused together	15.00
71 Autobots Surrender to Decepticons	17.00
72 Decepticon Civil War, I:Gravitron	17.00
73 I:Unicron,A:Neoknights	17.00
74 A:Unicron & Brothers of Chaos.	17.00
75 V:Thunderwing & Dark Matrix.	17.00
76 Aftermath of War	17.00
77 Unholy Alliance	17.00
78 Galvatron vs.Megatron	22.00
79 Decepticons Invade Earth.	22.00
80 Return of Optimus Prime,final	35.00

[2nd Regular Series]

1 Split Foil(c),A:Dinobots	3.00
2 A:G.I.Joe,Cobra	2.25
3	2.25
4 MaG,V:Jhiaxus	2.25
5	2.25
6 V:Megatron	2.25
7 V:Darkwing	2.25
8 V:Darkwing	2.25
9	2.25
10 Total War	2.25
11	2.25

TRANSFORMERS COMICS MAGAZINE
1986–88

1 Digest-size	2.25
2 thru 11	@2.25

TRANSFORMERS, THE MOVIE
Dec., 1986–Feb., 1987

1 thru 3 Animated movie adapt.	@2.25

TRANSFORMERS UNIVERSE
Dec., 1986

1	3.00
2 &3	@3.00
4 March, 1987	3.00

TRANSMUTATION OF IKE GARUDA
Epic, 1991

1 JSh,I:Ike Garuda	4.00
2 JSh,conclusion	4.00

Trouble #3
© Marvel Entertainment Group

TROUBLE
Marvel Epic, June, 2003

1 MMr(s),Tyd,Teenage Romance	3.50
2 MMr(s),Tyd,photo (c)	3.00
3 MMr(s),Tyd,consequences	3.00
4 MMr(s),TyD,consequences	3.00
5 MMr(s),TyD,concl.	3.00

TROUBLE WITH GIRLS: NIGHT OF THE LIZARD
Epic *Heavy Hitters*, 1993

1 BBI,AW,R:Lester Girls	2.75
2 BBI,AW,V:Lizard Lady	2.25
3 BBI,AW,V:Lizard Lady	2.25
4 BBI,AW,last issue	2.25

TRUE COMPLETE MYSTERY
See: COMPLETE MYSTERY

TRUE LIFE TALES
Marvel Comics, 1949

1 (8) Ph(c)	125.00
2 Ph(c)	125.00

TRUE SECRETS
Marvel Atlas, 1950–56
Previously LOVE DIARY or OUR LOVE, depending on who you believe.

3	150.00
4	100.00
5	100.00
6 BEv	110.00
7	100.00
8 thru 10	@100.00
11 thru 21	@90.00
22 BEv	100.00
23	90.00
24 ViC	100.00
25 thru 28	@90.00
29 thru 39	@75.00
40 Sept., 1956	75.00

TRUE WESTERN
Dec., 1949

1 Ph(c),Billy the Kid	200.00
2 Ph(c),Alan Ladd,Badmen vs. Lawmen	250.00

Becomes:

TRUE ADVENTURES

3 BP,MSy,Boss of Black Devil	200.00

Becomes:

MEN'S ADVENTURES

4 AvB,He Called me a Coward	400.00
5 AvB,Brother Act	250.00
6 AvB,Heat of Battle	225.00
7 AvB,The Walking Death	225.00
8 AvB,RH,Journey Into Death	225.00
9 AvB,Bullets,Blades and Death	150.00
10 BEv,The Education of Thomas Dillon	150.00
11 Death of A Soldier	150.00
12 Firing Squad	150.00
13 RH(c),The Three Stripes	150.00
14 GC,BEv,Steel Coffin	150.00
15 JMn(c)	150.00
16 AyB	150.00
17 AyB	150.00
18 AyB	150.00
19 JRo	125.00
20 GC,RH(c)	125.00
21 BEv(c),JSt,The Eye of Man	250.00
22 BEv,JR,Mark of the Witch	250.00
23 BEv(c),RC,The Wrong Body	275.00
24 RH,JMn,GT,Torture Master	250.00
25 SSh(c),Who Shrinks My Head	450.00
26 Midnight in the Morgue	250.00
27 BP,CBu(c),A:Capt.America, Human Torch,Sub-Mariner	1,500.00
28 BEv,A:Capt.America,Human Torch, Sub-Mariner,July, 1954	1,400.00

TRUTH: RED WHITE BLACK
Nov., 2002

1 (of 7) untold Capt. America	3.50
2 thru 7 KB	@3.50
GN Truth, Red White & Black	4.00

TRY-OUT WINNER BOOK
March, 1988

1 Spider-Man vs. Doc Octopus	15.00

TV STARS
Aug., 1978

1 A:Great Grape Ape	40.00
2	35.00
3 ATh,DSt	35.00
4 A:Top Cat,Feb., 1979	30.00

2-GUN KID
See: BILLY BUCKSKIN

MARVEL

Two-Gun Kid #28
© Marvel Entertainment Group

TWO-GUN KID

Atlas, March, 1948—April, 1977
1 SSh,B:Two-Gun Kid,The
Sheriff 1,800.00
2 Killers of Outlaw City 750.00
3 RH,SSh,A:Annie Oakley 600.00
4 RH,A:Black Rider 600.00
5 RH 700.00
6 . . . . 600.00
7 RH,Brand of a Killer 600.00
8 Secret of the Castle of Slaves 600.00
9 JSe,SSh,Trapped in Hidden
Valley, A:Black Rider 600.00
10 JK(c),The Horrible Hermit
of Hidden Mesa 600.00
11 JMn(c),GT,A:Black Rider. 350.00
12 JMn(c),GT,A:Black Rider 350.00
13 . . . . 300.00
14 . . . . 300.00
15 thru 24 . . . . @300.00
25 AW,JMn 300.00
26 DAy,JMn 200.00
27 DAy,JMn 200.00
28 JMn 200.00
29 . . . . 200.00
30 AW 200.00
31 thru 44 . . . . @150.00
45 JDa 100.00
46 JDa 100.00
47 JDa 100.00
48 . . . . 100.00
49 JMn 100.00
50 . . . . 100.00
51 AW 100.00
52 thru 59 . . . . @100.00
60 DAy,New O:Two-Gun Kid . . . 150.00
61 JK,DAy,The Killer and The Kid 100.00
62 JK,DAy,At the Mercy of Moose
Morgan 100.00
63 DAy,The Guns of Wild Bill
Taggert. 75.00
64 DAy,Trapped by Grizzly
Gordon. 75.00
65 DAy,Nothing Can Save Fort
Henry 75.00
66 DAy,Ringo's Raiders. 75.00
67 DAy,The Fangs of the Fox 75.00
68 DAy,The Purple Phantom 75.00
69 DAy,Badman Called Goliath . . . 75.00
70 DAy,Hurricane 75.00
71 DAy,V:Jesse James 75.00
72 DAy,V:Geronimo 75.00
73 Guns of the Galloway Gang . . . 75.00
74 Dakota Thompson. 75.00
75 JK,Remember the Alamo 100.00

76 JK,Trapped on the Doom 100.00
77 JK,V:The Panther 100.00
78 V:Jesse James 60.00
79 The River Rats 60.00
80 V:The Billy Kid 60.00
81 The Hidden Gun 60.00
82 BEv,Here Comes the Conchos. 60.00
83 Durango,Two-Gun
Kid Unmasked 60.00
84 Gunslammer 60.00
85 Fury at Falcon Flats,
A:Rawhide Kids. 60.00
86 V:Cole Younger. 60.00
87 OW,The Sidewinder and the
Stallion 60.00
88 thru 101 . . . . @50.00
102 thru 136 . . . . @40.00

TWO-GUN KID: SUNSET RIDERS

1995
1 FaN,R:Two-Gun Kid,64-pg. 7.00
2 FaN,concl. 64-pg. 7.00

TWO GUN WESTERN
See: CASEY–CRIME PHOTOGRAPHER

2001: A SPACE ODYSSEY

Oct., 1976
1 JK,FRg,Based on Movie 10.00

2001: A SPACE ODYSSEY

Dec., 1976—Sept., 1977
1 JK,Based on Movie 25.00
2 JK,Vira the She-Demon 15.00
3 JK,Marak the Merciless 15.00
4 JK,Wheels of Death. 15.00
5 JK,Norton of New York 15.00
6 JK,Immortality ...Death 15.00
7 JK,The New Seed 15.00
8 JK,Capture of X-51,I&O:Mr.
Machine(Machine-Man) 20.00
9 JK,A:Mr Machine 15.00
10 Hotline to Hades,A:Mr Machine 15.00

2010

April, 1985
1 TP,movie adapt 2.25
2 TP,movie adapt,May, 1985 . . . . . 2.25

2099 A.D.

1995
1 Chromium cover 4.00

2099 APOCALYPSE

1995
1 . . . . 5.00

2099 GENESIS

1996
1 Chromium Cover 4.00

2099: MANIFEST DESTINY

March, 1998
GN LKa,MMK,F:Miguel
O'Hara, 48-pg. 6.00

2099 SPECIAL: THE WORLD OF DOOM

1995
1 The World of Doom 2.25

2099 Unlimited #5
© Marvel Entertainment Group

2099 UNLIMITED

1993–96
1 DT,I:Hulk 2099,A:Spider-Man 2099,
I:Mutagen. 4.50
2 DT,F:Hulk 2099,Spider-Man 2099,
I:R-Gang 4.25
3 GJ(s),JJB,F:Hulk & SpM 2099. . . 4.25
4 PR(c),GJ(s),JJB,I:Metalscream
2099,Lachryma 2099. . . . . 4.25
5 GJ(s),I:Vulx,F:Hazarrd 2099 . . . . 4.25
6 . . . . 4.25

Becomes:

2099 A.D. UNLIMITED

7 . . . . 4.25
8 F:Public Enemy 4.25
9 One Nation Under Doom. 4.25
10 V:Chameleon 2099 . . . . 4.25
Spec. #1 The World of Doom 2.25

2099: WORLD OF TOMORROW

1996–97
1 . . . . 2.50
2 . . . . 2.50
3 MMk,MsM,ATi,F:Spider-Man,
X-Men 2.50
4 ATi,X-Men 2099 discover secret . 2.50
5 ATi 2.50
6 PFe&ATi(c),Phalanx's final
assault 2.50
7 Spider-Man 2099 searches for his
brother: Green Goblin 2.50
8 Phalanx invasion aftermath 2.50
9 Humanity vs. Lunatika 2.50

TYPHOID

1995–96
1 ANo,JVF,Painted series 4.00
2 ANo,JVF,Hunt for serial killer. . . . 4.00
3 ANo,JVF,sex,blood & videotapes. 4.00
4 ANo,JVF,conclusion 4.00

ULTIMATE ADVENTURES (OF HAWK-OWL & ZIPPY)

Sept., 2002
1 JQ designs,U-Decide. 2.25
2 DFg 2.25
3 DFg 2.25
4 DFg,Hawk-Owl & Zippy 2.25
5 & 6 DFg . . . . @3.00

ULTIMATE DAREDEVIL & ELEKTRA
Nov., 2002
1 (of 4) DaM, at Columbia U. . . . 5.00
2 SvL,DaM 3.50
3 SvL,DaM 3.50
4 SvL,concl. 3.50

ULTIMATE ELEKTRA
Aug., 2004
1 (of 5) SvL,Devil's Due,pt.1 . . . 2.25
2 SvL,Devil's Due,pt.2 . . . . 2.25
3 SvL,Devil's Due,pt.3 . . . . 2.25
4 SvL,Devil's Due,pt.4 . . . . 3.00
5 SvL,Devil's Due,pt.5 . . . . 3.00

ULTIMATE EXTINCTION
Jan., 2006
1 WEl,BPe 3.00
2 thru 5 . . . . @3.00

ULTIMATE FANTASTIC FOUR
Dec., 2003
1 BMB,AKu,The Fantastic,pt.1 . . . 5.00
2 BMB,AKu,The Fantastic,pt.2 . . . 5.00
3 BMB,AKu,The Fantastic,pt.3 . . . 4.00
4 BMB,AKu,The Fantastic,pt.4 . . . 4.00
5 BMB,AKu,The Fantastic,pt.5 . . . 4.00
6 BMB,AKu,The Fantastic,pt.6 . . . 4.00
7 WEl(s),SI,Doom,pt.1 . . . . 4.00
8 WEl(s),SI,Doom,pt.2 . . . . 2.50
9 WEl(s),SI,Doom,pt.3 . . . . 2.50
10 WEl(s),SI,Doom,pt.4 . . . . 2.50
11 WEl(s),SI,Doom,pt.5 . . . . 2.50
12 WEl(s),SI,Doom,pt.6 . . . . 2.50
13 WEl,AKu,N-Zone,pt.1 . . . . . . 2.25
14 WEl,AKu,N-Zone,pt.2 . . . . . . 2.25
15 WEl,AKu,N-Zone,pt.3 . . . . . . 2.25
16 WEl,AKu,N-Zone,pt.4 . . . . . . 2.25
17 WEl,AKu,N-Zone,pt.5 . . . . . . 2.25
18 WEl,AKu,N-Zone,pt.6 . . . . . . 2.25
19 JaL,Think Tank,pt.1 . . . . 2.25
20 JaL,Think Tank,pt.2 . . . . 2.50
21 MMr(s),Crossover,pt.1 . . . . . . 6.00
22 MMr(s),Crossover,pt.2 . . . . . . 8.00
23 MMr(s),Crossover,pt.3 . . . . . . 7.00
24 MMr(s),,Tomb of Namor,pt.1 . . 2.50
25 MMr(s),Tomb of Namor. 2.50
26 MMr(s),Tomb of Namor. 2.50
27 MMr(s),President Thor, pt.1 . . . 2.50
28 MMr(s),President Thor, pt.2 . . . 2.50
29 MMr(s),President Thor, pt.3 . . . 3.00
30 MMr(s),Frightful, pt.1 . . . . 7.00
31 MMr(s),Frightful, pt.2 . . . . 7.00
32 MMr(s),Frightful, pt.3 . . . . 3.00
33 PFe,God War, pt.1 . . . . 3.00
34 PFe,God War, pt.2 . . . . 3.00
35 PFe,God War, pt.3 . . . . 3.00
36 PFe,God War, pt.4 . . . . 3.00
37 PFe, God War, pt.5 . . . . 3.00
38 PFe, God War, pt.6 . . . . 3.00
39 MCy(s),Diablo, pt.1 . . . . 3.00
40 MCy(s),Devils, pt.2 . . . . 3.00
41 MCy(s),Diablo, pt.3 . . . . 3.00
42 MCy(s),PFe,Silver Surfer,pt.1 . . . 3.00
43 MCy(s),PFe,Silver Surfer,pt.2 . . . 3.00
44 MCy(s),PFe,Silver Surfer,pt.3 . . . 3.00
45 MCy(s),PFe,Silver Surfer,pt.4 . . . 3.00
46 MCy(s),PFe,Silver Surfer,pt.5 . . . 3.00
47 Ghosts, pt.1 (of 3). 3.00
48 MCy(s),Ghosts, pt. 2 . . . . 3.00
Ann. #1 Enter the Inhumans 4.00
Ann. #2 Nursery Two 4.00

ULTIMATE IRON MAN
March, 2005
1 (of 5) AKu, Orson Scott Card(s) . 6.00
1a Variant Foil (C). 6.00

---

2 AKu,O:Ultimate Iron Man. 3.00
3 AKu,F:Rhodey Rhodes 3.00
4 AKu 3.00
5 AKu 3.00

ULTIMATE MARVEL
Flipbook, June, 2005
1 Ultimate X-Men #1
    & Ultimate Fantastic Four #1. . . 4.00
2 Ult.X-Men#2 & Ult. F.Four#2 . . . . 4.00
3 Ult.X-Men#3 & Ult. F.Four#3 . . . . 4.00
4 Ult.x-men#4 & Ult. F.four#4 . . . . 4.00
5 Ult.X-Men#5 & Ult. F.Four#5 . . . . 4.00
6 thru 11 . . . . @4.00
12 thru 20 . . . . 5.00

ULTIMATE MARVEL TEAM-UP
Feb., 2001
1 Spider-Man & Wolverine 5.00
2 Spider-Man & The Hulk 4.00
3 Spider-Man & The Hulk 4.00
4 Spider-Man & Iron Man 4.00
5 Spider-Man & Iron Man,MiA 4.00
6 Spider-Man & Punisher,BSz 3.50
7 Spider-Man & Daredevil,BSz 3.50
8 Spider-Man,Daredevil,Punisher . . 3.50
9 Spider-Man & Fantastic Four. . . . 3.50
10 Spider-Man & Man-Thing 3.50
11 BMB(s),Spider-Man & X-Men . . . 3.50
12 Spider-Man & Dr. Strange. 3.50
13 Spider-Man & Dr. Strange. 3.50
14 Spider-Man & Black Widow 3.50
15 Spider-Man & Shang-Chi 3.50
16 Spider-Man & Shang-Chi 3.50

ULTIMATE MARVEL MAGAZINE
May, 2001
5 thru 11, 80-page, rep. . . . . @4.00

ULTIMATE NIGHTMARE
Aug., 2004
1 (of 5) Tunguska 2.25
2 WEl(s) 2.25
3 WEl(s) 2.25
4 WEl(s) 3.00
5 WEl(s) 3.00

Ultimate Nightmare #5
© *Marvel Entertainment Group*

ULTIMATE ORIGINS
Nov., 2007
1 (of 6) BMB 3.00
1a variant (c) 3.00

ULTIMATE POWER
Oct., 2006
1 BMB(s),V:Squadron Supreme . . . 3.00
1a Director's Cut. 4.00
2 BMB(s),V:Squadron Supreme . . . 3.00
3 BMB(s). 3.00
4 MSz(s). 3.00
5 MSz(s). 3.00
6 MSz(s). 3.00
7 JLb(s). 3.00
8 JLb(s). 3.00
9 finale 3.00

ULTIMATES, THE
Jan., 2002
1 MMr,BHi,Nick Fury, heroes 6.00
2 MMr,BHi,Search for Cap.Am. . . 10.00
3 MMr,BHi,Cap.America lives. 8.00
4 MMr,BHi,no one to fight. 8.00
5 MMr,BHi. 10.00
6 MMr,BHi,celebrities 5.00
7 MMr,BHi,new additions 5.00
8 MMr,Quicksilver&ScarletWitch. . . 3.00
9 MMr,BHi. 3.00
10 MMr,BHi,F:Hawkeye. 3.00
11 BHi,PNe 3.00
12 BHi,PNe 3.00
13 BHi,Chitauri,concl.48-pg. 3.50
Spec. Must Have rep. #1–#3 . . . . . 4.00
Vol. 2
1 BHi 3.00

ULTIMATE SECRET
Dec., 2004
1 (of 4) WEl(s) 3.00
2 Wel(s), Mahr Vehl 3.00
3 WEl(s),V:Kree 3.00
4 WEl(s), conc. 3.00

ULTIMATE SIX
Sept., 2003
1 BMB,JQ,F:Villains 3.00
2 BMB,Sinister Six 3.00
3 BMB,Ultimate Spidey. 3.00
4 BMB,F:The Ultimates. 3.00
5 BMB,Spidey kidnapped 3.00
6 BMB,V:Sinister Six. 3.00
7 BMB,Green Goblin. 3.00

ULTIMATE SPIDER-MAN
Sept., 2000
1 BMB,JQ,MBa,ATi,A:Mary Jane
    48-pg.red card(c) 110.00
1A variant white (c) 175.00
1B Dynamic Forces (c) 65.00
2A BMB,MBa,ATi,Dr.Otto Octopus,
    car 50.00
2B Dynamic Forces JaL(c),
    Spider-Man swinging 35.00
3 BMB,ATi,MBa,A:Mary Jane 35.00
4 BMB,ATi,MBa,D:Uncle Ben 35.00
5 BMB,ATi,MBa,hand of fate,
    scarce 75.00
6 BMB,ATi,MBa,V:Green Goblin . . . 40.00
7 BMB,ATi,MBa,V:Green Goblin . . . 25.00
8 BMB,ATi,MBa,V:Shocker 20.00
9 BMB,ATi,MBa,V:Kingpin 12.00
10 BMB,ATi,MBa,V:Kingpin 9.00
11 BMB,ATi,MBa,V:Kingpin 9.00
12 BMB,ATi,MBa,V:Kingpin 9.00
13 BMB,ATi,MBa,Mary Jane 11.00
14 BMB,MBa,ATi,Doctor Octopus . . 9.00
15 BMB,MBa,ATi,Doctor Octopus . . 8.00
16 BMB,MBa,ATi,F:Ock,Kraven. . . . 8.00

    All comics prices listed are for *Near Mint* condition.

17 BMB,MBa,ATi,F:Justin Hammer . 7.00	70 BMB,MBa,Sorcerer Supreme . . . 2.25	7 MMr,BHi,Wolf in the Fold 3.00
18 BMB,MBa,ATi,Doc Oc kicks butt 7.00	71 BMB,MBa,Sorcerer Supreme . . . 2.25	8 MMr,BHi,Grand Theft America . . . 3.00
19 BMB,MBa,ATi,Justin Hammer . . 7.00	72 BMB,MBa,Hobgoblin,pt.1 . . . . . 2.25	9 MMr,BHi,Grand Theft America . . . 3.00
20 BMB,MBa,ATi,Doc Oc,Kraven . . 7.00	73 BMB,MBa,Hobgoblin,pt.2 . . . . . 2.25	10 MMr,BHi,Grand Theft America . . 3.00
21 BMB,MBa,ATi,vs. the press . . . 7.00	74 BMB,MBa,Hobgoblin,pt.3 . . . . . 2.25	11 MMr,BHi,Grand Theft America . . 3.00
22 BMB,MBa,ATi,R:Green Goblin	75 BMB,MBa,Hobgoblin,pt.4 . . . . . 2.25	12 MMr,BHi,Grand Theft America . . 4.00
+ Chapter 1, 54-pg. 7.00	76 BMB,MBa,Hobgoblin,pt.5 . . . . . 2.25	13 BHi,Grand Theft America 4.00
23 BMB,MBa,ATi,G.Goblin,G.Stacy . 7.00	77 BMB,MBa,Hobgoblin,pt.6 . . . . . 2.25	Ann.#1 The Reserves (2005). 4.00
24 BMB,MBa,ATi,Green Goblin deal 4.00	78 BMB,MBa,I:Mark Raxton 2.50	Ann.#2 F:Arnim Zola (2006) 4.00
25 BMB,MBa,ATi 4.00	79 BMB,MBa,Warriors,pt.1 . . . . 3.00	Spec. Must Have, rep. #1–#3 . . . . . 5.00
26 BMB,MBa,ATi,S.H.I.E.L.D. 3.00	80 BMB,MBa,Warriors,pt.2 . . . . 2.50	
27 BMB,MBa,ATi 3.00	81 BMB,MBa,Warriors,pt.3 . . . . 2.50	**ULTIMATE VISION**
28 BMB,MBa,ATi 3.00	82 MBa,Warriors,pt.4, Gang War. . . 2.50	**Nov., 2006**
29 BMB,MBa,ATi 3.00	83 MBa,Warriors,pt.5, Gang War. . . 2.50	1-shot Visions 3.00
30 BMB,MBa,ATi 3.00	84 BMB,MBa,Warriors,pt.6 . . . . . . 2.50	1 (of 5) BPe 3.00
31 BMB,MBa,ATi 3.00	85 BMB,MBa,Warriors,pt.7 . . . . . . 2.50	2 BPe 3.00
32 BMB,MBa,ATi 3.00	86 BMB,MBa,Silver Sable,pt.1 . . . . 2.50	3 BPe 3.00
33 BMB,MBa,ATi,V:Venom 10.00	87 BMB,MBa,Silver Sable,pt.2 . . . . 2.50	4 BPe 3.00
34 BMB,MBa,ATi,V:Venom 8.00	88 BMB,MBa,Silver Sable,pt.3 . . . . 2.50	5 . . . . 3.00
35 BMB,MBa,ATi,V:Venom 8.00	89 BMB,MBa,Silver Sable,pt.4 . . . . 2.50	
36 BMB,MBa,ATi,V:Venom 5.00	90 BMB,MBa,Silver Sable,pt.5 . . . . 2.50	**ULTIMATE WAR**
37 BMB,MBa,ATi,V:Venom 5.00	91 BMB,MBa,Deadpool,pt.1 . . . . . . 2.50	**Marvel Dec. 2002**
38 BMB,MBa,ATi,V:Venom,concl. . . 5.00	92 BMB,MBa,Deadpool,pt.2 . . . . . . 2.50	1 (of 4) CBa,X-Men vs. Ultimates . . 5.00
39 BMB,MBa,ATi,F:Nick Fury 2.50	93 BMB,MBa,Deadpool,pt.3 . . . . . . 3.00	2 CBa 4.00
40 BMB,MBa,Irresponsible,pt.1 . . . . 2.50	94 BMB,MBa,Deadpool,pt.4 . . . . . . 3.00	3 CBa 4.00
41 BMB,MBa,Irresponsible,pt.2 . . . . 2.50	95 BMB,MBa,Morbius 3.00	4 CBa,concl. 4.00
42 BMB,MBa,Irresponsible,pt.3 . . . . 2.50	96 BMB,MBa,Morbius V:Blade 3.00	
43 BMB,MBa,Irresponsible,pt.4 . . . . 2.50	97 BMB,MBa,Clone Saga,pt.1. . . . . 3.00	**ULTIMATE**
44 BMB,MBa,Irresponsible,pt.5 . . . . 2.50	98 BMB,MBa,Clone Saga,pt.2. . . . . 3.00	**WOLVERINE VS. HULK**
45 BMB,MBa,Irresponsible,pt.6 . . . . 2.50	99 BMB,MBa,Clone Saga,pt.3. . . . . 4.00	**Dec., 2005**
46 BMB,MBa,F:S.H.I.E.L.D.,40-pg . 3.00	100 MBa,Clone Saga,pt.4, 64-pg. . . 4.00	1 . . . . 3.00
47 BMB,MBa,Unfair,pt.1 . . . . 2.50	100a variant (c) 10.00	2 . . . . 3.00
48 BMB,MBa,Unfair,pt.2 . . . . 2.25	101 BMB,MBa,Clone Saga,pt.5. . . . 3.00	3 . . . . 3.00
49 BMB,MBa,Unfair,pt.3 . . . . 2.25	102 BMB,MBa,Clone Saga,pt.6. . . . 3.00	
50 BMB,MBa,Claws,pt.1 . . . . 3.00	103 BMB(s),MBa,Clone Saga,pt.7. . 3.00	**ULTIMATE X-MEN**
51 BMB,MBa,Claws,pt.2 . . . . 2.50	104 BMB(s),MBa,Clone Saga,pt.8. . 3.00	**Dec., 2000**
52 BMB,MBa,Claws,pt.3 . . . . 2.50	105 BMB(s),MBa,Clone Saga 3.00	1 AKu,ATi,MMr,48-page, card (c) . 25.00
53 BMB,MBa,Claws,concl. 2.25	106 BMB(s),MBa,Ultimate Knights . 3.00	1A Dynamic Forces (c) 30.00
54 BMB,MBa,Goes Hollywood,pt.1 . 3.00	107 BMB(s),MBa,Ultimate Knights . 3.00	1B Preview 30.00
54a Arachnoman variant 12.00	108 BMB(s),MBa,Ultimate Knights . 3.00	2 AKu,ATi,MMr,F:Wolverine 15.00
55 BMB,MBa,Goes Hollywood,pt.2 . 2.25	109 BMB(s),MBa,Ultimate Knights . 3.00	3 AKu,ATi,MMr,V:Magneto 7.00
56 BMB,MBa,Goes Hollywood,pt.3 . 2.25	110 BMB(s),MBa,Ultimate Knights. . 3.00	4 AKu,ATi,MMr,V:Magneto 7.00
57 BMB,MBa,Goes Hollywood,pt.4 . 2.25	110a variant (c) 3.00	5 AKu,ATi,MMr,One traitor? 7.00
58 BMB,MBa,Goes Hollywood,pt.5 . 2.25	111 BMB(s),SI 3.00	6 AKu,ATi,MMr,V:Magneto 7.00
59 BMB,MBa,Goes Hollywood,pt.6 . 2.25	111a variant (c) 3.00	7 AKu,ATi,MMr,Weapon X,pt.1 . . 10.00
60 BMB,MBa,Carnage,pt.1 . . . . . . 6.00	112 BMB(s),SI,Death of a Goblin . . 3.00	8 AKu,ATi,MMr,Weapon X,pt.2 . . . 7.00
61 BMB,MBa,Carnage,pt.2 . . . . . . 3.50	113 BMB(s),SI,Death of a Goblin . . 3.00	9 MMr,TR,SHa,Weapon X,pt.3 . . . . 7.00
62 BMB,MBa,Carnage,pt.3 . . . . . . 5.00	114 BMB(s),SI,Death of a Goblin . . 3.00	10 MMr,TR,SHa,Weapon X,pt.4 . . . 7.00
63 BMB,MBa,Carnage,pt.4 . . . . . . 2.25	115 BMB(s),SI,Death of a Goblin . . 3.00	11 MMr,AKu,ATi,Weapon X,pt.5. . . 5.00
64 BMB,MBa,Carnage,pt.5 . . . . . . 2.25	116 BMB(s),SI,Death of a Goblin . . 3.00	12 MMr,AKu,Weapon X,pt.6 . . . . . 5.00
65 BMB,MBa,Carnage,pt.6 . . . . . . 2.25	Ann.#1 More than you	13 AKu(c),F:Gambit 5.00
66 BMB,MBa,Switcheroo,pt.1 . . . . 2.25	Bargained for (2005). 6.00	14 AKu(c),F:Gambit,pt.2 . . . . 4.00
67 BMB,MBa,Switcheroo,pt.2 . . . . 2.25	Ann.#2 (2006) 3.00	15 AKu,MMr,Xavier's teachings . . . 4.00
68 BMB,MBa,F:Johnny Storm 2.25	Spec.1 Collected, rep.#1–#3 . . . . . 4.00	16 AKu,MMr,to Scotland 4.00
69 BMB,MBa,F:Johnny Storm 2.25	Spec.#1-#2-#3, 96-pg. 4.00	17 AKu,MMr,Proteus Saga,pt.2 . . . 4.00
	Spec.#1 all-star artists, 54-pg. 3.50	18 AKu,MMr,World Tour 4.00
	Spec. Must Have, rep. 4.00	19 AKu,MMr,World Tour,concl. 4.00
		20 AKu,MMr,World Tour,epilogue. . . 3.75
	ULTIMATES SAGA	21 MMr,DaM,Hellfire & Brimstone . 3.75
	Nov., 2007	22 MMr,DaM,Hellfire & Brimstone . 3.75
	Spec. 4.00	23 MMr,DaM,Hellfire & Brimstone . 3.75
		24 MMr,DaM,Hellfire&Brimstone . . . 3.75
	ULTIMATE TALES	25 MMr,DaM,AKu(c), Hellfire &
	Flipbook, June, 2005	Brimstone, 48-pg. 5.00
	1 Ultimate Spider-Man #0	26 MMr,AKu,Professor-X 5.00
	& Ultimate Spider-Man #1 . . . . . 4.00	27 MMr,AKu,V:Brotherhood 5.00
	2 Ultimate Spider-Man #2 & #3 . . . 4.00	28 MMr,AKu,V:Brotherhood 5.00
	3 Ultimate Spider-Man #4 & #5 . . . 4.00	29 MMr,AKu,Missing X-Man 5.00
	4 Ultimate Spider-Man #6 & #7 . . . 4.00	30 MMr,AKu,Storm's gang. 5.00
	5 Ultimate Spider-Man #7 & #8 . . . 4.00	31 MMr,AKu,V:Magneto. 5.00
	6 thru 13 . . . . @4.00	32 MMr,AKu,Ultimate fate 4.50
	14 thru 18. . . . . @5.00	33 MMr,AKu,Return of the King. . . . 3.50
		34 BMB,Blockbuster,pt.1 . . . . 6.00
	ULTIMATES 2	35 BMB,Blockbuster,pt.2 . . . . 3.25
	Dec., 2004	36 BMB,Blockbuster,pt.3 . . . . 3.25
	1 MMr,BHi. 3.00	37 BMB,Blockbuster,pt.4 . . . . 3.25
	2 MMr,BHi,Gods & Monsters 3.00	38 BMB,Blockbuster,pt.5 . . . . 3.25
	3 MMr,BHi,Trial of Incredible Hulk . 3.00	39 BMB,Blockbuster,pt.6 . . . . 2.75
	4 MMr,BHi,Nick Fury vs. Thor. . . . 3.00	40 BMB,New Mutants,pt.1 . . . . 3.00
	5 MMr,BHi,v:Thor. 3.00	41 BMB,New Mutants,pt.2. . . . . 2.75
	6 MMr,BHi,F:Hank Pym 3.00	

Ultimate Spider-Man #82
© Marvel Entertainment Group

42 BMB,New Mutants,pt.3	3.50
43 BMB,New Mutants,pt.4	2.25
44 BMB,New Mutants,pt.5	4.00
45 BMB,New Mutants,pt.6	2.25
46 BPe,The Tempest,pt.1	2.25
47 BPe,The Tempest,pt.2	2.25
48 BPe,The Tempest,pt.3	2.25
49 BPe,The Tempest,pt.4	2.25
50 NKu,Cry Wolf,pt.1	4.00
51 NKu,Cry Wolf,pt.2	2.25
52 NKu,Cry Wolf,pt.3	2.25
53 NKu,Cry Wolf,pt.4	2.25
54 SI,Longshot, pt.1	2.25
55 SI,Longshot, pt.2	2.25
56 SI,Longshot, pt.3	2.25
57 SI,The Most Dangerous Game	2.25
58 SI, A Hard Lesson	2.25
59 SI,F:Wolverine pt.1	2.25
60 SI,F:Wolverine & Storm,pt.2	2.50
61 SI,Magnetic North,pt.1	15.00
62 SI,Magnetic North,pt.2	2.50
63 SI,Magnetic North,pt.3	2.50
64 SI,Magnetic North,pt.4	2.50
65 SI,Magnetic North,pt.5	2.50
66 TR,Date Night,pt.1	2.50
67 TR,Date Night,pt.2	2.50
68 TR,Date Night,pt.3	2.50
69 Phoenix, pt.1	3.00
70 Phoenix, pt.2	3.00
71 Phoenix, pt.3	3.00
72 TR,Magical,pt.1	3.00
73 TR,Magical,pt.2	3.00
74 TR,Magical,pt.3	3.00
75 TR,Ultimate Cable,pt.1	4.00
76 TR,Ultimate Cable,pt.2	4.00
77 F:Ultimate Cable,pt.3	3.00
78 F:Ultimate Cable,pt.4	3.00
79 Aftermath, pt.1	3.00
80 Aftermath	3.00
81	3.00
82 The Underneath, pt.1	3.00
83 The Underneath, pt.2	3.00
84 Sentinels, pt.1	3.00
85 Sentinels, pt.2	3.00
86 Sentinels, pt.3	3.00
87 Sentinels, pt.4	3.00
88 Sentinels, pt. 5	3.00
Ann.#1 Ultimate Sacrifice (2005)	4.00
Ann.#2 F:Dazzler (2006)	4.00
Spec. #1-#2-#3, 96-pg.	4.00
Spec. rep. Must Have #1–#3	4.00

ULTIMATE X-MEN/ FANTASTIC FOUR
Dec., 2005

1 x-over	3.00
1 Ultimate F.Four/X-Men x-over	3.00

ULTRAFORCE/AVENGERS

1 V:Loki,A:Malibu's Ultraforce	4.00

ULTRAGIRL
[Mini-series] 1996

1 BKs,I&O:Ultra Girl	2.25
2 and 3 BKs	@2.25

ULTRA X-MEN COLLECTION

1 Metallic(c), art from cards	3.00
2 thru 5 art from cards	@3.00

ULTRA X-MEN III

Preview	3.00

ULTRON
June, 1999

1-shot Ultron Unleashed, rep.	3.50

UNCANNY ORIGINS
Sept., 1996

1 F:Cyclops	2.25
2 F:Quicksilver	2.25
3 DHv,BAn,F:Archangel	2.25
4 F:Firelord	2.25
5 MHi,F:Hulk	2.25
6 F:Beast	2.25
7 F:Venom	2.25
8 F:Nightcrawler	2.25
9 F:Storm	2.25
10 F:Black Cat	2.25
11 F:Luke Cage	2.25
12 F:Black Knight	2.25
13 LWn,MCa,F:Doctor Strange	2.25
14 LWn,MCW,F:Iron Fist	2.25

UNCANNY TALES
Marvel Atlas, June, 1952

1 RH,While the City Sleeps	1,300.00
2 JMn,BEv	750.00
3 Escape to What	600.00
4 JMn,Nobody's Fool	600.00
5 Fear	600.00
6 He Lurks in the Shadows	600.00
7 BEv,Kill,Clown,Kill	600.00
8 JMn,Bring Back My Face	500.00
9 BEv,RC,The Executioner	500.00
10 JMn,RH(c),JR,The Man Who Came Back To Life	500.00
11 GC,The Man Who Changed	350.00
12 BP,BEv,Bertha Gets Buried	350.00
13 RH,Scared Out of His Skin	350.00
14 RH,TLw,Victims of Vonntor	350.00
15 RA,JSt,The Man Who Saw Death	350.00
16 JMn,GC,Zombie at Large	350.00
17 GC,TLw,I Live With Corpses	350.00
18 JF,BP,Clock Face(c)	350.00
19 DBr,RKr,TLw,The Man Who Died Again	350.00
20 DBr,Ted's Head	350.00
21	300.00
22 DAy	300.00
23 TLw	300.00
24	300.00
25 MSy	300.00
26 Spider-Man prototype story	450.00
27 RA,TLw	300.00
28 TLw	325.00
29 JMn	250.00
30	250.00

31	250.00
32 BEv	250.00
33	250.00
34 BP	250.00
35 TLw,JMn	250.00
36 BP,BEv	250.00
37 MD	250.00
38 BP	250.00
39 BEv	250.00
40	250.00
41	250.00
42 MD	250.00
43	225.00
44	225.00
45 MD	225.00
46 GM	225.00
47 TSe	225.00
48 BEv	225.00
49 JO	225.00
50 JO	225.00
51 GM	250.00
52 GC	225.00
53 JO,AT	225.00
54	225.00
55	225.00
56 Sept., 1957	250.00

UNCANNY TALES FROM THE GRAVE
Dec., 1973—Oct., 1975

1 RC,Room of no Return	35.00
2 DAy,Out of the Swamp	25.00
3 No Way Out	25.00
4 JR,SD,Vampire	25.00
5 GK,GT,Don't Go in the Cellar	25.00
6 JR,SD,The Last Kkrul	25.00
7 RH,SD,Never Dance With a Vampire	25.00
8 SD,Escape Into Hell	25.00
9 JA,The Nightmare Men	25.00
10 SD,DH,Beware the Power of Khan	25.00
11 SD,JF,RH,Dead Don't Sleep	25.00
12 SD,Final Issue	25.00

UNCANNY X-MEN
See: X-MEN

UNDERWORLD
Feb., 2006

1 F:Jackie Dio	3.00
2 thru 5	@3.00

UNION JACK
Oct., 1998

1 (of 3) BRa,F:Joey Chapman	3.00
2 BRa,V:Baroness	3.00
3 BRa,conclusion	3.00

UNION JACK
Sept., 2006

1	3.00
2 thru 4	@3.00

UNIVERSE X
July, 2000

0 AxR,DBw,48-pg.	4.00
1 (of 12) AxR,DBw,Capt.MarVell.	3.50
2 AxR,DBw,	3.50
3 AxR,DBw,	3.50
4 AxR,DBw,Cap.Am vs. Hydra	3.50
5 AxR,DBw,Mar-Vell vs.Death	3.50
6 AxR,DBw,Moonknight	3.50
7 AxR,DBw,Supreme Intelligence	3.50
8 AxR,DBw,Monster Generation	3.50
9 AxR,DBw,Supreme Intelligence	3.50
10 AxR,DBw,V:Mephisto	3.50
11 AxR,DBw,A:Belasco	3.50
12 AxR,DBw,V:Absorbing Man	3.50

Ultragirl #1
© Marvel Entertainment Group

All comics prices listed are for *Near Mint* condition.

Spec."4",F:Fantastic Four 4.00
Spec. Spidey,AxR,JG,JR,48-page . . 4.00
Spec. Beasts,AxR,48-page 4.00
Spec. Omnibus,AxR. 4.00
Spec. Iron Men, 48-page 4.00
Spec. Universe X:X 48-page 4.00

UNKNOWN WORLDS OF SCIENCE FICTION
Jan., 1975
(Black & White Magazine)
1 AW,RKr,AT,FF,GC 30.00
2 FB,GP 25.00
3 GM,AN,GP,GC 25.00
4 . . . . 25.00
5 GM,NC,GC 25.00
6 FB,AN,GC,Nov., 1975 . . . . 25.00
Spec.#1 AN,NR,JB. 30.00

UNTAMED
Epic *Heavy Hitters*, 1993
1 I:Griffen Palmer 2.75
2 V:Kosansui. 2.25
3 V:Kosansui. 2.25

Untold Legend of Captain Marvel #2
© *Marvel Entertainment Group*

UNTOLD LEGEND OF CAPTAIN MARVEL, THE
1997
1 (of 3) Early days of Captain
  Marvel 2.50
2 Early days of Captain Marvel . . . 2.50
3 V:Kree 2.50

UNTOLD TALES OF SPIDER-MAN
Sept., 1995 – Sept., 1997
1 F:Young Spider-Man 3.00
2 V:Batwing. 2.25
3 V:Sandman 2.25
4 V:J.Jonah Jameson 2.25
5 V:Vulture 2.25
6 A:Human Torch 2.25
7 . . . . 2.25
8 . . . . 2.25
9 A:Batwing,Lizard 2.25
10 KBk,PO,I:Commanda 2.25
11 KBk,PO, ... 2.25
12 KBk,PO, ... 2.25
13 KBk,PO, ... 2.25
14 KBk,PO, ... 2.25

15 KBk,PO,AV,Gordon's plan to
  control the Bugle 2.25
16 Re-I:Mary Jane Watson 2.25
17 KBk,PO,AV,V:Hawkeye. 2.25
18 KBk,PO,AV,A:Green Goblin,
  Headsman. 2.25
19 KBk,PO,AW,F:Doctor Octopus . . 2.25
20 KBk,PO,AW,V:Vulture 2.25
21 KBk,PO,AW,V:Menace,A:Original
  X-Men 2.25
22 KBk,PO,AW,V:Scarecrow,. 2.25
23 KBk,PO,AW,V:Crime Master,
  A:Green Goblin 2.25
24 KBk,PO,BMc, Fate of Batwing . . 2.25
25 LBI,PO,BMc, V:Green Goblin,
  final issue 2.25
Minus 1 Spec., RSt,JR, flashback,
  Peter's parents 2.25
Ann.'96 1 KBk,MiA,JSt,A date with
  Invisible Girl?. 2.25
Ann.'97 KBk,TL,A:everyone, 48-pg. 3.00
one-shot GN KBk,SL,Encounter,
  A:Dr. Strange 48-pg. 6.00

UNTOLD TALES OF THE NEW UNIVERSE
March, 2006
D.P. 7 #1 . . . . 3.00
Justice #1. . . . . 3.00
Nightmask #1. . . . . 3.00
Starbrand #1 . . . . 3.00
PSI-Force #1 . . . . 3.00

U.S.A. Comics #15
© *Marvel Entertainment Group*

U.S.A. COMICS
Marvel Timely, Aug., 1941
1 S&K(c),BW,AAv,SSh,Bondage(c),
  The Defender(c) 24,000.00
2 S&K(c),BW,SSh, Capt.
  Terror(c) 6,500.00
3 S&K(c),SSh,Capt.Terror(c) . . 4,800.00
4 SSh,Major Liberty 4,000.00
5 Hitler(c),O:AmericanAvenger 4,200.00
6 ASh(c),Capt.America(c) 5,000.00
7 BW,O:Marvel Boy 5,000.00
8 ASh(c),Capt.America (c). . . . 3,500.00
9 ASh(c),Bondage(c), Captain
  America 3,500.00
10 ASh(c),Bondage(c), Captain
  America 3,500.00
11 SSh(c),Bondage(c), Captain
  America 2,500.00
12 ASh(c),Capt.America 2,500.00

13 ASh(c),Capt.America 2,500.00
14 AyB(c),Capt.America 2,000.00
15 Capt.America. 2,000.00
16 ASh(c),Bondage(c),
  Capt.America 2,000.00
17 Bondage(c),Capt.America . . 2,000.00

U.S. 1
May, 1983–Oct., 1984
1 AM(c),HT,Trucking Down the
  Highway 3.00
2 HT,Midnight 3.00
3 FS,ME,Rhyme of the Ancient
  Highwayman 3.00
4 FS,ME 3.00
5 FS,ME,Facing The Maze 3.00
6 FS,ME 3.00
7 FS,ME 3.00
8 FS,ME 3.00
9 FS,ME,Iron Mike-King of
  the Bike 3.00
10 thru 12 FS,ME. . . . . @3.00

U.S. AGENT
June–Dec., 1993
1 V:Scourge,O:U.S.Agent. 2.25
2 V:Scourge 2.25
3 V:Scourge 2.25
4 last issue 2.25

U.S. AGENT
May, 2001
1 (of 3) JOy,KK,Maximum Security. 3.00
2 JOy,KK, ... 3.00
3 JOy,KK,A:Capt.America. 3.00

U.S. WAR MACHINE
Marvel Max, Sept., 2001
1 (of 12) Weekly series,24-page. . . 2.25
2 thru 12 . . . . @2.25

U.S. WAR MACHINE 2.0
June, 2003
1 (of 3) V:Iron Man 3.00
2 . . . . 3.00
3 concl. 3.00

VALKYRIE
1996
1-shot JMD 2.50

VAMPIRE TALES
Aug., 1973
(black & white magazine)
1 BEv,B:Morbius the Living
  Vampire 90.00
2 JSo,I:Satana 60.00
3 A:Satana 50.00
4 GK 50.00
5 GK,O:Morbius The Living
  Vampire 60.00
6 AA,I:Lilith 50.00
7 HC,PG 50.00
8 AA,A:Blade The Vampire
  Slayer 65.00
9 RH,AA 50.00
10 . . . . 50.00
11 June, 1975 . . . . 50.00
Ann.#1 . . . . 50.00

VAULT OF EVIL
Feb., 1973—Nov., 1975
1 GK,B:1950's reps,Come
  Midnight,Come Monster 35.00
2 The Hour of the Witch 25.00
3 The Woman Who Wasn't 25.00
4 Face that Follows 25.00
5 Ghost 25.00

Vault of Evil #6
© Marvel Entertainment Group

6 GT,The Thing at the Window . . 25.00
7 Monsters 25.00
8 The Vampire is my Brother 25.00
9 Giant Killer 25.00
10 MD,The Lurkers in the Caves. . 25.00
11 JK,BEv,Two Feasts For
a Vampire 25.00
12 Midnight in the
Haunted Mansion 25.00
13 Hot as the Devil 25.00
14 SD,Midnight in the Haunted
Manor 25.00
15 SD,Don't Shake Hands with
the Devil 25.00
16 A Grave Honeymoon. 25.00
17 Grave Undertaking 25.00
18 The Deadly Edge 25.00
19 Vengeance of Ahman Ra 25.00
20 SD 25.00
21 Victim of Valotorr. 25.00
22 SD 25.00
23 Black Magician Lives Again . . . 25.00

VENOM
April, 2003
1 SK(c),Shiver,pt.1 . . . . 3.00
2 Shiver,pt.2 . . . . 2.50
3 SK(c),Shiver,pt.3 . . . . 2.50
4 SK(c),Shiver,pt.4 . . . . 2.50
5 SK(c),Shiver,pt.5 . . . . 2.50
6 . . . . 2.50
7 SK(c) 2.50
8 SK(c) Run,pt.3,F:Wolverine 3.00
9 SK(c) Run,pt.4 . . . . 3.00
10 Run,pt.5 . . . . 3.00
11 Patterns,pt.1 . . . . 3.00
12 Patterns,pt.2 . . . . 3.00
13 Patterns,pt.3 . . . . 3.00
14 Twist,pt.1 . . . . 3.00
15 Twist,pt.2 . . . . 3.00
16 Twist,pt.3 . . . . 3.00
17 Twist,pt.4 . . . . 3.00
18 Twist,pt.5 . . . . 3.00

VENOM: ALONG
CAME A SPIDER
1996
1 LHA,GLz,V:New Spider-Man 3.00
2 LHa,JPi,V:New Spider-Man 3.00
3 . . . . 3.00
4 conclusion, 48-pg. 3.00

VENOM: CARNAGE
UNLEASHED
1995
1 Venom vs. Carnage. 3.00
2 Venom vs. Carnage. 3.00
3 No Spider-Help 3.00
4 JRu,Wld,LHa,cardstock(c). 3.00

VENOM:
THE ENEMY WITHIN
1994
1 BMc,Glow-in-the-dark(C),
A:Demogoblin,Morbius 3.25
2 BMc,A:Demogoblin,Morbius 3.25
3 BMc,V:Demogoblin,A:Morbius. . . 3.25

VENOM: FINALE
1997–98
1 (of 3) LHa, ... 3.00
2 LJa, ... 3.00
3 LJa 3.00

VENOM: FUNERAL PYRE
1993
1 TL,JRu,A:Punisher. 3.50
2 TL,JRu,AM,V:Gangs 3.50
3 TL,JRu,Last issue 3.50

VENOM: THE HUNGER
1996
1 thru 4 LKa,TeH,V:Dr. Paine . . . @2.25

VENOM: THE HUNTED
1996
1 LHa,3 part mini-series 3.00

VENOM:
LETHAL PROTECTOR
1993
1 MBa,A:Spider-Man.holo-grafx(c) . 7.00
1a Gold Ed. 25.00
2 MBa,A:Spider-Man. 3.50
3 MBa,Families of Venom's
victims 3.50
4 RLm,A:Spider-Man,V:Life
Foundation. 3.50
5 RLm,V:Five Symbiotes,A:SpM. . . 3.50
6 RLm,V:Spider-Man. 3.50
Super Size Spec.#1 Planet of
the Symbiotes,pt.3. . . . . 4.00
Venom:Deathtrap:The Vault,RLm,
A:Avengers,Freedom Force . . . 7.00

VENOM: LICENSE TO KILL
1997
1 (of 3) LHa,KHt, sequel to Venom
on trial 2.25
2 LHa,V:Dr. Yes 2.25
3 LHa,V:Dr. Yes 2.25

VENOM: THE MACE
1994
1 Embossed(c),CP(s),LSh,I:Mace . 3.25
2 CP(s),LSh,V:Mace 3.25
3 CP(s),LSh,V:Mace,final issue . . . 3.25

VENOM: THE MADNESS
1993–94
1 B:ANi(s),KJo,V:Juggernaut 3.50
2 KJo,V:Juggernaut 3.25
3 E:ANi(s),KJo,V:Juggernaut 3.25

VENOM: NIGHTS
OF VENGEANCE
1994
1 RLm,I:Stalkers,A:Vengeance 3.25
2 RLm,A:Vengeance,V:Stalkers . . . 3.25
3 RLm,V:Stalkers 3.25
4 RLm,final issue 3.25

VENOM: ON TRIAL
Jan.–May, 1997
1 LHa,Tries to break out 2.25
2 LHa,Defended by Matt Murdock
(Daredevil),A:Spider-Man 2.25
3 LHa,A:Spider-Man, Carnage,
Daredevil 2.25

VENOM:
SEED OF DARKNESS
1997
1 LKa,JFy,Flashback, early Eddie
Brock 2.25

VENOM:
SEPARATION ANXIETY
1994–95
1 Embossed(c) 3.00
2 V:Symbiotes. 3.00
3 . . . . 3.00
4 . . . . 3.00

VENOM: SIGN
OF THE BOSS
1997
1 (of 2) IV,TDr,V:Ghost Rider 2.25
2 (of 2) IV,TDr,conclusion 2.25

VENOM: SINNER
TAKES ALL
1995
1 LHa,GLz,I:New Sin-Eater 3.00
2 V:Sineater 3.00
3 Wrong Man 3.00
4 LHa,GLz,V:Sin-Eater 3.00
5 LHa, finale 3.00

VENOM: TOOTH
AND CLAW
1996–97
1 (of 3) LHa,JPi,AM, Dirtnap usurps
Venom's body 2.25
2 LHa,JPi,AM,V:Wolverine 2.25
3 LHa,JPi,AM,V:Wolverine,
Chimera. 2.25

VENOM VS. CARNAGE
June, 2004
1 (of 4) 3.00
2 F:Black Cat 3.00
3 . . . . 3.00
4 F:Toxin 3.00

VENUS
Marvel Atlas, Aug., 1948
1 B:Venus,Hedy Devine,HK,Hey
Look 2,000.00
2 Venus(c) 1,300.00
3 Carnival(c) 1,100.00
4 Cupid(c).HK,Hey Look 1,100.00
5 Serenade(c) 1,100.00
6 SSh(c),Wrath of a Goddess,
A:Loki. 900.00
7 Romance that Could Not Be . . 900.00
8 The Love Trap 900.00
9 Whom the Gods Destroy 900.00

Venus #6
© Marvel Entertainment Group

10 JMn,B:Science Fiction/Horror,
   Trapped On the Moon 1,200.00
11 RH,The End of the World. . . 1,300.00
12 GC,The Lost World 1,200.00
13 BEv,King o/t Living Dead . . . 1,200.00
14 BEv,The Fountain of Death . 1,200.00
15 BEv,The Empty Grave 1,200.00
16 BEv,Where Gargoyles Dwell 1,300.00
17 BEv,Tower of Death,
   Bondage(c) 1,200.00
18 BEv,Terror in the Tunnel . . . 1,200.00
19 BEv,PMo, Kiss Of Death . . . 1,200.00

VERY BEST OF MARVEL COMICS
1-shot reps Marvel Artists
   Favorite Stories 13.00

VIDEO JACK
Nov., 1987
1 KGi,O:Video Jack 3.00
2 KGi. 2.50
3 KGi. 2.50
4 KGi. 2.50
5 KGi. 2.50
6 KGi,NA,BWr,AW 2.50

VISION, THE
1994–95
1 BHs,mini-series 2.25
2 BHs 2.25
3 BHs 2.25
4 BHs 2.25

VISION & SCARLET WITCH
[1st Series] Nov., 1982
1 RL,V:Halloween 3.00
2 RL,V:Isbisa,D:Whizzer. 3.00
3 RL,A:Wonderman,V:GrimReaper 3.00
4 RL,A:Magneto,Inhumans. 3.00
   [2nd Series] 1985–86
1 V:Grim Reaper. 2.50
2 V:Lethal Legion,D:Grim Reaper. . 2.50
3 V:Salem's Seven 2.50
4 I:Glamor & Illusion 2.50
5 A:Glamor & Illusion 2.50
6 A:Magneto 2.50
7 V:Toad 2.50
8 A:Powerman 2.50
9 V:Enchantress 2.50
10 A:Inhumans. 2.50
11 A:Spider-Man. 2.50

---

12 Birth of V&S's Child 8.00

VISIONARIES
Star, Nov., 1987
1 thru 5 . . . . @2.50
6 Sept., 1988 . . . . 2.50

VOID INDIGO
Epic, Nov., 1984
1 VM,Epic Comics 2.50
2 VM,Epic Comics,March, 1985 . . . 2.50

WACKY DUCK
See: DOPEY DUCK

WALLY THE WIZARD
Star, April, 1985
1 . . . . 4.00
2 thru 11 . . . . @4.00
12 March, 1986. . . . . 4.00

WAR, THE
1989
1 Sequel to The Draft & The Pit . . 4.00
2 . . . . 4.00
3 . . . . 4.00
4 1990. . . . . 4.00

WAR ACTION
Marvel Atlas, April, 1952
1 JMn,RH,War Stories, Six Dead
   Men 250.00
2 GT 125.00
3 Invasion in Korea 100.00
4 thru 10 . . . . @100.00
11 and 12 . . . . @125.00
13 BK. 125.00
14 Rangers Strike,June, 1953 . . . 100.00

WAR ADVENTURES
Marvel Atlas, Jan., 1952
1 GT,Battle Fatigue 200.00
2 The Story of a Slaughter 125.00
3 JRo 100.00
4 RH(c) 100.00
5 RH,Violent(c) 100.00
6 Stand or Die 100.00
7 JMn(c) 100.00
8 BK 125.00
9 RH(c) 100.00
10 JRo(c),Attack at Dawn 100.00
11 Red Trap 100.00
12 . . . . 100.00
13 RH(c),The Commies Strike
   Feb., 1953 . . . . 100.00

WAR COMBAT
Marvel Atlas, March, 1952
1 JMn,Death of Platoon Leader . 175.00
2 . . . . 125.00
3 JMn(c) 100.00
4 JMn(c) 100.00
5 The Red Hordes 100.00
Becomes:

COMBAT CASEY
6 BEv,Combat Casey cont 175.00
7 . . . . 125.00
8 JMn(c) 100.00
9 . . . . 100.00
10 RH(c). 125.00
11 . . . . 100.00
12 . . . . 100.00
13 thru 19 . . . . @125.00
20 . . . . 100.00
21 thru 33. . . . . @100.00
34 July, 1957 . . . . 100.00

War Comics #3
© Marvel Entertainment Group

WAR COMICS
Marvel Atlas, Dec., 1950
1 You Only Die Twice 350.00
2 Infantry's War 200.00
3 . . . . 125.00
4 GC,The General Said Nuts . . 125.00
5 . . . . 125.00
6 The Deadly Decision of
   General Kwang 125.00
7 RH,JMn 125.00
8 RH,No Survivors 125.00
9 RH,JMn 125.00
10 . . . . 125.00
11 Flame thrower 150.00
12 thru 21 . . . . @100.00
22 . . . . 125.00
23 thru 37 . . . . @100.00
38 JKu 125.00
39 . . . . 100.00
40 . . . . 100.00
41 . . . . 100.00
42 JO 125.00
43 AT,MD 125.00
44 . . . . 100.00
45 . . . . 100.00
46 RC 125.00
47 . . . . 100.00
48 MD,JO. 100.00
49 Sept., 1957 . . . . 125.00

WARHEADS
Marvel UK, 1992–93
1 GEr,I:Warheads,A:Wolverine, . . . 2.25
2 GEr,V:Nick Fury 2.25
3 DTy,A:Iron Man 2.25
4 SCy,A:X-Force 2.25
5 A:X-Force,C:Deaths'Head II . . . 2.25
6 SCy,A:Death's Head II. 2.25
7 SCy,A:Death's Head II,S.Surfer. . 2.25
8 SCy,V:Mephisto 2.25
9 SCy,V:Mephisto 2.25
10 JCz,V:Mephisto. 2.25
11 A:Death's Head II 2.25
12 V:Mechanix 2.25
13 Xenophiles Reptiles 2.25
14 last issue. 2.25

WARHEADS: BLACK DAWN
1 A:Gh.Rider,Morbius 3.25
2 V:Dracula. 2.25

All comics prices listed are for *Near Mint* condition.

MARVEL

WAR IS HELL
Jan., 1973—Oct., 1975
1 BP,B:reps.,Decision at Dawn . . 35.00
2 Anytime,Anyplace,War is Hell . . 20.00
3 Retreat or Die 20.00
4 Live Grenade 20.00
5 Trapped Platoon 20.00
6 We Die at Dawn 20.00
7 While the Jungle Sleeps,A:Sgt
    Fury 20.00
8 Killed in Action,A;Sgt Fury 20.00
9 B:Supernatural,War Stories . . . 60.00
10 Death is a 30 Ton Tank. 20.00
11 thru 15 . . . . @20.00

Warlock #15
© *Marvel Entertainment Group*

WARLOCK
[1st Regular Series] Aug., 1972
1 MGr,GK,I:Counter Earth,
    A:High Evolutionary. 90.00
2 MGr,JB,TS,V:Man Beast 50.00
3 MGr,GK,TS,V:Apollo 50.00
4 MGr,JK,TS,V:Triax 25.00
5 MGr,GK,TS,V:Dr.Doom 25.00
6 MGr,TS(i),O:Brute 25.00
7 MGr,TS(i),V:Brute,D:Dr.Doom . . 25.00
8 MGr,TS(i),R:Man-Beast(cont.
    in Hulk #176). 25.00
9 MGr,JSn,1st`Rebirth'Thanos,
    O:Magnus,N:Warlock,
    I:In-Betweener 40.00
10 MGr,JSn,SL,O:Thanos,V:Magus,
    A:In-Betweener 50.00
11 MGr,JSn,SL,D:Magus,A:Thanos,
    In-Betweener 40.00
12 MGr,JSn,SL,O:Pip,V:Pro-Boscis
    A:Starfox 25.00
13 MGr,JSn,SL,I&O:Star-Thief. . . . 25.00
14 MGr,JSn,SL,V:Star-Thief. 25.00
15 MGr,JSn,A:Thanos,V:Soul-Gem 40.00

[2nd Regular Series] 1992
1 JSn,rep.Strange Tales #178-180
    Baxter Paper 5.00
2 JSn,rep.Strange Tales #180
    & Warlock #9. . . . . 4.00
3 JSn,rep.Warlock #10-#12 . . . . . 4.00
4 JSn,rep.Warlock #13-#15 . . . . . 4.00
5 JSn,rep.Warlock #15 . . . . 4.00
6 JSn,rep. 4.00

WARLOCK
[Limited Series]
1 Rep.Warlock Series 3.50
2 thru 6 Rep.Warlock Series . . . @3.00

WARLOCK
Sept., 1998
1 (of 4) TL,RJn,R:Adam Warlock . . 3.00
2 TL,murderer revealed 3.00
3 TL,V:Drax. 3.00
4 TL,Concl. 3.00

WARLOCK
Aug., 1999
1 LSi,PFe,Marvel Tech 3.00
2 LSi,PFe,A:Iron Man 2.50
2a variant PFe cover 2.50
3 LSi,PFe,MMo,F:Psiren. 2.50
4 LSi,PFe,MMo,V:Mole Man. 2.50
5 LSi,PFe,MMo. 2.50
6 LSi,PFe,MMo,A:Kitty Pryde 2.50
7 LSi,PFe,MMo,R:Wolfsbane,
    Magus 2.50
8 LSi,PFe,MMo,V:Bastion. 2.50
9 LSi,PFe,MMo,F:Bastion. 2.50

WARLOCK
Sept., 2004
1 CAd,F:Adam Warlock 3.00
2 CAd 3.00
3 CAd 3.00
4 CAd 3.00

WARLOCK AND THE
INFINITY WATCH
1992–95
1 AMe,Trial of the Gods(from
    Infinity Gauntlet) 3.00
2 AMe,I:Infinity Watch(Gamora,Pip,
    Moondragon,Drax & 1 other). . . 2.75
3 RL,TA,A:High Evolutionary,
    Nobilus,I:Omega 2.75
4 RL,TA,V:Omega. 2.50
5 AMe,TA,V:Omega. 2.50
6 AMe,V:Omega(Man-Beast) 2.50
7 TR,TA,V:Mole Man,A:Thanos . . 2.50
8 TR,TA,Infinity War,A:Thanos . . . 2.25
9 AMe,TA,Inf.War,O:Gamora 2.25
10 AMe,Inf.War,Thanos vs
    Doppleganger 2.50
11 O:Pip,Gamora,Drax,M'dragon. . 2.25
12 TR,Drax Vs.Hulk 2.25
13 TR,Drax vs Hulk 2.25
14 AMe,V:United Nations. 2.25
15 AMe,Magnus,Him 2.25
16 TGr,I:Count Abyss. 2.25
17 TGr,I:Maxam 2.25
18 AMe,Inf.Crusade,N:Pip 2.25
19 TGr,A:Hulk,Wolverine,Infinity
    Crusade 2.25
20 AMe,Inf.Crusade 2.25
21 V:Thor 2.25
22 AMe,Infinity Crusade. 2.25
23 JSn(s),TGb,Blood &
    Thunder#4 . . . . 2.25
24 JSn(s),TGb,V:Geirrodur 2.25
25 JSn(s),AMe,Die-Cut(c),Blood &
    Thunder #12 . . . . 3.50
26 A:Avengers 2.25
27 TGb,V:Avengers 2.25
28 TGb,V:Man-Beast. 2.25
29 A:Maya 2.25
30 PO. 2.25
31 . . . . 2.25
32 Heart & Soul 2.25
33 V:Count Abyss 2.25
34 V:Count Abyss 2.25
35 V:Tyrannus 2.25
36 . . . . 2.25
37 A:Zaharius. 2.25
38 . . . . 2.25
39 V:Domitron 2.25
40 A:Thanos. 2.25
41 Monster Island 2.25

42 Warlock vs. Maxam, Atlantis
    Rising, final issue 2.25

WARLOCK CHRONICLES
1993–94
1 TR,F:Adam Warlock,holo-grafx(c),
    I:Darklore,Meer'lyn 3.25
2 TR,Infinity Crusade,Thanos revealed
    to have the Reality Gem 2.25
3 TR,A:Mephisto. 2.25
4 TR,A:Magnus. 2.25
5 TR(c),Inf.Crusade 2.25
6 TR,Blood & Thunder,pt.#3 . . . . . 2.25
7 TR,Blood & Thunder,pt.#7 . . . . . 2.25
8 TR,Blood & Thunder,pt.#11 . . . . 2.25
9 TR 2.25
10 TR 2.25
11 TR 2.25

War Machine #12
© *Marvel Entertainment Group*

WAR MACHINE
1994–96
1 GG,Foil Embossed(c),B:LKa&StB,
    O:War Machine,V:Cable,
    C:Deathlok. 3.25
1a Newstand Ed. 2.25
2 GG,V:Cable,Deathlok,w/card . . . 3.25
3 GG,V:Cable,Deathlok. 3.25
4 GG,C:Force Works. 3.25
5 GG,I:Deachtoll 3.25
6 GG,V:Deathtoll 3.25
7 GG,A:Hawkeye 3.25
8 reg ed. 3.25
8a neon(c),w/insert print. 3.00
9 Hands of Mandarin,pt.2 . . . . 2.25
10 Hands of Mandarin,pt.5 . . . . . . 2.25
11 X-Mas Party 2.25
12 V:Terror Device. 2.25
13 V:The Rush Team 2.25
14 A:Force Works 2.25
15 In The Past of WWII 2.25
16 DAn,A:Rick Fury,Cap.America . . 2.25
17 The Man Who Won WWII. 2.25
18 DAn,N:War Machine 2.25
19 DAn,A:Hawkeye 2.25
20 DAn,The Crossing 2.25
21 DAn,The Crossing 2.25
22 DAn,V:Iron Man 2.25
23 DAn,Avengers:Timeslide. 2.25

WAR MAN
Epic, 1993
1 thru 2 CDi(s) 2.50

WEAPON X
1995
1 Wolverine After Xavier	4.00
2 Full Scale War	2.25
3 Jean Leaves	2.25
4 F:Gateway	2.25

WEAPON X
Aug., 2002
1-shot Wild Child #1, JWi	2.50
1-shot Sauron #1, JWi,KIK	2.50
1-shot Kane #1, JWi	2.50
1-shot Marrow #1, JWi	2.50
1-shot Agent Zero #1, JWi	2.50
1	2.25
2 F:Marrow	2.25
3	2.25
4 Hunt for Sabretooth	2.25
5 Evil plans,D.Maggot	3.00
6 NRd,special mission	2.25
7 The Underground,pt.1	2.25
8 The Underground,pt.2	3.00
9 The Underground,pt.3	3.00
10 The Underground,pt.4	3.00
11 The Underground,pt.5	3.00
12 The Underground,pt.6	3.00
13 The Underground,concl.	3.00
14 R:Mr. Sinister	3.00
15 Defection,pt.1,F:X-Man	3.00
16 Defection,pt.2	3.00
17 Defection,pt.3	3.00
18 Defection,pt.4	3.00
19 Countdown to Zero,pt.1	3.00
20 Countdown to Zero,pt.2	3.00
21 Countdown to Zero,pt.3	3.00
22 Mutant feared	3.00
23 TMd,War of the Programs,pt.1	3.00
24 TMd,War of the Programs,pt.2	3.00
25 TMd,War of the Programs,pt.3	3.00
26 TMd,Man and Superman,pt.1	3.00
27 TMd,Man and Superman,pt.2	3.00
28 TMd,Man and Superman,pt.3	3.00

WEAPON X:
DAYS OF FUTURE NOW
July, 2005
1 (of 5) BS	3.00
2 Bs.	3.00
3 BS(c),	3.00
4 BS,Lord Magnus	3.00
5 BS	3.00

WEAVEWORLD
Epic, 1991–92
1 MM, Clive Barker adaptation	5.00
2 MM,Into the Weave	5.00
3 MM.	5.00

WEB OF
SCARLET SPIDER
1995–96
1 TDF,Virtual Mortality,pt.1	2.00
2 TDF,CyberWar,pt.2	2.00
3 Nightmare in Scarlet,pt.1	2.00
4 Nightmare in Scarlet,pt.3	2.00

WEB OF SPIDER-MAN
April, 1985
1 JM,V:New Costume	20.00
2 JM,V:Vulture	15.00
3 JM,V:Vulture	15.00
4 JM,JBy,V:Dr.Octopus	7.00
5 JM,JBy,V:Dr.Octopus	7.00
6 MZ,BL,JM,Secret Wars II	7.00
7 SB,A:Hulk,V:Nightmare, C:Wolverine	7.00
8 V:Smithville Thunder	7.00
9 V:Smithville Thunder	7.00

10 JM,A:Dominic Fortune, V:Shocker	7.00
11 BMc,V:Thugs	7.00
12 BMc,SB,V:Thugs	7.00
13 BMc,V:J.JonahJameson	7.00
14 KB,V:Black Fox	7.00
15 V:Black Fox,I:Chance	6.00
16 MS,KB,V:Magma	6.00
17 MS,V:Magma	7.00
18 MS,KB,Where is Spider-Man?	10.00
19 MS,BMc,I:Solo,Humbug	7.00
20 MS,V:Terrorists	7.00
21 V:Fake Spider-Man	7.00
22 MS,V:Terrorists	7.00
23 V:Slyde	7.00
24 SB,V:Vulture,Hobgoblin	7.00
25 V:Aliens	7.00
26 V:Thugs	7.00
27 V:Headhunter	7.00
28 BL,V:Thugs	7.00
29 A:Wolverine,2nd App:New Hobgoblin	9.00
30 KB,O:Rose,C:Daredevil,Capt. America,Wolverine,Punisher	9.00
31 MZ,BMc,V:Kraven	8.00
32 MZ,BMc,V:Kraven	8.00
33 BSz(c),SL,V:Kingpin,Mad Dog Ward,pt.#1	6.00
34 SB,A:Watcher	6.00
35 AS,V:Living Brain	6.00
36 AS,V:Phreak Out,I:Tombstone	7.00
37 V:Slasher	7.00
38 AS,A:Tombstone,V:Hobgoblin	7.00
39 AS,V:Looter(Meteor Man)	6.00
40 AS,V:Cult of Love	6.00
41 AS,V:Cult of Love	6.00
42 AS,V:Cult of Love	6.00
43 AS,V:Cult of Love	6.00
44 AS,V:Warzone,A:Hulk	5.00
45 AS,V:Vulture	5.00
46 A:Dr.Pym,V:Nekra	5.00
47 AS,V:Hobgoblin	6.00
48 AS,O:New Hobgoblin's Demonic Power	10.00
49 VM,V:Drugs	5.00
50 AS,V:Chameleon(double size)	7.00
51 MBa,V:Chameleon,Lobo Bros.	5.00
52 FS,JR,O:J.Jonah Jameson V:Chameleon	5.00
53 MBa,V:Lobo Bros.,C:Punisher A:Chameleon	5.00
54 AS,V:Chameleon,V:Lobo Bros.	5.00
55 AS,V:Chameleon,Hammerhead, V:Lobo Bros.	5.00
56 AS,I&O:Skin Head, A:Rocket Racer	5.00
57 AS,D:SkinHead, A:Rocket Racer	5.00
58 AS,V:Grizzly	5.00
59 AS,Acts of Vengeance,V:Titania A:Puma,Cosmic Spider-Man	7.00
60 AS,A of V,V:Goliath	5.00
61 AS,A of V,V:Dragon Man	5.00
62 AS,V:Molten Man	5.00
63 AS,V:Mister Fear	3.00
64 AS,V:Graviton,Titania,Trapster	3.00
65 AS,V:Goliath,Trapster,Graviton	3.00
66 AS,V:Tombstone,A:G.Goblin	3.00
67 AS,A:GreenGoblin, V:Tombstone	3.00
68 AS,A:GreenGoblin, V:Tombstone	3.00
69 AS,V:Hulk	4.00
70 AS,I:The Spider/Hulk	4.00
71 A:Silver Sable	3.00
72 AM,A:Silver Sable	3.00
73 AS,A:Human Torch, Colossus,Namor	3.00
74 AS,I:Spark,V:Bora	3.00
75 AS,C:New Warriors	3.00
76 AS,Spidey in Ice	3.00
77 AS,V:Firebrand,Inheritor	3.00

Web of Spider-Man #103
© Marvel Entertainment Group

78 AS,A:Firebrand,Cloak&Dagger	3.00
79 AS,V:Silvermane	3.00
80 AS,V:Silvermane	3.00
81 I:Bloodshed	3.00
82 V:Man Mountain Marko	3.00
83 V:A.I.M. Supersuit	3.00
84 AS,B:Name of the Rose	3.00
85 AS,Name of the Rose	3.00
86 AS,I:Demogoblin	3.00
87 AS,I:Praetorian Guard	3.00
88 AS,Name of the Rose	3.00
89 AS,E:Name of the Rose, I:Bloodrose	3.00
90 AS,30th Ann.,w/hologram, polybagged,V:Mysterio	3.50
90a Gold 2nd printing	3.00
91 AS,V:Whisper And Pulse	3.00
92 AS,V:Foreigner	3.00
93 AS,BMc,V:Hobgoblin,A:Moon Knight,Foreigner	3.00
94 AS,V:Hobgoblin,A:MoonKnight	3.00
95 AS,Spirits of Venom#1,A:Venom, J.Blaze,GR,V:Hag & Troll	3.00
96 AS,Spirits of Venom#3, A:G.R, J.Blaze,Venom,Hobgoblin	3.00
97 AS,I:Dr.Trench,V:Bloodrose	3.00
98 AS,V:Bloodrose,Foreigner	3.00
99 I:Night Watch,V:New Enforcer	3.00
100 AS,JRu,V:Enforcers,Bloodrose, Kingpin(Alfredo),I:Spider Armor, O:Night Watch,Holografx(c).	4.00
101 AS,Total Carnage,V:Carnage, Shriek,A:Cloak and Dagger, Venom	3.00
102 Total Carnage#6,V:Carnage, A:Venom,Morbius	3.00
103 AS,Maximum Carnage#10, V:Carnage	3.00
104 AS,Infinity Crusade	2.50
105 AS,Infinity Crusade	2.50
106 AS,Infinity Crusade	2.75
107 AS,A:Sandman,Quicksand	2.50
108 B:TKa(s),AS,I:Sandstorm, BU:Cardiac	2.50
109 AS,V:Shocker,A:Night Thrasher, BU:D:Calypso	2.50
110 AS,I:Warrant,A:Lizard	2.50
111 AS,V:Warrant,Lizard	2.50
112 AS,Pursuit#3,V:Chameleon, w/card	2.50
113 AS,A:Gambit,Black Cat,w/cel	3.50
113a Newsstand Ed.	2.50
114 AS	2.50
115 AS,V:Facade	2.50

116 AS,V:Facade 2.50
117 Foil(c), flip book with
    Power & Responsibility #1 . . . . 5.00
117a Newsstand ed. 2.50
118 Spider-clone, V:Venom 3.00
119 Clone,V:Venom 3.00
119a bagged with Milestone rep.
    Amazing Sp-Man #150,checklist 8.00
120 Web of Life,pt.1. . . . . 2.50
121 Web of Life,pt.3. . . . . 2.50
122 Smoke and Mirrors,pt.1 . . . . . 2.50
123 The Price of Truth,pt.2 . . . . . . 2.25
124 The Mark of Kaine,pt.1 . . . . . . 2.00
125 R:Gwen Stacy. 3.00
125a 3-D Holodisk cover 4.25
126 The Trial of Peter Parker,pt.1 . . 2.25
127 Maximum Clonage,pt.2 . . . . . . 2.25
128 TDF,Exiled,pt.1 . . . . 2.50
129 Timebomb,pt.2 . . . . 3.00
Ann.#1 V:Future Max 7.00
Ann.#2 AAd,MMi,A:Warlock 10.00
Ann.#3 AS,DP,JRu,JM,BL 4.50
Ann.#4 AS,TM,RLm,Evolutionary
    Wars,A:Man Thing,V:Slug 5.00
Ann.#5 AS,SD,JS,Atlantis
    Attacks,A:Fantastic Four 4.00
Ann.#6 GK,SD,JBr,SB,A:Punisher. . 4.50
Ann.#7 Vibranium Vendetta #3 . 3.50
Ann.#8 Hero Killers#3,A:New
    Warriors,BU:Venom,Black Cat . 3.50
Ann.#9 CMa,I:Cadre,w/card. 3.50
Ann.#10 V:Shriek 4.00
Super Size Spec.#1 Planet of
    the Symbiotes,pt.5. . . . . 4.00

WEBSPINNERS: TALES
OF SPIDER-MAN
Nov., 1998

1 JMD,JR,MZi,A:Mysterio,seq.to
    Amaz.Sp-M#38, 48-page. 3.00
1a signed 7.00
2 JMD,JR,V:J.Jonah Jameson 2.50
2a variant SR cover 2.50
3 JMD, V:Mysterio, concl. 2.50
4 KG,ErS,seq.to Silver Surfer#18 . 2.50
5 KG,ErS,A:Silver Surfer. 2.50
6 KG,ErS,F:Silver Surfer,
    Psycho-Man & Annihilus 2.50
7 BS,MPn,V:Sandman 2.50
8 BS,MPn,V:Sandman 2.50
9 V:Sandman 2.50
10 V:Chameleon, pt.1 . . . . 2.50
11 V:Chameleon, pt.2 . . . . 2.50
12 conclusion, 48-pg. 3.50
13 . . . . 2.50
14 HMe,BS,A:Carnage 2.50
15 V:Vulture 2.50
16 V:Vulture 2.50
17 TDF, black costume 2.50
18 TDF, Silversable 2.50

WEIRD WONDERTALES
Dec., 1973

1 B:Reprints 45.00
2 I Was Kidnapped by a Flying
    Saucer 25.00
3 BP,The Thing in the Bog 25.00
4 SD,SK,It Lurks Behind
    the Wall 25.00
5 SD 25.00
6 The Man Who Owned a Ghost . 25.00
7 BP,The Apes That Walked
    like Men 25.00
8 JMn,Reap A Deadly Harvest . 25.00
9 The Murder Mirror 25.00
10 SD,SK,Mister Morgan's
    Monster 25.00
11 SD, SK,Slaughter in
    Shrangri-La 20.00
12 SD,MD,The Stars Scream
    Murder 20.00

13 SD,The Totem Strikes 20.00
14 Witching Circle 20.00
15 . . . . 20.00
16 GC,The Shark. 20.00
17 Creature From Krogarr 20.00
18 Krang 20.00
19 SD,A:Dr Druid. 20.00
20 SD,MD,The Madness 20.00
21 SD,A:Dr Druid 20.00
22 The World Below,May, 1975 . . . 20.00

WENDY PARKER COMICS
Marvel Atlas, 1953

1 . . . . 150.00
2 . . . . 100.00
3 . . . . 125.00
4 . . . . 125.00
5 . . . . 125.00
6 . . . . 125.00
7 . . . . 125.00
8 . . . . 125.00

WEREWOLF BY NIGHT
Sept., 1972

1 MP(cont from Marvel Spotlight)
    FullMoonRise..WerewolfKill. . 200.00
2 MP,Like a Wild Beast at Bay . . . 75.00
3 MP,Mystery of the Mad Monk . . 50.00
4 MP,The Danger Game 50.00
5 MP,A Life for a Death 50.00
6 MP,Carnival of Fear 40.00
7 MP,JM, Ritual of Blood 40.00
8 MP,Krogg,Lurker from Beyond . 40.00
9 TS,V:Tatterdemalion 40.00
10 TS,bondage cover 40.00
11 GK,TS,Full Moon..Fear Moon . 30.00
12 GK,Cry Monster 30.00
13 MP,ManMonsterCalledTaboo . 25.00
14 MP,Lo,the Monster Strikes 25.00
15 MP,(new)O:Werewolf,
    V:Dracula. 50.00
16 MP,TS,A:Hunchback of Notre
    Dame. 35.00
17 Behold the Behemoth 35.00
18 War of the Werewolves 35.00
19 V:Dracula 32.00
20 The Monster Breaks Free 30.00
21 GK(c),To Cure a Werewolf 15.00
22 GK(c),Face of a Friend 15.00
23 Silver Bullet for a Werewolf . . . 15.00
24 GK(c),V:The Brute 15.00
25 GK(c),Eclipse of Evil. 15.00
26 GK(c),A Crusade of Murder . . . 15.00

Werewolf by Night #36
© Marvel Entertainment Group

27 GK(c),Scourge o/t Soul-Beast . 15.00
28 GK(c),V:Dr.Glitternight 15.00
29 GK(c),V:Dr.Glitternight 15.00
30 GK(c),Red Slash across
    Midnight 15.00
31 Death in White 15.00
32 I&O:Moon Knight 160.00
33 Were-Beast..Moon Knight
    A:Moon Knight(2nd App) 160.00
34 GK(c),TS,House of Evil..House
    of Death. 15.00
35 TS,JS,BWi,Jack Russell vs.
    Werewolf 15.00
36 Images of Death 15.00
37 BWr(c),BW,A:Moon Knight,
    Hangman,Dr.Glitternight 20.00
38 . . . . 22.00
39 V:Brother Voodoo 22.00
40 A:Brother Voodoo,V:Dr.
    Glitternight. 15.00
41 V:Fire Eyes 15.00
42 A:IronMan,Birth of a Monster . . 15.00
43 Tri-Animal Lives,A:Iron Man . . . 15.00
G-Size#2,SD,A:Frankenstein
    Monster (reprint) 15.00
G-Size#3 GK(c),Transylvania 15.00
G-Size#4 GK(c),A:Morbius 15.00
G-Size#5 GK(c),Peril of
    Paingloss. 10.00

WEREWOLF BY NIGHT
Dec., 1997

1 PJe,F:Jack Russell returns 3.00
2 PJe,Search for wolf Amulet 3.00
3 PJe,Stuck between man & wolf . 3.00
4 PJe,to the depths of hell 3.00
5 PJe, confronts demon 3.00
6 PJe, visit Underworld nightclub . 3.00
Storyline continues in Strange Tales

WEST COAST AVENGERS
[Limited Series] Sept., 1984

1 BH,A:Shroud,J:Hawkeye,IronMan,
    WonderMan,Mockingbird,Tigra . 4.00
2 BH,V:Blank. 3.00
3 BH,V:Graviton 3.00
4 BH,V:Graviton 3.00

[Regular Series] 1985–89

1 AM,JSt,V:Lethal Legion 4.00
2 AM,JSt,V:Lethal Legion 3.00
3 AM,JSt,V:Kraven 3.00
4 AM,JSt,A:Firebird,Thing,I:Master
    Pandemonium 3.00
5 AM,JSt,A:Werewolf,Thing 3.00
6 AM,KB,A:Thing 3.00
7 AM,JSt,V:Ultron 3.00
8 AM,JSt,V:Rangers,A:Thing 3.00
9 AM,JSt,V:Master Pandemonium . 3.00
10 AM,JSt,V:Headlok,Griffen 3.00
11 AM,JSt,A:Nick Fury 3.00
12 AM,JSt,V:Graviton 3.00
13 AM,JSt,V:Graviton 3.00
14 AM,JSt,V:Pandemonium 3.00
15 AM,JSt,A:Hellcat 3.00
16 AM,JSt,V:Tiger Shark,
    Whirlwind 3.00
17 AM,JSt,V:Dominus' Minions . . . 3.00
18 AM,JSt,V:The Wild West 3.00
19 AM,JSt,A:Two Gun Kid 3.00
20 AM,JSt,A:Rawhide Kid 3.00
21 AM,JSt,A:Dr.Pym,Moon Knight . 3.00
22 AM,JSt,A:Fant.Four,Dr.Strange,
    Night Rider 3.00
23 AM,RT,A:Phantom Rider 3.00
24 AM,V:Dominus 3.00
25 AM,V:Abomination 3.00
26 AM,V:Zodiac 3.00
27 AM,V:Zodiac 3.00
28 AM,V:Zodiac 3.00
29 AM,V:Taurus,A:Shroud 3.00
30 AM,C:Composite Avenger 3.00

West Coast Avengers #1
© Marvel Entertainment Group

31 AM,V:Arkon 3.00
32 AM,TD,V:Yetrigar,J:Wasp 3.00
33 AM,O:Ant-Man,Wasp;
   V:Madam X,El Toro 3.00
34 AM,V:Quicksilver,J:Vision &
   Scarlet Witch 3.00
35 AM,V:Dr.Doom,Quicksilver 3.00
36 AM,V:The Voice 3.00
37 V:The Voice,A:Mantis 3.00
38 AM,TMo,V:Defiler 3.00
39 AM,V:Swordsman 3.00
40 AM,MGu,V:NightShift,
   A:Shroud 3.00
41 TMo,I:New Phantom Rider,
   L:Moon Knight 3.00
42 JBy,Visionquest#1,V:Ultron 3.50
43 JBy,Visionquest#2, ... 3.00
44 JBy,Visionquest#3,J:USAgent . . 3.00
45 JBy,Visionquest#4,
   I:New Vision. 3.50
46 JBy,I:Great Lakes Avengers 3.00
Ann. #1 MBr,GI,V:Zodiak 3.25
Ann. #2 AM,A:SilverSurfer,V:Death,
   Collector,R:Grandmaster 3.00
Ann. #3 AM,RLm,TD,Evolutionary
   Wars,R:Giant Man 3.50
Becomes:

AVENGERS WEST COAST

WESTERN GUNFIGHTERS
[2nd series] Aug., 1970
1 JK,JB,DAy,B:Ghost Rider
   A:Fort Rango,The Renegades
   Gunhawk 75.00
2 HT(c),DAy,JMn,O:Nightwind,
   V:Tarantula 35.00
3 DAy,MD,V:Hurricane, rep. 35.00
4 HT(c),DAy,TS,B:Gunhawk,
   Apache Kid,A;Renegades 45.00
5 DAy,FrG,A:Renegades 35.00
6 HT(c),DAy,SSh,Death of
   Ghost Rider 30.00
7 HT(c),DAy,SSh,O:Ghost Rider
   retold,E:Ghost Rider,Gunhawk 30.00
8 DAy,SSh,B:Black Rider,Outlaw
   Kid(rep) 25.00
9 DW,Revenge rides the Range. . 25.00
10 JK,JMn,O:Black Rider,B:Matt
   Slade,E:Outlaw Kid 25.00
11 JK,Duel at Dawn 25.00
12 JMn,O:Matt Slade 30.00
13 Save the Gold Coast Expires . . 25.00
14 JSo(c),Outlaw Town 25.00

15 E:Matt Slade,Showdown in
   Outlaw Canyon 25.00
16 B:Kid Colt,Shoot-out in Silver
   City 25.00
17 thru 20 . . . . @25.00
21 thru 24 . . . . @15.00
25 . . . . 15.00
26 F:Kid Colt,Gun-Slinger,
   Apache Kid 15.00
27 thru 32 . . . . @15.00
33 Nov., 1975. . . . . 15.00

WESTERN KID
[1st Series] Dec., 1954
1 JR,B:Western Kid,O:Western Kid
   (Tex Dawson) 250.00
2 JMn,JR,Western Adventure . . . 125.00
3 JMn(c),JR,Gunfight(c) 100.00
4 JMn(c),JR,The Badlands 100.00
5 JR 100.00
6 JR 100.00
7 JR 100.00
8 JR 100.00
9 JR,AW 100.00
10 JR,AW,Man in the Middle 125.00
11 thru 16 . . . . @100.00
17 Aug., 1957. . . . . 100.00

[2nd Series]
Dec., 1971–Aug., 1972
1 Reprints 35.00
2 . . . . 20.00
3 AW 25.00
4 . . . . 20.00
5 . . . . 20.00

WESTERN OUTLAWS
Marvel Atlas,
Feb., 1954–Aug., 1957
1 JMn(c),RH,BP,The Greenville
   Gallows,Hanging(c) 300.00
2 . . . . 150.00
3 thru 10 . . . . @125.00
11 AW,MD 150.00
12 JMn 100.00
13 MB,JMn. 125.00
14 AW 125.00
15 AT,GT 100.00
16 BP,JMn,JSe,AW 100.00
17 JMn,AW 100.00
18 JSe 100.00
19 JMn,JSe,RC 100.00
20 and 21 JSe . . . . @100.00

WESTERN OUTLAWS
& SHERIFFS
See: BEST WESTERN

WESTERN TALES
OF BLACK RIDER
See: ALL WINNERS COMICS

WESTERN TEAM-UP
Nov., 1973
1 Rawhide Kid/Dakota Kid 50.00

WESTERN THRILLERS
Nov., 1954
1 JMn,Western tales 200.00
2 . . . . 100.00
3 . . . . 100.00
4 . . . . 100.00
Becomes:

COWBOY ACTION
March, 1955–March, 1956
5 JMn(c),The Prairie Kid 150.00
6 . . . . 100.00
7 . . . . 100.00
9 . . . . 100.00

10 . . . . 100.00
11 MN,AW,The Manhunter, ... 125.00
Becomes:

QUICK-TRIGGER
WESTERN
May, 1956–Sept., 1957
12 Bill Larson Strikes 175.00
13 AW,The Man From Cheyenne 175.00
14 BEv,RH(c) 175.00
15 AT,RC 150.00
16 JK,JD 125.00
17 GT 125.00
18 GM 125.00
19 JSe 100.00

WESTERN TRAILS
Marvel Atlas, 1957
1 MMe,FBe,JSe(c),Ringo Kid . . . 165.00
2 MMe,FBe,JSe(c) 100.00

WESTERN WINNERS
See: ALL WINNERS COMICS

WHAT IF?
[1st Regular Series] Feb., 1977
1 Spider-Man joined Fant.Four . . . 25.00
2 GK(c),Hulk had Banner brain . . 15.00
3 GK,KJ,F:Avengers 12.00
4 GK(c),F:Invaders 12.00
5 F:Captain America 12.00
6 F:Fantastic Four. 12.00
7 GK(c),F:Spider-Man. 10.00
8 GK(c),F:Daredevil 10.00
9 JK(c),F:Avengers of the '50s . . . 10.00
10 JB,F:Thor 10.00
11 JK,F:FantasticFour 8.00
12 F:Hulk 8.00
13 JB,Conan Alive Today. 8.00
14 F:Sgt. Fury 6.00
15 CI,F:Nova 6.00
16 F:Master of Kung Fu 6.00
17 CI,F:Ghost Rider 6.00
18 TS,F:Dr.Strange 5.00
19 PB,F:Spider-Man 6.00
20 F:Avengers 5.00
21 GC,F:Sub-Mariner. 5.00
22 F:Dr.Doom. 5.00
23 JB,F:Hulk 5.00
24 GK,RB,Gwen Stacy had lived. . 10.00
25 F:Thor,Avengers,O:Mentor 5.00
26 JBy(c),F:Captain America 5.00
27 FM(c),Phoenix hadn't died 22.00

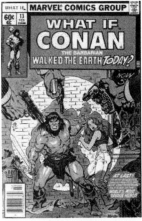

What If #13
© Marvel Entertainment Group

MARVEL

28 FM,F:Daredevil,Ghost Rider. . . 10.00
29 MG(c),F:Avengers. 6.00
30 RB,F:Spider-Man 10.00
31 Wolverine killed the Hulk 20.00
32 Avengers lost to Korvac 5.00
33 BL,Dazzler herald of Galactus . . 5.00
34 FH,FM,JBy,BSz:Humor issue . . . 5.00
35 FM,Elektra had lived. 6.00
36 JBy,Fant.Four had no powers. . . 5.00
37 F:Thing,Beast,Silver Surfer. . . . 5.00
38 F:Daredevil,Captain America . . . 5.00
39 Thor had fought Conan. 5.00
40 F:Dr.Strange 5.00
41 F:Sub-Mariner. 5.00
42 F:Fantastic Four 5.00
43 F:Conan 5.00
44 F:Captain America 5.00
45 F:Hulk,Berserk 5.00
46 Uncle Ben had lived 7.00
47 F:Thor,Loki 5.00
Spec.#1 F:Iron Man,Avengers . . . 6.00
Best of What IF? rep.#1,#24,
   #27,#28 . . . . 13.00

[2nd Regular Series]
1 RWi,MG,The Avengers had lost
   the Evolutionary War 5.00
2 GCa,Daredevil Killed Kingpin,
   A:Hobgoblin, The Rose 4.00
3 Capt.America Hadn't Given Up
   Costume,A:Avengers. 3.50
4 MBa,Spider-Man kept Black
   Costume,A:Avengers,Hulk 6.00
5 Vision Destroyed Avengers,
   A:Wonder Man. 3.50
6 RLm,X-Men Lost Inferno,
   A:Dr.Strange 6.00
7 RLd,Wolverine Joined Shield,
   A:Nick Fury,Black Widow 7.00
8 Iron Man Lost The Armor Wars,
   A:Ant Man 3.00
9 RB,New X-Men Died 6.00
10 MZ(c),BMc,Punisher's Family
   Didn't Die,A:Kingpin 3.00
11 TM(c),JV,SM,Fant.Four had the
   Same Powers,A:Nick Fury 3.50
12 JV,X-Men Stayed in Asgard,
   A:Thor,Hela 5.00
13 JLe(c),Prof.X Became
   Juggernaut,A:X-Men 3.50
14 RLm(c),Capt.Marvel didn't die
   A:Silver Surfer. 3.50
15 GCa,Fant.Four Lost Trial of
   Galactus,A:Gladiator 3.00
16 Wolverine Battled Conan,
   A:X-Men,Red Sonja. 5.00
17 Kraven Killed Spider-Man,
   A:Daredevil,Captain America . . 3.00
18 LMc,Fant.Four fought Dr.Doom
   before they gained powers 3.00
19 RW,Vision took over Earth,
   A:Avengers,Dr.Doom. 3.00
20 Spider-Man didn't marry Mary
   Jane,A:Venom,Kraven. 3.00
21 Spider-Man married Black Cat,
   A:Vulture,Silver Sable 3.00
22 RLm,Silver Surfer didn't escape
   Earth,A:F.F,Mephisto,Thanos . 4.00
23 New X-Men never existed,
   A:Eric the Red,Lilandra 3.00
24 Wolverine Became Lord of
   Vampires,A:Punisher. 3.00
25 Marvel Heroes lost Atlantis
   Attacks,double size 3.50
26 LMc,Punisher Killed Daredevil,
   A:Spider-Man. 3.00
27 Submariner Joined Fantastic
   Four,A:Dr. Doom 3.00
28 RW,Capt.America led Army of
   Super-Soldiers,A:Submariner . . 3.00
29 RW,Capt.America formed the
   Avengers 3.00

What If 2nd Series #27
© Marvel Entertainment Group

30 Inv.Woman's 2nd Child had
   lived,A:Fantastic Four 3.00
31 Spider-Man/Captain Universe
   Powers. 3.00
32 Phoenix Rose Again,pt.1 . . . . . 3.00
33 Phoenix Rose Again,pt.2 . . . . . 3.00
34 Humor Issue 3.00
35 B:Time Quake,F.F. vs.Dr. Doom
   & Annihilus. 3.00
36 Cosmic Avengers,V:Guardians
   of the Galaxy 3.00
37 X-Vampires,V:Dormammu 4.00
38 Thor was prisoner of Set 3.00
39 E:Time Quake,Watcher saved the
   Universe 3.00
40 Storm remained A thief? 3.00
41 JV,Avengers fought Galactus . . 3.00
42 KWe,Spidey kept extra arms . . 3.00
43 Wolverine married Mariko. 3.50
44 Punisher possessed by Venom . 3.00
45 Barbara Ketch became G.R. . . . 3.00
46 Cable Killed Prof.X,Cyclops &
   Jean Grey 3.00
47 Magneto took over USA 3.00
48 Daredevil Saved Nuke 3.00
49 Silver Surfer had Inf.Gauntlet? . 3.50
50 Hulk killed Wolverine 8.00
51 PCu,Punisher is Capt.America . 15.00
52 BHi,Wolverine led Alpha Flight . 3.50
53 F:Iron Man,Hulk 3.00
54 F:Death's Head 3.00
55 LKa(s),Avengers lose G.Storm . 3.00
56 Avengers lose G.Storm#2 . . . . . 3.00
57 Punisher a member of SHIELD . 3.00
58 Punisher kills SpM 3.00
59 Wolverine lead Alpha Flight . . . 3.50
60 RoR,Scott & Jean's Wedding . . 3.00
61 Spider-Man's Parents 3.00
62 Woverine vs Weapon X 3.50
63 F:War Machine,Iron Man 3.00
64 Iron Man sold out 3.00
65 Archangel fell from Grace. 3.00
66 Rogue and Thor 3.00
67 Cap.America returns. 3.00
68 Captain America story. 3.00
69 Stryfe Killed X-Men 3.00
70 Silver Surfer 3.50
71 The Hulk 3.00
72 Parker Killed Burglar. 3.00
73 Daredevil,Kingpin 3.00
74 Sinister Formed X-Men. 7.00
75 Gen-X's Blink had lived 3.00
76 Flash Thompson Spider-Man . . 3.00
77 Legion had killed Magneto 10.00

78 FF had stayed together 6.00
79 Storm had Phoenix's Power 3.00
80 KGa,Hulk was Cured 3.00
81 Age of Apocalypse didn't end . . 11.00
82 WML,J.JonahJameson
   adopted Spider-Man 3.00
83 Daredevil. 3.00
84 Shard 3.00
85 Magneto Ruled all mutants. 3.00
86 Scarlet Spider vs. Spider-Man . . 3.00
87 Sabretooth 3.00
88 Spider-Man 3.00
89 Fantastic Four. 3.00
90 Cyclops & Havok 3.00
91 F:Hulk, nice guy, Banner violent. 3.00
92 F:Cannonball,Husk 3.00
93 F:Wolverine 3.50
94 JGz,F:Juggernaut 3.00
95 IV,F:Ghost Rider 3.00
96 CWo,F:Quicksilver. 3.00
97 F:Black Knight. 3.00
98 F:Nightcrawler & Rogue 3.00
99 F:Black Cat. 3.00
100 IV,KJ,F:Gambit &
   Rogue, 48-pg. 7.00
101 ATi,F:Archangel. 3.00
102 F:Daredevil's Dad 3.00
103 DaF,F:Captain America. 3.00
104 F:Silver Surver,ImpossibleMan . 3.00
105 TDF,RF,F:Spider-Man and
   Mary Jane's Daughter 25.00
106 TDF,F:X-Men,Gambit
   sentenced to death 3.00
107 TDF,RF,BSz,F:Thor. 3.00
108 TDF,F:The Avengers 3.00
109 TA,F:Fantastic Four 3.00
110 TDF,F:Wolverine 3.00
111 TDF,F:Wolverine 3.00
112 F:Ka-Zar 3.00
113 F:Iron Man, Dr. Strange, ... 3.00
114 F:Secret Wars, 32-page,
   final issue 12.00
Minus 1 Spec., AOI, flashback,
   F:Bishop 3.00

WHAT IF
Dec., 2004
1-shot Aunt May Had Died Instead
   Of Uncle Ben. 3.00
1-shot Karen Page Had Lived . . . 3.00
1-shot Jessica Jones Had Joined
   The Avengers 3.00
1-shot Magneto Had Formed the
   X-Men with Professor X 3.00
1-shot Dr. Doom Had Become
   The Thing 3.00
1-shot General Ross Had Become
   The Hulk 3.00
1-shot Wha...Huh? (2005) 4.00

WHAT IF?
Dec., 2005
1 Fantastic Four were cosmonauts 3.00
2 Stephen Rogers/Captain America 3.00
3 Thor transformed into Herald
   of Galactus 3.00
4 Public Enemy Number One. 3.00
5 Namor grew up on land 3.00
6 Samurai Devil Who Dares 3.00

WHAT IF?
Nov., 2006
Avengers Disassembled #1. . . . . . 4.00
Spider-Man #1 . . . . 3.00
Wolverine Enemy of the State #1 . 3.00
X-Men Age of Apocalypse 3.00
X-Men Deadly Genesis 3.00
Planet Hulk. 4.00
Annihilation (2007). 3.00

WHAT THE -?!
[Parodies]
Aug., 1988

```
1 ................................ 5.00
2 JBy,JOy,AW,................. 4.00
3 TM,............................ 5.00
4 ................................ 3.00
5 EL,JLe,WPo,Wolverine ........ 5.00
6 Wolverine,Punisher ........... 3.00
7 ................................ 2.50
8 DK ............................. 2.50
9 ................................ 2.50
10 JBy,X-Men,Dr.Doom, Cap.
    America ..................... 2.50
11 DK,RLd(part)................. 2.50
12 Conan, F.F.,Wolverine. ....... 2.50
13 Silver Burper,F.F.,Wolverine.. . 2.50
14 Spittle-Man ................. 2.50
15 Capt.Ultra,Wolverina......... 2.50
16 Ant Man,Watcher ............ 2.50
17 Wulverean/Pulverizer,Hoagg/
    Spider-Ham,Sleep Gawker,F.F. . 2.50
18 ............................... 2.50
19 ............................... 2.50
20 Infinity Wart Crossover ........ 2.50
21 Weapon XX,Toast Rider ....... 2.50
22 F:Echs Farce ................. 2.50
23 ............................... 2.50
24 Halloween issue ............. 2.50
25 ............................... 2.50
26 Spider-Ham 2099 ............ 2.50
Summer Spec. ................. 2.50
Fall Spec. ...................... 2.50
```

WHERE CREATURES ROAM
July, 1970—Sept., 1971

```
1 JK,SD,DAy,B:Reprints
    The Brute That Walks ....... 40.00
2 JK,SD,Midnight/Monster ...... 25.00
3 JK,SD,DAy,Thorg ............ 25.00
4 JK,SD,Vandoom .............. 25.00
5 JK,SD,Gorgilla ............. 25.00
6 JK,SD,Zog ................. 25.00
7 SD ........................... 25.00
8 The Mummy's Secret,E:Reprints 25.00
```

WHERE MONSTERS DWELL
Jan., 1970

```
1 JK,SD,B:Reprints,Cyclops .... 50.00
2 JK,Sporr .................... 35.00
3 JK,Grottu .................. 35.00
4 ............................. 35.00
5 JK,Taboo .................. 35.00
6 JK,Groot .................. 35.00
7 JK,Rommbu ................ 35.00
8 JK,SD,The Four-Armed Men .. 35.00
9 JK,Bumbu ................. 35.00
10 JK,SD,Monster That Walks
    Like A Man............... 35.00
11 JK,Gruto ................. 35.00
12 JK,GC,SD,Orogo,giant-size ... 40.00
13 JK,The Thing That Crawl ..... 25.00
14 JK,The Green Thing ........ 25.00
15 JK,JSe,Kraa- The Inhuman ... 25.00
16 JK,Beware the Son Of Goom . . 25.00
17 SD,The Hidden Vampires . . . . . 25.00
18 SD,The Mask of Morghum . . . 25.00
19 SD,The Insect Man......... 25.00
20 Klagg .................... 25.00
21 Fin Fang Foom ............. 25.00
22 Elektro. ................... 25.00
23 SD,The Monster Waits For Me . 25.00
24 SD,The Things on
    Easter Island ............. 25.00
25 SD,The Ruler of the Earth .... 25.00
26 ............................. 25.00
27 ............................. 25.00
```

Where Monsters Dwell #31
© Marvel Entertainment Group

```
28 Droom,The Living Lizard...... 25.00
29 thru 37 Reprints ........... @25.00
38 AW,reprints, Oct., 1975....... 25.00
```

WHIP WILSON
See: BLAZE CARSON

WHITE TIGER
Nov., 2006

```
1 A Hero's compulsion ......... 3.00
2 a Hero's Compulsion ......... 3.00
3 ............................. 3.00
4 ............................. 3.00
5 ............................. 3.00
6 ............................. 3.00
```

WILD
Marvel Atlas, Feb., 1954

```
1 BEv,JMn,Charlie Chan
    Parody.................... 350.00
2 BEv,RH,JMn,Witches(c). .... 200.00
3 CBu(c),BEv,RH,JMn, ....... 175.00
4 GC,Didja Ever See a Cannon
    Brawl ................... 175.00
5 RH,JMn,Aug., 1954 ....... 175.00
```

WILD CARDS
Epic, Sept., 1990

```
1 JG ......................... 5.50
2 JG,V:Jokers ................. 4.50
3 A:Turtle..................... 4.50
```

WILDC.A.T.S/X-MEN: THE DARK AGE
Dec., 1997

```
1-shot MtB,WEI,V:Daemonites
    & Sentinels, 48-pg. .......... 4.50
1a variant cover MGo .......... 4.50
```

WILD THING
Marvel UK, 1993

```
1 A:Virtual Reality Venom and
    Carnage.................... 3.00
2 A:VR Venom and Carnage ..... 2.25
3 A:Shield ................... 2.25
4 ............................. 2.25
5 Virtual Reality Gangs ........ 2.25
6 Virtual Reality Villians ....... 2.25
7 V:Trask..................... 2.25
8 ............................. 2.25
9 ............................. 2.25
```

```
10 ............................. 2.25
11 ............................. 2.25
12 ............................. 2.25
13 ............................. 2.25
```

WILD THING
Aug., 1999

```
1 RLm,AM,LHa,F:Wolverine's
    daughter Rina ............. 2.25
2A RLm,AM,LHa,Bloody
    Reunions ................. 2.25
2B variant AW (c) ............. 2.25
3 RLm,AM,LHa,A:Rina ....... 2.25
4 RLm,AM,LHa ............. 2.25
5 RLm,AM,LHa,V:Robot monster . . 2.25
```

WILD WEST
Spring, 1948

```
1 SSh(c),B:Two Gun Kids,Tex
    Taylor,Arizona Annie....... 450.00
2 SSh(c),CCb, Captain Tootsie. . 300.00
```
Becomes:

WILD WESTERN
1948

```
3 SSh(c),B:Tex Morgan,Two Gun
    Kid,Tex Taylor,Arizona Annie 350.00
4 Rh,SSh,CCB,Capt. Tootsie.
    A:Kid Colt,E:Arizona Annie . . 250.00
5 RH,CCB,SSh,Captain Tootsie
    A;Black Rider,Blaze Carson . 300.00
6 A:Blaze Carson,Kid Colt ..... 200.00
7 Two-Gun Kid ............... 200.00
    Kid,Tex Taylor,Arizona Annie 350.00
8 RH ......................... 200.00
9 Ph(c),B:Black Rider,
    Tex Morgan. ............. 225.00
10 Ph(c), Black Rider. ........ 250.00
11 Black Rider ............... 200.00
12 Black Rider ............... 200.00
13 Black Rider ............... 200.00
14 Prairie Kid,Black Rider ....... 175.00
15 Black Rider ............... 175.00
16 thru 18 Black Rider ....... @175.00
19 Black Rider ............... 185.00
20 thru 29 Kid Colt .......... @150.00
30 JKa, Kid Colt. ............. 150.00
31 thru 40................... @100.00
41 thru 47.................. @100.00
48 AW ...................... 125.00
49 thru 53.................. @100.00
54 AW ...................... 125.00
55 AW ...................... 125.00
56 and 57 Sept., 1957 ....... @100.00
```

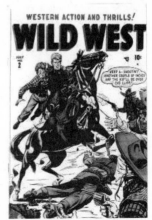

Wild Western #2
© Marvel Entertainment Group

MARVEL

MARVEL

WILLIAM SHATNER'S TEK WORLD
1992–94
1 LS,Novel adapt.	2.25
2 LS,Novel adapt.cont.	2.25
3 LS,Novel adapt.cont.	2.25
4 LS,Novel adapt.cont.	2.25
5 LS,Novel adapt.concludes	2.25
6 LS,V:TekLords	2.25
7 E:The Angel	2.25
8	2.25
9	2.25
10	2.25
11 thru 17	@2.25
18	2.25
19 Sims of the Father#1	2.25
20 Sims of the Father#2	2.25
21 Who aren't in Heaven	2.25
22 Father and Guns	2.25
23 We'll be Right Back	2.25
24	2.25

WILLIE COMICS
See: IDEAL COMICS

WILLIE THE WISE-GUY
Marvel Atlas, 1957
1 MMe	100.00

WILLOW
Aug., 1988
1 Movie adapt.	3.00
2 Movie adapt.	3.00
3 Movie adapt,Oct., 1988.	3.00

WINTER SOLDIER: WINTER KILLS
Dec., 2006
Civil War	3.00

WISDOM
Nov., 2006
1 F:Pete Wisdom	4.00
2 thru 6	4.00

WITCHES
June, 2004
1 MD2,F:Kale,Topaz,Satana	3.00
2 MD2,F:Kale,Topaz,Satana	3.00
3 MD2	3.00
4 MD2	3.00

WITNESS, THE
Sept., 1948
1	3,200.00

WOLFPACK
Aug., 1988
1 I:Wolfpack	8.00
2 thru 11	@2.50
12 July, 1988	2.50

WOLVERINE
[Limited Series] Sept., 1982
1 B:CCI(s),FM,JRu,A:Mariko, I:Shingen	75.00
2 FM,JRu,A:Mariko,I:Yukio	50.00
3 FM,JRu,A:Mariko,Yukio	50.00
4 B:CCI(s),FM,JRu,A:Mariko, D:Shingen	55.00

[Regular Series] 1988
1 JB,AW,V:Banipur	50.00
2 JB,KJ,V:Silver Samurai	25.00
3 JB,AW,V:Silver Samurai	10.00
4 JB,AW,I:Roughhouse, Bloodsport	10.00

Wolverine #3
© Marvel Entertainment Group

5 JB,AW,V:Roughhouse, Bloodsport	10.00
6 JB,AW,V:Roughhouse, Bloodsport	10.00
7 JB,A:Hulk	10.00
8 JB,A:Hulk	10.00
9 GC,Old Wolverine Story	10.00
10 JB,BSz,V:Sabretooth (1st battle)	30.00
11 JB,BSz,B:Gehenna Stone	10.00
12 JB,BSz,Gehenna Stone	10.00
13 JB,BSz,Gehenna Stone	10.00
14 JB,BSz,Gehenna Stone	10.00
15 JB,BSz,Gehenna Stone	10.00
16 JB,BSz,E:Gehenna Stone	10.00
17 JBy,KJ,V:Roughhouse	10.00
18 JBy,KJ,V:Roughhouse	10.00
19 JBy,KJ,A of V,I:La Bandera	10.00
20 JBy,KJ,A of V,V:Tigershark	7.00
21 JBy,KJ,V:Geist	7.00
22 JBy,KJ,V:Geist,Spore	7.00
23 JBy,KJ,V:Geist,Spore	7.00
24 GC,Snow Blind	6.00
25 JB,O:Wolverine(part)	6.00
26 KJ,Return to Japan	6.00
27 thru 30 Lazarus Project	6.00
31 MS,DGr,A:Prince o'Mandripoor	6.00
32 MS,DGr,V:Ninjas	6.00
33 MS,Wolverine in Japan	6.00
34 MS,DGr,Wolverine in Canada	6.00
35 MS,DGr,A:Puck	6.00
36 MS,DGr,A:Puck,Lady D'strike	6.00
37 MS,DGr,V:Lady Deathstrike	6.00
38 MS,DGr,A:Storm,I:Elsie Dee	6.00
39 MS,DGr,Wolverine Vs. Clone	6.00
40 MS,DGr,Wolverine Vs. Clone	6.00
41 MS,DGr,R:Sabretooth, A:Cable	8.00
41a 2nd printing	2.25
42 MS,DGr,A:Sabretooth,Cable	9.00
42a 2nd printing	6.00
43 MS,DGr,A:Sabretooth,C:Cable	7.00
44 LSn,DGr	6.00
45 MS,DGr,A:Sabretooth	7.00
46 MS,DGr,A:Sabretooth	7.00
47 V:Tracy	6.00
48 LHa(s),MS,DGr,B:Shiva Scenario	6.00
49 LHa(s),MS,DGr,	6.00
50 LHa(s),MS,DGr,A:X-Men,Nick Fury, I:Shiva,Slash-Die Cut(c)	7.00
51 MS,DGr,A:Mystique,X-Men	5.00
52 MS,DGr,A:Mystique,V:Spiral	5.00
53 MS,A:Mystique,V:Spiral,Mojo	5.00
54 A:Shatterstar	5.00

55 MS,V:Cylla,A:Gambit,Sunfire	5.00
56 MS,A:Gambit,Sunfire,V:Hand, Hydra	5.00
57 MS,D:Lady Mariko,A:Gambit	5.50
58 A:Terror	5.00
59 A:Terror	5.00
60 Sabretooth vs.Shiva, I:John Wraith	5.00
61 MT,History of Wolverine and Sabretooth,A:John Wraith	5.00
62 MT,A:Sabretooth,Silver Fox	5.00
63 MT,V:Ferro,D:Silver Fox	5.00
64 MPa,V:Ferro,Sabretooth	5.00
65 MT,A:Professor X	5.00
66 MT,A:X-Men	5.00
67 MT,A:X-Men	5.00
68 MT,V:Epsilon Red	5.00
69 DT,A:Rogue,V:Sauron,tie-in to X-Men#300	5.00
70 DT,Sauron,A:Rogue,Jubilee	5.00
71 DT,V:Sauron,Brain Child, A:Rogue, Jubilee	5.00
72 DT,Sentinels	5.00
73 DT,V:Sentinels	5.00
74 ANi,V:Sentinels	5.00
75 AKu,Hologram(c),Wolv.has Bone Claws,leaves X-Men	10.00
76 DT(c),B:LHa(s),A:Deathstrike, C:Puck	5.00
77 AKu,A:Vindicator,Puck,V:Lady Deathstrike	5.00
78 AKu,V:Cylla,Bloodscream	5.00
79 AKu,V:Cyber,I:Zoe Culloden	5.00
80 IaC,V:Cyber,	5.00
81 IaC,V:Cyber,A:Excalibur	5.00
82 AKu,BMc,A:Yukio,Silver Samurai	5.00
83 AKu,A:Alpha Flight	5.00
84 A:Alpha Flight	5.00
85 Phalanx Covenant, Final Sanction, V:Phalanx,holografx(c)	5.50
85a newsstand ed.	3.00
86 AKu,V:Bloodscream	3.00
87 AKu,deluxe,V:Juggernaut	3.00
87a newsstand ed.	3.00
88 AKu,deluxe ed.	3.00
88a newsstand ed.	3.00
89 deluxe ed.	3.00
89a newsstand ed.	2.00
90 V:Sabretooth, deluxe ed.	4.00
90a newsstand ed.	2.00
91 LHa,Logan's future unravels.	3.00
92 LHa,AKu,DGr,A:Sabretooth	3.00
93 R:Cyber.	3.00
94 Feral Wolverine	3.00
95 LHa,AKu,DGr,V:Dark Riders	3.00
96 LHa,Aku,DGr,Death of Cyber	3.00
97 LHa,AKu,DGr,A:Genesis	3.00
98 LHa,AKu,F:Genesis	3.00
99	3.00
100 LHa,AKu,DG,A:Elektra;double- size, Foil Hologram cover	12.00
100a regular edition	4.00
101 LHa,AKu,A:Elektra	3.00
102 LHa	3.00
103 LHa,Elektra,A:Onslaught	3.00
104 LHa,Gateway, Onslaught	3.00
105 LHa,Gateway, Elektra	3.00
106 LHa	3.00
107 LHa,VS,prologue to Elektra#1	3.00
108 LHa,back to Tokyo,A:Yukio	3.00
109 LHa,DG,	3.00
110 LHa,DG,Who's spying on Logan.	3.00
111 LHa,DG,Logan moves to NYC	3.00
112 LHa,DG,Logan in NYC	3.00
113 LHa,R:Ogun,A:Lady Deathstrike & Spiral	3.00
114 LHa,back in costume,V:Cyborg Donald Pierce	3.00
115 LHa,Zero Tolerance,V:Bastion	3.00
116 LHa,Zero Tolerance,	3.00

Wolverine #75
© *Marvel Entertainment Group*

117 LHa,Zero Tolerance, V:Prime
Sentinels 3.00
118 LHa,Zero Tolerance aftermath . 3.00
119 WEI,Pt.1 (of 4). 3.00
120 WEI,The White Ghost 3.00
121 WEI,Not Yet Dead, pt.3. . . . . . . 3.00
122 WEI,Not Yet Dead, pt.4. . . . . . . 3.00
123 TDF,DCw,R:Roughhouse,
Bloodscream 3.00
124 TDF,DCw,A:Captain America,
V:Rascal 3.00
125 CCl,V:Viper,48-pg. 7.50
125a Dynamic Forces (c). 6.50
126 CCl,V:Sabretooth 3.50
127 CCl,Sabretooth takes over 3.00
128 CCl,V:Hydra, The Hand 3.00
129 TDz,A:Wendigo 3.00
130 TDz,V:Viper. 3.00
131 TDz,V:Viper. 3.00
131a Uncensored. 12.00
132 TDz,Halloween in SalemCenter 3.00
133 EL,JMs,F:Warbird 3.00
133a variant EL cover (1:4) 6.00
134 EL,JMs,V:Big Apple heroes . . . 3.00
135 EL,JMs,Joins Starjammers 3.00
136 EL,JMs,on prison planet 3.00
137 EL,JMs,V:The Collector 3.00
138 EL,JMs,Great Escape concl. . . 3.00
139 EL,A:Cable 3.00
140 EL,Xavier paranoid 3.00
141 EL,Wolverine paranoid 3.00
142 EL,R:Alpha Flight 3.00
143 EL,A:Alpha Flight 3.00
144 EL,A:Hercules,V:Leader 3.00
145 EL,25th Anniv. 48-pg. 8.00
145A Foil Stamped (c) 20.00
146 EL,Ages of Apocalypse,pt.1 . 20.00
147 FaN,Ages of Apocalypse,pt.2 . 10.00
148 EL,Ages of Apocalypse,pt.3 . . . 7.00
149 EL,mutant no more? 3.00
150 X-Men: Revolution 5.00
150a variant (c) 8.00
151 SSr,V:Lord Haan. 3.00
152 SSr,Lord Haan, Gom 3.00
153 SSr,Kia 3.00
154 RLd,ErS,Deadpool 3.00
155 RLd,Watchtower,Siryn 3.00
156 RLd,IaC,F:Spider-Man 3.00
157 RLd,IaC,F:Spider-Man 3.00
158 RLd,IaC,V:Administrator 3.00
159 SCh,V:Mr.X 3.00
160 SCh,V:Lady Killers,Mr.X 3.00
161 SCh,V:Mr.X 3.00
162 SCh,A:Sabretooth 3.00

163 SCh,F:Beast 3.00
164 SCh,F:Beast 3.00
165 SCh,NRd,trapped 3.50
166 SCh,NRd,BWS,48-page 10.00
167 DaF,NRd,BWS(c),V:Viper 2.50
168 DaF,NRd,F:Patch 2.50
169 DaF,NRd,Bloodsport,concl. 2.50
170 SCh,NRd,Stay Alive,pt.1 . . . . . . 2.50
171 SCh,NRd,V:Wendigo,'Nuff Said 2.50
172 SCh,NRd,Stay Alive,pt.3 . . . . . . 2.50
173 SCh,NRd,in Las Vegas 2.50
174 SCh,NRd,Amiko & Yukio 2.50
175 SCh,NRd,Omega Red,48-pg. . . 4.00
176 SCh,NRd, ... 2.25
177 SCh,DaF,Shadow Pulpit,pt.1 . . 2.25
178 SCh,DaF,Shadow Pulpit,pt.2 . . 2.25
179 SCh&MRd(c),R:Alpha Flight . . . 2.25
180 AKu(c). 2.25
181 SCh, new direction 2.25
182 SCh,TP 2.25
183 SCh,, 48-pg. 3.50
184 SCh,When Animals Attack 2.25
185 SCh,When Animals Attack 2.25
186 SCh,V:Punisher, Round 2. . . . . 3.00
187 JMC 2.25
188 pt.1 . . . . 2.25
189 pt.2 . . . . 2.25
Ann. '97 JOs,V:Volk. 4.00
Ann.1999 F:Deadpool, 48-pg. 4.00
Ann.2000 48-page 4.00
Ann.2001 48-page 3.50
Spec. '95 LHa,F:Nightcrawler 4.00
Spec.Minus 1, LHa,CNn, flashback,
F:Weapon X. 2.25
Spec.Global Jeapordy,PDd(s) 3.00
Spec.Save the Tiger,rep. 3.00
Spec.Winter Spec. MWa B&W 3.00
Spec.JungleAdventure,MMi,deluxe . 5.50
1-shot Bloodlust,AD,V:Siberian
Were-Creatures 6.00
GN Acts of Vengeance, rep. 7.00
GN Black Rio, 48-page 6.00
GN Bloody ChoicesJB,A:N.Fury . . 13.00
GN Inner Fury,BSz,V:Nanotech
Machines 6.25
GN Killing, KSW,JNR. 6.00
GN Rahne of Terror, C:Cable 8.00
GN Scorpio Rising, T.U.Fury 6.00
GN Typhoid's Kiss,rep. 7.00
GN Bloodhungry SK 7.00

WOLVERINE
May, 2003
1 DaR,Brothers,pt.1, relaunch 3.50
2 DaR,Brothers,pt.2 . . . . 2.25
3 DaR,Brothers,pt.3 . . . . 2.25
4 DaR,Brothers,pt.4 . . . . 2.25
5 DaR,Brothers,pt.5 . . . . 2.25
6 DaR,F:Nightcrawler 2.25
7 Coyote Crossing,pt.1 . . . . 2.25
8 Coyote Crossing,pt.2 . . . . 2.25
9 Coyote Crossing,pt.3 . . . . 2.25
10 Coyote Crossing,pt.4 . . . . 2.25
11 Coyote Crossing,concl. 2.25
12 Dreams 2.25
13 DaR,Feral,pt.1. . . . . 2.25
14 DaR,Feral,pt.2. . . . . 2.25
15 DaR,Return of the Native,pt.3 . . . 2.25
16 DaR,Return of the Native,pt.4 . . . 2.25
17 DaR,Return of the Native,pt.5 . . . 2.25
18 DaR,Return of the Native,pt.6 . . . 2.25
19 DaR,Return of the Native,pt.7 . . . 2.25
20 JR2,Enemy of the State,pt.1 . . . . 3.00
21 JR2,Enemy of the State,pt.2 . . . . 3.00
22 MMr,JR2,Enemy of the State . . . 3.00
23 MMr,JR2,Enemy of the State . . . 2.25
24 MMr,JR2,Enemy of the State . . . 2.25
25 MMr,JR2,Enemy of the State . . . 2.25
26 MMr,JR2,Agent of S.H.I.E.L.D.. . 2.25
26a variant MS(c) 10.00
27 MMr,JR2,Agent of S.H.I.E.L.D.. . 2.25
28 MMr,JR2,Agent of S.H.I.E.L.D.. . 2.25

29 MMr,JR2,Agent of S.H.I.E.L.D.. . 2.50
30 MMr,JR2,Agent of S.H.I.E.L.D.. . 2.50
31 MMr,JR2,Agent of S.H.I.E.L.D.. . 2.50
32 MMr,Prisoner Number Zero 2.50
33 Chasing Ghosts,pt.1 . . . . 2.50
34 Chasing Ghosts,pt.2 . . . . 2.50
35 Chasing Ghosts,pt.3 . . . . 2.50
36 Origins and Endings,pt.1 . . . . . . 2.50
37 Origins and Endings,pt.2 . . . . . . 2.50
38 Origins and Endings,pt.3 . . . . . . 2.50
39 Origins and Endings,pt.4 . . . . . . 2.50
40 Origins and Endings,pt.5 . . . . . . 3.00
41 The Package, 48-pg. 4.00
42 Vendetta,pt.1, Civil War tie-in . . 10.00
43 Vendetta,pt.2, Civil War tie-in . . 6.00
44 Vendetta,pt.3, Civil War tie-in . . 4.00
45 Vendetta,pt.4, Civil War tie-in . . 4.00
46 Vendetta,pt.5, Civil War tie-in . . 4.00
47 Vendetta,pt.6, Civil War tie-in . . 3.50
48 Vendetta epilogue 3.00
49 Better to Give, 48-pgs. 4.00
50 JLb,Evolution, pt.1 . . . . 4.00
50a in B&W 4.00
51 JLb,Evolution, pt.2 . . . . 3.00
52 JLb,Evolution, pt.3 . . . . 3.00
53 . . . . 3.00
53 B&W 3.00
54 JLb 3.00
54a in B&W 3.00
55 JLb,V:Sabretooth 3.00
55a in B&W 3.00
56 HC,Man in the Pit, 48-pgs. 4.00
57 ScK 3.00
58 Logan Dies, pt.2 . . . . 3.00
59 Logan Dies, pt.3 . . . . 3.00
Ann. Deathsong 4.00
Spec. Marvel Must Have, rep.
#20–#22 Enemy of the State. . . 4.00

WOLVERINE & PUNISHER:
DAMAGING EVIDENCE
1993
1 B:CP(s),GEr,A:Kingpin. 3.00
2 GEr,A:Kingpin,Sniper. 3.00
3 GEr,Last issue 3.00

WOLVERINE/ CAPTAIN
AMERICA
March, 2004
1 Alien technology stolen 3.00
2 thru 4 . . . . 3.00

*Wolverine & Punisher: Damaging
Evidence #1 © Marvel Ent. Group*

WOLVERINE: DAYS OF FUTURE PAST
Oct., 1997
1 (of 3) JFM,JoB,JHo, Logan & Magneto in far future 2.50
2 JFM,JoB,JHo,with Jubilee 2.50
3 JFM,JoB,JHo,V:Council of the Chosen, concl 2.50

WOLVERINE: DOOMBRINGER
Nov., 1997
1-shot DgM,JP,F:Silver Samurai . . . 3.00

WOLVERINE/DOOP
May, 2003
1 (of 2) 3.00
2 . . . . 3.00

WOLVERINE ENCYCLOPEDIA
Vol. 1 AKu(c) 48-pg 8.50
Vol. 2 48-pg 6.50
Vol. 3 48-pg 6.50

WOLVERINE: THE END
Nov., 2003
1 (of 6) CCt 10.00
2 thru 3 CCt . . . . @5.00
4 thru 6 CCt . . . . @3.50

WOLVERINE/GAMBIT: VICTIMS
1995
1 Takes Place in London 3.00
2 Is Wolverine the Killer? 3.00
3 V:Mastermind 3.00
4 conclusion 3.00

WOLVERINE/HULK
Feb., 2002
1 (of 4) SK, and a girl named Po . . 3.50
2 SK,snowy wasteland 3.50
3 SK,ghostly little girl 3.50
4 SK,concl 3.50

WOLVERINE/NETSUKE
Sept., 2002
1 (of 4) GgP, Wolverine Samurai . . 3.00
2 GgP 4.00
3 GgP 4.00
4 GgP, concl 4.00

WOLVERINE ORIGINS
Apr., 2006
1 SDi 45.00
2 SDi 20.00
3 SDi,Born in Blood 10.00
4 SDi,Born in Blood 6.00
5 SDi,Born in Blood 6.00
6 SDi,Savior, pt.1 . . . . 6.00
7 SDi,Savior, pt.2 . . . . 4.00
8 SDi,Savior, pt.3 . . . . 4.00
9 SDi,Savior, pt.4 . . . . 3.00
10 SDi,Wolverine's son 3.00
10a variant (c) 3.00
11 SDi,Swift and Terrible, pt.1 . . . . 3.00
12 SDi,Swift and Terrible, pt.2 . . . . 3.00
13 SDi,Swift and Terrible, pt.3 . . . . 3.00
14 SDi,Swift and Terrible, pt.4 . . . . 3.00
15 SDi,Swift and Terrible, pt.5 . . . . 3.00
16 SDi,Our War, pt.1 . . . . 3.00
16a variant (c) 3.00
17 SDi,Our War, pt.2 . . . . 3.00
18 SDi,Our War, pt.3 . . . . 3.00
19 SDi,Our War, pt.4 . . . . 3.00

Ann. #1 Return to Madripoor 4.00

WOLVERINE/PUNISHER
March 2004
1 (of 5) LW 3.00
2 thru 5 LW . . . . @3.00

WOLVERINE/PUNISHER: REVELATION
Apr. 1999
1 (of 4) TSg,PtL,Revelation 3.00
1a signed 30.00
2 TSg,PtL,V:Revelation 3.00
3 TSg,PtL,V:Revelation 3.00
4 TsG,PtL,V:Revelation,concl 3.00

WOLVERINE SAGA
Sept., 1989
1 RLd(c), ... 6.50
2 . . . . 5.50
3 . . . . 5.50
4 Dec., 1989 . . . . 5.50

WOLVERINE: SNIKT!
May, 2003
1 (of 5) 3.00
2 alien landscape 3.00
3 . . . . 3.00
4 V:Mandate aliens 3.00
5 Concl 3.00

WOLVERINE: SOULTAKER
March, 2005
1 (of 5) Mark of Mana 3.00
2 Mark of Mana 3.00
3 V:demon-lord Ryuki 3.00
4 V:Hana,Ryuki 3.00
5 Finale 3.00

WOLVERINE: X-ISLE
April, 2003
1 (of 5) A:Amiko 2.50
2 thru 5 . . . . @2.50

WONDER DUCK
Sept., 1949
1 Whale(c) 200.00
2 . . . . 125.00
3 March, 1950 . . . . 125.00

WONDERMAN
March, 1986
1 KGa,one-shot special 3.00

WONDER MAN
Sept., 1991
1 B:GJ(s),JJ,V:Goliath 2.50
2 JJ,A:West Coast Avengers 2.25
3 JJ,V:Abominatrix,I:Spider 2.25
4 JJ,I:Splice,A:Spider 2.25
5 JJ,A:Beast,V:Rampage 2.25
6 JJ,A:Beast,V:Rampage 2.25
7 JJ,Galactic Storm,pt.4, A:Hulk & Rich Jones 2.25
8 JJ,GalacticStorm,pt.11,A:Vision . 2.25
9 JJ,GalacticStorm,pt.18,A:Vision . 2.25
10 JJ,V:Khmer Rouge 2.25
11 V:Angkor 2.25
12 V:Angkor 2.25
13 Infinity War 2.25
14 Infinity War,V:Warlock 2.25
15 Inf.War,V:Doppleganger 2.25
16 JJ,I:Armed Response, A:Avengers West Coast 2.25
17 JJ,A:Avengers West Coast 2.25
18 V:Avengers West Coast 2.25
19 . . . . 2.25

Wonder Man #3
© Marvel Ent. Group

20 V:Splice,Rampage 2.25
21 V:Splice,Rampage 2.25
22 JJ,V:Realm of Death 2.25
23 JJ,A:Grim Reaper,Mephisto 2.25
24 JJ,V:Grim Reaper,Goliath 2.25
25 JJ,N:Wonder Man,D:Grim Reaper, V:Mephisto 3.25
26 A:Hulk,C:Furor,Plan Master 2.25
27 A:Hulk 2.25
28 RoR,A:Spider-Man 2.25
29 RoR,A:Spider-Man 2.25
30 V:Hate Monger 2.25
31 . . . . 2.25
32 . . . . 2.25
33 . . . . 2.25
Spec.#1 (1985),KGa 3.00
Ann.#1 System Bytes #3 . . . . 2.25
Ann.#2 I:Hit-Maker,w/card 3.00

WONDER MAN
Dec., 2006
1 PDd,My Fair Super Hero 3.00
2 PDd,My Fair Super Hero 3.00
3 PDd,My Fair Super Hero 3.00
4 PDd, ... 3.00
5 . . . . 3.00

WORLD CHAMPIONSHIP WRESTLING
1 F:Lex Luger,Sting 2.25
2 . . . . 2.25
3 . . . . 2.25
4 Luger Vs El Gigante 2.25
5 Rick Rude Vs. Sting 2.25
6 F:Dangerous Alliance,R.Rude . . . 2.25
7 F:Steiner Brothers 2.25
8 F:Sting,Dangerous Alliance 2.25
9 Bunkhouse Brawl 2.25
10 Halloween Havoc 2.25
11 Sting vs Grapplers 2.25
12 F:Ron Simmons 2.25

WORLD OF FANTASY
Marvel Atlas, May, 1956
1 The Secret of the Mountain . . . 750.00
2 JMn,AW,Inside the Tunnel 400.00
3 DAy,SC, The Man in the Cave . 350.00
4 BEv(c),BP,JF,Back to the Lost City 275.00
5 BEv(c),BP,In the Swamp 275.00
6 BEv(c),BP,The Strange Wife of Henry Johnson 275.00
7 BEv(c),GM,Man in Grey 275.00

World of Fantasy #8
© Marvel Entertainment Group

8 GM,JO,MF,The Secret of the
Black Cloud 300.00
9 BEv,BK. 275.00
10 . . . . 275.00
11 AT 200.00
12 BEv(c). 200.00
13 BEv,JO 200.00
14 JMn(c),GM,JO,CI,JM 200.00
15 JK(c) 200.00
16 AW,SD,JK 275.00
17 JK(c),SD 275.00
18 JK(c) 275.00
19 JK(c),SD,Aug., 1959. . . . . 275.00

WORLD OF MYSTERY
Marvel Atlas, 1956–57
1 BEv(c),AT,JO,The Long Wait . 650.00
2 BEv(c),The Man From
Nowhere 250.00
3 SD,AT,JDa, The Bugs 300.00
4 SD(c),BP,What Happened in
the Basement 300.00
5 JO,She Stands in Shadows . . 250.00
6 AW,SD,GC,Sinking Man 300.00
7 GC,JSe,Pick A Door 250.00

WORLD OF SUSPENSE
Marvel Atlas, April, 1956
1 JO,BEv,JMn,A Stranger
Among Us 550.00
2 SD,LC,JMN(c),When Walks
the Scarecrow 300.00
3 AW,JMN(c),The Man Who
Couldn't Be Touched . . 300.00
4 Something is in This House . . 225.00
5 BEv,DH,JO. 225.00
6 BEv(c),BP 225.00
7 AW,The Face 300.00
8 Prisoner of the Ghost Ship . . 225.00

WORLD'S GREATEST SONGS
Marvel Atlas, 1954
1 Eddie Fisher, Frank Sinatra. . . 500.00

WORLDS UNKNOWN
May, 1973
1 GK,AT,The Coming of the
Martians,Reprints 25.00
2 GK,TS,A Gun For A Dinosaur . . 20.00
3 The Day the Earth Stood
Still. 20.00
4 JB,Arena 20.00

5 DA,JM,Black Destroyer 20.00
6 GK(c),The Thing Called It 20.00
7 GT,The Golden Voyage of
Sinbad,Part 1 . . . . 20.00
8 The Golden Voyage of
Sinbad,Part 2, Aug., 1974 . . . 20.00

WORLD WAR HULK
May, 2007
1 JR2 . . . . 4.00
2 thru 5 JR2,finale. . . . . @4.00
1a thru 4a variant JR2 (c). . . . . . @4.00
Spec. Prologue: World Breaker 4.00
Spec. Aftersmash. 4.00

WORLD WAR HULK: FRONT LINE
June, 2007
1 PJe. 3.00
2 thru 6 PJe 3.00

WORLD WAR HULK: GAMMA CORPS
July, 2007
1 . . . . 3.00
2 thru 4 finale 3.00
Spec. Gamma Files 4.00

WORLD WAR HULK: X-MEN
June, 2007
1 (of 3) 4.00
2 thru 3 . . . . @3.00

WYATT EARP
Marvel Atlas, Nov., 1955
1 JMn,F:Wyatt Earp 300.00
2 AW,Saloon(c). 150.00
3 JMn(c),The Showdown,
A:Black Bart 125.00
4 Ph(c),Hugh O'Brian,JSe,
India Sundown 125.00
5 Ph(c),Hugh O'Brian,DW,
Gun Wild Fever 125.00
6 BEv(c) 125.00
7 AW 125.00
8 JMn,Wild Bill Hickok 125.00
9 and 10 . . . . @125.00
11 . . . . 125.00
12 AW,JMn. 125.00
13 . . . . 100.00
14 . . . . 100.00
15 thru 20. . . . . @100.00
21 JDa(c). 100.00
22 thru 29. . . . . @100.00
30 AW,Reprints 35.00
31 thru 33 Reprints . . . . @30.00
34 June, 1973 . . . . 30.00

WYRMS
Feb., 2007
1 (of 6) Orson Scott Card adapt. . . 3.00
2 thru . . . . @3.00

XAVIER INSTITUTE ALUMNI YEARBOOK
GN 48-pg. (1996). 6.00

X-CALIBRE
1995
1 Excaliber After Xavier 4.00
2 V:Callisto & Morlock Crew 3.00
3 D:Juggernaut 3.00
4 Secret Weapon 3.00

X-Factor #18
© Marvel Entertainment Group

X-FACTOR
Feb., 1986
1 WS(c),JG,BL,JRu,I:X-Factor,
Rusty 8.00
2 JG,BL,I:Tower. 5.00
3 JG,BL,V:Tower 5.00
4 KP,JRu,V:Frenzy 5.00
5 JG,JRu,I:Alliance of Evil,
C:Apocalypse 7.00
6 JG,BMc,I:Apocalypse. 10.00
7 JG,JRu,V:Morlocks,I:Skids. . . . 5.00
8 MS,JRu,V:Freedom Force 5.00
9 JRu(i),V:Freedom Force
(Mutant Massacre). 5.00
10 WS,BWi,V:Marauders(Mut.Mass),
A:Sabretooth 6.00
11 WS,BWi,A:Thor(Mutant Mass) . . 5.00
12 MS,BWi,V:Vanisher. 4.00
13 WS,DGr,V:Mastermold 4.00
14 WS,BWi,V:Mastermold 5.00
15 WS,BWi,D:Angel. 5.00
16 DM,JRu,V:Masque 4.00
17 WS,BWi,I:Rictor. 5.00
18 WS,BWi,V:Apocalypse 4.00
19 WS,BWi,V:Horsemen of
Apocalypse 3.50
20 JBr,A:X-Terminators 3.50
21 WS,BWi,V:The Right. 3.50
22 SB,BWi,V:The Right 3.50
23 WS,BWi,C:Archangel 7.00
24 WS,BWi,Fall of Mutants,
I:Archangel 12.00
25 WS,BWi,Fall of Mutants 3.50
26 WS,BWi,Fall of Mutants,
N:X-Factor. 3.50
27 WS,BWi,Christmas Issue 3.50
28 WS,BWi,V:Ship. 3.50
29 WS,BWi,V:Infectia. 3.50
30 WS,BWi,V:Infectia,Free.Force . . 3.50
31 WS,BWi,V:Infectia,Free.Force . . 3.50
32 SLi,A:Avengers 3.50
33 WS,BWi,V:Tower & Frenzy,
R:Furry Beast 3.50
34 WS,BWi,I:Nanny,
Orphan Maker 3.50
35 JRu(i),WS(c),V:Nanny,
Orphan Maker 3.50
36 WS,BWi,Inferno,V:Nastirh. 3.50
37 WS,BWi,Inferno,V:Gob.Queen . . 3.50
38 WS,AM,Inferno,A:X-Men,D:
MadelynePryor(GoblinQueen). . 3.50
39 WS,AM,Inferno,A:X-Men,
V:Mr.Sinister 3.50

X-Factor #50
© Marvel Entertainment Group

40 RLd,AM,O:Nanny,Orphan Maker
　1st Liefeld Marvel work 6.00
41 AAd,AM,I:Alchemy 3.50
42 AAd,AM,A:Alchemy 3.50
43 PS,AM,V:Celestials. 3.50
44 PS,AM,V:Rejects. 3.50
45 PS,AM,V:Rask 3.50
46 PS,AM,V:Rejects. 3.50
47 KD,AM,V:Father 3.50
48 thru 49 PS,AM,V:Rejects 3.50
50 RLd&TM(c),RB,AM,A:Prof.X
　(double sized),BU:Apocalypse . 5.00
51 AM,V:Sabretooth,Caliban 4.00
52 RLd(c),AM,V:Sabretooth,
　Caliban 3.00
53 AM,V:Sabretooth,Caliban 3.00
54 MS,AM,A:Colossus,I:Crimson. . 3.00
55 MMi(c),CDo,AM,V:Mesmero. . . 3.00
56 AM,V:Crimson 3.00
57 NKu,V:Crimson 3.00
58 JBg,AM,V:Crimson 3.00
59 AM,V:Press Gang 3.00
60 JBg,AM,X-Tinction Agenda#3 . . 4.00
60a 2nd printing(gold) 2.50
61 JBg,AM,X-Tinction Agenda#6 . . 3.50
62 JBg,AM,JLe(c),E:X-Agenda . . . 3.50
63 WPo,I:Cyberpunks 3.50
64 WPo,ATb,V:Cyberpunks 3.00
65 WPo,ATb,V:Apocalypse 3.00
66 WPo,ATb,I:Askani,
　V:Apocalypse 3.00
67 WPo,ATb,V:Apocalypse,I:Shinobi
　Shaw,D:Sebastian Shaw 3.00
68 WPo,ATb,JLe(c),V:Apocalypse,
　L:Nathan,(taken into future). . . 3.00
69 WPo,V:Shadow King. 3.00
70 MMi(c),JRu,Last old team. 3.00
71 LSn,AM,New Team 4.00
71a 2nd printing 2.50
72 LSn,AM,Who shot Madrox
　revealed. 3.00
73 LSn,AM,Mob Chaos in D.C. . . . 3.00
74 LSn,AM,I:Slab. 3.00
75 LSn,AM,I:Nasty Boys(doub.sz). . 3.50
76 LSn,AM,V:Mutant Lib. Front. . . . 3.25
77 LSn,AM,V:Mutant Lib. Front . . . 3.25
78 LSn,AM,V:Helle's Belles 3.25
79 LSn,AM,V:Helle's Belles 3.25
80 LSn,AM,V:Helle's Belles,
　C:Cyber 3.25
81 LSn,AM,V:Helle's Belles,Cyber. . 3.25
82 JQ(c),LSn,V:Brotherhood of Evil
　Mutants,I:X-iles 3.25
83 MPa,A:X-Force,X-iles 3.25

84 JaL,X-Cutioners Song #2,
　V:X-Force,A:X-Men 3.25
85 JaL,X-Cutioners Song #6,
　Wolv.& Bishop,V:Cable 3.25
86 JaL,AM,X-Cutioner's Song#10,
　A:X-Men,X-Force,V:Stryfe 3.25
87 JQ,X-Cutioners Song
　Aftermath. 3.00
88 JQ,AM,V:2nd Genegineer,
　I:Random. 4.00
89 JQ,V:Mutates,Genosha. 3.00
90 JQ,AM,Genosha vs. Aznia 3.00
91 AM,V:Armageddon 3.00
92 JQ,AM,V:Fabian Cortez,
　Acolytes,hologram(c). 6.00
93 Magneto Protocols 3.00
94 PR,J:Forge 3.00
95 B:JMD(s),AM,Polaris
　Vs. Random. 3.00
96 A:Random 3.00
97 JD,I:Haven,A:Random 3.00
98 GLz,A:Haven,A:Random. 3.00
99 JD,A:Haven,Wolfsbane returns
　to human 3.00
100 JD,Red Foil(c),V:Haven,
　D:Madrox. 6.00
100a Newstand Ed. 3.00
101 JD,AM,Aftermath. 2.50
102 JD,AM,V:Crimson Commando,
　Avalanche 2.50
103 JD,AM,A:Malice 2.50
104 JD,AM,V:Malice,
　C:Mr. Sinister. 2.50
105 JD,AM,V:Malice. 2.50
106 Phalanx Covenant,Life Signs
　Holografx(c). 3.50
106a newsstand ed 2.50
107 A:Strong Guy. 2.50
108 A:Mystique, deluxe ed. 2.50
108a newsstand ed. 2.00
109 A:Mystique,V:Legion, deluxe. . 2.50
109a newsstand ed. 2.25
110 Invasion. 2.50
110a deluxe ed. 2.25
111 Invasion. 2.50
111a deluxe ed. 2.25
112 AM,JFM,SEp,F:Guido,Havok . 2.50
113 A:Mystique. 2.50
114 AM,Wild Child & Mystique. . . . 2.50
115 F:Wild Child,Havok 2.50
116 F:Wild Child. 2.50
117 HMe,AM,F:Cyclops 2.50
118 HMe,AM,A:Random,Shard . . . 2.50
119 HMe,AM,F:Sabretooth 2.50
120 A:Sabretooth 2.50
121 A:Sabretooth 2.50
122 HMe,SEp,AM,J:Sabretooth. . . 2.50
123 A:Hound 2.50
124 A:Onslaught 3.50
125 Onslaught saga, double size . . 4.00
126 Beast vs. Dark Beast. 2.50
127 Mystique 2.50
128 HMe,JMs,AM,Hound Program . 2.50
129 HMe,JMs,AM,Graydon Creed's
　campaign 2.50
130 HMe,JMs,AM,Assassination of
　Graydon Creed 2.50
131 HMe,JMs,ATi,Havok strikes
　back. 2.50
132 HMe,JMs,ATi,Break away from
　government 2.50
133 HMe,JMs,ATi,A:Multiple Man &
　Strong Guy 2.50
134 HMe,JMs,Ati,Operation X-Factor
　Underground, cont. 2.50
135 HMe,JMs,Strong Guy awakes . 2.50
136 HMe,JMs,ATi, A:Sabretooth . . 2.50
137 HMe,JMs,ATi, Final fate of
　Shard and Polaris 2.50
138 HMe,JMs,ATi,Sabertooth,
　V:Maberick. 2.50

139 HMe,ATi,Who killed Graydon
　Creed. 2.50
140 HMe,ATi,Who killed Graydon
　Creed, A:Mystique 2.50
141 HMe,ATi,Shard's Plan 2.50
142 ATi,F:Wild Child. 2.50
143 HMe,ATi,Havok vs.DarkBeast. . 2.50
144 HMe,ATi,V:Brotherhood,
　Dark Beast. 2.50
145 HMe,ATi,Havok vs. X.U.E. . . . 2.50
146 HMe,ATi,Havok, Multiple
　Man,V:Polaris 2.50
147 HMe,Havok v. Mandroids 2.50
148 F:Shard. 2.50
149 HMe,Polaris & Madrox rejoin . 3.50
Spec #1 JG,Prisoner of Love 5.00
Ann.#1 BL,BBr,V:CrimsonDynamo . 5.00
Ann.#2 TGr,JRu,A:Inhumans 4.00
Ann.#3 WS(c),AM,JRu,PC,TD,
　Evolutionary War 3.50
Ann.#4 JBy,WS,JRu,MBa,Atlantis
　Attacks,BU:Doom & Magneto . . 3.50
Ann.#5 JBg,AM,DR,GI,Days of Future
　Present,A:Fant.Four,V:Ahab. . . 4.00
Ann.#6 Flesh Tears Saga,pt.4,
　A:X-Force, New Warriors 4.00
Ann #7 JQ,JRu,Shattershot,pt.3 . . 4.00
Ann.#8 I:Charon,w/card 3.25
Ann.#9 JMD(s),MtB,V:Prof.Power,
　A:Prof.X,O:Haven 3.25
Minus 1 Spec., HMe,JMs,ATi,
　flashback,F:Havok. 2.50
GN X-Men: Wrath of Apocalypse,
　rep.X-Factor#65-#68 . . . . 5.00

X-FACTOR
April, 2002

1 (of 4) When will it stop. 2.50
2 FBI agents 2.50
3 in San Francisco 2.50
4 Concl.. . . . . 2.50

X-FACTOR
Dec., 2005

1 PDd(s) 4.50
2 PDd(s), Decimation tie-in. 3.00
3 PDd(s), Decimation tie-in. 3.00
4 PDd(s), Strong Guy & Wolfsbane 3.00
5 PDd(s) 3.00
6 PDd(s), The Butterfly Defect 3.00
7 PDd(s), Two Meetings 3.00
8 PDd(s), Civil War tie-in 5.00
9 PDd(s), Civil War tie-in 4.00
10 PDd(s). 3.00
11 PDd(s). 3.00
12 PDd(s), V:Mr. Tryp & Singularity. 3.00
13 PDd(s), Re-X-Aminations 3.00
14 PDd(s),F:Jamie Madrox 3.00
15 PDd(s),Agent of Hydra 3.00
16 PDd(s),The Multiple Man 3.00
17 PDd(s),I:X-MAD 3.00
18 . . . . 3.00
19 PDd(s). 3.00
20 PDd(s). 3.00
21 PDd(s), The Isolationist, pt.1 . . 3.00
22 PDd(s), The Isolationist, pt.2 . . 3.00
23 PDd(s), The Isolationist, pt. 3 . . 3.00
24 PDd(s), The Isolationist, pt.4 . . 3.00
25 Messiah Complex, pt.3 x-over . . 3.00

X-51
July, 1999

1 JQ&JP(c) Marvel Tech. 2.50
2 JoB,V:Brotherhood of Mutants. . . 2.50
2a variant cover 2.50
3 JoB,A:X.E.R.O. 2.50
4 JoB,A:Avengers 2.50
5 JoB,V:Vision. 2.50
6 JoB. 2.50
7 JoB,A:Sebastian Shaw 2.50
8 JoB,F:X-Men 2.50

9 JoB, ... 2.50
10 JoB,F:Machine Man 2.50
11 JoB,F:Celestial 2.50
12 JoB,final issue. 2.50

X-FORCE
Aug., 1991

1 RLd,V:Stryfe,Mutant Liberation
Front,bagged, white on black
graphics with X-Force Card. . . . 4.00
1a with Shatterstar Card. 4.00
1b with Deadpool Card. 4.00
1c with Sunspot & Gideon Card . . 4.00
1d with Cable Card. 5.00
1e Unbagged Copy. 2.75
1f 2nd Printing. 2.50
2 RLd,I:New Weapon X,V:
Deadpool 3.50
3 RLd,C:Spider-Man,
V:Juggernaut,Black Tom 3.00
4 RLd,SpM/X-Force team-up,
V:Juggernaut(cont.from SpM#16)
Sideways format 3.00
5 RLd,A:Brotherhood Evil Mutants . 3.00
6 RLd,V:Bro'hood Evil Mutants. . . . 3.00
7 RLd,V:Bro'hood Evil Mutants. . . . 3.00
8 MMi,O:Cable(Part). 3.50
9 RLd,D:Sauron,Masque 3.00
10 MPa,V:Mutant Liberation Front. . 3.00
11 MPa,Deadpool Vs Domino 3.00
12 MPa,A:Weapon Prime,Gideon . . 2.50
13 MPa,V:Weapon Prime 2.50
14 TSr,V:Weapon Prime,Krule. 2.50
15 GCa,V:Krule,Deadpool 2.50
16 GCa,X-Cutioners Song #4,
X-Factor V:X-Force 3.00
17 GCa,X-Cutioners Song#8,
Apocalypse V:Stryfe 3.00
18 GCa,X-Cutioners Song#12,
Cable vs Stryfe 3.00
19 GCa,X-Cutioners Song
Aftermath,N:X-Force 2.50
20 GCa,O:Graymalkin 2.50
21 GCa,V:War Machine,SHIELD . . . 2.50
22 GCa,V:Externals 2.50
23 GCa,V:Saul,Gigeon,A:Six Pack . 2.50
24 GCa,A:Six Pack,A:Deadpool . . . 2.50
25 GCa,A:Mageneto,Exodus,
R:Cable 5.00
26 GCa(c),MtB,I:Reignfire 2.50
27 GCa(c),MtB,V:Reignfire,MLF,
I:Moonstar,Locus 2.50
28 MtB,V:Reignfire,MLF. 2.50
29 MtB,V:Arcade,C:X-Treme 2.50
30 TnD,V:Arcade,A:X-Treme 2.50

X-Force #27
© *Marvel Entertainment Group*

31 F:Siryn. 2.50
32 Child's Play#1,A:New Warriors. . 2.50
33 Child's Play#3,A:New Warriors,
V:Upstarts 2.50
34 F:Rictor,Domino,Cable 3.00
35 TnD,R:Nimrod. 2.50
36 TnD,V:Nimrod 2.50
37 PaP,I&D:Absalom 2.50
38 TaD,Life Signs,pt.2,
I:Generation X, foil(c) 5.00
38a newsstand ed. 2.50
39 TaD 2.50
40 TaD, deluxe 2.50
40a newsstand ed. 2.50
41 TaD,O:feral,deluxe 2.50
41a newsstand ed. 2.25
42 Emma Frost, deluxe 2.50
42a newsstand ed. 2.25
43 Home is Where Heart 2.50
43a deluxe ed. 2.50
44 AdP,Prof.X,X-Mansion. 2.50
45 AdP,Caliban vs. Sabretooth 2.50
46 R:The Mimic 2.50
47 A:Deadpool 2.50
48 AdP,Siryn Takes Charge 2.50
49 ADp,MBu,Holocaust is here 2.50
50 AdP,MPn,F:Sebastian Shaw . . . 3.00
50a prismatic foil cover 4.50
50b variant RLd(c). 6.00
51 AdP,MPn,V:Risque. 2.50
52 A:Onslaught 3.50
53 . . . . 2.50
54 AdP, Can X-Force
protect X-Ternals? 2.50
55 V:S.H.I.E.L.D. 2.50
56 Deadpool, A:Onslaught. 4.00
57 Onslaught saga. 2.50
58 Onslaught saga. 2.50
59 Longshot, with card. 2.50
60 JLb,,F:Shatterstar,A:Long Shot. . 2.50
61 JLb,R:Longshot,O:Shatterstar . . 2.50
62 JLb,F:Sunspot. 2.50
63 JFM,AdP,F:Risque,Cannonball. . 2.50
64 JFM, AdP,In Latveria, searching
for Doctor Doom's weapons . . . 2.50
65 JFM, AdP,Warpath follows Risque
to Florida 2.50
66 JFM,AdP,A:Risque,James
Proudstar. 2.50
67 JFM,AdP,F:Warpath, Risque. . . . 2.50
68 JFM,AdP,Zero Tolerance. 2.50
69 JFM,AdP,Zero Tolerance
aftermath 2.50
70 JFM,AdP,new direction starts . . . 2.50
71 JFM,AdP,new direction 2.50
72 JFM,AdP,on the road 2.50
73 JFM,AdP,in New Orleans 2.50
74 JFM,ASm,Skids is back 2.50
75 JFM,AdP,A:Reignfire,
double size 3.00
76 JFM,AdP,F:Shatterstar 2.50
77 JFM,AdP,F:Sunfire & Meltdown . 2.50
78 JFM,AdP,Reignfire makes his
move 2.50
79 JFM,AdP,O:Reignfire 2.50
80 JFM,AdP,V:Reignfire. 2.50
81 JFM,AdP,trip to Hawaii,
V:Lava Men, AdP Poster 2.50
82 JFM,V:Griffin, Damocles
Foundation. 2.50
83 JFM,F:Cannonball. 2.50
84 JFM,V:Deviants. 2.50
85 JFM,Return of Skids 2.50
86 JFM,A:Hulk 2.50
87 JFM,V:new Hellions 2.50
88 JFM,V:new Hellions 2.50
89 JFM,prisoners of the Hellions . . . 2.50
90 JFM,Hellion War,concl. 2.50
91 JFM,home to San Francisco. . . . 2.50
92 JFM,F:Domino 2.50
93 JFM,Domino returns 2.50
94 JFM,destination Genosha 2.50

X-Force #Ann. #2
© *Marvel Entertainment Group*

95 JFM,F:Magneto. 2.50
96 JFM,A:Selene 2.50
97 JFM,V:Reignfire 2.50
98 . . . . 2.50
99 JFM,F:Dani Moonstar 2.50
100 JFM,Four Personas,48-pg. 3.00
101 new members,some gone 2.50
102 WPo,X-Men: Revolution 2.50
102a variant (c) 5.00
103 WPo,WEI,Games Without
Frontiers,pt.2 . . . . 2.50
104 WPo,WEI,Games,pt.3 . . . . 2.50
105 WPo,WEI,Games,pt.4 . . . . 2.50
106 WEI,IEd,WPo,Murder
Ballads,pt.1 . . . . 2.50
107 WEI,IEd,MurderBallads,pt.2 . . . 2.50
108 WEI,IEd,Ballads,pt.3 . . . . 2.50
109 WEI,IEd,Ballads,pt.4 . . . . 2.50
110 WEI,IEd,Rage War,pt.1 . . . . 2.50
111 WEI,IEd,Rage War,pt.2 . . . . 2.50
112 WEI,IEd,Rage War,pt.3 . . . . 2.50
113 WEI,IEd,Rage War,pt.4 . . . . 2.50
114 . . . . 2.50
115 IEd,final issue? 2.50
116 PrM,MiA,new team 5.00
117 PrM,MiA,new members. 5.00
118 PrM,MiA,F:U-Go Girl. 2.50
119 PrM,MiA,F:U-Go Girl. 2.50
120 PrM,MiA,A:Wolverine 2.50
121 PrM,MiA,I:Lacuna 2.50
122 PrM,MiA,F:Lacuna 2.50
123 PrM,MiA,'Nuff Said 2.50
124 PrM,Orphan & U-Go Girl 2.50
125 PrM,Anarchist, Doop. 2.50
126 PrM,MiA,one won't come home 2.50
127 PrM,MiA,who won't come home 2.50
128 PrM,MiA,body bag time 2.50
129 PrM,DFg,something
even worse 2.50
Ann.#1 Shattershot,pt1 . . . . 3.00
Ann.#2 JaL,LSn,I:X-Treme,w/card. . 3.25
Ann.#3 . . . . 2.50
Ann.1998 X-Force/Champions. 6.00
Ann.1999 R:Shatterstar & Rictor . . . 3.50
Spec.#102 Rough cut edition. 3.00
Minus 1 Spec., JFM,AdP, flashback,
F:John Proudstar. 2.50

X-FORCE
Aug., 2004

1 RLd,X-Men: Reload Wave. 3.00
2 RLd,Cable completes team 3.00
3 RLd,Cable vs. Cannonball. 3.00
4 RLd,F:Wolverine & Deadpool . . . 3.00

MARVEL

5 RLd,F:Fantastic Four 3.00
6 Fan,rld, V:skornn,concl. 3.00

X-FORCE: SHATTERSTAR
Feb., 2005
1 (of 4) RLd(c),MMy 3.00
2 Rld(c),Mmy 3.00
3 RLd(c),MMy 3.00
4 RLd(c),MMy,finale 3.00

X-MAN
March, 1995
1 Cable after Xavier 5.00
2 Sinister's Plan 4.00
3 V:Domino 3.00
4 V:Sinister 3.00
5 Into this World 3.00
6 V:X-Men 2.50
7 Evil from Age of Apocalypse 2.50
8 Crossover Adventure 2.50
9 F:Nate's Past 2.50
10 Nate's Past 2.50
11 Young Nate seeks out X-Men . . . 2.50
12 F:Excalibur 2.50
13 . . . . 2.50
14 . . . . 2.50
15 JOs,X-Men/Cable war aftermath 3.00
16 Holocaust,A:Onslaught 2.50
17 Holocaust,Quicksilver,Scarlet
    Witch, A:Onslaught 2.50
18 Onslaught saga 2.50
19 Onslaught saga 2.50
20 . . . . 2.50
21 TKa,RCz,F:Nate 2.50
22 TKa,RCz,F:Threnody,A:Madelyne
    Pryor 2.50
23 TKa,RCz,F:Bishop 2.50
24 TKa,RCz,Spider-Man vs. Nate . 2.50
25 TKa,RCz,Madelyne Pryor,
    double size 4.00
26 TKa,RCz,Nate limps to Muir
    Isle,A:Moira Mactaggert 2.50
27 TKa,RCz,Hellfire Club, concl. . . 2.50
28 TKa,RCz,Dark Beast's offer . . . 2.50
29 TKa,RCz,Back in New York, . . . 2.50
30 TKa,RCz,F:Nate Grey. 2.50
31 RL,DGr,F:Nate Grey 2.50
32 TKa,V:Jacknife 2.50
33 TKa,V:Jacknife 2.50
34 TKa,Secret of Nate's popularity . 2.50
35 TKa,Terrorists Strike 2.50
36 TKa,V:Purple Man 2.50

X-Man #49
© *Marvel Entertainment Group*

37 TKa,Nate leaves N.Y.,
    A:Spider-Man 2.50
38 TKa,A:Spider-Man, Gwen Stacy . 2.50
39 TKa,AOI,Nate & Madeline Pryor. 2.50
40 TKa,RPc,V:Great Beasts 2.50
41 TKa,RCz,Madelyne Pryor 2.50
42 TKa,RCz,hunted by leprechauns 2.50
43 TKa,RCz,Nate Grey–murderer?! 2.50
44 TKa,RCz,F:Nate Grey,Gauntlet . 2.50
45 TKa,prelude to X-Man/Cable
    x-over. 2.50
46 TKa,Cable x-over 2.50
47 TKa,Blood Brothers,pt.3 . . . . . . 2.50
48 LRs,V:Crusader 2.50
49 LRs,TKa,F:Nate 2.50
50 TKa,LRs,War of the
    Mutants,pt.2, 48-page 3.50
51 TKa,LRs,V:Psi-Ops. 2.50
52 TKa,LRs,V:Psi-Ops. 2.50
53 TKa,Strange Relations,pt.1 . . . . 2.50
54 TKa,Strange Relations,pt.2. . . . 2.50
55 TKa,M'Kraan Crystal. 2.50
56 TKa,Nate in Greyville 2.50
57 TKa,V:Mysterio 2.50
58 TKa,V:Threnody 2.50
59 TKa 2.50
60 TKa, ... 2.50
61 TKa, ... 2.50
62 TKa,trapped 2.50
63 WEI,X-Men: Revolution 2.25
63a variant(c) 2.25
64 WEI,No Direction Home,pt.2 . . . 2.25
65 WEI,No Direction Home,pt.3. . . . 2.25
66 WEI,No Direction Home,pt.4. . . . 2.25
67 WEI,Down the Spiral,pt.1 . . . . . 2.25
68 WEI,Down the Spiral,pt.2 . . . . . 2.25
69 WEI,Down the Spiral,pt.3 . . . . . 2.25
70 WEI,Down the Spiral,pt.4 . . . . . 2.25
71 AOI,StG,Fearful
    Symmetries,pt.1. . . . . 2.25
72 AOI,StG,Symmetries,pt.2 . . . . . 2.25
73 AOI,StG,Symmetries,pt.3 . . . . . 2.25
74 AOI,StG,Symmetries,pt.4 . . . . . 2.25
75 Anti-Man, final issue 3.00
Minus 1 Spec., TKa,RCz,
    flashback,O:Nate Grey 2.00
Spec.#1 X-Man '96 . . . . 3.50
Ann. '97 RBe, Nate, Sugar Man,
    Dark Beast, Holocaust. 3.00
Ann. '98 X-Man, The Hulk, Thanos,
    48-pg. 3.00
GNv X-Man,BRa,TyD, 48-pg. . . . 6.00

X-MEN
Sept., 1963
1 JK,O:X-Men,I:Professor X,Beast
    Cyclops,Marvel Girl,Iceman
    Angel,Magneto 17,000.00
2 JK,I:Vanisher. 5,000.00
3 JK,I:Blob 2,000.00
4 JK,I:Quicksilver,Scarlet Witch
    Mastermind,Toad 2,500.00
5 JK,V:Broth. of Evil Mutants . 1,500.00
6 JK,V:Sub-Mariner 1,000.00
7 JK,V:Broth. of Evil Mutants,
    Blob 1,000.00
8 JK,I:Unus,1st Ice covered
    Iceman 1,000.00
9 JK,A:Avengers,I:Lucifer . . . 1,100.00
10 JK,I:Modern Ka-Zar 1,100.00
11 JK,I:Stranger 900.00
12 JK,O:Prof.X,I:Juggernaut. . 1,200.00
13 JK,JSt,V:Juggernaut 650.00
14 JK,I:Sentinels 650.00
15 JK,O:Beast,V:Sentinels. . . . 650.00
16 JK,V:Mastermold,Sentinels. . . 650.00
17 JK,V:Magneto 400.00
18 V:Magneto. 400.00
19 I:Mimic. 400.00
20 V:Lucifer 400.00
21 V:Lucifer,Dominus. 250.00
22 V:Maggia 250.00

23 V:Maggia. 250.00
24 I:Locust(Prof.Hopper) 250.00
25 JK,I:El Tigre 250.00
26 V:El Tigre 230.00
27 C:Fant.Four,V:Puppet Master. 230.00
28 I:Banshee 400.00
29 V:Super-Apaptoid 225.00
30 JK,I:The Warlock. 225.00
31 JK,I:Cobalt Man 225.00
32 V:Juggernaut 225.00
33 GK,A:Dr.Strange,Juggernaut . 225.00
34 V:Tyrannus,Mole Man. 225.00
35 JK,A:Spider-Man,Banshee . . 225.00
36 V:Mekano 225.00
37 DH,V:Blob,Unus 225.00
38 DH,A:Banshee,O:Cyclops. . . 250.00
39 DH,GT,A:Banshee,V:Mutant
    Master,O:Cyclops 300.00
40 DH,GT,V:Frankenstein,
    O:Cyclops 250.00
41 DH,GT,I:Grotesk,O:Cyclops . 250.00
42 DH,GT,JB,V:Grotesk,
    O:Cyclops,D:Prof.X 150.00
43 GT,JB,V:Magneto,Quicksilver,
    Scarlet Witch,C:Avengers . . 200.00
44 V:Magneto,Quicksilver,Sc.Witch,
    R:Red Raven,O:Iceman . . . 200.00
45 PH,JB,V:Magneto,Quicksilver,
    Scarlet Witch,O:Iceman . . . 200.00
46 DH,V:Juggernaut,O:Iceman . 225.00
47 DH,I:Maha Yogi. 210.00
48 DH,V:Quasimodo. 210.00
49 JSo,DH,C:Magneto,I:Polaris,
    Mesmero,O:Beast 210.00
50 JSo,V:Magneto,O:Beast 200.00
51 JSo,V:Magneto,Polaris,
    Erik the Red,O:Beast. 200.00
52 DH,MSe,JSt,O:Lorna Dane
    V:Magneto,O:Beast 175.00
53 1st BWS,O:Beast 175.00
54 BWS,DH,I:Havok,O:Angel . . 175.00
55 BWS,DH,O:Havok,Angel . . . 175.00
56 NA,V:LivingMonolith,O:Angel . 175.00
57 NA,V:Sentinels,A:Havok . . . 175.00
58 NA,A:Havoc,V:Sentinels 250.00
59 NA,V:Sentinels,A:Havoc. . . . 225.00
60 NA,I:Sauron 200.00
61 NA,V:Sauron 200.00
62 NA,A:Ka-Zar,Sauron,Magneto 200.00
63 A:Ka-Zar,V:Magneto 200.00
64 DH,A:Havok,I:Sunfire 200.00
65 NA,MSe,A:Havok,Shield,
    Return of Prof.X. 200.00
66 SB,MSe,V:Hulk,A:Havok. . . . 200.00
67 rep.X-Men #12,#13 . . . . 150.00

X-Men #73
© *Marvel Entertainment Group*

68 rep.X-Men #14,#15 . . . . 150.00
69 rep.X-Men #16,#19 . . . . 150.00
70 rep.X-Men #17,#18 . . . . 150.00
71 rep.X-Men #20 . . . . 150.00
72 rep.X-Men #21,#24 . . . . 150.00
73 thru 93 rep.X-Men #25-45. . @125.00
94 GK(c),B:CCl(s),DC,BMc,B:2nd
  X-Men,V:Count Nefaria . . . 1,400.00
95 GK(c),DC,V:Count Nefaria,
  Ani-Men,D:Thunderbird 300.00
96 DC,I:Moira McTaggert,
  Kierrok 150.00
97 DC,V:Havok,Polaris,Eric
  the Red,I:Lilandra 150.00
98 DC,V:Sentinels,Stephen Lang 140.00
99 DC,V:Sentinels,S.Lang 140.00
100 DC,V:Stephen Lang 200.00
101 DC,I:Phoenix,Black Tom,
  A:Juggernaut 200.00
102 DC,O:Storm,V:Juggernaut,
  Black Tom 125.00
103 DC,V:Juggernaut,Bl.Tom . . . 125.00
104 DC,V:Magneto,I:Star
  Jammers,A:Lilandra 100.00
105 DC,BL,V:Firelord 90.00
106 DC,TS,V:Firelord 90.00
107 DC,DGr,I:Imperial Guard,Star
  Jammers,Gladiator,Corsair . . 100.00
108 JBy,TA,A:Star Jammers,
  C:Fantastic Four,Avengers . . . 125.00
109 JBy,TA,I:Vindicator 110.00
110 TD,DC,V:Warhawk 75.00
111 JBy,TA,V:Mesmero,A:Beast,
  Magneto. 75.00
112 GP(c),JBy,TA,V:Magneto,
  A:Beast 75.00
113 JBy,TA,V:Magneto,A:Beast . . 75.00
114 JBy,TA,A:Beast,R:Sauron . . . 90.00
115 JBy,TA,V:Sauron,Garokk,
  A:Ka-Zar,I:Zaladane 75.00
116 JBy,TA,V:Sauron,Garokk,
  A:Ka-Zar 75.00
117 JBy,TA,O:Prof.X,I:Amahl
  Farouk (Shadow King). 65.00
118 JBy,I:Moses Magnum,A:Sunfire
  C:Iron Fist,I:Mariko 65.00
119 JBy,TA,V:Moses Magnum,
  A:Sunfire 65.00
120 JBy,TA,I:AlphaFlight (Shaman,
  Sasquatch,Northstar,Snowbird,
  Aurora). 125.00
121 JBy,TA,V:Alpha Flight 100.00
122 JBy,TA,A:Juggernaut,Black
  Tom,Arcade,Power Man 65.00
123 JBy,TA,V:Arcade,A:SpM 60.00
124 JBy,TA,V:Arcade 60.00
125 JBy,TA:A:Beast,Madrox the
  Multiple Man,Havok,Polaris . . . 65.00
126 JBy,TA,I:Proteus,
  A:Havok,Madrox 65.00
127 JBy,TA,V:Proteus,A:Havok,
  Madrox. 65.00
128 GP(c),JBy,TA,V:Proteus,
  A:Havok,Madrox 65.00
129 JBy,TA,I:Shadow Cat,White
  Queen,C:Hellfire Club 90.00
130 JR2(c),JBy,TA,I:Dazzler
  V:White Queen 65.00
131 JBy,TA,V:White Queen,
  A:Dazzler. 65.00
132 JBy,TA,I:Hellfire Club,
  V:Mastermind 65.00
133 JBy,TA,V:Hellfire Club,
  Mastermind,F:Wolverine 65.00
134 JBy,TA,V:Hellfire Club,Master
  mind,I:Dark Phoenix,A:Beast . 75.00
135 JBy,TA,V:Dark Phoenix,C:SpM,
  Fant.Four,Silver Surfer 65.00
136 JBy,TA,V:Dark Phoenix,
  A:Beast 65.00
137 JBy,TA,D:Phoenix,V:Imperial
  Guard,A:Beast. 70.00

138 JBy,TA,History of X-Men,
  L:Cyclops,C:Shadow Cat 55.00
139 JBy,TA,A:Alpha Flight,R:Wendigo,
  N:Wolverine,J:Shadowcat 60.00
140 JBy,TA,V:Wendigo,A:Alpha
  Flight 55.00
141 JBy,TA,I:2nd Brotherhood of Evil
  Mutants,I:Rachel (Phoenix II) . 70.00
Becomes:

UNCANNY X-MEN
142 JBy,TA,V:Evil Mutants,
  A:Rachel (Phoenix II) 70.00
143 JBy,TA,V:N'Garai,I:Lee
  Forrester 50.00
144 BA,JRu,A:Man-Thing,
  O:Havok, V:D'Spayre. 20.00
145 DC,JRu,V:Arcade,A:DrDoom . 20.00
146 DC,JRu,V:Dr.Doom,Arcade . . 20.00
147 DC,JRu,V:Dr.Doom,Arcade . . 20.00
148 DC,JRu,I:Caliban,A:Dazzler
  Spiderwoman. 20.00
149 DC,JRu,A:Magneto. 20.00
150 DC,JRu,BWi,V:Magneto 22.00
151 JSh,BMc,JRu,V:Sentinels . . . 20.00
152 BMc,JRu,V:White Queen 20.00
153 DC,JRu,I:Bamf 20.00
154 DC,JRu,BWi,I:Sidrian Hunters
  A:Corsair,O:Cyclops(part) . . . 20.00
155 DC,BWi,V:Deathbird,I:Brood. . 20.00
156 DC,BWi,V:Death Bird,
  A:Tigra, Star Jammers. 20.00
157 DC,BWi,V:Deathbird 20.00
158 DC,BWi,2nd A:Rogue,
  Mystique 25.00
159 BSz,BWi,V:Dracula 20.00
160 BA,BWi,V:Belasco,I:Magik . . . 20.00
161 DC,BWi,I:Gabrielle Haller,
  O:Magneto,Professor X 20.00
162 DC,BWi,V:Brood. 25.00
163 DC,BWi,V:Brood. 20.00
164 DC,BWi,V:Brood,I:Binary 18.00
165 PS,BWi,V:Brood 20.00
166 PS,BWi,V:Brood,A:Binary,
  I:Lockheed 18.00
167 PS,BWi,V:Brood,A:N.Mutants . 22.00
168 PS,BWi,I:Madelyne Pryor . . . 20.00
169 PS,BWi,I:Morlocks 18.00
170 PS,BWi,A:Angel,V:Morlocks . . 18.00
171 WS,BWi,J:Rogue,V:Binary . . . 28.00
172 PS,BWi,V:Viper,Silver
  Samurai, ... 20.00
173 PS,BWi,V:Viper,Silver
  Samurai. 18.00
174 PS,BWi,A:Mastermind 20.00
175 PS,JR2,BWi,W:Cyclops and
  Madelyne,V:Mastermind 20.00
176 JR2,BWi,I:Val Cooper 12.00
177 JR2,AW,V:Brotherhood of
  Evil Mutants. 12.00
178 JR2,BWi,BBr,V:Brotherhood
  of Evil Mutants. 12.00
179 JR2,DGr,V:Morlocks 12.00
180 JR2,DGr,BWi,Secret Wars . . . 15.00
181 JR2,DGr,A:Sunfire 12.00
182 JR2,DGr,V:S.H.I.E.L.D. 12.00
183 JR2,DGr,V:Juggernaut 12.00
184 JR2,DGr,V:Selene,I:Forge . . . 16.00
185 JR2,DGr,V:Shield,U.S.
  Govt.,Storm loses powers . . . 12.00
186 BWS,TA,Lifedeath,
  V:Dire Wraiths 14.00
187 JR2,DGr,V:Dire Wraiths 12.00
188 JR2,DGr,V:Dire Wraiths 12.00
189 JR2,SL,V:Selene,A:Magma . . 12.00
190 JR2,DGr,V:Kulan Gath,A:SpM,
  Avengers,New Mutants 12.00
191 JR2,DGr,A:Avengers,Spider-Man,
  New Mutants,I:Nimrod. 12.00
192 JR2,DGr,V:Magus 12.00
193 JR2,DGr,V:Hellions,I:Firestar
  Warpath,20th Anniv. 20.00
194 JR2,DGr,SL,V:Nimrod 12.00

Uncanny X-Men #175
© *Marvel Entertainment Group*

195 BSz(c),JR2,DGr,A:Power
  Pack,V:Morlocks 12.00
196 JR2,DGr,J:Magneto 15.00
197 JR2,DGr,V:Arcade 12.00
198 BWS,F:Storm,Lifedeath II . . . 12.00
199 JR2,DGr,I:Freedom Force,
  Rachel becomes 2nd Phoenix 12.00
200 JR2,DGr,A:Magneto,I:Fenris . . 20.00
201 RL,WPo(i),I:Nathan
  Christopher (Cyclops son). . . . 22.00
202 JR2,AW,Secret Wars II 12.00
203 JR2,AW,Secret Wars II 12.00
204 JBr,WPo,V:Arcade 12.00
205 BWS,A:Lady Deathstrike 22.00
206 JR2,DGr,V:Freedom Force . . . 12.00
207 JR2,DGr,V:Selene. 12.00
208 JR2,DGr,V:Nimrod,
  A:Hellfire Club 12.00
209 JR2,CR,V:Nimrod,A:Spiral . . . 12.00
210 JR2,DGr,I:Marauders,
  (Mutant Massacre). 25.00
211 JR2,BBl,AW,V:Marauders,
  (Mutant Massacre). 25.00
212 RL,DGr,V:Sabretooth,
  (Mutant Massacre). 35.00
213 AD,V:Sabretooth (Mut.Mass) . 35.00
214 BWS,BWi,V:Malice,A:Dazzler. 12.00
215 AD,DGr,I:Stonewall,Super
  Sabre,Crimson Commando. . . 12.00
216 BWS(c),JG,DGr,V:Stonewall . . 12.00
217 WS(c),JG,SL,V:Juggernaut. . . 12.00
218 AAD(c),MS,DGr,V:Juggernaut 12.00
219 BBl,DGr,V:Marauders,Polaris
  becomes Malice,A:Sabertooth 12.00
220 MS,DGr,A:Naze 12.00
221 MS,DGr,I:Mr.Sinister,
  V:Marauders 24.00
222 MS,DGr,V:Marauders,Eye
  Killers,A:Sabertooth. 28.00
223 KGa,DGr,A:Freedom Force . . 12.00
224 MS,DGr,V:Adversary. 15.00
225 MS,DGr,Fall of Mutants
  I:1st US App Roma 16.00
226 MS,DGr,Fall of Mutants 16.00
227 MS,DGr,Fall of Mutants 16.00
228 RL,TA,A:OZ Chase 14.00
229 MS,DGr,I:Reavers,Gateway . . 14.00
230 RL,DGr,Xmas Issue 14.00
231 RL,DGr,V:Limbo 12.00
232 MS,DGr,V:Brood 12.00
233 MS,DGr,V:Brood 12.00
234 MS,JRu,V:Brood 15.00
235 RL,CR,V:Magistrates 12.00
236 MS,DGr,V:Magistrates 12.00

Uncanny X-Men #217
© *Marvel Entertainment Group*

237 RL,TA,V:Magistrates 12.00
238 MS,DGr,V:Magistrates 12.00
239 MS,DGr,Inferno,A:Mr.Sinister . 12.00
240 MS,DGr,Inferno,V:Marauders . 15.00
241 MS,DGr,Inferno,O:Madeline
   Pryor,V:Marauders 12.00
242 MS,DGr,Inferno,D:N'Astirh,
   A:X-Factor,Double-sized 12.00
243 MS,Inferno,A:X-Factor. 12.00
244 MS,DGr,I:Jubilee. 30.00
245 RLd,DGr,Invasion Parody. . . . 12.00
246 MS,DGr,V:Mastermold,
   A:Nimrod. 12.00
247 MS,DGr,V:Mastermold 12.00
248 JLe(1st X-Men Art),DGr,
   V:Nanny & Orphan Maker 30.00
248a 2nd printing 3.00
249 MS,DGr,C:Zaladane,
   V:Savage Land Mutates. 10.00
250 MS,SL,I:Zaladane. 10.00
251 MS,DGr,V:Reavers. 14.00
252 JLe,BSz(c),RL,SW,V:Reavers 10.00
253 MS,SL,V:Amahl Farouk 10.00
254 JLe(c),MS,DGr,V:Reavers . . . 10.00
255 MS,DGr,V:Reavers,D:Destiny. 10.00
256 JLe,SW,Acts of Vengeance,
   V:Manderin,A:Psylocke 15.00
257 JLe,JRu,AofV,V:Manderin 12.00
258 JLe,SW,AofV,V:Manderin 12.00
259 MS,DGr,V:Magistrates, ... 8.00
260 JLe(c),MS,DGr,A:Dazzler 8.00
261 JLe(c),MS,DGr,V:Hardcase &
   Harriers 8.00
262 KD,JRu,V:Masque,Morlocks . . . 8.00
263 JRu(i),O:Forge,V:Morlocks 8.00
264 JLe(c),MC,JRu,V:Magistrate . . 8.00
265 JRu(i),V:Shadowking 8.00
266 NKu(c),MC,JRu,I:Gambit 50.00
267 JLe,WPo,SW,V:Shadowking . . 20.00
268 JLe,SW,A:Captain America,
   Black Widow,V:The Hand,
   Baron Strucker. 20.00
269 JLe,ATi,Rogue V:Ms.Marvel . . 10.00
270 JLe,ATi,SW,X-Tinction Agenda
   #1, A:Cable,New Mutants 12.00
270a 2nd printing(Gold) 4.00
271 JLe,SW,X-Tinction Agenda
   #4,A:Cable,New Mutants. 10.00
272 JLe,SW,X-Tinction Agenda
   #7,A:Cable,New Mutants. 10.00
273 JLe,WPo,JBy,KJ,RL,MS,MGo,
   LSn,SW,A:Cable,N.Mutants . . 10.00
274 JLe,SW,V:Zaladane,A:Magneto,
   Nick Fury,Ka-Zar 10.00

275 JLe,SW,R:Professor X,A:Star
   Jammers,Imperial Guard 12.00
275a 2nd Printing (Gold) 3.00
276 JLe,SW,V:Skrulls,Shi'ar 10.00
277 JLe,SW,V:Skrulls,Shi'ar 10.00
278 PS,Professor X Returns to
   Earth,V:Shadowking 8.00
279 NKu,SW,V:Shadowking 7.00
280 E:CCl(s),NKu,A:X-Factor,
   D:Shadowking,Prof.X Crippled . 7.00
281 WPo,ATi,new team (From X-Men
   #1),D:Pierce,Hellions,V:Sentinels,
   I:Trevor Fitzroy,Upstarts 10.00
281a 2nd printing,red(c). 3.00
282 WPo,ATi,V:Fitzroy,C:Bishop . . 15.00
282a 2nd printing,gold(c) of #281
   inside 3.00
283 WPo,ATi,I:Bishop,Malcolm,
   Randall 15.00
284 WPo,ATi,SOS from USSR 5.00
285 WPo,I:Mikhail(Colossus'
   brother from Russia) 5.00
286 JLe,WPo,ATi,A:Mikhail 5.00
287 JR2,O:Bishop,
   D:Malcolm,Randall 6.00
288 NKu,BSz,A:Bishop 5.00
289 WPo,ATi,Forge proposes
   to Storm 5.00
290 WPo,SW,V:Cyberpunks,
   L:Forge 5.00
291 TR,V:Morlocks. 5.00
292 TR,V:Morlocks. 5.00
293 TR,D:Morlocks,Mikhail 5.00
294 BP,TA,X-Cutioner's Song#1,
   Stryfe shoots Prof X,A:X-Force,
   X-Factor,polybag.w/ProfX card . 5.00
295 BP,TA,X-Cutioners Song #5,
   V:Apocalypse. 5.00
296 BP,TA,X-Cutioners Song #9,
   A:X-Force,X-Factor,V:Stryfe . . . 5.00
297 BP,X-Cutioners Song
   Aftermath. 5.00
298 BP,TA,V:Acolytes 5.00
299 BP,A:Forge,Acolytes,I:Graydon
   Creed (Sabretooth's son) 5.00
300 JR2,DGr,BP,V:Acolytes,A:Forge,
   Nightcrawler,Holografx(c) 10.00
301 JR2,DGr,I:Sienna Blaze,
   V:Fitzroy 5.00
302 JR2,V:Fitzroy 5.00
303 JR2,V:Upstarts,D:Illyana 6.00
304 JR2,JaL,PS,L:Colossus,
   V:Magneto,Holo-grafx(c) 8.00
305 JD,F:Rogue,Bishop. 5.00
306 JR2,V:Hodge. 5.00
307 JR2,Bloodties#4,A:Avengers,
   V:Exodus,Cortez 6.00
308 JR2,Scott & Jean announce
   impending marriage. 5.00
309 JR2,O:Professor X & Amelia . 5.00
310 JR2,DG,A:Cable,V:X-Cutioner,
   w/card 5.00
311 JR2,DG,AV,V:Sabretooth,
   C:Phalanx 5.00
312 JMd,DG,A:Yukio,I:Phalanx,
   w/card 5.00
313 JMd,DG,V:Phalanx 5.00
314 LW,BSz,R:White Quen 5.00
315 F:Acolytes 5.00
316 V:Phalanx,I:M,Phalanx Covenant
   Generation Next,pt.1, holo(c) . . 5.00
316a newsstand ed. 3.00
317 JMd,V:Phalanx,prism(c) 5.00
317a newsstand ed. 3.00
318 JMd,L:Jubilee, deluxe 5.00
318a newsstand ed. 3.00
319 R:Legion, deluxe 5.00
319a newsstand ed. 3.00
320 deluxe ed. 5.00
320 newsstand ed. 3.00
321 R:Lilandra, deluxe ed 5.00
321 newsstand ed. 5.00

322 SLo,TGu,Rogue,Iceman run from
   Gambit's Secret. 8.00
323 I:Onslaught 5.00
324 SLo,F:Cannonball 5.00
325 R:Colossus 7.00
326 SLo,JMd,F:Gambit,Sabretooth . 4.00
327 SLo,JMd,Magneto's Fate 4.00
328 SLo,JMd,Sabretooth freed . . . 4.00
329 SLo,JMd,A:Doctor Strange . . . 4.00
330 Dr.Strange. 4.00
331 White Queen. 4.00
332 SLo,JMd, cont from
   Wolverine #100 . . . . 4.00
333 SLo,JMd, Operation: Zero
   Tolerance, Onslaught saga . . . 4.00
334 SLo,JMd, Onslaught saga 4.00
335 SLo,JMd, Onslaught saga 4.00
336 Apocalypse vs. Onslaught 4.00
337 Operation: Zero Tolerance 4.00
338 SLo,JMd,R:Angel 4.00
339 SLo,JMd,F:Cyclops, J.J.
   Jameson, Havok 4.00
340 SLo,JMd,F:Iceman 4.00
341 SLo,JMd,Rogue gets gift 4.00
342 SLo,JMd, Shi'ar Empire, pt.1 . 5.00
342a Rogue cover 12.00
343 SLo,JMd, Shi'ar Empire, pt.2 . 4.00
344 SLo,JMd, Shi'ar Empire, pt.3 . 4.00
345 SLo,JMd, trip home, A:Akron . 5.00
346 SLo,JMd,Zero Tolerance,
   A:Spider-Man 4.00
347 SLo,JMd,Zero Tolerance. 4.00
348 SLo,JMd,at Magneto's base . . 4.00
349 SLo,JMd,Maggot vs. Psylocke
   & Archangel 4.00
350 SSe,JMd,Trial of Gambit,
   double-sized 5.00
350a Gambit (c) 12.00
351 SSe,JMd,Dr. Cecilia Reyes. . . 3.00
352 SSe,EBe,Cyclops & Phoenix
   leave, Facade arrives 3.00
353 SSe,CBa,Rogues Anguish . . . 3.00
354 SSe,CBa,F:Rogue 10.00
354a Jean Gray (c) 12.00
355 SSe, CBa, North & South
   pt.2 x-over 5.00
356 SSe,CBa, originals V:Phoenix . 3.00
357 SSe,Cyclops & Phoenix 3.00
358 SSe,CBa,Phoenix collapses . . 3.00
359 SSe,CBa,Rogue 3.00
360A SSe,CBa, I:New X-Men, foil
   etched cover 5.00
360B regular cover 4.00
361 SSe,SSr,R:Gambit 3.50

Uncanny X-Men #374
© *Marvel Entertainment Group*

362 SSe,CBa,Hunt for Xavier,pt.1 . . 3.50
363 SSe,CBa,Hunt for Xavier,pt.3 . . 3.50
364 SSe,Hunt for Xavier,pt.5 . . . . . . 5.00
365 SSe,CBa,A:Professor X 3.00
366 AD,BPe,Magneto War,pt.1 . . . . 3.00
367 AD,Magneto War,pt.3 . . . . 3.00
368 AD,AKu,Requiem for an X-Man 3.00
368a signed 20.00
369 AD,AKu,V:Juggernaut 3.00
370 AD,AKu,in the past 3.00
371 AD,AKu(c),Rage Against
     the Machine, pt.1 x-over 3.00
371a signed 20.00
372 AKu,AD,The Shattering,pt.1 . . 3.00
373 AKu,AD,The Shattering,pt.2 . . 3.00
374 AKu,AD,The Shattering 3.00
375 AKu,AD,48-pg. 5.00
376 AKu,AD 7.00
377 AKu,AD,Apocalypse12,pt.5 . . . 7.00
378 AKu,AD,TTn,Ages of
     Apocalypse,pt.1,x-over 3.00
379 AKu,AD,TTn,mutants no more . 3.00
380 AD,TR,poly-bagged w/Genesis. 4.00
381 CCl,AKu,TTn,X-Men:
     Revolution 7.00
381a foil (c) 12.00
382 CCl,TTn,Shockwave Riders . . . 3.00
383 CCl,AKu,TTn,48-pg. 3.50
384 CCl,AKu,TTn,I:Killion 3.00
385 CCl,TR,Red Pirates 3.00
386 CCl,TR,Phoenix 3.00
387 CCl,TTn,Maximum Security . . . 3.00
388 CCl,SvL,Dream's End,pt.1 . . . . 5.00
389 CCl,SvL,F:Cecilia Reyes 3.00
390 CCl,SvL,Legacy Virus,
     D:Colossus 10.00
391 SLo,SvL,return 3.00
392 SLo,SvL,Eve of Destruction . . 3.00
393 SLo,SvL,Eve of Destruction . . . 5.00
394 JoC,IaC,F:Warp Savant 5.00
395A JoC,IaC,Poptopia,pt.1 . . . . . . 3.00
395B variant BWS(c) 3.00
396 JoC,IaC,Poptopia,pt.2 . . . . 3.00
397 JoC,IaC,Poptopia,pt.3 . . . . 3.00
398 JoC,IaC,Poptopia,pt.4 . . . . 3.00
399 JoC,SHa,X-Ranch 3.00
400 F:XStacy,48-page 5.00
401 JoC,RG,F:Banshee,'Nuff Said . 3.50
402 JoC,RG,vs.X-Corp. 2.50
403 JoC,AaL,DaM,X-Corp's secret . 2.50
404 JoC,RG,V:Multiple Men. 2.50
405 JoC,SeP,V:Banshee 2.50
406 JoC,AaL,X-Corps,concl. 2.50
407 JoC,SeP,Nightcrawler 2.50
408 JoC,SeP,V:Vanisher 2.50
409 JoC,SeP,V:Vanisher 2.50
410 RG,Hope 2.50
411 RG,Hope,pt.2. . . . . 2.50
412 RG,Hope,pt.3 . . . . 2.50
413 RG,Annie's Moving 2.50
414 Northstar Joins team. 2.50
415 SeP,F:Nightcrawler 2.50
416 KiA,F:Juggernaut 4.00
417 KiA,Dominant Species 3.00
418 KiA,Dominant Species 3.00
419 KiA,Archangel and Husk. 2.25
420 KiA,Dominant Species,concl. . . 2.25
421 RG,V:Alpha Flight,pt.1 . . . . 2.25
422 RG,V:Alpha Flight,pt.2,48-pg. . . 3.50
423 RG,Holy War,pt.1 . . . . 2.25
424 RG,Holy War,pt.2 . . . . 2.25
425 Sacred Vows,pt.1 . . . . 2.25
426 Sacred Vows,pt.2 . . . . 2.25
427 F:Jubilee, Angel, Husk 2.25
428 O:Nightcrawler,F:Mystique . . . 2.25
429 Draco,pt.1 . . . . 2.25
430 Draco,pt.2 . . . . 2.25
431 Draco,pt.3 . . . . 2.25
432 Draco,pt.4 . . . . 2.25
433 Draco,pt.5 . . . . 2.25
434 Draco,pt.6 . . . . 2.25
435 Trial of the Juggernaut,pt.1 . . . 2.25

436 Trial of the Juggernaut,pt.2 . . . . 2.25
437 She Lies With Angels,pt.1 . . . . . 2.50
438 She Lies With Angels,pt.2 . . . . . 2.25
439 She Lies With Angels,pt.3 . . . . . 2.25
440 She Lies With Angels,pt.4 . . . . . 2.25
441 She Lies With Angels,pt.5 . . . . . 2.25
442 Of Darkest Nights,pt.1 . . . . 2.25
443 Of Darkest Nights,pt.2 . . . . 2.25
444 The End of History,pt.1 . . . . 2.25
445 The End of History,pt.2 . . . . 2.25
446 The End of History,pt.3 . . . . 2.25
447 The End of History,pt.4 . . . . 2.25
448 CCl,Guess Who's Back,pt.1 . . . 2.25
449 CCl,Guess Who's Back,pt.2 . . . 2.25
450 CCl,AD,Cruelest Cut,pt.1 . . . . . 3.00
451 CCl,AD,Cruelest Cut,pt.2 . . . . . 2.25
452 CCl(s),Chasing Hellfire 2.25
453 CCl(s),Chasing Hellfire 2.25
454 CCl(s),Chasing Hellfire, concl. . 2.25
455 CCl(s),On Ice,pt.1 . . . . 2.25
456 CCl(s),On Ice,pt.2 . . . . 2.25
457 CCl(s),AD,On Ice 2.25
458 CCl(s),AD,On Ice,A:Ka-Zar. . . 2.25
459 CCl(s),AD,On Ice 2.50
460 CCl(s),TR,Mojo Rising,pt.1 . . . . 2.50
461 CCl(s),TR,Mojo Rising,pt.2. . . . 5.00
462 CCl(s),AD,Season of the Witch 2.50
463 CCl(s),AD,Season of the Witch 2.50
464 CCl,CBa,Season of the Witch . 2.50
465 CCl,CBa,Season of the Witch . 2.50
466 Grey's End, Decimation tie-in . 2.50
467 Grey's End, Decimation tie-in . 2.50
468 Grey's End, Decimation tie-in . 2.50
469 CCl,Wand'ring Star,pt.1 . . . . . . 2.50
470 CCl,Wand'ring Star,pt.2. . . . . . 2.50
471 CCl,Wand'ring Star,pt.3 . . . . . . 2.50
472 CCl,CBa,First Foursaken, pt.1 . 3.00
473 CCl,CBa,First Foursaken, pt.2 . 3.00
474 CCl,CBa,First Foursaken, pt.3 . 3.00
475 Rise and Fall of Shi'ar Empire . 3.00
476 Rise and Fall of Shi'ar Empire . 3.00
477 Rise and Fall of Shi'ar Empire . 3.00
478 Rise and Fall of Shi'ar Empire . 3.00
479 Rise and Fall of Shi'ar Empire . 3.00
480 Rise and Fall of Shi'ar Empire . 3.00
481 BTn,Rise & Fall Shi'ar Empire . 3.00
482 BTn,Rise & Fall Shi'ar Empire . 3.00
483 BTn,Rise & Fall Shi'ar Empire . 3.00
484 BTn,Rise & Fall Shi'ar Empire . 3.00
485 BTn,Rise & Fall Shi'ar Empire . 3.00
486 BTn,Rise & Fall Shi'ar Empire . 3.00
487 SvL,The Extremists,pt.1 . . . . . . 3.00
488 SvL,The Extremists,pt.2 . . . . . . 3.00
489 SvL,The Extremists,pt.3 . . . . . . 3.00
490 SvL,The Extremists,pt.4 . . . . . . 3.00
491 SvL,The Extremists,pt.5 . . . . . . 3.00
492 Messiah Complex, pt.2 x-over . 3.00
Ann.#1 rep.#9,#11 . . . . 200.00
Ann.#2 rep.#22,#23 . . . . 125.00
Ann.#3 GK(c),GP,TA,A:Arkon 50.00
Ann.#4 JR2,BMc,A:Dr.Strange . . 25.00
Ann.#5 BA,BMc,A:F.F. 20.00
Ann.#6 BSz,BWi,Dracula 20.00
Ann.#7 MGo,TMd,BWi,TA,BBr,
     BA,JRu,BBl,SL,AM,
     V:Impossible Man 15.00
Ann.#8 SL,Kitty's story. 15.00
Ann.#9 AAd,AG,MMi,Asgard,V:Loki,
     Enchantress,A:New Mutants . . 20.00
Ann.#10 AAd,TA,V:Mojo,
     J:Longshot,A:New Mutants . . . 18.00
Ann.#11 AD,V:Horde,A:CaptBrit. . . 7.00
Ann.#12 AAd,BWi,RLm,TD,Evol.
     War,V:Terminus,Savage Land. . 7.00
Ann.#13 MBa,JRu,Atlantis Attacks . 6.00
Ann.#14 AAd,DGr,BWi,AM,ATi,
     V:Ahab,A:X-Factor, ... 15.00
Ann.#15,TR,JRu,MMi(c),Flesh Tears,
     Pt.3,A:X-Force,New Warriors . . 6.00
Ann.#16 JaL,JRu,Shattershot
     Part.2. 5.00

X-Men King-Size Special #1
© Marvel Entertainment Group

Ann.#17 JPe,MFm,I:X-Cutioner,
     D:Mastermind,w/card. 5.00
Ann.#18 JR2,V:Caliban,
     BU:Bishop 4.00
Ann.1999 AD 3.50
Ann.2000 SLo,F:Professor X 3.50
Ann.2001 JoC,48-pg. 3.50
Ann. #1 (2006) 4.00
Marvel Milestone rep. #1 (1991) . . . 3.00
Marvel Milestone rep. #9 (1993) . . . 3.00
Marvel Milestone rep. #28 (1994) . . 3.00
G-Size #1,GK,DC,I:New X-Men
     (Colossus,Storm,Nightcrawler,
     Thunderbird,3rd A:Wolv.) . . 1,500.00
G-Size #2,rep.#57-59. . . . . 150.00
Marvel Milestone rep. Giant
     Size #1 (1991) 4.00
Spec.#1 X-Men: Earth Fall,
     rep. #232-#234 (1996) 3.00
Spec.#1 X-Men vs. Dracula, rep.
     X-Men Ann.#6 (1993) 2.00
GN X-Men: Days of Future Past
     rep. X-Men #141-142 . . . . 5.00
GN Pryde of the X-Men 11.00
GN God Loves,Man Kills,
     (1994) prestige 7.00
GN X-Men Firsts, I:Wolverine,Rogue,
     Gambit & Mr. Sinister, rep.
     Avengers Ann.#10, Uncanny
     X-Men 221,#266 & Incredible
     Hulk #181 (1996). 5.00
GN X-Men Rarities,F:Classic
     Stories (1995) 6.00

X-MEN

[2nd Regular Series] Oct., 1991
1A(c);Storm,Beast,B:CCl(s),JLe,SW
     I:Fabian Cortez,Acolytes,
     V:Magneto 5.00
1B(c);Colossus,Psylocke 8.00
1C(c);Cyclops,Wolverine 8.00
1D(c);Magneto 8.00
1E(c);Gatefold w/pin-ups 9.00
2 JLe,SW,V:Magneto Contd. 5.00
3 E:CCl(s),JLe,SW,V:Magneto . . . 5.00
4 JBy(s),JLe,SW,I:Omega Red,
     V:Hand 6.00
5 B:SLo(s),JLe,SW,V:Hand,
     Omega Red,I:Maverick 5.00
6 JLe,SW,V:Omega Red, Hand,
     Sabretooth. 5.00
7 JLe,SW,V:Omega Red,Hand,
     Sabretooth. 5.00
8 JLe,SW,Bishop vs. Gambit 5.00

MARVEL

9 JLe,SW,A:Ghost Rider,V:Brood . . 4.50
10 JLe,SW,MT,Longshot Vs. Mojo,
   BU:Maverick 4.50
11 E:SLo(s)JLe,MT,V:Mojo,
   BU:Maverick 4.50
12 B:FaN(s),ATb,BWi,I:Hazard 4.00
13 ATb,BWi,V:Hazard 4.00
14 NKu,X-Cutioners Song#3,A:X-Fact.
   X-Force,V:Four Horsemen . . 4.00
15 NKu,X-Cutioners Song #7,
   V:Mutant Liberation Front . . . 4.00
16 NKu,MPn,X-Cutioners Song #11,
   A:X-Force,X-Factor,V:Dark Riders,
   Apocalypse Vs.Archangel,IR:Stryfe
   is Nathan Summers 4.00
17 NKu,MPn,R:Illyana,A:Darkstar . . 4.00
18 NKu,MPn,R:Omega Red,V:Soul
   Skinner 4.00
19 NKu,MPn,V:Soul Skinner,
   Omega Red 4.00
20 NKu,MPn,J.Grey vs Psylocke . . 4.00
21 NKu,V:Silver Samurai,Shinobi . . 4.00
22 BPe,V:Silver Samurai,Shinobi . . 4.00
23 NKu,MPn,V:Dark Riders,
   Mr.Sinister 4.00
24 NKu,BSz,A Day in the Life 4.00
25 NKu,Hologram(c),V:Magneto,
   Wolverine's Adamantium skeleton
   pulled out. 15.00
25a Gold Edition 25.00
25b B&W cover 35.00
26 NKu,Bloodties#2,A:Avengers,
   I:Unforgiven 4.00
27 RiB,I:Threnody 4.00
28 NKu,MRy,F:Sabretooth 4.00
29 NKu,MRy,V:Shinobi 4.00
30 NKu,MRy,W:Cyclops&Jean Grey,
   w/card 6.00
31 NKu,MRy,A:Spiral,Matsuo,
   D:Kwannon 4.00
32 NKu,MRy,A:Spiral,Matsuo. 3.50
33 NKu,MRy,F:Gambit &
   Sabretooth 3.50
34 NKu,MRy,A:Riptide 3.50
35 LSh,A:Nick Fury 3.50
36 NKu,MRy,I:Synch,PhalanxCovenant
   Generation Next,pt.2, deluxe. . . 5.00
36a Newsstand ed. 2.25
37 NKu,MRy,Generation Next,pt.3
   foil(c) 5.00
37a newsstand ed. 2.50
38 NKu,MRy,F:Psylocke 3.50
38a newsstand ed. 3.00
39 X-Treme, deluxe 3.50
39a newsstand ed. 3.00
40 deluxe 3.50
40a newsstand ed. 3.00
41 V:Legion, deluxe 3.50
41a newsstand ed. 3.00
42 PS,PaN,Mysterious Visitor 3.00
43 Rogue and Iceman 3.00
44 FaN,Mystery of Magneto 3.00
45 20th Anniv.pt.2 . . . . 5.00
46 FaN,Aku,V:Comcast 3.00
47 SLo,AKu,CaS,F:Dazzler 3.00
48 SLo,AKu,CaS,F:Sabretooth 3.00
49 SLo,AKu,Bishop wanted 3.00
50 Onslaught(c) 7.00
50a regular edition 8.00
51 MWa,Onslaught 6.00
52 MWa,AKu,CaS,V:Sinister 6.00
53 Onslaught saga. 7.00
54 Onslaught saga. 5.00
54a Foil cover 25.00
55 Onslaught saga. 3.50
56 Onslaught saga. 3.50
57 Operation: Zero Tolerence 3.50
58 SLo,NKu 3.50
59 . . . . 3.50
60 SLo,NKu,F:Ororo, V:Candra . . . 3.50
61 SLo,CNn,F:Storm, V:Candra . . . 3.50

62 SLo,CPa,F:Sebastian Shaw,
   Shang Chi 3.50
62A variant Storm/Wolverine(c) . . . 15.00
63 SLo,CPa,ATi,A:Sebastian Shaw,
   Inner Circle 3.00
64 SLo,CPa,ATi,V:Hellfire Club . . . 3.00
65 SLo,CPa,ATi, No Exit prelude . . 3.00
66 SLo,CPa,ATi, Zero Tolerance,
   A:Bastion 3.00
67 SLo,CPa,ATi, Zero Tolerance,
   F:Iceman, Cecelia Reyes 3.00
68 SLo,CPa,ATi, Operation: Zero
   Tolerance. 3.00
69 SLo,CPa, Operation: Zero
   Tolerance, concl. 3.50
70 ATi,Who will join X-Men?,
   double-sized 5.00
71 ATi,Cyclops banished 4.00
72 ATi,Professor Logan's School of
   Hard Knocks 3.00
73 ATi,Marrow visits Callisto 3.00
74 ATi,Terror in Morlock Tunnels . . . 3.00
75 ATi,V:N'Garai, double size 4.00
76 CCI,V:Sabretooth, 35th anniv
   kickoff 3.00
77 ATi,A:Black Panther,Maggott . . . 3.00
78 Return of Professor X 3.00
79 ATi,Cannonball must leave team 3.00
80A BPe, ATi, cont. from Uncanny
   X-Men #360, etched foil (c) . . . 7.50
80B regular cover 6.00
81 AKu,MFm,Search for Prof.X 3.00
82 AKu,MFm,Hunt for Xavier 3.00
83 AKu,MFm,Hunt for Xavier,pt.4 . . 3.00
84 AJu,Hunt for Xavier,concl. 3.50
85 AD,MFm,R:Magneto 3.00
85a signed 30.00
86 AD,MFm,Magneto War,pt.2,
   O:Joseph 3.50
87 AD,MFm,Magneto War,pt.4. . . . . 3.50
88 AD,MFm,R:Juggernaut 3.00
89 AD,MFm,In the past 3.00
90 AD,MFm,In the past,concl. 3.00
91 AD,AKu,Rage Against
   the Machine, pt.2 x-over 3.00
91a signed 30.00
92 AD,MFm,The Shattering x-over . 3.00
93 AD,MFm,The Shattering x-over . 3.00
94 AD,MFm,Shattering,x-over 4.00
95 AD,TR,A:Death. 3.00
96 AD 9.00
97 AD,MFm,Apocalypse12,pt.7 . . . 8.00
97a variant (c) 20.00
98 AD,MFm,Ages of Apocalypse . . 9.00

X-Men 2nd Series #78
© Marvel Entertainment Group

99 AD,BBh,mutants no more? 3.00
100 CCI,X-Men:Revolution,48-pg. . . 6.00
100a variant covers 7.00
101 CCI,X-Men:Revolution 3.00
102 CCI,R:Wolverine 3.00
103 CCI,Wolverine v. Rogue 3.00
104 CCI,V:Killion 3.00
105 CCI,Archangel,Psylocke 3.00
106 CCI,Neo,Cecelia Reyes 3.50
107 CCI,Cadre K 4.00
108 CCI,Dream'sEnd,pt.4,x-over . . . 5.00
109 CCI,at X-Mansion, 100-page . . 4.00
110 SLo,F:Kitty Pryde 4.00
111 SLo,F:Trish Tilby 3.25
112 SLo,Eve of Destruction,pt.2 . . . 3.25
113 SLo,Eve of Destruction,pt.4 . . . 3.25
Becomes:

NEW X-MEN

114 GMo,E is for Extinction,pt.1 . . 8.00
115A GMo,E for Extinction,pt.2 . . . . 6.00
115B variant BWS(c) 4.00
116 GMo,E for Extinction,pt.3 . . . . . 3.50
117 GMo,F:Beast. 3.50
118 GMo,GermFreeGeneration,pt.1 3.50
119 GMo,Germ Free Gen.,pt.2 . . . . 3.50
120 GMo,Germ Free Gen.,concl. . . . 3.00
121 GMo,Xavier's mind,'Nuff Said. . . 3.00
122 GMo,Imperial,pt.1 . . . . 3.00
123 GMo,Imperial,pt.2 . . . . 2.50
124 GMo,Imperial,pt.3 . . . . 2.50
125 GMo,Imperial,pt.4 . . . . 2.50
126 GMo,Imperial,pt.5 . . . . 3.50
127 GMo,F:Xorn 3.00
128 GMo,Jean Grey, Emma Frost. . . 3.00
129 GMo,Weapon XII 3.00
130 GMo 2.50
131 GMo,JPL,BSz 2.50
132 GMo,PJ,F:Storm 2.25
133 . . . . 2.25
134 GMo,NRd,no Magneto 2.25
135 GMo,Riot At Xavier's 2.25
136 GMo,Riot At Xavier's 2.25
137 GMo,Riot At Xavier's 2.25
138 GMo,Riot At Xavier's,concl. 2.25
139 GMo,PJ,Murder at Mansion . . . 2.25
140 GMo,PJ,Murder at Mansion . . . 2.25
141 GMo,PJ,Murder at Mansion . . . 2.25
142 GMo,CBa,Weapon Plus,pt.1. . . 2.25
143 GMo,CBa,Weapon Plus,pt.2. . . 2.25
144 GMo,CBa,Weapon Plus,pt.3. . . 2.25
145 GMo,CBa,Weapon Plus,pt.4. . . 2.25
146 PJ,Planet X,pt.1 . . . . 2.25
147 PJ,Planet X,pt.2 . . . . 2.25
148 PJ,Planet X,pt.3 . . . . 2.25
149 PJ,Planet X,pt.4 . . . . 2.25
150 PJ,Planet X,finale,48-pg. 3.50
151 MS,Here Comes Tomorrow 2.25
152 MS,Here Comes Tomorrow 2.25
153 MS,Here Comes Tomorrow . . . 2.25
154 MS,Here Comes Tomorrow 2.25
155 SvL,Bright New Mourning,pt.1 . 2.25
156 SvL,Bright New Mourning,pt.2 . 2.25
becomes:

X-MEN

157 SvL,Day of the Atom,pt.1 . . . . . 2.25
158 SvL,Day of the Atom,pt.2 . . . . . 2.25
159 SvL,Day of the Atom,pt.3 . . . . . 2.25
160 SvL,Day of the Atom,pt.4 . . . . . 2.25
161 SvL,Heroes & Villains,pt.1 . . . . 2.25
162 SvL,Heroes & Villains,pt.2 . . . . 2.25
163 SvL,Heroes & Villains,pt.3 . . . . 2.25
164 SvL,Heroes & Villains,pt.4 . . . . 2.25
165 . . . . 2.25
166 SvL,Golgotha,pt.1 . . . . 2.25
167 SvL,Golgotha,pt.2 . . . . 2.25
168 SvL,Golgotha,pt.3 . . . . 2.25
169 SvL,Golgotha,pt.4 . . . . 2.50
170 SvL,Golgotha,pt.5, concl. 2.50
171 SvL,Bizarre Love Triangle,pt.1 . 2.50
172 SvL,Bizarre Love Triangle,pt.2 . 2.50
173 SvL,Bizarre Love Triangle,pt.3 . 2.50

X-Men Adventures #12
© Marvel Entertainment Group

174 SvL,Bizarre Love Triangle,pt.4 . 2.50
175 SvL,Wild Kingdom,x-over,pt.1. . 2.50
176 SvL,Wild Kingdom,x-over,pt.3. . 2.50
177 SvL,House Arrest, pt.1 . . . . 2.50
178 SvL,House Arrest, pt.2 . . . . 2.50
179 SvL,House Arrest, pt.3 . . . . 2.50
180 SvL,What Lorna Saw,pt.1 . . . . . 2.50
181 SvL,What Lorna Saw,pt.2 . . . . . 2.50
182 SvL,Blood of Apocalypse, pt.1 . 2.50
183 SvL,Blood of Apocalypse, pt.2 . 2.50
184 SvL,Blood of Apocalypse, pt.3 . 3.00
185 SvL,Blood of Apocalypse, pt.4 . 3.00
186 SvL,Blood of Apocalypse, pt.5 . 3.00
187 SvL,Blood of Apocalypse, after. 3.00
188 CBo,Supernovas,pt.1 . . . . 3.00
189 CBo,Supernovas,pt.2 . . . . 3.00
190 CBo,Supernovas,pt.3 . . . . 3.00
191 CBo,Supernovas,pt.4 . . . . 3.00
192 CBo,Supernovas,pt.5 . . . . 3.00
193 CBo,Supernovas,pt.6 . . . . 3.00
194 CBo,Primary Infection. 3.00
195 HuR,Primary Infection. 3.00
196 HuR,Primary Infection. 3.00
197 MCy,CBa,Condition Critical,pt.1 3.00
198 MCy,CBa,Condition Critical,pt.2 3.00
199 MCy,CBa,Condition Critical,pt.3 3.00
200 CBa,Blinded by the Light,pt.1 . 4.00
200a variant (c) 4.00
200b variant gatefold (c) 4.00
201 MCy,HuR. 3.00
202 MCy,HuR. 3.00
203 MCy,HuR. 3.00
204 Blinded by the Light 3.00
205 Messiah Complex, pt.5 x-over . 3.00
1-shot Endangered Species. 4.00
Ann.#1 JLe,Shattershot,pt.1,
    I:Mojo II 4.00
Ann.#2 I:Empyrean,w/card. 4.00
Ann.#3 F:Storm 4.00
Ann. Uncanny X-Men '97, V:Brother-
    hood, 48-pg. 3.50
Ann. '98 RMz, F:X-Men & Doctor
    Doom. 3.50
Ann. '98 X-Men/Fantastic Four, JoC,
    PaP, 48-pg. 3.50
Ann.1999 Rage Against the
    Machine, pt.3 x-over, 48-pg. . . 3.50
Ann.2000 CCI,SHa,SEa,48-pg. . . . 4.00
Ann. 2001 GMo,Marvelscope 7.50
Ann. 1 F:Northstar & Aurora (2007). 4.00
Uncanny X-Men'95 Spec. F:Husk . 4.00
Giant Size X-Men #3 (2005) 5.00
Giant Size X-Men #4 (2005) 5.00
Spec.X-Men'95, F:Mr.Sinister 5.00

Spec.X-Men'96 LHa, 64-pg., F:Gambit,
    Rogue, Magneto, Jubilee
    & Wolverine 4.00
Spec. X-Men'97,JFM,SEp,F:Gambit,
    Joesph & Phoenix 4.00
Minus 1 Spec. SLo, JMd,, flashback,
    discovery of mutants 2.00
Spec.#1 X-Men: Road to Onslaught
    (1996) 2.50
Spec. X-Men Universe: Past,
    Present and Future 3.00
Spec. X-Men:Year in Review 3.00
Spec.#1 X-Men (2000). 3.50
Spec. Millennial Visions 4.00
Spec.2001, Millennial Vision
    48-page 3.50
Spec. X-Men:Declassified,48-pg . . . 3.50
Spec. Unearthed Archives
    Sketchbook 3.00
Spec. X-Men/Sentry, PJe,MT. 3.00
Spec. God Loves, Man Kills. 5.00
Spec. rep. Must Have #114–#116 . 4.00
Chrom.Classics GN,TKa,AD,MFm,
    Age of Apocalypse. 3.00

X-MEN ADVENTURES
[1st Season] 1992–94
1 V:Sentinals, Based on TV
    Cartoon 6.00
2 V:Sentinals,D:Morph 5.00
3 V:Magneto,A:Sabretooth 4.00
4 V:Magneto 4.00
5 V:Morlocks. 4.00
6 V:Sabretooth 3.50
7 V:Cable,Genosha,Sentinels. . . . 3.00
8 A:Colossus,A:Juggernaut 3.00
9 I:Colossus(on cartoon),
    V:Juggernaut 3.00
10 A:Angel,V:Mystique. 3.00
11 I:Archangel(on cartoon) 2.50
12 V:Horsemen of Apocalypse. . . . 2.50
13 RMc(s),I:Bishop(on cartoon). . . . 2.50
14 V:Brotherhood of Evil Mutants . . 2.50
15 . . . . 2.50
[2nd Season] 1994–95
1 R:Morph,I:Mr. Sinister
    (on cartoon) 3.00
2 I:Nasty Boys (on cartoon) 2.50
3 I:Shadow King (on cartoon). 2.50
4 I:Omega Red (on cartoon). 2.50
5 I:Alpha Flight (on cartoon) 2.50
6 F:Gambit. 2.50
7 A:Cable,Bishop,Apocalypse. . . . 2.50
8 A:Cable,Biship,Apocalypse 2.50
9 O:Rogue 2.50
10 . . . . 2.50
11 F:Mojo,Longshot 2.50
12 Reunions,pt.1 . . . . 2.50
13 Reunions,pt.1 . . . . 2.50
[3rd Season] 1995–96
1 Out of the Past,pt.1 . . . . 3.00
2 V:Spirit Drinker. 2.50
3 Phoenix Saga,pt.1 . . . . 2.50
4 Phoenix Saga,pt.2 . . . . 2.50
5 Phoenix Saga,pt.3 . . . . 2.50
6 Phoenix Saga,pt.4 . . . . 2.50
7 Phoenix Saga,pt.5 . . . . 2.50
8 War in The Savage Land 2.50
9 F:Ka-Zar. 2.50
10 Dark Phoenix,Saga,pt.1 . . . . . . 2.50
11 Dark Phoenix Saga,pt.2 . . . . . . 2.50
12 Dark Phoenix Saga,pt.3 . . . . . . 2.50
13 Dark Phoenix Saga,pt.4 . . . . . . 2.50

X-MEN:
AGE OF APOCALYPSE
March, 2005
1-shot Age of Apocalypse, 48-pg. . 4.00
1 (Of 6) CBa 3.00
2 CBa 3.00

3 thru 5 CBa . . . . @3.00
6 CBa,finale 3.00

X-MEN: ALPHA
1994
1 Age of Apocalypse, double size. . 7.00
1a gold edition, 48pp 50.00

X-Men/Alpha Flight #1
© Marvel Entertainment Group

X-MEN/ALPHA FLIGHT
Jan., 1986
1 PS,BWi,V:Loki 5.00
2 PS,BWi,V:Loki 5.00

X-MEN/ALPHA FLIGHT:
THE GIFT
Jan., 1998
1-shot CCI,PS, rep. of limited series 6.00

X-MEN AND POWER PACK
Oct., 2005
1 (of 4) 3.00
2 thru 4 . . . . @3.00
Digest The Power of X. 8.00

X-MEN/ ANIMATION
SPECIAL
TV Screenplay Adapt. 11.00

X-MEN: APOCALYPSE/
DRACULA
Feb., 2006
1 . . . . 3.00
2 thru 4 . . . . 3.00

X-MEN ARCHIVES:
CAPTAIN BRITAIN
1995
1 AMo,AD,Secret History 3.00
2 AMo,AD,F:Captain Britain 3.00
3 AMo,AD,Trial of Captain Britain . . 3.00
4 AMo,AD,Trial cont. 3.00
5 AD,AMo,F:Captain Britain 3.00
6 AMo,AD,Final Apocalypse? 3.00
7 AMo,AD,conclusion 3.00

X-MEN: ASKANI'SON
1 SLo,GeH,sequel to Adventures of
    Cyclops & Phoenix 3.00

2 SLo,GeH,A:Stryfe 3.00
3 SLo,GeH 3.00
4 SLo,GeH,conclusion 3.00
Books of Askani, portraits (1995). . . 3.00

X-MEN AT STATE FAIR
1 KGa,Dallas Times Herald 65.00

X-MEN: BLACK SUN
Sept., 2000
1 (of 5) CCI,New X-Men 3.00
2 CCI,Storm 3.00
3 CCI,RT,Banshee & Sunfire 3.00
4 CCI,LSi,Colossus&Nightcrawler . 3.00
5 CCI,Wolverine & Thunderbird . . . 3.00

X-MEN: CHILDREN OF THE ATOM
Jan., 2000
1 (of 6) JoC,SR,O:X-Men 5.00
2 JoC,SR,F:Professor X 3.00
3 JoC,SR 3.00
4 JoC,SR 3.00
5 JoC,SR, ... 3.00
6 JoC,SR,concl. 3.00

X-MEN CHRONICLES
1995
1 X-Men Unlimited AX 5.00
2 V:Abbatoir 5.00

X-MEN/CLANDESTINE
1996
1 & 2 AD,MFm,48-pg. . . . . @3.00

X-Men Classics #1
© *Marvel Entertainment Group*

X-MEN CLASSICS
Dec., 1983
1 NA,rep. 7.00
2 NA,rep. 7.00
3 NA,rep. 7.00

CLASSIC X-MEN
Sept., 1986
1 AAd(c),JBo,New stories, rep.
  giant size X-Men 1 . . . . 9.00
2 rep.#94,JBo/AAd(c) 6.00
3 thru 9 rep#95-101,JBo/AAd(c) . @4.00
10 rep.#102,JBo/AAd(c),BU:Wolv.. 8.00
11 rep.#103,JBo/BL(c), ... 3.00

12 rep.#104,JBo/AAd(c),BU:
  O:Magneto. 7.00
13 thru 16 rep.,JBo/AAd(c) . . . @3.00
17 rep.#111,JBo/TA(c) 5.00
18 rep.#112,JBo/AAd(c). 4.00
19 rep.#113,JBo/AAd(c). 4.00
20 thru 22 rep.,JBo/AAd(c) . . . @3.00
23 thru 25 rep.,JBo/KGa(c) . . . @3.00
26 rep.#120,JBo/KGa(c). 4.00
27 thru 29 rep.,JBo/KD(c) . . . . @3.00
30 thru 35 rep.,JBo/SLi(c) . . . . @3.00
36 rep.#130,MBr/SLi(c) 3.00
37 rep.#131,RL/SLi(c) 3.00
38 rep.#132,KB/SLi(c) 3.00
39 rep.#133,2nd JLe X-Men/SLi(c) 11.00
40 thru 42 rep.,SLi(c) . . . . @3.00
43 rep.#137,JBy(c). 3.00
Becomes:

X-MEN CLASSICS
1990
44 rep.#138,KD/SLi(c). 3.00
45 thru 49 rep.#139-#145,SLi(c) . @3.00
50 thru 69 rep.#146-#165 . . . @3.00
70 thru 105 rep.#166-#201 . . . @2.50
106 Phoenix vs. Beyonder. 2.50
107 F:Rogue. 2.50
108 F:Nightcrawler. 2.50
109 Rep. Uncanny X-Men #205 . . 2.50
110 Rep. Uncanny X-Men #206 . . 2.50

X-MEN: COLOSSUS–BLOODLINE
Sept., 2005
1 (of 5) Colossus 3.00
2 Russia 3.00
3 thru 5 . . . . @3.00

X-MEN: DEADLY GENESIS
Nov., 2005
1 . . . . 4.00
2 Decimation tie-in 3.50
3 thru 5 . . . . @3.50

X-MEN: DIE BY THE SWORD
Oct., 2007
1 (of 5) 3.00
2 thru 3 . . . . @3.00

X-MEN: EMPEROR VULCAN
Sept., 2007
1 . . . . 3.00
2 thru 3 . . . . @3.00

X-MEN: THE END
Aug., 2004
1 Dreamers and Demons,pt.1 . . . . 3.00
2 thru 6 Dreamers and Demons . @3.00

X-MEN: THE END– HEROES AND MARTYRS
March, 2005
1 (of 6) CCI(s) 3.00
2 CCI(s). 3.00
3 CCI(s). 3.00
4 CCI(s). 3.00
5 & 6 CCI(s) . . . . @3.00

X-MEN: THE END– MEN AND X-MEN
Jan., 2006
1 CCI. 3.00
2 thru 6 CCI . . . . @3.00

X-MEN EVOLUTION
Nov., 2001
1 cartoon series tie-in 2.25
2 F:Cyclops 2.25
3 F:Jean Grey 2.25
4 F:Nigntcrawler, Shadowcat,
  Spyke, Rogue 2.25
5 F:Mystique, Rogue. 2.25
6 I:Mimic 2.25
7 new recruits, Beast 2.25
8 F:Angel, Storm. 2.25
9 F:Professor X, Brotherhood 2.25
10 . . . . 2.25
Digest. 6.00

X-MEN FAIRY TALES
May, 2006
1 Kitty's Fairy Tale. 3.00
2 Professor X and Magneto 3.00
3 Rogue and Gambit 3.00
4 Logan 3.00

X-MEN/FANTASTIC FOUR
Dec., 2004
1 (of 5) PtL 3.50
2 PtL 3.50
3 PtL 3.50
4 PtL,Brood attack 3.50
5 PtL,Finale. 3.50

X-MEN FIRST CLASS
Sept., 2006
1 . . . . 3.00
2 V:The Lizard 3.00
3 . . . . 3.00

X-MEN: FIRST CLASS
June, 2007
1 RCz 3.00
4 thru 6 RCz . . . . @3.00
Spec. 4.00

X-MEN FOREVER
Nov., 2000
1 (of 6) FaN,KM, ... 5.00
2 FaN,KM,displaced in time 4.00
3 FaN,KM, crucial points 4.00
4 FaN,KM,Toad. 3.50
5 FaN,KM,Prosh 3.50
6 FaN,KM, concl. 3.50

X-MEN: HELLFIRE CLUB
Nov., 1999
1 (of 4) AKu,BRa,CAd. 3.00
2 AKu,BRa,CAd,O:Inner Circle . . . 3.00
3 AKu,BRa,CAd,O:cont. 3.00
4 AKu,BRa,O:Concl. 3.00

X-MEN: THE HIDDEN YEARS
Oct., 1999
1 JBy,TP,Original team,48-pg. . . . 4.00
2 JBy,TP 3.00
3 JBy,TP, ... 3.00
4 JBy,TP,Savage Land concl. 3.00
5 JBy,TP,A:Candy Southern 3.00
6 JBy,TP,F:Storm 3.00
7 JBy,TP,V:Deluge 3.00
8 JBy,TP,Fant.Four 3.00
9 JBy,TP,Phoenix 3.00
10 JBy,TP,Candy Southern 3.00
11 JBy,TP,Beast. 3.00
12 JBy,TP,48-pg. 4.00
13 JBy,TP,Beast 3.00
14 JBy,TP,Beast,Angel. 3.00
15 JBy,X-Mansion 3.00
16 JBy,return, to new conflicts 3.00

17 JBy,Kraven,Beast 3.00
18 JBy,Tad Carter,Lorna Dane. 3.00
19 JBy,TP,Lorna,Angel,Promise . . . 3.00
20 JBy,TP,Sub-Mariner,Magneto . . . 3.00
21 JBy,TP,Namor,Magneto 3.00
22 JBy,TP,X-Men & Fant.Four 3.00

X-MEN ICONS: CHAMBER
Aug., 2002
1 (of 4) NRd 3.50
2 thru 4 NRd . . . . @3.00

X-MEN INDEX
**See: OFFICIAL MARVEL INDEX
TO THE X-MEN**

X-MEN: KITTY PRYDE–
SHADOW & FLAME
June, 2005
1 (of 5),Kitty Pryde & Lockhead . . . 3.00
2 thru 5 Finale. . . . . @3.00

X-MEN: LIBERATORS
Sept., 1999
1 (of 4) PJ,F:Wolverine,Nightcrawler
  & Colossus 3.00
2 PJ,V:Russian army 3.00
3 PJ,V:Nikolas. 3.00
4 PJ,V:Omega Red. 3.00

X-MEN: LOST TALES
1997
1 CCl,JBo,rep. from Classic X-Men 3.00
2 CCl,JBo,rep. from Classic X-Men 3.00

X-MEN: MAGIK
Oct., 2000
1 (of 4) DAn,ALa,LSh 3.00
2 DAn,ALa,LSh,V:Mephisto 3.00
3 DAn,ALa,LSh,F:Limbo 3.00
4 DAn,ALa,LSh,concl. 3.00

X-MEN:
MESSIAH COMPLEX
Oct., 2007
One-shot x-over, pt.1 . . . . 4.00

X-MEN/MICRONAUTS
Jan., 1984
1 JG,BWi,Limited Series 4.00
2 JG,BWi,KJo,V:Baron Karza 3.00
3 JG,BWi,V:Baron Karza. 3.00
4 JG,BWi,V:Baron Karza,Apr.1984 . 3.00

X-MEN: THE
MAGNETO WAR
Jan., 1999
1-shot AD, Joseph vs. Magneto. . . . 3.00
1a signed 20.00

X-MEN: THE MANGA
Jan., 1998
1 b&w,translated,F:Jubilee 4.00
2 Jubilee joins, V:Sentinels 3.00
3 Agent Gyrich strikes. 3.00
4 Beast captured, morph dead 3.00
5 Magneto attempts to rescue
  Beast. 3.00
6 Beast on trial, A:Sabretooth. 3.00
7 V:Magneto 3.00
8 V:Magneto 3.00
9 V:Morlocks 3.00
10 V:Morlocks, 40-pg. finale 3.00
11 Wolverine vs. Sabretooth 3.00
12 Wolverine vs. Sabretooth 3.00
13 F:Storm, Jubilee & Gambit 3.00

X-Men Manga #15
© Marvel Entertainment Group

14 &15 . . . . @3.00
16 A:Colossus,V:Juggernaut,
  double-size 4.00
17 F:Cable & Angel 3.00
18 Angel becomes Archangel 3.00
19 Angel becomes Death. 3.00
20 Rogue vs. Apocalypse 3.00
21 V:Four Horsemen 3.00
22 V:Sentinels 3.00
23 RGr(c),F:Bishop 3.00
24 RGr(c),V:Nimrod 3.00
25 Bishop vs. Gambit. 3.00
26 V:Brotherhood of Evil Mutants . . 3.00
27 Magneto Returns 3.00
28 V:Master Mold,A:Magneto 3.00
29 thru 32. . . . . @3.00

X-MEN: THE MOVIE
June, 2000
Magneto, photo(c) 6.00
Rogue, photo(c). 6.00
Wolverine, photo(c) 6.00
X-Men The Movie, photo(c) 6.00

X-MEN OMEGA
1995
1 FaN,Slo,After Xavier, concl. 7.00
1a Gold ed. Chromium(c) 48-pg. . 50.00

X-MEN: PHOENIX
Oct., 1999
1 (of 3) JFM,F:Rachel Summers . . 3.00
2 JFM 3.00
3 JFM,concl. 3.00

X-MEN: PHOENIX
May, 2003
1 (of 3) Legacy of Fire 3.00
2 Sword of Limbo 3.00
3 Concl. 3.00

X-MEN: PHOENIX
– ENDSONG
Jan., 2005
1 (of 5) Phoenix Force 5.00
2 thru 5 . . . . @5.00

X-MEN: PHOENIX
– WARSONG
Sept., 2006
1 (of 5) 5.00
2 thru 3 . . . . @5.00
4 . . . . 3.00
5 . . . . 3.00

X-MEN PRIME
1995
1 SLo,FaN,BHi,major plotlines for
  all X books begin, chromium(c). 9.00

X-MEN:
PRYDE & WISDOM
1 WEI,TyD,KIS 3.00
2 & 3 Wel,TyD,KIS3.00

X-MEN: RONIN
March, 2003
1 (of 5) manga mania 3.00
2 . . . . 3.00
3 . . . . 3.00
4 . . . . 3.00
5 . . . . 3.00

X-MEN: THE 198
Jan., 2006
1 Decimation tie-in 3.00
2 thru 5 . . . . @3.00

X-Man The Early Years #7
© Marvel Entertainment Group

X-MEN:
THE EARLY YEARS
1 rep. X-Men (first series) #1 . . . . . 2.50
2 rep. X-Men (first series) #2 . . . . . 2.50
3 rep. X-Men (first series) #3 . . . . . 2.50
4 thru 16 rep. X-Men (first series)
  #4 to #16 . . . . @2.50
17 Rep. X-Men #17 & #18. . . . . . . 2.50

X-MEN: THE RISE
OF APOCALYPSE
1 TKa,AdP, ancient history of
  X-Men 3.50
2 thru 4 TKa,AdP, ... @3.00

MARVEL

MARVEL

X-MEN: THE SEARCH FOR CYCLOPS
Oct., 2000

1A (of 4) TR,SHa,	5.00
1B variant AdP (c).	5.00
2A TR,SHa,Scott alive?	3.00
2B variant AdP(c)	3.00
3A TR,SHa,	3.00
3B variant AdP(c)	3.00
4A TR,SHa, concl.	5.00

X-MEN SPOTLIGHT ON STARJAMMERS
1990

1 DC,F:Starjammers,A:Prof.X.	5.00
2 DC,F:Starjammers,A:Prof.X.	5.00

X-MEN: TRUE FRIENDS
July, 1999

1 (of 3) CCl,RL,JP,F:Shadowcat	3.00
2 CCl,RL,JP,A:Kitty Pryde.	3.00
3 CCl,RL,JP,A:Wolverine,concl.	3.00

X-MEN 2099
1993–96

1 B:JFM(s),RLm,JP,I:X-Men 2099	4.00
1a Gold Ed.	5.00
2 RLm,JP,V:Rat Pack	3.00
3 RLm,JP,D:Serpentina	3.00
4 RLm,JP,I:Theatre of Pain.	3.00
5 RLm,JP,Fall of the Hammer#3.	3.00
6 RLm,JP,I:Freakshow	3.00
7 RLm,JP,V:Freakshow.	3.00
8 RLm(c),JS3,JP,N;Metalhead, I:2nd X-Men 2099	3.00
9 RLm,JP,V:2nd X-Men 2099	3.00
10 RLm,JP,A:La Lunatica	3.00
11 RLm,JP,V:2nd X-Men 2099.	3.00
12 RLm,JP,A:Junkpile	3.00
13 RLm,JP	3.00
14 RLm,JP,R:Loki	3.00
15 RLm,JP,F:Loki,I:Haloween Jack	3.00
16	3.00
17 X'ian	3.00
18 Haloween Jack	3.00
19 Conclusion Halloween Jack	3.00
Becomes:	

X-MEN 2099 A.D.

20 F:Bloodhawk	3.00
21 Doom Factor	3.00

X-Men 2099 #1
© Marvel Entertainment Group

22 One Nation Under Doom	3.00
23 V:Junkpile	3.00
24	3.00
25 X-Men Reunited	3.00
25a variant cover	4.25
26 V:Graverobber	3.00
27	3.00
28 X-Nation x-over.	3.00
29 X-Nation x-over.	3.00
30 & 31.	@3.00
32 V:Foolkiller	3.00
Spec.#1 Bros.Hildebrandt(c)	4.50
GN X-Men 2099: Oasis, rep., Greg Hildebrandt(c) 64-pg., (1998)	6.00

X-MEN 2: THE MOVIE
March, 2003

Prequel Wolverine, TMd	3.50
Prequel Nightcrawler.	3.50
Spec. Movie Adapt., 48-pg.	3.50

X-MEN UNIVERSE
Oct., 1999

1 rep. July 99 stories, 80-pg.	5.00
2 thru 11 rep., 80-pg.	@5.00
12 thru 17,rep., 80-pg.	@4.00

X-MEN UNLIMITED
1993

1 CBa,BP,O:Siena Blaze	7.00
2 JD,O:Magneto	6.00
3 FaN(s),BSz(c),MMK,Sabretooth joins X-Men,A:Maverick.	7.00
4 SLo(s),RiB,O:Nightcrawler,Rogue, Mystique,IR:Mystique is Nightcrawler's mother	5.00
5 JFM(s),LSh,After Shi'ar/ Kree War	4.50
6 JFM(s),PS,Sauron	4.50
7 JR2,HMe,O:Storm	4.50
8 Legacy Virus Victim	4.50
9 LHa,Wolverine & Psylocke	4.50
10 MWa,Dark Beast,Beast, double-size	8.00
11 Rogue & Magneto, double-size	8.00
12 Onslaught x-over,A:Juggernaut	3.00
13 GP,Binary gone berserk	3.00
14 TKa, Onslaught fallout	3.00
15 HMe,F:Wolverine, Iceman & Maverick	3.00
16 MvR,F:Banshee, White Queen, I:Primal	3.00
17 TKa,Wolverine vs. Sabretooth, minds are switched	4.00
18 TDF,V:Hydro Man	3.00
19 BRa,Nightcrawler v. Belasco	3.00
20 F:Generation X	3.00
21 TDz,Strong Guy returns	3.00
22 into Marrow's World	4.00
23 F:Professor X	3.00
24 F:Wolverine & Cecilia Reyes	3.00
25 BBh,48-pg.	3.00
26 BBh,Ages of Apocalypse,pt.4	7.00
27 BBh,X-Men: Revolution	3.00
28 BBh,Russia	3.00
29 BBh,Maximum Security	3.00
30 BBh,	3.00
31 MGo(c) three stories	3.00
32 JIT(c)	3.00
33 MK(c),Sabretooth,Blob	3.00
34 Marvel Girl vs. Sabretooth	3.50
35 F:Emma Frost, Jubilee	3.50
36 three stories	3.50
37 multiple dimensions, 48-pg.	3.50
38 DaR,F:Colossus	2.50
39 KIS,48-pg.	3.50
40 All evil issue, 48-pg.	3.50
41 I:MC Mystik,48-pg.	3.50
42 F:Prof. X, Jean Grey,48-pg.	3.50
43 CCl,BSz	2.50
44 animal cruelty	2.50

45 V:Alpha Flight	2.50
46 SB,F:Wolverine	2.50
47 Return of Psylocke	2.50
48 Mystique returns	2.50
49 F:Nightcrawler	2.50
50 PS,Japan connections	3.00

X-MEN UNLIMITED
March, 2004

1 TMd	3.00
2 F:Bishop.	3.00
3 F:Gambit	3.00
4 F:Juggernaut	3.00
5 F:Wolverine	3.00
6 Ladies of X.	3.00
7 F:nightcrawler, Kitty Pryde	3.00
8 F:Angel, Beast	3.00
9 F:Wolverine, Iceman	3.00
10 F:The Beast	3.00
11 MD2(c),Rachel & Havok	3.00
12 F:Wolverine.	3.00
13 Decimation tie-in	3.00
14 F:Colossus	3.00

X-MEN VS. AVENGERS
April, 1987

1 MS,JRu,V:Soviet SuperSoldiers	5.00
2 MS,JRu,V:Sov.Super Soldiers	3.50
3 MS,JRu,V:Sov.Super Soldiers	3.50
4 KP,JRu,BMc,AW,AM,V:Magneto July, 1987	3.50

X-MEN VS. THE BROOD
1996

1 and 2 Day of Wrath	@3.00

X-NATION 2099
1996

1	4.00
2	2.50
3 At Herod's Themepark	2.50

X.S.E.
Mini-Series 1996

1 (of 4) JOs,Bishop & Shard's secrets.	2.25
2 JOs, How did Shard die.	2.25
3 JOs, How Shard died.	2.25
4 JOs, conclusion	2.25

X-STATIX
July, 2002

1 PrM,MiA,super-team, 40-pg.	3.00
2 PrM,MiA,	2.50
3 PrM,MiA.	2.50
4 PrM,MiA, sex = death?	2.50
5 PrM,PPo	2.50
6 PrM,MiA,pt.1	2.50
7 PrM,MiA.	2.50
8 PrM,MiA,Orphan's New Love	2.50
9 PrM,MiA,	2.50
10 PrM,Diaries of Edie Sawyer.	3.00
11 PrM,F:Latino	3.00
12 PrM,If You Think I'm Sexy	3.00
13 PrM,MiA,Di Another Day,pt.1	3.00
14 PrM,MiA,Di Another Day,pt.2	3.00
15 PrM,MiA,Di Another Day,pt.3	3.00
16 PrM,MiA,Di Another Day,pt.4	3.00
16 PrM,MiA,Back from Dead,pt.4	3.00
17 PrM,MiA,Back from Dead,pt.5	3.00
18 PrM,MiA,Back from Dead,pt.6	3.00
19 PrM,MiA,The Cure,pt.1	3.00
20 PrM,MiA,The Cure,pt.2	3.00
21 PrM,MiA,V:Avengers,pt.1	3.00
22 PrM,MiA,V:Avengers,pt.2	3.00
23 PrM,MiA,V:Avengers,pt.3	3.00
24 PrM,MiA,V:Avengers,pt.4	3.00
25 PrM,MiA,V:Avengers,pt.5	3.00
26 PrM,MiA,finale.	3.00

X Terminators #3
© Marvel Entertainment Group

X-TERMINATORS
Oct., 1988—Jan., 1989
1 JBg,AW,AM,I:N'astirh. 4.00
2 JBg,AM,V:N'astirh 3.50
3 JBg,AM,V:N'astirh 3.00
4 JBg,AM,A:New Mutants. 3.00

X-TREME X-MEN
June, 2001
1 CCI,SvL,Destiny,48-page. 4.50
2A CCI,SvL,Guardia,Vargas 3.50
2B variant CPa(c) 3.50
3 CCI,SvL,V:Vargas 3.00
4 CCI,SvL,V:Vargas 3.00
5 CCI,SvL,F:Gambit 3.00
6 CCI,SvL,F:Gambit,Rogue 3.00
7 CCI,SvL 3.00
8 CCI,SvL,concl.'Nuff Said 3.00
9 CCI,SvL,V:Lady Mastermind . . . 3.00
10 CCI,SvL,Dimension X,pt.1 . . . . 3.00
11 CCI,SvL,Dimension X,pt.2 . . . . 3.00
12 CCI,SvL,V:Shaitan,Khan. 3.00
13 CCI,SvL,F:Gambit,Lifeguard . . . 3.00
14 CCI,SvL,F:Storm, Sage. 3.00
15 CCI,SvL,F:Storm,Rogue 3.00
16 CCI,SvL,F:Rogue, Gambit 3.00
17 CCI,SvL. 3.00
18 CCI,SvL,F:Jean Grey,Beast,
Nightcrawler. 3.00
19 CCI,F:Jean Grey. 3.00
20 CCI,SvL,Scism,pt.1 . . . . 3.00
21 CCI,SvL,Scism,pt.2 . . . . 3.00
22 CCI,SvL,Scism,pt.3 . . . . 3.00
23 CCI,SvL,Scism,pt.4 . . . . 3.00
24 CCI,SvL,R:Cannonball 3.00
25 CCI,SvL,God Loves,Man Kills2. . 3.00
26 CCI,SvL,God Loves,Man Kills2. . 3.00
27 CCI,SvL,God Loves,Man Kills2. . 3.00
28 CCI,SvL,God Loves,Man Kills2. . 3.00
29 CCI,SvL,God Loves,Man Kills2. . 3.00
30 CCI,SvL,God Loves,Man Kills2. . 3.00
31 CCI,SHa,Intifada,pt.1 . . . . 3.00
32 CCI,SHa,Intifada,pt.2 . . . . 3.00
33 CCI,SHa,Intifada,pt.3 . . . . 3.00
34 CCI,SHa,Intifada,pt.4 . . . . 3.00
35 CCI,SHa,Intifada,pt.5 . . . . 3.00
36 Storm: The Arena,pt.1. . . . . 3.00
37 Storm: The Arena,pt.2. . . . . 3.00
38 Storm: The Arena,pt.3. . . . . 3.00
39 Storm: The Arena,pt.4. . . . . 3.00
40 CCI,Bogan,pt.1,Prisoner of Fire . 3.00
41 CCI,Bogan,pt.2,Prisoner of Fire . 3.00
42 CCI,Bogan,pt.3,Prisoner of Fire . 3.00
43 CCI,Bogan,pt.4,Prisoner of Fire . 3.00
44 CCI,Prisoner of Fire,pt.5. . . . . . . 3.00
45 CCI,Prisoner of Fire,pt.6 . . . . 3.00
46 CCI,finale 3.50
Ann.2001 CCI,SvL,64-pg. 5.00

X-TREME X-MEN: SAVAGE LAND
July, 2001
1 (of 4) CCI,F:Rogue 3.50
2 CCI,Velociraptors & T-Rexes. . . . 3.00
3 CCI. 3.00
4 CCI,concl. 3.00

X-TREME X-MEN: X-POSE
Nov., 2002
1 (of 2) Ccl, two reporters. 3.00
2 CCI,Forbidden Mutant Love. 3.00

X-23
Jan., 2005
1 (of 6) BTn,Innocence Lost,pt.1 . . 6.00
2 Btn,o:x-23 . . . . 4.00
3 BTn,Innocence Lost. 3.00
4 BTn,Innocence Lost. 3.00
5 BTn,Innocence Lost. 3.00
6 BTn,Innocence Lost,concl. 3.00

X-23: TARGET X
Dec., 2006
1 (of 6) 3.00
2 thru 6 . . . . @3.00

X-UNIVERSE
1995
1 The Other Heroes 5.00
2 F:Ben Grimm,Tony Stark 5.00

YELLOW CLAW
Marvel Atlas, 1956
1 MMe 1,400.00
2 JK,JSe 1,200.00
3 BEv. 1,200.00
4 JK,JSe 1,200.00

YOGI BEAR
Nov., 1977
1 A:Flintstones 40.00
2 thru 9 March, 1979 . . . . @25.00

YOUNG ALLIES COMICS
Timely,
Summer, 1941—Oct., 1946
1 S&K,SSh,Hitler(c),I&O:Young Allies
1st meeting Capt. America &
Human Torch,A:Red Skull 30,000.00
2 S&K,A;Capt.America,Human
Torch. 7,500.00
3 Remember Pearl Harbor(c) . 5,500.00
4 A;Capt. America,Torch,Red Skull
ASh(c),Horror In Hollywood
A:Capt.America,Torch. 8,000.00
5 ASh(c),AAv,Capt.America . . . 3,500.00
6 ASh(c) 2,500.00
7 ASh(c),SSh 2,500.00
8 ASh(c),WW2,Bondage 2,500.00
9 ASh(c),Axis leaders(c),
B:Tommy Type,Hitler 2,800.00
10 ASh(c),O:Tommy Type. 2,500.00
11 ASh(c) 1,600.00
12 ASh(c),Decapitation 1,600.00
13 ASh(c) 1,600.00
14 ASh(c) 1,600.00
15 ASh(c),AAv. 1,600.00
16 ASh(c) 1,600.00
17 ASh(c),SSh 1,600.00

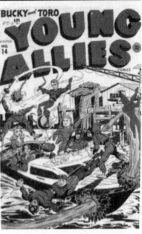

Young Allies #14
© Marvel Entertainment Group

18 ASh(c) 1,500.00
19 ASh(c),E:Tommy Type 1,500.00
20 SSh 1,500.00

YOUNG AVENGERS
Feb., 2005
1 Sidekicks 5.00
2 Sidekicks 3.00
3 Sidekicks 3.00
4 Sidekicks 3.00
5 Sidekicks 3.00
6 Sidekicks,concl. 3.00
7 Secret Identities,pt.1 . . . . 3.00
8 Secret Identities,pt.2 . . . . 3.00
9 New team member 3.00
10 Family Matters 3.00
11 Kree-Skrull War II 3.00
12 Family Matters 3.00
Spec. #1 Secret History (2005) 3.00

YOUNG HEARTS
Nov., 1949—Feb., 1950
1 . . . . 150.00
2 Feb., 1950 . . . . 100.00

YOUNG MEN
See: COWBOY ROMANCES

YUPPIES FROM HELL
1989
1 thru 3 Satire . . . . @3.00

ZIGGY PIG, SILLY SEAL
Marvel Timely, 1944
1 Funny Animals vs. Japs. 350.00
2 . . . . 175.00
3 thru 5 . . . . @125.00
6 . . . . 175.00

ZOMBIE
Sept., 2006
1 thru 4 . . . . @4.00

ZORRO
Marvel UK, 1990
1 Don Diego 3.00
2 thru 12 . . . . @3.00

GOLDEN AGE

A-1 COMICS
Magazine Enterprises, 1944
N# F:Kerry Drake,BU:Johnny
  Devildog & Streamer Kelly .. 300.00
1 A:Dotty Driple,Mr. EX,Bush
  Berry and Lew Loyal 165.00
2 A:Texas Slim & Dirty Dalton,
  The Corsair,Teddy Rich, Dotty
  Dripple,Inca Dinca,Tommy Tinker
  Little Mexico and Tugboat ... 100.00
3 same 100.00
4 same 100.00
5 same 100.00
6 same 100.00
7 same 100.00
8 same 100.00
9 Texas Slim Issue 125.00
10 Same characters as
  issues #2–#8 .... 100.00
11 Teena 150.00
12 Teena 100.00
13 JCr,Guns of Fact and Fiction,
  narcotics & junkies featured . 400.00
14 Tim Holt #1............. 1,100.00
15 Teena 100.00
16 Vacation Comics 75.00
17 Tim Holt #2, E:"A-1" on cover . 600.00
18 Jimmy Durante, Ph(c)...... 700.00
19 Tim Holt #3 .... 400.00
20 Jimmy Durante Ph(c) 600.00
21 OW,Joan of Arc movie adapt.. 400.00
22 Dick Powell (1949) 350.00
23 Cowboys N' Indians #6 ..... 175.00
24 FF(c),LbC,Trail Colt #1 ..... 600.00
25 Fibber McGee & Molly (1949). 125.00
26 LbC, Trail Colt #2 .... 500.00
27 GhostRider#1,O:GhostRider 1,700.00
28 Christmas (Koko & Kola #6)... 75.00
29 FF(c), Ghost Rider #2 ..... 1,200.00
30 BP, Jet Powers #1 .... 500.00
31 FF,Ghost Rider #3,O:Ghost
  Rider 1, 200.00
32 AW,GE,Jet Powers #2 ..... 500.00
33 Muggsy Mouse #1 .... 100.00
34 FF(c),Ghost Rider #4 ..... 1,100.00
35 AW,Jet Powers#3 .... 550.00
36 Muggsy Mouse #2 .... 150.00
37 FF(c),Ghost Rider #5...... 1,100.00
38 AW,WW,Jet Powers#4, Drugs 700.00
39 Muggsy Mouse #3 .... 75.00
40 Dogface Dooley #1........ 100.00
41 Cowboys 'N' Indians #7 .... 100.00
42 BP,Best of the West #1...... 650.00
43 Dogface Dooley#2 .... 75.00
44 Ghost Rider #6 .... 450.00
45 American Air Forces #5 .... 200.00
46 Best of the West #2 .... 400.00
47 FF,Thunda #1 .... 2,200.00
48 Cowboys N' Indians #8..... 150.00
49 Dogface Dooley #3......... 75.00
50 BP,Danger is Their
  Business #11 .... 200.00
51 Ghost Rider #7 .... 450.00
52 Best of the West #3 .... 300.00
53 Dogface Dooley #4 .... 75.00
54 BP,American Air Forces #6... 100.00
55 BP,U.S. Marines #5........ 100.00
56 BP,Thunda #2 .... 350.00
57 Ghost Rider #8, Drugs 500.00
58 American Air Forces #7 .... 100.00
59 Best of the West #4 .... 250.00
60 The U.S. Marines #6........ 100.00
61 Space Ace #5 .... 900.00
62 Starr Flagg, Undercover
  Girl #5 .... 600.00

63 FF,Manhunt #13 .... 550.00
64 Dogface Dooley #5......... 75.00
65 BP,American Air Forces #8... 100.00
66 Best of the West #5 .... 250.00
67 American Air Forces #9 .... 100.00
68 U.S. Marines #7 .... 100.00
69 Ghost Rider #9, Drugs 500.00
70 Best of the West #6 .... 200.00
71 Ghost Rider #10 .... 400.00
72 U.S. Marines #8 .... 100.00
73 BP,Thunda #3 .... 250.00
74 BP,American Air Forces #10.. 100.00
75 Ghost Rider #11 .... 350.00
76 Best of the West #7 .... 200.00
77 LbC,Grl,Manhunt #14 ...... 450.00
78 BP,Thunda #4 .... 250.00
79 American Air Forces #11..... 100.00
80 Ghost Rider #12, Bondage(c). 500.00
81 Best of the West #8 .... 200.00
82 BP,Cave Girl #11.......... 700.00
83 BP,Thunda #5 .... 225.00
84 Ghost Rider #13 .... 400.00
85 Best of the West #9 .... 200.00
86 BP,Thunda #6 .... 250.00
87 Best of the West #10 ...... 200.00
88 Bobby Benson's B-Bar-B #29. 150.00
89 BP,Home Run #3,Stan Musial. 275.00
90 Red Hawk #11 .... 200.00
91 BP,American Air Forces #12.. 100.00
92 Dream Book of Romance #5 . 175.00
93 BP,Great Western #8 ...... 300.00
94 FF,White Indian #11 .... 350.00
95 BP,Muggsy Mouse #5 ...... 75.00
96 BP,Cave Girl #12 .... 500.00
97 Best of the West #11 ...... 200.00
98 Starr Flagg Undercover
  Girl #6 .... 550.00
99 Muggsy Mouse #5 .... 75.00
100 Badmen of the West #1 .... 325.00
101 FF,White Indian #12 ...... 325.00
101(a) BP(c),FGu, Dream Book of
  Romance #6, Marlon Brando 300.00
103 BP,Best of the West #12.... 200.00
104 FF,White Indian #13 ...... 325.00
105 Great Western #9 .... 200.00
106 BP,Dream Book of Love #1 . 200.00
107 Hot Dog #1 .... 125.00
108 BP,LbC,Red Fox #15 ..... 350.00

A-1 Comics #98
© Magazine Enterprises

109 BP,Dream Book of Romance 150.00
110 Dream Book of Romance #8 150.00
111 BP,I'm a Cop #1 .... 200.00
112 Ghost Rider #14 .... 350.00
113 BP,Great Western #10 .... 175.00
114 Dream Book of Love #2 ... 150.00
115 Hot Dog #2 .... 100.00
116 BP,Cave Girl #13......... 500.00
117 White Indian #14......... 175.00
118 BP(c),Starr Flagg–
  Undercover Girl #7 .... 550.00
119 Straight Arrow's Fury #1 .... 225.00
120 Badmen of the West #2 .... 250.00
121 Mysteries of the
  Scotland Yard #1 .... 250.00
122 Black Phantom #1......... 550.00
123 Dream Book of Love #3 ... 125.00
124 Hot Dog #3 .... 100.00
125 BP,Cave Girl #14 .... 500.00
126 BP,I'm a Cop #2.......... 150.00
127 BP,Great Western 200.00
128 BP,I'm a Cop #3 .... 150.00
129 The Avenger #1 .... 600.00
130 BP,Strongman #1 .... 325.00
131 BP,The Avenger #2........ 400.00
132 Strongman #2 .... 300.00
133 BP,The Avenger #3........ 400.00
134 Strongman #3 .... 300.00
135 White Indian #15......... 175.00
136 Hot Dog #4 .... 100.00
137 BP,Africa #1 .... 350.00
138 BP,Avenger #4 .... 400.00
139 BP,Strongman #4, 1955 ... 300.00

ABBIE AN' SLATS
United Features Syndicate, March–Aug., 1948
1 RvB(c) 250.00
2 RvB(c) 175.00
3 RvB(c) 150.00
4 Aug., 1948 .... 150.00
N# 1940,Earlier Issue 600.00
N# 500.00

ABBOTT AND COSTELLO
St. John Publishing Co., Feb., 1948
1 PP(c), Waltz Time 900.00
2 Jungle Girl and Snake(c)..... 450.00
3 Outer Space (c) 300.00
4 MD, Circus (c) 250.00
5 MD,Bull Fighting (c) 250.00
6 MD,Harem (c) 250.00
7 MD,Opera (c)............. 250.00
8 MD,Pirates (c) 250.00
9 MD,Polar Bear (c) 250.00
10 MD,PP(c),Son of Sinbad tale . 325.00
11 MD. 200.00
12 PP(c), Movie issue 250.00
13 Fire fighters (c) 200.00
14 Bomb (c)............... 200.00
15 Bubble Bath (c).......... 200.00
16 thru 29 MD .... @175.00
30 thru 39 MD .... @150.00
40 MD,Sept., 1956. .... 150.00
3-D #1, Nov., 1953......... 500.00

ACE COMICS
David McKay Publications, April, 1937
1 JM, F:Katzenjammer Kids .. 5,500.00
2 JM, A:Blondie 1,500.00
3 JM, A:Believe It Or Not..... 1,000.00
4 JM, F:Katzenjammer Kids .. 1,000.00

        All comics prices listed are for *Near Mint* condition.

5 JM, A:Believe It Or Not 1,000.00
6 JM, A:Blondie 750.00
7 JM, A:Believe It Or Not 750.00
8 JM, A:Jungle Jim 750.00
9 JM, A:Blondie 750.00
10 JM, F:Katzenjammer Kids. . . . 700.00
11 I:The Phantom series. 1,200.00
12 A:Blondie, Jungle Jim 600.00
13 A:Ripley's Believe It Or Not . . 500.00
14 A:Blondie, Jungle Jim 500.00
15 A:Blondie. 500.00
16 F:Katzenjammer Kids 500.00
17 A:Blondie. 500.00
18 A:Ripley's Believe It Or Not . . 500.00
19 F:Katzenjammer Kids 500.00
20 A:Jungle Jim 500.00
21 A:Blondie. 450.00
22 A:Jungle Jim 450.00
23 F:Katzenjammer Kids 450.00
24 A:Blondie. 450.00
25 . . . . 450.00
26 O:Prince Valiant. 1,500.00
27 thru 36. . . . . @450.00
37 Krazy Kat Ends. 350.00
38 thru 40 . . . . @350.00
41 thru 59. . . . . @300.00
60 thru 69 . . . . @250.00
70 thru 89 . . . . @150.00
90 thru 99 . . . . @125.00
100 F:The Phantom. 165.00
101 thru 109. . . . . @125.00
110 thru 127 . . . . @100.00
128 Brick Bradford begins 100.00
129 thru 143. . . . . @100.00
144 Phantom covers begin 125.00
145 thru 150. . . . . @100.00
151 Oct.–Nov., 1949 . . . . 125.00

ACES HIGH
E.C. Comics, March–April, 1955
1 GE(a&c),JDa,WW,BK 500.00
2 GE(a&c),JDa,WW,BK 300.00
3 GE(a&c),JDa,WW,BK 250.00
4 GE(a&c),JDa,WW,BK 250.00
5 GE(c),JDa,WW,BK. 250.00

ADVENTURE IS MY CAREER
Street & Smith Publ., 1944
n# U.S.Coast Guard Academy. . . 300.00

ADVENTURES
St. John Publishing Co., Nov. 1949–Feb. 1950
1 Adventures in Romance 350.00
2 Spectacular Adventures 500.00

ADVENTURES IN 3-D
Harvey Publications, Nov. 1953–Jan 1954
1 with glasses. 350.00
1a rep. O'Dells Adventures
   in 3-D. 300.00
2 with glasses. 300.00

ADVENTURES INTO DARKNESS
Standard Pub., Aug., 1952
5 JK(c), ATh 650.00
6 GT, JK 450.00
7 JK(c) 450.00
8 ATh. 450.00
9 JK,ATh 450.00
10 JK,ATh,MSy 400.00
11 JK,ATh,MSy 400.00
12 JK,ATh,MSy 400.00
13 Cannibalism feature 550.00
14 Frozen Death 300.00

Adventures Into the Unknown #39
© American Comics Group

ADVENTURES INTO THE UNKNOWN!
American Comics Group, Fall 1948
1 FGu, Haunted House (c) . . . 4,000.00
2 Haunted Island (c) 1,500.00
3 AF, Sarcophagus (c). 1,500.00
4 Monsters (c). 750.00
5 Monsters (c). 750.00
6 Giant Hands (c) 600.00
7 Skeleton Pirate (c). 600.00
8 Horror. 600.00
9 Snow Monster 600.00
10 Red Bats. 600.00
11 Death Shadow 600.00
12 OW(c) 600.00
13 OW(c),Dinosaur 400.00
14 OW(c),Cave 400.00
15 Red Demons. 400.00
16 OW(c) 300.00
17 OW(c),The Thing Type 500.00
18 OW(c),Wolves. 400.00
19 OW(c),Graveyard 400.00
20 OW(c),Graveyard 400.00
21 OW(c),Bats and Dracula. . . . 300.00
22 Witches' Wrath 300.00
23 OW(c),Bats 300.00
24 Swamp Monster 300.00
25 The Were-Tiger of Assam. . . . 300.00
26 DW(s) 300.00
27 AW,RKu,OW(c) 400.00
28 thru 37. . . . . @300.00
38 A-Bomb 500.00
39 thru 49. . . . . @400.00
50 Giant fly (c) 400.00
51 H. Lazarus 500.00
52 H. Lazarus, 3-D-ish. 500.00
53 thru 55. . . . . @500.00
56 H. Lazarus 500.00
57 SMo,OW(c). 500.00
58 H. Lazarus 500.00
59 3-D-ish 400.00
60 Hospitality; Tomb for Titus. . . 200.00
61 OW,Rocket ship (c). 200.00
62 thru 69. . . . . @150.00
70 thru 79. . . . . @150.00
80 thru 90. . . . . @125.00
91 AW 150.00
92 thru 95. . . . . @100.00
96 AW 150.00
97 thru 99 . . . . @100.00
100 JB 125.00
101 thru 106. . . . . @100.00
107 AW 150.00

108 thru 115 . . . . @125.00
116 AW,AT. 150.00
117 thru 127 . . . . @125.00
128 AW,Forbidden Worlds. 125.00
129 thru 151. . . . . @125.00
152 JCr 125.00
153 A:Magic Agent. 125.00
154 O:Nemesis 150.00
155 Nemesis 125.00
156 A:Magic Agent. 125.00
157 thru 167 . . . . @125.00
168 JB,SD, Nemesis 125.00
169 Nemesis vs. Hitler. 150.00
170 thru 174, Aug., 1967 . . . . . @125.00

ADVENTURES IN WONDERLAND
Lev Gleason Publications, April, 1955
1 . . . . 150.00
2 . . . . 100.00
3 and 4 . . . . @75.00
5 Christmas. 125.00

ADVENTURES OF ALICE
Civil Service Publ., 1945–46
1 In Wonderland 200.00
2 Through the Looking Glass . . . 100.00
3 Monkey Island 100.00

THE ADVENTURES OF HOMER COBB
Say/Bart Prod., Sept. 1947
1 . . . . 500.00

ADVENTURES OF LITTLE ORPHAN ANNIE COMICS
Giveaway 1940–42
N#(1) 600.00
N#(2) 500.00
N#(3) 500.00

MIGHTY MOUSE ADVENTURES
St. John Publishing Co., Nov., 1951
1 Mighty Mouse Adventures 400.00
Becomes:

ADVENTURES OF MIGHTY MOUSE
St. John Publishing Co., Nov., 1951
2 Menace of the Deep 400.00
3 Storm Clouds of Mystery 300.00
4 Thought Control Machine 300.00
5 Jungle Peril 300.00
6 'The Vine of Destruction' 250.00
7 Space Ship(c) 250.00
8 Charging Alien(c). 250.00
9 Meteor(c) 150.00
10 'Revolt at the Zoo'. 150.00
11 Jungle(c). 150.00
12 A:Freezing Terror 150.00
13 A:Visitor from Outer Space . . 150.00
14 V:Cat. 150.00
15 . . . . 150.00
16 . . . . 150.00
17 . . . . 150.00
18 May, 1955 . . . . 150.00

ADVENTURES OF MIGHTY MOUSE
See: TERRY-TUNES COMICS

AGGIE MACK

**Four Star Comics/
Superior Comics, Jan., 1948**
1 AF,HR(c),Johnny Prep 600.00
2 JK(c) 300.00
3 AF,JK(c) 300.00
4 AF, Johnny Prep 400.00
5 AF,JK(c) 300.00
6 AF,JK(c) 275.00
7 AF,Burt Lancaster on cover . . . 325.00
8 AF,JK(c), Aug., 1949 . . . . 275.00

BILL BARNES

Street & Smith Publ.,July, 1940
1 (Bill Barnes Comics) 1,500.00
Becomes:

BILL BARNES,
AMERICA'S AIR ACE

Street & Smith Publ., 1940
2 Second Battle Valley Forge . . . 650.00
3 A:Aviation Cadets 500.00
4 Shotdown(c). 500.00
5 A:Air Warden, Danny Hawk . . . 500.00
6 A:Danny Hawk,RocketRodney. 400.00
7 How to defeat the Japanese . . 400.00
8 Ghost Ship 400.00
9 Flying Tigers, John Wayne . . . 425.00
10 I:Roane Waring. 400.00
11 Flying Tigers 400.00
12 War Workers. 400.00
Becomes:

*Air Ace Vol. 3 #8
© Street & Smith*

AIR ACE

Street & Smith Publ., Jan., 1944
2-1 Invades Germany 600.00
2-2 Jungle Warfare 350.00
2-3 A:The Four Musketeers . . . 200.00
2-4 A:Russell Swann. 200.00
2-5 A:The Four Musketeers . . . 200.00
2-6 Raft(c). 200.00
2-7 BP, What's New In Science . 200.00
2-8 XP-59 . . . . 200.00
2-9 The Northrop P-61 . . . . 200.00
2-10 NCG-14 . . . . 200.00
2-11 Whip Launch. 200.00
2-12 PP(c). 200.00
3-1 . . . . 150.00
3-2 Atom and Its Future 150.00
3-3 Flying in the Future. 150.00
3-4 How Fast Can We Fly 150.00
3-5 REv(c). 150.00
3-6 V:Wolves. 150.00
3-7 BP(c), Vortex of Atom Bomb 400.00

3-8 BP,Feb.–March, 1947 . . . . . 175.00

AIR FIGHTERS COMICS

Hillman Periodicals, Nov., 1941
1 I:Black Commander
  (only App) 4,500.00
2 O:Airboy A:Sky Wolf 7,000.00
3 O:Sky Wolf and Heap 3,500.00
4 A:Black Angel, Iron Ace 3,000.00
5 A:Sky Wolf and Iron Ace. . . . 2,200.00
6 Airboy's Bird Plane 2,700.00
7 Airboy Battles Kultur. 2,500.00
8 A:Skinny McGinty 2,200.00
9 A:Black Prince, Hatchet Man 2,200.00
10 I:The Stinger 2,200.00
11 Kida(c) 2,200.00
12 A:Misery. 2,200.00
2-1 A:Flying Dutchman 2,400.00
2-2 I:Valkyrie 2,700.00
2-3 Story Panels (c) 1,000.00
2-4 V:Japanese. 1,000.00
2-5 Air Boy in Tokyo 1,000.00
2-6 'Dance of Death'. 1,000.00
2-7 A:Valkyrie 1,000.00
2-8 Airboy Battles Japanese. . . 1,000.00
2-9 Airboy Battles Japanese. . . 1,000.00
2-10 O:Skywolf 1,200.00
Becomes:

AIRBOY COMICS

Hillman Periodicals, Dec., 1945
2-11 . . . . 1,200.00
2-12 A:Valkrie 800.00
3-1 . . . . 600.00
3-2 . . . . 600.00
3-3 Never published
3-4 I:The Heap 500.00
3-5 Airboy 500.00
3-6 A:Valkyrie 500.00
3-7 AMc,Witch Hunt 500.00
3-8 A:Condor. 550.00
3-9 O:The Heap 550.00
3-10 . . . . 500.00
3-11 . . . . 500.00
3-12 Airboy missing 650.00
4-1 Elephant in chains (c). 600.00
4-2 I:Rackman 450.00
4-3 Airboy profits on name 450.00
4-4 S&K 500.00
4-5 S&K,The American Miracle . 450.00
4-6 S&K,A:Heap and
  Flying Fool. 450.00
4-7 S&K 450.00
4-8 S&K,Girlfriend captured . . . 450.00
4-9 S&K,Airboy in Quick Sand . 450.00
4-10 S&K,A:Valkyrie 450.00
4-11 S&K,A:Frenchy. 450.00
4-12 FBe. 500.00
5-1 LSt 400.00
5-2 I:Wild Horse of Calabra . . . 400.00
5-3 . . . . 400.00
5-4 CI 400.00
5-5 Skull on cover. 400.00
5-6. . . . . 400.00
5-7. . . . . 400.00
5-8 Bondage (c) 400.00
5-9 Zoi,Row 400.00
5-10 A:Valykrie,O:The Heap. . . 450.00
5-11 Airboy vs. The Rats. 400.00
5-12 BK,Rat Army captures
  Airboy 400.00
6-1. . . . . 400.00
6-2. . . . . 400.00
6-3. . . . . 400.00
6-4 Airboy boxes. 500.00
6-5 A:The Ice People 400.00
6-6 . . . . 400.00
6-7 Airboy vs. Chemical Giant . . 400.00
6-8 O:The Heap 400.00
6-9 . . . . 400.00
6-10 . . . . 400.00
6-11 . . . . 400.00

6-12 . . . . 400.00
7-1 . . . . 350.00
7-2 BP. 350.00
7-3 BP. 350.00
7-4 I:Monsters of the Ice. 350.00
7-5 V:Monsters of the Ice 350.00
7-6 . . . . 350.00
7-7 Mystery of the Sargasso
  Sea 350.00
7-8 A:Centaur 350.00
7-9 I:Men of the StarlightRobot. . 350.00
7-10 O:The Heap 350.00
7-11 . . . . 350.00
7-12 Airboy visits India 350.00
8-1 BP,A:Outcast and Polo
  Bandits. 300.00
8-2 BP,Suicide Dive (c). 300.00
8-3 BK, I:The Living Fuse. 300.00
8-4 A:Death Merchants of
  the Air 300.00
8-5 A:Great Plane from Nowhere 300.00
8-6 . . . . 300.00
8-7 . . . . 300.00
8-8 . . . . 300.00
8-9 . . . . 300.00
8-10 A:Mystery Walkers 300.00
8-11 . . . . 300.00
8-12 . . . . 300.00
9-1 . . . . 300.00
9-2 A:Valkyrie 250.00
9-3 A:Heap (c). 250.00
9-4 A:Water Beast, Frog Headed
  Riders 300.00
9-5 A:Heap vs.Man of Moonlight 250.00
9-6 Heap (c) 250.00

*Airboy Vol. 4 #5
© Hillman Periodicals*

9-7 Heap (c) 250.00
9-8 Heap (c) 300.00
9-9 . . . . 300.00
9-10 Space (c) 300.00
9-11 . . . . 300.00
9-12 Heap (c) 300.00
10-1 Heap (c) 300.00
10-2 Ships on Space 250.00
10-3 . . . . 300.00
10-4 May, 1953 . . . . 300.00

AL CAPP'S
DOGPATCH COMICS

Toby Press, June, 1949
1 . . . . 350.00
2 A:Daisy. 250.00
3 . . . . 225.00
4 Dec., 1949 . . . . 225.00

GOLDEN AGE

AL CAPP'S SHMOO
Toby Press, July, 1949
1 100 Trillion Schmoos	600.00
2 Super Shmoo(c)	400.00
3	400.00
4	400.00
5 April, 1950	400.00

AL CAPP'S WOLF GAL
Toby Press, 1951
1 Pin-Up	500.00
2 1952	450.00

ALICE
Ziff-Davis Publ. Co., 1952
10 New Adventures in Wonderland	400.00
11 (#2)	350.00

ALLEY OOP
Standard Comics, Sept. 1947–Oct. 1949
10	350.00
11 thru 18	@300.00

(The Adventures of)
ALLEY OOP
Argo Publications, 1955–56
1	225.00
2	150.00
3	150.00

ALL-FAMOUS CRIME
Star Publications, May, 1951
1 LbC(c) (8)	350.00
2 LbC(c) (9)	500.00
3 LbC(c) (10)	325.00
4 LbC(c) (4) Law Crime	300.00
5 LbC(c) (5)	300.00
Becomes:

ALL-FAMOUS POLICE CASES
Feb., 1952
6 LbC(c)	325.00
7 LbC(c)	300.00
8 LbC(c) Marijuana	300.00
9 LbC(c)	250.00
10 thru 15 LbC(c)	@250.00
16 Sept., 1954	250.00

ALL GOOD COMICS
Fox Publications, 1946
1	400.00

ALL GOOD COMICS
R. W. Voight/ St. John Publishing, 1949
N# Giant	1,200.00

ALL GREAT
Fox Features, 1946
1 Crazy Horse, etc	500.00

ALL GREAT COMICS
See: DAGAR, DESERT HAWK

ALL HERO COMICS
Fawcett Publications, March, 1943
1 A:Capt. Marvel Jr.,Capt. Midnight,Ibis, Golden Arrow and Spy Smasher	3,000.00

All Great Comics #1
© *Fox Features*

ALL HUMOR COMICS
Comic Favorites, Inc. (Quality Comics) Spring 1946
1	350.00
2 PG Atomic Tot	200.00
3 I:Kelly Poole	125.00
4 thru 7	@ 125.00
8 PG	125.00
9	125.00
10	125.00
11 thru 17	@100.00

ALL-NEGRO COMICS
June,1947
1	9,000.00

ALL-NEW COMICS
Family Comics (Harvey Publ.) Jan., 1943
1 A:Steve Case, Johnny Rebel I:Detective Shane	5,000.00
2 JKu,O:Scarlet Phantom	2,000.00
3 Nazi War	1,800.00
4 AdH	1,500.00
5 Flash Gordon	1,800.00
6 ASh(c),I:Boy Heroes and Red Blazer	1,800.00
7 JKu,ASh(c),A:Black Cat & Zebra	1,800.00
8 JKu,A:Shock Gibson	1,800.00
9 JKu,A:Black Cat	1,800.00
10 ASh(c),JKu,A:Zebra	1,800.00
11 BP,A:Man in Black, Girl Commandos	1,800.00
12 JKu	1,400.00
13 Stuntman by S&K, A:Green Hornet&(c)	1,500.00
14 BP,A:Green Hornet	1,200.00
15 Smaller size, Distributed by Mail, March–April, 1947.	2,000.00

ALL PICTURE ALL TRUE LOVE STORY
St. John Publ. Co. 1952
1 MB,Romance on Route 202	800.00
2 MB	500.00

REAL SPORTS COMICS
Hillman Periodicals, 1948
1 BP,Boxing (c)	600.00
Becomes:

ALL SPORTS COMICS
Hillman Periodicals, 1949
2 BP,BK,Football (c)	550.00
3 Basketball (c)	450.00
Becomes:

ALL-TIME SPORTS COMICS
Hillman Periodicals, 1949
4 Auto Racing (c)	350.00
5 BP,Baseball (c), Ty Cobb	325.00
6 Horse Racing (c)	300.00
7 BK, Baseball (c), W. Johnson	300.00

ALL TOP COMICS
William H. Wise Co., 1944
N# 132pgs.,A:Capt. V,Red Robbins	500.00

ALL TOP COMICS
Fox Features Syndicate, Spring 1946
1 A:Cosmo Cat, Flash Rabbit	350.00
2	150.00
3 thru 6	@125.00
7	125.00
7a	125.00
8 JKa(c),I:Blue Beetle	4,500.00
9 JKa(c),A:Rulah	2,200.00
10 JKa(c),A:Rulah	2,200.00
11 A:Rulah,Blue Beetle	1,800.00
12 A:Rulah,Jo Jo,Blue Beetle	1,800.00
13 A:Rulah	1,800.00
14 A:Rulah,Blue Beetle	2,500.00
15 A:Rulah	2,100.00
16 A:Rulah,Blue Beetle	1,800.00
17 A:Rulah,Blue Beetle	1,800.00
18 A:Dagar,Jo Jo	1,300.00
Becomes:

MY EXPERIENCE
Fox Features Syndicate 1949–50
19 WW	450.00
20	125.00
21 WW	450.00
22 WW	400.00
Becomes:

JUDY CANOVA
Fox Features Syndicate, May, 1950–Sept., 1950
23 (1)WW(a&c)	400.00
24 (2)WW(a&c)	400.00
3 JO,WW(a&c)	400.00

ALL TOP COMICS
Green Publ., 1957–59
6 1957 Patoruzu the Indian	100.00
6 1958 Cosmo Cat	100.00
6 1959 Atomic Mouse	100.00
6 1959 Little Eva	100.00
6 Supermouse (c)	100.00

ALL-TRUE DETECTIVE CASES
Avon Periodicals, 1954
1 WW	350.00
2 EK(c),JKa	250.00
3 JKa	250.00
4 JKa	300.00
N# (5) JK,JKu	700.00

ALL YOUR COMICS
R.W. Voight, 1944
1 Red Robbins	350.00

All comics prices listed are for *Near Mint* condition.

GOLDEN AGE

ALL YOUR COMICS
Fox Features, 1946
1 . . . . 300.00

AMAZING ADVENTURE FUNNIES
Centaur Publ,. 1940
1 BEv,The Fantom of the Fair . 4,000.00
2 rep.After Fantoman 2,500.00
Becomes:

FANTOMAN
Aug., 1940
2 The Fantom of the Fair 3,000.00
3 . . . . 2,500.00
4 Red Blaze 2,500.00

AMAZING ADVENTURES
Ziff-Davis Publ., Co., 1950
1 MA,WW, Asteroid Witch 1,500.00
2 MA,ASh(c),Masters of Living
Flame. 700.00
3 MA,The Evil Men Do 700.00
4 Invasion of the Love Robots . . 700.00
5 MA,Secret of the Crater-Men. . 700.00
6 BK,Man Who Killed a World . . 750.00

AMAZING GHOST STORIES
See: WEIRD HORRORS

AMAZING-MAN COMICS
**Centaur Publications,
Sept., 1939–Feb., 1942**
5 BEv,O:Amazing Man. 35,000.00
6 BEv,FT,B:The Shark 7,000.00
7 BEv,I:Magician From Mars . . 5,000.00
8 BEv, Cat-Man as Woman . . . 4,000.00
9 BEv,FT,A:Eternal Monster. . . 4,000.00
10 BEv,FT 2,800.00
11 BEv,I:Zardi 2,800.00
12 SG(c) 2,500.00
13 SG(c) 2,500.00
14 FT,B:Reef Kinkaid, Dr. Hypo 2,000.00
15 FT,A:Zardi 2,000.00
16 AAv,Mighty Man's Powers
Revealed 2,000.00
17 FT,A:Dr. Hypo 2,000.00
18 FT,BLb(a),SG(c). 2,000.00
19 FT,BLb(a),SG(c). 2,000.00
20 FT,BLb(a),SG(c). 2,000.00
21 FT,O:Dash Dartwell 2,000.00

Amazing Man #8
© *Centaur Publications*

22 A:Silver Streak, The Voice . . 2,500.00
23 I&O:Tommy the AmazingKid 1,600.00
24 B:King of Darkness,
Blue Lady 1,600.00
25 A:Meteor Marvin. 2,500.00
26 A:Meteor Marvin,ElectricRay 2,500.00

AMAZING MYSTERY FUNNIES
Centaur Publications, 1938
1 Skyrocket Steele in Year X . . 7,500.00
2 WE,Skyrocket Steele 4,000.00
3 . . . . 2,500.00
(#4) WE,bondage (c) 2,400.00
2-1(#5) 2,200.00
2-2(#6) Drug use. 1,500.00
2-3(#7) Air Sub DX 1,500.00
2-4(#8) Sand Hog 1,500.00
2-5(#9) 2,500.00
2-6(#10) 1,500.00
2-7(#11) Fantom of Fair, scarce 7,000.00
2-8(#12) Speed Centaur 3,000.00
2-9(#13) 1,800.00
2-10(#14) 1,800.00
2-11(#15)Robot(c). 1,800.00
2-12(#16) BW,I:Space Patrol . 3,800.00
3-1(#17) I:Bullet 1,800.00
18 Fantom of Fair 1,800.00
19 BW,Space Patrol 2,000.00
20 . . . . 1,500.00
21 thru 24 BW,Space Patrol . @2,000.00

AMAZING WILLIE MAYS
Famous Funnies, 1954
1 Willie Mays(c) 1,500.00

AMERICA IN ACTION
Dell Publishing Co., 1942
1 . . . . 350.00

THE AMERICAN AIR FORCES
Flying Cadet Publ., 1944–45
1 War (c). 300.00
2 War (c). 400.00
3 War (c). 400.00
4 War (c) 250.00
Continues in *A-1 Comics.* See #45,
#54, #58, #65, #67, #74, #79, #91

AMERICAN GRAPHICS
Henry Stewart, 1954
1 Indian Legends 175.00
2 . . . . 125.00

AMERICAN LIBRARY
David McKay Publ., 1943
(#1) Thirty Seconds Over
Tokyo, movie adapt. 550.00
(#2) Guadalcanal Diary 400.00
3 Look to the Mountain 250.00
4 The Case of the Crooked
Candle (Perry Mason) 250.00
5 Duel in the Sun 250.00
6 Wingate's Raiders 250.00

AMERICA'S BEST COMICS
**Nedor/Better/Standard
Publications, Feb., 1942**
1 ASh(c),B:Black Terror, Captain Future,
The Liberator,Doc Strange . 4,500.00
2 O:American Eagle. 2,000.00
3 B:Pyroman 1,500.00
4 A:Doc Strange, Jimmy Cole . 1,100.00
5 ASh(c),A:LoneEagle,
Cap.Future. 1,100.00

6 A:American Crusader 1,100.00
7 ASh(c),A:Hitler,Hirohito 2,000.00
8 The Liberator ends 1,100.00
9 ASh(c),Fighting Yank 1,500.00
10 ASh(c),American Eagle 1,100.00
11 ASh(c) Hirihito & Tojo(c). . . . 1,500.00
12 Red Cross (c). 1,100.00
13 Fighting Yank. 1,100.00
14 Last American Eagle app. . . 1,100.00
15 ASh(c),Fighting Yank 1,100.00
16 ASh(c),Fighting Yank 1,100.00
17 ASh(c),Doc Strange
carries football 1,100.00
18 Fighting Yank,Bondage(c) . . 1,100.00
19 ASh(c),Fighting Yank 1,100.00
20 ASh(c),vs. the Black Market 1,100.00
21 ASh(c),Infinity (c) 1,100.00
22 A:Captain Future 1,000.00
23 B:Miss Masque 1,150.00
24 Miss Masque,Bondage (c). . . 1,150.00
25 A:Sea Eagle 750.00
26 A:The Phantom Detective . . . 750.00
27 Pyroman,ASh(c) 750.00
28 A:Commando Cubs,
Black Terror 750.00
29 ASh(c),A:Doc Strange. 750.00
30 ASh(c).Xela 750.00
31 ASh(c),Xela,July, 1949 . . . . . 750.00

AMERICA'S BIGGEST COMICS BOOK
William H. Wise, 1944
1 196 pgs. A:Grim Reaper, Zudo,
Silver Knight, Thunderhoof,
Jocko and Socko,Barnaby
Beep,Commando Cubs. 700.00
Becomes:

AMERICA'S FUNNIEST COMICS
William H. Wise, 1944
2 Funny Animal. 500.00
N# (3). 500.00

AMERICA'S GREATEST COMICS
Fawcett Publications, Fall 1941
1 MRa(c),A:Capt. Marvel,
Bulletman,Spy Smasher and
Minute Man. 6,500.00
2 F:Capt. Marvel 3,000.00
3 F:Capt. Marvel 2,500.00
4 B:Commando Yank. 2,000.00
5 Capt.Marvel in 'Lost Lighting' 2,000.00
6 Capt.Marvel fires
Machine Gun 2,000.00
7 A:Balbo the Boy Magician. . 1,800.00
8 A:Capt.Marvel Jr.,Golden
Arrow, Summer 1943 . . . . . 1,800.00

ANCHORS ANDREWS
St. John Publ. Co. 1953
1 MB,Navy Humor 275.00
2 thru 4 . . . . @100.00

ANDY COMICS
See: SCREAM COMICS

ANDY DEVINE WESTERN
Fawcett Publ. 1950
1 Photo (c) 900.00
2 . . . . 700.00

ANGEL
Dell Publishing Co., Aug., 1954
(1) *see Dell Four Color #576*
2 . . . . 90.00
3 thru 16 . . . . @75.00

ANIMAL ADVENTURES
Timor Publ./Accepted Publ.
1953–54
1 Funny Animal 90.00
1a rep.. . . . . 75.00
2 . . . . 75.00

ANIMAL ANTICS
Dell Publishing Co., 1946
1 B: Racoon Kids 650.00
2 . . . . 300.00
3 thru 10 . . . . @175.00
11 thru 23 . . . . @125.00

Animal Comics #17
© Dell Publishing

ANIMAL COMICS
Dell Publishing Co., 1942
1 WK,Pogo. 1,700.00
2 Uncle Wiggily(c),A:Pogo. . . . 1,000.00
3 Muggin's Mouse(c),A:Pogo . . . 750.00
4 Uncle Wiggily(c). 500.00
5 Uncle Wiggily(c). 750.00
6 Uncle Wiggily 500.00
7 Uncle Wiggily 500.00
8 WK,Pogo 600.00
9 WK,War Bonds(c),A:Pogo 600.00
10 WK,Pogo. 600.00
11 WK,Pogo. 400.00
12 WK,Pogo. 400.00
13 WK,Pogo. 400.00
14 WK,Pogo. 400.00
15 WK,Pogo. 400.00
16 Uncle Wiggily 250.00
17 WK,Pogo(c). 300.00
18 WK,Pogo(c). 300.00
19 WK,Pogo(c). 300.00
20 WK,Pogo. 250.00
21 WK,Pogo(c). 300.00
22 WK,Pogo. 200.00
23 WK,Pogo. 200.00
24 WK,Pogo(c). 200.00
25 WK,Pogo(c). 200.00
26 WK,Pogo(c). 200.00
27 thru 30 WK,Pogo(c) . . . . . . @200.00

ANIMAL FABLES
E.C. Comics, July–Aug., 1946
1 B:Korky Kangaroo,Freddy Firefly
  Petey Pig & Danny Demon . 750.00
2 B:Aesop Fables 400.00
3 . . . . 325.00
4 . . . . 325.00
5 Firefly vs. Red Ants 325.00
6 . . . . 325.00
7 O:Moon Girls,Nov.–Dec.1947 1,200.00

ANIMAL FAIR
Fawcett Publications,
March, 1946
1 B:Captain Marvel Bunny,
  Sir Spot 500.00
2 A:Droopy, Colonel Walrus . . . 350.00
3 . . . . 250.00
4 A:Kid Gloves, Cub Reporter . . 250.00
5 thru 7 . . . . @250.00
8 thru 10 . . . . @150.00
11 Feb., 1947 . . . . 200.00

ANIMATED COMICS
E.C. Comics, 1948
1 Funny Animal 1,250.00

ANNIE OAKLEY & TAGG
Dell Publishing Co., 1953
(1) see Dell Four Color #438
(2) see Dell Four Color #481
(3) see Dell Four Color #575
4 . . . . 250.00
5 . . . . 200.00
6 thru 10 . . . . @175.00
11 thru 18 . . . . @135.00

APACHE
Fiction House Magazines, 1951
1 . . . . 300.00

APACHE TRAIL
America's Best, 1957
1 . . . . 125.00
2 GT 85.00
3 . . . . 75.00
4 . . . . 75.00

APPROVED COMICS
St. John Publishing Co., 1954
1 The Hawk. 125.00
2 Invisible Boy 225.00
3 Wild Boy of the Congo. 100.00
4 Kid Cowboy 100.00
5 Flyboy 100.00
6 MB,BK,Daring Adventures. . . 150.00
7 The Hawk. 100.00
8 BP,Crime on the Run. 125.00
9 MB,Western Bandit Trails . . . 150.00
10 Dinky Duck 100.00
11 MB,Fighting Marines 175.00
12 Northwest Mounties 175.00

ARCHIE COMICS
MLJ Magazines,
Winter, 1942-43
1 I:Jughead & Veronica 30,000.00
2 rare 7,000.00
3 scarce 5,000.00
4 . . . . 2,600.00
5 . . . . 2,600.00
6 Christmas issue 2,000.00
7 thru 10 . . . . @2,200.00
11 thru 15 . . . . @1,500.00
16 thru 19 . . . . @1,200.00
Archie Publications, 1946
20 . . . . 1,200.00
21 . . . . 750.00
22 thru 31 . . . . @700.00
32 thru 42 . . . . @500.00
43 thru 50 . . . . @400.00
51 A:Katy Keene 250.00
52 thru 64 . . . . @225.00
65 thru 70 A:Katy Keene . . . . @225.00
71 . . . . 150.00
72 thru 74 A:Katy Keene . . . . @175.00
75 thru 99 . . . . @150.00
100 . . . . 150.00
101 thru 122 . . . . @150.00

123 UFO,Vampire 100.00
124 thru 130 . . . . @100.00
131 thru 145. . . . . @60.00
146 thru 182. . . . . @60.00
183 Caveman Archie 60.00
184 . . . . 60.00
185 I:The Archies Band 75.00
186 thru 195 . . . . @50.00
196 I:Cricket O'Dell 75.00
197 thru 200 . . . . @50.00
201 thru 228 . . . . @50.00
229 Lost Child 50.00
230 thru 260 . . . . @30.00
261 thru 300 . . . . @30.00

ARCHIE'S GIANT SERIES MAGAZINE
Archie Publications, 1954
1 . . . . 2,400.00
2 . . . . 1,400.00
3 . . . . 900.00
4 . . . . 850.00
5 . . . . 850.00
6 thru 10 . . . . @850.00
11 thru 20 . . . . @400.00
21 thru 29 . . . . @200.00
30 thru 35 . . . . @150.00

ARCHIE'S GIRLS BETTY AND VERONICA
Archie Publications, 1950
1 . . . . 3,600.00
2 . . . . 1,500.00
3 . . . . 900.00
4 . . . . 850.00
5 . . . . 850.00
6 thru 10 . . . . @750.00
11 thru 15 . . . . @550.00
16 thru 20 . . . . @400.00
21 . . . . 350.00
22 thru 29 . . . . @325.00
30 thru 40 . . . . @250.00
41 thru 50 . . . . @200.00
51 thru 60 . . . . @150.00
61 thru 70 . . . . @135.00
71 thru 74 . . . . @125.00
75 Devil 300.00
76 thru 90 . . . . @125.00
91 thru 99 . . . . @125.00
100 . . . . 125.00

ARCHIE'S JOKE BOOK MAGAZINE
Archie Publications, 1953
1 . . . . 1,700.00
2 . . . . 750.00
3 . . . . 600.00
15 thru 19 . . . . @350.00
20 thru 25 . . . . @250.00
26 thru 35 . . . . @200.00
36 thru 40 . . . . @175.00
41 1st NA art 400.00
42 & 43 TV Personalities . . . . @125.00
44 thru 48 NA. . . . . @150.00
49 thru 60. . . . . @75.00

ARCHIE'S MECHANICS
Archie Publications, 1954
1 . . . . 1,300.00
2 . . . . 750.00
3 . . . . 600.00

ARCHIE'S PAL, JUGHEAD
Archie Publications, 1949
1 . . . . 3,000.00
2 . . . . 1,500.00
3 . . . . 700.00

GOLDEN AGE

Archie's Pal Jughead #1
© *Archie Publications*

4 . . . . 650.00
5 . . . . 650.00
6 . . . . 500.00
7 thru 10 . . . . @450.00
11 thru 15 . . . . @300.00
16 thru 20 . . . . @300.00
21 thru 30 . . . . @250.00
31 thru 39 . . . . @150.00
40 thru 50 . . . . @150.00
51 thru 60 . . . . @100.00
61 thru 70 . . . . @100.00
71 thru 80 . . . . @45.00
81 thru 99 . . . . @40.00
100 . . . . 40.00

ARCHIE'S PALS 'N' GALS

Archie Publications, 1952–53
1 . . . . 1,400.00
2 . . . . 750.00
3 . . . . 500.00
4 . . . . 450.00
5 . . . . 450.00
6 . . . . 275.00
7 . . . . 275.00
8 thru 10 . . . . @275.00
11 thru 15 . . . . @150.00
16 thru 18 . . . . @125.00
19 Marilyn Monroe 275.00
20 thru 30 . . . . @100.00

ARCHIE'S RIVAL REGGIE

Archie Publications, 1950
1 . . . . 1,350.00
2 . . . . 700.00
3 . . . . 500.00
4 . . . . 450.00
5 . . . . 450.00
6 . . . . 350.00
7 thru 9 . . . . @250.00
10 thru 14 A: Katy Keen . . . . . @225.00
15 . . . . 200.00
16 Aug., 1954 . . . . 200.00

ARMY & NAVY COMICS
See: SUPERSNIPE COMICS

ARROW, THE

Centaur Publications, Oct., 1940–Oct., 1941
1 B:Arrow, BLb(c) 6,000.00

---

2 BLb(c) 2,500.00
3 O:Dash Dartwell,Human Meteor, Rainbow, Bondage(c) 2,500.00

ATOM-AGE COMBAT

St. John Publ. Co., 1952–53
1 Buck Vinson 1,000.00
1a rep. (1958) 500.00
2 Flying Saucer 500.00
3 . . . . 450.00
4 . . . . 500.00
5 Flying Saucer 350.00

ATOMAN

Spark Publications, Feb., 1946
1 JRo,MMe,O:Atoman,A:Kid Crusaders 1,300.00
2 JRo,MMe 700.00

ATOMIC BOMB

Jay Burtis Publ., 1945
1 . . . . 1,300.00

ATOMIC COMICS

Green Publishing Co., Jan., 1946
1 S&S,A:Radio Squad, Barry O'Neal 2,200.00
2 MB,A:Inspector Dayton, Kid Kane 1,100.00
3 MB,A:Zero Ghost Detective . . 800.00
4 JKa(c), July–Aug., 1946 . . . . . 800.00

ATOMIC COMICS

Daniels Publications, 1946 (Reprints)
1 A:Rocketman,Yankee Boy, Bondage (c),rep. 700.00

ATOMIC MOUSE

Capital Stories/ Charlton Comics, March, 1953
1 AFa,O:Atomic Mouse 500.00
2 AFa,Ice Cream (c) 150.00
3 AFa,Genie and Magic Carpet (c) 125.00
4 AFa 125.00
5 AFa,A:Timmy the Timid Ghost 125.00
6 thru 10 Funny Animal . . . . @100.00
11 thru 14 Funny Animal . . . @100.00
15 A:Happy the Marvel Bunny . . 100.00
16 Funny Animal,Giant 75.00
17 thru 30 Funny Animal . . . . . @75.00
31 thru 36 Funny Animal . . . . . @75.00
37 A:Atom the Cat 75.00
38 thru 40 Funny Animal . . . . . @50.00
41 thru 53 Funny Animal . . . . . @30.00
54 June, 1963 . . . . 30.00

ATOMIC THUNDERBOLT, THE

Regor Company, Feb., 1946
1 I:Atomic Thunderbolt, Mr. Murdo 1,200.00

ATOMIC WAR!

Ace-Junior Books, 1952–53
1 Atomic explosion (c) 1,700.00
2 . . . . 1,400.00
3 A-Bomb 1,400.00
4 . . . . 1,400.00

ATOM THE CAT
See: BO

ATTACK

Youthful Mag./Trojan, 1952
1 Violence 500.00
2 . . . . 250.00
3 Bondage 300.00
4 RKu 250.00
Becomes:

ATOMIC ATTACK

Youthful Magazines, 1953
5 . . . . 250.00
6 thru 8 . . . . @200.00

AUTHENTIC POLICE CASES

St. John Publ. Co., 1948
1 Hale the Magician 600.00
2 Lady Satan, Johnny Rebel . . . 350.00
3 A:Avenger 600.00
4 Masked Black Jack 350.00
5 JCo 350.00
6 JCo,MB(c) 650.00
7 thru 10 . . . . @275.00
11 thru 15 . . . . @275.00
16 thru 23 . . . . @175.00
24 thru 28 Giants . . . . @375.00
29 thru 38 . . . . @150.00

AVIATION CADETS

Street & Smith Publ., 1943
1 . . . . 200.00

AVON ONE-SHOTS

Avon Periodicals, 1949-1953
{Listed in Alphabetical Order}
1 Atomic Spy Cases 500.00
N# WW,Attack on Planet Mars . 1,500.00
1 Bachelor's Diary 600.00
1 Badmen of the West 500.00
N# Badmen of Tombstone 225.00
1 EK,Behind Prison Bars 375.00
2 Betty and Her Steady 125.00
N# EK,Blackhawk Indian Tomahawk War 250.00
1 EK,Blazing Sixguns 200.00
1 EK,Butch Cassidy 225.00
N# Chief Crazy Horse 250.00
N# FF,AW,EK,Chief Victorio's Apache Massacre 600.00
N# City of the Living Dead 750.00
1 Complete Romance 500.00
N# Custer's Last Fight 225.00
1 EK(c),Dalton Boys 225.00
N# GT(c),Davy Crockett 225.00
N# The Dead Who Walk 800.00
1 Diary of Horror,Bondage(c) . . . 700.00
N# WW,Earth Man on Venus . . 2,000.00
1 Eerie, bondage (c) 1,200.00
1 EK,Escape from Devil's Island 525.00
N# EK,Fighting Daniel Boone . . . 250.00
N# EK(c),For a Night of Love 375.00
1 WW,Flying Saucers 1,400.00
N# Flying Saucers 700.00
1 Going Steady with Betty 200.00
N# Hooded Menace 800.00
N# EK,King of the Badmen of Deadwood 200.00
1 King Solomon's Mines 500.00
N# EK(c),Kit Carson & the Blackfeet Warriors 100.00
N# EK,Last of the Comanches . . 200.00
N# EK,Masked Bandit 200.00
1 WW,Mask of Dr. Fu Manchu . 1,500.00
N# EK,Night of Mystery 600.00
1 WW,JKu,Outlaws of the Wild West 425.00
1 JKu,Out of this World 1,100.00
N# EK,Pancho Villa 300.00
1 EK,Phantom Witch Doctor 700.00

All comics prices listed are for Near Mint condition.

1 Pixie Puzzle Rocket
  to Adventureland 160.00
1 EK,Prison Riot,drugs 500.00
N# EK,Red Mountain Featuring
  Quantrell's Raiders 350.00
N# Reform School Girl 2,500.00
1 Robotmen of the Lost Planet 1,700.00
N# JO,WW(c),Rocket to
  the Moon 1,700.00
N# JKu,Secret Diary of
  Eerie Adventures 2,700.00
1 EK,Sheriff Bob Dixon's
  Chuck Wagon 175.00
1 Sideshow 425.00
1 JKu,Sparkling Love 300.00
N# Speedy Rabbit 100.00
1 EK(c)Teddy Roosevelt &
  His Rough Riders 225.00
N# The Underworld Story 350.00
N# EK(c),The Unknown Man 350.00
1 EK,War Dogs of the U.S. Army 175.00
N# EK(c),White Chief of the
  Pawnee Indians. 200.00
N# Women to Love 700.00

BABE
Prize/Headline Feature,
June–July, 1948
1 BRo 300.00
2 BRo 175.00
3 BRo 165.00
4 thru 9 BRo . . . . @150.00

BABE RUTH
SPORTS COMICS
Harvey Publications,
April, 1949
1 BP 600.00
2 BP,Baseball 350.00
3 BP,Joe DiMaggio(c) 400.00
4 BP,Bob Feller(c). 325.00
5 BP,Football(c) 325.00
6 BP,Basketball(c). 325.00
7 BP 275.00
8 BP,Yogi Berra. 325.00
9 BP,Stan Musial(c). 300.00
10 . . . . 300.00
11 Feb., 1951. . . . . 275.00

BADGE OF JUSTICE
See: CRIME AND JUSTICE

INDIAN BRAVES
Ace Periodicals, 1951
1 Green Arrow. 150.00
2 . . . . 75.00
3 . . . . 65.00
4 . . . . 65.00
Becomes:

BAFFLING MYSTERIES
Periodical House/
Ace Mag., 1951–55
5 GC,MSy 500.00
6 MSy 350.00
7 . . . . 325.00
8 LC 325.00
9 . . . . 325.00
10 . . . . 325.00
11 GC. 325.00
12 thru 15. . . . . @300.00
16 LC 300.00
17 LC 300.00
18 LC 300.00
19 . . . . 300.00
20 LC,Bondage 400.00
21 LC 300.00
22 LC,MSy 325.00
23 Bondage 325.00
24 reprint 200.00

25 reprint 200.00
Becomes:

HEROES OF
THE WILD FRONTIER
Ace Periodicals, 1956
27 (1) 100.00
2 . . . . 100.00

BANG-UP COMICS
Progressive Publ., 1941
1 CosmoMan, Lady Fairplay,
  O:Buzz Balmer 1,700.00
2 Buzz Balmer 1,000.00
3 Buzz Balmer 1,000.00

BANNER COMICS
Ace Magazines, Sept., 1941
3 B:Captain Courageous,
  Lone Warrior. 1,700.00
4 JM(c),Flag(c) 1,200.00
5 . . . . 1,200.00
Becomes:

CAPTAIN COURAGEOUS
COMICS
March, 1942
6 I:The Sword 1,500.00

THE BARKER
Quality Comics Group, 1946–49
1 Circus. 150.00
2 thru 14 . . . . @125.00
15 JCo 110.00

BARNEY BAXTER
Argo Publ., 1956
1 . . . . 125.00
2 . . . . 125.00

BARNEY GOOGLE &
SNUFFY SMITH
Toby Press, 1951–52
1 . . . . 150.00
2 . . . . 100.00
3 . . . . 100.00
4 HK 100.00

BARNYARD COMICS
Animated Cartoons, June, 1944
1 (fa) 300.00
2 (fa) 250.00
3 (fa) 150.00
4 (fa) 150.00
5 (fa) 150.00
6 thru 12 (fa) . . . . @125.00
13 FF(ti) 150.00
14 FF(ti) 150.00
15 FF(ti) 150.00
16 . . . . 125.00
17 FF(ti) 125.00
18 FF,FF(ti) 150.00
19 FF,FF(ti) 150.00
20 FF,FF(ti) 150.00
21 FF(ti) 125.00
22 FF,FF(ti) 150.00
23 FF(ti) 125.00
24 FF,FF(ti) 150.00
25 FF,FF(ti) 150.00
26 FF(ti) 125.00
27 FF(ti) 125.00
28 . . . . 100.00
29 FF(ti) 125.00
30 and 31 . . . . @100.00
Becomes:

DIZZY DUCK
32 Funny Animal 125.00
33 thru 39. . . . . @100.00

BASEBALL COMICS
Will Eisner Productions,
Spring, 1949
1 WE,A:Rube Rocky 1,100.00

Baseball Heroes N#
© Fawcett Publications

BASEBALL HEROS
Fawcett Publications, 1952
N# Babe Ruth (c) 1,500.00

BASEBALL THRILLS
Ziff-Davis Publ. Co., 1951
10 Bob Feller Predicts Pennant
  Winners 700.00
2 BP, Yogi Berra story 500.00
3 EK, Joe DiMaggio story,
  Summer 1952 . . . . 600.00

BASIL
St. John Publishing, 1953
1 F:Basil, The Royal Cat. 65.00
2 . . . . 40.00
3 . . . . 20.00
4 . . . . 20.00

BATTLE ATTACK
Stanmor Publications, 1952–55
1 War Combat. 150.00
2 thru 8 . . . . @100.00

BATTLE CRY
Stanmor Publications, 1952–55
1 Flame-thrower (c) 175.00
2 . . . . 125.00
3 . . . . 125.00
4 EC Copy 125.00
5 . . . . 125.00
6 thru 20 . . . . @100.00

BATTLEFIELD ACTION
See: DYNAMITE

BATTLE FIRE
Stamfor Publications, 1955
1 War 150.00
2 . . . . 100.00
3 thru 7 . . . . @100.00

BATTLEFRONT
Standard Comics, 1952
5 ATh. 175.00

BATTLE REPORT
Excellent Publ./
Ajax-Farrell, 1952—53
1 .... 150.00
2 thru 6 .... @100.00

BATTLE SQUADRON
Stanmor Publications, 1955
1 .... 125.00
2 .... 100.00
3 Iwo Jima flag 100.00
4 .... 100.00
5 .... 100.00

BATTLE STORIES
Fawcett Publications 1952–53
1 GE 200.00
2 .... 100.00
3 .... 100.00
4 .... 100.00
5 .... 100.00
6 thru 11 .... @100.00

BEANY & CECIL
Dell Publishing Co., Jan., 1952
1 .... 250.00
2 thru 5 .... @150.00

BEE 29,
THE BOMBARDIER
Neal Publications, 1945
1 Funny Animal............ 400.00

BEN BOWIE & HIS
MOUNTAIN MEN
Dell Publishing Co., 1952
(1) see Dell Four Color #443
(2 thru 6) see Dell Four Color
7 .... 150.00
8 thru 10 .... @125.00
11 I:Yellow Hair 100.00
12 thru 17 .... @100.00

BEST COMICS
Better Publications, Nov., 1939
1 B:Red Mask 2,000.00
2 A:Red Mask, Silly Willie 1,200.00
3 A:Red Mask 1,200.00
4 Cannibalism story,
  Feb., 1940 .... 1,500.00

Best Comics #1 © Better Publications

BEWARE
See: CAPTAIN SCIENCE

BEWARE TERROR TALES
Fawcett Publications, 1952–53
1 BP 900.00
2 RA,BP,MSy 700.00
3 .... 600.00
4 .... 600.00
5 .... 600.00
6 .... 600.00
7 .... 550.00
8 BP 750.00

THE BEYOND
Ace Magazines, 1950–55
1 Werewolf 650.00
2 .... 500.00
3 thru 10 .... @350.00
11 thru 20 .... @300.00
21 thru 30 .... @300.00

BIG CHIEF WAHOO
Eastern Color Printing,
1942–43
1 .... 600.00
2 BWa(c),Three Ring Circus ... 300.00
3 BWa(c) 225.00
4 BWa(c) 225.00
5 BWa(c),Wild West Rodeo 225.00
6 A:Minnie-Ha-Cha 175.00
7 .... 150.00
8 .... 100.00
9 .... 100.00
10 .... 125.00
11 thru 23 .... @100.00

BIG SHOT COMICS
Columbia Comics Group,
May, 1940
1 MBI,OW,Skyman,B:The Face,
  Joe Palooka, Rocky Ryan . 4,000.00
2 MBi,OW,Marvelo (c) 1,600.00
3 MBi,Skyman (c) 1,400.00
4 MBi,OW,Joe Palooka (c) ... 1,000.00
5 MBi,Joe Palooka (c) 800.00
6 MBi,Joe Palooka (c) 750.00
7 MBi,Elect Joe Palooka
  and Skyman 700.00
8 MBi,Joe Palooka and Skyman
  dress as Santa 700.00
9 MBi,Skyman 700.00

Big Shot Comics #10
© Columbia Comics Group

10 MBi,Skyman 700.00
11 MBi 600.00
12 MBi,OW................. 600.00
13 MBi,OW................. 600.00
14 MBi,OW,O:Sparky Watts..... 600.00
15 MBi,OW,O:The Cloak 800.00
16 MBi,OW................. 500.00
17 MBi(c),OW 500.00
18 MBi,OW................. 500.00
19 MBi,OW,The Face (c)...... 475.00
20 MBi,OW,OW(c),Skyman cov. . 475.00
21 MBi,OW,A:Raja the Arabian
  Knight 475.00
22 MBi,OW,Joe Palooka (c).... 475.00
23 MBi,OW,Sparky Watts (c) ... 400.00
24 MBi,OW,Uncle Sam (c)..... 700.00
25 MBi,OW,Hitler,Sparky Watts(c) 600.00
26 MBi,OW,Hitler,Devildog (c) ... 450.00
27 MBi,OW,Skyman (c)........ 450.00
28 MBi,OW,Hitler (c) 800.00
29 MBi,OW,I:Captain Yank 450.00
30 MBi,OW,Santa (c) 450.00
31 MBi,OW,Sparky Watts (c).... 400.00
32 MBi,OW,B:Vic Jordan
  newspaper reps........... 450.00
33 MBi,OW,Sparky Watts (c) ... 400.00
34 MBi,OW................. 400.00
35 MBi,OW................. 400.00
36 MBi,OW,Sparky Watts (c) ... 350.00
37 MBi,OW................. 350.00
38 MBi,Uncle Slap Happy (c) ... 350.00
39 MBi,Uncle Slap Happy (c) ... 350.00
40 MBi,Joe Palooka Happy (c) ... 350.00
41 MBi,Joe Palooka........... 300.00
42 MBi,Joe Palooka parachutes . 300.00
43 MBi,V:Hitler.............. 450.00
44 MBi,Slap Happy (c)........ 300.00
45 MBi,Slap Happy (c)........ 300.00
46 MBi,Uncle Sam (c),V:Hitler .. 450.00
47 MBi,Uncle Slap Happy (c) ... 300.00
48 MBi 300.00
49 MBi 250.00
50 MBi,O:The Face 250.00
51 MBi 250.00
52 MBi,E:Vic Jordan (Hitler cov)
  newspaper reps........... 400.00
53 MBi,Uncle Slap Happy (c) ... 225.00
54 MBi,Uncle Slap Happy (c) ... 225.00
55 MBi,Happy Easter (c)...... 225.00
56 MBi 225.00
57 MBi 225.00
58 MBi 225.00
59 MBi,Slap Happy 225.00
60 MBi,Joe Palooka.......... 225.00
61 MBi 200.00
62 MBi 200.00
63 MBi 200.00

64 MBi,Slap Happy 200.00
65 MBi,Slap Happy 200.00
66 MBi,Slap Happy 200.00
67 MBi 200.00
68 MBi,Joe Palooka. 200.00
69 MBi 200.00
70 MBi,OW,Joe Palooka (c) 200.00
71 MBi,OW. 200.00
72 MBi,OW. 200.00
73 MBi,OW,The Face (c). 200.00
74 MBi,OW. 200.00
75 MBi,OW,Polar Bear Swim
    Club (c) 200.00
76 thru 80 MBi,OW . . . . @175.00
81 thru 84 MBi,OW . . . . @175.00
85 MBi,OW,Dixie Dugan (c). 175.00
86 thru 95 MBi,OW . . . . @150.00
96 MBi,OW,X-Mas (c) 150.00
97 thru 99 MBi,OW . . . . @150.00
100 MBi,OW,Special issue. 175.00
101 thru 103 MBi,OW . . . . . . @150.00
104 MBi, Aug., 1949 . . . . 175.00

BIG-3
Fox Features Syndicate,
Fall 1940
1 B:BlueBeetle,Flame,Samson 4,200.00
2 A:BlueBeetle,Flame,Samson 1,800.00
3 same. 1,600.00
4 same. 1,500.00
5 same. 1,500.00
6 E:Samson, bondage (c) 1,400.00
7 A:V-Man, Jan., 1942 . . . . . . 1,400.00

THE BIG TOP COMICS
Toby Press, 1951
1 . . . . 135.00
2 . . . . 100.00

BILL BARNES,
AMERICA'S AIR ACE
See: AIR ACE

BILL BATTLE,
THE ONE-MAN ARMY
Fawcett Publications 1952–53
1 . . . . 200.00
2 . . . . 150.00
3 . . . . 150.00
4 . . . . 150.00

BILL BOYD WESTERN
Fawcett Publications, 1950
1 B:Bill Boyd, Midnite,Ph(c) 800.00
2 P(c) 500.00
3 B:Ph(c). 350.00
4 . . . . 300.00
5 . . . . 300.00
6 . . . . 300.00
7 thru 11 . . . . @250.00
12 thru 21 . . . . @235.00
22 E:Ph(c) 235.00
23 June, 1952 . . . . 250.00

BILL STERN'S
SPORTS BOOK
Approved Comics,
Spring-Summer, 1951
1 Ewell Blackwell 300.00
2 . . . . 250.00
2-2 EK Giant. 300.00

BILLY AND BUGGY BEAR
I.W. Enterprises, 1958
1 Funny animal. 100.00

BILLY BUNNY
Excellent Publications, 1954
1 . . . . 150.00
2 . . . . 100.00
3 . . . . 100.00
4 . . . . 100.00
Ann. #1 Christmas Frolics 225.00

BILLY THE KID
ADVENTURE MAGAZINE
Toby Press, Oct., 1950
1 AW(a&c),FF(a&c) 500.00
2 Photo (c) 200.00
3 AW,FF 500.00
4 . . . . 125.00
5 . . . . 125.00
6 FF,Photo (c) 250.00
7 Photo (c) 125.00
8 . . . . 125.00
9 HK Pot-Shot Pete 150.00
10 . . . . 125.00
11 . . . . 100.00
12 . . . . 100.00
13 HK. 100.00
14 AW,FF 150.00
15 thru 21. . . . . @100.00
22 AW,FF 125.00
23 thru 29. . . . . @100.00
30 1955 . . . . 100.00

BILLY THE KID
AND OSCAR
Fawcett Publications, 1945–46
1 Funny animal. 250.00
2 . . . . 200.00
3 . . . . 200.00

BILLY WEST
Visual Editions (Standard
Comics), 1949–51
1 . . . . 200.00
2 . . . . 150.00
3 thru 8 . . . . @100.00
9 . . . . 125.00

BINGO COMICS
Howard Publications, 1945
1 LbC,Drug 750.00

BLACK CAT COMICS
Harvey Publications
(Home Comics),
June–July, 1946
1 JKu 1,300.00
2 JKu,JSm(c) 700.00
3 JSm(c) 550.00
4 B:Red Demon 550.00
5 S&K 600.00
6 S&K,A:Scarlet Arrow,
    O:Red Demon 600.00
7 S&K 600.00
8 S&K,B:Kerry Drake 600.00
9 S&K,O:Stuntman 650.00
10 JK,JSm 550.00
11 . . . . 550.00
12 'Ghost Town Terror'. 550.00
13 LEI 500.00
14 LEI 500.00
15 LEI. 500.00
16 LEI 500.00
17 A:Mary Worth, Invisible
    Scarlet 500.00
18 LEI. 500.00
19 LEI. 500.00
20 A:Invisible Scarlet 500.00
21 LEI. 500.00
22 LEI thru 26. . . . . @500.00
27 X-Mas issue 450.00

Black Cat Mystery #31
© Harvey Publications

28 I:Kit,A:Crimson Raider 450.00
29 Black Cat bondage (c) 450.00
Becomes:

BLACK CAT MYSTERY
Aug., 1951
30 RP,Black Cat(c). 700.00
31 RP. 550.00
32 BP,RP,Bondage (c) 600.00
33 BP,RP,Electrocution (c). 600.00
34 BP,RP,Bondage. 450.00
35 BP,RP,OK, Atomic Storm 600.00
36 RP. 550.00
37 RP. 450.00
38 RP. 450.00
39 RP. 500.00
40 RP. 450.00
41 . . . . 450.00
42 . . . . 450.00
43 BP,Bondage 450.00
44 BP,HN,JkS,Oil Burning (c) . . . 600.00
45 BP,HN,Classic (c) 700.00
46 BP,HN 450.00
47 BP,HN 450.00
48 BP,HN 450.00
49 BP,HN 450.00
50 BP,Rotting Face 1,500.00
51 BP,HN,MMe 450.00
52 BP 400.00
53 BP 400.00
Becomes:

BLACK CAT WESTERN
Feb., 1955
54 A:Black Cat & Story 650.00
55 A:Black Cat 400.00
56 same. 400.00
Becomes:

BLACK CAT MYSTIC
Sept., 1956
58 JK,Starts Comic Code. 600.00
59 KB 400.00
60 JK 500.00
61 Colorama, HN. 400.00
62 . . . . 300.00
63 JK 350.00
64 JK 350.00
65 April, 1963. . . . . 350.00

BLACK COBRA
Farrell Publications (Ajax),
1954–55
1 . . . . 500.00
2 (6) 350.00
3 . . . . 300.00

GOLDEN AGE

Becomes:

BRIDES DIARY
Farrell Publications, 1955
4 . . . . 150.00
5 thru 8 . . . . @100.00
9 . . . . 125.00
10 . . . . 125.00

BLACK DIAMOND WESTERN
See: DESPERADO

UNCLE SAM QUARTERLY
Quality Comics Group, Fall, 1941
1 BE,LF(c),JCo,O:Uncle Sam . 7,000.00
2 LF&WE(c),DBe, Ray,
Black Condor 3,000.00
3 GT(a&c) 2,000.00
4 GT,GF(c). 1,900.00
5 RC,GT. 2,000.00
6 GT 1,900.00
7 Hitler, Tojo, Mussolini 2,000.00
8 GT 1,900.00
Becomes:

BLACKHAWK
Comic Magazines, Winter, 1944
9 Bait for a Death Trap 6,500.00
10 RC 1,850.00
11 RC 1,300.00
12 Flies to thrilling adventure . . 1,200.00
13 Blackhawk Stalks Danger . . 1,200.00
14 BWa 1,300.00
15 Patrols the Universe 1,200.00
16 RC,BWa,Huddles for
Action 1,200.00
17 BWa,Prepares for Action . . . 1,500.00
18 RC(a&c),BWa,One for All
and All for One 1,800.00
19 RC(a&c),BWa,Calls
for Action 2,000.00
20 RC(a&c),BWa,Smashes
Rugoth the Ruthless God. . 1,700.00
21 BWa,Battles Destiny
Written in Blood 1,200.00
22 RC(a&c),BWa,Fear battles
Death and Destruction 1,200.00
23 RC(a&c),BWa,Batters
Down Oppression. 1,200.00
24 RC(a&c),BWa 1,200.00
25 RC(a&c),BWa,V:The Evil
of Mung 1,200.00

Blackhawk #72
© *Comic Magazines*

26 RC(a&c),V:Menace of a
Sunken World 1,100.00
27 BWa,Destroys a War-Mad
Munitions Magnate 1,100.00
28 BWa,Defies Destruction in the
Battle of the Test Tube 1,100.00
29 BWa,Tale of the Basilisk
Supreme Chief 1,100.00
30 BWa,RC(a&c),The Menace
of the Meteors 1,100.00
31 BWa,RC(a&c),JCo,Treachery
among the Blackhawks . . . 1,000.00
32 BWa,RC(a&c),A:Delya,
Flying Fish 1,000.00
33 RC,BWa,A:The Mockers . . 1,000.00
34 BWa,A:Tana,Mavis. 1,000.00
35 BWa,I:Atlo,Strongest Man
on Earth 1,000.00
36 RC(a&c),BWa,V:Tarya 750.00
37 RC(a&c),BWa,V:Sari,The
Rajah of Ramastan 750.00
38 BWa 750.00
39 RC(a&c),BWa,V:Lilith 750.00
40 RC(a&c),BWa,Valley of
Yesterday. 750.00
41 RC(a&c),BWa 600.00
42 RC(a&c),BWa,V:Iron Emperor 600.00
43 RC(a&c),BWa,Terror
from the Catacombs 600.00
44 RC(a&c),BWa, King of Winds . 600.00
45 BWa,The Island of Death . . . 600.00
46 RC(a&c),BWa,V:DeathPatrol . 600.00
47 RC(a&c),BWa,War! 600.00
48 RC(a&c),BWa,A:Hawks of
Horror,Port of Missing Ships . 600.00
49 RC(a&c),BWa,A:Valkyrie,
Waters of Terrible Peace. . . . 600.00
50 RC(a&c),BWa,I:Killer Shark,
Flying Octopus 750.00
51 BWa,V:The Whip, Whip of
Nontelon 600.00
52 RC(a&c),BWa,Traitor in
the Ranks 600.00
53 RC(a&c),BWa,V:Golden
Mummy 600.00
54 RC(a&c),BWa,V:Dr. Deroski,
Circles of Suicide. 600.00
55 RC(a&c),BWa,V:Rocketmen. . 600.00
56 RC(a&c),BWa,V:The Instructor,
School for Sabotage 600.00
57 RC(a&c),BWa,Paralyzed City
of Armored Men. 600.00
58 RC(a&c),BWa,V:King Cobra,
The Spider of Delanza. 600.00
59 BWa,V:Sea Devil 600.00
60 RC(a&c),BWa,V:Dr. Mole and
His Devils Squadron 600.00
61 V:John Smith, Stalin's
Ambassador of Murder 500.00
62 V:General X, Return of
Genghis Kahn 500.00
63 RC(a&c),The Flying
Buzz-Saws. 500.00
64 RC(a&c),V:Zoltan Korvas,
Legion of the Damned. 500.00
65 Olaf as a Prisoner in Dungeon
of Fear. 500.00
66 RC(a&c),V:The Red
Executioner, Crawler. 500.00
67 RC(a&c),V:Future Fuehrer . . . 500.00
68 V:Killers of the Kremlin 400.00
69 V:King of the Iron Men,
Conference of the Dictators . 400.00
70 V:Killer Shark 400.00
71 V:Von Tepp, The Man Who
could Defeat Blackhawk
O:Blackhawk 500.00
72 V:Death Legion 400.00
73 V:Hangman,The Tyrannical
Freaks 300.00
74 Plan of Death 300.00

75 V:The Mad Doctor Baroc,
The Z Bomb Menace. 300.00
76 The King of Blackhawk Island 300.00
77 V:The Fiendish
Electronic Brain 300.00
78 V:The Killer Vulture,
Phantom Raider 300.00
79 V:Herman Goering, The
Human Bomb 300.00
80 V:Fang, the Merciless,
Dr. Death 300.00
81 A:Killer Shark, The Sea
Monsters of Killer Shark 300.00
82 V:Sabo Teur, the Ruthless
Commie Agent. 300.00
83 I:Hammmer & Sickle, V:Madam
Double Cross. 300.00
84 V:Death Eye,Dr. Genius,
The Dreaded Brain Beam . . . 300.00
85 V:The Fiendish Impersonator . 300.00
86 V:The Human Torpedoes 300.00
87 A:Red Agent Sovietta,V:Sea
Wolf, Le Sabre,Comics Code 300.00
88 V:Thunder the Indestructible,
The Phantom Sniper 300.00
89 V:The Super Communists. . . . 400.00
90 V:The Storm King, Villainess
Who Smashed the Blackhawk
Team 400.00
91 Treason in the Underground. . 400.00
92 V:The World Traitor. 400.00
93 V:Garg the Destroyer,
O:Blackhawk 350.00
94 V:Black Widow, Darkk the
Destroyer. 350.00
95 V:Madam Fury, Queen of the
Pirates 350.00
96 Doom in the Deep. 350.00
97 Revolt of the Slave Workers . . 300.00
98 Temple of Doom 300.00
99 The War That Never Ended . . 300.00
100 The Delphian Machine 325.00
101 Satan's Paymaster 275.00
102 The Doom Cloud 275.00
103 The Super Race 275.00
104 The Jet Menace 275.00
105 The Red Kamikaze Terror . 275.00
106 The Flying Tank Platoon . . . 275.00
107 The Winged Menace 275.00
Continued by: DC Comics

BLACK HOOD
See: LAUGH COMICS

BLACK KNIGHT, THE
Toby Press, 1953
1 Bondage 400.00

BLACK MAGIC
Crestwood Publ., 1950–51
1 S&K,MMe. 2,400.00
2 S&K,MMe 1,200.00
3 S&K,MMe 1,100.00
4 S&K,MMe 1,100.00
5 S&K,MMe 1,100.00
6 S&K,MMe 1,100.00
Volume 2, 1951
1 S&K,MMe. 600.00
2 MMe 500.00
3 . . . . 500.00
4 S&K,MMe 600.00
5 S&K,MMe 600.00
6 . . . . 500.00
7 S&K,MMe 600.00
8 MMe. 500.00
9 S&K,MMe. 600.00
10 . . . . 500.00
11 MMe 500.00
12 S&K,MMe 500.00
Volume 3, 1953
1 S&K,MMe. 500.00

2 S&K,MMe,AMc 500.00
3 S&K 500.00
4 S&K 500.00
5 S&K,MMe. 500.00
6 S&K,MMe. 500.00
Volume 4, 1954
1 S&K 500.00
2 S&K 500.00
3 S&K,SD(2nd work). 800.00
4 S&K,SD,eye damage. 650.00
5 S&K,SD 500.00
6 S&K,BP 400.00
Volume 5, 1956
1 S&K,MMe. 350.00
2 S&K,MMe. 350.00
3 S&K 350.00
4 S&K 350.00
5 S&K 350.00
6 S&K 350.00
Volume 6, 1957
1 JO 300.00
2 JO(c) 300.00
3 JO(c),GT 300.00
4 JO 300.00
5 JO(c) 300.00
6 JO(c) 300.00
Volume 7, 1958
1 LSt 300.00
2 JO 300.00
3 & 4 . . . . @300.00
5 AT,Hitler(c) 350.00
6 BP 250.00
Volume 8, 1961
1 BP 250.00
2 BP,SD 250.00
3 thru 5 BP . . . . @250.00

BLACKSTONE, MASTER MAGICIAN COMICS
Vital/Street & Smith Publ. 1946
1 . . . . 900.00
2 . . . . 700.00
3 . . . . 700.00

BLACKSTONE, THE MAGICIAN DETECTIVE
EC Comics, 1947
1 Happy Houlihans 750.00
See: Marvel Listings

BLACK TERROR
Better Publications/ Standard, Winter, 1942-43
1 Bombing (c) 5,000.00
2 V:Arabs,Bondage(c) 2,000.00
3 V:Nazis,Bondage(c) 1,200.00
4 ASh(c),V:Sub Nazis 1,000.00
5 V:Japanese 1,000.00
6 Air Battle 900.00
7 Air Battle,V:Japanese,
  A:Ghost 900.00
8 V:Nazis 900.00
9 V:Japanese,Bondage(c) 1,000.00
10 ASh(c),V:Nazis 900.00
11 & 12 . . . . @800.00
13 ASh(c) 725.00
14 ASh(c) 800.00
15 ASh(c) 725.00
16 ASh(c) 725.00
17 ASh(c),Bondage(c) 800.00
18 ASh(c) 700.00
19 & 20 ASh . . . . @700.00
21 ASh(c) 800.00
22 FF,ASh 700.00
23 ASh 700.00
24 Bondgae(c) 800.00
25 ASh 700.00
26 GT,ASh(c) 700.00
27 MME,GT,ASh 700.00

Black Terror #21
© Nedor Publications

BLAZING COMICS
Enwil Associates/Rural Home, June, 1944
1 B:Green Turtle, Red Hawk,
  Black Buccaneer 1,000.00
2 Green Turtle (c) 700.00
3 Green Turtle (c) 650.00
4 Green Turtle (c) 650.00
5 March, 1945 . . . . 650.00
5a Black Buccaneer(c),1955. . . . 400.00
6 Indian-Japanese(c), 1955 . . . . 400.00

BLAZING WEST
B & I Publ./American Comics 1948
1 . . . . 250.00
2 . . . . 150.00
3 . . . . 150.00
4 O&I: Little Lobo 125.00
5 thru 13 . . . . @100.00
14 O&I: The Hooded Horseman . 150.00
15 thru 20 . . . . @125.00
Becomes:

HOODED HORSEMAN
American Comics, 1952–54
21 . . . . 250.00
22 . . . . 200.00
23 . . . . 150.00
24 . . . . 150.00
25 . . . . 125.00
26 . . . . 150.00
27 . . . . 135.00

BLAZING WESTERN
Timor Publications, 1954
1 . . . . 200.00
2 thru 5 . . . . @100.00

BLONDIE COMICS
David McKay, Spring, 1947
1 . . . . 400.00
2 . . . . 200.00
3 . . . . 150.00
4 . . . . 150.00
5 . . . . 150.00
6 thru 10 . . . . @100.00
11 thru 15 . . . . @100.00
Harvey Publications, 1950
16 . . . . 150.00
17 thru 20 . . . . @125.00
21 thru 30 . . . . @100.00
31 thru 50 . . . . @100.00

51 thru 80 . . . . @100.00
81 thru 99 . . . . @100.00
100 . . . . 110.00
101 thru 124 . . . . @100.00
125 Giant, 80-pg. 125.00
126 thru 136 . . . . @100.00
137 Giant, 80-pg. 125.00
138 thru 139 . . . . @100.00
140 Giant, 80-pg. 125.00
141 thru 147 . . . . @100.00
148 Giant, 68-pg. 125.00
149 thru 154 . . . . @100.00
155 Giant, 68-pg. 125.00
156 . . . . 100.00
157 thru 159 Giant, 68-pg. . . . @125.00
160 . . . . 100.00
161 thru 163 Giant, 68-pg. . . . @125.00
See also: DAISY AND HER PUPS

BLOOD IS THE HARVEST
Catechetical Guild 1950
N# Comunist menace 1,800.00

BLUE BEETLE, THE
Fox Features Syndicate/ Holyoke Publ., Winter 1939
1 O:Blue Beetle,A:Master
  Magician 8,500.00
2 BP,Wonder World 2,500.00
3 JSm(c) 1,600.00
4 Mentions marijuana 1,500.00
5 GT,A:Zanzibar the Magician . 1,300.00
6 B:Dynamite Thor,
  O:Blue Beetle 1,300.00
7 A:Dynamo 1,200.00
8 E:Thor,A:Dynamo 1,200.00
9 BP(c),A:Black Bird,Gorilla . . 1,200.00
10 BP(c),A:Black Bird,
  bondage(c) 1,200.00
11 BP(c),A:Gladiator, Bondage . 1,000.00
12 A:Black Fury, Bondage 1,000.00
13 B:V-Man 1,000.00
14 JKu,I:Sparky. 1,000.00
15 JKu. 1,000.00
16 . . . . 1,000.00
17 AyB,A:Mimic. 1,000.00
18 JKu,E:V-Man,A:Red Knight . 1,000.00
19 JKu,A:Dascomb Dinsmore. . 1,000.00
20 I&O:Flying Tiger Squadron . 1,000.00
21 . . . . 800.00
22 A:Ali-Baba 800.00
23 A:Jimmy DooLittle 800.00
24 I:The Halo 800.00
25 . . . . 800.00
26 General Patton story 900.00

Blue Beetle #41
© Fox Features Syndicate

GOLDEN AGE

27 A:Tamoa	800.00
28	800.00
29	800.00
30 L:Holyoke	800.00
31 F:Fox.	775.00
32 Hitler (c)	900.00
33 Fight for Freedom	750.00
34 A:Black Terror,Menace of K-4	750.00
35 Threat From Saturn	750.00
36 The Runaway House	750.00
37 Inside the House	750.00
38 Revolt of the Zombies	750.00
39	750.00
40	750.00
41 A:O'Brine Twins	700.00
42	700.00
43	700.00
44	700.00
45	700.00
46 BP,A:Puppeteer, Bondage	700.00
47 JKa,V:Junior Crime Club	2,000.00
48 JKa,A:Black Lace	1,500.00
49 JKa.	1,500.00
50 JKa,The Ambitious Bride	1,500.00
51 JKa, Shady Lady	1,500.00
52 BP,JKa(c),Bondage (c)	1,900.00
53 JKa:A:Jack "Legs" Diamond,Bondage(c)	1,300.00
54 JKa,The Vanishing Nude	2,200.00
55 JKa.	1,250.00
56 JKa,Tri-State Terror	1,250.00
57 JKa,The Feagle Bros.	1,250.00
58	250.00
59	250.00
60 Aug., 1960	275.00

BLUE BEETLE
See: THING!, THE

Blue Bolt Vol 2 #6
© Funnies, Inc.

BLUE BOLT
Funnies, Inc./Novelty Press/
Premium Service Co, 1940

1 JSm,PGv,O:Blue Bolt	6,500.00
2 JSm,S&K	3,000.00
3 S&K,A:Space Hawk	2,500.00
4 S&K,BEv(c).	2,000.00
5 BEv,S&K,B:Sub Zero	2,000.00
6 JK,JSm	1,900.00
7 S&K,BEv	1,900.00
8 PGv,S&K(c)	1,900.00
9	1,700.00
10 PGv,S&K(c)	1,700.00
11 BEv(c)	1,700.00
12 PGv	1,700.00

2-1 BEv(c),PG,O:Dick Cole & V:Simba	700.00
2-2 BEv(c),FGu,O:Twister	550.00
2-3 PGv,Cole vs Simba	400.00
2-4 BD	400.00
2-5 I:Freezum.	400.00
2-6 PGv,O:Sgt.Spook, Dick Cole	350.00
2-7 BD,Lois Blake	350.00
2-8 BD	350.00
2-9 JW	350.00
2-10 JW	350.00
2-11 JW	350.00
2-12 E:Twister	350.00
3-1 A:115th Infantry	350.00
3-2 A:Phantom Sub	350.00
3-3	350.00
3-4 JW(c).	250.00
3-5 Jor	250.00
3-6 Jor	250.00
3-7 X-Mas (c)	250.00
3-8	250.00
3-9 A:Phantom Sub	250.00
3-10 DBa	250.00
3-11 April Fools (c).	250.00
3-12	250.00
4-1 Hitler,Tojo,Mussolini (c)	600.00
4-2 Liberty Bell (c)	200.00
4-3 What are You Doing for Your Country	200.00
4-4 I Fly for Vengence	200.00
4-5 TFH(c)	200.00
4-6 HcK	200.00
4-7 JWi(c).	200.00
4-8 E:Sub Zero	200.00
4-9	200.00
4-10	200.00
4-11	200.00
4-12	200.00
5-1 thru 5-12.	@175.00
6-1	175.00
6-2 War Bonds (c)	175.00
6-3	175.00
6-4 Racist(c).	300.00
6-5 Soccer (c)	175.00
6-6 thru 6-12.	@175.00
7-1 thru 7-12.	@175.00
8-1 Baseball (c)	175.00
8-2 JHa	175.00
8-3 JH	175.00
8-4 JHa	175.00
8-5 JH	175.00
8-6 JDo	175.00
8-7 LbC(c).	350.00
8-8	175.00
8-9 AMc(c)	175.00
8-10	175.00
8-11 Basketball (c).	200.00
8-12	175.00
9-1 AMc,Baseball (c)	175.00
9-2 AMc	175.00
9-3	175.00
9-4 JH	175.00
9-5 JH	175.00
9-6 LbC(c),Football (c).	300.00
9-7 JH	175.00
9-8 Hockey (c)	185.00
9-9 LbC(c),3-D effect	275.00
9-10	175.00
9-11	175.00
9-12	175.00
10-1 Baseball (c),3-D effect	200.00
10-2 3-D effect	200.00

Star Publications, 1949

102 LbC(c),Chameleon	550.00
103 LbC(c),same	500.00
104 LbC(c),same	500.00
105 LbC(c),O:Blue Bolt Space, Drug Story	900.00
106 S&K,LbC(c),A;Space Hawk	800.00
107 S&K,LbC(c),A;Space Hawk	800.00
108 S&K,LbC(c),A:Blue Bolt	800.00
109 BW,LbC(c).	800.00

110 B:Horror (c)s,A:Target	800.00
111 Weird Tales of Terror, A:Red Rocket	800.00
112 JyD	700.00
113 BW,JyD,A:Space Hawk.	700.00
114 LbC(C),JyD	700.00
115 LbC(c),JyD,A:Sgt.Spook	700.00
116 LbC(c),JyD,A:Jungle Joe	700.00
117 LbC(c),A:Blue Bolt,Jo-Jo.	700.00
118 WW,LbC(c),A:White Spirit.	700.00
119 LbC(c).	700.00

Becomes:

GHOSTLY WEIRD STORIES
Star Publications, Sept., 1953

120 LbC,A:Jo-Jo	750.00
121 LbC,A:Jo-Jo	700.00
122 LbC,A:The Mask,Sci-Fi.	750.00
123 LbC,A:Jo-Jo	600.00
124 LbC, Sept., 1954.	600.00

BLUE CIRCLE COMICS
Enwil Associates/
Rural Home, June, 1944

1 B:Blue Circle,O:Steel Fist	500.00
2	350.00
3 Hitler parody (c)	400.00
4	300.00
5 E:Steel Fist,A:DriftwoodDavey.	300.00
6	300.00

BLUE RIBBON COMICS
MLJ Magazines, Nov., 1939

1 JCo,B:Dan Hastings, Richy-Amazing Boy	7,000.00
2 JCo,B:Bob Phantom, Silver Fox	2,700.00
3 JCo,A:Phantom,Silver Fox.	2,000.00
4 O:Fox,Ty Gor,B:Doc Strong, Hercules	2,200.00
5 Gattling Gun (c)	1,500.00
6 Amazing Boy Richy (c)	1,400.00
7 A:Fox (c),Corporal Collins V:Nazis	1,400.00
8 E:Hercules	1,400.00
9 SCp,O&I:Mr. Justice	5,500.00
10 SCp,Mr. Justice (c)	2,500.00
11 CBi,MMe,SCp(c)	2,500.00
12 SCp,MMe,CBi,E:Doc Strong	2,500.00
13 CBi,IN,MMe,B:Inferno	2,500.00
14 MMe,CBi,SCp(c),A:Inferno	2,200.00
15 A:Inferno,E:Green Falcon	2,200.00
16 SCp(c),O:Captain Flag	3,000.00
17 Captain Flag, V:Black Hand.	2,200.00
18 SCp(c),Captain Flag	2,000.00
19 Captain Flag (c)	2,000.00
20 Captain Flag V:Nazis (c)	2,200.00
21 Captain Flag V:Death	2,000.00
22 Circus (c), March, 1942.	2,000.00

BLUE RIBBON COMICS
St. John Publications,
Feb., 1949

1 Heckle & Jeckle	150.00
2 MB(c),Diary Secrets	300.00
3 MB,MB(c),Heckle & Jeckle	150.00
4 Teen-age Diary Secrets	275.00
5 MB,Teen-age Diary Secrets.	350.00
6 Dinky Duck	100.00

BO
Charlton Comics, June, 1955

1	100.00
2	100.00
3 Oct., 1955	100.00

Becomes:

TOM CAT
Charlton Comics, 1956
4 Funny animal-cat 100.00
5 thru 8 . . . . @75.00
Becomes:

ATOM THE CAT
Charlton Comics, 1957–58
9 . . . . 100.00
10 . . . . 75.00
11 Atomic Mouse 125.00
12 Atomic Mouse 125.00
13 thru 17 . . . . @75.00

BOB & BETTY & SANTA'S WISHING WELL
Sears-Roebuck Co., 1941
N# Giveaway 300.00

BOBBY BENSON'S B-BAR-B RIDERS
**Parkway Publ. Co.
(M.E. Entertainment), 1950**
1 BP, Teen-age cowboy 750.00
2 BP 300.00
3 BP 250.00
4 BP,Lemonade Kid (c) 250.00
5 BP 250.00
6 BP 250.00
7 BP 250.00
8 BP 250.00
9 BP,FF(c) 500.00
10 BP 200.00
11 BP,FF(c) 500.00
12 BP 150.00
13 DAy,FF(c),A:Ghost Rider 500.00
14 DAy,A:Ghost Rider,bondage . . 400.00
15 DAy,A:Ghost Rider 350.00
16 photo(c) 200.00
17 . . . . 150.00
18 . . . . 150.00
19 . . . . 150.00

BOBBY COMICS
**Universal Phoenix
Features, 1946**
1 . . . . 150.00

BOB COLT
**Fawcett Publications,
Nov., 1950**
1 B:Bob Colt,Buck Skin 600.00
2 Death Round Train 400.00
3 Mysterious Black Knight of the
  Prairie 300.00
4 Death Goes Downstream 300.00
5 The Mesa of Mystery 300.00
6 The Mysterious Visitors 300.00
7 Dragon of Disaster 250.00
8 Redman's Revenge 250.00
9 Hidden Hacienda 250.00
10 Fiend from Vulture
  Mountain 250.00

BOB STEELE WESTERN
Fawcett Publications, 1950–52
1 Photo(c) 800.00
2 Ph(c); Dynamite Death 400.00
3 Ph(c); The Perilous Deadline . . 300.00
4 Ph(c); Six-Gun Menace 300.00
5 Ph(c); Murder on the Hoof 300.00
6 Ph(c); Range War 250.00
7 Ph(c); Tall Timber Terror 250.00
8 Ph(c); The Race of Death 250.00
9 Ph(c); Death Rides the Storm . 250.00
10 Ph(c); Draw...Or Die 250.00

BOB SWIFT
Fawcett Publications 1951–52
1 Boy sportsman 150.00
2 thru 5 . . . . @100.00

BOLD STORIES
Kirby Publishing Co., 1950
1 WW,Near nudity (c) 2,200.00
2 GI,Cobra's Kiss 1,800.00
3 WW,Orge of Paris 1,500.00
4 Case of the Winking Buddha . . 800.00
5 It Rhymes with Lust 800.00
6 Candid Tales, April, 1950 . . . . . 800.00

BOMBER COMICS
Elliot Publishing Co., 1944
1 B:Wonder Boy,Kismet,
  Eagle Evans 1,500.00
2 Wonder Boy(c) Hitler 1,100.00
3 Wonder Boy-Kismet (c) 650.00
4 Hitler,Tojo, Mussolini (c) 1,200.00

BOOK OF ALL COMICS
William H. Wise, 1945
1 A:Green Mask,Puppeteer 650.00

BOOK OF COMICS, THE
William H. Wise, 1945
N# A:Captain V 600.00

BOOTS AND HER BUDDIES
**Visual Editions
(Standard Comics), 1948–49**
5 Cowgirl 250.00
6 . . . . 200.00
7 . . . . 225.00
8 . . . . 200.00
9 FF 450.00

BORDER PATROL
P.L. Publishing Co., 1951
1 Wild West 200.00
2 . . . . 150.00
3 . . . . 150.00

THE BOUNCER
Fox Features Syndicate, 1944
N# (10) 500.00
11 O:The Bouncer 400.00
12 . . . . 300.00
13 . . . . 300.00
14 rep. #(10) 300.00

BOY COMICS
**Comic House, Inc.
(Lev Gleason Publ.) April, 1942**
3 O:Crimebuster,Bombshell,Young
  Robin, B:Yankee Longago,
  Swoop Storm 6,000.00
4 Hitler,Tojo,Mussolini (c) 2,200.00
5 Crimebuster saves day (c) . 1,600.00
6 O:Iron Jaw & Death of Son,
  B:Little Dynamite 5,000.00
7 Hitler,Tojo,Mussolini (c) 1,600.00
8 D:Iron Jaw 1,700.00
9 I:He-She 1,600.00
10 Iron Jaw returns 2,300.00
11 Iron Jaw falls in love 1,700.00
12 Crimebuster V:Japanese . . . 1,000.00
13 V:New,more terrible
  Iron Jaw 1,000.00
14 V:Iron Jaw 1,000.00
15 I:Rodent,D:Iron Jaw 1,200.00
16 Crimebuster V:Knight 600.00
17 Flag (c),Crimebuster
  V:Moth 600.00

*Boy Comics#18
© Comic House*

18 Smashed car (c) 550.00
19 Express train (c) 550.00
20 Coffin (c) 550.00
21 Boxing (c) 400.00
22 Under Sea (c) 400.00
23 Golf (c) 400.00
24 County insane asylum (c) 400.00
25 52 pgs 400.00
26 68 pgs 400.00
27 Express train (c) 450.00
28 E:Yankee Longago 450.00
29 Prison break (c) 450.00
30 O:Crimebuster,Murder (c) . . . 600.00
31 68 pgs 400.00
32 E:Young Robin Hood 400.00
33 . . . . 400.00
34 Suicide (c) & story 350.00
35 . . . . 300.00
36 . . . . 300.00
37 . . . . 300.00
38 . . . . 300.00
39 E:Little Dynamite 300.00
40 . . . . 300.00
41 thru 50 . . . . @275.00
51 thru 56 . . . . @250.00
57 B:Dilly Duncan 275.00
58 . . . . 250.00
59 . . . . 250.00
60 Iron Jaw returns 275.00
61 O:Iron Jaw,Crimebuster 300.00
62 A:Iron Jaw 275.00
63 thru 70 . . . . @200.00
71 E:Dilly Duncan 200.00
72 . . . . 200.00
73 . . . . 200.00
74 thru 79 . . . . @200.00
80 I:Rocky X 150.00
81 thru 88 . . . . @150.00
89 A:The Claw 175.00
90 same 175.00
91 same 175.00
92 same 175.00
93 The Claw(c),A:Rocky X 175.00
94 . . . . 125.00
95 . . . . 125.00
96 . . . . 125.00
97 . . . . 125.00
98 A:Rocky X 125.00
99 . . . . 125.00
100 . . . . 150.00
101 thru 118 . . . . @150.00
119 March, 1956 . . . . 150.00

All comics prices listed are for *Near Mint* condition.

GOLDEN AGE

BOY DETECTIVE
Avon Periodicals, 1951–52
1 F:Dan Tayler	300.00
2 Vice Lords of Crime	200.00
3 Spy Menace	200.00
4 The Death Trap	200.00

BOY EXPLORERS
See: TERRY AND THE PIRATES

BOYS' RANCH
Harvey Publications, 1950–51
1 S&K,F:Clay Duncan	1,000.00
2 S&K	750.00
3 S&K,MMe.	700.00
4 S&K	600.00
5 S&K,MMe.	400.00
6 S&K,MMe.	400.00

THE BRAIN
Sussex Publ. Co./Magazine Enterprises, 1956–58
1	150.00
2 thru 7	@100.00

BRENDA STARR
Four Star Comics Corp., 1947
13(1)	1,600.00
14(2) JKa,Bondage (c)	3,000.00

Superior Comics Ltd., 1948
2-3	2,000.00
2-4 JKa,Operating table (c).	2,000.00
2-5 Swimsuit (c)	1,500.00
2-6	1,500.00
2-7	1,500.00
2-8 Cosmetic (c)	1,500.00
2-9 Giant Starr (c)	1,500.00
2-10 Wedding (c)	1,500.00
2-11	1,500.00
2-12	1,500.00

Becomes:

BRENDA STARR REPORTER
Charlton Comics, 1955
13	800.00
14 & 15	@700.00

BRICK BRADFORD
Best Books (Standard Comics) July, 1949
5	300.00
6 Robot (c)	400.00
7 ASh(c)	150.00
8	150.00

BRIDES DIARY
See: BLACK COBRA

BROADWAY ROMANCES
Quality Comics Group, 1950
1 PG,BWa(a&c).	600.00
2 BWa,Glittering Desire	400.00
3 BL,Stole My Love.	200.00
4 Enslaved by My Past.	200.00
5 Flame of Passion,Sept.,1950	200.00

BRONCHO BILL
Visual Editions (Standard Comics) Jan., 1948
5	250.00
6 ASh(c)	125.00
7 ASh(c)	100.00
8	75.00
9 thru 13 ASh(c)	@100.00
14 and 15	@75.00
16 ASh(c)	100.00

AMERICA'S FAMOUS NEWSPAPER COMIC STRIP

JAN.

Bruce Gentry #1
© *Superior Comics*

BRUCE GENTRY
Four Star Publ./ Visual Editions/ Superior, Jan., 1948
1 B:Ray Bailey reprints	900.00
2 Plane crash (c)	500.00
3 E:Ray Bailey reprints	500.00
4 Tiger attack (c)	400.00
5	400.00
6 Help message (c)	400.00
7	400.00
8 End of Marriage (c),July, 1949	400.00

BUCCANEERS
See: KID ETERNITY

BUCK JONES
Dell Publishing Co., 1950
1 Buck Jones & Horse Silver	250.00
2	150.00
3 thru 8	@100.00

BUCK ROGERS
Eastern Color Printing, Winter 1940
1 Partial Painted(c)	6,500.00
2	2,300.00
3 Living Corpse from Crimson Coffin	2,000.00
4 One man army of greased lightning	1,900.00
5 Sky Roads	1,700.00
6 Sept., 1943	1,700.00

Toby Press
100 Flying Saucers	800.00
101	750.00
9 MA	750.00

BUDDIES IN THE U.S. ARMY
Avon Periodicals, 1952–53
1 Fightin' Guys & Fabulous Gals	200.00
2	125.00

BUFFALO BILL
Youthful Magazines, 1950–51
2 Annie Oakley	200.00
3 thru 9	@150.00

BUFFALO BILL PICTURE STORIES
Street & Smith Publ. 1949
1	250.00
2	250.00

BUFFALO BILL JR.
Dell Publishing Co., 1956
1	200.00
2 thru 6	@150.00
7 thru 13	@125.00

BUGHOUSE
Ajax/Farrell, 1954
1	250.00
2	150.00
3	150.00
4	150.00

BUG MOVIES
Dell Publishing Co., 1931
1	600.00

BUGS BUNNY
DELL GIANT EDITIONS
Dell Publishing Co.
Christmas
1 Christmas Funnies (1950)	350.00
2 Christmas Funnies (1951)	300.00
3 Christmas Funnies (1952)	250.00
4 Christmas Funnies (1953)	200.00
5 Christmas Funnies (1954)	200.00
6 Christmas Party (1955)	175.00
7 Christmas Party (1956)	185.00
8 Christmas Funnies (1957)	185.00
9 Christmas Funnies (1958)	185.00
1 County Fair (1957)	200.00

Halloween
1 Halloween Parade (1953)	200.00
2 Halloween Parade (1954)	175.00
3 Trick 'N' Treat Halloween Fun (1955)	185.00
4 Trick 'N' Treat Halloween Fun (1956)	185.00

Vacation
1 Vacation Funnies (1951)	325.00
2 Vacation Funnies (1952)	275.00
3 Vacation Funnies (1953)	250.00
4 Vacation Funnies (1954)	200.00
5 Vacation Funnies (1955)	200.00
6 Vacation Funnies (1956)	175.00
7 Vacation Funnies (1957)	175.00
8 Vacation Funnies (1958)	175.00
9 Vacation Funnies (1959)	175.00

BUGS BUNNY
Dell Publishing Co., 1942
see Four Color for early years
28 thru 30	@130.00
31 thru 50	@120.00
51 thru 70	@100.00
71 thru 85	@100.00
86 Giant-Show Time	125.00
87 thru 100	@100.00
101 thru 120	@75.00
121 thru 140	@50.00
141 thru 190	@50.00
191 thru 245	@50.00

BULLETMAN
Fawcett Publications, Summer, 1941
1 I:Bulletman & Bulletgirl	7,000.00
2 MRa(c)	2,800.00
3 MRa(c)	2,300.00
4 V:Headless Horror, Guillotine (c)	1,800.00

Bulletman #6
© *Fawcett Publications*

5 Riddle of Dr. Riddle.	2,300.00
6 V:Japanese	1,500.00
7 V:Revenge Syndicate	1,500.00
8 V:Mr. Ego	1,500.00
9 V:Canine Criminals	1,500.00
10 I:Bullet Dog	1,700.00
11 V:Fiendish Fiddler	1,100.00
12	1,000.00
13	1,000.00
14 V:Death the Comedian	1,000.00
15 V:Professor D.	1,000.00
16 VanishingElephant,Fall 1946	1,000.00

BULLS-EYE

Charlton Comics, 1954

1 S&K,Western Scout	750.00
2 S&K	650.00
3 thru 5 S&K	@500.00
6 S&K	450.00
7 S&K	500.00

Becomes:

CODY OF THE PONY EXPRESS

Charlton Comics, 1955

8 F:Buffalo Bill Cody	125.00
9	100.00
10	100.00

Becomes:

OUTLAWS OF THE WEST

BULLS-EYE
See: SCOOP COMICS

BUSTER BEAR

**Arnold Publications/
Quality Comics Group, 1953**

1 Funny animal	150.00
2	125.00
3 thru 10	@100.00

BUSTER BROWN COMICS

Brown Shoe Co., 1945–59

1	1,000.00
2	350.00
3	250.00
4 scarce	400.00
5	250.00
6	250.00
7	250.00
8	250.00
9	250.00
10	250.00

11 thru 20	@100.00
21 thru 24	@100.00
25 RC	150.00
26 thru 36	@100.00
37 RC	150.00
38	100.00
39	100.00
40 RC	150.00
41 RC	150.00
42	100.00
43	100.00

BUSTER BUNNY

**Animated Cartoons
(Standard)/Pines, 1949**

1 FF,Funny animal	150.00
2 thru 5	@100.00
6 thru 10	@100.00
11 thru 14	@100.00
15 racist(c)	125.00
16	100.00

BUSTER CRABBE

Famous Funnies, Nov., 1951

1 The Arrow of Death	650.00
2 AW&GE(c)	700.00
3 AW&GE(c)	750.00
4 FF(c)	900.00
5 AW,FF(a&c)	1,800.00
6 Sharks (c)	300.00
7 FF	350.00
8 Gorilla (c)	300.00
9 FF	350.00
10	250.00
11 Snakes (c)	200.00
12 Sept., 1953	200.00

BUSTER CRABBE

Lev Gleason Pub., 1953

1 Ph(c)	300.00
2 ATh	275.00
3 ATh	275.00
4 F. Gordon(c)	275.00

BUZ SAWYER

Standard Comics, June, 1948

1	300.00
2 I:Sweeney	250.00
3	250.00
4	250.00
5 June, 1949	250.00

CALLING ALL BOYS

**Parents Magazine Institute
Jan., 1946**

1 Skiing	200.00
2 Roy Rogers Story	150.00
3 Peril Out Post	150.00
4 Model Airplane	150.00
5 Fishing	150.00
6 Swimming	150.00
7 Baseball	175.00
8 School	150.00
9 The Miracle Quarterback	150.00
10 Gary Cooper (c)	200.00
11 Rin-Tin-Tin (c)	150.00
12 Bob Hope (c)	250.00
13 Bing Cosby (c)	225.00
14 J. Edgar Hoover (c)	150.00
15 Tex Granger (c).	125.00
16	125.00
17 Tex Granger (c), May, 1948	125.00

Becomes:

TEX GRANGER

June, 1948

18 Bandits of the Badlands	125.00
19 The Seven Secret Cities	100.00
20 Davey Crockett's Last Fight	100.00
21 Canyon Ambush	100.00

Calling All Boys #8
© *Parent Magazine Press*

22 V:Hooded Terror	100.00
23 V:Billy the Kid	100.00
24 A:Hector, Sept., 1949	100.00

CALLING ALL GIRLS

**Parent Magazine Press, Inc.,
Sept., 1941**

1	300.00
2 Virginia Weidler (c)	250.00
3 Shirley Temple (c)	300.00
4 Darla Hood (c)	150.00
5 Gloria Hood (c)	150.00
6	150.00
7	150.00
8	150.00
9 Flag (c)	150.00
10	150.00
11 Gary Cooper as Lou Gerrig	200.00
12 thru 20	@125.00
21 thru 39	@125.00
40 Liz Taylor	250.00
41	100.00
42	100.00
43 Oct., 1945	100.00

CALLING ALL KIDS

**Quality Comics, Inc.,
Dec./Jan., 1946**

1 Funny Animal stories	150.00
2	125.00
3 thru 5	@100.00
6 thru 10	@100.00
11 thru 25	@100.00
26 Aug., 1949.	100.00

CAMERA COMICS

**U.S. Camera Publishing Corp.,
July–Sept., 1944**

1 Airfighter,Grey Comet	350.00
2 How to Set Up a Darkroom	300.00
3 Linda Lens V:Nazi (c)	300.00
4 Linda Lens (c)	250.00
5 Diving (c)	250.00
6 Jim Lane (c)	250.00
7 Linda Lens (c)	250.00
8 Linda Lens (c)	250.00
9 Summer, 1946	250.00

CAMP COMICS

Dell Publishing Co., 1942

1 Ph(c),WK,A:Bugs Bunny.	1,500.00
2 Ph(c),WK,A:Bugs Bunny.	1,200.00
3 Ph(c),WK	1,000.00

GOLDEN AGE

CAMPUS LOVES
**Comic Magazines
(Quality Comics Group), 1949**
1 BWa,PGv 500.00
2 BWa,PGv 400.00
3 PGv,Photo(c) 250.00
4 PGv,Photo(c) 250.00
5 PGv,Photo(c) 250.00

CAMPUS ROMANCES
**Avon Periodicals/
Realistic Publ., 1949**
1 Walter Johnson 350.00
2 . . . . 300.00
3 . . . . 300.00

CANDY
William H. Wise, 1944–45
1 BW,Two-Scoop 600.00
1a rep.BW 100.00
2 BW 500.00
3 BW 500.00

CANDY
Quality Comics Group, 1947–56
1 JCo,PGv,Teen-age 375.00
2 JCo,PGv 300.00
3 JCo 150.00
4 JCo 150.00
5 JCo 150.00
6 thru 10 JCo . . . . @150.00
11 thru 20 JCo . . . . @125.00
21 thru 40 . . . . @100.00
41 thru 64 . . . . @100.00

CANNONBALL COMICS
Rural Home Publ. Co., 1945
1 Superhero, Crash Kid 1,400.00
2 Captive Prince 1,200.00

CANTEEN KATE
St. John Publishing Co., 1952
1 MB,Sexy babe 900.00
2 MB 600.00
3 MB 700.00

CAPTAIN AERO COMICS
Holyoke Publishing Co., 1941
1 B:Flag-Man&Solar,Master
 of Magic Captain Aero,
 Captain Stone 4,000.00

*Captain Aero Comics #6
© Holyoke Publishing Co.*

2 A:Pals of Freedom 1,600.00
3 JKu,B:Alias X,A:Pals of
 Freedom 1,600.00
4 JKu,O:Gargoyle,
 Parachute jump 1,600.00
5 JKu 1,500.00
6 JKu,Flagman,A:Miss Victory . 1,400.00
7 Alias X 900.00
8 O:Red Cross,A:Miss Victory . . 900.00
9 A:Miss Victory,Alias X 800.00
10 A:Miss Victory,Red Cross 750.00
11 A:Miss Victory 750.00
12 A:Miss Victory 750.00
13 A:Miss Victory 750.00
14 A:Miss Victory 750.00
15 AS(c),A:Miss Liberty 750.00
16 AS(c),Leather Face 500.00
17 LbC(c) 900.00
21 LbC(c) 900.00
22 LbC(c),I:Mighty Mite 900.00
23 LbC(c) 900.00
24 LbC(c) American Planes Dive
 Bomb Japan 1,200.00
25 LbC(c),Science Fiction(c) . . . 700.00
26 LbC(c) 1,500.00

CAPTAIN ATOM
**Nationwide Publishers, 1951
Mini-size**
1 Scientific adventure 550.00
2 thru 7 . . . . @250.00

CAPTAIN BATTLE
**New Friday Publ./
Magazine Press, Summer, 1941**
1 B:Captain Battle,O:Blackout 3,000.00
2 Pirate Ship (c) 1,700.00
3 Dungeon (c) 1,500.00
4 *.may not exist*
5 V:Japanese, Summer, 1943 . . 900.00

CAPTAIN BATTLE, Jr.
Comic House, Fall, 1943
1 Claw V:Ghost, A:Sniffer 2,500.00
2 Man who didn't believe
 in Ghosts 2,000.00

CAPTAIN COURAGEOUS
See: BANNER COMICS

CAPTAIN EASY
Standard Comics, 1939
N# Swash Buckler 1,500.00
10 . . . . 300.00
11 . . . . 150.00
12 . . . . 150.00
13 ASh(c) 150.00
14 . . . . 150.00
15 . . . . 150.00
16 ASh(c) 150.00
17 Sept., 1949 . . . . 150.00

CAPTAIN FEARLESS
COMICS
Helnit Publishing Co., 1941
1 O:Mr. Miracle,Alias X,Captain
 Fearless Citizen Smith,
 A:Miss Victory 1,500.00
2 A:Border Patrol, Sept.,1941 . . 800.00

CAPTAIN FLASH
Sterling Comics, Nov., 1954
1 O:Captain Flash 600.00
2 V:Black Knight 300.00
3 Beasts from 1,000,000 BC . . . 300.00
4 Flying Saucer Invasion 300.00

CAPTAIN FLEET
Approved Comics, Fall, 1952
1 Storm and Mutiny ...Typhoon . 250.00

CAPTAIN FLIGHT
COMICS
**Four Star Publications,
March, 1944–Feb.-March, 1947**
N# B:Captain Flight,Ace
 Reynolds, Dash the Avenger,
 ProfessorX 800.00
2 . . . . 450.00
3 . . . . 450.00
4 B:Rock Raymond Salutes
 America's Wartime Heroines . 450.00
5 Bondage (c),B:Red Rocket
 A:The Grenade 2,000.00
6 Girl tied at the stake 500.00
7 LbC(c),Dog Fight (c) 900.00
8 LbC(c),B:Yankee Girl,
 A:Torpedoman 900.00
9 LbC(c),Dog Fight (c) 900.00
10 LbC(c),Bondage (c) 900.00
11 LbC(c),Future(c) 2,000.00

CAPTAIN GALLANT
Charlton Comics, 1955
1 Ph(c),Buster Crabbe 200.00
2 . . . . 150.00
3 . . . . 150.00
4 Sept., 1956 . . . . 150.00

CAPTAIN JET
Four Star Publ., May, 1952
1 Factory bombing (c) 300.00
2 Parachute jump (c) 200.00
3 Tank bombing (c) 175.00
4 Parachute (c) 175.00
5 . . . . 175.00

CAPTAIN KIDD
**See: DAGAR,
DESERT HAWK**

CAPTAIN MARVEL
ADVENTURES
Fawcett Publications, 1941
N# JK, B:Captain Marvel &
 Sivana 55,000.00
2 GT,JK(c),Billy Batson (c) . . . 7,500.00
3 JK(c),Thunderbolt (c) 4,500.00
4 Shazam(c) 3,500.00
5 V:Nazis 2,500.00
6 Solomon, Hercules, Atlas, Zeus,
 Achilles & Mercury (c) . . . 2,000.00
7 Ghost of the White Room . . . 2,000.00
8 Forward America 2,000.00
9 A:Ibac the Monster, Nippo
 the Nipponese, Relm of
 the Subconscious 2,000.00
10 V:Japanese 2,000.00
11 V:Japanese and Nazis 1,500.00
12 Joins the Army 1,400.00
13 V:Diamond-Eyed Idol of
 Doom 1,400.00
14 Nippo meets his Nemesis . . 1,400.00
15 Big "Paste the Axis" contest. 1,400.00
16 Uncle Sam (c), Paste
 the Axis 1,400.00
17 P(c), Paste the Axis 1,200.00
18 P(c), O:Mary Marvel 3,600.00
19 Mary Marvel & Santa (c) . . . 1,500.00
20 Mark of the Black
 Swastika 6,000.00
21 Hitler 1,700.00
22 B:Mr. Mind serial,
 Shipyard Sabotage 1,500.00
23 A:Steamboat 1,100.00

Captain Marvel Adventures #21
© Fawcett Publications

24 Minneapolis Mystery 1,100.00
25 Sinister Faces (c). 1,100.00
26 Flag (c). 1,100.00
27 Joins Navy 800.00
28 Uncle Sam (c). 800.00
29 Battle at the China Wall 800.00
30 Modern Robinson Crusoe . . . 800.00
31 Fights his own Conscience. . . 800.00
32 V:Mole Men, Dallas. 800.00
33 Mt. Rushmore parody
   (c), Omaha 800.00
34 Oklahoma City 800.00
35 O:Radar the International
   Policeman, Indianapolis 700.00
36 Missing face contest,
   St. Louis. 700.00
37 V:Block Busting Bubbles,
   Cincinnati. 700.00
38 V:Chattanooga Ghost,
   Rock Garden City 700.00
39 V:Mr. Mind's Death Ray,
   Pittsburgh 700.00
40 V:Ghost of the Tower,Boston . 700.00
41 Runs for President, Dayton . . 600.00
42 Christmas special, St. Paul. . 600.00
43 V:Mr. Mind,I:Uncle Marvel,
   Chicago 600.00
44 OtherWorlds,Washington,D.C. 600.00
45 V:Blood Bank Robbers 600.00
46 E: Mr. Mind Serial, Tall
   Stories of Jonah Joggins. . . . 600.00
47 CCB,Shazam(c) 550.00
48 Signs Autographs (c) 550.00
49 V: An Unknown Killer 550.00
50 Twisted Powers 550.00
51 Last of the Batsons. 450.00
52 O&I:Sivana Jr.,V:Giant
   Earth Dreamer. 450.00
53 Gets promoted 450.00
54 Marooned in the Future,
   Kansas City 450.00
55 Endless String, Columbus . . . 450.00
56 Goes Crazy, Mobile 450.00
57 A:Haunted Girl, Rochester . . . 450.00
58 V:Sivana 450.00
59 CCB(c),PrC 450.00
60 Man who made Earthquakes . 450.00
61 I&V: Oggar, the Worlds
   Mightiest Immortal. 450.00
62 The Great Harness Race 450.00
63 Stuntman. 450.00
64 CCB(c&a),I:Lester the Imp . . . 450.00
65 V:Invaders from Outer Space . 450.00
66 Atomic War (c) 450.00
67 Hartford 350.00

68 Scenes from the Past,
   Baltimore 400.00
69 Gets Knighted. 350.00
70 Horror in the Box 350.00
71 Wheel of Death. 350.00
72 CCB,Empire State Bldg.Ph(c). 350.00
73 Becomes a Petrophile. 350.00
74 Who is the 13th Guest 350.00
75 V:Astonishing Yeast Menace . 350.00
76 A:Atom Ambassador 350.00
77 The Secret Life 350.00
78 O:Mr. Tawny 450.00
79 O:Atom,A:World's Worst
   Actor 400.00
80 Twice told story 900.00
81 A:Mr. Atom 800.00
82 A:Mr. Tawny 400.00
83 Indian Chief. 400.00
84 V:Surrealist Imp 400.00
85 Freedom Train 400.00
86 A:Mr. Tawny 400.00
87 V:Electron Thief 400.00
88 Billy Batson's Boyhood 400.00
89 V:Sivana 400.00
90 A:Mr. Tawny 400.00
91 A:Chameleon Stone 400.00
92 The Land of Limbo 400.00
93 Book of all Knowledge 400.00
94 Battle of Electricity 400.00
95 The Great Ice Cap 400.00
96 V:Automatic Weapon 400.00
97 Wiped Out. 400.00
98 United Worlds 400.00
99 Rain of Terror 400.00
100 V:Sivana,Plot against
   the Universe 750.00
101 Invisibility Trap 350.00
102 Magic Mix-up 350.00
103 Ice Covered World of
   1,000,000 AD. 350.00
104 Mr. Tawny's Masquerade . . . 350.00
105 The Dog Catcher 350.00
106 V:Menace of the Moon 350.00
107 V:Space Hunter. 350.00
108 V:Terrible Termites 350.00
109 The Invention Inventor 350.00
110 CCB(c),V:Sivana 350.00
111 The Eighth Sea,V:Vikings . . . 350.00
112 Worrybird. 350.00
113 Feud with Mr. Tawny 350.00
114 V:The Ogre 350.00
115 Mr. Tawny 350.00
116 Flying Saucer 450.00
117 Mr. Tawny bondage (c) 350.00
118 V:Weird Water Man. 350.00
119 Invisibility. 350.00
120 Voice heard round the world. 350.00
121 Origin retold 350.00
122 Atomic Fire 350.00
123 Dinosaur Dilemma 350.00
124 V:Discarded Instincts 350.00
125 V:Ancient Villain 350.00
126 The Creeping Horror. 350.00
127 Sivana's Voodoo Spell 350.00
128 . . . . 350.00
129 Robot Hunt 350.00
130 Double Doom 350.00
131 Station Whiz gets Atomic
   Powers. 350.00
132 V:Flood 350.00
133 The Pressure Peril 350.00
134 Sivana's Capsule Kingdom. . 350.00
135 Perplexing Past Puzzle. 325.00
136 Witch of Haven Street. 325.00
137 Seven Deadly Sins 325.00
138 V:Haunted Horror 400.00
139 V:Red Crusher 325.00
140 Hand of Horror 325.00
141 Man Without a World 325.00
142 The Beauty in Black 325.00
143 Great Stone Face on Moon . 325.00
144 Stolen Shazam Powers . . . 325.00

145 The Machines of Murder. . . . 325.00
146 The Unholy Spider 325.00
147 Thief From the Past 325.00
148 V:The World 325.00
149 Mr. Tawny Hermit 325.00
150 Captain Marvel's Wedding,
   Nov., 1953 . . . . 650.00

CAPTAIN MARVEL JR.
Fawcett Publications, 1942
1 MRa(c),O:Captain Marvel, Jr.,
   A:Capt. Nazi 9,700.00
2 MRa(c),O:Capt.Nippon,
   V:Capt. Nazi 3,500.00
3 MRa(c),Parade to
   Excitement 2,000.00
4 MRa(c),V:Invisible Nazi 1,800.00
5 MRa(c),V:Capt. Nazi 1,500.00
6 MRa(c),Adventure of Sabbac 1,300.00
7 MRa(c),City under the Sea . 1,300.00
8 MRa(c),Dangerous Double . 1,300.00
9 MRa(c),Independence (c) . . 1,400.00
10 Hitler (c). 1,600.00
11 MRa(c). 1,100.00
12 MRa(c),Scuttles the Axis
   Isle in the Sky. 1,200.00
13 MRa(c),V:The Axis,Hitler,(c). 1,600.00
14 MRa(c),X-Mas (c), Santa wears
   Capt. Marvel uniform 1,000.00
15 MRa(c),V:Capt. Nazi 1,100.00
16 MRa(c),A:Capt. Marvel,
   Sivana, Pogo 1,000.00
17 MRa(c),Meets his future self 1,000.00
18 MRa(c),V:Birds of Doom . . . 1,000.00
19 MRa(c),A:Capt. Nazi &
   Capt. Nippon 1,000.00
20 MRa(c),Goes on the Warpath 900.00
21 MRa(c),Buy War Stamps 700.00
22 MRa(c),Rides World's oldest
   steamboat 700.00
23 MRa(c) 700.00
24 MRa(c),V:Weather Man 700.00
25 MRa(c),Flag (c) 700.00
26 MRa(c),Happy New Year 700.00
27 MRa(c),Jungle Thrills 700.00
28 MRa(c),V:Sivana's Crumbling
   Crimes 700.00
29 MRa(c),Blazes a Wilderness
   Trail 700.00
30 MRa(c) 700.00
31 MRa(c) 500.00
32 Keeper of the Lonely Rock . . . 500.00
33 . . . . 500.00
34/35 I&O:Sivana Jr. 500.00
36 Underworld Tournament 500.00

Captain Marvel Jr. #23
© Fawcett Publications

Capt. Mavel Jr.–Catholic   **GOLDEN AGE**   **Comics Values Annual**

GOLDEN AGE

37 FreddyFreeman'sNews-stand. 500.00
38 A:Arabian Knight 500.00
39 V:Sivana Jr., Headline Stealer 500.00
40 Faces Grave Situation 500.00
41 I:The Acrobat 400.00
42 V:Sivana Jr. 400.00
43 BTh(c),V:Beasts on Broadway 400.00
44 Key to the Mystery 400.00
45 A:Icy Fingers 400.00
46 BTh(c&a) 400.00
47 BTh(c),V:Giant o/t Beanstalk . 400.00
48 Whale of a Fish Story 400.00
49 BTh(c),V:Dream Recorder . . . 400.00
50 Wanted: Freddy Freeman . . . 400.00
51 The Island Riddle 350.00
52 A:Flying Postman 350.00
53 Atomic Bomb on the Loose. . . 400.00
54 V:Man with 100 Heads 350.00
55 Pyramid of Eternity 350.00
56 Blue Boy's Black Eye 350.00
57 MRa(c),Magic Ladder 350.00
58 BTh(c),Amazing Mirror Maze . 350.00
59 MRa(c) 350.00
60 V:Space Menace 350.00
61 V:Himself. 300.00
62 V:Mr. Hydro. 300.00
63 V:Witch of Winter 300.00
64 thru 74 . . . . @300.00
75 V:Outlaw of Crooked Creek . . 300.00
76 thru 85 . . . . @300.00
86 Defenders of time 300.00
87 thru 89 . . . . @300.00
90 The Magic Trunk 300.00
91 thru 99 . . . . @300.00
100 V:Sivana Jr 300.00
101 thru 106 . . . . @300.00
107 The Horror Dimension 400.00
108 thru 118 . . . . @250.00
119 Condemned to Die, Electric
    Chair, June, 1953 . . . . 250.00

CAPTAIN MIDNIGHT
Fawcett Publications, 1942
1 O:Captain Midnight,
    Capt. Marvel (c) 6,000.00
2 Smashes Jap Juggernaut. . . 2,700.00
3 Battles Phantom Bomber . . . 2,400.00
4 Grapples the Gremlins 2,000.00
5 Double Trouble in Tokyo . . . 2,000.00
6 Blasts the Black Mikado . . . 1,400.00
7 Newspaper headline (c) 1,400.00
8 Flying Torpedoes
    Berlin-Bound 1,400.00
9 MRa(c), Subs in Mississippi 1,400.00
10 MRa(c), Flag (c). 1,500.00
11 MRa(c), Murder in Mexico . . 1,200.00
12 V:Sinister Angels 1,200.00
13 Non-stop around the World . 1,200.00
14 V:King of the Villains 1,200.00
15 V:Kimberley Killer. 1,200.00
16 Hitler's Fortress Breached . . 1,200.00
17 MRa(c), Hello Adolf 1,200.00
18 Death from the Skies 1,200.00
19 Hour of Doom for the Axis . . 1,200.00
20 Brain & Brawn against Axis 1,200.00
21 Trades with Japanese. 900.00
22 Plea for War Stamps. 900.00
23 Japanese Prison (c) 900.00
24 Rising Sun Flag (c) 900.00
25 Amusement Park Murder 900.00
26 Hotel of Horror 900.00
27 Death Knell for Tyranny 900.00
28 Gliderchuting to Glory. 900.00
29 Bomb over Nippon 900.00
30 . . . . 900.00
31 and 32. . . . . @500.00
33 V:Shark. 500.00
34 thru 40 . . . . @500.00
41 thru 63 . . . . @400.00
64 V:XOG, Ruler of Saturn. 400.00
65 . . . . 400.00
66 V:XOG. 400.00

Captain Midnight #27
© *Fawcett Publications*

67 Fall, 1948 . . . . 400.00
Becomes:

SWEETHEARTS
Oct., 1948
68 Robert Mitchum 250.00
69 thru 110 . . . . @125.00
111 Ronald Reagan story 175.00
112 thru 118 . . . . @125.00
119 WW,Marilyn Monroe 600.00
120 Atomic Bomb story . . . . . . @150.00
121 Liz Taylor. 200.00
122 Marjuana,1954 . . . . 150.00

CAPTAIN ROCKET
P.L. Publications, 1951
1 Sci-Fi 650.00

CAPTAIN SCIENCE
Youthful Magazines, 1950
1 WW,O:Captain Science,
    V:Monster God of Rogor . . 1,400.00
2 V:Cat Men of Phoebus,
    Space Pirates 600.00
3 Ghosts from the Underworld . 600.00
4 WW,Vampires 1,200.00
5 WW,V:Shark Pirates of
    Pisces 1,200.00
6 V:Invisible Tyrants,
    bondage (c). 700.00
7 Bondage(c) Dec., 1951 . . . . . 700.00
Becomes:

FANTASTIC
Feb., 1952
8 Isle of Madness 500.00
9 Octopus (c) 400.00
Becomes:

BEWARE
June, 1952
10 SHn,Doll of Death. 700.00
11 SHn,Horror Head 500.00
12 SHn,Body Snatchers 500.00
Becomes:

CHILLING TALES
Dec., 1952
13 MF,Screaming Skull 900.00
14 SHn,Smell of Death 600.00
15 SHn,Curse of the Tomb 700.00
16 HcK,Mark of the Beast
    Bondage(c) 600.00
17 MFc(c),Wandering Willie,
    Oct.,1953 . . . . 700.00

CAPTAIN STEVE SAVAGE
Avon Periodicals
[1st Series] 1950
N# WW 500.00
2 EK(c),The Death Gamble 300.00
3 EK(c),Crash Landing in
    Manchuria 250.00
4 EK(c),V:Red Raiders from
    Siang-Po 150.00
5 EK(c),Rockets of Death 150.00
6 Operation Destruction 150.00
7 EK(c),Flight to Kill 150.00
8 EK(c),V:Red Mystery Jet 150.00
9 EK(c) 150.00
10 . . . . 150.00
11 EK(c) 150.00
12 WW 225.00
13 . . . . 150.00

[2nd Series] Sept./Oct., 1954
5 . . . . 150.00
6 WW 200.00
7 thru 13 . . . . @150.00

CAPTAIN TOOTSIE
& THE SECRET LEGION
Toby Press, 1950
1 Sci-Fi 400.00
2 . . . . 250.00

CAPTAIN VIDEO
Fawcett Publications, 1951
1 GE,Ph(c) From TV series . . . 1,800.00
2 Time When Men Could Not
    Walk 1,200.00
3 GE,Indestructible Antagonist 1,000.00
4 GE,School of Spies 1,000.00
5 GE,Missiles of Doom,
    photo (c). 1,000.00
6 GE,Island of Conquerors,
    Photo (c); Dec., 1951 . . . . . 1,000.00

CAPTAIN WIZARD
Rural Home, 1946
1 Impossible Man 500.00

CARNIVAL
See: SCOOP COMICS

CASPER, THE
FRIENDLY GHOST
St. John Publishing, 1949
1 O:Baby Huey 3,500.00
2 . . . . 1,500.00
3 . . . . 1,400.00
4 . . . . 1,000.00
5 . . . . 1,000.00

Harvey Publications, 1952
7 Baby Huey 800.00
8 thru 9 Baby Huey . . . . @500.00
10 I:Spooky 550.00
11 A:Spooky 300.00
12 thru 18 . . . . @300.00
19 I:Nightmare 400.00
20 I:Wendy the Witch 2,000.00
21 thru 30 . . . . @250.00
31 thru 40 . . . . @200.00
41 thru 50 . . . . @150.00
51 thru 60 . . . . @150.00
61 thru 69 . . . . @150.00
70 July, 1958 . . . . 150.00

CATHOLIC COMICS
Catholic Publications, 1946–49
1 Sports. 550.00
2 Sports. 350.00
3 Sports. 300.00
4 thru 10 . . . . @300.00

11 thru 20	@250.00
21 thru 34	@275.00

CATMAN COMICS
Helnit Publ. Co./ Holyoke Publ. Co./ Continental Magazine, 1941

1 O:Deacon&Sidekick Mickey, Dr. Diamond & Ragman,A:Black Widow, B:Blaze Baylor	7,500.00
2 Ragman	2,800.00
3 B:Pied Piper	2,500.00
4 CQ	2,000.00
5 I&O: The Kitten	1,500.00
6 CQ	1,500.00
7 CQ	1,500.00
8 JKa, I:Volton	1,800.00
9 JKa	1,200.00
10 JKa,O:Blackout, B:Phantom Falcon	1,200.00
11 JKa,DRi,BF,PzF	1,200.00
12 Volton	1,000.00
13 rare	1,500.00
14 CQ	1,000.00
15 Rajah of Destruction	1,000.00
16 Bye-Bye Axis, Hitler	1,500.00
17 Buy Bonds and Stamps	1,000.00
18 Buy Bonds and Stamps	1,000.00
19 CQ,Hitler,Tojo &Mussolini(c)	1,500.00
20 CQ,Hitler,Tojo &Mussolini(c)	1,500.00
21 CQ	1,000.00
22 CQ	1,000.00
23 CQ	1,000.00
N# DRiV:Japanese,Bondage(c)	1,200.00
N# V:Demon	1,000.00
N# LbC(c),A:Leather Face	1,400.00
27 LbC(c),Flag (c),O:Kitten	1,500.00
28 LbC(c),Horror (c)	1,500.00
29 LbC(c),BF,RP	1,500.00
30 LbC(c),BF,Bondage(c)	1,600.00
31 LbC(c)	1,500.00
32 LbC(c),RP,Aug., 1946	1,500.00

CAVALIER COMICS
Sture Ashberg Publ. 1945

1 Historic adventure	250.00

CENTURY OF COMICS
Eastern Color Printing Co., 1933

N# Giveaway, very early	60,000.00

CHALLENGER, THE
Interfaith Publications, 1945

N# O:The Challenger Club	750.00
2 and 3 JKa	@600.00
4 JKa,BF	600.00

CHAMBER OF CHILLS
Harvey Publications/ Witches Tales, June, 1951

21 (1) AAv	900.00
22 (2) AAv	600.00
23 (3) Eyes Ripped Out	600.00
24 (4) LEI,Bondage (c)	700.00
5 LEI,Shrunken Skull, Operation Monster	700.00
6 LEI,Seven Skulls of Magondi	600.00
7 LEI,Pit of the Damned	600.00
8 LEI,Formula for Death	600.00
9 LEI,Bondage (c)	500.00
10 LEI,AAv,Cave of Death	500.00
11 AAv,Curse of Morgan Kilgane	400.00
12 AAv,Swamp Monster	400.00
13 AAv,The Lost Race	550.00
14 LEI,Down to Death	500.00
15 LEI,AAv,Nightmare of Doom	550.00
16 LEI,Cycle of Horror	550.00
17 LEI,Amnesia	550.00
18 LEI,Hair Cut-Atom Bomb	600.00

19 LEI,Happy Anniversary	500.00
20 Shock is Struck	500.00
21 LEI,BP,RP,Decapitation	600.00
22 LEI,Is Death the End?	550.00
23 LEI,BP,RP,Heartline	550.00
24 LEI,BP,Bondage(c)	600.00
25 LEI,	400.00
26 LEI,HN,AAv,Captains Return	400.00

Becomes:

CHAMBER OF CLUES
Feb., 1955

27 BP,A:Kerry Drake	250.00
28 A:Kerry Drake	150.00

CHAMPION COMICS
Worth Publishing Co., 1939

2 B:Champ, Blazing Scarab, Neptina, Liberty Lads, Jingleman	3,200.00
3	1,500.00
4 Bailout(c)	1,500.00
5 Jungleman(c)	1,500.00
6 MNe	1,500.00
7 MNe,Human Meteor	1,500.00
8 JK	3,000.00
9 JK,S&K	3,000.00
10 JK,Bondage (c)	3,000.00

Becomes:

CHAMP COMICS
Oct. 1940

11 Human Meteor	2,500.00
12 Human Heteor	2,200.00
13 Dragon's Teeth	2,000.00
14 Liberty Lads	2,000.00
15 RC,Liberty Lads	2,000.00
16 Liberty Lads	2,000.00
17 Liberty Lads	2,000.00
18 Liberty Lads	2,400.00
19 JSm,A:The Wasp	2,500.00
20 S&K,A:The Green Ghost	2,000.00
21 S&K	1,500.00
22 A:White Mask	1,500.00
23 Flag (c)	1,800.00
24 Hitler,Tojo & Mussolini	1,600.00
25 thru 29	@1,500.00

CHARLIE CHAN
Crestwood, 1948–55

1 S&K(c),CI,Detective	1,500.00
2 S&K	1,000.00
3 S&K	1,000.00
4 S&K	1,000.00
5 S&K	1,000.00

Charlton Comics, 1955

6 S&K	750.00
7	500.00
8	500.00
9	500.00

Becomes:

ZAZA THE MYSTIC
Charlton Comics, 1956

10 Psychic revelations	300.00
11	300.00

Becomes:

THIS MAGAZINE IS HAUNTED
Charlton Comics, 1957

12	450.00
13	650.00
14 The Green Man	400.00
15	350.00
16	700.00

Becomes:

OUTER SPACE
Charlton Comics, 1958

17 AS,WW,Sci-Fi	300.00
18 SD	450.00

Outer Space #25
© Charlton Comics

19 SD	450.00
20 SD	450.00
21 SD	450.00
22	300.00
23	300.00
24 SD Machine Men of Mars	300.00
25	300.00

CHARLIE McCARTHY
Dell Publishing Co., 1947

1 Ph(c)	300.00
2	200.00
3 thru 9	@200.00

CHEYENNE
Dell Publishing Co., 1956

1 Ph(c) all	350.00
2	200.00
3	150.00
4 thru 12	@135.00
13 thru 25	@125.00

CHIEF, THE
Dell Publishing Co., 1950

(1) see Dell Four Color #290	
2	125.00

CHILLING TALES
See: CAPTAIN SCIENCE

CHOICE COMICS
Great Comics, 1941

1 O:Secret Circle	2,800.00
2	1,500.00
3 The Lost City	2,100.00

CHRISTMAS CARNIVAL
Approved Comics (Ziff-Davis)/ St. John Publ., 1955

N# Santa	500.00
2	300.00

CHUCKLE THE GIGGLY BOOK OF COMIC ANIMALS
R. B. Leffing Well Co., 1944

1	300.00

All comics prices listed are for *Near Mint* condition.

CINEMA COMICS HERALD
**Paramount/Universal/RKO/
20th Century Fox
Giveaways, 1941-43**
N# Mr. Bug Goes to Town 200.00
N# Bedtime Story 150.00
N# Lady for a Night,J.Wayne . . . 325.00
N# Reap the Wild Wind 150.00
N# Thunderbirds 150.00
N# They All Kissed Me 150.00
N# Bombardier 175.00
N# Crash Dive 135.00
N# Arabian Nights. 150.00

CIRCUS COMICS
Farm Women's Publ., 1945
1 Clown, Funny Animal. 200.00
2 . . . . 150.00

CIRCUS COMICS
D.S. Publications, 1948
1 FF 400.00

CIRCUS OF FUN COMICS
A.W. Nugent Publ. Co., 1946
1 Funny animal. 250.00
2 . . . . 150.00
3 . . . . 150.00

CIRCUS THE COMIC RIOT
Globe Syndicate, June, 1938
1 BKa,WE,BW 10,000.00
2 BKa,WE,BW 6,000.00
3 BKa,WE,BW, Aug., 1938 . . . 5,000.00

CISCO KID COMICS
**Bernard Bailey/
Swappers Quarterly, 1944**
1 . . . . 700.00

*Cisco Kid Comics #7
© Dell Publishing Co.*

CISCO KID, THE
Dell Publishing Co., 1951
(1) *See Dell Four Color #292*
2 Jan., 1951 . . . . 500.00
3 thru 5 . . . . @300.00
6 thru 10 . . . . @250.00
11 thru 20 . . . . @225.00
21 thru 36 . . . . @175.00

37 thru 41 Ph(c)'s. . . . . @350.00

CLAIRE VOYANT
**Leader Publ./Visual Ed./
Pentagon Publ., 1946-47**
N# 1,100.00
2 JKa(c) 800.00
3 Case of the Kidnapped
Bride 1,000.00
4 Bondage (c) 800.00

CLAY CODY, GUNSLINGER
Better Publications, 1957
1 Western hero 100.00

CLEAN FUN, STARRING 'SHOOGAFOOTS JONES'
Specialty Book Co., 1945
N# 200.00

CLIMAX!
Gilmor Magazines, 1955
1 Mystery 250.00
2 . . . . 200.00

CLOAK AND DAGGER
**Approved Comics
(Ziff-Davis), Fall, 1952**
1 NS(c),Al Kennedy of the Secret
Service 400.00

CLOWN COMICS
Harvey Publications, 1945
N# 225.00
2 . . . . 150.00
3 . . . . 150.00

CLUE COMICS
Hillman Periodicals, 1943
1 O:Boy King,Nightmare,Micro-Face,
Twilight,Zippo. 2,700.00
2 rare 1,600.00
3 Boy King V:The Crane 1,100.00
4 V:The Crane 900.00
5 V:The Crane 900.00
6 Hells Kitchen 600.00
7 V:Dr. Plasma,Torture(c) 600.00
8 RP,A:The Gold Mummy King . 550.00
9 I:Paris 550.00
10 O:Gun Master 550.00
11 A:Gun Master 550.00
12 O:Rackman. 550.00
2-1 S&K,O:Nightro,A:Iron Lady. 1,100.00
2-2 S&K,Bondage(c). 1,600.00
2-3 S&K. 1,100.00
Becomes:

REAL CLUE CRIME STORIES
June, 1947
2-4 DBw,S&K,True Story of
Ma Barker. 1,100.00
2-5 S&K, Newface surgery(c) . . . 800.00
2-6 S&K, Breakout (c) 800.00
2-7 S&K, Stick up (c) 800.00
2-8 Kidnapping (c) 200.00
2-9 DBa,Boxing fix (c) 200.00
2-10 DBa,Murder (c) 200.00
2-11 Attempted bankrobbery (c) . 200.00
2-12 Murder (c) 200.00
3-1 thru 3-12. . . . . @200.00
4-1 thru 4-12. . . . . @200.00
5-1 thru 5-12. . . . . @150.00
6-1 thru 6-12. . . . . @150.00
6-10 Bondage(c) 200.00
7-1 thru 7-12. . . . . @135.00
8-1 thru 8-5, May, 1953 . . . . . @135.00

THE CLUTCHING HAND
American Comics, 1954
1 Horror. 600.00

CLYDE BEATTY
Commodore Productions, 1953
1 Photo(c). 400.00

C-M-O COMICS
**Comic Corp. of America
(Centaur), May, 1942**
1 Invisible Terror 2,000.00
2 Super Ann. 1,200.00

COCOMALT BIG BOOK OF COMICS
Harry A. Chesler, 1938
1 BoW,PGv,FGu,JCo,(Give away)
Little Nemo 4,000.00

CODY OF THE PONY EXPRESS
See: BULLS-EYE

*Cody of the Pony Express #1
© Fox Features Syndicate*

CODY OF THE PONY EXPRESS
Fox Features Syndicate, 1950
1 Western 200.00

COLOSSAL FEATURES MAGAZINE
Fox Features Syndicate, 1950
1 (33) Cody of the Pony Express 200.00
2 (34) Cody of the Pony Express 200.00
3 Crime. 200.00

COLOSSUS COMICS
**Sun Publications
March, 1940**
1 A:Colossus 10,000.00

COLUMBIA COMICS
William H. Wise Co., 1944
1 Joe Palooka,Charlie Chan . . . 450.00

COMIC BOOKS
Metropolitan Printing Co. 1950
1 Boots & Saddles 125.00

1 Green Lama-The Green Jet . . 500.00
1 My Pal Dizzy 60.00
1 Talullah. 150.00
1 New World 60.00

COMIC COMICS
Fawcett Publications, 1946
1 Captain Kidd 250.00
2 . . . . 275.00
3 thru 10 BW. . . . . @275.00

COMIC LAND
Fact and Fiction, 1946
1 Sandusky and the Senator . . . 250.00

COMICS, THE
**Dell Publishing Co.,
March, 1937**
1 I:Tom Mix & Arizona Kid 3,200.00
2 A:Tom Mix & Tom Beaty 2,700.00
3 A:Alley Oop 1,800.00
4 thru 11 same . . . . @1,800.00

THE COMICS CALENDAR
True Comics Press, 1946
1 . . . . 650.00

COMICS NOVEL
Fawcett Publications, 1947
1 Anarcho Dictator of Death 500.00

COMICS ON PARADE
**United Features Syndicate,
April, 1938–Feb., 1955**
1 B:Tarzan,Captain and the Kids,
  Little Mary, Mixup,Abbie & Slats,
  Broncho Bill,Li'l Abner 6,500.00
2 Circus Parade of all 2,800.00
3 . . . . 2,000.00
4 On Rocket. 1,500.00
5 All at the Store 1,500.00
6 All at Picnic. 1,000.00
7 Li'l Abner(c). 1,000.00
8 same. 1,000.00
9 same 1,000.00
10 same 1,000.00
11 same 900.00
12 same. 900.00
13 same. 900.00
14 Abbie n' Slats (c). 900.00
15 Li'l Abner(c). 900.00
16 Abbie n' Slats(c). 900.00
17 Tarzan,Abbie n' Slats(c). . . . 1,000.00
18 Li'l Abner(c). 900.00
19 same. 900.00
20 same. 900.00
21 Li'l Abner(c). 750.00
22 Tail Spin Tommy(c) 750.00
23 Abbie n' Slats(c) 750.00
24 Tail Spin Tommy(c) 750.00
25 Li'l Abner(c). 750.00
26 Abbie n' Slats(c) 750.00
27 Li'l Abner(c). 750.00
28 Tail Spin Tommy(c) 750.00
29 Abbie n' Slats(c) 750.00
30 Li'l Abner(c). 500.00
31 The Captain & the Kids(c) . . . 350.00
32 Nancy and Fritzi Ritz(c) 300.00
33 Li'l Abner(c). 400.00
34 The Captain & the Kids(c) . . . 300.00
35 Nancy and Fritzi Ritz(c) 300.00
36 Li'l Abner(c). 400.00
37 The Captain & the Kids(c) . . . 300.00
38 Nancy and Fritzi Ritz(c) 250.00
39 Li'l Abner(c). 400.00
40 The Captain & the Kids(c) . . . 300.00
41 Nancy and Fritzi Ritz(c) 200.00
42 Li'l Abner(c). 400.00
43 The Captain & the Kids(c) . . . 300.00

*Comics on Parade #16
© United Features Syndicate*

44 Nancy and Fritzi Ritz(c) 200.00
45 Li'l Abner(c). 300.00
46 The Captain & the Kids(c) . . . 200.00
47 Nancy and Fritzi Ritz(c) 200.00
48 Li'l Abner(c). 300.00
49 The Captain & the Kids(c) . . . 200.00
50 Nancy and Fritzi Ritz(c) 200.00
51 Li'l Abner(c). 300.00
52 The Captain & the Kids(c) . . . 200.00
53 Nancy and Fritzi Ritz(c) 200.00
54 Li'l Abner(c). 300.00
55 Nancy and Fritzi Ritz(c) 200.00
56 The Captain & the Kids(c) . . . 200.00
57 Nancy and Fritzi Ritz(c) 200.00
58 Li'l Abner(c). 300.00
59 The Captain & the Kids(c) . . . 200.00
60 thru 76 Nancy &
  Fritzi Ritz(c) . . . . @150.00
77 Nancy & Sluggo(c) 125.00
78 thru 104 Nancy & Sluggo(c) @125.00

COMICS REVUE
St. John Publ. Co., 1947
1 Ella Cinders and Blackie 200.00
2 Hap Hopper 125.00
3 Iron Vic. 125.00
4 Eva Cinders 125.00
5 Gordo 125.00

COMMANDER BATTLE
AND THE ATOMIC
SUBMARINE
American Comics Group, 1954
1 3-D(c) 1,100.00
2 . . . . 750.00
3 H-Bomb-3-D type. 800.00
4 . . . . 750.00
5 . . . . 750.00
6 . . . . 750.00
7 . . . . 750.00

COMPLETE BOOK OF
COMICS AND FUNNIES
William H. Wise & Co., 1945
1 Wonderman-Magnet 700.00

COMPLETE BOOK OF
TRUE CRIME COMICS
William H. Wise & Co., 1945
1 rep. Crime Does Not Pay . . . 2,000.00

CONFESSIONS
ILLUSTRATED
E.C. Comics, 1956
1WW,JO,JCr,JKa,Adult romance 400.00
2 JCr,RC,JKa,JO 300.00

CONQUEROR COMICS
**Albrecht Publications,
Winter, 1945**
1 . . . . 300.00

CONQUEST
Famous Funnies, 1955
1 Historical adventure 90.00

CONTACT COMICS
Aviation Press, July, 1944
N# LbC(c),B:Black Venus,
  Golden Eagle. 900.00
2 LbC(c),Peace Jet. 700.00
3 LbC(c),LbC,E:Flamingo 650.00
4 LbC(c),LbC 600.00
5 LbC(c),A:Phantom Flyer 650.00
6 LbC(c),HK 750.00
7 LbC(c),Flying Tigers. 600.00
8 LbC(c),Peace Jet. 600.00
9 LbC(c),LbC,A:Marine Flyers . . 600.00
10 LbC(c),A:Bombers of the AAF 600.00
11 LbC(c),HK,AF,Salutes Naval
  Aviation 700.00
12 LbC(c),A:Sky Rangers, Air Kids,
  May, 1946. . . . . 1,400.00

COO COO COMICS
**Nedor/Animated Cartoons
(Standard), Oct., 1942**
1 O&I:Super Mouse 500.00
2 . . . . 250.00
3 . . . . 200.00
4 . . . . 225.00
5 . . . . 225.00
6 thru 10 . . . . @150.00
11 thru 33 . . . . @150.00
34 thru 40 FF illustration . . . . @250.00
41 FF 400.00
42 FF 350.00
43 FF illustration 250.00
44 FF illustration 250.00
45 FF illustration 250.00
46 FF illustration 250.00
47 FF 350.00
48 FF illustration 250.00
49 FF illustration 250.00
50 FF illustration 250.00
51 thru 61 . . . . @125.00
62 April, 1952. . . . . 100.00

"COOKIE"
**Michel Publ./Regis Publ.
(American Comics Group)
April, 1946**
1 . . . . 350.00
2 . . . . 250.00
3 thru 5 . . . . @200.00
6 thru 20 . . . . @150.00
21 thru 30 . . . . @100.00
31 thru 54. . . . . @100.00
55 Aug., 1955. . . . . 100.00

COSMO CAT
Fox Features Syndicate, 1946
1 . . . . 325.00
2 . . . . 200.00
3 O:Cosmo Cat 225.00
4 thru 10 . . . . @150.00

GOLDEN AGE

COSMO
THE MERRY MARTIAN
Radio Comics/Archie Publ., 1958

1 Funny alien 250.00
2 thru 6 . . . . @200.00

COURAGE COMICS
J. Edward Slavin, 1945

1 . . . . 250.00
2 Boxing (c). 250.00
77 Naval rescue, PT99 (c) 250.00

COWBOY COMICS
See: STAR RANGER

COWBOYS 'N' INJUNS
Compix (M.E. Enterprises), 1946-47

1 Funny Animal Western 300.00
2 thru 5 . . . . @250.00
6 thru 8 See: A-1 Comics, #23,#41,#48

COWBOY WESTERN/ COMICS/HEROES
See: YELLOWJACKET

COW PUNCHER
Avon Periodicals/ Realistic Publ., Jan., 1947

1 JKu 650.00
2 JKu,JKa(c),Bondage (c) 550.00
3 AU(c) 350.00
4 . . . . 350.00
5 . . . . 350.00
6 WJo(c),Drug story 500.00
7 . . . . 350.00
1 JKu 350.00

CRACK COMICS
Comic Magazines (Quality Comics Group) 1940

1 LF,O:Black Condor,Madame
Fatal, Red Torpedo, Rock
Bradden, Space Legion,
B:The Clock,Wizard Wells . 9,000.00
2 Black Condor (c) 3,800.00
3 The Clock (c) 2,800.00
4 Black Condor (c) 2,500.00
5 LF,The Clock (c) 1,700.00
6 PG,Black Condor (c) 1,600.00
7 Clock (c) 1,600.00
8 Black Condor (c) 1,600.00
9 Clock (c) 1,600.00
10 Black Condor (c) 1,600.00
11 LF,PG,Clock (c) 1,400.00
12 LF,PG,Black Condor (c) 1,400.00
13 LF,PG,Clock (c) 1,400.00
14 AMc,LF,PG,Clack Condor(c) 1,400.00
15 AMc,LF,PG,Clock (c) 1,400.00
16 AMc,LF,PG,BlackCondor(c) 1,400.00
17 FGu,AMc,LF,PG,Clock (c) . 1,400.00
18 AMc,LF,PG,Black Condor(c) 1,400.00
19 AMc,LF,PG,Clock (c) 1,400.00
20 AMc,LF,PG,BlackCondor(c) 1,400.00
21 AMc,LF,PG,same 1,200.00
22 LF,PG,same 1,200.00
23 AMc,LF,PG,same 1,200.00
24 AMc,LF,PG,same 1,200.00
25 AMc,same 900.00
26 AMc,same 900.00
27 AMc,I&O:Captain Triumph . . 1,800.00
28 Captain Triumph (c) 1,000.00
29 A:Spade the Ruthless 1,000.00
30 I:Biff 800.00
31 Helps Spade Dig His Own
Grave. 500.00
32 Newspaper (c) 500.00

33 V:Men of Darkness 500.00
34 . . . . 500.00
35 V:The Man Who Conquered
Flame. 500.00
36 Good Neighbor Tour 500.00
37 V:The Tyrant of Toar Valley . . . 500.00
38 Castle of Shadows 500.00
39 V:Crime over the City 500.00
40 Thrilling Murder Mystery . . . 350.00
41 . . . . 350.00
42 All that Glitters is Not Gold . . . 350.00
43 Smashes the Evil Spell of
Silent 350.00
44 V:Silver Tip 350.00
45 V:King-The Jack of all Trades. 350.00
46 V:Mr. Weary 350.00
47 V:Hypnotic Eyes Khor 400.00
48 Murder in the Sky 400.00
49 . . . . 400.00
50 A Key to Trouble 400.00
51 V:Werewolf 400.00
52 V:Porcupine 400.00
53 V:Man Who Robbed the Dead 400.00
54 Shoulders the Troubles
of the World. 400.00
55 Brain against Brawn 400.00
56 Gossip leads to Murder 400.00
57 V:Sitok–Green God of Evil . . . 400.00
58 V:Targets. 300.00
59 A Cargo of Mystery 300.00
60 Trouble is no Picnic 300.00
61 V:Mr. Pointer-Finger of Fear . 300.00
62 V:The Vanishing Vandals 300.00
Becomes:

CRACK WESTERN
Nov., 1949–May, 1951

63 PG, I&O:Two-Gun Lil, B:Frontier
Marshal,Arizona Ames, ... 350.00
64 RC,Arizona AmesV:Two-
Legged Coyote 225.00
65 RC,Ames Tramples on
Trouble 225.00
66 Arizona Ames Arizona Raines,
Tim Holt,Ph(c) 150.00
67 RC, Ph(c),Randolph Scott . . 225.00
68 Ph(c) 150.00
69 RC. 150.00
70 O&I:Whip and Diablo 175.00
71 Bob Allen, Marshall,RC(c). . . 200.00
72 RC,Tim Holt,Ph(c). 150.00
73 Tim Holt,Ph(c). 100.00
74 RC(c). 150.00
75 RC(c). 150.00
76 RC(c),Stage Coach to
Oblivion 150.00
77 RC(c),Comanche Terror 150.00
78 RC(c),Killers of Laurel Ridge . 150.00
79 RC(c),Fires of Revenge 150.00
80 RC(c),Mexican Massacre . . . 150.00
81 RC(c),Secrets of Terror
Canyon 150.00
82 The Killer with a Thousand
Faces. 125.00
83 Rattlesnake Pete's Revenge . 125.00
84 PG(c),Revolt at Broke Creek . 125.00

CRACKAJACK FUNNIES
Dell Publishing Co., 1938

1 AMc,A:Dan Dunn,The Nebbs,
Don Winslow 4,000.00
2 AMc,same. 2,000.00
3 AMc,same. 1,500.00
4 AMc,same. 1,200.00
5 AMc,Naked Women(c) 1,400.00
6 AMc,same. 1,100.00
7 AMc,same. 1,100.00
8 AMc,same. 1,100.00
9 AMc,A:Red Ryder 3,000.00
10 AMc,A:Red Ryder 850.00
11 AMc,A:Red Ryder 750.00
12 AMc,A:Red Ryder 750.00

Crackajack Funnies #9
© Dell Publ. Co.

13 AMc,A:Red Ryder 750.00
14 AMc,A:Red Ryder 750.00
15 AMc,A:Tarzan 850.00
16 AMc. 700.00
17 AMc. 700.00
18 AMc,A:Stratosphere Jim . . . 700.00
19 AMc. 700.00
20 AMc. 700.00
21 AMc. 700.00
22 AMc. 700.00
23 AMc,A:Ellery Queen 700.00
24 AMc. 700.00
25 AMc,I:The Owl 1,500.00
26 AMc 1,000.00
27 AMc 1,000.00
28 AMc,A:The Owl 1,000.00
29 AMc,A:Ellery Queen. 1,000.00
30 AMc,A:Tarzan 1,000.00
31 AMc,A:Tarzan. 1,000.00
32 AMc,O:Owl Girl 1,100.00
33 AMc,A:Tarzan 900.00
34 AMc,same. 900.00
35 AMc,same 900.00
36 AMc,same 900.00
37 AMc. 900.00
38 AMc. 900.00
39 AMc,I:Andy Panada 1,100.00
40 AMc,A:Owl(c) 750.00
41 AMc 750.00
42 AMc. 750.00
43 AMc,Terry & The Pirates,
A:Owl(c). 700.00

CRASH COMICS
Tem Publishing Co., May, 1940

1 S&K,O:Strongman, B:Blue Streak,
Perfect Human, Shangra . . 6,000.00
2 S&K 3,000.00
3 S&K 2,400.00
4 S&K,O&I:Catman 6,000.00
5 S&K, Nov., 1940 . . . . 2,300.00

CRIME AND JUSTICE
Capitol Stories/ Charlton Comics 1951–55

1 . . . . 450.00
2 . . . . 250.00
3 . . . . 200.00
4 . . . . 200.00
5 . . . . 200.00
6 Negligee. 250.00
7 . . . . 200.00
8 . . . . 200.00
9 Comics vs. Crime story 350.00

Crime and Justice #20
© Charlton Comics

```
10 . . . . . . . . . . . . . . . . . . . . . . . 175.00
11 thru 13 Bondage . . . . . . . . @250.00
14 Woman Beheaded . . . . . . . . 300.00
15 Negligee . . . . . . . . . . . . . . . 250.00
16 . . . . . . . . . . . . . . . . . . . . . . . 200.00
17 . . . . . . . . . . . . . . . . . . . . . . . 200.00
18 SD . . . . . . . . . . . . . . . . . . . . 350.00
19 thru 21 . . . . . . . . . . . . @200.00
```
Becomes:

BADGE OF JUSTICE
Charlton Comics, 1955
```
22 (1) . . . . . . . . . . . . . . . . . . . . 200.00
23 (2) . . . . . . . . . . . . . . . . . . . . 150.00
24 (3) . . . . . . . . . . . . . . . . . . . . 150.00
25 (4) . . . . . . . . . . . . . . . . . . . . 150.00
```
Revived as:

CRIME AND JUSTICE
Charlton Comics, 1955
```
23 thru 26 . . . . . . . . . . . . . @150.00
```

CRIME AND PUNISHMENT
Lev Gleason Publications, April, 1948
```
1 CBi(c),Mr.Crime(c) . . . . . . . . . 500.00
2 CBi(c) . . . . . . . . . . . . . . . . . . . 250.00
3 CBi(c),BF . . . . . . . . . . . . . . . . 275.00
4 CBi(c),BF . . . . . . . . . . . . . . . . 200.00
5 CBi(c) . . . . . . . . . . . . . . . . . . . 200.00
6 thru 10 CBi(c) . . . . . . . . . . . @125.00
11 thru 15 CBi(c) . . . . . . . . . . @100.00
16 thru 27 CBi(c) . . . . . . . . . . @100.00
28 thru 38 . . . . . . . . . . . . . . @100.00
39 Drug issue . . . . . . . . . . . . . . 150.00
40 thru 44 . . . . . . . . . . . . . . @100.00
45 Drug issue . . . . . . . . . . . . . . 150.00
46 thru 58 . . . . . . . . . . . . . . @100.00
59 . . . . . . . . . . . . . . . . . . . . . . . 350.00
60 thru 65 . . . . . . . . . . . . . . @100.00
66 ATh . . . . . . . . . . . . . . . . . . . 550.00
67 Drug Storm . . . . . . . . . . . . . 600.00
68 ATh(c) . . . . . . . . . . . . . . . . . 400.00
69 Drug issue . . . . . . . . . . . . . . 150.00
74 Aug., 1955 . . . . . . . . . . . . . . 100.00
```

CRIME CLINIC
Approved Publ. (Ziff-Davis), 1951
```
1 (10) F:Dr. Tom Rogers . . . . . . . 375.00
2 (11) . . . . . . . . . . . . . . . . . . . . 250.00
3 . . . . . . . . . . . . . . . . . . . . . . . . 250.00
4 . . . . . . . . . . . . . . . . . . . . . . . . 250.00
5 . . . . . . . . . . . . . . . . . . . . . . . . 250.00
```

CRIME DETECTOR
Timor Publications, 1954
```
1 . . . . . . . . . . . . . . . . . . . . . . . . 300.00
2 . . . . . . . . . . . . . . . . . . . . . . . . 250.00
3 . . . . . . . . . . . . . . . . . . . . . . . . 200.00
4 . . . . . . . . . . . . . . . . . . . . . . . . 200.00
5 . . . . . . . . . . . . . . . . . . . . . . . . 250.00
```

CRIME DETECTIVE COMICS
Hillman Publications, March–April, 1948
```
1 BF(c),A:Invisible 6 . . . . . . . . 400.00
2 Jewel Robbery (c) . . . . . . . . . 200.00
3 Stolen Cash (c) . . . . . . . . . . . 175.00
4 Crime Boss Murder (c) . . . . . . 175.00
5 BK,Maestro (c) . . . . . . . . . . . 175.00
6 AMc,Gorilla (c) . . . . . . . . . . . 150.00
7 GMc,Wedding (c) . . . . . . . . . 150.00
8 . . . . . . . . . . . . . . . . . . . . . . . . 150.00
9 Safe Robbery (c) (a classic) . . 500.00
10 BP . . . . . . . . . . . . . . . . . . . . 150.00
11 BP . . . . . . . . . . . . . . . . . . . . 150.00
12 BK . . . . . . . . . . . . . . . . . . . . 150.00
2-1 GT,Bluebird Captured . . . . . 200.00
2-2 . . . . . . . . . . . . . . . . . . . . . . 150.00
2-3 . . . . . . . . . . . . . . . . . . . . . . 150.00
2-4 BK . . . . . . . . . . . . . . . . . . . 175.00
2-5 . . . . . . . . . . . . . . . . . . . . . . 150.00
2-6 . . . . . . . . . . . . . . . . . . . . . . 150.00
2-7 BK,GMc . . . . . . . . . . . . . . . 175.00
2-8 . . . . . . . . . . . . . . . . . . . . . . 150.00
2-9 . . . . . . . . . . . . . . . . . . . . . . 150.00
2-10 . . . . . . . . . . . . . . . . . . . . . 150.00
2-11 . . . . . . . . . . . . . . . . . . . . . 150.00
2-12 . . . . . . . . . . . . . . . . . . . . . 150.00
3-1 Drug Story . . . . . . . . . . . . . 150.00
3-2 thru 3-7 . . . . . . . . . . . . @150.00
3-8 May/June, 1953 . . . . . . . . . 100.00
```

CRIME DOES NOT PAY
See: SILVER STREAK COMICS

CRIME-FIGHTING DETECTIVE
See: CRIMINALS ON THE RUN

CRIME FILES
Standard Comics, 1952
```
5 ATh . . . . . . . . . . . . . . . . . . . . 300.00
6 . . . . . . . . . . . . . . . . . . . . . . . . 200.00
```

CRIME ILLUSTRATED
E.C. Comics, Nov.–Dec., 1955
```
1 Grl,RC,GE,JO . . . . . . . . . . . . 350.00
2 Grl,RC,JCr,JDa,JO . . . . . . . . 250.00
```

CRIME INCORPORATED
Fox Features Syndicate, 1950
(Formerly: WESTERN THRILLERS; MY PAST CONFESSIONS)
```
1 (12) Crimes Incorporated . . . . 300.00
2 . . . . . . . . . . . . . . . . . . . . . . . . 225.00
3 . . . . . . . . . . . . . . . . . . . . . . . . 225.00
```

CRIME MUST PAY THE PENALTY
Ace Magazines, 1948–56
```
1 "True cases of actual crimes" . 550.00
2 Violent . . . . . . . . . . . . . . . . . . 350.00
3 . . . . . . . . . . . . . . . . . . . . . . . . 300.00
4 . . . . . . . . . . . . . . . . . . . . . . . . 300.00
5 . . . . . . . . . . . . . . . . . . . . . . . . 200.00
6 . . . . . . . . . . . . . . . . . . . . . . . . 200.00
7 . . . . . . . . . . . . . . . . . . . . . . . . 200.00
8 Transvestite . . . . . . . . . . . . . . 300.00
```

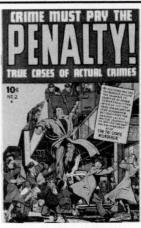

Crime Must Pay the Penalty #2
© Ace Magazines

```
9 . . . . . . . . . . . . . . . . . . . . . . . . 150.00
10 . . . . . . . . . . . . . . . . . . . . . . . 150.00
11 . . . . . . . . . . . . . . . . . . . . . . . 150.00
12 . . . . . . . . . . . . . . . . . . . . . . . 150.00
13 thru 19 . . . . . . . . . . . . . . @150.00
20 GC,Drugs . . . . . . . . . . . . . . 250.00
21 thru 32 . . . . . . . . . . . . . . @150.00
33 Drug story . . . . . . . . . . . . . . 225.00
34 thru 48 . . . . . . . . . . . . . . @150.00
```

CRIME MUST STOP
Hillman Periodicals, Oct., 1952
```
1 BK . . . . . . . . . . . . . . . . . . . 1,100.00
```

CRIME MYSTERIES
Ribage Publishing Corp., May, 1952
```
1 Transvestism,Bondage(c) . . . 1,000.00
2 A:Manhunter, Lance Storm,
    Drug . . . . . . . . . . . . . . . . . . . 750.00
3 FF-one page, A:Dr. Foo . . . . . 500.00
4 HcK,A:Queenie Star,
    BondageStar . . . . . . . . . . . . 850.00
5 Claws of the Green Girl . . . . . 450.00
6 . . . . . . . . . . . . . . . . . . . . . . . . 450.00
7 Sons of Satan . . . . . . . . . . . . 450.00
8 Death Stalks the Crown,
    Bondage(c) . . . . . . . . . . . . . 450.00
9 You are the Murderer . . . . . . . 375.00
10 The Hoax of the Death . . . . . 375.00
11 The Strangler . . . . . . . . . . . . 375.00
12 Bondage(c) . . . . . . . . . . . . . 450.00
13 AT,6 lives for one . . . . . . . . . 500.00
14 Painted in Blood . . . . . . . . . . 375.00
15 Feast of the Dead,Acid Face . 650.00
```
Becomes:

SECRET MYSTERIES
Nov., 1954
```
16 Hiding Place,Horror . . . . . . . . 400.00
17 The Deadly Diamond,Horror . . 300.00
18 Horror . . . . . . . . . . . . . . . . . . 350.00
19 Horror,July, 1955 . . . . . . . . . . 350.00
```

INTERNATIONAL COMICS
E.C. Publ. Co., Spring, 1947
```
1 KS,I:Manhattan's Files . . . . . 1,000.00
2 KS,A: Van Manhattan &
    Madelon . . . . . . . . . . . . . . . 750.00
3 KS,same . . . . . . . . . . . . . . . . 600.00
4 KS,same . . . . . . . . . . . . . . . . 600.00
5 I:International Crime-Busting
    Patrol . . . . . . . . . . . . . . . . . . 600.00
```
Becomes:

INTERNATIONAL CRIME PATROL

Spring, 1948

6 A:Moon Girl & The Prince . . 1,000.00

Becomes:

CRIME PATROL

Summer, 1948

7 SMo,A:Capt. Crime Jr.,Field
 Marshall of Murder 1,200.00
8 JCr,State Prison (c) 1,000.00
9 AF,JCr,Bank Robbery 1,000.00
10 AF,JCr,Wanted:James Dore. 1,000.00
11 AF,JCr. 1,000.00
12 AF,Grl,JCr,Interrogation(c) . . 1,000.00
13 AF,JCr 1,000.00
14 AF,JCr,Smugglers (c) 1,000.00
15 AF,JCr,Crypt of Terror 5,500.00
16 AF,JCr,Crypt of Terror 3,200.00

Becomes:

CRYPT OF TERROR

E.C. Comics, April, 1950

17 JCr(a&c),AF,'Werewolf
 Strikes Again' 5,000.00
18 JCr(a&c),AF,WW,HK
 'The Living Corpse' 3,000.00
19 JCr(a&c),AF,Grl,
 'Voodoo Drums' 2,900.00

Becomes:

TALES FROM THE CRYPT

Oct., 1950

20 JCr(a&c),AF,Gl,JKa
 'Day of Death'. 2,600.00
21 AF(a&c),WW,HK,Gl,'Cooper
 Dies in the Electric Chair . . 2,100.00
22 AF, JCr(c). 1,800.00
23 AF(a&c),JCr,JDa,Grl
 'Locked in a Mausoleum' . . 1,200.00
24 AF(c),WW,JDa,JCr,Grl
 'Danger...Quicksand' 1,200.00
25 AF(c),WW,JDa,JKa,Grl
 'Mataud Waxworks' 1,200.00
26 WW(c),JDa,Grl,
 'Scared Graveyard'. 1,100.00
27 JKa, WW(c), Guillotine (c) . . 1,100.00
28 AF(c),JDa,JKa,Grl,JO
 'Buried Alive'. 1,100.00
29 JDa(a&c),JKa,Grl,JO
 'Coffin Burier' 1,100.00
30 JDa(a&c),JO,JKa,Grl
 'Underwater Death' 1,100.00
31 JDa(a&c),JKa,Grl,AW
 'Hand Chopper' 1,200.00
32 JDa(a&c),GE,Grl,'Woman
 Crushed by Elephant'. 1,200.00
33 JDa(a&c),GE,JKa,Grl,'Lower
 Berth',O:Crypt Keeper 1,200.00
34 JDa(a&c),JKa,GE,Grl,'Jack the
 Ripper,'RayBradbury adapt. 1,200.00
35 JDa(a&c),JKa,JO,Grl,
 'Werewolf' 1,100.00
36 JDa(a&c),JKa,GE,Grl, Ray
 Bradbury adaptation 800.00
37 JDa(c),JO,BE 800.00
38 JDa(c),BE,RC,Grl,'Axe Man' . 800.00
39 JDa(a&c),JKa,JO,Grl,'Children
 in the Graveyard'. 800.00
40 JDa(a&c),GE,BK,Grl,
 'Underwater Monster' 1,200.00
41 JDa(a&c),JKa,GE,Grl,
 'Knife Thrower' 1,200.00
42 JDa(c),JO,Vampire (c) 1,200.00
43 JDa(c),JO,GE. 1,200.00
44 JO,RC,Guillotine (c). 1,100.00
45 JDa(a&c),JKa,BK,Gl,'Rat
 Takes Over His Life' 1,100.00
46 JDa(a&c),GE,JO,Gl,Werewolf
 man being hunted,Feb.'55 . 1,100.00

Crime Reporter #2
© St. John Publishing Co.

CRIME REPORTER

**St. John Publishing Co.,
Aug., 1948**

1 Death Makes a Deadline . . . 1,000.00
2 GT,MB(c),Matinee Murders . 1,100.00
3 GT,MB(c),Dec., 1948 . . . . . . 900.00

CRIMES BY WOMEN

**Fox Features Syndicate,
June, 1948**

1 Bonnie Parker 2,000.00
2 Vicious Female 1,300.00
3 Prison Break (c) 1,200.00
4 Murder (c) 1,200.00
5 . . . . 1,200.00
6 Girl Fight (c) 1,200.00
7 . . . . 900.00
8 . . . . 900.00
9 . . . . 900.00
10 Girl Fight (c) 800.00
11 . . . . 800.00
12 . . . . 800.00
13 ACME Jewelry Robbery (c) . . 800.00
14 Prison break (c) 800.00
15 Aug., 1951. . . . . 800.00

CRIME SMASHER

**Fawcett Publications,
Summer, 1948**

1 The Unlucky Rabbit's Foot . . . 750.00

CRIME SMASHERS

**Ribage Publishing Corp.,
Oct., 1950**

1 Girl Rape. 1,400.00
2 JKu,A:Sally the Sleuth, Dan
 Turner, Girl Friday, Rat Hale . 750.00
3 MFa 550.00
4 Zak(c) 550.00
5 WW 900.00
6 . . . . 450.00
7 Bondage (c),Drugs. 550.00
8 . . . . 450.00
9 Bondage (c). 550.00
10 . . . . 450.00
11 . . . . 450.00
12 FF, Eye Injury 550.00
13 . . . . 550.00
14 & 15. . . . . @450.00

CRIME ON THE WATERFRONT

See: FAMOUS GANGSTERS

CRIME SUSPENSTORIES

**L.L. Publishing Co.
(E.C. Comics), Oct.–Nov., 1950**

1a JCr,Grl 2,700.00
1 JCr,WW,Grl 2,000.00
2 JCr,JKa,Grl 1,500.00
3 JCr,WW,Grl,Poe Story 800.00
4 JCr,Gln,Grl,JDa 800.00
5 JCr,JKa,Grl,JDa. 800.00
6 JCr,JDa,Grl 600.00
7 JCr,Grl 600.00
8 JCr,Grl 600.00
9 JCr,Grl 600.00
10 JCr,Grl. 500.00
11 JCr,Grl. 500.00
12 JCr,Grl. 500.00
13 JCr,AW 550.00
14 JCr 500.00
15 JCr,Old Witch 500.00
16 JCr,AW 600.00
17 JCr,FF,AW, Ray Bradbury. . . 900.00
18 JCr,RC,BE. 550.00
19 JCr,RC,GE,AF(c) 550.00
20 RC,JCr, Hanging (c) 600.00
21 JCr 500.00
22 RC,JO,JCr(c),
 Severed head (c). 600.00
23 JKa,RC,GE 550.00
24 BK,RC,JO 500.00
25 JKa,(c),RC 600.00
26 JKa,(c),RC,JO. 700.00
27 JKa,(c),GE,Grl,March, 1955 . . 500.00

CRIMINALS ON THE RUN

**Premium Group of Comics,
Aug., 1948**

4-1 LbC(c) 500.00
4-2 LbC(c), A:Young King Cole . 400.00
4-3 LbC(c), Rip Roaring Action
 in Alps 400.00
4-4 LbC(c), Shark (c) 400.00
4-5 AMc 400.00
4-6 LbC,Dr. Doom 400.00
4-7 LbC 900.00
5-1 LbC 350.00
5-2 LbC 350.00
10 LbC 350.00

Becomes:

CRIME-FIGHTING DETECTIVE

April–May, 1950

11 LbC, Brodie Gang Captured . . 350.00
12 LbC(c), Jail Break Genius . . . 300.00
13 . . . . 250.00
14 LbC(c), A Night of Horror . . . 300.00
15 LbC(c). 300.00
16 LbC(c), Wanton Murder 300.00
17 LbC(c), The Framer
 was Framed. 300.00
18 LbC(c), A Web of Evil 300.00
19 LbC(c), Lesson of the Law . . . 300.00

Becomes:

SHOCK DETECTIVE CASES

**Star Publications,
Sept., 1952**

20 LbC(c), The Strangler 400.00
21 LbC(c), Death Ride. 400.00

Becomes:

SPOOK DETECTIVE CASES

**Star Publications,
Jan., 1953**

22 Headless Horror 500.00

Becomes:

GOLDEN AGE

SPOOK SUSPENSE AND MYSTERY

23 LbC,Weird Picture of Murder . 350.00
24 LbC(c),Mummy's Case 400.00
25 LbC(c),Horror Beyond Door . . 350.00
26 LbC(c),JyD,Face of Death 350.00
27 LbC(c),JyD,Ship of the Dead 350.00
28 LbC(c),JyD,Creeping Death . . 350.00
29 LbC(c),Solo for Death 350.00
30 LbC(c),JyD,Nightmare,
     Oct.,1954 . . . . 350.00

Crown Comics #1
© *Golfing*

CROWN COMICS

**Golfing/McCombs Publ.,
Winter 1944**

1 Edgar Allen Poe adapt. 700.00
2 MB,I:Mickey Magic 500.00
3 MB,Jungle adventure (c) 500.00
4 MB(c),A:Voodah. 550.00
5 MB(c),Jungle Adventure (c) . . 550.00
6 MB(c),Jungle Adventure (c) . . 550.00
7 JKa,AF,MB(c),Race Car (c) . . 550.00
8 MB 500.00
9 . . . . 300.00
10 Plane crash (c),A:Voodah. . . . 300.00
11 LSt,A:Voodah 250.00
12 LSt,AF,Master Marvin 250.00
13 LSt,AF,A:Voodah. 250.00
14 A:Voodah. 275.00
15 FBe,A:Voodah 250.00
16 FBe,A:Voodah,Jungle
     Adventure(c) 250.00
17 FBe,A:Voodah. 250.00
18 FBe,A:Voodah. 250.00
19 BP,A:Voodah,July, 1949 . . . . 250.00

CRUSADER FROM MARS

**Approved Publ.
(Ziff-Davis), Jan.–March, 1952**

1 Mission Thru Space, Death in
     the Sai 1,300.00
2 Beachhead on Saturn's Ring,
     Bondage(c),Fall, 1952 . . . . 1,000.00

CRYIN' LION, THE

**William H. Wise Co.,
Fall, 1944**

1 Funny Animal. 300.00
2 A. Hitler 200.00
3 Spring, 1945 . . . . 150.00

CRYPT OF TERROR
See: CRIME PATROL

CURLY KAYOE COMICS

**United Features
Syndicate, 1946–50**

1 Boxing 300.00
2 . . . . 250.00
3 thru 8 . . . . @200.00
1a United Presents . . . . . (1948) . . 200.00

CYCLONE COMICS

Bibara Publ. Co., June, 1940

1 O:Tornado Tom 2,800.00
2 . . . . 1,800.00
3 . . . . 2,000.00
4 Voltron. 1,200.00
5 A:Mr. Q,Oct., 1940 . . . . 1,600.00

DAFFY

**Dell Publishing Co.,
March, 1953**

(1) *see Dell Four Color #457*
(2) *see Dell Four Color #536*
(3) *see Dell Four Color #615*
4 thru 7 . . . . @125.00
8 thru 11 . . . . @75.00
12 thru 17 . . . . @60.00
Becomes:

DAFFY DUCK
July, 1959

18 . . . . 60.00
19 . . . . 60.00
20 . . . . 60.00
21 thru 30 . . . . @60.00

DAFFY TUNES COMICS

Four Star Publications, 1947

12 Funny Animal 125.00

ALL GREAT COMICS

**Fox Features Syndicate,
Oct., 1947**

12 A:Brenda Starr 1,200.00
13 JKa,O:Dagar, Desert Hawk . 1,300.00
Becomes:

DAGAR, DESERT HAWK
Feb., 1948

14 JKa,Monster of Mura 1,500.00
15 JKa,Curse of the Lost
     Pharaoh,Bondage 900.00
16 JKa,Wretched Antmen 800.00
19 Pyramid of Doom 700.00
20 . . . . 700.00
21 JKa(c),The Ghost of Fate,
     Bondage (c). 750.00
22 . . . . 700.00
23 Bondage (c) 750.00
Becomes:

CAPTAIN KIDD
June, 1949

24 Blackbeard the Pirate 250.00
25 Sorceress of the Deep 250.00
Becomes:

MY SECRET STORY
Oct., 1949

26 He Wanted More Than Love. . 250.00
27 My Husband Hated Me 200.00
28 I Become a Marked Women . . 200.00
29 My Forbidden Rapture,
     April, 1950 . . . . 200.00

DAGWOOD

Harvey Publications, 1950

1 . . . . 300.00
2 . . . . 200.00
3 . . . . 175.00
4 . . . . 175.00
5 . . . . 175.00

6 thru 10 . . . . @175.00
11 thru 20 . . . . @150.00
21 thru 30 . . . . @125.00
31 thru 50 . . . . @100.00
51 thru 70 . . . . @100.00
71 thru 109 . . . . @75.00
110 thru 140 . . . . @75.00

DAISY AND HER PUPS

**Harvey Publications,
1951–1954**

1 (21) F:Blondie & Dagwood's
     dog. 75.00
2 (22) 60.00
3 (23) 60.00
4 (24) 60.00
5 (25) 60.00
6 (26) 60.00
7 (27) 60.00
8 thru 18 . . . . @50.00

DAISY COMICS

**Eastern Color
Printing Co., 1936**

N# 750.00

DAISY HANDBOOK

Daisy Manufacturing Co., 1946

1 Buck Rogers, Red Ryder. 475.00
2 Capt. Marvel 475.00
N# (1955) 400.00

DANDY COMICS

E.C. Comics 1947–48

1 Funny Animal. 475.00
2 . . . . 325.00
3 thru 7 . . . . @250.00

DANGER

Comic Media, 1953–54

1 DH(c&a) 300.00
2 PMo 150.00
3 PMo 150.00
4 Marijuana (c) & story 200.00
5 PMo 150.00
6 Drug 175.00
7 . . . . 150.00
8 Torture (c) 225.00
9 thru 11 . . . . 150.00

Charlton Comics, 1955

12 . . . . 150.00
13 . . . . 125.00
14 . . . . 125.00
Becomes:

JIM BOWIE

15 . . . . 100.00
16 . . . . 100.00
17 . . . . 100.00
18 . . . . 100.00
19 April, 1957. . . . . 100.00

DANGER AND ADVENTURE
See: THIS MAGAZINE IS HAUNTED

DANGER IS OUR BUSINESS

**Toby Press/
I.W. Enterprises, 1953**

1 AW,FF,Men Who Defy Death
     for a Living. 750.00
2 Death Crowds the Cockpit . . . 300.00
3 Killer Mountain 250.00
4 . . . . 250.00
5 thru 9 . . . . @200.00
10 June, 1955 . . . . 250.00

GOLDEN AGE

DAN'L BOONE
Sussex Publ. Co. 1955–57
1 F:Dan'l Boone Greatest
  Frontiersman 200.00
2 . . . . 150.00
3 . . . . 100.00
4 thru 8 . . . . @100.00

DANNY BLAZE
Charlton Comics, 1955
1 . . . . 150.00
2 . . . . 125.00
Becomes:

NATURE BOY
3 JB,O:Blue Beetle 300.00
4 . . . . 125.00
5 Feb., 1957 . . . . 100.00

DAREDEVIL COMICS
**Lev Gleason Publications,
July, 1941**
1 Daredevil Battles Hitler, A:Silver
  Streak, Lance Hale, Dickey Dean,
  Cloud Curtis,V:The Claw,
  O:Hitler 25,000.00
2 I:The Pioneer, Champion of
  American,B:London,Pat
  Patriot,Pirate Prince 5,500.00
3 CBi(c),O:Thirteen 3,500.00
4 CBi(c),Death is the Referee . 3,000.00
5 CBi(c),I:Sniffer&Jinx, Claw
  V:Ghost,Lottery of Doom . . 2,700.00
6 CBi(c) 1,800.00
7 CBi(c), What Ghastly Sight Lies
  within the Mysterious Trunk 1,600.00
8 V:Nazis (c), E:Nightro 1,500.00
9 V:Double 1,500.00
10 America will Remember
  Pearl Harbor 1,500.00
11 Bondage (c), E:Pat
  Patriot, London 1,800.00
12 BW,CBi(c), O:The Law 2,200.00
13 BW,I:Little Wise Guys 1,700.00
14 BW,CBi(c) 1,200.00
15 BW,CBi(c), D:Meatball 1,400.00
16 BW,CBi(c) 1,100.00
17 BW,CBi(c), Into the Valley
  of Death 1,100.00
18 BW,CBi(c), O:Daredevil,
  double length story 2,000.00
19 BW,CBi(c), Buried Alive 900.00
20 BW,CBi(c), Boxing (c) 900.00
21 CBi(c), Can Little Wise Guys
  Survive Blast of Dynamite? 1,500.00
22 CBi(c) 750.00
23 CBi(c), I:Pshyco 750.00
24 CBi(c), Punch and Judy
  Murders 750.00
25 CBi(c), Baseball (c) 750.00
26 CBi(c) 700.00
27 CBi(c), Bondage (c) 750.00
28 CBi(c) 700.00
29 CBi(c) 700.00
30 CBi(c), Ann Hubbard White
  1922-1943 . . . . 700.00
31 CBi(c), D:The Claw 1,400.00
32 V:Blackmarketeers 500.00
33 CBi(c) 500.00
34 CBi(c) 500.00
35 B:Two Daredevil stories
  every issue 550.00
36 CBi(c) 550.00
37 CBi(c) 550.00
38 CBi(c), O:Daredevil 800.00
39 CBi(c) 500.00
40 CBi(c) 500.00
41 . . . . 500.00
42 thru 50 CBi(c) . . . . @500.00
51 CBi(c) 350.00
52 CBi(c),Football (c) 400.00

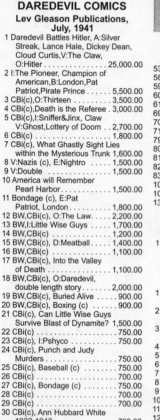

Daredevil #27
© *Lev Gleason Publications*

53 thru 57 . . . . @350.00
58 Football (c) 400.00
59 . . . . 350.00
60 . . . . 350.00
61 thru 68 . . . . @350.00
69 E:Daredevil 350.00
70 . . . . 250.00
71 thru 78 . . . . @150.00
79 B:Daredevil 250.00
80 . . . . 275.00
81 . . . . 150.00
82 . . . . 150.00
83 thru 99 . . . . @150.00
100 . . . . 175.00
101 thru 133 . . . . @150.00
134 Sept., 1956 . . . . 150.00

DARING LOVE
Gilmore Magazines, 1953
1 SD,1st work 900.00

DARK MYSTERIES
**Merit Publications,
June–July, 1951**
1 WW(a&c), Curse of the
  Sea Witch 1,800.00
2 WW(a&c), Vampire Fangs
  of Doom 1,200.00
3 Terror of the Unwilling
  Witch 800.00
4 Corpse that Came Alive 800.00
5 Horror of the Ghostly Crew . . . 650.00
6 If the Noose Fits Wear It! 650.00
7 Terror of the Cards of Death . . 650.00
8 Terror of the Ghostly Trail 650.00
9 Witch's Feast at Dawn 650.00
10 Terror of the Burning Witch . . . 650.00
11 The River of Blood 600.00
12 Horror of the Talking Dead . . . 600.00
13 Terror of the Hungry Cats 600.00
14 Horror of the Fingers of Doom 650.00
15 Terror of the Vampires Teeth . . 550.00
16 Horror of the Walking Dead . . 550.00
17 Terror of the Mask of Death . . 550.00
18 Terror of the Burning Corpse . 550.00
19 The Rack of Terror 750.00
20 Burning Executioner 650.00
21 The Sinister Secret 500.00
22 The Hand of Destiny 500.00
23 The Mardenburg Curse 350.00
24 Give A Man Enough Rope,
  July, 1955 . . . . 350.00

DARK SHADOWS
**Steinway Publications/Ajax
1957–58**
1 . . . . 350.00
2 and 3 . . . . @300.00

DATE WITH DANGER
**Visual Editions
(Standard Comics), 1952**
5 Secret Agent 150.00
6 Atom Bomb 175.00

DAVY CROCKETT
Avon Periodicals, 1951
1 . . . . 250.00

FRONTIER FIGHTER
Charlton Comics, 1955
1 JK,Davy Crocket-Buffalo Bill . . 150.00
2 JK 100.00
Becomes:

DAVY CROCKETT
Charlton Comics, 1956
3 thru 7 JK . . . . @100.00
8 Jan., 1957 JK 90.00
Becomes:

KID MONTANA

DEAD END
CRIME STORIES
**Kirby Publishing Co.,
April, 1949**
N# BP 750.00

DEAD-EYE
WESTERN COMICS
**Hillman Periodicals
Nov.–Dec., 1948**
1 BK 300.00
2 . . . . 250.00
3 . . . . 200.00
4 thru 12 . . . . @150.00
2-1 . . . . 125.00
2-2 . . . . 125.00
2-3 . . . . 150.00
2-4 . . . . 150.00
2-5 thru 2-12 . . . . @125.00
3-1 . . . . 125.00

DEADWOOD GULCH
Dell Publishing Co., 1931
1 . . . . 750.00

DEAR BEATRICE
FAIRFAX
**Best Books
(Standard Comics), Nov., 1950**
5 AsH(c) 200.00
6 thru 9 AsH(c) . . . . @125.00

DEATH VALLEY
**Comic Media/
Charlton Comics, 1953**
1 Cowboys & Indians 200.00
2 DH(c) 150.00
3 PMo 125.00
4 . . . . 125.00
5 PMo 125.00
6 . . . . 125.00
7 . . . . 125.00
8 BW 125.00
9 . . . . 125.00
Becomes:

All comics prices listed are for *Near Mint* condition.

FRONTIER SCOUT DANIEL BOONE
Charlton Comics
10 . . . . 150.00
11 thru 13 . . . . @100.00

DEBBIE DEAN, CAREER GIRL
Civil Service Publishing, April, 1945
1 . . . . 300.00
2 . . . . 250.00

Dell Giant Editions Moses and the Ten Commandments © Dell Publishing Co.

DELL GIANT EDITIONS
Dell Publishing Co., 1952-58
Abe Lincoln Life Story 175.00
Cadet Gray of West Point 175.00
Golden West Rodeo Treasury . . . 200.00
Life Stories of
  American Presidents 165.00
Lone Ranger Golden West 400.00
Lone Ranger Movie Story 850.00
Lone Ranger Western
  Treasury('53) 400.00
Lone Ranger Western
  Treasury('54) 500.00
Moses & Ten Commandments. . . 150.00
Nancy & Sluggo Travel Time 200.00
Pogo Parade 700.00
Raggedy Ann & Andy. 350.00
Santa Claus Funnies 200.00
Tarzan's Jungle Annual #1. . . . . . 350.00
Tarzan's Jungle Annual #2. . . . . . 225.00
Tarzan's Jungle Annual #3. . . . . 200.00
Tarzan's Jungle Annual #4. . . . . . 200.00
Tarzan's Jungle Annual #5. . . . . . 200.00
Tarzan's Jungle Annual #6. . . . . . 200.00
Tarzan's Jungle Annual #7. . . . . . 200.00
Treasury of Dogs 160.00
Treasury of Horses 160.00
Universal Presents-Dracula-
  The Mummy & Other Stories. 500.00
Western Roundup #1. . . . . 600.00
Western Roundup #2. . . . . 350.00
Western Roundup #3. . . . . 275.00
Western Roundup #4 thru #5 . . @250.00
Western Roundup #6 thru #10. @250.00
Western Roundup #11 thru #17 @225.00
Western Roundup #18. . . . . 225.00
Western Roundup #19 thru #25 @180.00

Woody Woodpecker Back
  to School #1 (1952). 250.00
Woody Woodpecker Back
  to School #2 (1953). 225.00
Woody Woodpecker Back
  to School #3 (1954). 225.00
Woody Woodpecker Back
  to School #4 (1955). 225.00
Woody Woodpecker County
  Fair #5 (1956) 225.00
Woody Woodpecker Back
  to School #6 (1957). 200.00
Woody Woodpecker County
  Fair #2 (1958) 200.00
Also See: Bugs Bunny; Marge's Little Lulu; Tom and Jerry, and Walt Disney Dell Giant Editions

DELL GIANT COMICS
Dell Publishing Co., Sept., 1959
21 M.G.M. Tom & Jerry
  Picnic Time 250.00
22 W.Disney's Huey, Dewey & Louie
  Back to School (Oct 1959) . . 500.00
23 Marge's Little Lulu &
  Tubby Halloween Fun 375.00
24 Woody Woodpeckers
  Family Fun. 275.00
25 Tarzan's Jungle World. 250.00
26 W.Disney's Christmas
  Parade,CB. 550.00
27 W.Disney's Man in
  Space (1960). 250.00
28 Bugs Bunny's Winter Fun . . . 250.00
29 Marge's Little Lulu &
  Tubby in Hawaii. 325.00
30 W.Disney's DisneylandU.S.A.. 300.00
31 Huckleberry Hound
  Summer Fun 300.00
32 Bugs Bunny Beach Party . . . 250.00
33 W.Disney's Daisy Duck &
  Uncle Scrooge Picnic Time . . 300.00
34 Nancy&SluggoSummerCamp. 200.00
35 W.Disney's Huey, Dewey &
  Louie Back to School 350.00
36 Marge's Little Lulu & Witch
  Hazel Halloween Fun 300.00
37 Tarzan, King of the Jungle . . . 250.00
38 W.Disney's Uncle Donald and
  his Nephews Family Fun . . . 350.00
39 W.Disney's Merry Christmas. . 350.00
40 Woody Woodpecker
  Christmas Parade 200.00
41 Yogi Bear's Winter Sports . . . 300.00
42 Marge's Little Lulu &
  Tubby in Australia 375.00
43 Mighty Mouse in OuterSpace . 550.00
44 Around the World with
  Huckleberry & His Friends . . 400.00
45 Nancy&SluggoSummerCamp. 150.00
46 Bugs Bunny Beach Party . . . 175.00
47 W.Disney's Mickey and
  Donald in Vacationland 250.00
48 The Flintstones #1
  (Bedrock Bedlam) 500.00
49 W.Disney's Huey, Dewey &
  Louie Back to School 325.00
50 Marge's Little Lulu &
  Witch Hazel Trick 'N' Treat . . 325.00
51 Tarzan, King of the Jungle . . . 200.00
52 W.Disney's Uncle Donald &
  his Nephews Dude Ranch . . 350.00
53 W.Disney's Donald Duck
  Merry Christmas 300.00
54 Woody Woodpecker
  Christmas Party. 225.00
55 W.Disney's Daisy Duck & Uncle
  Scrooge Show Boat (1961). . 250.00

DELL JUNIOR TREASURY
Dell Publishing Co., June, 1955
1 Alice in Wonderland. 175.00
2 Aladdin. 125.00
3 Gulliver's Travels 100.00
4 Adventures of Mr. Frog 125.00
5 Wizard of Oz 125.00
6 Heidi. 135.00
7 Santa & the Angel 135.00
8 Raggedy Ann. 135.00
9 Clementina the Flying Pig 125.00
10 Adventures of Tom Sawyer. . . 125.00

DENNIS THE MENACE
Visual Editions/Literary Ent. (Standard, Pines), Aug., 1953
1 . . . . 1,200.00
2 . . . . 500.00
3 . . . . 300.00
4 . . . . 300.00
5 thru 10 . . . . @200.00
11 thru 20. . . . . @175.00
21 thru 31. . . . . @150.00

Hallden (Fawcett Publications)
32 thru 40. . . . . @100.00
41 thru 50. . . . . @100.00
51 thru 60. . . . . @75.00
61 thru 70. . . . . @75.00
71 thru 90. . . . . @75.00
91 thru 140. . . . . @40.00
141 thru 166. . . . . @25.00

DESPERADO
Lev Gleason Publications, June, 1948
1 CBi(c) 275.00
2 CBi(c) 150.00
3 CBi(c) 200.00
4 CBi(c) 100.00
5 CBi(c) 100.00
6 CBi(c) 100.00
7 CBi(c) 100.00
8 CBi(c) 100.00
Becomes:

BLACK DIAMOND WESTERN
March, 1949
9 CBi(c) 300.00
10 CBi(c) 200.00
11 CBi(c) 150.00
12 CBi(c) 150.00

Black Diamond Western #15 © Lev Gleason Publications

All comics prices listed are for *Near Mint* condition.

13 CBi(c) 150.00
14 CBi(c) 150.00
15 CBi(c) 150.00
16 thru 28 BW,Big Bang Buster @150.00
29 thru 40 . . . . @175.00
41 thru 50 . . . . @125.00
51 thru 52 3-D Luse . . . . @250.00
53 thru 60 . . . . @100.00

Detective Dan Secret OP, 48
© Humor Publ. Co.

DETECTIVE DAN, SECRET OP, 48

Humor Publ. Co., 1933
N# 10"x13", 36 pg. b&w 25,000.00

DETECTIVE EYE

Centaur Publications, Nov., 1940
1 B:Air Man, The Eye Sees,
   A:Masked Marvel 3,500.00
2 O:Don Rance, Mysticape,
   Dec., 1940 . . . . 2,500.00

DETECTIVE PICTURE STORIES

Comics Magazine Co., Dec., 1936
1 The Phantom Killer 6,500.00
2 The Clock 3,000.00
3 . . . . 2,200.00
4 WE, Muss Em Up 2,200.00
5 Trouble, April, 1937 . . . . . . 2,400.00

DEVIL DOGS

Street & Smith Publ., 1942
1 U.S. Marines 500.00

DEXTER COMICS

Dearfield Publications, Summer, 1948–July, 1949
1 Teen Age 200.00
2 Sunie Prom 150.00
3 thru 5 . . . . @100.00

DICK COLE

Curtis Publ./ Star Publications, Dec.–Jan., 1949
1 LbC(a&c),CS,All sports(c) 425.00
2 LbC 250.00
3 LbC(a&c) 275.00
4 LbC(a&c),Rowing (c) 275.00

5 LbC(a&c) 275.00
6 LbC(a&c), Rodeo (c) 275.00
7 LbC(a&c) 250.00
8 LbC(a&c), Football (c) 250.00
9 LbC(a&c), Basketball (c) 250.00
10 Joe Louis 300.00
Becomes:

SPORTS THRILLS

Nov., 1950–Nov., 1951
11 Ted Williams & Ty Cobb 450.00
12 LbC, Joe DiMaggio & Phil
   Rizzuto, Boxing (c) 400.00
13 LbC(c),Basketball (c) 350.00
14 LbC(c),Baseball (c) 375.00
15 LbC(c),Baseball (c) 375.00

DICKIE DARE

Eastern Color Printing Co., 1941–42
1 BEv(c),M.Caniff 1,200.00
2 . . . . 500.00
3 . . . . 500.00
4 H. Scorcery Smith 550.00

DICK TRACY MONTHLY

Dell Publishing Co., Jan., 1948
1 ChG,AAv,Dick Tracy & the Mad
   Doctor' 800.00
2 ChG,A:MarySteele,BorisArson 450.00
3 ChG,A:Spaldoni,Big Boy 450.00
4 ChG,A:Alderman Zeld 450.00
5 ChG,A:Spaldoni,Mrs.Spaldoni . 375.00
6 ChG,A:Steve the Tramp 375.00
7 ChG,A:Boris Arson,Mary
   Steele 375.00
8 ChG,A:Boris & Zora Arson . . . 375.00
9 ChG,A:Chief Yellowpony 375.00
10 ChG,A:Cutie Diamond. 375.00
11 ChG,A:Toby Townly,
   Bookie Joe. 325.00
12 ChG,A:Toby Townly,
   Bookie Joe. 325.00
13 ChG,A:Toby Townly, Blake . . 350.00
14 ChG,A:Mayor Waite Wright. . 300.00
15 ChG,A:Bowman Basil 300.00
16 ChG,A:Maw,'Muscle'
   & 'Cut' Famon 300.00
17 ChG,A:Jim Trailer,
   Mary Steele 300.00
18 ChG,A:Lips Manlis,
   Anthel Jones 300.00
19 I:Sparkle Plenty. 350.00
20 'Black Cat Mystery' 300.00
21 'Tracy Meets Number One'. . . 300.00
22 'Tracy and the Alibi Maker' . . 275.00
23 'Dick Tracy Meets Jukebox' . . 275.00
24 'Dick Tracy and Bubbles' 275.00
Becomes:

DICK TRACY COMICS MONTHLY

Harvey, May, 1950
25 ChG,A:Flattop 300.00
26 ChG,A:Vitamin Flintheart. 200.00
27 ChG,'Flattop Escapes Prision' 200.00
28 ChG,'Case of the Torture
   Chamber'. 200.00
29 ChG,A:Brow,Gravel Gertie . . . 250.00
30 ChG,'Blackmail Racket'. 200.00
31 ChG,A:Snowflake Falls 175.00
32 ChG,A:Shaky,Snowflake Falls 175.00
33 ChG,'Strange Case
   of Measles' 225.00
34 ChG,A:Measles,Paprika 200.00
35 ChG,'Case of Stolen $50,000'. 200.00
36 ChG,'Case of the
   Runaway Blonde' 225.00
37 ChG,'Case of Stolen Money'. . 200.00

38 ChG,A:Breathless Mahoney . . 200.00
39 ChG,A:Itchy,B.O.Plenty. 200.00
40 ChG,'Case of Atomic Killer'. . . 200.00
41 ChG,Pt.1'Murder by Mail' 175.00
42 ChG,Pt.2'Murder by Mail' 175.00
43 ChG,'Case of the
   Underworld Brat' 175.00
44 ChG,'Case of the Mouthwash
   Murder' 175.00
45 ChG,'Case of the Evil Eyes' . . 175.00
46 ChG,'Case of the
   Camera Killers' 175.00
47 ChG,'Case of the
   Bloodthirsty Blonde'. 175.00
48 ChG,'Case of the
   Murderous Minstrel' 175.00
49 ChG,Pt.1 'Killer Who Returned
   From the Dead 175.00
50 ChG,Pt.2 'Killer Who
   Returned From the Dead' . . . 175.00
51 ChG, 'Case of the
   High Tension Hijackers'. 150.00
52 ChG, 'Case of the
   Pipe-Stem Killer. 150.00
53 ChG,Pt.1 'Dick Tracy Meets
   the Murderous Midget'. 150.00
54 ChG,Pt.2 'Dick Tracy Meets
   the Murderous Midget'. 150.00
55 ChG,Pt.3 'Dick Tracy Meets
   the Murderous Midget'. 150.00
56 ChG,'Case of the
   Teleguard Terror' 150.00
57 ChG,Pt.1 'Case of the
   Ice Cold Killer' 175.00
58 ChG,Pt.2 'Case of the
   Ice Cold Killer' 150.00
59 ChG,Pt.1 'Case of the
   Million Dollar Murder' 150.00
60 ChG,Pt.2 'Case of the
   Million Dollar Murder' 150.00
61 ChG,'Case of the
   Murderers Mask' 150.00
62 ChG,Pt.1 'Case of the
   White Rat Robbers'. 150.00
63 ChG,Pt.2 'Case of the
   White Rat Robbers'. 150.00
64 ChG,Pt.1 'Case of the
   Interrupted Honeymoon' 150.00
65 ChG,Pt.2 'Case of the
   Interrupted Honeymoon' 150.00
66 ChG,Pt.1 'Case of the
   Killer's Revenge' 150.00
67 ChG,Pt.2 'Case of the
   Killer's Revenge' 150.00
68 ChG,Pt.1'Case o/t TV Terror' . 150.00

Dick Tracy Comics Monthly #61
© Harvey Comics

69 ChG,Pt.2'Case o/t TV Terror' . 150.00
70 ChG,Pt.3'Case o/t TV Terror' . 135.00
71 ChG,A:Mrs. Forchune,Opal. . . 135.00
72 ChG,A:Empty Wiliams,Bonny . 135.00
73 ChG,A:Bonny Braids 135.00
74 ChG,A:Mr. & Mrs.
    Fortson Knox 135.00
75 ChG,A:Crewy Lou, Sphinx . . . 135.00
76 ChG,A:Diet Smith,Brainerd . . . 135.00
77 ChG,A:Crewy Lou,
    Bonny Braids 135.00
78 ChG,A:Spinner Records 135.00
79 ChG,A:Model Jones,
    Larry Jones 135.00
80 ChG,A:Tonsils,Dot View 135.00
81 ChG,A:Edward Moppet,Tonsils 135.00
82 ChG,A:Dot View,Mr. Crime . . . 135.00
83 ChG,A:RifleRuby,NewsuitNan. 135.00
84 ChG,A:Mr.Crime,NewsuitNan . 135.00
85 ChG,A:NewsuitNan, Mrs.Lava 135.00
86 ChG,A:Mr. Crime,Odds Zonn . 135.00
87 ChG,A:Odds Zonn,Wingy 135.00
88 ChG,A:Odds Zonn,Wingy 135.00
89 ChG,Pt.1'Canhead' 135.00
90 ChG,Pt.2'Canhead' 135.00
91 ChG,Pt.3'Canhead' 135.00
92 ChG,Pt.4'Canhead' 135.00
93 ChG,Pt.5'Canhead' 135.00
94 ChG,Pt.6'Canhead' 135.00
95 ChG,A:Mrs. Green,Dewdrop . . 135.00
96 ChG,A:Dewdrop,Sticks 135.00
97 ChG,A:Dewdrop,Sticks 135.00
98 ChG,A:Open-Mind Monty,
    Sticks 135.00
99 ChG,A:Open-Mind Monty,
    Sticks 150.00
100 ChG,A:Half-Pint,Dewdrop . . . 175.00
101 ChG,A:Open-Mind Monty . . . 150.00
102 ChG,A:Rainbow Reiley,
    Wingy 150.00
103 ChG,A:Happy,Rughead 150.00
104 ChG,A:Rainbow Reiley,
    Happy 150.00
105 ChG,A:Happy,Rughead 150.00
106 ChG,A:Fence,Corny,Happy . . 150.00
107 ChG,A:Rainbow Reiley 150.00
108 ChG,A:Rughead,Corny,
    Fence. 150.00
109 ChG,A:Rughead,Mimi,Herky . 150.00
110 ChG,A:Vitamin Flintheart. . . . 150.00
111 ChG,A:Shoulders,Roach 150.00
112 ChG,A:Brilliant,Diet Smith . . . 150.00
113 ChG,A:Snowflake Falls 150.00
114 ChG,A:'Sketch'Paree, ... 150.00
115 ChG,A:Rod & Nylon Hoze. . . 150.00
116 ChG,A:Empty Williams 150.00
117 ChG,A:Spinner Records 150.00
118 ChG,A:Sleet. 150.00
119 ChG,A:Coffyhead 150.00
120 ChG,'Case Against
    Mumbles Quartet' 150.00
121 ChG,'Case of the Wild Boys'. 150.00
122 ChG,'Case of the
    Poisoned Pellet'. 150.00
123 ChG,'Case of the Deadly
    Treasure Hunt'. 150.00
124 ChG,'Case of Oodles
    Hears Only Evil'. 150.00
125 ChG,'Case of the Desparate
    Widow' 150.00
126 ChG,'Case of Oodles'
    Hideout' 150.00
127 ChG,'Case Against
    Joe Period' 150.00
128 ChG,'Case Against Juvenile
    Delinquent'. 150.00
129 ChG,'Case of Son of Flattop' 150.00
130 ChG,'Case of Great
    Gang Roundup' 150.00
131 ChG,'Strange Case of
    Flattop's Conscience' 150.00

132 ChG,'Case of Flattop's
    Big Show' 150.00
133 ChG,'Dick Tracy Follows Trail
    of Jewel Thief Gang' 150.00
134 ChG,'Last Stand of
    Jewel Thieves'. 150.00
135 ChG,'Case of the
    Rooftop Sniper' 150.00
136 ChG,'Mystery of the
    Iron Room'. 150.00
137 ChG,'Law Versus Dick Tracy' 150.00
138 ChG,'Mystery of Mary X' 150.00
139 ChG,'Yogee the Merciless' . . 150.00
140 ChG,'The Tunnel Trap' 150.00
141 ChG,'Case of Wormy &
    His Deadly Wagon' 150.00
142 ChG,'Case of the
    Killer's Revenge' 150.00
143 ChG,'Strange Case of
    Measles' 150.00
144 ChG,'Strange Case of
    Shoulders' 150.00
145 ChG,'Case of the Fiendish
    Photographers'; April, 1961. . 150.00

DICK WINGATE
OF THE U.S. NAVY
**Superior Publ./
Toby Press, 1951**
N# 200.00
N# reprint 150.00

DIME COMICS
Newsbook Publ. Corp., 1945
1 LbC,A:Silver Streak 1,200.00

DING DONG
**Compix
(Magazine Enterprises), 1947**
1 (fa) 300.00
2 (fa) 150.00
3 thru 5 (fa) . . . . @100.00

DINKY DUCK
**St. John Publ. Co./Pines,
Nov., 1951**
1 . . . . 150.00
2 . . . . 125.00
3 thru 10 . . . . @100.00
11 thru 15 . . . . @100.00
16 thru 18 . . . . @75.00
19 Summer, 1958 . . . . 75.00

DIXIE DUGAN
**Columbia Publ./
Publication Enterprises,
July, 1942**
1 Boxing (c),Joe Palooka 500.00
2 . . . . 250.00
3 . . . . 175.00
4 . . . . 150.00
5 . . . . @150.00
6 thru 12 . . . . @100.00
13 1949 . . . . 100.00

DIZZY DON COMICS
**Howard Publications/
Dizzy Dean Ent., 1943**
1 B&W interior. 300.00
2 B&W interior 150.00
3 B&W Interior 125.00
4 B&W Interior 125.00
5 thru 21 . . . . @125.00
22 Oct., 1946 . . . . 275.00
1a thru 3a . . . . @300.00

DOC CARTER
V.D. COMICS
Health Publ. Inst., 1949
N# 350.00
N# 250.00

*Doc Savage Vol. 2 #4
© Street & Smith Publications*

DOC SAVAGE COMICS
Street & Smith Publ., May, 1940
1 B:Doc Savage, Capt. Fury, Danny
    Garrett, Mark Mallory, Whisperer,
    Capt. Death, Treasure
    Island, A: The Magician . . . 9,000.00
2 O:Ajax,The Sun Man,E:The
    Whisperer 3,000.00
3 Artic Ice Wastes 1,900.00
4 E:Treasure Island, Saves
    U.S. Navy 1,600.00
5 O:Astron, the Crocodile
    Queen, Sacred Ruby 1,500.00
6 E: Capt. Fury, O:Red Falcon,
    Murderous Peace Clan . . 1,000.00
7 V:Zoombas 1,000.00
8 Finds the Long Lost Treasure 1,000.00
9 Smashes Japan's Secret Oil
    Supply. 1,000.00
10 O:Thunder Bolt, The Living
    Dead A:Lord Manhattan . . . 1,000.00
11 V:Giants of Destruction 800.00
12 Saves Merchant Fleet from
    Complete Destruction 800.00
2-1 The Living Evil 800.00
2-2 V:Beggar King 800.00
2-3 . . . . 800.00
2-4 Fight to Death 800.00
2-5 Saves Panama Canal from
    Blood Raider 800.00
2-6 . . . . 800.00
2-7 V:Black Knight 800.00
2-8 Oct., 1943 . . . . 800.00

DR. ANTHONY KING
HOLLYWOOD LOVE
DOCTOR
Harvey, Publ., 1952
1 . . . . 250.00
2 . . . . 200.00
3 . . . . 200.00
4 BP,May, 1954 . . . . 200.00

GOLDEN AGE

DO-DO

Nationwide Publishers, 1950
1 Funny Animal Circus Humor . . 300.00
2 . . . . 150.00
3 . . . . 150.00
4 . . . . 150.00
5 thru 7 . . . . @150.00

Doll Man #11
© Quality Comics Group

DOLL MAN

**Comic Favorites
(Quality Comics Group),
Fall, 1941–Oct., 1953**
1 RC,B:Doll Man & Justine
  Wright 6,000.00
2 B:Dragon 2,200.00
3 Five stories 1,400.00
4 Dolls of Death, Wanted:
  The Doll Man 1,300.00
5 RC,Four stories 1,200.00
6 Buy War Stamps (c) 900.00
7 Four stories 900.00
8 BWa,Three stories,A:Torchy . 2,500.00
9 Torchy 900.00
10 RC,V:Murder Marionettes,
  Grim, The Good Sport 750.00
11 Shocks Crime Square in the
  Eye 750.00
12 Torchy 750.00
13 RC,Blows Crime Sky High . . . 750.00
14 Spotlight on Comics 750.00
15 Faces Danger 750.00
16 Torchy 550.00
17 Deals Out Punishment for
  Crime. 550.00
18 Redskins Scalp Crime 550.00
19 Fitted for a Cement Coffin . . 550.00
20 Destroys the Black Heart of
  Nemo Black 550.00
21 Problem of a Poison Pistol . . 500.00
22 V:Tom Thumb 500.00
23 V:Minstrel, Musician
  of Menace 500.00
24 V:Elixir of Youth. 500.00
25 V:Thrawn, Lord of Lightning . . 500.00
26 V:Sultan of Satarr &
  Wonderous Runt 500.00
27 Space Conquest 500.00
28 V:The Flame 500.00
29 V:Queen MAB 500.00
30 V:Lord Damion 500.00
31 I:Elmo, the Wonder Dog 450.00
32 A:Jeb Rivers 450.00
33 & 34. . . . . @450.00
35 Prophet of Doom. 450.00

36 Death Trap in the Deep 450.00
37 V:The Skull,B:Doll Girl,
  Bondage(c) 700.00
38 The Cult of Death 400.00
39 V:The Death Drug, Narcotics . 400.00
40 Giants of Crime 400.00
41 The Headless Horseman 300.00
42 Tale of the Mind Monster . . . 300.00
43 The Thing that Kills. 300.00
44 V:Radioactive Man 300.00
45 What was in the Doom Box? . 300.00
46 Monster from Tomorrow 300.00
47 V:Mad Hypnotist 300.00

FAMOUS GANG, BOOK OF COMICS

**Firestone Tire & Rubber Co.,
1942**
N# Porky Pig,Bugs Bunny 1,200.00
Becomes:

DONALD AND MICKEY MERRY CHRISTMAS

N# (2),CB, 1943. . . . . 1,200.00
N# (3),CB, 1944. . . . . 1,100.00
N# (4),CB, 1945. . . . . 1,700.00
N# (5),CB, 1946. . . . . 1,200.00
N# (6),CB, 1947. . . . . 1,200.00
N# (7),CB, 1948. . . . . 1,200.00
N# (8),CB, 1949. . . . . 1,100.00

DONALD DUCK

Whitman
W.Disney's Donald Duck ('35) . 6,000.00
W.Disney's Donald Duck ('36) . 5,000.00
W.Disney's Donald Duck ('38) . 5,000.00

DONALD DUCK GIVEAWAYS

Donald Duck Surprise Party (Icy
  Frost Ice Cream 1948)WK . 4,000.00
Donald Duck (Xmas Giveaway
  1944) 1,500.00
Donald Duck Tells About Kites
  (P.G.&E., Florida 1954). . . . 4,000.00
Donald Duck Tells About Kites
  (S.C.Edison 1954) 3,500.00
Donald Duck and the Boys
  (Whitman 1948) 1,200.00
Donald Ducks Atom Bomb
  (Cherrios 1947) 1,200.00

(WALT DISNEY'S) DONALD DUCK

**Dell Publishing Co.,
Nov., 1952**
(#1-#25) See Dell Four Color
26 CB;"Trick or Treat" (1952). . . . 800.00
27 CB(c);"Flying Horse"('53) 300.00
28 CB(c); Robert the Robot. 250.00
29 CB(c). 250.00
30 CB(c). 250.00
31 thru 39 . . . . @200.00
40 . . . . 150.00
41 . . . . 150.00
42 . . . . 150.00
43 . . . . 150.00
44 . . . . 150.00
45 CB. 400.00
46 CB; "Secret of Hondorica" 500.00
47 thru 51 . . . . @200.00
52 CB; "Lost Peg-Leg Mine" 400.00
53 . . . . 200.00
54 CB; "Forbidden Valley" 500.00
55 thru 59 . . . . @150.00
60 CB; "Donald Duck & the
  Titanic Ants". 400.00
61 thru 67 . . . . @150.00
68 CB. 225.00

69 thru 78. . . . . @150.00
79 CB (1 page) 200.00
80 . . . . 125.00
81 CB (1 page) 150.00
82 . . . . 125.00
83 . . . . 125.00
84 . . . . 125.00

DON FORTUNE MAGAZINE

**Don Fortune Publ. Co.,
Aug., 1946**
1 CCB 400.00
2 CCB 225.00
3 CCB,Bondage(c) 200.00
4 CCB 150.00
5 CCB 150.00
6 CCB, Jan., 1947 . . . . 150.00

DON NEWCOMBE

Fawcett Publications, 1950
1 Baseball Star 650.00

DON WINSLOW OF THE NAVY

**Fawcett Publ./
Charlton Comics, Feb., 1943**
1 Captain Marvel (c) 2,000.00
2 Nips the Nipponese in
  the Solomons 850.00
3 Single-Handed invasion of
  the Philippines 600.00
4 Undermines the Nazis! 500.00
5 Stolen Battleship Mystery 500.00
6 War Stamps for Victory,Flag(c) 500.00
7 Coast Guard 400.00
8 U.S. Marines 400.00
9 Fighting Marines 400.00
10 Fighting Seabees 400.00
11 . . . . 350.00
12 Tuned for Death 350.00
13 Hirohito's Hospitality 350.00
14 Catapults against the Axis . . . 350.00
15 Fighting Merchant Marine. . . . 300.00
16 V:The Most Diabolical Villain
  of all Time 300.00
17 Buy War Stamps (c) 300.00
18 The First Underwater Convoy. 300.00
19 Bonape Excersion. 300.00
20 The Nazi Prison Ship 300.00
21 Prisoner of the Nazis 225.00
22 Suicide Football 225.00
23 Peril on the High Seas 225.00
24 Adventures on the High Seas. 225.00
25 Shanghaied Red Cross Ship . 225.00
26 V:The Scorpion 225.00
27 Buy War Stamps 225.00
28 . . . . 225.00
29 Invitation to Trouble 225.00
30 . . . . 225.00
31 Man or Myth? 175.00
32 Return of the Renegade 175.00
33 Service Ribbons 175.00
34 Log Book. 175.00
35 . . . . 175.00
36 V:Octopus 175.00
37 V: Sea Serpent 175.00
38 Climbs Mt. Everest 175.00
39 Scorpion's Death Ledger 175.00
40 Kick Off! 175.00
41 Rides the Skis! 150.00
42 Amazon Island 150.00
43 Ghastly Doll Murder Case . . . 150.00
44 The Scorpions Web 150.00
45 V:Highwaymen of the Seas . . 150.00
46 Renegades Jailbreak 150.00
47 The Artic Expedition 150.00
48 Maelstrom of the Deep 150.00
49 The Vanishing Ship! 150.00
50 V:The Snake 150.00

GOLDEN AGE

Don Winslow of the Navy #36
© Fawcewtt Publications

51 A:Singapore Sal 150.00
52 Ghost of the Fishing Ships . . . 150.00
53 . . . . 150.00
54 . . . . 150.00
55 . . . . 150.00
56 Far East 150.00
57 A:Singapore Sal 150.00
58 thru 63 . . . . @150.00
64 MB. 150.00
65 Ph(c),Flying Saucer 250.00
66 Ph(c) 225.00
67 Ph(c) 225.00
68 Ph(c) 225.00
69 Ph(c), Jaws of Destruction . . . 225.00
70 . . . . 125.00
71 . . . . 125.00
72 . . . . 125.00
73 Sept., 1955 . . . . 125.00

DOROTHY LAMOUR
See: JUNGLE LIL

DOUBLE COMICS
Elliot Publications
1 ('40),Masked Marvel 4,000.00
2 ('41),Tornado Tim 3,000.00
3 ('42) 2,500.00
4 ('43) 2,000.00
5 ('44) 2,000.00

DOUBLE TALK
Feature Publications
1 Anti-communist 150.00

DOUBLE TROUBLE
St. John Publishing Co., 1957
1 Funny kids 100.00

DOUBLE UP
Elliot Publications, 1941
1 . . . . 1,600.00

DOWN WITH CRIME
**Fawcett Publications,
Nov., 1951**
1 A:Desarro 650.00
2 BP, A:Scanlon Gang 300.00
3 H-is for Heroin 300.00
4 BP, A:Desarro 275.00
5 No Jail Can Hold Me 275.00
6 The Puncture-Proof Assassin . 275.00
7 The Payoff, Nov., 1952 . . . . . . 275.00

DO YOU BELIEVE IN NIGHTMARES
St. John Publ. Co., 1957
1 SD 800.00
2 DAy 500.00

DUDLEY
**Prize Publications,
Nov.–Dec., 1952**
1 . . . . 175.00
2 . . . . 125.00
3 March–April, 1950 . . . . 100.00

DUMBO WEEKLY
The Walt Disney Co., 1942
1 Gas giveaways 1,500.00
2 thru 16 . . . . @600.00

DURANGO KID
**Magazine Enterprises,
Oct.–Nov., 1949**
1 FF, Charles Starrett photo (c)
  B:Durango Kid & Raider . . 1,200.00
2 FF, Charles Starrett Ph(c) 600.00
3 FF, Charles Starrett Ph(c) 500.00
4 FF, Charles Starrett Ph(c),
  Two-Timing Guns 450.00
5 FF, Charles Starrett Ph(c),
  Tracks Across the Trail 450.00
6 FF 300.00
7 FF,Atomic(c) 350.00
8 FF 300.00
9 FF 300.00
10 FF 300.00
11 FF 250.00
12 FF 250.00
13 FF 250.00
14 thru 16 FF . . . . @250.00
17 O:Durango Kid 300.00
18 FMe,DAy(c) 200.00
19 FMe,FGu 175.00
20 FMe,FGu 175.00
21 FMe,FGu 175.00
22 FMe,FGu 200.00
23 FMe,FGu,I:Red Scorpion 200.00
24 thru 30 FMe,FGu . . . . @200.00
31 FMe,FGu 200.00
32 thru 40 FGu . . . . @150.00
41 FGu,Oct., 1941 . . . . 150.00

DYNAMIC COMICS
**Dynamic Publications
(Harry 'A' Chesler),
Oct., 1941**
1 EK,O:Major Victory, Dynamic Man,
  Hale the Magician, A:Black
  Cobra 3,500.00
2 O:Dynamic Boy & Lady
  Satan,I:Green Knight,
  Lance Cooper 2,000.00
3 GT 1,800.00
8 Horror (c) 2,000.00
9 MRa,GT,B:Mr.E 2,000.00
10 . . . . 1,000.00
11 GT 900.00
12 GT 800.00
13 GT 900.00
14 . . . . 800.00
15 Sky Chief 800.00
16 GT,Bondage(c),Marijuana. . . . 900.00
17 . . . . 1,000.00
18 Ric. 700.00
19 A:Dynamic Man. 700.00
20 same,Nude Woman 1,500.00
21 same,Dinosaur(c) 700.00
22 same 700.00
23 A:Yankee Girl,1.0948 . . . . 700.00

DYNAMITE
**Comic Media/Allen Hardy Publ.,
May, 1953**
1 DH(c),A:Danger#6 . . . . 400.00
2 . . . . 200.00
3 PMo(a&c),B:Johnny
  Dynamite,Drug. 300.00
4 PMo(a&c),Prostitution 350.00
5 PMo(a&c) 200.00
6 PMo(a&c). 200.00
7 PMo(a&c),Prostitution 250.00
8 PMo(a&c) 200.00
9 PMo(a&c) 200.00
Becomes:

JOHNNY DYNAMITE
Charlton Comics, June, 1955
10 PMo(c) 150.00
11 . . . . 125.00
12 . . . . 125.00
Becomes:

FOREIGN INTRIGUES
1956
13 A:Johnny Dynamite. 150.00
14 same. 125.00
15 same. 125.00
Becomes:

BATTLEFIELD ACTION
Nov., 1957
16 . . . . 150.00
17 . . . . 100.00
18 . . . . 100.00
19 . . . . 100.00
20 . . . . 100.00
21 thru 30 . . . . @100.00

EAGLE, THE
**Fox Features Syndicate,
July, 1941**
1 B:The Eagle,A:Rex Dexter
  of Mars 3,500.00
2 B:Spider Queen 1,500.00
3 B:Joe Spook 1,200.00
4 Jan., 1942 . . . . 1,200.00

EAGLE
**Rural Home Publ.,
Feb.–March, 1945**
1 LbC 800.00
2 LbC,April–May, 1945 . . . . 500.00

EAT RIGHT TO WORK AND WIN
Swift Co., 1942
N# Flash Gordon,Popeye 750.00

EDDIE STANKY
Fawcett Publications, 1951
N# New York Giants 450.00

EERIE
**Avon Periodicals,
May–June, 1951–
Aug.–Sept., 1954**
1 JKa,Horror from the Pit,
  Bondage(c), 1947 . . . . 7,200.00
1a reprint, 1951 . . . . 1,200.00
2,WW(a&c), Chamber of Death 1,200.00
3 WW(a&c),JKa,JO
  Monster of the Storm 1,300.00
4 WW(c),Phantom of Reality . 1,200.00
5 WW(c), Operation Horror 900.00
6 Devil Keeps a Date 450.00
7 WW(c),JKa,JO,Blood for
  the Vampire 700.00
8 EK, Song of the Undead 400.00
9 JKa, Hands of Death 450.00

GOLDEN AGE

Eerie #17
© Avon Periodicals

10 EK,Castle of Terror 400.00
11 Anatomical Monster 400.00
12 Dracula 500.00
13 . . . . 400.00
14 Master of the Dead 400.00
15 Reprint #1 . . . . 300.00
16 WW, Chamber of Death 300.00
17 WW(c),JO,JKa, ... 350.00

EERIE ADVENTURES

**Approved Comics
(Ziff-Davis), Winter, 1951**
1 BP,JKa,Bondage 600.00

EGBERT

**Arnold Publications/
Comic Magazine, Spring, 1946**
1 I:Egbert & The Count 350.00
2 . . . . 250.00
3 . . . . 200.00
4 . . . . 200.00
5 . . . . 200.00
6 . . . . 250.00
7 thru 10 . . . . @200.00
11 thru 17 . . . . @150.00
18 1950 . . . . 150.00

EH!

**Charlton Comics,
Dec., 1953–Nov., 1954**
1 DAy(c),DG,Atomic Mouse 500.00
2 DAy(c) 300.00
3 DAy(c) 250.00
4 DAy(c),Sexual 275.00
5 DAy(c) 250.00
6 DAy(c),Sexual 275.00
7 DAy(c) 250.00

EL BOMBO COMICS

Frances M. McQueeny, 1945
1 . . . . 175.00

ELLA CINDERS

St. John Publishing Co. 1948
1 . . . . 200.00
2 . . . . 150.00
3 . . . . 100.00
4 . . . . 100.00
5 . . . . 100.00

ELLERY QUEEN

**Superior Comics,
May–Nov., 1949**
1 LbC(c),JKa,Horror 800.00
2 . . . . 550.00
3 Drug issue 650.00
4 The Crooked Mile 550.00

ELLERY QUEEN

**Approved Comics
(Ziff-Davis),
Jan.–March, 1952**
1 NS(c),The Corpse the Killed . . 650.00
2 NS,Killer's Revenge,
  Summer, 1952 . . . . 500.00

ELSIE THE COW

**D.S. Publishing Co.,
Oct.–Nov., 1949**
1 P(c) 450.00
2 Bondage(c) 300.00
3 July–Aug., 1950 . . . . 200.00

ENCHANTING LOVE

**Kirby Publishing Co.
Oct., 1949**
1 Branded Guilty, Ph(c) 200.00
2 Ph(c),BP 100.00
3 Ph(c),Utter Defeat was Our
  Victory; Jimmy Stewart 150.00
4 . . . . 100.00
5 Ph(c) GRi 200.00
6 . . . . 100.00

ERNIE COMICS

See: SCREAM COMICS

ESCAPE FROM FEAR

**Planned Parenthood
of America, 1956**
1 . . . . 150.00
2 (1962) 100.00

ETTA KETT

**Best Books, Inc.
(Standard Comics),
Dec., 1948**
11 . . . . 150.00
12 . . . . 100.00
13 . . . . 100.00
14 Sept., 1949 . . . . 100.00

EXCITING COMICS

**Better Publ./Visual Editions
(Standard Comics),
April, 1940**
1 O:Mask, Jim Hatfield,
  Dan Williams 7,000.00
2 B:Sphinx 3,500.00
3 V:Robot 2,500.00
4 V:Sea Monster 2,000.00
5 V:Gargoyle 2,000.00
6 . . . . 2,000.00
7 AS(c) 1,500.00
8 . . . . 1,500.00
9 O:Black Terror & Tim,
  Bondage(c) 17,000.00
10 A:Black Terror 5,000.00
11 same 2,800.00
12 Bondage(c) 2,200.00
13 Bondage(c) 2,200.00
14 O:Sphinx 2,000.00
15 O:Liberator 2,100.00
16 Black Terror 1,900.00
17 same 1,900.00
18 same 1,900.00
19 same 1,900.00
20 E:Mask,Bondage(c) 1,500.00

Exciting Comics #33
© Standard Comics

21 A:Liberator 1,500.00
22 O:The Eaglet,B:American
  Eagle 1,500.00
23 Black Terror 1,000.00
24 Black Terror 1,000.00
25 Bondage(c) 1,000.00
26 ASh(c) 1,000.00
27 ASh(c) 1,000.00
28 ASh(c),B:Crime Crusader . . 1,100.00
29 ASh(c) 1,000.00
30 ASh(c),Bondage(c). 1,100.00
31 ASh(c) 1,200.00
32 ASh(c) 1,200.00
33 ASh(c) 1,200.00
34 ASh(c) 1,200.00
35 ASh(c),E:Liberator 1,200.00
36 ASh(c) 1,200.00
37 ASh(c) 1,200.00
38 ASh(c) 1,200.00
39 ASh(c)O:Kara, Jungle
  Princess 1,800.00
40 ASh(c) 1,500.00
41 ASh(c) 1,500.00
42 ASh(c),B:Scarab 1,500.00
43 ASh(c) 1,000.00
44 ASh(c) 1,000.00
45 ASh(c),V:Robot 1,000.00
46 ASh(c) 1,000.00
47 ASh(c) 1,000.00
48 ASh(c) 1,000.00
49 ASh(c),E:Kara &
  American Eagle 1,000.00
50 ASh(c),E:American Eagle . . 1,000.00
51 ASh(c),B:Miss Masque 1,200.00
52 ASh(c),Miss Masque. 900.00
53 ASh(c),Miss Masque. 900.00
54 ASh(c),E:Miss Masque 900.00
55 ASh(c),O&B:Judy o/t Jungle . . 900.00
56 ASh(c). 900.00
57 ASh(c). 900.00
58 ASh(c). 900.00
59 ASh(c),FF,Bondage(c) 1,000.00
60 ASh(c),The Mystery Rider . . . 800.00
61 ASh(c). 800.00
62 ASh(c),CQ. 800.00
63 ASh(c). 800.00
64 ASh(c). 800.00
65 ASh(c),CQ. 800.00
66 . . . . 800.00
67 GT 800.00
68 . . . . 800.00
69 Sept., 1949 . . . . 800.00

EXCITING ROMANCES
Fawcett Publications, 1949
1 Ph(c)	200.00
2 Ph(c)	150.00
3 WW,Ph(c).	150.00
4 Ph(c)	150.00
5 thru 7	@100.00
8 thru 10 BP	@120.00
11 thru 12	@100.00

EXCITING WAR
**Visual Editions
(Standard Comics), 1952**
5 Korean war	150.00
6	100.00
7	100.00
8 ATh.	125.00

EXPLOITS OF DANIEL BOONE
**Comic Magazines
(Quality Comics Group), 1955**
1 Frontier hero	350.00
2	225.00
3 thru 6	@175.00

Explorer Joe #1
© Ziff-Davis

EXPLORER JOE
**Approved Comics
(Ziff-Davis), Winter, 1951**
1 NS,The Fire Opal of Madagascar	150.00
2 BK, Oct.–Nov., 1952	165.00

EXPOSED
**D.S. Publishing Co.,
March–April, 1948**
1 Corpses Cash and Carry	300.00
2 Giggling Killer	350.00
3 One Bloody Night	150.00
4 JO,Deadly Dummy	150.00
5 Body on the Beach	150.00
6 Fatal Masquerade	450.00
7 The Midnight Guest	450.00
8 Grl,The Secret in the Snow	450.00
9 The Gypsy Baron, July–Aug., 1949	450.00

EXTRA COMICS
Magazine Enterprises, 1947
1	900.00

EXTRA!
**E.C. Comics,
March–April, 1955**
1 JCr,RC,JSe	400.00
2 JCr,RC,JSe	300.00
3 JCr,RC,JSe	300.00
4 JCr,RC,JSe	300.00
5 Nov.–Dec., 1955	300.00

FACE, THE
**Publication Enterprises
(Columbia Comics), 1942**
1 MBi(c),The Face	1,700.00
2 MBi(c)	1,200.00
Becomes:

TONY TRENT
1948
3 MBi,A:The Face	350.00
4 1949	300.00

FAIRY TALE PARADE
Dell Publishing Co., 1942
1 WK,Giant	2,500.00
2 WK,Flying Horse	1,500.00
3 WK	1,000.00
4 WK	800.00
5 WK	800.00
6 WK	500.00
7 WK	500.00
8 WK	500.00
9 WK,Reluctant Dragon	500.00

FAIRY TALES
**Approved Comics
(Ziff-Davis), 1951**
10	300.00
11	250.00

FAMILY FUNNIES
Harvey Publications, 1950
1 Mandrake	200.00
2 Flash Gordon	150.00
3	125.00
4 Flash Gordon	125.00
5 Flash Gordon	125.00
6	125.00
7 Flash Gordon	125.00
8	125.00
Becomes:

TINY TOT FUNNIES
Harvey Publications, 1951
9 Dagwood (c),Flash Gordon	150.00
Becomes:

JUNIOR FUNNIES
Harvey Publications, 1951–52
10 Blondie, Popeye	100.00
11	100.00
12	100.00
13	100.00

FAMOUS COMICS
Whitman Publ. Co., 1934
1 3"x8", three per box	1,200.00
2	1,000.00
3	1,000.00

FAMOUS COMICS
Zain-Eppy Publ.
N# Joe Palooka	600.00

FAMOUS CRIMES
**Fox Features Syndicate,
June, 1948**
1 Cold Blooded Killer	700.00
2 Near Nudity (c)	550.00

3 Crime Never Pays	650.00
4	300.00
5	300.00
6	300.00
7 Drug issue	550.00
8 thru 19	@300.00
20 Aug., 1951	250.00
51 1952	180.00

FAMOUS FAIRY TALES
K.K. Publication Co., 1942
N# WK, Giveaway	600.00
N# WK, Giveaway	400.00
N# WK, Giveaway	400.00

FAMOUS FEATURE STORIES
Dell Publishing Co., 1938
1A:Tarzan, Terry and the Pirates Dick Tracy,Smilin' Jack	2,500.00

FAMOUS FUNNIES
**Eastern Color Printing Co.,
1933**
N# A Carnival of Comics	60,000.00
N# Feb., 1934, 1st 10-cent comic	50,000.00
1 July, 1934	35,000.00
2	15,000.00
3 B:Buck Rogers	12,000.00
4 Football (c)	5,000.00
5 Christmas	4,500.00
6	3,000.00
7	3,000.00
8	3,000.00
9	3,000.00
10	3,000.00
11 Four pages of Buck Rogers	1,500.00
12 Four pages of Buck Rogers	1,500.00
13	1,200.00
14	1,200.00
15 Football (c).	1,200.00
16	1,200.00
17 Christmas (c)	1,200.00
18 Four pages of Buck Rogers	1,500.00
19	1,200.00
20	1,200.00
21 Baseball	1,000.00
22 Buck Rogers	1,100.00
23	1,100.00
24 B: War on Crime	1,100.00
25	1,100.00
26	1,100.00
27 G-Men (c).	1,100.00

Famous Funnies #17
© Eastern Color Printing

---

28 . . . . 1,100.00
29 Christmas. 1,100.00
30 . . . . 1,100.00
31 . . . . 700.00
32 Phantom Magician 1,000.00
33 A:Baby Face Nelson &
   John Dillinger. 700.00
34 . . . . 700.00
35 Buck Rogers 800.00
36 . . . . 700.00
37 . . . . 700.00
38 Portrait,Buck Rogers. 800.00
39 . . . . 700.00
40 . . . . 700.00
41 thru 50. . . . . @600.00
51 thru 57. . . . . @500.00
58 Baseball (c). 500.00
59 . . . . 500.00
60 . . . . 500.00
61 . . . . 400.00
62 . . . . 400.00
63 . . . . 400.00
64 . . . . 400.00
65 JK 400.00
66 . . . . 400.00
67 . . . . 400.00
68 JK 400.00
69 . . . . 400.00
70 . . . . 400.00
71 BEv. 300.00
72 BEv,B:Speed Spaulding 300.00
73 BEv. 300.00
74 BEv. 300.00
75 BEv. 300.00
76 BEv. 300.00
77 BEv,Merry Christmas (c). 300.00
78 BEv. 300.00
79 BEv. 300.00
80 BEv,Buck Rogers 300.00
81 O:Invisible Scarlet O'Neil 325.00
82 Buck Rogers (c) 300.00
83 Dickie Dare 250.00
84 Scotty Smith 250.00
85 Eagle Scout,Roy Rogers 250.00
86 Moon Monsters 250.00
87 Scarlet O'Neil 250.00
88 Dickie Dare 250.00
89 O:Fearless Flint 250.00
90 Bondage (c) 350.00
91 . . . . 250.00
92 . . . . 250.00
93 . . . . 250.00
94 War Bonds 275.00
95 Invisible Scarlet O'Neil 200.00
96 . . . . 200.00
97 War Bonds Promo 200.00
98 . . . . 200.00
99 . . . . 200.00
100 Anniversary issue 200.00
101 thru 110 . . . . @200.00
111 thru 130 . . . . @125.00
131 thru 150. . . . . @100.00
151 thru 162. . . . . @100.00
163 Valentine's Day (c) 100.00
164 . . . . 100.00
165 . . . . 100.00
166 . . . . 100.00
167 . . . . 100.00
168 . . . . 100.00
169 AW 135.00
170 AW 135.00
171 thru 190. . . . . @150.00
191 thru 203. . . . . @135.00
204 War (c) 100.00
205 . . . . 100.00
206 . . . . 100.00
207 . . . . 100.00
208 . . . . 100.00
209 FF(c),Buck Rogers 2,500.00
210 FF(c),Buck Rogers. 2,500.00
211 FF(c),Buck Rogers. 2,500.00
212 FF(c),Buck Rogers. 2,500.00

Famous Funnies #212
© Easter Color Printing

213 FF(c),Buck Rogers. 2,500.00
214 FF(c),Buck Rogers. 2,500.00
215 FF(c),Buck Rogers. 2,500.00
216 FF(c),Buck Rogers. 2,500.00
217 . . . . 100.00
218 July, 1955 . . . . 100.00

FAMOUS GANGSTERS
Avon Periodicals, 1951
1 Al Capone, Dillinger,
  Luciano & Shultz 550.00
2 WW(c),Dillinger Machine-
  Gun Killer. 500.00
3 Lucky Luciano & Murder Inc. . . 500.00
Becomes:

CRIME ON
THE WATERFRONT
May, 1952
4 Underworld Gangsters who
  Control the Shipment of
  Drugs! 450.00

FAMOUS STARS
Ziff-Davis Publ. Co., 1950
1 OW,Shelley Winter,Susan
  Peters & Shirley Temple 800.00
2 BEv,Betty Hutton, Bing Crosby 600.00
3 OW,Judy Garland, Alan Ladd . 700.00
4 RC,Jolson, Bob Mitchum 600.00
5 BK,Elizabeth Taylor,
  Esther Williams 800.00
6 Gene Kelly, Spring, 1952 . . . 600.00

FAMOUS STORIES
Dell Publishing Co., 1942
1 Treasure Island 400.00
2 Tom Sawyer 375.00

FAMOUS WESTERN
BADMEN
See: REDSKIN

FANTASTIC
See: CAPTAIN SCIENCE

FANTASTIC COMICS
Fox Features Syndicate, 1939
1 LF(c),I&O:Samson, B:Star
  Dust, Super Wizard, Space
  Smith & Capt. Kid 9,000.00

2 BP,LF(c),Samson Destroyed the
  Battery & Routed the Foe. . 4,500.00
3 BP,LF(c),Slays the Iron
  Monster. 12,000.00
4 GT,LF(c),Demolishes the
  Closing Torture Walls 3,000.00
5 GT,LF(c),Crumbles the
  Mighty War Machine. 2,700.00
6 JSm(c),Bondage(c) 2,500.00
7 JSm(c) 2,500.00
8 GT,Destroys the Mask of
  Fire,Bondage(c) 1,600.00
9 Mighty Muscles saved the
  Drowning Girl 1,600.00
10 I&O:David. 1,600.00
11 Wrecks the Torture Machine
  to save his fellow American 1,500.00
12 Heaved the Huge Ship high
  into the Air 1,500.00
13 Samson(c) 1,500.00
14 Samson(c) 1,500.00
15 Samson(c) 1,500.00
16 E:Stardust 1,500.00
17 Samson(c) 1,500.00
18 I:Black Fury & Chuck. 1,500.00
19 Samson(c) 1,300.00
20 Samson(c) 1,300.00
21 B&I: The Banshee,Hitler(c) . 1,600.00
22 Hittler & Samson(c) 1,500.00
23 O:The Gladiator, Hitler (c)
  Nov., 1941 . . . . 1,800.00

FANTASTIC FEARS
Farrell Publications
(Ajax), 1953
(Formerly: CAPTAIN JET)
1 (7) Tales of Stalking Terror. . . . 700.00
2 (8) 450.00
3 . . . . 325.00
4 . . . . 325.00
5 SD,1st art 1,300.00
6 Decapitation. 850.00
7 . . . . 325.00
8 Decapitation 500.00
9 . . . . 325.00
Becomes:

FANTASTIC COMICS
Ajax, 1954
10 Tales of Enchantment 250.00
11 Amazing Adventures 300.00

FANTASTIC WORLDS
Visual Editions
(Standard Comics), 1952–53
5 ATh,Triumph Over Terror, Sci-fi 500.00
6 ATh,The Cosmic Terror 400.00
7 The Asteroid God 250.00

FANTOMAN
See: AMAZING
ADVENTURE FUNNIES

FARGO KID
See: JUSTICE TRAPS
THE GUILTY

FAST FICTION
Seaboard Publ.,
Oct., 1949
1 Scarlet Pimpernel 500.00
2 HcK,Captain Blood 400.00
3 She 500.00
4 The 39 Steps 350.00
5 HcK,Beau Geste 350.00
Becomes:

STORIES BY FAMOUS AUTHORS ILLUSTRATED
Famous Author Illustrated, Aug., 1950
1a Scarlet Pimpernel 400.00
2a Captain Blood 400.00
3a She 500.00
4a The 39 Steps 325.00
5a Beau Geste 300.00
6 HcK,MacBeth. 325.00
7 HcK,Window 275.00
8 HcK,Hamlet 300.00
9 Nicholas Nickleby 275.00
10 HcK,Romeo & Juliet 275.00
11 GS,Ben Hur. 290.00
12 GS,La Svengali. 275.00
13 HcK,Scaramouche 275.00

FAT AND SLAT JOKE BOOK
William H. Wise, 1944
N# 500.00

FAT AND SLAT
Fables Publ., Inc. (E.C. Comics), 1947
1 I&O:Voltage, Man of Lightning. 450.00
2 .... 300.00
3 .... 300.00
4 .... 300.00
Becomes:

GUNFIGHTER
Fables Publ., Inc. (E.C. Comics), 1948–50
5 JCr(c),Wild West 800.00
6 Grl,JCr(c),Moon Girl 700.00
7 AF,Grl. 600.00
8 AF,Grl. 600.00
9 AF,Grl. 600.00
10 JCr,AF,Grl. 600.00
11 AF,Grl 600.00
12 Grl. 600.00
13 JCr,WW,Grl. 625.00
14 JCr,WW,Grl,Bondage 650.00
Becomes:

HAUNT OF FEAR

FAVORITE COMICS
1934
1 Giveaways,Nebbs,Joe
  Palooka. 1,500.00
2 same. 1,000.00
3 same. 1,000.00

FAWCETT FUNNY ANIMALS
Fawcett Publications, Dec., 1942
1 I:Hoppy the Marvel Bunny,
  Captain Marvel (c) 1,000.00
2 X-Mas Issue 500.00
3 Spirit of '43 .... 400.00
4 and 5 .... @400.00
6 Buy War Bonds and Stamps . . 300.00
7 .... 300.00
8 Flag (c). 300.00
9 and 10 .... @300.00
11 thru 20 .... @200.00
21 thru 30 .... @150.00
31 thru 40 .... @150.00
41 thru 83 .... @125.00

Charlton Comics
84 .... 125.00
85 thru 91 Feb., 1956. .... @100.00

FAWCETT MINIATURES
Fawcett Publ. (Wheaties Giveaways), 1946
1 Capt. Marvel 250.00
2 Capt. Marvel 250.00
3 Capt. Marvel Jr. 250.00
4 Delecta of the Planets 400.00

FAWCETT MOVIE COMICS
Fawcett Publications, 1949
N# Dakota Lil 375.00
N#a Copper Canyon 300.00
N# Destination the Moon 1,200.00
N# Montana 300.00
N# Pioneer Marshal 300.00
N# Powder River Rustlers 450.00
N# Singing Guns 275.00
7 Gunmen of Abilene 325.00
8 King of the Bull Whip 450.00
9 BP,The Old Frontier 300.00
10 The Missourians 300.00
11 The Thundering Trail. 400.00
12 Rustlers on Horseback 325.00
13 Warpath. 250.00
14 Last Outpost,RonaldReagan . 550.00
15 The Man from Planet-X . . 3,500.00
16 10 Tall Men 200.00
17 Rose Cimarron 150.00
18 The Brigand 175.00
19 Carbine Williams. 175.00
20 Ivanhoe, Dec., 1952 .... 300.00

FEATURE BOOKS
David McKay Publications, May, 1937
N# Dick Tracy 15,000.00
N# Popeye 11,000.00
1 Zane Grey's King of the
  Royal Mounted 1,500.00
2 Popeye 1,400.00
3 Popeye and the "Jeep" ... 1,200.00
4 Dick Tracy 2,500.00
5 Popeye and his Poppa ... 1,100.00
6 Dick Tracy 1,500.00
7 Little Orphan Annie 1,500.00
8 Secret Agent X-9 .... 750.00
9 Tracy & the Famon Boys ... 1,500.00
10 Popeye & Susan 1,100.00
11 Annie Rooney 350.00
12 Blondie. 1,300.00
13 Inspector Wade. 400.00
14 Popeye in Wild Oats 1,400.00
15 Barney Baxter in the Air 600.00
16 Red Eagle. 400.00
17 Gang Busters. 1,100.00
18 Mandrake the Magician 1,100.00
19 Mandrake. 1,100.00
20 The Phantom 1,400.00
21 Lone Ranger 1,100.00
22 The Phantom 1,000.00
23 Mandrake in Teibe Castle . . 1,100.00
24 Lone Ranger 1,300.00
25 Flash Gordon on the
  Planet Mongo 1,800.00
26 Prince Valiant. 1,500.00
27 Blondie 300.00
28 Blondie and Dagwood. 300.00
29 Blondie at the Home
  Sweet Home 300.00
30 Katzenjammer Kids 275.00
31 Blondie Keeps the Home
  Fires Burning. 300.00
32 Katzenjammer Kids. 250.00
33 Romance of Flying 200.00
34 Blondie Home is Our Castle . . 300.00
35 Katzenjammer Kids. 250.00
36 Blondie on the Home Front. . 275.00
37 Katzenjammer Kids. 275.00
38 Blondie the ModelHomemaker 275.00

Feature Books #38
© *David McKay Publications*

39 The Phantom 800.00
40 Blondie 275.00
41 Katzenjammer Kids. 275.00
42 Blondie in Home-Spun Yarns . 275.00
43 Blondie Home-Cooked Scraps 275.00
44 Katzenjammer Kids in
  Monkey Business 275.00
45 Blondie in Home of the Free
  and the Brave 275.00
46 Mandrake in Fire World 750.00
47 Blondie in Eaten Out of
  House and Home 275.00
48 The Maltese Falcon 1,200.00
49 Perry Mason - The Case of
  the Lucky Legs 350.00
50 The Shoplifters Shoe,
  P. Mason 350.00
51 Rip Kirby - Mystery of
  the Mangler. 350.00
52 Mandrake in the Land of X . . 600.00
53 Phantom in Safari Suspense . 600.00
54 Rip Kirby - Case of the
  Master Menace 425.00
55 Mandrake in 5-Numbers
  Treasue Hunt. 600.00
56 Phantom Destroys the
  Sky Band. 600.00
57 Phantom in the Blue Gang,
  1948. .... 600.00

FEATURE FUNNIES
Harry A. Chesler Publ./ Comic Favorites, Oct., 1937
1 RuG(a&c),A:Joe Palooka,
  Mickey Finn, Bungles, Dixie
  Dugan, Big Top, Strange as
  It Seems, Off the Record . . 3,600.00
2 A: The Hawk 1,700.00
3 WE,Joe Palooka,The Clock . 1,400.00
4 RuG,WE,RuG(c),JoePalooka 1,200.00
5 WE, Joe Palooka drawing . . 1,200.00
6 WE, Joe Palooka (c) 1,200.00
7 WE,LLe, Gallant Knight story
  by Vernon Henkel 900.00
8 WE 900.00
9 WE, Joe Palooka story & (c) 1,200.00
10 WE,Micky Finn(c). 1,000.00
11 WE,LLe,The Bungles(c). ... 1,000.00
12 WE, Joe Palooka(c). 1,000.00
13 WE,LLe, World Series(c) . . . 1,100.00
14 WE,Ned Brant(c). 700.00
15 WE, Joe Palooka(c). 800.00
16 Mickey Finn(c) 700.00
17 WE 700.00
18 Joe Palooka (c). 800.00

Feature Comics #36
© Quality Comics Group

GOLDEN AGE

19 WE,LLe,Mickey Finn(c). 700.00
20 WE,LLe 700.00
Becomes:

FEATURE COMICS

**Quality Comics Group,
June. 1939–May, 1950**

21 Joe Palooka(c). 1,000.00
22 LLe(c),Mickey Finn(c). 650.00
23 B:Charlie Chan 650.00
24 AIA,Joe Palooka(c). 650.00
25 AIA,The Clock(c). 650.00
26 AIA,The Bundles(c). 650.00
27 WE,AIA,I:Doll Man 8,000.00
28 LF,AIA,The Clock(c). 2,800.00
29 LF,AIA,The Clock(c). 1,500.00
30 LF,AIA,Doll Man(c). 2,000.00
31 LF,AIA,Mickey Finn(c) 1,100.00
32 PGv,LF,GFx,Doll Man(c) . . . 1,000.00
33 PGv,LF,GFx,Bundles(c). 800.00
34 PGv,LF,GFx,Doll Man(c) . . . 1,000.00
35 PGv,LF,GFx,Bundles(c). 800.00
36 PGv,LF,GFx,Doll Man(c) . . . 1,000.00
37 PGv,LF,GFx,Bundles(c). 800.00
38 PGv,GFx,Doll Man(c) 750.00
39 PGv,GFx,Bundles(c). 750.00
40 PGv,GFx,WE(c),Doll Man(c) . 750.00
41 PGv,GFx,WE(c),Bundles(c) . . 550.00
42 GFx,Doll Man(c) 550.00
43 RC,GFx,Bundles(c). 425.00
44 RC,GFx,Doll Man(c). 800.00
45 RC,GFx,Bundles(c). 400.00
46 RC,PGv,GFx,Doll Man(c) . . . 600.00
47 RC,GFx,Bundles(c). 400.00
48 RC,GFx,Doll Man(c) 600.00
49 RC,GFx,Bundles(c). 400.00
50 RC,GFx,Doll Man(c) 600.00
51 RC,GFx,Bundles(c). 400.00
52 RC,GFx,Doll Man(c) 500.00
53 RC,GFx,Bundles(c). 325.00
54 RC,GFx,Doll Man(c) 500.00
55 RC,GFx,Bundles(c). 325.00
56 RC,GFx,Doll Man(c) 500.00
57 RC,GFx,Bundles(c). 325.00
58 RC,GFx,Doll Man (c) 500.00
59 RC,GFx,Mickey Finn(c) 325.00
60 RC,GFx,Doll Man(c) 500.00
61 RC,GFx,Bundles(c). 300.00
62 RC,GFx,Doll Man(c) 400.00
63 RC,GFx,Bundles(c). 300.00
64 BP,GFx,Doll Man(c) 400.00
65 BP,GFx(c),Bundles(c) 300.00
66 BP,GFx,Doll Man(c) 400.00
67 BP 300.00
68 BP,Doll Man vs.Bearded
    Lady. 400.00
69 BP,GFx(c),Devil (c) 350.00

70 BP,Doll Man(c) 500.00
71 BP,GFx(c) 350.00
72 BP,Doll Man(c) 400.00
73 BP,GFx(c),Bundles(c) 250.00
74 Doll Man(c) 400.00
75 GFx(c). 300.00
76 GFx(c). 300.00
77 Doll Man (c) until #140 . . . . . 400.00
78 Knows no Fear but the
    Knife Does. 300.00
79 Little Luck God 300.00
80 . . . . 300.00
81 Wanted for Murder 250.00
82 V:Shawunkas the Shaman . . . 250.00
83 V:Mechanical Man 250.00
84 V:Masked Rider, Death
    Goes to the Rodeo 250.00
85 V:King of Beasts 250.00
86 Is He A Killer?. 250.00
87 The Maze of Murder 250.00
88 V:The Phantom Killer 250.00
89 Crook's Goose 250.00
90 V:Whispering Corpse 250.00
91 V:The Undertaker 250.00
92 V:The Image 250.00
93 . . . . 250.00
94 V:The Undertaker 250.00
95 Flatten's the Peacock's Pride . 250.00
96 Doll Man Proves
    Justice is Blind. 250.00
97 V:Peacock. 250.00
98 V:Master Diablo 250.00
99 On the Warpath Again! 250.00
100 Crushes the City of Crime . 300.00
101 Land of the Midget Men!. . . 200.00
102 The Angle 200.00
103 V:The Queen of Ants 200.00
104 V:The Botanist 200.00
105 Dream of Death 200.00
106 V:The Sword Fish 200.00
107 Hand of Horror! 200.00
108 V:Cateye 200.00
109 V:The Brain 200.00
110 V:Fat Cat 200.00
111 V:The Undertaker 200.00
112 I:Mr. Curio & His Miniatures . 200.00
113 V:Highwayman 200.00
114 V:Tom Thumb 200.00
115 V:The Sphinx 200.00
116 V:Elbows 200.00
117 Polka Dot on the Spot. 200.00
118 thru 144 . . . . @ 200.00

A FEATURE PRESENTATION

Fox Features Syndicate, 1950
1 (5) The Black Tarantula 700.00
2 (6) WW,Moby Dick. 600.00
3 Jungle Thrills, bondage 500.00

FEDERAL MEN COMICS

Gerard Publ. Co., 1942
2 S&S,Spanking 800.00

FELIX THE CAT

**Dell Publishing Co.,
Feb.–March, 1948**
1 . . . . 550.00
2 . . . . 300.00
3 . . . . 200.00
4 . . . . 200.00
5 . . . . 200.00
6 thru 10 . . . . @150.00
11 thru 19 . . . . @150.00

Toby Press
20 thru 30 . . . . @350.00
31 . . . . 150.00
32 . . . . 350.00
33 . . . . 350.00
34 . . . . 150.00

Felix the Cat #36
© Toby Press

35 . . . . 150.00
36 . . . . 300.00
37 Giant, Christmas(c). 750.00
38 . . . . 300.00
39 . . . . 300.00
40 thru 60 . . . . @300.00
61 . . . . 275.00

Harvey, 1955

62 thru 80 . . . . @125.00
81 thru 99 . . . . @100.00
100 . . . . 125.00
101 thru 118 . . . . @100.00
Spec., 100 pgs, 1952. . . . . 350.00
Summer Ann., 100 pgs. 1953 . . 650.00
Winter Ann.,#2 100 pgs, 1954. . 600.00

FELIX AND HIS FRIENDS

Toby, 1953
1 F:Felix the Cat 350.00
2 . . . . 400.00
3 . . . . 400.00

FERDINAND THE BULL

Dell Publishing Co., 1938
1 . . . . 400.00

FIGHT AGAINST CRIME

Story Comics, May, 1951
1 Scorpion of Crime Inspector
    "Brains" Carroway 600.00
2 Ganglands Double Cross 350.00
3 Killer Dolan's Double Cross . 300.00
4 Hopped Up Killers - The
    Con's Slaughter,Drug issue . 350.00
5 FF,Horror o/t Avenging Corpse 350.00
6 Terror of the Crazy Killer 250.00
7 . . . . 250.00
8 Killer with the Two-Bladed
    Knife 250.00
9 Rats Die by Gas,Horror 600.00
10 Horror of the Con's Revenge . 600.00
11 Case of the Crazy Killer 600.00
12 Horror,Drug issue 700.00
13 The Bloodless Killer 600.00
14 Electric Chair (c) 700.00
15 Violence 600.00
16 RA,Bondage(c) 700.00
17 Knife in Neck(c) 700.00
18 Attempted Hanging (c) 700.00
19 Bondage(c) 700.00
20 Severed Head (c) 1,000.00
21 Violence 500.00
Becomes:

FIGHT AGAINST THE GUILTY
Dec., 1954
22 RA,Electric Chair 500.00
23 March, 1955 . . . . 350.00

FIGHT COMICS
Fiction House Magazines, Jan., 1940
1 LF,GT,WE(c),O:Spy Fighter . 6,500.00
2 GT,WE(c),Joe Lewis 2,500.00
3 WE(c),GT,B:Rip Regan,
   The Powerman 2,000.00
4 GT,LF(c) 1,500.00
5 WE(c) 1,500.00
6 GT,BP(c) 900.00
7 GT,BP(c),Powerman-Blood
   Money 900.00
8 GT,Chip Collins-Lair of
   the Vulture 900.00
9 GT,Chip Collins-Prey of the
   War Eagle 900.00
10 GT,Wolves of the Yukon 900.00
11 . . . . 800.00
12 RA,Powerman-Monster of
   Madness. 1,000.00
13 Shark Broodie-Legion
   of Satan 900.00
14 Shark Broodie-Lagoon
   of Death 900.00
15 Super-American-Hordes of
   the Secret Dicator. 1,200.00
16 B:Capt. Fight, Swastika
   Plague 1,200.00
17 Super-American-Blaster of
   the Pig-Boat Pirates 1,200.00
18 Shark Broodie-Plague of
   the Yellow Devils 1,200.00
19 E:Capt. Fight 1,200.00
20 . . . . 800.00
21 Rip Carson-Hell's Sky-Riders . 600.00
22 Rip Carson-Sky Devil's
   Mission 600.00
23 Rip Carson-Angels of
   Vengeance. 600.00
24 Baynonets for the Banzai
   Breed! Bondage(c) 800.00
25 Rip Carson-Samurai
   Showdown. 600.00
26 Rip Carson-Fury of
   the Sky-Brigade. 600.00
27 War-Loot for the Mikado
   Bondage(c) 800.00
28 Rip Carson 600.00

Fight Comics #43
© *Fiction House Magazines*

29 Rip Carson-Charge of the
   Lost Region 600.00
30 Rip Carson-Jeep-Raiders of
   the Torture Jungle 600.00
31 Gangway for the Gyrenes,
   Decapitation (c) 800.00
32 Vengeance of the Hun-
   Hunters, Bondage(c) 800.00
33 B:Tiger Girl 400.00
34 Bondage(c) 500.00
35 MB. 400.00
36 MB. 400.00
37 MB. 400.00
38 MB,Bondage(c). 500.00
39 MB,Senorita Rio-Slave Brand
   of the Spider Cult. 400.00
40 MB,Bondage (c) 500.00
41 MB,Bondage (c) 500.00
42 MB. 350.00
43 MB,Senorita Rio-The Fire-Brides of
   the Lost Atlantis, Bondage(c) 400.00
44 MB,R:Capt. Fight 500.00
45 MB,Tonight Don Diablo Rides. 500.00
46 MB. 500.00
47 MB,SenoritaRio-Horror's
   Hacienda 500.00
48 MB. 500.00
49 MB,JKa,B:Tiger Girl(c) 500.00
50 MB. 500.00
51 JKa,MB,O:Tiger Girl 700.00
52 JKa,MB,Winged Demons
   of Doom. 375.00
53 JKa,MB,Shadowland Shrine . . 375.00
54 JKa,MB,Flee the Cobra Fury . 375.00
55 JKa,MB,Jungle Juggernaut. . . 375.00
56 JKa,MB,Bondage 375.00
57 JKa,MB,Jewels of Jeopardy . 375.00
58 JKa,MB,Bondage 375.00
59 JKa,MB,Vampires of Crystal
   Cavern. 375.00
60 JKa,MB,Kraal of Deadly
   Diamonds 375.00
61 JKa,MB,Seekers of the Sphinx,
   O:Tiger Girl 500.00
62 JKa,MB,Graveyard of the
   Tree Tribe 400.00
63 JKa,MB,Bondage 400.00
64 JKa,MB,DawnBeast from
   Karama-Zan! 400.00
65 JKa,Beware the Congo Girl . . 300.00
66 JKa,Man or Ape! 300.00
67 Head-Hunters of Taboo Trek . 300.00
68 Fangs of Dr. Voodoo. 300.00
69 Cage of the Congo Fury 300.00
70 Kraal of Traitor Tusks 300.00
71 Captives for the Golden
   Crocodile 300.00
72 Land of the Lost Safaris 300.00
73 War-Gods of the Jungle 300.00
74 Advengers of the Jungle. . . . 300.00
75 Perils of Momba-Kzar. 300.00
76 Kraal of Zombi-Zaro 300.00
77 Slave-Queen of the Ape Man . 300.00
78 Great Congo Diamond
   Robbery. 400.00
79 A:Space Rangers 500.00
80 . . . . 200.00
81 E:Tiger Girl(c) 200.00
82 RipCarson-CommandoStrike . 200.00
83 NobodyLoves a Minesweeper 200.00
84 Rip Carson-Suicide Patrol . . . 200.00
85 . . . . 200.00
86 GE,Tigerman,Summer,1954 . . 250.00

FIGHTIN' AIR FORCE
Charlton Comics, 1956–60
3 . . . . 125.00
4 thru 10 . . . . @75.00
11 giant 100.00
12 US,Russia Nuclear attack. . . . 150.00
13 thru 20 . . . . @75.00
21 thru 30 . . . . @75.00

FIGHTING AMERICAN
Headline Publications (Prize), April–May, 1954
1 S&K,O:Fighting American &
   Speedboy 2,500.00
2 S&K(a&c) 1,200.00
3 S&K(a&c) 900.00
4 S&K(a&c) 850.00
5 S&K(a&c) 850.00
6 S&K(a&c),O:Fighting
   American 825.00
7 S&K(a&c), April–May, 1955 . . 750.00

FIGHTING FRONTS!
Harvey Publications, 1952–53
1 War 150.00
2 BP,violence 200.00
3 BP 125.00
4 . . . . 100.00
5 . . . . 100.00

FIGHTING DAVY CROCKETT
See: KIT CARSON

FIGHTING INDIANS OF THE WILD WEST
Avon Periodicals, March, 1952
1 EK,EL,Geronimo, Crazy Horse,
   Chief Victorio 250.00
2 EK,Same, Nov., 1952 . . . . 150.00

FIGHTING LEATHERNECKS
Toby Press, Feb., 1952
1 JkS,Duke's Diary 175.00
2 . . . . 125.00
3 . . . . 100.00
4 . . ● 100.00
5 . . . . 100.00
6 Dec., 1952 . . . . 100.00

THE FIGHTING MAN
Excellent Publications (Ajax/Farrell), 1952–53
1 War 175.00
2 . . . . 125.00
3 thru 8 . . . . @100.00
Ann.#1 (1952) 325.00

FIGHTIN' TEXAN
See: TEXAN, THE

FIGHTING UNDERSEA COMMANDOS
Avon Periodicals, 1952–53
1 Navy Frogmen. 200.00
2 . . . . 125.00
3 . . . . 100.00
4 BK 110.00
5 . . . . 100.00

FIGHTING WAR STORIES
Men's Publications, 1952
1 . . . . 150.00
2 thru 5 . . . . @100.00

FIGHTING YANK
Nedor Publ./Better Publ. (Standard Comics) Sept., 1942
1 JaB,B:Fighting Yank, A:Wonder
   Man, Mystico, bondage (c). 6,000.00
2 JaB 2,200.00
3 Shark, bondage (c). 2,000.00
4 ASh(c), bondage (c) 2,000.00

GOLDEN AGE

Fighting Yank #21
© *Nedor Publications*

5 ASh(c) 1,200.00
6 ASh(c) 1,200.00
7 ASh(c),Bomb(c) 1,100.00
8 ASh(c), bondage(c) 1,200.00
9 ASh(c) 1,100.00
10 ASh(c),bondage-torture(c) . 1,200.00
11 ASh(c), A:Grim Reaper,
   bondage (c) 1,100.00
12 ASh(c), Hirohito bondage (c) 1,100.00
13 ASh(c),kid bondage,snake(c)1,100.00
14 ASh(c) 900.00
15 ASh(c),bondage-torture(c) . . 1,100.00
16 ASh(c) 900.00
17 ASh(c),bondage(c) 1,100.00
18 ASh(c), A:American Eagle . . 1,000.00
19 ASh(c) 900.00
20 ASh(c) Shark. 900.00
21 ASh(c) A:Kara,Jungle
   Princess 900.00
22 ASh(c) A:Miss Masque-
   (c) story 1,000.00
23 ASh(c) Klu Klux Klan
   parody (c) 1,500.00
24 ASh(c),A:Miss Masque 800.00
25 ASh(c),JRo,MMe,A:Cavalier 1,100.00
26 ASh(c),JRo,MMe,A:Cavalier . . 800.00
27 ASh(c),JRo,MMe,A:Cavalier . . 800.00
28 ASh(c),JRo,MMe,AW
   A:Cavalier 900.00
29 ASh(c),JRo,MMe,Aug., 1949 . 900.00

FILM STAR ROMANCES
Star Publications, 1950
1 LbC(c), Rudy Valentino story . 650.00
2 Liz Taylor & Robert Taylor,
   photo (c) 800.00
3 May–June, 1950, photo(c). . . . 350.00

FIREHAIR COMICS
**Flying Stories, Inc.
(Fiction House Magazine),
Winter, 1948–Spring, 1952**
1 I:Firehair, Riders on the
   Pony Express 750.00
2 Bride of the Outlaw Guns 400.00
3 Kiss of the Six-Gun Siren! . . . 350.00
4 . . . . 350.00
5 . . . . 350.00
6 . . . . 325.00
7 War Drums at Buffalo Bend . . 250.00
8 Raid on the Red Arrows 250.00
9 French Flags and Tomahawks 250.00
10 Slave Maiden of the Crees . . . 250.00
11 Wolves of the Overland Trail. . 250.00

5 CENT COMICS
Fawcett Publications, 1940
1 B&W, I:Dan Dare, very rare 10,000.00

FLAME, THE
**Fox Feature Syndicate,
Summer, 1940**
1 LF,O:The Flame 6,000.00
2 GT,LF,Wing Turner 2,500.00
3 BP,Wonderworld 1,600.00
4 . . . . 1,600.00
5 GT 1,600.00
6 GT 1,600.00
7 A:The Yank 1,600.00
8 The Finger of the Frozen
   Death!, Jan., 1942 . . . . 1,600.00

FLAME, THE
Ajax/Farrell, 1954–55
1 (#5) superhero,O:Flame 650.00
2 . . . . 375.00
3 . . . . 350.00

FLAMING LOVE
**Comic Magazines
(Quality Comics Group),
Dec., 1949**
1 BWa,BWa(c),The Temptress
   I Feared in His Arms 600.00
2 Torrid Tales of Turbulent
   Passion 250.00
3 BWa,RC,My Heart's at Sea . . 350.00
4 One Women Who Made a
   Mockery of Love, Ph(c). 250.00
5 Bridge of Longing, Ph(c) 250.00
6 Men Both Loved & Feared Me,
   Oct., 1950 . . . . 250.00

FLAMING WESTERN ROMANCES
Star Publ., 1950
3 LbC,Robert Taylor Photo(c). . . 500.00

FLASH GORDON
**Harvey Publications,
Oct., 1950**
1 AR,Bondage(c) 600.00
2 AR 300.00
3 AR Bondage(c) 400.00
4 AR, April, 1951 . . . . 275.00

FLASH GORDON
Dell Publishing Co., 1953
2 . . . . 200.00
See also FOUR COLOR

FLIP
**Harvey Publications,
April, 1954**
1 HN 275.00
2 HN,BP,June, 1954 . . . . 275.00

FLY BOY
**Approved Comics
(Ziff-Davis) Spring, 1952**
1 NS(c),Angels without Wings . . 300.00
2 NS(c),Flyboy's Flame-Out,
   Oct.–Nov., 1952 . . . . 200.00

FLYING ACES
Key Publications, 1955–56
1 War 125.00
2 . . . . 100.00
3 . . . . 100.00
4 . . . . 100.00
5 . . . . 100.00

FLYING A'S RANGE RIDER, THE
**Dell Publishing Co.,
June–Aug., 1953**
(1) = *Dell Four Color #404*
2 Ph(c) all 200.00
3 . . . . 150.00
4 thru 10 . . . . @125.00
11 thru 16 . . . . @100.00
17 ATh 150.00
19 thru 24 . . . . @100.00

FLYING CADET
Flying Cadet Publ. Co., 1943
1 Aviation for student Airmen . . . 200.00
2 . . . . 150.00
3 Photo(c) 125.00
4 Photo(c) 125.00
5 Photo(c) 125.00
6a Photo(c) 125.00
6b Photo(c) 125.00
7 Photo(c) 125.00
8 Photo(c) 125.00
9 Photo(c) 125.00
10 thru 16 . . . . @100.00
17 nudity-woman 300.00

FLYIN' JENNY
Pentagon Publ. Co, 1946
N# 300.00
2 . . . . 350.00

FLYING MODELS
**Health-Knowledge
Publications, 1954**
1 . . . . 150.00

FOODINI
**Continental Publications,
March, 1950**
1 TV Puppet 300.00
2 Jingle Dingle 150.00
3 . . . . 100.00
4 Aug., 1950 . . . . 100.00

FOOTBALL THRILLS
**Approved Comics
(Ziff-Davis),
Fall-Winter, 1952**
1 BP,NS(c),Red Grange story . . 375.00
2 NS(c),Bronko Nagurski,
   Spring,1952 . . . . 250.00

FORBIDDEN LOVE
**Comic Magazine
(Quality Comics Group),
March, 1950**
1 RC,Ph(c),Heartbreak Road . 1,100.00
2 Ph(c),I Loved a Gigolo 900.00
3 Kissless Bride 550.00
4 BWa,Brimstone Kisses,
   Sept., 1950 . . . . 575.00

FORBIDDEN WORLDS
**American Comics Group,
July–Aug., 1951**
1 AW,FF 2,500.00
2 . . . . 1,200.00
3 AW,WW,JD 1,400.00
4 Werewolf (c) 750.00
5 AW 850.00
6 AW,King Kong (c) 750.00
7 . . . . 500.00
8 . . . . 500.00
9 Atomic Bomb 600.00
10 JyD 375.00
11 The Mummy's Treasure 300.00

All comics prices listed are for *Near Mint* condition.

GOLDEN AGE

Forbidden Worlds #21
© American Comics Group

97 thru 115 . . . . @125.00
116 OW(c)A:Herbie 150.00
117 . . . . 125.00
118 . . . . 125.00
119 . . . . 125.00
120 thru 124 . . . . @125.00
125 I:O:Magic Man 125.00
126 A:Magic Man 125.00
127 same 125.00
128 same 125.00
129 same 125.00
130 same 125.00
131 same 125.00
132 same 125.00
133 I:O:Dragona 125.00
134 A:Magic Man 125.00
135 A:Magic Man 125.00
136 A:Nemesis 125.00
137 SD,A:Magic Man 150.00
138 SD,A:Magic Man 150.00
139 A:Magic Man 125.00
140 SD,A:Mark Midnight 150.00
141 thru 145 . . . . @125.00

FOREIGN INTRIGUES
See: DYNAMITE

FOUR COLOR
Dell Publishing Co., 1939

N# Dick Tracy 15,000.00
N# Don Winslow of the Navy . . 2,500.00
N# Myra North 1,300.00
4 Disney's Donald Duck
   (1940) 25,000.00
5 Smilin' Jack 1,000.00
6 Dick Tracy 2,800.00
7 Gang Busters 700.00
8 Dick Tracy 1,500.00
9 Terry and the Pirates 1,000.00
10 Smilin' Jack 900.00
11 Smitty 650.00
12 Little Orphan Annie 800.00
13 Walt Disney's Reluctant
    Dragon (1941) 3,000.00
14 Moon Mullins 600.00
15 Tillie the Toiler 625.00
16 W.Disney's Mickey Mouse Outwits
    the Phantom Blob (1941) . 25,000.00
17 W.Disney's Dumbo the Flying
    Elephant (1941) 4,000.00
18 Jiggs and Maggie 650.00
19 Barney Google and
    Snuffy Smith 650.00
20 Tiny Tim 500.00
21 Dick Tracy 1,100.00
22 Don Winslow 600.00
23 Gang Busters 500.00
24 Captain Easy 700.00
25 Popeye 1,200.00

[Second Series, 1942]

1 Little Joe 1,000.00
2 Harold Teen 500.00
3 Alley Oop 900.00
4 Smilin' Jack 750.00
5 Raggedy Ann and Andy 900.00
6 Smitty 400.00
7 Smokey Stover 500.00
8 Tillie the Toiler 400.00
9 Donald Duck finds Pirate
   Gold! 20,000.00
10 Flash Gordon 1,800.00
11 Wash Tubs 550.00
12 Bambi 1,200.00
13 Mr. District Attorney 500.00
14 Smilin' Jack 600.00
15 Felix the Cat 1,400.00
16 Porky Pig 1,600.00
17 Popeye 900.00
18 Little Orphan Annie's
    Junior Commandos 700.00

Four Color (2nd Series) #10
© Dell Publishing

19 W.Disney's Thumper meets
    the Seven Dwarfs 1,200.00
20 Barney Baxter 500.00
21 Oswald the Rabbit 850.00
22 Tillie the Toiler 300.00
23 Raggedy Ann and Andy 650.00
24 Gang Busters 500.00
25 Andy Panda 950.00
26 Popeye 850.00
27 Mickey Mouse and the
    Seven Colored Terror 2,200.00
28 Wash Tubbs 375.00
29 CB,Donald Duck and the
    Mummy's Ring 12,000.00
30 Bambi's Children 900.00
31 Moon Mullins 325.00
32 Smitty 275.00
33 Bugs Bunny 2,200.00
34 Dick Tracy 750.00
35 Smokey Stover 300.00
36 Smilin' Jack 450.00
37 Bringing Up Father 350.00
38 Roy Rogers 4,200.00
39 Oswald the Rabbit 650.00
40 Barney Google and Snuffy
    Smith 400.00
41 WK,Mother Goose 400.00
42 Tiny Tim 300.00
43 Popeye 550.00
44 Terry and the Pirates 700.00
45 Raggedy Ann 550.00
46 Felix the Cat and the
    Haunted House 700.00
47 Gene Autry 800.00
48 CB,Porky Pig of the
    Mounties 2,000.00
49 W.Disney's Snow White and
    the Seven Dwarfs 1,400.00
50 WK,Fairy Tale Parade 450.00
51 Bugs Bunny Finds the
    Lost Treasure 650.00
52 Little Orphan Annie 500.00
53 Wash Tubbs 255.00
54 Andy Panda 550.00
55 Tillie the Toiler 250.00
56 Dick Tracy 650.00
57 Gene Autry 700.00
58 Smilin' Jack 400.00
59 WK,Mother Goose 350.00
60 Tiny Folks Funnies 275.00
61 Santa Claus Funnies 400.00
62 CB,Donald Duck in
    Frozen Gold 4,400.00
63 Roy Rogers-photo (c) 1,000.00
64 Smokey Stover 225.00

12 Chest of Death 300.00
13 Invasion from Hades 300.00
14 Million-Year Monster 300.00
15 The Vampire Cat 300.00
16 The Doll 300.00
17 . . . . 300.00
18 The Mummy 300.00
19 Pirate and the Voodoo Queen 300.00
20 Terror Island 300.00
21 The Ant Master 250.00
22 The Cursed Casket 250.00
23 Nightmare for Two 250.00
24 . . . . 250.00
25 Hallahan's Head 250.00
26 The Champ 250.00
27 SMo,The Thing with the
    Golden Hair 250.00
28 Portrait of Carlotta 250.00
29 The Frogman 250.00
30 The Things on the Beach . . . 250.00
31 SMo,The Circle of the
    Doomed 225.00
32 The Invasion of the
    Dead Things 225.00
33 . . . . 225.00
34 Atomic Bomb 300.00
35 Comics Code 275.00
36 thru 62 . . . . @175.00
63 AW 175.00
64 . . . . 125.00
65 . . . . 125.00
66 . . . . 125.00
67 . . . . 125.00
68 OW(c) 125.00
69 AW 175.00
70 . . . . 125.00
71 . . . . 125.00
72 . . . . 125.00
73 OW,I:Herbie 600.00
74 . . . . 125.00
75 JB 125.00
76 AW 175.00
77 . . . . 125.00
78 AW,OW(c) 150.00
79 thru 85 JB . . . . @125.00
86 Flying Saucer 160.00
87 . . . . 125.00
88 . . . . 125.00
89 . . . . 125.00
90 . . . . 125.00
91 . . . . 125.00
92 . . . . 125.00
93 . . . . 125.00
94 OW(c),A:Herbie 175.00
95 . . . . 125.00
96 AW 150.00

65 Smitty 225.00
66 Gene Autry 750.00
67 Oswald the Rabbit 300.00
68 WK,Mother Goose 325.00
69 WK,Fairy Tale Parade 450.00
70 Popeye and Wimpy 450.00
71 WK,Walt Disney's
    Three Caballeros 1,450.00
72 Raggedy Ann 450.00
73 The Grumps 250.00
74 Marge's Little Lulu 2,200.00
75 Gene Autry and the Wildcat . . 600.00
76 Little Orphan Annie 400.00
77 Felix the Cat 650.00
78 Porky Pig & the Bandit Twins . 700.00
79 Mickey Mouse in the Riddle
    of the Red Hat 2,400.00
80 Smilin' Jack 300.00
81 Moon Mullins 200.00
82 Lone Ranger 750.00
83 Gene Autry in Outlaw Trail . . . 550.00
84 Flash Gordon 900.00
85 Andy Panda and the
    Mad Dog Mystery 300.00
86 Roy Rogers-photo (c) 700.00
87 WK,DNo(c),Fairy Tale Parade 450.00
88 Bugs Bunny 400.00
89 Tillie the Toiler 250.00
90 WK,Christmas with
    Mother Goose 350.00
91 WK,Santa Claus Funnies . . . 300.00
92 WK,W.Disney's Pinocchio . . 1,100.00
93 Gene Autry 600.00
94 Winnie Winkle 200.00
95 Roy Rogers,Ph(c) 700.00
96 Dick Tracy 500.00
97 Marge's Little Lulu 900.00
98 Lone Ranger 600.00
99 Smitty 200.00
100 Gene Autry Comics-photo(c) 600.00
101 Terry and the Pirates 500.00
102 WK,Oswald the Rabbit 250.00
103 WK,Easter with
    Mother Goose 300.00
104 WK,Fairy Tale Parade 325.00
105 WK,Albert the Alligator 1,200.00
106 Tillie the Toiler 200.00
107 Little Orphan Annie 350.00
108 Donald Duck in the
    Terror of the River 3,200.00
109 Roy Rogers Comics 500.00
110 Marge's Little Lulu 600.00
111 Captain Easy 250.00
112 Porky Pig's Adventure in
    Gopher Gulch 600.00
113 Popeye 250.00
114 WK,Fairy Tale Parade 325.00
115 Marge's Little Lulu 600.00
116 Mickey Mouse and the
    House of Many Mysteries . . . 600.00
117 Roy Rogers Comics, Ph(c) . . 400.00
118 Lone Ranger 550.00
119 Felix the Cat 600.00
120 Marge's Little Lulu 600.00
121 Fairy Tale Parade 225.00
122 Henry 250.00
123 Bugs Bunny's Dangerous
    Venture 275.00
124 Roy Rogers Comics,Ph(c) . . 400.00
125 Lone Ranger 400.00
126 WK,Christmas with
    Mother Goose 250.00
127 Popeye 250.00
128 WK,Santa Claus Funnies . . . 250.00
129 W.Disney's Uncle Remus
    & His Tales of Brer Rabbit . . 500.00
130 Andy Panda 200.00
131 Marge's Little Lulu 550.00
132 Tillie the Toiler 200.00
133 Dick Tracy 400.00
134 Tarzan and the Devil Ogre . 1,200.00
135 Felix the Cat 450.00

136 Lone Ranger 375.00
137 Roy Rogers Comics 375.00
138 Smitty 175.00
139 Marge's Little Lulu 500.00
140 WK,Easter with
    Mother Goose 250.00
141 Mickey Mouse and the
    Submarine Pirates 500.00
142 Bugs Bunny and the
    Haunted Mountain 275.00
143 Oswald the Rabbit &
    Prehistoric Egg 175.00
144 Poy Rogers Comics,Ph(c) . . 400.00
145 Popeye 250.00
146 Marge's Little Lulu 500.00
147 W.Disney's Donald Duck
    in Volcano Valley 2,100.00
148 WK,Albert the Alligator
    and Pogo Possum 1,000.00
149 Smilin' Jack 175.00
150 Tillie the Toiler 150.00
151 Lone Ranger 325.00
152 Little Orphan Annie 250.00
153 Roy Rogers Comics 350.00
154 Andy Panda 200.00
155 Henry 200.00
156 Porky Pig and the Phantom . 600.00
157 W.Disney's Mickey Mouse
    and the Beanstalk 350.00
158 Marge's Little Lulu 500.00
159 CB,W.Disney's Donald Duck
    in the Ghost of the Grotto . 3,000.00
160 Roy Rogers Comics,Ph(c) . . 350.00
161 Tarzan & the Fires of Tohr . 1,000.00
162 Felix the Cat 325.00
163 Dick Tracy 325.00
164 Bugs Bunny Finds the
    Frozen Kingdom 275.00
165 Marge's Little Lulu 500.00
166 Roy Rogers Comics,Ph(c) . . 350.00
167 Lone Ranger 325.00
168 Popeye 250.00
169 Woody Woodpecker,Drug . . 400.00
170 W.Disney's Mickey Mouse
    on Spook's Island 350.00
171 Charlie McCarthy 450.00
172 WK,Christmas with
    Mother Goose 250.00
173 Flash Gordon 350.00
174 Winnie Winkle 150.00
175 WK,Santa Claus Funnies . . . 250.00
176 Tillie the Toiler 150.00
177 Roy Rogers Comics,Ph(c) . . 325.00
178 CB,W.Disney's Donald
    Duck Christmas on Bear
    Mountain 2,500.00

Four Color #167
© *Dell Publishing Co.*

179 WK,Uncle Wiggily 275.00
180 Ozark the Ike 200.00
181 W.Disney's Mickey Mouse
    in Jungle Magic 500.00
182 Porky Pig in Never-
    Never Land 600.00
183 Oswald the Rabbit 175.00
184 Tillie the Toiler 175.00
185 WK,Easter with
    Mother Goose 250.00
186 W.Disney's Bambi 300.00
187 Bugs Bunny and the
    Dreadful Bunny 200.00
188 Woody Woodpecker 200.00
189 W.Disney's Donald Duck in
    The Old Castle's Secret . . . 1,500.00
190 Flash Gordon 400.00
191 Porky Pig to the Rescue 500.00
192 WK,The Brownies 250.00
193 Tom and Jerry 400.00
194 W.Disney's Mickey Mouse
    in the World Under the Sea . . 500.00
195 Tillie the Toiler 125.00
196 Charlie McCarthy in The
    Haunted Hide-Out 300.00
197 Spirit of the Border 200.00
198 Andy Panda 200.00
199 W.Disney's Donald Duck in
    Sheriff of Bullet Valley 1,600.00
200 Bugs Bunny, Super Sleuth . . 225.00
201 WK,Christmas with
    Mother Goose 225.00
202 Woody Woodpecker 150.00
203 CB,W.Disney's Donald Duck in
    The Golden Christmas Tree 1,400.00
204 Flash Gordon 250.00
205 WK,Santa Claus Funnies . . . 275.00
206 Little Orphan Funnies 200.00
207 King of the Royal Mounted . . 250.00
208 W.Disney's Brer Rabbit
    Does It Again 200.00
209 Harold Teen 100.00
210 Tippe and Cap Stubbs 100.00
211 Little Beaver 150.00
212 Dr. Bobbs 90.00
213 Tillie the Toiler 125.00
214 W.Disney's Mickey Mouse
    and his Sky Adventure 400.00
215 Sparkle Plenty 200.00
216 Andy Panda and the
    Police Pup 150.00
217 Bugs Bunny in Court Jester . 200.00
218 W.Disney's 3 Little Pigs 225.00
219 Swee'pea 150.00
220 WK,Easter with
    Mother Goose 235.00
221 WK,Uncle Wiggly 175.00
222 West of the Pecos 125.00
223 CB,W.Disney's Donald Duck in
    Lost in the Andes 1,600.00
224 Little Iodine 200.00
225 Oswald the Rabbit 125.00
226 Porky Pig and Spoofy 400.00
227 W.Disney's Seven Dwarfs . . . 225.00
228 The Mark of Zorro 400.00
229 Smokey Stover 125.00
230 Sunset Press 125.00
231 W.Disney's Mickey Mouse
    and the Rajah's Treasure . . . 400.00
232 Woody Woodpecker 150.00
233 Bugs Bunny 200.00
234 W.Disney's Dumbo in Sky
    Voyage 250.00
235 Tiny Tim 90.00
236 Heritage of the Desert 125.00
237 Tillie the Toiler 125.00
238 CB,W.Disney's Donald Duck
    in Voodoo Hoodoo 1,300.00
239 Adventure Bound 100.00
240 Andy Panda 150.00
241 Porky Pig 300.00
242 Tippie and Cap Stubbs 90.00

243 W.Disney's Thumper
Follows His Nose. 200.00
244 WK,The Brownies 175.00
245 Dick's Adventures in
Dreamland. 100.00
246 Thunder Mountain. 90.00
247 Flash Gordon 500.00
248 W.Disney's Mickey Mouse
and the Black Sorcerer 275.00
249 Woody Woodpecker 150.00
250 Bugs Bunny in
Diamond Daze 225.00
251 Hubert at Camp Moonbeam . 100.00
252 W.Disney's Pinocchio 225.00
253 WK,Christmas with
Mother Goose 225.00
254 WK,Santa Claus Funnies,
A:Pogo. 250.00
255 The Ranger. 100.00
256 CB,W.Disney's Donald Duck in
Luck of the North 1,000.00
257 Little Iodine 150.00
258 Andy Panda and the
Ballon Race. 150.00
259 Santa and the Angel 100.00
260 Porky Pig, Hero of the
Wild West 250.00
261 W.Disney's Mickey Mouse
and the Missing Key 300.00
262 Raggedy Ann and Andy 175.00
263 CB,W.Disney's Donald Duck in
Land of the Totem Poles . . 1,000.00
264 Woody Woodpecker in
the Magic Lantern 150.00
265 King of the Royal Mountain . 150.00
266 Bugs Bunny on the Isle of
Hercules 175.00
267 Little Beaver 300.00
268 W.Disney's Mickey Mouse's
Surprise Visitor 300.00
269 Johnny Mack Brown,Ph(c) . . 400.00
270 Drift Fence 100.00
271 Porky Pig 250.00
272 W.Disney's Cinderella 225.00
273 Oswald the Rabbit 100.00
274 Bugs Bunny 175.00
275 CB,W.Disney's Donald Duck
in Ancient Persia 900.00
276 Uncle Wiggly. 175.00
277 PorkyPig in DesertAdventure 250.00
278 Bill Elliot Comics,Ph(c) 250.00
279 W.Disney's Mickey Mouse &
Pluto Battle the Giant Ants . . 300.00
280 Andy Panda in the Isle
of the Mechanical Men 150.00
281 Bugs Bunny in The Great
Circus Mystery. 175.00
282 CB,W.Disney's Donald Duck in
The Pixilated Parrot. 900.00
283 King of the Royal Mounted . . 150.00
284 Porky Pig in the Kingdom
of Nowhere 250.00
285 Bozo the Clown. 350.00
286 W.Disney's Mickey Mouse
and the Uninvited Guest 300.00
287 Gene Autry's Champion in the
Ghost of BlackMountain,Ph(c)200.00
288 Woody Woodpecker 150.00
289 BugsBunny in IndianTrouble. 175.00
290 The Chief 125.00
291 CB,W.Disney's Donald Duck in
The Magic Hourglass 900.00
292 The Cisco Kid Comics 450.00
293 WK,The Brownies 175.00
294 Little Beaver 75.00
295 Porky Pig in President Peg . . 250.00
296 W.Disney's Mickey Mouse
Private Eye for Hire 200.00
297 Andy Panda in The
Haunted Inn. 150.00
298 Bugs Bunny in Sheik
for a Day 175.00

Four Color #300
© Dell Publishing Co.

299 Buck Jones & the Iron Trail . 250.00
300 CB,W.Disney's Donald Duck in
Big-Top Bedlam. 900.00
301 The Mysterious Rider 100.00
302 Santa Claus Funnies 100.00
303 Porky Pig in The Land of
the Monstrous Flies 200.00
304 W.Disney's Mickey Mouse
in Tom-Tom Island 250.00
305 Woody Woodpecker 100.00
306 Raggedy Ann 125.00
307 Bugs Bunny in Lumber
Jack Rabbit 150.00
308 CB,W.Disney's Donald Duck in
Dangerous Disguise 800.00
309 Dollface and Her Gang 100.00
310 King of the Royal Mounted . 125.00
311 Porky Pig in Midget Horses
of Hidden Valley 200.00
312 Tonto 200.00
313 W.Disney's Mickey Mouse in
the Mystery of the Double-
Cross Ranch 250.00
314 Ambush. 90.00
315 Oswald Rabbit 100.00
316 Rex Allen,Ph(c). 275.00
317 Bugs Bunny in Hare Today
Gone Tomorrow 150.00
318 CB,W.Disney's Donald Duck in
No Such Varmint 800.00
319 Gene Autry's Champion 100.00
320 Uncle Wiggly 150.00
321 Little Scouts 75.00
322 Porky Pig in Roaring Rockies 150.00
323 Susie Q. Smith 75.00
324 I Met a Handsome Cowboy . 150.00
325 W.Disney's Mickey Mouse
in the Haunted Castle 250.00
326 Andy Panda 100.00
327 Bugs Bunny and the
Rajah's Treasure 150.00
328 CB,W.Disney's Donald Duck
in Old California. 850.00
329 Roy Roger's Trigger,Ph(c) . . 275.00
330 Porky Pig meets the
Bristled Bruiser 150.00
331 Disney's Alice in
Wonderland 275.00
332 Little Beaver 75.00
333 Wilderness Trek 90.00
334 W.Disney's Mickey Mouse
and Yukon Gold. 250.00
335 Francis the Famous
Talking Mule 200.00
336 Woody Woodpecker 100.00
337 The Brownies 100.00

338 Bugs Bunny and the
Rocking Horse Thieves 200.00
339 W.Disney's Donald Duck
and the Magic Fountain. 400.00
340 King of the Royal Mountain . 150.00
341 W.Disney's Unbirthday Party
with Alice in Wonderland 275.00
342 Porky Pig the Lucky
Peppermint Mine 150.00
343 W.Disney's Mickey Mouse in
Ruby Eye of Homar-Guy-Am 150.00
344 Sergeant Preston from
Challenge of the Yukon 250.00
345 Andy Panda in Scotland Yard 100.00
346 Hideout 100.00
347 Bugs Bunny the Frigid Hare . 150.00
348 CB,W.Disney's Donald Duck
The Crocodile Collector. 600.00
349 Uncle Wiggly. 125.00
350 Woody Woodpecker 100.00
351 Porky Pig and the Grand
Canyon Giant 150.00
352 W.Disney's Mickey Mouse
Mystery of Painted Valley . . . 200.00
353 CB(c),W.Disney'sDuckAlbum 300.00
354 Raggedy Ann & Andy 125.00
355 Bugs Bunny Hot-Rod Hair . . 150.00
356 CB(c),W.Disney's Donald
Duck in Rags to Riches. 500.00
357 Comeback. 75.00
358 Andy Panada 100.00
359 Frosty the Snowman. 175.00
360 Porky Pig in Tree Fortune . . 100.00
361 Santa Claus Funnies 100.00
362 W.Disney's Mickey Mouse &
the Smuggled Diamonds. . . . 250.00
363 King of the Royal Mounted . . 125.00
364 Woody Woodpecker 90.00
365 The Brownies 90.00
366 Bugs Bunny Uncle
Buckskin Comes to Town . . . 150.00
367 CB,W.Disney's Donald Duck in
A Christmas for Shacktown . . 800.00
368 Bob Clampett's
Beany and Cecil 500.00
369 Lone Ranger's Famous
Horse Hi-Yo Silver. 200.00
370 Porky Pig in Trouble
in the Big Trees 150.00
371 W.Disney's Mickey Mouse
the Inca Idol Case 200.00
372 Riders of the Purple Sage . . . 75.00
373 Sergeant Preston 150.00
374 Woody Woodpecker 75.00
375 John Carter of Mars 600.00
376 Bugs Bunny 200.00
377 Susie Q. Smith 75.00
378 Tom Corbett, Space Cadet . . 350.00
379 W.Disney's Donald Duck in
Southern Hospitality 300.00
380 Raggedy Ann & Andy 125.00
381 Marge's Tubby 375.00
382 W.Disney's Show White and
the Seven Dwarfs 200.00
383 Andy Panda 75.00
384 King of the Royal Mounted. . 100.00
385 Porky Pig 100.00
386 CB,W.Disney's Uncle Scrooge
in Only A Poor Old Man . . . 2,700.00
387 W.Disney's Mickey Mouse
in High Tibet 200.00
388 Oswald the Rabbit 100.00
389 Andy Hardy Comics 75.00
390 Woody Woodpecker 75.00
391 Uncle Wiggly. 125.00
392 Hi-Yo Silver. 100.00
393 Bugs Bunny 150.00
394 CB(c),W.Disney's Donald Duck
in Malayalaya 500.00
395 Forlorn River. 75.00
396 Tales of the Texas Rangers,
Ph(c) 200.00

397 Sergeant Preston o/t Yukon . 150.00
398 The Brownies 75.00
399 Porky Pig in the Lost
    Gold Mine 100.00
400 AMc,Tom Corbett 200.00
401 W.Disney's Mickey Mouse &
    Goofy's Mechanical Wizard. . 150.00
402 Mary Jane and Sniffles 100.00
403 W.Disney's Li'l Bad Wolf 150.00
404 The Ranger Rider,Ph(c) 200.00
405 Woody Woodpecker 75.00
406 Tweety and Sylvester 125.00
407 Bugs Bunny, Foreign-
    Legion Hare 125.00
408 CB,W.Disney's Donald Duck
    and the Golden Helmet 750.00
409 Andy Panda 75.00
410 Porky Pig in the
    Water Wizard. 100.00
411 W.Disney's Mickey Mouse
    and the Old Sea Dog. 150.00
412 Nevada 75.00
413 Disney's Robin Hood(movie),
    Ph(c) 200.00
414 Bob Clampett's Beany
    and Cecil 250.00
415 Rootie Kazootie 175.00
416 Woody Woodpecker 75.00
417 Double Trouble with Goober. . 75.00
418 Rusty Riley 75.00
419 Sergeant Preston 150.00
420 Bugs Bunny 125.00
421 AMc,Tom Corbett 200.00
422 CB,W.Disney's Donald Duck
    and the Gilded Man 750.00
423 Rhubarb 100.00
424 Flash Gordon 200.00
425 Zorro 250.00
426 Porky Pig 100.00
427 W.Disney's Mickey Mouse &
    the Wonderful Whizzix. 150.00
428 Uncle Wiggily 100.00
429 W.Disney's Pluto in
    Why Dogs Leave Home 200.00
430 Marge's Tubby 200.00
431 Woody Woodpecker 100.00
432 Bugs Bunny and the
    Rabbit Olympics 125.00
433 Wildfire 75.00
434 Rin Tin Tin,Ph(c). 300.00
435 Frosty the Snowman. 100.00
436 The Brownies 75.00
437 John Carter of Mars 400.00
438 W.Disney's Annie
    Oakley (TV). 275.00
439 Little Hiawatha 100.00
440 Black Beauty 75.00
441 Fearless Fagan. 75.00
442 W.Disney's Peter Pan 175.00
443 Ben Bowie and His
    Mountain Men 125.00
444 Marge's Tubby 200.00
445 Charlie McCarthy 100.00
446 Captain Hook and Peter Pan 175.00
447 Andy Hardy Comics 75.00
448 Beany and Cecil 300.00
449 Tappan's Burro 75.00
450 CB(c),W.Disney's Duck
    Album 200.00
451 Rusty Riley 65.00
452 Raggedy Ann and Andy 125.00
453 Susie Q. Smith 65.00
454 Krazy Kat Comics 65.00
455 Johnny Mack Brown Comics,
    Ph(c) 125.00
456 W.Disney's Uncle Scrooge
    Back to the Klondike 1,500.00
457 Daffy 150.00
458 Oswald the Rabbit 75.00
459 Rootie Kazootie 150.00
460 Buck Jones 175.00
461 Marge's Tubby 175.00

462 Little Scouts 50.00
463 Petunia 75.00
464 Bozo 175.00
465 Francis the Talking Mule 100.00
466 Rhubarb, the Millionaire Cat . . 75.00
467 Desert Gold. 75.00
468 W.Disney's Goofy 300.00
469 Beetle Bailey 175.00
470 Elmer Fudd 100.00
471 Double Trouble with Goober. . 40.00
472 Wild Bill Elliot,Ph(c). 150.00
473 W.Disney's Li'l Bad Wolf . . . 75.00
474 Mary Jane and Sniffles 125.00
475 M.G.M.'s the Two
    Mouseketeers 125.00
476 Rin Tin Tin,Ph(c). 150.00
477 Bob Clampett's Beany and
    Cecil 300.00
478 Charlie McCarthy 100.00
479 Queen o/t West Dale Evans . 400.00
480 Andy Hardy Comics 65.00
481 Annie Oakley and Tagg. 150.00
482 Brownies. 75.00
483 Little Beaver 75.00
484 River Feud 75.00
485 The Little People. 125.00
486 Rusty Riley 75.00
487 Mowgli, the Jungle Book. . . . 100.00
488 John Carter of Mars 350.00
489 Tweety and Sylvester 100.00
490 Jungle Jim 125.00
491 EK,Silvertip 150.00
492 W.Disney's Duck Album 150.00
493 Johnny Mack Brown,Ph(c) . . 125.00
494 The Little King. 175.00
495 CB, W.Disney's Uncle
    Scrooge 1,100.00
496 The Green Hornet. 750.00
497 Zorro, (Sword of). 250.00
498 Bugs Bunny's Album. 100.00
499 M.G.M.'s Spike and Tyke 90.00
500 Buck Jones 100.00
501 Francis the Famous
    Talking Mule 90.00
502 Rootie Kazootie 135.00
503 Uncle Wiggily 90.00
504 Krazy Kat 75.00
505 W.Disney's the Sword and
    the Rose (TV),Ph(c). 150.00
506 The Little Scouts 40.00
507 Oswald the Rabbit 75.00
508 Bozo 175.00
509 W.Disney's Pluto. 100.00
510 Son of Black Beauty 60.00
511 EK,Outlaw Trail 75.00
512 Flash Gordon 125.00

Four Color #488
© Dell Publishing Co.

513 Ben Bowie and His
    Mountain Men 60.00
514 Frosty the Snowman. 100.00
515 Andy Hardy 50.00
516 Double Trouble With Goober . 40.00
517 Walt Disney's Chip 'N' Dale . 200.00
518 Rivets 50.00
519 Steve Canyon 150.00
520 Wild Bill Elliot,Ph(c). 125.00
521 Beetle Bailey 100.00
522 The Brownies 75.00
523 Rin Tin Tin,Ph(c). 150.00
524 Tweety and Sylvester 100.00
525 Santa Claus Funnies 100.00
526 Napoleon. 50.00
527 Charlie McCarthy 100.00
528 Queen o/t West Dale Evans,
    Ph(c) 200.00
529 Little Beaver 75.00
530 Bob Clampett's Beany
    and Cecil 300.00
531 W.Disney's Duck Album 150.00
532 The Rustlers 60.00
533 Raggedy Ann and Andy 125.00
534 EK,Western Marshal. 125.00
535 I Love Lucy,Ph(c) 1,100.00
536 Daffy 100.00
537 Stormy, the Thoroughbred . . . 75.00
538 EK,The Mask of Zorro 250.00
539 Ben and Me 75.00
540 Knights of the Round Table,
    Ph(c) 150.00
541 Johnny Mack Brown,Ph(c) . . 125.00
542 Super Circus Featuring
    Mary Hartline 125.00
543 Uncle Wiggly. 100.00
544 W.Disney's Rob Roy(Movie),
    Ph(c) 150.00
545 The Wonderful Adventures
    of Pinocchio. 150.00
546 Buck Jones 100.00
547 Francis the Famous
    Talking Mule 90.00
548 Krazy Kat 75.00
549 Oswald the Rabbit 75.00
550 The Little Scouts 50.00
551 Bozo 175.00
552 Beetle Bailey. 100.00
553 Susie Q. Smith 60.00
554 Rusty Riley 70.00
555 Range War 70.00
556 Double Trouble with Goober. . 40.00
557 Ben Bowie and His
    Mountain Men 75.00
558 Elmer Fudd 75.00
559 I Love Lucy,Ph(c) 600.00
560 W.Disney's Duck Album 150.00
561 Mr. Magoo. 200.00
562 W.Disney's Goofy 150.00
563 Rhubarb, the Millionaire Cat. 100.00
564 W.Disney's Li'l Bad Wolf. . . . 100.00
565 Jungle Jim. 75.00
566 Son of Black Beauty 60.00
567 BF,Prince Valiant,Ph(c). 250.00
568 Gypsy Cat 90.00
569 Priscilla's Pop 75.00
570 Bob Clampett's Beany
    and Cecil 275.00
571 Charlie McCarthy 100.00
572 EK,Silvertip 90.00
573 The Little People. 100.00
574 The Hand of Zorro 225.00
575 Annie and Oakley and Tagg,
    Ph(c) 175.00
576 Angel. 60.00
577 M.G.M.'s Spike and Tyke 60.00
578 Steve Canyon 90.00
579 Francis the Talking Mule. 75.00
580 Six Gun Ranch 75.00
581 Chip 'N' Dale. 100.00
582 Mowgli, the Jungle Book. . . . 100.00
583 The Lost Wagon Train 75.00

        All comics prices listed are for *Near Mint* condition.

584 Johnny Mack Brown,Ph(c) .. 125.00
585 Bugs Bunny's Album....... 100.00
586 W.Disney's Duck Album 160.00
587 The Little Scouts........... 50.00
588 MB,King Richard and the
　　Crusaders,Ph(c) 175.00
589 Buck Jones 100.00
590 Hansel and Gretel......... 125.00
591 EK,Western Marshal....... 100.00
592 Super Circus............. 125.00
593 Oswald the Rabbit 60.00
594 Bozo 160.00
595 Pluto 75.00
596 Turok, Son of Stone...... 1,100.00
597 The Little King............ 100.00
598 Captain Davy Jones 90.00
599 Ben Bowie and His
　　Mountain Men 75.00
600 Daisy Duck's Diary 150.00
601 Frosty the Snowman....... 100.00
602 Mr. Magoo and the Gerald
　　McBoing-Boing 225.00
603 M.G.M.'s The Two
　　Mouseketeers 90.00
604 Shadow on the Trail 75.00
605 The Brownies 75.00
606 Sir Lancelot.............. 150.00
607 Santa Claus Funnies 100.00
608 EK,Silver Tip 75.00
609 The Littlest Outlaw,Ph(c). ... 125.00
610 Drum Beat,Ph(c) 175.00
611 W.Disney's Duck Album 150.00
612 Little Beaver 65.00
613 EK,Western Marshal....... 100.00
614 W.Disney's 20,000 Leagues
　　Under the Sea (Movie) 200.00
615 Daffy 100.00
616 To The Last Man.......... 75.00
617 The Quest of Zorro 225.00
618 Johnny Mack Brown,Ph(c) .. 125.00
619 Krazy Kat 65.00
620 Mowgli, Jungle Book 90.00
621 Francis the Famous
　　Talking Mule 65.00
622 Beetle Bailey............. 100.00
623 Oswald the Rabbit 65.00
624 Treasure Island,Ph(c) 150.00
625 Beaver Valley 125.00
626 Ben Bowie and His
　　Mountain Men 75.00
627 Goofy 150.00
628 Elmer Fudd 65.00
629 Lady & The Tramp with Jock 150.00
630 Priscilla's Pop 65.00
631 W.Disney's Davy Crockett
　　Indian Fighter (TV),Ph(c). ... 375.00
632 Fighting Caravans.......... 75.00
633 The Little People........... 75.00
634 Lady and the Tramp Album. . 100.00
635 Bob Clampett's Beany
　　and Cecil 300.00
636 Chip 'N' Dale............. 100.00
637 EK,Silvertip 75.00
638 M.G.M.'s Spike and Tyke 60.00
639 W.Disney's Davy Crockett
　　at the Alamo (TV),Ph(c)..... 300.00
640 EK,Western Marshal 100.00
641 Steve Canyon 110.00
642 M.G.M.'s The Two
　　Mouseketeers 80.00
643 Wild Bill Elliott,Ph(c) 75.00
644 Sir Walter Raleigh,Ph(c) 125.00
645 Johnny Mack Brown,Ph(c) .. 125.00
646 Dotty Dripple and Taffy 75.00
647 Bugs Bunny's Album....... 100.00
648 Jace Pearson of the
　　Texas Rangers,Ph(c)....... 100.00
649 Duck Album.............. 100.00
650 BF,Prince Valiant 125.00
651 EK,King Colt 75.00
652 Buck Jones 75.00
653 Smokey the Bear 200.00

Four Color #640
© Walt Disney

654 Pluto 75.00
655 Francis the Famous
　　Talking Mule 75.00
656 Turok, Son of Stone 650.00
657 Ben Bowie and His
　　Mountain Men 75.00
658 Goofy 150.00
659 Daisy Duck's Diary 125.00
660 Little Beaver 75.00
661 Frosty the Snowman....... 100.00
662 Zoo Parade 100.00
663 Winky Dink 150.00
664 W.Disney's Davy Crockett in
　　the Great Keelboat
　　Race (TV),Ph(c)........... 300.00
665 The African Lion 100.00
666 Santa Claus Funnies 100.00
667 EK,Silvertip and the Stolen
　　Stallion................. 100.00
668 W.Disney's Dumbo 325.00
668a W.Disney's Dumbo 300.00
669 W.Disney's Robin Hood
　　(Movie),Ph(c)............ 100.00
670 M.G.M.'s Mouse Musketeers . 75.00
671 W.Disney's Davey Crockett &
　　the River Pirates(TV),Ph(c) .. 275.00
672 Quentin Durward,Ph(c).... 125.00
673 Buffalo Bill Jr.,Ph(c) 150.00
674 The Little Rascals 150.00
675 EK,Steve Donovan,Ph(c) ... 150.00
676 Will-Yum!................. 60.00
677 Little King 100.00
678 The Last Hunt,Ph(c) 150.00
679 Gunsmoke................ 350.00
680 Out Our Way with the
　　Worry Wart 60.00
681 Forever, Darling,Lucile
　　Ball Ph(c)............... 225.00
682 When Knighthood Was
　　in Flower,Ph(c) 150.00
683 Hi and Lois 60.00
684 SB,Helen of Troy,Ph(c) 200.00
685 Johnny Mack Brown,Ph(c) .. 150.00
686 Duck Album.............. 150.00
687 The Indian Fighter,Ph(c) 150.00
688 SB,Alexander the Great,
　　Ph(c) 150.00
689 Elmer Fudd 75.00
690 The Conqueror,
　　John Wayne Ph(c)........ 300.00
691 Dotty Dripple and Taffy 50.00
692 The Little People........... 75.00
693 W.Disney's Brer Rabbit
　　Song of the South 175.00
694 Super Circus,Ph(c) 125.00
695 Little Beaver 75.00

696 Krazy Kat 75.00
697 Oswald the Rabbit 60.00
698 Francis the Famous
　　Talking Mule 75.00
699 BA,Prince Valiant 150.00
700 Water Birds and the
　　Olympic Elk 100.00
701 Jimmy Cricket 175.00
702 The Goofy Success Story . . . 135.00
703 Scamp.................. 175.00
704 Priscilla's Pop 60.00
705 Brave Eagle,Ph(c)........ 150.00
706 Bongo and Lumpjaw...... 100.00
707 Corky and White Shadow,
　　Ph(c) 135.00
708 Smokey the Bear 100.00
709 The Searchers,John
　　Wayne Ph(c)............ 700.00
710 Francis the Famous
　　Talking Mule 75.00
711 M.G.M.'s Mouse Musketeers . 60.00
712 The Great Locomotive
　　Chase, Ph(c) 135.00
713 The Animal World 60.00
714 W.Disney's Spin
　　& Marty (TV) 250.00
715 Timmy 75.00
716 Man in Space 150.00
717 Moby Dick,Ph(c) 150.00
718 Dotty Dripple and Taffy 50.00
719 BF,Prince Valiant......... 125.00
720 Gunsmoke,Ph(c)......... 175.00
721 Captain Kangaroo,Ph(c).... 325.00
722 Johnny Mack Brown,Ph(c) .. 125.00
723 EK,Santiago 175.00
724 Bugs Bunny's Album....... 75.00
725 Elmer Fudd 60.00
726 Duck Album.............. 100.00
727 The Nature of Things 110.00
728 M.G.M.'s Mouse Musketeers . 60.00
729 Bob Son of Battle 75.00
730 Smokey Stover 100.00
731 EK,Silvertip and The
　　Fighting Four 80.00
732 Zorro, (the Challenge of) ... 250.00
733 Buck Rogers 75.00
734 Cheyenne,C.Walker Ph(c) .. 300.00
735 Crusader Rabbit 575.00
736 Pluto 75.00
737 Steve Canyon 100.00
738 Westward Ho, the Wagons,
　　Ph(c) 200.00
739 MD,Bounty Guns 75.00
740 Chilly Willy 125.00
741 The Fastest Gun Alive,Ph(c). 150.00
742 Buffalo Bill Jr.,Ph(c) 100.00
743 Daisy Duck's Diary 110.00
744 Little Beaver 65.00
745 Francis the Famous
　　Talking Mule 65.00
746 Dotty Dripple and Taffy 50.00
747 Goofy 135.00
748 Frosty the Snowman....... 100.00
749 Secrets of Life,Ph(c) 100.00
750 The Great Cat 125.00
751 Our Miss Brooks,Ph(c) 150.00
752 Mandrake, the Magician 200.00
753 Walt Scott's Little People 75.00
754 Smokey the Bear 125.00
755 The Littlest Snowman 100.00
756 Santa Claus Funnies 100.00
757 The True Story of
　　Jesse James,Ph(c) 175.00
758 Bear Country............. 100.00
759 Circus Boy,Ph(c)......... 250.00
760 W.Disney's Hardy Boys(TV). 250.00
761 Howdy Doody 250.00
762 SB,The Sharkfighters,Ph(c) . 150.00
763 GrandmaDuck'sFarmFriends 150.00
764 M.G.M.'s Mouse Musketeers . 60.00
765 Will-Yum!................. 60.00
766 Buffalo Bill,Ph(c)......... 100.00

GOLDEN AGE

767 Spin and Marty 175.00
768 EK,Steve Donovan, Western
   Marshal,Ph(c) 125.00
769 Gunsmoke. 200.00
770 Brave Eagle,Ph(c) 65.00
771 MD,Brand of Empire 65.00
772 Cheyenne,C.Walker,Ph(c) . . 150.00
773 The Brave One,Ph(c) 100.00
774 Hi and Lois 50.00
775 SB,Sir Lancelot and
   Brian,Ph(c). 175.00
776 Johnny Mack Brown,Ph(c) . . 125.00
777 Scamp. 135.00
778 The Little Rascals 100.00
779 Lee Hunter, Indian Fighter . 100.00
780 Captain Kangaroo,Ph(c). . . . 275.00
781 Fury,Ph(c) 150.00
782 Duck Album. 100.00
783 Elmer Fudd 60.00
784 Around the World in 80
   Days,Ph(c). 125.00
785 Circus Boys,Ph(c) 250.00
786 Cinderella 125.00
787 Little Hiawatha 100.00
788 BF,Prince Valiant. 125.00
789 EK,Silvertip-Valley Thieves. . 100.00
790 ATh,The Wings of Eagles,
   J.Wayne Ph(c) 300.00
791 The 77th Bengal Lancers,
   Ph(c) 150.00
792 Oswald the Rabbit 65.00
793 Morty Meekle 50.00
794 SB,The Count of Monte
   Cristo 150.00
795 Jiminy Cricket 125.00
796 Ludwig Bemelman's
   Madeleine and Genevieve. . . 60.00
797 Gunsmoke,Ph(c). 175.00
798 Buffalo Bill,Ph(c). 100.00
799 Priscilla's Pop 60.00
800 The Buccaneers,Ph(c). 150.00
801 Dotty Dripple and Taffy 50.00
802 Goofy 150.00
803 Cheyenne,C.Walker Ph(c) . . 150.00
804 Steve Canyon 100.00
805 Crusader Rabbit 450.00
806 Scamp. 125.00
807 MB,Savage Range 65.00
808 Spin and Marty,Ph(c). 175.00
809 The Little People 75.00
810 Francis the Famous
   Talking Mule 65.00
811 Howdy Doody 200.00
812 The Big Land,A.Ladd Ph(c) . 225.00
813 Circus Boy,Ph(c). 225.00
814 Covered Wagon,A:Mickey
   Mouse 125.00
815 Dragoon Wells Massacre . . 150.00
816 Brave Eagle,Ph(c). 65.00
817 Little Beaver 65.00
818 Smokey the Bear 125.00
819 Mickey Mouse in Magicland . 100.00
820 The Oklahoman,Ph(c). 175.00
821 Wringle Wrangle,Ph(c) 150.00
822 ATh,W.Disney's Paul Revere's
   Ride (TV) 175.00
823 Timmy 50.00
824 The Pride and the Passion,
   Ph(c) 175.00
825 The Little Rascals 100.00
826 Spin and Marty and Annette,
   Ph(c) 425.00
827 Smokey Stover 90.00
828 Buffalo Bill, Jr,Ph(c). 90.00
829 Tales of the Pony Express,
   Ph(c) 90.00
830 The Hardy Boys,Ph(c) 175.00
831 No Sleep 'Til Dawn,Ph(c) . . . 125.00
832 Lolly and Pepper. 65.00
833 Scamp. 125.00
834 Johnny Mack Brown,Ph(c) . . 125.00
835 Silvertip- The Fake Rider 90.00

Four Color #811
© *Dell Publishing Co.*

836 Man in Fight 135.00
837 All-American Athlete
   Cotton Woods 65.00
838 Bugs Bunny's Life
   Story Album 75.00
839 The Vigilantes 125.00
840 Duck Album 100.00
841 Elmer Fudd 60.00
842 The Nature of Things 100.00
843 The First Americans 150.00
844 Gunsmoke,Ph(c). 175.00
845 ATh,The Land Unknown 225.00
846 ATh,Gun Glory 175.00
847 Perri 90.00
848 Marauder's Moon 65.00
849 BF,Prince Valiant. 125.00
850 Buck Jones 75.00
851 The Story of Mankind,
   V.Price Ph(c) 135.00
852 Chilly Willy 100.00
853 Pluto 75.00
854 Hunchback of Notre Dame,
   Ph(c) 250.00
855 Broken Arrow,Ph(c) 100.00
856 Buffalo Bill, Jr.,Ph(c) 100.00
857 The Goofy Adventure Story . 150.00
858 Daisy Duck's Diary 90.00
859 Topper and Neil. 80.00
860 Wyatt Earp,Ph(c) 200.00
861 Frosty the Snowman 75.00
862 Truth About Mother Goose . . 135.00
863 Francis the Famous
   Talking Mule 60.00
864 The Littlest Snowman 90.00
865 Andy Burnett,Ph(c) 175.00
866 Mars and Beyond 150.00
867 Santa Claus Funnies 100.00
868 The Little People. 90.00
869 Old Yeller,Ph(c). 110.00
870 Little Beaver 75.00
871 Curly Kayoe 60.00
872 Captain Kangaroo,Ph(c). . . . 250.00
873 Grandma Duck's
   Farm Friends. 90.00
874 Old Ironsides. 125.00
875 Trumpets West 60.00
876 Tales of Wells Fargo,Ph(c). . 175.00
877 ATh,Frontier Doctor,Ph(c) . . 175.00
878 Peanuts. 350.00
879 Brave Eagle,Ph(c). 60.00
880 MD,Steve Donovan,Ph(c) . . . 75.00
881 The Captain and the Kids 60.00
882 ATh,W.DisneyPresentsZorro . 300.00
883 The Little Rascals 100.00
884 Hawkeye and the Last
   of the Mohicans,Ph(c) 135.00

885 Fury,Ph(c) 125.00
886 Bongo and Lumpjaw. 90.00
887 The Hardy Boys,Ph(c) 175.00
888 Elmer Fudd 60.00
889 ATh,W.Disney's Clint
   & Mac(TV),Ph(c) 225.00
890 Wyatt Earp,Ph(c) 135.00
891 Light in the Forest,
   C.Parker,Ph(c) 135.00
892 Maverick,J.Garner Ph(c). . . . 475.00
893 Jim Bowie,Ph(c) 100.00
894 Oswald the Rabbit 60.00
895 Wagon Train,Ph(c) 200.00
896 Adventures of Tinker Bell . . . 150.00
897 Jiminy Cricket 125.00
898 EK,Silvertip 90.00
899 Goofy 100.00
900 BF,Prince Valiant 125.00
901 Little Hiawatha 90.00
902 Will-Yum! 60.00
903 Dotty Dripple and Taffy 50.00
904 Lee Hunter, Indian Fighter . . 60.00
905 W.Disney's Annette (TV),
   Ph(c) 550.00
906 Francis the Famous
   Talking Mule 60.00
907 Ath,Sugarfoot,Ph(c). 250.00
908 The Little People
   and the Giant. 75.00
909 Smitty 60.00
910 ATh,The Vikings,
   K.Douglas Ph(c) 150.00
911 The Gray Ghost,Ph(c). 150.00
912 Leave it to Beaver,Ph(c). . . . 300.00
913 The Left-Handed Gun,
   Paul Newman Ph(c) 175.00
914 ATh,No Time for Sergeants,
   Ph(c) 175.00
915 Casey Jones,Ph(c) 100.00
916 Red Ryder Ranch Comics . . 150.00
917 The Life of Riley,Ph(c). 225.00
918 Beep Beep, the Roadrunner. 200.00
919 Boots and Saddles,Ph(c) . . 135.00
920 Ath,Zorro,Ph(c) 225.00
921 Wyatt Earp.Ph(c) 135.00
922 Johnny Mack Brown,Ph(c) . . 135.00
923 Timmy 50.00
924 Colt .45,Ph(c) 200.00
925 Last of the Fast Guns,Ph(c) . 135.00
926 Peter Pan 75.00
927 SB,Top Gun 60.00
928 Sea Hunt,L.Bridges Ph(c) . . 225.00
929 Brave Eagle,Ph(c). 60.00
930 Maverick,J. Garner Ph(c) . . . 225.00
931 Have Gun, Will Travel,Ph(c) . 275.00
932 Smokey the Bear 100.00
933 ATh,W.Disney's Zorro 225.00
934 Restless Gun 225.00
935 King of the Royal Mounted . . 65.00
936 The Little Rascals 100.00
937 Ruff and Ready. 250.00
938 Elmer Fudd. 60.00
939 Steve Canyon 90.00
940 Lolly and Pepper 50.00
941 Pluto 75.00
942 Pony Express 90.00
943 White Wilderness 125.00
944 SB,7th Voyage of Sinbad . . . 250.00
945 Maverick,J.Garner Ph(c) . . . 250.00
946 The Big Country,Ph(c) 150.00
947 Broken Arrow,Ph(c) 90.00
948 Daisy Duck's Diary 90.00
949 High Adventure,Ph(c) 100.00
950 Frosty the Snowman 75.00
951 ATh,Lennon Sisters
   Life Story,Ph(c) 250.00
952 Goofy 90.00
953 Francis the Famous
   Talking Mule 60.00
954 Man in Space 150.00
955 Hi and Lois 50.00
956 Ricky Nelson,Ph(c) 375.00

GOLDEN AGE

957 Buffalo Bee 175.00
958 Santa Claus Funnies 90.00
959 Christmas Stories 75.00
960 ATh,W.Disney's Zorro 225.00
961 Jace Pearson's Tales of
    Texas Rangers,Ph(c). 90.00
962 Maverick,J.Garner Ph(c). . . . 250.00
963 Johnny Mack Brown,Ph(c) . . 125.00
964 The Hardy Boys,Ph(c) 175.00
965 GrandmaDuck'sFarmFriends . 90.00
966 Tonka,Ph(c). 150.00
967 Chilly Willy 90.00
968 Tales of Wells Fargo,Ph(c). . 150.00
969 Peanuts. 200.00
970 Lawman,Ph(c). 250.00
971 Wagon Train,Ph(c) 125.00
972 Tom Thumb. 175.00
973 SleepingBeauty & the Prince 250.00
974 The Little Rascals 125.00
975 Fury,Ph(c) 125.00
976 ATh,W.Disney's Zorro,Ph(c) . 225.00
977 Elmer Fudd 60.00
978 Lolly and Pepper. 50.00
979 Oswald the Rabbit 60.00
980 Maverick,J.Garner Ph(c) . . . 250.00
981 Ruff and Ready. 150.00
982 The New Adventures of
    Tinker Bell 150.00
983 Have Gun, Will Travel,Ph(c). 175.00
984 Sleeping Beauty's Fairy
    Godmothers. 165.00
985 Shaggy Dog,Ph(c) 150.00
986 Restless Gun,Ph(c). 150.00
987 Goofy 90.00
988 Little Hiawatha 90.00
989 Jimmy Cricket 125.00
990 Huckleberry Hound 235.00
991 Francis the Famous
    Talking Mule 60.00
992 ATh,Sugarfoot,Ph(c) 250.00
993 Jim Bowie,Ph(c) 90.00
994 Sea HuntL.Bridges Ph(c) . . . 150.00
995 Donald Duck Album 125.00
996 Nevada 75.00
997 Walt Disney Presents,Ph(c) . 150.00
998 Ricky Nelson,Ph(c) 375.00
999 Leave It To Beaver,Ph(c) . . . 300.00
1000 The Gray Ghost,Ph(c). 150.00
1001 Lowell Thomas' High
    Adventure,Ph(c). 90.00
1002 Buffalo Bee 125.00
1003 ATh,W.Disney's Zorro,Ph(c) 225.00
1004 Colt .45,Ph(c) 150.00
1005 Maverick,J.Garner Ph(c). . . 225.00
1006 SB,Hercules 175.00
1007 John Paul Jones,Ph(c) 90.00
1008 Beep, Beep, the
    Road Runner. 125.00
1009 CB,The Rifleman,Ph(c) . . . 475.00
1010 Grandma Duck's Farm
    Friends. 250.00
1011 Buckskin,Ph(c) 150.00
1012 Last Train from Gun
    Hill,Ph(c) 155.00
1013 Bat Masterson,Ph(c) 225.00
1014 ATh,The Lennon Sisters,
    Ph(c) 250.00
1015 Peanuts. 200.00
1016 Smokey the Bear 75.00
1017 Chilly Willy 90.00
1018 Rio Bravo,J.Wayne Ph(c) . . 450.00
1019 Wagoon Train,Ph(c) 125.00
1020 Jungle 60.00
1021 Jace Pearson's Tales of
    the Texas Rangers,Ph(c). . . . 90.00
1022 Timmy 55.00
1023 Tales of Wells Fargo,Ph(c) . 150.00
1024 ATh,Darby O'Gill and
    the Little People,Ph(c). 175.00
1025 CB,W.Disney's Vacation in
    Disneyland. 350.00
1026 Spin and Marty,Ph(c) 135.00

1027 The Texan,Ph(c) 150.00
1028 Rawhide,
    Clint Eastwood Ph(c). 450.00
1029 Boots and Saddles,Ph(c) . . 100.00
1030 Spanky and Alfalfa, the
    Little Rascals 100.00
1031 Fury,Ph(c) 125.00
1032 Elmer Fudd 55.00
1033 Steve Canyon,Ph(c) 90.00
1034 Nancy and Sluggo
    Summer Camp 75.00
1035 Lawman,Ph(c). 150.00
1036 The Big Circus,Ph(c). 125.00
1037 Zorro,Ph(c) 275.00
1038 Ruff and Ready. 150.00
1039 Pluto 75.00
1040 Quick Draw McGraw 275.00
1041 ATh,Sea Hunt,
    L.Bridges Ph(c) 150.00
1042 The Three Chipmunks 125.00
1043 The Three Stooges,Ph(c) . . 500.00
1044 Have Gun,Will Travel,Ph(c) 175.00
1045 Restless Gun,Ph(c). 150.00
1046 Beep Beep, the
    Road Runner. 100.00
1047 CB,W.Disney's
    GyroGearloose 350.00
1048 The Horse Soldiers
    J.Wayne Ph(c). 275.00
1049 Don't Give Up the Ship
    J.Lewis Ph(c). 150.00
1050 Huckleberry Hound 150.00
1051 Donald in Mathmagic Land. 150.00
1052 RsM,Ben-Hur 200.00
1053 Goofy 90.00
1054 Huckleberry Hound
    Winter Fun. 150.00
1055 CB,Daisy Duck's Diary 175.00
1056 Yellowstone Kelly,
    C.Walker Ph(c) 120.00
1057 Mickey Mouse Album 100.00
1058 Colt .45,Ph(c) 175.00
1059 Sugarfoot 175.00
1060 Journey to the Center of the
    Earth, P.Boone Ph(c) 225.00
1061 Buffalo Bill 125.00
1062 Christmas Stories 75.00
1063 Santa Claus Funnies 90.00
1064 Bugs Bunny's Merry
    Christmas 90.00
1065 Frosty the Snowman. 75.00
1066 ATh,77 Sunset Strip,Ph(c). . 235.00
1067 Yogi Bear 220.00
1068 Francis the Famous
    Talking Mule 60.00
1069 ATh,The FBI Story,Ph(c) . . . 175.00
1070 Soloman and Sheba,Ph(c) . 160.00
1071 ATh,TheRealMcCoys,Ph(c). 175.00
1072 Blythe 90.00
1073 CB,Grandma Duck's Farm
    Friends. 235.00
1074 Chilly Willy 90.00
1075 Tales of Wells Fargo,Ph(c) . 150.00
1076 MSy,The Rebel,Ph(c) 250.00
1077 SB,The Deputy,
    H.Fonda Ph(c). 350.00
1078 The Three Stooges,Ph(c) . . 250.00
1079 The Little Rascals 100.00
1080 Fury,Ph(c) 125.00
1081 Elmer Fudd 55.00
1082 Spin and Marty 150.00
1083 Men into Space,Ph(c) 150.00
1084 Speedy Gonzales 125.00
1085 ATh,The Time Machine. . . . 300.00
1086 Lolly and Pepper. 50.00
1087 Peter Gunn,Ph(c) 175.00
1088 A Dog of Flanders,Ph(c) . . . 90.00
1089 Restless Gun,Ph(c). 150.00
1090 Francis the Famous
    Talking Mule 60.00
1091 Jacky's Diary. 90.00
1092 Toby Tyler,Ph(c) 125.00

Four Color #1013
© Dell Publishing Co.

1093 MacKenzie's Raiders,Ph(c) 125.00
1094 Goofy 150.00
1095 CB,W.Disney's
    GyroGearloose 170.00
1096 The Texan,Ph(c) 150.00
1097 Rawhide,C.Eastwood Ph(c) 375.00
1098 Sugarfoot,Ph(c). 150.00
1099 CB(c),Donald Duck Album . 150.00
1100 W.Disney's Annette's
    Life Story (TV),Ph(c) 425.00
1101 Robert Louis Stevenson's
    Kidnapped,Ph(c) 125.00
1102 Wanted: Dead or Alive,
    Ph(c) 250.00
1103 Leave It To Beaver,Ph(c). . . 275.00
1104 Yogi Bear Goes to College . 150.00
1105 ATh,Gale Storm,Ph(c) 225.00
1106 ATh,77 Sunset Strip,Ph(c). . 175.00
1107 Buckskin,Ph(c) 125.00
1108 The Troubleshooters,Ph(c) . . 90.00
1109 This Is Your Life, Donald
    Duck,O:Donald Duck. 250.00
1110 Bonanza,Ph(c) 650.00
1111 Shotgun Slade. 125.00
1112 Pixie and Dixie
    and Mr. Jinks 150.00
1113 Tales of Wells Fargo,Ph(c) . 165.00
1114 Huckleberry Finn,Ph(c) 90.00
1115 Ricky Nelson,Ph(c) 300.00
1116 Boots and Saddles,Ph(c) . . . 90.00
1117 Boy and the Pirate,Ph(c) . . . 125.00
1118 Sword and the Dragon,Ph(c)135.00
1119 Smokey and the Bear
    Nature Stories 65.00
1120 Dinosaurus,Ph(c) 150.00
1121 RC,GE,HerculesUnchained 175.00
1122 Chilly Willy. 80.00
1123 Tombstone Territory,Ph(c) . . 175.00
1124 Whirlybirds,Ph(c). 165.00
1125 GK,RH,Laramie,Ph(c) 175.00
1126 Sundance,Ph(c) 125.00
1127 The Three Stooges,Ph(c) . . 350.00
1128 Rocky and His Friends 650.00
1129 Pollyanna,H.Mills Ph(c) . . . 150.00
1130 SB,The Deputy,
    H.Fonda Ph(c) 175.00
1131 Elmer Fudd 55.00
1132 Space Mouse 100.00
1133 Fury,Ph(c) 125.00
1134 ATh,Real McCoys,Ph(c) . . . 175.00
1135 M.G.M.'s Mouse Musketeers100.00
1136 Jungle Cat,Ph(c) 120.00
1137 The Little Rascals 100.00
1138 The Rebel,Ph(c) 165.00
1139 SB,Spartacus,Ph(c). 250.00
1140 Donald Duck Album 200.00

GOLDEN AGE

1141 Huckleberry Hound for
   President 150.00
1142 Johnny Ringo,Ph(c) 135.00
1143 Pluto 100.00
1144 The Story of Ruth,Ph(c) . . 150.00
1145 GK,The Lost World,Ph(c) . . 175.00
1146 Restless Gun,Ph(c) 150.00
1147 Sugarfoot,Ph(c) 175.00
1148 I aim at the Stars,Ph(c) . . . 135.00
1149 Goofy 125.00
1150 CB,Daisy Duck's Diary . . . 200.00
1151 Mickey Mouse Album 100.00
1152 Rocky and His Friends 400.00
1153 Frosty the Snowman 90.00
1154 Santa Claus Funnies 175.00
1155 North to Alaska 325.00
1156 Walt Disney Swiss
   Family Robinson 135.00
1157 Master of the World 125.00
1158 Three Worlds of Gulliver . . . 125.00
1159 ATh,77 Sunset Strip 170.00
1160 Rawhide 300.00
1161 CB,Grandma Duck's
   Farm Friends 300.00
1162 Yogi Bera joins the Marines . 135.00
1163 Daniel Boone 90.00
1164 Wanted: Dead or Alive . . . 175.00
1165 Ellery Queen 200.00
1166 Rocky and His Friends 475.00
1167 Tales of Wells Fargo,Ph(c) . 150.00
1168 The Detectives,
   R.Taylor Ph(c) 175.00
1169 New Adventures of
   Sherlock Holmes 300.00
1170 The Three Stooges,Ph(c) . . 275.00
1171 Elmer Fudd 60.00
1172 Fury,Ph(c) 125.00
1173 The Twilight Zone 425.00
1174 The Little Rascals 75.00
1175 M.G.M.'s Mouse Musketeers . 50.00
1176 Dondi,Ph(c) 75.00
1177 Chilly Willy 80.00
1178 Ten Who Dared 135.00
1179 The Swamp Fox,
   L.Nielson Ph(c) 150.00
1180 The Danny Thomas Show . 300.00
1181 Texas John Slaughter,Ph(c) . 135.00
1182 Donald Duck Album 100.00
1183 101 Dalmatians 225.00
1184 CB,W.Disney's
   Gyro Gearloose 165.00
1185 Sweetie Pie 75.00
1186 JDa,Yak Yak 145.00
1187 The Three Stooges,Ph(c) . . 250.00
1188 Atlantis the Lost
   Continent,Ph(c) 200.00
1189 Greyfriars Bobby,Ph(c) . . . 135.00
1190 CB(c),Donald and
   the Wheel 135.00
1191 Leave It to Beaver,Ph(c) . . . 400.00
1192 Rocky Nelson,Ph(c) 300.00
1193 The Real McCoys,Ph(c) . . . 150.00
1194 Pepe,Ph(c) 50.00
1195 National Velvet,Ph(c) 125.00
1196 Pixie and Dixie
   and Mr. Jinks 100.00
1197 The Aquanauts,Ph(c) 135.00
1198 Donald in Mathmagic Land . 125.00
1199 Absent-Minded Professor,
   Ph(c) 150.00
1200 Hennessey,Ph(c) 125.00
1201 Goofy 90.00
1202 Rawhide,C.Eastwood Ph(c) 300.00
1203 Pinocchio 100.00
1204 Scamp 75.00
1205 David & Goliath,Ph(c) 125.00
1206 Lolly and Pepper 40.00
1207 MSy,The Rebel,Ph(c) 175.00
1208 Rocky and His Friends 375.00
1209 Sugarfoot,Ph(c) 150.00
1210 The Parent Trap,
   H.Mills Ph(c) 175.00

Four Color #1244
© Dell Publishing Co.

1211 RsM,77 Sunset Strip,Ph(c) . 150.00
1212 Chilly Willy 80.00
1213 Mysterious Island,Ph(c) . . . 150.00
1214 Smokey the Bear 65.00
1215 Tales of Wells Fargo,Ph(c) . 135.00
1216 Whirlybirds,Ph(c) 135.00
1218 Fury,Ph(c) 125.00
1219 The Detectives,
   Robert Taylor Ph(c) 150.00
1220 Gunslinger,Ph(c) 150.00
1221 Bonanza,Ph(c) 350.00
1222 Elmer Fudd 60.00
1223 GK,Laramie,Ph(c) 125.00
1224 The Little Rascals 75.00
1225 The Deputy,H.Fonda Ph(c) . 175.00
1226 Nikki, Wild Dog of the North . 90.00
1227 Morgan the Pirate,Ph(c) . . . 135.00
1229 Thief of Bagdad,Ph(c) 125.00
1230 Voyage to the Bottom
   of the Sea,Ph(c) 225.00
1231 Danger Man,Ph(c) 200.00
1232 On the Double 75.00
1233 Tammy Tell Me True 125.00
1234 The Phantom Planet 135.00
1235 Mister Magoo 175.00
1236 King of Kings,Ph(c) 135.00
1237 ATh,The Untouchables,
   Ph(c) 400.00
1238 Deputy Dawg 200.00
1239 CB(c),Donald Duck Album . 150.00
1240 The Detectives,
   R.Taylor Ph(c) 150.00
1241 Sweetie Pies 50.00
1242 King Leonardo and
   His Short Subjects 225.00
1243 Ellery Queen 150.00
1244 Space Mouse 200.00
1245 New Adventures of
   Sherlock Holmes 250.00
1246 Mickey Mouse Album 100.00
1247 Daisy Duck's Diary 150.00
1248 Pluto 125.00
1249 The Danny Thomas Show,
   Ph(c) 300.00
1250 Four Horseman of the
   Apocalypse,Ph(c) 125.00
1251 Everything's Ducky 85.00
1252 The Andy Griffith Show,
   Ph(c) 700.00
1253 Spaceman 135.00
1254 'Diver Dan' 90.00
1255 The Wonders of Aladdin . . . 125.00
1256 Kona, Monarch of
   Monster Isle 135.00
1257 Car 54, Where Are You?,
   Ph(c) 175.00

1258 GE,The Frogmen 135.00
1259 El Cid,Ph(c). 135.00
1260 The Horsemasters,Ph(c) . . . 250.00
1261 Rawhide,C.Eastwood Ph(c) 300.00
1262 The Rebel,Ph(c) 175.00
1263 RsM,77 Sunset Strip,Ph(c) . 150.00
1264 Pixie & Dixie & Mr.Jinks . . . 175.00
1265 The Real McCoys,Ph(c) . . . 150.00
1266 M.G.M.'s Spike and Tyke . . . 50.00
1267 CB,GyroGearloose 125.00
1268 Oswald the Rabbit 60.00
1269 Rawhide,C.Eastwood Ph(c) 300.00
1270 Bullwinkle and Rocky 375.00
1271 Yogi Bear Birthday Party 90.00
1272 Frosty the Snowman 90.00
1273 Hans Brinker,Ph(c) 125.00
1274 Santa Claus Funnies 100.00
1275 Rocky and His Friends 375.00
1276 Dondi 50.00
1278 King Leonardo and
   His Short Subjects 225.00
1279 Grandma Duck's Farm
   Friends 75.00
1280 Hennessey,Ph(c) 110.00
1281 Chilly Willy 80.00
1282 Babes in Toyland,Ph(c). . . . 250.00
1283 Bonanza,Ph(c) 350.00
1284 RH,Laramie,Ph(c). 125.00
1285 Leave It to Beaver,Ph(c) . . . 300.00
1286 The Untouchables,Ph(c) . . . 275.00
1287 Man from Wells Fargo,Ph(c) 100.00
1288 RC,GE,The Twilight Zone . . 250.00
1289 Ellery Queen 150.00
1290 M.G.M.'s Mouse
   Musketeers 50.00
1291 RsM,77 Sunset Strip,Ph(c) . 150.00
1293 Elmer Fudd 55.00
1294 Ripcord 125.00
1295 Mr. Ed, the Talking Horse,
   Ph(c) 250.00
1296 Fury,Ph(c) 125.00
1297 Spanky, Alfalfa and the
   Little Rascals 75.00
1298 The Hathaways,Ph(c) 75.00
1299 Deputy Dawg 200.00
1300 The Comancheros 275.00
1301 Adventures in Paradise 100.00
1302 JohnnyJason,TeenReporter . 50.00
1303 Lad: A Dog,Ph(c). 75.00
1304 Nellie the Nurse 125.00
1305 Mister Magoo 150.00
1306 Target: The Corruptors,
   Ph(c) 100.00
1307 Margie 90.00
1308 Tales of the Wizard of Oz . . 225.00
1309 BK,87th Precinct,Ph(c) 175.00
1310 Huck and Yogi Winter
   Sports 150.00
1311 Rocky and His Friends 375.00
1312 National Velvet,Ph(c) 75.00
1313 Moon Pilot.Ph(c) 135.00
1328 GE,The Underwater
   City,Ph(c) 125.00
1330 GK,Brain Boy 225.00
1332 Bachelor Father 135.00
1333 Short Ribs 90.00
1335 Aggie Mack 60.00
1336 On Stage 75.00
1337 Dr. Kildare,Ph(c) 150.00
1341 The Andy Griffith Show,
   Ph(c) 675.00
1348 JDa,Yak Yak 150.00
1349 Yogi Berra Visits the U.N. . . 175.00
1350 Commanche,Ph(c) 90.00
1354 Calvin and the Colonel 150.00

FOUR FAVORITES
Ace Magazines, Sept., 1941
1 B:Vulcan, Lash Lighting, Magno
   the Magnetic Man, Raven,
   Flag (c),Hitler 2,700.00
2 A: Black Ace 1,300.00

4 Favorites #18
© Ace Magazines

3 E:Vulcan 1,000.00
4 E:Raven,B:Unknown
  Soldiers 900.00
5 B:Captain Courageous 900.00
6 A: The Flag, B: Mr. Risk 800.00
7 JM 800.00
8 . . . . 800.00
9 RP,HK 900.00
10 HK 1,000.00
11 HK,LbC,UnKnown Soldier . . 1,200.00
12 LbC 600.00
13 LbC 500.00
14 Fer 500.00
15 Fer. 500.00
16 Bondage(c) 600.00
17 Magno Lighting 500.00
18 Magno Lighting 500.00
19 RP(a&c) 400.00
20 RP(a&c) 400.00
21 RP(a&c) 400.00
22 RP(c). 350.00
23 RP(c). 350.00
24 RP(c). 350.00
25 RP(c). 350.00
26 RP(c). 350.00
27 RP(c). 300.00
28 . . . . 300.00
29 . . . . 300.00
30 thru 32 . . . . @250.00

4MOST
Novelty Publ./Star Publ.,
Winter 1941
1 The Target, The Cadet 2,500.00
2 The Target. 1,200.00
3 Dan'l Flannel, Flag(c) 700.00
4 Dr. Seuss (1pg.). 700.00
2-1 . . . . 400.00
2-2 . . . . 400.00
2-3 . . . . 400.00
2-4 Hitler,Tojo,Mussolini (c) 600.00
3-1 . . . . 300.00
3-2 . . . . 300.00
3-3 . . . . 300.00
3-4 . . . . 300.00
4-1 . . . . 250.00
4-2 Walter Johnson(c) 250.00
4-3 . . . . 250.00
4-4 . . . . 250.00
5-1 The Target, Football(c) 200.00
5-2 . . . . 200.00
5-3 . . . . 200.00
5-4 Football(c) 200.00
6-1 Skiing(c). 200.00
6-2 LbC(c) 500.00

6-3 Tennis(c) 200.00
6-4 Football(c) 200.00
6-5 . . . . 300.00
7-1 Basketball(c) 200.00
7-2 LbC(c) 500.00
7-3 . . . . 250.00
7-4 LbC(c) 500.00
7-5 . . . . 250.00
7-6 LbC(c) 500.00
Becomes:

FOREMOST BOYS
Jan., 1949
8-1 . . . . 250.00
8-2 LbC(c),Surfing(c) 500.00
8-3 LbC(c) 500.00
8-4 LbC 500.00
8-5 LbC(c) 500.00
8-6 LbC 500.00
38 LbC(c), Johnny Weismuller. . 500.00
39 LbC(c), Johnny Weismuller. . 500.00
40 LbC(c), White Rider 500.00
Becomes:

THRILLING CRIME CASES

FOXHOLE
Mainline Publ., 1954
1 JK. 700.00
2 JK. 500.00
3 JK(c) 400.00
4 JK(c) 400.00
Charlton Comics, 1955–56
5 JK(c) 400.00
6 JK. 400.00
7 . . . . 150.00

FOXY FAGAN
Dearfield Publ. Co., 1946–48
1 . . . . 175.00
2 . . . . 125.00
3 . . . . 100.00
4 . . . . 100.00
5 . . . . 100.00
6 Rocket 100.00
7 . . . . 100.00

FRANK BUCK
Fox Features Syndicate, 1950
1 (70) WW. 425.00
2 (71) WW. 225.00
3 . . . . 175.00

FRANKENSTEIN COMICS
Crestwood Publications
(Prize Publ.), Summer, 1945
1 B:Frankenstein,DBr(a&c) . . . 2,000.00
2 DBr(a&c) 1,000.00
3 DBr(a&c) 750.00
4 DBr(a&c) 750.00
5 DBr(a&c) 750.00
6 DBr(a&c),S&K 600.00
7 DBr(a&c),S&K 600.00
8 DBr(a&c),S&K 600.00
9 DBr(a&c),S&K 600.00
10 DBr(a&c),S&K 600.00
11 DBr(a&c)A:Boris Karloff 500.00
12 DBr(a&c). 500.00
13 DBr(a&c). 500.00
14 DBr(a&c). 500.00
15 DBr(a&c). 500.00
16 DBr(a&c). 500.00
17 DBr(a&c). 500.00
18 DBr,B:Horror 750.00
19 DBr 400.00
3-4 DBr. 350.00
3-5 DBr. 350.00
3-6 DBr. 350.00
4-1 thru 4-6 DBr. . . . . @350.00
5-1 thru 5-4 DBr. . . . . @350.00

Frankenstein Comics #24
© Crestwood Publications

5-5 DBr, Oct.–Nov., 1954 . . . . . . 350.00

FRANK MERRIWELL
AT YALE
Charlton Comics, 1955–56
1 . . . . 100.00
2 thru 4 . . . . @75.00

FREEDOM TRAIN
Street & Smith Publications
1 BP 250.00

FRISKY ANIMALS
ON PARADE
Ajax-Farrell Publ., 1957
1 LbC(c) 250.00
2 . . . . 125.00
3 LbC(c) 250.00

FRISKY FABLES
Novelty Press/Premium Group/
Star Publ., Spring, 1945
1 AFa 250.00
2 AFa 150.00
3 AFa 150.00
4 AFa 125.00
5 AFa 125.00
6 AFa 125.00
7 AFa,Flag (c) 150.00
2-1 AFa,Rainbow(c). 150.00
2-2 AFa 135.00
2-3 AFa 135.00
2-4 AFa 135.00
2-5 AFa 135.00
2-6 AFa 135.00
2-7 AFa 135.00
2-8 AFa,Halloween (c) 135.00
2-9 AFa,Thanksgiving(c) 125.00
2-10 AFa,Christmas (c) 135.00
2-11 AFa. 135.00
2-12 AFa,Valentine's Day (c) 125.00
3-1 AFa 125.00
3-2 AFa 125.00
3-3 AFa 135.00
3-4 AFa 125.00
3-5 AFa 125.00
3-6 AFa 125.00
3-7 AFa 125.00
3-8 AFa,Turkey (c) 125.00
3-9 AFa 125.00
3-10 AFa 125.00
3-11 AFa,1948(c) 125.00
3-12 AFa 125.00

GOLDEN AGE

GOLDEN AGE

4-1 thru 4-7 AFa . . . . @125.00	
5-1 AFa 125.00	
5-2 AFa 125.00	
5-3 . . . . 125.00	
5-4 Star Publications 125.00	
39 LbC(c). 300.00	
40 LbC(c), Christmas 300.00	
41 LbC(c). 300.00	
42 LbC(c). 300.00	
43 LbC(c). 300.00	
Becomes:	

FRISKY ANIMALS
Star Publications Jan., 1951

44 LbC, Super Cat. 300.00	
45 LbC 375.00	
46 LbC,Baseball. 275.00	
47 LbC 275.00	
48 LbC 275.00	
49 LbC 275.00	
50 LbC 275.00	
51 LbC(c). 275.00	
52 LbC(c), Christmas. 300.00	
53 LbC(c). 275.00	
54 LbC(c),Supercat(c) 275.00	
55 LbC(c),same 275.00	
56 LbC(c),same 275.00	
57 LbC(c),same 275.00	
58 LbC(c),same,July, 1954 . . . . 275.00	

FRITZI RITZ
**United Features Syndicate/
St. John Publications,
Fall, 1948**

N# Special issue 250.00	
2 . . . . 150.00	
3 . . . . 125.00	
4 and 5 . . . . @125.00	
6 A:Abbie & Slats 150.00	
7 . . . . 125.00	
Becomes:	

UNITED COMICS
United Features, 1950

8 thru 26 Bushmiller(c) . . . . . . @125.00
Becomes:

FRITZI RITZ
United Features, 1953

27 thru 59 . . . . @100.00

Fritzi Ritz #35
© *United Features*

FROGMAN COMICS
**Hillman Periodicals,
Jan.–Feb., 1952–May, 1953**

1 . . . . 200.00

---

2 . . . . 150.00	
3 . . . . 150.00	
4 MMe. 150.00	
5 BK,AT. 150.00	
6 thru 11 . . . . @100.00	

FROM HERE TO INSANITY
Charlton Comics, 1955

8 . . . . 350.00	
9 . . . . 250.00	
10 SD(c). 350.00	
11 JK 350.00	
12 JK 350.00	
3-1 . . . . 700.00	

FRONTIER FIGHTER
See: DAVY CROCKETT

FRONTIER ROMANCES
**Avon Periodicals,
Nov.–Dec., 1949**

1 She Learned to Ride and Shoot,	
and Kissing Came Natural . . 700.00	
2 Bronc-Busters Sweetheart,	
Jan.–Feb., 1950 . . . . 500.00	

FRONTIER SCOUT
DANIEL BOONE
See: DEATH VALLEY

FRONTIER TRAIL
See: RIDER, THE

FRONTLINE COMBAT
**Tiny Tot Publications
(E.C. Comics), ,
July–Aug., 1951**

1 HK(c),WW, JSe,JDa,Hanhung	
Changjn (c) 1,400.00	
2 HK(c),WW,Tank Battle (c) 650.00	
3 HK(c),WW,Naval Battleship	
fire (c) 800.00	
4 HK(c),WW, Bazooka (c) 600.00	
5 HK(c),JSe 800.00	
6 HK(c),WW,JSe. 450.00	
7 HK(c),WW,JSe,Document of the	
Action at Iwo Jima 450.00	
8 HK(c),WW,ATh 450.00	
9 HK(c),WW,JSe,Civil War iss. . 450.00	
10 GE,HK(c),WW,	
Crying Child (c) 400.00	
11 GE. 300.00	
12 GE,Air Force issue 300.00	
13 JSe,GE,WW(c), Bi-Planes (c). 300.00	
14 JKu,GE,WW(c) 300.00	
15 JSe,GE,WW(c), Jan., 1954 . . 300.00	

FRONT PAGE
COMIC BOOK
Front Page Comics, 1945

1 JKu,BP,BF(c),I:Man in Black . . 600.00

FUGITIVES FROM
JUSTICE
**St. John Publishing Co.,
Feb., 1952**

1 . . . . 300.00	
2 MB, Killer Boomerang 300.00	
3 GT 275.00	
4 . . . . 175.00	
5 Bondage (c), Oct., 1952 . . . . . 250.00	

FUNLAND
**Approved Comics
(Ziff-Davis), 1949**

N# 225.00

FUNLAND COMICS
Croyden Publ., 1945

1 Funny Animal. 250.00

FUNNIES, THE
(1ST SERIES)
Dell Publishing Co., 1929-30

1 B:Foxy Grandpa, Sniffy. 2,500.00	
2 thru 21 . . . . @700.00	
N#(22) thru (36) . . . . @800.00	

FUNNIES, THE
(2ND SERIES)
Dell Publishing Co., Oct., 1936

1 Tailspin Tommy,Mutt & Jeff,	
Capt. Easy,D.Dixon 5,500.00	
2 Scribbly 2,700.00	
3 . . . . 2,000.00	
4 Christmas issue 1,500.00	
5 . . . . 1,500.00	
6 thru 10 . . . . @1,200.00	
11 thru 22 . . . . 1,000.00	
23 thru 29 . . . . @800.00	
30 B:John Carter of Mars 2,700.00	
31 inc. Dick Tracy 1,500.00	
32 . . . . 1,500.00	
33 . . . . 1,500.00	
34 . . . . 1,500.00	
35 AMc,John Carter (c). 1,500.00	
36 AMc,John Carter (c). 1,500.00	
37 AMc,John Carter (c). 1,500.00	
38 Rex King of the Deep (c). . . 1,500.00	
39 Rex King (c). 1,500.00	
40 AMc,John Carter (c). 1,500.00	
41 Sky Ranger (c). 1,500.00	
42 Rex King (c). 1,500.00	
43 Rex King (c). 1,500.00	
44 Rex King (c). 1,500.00	
45 AMc,I&O:Phantasmo:Master	
of the World 1,600.00	
46 AMc,Phantasmo (c) 900.00	
47 AMc,Phantasmo (c) 800.00	
48 AMc,ShM,Phantasmo (c) . . . 800.00	
49 AMc,Phantasmo (c) 800.00	
50 AMc,Phantasmo (c) 800.00	
51 AMc,Phantasmo (c) 800.00	
52 AMc,Phantasmo (c) 750.00	
53 AMc,Phantasmo (c) 750.00	
54 AMc,Phantasmo (c) 750.00	
55 AMc,Phantasmo (c) 750.00	
56 AMc,Phantasmo (c)	
E:John Carter 750.00	
57 AMc,I&O:Captain Midnight. . 6,000.00	
58 AMc,Captain Midnight (c). . . 1,800.00	
59 AMc,Captain Midnight (c). . . 1,800.00	
60 AMc,Captain Midnight (c). . . 1,800.00	
61 AMc,Captain Midnight (c). . . 1,500.00	
62 AMc,Captain Midnight (c). . . 1,200.00	
63 AMc,Captain Midnight (c). . . 1,200.00	
64 B: Woody Woodpecker 1,650.00	
Becomes:	

NEW FUNNIES
Dell Publishing Co. July, 1942

65 Andy Panda, Raggedy Ann &	
Andy, Peter Rabbit 1,600.00	
66 same 750.00	
67 Felix the Cat 750.00	
68 . . . . 750.00	
69 WK, The Brownies 750.00	
70 . . . . 750.00	
71 . . . . 500.00	
72 WK 500.00	
73 . . . . 500.00	
74 . . . . 500.00	
75 WK,Brownies 500.00	
76 CB,Andy Panda, Woody	
Woodpecker 2,000.00	
77 same 500.00	
78 Andy Panda 500.00	

79	350.00
80	350.00
81	350.00
82 WK,Brownies	400.00
83 WK,Brownies	400.00
84 WK,Brownies	400.00
85 WK,Brownies	400.00
86	300.00
87 Woody Woodpecker	250.00
88 same	250.00
89 same	250.00
90 same	250.00
91 thru 99	@200.00
100	175.00
101 thru 110	@150.00
111 thru 118	@150.00
119 Christmas	150.00
120 thru 142	@150.00
143 Christmas (c)	150.00
144 thru 149	@150.00
150 thru 154	@100.00
155 Christmas (c)	150.00
156 thru 167	@100.00
168 Christmas (c)	150.00
169 thru 181	@100.00
182 I&O:Knothead & Splinter	100.00
183 thru 200	@100.00
201 thru 240	@100.00
241 thru 288	@75.00

THE FUNNIES ANNUAL
Avon Periodicals, 1959

1 Best newspaper strips	700.00

FUNNIES ON PARADE
Eastern Color Printing Co., 1933

N# Mutt & Jeff, Joe Palooka	18,000.00

FUNNY BOOK
Funny Book Publ. Corp., (Parents Magazine) Dec., 1952

1 Alec, the Funny Bunny, Alice in Wonderland	200.00
2 Gulliver in Giant-Land	150.00
3	125.00
4 Adventures of Robin Hood	100.00
5 thru 9	@100.00

FUNNY FILMS
Best Syndicated Features (American Comics Group), Sept.–Oct., 1949

1 B:Puss An' Boots, Blunderbunny	250.00
2	125.00
3 Christmas(c)	125.00
4 thru 10	@100.00
11 thru 20	@100.00
21 thru 28	@75.00
29 May–June, 1954	100.00

FUNNY FUNNIES
Nedor Publ. Co., April, 1943

1 Funny Animals	250.00

COMICS MAGAZINE
Comics Magazine/Centaur, May, 1936

1 S&S, Dr. Mystic	17,000.00
2 S&S, Federal Agent	4,000.00
3	3,000.00
4	3,000.00
5	3,000.00

Becomes:

FUNNY PAGES
Centaur, Nov., 1936

6 I:The Clock,1st masked hero	3,600.00

Funny Pages #34
© Centaur

7 WE	1,500.00
8 WE	1,500.00
9	1,500.00
10 WE	1,500.00
11	1,500.00
12	1,000.00
13 FGu,BoW	1,000.00
14 JCo,FGu,BoW	1,000.00
15 JCo	1,000.00
16 JCo,FGu	1,000.00
17 Centaur	1,500.00
18	1,000.00
19	1,000.00
20	1,000.00
21 B:The Arrow	6,000.00
22 BEv,GFx	2,000.00
23	2,000.00
24 BKa,B.Wayne prototype	2,600.00
25 JCo	1,800.00
26	1,800.00
27	1,800.00
28	1,800.00
29 JCo,BoW	1,800.00
30 BoW,The Arrow(c)	4,000.00
31	4,000.00
32 JCo,BoW	2,000.00
33 JCo,BoW,The Arrow(c)	3,000.00
34 JCo,The Arrow(c)	4,000.00
35 BoW,The Arrow(c)	4,000.00
36 Mad Ming (c)	2,000.00
37 JCo,Mad Ming (c)	2,000.00
38 Mad Ming(c)	2,000.00
39 The Arrow(c)	3,000.00
40 BoW,The Arrow(c)	3,000.00
41 BoW,The Arrow(c)	3,000.00
42 BoW,The Arrow(c)	3,000.00

FUNNY PICTURE STORIES
Comics Magazine/Centaur Publ., Nov., 1936

1 B:The Clock	6,000.00
2 The Spinner Talks	2,000.00
3 Tyrant Gold	1,300.00
4 WE,The Brothers Three	1,300.00
5 Timber Terror	1,300.00
6 War in Asia (c)	1,300.00
7 Racist Humor (c)	1,300.00

Vol 2

#1(10)	900.00
#2 (11) BoW	900.00
#3 (12)BoW	800.00
#4 (13) Christmas (c)	900.00
#5 (14) BoW	800.00
#6 (15) Centaur	1,200.00
#7 (16)	700.00

#8 (17)	700.00
#9 (18)	700.00
#10 (19)	700.00
#11 (20)	700.00

Vol 3

#1	700.00
#2	700.00
#3	700.00

Becomes:

COMIC PAGES
July, 1939

4 BoW	850.00
5	650.00
6	650.00

FUNNYMAN
Magazine Enterprises of Canada, Dec., 1947

1 S&K(a&c)	700.00
2 S&K(a&c)	400.00
3 S&K(a&c)	300.00
4 S&K(a&c)	300.00
5 S&K(a&c)	300.00
6 S&K(a&c), Aug., 1948	300.00

FUNNY TUNES
Avon Periodicals, July, 1953

1 (fa),Space Mouse, Peter Rabbit Merry Mouse,Cicero the Cat	150.00
2 same	100.00
3 same	100.00

Becomes:

SPACE COMICS
Avon Periodicals, March–April, 1954

4 (fa),F:Space Mouse	125.00
5 (fa),F:Space Mouse	100.00

FUTURE COMICS
David McKay Publications, June, 1940

1 Lone Ranger,Phantom	4,500.00
2 Lone Ranger	2,000.00
3 Lone Ranger	1,600.00
4 Lone Ranger,Sept., 1940	1,500.00

FUTURE WORLD COMICS
George W. Dougherty, Summer, 1946

1	600.00
2 Fall, 1946	500.00

GABBY HAYES WESTERN
Fawcett Publ., Nov., 1948

1 Ph(c)	750.00
2 Ph(c)	350.00
3 The Rage of the Purple Sage, Ph(c)	225.00
4 Ph(c)	225.00
5 Ph(c)	175.00
6 Ph(c)	175.00
7 Ph(c)	150.00
8 Ph(c)	150.00
9 Ph(c),V:The Kangaroo Crook	150.00
10 Ph(c)	150.00
11 Ph(c), Chariot Race	150.00
12 V:Beaver Ben, The Biting Bandit,Ph(c)	125.00
13 thru 50	@125.00

Charlton Comics

51	125.00
52 thru 59 Dec., 1954	@100.00

GOLDEN AGE

GANGSTERS AND GUN MOLLS

Realistic Comics (Avon), Sept., 1951

1 WW,A:Big Jim Colosimo,
  Evelyn Ellis 675.00
2 JKa, A:Bonnie Parker, The
  Kissing Bandit 500.00
3 EK, A:Juanita Perez, Crimes
  Homicide Squad 450.00
4 A:Mara Hite, Elkins Boys,
  June, 1952 .... 350.00

GANGSTERS CAN'T WIN

D.S. Publishing Co., Feb.–March, 1948

1 Shot Cop (c) 450.00
2 A:Eddie Bentz 250.00
3 Twin Trouble Trigger Man 200.00
4 Suicide on SoundStageSeven 250.00
5 Trail of Terror 200.00
6 Mystery at the Circus 200.00
7 Talisman Trail 150.00
8 .... 150.00
9 Suprise at Buoy 13,
  June–July, 1949 .... 150.00

GANG WORLD

Literary Enterprises (Standard Comics), Oct., 1952

5 Bondage (c) 300.00
6 Mob Payoff, Jan., 1953 ..... 150.00

GASOLINE ALLEY

Star Publications, Oct., 1950

1 .... 275.00
2 LBc 325.00
3 LBc(c), April, 1950 .... 250.00

GEM COMICS

Spotlight Publ. April, 1945

1 A:Steve Strong,Bondage(c) .. 700.00

GENE AUTRY COMICS

Fawcett Publications, Jan., 1942

1 The Mark of Cloven Hoof . 15,000.00
2 .... 2,500.00
3 Secret o/t Aztec Treasure .. 1,700.00
4 .... 1,600.00
5 Mystery of Paint Rock
  Canyon 1,600.00
6 Outlaw Round-up 1,300.00
7 Border Bullets 1,300.00
8 Blazing Guns 1,300.00
9 Range Robbers 1,300.00
10 Fightin' Buckaroo, Danger's
  Trail, Sept., 1943 .... 1,300.00
11 .... 1,200.00
12 .... 1,200.00

GENE AUTRY COMICS

Dell Publishing Co., May/June, 1946

1 .... 1,000.00
2 Ph(c) 600.00
3 Ph(c) 400.00
4 Ph(c),I:Flap Jack 400.00
5 Ph(c), all. 400.00
6 thru 10 .... @300.00
11 thru 19 .... @300.00
20 .... 275.00
21 thru 29 .... @200.00
30 thru 40, B:Giants ...... @175.00
41 thru 56 E:Giants .... @150.00
57 .... 150.00

Gene Autry Comics #62
© Dell Publishing Co.

58 Christmas (c) 125.00
59 thru 66 .... @125.00
67 thru 80, B:Giant .... @125.00
81 thru 90, E:Giant .... @100.00
91 thru 93 .... @100.00
94 Christmas (c) 100.00
95 thru 99 .... @100.00
100 .... 150.00
101 thru 111 .... @125.00
112 thru 121 .... @125.00

GENE AUTRY'S CHAMPION

Dell Publishing Co., Aug., 1950

(1) *see Dell Four Color #287*
(2) *see Dell Four Color #319*
3 .... 150.00
4 thru 19 .... @125.00

GENERAL DOUGLAS MACARTHUR

Fox Features Syndicate, 1950

N# True life story 275.00

GEORGE PAL'S PUPPETOON'S

Fawcett Publications, Dec., 1945

1 Captain Marvel (c) 700.00
2 .... 400.00
3 .... 300.00
4 thru 17 .... @250.00
18 Dec., 1947 .... 200.00

GERALD McBOING-BOING AND THE NEARSIGHTED MR. MAGOO

Dell Publishing Co., Aug.–Oct., 1952

1 .... 225.00
2 thru 5 .... @175.00

GERONIMO

Avon Periodicals, 1950

1 Massacre at San Pedro Pass . 250.00
2 EK(c), Murderous Battle
  at Kiskayah 150.00
3 EK(c) 150.00
4 EK(c),Apache Death Trap,
  Feb., 1952 .... 125.00

GET LOST

Mikeross Publications, Feb.–March, 1954

1 .... 400.00
2 .... 300.00
3 June–July, 1954 .... 225.00

GHOST

Fiction House Magazine, Winter, 1951–Summer, 1954

1 The Banshee Bells 1,400.00
2 I Woke In Terror 800.00
3 The Haunted Hand of X ... 700.00
4 Flee the Mad Furies 350.00
5 The Hex of Ruby Eye 600.00
6 The Sleepers in the Crypt .. 600.00
7 When Dead Rogues Ride ... 600.00
8 Curse of the Mist-Thing 600.00
9 It Crawls by Night,
  Bondage(c) 700.00
10 Halfway to Hades 600.00
11 GE, The Witch's Doll...... 600.00

GHOST BREAKERS

Street & Smith Publ., 1948

1 BP(a&c), A:Dr. Neff 800.00
2 BP(a&c), Breaks the Voodoo
  Hoodoo,Dec., 1948 .... 600.00

GHOSTLY WEIRD STORIES

See: BLUE BOLT

GIANT BOY BOOK OF COMICS

Newsbook Publ. (Lev Gleason), 1945

1 A:Crime Buster & Young
  Robin Hood 1,500.00

GIANT COMICS EDITION

St. John Publ., 1948

1 Mighty Mouse 750.00
2 Abbie and Slats 400.00
3 Terry Toons 600.00
4 Crime Comics 850.00
5 MB, Police Case Book 850.00
6 MB(a&c), Western
  Picture Story 700.00
7 Mopsy 450.00
8 Adventures of Mighty Mouse . 450.00
9 JKu,MB,Romance & Confession
  Stories,Ph(c) 750.00
10 Terry Toons 500.00
11 MB(a&c),JKu,Western
  Picture Stories 700.00
12 MB(a&c),Diary Secrets,
  Prostitute 2,000.00
13 MB,JKu, Romances 750.00
14 Mighty Mouse Album 500.00
15 MB(c),Romance 900.00
16 Little Audrey 550.00
N#, Mighty Mouse Album 500.00

GIANT COMICS EDITION

United Features Syndicate, 1945

1 A:Abbie & Slats, Jim Hardy,
  Ella Cinders,Iron Vic 600.00
2 Elmo, Jim Hardy, Abbie &
  Slats, 1945 .... 400.00

G.I. COMBAT

Quality Comics Group, 1952

1 RC(c), Beyond the Call
  of Duty 1,100.00
2 RC(c), Operation Massacre .. 500.00

G.I. Combat #26
© *Quality Comics Group*

3 An Indestructible Marine 400.00
4 Bridge to Blood Hill 400.00
5 Hell Breaks loose on
    Suicide Hill. 400.00
6 Beachhead Inferno 375.00
7 Fire Power Assault 300.00
8 RC(c),Death-trap Hill 300.00
9 Devil Riders 300.00
10 RC(c), Two-Ton Booby Trap . . 400.00
11 Hell's Heroes. 250.00
12 Hand Grenade Hero 250.00
13 Commando Assault. 250.00
14 Spear Head Assault 250.00
15 Vengeance Assault 250.00
16 Trapped Under Fire. 225.00
17 Attack on Death Mountain. . . . 225.00
18 Red Battle Ground 225.00
19 Death on Helicopter Hill 225.00
20 Doomed Legion-Death Trap . 225.00
21 Red Sneak Attack 200.00
22 Vengeance Raid 200.00
23 No Grandstand in Hell 200.00
24 Operation Steel
    Trap,Comics Code. 200.00
25 Charge of the Commie
    Brigade 200.00
26 Red Guerrilla Trap 200.00
27 Trapped Behind Commie
    Lines 200.00
28 Atomic Battleground 200.00
29 Patrol Ambush 200.00
30 Operation Booby Trap 200.00
31 Human Fly on Heartbreak
    Hill 200.00
32 Atomic Rocket Assault 225.00
33 Bridge to Oblivion 200.00
34 RC,Desperate Mission 225.00
35 Doom Patrol 200.00
36 Fire Power Assault 200.00
37 Attack at Dawn 200.00
38 Get That Tank 200.00
39 Mystery of No Man's Land . . . 200.00
40 Maneuver Battleground 200.00
41 Trumpet of Doom 200.00
42 March of Doom 200.00
43 Operation Showdown 200.00
       See: DC Comics

GIFT COMICS
**Fawcett Publications,
March, 1942**

1 A:Captain Marvel, Bulletman,
    Golden Arrow,Ibis, the
    Invincible, Spy Smasher. . . 4,000.00
2 . . . . 2,500.00

3 . . . . 1,800.00
4 A:Marvel Family, 1949 . . . . . 1,400.00

GIGGLE COMICS
**Creston Publ./
American Comics Group,
Oct., 1943**

1 (fa)same. 500.00
2 KHu 250.00
3 KHu 225.00
4 KHu 200.00
5 KHu 200.00
6 KHu 150.00
7 KHu 150.00
8 KHu 150.00
9 I:Super Katt 175.00
10 KHu. 125.00
11 thru 20 KHu . . . . @125.00
21 thru 30 KHu . . . . @125.00
31 thru 40 KHu. . . . . @100.00
41 thru 94 KHu. . . . . @100.00
95 A:Spencer Spook 100.00
96 KHu. 100.00
97 KHu. 100.00
98 KHu. 100.00
99 KHu. 100.00
100 and 101 March–April,1955 @100.00

G.I. IN BATTLE
Ajax/Farrell, 1952

1 War stories. 150.00
2 thru 9 . . . . @100.00
Ann #1 100 pgs. (1952) 350.00

Ajax, 1957

1 . . . . 125.00
2 . . . . 100.00
3 thru 6 . . . . @100.00

G.I. JANE
**Stanhall Publ.,
May, 1953**

1 . . . . 150.00
2 thru 6 . . . . @125.00
7 thru 9 . . . . @100.00
10 Dec., 1954 . . . . 100.00

G.I. JOE
**Ziff-Davis Publication Co.,
1950**

10 NS(c),Red Devils of Korea,
    V:Seoul City Lou 250.00
11 NS(c),The Guerrilla's Lair 125.00
12 NS(c). 125.00
13 NS(c),Attack at Dawn 125.00
14 NS(c),Temple of Terror,
    A:Peanuts the Great 135.00
2-6 It's a Foot Soldiers Job,
    I:Frankie of the Pump 125.00
2-7 BP,NS(c),The Rout at
    Sugar Creek 125.00
8 BP,NS(c),Waldo'sSqueezeBox 125.00
9 NS(c),Dear John 125.00
10 NS(c),Joe Flies the Payroll . . 125.00
11 NS(c),For the Love of Benny . 125.00
12 NS(c),Patch work Quilt 125.00
13 NS(c). 125.00
14 NS(c),The Wedding Ring 125.00
15 The Lacrosse Whoopee 125.00
16 Mamie's Mortar 125.00
17 A Time for Waiting. 125.00
18 Giant 300.00
19 Old Army Game..Buck Passer 125.00
20 General Confusion 125.00
21 Save 'Im for Brooklyn 125.00
22 Portrait of a Lady 125.00
23 Take Care of My Little Wagon 125.00
24 Operation 'Operation' 125.00
25 The Two-Leaf Clover 125.00
26 NS(c),Nobody Flies Alone
    Mud & Wings. 125.00

27 'Dear Son...Come Home' 125.00
28 They Alway's Come Back
    Bondage (c). 135.00
29 What a Picnic 100.00
30 NS(c),The One-Sleeved
    Kimono 125.00
31 NS(c),Get a Horse 100.00
32 thru 47. . . . . @100.00
48 Atom Bomb 125.00
49 thru 51 June, 1957 . . . . @100.00

GINGER
**Close-Up Publ.
(Archie Publications),
Jan., 1951**

1 GFs,Teen-age 200.00
2 . . . . 150.00
3 . . . . 125.00
4 . . . . 125.00
5 . . . . 100.00
6 . . . . 100.00
7 thru 9 . . . . @125.00
10 A:Katy Keene,Summer,1954. . 150.00

GIRLS IN LOVE
**Fawcett Publications,
May, 1950**

1 Ph(c) 150.00
2 Ph(c),July, 1950 . . . . 100.00

GOLDEN ARROW
**Fawcett Publications,
Spring, 1942**

1 B:Golden Arrow 1,250.00
2 . . . . 600.00
3 . . . . 425.00
4 . . . . 400.00
5 Spring, 1947 . . . . 400.00
6 BK 425.00
6a 1944 Well Known Comics
    (Giveaway) 450.00

GOLDEN LAD
**Spark Publications,
July, 1945–June, 1946**

1 MMe(a&c),A:Kid Wizards,
    Swift Arrow,B:Golden Ladd. 1,200.00
2 MMe(a&c) 600.00
3 MMe(a&c) 600.00
4 MMe(a&c), The Menace of
    the Minstrel 600.00
5 MMe(a&c),O:Golden Girl 600.00

GOLDEN WEST LOVE
**Kirby Publishing Co.,
Sept.–Oct., 1949**

1 BP,I Rode Heartbreak Hill,
    Ph(c) 300.00
2 BP 200.00
3 BP,Ph(c) 200.00
4 BP,April, 1950 . . . . 200.00

GOLD MEDAL COMICS
Cambridge House, 1945

N# Captain Truth, Lucky Man. . . 500.00

GOOFY COMICS
**Nedor Publ. Co./
Animated Cartoons
(Standard Comics),
June, 1943**

1 (fa) 400.00
2 . . . . 250.00
3 VP 250.00
4 VP 225.00
5 VP 225.00
6 thru 10 VP . . . . @225.00
11 thru 15 . . . . @200.00

15 thru 19 . . . . @200.00
20 thru 35 FF . . . . @150.00
36 thru 48 . . . . @100.00

GREAT AMERICAN COMICS PRESENTS– THE SECRET VOICE
4 Star Publ., 1944
1 Hitler,Secret Weapon 600.00

GREAT COMICS
Novak Publ. Co., 1945
1 LbC(c) 650.00

GREAT COMICS
Great Comics Publications, Nov., 1941
1 I:The Great Zarro,Madame
  Strange 2,500.00
2 Buck Johnson 1,100.00
3 The Lost City, Hitler,
  Jan., 1942 . . . . 5,000.00

GREEN GIANT COMICS
Pelican Publications, 1941
1 Black Arrow, Dr. Nerod
  O:Colossus, Green Giant . 19,000.00

GREEN HORNET COMICS
Helnit Publ. Co./ Family Comics (Harvey Publ.), Dec., 1940
1 B:Green Hornet,P(c) 10,000.00
2 Radio Stories 3,500.00
3 BWh(c) 2,500.00
4 BWh(c) 2,000.00
5 BWh(c) 2,000.00
6 . . . . 2,000.00
7 BP, O:Zebra, B:Robin
  Hood & Spirit of 76 . . . . . . 1,700.00
8 BP,Bondage (c) 1,800.00
9 BP,JK(c),Behind the (c) 2,000.00
10 BP 1,800.00
11 Who is Mr. Q? 1,500.00
12 BP,A:Mr.Q 1,500.00
13 Hitler (c) 1,800.00
14 BP,Spirit of 76-Twinkle
  Twins, Bondage(c) 1,200.00
15 ASh(c),Nazi Ghost Ship 1,200.00
16 BP,Prisoner of War 1,200.00
17 BP,ASh(c),Nazis' Last Stand 1,200.00

Green Hornet Comics #25
© Harvey Publications

18 BP,ASh(c),Jap's Treacherous
  Plot,Bondage (c) 1,200.00
19 BP,ASh(c),Clash with the
  Rampaging Japs. 1,200.00
20 BP,ASh(c),Tojo's
  Propaganda Hoax 1,400.00
21 BP,ASh(c),Unwelcome
  Cargo 1,000.00
22 ASh(c),Rendezvous with
  Jap Saboteurs 800.00
23 BF,ASh(c),Jap's Diabolical
  Plot #B2978 . . . . 800.00
24 BF,Science Fiction (c) 1,000.00
25 thru 29 . . . . @750.00
30 BP,JKu,AAv 750.00
31 BP,JKu 750.00
32 BP,JKu 600.00
33 BP,JKu,AAv 600.00
34 BP,JKu 600.00
35 BP,JKu 600.00
36 BP,JKu,Bondage (c) 800.00
37 BP,JKu,AAv,S&K 500.00
38 BP,JKu 500.00
39 S&K,AAv 800.00
40 thru 45 . . . . @500.00
46 Drug 600.00
47 AAv,Sept., 1949 . . . . 500.00

GREEN LAMA
Spark Publications/Prize Publ., Dec., 1944
1 I:Green Lama, Lt. Hercules
  & Boy Champions 2,200.00
2 MRa,Forward to Victory
  in 1945 . . . . 1,500.00
3 MRa,The Riddles of Toys . 1,200.00
4 MRa,Dive Bombs Japan . . . 1,100.00
5 MRa(a&c),Fights for
  the Four Freedoms 1,100.00
6 MRa,Smashes a Plot
  against America 1,100.00
7 MRa,Merry X-Mas 600.00
8 MRa,Smashes Toy Master
  of Crime, March, 1946. . . . . 600.00

GREEN MASK, THE
Fox Features Syndicate, Summer, 1940
1 LF(c),O:Green Mask &
  Domino 6,500.00
2 A:Zanzibar 2,200.00
3 BP 1,500.00
4 B:Navy Jones 1,200.00
5 . . . . 1,000.00
6 B:Nightbird,E:Navy Jones,
  Bondage (c) 800.00
7 B:Timothy Smith &
  The Tumbler 800.00
8 JSs 600.00
9 E:Nightbird, Death Wields
  a Scalpel! 600.00
10 . . . . 500.00
11 The Banshee of Dead
  Man's Hill 500.00
2-1 Election of Skulls 400.00
2-2 Pigeons of Death 400.00
2-3 Wandering Gold Brick 350.00
2-4 Time on His Hands 350.00
2-5 JFe,SFd 450.00
2-6 Adventure of the Disappearing
  Trains, Oct.–Nov., 1946. . . . 450.00

GUMPS, THE
Dell Publishing Co., 1945
1 . . . . 250.00
2 . . . . 200.00
3 thru 5 . . . . @150.00

GUNFIGHTER
See: FAT AND SLAT

GUNS AGAINST GANGSTERS
Curtis Publ./Novelty Press, Sept.–Oct., 1948
1 LbC(a&c),B:Toni Gayle 500.00
2 LbC(a&c) 400.00
3 LbC(a&c) 350.00
4 LbC(a&c) 350.00
5 LbC(a&c) 350.00
6 LbC(a&c),Shark 350.00
2-1 LbC(a&c),Sept.–Oct., 1949 . 350.00

GUNSMOKE
Western Comics, Inc., April–May, 1949
1 Grl(a&c),Gunsmoke & Masked
  Marvel,Bondage (c) 700.00
2 Grl(a&c) 400.00
3 Grl(a&c),Bondage(c) 350.00
4 Grl(c) 250.00
5 Grl(c) 250.00
6 . . . . 225.00
7 . . . . 150.00
8 . . . . 150.00
9 . . . . 150.00
10 . . . . 150.00
11 thru 15 . . . . @125.00
16 Horror, Jan., 1952. . . . . 150.00

GUNSMOKE
Dell Publishing Co., 1957
6 J.Arness Ph(c) all 200.00
7 . . . . 200.00
8 . . . . 200.00
9 . . . . 200.00
10 AW,RC 225.00
11 . . . . 200.00
12 AW 225.00
13 thru 27 . . . . @175.00

GUNSMOKE TRAIL
Four Star Comic. Corp (Ajax/Farrell), 1957
1 Western action. 125.00
2 . . . . 100.00
3 . . . . 100.00
4 . . . . 100.00

HA HA COMICS
Creston Publ. (American Comics Group), Oct., 1943
1 Funny Animal, all 450.00
2 . . . . 200.00
3 . . . . 150.00
4 . . . . 150.00
5 . . . . 150.00
6 thru 10 . . . . @125.00
11 . . . . 100.00
12 KHu 100.00
13 KHu 100.00
14 KHu 100.00
15 KHu 100.00
16 thru 20 KHu. . . . . @100.00
21 thru 30 KHu. . . . . @100.00
31 thru 101 . . . . @100.00
102 Feb.–March, 1955 . . . . 100.00

MISTER RISK
Humor Publ., Oct., 1950
1 (7) B:Mr. Risk 150.00
2 . . . . 150.00
Becomes:

MEN AGAINST CRIME
Ace Magazines, Feb., 1951
3 A:Mr. Risk, Case of the Carnival
    Killer 150.00
4 Murder-And the Crowd Roars 125.00
5 . . . . 125.00
6 . . . . 125.00
7 Get Them! 125.00
Becomes:

HAND OF FATE
Ace Magazines, Dec., 1951
8 MSy 600.00
9 LC 400.00
10 LC 400.00
11 Genie(c) 300.00
12 . . . . 275.00
13 MSy,Hanging(c) 400.00
14 MSy, ... 275.00
15 . . . . 275.00
16 . . . . 275.00
17 . . . . 275.00
18 . . . . 275.00
19 LC,Drug issue,Quicksand(c) . . 400.00
20 LC 300.00
21 LC,Drug issue 400.00
22 LC 300.00
23 LC,Graveyard(c) 400.00
24 LC,Electric Chair 500.00
25 Nov., 1954 . . . . 250.00
25a Dec., 1954 . . . . 275.00

HANGMAN COMICS
See: LAUGH COMICS

HAP HAZARD COMICS
**A.A. Wyn/Red Seal Publ./
Readers Research,
Summer, 1944**
1 Funny Teen 250.00
2 Dog Show 200.00
3 Sgr, ... 150.00
4 Sgr, ... 150.00
5 thru 10 Sgr, ... @150.00
11 thru 13 Sgr, ... @75.00
14 AF(c) 100.00
15 . . . . 75.00
16 thru 24 . . . . @75.00
Becomes:

REAL LOVE
April, 1949
25 Dangerous Dates 200.00
26 . . . . 150.00
27 LbC(c), Revenge Conquest . . 175.00
28 thru 40 . . . . @125.00
41 thru 66 . . . . @100.00
67 Comics code 75.00
68 thru 76, Nov., 1956 . . . . @75.00

HAPPY COMICS
**Nedor Publications/
Animated Cartoons,
Aug., 1943**
1 Funny Animal in all 400.00
2 . . . . 250.00
3 . . . . 150.00
4 . . . . 150.00
5 thru 10 . . . . @150.00
11 thru 20 . . . . @125.00
21 thru 31 . . . . @125.00
32 FF 300.00
33 FF 500.00
34 thru 37 FF . . . . @150.00
38 thru 40 . . . . @100.00
Becomes:

HAPPY RABBIT
Standard Comics, Feb., 1951
41 Funny Animal in all 100.00
42 thru 50 . . . . @75.00

HARVEY COMIC HITS
**Harvey Publications, Oct., 1951
(Formerly: JOE PALOOKA)**
51 Phantom 400.00
52 Steve Canyon's Air Power . . . 200.00
53 Mandrake 300.00
54 Tim Tyler's Tales of Jungle
    Terror 175.00
55 Love Stories of Mary Worth . . 125.00
56 Phantom, Bondage (c) 400.00
57 AR,Kidnap Racket 250.00
58 Girls in White 150.00
59 Tales of the Invisible 200.00
60 Paramount Animated Comics 600.00
61 Casper the Friendly Ghost . . . 750.00
62 Paramount Animated Comics,
    April, 1953 . . . . 225.00

HARVEY COMICS LIBRARY
Harvey Publications, 1952
1 Teen-age dope slaves 2,000.00
2 Sparkle Plenty 350.00

HAUNTED THRILLS
**Four Star Publ.
(Ajax/Farrell), June, 1952**
1 Ellery Queen 750.00
2 LbC,Ellery Queen 450.00
3 Drug Story 500.00
4 Ghouls Castle 400.00
5 Fatal Scapel 400.00
6 Pit of Horror 400.00
7 Trail to a Tomb, Hitler 350.00
8 Vanishing Skull 325.00
9 Madness of Terror 325.00
10 . . . . 325.00
11 Nazi Concentration Camp 400.00
12 RWb 325.00
13 . . . . 275.00
14 RWb, Jesus Christ 300.00
15 The Devil Collects 275.00
16 . . . . 275.00
17 Mirror of Madness 275.00
18 No Place to Go, Lingerie
    Nov.–Dec., 1954 . . . . 300.00

HAUNT OF FEAR
**Fables Publ. (E.C. Comics) ,
May–June, 1950**
15 JCr(a&c),AF,WW 5,000.00
16 JCr(a&c),AF,WW 2,500.00
17 JCr(a&c),AF,WW,O:Crypt
    of Terror,Vault of Horror
    & Haunt of Fear 2,400.00
4 AF(c),WW,JDa 1,500.00
5 JCr(a&c),WW,JDa,Eye Injury 1,200.00
6 JCr(a&c),WW,JDa. 1,000.00
7 JCr(a&c),WW,JDa. 1,000.00
8 AF(c),JKa,JDa,
    Shrunken Head 1,000.00
9 AF(c),JCr,JDa 1,000.00
10 AF(c),Grl,JDa 900.00
11 JKa,Grl,JDa 1,000.00
12 JCr,Grl,JDa 800.00
13 Grl,JDa 800.00
14 Grl(a&c),JDa,O:Old Witch . . . 900.00
15 JDa 700.00
16 Grl(c),JDa,Ray Bradbury
    adaptation 700.00
17 JDa,Grl(c),Classic
    Ghastly (c) 700.00
18 JDa,Grl(c),JKa,Ray Bradbury
    adaptation 700.00
19 JDa,Guillotine (c),
    Bondage (c) 900.00
20 RC,JDa,Grl(a&c) 900.00
21 JDa,Grl(a&c) 800.00
22 JDa,Grl(a&c) 700.00

23 JDa,Grl(a&c) 700.00
22 JDa,Grl(a&c) 700.00
23 JDa,Grl(a&c) 700.00
24 JDa,Grl(a&c) 700.00
25 JDa,Grl(a&c) 700.00
26 RC,JDa,Grl(a&c) 800.00
27 JDa,Grl(a&c), Cannibalism . . . 800.00
28 Dec., 1954 . . . . 750.00

HAWK, THE
**Approved Comics
(Ziff-Davis), Winter, 1951**
1 MA,The Law of the Colt,P(c) . 275.00
2 JKu,Iron Caravan of the
    Mojave, P(c) 125.00
3 Leverett's Last Stand,P(c) . . . 110.00
4 Killer's Town,P(c) 100.00
5 . . . . 100.00
6 . . . . 100.00
7 . . . . 100.00
8 MB(c),Dry River Rampage . . . 150.00
9 MB(a&c),JKu 150.00
10 MB(c) 150.00
11 MB(c) 150.00
12 MB(a&c), May, 1955 . . . . 150.00

HEADLINE COMICS
**American Boys Comics/
Headline Publ. (Prize Publ.),
Feb., 1943**
1 B:Jr. Rangers 1,000.00
2 JaB(a&c) 500.00
3 JaB(a&c) 450.00
4 . . . . 350.00
5 HcK 350.00
6 HcK 350.00
7 HcK,Jr. Rangers 350.00
8 HcK,Hitler (c) 1,000.00
9 HcK 350.00
10 HcK,Hitler story,Wizard(c). . . 400.00
11 . . . . 275.00
12 HcK,Heroes of Yesterday . . . 275.00
13 HcK,A:Blue Streak 275.00
14 HcK,A:Blue Streak 275.00
15 HcK,A:Blue Streak 275.00
16 HcK,O:Atomic Man 450.00
17 Atomic Man(c). 250.00
18 Atomic Man(c). 250.00
19 S&K,Atomic Man(c) 500.00
20 Atomic Man(c). 250.00
21 E:Atomic Man 250.00
22 HcK 200.00
23 S&K(a&c),Valentines Day
    Massacre 400.00

Headline Comics #23
© Prize Publications

GOLDEN AGE

GOLDEN AGE

24 S&K(a&c),You Can't Forget
   a Killer 400.00
25 S&K(a&c),Crime Never Pays . 400.00
26 S&K(a&c),Crime Never Pays . 400.00
27 S&K(a&c),Crime Never Pays . 400.00
28 S&K(a&c),Crime Never Pays . 400.00
29 S&K(a&c),Crime Never Pays . 400.00
30 S&K(a&c),Crime Never Pays . 400.00
31 S&K(a&c),Crime Never Pays . 400.00
32 S&K(a&c),Crime Never Pays . 400.00
33 S&K(a&c),Police and FBI
   Heroes. 400.00
34 S&K(a&c),same 400.00
35 S&K(a&c),same 400.00
36 S&K,same,Ph(c) 350.00
37 S&K,MvS,same,Ph(c) 400.00
38 S&K,same,Ph(c) 150.00
39 S&K,same,Ph(c) 150.00
40 S&K,Ph(c)Violent Crime 150.00
41 Ph(c),J.Edgar Hoover(c) 150.00
42 Ph(c) 125.00
43 Ph(c) 125.00
44 MMe,MvS,WE,S&K 250.00
45 JK 200.00
46 . . . . 150.00
47 . . . . 150.00
48 . . . . 150.00
49 MMe 150.00
50 . . . . 150.00
51 JK 150.00
52 . . . . 150.00
53 . . . . 150.00
54 . . . . 150.00
55 . . . . 150.00
56 S&K 250.00
57 . . . . 100.00
58 . . . . 100.00
59 . . . . 100.00
60 MvS(c). 100.00
61 MMe,MvS(c) 100.00
62 MMe(a&c) 100.00
63 MMe(a&c) 100.00
64 MMe(a&c) 100.00
65 MMe(a&c) 100.00
66 MMe(a&c) 100.00
67 MMe(a&c) 100.00
68 MMe(a&c) 100.00
69 MMe(a&c) 100.00
70 MMe(a&c) 100.00
71 MMe(a&c) 100.00
72 MMe(a&c) 100.00
73 MMe(a&c) 100.00
74 MMe(a&c) 100.00
75 MMe(a&c) 100.00
76 MMe(a&c) 100.00
77 MMe(a&c),Oct., 1956 . . . . . . 100.00

HECKLE AND JECKLE
St. John Publ./Pines,
Nov., 1951
1 Blue Ribbon Comics 300.00
2 Blue Ribbon Comics 150.00
3 . . . . 125.00
4 . . . . 125.00
5 . . . . 125.00
6 . . . . 125.00
7 . . . . 125.00
8 thru 14 . . . . @100.00
15 . . . . 125.00
16 thru 20 . . . . @100.00
21 thru 33 . . . . @100.00
34 June, 1959 . . . . 100.00

HELLO PAL COMICS
Harvey Publications,
Jan., 1943
1 B:Rocketman & Rocket Girl,
   Mickey Rooney, Ph(c) . . 1,500.00
2 Charlie McCarthy, Ph(c) . . . 1,200.00
3 Bob Hope, Ph(c), May, 1943 1,500.00

HE-MAN
Approved Comics
(Ziff-Davis)/Toby Press, 1952
1 "Real-Life Adventure". 200.00
1a 175.00
2a 175.00

HENRY
Dell Publishing Co.,
Oct., 1946
2 . . . . 150.00
3 thru 10 . . . . @150.00
11 thru 20 . . . . @125.00
21 thru 30 . . . . @125.00
31 thru 40 . . . . @100.00
41 thru 50 . . . . @75.00
51 thru 65 . . . . @50.00

HENRY ALDRICH COMICS
Dell Publishing Co.,
Aug.–Sept., 1950
1 . . . . 200.00
2 . . . . 150.00
3 . . . . 125.00
4 . . . . 125.00
5 . . . . 125.00
6 thru 10 . . . . @100.00
11 thru 22 . . . . @75.00

HEROES OF
THE WILD FRONTIER
See: BAFFLING MYSTERIES

Heroic Comics #9
© Eastern Color Printing

HEROIC COMICS
Eastern Color Printing Co./
Famous Funnies Aug., 1940
1 BEv(a&c),O:Hydroman,Purple
   Zombie, B:Man of India . . . 3,000.00
2 BEv(a&c),B:Hydroman (c)s. . 1,500.00
3 BEv(a&c) 750.00
4 BEv(a&c) 750.00
5 BEv(a&c) 650.00
6 BEv(a&c) 650.00
7 BEv(a&c),O:Man O'Metal 750.00
8 BEv(a&c) 500.00
9 BEv 500.00
10 BEv 500.00
11 BEv,E:Hydroman (c)s 500.00
12 BEv,B&O:Music Master 550.00
13 BEv,RC,LF 500.00
14 BEv 550.00
15 BEv,I:Downbeat 550.00

16 BEv,BTh,CCB(c),A:Lieut
   Nininger, Major Heidger,
   Lieut Welch,B:P(c). 350.00
17 BEv,A:JohnJames Powers,Hewitt
   T.Wheless, Irving Strobing. . . 350.00
18 HcK,BEv,Pass the Ammunition 350.00
19 HcK,BEv,A:Barney Ross. 350.00
20 HcK,BEv 350.00
21 HcK,BEv 250.00
22 HcK,BEv,Howard Gilmore. . . . 250.00
23 HcK,BEv 250.00
24 HcK,BEv 250.00
25 HcK,BEv, Rainbow Boy 250.00
26 HcK,BEv 250.00
27 HcK,BEv 250.00
28 HcK,BEv,E:Man O'Metal. 250.00
29 HcK,BEv,E:Hydroman. 250.00
30 BEv 250.00
31 BEv,CCB,Capt. Tootsie 125.00
32 ATh,CCB,WWII(c),
   Capt. Tootsie 150.00
33 ATh, ... 175.00
34 WWII(c) 125.00
35 Ath,B:Rescue(c) 175.00
36 HcK,ATh 150.00
37 same 75.00
38 ATh 150.00
39 HcK,ATh 125.00
40 ATh,Boxing 125.00
41 Grl(c),ATh 125.00
42 ATh 125.00
43 ATh 100.00
44 HcK,ATh 100.00
45 HcK 100.00
46 HcK 100.00
47 HcK 100.00
48 HcK 125.00
49 HcK 100.00
50 HcK 100.00
51 HcK,ATh,AW 150.00
52 HcK,AW 125.00
53 HcK 125.00
54 . . . . 125.00
55 ATh 125.00
56 ATh(c) 100.00
57 ATh(c) 100.00
58 ATh(c) 100.00
59 ATh(c) 100.00
60 ATh(c) 100.00
61 BEv(c) 100.00
62 BEv(c) 100.00
63 BEv(c) 100.00
64 GE,BEv(c) 100.00
65 HcK(c),FF,ATh,AW,GE 150.00
66 HcK(c),FF 125.00
67 HcK(c),FF,Korean War(c) 125.00
68 HcK(c),Korean War(c). 100.00
69 HcK(c),FF 150.00
70 HcK(c),FF,B:Korean War(c) . . . 100.00
71 HcK(c),FF 100.00
72 HcK(c),FF 150.00
73 HcK(c),FF 100.00
74 HcK(c) 100.00
75 HcK(c),FF 100.00
76 thru 80 HcK,HcK(c). . . . . . @100.00
81 FF,HcK(c) 100.00
82 FF,HcK(c) 100.00
83 FF,HcK(c) 100.00
84 HcK(c) 100.00
85 HcK(c) 100.00
86 FF,HcK(c) 120.00
87 FF,HcK(c) 100.00
88 HcK(c),E:Korean War (c)s . . . 100.00
89 HcK(c) 100.00
90 HcK(c) 100.00
91 HcK(c) 100.00
92 HcK(c) 100.00
93 HcK(c) 100.00
94 HcK(c) 120.00
95 HcK(c) 100.00
96 HcK(c) 100.00
97 HcK(c),E:P(c),June, 1955. . . . 100.00

HICKORY
**Comic Magazine
(Quality Comics Group),
Oct., 1949**

1 HSa,	250.00
2 HSa,	125.00
3 HSa,	100.00
4 HSa,	100.00
5 HSa,	100.00
6 HSa,Aug., 1950	100.00

HI-HO COMICS
Four Star Publications, 1946

1 LbC(c)	600.00
2 LbC(c)	300.00
3 1946	250.00

*H-Jinx #1
© American Comics Group*

HI-JINX
**B & I Publ. Co. (American
Comics Group),
July–Aug., 1947**

1 (fa) all	325.00
2	200.00
3	125.00
4 thru 7	@100.00
N#	150.00

HI-LITE COMICS
E.R. Ross Publ. Fall, 1945

1	300.00

HILLBILLY COMICS
Charlton Comics, 1955

1	125.00
2 thru 4 July 1956	@100.00

HI-SCHOOL ROMANCE
Harvey Publications, 1949–58

1 BP,Ph(c)	200.00
2 BP,Ph(c)	150.00
3 BP,Ph(c)	125.00
4 Ph(c)	125.00
5 BPPh(c)	125.00
6 and 7	@125.00
8 BP	125.00
9	125.00
10 Rare	150.00
11 thru 20 BP(in many)	@100.00
21 thru 50	@100.00
51 thru 75	@75.00

HI-SPOT COMICS
See: RED RYDER COMICS

HIT COMICS
**Comics Magazine
(Quality Comics Group),
July, 1940**

1 LF(c),O:Neon,Hercules,I:The Red Bee, B:Bob & Swab, Blaze Barton Strange Twins,X-5 Super Agent Casey Jones,Jack & Jill	12,000.00
2 GT,LF(c),B:Old Witch	4,000.00
3 GT,LF(c),E:Casey Jones	3,700.00
4 GT, LF(c),B:Super Agent & Betty Bates,E:X-5	3,500.00
5 GT,LF(c),B:Red Bee (c)	10,000.00
6 GT,LF(c)	3,000.00
7 GT,LF(c),E:Red Bee (c)	2,800.00
8 GT,LF(c),B:Neon (c)	2,800.00
9 JCo,LF(c),E:Neon (c)	2,800.00
10 JCo,RC,LF(c),B:Hercules(c)	2,800.00
11 JCo,RC,LF(c),A:Hercules	2,700.00
12 JCo,RC,LF(c),A:Hercules	2,200.00
13 JCo,RC,LF(c),A:Hercules	2,200.00
14 JCo,RC,LF(c),A:Hercules	2,200.00
15 JCo,RC,A:Hercules	1,700.00
16 JCo,RC,LF(c),A:Hercules	1,700.00
17 JCo,RC,LF(c),E:Hercules(c)	1,700.00
18 JCo,RC(a&c),O:Stormy Foster,B:Ghost of Flanders	1,800.00
19 JCo,RC(c),B:Stormy Foster(c)	1,450.00
20 JCo,RC(c),A:Stormy Foster	1,500.00
21 JCo,RC(c)	1,500.00
22 JCo.	1,500.00
23 JCo,RC(a&c)	1,400.00
24 JCo,E:Stormy Foster (c)	1,400.00
25 JCo,RP,O:Kid Eternity	2,700.00
26 JCo,RP,A:Black Hawk	1,500.00
27 JCo,RP,B:Kid Eternity (c)s	700.00
28 JCo,RP,A:Her Highness	700.00
29 JCo,RP	700.00
30 JCo,RP,HK,V:Julius Caesar and his Legion of Warriors	650.00
31 JCo,RP	650.00
32 JCo,RP,V:Merlin the Wizard	400.00
33 JCo,RP	375.00
34 JCo,RP,E:Stormy Foster	375.00
35 JCo,Kid Eternity Accused of Murder	375.00
36 JCo,The Witch's Curse	375.00
37 JCo,V:Mr. Silence	375.00
38 JCo	375.00
39 JCo,Runaway River Boat	375.00
40 PG,V:Monster from the Past	375.00
41 PG,Did Kid Eternity Lose His Power?	300.00
42 PG,Kid Eternity Loses Killer Cronson	300.00
43 JCo,PG,V:Modern Bluebeard	300.00
44 JCo,PG,Trips up the Shoe	300.00
45 JCo,PG,Pancho Villa against Don Pablo	300.00
46 JCo,V:Mr. Hardeel.	300.00
47 A Polished Diamond Can Be Rough on Rats	300.00
48 EhH,A Treasure Chest of Trouble	300.00
49 EhH,V:Monsters from the Mirror	300.00
50 EhH,Heads for Trouble	300.00
51 EhH,Enters the Forgotten World	250.00
52 EhH,Heroes out of the Past	250.00
53 EhH,V:Mr. Puny	250.00
54 V:Ghost Town Killer.	250.00
55 V:The Brute	250.00
56 V:Big Odds	250.00

*Hit Comics #58
© Quality Comics Group*

57 Solves the Picture in a Frame	250.00
58 Destroys Oppression!	250.00
59 Battles Tomorrow's Crimes Today!	250.00
60 E:Kid Eternity (c)s, V:The Mummy	250.00
61 RC(a&c),I:Jeb Rivers	300.00
62 RC(c).	250.00
63 RC(c),A:Jeb Rivers	300.00
64 RC,A:Jeb Rivers	300.00
65 Bondage (c),RC,July, 1950	350.00

HOLIDAY COMICS
Fawcett Publ., Nov., 1942

1 Captain Marvel (c)	2,700.00

HOLLYWOOD COMICS
**New Age Publishers,
Winter, 1944**

1 (fa)	225.00

HOLLYWOOD CONFESSIONS
**St. John Publ. Co.,
Oct., 1949**

1 JKu(a&c)	400.00
2 JKu(a&c), Dec., 1949	475.00

HOLLYWOOD DIARY
**Comics Magazine
(Quality Comics), Dec., 1949**

1	250.00
2 Photo (c)	200.00
3 Photo (c)	150.00
4	150.00
5 Photo (c), Aug., 1950	150.00

HOLLYWOOD FILM STORIES
**Feature Publications,
(Prize) April, 1950**

1 June Allison,Ph(c)	250.00
2 Lizabeth Scott,Ph(c)	175.00
3 Barbara Stanwick,Ph(c)	175.00
4 Beth Hutton, Aug., 1950	175.00

HOLLYWOOD SECRETS
**Comics Magazine
(Quality Comics Group),
Nov., 1949**

1 BWa,BWa(c)	450.00

2 BWa,BWa(c),RC 300.00
3 Ph(c) 200.00
4 Ph(c),May, 1950 . . . . 200.00
5 Ph(c) 200.00
6 Ph(c) 200.00

HOLYOKE ONE-SHOT
Tem Publ.
(Holyoke Publ. Co.), 1944
1 Grit Grady 300.00
2 Rusty Dugan 300.00
3 JK,Miss Victory,O:Cat Woman. 400.00
4 Mr. Miracle 250.00
5 U.S. Border Patrol 250.00
6 Capt. Fearless 250.00
7 Strong Man 300.00
8 Blue Streak 200.00
9 S&K, Citizen Smith 300.00
10 S&K, Capt. Stone 300.00

THE HOODED HORSEMAN
See: OUT OF THE NIGHT

HOORAY COMICS
Tendon Publishing Co., 1946
1 Funny animal 250.00

HOOT GIBSON WESTERN
Fox Features Syndicate, 1950
(Formerly: MY LOVE STORY)
1 (5) Ph(c). 350.00
2 (6) 325.00
3 WW 350.00

HOPALONG CASSIDY
Fawcett Publications,
Feb., 1943
1 B:Hopalong Cassidy & Topper,
   Captain Marvel (c) 9,000.00
2 . . . . 1,200.00
3 Blazing Trails 600.00
4 5-full length story 500.00
5 Death in the Saddle, Ph(c) . . . 450.00
6 . . . . 450.00
7 . . . . 450.00
8 Phantom Stage Coach,Ph(c) . 450.00
9 The Last Stockade 450.00
10 4-spine tingling adventures. . . 450.00
11 Desperate Jetters! Ph(c). 300.00
12 The Mysterious Message 300.00
13 The Human Target, Ph(c) 300.00
14 Land of the Lawless, Ph(c) . . . 300.00
15 Death holds the Reins, Ph(c) . 300.00
16 Webfoot's Revenge, Ph(c) . . . 300.00

Hopalong Cassidy #18
© Fawcett Publications

17 The Hangman's Noose, Ph(c) 300.00
18 The Ghost of Dude Ranch,
   Ph(c) 300.00
19 A:William Boyd,Ph(c) 300.00
20 The Notorious Nellie Blaine!,
   B:P(c). 225.00
21 V:Arizona Kid 225.00
22 V:Arizona Kid 225.00
23 Hayride Horror 225.00
24 Twin River Giant 225.00
25 On the Trails of the Wild
   and Wooly West 225.00
26 thru 30 . . . . @200.00
31 52 pages 150.00
32 36 pages 150.00
33 52 pages 150.00
34 52 pages 150.00
35 52 pages 150.00
36 36 pages 125.00
37 thru 40, 52 pages . . . . . . @150.00
40 36 pages 150.00
41 E:P(c) 150.00
42 B:Ph(c) 150.00
43 . . . . 150.00
44 . . . . 125.00
45 . . . . 135.00
46 thru 51 . . . . @125.00
52 . . . . 100.00
53 . . . . 125.00
54 . . . . 125.00
55 . . . . 100.00
56 . . . . 125.00
57 thru 70 . . . . @125.00
71 thru 84, Ph(c)s . . . . @100.00
85 E:Ph(c),Jan., 1954 . . . . 125.00

HOPPY THE
MARVEL BUNNY
Fawcett Publications,
Dec., 1945
1 A:Marvel Bunny 500.00
2 . . . . 250.00
3 . . . . 225.00
4 . . . . 225.00
5 . . . . 225.00
6 thru 14 . . . . @200.00
15 Sept., 1947 . . . . 200.00

HORRIFIC
Artful/Comic Media/
Harwell Publ./Mystery,
Sept., 1952
1 Conductor in Flames(c) 800.00
2 Human Puppets(c). 400.00
3 DH(c),Bullet hole in
   head(c) 900.00
4 DH(c),head on a stick (c) . . . 350.00
5 DH(c) 350.00
6 DH(c),Jack the Ripper 400.00
7 DH(c),Shrunken Skulls 350.00
8 DH(c),I:The Teller 450.00
9 DH(c),Claws of Horror, Wolves
   of Midnight 350.00
10 DH(c),The Teller-Four
   Eerie Tales of Horror 350.00
11 DH(c),A:Gary Ghoul,Freddie,
   Demon,Victor Vampire
   Walter Werewolf 300.00
12 DH(c),A:Gary Ghoul,Freddie
   Demon,Victor Vampire,
   Walter Werewolf 300.00
13 DH(c),A:Gary Ghoul,Freddie
   Demom,Victor Vampire,
   Walter Werewolf 300.00
Becomes:

TERRIFIC COMICS
Dec., 1954
14 Eye Injury 900.00
15 . . . . 400.00
16 B:Wonderboy 400.00

Becomes:
WONDERBOY
Ajax/Farrell Publ., May, 1955
17 The Enemy's Enemy. 700.00
18 Success is No Accident,
   July, 1955 . . . . 550.00

HORROR FROM
THE TOMB
See: MYSTERIOUS
STORIES

HORSE FEATHER
COMICS
Lev Gleason Publications,
Nov., 1947
1 BW 300.00
2 . . . . 200.00
3 . . . . 150.00
4 Summer, 1948 . . . . 150.00

HOT ROD AND
SPEEDWAY COMICS
Hillman Periodicals
Feb.–March, 1952
1 . . . . 375.00
2 BK 250.00
3 . . . . 200.00
4 . . . . 200.00
5 April–May, 1953 . . . . 200.00

HOT ROD COMICS
Fawcett Publications,
Feb., 1952–53
N# BP,BP(c),F:Clint Curtis 500.00
2 BP,BP(c),Safety comes First . . 275.00
3 BP,BP(c),The Racing Game . . 200.00
4 BP,BP(c),Bonneville National
   Championships 200.00
5 BP,BP(c), ... 200.00
6 BP,BP(c),Race to Death 200.00

HOT ROD KING
Approved Comics
(Ziff-Davis), Fall, 1952
1 P(c) 350.00

HOT RODS
AND RACING CARS
Motor Mag./
Charlton Comics, 1951
1 Speedy Davis. 375.00
2 . . . . 200.00
3 thru 10 . . . . @150.00
11 thru 20 . . . . @125.00
21 thru 70 . . . . @100.00

HOWDY DOODY
Dell Publishing Co.,
Jan., 1950
1 Ph(c) 1,900.00
2 Ph(c) 800.00
3 Ph(c) 450.00
4 Ph(c) 450.00
5 Ph(c) 450.00
6 P(c) 450.00
7 thru 10 . . . . @275.00
11 . . . . 250.00
12 . . . . 250.00
13 Christmas (c) 250.00
14 thru 20. . . . . @250.00
21 thru 38. . . . . @200.00

Howdy Doody #17
© *Dell Publishing Co.*

HOW STALIN HOPES WE WILL DESTROY AMERICA
Pictorial News, 1951
N# (Giveaway) 750.00

HOW TO SHOOT
Remington, 1952
N# (promotional) 100.00

HUMBUG
Harvey Kurtzman, 1957
1 JDa,WW,WE,End of the World 400.00
2 JDa,WE,Radiator........... 200.00
3 JDa,WE 150.00
4 JDa,WE,Queen Victoria(c). ... 150.00
5 JDa,WE 150.00
6 JDa,WE 150.00
7 JDa,WE,Sputnik(c). 175.00
8 JDa,WE,Elvis/George
   Washington(c) 150.00
9 JDa,WE 150.00
10 JDa,Magazine............. 250.00
11 JDa,WE,HK,Magazine 200.00

HUMDINGER
Novelty Press/Premium Service, May–June, 1946
1 B:Jerkwater Line,Dink,
   Mickey Starlight 500.00
2 .... 250.00
3 .... 200.00
4 .... 200.00
5 .... 200.00
6 .... 200.00
2-1 .... 175.00
2-2 July–Aug., 1947 .... 175.00

HUMPHREY COMICS
Harvey Publications, Oct., 1948
1 BP,Joe Palooka 200.00
2 BP 125.00
3 BP 110.00
4 BP,A:Boy Heroes.......... 125.00
5 BP 100.00
6 BP 100.00
7 BP,A:Little Dot 100.00
8 BP,O:Humphrey........... 100.00
9 BP 100.00
10 BP 100.00

11 thru 21 .... @100.00
22 April, 1952............. 100.00

HUNTED
Fox Features Syndicate, 1950
(Formerly: MY LOVE MEMOIRS)
1 (13) Famous Crime Cases ... 450.00
2 .... 200.00

HURRICANE COMICS
Cambridge House, 1945
1 F:Hurry Kane............. 350.00

HYPER MYSTERY COMICS
Hyper Publications, May, 1940
1 B:Hyper 3,200.00
2 June, 1940 .... 2,000.00

IBIS, THE INVINCIBLE
Fawcett Publications, Jan., 1942–Spring, 1948
1 MRa(c),O:Ibis 3,500.00
2 Bondage (c) 1,800.00
3 BW 1,500.00
4 BW,A:Mystic Snake People .. 900.00
5 BW,Bondage (c),The
   Devil's Ibistick 1,000.00
6 BW, The Book of Evil 1,000.00

IF THE DEVIL WOULD TALK
Catechetical Guild, 1950
N# Rare 1,200.00
N#, 1958 Very Rare 850.00

ILLUSTRATED STORIES OF THE OPERAS
B. Bailey Publ. Co., 1943
N# Faust 900.00
N# Aida 850.00
N# Carman 850.00
N# Rigoletto 850.00

I LOVED
See: ZOOT COMICS

I LOVE LUCY COMICS
Dell Publishing Co., 1954
(1) *see Dell Four Color #535*
(2) *see Dell Four Color #559*
3 Lucile Ball Ph(c) all 400.00
4 .... 350.00
5 .... 350.00
6 thru 10 .... @300.00
11 thru 20 .... @200.00
21 thru 35 .... @175.00

IMPACT
E.C. Comics, March–April, 1955
1 RC,GE,BK,Grl 400.00
2 RC,JDu,Grl,BK,JO......... 275.00
3 JO,RC,JDU,Grl,JKa,BK...... 250.00
4 RC,JO,JDa,GE,Grl,BK....... 250.00
5 Nov.–Dec., 1955 .... 250.00

INCREDIBLE SCIENCE FANTASY
See: WEIRD SCIENCE

INCREDIBLE SCIENCE FICTION
E.C. Comics, July–Aug., 1955
30 JDa,BK,JO,WW 800.00
31 AW,WW,BK 750.00
32 AW,JDa,BK,JO 750.00
33JDa,BK,JO,WW 750.00

INDIAN BRAVES
See: BAFFLING MYSTERIES

INDIAN CHIEF
Dell Publishing Co., July–Sept., 1951
3 P(c) all 125.00
4 .... 100.00
5 .... 100.00
6 A:White Eagle 100.00
7 .... 100.00
8 .... 100.00
9 .... 100.00
10 .... 100.00
11 .... 100.00
12 I:White Eagle 125.00
13 thru 29................ @100.00
30 SB 75.00
31 thru 33 SB.............. @75.00

INDIAN FIGHTER
Youthful Magazines, May, 1950
1 Revenge of Chief Crazy
   Horse 200.00
2 Bondage (c) 200.00
3 .... 100.00
4 Cheyenne Warpath 100.00
5 .... 100.00
6 Davy Crockett in Death Stalks
   the Alamo 100.00
7 Tom Horn-Bloodshed at
   Massacre Valley 100.00
8 Tales of Wild Bill Hickory,
   Jan., 1952 .... 100.00

INDIANS
Wings Publ. Co. (Fiction House), Spring, 1950
1 B:Long Bow, Manzar, White
   Indian & Orphan 400.00
2 B:Starlight 200.00
3 Longbow(c) 175.00
4 Longbow(c) 150.00
5 Manzar(c). 175.00
6 Captive of the Semecas 150.00
7 Longbow(c) 150.00
8 A:Long Bow 150.00
9 A:Long Bow 150.00
10 Manzar(c) 150.00
11 thru 16................ @125.00
17 Spring, 1953,Longbow(c) 125.00

INDIANS ON THE WARPATH
St. John Publ. Co., 1950
N# MB(c). 450.00

INDIAN WARRIORS
See: OUTLAWS, THE

INFORMER, THE
Feature Television Productions, April, 1954
1 MSy,The Greatest Social
   Menace of our Time! 200.00
2 MSy 150.00
3 MSy 100.00
4 MSy 100.00
5 Dec., 1954 .... 100.00

GOLDEN AGE

INSIDE CRIME
Hero Books/
Fox Feature Syndicate, 1950
1 . . . . 400.00
2 . . . . 300.00
N# 150.00

INTERNATIONAL COMICS
See: CRIME PATROL

INTERNATIONAL
CRIME PATROL
See: CRIME PATROL

INTIMATE
CONFESSIONS
Fawcett Publ./
Realistic Comics, 1951
1a P(c) all, Unmarried Bride . . 1,200.00
1 EK,EK(c),Days of Temptation...
    Nights of Desire 300.00
2 Doomed to Silence 300.00
3 EK(c), The Only Man For Me . 175.00
3a Robert Briffault 325.00
4 EK(c),Tormented Love 275.00
5 Her Secret Sin 275.00
6 Reckless Pick-up 275.00
7 A Love Like Ours,Spanking . . . 275.00
8 Fatal Woman, March, 1953 . . 250.00

INTRIGUE
Comics Magazine (Quality
Comics Group), 1955
1 LbC,Ghost Ship 450.00

INVISIBLE
SCARLET O'NEIL
Harvey Publications,
Dec., 1950
1 . . . . 200.00
2 . . . . 150.00
3 April, 1951 . . . . 150.00

IRON VIC
United Features Syndicate/
St. John Publ. Co., 1940
1-shot 500.00

IS THIS TOMORROW?
Catechetical Guild, 1950
1 Communist threat 250.00
2 (1) Canada. 150.00
3 (1) America 200.00
4 (1) Turkey. 100.00
5 (1) Australia 150.00

IT REALLY HAPPENED
William H. Wise/
Visual Editions, 1945
1 Benjamin Franklin, Kit Carson 300.00
2 The Terrible Tiddlers 200.00
3 Maid of the Margiris 150.00
4 Chaplain Albert J. Hoffman . . . 150.00
5 AS(c),Monarchs of the Sea,Lou
    Gehrig, Amelia Earhart 275.00
6 AS(c),Ernie Pyle 150.00
7 FGu,Teddy Roosevelt,Jefferson
    Davis,Story of the Helicopter. 150.00
8 FGu,Man O' War,Roy Rogers . 250.00
9 AS(c),The Story of
    Old Ironsides 150.00
10 AS(c),Honus Wagner, The
    Story of Mark Twain. 200.00
11 AS(c),MB,Queen of the Spanish
    Main, Oct., 1947 . . . . 175.00

IT'S FUN TO STAY ALIVE
Nat.'l Auto Dealers Assoc., 1947
1 Bugs Bunny 250.00

JACE PEARSON OF
THE TEXAS RANGERS
Dell Publishing Co., May, 1952
(1) *see Dell Four Color #396*
2 Ph(c),Joel McRae 150.00
3 Ph(c),Joel McRae 150.00
4 Ph(c),Joel McRae 150.00
5 Ph(c),Joel McRae 150.00
6 Ph(c),Joel McRae 150.00
7 Ph(c),Joel McRae 150.00
8 Ph(c),Joel McRae 150.00
9 Ph(c),Joel McRae 150.00
(10) *see Dell Four Color #648*
Becomes:

TALES OF JACE
PEARSON OF
THE TEXAS RANGERS
Feb., 1955
11 . . . . 125.00
12 . . . . 125.00
13 . . . . 125.00
14 . . . . 125.00
15 ATh 150.00
16 ATh 150.00
17 thru 20 . . . . @100.00

JACK ARMSTRONG
Parents' Institute,
Nov., 1947
1 Artic Mystery 700.00
2 Den of the Golden Dragon . . . 275.00
3 Lost Valley of Ice 200.00
4 Land of the Leopard Men 200.00
5 Fight against Racketeers of
    the Ring 200.00
6 . . . . 175.00
7 Baffling Mystery on the
    Diamond 175.00
8 . . . . 175.00
9 Mystery of the Midgets 175.00
10 Secret Cargo. 175.00
11 . . . . 175.00
12 Madman's Island, rare 200.00
13 Sept., 1949 . . . . 175.00

Jackie Gleason #4
© St. John Publishing Col

JACKIE GLEASON
St. John Publishing Co.,
Sept., 1955
1 Ph(c) 900.00
2 . . . . 550.00
3 . . . . 500.00
4 Dec., 1955 . . . . 500.00

JACKIE ROBINSON
Fawcett Publications,
May, 1950
N# Ph(c) all issues. 1,800.00
2 . . . . 1,000.00
3 . . . . 900.00
4 . . . . 900.00
5 . . . . 900.00
6 May, 1952 . . . . 900.00

JACK IN THE BOX
See: YELLOW JACKET
COMICS

JACKPOT COMICS
MLJ Magazines, Spring, 1941
1 CBi(c),B:Black Hood,Mr.Justice,
    Steel Sterling,Sgt.Boyle . . 5,500.00
2 SCp(c), ... 2,400.00
3 Bondage (c) 1,800.00
4 First Archie 7,000.00
5 Hitler(c) 2,500.00
6 Son of the Skull v:Black
    Hood, Bondage(c) 1,800.00
7 Bondage (c) 1,800.00
8 Sal(c), ... 1,500.00
9 Sal(c), ... 1,500.00
Becomes:

JOLLY JINGLES
Summer, 1943
10 Super Duck,(fa). 500.00
11 Super Duck 250.00
12 Hitler parody (c),A:Woody
    Woodpecker 350.00
13 thru 15 Super Duck . . . . @150.00
16 Dec., 1944 . . . . 150.00

JACK THE GIANT
KILLER
Bimfort & Co.,
Aug.–Sept., 1953
1 HcK,HcK(c) 300.00

JAMBOREE
Round Publishing Co.,
Feb., 1946
1 . . . . 350.00
2 March, 1946 . . . . 200.00

JANE ARDEN
St. John Publ. Co.,
March, 1948
1 . . . . 200.00
2 June, 1948 . . . . 150.00

JEEP COMICS
R.B. Leffingwell & Co.,
Winter, 1944
1 B;Captain Power 850.00
2 . . . . 500.00
3 LbC(c),March–April, 1948 . . . 650.00

JEFF JORDAN,
U.S. AGENT
D.S. Publ. Co., Dec., 1947
1 . . . . 250.00

JERRY DRUMMER
Charlton Comics, 1957
1 Revolutionary War 100.00
2 . . . . 100.00

JESSE JAMES
**Avon Periodicals/
Realistic Publ., Aug., 1950**
1 JKu,The San Antonio Stage
  Robbery 250.00
2 JKu,The Daring Liberty Bank
  Robbery 175.00
3 JKu,The California Stagecoach
  Robberies 175.00
4 EK(c),Deadliest Deed! 100.00
5 JKu,WW,Great Prison Break . . 175.00
6 JKu,Wanted Dead or Alive . . . 175.00
7 JKu,Six-Gun Slaughter at
  San Romano! 150.00
8 EK,Daring Train Robbery! 125.00
9 EK 100.00
10 thru 14 {Do not exist}
15 EK 125.00
16 EK, Butch Cassidy 100.00
17 EK, Jessie James 100.00
18 JKu 100.00
19 JKu 100.00
20 AW,FF,A:Chief Vic,Kit West . . 200.00
21 EK, Two Jessie James 100.00
22 EK,Chuck Wagon 100.00
23 EK 100.00
24 EK,B:New McCarty 100.00
25 EK 100.00
26 EK 100.00
27 EK,E:New McCarty 100.00
28 Quantrells Raiders 100.00
29 Aug., 1956. . . . . 100.00

JEST
Harry 'A' Chesler, 1944
10 J. Rebel,Yankee Boy 300.00
11 1944,Little Nemo 350.00

JET ACES
**Real Adventure Publ. Co.
(Fiction House), 1952**
1 Set 'em up in MIG Alley 200.00
2 Kiss-Off for Moscow Molly . . . 125.00
3 Red Task Force Sighted 125.00
4 Death-Date at 40,000, 1953 . . 125.00

JET FIGHTERS
**Standard Magazines,
Nov., 1953**
5 ATh,Korean War Stories 150.00
6 Circus Pilot 125.00
7 ATh, Iron Curtains for Ivan,
  March, 1953 . . . . 150.00

JETTA OF THE 21st CENTURY
Standard Comics, Dec., 1952
5 Teen Stories. 300.00
6 Robot (c) 250.00
7 April, 1953 . . . . 150.00

JIGGS AND MAGGIE
**Best Books (Standard)/
Harvey Publ., June, 1949**
11 . . . . 150.00
12 thru 21 . . . . @100.00
22 thru 25. . . . . @100.00
26 Part 3-D 200.00
27 Feb.–March, 1954. . . . . 100.00

JIM BOWIE
See: DANGER

JIM DANDY
**Dandy Magazine
(Lev Gleason), 1956**
1 Teen-age humor. 125.00
2 . . . . 100.00
3 . . . . 100.00

JIM HARDY
Spotlight Publ., 1944
N# Dynamite Jim,Mirror Man . . . 600.00

JIM RAY'S AVIATION SKETCH BOOK
Vital Publishers, Feb., 1946
1 Radar, the Invisible eye 550.00
2 Gen.Hap Arnold, May, 1946 . . 350.00

*Jingle Jangle Comics #6
© Eastern Color Printing*

JINGLE JANGLE COMICS
**Eastern Color Printing Co.,
Feb., 1942**
1 B:Benny Bear,Pie Face Prince,
  Jingle Jangle Tales,Hortense 700.00
2 GCn 350.00
3 GCn 300.00
4 GCn,Pie Face (c). 300.00
5 GCn,B:Pie Face. 300.00
6 GCn, ... 250.00
7 . . . . 250.00
8 . . . . 250.00
9 . . . . 250.00
10 . . . . 250.00
11 . . . . 200.00
12 . . . . 200.00
13 . . . . 200.00
14 . . . . 200.00
15 E:Pie Face. . . . . @200.00
16 thru 20. . . . . @175.00
21 thru 25. . . . . @150.00
26 thru 30. . . . . @150.00
31 thru 41. . . . . @100.00
42 Dec., 1949 . . . . 100.00

JING PALS
**Victory Publ. Corp.,
Feb., 1946**
1 Johnny Rabbit 250.00
2 . . . . 200.00
3 . . . . 200.00
4 Aug., 1948 . . . . 200.00

JOE COLLEGE
**Hillman Periodicals,
Fall, 1949**
1 BP,DPr 150.00
2 BP, Winter, 1949 . . . . 125.00

JOE LOUIS
**Fawcett Periodicals,
Sept., 1950**
1 Ph(c),Life Story 800.00
2 Ph(c),Nov., 1950 . . . . 500.00

JOE PALOOKA
**Publication Enterprises
(Columbia Comics Group) 1943**
1 Lost in the Desert 1,500.00
2 Hitler (c) 850.00
3 KO's the Nazis! 600.00
4 Eiffel tower (c), 1944 . . . . . . 450.00

JOE PALOOKA
**Harvey Publications,
Nov., 1945–March, 1961**
1 Joe Tells How He Became
  World Champ 700.00
2 Skiing (c) 350.00
3 . . . . 200.00
4 Welcome Home Pals! 200.00
5 S&K,The Great Carnival
  Murder Mystery 275.00
6 Classic Joe Palooka (c). 200.00
7 BP,V:Grumpopski 200.00
8 BP,Mystery of the Ghost Ship . 150.00
9 Drooten Island Mystery 150.00
10 BP 150.00
11 . . . . 125.00
12 BP,Boxing Course. 125.00
13 . . . . 110.00
14 BP,Palooka's Toughest Fight. . 110.00
15 BP,O:Humphrey 200.00
16 BP,A:Humphrey. 110.00
17 BP,I:Little Max,A:Humphrey . . 200.00
18 A:Little Max 110.00
19 BP,Freedom Train(c). 125.00
20 Punch Out(c). 110.00
21 . . . . 100.00
22 V:Assassin 100.00
23 Big Bathing Beauty Issue . . . 100.00
24 . . . . 100.00
25 . . . . 100.00
26 BP,Big Prize Fight Robberies . 100.00
27 BP,Mystery of Bal
  Eagle Cabin,A:Little Max 110.00
28 BP,Fights Out West, Babe
  Ruth. 100.00
29 BP,Joe Busts Crime
  Wide Open 100.00
30 BP,V:Hoodlums, Nude
  Painting 125.00
31 BP, Dizzy Dean. 125.00
32 BP,Fight Palooka Was Sure
  to Lose. 100.00
33 BP,Joe finds Ann. 100.00
34 BP,How to Box like a Champ . 100.00
35 BP,More Adventures of Little
  Max, Joe Louis 125.00
36 BP 100.00
37 BP,Joe as a Boy 100.00
38 BP 100.00
39 BP,Original Hillbillies with
  Big Leviticus 100.00
40 BP,Joe's Toughest Fight 100.00
41 BP,Humphrey's Grudge Fight . 100.00
42 BP. 100.00
43 BP 100.00
44 BP,M:Ann Howe, Markies 125.00
45 BP 90.00
46 Champ of Champs 90.00
47 BreathtakingUnderwaterBattle . 90.00
48 BP,Exciting Indian Adventure . . 90.00

All comics prices listed are for *Near Mint* condition.

49 BP	90.00
50 BP,Bondage(c)	90.00
51 BP, Babe Ruth	90.00
52 BP,V:Balonki	90.00
53 BP	90.00
54 V:Bad Man Trigger McGehee	90.00
55	90.00
56 Foul Play on the High Seas	90.00
57 Curtains for the Champ	90.00
58 V:The Man-Eating Swamp Terror	90.00
59 The Enemy Attacks	90.00
60 Joe Fights Escaped Convict	90.00
61	90.00
62 S&K, Boy Explorers	125.00
63	90.00
64	90.00
65	90.00
66 Drug	125.00
67 Drug	150.00
68	90.00
69 Torture	150.00
70 BP, Vs. "Gooks"	90.00
71 Bloody Bayonets	90.00
72 Tank	90.00
73 BP	90.00
74 thru 115	@90.00
116 thru 117 giants	@150.00
118 Giant, Jack Dempsey	@150.00
Giant 1 Body Building	150.00
Giant 2 Fights His Way Back	200.00
Giant 3 Visits Lost City	125.00
Giant 4 All in Family	150.00

JOE YANK
Visual Editions (Standard Comics), March, 1952

5 ATh,WE,Korean Jackpot!	150.00
6 Bacon and Bullets, G.I.Renegade	150.00
7 Two-Man War,A:Sgt. Glamour	100.00
8 ATh(c),Miss Foxhole of 1952,	125.00
9 G.I.'s and Dolls,Colonel Blood	75.00
10 A Good Way to Die, A:General Joe	75.00
11	75.00
12 RA	75.00
13	75.00
14	75.00
15	75.00
16 July, 1954	75.00

JOHN HIX SCRAPBOOK
Eastern Color Printing Co., 1937

1 Strange as It Seems	600.00
2 Strange as It Seems	400.00

JOHNNY DANGER
Toby Press, Aug., 1954

1 Ph(c),Private Detective	225.00

JOHNNY DYNAMITE
See: DYNAMITE

JOHNNY HAZARD
Best Books (Standard Comics), Aug., 1948

5 FR	250.00
6 FR,FR(c)	225.00
7 FR(c)	200.00
8 FR,FR(c), May, 1949	225.00

JOHNNY LAW, SKY RANGER
Good Comics (Lev Gleason), April, 1955

1	125.00
2	75.00
3	75.00
4 Nov., 1955	75.00

JOHNNY MACK BROWN
Dell Publishing Co., 1950–52

1 See: FOUR COLOR	
2 Western hero	225.00
3	175.00
4 thru 10	@125.00

JOHN WAYNE ADVENTURE COMICS
Toby Press, Winter, 1949

1 Ph(c),The Mysterious Valley of Violence	2,500.00
2 AW,FF,Ph(c)	1,200.00
3 AW,FF,Flying Sheriff	1,200.00
4 AW,FF,Double-Danger,Ph(c)	1,200.00
5 Volcano of Death,Ph(c)	750.00
6 AW,FF,Caravan of Doom, Ph(c)	900.00
7 AW,FF,Ph(c)	800.00
8 AW,FF,Duel of Death,Ph(c)	1,100.00
9 Ghost Guns,Ph(c)	525.00
10 Dangerous Journey,Ph(c)	500.00
11 Manhunt!,Ph(c)	500.00
12 HK,Joins the Marines,Ph(c)	500.00
13 V:Frank Stacy	450.00
14 Operation Peeping John	450.00
15 Bridge Head	450.00
16 AW,FF,Golden Double-Cross	450.00
17 Murderer's Music	450.00
18 AW,FF,Larson's Folly	550.00
19	400.00
20 Whale (c)	400.00
21	400.00
22 Flash Flood!	400.00
23 Death on Two Wheels	400.00
24 Desert	400.00
25 AW,FF,Hondo!,Ph(c)	550.00
26 Ph(c)	450.00
27 Ph(c)	450.00
28 Dead Man's Boots!	450.00
29 AW,FF,Ph(c),Crash in California Desert	500.00
30 The Wild One, Ph(c)	450.00
31 AW,FF,May, 1955	500.00

JO-JO COMICS
Fox Features Syndicate, Spring, 1946

N# (fa) JoJo	250.00
2 (fa) Electro	150.00
3 (fa)	150.00
4 (fa)	150.00
5 (fa)	150.00
6 (fa)	150.00
7 B:Jo-Jo Congo King	1,400.00
8 (7)B:Tanee,V:The Giant Queen	900.00
9 (8)The Mountain of Skulls	750.00
10 (9)Death of the Fanged Lady	750.00
11 (10)	750.00
12 (11)Bondage(c), Water Warriors	650.00
13 (12) Jade Juggernaut	625.00
14 The Leopards of Learda	625.00
15 The Flaming Fiend	700.00
16 Golden Gorilla,bondage(c)	625.00
17 Stark-Mad Thespian, bondage(c)	700.00
18 The Death Traveler	625.00
19 Gladiator of Gore	625.00

20	625.00
21	625.00
22	625.00
23	625.00
24	625.00
25 Bondage(c)	700.00
26	625.00
27	625.00
28	625.00
29 July, 1949	650.00

JOLLY JINGLES
See: JACKPOT

JON JUAN
Toby Press, 1950

1 ASh(c),Superlover	1,000.00

Journey Into Fear #14
© Superior Publications

JOURNEY INTO FEAR
Superior Publications, May, 1951–Sept., 1954

1 MB,Preview of Chaos	1,000.00
2 Debt to the Devil	650.00
3 Midnight Prowler	550.00
4 Invisible Terror	550.00
5 Devil Cat	375.00
6 Partners in Blood	375.00
7 The Werewolf Lurks	375.00
8 Bells of the Damned	375.00
9 Masked Death	375.00
10 Gallery of the Dead	375.00
11 Beast of Bedlam	350.00
12 No Rest for the Dead	350.00
13 Cult of the Dead	350.00
14 Jury of the Undead	350.00
15 Corpse in Make-up	375.00
16 Death by Invitation	325.00
17 Deadline for Death	325.00
18 Here's to Horror	325.00
19 This Body is Mine!	325.00
20 Masters of the Dead	325.00
21 Horror in the Clock	325.00

JUDGE PARKER
Argo, Feb., 1956

1	100.00
2	75.00

JUDO JOE
Jay-Jay Corp., Aug., 1952

1 Drug	150.00
2	100.00
3 Drug, Dec., 1953	125.00

JUDY CANOVA
See: ALL TOP COMICS

JUKE BOX
Famous Funnies, March, 1948

1 ATh(c),Spike Jones 600.00
2 Dinah Shore,Transvestitism. . . 400.00
3 Vic Damone, Peggie Lee. 300.00
4 Jimmy Durante. 300.00
5 . . . . 300.00
6 Jan., 1949,Desi Arnaz 325.00

JUMBO COMICS
Real Adventure Publ. Co. (Fiction House), Sept., 1938

1 LF,BKa,JK,WE(a&c),B:Sheena
   Queen of the Jungle,The Hawk
   The Hunchback 40,000.00
2 LF,JK,WE,BKa,BP,
   O:Sheena 18,000.00
3 JK,WE(a&c),BP,LF,BKa . . 10,000.00
4 WE(a&c),MMe,LF,BKa,
   O:The Hawk 9,000.00
5 WE(a&c),BP,BKa 8,000.00
6 WE(a&c),BP,BKa 7,000.00
7 WE,BKa,BP 7,000.00
8 LF(c),BP,BKa,World of
   Tommorow 7,000.00
9 LF(c),BP 6,000.00
10 WE,LF(c),BKa,Regular size
   issues begin 3,000.00
11 LF(c),WE&BP,War of the
   Emerald Gas 2,000.00
12 WE(c),WE&BP,Hawk in Buccaneer
   Vengeance,Bondage(c) . . 2,500.00
13 WE(c),BP,Sheena in The
   Thundering Herds. 2,000.00
14 WE(c),LF,BP,Hawk in Siege
   of Thunder Isle,B:Lightning 2,100.00
15 BP(a&c),Sheena(c) 1,200.00
16 BP(a&c),The Lightning
   Strikes Twice 1,500.00
17 BP(c), B:Sheena covers
   and lead stories 1,200.00
18 BP 1,200.00
19 BP(c),BKa,Warriors of
   the Bush 1,200.00
20 BP,BKa,Spoilers of the
   Wild. 1,200.00
21 BP,BKa,Prey of the
   Giant Killers. 900.00
22 BP,BKa,Victims of the
   Super-Ape,O:Hawk. 1,000.00
23 BP,BKa,Swamp of the
   Green Terror 1,000.00
24 BP,BKa,Curse of the Black
   Venom 1,000.00
25 BP,BKa,Bait for the Beast. . . . 900.00
26 BP,BKa,Tiger-Man Terror 900.00
27 BP,BKa,Sabre-Tooth Terror. . . 900.00
28 BKa,RWd,The Devil of
   the Congo 900.00
29 BKa,RWd,Elephant-Scourge . 900.00
30 BKa,RWd,Slashing Fangs . . . 900.00
31 BKa,RWd,Voodoo Treasure
   of Black Slave Lake. 800.00
32 BKa,RWd,AB,Captives of
   the Gorilla-Men 800.00
33 BKa,RWd,AB,Stampede
   Tusks. 800.00
34 BKa,RWd,AB,Claws of the
   Devil-Cat 800.00
35 BKa,RWd,AB,Hostage of the
   Devil Apes 800.00
36 BKa,RWd,AB,Voodoo Flames 800.00
37 BKa,RWd,AB,Congo Terror . . 800.00
38 BKa,RWd,AB,Death-Trap of
   the River Demons 800.00

Jumbo Comics #42
© Fiction House

39 BKa,RWd,AB,Cannibal Bait . . 800.00
40 BKa,RWd,AB,
   Assagai Poison 800.00
41 BKa,RWd,AB,Killer's Kraal,
   Bondage(c) 700.00
42 BKa,RWd,AB,Plague of
   Spotted Killers 700.00
43 BKa,RWd,AB,Beasts of the
   Devil Queen. 700.00
44 BKa,RWd,AB,Blood-Cult of
   K'Douma 700.00
45 BKa,RWd,AB,Fanged
   Keeper of the Fire-Gem 700.00
46 BKa,RWd,AB,Lair of the
   Armored Monsters. 700.00
47 BKa,RWd,AB,The Bantu
   Blood-Monster 700.00
48 BKa,RWd,AB,Red Meat for
   the Cat-Pack. 700.00
49 BKa,RWd,AB,Empire of the
   Hairy Ones 700.00
50 BKa,RWd,AB,Eyrie of the
   Leopard Birds 700.00
51 BKa,RWd.AB,Monsters with
   Wings. 500.00
52 BKa,RWd,AB,Man-Eaters
   Paradise 500.00
53 RWd,AB,Slaves of the
   Blood Moon 500.00
54 RWd,AB,Congo Kill. 500.00
55 RWd,AB,Bait for the Silver
   King Cat. 500.00
56 RWd,AB,Sabre Monsters of
   the Aba-Zanzi,Bondage(c). . . 700.00
57 RWd,AB,Arena of Beasts 500.00
58 RWd,AB,Sky-Atlas of the
   Thunder-Birds 500.00
59 RWd,AB,Kraal of Shrunken
   Heads 500.00
60 RWd,AB,Land of the
   Stalking Death 400.00
61 RWd,AB,King-Beast of
   the Masai. 400.00
62 RWd,AB,Valley of Golden
   Death. 400.00
63 RWd,AB,The Dwarf Makers . . 400.00
64 RWd,The Slave-Brand of Ibn
   Ben Satan,Male Bondage . . . 600.00
65 RWd,The Man-Eaters of
   Linpopo 400.00
66 RWd,Valley of Monsters 400.00
67 RWd,Land of Feathered Evil . 400.00
68 RWd,Spear of Blood Ju-Ju . . 400.00
69 RWd,AB,MB,Slaves for the
   White Sheik 400.00

70 RWd,AB,MB,The Rogue
   Beast's Prey 400.00
71 RWd,AB,MB,The Serpent-
   God Speaks. 350.00
72 RWd,AB,MB,Curse of the
   Half-Dead 350.00
73 RWd,AB,MB,War Apes of
   the T'Kanis. 350.00
74 RWd,AB,MB,Drums of the
   Voodoo God 350.00
75 RWd,AB,MB,Terror Trail of
   the Devil's Horn 350.00
76 RWd,AB,MB,Fire Gems of
   Skull Valley 350.00
77 RWd,AB,MB,Blood Dragons
   from Fire Valley 350.00
78 RWd,AB,MB,Veldt of the
   Vampire Apes 350.00
79 RWd,AB,MB,Dancing
   Skeletons. 350.00
80 RWd,AB,MB,Banshee
   Cats 350.00
81 RWd,MB,AB,JKa,Heads for
   King' Hondo's Harem. 300.00
82 RWd,MB,AB,JKa,Ghost Riders
   of the Golden Tuskers. 300.00
83 RWd,MB,AB,JKa,Charge of
   the Condo Juggernauts. . . . 300.00
84 RWd,MB,AB,JKa,Valley of
   the Whispering Fangs 300.00
85 RWd,MB,AB,JKa,Red Tusks
   of Zulu-Za'an 300.00
86 RWd,MB,AB,JKa,Witch-Maiden
   of the Burning Blade 300.00
87 RWd,AB,MB,JKa,Sargasso of
   Lost Safaris 300.00
88 RWd,AB,MB,JKa,Kill-Quest
   of the Ju-Ju Tusks. 300.00
89 RWd,AB,MB,JKa,Ghost Slaves
   of Bwana Rojo. 300.00
90 RWd,AB,MB,JKa,Death Kraal
   of the Mastadons 300.00
91 RWd,AB,MB,JKa,Spoor of
   the Sabre-Horn Tiger. 275.00
92 RWd,MB,JKa,Pied Piper
   of the Congo 275.00
93 RWd,MB,JKa,The Beasts
   that Dawn Begot 275.00
94 RWd,MB,JKa,Wheel of a
   Thousand Deaths 350.00
95 RWd,MB,JKa,Flame Dance
   of the Ju-Ju Witch 275.00
96 RWd,MB,JKa,Ghost
   Safari. 275.00
97 RWd,MB,JKa,Banshee Wail
   of the Undead,Bondage(c) . . 400.00
98 RWd,MB,JKa,Seekers of
   the Terror Fangs 300.00
99 RWd,MB,JKa,Shrine of
   the Seven Souls 300.00
100 RWd,MB,Slave Brand
   of Hassan Bey. 350.00
101 RWd,MB,Quest of the
   Two-Face Ju Ju. 300.00
102 RWd,MB,Viper Gods of
   Vengeance Veldt 300.00
103 RWd,MB,Blood for the
   Idol of Blades. 300.00
104 RWd,MB,Valley of Eternal
   Sleep 300.00
105 RWd,MB,Man Cubs from
   Momba-Zu. 350.00
106 RWd,MB,The River of
   No-Return 350.00
107 RWd,MB,Vandals of
   the Veldt 300.00
108 RWd,MB,The Orphan of
   Vengeance Vale. 300.00
109 RWd,MB,The Pygmy's Hiss
   is Poison 300.00
110 RWd,MB,Death Guards the
   Congo Keep 300.00

GOLDEN AGE

111 RWd,MB,Beware of the
Witch-Man's Brew 300.00
112 RWd,MB,The Blood-Mask
from G'Shinis Grave 275.00
113 RWd,MB,The Mask's of
Zombi-Zan 275.00
114 RWd,MB 275.00
115 RWd,MB,Svengali of
the Apes 275.00
116 RWd,MB,The Vessel of
Marbel Monsters 275.00
117 RWd,MB,Lair of the Half-
Man King 275.00
118 RWd,MB,Quest of the
Congo Dwarflings 275.00
119 RWd,MB,King Crocodile's
Domain 275.00
120 RWd,MB,The Beast-Pack
Howls the Moon 275.00
121 RWd,MB,The Kraal of
Evil Ivory 275.00
122 RWd,MB,Castaways of
the Congo 250.00
123 RWd,MB, ... 250.00
124 RWd,MB,The Voodoo Beasts
of Changra-Lo 250.00
125 RWd,MB,JKa(c),The Beast-
Pack Strikes at Dawn 250.00
126 RWd,MB,JKa(c),Lair of the
Swamp Beast 250.00
127 RWd,MB,JKa(c),The Phantom
of Lost Lagoon 250.00
128 RWd,MB,JKa(c),Mad Mistress
of the Congo-Tuskers 250.00
129 RWd,MB,JKa(c),Slaves of
King Simbas Kraal 250.00
130 RWd,MB,JKa(c),Quest of
the Pharaoh's Idol 250.00
131 RWd,JKa(c),Congo Giants
at Bay 250.00
132 RWd,JKa(c),The Doom of
the Devil's Gorge 250.00
133 RWd,JKa(c),Blaze the
Pitfall Trail 250.00
134 RWd,JKa(c),Catacombs of
the Jackal-Men 250.00
135 RWd,JKa(c),The 40 Thieves
of Ankar-Lo 250.00
136 RWd,JKa(c),The Perils of
Paradise Lost 250.00
137 RWd,JKa(c),The Kraal of
Missing Men 250.00
138 RWd,JKa(c),The Panthers
of Kajo-Kazar 250.00
139 RWd,JKa(c),Stampede of
the Congo Lancers 250.00
140 RWd,JKa(c),The Moon
Beasts from Vulture Valley . . 250.00
141 RWd,JKa(c),B:Long
Bow 275.00
142 RWd,JKa(c),Man-Eaters
of N'Gamba 250.00
143 RWd,JKa(c),The Curse of
the Cannibal Drum 250.00
144 RWd,JKa(c),The Secrets of
Killers Cave 250.00
145 RWd,JKa(c),Killers of
the Crypt 250.00
146 RWd,JKa(c),Sinbad of the
Lost Lagoon 250.00
147 RWd,JKa(c),The Wizard of
Gorilla Glade 250.00
148 RWd,JKa(c),Derelict of
the Slave King 250.00
149 RWd,JKa(c),Lash Lord of
the Elephants 250.00
150 RWd,JKa(c),Queen of
the Pharaoh's Idol 250.00
151 RWd,The Voodoo Claws
of Doomsday Trek 250.00
152 RWd,Red Blades of Africa . . 250.00

153 RWd,Lost Legions of the
Nile 250.00
154 RWd,The Track of the
Black Devil 250.00
155 RWd,The Ghosts of
Blow- Gun Trail 250.00
156 RWd,The Slave-Runners
of Bambaru 250.00
157 RWd,Cave of the
Golden Skull 250.00
158 RWd,Gun Trek to
Panther Valley 250.00
159 RWd,A:Space Scout 225.00
160 RWd,Savage Cargo,
E:Sheena covers 225.00
161 RWd,Dawns of the Pit 225.00
162 RWd,Hangman's Haunt 225.00
163 RWd,Cagliostro Cursed
Thee 225.00
164 RWd,Death Bars the Door . . 225.00
165 RWd,Day off from a Corpse . 225.00
166 RWd,The Gallows Bird 225.00
167 RWd,Cult of the Clawmen,
March, 1953 . . . . 225.00

JUNGLE COMICS
Glen Kel Publ./Fiction House,
Jan., 1940

1 HcK,DBr,LF(c),O:The White
Panther,Kaanga,Tabu, B:The
Jungle Boy,Camilla, all
Kaanga covers & stories . . 9,000.00
2 HcK,DBr,WE(c),B:Fantomah 2,500.00
3 HcK,DBr,GT,The Crocodiles
of Death River 2,200.00
4 HcK,DBr,Wambi in
Thundering Herds 2,000.00
5 WE(c),GT,HcK,DBr,Empire
of the Ape Men 2,400.00
6 WE(c),GT,DBr,HcK,Tigress
of the Deep Jungle Swamp 1,400.00
7 BP(c),DBr,GT,HcK,Live
Sacrifice,Bondage(c) 1,200.00
8 BP(c),GT,HcK,Safari into
Shadowland 1,200.00
9 GT,HcK,Captive of the
Voodoo Master 1,200.00
10 GT,HcK,BP,Lair of the
Renegade Killer 1,200.00
11 GT,HcK,V:Beasts of Africa's Ancient
Primieval Swamp Land 900.00
12 GT,HcK,The Devil's
Death-Trap 900.00
13 GT(c),GT,HcK,Stalker of
the Beasts 950.00
14 HcK,Vengeance of the
Gorilla Hordes 900.00
15 HcK,Terror of the Voodoo
Cauldron 900.00
16 HcK,Caveman Killers 900.00
17 HcK,Valley of the Killer-Birds . 900.00
18 HcK,Trap of the Tawny
Killer, Bondage(c) 1,000.00
19 HcK,Revolt of the Man-Apes . 900.00
20 HcK,One-offering to
Ju-Ju Demon 900.00
21 HcK,Monster of the Dismal
Swamp, Bondage(c) 750.00
22 HcK,Lair o/t Winged Fiend . . . 700.00
23 HcK,Man-Eater Jaws 700.00
24 HcK,Battle of the Beasts 700.00
25 HcK,Kaghis the Blood God,
Bondage(c) 750.00
26 HcK,Gorillas of the
Witch-Queen 700.00
27 HcK,Spore o/t Gold-Raiders . . 700.00
28 HcK,Vengeance of the Flame
God, Bondage(c) 750.00
29 HcK,Juggernaut of Doom 625.00
30 HcK,Claws o/t Black Terror . . 625.00
31 HcK,Land of Shrunken
Skulls 500.00

Jungle Comics #32
© Fiction House

32 HcK,Curse of the King-Beast . 500.00
33 HcK,Scaly Guardians of
Massacre Pool,Bondage(c) . . 600.00
34 HcK,Bait of the Spotted
Fury,Bondage(c) 600.00
35 HcK,Stampede of the
Slave-Masters 500.00
36 HcK,GT,The Flame-Death of
Ju Ju Mountain 500.00
37 HcK,GT,Scaly Sentinel of
Taboo Swamp 500.00
38 HcK,GT,Duel of the Congo
Destroyers 500.00
39 HcK,Land of Laughing Bones . 500.00
40 HcK,Killer Plague 500.00
41 Hck,The King Ape
Feeds at Dawn 450.00
42 Hck,RC,Master of the
Moon-Beasts 475.00
43 HcK,The White Shiek 450.00
44 HcK,Monster of the
Boiling Pool 450.00
45 HcK,The Bone-Grinders of
B'Zambi, Bondage(c). 500.00
46 HcK,Blood Raiders of
Tree Trail 450.00
47 HcK,GT,Monsters of the Man
Pool, Bondage(c). 500.00
48 HcK,GT,Strangest Congo
Adventure 400.00
49 HcK,GT,Lair of the King
-Serpent. 400.00
50 HcK,GT,Juggernaut of
the Bush 400.00
51 HcK,GT,The Golden Lion of
Genghis Kahn 400.00
52 HcK,Feast for the River
Devils, Bondage(c) 500.00
53 HcK,GT,Slaves for Horrors
Harem 375.00
54 HcK,GT,Blood Bride of
the Crocodile 350.00
55 HcK,GT,The Tree Devil 350.00
56 HcK,Bride for the
Rainmaker Raj 350.00
57 HcK,Fire Gems of T'ulaki 350.00
58 HcK,Land of the
Cannibal God 350.00
59 HcK,Dwellers of the Mist
Bondage(c) 450.00
60 HcK,Bush Devil's Spoor 400.00
61 HcK,Curse of the Blood
Madness 400.00
62 Bondage(c) 450.00
63 HcK,Fire-Birds for the
Cliff Dwellers 350.00

64 Valley of the Ju-Ju Idols 350.00
65 Shrine of the Seven Ju Jus,
   Bondage(c) 400.00
66 Spoor of the Purple Skulls . . . 350.00
67 Devil Beasts of the Golden
   Temple. 350.00
68 Satan's Safari 350.00
69 Brides for the Serpent King . . 350.00
70 Brides for the King Beast,
   Bondage(c) 400.00
71 Congo Prey,Bondage(c) 400.00
72 Blood-Brand o/t Veldt Cats . . . 350.00
73 The Killer of M'omba Raj,
   Bondage(c) 400.00
74 AgF,GoldenJaws,
   Bondage(c) 400.00
75 AgF,Congo Kill 350.00
76 AgF,Blood Thirst of the
   Golden Tusk 350.00
77 AgF,The Golden Gourds
   Shriek Blood,Bondage(c) . . . 400.00
78 AgF,Bondage(c) 400.00
79 AgF,Death has a
   Thousand Fangs 375.00
80 AgF,Salome of the
   Devil-Cats Bondage(c) 400.00
81 AgF,Colossus of the Congo . . 375.00
82 AgF,Blood Jewels of the
   Fire-Bird. 375.00
83 AgF,Vampire Veldt,
   Bondage(c) 400.00
84 AgF,Blood Spoor of the
   Faceless Monster 375.00
85 AgF,Brides for the Man-Apes
   Bondage(c) 400.00
86 AgF,Firegems of L'hama
   Lost, Bondage(c) 400.00
87 AgF,Horror Kraal of the
   Legless One,Bondage(c). . . . 400.00
88 AgF,Beyond the Ju-Ju Mists . . 375.00
89 AgF,Blood-Moon over the
   Whispering Veldt 350.00
90 AgF,The Skulls for the
   Altar of Doom,Bondage(c) . . 425.00
91 AgF,Monsters from the Mist
   Lands, Bondage(c) 425.00
92 AgF,Vendetta of the
   Tree Tribes 400.00
93 AgF,Witch Queen of the
   Hairy Ones 400.00
94 AgF,Terror Raid of
   the Congo Caesar. 400.00
95 Agf,Flame-Tongues of the
   Sky Gods. 400.00
96 Agf,Phantom Guardians of the
   Enchanted Lake,Bondage(c). 400.00
97 AgF,Wizard of the Whirling
   Doom,Bondage(c) 375.00
98 AgF,Ten Tusks of Zulu Ivory . . 450.00
99 AgF,Cannibal Caravan,
   Bondage(c) 375.00
100 AgF,Hate has a
   Thousand Claws 375.00
101 AgF,The Blade of
   Buddha, Bondage(c) 375.00
102 AgF,Queen of the
   Amazon Lancers 350.00
103 AgF,The Phantoms of
   Lost Lagoon. 350.00
104 AgF 350.00
105 AgF,The Red Witch
   of Ubangi-Shan 350.00
106 AgF,Bondage(c) 375.00
107 Banshee Valley. 375.00
108 HcK,Merchants of Murder. . . 375.00
109 HcK,Caravan of the
   Golden Bones 350.00
110 HcK,Raid of the Fire-Fangs . 350.00
111 HcK,The Trek of the
   Terror-Paws. 350.00
112 HcK,Morass of the
   Mammoths. 350.00

Jungle Comics #137
© Fiction House

113 HcK,Two-Tusked Terror 350.00
114 HcK,Mad Jackals Hunt
   by Night 350.00
115 HcK,Treasure Trove in
   Vulture Sky 350.00
116 HcK,The Banshees of
   Voodoo Veldt. 350.00
117 HcK,The Fangs of the
   Hooded Scorpion 350.00
118 HcK,The Muffled Drums
   of Doom. 350.00
119 HcK,Fury of the Golden
   Doom. 350.00
120 HcK,Killer King Domain 350.00
121 HcK,Wolves of the
   Desert Night 350.00
122 HcK,The Veldt of
   Phantom Fangs. 350.00
123 HcK,The Ark of the
   Mist-Maids 350.00
124 HcK,The Trail of the
   Pharaoh's Eye 350.00
125 HcK,Skulls for Sale on
   Dismal River 350.00
126 HcK,Safari Sinister 300.00
127 HcK,Bondage(c) 300.00
128 HcK,Dawn-Men of the
   Congo 300.00
129 HcK,The Captives of
   Crocodile Swamp 300.00
130 HcK,Phantoms of the Congo 300.00
131 HcK,Treasure-Tomb of the
   Ape-King 300.00
132 HcK,Bondage(c) 350.00
133 HcK,Scourge of the Sudan
   Bondage(c) 350.00
134 HcK,The Black Avengers of
   Kaffir Pass 300.00
135 HcK 300.00
136 HcK,The Death Kraals
   of Kongola 300.00
137 BWg(c),HcK,The Safari of
   Golden Ghosts 300.00
138 BWg(c),HcK,Track of the
   Black Terror Bondage(c) 350.00
139 BWg(c),HcK,Captain Kidd
   of the Congo 300.00
140 BWg(c),HcK,The Monsters
   of Kilimanjaro 300.00
141 BWg(c)HcK,The Death Hunt
   of the Man Cubs 300.00
142 BWg(c),Hck,Sheba of the
   Terror Claws,Bondage(c). . . . 350.00
143 BWg(c)Hck,The Moon of
   Devil Drums. 300.00

144 BWg(c)Hck,Quest of the
   Dragon's Claw. 300.00
145 BWg(c)Hck,Spawn of the
   Devil's Moon 300.00
146 BWg(c),HcK,Orphans of
   the Congo 300.00
147 BWG(c),HcK,The Treasure
   of Tembo Wanculu. 300.00
148 BWg(c),HcK,Caged Beasts
   of Plunder-Men,Bondage(c) . 350.00
149 BWg(c),HcK 275.00
150 BWg(c),HcK,Rhino Rampage,
   Bondage(c) 350.00
151 BWg(c),HcK 275.00
152 BWg(c),HcK,The Rogue of
   Kopje Kull 275.00
153 BWg(c),HcK,The Wild Men
   of N'Gara. 275.00
154 BWg(c),HcK,The Fire Wizard 275.00
155 BWg(c),HcK,Swamp of
   the Shrieking Dead 275.00
156 BWg(c),HcK 275.00
157 BWg(c),HcK 275.00
158 BWg(c),HcK,A:Sheena 275.00
159 BWg(c),HcK,The Blow-Gun
   Kill 275.00
160 BWg,HcK,King Fang. 275.00
161 BWg(c),HcK,The Barbarizi
   Man-Eaters 275.00
162 BWg(c) 275.00
163 BWg(c),Jackals at the
   Kill, Summer,1954 . . . . 275.00

JUNGLE JIM
Best Books
(Standard Comics), Jan., 1949
11 . . . . 125.00
12 Mystery Island. 100.00
13 Flowers of Peril. 100.00
14 thru 19. . . . . @100.00
20 1951 . . . . 100.00

JUNGLE JIM
Dell Publishing Co., Aug., 1953
(1) *see Dell Four Color #490*
(1) *see Dell Four Color #565*
3 P(c) all 125.00
4 . . . . 125.00
5 . . . . 125.00
6 . . . . 100.00
7 . . . . 100.00
8 thru 12 . . . . @100.00
13 'Mystery Island'. 100.00
14 'Flowers of Peril'. 100.00
15 thru 20. . . . . @100.00

JUNGLE JO
Hero Books
(Fox Features Syndicate),
March, 1950
N# Congo King. 650.00
1 WW,Mystery of Doc Jungle . . 650.00
2 Tangl 500.00
3 The Secret of Youth,
   Sept., 1950 . . . . 500.00

JUNGLE LIL
Hero Books, April, 1950
1 Betrayer of the Kombe Dead. . 500.00
Becomes:

DOROTHY LAMOUR
Fox Features Syndicate,
June 1950
2 WW,Ph(c)The Lost Safari 500.00
3 WW,Ph(c), Aug., 1950 . . . . . . 300.00

JUNGLE THRILLS
See: TERRORS OF
THE JUNGLE

All comics prices listed are for *Near Mint* condition.

JUNIE PROM
Dearfield Publishing Co.
Winter, 1947
1 Teenage Stories 150.00
2 .... 125.00
3 .... 100.00
4 .... 100.00
5 .... 100.00
6 June, 1949 .... 100.00

JUNIOR COMICS
Fox Features Syndicate,
Sept., 1947
9 AF(a&c) ,Teenage Stories... 1,500.00
10 AF(a&c) 1,400.00
11 AF(a&c) 1,400.00
12 AF(a&c) 1,400.00
13 AF(a&c) 1,400.00
14 AF(a&c) 1,400.00
15 AF(a&c) 1,400.00
16 AF(a&c),July,1948 ...... 1,400.00

JUNIOR FUNNIES
See: FAMILY FUNNIES

JUNIOR HOPP COMICS
Stanmor Publications,
Jan., 1952
1 Teen-age 125.00
2 .... 100.00
3 July, 1952 .... 100.00

JUNIOR MISS
Marvel Timely, 1944, 1947–50
1 F:Frank Sinatra &June Allyson 400.00
24 .... 150.00
25 thru 38 Cindy .... @125.00
39 HK..................... 150.00

JUSTICE TRAPS
THE GUILTY
Headline Publications,
(Prize) Oct.–Nov., 1947
2-1 S&K(a&c),Electric chair (c) . 900.00
2 S&K(a&c) 450.00
3 S&K(a&c) 400.00
4 S&K(a&c),True Confession
　of a Girl Gangleader 400.00
5 S&K(a&c) 400.00
6 S&K(a&c),JSe,AF 425.00
7 S&K(a&c) 400.00
8 S&K(a&c),WE,BK 400.00
9 S&K(a&c) 400.00
10 S&K(a&c),BK 400.00
11 S&K(a&c),JSe 175.00
12 .... 125.00
13 .... 150.00
14 JSe,WE................. 125.00
15 .... 125.00
16 .... 125.00
17 .... 125.00
18 S&K(a&c) 150.00
19 S&K(a&c) 150.00
20 .... 150.00
21 S&K.................... 175.00
22 S&K(c),MMe 175.00
23 S&K(c)................. 175.00
24 .... 100.00
25 .... 100.00
26 .... 100.00
27 S&K(c),MMe 175.00
28 .... 100.00
29 .... 100.00
30 S&K.................... 150.00
31 thru 49................ @100.00
50 .... 100.00
51 thru 54................ @100.00
55 .... 100.00
56 .... 100.00

57 .... 100.00
58 Drug 300.00
59 thru 92................ @100.00
Becomes:

FARGO KID
Headline Publications
(Prize),　June–July. 1958
93 AW,JSe,O:Kid Fargo 175.00
94 JSe 125.00
95 June–July, 1958,JSe 125.00

Ka'a'nga Comics #9
© Fiction House

KA'A'NGA COMICS
Glen-Kel Publ.
(Fiction House),
Spring, 1949–Summer, 1954
1 Phantoms of the Congo 800.00
2 V:The Jungle Octopus 400.00
3 .... 300.00
4 The Wizard Apes of
　Inkosi-Khan 350.00
5 A:Camilla 225.00
6 Captive of the Devil Apes .. 200.00
7 GT,Beast-Men of Mombassa . 200.00
8 The Congo Kill-Cry 200.00
9 Tabu-Wizard.............. 200.00
10 Stampede for Congo Gold ... 200.00
11 Claws of the Roaring Congo.. 150.00
12 Bondage(c).............. 250.00
13 Death Web of the Amazons .. 150.00
14 Slave Galley of the Lost
　Nile Bondage(c)........... 250.00
15 Crocodile Moon,Bondage(c).. 250.00
16 Valley of Devil-Dwarfs,Sheena 150.00
17 Tembu of the Elephants 125.00
18 The Red Claw of Vengeance . 125.00
19 The Devil-Devil Trail 125.00
20 The Cult of the Killer Claws .. 125.00

KASCO COMICS
Kasco Grainfeed
(Giveaway), 1945
1 BWo 250.00
2 1949,BWo 200.00

KATY KEENE
Archie Publications/Close-Up
Radio Comics, 1949
1 BWo 1,700.00
2 BWo 1,000.00
3 BWo 900.00
4 BWo 900.00

5 BWo 800.00
6 BWo 700.00
7 BWo 500.00
8 thru 12 BWo .... @500.00
13 thru 20 BWo .... @400.00
21 thru 29 BWo .... @300.00
30 thru 38 BWo .... @300.00
39 thru 62 BWo .... @300.00
Ann.#1 .... 900.00
Ann.#2 thru #6 .... @500.00

KATZENJAMMER KIDS
David McKay Publ., 1947–50
1 .... 250.00
2 .... 125.00
3 .... 100.00
4 .... 100.00
5 thru 11 .... @100.00
Standard Comics, 1950–53
12 thru 22 .... @100.00
Harvey Publ., 1953–54
22 thru 25 .... @100.00

KAYO
See: SCOOP COMICS

KEEN DETECTIVE
FUNNIES
Centaur Publications,
July, 1938
1-8 B:The Clock, ... 3,500.00
1-9 WE 1,300.00
1-10 .... 1,200.00
1-11 Dean Denton 1,200.00
2-1 The Eye Sees 1,100.00
2-2 JCo 1,100.00
2-3 TNT 1,100.00
2-4 MGv,Gabby Flynn 1,100.00
5 MGv 1,100.00
6 MGv,BEv................ 1,000.00
7 BEv,Masked Marvel 3,800.00
8 PGv,Gabby Flynn,Nudity
　Expanded 16 pages 1,400.00
9 BEv,Dean Denton 1,100.00
10 BEv 1,100.00
11 BEv,Sidekick 1,100.00
12 BEv,Masked Marvel(c)..... 1,400.00
3-1 Masked Marvel(c)....... 1,100.00
3-2 Masked Marvel(c)....... 1,100.00
3-3 BEv 1,100.00
16 BEv 1,100.00
17 JSm 1,100.00
18 The Eye Sees,Bondage(c).. 1,200.00
19 LFe 950.00
20 BEv,The Eye Sees........ 1,400.00
21 Masked Marvel(c)........ 950.00
22 Masked Marvel(c)........ 950.00
23 B:Airman 1,300.00
24 Airman 1,400.00

KEEN KOMICS
Centaur Publications,
May, 1939
1 Teenage Stories 1,400.00
2 PGv,JaB,CBu,Cut Carson 900.00
3 JCo,Saddle Sniffl 900.00

KEEN TEENS
Life's Romances Publ./Leader/
Magazine Enterprises, 1945
N# P(c),Claire Voyant........ 500.00
N# Ph(c),Van Johnson 350.00
3 Ph(c), ... 125.00
4 Ph(c),Glenn Ford 150.00
5 Ph(c),Perry Como 150.00
6 .... 125.00

KEN MAYNARD WESTERN

Fawcett Publications, Sept., 1950–Feb., 1952

1 B:Ken Maynard & Tarzan (horse)
   The Outlaw Treasure Trail . . 800.00
2 Invasion of the Badmen 500.00
3 Pied Piper of the West 350.00
4 Outlaw Hoax 350.00
5 Mystery of Badman City 350.00
6 Redwood Robbery 350.00
7 Seven Wonders of the West . . 350.00
8 Mighty Mountain Menace 350.00

KEN SHANNON

Quality Comics Group, Oct., 1951–April, 1953

1 RC, Evil Eye of Count Ducrie . 500.00
2 RC, Cut Rate Corpses 375.00
3 RC, Corpse that Wouldn't
   Sleep 275.00
4 RC, Stone Hatchet Murder . . . 275.00
5 RC, Case of the Carney Killer 275.00
6 Weird Vampire Mob 275.00
7 RC,Ugliest Man in the World . 225.00
8 Chinatown Murders,Drug. 350.00
9 RC, Necklace of Blood 225.00
10 RC, Shadow of the Chair 225.00

KEN STUART

Publication Enterprises, 1949

1 . . . . 150.00

KERRY DRAKE DETECTIVE CASES

Life's Romances/M.E., 1944

(1) see N# A-1 Comics
2 A:The Faceless Horror 250.00
3 . . . . 200.00
4 A:Squirrel, Dr. Zero, Caresse . 200.00
5 Bondage (c) 400.00

Harvey Publ., Jan., 1952

6 A:Stitches 250.00
7 A:Shuteye 275.00
8 Bondage (c) 350.00
9 Drug 350.00
10 BP,A:Meatball,Drug. 350.00
11 BP,I:Kid Gloves 150.00
12 BP 150.00
13 BP,A:Torso 125.00
14 BP,Bullseye Murder Syndicate 125.00
15 BP,Fake Mystic Racket. 125.00

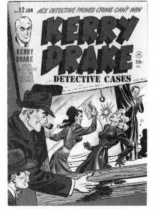

Kerry Drake Detective Cases #12
© Harvey Publications

16 BP,A:Vixen 100.00
17 BP,Case of the $50,000
   Robbery. 100.00
18 BP,A:Vixen 100.00
19 BP,Case of the Dope
   Smugglers 250.00
20 BP,Secret Treasury Agent. . . 100.00
21 BP,Murder on Record 100.00
22 BP,Death Rides the Air Waves 100.00
23 BP,Blackmailer's Secret
   Weapon. 100.00
24 Blackmailer's Trap 100.00
25 Pretty Boy Killer 100.00
26 . . . . 100.00
27 . . . . 100.00
28 BP 100.00
29 BP 100.00
30 Mystery Mine,Bondage(c) . . . 250.00
31 . . . . 100.00
32 . . . . 100.00
33 Aug., 1952. . . . . 100.00

KEWPIES

Will Eisner Publications, Spring, 1949

1 . . . . 650.00

KEY COMICS

Consolidated Magazines Jan., 1944

1 B:The Key, Will-O-The-Wisp . . 600.00
2 . . . . 300.00
3 . . . . 250.00
4 WJo(c) O:John Quincy,
   B:The Atom 275.00
5 HoK,Aug., 1946 . . . . 300.00

KEY RING COMICS

Dell Publishing Co., 1941

1 Sky Hawk,Viking Carter. 250.00
(1) Radior. 300.00

KID COWBOY

Approved Comics/ St. John Publ. Co., 1950

1 B:Lucy Belle & Red Feather . . 200.00
2 JMr,Six-Gun Justice 150.00
3 Shadow on Hangman's Bridge 125.00
4 Red Feather V:Eagle of Doom 100.00
5 Killers on the Rampage 100.00
6 The Stovepipe Hat 100.00
7 Ghost Town of Twin Buttes . . . 100.00
8 Thundering Hoofs 100.00
9 Terror on the Salt Flats 100.00
10 Valley of Death 100.00
11 Vanished Herds,Bondage(c). . 200.00
12 . . . . 100.00
13 . . . . 100.00
14 1954 . . . . 100.00

KIDDIE KARNIVAL

Approved Comics, 1952

N# Little Bit 500.00

KID ETERNITY

Comics Magazine, Spring, 1946

1 . . . . 1,500.00
2 . . . . 550.00
3 Follow Him Out of This World . 575.00
4 Great Heroes of the Past 350.00
5 Don't Kid with Crime 325.00
6 Busy Battling Crime 325.00
7 Protects the World 325.00
8 Fly to the Rescue 325.00
9 Swoop Down on Crime 325.00
10 Golden Touch from Mr. Midas. 325.00
11 Aid the Living by Calling
   the Dead 250.00

Buccaneers #20
© Quality Comics Magazine

12 Finds Death 250.00
13 Invades General Poschka. . . . 250.00
14 Battles Double 250.00
15 A: Master Man. 250.00
16 Balance Scales of Justice. . . . 225.00
17 A:Baron Roxx 225.00
18 A:Man with Two Faces 225.00
Becomes:

BUCCANEERS

Quality Comics Group, Jan., 1950

19 RC,Sword Fight(c) 750.00
20 RC,Treasure Chest 500.00
21 RC,Death Trap 550.00
22 A:Lady Dolores,Snuff,
   Bondage(c) 400.00
23 RC,V:Treasure Hungry
   Plunderers of the Sea 500.00
24 A:Adam Peril,Black Roger,
   Eric Falcon 350.00
25 V:Clews 350.00
26 V:Admiral Blood 350.00
27 RC(a&c)May, 1951 . . . . 500.00

KID ZOO COMICS

Street & Smith Publ., 1948

1 (fa) 350.00

KILLERS, THE

Magazine Enterprises, 1947

1 LbC(c),Thou Shall Not Kill . . 1,700.00
2 Grl,OW,Assassins Mad Slayers
   of the East,Hanging(c),Drug1,400.00

KILROYS, THE

B&L Publishing Co./ American Comics, June–July, 1947

1 Three Girls in Love(c) 300.00
2 Flat Tire(c) 150.00
3 Right to Swear(c) 125.00
4 Kissing Booth(c) 125.00
5 Skiing(c),Moronica 125.00
6 Prom(c) 100.00
7 To School 100.00
8 . . . . 100.00
9 . . . . 100.00
10 B:Solid Jackson solo. 100.00
11 . . . . 100.00
12 Life Guard(c). 100.00
13 thru 21. . . . . @100.00
22 thru 30. . . . . @100.00
31 thru 40. . . . . @100.00
41 thru 47. . . . . @100.00

GOLDEN AGE

GOLDEN AGE

48 3-D effect 200.00
49 3-D effect 200.00
50 thru 54, July, 1954. . . . . . . @100.00

KING COMICS

**David McKay Publications,
April, 1936
(all have Popeye covers)**

1 AR,EC,B:Popeye,Flash Gordon,B:
  Henry,Mandrake 20,000.00
2 AR,EC,Flash Gordon 4,000.00
3 AR,EC,Flash Gordon 2,500.00
4 AR,EC,Flash Gordon 2,000.00
5 AR,EC,Flash Gordon 1,500.00
6 AR,EC,Flash Gordon 1,100.00
7 AR,EC,King Royal Mounties 1,050.00
8 AR,EC,Thanksgiving(c) 1,000.00
9 AR,EC,Christmas(c) 1,000.00
10 AR,EC,Flash Gordon 1,000.00
11 AR,EC,Flash Gordon 800.00
12 AR,EC,Flash Gordon 800.00
13 AR,EC,Flash Gordon 800.00
14 AR,EC,Flash Gordon 800.00
15 AR,EC,Flash Gordon 800.00
16 AR,EC,Flash Gordon 800.00
17 AR,EC,Flash Gordon 750.00
18 AR,EC,Flash Gordon 750.00
Covers say: "Starring Popeye"
19 AR,EC,Flash Gordon 750.00
20 AR,EC,Football(c) 750.00
21 AR,EC,Flash Gordon 600.00
22 AR,EC,Flash Gordon 600.00
23 AR,EC,Flash Gordon 600.00
24 AR,EC,Flash Gordon 600.00
25 AR,EC,Flash Gordon 600.00
26 AR,EC,Flash Gordon 550.00
27 AR,EC,Flash Gordon 550.00
28 AR,EC,Flash Gordon 550.00
29 AR,EC,Flash Gordon 550.00
30 AR,EC,Flash Gordon 550.00
31 AR,EC,Flash Gordon 550.00
32 AR,EC,Flash Gordon 550.00
33 AR,EC,Skiing(c) 550.00
34 AR,Ping Pong(c) 450.00
35 AR,Flash Gordon 450.00
36 AR,Flash Gordon 450.00
37 AR,Flash Gordon 450.00
38 AR,Flash Gordon 450.00
39 AR,Baseball(c) 450.00
40 AR,Flash Gordon 450.00
41 AR,Flash Gordon 425.00
42 AR,Flash Gordon 425.00
43 AR,Flash Gordon 425.00
44 AR,Popeye golf(c). 425.00
45 AR,Flash Gordon 425.00
46 AR,B:Little Lulu 425.00
47 AR,Flash Gordon 425.00
48 AR,Flash Gordon 425.00
49 AR,Weather Vane 425.00
50 AR,B:Love Ranger 425.00
51 AR,Flash Gordon 300.00
52 AR,Flash Gordon 300.00
53 AR,Flash Gordon 300.00
54 AR,Flash Gordon 300.00
55 AR,Magic Carpet. 300.00
56 AR,Flash Gordon 300.00
57 AR,Cows Over Moon(c) 300.00
58 AR,Flash Gordon 300.00
59 AR,Flash Gordon 300.00
60 AR,Flash Gordon 300.00
61 AR,B:Phantom,Baseball(c) . . 300.00
62 AR,Flash Gordon 300.00
63 AR,Flash Gordon 250.00
64 AR,Flash Gordon 250.00
65 AR,Flash Gordon 250.00
66 AR,Flash Gordon 250.00
67 AR,Sweet Pea. 250.00
68 AR,Flash Gordon 250.00
69 AR,Flash Gordon 250.00
70 AR,Flash Gordon 250.00
71 AR,Flash Gordon 250.00
72 AR,Flash Gordon 250.00

King Comics #57
© David McKay Publications

73 AR,Flash Gordon 250.00
74 AR,Flash Gordon 250.00
75 AR,Flash Godron 250.00
76 AR,Flag(c). 250.00
77 AR,Flash Gordon 250.00
78 AR,Popeye,Olive Oil(c) 250.00
79 AR,Sweet Pea. 250.00
80 AR,Wimpy(c). 250.00
81 AR,B:Blondie(c). 250.00
82 thru 91 AR . . . . @200.00
92 thru 98 AR . . . . @200.00
99 AR,Olive Oil(c) 200.00
100 . . . . 200.00
101 thru 116 AR . . . . @175.00
117 O:Phantom 200.00
118 Flash Gordon 175.00
119 Flash Gordon 150.00
120 Wimpy(c). 125.00
121 thru 140. . . . . @125.00
141 Flash Gordon 125.00
142 Flash Gordon 125.00
143 Flash Gordon 125.00
144 Flash Gordon 125.00
145 Prince Valiant 100.00
146 Prince Valiant 100.00
147 Prince Valiant 100.00
148 thru 154. . . . . @75.00
155 E:Flash Gordon. 75.00
156 Baseball(c) 75.00
157 thru 159. . . . . @75.00

KING OF THE ROYAL MOUNTED

**Dell Publishing Co.,
Dec., 1948–1958**

(1) *see Dell Four Color #207*
(2) *see Dell Four Color #265*
(3) *see Dell Four Color #283*
(4) *see Dell Four Color #310*
(5) *see Dell Four Color #340*
(6) *see Dell Four Color #363*
(7) *see Dell Four Color #384*
8 Zane Grey adapt. 150.00
9 . . . . 125.00
10 . . . . 125.00
11 thru 28 . . . . @100.00

KIT CARSON

Avon Periodicals, 1950

N# EK(c) Indian Scout 200.00
2 EK(c),Kit Carson's Revenge,
  Doom Trail. 150.00
3 EK(c),V:Comanche Raiders . . 100.00
4 . . . . 100.00
5 EK(c),Trail of Doom 100.00

6 EK(c) 100.00
7 EK(c) 100.00
8 EK(c) 100.00
Becomes:

FIGHTING DAVY CROCKETT

Oct.–Nov, 1955

9 EK(c) 100.00

KO KOMICS

**Gerona Publications,
Oct., 1945**

1 . . . . 1,100.00

KOMIK PAGES

See: SCOOP COMICS

KRAZY KAT COMICS

**Dell Publishing Co.,
May–June, 1951**

1 . . . . 150.00
2 . . . . 100.00
3 . . . . 100.00
4 . . . . 100.00
5 . . . . 100.00

KRAZY LIFE

See: PHANTOM LADY

LABOR IS A PARTNER

**Catechetical Guild
Educational Society, 1949**

1 Anti-Communism 250.00

LADY LUCK

See: SMASH

LAFFY-DAFFY COMICS

**Rural Home Publ. Co.,
Feb., 1945**

1 (fa) 150.00
2 . . . . 150.00

LANCE O'CASEY

Fawcett, 1946–47

1 High Seas Adventure
  from Whiz comics 450.00
2 thru 4 . . . . @300.00

LAND OF THE LOST

**E.C. Comics,
July–Aug., 1946–Spring 1948**

1 Radio show adapt. 500.00
2 . . . . 300.00
3 thru 9 . . . . @250.00

LARGE FEATURE COMICS

Dell Publishing Co., 1939

1 Dick Tracy vs. the Blank 2,700.00
2 Terry and the Pirates 1,400.00
3 Heigh-Yo Silver!
  the Lone Ranger. 2,200.00
4 Dick Tracy gets his man 1,500.00
5 Tarzan of the Apes 2,600.00
6 Terry and the Pirates 1,400.00
7 Lone Ranger to the rescue. . 2,200.00
8 Dick Tracy, Racket Buster . . 1,500.00
9 King of the Royal Mounted . . . 800.00
10 Gang Busters. 1,000.00
11 Dick Tracy, Mad Doc Hump . 1,400.00
12 Smilin' Jack. 950.00
13 Dick Tracy and Scottie
  of Scotland Yard 1,300.00
14 Smilin' Jack helps G-Men 950.00

Large Feature Comics #14
© Dell Publishing Co.

15 Dick Tracy and	
the Kidnapped Princes	1,300.00
16 Donald Duck, 1st Daisy.	9,000.00
17 Gang Busters	700.00
18 Phantasmo The Master	
of the World	500.00
19 Walt Disney's Dumbo	4,500.00
20 Donald Duck	10,000.00
21 Private Buck	225.00
22 Nuts and Jolts	225.00
23 The Nebbs	300.00
24 Popeye in 'Thimble Theatre'	1,100.00
25 Smilin'Jack	900.00
26 Smitty	450.00
27 Terry and the Pirates	900.00
28 Grin and Bear It	250.00
29 Moon Mullins	500.00
30 Tillie the Toiler	450.00

[Series 2]

1 Peter Rabbit	900.00
2 Winnie Winkle	350.00
3 Dick Tracy	1,200.00
4 Tiny Tim	550.00
5 Toots and Casper	300.00
6 Terry and the Pirates	850.00
7 Pluto saves the Ship	2,500.00
8 Bugs Bunny	2,700.00
9 Bringing Up Father	425.00
10 Popeye	850.00
11 Barney Google&SnuffySmith	500.00
12 Private Buck	250.00
13 1001 Hours of Fun	400.00

LARRY DOBY, BASEBALL HERO
Fawcett Publications, 1950

1 Ph(c),BW	1,000.00

LARS OF MARS
Ziff-Davis Publishing Co., April–May, 1951

10 MA,'Terror from the Sky'	1,200.00
11 GC, The Terror Weapon	950.00

LASH LARUE WESTERN
Fawcett Publications, Summer, 1949

1 Ph(c),The Fatal Roundups	1,600.00
2 Ph(c),Perfect Hide Out	750.00
3 Ph(c),The Suspect	600.00
4 Ph(c),Death on Stage	600.00
5 Ph(c),Rustler's Haven	600.00
6 Ph(c)	500.00
7 Ph(c),Shadow of the Noose	425.00

8 Ph(c),Double Deadline	425.00
9 Ph(c),Generals Last Stand	425.00
10 Ph(c)	425.00
11 Ph(c)	350.00
12 thru 20 Ph(c)	@300.00
21 thru 29 Ph(c)	@250.00
30 thru 46 Ph(c)	@225.00
46 Ph(c),Lost Chance	225.00

LASSIE
Dell Publishing Co., Oct.–Dec., 1950

1 Ph(c) all	300.00
2	150.00
3 thru 10	@125.00
11	100.00
12 Rocky Langford	100.00
13	100.00
14	100.00
15 I:Timbu	100.00
16	100.00
17	100.00
18	100.00
19	100.00
20 MB	125.00
21 MB	125.00
22 MB	125.00
23 thru 38	@100.00
39 I:Timmy	100.00
40 thru 62	@100.00
63 E:Timmy	100.00
64 thru 70	@100.00

LATEST COMICS
Spotlight Publ./ Palace Promotions, March, 1945

1 Funny Animal-Super Duper	250.00
2	200.00

SPECIAL COMICS
MLJ Magazines, Winter, 1941

1 O:Boy Buddies & Hangman,	
D:The Comet	4,500.00

Becomes:

HANGMAN COMICS
Spring, 1942

2 B:Hangman & Boy Buddies	2,900.00
3 V:Nazis (c),Bondage(c)	1,900.00
4 V:Nazis (c)	1,600.00
5 Bondage (c)	1,600.00
6 HSa	1,600.00
7 BF,Graveyard (c)	1,600.00
8 BF	1,600.00

Becomes:

BLACK HOOD
Winter, 1943–44

9 BF, Hang Man	1,600.00
10 BF,A:Dusty, Boy Detective	1,000.00
11 Here lies the Black Hood	700.00
12	600.00
13 EK(c)	600.00
14 EK(c)	500.00
15 EK	500.00
16 EK(c)	500.00
17 Bondage (c)	650.00
18	600.00
19 I.D. Revealed	800.00

Becomes:

LAUGH COMICS
Archie Comics, Fall, 1946

20 BWo,B:Archie,Katy Keene	1,000.00
21 BWo	500.00
22 BWo	500.00
23 Bwo	500.00
24 BWo,JK,Pipsy	500.00
25 BWo	500.00

Laugh Comis #23
© Archie Comics

26 BWo	275.00
27 BWo	275.00
28 BWo	275.00
29 BWo	275.00
30 BWo	275.00
31 thru 40 BWo	@200.00
41 thru 50 BWo	@175.00
51 thru 60 BWo	@150.00
61 thru 80 BWo	@150.00
81 thru 99 BWo	@150.00
100 BWo	150.00
101 thru 126 BWo	@125.00
127 A:Jaguar	150.00
128 A:The Fly	150.00
129 A:The Fly	150.00
130 A:Jaguar	150.00
131 A:Jaguar	150.00
132 A:The Fly	150.00
133 A:Jaguar	150.00
134 A:The Fly	150.00
135 A:Jaguar	150.00
136 A:Fly Girl	150.00
137 A:Fly Girl	150.00
138 A:The Fly	150.00
139 A:The Fly	150.00
140 A:Jaguar	150.00
141 A:Jaguar	150.00
142 thru 144	@150.00

LAUGH COMIX
See: TOP-NOTCH COMICS

LAUREL AND HARDY
St. John Publishing Co., March, 1949

1	1,100.00
2	600.00
3	400.00
26 Rep #1	225.00
27 Rep #2	225.00
28 Rep #3	225.00

LAWBREAKERS
Law & Order Magazines (Charlton), March, 1951

1	600.00
2	300.00
3	250.00
4 Drug, White Death	300.00
5	225.00
6 LM(c)	250.00
7 Drug, Deadly Dopester	300.00
8	225.00
9 StC(c)	225.00

GOLDEN AGE

Becomes:

LAWBREAKERS
SUSPENSE STORIES
Jan., 1953

10 StC(c)	600.00
11 LM(c),Negligee(c)	1,550.00
12 LM(c)	350.00
13 DG(c)	350.00
14 DG(c),Sharks	350.00
15 DG(c),Acid in Face(c)	800.00

Becomes:

STRANGE SUSPENSE
STORIES
Jan., 1954

16 DG(c)	400.00
17 DG(c)	300.00
18 SD,SD(c)	550.00
19 SD,SD(c),Electric Chair	700.00
20 SD,SD(c)	600.00
21 SD,SD(c)	300.00
22 SD,SD(c)	450.00

Becomes:

THIS IS SUSPENSE
Feb., 1955

23 WW; Comics Code	350.00
24 GE,DG(c)	175.00
25 DG(c)	150.00
26 DG(c)	150.00

Becomes:

STRANGE SUSPENSE
STORIES
Oct., 1955

27	175.00
28	125.00
29	125.00
30	125.00
31 SD	300.00
32 SD	300.00
33 SD	300.00
34 SD	700.00
35 SD	300.00
36 SD	300.00
37 SD	300.00
38	125.00
39 SD	250.00
40 SD	300.00
41 SD	250.00
42	100.00
43	100.00
44	100.00

Strange Suspense Stories #22
© Charlton

45	100.00
46	100.00
47 SD	250.00
48 SD	250.00
49	100.00
50 SD	250.00
51 SD	250.00
52 SD	250.00
53 SD	250.00
54 thru 60	@100.00
61 thru 74	@100.00
75 SD,SD(c), Captain Atom	250.00
77 Oct 1965	125.00

LAW-CRIME
Essenkay Publications,
April, 1948

1 LbC,LbC-(c);Raymond Hamilton Dies In The Chair	1,100.00
2 LbC,LbC-(c);Strangled Beauty Puzzles Police	900.00
3 LbC,LbC-(c);Lipstick Slayer Sought; Aug., 1943	1,100.00

MISS LIBERTY
Burten Publishing, circa 1944

1 Reprints-Shield,Wizard	450.00

Becomes:

LIBERTY COMICS
Green Publishing, May, 1946

10 Reprints,Hangman	300.00
11 Wilbur in women's clothes	225.00
12 Black Hood, Skull(c)	900.00
14 Patty of Airliner	200.00
15 Patty of Airliner	200.00

LIBERTY GUARDS
Chicago Mail Order
(Comic Corp of America),
Circa 1942

1 PG(c),Liberty Scouts	500.00

Becomes:

LIBERTY SCOUTS
June, 1941–Aug., 1941

PG(a&c)O:Fireman,Liberty Scouts	2,000.00
3 PG,PG(c),O:Sentinel	1,500.00

LIFE STORY
Fawcett Publications,
April, 1949

1 Ph(c)	200.00
2 Ph(c)	150.00
3 Ph(c)	125.00
4 Ph(c)	125.00
5 Ph(c)	125.00
6 Ph(c)	125.00
7 Ph(c)	100.00
8 Ph(c)	100.00
9 Ph(c)	100.00
10 Ph(c)	100.00
11	100.00
12	100.00
13 WW, BP,Drug	250.00
14	100.00
15	100.00
16 thru 21	@100.00
22 Drug	200.00
23 BP	100.00
24 BP	100.00
25 thru 35	@100.00
36 Drug	200.00
37	100.00
38	100.00
39 BP,Drug	125.00
40	100.00
41	100.00
42	100.00

43 GE	125.00
44	100.00
45 1952	100.00

LIFE WITH
SNARKY PARKER
Fox Feature Syndicate,
Aug., 1950

1	350.00

SURE-FIRE
Ace Magazines, 1940

1 O:Flash Lightning	2,700.00
2 Whiz Wilson	1,250.00
3 The Raven,Sept., 1940	900.00
3a Ace McCoy,Oct., 1940	900.00

Becomes:

LIGHTNING COMICS
Dec., 1940

4 Sure-Fire Stories	1,600.00
5 JM	1,000.00
6 JM,Dr. Nemesis	1,000.00

Vol. 2

1 JM	800.00
2 JM,Flash Lightning	800.00
3 JM	800.00
4 JM	800.00
5 JM	800.00
6 JM, bondage(c)	900.00

Vol. 3

1 I:Lightning Girl	800.00

LINDA
Ajax/Farrell Publications, 1954

1	200.00
2 Lingerie	150.00
3	125.00
4	125.00

LINDA
See: PHANTOM LADY

LI'L ABNER
Harvey Publications,
Dec., 1947

61 BP,BW,Sadie Hawkins Day	500.00
62	300.00
63	300.00
64	300.00
65 BP	300.00
66	250.00
67	250.00
68 FearlessFosdick V:Any Face	300.00
69	300.00
70	250.00

Toby Press

71	200.00
72	200.00
73	200.00
74	200.00
75 HK	250.00
76	200.00
77 HK	250.00
78 HK	250.00
79 HK	250.00
80	225.00
81	200.00
82	200.00
83 Baseball	225.00
84	200.00
85	200.00
86 HK	250.00
87	200.00
88	200.00
89	200.00
90	200.00
91 Rep. #77	225.00
92	200.00

All comics prices listed are for *Near Mint* condition.

93 Rep. #71	225.00
94	200.00
95 Fearless Fosdick	225.00
96	200.00
97 Jan., 1955	200.00

LITTLE AL OF THE F.B.I.
**Approved Comics
(Ziff Davis) 1950**

10	225.00
11	150.00

LITTLE AL OF THE SECRET SERVICE
**Approved Comics
(Ziff Davis), 1951**

1	225.00
2	150.00
3	150.00

LITTLE ANGEL
Standard Comics, 1954–59

5	125.00
6 thru 16	@100.00

LITTLE ANNIE ROONEY
**St. John Publishing
Co./Standard, 1948**

1	225.00
2	125.00
3	125.00

LITTLE AUDREY
**St. John Publ. Co./
Harvey Comics, April, 1948**

1	700.00
2	350.00
3 thru 6	@250.00
7 thru 10	@175.00
11 thru 20	@150.00
21 thru 24	@125.00
25 B:Harvey Comics	250.00
26 A: Casper	150.00
27 A: Casper	150.00
28 A: Casper	150.00
29 thru 31	@125.00
32 A: Casper	125.00
33 A: Casper	125.00
34 A: Casper	125.00
35 A: Casper	125.00
36 thru 53	@100.00

LITTLE BEAVER
Dell Publishing Co., 1951

3	100.00
4 thru 8	@100.00

LITTLE BIT
**Jubilee Publishing Company,
March, 1949**

1	125.00
2 June, 1949	100.00

LITTLE DOT
**Harvey Publications,
Sept., 1953**

1 I: Richie Rich & Little Lotta	3,100.00
2	1,200.00
3	800.00
4	750.00
5 O:Dots on Little Dot's Dress	750.00
6 1st Richie Rich(c)	750.00
7	550.00
8	500.00
9	500.00
10	500.00
11 thru 20	@350.00

Little Dot #17
© Harvey Publications

21 thru 30	@250.00
31 thru 39	@200.00
40 thru 50	@150.00
51 thru 60	@150.00
61 thru 70	@150.00
71 thru 80	@150.00
81 thru 100	@150.00
101 thru 130	@100.00
131 thru 140	@100.00
141 thru 145, 52 pages	@100.00
146 thru 163	@75.00

LITTLE EVA
**St. John Publishing Co.,
May, 1952**

1	200.00
2	150.00
3	125.00
4	125.00
5 thru 10	@100.00
11 thru 30	@100.00
31 Nov., 1956.	100.00

LI'L GENIUS
Charlton Comics, 1955

1	125.00
2	80.00
3	80.00
4	80.00
5	80.00
6 thru 15	@80.00
16 Giants	125.00
17 Giants	125.00
18 Giants,100 pages	150.00
19 thru 40	@75.00
41 thru 54	@60.00
55 1965	50.00

LI'L GHOST
**St. John Publishing/
Fago Magazine Co.**

1	125.00
2a	75.00
3	75.00

LITTLE GIANT COMICS
**Centaur Publications,
July, 1938**

1 PG, B&W with Color(c)	1,200.00
2 B&W with Color(c)	800.00
3 B&W with Color(c)	800.00
4 B&W with Color(c)	800.00

LITTLE GIANT DETECTIVE FUNNIES
**Centaur Publications,
Oct., 1938–Jan., 1939**

1 B&W	1,200.00
2 B&W	800.00
3 B&W	800.00
4 WE	800.00

LITTLE GIANT MOVIE FUNNIES
**Centaur Publications,
Aug., 1938**

1 Ed Wheelan-a	1,200.00
2 Ed Wheelan-a, Oct., 1938	800.00

LITTLE GROUCHO
Reston Publ., Co. 1955

1	100.00
2	75.00

LITTLE IKE
**St. John Publishing Co.,
April, 1953**

1	100.00
2	75.00
3	75.00
4 Oct., 1953	75.00

LITTLE IODINE
**Dell Publishing Co.,
April, 1949**

1	175.00
2	125.00
3	125.00
4	125.00
5	125.00
6 thru 10	@100.00
11 thru 30	@100.00
31 thru 50	@100.00
51 thru 56	@100.00

LITTLE JACK FROST
Avon Periodicals, 1951

1	125.00

LI'L JINX
Archie Publications, 1956

11	150.00
12 thru 16	@125.00

LITTLE JOE
St. John Publishing Co., 1953

1	75.00

LITTLE LULU
See: MARGE'S LITTLE LULU

LI'L MENACE
Fago Magazine Co., 1958

1 Peter Rabbit	100.00
2	75.00
3	75.00

LITTLE MAX COMICS
**Harvey Publications,
Oct., 1949**

1 I: Little Dot,Joe Palooka(c)	300.00
2 A: Little Dot,Joe Palooka(c)	250.00
3 A: Little Dot,Joe Palooka(c)	150.00
4	100.00
5 C: Little Dot	100.00
6 thru 10	@100.00
11 thru 22	@75.00
23 A: Little Dot	75.00

24 thru 37 . . . . @60.00
38 Rep. #20 . . . . 60.00
39 thru 72. . . . . @50.00
73 A: Richie Rich; Nov.'61 . . . . . . 50.00

LITTLE MISS MUFFET
**Best Books
(Standard Comics),
Dec., 1948**
11 Strip Reprints. 100.00
12 Strip Reprints 75.00
13 Strip Reprints; Mar.'49 . . . . . 75.00

LITTLE MISS SUNBEAM
COMICS
**Magazine Enterprises,
June–July, 1950**
1 . . . . 200.00
2 . . . . 100.00
3 . . . . 100.00
4 Dec.–Jan., 1951 . . . . 100.00

LITTLE ORPHAN ANNIE
Dell Publishing Co., 1948
1 . . . . 250.00
2 Orphan Annie and the Rescue 150.00
3 . . . . 150.00
See also: *Four Color*

LI'L PAN
**Fox Features Syndicate,
Dec.–Jan., 1946-47**
6 . . . . 125.00
7 . . . . 100.00
8 April–May, 1947 . . . . 100.00

LITTLE ROQUEFORT
**St. John Publishing Co.,
June,1952**
1 . . . . 125.00
2 . . . . 100.00
3 thru 9 . . . . @100.00

Pines
10 Summer 1958 . . . . 100.00

LITTLE SCOUTS
**Dell Publishing Co.,
March, 1951**
(1) *see Dell Four Color #321*
2 . . . . 100.00
3 thru 6 . . . . @75.00

LITTLEST SNOWMAN
**Dell Publishing Co.,
Dec., 1956**
1 . . . . 100.00

LIVING BIBLE, THE
**Living Bible Corp.
Autumn, 1945**
1 LbC-(c) Life of Paul 525.00
2 LbC-(c) Joseph &His Brethern. 400.00
3 LbC-(c) Chaplains At War 575.00

LONE EAGLE
**Ajax/Farrell,
April–May, 1954**
1 . . . . 200.00
2 . . . . 150.00
3 Bondage(c) 200.00
4 Oct.–Nov., 1954 . . . . 150.00

LONELY HEART
**Excellent Publications
(Ajax/Farrell), 1955**
9 . . . . 150.00

10 thru 14 . . . . @100.00
Becomes:

DEAR HEART
Ajax/Farrell Publ., 1956
15 . . . . 100.00
16 . . . . 100.00

LONE RANGER
**Dell Publishing Co.,
Jan.–Feb., 1948**
1 B:Lone Ranger & Tonto
  B:Strip Reprint 1,400.00
2 . . . . 600.00
3 . . . . 400.00
4 . . . . 400.00
5 . . . . 400.00
6 . . . . 350.00
7 . . . . 350.00
8 O:Retold 400.00
9 . . . . 350.00
10 . . . . 350.00
11 B:Young Hawk 250.00
12 thru 20 . . . . @250.00
21 . . . . 200.00
22 . . . . 200.00
23 O:Retold 275.00
24 thru 30 . . . . @200.00
31 (1st Mask Logo) 250.00
32 thru 36 . . . . @175.00
37 (E:Strip reprints) 150.00
38 thru 50 . . . . @150.00
51 thru 75 . . . . @150.00
76 thru 99 . . . . @125.00
100 . . . . 150.00
101 thru 111 . . . . @150.00
112 B:Clayton Moore Ph(c) 350.00
113 thru 117 . . . . @200.00
118 O:Lone Ranger & Tonto
  retold, Anniv. issue 450.00
119 thru 144 . . . . @200.00
145 final issue,May/July, 1962. . 200.00

THE LONE RANGER'S
COMPANION TONTO
Dell Publishing Co., Jan., 1951
(1) *see Dell Four Color #312*
2 P(c) all 200.00
3 . . . . 150.00
4 . . . . 125.00
5 . . . . 125.00
6 thru 10 . . . . @125.00
11 thru 20 . . . . @100.00
21 thru 25 . . . . @100.00
26 thru 33 . . . . @100.00

THE LONE RANGER'S
FAMOUS HORSE
HI-YO SILVER
Dell Publishing Co., Jan., 1952
(1) *see Dell Four Color #369*
(1) *see Dell Four Color #392*
3 P(c) all 200.00
4 . . . . 125.00
5 . . . . 125.00
6 thru 10 . . . . @125.00
11 thru 36 . . . . @100.00

LONE RIDER
**Farrell (Superior
Comics), April, 1951**
1 . . . . 400.00
2 I&O: Golden Arrow; 52 pgs. . . 200.00
3 . . . . 175.00
4 . . . . 175.00
5 . . . . 175.00
6 E: Golden Arrow 175.00
7 G.Arrow Becomes Swift Arrow 175.00
8 O: Swift Arrow 200.00

9 thru 14 . . . . @100.00
15 O: Golden Arrow Rep. #2 . . 125.00
16 thru 19 . . . . @100.00
20 . . . . 100.00
21 3-D (c) 250.00
22 . . . . 100.00
23 A: Apache Kid 100.00
24 . . . . 100.00
25 . . . . 100.00
26 July, 1955 . . . . 100.00

LONG BOW
**Real Adventures Publ.
(Fiction House), Winter, 1950**
1 . . . . 250.00
2 . . . . 125.00
3 'Red Arrows Means War' 125.00
4 'Trial of Tomahawk' 125.00
5 . . . . 125.00
6 'Rattlesnake Raiders' 100.00
7 . . . . 100.00
8 . . . . 100.00
9 Spring, 1953 . . . . 100.00

LONG JOHN SILVER
AND THE PIRATES
See: TERRY
AND THE PIRATES

LOONEY TUNES AND
MERRIE MELODIES
Dell Publishing Co., 1941
1 B:&1st Comic App. Bugs Bunny
  Daffy Duck,Elmer Fudd . . 21,000.00
2 Bugs/Porky(c) 4,000.00
3 Bugs/Porky(c) B:WK,
  Kandi the Cave. 3,000.00
4 Bugs/Porky(c),WK 3,000.00
5 Bugs/Porky(c),WK,
  A:Super Rabbit. 2,400.00
6 Bugs/Porky/Elmer(c),E:WK,
  Kandi the Cave. 1,800.00
7 Bugs/Porky(c) 1,500.00
8 Bugs/Porky swimming(c),F:WK,
  Kandi the Cave. 1,800.00
9 Porky/Elmer car painted(c) . 1,300.00
10 Porky/Bugs/Elmer Parade(c) 1,300.00
11 Bugs/Porky(c),F:WK,
  Kandi the Cave. 1,300.00
12 Bugs/Porky rollerskating(c). . 900.00
13 Bugs/Porky(c) 900.00
14 Bugs/Porky(c) 900.00
15 Bugs/Porky X-Mas(c),F:WK
  Kandi the Cave. 1,000.00

*Loonie Tunes and Merrie Melodies #17
© Walt Disney*

---

16 Bugs/Porky ice-skating(c) . . 1,000.00
17 Bugs/Petunia Valentines(c) . 1,000.00
18 Sgt.Bugs Marine(c) 1,000.00
19 Bugs/Painting(c). 1,000.00
20 Bugs/Porky/ElmerWarBonds(c),
    B:WK,Pat,Patsy&Pete 1,000.00
21 Bugs/Porky 4th July(c). 1,000.00
22 Porky(c) 1,000.00
23 Bugs/Porky Fishing(c) 1,000.00
24 Bugs/Porky Football(c) 1,000.00
25 Bugs/Porky/Petunia Halloween
    (c),E:WK,Pat, Patsy & Pete 1,000.00
26 Bugs Thanksgiving(c) 750.00
27 Bugs/Porky New Years(c). . . . 750.00
28 Bugs/Porky Ice-Skating(c) . . . 750.00
29 Bugs Valentine(c) 750.00
30 Bugs(c). 750.00
31 Bugs(c). 600.00
32 Bugs/Porky Hot Dogs(c). 600.00
33 Bugs/Porky War Bonds(c) . . . 750.00
34 Bugs/Porky Fishing(c). 500.00
35 Bugs/Porky Swimming(c) 500.00
36 Bugs/Porky(c). 500.00
37 Bugs Halloween(c) 500.00
38 Bugs Thanksgiving(c) 500.00
39 Bugs X-Mas(c) 500.00
40 Bugs(c). 500.00
41 Bugs Washington's
    Birthday(c). 400.00
42 Bugs Magician(c) 400.00
43 Bugs Dream(c) 400.00
44 Bugs/Porky(c) 400.00
45 Bugs War Bonds(c). 400.00
46 Bugs/Porky(c) 400.00
47 Bugs Beach(c) 350.00
48 Bugs/Porky Picnic(c). 350.00
49 Bugs(c). 350.00
50 Bugs(c). 350.00
51 thru 60 . . . . @300.00
61 thru 80. . . . . @250.00
81 thru 86. . . . . @150.00
87 Bugs X-Mas(c) 175.00
88 thru 99 . . . . @150.00
100 . . . . 150.00
101 thru 110 . . . . @150.00
111 thru 125 . . . . @150.00
126 thru 150. . . . . @150.00
151 thru 165. . . . . @100.00
Becomes:

LOONEY TUNES
Aug., 1955
166 thru 200. . . . . @100.00
201 thru 245. . . . . @100.00
246 final issue,Sept.1962 . . . . . . 100.00

LOST WORLDS
Literary Enterprises
(Standard Comics),
Oct., 1952
5 ATh, Alice in Terrorland 600.00
6 ATh 450.00

LUCKY COMICS
Consolidated Magazines,
Jan., 1944–Summer 1946
1 Lucky Star 300.00
2 HcK(c) 200.00
3 . . . . 200.00
4 . . . . 200.00
5 Devil(c) 200.00

LUCKY DUCK
Standard Comics
(Literary Enterprises),
Jan.–Sept., 1953
5 IS(a&c) 125.00
6 IS(a&c) 100.00
7 IS(a&c) 100.00
8 IS(a&c) 100.00

LUCKY FIGHTS
IT THROUGH
Educational Comics, 1949
N# HK-a, V.D. Prevention 1,800.00

LUCKY "7" COMICS
Howard Publications, 1944
1 Bondage(c) Pioneer 600.00

LUCKY STAR
Nationwide Publications,
1950
1 JDa,B:52 pages western 225.00
2 JDa 150.00
3 JDa 150.00
4 JDa 125.00
5 JDa 125.00
6 JDa 125.00
7 JDa 125.00
8 thru 13 . . . . @100.00
14 1955,E:52 pages western. . . . 100.00

LUCY, THE REAL
GONE GAL
St. John Publishing Co.,
June, 1953
1 Negligee Panels,Teenage 250.00
2 . . . . 125.00
3 MD-a 100.00
4 Feb., 1954 . . . . 75.00
Becomes:

MEET MISS PEPPER
April, 1954
5 JKu-a 250.00
6 JKu (a&c), June,1954 . . . . 200.00

MAD
E.C. Comics, Oct.–Nov., 1952
1 JSe,HK(c),JDa,WW 12,000.00
2 JSe,JDa(c),JDa,WW. 3,500.00
3 JSe,HK(c),JDa,WW 2,200.00
4 JSe,HK(c),JDa-Flob Was
    A Slob,JDa,WW 2,100.00
5 JSe,BE(c).JDa,WW 3,000.00
6 JSe,HK(c),Jda,WW. 1,200.00
7 HK(c),JDa,WW 1,200.00
8 HK(c),JDa,WW 1,200.00
9 JSe,HK(c),JDa,WW 1,200.00
10 JSe,HK(c),JDa,WW 1,300.00
11 BW,BW(c),JDa,WW,Life(c). . 1,200.00
12 BK,JDa,WW. 1,000.00
13 HK(c),JDa,WW,Red(c). 1,000.00
14 RH,HK(c),JDa,WW,
    Mona Lisa(c). 1,000.00
15 JDa,WW,Alice in
    Wonderland(c) 1,000.00
16 HK(c),JDa,WW,
    Newspaper(c). 1,000.00
17 BK,BW,JDa,WW 1,000.00
18 HK(c),JDa,WW. 1,000.00
19 JDa,WW,Racing Form(c) 800.00
20 JDa,WW,Composition(c). 900.00
21 JDa,WW,1st A.E.Neuman(c) 1,000.00
22 BE,JDa,WW,Picasso(c) 1,000.00
23 Last Comic Format Edition,
    JDa,WW Think(c) 800.00
24 BK,WW, HK Logo & Border;
    1st Magazine Format 1,800.00
25 WW,AlJaffee Becomes Reg. 1,000.00
26 BK,WW,WW(c) 750.00
27 WWa,RH,JDa(c) 700.00
28 WW,BE(c),RH Back(c) 550.00
29 JKa,BW,WW,WW(c);
    1st Don Martin Artwork 550.00
30 BE,WW,RC; 1st A.E.
    Neuman(c) By Mingo 750.00
31 JDa,WW,BW,Mingo(c) 500.00

Mad Magazine #35
© E.C. Comics

32 MD,JO 1st as reg.;Mingo(c);
    WW-Back(c) 400.00
33 WWa,Mingo(c);JO-Back(c) . . . 500.00
34 WWa,Mingo(c);1st Berg
    as Reg. 400.00
35 WW,RC,Mingo
    Wraparound(c). 400.00
36 WW,BW,Mingo(c),JO,MD . . . 400.00
37 WW,Mingo(c)JO,MD 400.00
38 WW,JO,MD. 400.00
39 WW,JO,MD 400.00
40 WW,BW,JO,MD 400.00
41 WW,JO,MD 250.00
42 WW,JO,MD 250.00
43 WW,JO,MD 250.00
44 WW,JO,MD 250.00
45 WW,JO,MD 250.00
46 JO,MD 250.00
47 JO,MD 250.00
48 JO,MD 250.00
49 JO,MD 250.00
50 JO,MD 250.00
51 JO,MD 200.00
52 JO,MD 200.00
53 JO,MD 200.00
54 JO,MD 200.00
55 JO,MD 200.00
56 JO,MD 200.00
57 JO,MD 200.00
58 JO,MD 200.00
59 WW,JO,MD 250.00
60 JO,MD. 250.00

MAD HATTER, THE
O.W. Comics, 1946
1 Freddy the Firefly 1,300.00
2 V:Humpty Dumpty 600.00

MADHOUSE
Ajax/Farrell Publ., 1954
1 . . . . 400.00
2 . . . . 200.00
3 . . . . 200.00
4 . . . . 300.00

Second Series, 1957
1 . . . . 150.00
2 . . . . 125.00
3 . . . . 125.00

MAGIC COMICS
David McKay Publications,
Aug.,1939–Nov.-Dec., 1949
1 Mandrake the Magician, Henry,
    Popeye,Blondie, Barney Baxter,
    Secret Agent X-9, Bunky,
    Henry on(c) 4,200.00

GOLDEN AGE

GOLDEN AGE

2 Henry on(c). 1,500.00
3 Henry on(c) 1,100.00
4 Henry on(c),Mandrake-Logo . . 850.00
5 Henry on(c),Mandrake-Logo . . 750.00
6 Henry on(c),Mandrake-Logo . . 600.00
7 Henry on(c),Mandrake-Logo . . 600.00
8 B:Inspector Wade,Tippie 550.00
9 Henry-Mandrake Interact(c) . . 525.00
10 Henry-Mandrake Interact(c) . . 550.00
11 Henry-Mandrake Interact(c) . . 450.00
12 Mandrake on(c). 450.00
13 Mandrake on(c). 450.00
14 Mandrake on(c). 450.00
15 Mandrake on(c). 450.00
16 Mandrake on(c). 450.00
17 B:Lone Ranger 500.00
18 Mandrake on(c) 400.00
19 Mandrake/Robot on(c) 700.00
20 Mandrake on(c). 400.00
21 Mandrake on(c). 350.00
22 Mandrake on(c). 350.00
23 Mandrake on(c). 350.00
24 Mandrake on(c). 350.00
25 B:Blondie; Mandrake in
   Logo for Duration. 350.00
26 Blondie (c). 300.00
27 Blondie(c); HighSchoolHeroes 300.00
28 Blondie(c); HighSchoolHeroes 300.00
29 Blondie(c); HighSchoolHeroes 300.00
30 Blondie (c) 300.00
31 Blondie(c);High School
   Sports Page. 225.00
32 Blondie (c);Secret Agent X-9 . 225.00
33 C.Knight's-Romance of Flying 225.00
34 ClaytonKnight's-War in the Air 225.00
35 Blondie (c). 225.00
36 July'42; Patriotic-(c) 225.00
37 Blondie (c). 225.00
38 ClaytonKnight's-Flying Tigers 225.00
39 Blondie (c). 225.00
40 Jimmie Doolittle bombs Tokyo 225.00
41 How German Became
   British Censor 200.00
42 Joe Musial's-Dollar-a-Dither . . 200.00
43 Clay Knight's-War in the Air . . 200.00
44 Flying Fortress in Action 200.00
45 Clayton Knight's-Gremlins . . . 200.00
46 Adventures of Aladdin Jr. 200.00
47 Secret Agent X-9. . . . . 200.00
48 General Arnold U.S.A.F. 200.00
49 Joe Musial's-Dollar-a-Dither . . 200.00
50 The Lone Ranger 200.00
51 Joe Musial's-Dollar-a-Dither . . 150.00
52 C. Knights-Heroes on Wings . 150.00
53 C. Knights-Heroes on Wings . 150.00
54 High School Heroes 150.00
55 Blondie (c). 175.00
56 High School Heroes 150.00
57 Joe Musial's-Dollar-a-Dither . . 150.00
58 Private Breger Abroad 150.00
59 . . . . 150.00
60 . . . . 150.00
61 Joe Musial's-Dollar-a-Dither . . 125.00
62 . . . . 125.00
63 B:Buz Sawyer, Naval Pilot . . . 125.00
64 thru 70. . . . . @125.00
71 thru 80 . . . . @125.00
81 thru 90 . . . . @100.00
91 thru 99 . . . . @100.00
100 . . . . 125.00
101 thru 108. . . . . @100.00
108 Flash Gordon 125.00
109 Flash Gordon 125.00
110 thru 113 . . . . @125.00
114 The Lone Ranger 125.00
115 thru 119 . . . . @125.00
120 Secret Agent X-9 . . . . 150.00
121 Secret Agent X-9. . . . . 150.00
122 Secret Agent X-9. . . . . 150.00
123 Sec. Agent X-9 . . . . 150.00

GOLDEN AGE

MAJOR HOOPLE COMICS
Nedor Publications, 1942
1 Mary Worth,Phantom Soldier;
   Buy War Bonds On(c) 500.00

MAJOR INAPAK THE SPACE ACE
Magazine Enterprises, 1951
1 BP,Sci-Fi 200.00

MAJOR VICTORY COMICS
**H. Clay Glover Svcs./
Harry A. Chestler, 1944**
1 O:Major Victory,I:Spider
   Woman 950.00
2 A: Dynamic Boy 500.00
3 A: Rocket Boy 450.00

MAMMOTH COMICS
K.K. Publications, 1938
1 Alley Oop, Dick Tracy, etc. . . 3,000.00

MANHUNT!
Magazine Enterprises, 1953
1 LbC,FGu,OW(c);B:Red Fox,
   Undercover Girl, Space Ace . 750.00
2 LbC,FGu,OW(c);
   Electrocution(c) 550.00
3 LbC,FGu,OW,OW(c) 400.00
4 LbC,FGu,OW,OW(c) 400.00
5 LbC,FGu,OW,OW(c) 400.00
6 LbC,OW,OW(c) 375.00
7 LbC,OW; E:Space Ace 350.00
8 LbC,OW,FGu(c);B:Trail Colt . . 350.00
9 LbC,OW 350.00
10 LbC,OW,OW(c),Gwl 350.00
11 LbC,FF,OW;B:The Duke,
   Scotland Yard 550.00
12 LbC,OW 300.00
13 See: *A-1 Comics* #63
14 See: *A-1 Comics* #77

MAN OF WAR
**Comic Corp. of America
(Centaur Publ.), Nov., 1941**
1 PG,PG(c);Flag(c);B:The Fire-
   Man,Man of War,The Sentinel,
   Liberty Guards,Vapoman . . 2,700.00
2 PG,PG(c);I: The Ferret 2,100.00

MAN O'MARS
**Fiction House/
I.W. Enterprises, 1953**
1 MA, Space Rangers 650.00
1 MA, Rep. Space Rangers 100.00

MARCH OF COMICS
**K.K. Publications/
Western Publ., 1946
(All were Giveaways)**
N# WK back(c),Goldilocks 400.00
N# WK,How Santa got His
   Red Suit 375.00
N# WK,Our Gang 500.00
N# CB,Donald Duck;
   'Maharajah Donald' 10,000.00
5 Andy Panda 250.00
6 WK,Fairy Tales 250.00
7 Oswald the Lucky Rabbit . . . 225.00
8 Mickey Mouse 650.00
9 Gloomey Bunny 135.00
10 Santa Claus 125.00
11 Santa Claus. 100.00
12 Santa's Toys 100.00
13 Santa's Suprise. 100.00
14 Santa's Kitchen 100.00
15 Hip-It-Ty Hop. 100.00
16 Woody Woodpecker 175.00
17 Roy Rogers 300.00
18 Fairy Tales 125.00
19 Uncle Wiggily 100.00
20 CB,Donald Duck 5,200.00
21 Tom and Jerry 135.00
22 Andy Panda 125.00
23 Raggedy Ann and Andy 175.00
24 Felix the Cat; By
   Otto Messmer 275.00
25 Gene Autrey 275.00
26 Our Gang 275.00
27 Mickey Mouse. 500.00
28 Gene Autry 275.00
29 Easter 75.00
30 Santa 75.00
31 Santa. 75.00
32 Does Not Exist
33 A Christmas Carol. 75.00
34 Woody Woodpecker 150.00
35 Roy Rogers 325.00
36 Felix the Cat 250.00
37 Popeye 175.00
38 Oswald the Lucky Rabbit . . . 100.00
39 Gene Autry 275.00
40 Andy and Woody 100.00
41 CB,DonaldDuck,SouthSeas. 5,000.00
42 Porky Pig 100.00
43 Henry 100.00

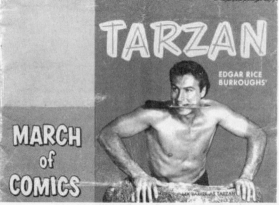

March of Comics #98 © Edgar Rice Burroughs

44 Bugs Bunny 125.00
45 Mickey Mouse. 350.00
46 Tom and Jerry 125.00
47 Roy Rogers. 250.00
48 Santa. 100.00
49 Santa. 100.00
50 Santa 100.00
51 Felix the Cat 200.00
52 Popeye 150.00
53 Oswald the Lucky Rabbit 100.00
54 Gene Autrey 250.00
55 Andy and Woody. 100.00
56 CB back(c),Donald Duck 400.00
57 Porky Pig 100.00
58 Henry 100.00
59 Bugs Bunny 125.00
60 Mickey Mouse 350.00
61 Tom and Jerry 100.00
62 Roy Rogers. 250.00
63 Santa. 75.00
64 Santa. 75.00
65 Jingle Bells 75.00
66 Popeye 125.00
67 Oswald the Lucky Rabbit 100.00
68 Roy Rogers. 225.00
69 Donald Duck 325.00
70 Tom and Jerry 100.00
71 Porky Pig 100.00
72 Krazy Kat 100.00
73 Roy Rogers. 225.00
74 Mickey Mouse 300.00
75 Bugs Bunny 100.00
76 Andy and Woody. 100.00
77 Roy Rogers. 200.00
78 Gene Autrey; last regular
    sized issue. 200.00
79 Andy Panda,5"x7" format 100.00
80 Popeye 100.00
81 Oswald the Lucky Rabbit 75.00
82 Tarzan. 200.00
83 Bugs Bunny 75.00
84 Henry 75.00
85 Woody Woodpecker 75.00
86 Roy Rogers. 150.00
87 Krazy Kat 75.00
88 Tom and Jerry. 75.00
89 Porky Pig 75.00
90 Gene Autrey 125.00
91 Roy Rogers and Santa 150.00
92 Christmas w/Santa 50.00
93 Woody Woodpecker 50.00
94 Indian Chief. 125.00
95 Oswald the Lucky Rabbit 50.00
96 Popeye 125.00
97 Bugs Bunny 75.00
98 Tarzan,Lex Barker Ph(c). 200.00
99 Porky Pig 50.00
100 Roy Rogers. 125.00
101 Henry 50.00
102 Tom Corbet,P(c) 150.00
103 Tom and Jerry 50.00
104 Gene Autrey 125.00
105 Roy Rogers. 125.00
106 Santa's Helpers. 50.00
107 *Not Published*
108 Fun with Santa 50.00
109 Woody Woodpecker 50.00
110 Indian Chief 50.00
111 Oswald the Lucky Rabbit 50.00
112 Henry. 50.00
113 Porky Pig. 50.00
114 Tarzan,RsM 200.00
115 Bugs Bunny. 50.00
116 Roy Rogers 125.00
117 Popeye 100.00
118 Flash Gordon, P(c) 150.00
119 Tom and Jerry 50.00
120 Gene Autrey 125.00
121 Roy Rogers. 125.00
122 Santa's Suprise. 50.00
123 Santa's Christmas Book 50.00
124 Woody Woodpecker 50.00

MaRCH OF COMiCS

The THREE STOOGES

March of Comics #304
© Western Publications

125 Tarzan, Lex Barker Ph(c) . . . 200.00
126 Oswald the Lucky Rabbit 50.00
127 Indian Chief. 75.00
128 Tom and Jerry 50.00
129 Henry 50.00
130 Porky Pig 50.00
131 Roy Rogers 125.00
132 Bugs Bunny 50.00
133 Flash Gordon,Ph(c) 125.00
134 Popeye 75.00
135 Gene Autrey 100.00
136 Roy Rogers 100.00
137 Gifts from Santa 40.00
138 Fun at Christmas 40.00
139 Woody Woodpecker 40.00
140 Indian Chief 75.00
141 Oswald the Lucky Rabbit 40.00
142 Flash Gordon 125.00
143 Porky Pig 40.00
144 RsM,Ph(c),Tarzan 175.00
145 Tom and Jerry 40.00
146 Roy Rogers,Ph(c) 125.00
147 Henry 40.00
148 Popeye 75.00
149 Bugs Bunny 40.00
150 Gene Autrey 100.00
151 Roy Rogers 100.00
152 The Night Before Christmas . . 40.00
153 Merry Christmas 40.00
154 Tom and Jerry 40.00
155 Tarzan,Ph(c) 175.00
156 Oswald the Lucky Rabbit 40.00
157 Popeye 75.00
158 Woody Woodpecker 40.00
159 Indian Chief. 75.00
160 Bugs Bunny 40.00
161 Roy Rogers 100.00
162 Henry 40.00
163 Rin Tin Tin. 125.00
164 Porky Pig 40.00
165 The Lone Ranger 100.00
166 Santa & His Reindeer 40.00
167 Roy Rogers and Santa 100.00
168 Santa Claus' Workshop 40.00
169 Popeye 75.00
170 Indian Chief 75.00
171 Oswald the Lucky Rabbit 40.00
172 Tarzan. 175.00
173 Tom and Jerry 40.00
174 The Lone Ranger 125.00
175 Porky Pig 40.00
176 Roy Rogers 125.00
177 Woody Woodpecker 40.00
178 Henry 40.00
179 Bugs Bunny 40.00
180 Rin Tin Tin 75.00

181 Happy Holiday 30.00
182 Happi Tim 40.00
183 Welcome Santa. 30.00
184 Woody Woodpecker 40.00
185 Tarzan, Ph(c) 150.00
186 Oswald the Lucky Rabbit 30.00
187 Indian Chief. 75.00
188 Bugs Bunny 30.00
189 Henry 30.00
190 Tom and Jerry 30.00
191 Roy Rogers. 100.00
192 Porky Pig 30.00
193 The Lone Ranger 125.00
194 Popeye 75.00
195 Rin Tin Tin. 100.00
196 *Not Published*
197 Santa is Coming 30.00
198 Santa's Helper 30.00
199 Huckleberry Hound 100.00
200 Fury 75.00
201 Bugs Bunny 50.00
202 Space Explorer 100.00
203 Woody Woodpecker 30.00
204 Tarzan. 125.00
205 Mighty Mouse 75.00
206 Roy Rogers,Ph(c) 100.00
207 Tom and Jerry 30.00
208 The Lone Ranger,Ph(c) 150.00
209 Porky Pig 30.00
210 Lassie 75.00
211 *Not Published*
212 Christmas Eve 30.00
213 Here Comes Santa 30.00
214 Huckleberry Hound. 125.00
215 Hi Yo Silver 100.00
216 Rocky & His Friends. 125.00
217 Lassie 75.00
218 Porky Pig 30.00
219 Journey to the Sun 100.00
220 Bugs Bunny 30.00
221 Roy and Dale,Ph(c) 125.00
222 Woody Woodpecker 30.00
223 Tarzan. 125.00
224 Tom and Jerry 30.00
225 The Lone Ranger 100.00
226 Christmas Treasury. 30.00
227 *Not Published*
228 Letters to Santa 30.00
229 The Flintstones 150.00
230 Lassie 75.00
231 Bugs Bunny 30.00
232 The Three Stooges 250.00
233 Bullwinkle 150.00
234 Smokey the Bear 40.00
235 Huckleberry Hound 100.00
236 Roy and Dale 100.00
237 Mighty Mouse 50.00
238 The Lone Ranger 100.00
239 Woody Woodpecker 30.00
240 Tarzan 125.00
241 Santa Around the World 30.00
242 Santa Toyland 30.00
243 The Flintstones 150.00
244 Mr.Ed,Ph(c). 75.00
245 Bugs Bunny 30.00
246 Popeye 50.00
247 Mighty Mouse 50.00
248 The Three Stooges 200.00
249 Woody Woodpecker 30.00
250 Roy and Dale 100.00

MARGE'S LITTLE LULU

Dell Publishing Co., 1948

1 B:Lulu's Diary 1,300.00
2 I:Gloria,Miss Feeny 600.00
3 . . . . 500.00
4 . . . . 500.00
5 . . . . 500.00
6 . . . . 400.00
7 I:Annie,X-Mas (c). 400.00
8 . . . . 400.00
9 . . . . 400.00

GOLDEN AGE

10 .... 400.00
11 thru 18 .... @350.00
19 I:Wilbur 350.00
20 I:Mr.McNabbem............ 350.00
21 .... 300.00
22 .... 300.00
23 .... 300.00
24 .... 300.00
25 .... 300.00
26 rep.Four Color #110 .... 300.00
27 thru 29 .... @300.00
30 Christmas (c) 300.00
31 thru 34 .... @250.00
35 B:Mumday Story 250.00
36 .... 250.00
37 .... 250.00
38 .... 250.00
39 I:Witch Hazel 275.00
40 Halloween (c) 250.00
41 .... 200.00
42 Christmas (c) 200.00
43 Skiing (c)................... 200.00
44 Valentines Day (c). 200.00
45 2nd A:Witch Hazel 200.00
46 thru 60 .... @200.00
61 .... 150.00
62 .... 150.00
63 I:Chubby 150.00
64 thru 67 .... @150.00
68 I:Professor Cleff 150.00
69 thru 77 .... @150.00
78 Christmas (c) 150.00
79 .... 150.00
80 .... 150.00
81 thru 89 .... @125.00
90 Christmas (c) 125.00
91 thru 99 .... @125.00
100 .... 150.00
101 thru 122................. @100.00
123 I:Fifi 110.00
124 thru 164................. @100.00
165 giant sized................ 200.00
166 giant sized................ 200.00

MARGE'S TUBBY
Dell Publishing Co., 1953
1 .... 400.00
2 .... 200.00
3 & 4 .... @175.00
5 thru 10 .... @150.00
11 thru 20 .... @125.00
21 thru 49 .... @100.00

MARK TRAIL
Standard Magazines/
Fawcett/Pines, 1955
1 .... 125.00
5 .... 75.00
A1 .... 150.00

MARMADUKE MOUSE
Quality Comics Group
(Arnold Publications), 1946
1 Funny Animal................ 250.00
2 Funny Animal................ 200.00
3 thru 8 Funny Animal ..... @125.00
9 Funny Animal................ 100.00
10 Funny Animal 100.00
11 thru 20 Funny Animal ..... @75.00
21 thru 30 Funny Animal ..... @60.00
31 thru 40 Funny Animal ..... @60.00
41 thru 50 Funny Animal ..... @60.00
51 thru 65 Funny Animal ..... @50.00

MARTIN KANE
Hero Books (Fox Features
Syndicate), June, 1950
1 WW,WW-(c)................ 400.00
2 WW,JO, Auguat, 1950 ...... 300.00

The Marvel Family #36
© Fawcett Publications

MARVEL FAMILY, THE
Fawcett Publications,
Dec., 1945–Jan., 1954
1 O:Captain Marvel,Captain Marvel Jr.,
  Mary Marvel,Uncle Marvel;
  V:Black Adam 2,700.00
2 Uncle Marvel............. 1,300.00
3 .... 900.00
4 The Witch's Tale 700.00
5 Civilization of a
  Prehistoric Race 600.00
6 .... 550.00
7 The Rock of Eternity,Shazam . 550.00
8 The Marvel Family
  Round Table 500.00
9 V: The Last Vikings 500.00
10 CCB(c),JaB,BTh,V:Sivana
  Family 500.00
11 V: The Well of Evil......... 400.00
12 V: The Iron Horseman 400.00
13 BTh,CCB,PrC(c)............ 400.00
14 Captain Marvel Invalid 400.00
15 V: Mr. Triangle............. 425.00
16 World's Mightiest Quarrell... 425.00
17 .... 425.00
18 .... 425.00
19 V: The Monster Menace 425.00
20 The Marvel Family Feud 425.00
21 V: The Trio of Terror 400.00
22 V: The Triple Threat 400.00
23 March of Independence (c). .. 425.00
24 V: The Fighting Xergos..... 400.00
25 Trial of the Marvel Family.... 400.00
26 V: Mr. Power............... 400.00
27 V: The Amoeba Men........ 400.00
28 .... 400.00
29 V: The Monarch of Money ... 400.00
30 A:World's Greatest Magician . 400.00
31 V:Sivana & The Great Hunger 300.00
32 The Marvel Family Goes
  Into Buisness.............. 300.00
33 I: The Hermit Family 300.00
34 V: Sivana's Miniature Menace 300.00
35 V: The Berzerk Machines 300.00
36 V: The Invaders From Infinity . 300.00
37 V: The Earth Changer....... 300.00
38 V: Sivana's Instinct
  Exterminator Gun 300.00
39 The Legend of Atlantis 300.00
40 Seven Wonders of the
  Modern World 300.00
41 The Great Oxygen Theft..... 300.00
42 V: The Endless Menace 250.00
43 .... 250.00
44 V: The Rust That Menaced
  the World................. 250.00

45 The Hoax City............. 250.00
46 The Day Civilization Vanished 250.00
47 V: The Interplanetary Thieves. 300.00
48 V: The Four Horsemen 250.00
49 ...Proves Human Hardness. .. 250.00
50 The Speech Scrambler
  Machine.................. 250.00
51 The Living Statues 275.00
52 The School of Witches 250.00
53 V:Man Who Changed World . . 250.00
54 .... 250.00
55 .... 250.00
56 The World's Mightiest Project. 250.00
57 .... 250.00
58 The Triple Time Plot 250.00
59 .... 250.00
60 .... 250.00
61 .... 250.00
62 .... 250.00
63 V: The Pirate Planet 250.00
64 .... 250.00
65 .... 250.00
66 The Miracle Stone.......... 250.00
67 .... 250.00
68 .... 250.00
69 V: The Menace of Old Age ... 250.00
70 V: The Crusade of Evil 250.00
71 .... 250.00
72 .... 250.00
73 .... 250.00
74 .... 250.00
75 The Great Space Struggle ... 250.00
76 .... 225.00
77 Anti-Communist............ 400.00
78 V: The Red Vulture 300.00
79 Horror 250.00
80 .... 250.00
81 .... 250.00
82 .... 250.00
83 V: The Flying Skull 250.00
84 thru 87 .... @250.00
88 Jokes of Jeopardy.......... 250.00
89 And Then There Were None.. 250.00

MARVELS OF SCIENCE
Charlton Comics, 1946
1 1st Charlton Book; Atomic
  Bomb Story 350.00
2 .... 250.00
3 .... 250.00
4 President Truman(c); Jun.'6 .. 250.00

MARY MARVEL COMICS
Fawcett Publications,
Dec., 1945
1 Intro: Mary Marvel......... 3,000.00
2 .... 1,100.00
3 .... 750.00
4 On a Leave of Absence 700.00
5 Butterfly (c) Bullet Girl 500.00
6 A:Freckles,Teenager of
  Mischief 500.00
7 The Kingdom Undersea 500.00
8 Holiday Special Issue 500.00
9 Air Race (c) 450.00
10 A: Freckles 450.00
11 A: The Sad Dryads 300.00
12 Red Cross Appeal on(c) 300.00
13 Keep the Homefires Burning . 300.00
14 Meets Ghosts (c) 300.00
15 A: Freckles 300.00
16 The Jukebox Menace 275.00
17 Aunt Agatha's Adventures... 275.00
18 .... 275.00
19 Witch (c) 275.00
20 .... 275.00
21 V: Dice Head............... 250.00
22 The Silver Slippers 250.00
23 The Pendulum Strikes....... 250.00
24 V: The Nightowl............ 250.00
25 A: Freckles 250.00

| All comics prices listed are for *Near Mint* condition.

26 A:Freckles dressed as Clown . 250.00
27 The Floating Oceanliner 250.00
28 Western, Sept., 1948 . . . . 250.00
Becomes:

MONTE HALE WESTERN
**Fawcett Publications,
Oct., 1948**
29 Ph(c),B:Monte Hale & His
   Horse Pardner 700.00
30 Ph(c),B:Big Bow-Little
   Arrow; CCB,Captain Tootsie . 300.00
31 Ph(c),Giant 250.00
32 Ph(c),Giant 250.00
33 Ph(c),Giant 250.00
34 Ph(c),E:Big Bow-Little
   Arrow;B:Gabby Hayes,Giant . 250.00
35 Ph(c),Gabby Hayes, Giant . . . 250.00
36 Ph(c),Gabby Hayes, Giant . . . 250.00
37 Ph(c),Gabby Hayes 200.00
38 Ph(c),Gabby Hayes, Giant . . . 200.00
39 Ph(c),CCB, Captain Tootsie;
   Gabby Hayes, Giant 200.00
40 Ph(c),Gabby Hayes, Giant . . . 200.00
41 Ph(c),Gabby Hayes 200.00
42 Ph(c),Gabby Hayes, Giant . . . 175.00
43 Ph(c),Gabby Hayes, Giant . . . 175.00
44 Ph(c),Gabby Hayes, Giant . . . 175.00
45 Ph(c),Gabby Hayes 175.00
46 Ph(c),Gabby Hayes, Giant . . . 200.00
47 Ph(c),A:Big Bow-Little Arrow;
   Gabby Hayes, Giant 200.00
48 Ph(c),Gabby Hayes, Giant . . . 200.00
49 Ph(c),Gabby Hayes 175.00
50 Ph(c),Gabby Hayes 175.00
51 Ph(c),Gabby Hayes, Giant . . . 135.00
52 Ph(c),Gabby Hayes, Giant . . . 135.00
53 Ph(c),A:Slim Pickens;
   Gabby Hayes. 125.00
54 Ph(c),Gabby Hayes, Giant . . . 135.00
55 Ph(c),Gabby Hayes, Giant . . . 135.00
56 Ph(c),Gabby Hayes, Giant . . . 125.00
57 Ph(c),Gabby Hayes 125.00
58 Ph(c),Gabby Hayes, Giant . . . 125.00
59 Ph(c),Gabby Hayes, Giant . . . 125.00
60 thru 79 Ph(c),Gabby Hayes @100.00
80 Ph(c),E: Gabby Hayes 100.00
81 Ph(c) 100.00
82 Final Ph(c) 125.00

Charlton Comics, Feb., 1955
83 R:G. Hayes Back B&W Ph(c) . 150.00
84 . . . . 100.00
85 . . . . 100.00
86 E: Gabby Hayes 100.00
87 . . . . 100.00
88 Jan., 1956. . . . . 100.00

MASK COMICS
**Rural Home Publications,
Feb.–March, 1945**
1 LbC,LbC-(c), Evil (c). 4,500.00
2 LbC-(c),A:Black Rider,The
  Collector The Boy Magician;
  Apr-May'45, Devil (c) 2,500.00

MASKED MARVEL
**Centaur Publications,
Sept., 1940**
1 I: The Masked Marvel 2,400.00
2 PG, ... 1,700.00
3 Dec., 1940 . . . . 1,600.00

THE MASKED RAIDER
Charlton Comics, 1955
1 . . . . 150.00
2 . . . . 125.00
3 . . . . 100.00
4 thru 7 . . . . @100.00
8 Billy the Kid 100.00

*Continued as Billy the Kid,
see Color Pub. section*

MASKED RANGER
**Premier Magazines,
April, 1954**
1 FF,O&B:The Masked Ranger,
  Streak the Horse,The
  Crimson Avenger. 600.00
2 . . . . 200.00
3 . . . . 200.00
4 B: Jessie James,Billy the Kid,
  Wild Bill Hickok,
  Jim Bowie's Life Story 200.00
5 . . . . 200.00
6 . . . . 200.00
7 . . . . 200.00
8 . . . . 200.00
9 AT,E:All Features; A:Wyatt
  Earp Aug., 1955. . . . . 225.00

MASTER COMICS
**Fawcett Publications,
March, 1940**
1-6 Oversized,7-Normal Format
1 O:Master Man; B:The Devil's
  Dagger, El Carin-Master of
  Magic, Rick O'Say, Morton
  Murch, White Rajah, Shipwreck
  Roberts, Frontier Marshall,
  Mr. Clue, Streak Sloan . . . 16,000.00
2 Master Man (c) 4,500.00
3 Master Man (c) Bondage . . . 3,600.00
4 Master Man (c) 3,500.00
5 Master Man (c) 3,500.00
6 E: All Above Features 3,600.00
7 B:Bulletman,Zorro,The Mystery
  Man, Lee Granger, Jungle
  King,Buck Jones 5,000.00
8 B:The Red Gaucho,Captain
  Venture, Planet Princess . . 3,000.00
9 Bulletman & Steam Roller . . 2,800.00
10 E: Lee Granger 4,000.00
11 O: Minute Man 5,500.00
12 Minute Man (c). 3,000.00
13 O:Bulletgirl; E:Red Gaucho . 3,500.00
14 B: The Companions Three. . 2,500.00
15 MRa, Bulletman & Girl (c) . . 2,500.00
16 MRa, Minute Man (c) 2,500.00
17 B:MRa on Bulletman 2,200.00
18 MRa, ... 2,200.00
19 MRa, Bulletman & Girl (c) . . 2,200.00
20 MRa,C:Cap.Marvel-
  Bulletman 2,200.00
21 MRa-(c),Capt. Marvel in
  Bulletman,I&O:Captain
  Nazi 9,000.00
22 MRa-(c),E:Mystery Man,Captain
  Venture; Bondage(c);Capt.
  Marvel Jr. X-Over In
  Bulletman; A:Capt. Nazi . . . 8,000.00
23 MRa(a&c),B:Capt. Marvel Jr.
  V:Capt. Nazi 4,800.00
24 MRa(a&c),Death By Radio . 2,200.00
25 MRa(a&c),The Jap Invasion 2,200.00
26 MRa(a&c),Capt. Marvel Jr.
  Avenges Pearl Harbor 2,200.00
27 MRa(a&c),V For Victory(c). . 2,200.00
28 MRa(a&c),Liberty Bell(c). . . . 2,200.00
29 MRa(a&c),Hitler &
  Hirohito(c). 2,900.00
30 MRa(a&c),Flag (c);Capt.
  Marvel Jr, V: Capt. Nazi . . 2,000.00
31 MRa(a&c),E:Companions
  Three,Capt.Marvel Jr,
  V:Mad Dr. Macabre 1,500.00
32 MRa(a&c),E: Buck Jones;
  CMJr Strikes Terror Castle . 1,500.00
33 MRa(a&c),B:Balbo the Boy
  Magician,Hopalong Cassidy 1,500.00

*Master Comics #46
© Fawcett Publications*

34 MRa(a&c),Capt.Marvel Jr
  V: Capt.Nazi 2,000.00
35 MRa(a&c),CMJr Defies
  the Flame 1,500.00
36 MRa(a&c),Statue Of
  Liberty(c). 1,500.00
37 MRa(a&c),CMJr Blasts
  the Nazi Raiders 1,500.00
38 MRa(a&c),CMJr V:the Japs . 1,500.00
39 MRa(a&c),CMJr Blasts
  Nazi Slave Ship 1,500.00
40 MRa(a&c),Flag (c) 1,500.00
41 MRa(a&c),Bulletman,Bulletgirl,
  CMJr X-over In Minuteman 1,500.00
42 MRa(a&c),CMJr V: Hitler's
  Dream Soldier 700.00
43 MRa(c),CMJr Battles For
  Stalingrad. 700.00
44 MRa(c),CMJr In Crystal City
  of the Peculiar Penguins . . . 700.00
45 MRa(c), ... 700.00
46 MRa(c) 700.00
47 MRa(c),A:Hitler; E: Balbo 750.00
48 MRa(c),I:Bulletboy;Capt.
  Marvel A: in Minuteman. 800.00
49 MRa(c),E: Hopalong Cassidy,
  Minuteman 700.00
50 I&O: Radar,A:Capt. Marvel,
  B:Nyoka the Jungle Girl . . . 700.00
51 MRa(c),CMJr V: Japanese . . 500.00
52 MRa(c),CMJr & Radar Pitch
  War Stamps on (c). 500.00
53 CMJR V: Dr. Sivana 500.00
54 MRa(c),Capt.Marvel Jr
  Your Pin-Up Buddy 500.00
55 . . . . 500.00
56 MRa(c) 400.00
57 CMJr V: Dr. Sivana 400.00
58 MRa(a&c), ... 400.00
59 MRa(c),A:The Upside
  Downies. 500.00
60 MRa(c) 500.00
61 CMJr Meets Uncle Marvel . . . 500.00
62 Uncle Sam on (c) 500.00
63 W/ Radar (c) 400.00
64 W/ Radar (c) 400.00
65 BTh(c),JkS 400.00
66 CMJr & Secret Of the Sphinx 400.00
67 Knight (c) 400.00
68 CMJr in the Range of
  the Beasts 400.00
69 . . . . 400.00
70 . . . . 400.00
71 CMJr,V:Man in Metal Mask. . . 350.00
72 CMJr V: Sivana & The Whistle
  That Wouldn't Stop 350.00

GOLDEN AGE

GOLDEN AGE

73 CMJr V: The Ghost of Evil . . . 350.00
74 CMJr & The Fountain of Age . 350.00
75 CMJr V: The Zombie Master. . 350.00
76 . . . . 350.00
77 BTh(c),BK,Pirate Treasure . . . 350.00
78 CMJr in Death on the Scenic
   Railway 350.00
79 CMJr V: The Black Shroud . . 350.00
80 CMJr-The Land of Backwards 350.00
81 CMJr & The Voyage 'Round
   the Horn. 300.00
82 CMJr,IN,Death at the
   Launching 300.00
83 . . . . 300.00
84 BTh(c&a) CMJr V: The Human
   Magnet. 300.00
85 CMJr-Crime on the Campus . 250.00
86 CMJr & The City of Machines . 250.00
87 CMJr & The Root of Evil 250.00
88 CMJr V: The Wreckers;
   B: Hopalong Cassidy. 250.00
89 . . . . 250.00
90 CMJr V: The Caveman 250.00
91 CMJr V: The Blockmen. 250.00
92 CMJr V: The Space Slavers . . 250.00
93 BK,CMJr,V:TheGrowingGiant . 250.00
94 E: Hopalong Cassidy 250.00
95 B: Tom Mix; CMJr Meets
   the Skyhawk 250.00
96 CMJr Meets the World's
   Mightiest Horse 250.00
97 CMJr Faces the Doubting
   Thomas 250.00
98 KKK Type 250.00
99 Witch (c) 250.00
100 CMJr V: The Ghost Ship. . . . 275.00
101 thru 105 . . . . @225.00
106 E: Bulletman 225.00
107 CMJr Faces the Disappearance
   of the Statue of Liberty 250.00
108 . . . . 250.00
109 . . . . 250.00
110 CMJr & The Hidden Death . . 250.00
111 thru 122 . . . . @250.00
123 CMJr V: The Flying
   Desperado. 250.00
124 . . . . 250.00
125 CMJr & The Bed of Mystery . 250.00
126 thru 131. . . . . @250.00
132 V: Migs 250.00
133 E: Tom Mix; April, 1953. . . . . 300.00

MAZIE
**Nationwide Publ./
Magazine Publ./
Harvey Publ., 1951–58**
1 . . . . 150.00
2 . . . . 75.00
3 . . . . 75.00
4 . . . . 75.00
5 . . . . 75.00
6 thru 10 . . . . @75.00
11 thru 20 . . . . @50.00
21 thru 28 . . . . @50.00

MD
**E.C. Comics,
April, 1955–Jan., 1956**
1 RC,GE,Grl,JO,JCr(c). 500.00
2 thru 5 RC,GE,Grl,JO,JCr(c). . . 350.00

MEDAL OF
HONOR COMICS
**Stafford Publication,
Spring, 1947**
1 True Stories of Medal of Honor
   Recipients 200.00

Meet Corliss Archer #3
© Fox Features Syndicate

MEET CORLISS
ARCHER
**Fox Features Syndicate,
March, 1948**
1 AF,AF(c), Teenage 1,500.00
2 AF(c) 750.00
3 . . . . 700.00
Becomes:

MY LIFE
Sept., 1948
4 JKa,AF, ... 550.00
5 JKa, ... 300.00
6 JKa,AF, ... 275.00
7 WW,Watercolor & Ink Drawing
   on(c) 325.00
8 . . . . 150.00
9 . . . . 150.00
10 WW, July, 1950. . . . . 300.00

MEET MERTON
Toby Press, Dec., 1953
1 DBe,Teen Stories. 125.00
2 DBe 75.00
3 DBe 75.00
4 DBe; June, 1954 . . . . 75.00

MEET THE NEW
POST GAZETTE
SUNDAY FUNNIES
Pittsburg Post Gazette, 1949
N# One Shot Insert F: Several
   Syndicated Characters in Stories
   Exclusive to This Edition . . 9,000.00

MEL ALLEN
SPORTS COMICS
Visual Editions, 1949
1 GT 300.00
2 Lou Gehrig. 200.00

MEN AGAINST CRIME
See: HAND OF FATE

MEN IN ACTION
Ajax/Farrell Publ., 1957
1 AyB 200.00
2 . . . . 100.00
3 RH 100.00
4 AyB 100.00
5 AyB,JMn. 100.00

6 AyB 100.00
7 RH. 75.00
8 SSh 75.00
9 . . . . 75.00

MEN OF COURAGE
Catechetical Guild
N# 100.00

MERRY COMICS
Carlton Comics, 1945
N# A:Boogeyman. 300.00

MERRY-GO-ROUND
COMICS
**LaSalle/Croyden/
Rotary Litho., 1944**
1 LaSalle Publications Edition . . 225.00
1a 1946, Croyden Edition 100.00
1b Sept-Oct.'47,Rotary Litho Ed. 125.00
2 . . . . 125.00

MERRY MOUSE
**Avon Periodicals,
June, 1953**
1 (fa),F. Carin (a&c) 150.00
2 (fa),F. Carin (a&c) 75.00
3 (fa),F. Carin (a&c) 75.00
4 (fa),F. Carin (a&c);Jan.'54 . . . . 75.00

METEOR COMICS
**Croyden Publications,
Nov., 1945**
1 Captain Wizard & Baldy Bean. 550.00

MICKEY FINN
**Eastern Color/
Columbia Comics Group, 1942**
1 . . . . 400.00
2 . . . . 250.00
3 A: Charlie Chan 200.00
4 . . . . 150.00
5 thru 9 . . . . @100.00
10 thru 15. . . . . @80.00

(WALT DISNEY'S)
MICKEY MOUSE
Dell Publishing Co., Dec., 1952
#1-#27 Dell Four Color
28 . . . . 125.00
29 . . . . 100.00
30 . . . . 100.00
31 . . . . 100.00
32 thru 34. . . . . @100.00
35 thru 50. . . . . @100.00
51 thru 73. . . . . @100.00
74 . . . . 125.00
75 thru 99. . . . . @100.00
100 thru 105 rep. . . . . @125.00
106 thru 120. . . . . @150.00
121 thru 130. . . . . @100.00
131 thru 146. . . . . @30.00
147 rep,Phantom Fires 30.00
148 rep. 100.00
149 thru 158. . . . . @60.00
159 rep. 60.00
160 thru 170. . . . . @60.00
171 thru 199. . . . . @25.00
200 rep. 25.00
201 thru 218. . . . . @25.00

MICKEY MOUSE
MAGAZINE
Kay Kamen, 1933
1 scarce. 20,000.00
2 . . . . 5,000.00

3 thru 8	@4,000.00
9	3,500.00

MICKEY MOUSE MAGAZINE
Kay Kamen, 1933–34

1 digest size (1933)	4,000.00
2 dairy give-away promo	2,000.00
3 dairy give-away promo	1,500.00
4 dairy give-away promo	1,500.00
5 dairy give-away promo	1,500.00
6 dairy give-away promo	1,500.00
7 dairy give-away promo	1,500.00
8 dairy give-away promo	1,500.00
9 dairy give-away promo	1,500.00
10 dairy give-away promo	1,500.00
11 dairy give-away promo	1,500.00
12 dairy give-away promo	1,500.00

Volume II, 1934–35

1 dairy give-away promo	1,500.00
2 Christmas issue	1,500.00
3 dairy give-away promo	1,500.00
4 dairy give-away promo	1,500.00
5 1st Donald Duck as Sailor	5,000.00
6 dairy give-away promo	1,500.00
7 dairy give-away promo	1,500.00
8 dairy give-away promo	1,500.00
9 dairy give-away promo	1,500.00
10 dairy give-awaypromo	1,500.00
11 dairy give-away promo	1,500.00
12 dairy give-awaypromo	1,500.00

MICKEY MOUSE MAGAZINE
K.K. Pub./Westen Pub., 1935

1 (1935) 13¼"x10¼"	35,000.00
2 OM, new size 11½"x8½"	6,000.00
3 OM	3,000.00
4 OM	3,000.00
5 (1936) Donald Duck solo	5,000.00
6 Donald Duck editor	4,500.00
7	3,000.00
8 Donald Duck solo	4,500.00
9 1st Minnie & Minnie	4,500.00
10	3,000.00
11 Mickey & Pluto	3,500.00
12	3,000.00

Volume II

1 OM	2,500.00
2 OM	2,500.00
3 OM,Christmas issue, 100pg	7,500.00
4 OM (1937) Roy Ranger adv.strip	2,000.00
5 Ted True strip	1,200.00
6 Mickey Mouse cut-outs	1,200.00
7 Mickey Mouse cut-outs	1,200.00
8 Mickey Mouse cut-outs	1,200.00
9 Mickey Mouse cut-outs	1,200.00
10 Full color	2,200.00
11	1,200.00
12 Hiawatha	1,500.00
13	1,200.00

Volume III

2 Big Bad Wolf (c)	1,700.00
3 CB,First Snow White	4,000.00
4 CB,(1938) Snow White	2,500.00
5 Snow White (c)	2,500.00
6 Snow White ends	1,600.00
7 CB,7 Dwarfs Easter (c)	1,400.00
8	1,200.00
9 CB,Dopey(c)	1,100.00
10 Goofy(c)	1,100.00
11 Mickey Mouse Sheriff	1,100.00
12 CB,A:Snow White	1,100.00

Volume IV

1 OM,Practile Pig & Brave Little Tailor	1,200.00
2 I:Huey,Louis & Dewey(c)	1,500.00
3 Ferdinand the Bull	1,200.00

4 (1939),B:Spotty	1,100.00
5 Pluto solo	1,200.00
7 Ugly Duckling	1,200.00
7a Goofy & Wilber	1,200.00
8 Big Bad Wolf(c)	1,200.00
9 CB,The Pointer	1,200.00
10 CB,July 4th	1,400.00
11 Slick, oversize	1,200.00
12 CB,Donald's Penguin	1,300.00

Volume V

1 Black Pete	1,300.00
2 Goofy(c),I:Pinocchio	1,500.00
3 Pinocchio	1,500.00
4 (1940)	1,200.00
5 Jiminy Cricket(c)	1,200.00
6 Tugboat Mickey	1,200.00
7 Huey, Louis & Dewey(c)	1,200.00
8 Figaro & Cleo	1,200.00
9 Donald(c),J.Cricket	1,300.00
10 July 4th	1,300.00
11 Mickey's Tailor	1,300.00
12 Change of comic format	8,000.00

becomes:
WALT DISNEY COMICS & STORIES

MICKEY MOUSE
Whitman

904 W.Disney's Mickey Mouse and His Friends (1934)	3,000.00
948 Disney'sMickeyMouse('34)	3,000.00

MIDGET COMICS
St. John Publishing Co., Feb., 1950

1 MB(c),Fighting Indian Stories	250.00
2 April, 1950;Tex West-Cowboy Marshall	150.00

MIDNIGHT
Ajax/Farrell, 1957

1 Voodoo & Strange Fantasy	175.00
2	125.00

MIGHTY ATOM, THE
See: PIXIES

MIGHTY MIDGET COMICS
4"x5" Format
Samuel E. Lowe & Co./ Fawcett, 1942-43

1 Bulletman	500.00
2 Captain Marvel	500.00
3 Captain Marvel Jr.	500.00
4 Golden Arrow	400.00
5 Ibis the Invincible	500.00
6 Spy Smasher	450.00
7 Balbo, The Boy Magician	250.00
8 Bulletman	300.00
9 Commando Yank	200.00
10 Dr. Voltz, The Human Generator	250.00
11 Lance O'Casey	250.00
12 Leatherneck the Marine	250.00
13 Minute Man	250.00
14 Mister Q	275.00
15 Mr. Scarlet & Pinky	250.00
16 Pat Wilson & His Flying Fortress	225.00
17 Phantom Eagle	250.00
18 State Trooper Stops Crime	250.00
19 Tornado Tom	250.00

MIGHTY MOUSE
St. John Publishing, Aug., 1947

5	500.00
6 thru 10	@250.00
11 thru 20	@200.00

Mighty Mouse #28
© St. John Publishing

21 thru 25	@150.00
26 thru 30	@125.00
31 thru 34	@100.00
35 Flying Saucer	150.00
36	100.00
37	100.00
38 thru 45 Giant 100 pgs	@250.00
46 thru 66	@100.00
67 P(c),	100.00

Pines

68 thru 81 Funny Animal	@100.00
82 Infinity (c)	100.00
83 June, 1959	100.00

MIGHTY MOUSE ADVENTURES
See: ADVENTURES OF MIGHTY MOUSE

MIGHTY MOUSE ADVENTURE STORIES
St. John Publishing Co., 1953

N# 384 Pages,Rebound	600.00

MIKE BARNETT, MAN AGAINST CRIME
Fawcett Publications, Dec., 1951

1 The Mint of Dionysosi	250.00
2 Mystery of the Blue Madonna	135.00
3 Revenge Holds the Torch	125.00
4 Special Delivery	125.00
5 Market For Morphine Drug	150.00
6 Oct., 1952	125.00

MILITARY COMICS
Comics Magazines (Quality Comics Group), Aug., 1941

1 JCo,CCu,FGu,BP,WE(c),O:Blackhawk, Miss America, Death Patrol, Blue Tracer; B:X of the Underground, Yankee Eagle,Q-Boat, Shot & Shell, Archie Atkins, Loops & Banks	20,000.00
2 JCo,FGu,BP,CCu,CCu(c),B: Secret War News	5,000.00
3 JCo,FGu,BP,AMc,CCu,CCu(c), I&O:Chop Chop	4,000.00
4 FGu,BP,AMc,CCu,CCu(c)	3,500.00
5 FGu,BP,AMc,CCu,CCu(c) B: The Sniper	3,000.00

Military Comics #14
© *Quality Comics Group*

6 FGu,BP,AMc,CCu,CCu(c) . . 2,500.00
7 FGu,BP,AMc,CCu,CCu(c)
  E:Death Patrol 2,500.00
8 FGu,BP,AMc,CCu,CCu(c) . 2,500.00
9 FGu,BP,AMc,CCu,CCu(c),
  B: The Phantom Clipper . . 2,500.00
10 FGu,BP,CCu,AMc,WE(c) . . 2,700.00
11 FGu,BP,CCu,AMc,
  WE(c),Flag(c) 2,200.00
12 FGu,BP,AMc,RC(a&c) 2,300.00
13 FGu,BP,AMc,RC(a&c),E:X of
  the Underground 2,000.00
14 FGu,AMc,RC(a&c),B:Private
  Dogtag 2,000.00
15 FGu,AMc,RC(a&c), ... 2,000.00
16 FGu,AMc,RC(a&c),E:The Phantom
  Clipper,Blue Tracer. 1,500.00
17 FGu,AMc,RC(a&c),
  B:P.T. Boat 1,500.00
18 FGu,AMc,RC(a&c), V:
  The Thunderer 1,500.00
19 FGu,RC(a&c), V:King Cobra 1,500.00
20 GFx,RC(a&c), Death Patrol 1,500.00
21 FGu,GFx 1,200.00
22 FGu,GFx 1,200.00
23 FGu,GFx 1,200.00
24 FGu,GFx,V: Man-Heavy
  Glasses. 1,200.00
25 FGu,GFx,V: Wang The Tiger 1,200.00
26 FGu,GFx,V: Skull 1,000.00
27 FGu,JCo,R:The Death Patrol 1,000.00
28 FGu,JCo, Dungeon of Doom 1,000.00
29 FGu,JCo,V: Xanukhara . . . 1,000.00
30 FGu,JCo,BWa(a&c),Blackhawk
  V: Dr. Koro 1,000.00
31 FGu,JCo,BWa,E:Death
  Patrol; I: Captain Hitsu 1,000.00
32 JCo,A: Captain Hitsu 900.00
33 W/ Civil War Veteran. 900.00
34 A: Eve Rice 900.00
35 Shipwreck Island. 900.00
36 Cult of the Wailing Tiger 900.00
37 Pass of Bloody Peace 900.00
38 B.Hawk Faces Bloody Death . 900.00
39 A: Kwan Yin. 900.00
40 V: Ratru 800.00
41 W/ Chop Chop (c). 800.00
42 V: Jap Mata Hari. 800.00
43 . . . . 800.00
Becomes:

MODERN COMICS
Nov., 1945
44 Duel of Honor. 1,000.00
45 V: Sakyo the Madman 750.00
46 RC, Soldiers of Fortune 750.00
47 RC,PG,V:Count Hokoy 750.00

48 RC,PG,V:Pirates of Perool . . . 750.00
49 RC,PG,I:Fear,Lady
  Adventuress. 750.00
50 RC,PG 750.00
51 RC,PG, Ancient City of Evil. . . 500.00
52 PG,BWa,V: The Vulture. 500.00
53 PG,BWa,B: Torchy 850.00
54 PG,RC,RC/CCu,BWa 500.00
55 PG,RC,RC/CCu,BWa 500.00
56 PG,RC/CCu,BWa 500.00
57 PG,RC,RC/CCu,BWa 500.00
58 RC,RC,RC/CCu,BWa,
  V:The Grabber. 500.00
59 PG,RC,RC/CCu,BWa 500.00
60 PG,RC/CCu,BWa,RC(c),
  V:Green Plague 500.00
61 PG,RC/CCu,BWa,RC(c) 475.00
62 PG,RC/CCu,BWa,RC(c) 475.00
63 PG,RC/CCu,BWa,RC(c) 450.00
64 PG,RC/CCu,BWa,RC(c) 450.00
65 PG,RC/CCu,BWa,RC(c) 450.00
66 PG,RC/CCu,BWa 450.00
67 PG,RC/CCu,BWa,RC(c) 450.00
68 PG,RC/CCu,BWa,RC(c);
  I:Madame Butterfly 450.00
69 PG,RC/CCu,BWa,RC(c) 450.00
70 PG,RC/CCu,BWa,RC(c) 450.00
71 PG,RC/CCu,BWa,RC(c) 450.00
72 PG,RC/CCu,BWa,RC(c) 450.00
73 PG,RC/CCu,BWa,RC(c) 450.00
74 PG,RC/CCu,BWa,RC(c) 450.00
75 PG,RC/CCu,BWa,RC(c) 450.00
76 PG,RC/CCu,BWa,RC(c) 450.00
77 PG,RC/CCu,BWa,RC(c) 450.00
78 PG,RC/CCu,BWa,JCo,RC(c) . 450.00
79 PG,RC/CCu,BWa,JCo,RC(c) . 450.00
80 PG,RC/CCu,BWa,JCo,RC(c) . 475.00
81 PG,RC/CCu,BWa,JCo,RC(c) . 475.00
82 PG,RC/CCu,BWa,JCo,RC(c) . 450.00
83 PG,RC/CCu,BWa,JCo,RC(c);
  E: Private Dogtag 450.00
84 PG,RC/CCu,BWa,RC(c) 450.00
85 PG,RC/CCu,BWa,RC(c) 450.00
86 PG,RC/CCu,BWa,RC(c) 450.00
87 PG,RC/CCu,BWa,RC(c) 450.00
88 PG,RC/CCu,BWa,RC(c) 450.00
89 PG,RC/CCu,BWa,RC(c) 450.00
90 PG,RC/CCu,GFx,RC(c) 450.00
91 RC/CCu,GFx,RC(c) 450.00
92 RC/CCu,GFx,RC(c) 450.00
93 RC/CCu,GFx,RC(c) 450.00
94 RC/CCu,GFx,RC(c) 450.00
95 RC/CCu,GFx,RC(c) 450.00
96 RC/CCu,GFx,RC/CCu(c) 450.00
97 RC/CCu,GFx,RC/CCu(c) 450.00
98 RC/CCu,GFx,RC/CCu(c) 450.00
99 RC/CCu,GFx,JCo,RC/CCu(c). 450.00
100 GFx,JCo,RC/CCu(c) 475.00
101 GFx,JCo,RC/CCu(c) 450.00
102 GFx,JCo,WE,BWa,
  RC/CCu(c). 600.00

MILT GROSS FUNNIES
Milt Gross, Inc., Aug., 1947
1 Gag Oriented Caricature 250.00
2 Gag Oriented Caricature 175.00

MINUTE MAN
Fawcett Publications,
Summer, 1941
1 V: The Nazis 3,000.00
2 V: The Mongol Horde 2,000.00
3 V: The Black Poet;Spr'42 . . 2,000.00

MIRACLE COMICS
E.C. Comics, Feb.,1940
1 B:Sky Wizard,Master of Space,
  Dash Dixon,Man of Might,Dusty
  Doyle,Pinkie Parker, The Kid
  Cop,K-7 Secret Agent,Scorpion
  & Blandu,Jungle Queen . . 2,700.00

2 . . . . 1,400.00
3 B:Bill Colt,The Ghost Rider . 1,400.00
4 A:The Veiled Prophet,
  Bullet Bob; Mar'41 . . . . 1,100.00

MISS CAIRO JONES
Croyden Publishers, 1944
1 BO,Rep. Newspaper Strip . . . 250.00

MISS LIBERTY
See: LIBERTY COMICS

MR. ANTHONY'S
LOVE CLINIC
Hillman Periodicals, 1945
1 Ph(c) 250.00
2 . . . . 150.00
3 . . . . 100.00
4 . . . . 100.00
5 Ph(c),Apr/May'50 . . . . 100.00

MR. MUSCLES
See: THING, THE

MISTER MYSTERY
Media Publ./SPM Publ./
Aragon Publ., Sept., 1951
1 HK,RA,Horror 1,400.00
2 RA,RA(c). 850.00
3 RA(c) 850.00
4 Bondage(c) 900.00
5 Lingerie(c) 800.00
6 Bondage(c) 800.00
7 BW,Bondage(c);The Brain
  Bats of Venus 1,800.00
8 Lingerie(c) 750.00
9 HN 750.00
10 . . . . 750.00
11 BW,Robot Woman 1,200.00
12 Flaming Object to Eye (c) . . 1,800.00
13 . . . . 600.00
14 . . . . 600.00
15 The Coffin & Medusa's Head . 600.00
16 Bondage(c) 600.00
17 Severed Heads. 600.00
18 BW,Bondage(c). 900.00
19 Reprints. 550.00

MISTER RISK
See: HAND OF FATE

MISTER UNIVERSE
Mr. Publ./Media Publ./
Stanmore, July, 1951
1 . . . . 275.00
2 RA(c);Jungle That time Forgot 150.00
3 Marijuana Story 150.00
4 Mr. Universe Goes to War 125.00
5 Mr. Universe Goes to War;
  April, 1952. . . . . 125.00

MODERN COMICS
See: MILITARY COMICS

MODERN LOVE
Tiny Tot Comics
(E.C. Comics), June–July, 1949
1 Grl,AF,Stolen Romance 1,100.00
2 Grl,JcR,AF(c),I Craved
  Excitement 700.00
3 AF(c);Our Families Clashed . . 650.00
4 AF(c);I Was a B Girl, panties . 800.00
5 RP,AF(c);Saved From Shame 800.00
6 AF(c);The Love That
  Might Have Been 800.00
7 Grl,WW,AF(c);They Won't Let
  Me Love Him 600.00
8 Grl,AF(c);Aug-Sept'50 . . . . . . 600.00

GOLDEN AGE

MOLLY O'DAY
Avon Periodicals,
Feb., 1945
1 GT;The Enchanted Dagger . . . 800.00

MONSTER
Fiction House Magazines, 1953
1 Dr. Drew. 750.00
2 . . . . 500.00

MONSTER CRIME COMICS
Hillman Periodicals,
Oct., 1952
1 52 Pgs,15 Cent (c) Price . . . 1,800.00

MONTE HALL WESTERN
See: MARY MARVEL COMICS

MONTY HALL OF THE U.S. MARINES
Toby Press, Aug., 1951
1 JkS,:Monty Hall,Pin-Up Pete;
    (All Issues) 150.00
2 JkS 125.00
3 thru 5 JkS. . . . . @100.00
6 JkS. 100.00
7 JkS,The Fireball Express 100.00
8 JkS. 100.00
9 JkS. 100.00
10 The Vial of Death 100.00
11 Monju Island Prison Break . . . 100.00

MOON GIRL AND THE PRINCE
E.C. Comics, Autumn, 1947
1 JCr(c),O:Moon Girl 1,400.00
Becomes:

MOON GIRL
E.C. Comics, 1947
2 JCr(c),Battle of the Congo . . . 800.00
3 . . . . 750.00
4 V: A Vampire 750.00
5 1st E.C. Horror-Zombie
    Terror 1,700.00
6 . . . . 900.00
Becomes:

MOON GIRL FIGHTS CRIME
E.C. Comics, 1949
7 O:Star;The Fiend Who
    Fights With Fire 900.00
8 True Crime Feature 900.00
Becomes:

A MOON, A GIRL ...ROMANCE
Sept.–Oct., 1949
9 AF,Grl,AF(c),C:Moon Girl;
    Spanking Panels 1,200.00
10 AF,Grl,WW,AF(c),Suspicious
    of His Intentions 900.00
11 AF,Grl,WW,AF(c),Hearts
    Along the Ski Trail 900.00
12 AF,Grl,AF(c),
    March–April, 1950 . . . . 1,100.00
Becomes:

WEIRD FANTASY

MOON MULLINS
Michael Publ. (American
Comics Group), 1948
1 . . . . 275.00
2 thru 8 . . . . @150.00

MOPSY
St. John Publishing Co.,
Feb., 1948
1 Paper Dolls Enclosed 800.00
2 . . . . 550.00
3 . . . . 550.00
4 Paper Dolls Enclosed 550.00
5 Paper Dolls Enclosed 550.00
6 Paper Dolls Enclosed 550.00
7 . . . . 525.00
8 Paper Dolls Enclosed;
    Lingerie Panels 550.00
9 . . . . 500.00
10 . . . . 500.00
11 . . . . 500.00
12 . . . . 500.00
13 Paper Dolls Enclosed 500.00
14 thru 18 . . . . @500.00
19 Lingerie(c);Paper
    Dolls Enclosed. 500.00

MOTION PICTURE COMICS
Fawcett Publications,
Nov., 1950
101 Ph(c),Monte Hale's-
    Vanishing Westerner 450.00
102 Ph(c),Rocky Lane's-Code
    of the Silver Sage 400.00
103 Ph(c),Rocky Lane's-Covered
    Wagon Raid. 400.00
104 BP,Ph(c),Rocky Lane's-
    Vigilante Hideout 400.00
105 BP,Ph(c),Audie Murphy's-
    Red Badge of Courage 500.00
106 Ph(c),George Montgomery's-
    The Texas Rangers 450.00
107 Ph(c),Rocky Lane's-Frisco
    Tornado 400.00
108 Ph(c),John Derek's-Mask
    of the Avenger 350.00
109 Ph(c),Rocky Lane's-Rough
    Rider of Durango 375.00
110 GE,Ph(c), When Worlds
    Collide 1,700.00
111 Ph(c),Lash LaRue's-The
    Vanishing Outpost 500.00
112 Ph(c),Jay Silverheels'-
    Brave Warrior 300.00
113 KS,Ph(c),George Murphy's-
    Walk East on Beacon 250.00
114 Ph(c),George Montgomery's-
    Cripple Creek;Jan, 1953 . . . . 250.00

MOTION PICTURES FUNNIES WEEKLY
1st Funnies Incorporated, 1939
1 BEv,1st Sub-Mariner 35,000.00
2 Cover Only 1,500.00
3 Cover Only 1,500.00
4 Cover Only 1,500.00

MOVIE COMICS
Fiction House Magazines,
Dec., 1946
1 Big Town on(c) 800.00
2 MB,White Tie & Tails 550.00
3 MB,Andy Hardy Laugh Hit . . 550.00
4 MB,Slave Girl 650.00

MOVIE LOVE
Famous Funnies Publ.,
Feb., 1950
1 Ph(c),Dick Powell(c) 200.00
2 Ph(c),Myrna Loy(c) 150.00
3 Ph(c),Cornell Wilde(c) 125.00
4 Ph(c),Paulette Goddard(c) . . . 125.00
5 Ph(c),Joan Fontaine(c) 125.00

Movie Love #16
© Famous Funnies

6 Ph(c),Ricardo Montalban(c) . . 125.00
7 Ph(c),Fred Astaire(c) 150.00
8 AW,FF,Ph(c),Corinne
    Calvert(c) 600.00
9 Ph(c),John Lund(c) 125.00
10 FF,Ph(c),Mona Freeman(c) . . 600.00
11 Ph(c),James Mason(c) 150.00
12 Ph(c),Jerry Lewis &
    Dean Martin(c). 200.00
13 Ph(c),Ronald Reagan(c). 300.00
14 Ph(c),Janet Leigh,Gene Kelly. 125.00
15 Ph(c),John Payne 125.00
16 Ph(c),Angela Lansbury 150.00
17 Ph(c),Leslie Caron 150.00
18 Ph(c),Cornel Wilde 125.00
19 Ph(c),John Derek 125.00
20 Ph(c),Debbie Reynolds 150.00
21 Ph(c),Patricia Medina 125.00
22 Ph(c),John Payne 125.00

MOVIE THRILLERS
Magazine Enterprises 1949
1 Ph(c),Burt Lancaster's-
    Rope of Sand 375.00

MURDER, INCORPORATED
Fox Features Incorporated,
Jan., 1948–Aug., 1951
1 For Adults Only-on(c) 750.00
2 For Adults Only-on(c);Male
    Bondage(c),Electrocution sty 500.00
3 Dutch Schultz-Beast of Evil . . 300.00
4 The Ray Hamilton Case,
    Lingerie(c) 300.00
5 . . . . 300.00
6 . . . . 300.00
7 . . . . 300.00
8 . . . . 325.00
9 Bathrobe (c) 350.00
9a Lingerie (c) 350.00
10 . . . . 250.00
11 . . . . 250.00
12 . . . . 250.00
13 . . . . 275.00
14 Bill Hale-King of the
    Murderers 250.00
15 . . . . 250.00
16(5),Second Series 200.00
17(2). 200.00
18(3), Bondage(c) with Lingerie. . 300.00

GOLDEN AGE

MURDEROUS GANGSTERS

Avon Periodicals/Realistic, July, 1951

1 WW,Pretty Boy Floyd,
  Leggs Diamond 650.00
2 WW,Baby Face Nelson,Mad
  Dog Esposito 400.00
3 P(c),Tony & Bud Fenner,
  Jed Hawkins 350.00
4 EK(c),Murder By Needle-
  Drug Story, June, 1952 . . . . . 400.00

MUTINY

Aragon Magazines, Oct., 1954

1 AH(c),Stormy Tales of the
  Seven Seas 200.00
2 AH(c) 150.00
3 Bondage(c),Feb., '55 . . . . . . 300.00

MY CONFESSION
See: WESTERN TRUE CRIME

MY PAST CONFESSIONS
See: WESTERN THRILLERS

My Secret Life #24
© Fox Features Syndicate

MY SECRET LIFE

Fox Features Syndicate, July, 1949

22 I Loved More Than Once 150.00
23 WW 250.00
24 Love Was a Habit 100.00
25 . . . . 100.00
Becomes:

ROMEO TUBBS

Dec., 1952

26 WW,That Lovable Teen-ager . 250.00

MY SECRET STORY
See: DAGAR, DESERT HAWK

MYSTERIES WEIRD AND STRANGE

Superior Comics/ Dynamic Publ., May, 1953

1 The Stolen Brain 600.00
2 The Screaming Room,
  Atomic Bomb 350.00

---

3 SD,The Avenging Corpse 300.00
4 SD,Ghost on the Gallows 300.00
5 SD,Horror a la Mode 300.00
6 SD,Howling Horror 300.00
7 SD,Demon in Disguise 275.00
8 SD,The Devil's Birthmark 275.00
9 SD 275.00
10 SD 300.00
11 SD 300.00

MYSTERIOUS ADVENTURES

Story Comics, March, 1951

1 WJo(c),Wild Terror of the
  Vampire Flag 1,000.00
2 Terror of the Ghoul's Corpse . 500.00
3 Terror of the Witche's Curse . . 450.00
4 The Little Coffin That Grew . . . 450.00
5 LC,Curse of the Jungle,
  Bondage(c) 500.00
6 LC,Ghostly Terror in the
  Cave 450.00
7 LC,Terror of the Ghostly
  Castle 600.00
8 Terror of the Flowers of Death. 700.00
9 The Ghostly Ghouls-
  Extreme Violence 500.00
10 Extreme Violence 450.00
11 The Trap of Terror 500.00
12 SHn,Vultures of Death-
  Extreme Violence 500.00
13 Extreme Violence 500.00
14 Horror of the Flame Thrower
  Extreme Violence 500.00
15 DW,Ghoul Crazy 600.00
16 Chilling Tales of Horror 600.00
17 DW,Bride of the Dead 600.00
18 Extreme Violence 600.00
19 The Coffin 600.00
20 Horror o/t Avenging Corpse . . 600.00
21 Mother Ghoul's Nursery
  Tales, Bondage (c) 600.00
22 RA,Insane 450.00
23 RA,Extreme Violence 450.00
24 KS 350.00
25 KS,Aug., 1955. . . . . 350.00

HORROR FROM THE TOMB

Premier Magazines, Sept., 1954

1 AT,GWb,The Corpse Returns . 550.00
Becomes:

MYSTERIOUS STORIES

Dec., 1954–Jan., 1955

2 GWb(c),Eternal Life 700.00
3 GWb,The Witch Doctor 450.00
4 That's the Spirit 400.00
5 King Barbarossa 400.00
6 GWb,Strangers in the Night. . . 450.00
7 KS,The Pipes of Pan;Dec'55 . . 400.00

MYSTERIOUS TRAVELER COMICS

Trans-World Publications, Nov., 1948

1 BP,BP(c),Five Miles Down 850.00

MYSTERY COMICS

William H. Wise & Co., 1944

1 ASh(c),B:Brad Spencer-Wonderman,
  King of Futeria,The Magnet, Zudo-
  Jungle Boy,Silver Knight. . . 1,700.00
2 ASh(c),Bondage (c) 1,100.00
3 ASh(c),Robot(c),Lance Lewis,
  Brad Spencer, Wonderman . . 900.00

---

4 ASh(c),E:All Features,
  KKK Type(c) 900.00

MYSTERY MEN COMICS

Fox Features Syndicate, Aug., 1939

1 GT,DBr,LF(c),Bondage(c);I:Blue
  Beetle,Green Mask,Rex Dexter
  of Mars,Zanzibar,Lt.Drake,D-13
  Secret Agent,Chen Chang,
  Wing Turner,Capt. Denny 18,000.00
2 GT,BP,DBr,LF(c),
  Rex Dexter (c) 6,000.00
3 LF(c) 7,000.00
4 LF(c),B:Captain Savage 4,000.00
5 GT,BP,LF(c),Green Mask (c) 4,000.00
6 GT,BP 3,500.00
7 GT,BP,Bondage(c),
  Blue Beetle(c). 4,000.00
8 GT,BP,LF(c),Bondage(c),
  Blue Beetle 3,500.00
9 GT,BP,DBr(c),B:The Moth. . . 2,000.00
10 GT,BP,JSm(c),A:Wing
  Turner; Bondage(c) 1,500.00
11 GT,BP,JSm(c),I:The Domino 1,500.00
12 GT,BP,JSm(c),BlueBeetle(c) 1,500.00
13 GT,I:The Lynx & Blackie . . . 1,000.00
14 GT,Male Bondage (c) 950.00
15 GT,Blue Beetle (c). 900.00
16 GT,Hypo(c),MaleBondage(c) . 950.00
17 GT,BP,Blue Beetle (c). 900.00
18 GT,Blue Beetle (c). 900.00
19 GT,I&B:Miss X 1,000.00
20 GT,DBr,Blue Beetle (c) 900.00
21 GT,E:Miss X 900.00
22 GT,CCu(c),Blue Beetle (c) . . 900.00
23 GT,Blue Beetle (c). 900.00
24 GT,BP,DBr, Blue Beetle (c). . . 900.00
25 GT,Bondage(c);
  A:Private O'Hara 950.00
26 GT,Bondage(c);B:The Wraith . 950.00
27 GT,Bondage(c),BlueBeetle(c) . 950.00
28 GT,Bondage(c);Satan's
  Private Needlewoman 950.00
29 GT,Bondage(c),Blue
  Beetle (c). 950.00
30 Holiday of Death 900.00
31 Bondage(c);Feb'42 . . . . 950.00

MY STORY
See: ZAGO, JUNGLE PRINCE

NANCY AND SLUGGO
See: SPARKLER COMICS

NAPOLEON AND UNCLE ELBY

Eastern Color Printing, 1942

1 . . . . 650.00

NATIONAL COMICS

Comics Magazines (Quality Comics Group), July, 1940

1 GT,HcK,LF(c),B:Uncle Sam,
  Wonder Boy,Merlin the Magician,
  Cyclone, Kid Patrol,Sally O'Neil-
  Police-woman, Pen Miller,
  Prop Powers,PaulBunyan 10,000.00
2 WE,GT,HcK,LF&RC(c) 4,200.00
3 GT,HcK,LF,WE&RC(c) 3,000.00
4 GT,HcK,LF&RC(c),E:Cyclone;
  Torpedo Islands of Death . . 3,100.00
5 GT,LF&RC(c),B:Quicksilver;
  O:Uncle Sam 2,800.00
6 GT,LF&RC(c) 2,100.00
7 GT,LF&RC(c) 3,500.00
8 GT,LF&RC(c) 2,100.00
9 JCo,LF&RC(c) 2,100.00
10 RC,JCo,LF&RC(c) 2,100.00

National Comics #33
© Quality Comics Group

11 RC,JCo,LF&RC(c) 2,100.00
12 RC,JCo,LF&RC(c) 1,600.00
13 RC,JCo,LF,LF&RC(c). 1,500.00
14 RC,JCo,LF,PG,LF&RC(c). . . 1,600.00
15 RC,JCo,LF,PG,LF&RC(c). . . 1,600.00
16 RC,JCo,LF,PG,LF&RC(c). . . 1,600.00
17 RC,JCo,LF,PG,LF&RC(c). . . 1,700.00
18 JCo,LF,PG,LF&RC(c),
   Pearl Harbor 2,200.00
19 JCo,LF,PG,RC(c),The Black
   Fog Mystery 1,700.00
20 JCo,LF,PG,LF&RC(c) 1,700.00
21 LF,JCo,PG,LF(c). 1,700.00
22 JCo,LF,PG,FGu,GFx,LF(c),
   E:Jack & Jill,Pen Miller,
   Paul Bunyan 1,700.00
23 JCo,PG,FGu,GFx,AMc,LF
   & GFx(c),B:The Unknown,
   Destroyer 171 . . . . 1,800.00
24 JCo,PG,RC,AMc,FGu,
   GFx,RC(c) 1,800.00
25 AMc,RC,JCo,PG,FGu,
   GFx,RC(c) 1,300.00
26 AMc,Jco,RC,PG,RC(c),
   E:Prop Powers,WonderBoy 1,300.00
27 JCo,AMc 1,300.00
28 JCo,AMc 1,300.00
29 JCo,O:The Unknown;U.Sam
   V:Dr. Dirge 1,400.00
30 JCo,RC(c) 900.00
31 JCo,RC(c) 1,000.00
32 JCo,RC(c) 1,000.00
33 JCo,GFx,RC(c),B:Chic Carter;
   U.Sam V:Boss Spring 1,000.00
34 JCo,GFx,U.Sam V:Big John
   Fales. 1,000.00
35 JCo,GFx,E:Kid Patrol 900.00
36 JCo 900.00
37 JCo,FGu,A:The Vagabond . . . 900.00
38 JCo,FGu,Boat of the Dead . . . 900.00
39 JCo,FGu,Hitler(c);U.Sam
   V:The Black Market 1,300.00
40 JCo,FGu,U.Sam V:The
   Syndicate of Crime 750.00
41 JCo,FGu 750.00
42 JCo,FGu,JCo(c),B:The Barker 600.00
43 JCo,FGu,JCo(c) 600.00
44 JCo,FGu 600.00
45 JCo,FGu,E:Merlin Magician . . 600.00
46 JCo,JCo(c),Murder is no Joke 600.00
47 JCo,JCo(c),E:Chic Carter 600.00
48 JCo,O:The Whistler 600.00
49 JCo,JCo(c),A Corpse
   for a Cannonball 600.00
50 JCo,JCo(c),V:Rocks Myzer . . 600.00

51 JCo,BWa,JCo(c),
   A:Sally O'Neil 700.00
52 JCo,A Carnival of Laughs 500.00
53 PG,V:Scramolo 500.00
54 PG,V:Raz-Ma-Taz 500.00
55 JCo,AMc,V:The Hawk 500.00
56 GFx,JCo,AMc,V:The Grifter . . 500.00
57 GFx,JCo,AMc,V:Witch Doctor. 500.00
58 GFz,JCo,AMc,Talking Animals 500.00
59 JCo,JCo,AMc,V:The Birdman. 500.00
60 GFx,JCo,AMc,V:Big Ed Grew 500.00
61 GFx,AMc,Trouble Comes in
   Small Packages. 300.00
62 GFx,AMc,V:Crocodile Man . . . 300.00
63 GFx,AMc,V:Bearded Lady . . . 300.00
64 GFx,V:The Human Fly 300.00
65 GFx,GFx(c)V:The King 300.00
66 GFx,GFx(c)V:The Man Who
   Hates the Circus 300.00
67 GFx,Gfx(c),A:Quicksilver;
   V:Ali Ben Riff Raff 300.00
68 GFx,GFx(c),V:Leo theLionMan 300.00
69 GFx,Gfx(c),A:Percy the
   Powerful. 300.00
70 GFx,GFx(c),Barker Tires
   of the Big Top 300.00
71 PG,GFx(c),V:SpellbinderSmith 300.00
72 PG,GFx(c),The Oldest Man
   in the World 300.00
73 PG,GFx(c),V:A CountrySlicker 300.00
74 PG,GFx(c),V:Snake Oil Sam. . 300.00
75 PG,GFx(c),Barker Breakes the
   Bank at Monte Marlo;Nov'49. 300.00

NAVY HEROES
Almanac Publ. Co., 1945
1 Propaganda 135.00

NAVY PATROL
Key Publications, 1955
1 . . . . 125.00
2 thru 4 . . . . @100.00

NAVY TASK FORCE
**Stanmor Publ./
Aragon Publ., 1953**
1 . . . . 125.00
2 thru 8 . . . . @75.00

NEGRO HEROES
National Urban League, 1947
1 . . . . 1,500.00
2 Jackie Robinson 2,000.00

NEGRO ROMANCE
**Fawcett Publications,
June, 1950**
1 GE,Ph(c), Love's Decoy 1,800.00
2 GE,Ph(c), A Tragic Vow 1,500.00
3 GE,Ph(c), My Love
   Betrayed Me 1,500.00
Charlton Comics
4 Rep.FawcettEd.#2;May,1955 1,200.00

NEW ROMANCES
**Standard Comics,
May, 1951**
5 Ph(c), The Blame I Bore 175.00
6 Ph(c), No Wife Was I 150.00
7 Ph(c), My Runaway Heart,
   Ray Miland 125.00
8 Ph(c) 125.00
9 Ph(c) 125.00
10 ATh,Ph(c) 150.00
11 ATh,Ph(c) of Elizabeth Taylor . 300.00
12 Ph(c). 125.00
13 Ph(c). 125.00
14 ATh,Ph(c) 150.00
15 Ph(c). 125.00

16 ATh,Ph(c) 150.00
17 Ath, ... 150.00
18 and 19 . . . . @125.00
20 GT, ... 125.00
21 April, 1954 . . . . 125.00

NICKEL COMICS
Dell Publishing Co., 1938
1 Bobby & Chip 1,200.00

Nickel Comics #4
© National Urban League

NICKEL COMICS
**Fawcett Publications,
May, 1940**
1 JaB(c),O&I: Bulletman 7,000.00
2 JaB(c), ... 2,000.00
3 JaB(c), ... 1,500.00
4 JaB(c), B: Red Gaucho 1,300.00
5 CCB(c),Bondage(c) 1,300.00
6 and 7 CCB(c) . . . . @1,200.00
8 CCB(c),Aug. 23, 1940,
   World's Fair 1,400.00

NIGHTMARE
See: WEIRD HORRORS

NIGHTMARE
Ziff-Davis Publishing Co., 1952
1 EK,GT,P(c),The Corpse That
   Wouldn't Stay Dead 900.00
2 EK,P(c),Vampire Mermaid . . . 550.00
St. John Publishing Co.
3 EK,P(c),The Quivering Brain . 450.00
4 P(c),1953 . . . . 350.00

NORTHWEST MOUNTIES
**Jubilee Publications/
St. John Publ. Co.,
Oct., 1948**
1 MB,BLb(c),Rose of the Yukon 650.00
2 MB,BLb(c),A:Ventrilo 500.00
3 MB, Bondage(c) 550.00
4 MB(c),A:Blue Monk,July'49 . . 500.00

NUTS!
**Premere Comics Group,
March, 1954**
1 . . . . 400.00
2 . . . . 300.00
3 Mention of "Reefers" 325.00
4 . . . . 250.00
5 Captain Marvel Spoof;Nov.'54 250.00

GOLDEN AGE

GOLDEN AGE

NUTTY COMICS
Harvey Publications, 1945
1 BW,Funny animal. 125.00
2 . . . . 125.00
3 . . . . 110.00
4 thru 8 . . . . @75.00

NUTTY LIFE
See: PHANTOM LADY

Nyoka The Jungle Girl #5
© Fawcett Publications

NYOKA THE JUNGLE GIRL
Fawcett Publications, Winter, 1945
2 Bondage(c);Partial Ph(c) of
   Kay Aldridge as Nyoka 800.00
3 . . . . 450.00
4 Bondage(c) 500.00
5 Barbacosi Madness;
   Bondage(c) 500.00
6 . . . . 275.00
7 North Pole Jungle;
   Bondage(c) 400.00
8 Bondage(c) 400.00
9 . . . . 250.00
10 . . . . 250.00
11 Danger! Death! in an
   Unexplored Jungle 250.00
12 . . . . 225.00
13 The Human Leopards 250.00
14 The Mad Witch Doctor;
   Bondage(c) 400.00
15 Sacred Goat of Kristan 225.00
16 BK,The Vultures of Kalahari . . 250.00
17 BK 250.00
18 BK,The Art of Murder 250.00
19 The Elephant Battle 250.00
20 Explosive Volcano Action 250.00
21 . . . . 175.00
22 The Weird Monsters 175.00
23 Danger in Duplicate 175.00
24 The Human Jaguar;
   Bondage(c) 400.00
25 Hand Colored Ph(c) 150.00
26 A Jungle Stampede 150.00
27 Adventure Laden 150.00
28 The Human Statues of
   the Jungle 150.00
29 Ph(c) 150.00
30 Ph(c) 150.00
31 thru 40 Ph(c) . . . . @125.00
41 thru 50 Ph(c) . . . . @135.00
51 thru 59 Ph(c) . . . . @100.00

60 Ph(c) 100.00
61 Ph(c),The Sacred Sword of
   the Jungle 100.00
62 & 63 Ph(c) . . . . @100.00
64 Ph(c), The Jungle Idol 100.00
65 Ph(c) 100.00
66 Ph(c) 100.00
67 Ph(c), The Sky Man 100.00
68 thru 74 Ph(c) . . . . @100.00
75 Ph(c), The Jungle Myth
   of Terror 100.00
76 Ph(c) 100.00
77 Ph(c),The Phantoms of the
   Elephant Graveyard;Jun'53 . . 100.00

OAKY DOAKS
Eastern Color Printing Co., July, 1942
1 Humor Oriented 450.00

OKAY COMICS
United Features Syndicate, 1940
1 . . . . 650.00

OK COMICS
United Features Syndicate, July, 1940
1 B:Pal Peyton,Little Giant, Phantom
   Knight,Sunset Smith,Teller Twins,
   Don Ramon, Jerrry Sly,Kip Jaxon,
   Leatherneck,Ulysses 1,200.00
2 O:Master Mist,Oct., 1940 . . . 1,300.00

OKLAHOMA KID
Ajax/Farrell Publ., 1957
1 . . . . 150.00
2 . . . . 125.00
3 . . . . 125.00
4 . . . . 125.00

100 PAGES OF COMICS
Dell Publishing Co., 1937
101 Alley Oop,OG,Wash Tubbs,
   Tom Mix,Dan Dunn 2,500.00

ON THE AIR
NBC Network Comics, 1947
1 Giveaway, no cover 300.00

ON THE SPOT
Fawcett Publications, Autumn, 1948
N# Bondage(c),PrettyBoyFloyd . . 450.00

OPERATION PERIL
American Comics Group (Michel Publ.), Oct.–Nov., 1950
1 LSt,OW,OW(c),B:TyphoonTyler,
   DannyDanger,TimeTravellers 550.00
2 OW,OW(c),War (c). 300.00
3 OW,OW(c),Horror 250.00
4 OW,OW(c), Flying Saucers . . . 300.00
5 OW,OW(c), Science Fiction . . . 300.00
6 OW, Tyr. Rex 275.00
7 OW,OW(c),Sabretooth 275.00
8 OW,OW(c) 250.00
9 OW,OW(c) 250.00
10 OW,OW(c),science fiction . . . 275.00
11 OW,OW(c), War 250.00
12 OW,OW(c),E: Time Travellers . 250.00
13 OW,OW(c),War Stories 150.00
14 OW,OW(c),War Stories 150.00
15 OW,OW(c),War Stories 150.00
16 OW,OW(c),April–May,1953,
   War Stories 150.00

OUR FIGHTING MEN IN ACTION
Ajax/Farrell, 1957
1 . . . . 125.00
2 thru 6 . . . . @100.00

OUR FLAG COMICS
Ace Magazines, Aug., 1941–April, 1942
1 MA,JM,B:Capt.Victory,Unknown
   Soldier,The Three Cheers . 3,900.00
2 JM,JM(c),O:The Flag 1,700.00
3 Tank Battle (c). 1,300.00
4 MA 1,300.00
5 I:Mr. Risk, Male Bondage . . . 1,400.00

Our Gang Comics #28
© Dell Publishing Co.

OUR GANG COMICS
Dell Publishing Co., Sept.–Oct., 1942
1 WK,Barney Bear, Tom &
   Jerry 1,700.00
2 WK 750.00
3 WK,Benny Burro 400.00
4 WK 400.00
5 WK 450.00
6 WK 750.00
7 WK 350.00
8 WK,CB,Benny Burro 900.00
9 WK,CB,Benny Burro 850.00
10 WK,CB,Benny Burro 600.00
11 WK,I:Benny Bear 850.00
12 thru 20 WK . . . . @350.00
21 thru 29 WK . . . . @300.00
30 WK,Christmas(c). 250.00
31 thru 34 WK . . . . @250.00
35 WK,CB 200.00
36 WK,CB 200.00
37 thru 40 WK . . . . @125.00
41 thru 50 WK . . . . @100.00
51 thru 56 WK . . . . @100.00
57 . . . . 100.00
58 Our Gang 100.00
59 Our Gang 100.00
Becomes:

TOM AND JERRY
July, 1949
60 . . . . 200.00
61 . . . . 150.00
62 . . . . 100.00
63 . . . . 100.00
64 . . . . 100.00
65 . . . . 100.00

66 Christmas (c) 120.00
67 thru 70. . . . . @125.00
71 thru 76. . . . . @125.00
77 Christmas (c) 125.00
78 thru 80. . . . . @125.00
81 thru 89. . . . . @100.00
90 Christmas (c) 125.00
91 thru 99. . . . . @100.00
100 . . . . 125.00
101 thru 120. . . . . @100.00
121 thru 150. . . . . @100.00
151 thru 212. . . . . @100.00

OUTER SPACE
See: CHARLIE CHAN

OUTLAWS
**D.S. Publishing Co.,
Feb.–March, 1948**
1 HcK,Western Crime Stories . . 500.00
2 Grl,Doc Dawson's Dilema . . . 500.00
3 Cougar City Cleanup 200.00
4 JO,Death Stakes A Claim 250.00
5 RJ,RJ(c),Man Who Wanted
 Mexico 200.00
6 AMc,RJ,RJ(c),The Ghosts of
 Crackerbox Hill 200.00
7 Grl,Dynamite For Boss Cavitt . 350.00
8 Grl,The Gun & the Pen 350.00
9 FF,Shoot to Kill;June–
 July, 1949 . . . . 650.00

WHITE RIDER AND
SUPER HORSE
**Star Publications,
Sept., 1950**
1 LbC(c) 250.00
2 LbC(c) 200.00
3 LbC(c) 200.00
4 LbC(c) 200.00
5 LbC(c),Stampede of Hard
 Riding Thrills 225.00
6 LbC(c),Drums of the Sioux . . . 225.00
Becomes:

INDIAN WARRIORS
June, 1951
7 LbC(C),Winter on the Great
 Plains 250.00
8 LbC(c) 225.00
Becomes:

WESTERN CRIME
CASES
Dec., 1951
9 LbC(c),The Card Sharp Killer . 275.00
Becomes:

OUTLAWS, THE
May, 1952
10 LbC(c),Federated Express . . . 275.00
11 LbC(c),Frontier Terror!!!. 225.00
12 LbC(c),Ruthless Killer!!! 225.00
13 LbC(c),The Grim Avengers . . . 225.00
14 AF,JKa,LbC(c),Trouble in
 Dark Canyon,April, 1954 . . . . 225.00

OUT OF THE NIGHT
**American Comics Group/
Best Synd. Feature,
Feb.–March, 1952**
1 AW 1,000.00
2 AW 700.00
3 . . . . 400.00
4 AW 550.00
5 . . . . 400.00
6 The Ghoul's Revenge 400.00
7 . . . . 400.00
8 The Frozen Ghost 400.00

9 Death Has Wings,
 Science Fiction 400.00
10 Ship of Death 400.00
11 . . . . 275.00
12 Music for the Dead 275.00
13 HN,From the Bottom of
 the Well 275.00
14 Out of the Screen 275.00
15 The Little Furry Thing 250.00
16 Nightmare From the Past 250.00
17 The Terror of the Labyrinth . . . 250.00
Becomes:

HOODED HORSEMAN
Dec., 1954–Jan., 1955
18 B: The Hooded Horseman . . . 125.00
19 The Horseman's Strangest
 Adventure 175.00
20 OW,O:Johnny Injun. 125.00
21 OW,OW(c). 175.00
22 OW 125.00
23 . . . . 125.00
24 . . . . 125.00
25 . . . . 100.00
26 O&I:Cowboy Sahib 125.00
27 Jan.–Feb., 1953 . . . . 110.00

OUT OF THE SHADOWS
**Visual Editions
(Standard Comics),
July, 1952–Aug., 1954**
5 ATh,GT,The Shoremouth
 Horror 800.00
6 ATh,JKz,Salesman of Death . . 500.00
7 JK,Plant of Death 400.00
8 Mask of Death 700.00
9 RC,Till Death Do Us Part 400.00
10 MSy,We Vowed,Till Death
 Do Us Part. 400.00
11 ATh,Fountain of Fear. 400.00
12 ATh,Hand of Death 500.00
13 MSy,The Cannibal 375.00
14 ATh,The Werewolf. 375.00

OXYDOL-DREFT
**Giveaways, 1950
The Set is More Valuable if the
Original Envelope is Present**
1 L'il Abner 150.00
2 Daisy Mae 150.00
3 Shmoo 200.00
4 AW&FF(c),John Wayne 200.00
5 Archie 200.00
6 Terry Toons Comics 150.00

OZARK IKE
**Visual Editions
(Standard Comics), 1948**
11 . . . . 175.00
12 thru 20 . . . . @100.00
21 thru 25 . . . . @100.00

OZZIE AND BABS
**Fawcett Publications,
Winter, 1946**
1 Humor Oriented, Teenage 150.00
2 Humor Oriented 100.00
3 thru 12 Humor Oriented . . . @100.00
13 Humor Oriented;1949 . . . . . . 100.00

PAGEANT OF COMICS
**St. John Publishing Co.,
Sept., 1947**
1 Rep. Mopsy 150.00
2 Rep. Jane Arden,Crime
 Reporter. 150.00

PANHANDLE PETE
AND JENNIFER
**J. Charles Lave
Publishing Co., July, 1951**
1 (fa) 125.00
2 (fa) 100.00
3 (fa),Nov.'51 . . . . 100.00

PANIC
**Tiny Tot Publications
(E.C. Comics), March, 1954
"Humor in a Jugular Vein"**
1 BE,JKa,JO,JDa,AF(c) 750.00
2 BE,JO,WW,JDa,A:Bomb 400.00
3 BE,JO,BW,WW,JDa,AF(c) . . 300.00
4 BE,JO,WW,JDa,BW(c),
 Infinity(c) 300.00
5 BE,JO,WW,JDa,AF(c) 250.00
6 BE,JO,WW,JDa,Blank (c) . . . 250.00
7 BE,JO,WW,JDa 250.00
8 BE,JO,WW,JDa,Eye Chart (c) . 200.00
9 BE,JO,WW,JDa,Ph(c),
 Confidential(c) 500.00
10 BE,JDa, Postal Package(c) . . 350.00
11 BE,WW,JDa,Wheaties parody
 as Weedies (c) 300.00
12 BE,WW,JDa,JDa(c);
 Dec.–Jan., 1955–56 . . . . 300.00

*Paramount Animate Comics #8
© Harvey Publications*

PARAMOUNT
ANIMATED COMICS
**Family Publications
(Harvey Publ.), June, 1953**
1 (fa),B:Baby Herman & Katnip,
 Baby Huey,Buzzy the Crow . 275.00
2 (fa) 125.00
3 (fa) 100.00
4 thru 6 (fa) . . . . @100.00
7 (fa), Baby Huey (c) 275.00
8 (fa), Baby Huey (c) 100.00
9 (fa), Infinity(c),Baby Huey (c). . 100.00
10 thru 21 (fa),Baby Huey(c) . . @100.00
22 (fa), July, 1956, Baby Huey (c) 100.00

PAROLE BREAKERS
**Avon Periodicals/Realistic,
Dec., 1951–July, 1952**
1 P(c),Hellen Willis,Gun
 Crazed Gun Moll 650.00
2 JKu,P(c),Vinnie Sherwood,
 The Racket King 400.00
3 EK(c),John "Slicer" Berry,
 Hatchetman of Crime 350.00

All comics prices listed are for *Near Mint* condition. **CVA Page 451**

PATCHES
Rural Home Publ./
Patches Publ.,
March–April, 1945
1 LbC(c),Imagination In Bed(c). . 600.00
2 Dance (c) 225.00
3 Rocking Horse (c) 200.00
4 Music Band (c). 200.00
5 LbC(c),A:Danny Kaye,Football 275.00
6 A: Jackie Kelk 200.00
7 A: Hopalong Cassidy 225.00
8 A: Smiley Burnettte 175.00
9 BK,A: Senator Claghorn 175.00
10 A: Jack Carson 175.00
11 A: Red Skeleton; Dec'47. . . . . 200.00

PAT THE BRAT
Radio Comics (Archie
Publications), 1955–59
1 . . . . 175.00
2 . . . . 150.00
3 . . . . 125.00
4 . . . . 125.00
15 thru 20. . . . . @75.00
21 thru 33 . . . . @75.00

PAUL TERRY'S COMICS
See: TERRY-TOONS
COMICS

PAWNEE BILL
Story Comics,
Feb.–July, 1951
1 A:Bat Masterson,Wyatt Earp,
   Indian Massacre
   at Devil's Gulch 150.00
2 Blood in Coffin Canyon 100.00
3 LC,O:Golden Warrior,Fiery
   Arrows at Apache Pass. 100.00

PAY-OFF
D.S. Publishing Co.,
July–Aug., 1948–
March–April, 1949
1 True Crime 1 & 2. . . . . 350.00
2 The Pennsylvania Blue-Beard 200.00
3 The Forgetful Forger 150.00
4 RJ(c),Lady and the Jewels . . . 150.00
5 The Beautiful Embezzeler 150.00

PEDRO
Fox Features Syndicate,
Jan., 1950
1 WW,WW(c),Humor Oriented . 300.00
2 Aug., 1950 . . . . 200.00

PENNY
Avon Publications, 1947
1 The Slickest Chick of 'em All . 175.00
2 . . . . 100.00
3 America's Teen-age
   Sweetheart 100.00
4 . . . . 100.00
5 . . . . 100.00
6 Perry Como Ph(c),Sept.–
   Oct., 1949 . . . . 125.00

PEP COMICS
MJL Magazines/
Archie Publications,
Jan., 1940
1 IN,JCo,MMe,IN(c),I:Shield,
   O:Comet,Queen of Diamonds,
   B:The Rocket,Press Guardian,
   Sergeant Boyle Chang,Bently
   of Scotland Yard. 17,000.00
2 CBi,JCo,IN,IN(c),O:Rocket . 4,500.00
3 JCo,IN,IN(c),Shield (c) 3,000.00

Pep Comics #6
© Archie Publications

4 Cbi,JCo,MMe,IN,IN(c),
   C:Wizard(not Gareb) 2,400.00
5 Cbi,JCo,MMe,IN,IN(c),
   C:Wizard. 2,400.00
6 IN,IN(c), Shield (c) 1,800.00
7 IN,IN(c),Bondage(c),Shield(c)1,800.00
8 JCo,IN, Shield (c) 1,800.00
9 IN, Shield (c). 1,800.00
10 IN,IN(c), Shield (c) 1,800.00
11 MMe,IN,IN(c),I:Dusty,
   Boy Detective 2,000.00
12 IN,IN(c),O:Fireball
   Bondage(c), E:Rocket,
   Queen of Diamonds 2,200.00
13 IN,IN(c),Bondage(c). 1,500.00
14 IN,IN(c). 1,500.00
15 IN,Bondage(c) 1,500.00
16 IN,O:Madam Satan 2,400.00
17 IN,IN(c),O:Hangman,
   D:Comet 6,000.00
18 IN,IN(c),Bondage(c) 1,500.00
19 IN 1,500.00
20 IN,IN(c),E:Fireball 1,500.00
21 IN,IN(c),Bondage(c),
   E: Madam Satan. 1,500.00
22 IN,IN(c)I:Archie,
   Jughead, Betty 30,000.00
23 IN,IN(c). 3,000.00
24 IN,IN(c). 2,000.00
25 IN,IN(c). 2,000.00
26 IN,IN(c),I:Veronica 3,000.00
27 IN,IN(c),Bill of Rights (c) . . . 1,500.00
28 IN,IN(c), V:Capt. Swastika. . 1,500.00
29 ASh (c). 1,500.00
30 B:Capt.Commando 1,500.00
31 Bondage(c) 1,500.00
32 Bondage(c) 1,200.00
33 . . . . 1,200.00
34 Bondage(c) 1,200.00
35 . . . . 1,200.00
36 1st Archie(c). 3,200.00
37 Bondage(c). 850.00
38 ASh(c). 800.00
39 ASh(c), Human Shield 800.00
40 . . . . 800.00
41 2nd Archie; I:Jughead. 600.00
42 F:Archie & Jughead 600.00
43 F:Archie & Jughead 600.00
44 . . . . 600.00
45 . . . . 600.00
46 . . . . 600.00
47 E:Hangman,Infinity(c) 600.00
48 B:Black Hood 600.00
49 . . . . 600.00
50 . . . . 600.00
51 . . . . 400.00
52 B:Suzie 400.00

53 . . . . 400.00
54 E:Captain Commando 400.00
55 . . . . 400.00
56 thru 58. . . . . @350.00
59 E:Suzie 350.00
60 B:Katy Keene 350.00
61 . . . . 300.00
62 I L'il Jinx 300.00
63 . . . . 300.00
64 . . . . 300.00
65 E:Shield. 300.00
66 thru 71. . . . . @200.00
72 thru 80. . . . . @175.00
81 thru 90. . . . . @150.00
91 thru 99. . . . . @125.00
100. . . . . 200.00
101 thru 110. . . . . @125.00
111 thru 120 . . . . @100.00
121 thru 130. . . . . @125.00
131 thru 140. . . . . @100.00
141 thru 150. . . . . @100.00
151 thru 160,A:Super Heroes . @100.00

PERFECT CRIME, THE
Cross Publications,
Oct., 1949
1 BP,DW 450.00
2 BP 250.00
3 . . . . 225.00
4 BP 225.00
5 DW 225.00
6 . . . . 225.00
7 B:Steve Duncan 225.00
8 Drug Story 300.00
9 . . . . 200.00
10 . . . . 200.00
11 Bondage (c) 300.00
12 . . . . 200.00
13 . . . . 200.00
14 Poisoning (c). 350.00
15 'The Most Terrible Menace,'
   Drug. 300.00
16 . . . . 150.00
17 . . . . 150.00
18 Drug (c). 400.00
19 . . . . 150.00
20 thru 25. . . . . @125.00
26 Drug w/ Hypodermic (c) 400.00
27 . . . . 150.00
28 . . . . 150.00
29 . . . . 150.00
30 E:Steve Duncan, Rope
   Strangulation (c) 400.00
31 . . . . 125.00
32 . . . . 125.00
33 . . . . 125.00

PETER PAUL'S 4 IN 1
JUMBO COMIC BOOK
Capitol Stories, 1953
1 F: Racket Squad in Action,
   Space Adventures,Crime &
   Justice,Space Western 500.00

PETER PENNY AND HIS
MAGIC DOLLAR
American Bakers Assn., 1947
1 History from Colonial
   America to the 1950's 200.00
2 . . . . 125.00

PETER RABBIT
Avon Periodicals, 1947
1 HCa 450.00
2 HCa 325.00
3 HCa 275.00
4 HCa 275.00
5 HC 275.00
6 HCa 275.00

GOLDEN AGE

7 thru 10 . . . . @100.00
11 . . . . 100.00

KRAZY LIFE
Fox Features Syndicate, 1945
1 (fa) 100.00
Becomes:

NUTTY LIFE
Summer, 1946
2 (fa) 100.00
Becomes:

WOTALIFE
**Fox Features Synd./
Green Publ., Aug.–Sept., 1946**
3 (fa)B:L'il Pan,Cosmo Cat 150.00
4 . . . . 100.00
5 thru 11 . . . . @100.00
12 July, 1947 . . . . 100.00
9a rep (1959) 100.00
Becomes:

Phantom Lady #20
© Fox Feature Syndicate

PHANTOM LADY
**Fox Features Syndicate,
Aug., 1947**
13(#1) MB,MB(c) Knights of
   the Crooked Cross 7,200.00
14(#2) MB,MB(c) Scoundrels
   and Scandals 3,900.00
15 MB,MB(c) The Meanest
   Crook In the World 3,900.00
16 MB,MB(c) Claa Peete The
   Beautiful Beast, Negligee . . 3,900.00
17 MB.MB(c) The Soda Mint
   Killer, Bondage (c) 10,000.00
18 MB,MB(c) The Case of
   Irene Shroeder 2,500.00
19 MB,MB(c) The Case of
   the Murderous Model 2,500.00
20 MB,MB(c) Ace of Spades. . . 2,200.00
21 MB,MB(c). 2,200.00
22 MB,JKa 2,200.00
23 MB,JKa Bondage (c) 2,200.00
Becomes:

MY LOVE SECRET
June, 1949
24 JKa, My Love Was For Sale. . 250.00
25 Second Hand Love 150.00
26 WW I Wanted Both Men 250.00
27 I Was a Love Cheat 125.00
28 WW, I Gave Him Love 250.00
29 . . . . 125.00

30 Ph(c) 125.00

LINDA
Ajax/Farrell, April–May, 1954
1 . . . . 200.00
2 Lingerie section 150.00
3 . . . . 100.00
4 Oct.–Nov.,1954 . . . . 100.00
Becomes:

PHANTOM LADY
Dec., 1954–Jan., 1955
5(1) MB 1,700.00
2 Last Pre-Code Edition 1,300.00
3 Comics Code 1,000.00
4 Red Rocket,June, 1955 . . . . 1,000.00

PHIL RIZZUTO
Fawcett Publications, 1951
Ph(c) The Sensational Story of
   The American League MVP 1,150.00

PICTURE CRIMES
1937
1 . . . . 1,500.00

PICTURE NEWS
**299 Lafayette Street Corp.,
Jan., 1946–Jan.-Feb., 1947**
1 Will The Atom Blow The
   World Apart 750.00
2 Meet America's 1st Girl Boxing
   Expert,Atomic Bomb 500.00
3 Hollywood's June Allison Shows
   You How to be Beautiful,
   Atomic Bomb 400.00
4 Amazing Marine Who Became
   King of 10,000 Voodoos,
   Atomic Bomb 450.00
5 G.I.Babies,Hank Greenberg. . . 400.00
6 Joe Louis(c) 450.00
7 Lovely Lady, Englands
   Future Queen 350.00
8 Champion of them All 350.00
9 Bikini Atom Bomb,
   Joe DiMaggio 400.00
10 Dick Quick, Ace Reporter,
   Atomic Bomb 400.00

PICTURE PARADE
Gilberton Co., 1953
1 A–Bomb 300.00
2 United Nations 150.00
3 American Indians 150.00
4 Christmas issue 150.00
Becomes:

PICTURE PROGRESS
Gilberton Co., 1954
5 1953 News. 100.00
6 Birth of America 100.00
7 Four Seasons 100.00
8 Paul Revere 100.00
9 Hawaian Islands 100.00
10 Flight 100.00
11 thru 20 . . . . @100.00

PICTURE SCOPE
JUNGLE ADVENTURES
Star Publications, 1954
7 LbC(c) 700.00

PICTURE STORIES FROM
AMERICAN HISTORY
E.C. Comics, 1946–47
1 . . . . 600.00
2 thru 4 . . . . @450.00

PICTURE STORIES
FROM SCIENCE
**Educational Comics,
Spring, 1947**
1 Understanding Air and Water . 500.00
2 Fall '47 Amazing Discoveries
   About Food & Health 400.00

PICTURE STORIES
FROM WORLD HISTORY
E.C. Comics, Spring, 1947
1 Ancient World to the
   Fall of Rome 400.00
2 Europes Struggle for
   Civilization 375.00

PINHEAD AND
FOODINI
**Fawcett Publications,
July, 1951–Jan., 1952**
1 Ph(c) 400.00
2 Ph(c) 200.00
3 Ph(c) Too Many Pinheads 150.00
4 Foodini's Talking Camel 150.00

PIN-UP PETE
Toby Publications, 1952
1 Loves of a GI Casanova 250.00

PIONEER PICTURE
STORIES
**Street & Smith Publ.,
Dec., 1941**
1 Red Warriors in Blackface 400.00
2 Life Story Of Errol Flynn 350.00
3 Success Stories of Brain
   Muscle in Action 250.00
4 Legless Ace & Boy Commando
   Raid Occupied France 250.00
5 How to Tell Uniform and
   Rank of Any Navy Man 250.00
6 General Jimmy Doolittle 300.00
7 Life Story of Admiral Halsey . . 300.00
8 Life Story of Timoshenko 250.00
9 Dec., '43,Man Who Conquered
   The Wild Frozen North 250.00

PIRACY
E.C. Comics, Oct.–Nov., 1954
1 WW,JDa,AW,WW(c),RC,AT . . 650.00
2 RC,JDa(c),WW,AW,AT. 500.00
3 RC,GE, RC(c),Grl 400.00
4 RC,GE,RC(c),Grl 350.00
5 RC,GE,BK(c),Grl 350.00
6 JDa,RC,GE,BK(c),Grl 350.00
7 Oct Nov GE(c),RC,GE,Grl . . . 350.00

PIRATES COMICS
Hillman Periodicals, Feb., 1950
1 . . . . 350.00
2 . . . . 250.00
3 . . . . 200.00
4 Aug–Sept., 1950 . . . . 200.00

PIXIES, THE
**Magazine Enterprises,
Winter, 1946**
1 Mighty Atom 150.00
2 thru 5 . . . . @100.00
Becomes:

MIGHTY ATOM, THE
1949
6 . . . . 125.00

Planet Comics #4
© *Fiction House Magazines*

PLANET COMICS

**Love Romance Publ.
(Fiction House Magazines),
Jan., 1940–Winter, 1953**

1 AB,DBr,HcK, Planet Comics,
  WE&LF,O:Aura,B:Flint Baker,
  Red Comet,Spurt Hammond,
  Capt. Nelson Cole 22,000.00
2 HcK,LF(c) 8,000.00
3 WE(c),HcK 5,000.00
4 HcK,B:Gale Allan and
  the Girl Squad 4,000.00
5 BP,HcK 3,800.00
6 BP,HcK,BP(c),The Ray
  Pirates of Venus 3,800.00
7 BP,AB,HcK,BP(c) B:Buzz
  Crandall Planet Payson . . . 3,200.00
8 BP,AB HcK 3,200.00
9 BP,AB,GT,HcK,B:Don
  Granville Cosmo Corrigan . 3,200.00
10 BP,AB,GT HcK 3,200.00
11 HcK, B:Crash Parker 3,200.00
12 Dri,B:Star Fighter 3,200.00
13 Dri,B:Reef Ryan 2,300.00
14 Dri B:Norge Benson 2,300.00
15 B: Mars,God of War 4,800.00
16 Invasion From The Void. . . . 2,200.00
17 Warrior Maid of Mercury . . . 2,200.00
18 Bondage(c) 2,300.00
19 Monsters of the Inner
  World 2,200.00
20 RP, Winged Man Eaters
  of the Exile Star 2,200.00
21 RP,B:Lost World
  Hunt Bowman 2,300.00
22 Inferno on the Fifth Moon . . 2,200.00
23 GT,Lizard Tyrant of
  the Twilight World 2,000.00
24 GT,Grl Raiders From
  The Red Moon 2,000.00
25 Grl,B:Norge Benson 2,000.00
26 Grl,B:The Space Rangers
  Bondage(c). 2,100.00
27 Grl, The Fire Eaters of
  Asteroid Z. 1,600.00
28 Grl, Bondage (c) 2,200.00
29 Grl,Dragon Raiders of Aztla. 2,600.00
30 GT,Grl City of Lost Souls. . . 2,000.00
31 Grl,Fire Priests of Orbit6X . . 1,600.00
32 Slaver's Planetoid 1,700.00
33 MA 1,600.00
34 MA,Bondage 1,700.00
35 MA B:Mysta of The Moon . . 1,600.00
36 MA Collosus of the
  Blood Moon 1,600.00

37 MA, Behemoths of the
  Purple Void 1,600.00
38 MA 1,400.00
39 MA.Death Webs Of Zenith 3 1,400.00
40 Chameleon Men from
  Galaxy 9 . . . . 1,400.00
41 MA,AgF,New O: Auro
  Bondage (c) 1,400.00
42 MA,AgF,E:Gale Allan 1,400.00
43 MA,AgF Death Rays
  From the Sun.. . . . . 1,400.00
44 MA,Bbl,B:Futura 1,400.00
45 MA,Bbl,Her Evilness
  from Xanado. 1,400.00
46 MA,Bbl,GE The Mecho-Men
  From Mars 1,400.00
47 MA,Bbl,GE,The Great
  Green Spawn 1,100.00
48 MA,GE 1,100.00
49 MA,GE, Werewolves From
  Hydra Hell. 1,100.00
50 MA,GE,The Things of Xeves 1,100.00
51 MA,GE, Mad Mute X-Adapts 1,000.00
52 GE,Mystery of the Time
  Chamber. 1,000.00
53 MB,GE,Bondage(c)
  Dwarflings From Oceania. . 1,000.00
54 MB,GE,Robots From Inferno 1,000.00
55 MB,GE,Giants of the
  Golden Atom. 1,000.00
56 MB,GE,Grl 900.00
57 MB,GE,Grl 900.00
58 MB,GE,Grl 900.00
59 MB,GE,Grl,LSe 900.00
60 GE,Grl,Vassals of Volta 900.00
61 GE,Grl, The Brute in the
  Bubble 800.00
62 GE,Musta,Moon Goddess . . 800.00
63 GE,Paradise or Inferno. 800.00
64 GE,Monkeys From the Blue . 800.00
65 The Lost World 800.00
66 The Plague of the
  Locust Men 800.00
67 The Nymphs of Neptune. . . . 800.00
68 Synthoids of the 9th Moon . . 800.00
69 The Mentalists of Mars 800.00
70 Cargo For Amazonia. 800.00
71 Sandhogs of Mars. 700.00
72 Last Ship to Paradise 700.00
73 The Martian Plague 700.00

PLASTIC MAN

**Comics Magazines
(Quality Comics Group),
Summer, 1943–Nov., 1956**

1 JCo(a&c)Game of Death . . . 7,000.00
2 JCo(a&c)The Gay Nineties
  Nightmare. 2,700.00
3 JCo(a&c). 1,700.00
4 JCo(a&c). 1,500.00
5 JCo(a&c). 1,400.00
6 JCo(a&c). 1,500.00
7 JCo(a&c). 1,500.00
8 JCo(a&c). 1,500.00
9 JCo(a&c). 1,500.00
10 JCo(a&c) 1,500.00
11 JCo(a&c) 1,500.00
12 JCo(a&c),V:Spadehead 1,500.00
13 JCo(a&c),V:Mr.Hazard 1,500.00
14 JCo(a&c),Words,Symbol
  of Crime 1,500.00
15 JCo(a&c),V:BeauBrummel. . 1,500.00
16 JCo(a&c),Money
  Means Trouble 1,500.00
17 JCo(a&c),A:The Last
  Man on Earth 1,200.00
18 JCo(a&c),Goes Back
  to the Farm. 1,200.00
19 JCo(a&c),V:Prehistoric
  Plunder. 1,200.00
20 JCo(a&c),A:Sadly,Sadly. . . . 1,200.00

21 JCo(a&c),V:Crime Minded
  Mind Reader 800.00
22 JCo(a&c), Which Twin
  is the Phony. 800.00
23 JCo(a&c),The Fountain
  of Age 800.00
24 JCo(a&c),The Black Box
  of Terror. 800.00
25 JCo(a&c),A:Angus
  MacWhangus 800.00
26 JCo(a&c),On the Wrong
  Side of the Law? 800.00
27 JCo(a&c),V:The Leader 800.00
28 JCo(a&c),V:Shasta 800.00
29 JCo(a&c),V:Tricky Toledo 800.00
30 JCo(a&c),V:Weightless
  Wiggins 800.00
31 JCo(a&c),V:Raka the
  Witch Doctor 600.00
32 JCo(a&c),V:Mr.Fission 600.00
33 JCo(a&c),V:The Mad
  Professor 600.00
34 JCo(a&c),Smuggler'sHaven . . 600.00
35 JCo(a&c),V:The Hypnotist . . 600.00
36 JCo(a&c),The Uranium
  Underground 600.00
37 JCo(a&c),V:Gigantic Ants 600.00
38 JCo(a&c),The Curse of
  Monk Mauley. 600.00
39 JCo(a&c),The Stairway
  to Madness 600.00
40 JCo(a&c),The Ghoul of
  Ghost Swamp 600.00
41 JCo(a&c),The Beast with
  the Bloody Claws. 500.00
42 JCo(a&c),The King of
  Thunderbolts 500.00
43 JCo(a&c),The Evil Terror . . . 500.00
44 JCo(a&c),The Magic Cup . . . 500.00
45 The Invisible Raiders 500.00
46 V:The Spider 500.00
47 The Fiend of a
  Thousand Faces 500.00
48 Killer Crossbones 500.00
49 JCo,The Weapon for Evil . . . 500.00
50 V:Iron Fist 500.00
51 Incredible Sleep Weapon . . . 500.00
52 V:Indestructible Wizard. 500.00
53 V:Dazzia,Daughter of
  Darkness 500.00
54 V:Dr.Quomquat. 500.00
55 The Man Below Zero 500.00
56 JCo, The Man Who Broke
  the Law of Gravity 500.00
57 The Chemist's Cauldron 500.00

Plastic Man #2
© *Quality Comics Group*

58 JCo,The Amazing
    Duplicating Machine 500.00
59 JCo,V:The Super Spy 500.00
60 The Man in the Fiery
    Disguise. 450.00
61 V:King of the Thunderbolts . . 450.00
62 V:The Smokeweapon 450.00
63 V:Reflecto 450.00
64 The Invisible Raiders 450.00

PLAYFUL LITTLE AUDREY
Harvey Publications, 1957

1 . . . . 450.00
2 . . . . 250.00
3 . . . . 135.00
4 . . . . 135.00
5 . . . . 135.00
6 thru 9 . . . . @100.00
10 thru 30 . . . . @100.00

POCAHONTAS
**Pocahontas Fuel Co.,
Oct., 1941**

N# 300.00
2 . . . . 275.00

POCKET COMICS
**Harvey Publications,
Aug., 1941**

1 100 pages,O:Black Cat,Spirit
    of '76,Red Blazer Phantom
    Sphinx & Zebra,B:Phantom
    Ranger,British Agent #99,
    Spin Hawkins,Satan 1,500.00
2 . . . . 1,000.00
3 . . . . 750.00
4 Jan.'42,All Features End 750.00

POGO POSSUM
Dell Publishing Co., 1949

1 WK,A:Swamp Land Band . . . 1,500.00
2 WK 1,000.00
3 WK. 600.00
4 WK. 600.00
5 WK. 600.00
6 thru 10 WK. . . . . @450.00
11 WK, Christmas (c). . . . . . . @400.00
12 thru 16 WK . . . . @500.00

POLICE AGAINST CRIME
Premier Magazines, 1954

1 JyD,Knife in Face 350.00
2 . . . . 165.00
3 . . . . 125.00
4 thru 9 . . . . @125.00

POLICE COMICS
**Comic Magazines
(Quality Comics Group),
Aug., 1941**

1 JCo,WE.PGv,RC,FGu,AB,
    GFx(a&c),B&O:Plastic Man
    The Human Bomb,#711,I&B,
    Chic Canter,The Firebrand
    Mouthpiece,Phantom Lady
    The Sword 13,000.00
2 JCo,PGv,WE,RC,FGu,
    GFx(a&c) 5,500.00
3 JCo,PGv,WE,RC,FGu,
    GFx(a&c) 3,500.00
4 JCo,GFx,PGv,WE,RC,FGu,
    GFx&WEC(c) 3,000.00
5 JCo,PGv,WE,RC,FGu,
    GFx(a&c) 3,000.00
6 JCo,PGv,WE,RC,FGu,
    GFx(a&c) 2,500.00
7 JCo,PGv,WE,RC,FGu,
    GFx(a&c) 2,500.00

8 JCo,PGv,WE,RC,FGu,
    GFx(a&c),B&O:Manhunter 3,000.00
9 JCo,PGv,WE,RC,FGu,
    GFx(a&c) 2,000.00
10 JCo,PGv,WE,RC,FGu,
    GFx(a&c) 2,000.00
11 JCo,PGv,WE,RC,FGu,GFx(a&c),
    B:Rep:Rep.Spirit Strips. . . . 3,500.00
12 JCo,GFx,PGv,WE,FGu,AB,
    RC(c) I:Ebony. 2,000.00
13 JCo,GFx,PGv,WE,FGu,AB,RC(c)
    E:Firebrand,I:Woozy Winks 2,000.00
14 JCo,PGv,WE,Jku,GFx(a&c). 1,500.00
15 JCo,PGv,WE,Jku,GFx(a&c)
    E#711,B:Destiny 1,500.00
16 JCo,PGv,WE,JKu. 1,500.00
17 PGv,WE,JKu,JCo(a&c) 1,500.00
18 PGv,WE,JCo(a&c) 1,500.00
19 PGv,WE,JCo(a&c) 1,500.00
20 PGv,WE,JCo(a&c),A:Jack
    Cole in Phantom Lady 1,500.00
21 PGv,WE,JCo(a&c) 1,400.00
22 PGv,WE,RP,JCo(a&c)
    The Eyes Have it 1,400.00
23 WE,RP,JCo(a&c),E:Phantom
    Lady 1,200.00
24 WE,HK,JCo(a&c),B:Flatfoot
    Burns 1,200.00
25 WE,HK,RP,JCo(a&c),The
    Bookstore Mysrery 1,200.00
26 WE,HK,JCo(a&c)E:Flatfoot
    Burns 1,200.00
27 WE,JCo(a&c). 1,200.00
28 WE,JCo(a&c). 1,200.00
29 WE,JCo(a&c). 1,200.00
30 WE,JCo(a&c),A Slippery
    Racket 1,200.00
31 WE,JCo(a&c),Is Plastic
    Man Washed Up?. 1,000.00
32 WE,JCo(a&c),Fiesta Turns
    Into a Fracas 1,000.00
33 JCo,WE 1,000.00
34 WE,JCo(a&c). 1,000.00
35 WE,JCo(a&c). 1,000.00
36 WE,JCo(a&c),Rest In Peace 1,000.00
37 WE,PGv,JCo(a&c),Love
    Comes to Woozy 1,000.00
38 WE,PGv,JCo(a&c). 1,000.00
39 WE,PGv,JCo(a&c). 1,000.00
40 WE,PGv,JCo(a&c). 1,000.00
41 WE,PGv,JCo(a&c),E:Reps.
    of Spirit Strip 900.00
42 LF&WE,PGv,JCo(a&c),
    Woozy Cooks with Gas. . . . 900.00
43 LF&WE,PGv,JCo(a&c) 900.00
44 PGv,LF,JCo(a&c) 900.00

Police Comics #55
© Quality Comics Group

45 PGv,LF,JCo(a&c) 900.00
46 PGv,LF,JCo(a&c) 900.00
47 PGv,LF,JCo(a&c),V:Dr.Slicer. . 900.00
48 PGv,LF,JCo(a&c),V:Big
    Beaver. 900.00
49 PGv,LF,JCo(a&c),V:Thelma
    Twittle 900.00
50 PGv,LF,JCo(a&c) 900.00
51 PGv,LF,JCo(a&c),V:The
    Granite Lady 700.00
52 PGv,LF,JCo(a&c) 700.00
53 PGv,LF,JCo(a&c),V:Dr.
    Erudite. 700.00
54 PGv,LF,JCo(a&c) 700.00
55 PGv,LF,JCo(a&c),V:The
    Sleepy Eyes 700.00
56 PGv,LF,JCo(a&c),V:The
    Yes Man. 700.00
57 PGv,LF,JCo(a&c),V:Mr.Misfist. . 700.00
58 PGv,LF,JCo(a&c),E:The
    Human Bomb 700.00
59 PGv,LF,JCo(a&c),A:Mr.
    Happiness 700.00
60 PGv,LF,JCo(a&c) 500.00
61 PGv,LF,JCo(a&c) 500.00
62 PGv,LF,JCo(a&c) 500.00
63 PGv,LF,JCo(a&c),V:The
    Crab. 500.00
64 PGv,LF,HK,JCo(a&c) 500.00
65 PGv,LF,JCo(a&c) 500.00
66 PGv,LF,JCo(a&c) Love
    Can Mean Trouble. 500.00
67 LF,JCo(a&c),
    V:The Gag Man. 500.00
68 LF,JCo(a&c) 500.00
69 LF,JCo(a&c),V:Strecho 500.00
70 LF,JCo(a&c) 500.00
71 PGv,LF,JCo(a&c) 400.00
72 LF,JCo(a&c),V:Mr.Cat 400.00
73 LF,JCo(a&c) 400.00
74 LF,JCo(a&c),V:Prof.Dimwit . . . 400.00
75 LF,JCo(a&c) 400.00
76 LF,JCo(a&c),V:Mr.Morbid 400.00
77 LF,JCo(a&c),V:Skull Face
    & Eloc 400.00
78 LF,JCo(a&c),A Hot Time In
    Dreamland. 400.00
79 LF,JCo(a&c),V:Eaglebeak. . . . 400.00
80 LF,JCo(a&c),V:Penetro 400.00
81 LF,JCo(a&c),V:A Gorilla 400.00
82 LF,JCo(a&c) 400.00
83 LF,JCo(a&c) 400.00
84 LF,JCo(a&c) 400.00
85 LF,JCo(a&c),V:Lucky 7 . . . . . 400.00
86 LF,JCo(a&c),V:The Baker 400.00
87 LF,JCo(a&c) 400.00
88 LF,JCo(a&c),V:The Seen 400.00
89 JCo(a&c),The Vanishers 350.00
90 LF,JCo(a&c),V:Capt.Rivers. . . 350.00
91 JCo(a&c),The Forest Primeval 400.00
92 LF,JCo(a&c),V:Closets
    Kennedy 400.00
93 JCo(a&c),V:The Twinning
    Terror 350.00
94 JCo(a&c),WE 600.00
95 JCo(a&c),WE,V:Scowls 600.00
96 JCo(a&c),WE,V:Black Widow. 600.00
97 JCo(a&c),WE,V:The Mime . . 600.00
98 JCo(a&c),WE. 600.00
99 JCo(a&c),WE 600.00
100 JCo(a&c). 700.00
101 JCo(a&c). 700.00
102 JCo(a&c),E:Plastic Man . . . 700.00
103 JCo,LF,B&I:Ken Shannon;
    Bondage(c) 550.00
104 The Handsome of Homocide 350.00
105 Invisible Hands of Murder. . . 350.00
106 Museum of Murder 350.00
107 Man with the Shrunken
    Head 350.00
108 The Headless Horse Player . 350.00

All comics prices listed are for *Near Mint* condition.   **CVA Page 455**

GOLDEN AGE

109 LF,Bondage(c),Blood on the
Chinese Fan 350.00
110 Murder with a Bang. 350.00
111 Diana, Homicidal Huntress . 350.00
112 RC,The Corpse on the
Sidewalk 400.00
113 RC(a&c), The Dead Man
with the Size 13 Shoe 400.00
114 The Terrifying Secret of
the Black Bear. 350.00
115 Don't Let Them Kill Me 350.00
116 Stage Was Set For Murder . . 350.00
117 Bullet Riddled Bookkeeper . . 350.00
118 Case of the Absent Corpse. . 350.00
119 A Fast & Bloody Buck 350.00
120 Death & The Derelict 350.00
121 Curse of the Clawed Killer . . 350.00
122 The Lonely Hearts Killer 350.00
123 Death Came Screaming 350.00
124 Masin Murder 350.00
125 Bondage(c),The Killer of
King Arthur's Court 400.00
126 Hit & Run Murders 350.00
127 Oct'53,Death Drivers 350.00

POLICE LINE-UP
**Avon Periodicals/
Realistic Comics, Aug., 1951**
1 WW,P(c). 500.00
2 P(c),Drugs 400.00
3 JKu,EK,P(c). 250.00
4 July, '52;EK 250.00

POLICE TRAP
Mainline, Sept., 1954
1 S&K(c) 400.00
2 S&K(c) 225.00
3 S&K(c) 225.00
4 S&K(c) 225.00

Charlton Comics, July, 1955
5 S&K,S&K(c). 300.00
6 S&K,S&K(c). 300.00
Becomes:

PUBLIC DEFENDER
IN ACTION
Charlton Comics, March, 1956
7 . . . . 150.00
8 and 9 . . . . @100.00
10 thru 12, ... @100.00

POPEYE
Dell Publishing Co., 1948
1 . . . . 500.00
2 . . . . 250.00
3 'Welcome to Ghost Island'. . . . 225.00
4 thru 10 . . . . @225.00
11 . . . . 200.00
12 . . . . 200.00
13 . . . . 200.00
14 thru 20. . . . . @200.00
21 thru 30. . . . . @150.00
31 thru 40 . . . . @135.00
41 thru 45. . . . . @125.00
46 O:Swee' Pea. 150.00
47 thru 50. . . . . @125.00
51 thru 65. . . . . @100.00

POPULAR COMICS
**Dell Publishing Co.,
Feb., 1936**
1 Dick Tracy, Little Orphan
Annie 9,000.00
2 Terry Pirates 4,000.00
3 Terry,Annie,Dick Tracy 3,000.00
4 . . . . 2,000.00
5 B:Tom Mix 2,000.00
6 I:Scribbu 1,800.00
7 . . . . 1,500.00

Popular Comics #14
© Dell Publishing Co.

8 Scribbu & Reg Fellers. . . . 1,500.00
9 . . . . 1,500.00
10 Terry,Annie,Tracy 1,500.00
11 Terry,Annie,Tracy 1,000.00
12 Christmas(c). 1,000.00
13 Terry,Annie,Tracy 1,000.00
14 Terry,Annie,Tracy 1,000.00
15 Terry,Annie,Tracy 1,000.00
16 Terry,Annie,Tracy 1,000.00
17 Terry,Annie,Tracy 1,000.00
18 Terry,Annie,Tracy 1,000.00
19 Terry,Annie,Tracy 1,000.00
20 Terry,Annie,Tracy 1,000.00
21 Terry,Annie,Tracy 750.00
22 Terry,Annie,Tracy 750.00
23 Terry,Annie,Tracy 750.00
24 Terry,Annie,Tracy 750.00
25 Terry,Annie,Tracy 750.00
26 Terry,Annie,Tracy 750.00
27 E:Terry,Annie,Tracy. 750.00
28 A:Gene Autry. 600.00
29 . . . . 600.00
30 . . . . 600.00
31 A:Jim McCoy 650.00
32 A:Jim McCoy 650.00
33 . . . . 650.00
34 . . . . 650.00
35 Christmas(c),Tex Ritter 650.00
36 . . . . 650.00
37 . . . . 650.00
38 B:Gang Busters 650.00
39 . . . . 550.00
40 . . . . 550.00
41 . . . . 550.00
42 . . . . 550.00
43 F:Gang Busters. 550.00
44 . . . . 450.00
45 Tarzan(c). 450.00
46 O:Martan the Marvel Man . . 550.00
47 F:Martan the Marvel Man . . . 450.00
48 F:Martan the Marvel Man . . . 450.00
49 F:Martan the Marvel Man . . . 425.00
50 . . . . 425.00
51 B&O:Voice. 425.00
52 A:Voice 425.00
53 F:The Voice. 425.00
54 F:Gang Busters,A:Voice 425.00
55 F:Gang Busters. 400.00
56 F:Gang Busters. 400.00
57 F:The Marvel Man. 400.00
58 F:The Marvel Man. 400.00
59 F:The Marvel Man. 400.00
60 O:Prof. Supermind 400.00
61 Prof. Supermind & Son 350.00
62 Supermind & Son 350.00
63 B:Smilin' Jack 350.00
64 Smilin'Jack,Supermind 350.00

65 Professor Supermind 350.00
66 . . . . 350.00
67 Gasoline Alley. 350.00
68 F:Smilin' Jack 350.00
69 F:Smilin' Jack 350.00
70 F:Smilin' Jack 350.00
71 F:Smilin' Jack 350.00
72 B:Owl,Terry & the Pirates . . . 550.00
73 F:Terry and the Pirates 400.00
74 F:Smilin' Jack 400.00
75 F:Smilin'Jack,A:Owl 400.00
76 Captain Midnight. 500.00
77 Captain Midnight. 500.00
78 Captain Midnight. 500.00
79 A:Owl. 350.00
80 F:Smilin' Jack,A:Owl 350.00
81 F: Terry&thePirates,A:Owl . . . 350.00
82 F:Smilin' Jack,A:Owl 350.00
83 F:Smilin' Jack,A:Owl 350.00
84 F:Smilin' Jack,A:Owl 350.00
85 F:ThreeLittleGremlins,A:Owl. . 350.00
86 F:Three Little Gremlins 250.00
87 F:Smilin' Jack 250.00
88 F:Smilin' Jack 250.00
89 F:Smokey Stover 250.00
90 F:Terry and the Pirates 250.00
91 F:Smokey Stover 250.00
92 F:Terry and the Pirates 250.00
93 F:Smilin' Jack 250.00
94 F:Terry and the Pirates 250.00
95 F:Smilin' Jack 250.00
96 F:Gang Busters. 250.00
97 F:Smilin' Jack 250.00
98 B:Felix Cat 250.00
99 F:Bang Busters 250.00
100 . . . . 275.00
101 thru 141 . . . . @175.00
142 E:Terry & the Pirates. 125.00
143 . . . . 125.00
144 . . . . 125.00
145 F:Harold Teen 125.00

POWER COMICS
Holyoke/Narrative Publ., 1944
1 LbC(c). 2,200.00
2 B:Dr.Mephisto,Hitler(c) . . . 2,300.00
3 LbC(c) 2,500.00
4 LbC(c) 2,200.00

PRIDE OF THE
YANKEES
Magazine Enterprises, 1949
1 N#,OW,Ph(c),The Life
of Lou Gehrig 1,250.00

PRISON BREAK
**Avon Periodicals/Realistic,
Sept., 1951**
1 WW(c),WW 600.00
2 WW(c),WW,JKu 400.00
3 JD,JO. 350.00
4 EK 275.00
5 EK,CI 275.00

PRIZE COMICS
**Feature Publications
(Prize Publ.), March, 1940**
1 O&B:Power Nelson,Jupiter.
B:Ted O'Neil,Jaxon of
the Jungle,Bucky Brady,
Storm Curtis, Rocket(c) . . . 5,000.00
2 B:The Owl. 2,500.00
3 Power Nelson(c). 2,100.00
4 Power Nelson(c). 2,100.00
5 A:Dr.Dekkar. 1,500.00
6 A:Dr.Dekkar. 1,500.00
7 S&K,DBr,JK(c),O&B DR Frost,
Frankenstein,B:GreenLama,
Capt Gallant,Voodini
Twist Turner 3,500.00

All comics prices listed are for *Near Mint* condition.

8 S&K,DBr 1,800.00
9 S&K,DBr,Black Owl(c) 1,700.00
10 DBr,Black Owl(c) 1,500.00
11 DBr,O:Bulldog Denny 1,200.00
12 DBr 1,200.00
13 DBr,O&B:Yank and
   Doodle,Bondage 1,400.00
14 DBr,Black Owl(c) 1,200.00
15 DBr,Black Owl(c) 1,200.00
16 DBr,JaB,B:Spike Mason 1,200.00
17 DBr,Black Owl(c) 1,200.00
18 DBr,Black Owl(c) 1,200.00
19 DBr,Yank&Doodle(c) 1,200.00
20 DBr,Yank&Doodle(c) 1,200.00
21 DBr,JaB(c),Yank&Doodle(c) . . 900.00
22 DBr,Yank&Doodle(c) 900.00
23 DBr,Uncle Sam(c) 900.00
24 DBr,Abe Lincoln(c) 900.00
25 DBr,JaB,Yank&Doodle(c) 900.00
26 DBr,JaB,JaB(c),Liberty
   Bell(c) 900.00
27 DBr,Yank&Doodle(c) 700.00
28 DBr,Yank&Doodle(c) 600.00
29 DBr,JaB(c)Yank&Doodle(c) . . . 600.00
30 DBr,Yank&Doodle(c) 700.00
31 DBr,Yank&Doodle(c) 600.00
32 DBr,Yank&Doodle(c) 600.00
33 DBr,Bondage(c),Yank
   & Doodle 700.00
34 DBr,O:Airmale;New
   Black Owl 700.00
35 DBr,B:Flying Fist & Bingo . . . 500.00
36 DBr,Yank&Doodle(c) 500.00
37 DBr,I:Stampy,Hitler(c) 550.00
38 DBr,B.Owl,Yank&Doodle(c) . . 500.00
39 DBr,B.Owl,Yank&Doodle(c) . . 500.00
40 DBr,B.Owl,Yank&Doodle(c) . . 500.00
41 DBr,B.Owl,Yank&Doodle(c) . . 500.00
42 DBr,B.Owl,Yank&Doodle(c) . . 300.00
43 DBr,B.Owl,Yank&Doodle(c) . . 300.00
44 DBr, B&I:Boom Boom
   Brannigan 300.00
45 DBr 300.00
46 DBr 300.00
47 DBr 300.00
48 DBr,B:Prince Ra;Bondage(c) . . 400.00
49 DBr,Boom Boom(c) 300.00
50 DBr,Frankenstein(c) 300.00
51 DBr 300.00
52 DBr, B:Sir Prize 300.00
53 DBr, The Man Who Could
   Read Features 300.00
54 DBr 300.00
55 DBr,Yank&Doodle(c) 300.00
56 DBr,Boom Boom (c) 300.00
57 DBr,Santa Claus(c) 300.00
58 DBr,The Poisoned Punch 300.00
59 DBr,Boom Boom(c) 300.00
60 DBr,Sir Prise(c) 300.00
61 DBr,The Man wih the
   Fighting Feet 300.00
62 DBr,Hck(c),Yank&Doodle(c) . . 300.00
63 DBr,S&K,S&K(c),Boom
   Boom(c) 350.00
64 DBr,Blackowl Retires 250.00
65 DBr,DBr(c),Frankenstein 250.00
66 DBr,DBr(c),Frankenstein 250.00
67 DBr,B:Brothers in Crime 250.00
68 DBr,RP(c) 250.00
Becomes:

PRIZE COMICS
WESTERN
Feature Publ., April–May, 1948
69 ACa(c),B:Dusty Ballew 175.00
70 ACa(c) 150.00
71 ACa(c) 150.00
72 ACa(c),JSe 150.00
73 ACa(c) 150.00
74 ACa(c) 150.00
75 JSe,S&K(c),6-Gun Showdown
   at Rattlesnake Gulch 160.00

Prize Comics Western #86
© *Prize Publications*

76 Ph(c),Randolph Scott 175.00
77 Ph(c),JSe,Streets of
   Laredo,movie 160.00
78 Ph(c),JSe,HK,Bullet
   Code, movie 250.00
79 Ph(c),JSe,Stage to
   China, movie 250.00
80 Ph(c),Gunsmoke Justice. 175.00
81 Ph(c),The Man Who Shot
   Billy The Kid 175.00
82 Ph(c),MBi,JSe&BE,Death
   Draws a Circle 175.00
83 JSe,S&K(c) 150.00
84 JSe 125.00
85 JSe,B:American Eagle 325.00
86 JSe 150.00
87 JSe&BE 150.00
88 JSe&BE 150.00
89 JSe&BE 150.00
90 JSe&Be 150.00
91 JSe&BE,JSe&BE(c) 150.00
92 JSe,JSe&BE(c) 150.00
93 JSe,JSe&BE(c), ... 150.00
94 JSe&BE,JSe&BE(c) 150.00
95 JSe,JSe&BE(c) 150.00
96 JSe,JSe&BE,JSe&BE(c). 150.00
97 JSe,JSe&BE,JSeBE(c) 150.00
98 JSe&BE,JSe&BE(c) 150.00
99 JSe&BE,JSe&BE(c) 150.00
100 JSe,JSe(c) 175.00
101 JSe 150.00
102 JSe 150.00
103 JSe 150.00
104 JSe 150.00
105 JSe 150.00
106 JSe 100.00
107 JSe 100.00
108 JSe 110.00
109 JSe&AW 125.00
110 JSe&BE. 125.00
111 JSe&BE 125.00
112 . . . . 100.00
113 AW&JSe 125.00
114 MMe,B:The Drifter 100.00
115 MMe 100.00
116 MMe 100.00
117 MMe 100.00
118 MMe,E:The Drifter 100.00
119 Nov/Dec'56 . . . . 100.00

PRIZE MYSTERY
Key Publications, 1955
1 . . . . 125.00
2 and 3 . . . . @100.00

PSYCHOANALYSIS
**E.C. Comics,
March–April, 1955**
1 JKa,JKa(c) 350.00
2 JKa,JKa(c) 250.00
3 JKa,JKa(c) 225.00
4 JKa,JKa(c) Sept.–Oct., 1955 . . 225.00

PUBLIC DEFENDER
IN ACTION
See: POLICE TRAP

PUBLIC ENEMIES
D.S. Publishing Co., 1948
1 AMc 325.00
2 AMc 275.00
3 AMc 200.00
4 AMc 200.00
5 AMc 200.00
6 AMc 175.00
7 AMc,Eye Injury 200.00
8 . . . . 175.00
9 . . . . 175.00

PUNCH AND JUDY
COMICS
Hillman Periodicals, 1944
1 (fa) 300.00
2 . . . . 250.00
3 . . . . 200.00
4 thru 12 . . . . @175.00
2-1 . . . . 150.00
2-2 JK 300.00
2-3 . . . . 150.00
2-4 . . . . 150.00
2-5 . . . . 150.00
2-6 . . . . 150.00
2-7 . . . . 150.00
2-8 . . . . 150.00
2-9 . . . . 150.00
2-10 JK. 300.00
2-11 JK 300.00
2-12 JK 300.00
3-1 JK. 300.00
3-2 . . . . 275.00
3-3 . . . . 100.00
3-4 . . . . 100.00
3-5 . . . . 100.00
3-6 . . . . 100.00
3-7 . . . . 100.00
3-8 . . . . 100.00
3-9 . . . . 100.00

PUNCH COMICS
Harry 'A' Chesler, Dec., 1941
1 B:Mr.E,The Sky Chief,Hale
   the Magician,Kitty Kelly . . . 2,500.00
2 A:Capt.Glory 2,000.00
3-8 Do Not Exist
9 B:Rocket Man & Rocket
   girl,Master Ken 2,000.00
10 JCo,A:Sky Chief. 1,200.00
11 JCo,O:Master Key,A:Little
   Nemo 1,200.00
12 A:Rocket Boy,Capt.Glory . . . 4,000.00
13 Ric(c) 1,200.00
14 GT 900.00
15 FSm(c) 900.00
16 . . . . 900.00
17 . . . . 900.00
18 FSm(c),Bondage(c),Drug. . . 1,200.00
19 FSm(c) 900.00
20 Women semi-nude(c) 1,200.00
21 Drug 1,200.00
22 I:Baxter,Little Nemo 500.00
23 A:Little Nemo 500.00

PUPPET COMICS
Dougherty, Co., Spring, 1946
1 Funny Animal 150.00
2 . . . . 125.00

PURPLE CLAW, THE
**Minoan Publishing Co./
Toby Press, Jan., 1953**
1 O:Purple Claw 450.00
2 and 3 . . . . @300.00

QUEEN OF THE WEST,
DALE EVANS
**Dell Publishing Co.,
July, 1953**
(1) see Dell Four Color #479
(1) see Dell Four Color #528
3 ATh, Ph(c) all 150.00
4 ATh,RsM 135.00
5 RsM 125.00
6 RsM 125.00
7 RsM 125.00
8 RsM 125.00
9 RsM 125.00
10 RsM 125.00
11 . . . . 90.00
12 RsM 100.00
13 RsM 100.00
14 RsM 100.00
15 RsM 100.00
16 RsM 100.00
17 RsM 100.00
18 RsM 100.00
19 . . . . 90.00
20 RsM 100.00
21 . . . . 90.00
22 RsM 100.00

Racket Squad in Action #17
© Charlton Comics

RACKET SQUAD
IN ACTION
**Capitol Stories/
Charlton Comics,
May–June, 1952**
1 Carnival(c) 350.00
2 . . . . 175.00
3 Roulette 175.00
4 FFr(c) 350.00
5 Just off the Boat 300.00
6 The Kidnap Racket 200.00
7 . . . . 150.00
8 . . . . 150.00
9 2 Fisted fix 150.00

10 Explosion Blast (c) 250.00
11 SD(a&c),Racing(c) 375.00
12 JoS,SD(c),Explosion(c). 900.00
13 JoS(c),The Notorious Modelling
　　Agency Racket,Acid 150.00
14 DG(c),Drug 200.00
15 Photo Extortion Racket 150.00
16 thru 28 . . . . @150.00
29 March, 1958 . . . . 150.00

RAGGEDY ANN
AND ANDY
Dell Publishing Co., 1946
1 Billy & Bonnie Bee 650.00
2 . . . . 350.00
3 DNo,B:Egbert Elephant 350.00
4 DNo,WK 400.00
5 DNo 300.00
6 DNo 300.00
7 Little Black Sambo 300.00
8 . . . . 300.00
9 . . . . 300.00
10 . . . . 300.00
11 thru 20 . . . . @250.00
21 Alice in Wonderland 300.00
22 thru 27 . . . . @200.00
28 WK 225.00
29 thru 39 . . . . @200.00

RAGS RABBIT
Harvey Publications, 1957
11 . . . . 75.00
12 thru 18 . . . . @60.00

RALPH KINER
HOME RUN KING
Fawcett Publications, 1950
1 N#, Life Story of the
　　Famous Pittsburgh Slugger 1,000.00

RAMAR OF THE
JUNGLE
**Toby Press/
Charlton Comics, 1954**
1 Ph(c),TV Show. 275.00
2 Ph(c) 200.00
3 . . . . 200.00
4 . . . . 200.00
5 Sept '56 . . . . 200.00

RANGE BUSTERS
Charlton Comics, 1955
8 . . . . 100.00
9 & 10 . . . . @75.00

RANGE ROMANCES
**Comics Magazines
(Quality Comics), Dec., 1949**
1 PGv(a&c) 350.00
2 RC(a&c) 350.00
3 RC,Ph(c) 300.00
4 RC,Ph(c) 250.00
5 RC,PGv,Ph(c) 250.00

RANGERS OF FREEDOM
**Flying Stories, Inc.
(Fiction House), Oct., 1941**
1 I:Ranger Girl & Rangers
　　of Freedom;V:Super-Brain . 5,000.00
2 V:Super -Brain 1,700.00
3 Bondage(c) The Headsman
　　of Hate 1,300.00
4 Hawaiian Inferno. 1,000.00
5 RP,V:Super-Brain 1,000.00
6 RP,Bondage(c);Bugles
　　of the Damned 1,000.00
7 RP,Death to Tojo's Butchers . . 750.00

Rangers #33
© Fiction House

Becomes:

RANGERS COMICS
Dec., 1942
8 RP,B:US Rangers 750.00
9 GT,BLb,Commando Steel
　　for Slant Eyes 750.00
10 BLb,Bondage (c). 750.00
11 Raiders of the
　　Purple Death 700.00
12 A:Commando Rangers 700.00
13 Grl,B:Commando Ranger. . . 800.00
14 Grl,Bondage(c) 850.00
15 GT,Grl,Bondage(c) 850.00
16 Grl,GT;Burma Raid 600.00
17 GT,GT,Bondage(c),Raiders
　　of the Red Dawn 750.00
18 GT 600.00
19 GE,BLb,GT,Bondage(c) 750.00
20 GT 600.00
21 GT,Bondage(c) 650.00
22 GT,B&O:Firehair 500.00
23 GT,BLb,B:Kazanda 450.00
24 Bondage(c) 450.00
25 Bondage(c) 450.00
26 Angels From Hell 400.00
27 Bondage(c) 500.00
28 BLb,E:Kazanda;B&O Tiger
　　Man 450.00
29 Bondage(c) 500.00
30 BLb,B:Crusoe Island 450.00
31 BLb,Bondage(c) 400.00
32 BLb 400.00
33 BLb,Drug. 550.00
34 BLb 300.00
35 BLb,Bondage(c) 400.00
36 BLb,MB 300.00
37 BLb,Mb 350.00
38 BLb,MB,GE,Bondage(c) 400.00
39 BLb,GE 500.00
40 BLb,GE,BLb(c) 300.00
41 BLb,GE, L:Werewolf Hunter . . 300.00
42 BLb,GE 300.00
43 BLb,GE 300.00
44 BLb,GE 300.00
45 BLb,GEl. 300.00
46 BLb,GE 300.00
47 BLb,JGr, Dr. Drew. 300.00
48 BLb,JGr, L:Glory Forces . . . 300.00
49 BLb,JGr. 300.00
50 BLb,JGr,Bondage(c) 350.00
51 BLb,JGr. 300.00
52 BLb,JGr,Bondage(c) 350.00
53 BLb,JGr,Prisoners of
　　Devil Pass 250.00

54 JGr,When The Wild
   Commanches Ride 250.00
55 JGr,Massacre Guns at
   Pawnee Pass 250.00
56 JGr, Gun Smuggler of
   Apache Mesa 250.00
57 JGr,Redskins to the
   Rescue 225.00
58 JGr,Brides of the
   Buffalo Men 225.00
59 JGr,Plunder Portage 225.00
60 JGr, Buzzards of
   Bushwack Trail 225.00
61 BWh(c)Devil Smoke at
   Apache Basin 200.00
62 BWh(c)B:Cowboy Bob 200.00
63 BWh(c) 200.00
64 BWh(c)B:Suicide Smith 200.00
65 BWh(c):Wolves of the
   Overland Trail,Bondage(c) . . 225.00
66 BWh(c) 200.00
67 BWh(c)B:Space Rangers 200.00
68 BWh(c);Cargo for Coje 200.00
69 BWh(c);Great Red Death Ray 200.00

REAL CLUE
CRIME STORIES
See: CLUE COMICS

REAL FUNNIES
Nedor Publishing Co.,
Jan., 1943
1 (fa) 400.00
2 and 3 (fa) . . . . @200.00

REAL HEROES COMICS
Parents' Magazine Institiute,
Sept., 1941
1 HcK,Franklin Roosevelt 400.00
2 J, Edgar Hoover. 250.00
3 General Wavell 200.00
4 Chiang Kai Shek, Churchill . . . 225.00
5 Stonewall Jackson 250.00
6 Lou Gehrig. 300.00
7 Chennault and his
   Flying Tigers 250.00
8 Admiral Nimitz 250.00
9 The Panda Man 200.00
10 Carl Akeley-Jungle
   Adventurer 200.00
11 Wild Jack Howard 200.00
12 General Robert L
   Eichelberger 200.00
13 HcK,Victory at Climback 200.00
14 Pete Gray 200.00
15 Alexander Mackenzie 200.00
16 Balto of Nome Oct '46 . . . . . . 200.00

REAL LIFE STORY
OF FESS PARKER
Dell Publishing Co., 1955
1 . . . . 150.00

REAL LIFE COMICS
Visual Editions/Better/
Standard/Nedor, Sept., 1941
1 ASh(c),Lawrence of
   Arabia,Uncle Sam(c) 1,200.00
2 ASh(c),Liberty(c) 450.00
3 Adolph Hitler(c) 2,000.00
4 ASh(c)Robert Fulton,
   Charles DeGaulle, Old Glory. 300.00
5 ASh(c)Alexander the Great . . . 300.00
6 ASh(c)John Paul Jones,CDR . 250.00
7 ASh(c)Thomas Jefferson 250.00
8 Leonardo Da Vinci 250.00
9 US Coast Guard Issue. 250.00
10 Sir Hubert Wilkens 250.00
11 ASh(c),Odyssey on a Raft. . . . 200.00

Real Life Comics #24
© Nedor

12 ASh(c),ImpossibleLeatherneck 200.00
13 ASh(c)The Eternal Yank 200.00
14 ASh(c),Sir Isaac Newton. 200.00
15 ASh(c),William Tell 200.00
16 ASh(c),Marco Polo 200.00
17 ASh(c),Albert Einstein. 250.00
18 ASh(c),Ponce De Leon 200.00
19 ASh(c),The Fighting Seabees. 200.00
20 ASh(c),Joseph Pulitzer 200.00
21 ASh(c),Admiral Farragut 200.00
22 ASh(c),Thomas Paine. 200.00
23 ASh(c),Pedro Menendez 200.00
24 ASh(c),Babe Ruth 350.00
25 ASh(c),CQ,Marcus Whitman. . 200.00
26 ASh(c),CQ,Benvenuto Cellini . 200.00
27 ASh(c),CQ,A-Bomb Story 300.00
28 ASh(c),CQ,Robert Blake. 200.00
29 ASh(c),CQ,Daniel DeFoe,
   A-Bomb 250.00
30 ASh(c),CQ,Baron Robert Clive 200.00
31 ASh(c),CQ,Anthony Wayne . . 200.00
32 ASh(c),CQ,Frank Sinatra 225.00
33 ASh(c),CQ,Frederick Douglas 150.00
34 ASh(c),CQ,P Revere,J.Stewart 175.00
35 ASh(c),CQ,Rudyard Kipling . 150.00
36 ASh(c),CQ,Story of the
   Automobile. 150.00
37 ASh(c),CQ,Francis Manion,
   Motion Picture, Bing Crosby . 150.00
38 ASh(c),CQ,Richard Henry
   Dana 150.00
39 ASh(c),CQ,Samuel FB Morse. 150.00
40 FGu,CQ,ASh(c),Hans Christian
   Anderson, Bob Feller. 250.00
41 CQ,Abe Lincoln,Jimmy Foxx . 200.00
42 Joseph Conrad,Fred Allen . . . 150.00
43 Louis Braille,O.W.Holmes. . . . 100.00
44 Citizens of Tomorrow 100.00
45 ASh(c),FrancoisVillon,
   Olympics, Burl Ives 200.00
46 ASh(c),The Pony Express. . . . 200.00
47 ASh(c),Montezuma, Gershwin 200.00
48 ASh(c) 200.00
49 ASh(c),Gene Bearden,
   Baseball. 200.00
50 FF,ASh(c),Lewis & Clark. 500.00
51 GE,ASh(c),Sam Houston 350.00
52 GE,FF,ASh(c),JSe&BE
   Leif Erickson 500.00
53 GT,JSe&BE,Henry Wells &
   William Fargo 250.00
54 GT,Alexander Graham Bell . . . 250.00
55 ASh(c),JSe&BE,The James
   Brothers. 250.00
56 JSe&BE. 250.00
57 JSe&BE. 250.00

58 JSe&BE,Jim Reaves 300.00
59 FF,JSe&BE,Battle Orphan
   Sept '52 . . . . 250.00

REAL SPORTS COMICS
See: ALL SPORTS COMICS

REAL WESTERN HERO
See: WOW COMICS

REAL WEST ROMANCES
Crestwood Publishing Co./
Prize Publ., April–May, 1949
1 S&K,Ph(c) 325.00
2 Ph(c),Spanking 150.00
3 JSe,BE,Ph(c) 150.00
4 S&K,JSe,BE,Ph(c) 250.00
5 S&K,MMe,JSe,Audie
   Murphy Ph(c) 225.00
6 S&K,JSe,BE,Ph(c) 150.00

RECORD BOOK OF
FAMOUS POLICE CASES
St. John Publishing Co., 1949
1 N#,JKu,MB(c) 500.00

RED ARROW
P.L. Publishing Co.,
May, 1951
1 Bondage(c) 350.00
2 . . . . 200.00
3 P(c) 200.00

RED BAND COMICS
Enwil Associates,
Nov., 1944
1 The Bogeyman 500.00
2 O:Bogeyman,same(c)as#1 . . . 350.00
3 A:Captain Wizard 300.00
4 May, '45,Repof#3,Same(c) . . 300.00

RED CIRCLE COMICS
Enwil Associates
(Rural Home Public),
Jan., 1945
1 B:Red Riot,The Prankster 550.00
2 LSt,A:The Judge 400.00
3 LSt(A&c). 300.00
4 LSt(a&c) covers of #4
   stapled over other comics . . . 300.00

TRAIL BLAZERS
Street & Smith Publ., Jan., 1942
1 Wright Brothers 500.00
2 Benjamin Franklin,Dodgers . . . 400.00
3 Red Barber,Yankees 500.00
4 Famous War song 250.00
Becomes:
RED DRAGON COMICS
Jan., 1943
5 JaB(c),B&O:Red Rover:
   B:Capt.Jack Commando
   Rex King&Jet,Minute Man . 1,500.00
6 O:Red Dragon. 3,700.00
7 The Curse of the
   Boneless Men. 3,000.00
8 China V:Japan 1,100.00
9 The Reducing Ray,Jan '44 . . 1,100.00

(2nd Series) Nov., 1947
1 B:Red Dragon 1,500.00
2 BP 925.00
3 BP,BP(c),I:Dr Neff 800.00
4 BP,BP(c) 1,100.00
5 MMe,BP,BP(c) 550.00
6 BP,BP(c) 550.00
7 MMe,BP,BP(c),May, 49 . . . . . 550.00

GOLDEN AGE

RED MASK
See: TIM HOLT

RED RABBIT
**Dearfield/
J. Charles Lave Publ. Co.,
Jan., 1941**
1 (fa)	200.00
2	125.00
3	100.00
4	100.00
5	100.00
6 thru 10	@100.00
11 thru 22	@75.00

RED RYDER COMICS
**Hawley Publ./
Dell Publ. Co. 1940**
1	4,700.00

Becomes:

HI-SPOT COMICS
Hawley Publications, 1940
2 Alley Oop, Capt. Easy	1,700.00

Becomes:

RED RYDER COMICS
**Hawley Publ./Dell
Publ. Co., 1941**
3 Alley Oop, Capt. Easy	2,000.00
4	900.00
5	900.00
6	900.00
7	650.00
8	650.00
9	650.00
10	650.00
11 thru 20	@500.00
21 thru 30	@400.00
31 thru 40	@300.00
41 thru 50	@250.00
51 thru 60	@200.00
61 thru 70	@200.00
71 thru 80	@200.00
80 thru 99	@100.00
100	150.00
101 thru 151	@100.00
Giant #1	100.00
Giant #2	100.00

RED SEAL COMICS
See: SCOOP

REDSKIN
**Youthful Magazines,
Sept., 1950**
1 WJo,Redskin,Bondage(c)	350.00
2 Apache Dance of Death	125.00
3 WJo(c),Daniel Boone	100.00
4 WJo(c),Sitting Bull- Red Devil of the Black Hills	100.00
5 DW	100.00
6 Geronimo- Terror of the Desert,Bondage	250.00
7 Firebrand of the Sioux	100.00
8	100.00
9	100.00
10 Dead Man's Magic	100.00
11 RP,DW	100.00
12 Quanah Parker,Bondage(c)	250.00

Becomes:

FAMOUS WESTERN BADMEN
Dec., 1952
13 Redskin- Last of the Comanches	150.00
14	100.00
15 The Dalton Boys Apr '52	100.00

REG'LAR FELLERS
Visual Editions (Standard), 1947
5	100.00
6	100.00

REMEMBER PEARL HARBOR
Street & Smith Publ., 1942
1 N# JaB,Battle of the Pacific,Uncle Sam(c)	700.00

RETURN OF THE OUTLAW
**Minoan Publishing Co.,
Feb., 1953**
1 Billy The Kid	125.00
2	100.00
3 thru 11	@75.00

REVEALING ROMANCES
**A.A. Wyn
(Ace Magazines), Sept., 1949**
1	150.00
2	125.00
3 thru 6	@100.00

REX ALLEN COMICS
**Dell Publishing Co.,
Feb., 1951**
(1) see Dell Four Color #316	
2 Western, Ph(c) all	200.00
3 thru 10	@150.00
11 thru 23	@125.00
24 ATh	135.00
25 thru 31	@125.00

Rex Dexter #1
© *Fox Features Syndicate*

REX DEXTER OF MARS
**Fox Features Syndicate,
Autumn, 1940**
1 DBr,DBr(c) Battle ofKooba	3,000.00

REX MORGAN, M.D.
Argo Publications, 1950
1	150.00
2	100.00

RIBTICKLER
Fox Features Syndicate, 1945
1	225.00
2	150.00
3 Cosmo Cat	125.00

4 thru 6	@100.00
7 Cosmo Cat	100.00
8 thru 9	@100.00

RICKY
Visual Editions (Standard Comics), 1953
1	75.00

THE RIDER
**Four Star Comics
(Ajax-Farrell Publ.), 1957**
1 Swift Arrow	150.00
2 thru 5	@100.00

Becomes:

FRONTIER TRAIL
Ajax-Farrell Publ., 1958
6	100.00

RIN TIN TIN
**Dell Publishing Co.,
Nov., 1952**
(1) see Dell Four Color #434	
(1) see Dell Four Color #476	
(1) see Dell Four Color #523	
4 thru 10 Ph(c) all	@100.00
11 thru 20	@125.00

RIPLEY's BELIEVE IT OR NOT!
Harvey Publications, 1953–54
1 BP	150.00
2 Li'l Abner	125.00
3	125.00
4	125.00

RIVETS
Argo Publications, 1956
1	100.00
2	75.00
3	75.00

ROBIN HOOD
Sussex Publ. Co (Magazine Enterprises), 1955
1 FBe	200.00
2 FBe	150.00
3 FBe	150.00
4 FBe	150.00
5 FBe	150.00
6 FBe,BP	150.00

Becomes:

ADVENTURES OF ROBIN HOOD
Magazine Enterprises, 1957
7 BP, Richard Green Ph(c)	200.00
8 Richard Green Ph(c)	200.00

ROBIN HOOD AND HIS MERRY MEN
See: THIS MAGAZINE IS HAUNTED

ROBIN HOOD TALES
Quality Comics Group, 1956
1 MB	450.00
2 MB	400.00
3 MB	400.00
4 MB	400.00
5 MB	400.00
6 MB	400.00

See: DC Comics

ROCKET COMICS

**Hillman Periodicals,
March, 1940**

1 O:Red Roberts;B:Rocket
  Riley,Phantom Ranger,Steel
  Shank,Buzzard Baynes,Lefty
  Larson,The Defender,Man
  with 1,000 Faces 4,500.00
2 . . . . 2,000.00
3 May, '40 E:All Features 2,500.00

Rocket Kelly #1
© *Fox Features Syndicate*

ROCKET KELLY

**Fox Features Syndicate,
Autumn, 1945–Oct., Nov., 1946**

N# 450.00
1 . . . . 350.00
2 A:The Puppeteer 325.00
3 thru 6 . . . . @300.00

ROCKETMAN

**Ajax/Farrell Publications,
June, 1952**

1 Space Stories of the Future . . . 550.00

ROCKET SHIP X

**Fox Features Syndicate,
Sept., 1951**

1 . . . . 900.00
2 N# Variant of Original 500.00

ROCKY LANE WESTERN

**Fawcett/Charlton Comics,
May, 1949**

1 Ph(c)B:Rocky Lane,Slim
  Pickins 1,500.00
2 Ph(c) 600.00
3 Ph(c) 500.00
4 Ph(c)CCB,Rail Riders
  Rampage,F Capt Tootsie. . . . 500.00
5 Ph(c)The Missing
  Stagecoaches 450.00
6 Ph(c)Ghost Town Showdown . 300.00
7 Ph(c)The Border Revolt. 350.00
8 Ph(c)The Sunset Feud 350.00
9 Ph(c)Hermit of the Hills 350.00
10 Ph(c)Badman's Reward 300.00
11 Ph(c)Fool's Gold Fiasco 250.00
12 Ph(c),CCB,Coyote Breed
  F:Capt Tootsie,Giant 250.00
13 Ph(c),Giant 250.00
14 Ph(c) 200.00

15 Ph(c)B:Black Jacks
  Hitching Post,Giant 225.00
16 Ph(c),Giant 200.00
17 Ph(c),Giant 200.00
18 Ph(c) 225.00
19 Ph(c),Giant 235.00
20 Ph(c)The Rodeo Rustler
  E:Slim Pickens 235.00
21 Ph(c)B: Dee Dickens 200.00
22 Ph(c) 175.00
23 thru 30 . . . . @200.00
31 thru 40 . . . . @175.00
41 thru 55 . . . . @175.00
56 thru 87 . . . . @150.00

ROD CAMERON WESTERN

**Fawcett Publications,
Feb., 1950**

1 Ph(c) 750.00
2 Ph(c) 350.00
3 Ph(c),Seven Cities of Cipiola . 300.00
4 Ph(c),Rip-Roaring Wild West . 250.00
5 Ph(c),Six Gun Sabotage 250.00
6 Ph(c),Medicine Bead Murders 250.00
7 Ph(c),Wagon Train Of Death . 250.00
8 Ph(c),Bayou Badman 250.00
9 Ph(c),Rustlers Ruse 250.00
10 Ph(c),White Buffalo Trail 250.00
11 Ph(c),Lead Poison 225.00
12 Ph(c) 225.00
13 Ph(c) 225.00
14 Ph(c) 225.00
15 Ph(c) 225.00
16 thru 19 Ph(c) . . . . @225.00
20 Phc(c),Great Army Hoax. 225.00

ROLY-POLY COMICS

Green Publishing Co., 1945

1 B:Red Rube&Steel Sterling . . 400.00
6 A:Blue Cycle 250.00
10 A:Red Rube 300.00
11 . . . . 250.00
12 Black Hood 250.00
13 . . . . 250.00
14 A:Black Hood, Decapitation . . 550.00
15 A:Steel Fist;1946. . . . . 400.00

ROMANCE AND CONFESSION STORIES

St. John Publishing Co., 1949

1 MB(c),MB. 600.00

ROMANTIC WESTERN

**Fawcett Publications,
Winter, 1949**

1 Ph(c) 300.00
2 Ph(c),AW,AMc 325.00
3 Ph(c) 250.00

ROOKIE COP

Charlton, 1955

27 . . . . 125.00
28 . . . . 100.00
29 . . . . 100.00
30 . . . . 100.00
31 thru 33 . . . . @100.00

ROUNDUP

**D.S. Publishing Co.,
July–Aug., 1948**

1 HcK 250.00
2 Drug 175.00
3 . . . . 150.00
4 . . . . 150.00
5 Male Bondage 175.00

ROY CAMPANELLA, BASEBALL HERO

Fawcett Publications, 1950

N# Ph(c),Life Story of the
  Battling Dodgers Catcher . . 1,000.00

ROY ROGERS COMICS

Dell Publishing Co., 1948

1 photo (c) 1,600.00
2 . . . . 600.00
3 . . . . 400.00
4 . . . . 400.00
5 . . . . 400.00
6 thru 10 . . . . @300.00
11 thru 18 . . . . @250.00
19 Chuck Wagon Charlie. 225.00
20 Trigger. 225.00
21 thru 30 . . . . @225.00
31 thru 46 . . . . @300.00
47 thru 50 . . . . @125.00
51 thru 56 . . . . @110.00
57 Drug 125.00
58 Drug 135.00
59 thru 80 . . . . @125.00
81 thru 91 . . . . @100.00
Becomes:

ROY ROGERS AND TRIGGER

Aug., 1955

92 . . . . 100.00
93 . . . . 100.00
94 . . . . 100.00
95 . . . . 100.00
96 thru 99 . . . . @100.00
100 Trigger Returns 125.00
101 thru 118 . . . . @100.00
119 thru 125 ATn . . . . @150.00
126 thru 131 . . . . @120.00
132 Dale Evans 150.00
133 thru 144 RsM . . . . @110.00
145 . . . . 150.00

ROY ROGER'S TRIGGER

**Dell Publishing Co.,
May, 1951**

(1) *see Dell Four Color #329*
2 Ph(c) 250.00
3 P(c) 100.00
4 P(c) 100.00
5 P(c) 100.00
6 thru 17 P(c) . . . . @100.00

RULAH, JUNGLE GODDESS

See: ZOOT COMICS

RUSTY, BOY DETECTIVE

**Good Comics/Lev
Gleason Publ., 1955**

1 . . . . 125.00
2 . . . . 100.00
3 . . . . 100.00
4 . . . . 100.00
5 . . . . 100.00

SAARI, THE JUNGLE GODDESS

**P.L. Publishing Co.,
Nov., 1951**

1 The Bantu Blood Curse 600.00

SABU, ELEPHANT BOY

**Fox Features Syndicate,
June, 1950**

1(30) WW,Ph(c) 350.00
2 JKa,Ph(c),Aug.'50 . . . . 250.00

GOLDEN AGE

HAPPY HOULIHANS
**Fables Publications
(E.C. Comics), Autumn, 1947**
1 O:Moon Girl 650.00
2 . . . . 350.00
Becomes:

SADDLE JUSTICE
Spring, 1948
3 HcK,JCr,AF 700.00
4 AF,JCr, Grl 600.00
5 AF,Grl 550.00
6 AF,Grl 500.00
7 AF,Grl 500.00
8 AF,Grl, ... 550.00
Becomes:

SADDLE ROMANCES
Nov., 1949
9 Grl(c),Grl 625.00
10 AF(c),WW,Grl 650.00
11 AF(c),Grl 625.00

SAD SACK COMICS
**Harvey Publications,
Sept., 1949**
1 I:Little Dot 1,000.00
2 Flying Fool 500.00
3 . . . . 400.00
4 . . . . 300.00
5 . . . . 300.00
6 thru 10 . . . . @250.00
11 thru 21 . . . . @175.00
22 Back in the Army Again,
   The Specialist 200.00
23 thru 50 . . . . @150.00
51 thru 100 . . . . @100.00

SAINT, THE
**Avon Periodicals,
Aug., 1947**
1 JKa,JKa(c),Bondage(c) 1,500.00
2 . . . . 800.00
3 Rolled Stocking Leg(c). 700.00
4 MB(c) Longerie 700.00
5 Spanking Panel 800.00
6 B:Miss Fury 800.00
7 WJo(c),Detective Cases(c) . . . 600.00
8 P(c),Detective Cases(c) 650.00
9 EK(c),The Notorious
   Murder Mob 650.00
10 WW,P(c),V:The Communist
   Menace 600.00
11 P(c),Wanted For Robbery 400.00
12 P(c),The Blowpipe Murders
   March, 1952 . . . . 400.00

SAM HILL PRIVATE EYE
Close-Up Publications, 1950
1 The Double Trouble Caper . . . 200.00
2 . . . . 150.00
3 . . . . 125.00
4 Negligee panels 200.00
5 . . . . 100.00
6 . . . . 100.00
7 . . . . 100.00

SAMSON
**Fox Features Syndicate,
Autumn, 1940**
1 BP,GT,A:Wing Turner 3,800.00
2 BP,A:Dr. Fung 1,400.00
3 JSh(c),A:Navy Jones 1,000.00
4 WE,B:Yarko 850.00
5 WE 750.00
6 WE,O:The Topper;Sept'41 . . . 750.00

SAMSON
**Ajax Farrell Publ
(Four Star), April, 1955**
12 The Electric Curtain 400.00
13 Assignment Danger 350.00
14 The Red Raider;Aug'55 . . . . . 350.00

SANDS OF THE SOUTH PACIFIC
Toby Press, Jan., 1953
1 2-Fisted Romantic Adventure . 300.00

SANTA CLAUS FUNNIES
Dell Publishing Co., 1942
N# WK 700.00
2 WK 450.00

SANTA CLAUS PARADE
**Approved Comics (Ziff-Davis)/
St. John Publ., 1951**
N# 400.00
2 . . . . 300.00
3 . . . . 250.00

SANTA'S CHRISTMAS COMICS
**Best Books (Standard
Comics), 1952**
N# Dizzy Duck 250.00

SCIENCE COMICS
**Fox Features Syndicate,
Feb., 1940**
1 GT,LF(c),O&B:Electro,Perisphere
  Payne,The Eagle,Navy Jones;
  B:Marga,Cosmic Carson,
  Dr. Doom; Bondage(c) . . . 8,000.00
2 GT,LF(c) 4,500.00
3 GT,LF(c),Dynamo 3,500.00
4 JK,Cosmic Carson 3,500.00
5 Giant Comiscope Offer
  Eagle(c) 2,000.00
6 Dynamop(c) 2,000.00
7 Bondage(c),Dynamo 2,200.00
8 Sept., 1940 Eagle(c). 2,000.00

SCIENCE COMICS
**Humor Publications,
Jan., 1946**
1 RP(c),Story of the A-Bomb . . . 250.00
2 RP(c),How Museum Pieces
  Are Assembled 125.00
3 AF,RP(c),How Underwater
  Tunnels Are Made 175.00
4 RP(c),Behind the Scenes at
  A TV Broadcast 100.00
5 The Story of the World's
  Bridges; Sept., 1946 . . . . . 100.00

SCIENCE COMICS
**Ziff-Davis Publ. Co.,
May, 1946**
N# Used For A Mail Order
  Test Market 500.00

SCIENCE COMICS
**Export Publication Enterprises,
March, 1951**
1 How to resurrect a dead rat. . . 125.00

SCOOP COMICS
**Harry 'A' Chesler Jr.,
Nov., 1941**
1 I&B:Rocketman&Rocketgirl;B:Dan
  Hastings;O&B:Master Key . 2,400.00

*Scoop Comics #2
© Harry A Chesler, Jr.*

2 A:Rocketboy,Eye Injury 2,500.00
3 Partial rep. of #2 . . . . 1,000.00
4 thru 7 do not exist
8 1945 . . . . 650.00
Becomes:

SNAP
Harry 'A' Chesler Jr., 1944
N# Humorous 175.00
Becomes:

KOMIK PAGES
Harry 'A' Chesler Jr., 1944
1(10) JK, Duke of Darkness 350.00
Becomes:

BULLS-EYE
Harry 'A' Chesler Jr., 1944
11 Green Knight, Skull (c) 600.00
Becomes:

KAYO
Harry 'A' Chesler Jr., 1945
12 Green Knight. 250.00
Becomes:

CARNIVAL
Harry 'A' Chesler Jr., 1945
(13) Guardineer 225.00
Becomes:

RED SEAL COMICS
**Harry 'A' Chesler, Jr./Superior,
Oct., 1945**
14 GT,Bondage(c),Black Dwarf 1,100.00
15 GT,Torture 650.00
16 GT. 900.00
17 GT,Lady Satan,Sky Chief 700.00
18 Lady Satan,Sky Chief 700.00
19 Lady Satan,Sky Chief 600.00
20 Lady Satan,Sky Chief 600.00
21 Lady Satan,Sky Chief 550.00
22 Rocketman 450.00

SCOOTER COMICS
Rucker Publications, 1946
1 . . . . 150.00

SCOTLAND YARD
Charlton Comics, 1955
1 . . . . 175.00
2 thru 4 . . . . @125.00

All comics prices listed are for *Near Mint* condition.

SCREAM COMICS
**Humor Publ./Current Books
(Ace Magazines),
Autumn, 1944**
1 . . . . 250.00
2 . . . . 150.00
3 thru 15 . . . . @125.00
16 I:Lily Belle 150.00
17 . . . . 125.00
18 Drug 225.00
19 . . . . 125.00
Becomes:

ANDY COMICS
June, 1948
20 Teenage 125.00
21 . . . . 125.00
Becomes:

ERNIE COMICS
Sept., 1948
22 Teenage 125.00
23 thru 25 . . . . @100.00
Becomes:

ALL LOVE ROMANCES
May, 1949
26 Ernie 125.00
27 LbC 200.00
28 thru 32 . . . . @100.00

(Capt. Silvers Log of...) SEA HOUND, THE
Avon Periodicals, 1945
N# The Esmerelda's Treasure . . 250.00
2 Adventures in Brazil 200.00
3 Louie the Llama 150.00
4 In Greed & Vengence;
Jan-Feb, 1946 . . . . 150.00

*Secret Missions #1
© St. John Publishing Co.*

SECRET MISSIONS
St. John Publishing Co., 1950
1 JKu 250.00

SECRET MYSTERIES
See: CRIME MYSTERIES

SELECT DETECTIVE
**D.S. Publishing Co.,
Aug.–Sept., 1948**
1 MB,Exciting New Mystery
Cases 400.00

2 MB,AMc,Dead Men 225.00
3 Face in theFrame;Dec-Jan'48 . 200.00

SENSATIONAL POLICE CASES
Avon Periodicals, 1952
N# JKu,EK(c) 500.00
2 . . . . 200.00
3 . . . . 200.00
4 . . . . 200.00

SERGEANT PRESTON OF THE YUKON
Dell Publishing Co., Aug., 1951
(1 thru 4) *see Dell Four Color #344;
#373, 397, 419*
5 P(c) 125.00
6 Bondage, P(c) 175.00
7 thru 11 P(c) 125.00
12 P(c) 125.00
13 P(c),O:Sergeant Preston 150.00
14 thru 17 P(c) . . . . @125.00
18 Yukon King,P(c) 125.00
19 thru 29 Ph(c) . . . . @150.00

SEVEN SEAS COMICS
**Universal Phoenix Features/
Leader Publ., April, 1946**
1 MB,RWb(c),B:South Sea
Girl, Captain Cutlass 1,400.00
2 MB,RWb(c) 1,200.00
3 MB,AF,MB(c) 1,100.00
4 MB,MB(c) 1,200.00
5 MB,MB(c),Hangman's
Noose 1,100.00
6 MB,MB(c);1947 . . . . 1,000.00

SHADOW COMICS
**Street & Smith Publ.,
March, 1940**
1-1 P(c),B:Shadow,Doc Savage,
Bill Barnes,Nick Carter,
Frank Merriwell,Iron Munro 8,000.00
1-2 P(c),B: The Avenger 3,000.00
1-3 P(c),A: Norgill the
Magician 2,000.00
1-4 P(c),B:The Three
Musketeers 1,500.00
1-5 P(c),E: Doc Savage 1,500.00
1-6 A: Captain Fury 1,300.00
1-7 O&B: The Wasp 1,400.00
1-8 A:Doc Savage 1,300.00
1-9 A:Norgill the Magician . . . 1,300.00
1-10 O:Iron Ghost;B:The Dead
End Kids 1,300.00
1-11 O:Hooded Wasp 1,300.00
1-12 Crime Does Not pay 1,200.00
2-1 . . . . 1,200.00
2-2 Shadow Becomes Invisible 2,200.00
2-3 O&B:Supersnipe;
F:Little Nemo 1,900.00
2-4 F:Little Nemo 1,200.00
2-5 V:The Ghost Faker 1,200.00
2-6 A:Blackstone the Magician 1,000.00
2-7 V:The White Dragon 1,000.00
2-8 A:Little Nemo 1,000.00
2-9 The Hand of Death 1,000.00
2-10 A:Beebo the WonderHorse 1,000.00
2-11 V:Devil Kyoti 1,000.00
2-12 V:Devil Kyoti 900.00
3-1 JaB(c),V:Devil Kyoti 900.00
3-2 Red Skeleton Life Story 900.00
3-3 V:Monstrodamus 900.00
3-4 V:Monstrodamus 900.00
3-5 V:Monstrodamus 900.00
3-6 V:Devil's of the Deep 900.00
3-7 V: Monstrodamus 900.00
3-8 E: The Wasp 900.00
3-9 The Stolen Lighthouse 900.00

*Shadow Comics Vol. 5 #7
© Street & Smith Publ.*

3-10 A:Doc Savage 900.00
3-11 P(c),V: Thade 900.00
3-12 V: Thade 900.00
4-1 Red Cross Appeal on (c) . . . 800.00
4-2 V:The Brain of Nippon 800.00
4-3 Little Men in Space 800.00
4-4 ...Mystifies Berlin 800.00
4-5 ...Brings Terror to Tokio 800.00
4-6 V:The Tarantula 800.00
4-7 Crypt of the Seven Skulls . . . 850.00
4-8 V:the Indigo Mob 800.00
4-9 Ghost Guarded Treasure
of the Haunted Glen 800.00
4-10 V:The Hydra 800.00
4-11 V:The Seven Sinners 800.00
4-12 Club Curio 1,000.00
5-1 A:Flatty Foote 1,000.00
5-2 Bells of Doom 1,000.00
5-3 The Circle of Death 1,000.00
5-4 The Empty Safe Riddle . . . 1,000.00
5-5 The Mighty Master Nomad . 1,200.00
5-6 ...Fights Piracy Among
the Golden Isles 750.00
5-7 V:The Talon 750.00
5-8 V:The Talon 750.00
5-9 V:The Talon 750.00
5-10 V:The Crime Master 750.00
5-11 The Clutch of the Talon 750.00
5-12 Most Dangerous Criminal . . 750.00
6-1 Double Z 600.00
6-2 Riddle of Prof.Mentalo 600.00
6-3 V:Judge Lawless 600.00
6-4 V:Dr. Zenith 600.00
6-5 . . . . 600.00
6-6 ...Invades the
Crucible of Death 600.00
6-7 Four Panel (c) 600.00
6-8 Crime Among the Aztecs . . . 600.00
6-9 I:Shadow Jr. 650.00
6-10 Devil's Passage 600.00
6-11 The Black Pagoda 600.00
6-12 BP,BP(c),Atomic Bomb
Secrets Stolen 650.00
7-1 The Yellow Band 650.00
7-2 A:Shadow Jr. 650.00
7-3 BP,BP(c),Crime Under
the Border 800.00
7-4 BP,BP(c),One Tree Island,
Atomic Bomb 900.00
7-5 A:Shadow Jr. 650.00
7-6 BP,BP(c),The Sacred Sword
of Sanjorojo 800.00
7-7 Crime K.O. 650.00
7-8 ...Raids Crime Harbor 650.00
7-9 BP,BP(c),Kilroy Was Here . . 800.00

7-10 BP,BP(c),The Riddle of
    the Flying Saucer 1,000.00
7-11 BP,BP(c),Crime
    Doesn't Pay 800.00
7-12 BP,BP(c)Back From
    the Grave. 800.00
8-1 BP,BP(c),Curse of the Cat . . 800.00
8-2 BP,BP(c),Decay,Vermin &
    Murder in the Bayou 800.00
8-3 BP,BP(c),The Spider Boy . . . 800.00
8-4 BP,BP(c),Death Rises
    Out of the Sea 800.00
8-5 BP,BP(c),Jekyll-
    Hyde Murders 800.00
8-6 Secret of Valhalla Hall . . 800.00
8-7 BP,BP(c),Shadow in Danger 800.00
8-8 BP,BP(c),...Solves a
    Twenty Year Old Crime 800.00
8-9 BP,BP(c),3-D Effect(c) 800.00
8-10 BP,BP(c),Up&Down(c) 800.00
8-11 BP,BP(c). 800.00
8-12 BP,BP(c),Arabs,Boat(c) 800.00
9-1 Airport(c) 800.00
9-2 BP,BP(c),Flying Cannon(c) . . 800.00
9-3 BP,BP(c),Shadow's Shadow . 800.00
9-4 BP,BP(c) 800.00
9-5 Death in the Stars;Aug'49 . . . 800.00

SHARP COMICS
H.C. Blackerby, Winter, 1945
1 O:Planetarian(c) 600.00
2 O:The Pioneer 500.00

SHEENA, QUEEN OF THE JUNGLE
Real Adventures (Fiction House) Spring, 1942–Winter, 1952
1 Blood Hunger 4,000.00
2 Black Orchid of Death 1,600.00
3 Harem Shackles 1,200.00
4 The Zebra Raiders 750.00
5 War of the Golden Apes 700.00
6 . . . . 625.00
7 They Claw By Night 600.00
8 The Congo Colossus 600.00
9 and 10 . . . . @550.00
11 Red Fangs of the Tree Tribe. . 550.00
12 . . . . 450.00
13 Veldt o/t Voo Doo Lions 450.00
14 The Hoo Doo Beasts of
    Mozambique 450.00
15 . . . . 450.00
16 Black Ivory 450.00
17 Great Congo Treasure Trek . . 450.00
18 Doom of the Elephant Drum . . 450.00

SHERLOCK HOLMES
Charlton Comics, 1955
1 . . . . 575.00
2 . . . . 500.00

SHIELD-WIZARD COMICS
MLJ Magazines, Summer, 1940
1 IN,EA,O:Shield 8,700.00
2 IN,O:Shield;I:Roy 4,000.00
3 IN,Roy,Child Bondage(c) . . . 2,400.00
4 IN,Shield,Roy,Wizard 2,000.00
5 IN,B:Dusty-Boy Dectective,
    Child Bondage 2,000.00
6 B:Roy the Super Boy,Child
    Bondage 1,900.00
7 Shield(c),Roy Bondage(c) . . 2,000.00
8 IN,Bondage(c) 1,900.00
9 IN,Shield/Roy(c) 1,400.00
10 IN,Shield/Roy(c). 1,400.00

Shield-Wizard Comics #1
© MLJ Magazines

11 IN,Shield/Roy(c) 1,400.00
12 IN,Shield/Roy(c). 1,400.00
13 Bondage (c);Spring'44 . . . . . 1,500.00

SHIP AHOY
Spotlight Publishers, Nov., 1944
1 LbC(c) 250.00

SHOCK DETECTIVE CASE(S)
See: CRIMINALS ON THE RUN

SHOCK ILLUSTRATED
E.C. Comics, 1955
1 Drugs 300.00
2 AW,GI,RC. 200.00
3 RC,Of Great Rarity 4,000.00

SHOCK SUSPENSTORIES
Tiny Tot Comics (E.C. Comics), Feb.–March, 1952
1 JDa,JKa,AF(c),ElectricChair. 2,000.00
2 WW,JDa,Grl,JKa,WW(c). . . . 1,500.00
3 WW,JDa,JKa,WW(c). 1,000.00
4 WW,JDa,JKa,WW(c). 1,000.00
5 WW,JDa,JKa,WW(c),
    Hanging 1,200.00
6 WW,AF,JKa,WW(c),
    Bondage(c) 1,300.00
7 JKa,WW,GE,AF(c),Face
    Melting 1,300.00
8 JKa,AF,AW,GE,WW,AF(c) . . . 900.00
9 JKa,AF,RC,WW,AF(c) 800.00
10 JKa,WW,RC,JKa(c),Drug . . . 800.00
11 JCr,JKa,WW,RC,JCr(c) 700.00
12 AF,JKa,WW,RC,AF(c)
    Drug(c). 800.00
13 JKa,WW,FF,JKa(c). 1,000.00
14 JKa,WW,BK,WW(c) 700.00
15 JKa,WW,RC,JDa(c)
    Strangulation 600.00
16 GE,RC,JKa,GE(c),Rape 600.00
17 GE,RC,JKa,GE(c). 400.00
18 GE,RC,JKa,GE(c);Jan'55 . . . 400.00

SHOCKING MYSTERY CASES
See: THRILLING CRIME CASES

SILVER STREAK COMICS
Your Guide/New Friday/ Comic House/Newsbrook Publications/Lev Gleason, Dec., 1939
1 JCo(a&c),I&B:The Claw,Red
    Reeves Capt.Fearless;B:Mr.Mid-
    night,Wasp;A:Spiritman . . 18,000.00
2 JSm,JCo,JSm(c) 6,500.00
3 JaB(c),I&O:Silver Streak;
    B:Dickie Dean,Lance Hale,
    Ace Powers,Bill Wayne,
    Planet Patrol 5,500.00
4 JCo,JaB(c)B:Sky Wolf;
    N:Silver Streak,I:Lance
    Hale's Sidekick-Jackie 2,500.00
5 JCo(a&c),Dickie Dean
    V:The Raging Flood 3,000.00
6 JCo,JaB,JCo(a&c),O&I:Daredevil
    [Blue & Yellow Costume];
    R:The Claw 24,000.00
7 JCo,N: Daredevil 15,000.00
8 JCo(a&c) 5,500.00
9 JCo,BoW(c) 3,000.00
10 BoW,BoW(c) 2,500.00
11 DRi(c) I:Mercury 2,000.00
12 DRi(c). 1,500.00
13 JaB,JaB(c),O:Thun-Dohr . . . 1,500.00
14 JaB,JaB(c),A:Nazi
    Skull Men 1,500.00
15 JaB,DBr,JaB(c),
    B:Bingham Boys. 1,200.00
16 DBr,BoW(c),Hitler(c) 1,600.00
17 DBr,JaB(c),E:Daredevil 1,200.00
18 DBr,JaB(c),B:The Saint 1,100.00
19 DBr,EA 900.00
20 BW,BEv,EA 900.00
21 BW,BEv. 900.00
Becomes:

CRIME DOES NOT PAY
June, 1942
22(23) CBi(c),The Mad Musician
    & Tunes of Doom 4,500.00
23 CBi(c),John Dillinger-One
    Man Underworld. 2,200.00
24 CBi(c),The Mystery of the
    Indian Dick 1,600.00
25 CBi(c),Dutch Shultz-King
    of the Underworld. 1,000.00
26 CBi(c),Lucky Luciano-The
    Deadliest of Crime Rats . . . 1,000.00
27 CBi(c),Pretty Boy Floyd 1,000.00
28 CBi(c). 1,000.00
29 CBi(c),Two-Gun Crowley-The
    Bad Kid with the Itchy
    Trigger Finger 950.00
30 CBi(c),"Monk"Eastman
    V:Thompson's Mob 950.00
31 CBi(c) The Million Dollar
    Bank Robbery 600.00
32 CBi(c),Seniorita of Sin 600.00
33 CBi(c),Meat Cleaver Murder. . 500.00
34 CBi(c),Elevator Shaft 500.00
35 CBi(c),Case o/t MissingToe . . 500.00
36 CBi(c) 550.00
37 CBi(c) 550.00
38 CBi(c) 500.00
39 FGu,CBi(c) 550.00
40 FGu,CBi(c) 550.00
41 FGu,RP,CBi(c),The Cocksure
    Counterfeiter 400.00
42 FGu,RP,CBi(c) 450.00
43 FGu,RP,CBi(c)Electrocution . . 500.00
44 FGu,CBi(c),The Most Shot
    At Gangster 250.00
45 FGu,CBi(c) 250.00
46 FGu,CBi(c),ChildKidnapping(c)300.00
47 FGu,CBi(c),ElectricChair. . . . 450.00
48 FGu,CBi(c) 250.00

Crime Does Not Pay #35
© Lev Gleason

49 FGu,CBi(c) 250.00
50 FGu,CBi(c) 250.00
51 FGu,GT,CBi(c),1st Monthly. . . 225.00
52 FGu,GT,CBi(c) 225.00
53 FGu,CBi(c) 225.00
54 FGu,CBi(c) 225.00
55 FGu,CBi(c) 225.00
56 FGu,GT,CBi(c) 225.00
57 FGu,CBi(c) 225.00
58 FGu,CBi(c) 225.00
59 FGu,Cbi(c) 225.00
60 FGu,CBi(c) 225.00
61 FGu,GT,CBi(c) 225.00
62 FGu,CBi(c),Bondage(c) 225.00
63 FGu,GT,CBi(c) 200.00
64 FGu,GT,CBi(c) 200.00
65 FGu,CBi(c) 200.00
66 FGu,CBi(c) 200.00
67 FGu,GT,CBi(c) 200.00
68 FGu,CBi(c) 200.00
69 FGu,CBi(c) 200.00
70 FGu,CBi(c) 200.00
71 FGu,CBi(c) 175.00
72 FGu,CBi(c) 175.00
73 FGu,CBi(c) 175.00
74 FGu,CBi(c) 175.00
75 FGu,CBi(c) 175.00
76 FGu,CBi(c) 175.00
77 FGu,CBi(c),Electrified Safe. . . 200.00
78 FGu,CBi(c) 175.00
79 FGu 175.00
80 FGu 175.00
81 FGu 175.00
82 FGu 175.00
83 FGu 175.00
84 FGu 175.00
85 FGu 175.00
86 FGu 175.00
87 FGu,P(c),The Rock-A-Bye
  Baby Murder 175.00
88 FGu,P(c),Death Carries Torch 175.00
89 FGu,BF,BF P(c),The Escort
  Murder Case 175.00
90 FGu,BF P(c),The Alhambra
  Club Murders 175.00
91 FGu,AMc,BF P(c),Death
  Watches The Clock 175.00
92 BF,FGu,BF P(c) 175.00
93 BF,FGu,AMc,BF P(c) 175.00
94 BF,FGu,BF P(c) 175.00
95 FGu,AMc,BF P(c) 175.00
96 BF,FGu,BF P(c),The Case of
  the Movie Star's Double 175.00
97 FGu,BF P(c) 175.00
98 BF,FGu,BF P(c),Bondage(c). . 200.00
99 BF,FGu,BF P(c) 175.00

100 FGu,BF,AMc,P(c),The Case
  of the Jittery Patient 175.00
101 FGu,BF,AMc,P(c) 125.00
102 FGu,BF,AMc,BF P(c) 125.00
103 FGu,BF,AMc,BF P(c) 125.00
104 thru 110 FGu . . . . @125.00
111 thru 120 . . . . @125.00
121 thru 140 . . . . @100.00
141 JKu 100.00
142 JKu,CBi(c). 100.00
143 JKu,Comic Code. 100.00
144 I Helped Capture "Fat Face"
  George Klinerz 80.00
145 RP,Double Barrelled Menace . 80.00
146 BP,The Con & The Canary . . . 80.00
147 JKu,BP,A Long Shoe On the
  Highway;July, 1955 . . . . 175.00

SINGLE SERIES
**United Features Syndicate,
1938**
1 Captain & The Kids 1,400.00
2 Bronco Bill 750.00
3 Ella Cinders 600.00
4 Li'l Abner 1,200.00
5 Fritzi Ritz 300.00
6 Jim Hardy 600.00
7 Frankie Doodle 450.00
8 Peter Pat 450.00
9 Strange As it Seems 450.00
10 Little Mary Mixup. 450.00
11 Mr. & Mrs. Beans 450.00
12 Joe Jinx. 400.00
13 Looy Dot Dope 400.00
14 Billy Make Believe. 400.00
15 How It Began 450.00
16 Illustrated Gags. 275.00
17 Danny Dingle 325.00
18 Li'l Abner 900.00
19 Broncho Bill. 650.00
20 Tarzan 1,700.00
21 Ella Cinders 450.00
22 Iron Vic 450.00
23 Tailspin Tommy 550.00
24 Alice In Wonderland 600.00
25 Abbie an' Slats 500.00
26 Little Mary Mixup. 450.00
27 Jim Hardy 450.00
28 Ella Cinders & Abbie AN'
  Slats 1942 . . . . 450.00

SIX GUN HEROES
Fawcett Publications, 1950
1 Rocky Lane,Hopalong Cassidy 650.00
2 . . . . 350.00
3 . . . . 250.00
4 . . . . 250.00
5 Lash Larue. 250.00
6 . . . . 175.00
7 . . . . 175.00
8 . . . . 175.00
9 . . . . 175.00
10 . . . . 175.00
11 thru 23 . . . . @125.00
Charlton Comics, 1954
24 . . . . 250.00
25 . . . . 125.00
26 thru 50 . . . . @100.00
51 thru 70 . . . . @100.00

SKELETON HAND
**American Comics Group,
Sept.–Oct., 1952**
1 . . . . 650.00
2 The Were-Serpent of Karnak. . 450.00
3 Waters of Doom 325.00
4 Black Dust 325.00
5 The Rise & Fall of the
  Bogey Man 325.00
6 July–Aug., 1953 . . . . 325.00

SKIPPY'S OWN BOOK OF COMICS
M.C. Gaines, 1934
N# 6,000.00

SKY BLAZERS
**Hawley Publications,
Sept., 1940**
1 Flying Aces,Sky Pirates 900.00
2 Nov., 1940 . . . . 600.00

SKYMAN
Columbia Comics Group, 1941
1 OW,OW(c),O:Skyman,Face . 1,900.00
2 OW,OW(c),Yankee Doodle . . . 900.00
3 OW,OW(c) 550.00
4 OW,OW(c),Statue of
  Liberty(c) 1948 . . . . 550.00

SKY PILOT
**Ziff-Davis Publishing Co.,
1950**
10 NS, P(c),Lumber Pirates. 200.00
11 NS, P(c),The 2,00 Foot Drop;
  April–May, 1951. . . . . 175.00

SKY ROCKET
**Home Guide Publ.
(Harry 'A' Chesler), 1944**
1 Alias the Dragon,Skyrocket . . . 400.00

SKY SHERIFF
**D.S. Publishing,
Summer, 1948**
1 I:Breeze Lawson & the Prowl
  Plane Patrol 150.00

SLAM-BANG COMICS
**Fawcett Publications,
Jan., 1940**
1 B:Diamond Jack,Mark Swift,
  Lee Granger,Jungle King . . 4,000.00
2 F:Jim Dolan Two-Fisted
  Crime Buster 1,800.00
3 A: Eric the Talking Lion 3,000.00
4 F: Hurricane Hansen-Sea
  Adventurer 1,500.00
5 . . . . 1,500.00
6 I: Zoro the Mystery Man;
  Bondage(c) 1,500.00
7 Bondage(c);Sept., 1940 . . . . 1,500.00

Slam-Bang Comics #1
© Fawcett Publications

All comics prices listed are for *Near Mint* condition.

SLAPSTICK COMICS
Comic Magazine Distrib., Inc., 1945
N# Humorous Parody 350.00

SLASH-D DOUBLECROSS
St. John Publishing Co., 1950
N# 300.00

SLAVE GIRL COMICS
Avon Periodicals, Feb., 1949
1 EL 1,500.00
2 EL 1,000.00

SLICK CHICK COMICS
Leader Enterprises, Inc., 1947
1 Teen-Aged Humor 150.00
2 Teen-Aged Humor 100.00
3 1947 . . . . 100.00

SLUGGER
Lev Gleason Publications, 1956
1 CBi(c) 75.00

SMASH COMICS
**Comics Magazine, Inc.
(Quality Comics Group),
Aug., 1939**
1 WE,O&B:Hugh Hazard, Bozo
  the Robot,Black X, Invisible
  Justice: B:Wings Wendall,
  Chic Carter 6,000.00
2 WE,A:Lone Star Rider 2,000.00
3 WE,B:Captain Cook, John
  Law 1,100.00
4 WE,PGv,B:Flash Fulton 1,000.00
5 WE,PGv,Bozo Robot 1,000.00
6 WE,PGv,GFx,Black X(c) 1,000.00
7 WE,PGv,GFx,Wings
  Wendell(c) 900.00
8 WE,PGv,GFx,Bozo Robot 900.00
9 WE,PGv,GFx,Black X(c) 900.00
10 WE,PGv,GFx,Bozo Robot(c) . 900.00
11 WE,PGv,GFx,BP,Black X(c) . . 900.00
12 WE,PGv,GFx,BP,Bozo(c) 900.00
13 WE,PGv,GFx,AB,BP,B:Mango,
  Purple Trio,BlackX(c). 900.00
14 BP,LF,AB,PGv,I:The Ray . . . 4,500.00
15 BP,LF,AB,PGv,The Ram(c) . 2,000.00
16 BP,LF,AB,PGv,Bozo(c). 1,900.00
17 BP,LF,AB,PGv,JCo,
  The Ram(c) 1,900.00

Smash Comics#21
© Quality Comics Group

18 BP,LF,AB,JCo,PGv,
  B&O:Midnight 2,500.00
19 BP,LF,AB,JCo,PGv,Bozo(c) . 1,400.00
20 BP,LF,AB,JCo,PGv,
  The Ram(c) 1,400.00
21 BP,LF,AB,JCo,PGv. 1,400.00
22 BP,LF,AB,JCo,PGv,
  B:The Jester 1,400.00
23 BP,AB,JCo,RC,PGv,
  The Ram(c) 1,300.00
24 BP,AB,JCo,RC,PGv,A:Sword,
  E:ChicCarter,
  N:WingsWendall 1,300.00
25 AB,JCo,RC,PGv,O:Wildfire . 1,300.00
26 AB,JCo,RC,PGv,Bozo(c) . . . 1,200.00
27 AB,JCo,RC,PGv,
  The Ram(c) 1,200.00
28 AB,JCo,RC,PGv,
  1st Midnight (c) 1,200.00
29 AB,JCo,Rc,PGv,B:
  Midnight(c) 1,200.00
30 AB,JCo,PGv 1,200.00
31 AB,JCo,PGv 900.00
32 AB,JCo,PGv 900.00
33 AB,JCo,PGv,O:Marksman . . 1,000.00
34 AB,JCo,PGv 900.00
35 AB,JCo,RC,PGv 900.00
36 AB,JCo,RC,PGv,
  E:Midnight(c) 900.00
37 AB,JCo,RC,PGv,Doc Wacky
  Becomes Fastest Human
  on Earth 900.00
38 JCo,RC,PGv,B:YankeeEagle 1,500.00
39 PGv,B:Midnight(c) 900.00
40 PGv,E:Ray 900.00
41 PGv 800.00
42 PGv,B:Lady Luck 2,200.00
43 PGv,A:Lady Luck 800.00
44 PGv 700.00
45 PGv,E:Midnight(c) 700.00
46 RC,Twelve Hours to Live . . . 700.00
47 Wanted Midnight,
  Dead or Alive 700.00
48 Midnight Meets the
  Menace from Mars 700.00
49 PGv,FGu,Mass of Muscle . . . 700.00
50 I:Hyram the Hermit 700.00
51 A:Wild Bill Hiccup 500.00
52 PGv,FGu,Did Ancient Rome Fall,
  or was it Pushed? 500.00
53 Is ThereHonorAmongThieves. 400.00
54 A:Smear-Faced Schmaltz . . . 450.00
55 Never Trouble Trouble until
  Trouble Troubles You 450.00
56 The Laughing Killer 450.00
57 A Dummy that Turns Into
  A Curse 450.00
58 . . . . 450.00
59 A Corpse that Comes Alive . . 450.00
60 The Swooner & the Trush 450.00
61 . . . . 400.00
62 V:The Lorelet 400.00
63 PGv 450.00
64 PGv,In Search of King Zoris . . 450.00
65 PGv,V:Cyanide Cindy 450.00
66 Under Circle's Spell 450.00
67 A Living Clue 450.00
68 JCo,Atomic Dice 450.00
69 JCo,V:Sir Nuts 450.00
70 . . . . 450.00
71 . . . . 300.00
72 JCo,Angela,the Beautiful
  Bovine 300.00
73 . . . . 300.00
74 . . . . 300.00
75 The Revolution 300.00
76 Bowl Over Crime. 300.00
77 Who is Lilli Dilli? 300.00
78 JCo,Win Over Crime. 300.00
79 V:The Men From Mars 300.00
80 JCo,V:Big Hearted Bosco . . . 300.00
81 V:Willie the Kid 300.00

82 V:Woodland Boy 300.00
83 JCo,Quizmaster 300.00
84 A Date With Father Time. . . . 300.00
85 JCo,A Singing Swindle 300.00
Becomes:

LADY LUCK
**Comics Magazine
(Quality Comics), 1949**
86 (1) 1,200.00
87 thru 90 . . . . @900.00

SMASH HITS SPORTS COMICS
**Essankay Publications,
Jan., 1949**
1 LbC,LbC(c) 400.00

SMILEY BURNETTE WESTERN
**Fawcett Publications,
March, 1950**
1 Ph(c),B:Red Eagle 650.00
2 Ph(c) 500.00
3 Ph(c) 500.00
4 Ph(c) 500.00

SMILIN' JACK
Dell Publishing Co., 1948
1 . . . . 175.00
2 thru 8 . . . . @100.00

SMITTY
Dell Publishing Co., 1948
1 . . . . 150.00
2 . . . . 125.00
3 thru 7 . . . . @100.00

SNAP
See: SCOOP COMICS

SNAPPY COMICS
**Cima Publications,
(Prize), 1945**
1 A:Animale 450.00

SNIFFY THE PUP
**Animated Cartoons
(Standard Comics), Nov., 1949**
5 FF,Funny Animal 125.00
6 thru 9 Funny Animal . . . . . . @100.00
10 thru 17 Funny Animal . . . . . @100.00
18 Sept., 1953 . . . . 100.00

SOLDIER AND MARINE COMICS
Charlton Comics, 1954
11 . . . . 125.00
12 thru 15 . . . . @100.00
Vol 2 #9 . . . . 100.00

SOLDIER COMICS
Fawcett Publications, Jan., 1952
1 Fighting Yanks on Flaming
  Battlefronts 200.00
2 Blazing Battles Exploding
  with Combat 150.00
3 . . . . 125.00
4 A Blow for Freedom 125.00
5 Only The Dead Are Free 125.00
6 Blood & Guts 125.00
7 The Phantom Sub 125.00
8 More Plasma! 135.00
9 Red Artillery 125.00
10 . . . . 125.00
11 Sept., 1953 . . . . 125.00

SOLDIERS OF FORTUNE
**Creston Publications
(American Comics Group),
Feb.–March, 1952**
1 OW(c),B:Ace Carter,
  Crossbones, Lance Larson . 300.00
2 OW(c) 175.00
3 OW(c) 125.00
4 . . . . 125.00
5 OW(c) 125.00
6 OW(c),OW,Bondage(c) 200.00
7 . . . . 125.00
8 OW thru 10. . . . . @125.00
11 OW,Format Change to War . . 100.00
12 . . . . 100.00
13 OW,Feb.–March, 1953 . . . . . . 100.00

SON OF SINBAD
**St. John Publishing Co.,
Feb., 1950**
1 JKu,JKu(c),The Curse of the
  Caliph's Dancer 500.00

Space Action #1
© *Ace Magazines*

SPACE ACTION
**Junior Books
(Ace Magazines),
June, 1952–Oct., 1952**
1 Invaders from a Lost Galaxy 1,200.00
2 The Silicon Monster from
  Galaxy X 900.00
3 Attack on Ishtar 900.00

SPACE ADVENTURES
**Capitol Stories/
Charlton Comics,
July, 1952**
1 AFa&LM(c) 800.00
2 . . . . 350.00
3 DG(c) 300.00
4 DG(c) 300.00
5 StC(c) 300.00
6 StC(c),Two Worlds 250.00
7 DG(c),Transformation 275.00
8 DG(c),All For Love 250.00
9 DG(c) 250.00
10 SD,SD(c). 800.00
11 SD,JoS 850.00
12 SD(c) 1,000.00
13 A:Blue Beetle 250.00
14 A:Blue Beetle 250.00
15 Ph(c) of Rocky Jones 250.00
16 BKa,A:Rocky Jones 300.00
17 A:Rocky Jones 225.00

18 A:Rocky Jones 225.00
19 . . . . 200.00
20 First Trip to the Moon 350.00
21 War at Sea 200.00
22 Does Not Exist
23 SD,Space Trip to the Moon. . . 300.00
24 . . . . 250.00
25 Brontosaurus. 250.00
26 SD,Flying Saucers 300.00
27 SD,Flying Saucers 300.00
28 Moon Trap. 200.00
29 Captive From Space 200.00
30 Peril in the Sky 200.00
31 SD,SD(c),Enchanted Planet . 250.00
32 SD,SD(c),Last Ship
  from Earth 250.00
33 Galactic Scourge,
  I&O:Captain Atom 700.00
34 SD,SD(c),A:Captain Atom. . . 275.00
35 thru 40 SD,SD(c),
  A:Captain Atom . . . . @275.00

SPACE BUSTERS
**Ziff-Davis Publishing Co.,
Spring, 1952**
1 BK,NS(c),Ph(c),Charge of
  the Battle Women 1,200.00
2 EK,BK,MA,NS(c),
  Bondage(c),Ph(c) 900.00
3 Autumn, 1952 . . . . 750.00

SPACE COMICS
See: FUNNY TUNES

SPACE DETECTIVE
**Avon Periodicals,
July, 1951**
1 WW,WW(c),Opium Smugglers
  of Venus 1,700.00
2 WW,WW(c),Batwomen of
  Mercury 1,200.00
3 EK(c),SeaNymphs ofNeptune 600.00
4 EK,Flame Women of Vulcan,
  Bondage(c) 650.00

SPACE MOUSE
**Avon Periodicals,
April, 1953**
1 Funny Animal 150.00
2 Funny Animal. 125.00
3 thru 5 Funny Animal . . . . . @100.00

SPACE PATROL
**Approved Comics
(Ziff-Davis),
Summer, 1952**
1 BK,NS,Ph(c), The Lady of
  Diamonds 1,400.00
2 BK,NS,Ph(c),Slave King of
  Pluto,Oct.–Nov., 1952 . . . . 1,000.00

SPACE THRILLERS
Avon Periodicals, 1954
N# Contents May Vary. 1,700.00

SPACE WESTERN
COMICS
**See: YELLOWJACKET
COMICS**

SPARKLE COMICS
**United Features
Syndicate, 1948**
1 Nancy, Li'l Abner 250.00
2 . . . . 150.00
3 . . . . 125.00
4 . . . . 125.00
5 . . . . 125.00

6 . . . . 125.00
7 . . . . 125.00
8 thru 10 . . . . @125.00
11 thru 20 . . . . @100.00
21 thru 32 . . . . @100.00
33 Peanuts. 125.00

SPARKLER COMICS
**United Features Syndicate,
July, 1940**
1 Jim Handy 500.00
2 Frankie Doodle,Aug., 1940 . . . 400.00

SPARKLER COMICS
**United Features Syndicate,
July, 1941**
1 BHg,O:Sparkman;B:Tarzan,Captain
  & the Kids,Ella Cinders,Danny
  Dingle,Dynamite Dunn, Nancy,
  Abbie an' Slats, Frankie
  Doodle,Broncho Bill 4,000.00
2 BHg, The Case of Poisoned
  Fruit 1,500.00
3 BHg 1,200.00
4 BHg,Case of Sparkman &
  the Firefly 1,200.00
5 BHg,Sparkman,Natch 1,000.00
6 BHg,Case of the Bronze
  Bees 1,000.00
7 BHg,Case of the Green
  Raiders 1,000.00
8 BHg,V:River Fiddler 1,000.00
9 BHg,N:Sparkman 1,000.00
10 BHg,B:Hap Hopper,
  Sparkman's ID revealed . . . 1,000.00
11 BHg,V:Japanese 700.00
12 BHg,Another N:Sparkman . . . 700.00
13 BHg,Hap Hopper Rides
  For Freedom 700.00
14 BHg,BHg(c),Tarzan
  V:Yellow Killer. 1,000.00
15 BHg 600.00
16 BHg,Sparkman V:Japanese . . 600.00
17 BHg,Nancy(c) 600.00
18 BHg,Sparkman in Crete 600.00
19 BHg,I&B:Race Riley,
  Commandos 600.00
20 BHg,Nancy(c) 600.00
21 BHg,Tarzan(c). 750.00
22 BHg,Nancy(c) 500.00
23 BHg,Capt&Kids(c). 500.00
24 BHg,Nancy(c) 500.00
25 BHg,BHg(c),Tarzan(c). 750.00
26 BHg,Capt&Kids(c). 500.00
27 BHg,Nancy(c) 500.00

Sparkler Comics #39
© *United Features Syndicate*

GOLDEN AGE

GOLDEN AGE

28 BHg,BHg(c),Tarzan(c)	750.00
29 BHg,Capt&Kids(c)	500.00
30 BHg,Nancy(c)	500.00
31 BHg,BHg(c),Tarzan(c)	750.00
32 BHg,Capt&Kids(c)	300.00
33 BHg,Nancy(c)	300.00
34 BHg,BHg(c),Tarzan(c)	750.00
35 BHg,Capt&Kids(c)	300.00
36 BHg,Nancy(c)	300.00
37 BHg,BHg(c),Tarzan(c)	750.00
38 BHg,Capt&Kids(c)	350.00
39 BHg,BHg(c),Tarzan(c)	800.00
40 BHg,Nancy(c)	350.00
41 BHg,Capt&Kids(c)	200.00
42 BHg,BHg,Tarzan(c)	500.00
43 BHg,Nancy(c)	200.00
44 BHg,Tarzan(c)	500.00
45 BHg,Capt&Kids(c)	200.00
46 BHg,Nancy(c)	200.00
47 BHg,Tarzan(c)	500.00
48 BHg,Nancy(c)	200.00
49 BHg,Capt&Kids(c)	200.00
50 BHg,BHg(c),Tarzan(c)	500.00
51 BHg,Capt&Kids(c)	200.00
52 BHg,Nancy(c)	200.00
53 BHg,BHg(c),Tarzan(c)	500.00
54 BHg,Capt&Kids(c)	200.00
55 BHg,Nancy(c)	200.00
56 BHg,Capt&Kids(c)	200.00
57 BHg,F:Li'l Abner	200.00
58 BHg,A:Fearless Fosdick	350.00
59 BHg,B:Li'l Abner	350.00
60 BHg,Nancy(c)	200.00
61 BHg,Capt&Kids(c)	200.00
62 BHg,Li'L Abner(c)	200.00
63 BHg,Capt&Kids(c)	200.00
64 BHg,Valentines (c)	200.00
65 BHg,Nancy(c)	200.00
66 BHg,Capt&Kids(c)	200.00
67 BHg,Nancy(c)	200.00
68 BHg,	200.00
69 BHg,B:Nancy (c)	200.00
70 BHg	200.00
71 thru 80 BHg	@150.00
81 BHg,E:Nancy(c)	150.00
82 BHg	150.00
83 BHg,Tarzan(c)	200.00
84 BHg	150.00
85 BHg,E:Li'l Abner	150.00
86 BHg	150.00
87 BHg,Nancy(c)	150.00
88 thru 96 BHg	@150.00
97 BHg,O:Lady Ruggles	350.00
98 BHg	100.00
99 BHg,Nancy(c)	100.00

100 BHg,Nancy(c)	125.00
101 thru 107 BHg	@100.00
108 & 109 BHg,ATh	150.00
110 BHg	100.00
111 BHg	100.00
112 BHg	100.00
113 BHg,ATh	125.00
114 thru 120 BHg	@100.00

Becomes:

NANCY AND SLUGGO
St. John/Dell Publ. 1955

121	150.00
122 thru 130	@125.00
131 thru 145	@100.00

SPARKLING STARS
Holyoke Publishing Co., June, 1944

1 B:Hell's Angels,Ali Baba,FBI, Boxie Weaver,Petey & Pop	300.00
2 Speed Spaulding	250.00
3 FBI	150.00
4 thru 12	@150.00
13 O&I:Jungo, The Man-Beast	175.00
14	150.00
15	150.00
16	150.00
17 thru 19	@150.00
20 I:Fangs the Wolfboy	150.00
21 thru 28	@150.00
29 Bondage(c)	300.00
30 thru 32	@100.00
33 March, 1948	100.00

SPARKMAN
Frances M. McQueeny, 1944

1 O:Sparkman	450.00

SPARKY WATTS
Columbia Comics Group, 1942

1 A:Skyman,Hitler(c)	1,200.00
2	500.00
3	350.00
4 O:Skyman	350.00
5 A:Skyman	300.00
6	200.00
7	200.00
8	250.00
9	200.00
10 1949	200.00

[STEVE SAUNDERS] SPECIAL AGENT
Parents Magazine/ Commended Comics, Dec., 1947

1 J. Edgar Hoover, Ph(c)	200.00
2	150.00
3 thru 7	@125.00
8 Sept., 1949	125.00

SPECIAL COMICS
See: LAUGH COMICS

SPECIAL EDITION COMICS
Fawcett Publications, Aug., 1940

1 CCB,CCB(c),F:Captain Marvel	18,000.00

A SPECTACULAR FEATURE MAGAZINE
Fox Features Syndicate, 1950

1 (11) Samson and Delilah	350.00

Becomes:

SPECTACULAR FEATURES MAGAZINE
Fox Features Syndicate, 1950

2 (12) Iwo Jima	360.00
3 True Crime Cases	275.00

SPECTACULAR STORIES MAGAZINE
Hero Books (Fox Features Syndicate), 1950

3 Actual Crime Cases	500.00
4 Sherlock Holmes	325.00

SPEED COMICS
Brookwood/Speed Publ. Harvey Publications, Oct., 1939

1 BP,B&O:Shock Gibson,B:Spike Marlin,Biff Bannon	5,500.00
2 BP,B:Shock Gibson(c)	1,700.00
3 BP,GT	1,200.00
4 BP	1,000.00
5 BP,DBr	1,000.00
6 BP,GT	800.00
7 GT,JKu,Bondage, B:Mars Mason	800.00
8 JKu	850.00
9 JKu	850.00
10 JKu,E:Shock Gibson(c)	850.00
11 JKu,E:Mars Mason	850.00
12 B:The Wasp	900.00
13 I:Captain Freedom;B:Girls Commandos,Pat Parker	900.00
14 AAv,Pocket sized-100pgs.	1,200.00
15 AAv,Pocket size	1,200.00
16 JKu,AAv,Pocket size	1,200.00
17 O:Black Cat	1,300.00
18 B:Capt.Freedom,Bondage(c)	1,100.00
19 S&K	1,000.00
20 S&K	1,000.00
21 JKu(c),Hitler & Tojo	1,200.00
22 JKu(c).	1,000.00
23 JKu(c),O:Girl Commandos.	1,000.00
24 Hitler,Tojo & Mussilini(c).	1,100.00
25	1,000.00
26 GT,Flag (c),Black Cat.	1,000.00
27 GT,Black Cat	1,000.00
28 E:Capt Freedom	1,000.00
29 Case o/t Black Marketeers	1,000.00
30 POW Death Chambers	1,000.00
31 ASh(c),Nazi Thrashing(c)..	1,200.00
32 ASh(c)	1,100.00
33 ASh(c)	1,100.00

Sparkler Comics #120
© United Features Syndicate

Speed Comics #19
© Harvey Publications

34 ASh(c) 1,100.00
35 ASh(c),BlackCat'sDeathTrap 1,150.00
36 ASh(c) 1,100.00
37 RP(c) 1,100.00
38 RP(c),War Bond Plea with Iwo
 Jima flag allusion(c) 1,100.00
39 RP(c),B:Capt Freedom(c) . . 1,200.00
40 RP(c) 1,200.00
41 RP(c) 1,200.00
42 JKu,RP(c). 1,200.00
43 JKu,AAv,E:Capt Freedom(c) 1,250.00
44 BP,JKu,Four Kids on a raft,
 Jan.–Feb., 1947 . . . . 1,300.00

SPEED SMITH
THE HOT ROD KING
Ziff-Davis Publishing Co., Spring, 1952
1 INS,Ph(c),A:Roscoe
 the Rascal 300.00

SPIRIT, THE
Will Eisner
(Weekly Coverless Comic Book), June, 1940
WE,O:SPirit 1,300.00
 6/9/40 WE 700.00
 6/16/40 WE,Black Queen . . . 400.00
 6/23/40 WE,Mr Mystic 250.00
 6/30/40 WE 250.00
 7/7/40 WE,Black Queen 250.00
 7/14/40 WE 200.00
 7/21/40 WE 200.00
 7/28/40 WE 200.00
 8/4/40 WE 200.00
 7/7/40-11/24/40,WE 165.00
 11/10/40 WE,Black Queen . . 150.00
 12/1/40 WE,Ellen
 Spanking(c) 225.00
 12/8/40-12/29/40 . . . . 125.00
1941 WE Each 125.00
 3/16 WE I:Silk Satin 200.00
 6/15 WE I Twilight 125.00
 6/22 WE Hitler 125.00
1942 WE Each. 100.00
 2-1 Duchess 125.00
 2-15 . . . . 100.00
 2-23 . . . . 150.00
1943 WE Each,LF,WE scripts . . 100.00
1944 JCo,LF 100.00
1945 LF Each, ... 100.00
1946 WE Each. 100.00
 1/13 WE,O:The Spirit. 125.00
 1/20 WE,Satin 125.00
 3/17 WE,I:Nylon 125.00
 4/21 WE,I:Mr.Carrion. 150.00
 7/7 WE,I:Dulcet Tone&Skinny 125.00
 10/6 WE,I:F:Gell 100.00
1947 WE Each 100.00
 7/13.,WE,Hansel &Gretel . . . 125.00
 7/20,WE,A:Bomb. 125.00
 9/28,WE,Flying Saucers 100.00
 10/5,WE, Cinderella 125.00
 12/7,WE,I:Power Puff 125.00
1948 WE Each 125.00
 1/11,WE,Sparrow Fallon 125.00
 1/25,WE,I:Last A Net 125.00
 3/14,WE,A:Kretuama. 125.00
 4/4,WE,A:Wildrice 125.00
 7/25,The Thing 100.00
 8/22,Poe Tale,Horror 125.00
 9/18, A:Lorelei 100.00
 11/7,WE,A:Plaster of Paris . . 100.00
1949 WE Each 100.00
 1/23 WE,I:Thorne 100.00
 8/21 WE,I:Monica Veto 100.00
 9/25 WE,A;Ice 100.00
 12/4 WE,I:Flaxen. 100.00
1950 WE Each 100.00
 1/8 WE,I:Sand Saref 150.00
 2/10, Horror Issue 100.00

Spirit Insert 8-8-43
© *Will Eisner*

1951 WE(Last WE 8/12/51) . . @100.00
 Non-Eisners. . . . . @25.00
1952 Non-Eisners. . . . . @25.00
 7/27 WW,Denny Colt. 500.00
 8/3 WW,Moon 500.00
 8/10 WW,Moon 500.00
 8/17 WW,WE,Heart 400.00
 8/24 WW,Rescue. 400.00
 8/31 WW,Last Man 400.00
 9/7 WW,Man Moon 550.00
 9/14 WE. 150.00
 9/21 WE Space 350.00
 9/28 WE Moon. 400.00
 10/5 WE Last Story 250.00

SPIRIT, THE
Quality Comics Group/ Vital Publ., 1944
N# Wanted Dead or Alive! . . . 1,300.00
N# ...in Crime Doesn't Pay,LF(c) 700.00
N# ...In Murder Runs Wild 600.00
4 ...Flirts with Death 500.00
5 ...Wanted Dead or Alive. 400.00
6 ...Gives You Triple Value 350.00
7 ...Rocks the Underworld 350.00
8 ...Cracks Down on Crime,LF(c) 350.00
9 ...Throws Fear Into the
 Heart of Crime 350.00
10 ...Stalks Crime,RC(c) 350.00
11 ...America's Greatest
 Crime Buster 325.00
12 WE(c),...The Famous Outlaw
 Who Smashes Crime 450.00
13 WE(c),...and Ebony Cleans Out
 the Underworld;Bondage(c) . 450.00
14 WE(c) 450.00
15 WE(c),Bank Robber at Large . 450.00
16 WE(c),The Case of the
 Uncanny Cat 450.00
17 WE(c),The Organ Grinding
 Bank Robber 550.00
18 WE,WE(c),'The Bucket
 of Blood 550.00
19 WE,WE(c),'The Man Who
 Murdered the Spirit' 550.00
20 WE,WE(c),'The Vortex' 550.00
21 WE,WE(c),'P'Gell of Paris' . . 550.00
22 WE(c),TheOctopus,Aug.1950. 900.00

SPIRIT, THE
Fiction House Magazines, 1952
1 Curse of Claymore Castle . . 600.00
2 WE,WE(c),Who Says Crime
 Doesn't Pay 550.00
3 WE/JGr(c),League of Lions . . 425.00

4 WE,WE&JGr(c),Last Prowl of
 Mr. Mephisto;Bondage (c) . . 450.00
5 WE,WE(c),Ph(c)1954 . . . . 500.00

SPIRITMAN
Will Eisner, 1944
1 3 Spirit Sections from
 1944 Bound Together 275.00
2 LF, 2 Spirit Sections
 from 1944 Bound Together . . 225.00

SPITFIRE COMICS
Harvey Publ., Aug., 1941
1 MKd(c),100-pgs.,Pocket-size 1,200.00
2 100-pgs.,Pocket-size,
 Oct., 1941 . . . . 1,100.00

SPITFIRE
Malverne Herald/ Elliot Publ. Co., 1944
132 & 133. . . . . @350.00

SPOOK COMICS
Baily Publications, 1946
1 A:Mr. Lucifer 400.00

SPOOK DETECTIVE CASES
And: SPOOK
SUSPENSE MYSTERY
See: CRIMINALS ON THE RUN

SPOOKY
Harvey Publications, Nov., 1955
1 Funny Apparition 800.00
2 same 500.00
3 . . . . 400.00
4 . . . . 400.00
5 . . . . 400.00
6 thru 10 same . . . . @300.00
11 thru 20 same . . . . @200.00
21 thru 30 same . . . . @100.00
31 thru 40 same . . . . @100.00
41 thru 70 same . . . . @75.00
71 thru 90 same . . . . @60.00

SPOOKY MYSTERIES
Your Guide Publishing Co., 1946
1 Rib-Tickling Horror 250.00

SPORT COMICS
See: TRUE SPORT PICTURE STORIES

SPORTS STARS
Sport Stars, Inc. (Parents' Magazine), 1946
1 Johnny Weissmuller. 600.00
2 Baseball Greats 350.00
3 . . . . 300.00
4 . . . . 300.00

SPORTS THRILLS
See: DICK COLE

SPOTLIGHT COMICS
Harry 'A' Chesler Jr. Publications, Nov., 1944
1 GT,GT(c),B:Veiled Avenger,
 Black Dwarf,Barry Kuda . . 1,200.00
2 . . . . 800.00
3 1945,Eye Injury 900.00

All comics prices listed are for *Near Mint* condition.

SPUNKY

**Standard Comics,
April, 1949**

1 FF,Adventures of a Junior
   Cowboy 125.00
2 FF 100.00
3 . . . . 75.00
4 . . . . 75.00
5 . . . . 75.00
6 . . . . 75.00
7 Nov., 1951 . . . . 75.00

SPY AND
COUNTERSPY

**Best Syndicated Features
(American Comics Group),
Aug.–Sept., 1949**

1 I&O:Jonathan Kent 350.00
2 . . . . 200.00
Becomes:

SPY-HUNTERS

Dec., 1949–Jan., 1950

3 Jonathan Kent 300.00
4 J.Kent. 150.00
5 J.Kent. 150.00
6 J.Kent. 150.00
7 OW(c),J.Kent. 150.00
8 OW(c),J.Kent. 150.00
9 OW(c),J.Kent. 150.00
10 OW(c),J.Kent. 150.00
11 . . . . 125.00
12 OW(c),MD. 125.00
13 and 14 . . . . @125.00
15 OW(c) 125.00
16 AW 175.00
17 . . . . 100.00
18 War (c) 100.00
19 and 20 . . . . @100.00
21 B:War Content 100.00
22 . . . . 100.00
23 Torture. 250.00
24 'BlackmailBrigade',July,1953 . 100.00

SPY SMASHER

**Fawcett Publications,
Autumn, 1941**

1 B;Spy Smasher 6,000.00
2 MRa(c) 2,600.00
3 Bondage (c) 2,000.00
4 1st ISb art 1,800.00
5 MRa,Mt. Rushmore(c) 1,800.00

Spy Smasher #8
© *Fawcett Publications*

6 MRa(a&c),V:The Sharks
   of Steel 1,500.00
7 MRa 1,500.00
8 AB 1,200.00
9 AB,Hitler,Tojo, Mussolini(c) . . 1,600.00
10 AB,Did Spy Smasher
    Kill Hitler? 1,500.00
11 AB,Feb., 1943 . . . . 1,200.00

STAMPS COMICS

**Youthful Magazines/Stamp
Comics, Inc.,
Oct., 1951**

1 HcK,Birth of Liberty 350.00
2 HcK,RP,Battle of White Plains 200.00
3 HcK,DW,RP,Iwo Jima 175.00
4 HcK,DW,RP 175.00
5 HcK,Von Hindenberg disaster . 200.00
6 HcK,The Immortal Chaplains . . 175.00
7 HcK,RKr,RP,B&O:Railroad . . . 250.00
Becomes:

THRILLING ADVENTURES
IN STAMPS

Jan., 1953

8 HcK, 100 Pgs. 1,000.00

STAR COMICS

**Comic Magazines/Ultem
Publ./Chesler
Centaur Publications,
Feb., 1937**

1 B:Dan Hastings 3,000.00
2 . . . . 1,300.00
3 African Blacks (c) 1,500.00
4 WMc(c),A:Little Nemo. 1,200.00
5 WMc(c),A:Little Nemo 1,200.00
6 CBi(c),FGu 1,200.00
7 FGu 1,000.00
8 BoW,BoW(c),FGu,A:Little
   Nemo,Horror 1,100.00
9 FGu,CBi(c) 1,000.00
10 FGu,CBi(c),BoW,A:Impyk . . 1,400.00
11 FGu,BoW,JCo 1,100.00
12 FGu,BoW,B:Riders of the
    Golden West 800.00
13 FGu,BoW 800.00
14 FGu,GFx(c). 800.00
15 CBu,B:The Last Pirate 800.00
16 CBu,B:Phantom Rider 900.00
2-1 CBu,B:Phantom Rider(c) . . 850.00
2-2 CBu,A:Diana Deane 750.00
2-3 GFx(c),CBu,Hollywood . . . 700.00
2-4 CBu 700.00
2-5 CBu 700.00
2-6 CBu,E:Phantom Rider 700.00
2-7 CBu,Jungle Queen,
    Aug., 1939 . . . . 700.00

STARLET O'HARA IN
HOLLYWOOD

**Standard Comics,
Dec., 1948**

1 The Terrific Tee-Age Comic . . 350.00
2 Her Romantic Adventures in
   Movie land 200.00
3 and 4, Sept., 1949 . . . . . . @150.00

STAR RANGER

**Comics Magazines/Ultem/
Centaur Publ.,
Feb., 1937**

1 FGu,I:Western Comic 3,000.00
2 . . . . 1,300.00
3 FGu 1,200.00
4 . . . . 1,200.00
5 . . . . 1,200.00
6 FGu 1,100.00
7 FGu 900.00

8 GFx,FGu,PGv,BoW 900.00
9 GFx,FGu,PGv,BoW 900.00
10 JCo,GFx,FGu,PGv,BoW . . . 1,300.00
11 . . . . 850.00
12 JCo(a&c),FGu,PGv. 850.00
Becomes:

COWBOY COMICS

July, 1938

13 FGu,PGv 1,000.00
14 FGu,PGv 900.00
Becomes:

STAR RANGER
FUNNIES

Oct., 1938

15 WE,PGv 1,400.00
2-1(16) JCo(a&c) 1,100.00
2-2(17) PGv,JCo,A:Night Hawk 1,000.00
2-3(18) JCo,FGu 900.00
2-4(19) A:Kit Carson 900.00
2-5(20) Oct., 1939 . . . . 900.00

STARS AND STRIPES
COMICS

**Comic Corp of America
(Centaur Publications),
May, 1941**

2 PGv,PGv(c),'Called to Colors',
   The Shark,The Voice 3,300.00
3 PGv,PGv(c),O:Dr.Synthe . . . 1,900.00
4 PGv,PGv(c),I:The Stars
   & Stripes 1,600.00
5 . . . . 1,200.00
6(5), Dec., 1941 . . . . 1,200.00

STAR STUDDED

Cambridge House, 1945

N# 25 cents (c) price;128 pgs.;
   32 F:stories 500.00
N# The Cadet,Hoot Gibson,
   Blue Beetle 350.00

STARTLING COMICS

**Better Publ./Nedor Publ.,
June, 1940**

1 WE,LF,B&O:Captain Future,
   Mystico, Wonder Man;
   B:Masked Rider 5,000.00
2 Captain Future(c) 2,000.00
3 same 1,500.00
4 same 1,400.00
5 same 1,300.00
6 same 1,300.00
7 same 1,300.00
8 ASh(c),Captain Future 1,300.00
9 Bondage(c) 1,300.00
10 O:Fighting Yank 7,000.00
11 Fighting Yank(c) 2,000.00
12 Hitler,Mussolini,Tojo (c) 1,800.00
13 JBi 1,500.00
14 JBi 1,500.00
15 Fighting Yank (c) 1,500.00
16 Bondage(c),O:Four
    Comrades. 1,500.00
17 Fighting Yank (c),
    E:Masked Rider 1,100.00
18 JBi,B&O:Pyroman 2,000.00
19 Pyroman(c) 1,000.00
20 Pyroman(c),B:Oracle 1,000.00
21 HcK,ASh(c)Bondage(c)
    O:Ape 1,200.00
22 HcK,ASh(c),Fighting Yank(c) 1,000.00
23 HcK,BEv,ASh(c),Pyroman(c) 1,000.00
24 HcK,BEv,ASh(c),Fighting
    Yank(c) 1,000.00
25 HcK,BEv,ASh(c),Pyroman(c) 1,000.00
26 BEv,ASh(c),Fighting Yank(c) 1,000.00
27 BEv,ASh(c),Pyroman(c). . . . 1,000.00
28 BEv,ASh(c),Fighting Yank(c) 1,000.00

Startling Comics #47
© Nedor Publications

29 BEv,ASh(c),Pyroman(c). . . . 1,000.00
30 ASh(c),Fighting Yank(c) 1,000.00
31 ASh(c),Pyroman(c). 1,000.00
32 ASh(c),Fighting Yank(c). . . . 1,000.00
33 ASh(c),Pyroman(c). 1,000.00
34 ASh(c),Fighting Yank(c),
　　O:Scarab 1,200.00
35 ASh(c),Pyroman(c). 1,000.00
36 ASh(c),Fighting Yank(c) 800.00
37 ASh(c),Bondage (c) 800.00
38 ASh(c),Bondage(c). 1,000.00
39 ASh(c),Pyroman(c). 1,000.00
40 ASh(c),E:Captain Future . . 1,000.00
41 ASh(c),Pyroman(c). 1,000.00
42 ASh(c),Fighting Yank(c) 1,000.00
43 ASh(c),Pyroman(c),
　　E:Pyroman 1,000.00
44 Grl(c),Lance Lewis(c) 1,200.00
45 Grl(c),I:Tygra 1,200.00
46 Grl,Grl(c),Bondage(c) 1,200.00
47 ASh(c),Bondage(c). 2,000.00
48 ASh(c),Lance Lewis(c). 1,000.00
49 ASh(c),Bondage(c),
　　E:Fighting Yank 7,500.00
50 ASh(c),Lance Lewis(c),
　　Sea Eagle. 1,100.00
51 ASh(c),Sea Eagle 1,100.00
52 ASh(c) 1,100.00
53 ASh(c),Sept., 1948. . . . . . . 1,100.00

STARTLING TERROR TALES
Star Publications, May, 1952
10 WW,LbC(c),The Story Starts 1,100.00
11 LbC(c),The Ghost Spider
　　of Death 2,200.00
12 LbC(c),White Hand Horror . . . 400.00
13 JyD,LbC(c),Love From
　　a Gorgor 425.00
14 LbC(c),Trapped by the
　　Color of Blood 400.00
4 LbC(c),Crime at the Carnival . 350.00
5 LbC(c),The Gruesome
　　Demon of Terror 350.00
6 LbC(c),Footprints of Death . . . 350.00
7 LbC(c),The Case of the
　　Strange Murder 350.00
8 RP,LbC(c),Phantom Brigade . . 350.00
9 LbC(c),The Forbidden Tomb . . 350.00
10 LbC(c),The Horrible Entity . . . 450.00
11 RP,LbC(c),The Law Will
　　Win, July, 1954 . . . . 350.00

STEVE CANYON COMICS
Harvey Publications, Feb., 1948–Dec., 1948
1 MC,BP,O:Steve Canyon. 275.00
2 MC,BP 175.00
3 MC,BP,Canyon's Crew 150.00
4 MC,BP,Chase of Death 150.00
5 MC,BP,A:Happy Easter 150.00
6 MC,BP,A:Madame Lynx. 165.00

STEVE ROPER
Famous Funnies, April, 1948
1 Reprints newspaper strips . . . 150.00
2 . . . . 75.00
3 . . . . 60.00
4 . . . . 60.00
5 Dec., 1948 . . . . 60.00

STORY OF HARRY S. TRUMAN, THE
Democratic National Committee, 1948
N# Giveaway-The Life of Our
　　33rd President 200.00

STRAIGHT ARROW
Magazine Enterprises, Feb.–March, 1950
1 OW,B:Straight Arrow & his
　　Horse Fury 1,000.00
2 BP,B&O:Red Hawk 400.00
3 BP,FF(c) 600.00
4 BP,Cave(c). 350.00
5 BP,StraightArrow'sGreatLeap . 350.00
6 BP 300.00
7 BP,The Railroad Invades
　　Comanche Country 300.00
8 BP 300.00
9 BP 300.00
10 BP 300.00
11 BP,The Valley of Time 350.00
12 thru 19 BP . . . . @350.00
20 BP,Straight Arrow's
　　Great War Shield. 300.00
21 BP,O:Fury 350.00
22 BP,FF(c) 375.00
23 BP 200.00
24 BP,The Dragons of Doom. . . . 250.00
25 BP, Secret Cave 200.00
26 BP,Red Hawk vs. Vikings 200.00
27 BP 150.00
28 BP,Red Hawk 150.00
29 thru 35 BP . . . . @150.00
36 BP Red Hawk, Drug 100.00
37 BP 100.00
38 BP 100.00
39 BP,The Canyon Beasts. 125.00
40 BP,Secret of the
　　Spanish Specters. 125.00
41 BP 100.00
42 BP 100.00
43 BP,I:Blaze 125.00
44 BP 100.00
45 thru 53 BP . . . . @100.00
54 BP,March, 1956 . . . . 100.00

STRANGE CONFESSIONS
Approved Publications (Ziff-Davis), Spring, 1952
1 EK,Ph(c) 750.00
2 Ph(c) 450.00
3 EK,Ph(c),Girls Reformatory . . . 450.00
4 Ph(c),Girls Reformatory. 450.00

STRANGE FANTASY
Farrell Publications/ Ajax Comics, Aug., 1952
(2)1 Jungle Princess. 700.00
2 Drug & Horror 500.00
3 The Dancing Ghost 500.00
4 Demon in the Dungeon,
　　A:Rocketman. 500.00
5 Visiting Corpse 350.00
6 . . . . 350.00
7 A:Madam Satan 450.00
8 A:Black Cat 350.00
9 S&K,SD, Black Cat 400.00
10 . . . . 350.00
11 Fearful Things Can Happen
　　in a Lonely Place. 400.00
12 The Undying Fiend 350.00
13 Terror in the Attic,
　　Bondage(c) 450.00
14 Monster in the Building,
　　Oct.–Nov., 1954. . . . . 350.00

STRANGE JOURNEY
America's Best, 1957
1 . . . . 250.00
2 Flying Saucer. 175.00
3 . . . . 150.00
4 . . . . 150.00

Strange Mysteries #19
© Superior Publications

STRANGE MYSTERIES
Superior Publ./Dynamic Publ., 1951
1 LKa,Horror 1,000.00
2 . . . . 500.00
3 thru 5 . . . . @425.00
6 . . . . 350.00
7 . . . . 350.00
8 . . . . 350.00
9 Bondage,3-D type 450.00
10 . . . . 300.00
11 thru 18 . . . . @250.00
19 MB 325.00
20 reprint #1, new (c). 250.00
21 reprint 250.00

UNKNOWN WORLD
Fawcett Publications, June, 1952
1 NS(c),Ph(c),Will You Venture
　　to Meet the Unknown 700.00
Becomes:

STRANGE STORIES FROM ANOTHER WORLD
Aug., 1952
2 NS(c),Ph(c),Will You?
  Dare You 750.00
3 NS(c),Ph(c),The Dark Mirror . . 500.00
4 NS(c),Ph(c),Monsters of
  the Mind 500.00
5 NS(c),Ph(c),Dance of the
  Doomed, Feb., 1953 . . . . . . 500.00

STRANGE SUSPENSE STORIES
Fawcett Publications, June, 1952
1 BP,MSy,MBi 1,500.00
2 MBi,GE 900.00
3 MBi,GE(c) 700.00
4 BP 700.00
5 MBi(c),Voodoo(c) 700.00
6 BEv 400.00
7 BEv 400.00
8 AW 400.00
9 . . . . 400.00
10 . . . . 500.00
11 thru 13 . . . . @300.00
14 . . . . 350.00
15 AW,BEv(c) 350.00

Charlton Comics
16 . . . . 350.00
17 . . . . 300.00
18 SD,SD(c) 500.00
19 SD,SD(c) 700.00
20 SD,SD(c) 500.00
21 . . . . 250.00
22 SD(c) 450.00
Becomes:

THIS IS SUSPENSE!
Feb., 1955
23 WW 400.00
24 . . . . 150.00
25 . . . . 100.00
26 . . . . 100.00
Becomes:

STRANGE SUSPENSE STORIES
Oct., 1955
27 . . . . 200.00
28 . . . . 175.00
29 . . . . 175.00

Strange Suspense Stories #22
© Charlton Comics

---

30 . . . . 175.00
31 SD(c) 300.00
32 SD 300.00
33 SD 300.00
34 SD,SD(c) 650.00
35 SD 300.00
36 SD,SD(c) 300.00
37 SD 325.00
38 . . . . 300.00
39 SD 350.00
40 SD 300.00
41 SD 300.00
42 thru 44 . . . . @125.00
45 SD 250.00
46 . . . . 125.00
47 SD 250.00
48 SD 250.00
49 . . . . 125.00
50 SD 250.00
51 SD 150.00
52 SD 150.00
53 SD 150.00
54 thru 60 . . . . @125.00
61 thru 74 . . . . @100.00
75 Capt. Atom 250.00
76 Capt. Atom 100.00
77 Capt. Atom 100.00

STRANGE SUSPENSE STORIES
See: LAWBREAKERS

STRANGE TERRORS
St. John Publishing Co., June, 1952
1 The Ghost of Castle
  Karloff, Bondage(c) 900.00
2 Unshackled Flight into Nowhere 600.00
3 JKu,Ph(c),The Ghost Who
  Ruled Crazy Heights 750.00
4 JKu,Ph(c),Terror from
  the Tombs 900.00
5 JKu,Ph(c),No Escaping
  the Pool of Death 750.00
6 LC,PMo,Bondage(c),Giant. . . . 900.00
7 JKu,JKu(c),Cat's Death,Giant 1,000.00

STRANGE WORLD OF YOUR DREAMS
Prize Group, Aug., 1952
1 S&K(c),What Do They Mean–
  Messages Rec'd in Sleep . 1,000.00
2 MMe,S&K(c),Why did I Dream
  That I Was Being Married
  to a Man without a Face? . . . 700.00
3 S&K(c) 500.00
4 MMe,S&K(c),The Story of
  a Man Who Dreamed a Murder
  that Happened 450.00

STRANGE WORLDS
Avon Periodicals, Nov., 1950
1 JKu,Spider God of Akka . . . 2,000.00
2 WW,Dara of the Vikings . . . 1,800.00
3 AW&FF,EK(c),WW,JO. 3,200.00
4 JO,WW,WW(c),The
  Enchanted Dagger 2,000.00
5 WW,WW(c),JO,Bondage(c);
  Sirens of Space 1,500.00
6 EK,WW(c),JO,SC,
  Maid o/t Mist 1,000.00
7 EK, Sabotage on
  Space Station 1 . . . . 700.00
8 JKu,EK,The Metal Murderer . . 700.00
9 The Radium Monsters 700.00
18 JKu 600.00
19 Astounding Super
  Science Fantasies 600.00

---

20 WW(c),Fighting War Stories . . 200.00
21 EK(c) 150.00
22 EK(c),Sept.–Oct., 1955 . . . . . 150.00

STRICTLY PRIVATE
Eastern Color Printing, July, 1942
1 You're in the Army Now-Humor . 275.00
2 F:Peter Plink, 1942 . . . . 250.00

STUNTMAN COMICS
Harvey Publications, April–May, 1946
1 S&K,O:Stuntman 1,900.00
2 S&K,New Champ of Split-
  Second Action 1,100.00
3 S&K,Digest sized,Mail Order
  Only, B&W interior,
  Oct.–Nov., 1946 . . . . 1,300.00

SUGAR BOWL COMICS
Famous Funnies, May, 1948
1 ATh,ATh(c),The Newest in
  Teen Age! 175.00
2 . . . . 100.00
3 ATh 125.00
4 . . . . 75.00
5 Jan., 1949 . . . . 75.00

SUN FUN KOMIKS
Sun Publications, 1939
1 F:Spineless Sam the
  Sweetheart 700.00

SUNNY, AMERICA'S SWEETHEART
Fox Features Syndicate, Dec., 1947
11 AF,AF(c) 1,800.00
12 AF,AF(c) 1,400.00
13 AF,AF(c) 1,400.00
14 AF,AF(c) 1,400.00

SUNSET CARSON
Charlton Comics, Feb., 1951–Aug., 1951
1 Painted, Ph(c);Wyoming
  Mail 1,200.00
2 Kit Carson-Pioneer 900.00
3 . . . . 700.00
4 Panhandle Trouble. 700.00

SUPER BOOK OF COMICS
Western Publishing Co., 1943
N# Dick Tracy 500.00
1 Dick Tracy, Smuggling 500.00
1a Smilin' Jack 250.00
2 Smitty,Magic Morro 250.00
3 Capt. Midnight 500.00
3a Moon Mullins 200.00
4 Red Ryder,Magic Morro 300.00
4a Smitty 200.00
5 Don Winslow, Magic Morro 300.00
5a Don Winslow,Stratosphere Jim 300.00
5a Terry & the Pirates 350.00
6 Don Winslow 300.00
6a King of the Royal Mounties . . 350.00
7 Little Orphan Annie 250.00
7a Dick Tracy 500.00
8 Dick Tracy 400.00
8a Dan Dunn 200.00
9 Terry & the Pirates 400.00
10 Red Ryder, Magic Morro 200.00

Super-Book of Comics 1st Series #7
© Western Publishing

SUPER-BOOK OF COMICS

Western Publishing Co., 1944

1 Dick Tracy (Omar)	300.00
1 Dick Tracy (Hancock)	200.00
2 Bugs Bunny (Omar)	200.00
2 Bugs Bunny (Hancock)	200.00
3 Terry & the Pirates (Omar)	250.00
3 Terry & the Pirates (Hancock)	250.00
4 Andy Panda (Omar)	100.00
4 Andy Panda (Hancock)	100.00
5 Smokey Stover (Omar)	100.00
5 Smokey Stover (Hancock)	100.00
6 Porky Pig (Omar)	200.00
6 Porky Pig (Hancock)	175.00
7 Smilin' Jack (Omar)	100.00
7 Smilin' Jack (Hancock)	100.00
8 Oswald the Rabbit (Omar)	100.00
8 Oswald the Rabbit (Hancock)	75.00
9 Alley Oop (Omar)	200.00
9 Alley Oop (Hancock)	175.00
10 Elmer Fudd (Omar)	100.00
10 Elmer Fudd (Hancock)	75.00
11 Little Orphan Annie (Omar)	100.00
11 Little Orphan Amnie (Hancock)	100.00
12 Woody Woodpecker (Omar)	125.00
12 WoodyWoodpecker(Hancock)	100.00
13 Dick Tracy (Omar)	200.00
13 Dick Tracy (Hancock)	175.00
14 Bugs Bunny (Omar)	200.00
14 Bugs Bunny (Hanock)	150.00
15 Andy Panda (Omar)	100.00
15 Andy Panda (Hancock)	75.00
16 Terry & the Pirates (Omar)	200.00
16 Terry & the Pirates (Hancock)	175.00
17 Smokey Stover (Omar)	100.00
17 Smokey Stover (Hancock)	75.00
18 Porky Pig (Omar)	150.00
18 Smokey Stover (Hancock)	75.00
19 Smilin' Jack (Omar)	75.00
N# Smilin' Jack (Omar)	50.00
20 Oswald the Rabbit (Omar)	50.00
N# Oswald the Rabbit (Hancock)	50.00
21 Gasoline Alley (Omar)	50.00
N# Gasoline Alley (Hancock)	50.00
22 Elmer Fudd (Omar)	75.00
N# Elmer Fudd (Hancock)	60.00
23 Little Orphan Annie (Omar)	75.00
N# Little Orphan Annie (Hancock)	60.00
24 Woody Woodpecker (Omar)	50.00
N# WoodyWoodpecker(Hancock)	50.00
25 Dick Tracy (Omar)	100.00
N# Dick Tracy (Hancock)	75.00
26 Bugs Bunny (Omar)	60.00
N# Bugs Bunny (Hancock)	50.00

27 Andy Panda (Omar)	50.00
27 Andy Panda (Hancock)	40.00
28 Terry & the Pirates (Omar)	50.00
28 Terry & the Pirates (Hancock)	100.00
29 Smokey Stover (Omar)	50.00
29 Smokey Stover (Hancock)	50.00
30 Porky Pig (Omar)	60.00
30 Porky Pig (Hancock)	50.00
N# Bugs Bunny (Hancock)	50.00

SUPER CIRCUS

Cross Publishing Co., Jan., 1951

1 Partial Ph(c)	200.00
2	125.00
3	100.00
4	100.00
5 1951	100.00

SUPER COMICS

Dell Publishing Co., May, 1938

1 Dick Tracy,Terry and the Pirates,Smilin'Jack,Smokey Stover,Orphan Annie,etc.	3,600.00
2	1,400.00
3	1,200.00
4	1,100.00
5 Gumps(c)	1,000.00
6	750.00
7 Smokey Stover(c)	750.00
8 Dick Tracy(c)	750.00
9	750.00
10 Dick Tracy(c)	750.00
11	600.00
12	600.00
13	600.00
14	600.00
15	600.00
16 Terry & the Pirates	500.00
17 Dick Tracy(c)	500.00
18	500.00
19	500.00
20 Smilin'Jack(c)	525.00
21 B:Magic Morro	400.00
22 Magic Morro(c)	450.00
23 all star(c)	400.00
24 Dick Tracy(c)	450.00
25 Magic Morro(c)	400.00
26	400.00
27 Magic Morro(c)	400.00
28 Jim Ellis(c)	450.00
29 Smilin'Jack(c)	400.00
30 inc.The Sea Hawk.	450.00
31 Dick Tracy(c)	400.00
32 Smilin' Jack(c)	425.00
33 Jim Ellis(c)	400.00
34 Magic Morro(c)	400.00
35 thru 40 Dick Tracy(c)	@400.00
41 B:Lightning Jim	350.00
42 thru 50 Dick Tracy(c)	@350.00
51 thru 54 Dick Tracy(c)	@250.00
55	250.00
56	250.00
57 Dick Tracy(c)	250.00
58 Smitty(c)	250.00
59	250.00
60 Dick Tracy(c)	275.00
61	235.00
62 Flag(c)	235.00
63 Dick Tracy(c)	235.00
64 Smitty(c)	225.00
65 Dick Tracy(c)	235.00
66 Dick Tracy(c)	235.00
67 Christmas(c)	235.00
68 Dick Tracy(c)	235.00
69 Dick Tracy(c)	235.00
70 Dick Tracy(c)	235.00
71 Dick Tracy(c)	200.00
72 Dick Tracy(c)	200.00
73 Smitty(c)	200.00

Super Comics #54
© Dell Publishing Co.

74 War Bond(c)	200.00
75 Dick Tracy(c)	200.00
76 Dick Tracy(c)	200.00
77 Dick Tracy(c)	200.00
78 Smitty(c)	150.00
79 Dick Tracy(c)	150.00
80 Smitty(c)	150.00
81 Dick Tracy(c)	150.00
82 Dick Tracy(c)	150.00
83 Smitty(c)	135.00
84 Dick Tracy(c)	150.00
85 Smitty(c)	135.00
86 All on cover	150.00
87 All on cover	150.00
88 Dick Tracy(c)	150.00
89 Smitty(c)	135.00
90 Dick Tracy(c)	150.00
91 Smitty(c)	135.00
92 Dick Tracy(c)	150.00
93 Dick Tracy(c)	150.00
94 Dick Tracy(c)	150.00
95 thru 99	@135.00
100	150.00
101 thru 115	@150.00
116 Smokey Stover(c)	100.00
117 Gasoline Alley(c)	100.00
118 Smokey Stover(c)	100.00
119 Terry and the Pirates(c)	110.00
120	100.00
121	100.00

SUPER-DOOPER COMICS

Able Manufacturing Co., 1946

1 A:Gangbuster	300.00
2	200.00
3 & 4	@150.00
5 A:Captain Freedom,Shock Gibson	150.00
6 & 7 same	@150.00
8 A:Shock Gibson, 1946	150.00

SUPER DUCK COMICS

MLJ Magazines/Close-Up (Archie Publ.), Autumn, 1944

1 O:Super Duck, Hitler	850.00
2	350.00
3 I:Mr. Monster	250.00
4 & 5	@225.00
6 thru 10	@200.00
11 thru 20	@150.00
21 thru 40	@125.00
41 thru 60	@100.00
61 thru 94	@75.00

GOLDEN AGE

SUPER FUNNIES
Superior Comics Publishers, March, 1954
1 Dopey Duck 500.00
2 Out of the Booby-Hatch 200.00
Becomes:

SUPER WESTERN FUNNIES
1954
3 F:Phantom Ranger 100.00
4 F:Phantom Ranger,Sept., 1954 100.00

SUPERIOR STORIES
Nesbit Publishing Co., 1955
1 Wells-The Invisible Man 300.00
2 Ingrahams-Pirate of the Gulf . . 125.00
3 Clark-Wreck of Grosvenor 125.00
4 O'Henry-Texas Rangers 125.00

SUPER MAGICIAN COMICS
Street & Smith Publ., May, 1941
1 B:The MysteriousBlackstone 1,000.00
2 V:Wild Tribes of Africa 550.00
3 V:Oriental Wizard 550.00
4 V:Quetzal Wizard,O:Transo . . 500.00
5 A:The Moylan Sisters 500.00
6 JaB,JaB(c),The Eddie
　Cantor story 500.00
7 In the House of Skulls 525.00
8 A:Abbott & Costello 550.00
9 V:Duneen the Man-Ape 525.00
10 V:Pirates o/t Sargasso Sea. . . 525.00
11 JaB(c),V:Fire Wizards 525.00
12 V:Baal 525.00
2-1 A:The Shadow 550.00
2-2 Temple of the 10,000 Idols . . 250.00
2-3 Optical Illusion on (c)-
　turn Jap into Monkey 250.00
2-4 V:Cannibal Killers 250.00
2-5 V:The Pygmies of Lemuriai . 250.00
2-6 V:Pirates & Indians 250.00
2-7 Can Blackstone Catch the
　Cannonball? 250.00
2-8 V:Marabout,B:Red Dragon . . 250.00
2-9 . . . . 250.00
2-10 Pearl Dives Swallowed By
　Sea Demons 250.00
2-11 Blackstone Invades
　Pelican Islands 250.00
2-12 V:Bubbles of Death 250.00
3-1 . . . . 275.00

Super Magician Vol. 8 #8
© Street & Smith

3-2 Bondage(c),Midsummers
　Eve 250.00
3-3 The Enchanted Garden 250.00
3-4 Fabulous Aztec Treasure . . . 250.00
3-5 A:Buffalo Bill 250.00
3-6 Magic Tricks to Mystify 250.00
3-7 V:Guy Fawkes 250.00
3-8 V:Hindu Spook Maker 250.00
3-9 . . . . 250.00
3-10 V:The Water Wizards 250.00
3-11 V:The Green Goliath 250.00
3-12 Lady in White 250.00
4-1 Cannibal of Crime 225.00
4-2 The Devil's Castle 225.00
4-3 V:Demons of Golden River . 225.00
4-4 V:Dr. Zero 225.00
4-5 Bondage(c) 225.00
4-6 V:A Terror Gang 225.00
4-7 . . . . 225.00
4-8 Mystery of the
　Disappearing Horse 225.00
4-9 A Floating Light? 225.00
4-10 Levitation 225.00
4-11 Lost, Strange Land
　of Shangri 225.00
4-12 I:Nigel Elliman 225.00
5-1 V:Voodoo Wizards of the
　Everglades,Bondage (c) 225.00
5-2 Treasure of the Florida
　Keys; Bondage (c) 225.00
5-3 Elliman Battles Triple Crime . 225.00
5-4 Can A Human Being Really
　Become Invisible 225.00
5-5 Mystery of the Twin Pools . . 225.00
5-6 A:Houdini 225.00
5-7 F:Red Dragon 500.00
5-8 F:Red Dragon,
　Feb.–March, 1947 . . . . 500.00

SUPERMOUSE
Standard Comics/Pines, Dec., 1948
1 FF,(fa) 400.00
2 FF,(fa) 200.00
3 FF,(fa) 150.00
4 FF,(fa) 150.00
5 FF,(fa) 150.00
6 FF,(fa) 150.00
7 thru 10 (fa) . . . . @125.00
11 thru 20 (fa) . . . . @125.00
21 thru 44 (fa) . . . . @100.00
45 (fa),Autumn, 1958 . . . . 100.00

SUPER-MYSTERY COMICS
Periodical House (Ace Magazines), July, 1940
1 B:Magno,Vulcan,Q-13,Flint
　of the Mountes 5,000.00
2 Bondage (c) 1,500.00
3 JaB,B:Black Spider 1,200.00
4 O:Davy;A:Captain Gallant . . . 850.00
5 JaB,JM(c),I&B:The Clown . . . 850.00
6 JM,JM(c),V:The Clown 750.00
2-1 JM,JM(c),O:Buckskin,
　Bondage(c) 750.00
2-2 JM,JM(c),V:The Clown 650.00
2-3 JM,JM(c),V:The Clown 650.00
2-4 JM,JM(c),V:The Nazis 650.00
2-5 JM,JM(c),Bondage(c) 650.00
2-6 JM,JM(c),Bondage(c),
　'Foreign Correspondent' 650.00
3-1 B:Black Ace 650.00
3-2 A:Mr, Risk, Bondage(c) 650.00
3-3 HK,HK(c),I:Lancer;B:Dr.
　Nemesis, The Sword 750.00
3-4 HK 1,000.00
3-5 HK,LbC,A:Mr. Risk 700.00
3-6 HK,LbC,A:Paul Revere Jr. . . 700.00
4-1 HK,LbC,A:Twin Must Die . . . 650.00
4-2 A:Mr. Risk 450.00

Super-Mystery Comics Vol. 5 #4
© Ace Magazines

4-3 Mango out to Kill Davey! . . . 450.00
4-4 Danger Laughs at Mr. Risk . . 450.00
4-5 A:Mr. Risk 450.00
4-6 RP,A:Mr. Risk 450.00
5-1 RP 450.00
5-2 RP,RP(c),The Riddle of the
　Swamp-Land Spirit 450.00
5-3 RP,RP(c),The Case of the
　Whispering Death 450.00
5-4 RP,RP(c) 450.00
5-5 RP,Harry the Hack 450.00
5-6 . . . . 450.00
6-1 . . . . 350.00
6-2 RP,A:Mr. Risk 350.00
6-3 Bondage (c) 375.00
6-4 E:Mango;A:Mr. Risk 350.00
6-5 Bondage(c) 375.00
6-6 A:Mr. Risk 350.00
7-1 . . . . 350.00
7-2 KBa(c) 350.00
7-3 Bondage(c) 375.00
7-4 . . . . 350.00
7-5 . . . . 350.00
7-6 . . . . 350.00
8-1 The Riddle of the Rowboat . . 300.00
8-2 Death Meets a Train 300.00
8-3 The Man Who Couldn't Die . 300.00
8-4 RP(c) 300.00
8-5 GT,MMe,Staged for Murder . 300.00
8-6 Unlucky Seven,July, 1949 . . 300.00

ARMY AND NAVY COMICS
Street & Smith Publ., May, 1941
1 Hawaii is Calling You,Capt.
　Fury,Nick Carter. 800.00
2 Private Rock V;Hitler 500.00
3 The Fighting Fourth 500.00
4 The Fighting Irish 500.00
5 I:Super Snipe 800.00
Becomes:

SUPERSNIPE COMICS
Oct., 1942
6 A "Comic" With A Sense
　of Humor 1,600.00
7 A:Wacky, Rex King 750.00
8 Axis Powers & Satan(c),
　Hitler(c). 1,300.00
9 Hitler Voodoo Doll (c) 1,350.00
10 Lighting (c) 750.00
11 A:Little Nemo. 750.00
12 Football(c). 750.00
2-1 B:Huck Finn 1,200.00

2-2 Battles Shark 650.00
2-3 Battles Dinosaur 500.00
2-4 Baseball(c). 500.00
2-5 Battles Dinosaur 500.00
2-6 A:Pochontas. 500.00
2-7 A:Wing Woo Woo 500.00
2-8 A:Huck Finn 500.00
2-9 Dotty Loves Trouble. 500.00
2-10 Assists Farm Labor
   Shortage 500.00
2-11 Dotty & the Jelly Beans 500.00
2-12 Statue of Liberty. 500.00
3-1 Ice Skating(c). 450.00
3-2 V:Pirates(c) 450.00
3-3 Baseball(c). 450.00
3-4 Jungle(c) 450.00
3-5 Learn Piglatin. 450.00
3-6 Football Hero 450.00
3-7 Saves Girl From Grisley 450.00
3-8 Rides a Wild Horse 450.00
3-9 Powers Santa's Sleigh. 450.00
3-10 Plays Basketball 450.00
3-11 Is A Baseball Pitcher 450.00
3-12 Flies with the Birds 450.00
4-1 Catches A Whale. 300.00
4-2 Track & Field Athlete 300.00
4-3 Think Machine(c). 300.00
4-4 Alpine Skiier. 300.00
4-5 Becomes a Boxer 300.00
4-6 Race Car Driver. 300.00
4-7 Bomber(c) 300.00
4-8 Baseball Star 300.00
4-9 Football Hero 300.00
4-10 Christmas(c) 300.00
4-11 Artic Adventure. 300.00
4-12 The Ghost Remover 300.00
5-1 Aug.–Sept., 1949 . . . . 300.00

SUPER SPY
**Centaur Publications,
Oct.–Nov., 1940**
1 O:Sparkler 1,500.00
2 A:Night Hawk, Drew Ghost, Tim
   Blain, S.S. Swanson the Inner
   Circle, Duke Collins, Gentlemen
   of Misfortune 900.00

SUPER WESTERN COMICS
Youthful Magazines, Aug., 1950
1 BP,BP,(c),B;Buffalo Bill,Wyatt
   .Earp,CalamityJane,SamSlade200.00
2 . . . . 100.00
3 . . . . 100.00

Sweet Sixteen #1
© Parents' Magazine Group

4 March, 1951 . . . . 100.00

SUPER WESTERN FUNNIES
See: SUPER FUNNIES

SUPERWORLD COMICS
**Komos Publications
(Hugo Gernsback), April, 1940**
1 FP,FP(c),B:MilitaryPowers,BuzzAllen
   Smarty Artie, Alibi Alige . . 13,000.00
2 FP,FP(c),A:Mario 7,000.00
3 FP,FP(c),V:Vest Wearing
   Giant Grasshoppers 5,500.00

SURE-FIRE COMICS
See: LIGHTNING COMICS

SURPRISE ADVENTURES
See: TORMENTED

SUSPENSE COMICS
**Et Es Go Mag. Inc.
(Continental Magazines),
Dec., 1945**
1 LbC, Bondage(c),B:Grey
   Mask. 6,500.00
2 DRi,I:The Mask. 4,000.00
3 LbC,ASh(c),Bondage(c) . . . 26,000.00
4 LbC,LbC(c),Bondage(c) 3,000.00
5 LbC,LbC(c) 3,000.00
6 LbC,LbC(c),The End of
   the Road 3,000.00
7 LbC,LbC(c) 2,700.00
8 LbC,LbC(c) 6,500.00
9 LbC,LbC(c) 2,700.00
10 RP,LbC,LbC(c). 2,700.00
11 RP,LbC,EL,LbC(c),Satan(c) . 5,000.00
12 LbC,LbC(c),Dec., 1946 . . . . 2,500.00

SUSPENSE DETECTIVE
**Fawcett Publications,
June, 1952**
1 GE,MBi,MBi(c),Death Poised
   to Strike 700.00
2 GE,MSy 400.00
3 A Furtive Footstep 350.00
4 MBi,MSy,Bondage(c),A Blood
   Chilling Scream 350.00
5 MSy,MSy(c),MBi,A Hair-Trigger
   from Death, March, 1953 . . . 350.00

SUZIE COMICS
See: TOP-NOTCH COMICS

SWEENEY
**Standard Comics,
June, 1949**
4 Buzz Sawyer's Pal 125.00
5 Sept., 1949 . . . . 100.00

SWEET SIXTEEN
**Parents' Magazine Group,
Aug.–Sept., 1946**
1 Van Johnson story 300.00
2 Alan Ladd story 200.00
3 Rip Taylor. 150.00
4 Elizabeth Taylor ph(c) 300.00
5 Gregory Peck story (c). 150.00
6 Dick Haymes(c) 150.00
7 Ronald Reagan(c) & story 300.00
8 Shirley Jones(c). 125.00
9 William Holden(c). 125.00
10 James Stewart(c) 150.00
11 . . . . 125.00
12 Bob Cummings(c). 125.00
13 Robert Mitchum(c) 150.00

SWIFT ARROW
**Farrell Publications (Ajax),
Feb.–March, 1954**
1 Lone Rider's Redskin Brother   200.00
2 . . . . 125.00
3 thru 4 . . . . @100.00
5 Oct.–Nov., 1954 . . . . 100.00

(2nd Series) April, 1957
1 . . . . 100.00
2 B:Lone Rider 100.00
3 Sept., 1957 . . . . 100.00

TAFFY
**Orbit Publications/Rural Home/
Taffy Publications,
March–April, 1945**
1 LbC(c),(fa),Bondage(c) 900.00
2 LbC(c),(fa) 400.00
3 (fa) 150.00
4 (fa) 150.00
5 LbC(c),A:Van Johnson 250.00
6 A:Perry Como 150.00
7 A:Dave Clark 150.00
8 A:Glen Ford 150.00
9 A:Lon McCallister 150.00
10 A:John Hodiak. 150.00
11 A:Mickey Rooney 165.00
12 Feb., 1948. . . . . 150.00

TAILSPIN
**Spotlight Publications,
Nov., 1944**
N# LbC(c),A:Firebird. 350.00

TALES FROM THE CRYPT
See: CRIME PATROL

TALES FROM THE GREAT BOOK
Famous Funnies, 1955
1 Samson 125.00
2 Joshua 100.00
3 Joash the Boy King 100.00
4 David 100.00

TALES OF HORROR
**Toby Press/Minoan Publ. Corp,
June, 1952–Oct., 1954**
1 Demons of the Underworld . . . 600.00
2 What was the Thing in
   the Pool?,Torture. 450.00
3 The Big Snake 300.00
4 The Curse of King Kala! 300.00
5 Hand of Fate 300.00
6 The Fiend of Flame 300.00
7 Beast From The Deep 300.00
8 The Snake that Held A
   City Captive 300.00
9 It Came From the Bottom
   of the World 350.00
10 The Serpent Strikes 300.00
11 Death Flower? 350.00
12 Guaranteed to Make Your
   Hair Stand on End,Torture. . . 350.00
13 Ghost with a Torch 350.00

TALES OF JACE PEARSON
See: JACE PEARSON

TALES OF TERROR
Toby Press, 1952
1 Just A Bunch of Hokey
   Hogwash 350.00

All comics prices listed are for *Near Mint* condition.

TALES OF TERROR ANNUAL
E.C. Comics, 1951
N# AF 8,000.00
2 AF 3,500.00
3 . . . . 2,700.00

TALLY-HO COMICS
Baily Publishing Co., 1944
N# FF,A:Snowman 700.00

TARGET COMICS
Funnnies Inc./Novelty Publ./ Premium Group/Curtis Circulation Co./Star Publications, Feb., 1940
1 BEv,JCo,CBu,JSm;B,O&I:Manowar, White Streak,Bull's-Eye;B:City Editor,High Grass Twins,T-Men, Rip Rory,Fantastic Feature Films, Calling 2-R 10,000.00
2 BEv,JSm,JCo,CBu,White Streak(c) 5,000.00
3 BEv,JSm,JCo,CBu 2,800.00
4 JSm,JCo 2,800.00
5 CBu,BW,O:White Streak . . . 8,000.00
6 CBu,BW,White Streak(c) . . . 3,500.00
7 CBu,BW,BW(c),V:Planetoid Stories,Space Hawk(c) . . . 10,000.00
8 CBu,BW,White Shark(c) . . . 2,800.00
9 CBu,BW,White Shark(c) . . . 2,500.00
10 CBu,BW,JK(c),The Target(c) 3,700.00
11 BW,The Target(c) 3,000.00
12 BW,same 2,800.00
2-1 BW,CBu 2,200.00
2-2 BW,BoW(c) 2,000.00
2-3 BW,BoW(c),The Target(c). . 1,500.00
2-4 BW,B:Cadet 1,500.00
2-5 BW,BoW(c),The Target(c) . . 1,500.00
2-6 BW,The Target(c) 1,200.00
2-7 BW,The Cadet(c) 1,200.00
2-8 BW,same 1,200.00
2-9 BW,The Target(c) 1,200.00
2-10 BW,same 1,800.00
2-11 BW,The Cadet(c) 1,200.00
2-12 BW,same 1,200.00
3-1 BW,same 1,200.00
3-2 BW 1,200.00
3-3 BW,The Target(c) 1,200.00
3-4 BW,The Cadet(c) 1,200.00
3-5 BW 1,200.00
3-6 BW,War Bonds(c) 1,800.00

Target Comics Vol. 4 #18
© Star Publications

3-7 BW 1,200.00
3-8 BW,War Bonds(c) 1,800.00
3-9 BW 1,200.00
3-10 BW 1,200.00
3-11 . . . . 400.00
3-12 . . . . 400.00
4-1 JJo(c) 200.00
4-2 ERy(c) 200.00
4-3 AVi 200.00
4-4 . . . . 200.00
4-5 APl(c),Statue of Liberty(c) . . 200.00
4-6 BW 200.00
4-7 AVi 200.00
4-8,Christmas(c) 200.00
4-9 . . . . 200.00
4-10 . . . . 200.00
4-11 . . . . 200.00
4-12 . . . . 200.00
5-1 . . . . 175.00
5-2 The Target 150.00
5-3 Savings Checkers(c) 150.00
5-4 War Bonds Ph(c) 150.00
5-5 thru 5-12 . . . . @150.00
6-1 The Target(c) 150.00
6-2 . . . . 150.00
6-3 Red Cross(c) 150.00
6-4 . . . . 150.00
6-5 Savings Bonds(c) 150.00
6-6 The Target(c) 200.00
6-7 The Cadet(c) 200.00
6-8 AFa 200.00
6-9 The Target(c) 200.00
6-10 . . . . 200.00
6-11 . . . . 200.00
6-12 . . . . 200.00
7-1 . . . . 200.00
7-2 Bondage(c) 200.00
7-3 The Target(c) 150.00
7-4 DRi,The Cadet(c). 150.00
7-5 . . . . 150.00
7-6 DRi(c). 150.00
7-7 The Cadet(c) 150.00
7-8 DRi(c). 150.00
7-9 The Cadet(c) 150.00
7-10 DRi,DRi(c) 150.00
7-11 . . . . 150.00
7-12 JH(c) 150.00
8-1 . . . . 125.00
8-2 DRi,DRi(c),BK 125.00
8-3 DRi,The Cadet(c) 125.00
8-4 DRi,DRi(c) 125.00
8-5 DRi,The Cadet(c). 125.00
8-6 DRi,DRi(c) 125.00
8-7 BK,DRi,DRi(c) 125.00
8-8 DRi,The Cadet(c). 125.00
8-9 DRi,The Cadet(c) 125.00
8-10 DRi,KBa,LbC(c) 600.00
8-11 DRi,The Cadet. 125.00
8-12 DRi,The Cadet. 125.00
9-1 DRi,LbC(c). 550.00
9-2 DRi. 125.00
9-3 DRi,Bondage(c),The Cadet(c) 200.00
9-4 DRi,LbC(c). 550.00
9-5 DRi,Baseball(c) 150.00
9-6 DRi,LbC(c). 550.00
9-7 DRi. 150.00
9-8 DRi,LbC(c). 550.00
9-9 DRi,Football(c). 150.00
9-10 DRi,LbC(c). 550.00
9-11,The Cadet 150.00
9-12 LbC(c),Gems(c). 550.00
10-1,The Cadet 150.00
10-2 LbC(c) 550.00
10-3 LbC(c) 550.00
Becomes:

TARGET WESTERN ROMANCES
Star Publications, Oct.–Nov., 1949
106 LbC(c),The Beauty Scar 500.00

107 LbC(c),The Brand Upon His Heart 450.00

TARZAN
Dell Publishing Co., Jan.–Feb., 1948
1 V:White Savages of Vari. . . . 2,500.00
2 Captives of Thunder Valley. . 1,000.00
3 Dwarfs of Didona 700.00
4 The Lone Hunter 700.00
5 The Men of Greed 700.00
6 Outlaws of Pal-ul-Don 600.00
7 Valley of the Monsters 600.00
8 The White Pygmies 600.00
9 The Men of A-Lur. 600.00
10 Treasure of the Bolgani 600.00
11 The Sable Lion 500.00
12 The Price of Peace 500.00
13 B:Lex Barker photo(c). 450.00
14 Lex Barker ph(c) 450.00
15 Lex Barker ph(c) 450.00
16 Lex Barker ph(c) 400.00
17 Lex Barker ph(c) 400.00
18 Lex Barker ph(c) 400.00
19 Lex Barker ph(c) 400.00
20 Lex Barker ph(c) 400.00
21 thru 24 Lex Barker ph(c) . . . @350.00
25 Brothers of the Spear 375.00
26 thru 54 E:L.Barker ph(c) . . . @300.00
55 thru 70 . . . . @250.00
71 thru 79 . . . . @200.00
80 thru 90 B:ScottGordonPh(c) @150.00
91 thru 99 . . . . @125.00
100 . . . . 150.00
101 thru 110 E:S.GordonPh(c). @150.00
111 thru 120 . . . . @125.00
121 thru 131 . . . . @100.00

TEENA
Standard Comics, 1949
20 . . . . 100.00
21 . . . . 100.00
22 . . . . 100.00

TEEN-AGE ROMANCES
St. John Publishing Co., Jan., 1949
1 MB(c),MB. 550.00
2 MB(c),MB. 350.00
3 MB(c),MB. 350.00
4 Ph(c) 300.00
5 MB,Ph(c) 300.00
6 MB,Ph(c) 300.00
7 MB,Ph(c) 300.00
8 MB,Ph(c) 300.00

Teen-Age Romances #7
© St. John Publishing Col

9 MB,MB(c),JKu 350.00
10 thru 27 MB,MB(c),JKu . . . . @250.00
28 . . . . 100.00
29 . . . . 100.00
30 . . . . 100.00
31 thru 34 MB(c) . . . . @125.00
35 thru 42 MB(c),MB . . . . @125.00
43 MB(c),MB,Comics Code 150.00
44 MB(c),MB 150.00
45 MB(c),MB 150.00

TEEN-AGE TEMPTATIONS
**St. John Publishing Co.,
Oct., 1952**

1 MB(c),MB. 650.00
2 MB(c),MB. 250.00
3 MB(c),MB. 350.00
4 MB(c),MB. 350.00
5 MB(c),MB. 350.00
6 MB(c),MB. 350.00
7 MB(c),MB. 350.00
8 MB(c),MB,Drug 400.00
9 MB(c),MB. 350.00
Becomes:

GOING STEADY
Dec., 1954

10 MB(c),MB 275.00
11 MB(c),MB 150.00
12 MB(c),MB 150.00
13 MB(c),MB 200.00
14 MB(c),MB 250.00

TEENIE WEENIES, THE
**Ziff-Davis Publishing Co.,
1951**

10 . . . . 250.00
11 . . . . 250.00

TEEN LIFE
See: YOUNG LIFE

TEGRA, JUNGLE EMPRESS
See: ZEGRA, JUNGLE
EMPRESS

TELEVISION COMICS
**Animated Cartoons
(Standard Comics), Feb., 1950**

5 Humorous Format,I:Willie Nilly 150.00
6 . . . . 100.00
7 . . . . 100.00
8 May, 1950 . . . . 100.00

TELEVISION PUPPET SHOW
Avon Periodicals, 1950

1 F:Sparky Smith,Spotty,
Cheeta, Speedy 250.00
2 Nov., 1950 . . . . 150.00

TELL IT TO THE MARINES
Toby Press, March, 1952

1 I:Spike & Pat 250.00
2 A:Madame Cobra 150.00
3 Spike & Bat on a
Commando Raid! 125.00
4 Veil Dancing(c) 125.00
5 . . . . 125.00
6 To Paris 100.00
7 Ph(c),The Chinese Bugle 100.00
8 Ph(c),V:Communists in
South Korea 100.00
9 Ph(c) 100.00
10 . . . . 100.00
11 . . . . 100.00
12 . . . . 100.00

13 John Wayne Ph(c) 200.00
14 Ph(c) 100.00
15 Ph(c),July, 1955 . . . . 100.00

TERRIFIC COMICS
See: HORRIFIC

TERRIFIC COMICS
**Et Es Go Mag. Inc./
Continental Magazines,
Jan., 1944**

1 LbC,DRi(c),F:Kid
Terrific Drug 5,500.00
2 LcC,ASh(c),B:Boomerang,
'Comics' McCormic 3,500.00
3 LbC,LbC(c) 3,500.00
4 LbC,RP(c) 6,500.00
5 LbC,BF,ASh(c),Bondage(c) . 9,000.00
6 LbC,LbC(c),BF,Nov.,1944 . . 3,200.00

TERRIFYING TALES
**Star Publications,
Jan., 1953**

11 LbC,LbC(c),'TyrantsofTerror'. . 800.00
12 LbC,LbC(c),'Bondage(c),
'Jungle Mystery'. 700.00
13 LbC(c),Bondage(c),'The
Death-Fire,Devil Head(c). . . . 800.00
14 LbC(c),Bondage(c),'The
Weird Idol' 650.00
15 LbC(c),'The Grim Secret',
April, 1954 . . . . 650.00
Becomes:

JUNGLE THRILLS
Star Publications, Feb., 1952

16 LbC(c),'Kingdom of Unseen
Terror' 750.00
Becomes:

TERRORS OF THE JUNGLE
Star Publications, May, 1952

17 LbC(c),Bondage(c) 750.00
18 LbC(c),Strange Monsters 500.00
19 JyD,LbC(c),Bondage(c),The
Golden Ghost Gorilla. 450.00
20 JyD,LbC(c),The Creeping
Scourge 450.00
21 LbC(c),Evil Eyes of Death! . . . 500.00
4 JyD,LbC(c),Morass of Death . 500.00
5 JyD,LbC(c),Bondage(c),
Savage Train 500.00
6 JyD,LbC(c),Revolt of the
Jungle Monsters 500.00
7 JyD,LbC(c) 500.00
8 JyD,LbC(c),Death's Grim
Reflection 500.00
9 JyD,LbC(c),Doom to
Evil-Doers 500.00
10 JyD,LbC(c),Black Magic,
Sept., 1954 . . . . 500.00

TERROR ILLUSTRATED
**E.C. Comics,
Nov.–Dec., 1955**

1 JCr,GE,Grl,JO,RC(c) 300.00
2 Spring, 1956 . . . . 200.00

BOY EXPLORERS
Harvey Comics, 1946

1 S&K(c),S&K,The Cadet 1,500.00
2 S&K(c),S&K 2,000.00
Becomes:

TERRY AND THE PIRATES
Harvey Comics, April, 1947

3 S&K,MC(c),MC,Terry and
Dragon Lady 550.00
4 S&K,MC(c),MC 300.00

Terry and the Pirates #3
© Harvey Comics

5 S&K,MC(c),MC,BP,
Chop-Chop(c) 175.00
6 S&K,.MC(c),MC 175.00
7 S&K,MC(c),MC,BP 175.00
8 S&K,MC(c),MC,BP 175.00
9 S&K,MC(c),MC,BP 175.00
10 S&K,MC(c),MC,BP 175.00
11 S&K,MC(c),MC,BP,
A:Man in Black 150.00
12 S&K,MC(c),MC,BP 150.00
13 S&K,MC(c),MC,Belly Dancers 150.00
14 thru 20 S&K,MC(c),MC . . . . @125.00
21 thru 26 S&K,MC(c),MC . . . . @110.00
27 Charlton Comics 100.00
28 . . . . 100.00
Becomes:

LONG JOHN SILVER AND THE PIRATES
Charlton Comics, 1956–57

30 . . . . 125.00
31 . . . . 125.00
32 . . . . 125.00

TERRY-BEARS COMICS
**St. John Publishing Co.,
June, 1952**

1 . . . . 125.00
2 & 3 . . . . @100.00

TERRY-TOONS COMICS
**Select, Timely, Marvel,
St. Johns, 1942**

1 Paul Terry (fa) 2,600.00
2 . . . . 1,000.00
3 thru 6 . . . . @700.00
7 Hitler,Hirohito,Mussolini(c) 750.00
8 thru 20 . . . . @500.00
21 thru 37 . . . . @300.00
38 I&(c):Mighty Mouse 2,200.00
39 Mighty Mouse 700.00
40 thru 49 All Mighty Mouse . . @300.00
50 I:Heckle & Jeckle 600.00
51 thru 60 . . . . 200.00
61 thru 70 . . . . @150.00
71 thru 86 . . . . @150.00
Becomes:

PAUL TERRY'S COMICS
St. John Publishing Co.

85a Mighty Mouse, etc. 150.00
86a 100.00
87 thru 100 . . . . @100.00
101 thru 125 . . . . @100.00
Becomes:

ADVENTURES OF MIGHTY MOUSE

St. John Publ. Co., 1955
126 thru 128 . . . . @150.00

Pines, 1956
129 thru 143 . . . . @150.00

Dell Publ. Co., 1959
144 thru 155 . . . . @125.00

TEXAN, THE

St. John Publishing Co., Aug., 1948
1 GT,F:Buckskin Belle,The Gay
  Buckaroo,Mustang Jack 200.00
2 GT 125.00
3 BLb(c) 100.00
4 MB,MB(c) 200.00
5 MB,MB(c),Mystery Rustlers
  of the Rio Grande 200.00
6 MB(c),Death Valley
  Double-Cross 125.00
7 MB,MB(c),Comanche Justice
  Strikes at Midnight 200.00
8 MB,MB(c),Scalp Hunters
  Hide their Tracks 200.00
9 MB(c),Ghost Terror of
  the Blackfeet 200.00
10 MB,MB(c),Treason Rides
  the Warpath 125.00
11 MB,MB(c),Hawk Knife 225.00
12 MB 300.00
13 MB,Doublecross at Devil'sDen 200.00
14 MB,Ambush at Buffalo Trail . 200.00
15 MB,Twirling Blades Tame
  Treachery 200.00
Becomes:

FIGHTIN' TEXAN

Sept., 1952
16 GT,Wanted Dead or Alive . . . 125.00
17 LC,LC(c);Killers Trail,
  Dec., 1952 . . . . 100.00

TEX FARRELL

D.S. Publishing Co., March–April, 1948
1 Pride of the Wild West 225.00

TEX GRANGER

See: CALLING ALL BOYS

TEX RITTER WESTERN

Fawcett Publications/ Charlton Comics, Oct., 1950–May, 1959
1 Ph(c),B:Tex Ritter, his Horse
  White Flash, his dog Fury, and
  his mom Nancy 1,000.00
2 Ph(c),Vanishing Varmints 450.00
3 Ph(c),Blazing Six-Guns 350.00
4 Ph(c),The Jaws of Terror 325.00
5 Ph(c),Bullet Trail 325.00
6 Ph(c),Killer Bait 250.00
7 Ph(c),Gunsmoke Revenge . . . 225.00
8 Ph(c),Lawless Furnace Valley 225.00
9 Ph(c),The Spider's Web 225.00
10 Ph(c),The Ghost Town 225.00
11 Ph(c),Saddle Conquest 225.00
12 Ph(c),Prairie Inferno 175.00
13 Ph(c) 175.00
14 Ph(c) 175.00
15 Ph(c) 175.00
16 thru 19 Ph(c) . . . . @175.00
20 Ph(c),Stagecoach To Danger . 175.00
21 Ph(c), ... 200.00
22 Panic at Diamond B 150.00
23 A:Young Falcon 125.00
24 A:Young Falcon 125.00
25 A:Young Falcon 125.00

26 thru 38 . . . . @100.00
39 AW,AW(c) 100.00
40 thru 46 . . . . @100.00

Thing #3
© *Charlton Comics*

THING!, THE

Song Hits/Capitol Stories/ Charlton Comics, Feb., 1952
1 Horror 2,000.00
2 Crazy King(c) 1,500.00
3 Green skinned creature 1,500.00
4 AFa(c),I Was A Zombie 1,100.00
5 LM(c),Severed Head(c) 1,100.00
6 . . . . 1,100.00
7 Fingernail to Eye(c) 1,200.00
8 . . . . 1,100.00
9 Severe cruelty 1,500.00
10 Devil(c) 900.00
11 SC,Cleaver, eye injury 1,100.00
12 SD,SD(c),Neck Blood
  Sucking 1,100.00
13 SD,SD(c) 1,100.00
14 SD,SD(c) torture 1,100.00
15 SD,SD(c) 1,100.00
16 Eye Torture 600.00
17 BP,SD(c) 1,100.00
Becomes:

BLUE BEETLE

Feb., 1955
18 America's Fastest Moving
  Crusader Against Crime 275.00
19 JKa,Lightning Fast 275.00
20 JKa 350.00
21 The Invincible 250.00
Becomes:

MR. MUSCLES

March, 1956
22 World's Most Perfect Man 150.00
23 Aug., 1956 . . . . 100.00

**THIS IS SUSPENSE
See: LAWBREAKERS**

**THIS IS SUSPENSE!
See: STRANGE
SUSPENSE STORIES**

THIS IS WAR

Standard Comics, July, 1952
5 ATh,Show Them How To Die . 200.00
6 ATh,Make Him A Soldier 125.00
7 One Man For Himself 100.00

8 Miracle on Massacre Hill 100.00
9 ATh,May, 1953 . . . . 125.00

THIS MAGAZINE IS HAUNTED

Fawcett Publications Oct., 1951
1 MBi,F:Doctor Death 1,000.00
2 GE 650.00
3 MBi,Quest of the Vampire . . . 450.00
4 BP,The Blind, The Doomed
  and the Dead 450.00
5 BP,GE,The Slithering Horror
  of Skontong Swamp! 650.00
6 Secret of the Walking Dead . . 350.00
7 The Man Who Saw Too Much . 350.00
8 The House in the Web 350.00
9 The Witch of Tarlo 350.00
10 I Am Dr Death,
  Severed Head(c) 575.00
11 BP,Touch of Death 350.00
12 BP 350.00
13 BP,Severed Head(c) 500.00
14 BP,Horrors of the Damned . . . 350.00

Charlton Comics, 1954
15 DG(c) 250.00
16 SD(c) 550.00
17 SD,SD(c) 700.00
18 SD,SD(c) 600.00
19 SD(c) 550.00
20 SMz(c). 300.00
21 SD(c) 500.00
Becomes:

DANGER AND ADVENTURE

Feb., 1955
22 The Viking King,F:Ibis the
  Invincible 150.00
23 F:Nyoka the Jungle Girl
  Comics Code. 125.00
24 DG&AA(c). 100.00
25 thru 27 . . . . @100.00
Becomes:

ROBIN HOOD AND HIS MERRY MEN

April, 1956
28 . . . . 150.00
29 thru 37 . . . . @100.00
38 SD,Aug., 1958 . . . . 150.00

**THIS MAGAZINE IS HAUNTED
See: CHARLIE CHAN**

3-D ANIMAL FUN

Premier Magazines, 1953
1 Ziggy Pig, Silly Seal,etc. 500.00

CAPTAIN 3-D

Harvey Publ, 1953
1 . . . . 150.00

CHERRIOS 3D CLASSICS

Walt Disney Productions, 1954
1 . . . . 150.00

3-D CIRCUS

Fiction House, 1953
1 . . . . 500.00

3-D DARING ADVENTURES

St. John Publ, 1953
1 . . . . 400.00

3-D-ELL
Dell Publishing Co., 1953
1 Rootie Kazootie 500.00
3 Flunkey Louise. 450.00

3-D DOLLY
Harvey Publ, 1953
1 Richie Rich 1,000.00

3-D EC CLASSICS
E.C. Comics 1954
1 . . . . 1,200.00
2 Tales from the Crypt of Terror 1,200.00

3-D FELIX THE CAT
Toby Press, 1953
N# 350.00

3-D FIRST CHRISTMAS
Fiction House, 1953
1 . . . . 250.00

3-D FUNNY MOVIES
Comic Media, 1953
1 Bugsey Bear 500.00

FUNNY 3-D
Harvey Publ., 1953
1 . . . . 350.00

3-D HAWK, THE
St. John Publ, 1953
1 MB,Western 400.00

3-D HOUSE OF TERROR
St. John Publ., 1953
1 . . . . 600.00

3-D I LOVE LUCY
1 Lucy, Desi, Ricky Jr. Ph(c). . . . 600.00

3-D INDIAN WARRIORS
Star Publications, 1953
1 . . . . 250.00

(3-D Features Presents) JET PUP
Dimensions Publ., 1953
1 . . . . 500.00

3-D JUNGLE THRILLS
Star Publications, 1953
1 . . . . 350.00

3-D KATY KEENE
Archie Publications, 1953
1 . . . . 500.00

3-D LITTLE EVA
St. John Publ, 1953
1 . . . . 350.00
2 . . . . 350.00

3-D LOVE
Steriographic Publications, 1953
1 . . . . 500.00

(Three Dimension Comics) MIGHTY MOUSE
St. John Publ, 1953
1 . . . . 350.00

3-D Funny 3-D #1
© Harvey Publications

2 . . . . 350.00
3 . . . . 350.00

3-D NOODNICK
Comic Media, 1953
1 . . . . 350.00

3-D ROMANCE
Steriographic Publ., 1954
1 . . . . 500.00

(Harvey 3-D Hits) SAD SACK
Harvey Publications, 1954
1 . . . . 400.00

3-D SHEENA, JUNGLE QUEEN
Fiction House, 1953
1 . . . . 1,000.00

3-D SPACE KAT-ETS
Power Publishing, 1953
1 . . . . 350.00

3-D SUPER ANIMALS
Star Publications, 1953
1 Pidgy and the Magic Glasses . 350.00

3-D SUPER FUNNIES
Superior Comics Publ., 1953
1 Dopey Duck 350.00

3-D THREE STOOGES
St. John Publ., 1953
1 . . . . 700.00
2 . . . . 650.00

3-D TRUE 3D
Harvey Publ., 1953
1 . . . . 400.00
2 . . . . 350.00

3-D WESTERN FIGHTERS
Star Publications, 1953
1 . . . . 350.00

THREE RING COMICS
Spotlight Publishers, March, 1945
1 Funny Animal 200.00

THREE STOOGES
Jubilee Publ., Feb., 1949
1 JKu,Infinity(c) 1,700.00
2 JKu,On the Set of the
'The Gorilla Girl' 1,200.00
St. John Publishing Co.
1:JKu,'Hell Bent for
Treasure,' Sept., 1953 . . . . 1,200.00
2 JKu. 900.00
3 JKu,3D. 900.00
4 JKu,Medical Mayhem 800.00
5 JKu,Shempador-Matador
Supreme 800.00
6 JKu, ... 800.00
7 JKu,Ocotber, 1954. . . . . 800.00

THRILLING COMICS
Better Publ./Nedor/ Standard Comics, Feb., 1940
1 B&O:Doc Strange,B:Nickie
Norton 5,000.00
2 B:Rio Kid,Woman in Red
Pinocchio 2,500.00
3 B:Lone Eagle,The Ghost . . . 2,000.00
4 Dr Strange(c) 1,400.00
5 Bondage(c) 1,500.00
6 Dr Strange(c) 1,400.00
7 Dr Strange(c) 1,500.00
8 V:Pirates 1,500.00
9 ASh,Bondage(c) 1,500.00
10 V:Nazis. 1,600.00
11 ASh(c),V:Nazis 1,300.00
12 ASh(c) 1,300.00
13 ASh(c),Bondage(c). 1,400.00
14 ASh(c) 1,000.00
15 ASh(c),V:Nazis 1,000.00
16 Bondage(c) 1,400.00
17 Dr Strange(c) 1,000.00
18 Dr Strange(c) 1,400.00
19 I&O:American Crusader. . . . 1,200.00
20 Bondage(c) 1,300.00
21 American Crusader(c) 1,000.00
22 Bondage(c) 1,200.00
23 American Crusader 1,000.00
24 I:Mike in Doc Strange 1,000.00
25 DR Strange(c) 1,000.00

Thrilling Comics #09
© Standard Comics

GOLDEN AGE

26 Dr Strange(c)	1,000.00
27 Bondage(c)	1,200.00
28 Bondage(c)	1,200.00
29 E:Rio Kid;Bondage(c)	1,200.00
30 Bondage(c)	1,200.00
31 Dr Strange(c)	800.00
32 Dr Strange(c)	800.00
33 Dr Strange(c)	800.00
34 Dr Strange(c)	800.00
35 Dr Strange.	800.00
36 ASh(c),B:Commando	900.00
37 BO,ASh(c).	800.00
38 ASh(c).	800.00
39 ASh(c),E:American Crusader	800.00
40 ASh(c).	800.00
41 ASh(c),F:American Crusader, Hitler.	1,800.00
42 ASh(c).	700.00
43 ASh(c).	700.00
44 ASh(c),Hitler(c).	1,400.00
45 EK,ASh(c).	600.00
46 ASh(c).	600.00
47 ASh(c).	600.00
48 EK,ASh(c).	600.00
49 ASh(c).	600.00
50 ASh(c).	600.00
51 ASh(c).	600.00
52 ASh(c),E:Th Ghost; Peto-Bondage(c).	900.00
53 ASh(c),B:Phantom Detective	700.00
54 ASh(c),Bondage(c).	900.00
55 ASh(c),E:Lone Eagle	700.00
56 ASh(c),B:Princess Pantha	700.00
57 ASh(c).	600.00
58 ASh(c).	600.00
59 ASh(c).	600.00
60 ASh(c).	600.00
61 ASh(c),Grl,A:Lone Eagle	600.00
62 ASh(c).	600.00
63 ASh(c),GT.	600.00
64 ASh(c).	600.00
65 ASh(c),E:Commando Cubs, Phantom Detective	600.00
66 ASh(c).	600.00
67 FF,ASh(c).	650.00
68 FF,ASh(c).	650.00
69 FF,ASh(c).	650.00
70 FF,ASh(c).	650.00
71 FF,ASh(c).	650.00
72 FF,ASh(c),Sea Eagle	650.00
73 FF,ASh(c).	650.00
74 ASh(c),E:Princess Pantha; B:Buck Ranger	500.00
75 B:Western Front	250.00
76 Western.	250.00
77 ASh(c).	250.00
78 Bondage(c).	350.00
79 BK.	250.00
80 JSe,BE,April, 1951	250.00

THRILLING CRIME CASES
Star Publications, June–July, 1950

41 LbC(c),The Unknowns	400.00
42 LbC(c),The Gunmaster	325.00
43 LbC,LbC(c),The Chameleon.	350.00
44 LbC(c),Sugar Bowl Murder	350.00
45 LbC(c),Maze of Murder.	350.00
46 LbC,LbC(c),Modern Communications	325.00
47 LbC(c),The Careless Killer	325.00
48 LbC(c),Road Black	325.00
49 LbC(c),The Poisoner.	650.00

Becomes:

SHOCKING MYSTERY CASES
Sept., 1952–Oct., 1954

50 JyD,LbC(c),Dead Man's Revenge	650.00

Shocking Mystery Cases #60
© Star Publications

51 JyD,LbC(c),A Murderer's Reward	450.00
52 LbC(c),The Carnival Killer.	450.00
53 LbC(c),The Long Shot of Evil	450.00
54 LbC(c),Double-Cross of Death	450.00
55 LbC(c),Return from Death	450.00
56 LbC(c),The Chase	500.00
57 LbC(c),Thrilling Cases	400.00
58 LbC(c),Killer at Large	400.00
59 LbC(c),Relentless Huntdown	400.00
60 LbC(c),Lesson of the Law.	400.00

THRILLING TRUE STORY OF THE BASEBALL GIANTS
Fawcett Publications, 1952

N# Partial Ph(c),Famous Giants of the Past, Willie Mays	1,200.00
2 Yankees Ph(c),Joe DiMaggio, Yogi Berra,Mickey Mantle, Casey Stengel	1,000.00

THRILLS OF TOMORROW
See: TOMB OF TERROR

TICK TOCK TALES
Magazine Enterprises, Jan., 1946

1 (fa) Koko & Kola	250.00
2 (fa) Calender	200.00
3 thru 10 (fa)	@150.00
11 thru 18 (fa)	@125.00
19 (fa),Flag(c)	125.00
20 thru 22 (fa)	@125.00
23 (fa),Mugsy Mouse	125.00
24 thru 33 (fa)	@125.00
34 (fa), 1951	125.00

TIM HOLT
Magazine Enterprises, Jan.–Feb., 1949

1 thru 3 see: *A-1 Comics* #14, #17, #19	
4 FBe,Ph(c)	1,200.00
5 FBe,Ph(c).	700.00
6 FBe,Ph(c),I:Calico Kid	600.00
7 FBe,Ph(c),Man-Killer Mustang	500.00
8 FBe,Ph(c)	500.00
9 FBe,DAy(c),TerribleTenderfoot	500.00
10 FBe,DAy(c),The Devil Horse	500.00
11 FBe,DAy(c),O&I:Ghost Rider	750.00
12 FBe,DAy(c),Battle at Bullock Gap.	250.00
13 FBe,DAy(c),Ph(c)	250.00

14 FBe,DAy(c),Ph(c),The Honest Bandits	250.00
15 FBe,DAy,Ph(c)	250.00
16 FBe,DAy,Ph(c)	250.00
17 FBe,DAy,Ph(c)	750.00
18 FBe,DAy,Ph(c)	300.00
19 FBe,DAy,They Dig By Night	175.00
20 FBe,DAy,O:Red Mask.	300.00
21 FBe,DAy,FF(c)	600.00
22 FBe,DAy	175.00
23 FF,FBe,DAy.	500.00
24 FBe,DAy,FBe(c)	175.00
25 FBe,DAy,FBe(c)	350.00
26 FBe,DAy,FBe(c)	175.00
27 FBe,DAy,FBe(c),V:Straw Man.	175.00
28 FBe,DAy,FBe(c),Ph(c)	175.00
29 FBe,DAy,FBe,Ph(c),	175.00
30 FBe,DAy,FBe(c),Lady Doom & The Death Wheel	200.00
31 FBe,DAy,FBe(c)	200.00
32 FBe,DAy,FBe(c)	200.00
33 FBe,DAy,FBe(c)	200.00
34 FBe,DAy,FBe(c)	250.00
35 FBe,DAy,FBe(c)	250.00
36 FBe,DAy,FBe(c),Drugs	350.00
37 FBe,DAy,FBe(c)	250.00
38 FBe,DAy,FBe(c)	250.00
39 FBe,DAy,FBe(c),3D Effect	200.00
40 FBe,DAy,FBe(c)	200.00
41 FBe,DAy,FBe(c)	200.00

Becomes:

RED MASK
June–July, 1954

42 FBe,DAy,FBe(c),3D	300.00
43 FBe,DAy,FBe(c),3D	250.00
44 FBe,DAy,FBe(c),Death at Split Mesa,3D	250.00
45 FBe,DAy,FBe(c),V:False Red Mask	250.00
46 FBe,DAy,FBe(c)	250.00
47 FBe,DAy,FBe(c)	250.00
48 FBe,DAy,FBe(c),Comics Code	250.00
49 FBe,DAy,FBe(c)	250.00
50 FBe,DAy	250.00
51 FBe,DAy,The Magic of 'The Presto Kid'.	250.00
52 FBe,DAy,O:Presto Kid	275.00
53 FBe,DAy	200.00
54 FBe,DAy,Sept., 1957	275.00

TIM McCOY
See: ZOO FUNNIES

TIM TYLER COWBOY
Standard Comics, Nov., 1948

11	150.00
12	100.00
13 The Doll Told the Secret	100.00
14 Danger at Devil's Acres	100.00
15 Secret Treasure	100.00
16	100.00
17	100.00
18 1950	100.00

TINY TOTS COMICS
Dell Publishing Co., 1943

1 WK,fairy tales.	500.00

TINY TOTS COMICS
E.C. Comics, March, 1946

N# Your First Comic Book B:Burton Geller(c) and art	500.00
2	275.00
3 Celebrate the 4th	250.00
4 Go Back to School	275.00
5 Celebrate the Winter	250.00
6 Do Their Spring Gardening	250.00
7 On a Thrilling Ride	250.00
8 On a Summer Vacation	250.00

9 On a Plane Ride 250.00
10 Merry X-Mas Tiny Tots
   E:Burton Geller(c)and art . . . 250.00

TIP TOP COMICS
United Features, St. John, Dell, 1936

1 HF,Li'l Abner 12,000.00
2 HF 3,000.00
3 HF,Tarzan(c) 2,500.00
4 HF,Li'l Abner(c) 1,500.00
5 HF,Capt&Kids(c) 1,100.00
6 HF 1,000.00
7 HF 1,000.00
8 HF,Li'l Abner(c) 1,000.00
9 HF,Tarzan(c) 1,400.00
10 HF,Li'L Abner(c) 1,000.00
11 HF,Tarzan(c) 1,000.00
12 HF,Li'l Abner 800.00
13 HF,Tarzan(c) 1,000.00
14 HF,Li'L Abner(c) 800.00
15 HF,Capt&kids(c) 800.00
16 HF,Tarzan(c) 1,000.00
17 HF,Li'L Abner(c) 800.00
18 HF,Tarzan(c) 1,000.00
19 HF,Football(c) 750.00
20 HF,Capt&Kids(c) 750.00
21 HF,Tarzan(c) 800.00
22 HF,Li'l Abner(c) 550.00
23 HF,Capt&kids(c) 550.00
24 HF,Tarzan(c) 800.00
25 HF,Capt&Kids(c) 550.00
26 HF,Li'L Abner(c) 550.00
27 HF,Tarzan(c) 800.00
28 HF,Li'l Abner(c) 550.00
29 HF,Capt&Kids(c) 550.00
30 HF,Tarzan(c) 800.00
31 HF,Capt&Kids(c) 550.00
32 HF,Tarzan(c) 800.00
33 HF,Tarzan(c) 800.00
34 HF,Capt&Kids(c) 800.00
35 HF 500.00
36 HF,HK,Tarzan(c) 800.00
37 HF,Tarzan 800.00
38 HF 500.00
39 HF,Tarzan 700.00
40 HF 500.00
41 Tarzan(c) 750.00
42 . . . . 450.00
43 Tarzan(c) 500.00
44 HF 450.00
45 HF,Tarzan(c) 500.00
46 HF 450.00
47 HF,Tarzan(c) 500.00
48 HF 450.00
49 HF 450.00

Tip Top #16
© United Features

50 HF,Tarzan(c) 500.00
51 . . . . 400.00
52 Tarzan(c) 500.00
53 . . . . 400.00
54 O:Minorman 500.00
55 . . . . 350.00
56 . . . . 350.00
57 BHg 400.00
58 . . . . 300.00
59 BHg 400.00
60 . . . . 300.00
61 and 62 BHg . . . . @400.00
63 thru 90 . . . . @200.00
91 thru 99 . . . . @150.00
100 . . . . 175.00
101 thru 150 . . . . @125.00
151 thru 188 . . . . @100.00
189 thru 225 . . . . @75.00

TIP TOPPER COMICS
United Features Syndicate, 1949

1 Abbie & Slats, Li'l Abner, etc. . . 200.00
2 . . . . 150.00
3 . . . . 125.00
4 . . . . 125.00
5 Fearless Fosdick 125.00
6 Fearless Fosdick 125.00
7 . . . . 100.00
8 . . . . 100.00
9 . . . . 100.00
10 . . . . 100.00
11 thru 16 . . . . @100.00
17 Peanuts (c) 150.00
18 thru 24 . . . . @100.00
25 Peanuts 110.00
26 Peanuts 110.00

T-MAN
Comics Magazines (Quality Comics Group), Sept., 1951

1 JCo,Pete Trask-the
  Treasury Man 600.00
2 RC(c),The Girl with Death
  in Her Hands 300.00
3 RC(a&c),Death Trap in Iran . . 300.00
4 RC(a&c),Panama Peril 300.00
5 RC(a&c),Violence in Venice . . 300.00
6 RC(c),The Man Who
  Could Be Hitler 275.00
7 RC(c),Mr. Murder & The
  Black Hand 275.00
8 RC(c),Red Ticket to Hell 275.00
9 RC(c),Trial By Terror 275.00
10 RC 275.00
11 The Voice of Russia 175.00
12 Terror in Tokyo 175.00
13 Mind Assassins 175.00
14 Trouble in Bavaria, Hitler 200.00
15 The Traitor,Bondage(c) 175.00
16 Hunt For a Hatchetman 175.00
17 Red Triggerman 175.00
18 Death Rides the Rails 175.00
19 Death Ambush 175.00
20 The Fantastic H-Bomb Plot. . . 200.00
21 The Return of Mussolini 150.00
22 Propaganda for Doom 165.00
23 Red Intrigue in Parid,H-Bomb . 150.00
24 Red Sabotage 150.00
25 RC,The Ingenious Red Trap . . 150.00
26 . . . . 125.00
27 . . . . 125.00
29 thru 33 . . . . @125.00
34 Hitler (c) 150.00
35 thru 37 . . . . @125.00
38 Dec., 1956 . . . . 125.00

T-Man #35
© Quality Comics Group

TNT COMICS
Charles Publishing Co., Feb., 1946

1 FBI story,YellowJacket 450.00

TOM AND JERRY
DELL GIANT EDITIONS
Dell Publishing Co., 1952–58

Back to School 300.00
Picnic Time 250.00
Summer Fun 1 . . . . 350.00
Summer Fun 2 . . . . 200.00
Winter Carnival 1 . . . . 500.00
Winter Carnival 2 . . . . 350.00
Winter Fun 3 . . . . 200.00
Winter Fun 4 . . . . 175.00
Winter Fun 5 . . . . 150.00
Winter Fun 6 . . . . 150.00
Winter Fun 7 . . . . 150.00

TOM AND JERRY
See: OUR GANG COMICS

TOMB OF TERROR
Harvey Publications, June, 1952

1 BP,The Thing From the
  Center of the Earth 750.00
2 RP,The Quagmire Beast 500.00
3 BP,RP,Caravan of the
  Doomed, Bondage(c) 500.00
4 RP,I'm Going to Kill You,
  Torture 400.00
5 RP 400.00
6 RP,Return From the Grave . . . 400.00
7 RP,Shadow of Death 400.00
8 HN,The Hive 400.00
9 BP,HN,The Tunnel 400.00
10 BP,HN,The Trial 400.00
11 BP,HN,The Closet 400.00
12 BP,HN,Tale of Cain 450.00
13 BP,What Was Out There 500.00
14 BP,SC,End Result 500.00
15 BP,HN,Break-up, Exploding
  Head 1,000.00
16 BP,Going,Going,Gone 600.00
Becomes:

THRILLS OF TOMORROW
Oct., 1954

17 RP,BP,The World of Mr. Chatt. 250.00
18 RP,BP,The Dead Awaken 200.00

All comics prices listed are for *Near Mint* condition.

19 S&K,S&K(c),A:Stuntman 500.00
20 S&K,S&K(c),A:Stuntman 500.00

TOM CAT See:BO

TOM CORBETT SPACE CADET

**Dell Publishing Co.,
Jan., 1952**
See also Dell Four Color
4 based on TV show 200.00
5 . . . . 150.00
6 . . . . 100.00
7 . . . . 100.00
8 . . . . 100.00
9 . . . . 100.00
10 and 11 . . . . @100.00

TOM CORBETT SPACE CADET

**Prize Publications,
May–June, 1955**
1 Robot(c) 450.00
2 . . . . 350.00
3 Sept.–Oct., 1955 . . . . 350.00

TOM MIX COMICS

**Ralston-Purina Co.,
Sept., 1940**
1 O:Tom Mix. 4,500.00
2 . . . . 1,500.00
3 . . . . 900.00
4 thru 9 . . . . @750.00
Becomes:

TOM MIX COMMANDOS COMICS

Nov., 1942
10 . . . . 750.00
11 Invisible Invaders 750.00
12 Terrible Talons Of Tokyo 750.00

TOM MIX WESTERN

**Fawcett Publications,
Jan., 1948**
1 Ph(c),Two-Fisted
   Adventures 1,500.00
2 Ph(c),Hair-Triggered Action . . 600.00
3 Ph(c),Double Barreled Action . 500.00
4 Ph(c),Cowpunching 500.00
5 Ph(c),Two Gun Action 500.00
6 CCB,Most Famous Cowboy . . 350.00
7 CCB,A Tattoo of Thrills 250.00
8 EK,Ph(c),Gallant Guns 325.00
9 CCB,Song o/t Deadly Spurs . . 325.00
10 CCB,Crack Shot Western . . . 325.00
11 CCB,EK(C),Triple Revenge . . 325.00
12 King of the Cowboys. 250.00
13 Ph(c),Leather Burns 250.00
14 Ph(c),Brand of Death 250.00
15 Ph(c),Masked Treachery. . . . 250.00
16 Ph(c),Death Sputing Guns . . 250.00
17 Ph(c),Trail of Doom. 250.00
18 Ph(c),Reign of Terror 225.00
19 Hand Colored Ph(c) 250.00
20 Ph(c),CCB,F:Capt Tootsie. . . 225.00
21 Ph(c) 225.00
22 Ph(c),The Human Beast. 225.00
23 Ph(c),Return of the Past 225.00
24 Hand Colored Ph(c),
   The Lawless City. 225.00
25 Hand Colored Ph(c),
   The Signed Death Warrant . . 225.00
26 Hand Colored Ph(c),
   Dangerous Escape 225.00
27 Hand Colored Ph(c),
   Hero Without Glory 225.00
28 Ph(c),The Storm Kings 225.00

Tom Mix #55
© Fawcett Publications

29 Hand Colored Ph(c),The
   Case of the Rustling Rose . . 225.00
30 Ph(c),Disappearance
   in the Hills 225.00
31 Ph(c) 175.00
32 Hand Colored Ph(c),
   Mystery of Tremble Mountain 175.00
33 . . . . 175.00
34 . . . . 175.00
35 Partial Ph(c),The Hanging
   at Hollow Creek. 175.00
36 Ph(c) 175.00
37 Ph(c) 175.00
38 Ph(c),36 pages 150.00
39 Ph(c) 175.00
40 Ph(c) 175.00
41 Ph(c) 175.00
42 Ph(c) 175.00
43 Ph(c) 150.00
44 Ph(c) 150.00
45 Partial Ph(c),The Secret
   Letter 150.00
46 Ph(c) 150.00
47 Ph(c) 150.00
48 Ph(c) 150.00
49 Partial Ph(c),Blind Date
   With Death. 150.00
50 Ph(c) 150.00
51 Ph(c) 150.00
52 Ph(c) 150.00
53 Ph(c) 150.00
54 Ph(c) 150.00
55 Ph(c) 150.00
56 Partial Ph(c),Deadly Spurs . . 150.00
57 Ph(c)5 . . . . 150.00
58 Ph(c) 150.00
59 Ph(c) 150.00
60 Ph(c) 150.00
61 Partial Ph(c),Lost in the
   Night,May, 1953. . . . . 175.00

TOMMY OF THE BIG TOP

**King Features/
Standard Comics, 1948**
10 Thrilling Circus Adventures . . . 150.00
11 . . . . 100.00
12 March, 1949 . . . . 100.00

TOM-TOM THE JUNGLE BOY

Magazine Enterprises, 1946
1 (fa) 200.00
2 (fa) 150.00

3 Winter 1947,(fa),X-mas issue . 125.00
1 . . . . 100.00

TONTO
See: LONE RANGER'S
COMPANION TONTO

TONY TRENT
See: FACE, THE

TOP FLIGHT COMICS

**Four Star/St. John Publ. Co.,
July, 1949**
1 . . . . 125.00
1 Hector the Inspector 100.00

TOPIX COMICS

Topix/Catechetical Guild, 1942
1 Catholic 350.00
2 . . . . 250.00
3 . . . . 250.00
4 . . . . 200.00
5 . . . . 200.00
6 . . . . 200.00
7 . . . . 200.00
8 . . . . 200.00
Volume 2, any, except #5 . . . . . 250.00
5 Pope Pius XII 250.00
Volume 3, any 200.00
Volume 4, any 175.00
Volume 5, any, except #12 . . . . . 150.00
12 Life of Christ 175.00
Volume 6, any 125.00
Volume 7, any 100.00
Volume 8, any #4 . . . . 150.00
4 Dagwood Splits Atom. 150.00
12 Christmas issue 100.00
Volume 10, any 100.00

TOP LOVE STORIES

**Star Publications,
May, 1951**
3 LbC(c) 300.00
4 LbC(c) 250.00
5 LbC(c) 250.00
6 LbC(c),WW 350.00
7 LbC(c) 250.00
8 LbC(c), WW Story 275.00
9 LbC(c) 250.00
10 thru 16 LbC(c) . . . . @250.00
17 LbC(c),WW 275.00
18 LbC(c) 250.00
19 LbC(c),JyD 250.00

TOP-NOTCH COMICS

**MLJ Magazines,
Dec., 1939**
1 JaB,JCo,B&O:The Wizard,
   B:Kandak,Swift of the Secret
   Service,The Westpointer,
   Mystic, Air Patrol,Scott
   Rand, Manhunter 12,000.00
2 JaB,JCo,B:Dick Storm,
   E:Mystic, B:Stacy Knight . . 5,000.00
3 JaB,JCo,EA(c),E:Swift of the
   Secret Service,Scott Rand 3,000.00
4 JCo,EA(c),MMe,O&I:Streak,
   Chandler 2,700.00
5 Ea(c),MMe,O&I:Galahad,
   B:Shanghai Sheridan 2,800.00
6 Ea(c),MMe,A:The Shield . . . 2,500.00
7 Ea(c),MMe,N:The Wizard . . 3,000.00
8 E:Dick Sorm,B&O:Roy The1
   Super Boy,The Firefly 2,500.00
9 O&I:Black Hood,
   B:Fran Frazier 10,000.00
10 A:Black Hood. 3,000.00
11 . . . . 2,000.00

Top-Notch Comics #4
© MLJ Magazines

12	2,000.00
13	2,000.00
14 Bondage(c)	2,000.00
15 MMe	2,000.00
16	1,800.00
17 Bondage(c)	2,000.00
18	1,800.00
19 Bondage(c)	2,000.00
20	1,800.00
21	1,500.00
22	1,500.00
23 Bondage(c)	1,700.00
24 Black Hood Smashes Murder Ring	1,500.00
25 E:Bob Phantom	1,500.00
26	1,500.00
27 E:The Firefly	1,500.00
28 B:Suzie,Pokey Okay, Gag Oriented	1,500.00
29 E:Kandak	1,500.00
30	1,500.00
31	700.00
32	700.00
33 BWo,B:Dotty&Ditto	700.00
34 BWo	700.00
35 BWo	700.00
36 BWo	700.00
37 thru 40 BWo	@700.00
41	700.00
42 BWo	700.00
43	700.00
44 EW:Black Hood,I:Suzie	700.00
45 Suzie(c)	800.00

Becomes:

LAUGH COMIX
Summer, 1944

46 Suzie & Wilbur	400.00
47 Suzie & Wilbur	300.00
48 Suzie & Wilbur	300.00

Becomes:

SUZIE COMICS
Spring, 1945

49 B:Ginger	400.00
50 AFy(c)	300.00
51 AFy(c)	300.00
52 AFy(c)	300.00
53 AFy(c)	300.00
54 AFy(c)	350.00
55 AFy(c)	350.00
56 BWo,B;Katie Keene	200.00
57 thru 70 BWo	@200.00
71 thru 79 BWo	@150.00
80 thru 99 BWo	@150.00
100 Aug., 1954, BWo	150.00

TOPS
**Tops Mag. Inc.
(Lev Gleason), July, 1949**

1 RC&BLb,GT,DBa,CBi(c),I'll Buy That Girl,Our Explosive Children	1,800.00
2 FGu,BF,CBi(c),RC&BLb	1,700.00

TOPS COMICS
Consolidated Book Publishers, 1944

2000 Don on the Farm	300.00
2001 The Jack of Spades V:The Hawkman	200.00
2002 Rip Raiders	150.00
2003 Red Birch	100.00

TOP SECRET
Hillman Publications, Jan., 1952

1 The Tricks of the Secret Agent Revealed	250.00

TOP SECRETS
Street & Smith Publ., Nov., 1947

1 BP,BP(c),Of the Men Who Guard the U.S. Mail	450.00
2 BP,BP(c),True Story of Jim the Penman	350.00
3 BP,BP(c),Crime Solved by Mental Telepathy	300.00
4 Highway Pirates	300.00
5 BP,BP(c),Can Music Kill	300.00
6 BP,BP(c),The Clue of the Forgotten Film	300.00
7 BP,BP(c),Train For Sale	450.00
8 BP,BP(c)	300.00
9 BP,BP(c)	300.00
10 BP,BP(c),July–Aug., 1949	350.00

TOPS IN ADVENTURE
Approved Comics (Ziff-Davis), Autumn, 1952

1 BP,Crusaders From Mars	700.00

TOP SPOT COMICS
Top Spot Publishing Co., 1945

1 The Duke Of Darkness	450.00

TOPSY-TURVY
R.B. Leffingwell Publ., April, 1945

1 I:Cookie	200.00

TOR
St. John Publishing Co., Sept., 1953

1 JKu,JKu(c),O;Tor,One Million Years Ago	150.00
2 JKu,JKu(c),3-D Issue	100.00
3 JKu,JKu(c),ATh,historic Life	125.00
4 JKu,JKu(c),ATh	125.00
5 JKu,JKu(c),ATh,Oct., 1954	125.00

TORCHY
Quality Comics Group, Nov., 1949

1 GFx,BWa(c),The Blonde Bombshell	2,400.00
2 GFx(a&c),Beauty at Its Best	1,100.00
3 GFx,GFx(c),You Can't Beat Nature	1,100.00
4 GFx,GFx(c),The Girl to Keep Your Eye On	1,400.00

5 BWa,GFx,BWa(c),At the Masquerade Party	1,700.00
6 Sept., 1950,BWa,GFx, BWa(c),The Libido Driven Boy Scout	1,700.00

TORMENTED, THE
Sterling Comics, July, 1954

1 Buried Alive	400.00
2 Sept., 1954,The Devils Circus	350.00

Becomes:

SURPRISE ADVENTURES
Sterling Comics, 1955

3 MSy	200.00
4	150.00
5 MSy	200.00

Toyland Comics #2
© Fiction House Magazines

TOYLAND COMICS
Fiction House Magazines, Jan., 1947

1 Wizard of the Moon	400.00
2 Buddy Bruin & Stu Rabbit	200.00
3 GT,The Candy Maker	250.00
4 July, 1947	200.00

TOY TOWN COMICS
Toytown Publ./Orbit Publ., Feb., 1945

1 LbC,LbC(c)(fa)	550.00
2 LbC,(fa)	300.00
3 LbC,LbC(c),(fa)	250.00
4 thru 7 LbC,(fa) May, 1947	@250.00

TRAIL BLAZERS
See: RED DRAGON COMICS

TRAPPED
Harvey Publications, 1951

N#	150.00

TRAPPED!
Periodical Magazines (Ace Magazines), 1954

1	125.00
2 and 3	@60.00

TREASURE CHEST
George A Pflaum Publ., Inc., 1946

1	325.00
2 thru 4	@150.00

GOLDEN AGE

5 Dr Styx 160.00
6 . . . . 150.00
Vol 2, 1 thru 20 . . . . @150.00
Vol 3, 1 thru 5 (1947–48) . . . . . @150.00
Vol 3, #6 Verne, Voyage to Moon, 135.00
Vol 3, 7 thru 20 . . . . @110.00
Vol 4, 1 thru 20 (1948–49) . . . . @135.00
Vol 5, 1 thru 20 (1949–50) . . . . @125.00
Vol 6, 1 thru 20 (1950–51) . . . . @125.00
Vol 7, 1 thru 20 (1951–52) . . . . @125.00
Vol 8, 1 thru 20 (1952–53) . . . . @125.00
Vol 9, 1 thru 20 (1953–54) . . . . @100.00
Vol 10, 1 thru 10 (1954–55) . . . @100.00
Vol 10, #11 BP 100.00
Vol 10, 12 thru 20 . . . . @100.00
Vol 11, 1 thru 20 (1955–56) . . . @100.00
Vol 12, 1 thru 20 (1956–57) . . . @100.00
Vol 13, 1 thru 20 (1957–58) . . . . @75.00
Vol 14, 1 thru 20 (1958–59) . . . . @75.00
Vol 15, 1 thru 20 (1959–60) . . . . @75.00
Vol 16, 1 thru 20 (1960–61) . . . . @75.00
Vol 17, 1 thru 20 (1962–63)
   odd #s . . . . @75.00
   even #s "Godless Communism"
2 RC 275.00
4 and 6 . . . . @275.00
8 thru 14 Stalin, WWII . . . . @275.00
14 thru 20 Kruschev . . . . @225.00

TREASURE COMICS
Prize Comics Group, 1943
1 S&K, Reprints of Prize Comics
   #7 through #11 . . . . 3,500.00

TREASURE COMICS
**American Boys Comics
(Prize Publications),
June–July, 1945**
1 HcK, B:PaulBunyan, MarcoPolo 700.00
2 HcK(a&c), B:Arabian Knight,
   Gorilla King, Dr.Styx 350.00
3 HcK 250.00
4 HcK 250.00
5 HcK, JK, Marco Polo 350.00
6 BK, HcK(a&c) 250.00
7 FF, HcK(a&c), Capt.Kidd, Jr. . . . 550.00
8 HcK, FF 550.00
9 HcK, DBa 250.00
10 JK, DBa, JK(c) 450.00
11 BK, HcK, DBa, The Weird
   Adventures of Mr. Bottle 300.00
12 DBa, DBa(c), Autumn, 1947 . . . 250.00

TREASURY OF COMICS
St. John Publishing Co., 1947
1 RvB, RvB(c), Abbie an' Slats . . 150.00
2 Jim Hardy 125.00
3 Bill Bimlin 125.00
4 RvB, RvB(c), Abbie an' Slats . . 125.00
5 Jim Hardy, Jan., 1948 . . . . 100.00

TREASURY OF COMICS
St. John Publishing Co., 1948
1 Abbott & Costello,
   Little Audrey 250.00
2 . . . . 125.00
3 thru 5 . . . . @110.00

TRIPLE THREAT
**Gerona Publications,
Winter, 1945**
1 F:King O'Leary, The Duke of
   Darkness, Beau Brummell . . . 400.00

TRUE ANIMAL PICTURE STORIES
True Comics Press, 1947
1 & 2 . . . . @125.00

TRUE AVIATION PICTURE STORIES
**Parents' Institute/P.M.I.,
Aug., 1942**
1 How Jimmy Doolittle
   Bombed Tokyo 250.00
2 Knight of the Air Mail 200.00
3 The Amazing One-Man
   Air Force 150.00
4 Joe Foss America's No. 1
   Air Force 150.00
5 Bombs over Germany 150.00
6 Flight Lt. Richard
   Hillary R.A.F. 150.00
7 "Fatty" Chow China's
   Sky Champ 150.00
8 Blitz over Burma 150.00
9 Off the Beam 150.00
10 "Pappy" Boyington 150.00
11 Ph(c) 150.00
12 . . . . 150.00
13 Ph(c), Flying Facts 150.00
14 . . . . 150.00
15 True Aviation Adventures 150.00
Becomes:

AVIATION AND MODEL BUILDING
Dec., 1946
16 . . . . 125.00
17 Feb., 1947. . . . . 150.00

TRUE COMICS
**True Comics/
Parents' Magazine Press,
April, 1941–Aug., 1950**
1 My Greatest Adventure-by
   Lowell Thomas, Churchill . . . 450.00
2 BEv, The Story of the
   Red Cross 200.00
3 Baseball Hall of Fame 225.00
4 Danger in the Artic 150.00
5 Father Duffy-the Fighting
   Chaplain, Joe Louis. 165.00
6 The Capture of Aquinaldo 175.00
7 JKa, Wilderness Adventures of
   George Washington 165.00
8 U.S. Army Wings 125.00
9 A Pig that Made History 125.00
10 Adrift on an Ice Pan 125.00
11 Gen. Douglas MacArthur. 110.00
12 Mackenzie-King of Cananda . . 110.00
13 The Real Robinson Crusoe. . . 110.00
14 Australia war base of
   the South Pacific 110.00
15 The Story of West Point 125.00
16 How Jimmy Doolittle
   Bombed Tokyo. 120.00
17 The Ghost of Captain Blig,
   B.Feller 125.00
18 Battling Bill of the
   Merchant Marine 135.00
19 Secret Message Codes. 110.00
20 The Story of India 100.00
21 Timoshenko the Blitz Buster . . 110.00
22 Gen, Bernard L. Montgomery. 100.00
23 The Story of Steel 100.00
24 Gen. Henri Giraud-Master
   of Escape 100.00
25 Medicine's Miracle Men 100.00
26 Hero of the Bismarck Sea. . . . 100.00
27 Leathernecks have Landed. . . 110.00
28 The Story of Radar 100.00
29 The Fighting Seabees. 100.00
30 Dr. Norman Bethune-Blood
   Bank Founder 100.00
31 Our Good Neighbor Bolivia,
   Red Grange 110.00
32 Men against the Desert 125.00
33 Gen.Clark and his Fighting 5th 150.00

True Comics #45
© *Parents' Magazine Press*

34 Angel of the Battlefield 125.00
35 Carlson's Marine Raiders 125.00
36 Canada's Sub-Busters 125.00
37 Commander of the Crocodile
   Fleet. 125.00
38 Oregon Trailblazer 125.00
39 Saved by Sub, FBI 125.00
40 Sea Furies 125.00
41 Cavalcade of England. 100.00
42 Gen. Jaques Le Clerc-Hero
   of Paris 100.00
43 Unsinkable Ship 100.00
44 El Senor Goofy, Truman 100.00
45 Tokyo Express 100.00
46 The Magnificent Runt 100.00
47 Atoms Unleashed,
   Atomic Bomb 175.00
48 Pirate Patriot 100.00
49 Smoking Fists 100.00
50 Lumber Pirates 100.00
51 Exercise Musk-Ox. 100.00
52 King of the Buckaneers 100.00
53 Baseline Booby. 100.00
54 Santa Fe Sailor. 100.00
55 Sea Going Santa 100.00
56 End of a Terror 100.00
57 Newfangled Machines 100.00
58 Leonardo da Vinci-500 years
   too Soon, Houdini 100.00
59 Pursuit Pirates, Bob Hope . . . 100.00
60 Emmett Kelly-The World's
   Funniest Clown 100.00
61 Peter Le Grand-
   Bold Buckaneer 100.00
62 Sutter's Gold. 100.00
63 Outboard Outcome 100.00
64 Man-Eater at Large. 100.00
65 The Story of Scotland Yard . . . 100.00
66 Easy Guide to Football
   Formations, Will Rogers 100.00
67 The Changing Zebra. 100.00
68 Admiral Byrd 100.00
69 FBI Special Agent Steve
   Saunders, Jack Benny 100.00
70 The Case of the Seven
   Hunted Men. 100.00
71 Story of Joe DiMaggio 150.00
72 FBI, Jackie Robinson. 125.00
73 The 26 Mile Dash-Story of
   the Marathon, Walt Disney . . 100.00
74 A Famous Coach's Special
   Football Tips, Amos & Andy . 100.00
75 King of Reporters 100.00
76 Story of a Buried Treasure . . . 100.00
77 France's Greatest Detective. . . 100.00
78 Cagliostro-Master Rogue 100.00

79 Ralph Bunche-Hero of Peace. 100.00
80 Rocket Trip to the Moon 250.00
81 Red Grange 250.00
82 Marie Celeste Ship of
   Mystery 175.00
83 Bullfighter from Brooklyn. 175.00
84 King of the Buccaneers 175.00

TRUE CONFIDENCES
Fawcett Publications,
Autumn, 1949
1 . . . . 225.00
2 and 3 . . . . @125.00
4 DP 125.00

TRUE CRIME COMICS
Magazine Village, Inc.,
May, 1947
2 JCo(c),James Kent-Crook,
   Murderer,Escaped Convict;
   Drug 2,300.00
3 JCo(a&c),Benny Dickson-
   Killer;Drug. 1,600.00
4 JCo(a&c),Little Jake-
   Big Shot 1,400.00
5 JCo(c),The Rat & the Blond
   Gun Moll;Drug 1,000.00
6 Joseph Metley-Swindler,
   Jailbird, Killer 800.00
2-1(7) ATh,WW,Ph(c),Phil
   Coppolla,Sept., 1949 . . . . . 1,300.00

TRUE LOVE PICTORIAL
St. John Publishing Co., 1952
1 Ph(c) 300.00
2 MB 350.00
3 MB(c),MB,JKu 600.00
4 MB(c),MB,JKu 600.00
5 MB(c),MB,JKu 600.00
6 MB(c) 300.00
7 MB(c) 300.00
8 MB(c) 275.00
9 MB(c) 275.00
10 MB(c),MB 275.00
11 MB(c),MB 275.00

TRUE MOVIE AND TELEVISION
Toby Press, Aug., 1950
1 Liz Taylor, Ph(c) 850.00
2 FF,Ph(c),John Wayne,
   L.Taylor 550.00
3 June Allyson,Ph(c) 400.00
4 Jane Powell,Ph(c),Jan.,1951. . 250.00

SPORT COMICS
Street & Smith Publ., Oct., 1940
1 F:Lou Gehrig 850.00
2 F:Gene Tunney 400.00
3 F:Phil Rizzuto 450.00
4 F:Frank Leahy 350.00
Becomes:

TRUE SPORT PICTURE STORIES
Street & Smith Publ.,
Feb., 1942–July-Aug., 1949
5 Joe DiMaggio 500.00
6 Billy Confidence 300.00
7 Mel Ott 325.00
8 Lou Ambers 300.00
9 Pete Reiser 300.00
10 Frankie Sinkwich. 300.00
11 Marty Serfo 300.00
12 JaB(c),Jack Dempsey 325.00
2-1 JaB(c),Willie Pep 300.00
2-2 JaB(c) 300.00
2-3 JaB(c),Carl Hubbell 325.00
2-4 Advs. in Football & Battle . . . 325.00

True Sport Picture Stories Vol. 4 #2
© Street & Smith Publications

2-5 Don Hutson 300.00
2-6 Dixie Walker. 325.00
2-7 Stan Musial 350.00
2-8 Famous Ring Champions
   of All Time 325.00
2-9 List of War Year Rookies . . . 350.00
2-10 Connie Mack 325.00
2-11 Winning Basketball Plays . . 300.00
2-12 Eddie Gottlieb 300.00
3-1 Bill Conn 300.00
3-2 Philadelphia Athletics 300.00
3-3 Leo Durocher 325.00
3-4 Rudy Dusek 275.00
3-5 Ernie Pyle 275.00
3-6 Bowling with Ned Day 275.00
3-7 Return of the Mighty (Home
   from War);Joe DiMaggio(c) . . 350.00
3-8 Conn V:Louis 325.00
3-9 Reuben Shark 275.00
3-10 BP,BP(c),Don "Dopey"
   Dillock 275.00
3-11 BP,BP(c),Death
   Scores a Touchdown 275.00
3-12 Red Sox V:Senators 275.00
4-1 Spring Training in
   Full Spring 275.00
4-2 BP,BP(c),How to Pitch 'Em
   Where They Can't Hit 'Em . . 275.00
4-3 BP,BP(c),1947 Super Stars . 250.00
4-4 BP,BP(c),Get Ready for
   the Olympics 235.00
4-5 BP,BP,(c),Hugh Casey 225.00
4-6 BP,BP(c),Phantom Phil
   Hergesheimer 225.00
4-7 BP,BP(c),How to Bowl Better 225.00
4-8 Tips on the Big Fight 235.00
4-9 BP,BP(c),Bill McCahan 225.00
4-10 BP,BP(c),Great Football
   Plays 225.00
4-11 BP,BP(c),Football. 225.00
4-12 BP,BP(c),Basketball. 225.00
5-1 Satchel Paige 250.00
5-2 History of Boxing 225.00

TRUE-TO-LIFE ROMANCES
Star Publications,
Nov.–Dec., 1949
3 LbC(c),GlennFord/JanetLeigh . 350.00
4 LbC(c) 250.00
5 LbC(c) 250.00
6 LbC(c) 250.00
7 LbC(c) 250.00
8 LbC(c) 250.00

9 LbC(c) 250.00
10 LbC(c) 250.00
11 LbC(c) 250.00
12 LbC(c) 250.00
13 LbC(c),JyD 250.00
14 LbC(c),JyD 250.00
15 LbC(c),WW,JyD 275.00
16 LbC(c),WW,JyD 275.00
17 LbC(c),JyD 250.00
18 LbC(c),JyD 250.00
19 LbC(c),JyD 250.00
20 LbC(c),JyD 250.00
21 LbC(c),JyD 250.00
22 LbC(c),JyD 250.00
23 LbC(c) 250.00

TRUE WAR EXPERIENCES
Harvey Publications, 1952
1 . . . . 150.00
2 thru 4 . . . . @100.00

TUBBY
See: MARGE'S TUBBY

TUFFY
Best Books, Inc.
(Standard Comics) 1949
5 . . . . 125.00
6 true 9 . . . . @100.00

TUROK, SON OF STONE
Dell Publishing Co.,
Dec., 1954
(1) see Dell Four Color #596
(2) see Dell Four Color #656
3 Cavemen 400.00
4 & 5 . . . . @300.00
6 & 7 . . . . @250.00
8 Dinosaur, Lost Valley 275.00
9 thru 16 . . . . @175.00
17 Prehistoric Pigmies 200.00
18 thru 29 . . . . @125.00

TV SCREEN CARTOONS
(see REAL SCREEN COMICS)

TV TEENS
Charlton Comics, 1954
1 Ozzie & Babs. 125.00
2 . . . . 100.00
3 . . . . 100.00
4 . . . . 100.00
5 . . . . 100.00
6 Don Winslow 100.00
7 B:Mopsy. 100.00
8 thru 13 . . . . @100.00

TWEETY AND SYLVESTER
Dell Publishing Co.,
June, 1952
(1) see Dell Four Color #406
(2) see Dell Four Color #489
(3) see Dell Four Color #524
4 thru 20 . . . . @125.00
21 thru 37 . . . . @100.00

TWINKLE COMICS
Spotlight Publications,
May, 1945
1 Humor Format 350.00

TWO-BIT WACKY WOODPECKER
Toby Press, 1952
1 . . . . 150.00
2 . . . . 120.00
3 . . . . 120.00

TWO-FISTED TALES

**Fables Publications
(E.C. Comics),
Nov.–Dec., 1950–March, 1955**

18 JCr,WW,JSe,HK(a&c)	1,700.00
19 JCr,WW,JSe,HK(a&c)	1,400.00
20 JDa,WW,JSe,HK(a&c)	800.00
21 JDa,WW,JSe,HK(a&c)	750.00
22 JDa,WW,JSe,HK(a&c)	750.00
23 JDa,WW,JSe,HK(a&c)	600.00
24 JDa,WW,JSe,HK(a&c)	500.00
25 JDa,WW,JSe,HK(a&c)	500.00
26 JDa,JSe,HK(c),Action at the Changing Reservoir	350.00
27 JDa,JSe,HK(c)	350.00
28 JDa,JSe,HK(c)	350.00
29 JDa,JSe,HK(c)	400.00
30 JSe,JDa(a&c)	400.00
31 JDa,JSe,HK(c),Civil War Story	350.00
32 JDa,JKu,WW(c)	350.00
33 JDa,JKu,WW(c),A-Bomb	400.00
34 JDa,JSe(a&c)	350.00
35 JSe,JDa(a&c),Civil War Story	350.00
36 JDa,JSe(a&c),A Difference of Opinion	400.00
37 JSe(a&c),Bugles & Battle Cries	400.00
38 JSe(a&c)	400.00
39 JSe(a&c)	400.00
40 JDa,JSe,GE(a&c)	400.00
41 JSe,GE,JDa(c)	400.00
Ann. 1952 (#1)	1,600.00
Ann. 1953 (#2) JDa(c)	1,300.00

UNCLE CHARLIE'S FABLES

**Lev Gleason Publications,
Jan., 1952**

1 CBi(c),Ph(c)	200.00
2 BF,CBi(c),Ph(c)	125.00
3 CBi(c),Ph(c)	135.00
4 CBi(c),Ph(c)	135.00
5 CBi,Ph(c),Sept., 1952	135.00

UNCLE JOE'S FUNNIES

Centaur Publications, 1938

1 BEv,Puzzles & Comics	900.00

UNCLE MILTY

**Victoria Publications
(True Cross Comic), 1950**

1 Milton Berle	800.00
2	500.00
3	400.00
4	375.00

UNCLE SAM

See: BLACKHAWK

UNCLE SCROOGE

**Dell Publishing Co.,
March, 1952**

(1) see Dell Four Color #386	
(2) see Dell Four Color #456	
(3) see Dell Four Color #495	
4 Gladstone Album #11	700.00
5 Gladstone Special	600.00
6	450.00
7 CB, Seven Cities of Cibola	400.00
8 thru 10	@350.00
11 thru 23	@300.00
24 Christmas issue	300.00
25 thru 30	@250.00
31 thru 39	@200.00

Underworld #7
© *D.S. Publishing Co.*

UNDERWORLD

**D.S. Publishing Co.,
Feb.–March, 1948**

1 SMo(c),Violence	750.00
2 SMo(c),Electrocution	600.00
3 AMc,AMc(c),The Ancient Club	500.00
4 Grl,The Beer Baron Murder	450.00
5 Grl,The Postal Clue	300.00
6 The Polka Dot Gang	250.00
7 Mono-The Master	250.00
8 The Double Tenth	250.00
9 Thrilling Stories of the Fight against Crime,June, 1953	250.00

UNDERWORLD CRIME

**Fawcett Publications,
June, 1952**

1 The Crime Army	500.00
2 Jailbreak	350.00
3 Microscope Murder	300.00
4 Death on the Docks	300.00
5 River of Blood	300.00
6 The Sky Pirates	300.00
7 Bondage & Torture(c)	500.00
8 and 9 June, 1953	@300.00

UNITED COMICS

See: FRITZI RITZ

UNITED STATES FIGHTING AIR FORCE

**Superior Comics, Ltd.,
Sept., 1952**

1 Coward's Courage	150.00
2 Clouds that Killed	125.00
3 Operation Decoy	100.00
4 thru 28	@100.00
29 Oct., 1959	100.00

UNITED STATES MARINES

**Wm. H. Wise/Magazine Ent/
Toby Press, 1943–52**

N# MBi,MBi(c),Hellcat out of Heaven	250.00
2 MBi,Drama of Wake Island, Tojo	600.00
3 A Leatherneck Flame Thrower, Tojo	500.00
4 MBi	150.00
5 BP	100.00
6 BP	100.00

7 BP	100.00
8 thru 11	@100.00

UNKEPT PROMISE

Legion of Truth, 1949

1 Anti:Alcoholic Drinking	150.00

UNKNOWN WORLDS

**See: STRANGE STORIES
FROM ANOTHER WORLD**

UNSEEN, THE

**Visual Editions
(Standard Comics), 1952**

5 ATh,The Hungry Lodger	600.00
6 JKa,MSy,Bayou Vengeance	400.00
7 JKz,MSy,Time is the Killer	400.00
8 JKz,MSy,The Vengeance Vat	300.00
9 JKz,MSy,Your Grave is Ready	450.00
10 JKz,MSy	400.00
11 JKz,MSy	300.00
12 ATh,GT,Till Death Do Us Part	400.00
13	300.00
14	300.00
15 ATh,The Curse of the Undead!, July, 1954	400.00

UNTAMED LOVE

**Comic Magazines
(Quality Comics Group),
Jan., 1950**

1 BWa(c),PGv	325.00
2 Ph(c)	200.00
3 PGv, Ph(c)	225.00
4 Ph(c)	200.00
5 PGv, Ph(c)	225.00

USA IS READY

Dell Publishing Co., 1941

1 Propaganda WWII	600.00

U.S. JONES

**Fox Features Syndicate,
Nov., 1941**

1 Death Over the Airways	1,900.00
2 Nazi (c),Jan., 1942	1,400.00

U.S. MARINES IN ACTION!

**Avon Periodicals,
Aug.–Dec., 1952**

1 On Land,Sea & in the Air	125.00
2 The Killer Patrol	100.00
3 EK(c),Death Ridge	100.00

U.S. PARATROOPS

Avon Periodicals, 1951

1 WW	200.00
2 EK	125.00
3	100.00
4 thru 6 EK	@125.00

U.S. TANK COMMANDOS

**Avon Periodicals,
June, 1952**

1 EK(c),Fighting Daredevils of the USA	150.00
2 EK(c)	100.00
3 EK,EK(c),Robot Armanda	100.00
4 EK,EK(c),March, 1953	100.00

VALOR

E.C. Comics, March, 1955

1 AW,AT,WW,WW(c),Grl,BK	700.00
2 AW(c),AW,WWGrl,BK	500.00

GOLDEN AGE

3 AW,RC,BK,JOc(c) 400.00
4 WW(c),RC,Grl,BK,JO 400.00
5 WW(c),WW,AW,GE,Grl,BK . . . 350.00

VARIETY COMICS

Rural Home Publ./
Croyden Publ. Co., 1944
1 MvS,MvS(c),O:Capt, Valiant . . 300.00
2 MvS,MvS(c) 250.00
3 MvS,MvS(c) 200.00
4 . . . . 150.00
5 1946 . . . . 150.00

VAULT OF HORROR
See: WAR AGAINST CRIME

V...COMICS

Fox Features Syndicate,
Jan., 1942
1 V:V-Man, Nazi(c) 1,800.00
2 The Horror of the
　Dungeons, March, 1942 . . 1,400.00

VERI BEST
SURE FIRE COMICS

Holyoke Publishing Co., 1945
1 Capt Aero, Miss Victory, Red
　Cross, Devil Dogs 600.00

VERI BEST
SURE SHOT COMICS

Holyoke Publishing Co., 1945
1 reprint Holyoke One-Shots . . . 500.00

VIC FLINT

St. John Publishing Co.,
Aug., 1948
1 ...Crime Buster 200.00
2 . . . . 175.00
3 . . . . 150.00
4 . . . . 150.00
5 April, 1949 . . . . 150.00

VIC FLINT

Argo Publ., 1956
1 . . . . 100.00
2 . . . . 100.00

VIC JORDAN

Civil Service Publications,
April, 1945
1 Escape From a Nazi Prison . . 150.00

VIC TORRY AND HIS
FLYING SAUCER

Fawcett Publications, 1950
1 Ph(c),Revealed at Last 1,000.00

VICTORY COMICS

Hillman Periodicals,
Aug., 1941
1 BEv,BEv(c),F:TheConqueror 5,000.00
2 BEv,BEv(c) 1,900.00
3 The Conqueror(c) 1,350.00
4 Dec., 1941 . . . . 1,300.00

VIC VERITY MAGAZINE

Vic Verity Publications,
1945
1 CCB,CCB(c),B:Vic Verity,Hot-
　Shot Galvan, Tom Travis . . . 300.00
2 CCB,CCB(c),Annual Classic
　Dance Recital 175.00
3 CCB 150.00

4 CCB,I:Boomer Young;The
　Bee-U-TiFul Weekend 150.00
5 CCB,Championship Baseball
　Game 150.00
6 CCB,High School Hero 150.00
7 CCB,CCB(c),F:Rocket Rex . . 150.00

VOODOO

Four Star Publ./Farrell/
Ajax Comics, May, 1952
1 MB,South Sea Girl 900.00
2 MB 700.00
3 Face Stabbing 500.00
4 MB,Rendezvous 500.00
5 Ghoul For A Day,Nazi 400.00
6 The Weird Dead,
　Severed Head 425.00
7 Goodbye World 400.00
8 MB, Revenge 500.00
9 Will this thing Never Stew? . . . 400.00
10 Land of Shadows & Screams . 400.00
11 Human Harvest 350.00
12 The Wazen Taper 350.00
13 Bondage(c),Caskets to
　Fit Everybody 375.00
14 Death Judges the
　Beauty Contest, Zombies . . . 350.00
15 Loose their Heads, Opium . . . 350.00
16 Fog Was Her Shroud 325.00
17 Apes Laughter,Electric Chair . 350.00
18 Astounding Fantasy 325.00
19 MB,Bondage(c);
　Destination Congo 450.00
Ann.#1 100-pg. 1,400.00
Becomes:

VOODA

April, 1955
20 MB,MB(c),Echoes of
　an A-Bomb. 500.00
21 MB,MB(c),Trek of Danger. . . . 450.00
22 MB,MB(c),The Sun Blew
　Away, Aug., 1955. . . . . 450.00

WALT DISNEY'S
COMICS & STORIES

Dell Publishing Co.
N# 1943 dpt.store giveaway 750.00
N# 1945 X-mas giveaway 350.00

WALT DISNEY'S
COMICS & STORIES

Dell Publishing Co.,
Oct., 1940
1 (1940)FGu,Donald Duck &
　Mickey Mouse 35,000.00
2 . . . . 12,000.00
3 . . . . 4,200.00
4 1st Huey, Dewey & Louie
　Christmas(c) 3,000.00
4a Promo issue 4,500.00
5 Goofy(c) 2,300.00
6 . . . . 1,900.00
7 . . . . 1,900.00
8 Clarabelle Cow(c) 1,900.00
9 . . . . 1,900.00
10 . . . . 1,900.00
11 2nd Huey,Louie,Dewey(c) . . 1,900.00
12 . . . . 1,500.00
13 . . . . 1,400.00
14 . . . . 1,400.00
15 3 Little Kittens 1,300.00
16 3 Little Pigs 1,300.00
17 The Ugly Ducklings 1,300.00
18 . . . . 1,100.00
19 . . . . 1,100.00
20 . . . . 1,100.00
21 . . . . 1,100.00
22 . . . . 950.00
23 . . . . 950.00

24 Flying Gauchito. 900.00
25 . . . . 900.00
26 . . . . 900.00
27 Jose Carioca. 900.00
28 . . . . 950.00
29 . . . . 900.00
30 . . . . 900.00
31 CB; Donald Duck 6,000.00
32 CB 2,500.00
33 CB 1,700.00
34 CB;WK; Gremlins. 1,500.00
35 CB;WK; Gremlins. 1,500.00
36 CB;WK; Gremlins. 1,500.00
37 CB;WK; Gremlins 800.00
38 CB;WK; Gremlins 1,000.00
39 CB;WK; Gremlins, X-mas . . 1,000.00
40 CB;WK; Gremlins. 1,000.00
41 CB;WK; Gremlins 900.00
42 CB 750.00
43 CB,Seven Dwarfs 750.00
44 CB 750.00
45 CB,Nazis in stories 750.00
46 CB,Nazis in stories 750.00
47 CB,Nazis in stories 750.00
48 CB,Nazis in stories 750.00
49 CB,Nazis in stories 750.00
50 CB,Nazis in stories 750.00
51 CB,Christmas 600.00
52 CB; Li'l Bad Wolf begins 600.00
53 CB 600.00
54 CB 600.00
55 CB 600.00
56 CB 600.00
57 CB 600.00
58 CB,Flag. 600.00
59 CB 600.00
60 CB 600.00
61 CB; Dumbo 500.00
62 CB 500.00
63 CB; Pinocchio 500.00
64 CB; Pinocchio, X-mas 500.00
65 CB; Pluto. 500.00
66 CB 500.00
67 CB 500.00
68 CB, Mickey Mouse 500.00
69 CB 500.00
70 CB 500.00
71 CB 400.00
72 CB 400.00
73 CB 400.00
74 CB 400.00
75 CB; Brer Rabbit. 400.00
76 CB; Brer Rabbit, X-mas 400.00
77 CB; Brer Rabbit. 400.00
78 CB 400.00
79 CB 400.00

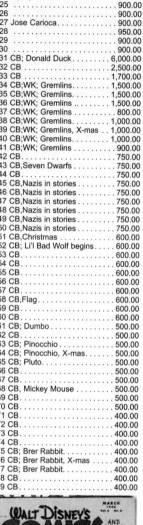

Walt Disney's Comics & Stories #66
© Walt Disney

80 CB 400.00
81 CB 400.00
82 CB;Bongo,Googy 400.00
83 CB;Bongo 400.00
84 CB;Bongo 400.00
85 CB 400.00
86 CB;Goofy & Agnes 400.00
87 CB;Goofy & Agnes 350.00
88 CB;Goofy & Agnes,
    I:Gladstone Gander 450.00
89 CB;Goofy&Agnes,Chip'n'Dale 350.00
90 CB;Goofy & Agnes 350.00
91 CB 300.00
92 CB 300.00
93 CB 300.00
94 CB 300.00
95 CB(c) 300.00
96 Little Toot 300.00
97 CB; Little Toot 300.00
98 CB; Uncle Scrooge 550.00
99 CB, Christmas(c) 300.00
100 CB 400.00
101 CB 300.00
102 CB 300.00
103 CB 275.00
104 . . . . 275.00
105 CB 300.00
106 CB 300.00
107 CB, Donald super-powers . . . 400.00
108 . . . . 275.00
109 . . . . 275.00
110 CB 300.00
111 CB 300.00
112 CB; drugs 400.00
113 CB 300.00
114 CB 300.00
115 WK(c) 300.00
116 Dumbo 150.00
117 . . . . 150.00
118 . . . . 150.00
119 . . . . 150.00
120 . . . . 150.00
121 Grandma Duck begins 150.00
122 . . . . 150.00
123 . . . . 200.00
124 CB,Christmas 250.00
125 CB;I:Junior Woodchucks . . . 300.00
126 CB 250.00
127 CB 200.00
128 CB 200.00
129 CB 200.00
130 CB 200.00
131 CB 200.00
132 CB A:Grandma Duck 200.00
133 CB 200.00
134 I:The Beagle Boys 400.00
135 CB 200.00
136 CB 200.00
137 CB 200.00
138 CB,Scrooge & Money 300.00
139 CB 200.00
140 CB; I:Gyro Gearloose 400.00
141 CB 150.00
142 CB 150.00
143 CB; Little Hiawatha 150.00
144 CB; Little Hiawatha 150.00
145 CB; Little Hiawatha 150.00
146 CB; Little Hiawatha 150.00
147 CB; Little Hiawatha 150.00
148 CB; Little Hiawatha 150.00
149 CB; Little Hiawatha 150.00
150 CB; Little Hiawatha 150.00
151 CB; Little Hiawatha 150.00
152 thru 200 CB . . . . @125.00
201 thru 203 CB . . . . @100.00
204 CB, Chip 'n' Dale & Scamp . . 100.00
205 thru 240 CB . . . . @100.00
241 CB; Dumbo x-over 100.00
242 CB 100.00
243 CB 100.00
244 CB 100.00
245 CB 100.00

Walt Disney's Comics & Stories #167
© Walt Disney

246 CB 100.00
247 thru 255 CB;Gyro
    Gearloose . . . . @100.00
256 thru 263 CB;Ludwig Von
    Drake & Gearloose . . . . . . @100.00

WALT DISNEY'S
DELL GIANT EDITIONS
Dell Publishing Co.

1 CB,W.Disney'sXmas
    Parade('49) 1,200.00
2 CB,W.Disney'sXmas
    Parade('50) 1,000.00
3 W.Disney'sXmas Parade('51) . 350.00
4 W.Disney'sXmas Parade('52) . 300.00
5 W.Disney'sXmas Parade('53) . 300.00
6 W.Disney'sXmas Parade('54) . 300.00
7 W.Disney'sXmas Parade('55) . 300.00
8 CB,W.Disney'sXmas
    Parade('56) 500.00
9 CB,W.Disney'sXmas
    Parade('57) 500.00
1 CB,W.Disney's Christmas in
    Disneyland (1957) 600.00
1 CB,W.Disney's Disneyland
    Birthday Party (1958) 600.00
1 W.Disney's Donald and Mickey
    in Disneyland (1958) 250.00
1 W.Disney's Donald Duck
    Beach Party (1954) 350.00
2 W.Disney's Donald Duck
    Beach Party (1955) 250.00
3 W.Disney's Donald Duck
    Beach Party (1956) 250.00
4 W.Disney's Donald Duck
    Beach Party (1957) 250.00
5 W.Disney's Donald Duck
    Beach Party (1958) 250.00
6 W.Disney's Donald Duck
    Beach Party (1959) 250.00
1 W.Disney's Donald Duck
    Fun Book (1954) 1,200.00
2 W.Disney's Donald Duck
    Fun Book (1954) 1,300.00
1 W.Disney's Donald Duck
    in Disneyland (1955) 350.00
1 W.Disney's Huey, Dewey
    and Louie (1958) 250.00
1 W.Disney's DavyCrockett('55). 400.00
1 W.Disney's Lady and the
    Tramp (1955) 650.00
1 CB,W.Disney's Mickey Mouse
    Almanac (1957) 600.00

1 W.Disney's Mickey Mouse
    Birthday Party (1953) 700.00
1 W.Disney's Mickey Mouse
    Club Parade (1955) 600.00
1 W.Disney's Mickey Mouse
    in Fantasyland (1957) 275.00
1 W.Disney's Mickey Mouse
    in Frontierland (1956) 300.00
1 W.Disney's Summer Fun('58) . 300.00
2 CB,W.Disney'sSummer
    Fun('59) 300.00
1 W.Disney's Peter Pan
    Treasure Chest (1953) 2,400.00
1 Disney Silly Symphonies('52) . 650.00
2 Disney Silly Symphonies('53) . 550.00
3 Disney Silly Symphonies('54) . 450.00
4 Disney Silly Symphonies('54) . 450.00
5 Disney Silly Symphonies('55) . 400.00
6 Disney Silly Symphonies('56) . 400.00
7 Disney Silly Symphonies('57) . 400.00
8 Disney Silly Symphonies('58) . 400.00
9 Disney Silly Symphonies('59) . 400.00
1 Disney SleepingBeauty('59) . 600.00
1 CB,W.Disney's Uncle Scrooge
    Goes to Disneyland (1957) . . 600.00
1 W.Disney's Vacation in
    Disneyland (1958) 275.00
1 CB,Disney's Vacation
    Parade('50) 2,000.00
2 Disney'sVacation Parade('51) . 600.00
3 Disney'sVacation Parade('52) . 350.00
4 Disney'sVacation Parade('53) . 350.00
5 Disney'sVacation Parade('54) . 350.00
6 Disney's Picnic Party (1955) . 300.00
7 Disney's Picnic Party (1956) . 300.00
8 CB,Disney's Picnic
    Party (1957) 500.00

WALT DISNEY'S
DELL JUNIOR TREASURY
1 W.Disney's Alice in Wonderland
    (1955) 250.00

WALT DISNEY
PRESENTS
Dell Publishing Co.,
June–Aug., 1952
1 Ph(c), Four Color 200.00
2 Ph(c) 150.00
3 Ph(c) 150.00
4 Ph(c) 150.00
5 and 6 Ph(c) . . . . @150.00

WAMBI
JUNGLE BOY
Fiction House Magazines,
Spring, 1942–Winter, 1952
1 HcK,HcK(c),Vengence of
    the Beasts 1,400.00
2 HcK,HcK(c),Lair of the
    Killer Rajah 750.00
3 HcK,HcK(c) 550.00
4 HcK,HcK(c),The Valley of
    the Whispering Drums 350.00
5 HcK,HcK(c),SwamplandSafari 300.00
6 Taming of the Tigress 275.00
7 Duel of the Congo Kings 275.00
8 AB(c),Friend of the Animals . . 275.00
9 Quest of the Devils Juju 275.00
10 Friend of the Animals 250.00
11 . . . . 250.00
12 Curse of the Jungle Jewels . . 250.00
13 New Adventures of Wambi . . . 175.00
14 . . . . 175.00
15 The Leopard Legions 175.00
16 . . . . 175.00
17 Beware Bwana! 175.00
18 Ogg the Great Bull Ape 175.00

WANTED COMICS

Toytown Comics/Orbit Publications, Sept.–Oct., 1947

9 Victor Everhart	350.00
10 Carlo Banone	200.00
11 Dwight Band	200.00
12 Ralph Roe	200.00
13 James Spencer;Drug	175.00
14 John "Jiggs" Sullivan;Drug	175.00
15 Harry Dunlap;Drug	125.00
16 Jack Parisi;Drug	135.00
17 Herber Ayers;Drug	135.00
18 Satan's Cigarettes;Drug	325.00
19 Jackson Stringer	125.00
20 George Morgan	125.00
21 BK,Paul Wilson	150.00
22 Strong violence	150.00
23 George Elmo Wells	125.00
24 BK,Bruce Cornett;Drug	150.00
25 Henry Anger	125.00
26 John Wormly	125.00
27 Death Always Knocks Twice	125.00
28 Paul H. Payton	125.00
29 Hangmans Holiday	125.00
30 George Lee	125.00
31 M Consolo	125.00
32 William Davis	125.00
33 The Web of Davis	125.00
34 Dead End	125.00
35 Glen Roy Wright	125.00
36 SSh,SSh(c),Bernard Lee Thomas	100.00
37 SSh,SSh(c),Joseph M. Moore	100.00
38 SSh,SSh(c)	100.00
39 The Horror Weed;Drug	250.00
40	100.00
41	100.00
42	100.00
43	100.00
44	100.00
45 Killers on the Loose;Drug	125.00
46 Charles Edward Crews	100.00
47	100.00
48 SSh,SSh(c)	100.00
49	100.00
50 JB(c),Make Way for Murder	150.00
51 JB(c),Dope Addict on a Holiday of Murder;Drug	135.00
52 The Cult of Killers; Classic Drug	135.00
53 April, 1953	100.00

WAR AGAINST CRIME

L.L. Publishing Co. (E.C. Comics), Spring, 1948

1 Grl, Stories from Police	1,200.00
2 Grl,Guilty of Murder	700.00
3 JCr(c)	700.00
4 AF,JCr(c)	600.00
5 JCr(c)	600.00
6 AF,JCr(c)	600.00
7 AF,JCr(c)	600.00
8 AF,JCr(c)	600.00
9 AF,JCr(c),The Kid	600.00
10 JCr(c),I:Vault Keeper	3,400.00
11 JCr(c)	2,200.00

Becomes:

VAULT OF HORROR, THE

April–May, 1950–Jan., 1955

12 AF,JCr(a&c),Wax Museum	8,000.00
13 AF,WW,JCr(c),Grl,Drug	2,400.00
14 AF,WW,JCr(c),Grl	2,000.00
15 AF,JCr(a&c),Grl,JKa	2,000.00
16 Grl,JKa,JCr(a&c)	1,500.00
17 JDa,Grl,JKa,JCr(a&c)	1,500.00
18 JDa,Grl,JKa,JCr(a&c)	1,400.00
19 JDa,Grl,JKa,JCr(a&c)	1,400.00
20 JDa,Grl,JKa,JCr(a&c)	1,200.00
21 JDa,Grl,JKa,JCr(a&c)	1,200.00
22 JDa,JKa,JCr(a&c)	1,200.00
23 JDa,Grl,JCr(a&c)	1,200.00
24 JDa,Grl,JO,JCr(a&c)	1,200.00
25 JDa,Grl,JKa,JCr(a&c)	1,200.00
26 JDa,Grl,JCr(a&c)	900.00
27 JDa,Grl,GE,JCr(a&c)	1,000.00
28 JDa,Grl,JCr(a&c)	1,000.00
29 JDa,Grl,JKa,JCr(a&c), Bradbury Adapt.	1,000.00
30 JDa,Grl,JCr(a&c)	1,000.00
31 JDa,Grl,JCr(a&c), Bradbury Adapt	800.00
32 JDa,Grl,JCr(a&c)	800.00
33 JDa,Grl,RC,JCr(c)	800.00
34 JDa,Grl,RC,JCr(a&c)	800.00
35 JDa,Grl,JCr(a&c),X-mas	800.00
36 JDa,Grl,BK,JCr(a&c),Drug	800.00
37 JDa,Grl,AW,JCr(a&c) Hanging	800.00
38 JDa,Grl,BK,JCr(a&c).	800.00
39 Grl,BK,RC,JCr(a&c) Bondage(c)	800.00
40 Grl,BK,JO,JCr(a&c)	900.00

WAR BATTLES

Harvey Publications, Feb., 1952

1 BP,Devils of the Deep	175.00
2 BP,A Present From Benny	125.00
3 BP	100.00
4	100.00
5	100.00
6 HN	100.00
7 BP	125.00
8	100.00
9 Dec., 1953	100.00

WAR BIRDS

Fiction House Magazines, 1952

1 Willie the Washout	225.00
2 Mystery MIGs of Kwanjamu	125.00
3 thru 6	@125.00
7 Winter, 1953,Across the Wild Yalu	125.00

WAR COMICS

Dell Publishing Co., May, 1940

1 AMc,Sky Hawk	900.00
2 O:Greg Gildam	500.00
3	350.00
4 O:Night Devils	400.00

WARFRONT

Fighting Forces Publ./ Harvey Publications

1 Korean War	200.00
2	150.00
3	125.00
4	125.00
5	125.00
6 thru 10	@125.00
11 thru 21	@100.00
22 HN	125.00
23 thru 33	@100.00
34 JK	100.00
35	100.00

WAR FURY

Comic Media/Harwell, 1952

1 DH,RP,hole in head	375.00
2 Violent	200.00
3 Violent	200.00
4 PMo,Violent	200.00

WAR HEROES

Dell Publishing Co., July–Sept., 1942

1 Gen. Douglas MacArthur (c)	400.00
2	300.00

3 Pro-Soviet	250.00
4 A:Gremlins	350.00
5	250.00
6	200.00
7	200.00
8 thru 11	@200.00

War Heroes #7
© *Ace Magazines*

WAR HEROES

Ace Magazines, May, 1952

1 Always Comin'	150.00
2 LC,The Last Red Tank	125.00
3 You Got it	100.00
4 A Red Patrol	100.00
5 Hustle it Up	100.00
6 LC,Hang on Pal	125.00
7 LC	125.00
8 LC, April, 1953	125.00

WARPATH

Key Publications/ Stanmore, Nov., 1954

1 Red Men Raid	125.00
2 AH(c),Braves Battle	100.00
3 April, 1955	100.00

WARRIOR COMICS

H.C. Blackerby, 1944

1 Ironman wing Brady	400.00

WAR REPORT

Excellent Publ. (Ajax/Farrell Publ.), 1952

1	150.00
2 Burning bodies	250.00
3	125.00
4	125.00
5	125.00

WAR SHIPS

Dell Publishing Co., 1942

1 AMc	250.00

WAR STORIES

Dell Publishing Co., 1942

5 O:The Whistler	350.00
6 A:Night Devils	250.00
7 A:Night Devils	250.00
8 A:Night Devils	250.00

WARTIME ROMANCES
St. John Publishing Co.,
July, 1951
1 MB(c),MB	500.00
2 MB(c),MB	300.00
3 MB(c),MB	275.00
4 MB(c),MB	275.00
5 MB(c),MB	250.00
6 MB(c),MB	250.00
7 thru 8 MB(c),MB	@250.00
9 thru 12 MB(c),MB	@200.00
13 thru 15 MB(c)	@125.00
16 MB(c),MB	200.00
17 MB(c)	125.00
18 MB(c),MB	200.00

WAR VICTORY COMICS
U.S. Treasury/War Victory/
Harvey Publ., Summer, 1942
1 Savings Bond Promo with Top Syndicated Cartoonists, benefit USO	650.00

Becomes:

WAR VICTORY ADVENTURES
Summer, 1942
2 BP,2nd Front Comics	300.00
3 BP,F:Capt Cross of the Red Cross	250.00

WASHABLE JONES AND THE SHMOO
Toby Press Publ., 1953
1 Super Shmoo	275.00

WEB OF EVIL
Comic Magazines, Inc.
(Quality Comics Group),
Nov., 1952
1 Custodian of the Dead	900.00
2 JCo,Hangmans Horror	600.00
3 JCo	600.00
4 JCo(a&c),Monsters of the Mist	600.00
5 JCo(a&c),The Man who Died Twice,Electric Chair(c).	700.00
6 JCo(a&c),Orgy of Death	600.00
7 JCo(a&c),The Strangling Hands	600.00
8 JCo,Flaming Vengeance	550.00
9 JCo,The Monster in Flesh	550.00
10 JCo,Brain that Wouldn't Die	550.00
11 JCo,Buried Alive	550.00
12 Phantom Killer	350.00
13 Demon Inferno	350.00
14 RC(c),The Monster Genie.	350.00
15 Crypts of Horror	350.00
16 Hamlet of Horror	350.00
17 Terror in Chinatown, Drug.	375.00
18 Scared to Death,Acid Face.	400.00
19 Demon of the Pit.	350.00
20 Man Made Terror	350.00
21 Dec., 1954, Death's Ambush	350.00

WEB OF MYSTERY
A.A. Wyn Publ.
(Ace Magazines), Feb., 1951
1 MSy,Venom of the Vampires	800.00
2 MSy,Legacy of the Accursed	450.00
3 MSy,The Violin Curse	400.00
4 GC	400.00
5	400.00
6 LC	400.00
7 MSy	400.00
8 LC,LC(c),MSy,The Haunt of Death Lake	400.00
9 LC,LC(c)	400.00

Web of Mystery #16
© Ace Magazines

10	400.00
11 MSy	400.00
12 LC	350.00
13 LC,LC(c)Surrealist	350.00
14 MSy	350.00
15	350.00
16	350.00
17 LC,LC(c)	350.00
18 LC	350.00
19 LC	350.00
20 LC, Beyond	350.00
21 MSy	350.00
22	350.00
23	350.00
24 LC	350.00
25 LC	350.00
26	350.00
27 LC, Beyond	350.00
28 RP,1st Comics Code issue	300.00
29 MSy,Sept., 1955	300.00

WEEKENDER, THE
Rucker Publishing Co.,
Sept., 1945
1-1 rep.(c), As Zip	250.00
1-2 thru 1-4	@275.00
2-1 rep.(c), As Dynamic	300.00
2-2 Jco,rep.(c), As Dynamic	275.00
2-3 WMc,Jan., 1946	275.00

WEIRD ADVENTURES
P.L. Publishing,
May, 1951–Oct., 1951
1 MB,Missing Diamonds	900.00
2 Puppet Peril	700.00
3 Blood Vengeance.	600.00

WEIRD ADVENTURES
Approved Comics
(Ziff-Davis)
July–Aug., 1951
10 P(c),Seeker from Beyond	550.00

WEIRD CHILLS
Key Publications,
July, 1954
1 MBi(c),BW	1,300.00
2 Eye Torture(c)	1,200.00
3 Bondage(c),Nov., 1954	750.00

WEIRD COMICS
Fox Features Syndicate,
April, 1940
1 LF(c),Bondage(c),B:Birdman, Thor,Sorceress of Doom, BlastBennett,Typhon,Voodoo Man, Dr.Mortal	8,500.00
2 LF(c),Mummy(c)	3,500.00
3 JSm(c)	1,800.00
4 JSm(c)	1,800.00
5 Bondage(c),I:Dart,Ace; E:Thor	1,900.00
6 Dart & Ace(c)	1,500.00
7 Battle of Kooba	1,500.00
8 B:Panther Woman,Dynamo, The Eagle	1,500.00
9 V:Pirates	1,200.00
10 A:Navy Jones	1,200.00
11 Dart & Ace(c).	900.00
12 Dart & Ace(c)	900.00
13 Dart & Ace(c)	900.00
14 The Rage(c)	900.00
15 Dart & Ace (c)	900.00
16 Flag,The Encore(c).	900.00
17 O:Black Rider	850.00
18	850.00
19	850.00
20 Jan., 1941,I'm The Master of Life and Death	1,200.00

WEIRD FANTASY
I.C. Publishing Co.
(E.C. Comics),
May–June, 1950
13(1)AF,HK,JKa,WW,AF(c), Roger Harvey's Brain	3,500.00
14(2)AF,HK, JKa,WW,AF(c),Cosmic Ray Brain Explosion	2,000.00
15(3)AF,HK,JKa,WW,AF(c),Your Destination is the Moon	1,500.00
16(4)AF,HK,JKa,WW,AF(c),	1,500.00
17(5)AF,HK,JKa,WW,AF(c),Not Made by Human Hands	1,100.00
6 AF,HK,JKa,WW,AF(c),Robot.	1,000.00
7 AF,JKa,WW,AF(c)	1,000.00
8 AF,JKa,WW,AF(c)	1,000.00
9 AF,Jka,WW,JO,AF(c)	1,000.00
10 AF,Jka,WW,JO,AF(c)	900.00
11 AF,Jka,WW,JO,AF(c)	1,000.00
12 AF,Jka,WW,JO,AF(c)	1,000.00
13 AF,Jka,WW,JO,AF(c)	1,000.00
14 AF,JKa,WW,JO,AW&FF, AF(c)	900.00
15 AF,JKa,JO,AW&RKr,AF(c), Bondage(c)	1,000.00
16 AF,JKa,JO,AW&RKr,AF(c).	1,500.00
17 AF,JOP,JKa,AF(c),Bradbury	1,000.00
18 AF,JO,JKa,AF(c),Bradbury.	1,000.00
19 JO,JKa,JO(c),Bradbury	1,000.00
20 JO,JKa,FF,AF(c)	1,000.00
21 JO,JKa,AW&FF(c)	1,200.00
22 JO,JKa,JO(c),Nov.,1953	700.00

With Weird Science, Becomes:

WEIRD SCIENCE FANTASY

WEIRD HORRORS
St. John Publishing Co.,
June, 1952
1 GT,Dungeon of the Doomed	900.00
2 Strangest Music Ever	500.00
3 PMo,Strange Fakir From the Orient, Drug	500.00
4 Murderers Knoll	400.00
5 Phantom Bowman	400.00
6 Monsters from Outer Space	700.00
7 LC,Deadly Double	700.00
8 JKu,JKu(c),Bloody Yesterday	600.00
9 JKu,JKu(c),Map Of Doom	600.00

Becomes:

NIGHTMARE
Dec., 1953
10 JKu(c),The Murderer's Mask . 800.00
11 BK,Ph(c),Fangs of Death 600.00
12 JKu(c),The Forgotten Mask . . 500.00
13 BP,Princess of the Sea 400.00
Becomes:

AMAZING GHOST STORIES
Oct., 1954
14 EK,MB(c),Pit & Pendulum. . . . 450.00
15 BP,Weird Thrillers 350.00
16 Feb., 1955, EK,JKu. 400.00

WEIRD JUNGLE TALES
Star Publications, 1953
202 . . . . 150.00

WEIRD MYSTERIES
Gilmore Publications, Oct., 1952
1 BW(c) 1,300.00
2 BWi, Robot Woman 1,700.00
3 Severed Heads(c) 900.00
4 BW,Human headed ants(c) . 1,650.00
5 BW,Brains From Head(c) . . . 1,700.00
6 Severed Head(c) 900.00
7 Used in "Seduction" 1,200.00
8 The One That Got Away 850.00
9 Epitaph,Cyclops, Violence. . . . 750.00
10 The Ruby 700.00
11 Voodoo Dolls. 650.00
12 Sept., 1954 . . . . 650.00

WEIRD SCIENCE
E.C. Comics, 1950
1 AF(a&c),JKu,HK,WW 4,500.00
2 AF(a&c),JKu,HK,WW,Flying
  Saucers(c) 2,000.00
3 AF(a&c),JKu,HK,WW 1,700.00
4 AF(a&c),JKu,HK 1,700.00
5 AF(a&c),JKu,HK,WW,
  Atomic Bomb(c) 1,500.00
6 AF(a&c),JKu,HK 1,500.00
7 AF(a&c),JKu,HK,Classic(c). . 1,500.00
8 AF(a&c),JKu 1,500.00
9 WW(c),JKu,Classic(c). 1,600.00
10 WW(c),JKu,JO,Classic(c) . . 1,500.00
11 AF,JKu,Space war. 800.00
12 WW(c),JKu,JO,Classic(c) . . . 800.00
13 WW(c),JKu,JO, ... 800.00
14 WW(a&c),JO. 900.00

Weird Science #17
© E.C. Comics

15 WW(a&c),JO,Grl,AW,
  RKr,JKa 900.00
16 WW(a&c),JO,AW,RKr,JKa . . . 800.00
17 WW(a&c),JO,AW,RKr,JKa . . . 800.00
18 WW(a&c),JO,AW,RKr,
  JKa,Atomic Bomb 800.00
19 WW(a&c),JO,A
  FF,Horror(c) 900.00
20 WW(a&c),JO,AW,FF,JKa 900.00
21 WW(a&c),JO,AW,FF,JKa 900.00
22 WW(a&c),JO,AW,FF 900.00
Becomes:

WEIRD SCIENCE FANTASY
March, 1954
23 WW(a&c),AW,BK 1,000.00
24 WW,AW,BK,Classic(c) 1,000.00
25 WW,AW,BK,Classic(c) 1,100.00
26 AF(c),WW,RC,
  Flying Saucer(c) 800.00
27 WW(a&c),RC 800.00
28 AF(c),WW 900.00
29 AF(c),WW,Classic(c) 2,500.00
Becomes:

INCREDIBLE SCIENCE FANTASY
July–Aug., 1955
30 WW,JDa(c),BK,AW,RKr,JO . . 700.00
31 WW,JDa(c),BK,AW,RKr 750.00
32 JDa(c),BK,WW,JO 750.00
33 WW(c),BK,WW,JO 750.00

WEIRD TALES OF THE FUTURE
S.P.M. Publ./ Aragon Publications, March, 1952
1 RA 1,700.00
2 BW,BW(c), Jumpin Jupiter . . 2,500.00
3 BW,BW(c) 2,500.00
4 BW,BW(c) 2,000.00
5 BW,BW(c),Jumpin' Jupiter
  Lingerie(c) 2,500.00
6 Bondage(c) 1,100.00
7 BW,Devil(c). 2,000.00
8 July–Aug., 1953 . . . . 2,200.00

WEIRD TERROR
Allen Hardy Associates (Comic Media), Sept., 1952
1 RP,DH,DH(c),Dungeon of the
  Doomed;Hitler 850.00
2 HcK(c),PMo, Torture 700.00
3 PMo,DH,DH(c),Strong
  Violence. 700.00
4 PMo,DH,DH(c),Severed Head. 700.00
5 PMo,DH,RP,DH(c),Hanging(c). 600.00
6 DH,RP,DH(c),Step into
  My Parlour, Severed Head . . 650.00
7 DH,PMo,DH(c),Blood o/t Bats . 650.00
8 DH,RP,DH(c),Step into
  My Parlour, Severed Head . . 625.00
9 DH,PMo,DH(c),The Fleabite . . 500.00
10 DH,BP,RP,DH(c) 500.00
11 DH,DH(c),Satan's Love Call . . 600.00
12 DH,DH(c),King Whitey 500.00
13 DH,DH(c),Wings of Death,
  Severed Head, Sept. 1954 . . 500.00

WEIRD THRILLERS
Approved Comics (Ziff-Davis), Sept.–Oct., 1951
1 Ph(c),Monsters & The Model 1,300.00
2 AW,P(c),The Last Man 1,000.00
3 AW,P(c),Princess o/t Sea . . 1,300.00
4 AW,P(c),The Widows Lover. . . 900.00

5 BP,Oct., 1952,AW,P(c),
  Wings of Death 850.00

Western Action Thrillers #1
© Dell Publishing

WESTERN ACTION THRILLERS
Dell Publishing Co., April, 1937
1 Buffalo Bill, Texas Kid. 1,400.00

WESTERN ADVENTURES COMICS
A.A. Wyn, Inc. (Ace Magazines), Oct., 1948
N#(1)Injun Gun Bait 300.00
N#(2)Cross-Draw Kid 175.00
N#(3)Outlaw Mesa 175.00
4 Sheriff, Sal 125.00
5 . . . . 125.00
6 Rip Roaring Adventure 125.00
Becomes:

WESTERN LOVE TRAILS
Nov., 1949
7 . . . . 150.00
8 Maverick Love 125.00
9 March, 1950 . . . . 100.00

WESTERN BANDIT TRAILS
St. John Publishing Co., Jan., 1949
1 GT,MB(c), Blue Monk 375.00
2 GT,MB(c) 300.00
3 GT,MB,MB(c),Gingham Fury . 300.00

WESTERN CRIME BUSTERS
Trojan Magazines, Sept., 1950–April, 1952
1 Gunslingin' Galoots 500.00
2 K-Bar Kate 250.00
3 Wilma West 250.00
4 Bob Dale 250.00
5 Six-Gun Smith 250.00
6 WW 450.00
7 WW,Wells Fargo Robbery . . . 450.00
8 . . . . 250.00
9 WW,Lariat Lucy 450.00
10 WW,Tex Gordon 500.00

WESTERN CRIME CASES
See: OUTLAWS, THE

WESTERNER, THE
**Wanted Comics Group/
Toytown Publ.,
June, 1948**

14 F:Jack McCall	250.00
15 F:Bill Jamett	200.00
16 F:Tom McLowery	200.00
17 F:Black Bill Desmond	200.00
18 BK,F:Silver Dollar Dalton	250.00
19 MMe,F:Jess Meeton	150.00
20	150.00
21 BK,MMe	200.00
22 BK,MMe	200.00
23 BK,MMe	200.00
24 BK,MMe	200.00
25 O,I,B:Calamity Jane	200.00
26 BK,F:The Widowmaker	250.00
27 BK	100.00
28 thru 31	@100.00
32 E:Calamity Jane	100.00
33 A:Quest	100.00
34	100.00
35 SSh(c)	100.00
36	100.00
37 Lobo-Wolf Boy	100.00
38	100.00
39	100.00
40 SSh(c)	100.00
41 Dec., 1951	100.00

WESTERN FIGHTERS
**Hillman Periodicals,
April–May, 1948**

1 S&K(c)	500.00
2 BF(c)	200.00
3 BF(c)	150.00
4 BK,BF	175.00
5	125.00
6	125.00
7 BK	150.00
8	125.00
9	125.00
10 BK	150.00
11 AMC&FF	400.00
2-1 BK	150.00
2-2 BP	125.00
2-3 thru 2-12	@100.00
3-1 thru 3-11	@100.00
3-12 BK	125.00
4-1	100.00
4-2 BK	150.00
4-3 BK	150.00
4-4 BK	150.00

*Western Fighters #16
© Hillman Periodicals*

4-5 BK	150.00
4-6 BK	150.00
4-7 March–April, 1953	100.00

WESTERN FRONTIER
**P.L. Publishers
(Approved Comics),
May, 1951**

1 Flaming Vengeance	150.00
2	125.00
3 Death Rides the Iron Horse	75.00
4 thru 6	@75.00
7 1952	75.00

WESTERN HEARTS
**Standard Magazine, Inc.,
Dec., 1949**

1 JSe, Whip Wilson, Ph(c)	300.00
2 AW,FF, Palomino, Ph(c)	300.00
3 Rex Allen, Ph(c)	200.00
4 JSe,BE, Ph(c)	175.00
5 JSe,BE,Ray Milland, Ph(c)	175.00
6 JSe,BE,Irene Dunn, Ph(c)	175.00
7 JSe,BE,Jock Mahoney Ph(c)	175.00
8 Randolph Scott, Ph(c)	175.00
9 JSe,BE, Whip Wilson, Ph(c)	200.00
10 JSe,BE, Bill Williams,Ph(c)	175.00

WESTERN HERO
See: WOW COMICS

WESTERN KILLERS
Fox Features Syndicate, 1948

N# Lingerie	300.00
60 Violence	325.00
61 JCo,LSe	250.00
62	225.00
63	225.00
64	225.00

WESTERN LOVE
**Feature Publications
(Prize Comics Group),
July–Aug., 1949**

1 S&K, Randolph Scott	450.00
2 S&K, Whip Wilson	325.00
3 JSe,BE, Reno Brown	225.00
4 JSe,BE	225.00
5 JSe,BE, Dale Robertson	325.00

WESTERN PICTURE STORIES
**Comics Magazine Co.,
Feb., 1937–June, 1937**

1 WE,Treachery Trail, 1st Western	3,000.00
2 WE,Weapons of the West	1,600.00
3 WE,Dragon Pass	1,400.00
4 CavemanCowboy	1,400.00

WESTERN ROUGH RIDERS
**Stanmor Publ.
(Gilmore Magazines), 1954**

1	125.00
2	100.00
3	100.00
4	100.00

WESTERN THRILLERS
**Fox Features Syndicate,
Aug., 1948**

1 Velvet Rose	700.00
2	300.00
3 GT,RH(c)	250.00
4	275.00
5 Butch Cassidy	275.00

6 June, 1949	250.00

Becomes:

MY PAST CONFESSIONS
Aug., 1949

7	225.00
8	150.00
9	150.00
10	150.00
11 WW	300.00
12 Crimes Inc.	125.00

WESTERN TRUE CRIME
**Fox Features Syndicate,
Aug., 1948**

1 (#15) JKa, Zoot 14.	450.00
2 (#16) JKa, Violence	350.00
3 JKa.	325.00
4 JCr	325.00
5	250.00
6	250.00

Becomes:

MY CONFESSION
Aug., 1949–Feb., 1950

7 WW	400.00
8 WW,My Tarnished Reputation	350.00
9 I:Tormented Men	150.00
10 I Am Damaged Goods	150.00

WHACK
**St. John Publishing Co.,
Dec., 1953**

1 3-D	425.00
2 Steve Crevice,Flush Jordan V:Bing (Crosby)The Merciful	300.00
3 F:Little Awful Fannie	250.00

WHAM COMICS
**Centaur Publications,
Nov., 1940**

1 PG,The Sparkler & His Disappearing Suit	2,400.00
2 Dec., 1940,PG,PG(C), Men Turn into Icicles	1,600.00

WHIRLWIND COMICS
**Nita Publications,
June, 1940**

1 F:The Cyclone	3,300.00
2 A:Scoops Hanlon,Cyclone(c)	1,600.00
3 Sept., 1940,A:Magic Mandarin,Cyclone(c)	1,500.00

WHITE PRINCESS OF THE JUNGLE
Avon Periodicals, July, 1951

1 EK(c),Terror Fangs	900.00
2 EK,EK(c),Jungle Vengeance	600.00
3 EK,EK(c),The Blue Gorilla	500.00
4 Fangs of the Swamp Beast	450.00
5 EK,Coils of the Tree Snake Nov., 1952	450.00

WHITE RIDER AND SUPER HORSE
See: OUTLAWS, THE

WHIZ COMICS
**Fawcett Publications,
Feb., 1940**

1 O:Captain Marvel,B:Spy Smasher, Golden Arrow,Dan Dare, Scoop Smith, Ibis the Invincible, Sivana	125,000.00
2	12,000.00
3 Make way for Captain Marvel	7,000.00

Whiz Comics #6
© *Fawcett Publications*

4 Captain Marvel
  Crashes Through 6,000.00
5 Captain Marvel
  Scores Again! 5,000.00
6 Circus of Death 3,700.00
7 B:Dr Voodoo,Squadron
  of Death 3,700.00
8 Saved by Captain Marvel! . . 3,700.00
9 MRa,Captain Marvel
  on the Job. 3,700.00
10 Battles the Winged Death . . 3,700.00
11 Hurray for Captain Marvel . . 2,500.00
12 Captain Marvel rides
  the Engine of Doom 2,500.00
13 Worlds Most Powerful Man!. 2,500.00
14 Boomerangs the Torpedo . . 2,500.00
15 O:Sivana 2,400.00
16 Dr. Voodoo. 2,300.00
17 Knocks out a Tank 2,300.00
18 V:Spy Smasher 2,300.00
19 Crushes the Tiger Shark . . . 1,900.00
20 V:Sivana 1,900.00
21 O:Lt. Marvels 2,000.00
22 Mayan Temple 1,300.00
23 GT,A:Dr. Voodoo 1,300.00
24 . . . . 1,300.00
25 O&I:Captain Marvel Jr., Stops
  the Turbine of Death. 12,000.00
26 . . . . 1,300.00
27 V:Death God of the
  Katonkas. 1,400.00
28 V:Mad Dervish of Ank-Har . . 1,400.00
29 Three Lt. Marvels (c), Pan
  American Olympics 1,400.00
30 CCB(c). 1,300.00
31 Douglass MacArthur
  & Spy Smasher(c) 1,100.00
32 Spy Smasher(c). 1,100.00
33 Spy Smasher(c). 1,400.00
34 Three Lt. Marvels (c) 700.00
35 Capt. Marvel and the
  Three Fates 1,000.00
36 Haunted Hallowe'en Hotel . . . 700.00
37 Return of the Trolls 700.00
38 Grand Steeplechase 700.00
39 A Nazi Utopia 700.00
40 A:Three Lt. Marvels, The
  Earth's 4 Corners 700.00
41 Captain Marvel 1,000 years
  from Now 600.00
42 Returns in Time Chair. 600.00
43 V:Sinister Spies,
  Spy Smasher(c). 600.00
44 Life Story of Captain Marvel . . 650.00
45 Cures His Critics. 600.00

46 . . . . 600.00
47 Captain Marvel needs
  a Birthday 600.00
48 . . . . 600.00
49 Writes a Victory song 600.00
50 Captain Marvel's most
  embarrassing moment 600.00
51 Judges the Ugly-
  Beauty Contest 500.00
52 V:Sivana, Chooses
  His Birthday 500.00
53 Captain Marvel fights
  Billy Batson 500.00
54 Jack of all Trades 500.00
55 Family Tree. 500.00
56 Tells what the Future Will Be . 500.00
57 A:Spy Smasher,Golden Arrow,
  Ibis. 500.00
58 . . . . 500.00
59 V:Sivana's Twin. 500.00
60 Missing Person's Machine . . . 500.00
61 Gets a first name 450.00
62 Plays in a Band. 450.00
63 Great Indian Rope Trick 450.00
64 Suspected of Murder 450.00
65 Lamp of Diogenes. 450.00
66 The Trial of Mr. Morris! 450.00
67 . . . . 450.00
68 Laugh Lotion, V:Sivana. 450.00
69 Mission to Mercury 650.00
70 Climbs the World's Mightiest
  Mountain 550.00
71 Strange Magician 500.00
72 V:The Man of the Future. 500.00
73 In Ogre Land. 500.00
74 Old Man River. 500.00
75 The City Olympics. 500.00
76 Spy Smasher becomes
  Crime Smasher 500.00
77 . . . . 500.00
78 Golden Arrow 500.00
79 . . . . 500.00
80 . . . . 500.00
81 . . . . 500.00
82 The Atomic Ship 500.00
83 Magic Locket. 500.00
84 . . . . 500.00
85 The Clock of San Lojardo 500.00
86 V:Sinister Sivanas. 500.00
87 The War on Olympia. 500.00
88 The Wonderful Magic Carpet . 500.00
89 Webs of Crime 500.00
90 . . . . 500.00
91 Infinity (c) 500.00
92 . . . . 500.00
93 Captain America become
  a Hobo?. 500.00
94 V:Sivana 500.00
95 Captain Marvel is grounded . . 500.00
96 The Battle Between Buildings. 500.00
97 Visits Mirage City 500.00
98 . . . . 500.00
99 V:Menace in the Mountains . . 500.00
100 Anniversary Issue 600.00
101 . . . . 500.00
102 A:Commando Yank 500.00
103 . . . . 500.00
104 Flag(c). 500.00
105 . . . . 500.00
106 A:Bulletman. 500.00
107 The Great Experiment 600.00
108 thru 114 . . . . @400.00
115 The Marine Invasion 400.00
116 . . . . 400.00
117 V:Sivana 400.00
118 thru 121 . . . . @400.00
122 V:Sivana 400.00
123 . . . . 400.00
124 . . . . 400.00
125 Olympic Games of the Gods 400.00
126 . . . . 400.00
127 . . . . 400.00

128 . . . . 400.00
129 . . . . 350.00
130 . . . . 350.00
131 The Television Trap. 350.00
132 thru 142 . . . . @350.00
143 Mystery of the Flying Studio . 350.00
144 V:The Disaster Master 350.00
145 . . . . 350.00
146 . . . . 350.00
147 . . . . 350.00
148 . . . . 350.00
149 . . . . 350.00
150 V:Bug Bombs 450.00
151 . . . . 450.00
152 . . . . 450.00
153 V:The Death Horror 600.00
154 Horror Tale, I:Dr.Death 600.00
155 V:Legend Horror,Dr.Death . . 650.00

WHODUNIT?
D.S. Publishing Co.,
Aug.–Sept., 1948
1 MB,Weeping Widow 350.00
2 Diploma For Death 150.00
3 Dec.–Jan., 1949 . . . . 150.00

WHO IS NEXT?
Standard Comics,
Jan., 1953
5 ATh,RA,Don't Let Me Kill 300.00

Wilbur Comics #14
© *Archie Comics*

WILBUR COMICS
MLJ Magazines
(Archie Publications),
Summer, 1944
1 F:Wilbur Wilkin-America's Song
  of Fun 750.00
2 . . . . 400.00
3 . . . . 300.00
4 . . . . 300.00
5 I:Katy Keene 1,500.00
6 F:Katy Keene 350.00
7 F:Katy Keene. 350.00
8 F:Katy Keene. 350.00
9 F:Katy Keene. 350.00
10 F:Katy Keene 350.00
11 thru 20 F:Katy Keene . . . . @300.00
21 thru 30 F:Katy Keene . . . . @250.00
31 thru 40 F:Katy Keene . . . . @150.00
41 thru 56 F:Katy Keene . . . . @125.00
57 thru 89. . . . . @100.00
90 Oct., 1965. . . . . 100.00

GOLDEN AGE

WILD BILL ELLIOT
**Dell Publishing Co.,
May, 1950**
(1) *see Dell Four Color #278*
2 . . . . 150.00
3 thru 5 . . . . @100.00
6 thru 10 . . . . @100.00
(11-12) *see Four Color #472, 520*
13 thru 17 . . . . @100.00

WILD BILL HICKOK
AND JINGLES
**See: YELLOWJACKET
COMICS**

WILD BILL HICKOK
**Avon Periodicals,
Sept.–Oct., 1949**
1 Grl(c),Frontier Fighter 350.00
2 Ph(c),Gambler's Guns 150.00
3 Ph(c),Great Stage Robbery . . 100.00
4 Ph(c),Guerilla Gunmen 100.00
5 Ph(c),Return of the Renegade 100.00
6 EK,EK(c),Along the Apache
   Trail 100.00
7 EK,EK(c)Outlaws of
   Hell's Bend 100.00
8 Ph(c),The Border Outlaws . . . 100.00
9 PH(c),Killers From Texas . . . 100.00
10 Ph(c) 100.00
11 EK,EK(c),The Hell Riders 100.00
12 EK,EK(c),The Lost Gold Mine 100.00
13 EK,EK(c),Bloody Canyon
   Massacre 125.00
14 . . . . 125.00
15 . . . . 100.00
16 JKa,Bad Men of Deadwood . . 100.00
17 JKa 100.00
18 JKa,Kit West 100.00
19 thru 23 . . . . @100.00
24 EK,EK(c) 100.00
25 EK,EK(c) 100.00
26 EK,EK(c) 100.00
27 EK,EK(c) 100.00
28 EK,EK(c),May–June, 1956 . . . 100.00

WILD BOY OF
THE CONGO
**Approved(Ziff-Davis)/
St. John Publ. Co.,
Feb.–March, 1951**
10(1)NS,PH(c),Bondage(c),The
   Gorilla God 400.00
11(2)NS,Ph(c),Star of the Jungle. 200.00
12(3)NS,Ph(c),Ice-Age Men. 200.00
4 NS.Ph(c),Tyrant of the Jungle 250.00
5 NS,Ph(c),The White Robe
   of Courage 150.00
6 NS,Ph(c) 150.00
7 MB,EK.Ph(c) 200.00
8 Ph(c),Man-Eater 150.00
9 Ph(c),Killer Leopard 150.00
10 . . . . 150.00
11 MB(c). 200.00
12 MB(c) 200.00
13 MB(c) 200.00
14 MB(c) 200.00
15 June, 1955 . . . . 150.00

WILD FRONTIER
Charlton Comics, 1955
1 Davy Crockett 125.00
2 same 100.00
3 thru 7 same . . . . @100.00
7 O:Cheyenne Kid 100.00
Becomes:

CHEYENNE KID

WILL ROGERS WESTERN
Fox Features Syndicate, 1950
1 (5) 500.00
2 Ph(c) 400.00

WINGS COMICS
**Wings Publ.
(Fiction House Magazines),
Sept., 1940**
1 HcK,AB,GT,Ph(c),B:Skull Squad,
   Clipper Kirk,Suicide Smith,
   War Nurse,Phantom Falcons,
   GreasemonkeyGriffin,Parachute
   Patrol,Powder Burns 5,000.00
2 HcK,AB,GT,Bomber Patrol . . 2,000.00
3 HcK,AB,GT 1,500.00
4 HcK,AB,GT,B:Spitfire Ace . . 1,500.00
5 HcK,AB,GT,Torpedo Patrol . 1,500.00
6 HcK,AB,GT,Bombs for Berlin 1,000.00
7 HcK,AB 1,000.00
8 HcK,AB,The Wings of Doom 1,000.00
9 Sky-Wolf 900.00
10 The Upside Down 900.00
11 . . . . 800.00
12 Fury of the fire Boards 800.00
13 Coffin Slugs For The
   Luftwaffe 800.00
14 Stuka Buster 800.00
15 Boomerang Blitz 800.00
16 O:Capt.Wings 900.00
17 Skyway to Death 700.00
18 Horsemen of the Sky 700.00
19 Nazi Spy Trap 700.00
20 The One Eyed Devil 700.00
21 Chute Troop Tornado 600.00
22 TNT for Tokyo 600.00
23 RP,Battling Eagles of Bataan . 600.00
24 RP,The Death of a Hero 600.00
25 RP,Suicide Squeeze 600.00
26 Tojo's Eagle Trap 600.00
27 BLb,Mile High Gauntlet. 600.00
28 BLb,Tail Gun Tornado 600.00
29 BLb,Buzzards from Berlin . . . 600.00
30 BLb,Monsters of the
   Stratosphere 550.00
31 BLb,Sea Hawks away. 550.00
32 BLb,Sky Mammoth 550.00
33 BLb,Roll Call of the Yankee
   Eagles 550.00
34 BLb,So Sorry,Mr Tojo 550.00
35 BLb,RWb,Hell's Lightning . . . 550.00
36 RWb,The Crash-Master 550.00
37 RWb,Sneak Blitz. 550.00
38 RWb,Rescue Raid of the
   Yank Eagle 550.00
39 RWb,Sky Hell/Pigboat Patrol . 550.00
40 RWb,Luftwaffe Gamble. 550.00
41 RWb,.50 Caliber Justice 500.00
42 RWb,PanzerMeat forMosquito 500.00
43 RWb,Suicide Sentinels 500.00
44 RWb,Berlin Bombs Away . . . 500.00
45 RWb,Hells Cargo 500.00
46 RWb,Sea-Hawk Patrol 500.00
47 RWb,Tojo's Tin Gibraltar 500.00
48 RWb 500.00
49 RWb,Rockets Away 500.00
50 RWb,Mission For a Madman . 500.00
51 RWb,Toll for a Typhoon 400.00
52 MB,Madam Marauder 400.00
53 MB,Robot Death Over
   Manhattan 400.00
54 MB,Juggernauts of Death . . . 400.00
55 MB. 400.00
56 MB,Sea Raiders Grave. 400.00
57 MB,Yankee Warbirds over
   Tokyo 400.00
58 MB. 400.00
59 MB,Prey of the Night Hawks. . 400.00
60 MB,E:Skull Squad,
   Hell's Eyes 400.00
61 MB,Raiders o/t Purple Dawn . 350.00

Wings #8
© Fiction House Magazines

62 Twilight of the Gods 350.00
63 Hara Kiri Rides the Skyways . 350.00
64 Taps for Tokyo 350.00
65 AB,Warhawk for the Kill 350.00
66 AB,B:Ghost Patrol. 350.00
67 AB 350.00
68 AB,ClipperKirkBecomesPhantom
   Falcon;O:Phantom Falcon. . . 350.00
69 AB,O:cont,Phantom Falcon . . 350.00
70 AB,N:Phantom Falcon;
   O:Final Phantom Falcon 350.00
71 Ghost Patrol becomes
   Ghost Squadron 350.00
72 V:Capt. Kamikaze 350.00
73 Hell & Stormoviks 350.00
74 BLb(c),Loot is What She
   Lived For 350.00
75 BLb(c),The Sky Hag 350.00
76 BLb(c),Temple of the Dead. . 350.00
77 BLb(c),Sky Express to Hell. . 350.00
78 BLb(c),Loot Queen of
   Satan's Skyway 350.00
79 BLb(c),Buzzards of
   Plunder Sky 350.00
80 BLb(c),Port of Missing Pilots . 350.00
81 BLb(c),Sky Trail of the
   Terror Tong 350.00
82 BLb(c),Bondage(c),Spider &
   The Fly Guy 400.00
83 BLb(c),GE,Deep Six For
   Capt. Wings 350.00
84 BLb(c),GE,Sky Sharks to
   the Kill 350.00
85 BLb(c),GE 350.00
86 BLb(c),GE,Moon Raiders . . . 350.00
87 BLb(c),GE 350.00
88 BLb(c),GE,Madmans Mission. 350.00
89 BLb(c),GE,Bondage(c),
   Rockets Away 500.00
90 BLb(c),GE,Bondage(c),The
   Radar Rocketeers 500.00
91 BLb(c),GT,Bondage(c),V-9 for
   Vengeance. 500.00
92 BLb(c),Death's red Rocket 350.00
93 BLb(c),GE,Kidnap Cargo 600.00
94 BLb(c),GE,Bondage(c),Ace
   of the A-Bomb Patrol 650.00
95 BLb(c),GE,The Ace of
   the Assassins 350.00
96 BLb(c),GE 350.00
97 BLb(c),GE,The Sky Octopus . 350.00
98 BLb(c),GE,The Witch Queen
   of Satan's Skyways 350.00
99 BLb(c),GE,The Spy Circus . . 350.00
100 BLb(c),GE,King o/t Congo . . 400.00

Wings #75
© *Fiction House Magazines*

101 BLb(c),GE,Trator of
the Cockpit 300.00
102 BLb(c),GE,Doves of Doom . . 300.00
103 BLb(c),GE 300.00
104 BLb(c),GE,Fireflies of Fury . . 300.00
105 BLb(c),GE 300.00
106 BLb(c),GE,Six Aces & A
Firing Squad 300.00
107 BLb(c),GE,Operation Satan . 300.00
108 BLb(c),GE,The Phantom
of Berlin 300.00
109 GE,Vultures of
Vengeance Sky 300.00
110 GE,The Red Ray Vortex 300.00
111 GE,E:Jane Martin 250.00
112 The Flight of the
Silver Saucers 250.00
113 Suicide Skyways 250.00
114 D-Day for Death Rays 250.00
115 Ace of Space 250.00
116 Jet Aces of Korea 250.00
117 Reap the Red Wind 250.00
118 Vengeance Flies Blind 250.00
119 The Whistling Death 250.00
120 Doomsday Mission 250.00
121 Ace of the Spyways 250.00
122 Last Kill Korea 250.00
123 The Cat & the Canaries 250.00
124 Summer, 1954, Death
Below Zero 250.00

WINNIE WINKLE
**Dell Publishing Co.,
1948**
1 . . . . 200.00
2 . . . . 150.00
3 thru 7 . . . . @150.00

WITCHCRAFT
**Avon Periodicals,
March–April, 1952**
1 SC,JKu,Heritage of Horror . . 1,100.00
2 SC,JKu,The Death Tattoo 800.00
3 EK,Better off Dead 600.00
4 Claws of the Cat,
Boiling Humans 650.00
5 Ph(c),Where Zombies Walk . . 700.00
6 March, 1953 Mysteries of the
Moaning Statue 800.00

WITCHES TALES
**Harvey Publications,
Jan., 1951**
1 RP,Bondage(c),Weird Yarns
of Unseen Terror 900.00

2 RP,AAv,We Dare You 600.00
3 RP,Bondage(c)Forest of
Skeletons 400.00
4 BP 400.00
5 BP,Bondage(c),Share
My Coffin 450.00
6 BP,Bondage(c),Servants of
the Tomb 400.00
7 BP,Screaming City 400.00
8 LEI(c),Bondage(c) 450.00
9 Fatal Steps 400.00
10 LEI,BP,IT!,Bondage 450.00
11 BP,Monster Maker 350.00
12 Bondage(c);The Web
of the Spider 350.00
13 The Torture Jar 350.00
14 AAv,Transformation 350.00
15 Drooling Zombie 350.00
16 LEI,Revenge of a Witch 350.00
17 LEI,Dimension IV 350.00
18 LEI,HN,Bird of Prey 400.00
19 LEI,HN,The Pact 400.00
20 LEI,HN,Kiss & Tell 400.00
21 LEI,HN,The Invasion 400.00
22 LEI,HN,A Day of Panic 400.00
23 LEI,HN,The Wig Maker 400.00
24 LEI,HN,The Undertaker 425.00
25 LEI,What Happens at 8:30 PM?
Severed Heads(c) 500.00
26 LEI,Up There 350.00
27 LEI,The Thing That Grew 350.00
28 AAv,Demon Flies 350.00
Becomes:

WITCHES WESTERN TALES
Feb., 1955
29 S&K(a&c),F:Davy Crockett . . . 350.00
30 S&K(a&c) 300.00
Becomes:

WESTERN TALES
Oct., 1955
31 S&K(a&c),F:Davy Crockett . . . 250.00
32 S&K(a&c),F:Davy Crockett . . . 250.00
33 S&K(a&c),July–Sept.,1956 . . . 250.00

WITH THE MARINES ON THE BATTLEFRONTS OF THE WORLD
Toby Press, June, 1953
1 Flaming Soul, John
Wayne, Ph(c) 400.00
2 Mar., 1954, Monty Hall, Ph(c) . 125.00

WITTY COMICS
**Irwin H. Rubin/Chicago Nite
Life News, 1945**
1 Pioneer, Jr. Patrol 400.00
2 1945 . . . . 200.00
3 thru 7 . . . . @150.00

WOMEN IN LOVE
**Fox Features Synd./
Hero Books/
Ziff-Davis, Aug., 1949**
1 . . . . 600.00
2 JKa,AF(c) 400.00
3 . . . . 250.00
4 WW 300.00

WOMEN OUTLAWS
**Fox Features Syndicate,
July, 1948**
1 Partial nudity 1,200.00
2 . . . . 900.00
3 . . . . 900.00
4 . . . . 700.00
5 . . . . 550.00

Women Outlaws #2
© *Fox Features Syndicate*

6 . . . . 550.00
7 . . . . 550.00
8 . . . . 550.00
N# Cody of the Pony Express . . . 400.00
Becomes:

MY LOVE MEMORIES
**Fox Features Syndicate,
Nov., 1949**
9 . . . . 250.00
10 . . . . 150.00
11 . . . . 175.00
12 WW 200.00

WONDERBOY
See: HORRIFIC

WONDER COMICS
**Great Publ./Nedor/
Better Publications,
May, 1944**
1 SSh(c),B:Grim Reaper,
Spectro Hitler(c) 2,500.00
2 ASh(c),O:Grim Reaper,B:Super
Sleuths,Grim Reaper(c) . . 1,500.00
3 ASh(c),Grim Reaper(c) 1,300.00
4 ASh(c),Grim Reaper(c) 800.00
5 ASh(c),Grim Reaper(c) 800.00
6 ASh(c),Grim Reaper(c) 800.00
7 ASh(c),Grim Reaper(c) 800.00
8 ASh(c),E:Super Sleuths,
Spectro 800.00
9 ASh(c),B:Wonderman 800.00
10 ASh(c),Wonderman(c) 850.00
11 Grl(c),B:Dick Devins 1,000.00
12 Grl(c),Bondage(c) 1,000.00
13 ASh(c),Bondage(c). 1,000.00
14 ASh(c),Bondage(c)
E:Dick Devins 1,000.00
15 ASh(c),Bondage(c),B:Tara . . 1,300.00
16 ASh(c),A:Spectro,
E:Grim Reaper 1,000.00
17 FF,ASh(c),A:Super Sleuth . . 1,400.00
18 ASh(c),B:Silver Knight 1,300.00
19 ASh(c),FF 1,300.00
20 FF,ASh(c),Oct., 1948 . . . . . . 1,500.00

WONDER COMICS
**Fox Features Syndicate,
May, 1939**
1 BKa,WE,WE(c),B:Wonderman,
DR.Kung,K-51 . . . . 28,000.00
2 WE,BKa,LF(c),B:Yarko the
Great,A:Spark Stevens 9,000.00
Becomes:

Wonderworld Comics #32
© *Fox Features Syndicate*

WONDERWORLD COMICS

**Fox Features Syndicate,
July, 1939–Jan., 1942**

3 WE,LF,BP,LF&WE,I:Flame . 14,000.00
4 WE,LF,BP,LF(c) 7,000.00
5 WE,LF,BP,GT,LF(c),Flame . . 3,500.00
6 WE,LF,BP,GT,LF(c),Flame . . 3,500.00
7 WE,LF,BP,GT,LF(c),Flame . . 5,500.00
8 WE,LF,BP,GT,LF(c),Flame . . 5,000.00
9 WE,LF,BP,GT,LF(c),Flame . . 3,500.00
10 WE,LF,BP,LF(c),Flame. 3,500.00
11 WE,LF,BP,LF(c),O:Flame . . 3,500.00
12 BP,LF(c),Bondage(c),Flame. 2,500.00
13 LF(c),E:Dr Fung,Flame . . . 2,500.00
14 JoS,Bondage(c),Flame 2,000.00
15 JoS&LF(c),Flame. 1,800.00
16 Flame(c). 1,500.00
17 Flame(c). 1,500.00
18 Flame(c). 1,500.00
19 Male Bondage(c),Flame . . . 1,600.00
20 Flame(c). 1,400.00
21 O:Black Club &Lion,Flame. . 1,300.00
22 Flame(c). 1,100.00
23 Flame(c). 1,000.00
24 Flame(c). 1,000.00
25 A:Dr Fung,Flame 1,000.00
26 Flame(c). 1,000.00
27 Flame(c). 1,000.00
28 Bondage(c)I&O:US Jones,
   B:Lu-nar,Flame. 1,500.00
29 Bondage(c),Flame 900.00
30 O:Flame(c),Flame 1,500.00
31 Bondage(c),Flame 900.00
32 Hitler(c),Flame. 1,200.00
33 Male Bondage(c) 900.00

WONDERLAND COMICS

**Feature Publications
(Prize Comics Group),
Summer, 1945**

1 (fa),B:Alex in Wonderland 250.00
2 . . . . 150.00
3 thru 8 . . . . @125.00
9 1947. . . . . 125.00

WONDERWORLD
See:WONDER COMICS

THE WORLD AROUND US

Gilberton Publications, 1958
1 GE,Dogs. 125.00
2 SC,Indians. 125.00
3 LbC,Horses. 125.00

4 LbC,Railroads 100.00
5 Grl,Space. 125.00
6 GE,The FBI 125.00
7 Grl,Pirates 100.00
8 GE,Grl,Flight 100.00
9 Grl,EK,Army. 100.00
10 EK,Navy 100.00
11 Marines 100.00
12 Grl,Coast Guard 100.00
13 JCo,Air Force 100.00
14 GE,EK,The French Revolution 125.00
15 AW,GM,EK,Prehistoric
   Animals 135.00
16 EK,The Crusades 100.00
17 GE,RC,Festivals 100.00
18 GE,RC,Great Scientists 100.00
19 AW,GM,The Jungle 125.00
20 RC,GE,AT,Communications . . 125.00
21 RC,GE,GM,American
   Presidents 125.00
22 GE,Boating 100.00
23 RC,GE,Great Explorers 100.00
24 GM,GE,Ghosts 125.00
25 GM,GE,Magic. 125.00
26 The Civil War 150.00
27 RC,GE,CM,AT,High Adventure 100.00
28 RC,GE,GM,AT,LbC(c),Whaling 110.00
29 RC,GE,AT,GM,Vikings 125.00
30 RC,GE,JK,AT,Undersea
   Adventures 125.00
31 RC,GE,Grl,EK,JK,Hunting . . . 100.00
32 GM,JK,RC,GE,For Gold
   and Glory. 100.00
33 AT,GE,RC,Famous Teens 110.00
34 RC,GE,Fishing 100.00
35 LcM,JK,GM,GE,Spies 110.00
36 JK,Fight For Life 100.00

WORLD FAMOUS HEROES MAGAZINE

**Comic Corp. of America
(Centaur) Oct., 1941**

1 BLb,Paul Revere 1,700.00
2 BLb,Andrew Jackson,V:
   Dickinson, Lou Gehrig 750.00
3 BLb,Juarez-Mexican patriot . . 700.00
4 BLb,Canadian Mounties 700.00

WORLD FAMOUS STORIES

Croyden Publ., 1945
1 Rip Van Winkle,Ali Baba 175.00

THE WORLD IS HIS PARISH

George A. Pflaum, 1953
N# Pope Pius XII 75.00

WORLD'S GREATEST STORIES

**Jubilee Publications
Jan., 1949**
1 F:Alice in Wonderland 450.00
2 F:Pinocchio 400.00

WORLDS BEYOND

Fawcett Publications, 1951
1 BP,BBa. 650.00
Becomes:

WORLDS OF FEAR

Fawcett Publications, 1952
2 BP,SMo(c). 900.00
3 GE,SMo(c). 700.00
4 BP,MSy,SMo(c). 650.00
5 BP,MSy,SMo(c) 650.00
6 SMo(c). 650.00
7 SMo(c). 650.00

World's of Fear #7
© *Fawcett Publications*

8 SMo(c). 650.00
9 . . . . 650.00
10 no-eyed man, eyeballs(c) . . 1,500.00

WORLD WAR III

**Ace Periodicals,
March–May, 1953**
1 Atomic Bomb (c). 1,400.00
2 The War That Will Never
   Happen 900.00

WOTALIFE COMICS
See: PHANTOM LADY

WOW COMICS

**David McKay/Henle Publ.,
July, 1936–Nov., 1936**
1 WE,DBr(c),Fu Manchu,
   Buck Jones. 5,000.00
2 WE,Little King 3,000.00
3 WE,WE(c), Popeye. 2,700.00
4 WE,BKa,AR,DBr(c),Popeye,
   Flash Gordon 3,500.00

WOW COMICS

**Fawcett Publications,
Winter, 1940**
N#(1)S&K,CCB(c),B&O:Mr Scarlett;
   B:Atom Blake,Jim Dolan,Rick
   O'Shay,Bondage(c) 27,000.00
2 B:Hunchback 4,500.00
3 V:Mummy Ray Gun 2,500.00
4 O:Pinky 2,600.00
5 F:Pinky the Whiz Kid 1,500.00
6 O:Phantom Eagle;
   B:Commando Yank 1,500.00
7 Spearhead of Invasion 1,000.00
8 All Three Heroes. 1,000.00
9 A:Capt Marvel,Capt MarvelJr.
   Shazam,B:Mary Marvel . . . 2,500.00
10 The Sinister Secret of
   Hotel Hideaway 1,200.00
11 . . . . 700.00
12 Rocketing adventures 700.00
13 Thrill Show 700.00
14 V:Mr Night. 600.00
15 Shazam Girl of America 800.00
16 Ride to the Moon 800.00
17 V:Mary Batson,Alter Ego
   Goes Berserk 800.00
18 I:Uncle Marvel,Infinity(c)
   V is For Victory 800.00
19 A Whirlwind Fantasy. 800.00
20 Mary Marvel's Magic Carpet. . 800.00

GOLDEN AGE

Wow Comics #22
© *Fawcett Publications*

21 Word That Shook the World . . 450.00
22 Come on Boys-
 Everybody Sing 450.00
23 Trapped by the Terror of
 the Future 450.00
24 Mary Marvel 450.00
25 Mary Marvel Crushes Crime . . 450.00
26 Smashing Star-
 Studded Stories 350.00
27 War Stamp Plea(c) 350.00
28 Pinky 350.00
29 . . . . 350.00
30 In Mirror Land 350.00
31 Stars of Action 300.00
32 The Millinery Marauders 300.00
33 Mary Marvel(c) 300.00
34 A:Uncle Marvel 300.00
35 I:Freckles Marvel 400.00
36 Secret of the Buried City 300.00
37 7th War loan plea 300.00
38 Pictures That Came to Life . . . 300.00
39 The Perilous Packages 300.00
40 The Quarrel of the Gnomes . . 300.00
41 Hazardous Adventures 250.00
42 . . . . 250.00
43 Curtain Time 250.00
44 Volcanic Adventure 250.00
45 Commando Yank 250.00
46 Commando Yank 250.00
47 Commando Yank 250.00
48 Commando Yank 250.00
49 Commando Yank 250.00
50 Mary Marvel/Commando Yank 250.00
51 Command Yank 225.00
52 . . . . 225.00
53 Murder in the Tall Timbers . . . 225.00
54 Flaming Adventure 225.00
55 Earthquake! 225.00
56 Sacred Pearls of Comatesh . . 225.00
57 . . . . 225.00
58 E:Mary Marvel;The Curse
 of the Keys 225.00
59 B:Ozzie the Hilarious
 Teenager 225.00
60 thru 64 . . . . @225.00
65 A:Tom Mix 225.00
66 A:Tom Mix 225.00
67 A:Tom Mix 225.00
68 A:Tom Mix 225.00
69 A:Tom Mix,Baseball 225.00
Becomes:

REAL WESTERN HERO
Sept., 1948
70 It's Round-up Time 500.00

---

71 CCB,P(c),A Rip
 Roaring Rodeo 300.00
72 w/Gabby Hayes 300.00
73 thru 75 . . . . @300.00
Becomes:

WESTERN HERO
March, 1949
76 Partial Ph(c)&P(c) 400.00
77 Partial Ph(c)&P(c) 200.00
78 Partial Ph(c)&P(c) 200.00
79 Partial Ph(c)&P(c),
 Shadow of Death 175.00
80 Partial Ph(c)&P(c) 200.00
81 CCB,Partial Ph(c)&P(c),
 F:Tootsie 200.00
82 Partial Ph(c)&P(c),
 A:Hopalong Cassidy 200.00
83 Partial Ph(c)&P(c) 200.00
84 Ph(c) 175.00
85 Ph(c) 175.00
86 Ph(c),The Case of the
 Extra Buddy, giant 175.00
87 Ph(c),The Strange Lands 175.00
88 Ph(c),A:Senor Diablo 175.00
89 Ph(c),The Hypnotist 175.00
90 Ph(c),The Menace of
 the Cougar, giant 150.00
91 Ph(c),Song of Death 150.00
92 Ph(c),The Fatal Hide-out,
 giant 150.00
93 Ph(c),Treachery at
 Triple T, giant 150.00
94 Ph(c),Bank Busters,giant 150.00
95 Ph(c),Rampaging River 150.00
96 Ph(c),Range Robbers,giant . . 150.00
97 Ph(c),Death on the
 Hook,giant 150.00
98 Ph(c),Web of Death,giant 150.00
99 Ph(c),The Hidden Evidence . . 150.00
100 Ph(c),A:Red Eagle,Giant . . . 150.00
101 Red Eagle, Ph(c) 150.00
102 thru 111 Ph(c) . . . . @150.00
112 Ph(c),March, 1952 . . . . 175.00

XMAS COMICS
Fawcett Publications, 1941
1 Whiz #21 . . . . 6,500.00
2 Capt. Marvel 2,500.00
7 Hoppy, Funny Animal 1,000.00
Second Series, 1949–52
4 Whiz, Capt. Marvel, Nyoka . . 1,100.00
5 . . . . 900.00
6 . . . . 900.00
7 Bill Boyd 900.00

X-VENTURE
Victory Magazines, 1947
1 Mystery Shadow, Atom
 Wizard 1,600.00
2 same 850.00

YANKEE COMICS
**Chesler Publications
(Harry A. Chesler),
Sept., 1941–March, 1942**
1 F:Yankee Doodle Jones . . . 2,600.00
2 The Spirit of '41 . . . . 1,300.00
3 Yankee Doodle Jones 900.00
4 JCo,Yankee Doodle Jones . . . 900.00

YANKS IN BATTLE
**Comic Magazine, Inc.
(Quality Comics Group), 1956**
1 CCv 125.00
2 CCv 100.00
3 CCv 100.00
4 CCv 100.00

THE YARDBIRDS
Ziff-Davis Publishing Co., 1952
1 . . . . 125.00

YELLOWJACKET COMICS
**Levy Publ./Frank Comunale/
Charlton, Sept., 1944**
1 O&B:Yellowjackets,B:Diana
 the Huntress 1,200.00
2 Rosita &The Filipino Kid 700.00
3 . . . . 650.00
4 Fall of the House of Usher 700.00
5 King of Beasts 700.00
6 . . . . 800.00
7 I:Diane Carter;The
 Lonely Guy 1,500.00
8 The Buzzing Bee Code 750.00
9 . . . . 700.00
10 Capt Grim V:The Salvage
 Pirates 750.00
Becomes:

JACK IN THE BOX
Charlton, Feb., 1946
11 Funny Animal,Yellow Jacket . . 300.00
12 Funny Animal 150.00
13 BW,Funny Animal 300.00
14 thru 16 Funny Animal . . . . . @150.00
Becomes:

COWBOY WESTERN COMICS
Charlton, July, 1948
17 Annie Oakley,Jesse James . . . 275.00
18 JO,JO(c) 200.00
19 JO,JO(c),Legends of Paul
 Bunyan 200.00
20 JO(c),Jesse James 125.00
21 Annie Oakley VisitsDryGulch . 125.00
22 Story of the Texas Rangers . . 125.00
23 . . . . 125.00
24 Ph(c),F:James Craig 125.00
25 Ph(c),F:Sunset Carson 125.00
26 Ph(c) 150.00
27 Ph(c),Sunset Carson movie . . 900.00
28 Ph(c),Sunset Carson movie . . 450.00
29 Ph(c),Sunset Carson movie . . 450.00
30 Ph(c),Sunset Carson movie . . 450.00
31 Ph(c) 100.00
32 thru 34 Ph(c) . . . . @100.00
35 thru 37 Sunset Carson . . . . @400.00
38 and 39 . . . . @100.00
Becomes:

SPACE WESTERN COMICS
Charlton Comics, Oct., 1952
40 Spurs Jackson,V:The
 Saucer Men 1,000.00
41 StC(c),Space Vigilantes 700.00
42 StC(c),Atomic Bomb 800.00
43 StC(c),Battle of
 Spacemans Gulch 700.00
44 StC(c),The Madman of Mars . 700.00
45 StC(c),The Moon Bat,Hitler . . . 900.00
Becomes:

COWBOY WESTERN COMICS
Oct., 1953
46 . . . . 300.00
Becomes:

COWBOY WESTERN HEROES
Dec., 1953
47 . . . . 150.00
48 . . . . 150.00
Becomes:

All comics prices listed are for *Near Mint* condition.   **CVA Page 497**

COWBOY WESTERN
May–June, 1954

49	125.00
50 F:Jesse James	125.00
51 thru 57	@100.00
58, Wild Bill Hickok, giant	125.00
59 thru 66	@100.00
67 AW&AT	150.00

Becomes:

WILD BILL HICKOK
AND JINGLES
Aug., 1958

68 AW	125.00
69 AW	100.00
70 AW	100.00
71	75.00
72	75.00
73	75.00
74 1960	75.00

YOGI BERRA
Fawcett, 1957

1 Ph(c)	1,100.00

Young Brides #2
© *Prize Comics*

YOUNG BRIDES
**Feature Publications (Prize
Comics), Sept.–Oct., 1952**

1 S&K,Ph(c)	500.00
2 S&K,Ph(c)	250.00
3 S&K,Ph(c)	200.00
4 S&K	200.00
5 S&K	200.00
6 S&K	200.00
2-1 S&K	200.00
2-2 S&K	100.00
2-3 S&K	150.00
2-4 S&K	150.00
2-5 S&K	150.00
2-6 S&K	150.00
2-7 S&K	150.00
2-8 S&K	100.00
2-9 S&K	100.00
2-10 S&K	175.00
2-11 S&K	175.00
2-12 S&K	175.00
3-1 thru 4-1	@100.00
4-2 S&K	200.00
4-3	100.00
4-4 S&K	175.00
4-5	100.00

YOUNG EAGLE
**Fawcett Publications/
Charlton Comics, Dec., 1950**

1 Ph(c)	250.00
2 Ph(c),Mystery of Thunder Canyon	125.00
3 Ph(c),Death at Dawn	100.00
4 Ph(c)	100.00
5 Ph(c),The Golden Flood	100.00
6 Ph(c),The Nightmare Empire	100.00
7 Ph(c),Vigilante Vengeance	100.00
8 Ph(c),The Rogues Rodeo	100.00
9 Ph(c),The Great Railroad Swindle	100.00
10 June, 1952, Ph(c),Thunder Rides the Trail,O:Thunder	100.00

YOUNG HEROES
**Titan Publ. (American
Comics Group), 1955**

35 Frontier Scout	125.00
36	125.00
37	125.00

YOUNG KING COLE
**Novelty Press/Premium
Svcs. Co., Autumn, 1945**

1-1 Detective Toni Gayle	500.00
1-2	250.00
1-3	200.00
1-4	200.00
2-1	150.00
2-2	150.00
2-3	150.00
2-4	150.00
2-5	150.00
2-6	150.00
2-7	150.00
3-1	175.00
3-2 LbC	250.00
3-3 The Killer With The Hat	150.00
3-4 The Fierce Tiger	150.00
3-5 AMc	150.00
3-6	175.00
3-7 LbC(c),Case of the Devil's Twin	300.00
3-8	150.00
3-9 The Crime Fighting King	150.00
3-10 LbC(c)	250.00
3-11 LbC(c)	250.00
3-12 July, 1948,AMc(c)	150.00

YOUNG LIFE
**New Age Publications,
Summer, 1945**

1 Partial Ph(c),Louis Prima	175.00
2 Partial Ph(c),Frank Sinatra	200.00

Becomes:

TEEN LIFE
Winter, 1945

3 Partial Ph(c),Croon without Tricks,June Allyson(c)	150.00
4 Partial Ph(c),Atom Smasher Blueprints,Duke Ellington(c)	125.00
5 Partial Ph(c), Build Your Own Pocket Radio, Jackie Robinson(c)	150.00

YOUNG LOVE
**Feature Publ.
(Prize Comics Group),
Feb.–March, 1949**

1 S&K,S&K(c)	650.00
2 S&K,Ph(c)	350.00
3 S&K,JSe,BE,Ph(c)	250.00
4 S&K,Ph(c)	175.00
5 S&K,Ph(c)	175.00
2-1 S&K,Ph(c)	250.00

2-2 Ph(c)	150.00
2-3 Ph(c)	150.00
2-4 Ph(c)	150.00
2-5 Ph(c)	150.00
2-6 S&K(c)	250.00
2-7 S&K(c),S&K	250.00
2-8 S&K	250.00
2-9 S&K(c),S&K	250.00
2-10 S&K(c),S&K	250.00
2-11 S&K(c),S&K	250.00
2-12 S&K(c),S&K	250.00
3-1 S&K(c),S&K	225.00
3-2 S&K(c),S&K	225.00
3-3 S&K(c),S&K	225.00
3-4 S&K(c),S&K	225.00
3-5 Ph(c)	175.00
3-6 BP,Ph(c)	175.00
3-7 Ph(c)	175.00
3-8 Ph(c)	175.00
3-9 MMe,Ph(c)	175.00
3-10 Ph(c)	175.00
3-11 Ph(c)	175.00
3-12 Ph(c)	175.00
4-1 S&K	175.00
4-2 Ph(c)	150.00
4-3 Ph(c)	150.00
4-4 Ph(c)	150.00
4-5 Ph(c)	150.00
4-5 Ph(c)	150.00
4-6 S&K,Ph(c)	150.00
4-7 thru 4-12 Ph(c)	@125.00
5-1 thru 5-12 Ph(c)	@125.00
6-1 thru 6-9	@75.00
6-10 thru 6-12	@75.00
7-1 thru 7-7	@75.00
7-8 thru 7-11	@75.00
7-12 thru 8-5	@75.00
8-6 thru 8-12	@75.00

YOUNG ROMANCE
COMICS
**Feature Publ./Headline/
Prize Publ., Sept.–Oct., 1947**

1 S&K(c),S&K	700.00
2 S&K(c),S&K	400.00
3 S&K(c),S&K	350.00
4 S&K(c),S&K	350.00
5 S&K(c),S&K	350.00
6 S&K(c),S&K	350.00
2-1 S&K(c),S&K	325.00
2-2 S&K(c),S&K	325.00
2-3 S&K(c),S&K	325.00
2-4 S&K(c),S&K	325.00
2-5 S&K(c),S&K	325.00
2-6 S&K(c),S&K	250.00
3-1 thru 3-12 S&K(c),S&K	@250.00
4-1 thru 4-12 S&K	@250.00
5-1 ATh,S&K	250.00
5-2	250.00
5-3	225.00
5-4 thru 5-12 S&K	@225.00
6-1	100.00
6-2	100.00
6-3	100.00

YOUR UNITED STATES
Lloyd Jacquet Studios, 1946

1N# Teeming Nation of Nations	300.00

ZAGO, JUNGLE PRINCE
**Fox Features Syndicate,
Sept., 1948**

1 A:Blue Beetle	1,000.00
2 JKa	750.00
3 JKa	600.00
4 MB(c)	600.00

Becomes:

MY STORY
May, 1949
5 JKa,Too Young To Fall in Love	275.00
6 I Was A She-Wolf	125.00
7 I Lost My Reputation	125.00
8 My Words Condemned Me	125.00
9 WW,Wayward Bride	250.00
10 WW,March, 1950,Second Rate Girl	250.00
11	125.00
12 Ph(c)	125.00

ZAZA THE MYSTIC
See: CHARLIE CHAN

TEGRA, JUNGLE EMPRESS
Fox Features Syndicate Aug., 1948
1 Blue Bettle,Rocket Kelly	850.00

Becomes:

ZEGRA, JUNGLE EMPRESS
Oct., 1948
2 JKa	1,000.00
3	700.00
4	700.00
5	700.00

Becomes:

MY LOVE LIFE
June, 1949–Aug., 1950
6 I Put A Price Tag On Love	200.00
7 An Old Man's Fancy	125.00
8 My Forbidden Affair	125.00
9 I Loved too Often	125.00
10 My Secret Torture	125.00
11 I Broke My Own Heart	125.00
12 I Was An Untamed Filly	125.00
13 I Can Never Marry You	100.00

ZIP COMICS
MLJ Magazines, Feb., 1940–Summer, 1944
1 MMe,O&B:Kalathar,The Scarlet Avenger,Steel Sterling,B:Mr Satan,Nevada Jones,War Eagle Captain Valor	9,000.00
2 MMe,CBi(c)B:Steel Sterling(c)	3,700.00
3 MMe,CBi(a&c)	3,000.00
4 MMe,CBi(a&c)	2,400.00
5 MMe,CBi(a&c)	2,400.00

Zip Comics #37
© MLJ Magazines

6 MMe,CBi(a&c)	2,200.00
7 MMe,CBi(a&c)	2,200.00
8 MMe,CBi(a&c),Bondage(c)	2,200.00
9 CMMe,CBi(a&c),E:Kalathar, Mr Satan;Bondage(c)	2,300.00
10 MMe,CBi(a&c),B:Inferno	2,200.00
11 MMe,CBi(a&c)	1,700.00
12 MMe,CBi(a&c),Bondage(c)	1,700.00
13 MMe,CBi(a&c),E:Inferno, Bondage(c),Woman in Electric Chair	1,900.00
14 MMe,CBi(a&c),Bondage(c)	1,600.00
15 MMe,CBi(a&c),Bondage(c)	1,900.00
16 MMe,CBi(a&c),Bondage(c)	1,600.00
17 CBI(a&c),E:Scarlet Avenger Bondage(c).	1,900.00
18 IN(c),B:Wilbur.	1,900.00
19 IN(c),Steel Sterling(c).	1,600.00
20 IN(c),O&I:Black Jack Hitler(c).	2,700.00
21 IN(c),V:Nazis	1,400.00
22 IN(c).	2,300.00
23 IN(c),Flying Fortress	1,500.00
24 IN(c),China Town Exploit	1,500.00
25 IN(c),E:Nevada Jones	1,500.00
26 IN(c),B:Black Witch, E:Capt Valor	1,500.00
27 IN(c),I:Web,V:Japanese	2,500.00
28 IN(C),O:Web,Bondage(c).	2,200.00
29 Steel Sterling & Web	1,100.00
30 V:Nazis.	1,000.00
31 IN(c)	800.00
32 Nazi Skeleton, WWII	1,000.00
33 Bondage(c)	1,000.00
34 I:Applejack;Bondage(c).	900.00
35 E:Zambini	800.00
36 I:Senor Banana.	800.00
37	800.00
38 E:Web.	800.00
39 O&B:Red Rube.	800.00
40 Red Rube	700.00
41	700.00
42 Red Rube	700.00
43 Steel Sterling(c).	700.00
44 Red Rube	700.00
45 E:Wilbur	700.00
46 Red Rube	700.00
47 Crooks Can't Win	750.00

ZIP-JET
St. John Publishing Co., Feb., 1953
1 Rocketman	1,200.00
2 April–May, 1953, Assassin of the Airlanes	750.00

ZIPPY THE CHIMP
Pines Comics, 1957
50	75.00
51	75.00

ZOO FUNNIES
Charlton Magazines, 1945
1 Funny Animals (1st Charlton)	300.00
2	200.00
3	125.00
4	125.00
5	125.00
6	100.00
7	100.00
8 Diana the Huntress	100.00
9	100.00
10	100.00
11 thru 15	@100.00

Becomes:

TIM MCCOY
Charlton Comics, 1948
16 Western Movie Stories, John Wayne.	700.00
17 Rocky Lane.	500.00

18 Rod Cameron	500.00
19 Jessie James	500.00
20 Jimmy Wakley.	500.00
21 Johnny Mack Brown	500.00

Becomes:

PICTORIAL LOVE STORIES
Charlton Comics, 1949
22 B:Me-Dan Cupid	250.00
23	250.00
24 Fred Astaire	275.00
25	250.00
26	250.00

ZOO FUNNIES
Charlton Comics, 1953–55
1 Timothy the Ghost	150.00
2 Leo the Lyin' Lion.	100.00
3 thru 7	@125.00
8 Nyoka	150.00
9 Nyoka	150.00
10 Nyoka	150.00
11 Nyoka	150.00
12 Nyoka	150.00
13 Nyoka	150.00

ZOOM COMICS
Carlton Publishing Co., Dec., 1945
N# O:Captain Milksop.	600.00

ZOOT COMICS
Fox Features Syndicate, Spring, 1946
N#(1)(fa)	300.00
2 A:Jaguar(fa)	250.00
3 (fa)	150.00
4 (fa)	150.00
5 (fa)	125.00
6 (fa)	125.00
7 B:Rulah.	1,500.00
8 JKa(c),Fangs of Stone	1,000.00
9 JKa(c),Fangs of Black Fury	1,000.00
10 JKa(c),Inferno Land	1,000.00
11 JKa,The Purple Plague, Bondage(c).	1,100.00
12 JKa(c),The Thirsty Stone, Bondage(c)	800.00
13 Bloody Moon.	700.00
14 Pearls of Pathos,Woman Carried off by Bird	950.00
15 Death Dancers	700.00
16	700.00

Becomes:

RULAH, JUNGLE GODDESS
Aug., 1948
17 JKa(c),Wolf Doctor.	1,500.00
18 JKa(c),Vampire Garden	1,100.00
19 JKa(c).	1,000.00
20	1,000.00
21 JKa(c).	1,000.00
22 JKa(c).	1,000.00
23	800.00
24	750.00
25	750.00
26	750.00
27	750.00

Becomes:

I LOVED
July, 1949–March, 1950
28	150.00
29 thru 31	@100.00
32 My Poison Love	100.00

DARK HORSE

ABE SAPIEN: DRUMS OF THE DEAD
Mar., 1998
1-shot Hellboy spin-off 3.00

ABYSS, THE
1989
1 MK,Movie Adaptation 2.50
2 MK, Movie Adaptation, pt.2 . . . . . 2.50

Accident Man #1
© Dark Horse Comics

ACCIDENT MAN
(B&W) 1993
1 I:Accident Man 2.50
2 thru 3 . . . . @2.50

ADVENTURES OF LUTHER ARKWRIGHT
DH/Valkyrie Press
(B&W) 1987–89
1 . . . . 2.50
2 thru 9 . . . . @2.50
(B&W) 1990
1 . . . . 2.50
2 thru 9 Rep . . . . @2.50

ADVENTURES OF THE MASK
1996
1 by Michael Eury & Marc
  Campos, TV cartoon adapt. . . . 2.50
2 thru 12 TV cartoon adapt. . . . . @2.50
Ash can (1995) 3.00

AEON FLUX
Oct., 2005
1 (of 4) Timothy Green art 3.00
2 thru 4 . . . . @3.00

AGE OF REPTILES
1993–94
1 DRd,Story on Dinosaurs 3.00
2 thru 4 DRd,Story on Dinosaurs @3.00

AGE OF REPTILES: THE HUNT
May, 1996
1 by Ricardo Delgado 3.00
2 thru 5 . . . . @3.00

AGENTS OF LAW
Comics' Greatest World, 1995
1 KG, I:Law 2.50
2 A:Barb Wire 2.50
3 KG,DLw,The Judgment Gate 2.50
4 Open Golden City 2.50
5 Who is the Mystery figure 2.50
6 V:Predator 2.50

ALIEN RESURRECTION
Oct., 1997
1 (of 2) movie adaptation 2.50
2 DMc(c) 2.50

ALIENS
(B&W) 1988
1 Movie Sequel,R:Hicks,Newt . . . 22.00
1a 2nd printing 3.00
1b 3rd printing 2.50
1c 4th printing 2.50
2 Hicks raids Mental Hospital 9.00
2a 2nd printing 2.50
2a 3rd printing 2.50
3 Realize Queen is on Earth 7.00
3a 2nd printing 2.50
4 Queen is freed, Newton on
  Aliens World 5.00
5 All out war on Aliens World 5.00
6 Hicks & Newt return to Earth 5.00

ALIENS (II)
[Mini-Series] 1989
1 DB,Hicks,Newt hijack ship 5.00
1a 2nd Printing 3.00
2 DB,Crazed general trains aliens . 3.00
2a 2nd Printing 3.00
3 DB,HicksV:General Spears 3.00
3a 2nd Printing 2.50
4 DB,Heroes reclaim earth
  from aliens 3.00

ALIENS
1-shot Earth Angel, JBy (1994) 3.00
1-shot Glass Corridor, DvL (1998) . . 3.00
1-shot Lovesick (1996) 3.00
1-shot Mondo Heat, I:Herk Mondo . 2.50
1-shot Mondo Pest (1995) 3.00
1-shot Pig, CDi,FH (1997) 3.00
1-shot Purge, IEd,PhH (1997) 3.00
1-shot Sacrifice, rep.Aliens UK
  (1993) 5.00
1-shot Salvation DGb,MMi,KN,
  F:Selkirk (1993) 5.00
1-shot Special (1997) 2.50
1-shot Stalker (1998) 2.50
1-shot Wraith (1998) 3.00
GN DNA War (2006) 7.00

ALIENS: ALCHEMY
Sept., 1997
1 (of 3) JAr,RCo 3.00
2 thru 3 . . . . @3.00

ALIENS: APOCALYPSE — DESTROYING ANGELS
Jan., 1999
1 (of 4) MSh 3.00
2 thru 4 MSh . . . . @3.00

ALIENS: BERSERKER
1995
1 I:Crew of the Nemesis 3.00
2 thru 4 . . . . @3.00

ALIENS: COLONIAL MARINES
1993
1 I: Lt. Joseph Henry 4.00
2 I: Pvt. Carmen Vasquez 3.00
3 thru 10 . . . . @3.00

ALIENS: EARTH WAR
1991
1 SK,JBo(c),Alien's War renewed . . 4.00
1a 2nd Printing 2.50
2 SK,JBo(c),To trap the Queen 4.00
3 SK,JBo(c) Stranded on
  Alien's planet 3.00
4 SK,JBo(c),Resolution,final 5.00

ALIENS: GENOCIDE
1991
1 Aliens vs. Aliens 3.50
2 Alien Homeworld 3.00
3 Search for Alien Queen 3.00
4 Conclusion, inc. poster 3.00

ALIENS: HAVOC
1997
1 (of 2) 'over 40 creators' 3.00
2 . . . . 3.00

ALIENS: HIVE
1992
1 KJo,I:Stanislaw Mayakovsky 4.00
2 KJo,A:Norbert 3.50
3 KJo,A:Julie,Gill 3.25
4 KJo,A:Stan,Final 3.00

ALIENS: KIDNAPPED
Dec., 1997–Feb., 1998
1 (of 3) 3.00
2 thru 3 . . . . @3.00

ALIENS: LABYRINTH
1993
1 F:Captured Alien 3.00
2 thru 4 . . . . @3.00

ALIENS: MUSIC OF THE SPEARS
1994
1 I:Damon Eddington 3.00
2 thru 4 TBd(c) . . . . @3.00

ALIENS: NEWT'S TALE
1992
1 How Newt Survived 5.50
2 JBo(c),Newt's point of view 5.50

All comics prices listed are for *Near Mint* condition.

ALIENS: ROGUE
1993
1 F:Mr.Kay 3.00
2 thru 4 V:Aliens . . . . @3.00

ALIENS: STRONGHOLD
1994
1 DoM,JP 3.00
2 thru 4 DoM,JP . . . . @3.00

ALIENS: SURVIVAL
Feb.–Apr., 1998
1 (of 3) TyH(c). 3.00
2 thru 3 . . . . @3.00

ALIENS/PREDATOR:
DEADLIEST OF
THE SPECIES
1993–95
1 B:CCl(s),JG,F:Caryn Delacroix . . 4.00
2 JG,V:Predator. 3.00
3 JG,F:Caryn Delacroix. 3.00
4 JG,V:Predator. 3.00
5 JG,Roadtrip 3.00
6 JG,in Space Station 3.00
7 thru 9 JG,EB. . . . . @3.00
10 CCl(s), Human Predators 3.00
11 CCl,EB,JBo(c),Delacroix vs.
   DeMatier 3.00
12 Caryn's Fate 3.00

ALIENS VS. PREDATOR
1996
0 PN,KS,Rep.DHP#34-36,(B&W) . . 7.00
1 Duel to the Death. 7.00
1a 2nd Printing 3.00
2 Dr. Revna missing 5.00
3 Predators attack Aliens 5.00
4 CW,F:Machiko & Predator 5.00
GN Thrill of the Hunt (2004) 7.00
GN Civilized Beasts (2007) 7.00
Ann.#1 (1999) 5.00
1-shot Booty, rep. *Previews* 3.00

ALIENS VS. PREDATOR:
DUEL
1995
1 Trap, JS 3.00
2 War 3.00

ALIENS VS. PREDATOR:
ETERNAL
June, 1998
1 (of 4) IEd,GF(c) 3.00
2 thru 4 IEd,GF(c) . . . . @3.00

ALIENS VS. PREDATOR:
WAR
1995
0 Prelude to New Series. 3.00
1 RSd,MM,RCo(c) F:Machiko. 3.00
2 thru 4 . . . . @3.00

ALIENS VS. PREDATOR:
XENOGENESIS
Dec., 1999
1 (of 4) MvR 3.50
2 thru 4 MvR,trapped . . . . @3.50

ALIENS VS. PREDATOR
VS. THE TERMINATOR
Apr., 2000
1 (of 4) MSh,MvR 3.50

Aliens Vs. Predator: Eternal #4
© Dark Horse Comics

2 MSh,MvR,V:Terminator-Alien
   hybrid. 3.50
3 MSh,MvR,on Predator ship 3.50
4 MSh,MvR,concl. 3.50

ALIENS: XENOGENESIS
Aug., 1999
1 DR 3.50
2 thru 4 . . . . @3.50

ALIEN 3
1992
1 thru 3 Movie Adaptation . . . . . @3.00

AMAZING ADVENTURES
OF THE ESCAPIST, THE
Dec., 2003
1 Michael Chabon, 80-pg. 9.00
2 thru 8 . . . . @9.00

AMAZING SCREW-ON
HEAD, THE
May, 2002
1-shot MMi 3.00

AMERICAN, THE
(B&W) 1987–89
1 CW,'Chinese Boxes,'D:Gleason . 5.00
2 CW,'Nightmares. 4.00
3 CW,Secrets of the American 4.00
4 CW,American vs.Kid America . . . 4.00
5 A:Kiki the Gorilla 4.00
6 Rashomon-like plot 3.50
7 Pornography business issue 3.50
8 Deals with violence issue 3.50
9 American Falls into a cult 3.50
Spec. (1990) 4.00

THE AMERICAN:
LOST IN AMERICA
1992
1 CMa, American joins a cult 2.50
2 CMa, V:'Feel-Good' cult. 2.50
3 CMa, 'Ape-Mask' cult. 2.50
4 CMa, Final issue 2.50
ColorSpec.#1 . . . . 3.00

AMERICAN SPLENDOR
1993–2000
1-shot Letterman by Harvey Pekar . 3.50
1-shot One Step Out of the
   Nest (1994) 3.50
1-shot On the Job (1997). 3.50
1-shot Comics Con, JZe (1996). . . . 3.50
1-shot Music Comics (1997) 3.50
1-shot Odds & Ends (1997). 3.50
1-shot Transatlantic Comics (1998). 3.50
1-shot Terminal (1999). 3.50
1-shot Bedtime Stories (2000) 4.50
1-shot Portrait of The Artist
   in his declining years (2001) . . . 4.00

AMERICAN SPLENDOR:
UNSUNG HERO
DH Maverick, Aug., 2002
1 (of 3) b&w 4.00
2 thru 3 . . . . @4.00

AMERICAN SPLENDOR:
WINDFALL
(B&W) 1995
1 Windfall Gained,pt.1 . . . . 4.25
2 Windfall Lost 4.25

ANCIENT JOE
DH Maverick, Oct., 2001
1 (of 3) B&W 3.00
2 . . . . 3.50
3 . . . . 3.50

ANGEL
1999–2001
1 Buffy spin-off 3.00
2 thru 9 . . . . @3.00
10 TSg 3.00
11 TSg 3.00
12 TSg,MMi(c) 3.00
13 TSg,demonic rats 3.00
14 TSg,Little Girl Lost 3.00
15 TSg,Past Lives,Buffy x-over 4.00
16 TSg,Past Lives,Buffy x-over 4.00
17 The Cordelia Special. 3.00
1–17a newsstand photo(c) . . . . . @4.00

ANGEL
2001–02
1 (of 4) 3.00
1a photo (c). 3.00
1b gold-foil (c). 13.00
1c gold-foil (c) signed 20.00
2 thru 4 . . . . @3.00
2a thru 4a photo (c) . . . . @3.00

ANIMAL CONFIDENTIAL
(B&W) 1992
1-shot parody. 2.50

APOCALYPSE NERD
(B&W) Feb., 2005
1 (of 6) Peter Bagge art 3.00
2 thru 5 . . . . @3.00

APPLESEED DATABOOK
(B&W–Manga) 1994
1 Flip Book, by Masamune Shirow . 5.00
1a 2nd printing 3.50
2 Flip Book 3.50

ARCHENEMIES
Apr., 2006
1 (of 4) by Drew Melbourne 3.00
2 thru 4 . . . . @3.00

DARK HORSE

DARK HORSE

ARMY OF DARKNESS
1992
1 . . . . 12.00
2 thru 3 . . . . @9.00

ATLAS
1994
1 BZ,I:Atlas 2.75
2 BZ,V:Sh'en Chui 2.75
3 BZ,V:Sh'en Chui 2.50
4 BZ, final issue 2.50

BABE
Legend, 1994
1 JBy(a&s) 3.00
2 thru 4 JBy(a&s) . . . . @2.50

BABE 2
Legend, 1995
1 V:Shrewmanoid 2.50
2 A:Abe Sapien 2.50

BACCHUS
COLOR SPECIAL
1995
1 A:Thor 3.00
2 A:Abe Sapien 2.50

BADGER:
SHATTERED MIRROR
1994
1 R:Badger 3.00
2 thru 4 . . . . @3.00

BADGER: ZEN POP
FUNNY ANIMAL VERSION
1 MBn,R:Badger (1994) 3.00
2 Ham 3.00

BADLANDER, THE
Oct., 2007
1 (of 4) 3.00

BADLANDS
(B&W) 1991
1 I:Connie Bremen 3.50
2 Anne Peck, C.I.A. 3.00
3 Assassination Rumor 2.50
4 Connie heads South 2.50
5 November 22, 1963, Dallas 2.50
6 Kennedy Assination aftermath . . . 2.50

BAKERS MEET
JINGLE BELL, THE
Dec., 2006
1-shot PDi,KB 3.00

BARB WIRE
Comics' Greatest World, 1994
1 Foil(c),I:Deathcard 3.00
2 DLw,I:Hurricane Max 3.00
3 V:Mace Blitzkrieg 3.00
4 Ghost,pt.1 . . . . 3.00
5 Ghost,pt.2 . . . . 3.00
6 Hardhide, Ignition. 3.00
7 A:Motorhead 3.00
8 V:Ignition 3.00
9 A:Mecha, V:Ignition 3.00
Movie Spec. (1996) 4.00

BARB WIRE:
ACE OF SPADES
1996
1 CW,TBd & DoM 3.00

2 thru 4 CW,TBd & DoM . . . . . . @3.00

BARRY WINDSOR-SMITH:
STORYTELLER
Oct., 1996
GNs 1 thru 9 9'x12½' . . . . @5.00

BASEBALL GREATS
1 Jimmy Piersall story 3.25
2 Bob Gibson 3.50
3 Harmon Killebrew 3.50

BASIL WOLVERTON'S
FANTASIC FABLES
(B&W) Oct., 1993
1 BW 2.50
2 BW 2.50

BASIL WOLVERTON'S
GN Gateway to Horror (1988) 5.00
TPB In Space, 240-pg. (1999) 17.00
GN Planet of Terror (1987) 5.00

BATMAN/ALIENS
DH/DC, Mar., 1997
1 (of 2) RMz,BWr 5.00
2 conclusion 5.00
TPB RMz,BWr 15.00

BATMAN/TARZAN: CLAWS
OF THE CATWOMAN
1999
1 (of 4) RMz,DvD(c),V:Dent,x-over. 3.00
2 thru 4 RMz,DvD(c) . . . . @3.00
TPB 96-pg.,DvD(c) 11.00

BATTLE GODS:
WARRIORS OF
THE CHAAK
Apr., 2000
1 (of 9) by Francisco Ruiz
    Velasco 3.00
2 the Lucha Libre 3.00
3 F:Takan, El Charro. 3.00
4 another tournament 3.00
5 The Chaak begins 3.00
6 Deathmatch: Takan vs. Chilbacan 3.00
7 sleeping god awakens 3.00
8 Hell breaks loose 3.00
9 concl. 3.00

Bettie Page Queen of the Nile #3
© Dark Horse Comics

BETTIE PAGE COMICS
1996–97
1-shot, some nudity (1996) 4.00
1-shot Bettie Page Comics: Spicy
    Adventure, by Jim Silke (1997) . 3.00
1 Queen of Hearts, movie adapt. . . 2.50

BETTIE PAGE:
QUEEN OF THE NILE
Dec., 1999
1 (of 3) low-budget time machine . . 3.00
2 and 3 concl. . . . . @3.00

BIG
1989
1 Movie Adaptation 3.00

BIG BLOWN BABY
(B&W) Aug., 1996
1 thru 4 by Bill Wray . . . . @3.00

BIG GUY AND
RUSTY THE ROBOT BOY
1995
1 V:Monster. 5.00
2 V:Monster. 5.00

BILLI 99
(B&W) 1991
1 'Pray for us Sinners' 4.50
2 'Trespasses'. 4.00
3 'Daily Bread'. 4.00
4 . . . . 4.00

BILLY THE KID'S
OLD-TIMEY ODDITIES
April, 2005
1 (of 4) KHt. 3.00
2 thru 4 KHt. . . . . @3.00

BLACKBURNE
COVENANT, THE
Apr., 2003
1 (of 4) FaN 3.00
2 thru 4 . . . . @3.00

BLACK CROSS
(B&W) 1987
1-shot special CW 3.00

BLACK CROSS:
DIRTY WORK
Apr., 1997
1-shot by Chris Warner 3.00

BLACK PEARL, THE
Sept., 1996
1 by Mark Hamill. 3.00
2 thru 5 . . . . @3.00

BLADE OF THE
IMMORTAL
(B&W–Manga) July, 1996
1 by Hiroaki Samura 9.00
Criminal Conquest
2 thru 4 pt. 2 thru pt.4 . . . . @6.00
Genius, Oct., 1996
5 & 6 . . . . @6.00
Fanatic, Jan., 1997
7 & 8 . . . . @6.00
Call of the Worm, Apr., 1997
9 thru 11 48-pg. . . . . @6.00
Dreamsong, July, 1997

All comics prices listed are for *Near Mint* condition.

Blade of the Immortal #19
© *Dark Horse Comics*

12 thru 18 . . . . @3.50
Rin's Bane, Mar., 1998
19 & 20 48-pg. . . . . @4.50
On Silent Wings, May, 1998
21 thru 25 . . . . @3.50
26 48-pg. 4.50
27 thru 28 . . . . @3.50
Dark Shadows, Jan., 1999
29 thru 33 . . . . @3.50
Food, June, 1999
34 48-pg. 4.50
Heart of Darkness, 1999
35 thru 42 . . . . @3.50
The Gathering, 2000
43 thru 57 . . . . @3.50
Secrets, 2001
58 thru 61, pt.1 thru pt.4 . . . . @3.50
62 Stigmata 3.50
63 Husk 3.50
64 Skin,pt.1 . . . . 3.50
65 Skin,pt.2 . . . . 3.50
Beasts, 2002
66 thru 72 Beasta pt.1 thru pt. 7 . @3.50
Fall Frost, 2002
73 thru 78 pt.1 thru pt. 6 . . . . . . @3.50
79 The Wind and the Heron 3.50
80 Petals on the Wind 3.50
81 Shadows 3.50
82 Mourning Shadows 3.50
83 Path of Shadows 3.50
84 Thorns 3.50
Mirror of the Soul, 2003
85 Mirror of the Soul,pt.1 . . . . 3.00
86 Mirror of the Soul,pt.2 . . . . 3.00
87 Mirror of the Soul,pt.3 . . . . 3.00
88 Light and Shadow 3.00
89 Crossroads 3.00
Last Blood, 2004
90 thru 95 Last Blood,pt.1–5 . . . . @3.00
95 Confession 3.00
Twilight, 2004
96 thru 98 Twilight,pt.1–3 . . . . . . @3.00
Trickster, 2005
99 thru 103 Trickster,pt.1–4 . . . . . @3.00
104 Forsaken 3.00
105 Duet 3.00
106 Cauldron 3.00
Shortcut, 2005
107 thru 111 Shortcut,pt.1–5 . . . . @3.00
On the Perfection of Anatomy, 2006
112 thru 117 On the Perfection
    of Anatomy . . . . @3.00
The Sparrow Net, 2006
118 thru 121 Sparrow Net, pt.1–4 . @3.00

Barefoot, 2007
122 thru 126 Barefoot, pt.1–5 . . . @3.00
Life in Death, 2007
127 Life in Death 3.00
Badger Hole, 2007
128 Badger Hole, pt.1 . . . . 3.00
129 Badger Hole, pt.2 . . . . 3.00
130 Badger Hole, pt.3 . . . . 3.00

BLAIR WHICH?
Dec., 1999
1-shot SA, Scary as heck 3.50

BLANCHE GOES TO HOLLYWOOD
(B&W) 1993
1 Turn of the Century N.Y. 3.00

BLANCHE GOES TO NEW YORK
(B&W) 1992
1 Turn of the Century Hollywood . . 3.00

BLAST CORPS
Sept., 1998
1-shot F:demolition experts 2.50

BLOOD WORLD
March 2003
1 (of 3) 3.00
2 . . . . 3.00

BLUE LILY
1993
1 . . . . 4.00
2 thru 3 . . . . @4.00

BMWFILMS.COM —THE HIRE
July, 2004
1 (of 6) MWg,Scandal 3.00
2 MWg,Precious Cargo 3.00
3 MWg,Hijacked 3.00
4 MWg,Tycoon 3.00

BODY BAGS
Aug., 1996
1 (of 4) 3.00
2 thru 4 . . . . @3.00

BOOK OF NIGHT
(B&W) 1987
1 CV 2.50
2 thru 3 CV . . . . @2.50

BORIS THE BEAR
(B&W) 1986
1 V:Funny Animals 3.00
1a 2nd printing 2.50
2 V:Robots 2.50
3 V:Super Heroes 2.50
4 thru 7 . . . . @2.50
8 LargeSize 2.50
9 thru 12 . . . . @2.50
See: B & W Pub. section

Color Classics 1987
1 . . . . 2.50
2 thru 7 . . . . @2.50

B.P.R.D.
2003
1-Shot Dark Waters, GyD 3.00
1-Shot Night Train, ScK 3.00
1-Shot The Soul of Venice,MMi 3.00

Boris the Bear #3
© *Dark Horse Comics*

1-Shot There's Something Under
    My Bed, AdP 3.00

B.P.R.D.: A PLAGUE OF FROGS
Mar., 2004
1 A Plague of Frogs 3.00
2 thru 5 A Plague of Frogs . . . . . @3.00

B.P.R.D.: THE BLACK FLAME
Aug., 2005
1 MMi,GyD 3.00
2 thru 6 MMi,GyD . . . . @3.00

B.P.R.D.: THE DEAD
2004–05
1 GyD,JAr,MMi 3.00
2 thru 5 . . . . @3.00

B.P.R.D.: GARDEN OF SOULS
Mar., 2007
1 (of 5) MMi,GyD,JAr 3.00
2 thru 5 . . . . @3.00

B.P.R.D.: KILLING GROUND
Aug., 2007
1 (of 5) MMi,GyD,JAr 3.00
2 thru 3 . . . . @3.00

B.P.R.D.: THE UNIVERSE MACHINE
April., 2006
1 MMi,GyD 3.00
2 thru 5 MMi,GyD . . . . @3.00

BRAVE
Mar., 1997
1 by Cully Hamner & Jason Martin . 3.00

BUBBLE GUM CRISIS: GRAND MAL
(Manga) 1994
1 thru 3 . . . . @2.75
4 final issue 2.50

DARK HORSE

BUFFY THE VAMPIRE SLAYER
Sept., 1998

1 JoB,AAd(c) Wu-Tang Fang	9.00
1a 2nd printing	4.00
1b gold foil logo	9.00
2 JoB, Halloween	6.00
3 JoB, Cold Turkey	6.00
4 White Christmas	6.00
5 Happy New Year	6.00
6 New Kid on the Block,pt.1	6.00
7 JoB, New Kid on the Block,pt.2	6.00
8 The Final Cut	6.00
9 Hey, Good Looking,pt.1	6.00
10 Hey, Good Looking,pt.2	6.00
11 A Boy Named Sue	6.00
12 A Nice Girl Like You	6.00
12a gold foil (c)	13.00
13 F:Cordelia Chase	5.00
14 Bad Blood,pt.5	5.00
15 Bad Blood,pt.6	5.00
16 Food Chain	5.00
17 Bad Blood,pt.7	4.00
18 Mardi Gras	3.00
19 Bad Blood, concl.	3.00
20 Angel heads to L.A.	3.00
21 Blood of Carthage,pt.1	3.00
22 Blood of Carthage,pt.2	3.00
23 Blood of Carthage,pt.3	3.00
24 Blood of Carthage,pt.4	3.00
25 Blood of Carthage,concl.	3.00
26 Heart of the Slayer,pt.1	3.00
27 Heart of the Slayer,pt.2	3.00
28 revenge	3.00
29 Past Lives,pt.2,Angel x-over	4.00
30 Past Lives,pt.4,Angel x-over	4.00
31 Lost and Found	4.00
32 hobo ghost	3.00
33 Demonic Entomology	3.00
34 Bug hunt, concl.	3.00
35 False Memories,pt.1	3.00
36 False Memories,pt.2	3.00
37 False Memories,pt.3	3.00
38 False Memories,pt.4	3.00
39 Night of a Thousand Vampires	3.00
40 JmP,Ugly Little Monsters,pt.1	3.00
41 JmP,Ugly Little Monsters,pt.2	3.00
42 JmP,Ugly Little Monsters,pt.3	3.00
43 JmP,Death of Buffy,pt.1	3.00
44 JmP,Death of Buffy,pt.2	3.00
45 JmP,Death of Buffy,pt.3	3.00
46 JmP,Withdrawal	3.00
47 Hellmouth to Mouth,pt.1	3.00
48 Hellmouth to Mouth,pt.2	3.00
49 Hellmouth to Mouth,pt.3	3.00
50 Hellmouth to Mouth,pt.4	3.50
51 SLo,FaN,Viva Las Buffy,pt.1	3.00
52 SLo,Viva Las Buffy, pt.2	3.00
53 SLo,Viva Las Buffy, pt.3	3.00
54 SLo,Viva Las Buffy, pt.4	3.00
55 Dawn and Hoopy the Bear	3.00
56 Slayer, Interrupted,pt.1	3.00
57 Slayer, Interrupted,pt.2	3.00
58 Slayer, Interrupted,pt.3	3.00
59 Slayer, Interrupted,pt.4	3.00
60 FaN,A Stake to the Heart,pt.1	3.00
61 FaN,A Stake to the Heart,pt.2	3.00
62 FaN,A Stake to the Heart,pt.3	3.00
63 FaN,A Stake to the Heart,pt.4	3.00
2a–63a newsstand photo(c)	@3.00
Ann. 1999, 64-pg.	5.00
Spec. 1-shot Spike and Dru	3.00
Spec. 1-shot Giles	3.00
Spec. 1-shot Giles, photo(c)	3.00
Spec. 1-shot Jonathan	3.00
Spec. 1-shotA photo (c).	3.00
Spec. 1-shot Lovers' Walk	3.00
Spec. 1-shot-A photo (c)	3.00
Spec. 1-shot Spike & Dru—The	
Queen of Hearts, photo (c)	3.00

Spec. 1-shot Spike & Dru—All'sFair	3.00
Spec. 1-shot Spike & Dru, ph(c)	3.00
Spec. 1-shot Willow & Tara	3.00
Spec. 1-shotA photo(c)	3.00
Spec. 1-shotB foil photo(c)	10.00
Spec. 1-shotC foil photo(c) sgn	20.00
Spec. 1-shotD red foil	17.00
Spec.1-shot Lost & Found, FaN	3.00
Spec.1-shotA photo (c)	3.00
Spec.1-shot Buffy the Vampire	
Slayer/Angel: Reunion (2002)	3.00
Spec.1-shotA photo (c)	3.00
Spec.1-shot Tales of the Slayers	
Broken Bottle of Djinn (2002)	3.50
Spec.1-shotA photo (c)	3.50
Spec. 1-shot Chaos Bleeds (2003)	3.00
Spec. Chaos Bleeds, photo(c).	3.00
Spec. 1/2 Wizard Mag. (1999)	10.00
GN Ring of Fire, photo(c)	10.00

BUFFY THE VAMPIRE SLAYER
Mar., 2007

1 JoW, sequel to TV series	3.00
1a later printings	@3.00
2 JoW,Terrorist Threat	3.00
2a later printings	@3.00
3 JoW,F:Willow	3.00
4 JoW,F:Willow	3.00
5 JoW, The Chain	3.00
5a&b variant (c)s	@3.00
6 F:Faith	3.00
7 Faith's Out to Kill a Slayer	3.00

BUFFY THE VAMPIRE SLAYER: ANGEL
May, 1999

1 (of 3)	3.00
2 & 3	@3.00
1a thru 3a newsstand, photo(c)	@3.00

BUFFY THE VAMPIRE SLAYER: HAUNTED
Dec., 2001

1 (of 4) deceased enemy's ghost	3.00
2 thru 4	@3.00
1a thru 4a photo (c)	@3.00

BUFFY THE VAMPIRE SLAYER: THE ORIGIN
Feb., 1999

1 (of 3) DIB,JoB	3.00
2 & 3	@3.00
2a & 3a newsstand, photo(c)	@3.00

BUFFY THE VAMPIRE SLAYER: OZ
July, 2001

1 (of 3)	3.00
1a photo(c)	3.00
1b gold foil photo (c)	13.00
1c gold foil photo(c) signed	25.00
1d fiery red foil photo(c)	17.00
2	3.00
2a photo(c)	3.00
3	3.00
3a photo(c)	3.00

Buffy the Vampire Slayer: The Origin #2
© Dark Horse Comics

BUFFY THE VAMPIRE SLAYER: WILLOW AND TARA — WILDERNESS
July, 2002

1 (of 2)	3.00
1a photo (c).	3.00
2 (of 2)	3.00
2a photo (c).	3.00

BY BIZARRE HANDS
(B&W) 1994

1 JLd(s).	2.50
2 JLd(s).	2.50
3 JLd(s).	2.50

CANNON GOD EXAXXION
Manga, Nov., 2001

1 Stage 1, part 1 (of 8)	3.00
2 thru 8 Stage One,pt.2 thru pt.8	@3.00
9 Stage Two,pt.1	3.00
10 Stage Two,pt.2	3.50
11 Stage Two,pt.3	3.50
13 thru 15.	@3.50
16 thru 20	@3.00

CARAVAN KIDD
(B&W–Manga) 1992

1 thru 10 by Johji Manabe	@2.50

[2nd Series] 1993

1 thru 10 F:Miam.	@2.50
Holiday Spec.	2.50
Valentine's Day Spec.	2.50

[3rd Series] 1994

1 thru 8	@2.50
Christmas Special	2.50

CATALYST: AGENTS OF CHANGE
Comics' Greatest World, 1994

1 JPn(c),V:US Army	2.50
2 JPn(c),I:Grenade	2.50
3 JPn(c),Rebel vs. Titan	2.50
4 JPn(c),Titan vs. Grace	2.50
5 JPn(c),V:Ape	2.50
6 and 7	@2.50

CHEVAL NOIR
(B&W) 1989

1 DSt(c)	4.00
2 thru 9	@3.50
10 80 pg.	4.50
11 80 pg.	4.50
12 MM(c)	4.50
13 thru 15	@4.50
16 thru 19 with 2-card strip	@4.50
20 Great Power o/t Chninkel	4.50
21 Great Power o/t Chninkel	4.50
22 Great Power o/t Chninkel,concl.	4.50
23 inc.'Rork','Forever War' concl.	4.50
24 In Dreams,pt.1	4.50
25 In Dreams,pt.2	4.50
26 In Dreams,pt.3	4.50
27 I:The Man From Ciguri (Airtight Garage sequel) Dreams,pt.4	3.50
28 Ciguri cont.	3.50
29 Ciguri cont.	3.50
30 Ciguri,cont.	3.50
31 Angriest Dog in the World.	3.50
32 thru 40	@3.50
41 F:Demon	3.50
42 F:Demon	3.50
43 F:Demon	3.50
44 F:Demon	3.50
45 thru 47	@3.50
48 SwM(c)	3.50
49 F:Rork	3.50
50 F:Rork	3.50

CHOSEN
Dec., 2003

1 (of 3) MMr,PrG	4.00
2	3.00
3	3.00

CHRONICLES OF CONAN
Sept., 2003

TPB Vol. 1 RTs,BWS reprints	16.00
TPB Vol. 2 Tower of the Elephant	16.00
TPB Vol. 3 Monster of Monoliths.	16.00
TPB Vol. 4 Red Nails	16.00
TPB Vol. 5 Shadow in the Tomb	16.00
TPB Vol. 6 Curse of Golden Skull	16.00
TPB Vol. 7 Dweller in the Pool	16.00
TPB Vol. 8 Brother of the Blade	17.00
TPB Vol. 9 Riders of the River-Dragons	17.00
TPB Vol. 10 When Giants Walk the Earth	17.00

Chronowar #6
© Dark Horse Comics

TPB Vol. 11 Dance of the Skull	17.00
TPB Vol. 12 Beast King of Abombi	17.00
TPB Vol. 13 Whispering Shadows	17.00

CHRONOWAR
(B&W) Aug., 1996

1 (of 9) by Kazumasa Takayama	3.00
2 thru 9	@3.00

CITY OF OTHERS
Feb., 2007

1 (of 4) BWr	3.00
2 thru 4	@3.00

CLASSIC STAR WARS
1992

1 AW,newspaper strip reps.	6.00
2 thru 7 AW,newspaper reps.	@4.00
8 AW,newspaper reps. w/card	4.00
9 AW,newspaper reps.	3.50
10 AW,newspaper reps.	3.50
11 thru 19 AW,newspaper reps.	@3.00
20 AW,newspaper strip reps., with trading card, final issue	4.00
TPB Vol. 1, In Deadly Pursuit	16.00
TPB Vol. 1, rep. 2nd edition.	17.00
TPB Vol. 2, Rebel Storm	17.00
TPB Vol. 3, Escape to Hoth	17.00

CLASSIC STAR WARS: A NEW HOPE
1994

1 AAd(c), rep.	4.25
2 AH(c), rep.	4.00
TPB Rep. #1–#2	10.00

CLASSIC STAR WARS: DEVILWORLDS
Aug., 1996

1 (of 2) by Alan Moore	2.50
2	2.50

CLASSIC STAR WARS: EARLY ADVENTURES
Aug., 1994–Apr., 1995

1 MiA(c), Gambler's World	3.00
2 RHo&MGr(c),Blackhole	2.50
3 EiS(c),Rebels of Vorzyd-5	2.50
3 bagged with trading card DH2.	5.00
4 RHo(c),Tatooine.	2.50
5 RHo(c),A:Lady Tarkin.	2.50
6 Weather Dominator	2.50
7 RHo(c),V:Darth Vader	2.50
8 KPI(c),X-Wing Secrets.	2.50
9 KPI(c),A:Boba Fett.	2.50
TPB RsM & AGw, AW(c)	20.00

CLASSIC STAR WARS: EMPIRE STRIKES BACK
1994

1 and 2 Movie Adaptation	@4.00
TPB Rep.#1–#2 AW&CG(c).	10.00
TPB reprint, Hildebrandt(c)	10.00

CLASSIC STAR WARS: HAN SOLO AT STAR'S END
Mar., 1997

1 thru 3 by Alfredo Alcala	@3.00
TPB rep. AW(c)	7.00

Classic Star Wars Return of the Jedi #1
© Dark Horse Comics

CLASSIC STAR WARS: A LONG TIME AGO
(B&W) Mar., 1999

1 thru 6 rep. Marvel comics	@6.00

CLASSIC STAR WARS: RETURN OF THE JEDI
1994

1 Movie Adaptation	4.00
2 Movie Adaptation	3.50
TPB Rep.#1–#2	10.00
TPB rep. Hildebrandt(c)	10.00

CLASSIC STAR WARS: VANDELHELM MISSION
1995

1-shot F:Han Solo, Lando	4.00

CLONEZONE
(B&W) 1989

Spec #1	2.50

CLOWNS, THE (PAGLIACCI)
Apr., 1998

1-shot B&W, CR.	3.00

COLORS IN BLACK
Comics From Spike, 1995

1 B:Passion Play.	3.00
2 Images	3.00
3 Back on the Bus	3.00
4 final issue.	3.00

COLUMBUS
(B&W) 1992

1-shot	2.50

COMIC BOOK

1 thru 4 9'x12' John Kricfalusi	@6.00

COMICS & STORIES
1996

1 (of 4) by Martin & Millionaire	3.00
2 thru 4	@3.00

DARK HORSE

Comics Greatest World, Hero Zero © Dark Horse Comics

COMICS' GREATEST WORLD

1993
(Arcadia)
1 B:MRi(s),FM(c),B:LW,B:O:Vortex, F:X,I:Seekers. 3.00
1a B&W proof ed. (1,500 made). . . 8.00
1b Hologram(c), with cards. 7.00
2 JoP,I:Pit Bulls 2.50
3 AH,I:Ghost 5.00
4 I:Monster 2.50

(Golden City)
1 B:BKs(s),JOy(c),I:Rebel, Amaz.Grace,V:WarMaker 2.50
1a Gold Ed. 5.00
2 I:Mecha 2.50
3 WS(c),I:Titan 2.50
4 E:BKs(s),GP(c),JD,I:Catalyst. . . . 2.50

(Steel Harbor)
1 B:CW(s),PG,I:Barb Wire, V:Ignition 2.50
2 MMi(c),TNa,I:Machine 2.50
3 CW(a&s),I:Wolf Gang 2.50
4 E:CW(s),VGi,I:Motorhead 2.50

(Vortex)
1 B:RSd(s),LW,DoM,I:Division 13. . 2.50
2 I:Hero Zero. 2.50
3 PC,I:King Tiger 2.50
4 B:RSd(s),E:MRi(s)BMc,E:LW, E:O:Vortex,C:Vortex 2.50
Sourcebook 10.00

CONAN
Feb., 2004
1 KBk,CNr,JLi(c) from R.E.Howard 9.00
1a JSC(c) 2nd printing 5.00
1b CNr(c) 3rd printing 3.00
2 Frost Giant's Daughter 4.00
3 Asgard 3.00
4 Hyperborea 3.00
5 Breaks out of slavery. 3.00
6 Rebel 3.00
7 Rebellion 3.00
8 Born on the Battlefield 3.00
9 KBk,CNr. 3.00
10 KBk,CNr,Death in the Temple. . . 3.00
11 KBk,CNr,God the the Bowl 3.00
12 KBk,CNr,The Widowmaker. 3.00
13 KBk,CNr,V:Thoth-Amon 3.00
14 KBk,CNr,V:Thoth-Amon 3.00
15 KBk,Wolves in the Woods 3.00

16 KBk,Horror on Uskuth Hill. 3.00
17 KBk,CNr,The City of Thieves . . . 3.00
18 KBk,CNr,Siren-Song of Death . . 3.00
19 KBk,CNr,Thing in the Temple . . . 3.00
20 KBk,CNr,Tower of the Elephant . 3.00
21 KBk,CNr,Tower of the Elephant . 3.00
22 KBk,CNr,Tower of the Elephant . 3.00
23 KBk, The War of the Dead 3.00
24 KBk,CNr,The Hall of the Dead . . 3.00
25 KBk,CNr,The Hand of the Mighty 3.00
26 KBk, TT,Seeds of Empire 3.00
27 KBk, TT,two stories 3.00
28 KBk, A night in Aquilonia. 3.00
29 MMi,CNr,The Hall of the Dead . . 3.00
30 MMi,CNr,The Hall of the Dead . . 3.00
31 MMi,CNr,The Hall of the Dead . . 3.00
32 KBk,Born on the Battlefield. 3.00
33 TT,CNr, pt.1, 40-pg. 3.00
34 TT,CNr, pt.2. . . . . 3.00
35 TT 3.00
36 TT Crom curse Picts & Prophets 3.00
37 TT,CNr,Honor Among Thieves . . 3.00
38 TT,CNr,Cursed and betrayed . . . 3.00
39 TT,CNr,Janissa Widowmaker . . . 3.00
40 TT,CNr,2 Wizards & a Funeral . . 3.00
41 TT,CNr,Rogues in the House . . . 3.00
42 TT,CNr,Rogues in the House . . . 3.00
43 TT,CNr,The Pits of Refuge 3.00
44 TT,CNr,The Pits of Refuge 3.00
45 KBk, Born on the Battlefield 3.00
Spec. #1 Daughters of Midora 5.00
0 Spec. KBk,CNr,Conan the Legend prologue (2003) 1.00

CONAN AND THE BOOK OF THOTH
March., 2006
1 (of 4) KBk,KJo,48-pg. 5.00
2 thru 5 KBk,KJo,48-pg. . . . . . . @5.00

CONAN AND THE DEMONS OF KHITAI
Oct., 2005
1 (of 4) 3.00
2 . . . . 3.00
3 contains nude ad 7.00
3a 2nd printing 3.50
4 . . . . 3.00

CONAN AND THE JEWELS OF GWAHLUR
April, 2005
1 CR 3.00
2 CR 3.00
3 CR 3.00

CONAN AND THE MIDNIGHT GOD
Jan., 2006
1 (of 5) 3.00
2 thru 5 . . . . @3.00

CONAN AND THE SONGS OF THE DEAD
July., 2006
1 (of 4) JLd(s),TT 3.00
2 thru 5 . . . . @3.00

CONCRETE
(B&W) 1987
1 PC,R:Concrete, A Stone among Stones 9.00
1a 2nd printing 3.00
2 PC, 'Transatlantic Swim' 6.00
3 PC 5.00
4 PC 4.00

5 PC, 'An Armchair Stuffed with Dynamite'. 4.00
6 PC,Concrete works on farm 4.00
7 PC,Concrete grows horns 4.00
8 PC,Climbs Mount Everest 4.00
9 PC,Mount Everest,pt.2. . . . . 4.00
10 PC,last Issue. 4.00
Spec. #1 Concrete ColorSpec.,PC (1989) 4.00
Spec. Concrete Celebrates Earth Day PC,Moebius (1990) 2.50
Spec. 1 A New Life, B&W rep., O: Concrete (1989) 3.50
Spec. Concrete: Land & Sea, rep. #1 & #2 (1989) 3.25
Spec. Concrete: Odd Jobs, rep. #5 & #6 (1990) 3.50

CONCRETE: ECLECTICA
1993
1 PC,The Ugly Boy 3.25
2 PC 3.25

CONCRETE: FRAGILE CREATURE
1991
1 PC,Rulers o/t Omniverse,pt.1 . . . 4.00
2 PC,Rulers o/t Omniverse,pt.2 . . . 3.00
3 PC,Rulers o/t Omniverse,pt.3 . . . 3.00
4 PC,Rulers o/t Omniverse,pt.3 . . . 3.00

CONCRETE: THE HUMAN DILEMMA
(B&W) Dec., 2004
1 (of 6) PC 3.50
2 thru 6 PC . . . . @3.50

CONCRETE: KILLER SMILE
DH Legend, 1994
1 PC 3.50
2 thru 4 PC . . . . @3.00

CONCRETE: STRANGE ARMOR
Dec., 1997–Apr., 1998
1 (of 5) 3.00
2 thru 5 . . . . @3.00

Concrete Strange Armor #5 © Dark Horse Comics

CONCRETE: THINK LIKE A MOUNTAIN
(B&W) 1996
1 thru 6 PC,GfD(c) . . . . @3.00

CORMAC MAC ART
July, 1989
1 Robert E. Howard adapt. 3.00
2 thru 4 . . . . @3.00

CORNY'S FETISH
April 1998
GN by Renee French, 64-pg. 5.00

COUTOO
(B&W) 1994
1 Lt. Joe Kraft 3.50

CREEPY
(B&W) 1992
1 KD,TS,GC,SL,Horror 4.00
2 TS,CI,DC,Demonic Baby 4.00
3 JM,TS,JG,V:Killer Clown 4.00
4 TS,Final issue 4.00

CREATURE FROM THE BLACK LAGOON
1 Movie Adaptation 5.00

CRIMINAL MACABRE
May, 2003
1 (of 5) F:Cal McDonald 4.00
2 thru 5 . . . . @3.00
1a & 2a 2nd printings . . . . @3.00
1-shot Feet of Clay (2006) 3.00

CRIMINAL MACABRE: MY DEMON BABY
Sept., 2007
1 (of 4) 3.00
2 . . . . 3.00

CRIMINAL MACABRE: TWO RED EYES
Dec., 2006
1 (of 4) 3.00
2 thru 4 . . . . @3.00

CRITICAL ERROR
1992
1 rep.Classic JBy story 2.75

CROMWELL STONE
(B&W) 1992
1-shot 3.50

[ANDREW VACHSS'] CROSS
1995
0 GfD(c),I:Cross,Rhino,Princess. . . 2.50
1 thru 7 . . . . @3.00

CRUSH
DH Rocket Comics, Oct., 2003
1 . . . . 3.00
2 thru 4 . . . . @3.00

CUD COMICS
(B&W) 1996
1 thru 8 by Terry LaBan . . . . @3.00

THE CURSE OF DRACULA
July, 1998
1 (of 3) MWn,GC 3.00
2 thru 3 . . . . @3.00

DAMN NATION
Feb., 2005
1 thru 3 . . . . @3.00

DANCE OF LIFEY DEATH, THE
(B&W) 1994
1-shot ECa 4.00

DANGER UNLIMITED
DH Legend, 1994
1 JBy(a&s),KD,I:Danger Unlimited,
  B:BU:Torch of Liberty 2.50
2 JBy(a&s),KD,O:DangerUnlimited. 2.50
3 JBy(a&s),KD,O:Torch of Liberty. . 2.50
4 JBy(a&s),KD,Final Issue 2.50

DARE DETECTIVES, THE
Oct., 2004
GN Vol. 1 The Snowpea Plot 6.00
GN Vol. 2 The Royal Treatment. . . . 7.00

DARK HORSE CLASSICS
(B&W) 1992
1 Last of the Mohicans 4.50
2 20,000 Leagues Under the Sea . 4.50

DARK HORSE CLASSICS: ALIENS VS. PREDATOR
Feb., 1997
1 thru 6 Rep. . . . . @3.00

DARK HORSE CLASSICS: GODZILLA, KING OF THE MONSTERS
July, 1998
1 RSd,SBi,now color. 3.00
2 rep. from 1995 . . . . 3.00
3 rep. from 1995 . . . . 3.00
4 rep. Godzilla #2, from 1995 . . . . . 3.00
5 & 6 . . . . @3.00

DARK HORSE CLASSICS: PREDATOR: JUNGLE TALES
1-shot Rep. 3.00

DARK HORSE CLASSICS: STAR WARS— DARK EMPIRE
1997
1 rep. by Tom Veitch,CK,DvD(c). . . 3.00
2 thru 6 rep., DvD(c) . . . . @3.00

DARK HORSE CLASSICS: TERROR OF GODZILLA
Aug., 1998
1 by Kazuhisa Iwata, AAd(c). 3.00
2 & 3 . . . . @3.00
4 rep. of 1988 B&W 3.00
5 & 6 AAd(c) . . . . @3.00

Dark Horse Comics #9
© *Dark Horse Comics*

DARK HORSE COMICS
1992
1 RL,CW,F:Predator,Robocop,
  I:Renegade,Time Cop,(double
  gatefold cover). 4.00
2 RL,CW,F:Predator,Robocop,
  Renegade,Time Cop 3.00
3 CW,F:Robocop,Time Cop,Aliens,
  Indiana Jones 3.00
4 F:Predator,Aliens,Ind.Jones. 3.00
5 F:Predator,E:Aliens 3.00
6 F:Robocop,Predator, E:Indiana
  Jones 3.00
7 F:Robocop,Predator,B:StarWars . 6.00
8 B&I:X,Robocop 8.00
9 F:Robocop,E:Star Wars 4.00
10 E:X,B:Godzilla,Predator,
   James Bond 3.50
11 F:Godzilla,Predator,James
   Bond,B:Aliens 2.75
12 F:Predator. 2.75
13 F:Predator,B:Thing 2.75
14 MiB(s),B:The Mark 2.75
15 MiB(s),E:The Mark,B:Aliens 2.75
16 B:Predator,E:Thing,Aliens. 2.75
17 B:Aliens,Star Wars:Droids. 2.75
18 E:Predator. 2.75
19 RL(c),B:X,E:Star Wars:Droids,
   Aliens. 2.75
20 B:Predator. 2.75
21 F:Mecha 2.75
22 B:Aliens, E:Mecha 2.75
23 B:The Machine 2.75
24 The Machine 2.75
25 Final issue. 2.75

DARK HORSE DOWNUNDER
(B&W) 1994
1 F:Australian Writers 2.50
2 Australian Writers 2.50
3 Australian Writers, finale 2.50

DARK HORSE MAVERICK
Ann.2000 48-pg. B&W 5.00
Ann.2001 48-pg. B&W 5.00

DARK HORSE MONSTERS
Feb., 1997
1-shot 3.00

DARK HORSE

DARK HORSE PRESENTS
(B&W) 1986

1 PC,I:Concrete 13.00
1a 2nd printing 3.00
2 PC,Concrete 6.00
3 Boris theBear,Concrete 5.00
4 PC,Concrete 5.00
5 PC,Concrete 5.00
6 PC,Concrete 5.00
7 I:MONQ 5.00
8 PC,Concrete 5.00
9 RSd 5.00
10 PC,Concrete, I:Masque 12.00
11 Masque 6.00
12 PC,Concrete, Masque 7.00
13 Masque 5.00
14 PC,Concrete, Masque 7.00
15 Masque 5.00
16 PC,Concrete, Masque 7.00
17 F:Roachmill 5.00
18 PC,Concrete, Mask. 7.00
19 Masque 5.00
20 double,Flaming Carrot 9.00
21 Masque 5.00
22 I:Duckman. 5.00
23 WiS,Filipino Massacre 5.00
24 PC,I:Aliens 15.00
25 thru 31 . . . . @3.00
32 A:Concrete 5.00
33 F:Mr. Monster 3.00
34 Aliens 4.00
35 Predator 4.00
36 Aliens vs.Predator 5.00
36a painted cover 8.00
37 The Heartbreakers 3.00
38 A:Concrete 4.00
39 Trekker 3.00
40 I:The Aerialist 3.00
41 Argosy 3.00
42 Aliens 5.00
43 Aliens 4.00
44 Crash 3.00
45 Predator 3.00
46 Predator 4.00
47 Monkers 3.00
48 with 2-card strip 3.00
49 with 2-card strip 3.00
50 inc.'Heartbreakers', with
    2-card strip 4.00
51 FM(c),inc.'Sin City' 8.00
52 FM,inc. 'Sin City' 7.00
53 FM,inc. 'Sin City' 7.00

Dark Horse Presents #14
© Dark Horse Comics

54 FM,Sin City;JBy Preview of
    Next Men,pt.1 . . . . 7.00
55 FM,Sin City;JBy Preview of
    Next Men (JBy),pt.2. . . . . 6.00
56 FM,Sin City,JBy,Next MenPt.3
    Aliens Genocide(prologue) 5.00
57 FM,SinCity;JBy Next Men,pt.4 . . 5.00
58 FM,Sin City,Alien Fire 5.00
59 FM,Sin City,Alien Fire 5.00
60 FM,Sin City 5.00
61 FM,Sin City 5.00
62 FM,E:Sin City 5.00
63 Moe,Marie Dakar 3.00
64 MWg,R:The Aerialist 3.00
65 B:Accidental Death 3.00
66 PC,inc.Dr.Giggles 3.00
67 B:Predator story (lead in to
    'Race War'),double size 4.50
68 F:Predator,Swimming Lessons
    (Nestrobber tie-in) 3.00
69 F:Predator. 3.00
70 F:Alec 3.00
71 F:Madwoman 3.00
72 F:Eudaemon 3.00
73 F:Eudaemon 3.00
74 F:Eudaemon 3.00
75 F:Chairman 3.00
76 F:Hermes Vs.the Eye,Ball Kid . . 2.50
77 F:Hermes Vs.the Eye,Ball Kid . . 2.50
78 F:Hermes Vs.the Eye,Ball Kid . . 2.50
79 B:Shadow Empires Slaves 2.50
80 AAd,I:Monkey Man & O'Brien . . 5.00
81 B:Buoy 3.00
82 B:Just Folks 3.00
83 Last Impression 3.00
84 MBn,F:Nexus,E:Hermes Vs.the
    Eye Ball Kid 3.00
85 Winner Circle, Eighth Woman . . 3.00
86 Eighth Woman 3.00
87 F:Concrete 4.00
88 Hellboy 3.00
89 Hellboy 4.00
90 Hellboy 3.00
91 Blackheart, Baden 3.00
92 Too Much Coffee Man. 6.00
93 Cud, Blackheart,Coffee Man. . . . 8.00
94 A:Eyeball Kid,Coffee Man 6.00
95 Too Much Coffee Man. 7.00
96 Kabuli Kid 3.00
97 F:Kabuki Kid 3.00
98 Pot Full of Noodles 3.00
99 Anthology title 3.00
100–#1 Lance Blastoff 4.50
100–#2 Hellboy 3.50
100–#3 Concrete 3.50
100–#4 Black Cross. 3.00
100–#5 Pan Fried Girl 3.00
101 BW,F:Aliens 3.00
102 F:Mr. Painter 3.00
103 F:The Pink Tornado 3.00
104 F:The Pink Tornado 3.00
105 F:The Pink Tornado 3.00
106 F:Godzilla 3.00
107 F:Rusty Razorclam 3.00
108 The Ninth Gland 3.00
109 The One Trick Ripoff. 3.00
110 F:Egg. 3.00
111 Ninth Gland 3.00
112 three stories, concl. 3.00
113 Trypto the Acid Dog 3.00
114 F:Star Slammers/Lance Blastoff 3.00
115 flip-book Dr. Spin/The Creep . . . 3.00
116 Fat Dog Mendoza 3.00
117 F:Aliens 3.00
118 Monkeyman O'Brien 3.00
119 Trout 3.00
120 'One Last Job'. 3.00
121 F: Imago 3.00
122 'Lords of Misrule'. 3.00
123 F: Jack Zero 3.00
124 F:Predator 3.00
125 F:Nocturnals 3.00

Dark Horse Presents Annual 1999
© Dark Horse Comics

126 flip book, 48-pg. 4.50
127 F:The Nocturnals 3.00
128 F:Dan & Larry 3.00
129 F:Hammer. 3.00
130 F:Wanted Man 3.00
131 F:Girl Crazy. 3.00
132 flip book 3.00
133 F:Tarzan 3.00
134 F:The Dirty Pair. 3.00
135 F:The Fall, concl. 4.00
136 The Ark 3.00
137 Predator 3.00
138 F:Terminators 3.00
139 F:Roachmill 3.00
140 F:Aliens. 3.00
141 F:Buffy the Vampire Slayer. 4.00
142 F:Lovecraftian tales. 3.00
143 F:Tarzan tales 3.00
144 F:Vortex. 3.00
145 F:Burglar Girls. 3.00
146 F:Aliens vs. Predator 3.00
147 F:Ragnok 3.00
148 The Nevermen 3.00
149 Wunderkind 3.00
150 F:Buffy, 48-pg. 5.00
151 F:Hellboy. 3.00
152 It! The Beast from Twenty
    Billion Years Beyond Earth 3.00
153 Helm of Harxis 3.00
154 Iron Reich 3000, flip-book. 3.00
155 Angel, flip-book 3.00
156 Witch's Son, flip-book 3.00
157 F:Witch's Son, final issue 15.00
Fifth Anniv. Special DGi,PC,
    SBi,CW,MW,FM,Sin City,
    Aliens,Give Me Liberty 20.00
Ann. 1997 F:Body Bags. 5.00
Ann. 1998 F:Hellboy 10.00
Ann. 1999 DHP, JR. 5.00
Ann. 2000 Girls Rule, 64-pg. 5.00
Milestone Ed.#1,rep.DHP#1 . . . . . . 2.50
Spec. Dark Horse 20 Years 1.00

DARK HORSE PRESENTS:
ALIENS

1 Rep. 5.00
1a Platinum Edition. 8.00

DARKNESS FALLS: THE TOOTH FAIRY— THE TRAGIC LIFE OF MATILDA DIXON
Jan., 2003
1-shot CAd 3.00

DEADFACE: DOING ISLANDS WITH BACCHUS
(B&W) 1991
1 rep. Bacchus apps. 3.00
2 rep. inc.'Book-Keeper of Atlantis . 3.00
3 rep. and new material 3.00

DEADFACE: EARTH, WATER, AIR & FIRE
(B&W) 1992
1 Bacchus & Simpson in Sicily 2.50
2 A:Don Skylla 2.50
3 Mafia/Kabeirol-War prep. 2.50
4 Last issue. 2.50

DEAD IN THE WEST
(B&W) 1993
1 TT,Joe Landsdale adapt. 5.00
2 TT,adapt. 5.00
Spec. #1 TT(c) 4.00

DEADLINE
(B&W) 1992
1 . . . . 4.00
2 thru 8 . . . . @4.00

DEADLINE USA
(B&W) 1991
1 rep. Deadline UK,Inc. Tank Girl
    Johnny Nemo 5.00
2 inc. Tank Girl,Johnny Nemo. 5.00
3 . . . . 5.00

DEAD OR ALIVE— A CYBERPUNK WESTERN
Apr., 1998
1 (of 4) by Tatjana and Alberto
    Ponticelli 2.50
2 thru 4 . . . . @2.50

DEAD TO RIGHTS
Oct., 2002
1-shot 64-pg. 6.00

DECADE OF DARK HORSE, A
1996
1 (of 4) inc. Star Wars, Nexus,
    Ghost. 3.00
2 thru 4 . . . . @3.00

[RANDY BOWEN'S] DECAPITATOR
June, 1998
1 (of 4) GEr,DoM 3.00
2 GEr 3.00
3 MMi,KJo,AAl 3.00
4 MMi, conclusion. 3.00

DEVIL CHEF
1994
1 I:Devil Chef 2.50

DEVIL'S FOOTPRINTS
March 2003
1 (of 4) 3.00
2 thru 4 . . . . @3.00

DIABLO: TALES OF SANCTUARY
Nov., 2001
1-shot 64-pg. 6.00

DIGIMON
June, 2000, Bi-weekly
1 . . . . 3.00
2 thru 6 . . . . @3.00
7 thru 12 ND(c) 3.00

DIRTY PAIR
(B&W–Manga) 1999
1-shot Start the Violence, AWa(c) . . 3.00
1-shot Start the Violence, JPn(c) . . . 3.00

DIRTY PAIR: FATAL BUT NOT SERIOUS
(Manga) 1995
1 R:Kei,Yuri 3.00
2 V:Kevin Sleet,Yuri 3.00
3 Anti Yuri 3.00
4 V:Terrorists 3.00
5 conclusion 3.00

DIRTY PAIR: RUN FROM THE FUTURE
Jan., 2000
1 (of 4) AWa(c) 3.00
1a AH(c) 3.00
2 AWa(c) 3.00
2a BSf(c) 3.00
3 AWa(c) 3.00
3a Bruce Timm(c) 3.00
4 AWa(c) 3.00
4a HuR(c) 3.00

DIRTY PAIR: SIM HELL
(B&W–Manga) 1993
1 thru 4 by Adam Warren . . . . . . @3.25

DIRTY PAIR: SIM HELL: REMASTERED
May, 2001
1 (of 4) full color, AWa 3.00
2 thru 4 AWa . . . . @3.00

DISNEY'S MONSTERS INC.
2001
1-shot movie adapt. 5.00

DISNEY'S TARZAN
June, 1999
1 and 2 Animated movie adapt. . . @3.00

DIVISION 13
Sept., 1994
1 & 2 . . . . @2.50
3 A:Payback 2.50
4 Carnal Genesis 2.50

DOC SAVAGE: CURSE OF THE FIRE GOD
1 R:Man of Bronze 3.00
2 Exploding Plane. 3.00
3 & 4 . . . . @3.00

DR. GIGGLES
1992
1 Horror movie adapt. 2.50
2 Movie adapt.contd. 2.50

DR. ROBOT
Apr., 2000
1-shot, by Bernie E. Mireault 3.00

DOMINION: CONFLICT 1 — NO MORE NOISE
(B&W–Manga) 1996
1 thru 6 by Masamune Shirow . . @3.00

DOMINION SPECIAL: PHANTOM OF THE AUDIENCE
(B&W–Manga)
1-shot by Masamune Shirow 2.50

DOMU: A CHILD'S DREAMS
(B&W–Manga)
1 Psychic Warfare. 6.00
2 Murders Continue 6.00
3 Psychic war conclusion 6.00

DRACULA
1 Movie Adaptation 5.00

DRAGON PRINCE
June, 2005
1 (of 5) RMz,JJ 3.00

DRAKUUN
(B&W) Feb., 1997
Rise of the Dragon Princess
1 (of 6) by Johji Manabe. 3.00
2 thru 6 . . . . @3.00
The Revenge of Gustav (Aug., 1997)
7 (1 of 6) by Johji Manabe 3.00
8 thru 12 pt.2 thru pt.6 . . . . @3.00
Shadow of the Warlock (Feb., 1998)
13 (1 of 6) by Johji Manabe. 3.00
14 thru 18 pt.2 thru pt.6 . . . . . . @3.00
The Hidden War (Sept., 1998)
19 (1 of 6) by Johji Manabe 3.00
20 thru 24 pt.2 thru pt.6 . . . . . . @3.00

Drakuun #9
© *Dark Horse Comics*

DARK HORSE

DARK HORSE

Flames of Empire (1999)
25 Flames of Empire (1 of 6)...... 3.00

DRAWING ON YOUR NIGHTMARES
Oct., 2003
1-shot Halloween 2003 Special 1 . . 4.00
1-shot Halloween Special 2 ...... 10.00

DROOPY
Oct., 1995
1 Dr. Droopenstein 2.50
2 Turkey For Dinner 2.50
3 Santa's Little Helpers......... 2.50

DUCKMAN
1990
1 by Everette Peck............. 2.50

DWIGHT T. ALBATROSS'S THE GOON NOIR
(B&W) Sept., 2006
1............................. 3.00
2 thru 3 .... @3.00

DYLAN DOG
(B&W) Bonelli Mar., 1999
1 (of 6) by Tiziano Di Sclavi & Angelo
 Stano, MMi(c), 96-pg. 5.00
2 thru 6 .... @5.00

EDGAR RICE BURROUGHS' RETURN OF TARZAN
Apr., 1997
1 adapted by Thomas Yeates
 & John Totleben............. 3.00
2 thru 3 .... @3.00

EDGAR RICE BURROUGHS' TARZAN
1996
Mugambi
1 Betrayed by 3 man-beasts...... 3.00
2 'Tarzan's Jungle Fury' 3.00
3 'Tarzan's Jungle Fury' 3.00
4 vs. the Tara virus 3.00
5 Cure to the Tara virus 3.00

Edgar Rice Burroughs' Tarzan #1
© Dark Horse Comics

6 .... 3.00
Tarzan and the Legion of Hate
7 pt.1....................... 3.00
8 pt.2....................... 3.00
9 pt.3....................... 3.00
10 pt.4, concl.................. 3.00
Le Monstre, June, 1997
11 pt.1 .... 3.00
12 pt.2 Bernie Wrightson(c)...... 3.00
Modern Prometheus, Aug., 1997
13 pt.1 MK(c) in New York........ 3.00
14 pt.2 MK(c).................. 3.00
Tooth and Nail, Oct., 1997
15 pt.1 MSh(c)................. 3.00
16 pt.2 .... 3.00
Tarzan vs. the Moon Men
17 TT,AW,TY 3.00
18 TT,AW,TY 3.00
19 TT,AW,TY 3.00
20 TT,AW,TY 3.00
Primeval
21 MGr....................... 3.00
22 MGr....................... 3.00
23 MGr....................... 3.00
24 MGr....................... 3.00
1-shot A Tale of Mugambi (1995)... 3.00

EDGAR RICE BURROUGHS' TARZAN: CARSON OF VENUS
May, 1998
1 (of 4) by Darko Macan and
 Igor Kordey, F:Carson Napier . . 3.00
2 thru 4 novels adapt.......... @3.00

EDGAR RICE BURROUGHS' TARZAN: THE LOST ADVENTURE
1995
1 Lost Manuscript 3.00
2 V:Gorgo the Buffalo........... 3.00
3 V:Bandits 3.00
4 V:Bandits 3.00

EDGAR RICE BURROUGHS' TARZAN: THE RIVERS OF BLOOD
Nov., 1999
1............................. 3.00
2 thru 8 .... @3.00

EDGAR RICE BURROUGHS' TARZAN— THE SAVAGE HEART
Apr., 1999
1 (of 4) MGr Jane is dead........ 3.00
2 thru 4 .... @3.00

EGON
Jan.–Feb., 1998
1 and 2 .... @3.00

EIGHTH WONDER, THE
Nov., 1997
1-shot by P. Janes & K. Plunkett... 3.00

ELRIC: STORMBRINGER
DH/Topps, 1996
1 by Michael Moorcock & CR..... 3.00
2 thru 7 (of 7) .... @3.00

EL ZOMBO
April 2004
1 (of 3) 3.00

2 and 3 .... @3.00

EMILY THE STRANGE
(B&W) Aug., 2007
1 The Death Issue 3.50
2 The Fake Issue 3.50

ENEMY
1994
1 MZ(c),StG(s),I:Enemy 2.75
2 MZ(c),StG(s),F:Heller.......... 2.75
3 MZ(c),StG(s),A:Heller 2.50
4............................. 2.50
5 final issue.................. 3.00

ESCAPISTS, THE
July, 2006
1............................. 3.00
2 thru 6 .... @3.00

EUDAEMON, THE
1993
1 Nel,I:New Eudaemon........... 3.00
2 Nel,V:Mordare 2.75
3 Nel,V:Mordare 2.75

EVIL DEAD III: ARMY OF DARKNESS
1 JBo,Movie adaptation 4.00
2 JBo,Movie adaptation 3.50
3 JBo,Movie adaptation 3.00

EXQUISITE CORPSE
1990
1-shot Green 3.00
1-shot Red 3.00
1-shot Yellow 3.00

EYEBALL KID
(B&W) 1992
1 I:Eyeball Kid................ 2.50
2 V:Stygian Leech............. 2.50
3 V:Telchines Brothers,last iss..... 2.50

FAFHRD AND THE GRAY MOUSER
Jan., 2007
1-shot HC,MMi 3.00

FAT DOG MENDOZA
(B&W) 1992
1 I&O:Fat Dog Mendoza......... 2.50

FEAR AGENT: THE LAST GOODBYE
June., 2007
1............................. 3.00
2 thru 4..................... @3.00

FEEDERS
Oct., 1999
1-shot MiA, prequel to Eyes
 to Heaven 3.00

FIERCE
June, 2004
1............................. 3.00
2 thru 4 .... @3.00

F5 ORIGIN
1-shot, rep................... 3.00

All comics prices listed are for Near Mint condition.

DARK HORSE

Flaming Carrot #25
© Dark Horse Comics

FLAMING CARROT
(B&W) 2001
Previous issues: see B&W section
18 Uncle Billy's mail-order bride . . . 4.00
18a Ash-Can-Limited 4.00
19 Hills Like White Elephants 4.00
20 Secret ice cream cult 4.00
21 Space Aliens 3.00
22 V:Space Aliens 3.00
23 Blipio appears 3.00
24 48-page 10th anniv. spec. 4.00
25 F:TMNT,Mysterymen, with
    2-card strip 3.00
26 A:TMNT 3.00
27 TM(c),A:TMNT conclusion 3.00
28 Injured bumblebee 3.00
29 Man in the Moon,Iron City 3.00
30 V:Man in the Moon 3.00
31 A:Fat Fury 3.00
Ann. 1 by Bob Burden 5.00

FLAXEN
1992
1 Based on Model,w/poster 3.00

FLOATERS
(B&W) 1993–94
1 thru 6 From Spike Lee . . . . @2.50

FOOT SOLDIERS, THE
1996
1 thru 4 by Jim Krueger 3.00
See also Image Comics

FORT: PROPHET OF
THE UNEXPLAINED
June, 2002
1 (of 4) F:Charles Fort 3.00
2 thru 4 . . . . @3.00

FRANKENSTEIN
1 Movie Adaptation 4.00

FRAY
2001
1 . . . . 8.00
1a 2nd printing 3.00
2 thru 3 . . . . @5.00
4 thru 5 . . . . @4.00
6 thru 8 . . . . @5.00

FREAKS' AMOUR
1992
1 . . . . 4.00
2 . . . . 4.00
3 . . . . 4.00

FREAKSHOW
1 JBo,DMc,KB, 'Wanda the Worm
  Woman,' 'Lillie'. 10.00

FREAKS OF THE
HEARTLAND
Jan., 2004
1 (of 6) horror 3.00
2 thru 6 . . . . @3.00

FUSED: THINK LIKE
A MACHINE
Dec., 2003
1 Robotic Cy-Bot. 3.00
2 . . . . 3.00
3 . . . . 3.00
4 . . . . 3.00

GALACTIC
DH Rocket Comics Aug., 2003
1 . . . . 3.00
2 & 3 . . . . @3.00
TPB 10.00

GAMERA
Aug., 1996
1 (of 4) by Dave Chipps &
  Mozart Couto 3.00
2 thru 4 . . . . @3.00

GARY GIANNI'S
MONSTERMEN
Aug., 1999
1-shot. 3.00

GHOST
Comics' Greatest World
Spec. AH(c) 4.00

GHOST
1995–98
1 by Eric Luke, R:Ghost 6.00
2 AH,MfM,Arcadia Nocturne,pt.2 . . 4.00
3 Arcadia Nocturn,pt.3 . . . . 4.00
4 . . . . 3.00
5 V:Predator 3.00
6 . . . . 3.00
7 Hell Night 3.00
8 thru 21 . . . . @3.00
22 The key is forever beyond
   your reach 3.00
23 I: The Goblins 3.00
24 X is dead. 3.00
25 double size 4.00
26 Fairytale version 3.50
27 . . . . 3.50
28 CW(c),Painful Music,pt.1 . . . . . 3.50
29 CW(c),Painful Music,pt.2 . . . . . 3.50
30 CW(c),Painful Music,pt.3 . . . . . 3.50
31 CW(c),Painful Music,pt.4 . . . . . 3.50
32 A Pathless Land 3.50
33 Jade Cathedral,pt.1 . . . . 3.50
34 Jade Cathedral,pt.2 . . . . 3.50
35 Jade Cathedral,pt.3 . . . . 3.50
36 Jade Cathedral,pt.4 . . . . 3.50
Spec.#2 Immortal Coil 4.50
Spec.#3 Scary Monsters 4.50

Ghost #8
© Dark Horse Comics

GHOST
1998–2000
1 CW,O:Ghost. 3.00
2 CW,V:Dr.Trouvaille 3.00
3 CW,V:Silhouette. 3.00
4 CW,The Devil Inside,O:pt.1 . . . . . 3.00
5 CW,Stare at the Sun,O:pt.2 . . . . . 3.00
6 CW,Stare at the Sun,O:pt.3 . . . . . 3.00
7 CW,Shifter,pt.1,F:King Tiger 3.00
8 CW,Shifter,pt.2 . . . . 3.00
9 CW,Shifter,pt.3 . . . . 3.00
10 CW,Shifter,pt.4 . . . . 3.00
11 CW,back in Arcadia. 3.00
12 Red Shadows,pt.1 (of 4). 3.00
13 Red Shadows,pt.2 . . . . 3.00
14 Red Shadows,pt.3 . . . . 3.00
15 Red Shadows,pt.4 . . . . 3.00
16 When the Devil Daydreams,pt.1. 3.00
17 When the Devil Daydreams,pt.2. 3.00
18 rogue agent. 3.00
19 Arcadia in chaos 3.00
20 F:Chris 3.00
21 F:Malcolm Greymater 3.00
22 final issue 3.00
Spec. Handbook #1 . . . . 3.00

GHOST/BATGIRL
Aug., 2000
1 (of 4) RBn,A:oracle 3.00
2 RBn,V:Two-Face 3.00
3 RBn,V:Carver, Greymater 3.00
4 RBn,concl 3.00

GHOST/HELLBOY
1996
1 & 2 MMi 3.50

GHOST AND
THE SHADOW
1995
Spec. 1-shot. 3.00

GHOST IN THE SHELL
(Manga) 1995
1 Manga Style. 25.00
2 Wetware Virus 20.00
3 Killer Robots 10.00
4 thru 8 . . . . @8.00

DARK HORSE

GHOST IN THE SHELL 2: MAN-MACHINE INTERFACE

Oct., 2002

1 40-pg.by Masamune Shirow 4.00
2 32-pg. 3.50
3 thru 11 . . . . @3.50
Spec. #1 Holographic Edition 5.00

GHOST IN THE SHELL 1.5: HUMAN ERROR PROCESSING

(B&W) Oct., 2006

1 by Shirow Masamune 3.00
2 thru 8 . . . . @3.00

G.I. Joe #1
© Dark Horse Comics

G.I. JOE

1995

1 by Mike Barr & Tatsuya Ishida . . . 3.00
2 thru 4 . . . . @3.00

Vol. 2 1996

1 . . . . 3.00
2 thru 4 . . . . @3.00

GIRL CRAZY

(B&W) May, 1996

1 GHe 3.00
2 and 3 GHe . . . . @3.00

GIVE ME LIBERTY

1990

1 FM/DGb, Homes & Gardens 6.00
2 FM/DGb 5.00
3 and 4 FM/DGb . . . . @5.00

GO BOY 7: HUMAN ACTION MACHINE

DH Rocket Comics, July, 2003

1 TPe 3.00
2 thru 8 . . . . @3.00

GODZILLA

(B&W) 1988

1 Japanese Manga 5.00
2 thru 6 . . . . @4.00
Spec #1 . . . . 3.00
TPB 2nd printing 18.00

GODZILLA COLOR SPECIAL

1992

1 AAd,R:Godzilla,V:Gekido-Jin 3.50
1a rep (1998) 3.00
Spec.1 Godzilla vs. Barkley MBn(s),
   JBt,DvD (1993) 3.50

GODZILLA

1995

0 RSd,The King of Monsters
   is back! 4.00
1 R:Godzill 4.00
2 V:Cybersaur 4.00
3 I:Bagorah the Bat Creature 4.00
4 V:Bagorah,Cybersaur 4.00
5 V:U.S. Army 4.00
6 thru 14 . . . . @4.00
15 'Thunder Downunder' 4.00
16 'Thunder in the Past'. 4.00
Spec.1 Godzilla vs. Hero Zero
   Tatsuya Ishida (1995) 2.50

GOON, THE

June, 2003

1 . . . . 6.00
2 . . . . 5.00
3 thru 9 . . . . @4.00
10 thru 20 . . . . @3.00
Spec. 25 Cent rep of #1. . . . . 1.00

GREEN LANTERN VS. ALIENS

Aug., 2000

1 RMz,RL,F:Hal Jordan, x-over . . . 3.00
2 (of 4) RMz,RL,F:Kyle Rayner . . . 3.00
3 RMz,RL, without ring 3.00
4 RMz,RL, V:Alien Queen. 3.00

GRENDEL

TPB Past Prime,MWg 15.00
Spec.1 Grendel Cycle, Grendel
   History (1995) 6.00
Spec.1 Devil Quest (1995). 5.00

GRENDEL: BEHOLD THE DEVIL

(B&W) July., 2007

0 MWg 16-pgs. 1.00

GRENDEL: BLACK, WHITE, AND RED

(B&W&R) Nov., 1998

1 (of 4) MWa, 48-pg. 5.00
2 thru 4 MWa, 48-pg. . . . . @4.00

GRENDEL CLASSICS

1995

1 Rep.#18–#19 Comico series 4.00
2 Rep. 4.00

GRENDEL: DEVIL BY THE DEED

1993

1 MWg,RRa 4.00
1 representation (1997) 4.00

GRENDEL: DEVIL CHILD

June, 1999

1 and 2 MWg 3.00

GRENDEL: THE DEVIL INSIDE

DH Maverick, Sept., 2001

1 (of 3) MWg. 3.00
2 . . . . 3.00
3 concl. 3.00

GRENDEL: DEVIL'S LEGACY

Aug., 1996

1 by Matt Wagner 3.00
2 thru 3 . . . . @3.00

DH/Maverick, Mar., 2000

1 (of 12) MWg, rep. from 1986 . . . . 3.00
2 thru 6 MWg . . . . @3.00
7 MWg,V:Tujiro XIV 3.00
8 MWg,back to N.Y. 3.00
9 MWg,F:Dominic Riley 3.00
10 MWg 3.00
11 MWg 3.00
12 MWg, concl. 3.00

GRENDEL: DEVIL'S REIGN

May, 2004

1 (of 7) MWg. 3.50
2 thru 7 . . . . @3.50

GRENDEL: GOD AND THE DEVIL

Jan., 2003

0 MWg,TSe. 3.50
1 MWg (of 10). 3.50
2 thru 9 MWg . . . . @3.50
10 MWg, concl., 48-pg. 5.00

GRENDEL: RED, WHITE, & BLACK

DH Maverick, Sept., 2002

1 (of 4) 48-pg. B&W 5.00
2 MWg,KJo,DIB 5.00
3 . . . . 5.00
4 MWg 5.00

GRENDEL TALES: DEVIL'S APPRENTICE

Sept., 1997

1 (of 3) 3.00
2 thru 3 . . . . @3.00

Grendel Tales, The Devil's Apprentice
#2 © Dark Horse Comics

GRENDEL TALES: DEVILS AND DEATHS
1994
1	3.00
2	3.00

GRENDEL TALES: DEVIL'S CHOICES
1995
1 F:Goran	3.00
2 thru 4	@3.00

GRENDEL TALES: FOUR DEVILS, ONE HELL
1 MWg(c),F:Four Grendels	3.50
2 MWg(c),F:Four Grendels	3.50
3 MWg(c),F:Four Grendels	3.50
4 MWg(c),F:Four Grendels	3.50
5 MWg(c),F:Four Grendels	3.50
6 MWg(c),last issue	3.25

GRENDEL TALES: HOMECOMING
1994
1 Babylon Crash	3.00
2 Babylon Crash,pt. 2	3.00
3 Too Dead To Die	3.00

GRENDEL TALES: THE DEVIL IN OUR MIDST
1994
1 MWg(c)	3.50
2 MWg(c)	3.25
3 thru 5	@3.00

GRENDEL TALES: THE DEVIL MAY CARE
1995
1 thru 6 mini-series	3.00

GRENDEL TALES: THE DEVIL'S HAMMER
1994
1 MWg(a&s),I:Petrus Christus	3.50
2 MWg(a&s),A:P.Christus	3.25
3 MWg(a&s),last issue	3.25

GRENDEL: WAR CHILD
1992
1 MWg	4.00
2 thru 9 MWg	3.00
10 MWg, final issue, dbl.size	4.00

GRIFTER AND THE MASK
Sept., 1996
1 by Seagle, Lima & Pimentel	2.50
2	2.50

GROO: HELL ON EARTH
Sept., 2007
1 (of 4) SA	3.00
2 SA	3.00
Spec. Groo 25th Anniv. Special	6.00

GUFF
Apr., 1998
1-shot by Sergio Aragones, flip book, with Meanie Babies card, B&W	2.50

GUNSMITH CATS
(B&W–Manga) 1995
1 I:Rally & Mini May	3.00
2 Revolver Freak	3.00
3	3.00
4 V:Bonnie and Clyde	3.00
5 V:Bonnie and Clyde	3.00
6 Hostage Situation	3.00
7 thru 10 (10 part series)	3.00

GUNSMITH CATS: BAD TRIP
(B&W) June, 1998
1 (of 6) by Kenichi Sonoda	3.00
2 thru 6	@3.00

GUNSMITH CATS: BEAN BANDIT
(B&W) June, 1998
1 (of 9) by Kenichi Sonoda	3.00
2 thru 9	@3.00

GUNSMITH CATS: GOLDIE VS. MISTY
(B&W) Nov., 1997
1 (of 7) by Kenichi Sonoda	3.00
2 thru 7	@3.00

GUNSMITH CATS: KIDNAPPED
Nov., 1999
1 (of 10) by Kenichi Sonoda	3.00
2 thru 10	@3.00

GUNSMITH CATS: MISTER V
(B&W) Oct., 2000
1 (of 11) by Kenichi Sonoda	3.50
2 thru 11	@3.50
Spec.	3.00

GUNSMITH CATS: SHADES OF GRAY
(B&W) May, 1997
1 (of 5) by Kenichi Sonoda	3.00
2 thru 5 (of 5)	@3.00

GUNSMITH CATS: THE RETURN OF GRAY
(B&W) Aug., 1996
1 thru 7 by Kenichi Sonoda	@3.00

HAMMER OF GOD: BUTCH
1994
1 thru 3 MBn	@2.50

HAMMER OF GOD: PENTATHLON
1994
1 MiB(s),NV	2.50

THE HAMMER: UNCLE ALEX
Aug., 1998
1-shot KJo	3.00

HAPPY BIRTHDAY MARTHA WASHINGTON
1995
1 Frank Miller	3.00

HARD BOILED
1990
1 GfD	7.00
2 and 3	@6.00

HARD LOOKS
(B&W) 1992
1 thru 10 AVs Adaptations	@2.50
Book One	15.00

HARLAN ELLISON'S DREAM CORRIDOR
1995
1 Various stories	3.00
2 Various stories	3.00
3 JBy, I Have No Mouth and I Must Scream & other stories	3.00
4 thru 6	@3.00
Spec.#1 Various stories	5.00
Spec. Quarterly, vol. 1	6.00
Spec. Quarterly, vol. 2	6.00

HAUNTED MAN, THE
Mar., 2000
1 (of 3) GJ,MBg	3.00
2 GJ,MBg	3.00
3	3.00

HEARTBREAKERS
1996
1	3.00
2 thru 4	@3.00

HEART OF EMPIRE: THE LEGACY OF LUTHER ARKWRIGHT
Apr., 1999
1 (of 9) BT	3.00
2 thru 5	@3.00
6 plot against royal family	3.50
7 countdown to cataclysm	3.50
8	3.50
9 conclusion	3.00

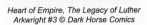

Heart of Empire, The Legacy of Luther Arkwright #3 © Dark Horse Comics

---

DARK HORSE

HELL
DH Rocket Comics, July, 2003
1 BAu 3.00
2 thru 4 BAu . . . . @3.00

HELLBOY
Christmas Special (1997) MMi,
  48-pg. 4.00
Spec. The Corpse and the
  Iron Shoes (1996) 3.00
Spec. The Wolves of St. August . . . 3.00
Hellboy Junior Halloween Special . . 4.00
Hellboy Junior Lurid Easter Special . 4.00
1-shot The Corpse 1.00
GN Animated Vol.1 Black
  Wedding Dress 7.00
GN Animated Vol. 2 Judgment Bell . 7.00
GN Animated Vol. 3 Menagerie 7.00

Hellboy: Almost Colossus #2
© Dark Horse Comics

HELLBOY:
ALMOST COLOSSUS
DH Legend, 1997
1 (of 2) MMi, sequel to *Wake the*
  Devil. 3.00
2 (of 2) 3.00

HELLBOY:
BOX FULL OF EVIL
Aug., 1999
1 (of 2) MMi 3.00
2 MMi, conclusion 3.00

HELLBOY:
CONQUEROR WORM
May, 2001
1 (of 4) MMi 3.00
2 thru 4 . . . . @3.00

HELLBOY:
DARKNESS CALLS
Apr., 2007
1 (of 6) MMi. . . . . @3.00
2 thru 6 . . . . @3.00

HELLBOY:
THE ISLAND
June, 2005
1 and 2 MMi . . . . @3.00

HELLBOY: MAKOMA
Feb., 2006
1 MMi,RCo 3.00
2 MMi,RCo 3.00

HELLBOY: SEEDS
OF DESTRUCTION
DH Legend, 1994
1 JBy,MMi,AAd,V:Vampire Frog,
  BU:Monkeyman & O'Brien 3.50
2 MMi(c),JBy,AAd,BU:Monkeyman
  & O'Brien 3.00
3 MMi(c),JBy,AAd,BU:Monkeyman
  & O'Brien 3.00
4 MMi(c),JBy,AAd,BU:Monkeyman
  & O'Brien 3.00

HELLBOY:
THE THIRD WISH
July, 2002
1 (of 2) MMi 3.00
2 . . . . 3.00

HELLBOY:
WAKE THE DEVIL
DH Legend, 1996
1 (of 5) MMi 3.00
2 thru 5 . . . . @3.00

HELLBOY: WEIRD TALES
Feb., 2003
1 FaN 3.00
2 thru 8 . . . . @3.00

HELLBOY JR.
October 1999
1 (of 2) MMi 3.00
2 . . . . 3.00

HELLGATE: LONDON
Oct., 2006
0 IEd 3.00
1 (of 4) IEd 3.00
2 thru 3 IEd . . . . @3.00

HELLHOUNDS
(B&W) 1994
1 I:Hellhounds 3.00
2 and 3 . . . . @3.00
Becomes:

HELLHOUNDS:
PANZER CORPS
3 thru 6 . . . . @3.00

HERBIE
1992
1 JBy,reps.& new material 3.00
2 Reps.& new material 2.50

HERETIC, THE
Nov., 1996
1 (of 4) by Rich DiLeonardo, Joe
  Phillips & Dexter Vines 3.00
2 thru 4 . . . . @3.00

HERMES VS. THE
EYEBALL KID
1994
1 thru 3 Symphony of Blood 3.00

HERO ZERO
1994
1 First and last issue. 2.50

HIEROGLYPH
Nov., 1999
1 RdD,F:Francisco Chavez. 3.00
2 thru 4 RdD . . . . @3.00

HOMICIDE
(B&W) 1990
Spec. JAr,DoM 2.50

THE HORROR OF
COLLIER COUNTY
Oct., 1999
1 (of 5) Halloween special 3.00
2 thru 5 concl. . . . . @3.00

HYPERSONIC
Nov., 1997
1 (of 4) DAn,GEr. 3.00
2 thru 4 . . . . @3.00

INCREDIBLES, THE
Nov., 2004
1 (of 4) 3.00
2 thru 4 . . . . @3.00

INDIANA JONES AND
THE ARMS OF GOLD
1994
1 In South America 2.75
2 In South America 2.75
3 V:Incan Gods 2.75
4 . . . . 2.50

Indiana Jones and the Fate of Atlantis
#2 © Dark Horse Comics

INDIANA JONES AND
THE FATE OF ATLANTIS
1991
1 DBa,Search for S.Hapgood with
  2-card strip 4.00
1a 2nd printing 3.00
2 DBa,Lost Dialogue of Plato with
  2-card strip 3.00
3 Map Room of Atlantis 3.00
4 Atlantis, Last issue 3.00

DARK HORSE

INDIANA JONES AND THE GOLDEN FLEECE
1994
1 SnW 2.75
2 SnW 2.50

INDIANA JONES AND THE IRON PHOENIX
1994
1 . . . . 2.50
2 V:Nazis 2.50
3 A:Nadia Kirov 2.50
4 V:Undead 2.50

INDIANA JONES AND THE SARGASSO PIRATES
1995
1 thru 4 . . . . @2.50

INDIANA JONES AND THE SHRINE OF THE SEA DEVIL
199
1 . . . . 2.50

INDIANA JONES AND THE SPEAR OF DESTINY
1995
1 I:Spear T/Pierced Christ 2.50
2 DSp, with Henry Jones 2.50
3 Search for the Shaft 2.50
4 concl 2.50

INDIANA JONES: THUNDER IN THE ORIENT
1993
1 DBa(a&s),in Tripoli 2.75
2 DBa(a&s),Muzzad Ram 2.75
3 DBa(a&s),V:Sgt.Itaki 2.75
4 DBa(a&s),In Hindu Kush 2.75
5 DBa(a&s),V:Japanese Army 2.75
6 DBa(a&s),last issue 2.75

INSANE
(B&W) 1988
1 . . . . 3.00
2 . . . . 3.00

INSTANT PIANO
(B&W) 1994
1 Offbeat humor 4.00
2 . . . . 4.00
3 Various stories 4.00
4 Devil Puppet 4.00

INVINCIBLE ED:
2003
1 The Beating of Ed 3.50
2 I'm Too Sexy 4.00
3 Lance Lundgrin Unleashes 3.00
4 The End 3.00
TPB 14.00

IRON EMPIRES
Dec., 2003
TPB Vol. 1 . . . . 18.00
TPB Vol. 2 Sheva's War 18.00

IRONHAND OF ALMURIC
(B&W) 1991
1 Robert E. Howard adaption 2.50

2 A:Cairn,V:Yagas 2.50
3 V:Yasmeena,The Hive Queen . . . 2.50
4 Conclusion 2.50
GN 11.00

JAMES BOND 007: QUASIMODO GAMBIT
1995
1 I:Maximillion Quasimodo 4.00
2 V:Fanatical Soldiers 4.00
3 V:Steel 4.00

JAMES BOND 007: SERPENT'S TOOTH
1992
1 PG,DgM,V:Indigo 5.50
2 PG,DgM,V:Indigo 5.00
3 PG,DgM 5.25
TPB 16.00

JAMES BOND 007: SHATTERED HELIX
1994
1 V:Cerberus 3.00
2 V:Cerberus 3.00

JAMES BOND 007: A SILENT ARMAGEDDON
1993
1 V:Troy 3.25
2 & 3 V:Omega . . . . @3.25

JINGLE BELLE
Nov., 2004
1 . . . . 3.00
2 thru 4 . . . . @3.00
1-shot-The Fight Before Christmas . 3.00

JOHN BOLTON'S STRANGE WINK
Mar., 1998
1 (of 3) 3.00
2 thru 3 . . . . @3.00

JOHNNY DYNAMITE
1994
1 . . . . 3.00
2 thru 4 . . . . @3.00

JOKER/MASK
May, 2000
1 (of 4) Batman x-over 3.00
2 Joker becomes Joker/Mask 3.00
3 A:Harley Quinn, Poison Ivy 3.00
4 three nuclear bombs, concl. 3.00

JONNY DEMON
1994
1 SL(c),KBk,NV 2.75
2 SL(c),KBk,NV 2.75
3 SL(c),KBk,NV, final issue 2.50

JOSS WHEDON'S FRAY
June, 2001
1 (of 8) 3.00
1a gold foil (c) 10.00
1b gold foil (c) signed 25.00
2 thru 8 . . . . @3.00
1 thru 6 2nd printings . . . . @3.00

JUDGE DREDD VS. ALIENS: INCUBUS
Mar., 2003
1 (of 4) 3.00
2 thru 4 . . . . @3.00

JUNIOR CARROT PATROL
(B&W) 1989
1 and 2 . . . . @3.00

KARAS
Nov., 2004
1-shot 3.00

KELLEY JONES' THE HAMMER
Sept., 1997
1 (of 4) KJo, horror series 3.00
2 thru 4 KJo, ... @3.00

KELLEY JONES' THE HAMMER: THE OUTSIDER
Feb., 1999
1 (of 3) KJo 3.00
2 and 3 . . . . @3.00

KELLEY JONES' THE HAMMER: UNCLE ALEX
1998
1-shot 3.00

KINGS OF THE NIGHT
1990
1 Robert E. Howard adapt 2.50
2 end Mini-Series 2.50

KING TIGER/MOTORHEAD
1996
1 (of 2) by D.G. Chichester, Karl
   Waller & Eric Shanower 3.00
2 . . . . 3.00

King Tiger/Motorhead #2
© Dark Horse Comics

DARK HORSE

KISS
July, 2002
1 JoC	4.00
2 thru 4 JoC	@3.00
5	3.00
6	3.00
7 thru 10 SLo	@3.00
11	3.00
12	3.00
13 MBn	3.00
1a thru 13a photo (c)	@3.00

KONG
Oct., 2005
TPB Kong: King of Skull Island	20.00
1 Movie adapt. (2005)	4.00
2 thru 3	@4.00

LAND OF NOD
(B&W) July, 1997
1 (of 4) by Jay Stephens	3.00
2 thru 4	@3.00

LAST TRAIN
TO DEADSVILLE
2004
1 (of 4) F:Cal McDonald	3.00
2 thru 4	@3.00

THE LEGEND OF
MOTHER SARAH
(B&W–Manga) 1995
1 I:Mother Sarah	4.00
2 Sarah and Tsutsu	4.00
3 Firing Squad	4.00
4 F:Toki	4.00
5 Yunnel Town	4.00
6 Kill or Be Killed	4.00
7 Firing Squad	4.00
8 Conclusion	4.00

THE LEGEND OF
MOTHER SARAH:
CITY OF THE ANGELS
(B&W–Manga) Oct., 1996
1 (of 9) by Katsuhiro Otomo and Takumi Nagayasu, 48-pg.	4.25
1 rep. (1997)	4.25
2 thru 4	4.25

Legend of Mother Sarah, City of the Angels #1 © Dark Horse Comics

2 thru 4 rep. (1997)	4.25
5 Tsue a victim	4.25
6 Mother Teres questioned	4.25
7 put in front trenches	4.25
8 Teres suicide run	4.25
9 concl., 32-pg.	3.25

THE LEGEND OF
MOTHER SARAH:
CITY OF THE CHILDREN
(B&W–Manga) 1996
1 thru 4 (7 part mini-series)	@4.25
5 thru 7	@4.00

LITTLE LULU
(B&W) May, 2005
1 My Dinner with Lulu	10.00
2 Sunday Afternoon	10.00
3 In The Doghouse	10.00
4 Lulu Goes Shopping	10.00
5 Lulu Takes a Trip	10.00
6 Letters to Santa	10.00
7 Lulu's Umbrella Service	10.00
8 Late for School	10.00
9 Luck Lulu	10.00
10 All Dressed Up	10.00
11 April Fools	10.00
12 Leave it to Lulu	10.00
13 Too Much Fun	10.00
17 The Valentine	10.00

LIVING WITH THE DEAD
Oct., 2007
1 (of 3) RCo(c)	3.00

LOBSTER JOHNSON:
THE IRON PROMETHEUS
Sept., 2007
1 (of 5) MMi	3.00
2	3.00

LONE
DH Rocket Comics, Sept., 2003
1	3.00
2 thru 6	@3.00

LONE GUNMEN, THE
June, 2001
1-shot	3.00
1-shot photo(c)	3.00
1-shot photo (c) lim ed.	7.00
1-shot photo (c) lim ed. signed	20.00

LONE WOLF 2100
May, 2002
1 (of 4) War Spore	4.00
2 thru 4 War Spore	@3.00
5 thru 11	@3.00
1-shot The Red File	3.00

LORDS OF MISRULE
(B&W) Jan., 1997
1 by DAn, PSj	3.00
2 thru 6	@3.00

LOST IN SPACE
Apr., 1998
1 (of 3) sequel to film	3.00
2 thru 3 GEr(c)	@3.00

LOVE ME TENDERLOIN
Jan., 2004
1-shot F:Cal McDonald	3.00

LUX AND ALBY
SIGN ON AND SAVE
THE UNIVERSE
(B&W) 1993
1	3.00
2 thru 9	@3.00

THE MACHINE
Comics Greatest World, 1994
1 (a) The Barb Wire spin	2.50
2 V:Salvage	2.50
3 Freak Show	2.50
4 I:Skion	2.50

MADMAN
DH Legend, 1994
1 MiA(s)	8.00
2 MiA(s)	6.00
3 MiA(s)	5.00
4 MiA(s),Muscleman	5.00
5 MiA(s),I:The Blast	4.00
6 MiA(s),A:Big Guy, Big Brain-o-rama,pt.1	12.00
7 MiA(s),FM,A:Big Guy, Big Brain-o-rama,pt.2	6.00
8 MiA(s)	4.00
9 Micro Madman	4.00
10	4.00
11	4.00
Yearbook '95 TPB	18.00
Yearbook '96 TPB	18.00
Yearbook '95 new printing (2003)	18.00
Apr., 1999
12 MiA	3.00
13 MiA	3.00
14 MiA	3.00
15 MiA	3.00
16 MiA	3.00
G-Men From Hell (Aug., 2000)	
17 Pt.1 MiA	3.00
18 Pt.2 MiA, Is Frank Einstein dead?	3.00
19 Pt.3 MiA	3.00
20 Pt.4 MiA, V:Mr.Monstadt	3.00

MADMAN/THE JAM
July, 1998
1 (of 2) MiA	3.00
2 MiA	3.00

MAGIC: THE GATHERING
Mar., 1998
1 (of 4) MGr,Initiation	3.00
2 MGr, Legacy	3.00
3 MGr, Crucible	3.00
4 MGr, Destiny	3.00

MAGNUS/NEXUS
DH/Valiant
1 MBn(s), SR	3.25
2 MBn(s), SR	3.25

MANGA DARKCHYLDE
Feb., 2005
1 (of 5)	3.00
2 thru 3	@3.00

MAN WITH
THE SCREAMING BRAIN
2005
1 (of 4)	3.00
2 thru 4	@3.00
1a thru 4a Variant(c)	@3.00

MARK, THE
1987–89
1 LSn 3.00
2 & 3 LSn . . . . @3.00
4 thru 6 . . . . @3.00

[Second Series] 1993
1 MiB(s),in America,V:Archon 3.00
2 MiB(s),V:Archon 3.00
3 MiB(s),V:Archon,A:Pierce 3.00
4 MiB(s),last issue 3.00

MARSHALL LAW
GN Super Babylon, KON (1992) . . . 5.00
1-shot Marshall Law: Cape Fear . . . 3.00

MARSHALL LAW:
SECRET TRIBUNAL
1993
1 KON 3.00
2 KON 3.00

M.A.R.S. PATROL
TOTAL WAR
Sept., 2004
TPB WW 13.00

MARTHA WASHINGTON
DIES
July., 2007
1-shot 3.50

MARTHA WASHINGTON
GOES TO WAR
DH Legend, 1994
1 FM(s),DGb, V:Fat Boys Corp. . . . 3.25
2 FM(s),DGb, V:Fat Boys Corp. . . . 3.25
3 FM(s),DGb, V:Fat Boys Corp. . . . 3.25
4 FM(s),DGb, V:Fat Boys Corp. . . . 3.25
5 FM(s),DBb, final issue 3.25

MARTHA WASHINGTON
SAVES THE WORLD
Dec., 1997
1 (of 3) FM,DGb 3.25
2 thru 3 . . . . @3.25

Martha Washington Saves the World #1
© Dark Horse Comics

MARTHA WASHINGTON
STRANDED IN SPACE
1995
1 . . . . 3.25

MARTIN MYSTRY
(B&W) DH/Bonelli, Mar., 1999
1 by Alfredo Castelli & Giancarlo
    Alessandrini, DGb(c) 92-pg. . . . 5.00
2 thru 6 . . . . @5.00

MASAKAZU KATSURA'S
SHADOW LADY
(B&W–Manga) Oct., 1998
Dangerous Love
1 (of 7) Masakazu Katsura 2.50
2 thru 7 . . . . @2.50
The Eyes of a Stranger, May, 1999
8 thru 12, pt.1–pt.5 . . . . @2.50
The Awakening
13 thru 19, pt.1–pt.7 . . . . @2.50
Sudden Death
20 thru 24, pt.1–pt.5 . . . . @2.50
Spec.48-pg. final issue 4.00

MASK, THE
1991
0 'Who's Laughing Now' (B&W) . . . 6.00
1 I:Lt.Kellaway Mask 5.00
2 V:Rapaz & Walter 5.00
3 O:Mask 5.00
4 final issue 5.00

MASK, THE
1994
1 Movie Adaptation 3.00
2 Movie Adaptation 2.50

MASK , THE
[Mini-series] 1995
The Mask Strikes Back (1995)
1 Mask Strikes Back,pt.1 . . . . 2.50
2 Mask Strikes Back,pt.2 . . . . 2.50
3 Mask Strikes Back,pt.3 . . . . 2.50
4 DoM,Mask Strikes Back,pt.4 . . . . 2.50
5 Mask Strikes Back,pt.5 . . . . 2.50
The Hunt for Green October (1995)
6 Pt.1 . . . . 2.50
7 Pt.2 Kellaway vs. Ray Tuttle 2.50
8 Pt.3 F:Emily Tuttle 2.50
9 Pt.4 final issue 2.50
World Tour (1995)
10 thru 13 Pt.1–Pt 4 . . . . @2.50
Southern Discomfort (1996)
14 Pt.1 Mardi Gras time 2.50
15 Pt.2 . . . . 2.50
16 Pt.3 . . . . 2.50
17 Pt.4 . . . . 2.50

MASK/MARSHALL LAW
Feb., 1998
1 (of 2) by Pat Mills and Kevin
    O'Neill 3.00
2 concl. 3.00

MASK RETURNS, THE
1992
1 inc.cut-out Mask 5.00
2 Mask's crime spree 4.00
3 . . . . 4.00
4 . . . . 4.00

MASK: TOYS IN
THE ATTIC
Aug., 1998
1 (of 4) 3.00

The Mask, Virtual Surreality
© Dark Horse Comics

2 thru 4 . . . . @3.00

MASK, THE:
VIRTUAL SURREALITY
1997
1-shot F: MMi,SA 3.00

MAXIMUM OVERLOAD
1 Masque (Mask) 12.00
2 thru 4 Mask . . . . @8.00

MAXIMUM OVERLOAD
1 thru 5 . . . . @4.00

MAYHEM
1989
1 F:The Mask, The Mark 5.00
2 thru 4 . . . . @4.00

MECHA
Comics Greatest World, 1995
1 color 3.00
2 color 3.00
3 thru 6 B&W . . . . @3.00
Spec.(#1) CW(c),color 3.00

MEDAL OF HONOR
1994
1 Ace of Aces 2.50
2 . . . . 2.50
3 Andrew's Raid 2.50
4 Frank Miller(c) 2.50
5 final issue 2.50
Spec. #1 JKu (1994) 2.50

MEZZ GALACTIC
TOUR 2494
1994
1 MBn,MV 2.50

MICHAEL CHABON
PRESENTS THE
AMAZING ADVENTURES
OF THE ESCAPIST
Dec., 2003
1 Michael Chabon, 80-pg. 9.00
2 thru 9 . . . . @9.00

DARK HORSE

MIKE MIGNOLA'S
B.P.R.D.: HOLLOW EARTH
Jan., 2002
1 (of 3) 3.00
2 . . . . 3.00
3 . . . . 3.00
TPB 120-pg. 18.00
1-shot Something Under My Bed . . 3.00
1-shot The Soul of Venice 3.00
1-shot Dark Waters 3.00
1-shot Night Train 3.00

MILKMAN MURDERS, THE
July, 2004
1 JoC,SvP. 3.00
2 thru 4 JoC,SvP. . . . . @3.00

MR. MONSTER
(B&W) 1988
1 . . . . 4.00
2 . . . . 3.00
3 Alan Moore story 3.00
4 . . . . 3.00
5 I:Monster Boy. 3.00
6 . . . . 3.00
7 . . . . 3.00
8 V:Vampires (giant size) 5.00

MONKEYMAN & O'BRIEN
DH Legend, 1996
1 by Arthur Adams 3.00
2 and 3 . . . . @3.00
Spec. 3.00

MONSTERS, INC.
Oct., 2001
1-shot 56-pg., Disney-Pixar 5.00

MORPHOS
THE SHAPE CHANGER
July, 1996
1-shot BHg. 5.00

MOTORHEAD
Comics Greatest World, 1995
1 V:Predator 2.50
2 Laughing Wolf Carnival 2.50
3 V:Jackboot 2.50
4 thru 6 . . . . @2.50

Morphos The Shape Changer
© Dark Horse Comics

Spec.#1 JLe(c),V:Mace Blitzkrieg
 (1994) 4.00

[BOB BURDEN'S
ORIGINAL]
MYSTERYMEN
July, 1999
1 . . . . 3.00
2 The Amazing Disc Man 3.00
3 F:Screwball 3.00
4 All Villain Comics #1 . . . . 3.50

MYSTERY MEN
July, 1999
1 (of 2) Movie adapt. 3.00
2 movie adaptation, concl. 3.00

MYST: THE BOOK OF
THE BLACK SHIPS
Aug., 1997
1 (of 4) from CD-Rom game 3.00
2 thru 4 . . . . @3.00

NAIL, THE
June, 2004
1 (of 4) 3.00
2 thru 4 . . . . @3.00

NATHAN NEVER
(B&W) DH/Bonelli, Mar., 1999
1 (of 6) by Michele Medda & Nicola
 Mari, AAd(c) 102-pg. 5.00
2 . . . . 5.00
3 . . . . 5.00
4 . . . . 5.00
5 . . . . 5.00
6 . . . . 5.00

NEVERMEN, THE
May, 2000
1 (of 4) GyD, V:Clockwork 3.00
2 GyD,V:Honshu 3.00
3 GyD,V:Clockwork. 3.00
4 GyD,V:League of Crows 3.00

NEVERMEN, THE:
STREETS OF BLOOD
Jan., 2003
1 (of 3) GyD 3.00
2 and 3 . . . . @3.00

NEW FRONTIER
(B&W) 1992
1 From series in Heavy Metal 2.75
2 Who Killed Ruby Fields? 2.75
3 Conclusion 2.75

NEW TWO FISTED
TALES: VOL II
1993
1 War stories. 5.00

[JOHN BYRNE'S]
NEXT MEN
1992
0 Rep Next Men from Dark Horse
 Presents 5.00
1 JBy,'Breakout'inc.trading card
 certificate 5.00
1a 2nd Printing Blue 3.00
2 JBy,World View 4.00
3 JBy,A:Sathanis. 4.00
4 JBy,A:Sathanis 4.00
5 JBy,A:Sathanis. 4.00

Next Men #10
© Dark Horse Comics

6 JBy,O:Senator Hilltop,
 Sathanis,Project Next Men 3.50
7 JBy,I:M-4,Next Men Powers
 explained 3.50
8 JBy,I:Omega Project,A:M-4 . . . . 3.00
9 JBy,A:Omega Project,A:M-4 . . . 3.00
10 JBy,V:OmegaProject,A:M-4 . . . 3.00
11 JBy,V:OmegaProject,A:M-4. . . 3.00
12 JBy,V:Dr.Jorgenson. 3.00
13 JBy,Nathan vs Jack 3.00
14 JBy,I:Speedboy 3.00
15 JBy,in New York 3.00
16 JBy,Jasmine's Pregnant 3.00
17 FM(c),JBy,Arrested 3.00
18 JBy,On Trial 3.00
Next Men: Faith (1993)
19 Faith, pt.1 JBy(a&s),V:Dr.
 Trogg, Blue Dahila. 3.25
20 Faith, pt.2 JBy,(a&s),F:Jack . . . 3.00
21 Faith,pt.3 MMi(c),JBy(a&s),
 I:Hellboy. 27.00
22 Faith,pt.4 JBy(a&s),Last issue . . 3.00
Next Men: Power (1994)
23 Power,pt.1, JBy(a&s) 2.75
24 Power,pt.2, JBy(a&s) 2.75
25 Power,pt.3, JBy(a&s) 2.75
26 Power,pt.4, JBy(a&s) concl. . . . 2.50
Next Men: Lies (1994)
27 Lies,pt.1,JBy 2.50
28 Lies,pt.2,JBy 2.50
29 Lies,pt.3,JBy 2.50
30 Lies,pt.4, JBy 2.50

NEXUS: ALIEN JUSTICE
1992
1 . . . . 4.25
2 . . . . 4.25
3 . . . . 4.00

NEXUS:
EXECUTIONER'S SONG
1996
1 (of 4) by Mike Baron, Steve
 Rude & Gary Martin 3.00
2 thru 4 . . . . @3.00

NEXUS: GOD CON
Apr., 1997
1 (of 2) 3.00
2 . . . . 3.00

All comics prices listed are for *Near Mint* condition.

DARK HORSE

NEXUS:
THE LIBERATOR
1992
1 'Waking Dreams' 3.00
2 Civil War,D:Gigo 3.00
3 Civil War contd. 3.00
4 Last issue. 3.00

NEXUS MEETS MADMAN
1996
1-shot 3.00

NEXUS:
NIGHTMARE IN BLUE
(B&W) July, 1997
1 (of 4) MBn,SR,GyM 3.00
2 thru 4 . . . . @3.00

NEXUS: THE ORIGIN
1995
1 SR,O:Nexus 5.00

NEXUS:
OUT OF THE VORTEX
1 R:Nexus 3.00
2 Zolot & Nexus Together 3.00
3 O:Vortex 3.00

NEXUS:
THE WAGES OF SIN
1995
1 The Client 3.00
2 V:Munson 3.00
3 SR(c&a) Murders in New Eden . . 3.00
4 . . . . 3.00

NIGHT BEFORE CHRISTMASK
1 Rick Geary 10.00

NINA'S NEW AND IMPROVED ALL-TIME GREATEST
1994
1 Anthology: Nina Paley 2.50

NINTH GLAND, THE
(B&W) Mar., 1997
1-shot by Renee French 4.00

NOCTURNALS: WITCHING HOUR
May, 1998
1-shot by Dan Brereton 5.00

NOSFERATU
(B&W) 1991
1 The Last Vampire 4.00
2 . . . . 3.00

OH MY GODDESS!
(B&W–Manga) 1994
1 by Kosuke Fujishima 5.00
2 & 3 . . . . @4.00
4 thru 6 . . . . @3.00
Part II, 1995
1 F:Keiichi 4.00
2 thru 9 . . . . @3.00
Part III, 1996
1 Wishes are Granted 3.00
2 Love Potion Number 9 . . . . 3.00

Oh My Goddess Part VI #3
© Dark Horse Comics

3 thru 5 . . . . @3.00
6 thru 11 Terrible Master Urd,
   pt.1 thru pt.6 . . . . @3.00
Part IV, 1996–97
1 Robot Wars 3.00
2 The Trials of Morisato,pt.1 . . . . . . 3.00
3 The Trials of Morisato,pt.2 . . . . . . 3.00
4 The Trials of Morisato,pt.3 . . . . . . 3.00
5 The Queen of Vengeance 3.00
6 Mara Strikes Back,pt.1,48-pg. . . . 4.00
7 Mara Strikes Back,pt.2 . . . . 3.00
8 Mara Strikes Back,pt.3 . . . . 3.00
Part V, 1997–98
1 The Forgotten Promise 3.00
2 The Lunch Box of Love 3.00
3 Meet Me by the Seashore, 48-pg. 4.00
4 You're So Bad, 48-pg. 3.00
5 Ninja Master,pt.1 . . . . 3.00
6 Ninja Master,pt.2, 48-pg. 4.00
7 Miss Keiichi,pt.1, 48-pg. 4.00
7 & 8 Miss Keiichi,pt.2 . . . . 3.00
9 It's Lonely at the Top 3.50
10 Fallen Angel, 48-pg. 4.00
11 Play the Game, 48-pg. 4.00
12 Sorrow, Fear Not. 4.00
Part VI, 1998–99
1 Devil in Miss Urd,pt.1, 40-pg. . . . 3.50
2 Devil in Miss Urd,pt.2 . . . . 3.00
3 Devil in Miss Urd,pt.3 . . . . 3.00
4 Devil in Miss Urd,pt.4 . . . . 3.00
5 Devil in Miss Urd,pt.5 . . . . 3.00
6 SuperUrd 3.00
Part VII, 1999
1 (of 8)The Fourth Goddess,pt.1 . . 3.50
2 The Fourth Goddess,pt.2 . . . . . . 3.00
3 The Fourth Goddess,pt.3 . . . . . . 3.00
4 The Fourth Goddess,pt.4,40-pg. . 3.50
5 The Fourth Goddess,pt.5,40-pg. . 3.50
Part VIII, 1999
1 (of 2) Childhood's End,
   by Kosuke Fujishima 3.50
2 Childhood's End,pt.2 . . . . 3.50
3 The Queen and the Goddess . . . 3.50
4 Hail to the Chief,pt.1 . . . . 3.50
5 Hail to the Chief,pt.2 . . . . 3.50
6 Hail to the Chief,pt.3 . . . . 3.50
Part IX, 2000
1 Pretty in Scarlet 3.00
2 The Goddess's Apprentice 3.00
3 Queen Sayoko,pt.1 . . . . 3.00
4 Queen Sayoko,pt.2 . . . . 3.50
5 Queen Sayoko,pt.3 (of 5) 3.00

6 Queen Sayoko,pt.4 . . . . 3.00
7 Queen Sayoko,pt.5 . . . . 3.50
PART X, Feb., 2001
1 The Secret of Speed 3.50
2 The Secret of Speed,concl. 3.00
3 one-shot. 3.50
4 Hand in Hand,pt.1 . . . . 3.50
5 Hand in Hand,pt.2 . . . . 3.50
PART XI, Aug., 2001
1 Banpei in Love,pt.1 (of 2) 3.50
2 Banpei in Love,pt.2 . . . . 3.50
3 Mystery Child,pt.1 (of 8) 3.00
4 Mystery Child,pt.2 . . . . 3.00
5 Mystery Child,pt.3 . . . . 3.00
6 Mystery Child,pt.4 . . . . 3.00
7 Mystery Child,pt.5 . . . . 3.50
8 Mystery Child,pt.6 . . . . 3.50
9 Mystery Child,pt.7 . . . . 3.00
10 Mystery Child,pt.8, 48-pg. 4.00
PART XII, July, 2002
1 (of 3) Learning to Love,pt.1 . . . . . 3.50
2 Learning to Love,pt.2 . . . . 3.50
3 Learning to Love,pt.3 . . . . 3.50
Continuing series (Oct., 2002)
91 Traveler,pt.1 (of 5). 3.00
92 Traveler,pt.2 . . . . 3.00
93 Traveler, pt.3 . . . . 3.00
94 Traveler, pt.4 . . . . 3.00
95 Traveler, pt.5 . . . . 3.50
96 The Phantom Racer, pt.1 . . . . . . 3.00
97 The Phantom Racer, pt.2 . . . . . . 3.00
98 The Phantom Racer, pt.3 . . . . . . 3.00
99 The Phantom Racer, pt.4 . . . . . . 3.00
100 Dr. Moreau, pt.1 . . . . 3.00
101 Dr. Moreau, pt.2 . . . . 3.00
102 Dr. Moreau, pt.3 . . . . 3.00
103 Dr. Moreau, pt.4 . . . . 3.00
104 Dr. Moreau, pt.5 . . . . 3.50
105 Sora Unchained,pt.1 . . . . 3.00
106 thru 110 Sora,pt.2–pt.6 . . . @3.00
111 and 112 Sora Unchained,
   pt.7–pt.8, 48-pg. . . . . @4.00

OKTANE
1995
1 R:Oktane 2.50
2 V:God Zero 2.50
3 V:God Zero 2.50
4 conclusion 2.50

ONE BAD RAT
1 BT 3.00
2 thru 4 . . . . @3.00

ORION
(B&W–Manga) 1993
1 SF by Masamune Shirow 2.50
2 F:Yamata Empire 3.00
3 thru 6 . . . . @3.00

OTIS GOES HOLLYWOOD
(B&W) Apr., 1997
1 (of 2) by Bob Fingerman 3.00
2 . . . . 3.00

OUTER ORBIT
Dec., 2006
1 (of 4) 3.00
2 thru 4 . . . . @3.00

OUT FOR BLOOD
(B&W) 1999
1 (of 4) GEr,F:Dan Sanger 3.00
2 The Wings; The Claws 3.00
3 . . . . 3.00
4 concl. 3.00

DARK HORSE

OUTLANDERS
(B&W–Manga) 1988
1	4.00
2	3.00
3 thru 7	@3.00
8 thru 20	@3.00
21 Operation Phoenix	3.00
22 thru 24	@3.00
25 thru 29 with 2-card strip	@3.00
30	2.75
31 Tetsua dying	2.75
32 D:The Emperor	2.75
33 Story finale	2.75
#0 The Key of Graciale	2.75

OUTLANDERS: EPILOGUE
(B&W) 1994
1	2.75

OUTLAW 7
Aug., 2001
1 (of 4)	3.00
2 thru 4	@3.00

Out of the Vortex #10
© Dark Horse Comics

OUT OF THE VORTEX
Comics' Greatest World, 1993
1 B:JOs(s),V:Seekers	2.50
2 MMi(c),DaW,A:Seekers	2.50
3 WS(c),E:JOs(s),DaW,A:Seeker, C:Hero Zero	2.50
4 DaW,A:Catalyst	2.50
5 V:Destroyers,A:Grace	2.50
6 V:Destroyers,A:Hero Zero	2.50
7 AAd(c),DaW,V:Destroyers, A:Mecha	2.50
8 DaW,A:Motorhead	2.50
9 DaW,V:Motorhead	2.50
10 MZ(c), A:Division 13	2.50
11 V:Reaver Swarm	2.50
12 Final issue	2.50

PENNY ARCADE
Dec., 2005
1 25-cent issue	1.00

PERHAPANAUTS, THE
Nov., 2005
1 (of 4) TDz	3.00
2 thru 4	@3.00

PERHAPANAUTS: SECOND CHANCES
Oct., 2005
1 (of 4) TDz	3.00
2 thru 4	@3.00

PI: THE BOOK OF ANTS
Artisan Entertainment, 1998
1-shot, movie adapt.	3.00

PLANET OF THE APES: THE HUMAN WAR
June, 2001
1 (of 3) IEd,with trading card	3.00
1a photo (c)	3.00
2 IEd,JSC	3.00
2a photo (c)	3.00
3 IEd,JSC	3.00
3a photo (c)	3.00

PLANET OF THE APES
Sept., 2001
1 IEd,MWg	3.00
1b gold foil photo(c)	9.00
1c gold foil photo(c) signed	25.00
2 IEd	3.00
3 IEd	3.00
4 DAn,IEd,Bloodlines,pt.1 (of 3)	3.00
5 DAn,IEd,Bloodlines,pt.2	3.00
6 DAn,IEd,Bloodlines,pt.3	3.00
1a thru 6a photo(c)	@3.00

PLANET OF THE APES (MOVIE)
1-shot Movie adaptation	7.00
1-shotA Movie adapt, foil (c)	9.00
1-shotB Movie, foil(c) signed	25.00

PRAIRIE MOON AND OTHER STORIES
(B&W) 1992
1-shot	2.50

PREDATOR
1989
1 CW,Mini Series	6.00
1a 2ndPrinting	3.00
2 CW	5.00
3 CW	4.00
4 CW	3.00
1 thru 4 later printings	@3.00

PREDATOR
1-shot Predator: Invaders from the Fourth Dimension (1994)	4.00
1-shot Predator Jungle Tales, Rite of Passage (1995)	3.00
1-shot Predator: Strange Roux (1995)	3.00
1-shot Predator: Captive (1998)	3.00
GN Predator Flesh and Blood	7.00

PREDATOR: BAD BLOOD
1993
1 CW,I:John Pulnick	3.00
2 CW,V:Predator	3.00
3 CW,V:Predator,C.I.A.	3.00
4 Last issue	3.00

PREDATOR: BIG GAME
1991
1 Corp.Nakai Meets Predator	3.50
2 Army Base Destroyed, with 2-card strip	3.50
3 Corp.Nakai Arrested, with 2-card strip	3.50
4 Nakai vs. Predator	3.50

PREDATOR: BLOODY SANDS OF TIME
1992
1 DBa,CW,Predator in WWI	3.50
2 DBa,CW, WWII cont'd.	3.25

PREDATOR: COLD WAR
1991
1 Predator in Siberia	3.50
2 U.S. Elite Squad in Siberia	3.25
3 U.S. vs. USSR commandos	3.25
4 U.S. vs. USSR in Siberia	3.00

Predator: Dark River #2
© Dark Horse Comics

PREDATOR: DARK RIVER
1996
1 thru 4 by Verheiden,RoR,RM	@3.00

PREDATOR: HELL & HOT WATER
1997
1 thru 3 MSh, GC & GWt	@3.00

PREDATOR: HELL COME A WALKIN'
Feb., 1998
1 (of 2) by Nancy Collins, Dean Ormston	3.00
2 concl.	3.00

PREDATOR: HOMEWORLD
Mar., 1999
1 (of 4)	3.00
2 thru 4	@3.00

PREDATOR: KINDRED
1996
1	3.00
2 thru 4	@3.00

PREDATOR: NEMESIS
Dec., 1997
1 (of 2) TTg(c). 3.00
2 . . . . 3.00

PREDATOR: PRIMAL
1997
1 (of 2) Kevin J. Anderson(s),
   ScK,Low 3.00
2 (of 2) 3.00

PREDATOR: RACE WAR
1993
0 F:Serial Killer. 3.00
1 V:Serial Killer. 3.00
2 D:Serial Killer. 3.00
3 in Prison. 3.00
4 Last Issue 3.00

PREDATOR 2
1991
1 DBy, Movie Adapt,pt1 . . . . 3.50
2 MBr, Movie Adapt.,pt2 with
   2-card strip 3.00

PREDATOR VS. JUDGE DREDD
Sept., 1997
1 (of 3) by John Wagner and
   Enrique Alcatena 3.00
2 thru 3 . . . . @3.00

PREDATOR VS. MAGNUS ROBOT FIGHTER
Valiant/Dark Horse 1992
1 LW,A:Tekla. 3.00
1a Platinum Ed. 5.00
1b Gold Ed. 3.00
2 LW,Magnus Vs. Predator, with
   2-card strip 3.00

PREDATOR: XENOGENESIS
Aug., 1999
1 (of 4) 3.00
2 IEd 3.00
3 IEd 3.00
4 . . . . 3.00

PRIMAL
Oct., 1992
1 Contd.from Primal:from the
   Cradle to the Grave. 3.00
2 A:TJ Cyrus 2.50
GN Primal From the Cradle
   to the Grave. 10.00

PROPELLER MAN
1993
1 I:Propeller Man 3.00
2 O:Propeller Man,w/2 card strip . . 3.00
3 V:Manipulator. 3.00
4 V:State Police,w/2 card strip 3.00
5 V:Manipulator. 3.00
6 V:Thing, w/2 card strip. 3.00
7 . . . . 3.00
8 Last issue,w/2 card strip 3.00

PUBO
DH Maverick, Nov., 2002
1 (of 3) by Leland Purvis, B&W 3.50
2 . . . . 3.50
3 . . . . 3.50

PUMPKINHEAD: THE RITES OF EXORCISM
1992
1 Based on the movie. 2.50
2 thru 4 . . . . @2.50

RACE OF SCORPIONS
(B&W) 1990
Book 1 short stories. 5.00
Book 2 . . . . 5.00

RACE OF SCORPIONS
(B&W) 1991
1 A:Argos,Dito,Alma,Ka 2.50
2 thru 4 . . . . @2.50

RACK & PAIN
1994
1 GCa(c),I:Rack,Pain 3.00
2 GCa(c),V:Web 3.00
3 GCa(c),V:Web 3.00
4 GCa(c),Final Issue. 3.00

RASCALS IN PARADISE
1994
1 I:Spicy Sanders 4.00
2 . . . . 4.00
3 last issue 4.00

Real Adventures of Jonny Quest #8
© Dark Horse Comics

REAL ADVENTURES OF JONNY QUEST, THE
Sept., 1996
1 . . . . 3.00
2 . . . . 3.00
3 thru 12 . . . . @3.00

REBEL SWORD
(B&W–Manga) 1994
1 by Yoshikazu Yashiko 2.50
2 . . . . 2.50
3 . . . . 2.50
4 V:Ruken 2.50
5 Choice of Jiro. 2.50
6 R:Ruken. 2.50

REDBLADE
1993
1 V:Demons 3.00

2 V:Tull 3.00
3 Last Issue 3.00

RED ROCKET 7
Aug., 1997
1 (of 7) MiA. 4.00
2 thru 7 . . . . @4.00

REID FLEMING/ FLAMING CARROT
(B&W) Jan., 2003
1-Shot Reid Fleming/Flaming
   Carrot 4.00

RETURN OF THE GREMLINS
Oct., 2006
1 (of 3) MRi. 3.00
2 thru 3 MRi . . . . @3.00

REVEAL
Oct., 2002
1 64-pg. 7.00

REVELATIONS
Aug., 2005
1 (of 6) PJe,HuR. 3.00
2 thru 6 . . . . @3.00

REX MUNDI
Aug., 2006
1 . . . . 3.00
2 thru 8 . . . . @3.00

RING OF ROSES
(B&W) 1991
1 Alternate world,1991 . . . . 2.50
2 Plague in London. 2.50
3 Plague cont.A:Secret Brother-
   hood of the Rosy Cross. 2.50
4 Conclusion. 2.50

RING OF THE NIEBELUNG, THE:
DH Maverick, 2000
RHINEGOLD, Feb., 2000
1 (of 4) CR 3.00
2 CR 3.00
3 CR 3.00
4 CR, concl. 3.00
VALKYRIE Aug., 2000
1 (of 3) CR 3.00
2 CR 3.00
3 CR, concl. 3.00
SIEGFRIED, Dec., 2000
1 (of 3) CR 3.00
2 CR 3.00
3 CR, concl. 3.00
GOTTERDAMMERUNG June, 2001
1 (of 4) CR 3.00
2 . . . . 3.00
3 . . . . 3.00
4 finale, 64-pg. 6.00

RIO AT BAY
1992
1 F:Doug Wildey art 3.00
2 F:Doug Wildey art 3.00

R.I.P.D.
Nov., 1999
1 (of 4) F:Rest in Peace Dept. 3.00
2 thru 4 . . . . @3.00

DARK HORSE

RIPLEY'S
BELIEVE IT OR NOT
June, 2002

1 (of 4) Into Thin Air 3.00
2 Grim Reaping 3.00
3 Human Wonders 3.00
4 Strange Invaders 3.00

ROACHMILL
(B&W) 1988

1 thru 8 . . . . @3.50
9 and 10 . . . . @3.00

Robocop: Mortal Coils #2
© Dark Horse Comics

ROBOCOP:
MORTAL COILS
1993

1 V:Gangs 2.75
2 V:Gangs 2.75
3 V:Coffin,V:Gangs 2.75
4 . . . . 2.75

ROBOCOP VERSUS
TERMINATOR
1992

1 FM(s),WS,w/Robocop cut-out . . . 3.50
2 FM(s),WS,w/Terminator cut-out . . 3.00
3 FM(s),WS,w/cut-out 3.00
4 FM(s),WS,Conclusion 3.00

ROBOCOP:
PRIME SUSPECT
1992

1 Robocop framed 2.75
2 thru 4 V:ZED-309s . . . . @2.50

ROBOCOP: ROULETTE
1993

1 V:ED-309s 2.75
2 I:Philo Drut 2.75
3 V:Stealthbot 2.75
4 last issue 2.75

ROBOCOP 3
1993

1 B:StG(s),Movie Adapt 2.75
2 V:Aliens,OCP 2.75
3 HNg,ANi(i) 2.75

ROCKETEER ADVENTURE
MAGAZINE
1988–95

1 and 2 . . . . @4.00
3 . . . . 3.00

ROCKSTAR GAMES' ONI
Feb., 2001

1 video-game tie-in 3.00
1a gold foil (c) 7.00
2 . . . . 3.00
3 concl. 3.00

THE SAFEST PLACE
IN THE WORLD
1995

SC, SD 2.50

SAMURAI:
HEAVEN AND EARTH
Dec., 2004

1 (of 5) 3.00
2 thru 5 . . . . @3.00
TPB 15.00

Vol. 2
1 (of 5) RMz 3.00
2 thru 5 RMz,LRs . . . . @3.00

SCARLET TRACES:
THE GREAT GAME
July, 2006

1 IEd 3.00
2 thru 4 . . . . @3.00

SCATTERBRAIN
June, 1998

1 (of 4) MMi 3.00
2 thru 4 . . . . @3.00

SCREWBALL SQUIRREL
July, 1995

1 . . . . 2.75
2 thru 3 . . . . @2.75

SCORPION KING, THE
Mar., 2002

1 (of 2) movie adapt. 3.00
1a photo (c). 3.00
2 (of 2) movie adapt. 3.00
2a photo (c). 3.00

SECRET, THE
Feb., 2007

1 (of 4) 3.00
2 thru 4 . . . . @3.00

SECRET OF
THE SALAMANDER
(B&W)

1 Jacquestardi, rep 3.00

SERENITY
July, 2005

1 movie adapt. 4.00
2 thru 3 . . . . @3.00
1a&b thru 3a&b variant(c) . . . . . @3.00

SERGIO ARAGONES
ACTIONS SPEAK
Jan., 2001

1 (of 6) 3.00
2 thru 6 . . . . @3.00

SERGIO ARAGONES'
BOOGEYMAN
(B&W) June, 1998

1 (of 4) 3.00
2 thru 4 . . . . @3.00

SERGIO ARAGONES'
DAY OF THE DEAD
Oct., 1998

1-shot 3.00

SERGIO ARAGONES'
GROO
Jan.–Apr., 1998

1 (of 4) 3.00
2 thru 4 . . . . @3.00

SERGIO ARAGONES'
GROO & RUFFERTO
Dec., 1998

1 (of 4) 3.00
2 thru 4 . . . . @3.00

SERGIO ARAGONES'
GROO: DEATH
AND TAXES
DH Maverick, Dec., 2002

1 (of 4) SA 3.00
2 thru 4 . . . . @3.00

SERGIO ARAGONES'
GROO: MIGHTIER THAN
THE SWORD
Jan., 2000

1 (of 4) SA 3.00
2 SA,V:Pipil Khan 3.00
3 SA,V:Relmihio 3.00
4 SA,concl. 3.00

SERGIO ARAGONES'
LOUDER THAN WORDS
(B&W) July–Dec., 1997

1 (of 6) SA 3.00
2 thru 6 . . . . @3.00

Sergio Aragones' Louder Than Words
#1 © Dark Horse Comics

DARK HORSE

SERGIO STOMPS STAR WARS
2000
1-shot SA, parody 3.00

SEX WARRIOR
1993
1 I:Dakini 2.50
2 V:Steroids 2.50

SHADOW, THE
1994
1 MK 3.00
2 MK 3.00

THE SHADOW AND DOC SAVAGE
1995
1 . . . . 3.50
2 The Shrieking Skeletons 3.50

THE SHADOW: HELL'S HEAT WAVE
1995
1 Racial War 3.00
2 MK,V:Ghost 3.00
3 Final issue 3.00

THE SHADOW: IN THE COILS OF LEVIATHAN
1993
1 MK,V:Monster 3.25
2 MK 3.25
3 MK,w/ GfD poster 3.25
4 MK,Final issue 3.25

THE SHADOW AND THE MYSTERIOUS 3
1994
1 Three stories 3.00

SHADOW EMPIRES: FAITH CONQURES
1994
1 CsM 3.00
2 thru 4 CsM . . . . @3.00

SHI: JUN-NEN
July 2004
1 BiT 3.00
2 thru 4 . . . . @3.00

SHINOBI
Nov., 2002
Spec.1-shot The Rise of Hotsuma . . 3.00

SHREK
Apr., 2003
1 (of 3) 3.00
2 and 3 . . . . @3.00
TPB 96-pg. 13.00

SILKE
Jan., 2001
1 TnD,F:Sandra Silke 3.00
1a variant(c) 3.00
2 TnD 3.00
3 TnD, The Hunt is on 3.00
4 TnD 3.00
4a variant(c) 3.00

SIN CITY:
DH-Legend
GN A Small Killing 14.00
GN Family Values (1997) 10.00
1-shot The Babe Wore Red (1994) . 6.00
1-shot The Babe Wore Red and other stories (1996) nudity 3.00
1-shot Lost Lonely, and Lethal, FM two-color 7.00
1-shot Sex and Violence, FM 6.00
1-shot Silent Night, FM (1995) 5.00

SIN CITY: A DAME TO KILL FOR
DH-Legend (B&W) 1993
1 FM(a&s),I:Dwight,Ava 6.00
2 FM(a&s),A:Ava 6.00
3 FM(a&s),D:Ava's Husband 6.00
1a thru 3a 2nd printings . . . . @3.00
4 thru 6 FM(a&s) . . . . @5.00

SIN CITY: HELL AND BACK
July, 1999
1 (of 9) FM 6.00
2 . . . . 5.00
3 . . . . 5.00
4 Five Foot Two, Eyes of Blue 5.00
5 . . . . 5.00
6 quest for Esther 5.00
7 & 8 . . . . @5.00
9 56-pg. 5.00

SIN CITY: JUST ANOTHER SATURDAY NIGHT
DH/Wizard
1/2 (Wizard, 24-pg.) 7.00
1/2 rep., Dark Horse, new (c) 3.00

SIN CITY: THAT YELLOW BASTARD
(B&W) 1996
1 F.Miller 5.00
2 thru 6 . . . . @5.00

SIN CITY: THE BIG FAT KILL
DH Legend, 1994
1 FM 5.00
2 FM 5.00
3 FM, Dump the Stiffs 5.00
4 FM, Town Without Pity 5.00
5 FM, final issue 5.00

SOCK MONKEY
(B&W) Sept., 1998
1 by Tony Millionaire 3.00
2 F:Uncle Gabby 3.00
VOLUME 2
1 and 2 . . . . @3.00
DH Maverick, Sept., 2002
Spec. #1 (of 2) 3.00
Spec. #2 . . . . 3.00
VOLUME 4, 2003
1 and 2 . . . . @3.00

SOCK MONKEY: THE INCHES INCIDENT
(B&W) Sept., 2006
1 (of 4) by Tony Millionaire 3.00
2 thru 4 . . . . @3.00

SOLO
1996
1 and 2 . . . . @1.00

SPACE CIRCUS
DH Maverick, July, 2000
1 (of 4) SA 3.00
2 thru 4 SA . . . . @3.00

SPACEHAWK
(B&W) 1989
1 BW reps. 3.50
2 thru 5 BW . . . . @3.50

SPACE PINCHY
Dec., 2005
1-shot Pleased Ta Meetya 3.00
1-shot Audrey's Super Power Pinch 3.00
1-shot The Laboratory of Love 3.00
1-shot Surrounded by Robots 3.00
1-shot The Pinch of the Illegal Brain Intrusion 4.00

SPACE USAGI
[Vol. 3] 1996
1 thru 3 Stan Sakai . . . . @3.00

SPEAK OF THE DEVIL
July., 2007
1 (of 6) GHe 3.00
2 . . . . 3.00

SPECIES
1995
1 Alien Human Hybrid 3.00
2 thru 4 SIL . . . . @3.00

Species: Human Race #4
© *Dark Horse Comics*

SPECIES: HUMAN RACE
1996
1 PhH 3.00
2 . . . . 3.00
3 SBi 3.00
4 . . . . 3.00

SPIRIT OF WONDER
(B&W) 1996
1 thru 5 by Kenji Tsuruia . . . . @3.00

DARK HORSE

DARK HORSE

SPYBOY
Oct., 1999
1 PDd,F:Alex Fleming 3.00
2 PDd 3.00
3 PDd,F:Bombshell 3.00
4 PDd,F:Judge and Jury 3.00
5 PDd,V:Judge and Jury 3.00
6 PDd,V:Barbie Q 3.00
7 PDd,V:Madam Imadam 3.00
8 PDd,V:Madam Imadam 3.00
9 PDd,V:Madam Imadam
   & Barbie Q. 3.00
10 PDd,death-defying action 3.00
11 PDd,V:Slackjaw. 3.00
12 PDd,V:Slackjaw. 3.00
13 PDd 3.00
14 PDd,F:SpyGirl. 3.00
15 PDd 3.00
15a variant TnD (c) 3.00
16 PDd 3.00
17 PDd 3.00
Spec. 1-shot 48-pg. 5.00
Spec. Motorola Spec. (2000) 2.50

SPYBOY: FINAL EXAM
May, 2004
1 PDd 3.00
2 thru 4 . . . . @3.00

SPYBOY 13: THE M.A.N.G.A. AFFAIR
Apr., 2003
1 (of 3) PDd(s) 3.00
2 and 3 . . . . @3.00

SPYBOY/YOUNG JUSTICE
Feb., 2002
1 PDd, x-over 3.00
2 and 3 . . . . @3.00

STAN SHAW'S BEAUTY & THE BEAST
1 Based on the book. 5.00

STAR KID
1998
1-shot 3.00

STARSHIP TROOPERS
Sept., 1997
1 (of 2) movie adaptation 3.00
2 movie adaptation, concl. 3.00

STARSHIP TROOPERS: BRUTE CREATIONS
1997
1-shot RbC. 3.00

STARSHIP TROOPERS: DOMINANT SPECIES
Aug., 1998
1 (of 4) 3.00
2 JoB,RyE. 3.00
3 & 4 . . . . @3.00

STARSHIP TROOPERS: INSECT TOUCH
1997
1 by Warren Ellis & Paolo Parente . 3.00
2 and 3 (of 3) . . . . @3.00

STAR SLAMMERS
1996
Spec. 1 . . . . 3.00

STARSTRUCK: THE EXPANDING UNIVERSE
(B&W) 1990
1 Book 1, with cards 3.00
2 Book 2, with 2-card strip 3.00
3 Book 3, with cards 3.00
4 Book 4, with cards 3.00

Star Wars #5
© Dark Horse Comics

STAR WARS
Dec., 1998
1 F:Ki-Adi-Mundi. 5.00
2 F:Ki-Adi-Mundi. 4.00
3 F:Ki-Adi-Mundi. 3.50
4 F:Sylvn. 3.50
5 V:Ephant Mon 6.00
6 V:Jabba the Hutt 6.00
7 Outlander 3.00
8 Outlander, A:Jabba the Hutt 3.00
9 A:Tusken Raiders 3.00
10 TT,RL,F:Ki-Adi-Mundi. 3.00
11 TT, RL,F:Aurra Sing 3.00
12 TT,Outlander,pt.6 . . . . 3.00
13 TT,TL,A'Sharad Hett 3.00
14 TT,TL,on Malastare 3.00
15 TT,TL,Podracing 3.00
16 TT,TL,V:Lannik terrorists. 3.00
17 TT,TL,V:Red Iaro terrorists 3.00
18 TT,TL,Smugglers Moon 3.00
19 JOs,JD,Twilight,pt.1 . . . . 3.00
20 JOs,JD,Twilight,pt.2 . . . . 3.00
21 JOs,JD,Twilight,pt.3 . . . . 3.00
22 JOs,JD,Twilight,pt.4 . . . . 3.00
23 Infinity's End,pt.1 . . . . 3.00
24 Infinity's End,pt.2 . . . . 3.00
25 Infinity's End,pt.3 . . . . 3.00
26 Infinity's End,pt.4 . . . . 3.00
27 Star Crash one-shot 3.00
28 Hunt for Aurra Sing,pt.1 . . . . . . 3.00
29 Hunt for Aurra Sing,pt.2 . . . . . . 3.00
30 Hunt for Aurra Sing,pt.3 . . . . . . 3.00
31 Hunt for Aurra Sing,pt.4 . . . . . . 3.00
32 Darkness,pt.1, JOs,JD 3.00
33 Darkness,pt.2, JOs,JD 3.00
34 Darkness,pt.3, JOs,JD 3.00
35 Darkness,pt.4, JOs,JD 3.00
36 Stark Hyperspace War,pt.1 . . . . 3.00
37 Stark Hyperspace War,pt.2 . . . . 3.00
38 Stark Hyperspace War,pt.3 . . . . 3.00
39 Stark Hyperspace War,pt.4 . . . . 3.00
40 The Devaronian Version,pt.1 . . . 3.00
41 The Devaronian Version,pt.2 . . . 3.00
42 Rite of Passage,pt.1 . . . . 3.00

43 Rite of Passage,pt.2 . . . . 3.00
44 Rite of Passage,pt.3 . . . . 3.00
45 Rite of Passage,pt.4 . . . . 3.00
becomes:

STAR WARS: REPUBLIC
Oct., 2002
46 Republic,pt.1 . . . . 3.00
47 Republic,pt.2 . . . . 3.00
48 Republic,pt.3 . . . . 3.00
49 Republic,pt.5 . . . . 3.00
50 Republic,pt.6, 64-page 6.00
51 Republic,pt.7 . . . . 3.00
52 Republic,pt.8 . . . . 3.00
53 Blast Radius 3.00
54 Jedi Fugitive 3.00
55 Battle of Jabiim,pt.1 . . . . 3.00
56 Battle of Jabiim,pt.2 . . . . 3.00
57 Battle of Jabiim,pt.3 . . . . 3.00
58 Battle of Jabiim,pt.4 . . . . 3.00
59 Enemy Lines 3.00
60 Origin of Asajj Ventress 3.00
61 Bail Organa. 3.00
62 On Hostile Ground 3.00
63 Quinlan Vos, Assassin 3.00
64 A Jedi's Tale 3.00
65 Mace Windu Unleashed,pt.1. . . . 3.00
66 Mace Windu Unleashed,pt.2. . . . 3.00
67 Great Power, Great Restraint . . . 3.00
68 Born to Fight 3.00
69 Dreadnaughts of Rendili,pt.1 . . . 3.00
70 Dreadnaughts of Rendili,pt.2 . . . 3.00
71 . . . . 3.00
72 Aayla Undercover 3.00
73 In the House of the Enemy. 3.00
74 Same War, New Clones 3.00
75 Siege of Saleucami. 3.00
76 Darkness, Light and Fire 3.00
77 Final Test of Quinlan Vos 3.00
78 Darth Vader, Right-hand Man . . . 3.00
79 Into the Unknown 3.00
80 Jedi...Fugitive 3.00
81 The Hidden Enemy,pt.1 . . . . 3.00
82 The Hidden Enemy,pt.2 . . . . 3.00
83 The Hidden Enemy,pt.3 . . . . 3.00
0 Spec. American Entertainment . 10.00

STAR WARS: A NEW HOPE— SPECIAL EDITION
Jan.–Apr., 1997
1 EB, AW 6.00
2 thru 4 . . . . @5.00
TPB Rep. #1–#4 Hildebrandt(c). . . 10.00
Spec. Edition boxed set 30.00

STAR WARS: BOBA FETT—
1-shot Bounty on Bar-Kooda,
   (1995) 48-pg. 9.00
1-shot When the Fat Lady Swings. . 7.00
1-shot Murder Most Foul (1997) . . . 7.00
1-shot Twin Engins of Destruction . . 6.00
1-shot Agent of Doom, CK (2000) . . 3.00
1-shot Overkill (2006) 3.00

STAR WARS: BOBA FETT— ENEMY OF THE EMPIRE
Jan., 1999
1 (of 4) V:Dark Lord of the Sith. . . . 3.00
2 thru 4 IG. . . . . @3.00

STAR WARS: BOUNTY HUNTERS
Aug., 1999
1-shot Aurra Sing, TT. 3.00
1-shot Kir Kanos, MRi,RSd 3.00

All comics prices listed are for *Near Mint* condition.

1-shot Scoundrel's Wages,
F:Dengar, 4-LOM & Bossk 3.00

STAR WARS: CHEWBACCA
Jan., 2000
1 (of 4) various tales 4.00
1 gold foil (c) 9.00
2 thru 4 . . . . @3.50

Star Wars: Crimson Empire, Council of Blood #1 © Dark Horse Comics

STAR WARS: CRIMSON EMPIRE
Dec., 1997–May, 1998
1 PG,CR,DvD(c) 9.00
3 PG,CR,DvD(c) 8.00
3 thru 5 PG,CR,DvD(c) . . . . @5.00

VOL II: COUNCIL OF BLOOD
1998
1 MRi,RSd,PG,DvD(c) 4.00
2 thru 6 RSd,PG,DvD(c) . . . . @3.00

STAR WARS: DARK EMPIRE
Dec., 1991
1 CK,Destiny of a Jedi 9.00
1a 2nd Printing 5.00
1b Gold Ed. 9.00
2 CK,Destroyer of worlds, very
low print run 9.00
2a 2nd Printing 5.00
2b Gold Ed. 9.00
3 CK,V:The Emperor 5.00
3a 2nd printing 4.00
3b Gold Ed. 9.00
4 CK,V:The Emperor 5.00
4a Gold Ed. 5.00
5 CK,V:The Emperor 5.00
5a Gold Ed. 9.00
6 CK,V:Emperor,last issue 5.00
6a Gold Ed. 8.00
Gold editions, foil logo set 35.00
Platinum editions, embossed set. 100.00
TPB Preview 32pg. 1.00
TPB rep.#1–#6. . . . . 20.00
TPB CK & Tom Veitch 2nd ed. . . . 18.00

STAR WARS: DARK EMPIRE II
1994
1 2nd chapter 6.00
2 F:Boba Fett 5.00
3 V:Darksiders 5.00
4 Luke Vs. Darksiders 5.00
5 Creatures 5.00
6 CK,DvD(c), save the twins. 5.00
Platinum editions, set. 50.00

STAR WARS: DARK FORCE RISING
May–Oct., 1997
1 thru 6 (of 6) MBn,TyD,KN . . . . @5.00

STAR WARS: DARK TIMES
Oct., 2006
1 The Path to Nowhere. 3.00
2 thru 5 Path to Nowhere . . . . . @3.00
6 Parallels, pt.1 . . . . 3.00
7 thru 8 Parallels. . . . . @3.00

STAR WARS: DARTH MAUL
Sept., 2000
1 (of 4) RMz,JD,Struzan(c) 3.00
1 photo (c). 5.00
2 Struzan(c),V:Black Sun 3.00
3 RMz,JD,Struzan(c) 3.00
4 RMz,JD,Struzan(c). 3.00
2 thru 4 photo(c) . . . . @3.00

STAR WARS: DROIDS
April–Sept., 1994
1 F:C-3PO,R2-D2 . . . . 5.00
2 V:Thieves. 3.00
3 on the Hosk moon 3.00
4 . . . . 3.00
5 A meeting. 3.00
6 final issue 3.00
Spec.#1 I:Olag Greck. 3.00

[2nd Series] Apr., 1995
1 Deputized Droids 3.00
2 Marooned on Nar Shaddaa 3.00
3 C-3PO to the Rescue 3.00
4 . . . . 3.00
5 Caretaker virus 3.00
6 Revolution 3.00
7 & 8 . . . . @3.00

STAR WARS: EMPIRE
Sept., 2002
1 Betrayal,pt.1 . . . . 3.50
2 Betrayal,pt.2. . . . . 3.50
3 Betrayal,pt.3. . . . . 3.50
4 Betrayal,pt.4. . . . . 3.00
5 National Public Radio adapt. . . . 3.00
6 Surrender or Die 3.00
7 Sacrifice! 3.00
8 Darklighter,pt.1 . . . . 3.00
9 Darklighter,pt.2. . . . . 3.00
10 Yavin Base,pt.1 . . . . 3.00
11 Yavin Base,pt.2 . . . . 3.00
12 Darklighter,pt.3 . . . . 3.00
13 What Sin Loyalty?. 3.00
14 The Savage Heart. 3.00
15 Darklighter,pt.4 . . . . 3.00
16 To the Last Man,pt.1 . . . . 3.00
17 To the Last Man,pt.2 . . . . 3.00
18 To the Last Man,pt.3 . . . . 3.00
19 To the Last Man,pt.3 . . . . 3.00
20 Rebel base 3.00
21 Rebel base,pt.2. . . . . 3.00
22 F:Deena Shan. 3.00

23 F:BoShek 3.00
24 Idiot's Array,pt.1 . . . . 3.00
25 Idiot's Array,pt.2 . . . . 3.00
26 Luke Skywalker Target 3.00
27 Promoted to General 3.00
28 Ghost Ship 3.00
29 In the Shadows of Their Fathers 3.00
30 Rebel vs. Rebel 3.00
31 The Price of Power 3.00
32 Ambush on Jabiim 3.00
33 Trapped on Jabiim 3.00
34 The Fate of a Planet. 3.00
35 Never Lie to Vader 3.00
36 thru 40 Wrong Side of the
War, pt.1–pt.5. . . . . @3.00

STAR WARS: EMPIRE'S END
Oct.–Nov., 1995
1 R:Emperor Palpatine 3.50
2 conclusion 3.50

Star Wars: Episode I: The Phantom Menace #4 © Dark Horse Comics

STAR WARS: EPISODE I THE PHANTOM MENACE
Apr., 1999
1 RdM,AW. 3.00
1a newsstand edition, photo (c) . . . 3.00
2 RdM,AW. 3.00
2a newsstand edition, photo (c) . . . 3.00
3 RdM,AW. 3.00
3a newsstand edition, photo (c) . . . 3.00
4 RdM,AW. 3.00
4a newsstand edition, photo (c) . . . 3.00
GN Phantom Menace RdM,AW. . . 13.00
Spec. Anakin Skywalker. 3.00
Spec. Anakin Skywalker, newsstand 3.00
Spec. Obi-Wan Kenobi. 3.00
Spec. Obi-Wan Kenobi, newsstand . 3.00
Spec. Queen Amidala 3.00
Spec. Qui-Gon Jinn 3.00

STAR WARS EPISODE II— ATTACK OF THE CLONES
Apr., 2002
1 (of 4) 48-pg. 4.00
2 thru 4 48-pg. . . . . @4.00
1A thru 4A photo (c) . . . . @4.00

STAR WARS: EPISODE III– REVENGE OF THE SITH
Mar., 2005
1 . . . . 3.00
2 thru 4 . . . . @3.00

STAR WARS: GENERAL GRIEVOUS
Mar., 2005
1 . . . . 3.00
2 thru 4 . . . . @3.00

Star Wars: Handbook #2, Crimson Empire © Dark Horse Comics

STAR WARS HANDBOOK
July, 1998
1 X-Wing Rogue Squadron 3.50
2 Crimson Empire 3.00
Dark Empire 3.00

STAR WARS: HEIR TO THE EMPIRE
Oct., 1995–Apr., 1996
1 I:Grand Admiral Thrawn 4.00
2 thru 6 . . . . @3.50

STAR WARS: INFINITIES — A NEW HOPE
May, 2001
1 (of 4) CW,TyH,Luke's attack fails,
    Death Star survives 3.00
1a gold foil photo (c) 9.00
2 CW,TyH 3.00
3 CW,TyH 3.00
4 CW,TyH, concl. 3.00

STAR WARS: INFINITIES — THE EMPIRE STRIKES BACK
July, 2002
1 (of 4) 3.00
2 thru 4 . . . . @3.00

STAR WARS: INFINITIES — RETURN OF THE JEDI
Nov., 2003
1 (of 4) 3.00
2 thru 4 . . . . @3.00

STAR WARS: JABBA THE HUTT—
1995–1996
1-shot The Garr Suppoon Hit 3.00
1-shot Hunger of Princess Nampi . . 3.00
1-shot The Dynasty Trap 3.00
1-shot Betrayal. 3.00
1-shot The Jabba Tape 3.00

STAR WARS: JANGO FETT
Dec., 2001
GN 64-pg..,RMz 6.00

STAR WARS: JANGO FETT—OPEN SEASONS
Apr., 2002
1 (of 4) 3.00
2 thru 4 . . . . @3.00

STAR WARS: JEDI
Feb., 2003
Spec. Mace Windu, JOs,JD,48-pg. . 5.00
Spec. Shaak Ti, JOs,JD, 48-pg. . . . 5.00
Spec. Aayla Secura, JOs,JD,48-pg. 5.00
Spec. Dooku,JOs,JD,48-pg. 5.00
Spec. Yoda, 48-pg. 5.00

STAR WARS: JEDI ACADEMY LEVIATHAN
Oct., 1998
1 (of 4) by Kevin J. Anderson 3.00
2 thru 4 . . . . @3.00

STAR WARS: JEDI COUNCIL — ACTS OF WAR
June, 2000
1 (of 4) RSd, V:Yinchorri 3.00
1b gold foil (c) 9.00
2 thru 4 RSd . . . . @3.00

STAR WARS: JEDI QUEST
Sept., 2001
1 . . . . 3.00
1a ruby red foil 9.00
1b ruby red foil, signed 25.00
2 thru 4 . . . . @3.00

STAR WARS: JEDI VS. SITH
Apr., 2001
1 (of 6) 3.00
1a gold foil, lim.e. 9.00
2 V:Darth Bane 3.00
3 thru 6 . . . . @3.00

STAR WARS: KNIGHTS OF THE OLD REPUBLIC
Jan., 2006
1 A Jedi Betrayed 6.00
2 F:Zayne Carrick 4.00
3 Ambush 4.00
4 The Noose Tightens 4.00
5 A Destroyer of Worlds 3.00
6 Commencement 3.00
7 Jedi vs. Mandalorians 3.00
8 Jedi vs. Mandalorians 3.00
9 Jedi vs. Mandalorians 3.00
10 . . . . 3.00

11 . . . . 3.00
12 . . . . 3.00
13 . . . . 3.00
14 . . . . 3.00
15 Days of Fear 3.00
16 Nights of Anger 3.00
17 Nights of Anger 3.00
18 Nights of Anger 3.00
19 Daze of Hate 3.00
20 Daze of Hate 3.00
21 Daze of Hate 3.00
22 Knights of Suffering 3.00
Spec. Knights/Rebellion flip-book . . 1.00

STAR WARS: THE LAST COMMAND
Nov., 1997–July, 1998
1 thru 6 MBn . . . . @3.50

STAR WARS LEGACY
June, 2006
0 The Future of Star Wars 3.00
1 The Sith born anew 6.00
2 The Future in Question 6.00
3 A Princess in Peril 4.00
4 thru 8 . . . . @3.00
9 Trust Issues, pt.1 . . . . 3.00
10 Trust Issues,pt.2 . . . . 3.00
11 The Ghosts of Ossus 3.00
12 The Ghosts of Ossus 3.00
13 Ready to Die 3.00
14 Dragon, pt. 1 . . . . 3.00
15 Dragon, pt. 2 . . . . 3.00
16 Dragon, pt. 3 . . . . 3.00
17 Dragon, pt. 4 . . . . 3.00

Star Wars: Mara Jade #4 © Dark Horse Comics

STAR WARS: MARA JADE— BY THE EMPEROR'S HAND
Aug., 1998
1 (of 6) by Timothy Zahn 5.00
2 thru 6 . . . . @4.00

STAR WARS: OBSESSION
Nov., 2004
1 (of 5) 3.00
2 thru 5 . . . . @3.00

DARK HORSE

STAR WARS: THE PROTOCOL OFFENSIVE
Sept., 1997
1-shot written by Anthony Daniels . . 5.00

STAR WARS: PURGE
Dec., 2005
1-shot Last Stand of the Jedi 3.00

STAR WARS: QUI-GON & OBI-WAN—LAST STAND ON ORD MANTELL
Jan., 2001
1 . . . . 3.00
1a variant TnD (c). 3.00
1c gold foil (c) 9.00
2 . . . . 3.00
3 . . . . 3.00
1a thru 3a photo(c) . . . . @3.00

STAR WARS: QUI-GON & OBI-WAN—THE AURORIENT EXPRESS
Feb., 2002
1 (of 2) 3.00
2 . . . . 3.00

STAR WARS: REBELLION
Apr., 2006
1 F:Janek Sunber 3.00
2 thru 5 My Brother, My Enemy . @3.00
6 The Ahakista Gambit 3.00
7 thru 10 The Ahakista Gambit . . @3.00

STAR WARS: RETURN OF TAG & BINK
March, 2006
1 & 2 . . . . @3.00

STAR WARS: THE RETURN OF THE JEDI
(B&W–Manga) June, 1999
1 (of 4) Shin-ichi Hiromoto,
  96-pg.. . . . . 9.00
2 thru 4 . . . . @9.00

STAR WARS: RIVER OF CHAOS
May–Nov., 1995
1 LSi,JBr,Emperor sends spies . . . 3.00
2 Imperial in Allies Clothing 3.00
3 . . . . 3.00
4 F:Ranulf 3.00

STAR WARS: SHADOWS OF THE EMPIRE
May, 1996
1 (of 6) by John Wagner, Kilian
  Plunkett & P. Craig Russell 3.50
2 thru 6 . . . . @3.50

STAR WARS: SHADOWS OF THE EMPIRE — EVOLUTION
Feb.–June, 1998
1 thru 5 . . . . @3.50

STAR WARS: SHADOW STALKER
Nov., 1997
1-shot from Star Wars Galaxy Mag. 3.50

STAR WARS: SPLINTER OF THE MIND'S EYE
Dec., 1995–June, 1996
1 thru 4 A.D.Foster novel adapt. . @3.50

STAR WARS: STARFIGHTER— CROSSBONES
Jan., 2002
1 (of 3) F:Nym, pirate captain. 3.00
2 from video game 3.00
3 . . . . 3.00

STAR WARS: TAG & BINK ARE DEAD
Oct., 2001
1 (of 2) 3.00
2 . . . . 3.00
1-shot Revenge of the Clone
  Menace 3.00

STAR WARS TALES
Sept., 1999
1 various authors, 64-pg. 9.00
2 thru 4, 64-pg. . . . . @6.00
5 F:Lando's Commandos 6.00
6 thru 9 . . . . @6.00
10 thru 24 . . . . @6.00
5a thru 24a photo(c) . . . . @6.00

STAR WARS: TALES FROM MOS EISLEY
1-shot, from Star Wars Galaxy
  Mag. #2–#4 . . . . 3.50

STAR WARS: TALES OF THE JEDI
Oct., 1993
1 RV,I:Ulic Qel-Droma. 6.00
2 RV,A:Ulic Qel-Droma 5.00
3 RV,D:Andur 5.00
4 RV,A:Jabba the Hut 4.00
5 RV,last issue 4.00

STAR WARS: TALES OF THE JEDI: DARK LORDS OF THE SITH
Oct., 1994–Mar., 1995
1 Bagged with card 3.00
2 . . . . 3.00
3 Krath Attack 3.00
4 F:Exar Kun. 3.00
5 V:TehKrath 3.00
6 Final battle 3.00

STAR WARS: TALES OF THE JEDI: THE FREEDON NADD UPRISING
Aug.–Sept., 1997
1 and 2 . . . . @3.00

STAR WARS: TALES OF THE JEDI: THE SITH WAR
Aug., 1995–Jan., 1996
1 F:Exar Kun. 3.00
2 F:Ulic Oel-Droma 3.00

3 F:Exar Kun. 3.00
4 thru 6 (6 part mini-series). . . . . @3.00

STAR WARS: TALES OF THE JEDI—THE FALL OF THE SITH EMPIRE
June–Oct., 1997
1 (of 5) 3.50
2 thru 5 . . . . @3.00

STAR WARS: TALES OF THE JEDI—THE GOLDEN AGE OF THE SITH
Oct., 1996–Feb., 1997
0 . . . . 2.50
1 thru 5 . . . . @3.50

STAR WARS: TALES OF THE JEDI— REDEMPTION
July, 1998
1 (of 5) by Kevin J. Anderson 3.50
2 thru 5 F:Ulic Qel-Droma . . . . . . @3.50

Star Wars: Underworld, The Yavin Vassilika #1 © Dark Horse Comics

STAR WARS: UNDERWORLD—THE YAVIN VASSILIKA
Dec., 2000
1 (of 5) F:Han Solo 3.00
2 thru 5 . . . . @3.00
1a thru 5a photo (c) . . . . @3.00

STAR WARS: UNION
Nov., 1999
1 (of 4) by Stackpole 3.00
1a gold foil (c) 9.00
2 the wedding approaches 3.00
3 almost there 3.00
4 wedding day 3.00

STAR WARS: VADER'S QUEST
Feb., 1999
1 (of 4) DGb,AMK 3.00
2 thru 4 . . . . @3.00

STAR WARS: A VALENTINE STORY
Feb., 2003
1-shot PC 3.50

STAR WARS: X-WING— ROGUE LEADER
Sept., 2005
1 thru 3 . . . . @3.00

*Star Wars: X-Wing Rogue Squadron
#35 © Dark Horse Comics*

STAR WARS: X-WING ROGUE SQUADRON
July, 1995
The Rebel Opposition
1 F:Wedge Antilles 5.00
2 . . . . 3.50
3 F:Tycho Clehu 3.50
4 F:Tycho Clehu 3.50
½ Wizard limited exclusive 6.00
The Phantom Affair
5 thru 8 . . . . @3.50
Battleground Tatooine
9 thru 12 . . . . @3.50
The Warrior Princess
13 thru 16 . . . . @3.50
Requiem for a Rogue
17 thru 20 . . . . @3.50
TPB rep 13.00
In the Empire's Service
21 thru 24 . . . . @3.50
Making of Baron Fell
25 . . . . 5.00
Family Ties
26 thru 27 . . . . @3.50
Masquerade
28 thru 31 . . . . @3.50
Mandatory Retirement
32 thru 35 . . . . @3.50

STAR WARS: ZAM WESELL
Feb., 2002
GN RMz, 64-pg 6.00

STEVE RUDE'S THE MOTH
Mar., 2004
1 thru 4 . . . . @3.00
Spec. Double sized 5.00

SUBHUMAN
Nov., 1998
1 (of 4) MSh 3.00
2 thru 4 MSh . . . . @3.00

SUPER MANGA BLAST
(B&W) Mar., 2000
1 128-pg 5.00
2 thru 6 128-pg . . . . @5.00
7 F:Oh My Goddess 5.00
8 F:Oh My Goddess 5.00
9 F:3x3 Eyes 5.00
10 F:Seraphic Feather 5.00
11 F:Oh My Goddess 5.00
12 F:Oh My Goddess 5.00
13 F:Club 9 . . . . 5.00
14 F:Club 9 . . . . 5.00
15 F:Club 9, 50-pg 6.00
16 F:3x3 Eyes 6.00
17 F:Club 9 . . . . 6.00
18 F:Club 9 . . . . 6.00
19 Seraphic Feather 6.00
20 What's Michael? 6.00
21 F:Club 9 . . . . 6.00
22 Club 9, 3x3 Eyes 6.00
23 Club 9, What's Michael? 6.00
24 F:Seraphic Feather 6.00
25 F:Appleseed 6.00
26 F:Shadow Star 6.00
27 F:What's Michael? 6.00
28 thru 59 . . . . @6.00

SUPERMAN/MADMAN HULLABALOO
June–Aug., 1997
1 (of 3) MiA 3.00
2 and 3 (of 3) . . . . @3.00

SUPERMAN/TARZAN: SONS OF THE JUNGLE
Oct., 2001
1 (of 3) CDi,HuR 3.00
2 CDi,HuR 3.00
3 CDi,HuR(c) 3.00

SUPERMAN VS. ALIENS
DC/Dark Horse, 1995
1 DJu,KN 6.00
2 V:Queen Alien 5.00
3 . . . . 5.00

SUPERMAN VS. ALIENS II
May, 2002
1 (of 4) CDi,JBg,KN, x-over 3.00
2 CDi,JBg,KN 3.00
3 CDi,JBg,KN 3.00
4 CDi,JBg,KN 3.00

SUPERMAN VS. THE TERMINATOR: DEATH TO THE FUTURE
Dec., 1999
1 (of 4) AIG,StP,x-over 3.00
2 AIG,StP,into the future 3.00
3 AIG,StP,A:Supergirl 3.00
4 AIG,StP,concl 3.00

SYN
Rocket Comics Aug., 2003
1 KG 3.00
2 thru 5 . . . . @3.00

TALE OF ONE BAD RAT
1994
1 BT 3.00

2 thru 4 . . . . @3.00

TALES OF ORDINARY MADNESS
(B&W) 1992
1 JBo(c),Paranoid 3.00
2 JBo(c),Mood 2.50
3 JBo(c),A Little Bit of Neurosis . . . 2.50
4 . . . . 2.50

TALES OF THE FEAR AGENTS: TWELVE STEPS IN ONE
Oct., 2007
1-shot 3.00

TALES OF THE VAMPIRES
Dec., 2003
1 Josh Whedon 3.00
2 thru 5 . . . . @3.00

TALES TO OFFEND
July, 1997
1-shot by Frank Miller 3.00

TANK GIRL
(B&W) 1991
1 Rep. from U.K.Deadline Mag.
  with 2-card strip 4.50
2 V:Indiana Potato Jones 4.00
3 On the Run 4.00
4 . . . . 4.00
[2nd Series] 1993
1 . . . . 3.50
2 thru 4 . . . . @3.00

TARZAN/JOHN CARTER: WARLORDS OF MARS
1996
1 (of 4) E.R.Burroughs adapt 3.00
2 thru 4 . . . . @3.00

TARZAN VS. PREDATOR AT THE EARTH'S CORE
1996
1 Tarzan vs. Predator 3.00
2 V:Predator 3.00

*Tarzan/John Carter, Warlords of Mars
#4 © Dark Horse Comics*

DARK HORSE

3 Tarzan on the Hunt 3.00
4 . . . . 3.00

TENTH, THE:
NIGHTWALKER
Apr., 2002

1 (of 4) TnD 3.00
2 thru 4 . . . . @3.00
1a thru 4a variant (c). . . . . @3.00

TENTH, THE:
RESURRECTED
Apr., 2001

1 TnD 3.00
1a variant(c) 7.00
1b variant(c) signed 15.00
2 TnD 3.00
3 TnD 3.00
4 TnD 3.00
3a and 4a variant (c)s . . . . @3.00

TERMINAL POINT
(B&W) 1993

1 . . . . 2.50
2 and 3 . . . . @2.50

TERMINATOR
1990

1 CW,Tempest 4.00
2 CW,Tempest 3.00
3 CW. 3.00
4 CW, conclusion 3.00

TERMINATOR
1-shot MW,3-D const(c2,
pop-up inside (1991) 5.00
Spec. AlG,GyD,GeD(1998) 3.00

TERMINATOR, THE
Sept., 1998

1 AlG,StP. 3.00
2 F:Sarah Connor. 3.00
3 F:Killerman. 3.00
4 F:D-800L & D-810X 3.00

TERMINATOR, THE:
THE DARK YEARS
Sept., 1999

1 (of 4) AlG,MvR,BWi 3.00
2 AlG,MvR,BWi,F:Jon Norden. 3.00
3 . . . . 3.00
4 AlG,MvR,concl.. . . . . 3.00

TERMINATOR:
END GAME
1992

1 JG,Final *Terminator* series. 3.00
2 JG,Cont.last Term.story 3.00
3 JG, Concl. 3.00

TERMINATOR:
ENEMY WITHIN
1991

1 cont. from Sec.Objectives 4.00
2 C890.L.threat contd. 3.00
3 Secrets of Cyberdyne 3.00
4 Conclusion. 3.00

TERMINATOR: HUNTERS
& KILLERS
1992

1 V:Russians. 3.00
2 V:Russians. 3.00
3 V:Russians. 3.00

TERMINATOR:
SECONDARY
OBJECTIVES
1991

1 cont. 1st DH mini-series 4.00
2 PG,A:New Female Terminator . . . 3.00
3 PG,Terminators in L.A.&Mexico . . 3.00
4 PG,Terminator vs Terminator 3.00

TERRITORY, THE
Jan., 1999

1 (of 4) JaD,DvL,F:Ishmael. 3.00
2 thru 4 . . . . @3.00

TEX AVERY'S DROOPY

1 Dr. Droopenstein 2.50
2 and 3 . . . . @2.50

TEX AVERY'S
SCREWBALL SQUIRREL

1 I:Screwball Squirrel 2.50
2 Cleaning House 2.50
3 School of Hard Rocks 2.50

THING, THE
1991

1 JHi, Movie adaptation 4.00
2 JHi, Movie adaptation 3.50

THING FROM
ANOTHER WORLD:
CLIMATE OF FEAR
1994

1 Argentinian Military Base
(Bahiathetis) 3.00
2 Thing on Base 3.00
3 Thing/takeover. 3.00
4 Conclusion. 3.00

THING FROM
ANOTHER WORLD:
ETERNAL VOWS
1993

1 PG,I:Sgt. Rowan 3.00
2 PG 3.00
3 PG,in New Zealand 3.00
4 PG,Last issue. 3.00

THIRTEEN O'CLOCK
(B&W)

1 Mr.Murmer,from Deadline USA . . 3.00

THE 13th SON
Oct., 2005

1 KJo, Worse Thing Waiting 3.00
2 thru 4 KJo. . . . . @3.00

3 X 3 EYES:
CURSE OF THE GESU
(B&W–Manga) 1995

1 I:Pai,Yakumo 3.00
2 thru 5 . . . . @3.00

300
May, 1998

1 (of 5) FM & Lynn Varley. 15.00
2 FM 12.00
3 FM 18.00
4 FM 15.00
5 FM . . . . @12.00

TIME COP
1994

1 Movie Adaptation 2.75
2 Movie Adaptation 2.50

TITAN
1994

Spec.#1 BS(c),I:Inhibitors 4.25

TITAN A.E.
May, 2000

1 (of 3) film prequel,pt.1 . . . . 3.00
2 thru 3 prequel,pt.2–pt.3 . . . . . @3.00

TONGUE*LASH
Aug., 1996

1 by Randy and Jean-Marc
Lofficier & Dave Taylor 3.00
2 . . . . 3.00

[VOL. II] 1999

1 (of 2) 3.00
2 . . . . 3.00

TONY MILLIONAIRE'S
SOCK MONKEY
VOL. 3

1 & 2. . . . . @3.00

Too Much Coffee Man Special
© Dark Horse Comics

TOO MUCH COFFEE MAN
(B&W) July, 1997

1-shot by Shannon Wheeler 3.00

TORCH OF LIBERTY
1995

Spec. 2.50

TREKKER
(B&W) 1987

1 thru 4 . . . . @3.00
5 thru 7 . . . . @3.00
8 O:Trekker. 3.00
9 . . . . 3.00
Spec.#1 Sins of the Fathers 3.00

TRIPLE X
(B&W) 1994

1 . . . . 4.00
2 V:Dr. Zemph. 4.00

DARK HORSE

3 . . . . 4.00
4 V:Rhine Lords 4.00
5 I:Klaar 4.00
6 Klaar captured 5.00
7 Revolution Consequences 5.00

Two Faces of Tomorrow #13
© Dark Horse Comics

TWO FACES OF TOMORROW, THE
(B&W–Manga) Aug., 1997
1 (of 13) from James P. Hogan
  novel, by Yukinobu Hoshino . . . 3.00
2 thru 4 . . . . @3.00
5 thru 13 . . . . @4.00

TWO FISTED TALES
Spec. WW,WiS 5.00

2112
GN JBy,A:Next Men 2.50
2nd Printing 5.00

ULTRAMAN TIGA
Aug., 2003
1 (of 10) 4.00
2 thru 4 . . . . @4.00
5 thru 10 . . . . @4.00

UMBRELLA ACADEMY: APOCALYPSE SUITE
Sept., 2007
1 (of 6) 4.00
2 . . . . 3.00

[ANDREW VACHSS'] UNDERGROUND
(B&W) 1993
1 AVs(s) 4.25
2 thru 5 AVs(s) . . . . @4.00

UNIVERSAL MONSTERS
1991
1 AAd,Creature From The
  Black Lagoon 5.50
1 Dracula 5.50
1 Frankenstein 5.50
1 The Mummy 5.50

URBAN LEGENDS
(B&W) 1993
1-shot 3.00

USAGI YOJIMBO
(B&W) 1996
1 by Stan Sakai 7.00
2 thru 9 . . . . @4.00
10 with Sergio Aragones 6.00
11 'The Lord of Owls' 6.00
12 'Vampire Cat of the Geishu' 3.00
13 thru 22 'Grasscutter,',pt.1
    thru pt. #10 . . . . @3.00
23 My Father's Sword 3.00
24 The Demon Flute 3.00
25 Momo-Usagi-Taro 3.00
26 The Hairpin Murders,pt.1 . . . . . . 3.00
27 The Hairpin Murders,pt.2 . . . . . . 3.00
28 Courtesan conspiracy,pt.1 . . . . . 3.00
29 Courtesan conspiracy,pt.2 . . . . . 3.00
30 Inspector Ishida mystery 3.00
31 The Haunted Inn of Moon
    Shadow Hill 3.00
32 Two stories 3.00
33 . . . . 3.00
34 Demon Mask,pt.1 . . . . 3.00
35 Demon Mask,pt.2 . . . . 3.00
36 Demon Mask,pt.3 . . . . 3.00
37 F:Sasuke the Demon Queller . . . 3.00
38 Priest Sanshobo's temple 3.00
39 Grasscutter II,pt.1 . . . . 3.00
40 V:Captain Quark 3.00
41 V:Neko Ninja 3.00
42 Grasscutter II,pt.4 . . . . 3.00
43 Grasscutter II 3.00
44 Grasscutter II 3.00
45 Grasscutter II 3.00
46 wraparound(c),pt.1 . . . . 3.00
47 wraparound(c),pt.2 . . . . 3.00
48 . . . . 3.00
49 Three seasons 3.00
50 Usagi dead? 3.00
51 The Shrouded Moon 3.00
52 Kitsune's youth 3.00
53 hunt for four ronin 3.00
54 Lone Goat and Kid 3.00
55 Lord Yoshikawa is dying 3.00
56 Katsuichi vs. Nakamura Joji 3.00
57 Crows,pt.1, renegade ronin 3.00
58 Crows,pt.2 . . . . 3.00
59 Crows,pt.3 . . . . 3.00
60 duel at Kitanoji 3.00
61 F:Chizu 3.00
62 Cursed woods 3.00
63 SS, return of Kitsune 3.00
64 SS, Tomago 3.00
65 SS 3.00
66 SS,giant monsters,pt.1 . . . . 3.00
67 SS,giant monsters,pt.2 . . . . 3.00
68 SS,giant monsters,pt.3 . . . . 3.00
69 SS,Fathers and Sons,pt.1 . . . . . 3.00
70 SS,Fathers and Sons,pt.2 . . . . . 3.00
71 to 99 SS . . . . @3.00
100 SS 3.50
101 thru 105 SS . . . . @3.00

USAGI YOJIMBO
1996
1 SS,color spec. 4.00
2 SS,color spec. 3.00
3 SS,color spec. 3.00
4 thru 6 . . . . @3.00

USAGI YOJIMBO COLOR SPECIAL: GREEN PERSIMMON
1-shot by Stan Sakai 3.00

VAMPIRELLA
(B&W) 1992
1 'The Lion and the Lizard'Pt.1 . . . . 4.50
2 'The Lion and the Lizard'Pt.2 . . . . 4.00
3 'The Lion and the Lizard'Pt.3 . . . . 4.00
4 'The Lion and the Lizard'Pt.3 . . . . 4.00
Spec. Vampirella's Summer Night . . 4.00

VAN HELSING
May, 2004
1-shot Movie tie-in 3.00

VENUS WARS
(B&W–Manga) 1991
1 Aphrodia V:Ishtar, with
  2-card strip 3.00
2 I: Ken Seno 2.50
3 Aphrodia V:Ishtar 2.50
4 Seno Joins Hound Corps. 2.50
5 SenoV:Octopus Supertanks 2.50
6 Chaos in Aphrodia 2.50
7 All Out Ground War 2.50
8 Ishtar V:Aphrodia contd. 2.50
9 Ishtar V:Aphrodia contd. 2.50
10 Supertanks of Ishtar Advance . . . 2.50
11 Aphrodia Captured 2.50
12 A:Miranda,48-pg. 2.75
13 Hound Brigade–Suicide Assault . 2.50
14 V:Army 2.50
15 . . . . 2.50

VENUS WARS II
1992
1 V:Security Police 2.75
2 Political Unrest 2.50
3 Conspiracy 2.50
4 A:Lupica 2.50
5 Love Hotel 2.50
6 Terran Consulate 2.50
7 Doublecross 2.50
8 D:Lupisa 3.00
9 A:Matthew 3.00
10 A:Mad Scientist 3.00
11 thru 15 V:Troopers . . . . @3.00

VERSION
(B&W–Manga) 1993
1.1 by Hisashi Sakaguchi 2.50
1.2 thru 1.8 . . . . @2.50

VERSION II
(B&W–Manga) 1993
2.1 by Hisashi Sakaguchi 2.50
2.2 thru 2.7 . . . . @2.50

VIRUS
1993
1 MP(c),F:The Wan Xuan & the
  crew of the Electra 3.00
2 MP(c),V:Captian Powell 3.00
3 MP(c),V:Virus 3.00
4 MP(c),Last issue 3.00

VORTEX, THE
1 . . . . 2.50

WACKY SQUIRREL
(B&W) 1987
1 thru 4 . . . . @2.75
Spec. Halloween Adventure 2.75
Spec. Summer Fun 2.75

WALTER: CAMPAIGN OF TERROR
1996
1 thru 4 . . . . @2.50

WARRIOR OF WAVERLY STREET, THE
Nov., 1996
1 (of 2) by M.Coto & J. Stokes 3.00
2 . . . . 3.00
1-shot Broodstorm 3.00

WARWORLD!
(B&W) 1989
1 . . . . 3.00

WHITE LIKE SHE
(B&W) 1994
1 by Bob Fingerman 3.00
2 thru 4 . . . . @3.00

WHO WANTS TO BE A SUPERHERO?
Oct., 2006
1 Feedback 3.50
Spec. Feedback (July 2007) 3.50

WILL TO POWER
Comics' Greatest World, 1994
1 BS, A:X 2.50
2 BS, A:X,Monster 2.50
3 BS, A:X 2.50
4 BS, In Steel Harbor 2.50
5 V:Wolfgang 2.50
6 V:Motorhead 2.50
7 JOy(c),V:Amazing Grace 2.50
8 V:Catalyst 2.50
9 Titan, Grace 2.50
10 Vortex alien, Grace 2.50
11 Vortex alien, King Titan 2.50
12 Vortex alien 2.50

WITCHBLADE/ALIENS/ DARKNESS/PREDATOR: MINDHUNTER
Dec., 2000
1 thru 3 . . . . @3.00
2a variant TnD (c) 3.00

WIZARD OF FOURTH STREET
(B&W) 1987
1 . . . . 3.00

Will To Power #8
© Dark Horse Comics

---

2 thru 4 . . . . @2.50

WOLF & RED
1995
1 Looney Tunes 2.50
2 Watchdog Wolf 2.50
3 Red Hot Riding Hood 2.50

WORLD BELOW, THE
Mar., 1999
1 PC 2.50
2 thru 4 PC . . . . @2.50

WORLD BELOW II, THE
Dec., 1999
1 (of 4) PC 3.00
2 thru 4 PC,Deeper and Stranger . . 3.00

X
Comics' Greatest World, 1994
1 B:StG(s),DoM,JP,I:X-Killer 3.00
2 DoM,JP,V:X-Killer 2.50
3 DoM,JP,A:Pit Bulls 2.50
4 DoM,JP 2.50
5 DoM,JP,V:Chaos Riders 2.50
6 Cyberassassins 2.50
7 Alamout 2.50
8 A:Ghost 2.50
9 War for Arcadia 2.50
10 War for Arcadia 2.50
11 I:Coffin, War 2.50
12 V:Coffin, A:Monster 2.50
13 D:X 2.50
14 conclusion to War 2.50
15 JS,SiG,war survivors 2.50
16 V:Headhunter 2.50
17 . . . . 2.50
18 V:Predator 2.50
19 V:Challenge 2.50
20 thru 25 . . . . @2.50
Spec. #1 One Shot to the Head 2.50

XENA: WARRIOR PRINCESS
Aug., 1999
1 . . . . 3.00
2 thru 9 . . . . @3.00
10 IEd,MD2,wayward viking 3.00
11 IEd,MD2,V:Lamia 3.00
12 IEd,MD2,Darkness Falls,concl. . . 3.00
13 IEd,MD2,F:Legion 3.00
14 conclusion 3.00
1 to 14 newsstand photo(c) . . . . . @3.00

YOUNG CYNICS CLUB
(B&W) 1993
1 by Glenn Wong 2.50

THE YOUNG INDIANA JONES CHRONICLES
1992
1 DBa,FS,TV Movie Adapt 3.25
2 DBa,TV Movie Adapt 2.75
3 DBa,GM 2.75
4 DBa,GM 2.75
5 DBa,GM 2.75
6 BBa,GM,WW1,French Army 2.75
7 The Congo 2.75
8 Africa,A:A.Schweitzer 2.50
9 Vienna,Sophie-daughter of Arch-
   Duke Ferdinand 2.50
10 In Vienna continued 2.50
11 Far East 2.50
12 Fever Issue 2.50

YOU'RE UNDER ARREST!
(B&W–Manga) 1995–96
1 by Kosuke Fujishima 3.00
2 thru 8 . . . . @3.00

ZERO KILLER
July., 2007
1 (of 6) 3.00
2 . . . . 3.00

ZOMBIEWORLD:
1-shot Eat Your Heart Out, KJo 3.00
1-shot Home for the Holidays 3.00

ZOMBIEWORLD: CHAMPION OF THE WORMS
Sept., 1997
1 (of 3) MMi 3.00
2 and 3 . . . . @3.00
Spec. Home for the Holidays 3.00

Zombie World: Dead End #2
© Dark Horse Comics

ZOMBIEWORLD: DEAD END
Jan., 1998
1 (of 2) by Stephen Blue 3.00
2 . . . . 3.00

ZOMBIEWORLD: THE TREE OF DEATH
May, 1999
1 (of 4) by P. Mills & J.Deadstock. . 3.00
2 thru 4 . . . . @3.00

ZOMBIEWORLD: WINTER'S DREGS
May, 1998
1 (of 4) by Fingerman & Edwards. . 3.00
2 thru 4 . . . . @3.00

ZONE, THE
(B&W) 1990
1-shot 3.00

IMAGE

AARON STRIPS
(B&W) Apr., 1997
1 thru 4 rep. from Sunday comic
   strips, by Aaron Warner . . . . . @3.00

ACTION PLANET
(B&W) Sept., 1997
Prev. Action Planet Comics
3 . . . . 4.00

ADRENALYNN
Aug., 1999
1 F:Sabina Nikoli. 2.50
2 TnD,V:Russian monster androids 2.50
3 TnD,V:last 2 Monster-cyborgs . . . 2.50
4 TnD,the real Sabina 2.50

ADVENTURES OF AARON
(B&W) March, 1997
by Aaron Warner
1 'Baby-sitter Gone Bad'. 3.00
2 'Thunder Thighs of the
   Terrordome' 3.00
3 'Baby-sitter Gone Bad,' concl. . . . 3.00
100 Super Special 3.00
Christmas Spectacular #1 . . . . 3.00

ADVENTURES OF
BARRY WEEN,
BOY GENIUS, THE
(B&W) March, 1999
1 (of 3) by Judd Winick 3.00
2 Growing Pains 3.00
3 School 3.00

ADVENTURES OF SPAWN
Jan., 2007
1 Director's Cut. 6.00

ADVENTURE STRIP
DIGEST
(B&W) April, 1998
1 by Randy Reynaldo 3.00
2 F:Rob Hanes, detective 3.00

AFTER THE CAPE
(B&W) Mar., 2007
1 (of 3) 3.00
2 Secret Life 3.00
3 Somewhere Below Rock Bottom. 3.00

AGENTS, THE
(B&W) April, 2003
1 thru 6 BDn . . . . @3.00

AGE OF BRONZE
(B&W) Nov., 1998
1 EiS,The Trojan War 3.00
2 EiS,Death of Paris 3.00
3 EiS,F:Herakles, Hektor 3.00
4 EiS,I:Helen 3.00
5 EiS,Achilles disguised 3.00
6 EiS,Helen gone 3.50
7 EiS,Odysseus mad? 3.50
8 EiS,Achilles missing. 3.50
9 EiS,Will war start? 3.50
10 EiS,Sacrifice,pt.1 . . . . 3.50
11 EiS,Sacrifice,pt.2 . . . . 3.50
12 EiS,You're not the Trojans? 3.50

13 thru 18 EiS,Sacrifice,pt.4–pt.9 @3.50
19 EiS,Sacrifice,pt.10. . . . . 3.50
20 Betrayal, pt.1. . . . . 3.50
21 Betrayal, pt 2 . . . . 3.50
22 Betrayal, pt.3 . . . . 3.50
23 Betrayal, pt.4 . . . . 3.50
24 Betrayal, pt.5 . . . . 3.50
25 Betrayal, pt.6 . . . . 3.50
26 Betrayal, pt.7 . . . . 3.50
Spec.1-shot Behind the Scenes . . . 3.50
Spec.#1 EiS, House of Horror 3.00
Spec.#2 . . . . 3.00

AGE OF HEROES, THE
(B&W) Halloween, 1996
1 JHI & JRy. 3.00
2 JHI & JRy. 3.00
3 JHI & JRy,Luko,Trickster &
   Aerwyn try to steal treasure . . . 3.00
4 JHI & JRy,Drake, the blind
   swordsman returns 3.00
5 JHI & JRy,O:Conor One-Arm. . . . 3.00
Spec. #1 rep. #1 & #2 . . . . 5.00
Spec. #2 rep. #3 & #4 . . . . 7.00

AGE OF HEROES: WEX
(B&W) Aug., 1998
1 by JHI,Vurtex 3.00

AGENCY, THE
Top Cow, July, 2001
1 (of 6) PJe. 4.00
1a variant(c) 4.00
1b variant MS(c) 4.00
2 PJe. 2.50
3 PJe. 2.50
4 PJe,A Virtual Secret. 3.00
5 PJe,Virtual 3.00
6 PJe,concl. 48-pg. 5.00

ALIEN PIG FARM 3000
Apr., 2007
1 (of 4) WiS(c) 3.00
2 MaS(c) 3.00
3 WiS(c) 3.00
4 MaS(c) 3.00

ALLEGRA
WildStorm, 1996
1 ScC,SSe 2.50
2 thru 4 . . . . @2.50

ALLEY CAT
July, 1999
1 BNa,MHw,F:Alley Baggett 2.50
1a variant painted cover (1:4). 3.50
2 BNa,MHw,women murdered 2.50
3 photo(c) 2.50
3a variant JJu cover (1:4). 2.50
4 into darkness 2.50
5 The Martyr,pt.1. . . . . 3.00
6 The Martyr,pt.2 . . . . 3.00
7 The Martyr,pt.3. . . . . 2.50
Wizard World Spec.#1 . . . . 2.50
Lingerie Edition 5.00

ALLIANCE, THE
Shadowline, 1995
1 JV,I:The Alliance, A Call
   to Arms 2.50
2 JV,Team comes together 'Like
   Pieces of a Puzzle' 2.50
3 I:Slash C 2.50

The Alliance #3
© *Shadowline*

4 . . . . 2.50
1a thru 4a variant covers . . . . . . @2.50

ALLIES, THE
Extreme, 1995
1 mini-series 2.50
2 thru 4 . . . . @2.50

ALTERATION
Feb., 2004
1 . . . . 3.00
1a variant (c) AAd 3.00
2 thru 4 . . . . @3.00
2a thru 4a variant (c)s . . . . @3.00

ALTERED IMAGE
April, 1998
1 JV,The Day Reality Went Wild. . . 2.50
2 JV,F:Everybody smooshed 2.50
3 JV,Middle Age Crisis, concl. 2.50

AMANDA AND GUNN
(B&W) April, 1997
1 JeR, Montana 2036 . . . . 3.00
2 (of 4) JeR. 3.00
3 (of 4) JeR. 3.00
4 (of 4) JeR, conclusion 3.00

AMAZING JOY
BUZZARDS, THE
(B&W) Dec., 2004
1 I was a Teenage Monster 3.00
2 The Island of Maru. 3.00
3 ...Go Hollywood 3.00
4 ...Go Hollywood,pt.2 . . . . 3.00
5 Ready...Set...Ignition 3.00
6 Here Come the Spiders,pt.2 . . . . 3.00
7 Go, El Campeon, Go, pt.1 . . . . . . 3.00
Vol. 2, 2005
1 Here Come the Spiders, pt.1 . . . . 3.00
2 thru 5 . . . . @3.00

ANGELA
TMP, 1994–95
1 NGa(s),GCa,A:Spawn	15.00
2 NGa(s),GCa,Angela's trial	14.00
3 NGa(s),GCa,In Hell	12.00
Spec. Pirate Spawn(c)	32.00
Spec. Pirate Angela(c) (1995)	30.00

ANGELA/GLORY: RAGE OF ANGELS
TMP/Extreme, 1996
1 x-over begins	5.00

ANGELUS, THE: PILOT SEASON
Top Cow, Oct, 2007
1	3.00

ANT
1	3.00
2	3.00
3 A:Spawn	3.00
4	3.00
5 thru 9 Moving On	@3.00
10	3.00
11	3.00
12 1992, Part Three	3.00
13	3.00

APHRODITE IX
Top Cow, Aug., 2000
1 by David Finch	4.00
1a variant JBz(c)	4.00
1a signed	15.00
1b variant Michale Turner(c)	4.00
1c variant MS(c)	4.00
2 amnesia	3.50
3 conspiracy	3.50
0 with pin-up & poster	3.00
4 Who is she? 48-pg.	5.50
Spec.1 Convention spec., signed	20.00
Preview ed., signed	5.00

ARCANUM
Top Cow, March, 1997
[Mini-series]
1 BPe, from Medieval Spawn/Witchblade	3.00
1a variant MS(s) (1:4)	2.50
2 BPe, Chi in Asylum	2.50
3 BPe, Ming Chang captive in Atlantis	2.50
4 BPe,'The End?'	2.50
5 BPe,Royale's secret journal	2.50
6 BPe,Safe Haven?	2.50
7 BPe,Egypt	2.50

AREA 52
Jan., 2001
1	3.00
2 The Gloves are off	3.00
3 Out of the Frying Pan and into the Fire	3.00
4 Beginning of the End	3.00

ARIA
Avalon, Nov., 1998
1 by Brian Holguin & Jay Anacleto	6.00
1a variant cover	8.00
2 A:Mad Gwynnion	3.00
3 English Countryside	3.00
4 V:Dark One	3.00
4a glow-in-the-dark(c)	10.00
5 London, 1966.	3.00
6 Subterranean Homesick Blues	3.00
7 Mad Gods and Irish Men	3.00

Preview ed. F:Kildare	3.00
Spec.#1 Blanc & Noir, sketchbook.	3.00
Spec.#1 alternate cover	7.00
Spec.#2 Blanc & Noir	2.50
Sketchbook by Jay Anacleto	6.00
Coll.Ed.#1, rep.#1–#2	6.00

ARIA/ANGELA: HEAVENLY CREATURES
Feb., 2000
1 (of 2) x-over	5.00
1a variant JQ(c) (1:4)	3.00
1b variant J.G. Jones(c) (1:4)	4.00
1c variant Jay Anacleto(c) (1:4)	3.00
1 B&W	3.00
2 x-over concl.	3.00
2a variant(c)	4.00
Museum edition	125.00

ARIA: THE SOUL MARKET
March, 2001
1 Legend continues	4.00
1a Museum edition	125.00
2 F:Robin Goodfellow	3.00
3 A Dark Rider Approaches	3.00
4 Auction of imprisoned souls	3.00
5 What price a soul?	3.00
6 Mortality	3.00
GN A Midwinter's Dream,40-pg.	5.00

ARIA: A SUMMER SPELL
March, 2002
1 (of 2) London, summer 1967	3.00
2 Kildare is in love	3.00

ARIA: THE USES OF ENCHANTMENT
Feb., 2003
1 thru 4	@3.00

ARKAGA
Sept., 1997
1 by Arnie Tang Jorgensen	3.00
2 Desire for revenge	3.00

ARMOR X
Mar., 2005
1 ASm	3.00
2 ASm	3.00
3 ASm	3.00
4 ASm, The End	3.00

ARMORY WARS, THE
June, 2007
1	3.00
1a variant (c)	3.00
2 thru 5	@3.00

ASCENSION
Top Cow, Sept., 1997
1 by David Finch,F:Angels	4.00
2 Andromeda fights alone	3.00
3 reunited with Lucien	3.00
4	3.00
5 Gregorieff and Dayak Army	3.00
6 Voivodul returns, concl.	3.00
7 Andy's problems worsen	2.50
8 revenge on Dayaks & Mineans	2.50
9 Andy exiled	2.50
10 A:D. Gavin Taylor	2.50
11 A:D. Gavin Taylor	2.50
12 A:turning point	2.50
13 A:Grigorieff, Petra	2.50
14 V:Marcus,A:Andromeda	2.50
15 Rowena's secrets	2.50
16 Petra joins Lucien	2.50
17 a schism	2.50

Ascension #19
© Top Cow

18 V:new entity	2.50
19 to Petra's Minean home	2.50
20 Resurrection,pt.1	2.50
21 Resurrection,pt.2	2.50
22 trapped	3.00
23 Andromeda's new outfit	3.00
Coll.Ed.#1, rep.#1–#2	5.00
Coll.Ed.#2	5.00

ASTOUNDING SPACE THRILLS
April, 2000
1 Ken Kelly(c),Cydonian Contant	3.00
2 The Criminal Code.	3.00
3 Gordo:Earthling Prime, flip-book	3.00
4 The Craving of Consumorr, flip-book	3.00
5 Attack of the Macrobes	3.00

ASTOUNDING WOLF-MAN
July, 2007
1a director's cut	4.00
2 thru 3	@3.50

ASTRO
April, 2006
1	7.00

ATHEIST, THE
(B&W) Feb., 2005
1 PhH,Incarnate	3.50
2 PhH,Incarnate,pt.2: The Tumor.	3.50
3 PhH,Incarnate,pt.3: Desperate Measures	3.50
4 PhH,Incarnate, pt.4: Sacrifice	3.50

ATHENA INC.
2002
1-shot Agents Roster,48-pg.	6.00
The Beginning, 48-pg.	6.00
1 reoffered	3.00
2 Gwen has a stalker	3.00
2a variant(c)	3.00
3 Gwen hearing voices	3.00
3a variant(c)	3.00
4 Revelations	3.00
4a variant(c)	3.00
5 The Belly of the Beast	3.00
6 All Hell Breaks Loose	3.00
5a– a variant (c)	@3.00

IMAGE

ATOMIC TOYBOX
April, 1999
Odyssey Line
1 AaL,F:Ken Logan 3.00
2 AaL,The Aliens are comming. . . . 3.00

AUTOMATION
Flypaper, 1998
1 Robots sent to Mars, and back . . 3.00
2 One goes mad. 3.00
3 Sherzad vs. Konak 3.00

AVIGON
(B&W) Oct., 2000
Spec. 56-pg. 6.00
GN 6.00
GN Gods and Demons (2005). . . . 20.00

THE AWAKENING
(B&W) Oct., 1997
1 (of 4) by Stephen Blue. 3.00
2 thru 4 . . . . @3.00

Backlash #21
© Wildstorm

BACKLASH
WildStorm, 1994–97
1 Taboo, 2 diff. covers 4.00
1a variant edition, 2 covers. 3.00
2 Savage Dragon 2.50
3 V:Savage Dragon 2.50
4 SRf,A:Wetworks. 2.50
5 SRf,A:Dane 2.50
6 BBh,SRf,A:Wetworks. 2.50
7 BBh,SRf,V:Bounty Hunters 2.50
8 RMz,BBh,BWS(c),WildStorm
  Rising,pt.8,w/2 cards 2.50
8a Newsstand ed. 2.50
9 F:Taboo,Dingo,V:Chasers 2.50
10 I:Crimson. 2.50
11 R:Bloodmoon 2.50
12 R:Taboo,Crimson's Costume . . . 3.00
13 Taboo to the Rescue. 2.50
14 A:Deathblow 2.50
15 F:Cyberjack. 2.50
16 F:Cole,Marc 2.50
17 F:Marc,Kink. 2.50
18 . . . . 2.50
19 Fire From Heaven,pt.2 . . . . 2.50
20 SRf,BBh,Fire From
  Heaven,pt.10. . . . . 2.50
21 SRf,BBh 2.50

22 SRf,BBh 2.50
23 SRf,BBh 2.50
24 SRf,BBh,return of Dingo 2.50
25 SRf,BBh,56-pg.. special 4.00
26 SRf,BBh,IR:Gramalkin 2.50
27 SRf,BBh 2.50
28 SRf,BBh,Backlash leads PSI
  team to Europe 2.50
29 SRf,BBh,Haroth raises the
  remnants of Atlantis. 2.50
30 SRf,BBh,Backlash confronts
  Kherubim lords 2.50
31 SRf,BBh,team returns to PSI . . . 2.50
32 SRf,BBh,earth-shattering
  final issue 2.50

BACKLASH/SPIDER-MAN
WildStorm/Marvel, 1996
1 x-over,pt.1 . . . . 2.50
1a variant cover 3.00
2 x-over,pt.2 . . . . 2.50

BADGER
(B&W) May, 1997
1 MBn,'Betelgeuse'. 3.00
2 MBn,'Beefalo don't like fences' . . 3.00
3 MBn,'Loose Eel'. 3.00
4 MBn,'Hot House' 3.00
5 MBn,Octopi in the hot tub 3.00
6 MBn,Prime Minister of
  Klactoveedesteen 3.00
7 MBn,Crime Comics 3.00
8 MBn,Root. 3.00
9 MBn 3.00
10 MBn,Tuesday Ruby 3.00
11 MBn,Watch the Skies 3.00
12 MBn,The Lady Cobras 3.00
13 MBn,Horse Police 3.00
14 MBn,Badger Sells Out 3.00

BAD IDEAS
Apr., 2004
1 (of 2) 48-pg. 6.00
2 48-pg. 6.00

BAD PLANET
Dec., 2005
1 (of 6) 3.00
1 new printing 3.00
2 Alien Death Spiders 3.00
3 Super-Terror 3D 3.50
4 . . . . 3.00
5 The Convict's Story 3.00

BADROCK
Extreme, 1995
1a RLd(p),TM(c),A:Dragon 2.50
1b SPa(ic),A:Savage Dragon 2.50
1c DF(ic) 2.50
2 RLd,ErS(s),V:Girth,A:Savage
  Dragon, flip-book-Grifter/
  Badrock #2 . . . . 2.50
3 RLd,ErS,V:The Overlord 2.50
Ann.#1 I:Gunner, 48-pg. 3.00
Super-Spec. #1 A:Grifter & The
  Dragon. 2.50

BADROCK AND COMPANY
Extreme, 1994–95
1 KG(s) 2.50
1a San Diego Comic Con ed. 3.00
2 RLd(c),Fuji 2.50
3 Overtkill,'Overt Operations' 2.50
4 TBm,MBm,TNu,A:Velocity 2.50
5 A:Grifter 2.50
6 Finale,A:ShadowHawk. 2.50

BALLISTIC
Top Cow, 1995
1 F:Wetworks 3.00
2 F:Wetworks,Jesters
  Transformation 3.00
3 F:Wetworks,final issue. 3.00

BALLISTIC ACTION
Top Cow, 1996
1 MSi(c), pin-ups. 3.00

BALLISTIC IMAGERY
Top Cow, 1995
1 F:Hellcop,Heavy Space,
  Cyberforce,anthology 3.00

BALLISTIC/WOLVERINE
Top Cow/Marvel, 1996
1 Devil's Reign,pt.4,x-over 4.00

BANISHED KNIGHTS
Dec., 2001
1 vampire civil war 3.00
1A variant(c) 3.00
1B holofoil(c). 5.00
2 F:Greyson & Belmiro 3.00

BASTARD SAMURAI
April, 2002
1 (of 3) 3.00
2 thru 3 F:Toshi . . . . @3.00

BATTLESTONE
Extreme, 1994
1 RLd,ErS,MMy,AV 2.50
1a variant cover 3.00
2 RLd,ErS,MMy,AV,I&D:Roarke,
  finale 2.50

BATTLE CHASERS
Cliffhanger, April, 1998
1 JMd, fantasy, team-up 9.00
1a Chromium ed. (5,000 made) . . 35.00
2 JMd,F:Gully 5.00
3 JMd,new ally 4.00
4 JMd,Red Monika 4.00
4a,b,c JMd variant covers . . . . . . @3.00
5 JMd,V:Lord August,with 8-pg.
  Planetary #0 . . . . 3.00
6 JMd 3.00

Battle Chasers #3
© Cliffhanger

IMAGE

6a variant AWa(c) 4.00

WildStorm/DC, Nov., 2000
7 JMd(c)(1:2) 3.00
7a variant JSC(c) (1:4) 4.00
7b variant HuR(c) (1:4) 7.00
8 JMd,V:Harvester 3.00
Prelude #1, JMd, 16-pg. 10.00

BATTLE HYMN
Dec., 2004
1 (of 5) 3.00
2 thru 5 . . . . @3.00

BATTLE OF THE PLANETS
Top Cow, July, 2002
1 AxR 3.00
1a-c variant(c)s . . . . @3.00
1d convention(c) 3.00
1e holofoil edition 6.00
2 AxR,attack on earth begins 3.00
3 AxR,The Firey Phoenix 3.00
4 Zoltar 3.00
5 Spectra connected to suicides. . . 3.00
6 Under A Blood Red Sky,pt.1 . . . . 3.00
7 Under A Blood Red Sky,pt.2 . . . . 3.00
8 Under A Blood Red Sky,pt.3 . . . . 3.00
9 Under A Blood Red Sky,pt.4 . . . . 3.00
10 Aftermath. 3.00
11 Second Encounters. 3.00
12 concl., 48-pg. 5.00
1-shot flip-book Thundercats 5.00
1-shot Mark 3.00
1-shot Battle Book 5.00
1-shot Hell, 48-pg. 5.00
2 animation (c) 5.00
1/2 reprint. 3.00

BATTLE OF THE PLANETS: COUP DE GRAS
Top Cow, June, 2005
1 (of 2) 3.00

BATTLE OF THE PLANETS: MANGA
Top Cow, Oct., 2003
1 . . . . 3.00
2 . . . . 3.00
3 finale 3.00

BATTLE OF THE PLANETS: PRINCESS
Top Cow, 2004
1 (of 6) 3.00
2 thru 6 Princess, pt.2–pt.6 . . . . . @3.00

BATTLE OF THE PLANETS: WITCHBLADE
Top Cow, Jan., 2003
1 48-pg.. . . . . 7.00

BATTLE POPE
June, 2005
1 . . . . 3.00
2 The Zombie Twins 3.00
3 . . . . 3.00
4 . . . . 3.00
5 . . . . 3.00
6 . . . . 3.00
7 Hellcorp in Shambles. 3.00
8 V:Brenda. 3.00
9 New Home. 3.00
10 Celebrity Status. 3.00
11 48-pg. 5.00
12 . . . . 3.50

13 . . . . 3.00
14 Vs. God, conclusion 3.50

BEDLAM
July, 2006
1-shot 48-page. 5.00

BEETLEBORGS
Extreme, Nov., 1996
1 from TV show 2.50

BERZERKERS
Extreme, 1995
1 F:Greylore,Hatchet,Psi-Storm,
  Cross,Wildmane,Youngblood#2 2.50
2 Into the Darkness 2.50
3 Slay Ride 2.50
4 final issue. 2.50

BEYOND AVALON
Jan., 2005
1 Wanderlust, pt.1 . . . . 3.00
2 Wanderlust, pt.2 . . . . 3.50
3 . . . . 3.50

BIG BANG COMICS
Big Bang Studios, 1996
(B&W) Prev.: Caliber
1 F:Mighty Man. 2.50
2 Silver Age Shadowhawk 2.50
3 . . . . 2.50
4 . . . . 3.00
5 Top Secret Origins 3.00
6 Round Table of America and
  Knights of Justice meet, orig.
  mini-series #3 (color). 3.00
7 . . . . 3.00
8 F:Mister U.S. 3.00
9 I:Peter Chefren 3.00
10 F:Galahad 3.00
11 Faulty Towers is destroying
  Midway City 3.00
12 F:The Savage Dragon 3.00
13 by Jeff Weigel, 40-pg.spec. . . . 3.00
14 RB,A:The Savage Dragon 3.00
15 SBi(c),F:Dr. Weird. 3.00
16 F:Thunder Girl. 3.00
17 . . . . 3.00
18 Savage Dragon on Trial 3.00
19 O:Beacon,Hummingbird 3.00
20 F:Knight Watchman,Blitz. 3.00
21 F:Shadow Lady. 3.00
22 The Bird-Man of Midway City . . . 3.00
23 Riddle of the Sphinx, sequel. . . . 3.00
24 History of Big Bang,Vol.1 . . . . . . 4.00
25 Anniv. iss. 4.00
26 Murder by Microphone, concl. . . 3.00
27 History of Big Bang,Vol.2 . . . . . . 4.00
28 Knight of the Living Dead,pt.1 . . 4.00
29 Knight of the Living Dead,pt.2 . . 4.00
30 F:Knight Watchman 4.00
31 F:Knight-Sprite 4.00
32 F:Pink Flamingo 4.00
33 Peril of Parallel Planets 4.00
34 To Save the Gods 4.00
35 Big Bang vs. 1963 . . . . 4.00
Giant Sz. Ann.#1 Ultiman. 5.00
Summer Spec.b&w, 48-pg. (2003). . 5.00
1-shot Round Table of America 3.00

BIG BANG PRESENTS: ULTIMAN FAMILY
Mar., 2005
1-shot F:The Ultimate Ape 3.50

BIG BRUISERS
WildStorm, 1996
1 F:Maul,Impact,Badrock 3.50

BIG HAIR PRODUCTIONS
(B&W) Feb., 2000
1 by Andy Suriano,F:Astro-Bug . . . 3.50
2 . . . . 3.50

Black and White #1
© Hack Studios

BLACK AND WHITE
Hack Studios, 1996
1 ATi,New heroes,'Beginnings' 2.50
2 ATi(p),apparent death 2.50
3 V:Chang. 2.50
Ashcan. 5.00

BLACK ANVIL
Top Cow, 1996
1 & 2 . . . . 2.50

BLACK FLAG
Extreme, 1994
1 B&W Preview. 3.00

BLACK FOREST, THE
Mar., 2004
GN 10.00
GN Book 2 The Castle of Shadows. 7.00

BLACKLIGHT
June, 2005
1 JV 3.00
2 . . . . 3.00
3 Light From A Dead Star 3.00
4 Suffer not a corpse to live, x-over 3.00

BLACK MIST
(B&W) Feb., 2007
1 (of 4) 4.00
2 . . . . 4.00
3 . . . . 4.00
4 . . . . 5.00

BLACK OPS
WildStorm, 1996
1 thru 5 . . . . @2.50

IMAGE

Black Ops #5
© WildStorm

BLACK TIDE
Nov., 2001
1 . . . . 3.00
1a variant(c) 3.00
1b variant(c) 3.00
2 Balance of Power 3.50
3 One Man's Enemy 3.50
4 Deception, Secrets and Lies . . . 3.50

BLAIR WITCH:
DARK TESTAMENTS
Oct., 2000
Spec. IEd,CAd 3.00

BLINDSIDE
Extreme, Aug., 1996
1 MMy & AV, F:Nucgaek Jeno 2.50
2 MMy & AV, Origin continues 2.50

BLISS ALLEY
(B&W) July, 1997
1 BML 3.00
2 BML,F:Wizard Walker 3.00
3 BML,Inky-Dinks 3.00

BLOKHEDZ
Nov., 2003
1 (of 4) 3.00
2 . . . . 3.00
Street Legends, 2004
3 thru 4 . . . . 3.00

BLOODHUNTER
Extreme, Nov., 1996
1 RV, Cabbot Stone rises from the
slab 3.00

BLOOD LEGACY
Top Cow, April, 2000
1 MHw,The Story of Ryan 2.50
1a variant Keu Cha(c). 2.50
1b variant Mike Turner(c) 2.50
2 thru 4 MHw, F:Dr. Ryerson . . . @2.50
1-shot The Young Ones (2003) 4.00

BLOOD NATION
Platinum, Feb., 2007
1 (of 4) 3.00
2 thru 4 . . . . @3.00

BLOODPOOL
Exteme, 1995
1 I:Seoul,Rubbe,Wylder,
'Discharged' 2.50
1a variant cover 2.50
2 The Hills Are Alive 2.50
3 Walk Like an Egyptian 2.50
4 final issue 2.50
[Regular Series] 1996
1 thru 3 JDy. . . . . @2.50

BLOODSTREAM
Jan., 2004
1 (of 4) 3.00
2 of 4 . . . . @3.00

BLOODSTRIKE
Extreme, 1993
1 A:Brigade, Rub the Blood(c)
Blood Brother prelude,x-over . . 3.50
2 I:Lethal, V:Brigade,BloodBrothers,
pt.2,B:BU:Knight 3.00
3 B:ErS(s),ATi(c),V:Coldsnap,Blood
Brothers,pt.4,'Turning Point' . . . 3.00
4 ErS(s). 3.00
5 KG,I:Noble,A:Supreme. 3.00
6 KG(s),CAx,C&J:Chapel,'Inside
Project:Born Again' 3.00
7 KG,RHe,A:Badrock,'Changing
of the Guard' 3.00
8 RHe,A:Spawn,Sleeping & Waking 3.00
9 RHe,Extreme Prejudice,pt.3,
I:Extreme Warrior,ATh,BU: Black
& White 3.00
10 Extreme Prejudice,pt.7,
V:Brigade, B:BU:Knight 3.00
25 I:Cabbot Bloodstrike 3.00
11 ErS(s),ATi(c),V:Coldsnap 3.00
12 ErS(s) 3.00
13 KG,A:Supreme,'BetterOffDead' . 3.00
14 KG(s),CAx,C&J:Chapel. 3.00
15 KG,RHe,A:Badrock,War Games,
pt.1,Extreme Sacrifice begins . 3.00
16 KG,RHe,War Games,pt.3,Extreme
Sacrifice ignites 3.00
17 KIA,V:The Horde. 3.00
18 ExtremeSacrifice,pt.3,x-over. . . 3.00
19 V:The Horde 3.00
20 R:Deadlock New Order. 3.00
21 KA,V:Epiphany New Order 3.00
22 V:The Horde, last issue 3.00
25 see above, after #10
Ashcan. 3.00

BLOODSTRIKE:
ASSASSIN
Extreme, 1995
0 R:Battlestone 3.00
1 Debut new series. 3.00
1a alternate cover. 3.00
2 V:M.D.K. Assassins 3.00
3 V:Persuasion 3.00

BLOODWULF
Extreme, 1995
1 RLd,R:Bloodwulf 2.50
1b Run OJ Run. 2.50
1c Alternate cover. 2.50
1d Alternate cover. 2.50
2 A:Hot Blood 2.50
3 Slippery When Wet 2.50
4 Darkness Gnaws at my Soul,
final issue 2.50
Summer Spec.#1 V:Supreme
Freeferall (1995) 2.50

Bloodwulf #4
© Image/Extreme

BLUE
Aug., 1999
1 Android teenager 2.50
2 by Greg Aronowitz 2.50
3 rescue mission. 2.50

BLUNTMAN
AND CHRONIC
Aug., 2001
GN MiA 15.00

BODY BAGS:
FATHER'S DAY
July, 2005
1 JPn,48-page 6.00
2 JPn,48-page 6.00
1-shot Three The Hard Way 6.00
1-shot One Shot (2006). 6.00

BODYCOUNT
March, 1996
1 KEa,SBs 2.50
2 thru 4 KEa,SBs . . . . @2.50

BOHOS
Flypaper (B&W) 1998
1 by Maggie Whorf & B.Penaranda 3.00
2 F:teenage bohemians 3.00
3 concl. 3.00

BOMB QUEEN
Feb., 2006
1 thru 4 . . . . @3.50
1-shot Bomb Queen vs. Blacklight . 3.50

BOMB QUEEN II
Oct., 2006
1 Queen of Hearts, pt.1 . . . . 3.50
2 . . . . 3.50
3 Queen of Hearts, pt.3 . . . . 3.50

BOMB QUEEN III
Mar., 2007
1 (0f 4) JV, The Good, The Bad
and the Lovely. 3.50
1a variant incentive JLi (c) 3.50
2 thru 4 . . . . @3.50

BOMB QUEEN IV
Aug, 2007
1 (of 4) Suicide Bomber 3.50
2 . . . . 3.50

BONDS
Aug., 2007
1 (of 3) Allegro 4.00
2 Adagio 4.00

BONE
(B&W) Dec., 1995
[Prev.: Cartoon Books]
21 thru 25 . . . . @4.00
26 The Turning. 4.00
27 end of Dragonslayer storyline. . . 4.00
Bone Sourcebook 1.00
reprints with new covers
#1 thru #9. . . . . @3.00
10 rep. 'Great Cow Race' 3.00
Cartoon Books
11 Aftermath of the Great Cow
   Race 3.00
12 . . . . 3.00
13 Thar she blows 3.00
14 . . . . 3.00
15 Double or nothing 3.00
16 hiding from the Rat Creatures . . 3.00
17 with 5 new pages 3.00
18 Betrayed 3.00
19 'Three cheers for Dragon-slayer
   Phoney Bone' 3.00
20 Phoney Bone vs. Lucius 3.00

BONE REST
July, 2005
1 . . . . 3.00
2 Opificium Dei, pt.1 . . . . 3.00
3 Opificium Dei,pt.2 . . . . 3.00
4 Opificium Dei, concl. 3.00
5 Second Coming, pt.1 . . . . 3.00
6 Second Coming, pt.2 . . . . 3.00
7 Second Coming, pt.3 . . . . 3.00
8 Second Coming, pt.4 . . . . 3.00

BOOF
TMP, 1994
1 . . . . 2.50
2 Meathook. 2.50
3 Joyride 2.50
4 thru 6 . . . . @2.50

BOOF AND THE
BRUISE CREW
TMP, 1994
1 . . . . 2.50
2 thru 5 . . . . @2.50
6 I:Mortar,O:Bruise Crew 2.50

BOOK OF SHADOWS
April, 2006
1 (of 2) 3.50
2 . . . . 3.50

BRASS
WildStorm, 1996
1 Rib,AWa,Folio Edition 3.50
2 Rib,AWa. 2.50
3 Rib,AWa,concl. 2.50

BRAWK
(B&W) Oct, 2007
1 (of 3) 3.00

BRIGADE
Extreme, 1993
[1st Series]
1 RLd(s),MMy,I:Brigade,Genocide . 3.50
1a Gold ed. 7.00
2 RLd(s),V:Genocide,w/coupon#4 . 4.00
2a w/o coupon 2.25
2b Gold ed. 4.00
3 I:Birds of Prey,V:Genocide. 2.50
4 CyP,Youngblood#5 flip 2.50
[2nd Series]
0 RLd(s),ATi(c),JMs,NRd,I:Warcry,
   A:Emp,V:Youngblood. 2.50
1 I:Boone,Hacker,V:Bloodstrike,
   Blood Brothers,pt.1 . . . . 2.75
1a Gold ed. 3.00
2 C:Coldsnap,Blood Brothers,pt.3 . 3.00
3 ErS(s),GP(c),MMy,NRd(i),I:Roman
   V:Bloodstrike,Blood Brothers,
   pt.5. 2.50
4 Rip(s),MMy,RHe,Changes,
   BU:Lethal. 2.50
5 Rip(s),MMy,It's A VeryDeepSea. . 2.50
6 Rip(s),MMy,I:Coral,Warlok,
   BU:Hackers Tale 2.50
7 Rip(s),MMy,V:Warlok 2.50
8 ErS(s),MMy,Extreme Prejudice,
   pt.2,BU:Black & White,pt.5 . . . . 2.50
9 ErS(s),MMy,Extreme Prejudice
   pt.6,ATh,BU:Black & White 2.50
25 ErS(s),MMy,D:Kayo,Coldsnap,
   Thermal 2.50
26 Images of Tomorrow 2.50
10 Extreme Prejudice 2.50
11 WildC.A.T.S. 2.50
12 Battlestone 2.50
13 Thermal. 2.50
14 Teamate deaths 2.50
15 MWm,R:Roman Birds of Prey . . . 2.50
16 ExtremeSacrifice,pt.4,x-over. . . . 2.50
17 MWn,I:New Team 2.50
18 I:The Shape New Order 2.50
19 MWn,F:Troll,Glory. 2.50
20 MWn,alien cult saga,concl. 2.50
21 F:ShadowHawk. 2.50
22 Supreme Apocalypse,pt.4 . . . . . . 2.50
23 . . . . 2.50
24 . . . . 2.50
25 & 26 see above
27 Extreme Babewatch 2.50
Sourcebook 3.00

Brigade #4
© Image/Extreme

BRIT
July, 2003
1-shot b&w, 48-pg. 5.00
1-shot Brit: Cold Death 5.00
1-shot Red,White,Black & Blue 5.00
Jan., 2007
1 . . . . 3.00
2 . . . . 3.00
3 . . . . 3.00

BUGBOY
(B&W) June 1998
1-shot, by Mark Lewis, 48-pg. 4.00

BULLETPROOF MONK
Flypaper, Nov., 1998
1 in San Francisco 3.00
2 N.Y. Chinatown 3.00
3 conclusion 3.00
1-shot Tales of the B P M 3.00

BURGLAR BILL
(B&W) Nov., 2004
1 (of 6) by Paul Grist 3.00
2 thru 6 . . . . @3.00

BUTCHER KNIGHT
Top Cow, July, 2000
1 DT,F:Luther Washington 2.50
1a variant(c) MS (1:3). 2.50
1b variant(c) DT (1:3) 2.50
2 DT 2.50
3 DT,Blood & Gore 2.50
4 DT,concl. 3.00

CAPES
Sept., 2003
1 thru 3 . . . . @3.00

CARVERS
Flypaper, Oct., 1998
1 F:five snowboarders 3.00
2 J:Crazy Jack 3.00
3 V:Evil Yeti. 3.00

CASANOVA
June, 2006
1 . . . . 2.50
2 thru 6 . . . . @2.50
7 thru 10 . . . . 2.00

CASEFILES:
SAM AND TWITCH
May, 2003
1 Have You Seen Me?,pt.1. . . . . . . 3.00
2 thru 6 Have You Seen
   Me?, pt.2 thru pt.6 . . . . @3.00
7 Skeletons,pt.1 . . . . 3.00
8 Skeletons,pt.2 . . . . 3.00
9 Skeletons,pt.3 . . . . 3.00
10 Skeletons,pt.4 . . . . 3.00
11 Skeletons,pt.5 . . . . 3.00
12 Skeletons,pt.6 . . . . 3.00
13 Cops and Robbers 2.50
14 Ancient Chinese Secret,pt.1 . . . . 2.50
15 Ancient Chinese Secret,pt.2 . . . . 2.50
16 Ancient Chinese Secret,pt.3 . . . . 2.50
17 Ancient Chinese Secret,pt.4 . . . . 2.50
18 Ancient Chinese Secret,pt.5 . . . . 2.50
19 Ancient Chinese Secret,pt.6 . . . . 2.50
20 Fathers and Daughters,pt.1 . . . . 2.50
21 Fathers and Daughters, pt.2 . . . . 2.50
22 Fathers and Daughters, pt.3 . . . . 2.50
23 . . . . 3.00
24 . . . . 3.00
25 Fathers and Daughters. 3.00

IMAGE

Casual Heroes #1
© Image/Motown

CASUAL HEROES
Motown, 1996
1 .... 2.50
2 thru 6 .... @2.50

CELESTINE
Extreme, 1996
1 .... 2.50
2 .... 2.50

CHANNEL ZERO
(B&W) 1998
1 by Brian Wood.............. 3.00
2 .... 3.00
3 gone global 3.00
4 Filter.................... 3.00
5 Brink of Millennium crash 3.00
6 Sound system 3.00

CHAPEL
Extreme, 1995
1 BWn,F:Chapel............... 3.50
2 V:Colonel Black 3.00
2a variant cover 2.50

[Regular Series]
1 BWn,F:Chapel 2.50
1a variant cover 2.50
2 V:Giger.................... 2.50
3 V:Giger.................... 2.50
4 Extreme Babewatch........... 2.50
5 Hell on Earth,pt.1............ 2.50
6 Hell on Earth,pt.2............ 2.50
7 Shadowhunt x-over,pt.2........ 2.50

CHASSIS
Nov., 1999
1 F:Chassis McBain 3.00
2 .... 3.00
2a variant Matt Busch(c)......... 3.00
3 Gizmotech Industries.......... 3.00
4 .... 3.00
4a Collector's variant(c) 4.00
5 Slic's One Shot, flip-cover 3.00

CHEMIST, THE
July, 2007
1. .... 3.50
2 .... 3.50

CHILDHOOD'S END
(B&W) Oct., 1997
1 (of 5) JCf,community playground. 3.00

THE C.H.I.X.
THAT TIME FORGOT
Studiosaurus, Aug., 1998
1 F:Good Girl 3.00

CHOLLY AND FLYTRAP
Nov., 2004
1 (of 4) by Arthur Suydam 5.00
2 Center City................. 5.00
3 .... 5.00
4 .... 5.00
Spec. Date With The Devil, 48-pg. . 6.00

CITY OF HEROES
Top Cow, May, 2005
1 Hard Crash, pt.1 .... 3.00
2 Hard Crash, pt.2 .... 3.00
3 Hard Crash, pt.3 .... 3.00
4 Smoke and Mirrors,pt.1........ 3.00
5 Smoke and Mirrors,pt.2........ 3.00
6 Smoke and Mirrors,pt.3........ 3.00
7 DJu 3.00
8 DJu 3.00
9 DJu 3.00
10 thru 16 .... @3.00
17 .... 3.00
18 Ladies Night 3.00
19 Portals................... 3.00
20 Threat from the Rikti,final issue . 3.00

CITY OF SILENCE
May, 2000
1 (of 3) WEI,GEr,F:Silencers 2.50
1a variant GEr,3-D(c)(1:4) 2.50
2 WEI,GEr................... 2.50
3 WEI,GEr................... 2.50

CLOCK MAKER, THE
Jan., 2003
1 (of 12) 2.50
2 thru 7 .... @2.50
5 to 7 (of 12) cancelled
Spec. Act One (#1ñ#4) 5.00
Spec. Act Two (#5ñ#7).......... 5.00
Spec. Act Three 5.00

CLOUDFALL
Nov., 2003
1-shot b&w 48-pg.............. 5.00
1-shot Cloudfall: Loose Ends...... 5.00

CODE BLUE
(B&W) April, 1998
1 by Jimmie Robinson 3.00
2 F.I.T.E. creates havoc 3.00

CODENAME:
STYKE FORCE
Top Cow, 1994
1A MS(s),BPe,JRu(i)............ 3.50
1B Gold Embossed Cover 6.00
1C Blue Embossed Cover 9.00
2 MS(s),BPe,JRu(i)............ 2.50
3 MS(s),BPe,JRu(i)............ 2.50
4 MS(s),BPe,JRu(i)............ 2.50
5 MS(s),BPe,JRu(i)............ 2.50
6 MS(s),BPe,JRu(i)............ 2.50
7 MS(s),BPe,JRu(i)............ 2.50
8A Cyblade poster (Tucci) 4.00
8B Shi poster (Silvestri) 4.00
8C Tempest poster (Tan) 2.50
9 New Teamate................ 2.50
10 SvG, B:New Adventure 2.50
11 F:Bloodbow................ 2.50
12 F:Stryker................. 2.50
13 SvG(s),F:Strkyer 2.50
14 New Jobs 2.50
Spec.#0 O:Stryke Force......... 2.50

COMBAT
Jan., 1996
1 .... 2.50
2 .... 2.50

COMMON FOE
May, 2005
1 (of 5) KG 3.50
2 thru 5 KG .... @3.50

COMMON GROUNDS
Top Cow, Jan., 2004
1 (of 6) DJu................. 4.00
2 DJu,SK................... 3.50
3 thru 6 DJu,SK.............. @3.00

COMPASS
Aug., 2007
1 .... 3.00
2 thru 3 .... @3.00

CONSUMED
Platinum, July, 2007
1 (of 4) JLi(c) 3.00
2 thru 4 .... @3.00

COSMIC RAY
June, 1999
1 by Stephen Blue 3.00
1a alternate cover (1:2) 3.00
2 F:Raymond Mann 3.00
3 F:Star Marshalls............. 3.00

COW, THE
Top Cow, April, 2000
1 Spring edition............... 3.00
2 Summer edition 3.00
3 Spring edition 2001 .... 3.00

CRAWL SPACE:
XXXOMBIES
Oct, 2007
1 .... 3.00

CREATURE FROM
THE DEPTHS
July, 2007
1-shot 4.00

CREECH, THE
TMP, Oct., 1997
1 GCa,DaM,F:Chirs Rafferty...... 2.50
2 GCa,DaM,F:Dennis Dross...... 2.50

[GREG CAPULLO'S
ORIGINAL] CREECH
TMP, Aug., 2001
1 A Vision of Death............. 2.50
2 Awakenings 2.50
3 The Resurrection............. 2.50

CREECH, THE:
OUT FOR BLOOD
July, 2001
1 GCa,Out for Blood, Book 1 ..... 5.00
2 GCa,48-pg. 5.00
3 GCa,Killing Machine perfected .. 5.00

IMAGE

CREED: UTOPIATE
Jan., 2002
1 (of 4) TKn. 3.50
2 TKn,disorder in dreamworld 3.00
3 TKn,fantasy vs. reality 3.00
4 TKn,Death of Creed. 3.00

CREEPS
Oct., 2001
1 (of 4) TMd 3.50
2 TMd,I:Gurgle,Chitter 3.00
3 TMd,Genesys Corporation. 3.00
4 TMd,through their eyes 3.00

Crimson #4
© Image/Cliffhanger

CRIMSON
Cliffhanger, May, 1998
1 BAu,HuR,F:Alex Elder, vampire
  'Dawn to Dusk' 5.00
1a variant AWa(c) 7.00
1b Chromium Edition 12.00
2 BAu,HuR,V:Jelly-Bats,
  'Unlife Story' 3.00
2a variant AAd(c) 6.00
3 BAu,HuR,V:Rose,Payment
  in Blood 4.00
4 BAu,HuR,F:Red Hood,Children
  of Judas,pt.1 . . . . 3.50
5 BAu,HuR,A:Red Hood,Children
  of Judas,pt.2 . . . . 3.50
6 BAu,HuR,A:Red Hood,Children
  of Judas,pt.3 . . . . 3.50
7 BAu,HuR,Christmas day 3.00
½ Dynamic Forces exclusive 4.00
WildStorm/DC, 1999
8 thru 23 BAu,HuR . . . . @2.50
24 BAu,HuR, final issue. 3.50
Spec.#1 Scarlet X: Blood on the
  Moon, BAu,HuR,one-shot 4.00
Spec. Crimson Sourcebook #1 . . . 3.00

CRIMSON PLAGUE
June, 2000
1 GP,64-pg. 3.00
2 GP,Sole Survivor 2.50
3 GP,Blood trail. 2.50
4 GP,Plague hits home 2.50

CROSS BRONX, THE
Sept., 2006
1 . . . . 3.00

1a & 2a variant (c) . . . . @3.00
2 thru 4 . . . . @3.00

CROW, THE
TMP, Feb., 1999
1 JMu,F:Eric Draven. 3.00
1a variant TP cover (1:4) 3.00
2 JMu,hunt for killers 3.00
3 JMu,justice for killers 3.00
4 JMu,Line Between Devil's Teeth . 3.00
5 JMu,Skin of an Angel,pt.1 . . . . . 3.00
6 JMu,Skin of an Angel,pt.2 . . . . . 3.00
7 JMu,Touch of Evil,pt.1 . . . . 3.00
8 JMu,Touch of Evil,pt.2 . . . . 3.00
9 JMu,Wings and Black Feathers. . 3.00
Crow Mag.#1, 56-pg. rep. 5.00
Crow Mag.#2 . . . . 5.00
Crow Mag.#3 . . . . 5.00

CRUSH, THE
Motown Jan., 1996
1 Mini-series 3.00
2 Let Me Light Your Fire 3.00
3 Million Dollar Smile 3.00
4 . . . . 3.00
5 The Hip Hop Slide 3.00

CRYPT
Extreme, 1995
1 A:Prophet. 2.50
1a variant cover 2.50
2 A:Prophet. 2.50

CRYPTICS, THE
June, 2006
1 . . . . 3.50
2 To Heck and Back 3.50

[JIM LEE'S]
C-23
WildStorm, April, 1998
1 BCi,JMi,F:Corben Helix 2.50
2 JMi,TC(c),V:Angelans 2.50
3 JMi,TC(c),with game card 2.50
4 JMi,Corbin, banished. 2.50
5 JMi,RCo(c),Queen Mother. 2.50
5a variant JLe(c) (1:4) 2.50
6 JMi,RCo(c),V:Hyper Shock
  Troopers 2.50
7 JMi,RCo(c),Hail to the Queen . . . 2.50
8 JMi,RCo(c),Long Live the King . . 2.50

C-23 #8
© WildStorm

CURSED
Top Cow, Sept., 2003
1 (of 4) It is Coming 3.00
2 The Walking Dead 3.00
3 The Nature of Curses 3.00
4 It is a Gift. 3.00

CURSE OF THE SPAWN
TMP, Sept., 1996
1 DT,DaM,F:Daniel Lianso 6.00
1a B&W variant. 16.00
2 DT,DaM,Dark Future,pt.2:
  Blood Lust 5.00
3 DT,DaM,Dark Future,pt.3:
  Corpse Candles. 5.00
4 DT,DaM 4.00
5 DT,DaM,Sam & Twitch search
  for Gretchen Culver. 3.00
6 DT,DaM,Sam & Twitch pursue
  Suture 3.00
7 DT,DaM,Suture is captured 3.00
8 DT,DaM,Suture escapes police
  custody 3.00
9 DT,DaM,Angela's secret origin . . 5.00
10 DT,DaM,Angela, Spawn Slayer. . 3.50
11 DT,DaM,Angela's story, concl. . . 3.50
12 DT,DaM,Jessica Priest, movie
  photo(c) 3.50
13 DT,DaM 'Heart of Darkness'. . . . 3.50
14 DT,DaM,Jessica, concl. 3.50
15 DT,DaM,Tempt an Angel,pt.1 . . . 3.50
16 DT,DaM,Tempt an Angel,pt.2 . . . 3.50
17 DT,DaM 3.50
18 DT,DaM,F:Tony Twist 3.50
19 DT,Curse & Tony Twist 3.50
20 DT,DaM,Monsters & Mythology . 3.50
21 DT,DaM,Zeus Must Die. 3.50
22 DT,F:Ryan Hatchett 3.50
23 DT,TM,R:Overkill 3.50
24 DT,TM,Pandemic 3.50
25 DT,TM,'Heart of Hell'. 2.50
26 DT,TM,V:The Crocodile. 2.50
27 DT,TM,F:Marc Simmons. 2.50
28 DT,TM,V:Suture 2.50
29 DT,TM,A:Jonathan Edward
  Custer 2.50

CYBERFORCE
Top Cow, 1992–93
[Limited Series]
0 WS,O:Cyber Force 2.50
1 MS,I:Cyberforce,w/coupon#3 . . . 5.00
1a w/o coupon 3.00
2 MS,V:C.O.P.S. 3.50
3 MS 2.50
4 MS,V:C.O.P.S,BU:Codename
  Styke Force. 2.50
[Regular Series] 1993
1 EcS(s),MS,SW. 2.50
1B Gold Foil Logo. 6.00
2 EcS(s),MS,SW,Killer Instinct
  #2,A:Warblade. 2.50
2B Silver Embossed Cover 6.00
3 EcS(s),MS,SW,Killer Instinct #4,
  A:WildC.A.T.S. 2.50
3B Gold Embossed Cover 6.00
4 EcS(s),MS,Ballistic 2.50
5 EcS(s),MS 2.50
6 EcS(s),MS,Ballistic's Past 2.50
7 S.H.O.C.s. 2.50
8 . . . . 2.50
9 A:Huntsman 2.50
10 A:Huntsman 2.50
10a Alternate Cover. 2.50
10b Silver Seal Oz-Con 500c 9.00
11 . . . . 2.50
12 T.I.M.M.I.E. goes wild 2.50
13 EcS,MS,O:Cyberdata 2.50
14 EcS,MSI,V:T.I.M.M.I.E. 2.50
15 New Cyberdata Threat 2.50

IMAGE

Cyberforce #4
© *Top Cow*

16 O:Ripclaw 2.50
17 Regrouping 2.50
18 thru 24 . . . . @2.50
25 . . . . 4.00
26 KWo 2.50
27 F:Ash. 2.50
27a variant JQ&JP(c) (1:4) 4.00
28 A:Gabriel 2.50
29 . . . . 2.50
30 ScL,'Devil's Reign' tie-in 2.50
31 The team in conflict 2.50
32 Cyblade leads rejuvenated team 2.50
33 KWo, Cheleene in midst of
    civil war 2.50
34 KWo,Royal Blood,pt.3. . . . . 2.50
35 BTn,Royal Blood, concl. 2.50
Ashcan 1 (San Diego) 4.00
Ashcan 1 (signed) 6.00
Sourcebook 1 . . . . 2.50
Sourcebook 2 I.W.Zero 2.50
Ann.#1 O:Velocity 2.50
Ann.#2 . . . . 3.00

Top Cow, March, 2006
0 MS 3.00
1 (of 2) RMz 3.00
2 . . . . 3.00
2a variant b&w (c). 3.00
3 . . . . 3.00
3a variant b&w (c). 3.00
4 . . . . 3.00
5 . . . . 3.00
5a variant (c). 3.00
6 Who will die 3.00
6a variant (c). 3.00
1-Shot Cyberforce/X-Men (2006). . . 4.00

CYBERFORCE/ CODE-NAME STRYKEFORCE: OPPOSING FORCES
Sept., 1995
1 V:Dangerous Threat. 2.50
2 Team vs. Team. 2.50

CYBERFORCE ORIGINS
Top Cow, 1995
1 O:Cyblade 2.50
1B Gold Seal 1000c 6.00
2 O:Stryker 2.50
3 O:Impact 2.50
4 Misery 3.00

CYBERFORCE UNIVERSE SOURCEBOOK
Top Cow, 1994–95
1 . . . . 2.50
2 MS,BTn 2.50

CYBERNARY
WildStorm, 1995–96
1 (of 5) mini-series 2.50
2 thru 5 . . . . @2.50

CYBERPUNX
Extreme, 1996
1 and 2 . . . . @3.00
3 RLe & Ching Lau,F:Drake 3.00

CYBLADE: PILOT SEASON
Top Cow, Sept., 2007
1 . . . . 3.00

CYBLADE/SHI
1995
1 The Battle for Independents 3.00

CY-GOR
TMP, July, 1999
1 RV,I:Fatima,Frankie & Zevon . . . 2.50
2 RV,Fire in the Mind,pt.2 . . . . 2.50
3 RV,Needles and Pins. 2.50
4 RV, Exquisite Corpse 2.50
5 RV 2.50
6 RV, the Terraplane 2.50
7 RV,Young Doctor Acula 2.50

DAMNED
Homage, June, 1997
1 (of 4) StG, MZ & DRo. 2.50
2 StG, MZ & DRo,F:Mick Thorne . . 2.50
3 StG, MZ & DRo 2.50
4 StG, MZ & DRo 2.50

DANGER GIRL
WildStorm/Cliffhanger 1998
1 JSC,AGo,'Dangerously Yours,'
    40-pg. 8.00
1a chromium edition, 40-pg. 42.00
1b Tour Edition 15.00
2 I:Johnny Barracuda,'Dangerous
    Liaisons'. 5.00
3 in Switzerland 4.00
3a variant AH(c) 5.00
3b variant TC(c) 5.00
4 I:Major Maxim 3.00
5 JSC,AGo 2.50
5a variant JMd(c) 9.00

WildStorm/DC, 1999
6 JSC,SW 2.50
6a variant JMd(c) 5.00
6b variant HuR(c) 4.00
7 JSC,SW,concl.,48-pg. 6.00

DARING ESCAPES
TMP, 1998
1 ANi,F:Harry Houdini 3.00
2 ANi,search for Mystical Heart . . . 2.50
3 A:Kimiel 2.50
4 conclusion 2.50

DARK ANGEL: PHOENIX RESURRECTION
May, 2000
1 by Kia Asamiya, color manga . . . 3.00
2 thru 4 . . . . @3.00
1a thru 3a variant(c) . . . . @3.00

Darkchylde #0
© *Homage*

DARKCHYLDE
See: Maximum, 1996
1 Image reoffer 5.00
1C flip-book-Glory/Angel,Angels in
    Hell,pt.1, San Diego Con. 4.00
1D remastered, RLd(c). 6.00
2 Image reoffer 5.00
2a variant cover 3.00
2b remastered, with poster 2.50
3 Image reoffer 3.50
3a remastered, with poster 2.50

Image, 1997
4 RQu,Ariel & Kauldron's past 5.00
5 RQu,No one here gets out alive . 4.00

Homage, 1998
0 RQu,Ariel's back, Ariel's past. . . 2.50

DARKCHYLDE/GLORY
Extreme
1-shot, four variant covers, by
    RLd, RQu, JDy & PtL 3.00

DARKCHYLDE: THE DIARY
May, 1997
1-shot, RQu et al,diary excerpts . . . 5.00

DARKCHYLDE: THE LEGACY
WildStorm, 1998
1 RQu,F:Ariel 2.50
2 RQu 2.50

WildStorm/DC, 1999
3 RQu,A:Silencer 2.50
4 RQu,Carnival of Fools 2.50
4a RQu,AAd(c), variant (c) 2.50
Summer Swimsuit Spectacular #1 . 4.00
Spec.Dreams of the Darkchylde #0 . 2.50

DARKCHYLDE/ WITCHBLADE
Top Cow, July, 2000
1 RQu,Nightmare City. 2.50

DARK CROSSINGS
Top Cow, May, 2000
Spec. #1 Dark Cloud Rising. 6.00
Spec. #2 Dark Cloud Overhead. . . 6.00

IMAGE

DARKER IMAGE
1993
1 BML,BCi(s),RLd,SK,JLe,I:Blood
 Wulf,Deathblow,Maxx 4.00
1a Gold logo(c). 8.00
1b White(c) 6.00
Ashcan 1 . . . . 4.00

DARKMINDS
1998
1 PtL,cyberpunk,detective 8.00
2 Neon Dragon 5.00
2a variant cover 2.50
3 PtL,A:Neon Dragons 2.50
4 PtL,Paradox killer. 2.50
5 PtL,Unlikely friends, enemies . . . 3.00
6 PtL,Aurora Industries. 3.00
7 PtL,V:Mamuro Hayabusa. 3.00
8 Conclusion,1st story arc 2.50
½ PtL,Cyborg dreams. 2.50
VOL. II Feb., 2000
1 JMd(c) one year later. 2.50
1a variant PtL(c). 2.50
1b variant Omar Dogan(c) 2.50
2 Changing Faces. 2.50
2a variant PtL(c). 2.50
2b variant Michael Turner(c). 2.50
2c variant(c) 2.50
3 PtL(c),F:Reiko Tetsunori 2.50
3a variant Omar Dogan(c) 2.50
3b variant JQ(c) 2.50
4 PtL,cyborg attack. 2.50
5 PtL,The Prize. 2.50
6 PtL,9mm Answers 2.50
7 PtL,The Hunger 2.50
8 PtL,Born Again. 2.50
9 PtL,A Million and One 2.50
10 PtL,concl. 2.50
#0 The Bullet 2.50
#0a variant(c). 2.50

DARKMINDS: MACROPOLIS
Jan., 2002
1 (of 8) PtL 3.00
1a variant(c) 3.00
2 F:Tiny. 3.00
2a variant PtL(c) 3.00

DARKNESS, THE
Top Cow, 1996
0 Preview edition,B&W 15.00
½ 15.00
½ variant cover 22.00
1/2 rep.+new story (2001),MS 3.00
1 GEn,MS,Coming of Age 20.00
1a Dark cover 10.00
1b Platinum cover. 25.00
2 GEn,MS 7.00
3 GEn,MS,Jackie pursued by
 many foes 6.00
4 GEn,MS,Jackie explores
 Darkness power 6.00
5 GEn,MS,New York gangs on
 verge of all-out war 5.00
6 GEn,MS,F:JackieEstacado,concl. 4.00
7 MS 4.00
7a variant(c) 9.00
8 JBz,retribution 3.00
8a MS(c)(1:4) 7.00
9 Family Ties,pt.2,x-over 5.00
10 Family Ties,pt.3,x-over 6.00
11 GEn,MS,Hearts of Darkness . . 3.50
11a Chromium(c) 19.00
11b variant(c). 5.00
12 GEn,Hearts of Darkness. 3.00
13 GEn,Hearts of Darkness 3.00
14 GEn,JBz,Hearts of Darkness . . . 3.00
15 JBz,Spear of Destiny,pt.1 . . . . 3.00

The Darkness #27
© Top Cow

16 JBz,Spear of Destiny,pt.2 . . . . . 3.00
17 JBz,Spear of Destiny,pt.3 . . . . . 3.00
18 JBz,aftermath 3.00
19 JBz,No Mercy,pt.1. . . . . 2.50
20 JBz,No Mercy,pt.2. . . . . 2.50
21 JBz,Wynnwood 2.50
22 JBz,Where is Jenny? 2.50
23 JBz,SLo,new characters. 2.50
24 JBz,SLo,road trip to Vegas . . . 2.50
25 JBz,SLo,48-pg. 3.50
26 JBz,SLo,A:Joey Scarpaggio 2.50
27 SLo,FBI continues assault 2.50
28 Darkness/Witchblade,pt.4,x-over 2.50
29 SLo,High Noon,pt.1 . . . . 2.50
30 SLo,High Noon,pt.2 . . . . 2.50
31 SLo,High Noon,pt.3 . . . . 2.50
32 SLo,Dark Days Ahead 2.50
33 SLo,Capris Castagliano,pt.1. . . . 2.50
34 SLo,Capris Castagliano,pt.2 . . . 2.50
35 SLo,tour of his life. 2.50
36 SLo,Ripclaw,pt.3 . . . . 2.50
37 SLo,F:Robert Bearclaw. 2.50
38 SLo,V:Conquistator. 2.50
39 SLo,Jackie & Capris combine. . . 2.50
40 DK,Darkness falls?. 2.50
40a variant MS(c) 2.50
various foil (c). . . . . @9.00
Coll.Ed.#1,rep. #1–#2 . . . . 5.00
Coll.Ed.#2,rep. #3–#4, 56-pg. 5.00
Coll.Ed.#3,rep. #5–#6, 56-pg. 5.00
Coll.Ed.#3, with slipcase. 10.00
Coll.Ed.#4,rep. #7–#8 . . . . 5.00
Coll.Ed.#1,deluxe,rep.#1–#6 . . . . 15.00
Coll.Ed.#5,rep.#11–#12 . . . . 6.00
Coll.Ed.#6,rep.#13–#14 . . . . 6.00
Spec. Infinity, SLo 3.50
Darkness/Witchblade,pt.3 x-over . . 4.00
Spec.#1, Dark Ages 5.00
Spec. Vol. 2 #1 raw (no color) 3.00
1-shot Darkness/Hulk. 3.00

DARKNESS
Top Cow, Nov., 2002
1 PJe,DK. 3.00
1a holofoil(c). 6.00
2 DK 3.00
2 Megacon edition 6.00
3 DK 3.00
4 Under Cover of Darkness 3.00
5 You Lose Some 3.00
6 As the World Turns 3.00
7 PJe,F:Ernie Palanco 3.00
7a alternate (c) 3.00

8 PJe,Law by Jackie Estacado. . . . 3.00
9 PJe,Search for Blue Goldfish . . . 3.00
10 RMz,Hong Kong 3.00
11 RMz,Dragons and darklings 3.00
12 RMz,Army of assassins 3.00
13 RMz,Mystical Dragons 3.00
14 Streets Run Red,pt.1 . . . . 3.00
15 Streets Run Red,pt.2 . . . . 3.00
16 Streets Run Red,pt.3 . . . . 3.00
17 Hell House, pt.1 . . . . 3.00
18 Hell House, pt.2 . . . . 3.00
19 Hell House, pt.3 . . . . 3.00
20 Hell House, pt.4 . . . . 3.00
21 The Reckoning 3.00
22 All in the Family ,pt.1 . . . . 3.00
23 All in the Family ,pt.2 . . . . 3.00
24 All in the Family, pt.3. . . . . 3.00
1-shot Wanted Dead (2004) 3.00
1-shot Black Sails (2005). 3.00
E3 variant (c) reprint 3.00
Spec. Darkness/Batman, SLo,MS,
 x-over (1999). 6.00
1-shot Darkness/Vampirella (2005) . 3.00
1-shot Darkness/Wolverine (2006) . 3.00

DARKNESS, THE:
Top Cow, Dec., 2006
Level 0 . . . . 3.00
Level 1 . . . . 3.00
Level 1a thru b variant (c)s . . . . . @3.00
Level 1c variant incentive (c) 3.00
Level 2 . . . . 3.00
Level 2a thru b variant (c)s . . . . . @3.00
Level 3 . . . . 3.00
Level 3a variant (c) 3.00
Level 4 . . . . 3.00
Level 4a variant (c) 3.00
Level 5 . . . . 3.00
Level 5a variant (c) 3.00

DARKNESS, THE/PITT
Top Cow, Dec., 2006
Spec. First Look 3.00
Spec. First Look Wizard World . . . 10.00

DARKNESS, THE/ SUPERMAN
DC/Top Cow, Dec., 2004
1 (of 2) RMz(s) 3.00
2 RMz(s). 3.00

DARKNESS AND TOMB RAIDER
Top Cow, Mar., 2005
1-shot JaL,BTn. 3.00
1-shotA B&W cover 3.00

DARKNESS VS. MR. HYDE
Top Cow, Aug., 2005
1-shot Monster War #4 x-over 3.00
1-shotA variant (c) 3.00

DARK REALM
Oct., 2000
1 by Taeson Chang. 3.00
2 S.F.P.D. in chaos 3.00
3 flip-book 3.00
4 Prophecy is fulfilled 3.00

DARK SECTOR ZERO
Top Cow, Aug., 2007
1-shot BSz 3.00

DART
1996
1 thru 3 Jozef Szekeres . . . . . . @3.00

Dart #2
© Image

DAVID AND GOLIATH
Sept., 2003
1	3.00
2	3.00
3	3.00

DAWN: THREE TIERS
June, 2003
1 thru 4 JLi	@3.00
5 Hell Hath No Fury	3.00
6	3.00

DEADLANDS
July, 1999
GN 1-shot role-play tie-in	7.00

DEADLY DUO, THE
Highbrow, 1994–95
1 A:Kill-Cat	2.50
2 A:Pitt, O:Kid Avenger	2.50
3 A:Roman, O:Kill-Cat	2.50

[Second Series] 1995
1 A:Spawn	2.50
2 A:Savage Dragon	2.50
3 A:Grunge, Gen13	2.50
4 Movie Mayhem	2.50

DEADWORLD
(B&W) Mar., 2005
1	3.50
2 thru 6	@3.50
7 Slaughterhouse, pt.1	4.00
8 Slaughterhouse, pt.2	4.00

DEATHBLOW
WildStorm, 1993–96
1 JLe,MN,I:Cybernary	3.00
2 JLe,BU:Cybernary	2.50
3 JLe(a&s),BU:Cybernary	3.00
4 JLe(s),TSe,BU:Cybernary	2.50
5 JLe(s),TSe,BU:Cybernary	2.50
5a different cover	5.00
6 Black Angel	2.50
7	2.50
8 Black Angel	2.50
9 The Four Horsemen	2.50
10 Michael Cray, Sister Mary	2.50
11 A:Four Horsemen	2.50
12 Final Battle	2.50
13 New Story Arc	2.50

14 A:Johnny Savoy	2.50
15 F:Michael Cray	2.50
16 TvS,BWS(c),WildStorm Rising,pt.6,w/2 cards	2.50
16a Newsstand ed.	2.50
17 V:Gammorran Hunter Killers	2.50
18 F:Cybernary	2.50
19 F:Cybernary	2.50
20 A:Gen 13	3.50
21 Brothers in Arms,pt.2,A:Gen13	3.50
22 Brothers in Arms,pt.3	2.50
23 Brothers in Arms,pt.4	2.50
24 Brothers in Arms,pt.5	3.00
25 Brothers in Arms,pt.6	2.50
26 Fire From Heaven prelude	2.50
27 Fire From Heaven,pt.8	3.00
28 Fire From Heaven,finale,pt.3	2.50
29 last issue	2.50
0 JLe (1996)	3.00
Ashcan 1	4.00

DEATHBLOW/WOLVERINE
WildStorm, Sept., 1996
1 RiB, AWs,x-over, set in San Francisco's Chinatown	2.50
2 RiB, AWs,concl	2.50

DEATH, JR.
Apr., 2005
1 (of 3)	5.00
2	5.00
3	5.00

Series 2, July, 2006
1 48-pg.	5.00
2 48-pg.	5.00
3 48-pg.	5.00

DEATHMATE X-OVER
See: COLOR PUB.

DECEPTION, THE
(B&W) Flypaper, Jan., 1999
1 (of 3) F:Jordan Risk, magician	3.00
2 Framed for murder	3.00
3 V:South American Drug Cartel	3.00

DEEP SLEEPER
Aug., 2004
1 & 2 See B&W section	
3 The Vacant	3.00
4 conclusion	3.00
Omnibus rep.#1 & #2	6.00

DEFCON 4
WildStorm, 1996
1 mini-series	2.50
2	2.50
3	2.50
4	2.50

DEFIANCE
Feb., 2002
1 The Messenger,pt.1	3.00
2 thru 4 The Messenger,pt.2–pt.4	@3.00
5 thru 8 The Scabbard,pt.1–pt.4	@3.00

DEITY: REQUIEM
Feb., 2005
1-shot 56-pages	7.00

DEITY: REVELATIONS
June, 1999
1 F:Jamie	3.00
2 F:Joe Tripoli	3.00
3 A legend reborn	3.00
3a variant cover (1:10)	3.00

Deity: Revelations #2
© Image

DEMONSLAYER
Nov., 1999
1 MMy	3.00
2 Jaclyn begins her quest	3.00
3 MMy, Michael & the Demon	3.00
Shadow Edition,pt.1 B&W	5.00

VOL II
1 MMy,Into Hell,pt.1	3.00
1a variant(c) (1:4)	3.00
2 MMy	3.00
3 MMy, enter Ebon	3.00

DERRING RISK
June, 1999
1 Fantasy Adventure	2.50
1a AWa variant(c)	2.50

DESPERADO
Dec., 2005
1-shot Primer	2.00
1-shot Second Chances, 64-pg.	5.00

DESPERADOES
Homage, Sept., 1997
1 by JMi & John Cassaday	7.00
2 V:Leander Peik	3.00
2a 2nd printing	2.50
3 V:Leander Peik	3.00
4 V:Leander Peik, concl	3.00
5 V:Gideon Brood,pt.1	3.00

DESPERATE TIMES
(B&W) June, 1998
1 by Chris Eliopoulos	3.00
2 Strip joint	3.00
3 EL(c)	3.00
4 Christmas special	3.00
5 EL(c), sideways	3.00
6	3.00

Jan., 2004
0	3.00
1	3.00

DETONATOR, THE
Nov., 2004
1 Big Bang Theory, pt.1, MBn	2.50
2	2.50
3	2.50
4	2.50
5 final issue	3.00

DEVASTATOR
(B&W) April, 1998
1 JHI and Greg Horn. 3.00
2 book 1,pt.2. . . . . 3.00
3 concl. to book 1 . . . . 3.00

DEVIL'S DUE STUDIOS
Mar., 2003
1-shot 2003 Preview 2.50

DISCIPLES, THE
April, 2001
1 The new magic 3.00
2 Recruit Her or Kill Her 3.00
3 Viva Las Vegas 3.00
4 The Apples of Sodom 3.00

A DISTANT SOIL
(B&W) Highbrow, Aug., 1993
Prev: Aria Comics
15 CDo,Ascension,pt.3 . . . . 3.00
16 CDo,A:Bast, Avatar. 3.00
17 CDo,D'mer & Bast conflict 3.00
18 CDo,'Ascension' finale 3.00
19 CDo,'Spires of Heaven,'pt.1 . . . . 3.00
20 CDo,Lord Merai's suicide
   weakens Hierachy. 3.00
21 CDo,'Exile for D'mer?' 3.00
22 CDo,Avatar's secrets,32-pg. 3.00
23 CDo,three stories 3.00
24 CDo,malfunctioning spacesuit . . 3.00
25 CDo,NGa,Troll Bridge,48-pg. . . . 4.00
26 CDo,B.U.:Red-Cloak by
   E.Kushner. 3.00
27 CDo,B.U.:Liaden tale 3.00
28 CDo,B.U.:Liaden tale, concl.. . . . 3.00
29 CDo,B.U.:Delia Sherman story. . 3.00
30 . . . . 4.00
31 Sometimes the good guys lose . 4.00
32 F:Prince D'mer 4.00
33 Rebellion's final stand. 4.00
34 CDo, 64-pg. 5.00
35 CDo, 32-pg. 4.00
36 CDo. 4.00
37 CDo. 4.00
38 CDo, 40-pg. 4.50
Images of A Distant Soil. 3.00

DIVINE RIGHT:
THE ADVENTURES OF
MAX FARADAY
WildStorm, Sept., 1997
1 JLe,SW,Blaze of Glory. 7.00
1a variant cover 7.50
1b variant, signed 30.00
1c Voyager pollybaged pack. 6.00
1d Spanish edition 5.00
2 JLe,SW,Disco Inferno 5.00
2a variant(c) 5.00
3 JLe,SW,F:Christie Blaze,Enemies
   of the State 4.00
4 JLe,SW,F:Lynch,The Love
   Connection 2.50
4a variant(c) 4.00
5 JLe,SW,V:Dominique Faust,Party
   Crashers 3.00
6 JLe,SW,Truth or Consequences,
   Susanna Chaste located 3.00
7 JLe,SW,Into the Hollow Realm . . 3.00
8 JLe,SW,Tobru,V:Acheron. 3.00
8a variant SW(c). 3.00
Preview edition, JLe(c) (1997). 5.00
Coll.Ed.#1 . . . . 6.00
Coll.Ed.#2 . . . . 6.00
WildStorm/DC, 1999
9 JLe,SWi,Final Stand in
   Hollow Realm 3.00
10 JLe,SWi. 3.00

Divine Right #5
© WildStorm

11 JLe,SWi,Divine Intervention 3.00
12 JLe,SWi,Divine Intervention 3.00
Coll.Ed.#3, rep.#5 & #6 . . . . 6.00

DOLL AND CREATURE
March, 2006
1 (of 4) 3.50
2 thru 4 . . . . @3.00

DOLLZ
April, 2001
1 RGr,TSg. 3.00
1a-1c variant(c)s. 3.00
2 RGr 3.00
3 RGr 3.00

DOMINION
Jan., 2003
1 KG 3.00
2 thru 5 KG . . . . @3.00

DOOM'S IV
Extreme, 1994
1 RL(s),MPa, I:Doom's IV. 2.50
1a variant(c),left side of art 2.50
1b variant(c),right side of art. 2.50
2 Rld(s),MPa,MECH-MAX 2.50
2a variant (c). 2.50
3 Dr. Lychee, Brick 2.50
4 Dr. Lychee, Syber-idol 2.50
Sourcebook 2.50

DOUBLE IMAGE
Feb., 2001
1 The Bod, flip-book, Codeflesh . . . 3.00
2 The Bod/Codeflesh 3.00
3 The Bod/Codeflesh 3.00
4 The Bod/Codeflesh 3.00
5 Trust in Me/Codeflesh 3.00

DOWN
Top Cow, Nov., 2005
1 (of 4) WEI,TyH 3.00
2 thru 4 . . . . @3.00

DRACULA VS. ZORRO
(B&W) Sept., 1998
1 DMG,RM 3.00
2 DMG, RM, conclusion 3.00

DRAGON, THE
March, 1995
1 rep. of Savage Dragon 2.50
2 thru 5 rep. of Savage Dragon . . @2.50

THE DRAGON:
BLOOD AND GUTS
Highbrow, 1995
1 I:Grip 2.50
2 JPn,KIS 2.50
3 JPn,KIS 2.50

DRAIN
Nov., 2006
1 Decades. 3.00
2 Bleed With Me 3.00
3 In a Flash. 3.00
4 Sole Survivor Guilt. 3.00
5 Crescendo 3.00
6 . . . . 3.00

DRAWING FROM LIFE
(B&W) May, 2007
1 JV 3.50

DUNCAN'S KINGDOM
(B&W) Oct., 1999
1 by Gene Yang & Derek Kirk 3.00
2 . . . . 3.00

DUST
July, 2007
1 (of 2) 4.00
1a variant (c) 4.00
2 . . . . 4.00
2a variant (c) 4.00

DUSTY STAR
(B&W) April, 1997
0 sci-fi,western,adventure. 3.00
1 thru 3 . . . . @3.00

DUSTY STAR
Aug., 2005
1 . . . . 3.50
2 . . . . 3.50

DV8
WildStorm, 1996
1 WEI(s),HuR,'Lust for Life' 4.00
1a JLe(c). 5.00
1b Kevin Nowlan(c). 4.00
2 WEI(s),HuR,Gen-active serial
   killers,'Some Weird Sin'. 3.00
3 WEI(s), Neighborhood Threat . . . 3.00
4 WEI(s),HuR,Miss Drugstore. . . . 3.00
5 Ivana sends DV8 to Japan 2.50
6 idle hands are the devil's tools . . 2.50
7 WEI(s),'Shades' 2.50
8 HuR,Sublime, Evo & Frostbite
   abandoned,'Three'. 2.50
9 MHs,'Evolution' 2.50
10 MHs,'In Service to Nothing' . . . 2.50
11 MHs,F:Copycat,'Facets' 2.50
12 MHs,F:Freestyle,V:Sen.Killory . . 2.50
13 MHs,'The Sad Tales of
   Senator Killory' 2.50
14 MHs,TR,New Horizon,TR(c),
   'Barely Legal'. 5.00
14a TC(c). 2.50
14b Voyager bagged pack. 3.50
15 MHs,F:Ivana Baiul,'Settling
   Accounts' 2.50
16 MHs,V:Dominique Faust
   'Intersection' 2.50
17 MHs,Gen-Passive. 2.50

IMAGE

DV8 #9
© *WildStorm*

18 MHs,Team 7,A:Grifter,'Same as
   It Ever Was' 2.50
19 MHs,First Mision,pt.1,'Larger
   Concerns' 2.50
20 MHs,First Mision,pt.2,'Lounging
   in the Ammo Dump' 2.50
21 MHs,First Mision,pt.3,V:Anthrax . 2.50
22 MHs,V:Copycat,'Choices' 2.50
22a variant(c) JMd(1:4) 2.50
23 MHs,F:Threshold,'Gone to
   Ground' 2.50
24 MHs,F:Sublime,'Slip Stream,'
   prologue 2.50
25 MHs,Slipstream,pt.1 . . . . 2.50
DV8 Rave,preview (1996) 3.00
Ann.#1 'Head Trips' (1998) 3.00

WildStorm/DC, 1999

26 MHs,TVs 2.50
27 MHs,TVs,V:Gen-Actives 2.50
28 MHs,TVs,F:Evo. 2.50
29 MHs,TVs 2.50
30 MHs,TVs,Things Fall Apart,pt.1 . 2.50
31 MHs,TVs,Things Fall Apart,pt.2 . 2.50
32 MHs,TVs,Things Fall Apart,pt.3 . 2.50
Ann.'99 Slipstream 3.50
#0 40-pg. 3.00

DV8 VS. BLACK OPS
WildStorm, Oct., 1997

1 Techromis Design,pt.1 . . . . 3.00
2 Techromis Design,pt.2 . . . . 3.00
3 Techromis Design,pt.3 . . . . 3.00

DYNAMO 5
Mar., 2007

1 F:Captain Dynamo 3.00
2 thru 3 . . . . @3.50
4 . . . . 3.50
5 . . . . 3.50
7 . . . . 3.50
8 F:Bonechill 3.00

ECHO
March, 2000

1 A Broken World 2.50
1a variant(c) 2.50
2 Sacrifices 2.50
2a variant PtL(c) 2.50
3 Deadly new echo 2.50
3a variant PtL(c) 2.50
4 PtL,Desperate Times 2.50
5 PtL,Welcoming Party 2.50

---

6 Conspiracy Theory 2.50
6a variant PtL(c) 2.50
7 Anarchy,pt.1 . . . . 2.50
8 A Life Worth Living 3.00
#0 Thick as Thieves 2.50
#0a variant(c) 2.50
#1 Holochrome edition 7.00

86 VOLTZ: DEAD GIRL
(B&W) Mar., 2005

1-shot 56-page 6.00

ELECTROPOLIS
May, 2001

1 DMt, Infernal Machine,pt.1 . . . . . 3.00
2 DMt, Infernal Machine,pt.2 . . . . . 3.00
3 DMt, Heavy Meddle 3.00
4 DMt, Infernal Machine,pt.4 . . . . . 3.00

ELEKTRA/CYBLADE
Top Cow/Marvel, 1997

1-shot 'Devil's Reign,'pt.7
   (of 8) x-over 3.00

ELEPHANTMEN
July., 2006

0 Unnatural Selection 3.00
1 See the Elephant 3.00
2 Behemoth & Leviathan, flip-book. 3.00
3 Hip Flask 3.00
4 Hazardous Materials, Wounded
   Animals, flip-cover 3.00
5 Exodus 3.00
5a variant (c) 3.00
6 Abandoned by God 3.00
7 Captain Stoneheart 3.00
7a variant (c) 3.00
8 Moxa Cautery 3.00
9 Local Hippo 3.00
10 Unicorn 3.00
11 Man of Peace 3.00
Spec. The Pilot 3.00

ELEPHANTMEN:
WAR TOYS
(B&W) Aug., 2007

1 (of 3) 3.00
1a variant (c) 3.00
2 . . . . 3.00
2a variant (c) 3.00
3 . . . . 3.00
3a variant (c) 3.00

EMISSARY
May, 2006

1 Revelations 1:4 . . . . 3.50
2 Revelations 2:4 . . . . 3.50
3 Revelations 3:4 . . . . 3.50
4 Revelations 4:4 . . . . 3.50
5 Revelations 2:1 . . . . 3.50
6 Revelations 2.2 . . . . 3.50
7 Revelations 2:3 . . . . 3.50
8 Revelations 3:3 . . . . 3.50

EMPIRE
May, 2000

1 MWa,BKi,F:Golgoth 5.00
2 MWa,BKi,F:Xanna 4.00
3 MWa,BKi,F:Lohkyn 4.00
4 MWa,BKi,Nature vs. nurture 4.00

ESPERS
April, 1997
(B&W) Vol. 3

1 JHI,A:Brian Marx,V:Architects . . . 3.00
1a 2nd printing 3.00
2 JHI 3.00

---

3 JHI,Black Magic 3.00
4 JHI,Black Magic, concl. 3.00
5 JHI,two stories 3.00
6 JHI,F:Simon Ashley,Alan Black . . 3.00
7 JHI,Feel the Rapture 3.00
8 JHI, trip to Hong Kong 3.00
9 JHI,V:Architects 3.00

E.V.E. Protomecha #3
© *Top Cow*

E.V.E. PROTOMECHA
Top Cow, Feb., 2000

1 . . . . 3.00
1a variant JMd(c) 3.00
1b variant David Finch(c) 3.00
2 Gunner Unleashed. 3.00
2a variant Michael Turner(c) 3.00
2b variant SPa(c) 3.00
3 thru 6 . . . . @3.00

[ADVENTURES OF]
EVIL AND MALICE
June, 1999

1 by Jimmie Robinson 3.50
2 F:Max 2000 . . . . 3.50
3 V:Cold Heart & Le'Chef 3.50
4 final showdown 3.50

EVO
Top Cow

1 MS,Endgame,pt.3 x-over 3.00

EXPATRIATE, THE
Feb., 2004

1 . . . . 3.00
2 thru 7 . . . . @3.00

EXPOSURE
July, 1999

1 F:Shawna & Lisa 2.50
2 Mirrors to the Soul 2.50
3 . . . . 2.50
2a & 3a alternate photo(c) (1:2) . @2.50
4 Spark-Spangled See-Through
   Girl 2.50
4a alternate photo(c) (1:2) 2.50
Prelude 16-pg 7.00
Prelude holo-foil 15.00

EXTREME ANTHOLOGY
1 . . . . 2.50

EXTREME CHRISTMAS SPECIAL
Various artists, new work 3.00

EXTREME DESTROYER
Extreme, 1996
1 prologue, x-over,bagged
with card 2.50
2 epilogue, x-over 2.50

EXTREME HERO
1 . . . . 3.00

EXTREME PREJUDICE
Extreme, Nov., 1994
0 Prelude to X-over 3.00

EXTREME SACRIFICE
Extreme, Jan., 1995
Prelude,x-over,pt.1, A:Everyone
with trading card 2.50
Epilogue, x-over,pt.8, conclusion
with trading card 2.50

EXTREME 3000
Prelude 2.50

EXTREME TOUR BOOK
Tour Book 1992 . . . . 3.00
Tour Book 1994 . . . . 25.00

EXTREMELY YOUNGBLOOD
Extreme, Sept 1997
1 TBm&MBm(s) 3.50

EXTREME ZERO
0 RLd,CYp,ATi(i),I:Cybrid, Law &
Order, Risk, Code 9, Lancers,
Black Flag 3.00
0a Variant cover 3.00

FACELESS, THE
Aug., 2005
GN 7.00

FACTION PARADOX
Aug., 2003
1 War in Heaven 3.00
2 . . . . 3.00

FALLING MAN
(B&W) Dec., 1997
1 (of 3) BMC,PhH 3.00
2 Floyd vs. Duncan 3.00
3 . . . . 3.00

FATHOM
Top Cow, 1998
1 by Michael Turner,F:Aspen 7.00
2 war beneath the waves 4.00
3 Life changed forever 3.50
4 Connection to water 3.00
5 Aspen's connection to water 3.00
6 Admiral's plans revealed 3.00
7 Finale,pt.1 . . . . 3.00
8 Finale,pt.2 . . . . 3.00
9 Finale, conclusion, end 3.00
9a green foil (c) 16.00
10 Fathom returns 3.00
11 Fathom returns,pt.2 . . . . 3.00
12 Tomb Raider & Witchblade
x-over,pt.1 . . . . 3.00
12a variant(c) 5.00
13 x-over,pt.2 . . . . 3.00
13a variant(c) 5.00

Fathom #3
© *Top Cow*

14 Aspen & Vana, concl. 3.00
14a variant(c) 5.00
15 Killian's Blue Sun 2.50
15a variant(c) 5.00
16 Admiral's subterfuge discovered . 2.50
#0 rep. new Mike Turner(c) 2.50
1/2 . . . . 4.00
Spec. Swimsuit ed. 4.00
Fathom 2000 swimsuit calendar . . . 4.00
Fathom 2000 smimsuit Spec. 4.00

FATHOM: KILLIAN'S TIDE
Top Cow, March, 2001
1 (of 4) 5.00
1a variant(c) 4.00
2 thru 4 . . . . @3.00

FEAR AGENT
Oct., 2005
1 . . . . 3.00
2 . . . . 3.00
3 . . . . 3.00
4 . . . . 3.00
5 . . . . 3.00
6 Reignition, conc. 3.00
7 Homecoming 3.00
8 . . . . 3.00
9 . . . . 3.00
10 . . . . 3.00
11 . . . . 3.00

FEAR EFFECT
Top Cow, March, 2000
1-shot MHw, video game tie-in 5.00
Spec. 1 Fear Effect Retro Helix 3.00

FEATHER
Aug., 2003
1 thru 4 . . . . @3.00
5 48-pg 6.00

FELL
Sept., 2005
1 WEI 15.00
2 WEI 12.00
3 WEI 5.00
4 thru 8 WEI . . . . @5.00
9 thru 10 WEI . . . . @4.00

FELON
Top Cow, Oct., 2001
1 (of 4) 3.00
2 . . . . 3.00
3 concl. 3.00
4 I:Elizabeth Freeh 3.00

FELT: TRUE TALES OF UNDERGROUND HIP HOP
(B&W) May, 2005
1-shot 3.00

FERRO CITY
(B&W) Aug., 2005
1 . . . . 3.00
2 thru 4 . . . . @3.00

F5
April, 2000
1 TnD,48-pg. 3.00
2 TnD,life or death 2.50
3 TnD 2.50
4 TnD, betrayed 2.50
Preview Book, TnD,24-pg. 2.50

FIREBIRDS
Nov., 2004
1-shot by Jay Faeber 6.00

FIREBREATHER
Jan 2003
1 (of 4) PhH(s) 3.00
2 thru 4 PhH(s) . . . . @3.00
1-shot Firebreather: The Iron
Saint, PhH (2004) 6.00

FIRE FROM HEAVEN
WildStorm, 1996
1 x-over,Chapter 1 . . . . 3.50
2 x-over,Finale 2 . . . . 2.50

FIRST BORN
Top Cow, June, 2007
Spec. First Look 2.00
1 (of 3) RMz, MS(c) 3.00
1a variant (c) 3.00
2 RMz,MS(c) 3.00
2a variant (c) 3.00
3 RMz 3.00
3a variant (c) 3.00

FIRSTMAN
April, 1997
1 ASm,LukeHenry becomesApollo . 2.50

FLAK RIOT
June, 2005
1 (of 4) 3.00
2 . . . . 3.00
3 . . . . 3.00
4 . . . . 3.00

FLAMING CARROT
(B&W) Dec., 2004
1 by Bob Burden, Crouching Carrot,
Hidden Hot Wing 3.00
2 . . . . 3.50
3 . . . . 3.50
4 . . . . 3.50
Spec. 3.50

FOOT SOLDIERS, THE
(B&W) Sept., 1997
Prev.: Dark Horse
1 by Jim Krueger, Graveyard of
　Forgotten Heroes 3.00
2 Tragedy o/t Travesty Tapestry . . . 3.00
3 Arch enemies,pt.3 . . . . 3.00
4 'It's a Wicked World Afterall' . . . 3.00
5 Loose Ends 3.00

FOREVER AMBER
(B&W) July, 1999
1 by Don Hudson 3.00
1a variant cover (1:2) 3.00
2 Lady fights back. 3.00
3 Amber sent to jail. 2.50
4 Amber's revenge, concl. 3.00

FORSAKEN
Aug., 2004
1 Light of Other Days,pt.1 . . . . 3.00
2 Light of Other Days,pt.2. . . . . . . 3.00
3 Light of Other Days,pt.3. . . . . . . 3.00
4 The Light of Other Days,pt.4 . . . 3.00
5 The Light of Other Days,pt.5 . . . 3.00
6 The Light of Other Days,pt.6 . . . 3.00

FRANKENSTEIN MOBSTER
Oct., 2003
0 . . . . 3.00
0a variant (c). 3.00
1 MkW,Friday the 13th 3.00
2 MkW. 3.00
3 MkW,mystic control 3.00
4 MkW. 3.00
5 MkW,Blood debt. 3.00
6 Escape from police 3.00
7 Made Man, concl. 3.00
1a thru 7a variant (c). . . . . @3.00

FRANK FRAZETTA'S DEATH DEALER
Apr., 2007
1 (of 6) FF(c),Shadows of Mirahan 8.00
1a & b variant (c)s . . . . @8.00
2 . . . . 7.00
2a & b variant (c)s . . . . @7.00
3 . . . . 4.00
3a & b variant (c)s. . . . . @4.00
4 . . . . 4.00

Freak Force #15
© Highbrow

4a & b variant (c)s. . . . . @4.00
5 . . . . 4.00
5a & b variant (c)s. . . . . @4.00
6 . . . . 4.00
6a & b variant (c)s. . . . . @4.00

FREAK FORCE
Highbrow, 1993–95
1 EL(s),KG 3.00
2 EL(s),KG 3.00
3 EL(s),KG 3.00
4 EL(s),KG,A:Vanguard. 3.00
5 EL(s),KG 3.00
6 EL(s),KG 3.00
7 EL(s),KG 3.00
8 EL(s),space ants 3.00
9 EL(s),Cyberforce 3.00
10 EL(s),Savage Dragon 3.00
11 EL(s),Invasion,pt.1 . . . . 3.00
12 EL(s),Invasion,pt.2 . . . . 3.00
13 EL(s),Invasion,pt.3 . . . . 3.00
14 EL(s),Team Defeated 3.00
15 EL(s),F:Barbaric 3.00
16 KG,EL(s),V:Chelsea Nirvana. . . 3.00
17 EL,KG,major plots converge . . . 3.00
18 Final Issue 3.00

[Series Two] March, 1997
1 EL,Star joins team,V:The
　Frightening Force 3.00
2 EL,Dart quits team 3.00
3 EL,'Lo there shall come..an
　ending'. 3.00

FREEDOM FORCE
Jan., 2005
1 (of 6) Founding Fathers 3.00
2 Casualty of War 3.00
3 Double Trouble 3.00
4 Mechanical Mayhem 3.00
5 Forbidden Fruit 3.00
6 Out of Time 3.00

FRESHMEN, THE
Top Cow, 2005
1 thru 3 Intro to Superpowers 101
　pt. 1 thru pt. 3 . . . . @3.00
4 What Time is it in Budapest? . . . 3.00
5 Deepest Level of Truth 3.00
6 Finals 3.00
Spec. Yearbook (2005) 3.00
1-shot Freshmen Yearbook 3.00
Vol. 2
2 Fundamentals of Fear 3.00
2a variant incentive (c) 3.00
3 Fundamentals of Fear 3.00
3a variant (c)s . . . . @3.00
4 Fundamentals of Fear 3.00
5 Fundamentals of Fear 4.00
5a variant (c). 4.00
6 Fundamentals of Fear 4.00
6a variant (c) 4.00
1 Fundamentals of Fear 3.00

FRIENDS OF MAXX
I Before E, April, 1996
1 thru 3 WML&SK . . . . @3.00

FUSED!
March, 2002
1 Canned Heat,pt.1 (of 4) 3.00
1a variant(c) 3.00
2 Canned Heat,pt.2. . . . . 3.00
3 Canned Heat,pt.3. . . . . 3.00
4 Canned Heat,pt.4. . . . . 3.00

GALAXY-SIZE ASTOUNDING SPACE THRILLS
March, 2001
1 Galaxy Size Showdown, 48-pg.
　flip-book. 5.00

GAMORRA SWIMSUIT SPECIAL
WildStorm, 1996
Spec.#1 . . . . 2.50

GAZILLION
Nov., 1998
1 HSm, Mars vs. Xof. 2.50
1a variant cover (1:4) 2.50

Gear Station #1
© Image

GEAR STATION, THE
March, 2000
1 DaF,Dominion of Souls 6.00
1a variant AxR(c) 2.50
1b variant PtL(c) 2.50
1c variant Michael Turner(c). 2.50
2 DaF,23rd Gear. 2.50
2a variant AAd(c) 2.50
3 DaF,Who is Fable 2.50
4 DaF,first showdown 2.50
5 DaF,Gear Station Prime 2.50
6 DaF 2.50

GEEKSVILLE
(B&W) Mar., 2000
#0 by R.Koslowski & G.Sassaman . 3.00
1 Breaking into the Biz,pt.1 . . . . . . 3.00
2 Breaking into the Biz,pt.2 . . . . . . 3.00
3 Back to the Con 3.00
4 Breaking into the Biz 3.00
5 Dark Sky 3.00
6 End of 3 Geeks 3.00

GEMINAR
(B&W) June, 2000
1 . . . . 5.00
2 F:Captain Champion 5.00

GEN^{13}
WildStorm, 1994
0 Individual Hero Stories. 4.00

1 JLe(s),BCi(s),I:Fairchild,Grunge,
  Freefall,Burnout. 12.00
1a 2nd printing 4.00
2 JLe(s),BCi(s) 9.00
3 JLe(s),BCi(s),A:Pitt,'Payback' . . 7.00
4 JLe(s),BCi(s),'Free for All' 6.00
5 Final issue . . . . '5.00
5a WP variant cover 8.00

[Regular Series] 1995

1a BCi(s),V:Mercenaries. 5.00
1b Common Cover 2 . . . . 5.00
1c Heavy Metal Gen 8.00
1d Pulp Fiction Parody 9.00
1e Gen 13 Bunch 8.00
1f Lin-Gen-re. 9.00
1g Lil Gen 13 . . . . 8.00
1h Friendly Neighbor Grunge 8.00
1i Gen 13 Madison Ave 9.00
1j Gen-Et Jackson 8.00
1k Gen Dress Up cover 8.00
1l Verti-Gen. 8.00
1m Do It Yourself Cover 8.00
2 BCi,BWS(c),WildStorm Rising,
  pt.4, w/2 cards 3.00
2a newstand ed. 2.50
3 BCi,'Magical Mystery Tour' 3.00
4 BCi,'Tourist Trap' 3.00
5 BCi,I:New Member,Family Feud . 3.00
6 BCi,JLe,I:The Deviants,
  'Roman Holiday' 3.00
7 BCi,JLe,European Vacation,pt.2
  'Veni, Vidi, Vici' 3.00
8 BCi,'Bewitched,Bothered
  and Bewildered' 3.00
9 . . . . 3.00
10 Fire From Heaven,pt.3 . . . . 3.00
11 Fire From Heaven,pt.9 . . . . 3.00
12 F:Caitlin,her dad 3.00
13 A, B & C, each . . . . @3.00
14 'Higher Learning'. 2.50
15 Fraternity and Sorority rush 2.50
16. . . . . 2.50
17 BCi,JSC,AGo,battle royale in
  Tower of Luv,'Toy Soldiers' 2.50
18 BCi,JSC,AGo,V:Keepers,
  'Hello & Good-Byes' 2.50
19 BCi,JSC,AGo,Lynch & kids flee
  to Antarctica,'Bon Voyage'. 2.50
20 BCi,JSC,AGo,'To Boldly Go' . . . 2.50
21 BCi,JSC,AGo,V:D'Rahn,'Lost
  in Space' 2.50
22 BCi,civil war,'Homecoming'. . . . 2.50
23 BCi,21st century 2.50
24 BCi,V:D'Rahn,'Judgment Day' . . 2.50
25 BCi,Homecoming,JsC(c). 3.50
25a TC(c),'Where Angels Fear
  to Tread' 3.50
25b Voyager bagged pack 3.50
26 JAr,GFr,CaS,When Worlds
  Collide 2.50
27 JAr,GFr,CaS,'Search & Seizure'. 2.50
28 JAr,GFr,CaS,'Remote Control' . . 2.50
29 JAr,GFr,CaS,I:Tindalos,
  'A Firm Grip on Reality' 2.50
30 JAr,GFr,CaS,'Stranger Than
  Fiction' 2.50
31 JAr,GFr,CaS,Roxy's Big Score,
  'Paradigm Shift' 2.50
32 JAr,GFr,CaS,'Red Skies at
  Morning'. 2.50
33 JAr,GFr,CaS,aftermaths, 'Burning
  the Candle at Both Ends',
  with 8-page Planetary #0. . . . . . 4.00
34 JAr,GFr,CaS,AAd,A:Roxy
  & Sarah,'Overture' 2.50
35 JAr,GFr,CaS,John Lynch resigns,
  'But You Can't Hide' 2.50
36 JAr,GFr,CaS,F:John Lynch,
  'That Was Then' 2.50
College Yearbook 1997, Superheroes
  at Large 2.50
Ann. #1 WEI,SDi'London'sBrilliant' . 3.00

Gen^{13} #29
© *WildStorm*

1-Shot Gen13:Unreal World (1996). 3.00
Gen13 3-D Special (1997). 5.00
3-D Spec. #1, (1997) 5.00
3-D Spec. #1, variant cover 5.00
3-D Spec. #1, (1998) 5.00

WildStorm/DC, 1999

37 JAr,GFr,CaS,Reaper 2.50
38 JAr,GFr,CaS,BU:Grunge. 2.50
38a variant cover 2.50
39 JAr,GFr,CaS,Genocide 2.50
40 JAr,GFr,CaS,V:Reaper 2.50
41 JAr,GFr,CaS 2.50
42 JoC(s),KM,pro wrestlers 2.50
43 AWa(s&c),F:Fairchild 2.50
44 AWa(s&c),A:Mr.Magestic 2.50
45 SLo,EBe,JSb,fashion show 2.50
46 SLo,EBe,JSb,MightyJoeGrunge . 2.50
47 SLo,EBe,JSb. 2.50
48 SLo,EBe,JSb. 2.50
49 SLo,EBe,JSb. 2.50
50 SLo,EBe,JSb,48-pg. 4.00
50a variant JLe,SW(c) (1:4). 4.00
51 SLo,breather 2.50
52 SLo,F:Caitlin Fairchild. 2.50
53 F:all Villains issue 2.50
54 SLo,EBe,SWi,F:Fairchild 2.50
55 EBe,Return to Pod 9,pt.2 . . . . . 2.50
56 EBe,Fairchild,pt.3 . . . . 2.50
57 BRa,EBe,Tokyo in danger. 2.50
58 BRa,EBe,mini-monster
  massacre. 2.50
59 BRa,EBe,V:Gaijin13 . . . . 2.50
60 AWa,Behind the Power. 2.50
61 AWa,Goin' back to Cali 2.50
62 AWa,fast food 2.50
63 AWa,EBe,sailboat outing 2.50
64 AWa,Superhuman Like You,pt.1 . 2.50
65 AWa,Superhuman Like You,pt.2 . 2.50
66 AWa,8 guest artists 2.50
67 AWa,EBe,ColdAir on MyBehind . 2.50
68 AWa,Slave to Love,pt.1. . . . . 2.50
69 AWa,Slave to Love,pt.2. . . . . 2.50
70 AWa,F:Sara Rainmaker 2.50
71 AWa,Think Like A Gun,pt.1. . . . . 2.50
72 AWa,Think Like A Gun,pt.2 . . . . . 2.50
73 AWa,Think Like A Gun,pt.3 . . . . . 2.50
74 AWa,Think Like A Gun,pt.4 . . . . . 2.50
75 AWa,How the Story Ends,pt.1. . . 2.50
76 AWa,How the Story Ends,pt.2. . . 2.50
77 AWa,Story Ends,pt.3, 40-pg. . . . 3.50
Annual'99 JAr(s) 3.50
Ann. 2000 #1, Devil's
  Night x-over,pt.1 . . . . 3.50
Spec. Wired 2.50
Spec.#1 3-D AAd 5.00

Spec.#1a variant(c) 5.00
Spec. Carny Folk 3.50
Spec. 1-shot Going West. 2.50
GN Grunge Saves the World. 6.00
GN Bootleg: Grunge— The Movie. 10.00
GN Medicine Song, 48-pg. 6.00
GN Gen13/Fantastic Four 6.00
GN Science Friction, 48-pg. 6.00
GN London,New York,Hell 7.00
GN A Christmas Caper (2002) 6.00

GEN^{13} BOOTLEG
WildStorm, Nov., 1996

1 MFm&AD,lost in the 'Linquist
  Fault,'pt.1. . . . . 3.00
1a signed 15.00
2 'Linquist Fault,'pt.2. . . . . 3.50
3 Gen13 Fairy Tale 3.50
4 WS&LSi,F:Valaria,'Little Girl
  Lost' 3.50
5 F:Fairchild,'Timesick,'pt.1 . . . . . . 3.50
6 F:Fairchild,'Timesick,'pt.2 . . . . . . 3.50
7 'Renaissance Ruckus' 3.50
8 AWa,'Grunge's Movie,'pt.1 . . . . . . 4.00
9 AWa,'Grunge's Movie,'pt.2. . . . . . 4.00
10 AWa,'Grunge's Movie,'pt.3 . . . . . 4.00
11 AaL,WS,Chupacabra,pt.1 . . . . . . 2.50
12 AaL,WS,Chupacabra,pt.2 . . . . . . 2.50
13 F:Grunge,'The Trickster' 2.50
14 JMi,JoP,GL,bad neighbors 2.50
15 KNo,V:Trance,'Hanging,'pt.1 . . . 2.50
16 KNo,V:Trance,'Hanging,'pt.2. . . . 2.50
17 'Virgil Chu's Reality. 2.50
18 MFm,'A Day at the Beach' 2.50
19 BKs,JhB,Satyr. 2.50
20 CAd,F:John Lynch,'Numbskulls' . 2.50
Ann.#1 WEI,SDi, to NYC 3.00

GEN^{13}: INTERACTIVE
WildStorm, Oct., 1997

1 vote via Internet. 4.00
2 & 3 MHs,vote via Internet . . . . @3.00

GEN^{13}/ GENERATION X
WildStorm, July, 1997

1 BCi&AAd,'Generation Gap' 3.00
1a variant JSC(c) 3.00
3-D edition, with glasses 5.00
3-Da variant cover, with glasses . . . 5.00

GEN^{13}: MAGICAL DRAMA QUEEN ROXY
WildStorm, Oct., 1998

1 (of 3) AWa,Mall of Doom 4.00
2 AWa,V:Caitlin 4.00
3 AWa,dream sequence concl. 4.00

GEN^{13}/THE MAXX
WildStorm, 1995

Spec.#1 BML,x-over 4.00

GEN^{13}/MONKEY MAN & O'BRIEN
WildStorm, June, 1998

1 (of 2) AAd. 3.00
1a chromium edition 4.50
2 AAd,alternate universe, concl. . . . 3.00
2a variant AAd(c) 2.50

GEN^{13}: ORDINARY HEROES
WildStorm, 1996

1 & 2 . . . . @3.00

Gen¹² #2
© WildStorm

GEN¹²

WildStorm, Feb., 1998

1 BCi,Team 7 tie-in,'The Legacy' . . 3.00
2 BCi,F:Morgan of I.O. 3.00
3 BCi,Dominique Faust. 3.00
4 BCi,F:Miles Craven 3.00
5 BCi,Team 7 re-unites 3.00

GHOSTING

Platinum, Aug., 2007

1 (of 4) 3.00
2 . . . . 3.00

GHOST SPY

May, 2004

1 (of 6) 3.00
2 thru 5 . . . . @3.00

GIFT, THE

2004

8 Sacrifice 3.00
9 Corrupt. 3.00
10 Unleashed. 3.00
11 Betrayal. 3.00
12 Death 3.00
13 The Dragon. 3.00
14 O:Ancient One 3.00
1a director's cut 4.00

G.I. JOE

Sept., 2001

1 JSC(c) Reinstated,pt.1 . . . . 15.00
1a 2nd printing 6.00
2 Reinstated,pt.2. . . . . 6.00
3 JSC(c),Reinstated,pt.3. . . . . 5.00
4 JSC(c),Reinstated,pt.4. . . . . 5.00
5 F:Duke 3.50
6 Reckonings,pt.1 . . . . 3.00
7 Storm Shadow 3.00
8 Destro & Cobra Commander. . . . 3.00
9 Snake-eyes vs. Storm Shadow . . 3.00
10 Dreadnoks. 3.00
11 Mob rule in Chicago 3.00
12 JBz(c),V:Android Trooper 3.00
13 JBz(c),V:Firefly 3.00
14 Cobra Suburbs Return 3.00
15 Reunion. 3.00
16 missing child 3.00
17 kidnap Flint & Baroness 3.00
18 search for Flint & Baroness 3.00
19 . . . . 3.00

20 Storm Shadow 3.00
21 Snake-Eyes. 4.00
22 Return of Serpentor,pt.1 . . . . . . 4.00
21a & 22a variant (c)s . . . . @9.00
23 Return of Serpentor,pt.2 . . . . . . 3.00
24 Return of Serpentor,pt.3 . . . . . . 3.00
24a variant(c). 3.00
25 . . . . 3.00
25a variant (c) 3.00
Spec. M.I.A., rep. #1 & #2 . . . . 5.00

Devil's Due 2004

26 thru 30 . . . . @3.00
31 . . . . 8.00
32 . . . . 3.00
33 . . . . 7.00
33 2nd printing 8.00
34 thru 41 . . . . @3.00
42 D:Lady Jaye 5.00

G.I. JOE: BATTLE FILES

April, 2002

1 (of 3) G.I. Joe, 48-pg. 6.00
2 F:Cobra 6.00
3 F:Vehicles and Tech 6.00

G.I. JOE FRONTLINE

Oct., 2002

1 LHa(s),DJu,BL,DvD(c). 3.00
2 DJu,BL,DvD(c) V:Destro 3.00
3 DJu,BL,DvD(c) V:Destro 3.00
4 DJu,BL,Silent Castle 3.00
5 Icebound 3.00
6 Icebound,pt.2. . . . . 3.00
7 Icebound,pt.3. . . . . 3.00
8 Icebound,pt.4. . . . . 3.00
9 Kansas City 3.00
10 . . . . 3.00
11 Chuckles 3.00
12 Chuckles 3.00
13 Chuckles 3.00
14 Chuckles 3.00
15 F:Stalker 3.00
16 Night Creepers 3.00
17 PJe,F:Beachhead 3.00
18 . . . . 3.00
18a variant (c) 3.00
16a–17a variant (c) . . . . @3.00

G.I. JOE VS. TRANSFORMERS

June, 2003

1 . . . . 4.00
1a 2nd printing 3.00
2 thru 6 . . . . @3.00
1a–6a variant (c) . . . . @5.00

GIRLS

May, 2005

1 . . . . 6.00
1a 2nd & 3rd printings. . . . . @3.00
2 . . . . 4.00
3 thru 10 . . . . @3.00
11 thru 24 . . . . 3.00

GLISTER

Aug., 2007

1 Glister Butterworth and the
 Haunted Teapot, 64-pgs. 6.00
2 House Hunting. 6.00

GLORY

Extreme, 1995

0 JDy. 2.50
1 JDy,F:Glory 4.00
1a variant cover 4.00
2 JDy,V:Demon Father 3.00
3 JDy,A:Rumble & Vandal. 2.50
4 Vandal vs. Demon Horde. 2.50

Glory #3
© Image/Extreme

4a JDy variant cover 3.00
5 Supreme Apocalypse,pt.3,
 F:Vandal 2.50
6 Drug Problem. 2.50
7 F:Superpatriot 2.50
8 Extreme Babewatch. 2.50
9 Extreme Destroyer,pt.5,
 x-over, bagged with card 2.50
10 . . . . 2.50
11 . . . . 2.50
12 JDy, EBe & JSb 3.50
13 JDy, EBe & JSb 2.50
14 JDy, EBe & JSb 2.50
15 JDy, EBe & JSb, Out for
 vengeance 2.50
continued: see Color Comics section

GLORY/ANGELA ANGELS IN HELL

Extreme, 1996

1 . . . . 4.00

GLORY/AVENGELYNE

Extreme, 1996

1 V:B'lial,I:Faith. 4.00
1a no chrome(c) 3.00

GLORY/AVENGELYNE: THE GODYSSEY

Extreme

1 RLd & JDy 3.00
1a photo(c) 4.00

GLORY/CELESTINE: DARK ANGEL

Extreme, Sept., 1996

1 (of 3) JDy,PtL,sequel to Rage of
 Angels, A:Maximage 2.50
2 JDy,PtL,'Doomsday+1'. 2.50
3 JDy,PtL, conclusion 2.50

GLORY & FRIENDS

Extreme, 1995

Bikini Fest #1 . . . . 2.50
Bikini Fest #2 . . . . 2.50
Lingerie Special #1 (1995). 3.00
Christmas Special #1 (1995) 2.50

G-MAN
Dec., 2004
1 Learning to Fly. 6.00

GODLAND
June, 2005
1 Cosmic Wheels in Motion . . . 3.00
2 Every Breath You Take 3.00
3 The seismic Shift 3.00
4 The Torture Never Stops 3.00
5 Combat Rock. 3.00
6 . . . . 3.00
7 Acid Raindrops. 3.00
8 The Origin of the Universe 3.00
9 Funky Buster Round 3.00
10 The March of Ides. 3.00
11 Never Say Janus. 3.00
12 High Noon, Tea Time, 32-pg. . . . 3.00
13 . . . . 3.00
13a variant (c) 3.00
14 . . . . 3.00
15 O Sister Where Art Thou 3.00
16 Strange But True. 0.60
17 The Infinity Protocols 3.00
18 Dance Hall Crash Hall 3.00
19 High Head Stung 3.00
20 Viv Las Vulgar. 3.00

GO GIRL!
Aug., 2000
1 TrR,F:Lindsay Goldman. 3.50
2 TrR,wonderful life?. 3.50
3 TrR,The Teacher from Hell 3.50
4 TrR,Vacation at dude ranch. 3.50
5 TrR,origin of powers 3.50

GRAVESLINGER
Oct, 2007
1 (of 4) 3.00

GRAY AREA, THE
June, 2004
1 (of 3) JR2,KJ,48-pg. 6.00
2 JR2,KJ,32-pg. 4.00
3 JRw,KJ,48-pg. 6.00

GREASE MONKEY
March, 1998
1 TEI 3.00
2 TEI 3.00
3 TEI, The Calling; Rewards. 3.00

GRIFTER
WildStorm, 1995–96
1 BWS(c), WildStorm
   Rising,pt.5,w/2 cards. 2.50
1a Newsstand ed. 2.50
2 V:Diabolik,pt.1 . . . . 3.00
3 V:Diabolik,pt.2 . . . . 3.00
4 R:Forgotten Hero. 3.00
5 Rampage of a Fallen Hero 3.00
6 V:Poerhouse 3.00
7 City of Angels,pt.1 . . . . 3.00
8 City of Angels,pt.2 . . . . 3.00
9 City of Angels,pt.3 . . . . 3.00
10 City of Angels,pt.4. . . . . 3.00

GRIFTER/BADROCK
Extreme, 1995
1 To Save Badrock's Mom 3.00
1a Variant cover 2.50
2 flip-book-Badrock #2 . . . . 3.00
3 double-size 3.50

GRIFTER-ONE SHOT
WildStorm, 1995
1 SS,DN 5.00

GRIFTER
WildStorm, 1996
1 StG. 4.00
2 StG,V:Joe the Dead 3.00
3 StG,captured by MadJackPower . 3.00
4 StG,vs. Condition Red 3.00

Grifter #9
© *WildStorm*

5 StG,Grifter meets his dad,
   F:Molly Ingram. 3.00
6 StG,A:Santini 3.00
7 StG,MtB,I:Charlatan 3.00
8 StG,MtB,Zealot
   disappears,V:Soldier 3.00
9 StG,Zealot captured?, secret
   history of Quiet Men 3.00
10 StG,Grifter & Soldier go to
   rescue Zealot. 3.00
11 StG, renegade former agent 3.00
12 StG,'Who is Tanager?'. 3.00
13 StG,F:Condition Red,'Family
   Feud' 3.00
14 StG,V:Joe the Dead 3.00

GRIFTER/SHI
WildStorm, 1996
1 BCi,JLe,TC 3.00
2 BCi,JLe,TC 3.00

GROO
1994–95
1 SA 3.50
2 A:Arba, Dakarba 3.50
3 The Generals Hat 3.50
4 A Drink of Water. 3.50
5 SA,A Simple Invasion 3.50
6 SA,A Little Invention 3.50
7 The Plight of the Drazils 3.50
8 . . . . 3.50
9 I:Arfetto 3.50
10 The Sinkes 3.50
11 The Gamblers 3.50
12 . . . . 3.50

GROUNDED
July, 2005
1 (of 6) 3.00
2 thru 5 . . . . @3.00
6 32-pg. 3.50

GRRL SCOUTS
Feb., 2003
1 (of 4) Work Sucks, b&w. 3.00
2 thru 4 . . . . @3.00

GUARDIAN ANGEL
May, 2002
1 (of 4) AWs,F:ChristianAngelos. . . 3.00
2 AWs,no place like home 3.00
3 AWs,Our onlyhope. 3.00
4 concl. 3.00

GUNCANDY
(B&W) July, 2005
1 (of 2) BSf 6.00
2 BSt. 6.00

GUTSVILLE
May, 2007
1 (of 6) 3.00
2 thru 6 . . . . @3.00

HAMMER OF THE GODS:
HAMMER HITS CHINA
Feb., 2003
1 thru 3 . . . . @3.00

HAWAIIAN DICK
Dec., 2002
1 thru 3 Hawaii in 1953. . . . . @3.00

HAWAIIAN DICK:
THE LAST RESORT
Aug., 2004
1 (of 4) 3.00
2 & 3 . . . . @3.00
4 concl. 3.00

HAWKSHAWS
March, 2000
1 by Dietrich Smith 3.00
1a variant movie poster(c) 3.00
2 and 3 . . . . @3.00

HAZARD
WildStorm, 1996
1 JMi,RMr 3.00
2 JMi,RMr 3.00
3 JMi,RMr 3.00
4 JMi,RMr 3.00
5 JMi,RMr,Hazard finds Dr. D'Oro . 3.00
6 JMi,RMr 3.00
7 JMi,RMr,Hazard meets Prism . . . 3.00

HEADHUNTERS
(B&W) April, 1997
1 ChM,V:Army of Wrath 3.00
2 ChM,V:undead militia. 3.00
3 ChM,'Slaughterground' 3.00

HEARTBREAKERS
Superdigest, July 1998
1 B&W and color 104-pg. 10.00

HEAVEN'S DEVILS
Sept., 2003
1 (of 4) 3.00
2 thru 4 . . . . @3.00

HEDGE KNIGHT, THE
Aug., 2003
1 (of 6) MsM 5.00
1a variant (c) 12.00
2 . . . . 5.00

2a cardstock(c) 10.00
3 . . . . 4.00
3a holofoil (c) 6.00
See also Color Comics section

HEIRS OF ETERNITY
Apr., 2003
1 (of 5) 3.00
2 . . . . 3.00
3 . . . . 3.00
4 . . . . 3.00
5 . . . . 3.00

HELLCOP
Avalon, Oct., 1998
1 JoC,F:Virgil Hilts 2.50
2 JoC,It's a small underwold
   after all 2.50
3 JoC,new circles of Hell 2.50
4 JoC,secrets of Hell revealed . . . 2.50
5 JoC,Hell & High Water. 2.50
5a variant cover 3.00

HELLHOLE
Top Cow, May, 1999
1 SLo,AdP,F:Michael Cabrini 2.50
2 SLo,AdP,The Devil's Candy. 2.50
3 SLo,AdP,power brokers 2.50

HELLHOUNDS
Aug., 2003
1 Hadean Gates 3.00
2 thru 5 . . . . @3.00
6 EL(c),F:Savage Dragon. 3.00
1a and 2a variant (c). . . . . @3.00
5a variant (c). 3.00

HELLSHOCK
1994
1 I:Hellshock. 3.50
2 Powers & Origin. 3.50
3 New foe 3.50
4 . . . . 3.50

HELLSHOCK
Jan., 1997
1 JaL,Something wrong with
   Daniel, 48-pg. 3.00
2 JaL,Daniel learns to control
   powers. 2.50
3 JaL,Daniel free of madness. 2.50
4 JaL,Daniel searches for his
   mother, Jonakand plans escape
   from Hell 2.50
5 JaL,Jonakand and fallen angels
   tear hell apart 2.50
6 JaL,'The Milk of Paradise' 2.50
7 JaL,'A Mother's Story',
   double size 4.00
8 JaL,House of Torture 2.50

HELLSPAWN
TMP, July, 2000
1 The Clown,pt.1. . . . . 4.00
2 The Clown,pt.2. . . . . 3.00
3 Hate Me 3.00
4 Hate You 3.00
5 Selling Fear 3.00
6 Angels 5.00
7 The Group 2.50
8 The Suicide Gate. 2.50
9 Chains 2.50
10 Clash. 2.50
11 Conflicts of Interest 2.50
12 Monsters and Miracles 2.50
13 Heaven & Hell. 2.50
14 Light of Day. 2.50
15 Blinded 2.50
16 Hellworld,pt.4 . . . . 2.50

17 The Killing Hand,pt.1 . . . . 2.50
18 The Killing Hand,pt.2 . . . . 2.50
19 The Killing Hand,pt.3 . . . . 2.50
20 The Collection. 2.50
21 The Collection,pt.2 . . . . 2.50
22 Love Lost,pt.1 . . . . 3.00
23 Love Lost,pt.2 . . . . 2.50
24 In the Grip of Shadows. 2.50
25 Remember Me? 2.50

HERO BY NIGHT
Platinum, Mar., 2007
1 thru 4 . . . . @3.00

HERO CAMP
May, 2005
1 (of 4) 3.00
2 I Still Haven't Found What I'm
   Looking For, pt.1 . . . . 3.00
3 . . . . 3.00
4 Parents Day 3.00

HIDING IN TIME
July, 2007
1 (of 4) 3.50
2 thru 3 . . . . @3.50

HOLY TERROR, THE
Aug., 2002
1 (of 4) PhH 3.00
2 thru 3 PhH . . . . @3.00

HOMAGE STUDIOS
April, 1993
Swimsuit Spec.#1 JLe,WPo, MS . . 2.50

HONG ON THE RANGE
**Matinee Entertainment/
Flypaper, Dec., 1997**
1 (of 3) by William Wu & Jeff
   Lafferty. 2.50
2 in Washout. 2.50
3 Duke Goslin 2.50

HUMAN KIND
Top Cow, Aug., 2004
1 TnD,F:Alia Sparrow 3.00
2 TnD 3.00
3 TnD,Roads to New Rome,pt.3 . . 3.00
4 All Roads Lead to (New) Rome. . 3.00
5 All Roads Lead to (New) Rome. . 3.00

Hong on the Range #2
© Image/Flypaper

HUNTER-KILLER
Top Cow, 2005
0 MWa,MS, B&W, 16-pg. 1.00
1 MWa,MS 3.00
2 MWa,MS 3.00
2a variant JLi 3.00
3 MWa,MS 3.00
4 thru 6 MWa,MS . . . . @3.00
7 . . . . 3.00
8 . . . . 3.00
9 . . . . 3.00
9a variant (c). 3.00
10 . . . . 3.00
11 The Deadly Game Continues . . . 3.00
11a variant b&w (c), rare 4.00
12 The End of Morningstar? 3.00
Script-book 40-pg. 5.00
1-shot Hunter-Killer Dossier. 3.00

HYSTERIA:
ONE MAN GANG
(B&W) March, 2006
1 . . . . 3.00
2 . . . . 3.00
3 All car chase issue. 3.00
4 . . . . 3.50

IMAGE COMICS
Dec., 2005
Spec. Holiday Spec. (2005) 10.00

IMAGE INTRODUCES:
Oct., 2001
1 Primate 3.00
1b variant AGo(c) 3.00
(2) Legend of Isis. 3.00
(3) The Believer 3.00
(4) Cryptopia 3.00
(5) Dog Soldiers. 3.00

IMAGE TWO-IN-ONE
(B&W) Mar., 2001
1 EL,48-pg. F:Herculian & Duncan. 3.00

IMAGE ZERO
1993
0 I:Troll,Deathtrap,Pin-ups,rep.
   Savage Dragon #4,O:Stryker,
   F:ShadowHawk 9.00

IMAGES OF
SHADOWHAWK
1993–94
1 KG,V:Trencher 2.50
2 thru 3 V:Trencher. 2.50

IMAGINARIES, THE
Mar., 2005
1 (of 4) 3.00
2 . . . . 3.00
2a variant (c). 3.00
3 & 4 . . . . @3.00

IMMORTAL TWO
May, 1997
(B&W) Half-Tone
1 MsM,F:Gaijin & Gabrielle. 2.50
2 MsM. 2.50
3 MsM. 2.50
4 MsM,V:Okami Red. 2.50
5 MsM,new drug epidemic 2.50
6 MsM,First Order, cont. 2.50
7 MsM,vs. impossible odds 2.50
7 MsM,flip photo cover 2.50

Immortal Two #1
© Image

IMPALER
Oct., 2006
1 . . . . 3.00
2 thru 5 . . . . @3.00

INDUSTRY OF WAR
(B&W) Nov., 2005
1-shot 8.00

INFERNO: HELLBOUND
Top Cow, Nov., 2001
1 MS,DT,Hell loose on Earth 2.50
1a-1f variant(c) . . . . @2.50
2 thru 4 MS . . . . @2.75
#0 MS 16-pg., signed. 20.00

IN HER DARKEST HOUR
Aug., 2007
1-shot 3.50

INNOCENTS, THE
Top Cow, July, 2006
1 . . . . 3.00
GN 10.00

INTIMIDATORS, THE
Dec., 2005
1 . . . . 3.50
2 . . . . 3.50
3 Who is Atrocity 3.50
4 Crash and Byrn 3.50
5 Prison Break 3.50
6 Last Best Hope 3.50
7 Blame Canada 3.50

INTRIGUE
Aug., 1999
1 F:Kirk Best 2.50
1a variant cover (1:4) 2.50
2 on the run from the law 2.50
3 V:NYPD SWAT team 2.50
3a variant HuR cover (1:4) 2.50
4 . . . . 2.50
5 . . . . 3.00
5a variant Mike Wieringo(c) 3.00

INVINCIBLE
Jan., 2003
1 O:Mark Grayson 15.00

2 . . . . 12.00
3 quality time 9.00
4 human bombs 7.00
5 It Came From Outer Space 6.00
6 . . . . 6.00
7 Guardians of the Globe 5.00
8 shperhero funeral 5.00
9 Perfect Strangers,pt.1 . . . . 5.00
10 Perfect Strangers,pt.2 . . . . 7.00
11 Perfect Strangers,pt.3 . . . . 7.00
12 Perfect Strangers,pt.4 . . . . 7.00
13 Perfect Strangers,epilogue 7.00
14 Alien invaders return 7.00
15 Aquaria 4.00
16 Immortal is back 3.00
17 High school graduation 3.00
18 Space flight to Mars 3.00
19 . . . . 3.00
20 Return of the Robot Zombie 3.00
21 Return to Midnight City 3.00
22 Mark and Amber at college 3.00
23 . . . . 3.00
24 Worst beating yet 3.00
25 A Different World, pt.1 . . . . 5.00
26 A Different World, pt.2 . . . . 3.00
27 A Different World, pt.3 . . . . 3.00
28 A Different World, pt.4 . . . . 3.00
29 . . . . 3.00
30 A Different World 3.00
31 Mark & Amber to Africa 3.00
32 Life with Amber and Eva 3.00
33 Angstrom Levy 3.00
34 Angstrom Levy 3.00
35 . . . . 3.00
36 Re-animen Strike 3.00
37 . . . . 3.00
38 . . . . 3.00
39 . . . . 3.00
40 . . . . 3.00
41 . . . . 3.00
42 . . . . 2.00
43 Space Fight 3.00
44 . . . . 3.00
45 In deep space 3.00
46 . . . . 3.00
47 . . . . 3.00
Spec. #0 . . . . 1.00
Spec. Official Handbook of the
   Invincible Universe, Vol. 1 . . . . . 5.00
Spec. Script Book 4.00

IRON GHOST
Apr., 2005
1 thru 6 CDi(s) . . . . @3.00

IRON WINGS
March, 2000
1 Legends of Iron Wings 2.50
1a variant Andy Park(c) 2.50
2 V:Amaxius 2.50
3 Nightmares 2.50

JACKIE CHAN'S
SPARTAN X
(B&W) March, 1998
1 MGo,RM,Hell-Bent Hero for Hire . 3.00
2 MGo,to Russia 3.00
3 MGo,V:Kenshi 3.00
4 MGo,RM, in Istanbul 3.00
5 MGo,RM, Mind of God 3.00
5a MGo,RM, photo cover 3.00
6 MGo,RM, The Armor of Heaven . 3.00
6a MGo,RM, photo cover 3.00

JACK STAFF
Feb., 2003
1 Britain's Greatest hero 3.00
2 thru 7 . . . . @3.00
8 thru 14 . . . . @3.50

Jackie Chan Spartan X #1
© Image

King-Size Spec. #1 Weird World
   of Jack Staff 6.00

JADE WARRIORS
Aug., 1999
1 MD2,Destruction of Japan 2.50
2 MD2,V:Ramthar 2.50
3 MD2,Blood of the Children 2.50
1a thru 3a photo(c) . . . . @2.50
3b movie poster style(c) 2.50

JINN
Jan., 2000
1 F:Karen Lane 3.00
2 and 3 . . . . @3.00
1a thru 2a variant cover . . . . @3.00

JINX
(B&W) June, 1997
1 by Brian Michael Bendis 3.00
1a 2nd printing 3.00
2 F:Jinx, female bounty hunter 3.00
3 thru 5 . . . . @4.00
Spec.#1 Buried Treasure 4.00
Spec.#1 True Crime Confessions . . 4.00

JINX: TORSO
(B&W) Aug., 1998
1 by Brian Michael Bendis, 48-pg. . . 4.00
2 search continues 4.00
3 Torso Killer 4.00
4 breaking the law 4.00
5 48-pg. 5.00
6 conclusion, 48-pg. 5.00
Spec. #@%!! short stories 4.00

JOHNNY DELGADO
IS DEAD
Spacedog, Sept., 2007
1 (of 2) 40-pgs. 4.00
2 . . . . 4.00

JOURNEYMAN
Aug., 1999
1 by Brandon McKinney 3.00
2 enemies become allies 3.00
3 V:Dragon King 3.00

IMAGE

All comics prices listed are for *Near Mint* condition.

J.U.D.G.E.
March, 2000
1 by Greg Horn,F:Victoria Grace	3.00
1a variant cover	3.00
2 V:John Lawson	3.00
3 Secret Rage,pt.3	3.00

JUNKBOTZ ROTOGIN
Feb., 2003
1	2.50

KABUKI
Sept., 1997
1 DMk,O:Kabuki	7.00
1a variant JSo(c).	7.00
2 DMk,O:Kabuki, pg.2.	5.00
3 DMk,surprise visitor	5.00
4 DMk,Akemi, romance	7.00
5 DMk,action	4.00
6 DMk	3.00
7 DMk	3.00
7a DMk variant cover (1:2)	3.00
8 DMk	3.00
9 DMk, finale.	3.00
GN Reflections #1, 48-pg.	5.00
GN Reflections #1 signed	8.00
GN Reflections #2 art & stories	5.00
GN Reflections,Vol.3	5.00
GN Reflections,Vol.4	5.00
Spec. 1-shot The Ghost Play	3.00
Spec. #2 Images, rep. #2 & #3	6.00
Kabuki 1/2 Wizard Mail-in	3.00
Kabuki 1/2 signed	6.00

KABUKI AGENTS
(B&W) Aug., 1999
1 DMk,F:Scarab	4.00
1a JQ(c), DMk signed.	7.00
2 DMk,F:Scarab, Tiger Lily	3.00
3 DMk,F:Scarab, Tiger Lily	3.00
4 DMk,F:Scarab, Tiger Lily	3.00
5 thru 8 DMk	@3.00
Artbook.	5.00
Kabuki Agents: Scarab #1 signed	6.00

KABUKI: THE ALCHEMY
Jan., 2004
1 (of 6) DMk	3.00
2 DMk	3.00

KABUKI CLASSICS
Feb., 1999
1 Fear the Reaper, rep.	9.00
2 Dance of Death	3.00
3 Circle of Blood, act 1, 48-pg.	6.00
4 Circle of Blood, act 2	4.00
5 Circle of Blood, act 3	3.00
6 Circle of Blood, act 4	3.00
7 Circle of Blood, act 5	3.00
8 Circle of Blood, conclusion	3.00
9 Masks of the Noh, Act 1	3.00
10 Masks of the Noh, Act 2	3.00
11 Masks of the Noh, Act 3	3.00
12 Masks of the Noh, concl.	3.00
Kabuki Classics #1 signed.	7.00

KARZA
Feb., 2003
1 thru 4 Micronauts spin-off	@3.00

KID SUPREME
Supreme 1996–97
1 & 2	2.50
3 DaF,ErS	2.50
4 DaF,ErS,Party time	2.50
5 DaF,ErS,'Birds of a Feather'	2.50
6 DaF,ErS,I: Sensational Spinner	2.50
7 DaF,ErS,Everything falls apart.	2.50

KID TERRIFIC
(B&W) Nov., 1998
1 A:Snedak & Manny Stellar	3.00

KILLER INSTINCT TOUR BOOK
1 All Homage Artist,I:Crusade.	5.00
1a signed	20.00

KILLING GIRL
Aug., 2007
1 (of 5)	3.00
2	3.00

KILLRAZOR SPECIAL
Aug., 1995
1 O:Killrazor	2.50

KIN
Top Cow, Feb., 2000
1 GFr,Neanderthal	3.00
2 GFr,F:McLoon	3.00
3 GFr,Alaska revenge	3.00
4 GFr.	3.00
5 GFr,Born Free	3.00
6 GFr,40-pg.,The End?	4.00
6a variant AAd(c)	4.00
1st 6 as set, signed GFr	25.00

Kindrid #2
© WildStorm

KINDRED
WildStorm, 1994
1 JLe,BCi(s),BBh,I:Knidred	5.00
2 JLe,BCi(s),BBh,V:Kindred	3.50
3 JLe,BCi(s),BBh,V:Kindred	3.00
3a WPo(c),Alternate(c)	6.00
4 JLe,BCi(s),BBh,V:Kindred	3.00

'KINI
Flypaper, Feb., 1999
1 KK,BKs,F:Kim Walters	2.50

KISS: THE PSYCHO CIRCUS
TMP, July, 1997
1 SvG,AMe	8.00
2 AMe, unearthly origins	6.00
3 AMe, Judgment o/t Elementals	5.00
4 AMe,Smoke and Mirrors,pt.1	4.00
5 AMe,Smoke and Mirrors,pt.2	4.00
6 AMe,Smoke and Mirrors, concl.	4.00
7 AMe,Creatures of the Night	3.00
8 AMe,Forever	3.00
9 AMe,Four Sides to Every Story	3.00
10 AMe,Destroyer,pt.1	3.00
11 AMe,Destroyer,pt.2	3.00
12 AMe,Destroyer,pt.3 (of 4)	3.00
13 AMe, Destroyer,pt.4	3.00
14 AMe, in Feudal Japan.	3.00
15 AMe, in Feudal Japan, choices.	2.50
16 AMe, Ticket for Terror	2.50
17 AMe, World Without Heroes,pt.2	2.50
18 AMe, Sunburst Finish	2.50
19 Fate of the Psycho Circus	2.50
20 Mr. Makebelieve	2.50
21 Don't Talk to Strangers	2.50
22 Twin sisters	2.50
23 Tribunal of souls	2.50
24 Cat's Eye	2.50
25	2.50
26 Nightingale's Song,pt.1	2.50
27 Nightingale's Song,pt.2	2.50
28 Perdition Blues	2.50
29 Shadow of the Moon,pt.1	2.50
30 Shadow of the Moon,pt.2	2.50
31 Sins of Omission	2.50
32 Gallery of God's Mistakes	2.50
33 Gallery of God's Mistakes,pt.2	2.50
34 Far Corners of Night	2.50

KISS 4K
Platinum, May, 2007
1	4.00
1a Destroyer edition oversize	50.00
2 & 3	@3.00

KNIGHTMARE
Extreme, 1995
0 O:Knightmare.	2.50
1 I:Knightmare MMy	2.50
2 I:Caine	2.50
3 RLd,AV,The New Order, F:Detective Murtaugh	2.50
4 RLd,AV,MMy,I:Thrillkill	2.50
5 V:Thrillkill	2.50
6 Extreme Babewatch.	2.50
7	2.50
8 I:Acid	2.50

KNIGHTS OF THE JAGUAR
Top Cow, Jan., 2004
Spec. super limited	2.50

KNIGHTSTRIKE
Extreme, 1996
1 Extreme Destroyer,pt.6 x-over, bagged with card	2.50

KNIGHT WATCHMAN
(B&W) May, 1998
1 by Gary Carlson & Chris Ecker	3.00
2 thru 4 Graveyard Shift,pt.2–pt.3	@3.00

KORE
Apr., 2003
1	3.00
1a variant (c).	3.00
2 thru 5	@3.00

KURT BUSIEK'S ASTRO CITY
Juke Box, 1995–96
1 I:Samaritan,'In Dreams'	12.00
1a 2nd printing	2.50
2 I:Silver Agent,V:Shirak the Devourer	10.00
3 F:Jack in the Box	10.00

IMAGE

Kurt Busiek's Astro City Vol. 2 #3
© Homage

4 I:Hanged Man,Safeguards 11.00
5 I:Crackerjack 12.00
6 O:Samaritan,F:Winged Victory . 14.00

[Vol. 2] Homage, 1996
½ F:Hanged Man (1996) 5.00
1 KBk(s),BA,Welcome to
  Astro City. 9.00
1a Trunk(c) 8.00
1b 2nd printing 2.50
2 KBk(s),BA,O:First Family,
  F:Astra, Everyday Life. 7.00
2b 2nd printing 2.50
3 KBk(s),BA,Adventures in
  Other Worlds 7.00
4 KBk,BA,Teenager seeks to
  become teen sidekick,pt.1 (of 6) 6.00
5 Learning the Game 5.00
6 V: creatures of Shadow Hill 5.00
7 Aliens invade Astro City. 4.00
8 The aliens are out there 4.00
9 Honor Guard vs. Aliens finale . . 4.00
10 meet the junkman 4.00
11 Serpent's Teeth 4.00
12 F:Jack-In-The-Box 3.00
13 F:Looney Leo 3.00
14 F:Steeljack 3.00
15 F:supervillains 3.00
3-D #1 . . . . 5.00

Homage/DC, 1999
16 KBk(s), El Hombre 3.00
17 KBk(s), Mock Turtle 3.00
18 KBk(s), F:Steeljack 3.00
19 KBk(s), F:Steeljack 3.00
20 KBk(s). 3.00
21 KBk(s),F:Crackerjack 3.00
22 KBk(s),F:Samaritan. 3.00
Spec.1/2 KBk(s) 3.00

LABMAN
1996
1 I:Labman 4.00
1a variant cover 4.00
2 & 3 . . . . @4.00

LADY PENDRAGON
Nov., 1998
1 MHw,Destiny's Embrace 2.50
1a remastered, new cover 2.50
1b Dynamic Forces variant cover. . 7.00
1c JeL(c) glow-in-the-dark 20.00
1d Tour Edition 5.00
2 MHw, Destiny's Embrace,pt.2. . . . 3.00

3 MHw,Destiny's Embrace,pt.3 . . . . 3.00
3a variant cover (1:4) 2.50
0 MHw, Secrets & Origins. 2.50
0a Eurosketch cover. 9.00
Preview (Wizard, Chicago Comicon) 5.00

LADY PENDRAGON: DRAGON BLADE
April, 1999
1 MHw,Merlin trains Jennifer 2.50
1a variant cover (1:4) 2.50
1b Chrome Edition 5.00
2 MHw,F:Morgana 2.50
2a variant cover (1:4) 2.50
3 MHw,B.U.I:Alley Cat 3.00
4 MHw,Morgana returns 2.50
5 MHw,Spear of Destiny 2.50
6 MHw,Jennifer Drake resigns 2.50
7 MHw,Future Prophecy,pt.1 . . . . . 4.00
8 MHw,Future Prophecy,pt.2 . . . . . 2.50
9 MHw,Future Prophecy,pt.3 . . . . . 2.50
10 MHw,Messianic Lineage,pt.1 . . . 2.50
11 MHw,Messianic Lineage,pt.2 . . . 2.50
12 MHw,Messianic Lineage,pt.3 . . . 2.50
1a Glow-in-the-dark JaL(c) 2.50
Gallery Ed.#1 . . . . 3.00
Gallery Ed.#1a photo(c). 3.00

LADY PENDRAGON: MORE THAN MORTAL
May, 1999
1 MHw,Pendragon vs. Protector. . . 2.50
1a variant cover (1:4) 7.00
1b Gold foil(c) 7.00

LADY SUPREME
Extreme, 1996
1 TMr. 2.50
2 TMr,Die & Let Die,pt.2 . . . . 2.50
3 TMr,V:Manassa 2.50
4 TMr,'Lady Supreme goes
  undercover' 2.50

LAST CHRISTMAS, THE
May, 2006
1 Twas the Fight Before Christmas 3.00
2 thru 5 . . . . @3.00

LAST SHOT
Aug., 2001
1 Foodchain,pt.1 . . . . 3.00
2 Metal in his Heart. 3.00
3 Six String Noose 3.00
4 Angel of Death 3.00

LAST SHOT: FIRST DRAW
May, 2001
1 First Draw Revolver 3.00

LAST STRAW MAN, THE
Feb., 2004
1 (of 3) 4.00
2 40-pg. 4.00

LAZARUS
Oct, 2007
1 (of 3) 3.50

LEAVE IT TO CHANCE
Homage, 1996–98
1 JeR,PS,I:Chance Falconer 5.00
2 JeR,PS,Dragons are a Girl's
  Best Friend 5.00

Leave it to Chance #2
© Image/Homage

Homage
3 JeR,PS,Chance and St. George
  race against time. 5.00
4 JeR,PS. 3.00
5 JeR,PS,'Trick or Threat'. 3.00
6 JeR,PS,Return of Cap'n Hitch. . . 3.00
7 JeR,PS,'And Not a Drop to Drink 3.00
8 JeR,PS,Phantom of the Mall 3.00
9 JeR,PS,Midnite Monster
  Madness 3.00
10 JeR,PS,'Destroy All Monsters' . . 3.00
11 JeR,PS,Dead Men Can't Skate . 3.00
12 JeR,PS,visits her friend Dash. . . 3.00
13 JeR,PS,Reunion,48-pg. 5.00

LEGACY
May, 2003
1 . . . . 3.00
2 . . . . 3.00
3 . . . . 3.00
4 . . . . 3.00
4a variant (c). 3.00

LEGACY OF KAIN: DEFIANCE
Jan., 2004
1-shot. 3.00
1-shotA variant (c) 3.00

LEGEND OF ISIS
Feb., 2002
1 Origin of Isis. 3.00

LEGEND OF SUPREME
Dec., 1994
1 KG(s),JJ,DPs,Revelations,pt.1 . . 2.50
2 Revelations,pt.2. . . . . 2.50
3 Conclusion 2.50

LETHAL
1996
1 & 2 . . . . @2.50

LEX TALIONIS: A JUNGLE TALE
Jan., 2004
1-shot 48-pg. 6.00

All comics prices listed are for *Near Mint* condition.

IMAGE

LIBERTY MEADOWS
July, 2002
27 comic book convention 4.00
28 Ralph's Genetic Breakthrough . . 4.00
29 Brandy's Christmas Surprise . . . 4.00
30 Long Cold Winter,pt.1 . . . . 4.00
31 Long Cold Winter,pt.2 . . . . 4.00
32 The Cow is Back. 3.50
33 Mad Cow, pt.2 . . . . 3.50
34 thru 37 . . . . @3.00
1-shot Sourcebook, 48-pg. 5.00

LIONS, TIGERS & BEARS
Jan., 2005
1 (of 4) Fear and Pride, pt.1 . . . . . 3.00
2 Fear and Pride, pt.2 . . . . 3.00
3 Fear and Pride, pt.3 . . . . 3.00
4 Fear and Pride, pt. 4 . . . . 3.00
Vol. 2
1 (of 4) Betrayal, pt.1 . . . . 3.00
2 thru 4 Betrayal, pt.2 thru pt.4 . . @3.00

LITTLE RED HOT: BOUND
July, 2001
1 (of 3) by Dawn Brown 3.00
2 . . . . 3.00
3 . . . . 3.00

LITTLE RED HOT: CHANE OF FOOLS
(B&W) Feb., 1999
1 (of 3) by Dawn Brown, F:Chane . 3.00
2 stranded in desert 3.00
3 Heaven vs. Hell 3.00

LOADED BIBLE
April, 2006
1-shot Jesus vs. Vampires 5.00
1-shot #2 Blood of Christ 5.00

LOOKING GLASS WARS: HATTER M
Dec., 2005
1 (of 4) 4.00
2 . . . . 4.00
3 . . . . 3.50
4 . . . . 4.00

LOST ONES, THE
March, 2000
1 by Ken Penders 3.00
2 . . . . 3.00

LOVEBUNNY & MR. HELL
Feb., 2003
1-shot 3.00
1-shot Savage Love 3.00

LOW ORBIT
Nov., 2006
1 64-pg. 7.00

LUCHA LIBRE
Sept., 2007
1 F:Luchadoritos, 48-pgs. 6.00

LULLABY: WISDOM SEEKER
Feb., 2005
1 (of 4) 3.00
2 thru 4 . . . . @3.00

LYNCH
WildStorm, June, 1997
1 TVs,'Terror in the Jungle' 2.50

MACE GRIFFIN: BOUNTY HUNTER
Top Cow, Apr., 2003
1-shot 3.00

MADAME MIRAGE
Top Cow, Apr., 2007
Spec. First Look 2.00
1 PDi(s) 3.00
1a variant (c) 5.00
2 thru 4 . . . . @3.00

MADMAN ATOMIC COMICS
Apr., 2007
1 MiA 3.00
2 MiA 3.00
3 MiA, Swiped From Dimension X . 3.00
4 thru 6 . . . . @3.00

MAGDALENA
Top Cow, March, 2000
1 JBz,Darkness spin-off 4.00
1a variant MS(c) 4.00
1b variant Michael Turner(c) 4.00
2 JBz,secret revealed 2.50
3 JBz,Blood Divine,pt.3 . . . . 2.50
Preview, Magdalena/Blood
   Legacy, 22 pg.(2000) 3.00
1/2 Magdalena/Angelus, The Light
   and the Glory 3.00

MAGDALENA
Top Cow, July, 2003
1 (of 4) 3.00
2 thru 4 . . . . @3.00
1a and 2a variant (c) . . . . @3.00
Spec. Con. Preview 2.50

MAGDALENA/ VAMPIRELLA
Top Cow, June, 2003
1-shot 3.00
1-shotA variant (c) 1:4 . . . . 3.00
1-shot (2004) 3.00
1-shot-A variant (c) (2004) 3.00

MAGDELENA VS. DRACULA
Top Cow, Apr., 2005
1 (of 4) Monster War x-over 3.00

MAGE: THE HERO DEFINED
1997
1 MWg,F:Kevin Matchstick 5.00
2 MWg,Kirby Hero, V:harpies 4.00
3 MWg,Isis, Gretch 3.00
4 MWg,Isis, drug 3.00
5 MWg,into Canada 3.00
6 MWg,V:Dragonslayer 2.50
7 MWg 2.50
8 MWg,V:Red Caps 2.50
9 MWg,Sibling Trio 2.50
10 MWg,enchanted by a succubus . 2.50
11 MWg,Joe Phat, missing 2.50
12 MWg,Pale Incanter's Lair 2.50
13 MWg,What color is magic 2.50
14 MWg,Man Mountain of???? . . . 2.50
15 MWg, 48-pg. concl. 6.00
Spec. 3-D #1 (1998) 5.00

Mage: The Hero Defined 3-D #1
© Image

MAN AGAINST TIME
Motown 1996
1 'Every Hero' 2.50
2 . . . . 2.50
3 'Pro Patria Mori' 2.50

MANIC
Feb., 2004
1-shot 3.00

MARS ATTACKS
1996
1 KG,BSz(of 4) 2.50
2 thru 4 . . . . @2.50

MASK OF ZORRO, THE
July, 1998
1 (of 4) DMG,RoW,RM,MGo(c), . . . 3.00
2 DMG,RoW,RM,MGo(c) 3.00
3 DMG,RoW,MGo(c) 3.00
4 DMG,RoW,MGo concl. 3.00
4a photo cover 3.00

MASTERS OF THE UNIVERSE
2002
1 He-Man returns 3.00
1b variant JSC(c) 3.00
1b variant EN(c) 3.00
2 thru 4 . . . . @3.00
2a–4a variant (c) . . . . @3.00
Volume II
1 . . . . 3.00
2 thru 8 . . . . @3.00
1a–2a variant (c) . . . . @3.00
3a–4a holofoil (c) . . . . @6.00
1-shot Icons of Evil: Beast Man 5.00

MAXIMAGE
Extreme, 1995–96
1 RLe(c) 2.50
2 Extreme Destroyer,pt.2,
   x-over, bagged with card 2.50
3 . . . . 2.50
4 A:Angela,Glory 2.50
5 thru 8 . . . . @2.50
9 BML, Sex Slaves of Bomba
   Island 2.50
10 BML, The King of Emotion is
   back 2.50

Maxx #2
© *Image*

MAXX, THE
1993

1/2 SK,from Wizard	10.00
1 SK,I:The Maxx	5.00
1a glow in the dark(c)	12.00
2 SK,V:Mr.Gone	4.00
3 SK,V:Mr.Gone	4.00
4 SK	4.00
5 SK	3.00
6 SK	3.00
7 SK,A:Pitt	3.50
8 SK,V:Pitt	3.50
9 SK	3.00
10 SK	3.00
11 SK	2.50
12 SK	2.50
13 Maxx Wanders in Dreams	2.50
14 R:Julie	4.00
15 Julia's Pregnant	4.00
16 SK,Is Maxx in Danger?	4.00
17 SK,Gardener Maxx	4.00
18 SK,'Beware The Hooley'	2.50
19 SK,V:Hooley,'Last Fairy Tale'	2.50
20 SK,Questions are answered	2.50
21 AM(s),SK	3.00
22 SK,'Other Peoples' Crap'	2.50
23 SK,'Having to Believe'	2.50
24 SK	2.50
25 SK,'Lost and Found'	2.50
26 SK	2.50
27 V:Iago the Killer Slug	2.50
28 Sara and Norberg look for Julie	2.50
29 Sara and Gone defeat Iago the Slug	2.50
30 Lil' Sara faces her fears	2.50
31 F:The Library girl	2.50
32 F:The Library girl,pt.2	2.50
33 Sara's back	2.50
34 Mark and Julia	2.50
35 who knows?	2.50
36 bumfuzzled	2.50
37 Megan's story concl	2.50
38 Mark,Julie,Larry,pt.1 (of 4)	2.50
Spec. Friends of Maxx,F:Dude Japan	3.00
The Maxx 3-D #1	5.00

MECH DESTROYER
March, 2001

1 (of 4) Battle for Earth	3.00
2 Face of the Enemy	3.00
3 rescue the captives	3.00
4 V:The Crimson Death	3.00

MEDIEVAL SPAWN/ WITCHBLADE
May, 1996

1 thru 3	@5.00

MEGADRAGON & TIGER
March, 1999

1 by Tony Wong, from Hong Kong	3.00
2 F:Red Tiger	3.00
3 V:Single-Minded Arhat	3.00
4 V:Fiery Lord	3.00
5 F:Gigi	3.00

Megahurtz #2
© *Image*

MEGAHURTZ
(B&W) Aug., 1997

1 JPi,I:Megahurtz	3.00
2 JPi,visit to Wonderland	3.00
3 JPi,V:N-Filtraitors	3.00
4 JPi,Liberaiders	3.00

MEGATON MAN: BOMBSHELL
July, 1999

1 DSs,V:Unleash	3.00

MEGATON MAN: HARDCOPY
Fiasco (B&W) Feb., 1999

1 by Don Simpson	3.00
2 with 6 new pages	3.00

MELTDOWN
Dec., 2006

1 (of 2) F:The Flare, 48-pgs	6.00
2	6.00

MESSENGER, THE
July, 2000

1-shot JOy, 48-pg	6.00

MICE TEMPLAR, THE
Sept., 2007

1 56-pgs	4.00

MICRONAUTS
June, 2002

1	3.00
2	3.00

3	3.00
4	3.00
5	3.00
6 Star Chamber,pt.1	3.00
7 Star Chamber,pt.2	3.00
8 Invasion Earth,pt.1	3.00
9 Invasion Earth,pt.2	3.00
10 Invasion Earth,pt.3	3.00
11 Invasion Earth,pt.4	3.00
Spec. 2002 Con Special	3.00

MIDNIGHT NATION
Top Cow, Sept., 2000

1 MSz	5.00
1a variant GrF(c)	9.00
2 MSz,GrF, on the run	4.00
3 MSz,GrF, To Hell and inbetween	4.00
4 MSz,GrF, V:Walkers	4.00
5 MSz,GrF, Find your soul	4.00
6 MSz,GrF, Halfway	4.00
7 MSz,GrF, Change has begun	4.00
8 MSz,GrF, Road gets worse	4.00
9 MSz,GrF, New York, New York	4.00
10 MSz,GrF, Soul's price	4.00
11 MSz,GrF, Still the Road to Hell	4.00
12 MSz,GrF, The End of the Road	4.00

MIKE CAREY'S ONE-SIDED BARGAINS
(B&W) Dec., 2006

1-shot 64-pgs	6.00

MIKE GRELL'S MAGGIE THE CAT
Jan., 1996

1 (of 4) Master Piece,pt.1	2.50
2 Master Piece,pt.2	2.50

MINISTRY OF SPACE
April, 2001

1 (of 3) WEI,CWn,World War II	3.00
2 WEI,CWn	3.00
3 WEI,CWn,concl	3.00
Omnibus #1 & #2	5.00
3	3.00

MISERY SPECIAL
Dec., 1995

1 Cyberforce Origins	3.00

MISPLACED
May, 2003

1	3.00
1a variant (c)s	3.00
2 & 3	@3.00

MONSTER FIGHTERS, INC.
April, 1999

1 Who you gonna call	3.00
2 Wake the dead	3.00
1-shot The Black Book	3.50

MONSTER FIGHTERS INC.: THE GHOSTS OF CHRISTMAS
Dec., 1999

1 The Fright Before Christmas	4.00

MONSTERMAN
(B&W) Sept., 1997

1 MM,from Action Planet	3.00
2 MM,Inhuman monsters	3.00
3 MM,King of Monsters	3.00
4 MM, conclusion	3.00

MORA
Feb., 2005
1 All Beasts will Show Their Teeth . 3.00
2 In the Gloaming 3.00
3 Dying Among the Shadows 3.00
4 Conslusion, pt.1 . . . . 3.00

MORE THAN MORTAL/ LADY PENDRAGON
June, 1999
1 MHw,x-over 2.50
Prev. Edition 16-pg., B&W 5.00

MORE THAN MORTAL: OTHERWORLDS
Liar Comics, July, 1999
1 F:Derdre & Morand 3.00
1a variant cover (1:2) 5.00
2 in Otherworld 3.00
2a variant cover (1:2) 4.00
3 Lady in white 3.00
3a variant Derdre cover (1:2) 3.00
4 Woman in white, concl. 3.00
5 Famine,pt.1 . . . . 3.00
6 Famine,pt.2 . . . . 3.00
7 Famine,pt.3 . . . . 3.00
Art Gallery #1 . . . . 3.50

MR. MONSTER VS. GORZILLA
(2 color) July, 1998
1-shot, MGi 3.00

MR. MONSTER'S GAL FRIDAY: KELLY
(B&W) Jan., 2000
1 MGi 3.50
2 MGi 3.50
3 MGi,AMo(s) 3.50

MR. RIGHT
Aug., 2001
1 TDF,RF,flip-book 3.00
2 TDF,RF,F:General Public 3.00

MOTH
July, 2003
1-shot 48-pg. 6.00

M-REX
Nov., 1999
1 by Joe Kelly & Duncan Rouleau . 3.00
2 thru 5 . . . . @3.00
4a and 5a variant cover . . . . @3.00
#1 Limited Tour Edition 5.00
Preview, B&W, 16-pg 5.00

MS. FORTUNE
(B&W) 1998
1 by Chris Marrinan 3.00
2 Carnage in the Caribbean 3.00
3 Doom at the Dawn of Time 3.00

MUTANT EARTH
May, 2002
1 (of 4) F:Trakk 3.00
2 F:Zeithian warlord, Gallowz 3.00
3 thru 4 . . . . @3.00
1a thru 4a variant (c) . . . . @3.00

MYTHSTALKERS
Mar., 2003
1 The Labyrinth,pt.1 . . . . 3.00
2 The Labyrinth,pt.2 . . . . 3.00

3 The Labyrinth,pt.3 . . . . 3.00
4 The Labyrinth,pt.4 . . . . 3.00
5 London Nights 3.00
6 London Nights,pt.2 . . . . 3.00
7 Gangs of London 3.00
8 London Nights 3.00

NAMELESS, THE
(B&W) May, 1997
1 PhH,I:The Nameless, protector of
Mexico City's lost children 3.00
2 thru 5 . . . . @3.00

NASH
July, 1999
1 MMy, by & starring Kevin Nash . . 2.50
1a variant cover (1:2) 3.00
2 MMy, the end of Nash? 2.50
2a variant cover (1:2) 2.50
#1 Photo-Split edition 3.00
Preview edition MMy,F:Kevin Nash . 2.50
Preview ed.A variant cover (1:2) . . . 2.50

Necromancer #1 (Wizard World cover)
© Top Cow

NECROMANCER, THE
Top Cow, Aug., 2005
1 Something in the way, pt.1 . . . . . 3.00
1a & 1b variant(c)s . . . . @3.00
2 Something in the way, pt.2 . . . . . 3.00
3 Something in the way, pt. 3 . . . . . 3.00
4 thru 6 . . . . @3.00
1 Pilot Season 3.00

NEGATIVE BURN
(B&W) May, 2006
1 64-pg. 6.00
2 thru 11 . . . . @6.00

NEON CYBER
July, 1999
1 F:Neon Dragons 2.50
1a variant cover (1:2) 2.50
1b glow-in-the-dark edition 7.00
2 gang alliance 2.50
2a variant cover (1:2) 2.50
3 Neon a suspect 2.50
4 who framed Neon? 2.50
5 thru 8 . . . . @2.50

NEWFORCE
Extreme, 1996
1 Extreme Destroyer,pt.8
x-over, bagged with card 2.50
2 . . . . 2.50
3 . . . . 2.50
4 Team disbands 2.50

NEWMAN
Extreme, 1996
1 Extreme Destroyer,pt.3
x-over, bagged with card 2.50
2 . . . . 2.50
3 . . . . 2.50
4 Shadowhunt x-over,pt.5 . . . . 2.50

NEWMEN
Extreme, 1994
1 JMs 3.00
2 JMs,I:Girth 2.50
3 JMs,V:Girth,I:Ikonna 2.50
4 JMs,A:Ripclaw 2.50
5 JMs,Ripclaw,V:Ikonn 2.50
6 JMs 2.50
7 JMs 2.50
8 JMs,Team Youngblood 2.50
9 ErS(s),JMs,Kodiak Kidnapped . . . 2.50
10 ExtremeSacrifice,pt.5,x-over 2.50
11 F:Reign 2.50
12 R:Elemental 2.50
13 ErS,I:Bootleg 2.50
14 ErS,Dominion's Secret 2.50
15 I:Time Guild 2.50
16 . . . . 2.50
16a variant cover 3.00
17 R:Girth 2.50
18 F:Byrd 2.50
19 I:Bordda Khan,Shepherd 2.50
20 Extreme Babewatch 2.50
21 ErS,CSp,(1 of 5) 2.50
22 ErS,CSp, Who Needs the
Newmen? 2.50
23 ErS,CSp,Who are the Newmen? 2.50

NEW SHADOWHAWK, THE
June, 1995
1 KBk,I:New ShadowHawk 3.00
2 KBk,V:Mutants 3.00
3 KBk,I:Trophy 3.00
4 KBk,V:Blowfish 3.00
5 KBk, ... 3.00
6 KBk, ... 3.00
7 KBk, ... 3.00

NIGHT CLUB, THE
Apr., 2005
1 (of 4) MBn 3.00
2 Junkyard Apocalypse 3.00
3 Helluva Party 3.00
4 . . . . 3.00

NIGHTLY NEWS, THE
Nov., 2006
1 (of 6) 3.00
2 The Voice 3.00
3 We Don't Need No Education . . . 3.00
4 Cults in Our Midst 3.00
5 True Believers 3.00
6 Revenge 3.00

NINE RINGS OF WU-TANG, THE
Nov., 1999
1 by Brian Haberlin 4.00
2 thru 5 . . . . @3.00
4a variant cover 3.00
#1 limited tour edition 5.00
Preview, B&W, 16-pg 5.00

IMAGE

NINE RINGS OF WU-TANG, THE: FATIMA'S REVENGE
May, 2000
1 by Brian Haberlin 3.00

1963 Book 5
© Image

1963
April, 1993
1 Mystery Incorporated, AnM(s),
  RV,DGb 2.50
1a Gold ed. 3.00
1b Bronze ed. 3.00
2 No One Escapes...The Fury,
  RV,SBi,DGb,JV,I:The Fury. 2.50
3 Tales of the Uncanny,
  RV,SBi,I:U.S.A. 2.50
4 Tales From Beyond
  JV,SBi,I:N-Man, Johnny Beyond 2.50
5 Horus, Lord of Light,
  JV,SBi,I:Horus 2.50
6 Tomorrow Syndicate,
  JV,SBi,C:Shaft 2.50
Ashcan #1 . . . . 3.00
Ashcan #2 . . . . 2.50
Ashcan #4 . . . . 2.00

NINE VOLT
Top Cow, 1997
1 ACh 3.00
1a Variant(c) 4.00
2 ACh 3.00
3 ACh,V:crazed junkie terrorists . . . 2.50
4 ACh,V:Rev. Cyril Gibson 2.50

NOBLE CAUSES
Sept., 2001
1-shot First Impressions 3.00
1 two stories 3.00
2 . . . . 3.00
2a variant RGr(c) 3.00
3 three's a crowd 7.00
3a variant Ccs(c). 7.00
4 In Sickness and in Health,pt.4 . . . 3.00
4a variant(c) 3.00
1-shot Extended Family, 80-pg. 5.00
July, 2004
1 . . . . 3.50
1a & 2a variant(c) . . . . @3.50
2 thru 4 . . . . @3.50
5 A:Invincible. 3.50
6 F:Liz Donnelly 3.50

7 A Day in the Life 3.50
8 V:Venture 3.50
9 F:Celeste 3.50
10 Wrong body 3.50
11 . . . . 3.50
12 Birth of Zephyr's Child 3.50
13 F:Blackthornes 3.50
14 . . . . 3.50
15 . . . . 3.50
16 thru 24 . . . . @3.50
25 48-pg. 5.00
25a variant (c) 5.00
26 thru 31 . . . . @3.50

NOBLE CAUSES: DISTANT RELATIVES
July, 2003
1 (of 4) 3.00
2 thru 4 . . . . @3.00

NOBLE CAUSES: FAMILY SECRETS
Oct., 2002
1 (of 4) F:Liz Donnelly-Noble 3.50
2 spin control 3.00
3 guest stars galore 3.00
4 . . . . 3.00
1a– 3a variant(c). . . . . @3.00

No Honor #1 © Top Cow

NO HONOR
Top Cow, Feb., 2001
1 (of 4) F:Tanne Yojimbo. 4.00
2 . . . . 4.00
3 . . . . 2.50
4 concl. 2.50
Prev. 16-pg. B&W 5.00

NO HONOR: MAKYO
Top Cow, Nov., 2001
1 . . . . 4.00

NORMALMAN
July, 2004
1-shot 20th Anniv. 3.00

NORMAL MAN/ MEGATON MAN SPECIAL
1 . . . . 2.50

NYC MECH
Apr., 2004
1 . . . . 3.00
2 thru 6 . . . . @3.00

NYC MECH: BETA LOVE
May, 2005
1 . . . . 3.50
2 . . . . 3.50
3 thru 6 . . . . @3.00

OBERGEIST: RAGNAROK HIGHWAY
Top Cow/Minotaur 2001
1 TyH 3.00
2 TyH 3.00
3 TyH 3.00
4 TyH 3.00
5 TyH,Ambushed 3.00
6 TyH,His memory, Abyss's flame . 3.00

OBERGEIST: THE EMPTY LOCKET
Top Cow/Minotaur, 2002
1 TyH 3.00

OBJECTIVE FIVE
July, 2000
1 biological weapons 3.00
2 F:Lark, Alexis & DJ 3.00
3 Airborne Virus 3.00
4 Reunion 3.00
5 Hidden Enemies 3.00
6 in China 3.00
7 Origins 3.00

OCCULT CRIMES TASKFORCE
July, 2006
1 . . . . 3.00
2 thru 4 . . . . @3.00

OPERATION KNIGHTSTRIKE
May, 1995
1 RHe,A:Chapel,Bravo,Battlestone 2.50
2 In Afganistan 2.50
3 final issue. 2.50

ORIGINAL ADVENTURES OF CHOLLY & FLYTRAP
Apr., 2005
1 (of 2) A Little Love, A Little Hate . 3.50
2 The Rites of Spring 3.50
Jan., 2006
1 (of 2) 48-pg. 6.00
2 The Rights of Spring, 48-pg. 6.00

OTHERS, THE
March, 1995
0 JV(s),From ShadowHawk 2.50
1 JV(s)V:Mongrel 2.50
2 JV,Mongrel takes weapons 2.50
3 War 2.50
4 O:Clone 2.50

OVERKILL
Top Cow, Oct., 2000
1 PJe,x-over,A:Aliens,Predator. . . . 6.00
2 PJe,x-over,A:Aliens,Predator. . . . 6.00

IMAGE

OXIDO
Sept., 2003
1 (of 6) LHa(s) 3.00
2 LHa(s) 3.00

PACT
1994
1 JV(s),WMc,I:Pact, C:Youngblood 2.50
2 JV(s),V:Youngblood 2.50
3 JV(s),V:Atrocity 2.50

PACT, THE
Mar., 2005
1 (of 4) Father's Day, JV 3.00
2 . . . . 3.00
3 . . . . 3.00
4 . . . . 3.00

PARADE
(WITH FIREWORKS)
Sept., 2007
1 (of 2) 3.50
2 . . . . 3.50

PARADIGM
Sept., 2002
1 F:Chris Howells, 48-pg. b&w 3.50
2 40-pg. b&w 3.50
3 40-pg. b&w 3.50
4 40-pg. 3.50
5 . . . . 3.00
6 All About the Community 3.00
7 40-pg. 3.00
8 Swirly Things 3.00
9 Real Swirly Things 3.00
10 . . . . 3.00
11 40-pg. 3.50
12 40-pg. 3.50

PARLIAMENT OF
JUSTICE, THE
Mar., 2003
1-shot b&w, 56-pg. 6.00

PARTS UNKNOWN:
KILLING ATTRACTION
(B&W) April, 2000
1 Sci-Fi/UFO adventure 3.00

PARTS UNKNOWN:
HOSTILE TAKEOVER
(B&W) June, 2000
1 by Beau Smith & Brad Gorby . . . 3.00
2 . . . . 3.00
3 & 4 . . . . @3.00

PATIENT ZERO
Mar., 2004
1 (of 4) Eternity's Past,pt.1 . . . . . . 3.00
2 thru 4 Eternity's Past,pt.2ñ4 . . . @3.00

PAUL JENKINS' SIDEKICK
June, 2006
1 . . . . 3.50
2 thru 5 . . . . @4.00
Spec. Super Summer Spectacular . . 3.50
Spec. Super Summer Spect. #2 . . . 3.50

PHANTOM FORCE
Dec., 1993
1 RLd,JK,w/card 2.75
2 JK,V:Darkfire 2.50
See also Color Comics section

Phantom Guard #1
© WildStorm

PHANTOM GUARD
WildStorm, Oct., 1997
1 by Sean Ruffner, Ryan Benjamin 3.00
1a variant cover 3.00
1b Voyager bagged pack 3.50
2 Martian wasteland 3.00
3 Lowell Zerium Mines 3.00
4 'Target Locked'. 3.00
5 V:Vanox. 3.00
6 Countdown to Armageddon 3.00

PHANTOM JACK
Mar., 2004
1 Roach Motel. 3.00
2 Back to Baghdad 3.00
3 Among the Enemy 3.00
4 Madison Blue, Who Are You 3.00
5 Sins of Saddam Hussein 3.00

PHONOGRAM
(B&W) Aug., 2006
1 Public Image 3.50
2 Can't Imagine World Without Me. 3.50
3 Faster. 3.50
4 . . . . 3.50
5 Kissing With Dry Lips. 3.50
6 Live Forever. 3.50

PIECES FOR MOM:
A TALE OF THE UNDEAD
Jan., 2007
1-shot Zombie story 4.00

PIGTALE
(B&W) Jan., 2005
1 Private Eye: Boston Booth. 3.00
2 The Smell of Taxx 3.00
3 Dark Neon Rain` 3.00
4 Salty Pork & Bacon Tarts. 3.00

PIRATES OF
CONEY ISLAND, THE
Oct., 2006
1 . . . . 3.00
1a variant (c). 3.00
2 . . . . 3.00
3 . . . . 3.50
3a variant (c) 3.50
4 thru 8 . . . . @3.00
4a thru 8a variant (c)s . . . . @3.00

PITT
Top Cow, 1993–95
1 DK,I:Pitt,Timmy 4.00
2 DK,V:Quagg. 3.00
3 DK,V:Zoyvod 4.00
4 DK,V:Zoyvod 3.00
5 DK 2.50
6 DK 2.50
7 DK 2.50
8 Ransom 2.50
9 DK,Artic Adventures. 2.50
Ashcan 1 . . . . 3.00

PORTENT, THE
Feb., 2006
1 Condemnation 3.00
2 A Road of My Own. 3.00
3 . . . . 3.00
4 Nezabudka. 3.00

POWER OF THE MARK
1 I:Ted Miller 2.50
2 V:The Fuse 2.50
3 TMB(s), The Mark 2.50
4 TMB,Mark's secrets revealed . . . 2.50

POWER RANGERS ZEO
Extreme, Sept., 1997
1 thru 3 TBm&MBm(s),TNu,NRd @2.50

POWER RANGERS ZEO
YOUNGBLOOD
Extreme, Oct., 1997
1 RLd,TBm,MBm 3.00
2 RLd,TBm,MBm 3.00

POWERS
April, 2000
1 Who killed Retro Girl,pt.1 . . . . . 15.00
2 Who killed Retro Girl,pt.2. . . . . . 20.00
3 Who killed Retro Girl,pt.3 . . . . . 15.00
4 . . . . 12.00
5 A murder solved. 10.00
6 . . . . 10.00
7 WEI, Ride Along. 7.00
8 Role Play,pt.1. . . . . 7.00
9 Role Play,pt.2. . . . . 7.00
10 Role Play,pt.3 . . . . 7.00
11 . . . . 5.00
12 Groupies 5.00
13 Groupies,pt.2 . . . . 5.00
14 Groupies,pt.3 . . . . 5.00
15 Supergroup,pt.1 . . . . 5.00
16 Supergroup. 5.00
17 incl. Bastard Samurai prequel . . 5.00
18 superhero wanted for murder . . 5.00
19 supergroup shocking concl. 5.00
20 supergroup explosive concl. 5.00
21 Anarchy,pt.1 . . . . 3.50
22 Anarchy,pt.2 . . . . 3.50
23 Anarchy,pt.3 . . . . 3.50
24 Anarchy,pt.4 . . . . 3.50
25 The Sellouts,pt.1 . . . . 3.50
26 The Sellouts,pt.2 . . . . 3.50
27 The Sellouts,pt.3 . . . . 3.00
28 The Sellouts,pt.4 . . . . 3.00
29 The Sellouts,pt.5 . . . . 3.00
30 The Sellouts,pt.6 . . . . 3.00
31 Forever,pt.1 . . . . 3.00
32 Forever,pt.2 . . . . 3.00
33 Forever,pt.3 . . . . 3.00
34 Forever,pt.4 . . . . 3.00
35 Forever,pt.5 . . . . 3.00
36 Forever,pt.6 . . . . 3.00
37 Forever,pt.7 . . . . 3.00
Spec.-1 Coloring & Activity Book . . . 3.00
1/2 Wizard story + new 3.00
Scriptbook 344-pg. 20.00

IMAGE

Powers #9
© Image

VOLUME 2 (2004)
1 Legends,pt.1 . . . . 3.00
2 Legends,pt.2 . . . . 3.00
3 Legends,pt.3 . . . . 3.00

PROOF
Oct, 2007
1 . . . . 3.00

PROPHET
Extreme, 1993–95
0 San Diego Comic-Con ed 4.00
1 RLd(s)DPs,O:Prophet,I:Mary
  McCormick 3.00
1a Gold ed 4.00
2 RLd(s),DPs,C:Bloodstrike 2.50
3 RLd(s),DPs, V:Bloodstrike,
  I:Judas 2.50
4 RLd(s),DPs,I:Omen,A:Judas . . . 2.50
4a SPa(c),Limited ed 3.00
5 SPa,Supreme Apocalypse,pt.2 . . 3.00
6 SPa 2.50
7 SPa War Games,pt.1 . . . . 2.50
8 SPa War Games,pt.2 . . . . 2.50
9 SPa,Extreme Sacrifice Prelude . . 2.50
10 ExtremeSacrifice,pt.7,x-over . . . 2.50
Sourcebook 3.00
Ashcan #1 . . . . 3.00
Ashcan #2 . . . . 3.00

[Second Series] 1995
1 SPI, New Series 3.50
2 SPI, New Direction 2.50
2a variant cover 2.50
3 True Nature 2.50
4 The Dying Factor 2.50
5 . . . . 2.50
6 . . . . 2.50
7 CDi,SPa 2.50
8 & 9 . . . . @2.50
Ann.#1 Supreme Apocalypse 2.50
Spec.#1 Babewatch special (1995) . 2.50

PROPHET/CHAPEL: SUPER SOLDIERS
May, 1996
1 . . . . 2.50
1A variant(c) b&w 2.50
2 . . . . 2.50

PSCYTHE
Sept., 2004
1 (of 2) MT 4.00
2 MT 4.00

PUFFED
July, 2003
1 (of 3) 3.00
2 & 3 . . . . @3.00

PVP
Mar., 2003
1 Player vs. Player 3.00
2 Lord of the Schwing 3.00
3 Lost and Found 3.00
4 V:Devilfish 3.00
5 Max Powers 3.00
6 Skull the Troll 3.00
7 Chilling events 3.00
8 Brent Sienna Dies 3.00
9 Skull in local Zoo 3.00
10 Skull hyper-intelligent 3.00
11 F:Savage Dragon 3.00
12 Halloween party 3.00
13 Christmas issue 3.00
14 A:Invincible 3.00
15 Geeks Gone Wild 3.00
16 . . . . 3.00
17 . . . . 3.00
18 . . . . 3.00
19 . . . . 3.00
20 . . . . 3.00
21 . . . . 3.00
22 . . . . 3.00
23 Caffeine Rage 3.00
24 . . . . 3.00
25 . . . . 3.00
26 thru 29 . . . . @3.00
30 Time Tunnel 3.00
31 Incorrigable PVP 3.00
32 Together They Fight Crive 3.00
33 Girls Night Out 3.00
34 Double Date 3.00
35 Kill Pussycat Kill 3.50
36 Sci-fi Con 3.50
37 . . . . 3.50
38 . . . . 3.50
Spec #0 16-page, B&W 1.00
Spec. Replay #1, rep.#1 & #2 . . . . . 5.00

PVP #19
© Image

Q-UNIT: REVENGE
Oct., 1999
1 KIA,BNa 3.00
1a variant cover (1:2) 3.00
2 KIA,BNa 3.00
2a variant cover (1:2) 3.00

RADISKULL AND DEVIL DOLL
Dec., 2002
1-shot b&w 2.50
1-shot Radiskull Hate Love 3.00

RADIX
Dec., 2001
1 mysterious new force 3.00
2 F:Val Fiores 3.00
3 . . . . 3.00
4 mysterious object 3.00

RAGMOP
(B&W)
Vol.2 #1 by Rob Walton 3.00
Vol.2 #2 . . . . 3.00

RANDY O'DONNEL IS THE MAN
May, 2001
1 TDF,RLm,flip-book 3.00
2 TDF,RLm,The Chosen 3.00
3 TDF,RLm,Terror of the
  Warrior Toads 3.00
4 TDF,Merciless are the Malok 3.00

REALM OF THE CLAW
Oct., 2003
1 (of 6) 3.00
1a variant (c) 3.00
2 . . . . 3.00
2a variant (c) 3.00

RED STAR, THE
June, 2000
1 by Christian Gossett 8.00
2 Project: Antares 6.00
3 Fall of the Red Fleet 4.00
4 Marcus' mystic revelation 4.00
5 A worker's Tale 4.00
6 War torn Nokgorka 3.00
7 Nokgorka,pt.2 . . . . 3.00
8 Nokgorka,pt.3 . . . . 3.00
9 Marcus Antares is alive 3.00
9a variant(c) 3.00
Spec.#1 3-D Transformation 3.00

REGULATORS
June, 1995
1 F:Blackjack,'Touch of Scandal' . . 2.50
2 F:Vortex 2.50
3 F:Arson 2.50
4 F:Scandal 2.50

REPLACEMENT GOD AND OTHER STORIES, THE
(B&W) May, 1997
1 Knute vs. King Ursus 3.00
2 by Zander Cannon 3.00
3 thru 5 . . . . @3.00

REPO
June, 2007
1 (of 5) 3.50
2 thru 5 . . . . @3.50

Replacement God and Other Stories #5
© Image

RESIDENT EVIL
Wildstorm March, 1998
1 comic/game magazine 56-pg. . . . 7.00
2 thru 4 comic/game mag. 56-pg. @5.50

RETRO ROCKET
March, 2006
1 (of 4) 3.00
2 thru 4 . . . . @3.00

RETURN OF
SHADOWHAWK, THE
Sept., 2004
1-shot JV 3.00

REX MUNDI
Aug., 2002
0 . . . . 4.00
1 Unexpected visitor 3.50
2 Puzzle in the Painting 3.50
3 The Archbiship and the Pimp . . . 3.50
4 Shadows Beneath the City 3.00
5 Shadows Beneath the City 3.00
6 Secrets Revealed 3.00
7 Father of Wisdom 3.00
8 Suspicion grows. 3.00
9 National library. 3.00
10 Holy Grail 3.00
11 Treasure of the Temple 3.00
12 The Swan Knight 3.00
13 The Lost Kings 3.00
14 City of the Dead 3.00
15 Most Beloved 3.00
16 Path to Empire 3.00
17 Vine of David 3.00
18 Europe at War 3.00

RIDE, THE
June, 2004
1 Wheels of Change,pt.1 . . . . 3.00
2 Wheels of Change,pt.2 . . . . 3.00
1a thru 2a signed . . . . @15.00
1-shot 2 for the Road, Shotgun;
   Big Plans (2004) 3.00
1-shot Foreign Parts,CDi & RMZs(s) . 3.00
1-shot Halloween Special (2007) . . . 3.50
1-shot The Ride: Savannah (2007) . 5.00

RIDE, THE:
CHAIN REACTION
(B&W) July, 2006
1 (of 4) BSz 3.00
2 . . . . 3.00

RIDE, THE:
DIE, VALKYRIE
(B&W) June, 2007
1 (of 3) BSf 3.00
2 thru 3 BSf . . . . @3.00

RIPCLAW
Top Cow, 1995
1/2 Prelude to Series (Wizard) 3.00
1/2a Con versions. 7.00
1 A:Killjoy, I:Shadowblade 3.00
2 Cyblade, Heatwave 3.00
3 EcS,BPe,AV,Alliance S.H.O.C.s . 3.00
4 conclusion 3.00
Spec.#1 I:Ripclaw's Brother 3.00

[1st Regular Series]
1 thru 5 . . . . @2.50
Top Cow, Aug., 2007
1 Pilot Season 3.00

RIPTIDE
1995
1 O:Riptide 2.50
2 O:Riptide 2.50

RISING STARS
Top Cow, March, 1999
1 A celestial event. 5.00
1a, b, & c variant covers 8.00
2 life & death of Peter Dawson 8.00
3 new special 8.00
4 . . . . 8.00
5 To the netherworld 8.00
6 Things Fall Apart,pt.1 . . . . 8.00
7 Things Fall Apart,pt.2. . . . . 8.00
8 Things Fall Apart,pt.3. . . . . 5.00
9 Act Two,pt.1 . . . . 5.00
10 years later. 3.50
11 Specials out of control. 3.00
12 War for Chicago 3.00
12a Monstermart edition 10.00
12b Monstermart gold foil 17.00
12c Monstermart holofoil 25.00
13 Brothers 3.00
14 Patriot vs. Matthew Bright. 3.00
15 The Secret 3.00
16 finale 3.00
17 campaign to change the world . . 3.00
18 will they change the world 3.00
19 MSz,government vs. Specials . . 3.00
20 MSz. 3.00
21 MSz. 3.00
22 Phoenix in Ascension,pt.1 . . . . . 3.00
23 BA,Phoenix in Ascension,pt.2. . . 3.00
24 BA,Phoenix in Ascension,pt.3. . 4.00
1/2 rep. 3.00
#0 rep. from Wizard 2.50
Preview MSz, 16-pg., B&W 5.00
Prelude 3.00

RISING STARS: BRIGHT
Top Cow, Feb., 2003
1 (of 3) 3.00
2 Authority. 3.00
3 Civilian Casualties 3.00

RISING STARS:
UNTOUCHABLE
Top Cow, Sept., 2003
1 Story of Laurel Darkhaven 3.00

RISING STARS:
UNTOUCHABLE
Top Cow, March, 2006
1 (of 5) 3.00
2 thru 5 . . . . @3.00

RISING STARS:
VOICES OF THE DEAD
Top Cow, Apr., 2005
1 (of 6) 3.00
2 . . . . 3.00
3 . . . . 3.00
4 . . . . 3.00
5 . . . . 3.00
6 . . . . 3.00

ROB ZOMBIE'S
SPOOK SHOW
2004
Int. Omnibus #1 48-pg. 5.00
Int. Omnibus #2 48-pg. 5.00
12 International 3.00

ROCKETO JOURNEY
TO THE HIDDEN SEA
Feb., 2006
7 Reunions 3.00
8 Histories. 3.00
9 Histories. 3.00
10 Histories 4.00
11 Illumination 4.00
12 . . . . 4.00

ROCK 'N' ROLL
(B&W) Nov., 2005
1-shot 3.50

ROMP
Dec., 2003
1-shot AdP 6.00

ROTOGIN: JUNKBOTZ
Apr., 2003
1 (of 8) 3.00
2 thru 4 . . . . @3.00
1a variant(c) 3.00

RTA: PERSONALITY
CRISIS
Aug., 2005
1-shot 3.50

RUMBLE GIRLS
(B&W) April, 2000
1 (of 8) Silky Warrior Tansie 3.50
2 . . . . 3.50
3 Sugar and Wax 3.50
4 Sapphire Bullets. 3.50
5 It's Not Romantic 3.50
6 Boy, Girl, Boy Girl 3.50
7 The Life of My Time, concl. 4.00

RUMBLE IN LA RAMBLA
May, 2006
1 (of 3) 3.00
2 You Snooze, You Lose. 3.00
3 Penthouse Massacre. 3.00

RUN!
Dec., 2003
1-shot MMr. 3.00

RUNES OF RAGNAN
Oct. 2006
1 Flames of Muspell, pt.1 . . . . . . 3.50
2 Flames of Muspell, pt.2 . . . . 3.50
3 Flames of Muspell, pt.3 . . . . 3.50
4 Flames of Muspell, pt.4 . . . . 3.00

RUSSIAN SUNSET
Nov., 2006
1 (of 5) RMz 4.00
2 . . . . 4.00

SAFFIRE
April, 2000
1 MtB,SRf,F:Melanie,Lyssa,
  Priscilla 3.00
1a variant JMd(c) 3.00
1b Mat Broome blue foil(c) 9.00
1c Joe Mac blue foil(c) 11.00
2 MtB,SRf,V:The Kraken 3.00
2a randy green(c) 9.00
2b signed & number 9.00
3 MtB,SRf,Hades Gate 3.00

SAINT ANGEL
2000
Preview 3.00
1 KIA,BNa,40-pg.,flip-book 4.00
1a variant(c) 4.00
2 KIA,BNa,40-pg.,flip-book 4.00
3 KIA,BNa,40-pg.,flip-book 4.00
4 KIA,BNa,40-pg.,flip-book 4.00

Sam & Twitch #18
© Todd McFarlane

SAM & TWITCH
TMP, Aug., 1999
1 AMe,Spawn tie-in 2.75
2 AMe,The Udaku,pt.2 . . . . 2.50
3 AMe,The Udaku,pt.3 . . . . 2.50
4 AMe,The Udaku,pt.4 . . . . 2.50
5 AMe,The Udaku,pt.5 . . . . 2.50
6 AMe,The Udaku,pt.6 . . . . 2.50
7 AMe,The Udaku,pt.7 . . . . 2.50
8 AMe,The Udaku,pt.8 . . . . 2.50
9 One Really Bad Day 2.50
10 Witch Hunter,pt.1 . . . . 2.50
11 Witch Hunter,pt.2 . . . . 2.50
12 Witch Hunter,pt.3 . . . . 2.50
13 Witch Hunter,pt.4 . . . . 2.50
14 Dumb Laws and Egg 2.50
15 Bounty Hunter Wars,pt.1 . . . . . . 2.50
16 Bounty Hunter Wars,pt.2 . . . . . . 2.50

17 Bounty Hunter Wars,pt.3 . . . . . . 2.50
18 Bounty Hunter Wars,pt.4 . . . . . . 2.50
19 Bounty Hunter Wars,pt.5 . . . . . . 2.50
20 Jon Doe Affair,pt.1 . . . . 2.50
21 Jon Doe Affair,pt.2 . . . . 2.50
22 Jon Doe Affair,pt.3 . . . . 2.50
23 Jon Doe Affair,pt.4 . . . . 2.50
24 Jon Doe Affair,pt.5 . . . . 2.50
25 Jon Doe Affair,pt.6 . . . . 2.50
26 Jon Doe Affair,pt.7 . . . . 2.50
27 Death Row Confessions 2.50

SAMMY: TOURIST TRAP
Feb., 2003
1 (of 4) 3.00
2 thru 4 . . . . @3.00

SAM NOIR:
RONIN HOLIDAY
(B&W) Feb., 2007
1 Life's a beach and then you die . 3.00
2 Rhino what you did last summer . 3.00
3 Wake Up and Smell the Coffin . 3.00

SAM NOIR:
SAMURAI DETECTIVE
(B&W) Sept., 2006
1 Payback is a Niche 3.00
2 Blood Thirst, Ask Question Later . 3.00
3 . . . . 3.00
Spec. #1 rep. #1–#3 . . . . 8.00

SAM STORIES: LEGS
Dec., 1999
1-shot SK, 24-pg 2.50

SAVAGE DRAGON
Highbrow, July, 1992
1 EL,I:Savage Dragon 3.00
2 EL,I:Superpatriot 3.50
3 EL,V:Bedrock,with coupon#6 . . . 3.00
3a EL,w/o coupon 3.00
Spec. Savage Dragon Versus Savage
  Megaton Man #1 EL,DSm 3.00
Gold ed. 12.00

[2nd Series] June, 1993
1 EL,I:Freaks 4.00
2 EL,V:Teen.Mutant Ninja Turtles,
  Flip book Vanguard #0 . . . . 3.00
3 EL,A:Freaks 3.00
4 EL,A:Freaks 3.00
5 EL,Might Man flip book 3.00
6 EL,A:Freaks 3.00
7 EL,Overlord 3.00
8 EL,V:Cutthroat,Hellrazor 3.00
9 EL 3.00
10 EL 3.00
11 EL,A:Overlord 3.00
12 EL, Enter She-Dragon 3.00
13 EL,Mighty Man,Star,I:Widow
  (appeared after issue #20) 3.00
13a Larsen version of 13 . . . . 3.00
14 Possessed,pt.1 . . . . 3.00
15 Possessed,pt.2 . . . . 3.00
16 Possessed,pt.3,V:Mace 3.00
17 V:Dragonslayer 3.50
18 R:The Fiend 3.00
19 V:The Fiend 3.00
20 Rematch with Overlord 3.00
21 V:Overlord 3.00
22 A:Teenage Mutant Turtles 3.00
23 Rapture vs. SheDragon 3.00
24 Gang War,pt.1 . . . . 3.00
25 Gang War,pt.2 double size 4.00
26 . . . . 3.00
27 . . . . 3.00
28 . . . . 3.00
29 . . . . 3.00

30 EL,'Overlord Reborn' 3.00
31 'The Dragon is trapped in Hell' . . 3.00
32 Kill-Cat vs. Justice 3.00
33 fatherhood 3.00
34 F:Hellboy,pt.1 . . . . 4.00
35 F:Hellboy,pt.2 . . . . 4.00
36 Dragon & Star try to rescue
  Peter Klaptin 3.00
37 mutants struggle in ruins of
  Chicago 3.00
38 Dragon vs. Cyberface 3.00
39 Dragon vs. Dung 3.00
40 'G-Man' 3.00
41 Wedding issue 3.00
42 V:Darklord 3.00
43 Stranded on another world 3.00
44 in flying saucer 3.00
45 . . . . 3.00
46 She-Dragon vs. Vicious Circle . . 3.00
47 A knight and a mummy 3.00
48 Unfinished Business,pt.1 . . . . . . 3.00
49 Unfinished Business,pt.2 . . . . . . 3.00
50 Unfinished Business,pt.3,
  some reps., 96-pg. 6.00
51 F:She-Dragon 3.00
52 F:She-Dragon,V:Hercules 3.00
53 EL,F:She Dragon 3.00
54 EL,V:imposter Dragon 3.00
55 EL,Dragon & She-Dragon 3.00
56 EL,Rita Medermade kidnapped . 3.00
57 EL,V:Overlord 3.00
58 EL,Dragon's Resurrection 3.00
59 EL,return of Savage Dragon 3.00
60 EL,R:Devastator 3.00
61 EL,R:Rapture 3.00
62 EL,Savage Dragon married . . . 3.00
63 EL,Dragon's honeymoon 3.00
64 EL,Overlord's secrets 3.00
65 EL,Possessed 3.00
66 EL,Dragon shrunk 3.00
67 EL,A:SuperPatriot 3.00
68 EL,V:PowerHouse 3.00
69 EL 3.00
70 EL, Hell on Earth 3.00
71 EL,End of the World,prequel . . . 3.00
72 EL,End of the World,prequel . . . 3.50
73 EL,End of the World,pt.1 . . . . . . 3.50
74 EL,End of the World,pt.2 . . . . . . 3.50
75 EL,End of the World,pt.3 . . . . . . 5.00
76 EL,Hell on Earth begins 3.50
77 EL,Wildstar Returns 3.50
77a Variant JOy(c) 3.50
78 EL,Mind-slaves of the
  Brain-Child 3.50

Savage Dragon #66
© Erik Larsen

79 EL,Girl Trouble 3.50
80 EL,Lurkers beneath Lake Fear . . 3.50
81 EL,The Land Down Under 3.50
82 EL,The Bug Riders 3.50
83 EL,F:Madman 3.50
84 EL,F:Madman 3.50
85 EL,Peril in Pittsburgh 3.50
86 EL,Mighty Man returns 3.50
87 EL,Havoc in the Hidden City. . . . 3.50
88 EL,To Challenge the Gods 3.50
89 EL,Panic in Detroit 3.50
90 EL,Return to Chicago 3.50
91 EL,Rapture returns 3.50
92 EL,Reclaim the Earth,pt.1 . . . . . 3.50
93 EL,Reclaim the Earth,pt.2. . . . . . 3.50
94 EL,V:CyberFace 3.50
95 EL,V:Sebastian Khan,concl. 3.50
96 EL,V:The Creator 3.50
97 EL,F:She-Dragon 3.50
98 EL,return home 3.50
99 EL,Evil Twins 3.50
100 EL, Torn Between Two
    Worlds, 100-pg. 10.00
101 EL,F:son of Dragon. 3.00
102 EL,V:Afterbirth. 3.00
103 EL,Dragon & son 3.00

Savage Dragon #127
© Erik Larsen

104 EL,secrets 3.00
105 EL,F:The Candyman. 3.00
106 EL,Dragon as Santa 3.00
107 EL,flipcover Major Damage . . . 4.00
108 EL,Flying Shoes Incident 3.00
109 EL,Danger in Dimension X . . . 3.00
110 EL,Lost in Dimension X 3.00
111 EL,Mako the man-shark 3.00
112 EL,V:Octopus & OpenFace. . . . 3.00
113 EL,Vicious Circle. 3.00
114 EL,Cutthroat 3.00
115 EL,concl.,80-pg. 7.00
116 I:Negate. 3.00
117 EL,Powerless 3.00
118 EL,R:Arachnid. 3.00
119 EL,Running Man,pt.1 . . . . 3.00
120 EL, The Running Man,pt.2 . . . . 3.00
121 EL, The Running Man,pt.3 . . . . 3.00
122 EL, Weapons of Mass
    Destruction, pt.1 . . . . 3.00
123 EL Regenerative Powers 3.00
124 EL, Dismal Dregs of Defeat . . . 3.00
125 EL, The Fly, 64-pg. 5.00
126 EL, Glum Lord. 3.00
127 EL, A World Against Him. 3.00
128 EL, Wanted. 3.00
129 EL, ... 3.00
130 EL, V: Solar Man & Universo . . 3.00

131 EL Vengeance. 3.00
132 Rock City Diner, 80-pgs 7.00
133 A desperate search 3.00
134 World Tour, pt.1. . . . . 3.00
135 Enter: Prism 3.00
Spec #0 O:Savage Dragon (2006) . 2.50
Spec. 1-shot Savage Dragon
    Companion,64-pg. 3.00
Spec. 1-shot Savage Dragon/
    Hellboy, collected ed. 6.00

SAVAGE DRAGON DESTROYER DUCK
Nov., 1996
1 SvG,ChM,EL 4.00

SAVAGE DRAGON: GOD WAR
2004
1 (of 4) 3.00
2 thru 4 . . . . @3.00

SAVAGE DRAGON, THE: RED HORIZON
Comics Feb., 1997
1 MsM 3.00
2 MsM,Dragon in the ER,A:Freak
    Force 3.00
3 (of 3) MsM,Freak Force beaten. . 3.00

SAVAGE DRAGON: MARSHAL LAW
(B&W) July, 1997
1 (of 2) PMs,KON,F:Marshal Law. . 3.00
2 PMs,KON, concl. 3.00

SAVAGE DRAGON: SEX & VIOLENCE
July, 1997
1 (of 2) TBm,MBm 3.00
2 TBm,MBm,AH, concl. 3.00

SAVANT GARDE
WildStorm, March, 1997
1 'A team without a rule book' 2.50
2 Between killer & killer cat 2.50
3 V: strange Tapestry 2.50
4 'Any super-villain can take
    over the world'. 2.50
5 'The Final Showdown' 2.50
6 BKs,Guilty until proven innocent . 2.50
7 BKs,death of John Colt 2.50
Fan Edition #1, with Fan #22. . . . . 3.00
Fan Edition #2, with Fan #23. . . . . 3.00
Fan Edition #3, with Fan #24. . . . . 3.00

SEA OF RED
Mar., 2005
1 Terror on the High Seas 5.00
2 . . . . 3.50
3 . . . . 3.00
4 . . . . 3.00
5 Origin issue 3.00
6 . . . . 3.00
7 . . . . 3.00
8 . . . . 3.00
9 Estimated Casualties,pt.1 . . . . . 3.00
10 Estimated Casualties, pt.2 . . . . 3.00
11 World in ruins 3.00
12 Golem from Mesopotamia 3.00
13 Conclusion 3.50

SEASON OF THE WITCH
Oct., 2005
0 B&W, 24-page 2.50

1 (of 4) Spring. 3.50
2 Summer. 3.50
3 Autumn. 3.50
4 Winter 3.50

SECTION ZERO
June, 2000
1 KK,TG,UFO's etc. 2.50
2 KK,TG,Sargasso sea 2.50
3 KK,TG,Curse of Sargasso 2.50
4 KK,TG,Ground Zero revealed . . 2.50
5 KK,TG,Sargasso vs. Crust. 3.00
6 KK,TG,Fire and Rain 3.00

SEVENTH SHRINE, THE
Jan., 2005
1 (of 2) 56-pg. Robert Silverberg(s) 6.00
2 . . . . 6.00

SHADOWHAWK
Shadowline, Aug., 1992
1 JV,I:ShadowHawk,Black Foil(c),
    Pin-up, with coupon#1. . . . . . . 4.00
1a w/o coupon 3.00
2 JV,V:Arsenal,A:Spawn, I:Infiniti . 3.00
3 JV,V:Arsenal,w/glow-in-the-
    dark(c) 3.50
4 V:Savage Dragon 2.50
Ashcan #1 . . . . 2.50
Ashcan #2 . . . . 2.50
Ashcan #3 . . . . 2.50
Ashcan #4 . . . . 2.50

[2nd Series] 1993
1 JV,Die Cut(c) 2.50
1a Gold ed. 3.00
2 JV,ShadowHawk I.D. 2.50
2a Gold ed. 3.00
3 Poster(c),JV,w/Ash Can 2.50

[3rd Series] 1993
0 Zero issue 2.50
1 JV,CWf,V:Vortex,Hardedge,
    Red Foil(c). 2.50
1a Gold ed. 3.00
1b signed 6.00
2 JV,CWf,MA,I:Deadline,
    BU&I:US Male. 2.50
3 JV(a&s),ShadowHawk has AIDS,
    V:Hardedge,Blackjak. 2.50
4 JV(a&s),V:Hardedge 2.50
Note: #5 to #11 not used; #12 below
is the next issue, the 12th overall.
12 Monster Within,pt.1. . . . . 2.50
13 Monster Within,pt.2. . . . . 2.50
14 Monster Within,pt.3. . . . . 2.50
15 Monster Within,pt.4. . . . . 2.50
16 Monster Within,pt.5. . . . . 2.50
17 Monster Within,pt.6. . . . . 2.50
18 JV,D:ShadowHawk 2.50
Spec.#1 . . . . 3.50
Gallery#1 . . . . 2.50

SHADOWHAWK
2005
1 JV(s) 3.00
2 Zapped. 3.00
3 JV(s),V:Nocturn 3.00
4 . . . . 3.00
5 Dead Man Walking, x-over 3.00
6 Suffer not a corpse to live 3.00
7 My World On Fire, pt.1 . . . . 3.00
8 My World On Fire, pt.2 . . . . 3.00
9 Rise, pt.1 . . . . 3.50
10 Rise, pt.2 . . . . 3.50
11 Rise, pt.3. . . . . 3.50
12 Rise, pt.4. . . . . 3.50
13 Past Lives 3.50
14 On the Rebound, pt.1 . . . . 3.50
15 On the Rebound, pt.2. . . . . 3.50
1-shot Great Responsibility 2.00

IMAGE

SHADOWHAWK/ VAMPIRELLA
Feb., 1995
Book 2 V:Kaul 5.00
Book #1: see Vampi/ShadowHawk

SHADOWHUNT SPECIAL
Extreme, 1996
1 Shadowhunt x-over,pt.1 . . . . 2.50

SHADOWS
Feb., 2003
1 . . . . 3.00
2 . . . . 3.00
3 . . . . 3.00
4 b&w 3.00
5 b&w 3.00

Shaman's Tears #10
© Image/Creative Fire

SHAMAN'S TEARS
Creative Fire, 1993–96
0 MGr 2.50
1 MGr,I:Shaman,B:Origin 3.00
1a Siver Prism ed. 5.00
2 MGr,Poster(c) 2.50
3 MGr,V:Bar Sinister 2.50
4 MGr,V:Bar Sinister,E:Origin 2.50
5 MGr,R:Jon Sable 2.50
6 MGr,V:Jon Sable 2.50
7 MGr,V:Rabids. 2.50
8 MGr,A:Sable 2.50
9 MGr,Becoming of Broadarrow . . . 2.50
10 Becoming of Broadarrow,pt.2 . . . 2.50
11 Becoming of Broadarrow,pt.3 . . . 2.50
12 Becoming of Broadarrow,pt.4 . . . 2.50
13 The Offspring,pt.1 . . . . 2.50

SHANGRI-LA
Jan., 2004
GN 8.00

SHARKY
1998
1 by Dave Elliott & Alex Horley 2.50
1a variant cover (5,000 made) 3.00
2 coma over 2.50
2a variant cover 3.00
3 R:Blazin' Glory 2.50
3a variant SBi(c) 2.50
4 tons of guest stars, concl. 2.50
4a variant DAy(c) 2.50

SHATTERED IMAGE
WildStorm, 1996
1 KBk,TnD,crossover 2.50
2 KBk 2.50
3 KBk 2.50
4 KBk,TnD,concl. 2.50

SHE-DRAGON
Feb., 2005
1-shot EL(s) 48-pg. 6.00

SHIDIMA
Jan., 2001
1 PtL, A Warlands saga 3.00
1a variant(c) 3.00
1b stormkote(c). 8.00
2 PtL 3.00
2a variant(c) 3.00
2b variant(c) 3.00
3 PtL 3.00
3a variant(c) 3.00
3b variant(c) 3.00
4 . . . . 3.00
5 . . . . 3.00
6 . . . . 2.50
0 24-pg. 2.50
0 variant(c) 2.50

SHIP OF FOOLS
(B&W) Sept., 1997
0 Bryan J.L. Glass, Michael
  Avon Oeming. 3.00
1 Death & Taxes,pt.1 . . . . 3.00
2 Death & Taxes,pt.2 . . . . 3.00
3 Death & Taxes,pt.3 . . . . 3.00
4 Death & Taxes,pt.4 . . . . 3.00

SHOCKROCKETS
April, 2000
1 (of 6) KBk,SI 2.50
2 KBk,SI,Command Decision 2.50
3 KBk,SI,The Triangle Trade 2.50
4 KBk,SI,Rocket Science 2.50
5 KBk,SI,sneak attack. 2.50
6 KBk,SI,Final Battle,flip-book 2.50

SHUT UP & DIE
(B&W) 1998
1 JHI and Kevin Stokes 3.00
2 JHI,Angry White Man. 3.00
3 JHI,Wife abducted 3.00

Sigma #3
© WildStorm

4 JHI 3.00
5 JHI,A:Earl Jackson. 3.00

SIEGE
WildStorm, 1997
1 JPe,AV,Nothing you believe
  is real. 2.50
2 JPe,AV,Omega goes to Hawaii
  for funeral 2.50
3 JPe,AV,Zontarian Crab Ships vs.
  Drop Ship 2.50
4 JPe,AV,Rescue of Omega Squad 2.50

SIGMA
WildStorm, 1996
1 BCi,Fire From Heaven prelude . . 2.50
2 BCi,Fire From Heaven,pt.6 . . . . . 2.50
3 BCi,Fire From Heaven,pt.14 . . . . 2.50

SILENCERS, THE
July, 2005
1 . . . . 3.00
2 . . . . 3.00

SILENT SCREAMERS
Oct., 2000
1 Nosferatu, 40-pg. 5.00

SIREN
(B&W) May, 1998
1 by J. Torres & Tim Levins 3.00
2 F:Zara Rush, private eye 3.00
3 cpmc;isopm 3.00

'68
Jan., 2007
1-shot 4.00
1-shot-a variant (c) 4.00

SKINNERS
TMP, July, 2000
1 MtB,JMd. 3.00
1a variant PtL(c) 3.00
1b variant Andy Park(c) 3.00
1c variant MtB(c) 2-D 3.00
1d limited ed. Broom(c) 8.00
1e limited ed., signed 9.00
2 MtB,SRf 3.00
2a variant JBz(c). 3.00

SMALL GODS
June, 2004
1 Killing Grin,pt.1 . . . . 3.00
2 Killing Grin,pt.2 . . . . 3.00
3 Killing Grin,pt.3 . . . . 3.00
4 Killing Grin,pt.4 . . . . 3.00
5 Dead Man's Hand, pt.1 . . . . 3.00
6 Dead Man's Hand, pt.2 . . . . 3.00
7 Dead Man's Hand, pt.3 . . . . 3.00
8 Dead Man's Hand, pt.4 . . . . 3.00
9 Dead Man's Hand, concl. 3.00
10 Nightingale, pt.1 . . . . 3.00
11 Nightingale, pt. 2. . . . . 3.00
12 Nightingale, pt. 3. . . . . 3.00
Spec. #1 Two Time 3.00
Vol. 2
1 (of 2) Innocence. 3.00

SOLAR LORD
March, 1999
1 by Khoo Fuk Lung 2.50
2 Nickson is Solar Lord. 2.50
3 V:5 enemies 2.50
4 V:5 enemies. 2.50
5 V:The Emperor of Darkness 2.50
6 O:Nickson 2.50
7 concl., book one 2.50

IMAGE

SOMETHING WICKED
Oct., 2003
1 (of 4) b&w 3.00
2 thru 4 Among the Living . . . . . @3.00

SORROW
(B&W) Aug., 2007
1 (of 4) 3.00
2 thru 3 . . . . @3.00

SOUL OF A SAMURAI
Apr., 2003
1 (of 4) b&w, 48-pg. 4.00
2 . . . . 4.00
3 48-pg 6.00
4 48-pg. 6.00

SOUL REAVER:
LEGACY OF KAIN
Top Cow, June, 2000
1-shot MHw,video game tie-in 2.50

SOUL SAGA
Top Cow, 2000
1 SPa,F:Aries, Soulblade 5.00
1a variant(c) JMd (1:4) 5.00
1b variant Michael Turner(c) (1:4) . 5.00
2 SPa,death in the family 3.50
2a variant David Finch(c) 3.50
2b variant Pat Lee(c) 3.50
3 SPa, Khan Hordes 2.50
4 SPa, Dominion vs. Khan 2.50
5 SPa, F:Ares 2.50
Coll.Ed.Vol.1 . . . . 6.00

SOULWIND
(B&W) March, 1997
1 quest for Soulwind begins 3.00
2 Nick becomes 'Captain Crash' . . 3.00
3 Captain Crash & Poke pursue
   Soulwind info 3.00
4 concl. of story arc 3.00
5 The Day I Tried to Live,pt.1 . . . . 3.00
6 The Day I Tried to Live,pt.2 . . . . 3.00
7 The Day I Tried to Live,pt.3 . . . . 3.00
8 The Day I Tried to Live,pt.4 . . . . 3.00

SPARTAN:
WARRIOR SPIRIT
July, 1995
1 thru 4 . . . . @3.00

SPARTAN X
(B&W) Sept., 1998
1 MGo,RM,'Plague Train' 3.00
2 MGo,RM,'Plague Train,'pt.2 . . . . . 3.00
3 MGo,RM,'Plague Train,'pt.3. . . . . 3.00

SPAWN
TMP, May, 1992
1 TM,I:Spawn,w/GP,DK pinups 9.00
1a black & white 25.00
2 TM,V:The Violator 9.00
3 TM,V:The Violator 9.00
4 TM,V:The Violator,+coupon #2 . . 7.00
4a w/o coupon 3.00
5 TM,O:Billy Kincaid 6.00
6 TM,I:Overt-Kill 5.00
7 TM,V:Overt-Kill. 5.00
8 TM,AMo(s),F:Billy Kincaid 5.00
9 NGa(s),TM,I:Angela. 6.00
10 DS(s),TM,A:Cerebus. 5.00
11 FM(s),TM, Home Story 4.00
12 TM,Chapel killed Spawn 4.00
13 TM,A:Youngblood 4.00
14 TM,A:The Violator 5.00

Spawn #10
© Todd McFarlane

15 TM, Myths II 4.00
16 GCa,I:Anti-Spawn 5.00
17 GCa,V:Anti-Spawn 5.00
18 GCa,ATi,D:Anti-Spawn 9.00
19 & 20 see after #25
21 TM,The Hunt,pt.1 . . . . 9.00
22 TM,The Hunt,pt.2 . . . . 3.00
23 TM,The Hunt,pt.3 . . . . 3.00
24 TM,The Hunt,pt.4 . . . . 3.00
25 Image X Book,MS,BTn 5.00
19 I:Houdini 5.00
20 J:Houdini 6.00
26 TM. 4.00
27 I:The Curse 4.00
28 Faces Wanda 4.00
29 Returns From Angela 4.00
30 A:KKK 4.00
31 R:Redeemer 4.00
32 TM,GCa,New Costume. 4.00
33 R:Violator 4.00
34 V:Violator. 4.00
35 F:Sam & Twitch. 4.00
36 Talks to Wanda 4.00
37 I:The Freak 4.00
38 . . . . 4.00
39 . . . . 4.00
40 V:Curse 4.00
41 V:Curse 4.00
42 thru 49 . . . . @4.00
50 48-pg. 4.00
51 . . . . 3.00
52 . . . . 3.00
53 A:Malebolgia 3.00
54 return to New York, alliance
   with Terry Fitzgerald 3.00
55 plans to defeat Jason Wynn . . . 3.00
56 efforts to defeat Jason Wynn . . 3.00
57 . . . . 3.00
58 sequel to Spawn #29 . . . . 3.00
59 . . . . 3.00
60 battle between Spawn and
   Clown cont. 3.00
61 battle with Clown concl. 3.00
62 Spawn is Al Simmons for 1 day . 3.00
63 Operation: Wynn fall,pt.1 . . . . . 3.00
64 Wynn falls, bagged with toy
   catalog 3.00
65 recap issue 2.50
66 TM,GCa,lives of alley bums . . . 2.50
67 TM,GCa,Sam and Twitch 2.50
68 TM,GCa,R:Freak. 2.50
69 TM,GCa,F:Freak. 2.50
70 TM,GCa 2.50
71 TM,GCa,Cold Blooded Truth . . . 2.50
72 TM,GCa,Haunting of the Heap . . 2.50

73 TM,GCa,R:The Heap 2.50
74 TM,GCa,pathway to misery . . . 2.50
75 TM,GCa,Deadly Revelations . . . 2.50
76 TM,GCa,Granny Blake 2.50
77 TM,GCa,confronts 2.50
78 TM,GCa,DaM,'Sins of Excess' . 2.50
79 TM,GCa,DaM,Killer in N.Y. 2.50
80 TM,GCa,DaM,F:Sam & Twitch . 2.50
81 TM,GCa,DaM,Sins are reborn . 2.50
82 TM,GCa,DaM,sea of self-doubt . 2.50
83 TM,GCa,V:Jason Wynn 2.50
84 TM,GCa,DaM,Helle's Belles . . . 2.50
85 TM,GCa,DaM,Legend of
   Hellspawn 2.50
86 TM,GCa,DaM,V:Al Simmons . . . 2.50
87 TM,GCa,DaM,Al Simmons fate . 2.50
88 TM,GCa,DaM,Seasons of
   change 2.50
89 TM,GCa,DaM,secrets revealed . 2.50
90 TM,GCa,DaM,three stories 2.50
91 TM,GCa,DaM,Black Cat
   Bones,pt.1 . . . . 2.50
92 TM,GCa,DaM,Black Cat
   Bones,pt.2 . . . . 2.50
93 TM,GCa,DaM,Devil's Banquet . . 2.50
94 TM,GCa,DaM,Children's Hour . . 2.50
95 TM,GCa,DaM,Cracks in the
   Foundation 2.50
96 TM,GCa,DaM,Rules of
   Engagement 2.50
97 TM,GCa,DaM,Heaven's Folly . . . 2.50
98 TM,GCa,DaM,The Trouble
   with Angels 2.50
99 TM,GCa,DaM,Edge of Darkness 2.50
100A TM,GCa,DaM,TM(c)She dies . 9.00
100B TM,GCa,DaM,FM(c). 5.00
100C TM,GCa,DaM,GCa(c). 6.00
100D TM,GCa,DaM,AshleyWood(c) 5.00
100E TM,GCa,DaM,MMi(c). 5.00
100F TM,GCa,DaM,AxR(c) 5.00
101 TM,AMe,DaM,The Speed
   of Night 9.00
102 TM,AMe,DaM,Remains. 2.50
103 TM,AMe,DaM,A Town Called
   Malice 2.50
104 TM,Retribution Overdrive,pt.1 . . 2.50
105 TM,Retribution Overdrive,pt.2 . . 2.50
106 TM,The Kingdom,pt.1 . . . . 2.50
107 TM,The Kingdom,pt.2 . . . . 2.50
108 TM,The Kingdom,pt.3 . . . . 2.50
109 TM,Hour of Cleansing
   Approaches 2.50
110 TM,The Kingdom,pt.4 . . . . 2.50
111 TM,The Kingdom,pt.5 . . . . 2.50
112 TM,The Kingdom,pt.6 . . . . 2.50
113 TM,The Kingdom,pt.7 . . . . 2.50
114 TM,The Bridge,pt.1 . . . . 2.50
115 TM,The Bridge,pt.2 . . . . 2.50
116 TM,Consequences 2.50
117 TM,A Season in Hell 2.50
118 TM,A Season in Hell,pt.2 . . . . . 2.50
119 TM,A Season in Hell,pt.3 . . . . . 2.50
120 TM,A Season in Hell,pt.4 . . . . . 2.50
121 TM,The Devil His Due 2.50
122 TM,Salvation Road 2.50
123 TM,Freedom in Nothingness . . 2.50
124 TM,Through These Eyes 2.50
125 TM,Wake Up Dreaming,pt.1 . . . 2.50
126 TM,Wake Up Dreaming,pt.2 . . . 2.50
127 TM Loose Threads,pt.1. . . . . . . 2.50
128 TM,Loose Threads,pt.2. . . . . . . 2.50
129 TM,Loose Threads,pt.3. . . . . . . 2.50
130 TM,Loose Threads,pt.4. . . . . . . 3.00
131 TM,God is a Bullet,pt.1 . . . . . . 3.00
132 TM,God is a Bullet,pt.2 . . . . . . 2.50
133 TM,God is a Bullet,pt.3 . . . . . . 2.50
134 TM,God is a Bullet,pt.4 . . . . . . 2.50
135 TM,Mad Shadows,pt.1 . . . . 2.50
136 TM,Mad Shadows,pt.2 . . . . 2.50
137 TM,Mad Shadows,pt.3 . . . . 2.50
138 TM,Mad Shadows,pt.4 . . . . 2.50
139 TM,Asunder,pt.1 . . . . 2.50

Spawn #78
© Todd McFarlane

140 TM,Asunder,pt.2 . . . . 2.50
138 TM,A Thousand Clowns,pt.5. . . 2.50
139 TM,Hellbound,pt.1. . . . . 2.50
140 TM(s),Hellbound,pt.2 . . . . 2.50
141 TM(s),Hellbound,pt.3 . . . . 2.50
142 TM(s),Devil to Pay, pt.1 . . . . . . 2.50
143 TM(s),Devil to Pay, pt.2 . . . . . . 2.50
144 TM(s),Devil to Pay, pt.3 . . . . . . 2.50
145 TM(s),Destination Anywhere. . 2.50
146 TM(s),Destination Anywhere. . 2.50
147 TM(s),Howl 2.50
148 TM(s),Random Patterns, pt.1 . 2.50
149 TM(s),Random Patterns, pt.2 . 2.50
150 TM(s),TM(c), 48-page. 5.00
150a thru 150c variant(c)s 25.00
151 Beginning of the End 10.00
152 Another Spawn? 3.00
153 . . . . 3.00
154 . . . . 3.00
155 Angel Zera 3.00
156 . . . . 3.00
157 . . . . 3.00
158 The Rapture 3.00
159 Spawn bares his heart 3.00
160 V:The Disciple. 3.00
161 Armageddon 3.00
162 Beyond Good and Evil 3.00
163 Reconstruction 3.00
164 New Beginnings 3.00
165 The Lodgers 3.00
166 The Return of the Clown. 3.00
167 V:The Clown 3.00
168 The Crucible of the Clown . . . 3.00
169 Hellhouse, pt. 1. . . . . 3.00
170 Hellhouse, pt. 2. . . . . 3.00
171 Poor Nyx 3.00
172 A Tale of Three Brothers 3.00
173 A Tale of Three Brothers 3.00
174 Gunslinger Spawn. 3.00
175 Showdown with Gunslinger . . 3.00
Ann.#1 Blood & Shadows, 64-pg. . 5.00
GN Spawn Movie adapt. 5.00
GN Spawn: Blood and Salvation . . 5.00
Fan Edition #1, with Fan #16. . . . . 3.00
Fan Edition #1a variant cover 4.00
Fan Edition #1b gold logo,retailer . 5.00
Fan Edition #2, with Fan #17. . . . . 3.00
Fan Edition #2a variant cover 4.00
Fan Edition #2b gold logo,retailer . 5.00
Fan Edition #2c platinum Foil logo . 5.00
Fan Edition #2, with Fan #18. . . . . 3.00
Fan Edition #2a variant cover 4.00
Fan Edition #3b gold logo,retailer . 5.00
1-shot Spawn: Simony, 64-pg. 8.00

1-shot Spawn: Godslayer, 64-pg.. . . 7.00
Spec. Spawn 1 in 3-D 6.00

SPAWN: ARCHITECTS OF FEAR
Sept., 2007
1 56-pgs. 7.00

SPAWN/BATMAN
Image/DC 1994
1 FM(s),TM 5.00

SPAWN BLOOD FEUD
June, 1995
1 V:Vampires. 4.00
2 . . . . 4.00
3 Hunted as a Vampire 4.00
4 V:Heartless John 4.00

SPAWN BIBLE
TMP, Aug., 1996
1 TM,GCa 15.00
2 Book of the Dead, 56-pg. 15.00

SPAWN: THE DARK AGES
TMP, March, 1999
1 GF,LSh, from 12th century. 2.50
1a variant TM(c) (1:4). 7.00
2 LSh,A:Black Knight 2.50
3 LSh,A:Black Knight 2.50
4 LSh,Lord Covenant 2.50
5 LSh,Lord Covenant 2.50
6 LSh,Sister Immaculata. 2.50
7 LSh,Cogliostro 2.50
8 LSh,Acts of Contrition 2.50
9 LSh 2.50
10 LSh,F:Lord Covenant 2.50
11 LSh,Ghost on the Hill 2.50
12 LSh,The Faithful 2.50
13 LSh,Blood and Glory. 2.50
14 LSh,The Innocent 2.50
15 LSh,New Beginnings 2.50
16 CWf,Heart of the HellSpawn. . . . 2.50
17 CWf,The Circle and the Worm . . 2.50
18 CWf,Crucified 2.50
19 CWf,Like Any Other Man 2.50
20 Voices in the Dark. 2.50
21 Sins of the Hellspawn 2.50
22 The Seedling. 2.50
23 The Beast 2.50
24 Bleed, Pagan, Bleed. 2.50
25 The Plague of Man 2.50
26 Lesion 2.50
27 Bubonic Nights 2.50
28 Stonehaven,pt.1 . . . . 2.50
29 Stonehaven,pt.2 . . . . 2.50
30 The Beast of the Wood. 2.50
31 Home to Roost 2.50

SPAWN GODSLAYER
May, 2007
1 The Winter King, pt.1. . . . . 3.00
2 The Winter King, pt.2. . . . . 3.00
3 The Winter King, pt.3. . . . . 3.00
4 The Winter, King, pt.4 . . . . 3.00
5 Dromo's Tale 3.00
6 Return to Endra-La 3.00

SPAWN THE IMPALER
TMP Oct., 1996
1 (of 3) MGr, fully painted 4.00
2 thru 3 MGr . . . . @4.00

SPAWN: THE UNDEAD
TMP, May, 1999
1 PJe,DT,CWf,F:Spawn 2.50
2 PJe,DT,CWf,F:Travis Ward 2.50

3 PJe,DT,CWf,Heaven vs. Hell. . . . 2.50
4 PJe,DT,CWf,suicide cult 2.50
5 PJe,DT,CWf,The Wind That
   Shakes the Barley. 2.50
6 PJe,DT,CWf. 2.50
7 PJe,DT,CWf,Up the Down Stairs 2.50
8 PJe,DT,CWf,One Lunch to Live. . 2.50
9 PJe,DT,CWf,Waiting 2.50
10 PJe,DT,CWf,How to Win Friends
   and Influence People. 2.50
11 PJe,DT,CWf,Heaven and Hell
   and In Between 2.50

SPAWN/WILDC.A.T.S
Jan., 1996
1 AMo(s),Devilday, pt.1, x-over. . . . 3.50
2 AMo(s),Devilday, pt.2. . . . . 3.50
3 AMo(s),Devilday, pt.3. . . . . 3.50
4 AMo(s),Devilday, pt.4. . . . . 3.50

SPECIAL FORCES
Aug., 2007
1 (of 6) KB 3.00
2 thru 3 . . . . @3.00

Spirit of the Tao #8
© Top Cow

SPIRIT OF THE TAO
Top Cow, May, 1998
1 BTn,F:Lance & Jasmine 2.50
2 BTn,mission to destroy base 2.50
3 BTn,V:Jaikap Clan. 2.50
4 BTn,F:Jasmine & Lance 2.50
5 BTn, Antidote to virus 2.50
6 BTn, Tao grows stronger 2.50
7 BTn, V:Menicus 2.50
8 BTn, A:Messiah 2.50
9 BTn, The Dragon is Loose 2.50
10 BTn, Jasmine out of control 2.50
11 BTn, Dragon ash race. 2.50
12 BTn, F:Disciple 2.50
13 BTn, friend or foe 2.50
14 BTn, must one die? 2.50
15 BTn,conclusion, 48-pg. 4.00

SPLITTING IMAGE
March, 1993
1 DsM,A:Marginal Seven 2.50
2 DsM,A:Marginal Seven 2.50

All comics prices listed are for *Near Mint* condition.

STAN WINSTON'S REALM OF THE CLAW
Aug., 2006
GN 17.00

STAR
June, 1995
1 F:Star from Savage Dragon 2.50
2 Buried Alive 2.50
3 A:Savage Dragon,Rapture 2.50
4 A:Savage Dragon,Rapture 2.50

STARCHILD: MYTHOPOLIS
(B&W) 1997
0 JOn, 'Prologue' 3.00
1 JOn, 'Pinehead' 3.00
2 JOn, 'Pinehead,'pt.2 . . . . 3.00
3 JOn, 'Pinehead,'pt.3 . . . . 3.00
4 JOn, 'Fisher King,'pt.1 . . . . 3.00
5 JOn, 'Fisher King,'pt.2 . . . . 3.00

STARDUST KID, THE
May, 2005
1 (of 4) JMD,MP 3.50
2 JMD,MP, The Woman 3.50
3 JMD 3.50
4 JMD 3.50

STAY PUFFED
Jan., 2004
1-shot 3.00
1-shot B variant (c) 3.00

STEVE NILES' STRANGE CASES
Aug., 2007
1 The Gathering 3.00
2 The Abattor 2.50

STONE
Avalon Sept., 1998
2 WPo,V:Rook 2.50
3 WPo,A:Bann 2.50
4 WPo, conclusion 2.50

[VOL. II] Aug., 1999
1 WPo 2.50
1a Chromium Edition 7.00
2 WPo, search for murderer 2.50
2 Stonechrome edition 15.00
3 WPo,Blood from a Stone 2.50
4 WPo,A Rose by Any Other Name 2.50
5 Wpo, series resumes 3.00

STORMWATCH
WildStorm, 1993
0 JSc(c),O:StormWatch,
   V:Terrorists,w/card 2.50
1 JLe(c&s),ScC,TvS(i),
   I:StormWatch 2.50
1a Gold ed. 4.00
2 JLe(c&s),ScC,TvS(i),I:Cannon,
   Winter,Fahrenheit,Regent 2.50
3 JLe(c&s),ScC,TvS(i),V:Regent,
   I:Backlash 3.00
4 V:Daemonites 2.50
5 SRf(s),BBh,V:Daemonites 2.50
6 BCi,ScC,TC,A:Mercs 2.50
7 BCi,ScC,TC,A:Mercs 2.50
8 BCi,ScC,TC,A:Mercs 2.50
9 BCi,I:Defile 2.50
10 V:Talos 2.50
10a variant(c) 5.00
11 RMz(s),the end? 2.50
12 RMz(s),V:Hellstrike,'Visions
   of Deathtrap' 2.50

StormWatch #44
© Wildstorm

13 V:M.A.D.-1 . . . . 2.50
14 Despot 2.50
15 Batallion, Flashpoint 2.50
16 V:Defile 2.50
17 D:Batallion 2.50
18 R:Argos 2.50
19 R:M.A.D.-1,L:Winter 2.50
20 F:Cannon,Winter,Bendix 2.50
21 V:Wildcats 2.50
22 RMz,BWS(c),WildStorm
   Rising,pt.9,w/2 cards 2.50
22a Newsstand ed. 2.50
23 RMz(s),R:Despot,Warguard 2.50
24 V:Despot 2.50
25 SSe,ScC,BCi,A:Spartan 2.75
25a 2nd printing 2.50
26 V:Despot 2.50
27 V:Despot,Rebuilding,'And in
   the End' 2.50
28 F:Blademaster,Swift,Flint,
   Comanche,New Adventures . . . 2.50
29 I:Prism,Reorganization 2.50
30 V:Heaven's Fist 2.50
31 V:Middle Eastern Terrorists 2.50
32 . . . . 2.50
33 inc. Winters Journey 2.50
34 . . . . 2.50
35 Fire From Heaven,pt.5 . . . . 2.50
36 Fire From Heaven,pt.12 . . . . . . 2.50
37 Double size,F:Weatherman One,
   I:Rose Tatoo 8.00
38 WEI(s) 5.00
39 WEI(s) 5.00
40 WEI(s),virus. 5.00
41 WEI(s) 5.00
42 WEI(s),Weatherman discovers a
   conspiracy 5.00
43 WEI(s) 5.00
44 WEI(s),history of Jenny Sparks . . 5.00
45 WEI(s),Battalion visits
   his family 5.00
46 WEI(s),secrets and more
   secrets, prologue 5.00
47 WEI(s), JLe, SW, dangerous
   experiment gone awry 5.00
48 WEI(s),'Change or Die'pt.1 . . . . 5.00
49 WEI(s),'Change or Die'pt.2 . . . . 5.00
50 WEI(s),'Change or Die' concl.
   large size 8.00
Sourcebok JLe(s),DT 2.75
Spec.#1 RMz(s),DT 4.25
Spec.#2 F:Fleshpoint 2.50
Ashcan 1 . . . . 3.00

STORMWATCH
WildStorm, Oct., 1997
1 WEI,bacterial horror,'Strange
   Weather,'pt.1,'Hard Rain' 5.00
1a Variant cover 5.00
1b Voyager bagged pack 5.00
2 WEI,Stormwatch Black team,
   'Strange Weather,'pt.2 . . . . 5.00
3 WEI,Black team,'Strange
   Weather,'pt.3,'A Storm Coming'. 5.00
4 WEI,A Finer World,pt.1 . . . . 5.00
5 WEI,A Finer World,pt.2 . . . . 5.00
6 WEI,A Finer World,pt.3 . . . . 5.00
7 WEI,Bleed,pt.1 . . . . 5.00
8 WEI,Bleed,pt.2 . . . . 5.00
9 WEI,Bleed,pt.3 . . . . 5.00
10 WEI,'No Reason' 10.00
11 WEI,BHi,PNe,F:Jackson King,
   'No Direction Home' 10.00

STRANGE EMBRACE
May, 2007
1 thru 6 . . . . @3.00

STRANGE GIRL
June, 2005
1 . . . . 3.00
1a variant MK(c) 3.00
2 thru 7 . . . . @3.00
8 Life after God, concl. 3.00
9 The End of the Road 3.00
10 Strange Girl returns 3.00
11 Detour to Hell 3.00
12 . . . . 3.00
13 . . . . 3.00
14 . . . . 3.50
15 . . . . 3.50
16 Golden Lights, pt.1 . . . . 3.50
17 Golden Lights, pt.2 . . . . 3.50
18 . . . . 3.00

STRANGERS
Mar., 2003
1 (of 6) 3.00
2 In the Inwards of the Night 3.00
3 Caresses such as Snakes Give . 3.00
4 The Livid Daylights 3.00
5 Icy till the Evening 3.00
6 Icy till the Evening 3.00
2a–6a variant (c) 3.00

STRANGERS IN PARADISE VOL. 3
Homage,1996–97
1 TMr 5.00
2 TMr 4.00
3 TMr,David & Katchoo fight 3.50
4 TMr,Katchoo makes startling
   discovery 3.50
5 TMr,Francine's college days 3.50
6 TMr,Katchoo searches for David . 3.50
7 TMr 3.50
8 TMr,demons of the past 3.50

STREET FIGHTER
Sept., 2003
1 Round One! Fight! 5.00
2 . . . . 4.00
3 . . . . 4.00
4 Brothers 3.00
4a variant (c) 4.00
5 M.Bison 3.00
5a variant (c) 3.00
5b Power Cel Acetate (c) 5.00
6 The Beginning 3.00
6a variant (c) 4.00
6b Power Foil (c) 4.00
1a–3a variant (c) . . . . @5.00

STRIKEBACK!
WildStorm, 1996
1 rep & new art 2.50
2 thru 5 . . . . @2.50

STRONGARM
(B&W) Feb., 2007
1 (of 5) 3.00
2 thru 5 . . . . @3.00

STRYKEFORCE
Apr., 2004
1 (of 5) 3.00
2 thru 5 . . . . @3.00

Stupid #1
© Image

STUPID COMICS
Sept., 2002
1-shot by Jim Mahfood,b&w 3.00
1-shot #2 . . . . 3.00
3 . . . . 3.00

SUBURBAN GLAMOUR
Sept., 2007
1 (of 4) 3.50

SUPER-PATRIOT
July, 1993
1 N:Super-Patriot 2.50
2 KN(i),O:Super-Patriot. 2.50
3 A:Youngblood. 2.50
4 . . . . 2.50

SUPER-PATRIOT:
LIBERTY AND JUSTICE
June, 1995
1 R:Covenant 2.50
2 Tokyo 2.50
3 Tokyo gets Trashed 2.50
4 Final issue 2.50

SUPERPATRIOT:
AMERICA'S FIGHTING
FORCE
July, 2002
1 (of 4) F:Johnny Armstrong 3.00
2 patriotic pandemonium 3.00
3 High Anxiety. 3.00

4 The Final Battle, concl. 3.00

SUPERPATRIOT:
WAR ON TERROR
July, 2004
1 (of 4) 3.00
2 thru 4 . . . . @3.00

SUPERSTAR:
AS SEEN ON TV
Jan., 2001
Spec. KBk,SI,48-pg. 6.00

SUPREME
Supreme, 1992
0 O:Supreme 2.50
1 B:RLd(s&i),BrM, V:Youngblood . . 3.00
1a Gold ed. 5.00
2 BrM,I:Heavy Mettle,Grizlock 3.00
3 BrM,I:Khrome. 3.00
4 BrM 3.00
5 BrM(a&s),Clv(i),I:Thor,V:Chrome. 2.50
6 BrM,Clv(i),I:Starguard,
  A:Thor,V:Chrome 3.00
7 Rip,ErS(s),SwM,A:Starguard,
  A:Thor 3.00
8 Rip(s),SwM,V:Thor. 3.00
9 Rip&KtH(s),BrM,Clv(i), V:Thor . . 3.00
10 KrH(s),BrM,JRu(i), BU:I:Black
  & White 3.00
11 Extreme Prejudice,pt.4,
  I:Newmen 3.00
12 SPa(c),RLd(s),SwM 4.00
25 SPa(c),RLd(s),SwM,V:Simple
  Simon,Images of Tomorrow. . . . 6.00
13 B:Supreme Madness 3.00
14 Supreme Madness,pt.2. . . . . . . 3.00
15 RLd(s)A:Spawn. 3.00
16 V:StormWatch 3.00
17 Supreme Madness,pt.5. . . . . . . 3.00
18 E:Supreme Madness 3.00
19 V:The Underworld. 3.00
20 V:The Unterworld 3.00
21 God Wars 3.00
22 RLd,CNn,God Wars, V:Thor. . . . 3.00
23 ExtremeSacrifice,pt.2,x-over. . . . 3.00
24 Identity Questions 3.00
#25, see above, after #12
26 F:Kid Supreme 3.00
27 Rising Son,I:Cortex. 3.00
28 Supreme Apocalypse:Prelude . . 3.00
29 Supreme Apocalypse,pt.1. . . . . . 3.00
30 Supreme Apocalypse,pt.5. . . . . . 3.00
31 V:Equinox 3.00
32 V:Cortex 3.00
33 Extreme Babewatch 3.00
34 She-Supreme 3.00
35 Extreme Destroyer,pt.7
  x-over, bagged with card 3.00
36 . . . . 3.00
37 . . . . 3.00
38 . . . . 3.00
39 AMo. 3.00
40 AMo. 3.00
41 AMo. 5.00
42 AMo,'Secret Origins' 5.00
43 AMo,'Secrets of the Citadel
  Supreme' 3.00
44 See Color Comics section
Ann.#1 TMB,CAd,KG,I:Vergessen . . 3.00
Ashcan #1 . . . . 3.00
Ashcan #2 . . . . 2.00

SUPREME: GLORY DAYS
Oct., 1994
1 Supreme in WWI 3.00
2 (of 2) BNa&KIA(s),DdW,GyM,
  A:Superpatriot 3.00

SWORD, THE
Oct., 2007
1 . . . . 3.00

Sword of Damocles #2
© WildStorm

SWORD OF DAMOCLES
WildStorm, 1996
1 prelude to Fire From Heaven
  x-over. 2.50
2 Fire From Heaven,Finale,pt.2 . . . 2.50

SWORD OF DRACULA
Oct., 2003
1 . . . . 3.00
2 The Elders,pt.2 . . . . 3.00
3 The Elders,pt.3 . . . . 3.00
4 The Elders,pt.4 . . . . 3.00
5 The Elders,pt.5 . . . . 3.00
6 Concl. 3.00

SYLVIA FAUST
Aug., 2004
1 (of 4) 3.00
2 . . . . 3.00
3 Fade. 3.00

TALES FROM
THE BULLY PULPIT
Aug., 2004
1-shot 64-pg. 7.00

TALES OF
THE DARKNESS
Top Cow, April, 1998
1 WPo,F:Jackie Estacado. 3.00
2 WPo,concl. first story. 3.00
3 Dungeon, Fire, and Sword,pt.1 . . . 3.00
4 Dungeon, Fire & Sword. 3.00
5 in Dark Ages 3.00
6 futuristic story. 3.00
1/2 . . . . 3.00

TALES OF TELLOS:
MAIDEN VOYAGE
March, 2001
1 48-pg. 4.00

IMAGE

All comics prices listed are for *Near Mint* condition.

TALES OF TELLOS
Oct., 2004
1 (of 3) F:Dyn Jessa 3.50
2 TDz 3.50
3 TDz 3.50

TALES OF THE WITCHBLADE
Top Cow, 1996
1 TnD,F:Anne Bonney 9.00
1a TnD, variant cover (1:4). 12.00
1a signed, variant 20.00
2 TnD,F:Annabella 6.00
3 WEI,BTn,future 6.00
4 WEI,BTn,future,pt.2 . . . . 5.00
5 RiB,past 5.00
6 RGr, time of Celts 3.00
7 in Ancient Egypt 3.00
7a variant cover (1:4) 8.00
8 ancient Egypt,pt.2 . . . . 3.00
9 ancient Egypt,pt.3 . . . . 3.00
Coll.Ed.#1, rep. #1–#2 . . . . 5.00
Coll.Ed.#2, rep.#3–#4 . . . . 6.00

TASK FORCE 1
July., 2006
1 . . . . 3.50
2 thru 4 . . . . @3.50

TEAM 1: STORMWATCH
June, 1995
1 I:First StormWatch Team 2.50
2 V:Helspont,D:Think Tank 2.50

TEAM 1: WILDC.A.T.S
July, 1995
1 I:First Wildcats Team 2.50
2 B:Cabal 2.50

TEAM 7
WildStorm, 1994–95
1 New team. 4.00
2 New powers 2.50
3 Members go insane 2.50
4 final issue,V:A Nuke 2.50
Ashcan 2.50

TEAM 7 OBJECTIVE: HELL
May, 1995
1 CDi,CW,BWS(c),WildStorm
  Rising,Prologue,w/2 cards 3.00
1a Newsstand ed. 2.50
2 Cambodia 2.50

TEAM 7: DEAD REACONING
Jan., 1996
1 CDi 3.00
2 thru 4 CDi . . . . @2.50

TEAM YOUNGBLOOD
Extreme, 1993
1 B:ErS(s),ATi(c),CYp,NRD(i),
  I:Masada,Dutch,V:Giger 2.50
2 ATi(c),CYp,NRd(i),V:Giger 2.50
3 RLd(s),CYp,NRd(i),C:Spawn,
  V:Giger 2.50
4 ErS(s) 2.50
5 ErS(s),CNn,I:Lynx 2.50
6 ErS(s),N:Psi-Fire,
  BU:Black&White 2.50
7 ErS(s),CYp,ATh,Extreme
  Prejudice,pt.1,I:Quantum,
  BU:Black & White 2.50

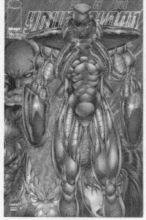

Team Youngblood #16
© Image/Extreme

8 ErS(s),CYp,ATh,Extreme Prejudice,pt.5, V:Quantum,
  BU:Black & White 2.50
9 RLd 2.50
10 ErS(s),CYp,ATh. 2.50
11 RLd,ErS,Cyp 2.50
12 RLd,ErS,Cyp 2.50
13 ErS,Cyp. 2.50
14 RLd,ErS,Cya 2.50
15 New Blood 2.50
16 RLd,ErS,TNu,I:New Sentinel,
  A:Bloodpool 2.50
17 ExtremeSacrifice,pt.6,x-over. . . 2.50
18 MS, membership drive 2.50
19 R:Brahma 2.50
20 Contact,pt.1 1000 yr Badrock . . 2.50
21 Contact,pt.2. . . . . 2.50
22 Shadowhunt x-over,pt.4 . . . . . . 2.50

TECH JACKET
2002
1 Origin issue 3.50
2 thru 8 . . . . @3.00

TEENAGE MUTANT NINJA TURTLES
(B&W) Highbrow, June, 1996
1 . . . . 4.00
2 . . . . 3.00
3 . . . . 3.00
4 Donatello resurrected 3.00
5 FFo,Warlord Komodo uses
  Splinter as guinea pig 3.00
6 FFo 3.00
7 FFo,Raphael joins Foot Clan? . . 3.00
8 FFo,Michelangelo tries to rescue
  Casey Jones' daughter 3.00
9 Enter: the Knight Watchman . . . 3.00
10 'Enter: The Dragon'. 3.00
11 V:DeathWatch,A:Vanguard 3.00
12 F:Raph, Foot Gang warfare . . . 3.00
13 Shredder is back! 3.00
14 Shredder vs. Splinter 3.00
15 F:Donatello. 3.00
16 reunited with Splinter 3.00
17 F:Leonardo 3.00
18 UFO Sightings 3.00
19 F:Leatherhead. 3.00
20 F:Triceraton 3.00
21 A:Pimiko 3.00
22 F:Lady Shredder. 3.00

23 F:Lady Shredder 3.00

TEKKEN FOREVER
Dec., 2001
1 (of 4) from Tekken 4 video game. 3.00
1a variant(c) 3.00
2 Iron Fist tournament 3.00

TELLOS
May, 1999
1 TDz, The Joining, part 1 . . . . . . 3.00
2 TDz, The Joining, part 2 . . . . . . 2.50
3 TDz, The Joining, part 3 . . . . . . 2.50
4 TDz,Hawke & Rikk. 2.50
4a variant JaL cover (1:4). 2.50
4b variant AAd cover (1:4) 2.50
4c variant RGr cover (1:4) 2.50
5 TDz,all-out battle 2.50
6 TDz,Aftermath 2.50
7 TDz,Darkness & Light 2.50
8 TDz,Tellos Joins Gorilla 2.50
8a variant Kia Asamiya(c). 2.50
8b variant HuR(c) 2.50
9 TDz,Jarek vs. Malesur. 2.50
10 TDz, concl. 3.00

TENTH, THE
Jan.,, 1997
1 BSt,TnD,Last stand against
  Hell on Earth 6.00
2 BSt,TnD,invasion of Darklon
  Corp. begins 5.00
3 BSt,TnD,Tenth & Espy team-up . . 4.00
4 BSt,TmD.confrontation with
  possible Armageddon 4.00

[Regular Series] Aug., 1997
1 TnD,BSt,V:Blackspell 5.00
2 TnD,BSt,V:Blackspell 4.00
3 TnD,BSt,Gozza,Eve 4.00
4 TnD,BSt,teleported to Japan . . . 4.00
5 TnD,BSt 3.50
6 TnD,BSt,CollateralDamage,pt.1. . 3.50
7 TnD,BSt,CollateralDamage,pt.2. . 4.00
8 TnD,BSt,Dark Wind At
  Your Back 3.00
9 TnD,BSt,F:Adrenalynn 3.00
10 TnD,pt.1 (of 3). 3.00
10a variant TnD(c) 3.00
11 TnD,Victor retains Tenth 3.00
11a variant cover 3.00
12 TnD,Black reign begins. 3.00
13 TnD,V:Rhazes Darkk 3.00
14 TnD,V:Rhazes Darkk 3.00

Tenth, Darkk Dawn © Image

IMAGE

Coll.Ed.Vol.1 rep. #1–#2 . . . . 5.00
Spec.Configuration#1, sourcebook . 2.50
1-shot The Tenth: Darkk Dawn,
   48-page O:The Tenth (2005). . . 5.00

TENTH, THE: BLACK EMBRACE
Feb., 1999
1 TnD,SLo, V:Gozza 4.00
1a variant cover (1:2) 9.00
2 TnD,SLo, F:Esperanza 2.50
3 TnD,SLo, F:Adrenalynn 2.50
4 TnD,SLo, conclusion 2.50

TENTH, THE: EVIL'S CHILD
Sept., 1999
1 TnD, F:Gozza 3.00
1a variant cover (1:3) 3.00
1b variant cover (1:3) 3.00
2 TnD, F:Twisted 3 . . . . 2.50
3 TnD 2.50
4 TnD, someone dies 2.50
Spec.Ed.#1, rep.#0 & #1/2. . . . . . 3.00

10TH MUSE, THE
Nov., 2000
1 MWn,KeL. 3.50
1a variant(c) 3.50
2 MWn,KeL,flip-book 3.50
2a variant(c) 3.50
2b photo(c) 3.50
3 MWn, critically wounded 3.50
3a variant(c) 3.50
3b photo(c) 3.50
4 MWn,Who is Medusa? 3.50
5 MWn,The Savage World 3.50
6 MWn,RCz,A:Serra 3.50
6 photo(c) 3.50
7 MWn,RCz,Maxwell Gideon 3.50
7a photo(c) 3.50
8 MWn,Assault on Olympus 3.50
8a photo(c) 3.50
9 MWn,San Francisco battle 3.50
9a photo(c) 3.50
10 MWn,RCr,I:The Odyssey 3.50
10a variant(c). 3.50
10b variant CBa(c). 3.50
11 RCr,The Endgame 3.50

TEXAS STRANGERS
Mar., 2007
1 Training Day, pt.1. . . . . 3.00
2 Training Day, pt. 2 . . . . 3.00
3 The Lone Stranger, pt.1 . . . . 3.00
4 The Lone Stranger, pt.2 . . . . 3.00

TIMESEEKERS
Aug., 2003
1 . . . . 3.00

TINCAN MAN
Jan., 2000
1 F:Alex Darkstar 3.00
1a variant GfD(c) (1:4) 3.00
2 no mercy 3.00
3 . . . . 3.00
Preview Book, 24-pg 3.00

TOMB RAIDER
Top Cow, Nov., 1999
1 DJu,JSb. 5.00
2 DJu,JSb,quest for Medusa Mask. 3.00
3 DJu,JSb,secret of Medusa Mask. 3.00
4 DJu,JSb,Medusa Mask found . . . 3.00
5 DJu,JSb,Ancient Futures. 3.00
6 DJu,JSb,Death Dance 3.00

7 DJu,JSb,Dead Center,pt.1(of4) . . 3.00
8 DJu,JSb,Dead Center,pt.2 . . . . . 3.00
9 DJu,JSb,Death by Midnight 3.00
9a variant(c) 7.00
10 DJu,JSb,Eye of Creation 3.00
11 DJu,BTn 3.00
12 DJu,BTn 3.00
13 DJu,JSb,Honduras,pt.1 . . . . . . 3.00
14 DJu,JSb,Honduras,pt.2. . . . . . . 3.00
15 DJu,JSb,Without Limit 3.00
16 DJu,JSb,Pieces of Zero,pt.1 . . . 3.00
17 DJu,JSb,Pieces of Zero,pt.2 . . . 3.00
18 DJu,JSb,Pieces of Zero,pt.3 . . . 3.00
19 DJu,Pieces of Eight,pt.1 . . . . . . 3.00
20 DJu,Pieces of Zero,pt.4 . . . . . . 3.00
21 Hunt for Black Mandala 3.00
22 The Trap,pt.2 . . . . 3.00
23 Path of the Tiger,pt.3 . . . . 3.00
24 Isle of Hydra 3.00
25 Endgame,pt.1 . . . . 3.00
26 Abyss,pt.1 . . . . 3.00
27 Abyss,pt.2 . . . . 3.00
28 Abyss,pt.3, Tempting Fate 3.00
29 V:Lord Vymes 3.00
30 Strange Flesh, 48-pg. 5.00
31 Conquista 3.00
32 Angel of Darkness,pt.1 . . . . 3.00
33 Angel of Darkness,pt.2 . . . . 3.00
34 Angel of Darkness,pt.3 . . . . 3.00
35 Black Legion,pt.1 . . . . 3.00
36 Black Legion,pt.2 . . . . 3.00
37 Black Legion,pt.3 . . . . 3.00
38 Bloodstone,pt.1 . . . . 3.00
39 Bloodstone,pt.2 . . . . 3.00
40 Risen. 3.00
41 Spirit Walker,pt.1 . . . . 3.00
42 Spirit Walker,pt.2. . . . . 3.00
43 Tower of Souls,pt.1 . . . . 3.00
44 Tower of Souls,pt.2 . . . . 3.00
45 Inner Demons 3.00
46 Gathering Storm,pt.1. . . . . 3.00
47 Gathering Storm,pt.2 . . . . 3.00
48 Gathering Storm, pt.3 . . . . 3.00
48a variant (c) 3.00
49 Vendetta 3.00
50 Alpha/Omega, 40-pg. 4.00
Spec. Gallery 3.00
Preview, B&W 16-pg. 2.50
0 Lara goes fishing 2.50
1/2 DJu, new(c). 3.00
Spec. Tomb Raider vs. Darkness . . 3.00
1-shot The Greatest Pleasure of
  All, Prelude, DJu,JJu (2002) . . . 5.00
1-shot Takeover 3.00
1-shot Epiphany 5.00
1-shot Arabian Nights 3.00
1-Shot The Greatest Treasure
  of All, DJu(s),JJu, 48-page 7.00
Spec. Covery Gallery (2006) 3.00

TOMB RAIDER: JOURNEYS
Top Cow, Dec., 2001
1 (of 12) more Lara Croft 3.00
1A variant AH(c) 3.00
2 washed ashore in El Dorado 3.00
3 Sodom and Gomorrah 3.00
4 Deja vu. 3.00
5 Who's in your yearbook? 3.00
6 . . . . 3.00
7 Maori Dream-Spear 3.00
8 way to the Underworld. 3.00
9 Akio 3.00
10 . . . . 3.00
11 . . . . 3.00
12 Settling Old Scores. 3.00

TOMB RAIDER VS. THE WOLF-MEN
Top Cow, May, 2005
2 (of 4) Monster War x-over 3.00

TOMB RAIDER/ WITCHBLADE
Top Cow, June, 2000
1/2 rep. 3.00

TOMB RAIDER/ WITCHBLADE REVISITED
Top Cow, Dec., 1998
1 Video game tie-in. 3.00

TOMB RAIDER/ WITCHBLADE/ MAGDALENA/ VAMPIRELLA
Top Cow, Aug., 2005
1-shot Special 3.00
1-shot Special variant (c)s . . . . . . @3.00

TOM JUDGE: END OF DAYS
Top Cow, Dec., 2002
1 PJe,40-pg. 4.00

TOOTH & CLAW
Aug., 1999
1 Reborn to rage. 3.00
2 MPa 3.00
3 MPa,Retribution,concl. 3.00

TOP COW
Top Cow, Feb., 1995–2006
Spec. Top Cow preview book 1.00
Spec. Freshmen, Necromance
  V.I.C.E. previews 1.00
Spec. Secrets: Winter Lingerie
  Specia (1996) 3.00l
Top Cow Bible 10.00
Top Cow/Ballistic Swimsuit Spec.#1
  MS(c) (1995) 4.00
Top Cow's California Christmas
  Spectacular Spec. Pin-ups 3.00

*Top Cow Secrets Winter Lingerie
Special © Top Cow*

TOP COW CLASSICS
Top Cow, 2000
Witchblade #1 B&W	3.00
The Darkness #1 B&W	3.00
Ascension #1	3.00
Fathom #1	3.00
Rising Stars #1 B&W	3.00
Cyberforce #1 B&W	3.00
Tomb Raider #1 B&W	3.00
Aphrodite IX #1, B&W	3.00
Midnight Nation #1, B&W	3.00
Witchblade #25, B&W	3.00
Magdalena #1 JBz,b&w	3.00
Tomb Raider/Wtchblace #1	3.00
Battle of the Planets #1	3.00
1-shot Book of Revelations (2003)	4.00

TOP COW/MARVEL:
UNHOLY UNION
Top Cow, June, 2007
1-shot 40-pgs.	4.00

A TOUCH OF SILVER
(B&W) Jan., 1997
1 JV,'Birthday'	3.00
2 JV,'Dance'	3.00
3 JV,'Bullies'	3.00
4 JV,'Separation'	3.00
5 JV,inc. Tomorrow Syndicate vs. Round Table of America, 12-pg. color section	3.00
6 JV 'Choices' Aug., 1963.	3.00

TRAKK: MONSTER HUNTER
Sept., 2003
1 (of 6)	3.00
1a variant (c).	3.00
2	3.00
2a variant (c).	3.00
2b variant SBs(c).	3.00
3	3.00
3a variant SBS(c).	3.00

TREKKER
May, 1999
1 RoR, in New Gelaph	3.00

TRENCHER
May, 1993
1 KG,I:Trencher	2.50
2 KG	2.50
3 KG,V:Supreme	2.50
4 KG,V:Elvis	2.50

TRIBE
March, 1993
1 TJn(s),LSn,I:The Tribe	2.50
1a Ivory(White) Editon	3.00
2	2.50
Ashcan 1	3.00

TRIPPER, THE
May., 2007
1-shot Movie Adapt. 48-pg.	6.00

TROLL
Extreme, Dec., 1993
1 RLd(s),JMs,I:Evangeliste, V:Katellan Command	2.50
2	2.50
Halloween Spec.#1	2.50
X-Mas Stocking Stuffer #1	3.00

TROLL: ONCE A HERO
Aug., 1994
1 Troll in WWII	2.50

TROUBLEMAN
Motown June, 1996
1 Charles Drost.	2.50
2	2.50

TRUE STORY, SWEAR TO GOD
(B&W) Sept., 2006
1 If This be Payday	3.00
2	3.00
3 Dog Day Afternoon	3.00
4 Flame On	3.00
5 The Big Apple	3.00
6 The Little Things	3.50
8	3.00
9	3.00

TRUTH, JUSTIN AND THE AMERICAN WAY
March., 2006
1 (of 5)	3.00
2	3.00
3	3.00
4 The Wedding is Off	3.00
5 Crashing the Party	3.00

TSUNAMI GIRL
Flypaper Jan., 1999
1 F:Michelle Vincent	3.00
2 Sorayama(c), A:Alan Poe	3.00
3 Sorayama(c), Surreal conspiracy	3.00

TUG & BUSTER
(B&W) June, 1998
1 MaH, humor, F:Stinkfinger	3.00

'21'
Top Cow, Feb., 1996
1 LWn,MDa	2.50
2 LWn,MDa	2.50
3 LWn,MDa	2.50
4 LWn,MDa,'Time Bomb,'pt.1	2.50
5 LWn,MDa,'Time Bomb,'pt.2	2.50
6 LWn,MDa,'Time Bomb,'pt.3 'Detonation'	2.50

TWO-BITS
Jan., 2005
1 Lullaby/Imaginaries flip-book	1.00

ULTRA
Aug., 2004
1 Seven Days, pt.1	3.00
2 Seven Days, pt.2	3.00
3 Seven Days, pt.3	3.00
4 Seven Days, pt.4	3.00
5 Seven Days, pt.5	3.00
6 Seven Days, pt.6	3.00
7 Seven Days, pt.7	3.00
8 Seven Days, concl.	3.00

UMBRA
(B&W) June, 2006
1 (of 3) 52-pg.	6.00
2	6.00
3	6.00

UNBOUND
(B&W) Jan., 1998
1 by Joe Pruett & Michael Peters	3.00
2	3.00
3 F:Marta & Erik	3.00

UNION
WildStorm, Feb., 1995
0 O:Union	2.50
0a WPo(c).	5.00
1 MT,I:Union,A:StormWatch	2.75
2 MT	2.75
3 MT	2.75
4 MT,Good Intentions	2.75

Regular Series 1995
1 R:Union, Crusade	2.50
2 V:Crusade & Mnemo	2.50
3 A:Savage Dragon.	2.50
4 JRo, BWS(c), WildStorm Rising,pt.3,w/2 cards	2.50
4a Newsstand ed.	2.50
5 V:Necros	2.50
6 V:Necros	2.50
7 Jill's Surprise	2.50
8 Regal Vengeance,pt.1	2.50
9 Regal Vengeance,pt.2	2.50
10 Regal Vengeance,pt.3	2.50
1-shot Final Vengeance, MHs, V:Regent (1997)	2.50

Trencher #2
© Image

Union #9
© WildStorm

UNION
WildStorm, 1996
1 MHs,RBn,'Knight of Faith'	2.50
2 MHs,RBn	2.50
3 MHs,RBn	2.50

UNIQUE
Platinum, Mar., 2007
1 (of 3) 48-pgs.	3.00
2 thru 3	@3.00

UNIVERSE
Top Cow, Aug., 2001
1 PJe,The Triad of Powers	2.50
1 variant foil(c)	12.00
2 PJe,Pilgrimage into the Inferno	2.50
3 PJe,Judge finds Hell	2.50
4 PJe,plan for mankind's fate	2.50
5 PJe,express train to hell	2.50
6 PJe,family held hostage	2.50
7 PJe,successor to the devil.	2.50
8 PJe, Stairway to Heaven,48-pg.	5.00

UNRAVEL
Apr., 2007
1 (of 4) Living in the Details	3.50
2 thru 3	@3.50

VAGABOND
Aug., 2000
1 RBn,SRf,F:Sharon Armstrong	3.00
1a variant(c)	3.00
1b deluxe	9.00
1c signed.	11.00
1d ruby red foil(c)	11.50
2 RBn,SRf.	3.00

VAGRANT STORY
Top Cow, Sept., 2000
1 video game tie-in	3.00

VAMPIRE'S CHRISTMAS
GN JLi 48-pg.	6.00

VANGUARD
Highbrow, 1993–94
1 EL(s),BU:I:Vanguard	3.00
2 EL(s),Roxann.	3.00
3 AMe	3.00
4 AMe	3.00
5 AMe,V:Aliens	3.00
6 V:Bank Robber	3.00
Spec. B&W 48-pg.	6.00

VANGUARD: STRANGE VISITORS
(B&W) 1996
1 (of 4) SEa,BAn,A:Amok,'Strange Visitors'	3.00
2 thru 4 SEa,BAn	@3.00

VELOCITY
Top Cow, 1995–95
1 V:Morphing Opponent	3.00
2 V:Charnel	3.00
3 thru 4	@3.00

Top Cow, Sept., 2007
1 Pilot Season.	3.00

VENTURE
Jan., 2003
1	3.00
2 thru 4	@3.00

V.I.C.E.
Top Cow, Oct., 2005
1	3.00
1a variant (c)s	@3.00
2	3.00
3	3.00
4	3.00
5	3.00

VICTORY
May, 2003
1 thru 4	@3.00
1a–4a variant (c)	@3.00

Vol. 2 Aug., 2004
1 (of 4)	3.00
2 thru 4	@3.00
2a–4a variant(c)s	@3.00

VIOLATOR
TMP, 1994
1 AMo(s),BS,I:Admonisher	5.00
2 AMo(s),BS	4.00
3 AMo(s),BS,last issue	4.00

VIOLATOR/BADROCK
Extreme, 1995
1 AMo(s),RLe(c),A:Celestine,'Rocks and Hard Places,'pt.1	2.50
2 AMo(s),RLe(c),V:Celestine,'Mondo Inferno'.	2.50
3 RLe(c),F:Dr. McAllister,'Where Angels Fear to Tread'	2.50
4 RLe(c),'Badrock's Bogus Journey,' final issue	2.50

VIOLENT MESSIAHS
June, 2000
1 F:Rankor Island	5.00
1a variant AMe(c) (1:4)	6.00
2	5.00
2a variant(c)	6.00
3 V:Citizen Pain	4.00
4 V:Jeremiah Parker.	3.00
5 flip-book	3.00
6 Tonight The Door Opens	3.00
7 In the Final Stretch	3.00
8 North End Mansion	3.00
Spec. Genesis, 56-pg.	5.00

VIOLENT MESSIAHS: LAMENTING PAIN
Sept., 2002
1 (of 4) F:Lt. Cheri Major	3.00
2 thru 4	@3.00
1a–4a variant (c)	@3.00

VOGUE
Extreme, 1995–96
1 F:Vogue,I:Redbloods	2.50
2	2.50
3 conclusion	2.50

VOLTRON: DEFENDER OF THE UNIVERSE
May, 2003
0	3.00
1 Revelations,pt.1	3.00
1a variant (c)s	3.00
2 thru 5 Revelations,pt.2–pt.5	@3.00

VOODOO
WildStorm, Nov., 1997
1 AMo(s),WildStorm universe	2.50
2 AMo(s),in old New Orleans	2.50
3 AMo(s),Samedi	2.50
4 AMo(s), Christian Charles	2.50

Voodoo #2
© WildStorm

WAHOO MORRIS
(B&W) Mar., 2000
1 Rock & Roll fantasy	3.00
2	3.00

WALKING DEAD
Oct., 2003
1	20.00
2 City of the Damned	15.00
3 Protection.	10.00
4 Guns	8.00
5 Zombies	6.00
6 Grave Situations	6.00
7 Snowbound	5.00
8 Search for shelter	4.00
9 Zombie hell-hole	4.00
10 Safer shelter	4.00
11 All Good Things.	4.00
12 Petty squabbles	4.00
13 CAd	4.00
14	3.00
15	3.00
16 CAd	3.00
17 CAd	3.00
18 CAd	3.00
19 CAd	3.00
20 CAd, Alone	3.00
21 CAd, Calm Before the Storm?	3.00
22 CAd	3.00
23 CAd	3.00
24 CAd	3.00
25	3.00
26	3.00
27	3.00
28	3.00
29 Zombie Attack	3.00
30 Near Death	3.00
31 New chapter begins	3.00
32 Surrounded.	3.00
33	3.00
34	3.00
35	3.00
36 Marriage proposal.	3.00
37 Ninth month begins.	3.00
38 Preparation for War.	3.00
39 Birth.	3.00
40 Beginning	3.00
41 Death surrounds them	3.00
42 The Time Has Come.	3.00
43	3.00
44	3.00
Script Book #1	4.00

WANTED

Top Cow, Dec., 2003

1 (of 6) MMr	7.00
1a variant (c)s	7.00
1b Death Row edition	4.00
2 thru 5	@4.00
#1 Death Row edition,32-pg.	4.00
#2 Death Row edition,32-pg.	4.00
#3 Death Row edition,32-pg.	3.00
#4 Death Row Edition,32-pg.	3.00
Spec. Wanted Dossier	3.00

WARBLADE: ENDANGERED SPECIES

WildStorm, 1995

1 I:Pillar	3.00
2 V:Ripclaw	2.50
3 I:Skinner	2.50
4 final issue	2.50

WARD OF THE STATE

May, 2007

1 (of 3)	3.50
2 thru 3	@3.50

WARLANDS

Aug., 1999

1 by Pat Lee	2.50
1a, b & c variant covers	2.50
1d Armore Chrome edition	9.00
2 help from the Elves?	2.50
2a variant cover (1:2)	2.50
3 the Dataran invasion	2.50
3a variant cover (1:2)	2.50
4	2.50
5 trapped between enemies	2.50
6 enemies clash	3.00
7 the Dataran Horde	2.50
8	2.50
9 final battle begins	2.50
10 flip-book	3.00
11	2.50
12 concl.	2.50
Spec. Three stories	6.00
Chronicles Vol.1, rep.#1–#3	8.00
Chronicles Vol.2, rep.#4–#6	8.00

WARLANDS: AGE OF ICE

July, 2001

1 Awakening	3.00
2 flip-book	3.00
3 thru 5	@3.00
1a and 2a variant covers	@3.00
Spec. #0 (2002)	3.00
Spec. #1/2 (2002)	3.00

WATERLOO SUNSET

(B&W) July, 2004

1 (of 4) B&W,56-pg.	7.00
2 Moving in High Places	7.00
3 Pilgrim Tale & Dog Parties	7.00
4 Within the Hollow Crown & Pragma	7.00

WEAPON, THE

Platinum, June, 2007

1 (of 4)	3.00
2 thru 4	@3.00

WEAPON ZERO

Top Cow, 1995

T-Minus-4 WS	8.00
T-Minus-3 Alien Invasion	5.00
T-Minus-2 Formation of a Team.	5.00
T-Minus-1 Alien Invasion	5.00
0 Whole Team Together	4.00

Weapon Zero #6
© TopCow

1	5.00
2	3.50
3	3.50
4 thru 9 WS,JBz	@3.00
10 WS,ScL,'Devil's Reign' tie-in.	3.00
11 WS,JBz,Weapon Zero & Lilith return to T'srii moonbase.	3.00
12 WS,JBz, What's wrong with Jamie.	3.00
13 WS,JBz,problems with Jamie	3.00
14 JBz,T'Srrii have returned	2.50
15 JBz,T'Srrii,concl.,48-pg.	3.50
Weapon Zero/Silver Surfer Spec. x-over (1997)	3.00

WEASEL GUY: ROADTRIP

(B&W) Aug., 1999

1 by Steve Buccellato	3.00
1a variant cover (1:4)	3.00
2 Peril in Pennsylvania	3.00
2a variant cover (1:4)	3.00
3 Don't Mess With Texas	3.00
3a variant cover (1:4)	3.00
4 48-pg, guest stars	5.00
4a variant KIA(c) (1:4).	5.00

WETWORKS

WildStorm, 1994

1 WPo,Rebirth	4.00
2 WPo,BCi,Brakken,Blood Queen	3.00
3 WPo,BCi,V:Vampire.	3.00
4 WPo,BCi,Dozer	2.50
5 WPo,BCi,Pilgrim's Turn	2.50
6 WPo,BCi,Civil War.	2.50
7 WPo,BCi,F:Pilgrim	2.50
8 WPo,SW,BWS(c), WildStorm Rising,pt.7,w/2 cards	2.50
8a Newsstand ed.	2.50
9 F:Jester,Pilgrim Dozer	2.50
10 R:Dozer to Action	2.50
11 Blood Queen Vs. Dane	2.50
12 V:Vampire Nation	2.50
13 WPo(c)	2.50
14	2.50
15	2.50
16 Fire From Heaven,pt.4	2.50
17 FTa,Fire From Heaven,pt.11	2.50
18 FTa	2.50
19 FTa	2.50
20 FTa	2.50
21 FTa	2.50
22 FTa,Dave vs.Bloodqueen concl.	2.50

23 FTa,Flattop & Crossbones, V:Lady Feign	2.50
24 FTa	2.50
25 FTa,Can Pilgrim withstand the beast that lurks within her, double size	4.50
26 team parts ways with Armand Waering	2.50
27 V:Craven, no rest for the weary	2.50
28 Vampire tracked in Pacific Northwest,A:Johnny Savoy	2.50
29 V:Soulbender,'Power Surge'	2.50
30 'Secret of the Siynn'	2.50
31 'Ashes to Ashes'	2.50
32 StG,PtL,V:Drakkar,'Sacrements of Damnation,'pt.1	2.50
32a Voyager pack, bagged with Phantom Guard preview	3.50
33 StG,PtL,Sacraments,pt.2.	2.50
34 StG,PtL,Sacraments,pt.3.	2.50
35 StG,PtL,Sacraments,pt.4.	2.50
36 StG,'Maximum Security'	2.50
37 StG,V:St.Crispin,'Diversionary Tactics,'pt.1	2.50
38 StG,'DiversionaryTactics,'pt.2	2.50
39 StG,'Symbiote Seizure'	2.50
40 StG,'Drawn Swords'	2.50
41 StG,V:Stormwatch,'Drawn Swords,' conclusion.	2.50
42 StG,'Flash Back,'pt.1.	2.50
43 StG,'Flash Back,'conclusion	2.50
3-D Spec.#1 (1998)	5.00
Sourcebook #1 (1994).	3.00
Hero Ashcan	3.00
Promo Ashcans #1,#2,#3	@3.00

WETWORKS/VAMPIRELLA

WildStorm, 1997

1 JMi & GK, x-over	3.00

WHIZ KIDS

Apr., 2003

1-shot b&w, 48-pg.	5.00

WICKED, THE

Dec., 1999

1 RMr,FTa,supernatural thriller	3.00
1a variant Jay Anacleto(c)(1:4).	3.00
2 thru 7	@3.00
3a & 4a variant covers	@3.00
Special Medusa's Tale	4.00

WILDC.A.T.S

WildStorm, 1992

1 B:BCi(s),JLe, SW(i), I:Wild-C.A.T.S.	6.00
1a Gold ed.	9.00
1b Gold and Signed	9.00
2 JLe,SW(i),V:Master Gnome, I:Wetworks, Prism foil(c), with coupon #5	5.00
2a w/o coupon	2.50
3 RLd(c),JLe,SW(i), V:Youngblood.	3.50
4 E:BCi(s),JLe,LSn,SW(i),w/card, A:Youngblood,BU:Tribe	3.50
4a w/red card	5.00
5 BCi(s),JLe,SW,V:Misery	3.00
6 BCi(s),JLe,SW,Killer Instinct, A:Misery,C:Ripclaw	3.00
7 BCi(s),JLe,SW, A:Cyberforce.	3.00
8 BCi(s),JLe,SW	4.00
9 BCi(s),JLe,SW	3.50
10 CCi(s),JLe,SW,I:Huntsman	3.00
11 CCi(s),JLe,SW,V:Triad, A:Huntsman.	3.00
11a WPo(c)	5.00
12 JLe,CCi,A:Huntsman	3.00
13 JLe,CCi,A:Huntsman	3.00
14 X book.	3.00
15 F:Black Razors	3.00

16 Black Razors. 3.00
17 A:StormWatch 3.00
18 R:Hightower 3.00
19 V:Hightower 3.00
20 TC,JeR,BWS(c),WildStorm
　　Rising,pt.2,w/2 cards 3.00
20a Newsstand ed. 3.00
21 Into Space Back Home 3.50
22 Space Adventures 3.50
23 F:Mr. Majestic's Team 3.50
24 O:Maul 3.50
25 double sized 5.00
26 AMo. 3.50
27 AMo. 3.50
28 AMo. 3.50
29 AMo,Fire From Heaven,pt.7 . . . . 3.50
30 AMo,BKs,Fire From
　　Heaven,pt.13 . . . . 3.50
31 AMo,BKs,'Cats & Dogs' 3.50
32 AMo,BKs,'Catharsis' 3.50
33 AMo,BKs,'Belling the Cat' 3.50
34 AMo,MtB,New York seconds
　　away from nuclear disaster 3.50
35 AMo,MtB,BKs,V:Crusade 3.00
36 AMo,MtB,BKs,V:Crusade,
　　A:Union,pt.2 . . . . 3.00
37 BCi,JPe,MtB,WildC.A.T.s
　　team divided 3.00
38 BCi,JPe,MtB,Puritans debut . . . 3.00
39 BCi,JPe,MtB,'C.A.T. Fight' 3.00
40 BCi,JPe,MtB,MtB(c),'Fight
　　of Flight' 3.50
40a variant cover by TC 5.00
41 BCi,JPe,MtB,backwards in time . 3.00
42 BCi,JPe,Mtb,in WWI 3.00
43 BCi,JPe,Mtb,in ancient China . . 3.00
44 BCi,JPe,Mtb,'Paradise Lost' . . . 3.00
45 BCi,JPe,Mtb,'Circus Maximus' . 3.00
46 BCi,JPe,Mtb,escape from
　　Rome 3.00
47 BCi,JPe,Mtb,time trip concl. . . . 3.00
47a variant JMd(c) 3.00
48 BCi,JPe,trapped in mothership . . 3.00
49 BCi,JPe,return to present 3.00
50 BCi,JPe,AMo,new
　　costumes,40-pg.(June, 1998) . . 4.00
Ann.#1 JRo,LSn (1998) 3.00
Spec.#1 SrG(s),TC,SW,I:Destine,
　　Pin-ups 3.50
Spec.#2 . . . . 2.50
3-D #1 rep. #1 (1997) 5.00
3-Da variant cover 5.00
Volume 2: See COLOR

WildC.A.T.s #40
© *WildStorm*

WILDC.A.T.S ADVENTURES
WildStorm, 1994
1 From animated TV series 3.00
2 Helspont,Troika 3.00
3 Caught in war 3.00
4 V:The President 3.00
5 I:Lonely 3.00
6 I:Majestics 3.00
7 . . . . 3.00
8 Betrayed 3.00
9 V:Black Razors 3.00
10 F:Voodoo. 3.00
Sourcebook (JS(c)) 3.00

WILDC.A.T.S/ALIENS
WildStorm, 1998
1-shot WEI,CSp,KN 6.00
1-shotA, variant GK&KN(c)(1:4) . . . 9.00

WILDC.A.T.S TRILOGY
June, 1993
1 BCi(s),JaL,V:Artemis 2.50
2 BCi(s),JaL,V:Artemis 2.50
3 BCi(s),JaL,V:Artemis 2.50

WILDC.A.T.S/X-MEN
WildStorm, Feb., 1997
1 (of 4) SLo,TC, giant Marvel/
　　Image x-over 5.00
1a alternate cover by JLe 5.00
2 & 4 see Marvel

WILDC.A.T.S/X-MEN
WildStorm/Marvel, 1997
Golden Age #1,SLo,TC 5.00
Golden Age #1a variant JLe(c) 5.00
3-D Golden Age #1, with glasses . . 5.00
3-D Golden Age #1, variant cover . . 5.00
Silver Age #1 SLo, JLe & SW,
　　x- over 4.50
Silver Age #1a NA&SW(c) 4.50
Silver Age #1b signed 20.00
Silver Age #1c signed, deluxe 30.00
3-D Silver Age #1, with glasses . . . 6.50
3-D Silver Age #1, NA(c) variant . . 6.50
Modern Age #1, JRo,AHu,MFm,
　　V:Hellfire Club 4.50
Modern Age #1a variant cover. . . . 4.50
3-D Modern Age #1, with glasses . . 5.00
3-D Modern Age #1, variant cover. . 5.00

WILDCORE
WildStorm, 1997–98
1 BBh,SRf,BBh(c), V:Drahn 2.50
1a variant TC(c) 2.50
1b Voyager bagged pack 3.00
2 BBh,SRf,Brawl joins. 2.50
3 BBh,SRf,V:D'rahn 2.50
4 BBh,SRf,A:Majestic 2.50
5 BBh,SRf,Tapestry 2.50
6 BBh,SRf,Zealot missing. 2.50
7 BBh,SRf,caught in fantasy world . 2.50
8 RBn,SRf,V:Tapestry 2.50
9 RBn,SRf,Zealot's soul restored . . 2.50
10 RBn,SRf,Trans-dimensional
　　trauma 2.50
GN Backlash & Taboo's African
　　Vacation. 6.00

WILDGUARD: CASTING CALL
Sept., 2003
1 (of 6) TNu 3.00
2 thru 6 TNu . . . . @3.00
1a–6a variant (c)s . . . . @3.00

WILDGUARD: FIRE POWER
Dec., 2004
1 . . . . 3.50

WILDGUARD: FOOL'S GOLD
July, 2005
1 (of 2) 3.50
2 . . . . 3.50

WILDSTAR: SKY ZERO
March, 1993
1 JOy,AG,I:WildStar. 2.50
1a Gold ed. 5.00
2 JOy,AG. 2.50
3 JOy,AG,V:Savage Dragon,
　　D:WildStar 2.50
4 JOy,AG,Last Issue,Pin-ups 2.50
[Regular Series] Sept., 1995
1 R:WildStar 2.50
2 V:Mighty Man 2.50
3 . . . . 2.50
Ashcan 2.50

WILDSTORM!
WildStorm, Aug., 1995
1 F:Spartan,Black Razors 2.50
2 F:Deathblow. 2.50
3 F:Taboo,Spartan 2.50
4 F:Nautika,Sunburst 2.50
Winter Wonderfest Spec.#1 . . . . . . 3.50
Spec.#1 Chamber of Horrors(1995) 3.50
Spec. Swimsuit Special '97 . . . . . . 2.50
Spec. Ultimate Sports Official
　　Program. 2.50
Sketchbook 3.00
Spec. Halloween '97 . . . . 2.50
GN Thunderbook #1 . . . . 7.00
GN Summer Spec., 48-pg. (DC) . . . 6.00

WILDSTORM ARCHIVES GENESIS
WildStorm, June, 1998
1 The #1 Collection, 238 pg 7.00

Wildstorm #1
© *WildStorm*

IMAGE

WILDSTORM RISING
WildStorm, May, 1995
1 JeR,BWS(c&a) WildStorm Rising,
  pt.1:Tricked by Defile,w/2 cards 2.50
1a Newsstand ed. 2.50
2 RMz,BBo,BWS(c) WildStorm
  Rising,pt.10,w/2 cards 2.50
2a Newsstand ed. 2.50
WildStorm Sourcebook #1 . . . . . . 2.50

WILDSTORM SPOTLIGHT
WildStorm, Feb., 1997
1 AMo,F:Majestic, at the end of
  time 2.50
2 StG,RMr,Loner returns 2.50
3 StG,RMr,Secret past of original
  Loner 2.50
4 F:Hellstrike,Stormwatch 2.50

WILDSTORM ULTIMATE SPORTS
WildStorm, 1997
Official Program #1 . . . . 2.50

WILDSTORM UNIVERSE '97
WildStorm, Nov., 1997
Sourcebook #1 thru #3 . . . . @2.50

WINGS OF ANANSI
Aug., 2005
GN 7.00

WITCHBLADE
Top Cow, 1995–96
1 I:Witchblade 35.00
1A Special retailer edition 35.00
1B Wizard Ace edition,acetate(c) . 20.00
2 . . . . 18.00
2 encore edition 7.00
3 . . . . 12.00
4 . . . . 9.00
5 . . . . 8.00
6 thru 8 . . . . @6.00
9 . . . . 7.00
9A variant cover 9.00
10 I:Darkness (Jackie Estacado) . . . 7.00
10a variant Darkness cover (1:4) . . 10.00
11 . . . . 6.00
12 Connection between Lisa,
  Microwave Murderer and
  Kenneth Irons 6.00
Witchblade 1/2 mail-in offer
  from Fan #8 . . . . 4.00

Top Cow, 1997
13 Dannette Boucher's secret past . 6.00
14 Sara searches for Microwave
  Murderer 5.00
15 'There is a war brewing...' 4.00
16 'Will Witchblade come between
  Sarah and Jake?' 4.00
17 New York City in shambles 4.00
18 Family Ties,pt.1,x-over 4.00
18a variant(c) 7.00
19 Family Ties,pt.4,x-over 4.00
20 Chief Siry, Ian Nottingham 3.00
21 another big surprise 3.00
22 F:Sara 3.00
22a special 9.00
23 F:Ian Nottingham 3.00
24 JPn,Sara learns truth 3.00
25 Save Jake's Life, 32 pg 3.50
26 'Grey' 3.00
27 A:Kenneth Irons 3.00
27a variant cover, all villains 9.00
28 A:Jackie Estacado 3.00
29 A:Kenneth Irons 3.00
30 Siry & Irons 3.00

Witchblade #16
© Top Cow

31 How Sara's father died 3.00
32 answers and questions 3.00
33 F:Eric 3.00
34 F:Tommy Gallo 3.00
35 Sara gets who she wants 3.00
36 The Darkness,pt.1 x-over 3.00
37 V:wicked creatures 3.00
38 V:Demons of the Underworld . . . 3.00
39 V:Demons of the Underworld . . . 3.00
40 PJe,RV 3.00
41 PJe,RV,arsonist 3.00
41a variant chrome (c) 5.00
42 PJe,pez dispensers 3.00
43 PJe,Impossible Murders 2.50
44 PJe,Impossible Murders 2.50
45 PJe 2.50
46 PJe 2.50
47 PJe 2.50
48 PJe 2.50
49 PJe,Firestarter is back 2.50
49a gold logo 7.00
50 PJe,48-pg. 5.50
50a variant DK(c). 9.00
50b variant MS(c) 9.00
50c variant(c) 9.00
51 PJe,What is the Witchblade? . . . 2.50
52 PJe,The Inferno is Coming 2.50
53 PJe 2.50
54 Ian Nottingham resurrected . . . 2.50
55 Tora No Shi 3.00
55a Battle of the Planets(c) 8.00
55b Battle(c) signed 8.00
56 Nottingham vs. Tora No Shi 2.50
57 Sonatine,pt.4 . . . . 2.50
58 Sara & Joe Siry 2.50
59 Jackie Estacado is dead? 2.50
60 Endgame,pt.2 x-over 3.00
61 Julie returns 3.00
61a sketch(c) 8.00
62 F:Magdalena 3.00
63 F:Magdalena 3.00
64 F:Magdalena 3.00
65 F:Magdalena,concl. 3.00
66 . . . . 3.00
67 Mother's Meat 3.00
68 Road Trip,pt.1 . . . . 3.00
69 Road Trip,pt.2 . . . . 3.00
70 return from trip 3.00
71 V:Shine 3.00
72 Level 42 . . . . 3.00
73 Level 42 . . . . 3.00
74 Death Pool 3.00
75 Death Pool, concl.,46-pg. 5.00
75a variant (c) 5.00

76 Death Pool follow-up 3.00
77 F:Celestine 3.00
78 TnD(c) 3.00
79 TnD(c) 3.00
80 Witch Hunt,pt.1 . . . . 3.00
81 Witch Hunt,pt.2 . . . . 3.00
82 Witch Hunt,pt.3 . . . . 3.00
83 Witch Hunt,pt.4 . . . . 3.00
84 Witch Hunt,pt.5 . . . . 3.00
85 Witch Hunt,pt.6 . . . . 3.00
86 Warrior Spirit 3.00
87 Heart of the City 3.00
88 Partners 3.00
89 Fugitive,pt.1 . . . . 3.00
90 Fugitive,pt.2 . . . . 3.00
91 Fugitive,pt.3 . . . . 3.00
92 48-pg. 5.00
93 . . . . 3.00
94 Artifacts, pt.1 . . . . 3.00
95 Artifacts, pt.2 . . . . 4.00
96 . . . . 3.00
97 . . . . 3.00
97a variant (c) 3.00
98 . . . . 3.00
99 . . . . 3.00
100 . . . . 6.00
100 a thru c variant (c) . . . . @9.00
100d variant JLi incentive (c) 9.00
101 . . . . 3.00
102 . . . . 3.00
103 . . . . 3.00
103a variant b&w (c), rare 4.00
104 . . . . 3.00
105 Magdalena returns 3.00
105a variant (c) 3.00
106 In New Orleans, pt.1 . . . . 3.00
106a variant (c) 3.00
107 Trip home 3.00
108 New Bearer, Old Foe 3.00
109 Awakened 3.00
110 RMz(s),First Born x-over 3.00
110a variant (c) 3.00
111 RMz(s),First Born x-over 3.00
112 RMz(s), First Born x-over 3.00
1-shot Witchblade/Punisher 4.00
Coll.Ed.Vol.#1 . . . . 5.00
Coll.Ed.Vol.#2 . . . . 5.00
Coll.Ed.Vol.#3 . . . . 5.00
Coll.Ed.Vol.#4, rep. #7 & #8 . . . . . 5.00
Coll.Ed.Vol.#5, rep. #9 & #10 . . . . 5.00
Coll.Ed.Vol.#6, rep. #11 & #12 . . . 5.00
Coll.Ed.Vol.#7, rep. #13 & #14 . . . 5.00
Coll.Ed.Vol.#8, rep. #15–#17 . . . . 7.00
Spec. Infinity SLo,AdP 3.50
Spec.#40 Preview book, B&W 5.00
Spec.#1 rep.movie photo cover . . . 2.50
Spec.Witchblade/Darkness,pt.2
  x-over, 48-pg. 4.00
Spec. Witchblade/Darkminds x-over 6.00
Gallery Edition #1 . . . . 3.00
Spec.1 Lady Death x-over 5.00
Spec. Tomb Raider 4.00
1/2 24-pg. 3.00
1-shot Nottingham, 48-pg. 5.00
1-shot Witchblade Animated 3.00
GN Witchblade/Darkminds:
  The Return of Paradox 7.00
1-shot Witchblade/Wolverine 3.00
1-shot Witchblade: Blood Oath 5.00
1-shot Witchblade and Tomb Raider,
  JaL,MT (2005) 3.00
1-shotA Witchblade and Tomb Raider,
  B&W cover (2005) 3.00
1-shot Art of Witchblade (2006) . . . 3.00
Spec. Bearers of the Blade (2006) . 3.00
Spec. Witchblade Tenth Anniv.
  Cover Gallery (2005) 3.00

WITCHBLADE: DESTINY'S CHILD
Top Cow, April, 2000
1 (of 3) O:Witchblade,pt.1 . . . . 3.00
2 O:Witchblade,pt.2 . . . . 3.00
3 O:Witchblade, concl. 3.00

WITCHBLADE TAKERU MANGA
Top Cow, Feb., 2007
1 . . . . 3.00
2 . . . . 3.00
2a variant (c) 3.00
3 . . . . 3.00
4 . . . . 3.00
5 thru 9 . . . . 3.00
5a thru 9a variant (c)s . . . . @4.00

WITCHBLADE VS. FRANKENSTEIN'S MONSTER
Top Cow, June, 2005
3 Monster War x-over 3.00

WITCHFINDER, THE
Liar, Oct., 1999
1 by R. Lugibihl & S. Scott 3.00
1a variant cover (1:2) 3.00
2 thru 3 . . . . @3.00

WOLVERINE/ WITCHBLADE
Top Cow, Jan., 1997
1-shot 'Devil's Reign'pt.5 (of 8) 4.00

WONDERLOST
(B&W) Dec., 2006
1 The Ups of the Downs,64-pgs. . . 6.00
2 . . . . 6.00

WOOD BOY, THE
Mar., 2005
1 (of 2) Raymond Feist (s) 3.00
2 . . . . 3.00

Wynonna Earp #5
© WildStorm

WORLD CLASS COMICS
Aug., 2002
1-shot, 40-pg. b&w. 5.00

WYNONNA EARP
WildStorm, 1996–97
1 BSt,'Violent Territory' 2.50
2 BSt,The Law comes to San
   Diablo 2.50
3 BSt,desperate to stop Hemo
   from going nationwide 2.50
4 BSt,goes to New York,
   V:ancient evil 2.50
5 BSt,battle with Raduk—Eater
   of the Dead concl. 2.50

YOUNGBLOOD
Extreme, April, 1992
0 RLd,O:Youngblood,w/coupon#7 . 3.00
0a without coupon. 1.50
0b gold coupon 9.00
1 RLd,I:Youngblood (flipbook) 5.00
1a 2nd print.,gold border 2.50
1b RLD,Silent Edition 13.00
2 RLd,I:ShadowHawk 5.00
3 RLd,I:Supreme,Showdown 3.00
4 RLd,DK,A:Prophet,BU:Pitt 3.00
5 RLd,Flip book,w/Brigade #4 . . . . 2.50
6 RLd(a&s),J:Troll,Knight Sabre,
   2nd Die Hard, Proposal to Girl
   friend 3.50
7 Badrock, V:Overtkill 2.50
8 Chapel, V:Spawn 2.50
9 . . . . 2.50
9a variant cover 5.00
10 Bravo, Badrock, Troll 2.50
Yr.Bk.#1 CYp,I:Tyrax,Kaman 2.75
Ashcan #1 . . . . 8.00
Ashcan #2 . . . . 4.00

[Volume 2] 1995
1 New Roster 2.50
2 The Program Continues 2.50
3 Extreme Babewatch. 2.50
4 Extreme Destroyer,pt.4
   x-over, bagged with card 2.50
5 . . . . 2.50
6 . . . . 2.50
7 Shadowhunt x-over,pt.3 . . . . 2.50
8 ErS,RCz. 2.50
9 ErS,RCz. 2.50
10 ErS,RCz 2.50
Spec. Baptism of Fire, F:Spawn . . 2.50
See Color Pub. section

YOUNGBLOOD BATTLEZONE
April, 1993
1 BrM 2.50
2 . . . . 3.00

YOUNGBLOOD STRIKEFILE
Extreme, 1993
1 JaL,RLd,I:Allies,A:Al Simmons
   (Spawn)I:Giger,Glory 3.00
1a Gold ed. 4.00
2 JaL,RLd,V:Super Patriot, Giger . . 3.00
2a Gold ed. 3.50
3 RLd,JaL,DaM(i), A:Super Partiot . 3.00
4 I:Overtkill 3.00
5 . . . . 3.00
6 and 7 flip books . . . . @3.00
8 Shaft 3.00
9 Knight Sabre 3.00
10 RLd,TNu,I:Bloodpool,Task,
   Psilence,Wylder,Rubble. 3.50

11 ExtremeSacrifice,pt.0,x-over
   O:Link Crypt 3.00
Ashcan. 3.00

YOUNGBLOOD/X-FORCE
Extreme/Marvel, 1996
1-shot Mojo visits Image x-over . . . 5.00
1-shot RLd variant cover 5.00

YOUNGBLOOD: YEAR ONE
1 KBk(s),RLd, the early years. 2.50
2 KBk(s),RLd,V:Giger,Cybernet . . . 2.50

Zealot #3 © WildStorm

ZEALOT
WildStorm, 1995
1 O:Zealot. 2.50
2 In Japan. 2.50
3 V:Prometheus 2.50

ZERO GIRL
WildStorm/Homage, 2000
1 thru 4 . . . . @3.00

ZOMBIE KING
(B&W) Apr., 2005
1 . . . . 3.00

ZORRO MANTANZAS
Sept., 1999
1 (of 4) DMG & Mike Mayhew 3.00
2 DMG,V:Machete. 3.00

ZORRO'S LADY RAWHIDE: OTHER PEOPLE'S BLOOD
(B&W) Feb., 1999
1 DMG,EM,JuB(c),cont. from Topps 3.00
2 DMG,EM,V:Scarlet Fever. 3.00
3 DMG,EM,V:Ansel Plague. 3.00
4 DMG,EM,V:Scarlet Fever. 3.00
5 DMG,EM,Whiplash. 3.00

All comics prices listed are for *Near Mint* condition.

COLOR COMICS

ABADAZAD

Crossgen Comics, 2003

1 . . . . 3.00
2 thru 6 . . . . @3.00

Hyperion Books, 2006

GN Vol. 1 Road to Inconceivable. . 10.00
GN Vol. 2 The Dream Thief 10.00

ABBOTT AND COSTELLO

Charlton Comics, 1968–71

1 . . . . 150.00
2 thru 9 . . . . @100.00
10 thru 21 . . . . @75.00
22 . . . . 60.00

ABC: A-Z

Wildstorm/DC, Sept., 2005

1-shot Tom Strong & Jack B. Quick. 4.00
1-shot Greyshirt & Cobweb 4.00
1-shot Terra Obscura & Splash
   Brannigan 4.00
1-shot Top 10 and Teams 4.00
1-shot Smax and First American . . . 4.00

ABIDING PERDITION

APC, 2005

1 . . . . 3.50
1a variant (c) 3.50
2 . . . . 3.50
2a variant (c) 3.50
1b SDCC edition 10.00
3 thru 4 . . . . @3.50

Markosia, 2005

5 thru 6 . . . . @3.50
5a thru 6a variant (c) . . . . @3.50

ACES HIGH

Gemstone, 1999

1 (of 5) EC Comics reprint 3.00
2 GE,BK,JDa 3.00
3 GE,BK,WW,JDa 3.00
4 GE,BK,WW,JDa 3.00
5 GE,BK,WW,JDa 3.00
Annual rep. #1–#5 . . . . 13.50

ACME NOVELTY LIBRARY

Fantagraphics, 1994–98

1 . . . . 6.00
2 thru 5 . . . . @6.00
6 thru 11 Jimmy Corrigan Meets
   His Dad, pt. 1 – pt. 6 (of 8) . . @4.50
12 Jimmy & Dad have lunch 5.00
13 Jimmy's Grandfather, 80-page . 11.00
14 F:Jimmy Corrigan 11.00
15 . . . . 10.00
1 thru 7, 2nd printings . . . . @4.00

ADAM-12

Gold Key, 1973–76

1 Photo(c), From TV show 100.00
2 thru 9 . . . . @50.00
10 . . . . 45.00

ADDAMS FAMILY

Gold Key, 1974–75

1 TV cartoon adapt. 175.00
2 . . . . 125.00
3 . . . . 100.00

ADLAI STEVENSON

Dell Publishing Co., 1966

1 Political Life Story 75.00

Acme Novelty Library #1
© Fantagraphics

ADRENALINE

A Wave Blue World, 2006

1 . . . . 3.00
2 thru 4 . . . . @3.00

ADVENT RISING: ROCK THE PLANET

360ep Inc., 2005

1 . . . . 2.25
2 thru 5 . . . . @2.25

ADVENTURES OF BIO BOY, THE

Speakeasy Comics, 2005

1 . . . . 3.00
2 thru 5 . . . . @3.00

THE ADVENTURES OF PIPSQUEAK

Archie Publications Sept. 1959–July 1960

34 . . . . 75.00
35 thru 39 . . . . @50.00

ADVENTURES OF ROBIN HOOD

Gold Key, 1974–75

1 From Disney cartoon 50.00
2 thru 7 . . . . @25.00

ADVENTURES OF THE FLY

Archie Publications/ Radio Comics, 1959–65

1 JSm/JK,O:Fly,I:SpiderSpry
   A:Lancelot Strong/Shield . . 1,000.00
2 JSm/JK,DAy,AW 600.00
3 JDa, O:Fly 500.00
4 V:Dazzler NA panel 300.00
5 A:Spider Spry 200.00
6 V:Moon Men 200.00
7 A:Black Hood 225.00
8 A:Lancelot Strong/Shield 225.00

9 A:Lancelot Strong/Shield
   I:Cat Girl 200.00
10 A:Spider Spry 200.00
11 V:Rock Men. 125.00
12 V:Brute Invaders 125.00
13 I:Kim Brand 125.00
14 I:Fly-Girl(Kim Brand) 150.00
15 A:Spider 125.00
16 A:Fly-Girl 125.00
17 A:Fly-Girl 125.00
18 A:Fly-Girl 125.00
19 A:Fly-Girl 125.00
20 O:Fly-Girl. 150.00
21 A:Fly-Girl. 100.00
22 A:Fly-Girl. 100.00
23 A:Fly-Girl,Jaguar 100.00
24 A:Fly-Girl 100.00
25 A:Fly-Girl 100.00
26 A:Fly-Girl,Black Hood 100.00
27 A:Fly-Girl,Black Hood 100.00
28 A:Black Hood 100.00
29 A:Fly-Girl,Black Hood 100.00
30 A:Fly-Girl,R:Comet 150.00
31 A:Black Hood, Shield, Comet . 150.00

Becomes:

FLYMAN

ADVENTURES OF THE JAGUAR

Archie Publications/ Radio Comics, 1961–63

1 I:Ralph Hardy/Jaguar 500.00
2 10 cent cover 200.00
3 Last 10 cent cover 175.00
4 A:Cat-Girl 150.00
5 A:Cat-Girl 150.00
6 A:Cat-Girl 150.00
7 . . . . 125.00
8 . . . . 125.00
9 . . . . 125.00
10 . . . . 125.00
11 . . . . 125.00
12 A:Black Hood 125.00
13 A:Cat-Girl,A:Black Hood 125.00
14 A:Black Hood 125.00
15 V:Human Octopus,last issue . 125.00

ADVENTURES OF YOUNG DR. MASTERS

Archie Comics, 1964

1 . . . . 50.00
2 . . . . 25.00

ADVENTUROUS UNCLE SCROOGE McDUCK

Gladstone, 1997

1 . . . . 3.00
2 Don Rosa, A Little Something
   Special 3.00
3 The Black Widow 3.00

AFTERMATH

Chaos! Comics, 2000

1 sequel to Armageddon 3.00
1 premium 8.00
Ashcan, Yellow 5.00
Ashcan, Blue 20.00

AGENT: AMERICA

Awesome Entertainment, 1997

1 RLe 2.50

2 RLe,JSb,JLb,F:Supreme,
  V:Smash 2.50

AIDEN MCKAIN CHRONICLES: BATTLE FOR EARTH
Digital Webbing, 2005
1 . . . . 3.00
3 . . . . 3.00

AIRBOY
Eclipse, 1986–89
1 TT/TY,D:Golden Age Airboy
  O:New Airboy 6.00
2 TT/TY,I:Marisa,R:SkyWolf 5.00
3 A:The Heap 5.00
4 A:Misery 5.00
5 DSt(c),R:Valkyrie 7.00
6 R:Iron Ace,I:Marlene 3.50
7 PG(c), ... 3.50
8 FH/TT(c) 3.50
9 thru 49 . . . . @3.00
50 AKu/NKu,double-size 4.00
Spec. Meets the Prowler 3.00
Spec. Mr. Monster 3.00
Spec. Vs Airmaidens 3.00

AIR FIGHTERS, SGT. STRIKE SPECIAL
Eclipse, 1988
1 A:Airboy,Valkyrie 3.00

AIRMAIDENS SPECIAL
Eclipse Comics, 1987
1 A:Valkyrie 3.00

Air War Stories #7
© Dell Publishing Co.

AIR WAR STORIES
Dell Publishing Co., 1964
1 . . . . 75.00
2 . . . . 50.00
3 thru 8 . . . . @40.00

ALAN MOORE'S AWESOME ADVENTURES
Awesome Entertainment, 1999
1 AMo 2.50
1a alternate AxR cover 7.00
2 F:Young Guns 3.00
Spec. Awesome Univ. Handbook . . . 3.00
Spec.A alternate AxR cover 3.00

ALAN MOORE'S GLORY
Comic Cavalcade, 2001
0 Park (c) 3.50
0a variant(c)s . . . . @3.50
0e Lush Lands edition 6.00
0f Finch Prism Foil (c). 13.00
Avatar Press, 2001
Preview B&W 16-page. 3.00
Preview signed gold (c) 9.00
1 (of 4) JLi(c) 3.50
1a variant(c)s . . . . @3.50
1g Finch Prism Foil (c) 13.00
1h Andy Park (c) 6.00
1i SSh(c) 6.00
1k Defender (c) 6.00
2 AMo,MMy, Finch (c) 3.50
2a variant(c)s . . . . @3.50
2e Glory Freedom (c) 6.00
2f Hall painted (c) 6.00

ALARMING ADVENTURES
Harvey Publications, 1962–63
1 AW,RC,JSe 150.00
2 AW,BP,RC,JSe 100.00
3 JSe 100.00

ALARMING TALES
Harvey Publications, 1957–58
1 JK,JK(c) 400.00
2 JK,JK(c) 250.00
3 JK. 200.00
4 JK,BP. 200.00
5 JK,AW 200.00
6 JK 200.00

ALBEDO, VOL. 3
Antarctic Press, 1994–95
Vol. 1 and II, See B&W
1 . . . . 3.00
2 thru 4 Various Artists . . . . @3.00

ALBION
Wildstorm/DC, June, 2005
1 (of 6) F:Old-time British heroes . . 3.00
2 . . . . 3.00
3 thru 6 . . . . @3.00

ALEISTER ARCANE
IDW Publishing, 2004
1 . . . . 4.00
2 . . . . 4.00
3 . . . . 4.00

ALIAS
Now Comics, 1990
1 BSz(c),Stranglehold 2.50
2 Stormfront 2.50
3 Firestorm 2.50
4 Blastpoint 2.50
5 Breakdown 2.50

ALIAS: AGENT BRISTOW
Arcade Comics, 2003
0 RLd 3.00
0a photo (c). 3.00
0b Dlx. Foil photo (c) 8.00
0c Chromium (c) 12.00
0d sgn art (c) 40.00
1 . . . . 3.00
1a photo (c). 3.00
1b Dlx. Foil photo (c) 6.00

ALICE IN WONDERLAND
Antarctic Press, 2006
1 (of 4) Rod Espinosa, Manga 3.50
2 thru 4 . . . . @3.50

ALIEN ARENA
Atomeka, 2002
1 (of 2) 3.00
2 . . . . 3.00
1a thru 2a variant (c). . . . . @3.00

ALIEN ENCOUNTERS
Eclipse Comics, 1985–87
1 . . . . 5.00
2 . . . . 4.00
3 I Shot the Last Martian 4.00
4 JBo(c) 4.00
5 RCo,Night of the Monkey 4.00
6 Now You See It,Freefall 4.00
7 . . . . 4.00
8 TY,Take One Capsule Every
  million Years,M.Monroe(c). 4.00
9 The Conquered 4.00
10 . . . . 4.00
11 TT,Old Soldiers 5.00
12 What A Relief,Eyes of
  the Sibyl. 5.00
13 GN,The Light at the End. 5.00
14 JRy,GN,TL,RT,Still born 5.00

ALIEN TERROR
Eclipse, 1986
3-D #1 Standard Procedure 3.00

ALIEN WORLDS
Pacific, 1982
1 AW,VM,NR. 7.00
2 DSt. 5.00
3 . . . . 4.00
4 DSt(i) 4.00
5 . . . . 4.00
6 . . . . 4.00
7 . . . . 4.00
3-D #1 AAd,DSt 7.00
Eclipse, 1985
8 AW 2.50
9 . . . . 2.50

[CAPTAIN JOHNER AND] ALIENS, THE
Gold Key, 1967
1 Rep. Magnus Robot Fighter . . . 90.00

ALIUS REX
Alias Enterprises, 2006
1 . . . . 3.50

ALL-ACTION CLASSICS
Sterling Publishing, 2006
GN Dracula 7.00
GN Tom Sawyer. 7.00

ALISTER THE SLAYER
Midnight Press, 1995
1 I:Alister The Slayer 2.50
2 V:Lady Hate 2.50
3 JQ&JP(c) V:Subterranean
  Vampire Bikers 2.50

ALL AMERICAN SPORTS
Charlton, 1967
1 . . . . 50.00

ALL HALLOWS EVE
Innovation, 1991
1 . . . . 5.00

ALLEY OOP
Dell Publishing Co., 1962–63
1 . . . . 125.00
2 . . . . 100.00

ALLEY OOP ADVENTURES
Antarctic Press, 1998
1	3.00
2	3.00
3 I:Granny Green	3.00

ALLIES
Awesome Entertainment, 1999
1 RLe,AMo	2.50
1a alternate RLe cover	7.00

ALL NEW EXILES
Malibu Ultraverse, 1995–96
Infinity F:Juggernaut,Blaze	2.50
1 TKa,KeL,Beginning the Quest	2.50
1a Computer painted cover (1:6)	2.50
1b signed edition	4.00
2 I:Hellblade, Phoenix flip issue	2.50
3 TKa,KeL,Phoenix Resurrection	2.50
4 thru 11	@2.50

ALPHA KORPS
Diversity Comics, 1996
1 I:Alpha Korps	3.00
2 The Price of Freedom, pt.2	2.50
3 The Price of Freedom, pt.3	2.50
1 thru 3 signed	@5.00
4 The Price of Freedom, pt.4	2.50

ALTER EGO
First, 1986
1 RTs, Ron Harris	2.50
2 thru 4	@2.50

Heroic Publishing, 2005
GN	18.00

ALVIN (& THE CHIPMUNKS)
Dell Publishing Co., 1962–73
1	175.00
2	150.00
3	125.00
4 thru 10	@125.00
11 thru 20	@100.00
21 thru 28	@100.00
1 Alvin for President & his pals in Merry Christmas with Clyde Crashcup & Leonardo	100.00

AMAZING CHAN & THE CHAN CLAN
Gold Key, 1973
1	60.00
2	40.00
3 and 4	@35.00

AMAZING HEROES SWIMSUIT ANNUALS
Fantagraphics, 1990–93
1990 Spec. A:Dawn	25.00
1990 2nd printing	15.00
1991 A: Dawn	20.00
1992 A: Dawn	20.00
1993 A: Dawn	20.00

AMAZON, THE
Comico, 1989
1	2.50
2	2.50
3 end mini-series	2.50

AMELIA RULES!
Renaissance Press, 2001
1 by Jimmy Gownley	3.00
2 thru 11	@3.00

AMELIA RULES!: SUPERHEROES
Renaissance Press, 2003
1 thru 6 (of 6)	@3.00
7 thru 16	@3.00
17 48-pgs.	5.00
18 thru 19	@3.00
Spec. Super Summer Special	5.00

American Flagg #3 © First

AMERICAN FLAGG
First, 1983–88
1 HC,I:American Flagg, Hard Times, pt.1	5.00
2 HC,Hard Times,pt.2	4.00
3 HC,Hard Times,pt.3	4.00
4 HC,Southern Comfort,pt.1	4.00
5 HC,Southern Comfort,pt.2	4.00
6 HC,Southern Comfort,pt.3	4.00
7 HC,State of the Union,pt.1	4.00
8 HC,State of the Union,pt.2	4.00
9 HC,State of the Union,pt.3	4.00
10 HC,Solidarity-For Now,pt.1 I:Luthor Ironheart	4.00
11 HC,Solidarity-For Now,pt.2	4.00
12 HC,Solidarity-For Now,pt.3	4.00
13 HC	4.00
14 PB	4.00
15 HC,American Flagg A Complete story,pt.1	4.00
16 HC,Complete Story,pt.2	4.00
17 HC,Complete Story,pt.3	4.00
18 HC,Complete Story,pt.4	4.00
19 HC,Bullets & Ballots, pt.1	4.00
20 HC,LSn,Bullets & Ballots,pt.2	4.00
21 AMo,HC,LSn,Bull&Ballots,pt.3	3.50
22 AMo,HC,LSn,Bull&Ballots,pt.4	3.50
23 AMo,HC,LSn,England Swings, pt.1	3.50
24 AMo,HC,England Swings,pt.2	3.50
25 AMo,HC,England Swings,pt.3	3.50
26 AMO,HC,England Swings,pt.4	3.50
27 AMo with Raul the Cat	3.50
28 BWg	3.50
29 JSon	3.50
30 JSon	3.50
31 JSon,O:Bob Violence	3.50
32 JSon,A:Bob Violence	3.50
33 A:Bob Violence	3.50
34 A:Bob Violence	3.50
35 A:Bob Violence	3.50
36 A:Bob Violence	3.50
37 A:Bob Violence	3.50

38 New Direction	3.50
39 JSon,A:Bob Violence	3.50
40 A:Bob Violence	3.50
41	3.50
42 F:Luther Ironheart	3.50
43	3.50
44	3.50
45	3.50
46 PS	3.50
47 PS	3.50
48 PS	3.50
49	3.50
50 HC,last issue	3.50
Special #1 HC,I:Time2	4.00

See Also: Howard Chaykin's American Flagg

AMERICAN FREAKSHOW
IDW Publishing, 2005
1	4.00
2 thru 3	@4.00

AMERICOMICS
AC Comics, 1983
1 GP(c),O:Shade	5.00
2	3.00
3 Blue Beetle	3.00
4 O:Dragonfly	3.00
5 and 6	@3.00
Spec.#1 Capt.Atom,BlueBeetle	3.00

AMERICA'S BEST COMICS
WildStorm/DC, 2000
Spec.#1 64-page	7.00
America's Best Comics Sketchbook	6.00

AMERICAN WASTELAND: BLOOD AND DIESEL
Arcana Studio, 2007
1	4.00
2 thru 3	@4.00

AMERICAN WAY, THE
Wildstorm/DC, Feb., 2006
1 (of 8) KSy,F:Civil Defense Corps.	5.00
2 KSy,A Hero Falls	3.00
3 KSy,I:New American	3.00
4 KSy,Battle with super-villain	3.00
5 KSy,V:Hellbent	3.00
6 KSy,Racial tensions	3.00
7 KSy,Super-hero civil war	3.00
8 KSy,finale	3.00

AMERICAN WOMAN
Antarctic Press, 1998
1 by Richard Stockton & Brian Denham	3.00
2	3.00
2a deluxe	6.00

ANDROMEDA
Andromeda, 1995
1 I:Andromeda	2.50
2 Andromeda vs. Elite Force	2.50

ANGEL FIRE
Crusade Comics, 1997
1 BiT, from Shi #12, BiT(c)	3.00
1a with Roberto Flores cover	3.00
1b with photo cover	3.00
2 F:Shi	3.00
3 F:Shi, concl.	3.00

ANGEL: AULD LANG SYNE
IDW Publishing, 2006
1	4.00
1a variant (c)	4.00

2 thru 5 . . . . @4.00
2a thru 5a variant (c) . . . . @4.00

ANGEL: MASKS
IDW Publishing, 2006
1-shot 48-pg. 7.50

ANGEL: OLD FRIENDS
IDW Publishing, 2005
1 . . . . 4.00
2 thru 5 . . . . @4.00
2a thru 5a variant (c) . . . . @4.00

ANGEL SPOTLIGHT
IDW Publishing, 2006
Spec. Connor 4.00
Spec. Connor variant (c) 4.00
Spec. Illyria. 4.00
Spec. Illyria variant (c) 4.00
Spec. Gunn 4.00
Spec. Gunn variant (c) 4.00
Spec. Wesley 4.00
Spec. Wesley variant (c) 4.00
Spec. Doyle 4.00
Spec. Doyle variant (c) 4.00

ANGEL: THE CURSE
IDW Publishing, 2005
1 Buffy spin-off 7.00
1a variant (c)s . . . . @7.00
1b 2nd printing 4.00
2 . . . . 5.00
3 thru 5 . . . . @4.00
Spec. Cover Gallery 4.00

ANIMAL MYSTIC: WATER WARS
Sirius, 1996
1 (of 6) DOe 4.00
2 thru 6 DOe . . . . @3.00

ANNE RICE'S THE TALE OF THE BODY THIEF
Sicilian Dragon, 1999
1 (of 12) 3.00
2 F:Lestat 3.00
3 thru 6 . . . . @3.00
7 F:Gretchen. 3.00

ANNIE OAKLEY AND TAGG
Gold Key, 1965
1 Ph(c), from TV show 90.00

ANT
Arcana Studios, 2004
1 . . . . 8.00
2 . . . . 5.00
3 . . . . 3.50
4 . . . . 3.50

A1/BLOODMOON
Atomeka, 2004
Spec. Mister Monster-Worlds War2 . 7.00
Spec. Mister Monster #2 . . . . 7.00

ANYTHING GOES
Fantagraphics, 1986
1 GK,FlamingCarot,Savage 4.00
2 S:AnM,JK,JSt,SK. 3.50
3 DS,NA(c),A:Cerebus 3.50
4 . . . . 3.50
5 A:TMNTurtles. 5.00
6 . . . . 3.00

APE NATION
Adventure Comics, 1991
1 Aliens land on Planet of
the Apes 3.00
2 General Ollo. 3.00
3 V:Gen.Ollo,Danada 2.50
4 D:Danada. 2.50

APOLLO SMILE
Eagle Wing, 1998
1 When the Levee Breaks 3.00
2 When the Levee Breaks, pt.2 . . . 3.00
3 When the Levee Breaks, pt.3 . . . 3.00

ARACHNAPHOBIA
Walt Disney, 1990
1 Movie Adapt. 6.00
1a Newsstand. 3.00

ARAKNIS
Mushroom Comics, 1995–96
1 I:Araknis, Shades of Evil pt.1 . . 3.50
2 Shades of Evil pt.2. . . . . 3.50
3 with pin-ups 2.50
4 . . . . 2.50
Mushroom Comics, 1996
0 Michael & Mario Ortiz 3.00
0 signed 4.00
1 . . . . 2.50
1 special edition 10.00
Mystic Comics
2 thru 6 . . . . @2.50

ARAKNIS: RETRIBUTION
Morning Star Productions, 1997
1 (of 4) by Michael & Mario Ortiz . . 2.50
1 signed 10.00
2 thru 4 . . . . @2.50

ARAKNIS: SHADES OF EVIL
Morning Star Productions
1 . . . . 2.50
2 thru 4 . . . . @2.50

ARCHAIC
Fenickx Productions, 2006
1 . . . . 3.00
2 thru 6 . . . . @3.00

ARCHANGELS: THE FALL
Cahaba Productions, 2005
1 . . . . 4.50
2 . . . . 4.50
3 . . . . 4.50

ARCHANGELS: THE SAGA
Eternal Studios, 1996
1 I:Cameron 2.50
2 V:Demons 2.50
3 and 4 . . . . @2.75
5 and 6 . . . . @2.50
7 . . . . 3.50
8 . . . . 4.50

ARCHARD'S AGENTS
Crossgen Comics, 2002
1 CDi(s) spin-off from Ruse 3.50

ARCHER & ARMSTRONG
Valiant, 1992
0 JiS(s),BWS,BL,I&O:Archer,
I:Armstrong,The Sec 3.00
0 Gold Ed. 5 . . . . 4.00
1 FM(c),B:JiS(s),BWS,BL,Unity #3,
A:Eternal Warrior. 2.50
2 thru 26 . . . . @2.50

Archard's Agents #1
© Crossgen Comics

ARCHIE
Archie Publications, 1981
1 thru 300 see Golden Age
301 thru 325 . . . . @6.50
326 Cheryl Blossom. 15.00
327 thru 335. . . . . @6.50
336 Michael Jackson 7.00
337 thru 400. . . . . @6.50
401 thru 429. . . . . @5.00
430 thru 529. . . . . @2.50
530 thru 552. . . . . @2.50
553 thru 580. . . . . @2.25
Archie's Christmas Stocking #4 . . . . 2.50
Archie's Christmas Stocking #5 . . . . 2.50
Archie's Christmas Stocking #6 . . . . 2.75
Archie's Christmas Stocking #7 . . . . 3.00
Archie's Spring Break Spec.1 . . . . . 2.50
Archie's Spring Break Spec.2 . . . . . 2.50
Archie's Spring Break Spec.3 . . . . . 2.75
Archie's Spring Break Spec.4(1999) 2.75
Archie's Spring Break Spec.5(2000) 2.75
Archie's Vacation Spec.#4 . . . . 2.50
Archie's Vacation Spec.#5 . . . . 2.50
Archie's Vacation Spec.#6 . . . . 2.50
Archie's Vacation Spec.#7 . . . . 2.50
Archie's Vacation Spec.#8 . . . . 2.50

ARCHIE AND FRIENDS
Archie Publications, 1992—98
1 thru 10 . . . . @5.00
11 thru 14 . . . . @4.00
15 Babewatch 6.00
16 thru 19 . . . . @4.00
20 Archies Band. 5.00
21 thru 48 . . . . @2.50
49 thru 56 Archie & Friends, Featuring
Josie and the Pussy Cats . . . @2.50
57 thru 86 . . . . @2.50
87 thru 114 . . . . @2.25

ARCHIE AND ME
Archie Publications, 1964–87
1 . . . . 325.00
2 . . . . 200.00
3 . . . . 125.00
4 . . . . 100.00
5 . . . . 100.00
6 thru 10 . . . . @75.00
11 thru 20 . . . . @40.00
21 thru 26 . . . . @50.00
27 Superheroes Groovymas 50.00
28 thru 100 . . . . @20.00
101 thru 162 . . . . @15.00

COLOR PUB.

ARCHIE AS PUREHEART THE POWERFUL
Archie Publications, 1966–67
1 superhero parody 200.00
2 . . . . 150.00
3 thru 6 Captain Pureheart . . . @125.00

ARCHIE AT RIVERDALE HIGH
Archie Publications, 1972
1 . . . . 100.00
2 . . . . 75.00
3 . . . . 50.00
4 . . . . 35.00
5 . . . . 35.00
6 thru 10 . . . . @30.00
11 thru 30 . . . . @25.00
31 thru 46 . . . . @20.00
47 in drag 14.00
48 thru 88 . . . . @10.00

Archie at Riverdale High #43
© Archie Publications

89 & 90 Cheryl Blossmos Band . @25.00
91 . . . . 8.00
92 Cheryl Blossom 14.00
93 thru 95 . . . . @8.00
96 Cheryl Blossom 14.00
97 & 98 . . . . @8.00
99 Cheryl Blossom 14.00
100 thru 102 . . . . @7.00
103 Archie Dates Cheryl Blossom . 14.00
104 thru 113 . . . . @8.00

ARCHIE COMICS DIGEST
Archie Comics Digest, 1973
1 . . . . 150.00
2 . . . . 75.00
3 . . . . 60.00
4 . . . . 60.00
5 . . . . 60.00
6 thru 10 . . . . 30.00
11 thru 32 . . . . @20.00
33 The Fly 25.00
34 thru 135 . . . . @6.00
136 Katy Keene 7.00
137 thru 204 . . . . @4.00
205 thru 230 . . . . @2.50

ARCHIE MEETS THE PUNISHER
Archie/Marvel, 1994
1-shot crossover, same contents
as Punisher meets Archie 7.00

ARCHIE'S MADHOUSE
Archie Publications, 1959–69
1 . . . . 500.00
2 . . . . 300.00
3 thru 5 . . . . @200.00
6 thru 10 . . . . @150.00
11 thru 16 . . . . @100.00
17 thru 21 . . . . @75.00
22 I:Sabrina 500.00
23 thru 25 Sabrina . . . . @200.00
26 thru 28 . . . . @100.00
29 thru 30 . . . . @50.00
31 thru 33 Sabrina . . . . @100.00
34 . . . . 50.00
35 B 70.00
36 Salem Cat & Sabrina 125.00
37 Sabrina 100.00
38 thru 66 . . . . 50.00

ARCHIE'S PAL JUGHEAD
SEE: JUGHEAD

ARCHIE'S SUPERHERO MAGAZINE
Archie Publications, 1979
1 JSm,SK,Rept.Double of Capt.
Strong #1,FLy,Black Hood 25.00
2 GM,NA/DG,AMc,I:'70's Black
Hood, Superhero rept. 30.00

ARCHIE'S TV LAUGH-OUT
Archie Publications, 1969–86
1 . . . . 200.00
2 giant 125.00
3 thru 6 giant . . . . @60.00
7 Josie 150.00
8 thru 22 . . . . @75.00
23 thru 41 . . . . @40.00
42 thru 80 . . . . @30.00
81 thru 90 . . . . @35.00
91 Cheryl Blossom 40.00
92 thru 99 . . . . @25.00
100 Michael Jackson 40.00
101 thru 106 . . . . @25.00

ARCHIE 3000
Archie Publications, 1989–1991
1 thru 16 . . . . 2.00

ARCHIE'S WEIRD MYSTERIES
Archie Comics, 1999
1 from animated series 4.00
2 Shriek 3.00
3 thru 25 . . . . @3.00
Becomes

ARCHIE'S MYSTERIES
Archie Comics, 2003
26 thru 34 . . . . @3.00

ARENA, THE
Alchemy, 1990
1 . . . . 2.50
1a signed, numbered, limited 3.00
2 . . . . 2.50

ARIANE & BLUEBEARD
Eclipse, 1988
Spec. CR 4.00

ARISTOKITTENS, THE
Gold Key, 1971–75
1 Disney 60.00
2 . . . . 50.00
3 . . . . 50.00
4 . . . . 50.00
5 thru 9 . . . . @50.00

ARKANIUM
Dreamwave, 2002
1 triple gatefold cover 3.00
2 thru 6 . . . . @3.00

ARMAGEDDON
Chaos! Comics, 1999
1 (of 4) F:Lady Death, Evil Ernie . . 3.00
1a Premium edition 8.00
2 O:Chaos 3.00
3 . . . . 3.00
4 concl 3.00

ARMAGEDDON FACTOR
AC Comics, 1987
1 Sentinels of Justice 2.50
2 . . . . 2.50
3 (1990) 4.00

ARMOR
Continuity, 1985
1 TGr,NA,A:Silver Streak,
silver logo 5.00
1a 2nd printing,red logo 3.00
2 TGr,NA(c) 3.00
3 TGr,NA(c) 3.00
4 TGr,NA(c) 3.00
5 BS,NA(c) 3.00
6 TVE,NA(c) 3.00
7 NA(c) 3.00
8 FS,NA(c) 3.00
9 FS,NA&KN(c) 3.00
10 FS,NA&KN(c) 3.00
11 SDr(i),KN(c) 3.00
12 KN(c) 3.00
13 NA(c),direct sales 3.00
14 KN(c), newsstand 3.00
[2nd Series]
1 V:Hellbender,Trading Card 3.00
[3rd Series, Deathwatch 2000]
1 Deathwatch 2000 pt.3,w/card . . 4.00
2 Deathwatch 2000 pt.9,w/card . . 3.00
3 Deathwatch 2000 pt.15,w/card . . 3.00
4 . . . . 3.00
5 Rise of Magic 3.00
6 Rise of Magic 3.00

ARMORED TROOPER VOTOMS
CPM Comics, 1996
1 TEI 3.00
2 thru 4 TEI . . . . @3.00
GN Supreme Survivor 17.00

ARMORINES
Valiant, 1994
0 (from X-O #25),Card Stock (c),
Diamond Dealer Meeting 2.50
0a Gold Ed 3.00
1 JGz(s),JCf,B:White Death 2.50
2 thru 12 . . . . @2.50
Yearbook I:Linoff 3.00
Vol. 2
1 48-pg 4.00
2 . . . . 4.00
3 and 4 . . . . @2.50

ARMORQUEST GENESIS
Alias Enterprises, 2005
1 (of 6) 3.00
2 . . . . 3.00
3 . . . . 3.00
4 thru 5 . . . . @3.50

ARMY ATTACK
Charlton, 1964
1 SG 75.00
2 SG 60.00

3 SG 50.00
4 . . . . 40.00
Vol. 2, 1965
38 thru 47 . . . . @40.00

ARMY OF DARKNESS:
D.E. (Dynamite Ent.) 2005
1 Ash vs. Re-Animator 3.00
1a signed 15.00
1b thru 2b Broomstick foil 15.00
2 thru 4 . . . . @3.00
5 Old School 3.00
5a glow-in-the-dark (c) . . . 15.00
5b variant glow-in-the-dark (c) . . . 18.00
6 Old School 3.00
6a variant (c) 3.00
6b Glow-in-the-dark (c) 15.00
7 Old School 3.00
7a variant (c)s . . . . @3.00
8 Ash vs. Dracula, pt.1 . . . . 3.00
8a variant (c)s . . . . @3.00
9 Ash vs. Dracula, pt. 2 . . . . 3.00
10 . . . . 3.00
10a variant (c)s . . . . @3.00
11 . . . . 3.00
11a variant (c) . . . . @3.00
12 . . . . 3.00
12a variant (c)s . . . . @3.00
13 Death of Ashley J. Williams . . . 3.00
13a variant (c)s . . . . @3.00
Tales of Army of Darkness, Vol. 1 . . 6.00

ARMY OF DARKNESS:
ASHES 2 ASHES
Devil's Due Publishing, 2004
1 . . . . 3.00
1a signed 18.00
1b director's cut 1-shot 5.00
2 thru 4 . . . . @3.00
D.E. (Dynamite Ent.) 2006
1b director's cut 5.00
1c director's cut foil (c) 18.00
1d photo (c) 7.00
2c variant glow-in-the-dark (c) . . . 18.00

ARMY OF DARKNESS:
FROM THE ASHES
D.E. (Dynamite Ent.) 2007
1 . . . . 3.50
2 thru 4 . . . . @3.50

ARMY OF DARKNESS:
SHOP TILL YOU
DROP (DEAD)
Devil's Due Publishing, 2004
1 . . . . 3.00
1a variant(c)s 3.00
2 thru 4 . . . . @3.00
D.E. (Dynamite Ent.) 2006
1 . . . . 3.00
1a variant glow-in-the-dark (c) . . . 18.00
1d exclusive (c) 7.00
1e enhanced photo (c) 18.00
2 . . . . 3.00
2a variant Fiery red foil(c) 15.00
2b variant special foil (c) 18.00
2c variant glow-in-the-dark (c) . . . 18.00
3 . . . . 3.00
3a variant Sabre foil (c) 15.00
3b variant glow-in-the-dark (c) . . . 18.00
4 . . . . 3.00
4a variant glow-in-the-dark (c) . . . 9.00

ARMY WAR HEROES
Charlton, 1963–70
1 . . . . 100.00
2 . . . . 40.00
3 thru 21 . . . . @30.00

22 GS,O&I:Iron Corporal 40.00
23 thru 38 . . . . @30.00

ARROW
Malibu, 1992
1 V:Dr.Sheldon,A:Man O'War 2.50

ARROWSMITH
Wildstorm/DC, 2003
1 (of 6) KBk(s),CPa 3.00
2 KBk(s),mystical aviator 3.00
3 KBk(s) thru 6 . . . . @3.00
Spec. Arrowsmith/Astro City 3.00

ARTESIA
Sirius, 1999
1 (of 6) by Mark Smylie 3.00
1a limited edition. 10.00
2 thru 6 . . . . @3.00
Ann.#1 . . . . 3.50
Ann.#2 . . . . 4.00

ARTESIA AFIELD
Sirius, 2000
1 (of 6) by Mark Smylie 3.00
1a Limited Ed. 6.00
2 thru 6 . . . . @3.00
Annual #3 Artesia. 5.00

ARTESIA AFIRE
Archaia Studios Press, 2003
1 (of 6) by Mark Smylie 4.00
2 . . . . 4.00
3 . . . . 4.00
4 . . . . 4.00
5 . . . . 4.00
6 . . . . 4.00

ARTESIA: BESIEGED
Archaia Studios, 2006
1 (of 6) The Calm Before 4.00
2 The Traitor King. 4.00
3 As I Lay Dying 4.00

ASH
Event Comics, 1994
1 JQ,JP,Fire and Crossfire,pt.1 . . 10.00
1a David Finch/Batt(c) 3.00
1b omnichrome commemorative . 12.00
1c omnichrom signed & numbered 25.00
2 JQ,JP,Fire and Crossfire,pt.2 . . . 7.00
2a David Finch/Batt (c). 3.00
3 JQ,JP,Secret of Origin 4.50
4 I:Actor 3.00
5 I:New Character. 3.00
6 V:Gabriel 3.00
0 Red Laser ed., Current Ash (c) . . 9.00
0 Red Laser ed., Future Ash (c) . . . 9.00

ASH:
CINDER AND SMOKE
Event Comics, 1997
1 MWa,BAu,HuR,JP 3.00
1a autographed virgin JQ cover . . 10.00
1b signed limited edition 12.00
2 HuR(c) 3.00
2 JQ(c) 3.00
3 (of 6) JQ&JP(c) 3.00
4 (of 6) JQ&JP(c) 3.00
5 (of 6) JQ&JP(c) 3.00
6 (of 6) JQ&JP(c) 3.00
3a thru 6a variant JP&HuR(c)s . . @3.00

ASH FILES, THE
Event Comics, 1997
1 JQ,JP 3.00
1 signed, limited 18.00

ASH: FIRE
AND CROSSFIRE
Event Comics, 1998
1 (of 5) JQ,JP 3.00
1a signed & numbered 20.00
2 . . . . 3.00

ASH: THE FIRE WITHIN
Event Comics, 1996
2 JQ,JP. 3.00
3 JQ,JP, Ash Rooftop cover 3.00
3a JQ,JP, Ash Firefighter cover . . . 3.00

ASH/22 BRIDES
Event Comics, 1996
1 FaN,HuR,JP. 3.00

Aspen #3 © Aspem

ASPEN
Aspen 2003
1 Fathom. 5.00
1a variant (c). 18.00
2 Fathom, Soulfire 3.50
2a San Diego 18.00
3 . . . . 3.00
3a Chicago 12.00
Aspen extended edition 9.00
Aspen Sketch Book 9.00
Aspen Swimsuit Special (2006) 9.00

ASPEN SEASONS
Aspen, 2005
1 Spring 2005 . . . . 3.00
1 Fall 2005 . . . . 3.00
1 Summer 2006 . . . . 3.00

ASSASSIN
Archangel Studios, 2003
1 (of 4) 3.00
1a variant (c). 3.00
2 . . . . 3.00

ASSASSINAUTS
Narwain Publishing, 2006
1 . . . . 3.50

ASSASSIN SCHOOL
APC, 2003
1 . . . . 3.50
2 thru 5 . . . . @3.50
S.O.S.(Super one-shot) 6.00

All comics prices listed are for *Near Mint* condition.

Vol. 2 (2004)

0 . . . . 3.00
1 . . . . 3.50
2 thru 8 . . . . @3.50
8a limited sketch (c) (1:10) 3.50

ASTER
Entity Comics, 1995

0 O:Aster the Celestial Knight 4.50
1 I:Celestial Knight 5.00
1b 2nd printing 3.00
2 . . . . 3.50
3 V:Tolmek 3.25
3a Variant cover 7.00
4 Final Issue 3.00

ASTER THE LAST
CELESTIAL KNIGHT
Entity Comics, 1995

1 R:Aster Chromium Cover 3.00
1a Clear Chromium Edition 4.00
1b Holo Chrome Edition 5.00
2 World Defender 3.00

Astro Boy #1
© Gold Key

ASTRO BOY
Gold Key, 1965

1 I:Astro Boy 1,000.00

ASTRO BOY
Now, 1989
Prev. Original Astro Boy

18 . . . . 3.00
19 . . . . 3.00
20 . . . . 3.00

ASTRO CITY
Wildstorm/DC, 2004

Astro City Spec. (2004) 4.00
Spec. A Visitor's Guide (2004) 6.00

ASTRO CITY:
THE DARK AGE
Wildstorm/DC, June, 2005

1 (of 16) KBk(s), BA,AxR(c) 3.00
2 KBk(s),BA,AxR(c) 3.00
3 KBk(s),BA,AxR(c) 3.00
4 KBk(s),BA,AxR(c) 3.00
Book 2, Oct., 2006
1 KBu,BA, Eyes of a Killer 3.00
2 KBu,BA 3.00
3 KBu,BA 3.00
4 KBu,BA, Gangwar erupts 3.00

COLOR PUB.

ASTRO CITY:
LOCAL HEROES
Homage/DC, 2003

1 (of 5) KBk,BA 3.00
2 thru 5 KBk,BA . . . . @3.00

ASTRO CITY: SAMARITAN
Wildstorm/DC, June, 2006

Spec. KBk, BA, 48-pg. 4.00

ASYLUM
Pendragon, 1995

1 . . . . 3.00
2 thru 3 . . . . @3.00

ASYLUM
Maximum Press, 1995

1 Warchild, Beanworld, Avengelyne,
    Battlestar Galactica 3.00
2 I:Deathkiss 3.00
3 . . . . 3.00
4 RLd,A:Cybrid 3.00
5 I:Black Seed 3.00
6 R:Steve Austin & Jaime
    Sommers 3.00
7 RLe,F:Bloodwulf 3.00
8 RLd 3.00
9 RLd 3.00
10 . . . . 3.00
11 . . . . 3.00
12 MMy,F:Blindside 3.00
13 . . . . 3.00

ATHENA VOLTAIRE:
FLIGHT OF THE FALCON
Speakeasy Comics, 2006

1 . . . . 3.00
2 thru 5 . . . . @3.00

ATHENA VOLTAIRE:
FLIGHT OF THE FLACON
Ape Entertainment, 2006

1 Ape edition, 48-pg. 4.50
2 . . . . 3.00
3 . . . . 4.50
4 . . . . 3.00

ATHENA VOLTAIRE:
THE LEGEND OF MU-KING
Ape Entertainment, 2007

1 (of 4) 3.50
2 thru 4 . . . . @3.50

ATLANTIS RISING
Platinum Studios 2007

1 (of 5) 3.00
2 . . . . 3.00
3 . . . . 3.00

ATLAS
Avatar Press, 2002

1 Gossett (c) 3.50
1b thru 1e variant (c)s . . . . @3.50
2 Brooks (c) 3.50
2b variant (c) 3.50

ATOM ANT
Gold Key, 1966

1 . . . . 550.00

ATOM-AGE COMBAT
Fago Magazines, 1959

2 Nuclear Sub,A-Bomb 325.00
3 Space Missile 225.00

ATOMIC RABBIT
Charlton Comics, 1955–58

1 . . . . 350.00
2 . . . . 150.00
3 thru 10 . . . . @100.00
11 . . . . 150.00
Becomes:

ATOMIC BUNNY
Charlton Comics, 1958

12 . . . . 150.00
13 thru 18 . . . . @100.00
19 Dec., 1959 . . . . 100.00

ATOMIC MOUSE
Charlton 1984, 1985

1 . . . . 15.00
10 thru 12 . . . . @12.00

ATOMICS, THE
AAA Pop Comics, 1999

1 by Mike Allred 3.00
2 Zapman 3.00
3 Mutant Street Beatniks 3.00
4 refugees from the Innerverse . . . 3.00
5 The Light 3.00
6 The Physical 3.00
7 I:The Skunk 3.00
8 F:The Laser 3.00
9 taken hostage 3.00
10 . . . . 3.00
11 Heroes divided 3.00
12 with poster 3.50
13 World of Savage Dragon 3.50
14 World of Savage Dragon,pt.4 . . 3.50
15 World of Savage Dragon,pt.5 . . 3.50
16 World of Savage Dragon,pt.6 . . 3.50
King Size Giant 10.00
King-Size Spec. Lessons in Light
    Lava & Lasers 9.00
King-Size Spec. Jigsaw 10.00
King-Size Vol. 3 . . . . 9.00
King-Size Vol. 4, 80-page 9.00

ATOMIKA
Speakeasy Comics, 2005

1 . . . . 3.00
1a signed 20.00
2 thru 6 . . . . @3.00
7 thru 9 God is Red . . . . @3.00

ATOMIK ANGELS
Crusade Entertainment, 1996

1 BiT 3.00
1 variant cover (1:25) 5.00
2 BiT 3.00
3 BiT 3.00
4 BiT, conclusion 3.00

ATOMIK MIKE
Alias Enterprises, 2006

1 . . . . 3.50
2 thru 4 . . . . @3.50

ATOMIK MIKE
Desperado Pub., 2007

1 thru 3 . . . . @4.00

ATTACK
Charlton Comics, 1958–59

54 100 pages 125.00
55 thru 60 . . . . @100.00

ATTACK
Charlton, 1962–64

#n 75.00
2 Jump Into Danger 50.00
3 SG, The Infiltrators 50.00

ATTACK
Charlton, 1971–75

1	35.00
2	20.00
3 thru 5	@12.00
6 thru 15	@10.00

Charlton, 1979

16 thru 20	@7.00
21 thru 48	7.00

ATTACK AT SEA
Charlton, 1968

1	30.00

AUGIE DOGGIE
Gold Key, 1963

1 Hanna-Barbera character	350.00

AUTHORITY, THE
WildStorm/DC, 1999

1 WEl(s),BHi,PNe	12.00
2 WEl(s),BHi,PNe,V:Kaizen Gamorra	10.00
3 WEl(s),BHi,PNe,destruction	10.00
4 WEl(s),BHi,PNe,save L.A.	10.00
5 WEl(s),BHi,PNe,Swiftships,pt.1	10.00
6 WEl(s),BHi,PNe	7.00
7 WEl(s),BHi,PNe	7.00
8 WEl(s),BHi,PNe	7.00
9 WEl(s),BHi,PNe,OuterDark,pt.1	7.00
10 WEl(s),BHi,PNe,OuterDark,pt.2	7.00
11 WEl(s),BHi,PNe,OuterDark,pt.3	7.00
12 WEl(s),BHi,PNe,OuterDark,pt.4	7.00
13 MMr(s),TvS,Nativity,pt.1	11.00
14 MMr(s),TvS,Nativity,pt.2	6.00
15 MMr(s),TvS,Nativity,pt.3	6.00
16 MMr(s),TvS,Nativity,pt.4	6.00
17 MMr(s),TvS,Earth Inferno,pt.1	6.00
18 MMr(s),TvS,Earth Inferno,pt.2	6.00
19 MMr(s),TvS,Earth Inferno,pt.3	6.00
20 MMr(s),TvS,Earth Inferno,pt.4	6.00
21 JMC,All Tomorrow's Parties	6.00
22 MMr(s),TvS,Brave New World, pt.1 (of 4)	6.00
23 TPe(s),Brave-World,pt.2	6.00
24 TPe(s),BU:Establishment,40-pg	3.50
25 TPe(s),Re-Space	3.50
26 TPe(s),F:Old Authority	3.50
27 MMr(s),New World Order,pt.2	3.50
28 MMr(s),AAd,F:Seth	3.50
29 New World Order,pt.4	3.50
Ann. 2000 #1, Devil's Night x-over, pt.2	5.00
GN The Authority: Kev (2002)	5.00
GN Scorched Earth	5.00

Volume 2

1 DT,F:Jack Hawksmoor, etc.	4.00
2 thru 13 DT	@3.00
14 WPo,Jack Hawksmore origin	3.00
Spec. #0, 40-pg.	3.00
X-Mas Spec. The Authority/Lobo x-over, 48-pg. (2003)	5.00
Spec. Authority/Lobo Spring Break Massacre, SBs, 48-page	5.00

AUTHORITY, THE
Wildstorm/DC, Oct., 2006

1 GMo	3.00
1a variant (c).	3.00
2 GMo	3.00

AUTHORITY: THE MAGNIFICENT KEVIN
Wildstorm, Sept., 2005

1 (of 5) GEn,F:Kev Hawkins	3.00
2	3.00
3	3.00
4	3.00
5	3.00

AUTHORITY, THE: MORE KEV
Wildstorm/DC, 2004

1 (of 4) GEn(s),GF	3.00
2 thru 4 GEn(s),GF	@3.00

AUTHORITY, THE: PRIME
Wildstorm/DC, Oct., 2007

1 DaR,Stormwatch vs. Authority	3.00

AUTHORITY, THE: REVOLUTION
Wildstorm/DC, 2004

1	3.00
2	3.00
3 America in Revolution	3.00
4 War in Washington	3.00
5 Nation's capitol in rubble	3.00
6 thru 12 concl.	@3.00

AUTOMATIC KAFKA
WildStorm/DC, 2002

1 JoC, Eye of the Storm	3.00
2 JoC,NPS agents	3.00
3 JoC,TV game show host	3.00
4 JoC,	3.00
5 JoC,	3.00
6 JoC,	3.00
7 JoC,who is Galaxia	3.00
8 thru 9 JoC	@3.00

Avengeblade #1 © Maximum Press

AVENGEBLADE
Maximum Press, 1996

1 RLe	3.00
2 RLe	3.00

AVENGELYNE
Maximum Press, 1995

1 RLd,I:Avengelyne Dir ed	12.00
1a Newstand Edition	5.00
1b Holochrome Edition	15.00
1 gold edition	10.00
2 V:B'Lial	4.00
3 I:Magogi	4.00
3 variant cover, pin-up	5.00

Regular Series, 1996

0 RLd,O:Avengelyne	5.00
1 RLd,BNa,F:Devlin	4.00
1 variant photo cover	4.00
2 I:Darkchylde	10.00
2a variant photo cover	12.00
3	3.50

4 A:Cybrid	3.50
5 A:Cybrid,	3.50
6 RLd,F:Divinity	3.50
7 RLd,F:Divinity	3.50
8 RLd,	3.50
9 RLd,	3.50
10 BNa,The Possession, pt.1	3.50
11 BNa,The Possession, pt.2	3.50
12 BNa,The Possession, pt.3	3.50
13 BNa,The Possession, pt.4	3.50
14 A:Bloodwulf	3.50
15 A:Glory, Prophet	3.50
Swimsuit Edition.	3.50
Swimsuit book, American Entertainment exclusive	7.50

AVENGELYNE
Awesome Entertainment, 1999

Prelude	3.00
1 RLe,RNa	3.00
1a, b & c variant covers	3.00
2 RLe,	3.00
3	3.00
Spec. Swimsuit, 1999	3.50
Spec.#1-shot Demonslayer (2000)	3.00
Spec.#1a Demonslayer variant (c)	3.00
Spec.#1b Demonslayer variant (c)	3.00
Spec.#1c Demonslayer variant (c)	3.00

AVENGELYNE: ARMAGEDDON
Maximum Press, 1996–97

1 (of 3) RLd	3.00
2 RLd	3.00
3 BNa,ScC, finale	3.00

AVENGELYNE: BAD BLOOD
Avatar, 2000

1 Matt Haley (c)	3.50
1a thru 1b variant(c)s	@3.50
1c prism foil (c) previews excl.	13.00
1d Al Rio velvet (c)	20.00
1e leather (c).	25.00
1f platinum (c)	8.00
1g Ruby Red ed..	20.00
2	3.50
2a variant(c)s	@3.50
Prelude Rick Lyon (c)	5.00
Prelude Al Rio (c).	5.00
Prelude Bikini (c)	6.00
Prelude prism foil(c) 16-page.	13.00
Prelude variant SSh(c).	6.00

AVENGELYNE BIBLE: REVELATIONS
Maximum Press

one-shot RLd,	3.50

AVENGELYNE: DARK DEPTHS
Avatar Press, 2001

1 (of 2) Rio(c)	3.50
1a MMy(c).	3.50
1b Martin (c)	3.50
1c blue velvet (c)	25.00
1d prism foil exclusive (c)	13.00
1e Heavenly Body edition	6.00
1f Royal Blue (c).	75.00
2 (of 2) Rio(c)	3.50
2a MMy(c).	3.50
2b Lyon (c)	3.50
2c Blue leather (c)	25.00
1/2 Rio (c) 16-page	5.00
1/2 Lloyd painted (c)	5.00
1/2 Frillion (c).	5.00
1/2 Midnight Prayer (c)	6.00
1/2 Prism foil exclusive (c)	13.00

AVENGELYNE: DEADLY SINS
Maximum Press, 1996
1 RLd (c) 3.00
1 photo (c) 3.00
2 RLd(c) 3.00

AVENGELYNE: DRAGON REALM
Avatar Press, 2001
1/2 Rio (c) 5.00
1/2 Carrie Hall (c) 5.00
1/2 Lloyd (c) 5.00
1/2 Martin (c) 5.00
1/2 Dying Breath ed 6.00
1/2 Prism foil ed 13.00
1 (of 2) Rio(c) 3.50
1a thru 1b variant(c)s . . . . @3.50
1c red leather (c) 25.00
1d bondage (c) 6.00
1e prism foil (c) 13.00
1f venomous edition 6.00
1g venomous emerald foil 14.00
1h Fearless edition 5.00
2 Rio(c) 3.50
2a thru 2b variant(c)s . . . . @3.50
2c Shaw (c) 3.50
2d Ron Adrian (c) 6.00

Avengelyne/Glory #1
© Maximum Press

AVENGELYNE/GLORY
Maximum Press, 1995
1 V:B'Lial 4.00
1a variant cover 5.00
Swimsuit Spec. #1 . . . . 3.00

AVENGELYNE/GLORY: THE GODYSSEY
Maximum Press, 1996
1 RLd,BNa 3.00
2 thru 5 RLd . . . . @3.00

AVENGELYNE/PANDORA
Avatar, 2000
Spec. x-over 3.50
Spec.Preview exclusive 3.50
Spec.Preview Bikini ed 6.00
Spec.McDaniel (c) 6.00
Spec.Previews exlusive Prism ed . . 13.00
Spec.Red Velvet 25.00
Spec.Ruby Red edition 20.00
Spec.Royal Blue 75.00

AVENGELYNE/POWER
Maximum Press, 1995–96
1 RLd,V:Hollywood 3.00
1 variant cover 3.50
2 RLd(c) 3.00
3 . . . . 3.00
3a photo (c) 3.00

AVENGELYNE/PROPHET
Maximum Press, 1996
1 RLd,BNa,MD2 . . . . 3.00
Awesome Entertainment, 2000
Rage of Furies #1 RLe(c) 3.00
#1a IaC(c) 3.00
#1b Grant(c) 3.00
#1c Walker Bros.(c) 3.00
#1d Wizard world ed. 5.00
#1e Wizard world, signed 10.00

AVENGELYNE: REVELATION
Avatar, 2000
1 Rio (c) 3.50
1a Haley (c) 3.50
1b Wraparound (c) 3.50
1c leather (c) 20.00
1d Matt Martin (c) 6.00
1e royal blue (c) 60.00
Previews prism foil (c) 13.00
Prelude Lyon (c) 6.00
Prelude platinum signed 11.00

AVENGELYNE: SERAPHACIDE
Avatar Press, 2001
1/2 Lyon (c) 5.00
1/2 Variant (c)s . . . . @5.00
1/2 Bound edition 6.00
1/2 Pax Romana (c) 6.00
1/2 Ron Adrian (c) 6.00
1 (of 2) Rio (c) 3.50
1a thru 1c variant (c)s . . . . @3.50
1d White Velvet (c) 20.00
1e Adam & Eve edition 6.00
1f Hard Woman (c) 6.00
1g Bikini (c) 6.00

AVENGELYNE/SHI
Avatar Press, 2001
1/2 RLd (c) 16-page 4.00
1/2 variant(c)s . . . . @4.00
1/2d Victory (c) 6.00
1/2e Sean Shaw, Cross cover 6.00
1 Finch (c) x-over 3.50
1a variant(c)s . . . . @3.50
1e Red Leather (c) 20.00
1f Prism foil (c) 13.00
1h Waller (c) 6.00
1i Face off cover 6.00
1j ruby red edition 25.00

AVENGELYNE/SUPREMA
Awesome Entertainment, 2000
Rage of Furies #1 (2000) 4.00
1a Wizard world ed. 5.00
1b signed 10.00

AVENGELYNE/ WARRIOR NUN AREALA
Maximum Press, 1997
Spec 3.00
Awesome Entertainment, 1997
Spec. #2 The Nazarene Affair 3.00

AVENGERS, THE
Gold Key, 1968
1 . . . . 500.00

AWESOME
Awesome Entertainment, 1997
Holiday Spec. #1 . . . . 2.50
Holiday Spec.'99 . . . . 5.00
Spring '99 Tourbook 5.00

AXA
Eclipse, 1987
1 The Adopted 4.00
2 The Donor 3.50

AXEL PRESSBUTTON
Eclipse, 1984
1 BB(c),Origin 3.00
2 SD,Wanted for Mass Murder 3.00
3 AD,Wanted for Mass Murder 3.00
4 TA, ... 3.00
5 AD,Slave of the Narco-Pollen . . . 2.50
6 TA,Days in Downtown Delta Five 2.50

AXIS ALPHA
Axis Comics, 1994
1 LSn,I:BEASTIES,Dethgrip,
  Shelter,W 3.00

AYA
Studio G, 2003
1 . . . . 3.00
2 thru 4 . . . . @3.00

AYA
AK Entertainment, 2006
1 Clone Order, pt.1 . . . . 3.00
2 Clone Order: Resurrection 3.00
3 Clone Order: A Pharaoh Reborn . 3.00
4 One Bullet 3.00
5 Zero Tolerance, pt. 2 . . . . 3.00
6 Zero Tolerance 3.00
7 thru 9 . . . . @3.00

AZTEC ACE
Eclipse, 1984
1 NR(i),I:AztecAce 3.50
2 NR(i) 3.50
3 thru 9 NR(i) . . . . @3.00
10 NR(i) 3.00
11 . . . . 3.50
12 thru 15 . . . . @2.50

BABES OF BROADWAY
Broadway, 1996
1 . . . . 3.00

BABY HUEY
Harvey, 1991
1 . . . . 7.00
2 . . . . 3.00
3 thru 9 . . . . @3.00

BABY HUEY, THE BABY GIANT
Harvey Publications, 1956–80
1 . . . . 900.00
2 . . . . 400.00
3 Anti-Pep Pills 300.00
4 . . . . 200.00
5 . . . . 200.00
6 thru 10 . . . . @150.00
11 thru 20 . . . . @100.00
21 thru 40 . . . . @75.00
41 thru 60 . . . . @50.00
61 thru 79 . . . . @40.00
80 . . . . 40.00
81 thru 95 giant size . . . . @50.00
96 Giant size 40.00
97 Giant size 40.00
98 . . . . 30.00

99	15.00
100	5.00
101	5.00

BABY HUEY AND PAPA
Harvey Publications, 1962–68

1	350.00
2	250.00
3	200.00
4	200.00
5	200.00
6 thru 10	@150.00
11 thru 20	@100.00
21 thru 33	@75.00

BABY HUEY DUCKLAND
Harvey Publications, 1962–66

1	250.00
2 thru 5	@100.00
6 thru 10	@75.00
11 thru 20	@50.00
21 thru 33	@40.00

BABY SNOOTS
Gold Key, 1970

1 F:Uptite Mouse	40.00
2	20.00
3 thru 10	@20.00
11 thru 22	@12.00

BACHELOR FATHER
Dell Publishing Co., 1962

1	150.00
2	125.00

BACK TO THE FUTURE
Harvey, 1991

1 Chicago 1927	3.00
2 Cretaceous Period	3.00
3 World War I	3.00
4 Doc Retires	3.00

BAD COMPANY
Quality, 1988

1	3.00
2 thru 19	@3.00

BAD EGGS
Acclaim, 1996

1 thru 4 BL,DP,That Dirty Yellow Mustard	@3.00

BADGER
Capital, 1983

1 JBt,I:Badger,Ham,Daisy Yak,Yeti.	5.00
2 JBt,I:Riley,A:YakYeti	4.00
3 JBt,O:Badger,Ham	4.00
4 JBt,A'Ham	4.00

First, 1984–91

5 thru 16 BR	@3.00
17 JBt,I:Lamont	3.50
18 thru 39	@3.00
40 thru 49 RLm,	@3.50
50 RLm,T:Roof off SuckerII	5.00
51 RLm,V:Demon	3.00
52 thru 54 TV	@4.00
55 thru 70	@3.00
Graphic Nov.BR,I:Mazis Sykes,D:Hodag	10.00
Badger Bedlam	5.00

BADGER GOES BERSERK
First, 1989

1 I:Larry,Jessie	4.00
2 MZ,V:Larry,Jessie	3.50
3 JBt/MZ,V:Larry,Jessie	3.00
4 JBt/MZ,V:Larry,Jessie	3.00

BAD GIRLS OF BLACKOUT
Blackout Comics, 1995

0	3.50
1 I:Ms. Cyanide, Ice	3.50
Ann.#1 Hari Kari, Lady Vampre	3.50
Ann.#1 Commemorative ed.	10.00

BAD KITTY
Chaos! Comics, 2001

1 BnP	3.00
1a premium edition	9.00
2	3.00
3	3.00
Ashcan	6.00
Script #1	5.00
Script #1 premium	20.00

BAD KITTY: MISCHIEF NIGHT
Chaos! Comics, 2001

1	3.00
1a premium edition	13.00
1b super premium edition	20.00

BAD KITTY: RELOADED
Chaos! Comics, 2001

1	3.00
1a premium ed.	9.00
2 F:Chastity	3.00
3	3.00
4	4.00
2a thru 4a variant (c).	@7.50

BAD MOON RISING
Avatar Press, 2006

1	4.00
1a variant (c)s	@4.00

BADROCK/WOLVERINE
Awesome Entertainment, 1997

Spec. #1 JV,CYp,V:Sauron,48pg	5.00

BAKER STREET
Caliber, 1989

1	3.00
2 thru 10	@3.00

BALLAD OF HALO JONES
Quality, 1987

1 IG Alan Moore story	2.50
1a IG rep.	2.50
2 thru 12	@2.50

BALLAD OF SLEEPING BEAUTY, THE
Beckett Comics, 2004

1	2.00
2 thru 4	@2.00
5 thru 8	@2.00

BALOO & LITTLE BRITCHES
Gold Key, 1968

1 From Disney's Jungle Book	50.00

BAMBI
Gold Key, 1963

1 From Disney movie	100.00

BAMM-BAMM & PEBBLES FLINTSTONE
Gold Key, 1964

1	200.00

Banana Splits #5
© Gold Key

BANANA SPLITS, THE
Gold Key, 1969

1 From Hanna-Barbera	200.00
2	150.00
3 thru 8	@150.00

BANZAI GIRL
Sirius Entertainment, 2002

Preview book, lim. ed.	5.00
1 (of 4) by Jinky Coronado	3.00
2 thru 4	@3.00
2a thru 4a lim.,signed,ph(c)	@12.00
3	3.00
4	3.00
Ann. #1	3.50
Fabulous Foto Book	4.00

BANZAI GIRLS
Arcana Studio, 2007

1	4.00
2 thru 4	@4.00

BARBARIANS, THE
Atlas, 1975

1 O: Andrax,F:Iron Jaw	50.00

BARBAROSSA AND THE LOST CORSAIRS
Kandora Publishing, 2005

1	3.50
2 thru 5	@3.50

BARBIE & KEN
Dell Publishing Co. 1962

1	800.00
2	650.00
3	650.00
4	650.00
5	675.00

BARBIE TWINS ADVENTURES, THE
Topps, 1995

1 I:Shane, Sia	3.00

BARBI TWINS ADVENTURES
Studio Chikara, 1998

Color Spec. The Roswell Incident	4.00

All comics prices listed are for *Near Mint* condition.

BARNEY AND
BETTY RUBBLE
Charlton Comics, 1973–76
1	60.00
2 thru 5	@30.00
6 thru 10	@25.00
11 thru 23	@20.00

BARNEY GOOGLE AND
SNUFFY SMITH
Gold Key, 1964
1	65.00

Charlton, 1970
1	35.00
2	20.00
3 thru 6	@20.00

BARRY M. GOLDWATER
Dell Publishing Co., 1965
1	75.00

BAR SINISTER
Acclaim Windjammer, 1995
1 From Shaman's Tears	2.50
2 V:SWAT Team	2.50
3 F: Animus Prime	2.50
4 MGe,RHo,V:Jabbersnatch	2.50

BART-MAN
Bongo, 1993
1 Foil(c),I:Bart-Man	4.00
2 I:Penalizer	2.50
3 When Bongos Collide,pt.3, with card	2.50
4 Crime-Time,pt.1	2.50
5 Bad Guys Strike Back	2.50

BART SIMPSON COMICS
Bongo Comics, 2000
1	3.00
2 thru 9	@3.00
10 thru 26	@3.00
27 thru 38	@3.00

BART SIMPSONS
TREEHOUSE OF HORROR
Bongo Comics, 1995
1 Bart People	3.00
2 thru 4	@3.00
5 48-pg.	3.50
6 and 7 64-page	@.50
8	@3.50
9 thru 13	@5.00
1-shot Treehouse of Terror	2.50

BASEBALL
Kitchen Sink, 1991
1 WE (c) reprint of 1949 orig.	4.00
2 Ray Gotto (c), w/4 BB cards	3.00

BAT, THE
Adventure
1 R:The Bat,inspiration for Batman says Bob Kane	3.00

BATMAN/DANGER GIRL
Wildstorm/DC, Dec. 2004
1-shot x-over, 48-page	5.00

BAT MASTERSON
Dell, 1960
1	225.00
2	125.00
3 thru 8	@125.00

BATTLEBOOKS
Battlebooks Inc., 1999
all BTi(c)
Bubba-Busters Battlebook	5.00
Captain America Battlebook	
Blue print, signed edition	9.00
Colossus Battlebook	4.00
Daredevil Battlebook BTi(c)	4.00
Daredevil Battlebook JQ&JP(c)	4.00
Darkchylde A Battlebook	4.00
Darkchylde B Battlebook	4.00
The Darkness Battlebook	4.00
Dr. Doom Battlebook	4.00
Elektra Battlebook	4.00
Blue print, signed edition	12.00
Elektra Battlebook, revised	4.00
Gambit Battlebook	4.00
Green Goblin Battlebook	4.00
Iron Man Battlebook	
Blue print, signed edition	12.00
Blue print, signed edition	12.00
The Incredible Hulk Battlebook	4.00
Blue print, signed edition	12.00
Magneto Battlebook	4.00
President Clinton Battlebook	5.00
Rogue Battlebook	4.00
Blue print, signed edition	12.00
Sabretooth Battlebook	4.00
Shi: The Spirit of Benkei Battlebook	4.00
Blue print, signed edition	9.00
Spider-Man Battlebook	
Blue print, signed edition	12.00
Storm Battlebook	4.00
The Thing Battlebook	4.00
Tomoe: Fan's of Fury Battlebook	4.00
Vampirella Hell on Earth Battlebook	4.00
White Queen Battlebook	4.00
Witchblade Battlebook	4.00
Wolverine Battlebook	4.00
Wolverine with Bone Claws Battlebook	
Blue print, signed edition	13.00

Battlefield Action #66
© Charlton

BATTLEFIELD ACTION
Charlton, 1960–66
16 thru 30 See Golden Age	
31 thru 62	@25.00

Charlton, 1980–84
63 thru 89	@

BATTLE OF
THE PLANETS
Gold Key, 1979
1 TV Cartoon	50.00
2 thru 5	@35.00

Whitman, 1980
6	20.00
7 thru 10	@20.00

BATTLER BRITTON
Wildstorm/DC, July 2006
1 GEn,CWi	3.00
2 thru 5 GEn,CWi	@3.00

BATTLESTAR GALACTICA
Maximum Press, 1995
1 Finds Earth	5.00
2 Council of Twelve	4.00
3 R:Adama	4.00
4 Pyramid Secrets	4.00
Spec. Ed. Painted Book (1997)	3.00
Battlestar Galactica: The Compendium #1 rep. from Asylum	3.00

BATTLESTAR GALACTICA
Realm Press, 1997
1 by Chris Scalf	4.00
1a variant cover	3.00
2 Law of Volhad	3.00
3 Prison of Souls, pt.1	3.00
3a alternate cover	3.00
4 Prison of Souls, pt.2	3.00
5	3.00
6 A Path of Darkness, pt.1	3.00
7 A Path of Darkness, pt.2	3.00
7a photo (c)	3.00
7b signed and numbered	6.00
8 Centurion Prime	3.00
Spec.#1 20 Yahren Reunion	5.00
Spec.#1 No Memory of Earth	3.00
Spec.#1 CenturionPrime,Scott(c)	3.00
Spec.#1 CenturionPrime,Parsons(c)	3.00
Spec.#2 Centurion Prime	3.00
Spec. 1999 Tourbook	3.00
Spec. 1999 Tourbook con. ed.	7.00
Spec. 1999 Tourbook sign.	30.00
Spec. Gallery #1	4.00
Tech Journal: The Galactica	4.00
Tech Journal: Ships of Fleet	4.00
Spec.No Man's Land	4.00
Spec.No Man's Land, deluxe	5.00
Cylon Dawn Spec. (2000)	4.00
Cylon Dawn Spec. deluxe	5.00
Darkest Night Spec. (2000)	4.00
Darkest Night Spec. variant (c)	5.00
Dire Prophecy Spec. (2000)	4.00
Dire Prophecy Spec. deluxe	5.00
Eve of Destruction Prelude(1999)	4.00
Spec.#1 Triad Triumph (2000)	4.00
Spec.#1a Triad Triumph,deluxe	5.00

BATTLESTAR GALACTICA
D.E. (Dynamite Ent.) 2006
0	1.00
1	3.00
1a photo foil	20.00
2 thru 5	@3.00
6 thru 12	@3.00
1a thru 12a variant (c)s	@3.00
2b thru 5b variant	
Cylon foil (c)s	@20.00

BATTLESTAR GALACTICA
APOLLO'S JOURNEY
Maximum Press, 1996
1 story by Richard Hatch	3.00
2	2.50
3	2.50

CYLON APOCALYPSE
Dynamite Entertainment, 2007
1	3.50
1a variant (c)s	@3.50
2 thru 4	@3.50
2a thru 4a variant (c)s	@3.50

THE ENEMY WITHIN
Maximum Press, 1996
1	3.00
2	2.50
3	2.50

JOURNEY'S END
Maximum Press, 1996
1 (of 4) RLd	3.00
2 RLd	3.00
3 RLd, the end of Galactica?	3.00
4 RLd, conclusion	3.00

PEGASUS
D.E. (Dynamite Ent.) 2007
1-shot	5.00

SEARCH FOR SANCTUARY
Realm Press, 1998
1 (of 4)	3.00
2 Path of Darkness	3.00
3 tensions grow	3.00
4	3.00

STARBUCK
Maximum Press, 1997
1 (of 3) RLd	3.00
2 RLd	3.00
3 RLd, the end of Galactica?	3.00

ZAREK
D.E. (Dynamite Ent.) 2006
1	3.50
1a photo foil (c)	5.00
2 thru 4	@3.50
2a thru 4a variant (c)s	@3.50

BATTLESTAR GALACTICA SEASON THREE
Real Press, 1999
1	3.00
1a alternate JaL(c)	5.00
1b Cylon Attack (c)	5.00
1c Cylon Attack (c) signed	30.00
2	3.00
2a alternate cover	5.00
2b pencil sketch cover	5.00
2c convention edition	5.00
3 Fire in the Sky	3.00
3a alternate cover	5.00
3b convention edition	5.00
4 Scott (c)	3.00
5 Busch (c)	3.00
6	3.00
4a thru 6a variant(c)	@3.00
7	3.00
8	3.00
7a & 8a deluxe	@5.00
Spec. 80-page Juggernaut	9.00
Tour Book Sketch ed	25.00

BATTLESTAR GALACTICA: SEASON ZERO
D.E. (Dynamite Ent.) 2007
1	3.00
1a variant (c)	3.00
2 thru 5	@3.00
2a thru 5a variant (c)s	@3.00

BATTLETECH
Blackthorne, 1987
1	3.00

---

2 thru 6	@3.00
(Changed to Black & White)	
1 3-D	3.00
2 3-D	3.00

BATTLETECH: FALLOUT
Malibu, Dec. 1994–Mar. 1995
0 Battletech	3.00
1 3 tales, Based on FASA game	3.00
1a gold foil limited edition	3.50
1b limited holographic editon	5.00
2 V:Clan Jade Falcon	3.00
3 R:Lea	3.00
4 Conclusion	3.00

BAY CITY JIVE
WildStorm/DC, 2001
1 (of 3) F:Sugah Rollins	3.00
1a variant (c) (1:4)	3.00
2 1976 streets of San Francisco	3.00
3 Hell on Earth, concl.	3.00

BEAGLE BOYS, THE
Gold Key, 1964–79
1	75.00
2 thru 5	@50.00
6 thru 10	@40.00
11 thru 20	@30.00
21 thru 47	@25.00

Beagle Boys vs. Uncle Scrooge #11
© Walt Disney

BEAGLE BOYS VERSUS UNCLE SCROOGE, THE
Gold Key, 1979
1 Case of the Missing Nuggets	20.00
2 There's Cash in the Trash	10.00
3 The Armored Car Caper	10.00
4 The Great Gift Grab	10.00
5 The Buccaneer's Map	10.00
6 The Foot Brake Fiasco	10.00
7 Vacation With Pay	10.00
8 Danger at Fifty Fathoms	10.00
9 The Bewitched Buck Baggers	10.00
10 The Frame-Up	10.00
11 Freebies Can be Costly	10.00
12 Number One Dollar	10.00

BEANIE THE MEANIE
Fago Publications, 1958
1	50.00
2 thru 3	@50.00

BEANY AND CECIL
Dell, 1962
1	250.00
2 thru 5	@58675.00

B.E.A.S.T.I.E.S.
Axis Comics, 1994
1 JS(a&s),I:Beasties	2.50

THE BEATLES, LIFE STORY
Dell Publishing Co., 1964
1	1,000.00

BEAUTIFUL KILLER
Black Bull Entertainment, 2001
1 JP(s)	5.00
1a variant (c).	4.00
2 JP(s)	4.00
3 JP(s)	4.00
Preview Edition, limited	5.00

BEAUTY, THE
Beckett Comics, 2004
1	2.00
2 thru 4	@2.00
5 thru 8	@2.00

BEAUTY AND THE BEAST
Innovation, 1993
1 From TV series	3.00
1a Deluxe	4.00
2 thru 7	@3.00

BEAUTY AND THE BEAST PORTRAIT OF LOVE
First, 1989–90
1 WP,TV tie in	9.00
2	8.00
Book II:Night of Beauty	6.00

BEAUTY AND THE BEAST
Walt Disney, 1992
Movie adapt.(Prestige)	5.00
Movie adapt.(newsstand)	3.00
mini-series	
1 Bewitched	3.00
2 Elsewhere	3.00
3 A:Catherine	3.00

BEDLAM!
Eclipse, 1985
1 SBi,RV,reprint horror	3.00
2 SBi,RV,reprint horror	3.00

BEEP BEEP
Dell, 1960
4	85.00
5	50.00
6 thru 14	@35.00

BEEP BEEP THE ROAD RUNNER
Gold Key, 1966
1	50.00
2 thru 5	@35.00
6 thru 9	@25.00
10 thru 88	@15.00
Whitman, 1980	
89	10.00
90 thru 105	@25.00

BEETLE BAILEY
Dell, 1956–62
5	75.00
6 thru 9	@50.00

Beetle Bailey #75
© Charlton

10 thru 38 . . . . @35.00
Gold Key, 1962–66
39 thru 53 . . . . @30.00
54 thru 65 . . . . @25.00
Charlton, 1969–76
67 . . . . 25.00
68 thru 119 . . . . @22.00
Gold Key, 1978
120 . . . . 7.00
121 thru 131 . . . . @7.00
Whitman, 1980
132 . . . . 7.00

BEETLE BAILEY
Harvey, 1992
1 F:Mort Walker's B.Bailey 4.00
2 Beetle builds a bridge 3.00
3 thru 12 . . . . @3.00

BEETLEJUICE
Harvey, 1991
1 EC,This is your lice 3.00
Holiday Special #1 . . . . 3.00

BEN CASEY
**Dell Publishing Co.,
June-July, 1962**
1 Ph(c) 125.00
2 Ph(c) 100.00
3 Ph(c) 75.00
4 Drug, Ph(c) 100.00
5 Ph(c) 75.00
6 thru 10 Ph(c) . . . . @75.00

BEOWULF
Speakeasy Comics, 2005
1 . . . . 3.00
2 thru 6 . . . . @3.00
7 Altered States. 3.00
8 Altered States. 3.00
9 Mortal Coil, pt.1 . . . . 3.00
10 Mortal Coil. pt.2. . . . . 3.00
11 Epochs, pt.1 . . . . 3.00
12 Epochs 3.00

BEOWULF
Antarctic Press, 2006
1 (of 3) 3.50
2 . . . . 3.50
3 . . . . 3.50

BEOWULF
IDW Publishing, 2007
1 . . . . 4.00
2 thru 4 . . . . @4.00

BERNI WRIGHTSON MASTER OF THE MACABRE
Pacific, 1983
1 BWr 6.00
2 BWr 4.00
3 BWr 3.50
4 BWr 3.50
Eclipse, 1984
5 BWr 3.50

BEST CELLARS
Out of the Cellers, 1995
1 Eric Powells (1) 20.00

BEST OF BUGS BUNNY
Gold Key, 1966–68
1 Both Giants 100.00
2 . . . . 75.00

BEST OF DENNIS THE MENACE, THE
**Hallden/Fawcett Publ.,
Summer, 1959–Spring, 1961**
1 . . . . 150.00
2 . . . . 100.00
3 thru 5 . . . . @100.00

BEST OF DONALD DUCK & UNCLE SCROOGE
Gold Key, 1964–67
1 . . . . 175.00
2 . . . . 125.00

BEST OF DONALD DUCK
Gold Key, 1965
1 . . . . 150.00

BETTI COZMO
Antarctic Press, 1999
1 (of 3) 3.00
2 . . . . 3.00
3 Raygun For Hire 3.00

BETTY
Archie Publications, 1992
1 . . . . @6.00
2 thru 39 . . . . @4.00
40 thru 60 . . . . @4.00
61 thru 80 . . . . @3.00
81 thru 100 . . . . @3.00
101 thru 119 . . . . @3.00
120 thru 142. . . . . @3.00
143 thru 170 . . . . @2.25

BETTY AND ME
Archie Publications, 1965–92
1 . . . . 175.00
2 . . . . 100.00
3 O:Superteen. 110.00
4 thru 8 Superteen . . . . @75.00
9 & 10 . . . . 60.00
11 thru 21 . . . . @50.00
22 Archie Band 50.00
23 thru 37 . . . . @40.00
38 Sabrina 60.00
39 Josie & Sabrina. 50.00
40 Archie & Betty in Cabin. 35.00
41 . . . . 35.00
42 Betty Vamp 35.00

43 thru 55. . . . . @30.00
56 thru 200. . . . . @15.00

BETTY AND VERONICA
Archie Publications, 1987
1 . . . . 10.00
2 thru 10 . . . . @6.00
11 thru 50 . . . . @5.00
51 thru 104 . . . . @4.00
105 thru 119 . . . . @3.00
120 thru 141 . . . . @5.00
142 thru 160 . . . . @3.00
161 thru 181 . . . . @3.00
182 thru 203 . . . . @3.00
204 thru 231 . . . . @2.25
Summer Fun Special #5 . . . . 3.00
Summer Fun Special #6 . . . . 3.00
Summer Fun Special #7 . . . . 3.00

BETTY & VERONICA SPECTACULAR
Archie Publications, 1992
1 thru 25 . . . . @3.00
26 thru 40 . . . . @3.00
41 thru 57 . . . . @3.00
58 thru 68 . . . . @3.00
69 thru 80 . . . . @2.25

BEVERLY HILLBILLYS
**Dell Publishing Co.,
April-June, 1963**
1 Ph(c) 300.00
2 Ph(c) 175.00
3 Ph(c) 150.00
4 Ph(c) 100.00
5 thru 9 Ph(c) . . . . @150.00
10 . . . . 100.00
11 thru 14 Ph(c) . . . . @150.00
15 thru 21 Ph(c) . . . . @100.00

BEWITCHED
**Dell Publishing Co.,
April-June, 1965**
1 Ph(c) 300.00
2 . . . . 200.00
3 thru 13 Ph(c) . . . . @125.00
14 . . . . 100.00

BEYOND THE GRAVE
Charlton Comics, 1975–76
1 SD,TS(c),P(c) 60.00
2 thru 6 . . . . @35.00
Charlton Comics, 1983–84
7 thru 17 . . . . @30.00

BIG BANG
Caliber Press, 1994
0 Whole Timeline inc. 3.00
1 . . . . 2.50
2 . . . . 2.50
3 . . . . 2.50
4 25 years after #3 . . . . 2.50

BIGFOOT
IDW Publishing, 2005
1 . . . . 4.00
2 thru 4 . . . . @4.00

BIG MAX
MR Comics, 2006
1 . . . . 3.00

BIG VALLEY, THE
Dell Publishing Co., 1966
1 Ph(c) 100.00
2 thru 6 . . . . @75.00

COLOR PUB.

BILL BLACK'S
FUN COMICS
AC Comics
1 Cpt.Paragon,B&W 3.00
2 and 3 B&W . . . . @2.50
4 Color 2.50

BILL
THE GALACTIC HERO
Topps, 1994
1 . . . . 5.00
2 thru 3 Harry Harrison adapt. . . @5.00

BILLY THE KID
Charlton Publ. Co., 1957–83
1 thru 8: MASKED RAIDER
(see Golden Age section)
9 DG(c),The Watergod 125.00
10 Rancho Malo. 100.00
11 O:Ghost Train 125.00
12 . . . . 100.00
13 AW,AT 125.00
14 No Limit Game 100.00
15 AW,O:Billy the Kid. 125.00
16 AW, The Fastest Gun 125.00
17 Home Town Hero 100.00
18 The Scared Squatter. 100.00
19 The Underdog. 100.00
20 JSe,3-Aces 125.00
21 JSe, The Kid's Last Meal 125.00
22 JSe, The Crisis 125.00
23 JSe, The Guilty Gunslinger. . . 125.00
24 JSe, Caught with the Cash. . . 125.00
25 JSe, Geronimo's Revenge . . . 125.00
26 JSe, Gambler's Greed 125.00
27 Winner's Luck 75.00
28 The Big Man 75.00
29 The Fall Guy 75.00
30 Masked Rider 100.00
31 thru 40. . . . . @75.00
41 thru 60. . . . . @35.00
61 thru 65. . . . . @30.00
66 Boundy Hunter 35.00
67 thru 87 . . . . @20.00
88 thru 153. . . . . @10.00

BIN4RY
APC, 2004
1 . . . . 3.50
2 thru 4 . . . . @3.50
5 The Virus,pt.1 . . . . 3.50
6 . . . . 3.50
7 . . . . 3.50
0a variant (c). 3.00

BIONEERS
Mirage/Next, 1994
1 New Heroes. 2.75
2 . . . . 2.75
3 All-out War 2.75

BIONIC WOMAN, THE
Charlton, 1977
1 Oct, 1977, TV show adapt. 30.00
2 thru 5 . . . . @20.00

BIONIX
Maximum Press, 1996
1 (of 3) RLd,F:Steve Austin &
  Jaime Sommers 3.00
2 RLd, ... 3.00

BIZARRE 3-D ZONE
Blackthorne, 1986
1 . . . . 3.00

BLACKBALL COMICS
Blackball Comics, 1994
1 KG,A:Trencher 3.25

[ORIGINAL] BLACK CAT
Recollections, 1988
1 thru 2 Reprints . . . . @3.00
3 thru 8 *see B&W Section*
9 thru 10 rep.. . . . . @3.00

BLACK DIAMOND
AC Comics, 1983
1 Colt B..U. story 4.00
2 thru 5 PG(c) . . . . @3.00

BLACK DIAMOND
AIT Planetlar, 2007
1 . . . . 3.00
2 thru 5 . . . . @3.00

BLACK ENCHANTRESS
Heroic Publishing, 2004
1 . . . . 3.00
2 thru 3 . . . . @3.00

BLACK FLAG
Maximum Press, 1995
1 Dan Fraga 3.00
2 I:New Character. 3.00
3 V:Network, I:Glitz 3.00
4 V:Glitz, Network 3.00
5 I:Jammers 3.00
6 I:Alphabots 3.00

BLACK FURY
Charlton Comics, 1955
1 . . . . 100.00
2 . . . . 75.00
3 thru 15 . . . . @75.00
16 thru 18 SD. . . . . @100.00
19 and 20. . . . . @60.00
21 thru 56. . . . . @60.00
57 March-April, 1966 . . . . 50.00

BLACK HARVEST
Devil's Due Publishing, 2005
1 (of 6) by Josh Howard 3.25
2 thru 6 . . . . @3.25

BLACK HOLE, THE
Whitman, 1980
1 & 2 movie adaptation . . . . @3.00

The Black Hole #3
© Whitman

3 & 4 new stories . . . . @3.00

BLACK HOOD
Archie/Red Circle, 1983
1 ATh,GM,DW 4.00
2 ATh,DSp,A:Fox 3.00
3 ATh,GM 3.00

BLACK JACK
Charlton Comics, 1957–59
20 . . . . 100.00
21 . . . . 75.00
22 . . . . 100.00
23 AW,AT 100.00
24 thru 26 SD . . . . @110.00
27 . . . . 75.00
28 SD 110.00
29 & 30. . . . . @75.00

BLACKJACK:
BLOOD & HONOR
Dark Angel, 1997
1 by Alex Simmons,JoB, 1930s
  Adventure, Hildebrandts(c) 3.00
2 KeL, ... 3.00
3 Tim Cheng disappears. 3.00
4 . . . . 3.00

BLACK PHANTOM
AC Comics, 1989
1 F:Red Mask 3.00
2 thru 3 F:Red Mask . . . . @3.00

BLACK PLAGUE
Boom! Studios, 2006
1-shot 4.00
1-shot Previews exclusive (c) 7.00

BLACK RAVEN
Mad Monkey Press, 1996
1 Blueprints pt.1 . . . . 3.00
2 Blueprints pt.2 . . . . 3.00
3 V:Temple Assassins 3.00
4 Blueprints pt.4 . . . . 3.00
GN#1 Blueprints. 7.00
GN#2 Blueprints. 5.00

BLACK SEPTEMBER
Malibu Ultraverse, 1995
Infinity End of Black September . . . 3.00

BLACK SUMMER
Avatar Press, 2007
0 (of 7) 1.00
0a variant wraparound (c) 1.00
1 . . . . 3.00
2 thru 4 . . . . @3.00
1a thru 4a wraparound (c) . . . . . @3.00

BLACK SUN
WildStorm/DC, 2002
Eye of the Storm
1 (of 6) TvS,F:Maggie Sun 3.00
2 thru 6 TvS . . . . @3.00

BLACK TERROR
Eclipse, 1989–90
1 . . . . 4.00
2 . . . . 4.00
3 . . . . 5.00

BLACK TIDE
Avatar Press, 2002
1A Park (c) 3.50
2 Miller (c). 3.50
3 Miller (c). 3.50
1a thru 3a variant (c)s . . . . @3.50

Angel Gate Press
4 thru 8	@3.50
4a thru 8a variant (c)	3.50
9 thru 12	@3.00
9a thru 11a variant (c)s	@3.00
GN Vol. 1 Enter the Game	8.00

BLACK TIGER: LEGACY OF FURY
Beyond Time Comics, 2004
1 (of 4)	3.00
2 thru 4	@3.00

BLACKBEARD LEGACY
Alias Enterprises, 2006
1	3.50
2 thru 4	@3.50

BLACKPOOL
Phenomenon Comics, 2005
1	3.00
2 thru 3	@3.00

BLACK WEB
Inks Comics
1	2.75
2 thru 3 V:Seeker	@2.75

BLADE OF KUMORI, THE
Devil's Due Publishing, 2004
1 RMz, Aftermath	3.00
1a variant (c)	3.00
2 thru 6 RMz, Aftermath	@3.00

BLAST-OFF
Harvey Publications, 1965
1 JK,AW	100.00

BLAZING COMBAT
Warren Publishing Co., 1965–66
1 FF(c)	400.00
2 FF(c)	150.00
3 FF(c)	125.00
4 FF(c)	150.00

BLAZING SIX-GUNS
Skywald Comics, 1971
1 F: Red Mask, Sundance Kid	35.00
2 Jesse James	25.00

BLONDIE AND DAGWOOD FAMILY
Harvey, 1963
1	75.00
2	50.00
3	50.00
4	50.00

BLONDIE COMICS
Harvey, 1963–65
142 thru 163 see golden age	@35.00

King, 1966–67
164 thru 175	@35.00

Becomes:

BLONDIE
Charlton, 1969–76
177	15.00
178 thru 222	@10.00

BLOOD & ROSES
Sky Comics, 1993
1 I:Blood,Rose	3.00

Blondie #219
© Charlton

BLOODBATH
Samson Comics
1 I:Alien,V:Starguile	3.00

BLOODCHILDE
Millennium, 1994
0 O:Bloodchilde	3.00
1 Neil Gaiman, Vampires	3.00
1 signed (lim. to 500)	5.00
2 Neil Gaiman, Vampires	3.00
3 Neil Gaiman, Vampires	3.00
4	3.00
5 Talk Show Host	3.00

BLOODFIRE
Lightning Comics, 1993
0 O:Bloodfire	3.00
1 JZy(s),JJn, red foil	5.00
1a Platinum foil Ed.	5.00
1b B&W Promo Ed. Silver ink	4.00
1c B&W Promo Ed. Gold ink	6.00
2 JZy(s),JJn,O:Bloodfire	4.00
3 JZy(s),JJn,I:Dreadwolf, Judgement Day,Overthrow	3.00
4 JZy(s),JJn,A:Dreadwolf,	3.00
5 JZy(s),JJn,I:Bloodstorm, w/card	3.00
6 SZ(s),TLw,V:Storman	3.00
7 SZ(s),TLw,A:Pres.Clinton	3.00
8 SZ(s),TLw,O:Prodigal	3.00
9 SZ(s),TLw,I:Prodigal (in Costume)	3.00
10 SZ(s),TLw,B:Rampage, I:Thorpe	3.00
11	3.00
12	3.00

BLOODFIRE/HELLINA
Lightning Comics, 1995
1 V:Slaughterhouse	3.00

BLOODLORE
Brave New Worlds
1 Dreamweavers	2.50
2 A Blow to the Crown	2.50

BLOODSCENT
Comico, 1988
1 GC	3.00

BLOODRAYNE
Digital Webbing, 2004
1-shot Skies Afire (2004)	10.00
1-shot Seeds of Sin (2005)	10.00

1-shot Lycan Rex (2005)	4.00
1-shot variant (c)	5.00
1-shot Dark Soul (2005)	4.00
1-shot Dark Soul variant (c)	5.00
1-shot Raw Convention Spec.	6.00
1-shot Twin Blades	8.00

BLOODRAYNE: PLAGUE OF DREAMS
Digital Webbing, 2006
1 (of 3)	4.00
1a variant (c)	4.00
2	4.00
3	4.00
3a variant (c)	4.00

BLOODRAYNE: RED BLOOD RUN
Digital Webbing, 2007
1 (of 3)	4.00
1a variant (c)	4.00
2 thru 3	@4.00
2a thru 3a variant (c)	@4.00

BLOODRAYNE: TIBETAN HEIGHTS
Digital Webbing, 2007
1	4.00
1a variant (c)	4.00

BLOODSHOT
Valiant, 1992
0 KVH(a&s),DG(i),Chromium (c), O:Bloodshot,A:Eternal Warrior	4.00
0a Gold Ed.,w/Diamond `Fall Fling' logo	10.00
1 BWS(c),B:KVH(s),DP,BWi, V:Mafia, I:Carboni,1st Chromium(c)	4.00
2 thru 6 DP	@2.50
7 thru 17 DP,JDx	@2.50
18 thru 39	@2.50
40 thru 49	@10.00
50	9.00
51	10.00
Yearbook #1 KVH,briefcase bomb.	4.25
Yearbook 1995 Villagers	3.00
Spec.GN Last Stand	10.00

Series Two
Acclaim, 1997
1 LKa(s),SaV, Behold, a Pale Horseman	2.50
1a variant cover	3.00
2 thru 16 LKa(s),SaV	@2.50

BLOOD SWORD
Jademan, 1988
1	3.00
2 thru 5	@3.00
6 thru 9	@3.00
10 thru 21	@3.00
22 thru 45	@3.00
46 V:Cannibal	3.00
47 thru 53	@3.00

BLOOD SWORD DYNASTY
Jademan, 1989
1	3.00
2 thru 6	@2.75
7 thru 18 MB	@2.75
19 thru 40	@2.75

BLUE BEETLE
Charlton Comics, 1964 (1st Silver Age Series)
1 O:Dan Garrett/BlueBeetle	150.00
2	125.00

3 V:Mr.Thunderbolt 150.00
4 V:Praying Mantis Man 125.00
5 V:Red Knight 125.00
(2nd S.A. Series), 1965
Previously: UNUSUAL TALES
50 V:Scorpion 125.00
51 V:Mentor 125.00
52 V:Magno 125.00
53 V:Praying Mantis Man. 125.00
54 V:Eye of Horus 125.00
Becomes:

GHOSTLY TALES
(3rd S.A. Series), 1967
1 SD,I:Question 150.00
2 SD,O:TedKord,D:DanGarrett . . . 75.00
3 SD,I:Madmen,A:Question 40.00
4 SD,A:Question 40.00
5 SD,VicSage(Question) app.
   in Blue Beetle Story. 40.00

BLUE PHANTOM, THE
Dell Publishing Co., 1962
1 . . . . 75.00

BLUE RIBBON
Archie/Red Circle, 1983
1 JK,AV,O:Fly rep. 7.00
2 TVe,Mr.Justice 6.00
3 EB/TD,O:Steel Sterling 6.00
4 . . . . 6.00
5 S&K,Shield rep. 6.00
6 DAy/TD,Fox. 6.00
7 TD,Fox. 6.00
8 NA,GM,Blackhood 7.00
9 thru 11 . . . . @6.00
12 SD,ThunderAgents 6.00
13 Thunderbunny. 6.00
14 Web & Jaguar. 6.00

BLUFF
Narwain Publishing, 2006
1 (of 3) 4.00
2 thru 3 . . . . @3.50

BOLD ADVENTURE
Pacific, 1987
1 & 2. @3.00
3 JSe 3.00

BOLT & STARFORCE SIX
AC Comics, 1984
1 . . . . 3.00
Bolt Special #1. . . . . 3.00

BOMBABY:
THE SCREEN GODDESS
Amaze Ink/Slave Labor
Graphics, 2003
1 (of 4) 3.50
2 . . . . 3.50
3 and 4 . . . . @4.00

BOMBAST
Topps, 1993
1 V:Savage Dragon,Trading Card . 3.25

BONANZA
Dell Publishing Co., 1960
1. . . . . 300.00
2 . . . . 250.00
3 thru 10 . . . . @200.00
11 thru 20 . . . . @150.00
21 thru 37. . . . . @150.00
Gold Key, 1962
1 Ph(c), from TV series. 350.00
2 . . . . 175.00
3 thru 9 . . . . @150.00
10 thru 37 . . . . @100.00

Bonanza #37
© Gold Key

BORIS KARLOFF
TALES OF MYSTERY
Gold Key, 1963–80
1 (Thriller) 175.00
2 (Thriller) 125.00
3 thru 8 . . . . @75.00
9 WW 100.00
10 JO 75.00
11 AW,JO 85.00
12 AT,AMc,JO 75.00
13 & 14. . . . . @50.00
15 RC,GE. 50.00
16 thru 20. . . . . @50.00
21 JJ,Screaming Skull 100.00
22 thru 50. . . . . @40.00
51 thru 74. . . . . @30.00
75 thru 97. . . . . @25.00

BOYS, THE
Wildstorm/DC, Aug., 2006
1 GEn,DaR,Watchers of the Supers 3.00
2 GEn,DaR. 3.00
3 GEn 3.00
4 GEn, DaR 3.00
5 GEn 3.00
6 GEn, DaR 3.00
7 GEn,DaR 3.00
8 GEn,DaR, Tek Knight 3.00
9 GEn,DaR, Tek Knight 3.00
10 GEn,DaR, ... 3.00
D.E.
11 thru 12 . . . . @3.00

BOZO
Innovation
1 1950's reprint stories 7.00

BOZO THE CLOWN
Blackthorne
1 3-D 3.00
2 3-D 3.00

BRADY BUNCH, THE
Dell Publishing Co., 1970
1 . . . . 250.00
2 . . . . 200.00

BRAIN BOY
Dell Publishing Co.,
April–June, 1962
1 . . . . 250.00
2 . . . . 200.00

3 . . . . 175.00
4 . . . . 175.00
5 . . . . 175.00
6 . . . . 175.00

BRAM STOKER'S
BURIAL OF THE RATS
Roger Corman's Comics, 1995
1 . . . . 2.50
2 thru 3 film adaptation . . . . @2.50

BRASS
WildStorm/DC, 2000
1 (of 6) JAr,RiB 2.50
2 JAr,RiB. 2.50
3 JAr,RiB. 2.50
4 JAr,RiB. 2.50
5 JAr,RiB,war is over 2.50
6 JAr,RiB,concl. 2.50

BRATH
Crossgen Comics, 2003
Prequel CDi(s) 3.00
1 CDi(s). 3.50
2 thru 10 CDi(s). . . . . @3.00
11 thru 17. . . . . @3.00

BREAKDOWN
Devil's Due Publishing, 2004
1 CDi. 3.00
1a variant (c). 3.00
2 thru 6 CDi,Aftermath . . . . @3.00

BREAK-THRU
Malibu Ultraverse, 1993–94
1 GJ(s),GP,AV(i),A:All Ultraverse
   Heroes. 2.75
1a Foil Edition. 7.50
2 GJ(s),GP,AV(i),A:All Ultraverse
   Heroes. 2.75

BREATHE
Markosia, 2007
1 (of 4) 3.00
2 thru 4 . . . . @3.00
1a thru 4a variant (c). . . . . @3.00

'BREED
Malibu Bravura
[Limited Series] 1994
1 JSn(a&s),Black (c),I:Stoner 3.00
2 JSn(a&s),I:Rachel 3.00
3 JSn(a&s),V:Rachel. 3.00
4 JSn(a&s),I:Stoner's Mom. 3.00
5 JSn(a&s),V:Rachel. 3.00
6 JSn(a&s),final issue. 3.00

'BREED II
Malibu Bravura
[Limited Series] 1994–95
1 JSn,The Book of Revelation . . . 3.00
1a gold foil edition. 4.00
2 JSn,A:Rachel 3.00
3 JSn,V:Actual Demon 3.00
4 JSn,Language of Demons 3.00
5 JSn,R:Rachael 3.00
6 JSn,final issue 3.00

BREEDING GROUND
Samson Comics
1 I:Mazit, Zero. 2.50

BRENDA LEE STORY, THE
Dell Publishing Co., 1962
1 . . . . 150.00

COLOR PUB.

All comics prices listed are for *Near Mint* condition.

BRENDA STARR REPORTER
Dell Publishing Co., 1963
1 . . . . 300.00

BRIAN BOLLAND'S BLACK BOOK
Eclipse, 1985
1 BB 3.00

BRIAN PULIDO'S BELLADONNA
Avatar Press, 2004
Preview 2.00
Preview variant (c)s 3.00
Convention Specials 3.00
1 . . . . 4.00
2 thru 5 . . . . @4.00
1a-b thru 5a-b variant (c)s . . . . . @4.00
1c Lioness (c) 6.00
1d Serpent (c) 6.00
1e Animal protectors (c) 6.00
1f Prism foil (c) 13.00
2c Cloud Burst (c) 6.00
2d Ferocious (c) 6.00
2e Pure Rage (c) 6.00
3c premium (c) 10.00
3d Back from Dead (c) 6.00
3e Leader of Pack (c) 6.00
4c premium (c) 10.00
4d Warrior Spirit (c) 6.00
4e Moonlight (c) 6.00
5c premium (c) 10.00
5d Raw Power (c) 6.00
5e Art Nouveau (c) 6.00

BRIAN PULIDO'S MEDIEVAL LADY DEATH
Avatar Press, 2005
1 . . . . 4.00
1a wraparound (c) 4.00
1b premium (c) 10.00
1c Fear Her Wrath (c) 6.00
1d portrait edition 6.00
2 thru 8 . . . . @4.00
2b thru 8b variant (c)s . . . . @6.00
2a thru 8a wraparound (c)s . . . . . @4.00
2c thru 8c premium (c)s . . . . . @10.00

BRIDES IN LOVE
Charlton Comics, 1956–65
1 . . . . 150.00
2 . . . . 125.00
3 thru 10 . . . . @75.00
11 thru 30 . . . . @75.00
31 thru 44 . . . . @60.00
45 . . . . 50.00

BRIGADE
Awesome Entertainment Vol II, 2000
1 A:Badrock 3.00

BRODIE'S LAW
Markosia, 2006
Prev. Black & White
7 thru 10 . . . . @3.50

BROTHERS OF THE SPEAR
Gold Key, 1972
1 . . . . 75.00
2 . . . . 30.00
3 thru 9 . . . . @25.00
10 thru 17 . . . . @20.00

Whitman, 1982
18 . . . . 20.00

BROTHERS: THE FALL OF LUCIFER
Markosia, 2006
1 (of 10) 3.50
1a variant (c)s . . . . @3.50
2 thru 5 . . . . @3.50

BRUCE LEE
Malibu, 1994
1 MBn(s), Stories of B.Lee 3.00
2 thru 6 . . . . @3.00

BRUTE, THE
Atlas, Feb.–July, 1975
1 . . . . 25.00
2 thru 3 . . . . @25.00

BUBBA
Silent Devil Productions, 2006
Super Sci-Fi Special 3.00

Buck Rogers #5
© Gold Key

BUCK ROGERS
Gold Key, 1964
1 P(c) 150.00
2 AMc,FBe,P(c),movie adapt 25.00
3 AMc,FBe,P(c),movie adapt 25.00
4 FBe,P(c) 25.00
5 AMc,P(c) 20.00
6 AMc,P(c) 20.00
Whitman
7 thru 9 AMc,P(c) . . . . @30.00
10 and 11 AMc,P(c) . . . . @20.00
12 and 13 P(c) . . . . @15.00
14 thru 16 . . . . @10.00

BUCK ROGERS IN THE 25TH CENTURY
Gold Key, 1979
2 from TV Series 20.00
3 thru 7 . . . . @25.00
8 . . . . 30.00
9 . . . . 30.00
10 not published
11 thru 16 . . . . @15.00

BUCK ROGERS
TSR, 1990–91
1 O:Buck Rogers 3.00

2 thru 3 O:Buck Rogers . . . . @3.00
4 thru 6 Black Barney . . . . @3.00
7 thru 10 The Martian Wars . . . . @3.00

BUCKY O'HARE
Continuity, 1991
1 MGo 2.75
2 thru 5 . . . . @2.50

BUDD'S BEAUTIES & BEASTS
Basement Comics, 2005
1-shot 5.00
2 (b&w) (2006) 3.25

BUFFALO BILL JR.
Gold Key, 1965
1 . . . . 75.00

BUGGED-OUT ADVENTURES OF RALFY ROACH
Bugged Out Comics
1 I: Ralfy Roach 3.00

BUGS BUNNY
Dell, 1952
28 thru 85 . . . . @100.00
Gold Key, 1962
86 . . . . 100.00
87 thru 218 . . . . @50.00
Spec. Winter Fun (1967) 75.00
Whitman, 1980
219 thru 245 . . . . @20.00

BUGS BUNNY AND PORKY PIG
Gold Key, 1965
1 . . . . 150.00

BULLWINKLE
Dell, 1962
1 . . . . 300.00

BULLWINKLE
Gold Key, 1962
1 Bullwinkle & Rocky 300.00
2 . . . . 200.00
3 thru 5 . . . . @150.00
6 and 7, rep. . . . . @150.00
8 thru 11 . . . . 150.00
12 rep. 75.00
13 and 14 . . . . @85.00
15 thru 19 . . . . @75.00
20 thru 24, rep. . . . . @35.00
25 . . . . 50.00

BULLWINKLE
Charlton Comics, 1970
1 . . . . 125.00
Becomes:

BULLWINKLE AND ROCKY
Charlton Comics, 1970–71
2 thru 7 . . . . @75.00

BULLWINKLE & ROCKY
Blackthorne, 1987
3-D 25.00

BULLWINKLE FOR PRESIDENT
Blackthorne, 1987
1 3-D Special 3.00

BURKE'S LAW
Dell Publishing Co., 1964
1 from TV Show 100.00
2 . . . . 75.00
3 . . . . 75.00

BUTTERNUT SQUASH
Speakeasy Comics, 2005
1 . . . . 4.00
2 . . . . 4.00

BUTCH CASSIDY
Skywald Comics, 1971
1 . . . . 30.00
2 & 3 . . . . @20.00

BUZZBOY:
SIDEKICKS RULE
Sky Dog Press, 2006
1 . . . . 3.00
2 thru 3 . . . . @3.00

CABBOT: BLOODHUNTER
Maximum Press, 1997
1 . . . .
2 thru 4 RV . . . . @2.50

CADILLACS
& DINOSAURS
Kitchen Sink, 1992
1 Rep. from Xenozoic Tales in 3-D . 6.00
Topps, 1994
BLOOD & BONES
1 thru 3 rep. Xenozoic Tales,
  all covers . . . . @3.00
MAN-EATER
1 thru 3, all covers 3.00
THE WILD ONES
1 thru 3, all covers 3.00

CAGES
Tundra, 1990
1 DMc 14.00
2 DMc 11.00
3 thru 4 DMc . . . . @7.50
5 thru 7 DMc 5.00

CAIN
Harris, 1993
1 B:DQ(s),I:Cain,Frenzy 5.00

Cain #2 © Harris

---

2 BSz(c),HBk,V:Mortatira 3.25

CAIN'S HUNDRED
**Dell Publishing Co.,
May-July, 1962**
1 . . . . 45.00
2 . . . . 30.00

CALIFORNIA RAISINS
Blackthorne, 1987
1 thru 4 3-D . . . . @2.50
5 3-D,O:Calif.Raisins 2.50
6 thru 8 3-D . . . . @2.50

CALVIN & THE COLONEL
**Dell Publishing Co.,
April-June, 1962**
1 . . . . 150.00
2 . . . . 100.00

CANNON BUSTERS
Devil's Due/UDON, 2004
1 . . . . 3.00
2 The Necklace. 3.00

CANNON HAWKE
Aspen, 2005
Prelude 2.50
1 . . . . 3.00
1a signed 25.00
2 . . . . 3.00
3 thru 5 . . . . @3.00

CAPCOM
SUMMER SPECIAL
Devil's Due, 2004
1 . . . . 12.00

CAP'N QUICK &
FOOZLE
Eclipse, 1984–85
1 . . . . 3.00
2 and 3 . . . . @3.00

CAPT. ELECTRON
Brick Computers Inc., 1986
1 . . . . 2.50
2 . . . . 2.50

CAPTAIN ATOM:
ARMAGEDDON
Wildstorm/DC, Oct., 2005
1 AxR(c) 3.00
1a variant JLe(c). 3.00
2 . . . . 3.00
3 Void's Death. 3.00
4 V:Wildcats 3.00
5 A:The Authority 3.00
6 F:Engineer 3.00
7 Looks into the future 3.00
8 V:Authority 3.00
9 Finale. 3.50

CAPTAIN ATOM
See: STRANGE
SUSPENSE STORIES

CAPTAIN CANUCK
Comely Comix, 1975–81
1 I:Blue Fox. 25.00
2 I:Red Coat 20.00
3 I:Heather 20.00
4 thru 14 . . . . 15.00
Summer Spec. #1 . . . . 15.00

CAPTAIN CANUCK:
LEGACY
Comely/Semple Comics, 2006
1 . . . . 3.00
1a special edition 8.00
2 . . . . 4.00

CAPTAIN CANUCK:
UNHOLY WAR
Comely Comix, 2004
1 (of 3) 2.50
2 thru 3 . . . . @2.50
4 . . . . 4.00

CAPTAIN GLORY
Topps, 1993
1 A:Bombast,Night Glider,
  Trading Card 3.25

CAPTAIN GRAVITY
Penny Farthing Press, 1998
1 by S.Vrattos & K. Martin 12.00
2 No one escapes Law of Gravity . 7.00
3 . . . . 5.00
4 . . . . 3.00
Spec. One True Hero. 3.00

CAPTAIN GRAVITY AND
THE POWER OF THE VRIL
Pennyfarthing Press, 2005
1 thru 6 . . . . @3.00

CAPTAIN HARLOCK:
FALL OF THE EMPIRE
Eternity, 1992
1 R:Captain Harlock 2.50
2 V:Tadashi 2.50
3 Bomb on the Arcadia 2.50
4 Final issue 2.50

CAPTAIN JOHNER
& THE ALIENS
Valiant, 1995
1 Rep. Magnus Robot Fighter #1–7
(Gold Key 1963–64). 3.00

CAPTAIN MARVEL
M. F. Enterprises, 1966
1 . . . . 75.00
2 . . . . 50.00
3 Fights The Bat 40.00
4 . . . . 40.00
5 Captain Marvel Presents the
  Terrible Five. 40.00

CAPTAIN NAUTICUS
Entity, 1994
1 V:Fathom 3.00
2 V:Fathom's Henchman 3.00
3 Surf's Up 3.00

CAPTAIN NICE
Gold Key, 1967
1 Ph(c) 125.00

CAPTAIN PARAGON
Americomics, 1983
1 thru 4 . . . . @3.00

CAPTAIN POWER
Continuity, 1988
1a NA,TVtie-in(direct sale) 3.00
1b NA,TVtie-in(newsstand). 3.00
2 NA 3.00

CAPTAIN STERN
Kitchen Sink Press, 1993–94
1 BWr,R:Captain Stern 5.25
2 BWr,Running Out of Time 5.00
3 thru 5 BWr,Running Out
   of Time . . . . @4.00

CAPTAIN THUNDER
AND BLUE BOLT
Hero Graphics, 1987
1 I:Capt.Thunder & Paul Fremont. . 2.50
2 Paul becomes Blue Bolt 2.50
3 O:Capt.Thunder 2.50
4 V:Iguana Boys 2.50
5 V:Ian Shriver, in Scotland 2.50
6 V:Krakatoa 2.50
7 V:Krakatoa 2.50
8 A:Sparkplug (from League
   of Champions) 2.50
9 A:Sparkplug 2.50
10 A:Sparkplug 2.50

CAPTAIN VENTURE
& THE LAND
BENEATH THE SEA
Gold Key, 1968
1 . . . . 75.00
2 . . . . 60.00

CAPTAIN VICTORY AND
THE GALACTIC RANGERS
Pacific, 1982
1 JK. 3.00
2 JK. 3.00
3 JK,BU:NA,I:Ms.Mystic 3.00
4 JK. 3.00
5 JK. 3.00
6 JK,SD. 3.00
7 thru 13 JK . . . . @3.00
Spec.#1 JK. 3.00

CAR 54,
WHERE ARE YOU?
Dell Publishing Co.,
March-May, 1962
1 Ph(c) 150.00
2 thru 7 Ph(c) . . . . @100.00

CARCA JOU
RENAISSANCE
1 and 2 . . . . @3.00

CARNOSAUR CARNAGE
Atomeka, 1993
GN 5.00

CAROLINE KENNEDY
Charlton Comics, 1961
1 . . . . 150.00

CASEY JONES
& RAPHAEL
Mirage, 1994
1 Family War. 2.75
2 Johnny Woo Woo 2.75
3 V:Johnny Woo Woo 2.75
4 9mm Raphael 2.75

CASPER & FRIENDS
Harvey, 1991
1 thru 4 . . . . @3.00
5 short stories, cont 3.00

CASPER AND SPOOKY
Harvey, 1972
1 . . . . 35.00
2 thru 7 . . . . @20.00

CASPER AND THE
GHOSTLY TRIO
Harvey, 1972
1 . . . . 35.00
2 thru 7 . . . . @20.00
Harvey, 1990
8 . . . . 6.00
9 thru 10 . . . . @6.00

CASPER & WENDY
Harvey, 1972–73
1 52-pg. giant 40.00
2 thru 5 . . . . @20.00
6 thru 8 . . . . @20.00

CASPER
ENCHANTED TALES
Harvey, 1992
1 short stories 3.00

CASPER
THE FRIENDLY GHOST,
1988
Blackthorne
1 3-D 3.00

CASPER GHOSTLAND
Harvey, 1992
1 short stories 3.00

CASPER'S GHOSTLAND
Harvey Publications,
Winter, 1958-59
1 giant 450.00
2 . . . . 250.00
3 thru 10 . . . . @150.00
11 thru 20 . . . . @100.00
21 thru 40 . . . . @75.00
41 thru 61 . . . . @60.00
62 thru 77 . . . . @50.00
78 thru 97 . . . . @40.00
98 Dec., 1979 . . . . 40.00

CASPER
THE FRIENDLY GHOST
Prev: The Friendly Ghost Casper
254 thru 260 . . . . @3.00
[Second Series], 1991–94
1 thru 14 . . . . @3.00
15 thru 28 . . . . @3.00

CASPER SPACE SHIP
Harvey, 1972
1 . . . . 40.00
2 thru 5 . . . . @25.00
Becomes:

CASPER IN SPACE
Harvey, 1973
6 . . . . 20.00
7 thru 8 . . . . @20.00

CASPER STRANGE
GHOST STORIES
Harvey, 1974
1 . . . . 40.00
2 . . . . 20.00
3 thru 15 . . . . @20.00

CASPER T.V. SHOWTIME
Harvey, 1980
1 . . . . 20.00
2 thru 5 . . . . @10.00

CASTLEVANIA:
THE BELMONT LEGACY
IDW Publishing, 2005
1 . . . . 4.00
2 thru 5 . . . . @4.00

CAST
Nautilus Comics, 2005
1 . . . . 3.00
2 thru 3 . . . . @3.00
4 . . . . 3.00

CATSEYE
Awesome/Hyperwerks, 1999
0 KIA,BNa,O:Catseye 3.00

CAULDRON
Real Comics, 1995
1 Movie Style Comic 3.00
1a Variat cover 3.00

Cave Kids #14
© Gold Key

CAVE KIDS
Gold Key, 1963
1 . . . . 125.00
2 . . . . 75.00
3 thru 5 . . . . @75.00
6 . . . . 60.00
7 A:Pebbles & Bamm Bamm 65.00
8 thru 10 . . . . @50.00
11 thru 16 . . . . @50.00

CAVEWOMAN
Avatar, 1999
Color Spec. 3.50
Color Spec. Fauna (c) 3.50
Color Spec. prism foil (c) 13.00
Color Spec. Royal Blue 75.00

CENTURY
Awesome Entertainment, 2000
1 RLe 3.00
1a Millennium edition 5.00
2 . . . . 3.00
2a Millennium edition 5.00
2b signed 13.00
3 . . . . 3.00

CHAINS OF CHAOS
Harris, 1994
1 Vampirella, Rook 5.00
2 V:Chaoschild 3.25
3 Final issue 3.25

CHAMPIONS
Eclipse, 1986–87
1 I:Flare,League of Champions
 Foxbat, Dr.Arcane 10.00
2 I:Dark Malice 10.00
3 I:Lady Arcane 8.00
4 O:Dark Malice 10.00
5 O:Flare 6.00
6 D:Giant Demonmaster 6.00
[New Series]
Hero Graphics, 1987–88
1 EL,I:Madame Synn,Galloping
 Galooper 5.00
2 I:Fat Man, Black Enchantress . . . 2.50
3 I:Sparkplug&Icicle,O:Flare 2.50
4 I:Exo-Skeleton Man 2.50
5 A:Foxbat. 2.50
6 I:Mechanon, C:Foxbat 2.00
7 A:Mechanon,J:Sparkplug,Icicle . . 2.00
8 O:Foxbat 2.00
9 Flare #0 (Flare preview) 2.00
10 Olympus Saga #1 . . . . 2.00
11 Olympus Saga #2 . . . . 2.00
12 Olympus Saga #3 . . . . 2.00
Ann.#1 O:Giant & DarkMalice 2.75
Ann.#2 . . . . 4.00

CHAMPIONS CLASSIC
Hero Graphics, 1993
1 GP(c),Rep.1st champions series . 2.50

CHAOS! BIBLE
Chaos! Comics, 1995
1 Character Profiles 3.50

CHAOS! CHRONICLES– THE HISTORY OF A COSMOS
Chaos! Comics, 1999
Spec. 3.50
Spec. signed premium 15.00

CHAOS EFFECT
Valiant, 1994
Alpha DJ(c), BCh, JOy, A:All
 Valiant Characters 2.50
Alpha Red (c). 60.00
Omega DJ(c), BCh, JOy, A:All
 Valiant Characters 2.50
Omega Gold(c) 3.50
Epilogue pt.1 . . . . 3.00
Epilogue pt.2 . . . . 3.00

CHAOS! GALLERY
Chaos! Comics, 1997
1 . . . . 3.00

CHAOS! NIGHTMARE THEATER
Chaos! Comics, 1997
1 (of 4) BWr(c) 2.50
2 BWr(c) 2.50
3 BWr(c) 2.50
4 BWr(c) 2.50

CHAOS QUARTERLY
Harris Comics, 1995
1 F:Lady Death 5.00
1a Premium Edition. 11.00
1b Signed,limited edition. 20.00

CHAPEL
Awesome Entertainment, 1997
1 BNa, from Spawn,Youngblood . . . 3.00

CHARLEMAGNE
Defiant, 1994
1 JiS(s),From Hero 3.00
2 JiS(s),I:Charles Smith 2.75
3 JiS(s),A:War Dancer 2.75
4 DGC(s),V:Dark Powers 2.75
5 Schism prequel 2.75
6 V:Wardancer 2.75
7 R:To Vietnam 2.75

CHARLIE CHAN
Dell Publishing Co., 1965
1 . . . . 100.00
2 . . . . 75.00

CHARLTON ACTION: FEATURING STATIC
Charlton, 1985
1 . . . . 8.00
2 . . . . 5.00

Charlton Bullseye #4 @ Charlton

CHARLTON BULLSEYE
Charlton, 1981–82
1 Blue Beetle, I:Rocket Rabbit 3.50
2 Capt. Catnip; Nell the Horse 2.50
3 Grundar 2.50
4 Vanguards 2.50
5 Warhund 2.50
6 Thunder-bunny 2.50
7 Captain Atom 2.50
8 weird stories. 2.50
9 . . . . 2.50
10 . . . . 2.50
Spec. #1 . . . . 2.00
Spec. #2 Atomic Mouse 2.00

CHARLTON BULLSEYE SPECIAL
Charlton, 1986
1 . . . . 9.00
2 . . . . 7.00

CHARLTON CLASSICS
Charlton, 1980
1 . . . . 7.00
2 . . . . 5.00
3 thru 9 . . . . @5.00

CHARLTON CLASSICS LIBRARY
Charlton, 1973
1 . . . . 25.00

CHARLTON PREMIERE
Charlton, 1967
1 . . . . 30.00
2 thru 5 . . . . @30.00

CHARLTON SPORT LIBRARY
Charlton, 1970
1 Professional Football 50.00

CHASE, THE
APC, 2004
1 (of 10) 3.50
2 . . . . 3.50
3 . . . . 3.50
4 . . . . 3.50

CHASSIS
Millennium/Expand, 1995
1 I:Chassis McBain, Aero Run 3.00
1 2nd printing 3.00
1 chrome cover. 10.00
2 . . . . 3.00
2a with racing card 5.00
2b Amanda Conner cover. 3.00
2c Amanda Conner cover, signed. 10.00
2d foil cover, signed 8.00
[Vol. 2] Hurricane Comics, 1998
0 by Joshua Dysart & Wm.O'Neill . 3.00
0a variant cover 3.00
1 . . . . 3.00
2 . . . . 3.00
3 . . . . 3.00

CHASTITY
Chaos! Comics, 2000
1/2 . . . . 3.00
1/2a premium ed., tattoo (c) 9.00
1/2b chromium edition 14.00
1 premium edition 9.00
Spec. #1 Reign of Terror (2000) . . . 3.00
Spec. #1 Reign of Terror, premium . 9.00
Spec. #1 Love Bites (2001) 3.00
Spec. #1 Love Bites, premium ed. . 9.00
Ashcan Love Bites (2001) 6.00

CHASTITY: CRAZYTOWN
Chaos! Comics, 2002
Ashcan b&w. 6.00
1 (of 3) 3.00
1a premium edition 9.00
1b foil edition. 15.00
2 thru 3 . . . . @3.00
2a and 3a variant (c). . . . . @7.50

CHASTITY: HEARTBREAKER
Chaos! Comics, 2002
1 . . . . 3.00
1a premium edition 9.00
1b super premium edition. 15.00

CHASTITY LUST FOR LIFE
Chaos! Comics, 1999
1 (of 4) PNu 3.00
1a alternate cover. 7.00
1b alternate cover, signed 20.00
1c premium edition 10.00
2 V:Hemlock 3.00
3 . . . . 3.00

CHASTITY: RE-IMAGINED
Chaos! Comics, 2002
1 Gothic tale	3.00
1a premium edition	10.00
1b super premium edition	20.00
Ashcan re-imagined b&w	6.00

CHASTITY ROCKED
Chaos! Comics, 1998
1 (of 4) PNu	3.00
1a & 1b variant covers	3.00
2 V:Jade	3.00
3 V:Jade	3.00
4 conclusion	3.00
Chastity/Cremator Preview	
Book, B&W	5.00

CHASTITY: SHATTERED
Chaos! Comics, 2001
1 BnP,LKa	3.00
1a premium edition	9.00
2	3.00
3	3.00
Ashcan	6.00

CHASTITY: THEATRE OF PAIN
Chaos! Comics, 1997
1 (of 3) BnP	6.00
1a premium edition	12.00
2	3.00
3	3.00
3a premium edition	15.00

CHECKMATE
Gold Key, 1962
1 Ph(c)	100.00
2 Ph(c)	75.00

CHERYL BLOSSOM
Archie Comics, 1996
1	2.50
2 thru 10	@2.50
11 thru 37	@2.50

CHERYL BLOSSOM GOES HOLLYWOOD
Archie Comics, 1996
1 (of 3) by Dan Parent &	
Bill Golliher	3.50
2 and 3	@3.50

CHEYENNE KID
Charlton, 1957
1 thru 7: WILD FRONTIER
(see Golden Age section)
8 DG(c), Stolen Empire	100.00
9 Ragin Bear's Revenge	75.00
10 AW,AT,SD(c),Custer's Last	
Stand	100.00
11 Giant size, Geronimo	100.00
12 AW,AT	100.00
13 AW,AT	100.00
14 AW	100.00
15	100.00
16	75.00
17 Peacemaker Colt	75.00
18 The Crumbling Idol	75.00
19 Their Last Battle	75.00
20 JSe, The Victim	75.00
21 JSe, The Blue-Eyed Braves	100.00
22 JSe, Rustlers Bait	100.00
23 The Gunless Wonder	60.00
24 JSe, The Indian Fighters	75.00
25 JSe, Fury of the Gods	75.00
26 JSe, Fat of the Land	75.00
27 Bad Medicine	60.00
28 The Alamo	60.00

Cheyenne Kid #79 © Charlton

29 Cheaters' Row	60.00
30 JSe, A Short Injun War	75.00
31 thru 98	@20.00
99 Nov., 1973	20.00

CHICKASAW ADVENTURES
Layne Morgan Media, 2005
1	3.00
2 The Battle of Akia	3.00
3 Tears at Fort Coffee	3.00
4 The Making of a Storyteller	3.00

CHI-CHIAN
Sirius, 1997
1 (of 6) by Voltaire	3.00
2 thru 6	@3.00

CHILD'S PLAY 2
Innovation
1 Movie Adapt Pt 1	2.50
2 Adapt Pt 2	2.50
3 Adapt Pt 3	2.50

CHILD'S PLAY 3
Innovation
1 Movie Adapt Pt 1	2.50
2 Movie Adapt Pt.2	2.50

CHILD'S PLAY: THE SERIES
Innovation
1 Chucky's Back	2.50
2 Straight Jacket Blues	2.50
3 M.A.R.K.E.D.	2.50
4 Chucky in Toys 4 You	2.50
5 Chucky in Hollywood	2.50

CHILDREN OF FIRE
Fantagor, 1987
1 thru 3 RCo	@4.00

CHILLING ADVENTURES IN SORCERY AS TOLD BY SABRINA
Archie, 1972–74
1	65.00
2	40.00
3 thru 5	@30.00

CHIMERA
Crossgen Comics, 2003
1 RMz,BPe	3.00
2 thru 4	@3.00

CHIP 'N DALE
Dell Publishing, 1955–66
4	125.00
5 thru 10	@100.00
11 thru 30	@100.00
Gold Key, 1967
1 reprints	75.00
2 thru 10	@30.00
11 thru 20	@20.00
21 thru 83	@15.00
Whitman, 1980
65	12.00
66 thru 69	@12.00
70 thru 83	@7.00

CHIP 'N DALE RESCUE RANGERS
Walt Disney, 1990
1 Rescue Rangers to the Rescue	4.00
2 pt.2	3.50
3 thru 7	@3.00
8 thru 18	@2.75

CHOO CHOO CHARLIE
Gold Key, 1969
1	150.00

CHOSEN, THE
Click Comics, 1995
1 I:The Chosen	2.50
2 I:Herman Cortez	2.50

CHRISTIAN
Maximum Press, 1996
1 and 2 (of 3) RLd	@3.00

CHROMA-TICK SPECIAL EDITION
New England Press, 1992
1 Rep.Tick#1,new stories	4.00
2 Rep.Tick#2,new stories	5.00
3 thru 8 Reps.& new stories	@3.50

CHROME
Hot Comics, 1986
1 Machine Man	3.50
2 thru 4	@3.00

CHROME WARRIORS IN A '59 CHEVY
Black Out Comics, 1998
0	3.00
1 Rob Roman & Tommy Castillo	3.00

CHROMIUM MAN, THE
Triumphant Comics, 1994
0 Blue Logo	6.00
0 Regular	2.50
1 I:Chromium Man,Mr.Death	3.50
2 I:Prince Vandal	3.00
3 thru 15	@2.50

CHROMIUM MAN: VIOLENT PAST
Triumphant Comics
1 thru 4 JnR(s)	@2.50

CHRONICLES OF CORUM
First, 1987–88
1 Michael Moorcock adapt	3.00

All comics prices listed are for *Near Mint* condition.

2	2.50
3	2.50
4 thru 12	@2.50

CHRONO MECHANICS
Alias Enterprises, 2005

GN ATi	7.00
Precious Metal Collection–	
Platinum.	3.50
Precious Metal Collection–Gold #2	3.50
Precious Metal Collection–Gold #3	3.50
Precious Metal Collection–	
Bronze #4	3.50

CHTULHU TALES
Boom! Studios, 2006

1	7.00

CHUCKY
Devil's Due, 2007

1	3.50
1a variant (c)	3.50
2 thru 5	@3.50
2a thru 5a variant (c)s	@3.50

CICERO'S CAT
Dell Publishing Co., 1959

1	100.00
2	75.00

CICI
Spilled Milk, 2002

1 (of 4)	3.00
2 thru 4	@2.50
1a Variant (c)	2.50

CIMMARON STRIP
Dell Publishing Co., 1968

1	75.00

CISCO KID, THE
Moonstone, 2004

1 (of 3)	3.00
2	3.00
3	3.00

CISCO KID, THE: GUNFIRE & BRIMSTONE
Moonstone Books, 2005

1	3.00
2	3.00
3	3.00

CITY KNIGHTS, THE
Windjammer 1995

1 I: Michael Walker	2.50
2 thru 4	@2.50

CITY OF HEROES
Blue King Studios, 2004

1	3.00
2 thru 12	@3.00

CITY OF TOMORROW
Wildstorm/DC, Apr., 2005

1 (of 6) HC	3.00
2 HC	3.00
3 thru 6 HC	@3.00

CITY KNIGHTS, THE
Windjammer, 1995

1 I:Michael Walker	2.50
2 I:Herald	2.50
3 V:Herald	2.50
4 V:Herald	2.50

CITY PERILOUS
Broadway Comics

1 GI,Remember the Future,pt.1	3.00
2 GI,Remember the Future,pt.2	3.00

Becomes:

KNIGHTS ON BROADWAY

3 thru 5 GI	@3.00

CLASH
Moonstone, 2007

1 (of 5)	3.50
2 thru 4	@3.50

CLASSIC BATTLESTAR GALACTICA
D.E. (Dynamite Ent.) 2006

1	3.50
1a Classic Cylon foil (c)	
2 thru 3	@3.00
2a thru 3a variant (c)	3.00
4	3.50
4a variant (c).	3.50
5	3.50
5a variant (c).	3.50

CLASSICS ILLUSTRATED
See Also: CLASSICS ILLUSTRATED SECTION

CLASSICS ILLUSTRATED
First, 1990

1 GW,The Raven	5.00
2 RG,Great Expectations	5.00
3 KB,Thru the Looking Glass	5.00
4 BSz,Moby Dick	5.00
5 SG,TM,KE, Hamlet.	5.00
6 PCr,JT, Scarlet Letter.	5.00
7 DSp,Count of Monte Cristo	5.00
8 Dr.Jekyll & Mr.Hyde	5.00
9 MP,Tom Sawyer.	5.00
10 Call of the Wild	5.00
11 Rip Van Winkle	5.00
12 Dr. Moreau	5.00
13 Wuthering Heights	5.00
14 Fall of House of Usher	5.00
15 Gift of the Magi	5.00
16 A: Christmas Carol	5.00
17 Treasure Island	5.00
18 The Devils Dictionary	5.00
19 The Secret Agent	5.00
20 The Invisible Man	5.00
21 Cyrano de Bergerac	5.00
22 The Jungle Book.	5.00
23 Swiss Family Robinson.	5.00
24 Rime of Ancient Mariner	5.00
25 Ivanhoe	5.00
26 Aesop's Fables	5.00
27 The Jungle	5.00

CLASSICS ILLUSTRATED
Acclaim 1997–98

A Christmas Carol	5.00
A Connecticut Yankee in	
King Arthur's Court	5.00
All Quiet on the Western Front	5.00
A Midsummer's Night Dream.	5.00
Around the World in 80 Days.	5.00
A Tale of Two Cities	5.00
The Call of the Wild	5.00
Captains Courageous	5.00
The Count of Monte Cristo	5.00
Crime and Punishment	5.00
Dr. Jekyll and Mr. Hyde	6.00
Don Quixote.	5.00
Frankenstein	6.00
From the Earth to the Moon.	5.00
Great Expectations	5.00
Gullivers Travels	5.00
Hamlet	5.00

Classics Illustrated: Frankenstein
© Acclaim

The House of the Seven Gables	5.00
Huckleberry Finn	5.00
The Hunchback of Notre Dame	5.00
The Illiad	5.00
The Invisible Man.	6.00
Jane Eyre.	5.00
Journey to the Center of the Earth	5.00
Kidnapped	5.00
The Last of the Mohicans	5.00
Les Miserables	5.00
Lord Jim.	5.00
Macbeth	5.00
The Master of Ballantrae	5.00
Moby Dick	5.00
Mysterious Island	5.00
The Odyssey	5.00
Oliver Twist	5.00
The Prince and the Pauper	5.00
The Red Badge of Courage.	5.00
Robinson Crusoe	5.00
Romeo & Juliet	5.00
Silas Mariner	5.00
Tom Sawyer	5.00
Wuthering Heights	5.00

CLASSICS ILLUSTRATED JUNIOR
Classics Illustrated Junior, 2003–2005

501 Show White & Seven Dwarfs	4.00
502 The Ugly Duckling.	4.00
503 Cinderella	4.00
504 The Pied Piper	4.00
508 Goldilocks & the Three Bears.	6.00
509 Beauty and the Beast	6.00
512 Rumplestiltskin	6.00
513 Pinocchio	6.00
514 Steadfast Tin Soldier.	4.00
515 Johnny Appleseed	4.00
519 Paul Bunyan	4.00
520 Thumbelina	4.00
530 The Golden Bird	4.00
535 The Wizard of Oz	4.00
536 The Chimney Sweep	4.00
539 The Enchanted Fish	4.00
540 Tinder Box.	4.00
546 The Elves and the Shoemaker.	4.00
548 Magic Pitcher	6.00
563 The Wishing Well	4.00
564 Salt Mountain	4.00
565 THe Silly Princess.	4.00
570 Pearl Princess.	4.00
571 How Fire Came to the Indians	4.00

COLOR PUB.

CLASSWAR
Com.X, 2001
1 . . . . 3.00
2 thru 3 . . . . @3.00
4 thru 6 . . . . @3.50
1 Metal edition 50.00

CLAUS
Draco, 1997
1 by Bowden & Guichardon 3.00
2 thru 4 . . . . @3.25

CLAW
THE UNCONQUERED
Wildstorm/DC, 2006
1 CDi, ASm 3.00
2 thru 6 CDi, ASm . . . . @3.00

CLIVE BARKER'S
TAPPING THE VEIN
Eclipse, 1989–92
1 . . . . 9.00
2 thru 5 . . . . @8.50

CLIVE BARKER'S THE
GREAT AND SECRET
SHOW
IDW Publishing, 2006
1 . . . . 4.00
1a variant (c) 4.00
2 thru 3 . . . . @4.00
4 Primal Scenes 4.00
5 The Devils Inside 4.00
6 Slaves and Lovers 4.00
7 . . . . 4.00
8 thru 12 . . . . @4.00

CLIVE BARKER'S THE
THIEF OF ALWAYS
IDW Publishing, 2005
1 . . . . 7.50
2 thru 3 . . . . @7.50

CLOCKWORK GIRL
Arcana Studio, 2007
0 . . . . 0.25
1 (of 4) 1.00
2 . . . . 2.00

Close Shaves of Pauline Peril #2
© Gold Key

COLOR PUB.

CLOSE SHAVES
OF PAULINE PERIL
Gold Key, 1970
1 . . . . 50.00
2 thru 4 . . . . @30.00

CLYDE CRASHCUP
Dell Publishing Co., 1963
1 . . . . 250.00
2 . . . . 200.00
3 thru 5 . . . . @175.00

COBALT BLUE
Innovation, 1989
Spec.#1 . . . . 3.00
Spec.#2 . . . . 3.00
1 and 2 . . . . @3.00

COBALT:
WARRIOR ANGEL
Mindchyld Comics, 2005
0 . . . . 4.00
1 . . . . 4.00
2 . . . . 4.00

CODE
Guardian Line, 2006
1 . . . . 3.00
2 thru 5 . . . . @3.00

CODENAME:
BLACK DEATH
Triumph Media, 2006
1 thru 4 . . . . @3.00

CODENAME: DANGER
Lodestone, 1985
1 RB/BMc,I:Makor 3.50
2 KB,I:Capt.Energy 3.00
3 PS/RB 3.00
4 PG 3.00

CODE NAME:
DOUBLE IMPACT
High Impact, 1997
1 RCI 3.00
1 variant cover 9.00
1 signed holofoil cover 12.00

CODENAME: FIREARM
Malibu Ultraverse, 1995
0 I:New Firearm 3.00
1 F:Alec Swan 3.00
2 Dual Identity 3.00
3 F:Hitch and Lopez 3.00
4 F:Hitch and Lopez 3.00
5 Working Together 3.00

CODENAME:
STRIKEFORCE
Spectrum, 1984
1 . . . . 3.00

COLD HEAT
Picturebox, 2006
1 thru 6 . . . . @5.00

COLOSSAL SHOW, THE
Gold Key, 1969
1 . . . . 75.00

COLOUR OF MAGIC
Innovation
1 Terry Pratchet novel adapt. 3.00

2 The Sending of Eight 3.00
3 Lure of the Worm 3.00
4 final issue 3.00

COLT .45
Dell Publishing Co., 1958
1 Ph(c) all 250.00
2 . . . . 225.00
3 . . . . 200.00
4 . . . . 200.00
5 . . . . 200.00
6 ATh 225.00
7 . . . . 200.00
8 . . . . 200.00
9 . . . . 200.00

COLT SPECIAL
AC Comics, 1985
1 . . . . 3.00
2 thru 3 . . . . @3.00

COMBAT
Dell Publishing Co., 1961
1 SG 100.00
2 SG 75.00
3 SG 75.00
4 JFK cover, Story 2-D 85.00
5 SG 75.00
6 SG 50.00
7 SG 50.00
8 SG 50.00
9 SG 50.00
10 SG 50.00
11 thru 27 SG . . . . @60.00
28 thru 40 SG . . . . @50.00

COMET, THE
Archie/Red Circle, 1983
1 AN,CI,O:Comet 3.00
2 AN,CI,D:Hangman 3.00

COMIC ALBUM
Dell Publishing Co.,
March-May, 1958
1 Donald Duck 175.00
2 Bugs Bunny 125.00
3 Donald Duck 150.00
4 Tom & Jerry 100.00
5 Woody Woodpecker 100.00
6 Bugs Bunny 100.00
7 Popeye 110.00
8 Tom & Jerry 100.00
9 Woody Woodpecker 100.00
10 Bugs Bunny 100.00
11 Popeye 110.00
12 Tom & Jerry 75.00
13 Woody Woodpecker 75.00
14 Bugs Bunny 75.00
15 Popeye 100.00
16 Flintstones 125.00
17 Space Mouse 100.00
18 3 Stooges,Ph(c) 125.00

COMIX INTERNATIONAL
Warren Magazines, 1974
1 . . . . 150.00
2 WW,BW 75.00
3 . . . . 40.00
4 RC 40.00
5 Spring, 1977 . . . . 40.00

CONCRETE JUNGLE:
THE LEGEND OF
THE BLACK LION
Acclaim, 1998
1 (of 6) CPr,JFy,F:Terry Smalls 2.50
2 CPr,JFy,Black Lion Order 2.50
3 CPr,JFy,The Man 2.50

4 CPr,JFy 2.50
5 CPr,JFy 2.50

CONNECT
Narwain Publishing, 2005
1 . . . . 4.00

CONTAINMENT
IDW Publishing, 2005
1 . . . . 4.00
2 thru 5 . . . . @4.00

CORBEN SPECIAL
Pacific, 1984
1 RCo 5.00

CORUM: THE BULL & THE SPEAR
First, 1989
1 thru 4 Michael Moorcock adapt.@2.50

COSMIC GUARD, THE
Devil's Due Publishing, 2004
1 JSn 3.00
2 thru 6 JSn . . . . @3.00

COUGAR, THE
Atlas, April–July, 1975
1 . . . . 25.00
2 O:Cougar 25.00

COUNTDOWN
WildStorm/DC, 2000
1 (of 8) JMi,AaL 2.50
2 thru 6 JMi,AaL . . . . @2.50
7 JMi,AaL,RyE,supercriminals . . . 2.50
8 JMi,AAl,RyE,concl. 3.00

COUNTER-OPS
Antarctic Press, 2003
1 . . . . 4.00
2 thru 5 . . . . @4.00

COUNTER-STRIKE
Infinity Comics, 2000
1 (of 4) 2.50
1a premium chroma-foil (c). 10.00
2 . . . . 2.50
3 . . . . 2.50
4 . . . . 2.50

COUP D'ETAT
Wildstorm/DC, 2004
1 (of 4) Sleeper, JLe 3.00
2 Stormwatch: Team Achilles 3.00
3 Wildcats Version 3.0 . . . . 3.00
4 The Authority, WPo 3.00
Spec. Afterword 3.00

COURTSHIP OF EDDIE'S FATHER
Dell Publishing Co., 1970
1 Ph(c) 100.00
2 Ph(c) 75.00

COVEN
Awesome Entertainment, 1997
1 IaC,JLb,JSb,V:The Pentad 7.00
1a variant covers 7.00
2 IaC,JLb,Who is Spellcaster? 5.00
3 IaC,JLb,V:The Pentad 5.00
4 IaC,JLb,Pentad, concl.. . . . . 4.00
5 IaC,JLb, ... 4.00
5 gold foil cover 8.00
6 IaC,JLb,Mardi Gras madness . . . 3.00
6 gold foil edition 8.00

7 IaC,JLb,V:Babylon 2.50
8 IaC,JLb,F:Thor, the God
of Thunder 2.50
9 IaC,JLb, ... 2.50
Coll.Ed. #1, rep. #1–#2,
new IaC(c) 5.00
Fan Appreciation #1, rep. #1,
new cover 2.50
Coven/Menace S.D.Con
preview book 5.00

VOL 2
1 IaC,JLb 2.50
1a, b & c variant covers 2.50
1d chrome edition 9.00
1e gold foil cover 8.00
2 IaC,JLb,V:Supreme 2.50
2a Lionheart (c). 8.00
2b signed 15.00
3 IaC,JLb, Long Flight Home 2.50
3 Ruby red edition 12.00
4 IaC,JLb 2.50
5 thru 7 . . . . @3.00
Coven Sourcebook #1 . . . . 3.00

COVEN 13
No Mercy Comics, 1997
1 by Rikki Rockett & Matt Busch . . 2.50
2 thru 4 . . . . @2.50

COVEN/RE:GEX
Awesome Entertainment, 1999
1 (of 2) RLe,JLb,IaC 2.50
1a alternate IaC cover 7.00
2 JLb, conclusion 2.50

COVEN: DARK ORIGINS
Awesome Entertainment, 1999
1 . . . . 2.50
1a & b variant covers 2.50

COVEN: DARK SISTER
Avatar Press, 2001
1/2 Rio (c) 4.00
1/2 Shaw (c) 4.00
1/2 Martin (c) 4.00
1/2 Raptor attack (c) 5.00
1/2 Previews Raptor prism foil (c) 13.00
1/2 Bad Vibes (c) 6.00
1 Park (c) 3.50
1a Rio (c) 3.50
1b Martin (c) 3.50
1c wraparound (c). 4.00
1d Blue leather (c) 25.00
1e Royal Blue edition, in case . . 75.00
1f Haunting Vision edition. 6.00
1g Prism foil edition 13.00
1h Embrace edition. 6.00
1i Embrace edition, emerald (c) . . 14.00
2 Adrian (c) edition 6.00

COVEN: SPELLCASTER
Avatar Press, 2001
1/2 Bewitched edition 6.00
1/2 Bikini edition 6.00
1/2 Rio Royal Blue (c). 60.00
1 Finch (c). 3.50
1a Rio (c) 3.50
1b Martin (c) 3.50
1c Wraparound (c) 4.00
1d Leather. 20.00
1e Finch Ruby Red(c). 20.00
1f Rio prism foil (c) 11.00
1g Royal Blue edition 60.00
2 Rio (c) 3.50
2a Shaw (c). 3.50
2b Martin (c) 3.50
2c Lyon (c) 3.50
Spec. #1 Free Spirit edition 5.96

COVEN: TOOTH & NAIL
Avatar Press, 2001
1 Adrian (c) 3.50
1a Rio (c) 3.50
1b Waller (c) 3.50
1c MMy(c). 3.50
1d Wraparound (c) 3.50
1e leather (c). 20.00
1f Royal Blue (c) 60.00
1g Bikini Edition (c) 6.00
1h Bad Ladies (c) 6.00
1i Prism exclusive (c) 11.00
1j Fantom (c) 6.00
1k Training Day (c) 6.00
1/2 Woman Scorned (c) 6.00
1/2a Prism Foil edition 11.00
1/2b Fantom edition 6.00
1/2c Adrian (c) 16-pg. 4.00
1/2d Waller (c) 4.00
1/2e MMy(c) 4.00
1/2f Martin (c) 4.00

COVER GIRL
Boom! Studios, 2007
1 . . . . 4.00
2 thru 5 . . . . @4.00

Cowboy in Africa #1
© Gold Key

COWBOY IN AFRICA
Gold Key, 1968
1 Chuck Conners,Ph(c) 100.00

CRACKED
Major Magazines, 1958
1 AW 300.00
2 . . . . 200.00
3 thru 6 . . . . @200.00
7 thru 10 . . . . @150.00
11 thru 20 . . . . @125.00
21 thru 30 . . . . @75.00
31 thru 36 . . . . @60.00
37 Beatles 75.00
38 thru 45 . . . . @60.00
46 Beatles 65.00
47 thru 50 . . . . @60.00
51 Beatles 65.00
52 Mysters 65.00
53 thru 56 . . . . @60.00
57 Rolling Stones 65.00
58 . . . . 60.00
59 Laurel & Hardy 65.00
60 & 61 . . . . @60.00
62 Beatles 65.00
63 thru 68 . . . . @60.00

69 Batman	65.00
70 Elvis	65.00
71 W.C. Fields	65.00
72 thru 99	@60.00
100	75.00
101 thru 103	@35.00
104 Godfather	75.00
105 thru 114	@35.00
115 M.A.S.H.	45.00
116 thru 118	@35.00
119 Kung Fu	40.00
120 Six Million Dollar Man	40.00
121 American Grafiti	40.00
122 thru 130	@23.00
131 Godfather	35.00
132 Baretta	35.00
133 Space:1999	40.00
134 Fonz	35.00
135 Bionic Woman	35.00
136 thru 145	@35.00
146 thru 148 Star Wars	@50.00
149 Star Wars	45.00
150 thru 162	@30.00
163 Mork & Mindy, Alien	45.00
164 thru 174	@25.00
175 thru 200	@20.00
201 thru 252	@15.00
253 thru 300	@15.00
301 thru 348	@10.00

[THE INCREDIBLE] CRASH DUMMIES
Harvey, 1993
1 thru 3, from the toy series .... @2.50

CRAZYMAN
Continuity, 1992
[1st Series]
1 Embossed(c),NA/RT(i), O:Crazyman ... 5.00
2 NA/BB(c) ... 2.50
3 DBa,V:Terrorists ... 2.50
[2nd Series], 1993
1 Die Cut(c) ... 2.50
2 thru 3 ... 2.50
4 In Demon World ... 2.50

CREATURE
Antarctic Press, 1997
1 (of 2) by D.Walker&J.Maranto . 3.00
2 concl ... 3.00

CREED/TEENAGE MUTANT NINJA TURTLES
Lightning Comics, 1996
1 ... 3.00
1 variant cover ... 3.00

CREED: CRANIAL DISORDER
Lightning Comics, 1996
1 (of 3) ... 3.00
1a variant cover, *Previews* exclusive ... 3.00
1b Platinum edition ... 8.00
1c Platinum edition, autographed 12.00
2 ... 3.00
2a variant cover ... 3.00

CREMATOR: HELL'S GUARDIAN
Chaos! Comics, 1998
1 (of 5) LJi ... 3.00
2 ... 3.00
3 V:Asteroth ... 3.00
4 ... 3.00
5 ... 3.00

CRIME MACHINE
Skywald Publications, 1971
1 JK ... 90.00
2 AT ... 50.00

CRIME PATROL
Gemstone, 2000
1 rep ... 2.50
2 rep. Fall 1948 ... 2.50
3 rep. Winter 1948 ... 2.50
4 rep. Feb. 1949 ... 2.50
5 rep ... 2.50
6 rep ... 2.50
7 rep ... 2.50
8 rep. Oct. 1949 ... 2.50
9 rep. Dec. 1949 ... 2.50
10 rep. Feb. 1950 issue ... 2.50

CRIME SUSPENSE STORIES
Russ Cochran, 1992
1 Rep. C.S.S. #1 (1950) ... 3.00
2 thru 7 Rep. C.S.S. ... @3.00
8 thru 15 Rep ... @3.00
Gemstone, 1996
16 thru 27 EC comics reprint ... @3.00

CRIMSON NUN
Antarctic Press, 1997
1 (of 4) ... 3.00
2 ... 3.00
3 ... 3.00
4 concl ... 3.00

CRIMSON PLAGUE
Event Comics, 1997
1 GP,F:DiNA: Simmons ... 3.00
2 GP ... 3.00

CROSSFIRE
Eclipse, 1984–86
1 DSp ... 3.00
2 thru 11 DSp ... @2.50
12 DSp,DSt(c),M.Monroe(c) & story 2.50
13 DSp ... 2.50
14 DSp ... 2.50
15 DSp,O:Crossfire ... 2.50
16 DSp,The Comedy Place ... 2.50
17 DSp,Comedy Place, Pt.2 ... 2.50
See B&W

CROSSFIRE & RAINBOW
Eclipse, 1986
1 DSp,V:Marx Brothers ... 2.50
2 DSp,PG(c),V:Marx Brothers ... 2.50
3 DSp,HC(c),A:Witness ... 2.50
4 DSp,DSt(c),This Isn't Elvis ... 3.50

CROSSGEN CHRONICLES
Crossgen Comics, 2000
1 RMz, 48-pg ... 4.50
2 RMz,GP ... 4.00
2a 2nd printing ... 11.00
3 BKs,GP, 48-page ... 5.00
4 MWa,GP, 48-page ... 4.00
5 RMz,GP ... 4.00
6 thru 8 ... @4.00

CROSSOVERS, THE
CG Entertainment, 2003
1 (of 6) Cross Currents ... 3.00
2 thru 11 ... @3.00

CROSSROADS
First, 1988
1 Sable,Whisper ... 4.00

Crossgen Chronicles #2
© *Crossgen Comics*

2 Sable, Badger ... 4.00
3 JSon,JAI,Badger/Luther Ironheart 4.00
4 Grimjack/Judah Macabee ... 4.00
5 LM,Grimjack/Dreadstar/Nexus... 4.00

CROW, THE: CITY OF ANGELS
Kitchen Sink, 1996
1 thru 3 movie adaptation ... @3.00
1 thru 3 movie adaptation, photo covers ... @3.00

CRUX
Crossgen Comics, 2001
1 MWa,SEp ... 7.00
2 MWa,SEp ... 5.00
3 thru 8 MWa,SEp ... @3.00
9 thru 20 ... @3.00
21 thru 33 ... @3.00

CRYBABY
Event Comics, 1999
1 GrL,SLo ... 3.00
1a limited, signed ... 10.00

CRYING FREEMAN III
Viz, 1991
1 A:Dark Eyes,Oshu ... 6.00
2 A:Dark Eyes, V:Oshu ... 5.25
3 Freeman vs. Oshu ... 5.25
4 Freeman Defeated ... 5.25
5 Freeman clones, A:Nitta ... 5.25
6 V:Nitta ... 5.25
7 ... 5.00
8 ... 5.00
9 ... 5.00

CRYING FREEMAN IV
Viz, 1992
1 B:The Pomegranate ... 5.00
2 thru 7 ... @3.00
8 E:The Pomegranate ... 3.00
[2nd Series]
1 The Festival ... 2.50

CRYPTIC WRITINGS OF MEGADETH
Chaos! Comics, 1997
1 BnP ... 3.00
1a Tour Edition, leather ... 20.00
1b Tour Edition, deluxe ... 30.00

COLOR PUB.

2 BnP 3.00
3 BnP 3.00
4 BnP 3.00

CSI: CRIME SCENE INVESTIGATION
IDW Publishing, 2003
1 (of 5) 5.00
1a photo(c) 8.00
2 thru 3 . . . . @5.00
4 thru 5 . . . . @4.00
GN Thicker Than Blood 7.00
GN Miami–Smoking Gun 7.00
GN Miami–Thou Shalt Not 7.00
GN Miami–Blood/Money 7.00

CSI: BAD RAP
IDW Publishing, 2003
1 (of 5) 4.00
2 . . . . 4.00
3 . . . . 4.00
5 . . . . 4.00

CSI: DEMON HOUSE
IDW Publishing, 2004
1 (of 5) 4.00
2 thru 5 . . . . @4.00

CSI: DOMINOS
IDW Publishing, 2004
1 . . . . 4.00
2 . . . . 4.00
3 . . . . 4.00
4 . . . . 4.00
5 . . . . 4.00

CSI: DYING IN THE GUTTERS
IDW Publishing, 2006
1 . . . . 4.00
2 thru 5 . . . . @4.00

CSI: MIAMI
IDW Publishing, 2003
GN Smoking Gun 7.00
GN Thou Shalt Not 7.00
GN Blood/Money 7.00

CSI: NY-BLOODY MURDER
IDW Publishing, 2005
1 . . . . 4.00
2 thru 5 . . . . @4.00

CSI: SECRET IDENTITY
IDW Publishing, 2005
1 . . . . 4.00
2 thru 5 . . . . @4.00

CURSE OF RUNE
Malibu Ultraverse, 1995
1A CU,Rune/Silver Surfer tie-in . . . 2.50
1B CU, alternate cover 2.50
2 COntrol of the Soul Gem 2.50
3 F:Marvel's Adam Warlock 2.50
4 N:Adam Warlock 2.50

CURSE OF THE BLOOD CLAN, THE
Dead Dog Comics, 2005
1 (of 3) by Mark Kidwell 5.00
1a variant (c) 5.00
2 thru 3 . . . . @5.00

CVO: AFRICAN BLOOD
IDW Publishing, 2006
1 thru 4 . . . . @4.00

CVO: COVERT VAMPIRIC OPERATIONS–ARTIFACT
IDW Publishing, 2003
1 . . . . 4.00
2 thru 3 . . . . @4.00
GN 6.00
1-shot Human Touch (2004) 4.00
GN 6.00

CVO: HUMAN TOUCH
IDW Publishing, 2004
1-shot 4.00

CVO: ROGUE STATE
IDW Publishing, 2004
1 thru 5 . . . . @4.00

CYBER CITY
CPM Comics, 1995
Part One
1 I:Oedo City 3.00
2 Sengoku 3.00
Part Two
1 Based on Animated Movie 3.00

CYBERCRUSH: ROBOTS IN REVOLT
Fleetway/Quality
1 inc.Robo-Hunter,Ro-Busters 2.50
2 and 3 . . . . @2.50
4 and 5 V:Terraneks . . . . @2.50

CYBERFROG
Harris, 1995
0 O:Cyberfrog 3.00
0 AAd(c), signed 18.00
0 Alternate AAd(c) 9.00
1 . . . . 2.50
2 thru 4 . . . . @3.00

CYBERFROG: RESERVOIR FROG
Harris, 1996
1 Preview Ashcan, signed
  & numbered 12.00
1 EL(c),V:the Swarm,
  Mr. Skorpeone 3.00
2 . . . . 3.00

CYBERHOOD
Entity Comics, 1995
1 R:Cyberhood 2.50
1a with PC Game 7.00

CYBERNARY 2.0
WildStorm/DC, 2001
1 (of 6) R:Yumiko Gamorra 3.00
2 F:MechaMax 3.00
3 F:Toshiro 3.00
4 secret race of cyborgs 3.00
5 revolution or evolution 3.00
6 Kaizen Gamorra, concl 3.00

CYBERPUNK
Innovation, 1989
1 . . . . 2.50
2 . . . . 2.50
Book 2,#1 . . . . 2.50
Book 2,#2 . . . . 2.50

CYBERPUNK: THE SERAPHIM FILES
Innovation, 1990
1 and 2 . . . . @2.50

CYBERPUNX
Maximum Press, 1997
1 MHw, ... 2.50

CYBERRAD
Continuity, 1991
1 NA layouts,I:Cyberran 3.00
2 NA I/o 2.50
3 NA I/o 2.50
4 NA I/o 2.50
5 NA I/o Glow in the Dark cov 5.00
6 NA I/o,Pullout poster 2.50
7 NA I/o,See-thru(c) 2.50
[2nd Series], 1992
1 Hologram cover 2.50
2 NA(c),The Disassembled Man . . . 2.50
[3rd Series]
1 Holo.(c),just say no 3.50
[4th Series], 1993
Deathwatch 2000]
1 Deathwatch 2000 pt.8,w/card . . . 2.50
2 Deathwatch 2000 pt. w/card 2.50

CYBRID
Maximum Press, 1995
1 F:Cybrid, I:The Clan 3.00

CYBRID
Maximum Press, 1997
0 RLd, 48pg 3.50
1 MsM,BNa 3.00
2 MsM,BNa 3.00

CYNDER
Immortelle Studios, 1996
1 thru 3: see B&W
Ann. #1 . . . . 3.00
Series II, 1997
1 A:Nira X 3.00

CYNDER/NIRA X
Immortelle Studios, 1996
1 x-over 3.00
1 variant cover 3.00
1 gold edition 10.00

DAEMONSTORM
Caliber, 1997
1 TM(c),JMt 4.00
1 signed 4.00

Daemonstorm #1
© Caliber

COLOR PUB.

DAEMONSTORM: DEADWORLD
Caliber
one-shot 4.00

DAEMONSTORM: OZ
Caliber, 1997
1 . . . . 4.00

DAFFY DUCK
Gold Key, 1962
1 . . . . 75.00
2 thru 10 . . . . @75.00
11 thru 40 . . . . @40.00
41 thru 75 . . . . @25.00
76 thru 97 . . . . @15.00
Whitman, 1980
128 thru 131 . . . . @15.00
134 thru 145 . . . . @15.00

DAGAR THE INVINCIBLE
Gold Key, 1972–82
1 O:Daggar;I:Villians Olstellon
  & Scorpio 50.00
2 . . . . 35.00
3 I:Graylon 25.00
4 . . . . 25.00
5 . . . . 25.00
6 1st Dark Gods story 20.00
7 thru 10 . . . . @20.00
11 thru 19 . . . . @15.00

DAI KAMIKAZE
Now, 1987–88
1 Speed Racer 7.00
1a 2nd printing 2.50
2 thru 12 . . . . @2.50

DAISY AND DONALD
Gold Key, 1973
1 . . . . 50.00
2 thru 5 . . . . @25.00
6 . . . . 20.00
7 thru 10 . . . . @15.00
11 thru 41 . . . . @12.00
Whitman, 1980
42 thru 46 . . . . @16.00
47 . . . . 80.00
48 thru 59 . . . . @22.00

Daisy and Donald #1
© Walt Disney

DAKTARI
Dell Publishing Co., 1967
1 Ph(c) 60.00
2 Ph(c) 40.00
3 Ph(c) 40.00
4 Ph(c) 40.00

DALGODA
Fantagraphics, 1984–86
1 . . . . 3.50
2 KN,I:Grinwood'Daughter 3.00
3 KN 2.50
4 thru 8 . . . . @2.50

DALKIEL: THE PROPHECY
Verotik, 1998
1-shot, prequel to Satanika 4.00

DAMAGED, THE
A-10 Comics, 2006
1 . . . . 3.00

DANGER GIRL: BACK IN BLACK
Wildstorm/DC, Nov., 2005
1 (of 4) 3.00
2 . . . . 3.00
3 Ruby 3.00
4 finale 3.00

DANGER GIRL: BODY SHOTS
Wildstorm/DC, Apr., 2007
1 (of 4) 3.00
2 thru 4 . . . . @3.00

DANGER GIRL: KAMIKAZE
WildStorm/DC, 2000
1 (of 2) 3.00
1a variant(c) 3.00
2 concl. 3.00
GN Viva Las Danger 5.00
Spec. Danger Girl 3-D 5.00
Spec. Hawaiian Punch 5.00

DANGER RANGER
Checker Comics, 1998
1 I:Kirby Jackson, BSz(c) 2.50
2 . . . . 2.50

DANIEL BOONE
Gold Key, 1965–69
1 . . . . 150.00
2 thru 5 . . . . @125.00
6 thru 14 . . . . @100.00
15 . . . . 75.00

DARE
Fantagraphics, 1991
1 F:Dan Dare 2.75
2 F:Dan Dare 2.75
3 and 4 F:Dan Dare . . . . @2.50

DARE THE IMPOSSIBLE
Fleetway/Quality
1 DGb,rep.Dan Dare from 2000AD 2.50
2 thru 14 DGb . . . . @2.50

DARK, THE
Continuum, 1990
1 LSn(c),MBr,V:Futura 4.00
2 LSn,Shot by Futura 3.00
3 MBr,Dark has amnesia 3.00

4 GT(c),MBr,O:The Dark. 3.00
Convention Book 1992 MBr,GP,
  MFm,MMi,VS,LSn,TV 5.00
Convention Book 1993 MBr,PC,
  ECh,BS,BWi,GP(c),Foil(c), . . 4.00
[2nd Series], 1994
1 Dark Regains Memory. 3.00
1a Signed, Foil Cover. 2.75
1 BS(c),Red Foil(c), ... 3.00
1a BS(c),newstand ed. 3.00
1b BS(c),Blue foil 3.00
2 War on Crime. 2.75
3 Geoffery Stockton 2.50
3 BS(c),Foil(c), ... 3.00
4 I:First Monster 2.50
4 GP(c),Foil(c),w/cards 3.00
5 thru 9 . . . . @2.50

DARK CHYLDE
Maximum Press, 1996
1 RQu. 9.00
1a Am.Entertainment edition. . . . 12.00
1b variant cover 9.00
2 RQu. 7.00
2 Variant cover 6.00
3 RQu 4.00
3 Variant cover 5.00
4 RQu 5.00
5 RQu,No One Here Gets Out
  Alive. 5.00
Spec. Dark Chylde/Avengelyne RLd,
  RQu,I:Witch Tower. 3.00
Spec. Dark Chylde/Glory RQu, . . 3.00
Darkchylde Entertainment, 2001
0 remastered, RQu (2001) 3.00
Last Issue special (2002) 4.00
Last issue exclusive variant(c). . . . 4.00

DARKCHYLDE REDEMPTION
Darkchylde Entertainment, 2001
1 RQu 3.00
2 thru 3 . . . . @3.00

DARK DAYS
IDW Publishing, 2003
1 (of 6) 4.50
2 thru 6 . . . . @4.25

DARK DOMINION
Defiant, 1993–94
1 SD,I:Michael Alexander 3.25
2 LWn(s),SLi(i), ... 2.75
3 LWn(s),SLi(i), ... 2.75
4 LWn(s),B:Hoxhunt 3.00
5 thru 7 LWn(s) . . . . @2.75
8 thru 12 LWn(s) . . . . @2.50

DARKEST HORROR OF MORELLA, THE
Verotik, 2006
1 . . . . 4.00
1 fan club (c) 9.00

DARKHAM VALE
APC, 2003
1 (of 10) by Jack Lawrence 3.50
2 thru 9 . . . . @3.50
10 finale 4.00
Spec. #0 . . . . 3.00

DARKHAM VALE: THE DRACOU IMPERATIVE
APC, 2004
1 . . . . 3.50
2 . . . . 3.50
3 . . . . 3.50
4 . . . . 3.50

COLOR PUB.

DARKHAM VALE: UPRISING
APC, 2005
1 (of 10) 3.50
2 thru 3 . . . . @3.50

DARKLON THE MYSTIC
Pacific, 1983
1 JSn. 2.50

DARKMAN VS. ARMY OF DARKNESS
D.E. (Dynamite Ent.) 2006
1 (of 4) Kbk,RSt,JFy 3.50
2 . . . . 3.50
1a thru 2a variant (c)s . . . . @3.50
3 thru 4 . . . . @3.50
3a thru 4a variant (c)s . . . . . . @3.50

DARKMINDS: MACROPOLIS
Dreamwave, 2002
1 . . . . 3.00
2 thru 4 . . . . @3.00
3a variant Pat Lee (c) 3.00
Vol. 2
1 thru 4 . . . . @3.00
PocketBook Vol. 1 . . . . 8.00

DARK MISTS
APC, 2005
1 (of 4) 3.50
Markosia, 2005
3 . . . . 3.50
4 . . . . 3.50

DARK ONE'S THIRD EYE
Sirius, 1996
one-shot Vol. 1 DOe 5.00
Vol. 2 DOe 5.00

DARK SHADOWS
Gold Key, 1969
1 W/Poster,Ph(c). 600.00
2 Ph(c) 250.00
3 W/Poster,Ph(c). 350.00
4 thru 7,Ph(c) . . . . @150.00
8 thru 10 . . . . @100.00
11 thru 20 . . . . @750.00
21 thru 35 . . . . @65.00

DARK SHADOWS
Innovation, 1992
1 Based on 1990's TV series 3.50
2 O:Victoria Winters 2.50
3 Barnabus Imprisoned. 2.50
4 V: Redmond Swann. 2.75
[2nd Series]
1 A:Nathan 2.75
2 thru 4 . . . . 2.75
Dark Shadows:Resurrected 16.00

DARK SIDE
Maximum Press, 1997
1 RLd,RQu 3.00

DARKSHRINE
Antarctic Press, 1999
1 by Shelby Robertson 3.00
1a deluxe 6.00
2 16-page 2.50

DARKSTALKERS
Devil's Due/UDON, 2004
1 . . . . 3.00
2 thru 6 . . . . @3.00

---

5 power foil (c) 4.00
6 evil foil (c) 4.00

DARKSTORM
Alias Enterprises, 2006
0 . . . . 3.50

DARKWING DUCK
Walt Disney, 1991
1 I:Darkwing Duck. 3.00
2 V:Taurus Bulba 3.00
3 Fowl Play 3.00
4 End o/t beginning,final issue 3.00

DARQUE PASSAGES
Acclaim, 1997
1 (of 4) sequal to Master Darque . . 2.50
1 signed edition. 4.00
2 . . . . 2.50
3 A:Pere Jean, Voodoo King. 2.50
4 conclusion 2.50

DAVID: THE SHEPHERD'S SONG
Alias Enterprises, 2005
1 (of 3) 3.00
2 thru 3 . . . . @3.00

*Davy Crockett King of the Wild Frontier
#1 (1969) © Gold Key*

DAVY CROCKETT KING OF THE WILD FRONTIER
Gold Key, 1963
1 . . . . 275.00
Gold Key, 1969
1 . . . . 80.00

DAWN
Sirius, 1995–97
1 JLi,R:Dawn 10.00
1a white trash edition 25.00
1b black light edition 15.00
1c look sharp edition 30.00
2 JLi, Trip to Hell. 7.00
2 variant cover 12.00
3 JLi 6.00
3 limited edition. 18.00
4 JLi,The Gauntlet 5.00
4a variant cover 10.00
5 JLi,Everybody Dies 4.00
5a variant cover 10.00
6 (of 6) JLi. 4.00
6a variant cover 9.00
10th Anniv. Spec. 3.00

10th Anniv. Spec, sgn,num. 5.00

DAWN: PIN-UP GODDESS
Linsner.com, 2001
Spec. 3.00
Spec. Limited, signed. 12.00

DAWN: THE RETURN OF THE GODDESS
Sirius, 1999
1 (of 4) JLi 3.00
1a limited, signed 25.00
2 A:Marinen 3.00
3 thru 4 . . . . @3.00
2a thru 4a deluxe . . . . @20.00

DAY OF THE DEAD: THE RISING OF BUB
Dead Dog Comics, 2006
1 (of 3) 5.00
2 thru 3 . . . . @5.00

DAZEY'S DIARY
Dell Publishing Co., 1962
1 . . . . 75.00

D-DAY
Charlton, 1963
1 . . . . 50.00
2 thru 6 . . . . @30.00

DEAD @ 17
Viper Comics, 2003
1 (of 4) 20.00
2 . . . . 15.00
3 . . . . 10.00
4 . . . . 10.00
Rough Cut #1 . . . . 12.00
Rough Cut #2 . . . . 5.00
Rough Cut #3 . . . . 5.00
Vol. 2 (2006)
1 . . . . 3.25
2 thru 3 . . . . @3.25

DEAD @ 17: BLOOD OF SAINTS
Viper Comics, 2004
1 (of 4) 10.00
2 thru 4 . . . . @4.00

DEAD @ 17: PROTECTORATE
Viper Comics, 2005
1 (of 3) 3.00
Vol. 2 (2006)
1 . . . . 3.25
2 thru 7 . . . . @3.25

DEAD @ 17: REVOLUTION
Viper Comics, 2004
1 (of 4) 3.00
2 thru 4 . . . . @3.00

DEAD BOYS: DEATH'S EMBRACE
London Night, 1996
1 EHr. 3.00
1 platinum edition 6.00

DEAD CLOWN
Malibu, 1996
1 I:Force America 2.50
2 I:Sadistic Six 2.50
3 TMs(s),last issue 2.50

DEADFORCE
Antarctic Press, 1999
1 (of 3) by Roy Burdine 3.00
2 . . . . 3.00
3 . . . . 3.00

DEAD KING
Chaos! Comics, 1997
1 (of 4) Burnt, pt.1, F:Homicide . . . 3.00
2 Burnt, pt.2 . . . . 3.00
3 Burnt, pt.3 . . . . 3.00
4 Burnt, pt.4, concl. 3.00

DEAD MEN TELL
NO TALES
Arcana Studio, 2005
1 (of 4) 4.00
2 thru 4 . . . . @4.00

DEADSIDE
Acclaim, 1998
1 (of 4) PJe, ... 2.50
2 thru 4 . . . . @2.50

DEAL WITH THE DEVIL
Alias Enterprises, 2005
1 (of 5) 1.00
2 thru 5 . . . . @3.00

Dear Nancy Parker #1
© Gold Key

DEAR NANCY PARKER
Gold Key, 1963
1 P(c) 60.00
2 P(c) 40.00

DEATH AND THE MAN
WHO WOULD NOT DIE
Silent Devil, 2007
1 (of 4) 3.00
2 . . . . 3.00

DEATHBLOW
Wildstorm/DC, Oct., 2006
1 . . . . 3.00
1a variant (c). 3.00
2 . . . . 3.00
3 . . . . 3.00
3a variant BSf (c) (1:10). 3.00
4 . . . . 3.00
4a variant BB (c). 3.00
5 V: U.S. government 3.00
6 . . . . 3.00
7 World's Deadliest Man 3.00

DEATHBLOW:
BY BLOWS
WildStorm/DC, 1999
1 (of 3) AMo,JBa. 3.00
2 AMo,JBa 3.00

DEATH COMES
TO DILLINGER
Silent Devil Productions, 2006
1 (of 2) 3.00
2 . . . . 3.00

DEATHDEALER
Verotika, 1995
1 FF(c), I:Deathdealer. 15.00
2 thru 4 FF(c) . . . . @12.00

DEATHMASK
Future Comics, 2003
1 DvM,DG,BL 3.00
2 thru 9 . . . . @3.00

DEATHMATE
Valiant/Image, 1993
Preview (Advanced Comics) 2.50
Preview (Previews) 2.50
Preview (Comic Defense Fund). . . . 4.00
Prologue BL,JLe,RLd,Solar meets
 Void 3.25
Prologue Gold 4.00
Blue SCh, HSn, F:Solar, Magnus,
 Battlestone, Livewire, Stronghold,
 Impact, Striker, Harbinger, Brigade,
 Supreme 3.00
Blue Gold Ed. 4.00
Yellow BCh,MLe,DP,F:Armstrong,
 H.A.R.D.C.A.T.S.,Ninjak,Zealot,
 Shadowman,Grifter,Ivar. 3.00
Yellow Gold Ed. 4.00
Black JLe,MS,F:Warblade,Ripclaw,
 Turok,X-O Manowar 4.00
Black Gold Ed. 6.00
Red RLd,JMs, ... 4.00
Red Gold Ed. 3.00
Epilogue 2.50
Epilogue Gold 3.00

DEATH OF HARI KARI
Blackout Comics, 1997
0 . . . . 3.00
0 super Sexy Kari Cover. 10.00
0 3-D super Sexy Kari Cover 15.00

DEATH OF
LADY VAMPRE
Blackout Comics, 1995
1 V:Baraclaw. 3.00
1 Commemorative Issue. 10.00

DEATHRACE 2020
Cosmic Comics, 1995
1 Pat Mills, Tony Skinner 2.50
2 V:Spyda, Sawmill Jones 2.50
3 O:Frankenstein 2.50
4 Deathrace cont. 2.50
5 F:Death Racers, D:Alchoholic . . . 2.50
6 V:Indestructiman 2.50
7 Smallville Mall 2.50

DEATH RATTLE
Kitchen Sink, 1985–88
1 . . . . 4.00
2 thru 7 . . . . @4.00
8 I:Xenozoic Tales. 9.00
9 thru 18 . . . . @3.00

DECOY
Pennyfarthing Press, 1999
1 (of 4) 2.75
2 . . . . 2.75
3 . . . . 2.75
4 . . . . 2.75

DECOY: STORM
OF THE CENTURY
Pennyfarthing Press, 2002
1 (of 4) 3.00
2 thru 4 . . . . @3.00

DEE SNIDER'S
STRANGELAND:
SEVEN SINS
Fangoria Comics, 2007
1 (of 4) 4.00
2 thru 4 . . . . @4.00

DEFENDERS, THE
Dell Publishing Co., 1962
1 . . . . 75.00
2 . . . . 50.00

DEFEX
Devil's Due Publishing, 2004
1 Aftermath 3.00
1a variant (c). 3.00
2 thru 6 Aftermath . . . . @3.00

DEFIANT:
ORIGIN OF A UNIVERSE
Defiant, 1993
1 Giveaway. 2.50

DEITY
Hyperwerks, 1997
0 . . . . 3.00
1 KIA. 5.00
1a Director's Cut. 3.00
2 thru 6 KIA . . . . @3.00
**VOL II Awesome/Hyperworks,
1998**
1 KIA,BNa, F:Jamie 3.00
1a Limited edition 8.00
1b Silver Foil edition 13.00
1c Gold Edition 20.00
2 KIA,BNa, A:Diamond Diaz 3.00
3 KIA,BNa, The Soul Crusher. 3.00
4 KIA,BNa, A:Ogden 3.00
5 KLa,BNa,V:Ma'Shiva 3.00

DEITY II: CATSEYE
Hyperwerks, 1998
1 KIA,BNa,F:Digby 3.00
2 KIA,BNa,A:II. 3.00
3 KIA,BNa,F:Catseye 3.00
4 KIA,BNa,conclusion 3.00

DELIVERER
Zion Comics
1 thru 3 . . . . @2.50
4 F:Gabriel 2.50
5 V:Division 2.50

DEMON-HUNTER
Atlas, 1975
1 The Harvester of Eyes 25.00

DEMONIQUE
London Night, 1996
0 Manga 3.00
1 EHr 3.00
2 EHr 3.00

DEMONSLAYER
Avatar Press, 2001
0 16-page, signed 6.00

DEMONSLAYER: FUTURE SHOCK
Avatar Press, 2002
1/2 Eradicate Edition 6.00

DEMONSLAYER: PATH OF TIME
Avatar, 2002
1 MMy 3.50
1a Medieval (c) 3.50
1b Ninja (c) 3.50
1c Western (c) 3.50
1d Matt Martin (c) 3.50
1e Serenity (c) 6.00
1f bondage (c) 6.00
1g Prism foil (c) 13.00
1/2 . . . . 4.00
1/2 Pirate (c) 4.00
1/2 Cave Girl (c) 4.00
1/2 Bikini (c) 4.00
1/2 Martin (c) 4.00

DEMONSLAYER: PROPHECY
Avatar Press, 2001
1 MMy 3.50
1a Celtic (c) 3.50
1b Hell on Wheels (c) 3.50
1c Leather (c) 20.00
1d lace edition 6.00
1e Bad Omens (c) 6.00
1f Mouth of Evil edition 6.00
1g Prism foil (c) 13.00

DEMONSLAYER: RAVE
Avatar Press, 2001
Spec. 3.50
Spec. Bad Schoolgirl (c) 3.50
Spec. Silent Moment (c) 3.50
Rave in Style (c) 6.00
Rave Previews prism foil (c) 13.00

DEMONSLAYER: REBIRTH
Awesome Entertainment, 2000
1 . . . . 3.00

DEMONSLAYER: VENGEANCE
Avatar Press, 2001
1 (of 2) MMy (c) 3.50
1a Park (c) 3.50
1b Wraparound (c) 4.00
1c Red Velvet (c) 20.00
1d prism foil (c) 13.00
1e fire (c) 6.00
1f ice (c) 6.00
1g Royal Blue edition 75.00
2 MMy, concl. 3.50
2a Bikini (c) 3.50
2b Jungle Girl (c) 3.50
2c Ruins edition 6.00

DEMONWARS: EYE FOR AN EYE
Crossgen Comics, 2003
1 thru 5 . . . . @3.00

DEMONWARS: THE DEMON AWAKENS
Devil's Due, 2007
1 . . . . 5.00

1a cardstock (c) 9.00
2 thru 3 . . . . @5.50
2a thru 3a cardstock (c) . . . . @9.50

DEMONWARS: TRIAL BY FIRE
Crossgen Comics, 2002
2 thru 5 . . . . @3.00

DEN
Fantagor, 1988
1 thru 10 RCo . . . . @2.50

DEN SAGA
Tundra/Fantagor, 1992–94
1 RCo,O:Den begins 5.00
2 thru 4 RCo . . . . @5.00

DENNIS THE MENACE
Fawcett, 1960-61
Fun Book #1 . . . . 75.00
And his Pal Joey #1 . . . . 50.00
And his Dog Ruff #1 . . . . 50.00
Television Special #1 . . . . 60.00
Triple Feature #1 . . . . 60.00
Television Special #2 . . . . 35.00

Dennis the Menace and His Friends #16 © Fawcett

DENNIS THE MENACE AND HIS FRIENDS
[VARIOUS SUBTITLES]
Fawcett, 1969–1980
1 thru 10 rep. . . . . @35.00
11 thru 20 rep. . . . . @20.00
21 thru 46 rep. . . . . @15.00

DENNIS THE MENACE GIANTS
[VARIOUS SUBTITLES]
Fawcett, 1955–69
N# Vacation Special 250.00
N# Christmas 200.00
2 . . . . 150.00
3 . . . . 150.00
4 . . . . 150.00
5 . . . . 150.00
6 thru 10 . . . . @150.00
11 thru 20 . . . . @100.00
21 thru 30 . . . . @75.00
31 thru 40 . . . . @60.00
41 thru 75 . . . . @60.00
Becomes:

DENNIS THE MENACE BONUS MAGAZINE
[VARIOUS SUBTITLES]
Fawcett, 1970–79
76 thru 100 . . . . @20.00
101 thru 120 . . . . @15.00
121 thru 185 . . . . @10.00
186 thru 196 Big Bonus Series . . @8.00
Becomes:

DENNIS THE MENACE
Fawcett, 1979–80
#16 Fun Fest 5.00
#17 Fun Fest 5.00
#10 Big Bonus Series 5.00
#11 Big Bonus Series 5.00

DEPUTY DAWG
Gold Key, 1965
1 . . . . 225.00

DER VANDALE
Innervision, 1998
1 (of 3) 2.50
2 (of 3) 2.50
3 (of 3) 2.50
3 variant cover 2.50

DESERT STORM JOURNAL
Apple Comics, 1991
1 Hussein on (c) 2.75
1a Schwartzkopf on (c) 2.75
2 thru 8 . . . . @2.75

DESOLATION JONES
Wildstorm/DC, May, 2005
1 WEI(s),JWi 3.00
2 WEI(s),JWi 3.00
3 WEI(s),JWi 3.00
4 WEI(s),JWi 3.00
5 WEI(s),JWi 3.00
6 WEI(s),JWi 3.00
7 WEI(s), To Be In England 3.00
8 WEI(s) 3.00
9 WEI(s) Sex, Lies, & Murder 3.00

DESPERADOES: BANNERS OF GOLD
IDW Publishing, 2004
1 thru 5 . . . . @4.00

DESPERADOES: BUFFALO DREAMS
IDW Publishing, 2007
1 . . . . 4.00
2 thru 4 . . . . @4.00

DESTROYER DUCK
Eclipse, 1982–84
1 JK,AA,SA,I:Groo 12.00
2 JK,AA,Starling 5.00
3 thru 7 JK. . . . . @5.00

DESTRUCTOR, THE
Atlas, 1975
1 thru 4 WW,SD . . . . @25.00

DETECTIVES, INC.
Eclipse, 1985
1 MR,rep.GraphicNovel 3.00
2 MR 2.50
[2nd Series]
1 GC,A Terror of Dying Dreams . . . 2.50
2 GC 2.50
3 GC,Cut to the Bone 2.50

DETONATOR
Chaos! Comics, 1994–95
1 I:Detonator	3.00
2 V:Messiah & Mindbender	3.00

DEVI
Virgin Comics, 2006
1 by Siddharth Kotian	3.50
2 thru 5	@3.25
6 thru 16	@3.00

Devo; Lods Starring Hot Stuff #16
© Harvey Publications

DEVIL KIDS
STARRING HOT STUFF
Harvey Publications, 1962–81
1	500.00
2	200.00
3 thru 10	@150.00
11 thru 20	@100.00
21 thru 30	@75.00
31 thru 40	@60.00
41 thru 50 68 pgs.	@50.00
51 thru 55 62 pgs.	@40.00
56 thru 70	@35.00
71 thru 100	@25.00
101 thru 107	@20.00

DEVILMAN
Verotika, 1995
1 Go Nagi	3.00
1a San Diego Con Gatefold edition	5.00
2 F:Devilman	3.00
3 Through History	3.00
4 French Revolution	3.00
5 Custer's Last Stand	3.00

DEVIL MAY CRY
Dreamwave, 2004
1 thru 4	@4.00
1a thru 4a variant (c)s	@4.00

DEVIL'S KEEPER
Alias Enterprises, 2005
1	1.00
2 thru 4	@3.00
2a variant (c)	3.00

DEVLIN
Maximum Press, 1996
1 A:Avengelyne,3-part mini-series	2.50
2 (of 3) RLd,BNa,A:Avengelyne	2.50

DICK TRACY
Blackthorne, 1986
1 3-D	3.00

DICK TRACY:
BIG CITY BLUES
1 Mini Series	4.00
2 Mini Series	6.00
3 Mini Series	6.00

DIGITAL GRAFFITI
APC, 2003
1	3.50
2 thru 4	@3.50

DINO ISLAND
Mirage, 1993
1	2.75
2	2.75

DINOSAUR REX
Upshot/Fantagraphics, 1987
1 thru 3 by Jan Strand & Henry Mayo	@3.00

DINOSAURS
Walt Disney
1 Citizen Robbie(From TV)	3.00

DINOSAURS ATTACK
Eclipse, 1991
1 HT,Based on Topps cards	3.50
2 and 3 HT,Based on cards	@3.50

DINOSAURS FOR HIRE
[1st Series] see: B&W
[2nd Series] Malibu, 1993–94
1 B:TMs(s),A:Reese,Archie, Lorenzo	3.00
2 thru 12	@2.50

DINO WARS:
EXTINCTION FILES
Antarctic Press, 2007
1	3.50

DINOWARS: JURASSIC
WAR OF THE WORLDS
Antarctic Press 2006
1 (of 4)	3.50
2 thru 4	@3.50

DISNEY ADVENTURES
Walt Disney
1	3.00
2	3.00
3 thru 13	@3.00
14 thru 28	@3.00

DISNEY COLOSSAL
COMICS COLLECTION
Walt Disney
1 inc.DuckTales, Chip'n'Dale	3.00
2 thru 9	@3.00

DISNEY COMICS IN 3-D
Walt Disney, 1992
1 F:Donald & Uncle Scrooge	3.00

DISNEY COMICS SPEC:
DONALD & SCROOGE
1 inc."Return to Xanadu"	9.00

DISNEY JUNIOR
Disney Press, 2006
GN #1 Finding Nemo	5.00
GN #2 Lilo & Stitch	5.00
GN #3 Disney's Tall Tails	5.00
GN #4 Kid Gravity	5.00

DISNEYLAND
BIRTHDAY PARTY
Gladstone, 1985
1 CB	15.00

DIVER DAN
Dell Publishing Co., Feb.-April, 1962
1	100.00
2	90.00

DIVINE INTERVENTION
WildStorm/DC, 1999
1	3.00
Wildcats, pt.2, JLe,SLo,RiB	3.00
Gen13, pt.3, JLe,SLo,RiB	3.00

DNAGENTS
Eclipse, 1983–85
1 O:DNAgents	4.00
2	3.00
3 thru 8	@2.50
9 DSp	2.50
10 thru 25	@2.50
See also: NEW DNAGENTS

DOC FRANKENSTEIN
Burlyman Entertainment, 2004
1	7.00
1a 2nd printing	4.00
2	5.00
3 thru 6	@3.50
3a thru 6a sketch (c)	@3.50

DOC SAVAGE
Gold Key, 1966
1	175.00

DOC SAVAGE
Millennium
1 V:Russians	2.50

DOC SAVAGE,
THE MAN OF BRONZE
Millennium, 1992
1 Monarch of Armageddon,pt.1	3.00
2 Monarch of Armageddon,pt.2	3.00
3 Monarch of Armageddon,pt.3	3.00
4 Monarch of Armageddon,pt.4	3.00

DOC SAVAGE:
DEVIL'S THOUGHTS
Millennium, 1992
1 V:Hanoi Shan	2.50
2 V:Hanoi Shan	2.50
3 Final issue	2.50

DOC SAVAGE:
DOOM DYNASTY
Millennium, 1991
1 and 2	@2.50

DOC SAVAGE:
MANUAL OF BRONZE
Millennium, 1992
1 Fact File	2.50

DOC SAVAGE: REPEL
Millennium, 1992
1 DvD(c) 2.50

DOCTOR BOOGIE
Media Arts, 1987
1 and 2 . . . . @2.50

DOCTOR CHAOS
Triumphant Comics, 1993
1 JnR(s),I:Doctor Chaos 2.50
2 JnR(s), ... 2.50
3 JnR(s),The Coming of
   the Cry,pt.1,I:Cry 2.50
4 JnR(s),The Coming of
   the Cry,pt.2,b:Ky'Li 2.50
5 JnR(s),E:Coming of the
   Cry,pt.3,V:Cry 2.50
6 Recovery 2.50
7 w/coupon 2.50
8 w/coupon 2.50
9 V:Mirth 2.50
10 Co. X #3 . . . . 2.50
11 Co. X #4 . . . . 2.50
12 A:Charlotte 2.50

DR. JJ
Narwain Publishing, 2006
1 The Devil's Psychologist 4.00

DR. KILDARE
Dell Publishing Co., April-June, 1962
1 . . . . 150.00
2 thru 9 . . . . @100.00

DOCTOR SOLAR MAN OF THE ATOM
Gold Key, 1962
1 BF,I:Dr. Solar 400.00
2 BF,I:Prof.Harbinger 150.00
3 BF,The Hidden Hands 125.00
4 BF,The Deadly Sea 125.00
5 BF,I:Dr.Solar in costume 150.00
6 FBe,I:Nuro 100.00
7 FBe,Vanishing Oceans 100.00
8 FBe,Thought Controller 100.00
9 FBe,Transivac The Energy
   Consuming Computer 100.00
10 FBe,The Sun Giant 100.00
11 FBe,V:Nuro 75.00
12 FBe,The Mystery of the
   Vanishing Silver 75.00
13 FBe,Meteor from 100 Mill.BC . . 75.00
14 FBe,Solar's Midas Touch 75.00
15 FBe O:Dr.Solar 100.00
16 FBe,V:Nuro 75.00
17 FBe,The Fatal Foe 75.00
18 FBe,The Mind Master 75.00
19 FBe,SolarV:Solar 75.00
20 AMc,Atomic Nightmares 75.00
21 AMc,Challenge from Outer
   Space. 50.00
22 AMc,Nuro,I:King Cybernoid . . . 50.00
23 AMc,A:King Cybernoid 50.00
24 EC,The Deadly Trio 50.00
25 EC,The Lost Dimension 50.00
26 EC,When Dimensions Collide. . 50.00
27 (1969) The Ladder to Mars . . . 50.00
28 (1981),1-pg AMc,The Dome
   of Mystery 40.00
29 DSp,FBe,Magnus 40.00
30 DSp,FBe,Magnus 40.00

DR. TOMORROW
Acclaim, 1997
1 (of 12) BL,Bart Simms finds
   Angel Computer 2.50

2 thru 12 BL . . . . @2.50

DOGS OF WAR
Defiant, 1994
1 F:Shooter,Ironhead 2.75
2 . . . . 2.50
3 Mouse Deserts 2.50
4 Schism Prequel 2.50
5 X-over 2.50
6 Aftermath 2.50

DOKTOR SLEEPLESS
Avatar Press, 2007
1 . . . . 4.00
2 thru 5 . . . . @4.00
1a thru 5a wraparound (c) . . . . . @4.00

DOLLMAN
Eternity, 1991
1 Movie adapt. sequel 2.50
2 V:Sprug & Braindead Gang 2.50
3 Toni Costa Kidnapped 2.50
4 . . . . 2.50

DOMINION
Boom! Studios, 2007
1 . . . . 4.00
2 thru 5 . . . . @4.00

Donald Duck #126 © Walt Disney

DONALD DUCK
Dell/Gold Key, 1962
85 thru 97 . . . . 75.00
98 rep. #46 CB 75.00
99 . . . . 65.00
100 . . . . 75.00
101 thru 111 . . . . @50.00
112 I:Moby Duck 60.00
113 thru 133 . . . . @50.00
134 CB rep. 50.00
135 CB rep. 50.00
136 thru 156 . . . . @40.00
157 CB rep. 40.00
158 thru 163 . . . . @40.00
164 CB rep. 40.00
165 thru 216 . . . . @30.00
Whitman, 1980
217 . . . . 30.00
218 . . . . 30.00
219 CB rep. 30.00
220 and 221 . . . . @50.00
222 scarce 300.00
223 thru 224 . . . . @75.00
225 thru 240 . . . . @30.00
241 thru 245 . . . . @35.00

Gladstone
246 CB,Gilded Man 25.00
247 CB 20.00
248 CB,Forbidden Valley 20.00
249 CB 20.00
250 CB,Pirate Gold 20.00
251 CB,Donald's Best Xmas 15.00
252 CB,Trail o/t Unicorn 8.00
253 CB 8.00
254 CB, in old Calif 9.00
255 CB 8.00
256 CB,Volcano Valley 8.00
257 CB,Forest Fire 8.00
258 thru 266 CB . . . . @8.00
267 thru 277 CB . . . . @8.00
278 CB 9.00
279 CB 9.00
280 thru 298 CB rep. . . . . @6.00
299 Life Guard Daze 5.00
300 Donald's 300th Triumph' 48pg . 6.00
301 The Gold Finder 5.00
302 Monkey Business 5.00
303 The Cantankerous Cat 5.00
304 Donald Duck Rants
   about Ants 5.00
305 Mockingbird Ridge 5.00
306 Worst Class Mail 5.00
307 Going to Sea. 5.00
308 Worst Class Mail 5.00

DONALD DUCK ADVENTURES
Gladstone, 1987
1 CB,Jungle Hi-Jinks 8.00
2 CB,Dangerous Disguise 6.00
3 CB,Lost in the Andes 6.00
4 CB,Frozen Gold 6.00
5 CB,Rosa 6.00
6 CB 3.00
7 CB 3.00
8 CB,Rosa 6.00
9 CB 3.00
10 CB 3.00
11 CB 3.00
12 CB,Rosa,Giant-size 6.00
13 CB,Rosa(c) 3.50
14 CB 3.00
15 CB 3.00
16 CB 3.00
17 CB 3.00
18 CB,No Such Varmint 3.00
19 CB 4.00
20 CB,Giant-size (1990) 4.00
21 CB,Rosa(c) (1993) 4.00
22 CB,The Pixilated Parrot 4.00
23 thru 30 . . . . @4.00
31 thru 40 . . . . @3.00
41 Bruce McDuck 3.00
42 The Saga of Sourdough Sam . . . 3.00
43 The Lost Charts of Columbus . . . 3.00
44 The Kitchy-Kaw Diamond 3.00
45 The Red Duck 3.00
46 . . . . 3.00
47 CB,Trick or Treat 3.00
48 The Saphead Factor 3.00

DONALD DUCK ADVENTURES
Walt Disney, 1990
1 Don Rosa, The Money Pit 6.00
2 CB 3.00
3 . . . . 3.00
4 CB 3.00
5 . . . . 3.00
6 . . . . 3.00
7 . . . . 3.00
8 . . . . 3.00
9 CB 3.00
10 Run-Down Runner 3.00
11 Whats for Lunch-Supper 3.00

12 Head of Rama Putra 3.00
13 JustAHumble,BumblingDuck . . . 3.00
14 CB,Day Gladstone's Luck
  Ran Out 4.00
15 A Tuft Luck Tale 3.00
16 Magica's Missin'Magic 3.00
17 CB,Secret of Atlantis 4.00
18 Crocodile Donald 3.00
19 Not So Silent Service 3.00
20 Ghost of Kamikaze Ridge 3.00
21 CB,The Golden Christmas Tree . 4.00
22 The Master Landscapist 5.00
23 The Lost Peg Leg Mine 3.00
24 On Stolen Time 4.00
25 Sense of Humor 3.00
26 CB,Race to the South Seas 4.00
27 CB,Nap in Nature 4.00
28 Olympic Tryout 3.00
29 CB,rep.March of Comics#20 . . . 4.00
30 A:The Vikings 3.00
31 The Sobbing Serpent of Loch
  McDuck 3.00
32 It Was No Occident 3.00
33 Crazy Christmas on Bear
  Mountain 3.00
34 Sup.Snooper Strikes Again 4.00
35 thru 38 CB rep . . . . @4.00

DONALD DUCK ALBUM
Dell Publishing Co.,
May-July, 1959
1 CB(c) 150.00
2 . . . . 100.00

DONALD DUCK
AND FRIENDS
Gemstone Publishing, 2003
308 thru 333 . . . . @3.00
334 thru 347 . . . . @3.00
348 . . . . 3.50

DONATELLO
Mirage, 1986
1 Teenage Mutant Ninja Turles . . . 10.00

DON BLUTH'S
DRAGON'S LAIR
Crossgen Comics, 2003
1 (of 6) Singe's Revenge 3.00
2 thru 3 . . . . @3.00

DON BLUTH'S
SPACE ACE
Crossgen Comics, 2003
1 (of 6) Defender of the Universe . . 3.00
2 thru 3 . . . . @3.00

DONE TO DEATH
Markosia, 2006
1 . . . . 3.50
2 thru 5 . . . . @3.50

DONNA MIA
Dark Fantasy Prod., 1995
1 I:Donna Mia 4.00
1a Deluxe Edition 5.00
1b signed & numbered
  (100 copies) 9.00
2 . . . . 3.00

DOOMSDAY + 1
Charlton, 1975–79
1 JBy,JBy(c) 35.00
2 JBy(c),P(c) 30.00
3 JBy,JBy(c),P(c) 25.00
4 JBy,JBy(c),P(c),I:Lok 25.00
5 and 6 JBy,JBy(c),P(c) . . . . . @25.00

7 thru 12 JBy,JBy(c),rep . . . . . @15.00

DOOMSDAY SQUAD
Fantagraphics, 1986
1 rep. JBy 3.00
2 rep. JBy 3.00
3 rep. SS,A:Usagi Yojimbo 3.00
4 thru 7, rep. JBy . . . . @3.00

Double-Dare Adventures #1
© Harvey Publications

DOUBLE DARE
ADVENTURES
Harvey Publications, 1966
1 I:B-man,Glowing Gladiator,
  Magicmaster 125.00
2 AW/RC rep. A:B-Man,Glowing
  Gladiator, Magicmaster 75.00

DOUBLE IMPACT
High Impact Studios, 1995–96
1 RCI,I:China & Jazz, chrome(c) . . 7.00
1 holographic rainbow (c) with
  certificate 12.00
1 rainbow (c), no certificate 9.00
1 chromium variant (c) 8.00
2 RCI,V:Castillo 3.00
2a signed, with certificate 4.00
3 China on cover 5.00
3a Jazzler on cover 3.00
3b Nikki on cover 3.00
3c Blondage 6.00
4 F:Mordred, The Rattler 3.00
4a Phoenix variant (c) 6.00
5 RCI 3.00
6 Buttshots 4.00
6a Jazz (c) 3.00
6a signed 6.00
7 I:Nikki Blade 3.00
8 . . . . 3.00
8a variant (c) 4.00
Gold edition, Lingerie special 3.00
Volume 2, 1996–97
0 RCI 3.00
1 RCI 3.00
1a deluxe edition 4.00
1b prism foil (c) 5.00
1c gold foil (c) 5.00
2 RCI 3.00
3 . . . . 3.00
3a special edition RCI(c) 8.00

DOROTHY
Illusive Arts Entertain., 2005
1 . . . . 5.00

1a 2nd printing 5.00
2 thru 4 . . . . @5.00
5 thru 8 . . . . @5.00

DOUBLE IMPACT: ALIVE
ABC Studios, 1999
1 RCI,F:China & Jazz 3.00
1a deluxe 7.00

DOUBLE IMPACT/
HELLINA
High Impact, 1996
1-shot RCI 3.00

DOUBLE IMPACT/
LETHAL STRYKE:
DOUBLE STRIKE
High Impact/London Night, 1996
1-shot RCI 3.00

DOUBLE IMPACT
SUICIDE RUN
High Impact, 1997
1 RCI 3.00
1 gold edition 10.00
1 platinum edition 20.00
2 . . . . 3.00
2a Suicide Cover 10.00

DOUBLE IMPACT: 2069
ABC Studios, 1999
1 RCI,Independent Day 3.00
1a premium edition 5.00
1b Sexy China ed. 5.00

DOUBLE LIFE OF
PRIVATE STRONG
Archie Publications, 1959
1 JSm/JK,I:Lancelot Strong/
  Shield, The Fly 1,100.00
2 JSm/JK,GT A:Fly 750.00

DRACULA
Dell, 1962
2 . . . . 60.00
3 thru 5 . . . . @40.00
6 thru 8 . . . . @25.00

DRACULA
Dell Publishing Co., 1966
1 see: Movie Classics
2 O:New Dracula (super-powers) . 75.00
3 Rain of Terror 50.00
4 The Origin of Fleeta 50.00
5 not published
6 rep. #2 (1972) 45.00
7 rep. #3 (1972) 35.00
8 rep. #4 (1973) 35.00

[BRAM STOKER'S]
DRACULA
Topps, 1992
1 MMi,Movie adaptation (trading
  cards in each issue) 5.00
1a Red Foil Logo 9.00
1b 2nd Print 3.00
2 MMi,Movie adapt.contd. 4.00
3 MMi,Movie adapt.contd. 4.00
4 MMi,Movie adapt.concludes 4.00

DRACULA CHRONICLES
Topps
1 True Story of Dracula 2.50
2 RTs,rep. Vlad #2 . . . . 2.50
3 RTs,rep. Vlad #3 . . . . 2.50

All comics prices listed are for *Near Mint* condition.

COLOR PUB.

DRACULA'S REVENGE
IDW Publishing, 2004
1 . . . . 4.00
2 . . . . 4.00

DRACULA VS CAPONE
Silent Devil Productions, 2006
1 (of 3) 3.00

DRACULA VS KING ARTHUR
Silent Devil Productions, 2005
1 . . . . 3.00
2 . . . . 3.00
3 . . . . 3.00
4 . . . . 5.00

DRACULA VS ZORRO
Topps, 1993
1 DMg(s),TY,Black(c), ... 3.25
2 DMg(s),TY,w/Zorro #0 . . . . 3.00

DRACULA: VLAD THE IMPALER
Topps, 1993
1 EM,I:Vlad Dracua, w/cards 3.25
1a Red Foil 10.00
2 EM, w/cards 3.25
3 EM,w/cards 3.00

DRAFTED
Devil's Due, 2007
Preview 1.00
1 . . . . 3.50
2 . . . . 3.50

DRAGONFLIGHT
Eclipse, 1991
1 Anne McCaffrey adapt. 5.00
2 novel adapt 5.00
3 novel adapt 5.00

DRAGONFLY
AC Comics, 1985
1 . . . . 3.50
2 thru 8 . . . . @2.00

DRAGONLANCE: CHRONICLES
Devil's Due Publishing, 2005
Vol. 1 Dragons of Autumn Twilight
1 (of 8) 3.00
1B signed edition 9.00
2 thru 3 . . . . @3.00
2a thru 3a collector's edition . . . @6.00
4 thru 8 . . . . @3.00
4a thru 8a collector's edition . . . . @6.00
Spec. rep. #1 & #2 . . . . 6.00
Vol. II Dragons of Winter Night
1 (of 4) 5.00
1a cardstock (c) 8.00
2 thru 4 . . . . @5.00
2a thru 4a cardstock (c) . . . . @9.00
Vol. III Dragons of Spring Dawning
1 . . . . 3.50
1a variant prestige (c) . . . . @5.50
2 thru 9 . . . . @3.50
2a thru 9a variant prestige (c) . . @5.50

DRAGONLANCE: THE LEGEND OF HUMA
Devil's Due Publishing, 2004
1 . . . . 3.00

1a variant (c) 3.00
2 thru 6 . . . . @3.00

DRAGONPRO
Antarctic Press, 2006
0 . . . . 3.50

DRAGONRING
Aircel, 1987–88, Vol. 2
1 . . . . 3.50
2 O:Dragonring 2.50
3 thru 15 . . . . @2.50
See also: B&W

DRAGON'S LAIR
Arcana Studio, 2006
1 . . . . 5.00
2 . . . . 3.00
3 thru 4 . . . . @4.00

Drag-Strip Hotrodders #6
© Charlton

DRAG-STRIP HOTRODDERS
Charlton 1963
1 . . . . 125.00
2 thru 5 . . . . @75.00
6 thru 16 . . . . @60.00
Becomes:

WORLD OF WHEELS
Charlton, 1967
17 thru 21 . . . . @40.00
22 thru 32 . . . . @35.00

DRAKKON WARS, THE
Realm Press, 1997
0 by Richard Hatch & Chris Scalf . . 3.00
1 . . . . 3.00

DREADSTAR
First, 1986–91
27 JSn,from Epic,traitor 3.00
28 thru 49 . . . . @3.00
50 JSn,AMe,Pawns 4.25
51 thru 64 . . . . @4.00

DREADSTAR
Malibu Bravura, 1994–95
1 JSn(c),PDd(s),EC,I:New Dreadstar (Kalla),w/stamp 2.75
2 JSn(c),PDd(s),EC,w/stamp 2.50
3 JSn(c),PDd(s),EC,w/stamp 2.75
4 PDd,EC,Kalla's origin,w/stamp . . 2.50

---

5 PDd,F:Vanth,w/stamp 2.50
6 PDd,w/stamp 2.50

DREAMLAND CHRONICLES, THE
Astonish Comics, 2003
1 . . . . 3.50
2 . . . . 3.50
Alias Enterprises, 2005
2 (of 4) 4.50
3 . . . . 4.50

DREAMS OF THE DARKCHYLDE
Darkchylde Entertainment, 2000
1 RQu,BPe 3.00
2 thru 6 . . . . @3.00
4a Fear 2001 edition 6.00

DREDD RULES
Fleetway/Quality, 1991–93
1 SBs(c),JBy,Prev.unpubl. in USA . 5.00
2 inc.Eldster Ninja Mud Wrestling Vigilantes 3.50
3 inc.That Sweet Stuff. 3.50
4 Our Man in Hondo City 3.50
5 thru 17 . . . . @3.25
18 F:Jonny Cool. 3.00
19 V:Hunter's Club 3.00
20 . . . . 4.00

DRIFT MARLO
Dell Publishing Co., May-July, 1962
1 . . . . 90.00
2 . . . . 70.00

DRUNKEN FIST
Jademan, 1988
1 . . . . 3.25
2 . . . . 2.50
3 thru 9 . . . . @2.00
10 thru 53 . . . . @2.00

DUCKMAN
Topps, 1994
1 USA Cartoon 2.50
2 XXX Files 2.50
3 I:King Chicken 2.50
4 V:Toys 2.50
5 F:Cornfed 2.50
6 Star Trek Parody 2.50
7 rep. 1990 B&W 1st app., now in color 2.50

DUCKMAN: THE MOB FROG SAGA
Topps, 1994
1 I:Mob Frog 2.50
2 D:Mob Frog 2.50
3 In the Name of the Duck 2.50

DUCK TALES
Gladstone, 1990
1 CB(r)I:LaunchpadMcQuck 7.00
2 CB(r) 4.00
3 . . . . 4.00
4 CB(r) 4.00
5 thru 11 . . . . @4.00
12 & 13 . . . . @5.00

DUCK TALES
Walt Disney, 1990
1 Scrooge's Quest:The Ice Demon 4.00
2 thru 19 . . . . @3.00

DUDLEY DO-RIGHT
Charlton Comics, 1970–71
1 From TV series 150.00
2 thru 7 . . . . @125.00

DUEL MASTERS
Dreamwave, 2003
1 . . . . 3.00
1a variant (c)s . . . . @3.00
2 thru 8 . . . . @3.00
Pocket Edition Vol. 2 . . . . 11.00

DUMMY'S GUIDE TO DANGER, A
Viper Comics, 2006
1 (of 4) 3.25
2 thru 4 . . . . @3.25

DUNC & LOO
Dell Publishing Co., 1961
1 . . . . 150.00
2 . . . . 125.00
3 thru 8 . . . . @75.00

DUNGEONS & DRAGONS: THE LOST CITY
Twenty First Century, 1999
1 (of 6) game tie-in 5.00
2 thru 6 . . . . @5.00

DUNGEONS & DRAGONS: AMBER CASTLE
Twenty First Century, 2000
1 (of 6) game tie-in 5.00

DUNGEONS & DRAGONS: TEMPEST'S GATE
Kenzer & Company, 2001
1 (of 4) Born of Fire 3.00
2 Forged in Tears 3.00
3 Tempered in Fellowship 3.00
4 Sheathed in Justice 3.00

DUNGEONS AND DRAGONS: WHERE SHADOWS FALL
Kenzer & Company, 2003
1 (of 5) 3.50
2 thru 5 . . . . @3.50

DWIGHT D. EISENHOWER
Dell Publishing Co., 1969
1 . . . . 75.00

DYNAMO
Tower Comics, 1966
1 WW,MSy,RC,SD,I:Andor . . . 150.00
2 WW,DA,GT,MSy,Weed solo
   story A:Iron Maiden 100.00
3 WW,GT,Weed solo story,
   A:Iron Maiden 100.00
4 WW,DA,A:Iron Maiden 100.00

DYNAMO JOE
First, 1986–87
1 . . . . 3.00
2 . . . . 2.50
3 thru 14 . . . . @2.50
Spec.#1 . . . . 2.50

EARTH 4
Continuity, 1993
1 Deathwatch 2000 Pt.6,w/card . . . 2.50
2 Deathwatch 2000 Pt.11,w/card . . 2.50

3 V:Hellbenders, w/card 2.50
[2nd Series]
1 WMc 2.50
2 thru 3 . . . . @2.50

EAST MEETS WEST
Innovation
1 . . . . 2.50
2 thru 3 . . . . @2.50

EBERRON: EYE OF THE WOLF
Devil's Due Publishing, 2006
1-shot 5.00
1-shot-a cardstock (c) 9.00

ECHO OF FUTUREPAST
Continuity, 1984–85
1 NA,MGo,I:Bucky O'Hare,
   Frankenstein 4.00
2 NA,MGo,A:Bucky O'Hare, Dracula,
Werewolf 3.50
3 NA,MGo,A:Bucky 3.50
4 NA,MGo,A:Bucky 3.50
5 NA,MGo,A:Drawla&Bucky 3.50
6 Ath,B:Torpedo 3.50
7 ATh 3.50
8 Ath, ... 3.25
9 Ath,Last issue 3.25

ECLIPSE GRAPHIC NOVELS
Eclipse
1 Axa 7.00
2 MR,I Am Coyote 7.00
3 DSt,Rocketeer 9.00
3a hard cover 30.00
4 Silver Heels 9.00
4a hard cover 30.00
5 Sisterhood of Steel 9.00
6 Zorro in Old Calif. 8.00

ECLIPSE MONTHLY
Eclipse, 1983–84
1 SD,DW,I:Static&Rio 2.50
2 GC,DW 2.50
3 thru 10 DW . . . . @2.50

EDGAR RICE BURROUGHS' A PRINCESS OF MARS
IDW Publishing, 2006
1 . . . . 4.00

EDGE
Malibu Bravura, 1994–95
1 GK,I:Edge 2.50
2 GK,STg,Gold Stamp 2.50
3 GK,The Ultimates 2.50
4 GK,V:Mr. Ultimate 2.50

EDGE OF CHAOS
Pacific, 1983
1 GM 2.50
2 GM 2.50
3 GM 2.50

EIGHT LEGGED FREAKS
WildStorm/DC, 2002
Spec. movie adapt. 64-pg. 7.00

87th PRECINCT
Dell Publishing Co., April-June, 1962
1 BK 200.00
2 . . . . 175.00

El Arsenal #2 © Arcana Studio

EL ARSENAL
Arcana Studio, 2005
1 (of 3) 3.00
2 thru 3 . . . . @3.00

EL CAZADOR
Crossgen Comics, 2003
1 CDi,SEp 3.00
2 thru 3 CDi,SEp . . . . @3.00
4 thru 8 . . . . @3.00
Spec. #1 Bloody Ballad of
   Blackjack Tom 3.00

ELEMENTALS
Comico, 1984–88
1 BWg,I:Destroyers 5.00
2 BWg 3.50
3 BWg 3.50
4 thru 12 BWg . . . . @3.00
13 thru 22 . . . . @3.00
23 thru 29 . . . . @3.00
Spec.#1 . . . . 3.00
Spec.#2 . . . . 3.00
[Second Series], 1989–94
1 . . . . 3.00
2 thru 4 . . . . @3.00
5 thru 28 . . . . @3.00
Spec.#1 Lingerie special 3.00
GN The Natural Order, rep. 10.00
GN Death & Resurrection 13.00
[Third Series], 1995
1 R:Elementals, polybagged with
   Chrysalis promo card 3.00
2 R:Original Monolith, polybagged
   with Chrysalis promo card 3.00
3A Destroy the Shadowspear 3.00
3B variant cover 3.00
4 Memoirs,pt.1 . . . . 3.00
5 Memoirs,pt.2 . . . . 3.00
GN Ghost of a Chance 6.00
Spec. Babes, photo multimedia
   bikini special 4.00
Spec. Hot Bikini Valentine 4.00
Spec. All New Summer Special . . . 5.00
Spec.#1 Lingerie Metalite 4.00

ELEMENTALS: HOW THE WAR WAS ONE
Comico, 1996
1 . . . . 3.00
2 . . . . 3.00
3 . . . . 3.00
4 . . . . 3.00

ELEMENTALS: THE VAMPIRE'S REVENGE
Comico, 1996–97
1 thru 4 . . . . @3.00

ELEMENTALS VS. THE CHARNEL PRIESTS
Comico, 1996
Spec. 1 (of 2) 3.00
2 . . . . 3.00

ELFLORD
Aircel, 1986–88
Volume 1: See B&W
Volume II
1 . . . . 3.50
2 . . . . 3.00
3 thru 20 . . . . @3.00
21 double size 5.00
22 thru 24 . . . . @3.00
Spec.#1 . . . . 3.00
25 thru 32, see B&W

ELFQUEST: BLOOD OF TEN CHIEFS
Warp Graphics, 1993–95
1 WP 3.00
2 WP 3.00
3 WP,B:Swift Spear pt. 1 . . . . 3.00
4 WP,B:Swift Spear pt. 2 . . . . 3.00
5 thru 20 . . . . @3.00

ELFQUEST: HIDDEN YEARS
Warp Graphics, 1992
1 WP 3.00
2 WP, w/coupon promo. 3.00
3 WP, w/coupon promo.Cont.sty.
    previewed in Harbinger#11 . . . . 3.50
4 WP,w/coupon 3.00
5 WP,O:Skywise 3.00
6 WP,F:Timmain 3.00
7 F:Timmain 3.00
8 Daughter's Day 3.00
9 WP(s),Enemy Face 3.00
9 1/2 WP,JBy,Holiday Spec. 3.50
10 thru 14 WP . . . . @3.00
15 WP Wolfrider Tribe Splits 3.50
16 thru 18 WP 3.00
19 thru 24 . . . . @3.00
25 B&W Wolfrider's Death 3.00
26 thru 29 B&W finale . . . . @3.00

ELFQUEST: JINK
Warp Graphics, 1994–96
1 Future 3.50
2 thru 7 . . . . @3.00
8 B&W V:Black Snakes 3.00
9 thru 12 . . . . 3.00

ELFQUEST: NEW BLOOD
Warp Graphics, 1992–96
1 JBy,artists try Elfquest 5.00
2 Barry Blair story 3.50
3 thru 5 . . . . @3.00
6 thru 31 . . . . @3.00
32 B&W Sorrow's End 3.00
33 thru 35 B&W 3.00
Summer Spec.1993 . . . . 4.25

ELFQUEST: THE REBELS
Warp Graphics, 1994–96
1 Aliens, set several hundred
    years in future 3.00
2 thru 8 . . . . @3.00

Elfquest: New Blood #17
© *Warp Graphics*

9 B&W Brother vs. Brother 3.00
10 thru 12 . . . . @3.00

ELFQUEST: SHARDS
Warp Graphics, 1994–96
1 Division 3.50
2 thru 5 . . . . @3.00
6 thru 11 . . . . @3.00
12 B&W F:High One Timmain 3.00
13 thru 16 B&W finale . . . . @3.00

ELFQUEST: WAVE DANCERS
Warp Graphics, 1993–96
1 Foil enhanced 3.50
2 thru 6 . . . . @3.00
Spec. #1 . . . . 3.00

ELIMINATOR COLOR SPECIAL
Eternity, 1991
1 DDo(c) set in the future 3.00

ELIMINATOR
Malibu Ultraverse, 1995
0 Man,DJa,MZ,Zothros tries to re-
    open passage to the Godwheel 3.00
1 MZ,Man,DRo, The Search for the
    Missing Infinity Gems,I:Siren . . . 3.00
1a Black Cover ed. 4.00
2 MZ 2.50
3 MZ, Infinity Gem tie-in,finale 2.50

ELK'S RUN
Hoarse and Buggy Prod., 2005
1 . . . . 3.00
2 thru 3 . . . . @3.00
Speakeasy Comics, 2005
4 thru 7 . . . . @3.00

ELRIC
Pacific, 1983–84
1 CR,MGi,Michael Moorcock adapt 4.00
2 CR,MGi,Elric of Melnibone 3.00
3 thru 6 CR,MGi . . . . @3.00

ELRIC (ONE LIFE)
Topps, 1996
0 NGa,CPR, One Life, based on
    Michael Moorcock character . . . 3.00

ELRIC, THE BANE OF THE BLACK SWORD
First, 1988–89
1 Michael Moorcock adapt 3.00
2 . . . . 3.00
3 thru 6 . . . . @3.00

ELRIC, SAILOR ON THE SEAS OF FATE
First, 1985–86
1 Michael Moorcock adapt 4.00
2 thru 7 . . . . @3.00

ELRIC, THE VANISHING TOWER
First, 1987–88
1 Michael Moorcock adapt 3.00
2 thru 6 . . . . @3.00

ELRIC, THE WEIRD OF THE WHITE WOLF
First, 1986–87
1 Michael Moorcock adapt 3.00
2 thru 5 . . . . @3.00
Graphic Novel CR 7.00

ELSINORE
Alias Enterprises, 2005
1 (of 9) 1.00
2 thru 7 . . . . @3.00
Elsinore Case Files #1: Arrivals 3.00

ELSINORE
Devil's Due Publishing, 2006
4 . . . . 4.00
5 thru 9 . . . . @3.25

ELVEN
Malibu Ultraverse, 1994
0 Rep.,A:Prime, double size 3.00
Mini-Series 1994–95
1 A:Prime, Primevil 2.50
2 AaL,R:Maxi-Man 2.50
3 AaL,V:Duey, Primevil 2.50
4 AaL,F:Primevil 2.50

E-MAN
Charlton Comics, 1973–75
1 JSon,O:E-Man 35.00
2 SD 20.00
3 . . . . 20.00
4 SD 20.00
5 SD,Miss Liberty Belle 20.00
6 JBy,Rog 2000 . . . . 20.00
7 JBy,Rog 2000 . . . . 20.00
8 J:Nova 25.00
9 JBy,Rog 2000 . . . . 20.00
10 JBy,Rog 2000 . . . . 20.00

E-MAN
First, 1983
1 JSon,O:E-Man & Nova, A:Rog
    2000, 1 pg. JBy 3.00
2 JSon,I:F-Men (X-Men satire) 1-
    page Mike Mist 2.50
3 thru 25 JSon . . . . @2.50
Spec. #1 . . . . 2.75

E-MAN
Comico, 1989–90
1 JSon 2.75
2 and 3 JSon . . . . @2.50

E-MAN
Alpha Productions, 1993
1 JSon 2.75

E-MAN: RECHARGED
Digital Webbing, 2006
1-shot 4.00

EMERGENCY
Charlton Comics, 1976
1 JSon(c),JBy 45.00
2 JSon 25.00
3 Thru 4 . . . . 25.00

ENCHANTED:
THE AWAKENING
Sirius, 1998
1 by Robert Chang 3.00
2 . . . . 3.00
3 conclusion 3.00

END OF STORY:
MITRABHED
Virgin Comics, 2007
1 . . . . 3.00
2 . . . . 3.00
3 Panchatantra 3.00

ENGINE
Shadow Planet, 2002
1 by Tim Tyler 3.50
1a signed sketch edition 10.00
2 thru 3 . . . . @3.00

ENIGMA CIPHER, THE
Boom! Studios, 2006
1 (of 5) 4.00
2 . . . . 4.00

ENIGMAS, THE
Digital Webbing, 2006
1-shot 6.00

ENSIGN O'TOOLE
Dell Publishing Co., 1962
1 . . . . 50.00
2 . . . . 40.00

EPSILON WAVE, THE
Independent, 1985
1 Darkest Before Dawn 3.00
2 Tango in Texas City 2.50
3 One More Step Toward Darkness 2.50
4 Afterlife 2.50
Elite Comics, 1986
5 thru 10 . . . . @2.50

ESC.(ESCAPE)
Comico, 1996
1 SPr. 3.00
2 thru 4 SPr. . . . . @3.00

ESC: NO EXIT
Comico, 1997
1 . . . . 3.00
1 medallion edition 10.00
2 . . . . 3.00

ESCAPE OF
THE LIVING DEAD
Avatar Press, 2005
1 . . . . 4.00
1a Wraparound (c) 4.00
1b Variant(c)s . . . . @4.00
2 thru 5 . . . . @4.00
2a thru 5a wraparound (c)s . . . . @4.00
2b thru 5b variant (c)s . . . . @4.00
Ann. #1 . . . . 5.00
Ann. #1a variant (c)s 5.00

ESCAPE OF THE
LIVING DEAD: AIRBORNE
Avatar Press, 2006
1 . . . . 4.00
2 thru 3 . . . . @4.00
1a thru 2a wraparound (c) 4.00
1b thru 3b variant (c)s . . . . @4.00

ESCAPE OF THE
LIVING DEAD: FEARBOOK
Avatar Press, 2006
1 . . . . 4.00
1a wraparound (c) 4.00
1b variant (c)s . . . . @4.00

ESPERS
Eclipse, 1986
1 I:ESPers. 3.00
2 JBo(c),V:Terrorists 3.00
3 V:Terrorists 3.00
4 Beirut 3.00
5 The Liquidators 3.00
6 V:Benito Giovanetti 3.00

Espionage #1
© Dell Publishing Co.

ESPIONAGE
Dell Publishing Co.,
May-July, 1964
1 . . . . 75.00
2 . . . . 50.00

ESTABLISHMENT, THE
WildStorm/DC, 2001
1 IEd,CAd,F:Charlie Arrows 2.50
2 IEd,CAd 2.50
3 IEd,CAd 2.50
4 IEd,CAd 2.50
5 IEd,CAd 2.50
6 IEd,CAd 2.50
7 IEd,CAd 2.50
8 IEd,CAd, in Russia 2.50
9 IEd,CAd, demon-god embryos . . 2.50
10 IEd,CAd, Charlie Arrows 2.50
11 IEd,CAd, DeadSpace 2.50
12 IEd,CAd, Moonbase Straker . . . 2.50
13 IEd,CAd, final issue 2.50

ESTANCIA
Hammock Entertainment, 2006
1 (of 17) 3.50
2 . . . . 3.50
3 thru 7 . . . . @3.50

ETERNAL WARRIOR
Valiant, 1992
1 FM(c),JDx,Unity #2,O:Eternal
  Warrior,Armstrong 4.00
1a Gold Ed. 12.00
1b Gold Foil Logo 20.00
2 thru 10 . . . . @3.00
11 thru 49 . . . . @3.50
50 . . . . 9.00
Yearbook #1 . . . . 4.25
Yearbook #2 . . . . 4.00
Wings of Justice WWI 2.50
Quarterly
Time and Treachery 4.00
Digital Alchemy 4.00
Spec. Blackworks AHo, ... 4.00

ETERNAL WARRIORS
Acclaim, 1997
Quarterly
Archer & Armstrong AHo 4.00
Mog AHo 4.00
The Immortal Enemy AHo 4.00

ETERNITY SMITH
Renegade, 1986
1 thru 5 . . . . @3.50
[Vol. 2] Hero, 1987
1 thru 9 . . . . @2.50
Heroic Publishing
1 Man Vs. Machine. 2.50
2 Man Vs. Machine. 2.50

EVA THE IMP
Red Top Comic/Decker, 1957
1 . . . . 50.00
2 . . . . 50.00

EVANGELINE
Comico, 1984
1 Guns of Mars 4.00
2 . . . . 3.00
Lodestone, 1986
1 . . . . 2.50
2 . . . . 2.50
First, 1988
1 . . . . 3.00
2 thru 9 . . . . @2.50
10 thru 12 . . . . @2.00

EVERQUEST
WildStorm/DC, 2001
GN The Ruins of Kunark, JLe 6.00
GN Transformation. 6.00

EVERYTHING'S ARCHIE
Archie Publications, 1969
1 Giant 125.00
2 Giant 75.00
3 thru 5 Giant . . . . @50.00
6 thru 10 Giant . . . . @35.00
11 thru 20 . . . . @25.00
21 thru 40 . . . . @15.00
41 thru 134 . . . . @10.00

EVIL ERNIE (THE SERIES)
Chaos! Comics, 1998
1 V:Purgatori 3.00
2 Search for Chastity, A:Savior. . . . 3.00
3 V:Purgatori 3.00
4 return to New Jersey 3.00
5 two beings 3.00
6 heart of America 3.00
7 Unholy Nights 3.00
8 Trauma,pt.1 . . . . 3.00
9 Trauma,pt.2 . . . . 3.00
10 Trauma,pt.3. . . . . 3.00

COLOR PUB.

EVIL ERNIE: DEPRAVED
Chaos! Comics, 1999
1 (of 3) 4.00
1a premium edition 9.00
2 . . . . 3.00
3 . . . . 3.00

Evil Ernie: Destroyer #8
© Chaos! Comics

EVIL ERNIE: DESTROYER
Chaos! Comics, 1997
Prev.#1 . . . . 3.00
1 (of 9) BnP 3.00
2 BnP 3.00
3 to Atlanta 3.00
4 siege of Atlanta 3.00
5 . . . . 3.00
6 Nuclear launch codes 3.00
7 Nuclear attack 3.00
8 Nuclear attack continues 3.00
9 New forms of living dead, concl. . 3.00

EVIL ERNIE IN SANTA FE
Devil's Due Publishing, 2005
1 . . . . 3.00
2 thru 4 . . . . @3.00

EVIL ERNIE: REVENGE
Chaos! Comics, 1994–95
1 SHu,BnP,A:LadyDeath,glow(c) . . 7.00
1a limited, glow-in-the-dark (c) . . . 15.00
1a Commemorative edition 12.00
2 SHu,BnP,Loses Smiley 6.00
3 SHu,BnP,V:Dr. Price 5.00
4 SHu,BnP,Final Issue 5.00

EVIL ERNIE:
STRAIGHT TO HELL
Chaos! Comics, 1995–96
1 Rampage in Hell, coffin(c) 4.00
1 limited, chromium edition 15.00
2 Cremator 4.00
3 . . . . 4.00
3a Chastity (c). 18.00
4 and 5 . . . . @4.00
Ashcan 1.50
Spec. 20.00

EVIL ERNIE:
THE RESURRECTION
Chaos! Comics, 1993–94
1 R:Evil Ernie 15.00

1a gold edition 35.00
2 Enhanced Cover 11.00
3 Massive Mayhem Lady Death
    poster 11.00
4 final issue, extra pages 11.00
Ashcan Resurrection (2001) 20.00

EVIL ERNIE VS.
THE MOVIE MONSTERS
Chaos! Comics
1 one-shot 3.00
1 omega edition 5.00
1 premium edition, signed 15.00

EVIL ERNIE VS.
THE SUPER-HEROES
Chaos! Comics, 1995
1 one-shot 3.50
1a foil (c) 30.00
1b limited 10.00
Spec. #2 by Hart Fisher
    & Steve Butler 3.00
Spec. #2, Premium edition 10.00

EVIL ERNIE:
WAR OF THE DEAD
Chaos! Comics, 1999
1 (of 3) 3.00
1a premium. 10.00
2 . . . . 3.00
3 concl. 3.00

EVIL ERNIE'S
BADDEST BATTLES
Chaos! Comics, 1996
1-shot, imaginary battles. 3.00

EXALTED
Udon Entertainment, 2005
1 . . . . 3.50
1 Power foil (c) 12.50
2 thru 4 . . . . @3.50
5 40-page 5.00
2a thru 5a Power foil (c)s . . . . . @12.50

EXECUTIONER
Innovation, 1993
1 Don Pendleton(s),F:Mack Bolan . 4.00
1a Collector's Gold Ed. 3.00
1b Tyvek cover 4.00
2 War against Mafia 2.75
3 War against Mafia,pt.3 . . . . 2.75

EXEMPLARS
1 and 2 . . . . @2.50

EXILES
Malibu Ultraverse, 1993
1 TMs(s),PaP,I:Exiles 4.00
1a w/out card 2.50
1b Gold hologram ed. 10.00
1c Ultra-limited 12.00
2 V:Kort. 3.00
3 BWS,Mastodon,BU:Rune 4.00
4 V:Kort 3.00

EX MACHINA
Wildstorm/DC, 2004
1 F:Mitchell Hundred,40-pg. 3.00
2 thru 5 State of Emergency . . . . @3.00
6 Tag, pt.1. . . . . 3.00
7 Tag, pt.2. . . . . 3.00
8 Tag, pt.3. . . . . 3.00
9 Tag, pt.4. . . . . 3.00
10 Tag, pt.5 . . . . 3.00
11 V:Fortune Tellers 3.00
12 Fact vs. Fiction, pt.1 . . . . 3.00

13 Fact vs. Fiction, pt.2 . . . . 3.00
14 Fact vs. Fiction, pt. 3 . . . . 3.00
15 Off the Grid, pt.1 . . . . 3.00
16 Off the Grid, pt.2 . . . . 3.00
17 March to War, pt.1 . . . . 3.00
18 March to War, pt.2 . . . . 3.00
19 March to War, pt.3 . . . . 3.00
20 March to War, pt.4 . . . . 3.00
21 Smoke, Smoke, pt.1 . . . . 3.00
22 Smoke, Smoke, pt.2 . . . . 3.00
23 Smoke, Smoke, pt.3 . . . . 3.00
24 Smoke, Smoke, pt.4 . . . . 3.00
25 Bradbury, Chief of Security. . . . 3.00
26 Power Down, Pt. 1 . . . . 3.00
27 Power Down, Pt. 2 . . . . 3.00
28 Power Down, Pt. 3 . . . . 3.00
29 Power Down, Pt. 4 . . . . 3.00
30 Ex Cathedra, pt.1 . . . . 3.00
31 Ex Cathedra, pt.2 . . . . 3.00
Spec. #1 Inside the Machine 3.00
Spec. Masquerade Special (2007). . 3.50
Spec. #1 Mayor Hundred's past. . . 3.00
Spec. #2 Life and Death 3.00

EX-MUTANTS
Malibu, Nov. 1992–Apr. 1994
1 I&O:Ex-Mutants 2.50
2 thru 18 . . . . @2.50

EXO-SQUAD
Topps, 1994
[Mini-Series]
0 . . . . 2.50
1 From Animated Series 2.50
2 F:Nara Burns 2.50
3 V:Neo-Sapiens 2.50

EXPLORERS
Explorer Press, 1995
1 I:Explorers 3.00
2 The Cellar 3.00

EXPOSURE SPECIAL
Avatar Press, 2000
1 . . . . 3.50
1a photo(c) 3.50

EXPOSURE:
SECOND COMING
Avatar Press, 2000
1 (of 2) Angel (c) 40-page 5.00

EXTINCTIONERS
Vision Comics, 1998
1 by Shawntae Howard &
    Malcolm Earle 4.00
2 . . . . 4.00

EXTINCTION EVENT
Wildstorm/DC, 2003
1 (of 5) BBh,humans vs. dinos 2.50
2 thru 5 BBh . . . . @2.50

EXTRA
Gemstone, 1999
1 (of 5) 2.50
2 thru 4 . . . . @2.50
5 final issue. 2.50

EXTREMES VIOLET
Blackout Comics, 1995
0 I:Violet 3.00
Becomes:

EXTREMES OF VIOLET
Blackout Comics, 1995
1 V:Drug Lords 3.00
2 A:Matt Chaney 3.00

EYE OF THE STORM
Rival Productions
1 I:Killian, Recon, Finesse, Stray . . 3.00
2 Conspiracy 3.00
3 3-D Comic Background 3.00
4 F:Recon 3.00
5 Sinclair & Rott 3.00
Ann. 48-pg. 5.00

EZRA
Arcana Studio, 2004
1 . . . . 3.00
2 thru 3 . . . . @3.00
4 . . . . 3.00

EZRA: EVOKED EMOTIONS
Arcana Studio, 2006
1 (of 3) 4.00
2 thru 3 . . . . @4.00

FADE FROM GRACE
Beckett Comics, 2004
1 . . . . 2.50
2 thru 5 . . . . @2.50

FALLEN ANGEL
IDW Publishing, 2005
2 PDd 4.00
3 thru 11 PDd . . . . @4.00
12 thru 21 . . . . @4.00

FALL OF CTHULHU, THE
Boom! Studios, 2007
0 . . . . 4.00
0a variant (c) 4.00
1 . . . . 4.00
1a 4.00
2 thru 9 . . . . @4.00
2a thru 9a variant (c) . . . . @4.00

FAMILY AFFAIR
Gold Key, 1970
1 W/Poster,Ph(c). 100.00
2 . . . . 50.00
3 Ph(c) 50.00
4 Ph(c) 50.00

FAMILY GUY
Devil's Due Publishing, 2006
1 100 Ways to Kill Lots 6.00

Fantastic Voyage #1
© Gold Key

2 Family Comes First 6.00
3 Books Don't Taste Very Good . . . 6.00
4 48-pgs. 6.00

FAMOUS INDIAN TRIBES
Dell Publishing Co., 1962
1 . . . . 27.00
2 . . . . 15.00

FANTASTIC VOYAGE
Gold Key, 1969
1 . . . . 90.00
2 . . . . 65.00

FANTASTIC VOYAGES OF SINBAD, THE
Gold Key, 1965
1 Ph(c) 125.00
2 June, 1967 . . . . 100.00

FANTASY FEATURES
AC Comics, 1987
1 . . . . 3.00
2 . . . . 3.00

FARO KORBIT
APC, 2003
1 (of 4) 3.50
2 thru 4 . . . . @3.50

FARSCAPE: WAR TORN
WildStorm/DC, 2001
1 (of 2) MWm, F:John Crichton . . . 5.00
2 MWm,48-page 5.00

FAT ALBERT
Gold Key, 1974–79
1 . . . . 50.00
2 . . . . 35.00
3 thru 10 . . . . @35.00
11 thru 29 . . . . @30.00

FATALE
Broadway, 1995
1 thru 6 JJo, Inherit the
  Earth, pt.5 . . . . @3.00
7 Fatale now Queen of the World. . 3.00
8 Crown of Thorns, pt.2 . . . . 3.00
9 Crown of Thorns, pt.3 . . . . 3.00

FATE'S FIVE
Innervision, 1998
1 (of 4) 2.50
1 variant cover 2.50
2 (of 4) 2.50
3 (of 4) 2.50

FATHOM
Comico, 1987
1 thru 3 From Elementals . . . . . . @2.50
[2nd Series], 1993
1 thru 3 . . . . @2.50
Aspen, 2005
0 . . . . 2.50
1 . . . . 3.00
1a signed 30.00
2 thru 4 . . . . @3.00
5 thru 11 . . . . @3.00
1-shot Fathom Beginnings 2.00

FATHOM: DAWN OF WAR
Aspen, 2003
0 . . . . 2.50
1 . . . . 3.00
2 thru 3 . . . . @3.00
Spec. Cannon Hawke #1 . . . . 3.00

FATHOM: KIANI
Aspen MLT, 2006
0 . . . . 2.50
1 thru 4 . . . . @3.00

FATHOM KILLIAN'S VESSEL
Aspen MLT, 2007
1 . . . . 3.00
1a variant (c) 3.00

FATMAN, THE HUMAN FLYING SAUCER
Lightning Comics, 1967
1 CCB,O:Fatman & Tin Man . . . 100.00
2 CCB 75.00
3 CCB,(Scarce). 80.00

FAUST: BOOK OF M
Avatar Press, 1999
1 (of 3) DQ,TV 4.00
1a (of 3) prism foil (c) 11.00
1b signed, leather cover 18.00
1c Royal Blue edition 60.00
2 . . . . 4.00
3 . . . . 4.00

FEARBOOK
Eclipse
1 SBi,RV,A Dead Ringer 2.50

FEAR THE DEAD
Boom! Studios, 2006
GN A Zombie Survivor's Journal . . . 6.00

FELIX THE CAT
Harvey, 1991
1 thru 4 . . . . @4.00
5 thru 7 . . . . @3.00

FELIX THE CAT: THE MOVIE
Felix Comics, 1998
1-shot, issued a mere 10 years
  after movie 4.00

FELIX'S NEPHEWS INKY & DINKY
Harvey Publications, 1957
1 . . . . 125.00
2 thru 7 . . . . @75.00

FEM 5
Entity, 1995
1 thru 4 five-part series . . . . @3.00
1 signed & numbered 13.00

FEMFORCE
AC Comics, 1985
1 O:Femforce 10.00
2 A:Captain Paragon. 5.00
3 Skin Game 5.00
4 Skin Game. 5.00
5 Back in the Past. 5.00
6 EL,Back in the Past 5.00
7 HB,O:Captain Paragon 5.00
8 V:Shade 5.00
9 V:Dr.Rivits 5.00
10 V:Dr.Rivits 5.00
11 D:Haunted Horsemen 4.00
12 V:Dr.Rivits 4.00
13 V:She-Cat 4.00
14 V:Alizarin Crimson 4.00
15 V:Alizarin Crimson 4.00
16 thru 56 See Black & White Pub.

57 V:Goat God 3.00
58 I:New Sentinels 3.00
59 I:Paragon 3.00
60 V:Sentinels 3.00
61 F:Tara 3.00
62 V:Valkyra 3.00
63 I:Rayda 3.00
64 thru 67 . . . . @3.00
68 Spellbound 3.00
69 She-Cat Possessed 3.00
70 Island Out of Time 3.00
71 Darkfire Returns 3.00
72 w/Sentinels of Justice 4.00
72a no extras 3.00
73 w/Compact Comic 4.00
73a Regular edition 3.00
74 Daughter of Darkness 4.00
74a Regular edition 3.00
75 Gorby Poster 5.00
75a Regular edition 3.00
76 Daughters pt. 3, polybagged
    with Compact Comic 4.00
76a no bag or comic 3.00
77 V:Sea Monster 3.00
78 V:Gorgana, bagged with comic . . 5.00
78a no bag or comic 3.00
79 V:Iron Jaw, polybagged
    with Index 5.00
79a no bag or index 3.00
80 polybagged with Index 6.00
80a F:Mr. Brimstone, Rad 3.00
81 polybagged with Index 6.00
81a Valentines Day Spec. 3.00
82 polybagged with Index 6.00
82a F:Ms. Victory 3.00
83 F:Paragon 3.00
84 The Death of Joan Wayne
    polybagged with index #4B 6.00
84a no bag or index 3.00
85 Synn vs. Narett, polybagged
    with card 5.00
85a no bag or card 3.00
86 polybagged with index #5 . . . . . . 5.00
86a unbagged, no suplements 3.00
87 Pandemonium in Paradise,
    polybagged with plate 9.00
87a unbagged, no plate 3.00
88 F:Garganta, polybagged with
    index #6 . . . . 6.00
89 polybagged with index 6.00
90 polybagged with index 6.00
91 polybagged with index 6.00
92 polybagged with index 6.00
88a thru 92a unbagged, no index @3.00
93 on see Black & White Pub.
Spec.#1 . . . . 2.50
Untold Origin Spec #1 . . . . 5.00

FEMFORCE: UP CLOSE
AC Comics, 1992–95
1 F:Stardust 4.00
2 F:Stardust 4.00
3 . . . . 4.00
4 . . . . 4.00
5 thru 8 with Sticker . . . . @4.00
5a thru 8a Regular Edition . . . . . @3.00
9 thru 11 . . . . @3.00

FERRET
Malibu, 1992
1 (From Protectors),DZ,V:Purple
    Dragon Tong,A:Iron Skull 2.50
[Regular Series] 1992–93
1 . . . . 2.50
2 thru 11 . . . . @2.50

FIGHT THE ENEMY
Tower Comics, 1966
1 BV,Lucky 7 . . . . 60.00
2 AMc 40.00
3 WW,AMc 40.00

FIGHTIN' ARMY
Charlton 1956–84
16 . . . . 40.00
17 thru 19 . . . . @50.00
20 SD 90.00
21 thru 23 . . . . @50.00
24 Giant 75.00
25 thru 50 . . . . @35.00
51 thru 74 . . . . @30.00
75 Lonely War 40.00
76 thru 88 . . . . @22.00
89 thru 92 SD . . . . @25.00
93 thru 99 . . . . @20.00
100 . . . . 25.00
101 thru 145 . . . . @20.00
146 thru 165 . . . . @10.00
166 thru 172 . . . . @10.00

FIGHTIN' FIVE
Charlton 1964
28 . . . . 100.00
29 thru 39 . . . . @50.00
40 . . . . 100.00
41 . . . . 75.00
Charlton 1981
42 . . . . 6.00
43 thru 497 . . . . @6.00

FIGHTING AMERICAN
Harvey, 1966
1 SK,Rep Fighting American
    from 1950's 150.00

FIGHTING AMERICAN
Awesome Entertainment
1 . . . . 7.00
1a variant (c) 4.00
1b Platinum (c) 12.00
2 . . . . 4.00
Coll.Ed.#1 rep.#1–#2 . . . . 5.00
Spec.#1 Fighting American: Cold War
    RLe,JLb 2.50

FIGHTING AMERICAN: DOGS OF WAR
Awesome Entertainment, 1998
1 JSn,SPa,F:John Flagg 2.50
1a Tour Edition, RLe cover 5.00
1b Tour Edition, signed 12.00
2 JSn,SPa,other super-soldiers . . 2.50
2a variant cover 2.50
3 A:Crimson Dragon 2.50
4 Who is No Name? 2.50
Spec.'98 Con preview,b&w,16-page 5.00

FIGHTING AMERICAN: RULES OF THE GAME
Awesome Entertainment, 1997
1 JLb 3.00
2 JLb 2.50
3 JLb, Baby Buzz Bomber 2.50

FIGHTIN' MARINES
Charlton 1955
14 . . . . 250.00
15 MB(c) 125.00
16 . . . . 50.00
17 MB 175.00
18 thru 24 . . . . @50.00
25 Giant 100.00
26 Giant, 100-pgs 165.00
27 thru 77 . . . . @40.00
78 Shot Gun Baker 30.00
79 thru 81 . . . . @30.00
82 Giant 75.00
83 thru 100 . . . . @25.00
101 thru 140 . . . . @20.00
141 thru 170 . . . . @8.00

Fightin' Marines #149
© Charlton

171 thru 176 scarce 10.00

FIGHTIN' NAVY
Charlton 1956
74 . . . . 90.00
75 thru 81 . . . . @50.00
82 giant 75.00
83 giant 100-pgs 100.00
84 thru 100 . . . . @40.00
101 UFO 45.00
102 thru 125 . . . . @25.00
Charlton 1983
126 thru 133 . . . . 25.00

FINAL DESTINATION: SPRING BREAK
Zenescope Entertainment, 2006
1 (of 5) 4.00
2 thru 5 . . . . @4.00

FINAL GIRL
Antarctic Press, 2007
1 . . . . 4.00
2 thru 5 . . . . @3.50

FIREARM
Malibu Ultraverse, 1993–95
0 w/video,I:Duet 3.00
1 I:Firearm,Alec Swan 2.50
1 silver foil, limited edition 4.00
2 BWS,A:Hardcase,BU:Rune 2.75
3 thru 10 . . . . @2.50
11 Ultraverse Premier #5,BU:Prime. 3.50
12 thru 18 . . . . @2.50

FIREBLAST: ADVENTURES IN THE 30TH CENTURY
Masterpiece Comics, 2006
1-shot 3.00

FIRST, THE
Crossgen Comics, 2000
1 BKs,BS 6.00
2 thru 13 BKs,BS . . . . @5.00
14 thru 25 . . . . @3.00
26 thru 36 . . . . @3.00
37 Atwaal returns 3.00

FIRST ADVENTURES
First, 1985
1 thru 5 . . . . @2.50

FIRST GRAPHIC NOVELS
First 1984

1 JBi,Beowolf	8.00
1a 2nd Printing	7.00
2 TT,Time Beavers	10.00
3 HC,American Flag Hard Times	12.00
4 Nexus,SR.	10.00
5 Elric,CR	20.00
6 Enchanted Apples of Oz	6.00
7 Secret Island of Oz	10.00
8 HC,Time 2	28.00
9 TMNT	20.00
10 TMNT II.	18.00
11 Sailor on the Sea	15.00
12 HC,American Flagg	15.00
13 Ice King.	10.00
14 TMNT III	14.00
15 Hex Breaker	10.00
16 Forgotten Forest	11.00
17 Mazinger	11.00
18 TMNT IV	13.00
19 O;Nexus	10.00
20 American Flagg.	16.00

FIRST WAVE: HEART OF A KILLER
Andromeda Entertainment, 2000

1 by Dan Parsons, TV tie-in	3.00
1a photo (c).	3.00
2	4.00
2a photo (c).	4.00
2b signed	10.00
2c sketch edition	20.00

FIRST WAVE: IN THE BEGINNING
Andromeda Entertainment, 2001

1	3.00
1a photo (c).	3.00

FIRST WAVE: JORDAN RADCLIFFE
Andromeda Entertainment, 2001

1 painted (c)	3.00
1a photo (c).	3.00
1b limited foil (c)	10.00

FISH POLICE
Comico, 1987

Vol 2 #6 thru #15 rep.	@2.50
Vol 2 #16 rep..	3.00
Vol 2 #17 rep.,AuA.	3.00
1 Color Special (July 1987)	3.50

FLAMEHEAD
JNCO Comics, 1998

1 I:Flamehead	2.50
2 thru 5	@2.50

FLARE
Hero Graphics

1 I:Darkon&Prof.Pomegranite	4.00
2 Blonde Bombshell,A:Galooper	3.00
3 I:Sky Marshall	3.00
Ann.#1	4.50
[2nd Series]	
1 A:Galloping Galooper.	3.00
2 A:Lady Arcane	3.00
3 I:Britannia.	3.00
4 A:Indigo	2.50
5 R:Eternity Smith,O:Die Kriegerin	4.00
6 I:Tigress	3.50
7 V:The Enemies	3.00
8 Morrigan Wars#4,A:Icicle Dragon	3.50
9 Morrigan Wars Pt.7 (B&W)	3.50

FLARE
Heroic Publishing, 2004

1	3.00
2	3.00
3 thru 9	@3.00
30	3.00
31 thru 32.	@3.00
33 thru 35.	@3.25
36 thru 37	@3.00

FLARE ADVENTURES
Hero Graphics, 1992

1 rep..	3.00
2 flipbook w/Champions Classics	3.00
3 flipbook w/Champions Classics	3.00
Becomes: B&W	

FLARE ADVENTURES
Heroic Publishing, 2005

1 The League of Champions	3.00
15	3.00
16 thru 18.	@3.25

Flash Gordon #14
© Charlton

19	4.50
19a variant (c)	4.50

FLASH GORDON
Gold Key, 1965

1	125.00

FLASH GORDON
King, 1966–69

1 AW,DH,A:Mandrake	150.00
1a Comp. Army giveaway.	125.00
2 FBe,A:Mandrake,R:Ming	100.00
3 RE,"Lost in the Land of The Lizardmen".	110.00
4 AW,B:Secret Agent X-9	120.00
5 AW	120.00
6 RC,On the Lost Continent of Mongo	110.00
7 MR, rep. In the Human Forest.	110.00
8 RC,JAp.	110.00
9 AR,rep	120.00
10 AR,rep.	120.00
11 RC	100.00
Charlton, 1969–70	
12 RC.	75.00
13 JJ	75.00
14	60.00
15	60.00
16	60.00
17 Brick Bradford story	60.00

18 MK,Attack of the Locust Men	60.00
Gold Key, 1975	
19 Flash returns to Mongo.	15.00
20 thru 30.	@10.00
31 thru 37 AW movie adapt	@10.00

FLESH AND BONES
UpShot, 1986

1 Moore.	3.00
2 thru 4 Moore.	@3.00

FLINTSTONES
Harvey

1	3.00
2 Romeo and Juliet.	3.00

FLINTSTONES
Archie, 1995

1 thru 10	@3.50
2 thru 14	@3.00
15 Frankenstone's Monster.	3.00
20 An Heir-Raising Tale.	3.00
21 King Fred The Last.	3.00
22 Something Gruesome This Way Comes.	3.00

FLINTSTONES, THE
Dell Publishing Co., 1961
#1 *see Dell Giant*

2	200.00
3 thru 6	@150.00
Gold Key, 1962	
7	150.00
8 A:Mr.& Mrs J. Evil Scientists	125.00
9 A:Mr.& Mrs.J. Evil Scientists	125.00
10 A:Mr.& Mrs.J. Evil Scientists	125.00
11 I:Pebbles.	150.00
12 The Too-Old Cowhand	100.00
13 thru 15.	@100.00
16 I:Bamm-Bamm	135.00
17 thru 20	@100.00
21 thru 23.	@70.00
24 I:Gruesomes	100.00
25 thru 29.	@100.00
30 Dude Ranch Roundup	100.00
31 Christmas(c).	100.00
32	65.00
33 A:Dracula & Frankenstein.	70.00
34 I:The Great Gazoo	125.00
35	65.00
36 The Man Called Flintstone	65.00
37 thru 60.	@65.00

FLINTSTONES, THE
Charlton Comics, 1970

1	150.00
2	90.00
3 thru 7	@60.00
8 Summer Vacation	100.00
9	60.00
10	60.00
11 thru 20	@50.00
21 thru 50.	@50.00

FLINTSTONES IN 3-D
Blackthorne

1	3.00
2	3.00
3 thru 5	@3.00

FLIPPER
Gold Key, 1966

1 Ph(c) from TV series	125.00
2 and 3 Ph(c)	@100.00

FLOOD RELIEF
Malibu Ultraverse, 1994

GN Ultraverse Heroes	5.00

FLY, THE
Archie/Red Circle, 1983
1 JSn,A:Mr.Justice 6.00
2 thru 9 RB,SD . . . . @5.00

FLYING SAUCERS
Dell, 1967
1 . . . . 75.00
2 thru 5 . . . . @50.00

FLYMAN
Archie Publications
{Prev: Adventures of the Fly}
31 I:Shield (Bill Higgins), A:Comet,
    Black Hood 100.00
32 I:Mighty Crusaders 85.00
33 A:Mighty Crusaders, R:Hangman
    Wizard 85.00
34 MSy,A:Black Hood,Shield,Comet
    Shield back-up story begins . . 75.00
35 O:Black Hood 75.00
36 O:Web,A:Hangman in Shield
    strip 75.00
37 A:Shield. 75.00
38 A:Web 60.00
39 A:Steel Sterling 60.00

FOOTSOLDIERS
Maximum Press, 1996
1 KJo,PhH, ... 3.00

FOOZLE
Eclipse, 1985
1 . . . . 2.50
2 . . . . 2.50
3 . . . . 2.50

FORBIDDEN PLANET
Innovation, 1992
1 Movie Adapt. 2.50
2 Movie adapt.contd. 2.50
3 Movie adapt.contd. 2.50
4 Movie adapt.contd. 2.50
GN rep.#1–#4 (1997). 9.00

FORCE OF THE BUDDHA'S PALM
Jademan, 1988–93
1 . . . . 3.00
2 thru 10 . . . . @2.50
11 thru 24. . . . . @2.50
25 thru 43. . . . . @2.50
44 D:White Crane 3.00
45 thru 55. . . . . @2.50

4-D MONKEY
Dr. Leung's, 1988–90
1 thru 11 . . . . @2.50

FOREVER WAR, THE
NBM
GN Vol. 1 Joe Haldeman adapt. . . . 9.00
GN Vol. 2 Joe Haldeman adapt. . . . 9.00
GN Vol. 3 Joe Haldeman adapt. . . . 9.00

FORGOTTEN REALMS: THE DARK ELF TRILOGY
Devil's Due Publishing, 2005
Book I: Homeland
1 (of 3) 5.00
1b convention special 9.00
2 thru 3 . . . . @5.00
2a thru 3a collector's edition . . . . @8.00
The Legend of Drizzt,
Book II: Exile
1 (of 3) 5.00

1a collector's edition 8.00
2 . . . . 5.00
2a collector's edition 8.00
3 . . . . 5.00
3a collector's edition 8.00
Book III Sojourn
1 (of 3) 5.00
1a variant (c) 8.00
2 thru 3 . . . . @5.00
2a thru 3a variant (c)s . . . . @9.00
Book IV The Crystal Shard
1 (of 3) 5.00
1a Card stock variant (c) 8.00
2 . . . . 5.00
2a Card stock variant (c) 8.00
3 . . . . 5.00
3a prestige (c) 9.00
Book V Streams of Silver
1a prestige (c) 9.50
2 thru 3 . . . . @5.50
2a thru 3a prestige (c) . . . . @9.50
The Halfling's Gem, 2007
1 . . . . 5.50
1a prestige (c) 9.50

FOUNDATION
Boom! Studios, 2007
1 . . . . 4.00
2 thru 4 . . . . @4.00

FOURTH HORSEMEN, THE
Fangoria Comics, 2007
1 (of 4) 4.00
2 thru 4 . . . . @4.00

FOXFIRE
Malibu Ultraverse, 1996
1 From Phoenix Resurrection 2.50
2 Fate of Mastodon revealed 2.50
3 . . . . 2.00
4 . . . . 2.00

FRANK
Nemesis, 1994
1 thru 4 DGc(s),GgP . . . . @3.00
1a thru 4a variant(c) . . . . @3.00

FRANK FRAZETTA FANTASY ILLUSTRATED
Frank Frazetta, 1998
1 . . . . 6.00
1a variant cover 8.00
3 thru 9 . . . . @6.00
3 Neil Gaiman signed &
    numbered 25.00
3 Daniel signed & numbered 20.00

FRANK FRAZETTA DEATH DEALER
Verotik, 1997
1 thru 4 by Glenn Danzig . . . . . . @7.00

FRANK MILLER'S ROBOCOP
Avatar Press/Pulsar Press, 2003
1 . . . . 3.50
1b robosteel (c). 15.00
2 thru 9 . . . . @3.50
1a thru 5a wraparound (c). . . . . @4.00
6a thru 9a wraparound (c). . . . . @3.50
2b Civic Duty edition 4.00
4b thru 8b special edition (c)s. . . @6.00
Pulsar Press, 2006
9 Savior (c) 6.00
Spec. Killing Machine. 3.00
Spec. Killing Machine variant (c) . . . 3.00
Spec. Killing Machine no escape
    variant(c) 6.00

FRANKENSTEIN
Dell Publishing Co., 1964
1 . . . . 125.00
2 . . . . 75.00
3 and 4 . . . . @60.00

FRANKENSTEIN
Caliber
Novel Adaptation 3.00

FRANKENSTEIN
Topps, 1994
1 thru 4 . . . . @3.00

FRANKENSTEIN
Malibu
1 thru 3 movie promo . . . . @2.50

FRANKENSTEIN DRACULA WAR
Topps, 1995
1 Frank Vs. Drac. 3.00
2 F:Saint Germaine. 3.00
3 Frank Vs. Drac. 3.00

FRANKENSTEIN JR.
Gold Key, 1967
1 . . . . 200.00

FREDDY
Dell Publishing Co., 1963
1 . . . . 50.00
2 and 3 . . . . @40.00

FREDDY'S DEAD: THE FINAL NIGHTMARE
Innovation
1 Movie adaption, Pt.1 . . . . 3.00
2 Movie adaption, Pt.2 . . . . 3.00
GN Movie Adapt. 7.00
3-D Special. 2.50

FRED PERRY'S S-GUILD
Antarctic Press, 2006
1 . . . . 3.50

FREE FALL
Narwain Publishing, 2005
1 thru 5 . . . . @4.00

Fred Perry's S-Guild #1
© Antarctic Press

All comics prices listed are for *Near Mint* condition.

FREEMIND
Future Comics, 2003
5 and 6 . . . . @3.50
7 thru 13 . . . . @3.00

FREEX
Malibu Ultraverse, 1993–95
1 I:Freex w/Ultraverse card 3.00
1a Ultra-Limited 4.00
1b Full Hologram (c) 5.00
2 L:Valerie,I:Rush 3.00
3 A:Rush 3.00
4 GJ(s),DdW,BWS,BU:Rune 2.75
5 thru 18 . . . . @2.50
Giant Size#1 A:Prime. 2.50

FRIDAY FOSTER
Dell Publishing Co., 1972
1 . . . . 45.00

FRIDAY THE 13th
Avatar Press, 2005
Spec. #1 . . . . 4.00
Spec. #1 variant (c)s 4.00
Spec. #1 variant special (c)s . . . . @6.00
Spec. #1 glow (c) 15.00
Spec. #1 Blood Red Con (c) 5.00
Spec. #1 Prism foil (c) 13.00
Spec. Fearbook #1 . . . . 4.00
Spec. Fearbook #1 variant (c)s . . @4.00
Spec. Fearbook #1 leather (c) . . . 20.00

FRIDAY THE 13TH
Wildstorm/DC, Dec., 2006
1 . . . . 3.00
1a variant (c) 3.00
2 . . . . 3.00
3 Secret of Crystal Lake 3.00
4 Camp Crystal Lake 3.00
5 Forest at Crystal Lake 3.00
6 Curse of Camp Crystal 3.00

FRIDAY THE 13TH:
BLOODBATH
Avatar Press, 2005
1 . . . . 4.00
2 thru 3 . . . . @4.00
1a thru 3a wraparound (c)s . . . . . @4.00
1b thru 3b variant (c)s. . . . . @4.00
2c thru 3c Die-dut (c)s . . . . @10.00
1d thru 3d Special (c)s . . . . @6.00
1e Leather (c) 20.00

FRIDAY THE 13TH:
HOW I SPENT MY
SUMMER VACATION
Wildstorm/DC, Sept, 2007
1 . . . . 3.00
2 Horror continues 3.00

FRIDAY THE 13th:
JASON VS. JASON X
Avatar Press, 2006
1 (of 2) by Mike WOlfer 4.00
1a wraparound (c) 4.00
1b variant (c)s . . . . @4.00
1c Nano steel (c) 15.00
1d Blood red convention (c) 5.00
1e Face Off (c) 6.00
2 . . . . 4.00
2a wraparound (c) 4.00
2b variant (c)s . . . . @4.00
2c Nano steel (c) 15.00
2d Blood red convention (c) 5.00

FRIDAY THE 13TH:
PAMELA'S TALE
Wildstorm/DC, July, 2007
1 Jason's Mother 3.00
2 finale 3.00

Friendly Ghost Casper #146
© Harvey Publications

FRIENDLY GHOST
CASPER, THE
Harvey Publications, 1958
1 . . . . 750.00
2 . . . . 500.00
3 thru 10 . . . . @400.00
11 thru 20 . . . . @250.00
21 thru 30 . . . . @100.00
31 thru 50 . . . . @75.00
51 thru 100 . . . . @60.00
101 thru 159 . . . . @50.00
160 thru 163 52 pgs. . . . . @35.00
164 thru 253 . . . . @20.00
Becomes:

CASPER
THE FRIENDLY GHOST

FRIGHT NIGHT
Now, 1988–90
1 thru 22 . . . . @2.50

FRIGHT NIGHT 3-D
Now, 1992
1 Dracula,w/3-D Glasses 3.00
2 . . . . 3.00

FRIGHT NIGHT II
Now
Movie Adaptation 4.00

FROGMEN, THE
Dell Publishing Co., 1962
1 GE,Ph(c) 150.00
2 GE,FF 100.00
3 GE,FF 100.00
4 . . . . 75.00
5 ATh 85.00
6 thru 11 . . . . @65.00

FROM HEAVEN TO HELL
Dead Dog Comics, 2005
1 . . . . 5.00
2 . . . . 5.00

FRONTLINE COMBAT
EC Comics, 1995
1 thru 4 rep. . . . . @3.00
Gemstone, 1996
5 thru 13 rep. . . . . @3.00
14 WW(c) 3.00
15 . . . . 3.00

F-TROOP
Dell Publishing Co., 1966
1 Ph(c) 175.00
2 thru 7 Ph(c) . . . . @100.00

FULL CIRKLE
Full Circle Publications, 2004
1 (of 3) SBs. 4.00
1a variant (c). 3.50
1b signed, either cover . . . . @10.00
1c 2nd printing 3.50
2 . . . . 3.50
2a variant (c). 3.50
2b 2nd printing 3.50
3 . . . . 4.00
3a variant (c) 3.50
1b and 3b Classic silver foil (c). . @8.00
Preview book 16-pg. 3.00
Preview book, signed. 5.00

FUN-IN
Gold Key, 1970–74
1 . . . . 125.00
2 . . . . 75.00
3 thru 6 . . . . @75.00
7 thru 10 . . . . @60.00
11 thru 15 . . . . @60.00

FUNKY PHANTOM
Gold Key, 1972–75
1 . . . . 100.00
2 . . . . 50.00
3 . . . . 50.00
4 . . . . 50.00
5 . . . . @50.00
6 thru 13 . . . . @35.00

FURIOUS FIST OF THE
DRUNKEN MONKEY:
ORIGIN OF THE SPECIES
SIlent Devil Productions, 2006
1 (of 3) 3.00
2 thru 3 . . . . @3.00

FURRY NINJA HIGH
SCHOOL STRIKES BACK
Shanda Fantasy Arts, 2003
1 (of 2) 5.00
2 . . . . 5.00

FUSED
Boom! Studios, 2005
1-shot 7.00

FUTURAMA COMICS
Bongo Comics, 2000
1 thru 6 . . . . @3.50
7 thru 10 . . . . @3.00
11 thru 21 . . . . @3.00
22 thru 34 . . . . @3.00
Spec. Futurama/Simpsons: Infinity
  Secret Crossover Crisis, pt.1 . . 2.50
Spec. Futurama/Simpsons Crossover
  Crisis, pt.2 . . . . 2.50

FUTURIANS
Lodestone, 1985
1 DC,I:Dr.Zeus 2.50

2 DC,I:MsMercury 2.50
3 DC 2.50
Eternity Graphic Novel, DC, Rep.
  +new material 10.00

GALACTICA:
THE NEW MILLENNIUM
Realm Press, 1999
1 Battlestar Galactica 3.00
1 convention edition 5.00
1a signed 12.00
2 Busch (c) 3.00
2a Scalf (c) 3.00
2b convention edition 5.00
3 . . . . 3.00
3a 3.00
4 . . . . 3.00
4a deluxe 5.00
Spec. Fangs of the Beast 4.00
Spec. Fangs of the Beast,deluxe . . 5.00
Tour Book, Conv. Ed., signed 15.00
Spec.Search for Sanctuary 4.00

GALL FORCE:
ETERNAL STORY
CPM, 1995
1 F:Solnoids 3.00
2 V:Paranoid 3.00
3 . . . . 3.00
4 Implant Secrets 3.00

GALLANT MEN, THE
Gold Key, 1963
1 RsM 50.00

GALLEGHER
BOY REPORTER
Gold Key, 1965
1 . . . . 50.00

GARGOYLES
Amaze Ink/Slave
Labor Graphics, 2006
1 . . . . 7.00
2 thru 3 . . . . @4.00
4 thru 5 . . . . @3.50
6 thru 8 . . . . @4.00

GARRISON'S GORRILLAS
Dell Publishing Co., 1968
1 Ph(c) 75.00
2 thru 5 Ph(c) . . . . @50.00

GARTH ENNIS'
CHRONICLES OF
WORMWOOD
Avatar Press, 2007
1 . . . . 4.00
1a variant wraparound (c) 4.00
2 thru 6 . . . . @4.00
2a thru 6a variant wraparound (c)@4.00

GARTH ENNIS'
STREETS OF GLORY
Avatar Press, 2007
Prev. 2.00

GARTH ENNIS'S 303
Avatar Press, 2004
1 (of 6) 4.00
1a wraparound (c). 4.00
1b gold foil (c) 7.00
2 thru 6 . . . . @4.00
2a thru 6a wraparound (c) 4.00

GASP!
American Comics Group
March, 1967
1 . . . . 75.00
2 thru 4, Aug. 1967 . . . . @50.00

GATE CRASHER
Black Bull Entertainment, 2000
1 (of 4) MWa,ACo,JP 2.50
1a variant (c). 5.00
2 MWa,ACo,JP 2.50
3 MWa,ACo,JP 2.50
3a variant JJu(c) 2.50
4 MWa,ACo,JP, concl. 2.50
4a variant JLi(c) 2.50

Gate Crasher (Ring of Fire) #1 variant
© Black Bull Entertainment

GATE CRASHER
Black Bull Entertainment, 2000
1 MWa,JP,ACo,F:Alex Wagner 2.50
1a variant Wizard World (c) 5.00
2 MWa,JP,ACo,Blue Tonya, Otmar . 2.50
3 MWa,JP,ACo,F:Hazard 2.50
4 MWa,JP,ACo,ACo(c) 2.50
5 MWa,JP,ACo,AAd(c) 2.50
6 MWa,JP,ACo 2.50
2a thru 6a variant (c)s . . . . @2.50

GATESVILLE COMPANY
Speakeasy Comics, 2005
1 . . . . 3.00
2 & 3 . . . . @3.00

GEARHEAD
Arcana Studio, 2007
1 (of 4) 4.00
2 thru 4 . . . . @4.00

G.E.I.
Cyberosia Publishing, 2004
1 . . . . 3.50
2 thru 3 . . . . @3.50

GEI
Narwain Publishing, 2006
1 . . . . 2.00

GEN-ACTIVE
WildStorm/DC, 2000
1 V:DV8,48-pg.quarterly 4.00
2 several stories 4.00

2a variant JPn (c) 4.00
3 BSz,JLe(c) 4.00
3a variant Lee Bermejo (c) 4.00
4 R:Wildcore 4.00
4a variant (c). 4.00
5 F:Sublime. 4.00
5a variant (c) (1:2) 4.00
6 Freakville 4.00

GENE FUSION
Beckett Entertainment, 2003
1 Monsters on Parade,pt.1 . . . . . . 3.00
2 Monsters on Parade,pt.2 . . . . . . 3.00
3 Monsters on Parade,pt.3 . . . . . . 3.00
4 Battle under the Big Tent 3.00

GENE RODDENBERRY'S
LOST UNIVERSE
Teckno-Comics, 1994
0 I:Sensua. 2.50
1 Gene Roddenberry's 2.50
2 Grange Discovered 2.50
3 Secrets Revealed 2.50
4 F:Penultra 2.50
5 I:New Alien Race 2.50
6 Two Doctor Granges 2.50
7 F:Alaa Chi Tskare 2.50

GENE RODDENBERRY'S
XANDER IN
LOST UNIVERSE
Teckno-Comics, 1995
1 V:Black Ghost 3.00
2 V:Walker. 3.00
3 V:Lady Sensua 3.00
4 thru 7 . . . . @3.00
8 F:Lady Sensua. 3.00
[Mini-Series], 1995
1 RoR,F:L.Nimoy's Primortals 3.00

GENE SIMMONS
DOMINATRIX
IDW, 2007
1 . . . . 4.00
2 thru 4 . . . . @4.00

GENE SIMMONS'
HOUSE OF HORRORS
Arcade/Simmons Comics
Group, 2006
1 . . . . 3.00
1a variant (c). 3.00

GENE SIMMONS'
JAZAN WILD
Arcade/Simmons Comics
Group, 2006
1 . . . . 3.00
1a variant (c)s . . . . @3.00
Spec House of Horrors, Halloween
  Edition #1, 90-pg. 6.00

GENE SIMMONS ZIPPER
IDW Publishing, 2007
1 . . . . 4.00

GENESIS
Malibu, 1993
0 GP,w/Pog,F:Widowmaker,
  A:Arrow 3.50
0a Gold Ed.. . . . . 5.00

GENESIS FIVE
Guardian Line, 2006
1 thru 5 . . . . @3.00

COLOR PUB.

GENSAGA: ANCIENT WARRIOR
Entity Comics, 1995
1 I:Gensaga	2.50
1a with Computer Games	2.50
2 V:Dinosaurs	2.50
3 V:Lord Abyss	2.50

GEN13
WildStorm/DC, 2002
1 CCI,Dylon & Ethan York	3.00
2 CCI,Herod strikes	3.00
3 CCI,Herod strikes	3.00
4 CCI,Hamza	3.00
5 CCI,V:Preston Kills	3.00
6 CCI,V:Purple Haze	3.00
7 CCI,V:The Chrome	3.00
8 CCI,V:The Chrome	3.00
9 CCI,the alter or the morgue	3.00
10 CCI,October Surprise,pt.4	3.00
11 CCI,Two Caitlins	3.00
12 CCI,G-Nome	3.00
13 CCI,G-Nome	3.00
14 CCI,F:Caitlin	3.00
15 CCI,V:The Clique	3.00
16 CCI,finale	3.00
See also Image Comics section	

GEN13
MOVIE ADAPTATION
WildStorm/DC, 2001
1 JMi, animated movie adapt	2.50

GEN13
Wildstorm/DC, Oct., 2006
1	3.00
1a variant (c)	3.00
2	3.00
2a variant (c)	3.00
3 On the Run	3.00
3a variant AWa (c)	3.00
4 Caught by a Psycho	3.00
4a variant (c) (1:10)	3.00
5 V:Heaven Zeleven	3.00
6 V:Heaven Zeleven	3.00
7 V:Flesh-eating dinosaurs	3.00
8	3.00
9 Tranquility	3.00
10 Tranquility	3.00
11 The Liberty Snots	3.00
12 Authori-teens	3.00
13 F:Megan	3.00

GENTLE BEN
Dell Publishing Co., 1968
1 Ph(c)	60.00
2	40.00
3 thru 5	@35.00

GEOMANCER
Valiant, 1994
1 RgM, I:Geomancer	3.00
2 thru 8	@2.50

GEORGE A ROMERO'S DAWN OF THE DEAD
IDW Publishing, 2004
1	4.00
1a variant photo (c)	4.00
2 thru 3	@4.00

GEORGE ROMERO'S NIGHT OF THE LIVING DEAD
Avatar Press, 2007
Spec. Just A Girl	3.00

Spec. Just A Girl variant (c)s	@3.00
Spec. Hunger	3.00
Spec. Hunger variant (c)s	@3.00

GEORGE A. ROMERO'S NIGHT OF THE LIVING DEAD: THE BEGINNING
Avatar Press, 2006
1	4.00
1a variant (c)s	@4.00
1b variant Splatter (c)	7.00
1c Leather (c)	20.00
2	4.00
2a variant (c)s	@4.00
2b variant splatter (c)	7.00

GEORGE OF THE JUNGLE
Gold Key, 1969
1 From animated TV show	250.00
2	200.00

GE ROUGE
Verotik, 1997
1 by Glenn Danzig & Calvin Irving	3.00
1 fan club cover (2000)	5.00
2 and 3	@3.00
Biz:GE Rouge #? SBs	3.00

GET SMART
Dell Publishing Co., 1966
1 Ph(c) all	200.00
2 SD	175.00
3 SD	150.00
4 thru 8	@125.00

[FILMATION'S] GHOSTBUSTERS
First, 1987
1 thru 4	@3.00

GHOST BUSTERS II
Now, 1989
1 thru 3 Mini-series	@3.00

GHOSTBUSTERS
88MPH Studios, 2004
1	3.00
1a variant (c)	3.50
2 thru 3	@3.25
88MPH Studios, 2005
1	4.00

GHOSTBUSTERS: LEGION
88MPH Studios, 2004
1 (of 4)	5.00
1a 2nd printing	3.00
2 thru 4	@3.00
1a thru 4a variant (c)s	@3.50

GHOSTING
Platinum Studios, 2007
1 (of 5)	3.00
2 thru 5	@3.00

GHOSTLY TALES
Charlton, 1966
Previously: Blue Beetle
55 I&O Dr. Graves	125.00
56 thru 70	@75.00
71 thru 100	@60.00
101 thru 169	@50.00

GHOST MANOR
Charlton, 1968
1	65.00
2 thru 19	@30.00

Ghost Manor #2
© Charlton

Becomes:

GHOSTLY HAUNTS
Charlton, 1971
20	20.00
21 thru 58	@15.00

GHOST MANOR
Charlton, 1971
1	60.00
2 thru 29	@30.00
30 thru 77	@20.00

GHOST STORIES
Dell Publishing Co., 1962
1	125.00
2	60.00
3 thru 10	@55.00
11	65.00
12 thru 19	@50.00
20	65.00
21 thru 33	@50.00
34 rep	50.00
35 rep	65.00
36 & 37 rep	@50.00

GIANT COMICS
Charlton Comics Summer, 1957
1 A:Atomic Mouse,Hoppy	250.00
2 A:Atomic Mouse	200.00
3	200.00

GIDGET
Dell Publishing Co., 1966
1 Ph(c),Sally Field	175.00
2 Ph(c),Sally Field	125.00

GIFT, THE
First, 1990
Holiday Special	6.00

GIFT, THE
Overcast Comics, 2003
1	6.00
2	4.00
3 thru 5	@3.50
6 thru 7	@3.00

GIGANTOR
Antarctic Press, 2000
1 (of 12) BDn	2.50
2 V:Red Reich	2.50
3	2.50

All comics prices listed are for *Near Mint* condition.

COLOR PUB.

4 Doppleganger,pt.1 . . . . 2.50
5 Doppleganger,pt.2 . . . . 2.50
6 Doppleganger,pt.3 . . . . 2.50
7 Rulers of the Sea 2.50
8 . . . . 2.50
9 Sting of the Spider 3.00
10 Sting of the Spider, pt.2 . . . . 3.00
11 Badge of Danger, pt.1 . . . . 3.00
12 Badge of Danger, pt.2, concl. . . . 3.00

G.I. JOE 3-D
Blackthorne, 1987
1 . . . . 3.00
2 thru 5 . . . . @2.50
Ann. #1 . . . . 2.50

G.I. JOE
Devil's Due Publishing, 2004
(Prev. Pub. by Image)
26 thru 35 . . . . @3.00
36 thru 41 Union of the Snake . . . @3.00
42 double size, 48-page 4.50
43 double size 4.50
31 Collector's club edition 10.00
Digest #1 G.I. Joe Arashikage
　Showdown 11.00

G.I. Joe: America's Elite #10
© *Devil's Due*

G.I. JOE: AMERICA'S ELITE
Devil's Due Publishing, 2005
0 . . . . 1.00
0 2nd printing, new cover 3.00
1 . . . . 1.00
1a signed 15.00
2 thru 4 . . . . @3.00
5 thru 6 48-pg. . . . . @4.50
7 thru 17 . . . . @3.00
18 thru 19 . . . . @3.00
20 . . . . 3.50
21 thru 24 Sins of the Mother . . . @3.50
25 thru 29 World War III, pt.1–pt.5 @3.50
13a cardstock (c) 6.00
1-shot Data Desk Handbook 3.00
1-shot Hunt for Cobra Commander . 1.00

G.I. JOE DECLASSIFIED
Devil's Due Publishing, 2006
1 (of 3) 5.00
1a variant cardstock (c) 9.00
2 thru 3 . . . . @5.00
2a thru 3a variant cardstock (c) . @9.00

G.I. JOE DREADNOKS: DECLASSIFIED
Devil's Due Publishing, 2006
1 (of 3) 5.00
1a cardstock (c) 9.00
2 (of 3) 5.00
2a cardstock (c) 9.00
3 . . . . 5.50
3a cardstock (c) 9.50

G.I. JOE: G.I. JOE REBORN
Devil's Due Publishing, 2004
Spec #1 . . . . 5.00

G.I. JOE: MASTER & APPRENTICE
Devil's Due Publishing, 2004
1 . . . . 3.00
1 Philly con. exclusive 9.00
2 thru 4 . . . . @3.00
Vol. II
1 thru 4 . . . . @3.00

G.I. JOE: RELOADED
Devil's Due Publishing, 2004
1 CDi 3.00
2 thru 14 . . . . @3.00
1-shot Cobra Reborn 5.00

G.I. JOE: SCARLETT DECLASIFIED
Devil's Due Publishing, 2006
1-shot 5.00

G.I. JOE: SIGMA 6
Devil's Due Publishing, 2005
1 thru 6 . . . . @3.00
Digest, 144-pg. 11.00

G.I. JOE: SPECIAL MISSIONS
Devil's Due Publishing, 2006
1-shot Manhattan 5.00
1-shot Toyko 5.00
1-shot Antarctica 5.00
1-shot Brazil 5.50
1-shot The Enemy 5.50

G.I. JOE: STORM SHADOW
Devil's Due, 2007
1 . . . . 3.50
2 thru 7 . . . . @3.50

G.I. JOE VS. TRANSFORMERS
Devil's Due Publishing, 2004
Vol. II
1 . . . . 5.00
1a variant (c) 5.00
2 thru 4 . . . . @3.00
2a thru 4a variant (c) . . . . @3.00

G.I. JOE VS TRANSFORMERS: THE ART OF WAR
Devil's Due Publishing, 2006
1 (of 5 . . . . 3.00
1a variant (c)s . . . . @3.00
2 thru 5 . . . . @3.00
2a thru 5a variant (c) . . . . @3.00

G.I. JOE VS. TRANSFORMERS IV: BLACK HORIZON
Devil's Due, 2007
1 (of 2) 3.00
1a variant (c) 3.00
2 . . . . 5.50
2a variant (c) 5.50

GIL THORP
Dell Publishing Co., 1963
1 . . . . 75.00

GIMOLES
Alias Enterprises, 2005
1 (of 4) 1.00
2 thru 4 . . . . @3.00

GINGER FOX
Comico, 1988
1 thru 4 . . . . @2.50

GIN-RYU
Believe In Yourself, 1995
1 F:Japanese Sword 2.75
2 Identity Revealed 2.75
3 . . . . 2.75
4 Manhunt For Gin-Ryu 2.75

G.I. R.A.M.B.O.T.
Wonder Color, 1987
1 thru 3 . . . . @2.50

GIRL FROM U.N.C.L.E.
Gold Key, 1967
1 The Fatal Accidents Affair 150.00
2 The Kid Commandos Caper . . 100.00
3 The Captain Kidd Affair 100.00
4 One-Way Tourist Affair 100.00
5 The Harem-Scarem Affair 100.00

GIRL GENIUS
Studio Foglio, 2001
0 Secret Blueprints Preview B&W . 1.50
1 by Phil & Kaja Foglio 3.00
2 and 3 . . . . @3.00
4 40-page 4.00
5 . . . . 3.00
6 40-page (cancelled?) 4.00
7 40-page 4.00

GLOBAL FREQUENCY
WildStorm/DC, 2002
1 (of 12) WEI. 3.00
2 WEI,SDi 3.00
3 WEI,LSh. 3.00
4 WEI,RMr 3.00
5 WEI,JMu 3.00
6 WEI, ... 3.00
7 WEI,Detonation 3.00
8 WEI,Miranda Zero disappears . . . 3.00
9 WEI,Cathedral Lung. 3.00
10 WEI,Superviolence 3.00
11 WEI,Aleph 3.00
12 WEI,concl. 3.00

GLOBAL FREQUENCY: GLOOM, THE
APC, 2005
1 . . . . 3.50
2 thru 6 . . . . @3.50

GLOOM, THE
Markosia, 2005
3 thru 5 . . . . @3.50

GLORY
Maximum Press, 1996
1–15 see Image
16 JDy 2.50
17 JDy 2.50
18 JDy 2.50
19 JDy,A:Demeter, Silverfall . . 2.50
20 JDy,A:Silverfall 2.50
21 JDy 2.50
22 JDy 2.50
23 A:Prophet 2.50
Awesome Entertainment, 1999
0 AMo 2.50
0a & b alternate covers. 2.50
0c Timeless Beauty MMy(c) 6.00
1 AMo & ATi 3.50
2 AMo & ATi 3.00

GLORY/CELESTINE: DARK ANGEL
Maximum Press, 1996
1 & 2 See: Image
3 (of 3) JDy. 2.50

GLORY/LIONHEART: RAGE OF FURIES
Awesome Entertainment, 2000
1 . . . . 3.00

GOAT, THE: H.A.E.D.U.S.
Acclaim, 1998
Spec. CPr,KG,F:Vincent Van Goat. . 4.00

GOBLIN LORD, THE
Goblin Studios, 1996
1 (of 6) sci-fi/fantasy 2.50
2 signed & numbered 10.00
3 . . . . 2.50
3a signed & numbered 10.00
4 thru 6 . . . . @2.50

GODS FOR HIRE
Hot Comics, 1986
1 . . . . 2.50
2 thru 7 . . . . @2.50

GODWHEEL
Malibu Ultraverse, 1995
0 R:Argus to Godwheel 2.50
1 I:Primevil 2.50
2 Hardcase new costume. 2.50
3 F:Lord Pumpkin 2.50

GODYSSEY
Maximum 1996
1 . . . . 3.50

GO-GO
Charlton Comics, 1966
1 Miss Bikini Luv. 125.00
2 Beatles. 150.00
3 Blooperman 60.00
4 . . . . 60.00
5 . . . . 60.00
6 JAp,Petula Clark, Ph(c) 75.00
7 Beach Boys 65.00
8 JAp,Monkees, Ph(c) 75.00
9 Ph(c),Oct., 1967 . . . . 50.00

GO-GO GORILLA & THE JUNGLE CREW
Ape Entertainment, 2005
Supper Spec. 3.00
Winter Fun Spec. 3.50

Go-Go #1
© Charlton Comics

GOLD DIGGER
Antarctic Press, 1999
VOL 2
1 by Fred Perry, F:Gina Diggers. . . 2.50
2 . . . . 2.50
3 by Fred Perry. 2.50
4 tinted glass is magical 2.50
5 . . . . 2.50
6 ancient cauldrons. 2.50
7 Halls of the Extremely Dead . . . 2.50
8 Gone Fishing 2.50
9 Fauntleroy..a God? 2.50
10 Arms Master of Jade. 2.50
11 Arms Master of Jade. 2.50
12 Arms Master of Jade. 3.00
13 Tournament of Arms 3.00
14 Tournament of Arms 3.00
15 . . . . 3.00
16 thru 26 . . . . @3.00
27 thru 37 . . . . @3.00
38 thru 42 . . . . @3.50
43 thru 57 . . . . @3.00
50a variant (c) 3.00
58 thru 68 . . . . @3.00
69 thru 74 . . . . @3.00
75 Heroes (c) 3.00
75a Villains (c) 3.00
76 thru 90 . . . . @3.00
Ann. 2003 B&W 5.00
Ann. 2004 B&W 5.00
Ann. 2005 B&W 4.50
Ann. 15th Special. 5.00
Ann., 2006 Special. 4.50
Anniv. Spec. #2 (2007). 5.00
Swimsuit Spec. #1 . . . . 4.50
Spec. Swimsuit 2001 . . . . 4.50
Spec. Swimsuit 2002 . . . . 4.50
Spec. Swimsuit 2003 . . . . 4.50
Spec. Swimsuit 2004 . . . . 4.50
Spec. Swimsuit Spec. 2005 . . . . 4.50
Spec. Swimsuit Spec. 2006 . . . . 4.50
Spec. Swimsuit Spec. 2007 . . . . 4.50
End of Summer Swimsuit (2002). . . 4.50
End of Summer Swimsuit (2003). . . 4.50
End of Summer Swimsuit (2004). . . 4.50
End of Summer Swimsuit (2005). . . 4.50
End of Summer Swimsuit (2006). . . 4.50
End of Summer Swimsuit (2007). . . 4.50
Spec. Halloween Spec. #1. . . . . . 3.00
Spec. Halloween Special, 2006 . . . 3.00
Spec. Peebo Tales (2007) 3.50
Spec. Peebo Tales #2 (2007) . . . 3.50
GN Perfect Memory Vol. 2. . . . . . 6.00
GN Perfect Memory Vol. 3 . . . . . 6.00
GN Perfect Memory Vol. 4. . . . . . 6.00

GN Perfect Memory, Vol. 5 . . . . . . 6.00
GN Pink Slip 10.00
Spec. Gold Digger Adventures #1
   O:Pink Avenger 3.00
Spec. Gold Digger color remix #1 . 3.00
Spec. Gold Digger color remix #2 . 3.00
Spec. Gold Digger color remix #3 . 3.00
Spec. Gold Digger color remix #4 . 3.00
Spec. Gold Digger Tangent #1 . . . 3.00
Spec. Gold Digger Tangent #2. . . 3.00

GOLD DIGGER BETA
Antarctic Press, 1998
Spec. 0 by Ben Dunn, Special
   Origin Issue, 24pg 2.00
1A bu Fred Perry, John Pound (c) . 3.00
1B Jeff Henderson (c). 3.00
2 and 3 . . . . @3.00

GOLD DIGGER SOURCEBOOK
Antarctic Press, 2007
1 . . . . 4.00
2 thru 11 . . . . @4.00

GOLDEN COMICS DIGEST
Gold Key, 1969–76
1 Tom & Jerry,Woody Woodpecker,
   Bugs Bunny 75.00
2 Hanna-Barbera,TV Fun
   Favorites 100.00
3 Tom & Jerry, Woody
   Woodpecker 50.00
4 Tarzan 50.00
5 Tom & Jerry, Woody Woodpecker,
   Bugs Bunny 30.00
6 Bugs Bunny 30.00
7 Hanna-Barbera,TV Fun
   Favorites 75.00
8 Tom & Jerry, Woody Woodpecker,
   Bugs Bunny 25.00
9 Tarzan 60.00
10 Bugs Bunny 25.00
11 Hanna-Barbera,TV Fun
   Favorites 75.00
12 Tom & Jerry,Bugs Bunny 25.00
13 Tom & Jerry. 25.00
14 Bugs Bunny,Fun Packed
   Funnies 25.00
15 Tom & Jerry, Woody
   Woodpecker, Bugs Bunny 25.00
16 Woody Woodpecker 25.00
17 Bugs Bunny 25.00
18 Tom & Jerry. 25.00
19 Little Lulu 45.00
20 Woody Woodpecker 25.00
21 Bugs Bunny Showtime 25.00
22 Tom & Jerry Winter Wingding. . . 25.00
23 Little Lulu & Tubby Fun Fling . . 40.00
24 Woody Woodpecker Fun
   Festival 22.00
25 Tom & Jerry. 22.00
26 Bugs Bunny Halloween Hulla-
   Boo-Loo,Dr. Spektor article . . . 22.00
27 Little Lulu & Tubby in Hawaii . . 45.00
28 Tom & Jerry. 22.00
29 Little Lulu & Tubby 45.00
30 Bugs Bunny Vacation Funnies . 22.00
31 Turk, Son of Stone 50.00
32 Woody Woodpecker
   SummerFun. 22.00
33 Little Lulu & Tubby Halloween
   Fun 45.00
34 Bugs Bunny Winter Funnies . . . 22.00
35 Tom & Jerry Snowtime Funtime 22.00
36 Little Lulu & Her Friends. 45.00
37 WoodyWoodpecker County Fair22.00
38 The Pink Panther 22.00
39 Bugs Bunny Summer Fun 22.00

40 Little Lulu 45.00
41 Tom & Jerry Winter Carnival . . . 22.00
42 Bugs Bunny 22.00
43 Little Lulu in Paris 45.00
44 Woody Woodpecker Family Fun
    Festival 22.00
45 The Pink Panther 22.00
46 Little Lulu & Tubby 45.00
47 Bugs Bunny 22.00
48 The Lone Ranger 22.00

GOLDEN PICTURE
STORY BOOK
Racine Press (Western), 1961
1 Huckleberry Hound 350.00
2 Yogi Bear 350.00
3 Babes In Toy Land 500.00
4 Walt Disney 450.00

GOLDEN PLATES, THE
AAA Pop Comics, 2004
1 (of 12) 8.00
1a 2nd printing 8.00
2 thru 4 . . . . @8.00

GOMER PYLE
Gold Key, 1966
1 Ph(c) from TV show 150.00
2 and 3 . . . . @100.00

GOOD GUYS
Defiant, 1993
1 JiS(s),I:Good Guys 3.75
2 JiS(s),V:Mulchmorg 3.25
3 V:Chasm 2.75
4 Seduction of the Innocent 3.25
5 I:Truc 3.00
6 A:Charlemagne 2.75
7 JiS(s),V:Scourge 2.50
8 thru 11 . . . . @2.50

GOOFY ADVENTURES
Walt Disney, 1990
1 Balboa de Goofy 3.00
2 . . . . 3.00
3 thru 17 . . . . @3.00

GOON
Albatross 2002
1 . . . . 40.00
2 . . . . 25.00
3 thru 5 b&w . . . . @12.00
Spec. Color special 7.00

GOOP, THE
JNCO Comics, 1998
1 . . . . 2.50
2 thru 4 . . . . @2.50

GORGO
Charlton Comics, 1961–65
1 SD,from Movie 450.00
2 SD(c&a),Return of Gorgo 250.00
3 SD(c&a) 200.00
4 SD(c) 150.00
5 The Day Manhattan Died 150.00
6 thru 11 . . . . @150.00
12 Monster's Rendezvous 150.00
13 thru 15 . . . . @125.00
16 SD,Menace from the Deep . . . 125.00
17 thru 23 . . . . @100.00

GORGO'S REVENGE
Charlton Comics, 1962
1 From movie 100.00
Becomes:

THE RETURN OF
GORGO

Gorgo #2
© Charlton Comics

THE RETURN OF GORGO
Charlton Comics, 1963
2 SD(c&a),Creature from
    Corpus III 75.00
3 Hidden Witness 75.00

GORILLA GORILLA
Disney Press, 2006
GN Vol. 1 . . . . 5.00

G.O.T.H.
Verotik, 1995
1 . . . . 3.00
2 . . . . 3.00
3 . . . . 3.00

THE GOTHIC SCROLLS,
DRAYVEN
Davdez Arts, 1997
1 16pg. 2.50
1a limited edition, new cover 3.00
2 and 3 . . . . @2.50
4 V:Lucifer 2.50
GN 13.00

GOVERNMENT BODIES
Speakeasy Comics, 2006
Vol. 2
1 (of 4) 3.00

GRATEFUL DEAD
COMIX
Kitchen Sink
1 TT,inc.DireWolf(large format) . . . 5.50
2 TT,inc.Jack Straw 5.00
3 TT,inc. Sugaree 5.00
4 TT,inc. Sugaree 5.00
5 TT,Uncle John's Band 5.00
6 TT,Eagle Mall #1 . . . . 5.00

GRAVESTONE
Malibu, July 1993–Feb. 1994
1 D:Gravestone,V:Wisecrack . . . 2.50
1a Newstand Ed. 2.50
2 A:Eternal Man, V:Night Plague . . 2.50
2a Newstand Ed. 2.50
3 Genesis Tie in,w/skycap 2.50
4 thru 9 . . . . @2.50

GREASE MONKEY
Kitchen Sink, 1997
1 by Tim Elred 3.50

2 by Tim Elred 3.50

GREAT AMERICAN
WESTERN
AC Comics, 1987
1 Santee, Dark Rider, Missourian . . 2.50
2 F:The Durango Kid 3.00
3 . . . . 3.00
4 F:Lash LaRue 3.50
5 Sunset Carson 5.00
6 King of the Bull Whip 6.00

GREEN HORNET, THE
Gold Key, 1967
1 Bruce Lee,Ph(c) 400.00
2 Ph(c) 300.00
3 Ph(c) 250.00

GREEN HORNET
Now, 1989
1 O:40's Green Hornet 7.00
1a 2nd Printing 4.00
2 O:60's Green Hornet 5.00
3 thru 5 . . . . @4.00
6 . . . . 3.00
7 BSz(c),I:New Kato 3.00
8 thru 12 . . . . @3.50
13 V:Ecoterrorists 3.50
14 V:Ecoterrorists 3.50
Spec.#1 . . . . 2.50
Spec.#2 . . . . 2.50
[2nd Series], 1991
1 V:Johnny Dollar Pt.1 . . . . 2.50
2 V:Johnny Dollar Pt.2 . . . . 2.50
3 V:Johnny Dollar Pt.3 . . . . 2.50
4 V:Ex-Con/Politician 2.50
5 V:Ex-Con/Politician 2.50
6 Arkansas Vigilante 2.50
7 thru 9 The Beast . . . . @2.50
10 Green Hornet-prey 2.50
11 F:Crimson Wasp 2.50
12 Crimson Wasp/Johnny Dollar
    Pt.1,polybagged w/Button 4.00
13 TD(i),Wasp/Dollar Pt.2 . . . . . . 2.50
14 TD(i),Wasp/Dollar Pt.3 . . . . . . 2.50
15 TD(i),Secondsight 2.50
16 A:Commissioner Hamiliton 2.50
17 V:Gunslinger 2.50
18 V:Sister-Hood 2.50
19 V:Jewel Thief 2.50
20 F:Paul's Friend 2.50
21 V:Brick Arcade 2.50
22 V:Animal Testers, with
    Hologravure card 4.00
23 with Hologravure card 4.00
24 thru 25 Karate Wars . . . . @2.50
26 B:City under Siege 2.50
27 with Hologravure card 4.00
28 V:Gangs 2.50
29 V:Gangs 2.50
30 thru 37 . . . . @2.50
38 R:Mei Li 2.50
39 Crimson Wasp 4.50
40 . . . . 4.50
41 . . . . 2.50
42 Baby Killer 2.50
43 Wedding Disasters 2.50
44 F:Amy Hamilton 2.50
45 Plane Hijacking 2.50
46 Airport Terrorists 2.50
Ann.#1 The Blue & the Green 2.50
1993 Ann 3.00

GREEN HORNET:
DARK TOMORROW
Now, 1993
1 thru 3 Hornet Vs Kato . . . . . . @3.00

GREEN HORNET: SOLITARY SENTINAL
Now, 1992
1 Strike Force 3.00
2 thru 3 . . . . @3.00

GREENHAVEN
Aircel, 1988
1 BaB,See Elford #18 . . . . 3.00
2 BaB,See Elford #19 . . . . 3.00
3 BaB,See Elford #20 . . . . 3.00

GREEN PLANET
Charlton, 1962
1 DG 125.00

GRENDEL
Comico, 1986–91
1 MW 8.00
1a 2nd printing 2.00
2 MW 5.00
3 thru 6 MW . . . . @4.00
7 MW 4.00
8 thru 12 MW . . . . @4.00
13 KSy(c) MW 3.50
14 KSy(c) MW 3.00
15 KSy(c) MW 3.00
16 MW,Mage 6.00
17 thru 19 MW,Mage . . . . @5.00
20 thru 32 MW . . . . @3.00
33 MW,giant-size 3.50
34 thru 36 MW . . . . @3.00
37 MW 6.00
38 MW 9.00
39 MW,D:Grendel 10.00
40 MW,D:Orion Assante 30.00

GREYLORE
Sirius, 1985–86
1 thru 5 . . . . @2.50

GREYSHIRT: INDIGO SUNSET
WildStorm/DC, 2001
America's Best Comics
1 (of 6) RV 3.50
2 RV 3.50
3 RV 3.50
4 RV, Star of Indigo. 3.50
5 RV, Fanman. 3.50
6 RV, Black Jack Hawkins 3.50

GRIFTER & MIDNIGHTER
Wildstorm/DC, Mar., 2007
1 (of 6) CDi. 3.00
2 thru 6 CDi. . . . . @3.00

GRIM GHOST, THE
Atlas, 1975
1 . . . . 20.00
2 . . . . 20.00
3 . . . . 20.00

GRIMJACK
First, 1984–91
1 TT Teenage suicide story. 3.00
2 thru 20 TT A:Munden's Bar . . . @2.50
21 thru 25. . . . . @2.50
26 1st color TMNTurtles. 10.00
27 thru 50. . . . . @2.50
51 thru 81. . . . . @2.50

GRIMJACK CASEFILE
First, 1990
1 thru 5 rep. . . . . @2.50

GRIMJACK: KILLER INSTINCT
IDW Publishing, 2005
1 JOs,TT. 4.00
2 thru 6 . . . . @4.00

GRIMM FAIRY TALES
Zenescope Entertainment, 2005
1 Little Red Riding Hood. 15.00
2 Cinderella. 35.00
3 Hansel & Gretel 12.00
4 Rumpelstilskin 12.00
5 Sleeping Beauty. 6.00
6 The Robber Bridegroom 4.00
7 Snow White 4.00
8 Jack and the Bean Stalk 4.00
9 Goldilocks 4.00
10 The Frog King. 4.00
11 Bluebeard 3.00
12 Pied Piper 3.00
13 Beauty and the Beast, pt.1 . . . 3.00
14 thru 21 . . . . @3.00
Ann. #1 . . . . 6.00

GRIMM FAIRY TALES: RETURN TO WONDERLAND
Zenescope Entertainment, 2007
0 . . . . 1.00
1 (of 7) 3.00
2 . . . . 3.00
3 . . . . 3.00
4 thru 6 . . . . @3.00

GRIMM'S GHOST STORIES
Gold Key/Whitman, 1972–82
1 . . . . 40.00
2 . . . . 25.00
3 . . . . 25.00
4 . . . . 25.00
5 AW 30.00
6 . . . . 15.00
7 . . . . 15.00
8 AW 20.00
9 . . . . 15.00
10 . . . . 15.00
11 thru 16 . . . . @12.00
17 RC 15.00
18 thru 60 . . . . @10.00

GRIMOIRE, THE
Speakeasy Comics, 2005
1 . . . . 3.00
2 thru 6 . . . . @3.00
7 thru 12 . . . . @3.00

GROO THE WANDERER
Pacific, 1982–84
1 SA,I:Sage,Taranto 25.00
2 SA,A:Sage 15.00
3 SA,C:Taranto 15.00
4 SA,C:Sage 15.00
5 SA,I:Ahax 15.00
6 SA,I:Gratic 18.00
7 SA,I:Chakaal 18.00
8 SA,A:Chakaal 18.00
Eclipse
Spec.#1 SA,O:Groo,rep Destroyer
 Duck #1 . . . . 23.00

GROUP LARUE, THE
Innovation, 1989
1 MBn 2.50
2 . . . . 2.50
3 . . . . 2.50

Groo the Wanderer #7
© Pacific

GRUMPY OLD MONSTERS
IDW Publishing, 2003
1 (of 4) 2.50
2 thru 4 . . . . @4.00

GRUNLAND
Narwain Publishing, 2006
GN 6.00

GRUNTS
Arcana Studio, 2006
1 (of 3) 4.00
2 thru 3 . . . . @4.00

GUARDIAN HEROES
Alias Enterprises, 2006
1-shot 3.50

GUILLOTIN
ABC, 1997
1 JQ(c) 3.00
1a RCI(c). 6.00
1b gold cover, polybagged with
 trading card 10.00
2 . . . . 3.00
2a Serpent (c). 6.00
2b Cold Series (c). 6.00

GULLIVER'S TRAVELS
Dell Publishing Co., 1965
1 . . . . 100.00
2 and 3 . . . . @75.00

GUMBY
Comico, 1987
1 AAd,Summer Fun Special 5.00
2 AAd,Winter Fun Special. 3.50

GUMBY IN 3-D
Blackthorne
Spec.#1 . . . . 4.00
2 thru 7 . . . . @3.00

GUMBY
Wildcard Production, 2006
1 . . . . 4.00
2 thru 4 . . . . @4.00

GUN FU: THE LOST CITY
Axiom, 2003
1 . . . . 3.50

1a variant (c). 6.00
2 thru 4 . . . . @3.50
2a thru 4a variant (c)s. . . . . . . @3.50
Preview signed edition. 3.00

Gunsomke #6
© Gold Key

GUNSMOKE
Gold Key, 1969
1 Ph(c), from TV series. 125.00
2 thru 6 . . . . @100.00

GUY RITCHIE'S
GAMEKEEPER
Virgin Comics, 2007
1 . . . . 3.00
2 thru 5 . . . . @3.00
1a variant (c) 3.00

HACK/SLASH
Devil's Due Publishing, 2004
1 . . . . 5.00
1-shot Girls Gone Dead. 5.00
1-shot variant(c). 5.00
1-shot Comic Book Carnage 5.00
1-shot Final Revenge of Evil Ernie . 5.00
1-shot Trailers 3.25
1-shot Slice Hard preview special. . 1.00
1-shot Slice Hard 5.00
1-shot Slice Hard variant (c) 5.00
1-shot Hack/Slash vs. Chucky. . . . 5.50
1-shot Hack/Slash vs. Chucky
  variant (c). . . . . @5.50

HACK/SLASH
Devil's Due, 2007
1 . . . . 3.50
1a variant (c) 3.50
2 thru 6 . . . . @3.50
2a thru 6a variant (c) . . . . @3.50

HACK SLASH:
LAND OF LOST TOYS
Devil's Due Publishing, 2005
1 (of 3) 3.25
2 thru 3 . . . . @3.25

HALL OF FAME
J.C. Productions, 1983
1 WW,GK,ThunderAgents 2.50
2 WW,GK,ThunderAgents 2.50
3 WW,Thunder Agents 2.50

HALLOWEEN
Chaos! Comics, 2000
1 premium glow-in-the-dark (c) . . . 13.00
1 chromium edition 16.00

HALLOWEEN:
BEHIND THE MASK
Chaos! Comics, 2000
1 photo (c). 3.00

HALLOWEEN II:
THE BLACKEST EYE
Chaos! Comics, 2001
Spec. 3.00
Spec. premium. 10.00

HALLOWEEN III:
THE DEVIL'S EYES
Chaos! Comics, 2001
Spec. 3.00
Spec. variant (c). 3.00
Spec. Previews exclusive 3.00

HALLOWEEN HORROR
Eclipse, 1987
1 . . . . 3.00

HALO:
AN ANGEL'S STORY
Sirius, 1996
1 by Chris Knowles. 3.00
2 . . . . 3.00
3 . . . . 3.00

HAMMER KID
Alias Enterprises, 2006
1-shot 3.50

HAMMER OF GOD
First, 1990
1 thru 4 . . . . @2.50
Deluxe #1 Sword of Justice Bk#1 . . 5.00
Deluxe #2 Sword of Justice Bk#2 . . 5.00

HAMSTER VICE
Blackthorne, 1985–87
1 thru 10 . . . . @2.50
3-D #1 . . . . 2.50

HAND OF FATE
Eclipse, 1988
1 I:Artemis Fate. 2.50
2 F:Artemis & Alexis 2.50
3 Mystery & Suspense 2.50

HANDS OF THE DRAGON
Atlas, 1975
1 . . . . 18.00

HANNA-BARBERA
ALL-STARS
Archie, 1995
1 . . . . 3.00
2 . . . . 3.00
3 . . . . 3.00
4 . . . . 3.00
5 . . . . 3.00

HANNA-BARBERA
BAND WAGON
Gold Key, 1962–63
1 . . . . 250.00
2 . . . . 160.00
3 . . . . 135.00

HANNA-BARBERA
PARADE
Charlton Comics, 1971–72
1 . . . . 150.00
2 thru 10 . . . . @75.00

HANNA-BARBERA
PRESENTS
Archie, 1995
1 thru 15 . . . . @3.00

HANNA-BARBERA
SUPER TV HEROES
Gold Key, 1968
1 B:Birdman,Herculiods,Moby Dick,
Young Samson & Goliath. 350.00
2 . . . . 250.00
3 thru 7 Oct. 1969 . . . . @225.00

HARBINGER
Valiant, 1992
0 DL,O:Sting,V:Harada, from TPB
  (Blue Bird Ed.). 25.00
0 from coupons. 4.00
1 DL,JDx,I:Sting,Torque,
  Zeppelin,Flamingo,Kris 20.00
2 DL,JDx,V:Harbinger Foundation,
  I:Dr.Heyward 10.00
3 DL,JDx,I:Ax,Rexo, V:Spider
  Aliens 10.00
4 DL,JDx,V:Ax,I:Fort,
  Spikeman,Dog,Bazooka 10.00
5 DL,JDx,I:Puff,Thumper,
  A:Solar,V:Harada. 10.00
6 DL,D:Torque,A:Solar,
  V:Harada,Eggbreakers 8.00
1a thru 6a w/o coupon. . . . . . . @2.00
7 DL,Torque's Funeral 8.00
8 thru 40 . . . . @2.50
41 V:Harbinger. 8.00

HARBINGER FILES:
HARADA
Valiant, 1994
1 BL,DC,O:Harada 2.75
2 Harada's ultimate weapon. 2.50

HARDCASE
Malibu Ultraverse, 1993–95
1 I:Hardcase,D:The Squad. 3.00
1a Ultra-Limited, silver foil 4.00
1b Full Hologram (c). 6.00
1c Platinum edition 3.50
2 w/Ultraverse card. 3.00
3 Hard decisions. 2.75
4 A:Strangers 2.75
5 BWS,V:Hardwire,BU:Rune 2.75
6 thru 15 . . . . @2.50
16 NIM-E 3.50
17 thru 24 . . . . @2.50
25 Mundiquest,concl. 3.00
26 Time Gem Disaster. 3.00

H.A.R.D. CORPS
Valiant, 1992
1 JLe(c),DL,BL,V:Harbinger
  Foundation,I:Flatline,D:Maniac . 2.50
1a Gold Ed.. . . . . 2.50
2 thru 30 . . . . @2.50

HARDY BOYS, THE
Gold Key, 1970
1 . . . . 100.00
2 thru 4 . . . . @60.00

COLOR PUB.

HARDY BOYS
NBM Books, 2004
1 The Ocean of Osyria, pt.1	3.00
2 The Ocean of Osyria, pt.2	3.00
3 The Ocean of Osyria, pt.3	3.00
4 Identity Theft, pt.1	3.00
5 Identity Theft, pt.2	3.00
GN Vol. 1 The Ocean of Osyria	8.00
GN Vol. 2 Identity Theft	8.00
GN Vol. 3: Madhouse	8.00

Papercutz, 2005
GN Vol. 4 Malled	8.00
GN Vol. 5 Sea You, Sea Me	8.00
GN Vol. 6 Hyde & Shriek	8.00
GN Vol. 7 Opposite Numbers	8.00

HARI KARI
Blackout Comics, 1995
0 I:Hari Kari	3.00
1	3.00
1a commemorative, variant(c)	10.00

Specials & 1-shots
1 The Beginning, O:Kari (1996)	3.00
1a The Beginning, commemorative, signed	10.00
1 Bloodshed (1996)	3.00
1a Bloodshed, deluxe, variant(c)	10.00
1 Live & Untamed! (1996)	3.00
1 Rebirth (1996)	3.00
0 The Silence of Evil (1996)	3.00
0 The Silence of Evil, limited, foil stamped	13.00
? The Diary of Kari Sun (1997)	3.00
? The Diary of Kari Sun, deluxe	10.00
0 Life or Death (1997)	3.00
0a Life or Death, super sexy parody edition	13.00
1 Passion & Death (1997)	3.00
1 Passion & Death, photo(c)	10.00
1 Possessed by Evil (1997)	3.00
1 Resurrection (1997)	3.00

HARLEM GLOBETROTTERS
Gold Key, 1972
1	75.00
2 thru 12, Jan. 1975	@50.00

HARRIERS
Entity, 1995
1 I:Macedon Arsenal, Cardinal	3.00
1a with Video Game	7.00
2 and 3 V:Kr'llyn	@2.50

HARSH REALM
Harris, 1994
1 thru 6 JHi(s)	@3.00

HARVEY HITS
Harvey Publications, 1957–67
1 The Phantom	500.00
2 Rags Rabbit	100.00
3 Richie Rich	3,000.00
4 Little Dot's Uncles	350.00
5 Stevie Mazie's Boy Friend	100.00
6 JK(c),BP,The Phantom	400.00
7 Wendy the Witch	700.00
8 Sad Sack's Army Life	200.00
9 Richie Rich's Golden Deeds	1,000.00
10 Little Lotta	300.00
11 Little Audrey Summer Fun	250.00
12 The Phantom	400.00
13 Little Dot's Uncles	300.00
14 Herman & Katnip	100.00
15 The Phantom	400.00
16 Wendy the Witch	800.00
17 Sad Sack's Army Life	200.00
18 Buzzy & the Crow	100.00
19 Little Audrey	200.00

Harvey Hits #3
© *Harvey Publications*

20 Casper & Spooky	200.00
21 Wendy the Witch	400.00
22 Sad Sack's Army Life	150.00
23 Wendy the Witch	400.00
24 Little Dot's Uncles	250.00
25 Herman & Katnip	100.00
26 The Phantom	350.00
27 Wendy the Good Little Witch	500.00
28 Sad Sack's Army Life	150.00
29 Harvey-Toon	150.00
30 Wendy the Witch	400.00
31 Herman & Katnip	100.00
32 Sad Sack's Army Life	150.00
33 Wendy the Witch	300.00
34 Harvey-Toon	100.00
35 Funday Funnies	100.00
36 The Phantom	300.00
37 Casper & Nightmare	200.00
38 Harvey-Toon	150.00
39 Sad Sack's Army Life	150.00
40 Funday Funnies	100.00
41 Herman & Katnip	100.00
42 Harvey-Toon	100.00
43 Sad Sack's Army Life	150.00
44 The Phantom	300.00
45 Casper & Nightmare	150.00
46 Harvey-Toon	100.00
47 Sad Sack's Army Life	100.00
48 The Phantom	300.00
49 Stumbo the Giant	250.00
50 Harvey-Toon	100.00
51 Sad Sack's Army Life	50.00
52 Casper & Nightmare	90.00
53 Harvey-Toons	40.00
54 Stumbo the Giant	100.00
55 Sad Sack's Army Life	40.00
56 Casper & Nightmare	75.00
57 Stumbo the Giant	100.00
58 Sad Sack's Army Life	40.00
59 Casper & Nightmare	75.00
60 Stumbo the Giant	100.00
61 Sad Sack's Army Life	40.00
62 Casper & Nightmare	75.00
63 Stumbo the Giant	90.00
64 Sad Sack's Army Life	40.00
65 Casper & Nightmare	60.00
66 Stumbo the Giant	75.00
67 Sad Sack's Army Life	40.00
68 Casper & Nightmare	60.00
69 Stumbo the Giant	75.00
70 Sad Sack's Army Life	40.00
71 Casper & Nightmare	60.00
72 Stumbo the Giant	75.00
73 Little Sad Sack	40.00
74 Sad Sack's Muttsy	40.00
75 Casper & Nightmare	55.00

76 Little Sad Sack	40.00
77 Sad Sack's Muttsy	40.00
78 Stumbo the Giant	75.00
79 Little Sad Sack	40.00
80 Sad Sack's Muttsy	40.00
81 Little Sad Sack	40.00
82 Sad Sack's Muttsy	40.00
83 Little Sad Sack	40.00
84 Sad Sack's Muttsy	35.00
85 Gabby Gob	35.00
86 G.I. Juniors	30.00
87 Sad Sack's Muttsy	35.00
88 Stumbo the Giant	65.00
89 Sad Sack's Muttsy	35.00
90 Gabby Goo	30.00
91 G.I. Juniors	30.00
92 Sad Sack's Muttsy	35.00
93 Sadie Sack	30.00
94 Gabby Goo	30.00
95 G.I. Juniors	30.00
96 Sad Sack's Muttsy	35.00
97 Gabby Goo	30.00
98 G.I. Juniors	30.00
99 Sad Sack's Muttsy	35.00
100 Gabby Goo	30.00
101 G.I. Juniors	25.00
102 Sad Sack's Muttsy	30.00
103 Gabby Goo	25.00
104 G.I. Juniors	25.00
105 Sad Sack's Muttsy	30.00
106 Gabby Goo	25.00
107 G.I. Juniors	25.00
108 Sad Sack's Muttsy	30.00
109 Gabby Goo	25.00
110 G.I. Juniors	25.00
111 Sad Sack's Muttsy	30.00
112 G.I. Juniors	25.00
113 Sad Sack's Muttsy	30.00
114 G.I. Juniors	25.00
115 Sad Sack's Muttsy	30.00
116 G.I. Juniors	25.00
117 Sad Sack's Muttsy	30.00
118 G.I. Juniors	25.00
119 Sad Sack's Muttsy	30.00
120 G.I. Juniors	25.00
121 Sad Sack's Muttsy	30.00
122 G.I. Juniors	25.00

HATE
Fantagraphics, 1990
1 thru 15, see B&W
16 thru 29	@3.00
30 48pg.	4.00
Ann.#1 48-page (2000)	4.00
Ann.#2 (2001)	4.00
Ann.#3 (2002)	4.00
Ann.#4 (2003)	5.00
Ann.#5 (2004)	5.00
Ann.#6 (2006)	5.00
Ann.#7 (2007)	5.00

HAUNTED
Charlton, 1971–84
1	65.00
2	30.00
3 thru 5	@30.00
6 thru 10	@25.00
11 thru 20	@20.00
21 thru 50	@15.00
51 thru 75	@10.00

HAUNTED, THE
Chaos! Comics, 2001
1 (of 4) PDd	3.00
1a variant Nat Jones (c)	3.00
1b premium ed.	10.00
2 PDd	3.00
2a variant Molenaar (c)	7.50
3 PDd	3.00
3a variant (c)	7.50
4	3.00

4a variant (c). 7.50
Ashcan, b&w 6.00

HAUNTED, THE:
GRAY MATTERS
Chaos! Comics, 2002
1 . . . . 3.00
1a premium edition 10.00

HAUNTED LOVE
Charlton, 1973–75
1 . . . . 75.00
2 . . . . 30.00
3 thru 5 . . . . @30.00
6 thru 11 . . . . @25.00

HAUNT OF FEAR
Gladstone, 1991
1 EC Rep. H of F #17,WS#28 . . . . 3.00
2 EC Rep. H of F #5,WS #29 . . . . . 3.00

HAUNT OF FEAR
Russ Cochran, 1991
1 EC Rep. H of F #15 . . . . 3.00
2 thru 5 EC Rep. H of F . . . . @3.00
Second Series, 1992
1 EC Rep. H of F #14,WS#13 . . . . 2.50
2 EC Rep. H of F #18,WF#14 . . . . 2.50
3 EC Rep. H of F #19,WF#18 . . . . 2.50
4 EC Rep. H of F #16,WF#15 . . . . 2.50
5 EC Rep. H of F #5,WF#22 . . . . . 2.50
6 EC Rep. H of F 2.50
7 EC Rep. H of F 2.50
8 thru 15 Rep. . . . . @2.50
Gemstone
16 thru 28 EC comics reprint . . . . @2.50

HAVE GUN, WILL TRAVEL
Dell Publishing Co., 1958
1 Richard Boone Ph(c) all. 250.00
2 . . . . 200.00
3 . . . . 200.00
4 thru 14 . . . . @150.00

HAWKMOON,
COUNT BRASS
First
1 Michael Moorcock adapt. 2.50
2 thru 4 . . . . @2.50

HAWKMOON
JEWEL IN THE SKULL
First, 1986
1 Michael Moorcock adapt. 3.00
2 thru 4 . . . . @2.50

HAWKMOON,
MAD GOD'S AMULET
First, 1987
1 Michael Moorcock adapt. 2.50
2 thru 4 . . . . @2.50

HAWKMOON,
SWORD OF THE DAWN
First, 1987
1 Michael Moorcock adapt. 2.50
2 thru 4 . . . . @2.50

HAWKMOON,
THE RUNESTAFF
First, 1988
1 Michael Moorcock adapt. 2.50
2 thru 4 . . . . @2.50

HEAVY METAL
MONSTERS
3-D-Zone, 1992
1 w/3-D glasses 4.00

HECTOR HEATHCOTE
Gold Key, 1964
1 . . . . 150.00

HEDG
Papyrus Media, 2002
1 by Patrick Sherman 3.00
1 signed 3.00
2 thru 4 . . . . @3.00

HEDGE KNIGHT, THE
Devil's Due Publishing, 2004
Previously published by Image
1 to 3 Collected edition, BV&JuB(c) 9.00
4 thru 6 . . . . @3.00
4a thru 6a variant (c)s . . . . @6.00

HELDEN
Caption Comics, 2001
1 (of 6) by Ralf Paul 3.00
2 thru 5 . . . . @3.00
6 concl. 52-pg. 4.00

HELIOS:
IN WITH THE NEW
Speakeasy Comics, 2005
1 & 2 (of 4) . . . . @3.00
Dakuwaka Productions, 2006
3 48-pg. 5.00

HELIOS:
UNDER THE GUN
Dakuwaka Productions, 2006
1 . . . . 3.00
2 thru 4 . . . . @3.00

HELLINA/
DOUBLE IMPACT
Lightning, 1996
1-shot JCy(c) 3.00
1-shot variant (c). 3.00

HELLINA:
HEART OF THORNS
Lightning Comics, 1996
1 . . . . 3.00
1 autographed edition 10.00
2 . . . . 3.00
2 variant cover 3.00
2 platinum edition 6.00

HELLINA: HELLBORN
Lightning, 1997
1 . . . . 3.00
1 autographed edition 10.00

HELLINA/NIRA X:
ANGEL OF DEATH
Lightning, 1996
1A cover A. 3.00
1B cover B 3.00
1C Platinum cover 9.00
1D signed 9.00

HELLINA/NIRA X:
CYBERANGEL
Lightning, 1996
1 autographed edition 10.00

HELIOS
Dakuwaka Productions, 2004
1 . . . . 3.00
2 thru 4 . . . . @3.00

HELL, MICHIGAN
FC9 Publishing, 2005
1 thru 4 . . . . @3.00

HERBIE
American Comics Group
April-May, 1964
1 . . . . 350.00
2 thru 4 . . . . @150.00
5 A:Beatles,Dean Martin, Frank
   Sinatra 200.00
6 . . . . 125.00
7 . . . . 125.00
8 O:Fat Fury 150.00
9 . . . . 125.00
10 . . . . 125.00
11 thru 13 . . . . @100.00
14 A:Nemesis,Magic Man 100.00
15 thru 22 . . . . @100.00
23 Feb., 1967. . . . . 100.00

HERCULES
Charlton Comics, 1967
1 . . . . 75.00
2 thru 7 . . . . @40.00
8 scarce 50.00
9 thru 13 Sept. 1969 . . . . @40.00

HERCULES: THE
LEGENDARY JOURNEYS
Topps, 1996
1 & 2 . . . . @3.00
3 RTs,JBt,SeM,The Shaper,pt.1 . . . 5.00
3a Xena Ph(c). 15.00
4 RTs,JBt,SeM,The Shaper,pt.2 . . . 5.00
5 RTs,JBt,SeM,The Shaper,pt.3 . . . 5.00

HERE COMES
THE BIG PEOPLE
Event Comics, 1997
1 ACo&JP(c) 3.00
1b JfD(c) 3.00
1c JQ&JP alternate (c) 10.00
1d JQ&JP alternate (c) signed . . . 30.00

HERO ALLIANCE
Wonder Color Comics, 1987
1 . . . . 2.50
Innovation, 1989–91
1 RLm,BS(c),R:HeroAlliance 6.00
2 RLm,BS(c),Victor vs.Rage 5.00
3 RLm,A:Stargrazers 4.00
4 BS(c),Fearful Symmetry 3.00
5 RLm(c) 2.50
6 BS(c),RLm pin-up 3.25
7 V:Magnetron 2.50
8 I:Vector 2.50
9 BS(c),V:Apostate 2.50
10 Living Legends, A:Sentry 2.50
11 Obligations, F:Kris Dunlop 2.50
12 Legacy, I:Bombshell 2.50
13 V:Bombshell 2.50
14 Kris Solo Story 2.50
15 JLA Parody Issue 2.50
16 V:Sepulchre 2.50
17 O:Victor,I&D:Misty 2.50
Annual #1 PS,BS,RLm 3.00
Spec.#1 Hero Alliance update 2.50
Spec.Hero Alliance & Justice Machine:
Identity Crises 2.50

HERO ALLIANCE: THE END OF THE GOLDEN AGE
Pied Piper, 1986
1 Bart Sears/Ron Lim 20.00
1a signed 25.00
1b 2nd printing 2.50
2 . . . . 12.00
3 . . . . 3.00
Graphic Novel 10.00
Innovation, 1989
1 RLm 5.00
1A 2nd printing 2.50
2 RLm 4.00
3 RLm 3.00

HERO ALLIANCE QUARTERLY
Innovation, 1991
1 Hero Alliance stories 2.75
2 inc. Girl Happy 2.75
3 inc. Child Engagement 2.75
4 . . . . 2.75

HERO AT LARGE
Speakeasy Comics, 2005
1 . . . . 3.00
2 . . . . 3.00
3 thru 4 . . . . @3.00

HERO SQUARED
Atomeka, 2004
Spec. #1 X-tra Sized, KG,JMD 4.00
Spec. #1 X-tra Sized, Previews 4.00
Boom! Studios, 2005
1 (of 3) KG,JMD 4.00
1a Pull My Finger (c) 4.00
2 thru 3 . . . . @4.00
4 . . . . 4.00
5 thru 7 ongoing series . . . . @4.00
Spec. #1 Brainless Sitcom (c) 7.00

HI-ADVENTURE HEROES
Gold Key, 1969
1 . . . . 75.00
2 . . . . 65.00

HIGH CHAPPARAL
Gold Key, 1968
1 . . . . 100.00

Hi-Adventure Heroes #1
© Gold Key

HIGHLANDER: THERE CAN BE ONLY ONE
D.E. (Dynamite Ent.) 2006
0 . . . . 1.00
1 . . . . 3.00
1a variant (c)s . . . . @3.00
1b variant Immortal gold foil (c) . . 20.00
2 . . . . 3.00
2a variant (c)s . . . . @3.00
3 thru 12 . . . . @3.00
3a thru 12a variant (c)s . . . . @3.00

HIGH ROADS
WildStorm/DC, 2002
Cliffhanger Productions
1 (of 6),SLo(s),F:Nick Highroad . . . 3.00
2 SLo(s),Paris 3.00
3 SLo(s),Nic Highroad 3.00
4 SLo(s),Iron Cross Brotherhood . . 3.00
5 SLo(s),Sloan,Bombridge 3.00
6 SLo(s),concl. 3.00

HIGH SCHOOL CONFIDENTIAL DIARY
Charlton Comics, 1960
1 . . . . 75.00
2 thru 11 . . . . @50.00
Becomes:

CONFIDENTIAL DIARY
12 . . . . 60.00
13 thru 17 March, 1963 . . . . @50.00

HIGH VOLTAGE
Blackout, 1996
O 3.00

HIGHWAYMEN, THE
Wildstorm/DC, June, 2007
1 (of 5) 3.00
2 . . . . 3.00
3 BSf(c) 3.00
4 BSf(c) 3.00
5 BSf(c),finale 3.00

HI-SCHOOL ROMANCE DATE BOOK
Harvey Publications, 1962
1 BP 90.00
2 . . . . 60.00
3 March, 1963 . . . . 65.00

HIS NAME IS ROG... ROG 2000
A Plus Comics
1 . . . . 2.50

HOBBIT, THE
Eclipse
1 . . . . 8.00
1a 2ndPrinting 6.00
2 . . . . 7.00
2a 2ndPrinting 5.00
3 . . . . 6.00

HOGAN'S HEROES
Dell Publishing Co., 1966
1 Ph(c) 150.00
2 Ph(c) 125.00
3 JD,Ph(c). 125.00
4 thru 8 Ph(c) . . . . @100.00
8 and 9 . . . . @100.00

HOLLYWOOD NOIR
Narwain Publishing, 2006
GN Vol. 1 . . . . 6.00

HONEY WEST
Gold Key, 1966
1 . . . . 200.00

HONEYMOONERS
Lodestone, 1986
1 . . . . 4.00
5 Mag. 3.00
[2nd Series] Triad, 1987
1 They Know What They Like. 5.00
2 The Life You Save 4.00
3 X-mas special,inc.Art Carney
   interview 4.00
4 In the Pink 4.00
5 Bang, Zoom, To the Moon 4.00
6 Everyone Needs a Hero inc.
   Will Eisner interview 4.00
7 . . . . 4.00
8 . . . . 4.00
9 Jack Davis(c). 5.00
10 thru 13 . . . . @4.00

HONG KONG
Blackout Comics, 1996
0 A:Hari Kari 3.00
0 limited commemorative edition . 10.00

HORROR SHOW
Dead Dog Comics, 2005
1 . . . . 5.00

HORRORWOOD
Ape Entertainment, 2006
1 thru 4 . . . . @3.50

HORSEMEN
Griot Enterprises, 2002
1 (of 3) 3.00
2 thru 3 . . . . @3.00
3.5 . . . . 3.00

HOT ROD RACERS
Charlton Comics, 1964
1 . . . . 150.00
2 thru 5 . . . . @100.00
6 thru 15 July, 1967 . . . . @75.00

HOTSPUR
Eclipse, 1987
1 RT(i),I:Josef Quist 3.00
2 RT(i),Amulet of Kothique Stolen . 3.00
3 RT(i),Curse of the SexGoddess . 3.00

HOT STUFF, THE LITTLE DEVIL
Harvey Publications, 1957
1	800.00
2 1st Stumbo the Giant	400.00
3 thru 5	@250.00
6 thru 10	@200.00
11 thru 20	@175.00
21 thru 40	@150.00
41 thru 60	@100.00
61 thru 100	@75.00
101 thru 105	@40.00
106 thru 112 52 pg Giants	@50.00
113 thru 139	@20.00
140 thru 177	@15.00

HOT STUFF SIZZLERS
Harvey Publications, 1960
1 F:Hot Stuff	350.00
2	150.00
3	125.00
4	125.00
5	125.00
6 thru 10	@100.00
11 thru 15	@90.00
16 thru 20	@85.00
21 thru 30	@60.00
31 thru 44	@50.00
45 E:68 pgs	50.00
46 thru 50	@40.00
51 thru 59	@30.00

HOWARD CHAYKIN'S AMERICAN FLAGG!
First, 1988
1 thru 9	@3.00
10 thru 12	@3.00

H.P.LOVECRAFT'S CTHULHU
Millennium, 1991
1 I:Miskatonic Project,V:Mi-Go	3.00
2 Arkham, trading cards	3.00
3	2.50

H.R. PUFNSTUF
Gold Key, 1970
1	350.00
2 & 3	@175.00
4 thru 8	@150.00

HUCK & YOGI JAMBOREE
Dell Publishing Co., March, 1961
1	175.00

HUCKLEBERRY HOUND
Charlton, 1970
1	100.00
2 thru 7	@75.00
8 Jan., 1972	80.00

HUCKLEBERRY HOUND
Dell Publishing Co., May-July, 1959
1	200.00
2	150.00
3 thru 7	@150.00
8 thru 10	@125.00
11 thru 17	@100.00

Gold Key, 1962
18 Chuckberry Tales	150.00
19 Chuckberry Tales	125.00
20 Chuckberry Tales	100.00
21 thru 30	@75.00
31 thru 43	@60.00

HUEY, DEWEY & LOUIE JUNIOR WOODCHUCKS
Gold Key, 1966
1	100.00
2 thru 5	@60.00
6 thru 17	@50.00
18	40.00
19 thru 25	@50.00
26 thru 30	@40.00
31 thru 57	@40.00
58	35.00
59	35.00
60 thru 80	@30.00
81 1984	30.00

HUNGER, THE
Speakeasy Comics, 2005
1	3.00
2 thru 5	@3.00
6 thru 8	@3.00

HUNK
Charlton, 1961
1	60.00
2 thru 11	@30.00

HUNTER'S MOON
Boom! Studios, 2007
1	4.00
1a variant (c)	4.00
2 thru 4	@4.00

Hybrids #3
© Continuity

HYBRIDS
Continuity, 1993
0 Deathwatch 2000 prologue	5.00
1 Deathwatch 2000 pt.4,w/card	3.00
2 Deathwatch 2000 pt.13,w/card	3.00
3 Deathwatch 2000 w/card	3.00
4 A:Valeria	3.00
5 O:Valeria	3.00

[2nd Series], 1994
1 Rise of Magic	3.00

HYBRIDS: ORIGIN
Continuity, 1993
1 thru 5	@3.00

HYDE-25
Harris, 1995
1 New Drug	3.00

HYPER-ACTIVES, THE
Alias Enterprises, 2005
0	1.00
1 (of 5)	3.50
2 thru 4	@3.50

I SPY
Gold Key, 1966
1 Bill Cosby Ph(c)	400.00
2 Ph(c)	300.00
3 thru 4 AMc,Ph(c)	@200.00
5 thru 6 Ph(c) Sept.1968	@200.00

I-BOTS
Big Comics, 1996
1 F:Lady Justice	2.50
2 thru 4	@2.50
5 StG(s),PB.	2.50
6 StG(s),PB.	2.50
7 PB,Rebirth,pt.1, triptych (c)	2.50
8 PB,Rebirth,pt.2, triptych (c)	2.50
9 PB,Rebirth,pt.3, Original I-Bots return, triptych (c)	2.50

ICICLE
Hero Graphics
1 A:Flare,Lady Arcane, V:Eraserhead	5.00
2 thru 5 see B&W section	

IDAHO
Dell, 1963
1	35.00
2 thru 8	20.00

I DREAM OF JEANNIE
Dell Publishing Co., 1965
1 Ph(c),B.Eden	300.00
2 Ph(c),B.Eden	200.00

I'M DICKENS – HE'S FENSTER
Dell Publishing Co., May-July, 1963
1 Ph(c)	100.00
2 Ph(c)	80.00

IMP
Slave Labor, 1994
1	2.50

IMPACT
Gemstone, 1999
1 EC Comic reprint	3.00
2 thru 5	@3.00
Annual #1 rep. #1–#5	13.50

IMPOSSIBLE TALES
After Hours, 2006
1 (of 2)	4.00
2	4.00

INCAL
Humanoids Publishing, 2001
1	3.00
2 thru 13	3.00

INDIA AUTHENTIC
Virgin Comics, 2007
1 Ganesha	3.00
2 Kaali	3.00
3 Indra, King of the Gods	3.00
4 Uma	3.00
5 Shiva	3.00
6 Vishnu – The Narasimha Avatar	3.00
7 Yama – The Lord of Death	3.00

INFANTRY
Devil's Due Publishing, 2004
1 Aftermath, JoC 3.00
1a variant (c) 3.00
2 thru 6 . . . . @3.00

INFINITEENS
FC9 Publishing, 2005
1 . . . . 3.00
1a variant (c) 3.00
2 thru 4 . . . . @3.00
Moonstone Books, 2006
1 . . . . 3.50
2 . . . . 3.00
3 thru 4 . . . . @3.50

INMATES:
PRISONERS OF SOCIETY
Delta Comics, 1997
1 (of 4) 3.00
2 thru 4 . . . . @3.00

INNER CIRCLE
Mushroom Comics, 1995
1.1 I:Point Blank 2.50
1.2 V:Deathcom 2.50
1.3 V:Deathcom 2.50
1.4 V:Deathcom 2.50

INNOCENTS
Radical Comics, 1995
1 I:Innocent 2.50

INNOVATORS
Dark Moon, 1995
1 I:Innovator, LeoShan 2.50
2 O:Mr. Void 2.50
3 I:Quill 2.50

INSANE CLOWN POSSE
Chaos Comics, 1999
1 . . . . 3.00
1 premium edition 9.00
1 Jeckel Brothers premium ed. 9.00
3 Raze the Desertz of Glass 3.00
3a variant (c) 9.00
Spec. The Amazing Jeckel Brothers 3.00

INSANE CLOWN POSSE:
DARK CARNIVAL
Chaos! Comics, 2002
1 . . . . 3.00
1a premium edition 9.00

INSANE CLOWN POSSE:
MR. JOHNSON'S HEAD
Chaos Comics, 2002
Ashcan 6.00
1 (of 2) 3.00
1a premium edition 9.00

INSANE CLOWN POSSE:
THE PENDULUM
Chaos! Comics, 2000
1 polybagged with CD single 6.00
1a variant (c) 9.00
2 polybagged 6.00
3 polybagged 6.00
4 polybagged 6.00
5 Road Rage, polybagged 6.00
6 . . . . 6.00
7 Pendulum's Promise 6.00
8 Sport hunting, with CD-ROM 6.00
9 Glimpse of Crystal Death 6.00
10 . . . . 6.00
11 with CD-ROM 6.00

12 . . . . 6.00
Spec. #1 Hallowicket 3.00

INSPECTOR, THE
Gold Key, 1974
1 BU:Pink Panther 45.00
2 BU:Pink Panther 30.00
3 thru 5 . . . . @25.00
6 . . . . 20.00
Becomes:

INSPECTOR AND THE
PINK PANTHER, THE
7 thru 19 . . . . @20.00

INTERVIEW WITH
A VAMPIRE
Innovation, 1991
1 based on novel,preq.to Vampire
   Chronicles 3.50
2 thru 11 . . . . @3.00

IN THE BLOOD
Boom! Studios, 2005
1 (of 4) 4.00
1a Previews exclusive (c) 7.00
2 . . . . 4.00
3 . . . . 4.00

INTIMATE
Charlton Comics, 1957
1 thru 3 . . . . @75.00
Becomes:

TEEN-AGE LOVE
4 . . . . 60.00
5 thru 9 . . . . @40.00
10 thru 35 . . . . @40.00
36 thru 96 . . . . @40.00

INTIMATES, THE
Wildstorm/DC, Nov., 2004
1 JoC(s),JLe 3.00
2 JoC(s),JLe 3.00
3 JoC(s),JLe,Blaster Pill Marathon . 3.00
4 JoC(s),JLe,School Dance 3.00
5 JoC(s),JLe,Hivejournal 3.00
6 JoC(s),JLe(c)F:Secret of Sykes. . 3.00
7 JoC(s),Last day of school year . . 3.00
8 JoC(s),Summer vacation 3.00
9 JoC(s),Summer vacation 3.00
10 JoC(s),Vacation's end 3.00
11 JoC(s),Back to School 3.00

The Intimates #1
© Wildstorm

12 JoC(s),Kids revolt 3.00

INTRUDER
TSR, 1990–91
1 thru 4 . . . . @3.00
5 thru 8 The Next Dimension . . . @3.00

INVADERS FROM HOME
Piranha Press, 1990
1 thru 6 . . . . @2.50

INVADERS, THE
Gold Key, 1967
1 Ph(c),DSp 200.00
2 Ph(c),DSp 150.00
3 Ph(c),DSp 150.00
4 Ph(c),DSp 150.00

INVINCIBLE FOUR OF
KUNG FU & NINJA
Dr. Leungs
1 . . . . 3.00
2 thru 4 . . . . @2.50
5 thru 11 . . . . @2.50

IO
Invictus Studios, 1994
1 I:IO 2.75
2 . . . . 2.75
3 V:Major Damage 2.75

IRON AND THE MAIDEN
Aspen MLT, 2007
1 . . . . 4.00
2 thru 4 . . . . @4.00
1a thru 4a variant (c)s . . . . @4.00

IRON HORSE
Dell Publishing Co.,
March, 1967
1 . . . . 50.00
2 . . . . 50.00

IRONJAW
Atlas, Jan.–July, 1975
1 NA(c),MSy 20.00
2 NA(c) 15.00
3 . . . . 15.00
4 O:IronJaw 15.00

IRON MARSHAL
Jademan, 1990
1 . . . . 2.50
2 thru 10 . . . . @2.50
11 thru 32 . . . . @2.50

ISAAC ASIMOV'S I-BOTS
Tekno-Comix, 1995
1 I:I-Bots 2.50
2 O:I-Bots 2.50
3 V:Black OP 2.50

IT'S ABOUT TIME
Gold Key, 1967
1 Ph(c) 75.00

ITCHY & SCRATCHY
Bongo Comics, 1993
1 DaC(s), ... 4.00
2 DaC(s), ... 3.50
3 . . . . 3.50

IVANHOE
Dell Publishing Co., 1963
1 . . . . 60.00

JACK HUNTER
Blackthorne, 1988
1 . . . . 2.50
2 . . . . 2.50
3 . . . . 2.50

JACKIE CHAN ADVENTURES
Tokyopop Press, 2003
GN Vol. 1 (of 3) Cine-Manga 8.00
GN Vol. 2 . . . . 8.00
GN Vol. 3 . . . . 8.00

JACKIE CHAN'S SPARTAN X
Topps, 1997
1 The Armor of Heaven, pt.1 . . . . . 3.00
2 The Armor of Heaven, pt.2 . . . . . 3.00
3 (of 6) 3.00

JADE
Chaos! Comics, 2001
1 . . . . 3.00
1a premium edition 9.00
2 . . . . 3.00
3 . . . . 3.00
4 . . . . 3.00
4a variant 7.50
Preview book 2.00
Preview book, premium 6.00
Ashcan Jade #1 . . . . 6.00

JADE FIRE
Kandora Publishing, 2005
1 . . . . 3.50
2 thru 4 . . . . @3.50

JADE: REDEMPTION
Chaos! Comics, 2001
1 (of 4) 3.00
1 premium edition 9.00
2 thru 4 . . . . @3.00
2a thru 4a variant (c). . . . . @6.00
Ashcan 5.00

JADEMAN COLLECTION
Jademan, 1989
1 . . . . 4.00
2 . . . . 3.00
3 thru 5 . . . . @2.50

JADEMAN KUNG FU SPECIAL
Jademan, 1988
1 I:Oriental Heroes, Blood
  Sword, Drunken Fist 5.00

JADE WARRIORS: SLAVE OF THE DRAGON
Avatar Press, 2000
1 (of 3) MD2, 40-page 3.50
1a photo (c). 3.50
1b wraparound (c). 3.50
2 MD2 . . . . 3.50
2a photo (c). 3.50

JAGUAR GOD
Verotika, 1995
1 Frazetta, I:Jaguar God. 3.00
2 V:Yi-Cha. 3.00
3 V:Yi-Cha. 3.00
4 V:Yi-Cha. 3.00
5 AOI 3.00
6 LSh,AOI 3.00
7 LSh,AOI 3.00
8 AOI 3.00

Spec.#1 Return to X'ibala,RCo 5.00
Spec. Jaguar God Illustrations. 4.00
Spec. fan club edition 10.00

JALILA
Studio G, 2003
1 . . . . 3.00
2 thru 4 . . . . @3.00
AK Entertainment, 2006
1 Overwhelmed, pt.1. . . . . 3.00
2 First Mission. 3.00
3 Overwhelmed. 3.00
4 Overwhelmed, pt. 2 . . . . 3.00
5 Overwhelmed, pt. 3 . . . . 3.00
6 War Crimes 3.00
7 thru 9 . . . . @3.00

JAMES BOND 007
Eclipse, 1991
1 MGr,PerfectBound 5.50
2 MGr 5.00
3 MGr,end series 5.00
GN Licence to Kill, MGr I/o 8.00

JAMES BOND: GOLDENEYE
Topps, 1995
1 Movie adaptation 3.00
2 thru 3 Movie adaptation . . . . . . @3.00

JASON GOES TO HELL
Topps, 1993
1 Movie adapt.,w/3 cards 3.25
2 thru 3 Movie adapt.,w/3 cards . @3.25

JASON VS. LEATHERFACE
Topps, 1995
1 Jason Meets Leatherface 15.00
2 SBi(c) Leatherface's family 10.00
3 SBi(c),conclusion 7.00

JASON X
Avatar Press, 2005
Spec. #1 . . . . 4.00
Spec. #1a Wraparound (c). 4.00
Spec. #1b Variant(c)s . . . . @4.00
Spec. 1c Blood red convention (c) . 5.00
Spec. 1d Extreme Force (c) 6.00
Spec. 1e Headless (c) 6.00
Spec. 1f Victim (c) 6.00

JAVA
Committed Comics, 2004
1 thru 3 . . . . @3.00

JAVERTS
Firstlight, 1994
1 thru 5 Pieces of an Icon. . . . . . @3.00

JAZAN WILD'S CARNIVAL OF SOULS
Markosia, 2005
1 (of 3) 3.50
2 . . . . 3.50
3 . . . . 3.50
3a variant (c)s . . . . @3.50

JENNA
Narwain Publishing, 2005
1 . . . . 4.00
2 . . . . 4.00
2a limited ed. with CD. 8.00
3 . . . . 4.00
1-shot Panic in New York. 3.00

JENNA MEETS 100 GIRLS
Narwain Publishing, 2006
1 (of 2) x-over 3.50

JENNY SPARKS: THE SECRET HISTORY OF THE AUTHORITY
WildStorm/DC, 2000
1 (of 5) MMr,JMC 8.00
1a variant (c) (1:4) 4.00
2 MMr,JMC 3.00
3 MMr,JMC,O:Jack Hawksmoor . . . 3.00
4 MMr,JMC 3.00
5 MMr,JMC,conclusion 3.00

JEREMIAH HARM
Boom! Studios, 2005
1 KG,AIG. 4.00
1a convention (c) 7.00
2 thru 5 . . . . @4.00

JET
WildStorm/DC, 2000
1 (of 4) DAn,ALa,F:Jodi Slayton. . . 2.50
2 DAn,ALa,Midnight to Midnight. . . 2.50
3 DAn,ALa,V:Timewaster 2.50
4 DAn,ALa,concl. 2.50

Jet Dream #1
© Gold Key

JET DREAM
Gold Key, 1968
1 . . . . 60.00

JETSONS, THE
Gold Key, 1963
1 . . . . 500.00
2 . . . . 300.00
3 thru 10 . . . . @200.00
11 thru 20 . . . . @150.00
21 thru 36 Oct. 1970 . . . . @125.00

JETSONS, THE
Charlton Comics, 1970
1 from Hanna-Barbera TV show. 150.00
2 . . . . 100.00
3 thru 10 . . . . @75.00
11 thru 20 Dec. 1973 . . . . @60.00

JETSONS, THE
Harvey Comics, 1991–92
1 thru 5 . . . . @3.00

All comics prices listed are for *Near Mint* condition.

JETSONS, THE
Archie, 1995
1 . . . . 3.00
2 thru 17 . . . . @3.00

JEZEBELLE
WildStorm/DC, 2001
1 (of 6) F:Harper Harrison 2.50
1a variant(c) (1:2) 2.50
2 BRa(s) 2.50
3 BRa(s) F:Harper Harrison 2.50
4 BRa(s),Seance&Sensibility,pt.1 . 2.50
5 BRa(s),Seance&Sensibility,pt.2 . 2.50
6 BRa(s),concl. 2.50

JEZEBEL JADE
Comico, 1988
1 AKu,A:Race Bannon 3.00
2 AKu 3.00
3 AKu 3.00

JIGSAW
Harvey Publications, 1966
1 . . . . 50.00
2 . . . . 40.00

JIMBO
Bongo Comics, 1995
1 R:Jimbo 3.00
2 thru 4 . . . . @3.00

JIM REAPER
Silent Devil Productions, 2006
1 Week One 4.00

JINDAI
Zenescope Entertainment, 2005
1 . . . . 3.00
2 thru 8 . . . . @3.00

JOE & MAX
Guardian Line, 2006
1 . . . . 3.00
2 thru 5 . . . . @3.00

J. N. WILLIAMSON'S MASQUES
Innovation, 1992
1 TV,From horror anthology 5.00
2 Olivia(c) inc.Better Than One . . . 5.00

JOHN BOLTON, HALLS OF HORROR
Eclipse, 1985
1 JBo 3.00
2 JBo 3.00

JOHN CARTER OF MARS
Gold Key, 1964
1 . . . . 150.00
2 . . . . 100.00
3 . . . . 100.00

JOHN DOE
Boom! Studios, 2006
Preview book 2.50

JOHN F. KENNEDY LIFE STORY
(WITH 2 REPRINTS)
Dell Publishing Co., 1964
1 . . . . 100.00
2 . . . . 75.00
3 . . . . 75.00

John Jakes Mullkon Empire #6
© Tekno Comix

JOHN JAKES MULLKON EMPIRE
Tekno Comix, 1995
1 I:Mulkons 2.50
2 O:Mulkons 2.50
3 D:Company Man 2.50
4 Disposal Problems 2.50
5 F:Granny 2.50
6 Where's Karma 2.50

JOHN LAW
Eclipse, 1983
1 WE 2.50

JOHNNY JASON TEEN REPORTER
Dell Publishing Co., 1962
1 . . . . 50.00
2 . . . . 40.00

JOHNNY NEMO
Eclipse, 1985–86
1 I:Johnny Nemo. 2.50
2 . . . . 2.50
3 F:Sindy Shade 2.50

JOHN STEELE SECRET AGENT
Gold Key, 1964
1 . . . . 150.00

JOHN WOO'S SEVEN BROTHERS
Virgin Comics, 2006
1 . . . . 3.00
1a variant (c) 3.00
2 . . . . 3.00
3 thru 8 . . . . @3.00
3a thru 8a variant (c) . . . . @3.00
Spec. Extended #1 & #2 . . . . 7.00

JONNY QUEST
Gold Key, 1964
1 TV show 700.00

JONNY QUEST
Comico, 1986
1 DW,SR,A:Dr.Zin 6.00
2 WP/JSon,O:RaceBannon 4.00
3 DSt(c) 4.00

4 TY/AW,DSt(i) 3.50
5 DSt(c)A:JezebelJade 3.00
6 AKu 3.00
7 . . . . 3.00
8 KSy 3.00
9 MA 3.00
10 King Richard III 3.00
11 JSon,BSz(c) 3.00
12 DSp 3.00
12 DSp 3.00
13 CI 3.00
14 thru 31 . . . . @3.00
Spec.#1 . . . . 3.00
Spec.#2 . . . . 3.00

JONNY QUEST CLASSICS
Comico, 1987
1 DW 3.00
2 DW,O:Hadji 3.00
3 DW 3.00

JON SABLE
First, 1983
1 MGr,A:President 4.50
2 MGr,Alcohol Issue 3.50
3 thru 6 MGr,O:Jon Sable . . . . . . @3.00
7 thru 24 MGr . . . . @2.50
25 thru 29 MGr,Shatter . . . . @3.00
30 thru 56 MGr . . . . @2.50

JON SABLE, FREELANCE: BLOODTRAIL
IDW Publishing, 2005
1 MGr 4.00
2 thru 6 . . . . @4.00

JONAS: TALES OF AN IRONSTAR
Codedeco Inc., 2004
1 . . . . 4.00
2 thru 6 . . . . @4.00

JOSIE
Archie Publications, 1963
1 . . . . 300.00
2 . . . . 150.00
3 . . . . 100.00
4 . . . . 100.00
5 . . . . 100.00
6 thru 10 . . . . @75.00
11 thru 20 . . . . @50.00
21 thru 30 . . . . @40.00
31 thru 40 . . . . @35.00
41 thru 54 . . . . @35.00
55 thru 74 . . . . @25.00
75 thru 105 . . . . @25.00
106 Oct., 1962 . . . . 25.00

JOVA'S HARVEST
Arcana Studio, 2005
1 (of 3) 5.00
2 . . . . 5.00
3 . . . . 3.50

JUDGE COLT
Gold Key, 1969
1 . . . . 50.00
2 . . . . 35.00
3 . . . . 35.00
4 Sept., 1970 . . . . 35.00

JUDGE DREDD
Eagle, 1983
1 BB,I:Judge Death(in USA) 9.00
2 BB(c&a),The Oxygen Board 7.00
3 BB(c),Judge Dredd Lives 6.00

4 BB(c),V:Perps 6.00
5 thru 10 BB(c),V:Perps . . . . @5.00
11 BB(c) 4.00
12 BB(c) 4.00
13 BB(c), The Day the Law
   Died, pt.5 . . . . 4.00
14 BB(c),Dredd vs. Dredd 4.00
15 thru 21 BB(c) . . . . @4.00
22 thru 27 BB(c),V:Perps . . . . @3.00
28 A:Judge Anderson,V:Megaman . 4.00
29 A:Monty, the guinea pig 3.00
30 V:Perps 3.00
31 Destiny's Angel, Pt. 1 . . . . 3.00
32 Destiny's Angel, Pt. 2 . . . . 3.00
33 V:League of Fatties 3.00
34 V:Executioner 3.00

JUDGE DREDD
Quality Press, 1986
1 Cry of the Werewolf Pt.1 . . . . 6.00
2 Cry of the Werewolf Pt.2 . . . . 5.00
3 Anti-smoking 4.00
4 Wreckers 4.00
5 Highwayman 4.00
6 thru 9 . . . . @3.00
10 thru 44 . . . . @3.00
45 thru 61 . . . . @2.50
Becomes:
JUDGE DREDD CLASSICS
62 thru 75 . . . . @2.50
76 Diary of a Mad Citizen 3.00
77 . . . . 3.00
Judge Dredd Special #1 . . . . 2.50

JUDGE DREDD:
AMERICA
Fleetway
1 I:America 3.50

JUDGE DREDD:
JUDGE CHILD QUEST
Eagle, 1984
1 thru 3 . . . . @3.00
4 BB(c) 3.00
5 . . . . 3.00

JUDGE DREDD'S
CRIME FILE
Eagle, 1984
1 Ron Smith, The Perp Runners . . 2.50
2 thru 6 . . . . @2.50
Quality (Prestige format), 1989
1 A:Rogue Trooper 6.50
2 IG,V:Fatties, Energy Vampires &
   Super Fleas 6.00
3 Battles foes from dead A:Judge
   Anderson 6.00

JUDGE DREDD'S
EARLY CASES
Eagle, 1986
1 Robot Wars, Pt.1 . . . . 4.00
2 Robot Wars, Pt.2 . . . . 3.00
3 V:Perps 3.00
4 IG, Judge Giant 3.00
5 V:Perps 3.00
6 V:Judge killing car Elvis 3.00

JUDGE DREDD'S
HARDCASE PAPERS
Fleetway/Quality
1 V:The Tarantula 7.50
2 Junkies & Psychos 6.50
3 Crime Call Vid. Show 6.50
4 Real Coffee,A:Johnny Alpha 6.50

JUDGE DREDD:
THE MEGAZINE
Fleetway/Quality, 1991
1 Midnite's Children Pt.1
   A:Chopper, Young Death 5.50
2 Midnite's Children Pt.2 . . . . 5.00
3 . . . . 5.00
23 thru 34 . . . . @4.00
35 thru 43 . . . . @5.50
44 thru 45 . . . . @7.00
Egmont Fleetway Limited
46 thru 75 . . . . @7.00

JUDGMENT DAY
Lightning Comics, 1993
1 B:JZy(s),KIK,V:Razorr,Rift,
   Nightmare, red prism(c) 5.00
1a Gold Prism(c) 5.00
1b Purple Prism(c) 7.00
1c Misprint,Red Prism(c), Bloodfire
   Credits inside 8.00
1d Misprint,Gold Prism(c), Bloodfire
   Credits inside 8.00
1e Misprint,Green Prism(c),
   Bloodfire Credits inside 8.00
1f B&W promo ed. Gold ink 5.00
1g B&W promo ed. platinum ed. . . 7.00
2 TLw,I:War Party,BU:Perg,
   w/Perg card 4.00
3 ErP,O:X-Treme 3.25
4 ErP,In Hell 3.25
5 TLw,In Hell 3.25
6 TLw,I:Red Front,O:Salurio 3.25
7 O:Safeguard 3.25
8 . . . . 3.00
9 . . . . 3.00
10 . . . . 3.00

JUDGMENT DAY
Maximum Press, 1997
Alpha AMo(s) 2.50
Alpha variant cover 2.50
Omega AMo(s) 2.50
Omega variant cover 2.50
Final Judgment AMo(s) 2.50
Final Judgment variant cover 2.50

JUDO GIRL
Alias Enterprises, 2005
1 (of 4) 3.00
2 thru 4 . . . . @3.00
2a thru 4a variant (c)s . . . . @3.00
Vol. 2
1 (of 4) 3.50
1a variant (c) 3.50
2 thru 4 . . . . @3.50

Jughead #173
© Archie Publications

JUDOMASTER
Charlton Comics, 1966
(Special War Series #4)
   I:Judomaster 60.00
89 FMc,War stories begin 50.00
89 (90) FMc,A:Thunderbolt 40.00
91 FMc,DG,A:Sarge Steel 40.00
92 FMc,DG,A:Sarge Steel 40.00
93 FMc,DG,I:Tiger 40.00
94 FMc,DG,A:Sarge Steel 40.00
95 FMc,DG,A:Sarge Steel 40.00
96 FMc,DG,A:Sarge Steel 40.00
97 FMc,A:Sarge Steel 40.00
98 FMc,A:Sarge Steel 40.00

JUGHEAD
**Archie Publications
1965–1987**
127 thru 130 . . . . @50.00
131 thru 150 . . . . @40.00
151 thru 160 . . . . @25.00
161 thru 200 . . . . @20.00
201 thru 250 . . . . @15.00
251 thru 300 . . . . @12.00
301 thru 352 . . . . @10.00

JUGHEAD
**Archie Publications
[2nd Series], 1987**
1 thru 45 . . . . @6.00
Becomes:
ARCHIE'S PAL JUGHEAD
June, 1993
46 thru 50 . . . . @3.50
51 thru 70 . . . . @2.50
71 thru 99 . . . . @2.50
100 A Storm Over Uniforms, x-over
   (Betty #57, Archie #467) 2.50
101 thru 122 . . . . @2.50
123 thru 161 . . . . @2.50
162 thru 185 . . . . @2.25

JUGHEAD AS
CAPTAIN HERO
Archie Publications, 1966
1 . . . . 100.00
2 . . . . 65.00
3 thru 7 . . . . @50.00

JUGHEAD'S FANTASY
Archie Publications, 1960
1 Sir Jugalot 300.00
2 Peter Goon 200.00
3 Superjughead 175.00

JUGHEAD'S FOLLY
Archie Publications, 1957
1 Jughead like Elvis 675.00

JUGHEAD'S JOKES
Archie Publications, 1967
1 . . . . 125.00
2 . . . . 75.00
3 thru 5 . . . . @40.00
6 thru 10 . . . . @35.00
11 thru 30 . . . . @25.00
31 thru 77 . . . . @10.00
78 Sept., 1982 . . . . 10.00

JUGHEAD WITH
ARCHIE DIGEST
**Archie Publications,
March, 1974**
1 . . . . 100.00
2 . . . . 60.00
3 thru 10 . . . . @50.00

11 thru 91 . . . . @20.00
92 thru 129 . . . . @15.00
130 thru 138 . . . . @10.00
139 thru 144 . . . . @10.00
145 thru 155 . . . . @7.00
156 thru 171 . . . . @5.00
172 thru 179 . . . . @5.00

JUMPER JUMPSCARS
Onipress, 2007
1 (of 4) 4.00
2 thru 3 . . . . @4.00

JUNCTION 17
Antarctic Press, 2003
1 color manga 3.50
2 thru 4 . . . . @3.00

JUNGLE ADVENTURES
Skywald, March–June, 1971
1 F:Zangar,Jo-Jo,Blue Gorilla 40.00
2 F:Sheena, Jo-Jo,Zangar 35.00
3 F:Zangar,Jo-Jo,White Princess . 35.00

JUNCTION 17
Antarctic Press, 2003
1 . . . . 3.50
2 thru 4 . . . . @3.00

JUNGLE BOOK
Gold Key, 1964
1 . . . . 75.00

JUNGLE COMICS
Blackthorne, 1988
1 DSt(c) 3.00
2 . . . . 3.00
3 . . . . 3.00
See B&W

JUNGLE JIM
Charlton, 1969–70
22 . . . . 60.00
23 . . . . 40.00
24 . . . . 40.00
25 . . . . 40.00
26 . . . . 40.00
27 . . . . 50.00
28 . . . . 50.00

JUNGLE TALES OF TARZAN
Charlton Comics, 1964
1 . . . . 100.00
2 . . . . 75.00
3 . . . . 75.00
4 July, 1965 . . . . 75.00

JUNGLE TWINS, THE
Gold Key, 1972
1 F:Tono and Kono 30.00
2 thru 5 . . . . @15.00
6 thru 17 . . . . @10.00

JUNGLE WAR STORIES
Dell Publishing Co., 1962
1 P(c) all 75.00
2 thru 11 . . . . @50.00
Becomes:
GUERRILLA WAR
12 thru 14 . . . . @50.00

JUNIOR WOODCHUCKS
Walt Disney, 1991
1 CB,Bubbleweight Champ. 3.00
2 CB,Swamp of no Return 3.00
3 Rescue Run-Around 3.00

TONO and KONO
THE JUNGLE TWINS

The Jungle Twins #7
© Gold Key

4 Cave Caper 3.00

JURASSIC PARK
Topps, 1993
1 Movie Adapt.,w/card 5.00
1a Newsstand Ed. 4.00
2 Movie Adapt.,w/card 3.25
3 Movie Adapt.,w/card 3.25
4 Movie Adapt.,w/card 3.25
2a thru 4a Newsstand Ed. . . . . . @2.75
Ann.#1 Death Lizards 4.00

JURASSIC PARK: ADVENTURES
Topps, 1994
1 thru 10 reprints titles . . . . @3.00

JURASSIC PARK: RAPTOR
Topps, 1993
1 SE w/Zorro #0 ashcan & cards . . . 3.25
2 w/3 cards 3.00

JURASSIC PARK: RAPTORS ATTACK
Topps, 1994
1 SEt(s), ... 2.75
2 thru 4 SEt(s), ... @2.75

JURASSIC PARK: RAPTOR HIJACK
Topps
1 SEt(s), ... 2.50
2 SEt(s), ... 2.50
3 SEt(s), ... 2.50
4 SEt(s), ... 2.50

[JURASSIC PARK:] THE LOST WORLD
Topps, 1997
1 (of 4) movie adapt 3.00
2 thru 4 . . . . @3.00

JUST A PILGRIM
Black Bull Entertainment, 2001
1 GEn,MT(c) 6.00
1a variant (c). 12.00
2 GEn,GF(c) 4.00
3 GEn,KN(c), Bloody Baskets 4.00
4 GEn,BSz(c) Firestarter 4.00
5 GEn,JMC(c). 4.00

Preview Ed. 8.00

JUST A PILGRIM: GARDEN OF EDEN
Black Bull Entertainment, 2002
1 GEn,JJu(c). 7.00
1a variant GF (c). 4.00
2 GEn,CE 4.00
3 GEn,CE 4.00
4 GEn,CE 4.00
Preview ed. limited. 7.00

JUSTICE CITY CHRONICLES
Ape Entertainment, 2005
1 (of 2) 3.50
2 . . . . 3.50

JUSTICE MACHINE
Noble Comics, 1981–85
1 JBy(c) Mag size,B&W 30.00
2 MGu,Mag size,B&W 16.00
3 MGu,Mag size,B&W 10.00
4 MGu,Bluecobalt 8.00
5 MGu 7.00
Texas Comics
Ann.#1:BWGI,I:Elementals,
  A: Thunder Agents. 5.00

JUSTICE MACHINE
[Featuring the Elementals]
Comico, 1986
1 . . . . 2.50
2 . . . . 2.50
3 . . . . 2.50
4 . . . . 2.50

JUSTICE MACHINE
Comico, 1987–89
1 MGu 2.50
2 MGu 2.50
3 thru 14 MGu . . . . @2.50
15 thru 27 MGu . . . . @2.50
28 MGu 2.50
29 MGu,IW. 2.50
Ann.#1 . . . . 2.50
SummerSpectacular 1 . . . . 2.75
MINI SERIES, 1990
1 thru 4 F:Elementals . . . . @2.50
Innovation, 1990
1 . . . . 2.50
2 thru 4 The Ragnarok Portfolio . @2.50
5 thru 7 Demon trilogy . . . . @2.50

JUSTICE MACHINE: CHIMERA CONSPIRACY
Millennium
1 AH,R&N:Justice Machine,
  wraparound cover 2.50

JUST MARRIED
Charlton Comics, 1958
1 . . . . 125.00
2 . . . . 75.00
3 thru 10 . . . . @50.00
11 thru 30 . . . . @35.00
31 thru 113 . . . . @25.00
114 Dec., 1976. . . . . 15.00

KABOOM
Awesome Entertainment, 1997
1 JLb,JMs, ... 5.00
1a variant (c)s 6.00
2 JLb,JMs, ... 3.00
3 JLb,JMs, ... 4.00
4 JLb,JMs,Kaboom the
  Barbarian,pt.1 (of 3) 2.50

COLOR PUB.

5 JLb,JMs,Barbarian,pt.2 . . . . 2.50
6 JLb,JMs,Barbarian,pt.3 . . . . 2.50

VOL II

1 (of 3) 2.50
2 JLe,JLb,F:Kyra. 2.50
3 JLe,JLb, conclusion 2.50
Collected #1 & #2 . . . . 6.00

KABUKI
Caliber Press, 1994–96
1 Color Gallery,32 paintings(1995) . 7.00
1-shot Color Special, inc.
  pin-up gallery (1996) 3.00
1-shot Fear the Reaper (1994). . . . 7.00

KABUKI: SKIN DEEP
Caliber, 1996
1 DMk 4.00
2 DMk(c) 3.50
2 AxR(c) 6.00
3 Origin issue 3.50
4 . . . . 3.50

KADE
Arcana Studios, 2003
1 . . . . 3.00
2 thru 5 . . . . @3.00

KADE: SHIVA'S SUN
Arcana Studio, 2007
0 . . . . 0.25
1 . . . . 4.00

KADE: SUN OF PERDITION
Arcana Studio, 2006
1 (of 4) 4.00
2 thru 4 . . . . @4.00

KAMIKAZE: 1946
Antarctic Press, 2000
1 Pickadon 3.00
2 Operation Olympic. 3.00
3 Queens of the Seas 3.00
4 Operation Coronet 3.00
5 Kaitens 3.00
6 Fortress Japan 3.00

KAMIKAZE
Wildstorm/DC, 2003
1 (of 5) extreme sport 3.00
2 thru 6 . . . . @3.00

KARMA INCORPORATED
Viper Comics, 2005
1 . . . . 3.00
2 . . . . 3.00
3 . . . . 3.00

KARNEY
IDW Publishing, 2005
1 . . . . 4.00
2 thru 4 . . . . @4.00

KATO OF THE GREEN HORNET
Now, 1991
1 BA,1st Kato solo story 2.50
2 BA,Kato in China contd. 2.50
3 Kato in China contd 2.50
4 Final Issue 2.50

KATO II
Now, 1992
1 VM,JSh,A:Karthage 2.50
2 VM,JSh,V:Karthage 2.50
3 VM,JSh,V:Karthage 2.50

Kato II #1
© Now

KATY KEENE FASHION BOOK MAGAZINE
Archie Publications, 1955
1 Woggon(a&c) 800.00
2 . . . . 500.00
3 thru 10 not published
11 thru 18 . . . . @350.00
19 . . . . 300.00
20 . . . . 300.00
21 . . . . 300.00
22 . . . . 300.00
23 Winter 1958-59 . . . . 300.00

KATY KEENE PINUP PARADE
Archie Publications, 1955
1 . . . . 750.00
2 . . . . 400.00
3 . . . . 350.00
4 . . . . 350.00
5 . . . . 350.00
6 . . . . 300.00
7 . . . . 300.00
8 . . . . 300.00
9 . . . . 300.00
10 Woggon art 300.00
11 Story on comics. 350.00
12 . . . . 300.00
13 . . . . 300.00
14 . . . . 300.00
15 Sept., 1961 . . . . 700.00

KEE-FU FIGHTERS
Roxbox Entertainment, 2006
1 . . . . 3.25
2 . . . . 3.25

KELLY GREEN
Eclipse
1 SDr,O:Kelly Green 2.50
2 SDr,One,Two,Three 2.50
3 SDr,Million Dollar Hit 2.50
4 SDr,Rare 4.00

KEN LASHLEY'S LEGENDS
DHJ Comics, 2002
1 (of 6) by Ken Lashley 3.00
1a variant (c). 3.00
1b previews exclusive. 5.00
2 . . . . 3.00

KEEP, THE
IDW Publishing, 2005
1 F.Paul Wilson (s) 4.00
2 . . . . 4.00
3 thru 5 . . . . @4.00

KID DEATH & FLUFFY
Event Comics, 1997
Spec.#1 Halloween Spec. John
  Cebollero(c) 3.00
Spec.#1a Halloween Spec. JQ(c) . . 3.00

KID MONTANA
Charlton Comics, 1957
Previously: DAVY CROCKETT
see Golden Age
9 . . . . 100.00
10 . . . . 85.00
11 . . . . 75.00
12 . . . . 75.00
13 AW 75.00
14 thru 20 . . . . @75.00
21 thru 35 . . . . @60.00
36 thru 49 . . . . @60.00
50 March, 1965 . . . . 60.00

KILLER INSTINCT
Acclaim
1 thru 3 . . . . @2.50
Spec. Brothers by Art Holcomb 2.50

KILLER 7
Devil's Due Publishing, 2006
1 . . . . 3.00
1a variant cardstock (c) 6.00
2 thru 4 . . . . @3.00
2a thru 4a variant cardstock (c) . @6.00

KILLERS, THE: WAR'S END
Speakeasy Comics, 2006
1 (of 5) 3.00
2 thru 3 . . . . @3.00

KILLER STUNTS, INC.
Alias Enterprises, 2005
1 (of 4) 1.00
2 thru 4 . . . . @3.00

KILLER TALES
Eclipse, 1985
1 Tim Truman 3.00

KILLER, THE
Archaia Studios, 2006
1 (of 10) 4.00
2 thru 6 . . . . @4.00

KILLZONE
Dreamwave, 2004
1 . . . . 3.00
2 . . . . 3.00
3 . . . . 3.00

KINDRED II
WildStorm/DC, 2002
1 (of 4) BBh 2.50
2 BBh 2.50
3 BBh,Backlash & Grifter 2.50
4 BBh,concl. 2.50

KING LEONARDO AND HIS SHORT SUBJECTS
Dell Publishing Co., 1961–62
1 . . . . 200.00
2 thru 4 . . . . @150.00

COLOR PUB.

KING LOUIE & MOWGLI
Gold Key, 1968
1 . . . . 60.00

KING OF DIAMONDS
Dell Publishing Co., 1962
1 Ph(c) 75.00

KING OF FIGHTERS: MAXIMUM IMPACT
Dr. Masters Publications, 2005
3 thru 6 . . . . 3.00
7 thru 8 . . . . @3.00

KING OF FIGHTERS, THE: NESTS SAGA
HK Comics, 2006
1 . . . . 3.00
1a variant (c)s . . . . @3.00

KISS KISS BANG BANG
Crossgen, 2004
1 . . . . 3.00
2 thru 7 . . . . @3.00

KIT KARTER
Dell Publishing Co., 1962
1 . . . . 50.00

KNIGHTHAWK
Windjammer, 1995
1 NA(c&a),I:Knighthawk the
  Protector,V:Nemo 2.75
2 NA(c&a),Birth of Nemo 2.50
3 NA,V:Nemo 2.50
4 NA,V:Nemo 2.50
5 I:Cannon, Brick 2.50
6 V:Cannon, Brick. 2.50

KNIGHTS OF THE ROUND TABLE
Dell Publishing Co.,1963-64
1 P(c) 60.00

KNUCKLES
Archie Comics, 1997
1 . . . . 2.50
2 thru 31 . . . . @2.50
32 thru 33 . . . . @2.50

KOLCHAK: TALES OF THE NIGHT STALKER
Moonstone, 2003
1 . . . . 3.50
2 thru 7 . . . . @3.50
GN Devil in the Details 7.00
1-shot Black & White & Red
  All Over 5.00

KOLCHAK TALES: THE FRANKENSTEIN AGENDA
Moonstone, 2007
1 (of 3) 3.50
2 thru 3 . . . . @3.50

KONA
Dell Publishing Co., 1962
1 P(c) all,SG 150.00
2 SG 75.00
3 SG 75.00
4 SG,B:Anak 75.00
5 thru 10 SG . . . . @75.00
11 thru 21 SG. . . . . @50.00

Konga #19
© Charlton

KONGA
Charlton Comics, 1960–65
1 SD,DG(c), movie adapt. 425.00
2 DG(c) 200.00
3 SD 150.00
4 SD 150.00
5 SD 150.00
6 thru 15 SD . . . . @100.00
16 thru 23 . . . . @75.00

KONGA'S REVENGE
Charlton Comics
2 Summer, 1962 . . . . 100.00
3 SD,Fall, 1964 . . . . 50.00
1 Dec., 1968 . . . . 35.00

KONG: KING OF SKULL ISLAND
Markosia, 2007
0 . . . . 2.00
1 (of 5) 4.00
1a variant (c) 4.50

KOOKIE
Dell Publishing Co., 1962
1 . . . . 150.00
2 . . . . 125.00

KORAK, SON OF TARZAN
Gold Key, 1964
1 . . . . 150.00
2 thru 11 . . . . @75.00
12 thru 21 . . . . @50.00
22 thru 30 . . . . @40.00
31 thru 40 . . . . @35.00
41 thru 44 . . . . @25.00
45 Jan., 1972. . . . . 25.00
Continued by DC

KORG: 70,000 B.C.
Charlton, 1975
1 . . . . 20.00
2 thru 9 . . . . @15.00

KRAZY KAT
Gold Key, 1964
1 . . . . 60.00

KROFFT SUPERSHOW
Gold Key, 1978
1 . . . . 40.00

2 thru 6 . . . . @25.00

KRUSTY COMICS
Bongo Comics, 1995
1 Rise and Fall of Krustyland 2.50
2 Rise and Fall of Krustyland 2.50
3 Rise and Fall of Krustyland 2.50

KULL IN 3-D
Blackthorne
1 . . . . 2.50
2 . . . . 2.50
3 . . . . 2.50

LAD: A DOG
Dell Publishing Co., 1961
1 . . . . 75.00
2 . . . . 60.00

LADY ARCANE
Hero Graphics, 1992
1 A: Flare,BU:O:Giant. 5.00
2 thru 4 . . . . @3.00

LADY DEATH
Chaos! Comics, 1994
1 BnP, A:Evil Ernie 15.00
1a signed gold foil. 20.00
2 BnP 15.00
3 BnP 10.00
Specials & 1-shots
1 Swimsuit Edition 10.00
1a Velvet Edition. 18.00
1 rep. with 8-page pin-up gallery . . 3.00
1 Lady Death in Lingerie,
  various artists 5.00
1 Lady Death & the Women of
  Chaos! Gallery, pin-ups (1996) . 2.50
1-shot Dragon Wars (1998) 3.00
1-shotA Dragon Wars, Premium Ed,
  Sketchbook cover 15.00
1-shot Retribution (1998) 3.00
1-shotA Retribution (1998) variant
  cover 3.00
1-shotB Retribution, premium ed. . 10.00

LADY DEATH
Chaos! Comics, 1998
? signed, limited 12.00
1 . . . . 3.00
1a signed, limited 9.00
2 R:Lady Demon 3.00
3 V:Levithia 3.00
4 V:Pagan 3.00
5 The Harrowing, pt.1 . . . . 3.00
6 V:Uriel 3.00
7 V:Moloch 3.00
8 time to sieze Hell 3.00
9 world scythe of the covenant. . . . 3.00
10 Goddess War,pt.2 x-over 3.00
11 V:Cremator 3.00
12 Unholy Nights 3.00
13 MD2,DQ,Inferno, pt.1 . . . . 3.00
13a signed 15.00
14 MD2,DQ,Inferno, pt.2 . . . . 3.00
15 MD2,DQ,Inferno, pt.3 . . . . 3.00
15a variant cover 6.00
16 MD2,DQ,Inferno, pt.4 . . . . 3.00
Swimsuit Spec.#1, signed 15.00

LADY DEATH
Chaos! Comics, 1999
1/2 Tribute Book 12.00
0 ashcan, yellow 9.00
0 ashcan, yellow, signed. 18.00
0 ashcan, blue 20.00
1 (of 12) by Steve Hughes 3.00
1a signed 12.00
1b deluxe Steve Hughes (c) 13.00

Spec. Swimsuit 2001 #1 . . . . 3.00
Spec. Swimsuit 2001 #1 premium . 10.00
Vol. 1 Lady Death's Black Book . . . 9.00
Vol. 1 Black Book,premium ed. . . . 12.00
Halloween Special Ashcan. 6.00
Halloween Spec. Ashcan, premium 20.00
Halloween Spec. #1 . . . . 3.00
Halloween Spec. #1a premium ed. 10.00
Halloween Spec. #1b
　super-premium edition. 20.00
Halloween Spec. 1c foil edition . . . 20.00

LADY DEATH

Crossgen Code 6 Comics, 2003
1 . . . . 3.00
2 thru 12 A Medieval Tale . . . . . . @3.00
GN Vol. 1 A Medieval Tale 10.00
Season Two, 2004
1 Spell Storm 3.00
2 thru 6 The Wild Hunt . . . . @3.00

LADY DEATH

Avatar, 2004
1 10th Anniv. Edition 4.00
1a painted (c) 4.00
1b premium (c) 10.00
1c variant (c)s . . . . @6.00
1d 10th Anniv. Prism foil (c) 13.00
Spec. Swimsuit 2005 . . . . 4.00
Spec. Swimsuit 2005 variant(c)s . @6.00
Spec. Swimsuit 2005 premium (c). 10.00
Spec. Swimsuit 2005 Prism foil (c) 13.00
Spec. Leather & Lace 2005
　Various (c)s . . . . @6.00
Spec. Bikini, 2005 . . . . 4.00
Spec. Bikini, 2005 variant (c)s . . @4.00
Spec. Bikini, 2005 variant (c)s . . @6.00
Ann. #1 . . . . 5.00
Ann. #1a variant (c)s . . . . @5.00
Ann. #1b premium (c) 10.00
Spec. 2006 Fetishes 4.00
Spec. 2006 Fetishes variant (c)s @4.00
Spec. 2006 Fetishes prem. (c)s . . @6.00
1-shot Dark Horizons 3.00
1-shot Dark Horizons variant (c)s @3.00
1-shot Dark Horizons premium (c) 10.00

LADY DEATH: ALIVE

Chaos! Comics, 2001
1 (of 4) 3.00
1a premium edition 10.00
2 . . . . 3.00
3 . . . . 3.00
4 . . . . 3.00
4a variant Scott Lewis (c) 7.50
Ashcan 6.00

LADY DEATH/BAD KITTY

Chaos! Comics, 2001
1 . . . . 3.00
1a premium ed. 9.00
2 . . . . 3.00

LADY DEATH BEDLAM

Chaos! Comics, 2002
1 BAu 3.00
1a premium edition 9.00

LADY DEATH II: BETWEEN HEAVEN & HELL

Chaos! Comics, 1995
1 V:Purgatori 5.00
1a Limited Edition 5,000c 25.00
1b premium velvet cover, signed . 30.00
2 Lives As Hope 4.00
3 V:Purgatori 4.00
4 final issue 4.00

LADY DEATH: BLACKLANDS

Avatar Press, 2006
½ 3.00
½ wraparound (c) 3.00
½ variant (c)s . . . . @3.00
½ premium 10.00
1 . . . . 4.00
1a wraparound (c) 4.00
1b variant (c)s . . . . @4.00
1c premium (c) 10.00
2 . . . . 4.00
2b variant premium (c) 10.00
3 . . . . 4.00
4 . . . . 4.00
2a thru 4a variant (c)s . . . . @4.00

LADY DEATH/CHASTITY

Chaos! Comics, 2001
1 x-over 3.00
1a premium edition 10.00

LADY DEATH/CHASTITY/ BAD KITTY: UNITED

Chaos! Comics, 2002
1 . . . . 3.00
1a premium edition 10.00

LADY DEATH/THE CROW

Chaos! Comics, 2002
1 . . . . 3.00
1a premium edition 10.00
1b super premium edition 20.00
Script #1 . . . . 5.00
Script #1 premium edition 20.00
Ashcan 6.00
Ashcan, premium edition 20.00
Preview book b&w 2.00
Preview book, premium edition 6.00

LADY DEATH: THE CRUCIBLE

Chaos! Comics, 1996
1 (of 6) BnP,SHu, ... 3.50
1 leather limited edition 15.00
2 BnP,SHu, ... 3.50
3 BnP,SHu, ... 3.50
4 BnP,SHu, ... 3.50
5 BnP,SHu, ... 3.50
6 BnP,SHu,V:Genocide,concl. 3.00
GN Collected ed. Vol. 1 . . . . 6.00

Lady Death: The Crucible #4
© Chaos! Comics

GN Collected ed. Vol. 2 . . . . 6.00
GN Collected ed. Vol. 3 . . . . 6.00
Spec. Script 5.00

LADY DEATH: DARK ALLIANCE

Chaos! Comics, 2002
Ashcan b&w 6.00
Ashcan premium edition 15.00
1 (of 5) F:everybody 3.00
1a premium edition 10.00
2 thru 5 . . . . @3.00
2a thru 5a Alternate cover (c) . . . @7.50

LADY DEATH: DARK MILLENNIUM

Chaos! Comics, 2000
1 (of 3) 3.00
1a premium edition 7.00
1a signed, limited 9.00
2 . . . . 3.00
3 . . . . 3.00
Preview Book B&W 5.00

LADY DEATH: DEATH BECOMES HER

Chaos! Comics, 1997
0 follows the *Crucible*, leads to
　Wicked Ways. 3.00

LADY DEATH/EVIL ERNIE

Chaos! Comics, 2002
Ashcan 6.00
Ashcan premium edition 15.00
1 BnP, sequel to Dark Alliance 3.50
1a premium edition 9.00
1b super premium edition 15.00
1c foil edition 15.00

LADY DEATH: THE GAUNTLET

Chaos! Comics, 2002
Ashcan b&w 6.00
1 (of 4) 3.00
1a premium edition 9.00
1b foil edition 15.00
2 . . . . 3.00
2a Variant JSC (c) 7.50

LADY DEATH: THE GODDESS RETURNS

Chaos! Chomics, 2002
1 (of 2) JOs 3.00
1a premium edition 9.00
2 . . . . 3.00
2a variant (c) 7.50

LADY DEATH: HEARTBREAKER

Chaos! Comics, 2002
1 . . . . 3.00
1a premium edition 9.00
1b super premium edition 15.00
1c foil (c) 15.00
1d MegaCon foil edition 20.00

LADY DEATH/JADE

Chaos! Comics, 2002
1 . . . . 3.00
1 premium edition 9.00

LADY DEATH: JUDGMENT WAR

Chaos! Comics, 1999
Prelude 3.00

1 (of 3)	3.00
1a premium	9.00
2	3.00
3 Hell is vanquished, concl.	3.00
Preview Book B&W	5.00

LADY DEATH:
LAST RITES
Chaos! Comics, 2001

1 (of 4) RCl(c)	3.00
1 premium ed. RCl(c)	12.00
2	3.00
2 variant DkG(c)	7.50
3	3.00
3a variant (c)	7.50
4	3.00
4a variant (c)	7.50

LADY DEATH:
LOST SOULS
Avatar Press, 2005

0	3.00
0a variant (c)s	@3.00
0b premium (c)	9.00
1 (of 2)	3.00
1a wraparound (c)	3.00
1b variant (c)s	@3.00
1c premium (c)	9.00
2	3.00
2a wraparound (c)	3.00
2b variant (c)s	@3.00
2c premium (c)	9.00

LADY DEATH:
LOVE BITES
Chaos! Comics, 2001

1	3.00
1 premium edition	9.00
Ashcan	6.00

LADY DEATH:
MASTERWORKS SPECIAL
Avatar Press, 2007

1-shot	5.00
1-shot variant (c)s	@5.00

LADY DEATH/
MEDIEVAL WITCHBLADE
Chaos! Comics, 2001

1 BAu,x-over	3.50
1a variant MS (c) (1:4)	3.50
1b premium edition	9.00
1c super premium	15.00
Preview book	2.00
Preview book, premium ed.	6.00
Ashcan 12-page, B&W	6.00

LADY DEATH:
MISCHIEF NIGHT
Chaos! Comics, 2001

1	3.00
1a premium edition	11.00
1b super premium edition	15.00

LADY DEATH:
PIRATE QUEEN
Avatar Press

Spec. 40-pgs.	5.00
Spec. variant (c)s	@5.00

LADY DEATH:
RE-IMAGINED
Chaos! Comics, 2002

1 Spanish Inquisition	3.00
1a premium edition	9.00

1b super premium edition	15.00
Ashcan Re-imagined (b&w)	6.00

LADY DEATH:
RIVER OF FEAR
Chaos! Comics, 2001

1	3.00
1a premium ed.	9.00

LADY DEATH:
SACRILEGE
Avatar Press, 2007

0 (of 2)	3.00
0a variant (c)s	@3.00
1	4.00
1a variant (c)s	@4.00
2	4.00
2a variant (c)s	@4.00

LADY DEATH/SHI
Avatar Press, 2006

Preview	2.50
Preview variant (c)	3.00
Preview variant Premium (c)	9.00
0	3.00
0a variant (c)s	@3.00
1	4.00
1a variant (c)s	@4.00
2	4.00
2a variant (c)s	@4.00

LADY DEATH:
THE MOURNING
Chaos! Comics, 2002

Ashcan	6.00
1 (of 2)	3.00
1a premium edition	9.00
2	3.00
2a variant (c).	7.50

Lady Death: The Odyssey#3
© Chaos! Comics

LADY DEATH:
THE ODYSSEY
Chaos! Comics, 1996

Sneak Peek Preview	2.00
1 embossed cover	5.00
1 SHu(c) premium edition	12.00
2	3.00
3	3.00
4	3.00
4a variant cover	12.00
Micro Premium Preview Book	12.00

LADY DEATH:
THE RAPTURE
Chaos! Comics, 1999

1 (of 4) BnP,V:Father Orbec	3.00
1a dynamic forces cover	7.00
1b dynamic forces, signed	12.00
1c premium edition	9.00
2 Heaven vs. Hell	3.00
3 V:Asteroth	3.00
4 BnP	3.00
Preview Book B&W	5.00
Collected ed. Vol. 1	6.00
Collected ed. Vol. 2	6.00

LADY DEATH:
THE WICKED
Avatar Press, 2005

½	3.00
½a variant (c)	@3.00
½b premium (c)	9.00
1	4.00
1a Wraparound (c)	4.00
1b Variant(c)s	@4.00
1c Premium (c)	9.00

LADY DEATH:
TRIBULATION
Chaos! Comics, 2000

1	3.00
1a premium edition, tattoo (c)	9.00
1b chromium (c)	13.00
1c chrome (c) signed	18.00
2	3.00
3	3.00
4 concl.	3.00
Ashcan B&W	6.66

LADY DEATH/
VAMPIRELLA:
DARK HEARTS
Chaos!/Harris, 1999

Spec. x-over, 40-page	3.50
Spec. Premium Edition	9.00

LADY DEATH
VS. PANDORA
Avatar Press, 2007

1	3.00
1a variat (c)s	3.00

LADY DEATH
VS. PURGATORI
Chaos! Comics, 2000

1 gold foil	30.00
1 premium ed.	9.00

LADY DEATH
VS. VAMPIRELLA II
Chaos!/Harris, 2000

1 x-over	3.50
1a premium ed.	9.00
1b Gold foil	25.00
1c Blue foil ed.	45.00

LADY DEATH:
WARRIOR TEMPTRESS
Avatar Press

Spec.	4.00
Spec. variant (c)s	@4.00

LADY DEMON
Chaos! Comics, 2000

1 (of 3)	3.00
1a premium ed.	9.00

2 . . . . 3.00
3 concl. 3.00
Preview book B&W 5.00

LADY PENDRAGON
Maximum Press, 1996
1 mini-series 2.50
2 . . . . 2.50
3 (of 3) MD2 . . . . 2.50

LADY RAWHIDE
Topps, 1995
1 All New Solo series 5.00
2 It Can't Happen Here,pt.2 . . . . . 3.50
3 . . . . 3.00
4 . . . . 3.00
5 conclusion 3.00
Spec.#1 Rep. Zorro #2-#3 . . . . 6.50

LADY RAWHIDE
Topps, 1996
Mini-Series
1 DMG 4.00
1a DMG,signed, numbered 9.00
2 DMG 3.00
3 DMG 3.00
4 DMG, EM, Intimate Wounds 3.00
5 DMG, EM 3.00
6 DMG 3.00
7 DMG 3.00

LADY RAWHIDE:
OTHER PEOPLE'S BLOOD
Topps, 1996
Mini-Series
1 DMG,EM,A Slice of Breast 3.00

LADY VAMPRE
Blackout, 1995
0 B&W 3.50
1 . . . . 3.00

LAI WAN,
DREAM WALKER
Moonstone Books, 2005
1 . . . . 3.00
2 . . . . 3.50

LANCELOT LINK,
SECRET CHIMP
Gold Key, 1971
1 . . . . 100.00
2 thru 8 . . . . @60.00

LANCELOT STRONG,
THE SHIELD
Red Circle, 1983
1 A:Steel Sterling 3.50
2 A:Steel Sterling 2.50
3 AN/EB,D:Lancelot Strong 2.50

LANCER
Gold Key, 1969
1 TV Adapt 60.00
2 . . . . 40.00
3 . . . . 40.00

LAND OF THE DEAD
IDW Publishing, 2005
2 . . . . 4.00
3 . . . . 4.00
4 . . . . 4.00
4a photo (c). 4.00
5 . . . . 4.00
5a photo (c) 4.00

Lancer #2
© Gold Key

LAND OF THE GIANTS
Gold Key, 1968
1 TV Adapt 125.00
2 thru 5 . . . . @75.00

LANDSALE & TRUMAN'S
DEAD FOLKS
Avatar Press, 2003
1 . . . . 3.50
1a wraparound (c). 4.00
2 thru 3 . . . . @3.50
2a thru 3a wraparound (c). . . . . . @4.00

LARAMIE
Dell, 1962
1 . . . . 125.00

LAREDO
Gold Key, 1966
1 TV Adapt 50.00

LARS OF MARS
Eclipse, 1987
1 3-D MA. 3.00

LASER ERASER &
PRESSBUTTON
Eclipse, 1985–87
1 GL,R:Laser Eraser 2.50
2 GL 2.50
3 GL,CK,Tsultrine' 2.50
4 MC,Death. 2.50
5 MC,JRy,Gates of Hell 2.50
6 Corsairs of Illunium 2.50
3-D#1 MC,GL(c),Triple Cross 2.50

LASH LARUE WESTERN
AC Comics
1 . . . . 3.50
Annual 3.00

LAST BASTION, THE
Speakeasy Comics, 2006
1 (of 6) 3.00
2 . . . . 3.00

LAST OF THE
VIKING HEROES
Genesis West, 1987
1 JK. 4.00

2 JK. 3.50
3 . . . . 3.50
4 . . . . 3.50
5A sexy cover 4.00
5B mild cover 3.50
6 . . . . 3.50
7 AA(c) 3.50
8 . . . . 3.50
9 Great Battle of Nidhogger 3.50
10 Death Among the Heroes 3.50
Summer Spec.#1 FF,JK. 3.50
Summer Spec.#2 . . . . 3.00
Summer Spec.#3,A:TMNT 2.50

LAUGH
Archie, 1987–91
1 . . . . 6.00
2 thru 10 . . . . @5.00
11 thru 29 . . . . @3.00

LAUREL AND HARDY
Dell Publishing Co., 1962
1 . . . . 125.00
2 . . . . 75.00
3 . . . . 75.00
4 . . . . 75.00

LAUREL & HARDY
Gold Key, 1967
1 . . . . 100.00
2 Oct., 1967 . . . . 75.00

LAURELL K. HAMILTON'S
ANITA BLAKE,
VAMPIRE HUNTER
Dabel Brothers Productions,
2006
1 . . . . 3.00
1a variant (c)s . . . . @6.00
2 Guilty Pleasures. 3.00
2a variant (c)s . . . . @6.00
3 . . . . 3.00
3a variant (c)s . . . . @6.00

LAWMAN
Dell Publishing Co., 1959
1 Ph(c) all 250.00
2 . . . . 150.00
3 ATh. 135.00
4 . . . . 100.00
5 thru 7 . . . . @100.00
8 thru 11 . . . . @100.00

LAW AND ORDER
Maximum Press, 1995
1 MMy,D:Law,I:New Law, Order . . . 2.50
2 V:Max Spur 2.50
3 V:Law's Murderer. 2.50

LAW OF DREDD
Quality
1 V:Perps 5.00
2 BB,Lunar Olympics 4.00
3 BB,V:Judge Death 3.00
4 thru 7 . . . . @3.00
Fleetway
8 Blockmania 3.00
9 BB,DGi,Framed for murders 3.00
10 thru 32 . . . . @2.50
33 League of Fatties,final issue. . . . 3.00

LAZARUS: THE MANY
REINCARNATIONS
Lodestone Publishing, 2000
1 by Zak Hennessey 3.00
2 . . . . 3.00
4 thru 7 . . . . @3.00

LEADING MAN
Oni Press, 2006
1 (of 5) 3.50
2 thru 5 . . . . @3.50

LEAGUE OF CHAMPIONS
Hero Graphics, 1990
{Cont. from Champions #12}
1 Olympus Saga #4 . . . . 3.00
2 Olympus Saga #5,O:Malice. . . . 3.00
3 Olympus Saga ends 3.00

LEAGUE OF EXTRA-ORDINARY GENTLEMEN
WildStorm/DC, 1999
America's Best Comics
1 (of 6) AMo(s),KON 3.00
2 thru 6 AMo(s),KON. . . . . @3.00
GN Collected Edition 6.00
Vol. II (July, 2002)
1 AMo(s),KON 3.50
2 AMo(s),KON,Martian marauders . 3.50
3 AMo(s),KON,traitor 3.50
4 AMo(s),KON, ... 3.50
5 AMo(s),KON, one dies. 3.50
6 AMo(s),KON,finale 3.50

LEFT ON MISSION
Boom! Studios, 2007
1 . . . . 4.00
2 thru 5 . . . . @4.00

LEGACY
Majestic, 1993
0 platinum 9.00
1 I:Legacy 2.50
2 . . . . 2.50

Legacy #1
© *Antarctic Press*

LEGACY
Antarctic Press, 1999
1 by Fred Perry. 3.00
2 thru 5 . . . . @3.00

LEGEND
Wildstorm/DC, Feb., 2005
1 (of 4) HC,RH, 48-page. 6.00
2 HC,RH 6.00
3 HC,RH, Vietnam war 6.00
4 HC,RH,concl. 6.00

LEGEND OF CUSTER, THE
Dell Publishing Co., 1968
1 Ph(c) 50.00

LEGEND OF ISIS, THE
Alias Enterprises, 2005
1 (of 4) 3.00
2 thru 6 . . . . @3.00
7 . . . . 3.00
8 . . . . 3.00
9 . . . . 3.50
10 God War x-over 3.50
11 Rise of Darkness 3.50
12 Rise of Darkness, pt.2 . . . . 3.50
13 Rise of Darkness, pt.3 . . . . 3.50
11 thru 12 . . . . @3.50

LEGEND OF ISIS
Bluewater Productions, 2007
1 . . . . 3.50
2 thru 4 . . . . @3.50
4a variant (c) 3.50

LEGEND OF THE ELFLORD
Davdez Arts, 1998
1 by Barry Blair & Colin Chan. 3.00
2 . . . . 2.50
3 . . . . 3.00
4 . . . . 3.00
GN Vol. 1 112-page 12.00

LEGEND OF THE SAGE
Chaos! Comics, 2001
1 (of 4) F:Victoria Noble 3.00
1a premium edition 9.00
2 . . . . 3.00
2a variant (c). 7.50
3 . . . . 3.00
3a variant (c). 7.50
4 . . . . 3.00
4a variant (c). 7.50
Preview Book. 2.00
Preview Book, premium edition 6.00

LEGENDS OF JESSE JAMES, THE
Gold Key, 1966
1 . . . . 50.00

LEGENDS OF LUXURA
Comic Cavalcade, 1998
Commemorative #1 by Kirk Lindo . . 6.00
Commemorative #1a deluxe 15.00

LEGENDS OF NASCAR
Vortex, 1990
1 HT,Bill Eliott ($1.50 cover Price)
   15,000 copies 10.00
1a ($2.00 cover price) 45,000
   copies 5.00
1b 3rd pr., 80,000 copies 4.00
2 Richard Petty. 4.00
3 Ken Schroder. 3.50
4 Bob Alison 3.00
5 Bill Elliott 3.00
6 Jr. Johnson 3.00
7 Sterling Marlin 3.00
8 Benny Parsons 3.00
9 Rusty Wallace 3.00
10 thru 14 . . . . @3.00

LEGENDS OF THE STARGRAZERS
Innovation, 1989
1 thru 5 . . . . @2.50

LEONARD NIMOY'S PRIMORTALS
Teckno-Comics, 1994
1 I:Primortals. 5.50
2 Zeerus Reveals Himself 4.00
3 thru 15 . . . . @2.50
Big Entertainment, 1996
0 SEa,MKb 2.50
1 thru 7 . . . . @2.50

LEONARDO
Mirage, 1986
1 TMNT Character 5.00

LEOPARD
Millennium
1 I:Leopard 3.00
1a Gold Cover. 4.00
2 O:Leopard,V:Razor's Edge 3.00

LETHAL INSTINCT
Alias Enterprises, 2005
1 (of 6) 1.00
2 thru 5 . . . . @3.00
6 . . . . 3.50

LETHAL STRYKE
London Night Studios, 1995
1 F:Stryke 3.00
1a commemorative (1999) 6.00
2 O:Stryke. 3.00
Ann. #1 EHr 3.00
Ann. #1 platinum edition 10.00

LETHAL STRIKE/ DOUBLE IMPACT: LETHAL IMPACT
London Night, 1996
1 by Jude Millien. 3.00
1 limited 5.00

LEXIAN CHRONICLES, THE: FULL CIRCLE
APC, 2005
1 . . . . 3.50
1a signed 15.00
1b red foil (c). 9.00
2 thru 5 . . . . @3.50
5a variant (c) 3.50
Markosia, 2005
6 thru 12 . . . . @3.50
7a thru 10a variant (c)s . . . . @3.50
11 . . . . 3.50
12 Full Circle 3.50
12a Commemorative sgn ed. 7.00

LIBERALITY FOR ALL
ACC Studios, 2005
1 (of 8) 3.00
2 . . . . 3.00
3 . . . . 3.00
3a variant (c) 3.00
4 . . . . 3.00
4a variant (c) 3.00

LIBERTY GIRL
Heroic Publishing, 2006
1 . . . . 3.25
2 . . . . 3.25
3 thru 4 . . . . @3.00

LIBERTY PROJECT, THE
Eclipse, 1987–88
1 I:Liberty Project 2.50
2 . . . . 2.50
3 V:Silver City Wranglers 2.50

4	2.50
5	2.50
6 F:Cimarron,Misery and Gin	2.50
7 I:Menace	2.50
8 V:Savage	2.50

LIDSVILLE
Gold Key, 1972

1	100.00
2	75.00
3 and 4	@75.00
5 Oct., 1973	75.00

LIEUTENANT, THE
**Dell Publishing Co.,
April-June, 1962**

1 Ph(c)	65.00

LIFE WITH ARCHIE
Archie Publications, 1958

1	500.00
2	250.00
3	175.00
4	175.00
5	175.00
6	125.00
7	125.00
8	125.00
9	125.00
10	125.00
11 thru 20	@100.00
21 thru 30	@75.00
31 thru 40	@65.00
41	60.00
42 B:Pureheart	125.00
43	75.00
44	75.00
45 R.I.V.E.R.D.A.L.E.	125.00
46 O:Pureheart	100.00
47 thru 59	@65.00
60 thru 100	@60.00
101 thru 200	@25.00
201 thru 285	@15.00

LIGHT FANTASTIC, THE
Innovation, 1992

1 Terry Pratchett adapt.	2.50
2 Adaptation continues	2.50
3 Adaptation continues	2.50
4 Adapt.conclusion	2.50

LIGHTNING COMICS PRESENTS
Lightning Comics, 1994

1 B&W Promo Ed.	3.50
1a B&W Promo Ed. Platinum	3.50
1b B&W Promo Ed. Gold	3.50

L'IL HELLIONS: DAY AT THE ZOO
Silent Devil Productions, 2006

1	4.00

LILLITH: DEMON PRINCESS
Antarctic Press, 1996

1 (of 3) from Warrior Nun Areala	3.00
1a Commemorative Edition (1999)	6.00
2 and 3	@3.00

LILO & STITCH
Disney Press, 2006

GN Vol. 1	5.00

LIMBO CITY
Dreamwave, 2002

1 BAu,BBh	3.00

---

2 thru 3	@3.00

LINCOLN-16
Skarwood Productions, 1997

1 GI	3.00
2 GI	3.00
3 GI	3.00

LINDA LARK
Dell Publishing Co., 1961

1	50.00
2 thru 8	@35.00

LINUS, THE LIONHEARTED
Gold Key, 1965

1	150.00

LIONHEART
Awesome Entertainment, 1999

1 IaC,JLb, from The Coven	3.00
1 Wizard World exclusive	5.50
2 IaC,JLb	3.00
2a variant cover	3.00
2b variant IaC cover	7.00
3 concl	3.00

LIPPY THE LION AND HARDY HAR HAR
Gold Key, 1963

1	175.00

LISA COMICS
Bongo Comics, 1995

1 F:Lisa Simpson	3.00

LITTLE AMBROSE
Archie Publications, 1958

1	175.00

Little Archie #137
© Archie Publications

LITTLE ARCHIE
Archie Publications, 1956

1	1,200.00
2	500.00
3	300.00
4	300.00
5	300.00
6 thru 10	@250.00
11 thru 20	@200.00
21 thru 30	@150.00
31 thru 40	@100.00
41 thru 60	@100.00

---

61 thru 80	@75.00
81 thru 100	@30.00
101 thru 180	@15.00

LITTLE ARCHIE MYSTERY
Archie Publications, 1963

1	225.00
2 Oct., 1963	150.00

LITTLE AUDREY & MELVIN
Harvey Publications, 1962

1	225.00
2 thru 5	@100.00
6 thru 10	@75.00
11 thru 20	@65.00
21 thru 40	@30.00
41 thru 50	@30.00
51 thru 53 52 pgs Giant size	@30.00
54 thru 60	@35.00
61 Dec., 1973	30.00

LITTLE AUDREY TV FUNTIME
Harvey Publications, 1962

1 A:Richie Rich	200.00
2 same	150.00
3 same	100.00
4	100.00
5	100.00
6 thru 10	@75.00
11 thru 20	@50.00
21 thru 32	@35.00
33 Oct., 1971	35.00

LITTLE DOT DOTLAND
Harvey Publications, 1962

1	200.00
2	150.00
3	100.00
4	100.00
5	100.00
6 thru 10	@75.00
11 thru 20	@60.00
21 thru 50	@50.00
51 thru 60	@40.00
61 Dec., 1973	40.00

LITTLE DOT'S UNCLES & AUNTS
Harvey Enterprises, 1961

1	300.00
2	200.00
3	200.00
4 thru 5	@150.00
6 thru 10	@125.00
11 thru 20	@100.00
21 thru 40	@75.00
41 thru 51	@50.00
52 April, 1974	50.00

LITTLE LOTTA
Harvey Publications, 1955

1 B:Richie Rich and Little Lotta	650.00
2	350.00
3	300.00
4	275.00
5	300.00
6 thru 10	@250.00
11 thru 20	@150.00
21 thru 40	@100.00
41 thru 60	@100.00
61 thru 80	@75.00
81 thru 99	@75.00
100 thru 103 52 pgs	@75.00
104 thru 120	@40.00
121 May, 1976	40.00

All comics prices listed are for *Near Mint* condition.

LITTLE LOTTA FOODLAND
Harvey Publications, 1963
1 68 pgs	300.00
2	200.00
3	150.00
4	200.00
5	200.00
6 thru 10	@200.00
11 thru 20	@100.00
21 thru 26	@75.00
27	50.00
28	25.00
29 Oct., 1972	50.00

LITTLE MERMAID
Walt Disney, 1992
1 based on movie	3.00
2 Serpent Teen	3.00
3 Guppy Love	3.00
4	3.00

LITTLE MONSTERS, THE
Gold Key, 1964
1	125.00
2	75.00
3 thru 10	@50.00
11 thru 20	@35.00
21 thru 43	@35.00
44 Feb., 1978	35.00

LITTLE MONSTERS
Now, 1990
1 thru 6	@2.50

LITTLE SAD SACK
Harvey Publications, 1964
1 Richie Rich(c)	100.00
2	75.00
3	75.00
4	75.00
5	75.00
6 thru 19 Nov. 1967	@75.00

LITTLE STOOGES, THE
Gold Key, 1972
1	75.00
2	50.00
3	45.00
4	45.00
5	45.00
6 and 7 March, 1974	@45.00

LIVING IN INFAMY
Ludovico Technique, 2005
1 (of 4)	3.00
2 thru 4	@3.00

LIZ
Narwain Publishing, 2006
1	4.00

LLOYD LLEWELLYN
Fantagraphics, 1987
Spec. #1	2.50

LOBO
Dell Publishing Co., 1965
1	60.00
2	50.00

LOCKE
Blackthorne
1 PO.Jones	2.50
2 TD	2.50
3 thru 5	@2.50

Lone Ranger #11
© *Gold Key*

LONE RANGER, THE
Gold Key, 1964
1	125.00
2	75.00
3	60.00
4	60.00
5	60.00
6 thru 10	@50.00
11 thru 18	@50.00
19 thru 27	@40.00
28 March, 1977	40.00

LONE RANGER, THE
D.E. (Dynamite Ent.) 2006
1	3.00
1a silver foil (c)	15.00
1b director's cut	5.00
2	3.00
3	3.00
4 thru 10	@3.00

LONE RANGER AND TONTO, THE
Topps, 1994
1 JLd,TT,RM,The Last Battle	2.50
2 JLd,TT,RM	2.50
3 JLd,TT,RM, O:Lone Ranger	2.50
4 JLd,TT,RM, It Crawls	2.50

LOOKERS
Avatar
Combo Spec. 16pg.	3.00
Combo Spec. Platinum	9.00

LOONEY TUNES
Dell, 1955
166	75.00
167 thru 246	@75.00

LOONEY TUNES AND MERRIE MELODIES
Dell, 1950
108	80.00
109 thru 153	@80.00
Becomes:

LOONEY TUNES AND MERRIE MELODIES COMICS
Dell, 1954
154	75.00
155 thru 165	@75.00
Becomes:

LOONEY TUNES
Dell, 1955
166	75.00
167 thru 246	@75.00

LOONEY TUNES
Gold Key, 1975
1 reprints	50.00
2 thru 10	@30.00
11 thru 30	@15.00
Whitman, 1980
31	15.00
32 thru 47	@15.00

LORD PUMPKIN
Malibu, Oct. 1994
0 Sludge	2.50

LORE
IDW Publishing, 2003
1	6.00
2	4.00
3	4.00
4	4.00

LOST BOOKS OF EVE, THE
Viper Comics, 2006
1	3.25
2 thru 4	@3.25

LOST HEROES
Davdez Arts, 1998
0 by Rob Prior, lost SF heroes	3.00
1 thru 5	@3.00
6	3.00
GN 5/6 56-page	8.00

LOST IN SPACE
Innovation, 1991
{based on TV series}
1 O:Jupiter II Project	3.50
2 Cavern of IdyllicSummersLost	3.00
2a Special Edition	3.00
3 Do Not Go Gently into that Good Night,Bill Mumy script	3.00
4 People are Strange	3.00
5 The Perils of Penelope	3.00
6 thru 12	@3.00
Project Krell	3.00
Ann.#1 (1991)	3.00
Ann.#2 (1992)	3.00
1Spec.#1 & #2 rep. Seduction of the Innocent	@3.00
GN Strangers among Strangers	6.00
1-shot Project Robinson, follows story in issue #12 (1993)	2.50
Becomes:

LOST IN SPACE: VOYAGE TO THE BOTTOM OF THE SOUL
Innovation, 1993–94
13 thru 18	@3.00

LOST PLANET
Eclipse, 1987–88
1 BHa,I:Tyler FLynn	2.50
2 BHa,R:Amelia Earhart	2.50
3 BHa	2.50
4 BHa,Devil's Eye	2.50
5 BHa,A:Amelia Earhart	2.50
6	2.50

LOVECRAFT
Adventure Comics
1 The Lurking Fear adapt.	3.00

COLOR PUB.

2 Beyond the Wall of Sleep 3.00
3 The Tomb. 3.00
4 The Alchemist 3.00

LOVE DIARY
Charlton Comics, 1958
1 . . . . 150.00
2 . . . . 125.00
3 thru 10 . . . . @100.00
11 thru 15 . . . . @100.00
16 thru 20. . . . . @100.00
21 thru 40. . . . . @75.00
41 thru 101. . . . . @20.00
102 Dec., 1976 . . . . 20.00

LOVE SHOWDOWN COLLECTION
Archie Comics, 1997
TPB x-over rep. Archie #429 (pt.1),
   Betty #19 (pt.2), Betty & Veronica
   #82, (pt.3), Veronica #39 (pt.4)
   Return of Cheryl Blossom 5.00

LUCIFER'S HAMMER
Innovation, 1993–94
1 thru 6 Larry Niven & Jerry
   Pournelle novel adaptation . . @2.50

LUCY SHOW, THE
Gold Key, 1963
1 Ph(c) 300.00
2 Ph(c) 250.00
3 thru 5 . . . . @200.00

LUDWIG VON DRAKE
Dell Publishing Co., 1961
1 . . . . 125.00
2 thru 4 . . . . @75.00

LUFTWAFFE 1946
Antarctic Press, 1998
1 color special, by Ted Namura . . . 3.00

LUGER
Eclipse, 1986–87
1 TY,I:Luger,mini-series 2.50
2 TY 2.50
3 TY,BHa,V:Sharks 2.50

LULLABY
Alias Enterprises, 2005
Vol. 2
1 . . . . 3.00
2 . . . . 3.00
3 . . . . 3.00
3a convention foil (c) signed. 15.00
4 . . . . 3.50
5 . . . . 3.50
5a variant (c) 5.00

LULLABY: ONCE UPON A TIME
Alias Enterprises, 2006
GN Vol. 1 Pied Piper of Hamelin . . . 6.00

LUNATIC FRINGE
Innovation, 1989
1 . . . . 2.50
2 . . . . 2.50

LURKERS
IDW Publishing, 2004
1 . . . . 4.00
2 . . . . 4.00
3 . . . . 4.00
4 . . . . 4.00

LUXURA
Comic Cavalcade, 1998
Commemorative #1 by Kirk Lindo . . 6.00
Commemorative #1a deluxe 15.00

LUXURA COLLECTION
Brainstorm
Commemorative edition, red foil
   cover, 48pg. 10.00

Lynch Mob #1
© Chaos! Comics

LYNCH MOB
Chaos! Comics, 1994
1 GCa(c), I:Mother Mayhem. 3.00
2 Lynch Mob Loses. 2.50
3 1994 Time Trip. 2.50
3a Gold cover 3.00
4 Mother Mayhem at UN 2.50

LYNDON B. JOHNSON
Dell Publishing Co., March, 1965
1 Ph(c) 50.00

M
Eclipse, 1990–91
1 thru 4 JMu . . . . @5.50

MACROSS
Comico
1 . . . . 35.00
Becomes:

ROBOTECH, THE MACROSS SAGA

MAD FOLLIES
E.C. Comics, 1963
(N#). 450.00
2 1964. 350.00
3 1965. 250.00
4 1966. 275.00
5 1967. 200.00
6 1968. 175.00
7 1969. 175.00

MAD HOUSE
Red Circle, 1974–82
95 thru 97 Horror stories . . . . . @22.00
98 thru 130 Humor stories . . . . . @15.00
Annual #8 thru #11 . . . . @18.00

MADMAN
Tundra, 1992
1 . . . . 15.00
2 . . . . 12.00
3 . . . . 7.00
Oni Press, 2003
King-Size Super Special 7.00

MADMAN ADVENTURES
Tundra, 1992
1 R & N:Madman 15.00
2 . . . . 9.00
3 . . . . 8.00

MADMAN PICTURE EXHIBITION
AAA Pop Comics, 2002
1 (of 4) 4.00
2 thru 4 . . . . 4.00

MADRAVEN HALLOWEEN SPECIAL
Hamilton Comics, 1995
1 Song of the Silkies. 3.00

MAD SPECIAL
E.C. Publications, Inc., 1970
1 . . . . 200.00
2 . . . . 125.00
3 . . . . 100.00
4 thru 8 . . . . @100.00
9 thru 13 . . . . @75.00
14 . . . . 60.00
15 . . . . 60.00
16 . . . . 50.00
17 . . . . 50.00
18 . . . . 50.00
19 thru 21. . . . . @50.00
22 thru 31. . . . . @35.00
32 . . . . 35.00
33 thru 58. . . . . @20.00

MAGE
Comico, 1984–86
1 MWg,I:Kevin Matchstick 10.00
2 MWg,I:Edsel. 11.00
3 MWg,V:Umbra Sprite. 9.00
4 MWg,V:Umbra Sprite. 9.00
5 MWg,I:Sean (Spook) 9.00
6 MWg,Grendel begins. 12.00
7 MWg,Grendel. 9.00
8 MWg,Grendel. 6.00
9 MWg,Grendel. 6.00
10 MWg,Grendel,Styx 6.00
11 MWg,Grendel,Styx 6.00
12 MWg,D:Sean,Grendel. 6.00
13 MWg,D:Edsel,Grendel 5.00
14 MWg,Grendel,O:Kevin 5.00
15 MWg,D:Umbra Sprite 11.00

MAGE KNIGHT: STOLEN DESTINY
IDW Publishing, 2002
1 (of 5) by TDz & D.Cabrera. 3.50
2 thru 5 . . . . @3.50

MAGIC FLUTE
Eclipse, 1989
1 CR 5.00

MAGIC THE GATHERING:
Acclaim
GN Serra Angel + card 6.00
GN Legend of the Fallen Angel +
   card 6.00
GN Dakkon Blackblade + card 6.00

...ANTIQUITIES WAR
Acclaim Armada, 1995
1 Based on the Antiquities Set 2.75
2 F:Urza, Mishra. 2.50
3 I:Tawnos, Ashod. 2.50
4 The War Begins. 2.50

...ARABIAN KNIGHTS
Acclaim Armada, 1995
1 Based on Rare Card set 2.75
2 V:Queen Nailah 2.50

...CONVOCATIONS
Acclaim Armada, 1995
1 Gallery of Art from Game. 2.50

...FALLEN EMPIRES
Acclaim Armada, 1995
1 with pack of cards 2.75
2 F:Tymolin 2.50

...HOMELANDS
Acclaim Armada, 1995
1 I:Feroz, Serra. 6.00

...ICE AGE
Acclaim Armada, 1995
1 Dominaia, from card game 3.00
2 Ice Age Adventures 2.50
3 CV(c) Planeswalker battles 2.50
4 final issue. 2.50

...SHADOW MAGE, THE
Acclaim Armada, 1995
1 I:Jared 3.00
2 F:Hurloon the Minotaur 2.75
3 VMk(c&a),V:Juggernaut. 2.50
4 Final issue 2.50

...URZA-MISHRA WAR, THE
Acclaim Armada
1 & 2 with Ice Age II card 6.00

...WAYFARER
Acclaim Armada, 1995
1 R:Jared 2.75
2 I:New Land. 2.50
3 R:Liana, Ravidel 2.50
4 I:Golthonor. 2.50
5 Final Issue 2.50

...THE LEGENDS OF:
THE ELDER DRAGONS
1 & 2 . . . . @2.50
JEDIT OJANEN
1 & 2 . . . . @2.50
SHANDALAR
1 & 2 . . . . @2.50

MAGILLA GORILLA
Gold Key, 1964
1 . . . . 175.00
2 thru 10 Dec. 1968 . . . . @125.00

MAGILLA GORILLA
Charlton Comics, 1970
1 . . . . 100.00
2 thru 5 . . . . @60.00

MAGIQUE
WildStorm/DC, 2000
Ann. 2000 #1, Devil's
  Night x-over, pt.4 . . . . 3.50

MAGNUS:
ROBOT FIGHTER
Gold Key, 1963
1 RM,I:Magnus,Teeja,A-1,
  I&B:Capt.Johner&aliens 500.00
2 RM,I:Sen.Zeremiah Clane 250.00
3 RM,I:Xyrkol 250.00
4 RM,I:Mekamn,Elzy. 150.00

---

5 RM,The Immortal One 150.00
6 RM,I:Talpa 125.00
7 RM,I:Malev-6,ViXyrkol 175.00
8 RM,I:Outsiders(Chet, Horio,
  Toun, Malf). 140.00
9 RM, I:Madmot 140.00
10 RM,Mysterious Octo-Rob 140.00
11 RM,I:Danae,Neo-Animals 125.00
12 RM,The Volcano Makers 125.00
13 RM,I:Dr Lazlo Noel 130.00
14 RM,The Monster Robs 125.00
15 RM,I:Mogul Radur. 125.00
16 RM,I:Gophs. 125.00
17 RM,I:Zypex 125.00
18 RM,I:V'ril Trent 125.00
19 RM,Fear Unlimited 125.00
20 RM,I:Bunda the Great. 125.00
21 RM, Space Spectre 125.00
22 Rep. #1 . . . . 100.00
23 DSp,Mission Disaster 100.00
24 Pied Piper of North Am 100.00
25 The Micro Giants 100.00
26 The Venomous Vaper 100.00
27 Panic in Pacifica 100.00
28 Threats from the Depths 100.00
29 thru 46 rep. . . . . @40.00

MAGNUS:
ROBOT FIGHTER
Valiant, 1991
0 PCu,BL,Emancipator,w/ BWS
  card 9.00
0a PCu,BL,w/o card 3.00
1 ANi,BL,B:Steel Nation 9.00
2 ANi,BL,Steel Nation #2 . . . . 7.00
3 ANi,BL,Steel Nation #3 . . . . 7.00
4 ANi,BL,E:Steel Nation 7.00
5 DL,BL(i),I:Rai(#1),V:Slagger
  Flipbook format 7.00
6 DL,A:Solar,V:Grandmother
  A:Rai(#2) 6.00
7 DL,EC,V:Rai(#3) 6.00
8 DL,A:Rai(#4),Solar,X-O
  Armor.E:Flipbooks 3.50
1a thru 8a w/o coupon . . . . @2.00
9 EC,V:Xyrkol,E-7 . . . . 3.50
10 V:Xyrkol. 3.50
11 V:Xyrkol. 3.50
12 I:Turok,V:Dr. Noel,
  I:Asylum,40pgs, ... 15.00
13 thru 20 . . . . @2.50
21 JaB,R:Malevalents, Grand-
  mother 3.00
21a Gold Ed. 4.00
22 JaB,D:Felina,V:Malevalents,
  Grandmother 2.50
23 V:Malevolents 2.50
24 V:Malevolents 2.50
25 N:Magnus,R:1-A,silver-foil(c) . . . 3.00
26 thru 63 . . . . @2.50
64 Ultimatum, F:Destroyer 12.00
Yearbook #1. . . . . 4.00

MAGNUS
(ROBOT FIGHTER)
Acclaim, 1997
1 Magnus back from the future. . . . 3.00
2 thru 7 . . . . @2.50
8 thru 18 TPe . . . . @2.50

MAJESTIC
Wildstorm/DC, Jan., 2005
1 DAn&ALa(s),A:Superman 3.00
1a variant (c). 3.00
2 DAn&ALa(s),Earth life abducted . 3.00
3 DAn&ALa(s),Earth life abducted . 3.00
4 DAn&ALa(s),Earth life abducted . 3.00
5 DAn&ALa(s),Demon Night. 3.00
6 DAn&ALa(s),V:old friend 3.00
7 DAn&ALa(s),Daemonites. 3.00

---

8 DAn&ALa(s),present day. 3.00
9 DAn&ALa(s),A:Zealot 3.00
10 DAn&ALa(s),Kherubim secrets. . 3.00
11 DAn&ALa(s) 3.00
12 DAn&ALa(s) 3.00
13 DAn&ALa(s),A:Zealot 3.00
14 DAn,ALa(s),V:Javen 3.00
15 DAn,ALa(s),Imperitor V. Shapers . 3.00
16 DAn,ALa(s),Duel of his life 3.00
17 DAn,ALa(s), final issue 3.00

MAJOR DAMAGE
Invictus Studios, 1994
1 I:Major Damage 2.50
2 V:Godkin 2.50
3 First Contact Conclusion 2.50

MAN CALLED A-X
Malibu Bravura, 1994–95
[Limited Series]
0 1st Puzzle piece 3.00
1 MWn,SwM 3.00
1a Gold foil Edition 4.00
2 MWn,SwM,VLElectobot 3.00
3 MWn,SwM,Mercy Island 3.00
4 MWn,SwM,One Who Came
  Before 3.00
5 MWn,SwM,Climax 3.00

MAN CALLED KEV, A
Wildstorm/DC, July, 2006
1 (of 5) GEn(s) 3.00
2 thru 5 GEn(s) . . . . @3.00

MANDRAKE
THE MAGICIAN
King Comics, 1966
1 . . . . 100.00
2 . . . . 75.00
3 . . . . 75.00
4 A:Girl Phantom. 75.00
5 Cape Cod Caper 75.00
6 . . . . 75.00
7 O:Lothar. 75.00
8 . . . . 75.00
9 A:Brick Bradford. 75.00
10 A:Rip Kirby 90.00

Man From Uncle #12
© *Gold Key*

MAN FROM U.N.C.L.E.
Gold Key, 1965
1 The Explosive Affair. 400.00
2 The Forthur Cookie Affair 200.00
3 The Deadly Devices Affair 100.00
4 The Rip Van Solo Affair 100.00

---

5 Ten Little Uncles Affair 100.00
6 The Three Blind Mice Affair . . . 100.00
7 The Pixilated Puzzle Affair
   I:Jet Dream (back-up begins) 110.00
8 The Floating People Affair 100.00
9 Spirit of St.Louis Affair 100.00
10 The Trojan Horse Affair 100.00
11 Three-Story Giant Affair 100.00
12 Dead Man's Diary Affair 100.00
13 The Flying Clowns Affair 100.00
14 Great Brain Drain Affair 100.00
15 The Animal Agents Affair 100.00
16 Instant Disaster Affair 100.00
17 The Deadly Visions Affair 100.00
18 The Alien Affair 100.00
19 Knight in Shining
   Armor Affair 100.00
20 Deep Freeze Affair 100.00
21 rep. #10 . . . . 75.00
22 rep. #7 . . . . 75.00

MAN FROM U.N.C.L.E.
Entertainment, 1987
1 thru 11 . . . . @3.00

MAN FROM U.N.C.L.E.
Millennium, 1993
1 The Birds of Prey Affair,pt.1 . . . . . 3.00
2 The Birds of Prey Affair,pt.2 . . . . . 3.00

MANGA SHI, 2000
Crusade Entertainment 1997
1 (of 3) BiT, Final Jihad, flip-book
   Shi: Heaven and Earth 3.00
2 BiT, flip-book Tomoe:
   Unforgettable Fire preview 3.00
3 BiT, conclusion 3.00

MANIFEST ETERNITY
Wildstorm/DC, June, 2006
1 SLo 3.00
2 thru 6 SLo . . . . @3.00

MAN IN BLACK
Harvey Publications, 1957
1 BP 250.00
2 BP 175.00
3 BP 175.00
4 BP, March, 1958 . . . . 175.00

MANIK
Millennium/Expand, 1995
1 I:Macedon, Arsenal,Cardinal 3.00

MANKIND
Chaos! Comics, 1999
1-shot StG 3.00
1-shotA photo cover 3.00
1-shotB variant cover 7.00
1-shotC variant cover, signed 50.00

MAN OF THE ATOM
Valiant Heroes Special Project
Acclaim, 1997
Spec. 4.00

MAN OF WAR
Eclipse, 1987–88
1 thru 3 . . . . @2.50

MAN OF WAR
Malibu, 1993–94
1 thru 3 V:Lift 2.50
1a thru 5a Newsstand Ed. 2.50
4 w/poster 2.50
5 V:Killinger 2.50
6 KM,Genesis Crossover 2.50
7 DJu,Genesis Crossover. 2.50

8 TMs(s),A:Rocket Ranger 2.50
9 thru 12 . . . . @2.50

MANTECH ROBOT WARRIORS
Archie Publications 1984–85
1 thru 4 . . . . @5.00

MANTRA
Malibu Ultraverse, 1993–95
1 AV,I:Mantra,w/Ultraverse card . . . 3.00
1a Full Hologram (c) 9.00
1b Silver foil (c) 5.00
2 AV,V:Warstrike 3.00
3 AV,V:Kismet Deadly 3.00
4 BWS,Mantra's marriage,
   BU:Rune story 2.50
5 thru 9 . . . . @2.50
10 NBy(c),DaR,B:Archmage Quest,
   Flip/UltraversePremiere #2 . . . . 3.00
11 thru 24 . . . . @2.50
Giant Sized#1 GP(c),I:Topaz 2.50
Ashcan #1 . . . . 2.50

MANTRA
Malibu Ultraverse, 1995–96
Infinity N:Mantra 2.50
1 Mantra in all Female Body 2.50
1a Computer Painted Cover 2.50
2 Phoenix flip issue 2.50
3 thru 7 . . . . @2.50

MANTRA: SPEAR OF DESTINY
Malibu Ultraverse, 1995
1 Search for Artifact 2.50
2 MiB,Eden vs. Aladdin 2.50

MANY GHOSTS OF DOCTOR GRAVES, THE
Charlton 1967
1 . . . . 90.00
2 thru 10 . . . . @40.00
11 thru 18 . . . . @30.00
19 thru 36 . . . . @25.00
37 thru 72 . . . . @15.00
Becomes:

DR. GRAVES
Charlton 1985
73 thru 75 . . . . @10.00

Many Ghosts of Doctor Graves #66
© Charlton

MANY WORLDS OF TESLA STRONG, THE
Wildstorm/DC, 2003
1 through the dimensions 6.00

MARCH HARE, THE
Boom! Studios, 2005
1-shot 4.00

MARCO POLO
Charlton, 1962
nn 175.00

MARGE'S LITTLE LULU
Gold Key, 1962
See Dell series
165 thru 166 giant . . . . @200.00
167 thru 169 . . . . @50.00
170 thru 207 . . . . @30.00
Becomes:

LITTLE LULU
Gold Key, 1972
207 thru 220 . . . . @20.00
221 thru 257 . . . . @10.00

MARINE WAR HEROES
Charlton, 1964
1 . . . . 50.00
2 thru 18 . . . . @25.00

MARINES ATTACK
Charlton, 1964
1 . . . . 50.00
2 thru 9 . . . . @25.00

MARK OF CHARON
Grossgen Comics, 2003
1 thru 5 JoB. . . . . @3.00

MARK RAND'S SKY TECHNOLOGIES INC.
Red Mercenary, 1995
1 I:Jae,Elliot,Firnn 3.00

MARKSMAN, THE
Hero Graphics, 1988
1 O:Marksman, Pt.#1 . . . . 2.50
2 O:Marksman, Pt.#2 . . . . 2.50
3 O:Marksman ends.I:Basilisk 2.50
4 A:Flare 2.50
5 I:Radar,Sonar. 2.50
Ann. #1, A:Champions 2.50

MARRIED... WITH CHILDREN
Now, 1990
1 . . . . 4.00
1a 2nd printing 2.50
2 Ph(c) 3.00
3 Kelly Ph(c) 3.00
4 thru 7 Ph(c) . . . . @2.50
   [2nd Series], 1991
1 Peg-Host of Radio Show 2.50
2 The Bundy Invention 2.50
3 Psychodad,(photo cover). 2.50
4 Mother-In-Law,(photo cover) 2.50
5 Bundy the Crusader 2.50
6 Bundy J: The Order of the
   Mighty Warthog 2.50
7 Kelly the VJ 2.50
Spec. Ph(c) (1992). 2.50
Spec. Bud Bundy, Fanboy in
   Paradise 3.00
3-D Spec.(1993). 2.50
1-shot Buck's Tale (1994) 2.50
Annual 1994 . . . . 3.50

...DYSFUNCTIONAL FAMILY
Now
1 I:The Bundies. 2.50
2 TV Appearance 2.50
3 Morally Pure Bundys 2.50

...FLASHBACK SPECIAL
Now, 1993
1 Peg and Al's first date 2.50
2 and 3 . . . . @2.50

...KELLY BUNDY SPECIAL
Now, 1992
1 with poster 2.50
2 and 3 with poster . . . . @2.50

...KELLY GOES TO KOLLEGE
Now, 1994
1 thru 3 . . . . @2.50

...LOTTO FEVER
Now, 1994
1 thru 3 . . . . @2.50

...QUANTUM QUARTET
Now, 1993
1 thru 4 Fantastic Four parody . . @2.50
Fall 1994 Spec., flip book 2.50

MARRIED WITH CHILDREN 2099
Mirage, 1993
1 thru 3 Cable Parody . . . . @2.50

MARS
First, 1984
1 thru 12 . . . . @2.50

MARS ATTACKS
Topps, 1994
1 KG(s) 5.00
2 thru 6 KG(s) . . . . @4.00
[Series 2], 1995
1 Counterstrike 3.50
2 Counterstrike,pt.2 . . . . 3.00
3 Counterstrike,pt.3 . . . . 3.00
4 Counterstrike,pt.4 Convictions. . . 3.00
5 Counterstrike concl. 3.00
6 Rescue of Janice Brown,pt.1. . . 3.00
7 Rescue of Janice Brown,pt.2. . . 3.00
8 . . . . 3.00
Spec. Baseball 3.00

MARS ATTACKS HIGH SCHOOL
Topps, 1997
Spec. #1 (of 2) BSz(c) 3.00
Spec. #2 . . . . 3.00

MARS ATTACKS THE SAVAGE DRAGON
Topps, 1996
1 thru 4 . . . . @3.00

MARSHAL
Dabel Brothers Productions, 2006
1 thru 4 . . . . @4.00

MARVEL/ULTRAVERSE BATTLEZONES
Malibu Ultraverse, 1996
1 DPs(c),The Battle of the Heroes . 4.00

MASKED MAN
Eclipse, 1985–88
1 . . . . 3.00

2 thru 10 . . . . @2.50

MASKS: TOO HOT FOR TV
Wildstorm/DC, 2003
Spec. 5.00

Master Darque #1
© Acclaim

MASTER DARQUE
Acclaim, 1997
Spec. F:Brixton Sound, 48pg. 4.00

MASTERS OF HORROR
IDW Publishing, 2005
1 . . . . 4.00
1a variant (c) 3.00
2 thru 4 . . . . @4.00

MASTERS OF THE UNIVERSE
Crossgen Comics, 2003
Spec. The Power of Fear. 3.00
1 Rise of the Snake Men 3.00
TPB Traveler #1 Shard of
  Darkness 10.00
Encyclopedia, Vol. 1 . . . . 3.00

MASTERS OF THE UNIVERSE
MVCreations, 2004
Vol. 3
1 . . . . 3.00
2 thru 6 . . . . @3.00
1a Quadruple Gatefold. 9.00
Season One Encyclopedia #4 . . . . 3.00
Season One Encyclopedia #5 . . . . 3.50

MASTERS OF THE UNIVERSE: ICONS OF EVIL
Crossgen Comics, 2003
Spec. Tri-Klops. 3.00
1 Mer-Man 5.00
1 Trapjaw 5.00

MASTERWORK SERIES
Seagate DC, 1983
1 FFrep.DC,Shining Knight 4.00
2 FFrep.DC,Shining Knight. 4.00
3 BWr,Horror DC rep. 4.00

MATADOR
Wildstorm/DC, May, 2005
1 (of 6) BSf,F:Lt. Isabel Cardona . . 3.00
2 thru 6 BSf. . . . . @3.00

MATT BUSCH'S DARIA JONTAK
Realm Press, 2000
1 sexy sci-fi. 4.00
1a deluxe 5.00
2 . . . . 4.00
2a deluxe 5.00
Companion Book 3.00
Companion Book, deluxe 4.00
Andromeda Entertainment/ PlanetMatt, 2001
Spec. Where Angels Fear to Tread . 4.00
Spec. deluxe 5.00

MAVERICK
Dell Publishing Co., 1958
1 Ph(c) Garner photos 500.00
2 Ph(c) 250.00
3 Ph(c) 250.00
4 Ph(c) 250.00
5 Ph(c) 250.00
6 thru 14 Ph(c) last Garner . . . @200.00
15 thru 19 Ph(c) R. Moore . . . . @175.00

MAVERICK MARSHALL
Charlton Comics, 1958
1 . . . . 100.00
2 thru 6 . . . . @75.00
7 May, 1960 . . . . 75.00

MAVERICKS
Dagger, 1994
1 PuD,RkL, I:Mavericks 3.00
2 PuD,RkL 3.00
3 thru 5 . . . . @3.00

MAXIMORTAL
King Hell/Tundra, 1992
1 RV,A:True-Man 4.50
2 Crack in the New World. 4.25
3 RV,Secret of the Manhattan
  Project revealed 4.25
4 . . . . 4.25
5 A:True Man 3.25
6 A:El Guano. 3.25

MAXIMUM FORCE
Atomeka, 2002
Spec. #1 SBs, ... 3.00

MAYA
Dell, 1967
1 . . . . 35.00
Gold Key, 1968
1 . . . . 50.00

MAZE AGENCY
Comico, 1988–91
1 O:Maze Agency 3.00
2 thru 6 . . . . @2.50
7 . . . . 2.75
8 thru 11 . . . . @2.50
12 . . . . 2.50
13 thru 15 . . . . @2.50
16 thru 23 . . . . @2.50
Spec. #1. . . . . 2.75

MAZE AGENCY, THE
IDW Publishing, 2005
1 MiB. 4.00
2 thru 4 . . . . @4.00

McHALE'S NAVY
Dell Publishing Co.
May-July, 1963
1 Ph(c) from TV show 150.00
2 Ph(c) 100.00
3 Ph(c) 100.00

McKEEVER & THE COLONEL
Dell Publishing Co., 1963
1 Ph(c) 125.00
2 Ph(c) 90.00
3 Ph(c) 90.00

M.D.
Gemstone, 1999
1 (of 5) New Direction 3.00
2 thru 4 . . . . @3.00
Annual #1 . . . . 13.50

M.D. GEIST
CPM, 1995
1 Cartoon Adaptation 3.00
2 J:Army 3.00
3 V:Final Terminator 3.00

M.D. GEIST: GROUND ZERO
CPM, 1996
1 thru 3 . . . . @3.00

MECHANICS
Fantagraphics, 1985
1 HB,rep.Love & Rockets 3.00
2 HB,rep.Love & Rockets 2.50
3 HB,rep.Love & Rockets 2.50

MEDIEVAL LADY DEATH
Avatar Press, 2006
Sourcebook 4.00
Sourcebook, wraparound (c) 4.00
Sourcebook, premium (c) 9.00

MEDIEVAL LADY DEATH: BELLADONNA
Avatar Press, 2005
½ 3.00
½ variant (c)s . . . . @3.00
1 . . . . 4.00
1a variant (c)s . . . . @4.00
1b Special (c)s . . . . @6.00

MEDIEVAL LADY DEATH: WAR OF THE WINDS
Avatar Press, 2006
1 (of 8) 4.00
1a wraparound (c) 4.00
1b variant premium (c) 9.00
1c Special (c)s . . . . @6.00
2 thru 5 . . . . @4.00
2a thru 4a wraparound (c)s . . . . @4.00
2b thru 4b premium (c)s . . . . . . @9.00
5a variant (c)s . . . . @4.00
5b variant premium (c) 9.00
6 . . . . 4.00
6a variant (c)s . . . . @4.00

MEDIA STARR
Innovation, 1989
1 thru 3 . . . . @2.50

MEGACITY 909
Devil's Due/Studio ICE, 2004
1 thru 8 . . . . @3.00
1a thru 6a variant (c) . . . . @3.00

MEGA DRAGON & TIGER
Comicsone.com, 2002
GN #3 thru #6 . . . . @14.00
GN #7 . . . . 15.00

MEGALITH
Continuity, 1990
1 MT 6.00
2 MT 4.00
3 MT, Painted issue 3.00
4 NA,TVE 3.00
5 NA,TVE 3.00
6 MN 3.00
7 MN 3.00
8 . . . . 3.00
9 SDr(i) 3.00
10 . . . . 3.00
[2nd Series], 1993
Deathwatch, 2000
0 Deathwatch 2000 prologue 5.00
1 Deathwatch 2000 Pt.5,w/card . . 3.00
2 Deathwatch 2000 Pt.10,w/card . . 3.00
3 pt.16,Indestructible(c),w/card . . . 3.00
4 & 5 Rise of Magic . . . . @3.00
6 & 7 . . . . @3.00

MEGAMAN
Dreamwave, 2003
1 . . . . 3.00
1a holofoil (c) 6.00
2 thru 4 . . . . @3.00
Pocket edition 11.00

MEGATON
Entity Comics, 1993
Holiday Spec. w/card 3.00

MEGATON EXPLOSION
1 RLd,AMe,I:Youngblood preview 25.00

MEGATON MAN
Kitchen Sink, 1984
1 Don Simpson art,I:MegatonMan . 6.00
1a rep. B&W 3.00
2 . . . . 4.00
3 and 4 . . . . @3.00
5 . . . . 3.00
6 Border Worlds 3.00
7 Border Worlds 3.00
8 Border Worlds 3.00
9 Border Worlds 3.00
10 final issue, 1986 . . . . 3.00

Megaton Man #4
© Kitchen Sink

MEK
DC/Homage, 2002
2 WEI 3.00
3 WEI, concl 3.00

MELTING POT
Kitchen Sink, 1993
1 . . . . 4.00
2 and 3 . . . . @3.00
4 . . . . 3.50

MELVIN MONSTER
Dell Publishing Co.1965
1 . . . . 175.00
2 thru 10 . . . . @150.00

[Katshuiro Otomo's] MEMORIES
Epic, 1992
1 . . . . 2.50

MEN FROM EARTH
Future Fun
1 based on Matt Mason toy 6.50

MENACE
Awesome Entertainment, 1998
1 by Jada Pinkett & Don Fraga . . 2.50
1a signed 15.00
2 . . . . 2.50
3 . . . . 2.50

MENDY AND THE GOLEM
The Golem Network, 2003
1 The Key 3.00
2 Blackout 3.00
3 . . . . 3.00
4 Meltdown 3.00
5 Beyond Control 3.00

MERCHANTS OF DEATH
Eclipse, 1988
1 King's Castle, The Hero 3.50
2 King's Castle,Soldiers of Fortune 3.50
3 Ransom, Soldier of Fortune 3.50
4 ATh(c),Ransom, Men o/t Legion . 3.50
5 Ransom,New York City Blues . . . 3.50

MENDY AND THE GOLEM
The Golem Network, 2003
1 The Key 3.00
2 Blackout 3.00
3 . . . . 3.00
4 Meltdown 3.00
5 Beyond Control 3.00

MERIDIAN
Crossgen Comics, 2000
1 BKs 4.50
2 BKs 4.50
3 BKs 4.00
4 BKs 4.00
5 BKs 4.00
6 thru 11 BKs . . . . @3.50
12 thru 18 BKs . . . . @3.00
19 thru 30 BKs . . . . @3.00
31 thru 44 BKs . . . . @3.00

MERLIN REALM
Blackthorne, 1985
1 3-D 2.50

METABARONS
Humanoids Publishing, 2000
1 . . . . 3.00
2 thru 9 . . . . @3.00
10 thru 17 . . . . @3.00

META DOCS
Antarctic Press, 2005
1-shot Type A 3.00
1-shot Code Black 3.50

META 4
First 1990
1 IG 4.50
2 IG 2.50
3 IG/JSon,final monthly 2.50

METAL GEAR SOLID
IDW 2004
1 Video Game tie-in 15.00
1a retail edition 6.00
2 thru 12 . . . . @4.00

METAL GEAR SOLID:
SONS OF LIBERTY
IDW Publishing, 2005
0 . . . . 4.00
1 . . . . 4.00
1a variant (c) 4.00
2 thru 9 . . . . @4.00
2a thru 9a variant (c) . . . . @4.00
9 thru 12 . . . . @4.00
9a thru 12a variant (c)s . . . . @4.00

METAL LOCUS:
HARD DRIVE
Speakeasy Comics, 2006
1 (of 4) 3.00
2 . . . . 3.00
3 . . . . 3.00

METALLIX
Future Comics, 2003
0 Tag-Team Super-Hero 3.50
1 . . . . 3.50
2 . . . . 3.50
3 thru 5 . . . . @3.50
6 thru 12 . . . . @3.00

METAL MILITIA
Entity Comics, 1995
1 I:Metal Militia 2.50
1a with Video Game 7.00
2 ICO 2.50
3 F:Detective Calahan 2.50
Ashcan 2.50

METAMORPHOSIS
Narwain Publishing, 2006
1 (of 3) 4.00

METAPHYSIQUE
Malibu Bravura, 1995
1 NBy,I:Metaphysique 3.00
1a Gold foil edition 4.00
2 NBy,Mandelbrot malfunctions . . . 3.00
3 I:Harridas 3.00
4 D:Maj.Character,B:Superious . . . 3.00
5 V:Astral Kid 3.00
6 Apocalyptic Armageddon, finale . 3.00
Ashcan NBy,B&W 2.00

MICHAELANGELO
Mirage
1 TMNT Character 15.00

MICHAEL LENT'S PREY:
ORIGIN OF THE SPECIES
Dabel Brothers Productions,
2006
1 . . . . 3.00
2 thru 4 . . . . @3.00

COLOR PUB.

MICHAEL TURNER'S
FATHOM
D.E. (Dynamite Ent.) 2006
Prelude #1 . . . . 3.00
Prelude #1 variant (c)s . . . . @3.00

MICKEY & DONALD
Gladstone, 1988
1 1449 Firestone 8.00
2 . . . . 4.00
3 Man of Tomorrow 3.00
4 thru 15 . . . . @3.00
16 giant-size 3.00
17 . . . . 3.00
18 . . . . 4.00
Becomes:

DONALD AND MICKEY
19 thru 26 . . . . @3.00

MICKEY MANTLE COMICS
Magnum, 1991
1 JSt,Rise to Big Leagues 4.00

Mickey Mouse #61
© Walt Disney

MICKEY MOUSE
Dell
85 thru 156 . . . . @35.00
157 thru 158 . . . . @25.00
159 thru 179 . . . . @15.00
180 thru 204 . . . . @10.00
Gold Key 1962
Mickey Mouse Album (1963) 40.00
Mickey Mouse Club (1964) 45.00
Mickey Mouse Surprise
  Party (1979) 45.00
Whitman, 1980
205 thru 207 . . . . @40.00
208 Scarce 125.00
209 thru 218 . . . . @20.00

MICKEY MOUSE
Gladstone, 1986
219 FG,Seven Ghosts 20.00
220 FG,Seven Ghosts 10.00
221 FG,Seven Ghosts 10.00
222 FG,Editor in Grief 5.00
223 FG,Editor in Grief 4.00
224 FG,Crazy Crime Wave 4.00
225 FG,Crazy Crime Wave 4.00
226 FG,Captive Castaways 4.00
227 FG,Captive Castaways 4.00
228 FG,Captive Castaways 4.00
229 FG,Bat Bandit 4.00
230 FG,Bat Bandit 3.00
231 FG,Bobo the Elephant 3.00

232 FG,Bobo the Elephant 3.00
233 FG,Pirate Submarine 3.00
234 FG,Pirate Submarine 3.00
235 FG,Photo Racer 3.00
236 FG,Photo Racer 3.00
237 FG,Race for Riches 3.00
238 FG,Race for Riches 3.00
239 FG,Race for Riches 3.00
240 FG,March of Comics 3.00
241 FG 4.00
242 FG 3.00
243 FG 3.00
244 FG,60th Anniv 5.00
245 FG,Giant Ants 4.00
246 FG 3.00
247 FG 3.00
248 FG 3.00
249 FG 5.00
250 FG 3.00
251 FG 3.00
252 FG 3.00
253 FG 3.00
254 FG 3.00
255 FG 4.00
256 FG 4.00

MICKEY MOUSE
Walt Disney, 1990
1 The Phantom Gondolier 4.00
2 . . . . 3.50
3 thru 19 . . . . @3.00

MICKEY MOUSE
AND FRIENDS
Gemstone Publishing, 2003
257 thru 270 . . . . @3.25
271 thru 296 . . . . @3.00
297 . . . . 3.50
1-shot Mickey Mouse meets
  Blotman (2005) 6.00

MICKEY MOUSE
MEETS BLOTMAN
Gemstone Publishing, 2005
1-shot 6.00
1-shot Blotman Returns (2006) . . . 6.00

MICKEY'S TWICE
UPON A CHRISTMAS
Gemstone Publishing, 2004
Spec. video adapt 4.00

MICKEY SPILLANE'S
MIKE DANGER
Tekno Comix, 1995
1 I:Mike Danger 3.00
2 thru 11 . . . . @2.50
Big Entertainment, 1996
1 . . . . 2.50
2 thru 10 . . . . @2.50

MICROBOTS, THE
Gold Key, 1971
1 . . . . 30.00

MICRONAUTS
Devil's Due Publishing, 2004
1 . . . . 3.00
2 thru 4 . . . . @3.00

MIDNIGHTER
Wildstorm/DC, Nov., 2006
1 GEn,CSp,KIS 3.00
1a & b variant (c)s . . . . @3.00
2 GEn,CSp,KIS 3.00
2a variant AAd (c) 3.00
3 GEn,CSp,KIS 3.00

3a variant JPe (c) (1:10) 3.00
4 GEn,CSp,KIS,To Kill Hitler 3.00
4a variant GF (c) (1:10) 3.00
5 GEn,CSp,KIS,Killing Machine . . . 3.00
6 GEn,GF,KIS,Feudal Japan. 3.00
7 DaR,KIS 3.00
8 JPL,Hawksmoor challenge 3.00
9 JP,BSf,Space station virus 3.00
10 KG,CSp,KIS, ... 3.00
11 A sultry siren 3.00
12 Back in New York 3.00

MIDNIGHTER: ARMAGEDDON
Wildstorm/DC, Oct., 2007
1 London destroyed by Carrier. . . . 3.00

MIDNIGHT EYE: GOKU PRIVATE INVESTIGATOR
Viz
1 A.D. 2014: Tokyo city 5.25
2 V:Hakuryu,A:Yoko 5.00
3 A:Ryoko,Search for Ryu 5.00
4 Goku vs. Ryu 5.00
5 Leilah Abducted 5.00
6 Lisa's I.D. discovered 5.00

MIDNIGHT KISS
APC, 2005
1 . . . . 3.50
2 & 3 . . . . @3.50
Markosia, 2005
4 & 5 . . . . @3.50
5a variant (c) 3.50

MIDNIGHT TALES
Charlton, 1972
1 . . . . 25.00
2 thru 18 . . . . @15.00

MiGHTY COMICS
Archie, 1966
{Prev: Flyman}
40 A:Web 60.00
41 A:Shield, Black Hood 50.00
42 A:Black Hood 50.00
43 A:Shield, Black Hood,Web 50.00
44 A:Black Hood, Steel Sterling
    Shield. 50.00
45 Shield-Black Hood team-up
    O:Web 50.00
46 A:Steel Sterling, Black
    Hood, Web. 50.00
47 A:Black Hood & Mr.Justice . . . 50.00
48 A:Shield & Hangman. 50.00
49 Steel Sterling-Black Hood
    team-up, A:Fox 50.00

[ALL NEW ADVENTURES OF] THE MIGHTY CRUSADERS
Archie/Red Circle, 1965
[1st Series]
1 O:Shield (Joe Higgins & Bill
    Higgins) 125.00
2 MSy,O:Comet 75.00
3 O:Fly-Man 65.00
4 A:Fireball,Jaguar,Web,Fox,
    Blackjack Hangman & more
    Golden Age Archie Heroes . . . 70.00
5 I:Ultra-Men&TerrificThree. 65.00
6 V:Maestro,A:Steel Sterling 65.00
7 O:Fly-Girl,A:Steel Sterling 65.00
[2nd Series], 1983
1 RB,R:Joe Higgins & Lancelot
    Strong as the SHIELD, Mighty
    Crusaders, A:Mr.Midnight 7.00

2 RB,V:Brain Emperor & Eterno . . . 5.00
3 RB,I:Darkling 5.00
4 DAy,TD. 4.00
5 . . . . 4.00
6 DAy,TD,Shield 4.00
7 . . . . 4.00
8 . . . . 4.00
9 Trial of the Shield 4.00
10 . . . . 4.00
11 DAy,D:Gold Age Black Hood, I:
    Riot Squad, series based on
    toy lines 5.00
12 DAy,I:She-Fox 5.00
13 Last issue 5.00

The Mighty Hercules #1
© Gold Key

MIGHTY HERCULES, THE
Gold Key, 1963
1 . . . . 275.00
2 . . . . 250.00

MIGHTY MAGNOR, THE
Malibu, 1993
1 SA 2.50
2 thru 6 SA . . . . @2.50

MIGHTY MORPHIN POWER RANGERS
Hamilton, 1994–95
1 From TV Series 2.75
2 Switcheroo 2.50
3 . . . . 2.50
4 F:White Ranger 2.50
5 F:Pink Ranger 2.50
6 V:Garganturon 2.50
[Series 2], 1995
1 Unstoppable Force 2.50
2 V:Mechanical Octopus. 2.50
3 . . . . 2.50
4 Lost Ranger. 2.50
[Series 3], 1995
1 O:Green Ranger 2.50
2 O:Green Ranger 2.50
3 I:New Megazords 2.50

MIGHTY MOUSE
Dell, 1966
166 . . . . 45.00
167 thru 172. . . . . 45.00

ADVENTURES OF MIGHTY MOUSE
Gold Key, 1962
1 . . . . 50.00
Becomes:

MIGHTY MOUSE
Gold Key, 1964
161 thru 165. . . . . @75.00
Also continued as:

ADVENTURES OF MIGHTY MOUSE
Gold Key, 1979
166 thru 172 . . . . @10.00

MIGHTY MOUSE
Spotlight, 1987
1 FMc,PC(c) 3.00
2 FMc,CS(c) 3.00
1 Holiday Special 3.00

MIGHTY MUTANIMALS
Archie Publications, 1991
[Mini-Series]
1 Cont.from TMNT Adventures#19,
    A:Raphael, Man Ray, Leather-
    head, Mondo Gecko,Deadman,
    Wingnut & Screwloose 2.50
2 V:Mr.Null,Malinga,Soul and Bean
    and the Malignoid Army. 2.50
3 Alien Invasion help off, Raphael
    returns to Earth 2.50
Spec.#1 rep. all #1-3 +SBi pin-ups . 3.00

MIGHTY MUTANIMALS
Archie, 1992
1 Quest for Jagwar's Mother 2.50
2 V:Snake Eyes 2.50
3 . . . . 2.50
4 Days of Future Past. 2.50
5 Into the Sun 2.50
6 V:Null & 4 Horsemen Pt#2. . . . . 2.50
7 Jaws of Doom 2.50

MIGHTY SAMSON
Gold Key, 1964–82
1 O:Mighty Samson 160.00
2 . . . . 125.00
3 . . . . 125.00
4 . . . . 125.00
5 . . . . 125.00
6 thru 10 . . . . @80.00
11 thru 20 . . . . @75.00
21 thru 32. . . . . @50.00

MIKE GRELL'S SABLE
First, 1990
1 thru 8 rep. . . . . @2.50
9 . . . . 2.50
10 Triptych 2.50

MIKE SHAYNE PRIVATE EYE
Dell Publishing Co., 1961-62
1 . . . . 75.00
2 . . . . 50.00
3 . . . . 50.00

MILLENNIUM INDEX
Independent Comics, 1988
1 . . . . 2.50
2 . . . . 2.50

MILLIE THE LOVABLE MONSTER
Dell, 1962
1 . . . . 75.00
2 . . . . 65.00
3 . . . . 50.00
4 thru 6 . . . . @25.00

COLOR PUB.

MILTON THE MONSTER
& FEARLESS FLY
Gold Key, 1966
1 . . . . 175.00

MIRACLE BRIGADE, THE
Counteractive Comics, 2006
1 . . . . 3.00

MIRACLEMAN
Eclipse, 1985–94
1 R:Miracleman. 15.00
2 AD,Moore,V:Kid Miracleman . . . 10.00
3 AD,Moore,V:Big Ben 10.00
4 AD,Moore,R:Dr.Gargunza 10.00
5 AD,Moore,O:Miracleman 10.00
6 Moore,V:Miracledog, D:Evelyn
   Cream 10.00
7 Moore,D:Dr.Gargunza 9.00
8 Moore. 9.00
9 RV,Moore,Birth of Miraclebaby . . 9.00
10 JRy,RV,Moore 9.00
11 JTo,Moore,Book III,
   I:Miraclewoman 9.00
12 thru 14 Moore . . . . @20.00
15 Moore 80.00
16 Moore 30.00
17 Golden Age 15.00
18 . . . . 12.00
19 thru 22. . . . . @14.00
23 Silver Age 25.00
24 BWS(c),NGa(s), ... 32.00
25 . . . . 9.00
26 thru 28 . . . . @3.00
3-D Special #1 . . . . 5.00

MIRACLEMAN
APOCRYPHA
Eclipse, 1991–92
1 inc. Rascal Prince 8.00
2 Miracleman, Family Stories 8.00
3 . . . . 8.00

MIRACLEMAN FAMILY
Eclipse, 1988
1 British Rep.,A:Kid Miracleman. . 12.00
2 Alan Moore (s) 12.00

MIRACLE SQUAD, THE
Upshot/Fantagraphics, 1986
1 Hollywood 30's. 2.50

Mischief Night #1
© Avatar

2 thru 4 . . . . @2.50

MISCHIEF NIGHT
Avatar Press, 2006
1 . . . . 4.00
1a wraparound (c). 4.00
1b variant (c)s . . . . @4.00
1c variant Splatter (c) 7.00
1d variant Ruby Red Foil Con. (c) . 5.00
1e variant Damned Duo (c) 4.00

MISERERE
Narwain Publishing, 2006
1 (of 3) 3.50
2 thru 3 . . . . @3.50

MISS FURY
Adventure Comics, 1991
1 O:Cat Suit 3.00
2 Miss Fury impersonator 3.00
3 A:Three Miss Fury's. 3.00
4 conclusion 3.00

MISSION IMPOSSIBLE
Dell Publishing Co., 1967
1 Ph(c) 150.00
2 Ph(c) 125.00
3 Ph(c) 100.00
4 Ph(c) 100.00
5 Ph(c) 100.00

MISSIONS IN TIBET
Dimension Comics, 1995
1 I:New Series 2.50
2 F:Orlando,Ting,Alex. 2.50
3 Two Worlds Collide 2.50
4 V:Sada. 2.50

MISS PEACH
(& SPECIAL ISSUES)
Dell Publishing Co., 1963
1 . . . . 150.00

MISPLACED
Devil's Due Publishing, 2004
3 and 4 . . . . @3.00
1-shot Misplaced@17 . . . . 5.00

MR. AND MRS. J.
EVIL SCIENTIST
Gold Key, 1963
1 . . . . 150.00
2 . . . . 100.00
3 . . . . 100.00
4 . . . . 100.00

MISTER ED,
THE TALKING HORSE
Gold Key, 1962
1 From TV show 150.00
2 thru 6 . . . . @90.00

MR. MAGOO
Dell, 1963
3 . . . . 125.00
4 thru 5 . . . . @125.00

MR. MAJESTIC
WildStorm/DC, 1999
1 JoC,A:Desmond. 2.50
1a variant cover 3.00
2 JoC,time gone berserk 2.50
3 JoC,F:Maxine Manchester. 2.50
4 JoC,F:Junior Majestic 2.50
5 JoC 2.50
6 JoC,F:Desmond. 2.50

7 JoC,Universal Law,pt.1 . . . . 2.50
8 JoC,Universal Law,pt.2 . . . . 2.50
9 JoC,Universal Law,pt.3 . . . . 2.50

MR. MONSTER
Eclipse, 1985–87
1 I:Mr. Monster 7.00
2 DSt(c). 5.00
3 V:Dr. NoZone. 3.50
4 Trapped in Dimension X 3.00
5 V:Flesh-eating Amoebo 3.00
6 KG,SD,reprints 3.00
7 . . . . 3.00
8 V:Monster in the Atomic Telling
   Machine. 3.00
9 V:Giant Clams 3.00
10 R:Dr.No Zone, 3-D 3.00

MR. MONSTER
ATTACKS
Tundra, 1992
1 DGb,SK,short stories. 4.25
2 SK,short stories cont. 4.25
3 DGb,last issue 4.25

MR. MONSTER
SUPERDUPER SPECIAL
Eclipse, 1986–87
1 . . . . 3.00
2 . . . . 3.00
3 . . . . 3.00
4 . . . . 3.00
5 . . . . 3.00
6 . . . . 3.00
Hi-Voltage Super Science 4.00
3-D Spec. Hi-Octane Horror,JKu,
   Touch of Death reprint. 5.00
Triple Treat. 4.00

MR. MONSTER
TRUE CRIME
Eclipse, 1986
1 . . . . 3.00
2 . . . . 3.00
3-D Spec. #1 . . . . 3.00

MR. MUSCLES
Charlton Comics, 1956
22 . . . . 100.00
23 . . . . 75.00

MR. MYSTIC
Eclipse
1 . . . . 2.50
2 . . . . 2.50
3 . . . . 2.50

MR. T
APC, 2005
1 . . . . 3.50
1a foil (c). 6.00
1b foil (c), signed 12.00
1c sketch edition. 40.00
1d Comix Shop (c) 7.00
2 . . . . 3.50
3 . . . . 3.50
4 . . . . 3.50
5 . . . . 3.50

MR. T AND THE T FORCE
Now, 1993
1 NA,R:Mr.T,V:Street Gangs 2.50
1a Gold Ed.. . . . . 9.00
2 NA,V:Demons 2.50
3 NBy,w/card 2.50
4 NBy,In Urban America 2.50
5 thru 10, with card . . . . @2.50

MISTER X
Vortex, 1984
1 HB	7.00
2 HB	5.00
3 HB	3.50
4 HB	3.00
5 thru 10	@3.00
11 thru 13	@3.00
14	3.00

MOBY DUCK
Gold Key, 1967–70
1 Walt Disney	50.00
2 thru 6	@25.00
7 thru 11	@20.00

Gold Key, 1973
12 thru 30	@15.00

MODERN MAN
Narwain Publishing, 2006
1 (of 4)	4.00
2	4.00

MODNIKS, THE
Gold Key, 1967
1	50.00
2	30.00

MOD SQUAD
Dell Publishing Co., 1969–71
1	125.00
2 thru 8	@75.00

MOD WHEELS
Gold Key, 1971–76
1	75.00
2 thru 18	@50.00
19	40.00

MONARCHY
WildStorm/DC, 2001
1 JMC,V:Young Authoritans	2.50
2 JMC,F:Union	2.50
3 JMC,Vox Populi,pt.1	2.50
4 JMC,Vox Populi,pt.2	2.50
5 JMC,Boy Who Talked to Spiders	2.50
6 JMC,Making the Metropolitan	2.50
7 JMC,Making the Metropolitan	2.50
8 JMC,Making the Metropolitan	2.50
9 JMC,Metropolitan epilog	2.50
10 JMC,V:Chimera	2.50
11 JMC,V:Higher Power	2.50
12 JMC,final issue	2.50

MONKEE'S, THE
Dell Publishing Co., 1967
1 Ph(c)	200.00
2 Ph(c)	150.00
3 Ph(c)	150.00
4 Ph(c)	150.00
5	125.00
6 Ph(c)	125.00
7 Ph(c)	125.00
8 and 9	@120.00
10 Ph(c)	125.00
11 thru 17	@100.00

MONOLITH
Comico, 1991
1 From Elementals	2.50
2 Seven Levels of Hell	2.50
3 Fugue and Variation	2.50
4 Fugue and Variation	2.50

MONROE'S, THE
Dell Publishing Co., 1967
1 Ph(c)	50.00

MONSTER CLUB
Autumn Press, 2003
1	3.50
2 thru 11	@3.50
12 40-pg.	3.50

Vol. 2
0	3.00
1 thru 6	@3.50
Preview ed.	3.00

Monster Hunters #1
© Charlton

MONSTER HUNTERS
Charlton, 1975–79
1 TS,The Boar's Head Beast	40.00
2 TS,Fish Fry; The Kukulkaton	30.00
3 TS,The Dictator	20.00
4 TS,Hidden Paradise	20.00
5 TS,The Last Monster Hunter	20.00
6 SD,MZ,The Beast or the Burden	25.00
7 MZ,TS,Blood Oath	20.00
8 TS,SD,Wormholes	25.00
9 MZ,Hour of the Werewolf	15.00
10 SD,The Conglomerate	25.00
11 The Montego Frame	15.00
12 Snake Charmer	15.00
13 SD,JSon,A Little Witchcraft	20.00
14 SD,Giant from the Unknown	40.00
15 SD,reps	20.00
16 TS,The Kilgore Monster	15.00
17 TS,reps from issue #3	15.00
18 SD,Incident at Soulbridge	20.00

Modern, 1977
1 & 2 rep issues 1 and 2	@3.00

MONSTER MASSACRE
Atomeka
1 SBs, DBr,DGb	8.50
1a Black Edition	35.00

MONSTER MAYHEM SERIES
Dead Dog Comics, 2005
1 Frankenstein	6.00
1a variant (c)	6.00
1 Creature	6.00
1a variant (c)	6.00

MONSTER WORLD
WildStorm/DC, 2001
1 (of 4) SLo	3.00
2 SLo, 5 young heroes	3.00
3 SLo,	3.00
4 SLo,concl.	3.00

MONTE COOK'S PTOLUS
Dabel Brothers Productions, 2006
1 (of 6)	3.00
2 thru 5	@3.00

MORBID ANGEL
London Night, 1996
? Angel's Tear, signed	10.00
1 Commemorative (1999)	10.00

MORBID ANGEL: PENANCE
London Night, 1996
Revised Color Spec., double size	4.00

MORE THAN MORTAL
Liar Comics, 1997
1	3.00
1a 2nd printing	3.00
1b convention, sign, num	9.00
2 Derdre vs. the Host	3.00
2a variant painted cover	6.00
3 MS(c)	3.00
4 thru 6	@3.00

MORE THAN MORTAL: SAGAS
Liar Comics, 1998
1 by Sharon Scott & Romano Molenaar	3.00
1a variant Tim Vigil(c)	3.00
1b variant JLi(c)	9.00
2 thru 3	@3.00

MORE THAN MORTAL: TRUTHS AND LEGENDS
Liar Comics, 1998
1 by Sharon Scott, Steve Firchow, Mark Prudeaux, O:Witchfinder	4.00
1a signed	9.00
2 thru 5	@3.00
5a variant cover (1:4)	3.00
6	3.00

MORLOCK 2001
Atlas, Feb.–July, 1975
1 thru 2 O:Morlock	@15.00
3 SD,BW,F:Midnight Men	20.00

MORRIGAN
Sirius, 1997
1 by Lorenzo Bartoli & Saverio Tenuta	3.00
2 and 3	@3.00
GN rep. #1–#3	10.00

MORTAL KOMBAT
Malibu, 1994
0 Four stories	3.00
1 Based on the Video Game	3.00
1a Foil Ed	4.00
1b with new material	3.00
2	3.00
3	3.00
4	3.00
5 I:Mortal Kombat II	3.00
6 Climax	3.00
Spec. #1 Tournament edition	4.00
Spec. #2 Tournament edition II	4.00
Spec #1 Baraka, V:Scorpion	3.00

...BATTLEWAVE
Malibu, 1995
1 New series	3.00
2 Action, Action, Action	3.00
3 The Gathering	3.00

4 F:Goro	3.00
5 F:Scorpion	3.00
6 final issue	3.00

...GORO, PRINCE OF PAIN
Malibu, 1994

1 Goro	3.00
1a Platinum Edition	6.25
2 Goro, V:Kombatant	3.00
3 Goro, V:God of Pain	3.00

...KITANA & MILEENA
Malibu, 1995

1 Secrets of Outworld	3.00

...KUNG LAO
Malibu, 1995

1 one-shot Battlewave tie-in	3.00

...RAYDEN AND KANO
Malibu, 1995

1 J:Rayden Kano	3.00
1a Deluxe Edition	5.00
2 A:Reptile	3.00
3 Kano, conclusion	3.00

...U.S. SPECIAL FORCES
Malibu, 1995

1 V:Black Dragon	3.50
2 V:Black Dragon	3.00

MORTAL KOMBAT: DECEPTION
Atomeka, 2005

0	4.00
0a chrome	10.00

MOSTLY WANTED
WildStorm/DC, 2000

1 (of 4) SLo,F:Sister Crenn	2.50
2 SLo(s),F:Andi Mooncrest	2.50
3 SLo(s)	2.50
4 SLo(s),conclusion	2.50

MOUSE GUARD
Archaia Studio Press, 2006

1 Belly of the Beast	22.00
1a 2nd printing	8.00
2 Shadows Within	15.00
2a 2nd printing	5.00
3 Rise of the Axe	8.00
3 (2nd printing)	4.00
4 The Dark Ghost	4.00
5 Midnight's Dawn	4.00

MOUSE GUARD: WINTER 1152
Archaia Studios Press

1	3.50
2 thru 6	@3.50

MOVIE CLASSIC
Dell, 1961–69

Around the World Under the Sea	50.00
Battle of the Bulge	50.00
Bon Voyage	30.00
The Cat	45.00
The Castilian	45.00
Cheyenne Autumn	90.00
Circus World	175.00
The Creature	150.00
Countdown	50.00
David Ladd's Life Story	125.00
Die, Monster, Die	90.00
The Dirty Dozen	75.00
Dr. Who and the Daleks	175.00
Dracula	125.00
El Dorado	225.00
Ensign Pulver	50.00
Frankenstein	125.00

Frankenstein, 2nd printing	50.00
The Great Race	75.00
The Hallelujah Trail	75.00
Hatari	125.00
The Horizontal Leiutenant	45.00
The Incredible Mr. Limpet	75.00
Jack the Giant Killer	135.00
Jason and the Argonauts	150.00
Lancelot and Guinevere	80.00
Lawrence of Arabia	100.00
Lion of Sparta	55.00
Mad Monster Party	150.00
The Masque of the Red Death	100.00
Maya	60.00
The Magic Sword	85.00
McHale's Navy	75.00
Merrill's Marauders	50.00
The Mouse on the Moon	50.00
The Mummy	125.00
The Music Man	60.00
The Naked Prey	90.00
The Night of the Grizzly	60.00
Operation Crossbow	50.00
Operation Bikini	50.00
The Prince and the Pauper	55.00
The Raven	100.00
Ring of Bright Water	60.00
The Runaway	50.00
Santa Claus Conquers the Martians	150.00
Ski Party	75.00
Smoky	45.00
Six Black Horses	50.00
Tales of Terror	40.00
Three Stooges Meet Hercules	165.00
Tomb of Ligeia	90.00
Twice Told Tales	100.00
Treasure Island	60.00
Two on a Guillotine	60.00
The Valley of Gwangi	150.00
War Gods of the Deep	50.00
The War Wagon	150.00
The Wolf Man	140.00
Who's Minding the Mint	50.00
Zulu	125.00

Movie Comics: Bambi
© Gold Key

MOVIE COMICS
Gold Key/Whitman, 1962–70

Alice in Wonderland	60.00
Aristocats	150.00
Bambi 1	100.00
Bambi 2	75.00
Beneath the Planet of the Apes	150.00
Big Red	60.00
Blackbeard's Ghost	60.00

Buck Rogers Giant Movie Edition	75.00
Bullwhip Griffin	60.00
Captain Sinbad	125.00
Chitty, Chitty Bang Bang	150.00
Cinderella	75.00
Darby O'Gill & the Little People	80.00
Dumbo	75.00
Emil & the Detectives	50.00
Escapade in Florence	150.00
Fall of the Roman Empire	60.00
Fantastic Voyage	100.00
55 Days at Peking	60.00
Fighting Prince of Donegal	60.00
First Men of the Moon	75.00
Gay Purr-ee	100.00
Gnome Mobile	60.00
Goodbye, Mr. Chips	60.00
Happiest Millionaire	60.00
Hey There, It's Yogi Bear	125.00
Horse Without a Head	50.00
How the West Was Won	125.00
In Search of the Castaways	125.00
Jungle Book, The	150.00
Kidnapped	60.00
King Kong	75.00
King Kong N#	125.00
Lady and the Tramp	60.00
Lady and the Tramp 1	100.00
Lady and the Tramp 2	50.00
Legend of Lobo, The	50.00
Lt. Robin Crusoe	50.00
Lion, The	50.00
Lord Jim	50.00
Love Bug, The	60.00
Mary Poppins	100.00
Mary Poppins 1	125.00
McLintock	225.00
Merlin Jones as the Monkey's Uncle	125.00
Miracle of the White Stallions	50.00
Misadventures of Merlin Jones	125.00
Moon-Spinners, The	135.00
Mutiny on the Bounty	60.00
Nikki, Wild Dog of the North	50.00
Old Yeller	60.00
One Hundred & One Dalmatians	75.00
Peter Pan 1	75.00
Peter Pan 2	50.00
P.T. 109	75.00
Rio Conchos	60.00
Robin Hood	50.00
Shaggy Dog & the Absent-Minded Professor	60.00
Sleeping Beauty	135.00
Snow White & the Seven Dwarfs	60.00
Son of Flubber	60.00
Summer Magic	135.00
Swiss Family Robinson	60.00
Sword in the Stone	135.00
That Darn Cat	135.00
Those Magnificent Men in Their Flying Machines	60.00
Three Stooges in Orbit	200.00
Tiger Walks, A	75.00
Toby Tyler	60.00
Treasure Island	60.00
20,000 Leagues Under the Sea	60.00
Wonderful Adventures of Pinocchio	75.00
Wonderful World of Brothers Grimm	60.00
X, the Man with the X-Ray Eyes	135.00
Yellow Submarine w/poster	450.00

MS. MYSTIC
Pacific

1 NA,Origin	7.00
2 NA,Origin,I:Urth 4	6.00

Continuity, 1988

1 NA,Origin rep.	3.00
2 NA,Origin,I:Urth 4 rep	3.00
3 NA,New material	3.00

4 TSh	3.00
5 DT	3.00
6	3.00
7	3.00
8 CH/Sdr,B:Love Story	3.00
9 DB	3.00
9a Newsstand(c)	3.00

[3rd Series], 1993

1 O:Ms.Mystic	2.50
2 A:Hybrid	2.50
3 thru 4	@2.50

[4th Series, Deathwatch 2000]

1 Deathwatch 2000 pt.8,w/card	2.50
2 Deathwatch 2000 w/card	2.50
3 Indestructible cover, w/card	2.50

MS. TREE'S THRILLING DETECTIVE ADVENTURES
Eclipse, 1983

1 Miller pin up	5.00
2	4.00
3	4.00

Becomes:

MS. TREE
Eclipse, 1983

4 thru 6	@4.00
7	4.00
8	8.00
9	4.00

Aardvark–Vanaheim, 1984

10	4.00

Renegade

1 3-D	4.00

MS. VICTORY GOLDEN ANNIVERSARY
AC Comics

1 Ms.Victory celebration	5.00

MS. VICTORY SPECIAL
AC Comics, 1985

1	2.50

MU
Devil's Due/Studio ICE, 2004

1	3.00
1a variant (c)	3.00
2 thru 4	@3.00
2a thru 4a variant (c)	@3.00

MUMMY ARCHIVES
Millennium, 1992

1.JM,Features,articles	2.50

MUMMY, OR RAMSES THE DAMNED, THE
Millennium, 1992

1 Anne Rice Adapt	5.00
2 JM,Mummy in Mayfair	3.75
3 JM	3.25
4 JM, To Egypt	3.00
5 JM,The Mummy's Hand	2.50
6 JM,20th Century Egypt	2.50
7 JM,More Ramses Past Revealed	2.50
8 JM,Hunt for Cleopatra	2.50
9 JM,Cleopatra's Wrath contd.	2.50
10 JM,Subterranian World	2.50
11 JM	2.50

MUMMY, THE: VALLEY OF THE GODS
Chaos! Comics, 2001

1 (of 3) MWn,MtB, movie tie-in	3.00
1a variant (c)	3.00
1b premium	9.00
2	3.00
2a Scorpion King photo (c)	3.00

3	3.00
3a Imhotep phoco (c)	3.00
Ashcan	6.00

MUNDEN'S BAR ANNUAL
First, 1988

1 BB,JOy,JSn,SR	3.00

MUNSTERS, THE
Gold Key, 1965–68

1	350.00
2	200.00
3 thru 5	@175.00
6 thru 16	@150.00

MUPPET BABIES
Harvey, 1993

1 Return of Muppet Babies	2.50

MURCIELAGA/SHE-BAT
Studio G, 2001

1 by D.Gross & R.Lopez	3.00
2 thru 4	@3.00

MUSH MOUSE AND PUNKIN PUSS
Gold Key, 1965

1 Hanna-Barbera	150.00

MUTANT CHRONICLES— GOLGOTHA
Valiant

1 thru 4 + game trading card	@3.00

MUTATION
Speakeasy Comics, 2005

1	3.00
2 thru 5	@3.00
TPB Vol. 1	15.00

MUTATION
Markosia, 2006

1	3.50
1a variant (c)	3.50
2 thru 4	@3.50

MY FAVORITE MARTIAN
Gold Key, 1964–66

1	275.00
2	150.00

My Favorite Martian #4
© Gold Key

3	125.00
4	125.00
5	125.00
6 thru 9	@125.00

MY LITTLE MARGIE
Charlton Comics, 1954–65

1 Ph(c)	500.00
2 Ph(c)	250.00
3 thru 8	@150.00
9	135.00
10	125.00
11 thru 19	@100.00
20 Giant Size	175.00
21 thru 35	@100.00
36 thru 53	@100.00
54 Beatles (c)	300.00

MY LITTLE MARGIE'S BOY FRIEND
Charlton Comics, 1955–58

1	200.00
2	150.00
3 thru 11	@100.00

MYSTERIES OF UNEXPLORED WORLDS/ SON OF VULCAN
Charlton Comics, 1956

1	500.00
2	275.00
3 SD,SD(c)	400.00
4 SD,Forbidden Room	450.00
5 SD,SD(c)	450.00
6 SD	450.00
7 SD, giant	500.00
8 SD	425.00
9 SD	425.00
10 SD,SD(c)	425.00
11 SD,SD(c)	425.00
12 SD,Charm Bracelet	300.00
13 thru 18	@150.00
19 SD(c)	300.00
20	150.00
21 thru 24 SD	@300.00
25	100.00
26 SD	300.00
27 thru 30	@100.00
31 thru 45	@80.00
46 I:Son ofVulcan,Dr.Kong(1965)	100.00
47 V:King Midas	80.00
48 V:Captain Tuska	80.00

Becomes:

SON OF VULCAN

49 DC redesigns costume	75.00
50 V:Dr.Kong	75.00

MYSTERIOUS SUSPENSE
Charlton, 1968

1 SD,F:Question	125.00

MYSTERY COMICS DIGEST
Gold Key, 1972–75

1 WW,Riley's Believe It Or Not	60.00
2 WW,Boris Karloff	60.00
3 RC,GEv,Twilight Zone	60.00
4 Ripley's Believe It or Not	50.00
5 Boris Karloff	50.00
6 Twilight Zone	50.00
7 Believe It Or Not	50.00
8 RC,AW,Boris Karloff	50.00
9 Twilight Zone	50.00
10 thru 13	@50.00
14 1st Xorkon	50.00
15 thru 20	@50.00
21 thru 26	@40.00

MYSTIC
Crosgen Comics, 2000
1 RMz,BPe	6.00
2 RMz,BPe	5.00
3 RMz,BPe	4.00
4 RMz,BPe	3.25
5 RMz,BPe	3.25
6 thru 10	@3.25
11	4.00
12 thru 30	@3.00
31 thru 43	@3.00

MYSTIC EDGE
Antarctic Press, 1998
1 by Ryan Kinnaird, F:Risa & Symattra	3.00

NANCY & SLUGGO
Dell Publishing Co., 1957
146 B:Peanuts	150.00
147 Peanuts	125.00
148 Peanuts	125.00
149 Peanuts	125.00
150 thru 161	@125.00
162 thru 165	@200.00
166 thru 176 A:OONA	@200.00
177 thru 180	@125.00
181 thru 187	@125.00

NARWAIN PREVIEW
Narwain Publishing, 2005
Spec.	2.50
Spec. variant (c).	2.50

NASCAR HEROES
Nascar Comics, 2007
1	4.00
2	4.00

NATIONAL VELVET
Dell Publishing Co., 1961
1 Ph(c)	150.00
2 Ph(c)	75.00

NEAT STUFF
Fantagraphics, 1986
1	4.50
2	3.00
3 thru 7	@2.50

NECROMANTRA/ LORD PUMPKIN
Malibu Ultraverse, 1995
1 A:Loki (from Marvel)	3.00
2 MiB,V:Godwheel, flipbook	3.00
3 O:Lord Pumpkin	3.00
4 Infinity Gem tie-in	3.00
4a variant cover	3.50

NECROPOLIS THE JUDGE DEATH INVASION
Fleetway, 1991
1 SBs(c),CE,A:Dark Judges/ Sisters Of Death	3.00
2 thru 9	@3.00

NECROSCOPE
Malibu, 1992
1 Novel adapt., holo(c)	3.25
1a 2nd printing	3.00
2 thru 4 Adapt. cont.	@3.00

Book II, Oct. 1994
1	3.00
2 thru 5	3.00

NECROWAR
Dreamwave, 2003
1	3.00
2 thru 4	@3.00

NEGATION
Crosgen Comics, 2001
1 MWa,PaP,F:Obregon Kaine	3.00
2 MWa,PaP,Kaine's master-plan	3.00
3 MWa,PaP,F:Captain Fluxor	3.00
4 thru 12 PaP	@3.00
13 thru 27	@3.00
Spec. #1 Negation: Lawbringer	3.00
Prequel MWa,PaP	3.00

NEGATION WAR
Crosgen Comics, 2004
1	3.00
2 thru 6	@3.00

NEGATIVE EXPOSURE
Humanoids Publishing, 2001
1 by Enrico Mirini	3.00
2	3.00
3 thru 4	@3.00

NEIL GAIMAN'S LADY JUSTICE
Tekno Comix (1995)
1 I:Lady Justice	2.50
1a	6.00
2 V:Blood Pirate	2.50
3 V:Blood Pirate	2.50
4 New Story Arc	2.50
5 Street Gang War	2.50
6 Street Gang War	2.50
7 thru 11	@2.50

Big Entertainment, April, 1996
1 thru 4	@2.50
5 DIB(s)	2.50
6 DIB(s),Woman About Town, pt.1	2.50
7 DIB(s),Woman About Town, pt.2	2.50
8 DIB(s),Woman About Town, pt.3	2.50

NEIL GAIMAN'S MR. HERO THE NEWMATIC MAN
Tekno-Comics, 1994
1 I:Mr. Hero, Tecknophage	2.50
2 A:Tecknophage	2.50

Neil Gaiman's Mr. hero #16
© Tekno-Comics

3 I:Adam Kaine	2.50
4 I:New Body	2.50
5 Earthquake	2.50
6 I:New Character	2.50
7 I:Deadbolt, Bloodboil	2.50
8 V:Avatar	2.50
9 in London	2.50
10 V:Demon	2.50
11 V:Monster	2.50
12 The Great Goward	2.50
13 thru 17	@2.50

NEIL GAIMAN'S PHAGE
Tekno-Comics, 1996
1	2.50

NEIL GAIMAN'S PHAGE: SHADOW DEATH
Big Entertainment, 1996
1 thru 4	@2.50
5 O:Orlando Holmes,A:Lady Messalina	2.50
6 conclusion	2.50

NEIL GAIMAN'S TECKNOPHAGE
Teckno-Comics, 1995
1 I:Kalighoul, Tom Vietch	2.50
1a Steel Edition	4.00
2 F:Mayor of New Yorick	2.50
3 Phange Building	2.50
4 Horde eevils	2.50
5 Middle Management	2.50
6 Escape from Phange	2.50
7 Mecca	2.50

NEIL GAIMAN'S WHEEL OF WORLDS
Teckno-Comics, 1995
0 Deluxe Edition w/Posters	3.00
0a I:Lady Justice	2.50
1	3.25

NEMESIS THE WARLOCK
Eagle, 1984
1 thru 8	@2.50

NEO DAWN
Committed Comics, 2004
1 thru 3	@3.00

NEOTOPIA
Antarctic Press, 2003
1 Princess for a Day	4.00
2 Philios to the Rescue	4.00
3 thru 5	@4.00

Vol. 2
1 (of 6)	3.00
2	3.00
3	4.00
4 thru 5	@3.00

Vol. 3
1 thru 5	@3.00

Vol. 4
1	3.00
2 thru 5	@3.00

NEPTUNE
Narwain Publishing, 2006
1-shot 48-pg. JP	6.00

NEUTRAL WORLD
APC, 2003
1 thru 4	@3.50

NEUTRO
Dell, 1967
1 .... 75.00

NEW ADVENTURES OF FELIX THE CAT
Felix Comics, Inc., 1992
1 New stories 2.50
2 The Magic Paint Brush 2.50

NEW ADVENTURES OF PHANTOM BLOT, THE
Gold Key, 1964
1 Disney 100.00
2 .... 80.00
3 thru 7 .... @50.00

NEW ADVENTURES OF PINOCCHIO
Dell Publishing Co., 1962
1 .... 150.00
2 and 3 .... @125.00

NEW ADVENTURES OF SPEED RACER
Now, 1993
0 Premiere, 3-D cover 2.50
1 thru 11 .... @2.50

NEW AMERICA
Eclipse, 1987–88
1 A:Scout 2.50
2 A:Scout 2.50
3 A:Roman Catholic Pope 2.50
4 A:Scout 2.50

NEW DNAGENTS, THE
Eclipse, 1985–87
1 R:DNAgents 2.50
2 thru 17 .... @2.50
3-D #1 .... 2.50

NEW JUSTICE MACHINE
Innovation, 1989
1 and 2 .... @2.50
2 .... 2.50

NEW KABOOM
Awesome Entertainment, 1999
1 RLe,JLb 2.50

NEW LINE CINEMA'S TALES OF HORROR
Wildstorm/DC, Sept., 2007
1 .... 3.00

NEWMEN
Maximum Press, 1997
1–22 see Image
23 ErS,CSp,AG,Anthem, pt.3 ...... 2.50
24 ErS,CSp,AG,Anthem, pt.4 ...... 2.50
25 ErS,CSp,AG,Anthem, pt.5 ...... 2.50

NEW ORLEANS SAINTS
1 Playoff season(football team) ... 6.00

NEWSTRALIA
Innovation, 1989
1 and 2 .... @2.50
3 .... 2.50

NEW TERRYTOONS
Dell Publishing Co., 1960–61
1 .... 100.00

New Terrytoons #44
© Gold Key

2 thru 8 .... @60.00
Gold Key, 1962
1 F:Heckle & Jeckle 150.00
2 .... 125.00
3 thru 10 .... @50.00
11 thru 20 .... @40.00
21 thru 30 .... @25.00
31 thru 40 .... @20.00
41 thru 54 .... @15.00

NEW WAVE, THE
Eclipse, 1986–87
1 Error Pages 2.50
1a Correction 2.50
2 .... 2.50
3 Space Station Called Hell 2.50
4 Birth of Megabyte 2.50
5 PG(c),O:Avalon 2.50
6 O:Megabyte 2.50
7 Avalon disappears 2.50
8 V:Heap,V:Druids 2.50
9 .... 2.50
10 V:Heap Team 2.50
11 .... 2.50
12 .... 2.50
13 V:Volunteers 2.50
14 1/3 issue 2.50

NEW WAVE vs. THE VOLUNTEERS
Eclipse, 1987
1 3-D,V:Volunteers 2.50
2 3-D,V:Volunteers 2.50

NEXT MAN
Comico, 1985
1 I&O:Next Man 2.50
2 .... 2.50
3 .... 2.50
4 .... 2.50
5 .... 2.50

NEXT NEXUS
First, 1989
1 SR 2.50
2 SR 2.50
3 SR 2.50
4 SR 2.50

NEXUS
Capital, 1983
1 SR,I:Judah Maccabee 5.00
2 SR,Origin,V:Bellows 4.00

3 SR,Sundra Captive 4.00
4 SR,V:Ziggurat 4.00
5 SR,I'm Bored! 4.00
6 SR,A:Badger,TrialogueTrilogy#1 . 4.00
First, 1985
7 SR,A:Badger,TrialogueTrilogy#2 . 4.00
8 SR,A:Badger,TrialogueTrilogy#3 . 3.00
9 thru 49 .... @2.50
50 SF,double size,A:Badger Pt.6
  Crossroads tie-in 3.50
51 thru 80 .... @2.50

NEXUS
Rude Dude Prod.
99 Space Opera, Act. 1 .... 3.00
100 Space Opera, Act 2, 48-pgs.... 6.00
101 Space Opera, Act. 3 .... 3.00
102 Space Opera, Act. 4 .... 3.00
1-shot Nexus' Greatest Hits (2007) . 2.00
1-shot Nexus: The Origin........ 4.00

NEXUS LEGENDS
First, 1989
1 thru 23 .... @2.50

NICKI SHADOW
Relentless Comics, 1997
1 by Eric Burnham & Ted Naifeh .. 2.50
2 Killing Zone, pt.2 .... 2.50
3 Killing Zone, pt.3 .... 2.50
4 Killing Zone, concl. 2.50

NIGHT GLIDER
Topps, 1993
1 V:Bombast,C:Captain Glory,
  Trading Card 3.25

NIGHTHUNTER
Empire Comics, 2001
1 (of 12) 3.75
2 thru 4 .... @3.75

NIGHTJAR
Avatar Press, 2004
1 (of 4) 3.50
2 thru 4 .... @3.50
1a and 4a wraparound (c)s..... @3.50

NIGHTJAR: HOLLOW BONES
Avatar Press, 2004
1 .... 4.00
1a wraparound (c)............. 4.00

NIGHT MAN, THE
Malibu Ultraverse, 1993–95
1 I:Night Man,Deathmask........ 2.75
1a Silver foil (c)............... 4.00
2 thru 15 .... @2.50
16 I:Bloodfly................. 3.50
17 thru 23 .... @2.50
Ann.#1 V:Pilgrim, 64pg........ 4.00
Malibu Ultraverse, 1995
Infinity Night Man vs. Night Man ... 2.50
1 Discovers New powers 2.50
1a Computer Painted Cover...... 2.50
2 thru 4 .... @2.50

NIGHT MAN/GAMBIT
Malibu, 1996
1 .... 2.50
2 .... 2.50
3 .... 2.50

NIGHTMARE
Innovation, 1989
1 AN 2.50

NIGHTMARE AND CASPER
Harvey Publications, 1963
1 . . . . 125.00
2 . . . . 75.00
3 . . . . 75.00
4 . . . . 75.00
5 . . . . 75.00
Becomes:

CASPER AND NIGHTMARE
6 B:68 pgs. 100.00
7 . . . . 75.00
8 . . . . 75.00
9 . . . . 75.00
10 . . . . 75.00
11 thru 20 . . . . @50.00
21 thru 30 . . . . @30.00
31 . . . . 30.00
32 E:68 pgs 30.00
33 thru 45 . . . . @25.00
46 Aug., 1974. . . . . 25.00

NIGHTMARE ON ELM STREET
Blackthorne, 1991
1 3-D. 2.50
2 3-D. 2.50
3 3-D. 2.50

NIGHTMARE ON ELM ST.: PARANOID
Avatar Press, 2005
1 . . . . 4.00
1a wraparound (c) 4.00
1b variant (c)s . . . . @4.00
1c leather (c) 15.00
2 . . . . 4.00
2a Wraparound (c) 4.00
2b Variant(c)s . . . . @4.00
2c Die-cut (c) 9.00

NIGHTMARE ON ELM STREET, A
Avatar Press, 2005
Spec. #1 . . . . 4.00
Spec. #1 variant (c)s 4.00
Spec. #1 glow (c) . . . . @4.00
Spec. #1 Blood Red Con (c) 5.00
Spec. #1 Painted (c) 6.00
Spec. #1 Carcass (c) 6.00

NIGHTMARE ON ELM STREET, A
Wildstorm/DC, Oct., 2006
1 CDi. 3.00
1a variant (c). 3.00
2 CDi. 3.00
3 CDi. 3.00
4 CDi. 3.00
5 CDi, Aztec secrets 3.00
6 CDi,Aztec Manuscript 3.00
7 CDi,Freddy vs. demon. 3.00
8 CDi,Fast food and Freddy. 3.00

NIGHTMARES ON ELM STREET
Innovation, 1991
1 Yours Truly, Freddy Krueger Pt.1 3.00
2 Yours Truly ,Freddy Krueger Pt.2 2.50
3 Loose Ends Pt.1,Return to
 Springwood 2.50
4 Loose Ends Pt 2 . . . . 2.50
5 . . . . 2.50
6 . . . . 2.50

NIGHTMARE ON ELM STREET, A
Avatar Press, 2005
Spec. #1 . . . . 4.00
Spec. #1 variant (c)s 4.00
Spec. #1 premium (c)s . . . . . . @6.00
Spec. Fearbook #1 . . . . 4.00
Spec. Fearbook #1 variant (c)s . . @4.00

NIGHTMARE ON ELM ST.: PARANOID
Avatar Press, 2005
1 thru 3 . . . . @4.00
1a thru 3a wraparound (c)s . . . . @4.00
1b thru 3b variant (c)s . . . . . . @4.00
1c Special (c)s. . . . . @6.00

NIGHTMARES
Eclipse, 1985
1 . . . . 2.50
2 . . . . 2.00

NIGHT MARY
IDW Publishing, 2005
1 . . . . 4.00
2 . . . . 4.00
3 thru 5 . . . . @4.00

NIGHT MUSIC
Eclipse, 1984–88
1 . . . . 2.50
2 . . . . 2.50
3 CR, Jungle Bear 3.00
4 Pelias & Melisande 2.00
5 Pelias 2.00
6 same as Salome #1
7 same as Red Dog #1
Graphic Novel 8.00

NIGHTS INTO DREAMS
Archie Comics, 1997
1 based on Sega game 2.00
2 . . . . 2.00
3 thru 6 . . . . @2.00

NIGHT OF THE LIVING DEAD
Dead Dog Comics, 2004
1 Barbara's Zombie Chronicles . . . 5.00
1a gold foil (c) 5.00
2 Barbara's Zombie Chronicles . . . 5.00
3 . . . . 5.00

NIGHT OF THE LIVING DEAD: BACK FROM THE GRAVE
Avatar Press, 2006
1-shot 3.00
1-shot variant (c)s . . . . @3.00
1-shot Splatter (c) 6.00
1-shot Head shot (c) 6.00
1-shot Haunting (c) 6.00
1-shot Necro-foil (c) 20.00
1-shot Sketch (c) 30.00

NIGHTSHADE
No Mercy Comics, 1997
1 by Mark Williams 2.50
2 . . . . 2.50
3 . . . . 2.50

NIGHT TRIBES
WildStorm/DC, 1999
1-shot Night Tribes unite 5.00

Nightveil #1
© AC Comics

NIGHTVEIL
AC Comics, 1984
1 . . . . 3.50
2 . . . . 2.50
3 thru 7 . . . . @2.50
Spec.#1 . . . . 2.50

9 LIVES OF FELIX
Harvey, 1991
1 . . . . 2.50
2 . . . . 2.50
3 . . . . 2.50
4 . . . . 2.50

NINJA BOY
WildStorm/DC, 2001
1 Ancient Japan, 40-pg. 3.50
2 . . . . 3.00
3 . . . . 3.00
4 . . . . 3.00
5 . . . . 3.00
6 Bishamon, God of War 3.00

NINJA HIGH SCHOOL
Eternity, 1992
1 Reps.orig.N.H.S.in color 2.50
2 thru 13 reprints. . . . . @2.50

NINJA HIGH SCHOOL
Antarctic Press, 2000
1 thru 74 see B&W
75 . . . . 3.00
76 Quagmire gang 3.00
77 . . . . 3.00
78 World Domination Tour 3.00
79 Dog Supreme 3.00
80 Jeremy Feeple is back 3.00
81 F:Diamond Diane 3.00
82 F:Quagmire Koalas. 3.00
83 Time passes 3.00
84 Past, Present, Future 3.00
85 Time has past 3.00
86 Queen of the Conglomerate . . . 3.00
87 Invaded by the Shallrams 3.00
88 Battle Chef battle 3.00
89 Sammie's secret 3.00
90 Earth's champion 3.00
91 The Toughest Contest. 3.00
92 Round 2 . . . . 3.00
93 Round 3 . . . . 3.00
94 F:Red Ninja,V:Lendo Rivalsan . 3.00
95 Ichi in a new place 3.00

All comics prices listed are for *Near Mint* condition.

COLOR PUB.

96 Dash the Impede 3.00
97 F:Asrial, Jeremy 3.00
98 Asrial found 3.00
99 F:Lendo Rivalson dies 3.00
100 F:Asrial, Jeremy, & Ichi
  BDn(c) 48-pg. 5.00
100a Fred Perry (c) 5.00
100b Robert Dejesus (c) 5.00
100c Rod Espinosa (c) 5.00
101 thru 110 . . . . @3.50
111 . . . . 3.50
112 . . . . 3.50
113 . . . . 3.50
114 . . . . 3.50
115 thru 140 . . . . @3.00
141 . . . . 1.00
142 thru 144 . . . . @3.00
Yearbook 2001 . . . . 4.00
Yearbook 2002 . . . . 4.00
Yearbook 2003 . . . . 5.00
Yearbook 2004 . . . . 5.00
Yearbook, 2005 . . . . 5.00
Yearbook, 2006 . . . . 4.50
Spec. Swimsuit special 2002 . . . . 4.00
Spec. Prom Formula (2004) B&W . . 6.00
Class Reunion Spec. (2007) 5.00

NINJA HIGH SCHOOL VERSION 2
Antarctic Press, 1999
1 by Ben Dunn 6.00
2 . . . . 5.00
3 . . . . 4.00
4 . . . . 3.00
5 thru 8 . . . . @2.50
9 Yumei strikes back 2.50
10 . . . . 2.50
11 Time & space distorted 2.50
12 When Worlds Colide, last issue . 2.50

NINJA HIGH SCHOOL FEATURING SPEED RACER
Eternity, 1993
1B 3.00
2B 3.00

NINJA SCROLL
Wildstorm/DC, Sept., 2006
1 Anime 3.00
1a variant JLe (c) 3.00
2 . . . . 3.00
3a, variant JLe (c) 3.00
3 . . . . 3.00
4 thru 12 . . . . @3.00

NINJAK
Valiant, 1994
0: O:Ninjak, Pt. 1 . . . . 2.50
00: O:Ninjak, Pt.2 . . . . 2.50
1 B:MMo(s),JQ,JP,Chromium(c),
  I:Dr.Silk,Webnet 3.00
1a Gold Ed 4.00
2 thru 28 . . . . @2.50
Yearbook #1, Dr. Silk 4.00

NINJAK
Acclaim, 1996
1 KBk(s), Denny Meechum
  becomes Ninjak 2.50
2 thru 12 KBk(s) . . . . @2.50

N.I.O.
Acclaim, 1998
1 (of 4) by Shon Bury & JPi 2.50
2 . . . . 2.50
3 . . . . 2.50
4 . . . . 2.50

NIRA X: ANIME
Entity Comics, 1997
1 BMs 3.00
1a deluxe, foil cover 3.50
2 BMs 3.00
2a deluxe, foil cover 3.50
Swimsuit #0 . . . . 2.75
Swimsuit #0 Manga (c) 2.75

NIRA X: CYBERANGEL
Entity, 1994
1 From pages of Zen 3.00
1a 2nd printing 2.75
2 V:Parradox 2.50
3 In Hydro-Dams 2.50
4 final issue 2.50
4a with computer game 7.00
Ashcan 2.50
[Series 2], 1995
1 R:Nira X 4.00
1a Clear Chromium Edition 7.00
1b Holo-Chrome edition 9.00
2 Alien Invasion 2.50
3 Mecha New York 2.50
4 Final Issue 2.50
[Series 3], 1996
0 . . . . 2.75
0a signed & numbered 7.00
1 . . . . 2.50
1a gold edition, signed & numb . . . 5.00
2 . . . . 2.50
3 . . . . 3.00

NIRA X/CYNDER: ENDANGERED SPECIES
Entity Comics, 1996
1 . . . . 3.00
1a gold ink enhanced, bagged . . . 11.00

NITROGEN: PROPHET
Arcade Comics, 2006
1 . . . . 4.00
1a variant (c)s . . . . @4.00

NJPW: THE RISE OF THE TIGER
Narwain Publishing, 2006
1 (of 5) 4.00
2 . . . . 4.00

NoMan #2
© Cower Comics

NOCTURNALS
Malibu Bravura, 1995
1 DIB,I:Nocturnals 3.00
1a Glow-in-the-Dark 4.00
2 DIB,I:Komodo, Mister Fane 3.00
3 DIB,F:Raccoon 3.00
4 DIB,I:The Old Wolf 3.00
5 Discovered by Police 3.00
6 DIB 3.00

NOCTURNALS: THE DARK FOREVER
Oni Press, 2001
1 by Dan Brereton 3.00
2 . . . . 3.00
3 . . . . 3.00

NOMAN
Tower Comics, 1966
1 GK,OW,WW,AW 150.00
2 OW,WW,A:Dynamo 100.00

NO TIME FOR SERGEANTS
Dell Publishing Co., 1958
1 Ph(c) 175.00
2 Ph(c) 100.00
3 Ph(c) 100.00

NOVA HUNTER
Ryal Comics
1 thru 3 . . . . @2.50
4 Climax 2.50
5 Death and Betrayal 2.50

NUKLA
Dell, 1965
1 . . . . 75.00
2 thru 4 . . . . @50.00

NURSES, THE
Gold Key, April, 1963
1 . . . . 75.00
2 . . . . 60.00
3 . . . . 60.00

NYOKA, JUNGLE GIRL
Charlton Comics, 1955–57
14 . . . . 150.00
15 thru 22 . . . . @125.00

NYOKA, THE JUNGLE GIRL
AC Comics, 1988
1 and 2 Further Adventures of
  Nyoka, the Jungle Girl . . . . . . @2.50

OBLIVION
Comico, 1995
1 R:The Elementals 2.50
2 I:Thunderboy, Lilith 2.50
3 I:Fen, Ferril 2.50
4 War 3.00
5 The Unholy Trilogy 3.00

OCCULT FILES OF DR. SPEKTOR
Gold Key, April, 1973
1 I:Lakot 75.00
2 thru 5 . . . . @30.00
6 thru 10 . . . . @30.00
11 I:Spertor as Werewolf 30.00
12 and 13 . . . . @25.00
14 A:Dr. Solar 50.00
15 thru 24 . . . . @20.00

COLOR PUB.

Whitman
25 rep. 20.00

OCEAN
Wildstorm/DC, 2004
1 (of 6) WEI(s),CSp,KIS 3.00
2 WEI,CSp,KIS 3.00
3 WEI,CSp,KIS 3.00
4 WEI,CSp,KIS 3.00
5 WEI,CSp,KIS 3.00
6 WEI,CSp,KIS,48-pg., concl. 4.00

ODYSSEY, THE
Avatar/TidalWave Studios, 2002
1A RCz (c) 3.50
1B MMy (c) 3.50
1C Parajullo (c) 3.50
1D Murphy (c) 3.50

ODYSSEY PRESENTS: VENUS
Alias Enterprises, 2006
1 . . . . 3.50

ODYSSEY, THE: ABSOLUTE POWER
Alias Enterprises, 2006
1-shot 5.00

OF BITTER SOULS
Speakeasy Comics, 2005
1 . . . . 3.00
2 thru 3 . . . . @3.00
4 thru 6 . . . . @3.00
Vol. 2, Markosia, 2006
1 . . . . 3.50
1a variant (c)s . . . . @3.50
2 . . . . 3.50
3 . . . . 3.50
3a variant (c) 3.50
4 . . . . 3.50
4a limited variant (c) 6.00

O.G. WHIZ
Gold Key, 1971–79
1 . . . . 100.00
2 . . . . 60.00
3 thru 6 . . . . @50.00
7 thru 11 . . . . @40.00

OINK: BLOOD AND CIRCUS
Kitchen Sink, 1997
1 (of 4) by John Mueller 5.00
2 thru 4 . . . . @5.00

OLYMPUS HEIGHTS
IDW Publishing, 2004
1 . . . . 4.00
2 thru 5 . . . . @4.00

O'MALLEY AND THE ALLEY CATS
Gold Key, 1971–74
1 . . . . 45.00
2 thru 9 . . . . @40.00

OMEGA 7
Omega 7
1 V:Exterminator X. 4.00
? by Alonzo L. Washington 4.00
0 . . . . 3.00

OMEGA SAGA, THE
Southpaw Publishing, 1998
0 by Mike Gerardo & Chris Navetta 3.00

---

1 Episode One, pt.1 . . . . 3.00
2 Episode One, pt.2 . . . . 3.00
Axess Comics
3 by Mike Gerardo, Heroes (c). . . . 3.00
3b Villains (c) 3.00

OMEN, THE
Chaos! Comics, 1998
Preview Book, BnP 2.50
1 by PNu & Justiniano 3.00
2 thru 5 . . . . @3.00
1-shot The Omen Vexed 3.00

On A Pale Horse #3
© Innovation

ON A PALE HORSE
Innovation
1 Piers Anthony adapt 5.00
2 Magician,I:Kronos 5.00
3 . . . . 5.00
4 VV 5.00
5 . . . . 5.00
6 . . . . 5.00

ONE-ARM SWORDSMAN
Dr. Leung's
1 . . . . 3.00
2 . . . . 3.00
3 . . . . 2.75
4 thru 11 . . . . @2.50

100 GIRLS
Arcana Studio, 2004
1 thru 7 . . . . @3.00
1a 2nd printing 3.00

100 GIRLS/JENNA
Arcana Studio, 2006
1 (of 2) 4.00

OPERATION: STORMBREAKER
Acclaim Special Event, 1997
Spec. F:Teutonic Knight 4.00

OPPOSITE FORCES
Alias Enterprises, 2005
Vol. 2
1 (of 4) 2.00
2 . . . . 3.00
3 . . . . 3.00
4 . . . . 3.00

ORBIT
Eclipse, 1990
1 DSt(c) 4.00
2 . . . . 4.00
3 . . . . 5.00

ORIENTAL HEROES
Jademan, 1988–92
1 by Tony Wong & MBn 2.50
2 . . . . 2.50
3 thru 13 . . . . @2.50
14 thru 40 . . . . @2.50
41 thru 44 . . . . 2.00
45 thru 53 . . . . @2.50

ORIGINAL ASTRO BOY
Now, 1987
1 KSy 3.00
2 thru 17 KSy . . . . @3.00

ORIGINAL CAPTAIN JOHNAR AND THE ALIENS
Valiant, 1995
1 Reprint from Magnus 3.00
2 Russ Manning rep. 3.00

ORIGINAL DICK TRACY
Gladestone, 1990
1 rep.V:Mrs.Pruneface 2.50
2 rep.V:Influence. 2.50
3 rep.V:TheMole 2.50
4 rep.V:ItchyOliver 2.50
5 rep.V:Shoulders 2.50

ORIGINAL DR. SOLAR MAN OF THE ATOM
Valiant, 1995
1 Reprint 3.00
2 Reprints 3.00
3 Reprints 3.00

ORIGINAL E-MAN
First, 1985
{rep. Charlton stories}
1 JSon,O:E-Man & Nova 2.50
2 JSon,V:Battery,SamuelBoar . . . 2.50
3 JSon,City in the Sand 2.50
4 JSon,A:Brain from Sirius 2.50
5 JSon,V:T.V. Man 2.50
6 JSon,I:Teddy Q 2.50
7 JSon,Vamfire 2.50

ORIGINAL MAGNUS ROBOT FIGHTER
Valiant, 1995
1 Reprint 3.00
2 Russ Manning Art 3.00
3 Russ Manning 3.00

ORIGINAL SHIELD
Archie, 1984
1 DAy/TD,O:Shield 2.50
2 DAy,O:Dusty 2.50
3 DAy 2.50
4 DAy 2.50

ORIGINAL TUROK, SON OF STONE
Valiant, 1995
1 Reprint 3.00
2 Alberto Gioletti art 3.00
3 Alberto Gioletti 3.00
4 Reprints 3.00

COLOR PUB.

ORIGIN OF THE DEFIANT UNIVERSE
Defiant, 1994
1 O:Defiant Characters 2.50

ORIGINS
Malibu Ultraverse,
1 O:Ultraverse Heroes 2.50

ORION THE HUNTER
Alias Enterprises, 2006
1 (of 4) 3.00
2 . . . . 3.00
3 . . . . 3.50
4 . . . . @3.50

ORSON SCOTT CARD'S WYRMS
Dabel Brothers Prod., 2006
1 . . . . 3.00
1a variant (c) 6.00
2 thru 5 . . . . @3.00
2a thru 5a variant (c)s . . . . @6.00

OUTBREED 999
Blackout Comics, 1994
1 thru 4 . . . . @3.00
5 Search For Daige 3.00

OUTCAST SPECIAL
Valiant, 1995
1 R:The Outcast. 2.50

OUTER LIMITS, THE
Dell Publishing Co., 1964
1 P(c) 250.00
2 thru 5 P(c) . . . . @125.00
6 thru 10 P(c) . . . . @100.00
11 thru 18 P(c) . . . . @75.00

OUTER SPACE
Charlton, 1968
1 . . . . 80.00

OUTLAW SCORN: 3030AD
Arcana Studio, 2006
1 (of 6) 4.00
2 . . . . 4.00
2a sketch (c) 15.00
3 thru 4 . . . . @3.00

OUTLAWS OF THE WEST
Charlton Comics, 1957–70
1 thru 10: CODY OF THE PONY
EXPRESS (see Golden Age section)
11 . . . . 100.00
12 . . . . 75.00
13 . . . . 75.00
14 Giant size 125.00
15 . . . . 75.00
16 . . . . 75.00
17 . . . . 75.00
18 SD. 135.00
19 . . . . 60.00
20 thru 40. . . . . @60.00
41 thru 50. . . . . @40.00
51 thru 70. . . . . @25.00
71 thru 81. . . . . @20.00
Charlton, 1979
82 . . . . 150.00
83 thru 88. . . . . @100.00

OUT OF THIS WORLD
Charlton Comics, 1956–59
1 . . . . 400.00

Out of tthis World #15
© Charlton

2 . . . . 200.00
3 SD 500.00
4 SD 500.00
5 SD 500.00
6 SD 500.00
7 SD,SD(c) 550.00
8 SD 450.00
9 SD 350.00
10 SD,Perfect Forcaster 350.00
11 SD 400.00
12 SD. 350.00
13 thru 15. . . . . @200.00
16 . . . . 400.00

OUTPOSTS
Blackthorne, 1997
1 thru 6 . . . . @2.50

OUT THERE
WildStorm/DC, 2001
1 HuR, Cliffhanger 2.50
2 HuR, ... 2.50
3 HuR 2.50
4 HuR 2.50
5 HuR 2.50
6 HuR 2.50
7 HuR,Road to El Dorado,pt.1 . . . . 2.50
8 HuR,Road to El Dorado,pt.2 . . . . 2.50
9 HuR,Road to El Dorado,pt.3 . . . . 2.50
10 HuR,Road to El Dorado,pt.4 . . . 3.00
11 HuR,Road to El Dorado,pt.5 . . . 3.00
12 HuR,Road to El Dorado,pt.6 . . . 3.00
13 HuR,The War in Hell,pt.1 . . . . . 3.00
14 HuR,The War in Hell,pt.2 . . . . . 3.00
15 HuR,Draedalus's Domain 3.00
16 HuR,Dreadrealm. 3.00
17 HuR,all-silent issue 3.00
18 HuR,V:Draedalus 3.00

OWL, THE
Gold Key, April, 1967
1 . . . . 125.00
2 April, 1968 . . . . 90.00

OZ/WONDERLAND CHRONICLES, THE
Buymetoys.com, 2005
0 . . . . 3.00
Preview (B&W). 3.00
1 JJu (c) 3.50
1a variant (c) 3.50
2 . . . . 3.50
2a variant (c) 3.50

OZF5 GALE FORCE
Alias Enterprises, 2005
1-shot 5.00
1-shot signed convention edition . . 15.00

PACIFIC PRESENTS
Pacific, 1992
1 DSt,Rocketeer,(3rd App.). 12.00
2 DSt,Rocketeer,(4th App.). 9.00
3 SD,I:Vanity. 2.50
4 and 5 . . . . @2.50

P.A.C.
Artifacts Inc., 1993
1 I:P.A.C.. . . . . 2.50

PAINKILLER JANE
Event Comics, 1997
1 JQ(c) 3.00
1 RL(c) 3.00
1 Red foil logo, signed 20.00
2 JQ&JP(c) 3.00
2 JP&RL(c) 3.00
3 JQ&JP(c) 3.00
3a JP&RL(c) 3.00
4 JQ&JP(c) A Too Bright Place
  For Dying. 3.00
4a RL&JP(c) 3.00
5 JQ&JP(c) Purgatory
  Station—Next Stop Hell 3.00
5a RL&JP(c) 3.00
6 RL&JP(c) Blood Harvest 3.00
6a BSz&JP(c) 3.00
7 Jane in the Jungle,
  pt.1,BiT&JP(c) 3.00
7a RL&JP(c) 3.00
Spec.#0 O:Painkiller Jane,48-pg. . . 4.00
Spec.#0A signed 25.00
Spec. Painkiller Jane/Hellboy
  Ancient Laughter (1998) 3.00
Spec. Painkiller Jane/Hellboy,
  signed 18.00
Spec. Painkiller Jane/The Darkness,
  signed, limited edition, JQ(c). . 25.00

PAINKILLER JANE
D.E. (Dynamite Ent.) 2006
0 . . . . 1.00
0a variant (c) 1.00
1 JP. 3.50
1a variant AH(c) 3.50
1b variant Blood Red foil (c). . . . 15.00
1c variant wraparound (c) 9.00
2 JP. 3.50
2a variant b&w (c) 12.00
3 JP. 3.50
3a variant (c)s . . . . @3.50

PAINKILLER JANE/ DARKCHYLDE
Event Comics, 1998
1 BAu,RQu 3.00
1a signed & numbered 25.00
1b Omnichrome edition. 12.00
1c Omnichrome, signed 25.00
1d Dynamic Forces cover. 7.00

PAINKILLER JANE VS. THE DARKNESS: STRIPPER
Event Comics, 1997
1 GEn,JP,x-over, Amanda Connor
  cover 3.00
1a Greg & Tim Hildebrandt 3.00
1b MS(c) 3.00
1c JQ(c) 3.00

COLOR PUB.

PAKKINS' LAND
Alias Enterprises, 2005
Vol. 2
1 . . . . 3.00
2 thru 8 . . . . @3.00

PANDEMONIUM: DELIVERANCE
Chaos! Comics, 1998
1-shot by Jesse Leon McCann &
  Jack Jadson 3.00

PANIC
Gemstone, 1997
1 thru 12 EC Comics reprint . . . . @2.50

PANTERA
Rock-it Comix, 1994
1 . . . . 4.00
1a Gold Ed. 20.00

PANTHA
Harris Comics, 1997
1 (of 2) MT 3.50
1 Marilyn Monroe MT alt.cov. 10.00
2 MT alternate (c) 10.00
2 photo (c). 10.00

PARA
Pennyfarthing Press, 2004
1 . . . . 3.00
2 thru 6 . . . . @3.00

PARADAX
Vortex, 1987
1 . . . . 2.50

PARADISE
Twenty First Century, 2000
1 thru 7 . . . . @3.00

PARADOX
Arcana Studio, 2005
1 (of 4) 3.00
2 . . . . 3.00
3 . . . . 3.00

PARAGON DARK APOCALYPSE
AC, 1993
1 thru 4, Fem Force crossover . . @3.00

PARANOIA
Adventure Comics, 1991
1 (based on video game) Clone1 . . 3.25
2 King-R-Thr-2 . . . . 3.00
3 R:Happy Jack,V:N3F 3.00
4 V:The Computer 3.00
5 V:The Computer 3.00
6 V:Lance-R-Lot,last issue 3.00

PARIAH
Revolution Comics, 2006
1 . . . . 3.00
2 thru 4 . . . . @3.00
4a variant (c) 3.00

PARTRIDGE FAMILY, THE
Charlton Comics, 1971–73
1 . . . . 125.00
2 thru 4 . . . . @60.00
5 Summer Special 125.00
6 thru 21 . . . . @50.00

PASSOVER
Maximum Press, 1996
1 (of 2) BNa 3.00
2 BNa,A:Avengelyne 3.00

PATH, THE
Crossgen Comics, 2002
1 RMz,BS 5.00
2 thru 4 RMz,BS . . . . @3.00
9 thru 23 . . . . @3.00
Prequel 48-pg. 5.00

PATHWAYS TO FANTASY
Pacific, 1984
1 BS,JJ art 3.00

PATRIOTS, THE
WildStorm/DC, 1999
1 BCi&JPe(s) 2.50
2 BCi&JPe(s) 2.50
3 thru 7 BCi&JPe(s) . . . . @2.50
8 BCi&JPe(s),V:Stealthers 2.50
9 BCi&JPe(s) 2.50
10 JPe(s),final issue 2.50

PAT SAVAGE: WOMAN OF BRONZE
Millennium, 1992
1 F:Doc Savage's cousin 2.50

PEACEKEEPER
Future Comics, 2003
1 . . . . 3.00
2 thru 5 . . . . @3.00

Peacemaker #3
© Charlton

PEACEMAKER
Charlton, 1967
1 A:Fightin' 5 . . . . 5.00
2 A:Fightin' 5 . . . . 3.00
3 A:Fightin' 5 . . . . 3.00
4 O:Peacemaker,A:Fightin' 5 . . . . 4.00
5 A:Fightin' 5 . . . . 2.50

PEANUTS
Dell Publishing Co., 1958
1 . . . . 300.00
2 . . . . 300.00
3 . . . . 250.00
4 . . . . 200.00
5 thru 13 . . . . @175.00

PEANUTS
Gold Key, 1963
1 . . . . 225.00
2 thru 4 . . . . @175.00

PEARL HARBOR
Antarctic Press, 2001
1 by Ted Nomura, Movie tie-in 4.00
2 movie tie-in, concl. 4.00
Spec. 60th Anniv. spec., 64-pg. . . 13.00
Spec. 60th Anniv., Japanese (c) . . 13.00

PEBBLES & BAMM-BAMM
Charlton Comics, 1972–76
1 . . . . 100.00
2 thru 10 . . . . @50.00
11 thru 36 . . . . @45.00

PEBBLES FLINTSTONE
Gold Key, 1963
1 A Chip off the old block 175.00

PENNY AND AGGIE
Alias Enterprises, 2005
1 . . . . 3.00
2 . . . . 3.00
3 . . . . 3.00
4 . . . . 3.00

PERFECT DARK: JANUS' TEARS
Prima Publishing, 2006
1 . . . . 3.50
2 thru 3 . . . . @3.50
4 thru 6 . . . . @3.50

PERFECT DARK ZERO
Prima Publishing, 2006
1 (of 6) 3.50

PERG
Lightning Comics, 1993
1 Glow in the dark(c),JS(c),
  B:JZy(s),KIK,I:Perg 3.75
1a Platinum Ed. 5.00
1b Gold Ed. 7.00
1 gold edition, glow-in-the-dark
  flip cover 25.00
2 KIK,O:Perg. 3.25
2a Platinum Ed. 5.00
3 Flip Book (c), ... 3.25
3a Platinum Ed 5.00
4 TLw,I:Hellina 9.00
4a Platinum Ed 5.00
5 A:Hellina. 3.25
6 PIA,A:Hellina 3.25
7 . . . . 3.00
8 V:Police 3.00

PERRY MASON MYSTERY MAGAZINE
Dell Publishing Co., 1964
1 . . . . 150.00
2 Ray Burr Ph(c). 100.00

PETER PAN: RETURN TO NEVERNEVER LAND
Adventure
1 Peter in Mass. 2.50
2 V:Tiger Lily. 2.50

PETER POTAMUS
Gold Key, 1965
1 . . . . 175.00

COLOR PUB.

PETTICOAT JUNCTION
Dell Publishing Co., 1964
1 Ph(c) 150.00
2 Ph(c) 100.00
3 Ph(c) 100.00
4 . . . . 100.00
5 Ph(c) 100.00

PHANTOM, THE
Gold Key, 1962
1 RsM 300.00
2 B:King, Queen & Jack 200.00
3 . . . . 150.00
4 . . . . 150.00
5 . . . . 150.00
6 . . . . 150.00
7 The Super Apes 150.00
8 . . . . 150.00
9 . . . . 150.00
10 The Sleeping Giant 150.00
11 E:King,Queen and Jack 125.00
12 B:Track Hunter 125.00
13 . . . . 125.00
14 The Historian 125.00
15 . . . . 125.00
16 . . . . 125.00
17 Samaris 125.00
King Comics, 1966
18 The Treasure of the Skull
  Cave;BU:Flash Gordon 100.00
19 The Astronaut & the Pirates . . . 75.00
20 A:GirlPhantom,E:FlashGordon . 75.00
21 BU:Mandrake 75.00
22 Secret of Magic Mountain 75.00
23 . . . . 75.00
24 A:Girl Phantom 75.00
25 . . . . 60.00
26 . . . . 60.00
27 . . . . 60.00
28 . . . . 60.00
29 *never published*

The Phantom #47
© *Charlton*

Charlton Comics, 1969–77
30 . . . . 50.00
31 JAp,Phantom of Shang-Ri-La . . 50.00
32 JAp,The Pharaoh Phantom . . . 50.00
33 The Jungle People 50.00
34 thru 39 . . . . @45.00
40 The Ritual 45.00
41 thru 43 . . . . @35.00
44 To Right A Wrong 35.00
45 . . . . 35.00
46 I:Piranha 30.00
47 thru 72 . . . . @30.00
73 . . . . 25.00

74 . . . . 30.00

PHANTOM
Wolf Publishing, 1992
1 Drug Runners 2.50
2 Mystery Child of the Sea 2.50
3 inc.feature pages on
  Phantom/Merchandise 2.50
4 TV Jungle Crime Buster 2.50
5 Castle Vacula-Transylvania 2.50
6 The Old West 2.50
7 Sercet of Colussus 2.75
8 Temple of the Sun God 2.75

PHANTOM, THE
Moonstone, 2002
1 CDi 3.50
2 thru 8 . . . . @3.50
9 thru 13 . . . . @3.50
14 thru 20 . . . . @3.50
12a Limited ed. (c) 4.50
17a thru 19a limited ed . . . . . . @4.50
Ann. #1 . . . . 6.50
Ann. #1 Limited Ed. 9.00

PHANTOM BOLT, THE
Gold Key, 1964–66
1 A:Mr X 125.00
2 Super Goof 100.00
3 thru 7 . . . . @75.00

PHANTOM FORCE
Genesis West, 1994
Previously: Image
0 JK/JLe(c) 3.00
3 thru 10 . . . . @3.00

PHANTOM JACK: THE NOWHERE MAN AGENDA
Speakeasy Comics, 2006
1 . . . . 3.00
2 thru 3 . . . . @3.00

PHAZE
Eclipse, 1988
1 BSz(c),Takes place in future 2.50
2 PG(c),V:The Pentagon 2.50
3 Schwieger Vs. Mammoth 2.50

PHOENIX
Atlas, 1975
1 thru 4 . . . . @20.00

PHOENIX RESURRECTION
Malibu Ultraverse, 1995–96
0 Intro to Phoenix Resurrection . . . 2.50
Genesis, A:X-Men 4.00
Revelations, A:X-Men 4.00
Aftermath, A:X-Men 4.00

PIERCE
Imperium Comics, 2006
1 . . . . 3.00
2 thru 4 . . . . @3.00

PINK PANTHER, THE
Gold Key, April, 1971
1 . . . . 100.00
2 thru 10 . . . . @75.00
11 thru 30 . . . . @50.00
31 thru 74 . . . . @30.00
75 thru 80 . . . . @50.00
81 thru 87 . . . . @35.00

PIRACY
Gemstone, 1998
1 EC comics reprint 2.50

2 thru 7 EC comics reprints . . . . @2.50

PIRATE CORP.
Eternity
1 thru 5 . . . . @2.50

PIRATES VS. NINJAS II: UP THE ANTE
Antarctic Press, 2007
1 . . . . 3.50
1a variant (c) 3.50
2 thru 5 . . . . @3.50

PIRATE TALES
Boom! Studios, 2006
1 . . . . 7.00

P.I.'S, THE
First, 1985
1 JSon,Ms.Tree,M Mauser 2.50
2 JSon,Ms.Tree,M Mauser 2.50
3 JSon,Ms.Tree,M Mauser 2.50

PISTOLFIST: REVOLUTIONARY WARRIOR
Alias Enterprises, 2006
1 (of 4) 3.50
2 . . . . 3.50
3 thru 4 . . . . @3.50

PITT
Full Bleed Studios, 1996
1 thru 9, see Image
10 thru 14 DK . . . . @2.50
14a variant cover 7.00
15 DK 2.50
16 DK, Ugly Americans, pt.1 . . . . . 2.50
17 DK, Ugly Americans, pt.2 . . . . . 2.50
18 DK, Ugly Americans, pt.3, concl. 2.50
19 by Brian Dawson 3.00
20 DK, Urgral Thul 2.50
Spec. In the Blood 2.50

PITT CREW
Full Bleed Studios, 1998
1 Monster 2.50
2 F:Rai-Kee 2.50
3 Tyrants 2.50
4 The Slayer 2.50
5 . . . . 2.50

PITT: BIOGENESIS
Full Bleed Studios, 2000
1 (of 3) DK 2.50
2 DK 2.50

PIXIE AND DIXIE AND MR. JENKS
Gold Key, 1963
1 . . . . 100.00

PLAGUE OF THE LIVING DEAD
Avatar Press, 2007
Spec. #1 40-pgs. 5.00
Spec. #1 variant (c)s 5.00
1 . . . . 2.50
1a variant (c)s . . . . @3.00
2 thru 6 . . . . @2.50
2a thru 6a variant (c)s . . . . @3.00

PLANETARY
WildStorm/DC, 1999
1 WEI 9.00

---

2 thru 12 WEI . . . . @5.00
13 WEI,secret history of
Elijah Snow 4.00
14 WEI,The Four vs. Planetary 4.00
15 WEI,in Australia. 4.00
16 WEI 4.00
17 WEI Elijah Snow's past 3.00
18 WEI,The Gun Club 3.00
19 WEI,Mystery in Space 3.00
20 WEI,Mystery in Space,pt.2 . . . . 3.00
21 WEI 3.00
22 WEI(s),Torture of William Leather 3.00
23 WEI(s),F:The Drummer 3.00
24 WEI(s),Dark Secrets 3.00
25 WEI(s),A Trap for the Four 3.00
26 WEI(s) 3.00

PLAN 9 FROM
OUTER SPACE
Malibu
GNv Movie Adapt. 5.00

PLANETARY BRIGADE
Boom! Studios, 2006
1 . . . . 3.00
2 . . . . 3.00

PLANETARY BRIGADE:
ORIGINS
Boom! Studios, 2006
1 Old School (c) 4.00
1a New School (c) 4.00
2 . . . . 4.00
3 . . . . 4.00

PLANET COMICS
Blackthorne, 1988
1 DSt(c) 3.00
2 . . . . 3.00
3 . . . . 3.00
4 . . . . 3.00

PLANET OF VAMPIRES
Atlas, Feb.–July, 1975
1 NA(c),1st PB 25.00
2 NA(c) 25.00
3 RH 25.00

POGZ N SLAMMER
Blackout Comics, 1995
1 I:Pogz N Slammer 2.50
2 Contact Other Schools 2.50

POINT BLANK
WildStorm/DC, 2002
Eye of the Storm
1 (of 5) CWi, super-hero noir 3.00
2 CWi, ... 3.00
3 CWi,F:Jack Hawksmoor 3.00
4 CWi, ... 3.00
5 CWi,concl. 3.00

POISON ELVES
Sirius Entertainment, 1998
Color Special #1 by Drew Hayes . . . 3.00
Color Spec.#1 limited 10.00

POIZON
London Night Studios, 1995
0 . . . . 3.00
0 signed gothchik edition 9.00
? O:Poizon 3.00
?a Commemorative (1999) 6.00
1 and 2 EHr . . . . @3.00
1a signed 7.00

POIZON: CADILLACS
AND GREEN TOMATOES
London Night, 1997
2 thru 3 . . . . @3.00
6 deluxe 5.00

POIZON: DEMON HUNTER
London Night, 1998
1 . . . . 3.00
1 Green Death edition 12.00

POIZON: LOST CHILD
London Night Studios, 1996
0 . . . . 3.00
1 mini series 3.00
1 signed 9.00
1 Green Death edition 12.00
2 thru 3 . . . . @3.00

POKEMAN TALES:
Viz Communications, 1999
1 thru 16 boardbooks . . . . @5.00
Gift Set Vol. 1 . . . . 20.00
Gift Set Vol. 2 . . . . 20.00
Movie Spec 5.00

POKEMAN THE MOVIE
2000: REVELATION LUGIA
Viz Communications, 2000
1 . . . . 4.00
2 & 3 . . . . @4.00
Spec. Pikachu's Rescue Adventure . 4.00
Art of Pokeman The Movie 2000 . . 10.00

POKEMAN:
THE FIRST MOVIE
Viz Communications, 1999
1 (of 4) Mewtwo Strikes Back 4.00
2 . . . . 4.00
3 . . . . 4.00
4 conclusion 4.00
Spec. Pikachu's Vacation 4.00
Art of Pokeman: First Movie 9.00

POPEYE
Gold Key, 1962
1-65 See Golden Age Section
66 . . . . 125.00
67 . . . . 100.00
68 thru 80 . . . . @75.00

King Comics, 1966
81 thru 92 . . . . @60.00

Popeye #77
© *Gold Key*

The Sea Hag creates a spinach shortage to get Popeye in her power!

Charlton, 1969
94 thru 99 . . . . @60.00
100 . . . . 75.00
101 thru 138 . . . . @35.00

Gold Key, 1978
139 thru 143 . . . . @25.00
144 50th Aniv. Spec. 30.00
155 . . . . @25.00

Whitman, 1980
156 thru 157 . . . . @25.00
158 thru 159 . . . . @35.00
162 thru 168 . . . . @25.00
169 thru 171 . . . . @30.00

POPEYE
Harvey Comics, 1993–94
1 thru 7 . . . . @2.50
Summer Spec.#1 . . . . 2.50

POPEYE SPECIAL
Ocean, 1987–88
1 & 2 . . . . @2.50

PORKY PIG
Gold Key, 1965
1 . . . . 75.00
2 thru 10 . . . . @40.00
11 thru 30 . . . . @25.00
31 thru 55 . . . . @20.00
56 thru 70 . . . . @15.00
71 thru 93 . . . . @10.00

Whitman, 1979
94 thru 96 . . . . @12.00
97 scarce 50.00
98 thru 109 . . . . @12.00

POSSESSED, THE
Wildstorm/DC July, 2003
1 (of 6) LSh,demons 3.00
2 thru 5 LSh,demon-infested. . . . @3.00
6 LSh,concl. 3.00

POTTER'S FIELD
Boom! Studios, 2007
1 (of 3) 4.00
2 thru 3 . . . . @4.00

POWER & GLORY
Malibu Bravura, 1994
1A HC(a&s),I:American
Powerhouse 3.00
1B alternate cover. 3.00
1c Blue Foil (c) 5.00
1d w/seirgraph 5.00
1e Newsstand 3.00
2 HC(a&s), O:American
Powerhouse 2.75
3 HC(a&s) 2.50
4 HC(a&s) 2.50
Winter Special 3.00

POWER AND THE
GLORY, THE
Narwain Publishing, 2005
1 . . . . 7.50

POWER FACTOR
Wonder Color Comics, 1986
1 . . . . 4.00
2 thru 3 . . . . @3.00

POWER FACTOR
Innovation, 1990
1 thru 4 . . . . @2.50

POWERKNIGHTS
Amara, 1995
P I:Powerknights 2.50

All comics prices listed are for *Near Mint* condition.

POWERMARK
Quest Ministries International, 2004
1 The Mission 3.00
2 Wake of Leviathan 3.00
3 Under Fire 3.00
4 Betrayal 3.00
5 Face Off. 3.00
6 They All Fall Down. 3.00
7 High & Mighty 3.00

POWER OF PRIME
Malibu Ultraverse, 1995
1 O:Prime Powers,Godwheel tie-in 2.50
2 V:Doc Gross, Godwheel tie-in . . . 2.50
3 F:Prime Phade. 2.50
4 F:Elven,Turbocharge 2.50

POWER OF THE VALKYRIE
Arcana Studio, 2006
1 . . . . 4.00
2 . . . . 4.00

POWER RANGERS ZEO/YOUNGBLOOD
Maximum Press, 1997
1 TNu,NRd 3.00

POWERS THAT BE
Broadway Comics
Preview Editions, 1995
1 thru 3 B&W. . . . . @2.50
Regular Series, 1995
1 JiS,I:Fatale, Star Seed 3.00
2 . . . . 3.00
3 . . . . 3.00
4 . . . . 3.00
5 It's the End of the World As We
    Know It,pt.1 . . . . 3.00
6 End/World As We Know It,pt.2 . . 3.00
Becomes:
STAR SEED
7 End/World As We Know It,pt.3 . . 3.00
8 End/World As We Know It,pt.4 . . 3.00
9 End/World As We Know It,pt.5 . . 3.00
10 End/World As We Know It,pt.6. . 3.00
11 End/World As We Know It,pt.7. . 3.00

PRIEST
Maximum Press, 1996
1 RLd, F:Michael O'Bannon 3.00
2 RLd,BNa, ... 3.00
3 RLd 3.00

PRIMAL RAGE
Sirius, 1996
1 TAr,from video game 3.00
1 foil cover, limited edition 3.00
2 TAr,DOe(c). 3.00

PRIME
Malibu Ultraverse, 1993–95
1 B:GJ(s),I:Prime 4.00
1a Ultra-Limited 5.00
1b Full Hologram (c). 5.00
2 V:Organism 8, with Ultraverse
    card 3.00
3 NBy,I:Prototype 3.00
4 NBy,V:Prototype. 3.00
5 NBy,BWS,I:Maxi-Man, BU:Rune . 3.00
6 NBy,A:Pres. Clinton 2.75
7 thru 11 . . . . @2.50
12 NBy,(Ultraverse Premiere#3)
    I:Planet Class 3.50
13 NBy,V:Kutt,Planet Class 3.00
14 thru 26. . . . . @2.50

Prime #12
© *Malibu*

Ashcan (first) 7.00
Ashcan #1 BV(c),B&W. 2.00
Ann.#1 R:Doc Gross 4.00

PRIME
Malibu Ultraverse, 1995–96
Infinty I:Spider-Prime 3.00
1 Spider-Prime vs. Lizard 2.50
1a Computer painted cover 2.50
2 thru 8 . . . . @2.50
9 and 10 . . . . @2.00
11 thru 15. . . . . @2.50

PRIME/CAPTAIN AMERICA
Malibu Ultraverse, 1996
1 GJ,NBy 4.00

PRIME VS. HULK
Malibu, 1995
0 . . . . 9.00
0a signed premium edition 12.00

PRIMER
Comico, 1982–84
1 . . . . 15.00
2 I:Grendel 100.00
3 . . . . 10.00
4 C:Maxx. 10.00
5 I:Maxx 45.00
6 I:Evangelyne 18.00
[Volume 2], 1996
1 F:Lady Bathory 3.00

PRIMUS
Charlton Comics, 1972
1 . . . . 25.00
2 thru 5 . . . . @15.00
6 thru 7 . . . . @12.00

PRINCESS SALLY
Archie Comics, 1995
1 Sonic tie-in 3.00
2 . . . . 3.00
3 . . . . 3.00

PRINCE VANDAL
Triumphant
1 JnR(s), ... 2.50
2 JnR(s), ... 2.50
3 JnR(s),ShG,I:Claire,V:Nicket,
    Vandal goes to Boviden. 2.50
4 JnR(s),ShG,Game's End 2.50

5 JnR(s),ShG,The Sickness, the
    rat appears 2.50
6 JnR(s),ShG,B:Gothic 2.50

PRIORITY: WHITE HEAT
AC Comics, 1986
1 thru 2 miniseries. . . . . @2.50

PROFESSIONAL: GOGOL 13
Viz
1 . . . . 5.00
2 . . . . 5.00
3 . . . . 5.00

PROFESSOR COFFIN
Charlton, 1985
19 From Midnight Tales 10.00
20 . . . . 10.00
21 . . . . 10.00

PROFESSOR OM
Innovation, 1990
1 I:Rock Warrior 2.50
2 Samurai Drama 2.50

PROGRAMME, THE
Wildstorm/DC, July, 2007
1 (of 12) PrM(s) 3.00
1a variant (c) (1:10) 3.00
2 thru 4 PrM(s) . . . . @3.00

PROJECT A-KO 0
Antarctic Press, 1994
0 digest size 5.00
Malibu, 1994
1 thru 4 Based on anime movie . @3.00

PROJECT A-KO 2
CPM, 1995
1 Space Saga 3.00
2 Space Saga 3.00
3 Queen Margarita 3.00

PROJECT A-KO: VERSUS THE UNIVERSE
CPM, 1995
1 Based on Animation. 3.00
2 strange magician 3.00
3 . . . . 3.00
4 (of 5) TEI 3.00

PROJECT EON
Speakeasy Comics, 2005
1 (of 2) 6.00
Markosia, 2006
1 . . . . 5.00
2 thru 3 . . . . @3.50

PROMETHEA
WildStorm/DC, 1999
America's Best Comics
1 AMo(s),F:Sophie Bangs,40-pg. . . 3.50
2 AMo(s),Judgment of Solomon . . 3.00
3 AMo(s),Misty Magic Land 3.00
4 AMo(s),CV,JWi. 3.00
5 AMo(s),JWi,F:WW1 . . . . 3.00
6 AMo(s),JWi,F:Grace Brannagh . . 3.00
7 AMo(s),JWi,F:Sophie Bangs . . . 3.00
8 AMo(s),JWi,V:Goetic demons . . 3.00
9 AMo(s),JWi,The Temple. 3.00
10 AMo(s),JWi,Sex, Stars
    and Serpents. 3.00
11 AMo(s),JWi,giant monster. 3.00
12 AMo(s),JWi,flip-book. 3.00
13 AMo(s),JWi,. 3.00
14 AMo(s),JWi, Lunar Realm. 3.00

15 AMo(s),JWi,. 3.00
16 AMo(s),JWi,Five Swell Guys. . . . 3.00
17 AMo(s),JWi,Stacia vs. Hell 3.00
18 AMo(s),JWi,double demonic. . . . 3.00
19 AMo(s),JWi,Tree of Life 3.00
20 AMo(s),JWi,edge of existence . . 3.00
21 AMo(s),JWi,Binah 3.00
22 AMo(s),JWi,Jack Foust 3.00
23 AMo(s),JWi,40-pg. 3.50
24 AMo(s),JWi 3.00
25 AMo(s),JWi,A Higher Court. 3.00
26 AMo(s),JWi,Later 3.00
27 AMo(s),JWi,Tom Strong 3.00
28 AMo(s),JWi,Jack Faust 3.00
29 AMo(s),JWi 3.00
30 AMo(s),JWi,Painted Doll 3.00
31 AMo(s),JWi 3.00
32 AMo(s),JWi, final issue 4.00
32a variant edition, on posters,
   plus signed book 50.00

PROPHECY
Immortelle Studios, 1998
1 by Hawk, Lovalle, & Wong,
   F:Cynder & War Dragon 3.00
2 . . . . 3.00

PROPHECY OF
THE SOUL SORCERER
Arcane Comics, 1999
1 (of 4) by Eric Dean Seaton 3.00
2 . . . . 3.00
3 . . . . 3.00
3a variant (c). 3.00
4 . . . . 3.00
4a variant (c). 3.00
5 . . . . 3.00
5a variant (c). 3.00
6 Nighthawk vs. Morbid 3.00
6a variant (c). 3.00
7 . . . . 3.00

PROPHET II
Awesome Entertainment, 1999
1 . . . . 3.00
1a holochrome wraparound (c). . . 12.00

PROPHET: LEGACY
Awesome Entertainment, 1999
1 RLe 3.00
2 . . . . 3.00
2a variant (c). 3.00
3 . . . . 3.00

PROPHET/CABLE
Maximum, 1997
1 (of 2) RLd x-over 3.50
2 RLd x-over,A:Domino, Kirby,
   Blaquesmith. 3.50

PROPHET OF DREAMS
Broken Tree Publications, 2002
1 (of 6) by Lawler & Vasquez 3.50
2 thru 6 . . . . @3.00

PROTECTORS
Malibu, 1992–94
1 I:Protectors, inc. JBi poster
   (direct) 3.00
1a thru 12a Newsstand . . . . @2.00
2 thru 20 . . . . @2.50
Protectors Handbook 2.50

PROTOTYPE
Malibu Ultraverse, 1993–95
1 V:Ultra-Tech,w/card 2.50
1a Ultra-lim. silver foil(c) 5.00
1b Hologram 6.00

Prototype #9
© *Malibu*

2 thru 18 . . . . @2.50
G-Size, Hostile Takeover 2.50
Spec.#0 LeS,JQ/JP(c) 2.50

PROTOTYPE: TURF WAR
Malibu Ultraverse,
1 LeS,V:Techuza. 2.50
2 LeS,F:Ranger,Arena 2.50
3 . . . . 2.50

PROWLER
Eclipse, 1987
1 I:Prowler. 2.50
2 GN,A:Original Prowler 2.50
3 GN 2.50
4 GN 2.50
5 GN, adaption of Vampire Bat. . . . 2.50
6 w/flexi-disk record 2.50

PROWLER IN
`WHITE ZOMBIE', THE
Eclipse, 1988
1 . . . . 2.50

PRUDENCE &
CAUTION
Defiant, 1994
1 CCI(s). 4.00
2 CCI(s). 2.50
3 CCI(s). 2.50
4 thru 5 CCI(s). . . . . @2.50
1a Spanish Version 3.25
2a thru 5a Spanish Version . . . . . @2.50

PSI-LORDS: REIGN OF
THE STARWATCHERS
Valiant, 1994
1 MLe,DG,Chromium(c),Valiant
   Vision,V:Spider Aliens 3.00
2 MLe,DG,V:Spider Aliens 2.50
3 MLe,DG,Chaos Effect-Epsilon#2,
   A:Solar. 2.50
becomes:

PSI-LORDS
4 V:Ravenrok 2.50
5 V:Ravenrok 2.50
6 . . . . 2.50
7 Micro-Invasion 2.50
8 A:Solar the Destroyer 2.50
9 Frozen Harbingers 2.50
10 F:Ravenrok 2.50

PSYCHO
Innovation
1 Hitchcock movie adapt 2.50
2 & 3 continued . . . . @2.50

PSYCHOANALYSIS
Gemstone, 1999
1 (of 4) 2.50
2 thru 3 . . . . @2.50

PSYCHOBLAST
First, 1987
1 thru 9 . . . . @2.50

PUBLIC ENEMY
American Mule Ent., 2006
0 . . . . 3.00
1 . . . . 4.00
2 thru 5 . . . . @3.00

PUDGY PIG
Charlton Comics, 1958
1 . . . . 100.00
2 . . . . 75.00

PUNCTURE
Com.X, 2001
1 (of 12) by R. Uttley & B.Oliver. . . 3.00
2 thru 4 . . . . @3.00
3 thru 6 . . . . @4.00

PUNX
Windjammer, 1995
1 KG,I:Punx 2.50
2 KG,A:Harbinger. 2.50
3 KG,F:P.M.S 2.50
4 KG,final issue 2.50
Spec.#1 . . . . 2.50

PUNX
Acclaim, 1997
One Shot Spec. F:Big Max 2.50

PUPPET MASTER
Eternity
1 Movie Adapt.Andre Toulon. 2.50
2 Puppets Protecting Diary. 2.50
3 R:Andre Toulon 2.50
4 . . . . 2.50

PUPPET MASTER:
CHILDREN OF THE
PUPPET MASTER
Eternity
1 Killer Puppets on the loose 2.50
2 concl. 2.50

PURGATORI
Chaos! Comics, 1998
1 DQ from slave to Goddess? 3.00
2 Goddess War,pt.1, x-over 3.00
3 Goddess War, epilog 3.00
4 Unholy Nights 3.00
5 V:Karmilla. 3.00
6 . . . . 3.00
7 V:Dracula 3.00
1-shot prelude 3.00
1-shot signed, limited + print 15.00
Coll. Vol. 1 thru Vol. 4 . . . . @6.00

PURGATORI
Chaos! Comics, 2000
1/2 . . . . 3.00
1/2 premium edition, tattoo(c). 9.00
1/2 chromium (c). 12.00
1/2 chromium signed 15.00

1/2 Ashcan 7.00
0 . . . . 3.00
0 premium edition 9.00
0 Ashcan 7.00

PURGATORI
Devil's Due Publishing, 2005
1 . . . . 3.00
2 . . . . 3.00
3 thru 6 . . . . @3.00

PURGATORI:
DARKEST HOUR
Chaos! Comics, 2001
1 . . . . 3.00
1a premium ed. RCl(c) 9.00
2 . . . . 3.00
2a variant (c). 7.50

PURGATORI:
THE DRACULA GAMBIT
Chaos! Comics, 1997
1 DQ & Brian LeBlanc 3.00
1a signed 15.00
1b premium 9.00
Sketchbook, b&w 3.50

PURGATORI: EMPIRE
Chaos! Comics, 2000
1 (of 3) 3.00
1a premium 9.00
1b Comic Legal Defense
Fund ed. 9.00
2 thru 3 . . . . @3.00
Preview Book B&W 5.00

PURGATORI:
GODDESS RISING
Chaos! Comics, 1999
1 (of 4) MD2 . . . . 3.00
1a premium edition 9.00
2 . . . . 3.00
3 . . . . 3.00
4 . . . . 3.00
Preview Book B&W 5.00

PURGATORI:
GOD HUNTER
Chaos! Comics, 2002
Ashcan b&w 6.00
1 (of 2) 3.00
1a premium edition 9.00
2 . . . . 3.00
2a variant Rio & Broeker (c) 7.50

PURGATORI: GOD KILLER
Chaos! Comics, 2002
1 (of 2) 3.00
1a premium edition 9.00
2 . . . . 3.00
2a variant (c). 7.50

PURGATORI:
HEARTBREAKER
Chaos! Comics, 2002
1 . . . . 3.00
1a premium edition 9.00
1b super premium edition 20.00
1c MegaCon foil edition 25.00

PURGATORI: LOVE BITES
Chaos! Comics, 2001
1 . . . . 3.00
1 premium edition 9.00
Ashcan 6.00

PURGATORI:
MISCHIEF NIGHT
Chaos! Comics, 2001
1 . . . . 3.00
1a premium edition 12.00
1b super premium edition 15.00

PURGATORI:
THE HUNTED
Chaos! Comics, 2001
1 . . . . 3.00
1a premium edition 9.00
2 . . . . 3.00
2a variant (c). 7.50
Ashcan 6.00

PURGATORI: RAVENOUS
Chaos! Comics, 2002
Ashcan b&w 6.00
1 (of 2) 3.00
1a premium edition 9.00

PURGATORI:
RE-IMAGINED
Chaos! Comics, 2002
1 Salem witch trials. 3.00
1a premium edition 9.00
1b super premium edition 15.00
Ashcan Purgatori re-imagined 6.00

PURGATORI: SANCTIFIED
Chaos! Comics, 2002
1 BnP 3.00
1 premium edition 9.00

PURGATORI:
TRICK OR TREAT
Chaos! Comics, 2002
1 . . . . 3.00
1a premium edition 9.00
1b super premium edition 20.00

PURGATORI:
THE VAMPIRES MYTH
Chaos! Comics, 1996
1 (of 3) 4.00
1-shot limited chromium edition . . 15.00
2 BnP,JBa 3.00
3 BnP,JBa, final issue 3.00

Quantum & Woody #2
© *Acclaim*

PURGATORI VS.
CHASTITY
Chaos! Comics, 2000
1 Alpha ending 3.00
1a Omega ending 3.00
1b deluxe 10.00

PURGATORI VS.
LADY DEATH
Chaos! Comics, 2000
1 . . . . 3.00
1a premium edition 9.00
Ashcan B&W 7.00

PURGATORI VS.
VAMPIRELLA
Chaos! Comics, 2000
1 . . . . 3.00
1 premium. 9.00

QUANTUM & WOODY
Acclaim, 1997
1 CPr(s),MBr Woodrow Van
Chelton & Eric Henderson
become unlikely superheros . . . 4.00
1a Variant (c) 5.00
2 CPr(s),MBr,World's worst
superhero team 3.00
3 CPr(s),MBr,Woody buys a goat . . 3.00
4 CPr(s),MBr. 3.00
5 thru 10 CPr(s) . . . . @2.75
11 thru 17 CPr(s) . . . . @2.50
18 thru 27. . . . . @2.50

QUANTUM LEAP
Innovation, 1991
{based on TV series}
1 1968 Memphis 3.50
1a Special Edition 2.50
2 Ohio 1962,Freedom of
the Press 3.00
3 1958, The $50,000 Quest 3.00
4 Small Miracles 2.50
5 . . . . 2.50
6 . . . . 2.50
7 Golf Pro,School Bus Driver 2.50
8 1958,Bank Robber. 2.50
9 NY 1969,Gay Rights 2.50
10 1960s' Stand-up Comic. 2.50
11 1959,Dr.(LSD experiments). . . . 2.50
12 . . . . 2.50

QUANTUM LEAP
Acclaim, 1997
1 BML(s),Into the Void, pt.1 . . . . . . 2.50
2 BML(s),Into the Void, pt.2 . . . . . . 2.50
3 BML(s),Into the Void, pt.3 . . . . . . 2.50
Spec. The Leaper Before. 4.00

QUEEN OF THE
DAMNED
Innovation, 1991
1 Anne Rice Adapt.On the Road
to the Vampire Lestat 3.50
2 Adapt. continued 2.50
3 The Devils Minion 2.50
4 Adapt.continued 2.50
5 Adapt.continued 2.50
6 Adapt.continued 2.50
7 Adapt.continued 2.50
8 Adapt.continued 2.50

QUICK-DRAW MCGRAW
Dell, 1960
2 . . . . 125.00
3 . . . . 125.00

---

4 Snaggle Pus	150.00
5	125.00
6	125.00
7 thru 11	@100.00

Gold Key, 1962

12	140.00
13	140.00
14	75.00
15	75.00

QUICK-DRAW McGRAW
Charlton Comics, 1970–72

1 TV Animated Cartoon	100.00
2	75.00
3	75.00
4 thru 8	@75.00

Q-UNIT
Harris

1 I:Q-Unit,w/card	3.25

RACE AGAINST TIME
Dark Ange., 1997

1	2.50
2	2.50

RACE FOR THE MOON
Harvey Publications, 1958

1 BP	250.00
2 JK,AW,JK/AW(c)	400.00
3 JK,AW,JK/AW(c)	500.00

RACER-X
Premiere

Spec.#1	5.00

Now, 1988

1 thru 3	@2.50
4 thru 11	@2.50

[2nd Series], 1989

1 thru 10	@2.50

RACER X
WildStorm/DC, 2000

1 (of 3) Rex Racer's secrets	2.50
1a variant (c) (1:4)	2.50
2 racing thrills	2.50
3 conclusion	3.00

RACK & PAIN: KILLERS
Chaos! Comics, 1996

1 (of 4) JaL(c)	3.00
2 BnP,LJi,JaL(c)	3.00

Racer X #3
© WildStorm

3 (of 4) BnP,LJi,	3.00
4 BnP,LJi, final issue	3.00

RADICAL DREAMER
Blackball, 1994

0	2.50
1 thru 5 V:Jorge Futran	@2.50

RADIOACTIVE MAN
Bongo, 1993

1 I:Radioactive Man	4.00
1 80pg offered again	3.25
88 V:Lava Man	2.50
212 V:Hypno Head	2.50
412 V:Dr. Crab, with trading card	2.50
679 with trading card	2.50
1000 Final issue	2.50

RADIOACTIVE MAN
Bongo Comics, 2000

100	2.50
136	2.50
222	2.50
4	2.50
575 new Radioactive Man born	2.50
106 new Radioactive Man insane	2.50
7	2.50
8 Official Movie Adaptation	3.00
199	3.00
Spec. Movie Adaptation	3.00

RAGGEDY ANN AND ANDY
Dell, 1964

1	75.00
2 thru 4	@50.00

RAGGEDY ANN AND ANDY
Gold Key, 1971

1	50.00
2 thru 6	@35.00

RAI
Valiant, 1991

0 DL,O:Bloodshot,I:2nd Rai,D:X-O, Archer,Shadowman,F:all Valiant heroes,bridges Valiant Universe 1992-4001	7.00
1 V:Grandmother	9.00
2 V:Icespike	10.00
3 V:Humanists,Makiko	30.00
4 V:Makiko,rarest Valiant	15.00
5 Rai leaves earth, C:Eternal Warrior	10.00
6 FM(c),Unity#7,V:Pierce	6.00
7 WS(c),Unity#15,V:Pierce, D:Rai,A:Magnus	6.00
8 Epilogue of Unity in 4001	6.00

Becomes:

RAI AND THE FUTURE FORCE
Valiant, 1993

9 F:Rai,E.Warrior of 4001,Tekla, X-O Commander,Spylocke	4.00
9a Gold Ed.	15.00
10 thru 26	@3.00

Becomes:

RAI
Valiant, 1994

27 thru 33	@3.00

RAISE THE DEAD
D.E. (Dynamite Ent.) 2007

1	3.50
1a variant (c)	3.50

2 thru 4	@3.50
2a thru 4a variant (c)	@3.50

RAKAN
Studio G, 2003

1	3.00
2 Den of Thieves	3.00
3	3.00
4	3.00

RAKAN
AK Entertainment, 2006

1 Sabretooth	3.00
2 Chessmaster	3.00
3 The Sword of Majido	3.00
4 The Devil's Axe	3.00
5 Den of Thieves, pt.1	3.00
6 Den of Thieves, pt. 2	3.00
7 thru 9	@3.00

RALPH SNART ADVENTURES
Now
[Volumes 1 & 2]
see B&W

9 and 10, color	2.50

[Volume 3], 1988

1	4.00
2 thru 10	@3.00
11 thru 21	@2.50
22 thru 26	@2.50

[Volume 4], 1992

1 thru 3, with 1 of 2 trading cards	2.50

[Volume 5], 1993

1 thru 5, with 1 of 2 trading cards	2.50
3-D Spec.#1 with 3-D glasses and 12 trading cards	3.50

RAMAYAN REBORN
Virgin Comics, 2006

1	3.00
2 thru 3	@3.00

RANDOM ENCOUNTER
Viper Comics

1 (of 4)	3.00
2 thru 4	@3.00

RANDOM 5
Amara Inc., 1995

1 I:Random 5	2.50

RANGO
Dell Publishing Co., 1967

1 Tim Conway Ph(c)	60.00

RANMA 1/2
Viz, 1992

1 I:Ranma	50.00
2 I:Upperclassmen Kuno	30.00
3 F:Upperclassmen Kuno	25.00
4 Confusion	5.00
5 A:Ryoga	5.00
6 Ryoga plots revenge	9.00
7 Conclusion	5.00

[Part 2], 1992

1	8.00
2	5.00
3 thru 7	@4.00
8	5.00
9	4.00
10 and 11	@3.00

continued, see B&W Pub.

RAPHAEL
Mirage, 1987

1 TMNTurtle characters	8.00

RARE BREED
Dark Moon Productions, 1995
1 V:Anarchy 2.50
2 V:Anarchy 2.50

RASH
Narwain Publishing, 2005
1 . . . . 4.00
2 . . . . 4.00

RAT BASTARD
Crucial Comics, 1997
1 by The Huja Brothers. 2.50
2 thru 6 . . . . @2.50

RAT PATROL, THE
Dell Publishing Co., 1967
1 Ph(c) 125.00
2 . . . . 100.00
3 thru 6 Ph(c) . . . . @75.00

RAVEN
Renaissance Comics, 1993
1 I:Raven 2.50
2 V:Macallister 2.50
3 . . . . 2.50
4 . . . . 2.50
5 . . . . 2.50
6 V:Nightmare Creatures 2.75

RAVEN HOUSE
Crossgen Comics, 2004
1 . . . . 3.00
2 . . . . 3.00

RAVENING
Avatar, 1998
1/2 Busch (c) F:Ravyn & Glyph . . . 3.00
1/2a Meadows(c) 3.00
1/2d Sketched Edition. 35.00
1/2e Blood Red Foil, signed 9.00

RAVENS AND RAINBOWS
Pacific, 1983
1 . . . . 2.50

RAVER
Malibu, 1993
1 Prism cover 3.00
1a Newsstand 2.50

Ravens & Rainbows #1
© Pacific

---

2 . . . . 2.50
3 Walter Koenig(s) 2.50
4 . . . . 2.00
5 . . . . 2.00

RAWHIDE
Dell, 1962
1 . . . . 250.00

RAWHIDE
Gold Key, 1963
1 From TV series 250.00
2 . . . . 225.00

RAY BRADBURY CHRONICLES
Byron Press
1 short stories 10.00
2 short stories 10.00
3 short stories 10.00

RAY BRADBURY COMICS
Topps, 1993–94
1 thru 5 with Trading Card . . . . @3.25
Spec.#1 The Illustrated Man 3.00
Spec. Trilogy of Terror 2.50
Spec. The Martian Chronicles . . . 3.00

RAYMOND E. FEIST'S MAGICIAN: APPRENTICE
Dabel Brothers Prod., 2006
1 (of 6) 3.00
1a variant Don Maitz (c) 6.00
2 thru 6 . . . . @3.00
2a thru 6a variant (c)s . . . . @6.00

RAZOR
London Night Studios, 1992
0 . . . . 9.00
0a 2nd printing (Fathom 1992) 4.00
0b reprint (1995) 3.00
1 I:Stryke (Fathom 1992) 8.00
1a second printing 3.00
2 J.O'Barr (c) 9.00
2a limited ed., red & blue 15.00
2b platinum ed. 16.00
3 Jim Balent (c). 7.00
3a with poster 12.00
4 . . . . 4.00
4a with poster 9.00
5 . . . . 7.00
5a platinum ed. 12.00
6 . . . . 5.00
7 . . . . 4.00
8 thru 10 . . . . @3.00
11 & 12 B&W, Rituals,pt.1&2 . . . . @3.00
1/2 (1995). 5.00
Ann.#1 I:Shi (1993) 25.00
Ann.#2 O:Razor B&W (1994) 35.00
Becomes:

RAZOR UNCUT
See: B&W Section

RAZOR
Volume 2
London Knight, 1996
1 DQ, ... 3.00
1a holochrome edition 5.00
2 DQ 3.00
2a holochrome edition 4.00
3 thru 7 . . . . @3.00
Razor Analog Burn. 2.50

RAZOR AND SHI SPECIAL
London Night Studios, 1994
1 Rep. Razor Ann.#1 + new art . . . 5.00
1a platinum version. 9.00

RAZOR ARCHIVES
London Night, 1997
1 & 2 see B&W
3 rep. Razor #10–12. . . . . 7.00

RAZOR BURN
London Night Studios, 1994
1 V:Styke. 3.00
1a signed 5.00
2 Searching for Styke 3.00
2a Platinum. 7.00
3 Stryke's War. 3.00
4 D:Razor, bagged 3.00
5 Epilogue. 3.00

RAZOR: CRY NO MORE
London Night Studios, 1995
1-shot 3.00
1a variant 4.00
1b Commemorative (1999). 6.00

RAZOR: HEX & VIOLENCE
EH! Productions, 2000
0 EHr. 3.00

RAZOR/MORBID ANGEL: SOUL SEARCH
London Night, 1996
1 (of 3) 3.00
1 platinum edition 5.00
1 Chromium edition. 7.00
2 . . . . 3.00
3 . . . . 3.00

RAZOR/POISON/ AREALA WARRIOR NUN: LITTLE BAD ANGELS
London Night, 1999
Spec. x-over Raxor cover 4.00
Spec.A Poison cover 4.00
Spec.B Areala cover 4.00

RAZOR THE RAVENING
Avatar
1 . . . . 3.50
1a Previews cover 3.50
1b Bondage cover. 6.00

RAZOR'S EDGE, THE: REDBIRD
Wildstorm/DC, March, 2005
1 (of 5) JPn. 3.00
2 JPn. 3.00
3 JPn. 3.00

RAZOR'S EDGE, THE: WARBLADE
Wildstorm/DC, 2004
1 SBs 3.00
2 SBs 3.00
3 SBs 3.00
4 SBs 3.00
5 SBs 3.00

RAZOR: THE SUFFERING
London Night Studios, 1994
1 . . . . 4.00
1a Director's cut 3.00
1b signed, limited 9.00
2 . . . . 3.00
2a Director's cut 2.50
3 final chapter. 3.00

COLOR PUB.

All comics prices listed are for *Near Mint* condition.

RAZOR: TORTURE
London Night Studios, 1995
0 Razor back from dead 4.00
0a signed edition. 7.00
1 . . . . 3.00
1a Commemorative (1999). 6.00
2 . . . . 3.00
3 EHr. 3.00
4 . . . . 3.00
5& 6 alt. cover, signed . . . . @4.00
7 . . . . 3.00

RAZOR SWIMSUIT SPECIAL
London Night Studios, 1995
1 pin-ups 3.00
1a platinum version. 7.00
1b commemorative edition 4.00

RAZOR/WARRIOR NUN AREALA: DARK MENACE
London Night, 1999
Spec. x-over 4.00
Spec.A x-over, variant cover 4.00

RAZOR/WARRIOR NUN AREALA: FAITH
London Night, 1996
1 by Jude Millien 3.00
1a variant cover 4.00

REAL GHOSTBUSTERS
Now, 1988
1 KSy(c) 4.50
2 thru 7 . . . . @2.50
8 thru 24 . . . . @2.00
[2nd Series], 1991
1 Halloween Special 2.50
Ann. 3-D w/glasses & pinups. 3.00

[Super Information Hijinks:] REALITY CHECK!
Sirius, 1996
1 by Tavisha Wolfgarth 3.00
2 Surfing the Internet 3.00
3 E is for Europa. 3.00
4 thru 8 . . . . @3.00
9 Nonesuch Nonsense, pt.1 . . . . . 3.00
10 Nonesuch Nonsense, pt.2 . . . . 3.00
11 Nonesuch Nonsense, pt.3 . . . . 3.00
12 Nonesuch Nonsense, pt.4 . . . . 3.00

REAL WAR STORIES
Eclipse, 1987–91
1 BB 3.00
1a 2nd printing 2.50
2 . . . . 5.00

RE-ANIMATOR
Adventure Comics, 1991
1 movie adaption 3.00
2 movie adaption 3.00

RE-ANIMATOR
Adventure
1 Prequel to Orig movie 2.50

RE-ANIMATOR: DAWN OF THE RE-ANIMATOR
Adventure, 1992
1 Prequel to movie 2.50
2 . . . . 2.50
3 . . . . 2.50
4 V:Erich Metler 2.50

RE-ANIMATOR: TALES OF HERBERT WEST
Adventure Comics
1 H.P.Lovecraft stories 5.00

RED
DC Wildstorm July, 2003
America's Best Comics
1 (of 3) WEI,CHm 3.00
2 WEI,CHm. 3.00
3 WEI,CHm. 3.00

RED DOG
Eclipse, 1988
1 CR,Mowgli Jungle Book story . . . 2.50

RED DRAGON
Comico, 1995
1 SBs,I:Red Dragon 2.50
2 How Soon is Nau? 3.00

REDEEMER, THE
Black Library, 2002
1 . . . . 3.50
2 thru 4 . . . . @3.50

REDEEMERS
Antarctic Press, 1997
1 (of 5) by Herb Mallette
  & Patrick Blain 3.00
2 . . . . 3.00

RED MENACE
Wildstorm/DC, Nov., 2006
1 (of 6) JOy,AV 3.00
1a variant (c). 3.00
2 JOy,AV. 3.00
2a variant MK (c) 3.00
3 JOy,AV. 3.00
4 JOy, AV, Under house arrest . . . 3.00
5 JOy,AV,Imprisoned on Alcatraz . 3.00
6 JOy,AV,finale 3.00

RED PROPHET: TALES OF ALVIN MAKER
Dabel Brothers Prod., 2006
1 (of 6) 3.00
1a variant (c) 6.00
2 thru 3 . . . . @3.00
2a thru 3a variant (c)s . . . . @6.00

Red Prophet: Tales of Alvin Maker #1
© Dabel Brothers

RED SONJA in 3-D
Blackthorne
1 thru 3 . . . . @2.50

RED SONJA
Cross Plains Comics, 1999
1 Death in Scarlet,pt.1 . . . . 3.00
1a photo (c). 3.00
2 Death in Scarlet,pt.2 . . . . 3.00
3 Death in Scarlet,pt.3 . . . . 3.00

RED SONJA
D.E. (Dynamite Entertain.), 2005
0 . . . . 2.00
1 . . . . 3.00
1a thru 1e variant (c)s. . . . . @3.00
2 thru 7 . . . . @3.00
8 Arrowsmith 3.00
9 Arrowsmith 3.00
10 Arrowsmith 3.00
11 Arrowsmith 3.00
12 Return of Kulan
  Gath, pt. 1, JLe(c) 3.00
13 Return of Kulan Gath, pt. 2. . . . 3.00
14 Return of Kulan Gath, pt. 3. . . . 3.00
15 Return of Kulan Gath, pt. 4. . . . 3.00
16 Return of Kulan Gath, pt. 5. . . . 3.00
17 Return of Kulan Gath 3.00
18 thru 29 . . . . @3.00
2a thru 17a variant (c)s . . . . @3.00
18 thru 29a variant (c)s . . . . @3.00
Ann. #1 (2006). 3.50
Giant Size #1 . . . . 5.00
Giant Size #1a variant (c) 5.00
1-shot Red Sonja Goes East 5.00
1-shot Red Sonja Goes East
  power foil (c) 15.00
1-shot One More Day 5.00
1-shot Monster Isle 5.00
1-shot Monster Isle variant (c) 5.00
1-shot Red Sonja/Claw 5.00
Spec. Vacant Shell 5.00
Spec. Vacant Shell variant (c) 5.00

RED SONJA/CLAW THE UNCONQUERED: DEVIL'S HANDS
Wildstorm/DC, March, 2006
1 (of 4) ASm 3.00
1a variant JLe (c) 3.00
2 ASm. 3.00
2a variant JLe (c) 3.00
3 ASm, Imprisoned 3.00
3a variant JLe (c) 3.00
4 ASm,Claw embraces evil. 3.00
4a variant JLe(c). 3.00

RED SONJA VS. THULSA DOOM
D.E. (Dynamite Ent.) 2001
1 (of 4) 3.50
2 . . . . 3.50
3 . . . . 3.50
4 . . . . 3.50
1a thru 3a variant (c) . . . . @3.50
1b thru 2b Fiery red Foil editions . 20.00

RED STAR, THE
Archangel Studios, 2002
Vol. 2
2 . . . . 3.00
3 . . . . 3.00
4 . . . . 3.00
5 . . . . 3.00
6 . . . . 3.00
Annual #1 foil (c) signed 10.00
Spec. Red Star: Sword of Lies. . . . 4.50

REESE'S PIECES
Eclipse, 1985
1 reprint from Web of Horror 2.50
2 reprint from Web of Horror 2.50

RE: GEX
Awesome Entertainment, 1998
0 RLe, ... 2.50
0a Red Foil variant 4.00
1 RLe,JLb 2.50
1a Platinum cover. 7.00
1b Red Foil cover 10.00
1c Variant RL cover 4.00
1d prime 3.00
1e prime millennium ed. 5.00
2 RLe,JLb 2.50
2a prime 3.00
2b Millennium edition 5.00
3 RLe,A:The Coven,V:Youngblood . 2.50
Con Spec. '98 . . . . 5.00
Orlando Megacon ashcan 9.00
Orlando Megacon ashcan, signed. 20.00

REGGIE
Archie Publications, 1963–65
15 thru 18 . . . . @75.00
Becomes:

REGGIE AND ME
Archie Publications, 1966–80
19 . . . . 60.00
20 thru 23 . . . . @50.00
24 thru 40 . . . . @35.00
41 thru 50 . . . . @25.00
51 thru 99 . . . . @20.00
100 . . . . 25.00
101 thru 126 . . . . @15.00

REGGIE'S WISE GUY JOKES
Archie Publications, April, 1968
1 . . . . 75.00
2 . . . . 40.00
3 . . . . 40.00
4 . . . . 40.00
5 thru 15 Giants . . . . @40.00
16 thru 28 Giants . . . . @35.00
29 thru 40 . . . . @25.00
41 thru 60 . . . . @20.00
11 thru 59 . . . . @15.00
60 Jan., 1982 . . . . 15.00

RELOAD
DC Homage, 2003
1 (of 3) WEI,JP 3.00
2 WEI,JP 3.00
3 WEI,JP, concl. 3.00

REMAINS
IDW Publishing, 2004
1 thru 5 . . . . @4.00

REPTILICUS
Charlton Comics, 1961
1 . . . . 400.00
2 . . . . 250.00
Becomes:

REPTISAURUS
1962
3 . . . . 150.00
4 thru 7 . . . . @125.00
8 Summer, 1963 . . . . 125.00

RESIDENT EVIL: FIRE & ICE
WildStorm/DC, 2000
1 (of 4) from videogame 2.50

---

2 . . . . 2.50
3 . . . . 2.50
4 concl. 2.50

RESISTANCE, THE
WildStorm/DC, 2002
1 JP(s),techno sci-fi 3.00
2 JP(s) 3.00
3 JP(s) 3.00
4 JP(s) 3.00
5 JP(s),V:Sampizi 3.00
6 JP(s),V:Sampizi & GCC 3.00
7 JP(s),F:Version Mary 3.00
8 JP(s),F:Version Mary 3.00

RETURN OF GORGO, THE
Charlton, 1963
2 thru 3 . . . . 125.00

RETURN OF KONGA, THE
Charlton Comics, 1962
N# 125.00

RETURN OF MEGATON MAN
Kitchen Sink, 1988
1 Don Simpson art (1988) 2.50
2 Don Simpson art 2.50
3 Don Simpson art 2.50

Return to Jurassic Park #3
© *Topps*

RETURN TO JURASSIC PARK
Topps, 1995
1 R:Jurassic Park 3.00
2 V:Blosyn Team, Army 3.00
3 The Hunted 3.00
4 Army 3.00
5 Heirs to the Thunder,pt.1 . . . . . . 3.00
6 Heirs to the Thunder,pt.2 . . . . . . 3.00
7 Inquiring Minds,pt.1 . . . . 3.00
8 Photo Finish, concl. 3.00
9 Jurassic Jam issue 3.00

REVENGE OF THE PROWLER
Eclipse, 1988
1 GN,R:Prowler. 2.50
2 GN,A:Fighting Devil Dogs with
    Flexi-Disk. 2.50
3 GN,A:Devil Dogs 2.50
4 GN,V:Pirahna. 2.50

REVENGERS
Continuity, 1985
1 NA,O:Megalith,I:Crazyman 4.00
2 NA,Megalith meets Armor & Silver
Streak,Origin Revengers#1 . . . . . . 2.50
3 NA/NR,Origin Revengers #2 . . . . 2.50
4 NA,Origin Revengers #3 . . . . 2.50
5 NA,Origin Revengers #4 . . . . 2.50
6 I:Hybrids. 3.00
Spec. #1 F:Hybrids 5.00

REVERE
Alias Enterprises, 2006
1 (of 4) 3.50
2 . . . . 3.50
3 . . . . 3.50
4 . . . . 3.50

REVOLUTION ON THE PLANET OF THE APES
MR Comics, 2005
1 (of 6) 4.00
2 thru 6 . . . . @4.00

RIBIT
Comico
thru 4 FT,Mini-series . . . . @3.00

RICHIE RICH
Harvey Publications, 1960–91
1 Inc.Casper,Little Dot 5,000.00
2 Inc. Little Dot, Little Lotta . . . 1,500.00
3 Inc. Little Dot, Little Lotta. 750.00
4 Inc. Little Dot, Little Lotta. 750.00
5 . . . . 750.00
6 . . . . 600.00
7 . . . . 600.00
8 Christmas(c) 600.00
9 . . . . 600.00
10 . . . . 600.00
11 thru 20 . . . . @500.00
21 thru 41 . . . . @500.00
42 Flying Saucer 500.00
43 thru 55 . . . . @250.00
56 Super Richie 150.00
57 . . . . 100.00
58 . . . . 100.00
59 Buck 125.00
60 thru 80 . . . . @100.00
81 thru 99 . . . . @50.00
100 Irona-Robot Maid 60.00
101 thru 111 . . . . @40.00
112 thru 116 52 pg Giants . . . . @50.00
117 thru 120 . . . . @40.00
121 thru 136 . . . . @30.00
137 Mr. Cheepers 30.00
138 thru 160 . . . . @20.00
161 thru 180 . . . . @15.00
181 thru 236 . . . . @12.00
237 Money Monster. 12.00
238 thru 254 . . . . @7.00

RICHIE RICH
Harvey, 1991
1 thru 15 . . . . @3.00
16 thru 28 . . . . @3.00

RICHIE RICH AND CADBURY
Harvey, 1977
1 . . . . 25.00
2 thru 10 . . . . @15.00
11 thru 29 . . . . @10.00

RICHIE RICH & CASPER
Harvey, 1974
1 . . . . 50.00
2 thru 5 . . . . @30.00

---

6 thru 10 . . . . @20.00
11 thru 25 . . . . @15.00
26 thru 45 . . . . @10.00

RICHIE RICH AND DOLLAR THE DOG
Harvey, 1977

1 . . . . 25.00
2 thru 10 . . . . @15.00
11 thru 24 . . . . @10.00

RICHIE RICH AND GLORIA
Harvey, 1977

1 . . . . 25.00
2 thru 10 . . . . @15.00
11 thru 25 . . . . @10.00

RICHIE RICH AND HIS GIRLFRIENDS
Harvey, 1979

1 . . . . 20.00
2 thru 10 . . . . @15.00
11 thru 16 . . . . @10.00

RICHIE RICH AND HIS MEAN COUSIN REGGIE
Harvey, 1979

1 . . . . 20.00
2 thru 3 . . . . @15.00

RICHIE RICH BANK BOOKS
Harvey, 1972–82

1 . . . . 75.00
2 Money Monster 55.00
3 thru 5 . . . . @50.00
6 thru 10 . . . . @35.00
11 thru 20 . . . . @25.00
21 thru 30 . . . . @15.00
31 thru 40 . . . . @10.00
41 thru 59 . . . . @8.00

RICHIE RICH BILLIONS
Harvey, 1974–82

1 . . . . 50.00
2 thru 5 . . . . @30.00
6 thru 10 . . . . @25.00
11 thru 20 . . . . @15.00
21 thru 30 . . . . @10.00
31 thru 48 . . . . @8.00

RICHIE RICH CASH
Harvey, 1974

1 . . . . 50.00
2 thru 10 . . . . @25.00
11 thru 20 . . . . @15.00
21 thru 47 . . . . @10.00

RICHIE RICH DIAMONDS
Harvey, 1972–82

1 . . . . 75.00
2 thru 5 . . . . @35.00
6 thru 10 . . . . @30.00
11 thru 20 . . . . @25.00
21 thru 30 . . . . @12.00
31 thru 59 . . . . @10.00

RICHIE RICH DOLLARS & CENTS
Harvey Publications, 1963–82

1 . . . . 400.00

2 . . . . 200.00
3 thru 5 . . . . @150.00
6 thru 10 . . . . @100.00
11 thru 24 . . . . @70.00
25 Nurse Jenny 75.00
26 thru 30 . . . . @60.00
31 thru 43 . . . . @50.00
44 thru 60 . . . . @40.00
61 thru 70 . . . . @30.00
71 thru 99 . . . . @20.00
100 Anniversary 25.00
102 thru 109 . . . . @20.00

Richie Rich Fortunes #10
© Harvey

RICHIE RICH FORTUNES
Harvey, 1971–82

1 . . . . 75.00
2 thru 5 . . . . @50.00
6 thru 10 . . . . @40.00
11 Orion 25.00
12 thru 20 . . . . @20.00
21 thru 30 . . . . @10.00
31 thru 63 . . . . @8.00

RICHIE RICH GEMS
Harvey, 1974–82

1 . . . . 50.00
2 thru 5 . . . . @30.00
6 thru 10 . . . . @25.00
11 thru 20 . . . . @20.00
21 thru 30 . . . . @10.00
31 thru 35 . . . . @8.00
36 Orion 10.00
37 . . . . 8.00
38 Stone-Age Riches 10.00
39 thru 43 . . . . @8.00

RICHIE RICH GOLD AND SILVER
Harvey, 1975–82

1 . . . . 50.00
2 . . . . 30.00
3 . . . . 30.00
4 . . . . 30.00
5 . . . . 30.00
6 thru 10 . . . . @25.00
11 thru 20 . . . . @20.00
21 thru 30 . . . . @10.00
31 thru 33 . . . . @8.00
34 Stone-Age Riches 10.00
35 thru 42 . . . . @8.00

RICHIE RICH INVENTIONS
Harvey, 1977

1 . . . . 25.00
2 thru 10 . . . . @15.00
11 thru 26 . . . . @12.00

RICHIE RICH JACKPOTS
Harvey, 1974–82

1 . . . . 75.00
2 thru 5 . . . . @50.00
6 thru 15 . . . . @30.00
16 Super Richie 32.00
17 thru 20 . . . . @25.00
21 thru 30 . . . . @12.00
31 thru 58 . . . . @10.00

RICHIE RICH MILLIONS
Harvey Publications, 1961–82

1 . . . . 400.00
2 . . . . 250.00
3 thru 10 . . . . @150.00
11 thru 20 . . . . @100.00
21 thru 30 . . . . @75.00
31 Orion, giant 50.00
32 thru 60 . . . . @45.00
61 thru 67 . . . . @35.00
68 Super Richie 35.00
69 thru 74 . . . . @25.00
75 thru 94 . . . . @20.00
95 thru 113 . . . . @15.00

RICHIE RICH MONEY WORLD
Harvey, 1972–82

1 Mayda Monny 85.00
2 Super Richie 60.00
3 thru 5 . . . . @50.00
6 thru 10 . . . . @35.00
11 thru 20 . . . . @18.00
21 thru 30 . . . . @10.00
31 thru 59 . . . . @8.00

RICHIE RICH PROFITS
Harvey, 1974–82

1 . . . . 60.00
2 thru 5 . . . . @30.00
6 thru 10 . . . . @25.00
11 thru 20 . . . . @20.00
21 thru 30 . . . . @10.00
31 thru 47 . . . . @8.00

RICHIE RICH RICHES
Harvey, 1972–82

1 Money Monster 90.00
2 thru 5 . . . . @50.00
6 thru 10 . . . . @30.00
11 thru 16 . . . . @20.00
17 Super Richie 22.00
18 thru 30 . . . . @15.00
31 thru 59 . . . . @10.00

RICHIE RICH SUCCESS STORIES
Harvey Publications, 1964–82

1 . . . . 500.00
2 thru 5 . . . . @250.00
6 thru 10 . . . . @125.00
11 thru 26 . . . . @100.00
27 Penny Van Dough 75.00
28 thru 43 . . . . @65.00
44 Super Richie 35.00
45 thru 55 . . . . @35.00

56 thru 66 . . . . @30.00
67 thru 105 . . . . @20.00

RICHIE RICH
VAULT OF MYSTERY
Harvey, 1974–82
1 . . . . 50.00
2 thru 5 . . . . @30.00
6 thru 10 . . . . @15.00
11 thru 20 . . . . @10.00
21 thru 30 . . . . @10.00
31 thru 47 . . . . @10.00

RICHIE RICH
ZILLIONZ
Harvey, 1976–82
1 . . . . 35.00
2 thru 5 . . . . @20.00
6 thru 10 . . . . @15.00
11 thru 20 . . . . @10.00
21 thru 33 . . . . @8.00

RIFLEMAN, THE
Dell Publishing Co., 1959
1 Chuck Connors Ph(c) all 500.00
2 Ph(c) 300.00
3 ATh,Ph(c) 275.00
4 Ph(c) 250.00
5 Ph(c) 250.00
6 ATh 275.00
7 thru 10 Ph(c) . . . . @225.00
11 thru 12 . . . . @200.00
Gold Key, 1962
13 thru 20 . . . . @150.00

RIN TIN TIN AND RUSTY
Dell, 1957
21 . . . . 75.00
22 thru 38 . . . . @75.00

RIN TIN TIN AND RUSTY
Gold Key, 1963
1 . . . . 100.00

RIOT
Riot Media, 2005
1 . . . . 3.00
2 . . . . 3.00

RIOT GEAR
Triumphant, 1993
1 JnR(s),I:Riot Gear 2.50
2 JnR(s),I:Rabin 2.50
3 JnR(s),I:Surzar 2.50
4 JnR(s),D:Captain Tich 2.50
5 JnR(s),reactions 2.50
6 JnR(s),Tich avenged 2.50
7 JnR(s),Information Age 2.50
8 JnR(s), ... 2.50

RIOT GEAR:
VIOLENT PAST
Triumphant, 1994
1 . . . . 2.50
2 . . . . 2.50

R.I.P.
TSR, 1990–91
1 thru 4 . . . . @3.00
5 thru 8 Brasher, Avenger of the
Dead . . . . @3.00

RIPFIRE
Malibu, 1995
0 Prequel to Ripfire Series 2.50

RIPLEY'S BELIEVE IT
OR NOT!
Gold Key, 1965–80
1 . . . . 150.00
2 thru 3 . . . . @125.00
4 Ph(c),AMc 75.00
5 GE,JJ 60.00
6 AMc 60.00
7 . . . . 50.00
8 . . . . 60.00
9 . . . . 50.00
10 GE 60.00
11 . . . . 40.00
12 . . . . 40.00
13 . . . . 40.00
14 . . . . 40.00
15 GE 45.00
16 thru 20 . . . . @40.00
21 thru 30 . . . . @25.00
31 thru 38 . . . . @22.00
39 RC 22.00
40 thru 50 . . . . @20.00
51 thru 94 . . . . @15.00

RISE OF THE SNAKEMEN
Crossgen Comics 2003
1 . . . . 3.00
2 thru 3 . . . . @3.00

RISK
Maximum Press, 1995
1 V:Furious 2.50

ROAD TO HELL
IDW Publishing, 2006
1 . . . . 4.00
2 thru 3 . . . . @4.00

ROB
Awesome Entertainment, 1999
1 RLe 2.50

ROBERT JORDAN'S
NEW SPRING
Red Eagle Publishing, 2005
1 . . . . 4.00
2 thru 4 . . . . @4.00
5 thru 8 CDi . . . . @4.00

ROBERT E. HOWARD'S
Cross Plains Comics, 1999
GN Marchers of Valhalla 7.00
GN Wolfshead 7.00
GN Worms of the Earth 10.00

ROBIN HOOD
Dell, 1963
1 . . . . 40.00

ROBIN HOOD
Eclipse, 1991
1 TT,Historically accurate series . . . 2.75
2 and 3 TT . . . . @2.75

ROBINSON CRUSOE
Dell, 1964
1 . . . . 30.00

ROBOCOP: WAR PARTY
Avatar Press, 2005
1 . . . . 4.00
1a variant (c)s . . . . @4.00
1b Matt Martin (c) 6.00
1c ED-209 photo (c) 6.00
2 . . . . 4.00
2a wraparound (c) 4.00

3 . . . . 4.00
3a wraparound (c) 4.00
2b thru 3b variant (c) . . . . @4.00

ROBOCOP: WILD CHILD
Avatar Press, 2005
1 16-page 3.00
1a photo (c) 3.00
1b variant (c) 3.00
1c wraparound (c) 3.00
1d Heaven Above (c) 6.00
1e Detroit's Finest (c) 6.00

ROBO DOJO
WildStorm/DC, 2002
1 (of 6) MWn, 40-pg 3.50
2 MWn, ... 3.00
3 MWn, ... 3.00
4 MWn,Techno Council 3.00
5 MWn,Robojin revolt 3.00
6 MWn,traitor revealed, concl. 3.00

ROBO HUNTER
Eagle
1 . . . . 2.50
2 thru 5 . . . . @2.50

Robotech #7
© Antarctic Press

ROBOTECH
Antarctic Press, 1997
1 by Fred Perry & BDn 3.00
2 . . . . 3.00
3 . . . . 3.00
4 Rolling Thunder, pt.1 . . . . 3.00
5 Rolling Thunder, pt.2 . . . . 3.00
6 Rolling Thunder, pt.3 . . . . 3.00
7 Rolling Thunder, pt.4 . . . . 3.00
8 Variants, pt.1 . . . . 3.00
9 Variants, pt.2 . . . . 3.00
10 Variants, pt.3 . . . . 3.00
11 Variants, pt.4 . . . . 3.00
GN Megastorm by Fred Perry
& Ben Dunn 8.00
Spec.1-shot Robotech: Final Fire . . 3.00
Spec.1-shot Robotech: Class
Reunion 3.00

ROBOTECH
Wildstorm/DC, 2002
0 JLe 2.50
1 (of 6) JLe 3.00
2 thru 5 . . . . @3.00
6 SeP, concl. 3.00
Spec. Robotech Sourcebook 3.00

COLOR PUB.

ROBOTECH: GENESIS
THE LEGEND OF ZOR
Eternity
1 O:Robotech w/cards 3.00
1a Limited Edition,extra pages
   with cards #1 & #2. . . . . 6.00
2 thru 6, each with cards. . . . . . . @2.50

ROBOTECH IN 3-D
Comico, 1985
1 . . . . 2.50

ROBOTECH: INVASION
Wildstorm/DC, 2004
1 (of 5) 3.00
2 thru 5 . . . . @3.00

ROBOTECH:
LOVE AND WAR
Wildstorm/DC July, 2003
1 (of 6) Max and Miriya. 3.00
2 flight school 3.00
3 Max and Miriya meet 3.00
4 Max and Miriya fight 3.00
5 Dixon dead. 3.00
6 conclusion 3.00

Robotech The Macross Saga #7
© Comico

ROBOTECH,
THE MACROSS SAGA
Comico, 1985–89
(formerly Macross)
2 . . . . 5.00
3 . . . . 4.00
4 . . . . 3.50
5 . . . . 3.50
6 J:Rick Hunter 3.50
7 V:Zentraedi 3.00
8 A:Rick Hunter 3.00
9 V:Zentraedi 3.00
10 Blind Game. 3.00
11 V:Zentraedi 3.00
12 V:Zentraedi 3.00
13 V:Zentraedi 3.00
14 Gloval's Reports 3.00
15 V:Zentraedi 3.00
16 V:Zentraedi 3.00
17 V:Zentraedi 3.00
18 D:Roy Fokker 3.00
19 V:Khyron 3.00
20 V:Zentraedi 3.00
21 A New Dawn 3.00

22 V:Zentraedi 3.00
23 Reckless 3.00
24 HB,V:Zentraedi 3.00
25 Wedding Bells. 3.00
26 The Messenger 3.00
27 Force of Arms 3.00
28 Reconstruction Blues 3.00
29 Robotech Masters. 3.00
30 Viva Miriya 3.00
31 Khyron's Revenge 3.00
32 Broken Heart. 3.00
33 A Rainy Night 3.00
34 Private Time 3.00
35 Season's Greetings 3.00
36 last issue. 3.00
Graphic Novel #1 . . . . 6.00

ROBOTECH MASTERS
Comico, 1985–88
1 . . . . 4.00
2 . . . . 3.00
3 Space Station Liberty. 3.00
4 V:Bioroids. 2.50
5 V:Flagship 2.50
6 Prelude to Battle 2.50
7 The Trap 2.50
8 F:Dana Sterling 2.50
9 Star Dust 2.50
10 V:Zor. 2.50
11 A:De Ja Vu 2.50
12 2OR. 2.50
13 . . . . 2.50
14 Clone Chamber,V:Zor. 2.50
15 Love Song. 2.50
16 V:General Emerson 2.50
17 Mind Games 2.50
18 Dana in Wonderland 2.50
19 . . . . 2.50
20 A:Zor,Musica 2.50
21 Final Nightmare 2.50
22 The Invid Connection 2.50
23 Catastrophe, final issue 2.50

ROBOTECH:
THE NEW GENERATION
Comico, 1985–88
1 . . . . 4.00
2 The Lost City 3.00
3 V:Yellow Dancer. 3.00
4 A:Yellow Dancer. 3.00
5 SK(i),A:Yellow Dancer 3.00
6 F:Rook Bartley. 3.00
7 Paper Hero 3.00
8 . . . . 3.00
9 KSy,The Genesis Pit 3.00
10 V:The Invid 3.00
11 F:Scott Bernard 3.00
12 V:The Invid 3.00
13 V:The Invid 3.00
14 Annie's Wedding. 3.00
15 Seperate Ways 3.00
16 Metamorphosis 3.00
17 Midnight Sun. 3.00
18 . . . . 3.00
19 . . . . 3.00
20 Birthday Blues. 3.00
21 Hired Gun 3.00
22 The Big Apple 3.00
23 Robotech Wars 3.00
24 Robotech Wars 3.00
25 V:Invid, last issue 3.00

ROBOTECH:
PRELUDE TO THE
SHADOW CHRONICLES
Wildstorm/DC, Oct., 2005
1 (of 5) JWp,JWt. 3.50
2 thru 5 . . . . @3.50

ROBOTECH SPECIAL
DANA'S STORY
Eclipse
1 . . . . 5.00

ROBOTECH II:
THE SENTINELS
Eternity
Swimsuit Spec.#1 . . . . 3.00

ROBOTIKA
Archaia Studio Press, 2006
1 . . . . 4.00
2 . . . . 4.00
3 . . . . 4.00
4 . . . . 4.00

ROB ZOMBIE'S
SPOOKSHOW
INTERNATIONAL
Crossgen Comics, 2003
1 (of 5) 3.50
2 . . . . 3.00
3 . . . . 3.00
MVCreations (2004)
4 thru 10 . . . . @3.00

ROCK 'N' ROLL
Revolutionary, 1990
Prev: Black & White
15 Poison 6.00
16 Van Halen 5.00
17 Madonna 6.00
18 AliceCooper. 5.00
19 Public Enemy, 2 Live Crew. . . . 5.00
20 Queensryche. 5.00
21 Prince 5.00
22 AC/DC. 5.00
23 Living Color. 5.00
24 Anthrax 5.00
25 Z.Z.Top 5.00
26 Doors 5.00
27 Doors 5.00
28 Ozzy Osbourne. 6.00
29 The Cure 5.00
30 . . . . 5.00
31 Vanilla Ice 5.00
32 Frank Zappa 5.00
33 Guns n' Roses 5.00
34 The Black Crowes. 5.00
35 R.E.M. 5.00
36 Michael Jackson 5.00
37 Ice T 5.00
38 Rod Stewart 5.00
39 New Kids on the Block 5.00
40 N.W.A./Ice Cube 5.00
41 Paula Abdul. 5.00
42 Metallica II. 5.00
43 Guns 'N' Roses 5.00
44 Scorpions 5.00
45 Greatful Dead 5.00
46 Grateful Dead 5.00
47 Grateful Dead 5.00
48 (now b/w),Queen 5.00
49 Rush 5.00
50 Bob Dylan Pt.1 . . . . 5.00
51 Bob Dylan Pt.2 . . . . 5.00
52 Bob Dylan Pt.3 . . . . 5.00
53 Bruce Springsteen 5.00
54 U2 Pt.1 . . . . 5.00
55 U2 Pt.2 . . . . 5.00
56 David Bowie 5.00
57 thru 58 . . . . @4.00
59 Eric Clampton 5.00
60 thru 63 . . . . @4.00
64 San Francisco 4.00
65 Pink Floyd 4.00

ROCK 'N' ROLL HIGH SCHOOL
Cosmic Comics, 1995
1 Sequel to the movie.......... 2.50

ROCKETEER
Walt Disney, 1991
1 DSt(c)RH,MovieAdaptation 7.00
Newsstand Version 3.25

ROCKETEER ADVENTURE MAGAZINE
Comico, 1988
1 DSt,MK,Rocketeer(6thApp.) ... 10.00
2 DSt,MK,Rocketeer(7thApp.) 8.00

ROCKETEER SPECIAL
Eclipse, 1984
1 DSt, Rocketeer(5th App.)...... 15.00

ROCKET MAN: KING OF THE ROCKET MEN
Innovation, 1991
1 thru 4 Adapts movie series ... @2.50

ROCKETO
Speakeasy Comics, 2005
1 .... 9.00
2 thru 3 .... @8.00
4 thru 6 .... @5.00

ROCKET RANGER
Adventure Comics, 1991
1 (of 12) from computer game 3.00

ROCKY AND HIS FIENDISH FRIENDS
Gold Key, 1962
1 .... 350.00
2 .... 250.00
3 .... 250.00
4 .... 200.00
5 .... 200.00

ROCKY HORROR PICTURE SHOW
Calibre/Tome, 1990
1 .... 6.00
1a 2nd printing 3.25
2 .... 3.50
3 The Conclusion 3.25
Rocky Horror Collection reps... 5.00

ROG 2000
Pacific, 1982
1 One-Shot, JBy 2.50

ROGER RABBIT
Walt Disney, 1990
1 I:Rick Flint, The Trouble
  with Toons 5.50
2 .... 3.50
3 .... 3.00
4 .... 3.00
5 .... 3.00
6 thru 9 .... @3.00
10 Tuned-in-toons 3.00
11 Who Framed Rick Flint 3.00
12 Somebunny to Love 3.00
13 Honey,I Stink with Kids 3.00
14 Who Fired Jessica Rabbit...... 3.00
15 The Great Toon Detective...... 3.00
16 See you later Aviator 3.00
17 Flying Saucers over Toontown .. 3.00
18 I Have Seen the Future 3.00

Roger Rabbit #7
© Walt Disney

ROGER RABBIT'S TOONTOWN
Walt Disney, 1991
1 Baby Herman,Jessica stories ... 2.50
2 Pre-Hysterical Roger 2.50
3 Lumberjack of tomorrow 2.50
4 The Longest Daze 2.50

ROGUES
Dark Planet Productions, 2004
1 .... 3.00
2 thru 5 .... @3.00
6 .... 5.50

ROGUE TROOPER
Fleetway/Quality, 1986
1 thru 5 .... @2.50
6 thru 21 .... @2.50
22/23 .... 2.50
24 .... 2.50
25/26 .... 2.50
27 thru 43 .... @2.50

ROGUE TROOPER: THE FINAL WARRIOR
Fleetway
1 RS,Golden Rebellion,pt 1 ..... 3.00
2 thru 3 .... @3.00
4 Saharan Ice-Belt War 3.00

ROKKIN
Wildstorm/DC, July, 2006
1 .... 3.00
2 thru 6 .... @3.00

ROLAND: DAYS OF WRATH
Terra Major, 1999
1 (of 4) 3.00
2 thru 4 .... @3.00

ROMAN HOLIDAYS, THE
Gold Key, 1973
1 .... 75.00
2 thru 4 .... @50.00

ROOK, THE
Harris Comics, 1995
0 O:Rook.................... 3.00
1 N:Rook.................... 3.00

2 I:Coffin 3.00
3 The Spider Obsidian 3.00

ROOM 222
Dell Publishing Co., 1970
1 .... 100.00
2 .... 75.00
3 Drug..................... 75.00
4 Ph(c) 60.00

ROSE
Cartoon Books, 2000
1 (of 3) 48-pg................. 6.00
2 JSi,CV,48-pg................ 6.00
3 JSi,CV,48-pg., concl.......... 6.00

ROSWELL
Bongo Comics, 1996
1 by Bill Morrison,The Story
  of the Century 3.00
2 The Untold Story 3.00
3 The Untold Story, concl........ 3.00
4 V:Mutato................... 3.00
5 .... 3.00
6 time-traveling comic collector ... 3.00

ROUTE 666
Crossgen Comics, 2002
1 .... 3.00
2 thru 5 .... @3.00
6 thru 24 .... @3.00

ROY ROGERS AND TRIGGER
Gold Key, 1967
1 .... 275.00

ROY ROGERS WESTERN CLASSICS
AC Comics, 1989
1 .... 3.00
2 .... 3.00
3 .... 3.00
4 .... 4.00

ROY THOMAS' ANGHEM
Heroic Publishing, 2006
1 .... 3.25
2 thru 3 .... @3.25

RUFF AND READY
Dell Publishing Co., 1958
1 .... 300.00
2 .... 200.00
3 .... 200.00
4 thru 12 .... @125.00

RUGRATS COMIC ADVENTURES
New England Comics, 1999
VOL. 1
1 thru 10 .... @3.00
VOL. 2
1 thru 10 .... @3.00
VOL. 3
1 .... 3.00
2 thru 9 .... @3.00

RUN, BUDDY, RUN
Gold Key, 1967
1 .... 60.00

RUNE
Malibu Ultraverse, 1994–95
0 BWS(a&s) 4.00
1 BWS(a&s),from Ultraverse 2.50

1a Foil cover	4.00
2 CU(s),BWS,V:Aladdin	2.50
3 DaR,BWS,(Ultraverse Premiere #1), Flip book.	3.75
4 thru 9	@2.50
G-Size #1	2.50

RUNE
Malibu Ultraverse, 1995–96

Infinity V:Annihilus	2.50
1 A:Adam Warlock	2.50
1a Computer painted cover	2.50
2 thru 6	@2.50

RUNE: HEARTS OF DARKNESS
Malibu Ultraverse, 1996

1 DgM(s),KHt,TBd, flip book	2.50
2 DgM,KHt,TBd, flip book	2.50
3 DgM,KHt,TBd, flip book	2.50

RUNE/SILVER SURFER
Ultravrse 1995

1 BWS(c),A:Adam Warlock	6.00
1a Lim. edition (5,000 made)	8.00
1b Standard ed.newsprint	3.00

RUNES OF RAGNAN
Silent Devil Productions, 2005

1	3.00
2 thru 4	@3.00

RUSE
Crossgen Comics, 2001

1 MWa.	8.00
2 MWa.	3.50
3 thru 14	@3.00
15 thru 27	@3.00
Spec. Archard's Agents, Deadly Dare (2004)	3.00

RUST
Now, 1987

1	4.00
2	3.00
3	2.50
4	2.50
5 thru 11	@2.50
12 I:Terminator	9.00
13 thru 15	@2.50

[Volume 2], 1989

1 thru 10	@2.50

RUST
Malibu

1 O:Rust	3.00
2 V:Marion Labs	3.00
3 I:Ashe Sapphire,5th Anniv.	3.00
4 I:Rustmobile.	3.00

RUULE: GANGLORDS OF CHINATOWN
Beckett Entertainment, 2003

1	6.00
2 thru 3	@6.00
4 thru 5	@3.00

RUULE: KISS & TELL
Beckett Entertainment, 2004

1	3.00
2 thru 5	@3.00
6 thru 8	@2.00

SABLE
First, 1988–90

1 AIDS story	2.50
2 thru 28	@2.50

SABRE
Eclipse, 1982–85

1 PG	2.50
2 PG	3.00
3 thru 14	@2.50

SABRINA, THE TEENAGE WITCH
Archie Publications, 1971–83

1	300.00
2 Archie	150.00
3 Archie	125.00
4	100.00
5	100.00
6 thru 10	@100.00
11 thru 30	@75.00
31 thru 40	@40.00
41 thru 76	@25.00
77	30.00

Sabrina The Teenage Witch #20
© Archie Comics

SABRINA THE TEENAGE WITCH
Archie Comics, 1996

one-shot photo cover	7.00
1 photo cover	5.00
2 Trouble in Time	5.00
3 photo cover	5.00
4 photo cover	5.00
5 Driver's License	5.00
6 Treasure Troubles	5.00
7 The Sculpture Switch	5.00
8 The Cable Girl, photo (c)	5.00
9 Farewell Feline	5.00
10 No Brain, No Pain.	5.00
11 thru 17	@3.00
18 thru 33 photo (c)	@3.00

[Volume 2], 2000

1 thru 3 from animated series	@2.50
4 thru 13	@2.50
14 thru 62	@2.50
63 thru 89	@2.25
Halloween Spooktacular #1	2.50
Halloween Spooktacular #2	2.50
Holiday Spectacular #3	2.50
GN The Magic Revisited	7.50

SAD SACK AND THE SARGE
Harvey Publications, 1957–82

1	300.00
2	150.00
3	100.00

4	100.00
5	100.00
6 thru 10	@100.00
11 thru 20	@75.00
21 thru 40	@50.00
41 thru 50	@35.00
51 thru 90	@25.00
91 thru 96 52 pg Giants	@15.00
97 thru 155	@15.00

SAD SACK'S ARMY LIFE
Harvey Publications, 1963–76

1	150.00
2 thru 10	@75.00
11 thru 20	@50.00
21 thru 30	@40.00
31 thru 50	@30.00
51 thru 61	@25.00

SAD SACK'S FUNNY FRIENDS
Harvey Publications, 1955–69

1	250.00
2 thru 10	@100.00
11 thru 20	@75.00
21 thru 30	@50.00
31 thru 40	@35.00
41 thru 75	@30.00

SAD SACK LAUGH SPECIAL
Harvey Publications, 1958

1	160.00
2	120.00
3 thru 10	@100.00
11 thru 20	@100.00

SAD SACK in 3-D
Blackthorne

1 and 2	@2.50

SAD SACK SACK WORLD
Harvey, 1964

1	100.00
2 thru 20	@50.00
21 thru 31	@30.00
32 thru 46	@15.00

SAD SACK USA
Harvey, 1972

1	30.00
2 thru 7	@20.00

SADHU
Virgin Comics, 2006

1 thru 5	@3.00

SAFETY-BELT MAN ALL HELL
Sirius, 1996

1	3.00
2	3.00
3	3.00
4 Linsner back (c)	4.00
5	3.00

SAGA OF THE METABARONS
Humanoids Publishing, 1999

1 (of 16) Sci-fi	3.00
2 thru 9	@3.00

SAINT LEGEND
Comicsone.com, 2002

GN #3 thru #6	@14.00
GN #7 thru GN #10	@15.00

SAM AND MAX, FREE-LANCE POLICE SPECIAL
Comico, 1987–89
1 .... 3.00

SAM SLADE ROBOHUNTER
Quality, 1986–89
1 .... 2.50
2 thru 10 .... @2.50
11 thru 21 .... @2.50
22/23 .... 2.50
24 .... 2.50
25/26 .... 2.50
27 thru 33 .... @2.50

SAMSONS
Samsons Comics, 1995
1/2 Various Artists 2.50

SAMUREE
Windjammer, 1995
1 I:Samuree 2.50
2 V: The Dragon 2.50
3 V: The Dragon 2.50

SAMURAI
Eclipse
1 .... 2.50
2 .... 2.50
3 thru 5 .... @2.50

SAMURAI GUARD
Colburn Comics, 2000
1 by Kirk C. Abrigo 2.50
2 .... 2.50
3 thru 6 .... @3.00

SAMUREE
Continuity, 1987
1 NA,A:Revengers 2.50
2 A:Revengers 2.50
3 NA,A:Revengers 2.50
4 A:Revengers 2.50
5 BSz(c),A:Revengers 2.50
6 A:Revengers 2.50
7 .... 2.50
8 Drug story 2.50
9 Drug story 2.50
[2nd Series], 1993
1 thru 3 Rise of Magic........ @2.50

SANDSCAPE
Dreamwave, 2003
1 .... 3.00
2 thru 4 .... @3.00

SANTANA
Rock-it Comix, 1994
1 TT(c&s),TY................. 4.00

SARGE STEEL/ SECRET AGENT
Charlton, 1964–66
1 DG,I:SargeSteel & IvanChung .. 75.00
2 DG,I:Werner Von Hess 50.00
3 DG,V:Smiling Skull........... 50.00
4 DG,V:Lynx 50.00
5 FMc,V:Ivan Chung........... 50.00
6 FMc,A:Judomaster........... 60.00
7 DG 50.00
8 V:Talon................... 50.00
Becomes:
SECRET AGENT
9 DG,A:The Lynx.............. 75.00
10 DG,JAp,A:Tiffany Sinn 50.00

SATANIKA
Verotik, 1995
0 .... 3.00
1 New ongoing series.......... 4.00
2 Femininity 3.50
3 thru 5 .... @3.00
6 thru 10 .... @3.00
10a Wingbird variant cover 5.00
11 SBi,final issue 4.00
11a Jason Blood variant (c)...... 10.00
11b Superfest 99 limited 15.00
1-shot Satanika X (adult)........ 5.00
1-shot Satanika vs.Shilene 10.00

SATANIKA TALES
Verotik, 2005
2 .... 4.00
2a variant (c).................. 5.00
2b Limited fan (c) 10.00

SATAN'S SIX
Topps, 1993
1 F:Satan's Six,w/3 cards........ 3.25
2 V:Kalazarr,w/3 cards 3.00
3 w/3 cards................... 3.00
4 w/3 cards................... 3.00

SAURIANS: UNNATURAL SELECTION
Crossgen Comics, 2002
1 (of 2) 3.00
2 .... 3.00

SAVAGE BROTHERS
Boom! Studios, 2006
1 (of 3) 3.50
2 thru 3 .... @3.50

SAVAGE COMBAT TALES
Atlas, Feb.–July, 1975
1 F:Sgt Strykers Death Squad ... 20.00
2 ATh,A:Warhawk 30.00
3 final issue................. 15.00

SAVAGE DRAGON/ TEENAGE MUTANT NINJA TURLTES CROSSOVER
Mirage, 1993
1 EL(s)....................... 3.00

SAVAGE RED SONJA QUEEN OF THE FROZEN WASTES
D.E. (Dynamite Ent.) 2006
1 (of 4) 3.50
1a foil (c) 4.00
2 thru 4 .... @3.50
2 thru 4a variant (c)s .... @3.50

SAVAGE TALES
D.E. (Dynamite Ent.) 2007
1 .... 5.00
1a variant (c)s .... @5.00
2 .... 5.00
3 .... 5.00
4 .... 5.00
5 .... 5.00

SAVAGE WORLD
Kandora Publishing, 2005
1 .... 3.50
2 .... 3.50
3 .... 3.50

SAVED BY THE BELL
Harvey, 1992
1 based on TV series 2.50
2 thru 5 .... @2.50

SAWED-OFF MOJO
Speakeasy Comics, 2006
1 (of 6) 3.00
2 thru 3 .... @3.00

Scamp #6
© Walt Disney

SCAMP
Dell, 1958
5 .... 75.00
6 thru 16 .... @60.00

SCAMP
Gold Key, 1967
1 Disney 60.00
2 thru 10 .... @25.00
11 thru 20 .... @20.00
21 thru 45.................. @10.00

SCARFACE: DEVIL IN DISGUISE
IDW, 2007
1 .... 4.00
2 thru 4 .... @4.00

SCARFACE: SCARRED FOR LIFE
IDW Publishing, 2006
1 .... 4.00
2 thru 5 .... @4.00
1a thru 5a variant (c)s .... @4.00

SCARLET CRUSH
Awesome Entertainment, 1998
1 by John Stinsman 2.50
2 .... 2.50
3 Icaria's decision 2.50
4 Nirasawa arrives 2.50

SCARY TALES
Charlton, 1975
1 JSon....................... 50.00
2 .... 25.00
3 SD,P(c) 25.00
4 TS,SD,JSon,P(c) 40.00
5 SD 40.00
6 .... 25.00
7 SD 30.00
8 SD 30.00

All comics prices listed are for *Near Mint* condition.

9 TS 40.00
10 . . . . 25.00
11 SD 30.00
12 SD 25.00
13 . . . . 20.00
14 SD 25.00
15 SD 25.00
16 SD 20.00
17 . . . . 20.00
18 BP 25.00
19 SD 25.00
20 JSon 18.00
21 SD 25.00
22 . . . . 15.00
23 thru 28 . . . . @14.00
30 thru 37 . . . . @12.00
38 Mr. Jigsaw 15.00
39 SD 20.00
40 thru 46 . . . . @15.00

SCATTERBRAIN
APC, 2005
1 . . . . 3.50
2 thru 4 . . . . @3.50

SCATTERBRAIN
Markosia, 2006
1 . . . . 3.50
1a variant (c)s . . . . @3.50
2 thru 4 . . . . @3.50
3a variant (c) 3.50

SCAVENGERS
Quality, 1988–89
1 thru 7 . . . . @2.50
8 thru 14 . . . . @2.50

SCAVENGERS
Triumphant Comics, 1993–94
0 Fso(c),JnR(s), ... 2.50
0a `Free Copy' 2.50
0b Red Logo 2.50
1 JnR(s),I:Scavengers,Ximos,
　C:Doctor Chaos 2.50
1a 2nd Printing 2.50
2 JnR(s), ... 2.50
3 JnR(s),I:Lurok 2.50
4 JnR(s), ... 2.50
5 Fso(c),JnR(s),D:Jack Hanal 2.50
6 JnR(s), ... 2.50
7 JnR(s),I:Zion 2.50
8 JnR(s),Nativity 2.50
9 JnR(s),The Challenge 2.50
10 JnR(s),Snowblind 2.50

SCHISM
Defiant
1 thru 4 Defiant's x-over . . . . @3.25

SCION
Crossgen Comics, 2000
1 RMz 5.00
2 RMz 5.00
3 RMz 4.50
4 . . . . 3.00
5 . . . . 3.00
6 . . . . 4.00
7 thru 18 . . . . @3.00
19 thru 30 RMz . . . . @3.00
31 thru 44 RMz . . . . @3.00

SCI-TECH
WildStorm/DC, 1999
1 (of 4) BCi,Ebe, ... 2.50
2 BCi,EBe, ... 2.50
3 BCi,EBe 2.50
4 BCi,EBe,concl 2.50

Scooby Doo #5
© Gold Key

SCOOBY DOO
Gold Key, 1970–75
1 . . . . 250.00
2 . . . . 175.00
3 . . . . 150.00
4 . . . . 150.00
5 . . . . 150.00
6 thru 20 . . . . @100.00
21 thru 30 . . . . @75.00

SCOOBY DOO
Charlton Comics, 1975–76
1 . . . . 150.00
2 thru 5 . . . . @75.00
6 thru 11 . . . . @60.00

SCOOBY-DOO
Harvey, 1992
1 . . . . 7.00
2 thru 3 . . . . @6.00

SCOOBY DOO
Archie, 1995
1 . . . . 6.00
2 thru 10 . . . . @5.00
11 thru 21 . . . . @4.00

SCOOBY DOO
MYSTERY COMICS
Gold Key, 1973
17 thru 30 . . . . @55.00

SCORCHED EARTH
Tundra, 1991
1 Earth 2025,I:Dr.EliotGodwin 3.50
2 Hunt for Eliot 3.00
3 Mystical Transformation 3.00

SCORPION, THE
Atlas, 1975
1 HC, bondage cover 30.00
2 HC,BWi,MK 25.00
3 . . . . 20.00

SCORPION CORP.
Dagger, 1993
1 PuD,JRI,CH, ... 2.75
2 PuD,JRI,CH,V:Victor Kyner 2.75
3 PuD,BlH,V:Victor Kyner 2.75

SCORPIO ROSE
Eclipse, 1983
1 MR/TP,I:Dr.Orient 2.50
2 MR/TP 2.50

SCOUT
Eclipse, 1985–87
1 TT,I:Scout,Fash.In Action 6.00
2 TT,V:Buffalo Monster 3.00
3 thru 18 TT . . . . @2.50
19 TT,w/Record,V:Lex Lucifer 3.00
20 thru 24 TT . . . . @2.50

SCOUT: WAR SHAMAN
Eclipse, 1988–89
1 TT,R:Scout (now a father) 2.50
2 thru 16 TT . . . . @2.50

SEADRAGON
Elite, 1986–87
1 . . . . 3.00
1a 2nd printing 2.50
2 thru 8 . . . . @2.50

SEA HUNT
Dell Publishing Co., 1958
1 L.BridgesPh(c) all 275.00
2 . . . . 200.00
3 ATh 225.00
4 RsM 200.00
5 RsM 200.00
6 RsM 200.00
7 . . . . 150.00
8 RsM 200.00
9 RsM 200.00
10 RsM 200.00
11 RsM 200.00
12 . . . . 200.00
13 RsM 200.00

SEAQUEST
Nemesis, 1994
1 HC(c),DGC,KP,AA,Based on
　TV Show 2.50

SEASON OF THE REAPER,
THE: WINTER
Speakeasy Comics, 2005
1 (of 3) 3.00
2 . . . . 3.00
3 . . . . 3.00

SEBASTIAN
Walt Disney
1 From Little Mermaid 2.50
2 While da Crab's Away 2.50

SECOND LIFE
OF DR. MIRAGE, THE
Valiant, 1993
1 B:BL(s),BCh,V:Mast.Darque 2.50
1a Gold Ed 3.00
2 thru 19 . . . . @2.50

SECOND STAGE
TURBINE BLADE
Eve Ink 2004
1 . . . . 25.00
1a Diamond 10.00
2 . . . . 10.00

SECRET AGENT
Gold Key, 1966
1 . . . . 250.00
2 . . . . 200.00

SECRET CITY SAGA
Topps, 1993
0 JK.	3.25
0 Gold Ed.	15.00
0 Red	10.00
1 thru 4 with 3 cards	@3.25

SECRET HISTORY, THE
Archaia Studios, 2007
1 (of 7)	6.00
2 thru 6	@6.00

SECRET SKULL
IDW Publishing, 2004
1	4.00
2 thru 4	@4.00

SECRETS OF THE VALIANT UNIVERSE
Valiant, 1994
1 from Wizard	2.50
2 BH,Chaos Effect-Beta#4,A:Master Darque,Dr.Mirage,Max St.James, Dr. Eclipse	2.50

SECRET SQUIRREL
Gold Key, 1966
1	225.00

Secret Weapons #4
© Valiant

SECRET WEAPONS
Valiant, 1993
1 JSP(a&s),BWi(i),I:Dr.Eclipse, A:Master Darque,A:Geoff, Livewire,Stronghold,Solar,X-O, Bloodshot,Shadowman	2.75
1a Gold Ed.	4.00
2 thru 23	@2.50

SECRET WEAPONS: PLAYING WITH FIRE
Valiant
1 & 2	@2.50

SEDUCTION OF THE INNOCENT
Eclipse, 1985–86
1 ATh,Hanged by the Neck, reps.	3.00
2	3.00
3 ATh,The Crushed Gardenia	3.00
4 ATh,NC,World's Apart	3.00

5 ATh,The Phantom Ship	3.00
6 ATh,RA,Hands of Don Jose	3.00
3-D #1 DSt(c)	5.00
3-D #2 ATh,MB,BWr,Man Who Was Always on Time	5.00

SEEKER
Sky Comics, 1995
1 JMt(s),I:Seeker	2.50

SENSEI
First, 1989
1 Mini-Series	2.75
2	2.75
3	2.75
4	2.75

SENTINELS OF JUSTICE
AC Comics, 1990
1 Capt.Paragon.	2.50
2	2.50
3 EL art	2.50
4 EL art	2.50
5	2.50
6	2.50
7	2.50

SENTRY: SPECIAL
Innovation, 1991
1	2.75

SERAPHIM
Innovation, 1990
1 and 2	@2.50

SERINA
Antarctic, 1996
1	3.00

SERPENTINA
Lightning, 1997
1	3.00
1a variant cover	3.00

SE7EN
Zenescope Entertainment, 2006
1 (of 7) Gluttony	4.00
2 Greed	4.00
3 Sloth	4.00
4 Lust	4.00
5 Pride	4.00
6 Envy	4.00
7 Wrath	4.00

SEVEN SISTERS
Zephyr Comics, 1997
1 by Curley, Cruickshank & Garcia.	3.00
2	3.00
3	3.00
4	3.00

SEVENTH SHRINE, THE
Devil's Due Publishing, 2004
1 (of 2) R.Silverberg adapt.	6.00
2	6.00

77 SUNSET STRIP
Dell Publishing Co., 1960
1 Ph(c)	150.00
2 Ph(c),RsM	150.00

77 SUNSET STRIP
Gold Key, 1962
1 from TV series, Ph(c).	150.00
2	150.00

SHADE SPECIAL
AC Comics, 1984
1	2.50

SHADOW, THE
Archie Comics, 1964–65
1	150.00
2	100.00
3	100.00
4	100.00
5	100.00
6 and 8	@75.00

SHADOW MAN
Valiant, 1992
0 BH,TmR,Chromium (c),O:Maxim St.James,Shadowman.	4.00
0a Newstand ed.	5.00
0b Gold Ed.	15.00
1 DL,JRu,I&O:Shadowman.	8.00
2 DL,V:Serial Killer	5.00
3 V:Emil Sosa	5.00
4 DL,FM(c),Unity#6,A:Solar	5.00
5 DL,WS(c),Unity#14, A:Archer & Armstrong	5.00
6 SD,L:Lilora	3.00
7 DL,V:Creature	3.00
8 JDx(i),I:Master Darque.	3.50
9 JDx(i),V:Darque's Minions	3.50
10 BH,I:Sandria	3.00
11 BH,N:Shadowman.	3.00
12 BH,V:Master Darque.	3.00
13 BH,V:Rev.Shadow Man	3.00
14 BH,JDx,V:Bikers	3.00
15 BH,JDx,V:JB,Fake Shadow Man,C:Turok	3.00
16 BH,JDx,I:Dr.Mirage, Carmen	3.50
17 BH,JDx,A:Archer & Armstrong	2.50
18 BH,JDx,A:Archer & Armstrong	2.50
19 BH,A:Aerosmith	2.50
20 BH,A:Master Darque, V:Shadowman's Father	2.50
21 BH,I:Maxim St.James (1895 Shadowman)	2.50
22 V:Master Darque.	2.50
23 BH(a&s),A:Doctor Mirage, V:Master Darque.	2.50
24 BH(a&s),V:H.A.T.E.	2.50
25 RgM,w/Valiant Era card	2.50
26 w/Valiant Era card.	3.00
27 BH,V:Drug Lord.	2.50
28 BH,A:Master Darque.	2.50
29 Chaos Effect-Beta#1,V:Master Darque.	2.50
30 R:Rotwak	2.50
31 thru 33	@2.50
34 Voodoo in Carribean	2.50
35 A:Ishmael	2.50
36 F:Ishmael	2.50
37 A:X-O, V:Blister	2.50
38 V:Ishmael, Blister	2.50
39 BH,TmR,Explores Powers	2.50
40 BH,TmR,I,Vampire!	2.50
41 A:Steve Massarsky	2.50
42	2.50
43 V:Smilin Jack	8.00

SHADOWMAN
Acclaim, 1996
1 GEn(s),Deadside, pt.1	4.00
2 GEn(s),Deadside, pt.2	4.00
3 GEn(s),Deadside, pt.3	4.00
4 GEn(s),Deadside, pt.4	4.00
5 thru 19 JaD,CAd	@4.00
20 Deadside vortes	7.00

VOLUME 3 (1999)
1 DAn,ALa,48-page	10.00
2	12.00
3 Flip-book	12.00
4 Flip-book	15.00

COLOR PUB.

---

5 . . . . 15.00
6 . . . . 15.00
7 final issue 30.00

SHADOWMANCER
Markosia, 2005
1 . . . . 3.50
1a variant (c)s . . . . @3.50
2 thru 10 . . . . @3.50
2a thru 10a variant (c) . . . . @3.50

SHADOW OF THE TORTURER, THE
Innovation, 1991
1 thru 6 Gene Wolfe adapt. . . . . @2.50

SHADOWPLAY
IDW Publishing, 2005
1 . . . . 4.00
1a variant (c) 4.00
2 . . . . 4.00
3 . . . . 4.00
3a variant (c). 4.00
4 . . . . 4.00
4a variant (c). 4.00

SHADOW REAVERS
Black Bull Entertainment, 2001
1 Nel,KM(c). 5.00
1a variant TDr(c). 9.00
2 Nel,GF(c). 3.00
2a variant TDr(c). 5.00
3 Nel 3.00
3a variant TDr(c). 5.00
4 Nel 3.00
4a variant limited master edition . . 5.00
5 Nel 3.00
5a variant limited master edition. . 5.00
Preview Edition 3.00
Preview Edition, limited 5.00

SHADOW STATE
Preview Editions
1 and 2 B&W. . . . . @2.50
Broadway, 1995
1 thru 4 F:BloodS.C.R.E.A.M. . . @2.50
5 JiS, Image Isn't Everything,
concl. 2.50
6 Anger of Lovers, pt.1 . . . . 2.50
7 Anger of Lovers, pt.2 . . . . 3.00

SHAIANA
Entity, 1995
1 R:Shaiana from Aster 3.75
1a clear chromium 8.00
1b Holochrome 9.00
2 Guardians of Earth 2.50

SHAOLIN
Black Tiger Press
1 I:Tiger. 3.00
2 I:Crane. 3.00

SHAOLIN COWBOY
Burlyman Entertainment, 2004
1 . . . . 3.50
2 thru 5 . . . . @3.50
6 . . . . 3.50
7 . . . . 3.50
3a thru 7a variant (c)s . . . . @3.50

SHARK-MAN
Thrill House, 2006
1 . . . . 4.00

SHATTER
First, 1985–88
1 . . . . 3.00

2 . . . . 2.50
3 . . . . 2.50
4 thru 14 . . . . @2.50
Spec. #1 Computer Comic. 5.00
#1a 2nd Printing. 2.00

SHAUN OF THE DEAD
IDW Publishing, 2005
1 . . . . 4.00
2 thru 4 . . . . @4.00

SHAUN THE SHEEP
Titan Publishing, 2007
1 . . . . 5.00
2 thru 9 . . . . @5.00

SHE-DEVILS ON WHEELS
Aircel
1 V:Man-Eaters. 3.00
2 V:Man-Eaters. 3.00
3 V:Man-Eaters. 3.00

SHEENA
Devil's Due, 2007
Preview Spec. 1.00
Priview Spec. variant (c) 1.00
1 . . . . 3.50
1a variant (c)s . . . . @3.50
2 thru 6 . . . . @3.50
2a & b thru 6 a & b variant (c)s. . @3.50

SHEENA: QUEEN OF THE JUNGLE
London Night
0 by Gabriel Cain & Wilson 3.00
0a Zebra Edition 5.00
0b Leopard Edition 5.00
0c Alligator Edition 5.00

SHEENA: QUEEN OF THE JUNGLE: BOUND
London Night, 1998
1 (of 4) by Everette Hartsoe
& Art Wetherell 3.00
1 ministry ed. 5.00
1 Leather retro edition 12.00

SHERIFF OF TOMBSTONE
Charlton Comics, 1958–61
1 AW,JSe 150.00
2 . . . . 100.00
3 thru 10 . . . . @100.00
11 thru 17 . . . . @75.00

SHIELD, THE: SPOTLIGHT
IDW Publishing, 2004
1 . . . . 4.00
2 thru 5 . . . . @4.00

SHI (THE WAY OF THE WARRIOR)
Crusade Comics, 1994–97
1 BiT,HMo,I:Shi 9.00
2 BiT 5.00
2a BiT, reissue, new cover 3.00
3 BiT 5.00
4 BiT 4.00
5 V:Arashi 3.00
5a variant cover 6.00
6 V:Tomoe. 3.00
7 V:Nara Warriors 3.00
8 New costume 3.00
9 thru 11 . . . . @3.00

Shi The Way of the Warrior #7
© Crusade Comics

12 Way of the Warrior, concl, flip-
book Angel Fire. 3.00
Spec. #1 Shi/Cyblade,Battle of the
Independents (1995) 4.00
Spec.#1a Shi/Cyblade,variant(c) . . . 6.00
Ashcan #1, sign & num. (2000) . . . 10.00
Spec. #1 10th Anniv. Edition (2004). 3.00
Crusade Entertainment, 2004
1 10th Anniv. Edition (2004) 3.00
1 10th Anniv. Graphite ed. 20.00

SHI: THE SERIES
Crusade Entertainment, 1997
1 sequel to *Shi: Heaven and Earth*,
F:Tomoe. 3.50
2 Unforgettable Fire, concl. 3.00
3 A Rock and a Hard Place, pt.1 . . 3.00
4 A Rock and a Hard Place, pt.2 . . 3.00
5 A Rock and a Hard Place, pt.3 . . 3.00
6 . . . . 3.00
7 Photographer's lucky picture . . . 3.00
8 V:Gemini Dawn twins 3.00
9 Bad Blood, pt.1 . . . . 3.00
9a variant BTi(c) 3.00
9b variant Ahn (c) 3.00
9c variant Kevin Lau (c) 3.00
10 Bad Blood, pt.2 . . . . 3.00
10a variant BTi(c) 3.00
10b variant Ahn (c) 3.00
10c variant Kevin Lau (c) 3.00
11 Bad Blood, pt.3 . . . . 3.00
12 The Dark Crusade, pt.1 (of 8). . . 3.00
13 The Dark Crusade, pt.2 (of 8). . . 3.00
14 The Dark Crusade, pt.3 (of 8). . . 3.00
15 The Dark Crusade, pt.4 (of 8). . . 3.00
16 The Dark Crusade, pt.5 (of 8). . . 3.00
1-shot The Essential Dark Crusade. 3.00
1-shot Shi:Five Year Celebration . . . 5.00
1-shotA,B,C,&D variant covers 5.00
#0 & Wolverine/Shi flip book 3.00
Spec. Shi/Vampirella,x-over(1997). . 3.00
Spec. Shi: Nightstalkers, VMk,
F:T.C.B. (1997) 3.50
Spec. Shi: Masquerade (1997) . . . 3.50
Spec. Shi: Art of War Tour Book
Wizard Chicago con (1998). . . . 6.00
G.I. Preview Edition (2001) 5.00
Spec. Through the Ashes (2001). . . 3.00

SHI: AKAI
Crusade Entertainment, 2001
1 BTi, I:RAF Victoria Cross. 3.00
1 antiques edition 25.00
Ashcan, signed & numbered 9.00

SHI: BLACK WHITE & RED
Crusade Entertainment, 1998
1 Night of the Rat, pt.1 . . . . 3.00
2 Night of the Rat, pt.2 . . . . 3.00
Coll. Ed. rep. #1–#2 . . . . 7.00

SHI: EAST WIND RAIN
Crusade Entertainment, 1997
1 BiT,MSo, fully painted 3.50
2 BiT, concl. 3.50

SHI: HEAVEN AND EARTH
Crusade Entertainment, 1997
1 (of 3) BiT 3.00
1 variant cover 3.00
2 BiT 3.00
3 BiT 3.00
4 BiT 3.00

SHI: HOT TARGET
Crusade Entertainment, 2003
1 . . . . 3.00

SHI: PANDORA'S BOX
Avatar Press, 2003
Preview Edition 16-pg. B&W 6.00
Preview BiT(c) 2.00
Preview prism foil (c) 11.00
1/2 prism foil (c) 11.00
1/2 royal blue (c) 60.00
1 BiT(c) 3.50
1a variant (c)s . . . . @3.50
1b prism foil (c) 11.00
1 royal blue edition 60.00

SHI: POISONED PARADISE
Avatar, 2002
Preview 16-pg., b&w 2.00
Preview, Ron Adrian (c) 6.00
Preview, prism foil edition 11.00
1 (of 2) BiT,Karl Waller,Martin(c). . . 3.50
1a BiT(c) 3.50
1b Waller (c) 3.50
1c Wraparound exclusive (c) 3.50
1d Angel of Death (c) 6.00
1e Angel of Death ruby foil (c) . . . 9.00
1f prism (c) 11.00
2 BiT(c) 3.50
2a-2c variant(c)s . . . . @3.50
1/2 Blossom (c) 6.00
1/2 variant (c)s . . . . @4.00
1/2 Royal Blue foil 75.00

SHI: REKISHI
Crusade Entertainment, 1997
1 (of 2) BiT 3.00
2 BiT, conclusion. 3.00
Coll.Ed. Shi:Reshiki, sourcebook,
  MS(c) 5.00

SHI VS 10TH MUSE
Bluewater Productions, 2007
1-shot x-over 3.50

SHI VS. TOMOE
Crusade, April, 1996
Spec. #1 BiT, double size 4.00
GN Unforgettable Fire, rep. 7.00

SHI-SENRYAKU
Crusade, 1995
1 BiT,R:Shi 3.00
1a variant cover 5.00
1 (of 3) 2nd edition 2.50
2 BiT,Arts of Warfare. 3.00
2 2nd edition 2.50

3 BiT 3.00
3 2nd edition 2.50

SHI – YEAR OF THE DRAGON
Crusade Entertainment, 2000
1 (of 3) BiT 3.00
1a variant (c). 3.00
1b signed & numbered 9.00
1c true colors ed. BiT 6.00
1d true colors ed. ruby red 25.00
2 Ana Tears (c) BiT 3.00
2a Death Incarnate (c) BiT 3.00
3 BTi, concl. 3.00
Ashcan, signed & numbered 9.00
Coll. Ed. Black,White,Red 7.00
GN #1 & #2 Black,White,Red 6.00
Poster Book 3.00

SHOCK SUSPENSE STORIES
Russ Cochran Press, 1992
1 reps.horror stories 2.50
2 inc.Kickback. 2.50
3 thru 4 . . . . @2.50
5 thru 7 reps.horror stories . . . . . @2.50
8 reps.horror stories 2.50
Gemstone
18 EC comics reprint 2.50

SHOCK THE MONKEY
Millennium/Expand, 1995
1 Shock therapy 3.00

SHON C. BURY'S NOX
Narwain Publishing, 2006
2 . . . . 4.00

SHOTGUN MARY
Antarctic Press, 1995
1 I:Shotgun Mary 3.00
1a with CD Soundtrack. 9.00
1b Red Foil cover 8.00
2 . . . . 3.00
Spec. Shooting Gallery 3.00
Spec. Deviltown 3.00
Spec. Deviltown, commem. (1999) . 6.00

SHOTGUN MARY
Antarctic Press, 1998
1 by Herb Mallette & Kelsey
  Shannon 3.00
2 Early Days, pt.2 . . . . 3.00
3 Early Days, pt.3 . . . . 3.00

SHOTGUN MARY: BLOOD LORE
Antarctic Press, 1997
1 (of 4) by Herb Mallette
  & Neil Googe 3.00
2 . . . . 3.00
3 . . . . 3.00
4 concl. 3.00

SHOTGUN MARY: SON OF THE BEAST, DAUGHTER OF LIGHT
Antarctic Press, 1997
1 . . . . 3.00

SHOTGUN WEDDING
Speakeasy Comics, 2005
1 . . . . 3.00
2 . . . . 3.00

Shrugged #0
© Aspin MLT

SHRUGGED
Aspen MLT., 2006
Spec. Beginnings 3.00
0 . . . . 7.00
1 . . . . 5.00
2 thru 5 . . . . @3.00
6 thru 8 . . . . @3.00

SICK
Charlton, 1976
109 . . . . 20.00
110 thru 134. . . . . 20.00
Annual #1. . . . . 40.00
Annual #2. . . . . 40.00

SIEGEL & SHUSTER
Eclipse, 1984–85
1 . . . . 2.50
2 . . . . 2.50

SIGIL
Crossgen Comics, 2000
1 BKs 5.00
2 BKs 3.25
3 thru 5 BKs . . . . @3.50
6 thru 12 BKs . . . . @3.25
13 thru 18 MWa,SEa . . . . @3.00
19 thru 30 SEa . . . . @3.00
31 thru 43 CDi(s) . . . . @3.00

SILENCERS, THE
Moonstone, 2003
1 . . . . 3.50
2 . . . . 3.50
3 . . . . 3.00
4 . . . . 3.50
1-shot Bitter Fruit, Bumper Edition . 5.00

SILENT DRAGON
Wildstorm/DC, July, 2005
1 (of 6) 3.00
2 thru 6 . . . . @3.00

SILENT GHOST
Speakeasy Comics, 2005
1 . . . . 3.00
2 . . . . 3.00
Markosia, 2006
1 . . . . 3.50
2 . . . . 3.50
3 thru 4 . . . . @3.50
4a variant (c) 3.50

All comics prices listed are for *Near Mint* condition.

SILENT HILL
IDW Publishing, 2005
1 Paint it Black 7.50
GN Among the Damned. 7.50
GN The Grinning Man 7.50

SILENT HILL: DEAD/ALIVE
IDW Publishing, 2005
1 . . . . 4.00
1a 4.00
2 thru 5 . . . . @4.00
2a thru 5a variant (c) 4.00

SILENT HILL: DYING INSIDE
IDW Publishing, 2004
1 . . . . 5.00
2 thru 5 . . . . @4.50

SILENT MOBIUS
Viz, 1991–92
1 Katsumi 5.75
2 Katsumi vs. Spirit 5.25
3 Katsumi trapped within entity. . . . 5.00
4 Nami vs. Dragon 5.00
5 Kiddy vs. Wire 5.00
6 Search for Wire 5.00

SILENT MOBIUS II
Viz, 1991
1 AMP Officers vs. Entities cont . . . 5.00
2 Entities in Amp H.Q. 5.00
3 V:Entity. 5.00
4 The Esper Weapon 5.00
5 Last issue. 5.00

SILENT MOBIUS III
Viz, 1992
1 F:Lebia/computer network 2.75
2 Lebia/computer link cont. 2.75
3 Lebia in danger 2.75
4 Return to Consciousness 2.75
5 Conclusion 2.75

SILKEN GHOST, THE
Crossgen Comics, 2003
1 (of 5) CDi 3.00
2 thru 5 . . . . @3.00
Vol. 1 Silken Ghost Traveler 10.00

SILVERBACK
Comico, 1989–90
1 thru 3 . . . . @2.50

SILVER CROSS
Antarctic Press, 1997
1 (of 3) by Ben Dunn 3.00
2 . . . . 3.00

SILVERHEELS
Pacific, 1983–84
1 and 3 . . . . @2.50

SILVER STAR
Pacific, 1983–84
1 thru 6 JK. . . . . @2.50

SILVER STAR
Topps, 1993
1 w/Cards 3.00

SILVER STORM
Silverline, 1998
1 . . . . 2.50
2 . . . . 2.50
3 . . . . @2.50

SIMPSONS COMICS
Bongo Comics, 1993
1 Colossal Horner 12.00
2 A:Sideshow Bob. 7.00
3 F:Bart 7.00
4 F:Bart 5.00
5 A:Itchy & Scratchy 5.00
6 F:Lisa 5.00
7 Circus in Town 5.00
8 Mr. Burns Voyage 5.00
9 Autobiographies 5.00
10 Tales of the Kwik-E-Mart. 5.00
11 Ned Flanders Public Enemy 4.00
12 In the Blodome 4.00
13 F:Bart & Millhouse 4.00
14 Homer owns beer company 4.00
15 Waltons parody 4.00
16 thru 49 . . . . @4.00
50 80-pg. 6.00
51 thru 99 . . . . @3.00
100 SA,100-pg. 7.00
101 thru 111 . . . . @3.00
112 thru 136 . . . . 3.00
Spec. Simpsons Classics #1
   thru #14 . . . . @4.00
Spec. #1 Winter Wingding 5.00
Simpsons Super Spectacular #1 . . 5.00
Simpsons Super Spectacular #2
   thru #5 . . . . @3.00
Spec. Summer Shindig #1 . . . . . . 5.00

SIMPSONS COMICS & STORIES
Welsh Publishing, 1993
1 with poster 4.00
1a without poster 2.50
Bongo Comics, 1998
1 F:Bartman, Itchy & Scratchy 3.00

SIMPSONS/FUTURAMA CROSSOVER CRISIS
Bongo Comics, 2005
Part II
1 (of 2) 3.00
2 . . . . 3.00

SINBAD JR
Dell, 1965
1 . . . . 60.00
2 thru 3 . . . . @45.00

SINGULARITY SEVEN
IDW Publishing, 2004
1 . . . . 4.00
2 thru 4 . . . . @4.00

SINS OF THE FALLEN: THE NIGHTSTALKER
Zenescope Entertainment, 2005
1 . . . . 3.00
2 thru 5 . . . . @3.00

SINTHIA
Lightning, 1997
1A by Joseph Adam, Daughter
   of Lucifer 3.00
1B 3.00
1c Platinum Edition 9.00
1d Autographed Edition 9.00
2 Sisters of Darkness 3.00
2a variant cover 3.00
3 Wagner(c) 3.00
3a variant Abrams cover 3.00
3b deluxe variant cover 9.00
4 Wagner(c) 3.00
4a variant John Cleary cover 3.00

SIRE, THE
After-Shock Comics, 2006
1 (of 3) 3.00
2 . . . . 3.00
3 Revelations 3.50

Siren #3
© Malibu

SIREN
Malibu Ultraverse, 1995
Infinity V:War Machine 2.50
1 V:War Machine 2.50
1a Computer painted cover 2.50
2 Phoenix flip issue 2.50
3 Phoenix Resurrection 2.50
Spec. #1 O:Siren 2.50

SISTERS OF MERCY
Maximum, 1995–96
1 . . . . 2.50
1a variant(c) 2.50
2 . . . . 2.50
3 . . . . 2.50
   No Mercy Comics
4 . . . . 2.50
5 . . . . 2.50

SISTERS OF MERCY: PARADISE LOST
London Night, 1997
1 by Ricki Rockett & Mark Williams 2.50
2 . . . . 2.50
3 . . . . 2.50
4 . . . . 2.50

SISTERS OF MERCY: WHEN RAZORS CRY CRIMSON TEARS
No Mercy Comics, 1996
1 . . . . 2.50

SIX-GUN HEROES
Charlton, 1960
7 . . . . 175.00
8 thru 10 . . . . @175.00

SIX-GUN SAMURAI
Alias Enterprises, 2005
1 . . . . 2.00
2 . . . . 3.00
3 . . . . 3.00
4 thru 6 . . . . @3.00

SIX MILLION DOLLAR MAN, THE
Charlton, 1976
1 JSon,Lee Majors Ph(c) 35.00
2 NA(c),JSon,Ph(c). 20.00
3 Ph(c) HC,NA 22.00
4 thru 9 Ph(c) . . . . @20.00

666 The Mark of the Beast #3
© Fleetway/Quality

666: MARK OF THE BEAST
Fleetway/Quality, 1986
1 I:Fludd, BU:Wolfie Smith 2.50
2 thru 18. . . . . @2.50

SIX STRING SAMURAI
Awesome Entertainment, 1998
1 RLe 3.00

SKATEMAN
Pacific, 1983
1 NA 2.50

SKYE RUNNER
Wildstorm/DC, April, 2006
1 . . . . 3.00
1a variant JLe (c) 3.00
2 thru 5 . . . . @3.00
6 finale 3.00

SKY SHARKS
Antarctic Press, 2007
1 (of 5) 3.50
2 thru 4 . . . . @3.50

SKY WOLF
Eclipse, 1988
1 V:Baron Von Tundra 2.50
2 TL,V:Baron Von Tundra 2.50
3 TL,cont. in Airboy #41 . . . . 2.50

SLAINE THE BERSERKER
Quality, 1987–89
1 thru 14 . . . . @2.50
15/16 . . . . 2.50
17 . . . . 2.50
18/19 . . . . 2.50
20 . . . . 2.50
Becomes:

SLAINE THE KING
Quality, 1989
21 thru 26 . . . . @2.50

SLAINE
Fleetway
1 thru 4 SBs,From 2000 AD . . . . @5.00

SLAINE THE HORNED GOD
Egmont Fleetway, 1998
1 (of 3) Pat Millagan & SBs, 68pg. . 7.00
2 (of 3) Pat Millagan & SBs, 68pg. . 7.00
3 68-pg., conclusion 7.00

SLAUGHTER
APC, 2003
1 . . . . 3.50
2 and 3 . . . . @3.50

SLEEPER
Wildstorm/DC, 2003
1 SeP,F:Holden Carver. 3.00
2 SeP 3.00
3 SeP,O:Miss Misery. 3.00
4 SeP,behind the curtain. 3.00
5 SeP,F:Holden Carver. 3.00
6 SeP,Holden's past 3.00
7 SeP,things get worse 3.00
8 SeP,Doppelganger. 3.00
9 SeP,secret records. 3.00
10 thru 12 SeP . . . . @3.00
Season Two (2004)
1 (of 12) SeP 3.00
2 thru 5 SeP . . . . @3.00
6 SeP 3.00
7 SeP 3.00
8 SeP,All-girl spy extravaganza . . . 3.00
9 SeP 3.00
10 SeP 3.00
11 SeP 3.00
12 SeP 3.00

SLIDERS
Valiant, 1996
1 & 2 . . . . @2.50

SLIDERS: DARKEST HOUR
Acclaim, 1996
1 DGC,DG. 2.50
2 DGC,DG. 2.50
3 DGC,DG, Concl.. . . . . 2.50
Spec. RgM, Montezuma IV rules the
    world 4.00
Spec. #2 Secrets 4.00

SLIDERS: ULTIMATUM
Valiant, 1996
1 & 2 . . . . @2.50

SLIMER
Now, 1989
1 thru 15 . . . . @2.50
Becomes:

SLIMER & REAL GHOSTBUSTERS
16 thru 18. . . . . @2.50

SLUDGE
Malibu Ultraverse, 1993–94
1 BWS,I:Sludge,BU:I:Rune. 2.75
1a Ultra-Limited 5.00
2 thru 13 AaL. . . . . @2.50
Red X-Mas 2.50

SMAX
Wildstorm/DC, 2003
1 (of 5) AMo,F:Jeff Smax 3.00
2 AMo,O:Smax 3.00
3 AMo,funeral 3.00
4 . . . . 3.00
5 AMo,V:Morningbright 3.00

SMILEY
Chaos! Comics, 1998
1 the Psychotic Button 3.00
Spec. Smiley Anti-Holiday Spec. . . . 3.00
Spec. Smiley Psychotic Button's
    Spring Break Road Trip. 3.00
Spec. Whacky Wrestling Spec. 3.00

SMOKE
What's Next Entertainment, 2000
1 (of 12) by Ty Rawls 3.00
2 . . . . 3.25
3 . . . . 3.25
4 . . . . 3.00
5 . . . . 3.25

SMOKE
IDW Publishing, 2005
1 Good Boys Grow Up 7.50
2 The Judas 7.50
3 The Men on the Chessboard. . . . 7.50

SMOKE AND MIRROR
Speakeasy Comics, 2005
1 . . . . 3.00
2 . . . . 3.00
3 thru 6 . . . . @3.00

SMOKE & MIRROR
Markosia, 2006
Vol. 2
1 . . . . 3.50
1a variant (c)s . . . . @3.50
2 thru 3 . . . . @3.50
2a thru 3a variant (c)s . . . . @3.50
4 . . . . 3.50

SMOKEY BEAR
Gold Key, 1970
1 . . . . 45.00
2 thru 6 . . . . @25.00
3 thru 13 . . . . @15.00

SNAGGLEPUSS
Gold Key, 1962–63
1 . . . . 150.00
2 . . . . 125.00
3 . . . . 125.00
4 . . . . 125.00

SNAKE EYES DECLASSIFIED
Devil's Due Publishing, 2005
1 . . . . 3.00
2 thru 3 . . . . @3.00
4 thru 6 . . . . @3.00

SNAKE PLISSKEN CHRONICLES
Crossgen Comics, 2003
1 . . . . 3.00
2 . . . . 3.00
3 . . . . 3.00

SNAKES ON A PLANE
Wildstorm/DC, Sept., 2006
1 CDo, movie adapt., ph(c). 3.00

2 CDo, movie adapt., ph(c). 3.00
1a & 2a, variant (c)s . . . . @3.00

SNAKEWOMAN
Virgin Comics, 2006

0 . . . . 1.00
1 . . . . 4.00
2 thru 5 . . . . @3.50
6 thru 10 . . . . @3.00

SNAKE WOMAN: TALE OF THE SNAKE CHARMER
Virgin Comics, 2007

1 . . . . 3.00
2 thru 6 . . . . @3.00

SNAK POSSE
HCom, 1994

1 . . . . 2.50
2 . . . . 2.50

SNOOPER AND BLABBER DETECTIVES
Gold Key, 1962–63

1 . . . . 150.00
2 . . . . 125.00
3 . . . . 125.00

SNOW WHITE & THE SEVEN DWARFS
Gold Key, 1963

1 . . . . 10.00

SNOW WHITE & SEVEN DWARFS GOLDEN ANNIVERSARY
Gladstone, 1987

1 w/poster & stickers 24.00

SNOWYBROOK INN
Counteractive Comics, 2006

1 . . . . 3.00

Soap Opera Love #1
© *Charlton*

SOAP OPERA LOVE
Charlton, 1983

1 . . . . 40.00
2 thru 3 . . . . @40.00

SOAP OPERA ROMANCES
Charlton, 1982–83

1 . . . . 40.00
2 thru 5 . . . . @30.00

SO DARK THE ROSE
CFD, 1995

1 Fully Painted 3.00

SOJOURN
Dreamer Comics, 1998

1 by Jim Somerville, Stranger
  & Stranger, pt.1 . . . . 3.00
2 Stranger & Stranger, pt.2 . . . . . 3.00
3 Malice in Wonderland 3.00
4 A Game of Conscience, pt.1 . . . 3.00
5 A Game of Conscience, pt.2 . . . 2.50
6 A Game of Conscience, pt.3 . . . 3.25
7 A Game of Conscience, pt.4 . . . 3.25
8 The Hunt 3.25
9 The Hunt, pt.2 . . . . 3.25
10 The Hunt, Bloodied 3.25

SOJOURN
Crossgen Comics, 2001

1 RMz 7.00
2 thru 5 RMz . . . . @5.00
6 thru 17 RMz 3.00
18 thru 24 . . . . @3.00
25 IEd 2.50
26 thru 37 . . . . @3.00
Collected Ed. #1 . . . . 4.00
Prequel RMz 3.00

SOJOURN/LADY DEATH
Crossgen Comics, 2004

1 (of 2) 3.00
2 . . . . 3.00

SOLAR: HELL ON EARTH
Acclaim, 1997

1 (of 4) CPr,DCw,Seleski twins
  have power of God 2.50
2 CPr,Goat Month prelude 2.50
3 CPr,RT,V:Jimmy Six 2.50
4 CPr, ... 2.50

SOLAR: MAN OF THE ATOM
Valiant, 1991

1 BWS,DP,BL,B:2nd Death B:Alpha
  & Omega 8.00
2 BWS,DP,BL,V:Dr Solar 7.00
3 BWS,DP,BL,V:Harada I:Harbinger
  Foundation 8.00
4 BWS,DP,BL,E:2nd Death V:Dr
  Solar 6.00
5 BWS,EC,V:Alien Armada 6.00
6 BWS,DP,SDr, V:Alien Armada X-
  O Armor 6.00
7 BWS,DP,SDr, V:Alien Armada X-
  O Armor 6.00
8 BWS,V:Dragon of Bangkok 6.00
9 BWS,DP,SDr, V:Erica's Baby . . . 7.00
10 BWS,DP,SDr,JDx,I:Eternal
  Warrior,E:Alpha&Omega 15.00
10a 2nd printing 7.00
11 SDr,A:Eternal Warrior, Prequel
  to Unity #0 . . . . 3.00
12 SDr,FM(c),Unity#9,O:Pierce,
  Albert 2.50
13 DP,SDr,WS(c),Unity #17,
  V:Pierce 2.50
14 DP,SDr,I:Bender (becomes
  Dr.Eclipse) 3.00
15 SD,V:Bender 3.00
16 thru 57 . . . . @2.50
58 I:Atman, The Inquisitor 5.00
59 and 60 KG . . . . @6.00

SOLITAIRE
Malibu Ultraverse, 1993–94

1 black baged edition with playing
  card: Ace of Clubs, Diamonds,
  Hearts or Spades 2.75
1d Newsstand edition,no card . . . 2.50
2 thru 12 . . . . @2.50

SOLOMON KANE
Blackthorne

1 3-D Special 2.50
2 3-D Special 2.50
1 thru 4 . . . . @2.50

SOLUS
Crossgen Comics, 2003

1 BKs,GP,RM,48-pg 3.00
2 thru 10 . . . . @3.00

SOLUTION
Malibu Ultraverse, 1993–95

0 DaR,O:Solution 4.00
1 DaR,I:Solution 2.50
1a foil cover 4.00
2 thru 17 . . . . @2.50

SOMERSET HOLMES
Pacific, 1983–84

1 BA,AW,I:Cliff Hanger &
  Somerset Holmes 2.50
2 thru 4 BA,AW . . . . @2.50

Eclipse, 1984

5 BA,AW 2.50
6 BA 2.50

SONIC THE HEDGEHOG
Archie Publications 1993
Mini-series

1 . . . . 35.00
2 . . . . 25.00
3 . . . . 25.00

SONIC THE HEDGEHOG
Archie Publications, 1993

1 A:Mobius,V:Robotnik 35.00
2 . . . . 25.00
3 thru 6 . . . . @15.00
7 thru 10 . . . . @15.00
11 thru 30 . . . . @15.00
31 thru 39 . . . . @7.00
40 thru 54 . . . . @7.00
55 thru 78 . . . . @4.00
79 and 80 . . . . @4.00
81 thru 99 . . . . @10.00
100 . . . . 2.50
101 thru 116 . . . . @2.50
117 thru 142 . . . . @2.50
143 thru 182 . . . . @2.25
GN Sonic Firsts, rep.#0, #1/4
  ashcan,#3,#4,#13 . . . . 5.00
Sonic Live Spec.#1 . . . . 2.50

SONIC QUEST: THE DEATH EGG SAGA
Archie Comics, 1997

1 (of 3) by Mike Gallagher & MaG,
  cont. from Sonic the Hedgehog
  #41 . . . . 2.50
2 and 3 . . . . @2.50

SONIC THE HEDGEHOG PRESENTS KNUCKLES CHASTIC
Archie Comics, 1995

1 I:New Heroes 2.50
Sonic Versus Knuckles Battle Royal
  Spec.#1 . . . . 2.50

All comics prices listed are for *Near Mint* condition.

COLOR PUB.

SONIC THE HEDGEHOG PRESENTS TAILS
Archie Comics, 1995
1 F:Tails 2.50
2 F:Tails 2.50

SONIC'S FRIENDLY NEMESIS: KNUCKLES
Archie Comics, 1996
1 . . . . 2.50

SONIC SUPER SPECIAL
Archie Comics, 1997
1 Brave New World. 2.50
3 Sonic Firsts 2.50
4 The Return of the King 2.50
5 Sonic Kids 2.50
6 Expanded Sonic #50, 48pg 2.50
7 F:Shadowhawk, The Maxx,
    Savage Dragon 2.50
8 four stories, 48-pg. 2.50
9 R:Sonic Kids 2.50
10 Some Enchanta Evening. 2.50
11 . . . . 2.50
12 48-pg. 2.50
13 thru 15 . . . . @2.50

SONIC X
Archie Comics, 2005
1 (of 4) 2.25
2 See Sonic; Sea Battle 2.25
3 thru 27 . . . . @2.25

SOULCATCHER
Moonstone, 2004
1 (of 2) 3.50
2 . . . . 3.50

SOULFIRE
Aspen Entertainment, 2003
0 The Day the Magic Died 8.00
1 . . . . 8.00
1a previews exclusive (c) 7.00
1b signed 25.00
2 . . . . 10.00
3 . . . . 10.00
4 . . . . 10.00
4a thru 4c variant (c) . . . . @9.00
5 . . . . 5.00
6 . . . . 5.00
7 . . . . 4.00
8 . . . . 3.00
9 . . . . 3.00
10 . . . . 4.00
Coll. Ed. #1 . . . . 7.00

SOULFIRE: CHAOS REIGN
Aspen MLT, 2006
Spec. Beginnings. 2.00
0 . . . . 2.50
1 . . . . 3.00
2 thru 3 . . . . @3.00

SOULFIRE: DYING OF THE LIGHT
Aspen, 2005
0 . . . . 2.50
0a signed 20.00
1 . . . . 3.00
1a signed edition. 35.00
2 . . . . 3.00
3 . . . . 3.00
4 . . . . 3.00
5 . . . . 3.00

SOULFIRE: NEW WORLD ORDER
Aspen MLT, 2007
0 . . . . 2.50
1 . . . . 3.00
1a variant (c) 3.00
2 . . . . 3.00

SOULMAN
Quantum Comics, 1998
1 . . . . 3.00
2 . . . . 3.00
3 16-pg. 3.00
4 16-pg. 3.00
5 24-pg. 3.00

SOUPY SALES COMIC BOOK
Archie Publications, 1965
1 . . . . 150.00

SPACE ADVENTURES
Charlton, 1967–79, Volume 3
1 (#60) O&I:Paul Mann & The
    Saucers From the Future . . . 100.00
2 thru 8 (1968–69) . . . . @75.00
9 thru 13 (1978–79) . . . . @30.00

SPACE: ABOVE AND BEYOND
Topps, 1995
1 thru 3 TV pilot adaptation. . . . @3.00

SPACE: ABOVE AND BEYOND— THE GAUNTLET
Topps, 1996
1 . . . . 3.00
2 (of 2) 3.00

SPACE ADVENTURES
Charlton, 1958
23 From Nyoka 300.00
24 thru 27 . . . . @250.00
28 thru 32 . . . . @100.00
33 SD, Capt. Atom 700.00
34 thru 40 Capt. Atom . . . . @300.00
41 thru 59 . . . . @50.00

Space Adventures #58
© Charlton

SPACE ARK
AC Comics, 1985–87
1 . . . . 3.00
2 . . . . 2.50

SPACE FAMILY ROBINSON
Gold Key, 1962–69
1 DSp 500.00
2 . . . . 250.00
3 . . . . 175.00
4 . . . . 175.00
5 . . . . 175.00
6 B:Captain Venture 150.00
7 . . . . 150.00
8 . . . . 150.00
9 . . . . 150.00
10 . . . . 150.00
11 thru 20 . . . . @100.00
21 thru 36 . . . . @75.00

SPACE GHOST
Gold Key, 1967
1 . . . . 600.00

SPACE GHOST
Comico, 1987
1 SR,V:Robot Master 10.00

SPACE GIANTS, THE
Pyramid Comics, 1997
0 . . . . 2.50
0a deluxe 2.50
1 . . . . 2.50
3 by Jeff Newman. 2.50

SPACE MAN
Dell Publishing Co., 1962–72
1 . . . . 125.00
2 . . . . 75.00
3 . . . . 75.00
4 thru 10 . . . . @50.00

SPACE: 1999
Charlton, 1975–76
1 . . . . 30.00
2 JSon,Survival. 25.00
3 JBy,Bring Them Back Alive 20.00
4 JBy 20.00
5 JBy. 20.00
6 JBy. 20.00
7 . . . . 20.00
8 B&W. 20.00

SPACE: 1999
A Plus Comics
1 GM,JBy 2.50

SPACE USAGI
Mirage, 1993
1 thru 3 From TMNT . . . . @2.75

SPACE WAR
Charlton Comics, 1959
1 . . . . 250.00
2 . . . . 150.00
3 . . . . 125.00
4 SD,SD(c) 250.00
5 SD,SD(c) 250.00
6 SD 250.00
7 . . . . 100.00
8 SD,SD(c) 250.00
9 . . . . 100.00
10 SD,SD(c). 250.00
11 . . . . 100.00
12 thru 15. . . . . @100.00
16 thru 27. . . . . @100.00

Becomes:

FIGHTIN' FIVE
28 SD,SD(c)............ 100.00
29 SD,SD(c)............ 100.00
30 SD,SD(c)............ 125.00
31 SD,SD(c)............ 125.00
32 .... 35.00
33 SD,SD(c)............ 125.00
34 Sd,SD(c)............ 125.00

SPACE WAR
Charlton, 1978
28 .... 15.00
29 thru 34.............. 10.00

SPECIAL EDUCATION
National Press Comics, 2006
1 thru 4 .... @3.00

Special War Series #4
© *Charlton*

SPECIAL WAR SERIES
Charlton, 1965
1 D-Day................. 50.00
2 The Company of the Dead 30.00
3 War and Attack 25.00
4 Judo Master............ 75.00
Becomes:

ATTACK!
Charlton, 1966
3 SG, Green Inferno of Viet Nam . 30.00
4 SG, Frozen Rendezvous 30.00
Becomes:

ATTACK AT SEA
Charlton, 1968
5 Channel Tag............... 30.00

SPECIES
Avatar Press/Pulsar Press, 2005
Spec. #1 .... 4.00
Spec. #1a Wraparound (c)........ 4.00
Spec. #1b Variant(c)s......... @4.00

SPECTER 7
Antarctic Press, 2002
1 (of 3) by Craig Babiar 5.00
2 and 3 .... @5.00

SPECWAR
Peter Four Productions, 2002
1 .... 3.25

2 thru 5 .... @3.25
6 thru 8 .... @3.25

SPEED BUGGY
Charlton, 1975
1 .... 30.00
2 thru 9 .... @25.00

SPEED DEMONS
Charlton, 1957
5 .... 50.00
6 thru 10 .... @50.00
Becomes:

SUBMARINE ATTACK
Charlton, 1958
11 .... 50.00
12 thru 30 .... @40.00
31 thru 54 .... @30.00

SPEED RACER
Now, 1987–90
1 .... 3.50
1a 2nd printing 2.50
2 thru 33 .... @2.50
34 thru 38 .... @2.50
Spec. #1 .... 2.50
#1 2nd printing............ 2.00
Spec. #2................. 3.50
Classics, Vol #2 .... 4.00
Classics, Vol #3 .... 4.00
[2nd Series]
1 R:Speed Racer 2.50
2 .... 2.50
3 V:Giant Crab 2.50
4 .... 2.50
5 Racer-X 2.50
6 .... 2.50
7 .... 2.50

SPEED RACER
WildStorm/DC, 1999
1 Demon on Wheels........... 2.50
2 .... 2.50
3 concl.................. 2.50

SPELLBINDERS
Quality, 1986–88
1 Nemesis the Warlock......... 2.50
2 thru 12 Nemesis the Warlock.. @2.50

SPELLGAME
Speakeasy Comics, 2005
2 .... 3.00
3 .... 3.00
4 thru 7 .... @3.00

S.P.I.C.E.
Awesome Entertainment, 1998
1 RLe,JLb,F:Kaboom 2.50

SPIDER
Eclipse, 1991
1 TT,Blood Dance 7.00
2 TT,Blood Mark 6.00
3 TT,The Spider Unmasked 5.50

SPIDER: REIGN OF THE VAMPIRE KING
Eclipse, 1992
1 TT,I:Legion of Vermin......... 5.25
2 thru 4 TT .... @2.50

SPIDER-MAN/BADROCK
Maximum Press, 1997
1 (of 2) DJu,MMy x-over......... 3.00
2 DJu,DaF x-over 3.00

SPIKE
IDW Publishing, 2005
1-shot Spike: Old Times,
  Buffy spin-off 7.50
1-shotA variant (c) 7.50
1-shot Old Wounds 7.50
1-shot Lost & Found 7.50
1-shot Lost & Found, variant (c) ... 7.50

SPIKE: ASYLUM
IDW Publishing, 2006
1 .... 4.00
1a variant (c)............... 4.00
2 thru 5 .... @4.00
2a thru 5a variant (c) .... @4.00

SPIKE: SHADOW PUPPETS
IDW, 2007
1 .... 4.00
2 thru 4 .... @4.00
1a thru 4a variant (c) .... @4.00

SPIKE VS. DRACULA
IDW Publishing, 2006
1 PDd 4.00
1a variant (c)s 4.00
2 thru 5 .... @4.00
2a thru 5a variant (c) .... @4.00

SPINE-TINGLING TALES
Gold Key, 1975
1 .... 20.00
2 thru 4 .... @12.00

SPIRAL PATH
Eclipse, 1986
1 V:Tairngir 2.50
2 V:King Artuk 2.50

SPIRIT, THE
Harvey, 1966
1 WE,O:Spirit 150.00
2 WE,O:The Octopus 100.00

SPIRIT, THE
Kitchen Sink, 1983–92
1 WE(c) (1983) 5.25
2 WE(c) 4.25
3 WE(c) (1984) 4.00
4 WE(c) 4.00
5 thru 7 WE(c) .... @3.00
8 thru 11 WE(c) (1985) .... @3.00
See: B&W Pub. section

SPIRIT, THE: THE NEW ADVENTURES
Kitchen Sink, 1997
1 AMo,DGb................ 4.00
2 Eisner/Stout cover 3.50
2a Eisner/Schultz cover 3.50
3 AMo,Last Night I Dreamed of
  Dr. Cobra............... 3.50
4 Dr. Broca von Bitelbaum 3.50
5 Cursed Beauty 3.50
6 Swami Vashti Bubu 3.50
7 Central City 3.50
8 by Joe Lansdale 3.50
9 .... 3.50
10 CAd,BRa............... 3.50

SPIRIT OF THE AMAZON
NW Studios, 2002
1 .... 3.00
2 .... 3.00
3 thru 7 .... @3.00

SPOOKY HAUNTED HOUSE
Harvey Publications, 1972–75
1 . . . . 50.00
2 . . . . 40.00
3 thru 5 . . . . @40.00
6 thru 10 . . . . @30.00
11 thru 15 . . . . @25.00

SPOOKY SPOOKTOWN
Harvey Publications, 1966–76
1 B:Casper,Spooky,68 pgs 300.00
2 . . . . 175.00
3 . . . . 150.00
4 . . . . 150.00
5 . . . . 150.00
6 thru 10 . . . . @100.00
11 thru 20 . . . . @75.00
21 thru 30 . . . . @75.00
31 thru 39 E:68 pgs . . . . @60.00
40 thru 45 . . . . @40.00
46 thru 66 . . . . @30.00

SPOONER
Astonish Comics, 2004
1 . . . . 3.00
2 thru 4 . . . . @3.00

SPRINGHEELED JACK
Full Circle Publications, 2006
1 new printing 4.00
2 new printing 4.00
3 new printing 4.00

Spyman #3
© Harvey

SPYMAN
Harvey, 1966
1 GT,JSo,1st prof work,
  I:Spyman 150.00
2 DAy,JSo,V:Cyclops 100.00
3 . . . . 75.00

SQUAD, THE
Malibu
0-A Hardcase's old team 2.50
0-B 2.50
0-C L.A.Riots 2.50

SQUALOR
First, 1989
1 . . . . 2.75

2 . . . . 2.75
3 . . . . 2.75

STAINLESS STEEL RAT
Eagle, 1986
1 Harry Harrison adapt. 2.50
2 thru 6 . . . . @2.50

STAR BLAZERS
Comico, 1989
1 . . . . 3.00
2 . . . . 3.00
3 . . . . 3.00
4 . . . . 3.00

[2nd Series]
1 . . . . 3.00
2 . . . . 3.00
3 thru 5 . . . . @3.00

STARBLAZERS
Argo Press, 1995
0 Battleship Yamato 3.00
1 F:Dereck Wildstar 3.00
2 After the Comet War 3.00
3 . . . . 3.00
4 TEI 3.00
5 thru 12 . . . . @3.00

STARDUST KID
Boom! Studios, 2006
4 . . . . 3.50
5 . . . . 3.50

STARFORCE SIX SPECIAL
AC Comics, 1984
1 . . . . 2.50

STARGATE
Entity Comics, 1996
1 . . . . 3.00
2 . . . . 3.00
3 . . . . 3.00
4 . . . . 3.00
4a deluxe limited edition 3.50

STARGATE ATLANTIS: WRAITHFALL
Avatar Press/Pulsar Press, 2006
1 . . . . 4.00
1a variant (c)s . . . . @4.00
1b variant photo (c)s . . . . @4.00
2 . . . . 4.00
2a variant (c)s . . . . @4.00
2b variant photo (c)s . . . . @4.00
3 . . . . 4.00
3a variant (c)s . . . . @4.00

STARGATE: DOOMSDAY WORLD
Entity Comics, 1996
1 new crew explores 2nd StarGate 3.00
1 prism-foil edition. 3.50
2 . . . . 3.00
3 . . . . 3.00
3 deluxe 3.50

STARGATE SG–1
Avatar, 2003
Convention Spec. 3.00
Convention Spec. Photo (c). 4.00
Spec. First Prime Edition 6.00
Convention Spec. 2004 . . . . 3.00
Convention Spec. 2004, ph(c). 4.00
2005 Convention Special 3.00
2005 Convention Special
  variant (c)s . . . . @3.00

2006 Convention Special 3.00
2006 Convention Special
  variant (c)s . . . . @3.00
2007 Special 3.00
2007 Special variant (c)s . . . . @3.00

STARGATE SG-1: ARIS BOCH
Avatar, 2004
1 . . . . 3.00
1a photo (c). 3.00
1b wraparound (c). 3.00

STARGATE SG-1: DANIEL'S SONG
Avatar Press/Pulsar Press, 2005
1 . . . . 3.00
1a photo(c) 3.00
1b wraparaound (c). 3.00

STARGATE SG-1: FALL OF ROME
Avatar, 2004
Prequel. 3.00
Prequel wraparound (c) 3.00
Prequel photo(c) 3.00
1 . . . . 4.00
2 thru 3 . . . . @4.00
1a thru 3a photo (c)s. . . . . @4.00
1b thru 3b wraparound (c)s. . . . . @4.00

STARGATE SG-1: P.O.W.
Avatar, 2004
1 . . . . 3.50
1a wraparound (c). 3.50
1b photo (c). 3.50
2 . . . . 3.50
2a wraparound (c). 3.50
2b photo (c). 3.50
3 . . . . 3.50
3a wraparound (c). 3.50
3b photo (c). 3.50

STARGATE SG-1: RA REBORN
Avatar Press/Pulsar Press, 2005
Prequel 3.00
Prequel variant (c)s . . . . @3.00
Prequel Carter painted (c) 6.00

STARGATE SG-1: RED DAWN
Avatar Press/Pulsar Press, 2006
Spec., 2006 convention (c) 6.00

STARGODS
Antarctic Press, 1998
1 by Zachary, Clark & Beaty 3.00
1a deluxe 6.00
2 The Golden Bow 3.00
2a deluxe, with poster. 6.00
Spec. Stargods Visions 3.00

STARK RAVEN
Hardline Studios, 2000
1 The Screaming Rain,pt.1 . . . . . . 3.00
2 The Screaming Rain,pt.2 . . . . . . 3.00
3 . . . . 3.00

Endless Horizons, 2000
4 . . . . 3.00
5 . . . . 3.00
6 Ken Kelly (c) 3.00
7 . . . . 3.00
8 . . . . 3.00

COLOR PUB.

STARKWEATHER
Arcana Studio, 2004
1 . . . . 3.00
2 thru 5 . . . . @3.00

STARKWEATHER: IMMORTAL
Archaia Studios, 2007
0 . . . . 5.00
1 (of 4) 4.00
2 . . . . 4.00

STAR MASTERS
AC Comics, 1994
1 . . . . 2.50

STAR REACH CLASSICS
Eclipse, 1984
1 JSn,NA(r) 2.50
2 AN 2.50
3 HC 2.50
4 FB(r) 2.50
5 . . . . 2.50
6 . . . . 2.50

STAR SEED
See: POWERS THAT BE

STARSHIP TROOPERS
Markosia, 2006
0 Previews exclusive 3.00
0a signed edition. 9.00
0 . . . . 5.00
1 Alamo Bay. 3.50
1a variant (c)s . . . . @3.50
1b director's cut 3.50
2 thru 4 Alamo Bay, pt. 2–pt. 4 . . @3.50
2a thru 4a variant (c)s . . . . @3.50

STARSHIP TROOPERS: DAMAGED JUSTICE
Markosia, 2006
1 . . . . 3.00
1a variant (c)s . . . . @3.00
1b variant sketch (c) signed 9.00
1c director's cut 3.50
2 thru 4 . . . . @3.50
2a thru 4a variant (c) . . . . @3.50

STARSHIP TROOPERS: DEAD MAN'S HAND
Markosia, 2006
1 (of 4) 4.00
1a variant (c)s . . . . @4.00
1b Ltd. Sketch (c) signed 9.00
1c Re-marked Previews exclusive 35.00
2 thru 4 . . . . @3.50
2a thru 4a variant (c)s . . . . @3.50
2b thru 4b signed Previews
  exclusives . . . . @9.00

STAR SLAMMERS
Malibu Bravura, 1994
1 WS(a&s) 2.75
2 WS(a&s),F:Meredith 2.75
3 WS(a&s) 2.50
4 WS(a&s) 2.50
5 WS,Rojas Choice. 2.50

STARSLAYER
Pacific, 1982–83
1 MGr,O:Starslayer 4.00
2 MGr,DSt,I:Rocketeer 9.00
3 DSt,MGr,A:Rocketeer(2ndApp.). . 6.00
4 MGr,Baraka Kuhr 2.50
5 MGr,SA,A:Groo 7.00
6 MGr,conclusion story 2.50

First, 1983–85
7 MGr layouts 2.50
8 MGr layouts, MG 2.50
9 MGr layouts, MG 2.50
10 TT,MG,I:Grimjack 4.00
11 thru 34 . . . . @2.50
Graphic Novel 10.00

STARSLAYER DIRECTORS CUT
Windjammer, 1995
1 R:Starslayer, Mike Grell 2.50
2 I:New Star Slayer. 2.50
3 Jolly Rodger. 2.50
4 V:Battle Droids. 2.50
5 I:Baraka Kuhi 2.50
6 V:Valkyrie 2.50
7 MGr(c&a),Can Torin destroy? . . . 2.50
8 MGr(c&a),JAI, Can Torin live with
  his deeds?,final issue 2.50

Star Trek #3
© Gold Key

STAR TREK
Gold Key, 1967–79
1 Planet of No Return 1,500.00
2 Devil's Isle of Space 1,000.00
3 Invasion of City Builders 500.00
4 Peril of Planet Quick Change . 500.00
5 Ghost Planet 500.00
6 When Planets Collide 300.00
7 Voodoo Planet 300.00
8 Youth Trap 250.00
9 Legacy of Lazarus 250.00
10 Sceptre of the Sun 200.00
11 Brain Shockers 200.00
12 Flight of the Buccaneer 150.00
13 Dark Traveler 150.00
14 Enterprise Mutiny 150.00
15 Museum a/t End of Time. 150.00
16 Day of the Inquisitors 150.00
17 Cosmic Cavemen 150.00
18 The Hijacked Planet 150.00
19 The Haunted Asteroid 150.00
20 A World Gone Mad 150.00
21 The Mummies of Heitus VII . . 125.00
22 Siege in Superspace. 125.00
23 Child's Play 125.00
24 The Trial of Capt. Kirk. 125.00
25 Dwarf Planet 125.00
26 The Perfect Dream 125.00
27 Ice Journey 125.00
28 The Mimicking Menace. 125.00
29 rep. Star Trek #1 . . . . 125.00
30 Death of a Star 100.00
31 The Final Truth. 100.00

32 The Animal People 100.00
33 The Choice 100.00
34 The Psychocrystals. 100.00
35 rep. Star Trek #4 . . . . 100.00
36 A Bomb in Time. 100.00
37 rep. Star Trek #5 . . . . 75.00
38 One of our Captains
  is Missing. 75.00
39 Prophet of Peace 75.00
40 AMc,Furlough to Fury, A:
  Barbara McCoy 75.00
41 AMc,The Evictors 75.00
42 World Against Time. 75.00
43 World Beneath the Waves 75.00
44 Prince Traitor 75.00
45 rep. Star Trek #7 . . . . 75.00
46 Mr. Oracle 75.00
47 AMc,This Tree Bears Bitter
  Fruit 75.00
48 AMc,Murder on Enterprise . . . 75.00
49 AMc,A Warp in Space 75.00
50 AMc,The Planet of No Life . . . 75.00
51 AMc,DestinationAnnihilation6 . . 60.00
52 AMc,And A Child Shall
  Lead Them 60.00
53 AMc,What Fools..Mortals Be . . 60.00
54 AMc,Sport of Knaves 60.00
55 AMc,A World Against Itself . . . 60.00
56 AMc,No Time Like The Past,
  A:Guardian of Forever. 60.00
57 AMc,Spore of the Devil 60.00
58 AMc,Brain Damaged Planet . . 60.00
59 AMc,To Err is Vulcan. 60.00
60 AMc,The Empire Man 60.00
61 AMc,Operation Con Game . . . 60.00

STAR TREK: ALIENS SPOTLIGHT
IDW Publishing 2007
Gorn spec. 4.00
Gorn spec. variant (c) 4.00
Vulcans spec. 4.00
Vulcans spec. variant (c) 4.00
Andorians spec. 4.00
Andorians spec. variant (c) 4.00

STAR TREK: ALL OF ME
WildStorm/DC, 2000
1-shot AaL,RyE 6.00

STAR TREK: DEEP SPACE NINE
Malibu, 1993
1 Direct ed. 3.25
1a Photo(c). 3.00
1b Gold foil 5.00
2 w/skycap 3.50
3 thru 9 . . . . @2.75
10 Descendants 2.50
11 A Short Fuse 2.75
12 Baby on Board 2.50
13 Problems with Odo 2.75
14 on Bejor 2.75
15 mythologic dilemma 2.75
16 thru 32 . . . . @2.50
Ann.#1 Looking Glass 4.00
Spec. #1 Collision Course 3.50
Spec. #0 Terok Nor 3.00

CELEBRITY SERIES: BLOOD AND HONOR
Malibu, 1995
1 Mark Lenard(s) 3.00
2 Rules of Diplomacy 3.00

LIGHTSTORM
Malibu, 1994
1 Direct ed. 3.50
1a Silver foil 8.00

HEARTS AND MINDS
Malibu, 1994
1 . . . . 3.00
2 . . . . 2.50
3 Into the Abyss,X-over preview . . . 2.50
4 final issue 2.50

THE MAQUIS
Malibu, 1995
1 Federation Renegades 2.50
1a Newsstand, photo(c) 2.50
2 Garack 2.50
3 F:Quark, Bashir 2.50

THE NEXT GENERATION
Malibu, 1994
1 Prophet & Losses, pt.2 . . . . 2.50
2 Prophet & Losses, pt.4 . . . . 2.50

STAR TREK:
DEEP SPACE NINE
N-VECTOR
WildStorm/DC, 2000
1 (of 4),F:Kira 2.50
2 sabotage 2.50
3 N-Vector viroid 2.50
4 F:Quark,concl. 2.50

STAR TREK:
DIVIDED WE FALL
WildStorm/DC, 2001
1 (of 4) TNG & DS9 x-over 3.00
2 thru 4 . . . . @3.00

STAR TREK:
ENTER THE WOLVES
WildStorm/DC, 2001
1-shot, 48-pg. 6.00

STAR TREK: KLINGONS:
BLOOD WILL TELL
IDW Publishing, 2007
1 . . . . 4.00
2 thru 5 . . . . @4.00
1a final 5a variant (c). . . . . @4.00
1b Klingon-Language variant 5.00

STAR TREK: THE
NEXT GENERATION —
THE KILLING SHADOWS
WildStorm/DC, 2000
1 (of 4) V:Bodai Shin, assassin . . 2.50
2 thru 4 V:Bodai Shin . . . . @2.50

STAR TREK: THE
NEXT GENERATION —
PERCHANCE TO DREAM
WildStorm/DC, 1999
1 (of 4) 2.50
2 thru 4 . . . . @2.50

STAR TREK:
THE NEXT GENERATION:
THE SPACE BETWEEN
IDW Publishing, 2007
1 . . . . 4.00
2 thru 6 . . . . @4.00
1a thru 6a variant (c). . . . . @4.00

STAR TREK: VOYAGER
WildStorm/DC, 2000
Spec. Elite Force 6.00
Spec. Avalon Rising 6.00

STAR TREK: VOYAGER
Malibu
A V:Maquis 2.75
Aa Newsstand, photo(c) 2.50
B conclusion. 2.75
Ba Newsstand, photo(c) 2.50

STAR TREK: VOYAGER —
PLANET KILLER
WildStorm/DC, 2001
1 (of 3) F:Kirk,Janeway 3.00
2 Doomsday Machine 3.00
3 concl. 3.00

STAR TREK: YEAR FOUR
IDW Publishing, 2007
1 . . . . 4.00
2 thru 5 . . . . @4.00
1a thru 5a variant (c)s. . . . . @4.00
Spec. IDW Focus On Star Trek 3.00

STAR WARS IN 3-D
Blackthorne, 1987
1 thru 7 . . . . @4.00

STARWATCHERS
Valiant
1 MLe,DG,Chromium(c),Valiant
  Vision, ... 3.50

S.T.A.T.
Majestic, 1993
1 FdS(s),PhH,I:S.T.A.T. 2.50

STATIC-X
Chaos! Comics, 2002
1 by BnP, with CD-Rom 6.00
1a photo (c) with CD-Rom 6.00
1b collector's edition 15.00
Vol. 2
1 with CD-Rom 6.00
1a collector's edition 15.00

STEALTH SQUAD
Petra Comics, 1993
1 I:Stealth Squad 2.50

STEAMPUNK
WildStorm/DC Cliffhanger, 2000
1 CBa 2.50
1 chromium edition . . . .
2 CBa,V:Absinthe 2.50
3 CBa,F:Cole Blaquesmith 2.50
4 CBa,CBa(c) 2.50
4a variant JSC (c) (1:4) 2.50
4b variant JMd (c) (1:4) 2.50
4c variant HuR (c) (1:4) 2.50
5 CBa,V:Abbey Monsters 2.50
6 Mechanica Sundown,pt.1 . . . . . . 2.50
7 Mechanica Sundown,pt.2 . . . . . . 2.50
8 Mechanica Sundown,pt.3 . . . . . . 2.50
9 Mambutu X, pt.1 . . . . 2.50
10 Mambutu X, pt.2 . . . . 2.50
11 CBa, Stonehenge secret 2.50
12 CBa, 40-pg. final issue 3.50

STEED & MRS. PEEL
Eclipse, 1990
1 IG,The Golden Game 5.00
2 IG,The Golden Game 5.00
3 IG,The Golden Game 5.00

STEEL CITY HAWK
Narwain Publishing, 2006
1 (of 4) 4.00
2 . . . . 4.00

Steed & Mrs. Peel #3
© Eclipse

STEEL CLAW
Quality, 1986
1 H:Ken Bulmer 4.00
2 . . . . 4.00
3 . . . . 4.00
4 . . . . 4.00

STEEL STERLING
Archie Publications, 1984
(formerly LANCELOT STRONG)
4 EB 4.00
5 EB 4.00
6 EB 4.00
7 EB 4.00

STEVE CANYON 3-D
Kitchen Sink, 1986
Milton Caniff & Peter Poplaski(c),
  w/glasses (1985) 6.00

STEVE ZODIAC
& THE FIREBALL XL-5
Gold Key, 1964
1 . . . . 150.00

STING OF THE
GREEN HORNET
Now, 1992
1 Polybagged w/trading card 2.75
2 inc.Full color poster 2.75
3 inc.Full color poster 2.75

STONE COLD
STEVE AUSTIN
Chaos! Comics, 1999
1 (of 4) Whoop Ass personified . . . 3.00
1b Premium 9.00
2 . . . . 3.00
3 . . . . 3.00
4 . . . . 3.00
1a thru 4a photo (c) . . . . @3.00

STORMBRINGERS
Stormbringer Studios, 2007
1 . . . . 5.00
2 . . . . 3.00
3 . . . . 3.00

COLOR PUB.

STORMQUEST
Caliber, 1994
1 I:Stormquest	2.50
2 Time Stone	2.50
3 BU:Seeker	2.50
4 F:Shalimar	2.50
5 Reunion	2.50
6 V:Samuroids	2.50

STORMWATCH: TEAM ACHILLES
WildStorm/DC, 2002
Eye of the Storm
1 WPo,SW,new team	3.00
2 WPo,SW,extremists vs. U.N.	3.00
3 WPo,SW,military action	3.00
4 WPo,SW,hunt for Ivana Baiul	3.00
5 WPo,F:The Authority	3.00
6 WPo,F:The Authority	3.00
7 MT,V:Ivana Baiul	3.00
8 F:Jukko Hamalainen	3.00
9 WPo,V:super-human	3.00
10 WPo	3.00
11 WPo	3.00
12 WPo,funeral	3.00
13 BSz,The Suiciders	3.00
14 WPo,Citizen Soldier	3.00
15 The Suiciders	3.00
16 V:Citizen Soldier	3.00
17 V:Citizen Soldier	3.00
18 O:Citizen Soldier	3.00
19 Citizen Soldier,concl.	3.00
20	3.00
21	3.00
22 Hallibastard	3.00
23 Baron Chaos	3.00
24 Project Entry Universe	3.00

STORMWATCH: PHD
Wildstorm/DC, Nov., 2006
1 DoM	3.00
1 a & b variant (c)s	@3.00
2 DoM, The Walking Ghost.	3.00
2a variant (c).	3.00
3 DoM, in Las Vegas	3.00
3a variant (c) (1:10)	3.00
4 DoM,Ladies night out.	3.00
4a variant (c) (1:10)	3.00
5 DoM,Secrets revealed	3.00
6 DoM,Jackson King's secrets	3.00
7 DoM,Assault on Precinct 18	3.00
8 ASm,F:StormWatch Prime	3.00

Strangers #9
© Malibu

9 ASm,Dying cast member	3.00
10 ASm,Slaughterhouse Smith	3.00
11 ASm,The real Assassin	3.00
12 ASm,The Walking Ghost	3.00

STRANGE DAYS
Eclipse, 1984–85
1	4.00
2	3.00
3	3.00

STRANGERS, THE
Malibu Ultraverse, 1993–95
1 I:Strangers	3.00
1a Ultra-Limited	4.00
1b Full Hologram (c)	5.00
2 A:J.D.Hunt,w/Ultraverse card	3.00
3 I:TNTNT	2.50
4 thru 12	@2.50
13 (Ultraverse Premiere#4)	3.50
14 thru 26	@2.50
Ann.#1 Death	4.00
Ashcan 1 (signed)	8.00
Ashcan 1 (unsigned)	8.00

STRANGE SUSPENSE STORIES
Charlton, 1967
1	45.00
2 thru 9	@35.00

STRANGE SUSPENSE STORIES/ CAPTAIN ATOM
Charlton Comics, 1965
75 SD,O:CaptainAtom,1960Rep.	250.00
76 SD, Capt.Atom,1960Rep.	150.00
77 SD, Capt.Atom,1960Rep.	150.00
Becomes:	

CAPTAIN ATOM
Charlton Comics, 1965–67
78 SD, new stories begin.	150.00
79 SD,I:Dr.Spectro	100.00
80 SD	100.00
81 SD,V:Dr.Spectro	100.00
82 SD,I:Nightshade,Ghost	100.00
83 SD,I:Ted Kord/Blue Beetle	75.00
84 SD,N:Captain Atom.	75.00
85 SD,A:Blue Beetle,I:Punch & Jewelee	75.00
86 SD,A:Ghost, Blue Beetle	75.00
87 SD,JAp,A:Nightshade	75.00
88 SD/FMc,JAp,A:Nightshade	75.00
89 SD/FMc,JAp,A:Nightshade, Ghost, last issue Dec.,1967	75.00

STREET FIGHTER
Ocean, 1986–87
1 thru 3	@3.00

STREET FIGHTER
Malibu, 1993
1 based on Video Game.	3.00
2 thru 3 Based on Video Game	@3.00

STREET FIGHTER
Devil's Due/UDON, 2004
7	4.50
7a variant (c).	4.50
8 thru 14	@3.00
8a thru 14a variant (c)s	@3.00

STREET FIGHTER II
Udon Entertainment, 2005
0	2.00
6	3.00
6a variant (c)	3.00

STREET FIGHTER LEGENDS: SAKURA
Udon Entertainment, 2006
1	4.00
1a variant (c)	4.00
2 thru 4	@4.00
2 thru 4a variant (c)	@4.00

STREET SHARKS
Archie Comics, 1995
1 & 2 Based on Cartoons	@2.50

STRIKE!
Eclipse, 1988
1 TL,RT,I&O:New Strike	2.50
2 TL,RT	2.50
3 TL,RT	2.50
4 TL,RT,V:Renegade CIA Agents	2.50
5 TL,RT,V:Alien Bugs	2.50
6 TL,RT,Legacy of the Lost.	2.50
Spec. #1 Strike vs. Sgt. Strike TL,RT,The Man	2.50

STRIKEBACK
Malibu Bravura, 1994–95
1	3.00
2	3.00
3 V:Doberman.	3.00
4 V:Dragonryder Island.	3.00
Spec.#1 KM,JRu,V:Dragon	3.50

STRIKEFORCE AMERICA
Comico, 1995
1 ScC,SK(c),I:StrikeforceAmerica.	2.50
2 V:Superior-prisoner	3.00
3 Breakout, pt.2	3.00
[Volume 2], 1995
1 ScC,polybagged with Chrysalis promo card	3.00

STRONTIUM DOG
[Mini Series]
Eagle, 1985
1	3.00
2 thru 4	@3.00
[Regular Series]
Quality, 1988
Story line continued from 2000 A.D.
7 thru 14	@2.50
15/16	2.50
17	2.50
18/19	2.50
20 thru 29	@2.50
Spec.#1	2.50
[2nd Series], 1997
1 thru 6	@2.50

STRYKE
London Night Studios, 1995
0 I:Stryke.	5.00
1	4.00

STUMBO TINYTOWN
Harvey Publications, 1963–66
1	300.00
2	150.00
3	125.00
4	125.00
5	125.00
6 thru 13	@100.00

STUPID HEROES
Next, 1994
1 PeL(s),w/ 2 card-strip	2.75
2	2.75
3 F:Cinder.	2.75

All comics prices listed are for *Near Mint* condition.

COLOR PUB.

SUBSPECIES
Eternity, 1991
1 Movie Adaptation	3.00
2 Movie Adaptation	2.50
3 Movie Adaptation	2.50
4 Movie Adaptation	2.50

SULLENGRAY
Ape Entertainment, 2005
1 (of 4)	3.50
2 thru 4	@3.50

SUNDOWN
Arcana Studio, 2005
1 (of 3)	3.00
2 thru 3	@3.00

SUN GLASSES AFTER DARK
Verotik, 1995
1	3.00
2 and 3	@3.00
4 thru 6	@4.00
6 fan club cover	5.00
? prequel, San Diego Con ed.	3.00

SUN-RUNNERS
Pacific, 1984
1	2.50
2	2.50
3	2.50

Eclipse, 1984–86
4 thru 7	@2.50
Summer Special #1	2.50

SUNSET CARSON
AC Comics
1 Based on Cowboy Star	5.00

SUPERBABES: FEMFORCE
AC Comics
1 Various Artists	5.00

SUPER BAD JAMES DYNOMITE
IDW Publishing, 2005
1 (s) by Wayans brothers	4.00
2	4.00
3	4.00
4	4.00
5	4.00

SUPER CAR
Gold Key, 1962–63
1	450.00
2	200.00
3	200.00
4	225.00

SUPERCOPS
Now, 1990
1 thru 4	@2.50

SUPER CRAZY TNT BLAST
Speakeasy Comics, 2005
1	3.00
2	3.00
3 thru 5	@3.00

SUPER FXXXXXS
Top Shelf Productions, 2005
1 by James Kochalka	7.00
2	5.00

3	5.00
4	5.00

SUPER GOOF
Gold Key, 1965–82
1	75.00
2 thru 10	@50.00
11 thru 20	@35.00
21 thru 30	@30.00
31 thru 74	@25.00

SUPERHEROES
Dell, 1967
1	60.00
2 thru 4	@35.00

SUPER HEROES VERSUS SUPERVILLIANS
Archie Publications, 1966
1 A:Flyman,Black Hood,The Web, The Shield	100.00

SUPERHUMAN SAMURAI SYBER SQUAD
Hamilton Comics, 1995
0 Based on TV Show	3.00

SUPER MARIO BROS.
Valiant, 1991
1 thru 6	@2.50
Spec. #1	2.50

SUPERMARKET
IDW Publishing, 2006
1	4.00
2	4.00
3	4.00
4	4.00

SUPERNATURAL FREAK MACHINE
IDW Publishing, 2005
1 A Cal McDonald Mystery	4.00
1a signed	15.00
2 thru 5	@4.00

SUPERNATURAL: ORIGINS
Wildstorm/DC, May, 2007
1 PHe, from TV show	3.00
2	3.00
3 Harvelle's Roadhouse Bar	3.00
4 South Dakota priest	3.00
5 American Southwest	3.00
6 His greatest Test	3.00

SUPERNAUT
Anarchy, 1997
1 (of 3)	3.00
1 gold logo	6.00
2 by Rob Hand, Hand of Doom	3.00
2a gold logo	6.00

SUPER REAL
Super Real Graphics, 2005
1 by Jason Martin	3.25
2	3.25
2a variant (c)	3.25
3	3.50
3a variant (c)	3.50
4	3.50

SUPER TEEN*TOPIA
Alias Enterprises, 2006
0	2.00
1	3.50

2 thru 4	@3.50

SUPREME
Maximum Press, 1997
#1–#43 see Image
44 AMo, JoB, A:Glory	3.00
45 AMo, JoB, A:Glory	3.00
46 AMo,Suprema	3.00
47 AMo	3.00
48 AMo	2.50
49 AMo	2.50
50 double size	4.00
51	3.50
52A AMo, Book 1	3.50
52B AMo, Book 2, continuation	3.50
53 AMo,CSp,AG,V:Omniman	3.00
54 AMo,CSp,AG,Ballad of Judy Jordan	3.00
55 AMo,CSp,AG,Silence At Gettysburg	3.00
56 AMo,CSp,AG,Reflections,pt.1	3.00
57 AMo,CSp,AG,Reflections,pt.2	3.00
58 AMo,CSp,AG,A World of His Own	3.00
59 AMo,CSp,AG,Professor Night of the Prism World	3.00
60 AMo,CSp,AG,F:Radar in Puppy Love	3.00
61 AMo,CSp,AG,Meet Mr. Meteor	3.00

SUPREME: THE RETURN
Awesome Entertainment, 1999
1 AMo,CSp,AG	3.00
1a variant AxR cover	7.00
2 AMo,JSn,	3.00
3 thru 8	@3.00

SUPREMA/SUPREME SACRIFICE
Arcade Comics, 2006
Flipbook	4.00

Surf 'N' Wheels #1
© Charlton

SURF 'N' WHEELS
Charlton, 1969
1	45.00
2 thru 6	@30.00

SURGE
Eclipse, 1984
1 A:DNAgents	3.00
2 A:DNAgents	3.00
3 A:DNAgents	3.00
4 A:DNAgents	3.00

SURROGATES
Top Shelf Productions, 2005
1 (of 5) 3.00
2 . . . . 3.00
3 thru 5 . . . . @3.00

SURVIVORS
Spectrum, 1984
1 Mag. size, (B&W). 5.00
2 A Hunter's Rage. 3.50
3 The Old One 2.50
4 Face-Off. 2.50

SUSPIRA:
THE GREAT WORKING
Chaos! Comics, 1997
1 (of 4) PNa 3.00
2 PNa 3.00
3 PNa 3.00
4 PNa 3.00

SWORD OF DRACULA/
VAMPIRELLA:EXTENDED
AND DANGEROUS
Digital Webbing, 2007
1-shot. 4.00
1-shot variant (c) 4.00

SWORD OF RED SONJA,
THE: DOOM OF THE GODS
D.E. (Dynamite Ent.) 2007
1 . . . . 3.50

SWORD OF VALOR
A Plus Comics
1 . . . . 2.50
2 . . . . 2.50
3 . . . . 2.50
4 . . . . 2.50

SWORDS OF TEXAS
Eclipse, 1987
1 FH,New America 2.50
2 FH,V:Baja Badlands 2.50
3 FH,TY(c),V:Dogs of Danger. 2.50
4 FH,V:Samurai Master 2.50

SYMBIOTES, THE
Drive Comics, 2004
1 (of 8) 3.00
2 thru 5 . . . . @3.00

SYMBOLS OF JUSTICE
High Impact Studios, 1995
1 I:Granger,Justice,Rayven 3.00
2 V:Devil's Brigade 3.00

SYPHONS
Now, 1988
1 . . . . 2.50
2 thru 7 . . . . @2.50

SYPHONS: COUNTDOWN
Now, 1994
1 F:Brigade 3.00
2 Led By Cross. 3.00
3 Blown Cover 3.00
1995 Ann. Doomsday Device 3.00

SYPHONS: THE
STARGATE STRATAGEM
Now, 1994
1 . . . . 3.00
2 . . . . 3.00
3 . . . . 3.00

TAD WILLIAMS
BURNING MAN
Alias Enterprises, 2005
1 (of 3) 3.00
2 thru 3 . . . . @3.00

TAG
Boom! Studios, 2006
1 (of 3) KG 4.00
2 . . . . 4.00
3 . . . . 4.00

TAG: CURSED
Boom! Studios, 2007
1 . . . . 4.00
2 thru 5 . . . . @4.00
2a variant (c) 4.00

TALENT
Boom! Studios, 2006
1 . . . . 4.00
1a 2nd printing 4.00
2 . . . . 3.00
3 . . . . 4.00
4 . . . . 4.00

TALES CALCULATED
TO DRIVE YOU BATS
Archie Publications, 1961–62
1 . . . . 250.00
2 . . . . 150.00
3 . . . . 100.00
4 . . . . 100.00
5 . . . . 100.00
6 . . . . 100.00

TALES FROM
THE CRYPT
Gladstone, 1990–91
1 E.C.rep.AW/FF,GS. 5.00
2 rep.. . . . . 4.00
3 rep. 3.50
4 rep. 3.00
5 rep.TFTC #45 . . . . 3.00
6 rep.TFTC #42 . . . . 3.00

TALES FROM
THE CRYPT
Russ Cochran Publ, 1992
1 rep. TFTC #31,CSS#12. . . . . 3.00
2 rep. TFTC #34,CSS#15. . . . . 3.00
3 rep. TFTC, CSS. 3.00
4 rep. TFTC #43,CSS#18. . . . . 3.00
5 rep. TFTC,CSS#23 . . . . 3.00
[2nd Series]
1 rep.horror stories 3.00
2 inc.The Maestro's Hand. 3.00
3 thru 6 . . . . @3.00
7 thru 8 . . . . @3.00
Gemstone, 1996
16 thru 30 EC comics reprint . . . . @3.00

TALES OF ALVIN MAKER:
RED PROPHET
Dabel Brothers Prod., 2006
1 . . . . 3.00
1a 6.00
2 thru 6 . . . . @3.00
2a thru 6a variant (c) . . . . @6.00

TALES OF BLOODY MARY
Bloody Mary Comics, 2005
1 (of 8) 3.00
2 thru 4 . . . . @3.00
5 thru 8 . . . . @3.00

Tales of Evil #3
© Atlas Comics

TALES OF EVIL
Atlas Comics, 1975
1 Werewolf 25.00
2 Bog Beast 20.00
3 Man-Monster 20.00

TALES OF MIDNIGHT
Beyond Starlight, 2006
Vol. 2
1 . . . . 3.00
2 thru 3 . . . . @3.00

TALES OF TERROR
Eclipse, 1985–87
1 . . . . 3.00
2 Claustrophobia' 3.00
3 GM,Eyes in the Darkness 3.00
4 TT,TY,JBo(c),The Slasher 3.00
5 Back Forty,Shoe Button Eyes . . . 3.00
6 Good Neighbors. 3.00
7 SBi,JBo,SK(i),Video. 3.00
8 HB,Revenant,Food for
  Thought 3.00
9 . . . . 3.00
10 . . . . 3.00
11 TT,JBo(c),Black Cullen 3.00
12 JBo,FH,Last of the Vampires . . . 3.00
13 . . . . 3.00

TALES OF THE
CHAMPIONS
Heroic Publishing, 2005
1 . . . . 3.00
2 . . . . 3.00
3 F:Tigress 3.00
4 . . . . 3.25

TALES OF THE
GREEN BERET
Dell Publishing Co., 1967
1 SG 60.00
2 thru 5 . . . . @50.00

TALES OF THE
GREEN HORNET
Now, 1990
1 NA(c),O:Green Hornet Pt.1 . . . . . 3.00
2 O:Green Hornet Pt.2 . . . . 2.50
3 Gun Metal Green 2.50
4 Targets. 2.50

TALES OF THE MYSTERIOUS TRAVELER
Charlton Comics, 1956

1 DG	700.00
2 SD	600.00
3 SD,SD(c)	500.00
4 SD,SD(c)	600.00
5 SD,SD(c)	600.00
6 SD,SD(c)	600.00
7 SD	550.00
8 SD	550.00
9 SD	550.00
10 SD,SD(c)	575.00
11 SD,SD(c)	575.00
12	300.00
13	325.00
14 (1985)	25.00
15 (1985)	20.00

TALES OF THE REALM
Crossgen Comics, 2003

1 (of 6)	3.00
2	3.00

TALES OF THE SUN RUNNERS
Sirius Comics, 1986

1	2.50
2 and 3	@2.50

TALESPIN
Walt Disney, 1991
(Reg.-Series)

1 Sky-Raker, Pt.1	2.50
2 Sky-Raker, Pt.2	2.50
3 Idiots Abroad	2.50
4 Contractual Desperation	2.50
5 The Oldman & the Sea Duck	2.50
6 F'reeze a Jolly Good Fellow	2.50

TALESPIN
Walt Disney, 1991
[Mini-Series]

1 Take-off Pt.1	3.00
2 Take-off Pt 2	3.00
3 Take-off Pt 3,Khan Job	3.00
4 Take-off pt 4	3.00

TALEWEAVER
WildStorm/DC, 2001

1 (of 6) 40-pg.	3.50
2	3.00
2a variant (c).	3.00
3 thru 6	@3.00

TALISMEN
Atlantis Studios, 2005

1 (of 4)	3.00
2 thru 4	@3.00

TANK GIRL: THE GIFTING
IDW Publishing, 2007

1	4.00
2 thru 4	@4.00
1a thru 4a variant (c)	4.00

TAOLAND
Severe Reality Productions

4 1st full color issue	6.00
5 48pg.	6.00

TAOLAND ADVENTURES
Antarctic Press, 1999

1 by Jeff Amano	3.00
2	3.00

TARGET AIRBOY
Eclipse, 1988

1 SK,A:Clint	2.50

TARGITT
Atlas, 1975

1 thru 3	@20.00

TAROT WITCH OF THE BLACK ROSE
Broadsword Comics, 2000

1 JBa(c)	3.00
2	3.00
3	3.00
4	3.00
5 JBa	3.00
6 Goulish Intentions	3.00
7 Return of the Dark Witch,pt.1	3.00
8 Return of the Dark Witch,pt.2	3.00
9 Return of the Dark Witch,pt.3	3.00
2a thru 16a signed	@10.00
1b, 4b, 6b, 8b deluxe	@20.00
7b double-deluxe edition.	25.00
9b thru 23b deluxe	@20.00
10 Quest for the Black Rose Sword	3.00
11 Black Rose Sword,pt.2	3.00
12	3.00
13	3.00
13b previews exlusive (c)	15.00
14	3.00
15	3.00
16	3.00
17 Cold Spell	3.00
18 Diary of a Witch	3.00
19 Mists of Darkness, pt.1	3.00
19a photo (c)	10.00
20 Mists of Darkness, pt.2	3.00
21 Mists of Darkness, pt.3	3.00
22 Mists of Darkness, pt.4	3.00
23 Ghouls Gone Wild	3.00
24 Ghouls Gone Wild,pt.2	3.00
25 thru 28	@3.00
18a thru 23a deluxe	@20.00
24a thru 28a deluxe	@20.00
29	3.00
19b exclusive previews (c)	10.00
29a deluxe	20.00
30 thru 34	@3.00
31b variant (c)	3.00
31d variant (c)	10.00
32b signed	10.00
35 thru 47	@3.00
30b signed	10.00
30a thru 34a deluxe	@20.00
35a thru 40a Deluxe	@20.00

Tarzan, Lord of the Jungle #1
© Gold Key

37b photo (c)	15.00
31c with photo	15.00

TARZAN, LORD OF THE JUNGLE
Gold Key, 1965

1	150.00

TARZAN OF THE APES
Gold Key, 1962–72
prev. Dell (see Golden Age)

132	100.00
133	80.00
134	80.00
135	90.00
136	80.00
137	80.00
138	80.00
139 I:Korak.	90.00
140 thru 154	@80.00
155 O:Tarzan	100.00
156 thru 161	@60.00
162 TV photo (c)	80.00
163	60.00
164	60.00
165 TV photo (c)	80.00
166	60.00
167	60.00
168 TV photo (c)	80.00
169 A:Leopard Girl	60.00
170	60.00
171 TV photo (c)	100.00
172 thru 177	@50.00
178 O:Tarzan, rep. #155	50.00
179 thru 191	@50.00
192 Tarzan and the Foreign Legion adaptation	50.00
193 thru 199	@50.00
200	60.00
201 thru 205	@50.00
206 last issue.	50.00
Continued by DC; see also Marvel	

TARZAN: THE BECKONING
Malibu, 1992

1 TY,I:The Spider Man	2.75
2 TY,Going back to Africa	2.50
3 thru 6	2.50

TARZAN THE WARRIOR
Malibu, 1992

1 SBs(c),O:Tarzan	3.50
2 & 3	@2.75
4 Wom'cha's Ship	2.75
5	2.75

TARZAN: LOVE, LIES, AND THE LOST CITY
Malibu, 1992

1 MWg&WS(s),Short Stories	4.00
2 The lost city of Opar	2.50
3 Final issue	2.50

TASMANIAN DEVIL & HIS TASTY FRIENDS
Gold Key, 1962

1	300.00

TASTEE-FREEZ COMICS
Harvey Comics, 1957

1 Little Dot.	400.00
2 Rags Rabbit.	75.00
3 Casper.	100.00
4 Sad Sack.	75.00
5 Mazie.	75.00
6 Dick Tracy	100.00

COLOR PUB.

TEAM ANARCHY
Anarchy, 1993
1 I:Team Anarchy 2.75
2 thru 3 . . . . 2.75
4 PuD,MaS,I:Primal 2.75

Team Yankee #5
© First

TEAM YANKEE
First, 1989
1 Harold Coyle novel adapt. 2.50
2 thru 6 . . . . @2.50

TEAM ZERO
Wildstorm/DC, Dec., 2006
1 CDi(s),DoM,World War II 3.00
2 Deathblow gathers his team 3.00
3 CDi(s),DoM,Peenemunde 3.00
4 CDi(s),DoM,V: Red Army 3.00
5 CDi(s),DoM,V: Red Army 3.00
6 CDi(s),DoM, conclusion 3.00

TEEN-AGE CONFIDENTIAL CONFESSIONS
Charlton Comics, 1960–64
1 . . . . 75.00
2 thru 5 . . . . @50.00
6 thru 10 . . . . @40.00
11 thru 22 . . . . @30.00

TEENAGE HOTRODDERS
Charlton Comics, April, 1963
1 . . . . 100.00
2 thru 5 . . . . @60.00
6 thru 10 . . . . @50.00
11 thru 23 . . . . @50.00
24 . . . . 50.00
Becomes:
TOP ELIMINATOR
25 thru 29 . . . . @50.00
Becomes:
DRAG 'N' WHEELS
30 . . . . 100.00
31 thru 39 . . . . 60.00
40 thru 50 Scot Jackson 50.00
51 thru 59 May, 1973 . . . . 40.00

TEENAGE MUTANT NINJA TURTLES
First
1 . . . . 6.00
2 . . . . 4.50

TEENAGE MUTANT NINJA TURTLES
Archie, 1988
(From T.V. Series)
1 O:TMNT,April O'Neil,Shredder
Krang 6.00
2 V:Shredder,O:Bebop &
Rocksteady 4.00
3 V:Shredder & Krang 3.00

TEENAGE MUTANT NINJA TURTLES
Mirage, 1993
1 A:Casey Jones 3.00
2 JmL(a&s) 3.00
3 thru 13 . . . . @2.75

TEENAGE MUTANT NINJA TURTLES ADVENTURES
Archie, 1988 [2nd Series]
1 Shredder,Bebop,Rocksteady
return to earth 5.00
2 I:Baxter Stockman 3.00
3 Three Fragments #1 . . . . 3.00
4 thru 9 . . . . @2.50
10 thru 25 . . . . @2.50
26 thru 40 . . . . @2.50
41 thru 70 . . . . @2.50
1990 Movie adapt(direct) 5.50
1990 Movie adapt(newsstand) 2.50
1991 TMNT meet Archie 2.50
1991 Movie Adapt II 2.50
Spec.#2 Ghost of 13 Mile Island . . 2.50
Spec.#3 Night of the Monsterex . . 2.50
TMNT Mutant Universe Sourcebook 2.00

TEENAGE MUTANT NINJA TURTLES ANIMATED
Dreamwave, 2003
1 . . . . 3.00
2 thru 9 . . . . @3.00

TEENAGE MUTANT NINJA TURTLES/ FLAMING CARROT
Mirage/Dark Horse, 1993
1 JmL 3.00
2 JmL 3.00
3 JmL 3.00
4 JmL 3.00

TMNT PRESENTS:
Archie, 1993
...APRIL O'NEIL
1 A:Chien Khan,Vid Vicious 2.50
2 V:White Ninja,A:V.Vicious 2.50
3 V:Vhien Khan,concl. 2.50
Spec. April O'Neil, May East Saga . 2.50
...DONATELLO AND LEATHERHEAD
1 . . . . 2.50
2 . . . . 2.50
...MERDUDE VS. RAY FILLET
1 . . . . 2.50
2 . . . . 2.50
3 . . . . 2.50

TMNT: THE MALTESE TURTLE
Mirage
Spec. F:Raphael Detective 3.00

TMNT: YEAR OF THE TURTLE
Archie Comics, 1995
1 All New Era 2.50

[JACK KIRBY'S] TEENAGENTS
[Mini-Series] Topps, 1993
1 WS,AH,w/3 cards. 3.00
2 NV,w/3 cards 3.00
3 NV,w/3 cards 3.00
4 NV,w/3 leftover? cards. 3.00

TEEN CONFESSIONS
Charlton Comics, 1959–76
1 . . . . 150.00
2 . . . . 125.00
3 . . . . 100.00
4 . . . . 100.00
5 . . . . 100.00
6 . . . . 100.00
7 . . . . 100.00
8 . . . . 100.00
9 . . . . 100.00
10 thru 30 . . . . @100.00
31 Beatles cover 225.00
32 . . . . 25.00
33 . . . . 25.00
34 . . . . 25.00
35 . . . . 25.00
36 . . . . 25.00
37 Beatles cover,Fan Club story . 250.00
38 thru 97 . . . . @20.00

TEEN SECRET DIARY
Charlton Comics, 1959–61
1 . . . . 100.00
2 . . . . 75.00
3 . . . . 75.00
4 . . . . 75.00
5 . . . . 75.00
6 thru 11 . . . . @75.00

TEKKEN 2
Knightstone, 1997
1 (of 4) Tekken Saga, pt.3 . . . . 3.00
2 . . . . 3.00
2a photo cover 3.00
3 . . . . 3.00
3a photo cover 3.00

TEKKEN SAGA
Knightstone, 1997
1 . . . . 4.00
2 . . . . 3.00
3 . . . . 3.00
4 Paul vs. Kazuya 3.00
5 Paul a prisoner 3.00
Nightstone Unlimited & Tekken ?. . . 3.00

TEMPEST
Alias Enterprises, 2006
1-shot 3.50

TEMPLAR CHRONICLES, THE: THE HERETIC
Markosia, 2007
1 . . . . 3.50
2 . . . . 3.50
3 . . . . 3.50
4 . . . . 3.50
2a thru 4a sketch (c) . . . . @6.00

10
Boom! Studios 2005
1-shot 7.00

COLOR PUB.

TENSE SUSPENSE
Fago Publications, 1958–59
1	150.00
2	100.00

10TH MUSE
Avatar/Tidal Wave Studios, 2002
1A MWn,RCz, Andy Park (c)	3.50
1B CBa(c)	3.50
1C RCz(c)	3.50
1D Mark Brooks (c)	3.50
1E Valdez (c)	3.50
2 RCz(c)	3.50
2a Caldwell (c)	3.50
2b Rousseau (c)	3.50
2 RCz(c)	3.50
2a Green (c)	3.50
2b Grant (c)	3.50

Angel Gate, 2003
1-shot Book of Lights	3.00

Alias Enterprises, 2005
Volume 2
1	3.00
1a foil (c)	5.00
1b signed, foil (c)	25.00
2 thru 9	@3.00
2a thru 9a variant (c)s	@3.00
2b foil, photo (c)	5.00
5a variant (c) signed	15.00
10	3.50
10a variant (c)	3.50
11 God War x-over	3.50
12 God War x-over, pt.5	3.50
13 Who killed Wonder Boy?	3.50
14	3.50
15 thru 17	@3.50

Bluewater Productions, 2007
1-shot giant	6.00

10th MUSE/EZRA
Arcana Studios, 2006
1	4.00
1a variant signed photo (c)	15.00

Terminator #17
© Now

TERMINATOR, THE
Now, 1988–89
1	9.00
2	5.00
3	4.00
4 thru 11	@3.50
12 I:JohnConnor($1.75,cov,dbl.sz)	3.50
13 thru 17	@3.50
Spec. #1	3.50

TERMINATOR: ALL MY FUTURES PAST
Now, 1990
1 Painted Art	3.00
2 Painted Art	3.00

TERMINATOR: THE BURNING EARTH
Now, 1990
1	12.00
2	10.00
3	9.00
4	9.00
5	9.00

TERMINATOR 2: CYBERNETIC DAWN
Malibu, 1995–96
1 thru 4	@2.50
0 flip-book/T2 Nuclear Twilight	2.50

TERMINATOR 2: INFINITY
D.E. (Dynamite Ent.) 2007
1	3.50
1a variant (c)s	@3.50
2 thru 5	@3.50

TERMINATOR 2: NUCLEAR TWILIGHT
Malibu, 1995–96
1 thru 4	@2.50
0 flip-book, see above	

TERMINATOR 3
Beckett Entertainment, 2003
1 Before the Rise	6.00
2 Before the Rise	6.00
3 Eyes of the Rise	6.00
4 Eyes of the Rise	6.00
5 Fragmented	6.00
6 Fragmented	6.00

TERRAFORMERS
Wonder Comics, 1987
1	3.00
2	3.00
3	3.00
4	3.00

TERRANAUTS
Fantasy General, 1986
1	3.00
2	3.00

TERRA OBSCURA
Wildstorm/DC June, 2003
America's Best Comics
1 (of 6) AMo(s)	3.00
2 AMo(s),F:Grant Halford	3.00
3 thru 5 AMo(s)	@3.00
6 AMo(s),concl.,40-pg.	4.00

Vol. 2, 2004
1 AMo(s)	3.00
2 AMo(s)	3.00
3	3.00
4 AMo(s),KIS	3.00
5 AMo(s),KIS	3.00
6 AMo(s),KIS, Showdown in space	3.00

TERRITORY 51
Lawdog Comics, 2004
1	3.00
1 convention edition, signed	11.00
2	4.00

TEXAS CHAINSAW MASSACRE
Avatar Press, 2005
Spec. #1	4.00
Spec. #1 variant (c)s	4.00
Spec. #1 glow (c)	12.00
Spec. #1 Bloodbath (c)	6.00
Spec. #1 Blood Red Con (c)	5.00
Spec. #1 painted (c)	6.00
Spec. #1 Lurking (c)	6.00
Spec. #1 Prism foil (c)	11.00
Spec. Fearbook #1	4.00
Spec. Fearbook #1 variant (c)s	@4.00
Spec. Fearbook #1 leather (c)	20.00

TEXAS CHAINSAW MASSACRE: THE GRIND
Avatar Press, 2005
1	4.00
1a Wraparound (c)	4.00
1b Variant(c)s	@4.00
1c leather (c)	15.00
1d Red foil convention (c)	5.00
2	4.00
2a Wraparound (c)	4.00
2b Variant(c)s	@4.00
2c Die-cut (c)	9.00
3a Wraparound (c)	4.00
3b variant (c)s	4.00
3c Die-cut (c)	10.00

TEXAS CHAINSAW MASSACRE
Wildstorm/DC, Nov., 2006
1 DAn,ALa	3.00
1a varaint (c)	3.00
2 DAn,ALa	3.00
3 DAn,ALa	3.00
4 DAn,ALa	3.00
5 DAn,ALa	3.00
6 DAn,ALa, Who lives?	3.00
Spec. Cut	3.00

TEXAS CHAINSAW MASSACRE: ABOUT A BOY
Wildstorm/DC, July, 2007
1 DAn,ALa,O:Leatherface	3.00

TEXAS CHAINSAW MASSACRE: BY HIMSELF
Wildstorm/DC, Aug., 2007
1 DAn,ALa,Hewitt Clan	3.00

TEXAS RANGERS IN ACTION
Charlton Comics, 1956–70
5	150.00
6 and 7	@100.00
8 SD	200.00
9 and 10	@100.00
11 AW	175.00
12	100.00
13 AW	150.00
14 thru 20	@100.00
21 thru 30	@60.00
31 thru 59	@50.00
60 B:Riley's Rangers	60.00
61 thru 79	@30.00

THAT WILKIN BOY
Archie Publications, 1969
1	70.00
2 thru 10	@50.00

All comics prices listed are for *Near Mint* condition.

11 thru 20	@30.00
21 thru 26 E:Giant size	@25.00
27 thru 52	@25.00

THESPIAN
Dark Moon, 1995

1 I:Thespian	2.50
2 V:Lemming	2.50
3 Lord of Manhattan	2.50

THIRD WORLD WAR
Fleetway, 1990–91

1 HamburgerLady	2.50
2	2.50
3 The Killing Yields	2.50
4 thru 6	@2.50

13: ASSASSIN
TSR, 1990–91

1 thru 4 from game	@3.00
5 thru 8 The Search for Maggie Darr	@3.00

30 DAYS OF NIGHT
IDW Publishing, 2002

1 by S.Niles & B.Templesmith	60.00
1a 2nd printing	7.00
2	40.00
3	16.00
Spec. Bloodsucker Tales (2004)	4.00
Annual 2004	5.00
Annual 2005	7.50

30 DAYS OF NIGHT: BEYOND BARROW
IDW Publishing, 2007

1	4.00
2	4.00

30 DAYS OF NIGHT: BLOODSUCKER TALES
IDW Publishing, 2004

1	4.00
2 thru 10	@4.00

30 DAYS OF NIGHT: DEAD SPACE
IDW Publishing 2005

1	4.00
2	4.00
3	4.00

30 DAYS OF NIGHT: EBEN AND STELLA
IDW Publishing, 2007

1	4.00
2 thru 4	@4.00

30 DAYS OF NIGHT: RED SNOW
IDW Publishing

1	4.00
2 thur 3	4.00

30 DAYS OF NIGHT: RETURN TO BARROW
IDW Publishing, 2004

1	4.00
2 thru 6	@4.00

30 DAYS OF NIGHT: SPREADING THE DISEASE
IDW Publishing, 2006

1	4.00

2 thru 5	@4.00
1a thru 5a variant (c)s	@4.00

THOSE ANNOYING POST BROTHERS
Vortex, 1985

1	3.00
2 thru 5	@2.50
6 thru 18	@2.50
See also B&W listings	

3-D ZONE PRESENTS
Renegade, 1987–89

1 Dr. Jekyll and Mr. Hyde	2.50
2 Weird Tales of Basil Wolverton	2.50
3 thru 10	@2.50
11 3-D Danse Macabre	2.50
12 3-D Presidents	2.50
13 Flash Gordon	2.50
14 Tyranostar	2.50
15 3-Dementia	2.50
16 Space Vixens	2.50
17 thru 20	2.50

3 LITTLE KITTENS
Broadsword Comics, 2002

1 JBa, Purrr-fect weapons	3.00
2 Puss N Bullets	3.00
3 Purrr-Fect Weapons	3.00
1a thru 3a deluxe	@15.00
1b thru 3b signed	@9.00

THREE STOOGES
Dell Publishing Co., 1959

6 Ph(c),B:Prof. Putter	300.00
7 Ph(c)	300.00
8 Ph(c)	300.00
9 Ph(c)	300.00

Gold Key, 1962

10 Ph(c)	250.00
11 Ph(c)	250.00
12 Ph(c)	250.00
13 Ph(c)	250.00
14 Ph(c)	200.00
15 Ph(c) Go Around the World	250.00
16 Ph(c),E:Prof. Putter	200.00
17 Ph(c),B:Little Monsters	200.00
18 Ph(c)	200.00
19 Ph(c)	200.00
20 Ph(c)	200.00
21 Ph(c)	200.00
22 Ph(c),Movie Scenes	200.00
23 thru 30 Ph(c)	@175.00
31 thru 50 Ph(c)	@150.00

Three Stooges #23
© Gold Key

51	150.00
52 thru 55 Ph(c)	@150.00

THREE STOOGES 3-D
Eclipse, 1991

1 thru 3 reprints from 1953	@2.50
4 reprints from 1953	3.50

THRESHOLD
Narwain Publishing, 2006

1 (of 5)	4.00

THRILL-O-RAMA
Harvey Publications, 1965–66

1 A:Man in Black(Fate),DW,AW	100.00
2 AW,A:Pirana,I:Clawfang, The Barbarian	75.00
3 A:Pirana, Fate	60.00

THRUD THE BARBARIAN
Thrud Comics, 2006

1	3.00
2 Phalanx of frosty foes	4.00
3 thru 5	@4.00

THUNDER AGENTS
Tower, 1965–69

1 WW,RC,GK,MSy,GT,I:Thunder Agents,IronMaiden,Warlord	350.00
2 WW,MSy,D:Egghead	200.00
3 WW,DA,MSy,V:Warlords	150.00
4 WW,MSy,RC,I:Lightning	150.00
5 WW,RC,GK,MSy	150.00
6 WW,SD,MSy,I:Warp Wizard	125.00
7 WW,MSy,SD,D:Menthor	125.00
8 WW,MSy,GT,DA,I:Raven	125.00
9 OW,WW,MSy,A:Andor	125.00
10 WW,MSy,OW,A:Andor	125.00
11 WW,DA,MSy	100.00
12 SD,WW,MSy	100.00
13 WW,OW,A:Undersea Agent	100.00
14 SD,WW,GK,N:Raven,A:Andor	100.00
15 WW,OW,GT,A:Andor	90.00
16 SD,GK,A:Andor	90.00
17 WW,OW,GT	90.00
18 SD,OW,RC	75.00
19 GT,I:Ghost	75.00
20 WW,RC,MSy,all reprints	75.00

T.H.U.N.D.E.R. AGENTS
J.C. Productions, 1983

1 MA,Centerfold	5.00
2 I:Vulcan	5.00

T.H.U.N.D.E.R. AGENTS
Maximum, 1995

1	3.00
2	3.00

THUNDERBIRD
Atlantis Studios, 2005

1	3.00
2	3.00

THUNDERBOLT
Charlton Comics, 1966–67

1 PAM,O:Thuderbolt	75.00
Prev: Son of Vulcan	
51 PAM,V:Evila	50.00
52 PAM,V:Gore the Monster	35.00
53 PAM,V:The Tong	35.00
54 PAM,I:Sentinels	35.00
55 PAM,V:Sentinels	35.00
56 PAM,A:Sentinels	35.00
57 A:Sentinels	35.00
58 PAM,A:Sentinels	35.00
59 PAM,A:Sentinels	35.00
60 PAM,JAp,I:Prankster	40.00

COLOR PUB.

THUNDERBOLT JAXON
Wildstorm/DC, Feb., 2006
1 (of 5) DGb,JHi 3.00
2 thru 5 DGb,JHi . . . . @3.00

THUNDERCATS
WildStorm/DC, 2002
0 JSC, preview issue 5.00
1a (of 5) King Lion-O 5.00
1b variant AAd (c) 3.50
2a V:Mumm-ra 3.00
2b variant JLe(c) 3.00
3 F:Lion-O 3.00
3a variant JMd(c) 3.00
4 F:New Thundera 3.00
5 concl. 3.00
GN Thundercats/Battle
  of the Planets 5.00
Sourcebook 3.00

THUNDERCATS: DOGS OF WAR
Wildstorm/DC June, 2003
1 (of 5) 10 years in future 3.00
2 New Thundera 3.00
3 BBh,AV 3.00
4 BBh,AV 3.00
5 BBh,AV 3.00

THUNDERCATS: ENEMY'S PRIDE
Wildstorm/DC June, 2004
1 Cat vs. Cat 3.00
2 . . . . 3.00
3 . . . . 3.00
4 . . . . 3.00
5 . . . . 3.00

THUNDERCATS: HAMMERHAND'S REVENGE
Wildstorm/DC, 2003
1 (of 5) 3.00
2 F:Lion-O 3.00
3 . . . . 3.00
4 (two covers) 3.00
5 (two covers) 3.00
Spec. Superman/Thundercats 6.00

THUNDERCATS: ORIGINS
Wildstorm/DC, 2003
Spec. Heroes & Villains,pt.1 . . . . 3.50
Spec. Villains & Heroes,pt.1 . . . . 3.50

THUNDERCATS: THE RETURN
Wildstorm/DC, 2003
1 (of 5) EBe,F:Lion-O 3.00
2 EBe,V:Mumm-Ra 3.00
3 EBe 3.00
4 EBe,Wilykat 3.00
5 EBe, concl. 3.00

TICK, THE
New England Comics, 2001
1 all new, all color 4.00
1a variant (c). 4.00
2 thru 5 . . . . @4.00
6 return of Proto-Tick 4.00
Spec. Big Halloween 2000 . . . . . . 3.50
Spec. Big Halloween 2001 . . . . . . 4.00
Spec. Introducing the Tick (2002) . . 4.00
Spec. Circus Maximus Update 4.00
Spec. Comic Con Extravaganza . . . 4.00
Spec. 20th Anniv. Special 6.00

TICK & ARTIE
New England Comics, 2002
1 . . . . 3.50
2 BEd(c) 3.50

TICK, THE: BIG XMAS TRILOGY
New England Comics, 2002
1 . . . . 4.00
2 . . . . 4.00
3 . . . . 4.00

TICK, THE: DAYS OF DRAMA
New England Comics, 2005
1 . . . . 5.00
2 . . . . 4.00
3 thru 6 . . . . @4.00

TICK'S INCREDIBLE INTERNET COMIC, THE
New England Comics, 2001
1 . . . . 4.00

TIGER GIRL
Gold Key, 1968
1 . . . . 50.00

TIGER-MAN
Atlas, 1975
1 thru 3 . . . . @15.00

TIGERS OF TERRA
Antarctic Press, 2000
Vol. 3
1 (of 4) War Against the Sun 3.00
2 Night of the Amazons 3.00
3 . . . . 3.00
4 Planet of War. 3.00
Spec. 4.00

TIME TUNNEL, THE
Gold Key, 1967
1 from TV show 150.00
2 . . . . 100.00

TIME TWISTERS
Quality, 1987–89
1 AMo(s),AD,DGb 2.50
2 AMo(s),DGb,Wheels of Fury 2.50
3 AMo(s),The Wages of Sin 2.50
4 AMo(s),Bad Timing 2.50
5 PrM(s),The Collector 2.50
6 AMo(s),AIG 2.50
7 AMo(s),Twist Ending 2.50
8 thru 21 . . . . @2.50

TIMEWALKER
Valiant, 1994
0 BH,DP,O:3 Immortals 3.00
1 DP, BH 2.50
2 thru 15 . . . . @2.50
Yearbook F:Harada 3.00

TIPPY'S FRIENDS GO-GO & ANIMAL
Tower Comics, 1966–69
1 . . . . 150.00
2 . . . . 75.00
3 . . . . 75.00
4 . . . . 75.00
5 thru 7 . . . . @75.00
8 Beatles on cover & back 150.00
9 thru 15 . . . . @75.00

TIPPY TEEN
Tower Comics, 1965–70
1 . . . . 200.00
2 thru 27 . . . . @100.00

TOHUBOHU
New Breed Comics, 1999
1 . . . . 3.25
2 thru 5 . . . . @3.00
6 A Serpent in the Garden 3.25

TOKA
Dell, 1964
1 Jungle King 70.00
2 thru 10 . . . . @30.00

TOKYO STORM WARNING
Wildstorm/DC June, 2003
1 (of 3) giant robots 3.00
2 WEI 3.00
3 WEI 3.00

Tom and Jerry, The Mouse From T.R.A.P. #1 © Gold Key

TOM AND JERRY
Gold Key, 1962–75
213 thru 214 giants . . . . @125.00
215 thru 240 . . . . @40.00
241 thru 291 . . . . @25.00
Tom & Jerry Summer Fun (1967) . 75.00
Giant #1 Tom & Jerry, the Mouse
  from T.R.A.P. 75.00
Gold Key, 1977–80
292 thru 300 . . . . @20.00
301 thru 327 . . . . @15.00
Whitman, 1980
328 thru 341 scarce . . . . @45.00
342 thru 344 . . . . @25.00

TOM & JERRY
Harvey, 1991–94
1 . . . . 2.50
2 thru 18 . . . . @2.00

TOM MIX WESTERN
AC Comics, 1988
1 . . . . 3.00

TOMMI-GUNN
London Night, 1997
0 . . . . 3.00
1 signed 12.00
1a, chromium, elite edition 15.00
2 . . . . 3.00
3 . . . . 3.00

TOMMI-GUNN: KILLER'S LUST
London Night, 1997
```
1 . . . . . . . . . . . . . . . . . . . . . . . 3.00
1 Japanese Chromium edition . . . 10.00
2 . . . . . . . . . . . . . . . . . . . . . . . 3.00
```

TOMOE
Crusade Entertainment, 1996
```
0 BiT . . . . . . . . . . . . . . . . . . . . 3.00
1 BiT,Fan Appreciation Edition . . . . 3.00
2 . . . . . . . . . . . . . . . . . . . . . . . 3.00
```

TOMOE/WITCHBLADE: FIRE SERMON
Crusade Entertainment, 1996
```
1 . . . . . . . . . . . . . . . . . . . . . . . 5.00
1a Gold foil . . . . . . . . . . . . . . . . 9.00
```

TOMOE: UNFORGETTABLE FIRE
Crusade Entertainment, 1997
```
1 (of 3) . . . . . . . . . . . . . . . . . . . 3.00
```

TOMORROW STORIES
WildStorm/DC, 1999
America's Best Comics
```
1 AMo,AxR(c) anthology . . . . . . . . 4.00
1a AxR(c),variant cover . . . . . . . . 3.50
2 AMo(s),KN,RV,JBa . . . . . . . . . 3.00
3 AMo(s),KN,RV,JBa . . . . . . . . . 3.00
4 AMo(s),KN,RV,JBa . . . . . . . . . 3.00
5 AMo(s),KN,RV,JBa . . . . . . . . . 3.00
6 AMo(s),RV,JBa . . . . . . . . . . . . 3.00
7 AMo(s),RV,JBa . . . . . . . . . . . . 3.00
8 AMo(s),RV,JBa . . . . . . . . . . . . 3.00
9 AMo(s),RV,JBa . . . . . . . . . . . . 3.00
10 AMo(s),RV,JBa,Jack B. Quick. . 3.00
11 AMo(s),RV,JBa,AAd,F:Cobweb. . 3.00
12 AMo(s),RV,JBa, x-over . . . . . . . 3.00
Spec. #1 AMo(s) 64-page . . . . . . . 7.00
Spec. #2 AMo(s) . . . . . . . . . . . . . 7.00
```

TOM STRONG
WildStorm/DC, 1999
America's Best Comics
```
1 AMo(s),CSp,40-pg. . . . . . . . . . . 4.00
2 AMo(s),CSp,Millennium City . . . . 3.00
3 AMo(s),CSp,Millennium City . . . . 3.00
4 AMo,CSp,Aztec,Berlin in WW2 . . 3.00
5 AMo,JOy,CSp,Memories of
  Pangea . . . . . . . . . . . . . . . . . . 3.00
6 AMo,CSp,DGb, Dead
  Man's Hand . . . . . . . . . . . . . . . 3.00
7 AMo,CSp,GFr . . . . . . . . . . . . . 3.00
8 AMo,CSp,Lost Mesa . . . . . . . . . 3.00
9 AMo,CSp, . . . . . . . . . . . . . . . . 3.00
10 AMo,CSp,F:Warren Strong . . . . 3.00
11 AMo,CSp,F:Tom Strange . . . . . 3.00
12 AMo,CSp,F:Tom Strange,pt.2 . . 3.00
13 AMo,CSp,Warren Strong . . . . . 3.00
14 AMo,CSp,Space Family Strong. . 3.00
15 AMo,CSp,Val Var Garm . . . . . . 3.00
16 AMo(s),CSp,KIS,Modular Man . . 3.00
17 AMo(s),CSp,KIS,Weird Rider . . 3.00
18 AMo(s),CSp,KIS,Weird Rider . . . 3.00
19 AMo(s),CSp,KIS . . . . . . . . . . . 3.00
20 AMo(s),CSp,KIS,JOy,pt.1 . . . . . 3.00
21 AMo(s),CSp,KIS,JOy,pt.2 . . . . . 3.00
22 AMo(s),CSp,KIS,JOy,pt.3 . . . . . 3.00
23 CSp,KIS,rescue mission . . . . . . 3.00
24 CSp,KIS . . . . . . . . . . . . . . . . 3.00
25 JPL,F:Strongmen of America . . . 3.00
26 MSh(s),PFe . . . . . . . . . . . . . . 3.00
27 SwM . . . . . . . . . . . . . . . . . . . 3.00
28 . . . . . . . . . . . . . . . . . . . . . . 3.00
29 DFg . . . . . . . . . . . . . . . . . . . 3.00
30 DFg,Terrible Life of Tom Strong . 3.00
```

Tom Strong #11
© *WildStorm/ABC*

```
31 JOy, Michael Moorcock(s) . . . . . 3.00
32 JOy, Michael Moorcock(s) . . . . . 3.00
33 JOy, F:Pneuman . . . . . . . . . . . 3.00
34 JP,PG, central China . . . . . . . . . 3.00
35 CSp,KIS, Snow Queen sequel . . 3.00
36 AMo(s),CSp,KIS,End of World . . 3.00
```

TOM STRONG'S TERRIFIC TALES
WildStorm/DC, 2001
America's Best Comics
```
1 AMo,AAd . . . . . . . . . . . . . . . . 3.50
2 AMo,AAd . . . . . . . . . . . . . . . . 3.00
3 AMo,AAd,JOy . . . . . . . . . . . . . 3.00
4 AMo(s),AAd,Jonni Future . . . . . . 3.00
5 AMo(s),SA,AAd(c) . . . . . . . . . . 3.00
6 AMo(s),JOy,AAd . . . . . . . . . . . 3.00
7 AMo(s),AAd . . . . . . . . . . . . . . 3.00
8 AMo(s),AAd, young Tom . . . . . . 3.00
9 AMo(s),three stories . . . . . . . . . 3.00
10 AMo(s),three stories . . . . . . . . 3.00
11 AMo(s), . . . . . . . . . . . . . . . . . 3.00
12 AMo(s),AAd, final issue . . . . . . 3.00
```

TOM SULLIVAN'S BOOKS OF THE DEAD
Dead Dog Comics, 2005
```
1 Devilhead . . . . . . . . . . . . . . . . 5.00
1a variant (c) . . . . . . . . . . . . . . . 5.00
2 . . . . . . . . . . . . . . . . . . . . . . . 5.00
3 . . . . . . . . . . . . . . . . . . . . . . . 5.00
4 . . . . . . . . . . . . . . . . . . . . . . . 5.00
```

TOM TERRIFIC!
Pines Comics
Summer, 1957
```
1 . . . . . . . . . . . . . . . . . . . . . 300.00
2 . . . . . . . . . . . . . . . . . . . . . 250.00
3 thru 5 . . . . . . . . . . . . . . . . @250.00
6 Fall, 1958 . . . . . . . . . . . . . . 250.00
```

TONY LOCO
Illusive Arts, 2006
```
1 . . . . . . . . . . . . . . . . . . . . . . . 3.50
2 thru 3 . . . . . . . . . . . . . . . . . @3.50
```

TOP CAT
Dell, 1961
```
1 . . . . . . . . . . . . . . . . . . . . . 275.00
2 thru 3 . . . . . . . . . . . . . . . . @135.00
```
Gold Key, 1962
```
4 . . . . . . . . . . . . . . . . . . . . . 125.00
5 . . . . . . . . . . . . . . . . . . . . . 125.00
```

```
6 thru 10 . . . . . . . . . . . . . . . @100.00
11 thru 20 . . . . . . . . . . . . . . . @75.00
21 thru 31 . . . . . . . . . . . . . . . @50.00
```

TOP CAT
Charlton Comics, 1970–73
```
1 . . . . . . . . . . . . . . . . . . . . . 125.00
2 thru 10 . . . . . . . . . . . . . . . . @75.00
11 thru 20 . . . . . . . . . . . . . . . @50.00
```

TOP TEN
WildStorm/DC, 1999
America's Best Comics
```
1 AMo(s),GeH,40-pg. . . . . . . . . . 3.50
2 AMo(s),GeH . . . . . . . . . . . . . . 3.00
3 thru 9 AMo(s),GeH . . . . . . . . @3.00
10 AMo(s),GeH,killer revealed . . . . 3.00
11 AMo(s),GeH,aftermath . . . . . . . 3.00
12 AMo(s),GeH,season finale . . . . 3.00
```

TOP TEN: BEYOND THE FARTHEST PRECINCT
Wildstorm/DC, Aug., 2005
```
1 (of 5) JOy . . . . . . . . . . . . . . . . 3.00
2 JOy . . . . . . . . . . . . . . . . . . . . 3.00
3 thru 5 JOy . . . . . . . . . . . . . . @3.00
```

TOP THAT! PUZZLE ADVENTURES
Top That! Publishing, 2005
```
1 Halfpipe Heroes . . . . . . . . . . . . 4.00
2 Freaky Fredas Ghost . . . . . . . . . 4.00
3 Chinese Mystery . . . . . . . . . . . . 4.00
4 Aztec Madness . . . . . . . . . . . . 4.00
5 Shadow on the Wall . . . . . . . . . 4.00
6 Celtic Double Cross . . . . . . . . . . 4.00
```

TOR IN 3-D
Eclipse, 1986
```
1 JKu . . . . . . . . . . . . . . . . . . . . 3.00
1a B&W limited 100 sign . . . . . . . 5.00
2 JKu . . . . . . . . . . . . . . . . . . . . 3.00
```

TORMENTRESS: MISTRESS OF HELL
Blackout Comics, 1977
```
0 . . . . . . . . . . . . . . . . . . . . . . . 3.00
```

TOTAL ECLIPSE
Eclipse, 1988–89
```
1 BHa,BSz(c),A:Airboy,Skywolf . . . 4.00
2 BHa,BSz(c),A:New Wave, Liberty
  Project . . . . . . . . . . . . . . . . . . 4.00
3 BHa,BSz(c),A:Scout,Ms.Tree . . . 4.00
4 BHa,BSz(c),A:Miracleman,
  Prowler . . . . . . . . . . . . . . . . . 4.00
5 BHa,BSz(c),A:Miracleman, Aztec
  Ace . . . . . . . . . . . . . . . . . . . . 4.00
```

TOTAL ECLIPSE, THE SERAPHIM OBJECTIVE
Eclipse, 1988
```
1 tie-in Total Eclipse #2 . . . . . . . . 2.50
```

TOTAL WAR
Gold Key, 1965
```
1 WW . . . . . . . . . . . . . . . . . . 150.00
2 WW . . . . . . . . . . . . . . . . . . 125.00
Becomes:
```

M.A.R.S. PATROL
```
3 WW . . . . . . . . . . . . . . . . . . 125.00
4 . . . . . . . . . . . . . . . . . . . . . 100.00
5 . . . . . . . . . . . . . . . . . . . . . 100.00
6 thru 10 . . . . . . . . . . . . . . . @100.00
```

TOY BOX
Alias Enterprises, 2006
0 . . . . 3.50

TOY BOY
Continuity, 1986–91
1 NA.I&O:Toy Boy,A:Megalith 3.00
2 TVE 3.00
3 TVE 3.00
4 TVE 3.00
5 TVE 3.00
6 TVE 3.00
7 MG 3.00

TRAILOR PARK OF TERROR
Imperium Comics, 2006
Vol. 2
1 . . . . 4.00
1 variant(c) 4.00
2 . . . . 4.00
3 . . . . 4.00
4 . . . . 4.00
5 . . . . 3.00
6 thru 8 . . . . @4.00
Spec. Halloween Special 4.00
Spec. Halloween Special #2 . . . 4.00

TRANQUILITY
Wildstorm/DC, Dec., 2006
1 . . . . 3.00
1a variant JSC (c) 3.00
2 . . . . 3.00
2a variant (c) (1:10) 3.00
3 Mr. Articulate's murder 3.00
3a variant (c) (1:10) 3.00
Becomes:

WELCOME TO TRANQUILITY
Wildstorm/DC, Mar., 2007
4 . . . . 3.00
4a variant (c) 3.00
5 Battle to the death 3.00
6 Who killed Mr. Articulate? 3.00
7 F:Sheriff Lindo 3.00
8 Three tales 3.00
9 Paradox Box 3.00
10 Secrets revealed 3.00
11 Plague of the undead 3.00

TRANSFORMERS
1 Robotics 2.50
2 . . . . 2.50
3 . . . . 2.50

TRANSFORMERS
IDW Publishing, 2005
0 . . . . 2.00
1 Infiltration 3.00
1a variant (c)s . . . . @3.00
2 thru 6 Infiltration 3.00
2a thru 6a variant (c)s . . . . @3.00
Spec. Animated movie adaptation . . 4.00
Spec. Anim. movie adapt. variant (c) 4.00
Cover Gallery 6.00

TRANSFORMERS: ARMADA
Dreamwave, 2002
1 . . . . 4.00
2 . . . . 3.00
3 thru 17 . . . . @3.00
18 thru 32 Energon . . . . @3.00
Spec. Summer Special #1 . . . . 5.00
2005 Annual 6.00
Energon Official Guidebook #1 . . . . 5.00

TRANSFORMERS BEAST WARS
Dreamwave, 2005
1 . . . . 3.00
2 . . . . 3.00

TRANSFORMERS EVOLUTIONS: HEARTS OF STEEL
IDW Publishing, 2006
1 CDi 3.00
1a variant (c) 3.00
2 thru 4 CDi . . . . @3.00
2a thru 4a variant (c) . . . . @3.00

Transformers: Generation One #4
© *Dreamwave*

TRANSFORMERS: GENERATION ONE
Dreamwave, 2002
1 . . . . 7.00
1a exclusive holofoil (c) 20.00
2 thru 6 . . . . @3.00
5a thru 6a variant (c) . . . . @3.00
7 thru 10 . . . . @3.00
0 . . . . 3.00
Preview book, exclusive (c) 4.00
Vol. 2
1 (of 6) 3.50
1a chrome edition 6.00
2 thru 14 . . . . @3.00
GN More than meets the Eye, guide 5.25
GN More than meets the Eye #3 . . . 5.25
2004 Datatracks 2.50

TRANSFORMERS: GENERATIONS
IDW Publishing, 2006
1 . . . . 2.00
1a variant (c) 2.00
2 . . . . 2.00
2a variant (c) 2.00
3 thru 9 . . . . @2.50
3a thru 9a variant (c) . . . . @2.50
10 thru 12 . . . . @3.00
10a thru 12a variant (c) . . . . @3.00

TRANSFORMERS/G.I. JOE
Dreamwave, 2003
1 . . . . 3.00
1a holofoil (c) 6.00
2 thru 6 . . . . @3.00
1-shot Divided Front 3.00

TRANSFORMERS/G.I. JOE: DIVIDED FRONT
Dreamwave, 2004
1 . . . . 3.00
2 thru 6 . . . . @3.00

TRANSFORMERS, THE: MEGATRON ORIGIN
IDW Publishing, 2007
1 . . . . 4.00
2 thru 4 . . . . 4.00
1a thru 4a variant (c) . . . . @4.00

TRANSFORMERS: MICROMASTERS
Dreamwave, 2004
1 (of 4) 3.00
2 thru 3 . . . . @3.00

TRANSFORMERS: MORE THAN MEETS THE EYE
Dreamwave, 2003
1 (of 8) 5.25
2 thru 7 . . . . @5.25
8 final issue 6.00
Vol. 2 Transformers Armada
1 thru 3 More than Meets
the Eye . . . . @5.00

TRANSFORMERS SPOTLIGHT
IDW Publishing, 2006
1-shot Hot Rod 4.00
1-shot Hot Rod variant (c) 4.00
1-shot Nightbeat 4.00
1-shot Nightbeat variant (c) 4.00
1-shot Shockwave 4.00
1-shot Shockwave variant (c) 4.00
Spec. Kup 4.00
Spec. Galvatron 4.00
Spec. Optimus Prime 4.00
Spec. Six Shot 4.00
Spec. Ultra Magnus 4.00
Spec. Ramjet 4.00
Spec. Soundwave 4.00
Specials variant (c)s . . . . @4.00

TRANSFORMERS: TARGET: 2006
IDW Publishing, 2007
1 . . . . 4.00
2 thru 5 . . . . @4.00
1a thru 5a variant (c) . . . . @4.00

TRANSFORMERS, THE: BEAST WARS
IDW Publishing, 2006
1 . . . . 3.00
1a variant (c) 3.00
2 . . . . 3.00
3 . . . . 3.00
4 . . . . 3.00
2a thru 4a variant (c) 3.00

TRANSFORMERS, THE: BEAST WARS: THE ASCENDING
IDW, 2007
1 . . . . 4.00
2 . . . . 4.00
1a thru 2a variant (c) . . . . @4.00
3 . . . . 4.00
4 . . . . 4.00
Spec. Sourcebook #1 . . . . 7.00

TRANSFORMERS, THE: BEST OF UK: DINOBOTS
IDW, 2007
1 . . . . 4.00
2 . . . . 4.00
3 . . . . 4.00

TRANSFORMERS, THE: DEVASTATION
IDW, 2007
1 . . . . 4.00
2 . . . . 4.00
3 . . . . 4.00

TRANSFORMERS, THE: ESCALATION
IDW Publishing, 2006
1 . . . . 4.00
1a variant b&w (c) 4.00
2 thru 6 . . . . @4.00
2a thru 6a variant (c)s . . . . @4.00

TRANSFORMERS, THE: ANIMATED MOVIE ADAPTATION
IDW, 2006
3 . . . . 4.00
4 . . . . 4.00

TRANSFORMERS, THE: MOVIE ADAPTATION
IDW, 2007
1 . . . . 4.00
2 thru 4 . . . . @4.00

TRANSFORMERS, THE: MOVIE PREQUEL
IDW, 2007
2 thru 4 . . . . @4.00
2a thru 4a variant (c) . . . . @4.00

TRANSFORMERS, THE: STORMBRINGER
IDW Publishing, 2006
1 . . . . 3.00
1a variant (c) 3.00
2 . . . . 3.00
3 . . . . 3.00
4 . . . . 3.00
2a thru 4a variant (c) . . . . @3.00

TRANSFORMERS: THE WAR WITHIN
Dreamwave, 2002
1 . . . . 3.00
2 thru 6 . . . . @3.00
Vol. 2 The Dark Ages
1 . . . . 3.00
2 . . . . 3.00
3 thru 6 . . . . @3.00
Vol. 3 The Age of Wrath
1 . . . . 3.00
2 thru 6 . . . . @3.00

TRANSFORMERS in 3-D
Blackthorne
1 thru 5 . . . . @2.50

TRANSFORMERS: TIMELINES
Fun Publications, 2006
1-shot Beast Wars 5.00
1-shot Summer Special (2007) 5.00

TRAVEL OF JAMIE McPHEETERS, THE
Gold Key, 1963
1 Kurt Russell 60.00

TRAVELLER
Maximum Press, 1996
1 (of 3) RLd,MHw, ... 3.00

TRIAL BY FIRE
Crossgen Comics, 2002
1 (of 5) 3.00

TRIBE
Axis Comics, 1993–94
1 see Image Comics section
2 TJn(s),LSn,V:Alex 2.50
3 TJn(s),LSn, ... 2.50
   Good Comics, 1996
0 TJn,LSn 3.00
1 TJn,LSn,Choice and
  Responsibility 3.00
2 TJn,LSn,Choice and
  Responsibility 3.00

TRIBULATION FORCE
Tyndale House, 2002
GN Vol. #1 . . . . 6.00
GN Vol. #2 thru Vol. 5 . . . . @6.00

TRICK 'R TREAT
Wildstorm/DC, Oct., 2007
1 . . . . 3.00
2 thru 4 . . . . @3.00

Trinity Angels #10
© Acclaim

TRINITY ANGELS
Acclaim, 1997
1 KM,DPs, Maria, Gianna &
  Theresa Barbella become Trinity
  Angels 2.50
2 thru 12 KM . . . . @2.50

TROLL LORDS
Comico, 1989–90
Spec. #1 . . . . 2.50
1 . . . . 2.50
2 thru 4 . . . . @2.50

TRON
Amaze Ink
3 thru 6 . . . . @4.00

TRON: DEREZZED
88MPH Studios, 2004
1 (of 4) 3.00
2 thru 3 . . . . @3.00
1a thru 3a variant (c)s . . . . @3.50

TRON: THE GHOST IN THE MACHINE
Amaze Ink/SLG, 2006
1 . . . . 3.50
2 . . . . 3.50

TROUBLEMAKERS
Acclaim, 1996
1 FaN(s) 2.50
2 thru 19 FaN(s) . . . . @2.50

TROUBLE WITH GIRLS
Comico, 1987–88
1 . . . . 3.00
2 thru 4 . . . . @2.50

TRUE LOVE
Eclipse, 1986
1 ATh,NC,DSt(c),reprints 3.00
2 ATh,NC,BA(c),reprints 3.00

TRUE ROMANCE
Pyramid Comics, 1997
1 . . . . 2.50
1a deluxe 3.00
2 thru 4 . . . . @2.50

TUFF GHOSTS STARRING SPOOKY
Harvey Publications, 1962–72
1 . . . . 250.00
2 thru 5 . . . . @150.00
6 thru 10 . . . . @100.00
11 thru 20 . . . . @75.00
21 thru 30 . . . . @50.00
31 thru 39 . . . . @40.00
40 thru 42 52 pg. Giants . . . . . @45.00
43 . . . . 45.00

TURISTAS: THE OTHER SIDE OF PARADISE
IDW Publishing, 2006
Book 1 . . . . 4.00

TUROK
Acclaim, 1998
1 FaN 3-D cover 2.50
2 FaN,A:Armorines 2.50
3 FaN,Lazarus Concordance 2.50
4 FaN, real President? 2.50

TUROK: CHILD OF BLOOD
Acclaim, 1997
1-shot FaN, 48pg 4.00

TUROK: COMIC BOOK MAGAZINE
Acclaim, 1998
Seeds of Evil 5.00
Adon's Curse 5.00
Turok/Shadowman 5.00

TUROK: DINOSAUR HUNTER
Valiant, 1993
1 BS,Chromium(c),O:Turok
  retold,V:Monark 3.00
1a Gold Ed. 4.00
2 thru 13 . . . . @2.75

14 V:Dino-Pirate. 2.50
15 RgM,V:Dino-Pirate 2.50
16 Chaos Effect-Beta#3, V:Evil
   Shaman 2.75
17 thru 47. . . . . @2.50
Yearbook #1 MBn(s),DC, N&V:Mon
   Ark 4.25
Yearbook 1995 MGr,The Hunted . . . 3.00
Spec. Tales of the Lost Land 4.00

TUROK QUARTERLY— REDPATH
Acclaim, 1997
March 1997, FaN(s),Spring Break
   in the Lost Land. 4.00
June 1997, FaN(s), Killer loose in
   Oklahoma City. 4.00

TUROK/SHADOWMAN
Acclaim, 1999
1-shot 4.00

TUROK 3: SHADOW OF OBLIVION
Acclaim, 2000
Spec. 48-page 5.00

TUROK/SHAMAN'S TEARS
Valiant, 1995
1 MGr,Ghost Dance Pt. 1 . . . . 2.50
2 MGr,JAl,White Buffalo
   kidnapped,V:Bar Sinister. 2.50
3 V:Supremeists/Circle Sea 2.50

TUROK: SON OF STONE
Gold Key, 1962
1 thru 29 see Golden Age
30 . . . . 150.00
31 Drug 165.00
32 thru 40. . . . . @125.00
41 thru 50. . . . . @100.00
51 thru 60. . . . . @75.00
61 thru 75. . . . . @65.00
76 thru 91. . . . . @50.00
Whitman
92 thru 130. . . . . @50.00
Giant #1 . . . . 200.00

TUROK: THE HUNTED
Valiant, 1996
1 & 2 . . . . 2.50

TUROK/TIMEWALKER
Acclaim, 1997
1 of 2 FaN(s),Seventh Sabbath . . . 2.50
2 of 2 FaN(s),Seventh Sabbath . . . 2.50

TURTLE SOUP
Millennium, 1991
1 Book 1, short stories 2.50
2 thru 4 . . . . @2.50

TV CASPER & COMPANY
Harvey Publications, 1963–74
1 B:68 pg. Giants 250.00
2 . . . . 150.00
3 . . . . 150.00
4 . . . . 150.00
5 . . . . 150.00
6 . . . . 100.00
7 . . . . 100.00
8 . . . . 100.00
9 . . . . 100.00
10 . . . . 100.00
11 thru 20. . . . . @75.00
21 thru 31 E:68 pg. Giants. . . . . @50.00

Tweety and Sylvester #105
© Whitman

32 thru 46. . . . . @40.00

TWEETY AND SYLVESTER
Gold Key, 1963–84
1 . . . . 75.00
2 thru 10 . . . . @60.00
11 thru 30 . . . . @40.00
31 thru 121. . . . . @15.00
Whitman, 1980
103 thru 104 . . . . @15.00
105 thru 107 scarce . . . . @40.00
108 thru 121 . . . . @25.00

12 O'CLOCK HIGH
Dell, 1965
1 . . . . 100.00
2 . . . . 75.00

24: NIGHTFALL
IDW Publishing, 2006
1 . . . . 3.00
1a variant (c) 3.00
2 . . . . 4.00
3 . . . . 4.00
4 . . . . 4.00
5 . . . . 4.00
2a thru 5a variant (c) . . . . @4.00

21 DOWN
WildStorm/DC, 2002
1 JP,JJu(c),F:Preston Kills 3.00
2 JP,JJu(c),Herod 3.00
3 JP,JJu(c),Bear Mountain 3.00
4 JP,JJu(c) 3.00
5 JP,JJu(c) 3.00
6 JP,JJu(c),The Conduit 3.00
7 JP,JJu(c),secret of Herod 3.00
8 JP,Roadside Attractions,pt.1 . . . . 3.00
9 JP,Roadside Attractions,pt.2 . . . . 3.00
10 JP,Roadside Attractions,pt.3 . . . 3.00
11 JP,Roadside Attractions,pt.4 . . . 3.00
12 JP,Roadside Attractions,concl. . . 3.00

TWILIGHT EXPERIMENT
Wildstorm/DC, Feb., 2005
1 (of 6) JP(s) 3.00
2 JP(s) 3.00
3 JP(s) 3.00
4 JP(s) 3.00
5 JP(s) 3.00
6 JP(s) 3.00

TWILIGHT MAN
First, 1989
1 Mini-Series. 2.75
2 Mini-Series. 2.75
3 Mini-Series. 2.75
4 Mini-Series. 2.75

TWILIGHT MEN
Markosia, 2006
0 . . . . 0.50
1 . . . . 3.50
2 thru 4 . . . . @3.50

TWILIGHT X-TRA
Antarctic Press, 1999
1 (of 3) by Joe Wright 2.50
2 . . . . 2.50
3 conclusion 2.50

TWILIGHT X: WAR
Antarctic Press, 2005
1 (of 7) by Joe Wight, Manga 3.00
2 thru 7 . . . . @3.00

TWILIGHT ZONE
Dell, 1961
1 . . . . 150.00
2 . . . . 150.00

TWILIGHT ZONE, THE
Gold Key, 1962
See also: Four Color #1173 & #1288
1 RC,FF,GE,P(c) all 250.00
2 . . . . 150.00
3 ATh,MSy 125.00
4 ATh. 125.00
5 . . . . 110.00
6 . . . . 110.00
7 . . . . 110.00
8 . . . . 110.00
9 ATh. 125.00
10 . . . . 100.00
11 . . . . 100.00
12 AW 100.00
13 AW,RC,FBe,AMc. 100.00
14 RC,JO,RC,AT 100.00
15 RC,JO. 100.00
16 . . . . 75.00
17 . . . . 75.00
18 . . . . 75.00
19 JO 75.00
20 . . . . 70.00
21 RC. 70.00
22 JO 70.00
23 JO 70.00
24 . . . . 60.00
25 GE,RC,ATh 60.00
26 RC,GE. 60.00
27 GE. 60.00
28 thru 31 . . . . @50.00
32 GE. 55.00
33 thru 38 . . . . @50.00
39 WMc 50.00
40 . . . . 35.00
41 . . . . 35.00
42 . . . . 35.00
43 RC. 40.00
44 thru 49 . . . . @35.00
50 FBe,WS. 35.00
51 AW 40.00
52 thru 56 . . . . @30.00
57 FBe 30.00
58 . . . . 30.00
59 FBe,AMc. 35.00
60 thru 70. . . . . @25.00
71 rep. 20.00
72 . . . . 25.00
73 rep. 20.00
74 . . . . 25.00
75 . . . . 25.00

COLOR PUB.

76 . . . . 25.00
77 FBe 30.00
78 FBe,AMc,The Missing Mirage. 230.00
79 rep 20.00
80 FBe,AMc 30.00
81 . . . . 30.00
82 AMc 35.00
83 FBe,WS 35.00
84 FBe,AMc 35.00
85 . . . . 30.00
86 rep 25.00
87 thru 91 . . . . @30.00

TWILIGHT ZONE
Now, 1990
1 NA,BSz(c) 8.00
1a 2nd printing Prestige +Harlan
  Ellison story 6.00
[Volume 2]
#1 The Big Dry (direct) 3.00
#1a Newsstand 2.50
2 Blind Alley 2.50
3 Extraterrestrial 2.50
4 The Mysterious Biker 2.50
5 Queen of the Void 2.50
6 Insecticide 2.50
7 The Outcasts,Ghost Horse 2.50
8 Colonists on Alcor 2.50
9 Dirty Lyle's House of Fun
  (3-D Holo) 3.00
10 Stairway to Heaven,Key
  to Paradise 2.50
11 TD(i),Partial Recall 2.50
3-D Spec. 2.50
Ann. #1 . . . . 2.75
[Volume 3]
1 thru 2 . . . . @2.50

TWIN BLADES:
KILLING WORDS
Alias Enterprises, 2006
1 . . . . 3.50
1a variant (c) 3.50
2 . . . . 3.50
3 . . . . 3.50

TWISTED TALES
Pacific, 1982–84
1 RCo. Infected 5.00
2 thru 8 . . . . @4.00
Eclipse
9 . . . . 4.00
10 GM,BWr 5.50

TWISTED TALES OF
BRUCE JONES
Eclipse, 1982–84
1 . . . . 3.00
2 . . . . 3.00
3 . . . . 3.00
4 . . . . 3.00

TWO FISTED TALES
Russ Cochran, 1992
1 JSe,HK,WW,JCr,reps 2.50
2 Reps inc.War Story 2.50
3 rep. 2.50
4 thru 6 rep . . . . @2.50
7 thru 8 rep. . . . . @2.50
Gemstone
17 thru 24 EC comics reprints . . . @2.50

TWO GUNS
Boom! Studios, 2007
1 (of 4) 4.00
2 thru 3 . . . . @4.00
2a thru 3a variant (c) . . . . @4.00
4 . . . . 4.00
5 . . . . 4.00

TWO-STEP
Wildstorm/DC Oct. 2003
1 (of 3) WEl(s),ACo,JP 3.00
2 WEl(s),ACo,JP 3.00
3 WEl(s),ACo,JP,concl. 3.00

2000 A.D. MONTHLY
Eagle, 1985
1 A:JudgeDredd 4.00
2 A:JudgeDredd 3.00
3 A:JudgeDredd 2.50
4 A:JudgeDredd 2.50
5 . . . . 2.50
6 . . . . 2.50
[2nd Series]
1 thru 4 . . . . @2.50
Quality
5 thru 27 . . . . @2.50
28/29 . . . . 2.50
30 . . . . 2.50
31/32 . . . . 2.50
33 thru 37 . . . . @2.50
Becomes:

2000 A.D. SHOWCASE
38 thru 54 . . . . @2.50
Rebellion, 2003
1 . . . . 2.50
2 . . . . 2.50
3 . . . . 2.50

2 TO THE CHEST
Dark Planet Productions, 2004
1 thru 5 . . . . @3.00

TZU THE REAPER
Murim Studios, 1997
1 by Gary Cohn & C.S. Chun 3.00
2 . . . . 3.00
3 . . . . 3.00
4 . . . . 3.00
5 . . . . 3.00

TZU: SPIRITS OF DEATH
Murim Studios, 1997
1 . . . . 3.00

UFO FLYING SAUCERS
Gold Key, 1968
1 . . . . 75.00
2 . . . . 50.00
3 thru 13 . . . . @35.00
Becomes:

UFO & Outer Space #17
© Gold Key

UFO & OUTER SPACE
Gold Key, 1978
14 thru 25 . . . . @20.00

ULTIMATE SPORTS
FORCE PRESENTS:
Ultimate Sports Entertainment
2004
1 Hardwood Heroes 4.00
1 The Guardians 4.00
1 The Zone 4.00
1 Air and Space 4.00

ULTRAFORCE
Malibu Ultraverse, 1994–95
1 Prime, Prototype 2.50
2 thru 10 . . . . @2.50
Spec.#0 . . . . 2.50
[2nd Series], 1995–96
Infinity Fant. Ultraforce Four 2.50
1 George Perez cover 2.50
1a Computer painted cover 2.50
2 thru 15 . . . . @2.50

ULTRAFORCE/
AVENGERS
Malibu Ultraverse, Aug. 1995
1 GP 4.00

ULTRAFORCE/
SPIDER-MAN
Malibu Ultraverse, 1996
1 . . . . 4.00

ULTRAMAN
Nemesis, 1994
1 EC,O:Ultraman 2.50
2 . . . . 2.50
3 . . . . 2.50
4 V:Blue Ultraman 2.50

ULTRAMAN
Harvey, 1993
1 . . . . 5.00
2 . . . . 5.00
3 . . . . 5.00

ULTRAMAN
Harvey/Ultracomics, 1993
1 with 1 of 3 cards 2.50
2 with 1 of 3 cards & virgin cover . . 2.50
3 with 1 of 3 cards & virgin cover . . 2.50

ULTRAVERSE
DOUBLE FEATURE
Malibu Ultraverse, 1995
1 F:Prime, Solitaire 4.00

ULTRAVERSE
FUTURE SHOCK
Malibu Ultraverse, 1996
1 one-shot,MPc,alternate futures . . 2.50

ULTRAVERSE ORIGINS
Malibu Ultraverse, 1994
1 O:Ultraverse Heroes 2.50
1a Silver foil cover 12.50

ULTRAVERSE UNLIMITED
Malibu Ultraverse, 1996
1 F:Warlock 2.50
2 LWn,KWe, A:All-New Exiles,
  V:Maxis 2.50

COLOR PUB.

ULTRAVERSE: YEAR ZERO: THE DEATH OF THE SQUAD
Malibu Ultraverse, 1995
0-A Hardcase's old team	2.50
0-B	2.50
0-C L.A. Riots	2.50
1 JHI,A:Squad, Mantra	3.00
2 JHI,DaR(c) prequel to Prime#1	3.00
3 Cont. Year Zero Story	3.00
4 I:NM-E	3.00

ULTRAVERSE: YEAR ONE
Malibu Ultraverse, 1995
1 Handbook, double size	5.00
2 Prime	2.50

ULTRAVERSE: YEAR TWO
Malibu Ultraverse, 1996
1 Marvel/Ultraverse/Info	5.00

UNCLE SCROOGE
Dell/Gold Key, 1962
40 CB,X-Mas	250.00
41	225.00
42	225.00
43 CB	225.00
44 CB	225.00
45 CB	225.00
46 Lost Beneath the Sea	225.00
47 CB	225.00
48 CB	225.00
49 CB,Loony Lunar Gold Rush	225.00
50 CB,Rug Riders in the Sky	225.00
51 CB,How Green Was my Lettuce	200.00
52 CB,Great Wig Mystery	200.00
53 CB,Interplanetary Postman	200.00
54 CB,Billion-Dollar Safari!	200.00
55 CB,McDuck of Arabia	200.00
56 CB,Mystery of the Ghost Town Railroad	200.00
57 CB,Swamp of No Return	200.00
58 CB,Giant Robot Robbers	200.00
59 CB,North of the Yukon	200.00
60 CB,Phantom of Notre Duck	150.00
61 CB,So Far and No Safari	150.00
62 CB,Queen of the Wild Dog Pack	150.00
63 CB,House of Haunts!	150.00
64 CB,Treasure of Marco Polo!	250.00
65 CB,Micro-Ducks from OuterSpace	150.00
66 CB,Heedless Horseman	150.00
67 CB rep.	150.00
68 CB,Hall of the Mermaid Queen!	150.00
69 CB,Cattle King!	150.00
70 CB,The Doom Diamond!	150.00
71 CB	150.00
72 CB rep.	150.00
73 CB rep.	150.00
74 thru 110	@100.00
111 thru 148	@40.00
149	35.00
150 thru 168	@35.00
169 thru 173	@35.00

Whitman, 1980
174 thru 176	@35.00
177 and 178	@40.00
179 Rare	700.00
180 thru 182	@60.00
183 thru 195	@25.00
196 and 197	@30.00
1981 thru 209	@35.00

Gladstone, 1986
210 CB,Beagle Boys	20.00
211 CB,Prize of Pizzaro	18.00
212 CB,city-golden roofs	18.00
213 CB,city-golden roofs	18.00

214 CB	18.00
215 CB, a cold bargain	18.00
216 CB	18.00
217 CB,7 cities of Cibola	18.00
218 CB	18.00
219 Don Rosa,Son of Sun	30.00
220 CB,Don Rosa	10.00
221 CB,A:BeagleBoys	4.00
222 CB,Mysterious Island	4.00
223 CB	4.00
224 CB,Rosa,Cash Flow	7.00
225 CB	4.00
226 CB,Rosa	5.00
227 CB,Rosa	5.00
228 CB	4.00
229 CB	4.00
230 CB	5.00
231 CB,Rosa(c)	4.00
232 CB	4.00
233 CB	4.00
234 CB	4.00
235 Rosa	7.00
236 CB	4.00
237 CB	4.00
238 CB	4.00
239 CB	4.00
240 CB	4.00
241 CB,giant	7.00

Uncle Scrooge #252
© Walt Disney

242 CB,giant	7.00

Walt Disney, 1990
243 CB,Pie in the Sky	4.00
244	3.50
245	3.50
246	3.50
247	3.50
248	3.50
249	3.50
250 CB	5.00
251	3.00
252 No Room For Human Error	3.00
253 Fab.Philosophers Stone	3.00
254 The Filling Station	3.00
255 The Flying Dutchman	3.00
256 CB,Status Seeker	3.00
257 Coffee,Louie or Me	3.00
258 CB,Swamp of no return	3.00
259 The only way to Go.	3.00
260 The Waves Above, The Gold Below	3.00
261 Rosa,Return to Zanadu, Pt.1	6.00
262 Rosa,Return to Zanadu, Pt.2	6.00
263 Rosa,Treasure Under Glass	6.00
264 Snobs Club	3.00
265 CB,Ten Cent Valentine	3.00

266 The Money Ocean,Pt.1	3.00
267 The Money Ocean,Pt 2	3.00
268 CB,Rosa,Island in the Sky	3.00
269 The Flowers	3.00
270 V:Magica DeSpell	3.00
271 The Secret o/t Stone	3.00
272 Canute The Brute's Battle Axe	3.00
273 CB,Uncle Scrooge-Ghost	3.25
274 CB,Hall of the Mermaid Queen.	3.25
275 CB,Rosa,Christmas Cheers,inc. D.Rosa centerspread	3.25
276 Rosa, thru 277	@7.00
278 thru 280	@3.00

Gladstone, 1993
281 Rosa	7.00
282 thru 284	@3.00
285 Rosa, Life & Times	11.00
286 thru 293 Rosa, Life & Times	@6.00
294 thru 299	@3.00
300 Rosa & Barks	5.00
301 Statuesque Spendthrifts	3.00
302	3.00
303 Rocks to Riches	3.00
304 My Private Eye	3.00
305 Vigilante of Pizen Bluff	3.00
306	3.00
307 Temper Temper	3.00
308 Revenge of the Witch	3.00

Prestige format, 64pg.
309 Whadalottajargon	8.00
310 The Sign of the Triple Distelfink	8.00
311 The Last Lord of Eldorado	8.00
312 The Hands of Zeus	8.00
313 The Fantastic River Race	8.00
314	8.00
315 The Flying Scot, pt.1	8.00
316 The Flying Scot, pt.2	8.00
317 Pawns of the Lamp Garou	8.00
318 Cowboy Captain of Cutty Sark	8.00
319 The Horse Radish Story	8.00
320 The Mysterious Stone Ray	8.00
321 The Giant Robot Robbers	8.00
322 Secret of the Lost Dutchman's Mine	8.00

UNCLE SCROOGE
Gemstone Publishing, 2003
319 thru 347	@7.00
348 thru 361	@7.00
362 thru 366	@7.50
367 thru 372	@8.00

UNCLE SCROOGE ADVENTURES
Gladstone, 1987
1 CB,McDuck of Arabia	9.00
2 translated from Danish	5.00
3 translated from Danish	5.00
4 CB	5.00
5 Rosa	5.00
6 CB	3.50
7 CB	3.00
8 CB	3.00
9 Rosa	3.50
10 CB	3.00
11 CB	3.00
12 CB	3.00
13 CB	3.00
14 Rosa	3.50
15 CB	3.00
16 CB	3.00
17 CB	3.00
18 CB	3.00
19 CB,Rosa(c)	3.50
20 CB,giant	6.00
21 CB,giant	6.00
22 Rosa(c)	6.00
23 CB,giant	4.00
24 thru 26	@2.50
27 Rosa,O:Jr. Woodchuck	4.00

28 giant 4.00
29 . . . . 2.50
30 giant 5.00
31 thru 32 . . . . @3.00
33 Barks 5.00
34 thru 40 . . . . @3.00
41 . . . . 2.50
42 The Dragon's Amulet 2.50
43 Queen of the Wild Dog Pack . . . 2.50
44 . . . . 2.50
45 Secret of the Duckburg Triangle. 2.50
46 The Tides Turn 2.50
47 The Menehune Mystery 2.50
48 The Tenth Avatar. 2.50
49 Dead-Eye Duck. 2.50
50 CB,The Secret of Atlantis 3.00
51 . . . . 2.50
52 The Black Diamond 2.50
53 Secret of the Incas 2.50
54 Secret of the Incas, pt.2 . . . . . . 2.50

UNCLE SCROOGE ADVENTURES
Gladstone, 1997–98
Don Rosa Specials
Spec.#1 (of 4). 11.00
Spec.#2 thru #4 . . . . @10.00
Van Horn Specials
Spec.#1 . . . . 10.00
Spec.#2 . . . . 10.00
Spec.#3 . . . . 10.00
Spec.#4 . . . . 10.00

UNCLE SCROOGE ADVENTURES IN COLOR
Gladstone, 1987–98
Carl Barks reprints
1 thru 32 . . . . @10.00
33 thru 35. . . . . @11.00
36 32pg. 9.00
37 thru 53. . . . . @10.00
54 Hall of the Mermaid Queen. . . . 10.00
55 The Doom Diamond 10.00
56 two adventures 10.00

UNCLE SCROOGE & DONALD DUCK
Gold Key, 1965
1 rep. 150.00

UNCLE SCROOGE AND DONALD DUCK
Gladstone, 1997
1 . . . . 2.50
2 Christmas stories. 2.50
3 Back to Long Ago 2.50

UNCLE SCROOGE AND MONEY
Gold Key, 1967
1 . . . . 135.00

UNCLE SCROOGE GOES TO DISNEYLAND
Gladstone, 1985
1 CB,etc. 100pp 13.00

UNDEAD, THE
Chaos! Comics Black Label,, 2001
Ashcan 6.00
Ashcan, premium edition 15.00
1 zombie wasteland 5.00
1a previews exclusive (c) 5.00
1b signed edition. 12.00
1c premium edition 9.00

1d super-premium edition. 15.00
1e foil (c). 15.00

UNDERDOG
Charlton, 1970
1 Planet Zot 150.00
2 Simon Sez/The Molemen 100.00
3 Whisler's Father. 100.00
4 The Witch of Pycoon 100.00
5 The Snowmen 100.00
6 The Big Shrink. 100.00
7 The Marbleheads. 100.00
8 The Phoney Booths. 100.00
9 Tin Man Alley 100.00
10 Be My Valentine (Jan., 1972) . 100.00

Underdog #1
© Gold Key

UNDERDOG
Gold Key, 1975
1 The Big Boom 125.00
2 The Sock Singer Caper 75.00
3 The Ice Cream Scream 75.00
4 . . . . 75.00
5 . . . . 75.00
6 Head in a Cloud. 75.00
7 The Cosmic Canine. 75.00
8 . . . . 75.00
9 . . . . 75.00
10 Bouble Trouble Gum. 75.00
11 The Private Life of
  Shoeshine Boy 50.00
12 The Deadly Fist of Fingers 50.00
13 . . . . 50.00
14 Shrink Shrank Shrunk. 50.00
15 Polluter Palooka 50.00
16 The Soda Jerk 50.00
17 Flee For Your Life 50.00
18 Rain Rain Go Away...Okay 50.00
19 Journey To the Center of
  the Earth 50.00
20 The Six Million Dollar Dog 50.00
21 Smell of Success 55.00
22 Antlers Away 55.00
23 Wedding Bells In Outer Space
  (Feb.,1979) 55.00

UNDERDOG
Whitman, 1975
1 . . . . 100.00
2 thru 10 . . . . @50.00
11 thru 23 . . . . @40.00

UNDERDOG
Spotlight, 1987
1 FMc,PC(c),The Eredicator. 5.00

2 FMc,CS(c), Prisoner of Love/
  The Return of Fearo 5.00

UNDERDOG
Harvey, 1993
1 . . . . 5.00
2 thru 5 . . . . @4.00

UNDERDOG IN 3-D
Blackthorne
1 Wanted Dead or Alive 2.50

UNDERSEA AGENT
Tower, 1966–97
1 F:Davy Jones,UnderseaAgent. 150.00
2 thru 4 . . . . @125.00
5 O&I:Merman 125.00
6 GK,WW(c) 125.00

UNDERTAKER
Chaos! Comics, 1999
Preview BSt, WWF character 2.50
Preview, photo (c). 2.50
1 Prophecy of the Dead 3.00
1a photo cover 3.00
2 V:Embalmer & Paul Bearer 3.00
3 O:Undertaker 3.00
4 Kane 3.00
5 Jezebel 3.00
6 thru 12 . . . . @3.00
2a thru 12a photo covers . . . . . . @3.00
Halloween Spec. 3.00
Halloween Spec. photo(c) 3.00

UNDERWORLD: RED IN TOOTH AND CLAW
IDW Publishing, 2004
1 . . . . 4.00
2 thru 3 . . . . @4.00

UNEARTHLY SPECTACULARS
Harvey, 1965
1 DW,AT,I:Tiger Boy 100.00
2 WW,AW,GK,I:Earthman,Miracles,
  Inc. A:Clawfang,TigerBoy 75.00
3 RC,AW,JO,A:Miracles,Inc. 65.00

U.N. FORCE
Gauntlet Comics, 1995
0 BDC(s) 3.00
1 B:BDC(s),I:U.N.Force 3.00
2 O:Indigo 3.00
3 . . . . 3.00
4 A:Predator 3.00
5 B:Critical Mass. 3.00

U.N. FORCE FILES
Gauntlet Comics
1 KP(c),F:Hunter Seeker, Lotus . . . 3.00

UNHUMAN
Narwain Publishing, 2006
1 BAu,TMd 4.00

UNION OF JUSTICE
Quantum Comics, 1998
1 by David Watkins & Steve Kurth . 3.00
2 . . . . 3.00
3 A:Golden Age Union 3.00

UNIQUE
Platinum Studios, 2007
1 (of 3) 3.00
2 . . . . 3.00
3 . . . . 3.00

All comics prices listed are for *Near Mint* condition.

COLOR PUB.

UNITY
Valiant, 1992
0 BWS,BL,Chapter#1,A:All Valiant
   Heroes,V:Erica Pierce 4.00
0a Red ed.,w/red logo 45.00
1 BWS,BL,Chapter#18,A:All Valiant
   Heroes,D:Erica Pierce 4.00

UNITY 2000
Acclaim, 1999
1 (of 6) 7.00
2 . . . . 9.00
3 . . . . 15.00

UNIT ZERO:
MARQUIS FILES
Marquis Models, 2004
1 . . . . 4.00
2 thru 5 . . . . 4.00

UNIVERSAL SOLDIER
Now, 1992
1 Based on Movie,Holo.(c) 2.75
2 Luc & Ronnie on the run
   from UniSols 2.50
2a Photo cover 2.50
3 Photo(c) 2.50

UNKNOWN WORLDS
OF FRANK BRUNNER
Eclipse, 1985
1 and 2 FB . . . . @4.00

UNTAMED LOVE
Fantagraphics, 1987
1 FF 3.00

UNTOLD TALES OF
Chaos! Comics, 2000
Purgatori #1 . . . . 3.00
Purgatori #1 premium ed. 13.00
Chastity #1 . . . . 3.00
Chastity premium #1 . . . . 13.00
Lady Death #1 . . . . 3.00
Lady Death #1 premium 13.00
Lady Death #1 chromium ed. 16.00

UNUSUAL TALES
Charlton Comics, 1955–65
1 . . . . 500.00
2 . . . . 300.00
3 thru 5 . . . . @200.00
6 SD,SD(c) 400.00
7 SD,SD(c) 450.00
8 SD,SD(c) 450.00
9 SD,SD(c) 500.00
10 SD,SD(c). 550.00
11 SD 500.00
12 SD 400.00
13 . . . . 200.00
14 SD 350.00
15 SD,SD(c). 425.00
16 thru 20 . . . . @150.00
21 . . . . 100.00
22 SD 125.00
23 . . . . 100.00
24 . . . . 100.00
25 thru 27 SD . . . . @225.00
28 . . . . 100.00
29 SD 225.00
30 thru 49 . . . . @85.00

URTH 4
Continuity, 1990
1 TVE,NA(c) 2.50
2 thru 3 TVE,NA . . . . @2.50
4 NA,Last issue. 2.50

Usagi Yojimbo #16
© Mirage

USAGI YOJIMBO
Mirage, 1993
1 A:TMNT 6.00
2 thru 16 . . . . @5.00
17 . . . . 8.00

U.S. AIR FORCE COMICS
Charlton, 1958
1 . . . . 100.00
2 . . . . 50.00
3 thru 20 . . . . @40.00
21 thru 37 . . . . @30.00

U.S. MARINES
Charlton, 1964
1 . . . . 45.00

U. T. F., THE
Speakeasy Comics, 2006
1 (of 3) 3.00
2 . . . . 3.00

U. T. F.:
UNDEAD TASK FORCE
Ape Entertainment, 2006
1 . . . . 3.00
3 . . . . 3.00

VALERIA, THE SHE BAT
Continuity, 1993
1 NA,I:Valeria 9.00
2 thru 4 . . . . [Not Released]
5 Rise of Magic. 2.50

VALERIA, THE SHE-BAT
Windjammer, 1995
1 (of 2) NA,Valeria & 'Rilla 2.50
2 (of 2) NA,BSz, final issue 2.50

VALHALLA
Antarctic Press, 1999
1 BDn set in 1939. . . . . 3.00

VALIANT READER:
GUIDE TO THE VALIANT
UNIVERSE
Acclaim, 1993
1 O:Valiant Universe 2.50

VALIANT VISION
STARTER KIT
Valiant, 1993
1 w/3-D Glasses 3.00
2 F:Starwatchers 3.00

VALKYRIE
Eclipse, 1988
1 PG,I:Steelfox,C:Airboy, Sky Wolf . 3.00
2 PG,O:New Black Angel 2.50
3 PG 2.50
[2nd Series]
1 BA,V:Eurasian Slavers 2.50
2 BA,V:Cowgirl 2.50
3 BA,V:Cowgirl 2.50

VALKYRIES
Alias Enterprises, 2006
1 . . . . 3.50
2 . . . . 3.50

VALLEY OF
THE DINOSAURS
Charlton, 1975
1 Hanna-Barbera TV adapt. 30.00
2 thru 11 . . . . @20.00

VALOR
Gemstone, 1998
1 EC comics reprint 2.50
2 . . . . 2.50
3 AW, The Cloak of Command 2.50
4 WW(c) 2.50
5 final issue 3.50

VAMPEROTICA
Brainstorm, 1996
1–16 see B&W
17 . . . . 3.00
17a signed 5.00
17 Holochrome cover. 30.00
18 Blood of the Damned (color). . . . 3.00
18a signed 5.00
19 Hunter's Blood 3.00
19a deluxe 3.00
20 Vampire Quest 3.00
21 hunting & feeding 3.00
22 . . . . 3.00

VAMPEROTICA LINGERIE
Comic Cavalcade, 1998
Commemorative #1 by Kirk Lindo . . 6.00
Commemorative #1a deluxe 15.00

VAMPI
Harris Comics, 2000
1/2 24-pg. 9.00
1/2 variant edition 18.00
1 Switchblade Kiss,pt.1. . . . . 3.00
1c signed & numbered 15.00
1d gold foil 25.00
1e convention special, B&W 10.00
1g limited holochrome edition. . . . 20.00
1g royal blue edition 40.00
1h Platinum edition 15.00
1i limited edition 9.00
2 Switchblade Kiss,pt.2. . . . . 8.00
1b thru 2b limited chrome (c) . . @12.00
2c limited holochrome edition 20.00
3 Switchblade Kiss,pt.3. . . . . 5.00
4 Dark Angel Rising,pt.1 . . . . 3.00
5 Dark Angel Rising,pt.2 . . . . 3.00
6 Dark Angel Rising,pt.3 . . . . 3.50
7 Underworld, pt.1 (of 3). 3.00
8 Underworld, pt.2 . . . . 3.00
9 Underworld, pt.3 . . . . 3.00
1a thru 9a deluxe . . . . @9.00

Vampi #10
© Anarchy Studios

Ashchan Vampi Dark Angel Rising
   platinum leather limited B&W . 15.00
Ashchan Vampi Underworld preview . 6.00
Ashchan Tainted Love 6.00
Vampi #1 preview 3.00
Anarchy Studios, 2001
10 . . . . 3.00
10b convention ed. 9.00
10c convention ed., signed 15.00
11 . . . . 3.00
12 . . . . 3.00
12b holo-fx chrome ed. 12.00
12c gold-fx chrome 20.00
13 . . . . 3.00
14 framed, I:Xenocyde 3.00
15 V:Xenocyde. 3.00
16 saved by Xenocide 3.00
17 Ultimatrix, pt.2 . . . . 3.00
18 Ultimatrix, pt.3 . . . . 3.00
19 Serpent's Kiss, pt.1 . . . . 3.00
20 Serpent's Kiss, pt.2 . . . . 3.00
21 Serpent's Kiss, pt.3 . . . . 3.00
22 Serpent's Kiss, pt.4 . . . . 3.00
23 Fallout, pt.1 . . . . 3.00
24 Fallout, pt.2 . . . . 3.00
25 . . . . 3.00
10a thru 16a deluxe . . . . @3.00
14a thru 25a limited . . . . @9.00
Sketchbook platinum leather 15.00
Ashchan Vampi:End Game 6.00
Ashchan Vampi #19–#21 . . . . 6.00
Ashchan Ultimatrix Leather Gold . . 15.00
Ashchan Vampi: Anarchy in the USA
   giant-sized, limited (2001) 6.00

VAMPI (DIGITAL)
Harris Comics, 2001
1 digital art 3.00
1a limited ed. 9.00
Preview edition, digital 3.00
Ashchan, Underworld gold leather. . 15.00

VAMPI VICIOUS
Anarchy Studios, 2003
Prototype Convention edition 9.00
1 . . . . 3.00
1a variant (c). 3.00
1 royal blue edition 40.00
1 gold foil edition 30.00
2 . . . . 3.00
3 . . . . 3.00
2a thru 3a variant (c) 3.00

VAMPI VICIOUS CIRCLE
Anarchy Studios, 2004
Ashchan Vicious Circle 6.00
1 . . . . 3.00
2 thru 3 . . . . @3.00
1a thru 3a variant (c). . . . . @9.00

VAMPI VICIOUS: GEMINI EFFECT
Anarchy Studios, 2005
1 . . . . 3.00
1a limited 9.00
2 . . . . 3.00
2a limited 9.00

VAMPI: VICIOUS RAMPAGE
Anarchy Studios, 2004
1 . . . . 3.00
1a limited 9.00
2 . . . . 3.00
2a limited 9.00

VAMPI VS. XIN
Anarchy Studios, 2004
1 & 2 . . . . @3.00
1a thru 2a limited . . . . @9.00

VAMPIRE LESTAT
Innovation, 1990–91
1 Anne Rice Adapt. 15.00
1a 2nd printing 4.00
1b 3rd printing. 2.50
2 . . . . 9.00
2a 2nd printing 4.00
2b 3rd printing. 2.50
3 . . . . 5.00
3a 2nd printing 2.50
4 . . . . 5.00
4a 2nd printing 2.50
5 . . . . 5.00
6 . . . . 5.00
7 . . . . 5.00
8 . . . . 5.00
9 scarce 8.00
9a 2nd Printing 3.00
10 . . . . 5.00
11 Those Who Must Be Kept 4.00
12 conclusion 4.00
Vampire Companion #1 . . . . 4.00
Vampire Companion #2 (preview
   Interview With The Vampire . . . 3.00
Vampire Companion #3 . . . . 3.00
GN rep.#1-#12 (Innovation) 25.00
GN rep.#1-#12 (Ballantine) 25.00

VAMPIRELLA
Warren Publishing Co., 1969–83
1 NA,FF(c),I:Vampirella 750.00
2 B:Amazonia 300.00
3 Very scarce 700.00
4 . . . . 250.00
5 FF(c) 265.00
6 . . . . 250.00
7 FF(c) 275.00
8 B:horror 225.00
9 BWS,BV(c),WW 225.00
10 No Vampirella,WW 100.00
11 TS,FF(c)O&I Pendragon. 200.00
12 WW 200.00
13 . . . . 175.00
14 . . . . 175.00
15 . . . . 175.00
16 . . . . 175.00
17 B:Tomb of the Gods 175.00
18 . . . . 175.00
19 WW,1973 Annual 150.00

20 thru 25 . . . . @125.00
26 . . . . 100.00
27 1974 Annual 120.00
28 thru 30 . . . . @100.00
31 FF(c) 120.00
32 thru 36 . . . . @75.00
37 1975 Annual 80.00
38 . . . . 75.00
39 . . . . 75.00
40 . . . . 75.00
41 thru 45 . . . . @50.00
46 O:Vampirella 65.00
47 thru 99 . . . . @50.00
100 Double Size 125.00
101 thru 110 . . . . @75.00
111 Giant Edition 100.00
112 . . . . 75.00
Ann. #1 WW. 450.00
Special #1 . . . . 300.00
Harris, 1998
113 Low distribution 500.00

VAMPIRELLA
Harris, 1992
0 Dracula Wars 5.00
0a Blue version 18.00
1 V:Forces of Chaos, w/coupon for
   DSt poster 15.00
1a 2nd printing 5.00
2 AH(c) 14.00
3 A:Dracula 7.00
4 A:Dracula 6.00
5 . . . . 6.00
Spec. #1 Vampirella/Shadowhawk:
   Creatures of the Night (1995) . . 5.50
Harris Comics, 1996
0 gold foil signed & numbered . . . 18.00
1 Commemorative Edition 3.00
1a Commemorative Edition,
   sgn & num. 9.00
25th Anniv. Spec., FF(c). 6.00
25th Anniv. Spec., lim. 7.00
Spec. Death of Vampirella,
   memorial, chromium cover . . . 15.00
Spec. 1-shot Vampirella/Cain,
   flipbook, 72-pg. (1996) 7.00
Spec. Vampirella Pin-up (1995) . . 3.50

VAMPIRELLA (MONTHLY)
Harris Comics, 1998–2000
1 Ascending Evil, pt.1 . . . . 3.00
1a ultra-violent cover 3.00
1b JaL(c). 9.00
2 Ascending Evil, pt.2 . . . . 3.00
2a JaL(c). 9.00
3 Ascending Evil, pt.3 . . . . 3.00
3a JaL(c). 9.00
4 Holy War, pt.1 . . . . 3.00
4a Crimson ed., Joe Linsner (c) . . . 3.00
5 Holy War, pt.2 . . . . 3.00
6 Holy War, pt.3 . . . . 3.00
7 Queen's Gambit, pt.1 . . . . 3.00
7a chromium Edition 9.00
8 Queen's Gambit, pt.2 . . . . 3.00
9 Queen's Gambit, pt.3, concl. 3.00
10 Hell on Earth, pt.1, V:Nyx 3.00
10a variant JaL cover 9.00
11 Hell on Earth, pt.2 . . . . 3.00
12 Hell on Earth, pt.3,
   New costume 3.00
12a variant cover, new costume . . . 3.00
12b chromium cover 9.00
13 World's End,pt.1 . . . . 3.00
13b Pantha cover. 9.00
14 World's End,pt.2 . . . . 3.00
15 World's End,pt.3 . . . . 3.00
13a thru 15a variant (c)s . . . . @3.00
16 Pantha #1 . . . . 3.00
17 Pantha #2 . . . . 3.00
16b limited photo ed. 9.00

16a thru 17a Phantha photo(c)s . @3.00
18 Rebirth, pt.1,JaL(c) 3.00
19 Rebirth, pt.2, ... 3.00
20 Rebirth, pt.3 . . . . 3.00
21 Dangerous Games,pt.1 . . . . 3.00
21c Millennium ed. 15.00
22 Dangerous Games,pt.2 . . . . 3.00
22a Dorian (c) 9.00
16c thru 22c Julie Strain (c)s . . . . @9.00
23 Vampirella/Lady Death:
    The Revenge, pt.1 . . . . 3.00
23a limited ed. 9.00
21b thru 23b limited chrome ed. @15.00
24 Death Valley, Vampirella (c) 3.00
24a Pantha (c) 3.00
25 Death Valley, vol.2 . . . . 3.00
25a alternate (c) 3.00
25b Monte Moore (c) 15.00
26 The End #1 . . . . 3.00
26a alternate (c) 9.00
26b platinum ed. 20.00
Ashcan, Ascending Evil, b&w, 16pg. 1.50
Ashcan, Ascending Evil, b&w,
    signed, limited 25.00
Ashcan, Queen's Gambit,B&W 6.00
Ashcan, Queen's Gambit,signed . . . 25.00
Ashcan World's End, B&W,16pg. . . . 6.00
Ashcan Rebirth preview,B&W,16-pg 6.00
Vampirella/Lady Death Limited
    Preview Ashcan, B&W. 6.00
Vampirella, Queen's Gambit #1
    special edition, alternate (c) . . . 9.00
    Chromium Edition 10.00
Spec.#0 A:Lady Death,B.U.:Pantha. 3.00
Spec.#0a Pantha(c) 3.00
Spec.#0b Vampirella(c) 9.00
Spec.#0c Vampirella(c), signed . . . 30.00
Spec.#0d Pantha(c) 9.00
Spec. Vampirella/Dracula: The
    Centennial, A:Pantha,16pg. . . . 2.00
Spec. Vampirella/Dracula: The
    Centennial, 48pg. (1997). 5.00
Spec.#1 Dangerous Games,
    holochrome (2001) 15.00
Ann.Ed.#2 Rebirth 10.00
Ann.Ed.#3 Rebirth,Bruce Timm(c). 10.00
Julie Strain Special. 4.00
Julie Strain Special variant(c) 10.00
Julie Strain Spec. chrome (c) 15.00
Julie Strain Spec. holochrome(c). . 25.00

VAMPIRELLA
Harris Comics, 2001

0 Gold edition 15.00
1 Nowheresville, Mayhew (c) 3.00
1a JSC (c). 3.00
1b Anacleto (c) 3.00
1c JaL (c) 3.00
1d commemorative ed. B&W, FF(c) 5.00
1e Chicago convention edition 9.00
1f Chicago convention, limited . . . 15.00
1g photo edition, limited 9.00
1h gold edition 25.00
1i holographic chrome (c) 12.00
1j royal blue edition. 50.00
1k gold-fx chrome (c) 20.00
1l Ascending evil gold (c) 15.00
2 thru 4 . . . . @3.00
4c holo FX chrome (c) 12.00
4d gold-fx chrome 30.00
2a thru 22a limited . . . . @9.00
2b thru 22b photo (c) . . . . @9.00
5 thru 22 . . . . @3.00
7c thru 10c limited Pantha
    MT(c). . . . . @9.00
7d Pantha holo fx MC(c). 15.00
Ashcan #1 giant-size 6.00
Ashcan #4–#6 giant-size, 16-pg. . . 6.00
Preview #7–#9 16-pg. 3.00
Ashcan #7–#9 giant-size,16-pg. . . . 6.00
Ashcan #11–#13 . . . . 6.00
1-shot Vampirella Genesis (2001) . . 3.00

1-shot Vampirella Genesis,
    variant 9.00
Spec. Model Search. 10.00
Spec. Halloween 2004 . . . . 5.00

VAMPIRELLA:
BLOOD LUST
Harris, 1997

1 (of 2) JeR & JJu. 5.00
2 JJu(c). 5.00
Book 1, JJu(c) Virgin edition 11.00
Book 2, JJu(c) Virgin edition 11.00

VAMPIRELLA CLASSIC
Harris Comics, 1995

1 Dark Angel. 3.50
2 V:Demogorgon. 3.25
3 V:Were Beast. 3.25
4 R:Papa Voodoo 3.25
5 . . . . 3.00

VAMPIRELLA:
CROSSOVERS
Harris, 1996–98

1-shot Vampirella vs.
    Eudaemon (1996) 9.00
1-shot StG,SSh,Vampirella/
    Wetworks, image x-over (1997) 3.00
1-shotA Vamp/Wetworks,
    SS&KN(c) 9.00
1-shot Vampirella/Shi (1997) 3.00
1-shotA Vamp/Shi, Chromium ed.. . 7.00
1-shotA Vamp/Shi, penciled(c). . . . 9.00
Ashcan #1, Vamp/Shi, 16pg 3.00
1-shot Vampirella/Painkiller
    Jane, foil JQ(c) (1998). 3.50
1-shotA Vampirella/Painkiller
    Jane, alternate RL&JP(c) 9.00
1 Crossover art gallery 3.00
1a Art gallery, chromium ed. 9.00
1b Art gallery, holochrome(c) 20.00

VAMPIRELLA: DEATH
AND DESTRUCTION
Harris

1 limited preview ashcan 4.00
1a The Dying of the Light 3.00
1b signed & numbered 3.00
1c satin edition 22.00
1d Lim. Ed., Mark Beachum (c) . . . 9.00
2 The Nature of the Beast 3.00
3 TSg,ACo,JP,JJu(c),Mistress
    Nyx kills Vampi 3.00

VAMPIRELLA/
LADY DEATH
Harris/Chaos!, 1999

1 x-over. 3.50
1a Valentine ed. 9.00
1b signed and numbered 15.00
1c gold edition. 25.00
1d penciled edition 9.00
Spec.#1 TheEnd,chrome(c)(2000). 12.00
Spec.#1a The End,holochrome(c). 20.00
Spec.#1 Revenge, chrome(c)
    (2000) 12.00
Spec.#1a Revenge,holochrome(c) 20.00

VAMPIRELLA LIVES
Harris, 1996–97

1 Linen Edition 7.00
1a Censored Photo cover edition . . 8.00
2 Vengeance edition 3.00
2a alternate edition, AH(c) 9.00
3 WEl(s),ACo,JP,Graveyard edition,
    JSC(c) 3.00
2b thru 3b Model photo edition . . @3.00

Vampirella Lives #2
© *Harris Comics*

VAMPIRELLA
OF DRAKULON
Harris Comics, 1996

1 V:assassin 3.00
1a alternate MiB(c) 9.00
2 Dracula returns 3.00
3 thru 5 . . . . @3.00

VAMPIRELLA:
SAD WINGS OF DESTINY
Harris, 1996

1 DQ(s),JJu(c) 4.00
1 signed & numbered (#1,500). . . . 5.00
Gold Emblem Seal Edition. 4.00

VAMPIRELLA STRIKES
Harris Comics, 1995

1 The Prize,pt.1 . . . . 3.00
1a limited, signed & numbered. . . . 9.00
1b full moon background 3.50
2 V:Dante Corp.,A:Passion. 3.00
3 V:subway stalker. 3.00
4 IEd,RN, Soul Food. 3.00
5 DQ,RN,F:Eudaemon 3.00
5 signed & numbered, (200). 9.00
6 . . . . 3.00
6 signed, alternate cover 9.00
6 signed & numbered 11.00
7 silver special flip book 3.00
Ann. #1 new cover 9.00

VAMPIRELLA
VS. HEMORRHAGE
Harris, 1997

1 IEd,MIB 3.50
1 signed & numbered 10.00
1 Linen edition, signed & numb. . . 20.00
1 MIB alternate cover 9.00
2 IEd,MIB 3.50
3 (of 3) IEd,MIB. 3.50

VAMPIRELLA VS. PANTHA
Harris, 1997

Showcase #1 preview 2.00
1 MMr,MT, MT(c) Vampirella vs.
    Pantha 3.50
1 MMr,MT, MT(c) Pantha vs.
    Vampirella 3.50
1a MMr,MT, MT(c). 9.00

All comics prices listed are for *Near Mint* condition.

COLOR PUB.

VAMPIRELLA/ WITCHBLADE
Harris Comics, 2003
1 . . . . 3.00
1a variant (c) 9.00
Spec. Union of the Damned 3.00
Spec. Variant (c) 9.00
Anarchy Studios/Harris Comics
Ashcan San Diego Comic Con
B&W, 16-page 5.00

VAMPIRELLA/ WITCHBLADE: FEAST
Anarchy Studios/Harris Comics, 2005
1 . . . . 3.00
1a & 1b variant (c)s . . . . @9.00

VAMPIRE THE MASQUERADE
Moonstone, 2001
1-shot Toreador 6.00
1-shot Nosferatu (2002) 7.00
1-shot Beckett 7.00
1-shot Ventrue 7.00
1-shot Calebros 6.00
1-shot Giovanni 5.50
1-shot Assamite 5.50
1-shot Lasombra 5.50
1-shot Isabel 5.00
1-shot Lucita 5.00

VAMPRESS LUXURA, THE
Brainstorm, 1996
1 . . . . 3.00
1a gold edition 9.00
2 . . . . 3.00
2a gold foil 9.00

VANDALA
Chaos! Comics, 2000
1 . . . . 3.00
1 premium 9.99

VANDALA II
Chaos! Comics, 2001
1 PDa,EBe 3.00
1a premium ed. Matt Hughes (c) . . 9.00

VANGUARD ILLUSTRATED
Pacific, 1983
1 . . . . 3.00
2 DSt(c) 3.00
3 thru 5 SR . . . . @3.00
6 GI 3.00
7 GE,I:Mr.Monster 6.00

VARICK: CHRONICLES OF THE DARK PRINCE
Q Comics, 1999
1 by Nick Marcari & Major Fareed . 2.50
2 32-pg. 2.50
3 thru 6 . . . . @2.50

VARUK
Counteractive Comics, 2006
1 . . . . 3.00

VAULT OF HORROR
Gladstone, 1990–91
1 Rep.GS,WW 5.00
2 Rep.VoH #27 & HoF #18 . . . . . . 3.00
3 Rep.VoH #13 & HoF #22 . . . . . . 3.00
4 Rep.VoH #23 & HoF #13 . . . . . . 3.00

5 Rep.VoH #19 & HoF #5 . . . . 3.00
6 Rep.VoH #32 & WF #6 . . . . 3.00
7 Rep.VoH #26 & WS #7 . . . . 3.00

VAULT OF HORROR
Russ Cochran Publ., 1991–92
1 Rep.VoH #28 & WS #18 . . . . . . 4.00
2 Rep.VoH #33 & WS #20 . . . . . . 3.00
3 Rep.VoH #26 & WS #7 . . . . 3.00
4 Rep.VoH #35 & WS #15 . . . . . . 3.00
4 Rep.VoH #18 & WS #11 . . . . . . 3.00
5 Rep.VoH #18 & WS #11 . . . . . . 3.00
2nd Series
1 thru 7 Rep.VoH . . . . @3.00
8 . . . . 3.00
Gemstone
17 thru 29 EC comics reprints . . . @3.00

VECTOR
Now, 1986
1 . . . . 3.00
2 thru 5 . . . . @3.00

VEGAS KNIGHTS
Pioneer, 1989
1 . . . . 2.50
2 . . . . 2.50
3 . . . . 2.50

Vengeance of Vampirella #24
© Harris

VENGEANCE OF VAMPIRELLA
Harris, 1994
1 Hemmorhage 6.00
1a Gold Edition 9.00
1 gold edition, signed, numbered . 12.00
2 Dervish 3.00
3 On the Hunt 3.00
4 Teenage Vampries 3.00
5 Teenage Vampires 3.00
6 . . . . 3.00
7 . . . . 3.00
8 bagged w/card 3.00
9 . . . . 3.00
10 Bad Jack Rising 3.00
11 Pits of Hell, w/card 3.00
12 V:Passion 3.00
13 V:Passion 3.00
14 Prelude to the Walk,pt.2 . . . . . . 3.00
15 The Mystery Walk,pt.1 . . . . 3.25
16 The Mystery Walk,pt.2 . . . . 3.25
17 The Mystery Walk,pt.3 . . . . 3.25
18 The Mystery Walk,pt.4 . . . . 3.00
19 The Mystery Walk,pt.5 . . . . 3.00
20 Mystery Walk epilog 3.00
14a thru 19a Buzz . . . . @5.00

21 thru 24 . . . . @3.00
25 The End 3.00
25 variant cover, signed &
numbered 8.00
25 signed & numbered (2,500) 8.00
25 gold edition, signed & numb. . . 15.00
25 alternate cover, signed by Jae
Lee & numbered (#1,500) 12.00
Mini-comic gold foil, signed 15.00

VENTURE
AC Comics, 1986
1 . . . . 3.00
2 thru 4 . . . . @3.00

VERONICA
Archie Publications, April, 1989
1 . . . . @7.00
2 thru 10 . . . . @5.00
11 thru 38 . . . . @4.00
39 Love Show Dolon 6.00
40 thru 50 . . . . @4.00
51 thru 71 . . . . @3.50
72 thru 93 . . . . @3.00
94 thru 97 . . . . @2.50
98 thru 120 . . . . @2.50
121 thru 133 . . . . @2.50
134 thru 156 . . . . @2.50
157 thru 185 . . . . @2.25

VEROTIKA
Verotika, 1995
1 thru 3 Jae Lee, Frazetta . . . . . @3.00
4 thru 9 . . . . @3.00
1-shot Rogues Gallery of Villians
(1998) 4.00

VEROTIK ILLUSTRATED
Verotik, 1997
1 48pg. 7.00
2 . . . . 7.00
3 . . . . 7.00
3a alternate cover 7.00
3 variant cover 9.00

VEROTIK WORLD
Verotik, 2004
2 . . . . 4.00
3 . . . . 4.00
2a variant (c) 9.00
2b Parody (c) 5.00
3a variant (c) 9.00
3b Shrunken Head (c) 9.00

VESPER
Acetylene Comics, 2001
Preview B&W 3.00
1 Girls Night Out 2.50
1a JOb (c) 2.50
2 . . . . 2.50
2a variant Wizardworld 2001(c) . . . 5.00
3 The Word for the Day 2.50
3a variant HbK(c) 2.50
4 . . . . 2.50
5 Soul Harvest 2.50
6 . . . . 2.50
6a variant (c) 2.50
7 Return of Gruel 3.00

VICKI
Atlas, 1975
1 Rep 75.00
2 thru 4 . . . . @40.00

VICTORIAN
Penny Farthing Press, 1999
1 . . . . 3.00
2 thru 5 . . . . @3.00
6 thru 13 . . . . @3.00

All comics prices listed are for *Near Mint* condition.

14 thru 17 . . . . @3.00
18 thru 24 . . . . @3.00
25 74-pg. 6.00

VICTORIA'S SECRET SERVICE
Alias Enterprises, 2005
0 . . . . 2.00
1 . . . . 3.00
2 . . . . 3.50
3 . . . . 3.50
4 . . . . 3.50
5 . . . . 3.50

VILLAINS
Viper Comics, 2006
1 (of 4) 3.25
2 . . . . 3.25
3 . . . . 3.25
4 . . . . 3.25

VILLAINS & VIGILANTES
Eclipse, 1986–87
1 A:Crusaders,Shadowman 3.00
2 A:Condor 3.00
3 V:Crushers 3.00
4 V:Crushers 3.00

VINTAGE MAGNUS ROBOT FIGHTER
Valiant, 1992
1 rep. Gold Key Magnus #22
(which is #1) 5.00
2 rep. Gold Key Magnus #3 . . . . . . 4.50
3 rep. Gold Key Magnus #13 . . . . . 3.50
4 rep. Gold Key Magnus #15 . . . . . 3.50

VIP
TV Comics, 2000
1 (of 3) 3.00
2 thru 3 . . . . @3.00
1a thru 3a photo (c) . . . . @3.00
Preview Edition 6.00

VIRGINIAN, THE
Gold Key, 1963
1 . . . . 100.00

VIRTEX
Oktomica Entertainment, 1998
0 16-pg. 2.50
1 V:Ripnun 2.50
2 V:Ripnun 2.50
3 alternate endings 2.50
4 Night of the Ninjella,pt.1 . . . . . . 2.50
5 Night of the Ninjella,pt.2 . . . . . . 3.00
6 All My Sins Remembered 3.00

VIRTUA FIGHTER
Malibu, 1995
1 New Video Game Comic 3.00

VISITOR
Valiant, 1994
1 New Series 2.50
2 thru 13 . . . . @2.50

VISITOR VS. VALIANT
Valiant, 1994
1 V:Solar 3.00
2 . . . . 3.00

VOLTRON
Solson, 1985
1 TV tie-in 4.00
2 . . . . 4.00
3 . . . . 4.00

VOLTRON: DEFENDER OF THE UNIVERSE
Devil's Due/UDON, 2004
Vol 2
1 . . . . 3.00
2 thru 12 . . . . @3.00

VOODOO CHILD
Virgin Comics, 2007
1 . . . . 3.00
2 thru 5 . . . . @3.00

VORTEX
Vortex, 1982–88
1 Peter Hsu art 9.00
2 Mister X on cover. 6.00
3 thru 4 . . . . @4.00
5 thru 8 . . . . @3.00
9 thru 13 . . . . @2.00

VORTEX
Comico, 1991
1 SBt,from Elementals 2.50
2 SBt, ... 2.50

VORTEX: THE SECOND COMING
Entity, 1996
1 (of 6) 3.00
1a variant cover 3.00
2 . . . . 3.00

Voyage to the Bottom of the Sea #8
© Gold Key

VOYAGE TO THE BOTTOM OF THE SEA
Gold Key, 1964–70
1 . . . . 200.00
2 thru 5 . . . . @125.00
6 thru 14 . . . . @75.00
15 and 16 reprints . . . . @50.00

VOYAGE TO THE DEEP
Dell Publishing Co., 1962
1 P(c) 125.00
2 P(c) 75.00
3 P(c) 75.00
4 P(c) 75.00

VSS: NEMESIS RISING
Bluewater, 2007
1 . . . . 3.50
2 thru 5 . . . . @3.50

WACKY ADVENTURES OF CRACKY
Gold Key, 1972–75
1 . . . . 30.00
2 thru 11 . . . . @25.00
12 . . . . 20.00

WACKY WITCH
Gold Key, 1971–75
1 . . . . 75.00
2 . . . . 30.00
3 thru 20 . . . . @25.00
21 . . . . 20.00

WAGON TRAIN
Dell, 1960
4 . . . . 100.00
5 ATh 125.00
6 thru 13 . . . . 100.00

WAGON TRAIN
Gold Key, 1964
1 . . . . 125.00
2 . . . . 100.00
3 . . . . 100.00
4 . . . . 100.00

WAKE THE DEAD
IDW Publishing, 2003
1 (of 5) 4.00
2 . . . . 4.00
3 thru 5 . . . . @4.00

WALK-IN
Virgin Comics, 2006
1 . . . . 3.00
2 thru 6 . . . . @3.00

WALLACE & GROMIT
Titan Publishing 2002
GN Catch of the Day 9.00
GN The Whippet Vanishes 9.00
GN The Bootiful Game 9.00
11 . . . . 6.00
13 thru 16 . . . . @6.00
GN A Pier too Far 9.00
Yearbook 2007 . . . . 10.00

WALLY
Gold Key, 1962–63
1 . . . . 60.00
2 . . . . 50.00
3 . . . . 50.00
4 . . . . 50.00

WALLY WOOD'S THUNDER AGENTS
Delux, 1984–86
1 GP,KG,DC,SD,I:New Menth. 6.00
2 GP,KG,DC,SD,The Raven 5.00
3 KG,DC,SD 5.00
4 GP,KG,RB,DA 5.00
5 JOy,KG,A:CodenamDangr 5.00

WALT DISNEY ANNUALS
Walt Disney's Autumn Adventure. . . 4.00
Walt Disney's Holiday Parade #1 . . 3.50
Walt Disney's Spring Fever 3.50
Walt Disney's Summer Fun 3.50
Walt Disney's Holiday Parade #2 . . 3.50

WALT DISNEY'S AUTUMN ADVENTURE
Disney, 1990
1 Rep. CB. 4.00

COLOR PUB.

WALT DISNEY'S CHRISTMAS PARADE
Gemstone Publishing, 2003
1 . . . . 9.00

WALT DISNEY'S COMICS AND STORIES
Dell/Gold Key, 1962

264 CB,Von Drake & Gearloose . . 75.00
265 CB,Von Drake & Gearloose . . 75.00
266 CB,Von Drake & Gearloose . . 75.00
267 CB,Von Drake & Gearloose . . 75.00
268 CB,Von Drake & Gearloose . . 75.00
269 CB,Von Drake & Gearloose . . 75.00
270 CB,Von Drake & Gearloose . . 75.00
271 CB,Von Drake & Gearloose . . 75.00
272 CB,Von Drake & Gearloose . . 75.00
273 CB,Von Drake & Gearloose . . 75.00
274 CB,Von Drake & Gearloose . . 75.00
275 CB 70.00
276 CB 70.00
277 CB 70.00
278 CB 70.00
279 CB 70.00
280 CB 70.00
281 CB 70.00
282 CB 70.00
283 CB 70.00
284 . . . . 40.00
285 . . . . 40.00
286 CB 50.00
287 . . . . 40.00
288 CB 50.00
289 CB 50.00
290 . . . . 40.00
291 CB 50.00
292 CB 50.00
293 CB; Grandma Duck's Farm
    Friends 50.00
294 CB 50.00
295 . . . . 40.00
296 . . . . 40.00
297 CB; Gyro Gearloose 50.00
298 CB; Daisy Duck's Dairy 50.00
299 CB rep. 50.00
300 CB rep. 50.00
301 CB rep. 50.00
302 CB rep. 50.00
303 CB rep. 50.00
304 CB rep. 50.00
305 CB rep. Gyro Gearloose 50.00
306 CB rep. 50.00
307 CB rep. 50.00
308 CB 50.00
309 CB 50.00
310 CB 50.00
311 CB 50.00
312 CB 50.00
313 thru 327 . . . . @30.00
328 CB 40.00
329 . . . . 30.00
330 . . . . 30.00
331 . . . . 30.00
332 . . . . 30.00
333 . . . . 30.00
334 . . . . 30.00
335 CB rep. 40.00
336 . . . . 30.00
337 . . . . 30.00
338 . . . . 30.00
339 . . . . 30.00
340 . . . . 30.00
341 . . . . 30.00
342 thru 350 CB rep. . . . . @30.00
351 thru 361 CB rep. with poster @60.00
351a thru 361a. without poster . @30.00
361 thru 400 CB rep. . . . . @50.00
401 thru 409 CB rep. . . . . @30.00
410 CB rep. Annette Funichello . . 30.00
411 thru 429 CB rep. . . . . @30.00

Walt Disney's Comics and Stories #305
© Gold Key

430 . . . . 20.00
431 CB rep. 25.00
432 CB rep. 25.00
433 . . . . 20.00
434 CB rep. 25.00
435 CB rep. 25.00
436 CB rep. 25.00
437 . . . . 20.00
438 . . . . 20.00
439 CB rep. 22.00
440 CB rep. 22.00
441 . . . . 20.00
442 CB rep. 22.00
443 CB rep. 22.00
444 . . . . 20.00
445 . . . . 20.00
446 thru 465 CB rep. . . . . @22.00
466 . . . . 22.00
467 thru 473 CB rep. . . . . @22.00

Whitman, 1980

474 thru 478 CB rep. . . . . @20.00
479 CB 50.00
480 CB Rare 150.00
481 thru 484 . . . . @50.00
485 thru 505 . . . . @25.00
506 . . . . 20.00
507 CB rep. 22.00
508 CB rep. 22.00
509 CB rep. 22.00
510 CB rep. 22.00

Gladstone, 1986

511 translation of Dutch 30.00
512 translation of Dutch 25.00
513 translation of Dutch 25.00
514 translation of Dutch 11.00
515 translation of Dutch 11.00
516 translation of Dutch 11.00
517 translation of Dutch 6.00
518 translation of Dutch 6.00
519 CB,Donald Duck 6.00
520 translation of Dutch, Rosa . 11.00
521 Walt Kelly 6.00
522 CB,WK,nephews 6.00
523 Rosa,Donald Duck 15.00
524 Rosa,Donald Duck 15.00
525 translation of Dutch 15.00
526 Rosa,Donald Duck 10.00
527 CB 6.00
528 Rosa,Donald Duck 15.00
529 CB 6.00
530 Rosa,Donald Duck 7.00
531 WK(c),Rosa,CB 7.00
532 CB 6.00
533 CB 6.00
534 CB 6.00
535 CB 6.00

536 CB 6.00
537 CB 6.00
538 CB 6.00
539 CB 6.00
540 CB new art 6.00
541 double-size,WK(c). 6.00
542 CB 7.00
543 CB,WK(c) 6.00
544 CB,WK(c) 6.00
545 CB 6.00
546 CB,WK,giant 7.00
547 CB,WK,Rosa,giant 15.00

Walt Disney, 1990

548 CB,WK,Home is the Hero. . 10.00
549 CB, ... 5.00
550 CB,prev.unpub.story! 8.00
551 . . . . 5.00
552 . . . . 5.00
553 . . . . 5.00
554 . . . . 5.00
555 . . . . 5.00
556 . . . . 5.00
557 . . . . 5.00
558 Donald's Fix-it Shop 5.00
559 Bugs 5.00
560 CB,April Fools Story 5.00
561 CB,Donald the Flipist 5.00
562 CB,3DirtyLittleDucks 5.00
563 CB,Donald Camping 5.00
564 Dirk the Dinosaur 5.00
565 CB,DonaldDuck,TruantOfficer. . 5.00
566 CB,Will O' the Wisp 5.00
567 CB,Turkey Shoot 5.00
568 CB,AChristmas Eve Story. . . . 5.00
569 CB, New Years Resolutions . . . 5.00
570 CB,Donald the Mailman
    +Poster 5.00
571 CB,Atom Bomb 8.00
572 CB,April Fools. 5.00
573 TV Quiz Show. 5.00
574 Pinnochio,64pgs 6.00
575 Olympic Torch Bearer, Li'l
    Bad Wolf,64 pgs. 6.00
576 giant 6.00
577 A:Truant Officers,64 pgs. 6.00
578 CB,Old Quacky Manor 5.00
579 CB,Turkey Hunt 5.00
580 CB,The Wise Little Red Hen,
    64 pg.-Sunday page format. . 5.50
581 CB,Duck Lake. 5.00
582 giant 5.50
583 giant 5.50
584 . . . . 5.00
585 CB, giant. 5.50

Gladstone, 1993

586 . . . . 5.00
587 thru 599. . . . . @5.00
600 CB 6.00
601 thru 605 prestige format . . . . @7.00
606 Winging It 7.00
607 Number 401 . . . . 7.00
608 Sleepless in Duckburg 7.00
609 . . . . 7.00
610 Treasures Untold 7.00
611 Romance at a Glance 7.00
612 The Sod Couple 7.00
613 Another Fine Mess 7.00
614 Airheads 7.00
615 Backyard Battlers 7.00
616 . . . . 7.00
617 Tree's A Crowd 7.00
618 A Dolt from the Blue 7.00
619 Queen of the Ant Farm 7.00
620 Caught in the Cold Rush 7.00
621 Room and Bored. 7.00
622 . . . . 7.00
623 All Quacked Up. 7.00
624 Their Loaded Forebear 7.00
625 Mummery's the Word 7.00
626 A Real Gone Guy 7.00
627 To Bee or Not to Bee 7.00
628 Officer for a Day 7.00

COLOR PUB.

629 The Ghost Train 7.00
630 two Donald Duck stories 7.00
631 Music Hath Charms 7.00
632 A Day in a Duck's Life 7.00
633 All Donald issue 7.00
634 The Runaway Train 7.00
635 Volcano Valley 7.00
636 Mission to Codfish Cove 7.00
637 Pizen Springs Dude Ranch 7.00

WALT DISNEY'S COMICS AND STORIES
Gemstone Publishing, 2003

634 thru 650 . . . . @7.00
651 thru 662 . . . . @7.00
663 thru 676 . . . . @7.00
677 thru 681 . . . . @7.50
682 thru 687 . . . . @8.00
Spec. Walt Disney's Vacation
  Parade 9.00
Spec. Vacation Parade #2 . . . . . . 9.00
Spec. Vacation Parade #3 . . . . . . 9.00
Spec. Vacation Parade #5 . . . . . . 10.00
Spec. Christmas Parade 9.00
Spec. Christmas Parade #1 . . . . . 9.00
Spec. Christmas Parade #2 . . . . . 9.00
Spec. Christmas Parade #3 . . . . . 9.00
Spec. Christmas Parade #4 . . . . . 7.00
Spec. Christmas Parade #5 . . . . . . 9.50

WALT DISNEY COMICS DIGEST
Gold Key, 1968–76
[All done by Carl Barks]

1 Rep,Uncle Scrooge 125.00
2 CB,ATh 75.00
3 CB,ATh 75.00
4 CB,ATh 75.00
5 CB,Daisy Duck 125.00
6 thru 13 CB,ATh . . . . @60.00
14 ATh 35.00
15 ATh 35.00
16 ATh,rep.Donald Duck #26 . . . . 60.00
17 CB,ATh 45.00
18 CB,ATh 45.00
19 CB,ATh 45.00
20 CB,ATh 45.00
21 CB,ATh 35.00
22 CB,ATh 35.00
23 CB,ATh 35.00
24 CB,ATh,Zorro 35.00
25 thru 31 CB,ATh . . . . @35.00
32 ATh 30.00
33 ATh 35.00
34 ATh,rep.Four Color #318 . . . . . 35.00
35 ATh 35.00
36 ATh 35.00
37 ATh 35.00
38 ATh,rep.Disneyland#1 . . . . 35.00
39 ATh 35.00
40 ATh,FG 30.00
41 ATh 25.00
42 CB 30.00
43 CB 30.00
44 Rep. Four Color #29 & others . 75.00
45 . . . . 25.00
46 CB 25.00
47 . . . . 25.00
48 . . . . 25.00
49 . . . . 25.00
50 CB 25.00
51 rep.Four Color #71 . . . . 35.00
52 CB 25.00
53 . . . . 25.00
54 . . . . 25.00
55 . . . . 25.00
56 CB,rep. Uncle Scrooge #32 . . . 30.00
57 CB 25.00

WALT DISNEY SHOWCASE
Gold Key, 1970–80

1 Boatniks (photo cover) 40.00
2 Moby Duck 30.00
3 Bongo & Lumpjaw 25.00
4 Pluto 25.00
5 $1,000,000 Duck (photo cover) . 30.00
6 Bedknobs & Broomsticks 25.00
7 Pluto 25.00
8 Daisy & Donald 25.00
9 101 Dalmatians rep. 35.00
10 Napoleon & Samantha 30.00
11 Moby Duck rep 20.00
12 Dumbo rep 25.00
13 Pluto rep 25.00
14 World's Greatest Athlete 30.00
15 3 Little Pigs rep 25.00
16 Aristocats rep 30.00
17 Mary Poppins rep 30.00
18 Gyro Gearloose rep 40.00
19 That Darn Cat rep 35.00
20 Pluto rep 25.00
21 Li'l Bad Wolf & 3 Little Pigs . . . 20.00
22 Unbirthday Party rep 30.00
23 Pluto rep 25.00
24 Herbie Rides Again rep 25.00
25 Old Yeller rep 25.00
26 Lt. Robin Crusoe USN rep 25.00
27 Island at the Top of the World . 30.00
28 Brer Rabbit, Bucky Bug rep . . . 25.00
29 Escape to Witch Mountain 30.00
30 Magica De Spell rep 45.00
31 Bambi rep 25.00
32 Spin & Marty rep 25.00
33 Pluto rep 20.00
34 Paul Revere's Ride rep 20.00
35 Goofy rep 20.00
36 Peter Pan rep 20.00
37 Tinker Bell & Jiminy Cricket rep. 20.00
38 Mickey & the Sleuth, Pt. 1 . . . 20.00
39 Mickey & the Sleuth, Pt. 2 . . . 20.00
40 The Rescuers 20.00
41 Herbie Goes to Monte Carlo . . 20.00
42 Mickey & the Sleuth 20.00
43 Pete's Dragon 25.00
44 Return From Witch Mountain
   & In Search of the Castaways. 25.00
45 The Jungle Book rep 25.00
46 The Cat From Outer Space . . . 20.00
47 Mickey Mouse Surprise Party . . 20.00
48 The Wonderful Adventures of
   Pinocchio 20.00
49 North Avenue Irregulars; Zorro . 20.00
50 Bedknobs & Broomsticks rep. . 20.00
51 101 Dalmatians 20.00

Walter Lantz Woody Woodpecker
Summer Fun #1 © Gold Key

52 Unidentified Flying Oddball 20.00
53 The Scarecrow 20.00
54 The Black Hole 20.00

WALTER LANTZ WOODY WOODPECKER
Dell, 1952

72 . . . . 40.00
Gold Key, 1962
73 thru 75 . . . . @75.00
76 thru 120 . . . . @25.00
121 thru 186 . . . . @15.00
Spec. Summer Fun (1966) 30.00
Whitman, 1980
188 thru 189 . . . . @15.00
190 thru 191 scarce . . . . @40.00
193 thru 201 . . . . @25.00

WALT KELLY'S CHRISTMAS CLASSICS
Eclipse, 1987

1 . . . . 5.00

WALT KELLY'S SPRINGTIME TALES
Eclipse, 1988

1 . . . . 5.00

WAR
Charlton, 1975

1 . . . . 25.00
2 thru 10 . . . . @15.00
11 thru 48 . . . . @8.00

WAR AGAINST CRIME
Gemstone, 2000

1 rep. 2.50
2 rep. Summer 1942 . . . . 2.50
3 rep. Fall 1948 . . . . 2.50
4 rep. Winter 1948 . . . . 2.50
5 rep. Feb. 1949 . . . . 2.50
6 rep. June 1949 . . . . 2.50
7 rep. 2.50
8 rep. Aug. 1949 . . . . 2.50
9 rep. Oct. 1949 . . . . 2.50
10 rep. Dec. 1949 issue 2.50
11 rep. Feb. 1950 issue 2.50

WAR AND ATTACK
Charlton, 1964

1 WW 75.00

WAR AT SEA
Charlton, 1957

22 . . . . 50.00
23 thru 30 . . . . @40.00
31 thru 42 . . . . @30.00

WARCAT SPECIAL
Entity Press, 1995

1 I:Warcat 3.00

WARCHILD
Maximum Press, 1995

1 I:Sword, Stone 3.50
2 I:Morganna Lefay 3.00
3 V: The Black Knight 2.50
4 Rescue Merlyn 2.50
[2nd Series]
1 . . . . 2.50

WAR DANCER
Defiant, 1994

1 B:JiS(s),I:Ahrq Tsolmec 2.75
2 I:Massakur 2.75
3 V:Massakur 2.75
4 JiS(s),A:Nudge 3.25

COLOR PUB.

Warfront #36
© Harvey

WARFRONT
Harvey, 1965
36 . . . . 75.00
37 thru 39 . . . . @75.00

WARHAWKS
TSR, 1990–91
1 thru 6 from game . . . . @3.00
7 thru 10 The Battle of Britain . . . @3.00

WARHAWKS 2050
TSR
1 Pt.1 . . . . 3.00

WARHAMMER 40K
Boom! Studios, 2006
0 . . . . 3.00
0a previews variant (c) 3.00
1 . . . . 3.00
1a previews exclusive. 3.00
2 thru 5 . . . . @3.00
3a theu 5a variant (c) . . . . @3.00

WARHAMMER 40K:
DAMNATION CRUSADE
Boom! Studios
2 . . . . 3.00
2a variant Previews exclusive (c) . 3.00
6 . . . . 3.00
3a variant (c) 3.00

WARHAMMER 40K:
BLOOD AND THUNDER
Boom! Studios, 2007
1 . . . . 4.00
1a variant (c) 4.00
2 thu 3 . . . . @4.00
2a thru 3a variant (c) . . . . @4.00

WARHAMMER 40K:
INQUISITOR
Boom! Studios, 2007
1 (of 5) 3.00
1a variant (c) 3.00

WARHAMMER:
FORGE OF WAR
Boom! Studios, 2007
1 . . . . 3.00
1a variant (c) 3.00

2 thru 5 . . . . @3.00
2a thru 5a variant (c) . . . . @3.00

WAR HEROES
Charlton Comics, 1963–67
1 . . . . 75.00
2 J.F.Kennedy. 60.00
3 thru 10 . . . . @35.00
11 thru 26 . . . . @30.00
27 Devils Brigade. 45.00

WARLASH
CFD, 1995
1 Project Hardfire 3.00

WARLANDS:
MALAGEN'S CAMPAIGN
Dreamwave, 2005
1 . . . . 3.00
2 thru 3 . . . . @3.00
Pocketbook Vol. 1 . . . . 10.00

WARMASTER
1 and 2 . . . . @4.00

WAR OF THE UNDEAD
IDW Publishing, 2007
1 . . . . 4.00
2 thru 3 . . . . @4.00

WAR OF THE WORLDS:
SECOND WAVE
Boom! Studios, 2006
1 . . . . 3.00
2 thru 6 . . . . @3.00

WARP
First, 1983
1 FB,JSon,I:Lord Cumulus & Prince
Chaos, play adapt pt.1 . . . . . . 4.00
2 thru 10 . . . . @3.00
11 thru 19 . . . . @2.50
Spec. #1 HC,O:Chaos 2.50
Spec. #2 MS/MG,V:Ylem 2.50
Spec. #3 . . . . 2.50

WARREN ELLIS'
BLACK GAS
Avatar Press, 2006
1 . . . . 4.00
1a wraparound (c) 4.00
1b variant (c)s . . . . @4.00
2 . . . . 4.00
2a wraparound (c) 4.00
2b variant (c)s . . . . @4.00
2c Auxiliary edition 4.00
3 . . . . 4.00
3a wraparound (c) 4.00
3b variant (c)s . . . . @4.00
Spec. #1 thru #3 Auxiliary ed. . . . @4.00
Vol. 2
1 . . . . 4.00
1a wraparound (c) 4.00
1b variant (c)s . . . . @4.00
1c Blood red concention (c) 5.00
2 . . . . 4.00
2a wraparound (c) 4.00
2b variant (c)s . . . . @4.00
3 . . . . 4.00
3a variant (c)s . . . . @4.00

WARREN ELLIS'
CHRONICLES OF
WORMWOOD
Avatar Press, 2006
Preview 2.00

WARREN ELLIS'
WOLFSKIN
Avatar Press, 2006
1 . . . . 4.00
1a wraparound (c) 4.00
1b variant (c)s . . . . @4.00
1c Blood Red convention (c) 5.00
1d Variant Bloodlust (c) 6.00
1e auxiliary ed. 4.00
2 . . . . 4.00
2a wraparound (c) 4.00
2b variant (c)s . . . . @4.00
3 . . . . 4.00
3a wraparound (c) 4.00
3b variant (c)s . . . . @4.00

WARRIOR BUGS, THE
Artcoda Productions, 2002
1 . . . . 3.00
2 . . . . 3.00
3 . . . . 3.00
4 . . . . 3.00
5 . . . . 3.00

WARRIOR NUN AREALA
Antartic Press, 1995
1 V:Lilith 4.00
1a limited edition. 8.00
2 V:Lilith 3.00
3 V:Hellmaster 3.00
3 silver edition. 12.00
BOOK II: RITUALS, 1996
1 Land of Rising Sun 3.00
1 Red edition. 9.00
1 signed 9.00
2 I:Cheetah 3.00
3 Iraq, 1989. . . . . 3.00
4 . . . . 3.00
5 Rituals,pt.5 . . . . 3.00
6 . . . . 3.00
Spec. Warrior Nun Portraits 4.00
Spec. Warrior Nun Portraits
Commemorative Edition (1999). 6.00
BOOK III, 1997
1 The Hammer & the Holocaust . . . 3.00
2 Hammer & the Holocaust,pt.2 . . . 3.00
3 Hammer & the Holocaust,pt.3 . . . 3.00
4 Holy Man, Holy Terror,pt.1 . . . . . 3.00
5 Holy Man, Holy Terror,pt.2 . . . . . 3.00
6 by Barry Lyga & Ben Dunn 3.00
Spec. Warrior Nun Areala/Glory
by Ben Dunn 3.00
Spec. poster edition 6.00
Spec. Warrior Nun Areala vs. Razor,
BDn,JWf x-over 4.00
Spec.Warrior Nun Areala vs. Razor
commemorative (1999) 6.00
Spec.Warrior Nun Areala/Avengelyne
comm. edition (1999). 6.00
VOL 3
1 F:Sister Shannon Masters 2.50
2 . . . . 2.50
3 . . . . 2.50
4 Antichrist arrives 2.50
5 . . . . 2.50
6 Crimson Nun 2.50
7 V:Ruprecht Marsh 2.50
8 V:Mr.Zhu 2.50
9 in the Vatican 2.50
10 V:Nebelhexa 2.50
11 A:Demoness Lillith 2.50
12 F:Lillith. 3.50
13 V:Julius Salvius 3.00
14 Rebirth, pt.2 . . . . 3.00
15 Rebirth, pt.3 . . . . 3.00
16 Rebirth, pt.4 . . . . 3.00
17 Seven Deadly Sins, pt.1 . . . . . . 3.00
18 Seven Deadly Sins, pt.2 . . . . . . 3.00
19 Seven Deadly Sins, pt.3 . . . . . . 3.00
Ann.2000 b&W. 4.00

WARRIOR NUN AREALA: SCORPIO ROSE
Antarctic Press, 1996
1 SEt & BDn 3.00
1a commemorative (1999) 6.00
2 thru 4 (of 4) . . . . @3.00

WARRIOR NUN DEI: AFTERTIME
Antarctic Press, 1997
1 (of 3) by Patrick Thornton 3.00
1 Commemorative edition (1999) . . 6.00
2 . . . . 3.00
3 . . . . 3.00

WARRIOR NUN: FRENZY
Antarctic Press, 1998
1 (of 2) by Miki Horvatic
& Esad T. Ribic 3.00
2 . . . . 3.00

WARRIOR NUN LAZARUS
Antarctic Press, 2006
0 . . . . 3.50

WARRIOR NUN: NO JUSTICE
Antarctic Press, 2002
1 F:Areala,V:The Judge 4.00

WARRIOR NUN: RESURRECTION
Antarctic Press, 1998
1 by Ben Dunn 3.00
1a deluxe 6.00
2 quest for lost God Armor 3.00
3 . . . . 3.00

WARRIORS OF PLASM
Defiant, 1993–95
1 JiS(s),DL,A:Lorca. 3.25
2 JiS(s),DL,Sedition Agenda. 3.25
3 JiS(s),DL,Sedition Agenda. 3.25
4 JiS(s),DL,Sedition Agenda. 3.25
5 JiS(s),B:The Demons of
Darkedge. 2.75
6 JiS(s),The Demons of
Darkedge,pt.2 . . . . 2.75
7 JiS(s),DL,. 2.75
8 JiS(s),DL,40-pg.. . . . . 3.00
9 JiS(s),LWn(s),DL,40-pg. 3.00
10 DL, ... 2.50
GN Home for the Holidays. 6.00

WARRIOR'S WAY
Bench Press Studios, 1998
1 . . . . 3.00
2 thru 7 . . . . @3.00

WARSTRIKE
Malibu Ultraverse, 1994–95
1 HNg,TA,in South America 2.50
2 HNg,TA,Gatefold(c) 2.50
3 in Brazil 2.50
4 HNg,TA,V:Blind Faith. 2.50
5 . . . . 2.50
6 Rafferty 2.50
7 Origin 2.50

WARSTRIKE: PRELUDE TO GODWHEEL
Malibu Ultraverse, 1994
1 Blind Faith/Lord Pumpkin 2.50

Warrior's Way #3
© Bench Press Studios

WART AND THE WIZARD
Gold Key, 1964
1 . . . . 75.00

WAR WINGS
Charlton, 1968
1 . . . . 30.00

WATCH, THE: CASUS BELLI
Phosphorescent Comics, 2004
1 . . . . 3.25
2 thru 3 . . . . @3.25

WATERDOGS
Roaring Studio, 2002
1 (of 3) 3.00
2 thru 3 . . . . @3.00

WATERWORLD
Acclaim, 1997
1 of 4 V:Leviathan. 2.50
2 of 4 Children of Leviathan 2.50
3 of 4 KoK. 2.50
4 of 4 KoK Children of Leviathan . . 2.50

WAVE WARRIORS
Astroboys
1 . . . . 2.50
2 . . . . 2.50

WAYFARERS
Eternity
1 . . . . 2.50
2 . . . . 2.50

WAY OF THE RAT
Crossgen Comics, 2002
1 CDi 4.00
2 thru 4 . . . . @3.00
5 thru 7 CDi. . . . . @3.00
8 thru 24 CDi. . . . . @3.00

WEASEL GUY WITCHBLADE
Hyperwerks, 1998
1-shot by Steve Succellato 3.00
1a variant Jeff Matsuda(c) 5.00

1b variant Karl Altstoeter(c) 8.00

WEB OF HORROR
Major Magazines, 1969
1 JJ(c),Ph(c),BWr 150.00
2 JJ(c),Ph(c),BWr 125.00
3 BWr,April, 1970 . . . . 125.00

WEAPON, THE
Platinum Studios, 2007
1 (of 4) 4.00
2 thru 4 . . . . @3.00

WEDDING OF POPEYE AND OLIVE, THE
Ocean Comics, 1999
1 PDa,. 2.75
1a signed, numbered 14.00
Spec. Sketch edition 40.00

WEIRD FANTASY
Russ Cochran, 1992
1 Reps 3.50
2 Reps.inc.The Black Arts. 3.00
3 thru 4 rep.. . . . . @3.00
5 thru 7 rep. 3.00
8 . . . . 3.00
Gemstone
9 thru 22 EC comics reprint . . . . @3.00

WEIRD SCIENCE
Gladstone, 1990–91
1 Rep. #22 + Fantasy #1 . . . . 4.00
2 Rep. #16 + Fantasy #17 . . . . . . 3.50
3 Rep. #9 + Fantasy #14 . . . . 3.50
4 Rep. #27 + Fantasy #11 . . . . . . 3.00
Russ Cochran/Gemstone, 1992
1 thru 21 EC comics reprint . . . . @3.00

WEIRD SCIENCE–FANTASY
Russ Cochran/Gemstone, 1992
1 Rep. W.S.F. #23 (1954). 3.50
2 Rep. Flying Saucer Invasion 3.00
3 Rep. 3.00
4 thru 6 Rep. . . . . @3.00
7 rep #29. . . . . 3.00
8 . . . . 3.00

WEIRD SUSPENSE
Atlas, Feb.–July, 1975
1 thru 3 F:Tarantula. . . . . @25.00

WEIRD TALES ILLUSTRATED
Millennium, 1992
1 KJo,JBo,PCr,short stories 5.00

WENDY, THE GOOD LITTLE WITCH
Harvey Publications, 1960–76
1 . . . . 450.00
2 . . . . 225.00
3 thru 10 . . . . @150.00
11 thru 20 . . . . @100.00
21 thru 30 . . . . @75.00
31 thru 50 . . . . @50.00
51 thru 64 . . . . @30.00
65 O:Wendy 50.00
66 thru 69 . . . . @25.00
70 thru 74 giants . . . . @30.00
75 thru 97 . . . . @8.00

WENDY WITCH WORLD
Harvey Publications, 1961–74
1 . . . . 300.00

2 thru 5 . . . . @150.00
6 thru 10 . . . . @100.00
11 thru 20 . . . . @75.00
21 thru 30 . . . . @60.00
31 thru 39 . . . . @50.00
40 thru 50 . . . . @40.00
51 thru 53 . . . . @30.00

WENDY AND THE NEW KIDS ON THE BLOCK
Harvey, 1991
1 . . . . 3.00
2 thru 3 . . . . @3.00

WEREWOLF
Dell, 1966
1 . . . . 50.00
2 thru 3 . . . . @30.00

WEREWOLVES: CALL OF THE WILD
Moonstone Books, 2006
1 . . . . 3.00
2 . . . . 3.50
3 . . . . 3.50

WESTERN ACTION
Atlas, 1975
1 F:Kid Cody,Comanche Kid 25.00

WESTWYND
Westwynd, 1995
1 I:Sable,Shiva,Outcast,Tojo. 2.50

WETWORKS: WORLDSTORM
Wildstorm/DC, Sept., 2006
1 WPo 3.00
1a variant (c). 3.00
1b variant WPo (c) 3.00
2 WPo 3.00
3 WPo 3.00
4 WPo, ... 3.00
4a variant (c). 3.00
5 WPo,Blood Box 3.00
6 WPo,Night Tribes 3.00
7 WPo,PrG 3.00
8 WPo,PrG 3.00
9 DaR,V:Vampires 3.00
10 JMD(s),Can a cyborg die? 3.00
11 JMD(s),Mother One 3.00
12 JMD(s),Red's story 3.00
13 JMD(s),WPo(c),Team reunited . . 3.00
14 JMD(s),WPo(c),V:Vampires 3.00

WHAT WERE THEY THINKING?
Boom! Studios, 2005
1-shot Keith Giffen remix 4.00
1-shot Some People Never Learn . . 4.00
1-shot Monster Mash-Up 4.00
Go West Young Man 4.00
Some People Never Learn 4.00
Monster Mash-up 4.00

WHEELIE AND THE CHOPPER BUNCH
Charlton, 1975
1 . . . . 40.00
2 thru 7 . . . . @30.00

WHERE'S HUDDLES
Gold Key, 1971
1 Hanna-Barbera 45.00
2 . . . . 30.00
3 . . . . 30.00

WHISPER
Capital, 1983–84
1 MG(c) 8.00
2 . . . . 6.00
First
1 . . . . 2.50
2 thru 10 . . . . @2.50
11 thru 19 . . . . @2.50
20 O:Whisper 2.50
21 thru 26 . . . . @2.50
27 Ghost Dance #2 . . . . 2.50
28 Ghost Dance #3 . . . . 2.50
29 thru 37 . . . . @2.50
Spec. #1 . . . . 4.00

WHISPER
Boom! Studios, 2006
1 . . . . 4.00

WHITE FANG
Walt Disney, 1990
1 Movie Adapt. 6.00

WHITE PICKET FENCES
Ape Entertainment, 2007
1 (of 3) 3.50
2 thru 3 . . . . @3.50

White Trash #1
© *Tundra*

WHITE TRASH
Tundra
1 I:Elvis & Dean 4.00
2 Trip to Las Vegas contd. 4.00
3 V:Purple Heart Brigade 4.00

WHODUNNIT
Eclipse, 1986–87
1 DSp,A:Jay Endicott 3.00
2 DSp,Who Slew Kangaroo? 3.00
3 DSp,Who Offed Henry Croft . . . 3.00

WIDOW MADE IN BRITAIN
N Studio
1 I:Widow 2.75
2 F:Widow 2.75
3 Rampage 2.75
4 In Jail 2.75

WIDOW METAL GYPSIES
London Night Studios, 1995
1 I:Emma Drew 3.00
2 Father Love 3.00
3 Final issue 3.00

WILD ANIMALS
Pacific, 1982
1 . . . . 3.00

WILD BOYS
Masterpiece Comics, 2007
1 . . . . 3.00
2 thru 4 . . . . @3.00

WILDCATS
WildStorm/DC, 1999
Previously from Image
VOLUME 2
1 SLo,TC, ... 2.50
1a variant cover 2.50
1b variant cover 2.50
1c variant cover 2.50
1d variant cover 2.50
1e variant cover 2.50
2 SLo,TC. 2.50
3 SLo,TC,F:Grifter 2.50
4 SLo,TC, ... 2.50
5 SLo,BHi,PNe, ... 2.50
6 SLo, ... 2.50
7 SLo,R:Pike 2.50
8 JoC(s),SeP,TC(c). 2.50
8a variant JLe&SW(c) (1:4) 2.50
9 JoC(s),SeP,TC(c),Las Vegas . . . 2.50
10 JoC(s),SeP,TC(c),Las Vegas . . 2.50
11 JoC(s),SeP,TC(c),R:Ladytron . . . 2.50
12 JoC(s),SeP,TC(c),go west 2.50
13 JoC(s),SeP,F:Void. 2.50
14 JoC(s),SeP,Serial Boxes,pt.1 . . . 2.50
15 JoC(s),SeP,Serial Boxes,pt.2 . . . 2.50
16 JoC,SeP,Serial Boxes,pt.3 . . . . . 2.50
17 JoC,SeP,Serial Boxes,pt.4 . . . . . 2.50
18 JoC,SeP,Serial Boxes,pt.5 . . . . . 2.50
19 JoC,SeP,Serial Boxes,pt.6 . . . . . 2.50
20 JoC,SDi,F:Grifter, Maul. 2.50
21 JoC,SDi,F:Grifter, Maul, pt.2 . . . 2.50
22 JoC,SeP,R:Grifter 2.50
23 JoC,SeP,F:Grifter 2.50
23a variant WPo(c) (1:4) 2.50
24 JoC,SeP,F:Voodoo 2.50
25 JoC,SeP, 40-pg. 3.50
26 JoC,SeP, control of Halo. 2.50
27 JoC,SeP,Grifter vs. Zealot 2.50
28, JoC,SeP,Voodoo,final issue . . . 2.50
Spec. WildC.A.T.s: Mosaic. 4.00
Ann. 2000 #1, Devil's
   Night x-over, pt.3 . . . . 3.50
GN Ladytron 6.00

WILDCATS: NEMESIS
Wildstorm/DC, Sept., 2005
1 (of 9) Zealot and Coda sisters . . . 3.00
2 . . . . 3.00
3 thru 9 . . . . @3.00

WILDCATS VERSION 3.0
Wildcats/DC, 2002
Eye of the Storm
1 JoC,old and new team members. 3.00
2 JoC,Jack Marlowe,Halo corp. . . . 3.00
3 JoC 3.00
4 JoC, ... 3.00
5 JoC 3.00
6 JoC 3.00
7 JoC,I:Beef Boys 3.00
8 JoC,BU:The Authority,pt.3 . . . . . 3.00
9 JoC,new Grifter 3.00
10 JoC,new Grifter 3.00
11 JoC,Lights Out in Garfield. 3.00
12 JoC,Jack Marlowe 3.00
13 JoC,Mister Wax. 3.00
14 JoC,Halo Corp. 3.00
15 JoC,Car of tomorrow. 3.00
16 JoC,new assassin. 3.00
17 JoC,SeP 3.00

18 JoC 3.00
19 JoC(s) 3.00
20 JoC(s),new team. 3.00
21 JoC(s),Grifter's team. 3.00
22 JoC(s),Coda War One 3.00
23 JoC(s),Coda War One 3.00
24 JoC(s),final issue 3.00

WILDCATS: WORLDSTORM
Wildstorm/DC, Sept., 2006
1 GMo,JLe,SWi. 3.00
1a variant TM,JLe (c) 3.00
1b variant JLe (c) 3.00
2 GMo,JLe,SW 3.00
2a variant EL (c) 3.00

WILDFIRE
Zion Comics
1 thru 3 V:Mr. Reeves . . . . @2.50
4 Lord D'Rune. 2.50

WILD GIRL
Wildstorm/DC, Nov., 2004
1 (of 6) SwM 3.00
2 SwM 3.00
3 SwM 3.00
4 SwM 3.00
5 SwM,JWi 3.00
6 SwM,JWi 3.00

WILDSIDERZ
Wildstorm/DC, Aug., 2005
0 JSC 2.00
1 (of 5) JSC, 40-page 3.50
2 JSC 3.50
3 JSC 3.50

WILDSTORM
Wildstorm/DC, 2005
Spec. Winter special 5.00

WILDSTORM FINE ARTS SPOTLIGHT
Wildstorm/DC, Dec., 2006
1-shot Jim Lee 3.50
1-shot J. Scott Campbell 3.50

WILD TIMES
WildStorm/DC, 1999
Deathblow 2.50
DV8 . . . . 2.50
Gen13 . . . . 2.50
Grifter 2.50
Wetworks 2.50

WILD WEST
Charlton, 1966
58 From Black Fury 25.00

WILD WEST C.O.W.- BOYS OF MOO MESA
Archie, 1992–93
1 Based on TV cartoon. 2.50
2 Cody kidnapped. 2.50
3 Law of the Year Parade,
    last issue 2.50
(Regular series)
1 Valley o/t Thunder Lizard 2.50
2 Plains, Trains & Dirty Deals 2.50

WILD WESTERN ACTION
Skywald, 1971
1 . . . . 35.00
2 . . . . 35.00
3 . . . . 35.00

WILD WILD WEST
Gold Key, 1966–69
1 TV show tie-in 300.00
2 . . . . 250.00
3 thru 7 . . . . @200.00

WILD WILD WEST
Millennium, 1990–91
1 . . . . 3.00
2 thru 4 . . . . @3.00

WILL EISNER'S 3-D CLASSICS
Kitchen Sink, 1985
WE art, w/glasses (1985). 3.00

WIN A PRIZE COMICS
Charlton Comics, 1955
1 S&K,Edgar Allen Poe adapt.. 1,100.00
2 S&K 800.00
Becomes:

TIMMY THE TIMID GHOST
Charlton Comics, 1957
3 . . . . 150.00
4 . . . . 125.00
5 . . . . 125.00
6 thru 10 . . . . @100.00
11 giant 125.00
12 giant 125.00
13 thru 19 . . . . @100.00
20 thru 25. . . . . @100.00
26 thru 44. . . . . @25.00
45 1966 . . . . 25.00

Winnie-The-Pooh #22
© Whitman

WINNIE-THE-POOH
Gold Key, 1977
1 . . . . 35.00
2 thru 5 . . . . @20.00
6 thru 17 . . . . @15.00
Whitman, 1980
18 thru 19 . . . . @20.00
20 thru 21 scarce . . . . @40.00
22 very scarce 50.00
23 thru 33 . . . . @20.00

WINTER MEN, THE
Wildstorm/DC, Aug., 2005
1 (of 8) JPL, U.S.S.R. soldiers 3.00
2 . . . . 3.00
3 . . . . 3.00
4 . . . . 3.00

5 . . . . 3.00

WINTERWORLD
Eclipse, 1987–88
1 JZ,I:Scully, Wynn 3.00
2 JZ,V:Slave Farmers 3.00
3 JZ,V:Slave Farmers 3.00

WISP
Oktomica Entertainment, 1999
1 All Along the Watchtower,pt.1 . . 2.50
2 All Along the Watchtower,pt.2 . . 2.50
3 All Along the Watchtower,pt.3 . . 3.00
4 The Acheron Protocol 3.00

W.I.T.C.H.
Hyperion Books, 2005
GN Vol. 1 . . . . 5.00
GN Vol. 2 . . . . 5.00
GN Vol. 3 . . . . 5.00
GN Vol. 4 . . . . 5.00
GN Vol. 5 Legends Revealed 5.00
GN Vol. 6 Forces of Change 5.00

WITCHBLADE: SHADES OF GRAY
D.E. (Dynamite Ent.) 2007
1 (of 4) 3.50
2 thru 4 . . . . @3.50
1a thru 4a variant (c)s . . . . @3.50

WITCHGIRLS, INC.
Heroic Publishing Inc., 2005
1 . . . . 4.00
2 . . . . 3.00
3 thru 4 . . . . @3.25
5 . . . . 4.50
5a variant (c). 4.50

WITCHING HOUR, THE
Millennium/Comico, 1992
1 Anne Rice adaptation 2.50
2 thru 5 . . . . @2.50

WITCHMAN
Avatar Press, 2006
1 . . . . 4.00
1a wraparound (c) 4.00
1b variant (c)s . . . . @4.00

WOLFMAN
Dell, 1964
1 . . . . 140.00

WONDERLAND
Amaze Ink/Slave Labor Graphics, 2006
1 . . . . 3.50
2 thru 4 . . . . @3.50
5 . . . . 4.00

WOOD BOY, THE
Devil's Due Publishing, 2004
1 (of 2) 3.00
2 . . . . 3.00

WOODSY OWL
Gold Key, 1973
1 . . . . 25.00
2 thru 10 . . . . @15.00

WOODY WOODPECKER AND FRIENDS
Harvey, 1991
1 . . . . 3.00
2 thru 4 . . . . @3.00

WOODY WOODPECKER
Harvey, 1991–93
1 thru 5 . . . . @2.50

WORLD OF ADVENTURE
Gold Key, 1963
1 . . . . 50.00
2 . . . . 30.00
3 . . . . 30.00

WORLD OF ARCHIE
Archie, 1992
1 thru 22 . . . . @2.50

WORLD OF WOOD
Eclipse, 1986–87
1 WW 4.00
2 WW,DSt(i) 4.00
3 WW 4.00
4 WW 4.00

WORLDSTORM
Wildstorm/DC, Oct., 2006
1-shot Preview 3.00
2 . . . . 3.00

WORLD WAR STORIES
Dell, 1965
1 . . . . 60.00
2 thru 3 . . . . @40.00

WORLD WAR II: 1946
Antarctic Press, 1999
1 by Ted Nomura 4.00
2 Born to Die 4.00
3 Battle for Moscow 4.00
4 Flying Tigers 4.00
5 . . . . 4.00
6 The Hunley vs. the Potsdam 4.00
7 The Yamato 4.00
8 Tuskegee Airmen 4.00
9 Firestorm 4.00
10 Destination: Space 4.00
11 Night Witches 4.00
12 Korea 4.00
Ann. 2000 b&w 4.00

WORLD-WATCH
Wild & Wolly Press, 2004
1 . . . . 12.00
2 . . . . 8.00
3 . . . . 5.00

WORMWOOD: GENGLEMAN CORPSE
IDW Publishing, 2006
1 . . . . 4.00
2 thru 7 . . . . @4.00

WRAITHBORN
Wildstorm/DC, Sept., 2005
1 (of 6) JBz 3.00
2 JBz 3.00

WRATH
Malibu Ultraverse, 1994–95
1 B:MiB(s),DvA,JmP,C:Mantra 2.50
1a Silver foil 3.00
2 DvA,JmP,V:Hellion 2.50
3 DvA,JmP,V:Radicals, I:Slayer . . . 2.50
4 DvA,JmP,V:Freex 2.50
5 DvA,JmP,V:Freex 2.50
6 DvA,JmP 2.50
7 DvA,JmP,I:Pierce,Ogre, Doc Virtual 2.50
8 . . . . 2.50
9 A:Prime 2.50

COLOR PUB.

G-Size #1 . . . . 2.50

WRAITHBORN
Wildstorm/DC, Sept., 2005
3 thru 6 JBz . . . . @3.00

WULF THE BARBARIAN
Atlas, 1975
1 O:Wulf 15.00
2 NA,I:Berithe The Swordsman . . 12.00
3 & 4 . . . . @8.00

WWF BATTLEMANIA
Valiant
1 WWF Action 2.50
2 thru 5 . . . . @2.50

Wyatt Earp #6
© Dell Publishing Co.

WYATT EARP
Dell Publishing Co., 1957
1 RsM 200.00
2 RsM 150.00
3 RsM 135.00
4 . . . . 100.00
5 Ph(c) 100.00
6 . . . . 100.00
7 . . . . 100.00
8 . . . . 100.00
9 . . . . 100.00
10 . . . . 100.00
11 . . . . 90.00
12 RsM 90.00
13 AT 90.00

WYATT EARP FRONTIER MARSHAL
Charlton, 1956
12 From Range Busters 100.00
13 thru 19 . . . . @60.00
20 AW 100.00
21 thru 30 . . . . @40.00
31 thru 60 . . . . @25.00
61 thru 72 . . . . @15.00

WYNONNA EARP: HOME ON THE STRANGE
IDW Publishing, 2003
1 . . . . 4.00
2 thru 3 . . . . @4.00
1a thru 2a variant (c)s . . . . @4.00

XANADU
Eclipse, 1988
1 . . . . 2.50

XENYA
Sanctuary Press, 1994
1 Hildebrandt Brothers 4.00
2 . . . . 3.25
3 . . . . 3.25
4 conclusion, Homecoming 3.00

XENA: WARRIOR PRINCESS
Topps, 1997
1 RTs,Revenge of the Gorgons, pt.1 . . . . 5.00
1a photo (c) 8.00
2 (of 2) rescue of Gabrielle 4.00
[VOL 2]
0 AaL Temple of the Dragon God . . 3.00
1 (of 3) Joxer, Warrior Prince, pt.1 . 5.00
1a deluxe 8.00
2 Joxer, Warrior Prince, pt.2 . . . . . 4.00
2a photo (c) 4.00

XENA, WARRIOR PRINCESS
D.E. (Dynamite Ent.) 2006
1 . . . . 3.50
1a variant (c)s . . . . @3.50
1a photo foil (c) 15.00
2 Pantheon Pandemonium 3.50
3 Stalk Like an Egyptian 3.50
4 Contest of Pantheons 3.50
5 thru 8 . . . . @3.50
2a thru 4a variant (c)s . . . . @3.50
5a thru 8a variant (c)s . . . . @3.50
Ann. #1 Strange Visitor 5.00
Ann. #1 variant (c)s . . . . @5.00

XENA: WARRIOR PRINCESS: BLOOD LINES
Topps, 1997
1 (of 3) ALo 3.00
1a photo (c) 3.00
2 (of 3) ALo 3.00
2a photo (c) 3.00

XENA: WARRIOR PRINCESS: CALLISTO
Topps, 1997
1 (of 3) RTs 3.00
1a photo (c) 3.00
2 (of 3) RTs 3.00
2a photo (c) 3.00
3 (of 3) RTs 3.00
3a photo (c) 3.00

XENA: WARRIOR PRINCESS: ORPHEUS
Topps, 1998
1 (of 3) 3.00
2 thru 3 (of 3) . . . . @3.00
1a thru 3a photo (c)s . . . . @3.00

XENA: WARRIOR PRINCESS: THE ORIGINAL OLYMPICS
Topps, 1998
1 (of 3) 3.00
1a photo cover 3.00
2 F:Hercules 3.00
2a photo cover 3.00
3 . . . . 3.00
3a photo cover 3.00

XENA:
WARRIOR PRINCESS:
THE WEDDING OF XENA
& HERCULES
Topps, 1998

1-shot 3.00
1-shot photo (c) 3.00

XENA,
WARRIOR PRINCESS:
THE WRATH OF HERA
Topps, 1998

1 (of 2) 3.00
1a photo cover edition 3.00
2 conclusion 3.00
2a photo cover edition 3.00

XENA:
WARRIOR PRINCESS:
XENA AND THE
DRAGON'S TEETH
Topps, 1997

1 (of 3) RTs, ... 3.00
1a photo (c). 3.00
2 (of 3) RTs, ... 3.00
2a photo (c). 3.00
3 (of 3) RTs, ... 3.00
3a photo (c). 3.00

XENOTECH
Mirage, 1993–94

1 I:Xenotech 2.75
2 . . . . 2.75
3 w/2 card strip 2.75

X-FILES
Topps, 1994–97

1 From Fox TV Series 35.00
1a Newstand 25.00
2 Aliens Killing Witnesses. 20.00
3 The Return. 18.00
4 Firebird,pt.1 . . . . 12.00
5 Firebird,pt.2 . . . . 9.00
6 Firebird,pt.3 . . . . 8.00
7 Trepanning Opera 7.00
8 Silent Cities of the Mind,pt.1 . . . . 6.00
9 Silent Cities of the Mind,pt.2 . . . . 5.00
10 Feeling of Unreality,pt.1 . . . . 5.00
11 Fealing of Unreality,pt.2 . . . . 5.00
12 Fealing of Unreality,pt.3 . . . . 5.00
13 A Boy and His Saucer. 5.00
14 . . . . 4.00
15 Home of the Brave 4.00
16 Home of the Brave,pt.2. . . . . 3.50
17 DgM,CAd 3.50
18 thru 21 . . . . @3.50
22 JRz,CAd,The Kanishibari 3.00
23 JRz,CAd,Donor. 3.00
24 JRz,Silver Lining 3.00
25 JRz,CAd,Remote Control,pt.1 . . 3.00
26 JRz,CAd,Remote Control,pt.2 . . 3.00
27 JRz,CAd,Remote Control,pt.3 . . 3.00
28 JRz,Be Prepared, pt.1,
    V:Windigo 3.00
29 JRz,Be Prepared, pt.2 . . . . 3.00
30 JRz,Surrounded, pt.1 . . . . 3.00
31 JRz,Surrounded, pt.2 (of 2) 3.00
32 . . . . 3.00
33 widows on San Francisco. 3.00
33 variant photo (c) 3.00
34 Project HAARP 3.00
35 Near Death Experience 3.00
36 Near Death Experience, pt.2 . . . 3.00
37 JRz,The Face of Extinction. 3.00
38 JRz,. 3.00
39 JRz, Widow's Peak. 3.00

40 Devil's Advocate 3.00
40a photo cover. 3.00
41 Severed. 3.00
41a photo cover. 3.00
Ann.#1 Hollow Eve 5.00
Ann.#2 E.L.F.S. 4.50
Spec.#1 Rep. #1-#3 . . . . 6.00
Spec.#2 Rep. #4-#6 Firebird 5.00
Spec.#3 Rep. #7-#9 . . . . 5.00
Spec.#4 Rep. 5.00
GN Afterflight 6.00
GN Official Movie Adapt. (1998) . . 6.00

X-FILES DIGEST
Topps, 1995

1 All New Series, 96pg. 4.00
2 and 3 . . . . 4.00

X-FILES, THE:
GROUND ZERO
Topps, 1997

1 (of 4) based on novel 3.00
2 thru 4 . . . . @3.00

X-FILES, THE:
SEASON ONE
Topps, 1997

1 RTs,JVF(c) Deep Throat 5.00
Deep Throat, variant (c). 7.50
2 RTs,JVF(c) Squeeze 4.00
Squeeze, RTs, JVF(c) 5.00
3 RTs,SSc,Conduit 4.00
Conduit, RTs 5.00
4 RTs,The Jersey Devil. 4.00
5 RTs,Shadows. 4.00
Shadows JVF(c). 5.00
6 Fire. 4.00
Fire. 5.00
7 RTs,JVF,Ice 4.00
Ice 5.00
8 RTs,Space 4.00
Space JVF(c). 5.00
Spec. Pilot Episode RTs,JVF
    new JVF(c) 5.00
Beyond the Sea JVF(c) 5.00

XIMOS: VIOLENT PAST
Triumphant, 1994

1 JnR(s) 2.50
2 JnR(s) 2.50

XIN
Anarchy Studios, 2002

Alpha Preview edition 2.50
Alpha Preview, collector's ed. 9.00
Ashcan limited edition 6.00
Ashcan gold foil leather 12.00
1 Legend of the Monkey King. 3.00
1a variant JMd(c) 3.00
1b Royal blue edition 25.00
1c gold foil edition. 25.00
1d holo foil fx edition. 9.00
2 thru 3 . . . . @3.00
2a thru 3a variant limited (c). . . . @9.00

XIN: JOURNEY OF
THE MONKEY KING
Anarchy Studios, 2003

1 . . . . 3.00
1a variant (c). 3.00
2 thru 3 . . . . @3.00
2a thru 3a variant (c) 3.00
1b thru 3b limited edition. . . . . . . @9.00

X ISLE
Boom! Studios, 2006

1 (of 5) 3.00
2 thru 5 . . . . @3.00

X-O MANOWAR
Valiant, 1992

0 JQ,O:Aric,1st Full Chromium(c). . 5.00
0a Gold Ed. 20.00
1 BL,BWS,I:Aric,Ken. 9.00
2 BL(i),V:Lydia,Wolf-Class Armor . . 6.00
3 I:X-Caliber,A:Solar 6.00
4 MM,A:Harbinger,C:Shadowman
    (Jack Boniface) 7.00
5 thru 13 . . . . @3.00
14 BS,A:Turok,I:Randy Cartier 3.50
15 BS,A:Turok 2.50
15a Red Ed. 7.00
16 thru 24. . . . . @2.50
25 JCf,JGz,PaK,I:Armories,
    BU:Armories#0 . . . . 3.00
26 JGz(s),RLv,F:Ken 2.50
27 JGz,RLe,A:Turok,Geomancer,
    Stronghold,Livewire 2.50
28 JGz,RLe,D:X-O,V:Spider
    Aliens,w/Valiant Era card. 2.75
29 thru 66. . . . . @2.50
67 thru 68 . . . . @8.00

X-O MANOWAR
Series Two, Acclaim, 1997

1 Rand Banion v. R.A.G.E. 2.50
2 thru 20 . . . . @2.50

XOMBIE
Devil's Due, 2007

1 . . . . 3.50
1a variant (c) 3.50
2 thru 6 . . . . @3.50
2a thru 6a variant (c) . . . . @3.50

XIII
Alias Enterprises, 2005

1 Day of the Black Sun. 1.00
2 thru 5 . . . . @3.00
6 . . . . 3.00

YAKKY DOODLE
& CHOPPER
Gold Key, 1962

1 . . . . 150.00

YANG
Charlton, 1973–76

1 . . . . 25.00
2 thru 13 . . . . @12.00

Yang #1
© *Charlton*

COLOR PUB.

All comics prices listed are for *Near Mint* condition.   **CVA Page 715**

Charlton, 1985
14 . . . . 7.00
15 thru 17 . . . . @5.00

YEAH!
Homage/DC, 1999
1 GHe 3.00

YENNY
Alias Enterprises, 2005
1 . . . . 2.00
1a variant (c) 3.00
2 thru 4 . . . . @3.00
5 thru 10 . . . . @3.50

YIN FEI
Leung's Publications, 1988–90
5 . . . . 3.00
6 thru 11 . . . . @3.00

YOGI BEAR
Dell, 1962
#1 thru #6, See Dell Four Color
7 thru 9 . . . . 125.00
Gold Key, 1962
10 . . . . 150.00
11 Jellystone Follies 135.00
12 . . . . 100.00
13 Surprise Party 135.00
14 thru 19 . . . . @100.00
20 thru 29 . . . . @50.00
30 thru 42 . . . . @45.00

YOGI BEAR
Charlton Comics, 1970–76
1 . . . . 75.00
2 thru 10 . . . . @50.00
11 thru 35 . . . . 40.00

YOGI BEAR
Harvey, 1992
1 . . . . 4.00
2 thru 6 . . . . @3.00

YOGI BEAR
Archie Comics, 1997
1 . . . . 2.50

YOSEMITE SAM
Gold Key/Whitman, 1970–84
1 . . . . 75.00
2 thru 10 . . . . @35.00
11 thru 40 . . . . @25.00
41 thru 81 . . . . @20.00

YOU'LL HAVE THAT
Viper Comics, 2006
1-shot 3.25

YOUNGBLOOD
Maximum Press/Extreme
Volume 2, 1996
Vol. 1 & Vol. 2 #1–#10, see Image
11 RLd,RCz, ... 2.50
12 Rle, V:Lord Dredd,A:New
    Man,double size 3.50
13 RLd,RCz,F:Die-Hard. 2.50
14 RLd,RCz, ... 2.50
Super Spec.#1 ErS,CSp,AG 3.00

YOUNGBLOOD
Awesome Entertainment, 1998
1 AMo,SSr. 2.50
1a variant covers, 7 different. . . @2.50
1b foil logo 6.00
1c plus custom illustration 60.00
2 AMo,SSr,Baptism of Fire 2.50

3 AMo,SSr,V:Professor Night 2.50
4 AMo,SSr,Young Guns 2.50
5 AMo,SSr,Young Guns 2.50
1-shot, Youngblood/X-Force
    x-over,48pg. (1998) 5.00

YOUNGBLOOD:
BLOODSPORT
Arcade Comics, 2002
1 MMr,RLd, RLd(c) 5.00
1a variant Quietly (c) 6.00
1b variant Park (c) 4.00
1c Foil ed. 9.00
1d Foil ed., signed 15.00
1e convention sketch ed. 40.00
1f San Diego con lim. ed. 9.00
1g San Diego con lim. signed. . . . 15.00
1h ltd (c) 15.00
2 MMr,RLd, RLd(c) 3.00
2a variant Quietly (c) 3.00
2b variant Park (c) 3.00
2c Foil ed. 9.00
2d Foil ed., signed 15.00
Spec. Imperial #1 Dossier 4.00
Spec. Imperial #1 Max edition 9.00
Spec. Imperial #1 signed 9.00

YOUNGBLOOD CLASSICS
Image/Extreme, 1996
1 RLd,ErS,series rewritten &
    redrawn, new cover 2.50
2 RLd,ErS 2.50
3 RLd,ErS 2.50

YOUNGBLOOD GENESIS
Awesome Entertainment, 2000
1 . . . . 4.00
1a signature edition 9.00
Arcade Comics, 2004
2 . . . . 4.00
2a RLd(c) 9.00

YOUNGBLOOD: IMPERIAL
Arcade Comics, 2004
0 . . . . 4.00
0a max edition 9.00
1 (of 12) Mmy,RLd(c) 3.00
1a max edition 12.00
1b premium, signed edition 20.00
2 Rld,MMy. 3.00
2a max edition 12.00
2b Authentic sign ed. 20.00

The Young Doctors #3
© Charlton

YOUNG DOCTORS, THE
Charlton, 1963
1 . . . . 50.00
2 thru 6 . . . . @30.00

YOUNG LAWYERS, THE
Dell, 1971
1 . . . . 40.00
2 . . . . 30.00

YOUNG REBELS, THE
Dell, 1971
1 . . . . 30.00

ZAK RAVEN, ESQ.
Avatar/Tidalwave Studios, 2002
1A Cha (c). 3.50
1B Arlem (c) 3.50
1C Miller (c) 3.50
1D Murphy (c). 3.50

ZANE GREY'S STORIES
OF THE WEST
Dell, 1955
27 thru 39 . . . . @75.00
Gold Key, 1964
1 . . . . 50.00

ZEIN
AK Entertainment, 2006
1 Enter the Scarab 3.00
2 Origins 3.00
3 The Rise of Anubis 3.00
4 Year of the Beast 3.00
5 Judgment Day 3.00
7 thru 9 . . . . @3.00

ZEIN GHOSTS
OF HELIOPOLIS
Studio G, 2003
1 . . . . 3.00
2 thru 4 . . . . @3.00

ZEN
Zen Comics, 2003
0 . . . . 3.00
1 . . . . 3.00
2 thru 4 . . . . @3.00

ZENDRA
Pennyfarthing Press, 2001
Volume 2
1 (of 6) Windmills of the World 3.00
2 All the Flesh Inherits 3.00
3 thru 5 . . . . @3.00
6 . . . . 3.00

ZEN INTERGALACTIC
NINJA
Archie, 1992
1 Rumble in the Rain Forest
    prequel, inc.poster. 3.00
2 Rumble in Rain Forest #1 . . . . . 3.00
3 Rumble in Rain Forest #2 . . . . . 3.00
Entity Comics, 1994
0 Chromium (c),JaL(c) 4.00
1 Joe Orbeta. 3.00
1a Platinum Edition. 20.00
2 Deluxe Edition w/card 5.00
3 V:Rawhead 3.00
4 thru 7 . . . . @3.25
GN A Fire Upon The Earth. 13.00
[2nd Series]
1 Joe Orbeta 5.00
2 . . . . 5.00
3 thru 5 . . . . @2.50

Zen Comics, 1998
Commemorative Ed. #1 . . . . 6.00

ZEN INTERGALACTIC NINJA
Studio Chikara, 1999
1 . . . . 4.00
1 variant (c). 10.00
2 . . . . 4.00
3 . . . . 4.00

ZEN/NIRA X: HELLSPACE
Zen Comics
1 . . . . 3.00

ZEN: NOVELLA
Eternity Comics
1 thru 8 . . . . @3.00

ZEN SPECIALS
Eternity
Spring#1 V:Lord Contaminous 2.50
April Fools#1 parody issue 2.50
Color Spec.#0 . . . . 3.50

ZEN: WARRIOR
Eternity Comics, 1994
1 vicious video game 3.00

ZENDRA
Pennyfarthing Press, 2001
1 (of 6) 3.00
2 thru 6 . . . . @3.00

ZENITH PHASE I
Fleetway
1 thru 3 . . . . @2.50

ZENITH PHASE II
Fleetway
1 thru 2 . . . . @2.50

ZERO GIRL: FULL CIRCLE
DC/Homage, 2002
2 SK 3.00
3 SK 3.00
4 SK 3.00
5 SK, concl.. . . . . 3.00

ZERO PATROL
Continuity, 1984–90
1 EM,NA,O&I:Megalith 4.00
2 EM,NA 4.00
3 EM,NA,I:Shaman. 3.00
4 EM,NA 3.00
5 EM 3.00
6 thru 8 EM . . . . @3.00

ZERO TOLERANCE
First, 1990–91
1 TV 3.50
2 TV 3.00
3 TV 3.00
4 TV 3.00

ZODY, THE MOD ROB
Gold Key, 1970
1 . . . . 40.00

ZOMBIE-PROOF
Moonstone 2007
1 . . . . 3.50
2 . . . . 3.50

Zero Tolerance #1 © First

ZOMBIES!
IDW Publishing, 2006
1 . . . . 4.00
2 thru 4 . . . . @4.00
3a thru 4a variant (c)s . . . . @4.00

ZOMBIE-SAMA
Crusade Entertainment, 2007
1 . . . . 5.00

ZOMBIES!: ECLIPSE OF THE UNDEAD
IDW Publishing, 2006
1 . . . . 4.00
2 thru 4 . . . . @4.00

ZOMBIES!: FEAST
IDW Publishing, 2006
1 . . . . 4.00
2 . . . . 4.00
3 . . . . 4.00
4 . . . . 4.00
5 . . . . 4.00

ZOMBIES VS. ROBOTS
IDW Publishing, 2006
1 . . . . 4.00
2 . . . . 4.00

ZOMBIES VS. ROBOTS VS. AMAZONS
IDW 2007
1 . . . . 4.00
2 . . . . 4.00
3 . . . . 4.00

ZOMBIE TALES: THE DEAD
Boom! Studios, 2006
1 . . . . 7.00

ZOOM SUIT
Superverse Productions, 2006
1 (of 4) 3.00
2 thru 4 . . . . @3.00
1a thru 4a variant (c)s . . . . @3.00
1b thru 4b variant sketch (c)s . . @9.00
1 Suspended Animation Edition . . . 3.00
2 Fantasticreal.com edition. 9.00

ZOONIVERSE
Eclipse, 1986–87
1 I:Kren Patrol,wrap-around(c) 3.00
2 . . . . 3.00
3 . . . . 3.00
4 V:Wedge City. 3.00
5 Spak vs. Agent Ty-rote. 3.00
6 last issue 3.00

ZORRO
Dell Publ. Co., 1959–61
1 thru 8, see Dell 4-Color
8 . . . . 200.00
9 . . . . 225.00
10 . . . . 200.00
11 . . . . 200.00
12 ATh 225.00
13 . . . . 150.00
14 . . . . 150.00
15 . . . . 150.00

ZORRO
Gold Key, 1966–68
1 ATh,Rep. 150.00
2 Rep. 100.00
3 Rep. 100.00
4 Rep. 100.00
5 Rep. 100.00
6 Rep. 100.00
7 Rep. 100.00
8 Rep. 100.00
9 Rep. 100.00

ZORRO
Topps, Nov., 1993
0 BSf(c),DMG(s), came bagged
   with Jurassic Park Raptor #1 and
   Teenagents #4. . . . . 4.00
1 DMG(s),V:Machete 3.00
2 DMG(s) 5.00
3 DMG(s) I:Lady Rawhide 12.00
4 MGr(c),DMG(s),V:Moonstalker . . 3.00
5 MGr,DMG(s),V:Moonstalker. 3.00
6 A:Lady Rawhide. 8.00
7 A:Lady Rawhide. 7.00
8 MGr(c),DMG(s) 3.00
9 A:Lady Rawhide. 4.00
10 A:Lady Rawhide 4.50
11 A:Lady Rawhide 8.00

ZORRO
Papercutz, 2005
1 Scars 3.00
2 Scars 3.00
3 Scars 3.00
4 Drownings 2.00
5 Drownings 3.00
6 Drownings 3.00
7 thru 10 . . . . @3.00
GN Vol. 1 Scars 8.00
GN Vol. 2 Drownings 8.00
GN Vol. 3 Vultures 8.00

ZOT!
Eclipse, 1984–85
1 by Scott McCloud 7.00
2 . . . . 4.00
3 Art and Soul. 4.00
4 Assault on Castle Dekko 3.00
5 Sirius Business 3.00
6 It's always darkest. 3.00
7 Common Ground. 3.00
8 Through the Door 3.00
9 Gorilla Warfare. 3.00
10 T.K.O. The Final Round 3.00
10a B&W 6.00
10b 2nd printing 3.00
Original Zot! Book 1. . . . . 10.00
(Changed to B & W)

All comics prices listed are for *Near Mint* condition.

B&W COMICS

A1
Atomeka Press, 1989–92
1 BWS,A:Flaming Carrot,Mr.X.... 10.00
2 BWS,JHw,ECa............. 10.00
3 BBo(c),ECa................ 10.00
4 SBs(c),JHw............... 6.00
5 WiS(c),NGa(s),KJo........ 7.00
6A JHw,F:Tank Girl......... 5.00

AARDWOLF
Aardwolf, 1994
1 DC,GM(c)................. 3.00
1a Certificate ed. signed....... 12.00
2 World Toughest Milkman....... 3.00
3 R.Block(s),O:Aardwolf........ 3.00

AARON STRIPS
Amazing Aaron Prod., 1999
1 thru 4, see Image
5 thru 9 .... @3.00
10 48-pg. 4.00

A.B.C. Warriors #6
© Fleetway Quality

A.B.C. WARRIORS
Fleetway/Quality, 1990
1 .... 2.50
2 thru 8 .... @2.25

ABSOLUTE ZERO
Antarctic Press, 1995
1 .... 3.00
2 Rooftop,Athena 3.00
3 Stan Sakai 3.50
4 3-D Man and Kirby.......... 3.00
5 Super Powers 3.00
6 Super Powers 3.00

AC ANNUAL
AC Comics, 1990
1 F:She-Cat; Tara; Nyoka........ 4.00
2 F:Yankee Girl; Ms.Victory 5.00
3 Vault of Heroes; Jet Girl 3.50
4 F:Sentinels of Justice 4.00

ACE COMICS PRESENTS
Ace, 1987
1 thru 7 .... @3.00

ACE McCOY
ACG Comics, 1999
1 thru 4 FF .... @3.00

ACE OF DIAMONDS
Lone Star Press, 2000
0 .... 3.00
1 .... 4.00
2 .... 3.00
3 .... 3.00

ACES
Eclipse, 1988
1 thru 5, mag. size .... @3.00

ACG'S AMAZING COMICS
ACG Comics, 2000
1 thru 5 F:Dragon Lady........ @3.00

ACHILLES STORM
Brainstorm, 1997
1 by Sandra Chang............. 3.00

DARK SECRET
Brainstorm, 1997
1 by Sandra Chang............. 3.00
2 .... 3.00
2a luxury edition 5.00

ACME
Fandom House, 1985–89
1 thru 9 .... @3.00

ACOLYTE CHRONICLES
Azure Press, 1995
1 I:Korath 3.00
2 V:Korath................. 3.00

A COP CALLED TRACY
ACG Comics, 1998
1 by Chester Gould............ 3.00
2 thru 9 .... @3.00
9a deluxe 3.00
10 thru 18................. @3.00
19 thru 24 giant-size,64-pg...... @6.00
Ann.#1 .... 3.00

ACTION GIRL COMICS
Slave Labor Graphics, 1994
1 thru 7 .... @3.00
1 thru 7, later printings .... @2.75
8 thru 12 .... @3.00
13 Halloween issue 3.00
14 F:Elizabeth Lavin 3.00
15 .... 3.00
16 GoGo Gang,pt.1 .... 2.75
17 GoGo Gang,pt.2 .... 2.75
18 Blue Monday.............. 3.00
19 Halloween 3.00

ACTION PHILOSOPHERS
Evil Twin Comics, 2005
1 Plato..................... 3.00
1a 2nd printing 3.00
(2) Spec. All-Sex Special #1 ...... 3.00
(3) Spec. Self-help for Stupid

Ugly Losers 3.00
Spec. World Domination Handbook. 3.00
Spec. Hate the French #1 .... 3.00
Spec. The People's Choice 3.00
Spec. It's All Greek to You 3.00
8 Senseless Violence Spectacular . 3.00
9 The Lightning Round 3.00

ADAM AND EVE A.D.
Bam, 1985–87
1 .... 3.00
2 thru 10 .... @3.00

ADDAM OMEGA
Antarctic Press, 1997
1 (of 4) by Bill Hughes 3.00
2 thru 4 .... @3.00

ADOLESCENT RADIOACTIVE BLACK-BELT HAMSTERS
Eclipse, 1986
1 I:Bruce,Chuck,Jackie,Clint...... 3.00
1a 2nd printing 2.50
2 A parody of a parody 2.50
3 I:Bad Gerbil 2.50
4 A:Heap (3-D),Abusement Park .. 2.50
5 Abusement Park #2 .... 2.50
6 SK,Abusement Park #3 .... 2.50
7 SK,V:Toe-Jam Monsters 2.50
8 SK 2.50
9 All-Jam last issue............. 2.50

[2nd Series] Parody Press
1 .... 2.50
2 Hamsters Go Hollywood 2.50

ADVENTURERS
Aircel/Adventure, 1986
0 Origin Issue 3.00
1 with Skeleton............... 7.00
1a Revised cover 5.00
1b 2nd printing 3.00
2 thru 6 Peter Hsu (c) .... @3.00
7 .... 3.00
8 .... 3.00
9 .... 3.00

ADVENTURERS BOOK II
Adventure Publ., 1987
0 O:Man Gods 3.00
1 .... 3.00
2 thru 9 .... @3.00

ADVENTURERS BOOK III
Adventure Publ., 1989
1A Lim.(c)Ian McCaig........... 2.50
1B Reg.(c)Mitch Foust 2.50
2 thru 6 .... @2.50

ADVENTURES INTO THE UNKNOWN
A Plus Comics, 1990
1 AW,WW, rep. classic horror..... 3.00
2 AW 3.00
3 AW 3.00
Halloween Spec. reps. Charlton & American Comics GroupHorror. 2.50
ACG Comics, 1997
1 FF,AW, Charlton comics reprint.. 3.00

ADVENTURES OF BARRY WEEN BOY GENIUS
Oni Press, 2000
1 (of 6) by Judd Winick 3.00
2 Monkey Tales,pt.2 . . . . 3.00
3 Monkey Tales,pt.3 . . . . 3.00
4 Monkey Tales,pt.4 . . . . 3.00
5 Monkey Tales,pt.5 . . . . 3.00
6 Monkey Tales,pt.6 . . . . 3.00

ADVENTURES OF CHRISSY CLAWS, THE
Heroic, 1991
1 thru 2 . . . . @3.25

ADVENTURES OF CHUK THE BARBARIC
White Wolf, 1987
1 & 2 . . . . @3.00

ADVENTURES OF HERCULES
ACG Comics, 1998
1 by Sam Glanzman 3.00
ACG Comics, 2002
1 reprint of 2 Charlton comics 6.00
1a deluxe 16.00
2 64-page 6.00

ADVENTURES OF LIBERAL MAN, THE
Political Comics, 1996
1 by Marcus Pierce & Pete Garcia . 3.00
2 V:Right Wing talk show hosts . . . 3.00
3 Contract with America,'pt.2 . . . . . 3.00
4 Terminate with Extreme
   Prejudice,'pt.2 . . . . 3.00
5 Extreme Prejudice,pt.3 . . . . 3.00
6 . . . . 3.00
7 1996 Election issue 3.00
9 . . . . 3.00
10 The Last Boy Scouts,pt.2 . . . . . 3.00

ADVENTURES OF LUTHER ARKWRIGHT
Valkyrie Press, 1987–89
1 thru 9 . . . . @3.00
See Also: Dark Horse section

ADVENTURES OF THE AEROBIC DUO
Lost Cause Productions
1 thru 3 . . . . @2.25
4 Gopher Quest 2.25
5 V:Stupid Guy 2.25

ADVENTURES OF THEOWN
Pyramid, 1986
1 thru 3, Limited series . . . . . . @3.00

AESOP'S FABLES
Fantagraphics, 1991
1 Selection of Fables 2.25
2 Selection of Fables 2.25
3 inc. Boy who cried wolf 2.25

AETOS
Hall of Heroes, 1997
1 by Dan Parsons 2.50
1 variant cover 4.00
2 . . . . 2.50

AETOS THE EAGLE
Ground Zero, 1997
1 (of 3) by Dan Parsons 3.00
2 . . . . 3.00
3 concl. 3.00

AETOS 2: CHILDREN OF THE GRAVES
Orphan Underground, 1995
1 A:Nightmare 2.50

Agent Unknown #3
© Renegade

AGENT UNKNOWN
Renegade, 1987
1 thru 3 . . . . @3.00

AGE OF HEROES, THE
Halloween Comics, 1996
1 JHI 3.50
1A signed 7.00
2 JHI 3.50
2A signed 7.00

AGONY ACRES
AA2 Entertainment, 1995
1 thru 3 . . . . @2.50
4 and 5 . . . . @3.00

AIRFIGHTERS CLASSICS
Eclipse, 1987
1 O:Airboy,rep.Air Fighters#2 . . . . 4.00
2 rep.Old Airboy appearances 4.00
3 thru 6 . . . . @4.00

AIRWAVES
Caliber, 1990
1 Radio Security 2.50
2 A:Paisley,Ganja 2.50
3 Formation of Rebel Alliance 2.50
4 Big Annie,pt. 1 . . . . 2.50
5 Big Annie,pt 2 . . . . 2.50

AKIKO
Sirius, 1996–2004
1 MCi, Akiko on the Planet Smoo. . 6.00
2 MCi,Captife of SKy Pirates 4.00
3 thru 17 MCi . . . . @3.00
18 MCi,Alia Rellapor, concl. 3.00
19 MCi,The Story Tree,pt.1 . . . . . . 3.00
20 MCi,F:Mr. Beeba 3.00
21 MCi,On the Road 3.00

22 MCi,On the Transport Ship 3.00
23 MCi,Follow me,pt.1 . . . . 3.00
24 MCi,Follow me,pt.2 . . . . 3.00
25 MCi,Done in One, 32pg 3.00
26 MCi,Bornstone's Elixir,pt.1 . . . . 3.00
27 MCi,Bornstone's Elixir,pt.2 . . . . 3.00
28 MCi,Bornstone's Elixir,pt.3 . . . . 3.00
29 MCi,Bornstone's Elixir,pt.4 . . . . 3.00
30 MCi,Bornstone's Elixir,pt.5 . . . . 3.00
31 MCi,Bornstone's Elixir, concl. . . . 3.00
32 MCi,On Planet Earth,pt.1 . . . . . 3.00
33 MCi,On Planet Earth,pt.2 . . . . . 3.00
34 MCi,On Planet Earth,pt.3 . . . . . 3.00
35 Moonshopping,pt.1 . . . . 3.00
36 Moonshopping,pt.2 . . . . 3.00
37 Moonshopping,pt.3 . . . . 3.00
38 Moonshopping,pt.4 . . . . 3.00
39 Big Bag of This and That 3.00
40 Battle of Boach's Keep,pt.1 . . . . 3.00
41 Battle of Boach's Keep,pt.2 . . . . 3.00
42 Battle of Boach's Keep,pt.3 . . . . 3.00
43 Battle of Boach's Keep,pt.4 . . . . 3.00
44 Battle of Boach's Keep,pt.5 . . . . 3.00
45 Battle of Boach's Keep,pt.6 . . . . 3.00
46 Battle of Boach's Keep,pt.7 . . . . 3.00
47 Battle of Boach's Keep,pt.8 . . . . 3.00
48 Akiko on Planet Earth,pt.1 . . . . . 3.00
49 Akiko on Planet Earth,pt.2 . . . . . 3.00
50 MCi,44-pg. 3.50
51 MCi,Quality Assortment 3.00
52 MCi 3.00
1-shot Akiko on the Planet Smoo . 4.00
1-shot Akiko on the Planet Smoo,
   signed & numbered, color 6.00

ALAN MOORE'S HYPOTHETICAL LIZARD
Avatar Press, 2004
Preview 2.00
Preview, wraparound (c) 3.00
Preview, convention (c) 6.00
1 (of 4) 4.00
1a wraparound (c). 4.00
1b Tarot (c) 4.00
2 thru 4 . . . . @3.50
2a thru 4a wraparound (c). . . . . . @3.50
2b thru 4b Tarot (c) . . . . @4.00

ALAN MOORE'S THE COURTYARD
Avatar Press, 2003
1 . . . . 3.50
2 . . . . 3.50
1a thru 2a wraparound (c). . . . . . @4.00

ALAN MOORE'S YUGGOTH CULTURES
Avatar Press, 2003
1 thru 3 . . . . @3.50
1 thru 3a wraparound (c) 4.00
Necrocomicon ashcan, 16-pg. 5.00

ALBEDO
Thoughts & Images, 1985–89
0 white cover, yellow drawing table
   Blade Runner 200.00
0a white(c) 100.00
0b blue(c),1st ptg 75.00
0c blue(c),2nd ptg 35.00
0d blue(c),3rd ptg 20.00
0e Photo(c),4th ptg.,inc. extra
   pages 15.00
1 SS,I:Nilson Groundthumper,
   dull red cover 75.00
1a bright red cover 50.00
2 SS,I:Usagi Yojimbo 400.00
3 SS,Erma, Usagi 30.00
4 SS,Usagi 35.00

5 Nelson Groundthumper 7.00
6 Erma, High Orbit 4.00
7 . . . . 4.00
8 Erna Feldna 4.00
9 High Orbit,Harvest Venture 4.00
10 thru 14 . . . . @4.00

ALBEDO VOL. II
Antarctic Press, 1991–93
1 New Erma Story 3.00
2 E.D.F. HQ. 3.00
3 Birth of Erma's Child 3.00
4 Non action issue 3.00
5 The Outworlds 3.00
6 War preparations 3.00
7 Ekosiak in Anarchy 3.00
8 EDF High Command 3.00
Spec. Color 3.00

VOL. III
1 . . . . 3.50

Vol 5 Anthropomorphics
Shanda Fantasy Arts, 2004
1 . . . . 5.00
3 Menace From Space 5.00

ALBERT
Narwain Publishing, 2006
1 (of 4) 3.00
2 thru 4 . . . . @3.00

ALICE IN THE LOST LAND
Radio Comix, 2000
1 (of 4) by Shuzilow Ha 3.00
2 thru 4 . . . . @3.00

ALIEN FIRE
Kitchen Sink Press, 1987
1 Eric Vincent art 3.50
2 Eric Vincent art 3.00
3 Eric Vincent art 3.00

Alien Nation, The Public Enemy #1
© Adventure Comics

ALIEN NATION:
A BREED APART
Adventure Comics, 1990
1 Friar Kaddish 3.00
2 Friar Kaddish 2.50
3 The `Vampires' Busted 2.50
4 Final Issue 2.50

ALIEN NATION:
THE FIRSTCOMERS
Adventure Comics, 1991
1 New Mini-series 2.50
2 Assassin 2.50
3 Search for Saucer 2.50
4 Final Issue 2.50

ALIEN NATION:
THE PUBLIC ENEMY
Adventure Comics, 1991
1 `Before the Fall' 2.50
2 Earth & Wehlnistrata 2.50
3 Killer on the Loose 2.50

ALIEN NATION:
THE SKIN TRADE
Adventure Comics, 1991
1 `Case of the Missing Milksop' . . . 2.50
2 `To Live And Die in L.A' 2.50
3 A:Dr. Jekyll 2.50
4 D.Methoraphan Exposed 2.50

ALIEN NATION:
THE SPARTANS
Adventure Comics, 1990
1 JT/DPo,Yellow wrap 4.00
1a JT/DPo,Green wrap 4.00
1b JT/DPo,Pink wrap 4.00
1c JT/DPo,blue wrap 4.00
1d LTD collectors edition 7.00
2 JT,A:Ruth Lawrence 2.50
3 JT/SM,Spartians 2.50
4 JT/SM,conclusion 2.50

ALISON DARE,
LITTLE MISS
ADVENTURES
Oni Press, 2001
1 (of 3) 3.00
Vol. 2
1 (of 2) Heart of the Maiden 3.00
2 Heart of the Maiden 3.00
1-shot 48-pg. (2000) 4.50

ALL-PRO SPORTS
All Pro Sports
1 Unauthorized Bio-Bo Jackson . . . 2.50
2 Unauthorized Bio-Joe Montana . . 2.50

ALLURA AND
THE CYBERANGELS
Avatar Press, 1998
Spec.#1 by Bill Maus 4.00

ALLY
Ally Winsor Productions, 1995
1 I&O: Ally 3.00
2 and 3 . . . . @3.00

ALONG THE CANADIAN
Obion Comics, 2004
1 thru 6 . . . . @3.00

ALTERNATE HEROES
Prelude Graphics, 1986
1 and 2 . . . . @3.00

AMAZING COMICS
PREMIERES
Amazing, 1987
1 thru 9 . . . . @3.00

AMAZON WOMAN
Fantaco, 1994
1 . . . . 3.00
2 . . . . 3.00
VOL. 2 (1996)
1 thru 4 . . . . @3.00
Christmas Spec. 5.00
Beach Party 6.00
Amazing Colossal Amazon
    Woman #1 . . . . 8.00
Amazing Colossal Amazon Album . 13.00
Jungle Annual #1 . . . . 6.00
Jungle Album 10.00
Spec. Invaders of Terror (1996) . . . 6.00
1-shot Attack of the Amazon Girls,
    cont. nudity 5.00

AMERICAN SPLENDOR
Harvey Bekar, 1976–90
1 thru 15 . . . . @3.25
Tundra, 1991
16 . . . . 4.00

AMERICAN WOMAN
Antarctic Press, 1998
1 by B.Denham & R.Stockton 3.00

AMERICA'S GREATEST
COMICS
AC Comics, 2002
1 F:Phantom Lady, golden-age rep. 7.00
2 F:Mysta on the Moon 7.00
3 F:Spy Smasher 7.00
4 F:Yarko, Master Magician 7.00
5 F: Captain Science 7.00
6 thru 13 . . . . @7.00
14 thru 16 . . . . @7.00

AMUSING STORIES
Blackthorne
1 thru 3 . . . . @2.25

ANATOMIC BOMBS
Brainstorm, 1998
1 Angelissa, by Mike James 3.00
1a Bad Tabitha, by Mike James . . . 3.00
1b Bad Tabitha, photo cover edition 4.00

ANGEL GIRL
Angel Entertainment, 1997
0 by David Campiti & Al Rio 3.00
1 by D.Campiti & R.Fraga 3.00
1 deluxe 6.00
Spec. #1 Angels Illustrated Swimsuit
    Special 5.00
1-shot Against All Evil 3.00
1-shot Before the Wings 3.00
1-shot Demonworld, by Ellis Bell &
    Mark Kuettner 3.00
1-shot Doomsday, by Ellis Bell &
    Mark Kuettner 3.00

ANGEL GIRL:
HEAVEN SENT
Angel Entertainment, 1997
0 by David Campiti & Al Rio 3.00
1 . . . . 3.00

ANGEL HEAT:
THE NINTH ORDER
Amazing Comics, 1997
1 . . . . 3.00
2 "Book of Revelations" 3.00
1a signed 3.00
3 Helcio the Redeemer 3.00

ANGEL OF DEATH
Innovation, 1991
1 thru 4 . . . . @2.25

ANGEL SCRIPTBOOK
IDW Publishing, 2006
1 City Of 4.00
1a variant (c) 4.00
2 A Hole in the World 4.00
3 Spin the Bottle 4.00
4 Waiting in the Wings 4.00
5 Five by Five 4.00
6 Sanctuary 4.00
7 Smile Time 4.00
2a thru 7a variant (cs) . . . . @4.00

ANGELS 750
Antarctic Press, 2004
1 (of 9) 3.00
2 thru 5 . . . . @3.00

ANGRY YOUTH COMIX
Fantagraphics Books, 2000
1 by Johnny Ryan 3.00
2 thru 5 . . . . 3.00
6 thru 9 . . . . @3.50
10 48-page 5.00
11 thru 13 . . . . @3.50

ANIMAL MYSTIC
Cry For Dawn/Sirius, 1993–95
1 DOe 25.00
1a variant, signed 35.00
1b 2nd printing, new (c) 7.00
2 I:Klor 25.00
2a 2nd printing, new (c) 6.00
3 . . . . 12.00
3a 2nd printing 5.00
4 last issue 4.00
4a special 15.00

ANIMAL MYSTIC: KLOR
Sirius, 1999
1 thru 3 DOe . . . . @3.00

ANTARES CIRCLE
Antarctic Press, 1990
1 . . . . 2.25
2 . . . . 2.25

ANUBIS
Unicorn Books
1 I:Anubis 2.50
2 F:Anubis 2.50
3 . . . . 2.50
Didactic Chocolate Press
3 by Scott Berwanger 2.75
4 thru 6 . . . . @2.75
Adventure Comics
7 `Sandy's Plight' 2.75
8 . . . . 3.00

A-OK
Antarctic Press, 1993
1 Ninja H.S. spin-off series 2.50
2 F:Paul,Moniko,James 2.50
3 Confrontation 2.50
4 . . . . 2.50

APATHY KAT
Entity, 1995
1 . . . . 2.75
1 signed, numbered 10.00
1a & 2a 2nd printings . . . . @2.75
2 . . . . 2.75
3 & 4 . . . . 2.75

APE CITY
Adventure Comics, 1990
1 Monkey Business 3.00
2 thru 4 . . . . @2.50

APOCALYPSE PLAN, THE
Narwain Publishing, 2006
1 (of 3) 3.50
2 . . . . 3.00

APPARITION, THE
Caliber, 1995
1 thru 4 . . . . @3.00
5 `Black Clouds' 3.00

APPLESEED
Eclipse, 1988
1 MSh,rep. Japanese comic 8.00
2 MSh,arrival in Olympus City . . . 6.00
3 MSh,Olympus City politics 5.00
4 MSh,V:Director 5.00
5 MSh,Deunan vs. Chiffon 5.00
Book Two, 1989
1 MSh,AAd(c),Olympus City 4.00
2 MSh,AAd(c),Hitomi vs.EswatUnit 4.00
3 MSh,AAd(c),Deunan vs.Gaia. . . 4.00
4 MSh,AAd(c),V:Robot Spiders . . . 4.00
5 MSh,AAd(c),Hitome vs.Gaia . . . 4.00
Book Three, 1989
1 MSh,Brigreos vs.Biodroid 5.00
2 MSh,V:Cuban Navy 4.00
3 MSh,`Benandanti' 4.00
4 MSh,V:Renegade biodroid. 4.00
5 MSh 4.00
Book Four, 1990
1 MSh,V:Munma Terrorists 3.50
2 MSh,V:Drug-crazed Munma . . . 3.50
3 Msh,V:Munma Drug Addicts . . . 3.50
4 MSh,Deunan vs. Pani 3.50

ARAMIS
Comics Interview, 1988
1 mini-series 2.25
2 & 3 . . . . @2.25

AREA 88
Eclipse, 1987
1 I:Shin Kazama 3.00
1a 2nd printing 2.50
2 Dangerous Mission 2.50
2a 2nd printing 2.50
3 O:Shin,Paris '78 . . . . 2.50
4 thru 8 . . . . @2.50
9 thru 36 . . . . @2.50
Viz Communications, 1988
37 thru 42 . . . . @2.50

AREALA, ANGEL OF WAR
Antarctic Press, 1998
1 F:Warrior Nun Areala, color 3.00
2 color 3.00
3 b&w 3.00
4 b&w, conclusion 3.00

ARGONAUTS
Eternity
1 thru 5 . . . . @2.25

ARIK KHAN
A Plus Comics
1 I:Arik Khan 2.50
2 . . . . 2.50
ACG Comics, 1998
1 by Frank Reyes, heroic fantasy . 3.00

Aristocratic X-traterrestrial Time
Traveling Thieves #2 © Fictioneer

ARISTOCRATIC X-TRA-TERRESTRIAL TIME-TRAVELING THIEVES
Fictioneer Books, 1987
1 V:IRS 2.50
2 V:Realty 2.50
3 V:MDM 2.50
4 thru 12 . . . . @2.50

ARIZONA: A SIMPLE HORROR
London Night/EH Prod., 1998
1 (of 3) by Joe Kennedy &
　Jerry Beck 3.00
2 double sized 3.00
3 . . . . 3.00
1-shot Wild at Heart, signed
　alternate cover 9.00

A.R.M.
Adventure Comics, 1990
1 Larry Niven adapt. Death by
　Ecstasy,pt.1 . . . . 2.50
2 Death by Ecstasy,pt.2 . . . . 2.50
3 Death by Ecstasy,pt.3 . . . . 2.50

ARMAGEDDON PATROL
Alchemy Texts, 1999
Spec. The Shot 3.00
1 (of 2) Cherries 3.00
2 Cherries 3.00
Spec. Maiden America (2002) 3.00
Spec. Fatal Mistakes 3.00
Spec. Life and Death 3.50
Spec. First Mission #1 . . . . 3.50
Spec. First Mission #2 . . . . 3.50
Spec. First Mission #3 . . . . 3.50

ARMED & DANGEROUS
Valiant, 1995
1 thru 4 . . . . @3.00
Spec.#1 . . . . 3.00

ARMED & DANGEROUS
Acclaim (Armada), 1996
1 BH,Hell's Slaughterhouse, pt.1 . 3.00
2 BH,Hell's Slaughterhouse, pt.2 . 3.00
3 BH,Hell's Slaughterhouse, pt.3 . 3.00
4 BH,Hell's Slaughterhouse, pt.4 . 3.00

B & W PUB.

ARMED & DANGEROUS
No. 2
Acclaim, 1996
1 BH,When Irish Eyes are
Dying, pt.1 . . . . 3.00
2 BH,When Irish Eyes, pt.2 . . . . . 3.00
3 BH,When Irish Eyes, pt.3 . . . . . 3.00
4 BH,When Irish Eyes, pt.4 . . . . . 3.00

ARROW SPOTLIGHT
Arrow Comics, 1998–99
Advendures of Simone & Ajax 3.00
Allison Chains 3.00
Descendants of Toshin. 3.00
Max Velocity, by Jack Snider 3.00
Red Vengeance, by Chris Kemple . . 3.00
Talonback 3.00

ARSENIC LULLABY
A Silent Comics, 1999
Spec. May '99 . . . . 2.50
Spec. July '99. . . . . 2.50
Spec. Sept.'99 . . . . 2.50
Spec. Jan. 2000. . . . . 2.50
8 thru 15 . . . . @2.50
Sept. 2001 . . . . 2.50
Nov. 2001. . . . . 2.65
Christmas 2001 . . . . 2.65
Spec. Christmas Special 2.50
Spec. Halloween Special 2.75
Volume 2, 2002
1 by Douglas Paszkiewicz 3.00
2 . . . . 3.00
3 . . . . 3.00
4 . . . . 3.00
AAA Milwaukee Publishing
Lost issue, signed (2002). 4.00
15 thru 16 . . . . @3.00
17 . . . . 3.00
Arsenic Lullaby Pub., 2005
18 thru 20 . . . . @3.00

ASHES
Caliber, 1990–91
1 thru 6 . . . . @2.50

ASHLEY DUST
Knight Press, 1995
1 thru 3 . . . . @2.50
4 V:Allister Crowley. 2.50
5 Metaphysical Adventure. 2.50

A SORT OF HOMECOMING
Alternative Comics 2003
1 (of 3) 3.50
2 and 3 . . . . @3.50

ASRIAL VS. CHEETAH
Antarctic Press, 1995–96
1 & 2 Ninja High School Gold
Digger x-over . . . . @3.00

ASSASSINATE HITLER!
New England Comics, 2001
1 (of 3) by Ron Ledwell 3.75
2 thru 3 . . . . @3.75

ASSASSINETTE
Pocket Change Comics, 1994
1 thru 4 . . . . @2.50
5 V:Nemesis 2.50
6 The Second Coming,pt.2 . . . . . . 2.50
7 The Second Coming,pt.3 . . . . . . 2.50
8 V:Crazy Actor. 2.50
9 . . . . 2.50
10 final issue. 2.50

Spec. Assassinette Returns 2.50
Spec. Assassinette Violated 2.50
Deluxe Assassinette Violated 4.25

ASSASSINETTE:
HARDCORE 1995
Pocket Change Comics
1 By Shadow Slasher Team 2.50
2 V:Bolero 2.50

AS TOLD BY...
NDP Comics, 2004
1 Rapunzel 3.00
2 Sleeping Beauty. 3.00
3 Goldilocks 3.00

ASSEMBLY
Antarctic Press, 2003
1 (of 4) 3.00
2 thru 4 . . . . @3.50

ASTOUNDING
SPACE THRILLS
Day One Comics, 1998
1 by Steve Conley, The Codex
Reckoning,pt.1. . . . . 3.00
2 Bros. Hildebrandt (c) 3.00
3 Aspects of Iron 3.00
4 The Robot Murders 3.00
5 Gordo returns. 3.00

ASTOUNDING SPACE
THRILLS: BLOOP
Day One Comics, 2004
1 . . . . 3.00
2 . . . . 3.00

ASTRA
CPM Manga, 2001
1 . . . . 3.00
1a variant JBa (c) 3.00
1b variant JBa(c) signed 30.00
2 thru 5 . . . . @3.00
6 thru 8 . . . . @3.00

ASTRONAUTS
IN TROUBLE:
LIVE FROM THE MOON
Gun Dog Comics, 1999
1 (of 5) 3.00
2 thru 5 . . . . @3.00
AIT Comics, 1999
Spec.#1 Cool Ed's 3.00
Spec.#1 CAd, One Shot, One Beer. 8.00

ASTRONAUTS IN
TROUBLE: SPACE:, 1959
AIT/Planetlar, 2000
1 (of 3) by Larry Young, CAd 3.00
2 . . . . 3.00
3 . . . . 3.00

ATHENA
A.M. Works, 1995
1 thru 14 by Dean Hsieh . . . . . . @3.00
Antarctic Press, 1996
0 . . . . 4.00

ATOMIC CITY TALES
Kitchen Sink, 1996
1 by Jay Stephens 3.50
2 thru 4 . . . . @3.50

Athena #10
© *A.M. Works*

ATOMIC COMICS
1 . . . . 2.75
Becomes:
MARK I

ATOMIC MAN
Blackthorne, 1986
1 . . . . 3.00
2 & 3 . . . . @2.50

ATOMIC MOUSE
A Plus Comics, 1990
1 A:Atomic Bunny 2.50

ATOMIC OVERDRIVE
Caliber
1 by Dave Darrigo & PGr 3.00
2 & 3 . . . . @3.00

A TRAVELLER'S TALE
Antarctic Press
1 I:Goshin the Traveller 2.50
2 . . . . 2.50

ATTACK OF THE
MUTANT MONSTERS
A Plus Comics, 1991
1 SD,rep.Gorgo(Kegor). 2.50

AUGUST
Arrow Comics, 1998
1 . . . . 3.00
2 thru 4 . . . . @3.00

AUTUMN
Caliber Press, 1995
1 I:James Turell 3.00

AUTUMN
Amaze Ink/SLG, 2004
1 . . . . 3.00
2 thru 5 . . . . @3.00

AVALON
Harrier, 1987
1 . . . . 2.50
2 thru 3 . . . . @2.50

AVANT GUARD
Day 1 Comics, 1994
1 thru 4 F:Feedback . . . . @2.50

AVATARS
Avatar Press, 1998
1 (of 2) by Gregory & Holaso 4.00
2 F:Pandora & Atlas 3.50

AV IN 3D
Aardvark–Vanaheim, 1984
1 Color,A:Flaming Carrot 6.00

AVELON
Drawbridge Studios, 1998
1 The Scrolls of Dyom, pt. 1 . . . . . 3.00
2 The Scrolls of Dyom, pt. 2 . . . . . 3.00
3 The Scrolls of Dyom, pt. 3 . . . . . 3.00
4 The Scrolls of Dyom, pt. 4 . . . . . 3.00
5 Way of the Wylden, 112-page . . . 6.00

AVELON
Kenzer & Company, 1998
1 . . . . 3.00
2 thru 11 Legacy of Thrain . . . . . @3.00
11 & 12 Heir to Legend . . . . @3.00

AVENUE X
Innovation, 1992
1 Based on NY radio drama 2.50
Purple Spiral
3 signed & numbered 3.00

AWAKENING COMICS
Awakening Comics, 1997
1 by Steve Peters 3.50
2 . . . . 3.50
3 thru 4 . . . . @3.00
Awakening Comics, 1999
1 by Steve Peters 3.50
Spec. Millennium Bug Fever 3.00

AWAKENINGS
Eighth Day Entertainment, 2004
1 (of 6) 3.00
2 thru 5 . . . . @3.00

AWESOME COMICS
1 thru 3 . . . . @2.25

AXED FILES, THE
Entity Comics, 1995
1 X-Files Parody 2.50
1 3rd printing, parody 2.75

B-MOVIE PRESENTS
B-Movie Comics, 1986
1 Captain Daring 2.50
2 The World of X-Ray 2.50
3 Tasma, Queen of the Jungle 2.50
4 Matrix the Accellerator 2.50

B.A.B.E. FORCE
Comics Conspiracy, 2002
1 . . . . 3.00
2 thru 3 . . . . @3.00
Basement Comics, 2003
4 . . . . 3.00
4a special ed. 8.95

B.A.B.E. FORCE:
BACK TO SCHOOL
Forcewerks Productions, 2004
1 . . . . 2.50

2 . . . . 2.50

B.A.B.E. FORCE:
JURASSIC TRAILER PARK
Forcewerks Productions, 2004
1 . . . . 2.50
2 . . . . 2.50

BABES OF AREA 51
Blatant Comics, 1997
1 . . . . 3.00

BABY ANGEL X
Brainstorm, 1996
1 . . . . 3.00
2 . . . . 3.00
3 gold edition 5.00
3a signed edition. 9.00

BABY ANGEL X:
SCORCHED EARTH
Brainstorm, 1997
1 by Scott Harrison 3.00
2 . . . . 3.00

BABYLON CRUSH
Boneyard Press, 1995
1 I:Babylon Crush 3.00
2 V:A Gang 3.00
3 V:Mafiaso Brothers 3.00
4 & 5 . . . . @3.00
CFD
6 & 7 . . . . @4.00
Boneyard, 1998
1-shot Buddha, F:Lesbian dominatrix
  vigilante 5.00
Spec. Babylon Bondage Christmas . 3.00
Spec. Girlfriends. 3.00
Spec. The Last Shepherd 3.00

BAD APPLES
High Impact, 1997
1 . . . . 3.00
1 Bad Candies cover 9.00
2 . . . . 3.00
2 deluxe 12.00
3 by Billy Patton 3.00
Vol. 2, ABC Studios, 1999
1 RCI. 3.00
1a deluxe variant 8.00

Baker Street #10
© *Caliber*

BAD APPLES:
HIGH EXPECTATIONS
ABC Studios, 1999
1 . . . . 3.00
1a Beach Fun (c) 8.00
2 . . . . 3.00
2a deluxe 8.00

BAKER STREET
(Prev. color)
Caliber, 1989
3 . . . . 3.25
4 . . . . 2.50
5 & 6 Children of the Night . . . . . @2.50
7 thru 10 Children of the Night . . @2.50

BAKER STREET:
GRAPHITTI
Caliber
1 'Elementary, My Dear' 2.50

BALANCE OF POWER
MU Press, 1990–91
1 thru 4 . . . . @2.50

BALLAD OF UTOPIA
Black Daze, 2000
1 by B.Buchanan & M.Hoffman . . . 3.00
2 thru 5 . . . . @3.00
Antimatter/Hoffman Int., 2003
7 thru 8 . . . . @3.00

BANANA SUNDAY
Oni Press Inc., 2005
1 (of 4) 3.00
2 thru 4 . . . . @3.00

BANDY MAN, THE
Caliber, 1996
1 SPr,CAd. 3.00
2 SPr,CAd,JIT. 3.00
3 SPr,CAd,JIT, conclusion. 3.00

BAOH
Viz, 1990
1 thru 8 . . . . @3.00

BARABBAS
Slave Labor, 1986
1 . . . . 4.50
2 thru 4 . . . . @2.50

BARBARIANS
ACG Comics
1 by Jeff Jones, Mike Kaluta,
  Wayne Howard 3.00
2 WW 3.00

BARBARIC TALES
Pyramid, 1986
1 . . . . 3.00
2 and 3 . . . . @2.25

BARBAROUS
I:Ron, 1998
1 by Ron Riley, 'Tween A Roch
  and a Hard Place, pt.1 . . . . 2.75

Vol 3
1 by Greg Narvasa 3.00
1a gold manga 9.00

2 'Tween A Roch and a Hard
 Place, pt.2 (of 2) 2.75
3 The Fifth Kind, pt.1 (of 2). 2.75
4 The Fifth Kind, pt.2 . . . . 2.75

BASEBALL SUPERSTARS
Revolutionary, 1991–93
1 Nolan Ryan 2.50
2 Bo Jackson 2.50
3 Ken Griffey Jr. 2.50
4 Pete Rose 2.50
5 Rickey Henderson 2.50
6 Jose Canseco 2.50
7 Cal Ripkin Jr. 2.50
8 Carlton Fisk 2.50
9 George Brett 2.50
10 Darryl Strawberry 2.50
11 Frank Thomas. 2.50
12 Ryne Sandberg (color) 2.75
13 Kirby Puckett (color) 2.75
14 Roberto & Sandy Alomar (color). 2.75
15 Roger Clemens (color) 2.75
16 Mark McGuire 3.00
17 Avery & Glavin 3.00
18 Dennis Eckersley 3.00
19 Dave Winfield 3.00
20 Jim Abbott. 3.00

BASTARD!!
Viz Communications, 2001
1 thru 2 Wizard . . . . @4.00
3 thru 5 Ninja. . . . . @4.00
6 thru 8 Fighter . . . . @4.00
9 thru 10 Vampire . . . . @4.00
11 thru 12 Empress . . . . @4.00
13 thru 15 Empress . . . . @4.00

BATTLE ANGEL ALITA
Viz, 1992
1 I:Daisuka,Alita 8.00
2 Alita becomes warrior 6.00
3 A:Daiuke,V:Cyborg. 4.00
4 Alita/Cyborg,A:Makaku 4.00
5 The Bounty Hunters' Bar 4.00
6 Confrontation 4.00
7 Underground Sewers,A:Fang . . . 3.00
8 & 9 . . . . @2.75
Part Two, 1993
1 V:Zapan 3.00
2 V:Zapan 3.00
3 F:Ido. 2.75
4 thru 7 V:Zapan . . . . @2.75
Part Three, 1993
1 thru 5 . . . . @2.75
6 . . . . 5.00
7 thru 13 . . . . @2.75
Part Four, 1994
1 . . . . 2.75
2 thru 7 . . . . @2.75
Part Five, 1995
1 thru 6 . . . . @2.75
7 . . . . 3.00
Part Six, 1995–96
1 . . . . 3.00
2 thru 8 YuK . . . . @3.00
Part Seven, 1996
1 thru 8 YuK . . . . @3.00
Part Eight, 1997
1 thru 9 YuK . . . . @3.00

BATTLE ANGEL ALITA: LAST ORDER
Viz Communicatons, 2002
Part 1
1 by Yukito Kishiro 3.00
2 thru 6 . . . . @3.00

BATTLE ARMOR
Eternity, 1988
1 thru 4 . . . . @2.50

BATTLE BEASTS
Blackthorne, 1988
1 thru 4 . . . . @2.50

BATTLE GIRLZ
Antarctic Press, 2002
1 by Rod Espinosa 3.00
2 thru 6 . . . . @3.00

BATTLEGROUND EARTH
Best Comics, 1996
1 . . . . 2.50
2 . . . . 2.50
3 'Destiny Quest: The Vengeance'
 concl. 2.50
4 V:Conjura. 2.50
5 'The Pit of Black Death'. 2.50

BATTLE POPE
Funk-O-Tron, 2000
1 . . . . 3.00
2 thru 4 . . . . @3.00
Spec.#1 Shorts. 5.00
Spec.#2 Shorts. 5.00
Spec.#3 Shorts. 3.00
Spec.#1 Christmas Popetacular . . 5.00

BATTLE POPE MAYHEM
Funk-O-Tron, 2001
1 (of 2) 3.00
2 . . . . 3.00

BATTLE POPE PRESENTS: SAINT MICHAEL
Funk-O-Tron, 2001
1 thru 3 . . . . @3.00

BATTLE POPE: WRATH OF GOD
Funk-O-Tron, 2002
1 (of 3) by R.Kirkman & T.Moore . . 3.50
2 thru 3 . . . . @3.50

BATTLESTAR BLACK & WHITE
Realm Press, 2000
1-shot Battlestar Galactica. 3.00

BATTLETECH
Blackthorne, 1987
(Prev. Color)
7 thru 12 . . . . @2.50
Ann.#1 . . . . 4.50

BATTRON
NEC
1 thru 2 WWII story. . . . . @2.75

BEAR
Amaze Ink/SLG, 2003
1 by Jamie Smart 3.00
2 thru 10 . . . . @3.00

BEAST WARRIOR OF SHAOLIN
Pied Piper, 1987
1 thru 5 . . . . @2.50

THE BEATLES EXPERIENCE
Revolutionary, 1991–92
1 Beatles 1960's 3.00
2 Beatles 1964-1966. . . . . 2.50
3 . . . . 2.50
4 Abbey Road, Let it be 2.50
5 The Solo Years 2.50
6 Paul McCartney & Wings. 2.50
7 The Murder of John Lennon 2.50
8 final issue. 2.50

BECK AND CAUL
Gauntlet, 1994
1 I:Beck and Caul 3.00
2 thru 6 . . . . @3.00
Ann.#1 A Single Step. 3.50

Belle Starr, Queen of Bandits #2
© Moonstone

BELLE STAR: QUEEN OF BANDITS
Moonstone, 2005
1 . . . . 3.00
2 . . . . 3.00

BENZINE
Antarctic Press, 2000
1 manga, by Ben Dunn. 5.00
2 thru 7 . . . . @5.00

BERLIN
Drawn & Quarterly, 1999
1 by Jason Lutes 3.00
2 thru 8 . . . . @3.00
9 thru 10 . . . . @3.50
11 thru 13 . . . . @4.00

BERZERKER
Gauntlet (Caliber), 1993
1 thru 6 . . . . @3.00

BEST OF THE WEST
AC Comics, 1998
1 F:Durango Kid 5.00
2 F:The Haunted Horseman. 5.00
3 F:The Haunted Horseman. 5.00
4 F:Roy Rogers, 44-pg. 6.00
5 F:Durango Kid 6.00
6 F:Durango Kid 6.00
7 F:Monte Hale 6.00
8 . . . . 6.00

9 F:Sunset Carson	6.00
10 F:Durango Kid	6.00
11 F:Black Diamond	6.00
12 F:Latigo Kid	6.00
13 F:The Durango Kid	6.00
14 F:Haunted Horseman	6.00
15 F:Roy Rogers	6.00
16 O:The Whip	6.00
17 F:Lone Ranger	6.00
18 F:Black Bull	6.00
19 F:Rocky Lane	6.00
20 F:Durango Kid	6.00
21 F:Masked Marvel	6.00
22 F:Ken Maynard	6.00
23 F:Freaks of Fear	6.00
24 F:Redmask, Black Phantom	6.00
25 FF(c),F:Haunted horsemen	6.00
26 F:Lazo Kid, Lemonade Kid	6.00
27 F:Roy Rogers	6.00
28 F:Red Mask	6.00
29 F:Jim Bowie	6.00
30 F:The Durango Kid	6.00
31 F:Haunted Horseman	6.00
32 F:Haunted Horseman	6.00
33 F:Zorro	7.00
34 Roy Rogers	7.00
35 The Haunted Horseman	7.00
36 Gene Autry	7.00
37 Origins Issue	7.00
38 Durango Kid	7.00
39 Roy Rogers	7.00
40 Redmask	7.00
41 The Haunted Horseman	7.00
42 Black Diamond	7.00
43 The Haunted Horseman	7.00
44 The Hooded Horseman	7.00
45 The Haunted Horsean	7.00
46 The Durango Kid	7.00
47 The Durango Kid	7.00
48 The Durango Kid	7.00
49 The Crimson Cavalier	7.00
50 Frankenstein Goes West	7.00
51 Redmask	7.00
52 Wild Bill Pecos	7.00
53 The Durango Kid	7.00
54 The Durango Kid	7.00
55 Strawman vs. Redmask	7.00
56 Haunted Horseman	7.00
57 Firehair	7.00
58 Haunted Horseman	7.00
59 Monte Hale	7.00
60 thru 64	@7.00

BETHANY THE VAMPFIRE
Brainstorm, 1997

0 O:Bethany	3.00
1 by Holly Galightly	3.00
1a luxury edition	5.00
2 & 3	@3.00

BETTIE PAGE
THE '50s RAGE
Illustration Studio, 2001

1 revised edition, Steve Woron	3.25
2 all pin-up layout	3.25
2 tame cover	3.25
Ann.#1 revised	3.25

BEYOND MARS
Blackthorne, 1989

1 thru 5	@2.25

BIG BANG PRESENTS
Big Bang Comics, 2006

1 Protoplasm	3.00
2 Super Frankenstein	3.00
3	4.00
4 Protoplasman	4.00
5 Tennrex	4.00

6 Agents of Badge, 64-pgs.	8.00

BIGGER
Free Lunch Comics, 1998

Spec.#1	3.50
1 (of 4) The Devil's Concubine	3.00
2 thru 4 Devil's Concubine,pt.2–4	@3.00

BIG NUMBERS
Mad Love

1 BSz,AMo(s)	6.00
2 BSz,AMo(s)	5.50

BILL THE BULL:
BURNT CAIN
Boneyard, 1992

1 I:Bill the Bull	3.00
2 & 3 For Hire	@3.00

BILL THE BULL:
ONE SHOT, ONE
BOURBON, ONE BEER
Boneyard, 1994

1	3.00
2	3.00

BILLY DOGMA
Millennium, 1997

1 by Dean Haspiel	3.00
1a signed print edition	5.00
2	3.00
3	3.00
4 They Found A Sawed-Off in My Afro	3.00

BILLY NGUYEN
PRIVATE EYE
Caliber, 1990

1	2.25
1a 2nd printing	2.25
2 thru 6	@2.25

BIO-BOOSTER
ARMOR GUYVER
Viz Communications
Part One, 1993

1 by Yoshiki Takaya	4.00
2 thru 12	@3.00

Bio-Booster Armor Guyver #3
© Viz Communications

Part Two, 1994–95

1 F:Sho	2.75
2 thru 7	@2.75

Part Three, 1995

1 Sho Unconscious	2.75
2 thru 7	@2.75

Part Four, 1995–96

1 thru 7	@3.00

Part Five, 1996

1 thru 7	@3.00

Part Six, 1996–97

1 thru 6 by Yoshiki Takaya	@3.00

BIRTHDAY BOY, THE
Beetlebomb Books, 1997

1 by Jason Lethcoe	3.00
2	3.00
3	3.00
4 16-pg.	3.00

VOL 2

1 16-pg.	3.00

BIZARRE HEROES
Kitchen Sink, 1990

1 DSs, parody	2.50

Fiasco Comics

1 DSs, reprint	3.00

BLACK BELT CLUB
Blue Sky Press 2006

1 Seven Wheels of Power	5.00
2 Night of the Mountain of Fear	5.00

[Original] BLACK CAT
Recollections, 1991

4 rep.	2.25
5 A:Ted Parrish	2.25
6 50th Anniv. Issue	2.25
7 rep.	2.25

BLACK COAT:
CALL TO ARMS
Speakeasy Comics, 2006

1 (of 4)	3.00
2 thru 3	@3.00

Ape Entertainment, 2006

4	3.00

BLACK COAT, THE:
OR GIVE ME DEATH
Ape Entertainment, 2007

1 (of 4)	3.50
2 thru 4	@3.50

BLACKENED
Enigma

1 V:Killing Machine	3.00
2 V:Killing Machine	3.00
3 Flaming Altar	3.00

BLACK-EYED SUSAN
Mad Yak Press, 2004

1	3.50
2 thru 4	@3.00

BLACK HEART
IRREGULARS, THE
Blue King Studios, 2005

1	3.00
2	3.00
3 Who's your Bagdaddy	3.00
4	3.00
5	3.00

BLACK HOLE
Kitchen Sink, 1995

1 by Charles Burns	3.50
1 new printing	4.50
2	3.50
3	3.50
3 2nd printing	4.50

Fantagraphics Books, 2000

5 by Charles Burns	4.00
6 thru 10	@4.50
11 thru 12	@5.00

BLACK KISS
Vortex, 1988

1 HC,Adult	7.00
1a 2nd printing	4.00
1b 3rd printing	2.50
2 HC	6.00
2a 2nd printing	3.00
3 HC	5.00
4 HC	4.00
5 & 6 HC	@2.50
7 thru 12 HC	@2.50

BLACKMASK
Eastern Comics, 1988

1 thru 6	@2.50

Black Mist Blood of Kali #1
© Caliber

BLACK MIST
Caliber Core, 1998

1 by James Pruett & Mike Perkins, Blood of Kali,pt.1	3.00
1a variant MV(c)	3.00
1b variant Jordan Raskin(c)	3.00
1c variant GyD(c)	3.00
1d premium edition, signed	10.00
2 thru 5 Blood of Kali,pt.2–pt.5	@3.00
Spec. Dawn of Armageddon, Blood of Kali,pt.6 & pt.7, 48-pg.	4.00

BLACK SCORPION
Special Studio, 1991

1 Knight of Justice	2.75
2 A Game for Old Men	2.75
3 Blackmailer's Auction	2.75

BLACKTHORNE 3 in 1
Blackthorne, 1987

1 & 2	@2.50

BLACK ZEPPELIN
Renegade, 1985

1 GD	3.00
2 thru 6 GD	@2.50

BLADE OF SHURIKEN
Eternity, 1987

1 thru 8	@2.50

BLAIR WITCH PROJECT
Oni Press, 1999

Spec. Movie adapt.	3.00

BLAIR WITCH CHRONICLES
Oni Press, 2000

1 (of 4) by Jen Van Meter & Guy Davis	3.00
2 thru 4	@3.00

BLIND FEAR
Eternity

1 thru 4	@2.50

BLONDE AVENGER
Blonde Avenger Comics, 1998

25 flip-book, Full Metal Corset	4.00
27 Full Metal Corset,pt.2	4.00
Spec. Short Blonde Girl with the Two Big Boobs	4.00

BLONDE AVENGER: DANGEROUS CONCLUSIONS
Brainstorm, 1997

1 V:Victor Von Fuchs	3.00
1a photo deluxe cover	4.00
2	3.00
2a photo deluxe cover	4.00

BLOOD & ROSES ADVENTURES
Knight Press, 1995

1 F:Time Agents	3.00
2 F:Time Agents	3.00
3 Search for Time Agents	3.00
4 Time Adventures	3.00

BLOOD 'N' GUTS
Aircel, 1990

1 thru 3	@2.50

BLOODBROTHERS
Eternity, 1988

1 thru 4	@2.50

BLOOD IS THE HARVEST
Eclipse, 1992

1 I:Nikita,Milo	4.50
2 V:M'Raud D:Nikita?	2.50
3 Milo captured	2.50
4 F:Nikita/Milo	2.50

BLOOD JUNKIES
Eternity, 1991

1 Vampires on Capitol Hill	2.50
2 final issue	2.50

BLOODLETTING
Fantaco

1 A Shilling for a Redcoat	3.00
2	3.00
3 Flee	3.00

4 thru 10 (of 11) by Chynna Clugston	@4.00

BLOOD OF DRACULA
Apple, 1987–90

1	3.00
2 thru 7	@3.00
8 thru 14	@3.00
15 with Record & Mask	4.00
16	5.00
17 thru 20	@4.50

BLOOD OF THE INNOCENT
Warp Graphics, 1986

1	3.00
2 thru 4	@3.00

BLOOD ORANGE
Fantagraphics Books, 2004

1	6.00
2 thru 4	@6.00

BLOODSHED
Damage, 1993

1 Little Brother	3.00
1a Commemorative issue	4.00
1b Encore edition, gold foil(c)	3.50
2 Little Brother	3.00
3 O:Bloodshed	3.00
3 `The Wastelands,' cont.	3.50
4 The City	3.50
5 the end is near.	3.50
6	3.50
7 Lies, concl.	3.50
`M'	3.50
`M' deluxe	5.00
Spec. Lunatics Fringe	3.50
Spec. Lies Epilogue, final issue	3.50
Spec. Chris Mass #1	3.50
Spec. Requiem	3.50

BLOODTHIRSTY PIRATE TALES
Black Swan Press, 1995

1	2.50
2	2.50
3	2.50
4 `Blockade of Charleston Harbor'.	2.50
5 `The Queen Anne's Revenge'	2.50
6 Blackhand's Party	2.50
7 Battle of Ocracoke Inlet	3.00
8 final issue	3.00

BLOODWING
Eternity, 1988

1	2.50
2 thru 5	@2.50

BLOODY SCHOOL
Curtis Comics, 2002
Vol. 1 Manga

1 by S.Yang & K. Yoo	3.00
2 thru 5	@3.00

BLUDGEON
Aardwolf, 1997

1 by JPi & David Chylsetk	3.00
2 `Alise in Wonderland'.	3.00
3 `Seeing Red'	3.00

BLUE BULLETEER
AC Comics, 1989

1	2.50

B & W PUB.

BLUE MONDAY: ABSOLUTE BEGINNERS
Oni Press, 2000
1 (of 4) 3.00
2 thru 4 . . . . @3.00
Spec. Nobody's Fool 3.00
Spec. Lovecats (2002) 3.00
Spec. Dead Man's Party (2002) 3.00

BLUE MONDAY: THE KIDS ARE ALRIGHT
Oni Press, 2000
1 by Chynna Clugston-Major 3.00
2 . . . . 3.00
3 concl. 3.00

BLUE MONDAY: PAINTED MOON
Oni Press, 2004
1 (of 4) 3.00
2 thru 4 . . . . @3.00

BOGIE MAN: CHINATOON
Atomeka
1 I:Francis Claine 3.00
2 F:Bogie Man 3.00
3 thru 4 F:Bogie Man 3.00

BOGIE MAN: MANHATTEN PROJECT
Apocalypse
1-shot D.Quale Assassination Plot . 4.00

BONAFIDE
Bonafide Productions
1 F:Doxie 'th Mutt 3.50
2 F:Doxie 'th Mutt 3.50
3 F:Doxie 'th Mutt 3.50

BONE
Cartoon Books, 1991
1 by Jeff Smith,I:Bone 95.00
1a 2nd printing 10.00
1b 3rd Printing 8.00
2 JSi,I:Thorn 40.00
2a 2nd printing 7.00
3 JSi 30.00
3a 2nd printing 5.00
4 JSi 18.00
5 JSi 15.00
6 JSi 15.00
7 JSi 12.00
8 JSi,The Great Cow Race,pt.1 . . . 9.00
9 JSi,The Great Cow Race,pt.2 . . . 8.00
1c thru 9a later printings . . . . @3.00
10 JSi,The Great Cow Race,pt.3 . . 8.00
11 JSi 4.00
12 JSi 4.00
13 JSi 8.00
14 thru 20 JSi, ... @4.00
21 thru 27, see Image
21 thru 27 reprints . . . . @3.00
28 JSi,'Rockjaw: Master of the
    Eastern Border' 3.00
29 JSi 3.00
30 JSi 3.00
31 JSi 3.00
32 JSi,Bartleby the Rat Creature Cub
    saga, concl. 3.00
33 JSi,Phoney's fate 3.00
34 JSi,Kingdok Slayer 3.00
35 JSi,Return of Gran'ma Ben. . . . 3.00
36 JSi,Return of Rockjaw 3.00
37 JSi,Extravaganza Issue 3.00
38 JSi,48-pg. 5.00
39 JSi,Ghost Circles 3.00

Bone #19
© Cartoon Books

40 JSi,wrap-around cover 3.00
41 JSi,Deep in enemy territory 3.00
42 JSi, ... 3.00
43 JSi,sacred wall 3.00
44 JSi,rooftop eatery 3.00
45 JSi,Inner Circle of Power 3.00
46 JSi,Rat Creature Army 3.00
47 JSi,Making money 3.00
48 JSi,Surrender or Die 3.00
49 JSi,The usurper Tarsil 3.00
50 JSi,War, Rat Creatures 3.00
51 JSi,Casualties 3.00
52 thru 53 . . . . @3.00
54 This Mortal Coil 3.00
55 Final issue 3.00
Spec.10th Anniv. Ed.with PVC fig. . 6.00

BONESHAKER
Caliber Press
1 Suicidal Wrestler 3.50

BONEYARD
NBM Books, 2001
1 by Richard Moore 3.00
2 thru 4 . . . . @3.00
5 thru 19 . . . . @3.00
20 thru 26 . . . . @3.00
Spec. Swimsuit Issue. 3.00

BOOK, THE
DreamSmith Studios, 1998
1 epic fantasy 72pg. 3.50
2 . . . . 3.50
3 thru 7 . . . . @4.00
Ashcan Preview, 24-pg. 5.00
Ashcan Preview, GP(c) 9.00
Handbook, 32-pg. 2.25

BOOK OF BALLADS AND SAGAS
Green Man Press, 1995
1 False Knight in the Road 3.00
2 thru 4 . . . . 3.00
5 . . . . 3.50

BOOK OF THE TAROT
Caliber Tome Press, 1998
1 History/Development o/t Tarot . . . 4.00
1a 64pg. 5.00
1b signed 5.00

BOOKS OF LORE
Peregrine
Spec.#1 fantasy anthology. 3.00
Spec.#2 . . . . 3.00
Spec.#3 . . . . 3.00
1-shot Shattered Lives 3.00

BOOKS OF LORE: THE KAYNIN GAMBIT
Peregrine, 1998
0 by Kevin Tucker
    & David Napoliello 3.00
1 (of 4) 3.00
1a Xavier (c) 3.00
2 thru 4 . . . . @3.00

BOOKS OF LORE: THE SHAPE OF EVIL
Peregrine Entertainment, 1999
1 (of 2) 3.00
2 . . . . 3.00

BOOKS OF LORE: THE STORYTELLER
Peregrine Entertainment, 2000
1 (of 3) by K.Tucker & P.Xavier . . . 3.00
2 & 3 . . . . @3.00

BOOKS WITH PICTURES
Very Dynamic Comics, 2007
1 . . . . 3.00
2 thru 6 . . . . @3.00

BOONDOGGLE
Knight Press, 1995
1 Waffle War 3.00
2 thru 3 Waffle War . . . . @3.00

BOONDOGGLE
Caliber Tapestry, 1997
Spec. 3.00
Spec., signed 3.00
1 thru 4 . . . . @3.00

BORDER WORLDS
Kitchen Sink, 1986
1 adult. 3.00
2 thru 7 . . . . @3.00
Spec.#1 Border Worlds: Marooned . 3.00

BORIS' ADVENTURE MAGAZINE
Nicotat, 1988
1 & 2 . . . . @2.50
3 thru 6 . . . . @3.00

BORIS THE BEAR
Nikotat, 1987
1–12: See Dark Horse section
13 thru 29. . . . . @2.50
30 thru 34 . . . . @2.50

BORN TO KILL
Aircel, 1991
1 thru 3 . . . . @2.50

BOSTON BOMBERS
Caliber
1 . . . . 2.25
2 . . . . 2.50
Spec.#1 . . . . 4.00
*Note: other issues are flip-books with:
Oz #17; The Searchers #5; Raven
Chronicles #12; & LegendLore #6*

B & W PUB.

BOUNTY
Caliber, 1991
1 'Bounty,''Navarro,'pt.1 . . . . 2.50
2 & 3'Bounty,''Navarro,'pt.2–pt3 @2.50

BOUNTY KILLER
Americanime Productions 2006
1 . . . . 3.50
1a variant (c) 3.50
2 . . . . 3.50
3 . . . . 4.00
1 Manga 4.00
2 thru 4 . . . . @4.00

BOX OFFICE POISON
Antarctic Press, 1996
1 by Alex Robinson. 8.00
2 . . . . 6.00
3 thru 5 . . . . @4.00
6 thru 10 . . . . @3.00
11 thru 21 . . . . @3.00
Big Super Spec.#1 . . . . 5.00

BRADLEYS, THE
Fantagraphics, 1999
1 (of 6) by Peter Bagge 3.00
2 thru 6 . . . . @3.00

BRAT PACK
King Hell Publications, 1990
1 . . . . 6.00
1a 2nd printing 3.00
2 thru 5 . . . . @4.00
Brat Pack Collection 13.00

BRATPACK/MAXIMORTAL
King Hell, 1996
Super Spec.#1 RV 3.00
Super Spec.#2 RV 3.00

BREAKFAST
AFTER NOON
Oni Press, 2000
1 (of 6) by Andi Watson 3.00
2 thru 6 . . . . @3.00

BREAKNECK BLVD.
Slave Labor Graphics, 1995–96
1 thru 3 Jhonen Vasques art. . . . @3.00
4 by Timothy Markin 3.00
5 & 6 . . . . @3.00

BRENDA STARR,
ACE REPORTER
ACG Comics, 1998
1 by Dale Messick, Charlton rep. . . 3.00
2 . . . . 3.00
Spec.#1 Pin-ups,rep. from 40s
  and 50s (1998) 3.00

BRIAN PULIDO'S GYPSY
Avatar Press, 2004
Preview 2.00
Preview variant (c)s 3.00
Preview Starlight (c) 6.00
Preview Holy Grail (c) 6.00
1 . . . . 3.50
1a variant (c)s . . . . @3.50
1b premium (c) 10.00
1c defensive (c) 6.00

BRIAN PULIDO'S
KILLER GNOMES
Avatar Press, 2004
1 . . . . 3.50

1a wraparound (c). 3.50

BRIAN PULIDO'S
LADY DEATH:
ABANDON ALL HOPE
Avatar Press, 2004
1/2 Spec. 16-page 3.00
1/2 Spec. variant (c)s 3.00
1/2 Spec. Premium (c). 9.00
1/2 Spec. Vengeance edition 6.00
1/2 Spec. Empress (c) 6.00
1 (of 4) 4.00
2 . . . . 4.00
3 . . . . 4.00
4 . . . . 4.00
1a thru 4a variant (c). . . . . @4.00
1b thru 4b premium (c) . . . . @10.00

BRIAN PULIDO'S
LADY DEATH:
DEAD RISING
Avatar Press, 2004
Spec. 16-page 2.50
Spec.A Medieval (c). 6.00
Spec.B Classic (c) 6.00
Spec C Leather (c) 25.00
Spec. D Sketch (c) 30.00
Spec. prism (c). 13.00

BRIAN PULIDO'S
UNHOLY
Avatar Press, 2004
Preview 2.00
Preview variant (c)s 3.00
1 (of 3) 3.50
2 . . . . 3.50
3 . . . . 3.50
1a thru 3a variant (c). . . . . @3.50
1b thru 3b wraparound (c). . . . . . @3.50
1c thru 3c premium (c) . . . . @10.00
Preview Rock & Roll (c). 6.00

BRIAN PULIDO'S
WAR ANGEL
Avatar Press, 2005
1 . . . . 3.50
1a variant (c)s 3.50
1b premium (c) 9.00
1c Fiery Reaper edition 6.00
1d Hells Belle (c) 6.00
2 . . . . 3.50
2a variant (c)s . . . . @3.50
2b premium (c) 9.00
3 . . . . 3.50
3a variant (c)s . . . . @3.50
3b premium (c) 9.00

BRIAN PULIDO'S
WAR ANGEL:
BOOK OF DEATH
Avatar Press, 2004
Spec. 2.50
Spec. variant(c)s . . . . @3.00
Spec. Attitude ed. 6.00
Spec. Feral (c) 6.00
Spec. Bad Omen (c) 6.00
1 . . . . 3.50
2 thru 3 . . . . @3.50
1a thru 3a variant (c)s . . . . @3.50
1b thru 3b premium (c) . . . . @9.00

BRILLIANT BOY
Circus Comics, 1997
1 . . . . 3.00
2 Drake,pt.1 (of 5). 3.00

3 Drake,pt.2 . . . . 2.50
4 Drake,pt.3 . . . . 2.50
5 Drake,pt.4 . . . . 2.50
6 Drake,pt.5 . . . . 2.50
7 & 8 The Great Thunder,pt.1–2. @2.50

BRODIE'S LAW
Studio G, 2004
1 (of 6) 3.00
2 thru 6 . . . . @3.00

BROID
Eternity, 1990
1 thru 4 . . . . @2.25

BROKEN HALO: IS
THERE NOTHING SACRED
Broken Halos Comics, 1998
1 by Donald J. Vigil & Tim Vigil. . . 3.00
2 . . . . 3.00
3 . . . . 3.00
Ashcan, limited ed. 16-pg. 7.00

BROKEN HEROES
Sirius, 1998
1 by Fillback Bros. 2.50
2 The Neon Graveyard 2.50
3 Rocket Man 2.50
4 thru 12 final issue. . . . . @2.50

BRONX
Eternity, 1991
1 A.Saichann Short Stories. 2.50
2 & 3 . . . . @2.50
Aircel
Reprint 3.00

BROTHER MAN
New City Comics
1 . . . . 5.00
1a 2.25
2 thru 7 . . . . @2.25

BRUCE JONES':
OUTER EDGE
Innovation, 1993
1 All reprints 2.50

Bruce Jones': Outer Edge #1
© *Innovation*

BRUCE JONES':
RAZOR'S EDGE
Innovation, 1993
1 All reprints	2.50
2 D:Grimm, Gritty	2.50

BRU-HED
Schism Comics, 1994
1 Blockhead	3.00
1a 2nd printing	2.75
2 Blockhead	3.00
Vol. 1 Bru-Hed's Bunnies, Baddies & Buddies (1998)	2.50
Vol. 1 Bru-Hed's Guide to Gettin' Girls Now	2.50
Vol. 2 Bru-Hed's Guide	2.50

BRUTAL PLANET
Neko Press, 2002
1 by Matt Kimball & Dark One	3.00
2	3.00
1a mini-print edition	5.00
3	3.00
4	3.00

BUBBA THE REDNECK
WEREWOLF
Brass Ball Comics 2003
1	3.00
2 thru 3	@3.00
4 thru 7	@3.00

BUCE-N-GAR
RAK, 1996
1	2.25
2	2.25
3	2.25

BUCKAROO BANZAI
Moonstone Books, 2005
Preview	1.00
1 Return of the Screw	3.50
1a variant (c)	3.50
1b Special edition (c)	4.50
2 thru 3	@3.50
2a thru 3a variant (c)s	@3.50
2b Dorman Special Ed (c)	4.50
3b Nestler Special Ed (c)	4.50

BUCK GODOT:
ZAP GUN FOR HIRE
Palliard Press, 1993
1 I:Buck Godot	3.00
2 thru 6	@3.00

Studio Foglio, 1997
7 by Phil Foglio & Barb Kaalberg	3.00
8 finale	3.50

BUFFALO WINGS
Antarctic Press, 1993
1	2.50
2	2.50

BUG
Planet X Productions, 1997
1	2.25
2	2.25

B.U.G.G.S
Acetylene Comics, 2001
1	2.50
1a variant San Diego Con (c)	3.00
2 thru 5	@2.50
3a variant (c)	2.50

Buck Godot, Zap Gun For Hire #5
© Palliard Press

BUGTOWN
Aeon, 2004
1 (of 6) MHo	3.00
2 thru 6	@3.00

BULLET CROW
Eclipse, 1987
1 & 2 Fowl of Fortune	@2.50

BULWARK
Millennium, 1995
1 I:Bulwark	3.00
2 O:Bulwark	3.00

BUREAU OF MANA
INVESTIGATION
Radio Comix, 2002
1 by C.Hanson & E.Garcia	3.00
2 thru 5	@3.00

BURGLAR BILL
Dancing Elephant Press, 2003
1 (of 6) by Paul Grist	3.00
2 thru 5	@3.00

BURNING BLUE, THE
Crusade Entertainment, 2001
1 BTi	3.00
1a computer gen (c)	3.00

BUSHIDO
Eternity, 1988
1 thru 6	@2.50

BUSHIDO
Americanime Productions 2006
1 Manga	3.50
2 thru 3	@4.00

BUZZ
Kitchen Sink
1 Mark Landman (c) (1990)	3.00
2 Mark Landman (c)	3.00
3 Mark Landman (c) (1991)	3.00

BUZZARD
Cat Head Comics, 1990–95
1 thru 9	@3.00
10 thru 20	@3.50

BUZZBOY
Sky Dog Press, 1998
1 (of 4) by John Gallagher & Tim Ogline	3.00
2 by John Gallagher & Steve Hauk	3.00
3	3.00
4 conclusion	3.00

CABLE TV
Parody Press
1 Cable Satire	2.50

CADILLACS
AND DINOSAURS
Kitchen Sink, 1992
3-D comic	4.00

CALIBER CORE
Caliber, 1998
0 48pg	3.00
1 Gestalt cover	3.00
1a Rain People cover	3.00
1b Spiral cover	3.00
2 F:Al-Haquat	3.00

CALIBER DOUBLE
FEATURE
Caliber, 2000
1 48-pg	4.00
2	4.00
3	4.00

CALIBER FOCUS
Caliber, 2000
1 48-pg	4.00
2 thru 4	@4.00

CALIBER PRESENTS
Caliber, 1989
1 TV,I:Crow	70.00
2 Deadworld	10.00
3 Realm	4.00
4 Baker Street	4.00
5 TV,Heart of Darkness, Fugitive	3.50
6 TV,Heart of Darkness, Fugitive	3.50
7 TV,Heart of Darkness, Dragonfeast	3.50
8 TV,Cuda,Fugitive	3.50
9 Baker Street,Sting Inc.	3.50
10 Fugitive, The Edge	3.50
11 Ashes,Random Thoughts	3.50
12 Fugitive,Random Thoughts	3.50
13 Random Thoughts,Synergist	3.50
14 Random Thoughts,Fugitive	3.50
15 Fringe, F:The Crow	4.00
16 Fugitive, The Verdict	3.50
17 Deadworld, The Verdict	3.50
18 Orlak,The Verdict	3.50
19 Taken Under,Go-Man	3.50
20 The Verdict,Go-Man	3.50
21 The Verdict,Go-Man	3.50
22 The Verdict,Go-Man	3.50
23 Go-Man,Heat Seeker	3.50
24 Heat Seeker,MacktheKnife	3.50
Christmas Spec. A:Crow,Deadworld Realm,Baker Street	10.00
Summer Spec. inc. the Silencers, Swords of Shar-Pei (preludes)	4.00
1-Shot	3.00
1-shot Hybrid	3.00

CALIBER SPOTLIGHT
Caliber, 1995
1 F:Kabuki,Oz	3.00

CALIBRATIONS
Caliber, 1996
1 WEI,MCy,`Atmospherics,'pt.1 . . . 3.00
2 WEI,MCy,`Atmospherics,'pt.2 . . . 3.00
3 WEI,MCy,`Atmospherics,'pt.3 . . . 3.00
4 WEI,MCy,`Atmospherics,'pt.4 . . . 3.00
5 WEI,MCy,`Atmospherics,' concl. . 3.00

CALIFORNIA GIRLS
Eclipse, 1987
1 . . . . 2.50
2 thru 8 . . . . @2.50

CALIGARI 2050
Monster
1 Gothic Horror 2.25
2 &3 Gothic Horror . . . . @2.25

CALL ME PRINCESS
CPM Manga, 1999
1 by Tomoko Taniguchi 3.00
1a variant cover 3.00
2 thru 6 . . . . @3.00

CAMELOT ETERNAL
Caliber, 1990
1 . . . . 3.00
2 . . . . 2.50
3 . . . . 2.50
4 Launcelot & Guinevere 2.50
5 Mordred Escapes. 2.50
6 MorganLeFay returns from dead. 2.50
7 Revenge of Morgan 2.50
8 Launcelot flees Camelot 2.50

CANDYAPPLEBLACK
Good Intentions Paving, 2004
1 . . . . 3.50
2 thru 7 . . . . @3.50

CANTON KID
Millennium, 1997
1 . . . . 2.50
Blam Comics, 2005
1 (of 4) 3.50
2 thru 4 . . . . @3.50

CAPTAIN CANUCK
REBORN
Semple Comics, 1993–96
0 thru 3 by Richard Comely . . . . @2.50

CAPT. CONFEDERACY
Steel Dragon, 1985–88
1 adult. 6.00
2 . . . . 2.50
3 . . . . 2.50
4 . . . . 2.50
4a 2.50
5 thru 12 . . . . @2.50

CAPT. ELECTRON
Brick Computers Inc., 1986
1 . . . . 2.50
2 . . . . 2.50

CAPTAIN HARLOCK
Eternity, 1989
1 BDn. 3.00
1a 2nd printing 2.50
2 thru 3 . . . . @2.50
4 thru 13 . . . . @2.25
Christmas special. 2.50
Spec.#1 The Machine People 2.50

Captain Confederacy #3
© *Steel Dragon*

CAPTAIN HARLOCK DEATHSHADOW RISING
Eternity, 1991
1 . . . . 2.75
2 . . . . 2.50
3 . . . . 2.25
4 Harlock/Nevich Truce. 2.25
5 Reunited with Arcadia Crew 2.25
6 . . . . 3.00

CAPTAIN HARLOCK: FALL OF THE EMPIRE
Eternity, 1992
1 . . . . 2.50
2 thru 4 . . . . @2.50

[ADVENTURES OF] CAPTAIN JACK
Fantagraphics, 1986
1 . . . . 4.00
2 & 3 . . . . @2.50
4 thru 12 . . . . @2.50

CAPTAIN KOALA
Koala Comics, 1997
1 . . . . 3.00
2 thru 7 . . . . @2.50

CAPTAIN STERNN: RUNNING OUT OF TIME
Kitchen Sink, 1993
1 BWr(c) (1993) 6.00
2 BWr(c) 6.00
3 BWr(c) (1994) 6.00
4 BWr(c) 6.00

CAPTAIN THUNDER AND BLUE BOLT
Hero Graphics, 1987
1 New stories 3.50
2 Hard Targets 3.50

CARDCAPTOR SAKURA
Mixx Entertainment, 1999
1 . . . . 3.00
2 thru 6 by Clamp . . . . @3.00
Tokyopop.Com, 2000
7 thru 25 . . . . @3.00
26 thru 34 . . . . @3.00

CARTOON HISTORY OF THE UNIVERSE
Rip Off Press, 1987
1 Gonick art 2.50
2 Sticks & Stones 2.50
3 River Realms. 2.50
4 Old Testament 2.50
5 Brains & Bronze. 2.50
6 These Athenians 2.50
7 All about Athens. 2.50
8 and 9 . . . . @2.50

CASES OF SHERLOCK HOLMES
Renegade, 1986
1 . . . . 2.50
2 thru 19 . . . . @2.50

CASTLE WAITING
Olio, 1997
1 by Linda Medley 10.00
1a 2nd printing 3.00
2 . . . . 5.00
2a 2nd printing 3.00
3 Labors of Love 3.00
4 birth of Lady Jain's baby 3.00
5 . . . . 3.00
6 City Mouse, Country Mouse,pt.1 . 3.00
7 City Mouse, Country Mouse,pt.2 . 3.00
Spec. The Curse of Brambly
Hedge (1996) 3.00
Spec. Curse of Brambly Hedge,
revised 1998, 96-pg. 9.00
VOL. 2, 2000
1 by Linda Medley 3.00
2 Solicitine,pt.1 . . . . 3.00
3 thru 7 . . . . @3.00
#13 (Vol. 2, #6) 3.00
#14 (Vol. 2, #7) 3.00
#15 thru #16 . . . . @3.00
Fantagraphics Books, 2006
Vol. 2
1 64-pg.. . . . . 6.00
2 . . . . 5.00
3 thru 9 . . . . @4.00

CAT & MOUSE
Aircel, 1989–92
1 . . . . 4.00
2 . . . . 3.00
3 thru 8 . . . . @2.50
9 Cat Reveals Identity 2.50
10 Tooth & Nail 2.50
11 Tooth & Nail. 2.50
12 Tooth & Nail, Demon. 2.50
13 `Good Times, Bad Times' 2.50
14 Mouse Alone 2.50
15 Champion ID revealed 2.50
16 Jerry Critically Ill 2.50
17 Kunoichi vs. Tooth. 2.50
18 Search for Organ Donor 2.50
Graphic Novel 10.00

CAT CLAW
Eternity, 1990
1 O:Cat Claw 2.75
1a 2nd printing 2.50
2 thru 9 . . . . @2.50

CATFIGHT
Lightning Comics, 1996
1 V:Prince Nightmare 4.00
1a Gold Edition 6.00
Spec.#1 Dream Warrior,
V:The Slasher 2.75
Spec.#1 Dream intoAction,A:Creed . 3.00
Spec.#1a signed and numbered . . . 8.00

Catfight, Escape From Limbo #1
© Lightning Comics

Spec.#1 Escape From Limbo 2.75
Spec.#1a variant cover (1996). 2.75
Spec.#1b platinum cover 6.00
Spec.#1d variant nude cover 8.00
Spec.#1 Sweet Revenge (1997) . . . 3.00
Spec.#1a variant cover 3.00

CAT-MAN RETRO COMIC
AC Comics, 1997
0 by Bill Black & Mark Heike 6.00
1 thru 3 . . . . @6.00
Ashcan #1 I:Catman & Kitten 6.00

CAVEWOMAN
Basement/Caliber, 1994–95
1 . . . . 70.00
1a by Budd Root 2nd printing 4.00
1b 3rd printing, new cover 3.00
2 . . . . 40.00
2a 2nd printing 3.00
2 3rd printing, new cover 3.00
3 and 4 . . . . @35.00
5 Cavewoman vs. Klyde,
   Round Two 25.00
6 . . . . 25.00

CAVEWOMAN
Basement Comics 2002
1-shot Movie special edition 9.00
1-shot movie oscar-gold edition. . . 10.00
1-shot Summer Spec. My Kylde
   has Fleas (2004) 3.50
1-shot Prehistoric Pin-ups #4. . . . . 3.50
Spec. Meriem's Gallery #4. . . . . . . 3.25
Spec. Meriem's Gallery #4 spec.ed. 9.00
1-shot flip book Cavewoman Jungle
   Tales #3/ Blonde Medusa #1 . . 3.75
1-shot Jungle Jam 3.50
1-shot Jungle Jam special ed. 7.00

CAVEWOMAN
INTERVENTION
Basement Comics, 2000
1 by Devon Massey 3.00
1a variant Budd Root (c). 8.00
1b gold foil alternate (c) 9.00
2 . . . . 3.00
2a variant (c). 8.00
2b Purple foil (c) 9.00
Spec. Klyde & Meriem 1-shot 9.00
Spec. Klyde & Meriem, KDM(c). . . 9.00
Spec. Klyde & Meriem green foil . . 9.00

Spec. Klyde & Meriem, Beauty,
   Blizzard & the Beast 8.00
Spec. Beauty, Blizzard, gold foil . . . 9.00
Spec. Prehistoric Pin-ups 4.50
Spec. Prehistoric Pin-ups gold foil . . 9.00
Spec. Prehistoric Pin-ups, Book 2 . . 4.50
Spec. Prehistoric Pin-ups 2,lim. . . . 8.00
Spec. Prehistoric Pin-ups 2,
   gold foil 9.00
Spec. Prehistoric Pin-ups 3 . . . . . 4.50
Spec. Prehistoric Pin-Ups 3 Spec. . 9.00
Cavewoman Cover Gallery, 48-pg. . 4.50
Cavewoman Cover Gallery spec. . . 9.00
1-shot He Said, She Said 3.50
1-shot He Said, She Said special . . 9.00
1-shot Cavewoman The Movie 3.25

CAVEWOMAN:
JUNGLE TALES
Basement Comics, 2000
1 by Budd Root 3.00
1a Frank Cho (c). 9.00
2 . . . . 3.00
2a spec. edition 8.00

CAVEWOMAN:
MERIEM'S GALLERY
Basement Comics, 2001
1 . . . . 3.50
1a Spec. lim. ed. 8.00
1b Gold foil edition 9.00
2 pin-up book 3.50
2a Special edition 8.00
2b gold special edition 9.00
3 . . . . 3.00
3a 9.00
4 . . . . 3.25
4a special ed. 9.00

CAVEWOMAN:
MISSING LINK
Basement Comics, 1997
1 (of 4) 3.00
2 thru 4 . . . . @3.00

CAVEWOMAN: ODYSSEY
Caliber, 1999
1 (of 5) 3.00
2 thru 4 . . . . @3.00
Basement Comics, 2000
1a front row seat (c) by Budd Root 8.00
1b foil (c). 9.00
2a variant (c). 6.00
2b jungle green foil (c) 9.00
1-shot spec. 3.00
1-shot spec. variant (c) 8.00
1-shot spec. foil (c) 9.00

CAVEWOMAN:
PANGAEAN SEA
Basement Comics, 1999
0 Origin issue 3.00
0 variant AAd (c). 8.00
0 special Root (c) 9.00
0 green foil (c). 9.00
0 alternate gold foil (c) 9.00
1 by Bud Root. 5.00
1a variant Massey (c). 8.00
1b Root Sea Blue foil (c) 9.00
1c Cho Sea Blue Foil (c) 9.00
2 . . . . 3.00
2 Blue Foil (c) 9.00
3 . . . . 3.25
3 silver foil (c) 9.00
4 . . . . 3.25
4b red foil edition 9.00
5 . . . . 3.25

5 red foil edition 9.00
6 . . . . 3.25
6b red foil (c). 8.00
7 . . . . 3.25
7a gold foil (c). 8.00
8 . . . . 3.25
9 . . . . 3.50
10 . . . . 3.25
2a thru 9a special edition (c). . . . @8.00
Spec. #1 Prehistoric Pin-ups 4.50
Prologue. 3.00

CAVEWOMAN: RAIN
Caliber, 1996
1 by Budd Root. 7.00
1a 2nd printing 3.00
2 . . . . 5.00
2a 2nd printing 3.00
3 . . . . 4.00
4 . . . . 4.00
5 . . . . 3.50
3a thru 5a 2nd editions, new (c)s @3.00
6 thru 8 . . . . @3.00

CAVEWOMEN: RAPTOR
Basement Comics, 2002
1 (of 2) 3.25
1a special edition 8.00
1b red foil edition 9.00
2 . . . . 3.25
2a special edition 8.00
2b Purple foil (c) 9.00

CAVEWOMAN: RELOADED
Basement Comics, 2005
1 thru 5 . . . . @4.00
2a thru 3a special edition . . . . . @7.00

CECIL KUNKLE
Darkline Comics, 1987
1 . . . . 2.50

CELESTIAL MECHANICS
Innovation, 1990
1 thru 3 . . . . @2.25

CELESTIAL ZONE
Asiapac Books, 2000
1 by Wee Tian Beng 9.00
2 thru 8 . . . . @9.00
9 152-pg. 9.00
11 Fantasy on Moonlit Lotus 9.00
12 THe Battle of Maling 9.00
13 Assault on Mt. Dream-Cloud. . . 10.00
14 An Onerous Battle. 10.00
15 Capturing Mt. Dream-Cloud . . . 10.00
16 Chi Xue & Xuan Hua injured . . 10.00
TCZ Studio, 2002
17 thru 25 152-pg. . . . . @10.00
Vol. 2
1 . . . . 10.00
2 thru 16 . . . . @9.50

CEMENT SHOOZ
Horse Feathers, 1991
1 with color pin-up 2.50

CEMETARIANS, THE
Amaze Ink/SLG, 2006
1 . . . . 3.00
2 thru 6 . . . . @3.00

CEREBUS
Aardvark–Vanaheim, 1977
0 . . . . 3.00
0a Gold Ed. 10.00

Cerebus #17
© Aardvark-Vanaheim

1 B:DS(s&a),I:Cerebus	500.00
1a Counterfeit	10.00
2 DS,V:Succubus	110.00
3 DS,I:Red Sophia	125.00
4 DS,I:Elrod	75.00
5 DS,A:The Pigts	60.00
6 DS,I:Jaka	60.00
7 DS,R:Elrod	45.00
8 DS,A:Conniptins	45.00
9 DS,I&V:K'cor	45.00
10 DS,R:Red Sophia	45.00
11 DS,I:The Cockroach	30.00
12 DS,R:Elrod	30.00
13 DS,I:Necross	25.00
14 DS,V:Shadow Crawler	25.00
15 DS,V: Shadow Crawler	25.00
16 DS, at the Masque	20.00
17 DS,'Champion'	20.00
18 DS,Fluroc	20.00
19 DS,I:Perce & Greet-a	20.00
20 DS,Mind Game	20.00
21 DS,A:CaptCockroach,rare	40.00
22 DS,D:Elrod	20.00
23 thru 29 DS	@10.00
30 DS,Debts	15.00
31 DS,Chasing Cootie	15.00
32 DS	8.00
33 DS,Friction	5.00
34 thru 50 DS	@6.00
51 DS,(scarce)	12.00
52 DS	5.00
53 DS,C:Wolveroach	7.00
54 DS,I:Wolveroach	9.00
55 DS,A:Wolveroach	8.00
56 DS,A:Wolveroach	8.00
57 DS	5.00
58 DS	5.00
59 DS,Memories,pt.V	5.00
60 DS,more vignettes	5.00
61 DS,A:Flaming Carrot	6.00
62 DS,A:Flaming Carrot	6.00
63 thru 66 DS	@5.00
67 thru 70 DS	@5.00
71 thru 81 DS	@4.00
82 thru 100 DS	@3.50
101 thru 125 DS	@3.00
126 thru 130 DS	@2.50
131 thru 146 DS	@4.00
147 Neil Gaiman, DS	6.00
148 thru 150 DS	@3.00
151 DS,B:Mothers & Daughters, Book 1: Flight,pt.1	4.00
152 thru 155 DS,Flight,pt.2–pt.5	@4.00
151a thru 53a 2nd printings	@2.50
156 thru 160 DS,Flight,pt.6–pt.10	@3.00
161 DS,Flight,pt.11, Bone story	15.00

162 DS,E:M&D,Bk.1:Flight pt.12	3.00
163 DS, Book 2: Women,pt.1	2.75
164 thru 174 Women,pt.2–12	@3.00
175 thru 186 Reads,pt.1–12	@3.00
187 DS, Book 4:Minds,pt.1	3.00
188 thru 199 Minds,pt.2–13	@3.00
200	3.50
201 thru 219 Guys,pt.1 to pt.19	@3.00
220 thru 231 Rick'sStory,pt.1–12	@3.00
232 thru 265 GoingHome,pt.1–34	@2.50
266 thru 296 LatterDays,pt.1– pt.31	@2.50
297 Latter Days, pt.32	2.50
298 Latter Days, pt.33	2.50
299 Latter Days, pt.34	2.50
300 Latter Days, pt.35, finale	2.50
Spec.#1 Cerebus Companion	3.50
Spec. Following Cerebus #1	4.00
Spec. Following Cerebus #2	4.00
Spec. Following Cerebus #3	4.00
Spec. Following Cerebus #4	4.00
Spec. Following Cerebus #5	4.00
Spec. Following Cerebus #6 thru #10	@4.00

CEREBUS CHURCH & STATE
Aardvark–Vanaheim, 1991

1 DS rep #51	2.50
2 thru 30 DS rep #52-#80	@2.50

CEREBUS HIGH SOCIETY
Aardvark–Vanaheim, 1990

1 thru 14 DS (biweekly)	@2.50
15 thru 24 DS rep	@2.50
25 DS rep. #50, final	2.50

CEREBUS JAM
Aardvark–Vanaheim, 1985

1 MA,BHa,TA,WE,A:Spirit	9.00

CEREBUS REPRINTS
Aardvark–Vanaheim

1A thru 28A DS rep	@2.50

See also: Church & State
See also: Swords of Cerebus

CHAINSAW VIGILANTE
New England Press

1 Tick Spinoff	3.25
2 & 3	@2.75

CHAMPION OF KITARA:
DUM DUM & DRAGONS
MU Press, 1992

1 Dragons Secret	3.00
2 Dragons Secret	3.00
3 Dragons Secret	3.00

CHANGE COMMANDER
GOKU II
Antarctic Press, 1996

1 (of 4) by Ippongi Bang	3.00
2 thru 3	@3.00

CHARLIE CHAN
Eternity, 1989

1 thru 6	@2.50

CHARM SCHOOL
Amaze Ink/SLG, 2000

1 by Elizabeth Watasin	3.00
2	3.00
4 Vampire Dragster Dean	3.00
5 Vampire Dragster Dean	3.00
6 fight to the death	3.00

7 thru 9	3.00
10	10.00

CHASER PLATOON
Aircel, 1990–91

1 Interstellar War	2.25
2 Ambush	2.25
3 New Weapon	2.25
4 Saringer Battle Robot	2.25
5 Behind Enemy Lines	2.25
6 Operation Youthtest	2.25

CHERUBS:
PARADISE LOST
Desperado Publishing, 2007

1 (of 4)	4.00
2 thru 4	@4.00

CHESTY SANCHEZ
Antarctic Press, 1995

1 & 2	@3.00
Giant Size Spec. #1 (1999)	6.00

CHIBI-POP MANGA
Chibi-Pop (1998)

2 thru 6 64-pg	@4.00

VOL 2

1 72-pg	4.00
2 thru 6	@4.00

CHICANOS
IDW Publishing, 2005

1	4.00
2 thru 9	@4.00

CHILDREN OF THE GRAVE
Shooting Star Comics, 2005

1 (of 4)	3.00
2 thru 4	@3.00

CHINA & JAZZ
ABC Comics, 1999

1 RCl	3.00

VOL. 2

1 (of 3) RCl	3.00
2 RCl	3.00
Spec. Raising Hell	5.00

CHINA & JAZZ
CODE NAME
DOUBLE IMPACT
High Impact, 1996

1 and 2	@3.00

CHINA & JAZZ:
TRIGGER HAPPY
ABC Comics, 1998

1 (of 4) by Clayton Henry	3.00
1a Jazz Bikini cover	4.00
1b China Bikini cover	6.00
1c gold variant cover	6.00
2	3.00
2a Playtoy edition	6.00
2b Mercenary edition	6.00
2c Gold edition	6.00
Spec. Trigger Happy Special	3.00
Spec.A manga cover	8.00
Spec. China & Jazz	3.00

CHINA & JAZZ:
SUPERSTARS
ABC Studios, 1999

1 (of 3)	3.00
Spec. China Platinum	3.00

CHIRALITY
CPM Manga Comics, 1997
6 by Satoshi Urushihara, SS(c) . . . 3.00
7 final battle for Shiori's life 3.00
8 thru 18 . . . . @3.00
Spec. Gallery, pin-up book. 4.00

CHIRALITY:
TO THE PROMISED LAND
CPM Comics, 1997
1 by Satoshi Urushihara 3.00
2 thru 4 . . . . @3.00

CHIRON
Annurel Studio Graphics
1 . . . . 2.50
1a 2nd printing 2.50
2 Transported to Doran. 2.50
3 Transported to Doran. 2.50
3a Gold Edition 4.00

CHISUJI
Antarctic Press, 2005
1 (of 6) 3.00
2 thru 3 . . . . @3.00

CIRCLE WEAVE, THE
Indigo Bean Productions, 1995
1 Apprentice to a God. 2.25
2 Apprentice to a God,pt.2 . . . . . . 2.25
3 Apprentice to a God,pt.3 . . . . . . 2.25
4 Apprentice to a God,pt.4 . . . . . . 2.25
5 Apprentice to a God,pt.5 . . . . . . 2.50

CLAN APIS
Active Synapse, 1998
1 (of 5) by Jay Hosler, F:Bees 3.00
2 F:Nyuki, Zambur 3.00
3 . . . . 3.00
4 . . . . 3.00
5 conclusion 3.00

CLANDE, INC.
Domain Publishing
1 I:Sam Davidson, Jeremy Clande. 3.00
2 V:Dias 3.00

CLERKS:
THE COMIC BOOK
Oni Press, 1998
1 KSm & Jim Mahfood 12.00
1a 2nd printing 4.00
Spec. The Lost Scene 5.00
Holiday Special 5.00

CLIFFHANGER COMICS
AC Comics, 1990
1 Masked Marvel, rep. 2.50
2 Don Winslow, rep. 2.50
1A & 2A . . . . @3.00

CLINT THE HAMSTER
Eclipse
1 . . . . 2.50
2 . . . . 2.50

COBB: OFF THE LEASH
IDW Publishing, 2006
1 . . . . 4.00
2 thru 3 . . . . @4.00

COBRA
Viz, 1990–91
1 thru 6 . . . . @3.00

Cliffhanger Comics 2A
© AC Comics

7 . . . . 3.25
8 V:SnowHawks 3.25
9 Zados. 3.25
10 thru 12 . . . . @3.25

COCOPIAZO
Amaze Ink/SLG, 2004
1 . . . . 3.00
2 thru 6 . . . . @3.00

COFFIN
Oni Press, 2000
1 . . . . 3.00
2 thru 4 . . . . @3.00

COLD BLOODED
CHAMELEON
COMMANDOS
Blackthorne, 1986
1 thru 7 . . . . @2.50

COLD EDEN
Legacy, 1995
1 Last City on Earth 2.35
2 V:Mutant Hunting Pack 2.35
3 D6 Tower 2.35

COLE BLACK
Rocky Hartberg, 1980
1 Newspaper strip format 15.00
2 . . . . 10.00
3 . . . . 10.00
4 . . . . 10.00
5 . . . . 12.00

Vol. 2, 1985
1 . . . . 3.50
2 & 3 . . . . @2.25

COLONEL KILGORE
Special Studios
1 WWII stories 2.50
2 Command Performance. 2.50

COLT
K-Z Comics
1 . . . . 4.00
2 pin-up by Laird. 6.00
2 pin-up by Henbeck. 2.25
3 thru 5 . . . . @2.25

COMIC BOOK HEAVEN
Amaze Ink/SLG, 2001
Vol. 2
1 . . . . 2.25
2 thru 5 . . . . @2.25
6 thru 9 . . . . @2.25
10 48-pg. 3.50

COMICS EXPRESS
Eclipse, 1989
1 thru 4 . . . . @3.00
5 thru 11 . . . . @4.00

COMING OF APHRODITE
Hero Graphics
1 Aphrodite/modern day 4.00

COMMAND REVIEW
Thoughts & Images, 1986
1 rep. Albedo #1-4 . . . . 6.00
2 rep. Albedo #5-8 . . . . 4.00
3 rep. Albedo #9-13 . . . . 4.00

CONDOM-MAN
Aaaahh!! Comics
1 I:Condom Man. 3.50
2 F:Condom Man 3.50
3 V:Alien Army 3.50
4 Brother bought back to life 3.50
5 O:Condom-Man (Chris Swafford) 3.50

CONQUEROR
Harrier, 1984–86
1 . . . . 3.50
2 thru 4 . . . . @2.50
5 thru 9 . . . . @2.50

CONSPIRACY COMICS
Revolutionary, 1991
1 Marilyn Monroe. 2.50
2 Who Killed JFK 2.50
3 Who Killed RFK 2.50

CONSTELLATION
GRAPHICS
Stages Comics 1986
1 thru 2 . . . . @2.25

CONSTRUCT
Caliber New Worlds, 1996
1 (of 6) PJe,LDu, sci-fi,48pg 4.00
2 PJe,LDu 3.00
3 PJe,LDu 3.00
4 PJe,LDu 3.00
5 PJe,LDu 3.00
6 PJe,LDu, conclusion 3.00

CORPORATE NINJA
Amaze Ink/SLG, 2005
1 . . . . 3.00
2 thru 3 . . . . @3.00

CORRECTOR YUI
Tokyopop Press, 2001
1 48-pg. 3.00
2 . . . . 3.00
3 . . . . 3.00
4 . . . . 3.00

CORTO MALTESE:
BALLAD OF
THE SALT SEA
NBM, 1997
1 by Hugo Pratt. 3.00

1 a 2nd printing 3.00
2 by Hugo Pratt. 3.00
3 Escondida 3.00
4 . . . . 3.00
5 . . . . 3.00
6 . . . . 3.00
7 final issue 3.00

COSMIC HEROES
Eternity, 1988
1 Buck Rogers rep. 2.50
2 thru 6 Buck Rogers rep. . . . . . @2.50
7 thru 9 Buck Rogers rep. . . . . . @2.50
10 . . . . 3.50
11 . . . . 4.00

Counter Parts #2
© Tundra

COUNTER PARTS
Tundra, 1993
1 thru 3 . . . . @3.00

COURTNEY CRUMRIN & THE COVEN OF MYSTICS
Oni Press, 2003
1 (of 4) by Ted Naifeh 3.00
2 thru 4 . . . . @3.00

COURTNEY CRUMRIN & THE NIGHT THINGS
Oni Press, 2002
1 (of 4) by Ted Naifeh 3.00
2 thru 4 . . . . @3.00

COURTNEY CRUMRIN AND THE PRINCE OF NOWHERE
Oni Press, 2007
1-shot. 6.00

COURTNEY CRUMRIN IN THE TWILIGHT KINGDOM
Oni Press, 2003
1 (of 4) 3.00
2 thru 4 . . . . @3.00

COVENTRY
Fantagraphics, 1996
1 BWg, `The Frogs of God' 4.00
2 BWg, `Thirteen Dead Guys
    Named Bob' 4.00

3 BWg. 4.00
4 . . . . 4.00

COWBOY BEBOP
Tokyopop Press, 2002
1 (of 4) by Yukata Nanten. 3.00
2 thru 4 . . . . @3.00
Spec. Complete Anime Guide #1. 13.00
Spec. Complete Anime
    Guide #2–#6 . . . . @13.00

CRAY BABY ADVENTURES, THE
Electric Milk, 1997
1 by Art Baltazar 3.00
TV Comics, 1997
1 2nd printing 3.00
2 . . . . 3.00
4 Captain Camel. 3.00
5 . . . . 3.00
Advent.Spec.San Diego Con
    lim. ed.. . . . . 5.00

CRAY BABY ADVENTURES: WRATH OF THE PEDDIDLERS
TV Comics, 1998
1 (of 3) by Art Baltazar 3.00
2 . . . . 3.00
3 concl. 3.00

CREATURES OF THE ID
Caliper, 1990
1 F. Einstein(a) 30.00

CREED
Hall of Heroes, 1994
1 TKn,I:Mark Farley 18.00
1A Wizard Ace edition rep. 15.00
2 TKn,Camping. 20.00

CREED
Lightning Comics, 1995
1-shot TKn retelling of #1&#2 . . . . 2.75
See also: Color

CREED/TEENAGE MUTANT NINJA TURTLES
Lightning Comics, 1996
1 TKn(c) 3.00
2 TKn(c) 3.00
1 Gold Collector's Edition 6.00
1 Platinum Edition. 10.00

CREED: CRANIAL DISORDER
Lightning Comics, 1996
1 . . . . 4.00
1A Previews variant cover 3.00
1B Platinum Edition. 6.00
1C signed platinum edition 8.00
2 . . . . 3.00
2b variant cover 3.00
3 . . . . 3.00
3b variant cover 3.00
3c limited edition 10.00

CREED: THE GOOD SHIP & THE NEW JOURNEY HOME
Lightning Comics, 1998
1 . . . . 3.00
1a variant cover 3.00
1b limited edition. 10.00

CREED: MECHANICAL EVOLUTION
Gearbox Press, 2000
1 (of 2) 3.00
1a variant (c). 3.00
1b signed 10.00
2 . . . . 3.00

CREED: USE YOUR DELUSION
Avatar Press, 1998
1 (of 2) by Trent Kaniuga 3.00
1 white leather 30.00
2 . . . . 3.00
2 deluxe 5.00
GN rep. #1–#2 . . . . 4.00

CRIME BUSTER
AC Comics
0 from FemForce 3.00
1 Rep. From Boys Illustrated 4.00

CRIMEBUSTER
ACG Comics, 2000
1 (of 3) F:Dick Tracy 3.00
2 & 3 . . . . @3.00

CRIME CLASSICS
Eternity, 1988
1 thru 11 rep. Shadow comic
    strip . . . . @2.50
12 . . . . 2.50

CRIMSON DREAMS
Crimson
1 thru 11 . . . . @2.25

CRITTERS
Fantagraphics Books, 1986–90
1 SS,Usagi Yojimbo,Cutey 7.00
2 Captain Jack,Birthright. 6.00
3 SS,Usagi Yojimbo,Gnuff 5.00
4 Gnuff,Birthright. 5.00
5 Birthright 5.00
6 SS,Usagi Yojimbo,Birthright. . . . 5.00
7 SS,Usagi Yojimbo,Jack Bunny . 5.00
8 SK,Animal Graffiti,Lizards 5.00
9 Animal Graffiti 5.00
10 SS,Usagi Yojimbo 5.00
11 SS,Usagi Yojimbo, ... 3.00
12 Birthright II 2.50
13 Birthright II,Gnuff. 2.50
14 SS,Usagi Yojimbo,BirthrightII . . 3.00
15 Birthright II,CareBears 2.50
16 SS,Groundthumper,Gnuff 2.50
17 Birthright II,Lionheart 2.50
18 Dragon's 2.50
19 Gnuff,Dragon's 2.50
20 Gnuff. 2.50
21 Gnuff 2.50
22 Watchdogs,Gnuff 2.50
23 Flexi-Disc,X-Mas Issue 4.00
24 Angst,Lizards,Gnuff. 2.50
25 Lionheart,SBi,Gnuff. 2.50
26 Angst,Gnuff. 2.50
27 SS,Ground Thumper. 2.50
28 Blue Beagle,Lionheart 2.50
29 Lionheart,Gnuff 2.50
30 Radical Dog,Gnuff 2.50
31 SBi,Gnuffs,Lizards 2.50
32 Lizards,Big Sneeze 2.50
33 Gnuff,Angst,Big Sneeze 2.50
34 Blue Beagle vs. Robohop 2.50
35 Lionheart,Fission Chicken 2.50
36 Blue Beagle,Fission Chicken . . . 2.50
37 Fission Chicken 2.50
38 SS,double size,Usagi Yojimbo . . 4.00

39 Fission Chicken	2.50
40 Gnuff	2.50
41 Duck'Bill Platypus	2.50
42 Glass Onion	2.50
43 Lionheart	2.50
44 Watchdogs	2.50
45 Ambrose the Frog	2.50
46 Lionheart	2.50
47 Birthright	2.50
48 Birthright	2.50
49 Birthright	2.50
50 SS,Neil the Horse, UsagiYojimbo	5.00
Spec.1 Albedo,rep+new 10pgStory	2.50

CROSSFIRE
Eclipse, 1987
Prev. Color

18 thru 26 DSp . . . . @2.50

CROW, THE
Caliber, 1989

1	55.00
1a 2nd Printing	6.00
1b 3rd Printing	5.00
2	35.00
2a 2nd Printing	4.00
2b 3rd Printing	4.00
3	25.00
3a 2nd Printing	4.00
4	25.00

Tundra, 1992

1 reps. Crow #1, #2	15.00
2	8.00
3	10.00

CROW, THE: DEAD TIME
Kitchen Sink, 1996

1	5.00
2	4.00
3	3.00

CROW, THE: DEMON IN DISGUISE
Kitchen Sink, 1997

1 (of 4) by John J. Miller & Dean Ormston	3.00
2	3.00
3	3.00

CROW, THE: FLESH AND BLOOD
Kitchen Sink, 1996

1 thru 3 . . . . @3.00

CROW, THE: WAKING NIGHTMARES
Kitchen Sink, 1997

1 PhH	3.00
2 thru 4 PhH	@3.00

CROW, THE: WILD JUSTICE, 1996
Kitchen Sink

1 thru 3 CAd . . . . @3.00

CROW/RAZOR: KILL THE PAIN
London Night, 1998

1 (of 3) JOb,EHr,	3.00
1b EHr & Jerry Beck, Director's Cut, 40pg	5.00
1c black leather, signed & numbered	25.00
1d Ministry of Night (c)	5.00

The Crow/Razor: Kill the Pain #0
© London Night

1e Ministry (c) signed	12.00
1f black leather, red foil logos	15.00
2	3.00
2a Ministry of Night (c)	5.00
2b Leather edition	9.00
3	3.00
3a Ministry of Night (c)	5.00
4	3.00
4a Ministry of Night (c)	6.00
4b Leather edition	12.00
4c Leather edition, signed	12.00
Spec. Finale	3.00
Spec. Finale, Ministry (c)	5.00
0	3.00
0a Ministry (c)	5.00
0b Red Velvet Elite	15.00
1-shotA Tour Book, cover A	5.00
1-shotB Tour Book, cover B	5.00
1-shotC Tour Book, cover C	5.00
1-shotD Tour Book, ministry edition	5.00
1-shotE Tour Book, limited black leather	12.00
1-shotF Tour Book, signed	15.00
Spec. Nocturnal Masque 48-pg.	6.00

EH! Productions, 1999

Spec. The Lost Chapter	5.00
Spec. The Lost Chapter, Elite Fan Ed.	6.00

CROW OF THE BEAR CLAN
Blackthorne, 1986

1	2.50
2 thru 6	@2.50

CRUSADERS
Guild, 1982

1 Southern Knights, Mag. size . . . 10.00

CRUSHER JOE
Ironcat, 1999

1 by Haruka Takachiho	3.00
2 thru 6	@3.00

CRY FOR DAWN
Cry For Dawn, 1989–90

1	95.00
1a 2nd Printing	35.00
1b 3rd Printing	22.00
2	55.00
2a 2nd Printing	18.00

3	38.00
4	18.00
5	18.00
6	18.00
7 Corporate Ladder,Rock A Bye Baby	12.00
8 Decay,This is the Enemy	12.00
9	12.00
1-shot Subtle Violents,F:Ryder	3.00

CRYING FREEMAN
Viz, 1989

1	4.00
2	3.50
3 thru 5	@3.50
6 thru 8	@3.00

CRYING FREEMAN II
Viz, 1990–91

1	4.00
2	3.50
3	3.50
4 thru 6	@3.00
7 V:Bugnug	3.00
8 Emu & The Samurai Sword	3.00
9 Final Issue	3.00

CRYING FREEMAN III
Viz, 1991

1 thru 10 . . . . @4.00

CRYING FREEMAN IV
Viz, 1992

1 thru 3	@4.00
4 thru 8	@2.75

CRY FREEMAN V
Viz, 1993

1 Return to Japan	4.00
2 A:Tateoka-assassin	4.00
3	4.00
4 A:Bagwana	4.00
5 V:Tsunaike	4.00
6 V:Aido Family	4.00
7 V:Tsunaike	4.00
GN:Taste of Revenge	15.00

CRYPT OF DAWN
Sirius, 1996

1 JLi(c)	6.00
1 variant cover	9.00
2 JLi(c)	4.00
3	3.00
4 JLi(c)	3.00
5 JLi(c)	3.00
6 Vanguard of Comics	3.00

CRYPTOZOO CREW
NBM Books, 2005

1	3.00
2 The Improbable Snowman	3.00
Spec. Mothman con edition	3.00

CRYSTAL BREEZE
High Impact, 1996

1 thru 3	@3.00
Spec.#1 Crystal Breeze Unleashed	3.00
Spec.#1 Crystal Breeze Revenge	3.00
Spec.#1a gold edition cover	10.00

CSI: DYING IN THE GUTTERS
IDW Publishing, 2006

1	4.00
2 thru 3	@4.00

CUBE
Class Enterpriese, 1998
1 by Patrick Fillion 3.00
2 . . . . 3.00
3 . . . . 3.00
4 . . . . 3.00
5 . . . . 3.00

CUDA
Rebel Studios
1 I:Cuda,Zora,V:Shanga Bai 2.25
CUDA B.C. (Rebel Studios) signed 13.00
Avatar Press, 1998
1 (of 4) by Tim & Joe Vigil 3.50
1b Leather cover. 15.00
1c signed 11.00
1d Royal Blue edition 40.00
2 . . . . 3.50
3 . . . . 3.50
4 . . . . 3.50
1 thru 4 gore (c) . . . . @6.00
0 80-pg. 8.00
0a Gore (c) 9.00
0c prism foil (c) 13.00
0d Royal blue 75.00

CUTEY BUNNY
Army Surplus Comix, 1982
1 . . . . 7.00
2 . . . . 4.00
3 . . . . 4.00
4 . . . . 4.00
Eclipse, 1985
5 X-Men, Batman parody 3.00

CUTIE HONEY
Ironcat, 1997
1 crime fighting android 3.00
2 . . . . 3.00
3 Wonderful Mask. 3.00
4 thru 6 . . . . @3.00
VOL 2, 1998
CUTIE HONEY '90
1 Sorayama cover. 3.00
2 thru 6 . . . . @3.00

CYBER 7
Eclipse, 1989
1 by Shuho Itahashi 2.50
2 thru 7 . . . . @2.50
Book 2: Rockland, 1990
1 . . . . 2.25
2 thru 7 . . . . @2.25
8 thru 10 . . . . @2.50

CYBERFROG
Hall of Heroes, 1994
1 I:Cyberfrog. 5.00
1a 2nd printing 2.50
2 V:Ben Riley 4.00
2a 2nd printing 2.50

CYBERFROG
Harris, 1997
1 3rd Anniv. Special 3.00
1a Walt Simonson(c) 6.00
1b signed & numbered 9.00
2 . . . . 3.50
2a variant cover 4.00
3 . . . . 3.50
4 . . . . 3.50
4a signed 9.00
Ashcan Cyberfrog: Amphibionix. . . 6.00
Spec. Cyberfrog Amphibionix(2001) 3.00

CYBERFROG VS CREED
Harris, 1997
1 . . . . 3.50
1 Creed vs. Cyberfrog, alternate
  edition 9.00

CYBERZONE
Jet Black Grafiks, 1994
1 thru 8 Never-never Land . . . . . @2.50

CYCLONE BILL
AND THE TALL TALES
Moonstone Books, 2004
1 . . . . 3.00
2 thru 3 . . . . @3.00

CYCLOPS
Blackthorne
1 Mini-series 2.50
2 . . . . 2.50
3 . . . . 2.50

Cycops #1
© Comics Interview

CYCOPS
Comics Interview, 1988
1 Mini-series, BSz. 2.50
2 . . . . 2.50
3 . . . . 2.50

CYGNUS X-1
Twisted Pearl Press
1 V:Yag'Nost 2.50
2 F:Rex and Bounty Hunters 2.50

CYNDER
Immortelle Studios, 1995
1 I:Cynder 5.00
2 . . . . 3.00
3 conclusion 2.50
Second Series, 1996
1 thru 3 . . . . 3.00

CYNDER/HELLINA
Immortelle Studios, 1996
Spec. 1 x-over 3.00

DAEMONIFUGE:
THE SCREAMING CAGE
Black Library, 2002
1 by Kev Walker 2.50

2 and 3 . . . . @2.50

DAIKAZU
Ground Zero
1 . . . . 5.00
2 . . . . 3.00
3 . . . . 3.00
1a thru 3a 2nd Printings . . . . @2.50
4 thru 8 . . . . @2.25

DAISY KUTTER
Viper Comics, 2004
1 . . . . 4.00
2 thru 4 . . . . @4.00

DA'KOTA
Millennium, 1997
1 by Pavlet & Petersen 3.00
1 signed 5.00
1 foil edition. 9.00
2 . . . . 3.00
2 foil edition. 5.00
3 . . . . 3.00
3a variant cover 3.00
3b foil deluxe edition. 7.00
Spec.#1 Orig.Art Edition 10.00

DAMNED, THE
Oni Press, 2006
1 . . . . 3.50
2 thru 5 . . . . @3.50

DAMONSTREIK
Imperial Comics
1 I:Damonstreik. 2.25
2 V:Sonix. 2.25
3 V:Sonix. 2.25
4 J:Ohm 2.25
5 V:Drakkus 2.25

DAMPYR
IDW Publishing, 2005
GN #1 Devil's Son 8.00
GN #2 Night Tribe 8.00
GN #3 Sand Specters 8.00
GN #4 Nocturne in Red 8.00
GN #5 Under the Stone Bridge 8.00
GN #6 Lamiah 8.00
GN #7 From the Darkness. 8.00
GN #8 Coast of Skeletons 8.00
GN #9 Forbidden Zone 8.00
GN #10 House of Blood. 8.00

DANGEROUS TIMES
Evolution, 1989
1 MK 2.50
2 MA(c) 2.25
2a 2nd printing 2.25
3 MR(c). 2.25
3a 2nd printing 2.25
4 thru 6 GP(c) . . . . @2.25

DAN TURNER
HOLLYWOOD DETECTIVE
Eternity, 1991
1 `Darkstar of Death' 2.50
Spec.#1 Dan Turner, Homicide
  Hunch, Dan Turner Framed . . . 2.50
Spec.#1 Dan Turner, The Star
  Chamber, Death of Folly
  Hempstead 2.50

DARK ANGEL
Boneyard, 1991
1 by Hart Fisher 2.25
2 . . . . 2.25

DARK ANGEL
Boneyard, 1997
1 by H.Fisher & J.Helkowski 2.25
2 . . . . 2.25
3 by Hart Fisher & John Cassaday. 2.25
4 The Quiet Demon 2.25
Spec.#1 Dark Angel/Bill the Bull,
    48-pg. (1998). 5.00
Spec. 1999 . . . . 5.00
GN Last Decade Dead Century. . . 16.00
GN deluxe 20.00

DARK ANGEL
CPM Manga, 1999
1 by Kia Asamiya 3.00
2 thru 9 . . . . @3.00
10 thru 31 . . . . @3.00

DARK ASSASSIN
Silverwolf, 1987
1 thru 3 . . . . @2.50
Vol. 2
1 thru 5 . . . . @2.50

DARK CITY ANGEL
Freak Pit Productions
1 I:Lt.Michelle Constello 3.50
2 . . . . 3.50
3 Sex Doll is Prime Suspect 3.50

DARK FANTASIES
Dark Fantasy, 1994–97
0 Donna Mia foil (c) 8.00
0 Destiny Angel foil (c) 7.50
1 Jli (c) 8.00
1a test print Jli (c) 9.00
1 2nd printing 4.00
1 signed & numbered 8.00
2 Kevin J. Taylor Girl (c) 4.00
2a foil stamped 3.00
3 JOb Crow (c) 4.00
3a foil stamped 3.50
4 . . . . 4.00
4a foil stamped 3.50
5 . . . . 4.00
5a foil stamped 3.50
6 Angel Destiny 4.00
6a foil stamped 3.50
7 . . . . 4.00
7a foil stamped 3.50
8 . . . . 4.00
8 Blue cover 3.50
8 Red cover 3.50
8 deluxe foil-enhanced 4.00
9 Destiny Angel (c) 3.50
9a Destiny Angel, red foil (c) 4.00
9b Horror (c) 3.50
9c Horror, red foil (c). 4.00
10 . . . . 3.50
10a red foil (c) 4.00
Spec.#1 Summers Eve Pin-up. . . . 3.00
Spec.#1 foil-stamped 3.50

DARK FRINGE
Brainstorm, 1996
1 . . . . 3.00

DARK FRINGE:
SPIRITS OF THE DEAD
Brainstorm, 1997
1 by Eman Torre & John Kisse 3.00
2 concl 3.00

DARK ISLAND
Davdez Arts, 1998
1 by Barry Blair & Colin Chan 2.50
2 thru 4 . . . . @2.50

DARKLIGHT: PRELUDE
Sirius, 2000
1 (of 3) by Teri Sue Wood 3.00
2 . . . . 3.00
3 concl 3.00

DARK LORD
RAK
1 thru 3 . . . . @2.25

DARK MANGA
London Night
1 Featuring Demonique 5.00

DARK MUSE
Dark Muse Productions
1 with mini-comic 3.50
1a with mini-comic 5.00
2 . . . . 4.00
3 F:Coffin Joe 4.00

Dark Oz #2
© Arrow Comics

DARK OZ
Arrow Comics, 1997
1 (of 5) by Griffith, Kerr & Bryan . . . 2.75
2 thru 5 . . . . @2.75
Spec. Bill Bryan's Oz Collection . . . 3.00

DARK PERIL
Quantum Comics, 1998
1 . . . . 3.00
2 . . . . 3.00
3 . . . . 3.00
4 . . . . 3.00

DARK REGIONS
White Wolf, 1987
1 . . . . 2.50
2 . . . . 2.50
3 Scarce 3.00
4 and 5 . . . . @2.50

DARK STAR
Rebel
1 I:Ran 2.25
2 thru 3 . . . . @2.25

DARK VISIONS
Pyramid, 1987
1 I:Wasteland Man 2.50
2 thru 4 . . . . @2.50

DARK WOLF
Eternity, 1988
1 and 2 . . . . @2.50
Volume 2
1 thru 14 . . . . @2.50
Ann. #1. . . . . 2.50

DARQUE RAZOR
London Night, 1996
? by Dan Membeila & Albert Holaso,
    Dark Birth 2.25
? necro-embossed edition 10.00
1 thru 3 . . . . @3.00

DAYS OF DARKNESS
Apple, 1992
1 From Pearl Harbor
    to Midway. 2.75
2 Pearl Harbor Attack,cont 2.75
3 Japanese Juggernaut 2.75
4 Bataan Peninsula. 2.75
GN 15.00

DEADBEATS
Claypool Comics, 1993
1 thru 13 . . . . @2.50
14 New Ways to Dream. 2.50
15 thru 25 . . . . @2.50
26 by Richard Howell & Ricardo
    Villagran, The Southland
    Family Saga 2.50
27 Christine transformed into
    Predator. 2.50
28 . . . . 2.50
29 forbidden antiquities 2.50
30 V:Dracula 2.50
31 Reconstructing Deadbeats 2.50
32 New generation of Deadbeats . . 2.50
33 Quiet Night in Fear City 2.50
34 Dagger of Deliverance 2.50
35 Deadbeats of Danger Street . . . 2.50
36 By His Majesty's Request 2.50
37 Carnival of Goals 2.50
38 HorrorFest begins 2.50
39 HorrorFest 2.50
40 HorrorFest. 2.50
41 Guys Night Out 2.50
42 Dark Dealings 2.50
43 Dodging the Bullet 2.50
44 Town for Sale 2.50
45 thru 50 . . . . @2.50
51 thru 74 . . . . @2.50
75 thru 82 . . . . @2.50

DEAD EYES OPEN
Amaze Ink/SLG, 2005
1 . . . . 3.00
2 . . . . 3.00
3 thru 6 . . . . @3.00

DEADKILLER
Caliber
1 Rep Deadworld 19 thru 21 . . . . . 3.00

DEAD SONJA:
SHE-ZOMBIE WITH
A SWORD
Blatant Comics, 2006
1 spoof 4.00
1a Zombie Bloodbath (c) 4.00
1b Dead Sexy (c) 10.00

DEADTIME STORIES
New Comics, 1987
1 AAd,WS 2.50

All comics prices listed are for *Near Mint* condition.   **CVA Page 737**

DEADWORLD
Arrow, 1986

1 Arrow Pyb	5.00
2	4.00
3 V:King Zombie	3.50
4 V:King Zombie	3.50
5 Team Rests	3.50
6 V:King Zombie	3.50
7 F:KZ & Deake, Graphic(c)	3.50
8 V:Living Corpse, Graphic(c).	2.50
9 V:Sadistic Punks, Graphic(c)	2.50
10 V:King Zombie, Graphic(c)	2.50
7a thru 10a Tame cover	@2.50
11 V:King Zombie, Graphic(c)	3.00
12 I:Percy, Graphic(c)	3.00
13 V:King Zombie, Graphic(c)	3.00
14 V:Voodoo Cult,Graphic(c)	3.00
15 Zombie stories,Graphic(c)	3.00
11a thru 15a Tame cover	@2.50
16 V:`Civilized' Community	2.50
17 V:King Zombie	2.50
18 V:King Zombie	2.50
19 V:Grakken	2.50
20 V:King Zombie	2.50
21 Dead Killer	2.50
22 L:Dan & Joey	2.50
23 V:King Zombie	2.50
24	2.50
25 (R:Vince Locke)	2.50
26	2.50

Caliber

1 thru 11	@3.00
12 thru 15 Death Call	@3.00
Spec. Deadworld Archives, rep.	2.50
Spec. Bits & Pieces, rep.	
Caliber Presents #2&#8	2.50
Spec. To Kill A King,R:Deadkiller	3.00

DEADWORLD: FROZEN OVER
Desperado, 2006

1 (of 4)	4.00
2 thru 3	@4.00

DEATH ANGEL
Lightning, 1997

1 by J. Cleary & Anderson	3.00
1 variant cover	3.00
1 limited edition A	9.00
1 limited edition B	9.00

DEATHDREAMS OF DRACULA
Apple

1 Selection of short stories	2.50
2 short stories	2.50
3 Inc. Rep. BWr,'Breathless'	2.50
4 short stories	2.50

DEATH HUNT
Eternity

1 & 2	@2.25

DEATHMARK
Lightning Comics, 1994

1 O:War Party	2.75

DEATH OF ANGEL GIRL
Angel Entertainment, 1997

1 by E.Bell & C.Forrest,F:Michelle	3.00

DEATH OF BLOODFIRE
Lightning

1	3.00
1a variant cover	3.00

DEATH RATTLE
Kitchen Sink, 1995
(Prev. Color)

1 thru 3	@3.50
4	3.00
5	2.50
6 Steve Bissette(c)	2.25
7 Ed Gein	2.25
8 I:Xenozoic Tales.	9.00
9 BW,rep.	2.25
10 AW,rep.	2.25
11 thru 15	@2.25
16 BW,Spacehawk	2.25
17 Rand Holmes(c)	2.25
18 FMc.	2.25

DEATH'S HEAD
Crystal

1 thru 3	@2.25

DEATHWORLD
Adventure Comics, 1990

1 Harry Harrison adapt.	2.50
2 thru 4	@2.50

BOOK II, 1991

1 Harry Harrison adapt.	2.50
2 thru 4	@2.50

BOOK III, 1991

1 H.Harrison adapt.,colonization.	2.50
2 Attack on the Lowlands	2.50
3 Attack on the Lowlands contd.	2.50
4 last issue	2.50

DEE VEE
Dee Vee, 1997

1 ECa, F:Alex	3.00
2 ECa	3.00
3 ECa	3.00
4 thru 14	@3.00
Spec. #1 Life is Cheap.	3.00
Spec., 2001, 64-page.	5.00

DEEP SLEEPER
Oni Press, 2004

1 (of 4)	3.50
2 thru 4	@3.50

DEFENSELESS DEAD
Adventure Comics, 1991

1 Larry Niven adapt. A:Gil	2.50

Defenseless Dead #3
© Adventure Comics

2 A:Organlegger	2.50
3 A:Organlegger	2.50

DELETE
Digital Noixe, 2004

1	3.00
2 thru 5	@3.00

DELTA TENN
Entertainment, 1987

1 thru 11	@2.50

DEMO
AIT/Planet Lar, 2003

1 (of 12)	4.00
2 thru 12	@3.00

DEMON BABY
SQP/666 Comics, 1997

1 by Rich Larson, seq. to Hell on Heels	3.00
2 & 3	@3.00
1a thru 3a deluxe	@9.00

DEMON BITCH
Forbidden, 1997–98

1-shot	3.00
Spec.#1 Demon Bitch vs. Angel Girl.	3.00
Spec.#1 Demon Bitch: Devilspawn, by Angela Benoit & Nirut Chaswan	3.00
Spec.#1 Demon Bitch: Hellslave, Free on Earth cover	3.00
Spec.#1 Demon Bitch: Tales of the Damned	3.00

DEMONGATE
Sirius, 1996–97

1 thru 12 by Bao Lin Hum & Colin Chan	@2.50

DEMON GUN
Crusade Entertainment, 1996

1 thru 3 GCh,KtH	@3.00

DEMON HUNTER
Aircel, 1989

1 thru 4	@2.50

DEMON HUNTER
Davdez Arts, 1998

1 by Barry Blair & Colin Chan	2.50
2 F:Hunter Gordon	2.50
3	2.50

DEMONIQUE
London Night, 1997

? by SKy Owens, A:Anvil	3.00
1 by Membeila & Owens.	3.00
2 F:Viper	3.00
3 Mayhem	3.00
4 Final issue	3.00

DEMONIQUE: ANGEL OF NIGHT
London Night, 1997

1 (of 3) by Skylar Owens	3.00
2	3.00
3 final issue	3.00

DEMONSLAYER: LORDS OF NIGHT
Avatar Press, 2003

1/2 Fire Edition	6.00
1/2 Ice Edition	6.00

1/2 Attitude Edition 6.00
Preview 2.25
Preview variant (c)s 6.00
1 . . . . 3.50
1a variant (c)s 3.50
1b wraparound (c) 4.00

DEMON'S TAILS
Adventure
1 . . . . 2.50
2 A:Champion 2.50
3 V:Champion 2.50
4 V:Champion 2.50

DEMON WARRIOR
Eastern, 1987
1 thru 12 . . . . @2.50
13 and 14 . . . . @2.50

DENIZENS OF
DEEP CITY
Jabberwocky, 1988
1 thru 8 . . . . @2.50

DERRECK WAYNE
JACKSON'S STRAPPED
Gothic Images, 1994
1 Confrontational Factor 2.25
2 thru 6 . . . . @2.25

DESCENDING ANGELS
Millennium, 1995
1 I:3 Angels 2.25
2 F:Jim Johnson 3.00
3 F:Jim Johnson 3.00

DESERT PEACH
Thoughts & Images, 1988
1 thru 4 . . . . @2.50

DESTINY ANGEL
Dark Fantasy, 1996
1 (of 3) 4.00
1 2nd printing 4.00
1a deluxe 4.50
2 `Sunless Garden' 3.50
2a foil cover 4.00
2b photo cover 4.00

DESTROY
Eclipse, 1986
1 Large Size 5.00
2 Small Size,3-D 5.00

DETECTIVE, THE
Caliber, 1998
1 by Gerard Goffaux 3.00
2 . . . . 3.00
3 Clutches of the Past 3.00

DEVIL JACK
Doom Theatre, 1995
1 I:Devil Jack 3.00
1a Directors Cut 3.00
2 V:Belegosi 3.00
3 . . . . 3.00

DEVIL'S PANTIES, THE
Silent Devil Productions, 2006
1 by Jennie Breeden 5.00
2 thru 14 . . . . @5.00

DEVIL'S WORKSHOP
Blue Comet Press, 1995
1 Iron Cupcakes 3.00

DIABOLIK
Scorpion Productions, 1999
VOL. 1
1 Terror Aboard The Karima 6.00
2 Fight Against Time 6.00
3 Crumbs for the Scum. 6.00
4 Family with no morals 6.00
5 & 6 . . . . @6.00
VOL. 2
1 Target: Diabolik 6.00
2 One Crazy Love. 6.00
3 . . . . 6.00
4 Interrupted Game. 6.00

DICK DANGER
Olsen Comics, 1998
1 by W.W. Olsen 3.00
2 F:Red Olga 3.00
3 The Angel Murder 3.00
4 Is Hitler Still Alive? 3.00
5 Nikita, The Cat Girl 3.00

DICKS
Caliber, 1997
1 (of 4),GEn,JMC, ... 3.00
2 thru 4 GEn,JMC . . . . @3.00

DICK TRACY
CRIMEBUSTER
ACG Comics, 1998
1 by M.A.Collins & D.Locher 3.00
2 thru 9 . . . . @3.00

DICK TRACY DETECTIVE
ACG Comics, 1999
1 (of 4) by Chester Gould 3.00
2 thru 4 . . . . @3.00

DICK TRACY MAGAZINE
1 V:Little Face Finnyo 4.00

DICK TRACY
Blackthorne, 1984–89
1 thru 12 . . . . @6.50
13 thru 25 . . . . @7.50
Becomes:

DICK TRACY
MONTHLY/WEEKLY
Blackthorne, 1988
1 thru 25 monthly . . . . @3.00
26 thru 108 weekly . . . . @4.00
Unprinted Stories #3 . . . . 3.00
1 3-D Special 3.00
Spec. #1. . . . . 3.00
Spec. #2. . . . . 3.00
Spec. #3. . . . . 3.00

DICK TRACY:
THE EARLY YEARS
Blackthorne, 1987
1 thru 3, 78-pg. . . . . @7.50
4 thru 6 . . . . @3.50
7 and 8 . . . . @4.00

DICK TRACY
UNPRINTED STORIES
Blackthorne, 1987
1 thru 4 . . . . @3.00

DICTATORS
Antarctic Press, 2004
Hitler #1 (of 4) 3.00
Hitler #2 thru #4 . . . . @3.00

Saddam Hussein #1 . . . . 4.00
Saddam Hussein #2 . . . . 4.00

DIGITAL DRAGON
Peregrine Entertainment, 1999
1 by Bryan Heyboer 3.00
2 thru 4 . . . . @3.00

DIGITAL WEBBING
PRESENTS
Digital Webbing 2001
1 thru 5 . . . . 3.00
6 thru 18 . . . . @3.00
19 thru 25 . . . . @3.50
26 . . . . 6.00
27 thru 31 . . . . @4.00

DIM-WITTED DARRYL
Slave Labor Graphics, 1998
1 by Michael Bresnahan 3.00
2 thru 5 . . . . @3.00

DINOSAURS FOR HIRE
Eternity, 1988
1 . . . . 3.00
1a Rep. 2.50
2 thru 9 . . . . @2.50
Fall Classic #1 . . . . 2.50
GN Guns 'N' Lizards 10.00
Malibu, 1993
#1 3-D special 3.50

DIRTY PAIR
Eclipse, 1988
1 . . . . 8.00
2 . . . . 7.00
3 . . . . 6.00
4 end mini-series 6.00
Vol. 2, 1989
1 thru 5 . . . . @5.00
Vol. 3, 1990
1 thru 5 . . . . @5.00

DIRTY PAIR:
SIM EARTH
Eclipse
1 . . . . 4.00
2 thru 4 . . . . @4.00

Dirty Pair #1
© Eclipse

DISCIPLES
Caliber Core, 1998
1 Climate of fear 3.00
2 . . . . 3.00

A DISTANT SOIL
Warp Graphics, 1983
1 A:Panda Khan 9.00
2 . . . . 5.00
3 . . . . 4.00
4 . . . . 3.00
5 thru 9 . . . . @3.00
Aria Press, 1991
1 F:Seasons of Spring 6.00
1a-2nd to 4th printing 2.50
2 Seasons of Spring,pt.2 . . . . 5.00
3 . . . . 3.00
4 . . . . 3.00
5 thru 8 . . . . @3.00
9 thru 11 Knights of the Angel . . . @3.00
12 thru 14 . . . . @3.00
GN Knights of the Angel, deluxe . . 16.00
GN Immigrant Song rep.#1–#3 . . . . 7.00
See Image Comics

DITKO'S WORLD: STATIC
Renegade, 1986
1 . . . . 2.25
2 thru 3 SD . . . . @2.25

DOCTOR
Ironcat, 1997
1 (of 5) by Bang Ippongi 3.00
2 . . . . 3.00
4 . . . . 3.00
5 Pay Back in the City of
   Santa La Paz 3.00
6 final issue 3.00

DR. BLINK: SUPERHERO SHRINK
Dork Storm Press, 2004
0 . . . . 3.00
1 . . . . 3.00
2 thru 3 . . . . @3.50

DR. GORPON
Eternity, 1991
1 I:Dr.Gorpon,V:Demon 2.25
2 A:Doofus,V:ChocolateBunny 2.50
3 D:Dr.Gorpon 2.50

DR. RADIUM
Silverline
1 . . . . 3.00
2 thru 4 . . . . @2.25

DR. RADIUM: MAN OF SCIENCE
Slave Labor, 1992
1 And Baby makes 2, BU: Dr.
   Radiums' Grim Future 2.50

DOC WEIRD'S THRILL BOOK
1 AW 2.25
2 & 3 . . . . @2.25

DOCTOR WEIRD
Caliber Press, 1994
1 V:Charnogg 2.50
2 V:Charnogg 2.50

DR. WONDER
Old Town Publishing, 1996
1 thur 5 . . . . @3.00

DODEKAIN
Antarctic Press, 1994
1 and 2 by Masayuki Fujihara . . . @3.00
3 Rampage Vs. Zogerians 3.00
4 V:Zogerians 3.00
5 F:Takuma 3.00
6 Dan vs. Takuma 2.75
7 V:Okizon 2.75
8 V:Okizon 3.00

DOGAROO
Blackthorne, 1988
1 . . . . 2.50

The Dogs O'War #3
© Crusade Entertainment

DOGS O'WAR, THE
Crusade Entertainment, 1996–97
1 (of 3) 3.00
2 thru 3 . . . . @3.00

DOGWITCH
Sirius Entertainment 2002
1 . . . . 3.50
1a signature plate edition 10.00
2 thru 17 . . . . @3.00
18 Finale special 3.50
18a Signature plate edition 12.00

DOLLS
Sirius, 1998
1-shot science fiction 3.00

DOMINION
Eclipse Manga, 1990
1 by Masamune Shirow 3.00
2 thru 6 . . . . @2.25

DOMINO CHANCE
Chance, 1982
1 1,000 printed 10.00
1a 2nd printing 3.50
2 thru 6 . . . . @3.00
7 I:Gizmo 7.00
8 A:Gizmo 11.00
9 . . . . 2.50

[2nd Series]
1 . . . . 3.00
2 and 3 . . . . @2.50

DONATELLO
Mirage, 1986
1-shot A:TMNTurtles 12.00

DONNA MIA
Avatar Press, 1997
0 by Tevlin Utz 3.00
0b leather cover 15.00
0c signed 8.00
1 . . . . 4.00
1a signed 8.00
1b Royal Blue edition 40.00
2 . . . . 4.00
2a deluxe 4.50
3 (of 3) 3.00
3a deluxe 8.00
Giant Size #1 . . . . 3.00
Giant Size #1 leather cover 15.00
Giant Size #1 signed 8.00
Giant Size #2 . . . . 4.00
Giant Size #2 Deluxe 10.00
Spec. Infinity 3.00
Spec.#1 Pin-up (1997) 3.00

DON SIMPSON'S BIZARRE HEROES
Fiasco Comics, 1990
0 thru 7 . . . . 3.00
8 V:Darkcease 3.00
9 R:Yan Man 3.00
10 F:Mainstreamers 3.00
11 Search for Megaton Man 3.00
12 . . . . 3.00
13 House of Megaton Man 3.00
14 Cec Vs. Dark Cease 3.00

DOOMED
IDW Publishing, 2005
1 . . . . 7.00
1a variant (c) 7.00
2 thru 3 . . . . @8.00
2a thru 3a variant (c) . . . . @8.00
4 . . . . 10.00
4a variant (c) 10.00

DOOMSDAY + 1
ACG Comics, 1998
1 by JBn rep. Charlton 3.00
2 A Faceless Foe 3.00
3 . . . . 3.00
4 The Hidden Enemy 3.00
5 Rule of Fear 3.00
6 . . . . 3.00
7 NA(c), final issue 3.00

DORK
Amaze Ink/SLG, 1993–2001
1 EDo 3.00
2 EDo 3.00
3 EDo 3.00
1 thru 3 2nd printings . . . . @3.00
4 thru 7 . . . . @3.00
8 . . . . 3.50
9 thru 11 . . . . @3.00

DORK TOWER
Corsair Publishing, 1998
1 by John Kovalic 3.00
2 thru 8 . . . . @3.50
Dork Storm, 2000
9 Angry Young Fan 3.00
10 Road Rules 3.00
11 World of Dorkness 3.00
12 . . . . 3.00
13 . . . . 3.00
14 Gilly, Warrior Princess 3.00
15 . . . . 3.00
16 Trader of the Last Orc 3.00

Dork #7
© *Amaze Ink/SGL*

17 Halloween in Mud Bay 3.00
17 At the Big Con. 3.00
18 Understanding Games 3.00
19 Junk Food Issue 3.00
20 Featuring Gilly. 3.00
21 20th Century Boy 3.00
22 Daily Carson 3.00
23 Dork Tower Frag 3.00
24 . . . . 3.00
25 . . . . 4.00
26 thru 32 . . . . @3.00
33 thru 35 . . . . @3.50
Spec. Lord of the Rings 3.00
Swimsuit Special #1 . . . . 3.00
Best of Dork Tower #1 . . . . 2.25
1-shot Wizkids Special 3.00

DOUBLE EDGE DOUBLE
Double Edge
1 thru 3 . . . . 3.50
4 Heroes Inc. Rep.#1-#2 . . . . 3.00

DOUBLE IMPACT
High Impact Studios, 1995–96
1 I: China & Jazz 5.00
1a Chromium (c) variant, signed . . 6.00
1b Rainbow (c) w/certificate 12.00
1c Rainbow (c) w/o certificate. 9.00
2 Castilo's Crime. 3.00
2b silver version 9.00
2c signed, w/certificate 5.00
3 . . . . 5.00
3a Bondage (c). 12.00
4 . . . . 5.00
4a Phoenix (c). 12.00
5 . . . . 5.00
6 China cover 3.00
6a Jazz cover 3.00
6b signed China or Jazz(c). 12.00
6c bondage(c). 9.00
7 & 8 . . . . @3.00
8a variant (c). 8.00

2nd Series, 1996–97
0 . . . . 3.00
1 . . . . 3.00
1a chromium (c) 4.00
1b Chromium variant edition. 12.00
1c Christmas (c) 9.00
2 . . . . 3.00
2a Sweedish Erotica(c) 9.00
Spec.#1 Double Impact/Lethal Strike:
   Double Strike, x-over 3.00

Spec.#1 Double Impact/Nikki Blade:
   Hard Core x-over (1997) 3.00
   Platinum variant RCI(c) 9.00
   Gold Metal variant RCI(c) 15.00
Spec.#1 Raising Hell, RCI,RkB . . . 3.00

ABC Comics, 1998
1 encore 3.00
1a encore, Chicago cover. 6.00
1b encore, San Diego nude cover . 6.00
Spec. Double Impact/Luxura (1998) 3.00
Spec. Vampeurotica edition. 6.00
Bikini Spec. 3.00
Christmas Spec. 3.00
Christmas Spec., gold foil 9.00
Coll.#1 . . . . 3.00
Coll.#1a x-mas 8.00
Spring Spec.#1. . . . . 3.00
Spring Spec.#1a manga cover 8.00
Summer Bikini Spec. 1999 . . . . 3.00
Gallery Collection #1 . . . . 5.00
Lingerie Special 3.00

DOUBLE IMPACT ALIVE
ABC Comics, 1999
1 (of 3) Double Impact Alive 2000 . 3.00
1a Double Impact Alive 2000,
   gold foil ed. 8.00
1b Red Leather. 12.00
2 RCI. 3.00
2a Manga cover 8.00
2c silver embossed foil 9.00

DOUBLE IMPACT:
ASSASSINS FOR HIRE
High Impact, 1997
1 RCI,RkB 3.00
2 . . . . 3.00

ABC Comics, 1998
1 . . . . 3.00

DOUBLE IMPACT:
FROM THE ASHES
ABC Comics, 1998
1 (of 2) RCI 3.00
2 RCI. 3.00
2A variant cover A 6.00
2B variant cover B 6.00

DOUBLE IMPACT:
HOT SHOTS
ABC Studios, 1999
1 RCI. 3.00
2 . . . . 3.00

DOUBLE IMPACT MERCS
ABC Comics, 1999
1 (of 3) RCI 3.00
1a deluxe 8.00
2 RCI. 3.00
2a deluxe 9.00

DOUBLE IMPACT:
ONE STEP BEYOND
ABC Comics, 1998
1 (of 2) RCI 3.00
1a Leather cover. 15.00

DOUBLE IMPACT RAW
ABC Comics, 1997
1 (of 3) RCI, adult 3.00
1b Star photo (c) 9.00
1A Wraparound cover A 6.00
1B Wraparound cover B 6.00
2 thru 3 . . . . @3.00
3A Variant cover A 6.00

VOL. 2
1 (of 3) adult material 3.00

DOUBLE IMPACT/RAZOR
ABC Studios, 1999
1 (of 3) 3.25
1b Previews exclusive 8.00
1c Manga alt.(c) 8.00
2 . . . . 3.25

DOUBLE IMPACT
SUICIDE RUN
ABC Comics, 1998
1 (of 2) RCI 3.00
1b Leather cover. 12.00
2 adult material 3.00
Collected edition 3.00
Collected, gold foil 9.00

DOUBLE IMPACT 2069
ABC Comics, 1999
1 Virgin Encore Edition 3.00
1a Deluxe Erotica edition 8.00
Christmas Spec. 3.00
Christmas Spec. Previews (c) 8.00

DOUBLE IMPACT X
ABC Comics, 2000
1 . . . . 6.00
1a alternate (c) 6.00
2 . . . . 6.00
2 deluxe, vinyl (c) 15.00
Intro 15.00

DRACULA
Eternity
1 . . . . 3.75
1a 2nd printing 2.50
2 thru 4 . . . . @2.50

DRACULA IN HELL
Apple, 1992
1 O:Dracula. 2.50
2 O:Dracula contd. 2.50

DRACULA: SUICIDE CLUB
Adventure, 1992
1 I:Suicide Club in UK. 2.50
2 Dracula/Suicide Club cont. 2.50
3 Club raid,A:Insp.Harrison. 2.50
4 Vision of Miss Fortune 2.50

DRACULA: THE LADY
IN THE TOMB
Eternity
1 . . . . 2.50

DRACULA'S
COZY COFFIN
Draculina Publishing, 1995
1 thru 4 Halloween issue . . . . . . @3.00

DRAGON ARMS
Antarctic Press 2002
1 48-pg. 5.00
2 thru 6 . . . . @3.50
1-shot Stand Alone Special 3.00

DRAGON ARMS:
CHAOS BLADE
Antarctic Press, 2004
1 . . . . 3.00
2 thru 6 . . . . @3.00

DRAGONBALL
Viz Communications, 1998
1 (of 12) by Akira Toriyama 8.00
2 thru 4 . . . . @5.00
5 thru 12 . . . . @3.00
PART TWO, 1999
1 (of 15) by Akira Toriyama 5.00
2 thru 4 . . . . @4.00
5 thru 15 . . . . @3.00
PART THREE, 2000
1 (of 14) by Akira Toriyama 3.00
2 thru 5 . . . . @3.00
8 thru 14 . . . . @3.00
PART FOUR, 2001
1 thru 4 (of 10) . . . . @3.00
5 thru 10 . . . . @3.00
PART FIVE, 2002
1 (of 7) 3.00
2 thru 6 . . . . @3.00
7 . . . . 3.00
Part 6
1 . . . . 3.50
2 . . . . 3.50

DRAGONBALL Z
Viz Communications, 1998
1 (of 9) by Akira Toriyama 11.00
2 thru 9 . . . . @5.00
PART TWO (1998)
1 (of 14) by Akira Toriyama 4.00
2 thru 9 . . . . @3.50
10 thru 14 . . . . @3.50
PART THREE (1999)
1 (of 10) by Akira Toriyama 3.50
2 thru 10 . . . . @3.00
PART 4 (2000)
1 thru 13 (of 15) . . . . @3.00
PART 5 (2001)
1 (of 12) 3.00
2 thru 10 . . . . @3.00

DRAGONFORCE
Aircel, 1988
1 DK 6.00
2 thru 7 DK . . . . @4.00
8 thru 12 . . . . @4.00
13 . . . . 2.50

DRAGONFORCE CHRONICLES
Aircel, 1988
Vol. 1 thru Vol. 5 rep. . . . . @3.00

DRAGON KNIGHTS
Tokyopop Press, 2001
1 by Mineko Ohkami. 3.00
2 thru 6 . . . . @3.00

DRAGONMIST
Raised Brow Publications
1 I:Dragonmist 2.75
2 F:Assassin 2.75

DRAGON OF THE VALKYR
Rak
1 . . . . 2.25
2 thru 4 . . . . @2.25

DRAGON QUEST
Silverwolf, 1986
1 TV 10.00
2 TV 6.00
3 TV 5.00

DRAGONRING
[1st Series]
1 B.Blair,rare 110.00
Aircel, 1986
1 . . . . 3.50
2 . . . . 2.50
3 thru 6 . . . . @2.50
See Also Color Comics

DRAGONROK SAGA
Hanthercraft
1 . . . . 2.50
2 thru 12 . . . . @2.50

Dragonrok Saga #2
© Hanthercraft

DRAGON WARS
Ironcat, 1998
1 by Ryukihei 3.00
2 thru 11 . . . . @3.00

DRAGON WEEKLY
1 Southern Knights 2.25
2 and 3 . . . . @2.25

DREAD OF NIGHT
Hamilton, 1991
1 Horror story collection 4.00
2 Json, inc.`Genocide' 4.00

DREAM ANGEL AND ANGEL GIRL
Angel Entertainment, 1998
1 . . . . 3.00

DREAM ANGEL: THE QUANTUM DREAMER
Angel Entertainment, 1997
1 by Mort Castle & Adriana Melo . . 3.00
2 . . . . 3.00

DREAM ANGEL: WORLD WITHOUT END
Angel Entertainment, 1998
1 Dream world cover 3.00

DREAMERY
Eclipse, 1986
1 . . . . 2.50
2 thru 13 . . . . @2.50

DREAMGIRL
Angel Entertainment, 1996
0 by David Campitti & Al Rio 3.00
1 . . . . 3.00
1 deluxe 6.00
1 Manga cover 5.00

DREAMLANDS
Caliber New Worlds, 1996
1 . . . . 3.00
2 flip book with Boston Bombers #3 3.00

DREAMTIME
Blind Rat, 1995
1 Young Deserter 3.00
2 Gypsy Trouble 2.50

DREAMWALKER
Caliber Tapestry, 1997
1 . . . . 3.00
2 thru 4 . . . . @3.00
5 by Jenni Gregory, 2nd story arc. . 3.00
6 2nd story arc, concl. 3.00

DREAMWALKER: CAROUSEL
Avatar, 1998
0 . . . . 3.00
1 by Jenni Gregory 3.00
2 conclusion 3.00

DREAMWALKER: SUMMER RAIN
Avatar, 1999
1 by Jenni Gregory 3.00

DREAMWALKER: AUTUMN LEAVES
Avatar, 1999
1 by Jenni Gregory 3.00
2 conclusion 3.00

DREAMWOLVES
Dramenon Studios, 1994
1 . . . . 3.00
2 . . . . 3.00
3 F:Desiree 3.00
4 and 5 V:Venefica . . . . @3.00
6 R:Carnifax 3.00
7 . . . . 3.00
8 F:Wendy Bascum 3.00

DRIFTERS
Infinity Graphics, 1986
1 . . . . 2.50

DROWNERS, THE
New Flame Publishing, 2004
1 (of 4) 3.00
2 thru 4 . . . . @3.00

DRYWALL AND OSWALD SHOW, THE
Fireman Press, 1998
1 by Mandy Carter,Trent Kaniuga . 3.00

DUEL
Antarctic Press, 2005
0 . . . . 3.00
1 (of 4) Rise of the Blackhawk . . . 3.00
2 Jet War in the South Atlantic 3.50
3 Germany 1945 . . . . 3.00

DUNGEON
NBM Books 2002
1 by L. Trondheim & J. Star 3.00
2 thru 8 . . . . @3.00

DUNGEON:
THE EARLY YEARS
NBM Books, 2004
1 thru 2 . . . . @3.00

DUNGEONEERS
Silverwolf, 1986
1 thru 8 . . . . @2.50

DUNGEONS & DRAGONS:
BLACK & WHITE
Kenzer & Company, 2002
1 (of 8) by J.Limke & R.Pereira . . . 3.00
2 thru 6 . . . . @3.00

DUNGEONS & DRAGONS
IN SHADOW OF DRAGONS
Kenzer & Company, 2001
1 (of 8) The Last of My Father 3.00
2 thru 8 . . . . @3.00

DWELLING, THE
**Chaos! Comics/Black Label
Graphics, 2002**
Ashcan 6.00
1 BnP 5.00
1a premium edition 9.00
1b super premium edition 15.00
1c signed edition. 12.00
Spec. #1 script edition 5.00
Spec. #1 premium script edition . . 20.00

EAGLE
Crystal, 1986
1 . . . . 3.00
1a signed & limited 5.00
2 thru 5 . . . . @2.75
6 thru 17 . . . . @2.50

Apple, 1988
18 thru 26 . . . . @2.50

EAGLE
Viz Communications, 2000
1 (of 14) The Candidate,112-pg. . . . 7.00
2 Scandal 7.00
3 The Vice-President 7.00
4 New Hampshire 7.00
5 On the Battlefield 7.00
6 King of New York 7.00
7 Pandora's Box 7.00
8 The Debate 7.00
9 Passion 7.00
10 Gone to Texas 7.00
11 Super Tuesday 7.00
12 Suspicion 7.00
13 Illegitimate child 7.00
14 Confession 7.00
15 The Nomination 7.00
16 The General 7.00
17 Coming Home 7.00
18 Frame Up 7.00
19 Fires in the Plain 7.00
20 Someone You Can Trust 7.00
21 End of the Trail 7.00
22 Father & Son 7.00

EAGLE: DARK MIRROR
Comic Zone
1 A:Eagle, inc reps 2.75
2 In Japan, V:Lord Kagami 2.75

3 . . . . 3.00
4 . . . . 3.00

EAGLES DARE
Aager Comics, 1994
1 thru 4 . . . . 2.25
5 V:Dragon 2.25

EARTH LORE: LEGEND
OF BEK LARSON
Eternity
1 . . . . 2.25

EARTH LORE: REIGN
OF DRAGON LORD
1 . . . . 2.25
2 . . . . 2.25

EARTH WAR
Newcomers Publishing, 1995
1 and 2 from Newcomers Illus. 3.00

EARTH: YEAR ZERO
Eclipse
1 thru 4 . . . . @2.25

EASY WAY
IDW Publishing, 2005
1 . . . . 4.00
2 thru 4 . . . . @4.00

EAT-MAN
Viz Communications, 1997
1 (of 6) by Akihito Yoshitami 3.00
2 thru 6 . . . . @3.00

PART TWO, 1998
1 (of 5) by Akihito Yoshitami 3.00
2 (of 5) 3.50
3 thru 5 . . . . @3.25

EB'NN THE RAVEN
Now
1 . . . . 5.00
2 . . . . 3.00
3 . . . . 2.50
4 . . . . 2.25
5 thru 9 . . . . @2.25

EBONIX-FILES, THE
Blatant Comics, 1998
1A TV parody, cover A 4.00
1B TV parody, cover B 4.00

ED THE HAPPY CLOWN
Drawn & Quarterly, 2005
1 (of 9) 3.00
2 thru 3 . . . . @3.00
4 thru 9 . . . . @3.00

EDDIE CAMPELL'S
BACCHUS
Eddie Campell Comics, 1995
1 V:Telchines. 7.00
1 2nd printing 3.00
2 thru 10 V:Telchines 4.00
11 thru 26 ECa . . . . @3.00
27 thru 37 ECa . . . . @3.00
38 thru 46 . . . . @3.00
47 thru 56 . . . . @3.00
57 thru 60 . . . . @3.00

EDDY CURRENT
Mad Dog, 1987
1 thru 12 . . . . @2.50

EDGAR ALLAN POE
Eternity, 1988
1 Black Cat 2.50
2 Pit & Pendulum 2.50
3 Masque of the Red Death 2.50
4 Murder in the Rue Morgue 2.50
5 Tell Tale Heart 2.50

EDGE
1 . . . . 3.00
Vol 2 #1 thru #3 . . . . @3.00
Vol 2 #4 thru #6 . . . . @2.50

Eightball #1
© Fantagraphics

EIGHTBALL
Fantagraphics, 1989
1 . . . . 11.00
2 . . . . 8.00
3 . . . . 7.00
4 . . . . 6.00
1a thru 4a later printings . . . . @3.00
5 thru 8 . . . . @6.00
9 thru 10 . . . . @4.00
11 A:Ghost World 4.00
12 F:Ghost World 4.00
13 thru 19 . . . . @4.00
20 . . . . 5.00
21 48-pg. 5.00
22 . . . . 7.00
23 . . . . 7.00

ELFLORD
Aircel, 1986
1 I:Hawk 5.00
1a 2nd printing 3.50
2 . . . . 3.00
2a 2nd printing 2.50
3 V:Doran 3.00
4 V:Doran 3.00
5 V:Doran 2.50
6 V:Nendo 2.50
Compilation Book 5.00

(Vol 2), #1 to #24, see Color
25 thru 31 . . . . @2.50
32 . . . . 2.50

ELFLORD:
RETURN OF THE KING
Nightwynd, 1992
1 . . . . 2.50
2 thru 4 . . . . @2.50

B & W PUB.

ELFLORD: SUMMER MAGIC
Nightwynd, 1993
thru 4 . . . . @2.50

ELFLORD
Warp Graphics, 1997
1 (of 4) by Barry Blair & Colin Chan 3.00
2 thru 4 . . . . @3.00

ELFLORD: ALL THE LONELY PLACES
Warp Graphics, 1997
1 (of 4) Barry Blair & Colin Chan . . . 3.00
Becomes:

HAWK AND WINDBLADE: ALL THE LONELY PLACES
2 (of 2) 3.00

ELFLORD CHRONICLES
Aircel, 1990
1 (of 12) thru 8 rep B.Blair . . . . . @2.50

ELFLORD CUTS LOOSE
Warp Graphics, 1997
1 by Barry Blair and Colin Chan . . . 3.00
2 F:Hawk Erik-san 3.00
3 . . . . 3.00
4 all out attack 3.00
5 north to safety 3.00
6 homeward 3.00
7 back to Greenhaven 3.00
8 Greenhaven Siege 3.00
9 Felines, Nothing More Than
　Felines 3.00

ELFLORD: HAWK
China Winds, 1998
1-shot by Barry Blair and
　Colin Chan 3.50

ELFLORE: THE HIGH SEAS
Raw Comics
4 by Barry Blair (500 copies) 5.00

ELFQUEST
Warp Graphics, 1979–85
1 WP 30.00
1a WP,2nd printing 9.00
1b WP,3rd printing 5.00
1c WP,4th printing (1989) 4.00
2 WP 16.00
3 WP 12.00
4 WP 12.00
5 WP 12.00
6 WP 12.00
2a thru 6a WP,2nd printing . . . . . @4.00
7 WP 10.00
8 WP 10.00
9 WP 10.00
2a thru 9a WP,later printings . . . . @3.00
10 thru 15 . . . . @6.00
16 WP,I:DistantSoil 8.00
17 thru 21 WP . . . . @5.00
Warp Graphics, 1996
4 thru 14 ed. RPi . . . . @5.00
15 . . . . 5.50
16 What if Cutter never
　became chief 5.50
17 F:Fire-Eye 5.50
18 Dreamtime, concl. 5.50
19 Wolfrider begins 5.50
20 . . . . 5.50

21 20th anniv. 5.50
22 F:Wolfrider 5.00
23 F:WaveDancers 5.00
24 F:Wolfrider 5.00
25 F:Wolfrider 5.00
26 Wild Hunt 5.00
27 . . . . 5.00
28 F:Ember & Teir 5.00
29 three new stories 5.00
30 new stories 5.00
31 new stories 5.00
32 Wild Hunt,pt.1, 24-pg. 3.50
33 Wild Hunt,pt.2 . . . . 3.50
34 Wild Hunt,pt.3 . . . . 3.50
35 Wild Hunt,pt.4 . . . . 3.50
Spec.#1 Worldpool,pt.1 (1997) . . . 3.50
Spec.#2 Worldpool,pt.2 (1997) . . . 3.50
Spec. Metamorphosis, WP,
　RPi (1996) 3.00
Spec. Elfquest: Wolfrider 3.00
Summer Spec. 2001 Recognition . . 3.00
Summer Spec. 2001 Wolfshadow . . 4.00

ELFQUEST: KAHVI
Warp Graphics, 1995
1 thru 6 I:Kahvi . . . . @2.25

ELFQUEST: KINGS OF THE BROKEN WHEEL
Warp Graphics, 1990–92
1 thru 9 WP . . . . @2.25

Elfquest: Seige at Blue Mountain #1
© Warp Graphics/Apple

ELFQUEST: SEIGE AT BLUE MOUNTAIN
Warp Graphics/Apple Comics, 1987–88
1 WP,JSo 7.00
1a 2nd printing 3.00
2 WP 6.00
2a 2nd printing 3.00
3 WP 5.00
3a 2nd printing 2.50
4 thru 8 WP . . . . @5.00

ELFQUEST: TWO SPEAR
Warp Graphics, 1995
1 thru 3 (of 5) Two-Spears past . @2.25

ELFQUEST: WORLDPOOL
Warp Graphics, 1997
Spec.#1 & 2 (of 2) . . . . @3.00

ELFTREK
Dimension, 1986
1 Elfquest's Star Trek parody 2.50
2 . . . . 2.50

ELF WARRIOR
Adventure, 1987
1 . . . . 3.00
2 thru 5 . . . . @2.50

EL HAZARD: THE MAGNIFICENT WORLD
Viz Communications, 2000
1 by Hidetomo Tsubura 3.00
2 thru 5 . . . . @3.00
Part 2, 2001
1 . . . . 3.00
2 thru 5 . . . . @3.00
Part 3, 2001
1 (of 6) 3.00
2 thru 6 . . . . @3.00

ELIMINATOR
Eternity
1 `Drugs in the Future' 2.50
2 . . . . 2.50

ELVIRA, MISTRESS OF THE DARK
Claypool Comics, 1993
1 . . . . 6.00
2 thru 35 . . . . @4.00
36 thru 74 photo covers . . . . @3.50
75 Mistress of the Jungle,pt.1 . . . . 3.50
76 Mistress of the Jungle,pt.2 . . . . 3.50
77 Rome on the Range 3.50
78 thru 90 photo covers . . . . @3.50
91 thru 103 . . . . @3.00
104 thru 127 . . . . @3.00
128 thru 138 . . . . @2.50
139 thru 150 . . . . @2.50
151 thru 166 . . . . @2.50

ELVIRA
Eclipse
1 Rosalind Wyck 2.50

EMBRACE: HUNGER OF THE FLESH
London Night, 1997
1 DQ,last of the original
　vampire race 3.00
1a DQ,deluxe 6.00
1b signed by Kevin West 12.00
2 DQ 3.00
2a DQ,deluxe 6.00
3 by Dan Membiela & Kevin
　West, concl. 3.00

EMERALDAS
Eternity, 1990
1 thru 4 . . . . @2.25

EMMA DAVENPORT
Lohamn Hill Press, 1995
1 I:Emma Davenport 2.75
2 . . . . 2.75
3 O:Hammerin Jim 2.75
4 Cookie Woofer War 2.75

EMO BOY
Amaze Ink/SLG, 2005
1 . . . . 3.00
2 thru 11 . . . . @3.00

EMPIRE
Eternity, 1988
1 . . . . 2.50
2 thru 4 . . . . @2.50

Empire Lanes #4
© Northern Lights

EMPIRE LANES
Northern Lights, 1986–87
1 . . . . 2.50
2 thru 4 . . . . @2.50

EMPTY ZONE
Sirius, 1998
1 by Jason Alexander 3.00
1a limited edition. 5.00
2 thru 4 . . . . 2.50
VOL. 2 TRANSMISSIONS, 1999
1 by Jason Alexander 3.00
2 thru 7 . . . . @3.00
8 History Lessions,pt.1 . . . . 3.00

EMPTY ZONE: CONVERSATIONS WITH THE DEAD
Sirius Entertainment, 2002
1 (of 5) by Jason Alexander 3.00
2 thru 3 . . . . @3.00

ENCHANTED
Sirius, 1997
1 (of 3) by Robert Chang 3.00
2 and 3 . . . . @3.00

ENCHANTED VALLEY
Blackthorne, 1987
1 . . . . 2.25
2 . . . . 2.25

ENCHANTER
Eclipse, 1987
1 . . . . 2.50
2 thru 3 . . . . @2.50

ENCHANTER: APOCALYPSE WIND NOVELLA
Entity
1 Foil Enhanced Cover. 3.00

ENFORCERS
Dark Visions Publishing, 1995
0 From Anthology Title 2.50

ENNIS AND MCCREA'S BIGGER DICKS
Avatar Press, 2002
1 (of 4) GEn,JMC,F:Dougie & Ivor . 5.00
1a Guaranteed to Offend cover . . . 5.00
2 thru 4 . . . . @5.00
2a thru 4a offensive (c) . . . . @5.00

ENNIS AND MCCREA'S DICKS 2
Avatar Press, 2002
1 (of 4) 3.50
2 thru 4 . . . . @3.50
1a thru 4a offensive (c) . . . . @4.00
X-Mas Spec. #1 . . . . 3.50
X-Man Spec. #1 offensive (c) 4.00

ENTROPY TALES
Entropy
1 . . . . 2.25
2 Domino Chance. 2.25
3 thru 5 . . . . @2.25

EPSILON WAVE
Elite
1 . . . . 3.00
2 thru 5 . . . . @2.25

EQUINE THE UNCIVILIZED
GraphXpress
1 . . . . 4.00
2 . . . . 2.50
3 thru 6 . . . . @2.25

EQUINOX CHRONICLES
Innovation, 1991
1 I:Team Equinox, Black Avatar . . . 2.25
2 Black Avatar Plans US conquest. 2.25

ERADICATORS
Greater Mercury, 1990–91
1 RLm (1st Work) 5.00
1a 2nd printing 2.25
2 . . . . 2.50
3 Vigil 2.25
4 thru 8 . . . . @2.25

ERIC PRESTON IS THE FLAME
B-Movie Comics, 1987
1 Son of G.A.Flame 2.50

ESCAPE TO THE STARS
Visionary
1 . . . . 2.25
2 thru 7 . . . . @2.25
[2nd Series]
1 . . . . 2.25
2 . . . . 2.25

ESCAPE VELOCITY
Escape Velocity Press, 1986
1 and 2 . . . . @2.50

ESMERALDAS
Eternity
1 . . . . 2.25
2 thru 4 . . . . 2.25

ESP
Curtis Comics, 2002
Vol. 1 Manga
1 by Jihoon Park & Takyoung Lee . 3.00
2 thru 5 . . . . @3.00
Vol. 2
1 . . . . 3.00

ESPERS
Halloween Comics, 1996
1 JHI, R:ESPers 3.00
1 JHI,signed 3.00
2 JHI,signed 3.00
3 JHI, ... 3.00
3 JHI,signed 3.00
4 thru 6 JHI, conclusion . . . . @3.00
Volume 2
1 `Undertow' 3.00
2 . . . . 3.00

ETERNITY TRIPLE ACTION
Malibu B&W
1 F:Gazonga. 2.25
2 F:Gigantor 2.50

EVENFALL
Amaze Ink/SLG, 2003
3 . . . . 3.00
4 . . . . 3.00
5 . . . . 3.00
6 thru 8 . . . . @3.00

EVENT PRESENTS THE ASH UNIVERSE
Event Comics, 1998
1-shot JQ,JP, 48pg 3.00

EVERETTE HARTSOE'S RAZOR
EH! Productions, 2000
1 . . . . 3.50
1a Ruby Foil 5.00
2 . . . . 4.00

EVIL ERNIE
Eternity, 1991–92
1 SHu,BnP,I&O:Evil Ernie,
  Lady Death 65.00
1a Spec. 1992 reprint, 16 extra
  pages. 24.00
2 Death & Revival of Ernie,
  A:Lady Death, 1st (c) 25.00
3 Psycho Plague, A:Lady Death . . 22.00
4 A:Lady Death 20.00
5 A:Lady Death 20.00

EVIL ERNIE
Chaos! Comics
1 thru 5 reprints . . . . @3.00
Spec. Youth Gone Wild, die-cut
  cover, Director's cut. 5.00
Chaos! Comics, 1996
1 encore presentation 3.00
2 thru 5 encore presentation. 3.00
TPB Revenge. 13.00
Preview Book Depraved 5.00
Pieces of Me Script 5.00

EVIL ERNIE: THE HORROR
Chaos! Comics, 2002
Ashcan b&w. 6.00
1 BnP 4.50
1a premium edition 10.00

B & W PUB.

1b signed edition. 15.00
1c super-premium edition. 20.00
Spec. Script edition. 5.00
Spec. Script Edition, premium 20.00

EVIL ERNIE: MANHATTAN DEATH TRIP
Chaos! Comics, 2002
1 BnP 3.50
1a premium edition. 10.00
1b super-premium edition. 20.00
Spec. #1 script. 5.00
Spec. #1 script, premium edition . . 20.00

EVIL ERNIE RETURNS
Chaos! Comics, 2001
1 BnP 4.00
1a premium edition. 9.00
1b super premium edition. 15.00
1c signed ed.. . . . . 11.00
Ashcan 6.00
Script #1 . . . . 5.00
Script #1 premium edition 15.00

EVIL EYE
Fantagraphics, 1998
1 by Richard Sala 3.00
2 Glass Scorpion,pt.2 . . . . 3.00
3 thru 7 . . . . @3.00
8 thru 11 . . . . @3.50
12 . . . . 4.00

EXIT
Caliber, 1995
1 I:New series 3.00
2 thru 4 `The Traitors,'pt.2–pt.4 . . 3.00
Epilogue. 3.00

EX LIBRIS
Amaze Ink/SLG, 2005
1 by James Turner 3.00
2 thru 6 . . . . @3.00

Ex-Mutants #4
© Amazing Comics

EX-MUTANTS
Amazing Comics, 1986
1 AC/RLm. 5.00
1a 2nd printing 2.25
2 and 3 . . . . @3.00
4 and 5 . . . . @2.25
Ann. #1. . . . . 2.25
Pin-Up Spec. #1. . . . . 2.25

Pied Piper Comics
6 thru 8 . . . . 2.25

EX-MUTANTS: THE SHATTERED EARTH CHRONICLES
Eternity, 1988
1 thru 3 . . . . @2.25
4 & 5 RLd(c) . . . . @2.75
6 thru 14 . . . . @2.25
Winter Special #1 . . . . 2.25

EXPERTS, THE
Near Mint Press, 2006
1 . . . . 3.00
2 . . . . 3.00
3 . . . . 3.50

EXPLORERS
Caliber Tapestry, 1997
1 . . . . 3.00
2 . . . . 3.00
3 `Nahuatl' 3.00
4 `The Sky is Falling' 3.00

EXTINCTIONERS
Shanda Fantasy Arts VOL 2, 1999
1 . . . . 3.00
2 thru 9 . . . . @3.00
10 thru 15 48-pg. . . . . @5.00
Spec. #2 Tales of the Endangered. . 5.00
Spec. #3 Tales of the Endangered. . 5.00

EXTREMELY SILLY
Antarctic Press
1 . . . . 4.00
Vol. II, 1996
1 . . . . 2.25
2 . . . . 2.25

EYE OF MONGOMBO
Fantagraphics Books, 1990–91
1 . . . . 3.00
2 thru 7 . . . . @2.25

FADE FROM BLUE
Second to Some Studios 2002
1 by Murphy & Dalrymple. 2.50
1a second printing 2.00
2 thru 8 . . . . @2.00
9 . . . . 2.00
10 concl. 48-pg. 5.00

FAITH
Lightning Comics, 1997
1 (of 2) 3.00
1a variant cover 3.00
1b Limited, cover A. 9.00
1c Limited, cover B. 9.00
1d signed & numbered 9.00
1 encore edition 3.00
1a encore, cover B 3.00
1b deluxe encore edition, cover A . 9.00
1c deluxe encore edition, cover B . 9.00

FAMILY BONES
King Tractor, 2006
1 (of 10) 3.50
2 thru 4 . . . . @3.50
5 . . . . 2.75

FANG: TESTAMENT
Sirius, 1997
1 by Kevin J. Taylor 2.50

2 . . . . 2.50
3 . . . . 2.50
4 (of 4) 2.50

FANGS OF THE WIDOW
London Night Studios, 1995
1 O:The Widow. 3.00
1a platinum edition. 5.00
2 Body Count 3.00
3 Emma Revealed 3.00
4 and 5 . . . . @3.00
Ground Zero, 1995
7 thru 9 `Metal Gypsies,'pt.#1–#3 @3.00
10 thru 13 rep. Widow: Bound by
Blood #1–#4 + additional
material 3.50
14 `Search and Destroy'pt.1 . . . . 3.00
15 `Search and Destroy'pt.2 . . . . 3.00
Ann. #1 Search and Destroy 6.00

FANTASCI
Warp Graphics-Apple, 1986
1 . . . . 2.50
2 and 3 . . . . @2.25
4 . . . . 4.00
5 thru 8 . . . . @2.25
9 `Apple Turnover' 2.25

FANTASTIC ADVENTURES
1 thru 5 . . . . @2.25

FANTASTIC FABLES
Silver Wolf, 1987
1 and 2 . . . . @2.25

FANTASTIC PANIC
Antarctic, 1993–94
1 thru 8 Ganbear. . . . . @2.75
Vol. 2, 1995
1 thru 4 . . . . @2.75
4 thru 9 . . . . @3.00
10 concl. 3.50

FANTASTIC STORIES
Basement Comics, 2001
1 F:Grakoom, the Forgotten God . . 3.00
1a special edition 9.00
2 Lost Women of the Moon 3.00
2a special edition 9.00
3 . . . . 3.00
3a special edition 9.00

FANTASTIC WORLDS
Flashback Comics, 1995
1 Space Opera 3.00
2 F:Attu, Captain Courage 3.00

FANTASY QUARTERLY
Independent, 1976
1 1978 1st Elfquest. 65.00

FART WARS: SPECIAL EDITION
Entity Comics, 1997
1 Star Wars trilogy parody,A:Nira X 2.75
1a Empire Attacks Back cover . . . 2.75
1b Return of the One-Eye cover. . . 2.75

FAR WEST
Antarctic Press, 1998
1 (of 4) by Richard Moore. 3.00
2 thru 4 . . . . @3.00
VOL. 2
1 (of 4) 3.00
2 . . . . 2.50

FASTLANE ILLUSTRATED
Fastlane Studios, 1994
1 Super Powers & Hot Rods 2.50
2 & 3 . . . . @2.50

FATALIS
Caliber Core, 1998
1 by Mark Chadbourn
  & Vince Danks. 3.00
1a signed & numbered 7.00
2 . . . . 3.00

FAT NINJA
Silver Wolf Comics, 1985–86
1 . . . . 2.50
2 Vigil 2.50
3 thru 8 . . . . @2.50

FAUST
Northstar, 1985
1 Vigil 25.00
1a Vigil,2nd Printing 4.00
1b Vigil,3rd Printing. 3.00
1c Tour Edition 25.00
2 Vigil 13.00
2a Vigil,2nd Printing 3.00
2b Vigil,3rd Printing. 2.50
3 Vigil 10.00
3a Vigil,2nd Printing 2.50
4 Vigil 5.00
5 Vigil 5.00
6 Vigil 5.00

Rebel Studios
7 Vigil 5.00
8 TV 3.50
9 TV,Love of the Damned 3.50
10 E:DQ(s),TV,Love o/t Damned . . . 3.50

VOL. II
1 TV,Love of the Damned 2.50

FAUST/777: THE WRATH
Avatar Press, 1998
0 by David Quinn & Tim Vigil,
  Darkness in Collision x-over . . . 3.00
0a wrap 4.00
0b leather cover 15.00
0c Royal Blue edition 50.00
0d Platinum edition 12.00
1 (of 4) 3.50
2 Darkness in Collision,pt.3 . . . . . 3.50
3 . . . . 3.50
4 . . . . 3.50
Faust Hornbook 5.00

FAUST: SINGHA'S TALONS
Avatar, 2000
1/2 . . . . 3.50
1/2 wraparound (c). 4.00
1/2 Beachum (c) 6.00
1/2 prism foil 11.00
1/2 royal blue edition 60.00
1/2 Blood Curse 5.00
1 (of 4) 4.00
1a wraparound (c). 4.50
1c red foil leather 25.00
1d prism foil 13.00
1 commemorative 6.00
2 . . . . 4.00
3 . . . . 4.00
4 . . . . 4.00
2a thru 4a previews exclusive . . . @4.50
Preview Book 6.00

FELIX THE CAT
Felix Comics, 1997
1 inc. Felix's Cafe 2.25

2 Crusin' for a Brusin' 2.25
3 Ah Choo 2.25
4 inc. Spaced Out 2.25
5 Holiday/Winter issue 2.25
6 The Felix Force 2.25
7 A Rash of Trash 2.25
8 Halloween 2.25
Cat-A-Strophic Wrestling Spec.#1 . . 2.25
Felix Summer Splash #1 . . . . 2.50

FELIX THE CAT TRUE CRIME STORIES
Felix Comics, 2000
1 . . . . 2.50
Spec.#1 Blockbuster movie
  bonanza. 2.50
Spec. Felix Jurassic Jamboree 2.50
Spec. Felix Magic Bag of Tricks . . . 2.50
Spec. Felix Laff-A-Palooza 2.50
1-shot Felix's Totally Wacky News. . 2.50
1-shot Halloween Spectacular #13 . 2.50
1-shot House of 1000 Ha Ha's 2.50
1-shot Felix the Cat's TV
  Extravaganza (2002) 2.50
1-shot Buy This Comic. 2.50
1-shot Amazing Colossal
  Felix the Cat 2.50
1-shot Silly Stories #1 . . . . 2.50

FEM FANTASTIQUE
AC Comics, 1988
1 . . . . 2.50

FEMFORCE
AC Comics, 1987
1 thru 15 See Color
16 I:Thunder Fox 3.00
17 F:She-Cat,Ms.Victory, giant . . . 3.00
18 double size 3.00
19 . . . . 3.00
20 V:RipJaw, Black Commando . . . 3.00
21 V:Dr.Pretorius 3.00
22 V:Dr.Pretorius 3.00
23 V:Rad 3.00
24 A:Teen Femforce. 3.00
25 V:Madame Boa 3.00
26 V:Black Shroud 3.00
27 V:Black Shroud 3.00
28 A:Arsenio Hall 3.00
29 V:Black Shroud 3.00
30 V:Garganta 3.00
31 I:Kronon Captain Paragon 3.00
32 V:Garganta 3.00
33 Personal Lives of team 3.00
34 V:Black Shroud 3.00
35 V:Black Shroud 3.00
36 giant,V:Dragonfly,Shade 3.00
37 A:Blue Bulleteer,She-Cat 3.00
38 V:Lady Luger. 3.00
39 F:She-Cat 3.00
40 V:Sehkmet 3.00
41 V:Captain Paragon 3.00
42 V:Alizarin Crimson 3.00
43 V:Glamazons of Galaxy G 3.00
44 V:Lady Luger,F:Garganta 5.00
45 Nightveil Rescued 3.00
46 V:Lady Luger. 3.00
47 V:Alizarin Crimson 3.00
48 . . . . 3.00
49 I:New Msw.Victory 3.00
50 Ms.Victory Vs.Rad,flexi-disc . . . 3.00
51 . . . . 3.00
52 V:Claw & Clawites 3.00
53 I:Bulldog Deni,V:(Dick
  Briefer's)Frightenstein 3.00
54 The Orb of Bliss 3.00
55 R:Nightveil. 3.00
56 V:Alizarin Crimson 3.00
57 thru 92 See Color
93 `Shattered Memories,'pt.2 . . . 3.00

Femforce #88
© AC Comics

93a deluxe 6.00
94 `Shattered Memories,'pt.3 . . . . . 3.00
94a deluxe 6.00
95 . . . . 3.00
95a deluxe 6.00
96 . . . . 3.00
96a deluxe 6.00
97 . . . . 3.00
98 deluxe 6.00
98 . . . . 3.00
98 deluxe 6.00
99 . . . . 3.00
99 deluxe 6.00
100 Anniv. issue, with poster 8.00
100A signed, with poster 11.00
100B no poster, not signed 4.00

THE YESTERDAY SYNDROME
101 Pt.1 . . . . 5.00
102 Pt.2 . . . . 5.00
103 Pt.3 . . . . 5.00

RETURN FROM THE ASHES
104 pt.1 Firebeam, 44pg 5.00
105 pt.2 . . . . 5.00
106 pt.3 concl. 5.00

DARKGODS: RAMPAGE
107 Darkgods: Rampage,pt.1 . . . . . 5.00
108 Darkgods: Rampage,pt.2 . . . . . 5.00
109 Darkgods: Rampage,pt.3 . . . . . 6.00
110 thru 117 . . . . @6.00
118 44-pg. 7.00
118a spec. edition, 60-pg. 9.00
119 The Missing Mask. 7.00
120 Superbabes,pt.1 . . . . 7.00
121 Superbabes,pt.2 . . . . 7.00
121a Femme Noir (c). 10.00
122 Superbabes,pt.3 . . . . 7.00
122a spec. editions, variant(c). . . @9.00
123 . . . . 7.00
124 . . . . 7.00
125 Firebeam Rising 7.00
126 Totally Absorbed 7.00
127 No Return 7.00
128 Halloween Special 7.00
129 Shorty 7.00
130 20th Anniversary issue 7.00
131 F:Rad and the Black Terror. . . . 7.00
132 Buckaroo Betty Bates. 7.00
133 Too Tall Tara 7.00
134 Generation Gap 7.00
135 Multitude of foes 7.00
136 Welcome to the Jungle 7.00
137 . . . . 7.00
138 thru 142 . . . . @7.00

Spec.#1 FemForce Timelines,
O:Femforce (1995) 3.00
Spec.#1 FemForce:Frightbook,
Horror tales by Briefer,
Ayers, Powell 3.00
Spec.#2 (2001) 6.00
Spec.#1 Femforce:Uncut (2001) . . 10.00
Untold Origin of FemForce 5.00
Secret Files of Femforce, deluxe. . . 5.00
Pulp Fiction Portfolio #2. . . . . 18.00
Spec. #1 Femforce vs. The Claw. . . 7.00
Spec. #1 Rampaging She-Cat 7.00
1-shot Claws of the She-Cat 5.00
Features #1: Giantess 7.00

FEMFORCE SPECIAL
AC Comics, 1999
1 Femforce Special: Rayda–
The Cyberian Connection 3.00
1a Variant cover 3.00
1b Variant cover, signed 9.00
2 . . . . 3.00
3 conclusion 4.00

FEVER, THE
Dark Vision Publishing, 1995
1 O:The Fever. 2.50
2 Fever's Father 2.50
3 thru 5 . . . . @2.50

FIFTIES TERROR
Eternity, 1988
1 thru 6 . . . . @2.50

FIGHTING YANK
AC Comics, 2001
1 by Hack Koilby. 6.00
2 . . . . 6.00
3 Cave Girl 6.00
4 . . . . 6.00
5 Three Chambers of Horror 6.00

FINAL CYCLE
Sirius
Graphic Novel 4.00
1 thru 4 . . . . @2.25

FINDER
Lightspeed Comics, 1996
1 thru 5 by Carla Speed McNeil . @3.00
6 thru 19 . . . . @3.00
20 thru 24 . . . . @3.00
25 thru 38 . . . . @3.00

FINDER FOOTNOTES
Lightspeed Press
1 thru 4 . . . . @6.00

FIRE TEAM
Aircel, 1990
1 thru 3 by Don Lomax . . . . @2.50
4 V:Vietnamese Gangs 2.50
5 Cam in Vietnam 2.50
6 . . . . 2.50

FIRST WAVE
Andromeda Entertainment, 2001
1 Patriot or Traitor. 3.00
1a signed 9.00
GN Through Alien Eyes 8.00

FIRST WAVE:
DOUBLE VISION
Andromeda Entertainment, 2001
1 (of 2) 3.00
1a photo (c). 3.00

FIRST WAVE: GENESIS
OF A GENIUS
Andromeda Entertainment, 2001
Spec. painted (c) 3.00
Spec. photo (c). 3.00

FISH POLICE
Fishwrap Productions, 1985
1 1st printing 7.00
1a 2nd printing 3.00
Becomes:

INSPECTOR GILL
OF THE FISH POLICE
2 . . . . 5.00
3 thru 11 . . . . @4.00

[Vol 2]
Comico Publ., 1987
5 thru 12 . . . . @3.50
13 thru 17 **see Color issues**
Apple Publ.
18 thru 24 . . . . @2.50

FISH SHTICKS
Apple, 1991
1 and 2 Fish Police . . . . @2.75
3 and 4 . . . . @2.50

FIST OF GOD
Eternity, 1988
1 thru 4 . . . . @2.50

FIST OF THE
NORTH STAR
Viz Select, 1996
1 thru 3 . . . . @3.25
4 . . . . 2.25
5 . . . . 3.25
6 . . . . 3.00
7 . . . . 3.00

Part Three
1 thru 5 by Buronson
& Tetsuo Hara . . . . @3.00

Part Four, 1996
1 thru 7 . . . . @3.00

FLAG FIGHTERS
Ironcat, 1997
1 by Masaomi Kanzaki 3.00

Flaming Carrot #1
© Aardvark-Vanaheim

2 Student Flagger,pt.1 . . . . 3.00
3 Student Flagger,pt.2 . . . . 3.00
4 Student Flagger,pt.3 . . . . 3.00
5 . . . . 3.00
6 Death Window 3.00
7 F:Murasame 3.00

FLAMING CARROT
Aardvark–Vanaheim, 1984
1 1981 Killian Barracks. 50.00
1a 1984. . . . . 25.00
2 . . . . 20.00
3 . . . . 17.00
4 thru 6 . . . . @12.00
Renegade
7 . . . . 10.00
8 . . . . 9.00
9 & 10 . . . . @8.00
11 & 12. . . . . @6.00
13 thru 15. . . . . @5.00
15a variant without cover price . . . 8.00
16 and 17. . . . . @5.00
See: Dark Horse

FLARE
Hero Graphics, 1990
1 thru 7 See Color
8 thru 14 . . . . 3.00

FLARE FIRST EDITION
Hero Graphics, 1993
1 Flare as teenager 5.00
2 . . . . 4.00
3 thru 11 . . . . @3.50

FLARE VS. TIGRESS
Hero Graphics
1 and 2 . . . . @3.50

FORBIDDEN KINGDOM
Eastern Comics, 1987
1 thru 11 . . . . @2.25

FORBIDDEN
VAMPIRE TALES
Forbidden, 1997
0 . . . . 3.00
1 sexy vampire 3.00
2 thru 7 . . . . @3.00
Spec.#1 Vault of Innocents 3.00

FORBIDDEN WORLDS
ACG, 1996
1 SD,JAp,rep. 2.50

FORCE SEVEN
Lone Star Press, 1999
1 . . . . 3.00
2 thru 7 . . . . @3.00

FORCE 10
Crow Comics, 1995
0 Ash Can Preview 1.00
1 I:Force 10. . . . . 2.50
2 Children of the Revolution,pt#2 . . 2.50
3 Against all Odds. 2.50

FORETERNITY
Antarctic Press, 1997
1 by Rod Espinoza 3.00
2 and 3 . . . . @3.00

FOREVER WARRIORS
Aardwolf, 1996
1 (of 3) RTs,RB. 3.00

All comics prices listed are for *Near Mint* condition.

2 RTs,RB. 3.00
3 RTs,RB, concl. 3.00

FOREVER WARRIORS
CFD, 1997
1 RB,RTs. 3.00
2 RB,RTs,KN. 3.00
3 RB, RTs, finale 3.00

FORGIVE ME FATHER
High Impact, 2004
1 . . . . 3.00
2 . . . . 3.00
1a thru 2a variant (c)s . . . . @6.00
Bulletproof Comics
3 . . . . 3.00

FORTY WINKS
Oddjobs Limited, 1997
1 (of 4) by Sneed & Peters 3.00
2 Everything Right is Wrong Again . 3.00
3 Where Your Eyes Don't Go 3.00
4 There Might be Giants 3.00
Peregrine Entertainment, 1998
Christmas Spec. 3.00
TV Party Spec. 3.00
Spec.#1 Buzzboy (2000) 3.00

FORTY WINKS:
MR. HORRIBLE
Peregrine Entertainment, 2000
1 . . . . 3.00
2 . . . . 3.00

FORTY WINKS:
THE FABLED PIRATE
QUEEN OF THE SOUTH
CHINA SEA
Peregrine Entertainment, 1999
1 by Vincent Sneed & Martinez . . . 3.00
2 . . . . 3.00
3 . . . . 3.00

FOUR KUNOICHI:
ENTER THE SINJA
Lightning Comics, 1997
1 . . . . 3.00

FOX COMICS
1 Spec. 3.00
25 . . . . 3.00
26 . . . . 3.50

FRAGILE PROPHET
Lost in the Dark Press, 2005
1 . . . . 3.00
2 . . . . 3.00
3 . . . . 3.00

FRANK
Fantagraphics
1 JWo 3.00
2 JWo 4.00
3 . . . . 4.00
4 . . . . 4.00

FRANKENSTEIN
Eternity
1 . . . . 2.25
2 . . . . 2.25
3 . . . . 2.25

FRANKIES FRIGHTMARES
1 Celebrates Frank 60th Anniv. . . . 2.25

FRANK THE UNICORN
Fish Warp
1 thru 7 . . . . @2.25

FREAK-OUT ON
INFANT EARTHS
Blackthorne, 1987
1 Don Chin 2.50
2 Don Chin 2.50

FREAKS
Monster Comics
1 Movie adapt. 2.50
2 Movie adapt.cont. 2.50
3 thru 4 Movie adapt. . . . . @2.50

FREAKSHOW
Atomic Diner, 2004
1 . . . . 3.00
2 thru 12 . . . . @3.00

FRED THE
POSSESSED FLOWER
Happy Predator, 1998
1 The Plant Behind the Scenes . . . 3.00
2 . . . . 3.00
3 Interview with a Demon 3.00
4 The People vs. Hell 3.00
5 . . . . 3.00
6 The Origin of Fred 3.00

French Ice #1
© Renegade Press

FRENCH ICE
Renegade Press, 1987
1 thru 15 . . . . @2.50

FRIENDS
Renegade, 1987
1 thru 5 . . . . @2.50

FRIGHT
Eternity
1 . . . . 2.25
2 thru 13 . . . . @2.25

FRINGE
Caliber
1 . . . . 2.50
2 thru 7 . . . . @2.50

FROM BEYOND
Studio Insidio
1 Short stories-horror 2.50
2 inc.Clara Mutilares. 2.50
3 inc.The Experiment 2.50
4 inc.Positive Feedback 2.50

FROM HELL
Tundra, 1991
1 . . . . 20.00
1a 2nd printing 10.00
2 . . . . 10.00
Kitchen Sink
Volume Three
1 AMo,ECa 10.00
2 AMo,ECa 7.00
2a 2nd printing 6.00
3 . . . . 7.00
3a 2nd printing 6.00
4 . . . . 7.00
4 new printing 5.00
5 . . . . 7.00
5 new printing 5.00
6 . . . . 7.00
7 . . . . 7.00
8 . . . . 7.00
8 AMo,ECa,new printing 5.00
9 AMo,ECa 7.00
9 new printing 5.00
10 AMo,ECa. 7.00
10 new printing 5.00
Spec. Dance of the Gull Catchers . . 5.00

FROM THE DARKNESS
Adventure Comics, 1990
1 JBa. 20.00
2 . . . . 25.00
3 and 4 . . . . @9.00

FROM THE DARKNESS II
BLOOD VOWS
Cry For Dawn
1 R:Ray Thorn,Desnoires 9.00
2 V:Desnoires 8.00
3 . . . . 8.00

FROM THE VOID
1 1st B.Blair,1982 . . . . 60.00

FROST:
THE DYING BREED
Caliber
1 thru 3 Vietnam Flashbacks . . . @3.00

F–III BANDIT
Antarctic Press, 1995
1 F:Akira, Yoohoo 3.00
2 F:Yukio 3.00
3 F:Were-Women 3.00
4 . . . . 3.00
5 Romeo & Juliet story 3.00
6 thru 8 . . . . @3.00

FUGITOID
Mirage
1-shot TMNT Tie-in 8.00

FULL METAL FICTION
London Night, 1997
1 EHr 4.00
1a Nun with a Gun edition 9.00
1b dark room edition cover 4.00
2 . . . . 4.00
2a signed 9.00
3 'Hellborne' concl. 4.00
4 thru 8 . . . . @4.00

FURIES
Carbon-Based, 1996
1 thru 6 . . . . @2.75

FURRLOUGH
Antarctic Press, 1991
1 Funny Animal Military stories. . . . 3.00
2 thru 10 . . . . @2.50
11 thru 20. . . . . @2.75
21 thru 33. . . . . @2.75
34 . . . . 3.00
35 48pg 4.00
36 thru 40 . . . . @3.00
41 thru 51 . . . . @3.00
Best of Furlough, Vol.1 . . . . 5.00
Best of Furlough, Vol.2 . . . . 5.00
Radio Comix, 1997
52 thru 75. . . . . @3.00
76 thru 99. . . . . @3.00
100 80-pg. 6.00
101 . . . . 3.00
102 . . . . 3.00
103 thru 139. . . . . @3.00
140 thru 153 . . . . @3.50
154 thru 177. . . . . @3.50
178 . . . . 4.00
Furrlough's Finest Vol. 1 . . . . 6.00
Furrlough's Finest Vol. 2 . . . . 6.00
Furrlough Presents Sex Kitten #1 . . 5.00

FURRY NINJA HIGH SCHOOL
Shanda Fantasy Arts, 2002
1 (of 2) x-over (self) parody 5.00
2 x-over, concl. 5.00

FURY
Aircel
1 thru 3 . . . . @2.25

FURY OF HELLINA, THE
Lightning Comics, 1995
1 V:Luciver 3.50
1a limited & signed 8.00
1b platinum 8.00

FUSION
Eclipse, 1987
1 . . . . 2.50
2 thru 17 . . . . @2.50

FUTABA-KUN CHANGE
Ironcat, 1998
1 by Hiroshi Aro 3.00
2 thru 6 . . . . @3.00
VOL. 2
1 . . . . 3.00
2 thru 6 . . . . @3.00
VOL. 3, 1999
1 . . . . 3.00
2 thru 6 . . . . @3.00
VOL. 4, 2000
1 . . . . 3.00
2 thru 6 . . . . @3.00
VOL. 5, 2000
1 by Hiroshi Aro 3.00
2 thru 6 . . . . @3.00
VOL. 6, 2001
1 . . . . 3.00
2 thru 6 . . . . @3.00
VOL. 7, 2001
1 . . . . 3.00
2 thru 6 . . . . @3.00
VOL. 8
1 thru 6 . . . . @3.00

Futurama #1
© Slave Labor

FUTURAMA
Slave Labor, 1989
1 thru 4 . . . . @2.50

FUTURETECH
Mushroom Comics, 1995
1 Automotive Hi-Tech 3.50
2 Cyber Trucks 3.50

FUTURIANS
Aardwolf, 1995
0 DC R:Futurians, sequel to
  Lodestone color series 3.00
0 second printing, DC 3.00

GAIJIN
Caliber, 1990
1-shot, 64pg. 3.50
1 thru 3 . . . . @2.25

GALAXION
Helikon, 1997
1 by Tara Jenkins, science fiction . . 2.75
2 . . . . 2.75
3 . . . . 2.75
4 Choices 2.75
5 . . . . 2.75
6 Communication 2.75
7 Song of Hiawatha 2.75
8 Persuasion 2.75
9 Deal with the Devil 2.75
10 . . . . 2.75
11 . . . . 2.75
Spec. #1, 16pg. 2.00
GN Vol 1 . . . . 16.00
Spec. Flip Book Galaxion
  & Amy Unbound 2.75

GATEKEEPER
GK Publishing, 1987
1 . . . . 2.50
2 and 3 . . . . @3.00

GATES OF THE NIGHT
Jademan
1 thru 4 . . . . @3.50

GEAR
Fireman Press, 1998
1 (of 6) by Douglas TenNaple 3.00
2 thru 6 . . . . @3.00

GEISHA
Oni Press, 1998
1 (of 4) by Andi Watson 3.00
2 . . . . 3.00
3 . . . . 3.00
4 . . . . 3.00

GEMS OF THE SAMURAI
Newcomers Publishing
1 I:Master Samurai 3.00

GENERIC COMIC BOOK
Comics Conspiracy, 2001
1 thru 4 . . . . @2.25
5 . . . . 2.25
5a Hyper Fanboy variant edition. . . 6.00
6 thru 13 . . . . @2.25

GENOCYBER
Viz, 1993
1 I:Genocyber 2.75
2 thru 5 . . . . @2.75

GEOBREEDERS
CPM Manga, 1999
1 by Akhiro Ito 3.00
2 thru 10 . . . . @3.00
11 thru 36 . . . . @3.00

GERIATRIC GANGRENE JUJITSU GERBILS
Planet X Productions
1 . . . . 2.50
2 . . . . 2.25

GHOSTS OF DRACULA
Eternity
1 A:Dracula & Houdini 2.50
2 A:Sherlock Holmes 2.50
3 A:Houdini 2.50
4 Count Dracula's Castle 2.50
5 Houdini, Van Helsing, Dracula
  team-up 2.50

GI GOVERNMENT ISSUED
Paranoid Press, 1994
1 thru 7 F:Mac, Jack . . . . @2.25

GIANT SHANDA ANIMAL
Shanda Fantasy Arts, 1998
1 . . . . 5.00
2 . . . . 5.00
3 . . . . 5.00
4 . . . . 4.50
5 thru 12 . . . . @5.00

GIDEON HAWK
Big Shot Comics, 1995
1 I:Gideon Hawk, Max 9471 . . . . . 2.25
2 The Jewel of Shamboli,pt.2 . . . . . 2.25
3 The Jewel of Shamboli,pt.3 . . . . . 2.25
2 The Jewel of Shamboli,pt.4 . . . . . 2.50
3 The Jewel of Shamboli,pt.5 . . . . . 2.50

GIGANTOR
Antarctic Press, 2000
1 (of 12) by Ben Dunn 3.00
2 thru 8 . . . . @3.00

GIRL GENIUS
Studio Foglio, 2001
1 thru 5 . . . . @3.00
Airship Entertainment, 2002
6 thru 10 . . . . @4.00
11 thru 14 . . . . @4.00

GIRLS OF NINJA HIGH SCHOOL, 1997
Antarctic Press
Spec. 4.00
Spec. 1998 cover A 3.00
Spec. 1998 cover B 3.00
Spec. 1999 . . . . 3.00

GIZMO
Chance, 1986
1 . . . . 7.50

GIZMO
Mirage, 1987
1 . . . . 5.50
2 . . . . 3.00
3 . . . . 2.50
4 thru 7 . . . . @2.50

GIZMO & THE FUGITOID
Mirage, 1989
1 and 2 . . . . @2.50

GLOOM COOKIE
Slave Labor Graphics, 1999
1 by Serena Valentino
  & Ted Naifeh 3.00
2 . . . . 3.00
3 . . . . 3.00
4 . . . . 3.00
5 . . . . 3.00
6 Sebastian's Search 3.00
7 thru 9 . . . . @3.00
10 thru 25 . . . . @3.00
26 thru 29 . . . . @3.00
Color Spec. A Monster's Christmas . 4.00

GNATRAT
Prelude, 1986
1 . . . . 5.00
2 Early Years 2.25

GNATRAT: THE MOVIE
Innovation, 1990
1 . . . . 2.25

GOBBLEDYGOOK
Mirage, 1986
1 1st series, Rare 1,100.00
2 1st series, Rare 550.00
1 TMNT series reprint 6.00

GOJIN
Antarctic Press, 1995
1 F:Terran Defense Force 3.00
2 F:Terran Defense Force 3.00
3 V:Alien Monster 3.00
4 Aliens Bone 3.00
5 thru 8 . . . . @3.00

GOLD DIGGER
Antarctic Press, 1992
[Limited Series]
1 Geena & Cheetah in Peru 8.00
2 Adventures contd. 6.00
3 Adventures contd 6.00
4 Adventures contd 5.00

[Volume 2], 1993
1 by Fred Perry 10.00
2 Fred Perry 8.00
3 Fred Perry 8.00
4 Fred Perry 6.00
5 misnumbered as #0 . . . . 5.00
6 thru 8 by Fred Perry . . . . @4.00
9 and 10 by Fred Perry . . . . @3.50

Gold Digger #11
© Antarctic Press

11 thru 27 by Fred Perry . . . . @3.00
28 and 29 by Fred Perry . . . . @3.00
30 thru 39 . . . . @3.00
40 Wedding day 3.00
41 Gold Digger Beta 3.00
42 . . . . 3.00
43 Beta Phase phenomenon 3.00
44 Beta tool 3.00
45 F:Priestess Tanya 3.00
46 Agent M. 3.00
47 Old Dirty Bastard 3.00
48 . . . . 3.00
49 The Library of Time 3.00
50 . . . . 3.00
50a deluxe 6.00
Ann. 1995, 48-pg. 4.00
Ann. 1996 . . . . 4.00
Ann. 1997 . . . . 4.00
Ann. 1998 . . . . 4.00
Ann. 2000 b&w 4.00
Ann. 2001 . . . . 4.00
Ann. 2002 B&W 4.00
Best of Gold Digger Ann. Vol. 1 . . . 3.00
Mangazine Spec. #1 . . . . 3.00

GOLD DIGGER/ NINJA HIGH SCHOOL
Antarctic Press, 1998
Spec. Asrial vs. Cheetah Compilation,
  x-over rep. 5.00
Spec. Science Fair Compilation,
  x-over rep. 5.00

GOLD DIGGER: EDGE GUARD
Radio Comix, 2000
1 (of 4) by John Barrett 3.00
2 thru 6 . . . . @3.00
7 finale 3.00

GOLD DIGGER: THRONE OF SHADOWS
Antarctic Press, 2006
1 Manga 3.00
2 thru 4 . . . . @3.00

GOLDEN AGE GREATS
AC Comics, 1995
Vol.#1 thru #6 40s and 50s . . . . @10.00
Vol. 7 Best of the West 10.00

Vol. 8 F:Phantom Lady, Miss
  Victory 10.00
Vol. 9 Fabulous Femmes of Fiction
  House 10.00
Vol. 11 Roy Rogers & The Silver
  Screen Cowboys 12.00
Vol. 12 Thrilling Science Fiction . . . 10.00
Vol. 13 . . . . 10.00
Vol. 14 The Comic Book Jungle . . 12.00

GOLDEN-AGE MEN OF MYSTERY
AC Comics, 1996
5 . . . . 7.00
7 . . . . 6.00
8 . . . . 6.00
9 . . . . 6.00
10 Masked comic book
  heroes, 52 pg. 7.00
11 rep. Cat-Man comics 7.00
12 Espionage, WE 7.00
13 F:Daredevil vs. The Claw 7.00
14 F:Commando Yank 7.00
15 F:Captain 3-D 7.00
16 F:Mr. Scarlet, Airboy 7.00
Becomes:

MEN OF MYSTERY
AC Comics, 1999
17 F:Stuntman 7.00
18 . . . . 7.00
19 Space edition 7.00
19a spec. ed. 68-pg. 9.00
20 F:Phantom Lady 7.00
21 Fawcett superheroes 7.00
22 Manhunter 7.00
23 Skyman 7.00
24 Captain Flash 7.00
25 . . . . 7.00
26 Emerald 7.00
27 The Fog Robbers 7.00
28 F:Black Terror,Miss Masque 7.00
29 The Lynx, Wildfire 7.00
30 War Years 7.00
31 Speed and Space 7.00
32 Phantom Lady 7.00
33 Red white and blue 7.00
34 Halloween Issue 7.00
35 F:Spy Smasher 7.00
36 F:Captain Flash 7.00
37 F:Cat-Man and Kitten 7.00
38 Spy Smasher vs. Iron Mask 7.00
39 Spy Smasher, Airboy 7.00
40 The Black Terror 7.00
41 Bulletman 7.00
42 Blue Bolt 7.00
43 The Flame 7.00
44 Cat-Man and Bulletman 7.00
45 thru 55 . . . . @7.00
56 thru 69 . . . . @7.00
Coll. Ed. #7 . . . . 20.00
Digest Spec. #1 . . . . 16.00
Spotlight Spec. #1 . . . . 15.00
Ann. #1 Spy Smasher Special 8.00

GOLDEN WARRIOR
Industrial Design, 1997
1 by Eric Bansen & RB 3.00
2 . . . . 3.00
3 . . . . 3.00

GOLDEN WARRIOR ICZER ONE
Antarctic, 1994
1 thru 5 . . . . @3.00

GOLDWYN 3-D
Blackthorne
1 . . . . 2.25

GO-MAN
Caliber
1 . . . . 2.25
2 thru 4 . . . . @2.25
Graphic Novel `N' 10.00

GOOD GIRL COMICS
AC
1 F:Tara Fremont 4.00

GOOD GIRLS
Fantagraphics, 1987
1 adult. 2.50
2 thru 4 . . . . @2.50

GOON, THE
Avatar Press, 1999
1 by Eric Powell 40.00
2 . . . . 20.00
3 . . . . 20.00

GORE SHRIEK
Fantaco, 1986
1 . . . . 2.50
2 and 3 . . . . @2.50
4 +Mars Attacks 3.00
5 . . . . 3.00
6 . . . . 3.50
Vol 2 #1 . . . . 2.50

GORI LORI
Chanting Monks 2006
1 . . . . 2.50
2 thru 3 . . . . @2.50

GOTHESS:
DARK ECSTASY
SCC Entertainment, 1997
1 (of 3) 3.00
2 . . . . 3.00
3 . . . . 3.00

GRACKLE, THE
Acclaim, 1996
1 MBn,PG,Double Cross, pt.1 . . . . 3.00
2 MBn,PG,Double Cross, pt.2 . . . . 3.00
3 MBn,PG,Double Cross, pt.3 . . . . 3.00
4 MBn,PG,Double Cross, pt.4 . . . . 3.00

The Grackle #4
© *Acclaim*

GRAPHIC STORY
MONTHLY
Fantagraphics
1 thru 7 . . . . @3.00

GRAPHIQUE MUSIQUE
Slave Labor, 1989–90
1 . . . . 35.00
2 . . . . 30.00
3 . . . . 25.00

GRAVEDIGGERS
Acclaim, 1996
1 (of 4) 3.00
2 thru 4 . . . . @3.00

GRAVE TALES
Hamilton, 1991
1 JSon,GM, mag. size 8.00
2 JSon,GM,short stories 6.00
3 JSon,GM, inc.`Stake Out' 6.00

GREAT DETECTIVE
STARRING SHERLOCK
HOLMES
ACG Comics, 1999
1 by Otto Lagoni 3.00
2 thru 5 . . . . @3.00

GREEN BERETS
ACG, 2000
1 JKu. 3.00
2 thru 7 JKu, Robin Moore . . . . . @3.00

GREENLEAF IN EXILE
Cat's Paw Comics, 1998
1 by Doug Anderson 3.00
2 thru 7 . . . . @3.00

GREMLIN TROUBLE
Anti-Ballistic Pixelation, 1995
1 & 2 Airstrike on Gremlin Home @3.00
1 new printing 3.00
3 thru 5 . . . . @3.00
6 `Fun with Electricity' 3.00
7 `Cypher in Fairyland' 3.00
8 . . . . 3.00
9 F:Candy Tsai 3.00
10 The Tuberians are coming 3.00
11 V:X-the-Unmentionable 3.00
12 preemptive strike on Site X 3.00
13 Gremlin-Goblin war 3.00
14 . . . . 3.00
15 Battle of 5 Armies 3.00
16 . . . . 3.00
17 kidnapped to Fairyland 3.00
18 . . . . 3.00
19 The Sky Stone 3.00
20 Ring Fortress 3.00
21 A-Girls 3.00
22 Gremlin Guild 3.00
23 escape from Mordovania 3.00
24 thru 30 . . . . @3.00
Spec. #1 Super Special 3.00
Super Special Final (2004) 3.25

GRENDEL
Comico, 1983
1 MW,O:Hunter Rose, rare 165.00
2 MW,O:Argent, rare. 125.00
3 MW,rare 125.00

GRENUORD
Fantagraphics Books, 2005
1 (of 6) 5.00

2 . . . . 5.00
3 . . . . 5.00

GREY
Viz Select, 1989
Book 1 . . . . 5.00
Book 2 scarce 5.50
Book 3 . . . . 3.00
Book 4 . . . . 3.00
Book 5 . . . . 3.00
Book 6 thru Book 9 . . . . @2.50

GREYMATTER
Alaffinity Studios, 1993
1 thru 14 by Marcus Harwell . . . @3.00

GRIFFIN, THE
Slave Labor, 1988
1 . . . . 2.50
1a 2nd printing 2.50
2 thru 4 . . . . @2.50
5 . . . . 2.50

Amaze Ink, 1997
1 by DVa & Phil Allora 3.00
2 by DVa & Paul Way 3.00

GRIPS
Silver Wolf, 1986
1 Vigil 12.00
2 Vigil 9.00
3 Vigil 8.00
4 Vigil 7.00
Vol 1 #1 rep 2.50

Volume 2
1 . . . . 2.50
2 . . . . 2.50
3 thru 8 . . . . @2.50
9 thru 12 . . . . @2.50

GROUND ZERO
Eternity
1 Science Fiction mini-series 2.50
2 Alien Invasion Aftermath 2.50

GRRL SCOUTS
Oni Press, 1999
1 (of 4) by Jim Mahfood 3.00
2 thru 4 . . . . @3.00

Amazing Aaron, 1999
1 Aaron Warner. 3.00
2 . . . . 3.00

GUERRILLA GROUNDHOG
Eclipse, 1987
1 . . . . 2.50
2 . . . . 2.50

GUILLOTIN
High Impact, 1997
Preview JQ,RCI 5.00
ABC Studios, 1999
Spec. Ed. 3.00
Spec. Ed. Serpent Ed. 8.00

GUILLOTINE
Silver Wolf, 1987
1 . . . . 2.25
2 . . . . 2.25

GUN CRISIS
Ironcat, 1998
1 (of 3) by Masoami Kanzaki 3.00
2 & 3 . . . . @3.00

Guillotine #1
© Silver Wolf

GUNDAM WING
Mixx Entertainment, 2000
1 . . . . 5.00
2 thru 4 . . . . @4.00
Tokyopop.Com, 2000
5 thru 12 . . . . @3.00

GUNDAM WING: BATTLEFIELD OF PACIFISTS
Tokyopop Press, 2001
1 48-pg. 3.00
2 thru 5 . . . . @3.00

GUNDAM WING: ENDLESS WALTZ
Tokyopop Press, 2002
1 (of 5) 3.00
2 thru 4 . . . . @3.00

GUNDAM WING: G-UNIT
Tokyopop Press, 2002
1 (of 12) 3.00
2 . . . . 3.00

GUNDAM WING: THE LAST OUTPOST
Tokyopop Press, 2002
1 (of 12) 3.00
2 thru 4 . . . . @3.00

GUNDAM: THE ORIGIN
Viz Communications, 2002
GN #1 by Yoshikazu Yasuhiko. . . . 8.00
GN #2 thru #12 . . . . @8.00

GUNFIGHTERS IN HELL: ORIGINAL SIN
Broken Halos, 2001
1 . . . . 4.00
1a variant (c). 6.00
1 limited edition 16-pg. 7.00
2 24-pg. 4.00
2a cardstock (c) 4.50
2b limited edition. 6.00

GUN FURY
Aircel, 1989
1 thru 10 . . . . @2.50

GUN FURY RETURNS
Aircel, 1990
1 . . . . 3.00
2 . . . . 3.00
3 V:The Yes Men 2.25
4 . . . . 2.25

GUNNER
Gun Dog Comics, 1999
1 . . . . 3.00
2 thru 7 by Eric Yonge. . . . . @3.00

GUNS OF SHAR-PEI
Caliber
1 The Good,the Bad & the Deadly . 3.00
2 & 3 . . . . @3.00

GUTWALLOW
Numbskull Press, 1998
1 by Dan Berger 3.00
2 thru 7 The Gingerbread Man . . @3.00
Digital Webbing 2002
1 (of 3) 3.00
2 Fury of the Furry 3.00
3 concl. 3.00

GUNWITCH, THE: OUTSKIRTS OF DOOM
Oni Press, 2001
1 by DIB 3.00
2 . . . . 3.00
3 . . . . 3.00

GYPSY
Avatar Press, 2005
1 . . . . 3.50
1a Wraparound (c) 3.50
1b Variant(c)s . . . . @3.50
1c Die-cut (c) 10.00
2 . . . . 4.00
2a wraparound (c). 4.00
2b Variant(c)s . . . . @4.00
2c premium (c) 10.00

GYRE
Abaculus, 1997
1 by Martin Shipp & Marc Laming . 3.00
2 . . . . 3.00
3 Soul Keeper, pt. 3.00
4 thru 6 . . . . @3.00
Spec. Edition 56-pg.. . . . . 4.50

HADES
Domain Publishing, 1995
1 F:Civil War Officer 3.00

HALL OF HEROES
Hall of Heroes, 1993
1 I:Dead Bolt. 10.00
2 and 3 . . . . @4.50
Ashcan, 8-pg. 6.00
Halloween Horror Special 2.50
Halloween Horror Special '98 . . . . . 2.50

HALL OF HEROES PRESENTS
Hall of Heroes, 1996–97
0 by Doug Brammer & Matt Roach,
    'Slingers' by Matt Martin 2.50
1 . . . . 2.50
1a signed & numbered 4.00
2 'The Last Days' 2.50
3 'The Power of the Golem' 2.50
4 F:Turaxx the Trobbit. 2.50
5 . . . . 2.50

HALLOWIENERS
Mirage
1 . . . . 2.25
2 . . . . 2.25

HALO BROTHERS
Fantagraphics
Special #1 . . . . 2.25

HAMMER GIRL
Brainstorm, 1996
1 dinosaur, sci-fi adventure. 3.00
2 . . . . 3.00
2a deluxe 5.00

HAMSTER VICE
Blackthorne, 1986
1 . . . . 3.50
2 . . . . 2.50
3 thru 11 . . . . @2.50
New Series
Eternity, 1989
1 and 2 . . . . @2.50

HANGED MAN
Caliber, 1998
1 (of 2) by AIG & Arthur Ranson. . . 3.00
2 (of 2) 3.00

HARD BOILED COMICS
Goodbum Studios 2006
1 . . . . 3.00
2 thru 4 . . . . @3.00

HARD ROCK COMICS
Revolutionary, 1992
1 Metallica-The Early Years 6.00
2 Motley Crew. 4.00
3 Jane's Addiction. 3.50
4 Nirvana 4.00
5 Kiss 9.00
5a 2nd printing 5.00
6 Def Leppard II 3.00
7 Red Hot Chili Peppers. 3.00
8 Pearl Jam. 3.00
9 Queen II. 3.00
10 Birth of Punk. 3.00
11 Pantera 3.00
12 Hendrix 3.00
13 Dead Kennedys 3.00
14 Van Halen II 2.50
15 Megadeath 2.50
16 Joan Jett. 2.50
17 Not printed
18 Queensryche. 2.50
19 Tesla 2.50
20 The Sweet. 2.50

HARI KARI
Blackout, 1995
1 . . . . 3.00
1a platinum 8.00
1-shot Possessed by Evil(1997) . . 3.00
1-shot Hari Kari Goes Hollywood
    (1997) 3.00
    Deluxe 15.00
Spec #1 Sexy Summer Rampage,
    gallery issue (1997). 3.00
    Deluxe, super sexy cover 10.00
1-shot Cry of Darkness (1998) 3.00
    Variant photo ultra sexy ed.. . . 10.00
1-shot The Last Stand (1998) 3.00
    Ultra sexy edition. 10.00
    Deluxe 15.00

HARI KARI MANGA
Blackout Comics, 1998
Spec. 0 Sex, Thugs & Rock 'n' Roll   3.00
1-shot Manga Adventures (1997) . . 3.00
1-shot Deadly Exposure, by Rob
   Roman & Nigel Tully 3.00
   Deluxe 15.00
1-shot Deadtime Stories, by Rob
   Roman & Nigel Tully 3.00
   Deluxe edition 15.00
1-shot Manga To Die For 3.00
   Deluxe 15.00
1-shot Running From Poison 3.00

HARPY:
PRIZE OF THE OVERLORD
Ground Zero, 1996
1 (of 6) 3.00
2 thru 6 . . . . @3.00
1-shot Harpy Preview, prequel. 3.00
Peregrine, 1998
Spec. Harpy Pin-up Book 3.00

Harte of Darkness #1
© Eternity

HARTE OF DARKNESS
Eternity, 1991
1 I:Dennis Harte,Vampire
   private-eye 2.50
2 V:Satan's Blitz St.Gang 2.50
3 Jack Grissom/Vampire. 2.50
4 V:Jack Grissom, conc.. . . . . 2.50

HARVEST KING
Caliber, 1998
1 by Joe Casey & Mike
   Macropoulos 3.00
2 . . . . 3.00
3 . . . . 3.00

HARVY FLIP BOOK
Blackthorne
1 thru 3 . . . . @2.25

HATE
Fantagraphics, 1990
1 . . . . 15.00
2 . . . . 10.00
3 . . . . 9.00
4 . . . . 8.00
5 . . . . 8.00
6 . . . . 8.00
7 . . . . 7.00

8 thru 10 . . . . @6.00
11 and 12 . . . . @5.00
1a to 12a reprints . . . . @2.50
13 thru 15 . . . . @4.00
Hate Jamboree, 64-pg. 4.00
See Color

HAVOC, INC.
Radio Comix, 1998
1 by Mark Barnard & Terrie Smith . 3.00
2 thru 9 . . . . @3.00
10 . . . . 3.50

HEAD, THE
1 Old Airboy (1966). 2.25

HEAVEN SENT
Antarctic Press, 2004
1 BDn 3.00
2 thru 5 . . . . @3.00
6 thru 11 . . . . @3.00
Stand Alone Special (2005) 3.00

HEAVY METAL
MONSTERS
Revolutionary, 1992
1 `Up in Flames' 2.25

HE IS JUST A RAT
Exclaim Bound Comics, 1995
1 & 2 V:Jimmy and Billy Bob 2.75

HELLGIRL
Knight Press, 1995
1 I:Jazzmine Grayce 3.00
1-shot Demonseed II, Bob Hickey &
   Bill Nichols (1997) 3.00
1-shot Demonsong, Bob Hickey &
   Bill Nichols (1997) 3.00
1-shot Purgatory (1997) 3.00

HELLINA
Lightning Comics, 1994
1-shot I&O:Hellina 5.00
   Commemorative 10.00
   1996 rep. gold 5.00
Spec. Hellina: Genesis with poster
   (1996) 3.00
   Platinum edition. 4.00
Spec. Hellina: In the Flesh (1997)
   two diff. mild covers . . . . @3.00
Spec. Hellina: Naked Desire (1997) 3.00
   Cover B 3.00
   Signed, ... 3.00
Spec. Hellina: Taking Back the Night
   (1995) V:Michael Naynar. 3.00
Spec. Hellina: Wicket Ways (1995)
   A:Perg 2.75
   Encore editions 3.00
   Encore variant (c) 3.00
Spec. Hellina: X-Mas in Hell (1996)
   two different covers . . . . @3.00
   Platinum edition. 5.00
Spec. Hellina: The Relic 3.00
   Variant cover 3.00
Spec. 1997 Pin-up 3.50
   1997 Pin-up, cover B. 3.50
X-Over Hellina/Catfight (1995)
   V:Prince of Sommia. 2.75
   Gold 4.00
   Encore edition, mild covers,
   2 different . . . . @3.00
X-Over Hellina/Cynder (1997) covA 3.00
   Cover B 3.00
Spec Hellina #1 Skybolt Toyz
   lim. ed. (1997) 2.25

HELLINA
Avatar Press, 2003
0 . . . . 3.50
0a variant (c). 3.50
0b wraparound (c). 4.00
0c Hard Ruler Edition 6.00
0d Prism foil edition 13.00

HELLINA:
HEART OF THORNS
Lightning Comics, 1996
1 (of 2) 3.00
1b autographed. 5.00
2 . . . . 2.75
2a variant cover 2.75
2b platinum edition. 6.00

HELLINA: HELL'S ANGEL
Lightning Comics, 1996
1 . . . . 2.75
1a platinum edition 8.00
1a platinum edition, signed. 9.00
1c nude platinum edition. 12.00
2 . . . . 2.75
2a platinum edition 8.00
1 encore edition, cover A 3.00
1a encore edition, cover B 3.00
1b deluxe encore edition, cover A . 5.00
1c deluxe encore edition, cover B . 5.00

HELLINA: KISS OF DEATH
Lightning Comics, 1995
1-shot A:Perg 4.00
1-shot gold edition 9.00
1-shot Encore editions 3.00
Lightning, 1997
1A 3.00
1B variant cover 3.00
1 encore, signed & numbered 5.00

HELLINA: SEDUCTION
Avatar Press, 2003
1/2 Carnage Edition 6.00
1/2 Statuesque Edition. 6.00
Preview 2.25
Preview variant (c) 6.00
Preview Bad Girl edition 6.00
1 . . . . 3.50
1a wraparound (c). 4.00

HELLINA VS PANDORA
Avatar Press, 2003
0 16-pg. 2.50
0a variant (c)s. . . . . @4.00
1 (of 3) 3.50
2 thru 3 . . . . @3.50
1a thru 3a variant (c)s. . . . . @3.50
Preview 2.25
Preview variant (c) 6.00
Preview Hellina's Army variant (c). . 6.00

HELSING
Caliber Core, 1998
1W by Gary Reed & Low,
   Wozniak(c). 3.00
1L Loudon (c) 3.00
1 variant cover 8.00
1 premium, signed 9.00
2 . . . . 3.00
3 . . . . 3.00
4 Secrets and Lies 3.00
Spec. Dawn of Armageddon, Secrets
   & Lies, concl. 48-pg. 4.00

HELTER SKELTER
Rog Heavy Industries, 1996
1 . . . . 3.00

2	3.00

Antarctic Press, 1997

0 by Mike Harris & Duc Tran	3.00
1 (of 4)	3.00
2 thru 6	@3.00

HEPCATS
Double Diamond, 1989

1	15.00
2	12.00
3 Snow Blind	12.00
4 thru 9	@9.00
10 thru 13	@3.50
14 Chapter 12	3.00
15 Snowblind Chp. 13	3.00

Hepcats #6
© *Antarctic Press*

Antarctic Press, 1996

0	3.00
1 by Martin Wagner	3.00
2 `Trial by Intimacy'	3.00
3 Snowblind,pt.1	3.00
4 Snowblind,pt.2	3.00
5 Snowblind,pt.3	3.00
6 Snowblind,pt.4	3.00
7 Snowblind,pt.5 Intrusion	3.00
8 Snowblind,pt.6 Super Heroes	3.00
9 Snowblind,pt.7 Kevin & Kathryn	3.00
10 Snowblind,pt.8 Exorcism, Prelude	3.00
11 Snowblind,pt.10 Exorcism(a)	3.00
12 Snowblind,pt.10 Exorcism(b)	3.00

HERCULES
A Plus Comics

1 Hercules Saga	2.50

HERCULES
Blatant Comics, 1997

1 TV parody (c)	3.00
1a Movie parody (c)	3.00
1b 3-D Rendered (c)	3.00

HERCULES PROJECT
Monster Comics, 1991

1 Origin issue,V:Mutants	2.25

HEROBEAR AND THE KID
Astonish Comics, 2000

1	12.00
1a 2nd printing	3.50
2	10.00
2a 2nd printing	3.50

3	3.50
4	3.50
5 Belief	3.50

HEROBEAR AND THE KID: SAVING TIME
Astonish Comics, 2004

1 (of 3) partial color	3.50

HEROES
Blackbird, 1987

1	5.00
2	3.00
3	2.50
4 comic size	2.50
5 thru 7	@2.50

HEROES ANONYMOUS
Bongo Comics, 2003

1 (of 6)	3.00
2 thru 6	@3.00

HEROES FROM WORDSMITH
Special Studios

1 WWI,F:Hunter Hawke	2.50

HEROES INCORPORATED
Double Edge Publishing

1 I:Heroes, Inc.	3.00
2 Betrayal	3.00

HEROIC TALES
Lone Star Press, 1997

1 by Robb Phipps & Bill Williams	2.50
2 Steel of a Soldier's Heart,pt.2	2.50
3 Steel of a Soldier's Heart,pt.3	2.50
4	2.50
5	2.50
6 The Belles of Freedom, prequel	2.50
7 The Children of Atlas,pt.1	2.50
8 by B.Williams & J.Parker, I:Atlas	2.50

HEROINES, INC.
Avatar

1 thru 5	@2.25

HERO SANDWICH
Slave Labor, 1987

1 thru 4	@2.50
5 thru 8	@2.50
9	2.50
GN	8.00

HEY MISTER
Insomnia Comics, 1997

1	2.50
2	2.50

Top Shelf

3 by Pete Sickman-Garner	3.00
4	3.00
Spec. Behind the Green Door	3.00
Spec. The Trouble With Jesus	3.00
Spec. Eyes on the Prize	3.00
Spec. Dial "M" for Mister	3.50

HICKEE
Alternative Comics 2003
Vol. 2

1	5.00
2	5.00

Vol. 3

1	3.00
2	3.00

HIGH CALIBER
Caliber, 1997

1 64pg.	4.00
1 signed edition	4.00
2 64pg.	4.00
3 48pg.	4.00
4	4.00

HIGH SCHOOL AGENT
Sun Comics, 1992

1 I:Kohsuke Kanamori	2.50
2 Treasure Hunt at North Pole	2.50
3 and 4	@2.50

HIGH SHINING BRASS
Apple

1	2.75
2 thru 4	@2.75

HIGH SOCIETY
Aardvark–Vanaheim

1 DS,Cerebus	25.00

HIGHWAY 13
Amaze Ink/SLG, 2000

1 thru 11 by Les McClaine	@3.00

HILLY ROSE'S SPACE ADVENTURES
Astro Comics, 1995

1 confronts Steeltrap	6.00
1 2nd & 3rd pr. by B.C. Boyer	3.00
2	5.00
2 2nd & 3rd printing	3.00
3	3.50
3 2nd printing	3.00
4 thru 9	@3.00

HIT THE BEACH
Antarctic, 1993

1	3.00
1a deluxe edition	5.00
2 & 3	@3.00
Spec. funny animal	3.00
Spec. 32 pg	3.00
Spec. deluxe	4.00
Spec. deluxe poster edition	5.00
Spec. 48-pg., 1999.	4.00
Spec. (#7) 48-pg., 2000	4.00
Ann. 2001.	4.00
Ann. 2002.	4.00
1-shot Hit the Beach 2003	5.00
1-shot Hit the Beach 2004	5.00
1-shot Hit the Beach 2005	5.00
1-shot Hit the Beach 2006	6.00
Spec. 2007	6.00

HITOMI AND HER GIRL COMMANDOS
Antarctic Press, 1992

1 Shadowhunter,from Ninja HS	2.50
2 Synaptic Transducer	2.50
3 Shadowhunter in S.America	2.50
4 V:Mr.Akuma,last issue	2.50

[Series II]

1	2.75
2 thru 10	@2.75

HOAX
Mental Note Press, 2005

1	3.00
2 thru 3	@3.00

Fantagraphics Books 2006

4	4.00

B & W PUB.

HOLLIDAY
Saddle Tramp Press 2002
1 F: Doc Holliday 2.50
2 thru 3 . . . . @2.50
4 thru 7 . . . . @3.00

HOLLYWOOD'S GOLDEN ERA, 1930S
A-List Comics, 1999
1 (of 3) 3.00
2 . . . . 3.00
3 . . . . 3.00

HOLO BROTHERS, THE
Monster Comics, 1991
1 thru 10 . . . . @2.25
Fantagraphics
Spec.#1 . . . . 2.25

HOLY KNIGHT
Pocket Change Comics
1 thru 3 . . . . @2.50
4 V:His Past 2.50
5 V:Souljoiner 2.50
6 V:Demon Priest 2.50
7 Silent Scream,pt.2 . . . . 2.50
8 'Dragon Quest,'pt.1 . . . . 2.50
9 'Dragon Quest,'pt.2 . . . . 2.50
10 'Dragon Quest,'pt.3 . . . . 2.50
11 'Dragon Quest,'pt.4 . . . . 2.50

Honk #3
© *Fantagraphics*

HONK
Fantagraphics, 1986
1 Don Martin 2.75
2 . . . . 2.75
3 . . . . 2.75

HONOR AMONG THIEVES
Gateway Graphics, 1987
1 and 2 . . . . @2.50

HONOR BRIGADE
Spinner Rack Comics, 2007
1 . . . . 3.00
2 thru 5 . . . . @3.00

HONOR OF THE DAMNED
Americanime Productions, 2005
1 Manga by Nevin Arnold 3.50
2 . . . . 3.50
3 . . . . 3.50
4 . . . . 4.00

HOON
Eenieweenie Comics, 1995
1 I:Hoon 2.50
2 Calazone Disaster 2.50
3 Reality Check. 2.50
4 thru 8 . . . . @2.50

HOON, THE
Caliber Tapestry, 1996
1 . . . . 3.00
2 & 3 . . . . @3.00

HOPELESS SAVAGES
Oni Press, 2001
1 . . . . 3.00
2 thru 4 . . . . @3.00

HOPELESS SAVAGES: GROUND ZERO
Oni Press, 2002
1 (of 4) 3.00
2 thru 4 . . . . @3.00

HOROBI
Viz, 1990
1 . . . . 4.00
2 thru 8 . . . . @3.75
Book 2, 1990–91
1 by Yoshihisa Tagami 3.50
2 D:Okado,Shoko Kidnapped 4.25
3 Madoka Attacks Zen 4.25
4 D:Abbess Mitsuko 4.25
5 Catharsis! 4.25
6 Shuichi Vs. Zen 4.25
7 Shuichi vs. Zen, conc. 4.25

HORROR IN THE DARK
Fantagor
1 RCo,Inc.Blood Birth 2.25
2 RCo,Inc.Bath of Blood 2.25
3 RCo 2.25
4 RCo,Inc.Tales of the
   Black Diamond 2.25

HORROR SHOW
Caliber
1 GD,1977-80 reprint horror 3.50

HOUSE OF FRIGHTENSTEIN
AC Comics
1 . . . . 3.00

HOUSE OF HORROR
AC Comics
1 . . . . 2.50

HOWL
Eternity
1 & 2 . . . . @2.25

H.P. LOVECRAFT'S THE CALL OF CTHULHU AND OTHERS
Cross Plains Comics, 1999
1-shot RTs,EM 6.00

H.P. LOVECRAFT'S THE DREAM-QUEST OF UNKNOWN KADATH
Mock Man Press, 1997
1 (of 5) by Jason Thompson 3.00

1 2nd printing 3.00
2 thru 5 . . . . @3.00

H.P. LOVECRAFT'S THE RETURN OF CTHULHU
Cross Plains Comics, 2000
1-shot RTs & EM 6.00

HSU AND CHAN
Amaze Ink/SLG, 2003
1 thru 5 . . . . @3.00
6 thru 7 . . . . @3.00

HUGO
Fantagraphics, 1985
1 . . . . 4.00
2 thru 4 . . . . @2.50

HUMAN GARGOYLES
Eternity, 1988
Book one 2.50
Book two 2.50
Book three 2.50
Book four 2.50

HUNT AND THE HUNTED, THE
Newcomers Publishing
1 I:Aramis Thiron 3.00
2 V:Werewolves 3.00
3 Rio De Janero 3.00
4 F:Aramis Thiron 3.00

HURRICANE GIRLS
Antarctic Press, 1995
1 & 2 Tale of Dinon . . . . @3.50
3 thru 7 seven part series . . . . . . @3.00

HUZZAH
1 I:Albedo's Erma Felna 50.00

HY-BREED
Division Publishing
1 thru 3 F:Cen Intel . . . . @2.25
4 thru 9 . . . . @2.50

HYPER DOLLS
Ironcat Manga, 1998
1 by Shinpei Itoh, F:Miyu & Maika . 3.00
2 thru 6 . . . . @3.00
VOL 2
1 . . . . 3.00
2 thru 6 . . . . @3.00
VOL 3
1 . . . . 3.00
2 thru 6 . . . . @3.00
VOL 4, 2000
1 . . . . 3.00
2 thru 6 . . . . @3.00
VOL 5, 2000
1 . . . . 3.00
2 thru 6 . . . . @3.00

I.F.S. ZONE
1 thru 6 . . . . @2.25

I AM LEGEND
Eclipse, 1991
1 Novel adapt. aka Omega Man . . . 6.00
2 thru 3 68-pg. . . . . @6.00

ICARUS
Aircel, 1987
1 thru 9 . . . . @2.50

ICON DEVIL
Spider
1 by Neil Hanson 2.25
2 . . . . 2.25
2nd Series
1 thru 5 . . . . @2.25

I DREAM OF JEANNIE
Airwave Comics, 2002
1 JJu(c) 3.00
1 special edition 6.00
2 . . . . 3.00
2a variant photo (c). 3.00
3 . . . . 3.00
Preview Book #1 . . . . 7.00
Spec. Trick-or-Treats Annual #1 . . . 3.50
Spec.#1 Wishbook (2001) 3.00
Spec.#1 Wishbook, photo (c). 3.00
Spec. Spring Spectacular 3.50
Spec. Spring Spectacular, photo(c) . 3.50

I HUNT MONSTERS
Antarctic Press 2004
1 . . . . 3.00
2 thru 9 . . . . @3.00
Vol. 2
1 by Rod Espinosa 3.00
2 thru 9 . . . . @3.00
Spec. Tales From Sleepy Hollow . . . 3.00

ILIAD
Amaze Ink, 1997
1 by Darren Brady & Alex Ogle . . . 3.00
2 thru 7 . . . . @3.00

ILIAD II
MicMac
1 . . . . 3.00
1a 2nd cover variation 3.00
2 . . . . 2.25
3 . . . . 2.25
4 . . . . 2.25

ILLUMINATUS
Rip Off, 1990
1 . . . . 2.25
2 . . . . 2.50
3 . . . . 2.50

INDUSTRIACIDE
Broken Tree Publications, 2002
1 (of 6) by Sean Dietrich 3.00
2 thru 6 . . . . @3.00

INFERNO
Caliber Press, 1995
1 I:City of Inferno 3.00
2 Search for Identity 3.00
3 V:Malateste 3.00
4 by MCy and Michael Gaydos . . . 3.00
5 . . . . 3.00

INTERZONE
Brainstorm Comics
1 w/4 cards 2.50
2 w/4 cards 2.50

INTO THE STORM
Curtis Comics, 2002
Vol. 1 Manga
1 by Jihoon Park & Takyoung Lee . 3.00
2 thru 4 . . . . @3.00
Vol. 2
1 . . . . 3.00

INU YASHA
Viz Communications, 1997
1 thru 5 (of 10) by Rumiko
  Takahashi . . . . @3.00
PART TWO:
A FEUDAL FAIRY TALE
Viz Communications, 1998
1 (of 9) by Rumiko Takahashi 3.00
2 thru 7 . . . . @3.00
8 thru 15 (of 15) . . . . @3.25
PART THREE, 1999
1 (of 7) thru 7 . . . . @3.25
PART FOUR, 1999
1 (of 7) by Rumiko Takahashi 3.25
2 thru 7 . . . . @3.25
PART FIVE, 2000
1 (of 11) by Rumiko Takahashi 3.00
2 thru 11 . . . . @3.00
PART SIX, 2001
1 (of 15) 3.00
2 thru 7 . . . . @3.00
8 thru 15 . . . . @3.00
PART SEVEN, 2002
1 (of 8) by Rumiko Takahashi 3.00
2 thru 7 . . . . @3.00

INVADERS FROM MARS
Eternity, 1990
1 . . . . 2.50
2 . . . . 2.50
3 . . . . 2.50
BOOK II, 1991
1 Sequel to '50's SF classic 2.50
2 Pact of Tsukus/Humans 2.50
3 Last issue 2.50

INVASION '55
Apple, 1990
1 . . . . 2.25
2 . . . . 2.25
3 . . . . 2.25

INVISIBLE PEOPLE
Kitchen Sink
1 WE,I:Peacus Pleatnik 3.00
2 WE,The Power 3.00
3 WE,Final issue 3.00

ISLAND
Tokyopop Press, 2001
1 48-pg. 3.00
2 thru 4 . . . . @3.00
2nd Series, 2002
1 thru 7 . . . . @3.00

ISMET
Canis
1 Cartoon Dog 8.00
2 . . . . 5.00
3 Rare 5.00
4 . . . . 5.00

IT'S SCIENCE
WITH DR. RADIUM
Slave Labor, 1986
1 . . . . 2.50
2 thru 9 . . . . @2.50
Spec #1 . . . . 3.00

JACKAROO, THE
Eternity, 1990
1 GCh 2.25
2 & 3GCh . . . . @2.25

The Jackaroo #1
© Eternity

JACK HUNTER
Blackthorne, 1987
1 . . . . 3.50
2 thru 3 . . . . @3.50

JACK OF NINES
1 . . . . 2.25
2 thru 4 . . . . @2.25
5 . . . . 2.25

JACK STAFF
Dancing Elephant Press, 2000
1 by Paul Grist 3.00
2 thru 4 . . . . @3.00
5 . . . . 3.00
6 . . . . 3.00
7 . . . . 3.00
8 36-pg. 4.50
9 thru 12 . . . . @3.00

JACK THE LANTERN
Castle Rain Entertainment 2002
0a signed and numbered 8.00
1 thru 3 . . . . @3.00
4 The quest 3.00
5 The quest 3.50
1-shot 1942 . . . . 4.00

JACK THE LANTERN:
GHOSTS
Castle Rain Entertainment, 2006
1 . . . . 2.50
2 . . . . 2.00

JACK THE RIPPER
Eternity
1 thru 4 . . . . @2.25

JAM, THE
Slave Labor, 1989
1 . . . . 3.00
2 thru 5 . . . . @3.00
Dark Horse, 1993
6 thru 8 . . . . 3.00
Caliber, 1995
9 . . . . 3.00
9 signed edition 3.00
10 It's a Kafka Thing 3.00
11 thru 14 . . . . @3.00
15 `The Kinetic,'pt.3 . . . . 3.00

JAMES O'BARR ORIGINAL SINS
ACG Comics, 2000
1 . . . . 3.00
2 . . . . 3.00

JAMES O'BARR TASTY BITES
ACG Comics, 1999
1 . . . . 3.00
1a signed 10.00

JANE'S WORLD
Girl Twirl, 2003
1 by Paige Braddock 3.00
2 thru 12 . . . . @3.00
13 thru 20 56-pg. . . . . @6.00
21 thru 24 . . . . @5.00

JASON AND THE ARGONAUTS
Caliber
1 . . . . 2.50
2 thru 5 . . . . @2.50

Jay & Silent Bob #2
© Oni Press

JAY & SILENT BOB
Oni Press, 1998
1 (of 4) by Kevin Smith & Duncan
Fregedo 5.00
1a Ph(c) 7.00
1b 2nd printing 3.00
2 thru 4 . . . . @4.00

JAZZ
High Impact, 1996
1 . . . . 3.00
1 Gold variant edition RCl(c) 9.00
2 . . . . 3.00
2a deluxe edition 9.00
3 . . . . 3.00
3a variant (c). 9.00

JAZZ THE SERIES
ABC Comics, 1999
1 RCl(c). 3.00
1a DOe(c). 3.00
2 . . . . 3.00

JAZZ: SOLITAIRE
ABC Comics, 1998
1 (of 4) by Jose Varese 3.00
1a photo cover 6.00
2 . . . . 3.00
2a Variant Exotika (c) 6.00
2b Variant Naughty (c) 6.00
3 . . . . 3.00
Collected Ed. 5.00

JAZZ: SUPERSTAR
ABC Comics, 1998
1 (of 3) by Jose Varese 3.00
1a JQ cover 6.00

JAZZ AGE CHRONICLES
Caliber, 1990
1 thru 6 . . . . @2.25
7 . . . . 2.50

JCP FEATURES
J.C. Productions, 1982
1 1st MT;S&K,NA/DG rep.
A:T.H.U.N.D.E.R.Agents,
TheFly, Black Hood Mag.Size . 11.00

JENNA AND NINJA HIGH
Narwain Publishing, 2006
1 (of 3) Ninja High School x-over . . 3.50
2 BDn 3.50
3 . . . . 3.50

JENNY FINN
Oni Press, 1999
1 (of 4) by MMi & Troy Nixey 3.00
2 MMi 3.00
3 MMi 3.00
4 MMi, concl.. . . . . 4.00

JEREMIAH
Fantagraphics, 1982–83
GN #1. . . . . 35.00
GN #2. . . . . 32.00

JEREMIAH: BIRDS OF PREY
Adventure Comics, 1991
1 I: Jeremiah,A:Kurdy 4.00
2 conclusion 4.00

JEREMIAH: EYES LIKE BURNING COALS
Adventure Comics, 1991
1 & 2 fourth series. . . . . @4.00

JEREMIAH: A FISTFUL OF SAND
Adventure Comics
1 A:Captain Kenney 4.00
2 conclusion 4.00

JEREMIAH: THE HEIRS
Adventure Comics, 1991
1 Nathanial Bancroft estate 4.00
2 conclusion 4.00

JERRY IGERS FAMOUS FEATURES
Blackthorne
1 . . . . 3.00
2 thru 4 . . . . @2.25
Pacific
5 thru 8 . . . . @2.25

JETCAT CLUBHOUSE
Oni Press, 2001
1 by Jay Stephens 3.25
2 thru 5 . . . . @3.25

JIM
Fantagraphics, 1987–90
1 . . . . 15.00
2 . . . . 12.00
3 and 4 . . . . @8.00
Second Series, 1994
1 . . . . 4.00
1a 2nd printing 3.00
2 . . . . 3.50
2a 2nd printing 3.00
3 thru 5 . . . . @3.00

JINGLE BELLE
Oni Press, 1999
1 (of 2) by PDi. 3.00
2 PDi 3.00
All-Star Holiday Hullabaloo 5.00
1-shot Jingle Belle Jubilee. 3.00
1-shot The Mighty Elves 3.00
1-shot Winter Wingding 3.00

J. O'BARR's THE CROW
Kitchen Sink, 1998
0 F:Eric Draven, 48-pg. 3.50
1 . . . . 3.50
2 Demon in Disguise 3.50

JOE PSYCHO & MOO FROG
Goblin Studios, 1996
1 Fanatics Edition 2.50
1 Fanatics signed and numbered
Edition 9.00
2 . . . . 2.50
2 signed & numbered 9.00
3 . . . . 2.50
4 . . . . 2.50
4B San Diego Con cover 5.00
5 . . . . 2.50
Spec. Psychosis Abnormalis 2.50

JOE R. LANSDALE'S BY BIZARRE HANDS
Avatar Press, 2004
1 . . . . 3.50
2 thru 6 . . . . 3.50
1a thru 6a wraparound (c)s. . . . . @3.50
4 thru 6 connecting covers . . . . . @6.00

JOE R. LANSDALE'S THE DRIVE-IN
Avatar Press, 2003
1 (of 4) 3.50
2 thru 4 . . . . @3.50
1a thru 4a wraparound (c). . . . . @4.00
Vol. 2, 2006
1 (of 4) 3.50
2 thru 4 . . . . @3.50
1a thru 4a wraparound (c). . . . . @3.50

JOE SINN
Caliber
1 I:Joe Sinn,Nikki 3.00
2 . . . . 3.00

JOHNNY ATOMIC
Eternity
1 I:Johnny A.Tomick 2.50
2 Project X-contingency plan 2.50
3 . . . . 2.50

JOHNNY COMET
ACG Comics, 1999
1	3.00
2	3.00
3 FF, rep.	3.00
4 FF, rep.	3.00
5 FF, rep.	3.00

JOHNNY DARK
Double Edge
1 V:Biker Gang	3.00

JOHNNY HIRO
Adhouse Books, 2007
1	3.00
2 thru 3	3.00

JOHNNY RAYGUN
Jetpack Press, 2003
1	3.00
2 thru 6	@3.00
Spec. Quarterly #1	3.00

JOHNNY
THE HOMICIDAL MANIAC
Slave Labor, 1996
1 by Jhonen Vasquez	28.00
1 3rd printing	15.00
1 signed, limited	15.00
2	12.00
2 3rd printing	12.00
3	10.00
3 3rd printing	6.00
4	5.00
4 2nd & 3rd printing	3.00
5	4.00
5 2nd printing	3.00
6	3.00
7	3.00

JOURNEY
Aardvark–Vanaheim, 1983
1	7.00
2	6.00
3	5.00
4	3.00
5 thru 7	@3.00
8 thru 14	@2.50
Fantagraphics, 1985
15	2.50
16 thru 28	@2.50

JR. JACKALOPE
1 orange cover, 1981	8.00
1a Yellow cover, 1981	10.00
2	8.00

JULIE'S JOURNEY/
GRAVITY
Paper Live Studios, 1998
1 by David Keye	2.50
2 thru 6	@2.50

JUNGLE COMICS
Blackthorne, 1988
4 thru 6	@2.50

JUNGLE COMICS
A-List Comics, 1997
1 reprint of golden age	3.00
2 thru 6	@3.00

JUNGLE FANTASY
Avatar Press, 2002
Preview	2.25

Preview, Fauna (c)	2.25
Preview, Wild (c)	6.00
1	3.50
1b wraparound (c)	4.00
2	3.50
3	3.50
3b Back to the Hunt Edition	6.00
4	3.50
4b volcanic edition	6.00
1a thru 4a variant (c)s	@3.50
5	3.50
5a wraparound (c)	3.50
1/2 Winged Death Edition	6.00
Ann. #1	5.00
Ann. #1a variant (c)s	@5.00

Jungle Girls #9
© AC Comics

JUNGLE GIRLS
AC Comics, 1989–93
1 incGold.Age reps.	3.00
2 Tara, Nyoka, Cave Girl	3.00
3 Greed,A:Tara	3.00
4 CaveGirl	3.00
5 Camilla	3.00
6 TigerGirl	3.00
7 CaveGirl	3.00
8 Sheena Queen o/t Jungle	3.00
9 Wild Girl,Tiger Girl,Sheena	3.00
10 F:Tara,Cave Girl,Nyoka	3.00
11 F:Sheena,Tiger Girl,Nyoka	3.00
12 F:Sheena,Camilla,Tig.Girl	3.00
13 F:Tara, Tiger Girl	3.00
14 Wildside	3.00
15 Wildside	3.00
16 Wildside	3.00

JUNIOR
Fantagraphics, 2000
1 (of 5) by Peter Bogge	3.00
2 thru 5	@3.00

JUPITER
Sandberg Publishing, 1999
1 by Jason Sandberg	3.00
2 thru 10	@3.00

JURASSIC JANE
London Night, 1997
1 by Sky Owens, F:Tira, elf princess of Atlantis	3.00
2 Sky Owens	3.00
3 Sky Owens	3.00

4 EHr, Sky Owens	3.00
5 by Preston Owens	3.00
6 by Sky Owens	3.00
7 by Sky Owens	3.00
Coll. Ed.	5.00

JUSTICE
Newcomers Publishing, 1995
1 I:Judiciary Urban Strike Team	3.00

JUSTY
Viz Communications, 1988
1 thru 9	@2.50

KABUKI:
CIRCLE OF BLOOD
Caliber Press, 1995
1 R:Kabuki	6.00
2 Kabuki Goes Rogue	5.00
3 V:Noh Agents	5.00
4 V:Noh Agents	3.50
5 V:Kai	3.00
6	3.00

KABUKI:
DANCE OF DEATH
London Night Studios, 1995
1 1st Full series	8.00

KABUKI:
MASKS OF THE NOH
Caliber, 1996
1A JQ(c)	3.00
1B Mays/Mack(c)	3.00
1C Buzz(c)	3.00
2	3.00
3 DMk	3.00
4 epilog	3.00

KAFKA
Renegade, 1987
1 thru 6	@2.50
The Execution Spec.	2.50

KAMUI
Eclipse, 1987
1 Sanpei Shirato Art	4.00
1a 2nd printing	2.50
2 Mystery of Hanbie	3.00
2a 2nd printing	2.50
3 V:Ichijiro	2.50
3a 2nd printing	2.50
4 thru 15	@2.50
16 thru 19	@2.50
20 thru 37	@2.50

KANE
Dancing Elephant, 1993
1 by Paul Grist	5.00
2 thru 13	@4.00
14 thru 17	@3.50
18 thru 22	@3.50
23 thru 33	@3.00

KANSAS THUNDER
Red Menace, 1997
1	3.00

KAOS MOON
Caliber, 1996
1 by DdB	3.50
1a 2nd edition	3.00
2	3.50
2a 2nd edition, new cover	3.00
3	5.00

4 Anubian Nights, Chapter 2. . . . . . 5.00
GN Full Circle, rep #1–#2 . . . . 6.00

KAPTAIN KEEN AND KOMPANY
Vortex, 1986
1 thru 3 . . . . @2.50
4 and 5 . . . . @2.50
6 and 7 . . . . @2.50

KATHARSIS
Americanime Corp. 2006
1 Manga 3.50
2 thru 3 . . . . @3.50

KATMANDU
Antarctic Press, 1993
1 thru 3 . . . . @2.75
4 & 5 Woman of Honor. 2.75
6 F:Laska 2.75

Med Systems
7 and 8 . . . . @2.25

Vision Comics, 1996
9 `When Warriors Die,'pt.3(of 3). . . 2.25
10 `The Curse of the Blood,'pt.1 . . . 2.50
11 `The Curse of the Blood,'pt.2 . . . 2.50
12 `The Curse of the Blood,' concl . . 3.00
13 `The Search For Magic,'pt.1 . . . . 3.00

Shanda Fantasy Arts
14 `The Search For Magic,'pt.2 . . . . 3.00
15 `The Search For Magic,'pt.3 . . . . 3.00
16 `Ceremonies,'pt.1 (of 3) 3.00
17 `Ceremonies,'pt.2 . . . . 3.00
18 `Ceremonies,'pt.3 . . . . 3.00
19 `Peace Keeper,'pt.1 . . . . 3.00
20 `Peace Keeper,'pt.2 . . . . 3.00
21 `Peace Keeper,'pt.3 . . . . 3.00
22 . . . . 3.00
23 and 24 . . . . @3.00
25 thru 36 48-pg. . . . . @5.00
Ann. #1 48-pg. 5.00
Ann. #2 . . . . 5.00
Ann. #3. . . . . 5.00
Ann. #4 . . . . 5.00
Ann. #5 . . . . 5.00
Ann. #6 . . . . 5.00
Spec. Katmandu 5.00

KEIF LLAMA
Fantagraphics
1 thru 6 . . . . @3.00

KEIF LLAMA: GAS WAR
Oni Press, 1999
1 by Matt Howarth 3.00

KEIF LLAMA: XENOTECH
Aeon, 2005
1 (of 6) by Matt Howarth 3.00
2 thru 6 . . . . @3.00

KELLEY BELLE, POLICE DETECTIVE
Newcomers Publishing
1 Debut issue 3.00
2 Case of the Jeweled Scarab 3.00
3 Case o/t Jeweled Scarab,pt.2 . . . 3.00

KICKASS GIRL: SKELETONS IN THE CLOSET
Neko Press 2003
1 . . . . 3.00

1a variant (c). 3.00
1b mini-print edition 5.00
2 thru 4 . . . . @3.00

KID CANNIBAL
Eternity, 1991
1 I:Kid Cannibal 2.50
2 Hunt for Kid Cannibal 2.50
3 A:Janice 2.50
4 final issue 2.50

Kiku San #3
© Aircel

KIKU SAN
Aircel, 1988
1 thru 6 . . . . @2.50

KILLBOX
Antarctic Press, 2002
1 . . . . 5.00
2 thru 3 . . . . @5.00

KILLING STROKE
Eternity, 1991
1 British horror tales 2.50
2 inc.`Blood calls to Blood' 2.50
3 and 4 . . . . @2.50

KILROY
Caliber Core, 1998
1C by Joe Pruett & Feliciano
   Zecchin, John Cassaday(c). . . . 3.00
1P JoP (c). 3.00
1a premium edition 9.00
2 . . . . 3.00
3 . . . . 3.00
4 O:Kilroy 3.00
Spec. Dawn of Armageddon,
   x-over, 48-pg. 4.00
Spec.#1 The Origin 5.00
Spec.#2 The Origin,pt.2 . . . . 5.00

KILROY IS HERE
Caliber Press, 1995
1 Kilroy Rescues Infant. 3.00
2 Reflections,pt.2 . . . . 3.00
3 Reflections,pt.3 . . . . 3.00
4 Lincoln Memorial 3.00
5 thru 8 . . . . @3.00
9 and 10 . . . . @3.00
11 WEI,RPc,`Screen' 3.00
12 Khymer Rouge 3.00
Spec. Kilroy: Daemonstorm (1997) . 3.00

KIMBER, PRINCE OF FEYLONS
Castle Graphics 1991
1 . . . . 3.50
Antarctic Press, 1992
1 I:Kimber. 2.50
2 V:Lord Tyrex. 2.50

KINDERGOTH
Bloodfire, 2004
1 . . . . 3.00
2 thru 4 . . . . @3.00

KINGDOM OF THE WICKED
Caliber, 1996
1 IEd 3.00
2 IEd 3.00
3 IEd 3.00
4 IEd 3.00

KING KONG
Monster Comics, 1991
1 thru 6 . . . . @2.50

KINGS IN DISGUISE
Kitchen Sink, 1988
1 thru 5 . . . . @2.50
6 end Mini-series 2.50

KING ZOMBIE
Caliber, 1998
1L by Tom Sniegoski & Jacen
   Burroughs, VcL(c) 3.00
1M Meadows (c). 3.00
2 . . . . 3.00
3 . . . . 3.00

KIRBY KING OF THE SERIALS
Blackthorne, 1989
1 . . . . 2.50
2 . . . . 2.50
3 . . . . 2.50
4 . . . . 2.50

KISSING CHAOS
Oni Press, 2001
1 (of 8) by Arthur Dela Cruz 2.50
2 16-pg.. . . . . 2.50
3 16-pg.. . . . . 2.50
4 . . . . 3.00
5 16-pg. 2.50
6 16-pg. 2.50
7 16-pg. 2.50
8 24-pg. 2.50

KISSING CHAOS: NONSTOP BEAUTY
Oni Press, 2002
1 (of 4) by Arthur Dela Cruz 3.00
2 . . . . 3.00
3 thru 4 . . . . @3.00
1-shot 1000 Words 3.00
1-shot Nine Lives 3.00
1-shot Sweet Nothings 3.50

KITZ 'N' KATZ
Phantasy
1 . . . . 3.50
Eclipse
2 . . . . 2.25
3 . . . . 2.25
4 and 5 . . . . @2.25

KLOR
Sirius 1999
1 . . . . 3.00

KLOWN SHOCK
North Star
1 Horror Stories. 2.75

KNEWTS OF
THE ROUND TABLE
Pan Entertainment, 1998
1 . . . . 2.50
2 thru 6 . . . . @2.50

KNIGHTMARE
Antarctic Press, 1994
1 . . . . 2.75
2 . . . . 2.75
3 Wedding Knight,pt.1 . . . . 2.75
4 Wedding Knight,pt.2 . . . . 2.75
5 F:Dream Shadow. 2.75
6 V:Razorblast 2.75

KNIGHT MASTERS
1 thru 7 . . . . @2.25

Knights of the Dinner Table #57
© Kenzer & Company

KNIGHTS OF
THE DINNER TABLE
Alderac Group, 1994
1 . . . . 40.00
2 . . . . 25.00
3 . . . . 15.00
Kenzer & Company, 1997
4 Have Dice Will Travel 12.00
5 Master of the Game. 12.00
6 on the high seas 9.00
7 Lord of Steam 9.00
8 A:magic cow. 5.00
9 To Dice for Sister Sara 5.00
16 thru 18 . . . . @5.00
19 thru 49. . . . . @3.00
50 double-size 5.00
51 thru 69 . . . . @3.00
70 thru 99. . . . . @4.00
100 giant 136-pg. 8.00
101 thru 108. . . . . @4.00
109 thru 133 . . . . @5.00
Spec. Black Hands Gaming Society 3.00
Spec. Origins 2003 . . . . 3.00

Spec #2 Black Hands Gaming. 3.00
Spec. Origins 2004 . . . . 3.00

KNIGHTS OF THE DINNER
TABLE: EVERKNIGHTS
Kenzer & Company, 2002
1 . . . . 3.00
2 thru 14 . . . . @3.00
Spec. Vs. King Arthur (2004). 3.00

KNIGHTS OF THE
DINNER TABLE/FAANS
Six-Handed Press, 1999
X-over Spec. 3.00

KNIGHTS OF THE DINNER
TABLE: HACKMASTERS
Kenzer & Company, 2000
1 . . . . 3.00
2 thru 8 . . . . @3.00
9 and 11 . . . . @3.00
11 . . . . 3.00
Becomes:

KNIGHTS OF THE DINNER
TABLE: HACKMASTERS
OF EVERKNIGHT
11 thru 15 . . . . @3.00

KNIGHTS OF THE DINNER
TABLE ILLUSTRATED
Kenzer & Company, 2000
1 . . . . 3.00
2 thru 8 . . . . @3.00
9 thru 41 . . . . @3.00
Travelers Special #1 . . . . 3.00

KNIGHTS OF THE DINNER
TABLE MINI-SERIES
Kenzer & Company, 2003
Vol. 1
1 (of 3) 3.00
2 thru 3 . . . . @3.00
1a thru 3a variant (c). . . . . @3.00

KNIGHT WATCHMAN
Caliber Press, 1994
1 Graveyard Shift,pt. 1 . . . . 3.00
2 Graveyard Shift,pt. 2 . . . . 3.00

KODOCHA:
SANA'S STAGE
Tokyopop Press, 2002
1 (of 5) by Miho Obana. 3.00
2 . . . . 3.00
3 thru 5 . . . . @3.00

KOMODO &
THE DEFIANTS
Victory
1 . . . . 2.25
2 thru 6 . . . . @2.25

KONI WAVES
Arcana Studio, 2006
1 (of 3) 3.00
2 thru 3 . . . . @3.00

KORVUS
Human Monster Press, 1997
1 by Mick Fernette 3.00
2 . . . . 3.00

Arrow Comics, 1998
3 . . . . 3.00
VOL 2
1 & 2 . . . . @3.00

KUNG FU WARRIORS
(Prev. ROBOWARRIORS)
CFW
12 . . . . 2.25
13 thru 19. . . . . @2.25

KUNOICHI
Lightning Comics, 1996
1 2 diff. mild covers. 3.00
1 platinum edition. 6.00
1 autographed edition. 9.00

KYRA
Elsewhere, 1989
1 thru 5 by Robin Ator. . . . . @2.50

L33T: COMICS
FOR GAMERS
Keenspot Entertainment, 2002
1 . . . . 5.00
2 thru 4 . . . . @5.00
5 24-pg. 3.00
6 thru 11 . . . . @5.00

LABOR FORCE
Blackthorne, 1986
1 thru 4 . . . . @2.50
5 thru 8 . . . . @2.50

LA COSA NOSTROID
Fireman Press, 1997
1 by Don Harmon & Rob Schrab . . 3.00
2 by Don Harmon & Edvis 3.00
3 . . . . 3.00
4 . . . . 3.00
5 . . . . 3.00
6 x-over madness 3.00
7 . . . . 3.00
8 . . . . 3.00
9 . . . . 3.00
10 final issue of Volume 1 . . . . 3.00

LACUNAE
CFD Productions, 1995
1 thru 4 F:Monkey Boys 2.50
5 thru 10 . . . . @2.50
11 HMo 2.50
12 HMo 2.50

LADIES OF
LONDON NIGHT
London Night, 1997
Fall Special. 5.00
Winter Special 5.00
    Winter Wonderland Edition 7.00
Spring 98 Special. 5.00
Spotlight: Devon Michaels 4.00

LADY DEATH:
DEATH GODDESS
Chaos! Comics
Spec. 16-page 2.50
Spec. variant (c). 6.00
Spec. premium (c) 10.00

LADY ARCANE
Heroic Publishing, 1992
1 color 4.00
2 thru 4 . . . . @3.50

LADY DEATH: INFERNAL SINS
Avatar Press, 2006

1-shot	2.50
1-shot wraparound (c)	3.00
1-shot variant (c)s	@3.00
1-shot premium (c)	10.00
0 blood red foil convention (c)	5.00
0 Repos (c)	6.00

LADY DEATH: QUEEN OF THE DEAD
Avatar Press, 2007

1-shot	3.00
1-shot variant (c)s	@3.00

LADY VAMPRE
Blackout Comics, 1996

0 (1995)	2.75
1 flip-book	3.00
0 Immortal No More (1998)	3.00
Spec.#1 In the Flesh (1996)	3.00
Spec.#1a photo sexy cover	10.00

LADY VAMPRE RETURNS
Blackout Comics, 1998

1 by Rob Roman & Kirk Manley	3.00
1a Deluxe edition	15.00

LAFFIN GAS
Blackthorne, 1986

1	2.50
2 thru 12	@2.50

LANCE STANTON WAYWARD WARRIOR

1 and 2	@2.25

LAND, THE
Caliber, 1999

1 by Donald Marquez	3.00
2	3.00
3	3.00
4 conclusion	3.00

LANDER
Mermaid Producions

1 Power of the Dollar,pt.1	2.25
2 Power of the Dollar,pt.2	2.25
3 Power of the Dollar,pt.3	2.25

Vol. 2

1 `By Whose Authority,'pt.1	2.75
2 `By Whose Authority,'pt.2	2.75

LAND OF OZ
Arrow Comics, 1998

1 by Gary Bishop & Bill Bryan	3.00
2 thru 6	@3.00

LAST DITCH
Edge Press

1 CCa(s),THa,	2.50

LAST GENERATION
Black Tie Studios, 1987

1	5.00
2	4.00
3 thru 5	@2.50
Book One Rep.	7.00

LAST MINUTE
Aces & Eights Publ., 2004

1	3.00
2 thru 6	6.00

LAST SIN OF MARK GRIM, THE
Sllent Devil Productions, 2006

1 (of 4)	3.00
2 thru 3	@3.00

Shanda Fantasy Arts, 2006

4	3.00

LATEX ALICE
Basement Comics, 2003

0	3.00
0a special edition	8.00
1 Blonde Ambition	3.00
1a Blonde Ambition, special	9.00
Spec. Papercuts	3.00
Spec. #1 Paper Cuts	9.00
Bikini Bash Gallery #1 spec.	9.00

LAZARUS CHRONICLES
Basement Comics 2006

1	3.50
1 special edition	
2	3.25

LEAGUE OF CHAMPIONS
Hero Comics, 1990
(cont. from Innovation L.of C. #3)

1 GP,F:Sparkplug,Icestar	3.50
2 GP(i),F:Marksman,Flare,Icicle	3.50
3	3.50
4 F:Sparkplug,League	3.50
5 Morrigan Wars,pt.#1	3.50
6 Morrigan Wars,pt.#3	3.50
7 Morrigan Wars,pt.#6	3.50
8 Morrigan Wars Conclusion	3.50
9 A:Gargoyle	3.50
10 A:Rose	3.50
11 thru 12	4.00
13 V:Malice	4.00
14 V:Olympians	4.00
15 V:Olympians	3.00

LE FEMME VAMPRIQUE
Brainstorm, 1997

1	3.50

LEGENDLORE
Caliber New Worlds

1 JMt signed	3.00
3 JMt	3.00
4 JMt	3.00
5 JMt	3.00
6 flip book w/Boston Bombers #4	3.00
7 JMt	3.00
8 JMt	3.00

LEGENDLORE: REALM WARS
Caliber New Worlds

1 by Joe Martin & Philip Xavier, Fawn cover by Xavier	3.00
1a Falla cover by Boller	3.00
1b signed	3.00
2	3.00
3	3.00
4 concl.	3.00

LEGENDLORE: WRATH OF THE DRAGON
Caliber Fantasy, 1998

1 by JMt & Philip Xavier	3.00
1 variant Philip Xavier(c)	3.00
2	3.00
3	3.00
4	3.00
5 Prisoner set free	3.00

Spec. Handbook	4.00
1-shot Legendlore: Slave of Fate by JMt & Philip Xavier	3.00
1-shot The Wind Spirits, 48-pg.	4.00
Giant Size Spec. 48-pg.	4.00

LEGEND OF LEMNEAR
CPM Manga, 1997

1	3.00
2 thru 18	@3.00

LEGENDS FROM DARKWOOD
Antarctic Press, 2003

1	3.50
2 thru 3	@3.50
4	3.00
Summer Fun Spec.	3.00
Special	3.00

LEGENDS OF CAMELOT
Caliber Fantasy, 1999

Excalibur	3.00
Quest For Honor	3.00
Merlin	3.00
The Enchanted Lady	3.00
Sir Balin & The Dolorous Stroke	3.00

LEGEND OF THE EIGHT DRAGON GODS
Komics, Inc., 2000

GN Vol. 1	10.00
GN Vol. 2 thru Vol. 6	@10.00

Legends of Luxura #3 #3
© Brainstorm

LEGENDS OF LUXURA
Brainstorm, 1996

1 platinum edition	5.00
2 gold edition	5.00
3	3.00

LEGION ANTHOLOGY
Limelight, 1997

1 four stories	3.00
2	3.00
3 F:Binary Angel	3.00
4	3.00
5 Binary Angel	3.00

B & W PUB.

LEGION X-I
Greater Mercury
1 McKinney 5.00
2 McKinney,rare 15.00
Volume 2, 1989
1 thru 4 . . . . @2.50

LEGION X-2
Vol 2 #1 . . . . 2.50
Vol 2 #2 . . . . 2.50
Vol 2 #3 . . . . 2.50
Vol 2 #4 . . . . 2.50

LENORE
Slave Labor, 1998
1 by Roman Dirge 3.00
2 thru 12 . . . . @3.00

LENSMAN
Eternity, 1990
1 E.E.`Doc' Smith adapt. 2.25
2 . . . . 2.25
3 . . . . 2.25
4 . . . . 2.25
5 On Radelix 2.25
6 . . . . 2.25
Collectors Spec #1, 56 pgs 4.00

LENSMAN:
GALACTIC PATROL
Eternity, 1990
1 thru 7 E.E. `Doc' Smith adapt. . @2.25

LENSMAN:
WAR OF THE GALAXIES
Eternity, 1990
1 thru 7 . . . . @2.25

LEONARDO
Mirage, 1986
1-shot TMNTurtles 13.00

LETHAL LADIES
OF BRAINSTORM
Brainstorm, 1997
1 F:Luxura, Vampfire, etc 3.00
1 luxury edition 5.00

LETHAL STRIKE
ARCHIVES
London Night, 1997
1 rep. Razor #7, #10 & Uncut
  #19–#21 . . . . 3.00

LETHAL STRIKE:
SHADOW VIPER
London Night, 1998
1 (of 2) from Razor: Torture #4 . . . 3.00
1 leather 15.00

LETHARGIC LAD
ADVENTURES
Crusade Entertainment, 1997
1 by Greg Hyland 3.00
2 . . . . 3.00
Becomes:

LETHARGIC LAD
TV Comics, 1997
3 by Greg Hyland 3.00
4 . . . . 3.00
5 . . . . 3.00
TPB Big Book of Lethargic Lad . . . 16.00

Lethargic Comics
6 by Greg Hyland 3.00
7 thru 14 . . . . @3.00
Dork Storm Press, 2002
Ann. #1 Jumbo-sized 4.00
Ann. #2 Jumbo-sized 4.00
Ann. #3 Jumbo-sized 4.00

LEVEL X
Caliber, 1997
1 . . . . 3.00
2 32pg 3.00
3 48pg 4.00

LEVEL X:
THE NEXT REALITY
Caliber, 1997
1 (of 2) by Dan Harbison & Randy
  Buccini, 64pg 4.00
2 48pg 4.00

LIBBY ELLIS
Eternity, 1988
1 . . . . 2.50
2 thru 4 . . . . @2.50

LIBERATOR
Eternity
1 . . . . 2.25
2 thru 6 . . . . @2.25

LIBERTY FROM HELL
Radio Comix, 2003
1 . . . . 3.00
2 thru 6 . . . . @3.00

LIBERTY MEADOWS
Insight Studios, 1999
1 by Frank Cho 25.00
2 . . . . 15.00
3 . . . . 8.00
4 thru 6 . . . . @8.00
7 thru 10 . . . . @7.00
11 thru 20 . . . . @6.00
21 thru 23 . . . . @5.00
24 Virtual Reality Adventure 5.00
25 Pool Party 5.00
26 Fossil Dinosaurs 5.00
Spec. Wedding Album 10.00

Liberty Meadows #10
© Insight Studios

L.I.F.E. BRIGADE
Blue Comet
1 A:Dr. Death 2.25
1a 2nd printing 2.25
2 . . . . 2.25

LIFE OF A FETUS
Slave Labor, 1999
1 by Andy Ristaino 3.00
2 thru 7 . . . . @3.00

LIFEQUEST
Caliber, 1997
1 by Matt Vanderpol 3.00
2 thru 6 . . . . @3.00

LITTLE GLOOMY
Amaze Ink/SLG, 1999
1 by Landry Walker & Eric Jones . . 3.00
2 thru 6 . . . . @3.00
Halloween Spec. 3.50

LITTLE GLOOMY'S SUPER
SCARY MONSTER SHOW
Amaze Ink/SLG, 2005
1 . . . . 3.00
2 . . . . 3.00
3 . . . . 3.00

LITTLE SCROWLIE
Amaze Ink/SLG, 2003
4 thru 7 . . . . @3.00
8 thru 15 . . . . @3.00

LITTLE STAR
Oni Press, 2005
1 . . . . 3.00
2 thru 6 . . . . @3.00

LITTLE WHITE MOUSE
(THE SERIES)
Caliber, 1998
1 by Paul Sizer 3.00
2 Fever Dreams 3.00
3 Filthy Jake 3.00
4 . . . . 3.00

LITTLE WHITE MOUSE:
ENTROPY DREAMING
Blue Line Pro Comics, 2001
1 by Paul Sizer 3.00
2 Nuts and Bolts 3.00
3 . . . . 3.00
4 concl. 3.00

LITTLE WHITE MOUSE:
OPEN SPACE
Blue Line Pro Comics, 2002
1 (of 4) by Paul Sizer 3.00
2 thru 4 . . . . @3.00

LIVINGSTONE MOUNTAIN
Adventure Comics, 1991
1 I:Scat,Dragon Rax 2.50
2 Scat & Rax Create Monsters 2.50
3 Rax rescue attempt 2.50
4 Final issue 2.50

LLOYD LLEWELLYN
Fantagraphics, 1986
1 Mag Size 4.00
2 thru 6 Mag Size . . . . @2.50
7 Regular Size 2.50

All comics prices listed are for *Near Mint* condition.   **CVA Page 763**

LOCAL
Oni Press, 2005
1 (of 12) 3.00
1a 2nd printing 3.00
2 Polaroid Boyfriend 3.00
3 Thories and Defenses 3.00
4 The Two Brothers 3.00
5 Last Lonely Days at the
   Oxford Theater 3.00
6 Megan and Gloria, Apartment 5A 3.00
7 Smash the State 3.00
8 Food as Substitute. 3.00
9 Wish You Were Here 3.00
10 The Process 3.00
11 thru 12 . . . . @3.00

LOCO VS. PULVERINE
Eclipse, 1992
1 Parody 2.50

LODOSS WAR:
CHRONICLES OF THE
HEROIC KNIGHT
CPM Manga, 2000
1 by Ryo Mizuno & M. Natsumoto . 3.00
2 thru 19 . . . . @3.00

LODOSS WAR:
DEELIT'S TALE
CPM Manga, 2001
1 by R. Mizuno & S. Yoneyama . . . 3.00
1a signed & numbered 15.00
2 thru 4 . . . . @3.00
5 thru 8 . . . . @3.00

LODOSS WAR:
THE GREY WITCH
CPM Manga, 1998
1 by Ryo Mizuno & Yoshihiko Ochi. 3.00
2 by Ryo Mizuno & Akikiro Yamada 3.00
3 thru 10 . . . . @3.00
11 thru 22 . . . . @3.00

LODOSS WAR:
THE LADY OF PHARIS
CPM Manga, 1999
1 by Ryo Mizuno & Akihiro Yamada 3.00
2 thru 7 . . . . @3.00

LOGAN'S RUN
Adventure Comics, 1990
1 thru 6 Novel adapt. . . . . @2.50

LOGAN'S WORLD
Adventure Comics, 1991
1 Seq. to Logan's Run 2.50
2 thru 6 . . . . @2.50

LONER
Fleetway
1 Pt.1 (of 7). 2.25
2 thru 6 Pt.2 thru Pt.6 . . . . @2.25

LONE WOLF & CUB
First, 1987–91
1 FM(c) 8.00
1a 2nd printing 2.50
1b 3rd printing. 2.50
2 . . . . 4.00
2a 2nd printing 2.50
3 . . . . 4.00
4 thru 10 . . . . @4.00
11 thru 17 . . . . @3.00
18 thru 25. . . . . @3.00

Lone Wolf & Cub #2
© First

26 thru 36. . . . . @3.00
37 and 38 . . . . @4.00
39 120-pg. 6.00
40 . . . . 3.25
41 MP(c), 60-pg. 4.00
42 thru 45 MP(c) . . . . @3.25

LOOKERS
Avatar Press, 1997
1 . . . . 3.00
1 deluxe 5.00
1 signed 12.00
2 . . . . 3.00
2 Deluxe cover 8.00
Spec. #1. . . . . 3.00
Spec. #1 signed 8.00
Spec. Allure of the Serpent (1999) 3.50
Spec. Slaves of Anubis (1998). . . . 3.50

LORD OF THE DEAD
Conquest
1 R.E.Howard adapt. 3.00

LORELEI
Power Comics, 1996
2 'Building the Perfect Beast,'pt.7 . 2.50
3 'Building the Perfect Beast,'pt.8 . 2.50
Vol.2
0 2nd printing 2.50
1 . . . . 2.50
1a deluxe 4.00
1b signed 8.00

LORI LOVECRAFT
Caliber, 1997
1 MV, 48pg 4.00
1a signed 4.00
1-shot The Dark Lady (1997) 3.00
1-shot Repression (1998). 3.00
Spec. The Big Comeback (1998). . . 3.00
AV Publications, 2000
1 by P.Ventrella & M.Vosburg 3.00
2 into the past 3.00

LOST, THE
Caliber, 1996
1 . . . . 3.00
1a special ed. 7.00
1b signed 3.00
2 thru 4 . . . . @3.00

LOST CONTINENT
Eclipse, 1990
1 thru 5, Manga. . . . . @3.50

LOST SQUAD
Devil's Due Publishing, 2005
1 thru 6 . . . . @3.00

LOST STORIES
Creative Frontiers, 1998
1 . . . . 3.00
2 . . . . 3.00
3 . . . . 3.00
4 The Big Horn Bruhaha. 3.00
5 Strike Force O'Shea,pt.1 . . . . . . 3.00
6 Strike Force O'Shea,pt.2 . . . . . . 3.00
7 Gnome for a Day 3.00
8 A Vampire Too Far. 3.00
9 The Undertroll Saga,pt.1 . . . . . . 3.00

LOST WORLD, THE
Millennium, 1996
1 & 2 Arthur Conan Doyle adapt. @3.00

LOTHAR
Powerhouse Graphics
1 I:Lothar,Galactic Bounty Hunter. . 2.50
2 I:Nightcap. 2.50

LOUIS RIEL
Drawn & Quarterly, 1999
1 (of 10) by Chester Brown 3.00
2 thru 5 . . . . @3.00
6 thru 10 . . . . @3.00

LOVE AND ROCKETS
Fantagraphics Books, 1982–96
1 HB,B&W cover, adult. 30.00
1a HB,Color cover 20.00
1b 2nd printing 4.00
2 HB 10.00
3 HB 6.00
4 HB 6.00
5 HB 6.00
6 HB 5.00
7 HB 6.00
8 HB 6.00
9 HB 5.00
10 HB 5.00
11 thru 21 HB . . . . @3.00
22 thru 39 HB . . . . @3.00
40 thru 50 . . . . @3.00
Bonanza rep. 3.00
Vol. 2, 2001
1 GHe,JHr, ... 4.00
1a 2nd printing 4.00
2 thru 9 . . . . @4.00
10 . . . . 6.00
11 thru 19 . . . . @4.50
20 . . . . 7.00

LOVE FIGHTS
Oni Press, 2003
1 . . . . 3.00
2 thru 4 . . . . @3.00
5 . . . . 6.00
6 thru 12 . . . . @3.00

LOVE HINA
Tokyopop Press, 2002
1 (of 4) by Ken Akamatsu 3.00
2 thru 4 . . . . @3.00

LOVE IN TIGHTS
Amaze Ink, 1998
1 . . . . 3.00

Spec. Valentine's Day Special 3.00
Spec. Spring Fling 3.00
Anniv. #1 . . . . 3.00
6 & 7 . . . . @3.00

LOVELY PRUDENCE
Millennium, 1997
1 by Maze 3.00
2 . . . . 3.00
3 Nightmares of Breeding. 3.00
#M 24-pg. 2.25
#M 24-pg., signed 3.00
Spec. Swimsuit Special 3.00
Christmas Misery Spec.#1 . . . . 3.00

LOVE THE WAY YOU LOVE
Oni Press 2006
1 . . . . 6.00
2 . . . . 6.00
3 thru 6 . . . . @6.00

LUBA
Fantagraphics, 1998
1 by Gilbert Hernandez 3.00
2 thru 5 . . . . @3.00
6 thru 10 . . . . @3.50

LUBA'S COMICS & STORIES
Fantagraphics, 2000
1 by Gilbert Hernandez. 3.00
2 GHe 3.50
3 GHe, Ofelia 3.50
4 GHe, The Light of Venus 3.50
5 GHe, Lovers and Hector 3.50
6 GHe 3.50
7 GHe, Fritz After Dark 3.50

LUFTWAFFE 1946
[Mini-Series]
Antarctic Press, 1996
1 . . . . 5.00
2 thru 4 . . . . @4.00
Antarctic Press, 1997
1 by Ted Namura & BDn. 3.00
2 Luftsturm,pt.2 . . . . 3.00
3 Luftsturm,pt.3 . . . . 3.00
4 Luftsturm,pt.4 . . . . 3.00
5 new weapons 3.00
6 Projekt Saucer,pt.1 . . . . 3.00
7 Projekt Saucer,pt.2 . . . . 3.00
8 Projekt Saucer,pt.3 . . . . 3.00
9 Projekt Saucer,pt.4 . . . . 3.00
10 Projekt Saucer,pt.5 . . . . 3.00
11 Projekt Saucer, epilogue 3.00
12 Richthofen's Flying Circus,pt.1 . . 3.00
13 Richthofen's Flying Circus,pt.2 . . 3.00
14 Jagdeschwader,pt.2 . . . . 3.00
15 Jagdeschwader,pt.3 . . . . 3.00
16 Jagdeschwader,pt.4 . . . . 3.00
17 Jagdeschwader,pt.5 . . . . 3.00
18 Schweinfurt 3.00
Tech Manual Vol. 1 . . . . 4.00
Tech Manual Vol. 2 . . . . 4.00
Tech Manual Vol. 3 Rocket Fighters 4.00
Tech Manual Vol. 4 Amerika
   Bombers 4.00
Tech Manual Vol. 5 Wonder
   Weapons 4.00
Tech. Manual Vol. 6 . . . . 6.00
Spec.#1 Triebflugel 3.00
Spec.#1 World War II: 1946 . . . . . . 4.00
Ann. #1 prototype artwork 3.00
New Volume (2002)
1 Tigers of the Luftwaffe 6.00
2 thru 18 . . . . @6.00

Volume 5
1 . . . . 6.00
2 thru 3 . . . . @6.00
Annual #2. 5.00
Annual #2. 5.00
TPB Technical Manual 22.00
TPB Vol. 1 Sourcebook 6.00

LUM*URUSEI YATSURA
Viz Communications
1 Art by Rumiko Takahashi 3.00
2 . . . . 3.00
3 . . . . 3.00
4 . . . . 3.00
5 . . . . 3.25
6 thru 8 . . . . @3.00

LUNAR DONUT
Cosmic Lunchbox Comics, 1996
1 by Parham & Tucker 3.00
2 thru 4 . . . . @3.00
Lunar Donut
5 . . . . 3.00
6 Powdered Sugar 3.00

LURID
IDW Publishing, 2002
1 by Paul Lee & Adam Huntley. . . . 3.00
2 . . . . 3.00
3 . . . . 3.00

LUST FOR LIFE
Slave Labor, 1997
1 by Jeff LeVine 3.00
2 . . . . 3.00
3 . . . . 3.00
4 . . . . 3.00

LUXURA
Brainstorm, 1996
Convention Book 2 . . . . 3.00
Ann.#1 48pg (1998) 4.00
Pin-up mag. Luxura: The Good, The
   Bad and the Beautiful (1999) . . 4.00
Spec.1 Luxura & Vampfire, x-over
   by Fauve (1997) 3.00
Luxura Leather, Platinum edition . . . 5.00
Luxura Leather, Signed edition 8.00

LUXURA/BABY ANGEL X
Brainstorm, 1996
Spec. x-over 3.00
Spec. deluxe 5.00
Luxury edition. 8.00
Deluxe luxury edition 12.00

LUXURA/WIDOW: BLOOD LUST
Brainstorm
Omega x-over pt.2 concl. 3.00
Omega Fusion cover 5.00
Luxury edition. 8.00
Deluxe luxury edition 12.00
See: Widow/Luxura for pt.1

LYNX: AN ELFLORD TALE
Peregrin, 1999
1 by Barry Blair 3.00
2 by Barry Blair & Colin Chan. 3.00
3 & 4 . . . . @3.00

M.A.C.H. 1
Fleetway
1 I:John Probe-Secret Agent 2.25
2 thru 9 . . . . @2.25

Mackenzie Queen #3
© Matrix

MACKENZIE QUEEN
Matrix, 1985
1 . . . . 3.75
2 thru 5 . . . . @3.75

MACROSS II
Viz Comics, 1992
1 Macross Saga sequel 2.75
2 A:Ishtar. 2.75
3 F:Reporter Hibiki,Ishtar 2.75
4 V:Feff,The Marduk 2.75
5 . . . . 2.75
6 . . . . 2.75
7 Sylvie Confesses 2.75
8 F:Ishtar. 2.75
9 V:Marduk Fleet 2.75
10 . . . . 2.75

MACROSS II: THE MICRON CONSPIRACY
Viz, 1994
1 Manga 2.75

MAD DOGS
Eclipse, 1992
1 I:Mad Dogs(Cops) 2.50
2 V:Chinatown Hood 2.50
3 . . . . 2.50

MAD RACCOONS
MU Press, 1991
1 thru 7 by Cathy Hill, Angst of
   an Artist . . . . @3.00

MAELSTROM
Aircel, 1987
1 thru 13 . . . . @2.50

MAGGOTS
Hamilton, 1991
1 JSon, mag size 4.00
2 JSon, mag size 4.00
3 GM/JSon,inc.'Some Kinda
   Beautiful' 4.00

MAGICAL MATES
Antarctic Press, 1995
1 & 2 Manga, by Mio Odagi . . . . @3.00
3 thru 8 (of 8) . . . . @3.00

MAGICAL POKEMON JOURNEY
Viz Communications, 2000
1 How Do You Do, Pikachu	5.00
2 Cooking with Jigglypuff	5.00
3 Pokemon Holiday	5.00
4 Fun at the Beach	5.00

PART 2, 2000
1 thru 4	@5.00

PART 3, 2000
1 thru 4	@5.00

PART 4, 2001
1 thru 4 Love Potion Pursuit	@5.00

PART 5, 2001
1 thru 4	@5.00

PART 6, 2001
1 (of 4)	5.00
2 thru 4	@5.00

PART 7, 2002
1	5.00
2 thru 4	@5.00

MAGIC PRIEST
Antarctic Press, 1998
1 (of 3) by B.Lyga & N.Googe	3.00
2	3.00

MAGIC WHISTLE
Alternative Press
Vol 2
1 by Sam Henderson	3.00
2 thru 8	@3.00
9 96-pg.	9.00
10	9.00

MAGUS
Caliber Core, 1998
1L by Gary Reed & Craig Brasfield, VcL(c)	3.00
1D GyD(c)	3.00
1 premium edition, signed	9.00
2 Magus secrets	3.00
3 Lilith & Beezlebub	3.00
1-shot Magus: The Forever King	3.00
Spec. Dawn of Armageddon, x-over, 48-pg.	3.00

MAI, THE PSYCHIC GIRL
Eclipse, 1987
1 I:Mai,Alliance of 13 Sages	3.75
1a 2nd printing	2.50
2 V:Wisdom Alliance	2.50
2a 2nd printing	2.50
3 V:Kaieda,I:Ojii-San.	2.50
4	2.50
5 thru 19	@2.50
20 thru 28	@2.50

MAID ATTACK
White Lightning Productions, 2003
1 (of 4)	4.00
2 thru 4	@4.00

MAINTENANCE
Onipress, 2006
1	3.50
2 thru 7	3.50

MAISON IKKOKU
Viz Comics, 1993
1 thru 7 Manga	3.00

[Part Two]
1 thru 6	3.00

[Part Three]
1 thru 6	3.00

[Part Four]
1 thru 6 F:Kyoko	3.00
7 thru 10	@3.00

[Part Six], 1996
1 thru 11 by Rumiko Takahashi	@3.50

[Part Seven], 1997
1 thru 8 by Rumiko Takahashi	@3.25
9 thru 13	@3.50

[Part Eight], 1998
1 (of 8)	3.25
2	3.50
3 thru 8	@3.25

[Part Nine], 1999
1 (of 10)	3.25
2 thru 10	@3.25

MANDRAKE
1	4.00
2	4.00
3	4.00
Ultimate Mandrake	15.00

MANDRAKE MONTHLY
1	4.00
2	4.00
3	5.00
4	5.00
5	5.00
6	7.00
Special #1	7.00

Man-Eating Cow #1
© New England Comics

MAN-EATING COW
New England Comics, 1992
1 Spin-off from the Tick	3.25
2 O:Mr.Krinkles,A:Lt.Valentine	2.75
3 Final issue	2.75
Bonanza #1, 128pg (1996)	5.00
Bonanza #2, 100pg.	5.00

MAN-ELF
3 A:Jerry Cornelius	2.25

MAN FROM U.N.C.L.E.
Entertainment Publ., 1987
1 `Number One with a Bullet Affair	3.50
2 `Number One with a Bullet Affair	3.00
3 `The E-I-E-I-O Affair'	3.00
4 `The E-I-E-I-O Affair,' concl.	3.00
5 `The Wasp Affair'	3.00
6 `Lost City of THRUSH Affair'	3.00
7 `The Wildwater Affair'	3.00
8 `The Wilder West Affair'	3.00
9 `The Canhadian Lightning Affair'	3.00
10 `The Turncoat Affair'	3.00
11 `Craters of the Moon Affair'	3.00

MANGA EX
Antarctic Press, 2001
1	7.00
2 thru 6	@7.00

MANGAPHILE
Radio Comix, 1999
1	3.00
2 thru 5	@3.00
6 thru 11	@3.00
12 48-pg.	4.00
13 48-pg.	4.00
14 thru 21 48-pg.	4.00
22 thru 25	@5.00

MANGA VIZION
Viz Communications
Vol. 1, 1995
1 thru 10 Ogre Slayer	@5.00

Vol. 2, 1996
1 thru 12	@5.00

Vol. 3, 1997
1 thru 8	@5.00

Vol. 4
1 thru 8	@5.00

MANGAZINE
Antarctic Press, 1985
1 newsprint cover	12.00
1a reprint	3.00
2	9.00
3	8.00
4	8.00
5	8.00

New Series
1	3.00
2	3.00
3	2.25
4	2.25
5 thru 7	@2.25
8 thru 13	@2.25
14 New Format	3.00
15 thru 44	@3.00

VOL. 3, 1999
1 thru 15	@9.00
16 thru 27 140+-pg.	@9.00
28 thru 39	@9.00
40 thru 70	@10.00

MANIMAL
Renegade, 1986
1 EC,rep.	2.50

MAN OF RUST
Blackthorne, 1986
1 Cover A	2.50
1 Cover B	2.50

MANSLAUGHTER
Brainstorm, 1996
1	3.00
1a gold foil edition	5.00

MANTUS FILES
Eternity
1 Sidney Williams novel adapt	2.50
2 Vampiric Figures	2.50
3 Secarus' Mansion	2.50
4 A:Secarus	2.50

MARCANE
Eclipse
1 Book 1,JMu 6.00

MARK I
(Prev.: Atomic Comics)
2 . . . . 2.25

MARK MILLAR'S
THE UNFUNNIES
Avatar, 2003
1 . . . . 3.50
2 thru 3 . . . . @3.50
1a Platinum (c) 6.00
1a thru 3a offensive (c) . . . . @3.50

MARMALADE BOY
Tokyopop Press, 2001
1 (of 5) by Wataru Yoshizumi 3.00
2 thru 5 . . . . 3.00

MARQUIS, THE
Caliber, 1997
1 GyD 3.00
1 spec. double gatefold cover 6.00
2 Marquis cover by Vincent Locke . 3.00
2a Marquis view of world GyD(c) . . 3.00
3 . . . . 3.00
Spec. The Marquis, Gallery of
  Hell, GyD 4.00
Spec. The Marquis: Les Preludes,
  GyD prelude edition (1996) 3.00
Spec.A Les Preludes, signed 3.00

MARQUIS, THE:
A SIN OF ONE
Oni Press, 2003
1 GyD 3.00

MARQUIS, THE:
DANSE MACABRE
Oni Press, 2000
1 (of 5) by Guy Davis 3.00
2 . . . . 3.00
3 thru 5 . . . . @3.00

MARTIAN SUCCESSOR
NADESICO
CPM Manga, 1999
1 by Kia Asamiya 3.00
2 . . . . 3.00
3 . . . . 3.00
4 thru 15 . . . . @3.00
16 thru 26 . . . . @3.00

MASKED WARRIOR X
Antarctic Press, 1996
1 (of 6) by Masayuki Fujihara 3.50
2 . . . . 3.00
3 The Girls of Olympus,' pt.2 . . . . . 3.00
4 'Protect the Silver Fortress' 3.00

MASQUERADE
Eclipse
1 . . . . 2.25
2 . . . . 2.25
3 . . . . 2.25

MATAAK
K-Blamm, 1995
1 I:Mataak 2.50
2 Spirit of Peace 2.50

MATT CHAMPION
Metro
1 EC 2.25
2 EC 2.25

MAVIS
Exhibit A, 1998
1 BLs, F:Wolff & Byrd's secretary . . 3.00
2 . . . . 3.00

MAX HAMM
FAIRY TALE DETECTIVE
Nite Owl Comix 2002
1 by Frank Cammuso 5.00
Vol. 2
1 (of 3) 5.00
2 thru 3 . . . . @5.00

MAXION
CPM, 1999
1 by Takeshi Takebayashi 3.00
2 thru 11 . . . . @3.00
12 thru 24 . . . . @3.00
25 . . . . 3.00
26 . . . . 3.00

MAX OF THE
REGULATORS
Atlantic
1 . . . . 4.00
2 thru 4 . . . . @3.50

MAXWELL MOUSE
FOLLIES
Renegade, 1986
1 Large format (1981) 4.00
1a Comic Size(1986) 3.00
2 thru 6 . . . . @2.50

MAYHEM
1 Mask(c) 9.00
2 thru 6 . . . . @8.00

MAZE AGENCY
Caliber, 1997
1 The Death of Justice Girl
  reprint series 3.00
1a signed 3.00
2 and 3 . . . . @3.00
2a and 3a variant AH(c)s . . . . . . @3.00

MEASLES
Fantagraphics, 1998
1 by Gilbert Hernandez 3.00
2 thru 8 . . . . @3.00

MEAT CAKE
Fantagraphics, 1995
1 thru 4 . . . . @2.50
5 thru 8 . . . . @3.00
9 thru 16 . . . . @4.00

MECHANOIDS
Caliber, 1991
1 . . . . 2.50
2 thru 5 . . . . @3.50

MECHARIDER: THE
REGULAR SERIES
Castle
1 . . . . 3.00
2 thru 3 F:Winter 3.00
Spec.#1 Limited Edition 3.00

MEDABOTS
Viz Communications, 2002
Part 1
1 (of 4) by Rin Horuma 2.75
2 thru 4 . . . . @2.75
Part 2
1 (of 4) New Challenges 2.75
2 thru 4 . . . . @2.75
Part 3
1 (of 4) 2.75
2 thru 4 . . . . @2.75
Part 4
1 by Horumarin 2.75
2 thru 4 . . . . 2.75

Megaton #3
© Megaton

MEGATON
Megaton, 1983
1 JG(c),EL(1stProWork),GD,MG,
  A:Ultragirl,Vanguard 14.00
2 EL,JG(pin-up),A:Vanguard 11.00
3 MG,AMe,JG,EL,I:Savage
  Dragon 18.00
4 AMe,EL,2nd A:Savage Dragon
  (inc.EL profile) 9.00
5 AMe,RLd(inside front cover) 5.00
6 AMe,JG(inside back cover),
  EL(Back cover) 5.00
7 AMe 5.00
8 RLd,I:Youngblood(Preview) 18.00

MEGATON MAN MEETS
THE UNCATEGORIZABLE
X-THEMS
Jabberwocky, 1989
1 . . . . 2.50

MEGATON MAN VS.
FORBIDDEN
FRANKENSTEIN
Fiasco Comics, 1996
1 by Don Simpson & Anton Drek . . 3.00

MELISSA MOORE:
BODYGUARD
Draculina Publishing, 1995
1 . . . . 3.00
2 thru 3 V:Machine Gun Eddie . . @3.00

MEMORY MAN
Emergency Stop Press, 1995
1 thru 2 Some of the Space Man . . 3.00

MEN IN BLACK
Aircel, 1991
1 by Lowell Cunningham & Sandy
  Carruthers, basis of Movie . . . 40.00
2 . . . . 22.00
3 F:Jay, Arbiter Doran 22.00

[Book II], 1991
1 . . . . 25.00
2 thru 3 . . . . @12.00

MEN IN BLACK:
THE ROBORG INCIDENT
Castle
1 thru 3 . . . . @3.00

MEN'S ALTERED WARS
CHRONICLES
Antarctic Press, 2001
Ann. #1 Magazine 6.00
Ann. #2 . . . . 6.00

Antarctic Press, 2003
1 . . . . 5.00
2 thru 3 . . . . @5.00

MERCEDES
Angus Publishing, 1995
8 thru 15 by Mike Friedland
  & Grant Fuhst . . . . @3.00

VOL. 4
1 thru 4 . . . . @3.00

VOL. 5, 1997
1 . . . . 3.00
2 . . . . 3.00
3 . . . . 3.00
Spec. Senseless Acts of
  Beauty (1998) 3.00

MERCHANTS OF DEATH
Eclipse, 1988
1 . . . . 2.50
2 thru 5 . . . . @2.50

MERCY
Avatar Press, 1997
0 O:Mercy 3.00
0b leather cover 25.00
1 (of 2) by Bill Maus 3.00
1 leather cover 22.00
1 signed 10.00

MERLIN
Adventure Comics, 1990
1 BMC,Merlin's Visions 2.50
2 V:Warlord Carados 2.50
3 . . . . 2.50
4 Ninevah 2.50
5 D:Hagus. 2.50
6 Final Issue 2.50

[2nd Series]
1 Journey of Rhiannon & Tryon . . . 2.50
2 Conclusion 2.50

MERMAID'S GAZE
Viz Comics, 1995
1 thru 3 V:Shingo 2.75
4 final issue. 2.75

METACOPS
Monster Comics, 1991
1 and 2 . . . . @2.25

Metal Guardian Faust #8
© Viz Communications

METAL GUARDIAN FAUST
Viz Communications, 1997
1 by Tetsuo Ueyama . . . . @3.00
2 thru 8 . . . . @3.00

METAL HURLANT
Humanoids Publishing, 2002
1 . . . . 4.00
2 thru 3 . . . . @4.00
4 thru 9 . . . . @4.00

METROPOLIS
Caliber, 1997
0 movie adaptation, series
  prequel,48pg 4.00
1 The Last Fredersen, pt.1 . . . . . . 3.00
2 The Last Fredersen, pt.2 . . . . . . 3.00
3 The Last Fredersen, pt.3 . . . . . . 3.00

METAPHYSIQUE
Eclipse
1 NB,Short Stories 2.50
2 NB,Short Stories 2.50

MIAMI MICE
Rip Off Press, 1986
1 1st printing 3.00
1a 2nd printing 2.50
3 . . . . 2.50
4 Record,A:TMNT 3.00

MICHELANGELO
Mirage, 1986
1 TMNT 17.00
1a 2nd Printing 4.50

MICRA
Fictioneer, 1986
1 . . . . 4.00
2 . . . . 3.00
3 . . . . 3.00
4 . . . . 2.50
5 . . . . 2.50
6 . . . . 2.50
7 . . . . 2.50
8 . . . . 2.50

MIDDLEMAN, THE
Viper Comics, 2005
1 . . . . 3.00

2 thru 4 . . . . @3.00

Vol. 2, 2006
1 . . . . 1.00
2 thru 4 . . . . @3.00

MIDNIGHT
Blackthorne
1 thru 4 . . . . @2.25

MIDNIGHT MOVER
Oni Press, 2003
1 (of 4) 3.00
2 thru 4 . . . . @3.00

MIDNIGHT PANTHER
CPM Comics, 1997
1 Manga, translated 3.00
2 . . . . 3.00
3 . . . . 3.00
4 . . . . 3.00
5 . . . . 3.00
6 Den of Scoundrels 3.00
7 The Sleeping Town 3.00
8 to Reincarnation City 3.00
9 O:Midnight Panthers 3.00
10 . . . . 3.00
11 . . . . 3.00
12 . . . . 3.00
Spec. Breaking Up is Hard to Do . . . 3.00

MIDNIGHT PANTHER:
FEUDAL FANTASY
CPM Manga, 1998
1 by Yu Asagiri 3.00
2 thru 5 . . . . @3.00

MIDNIGHT PANTHER:
SCHOOL DAZE
CPM Comics, 1998
1 (of 5) by Yu Asagiri 3.00
2 thru 5 . . . . @3.00

MIDNIGHT SUN
Amaze Ink/SLG, 2006
1 (of 5 . . . . 3.00
2 thru 3 . . . . @3.00

MIDNITE SKULKER
Target, 1986
1 thru 7 . . . . @2.50

MIGHTY GUY
C&T, 1987
1 . . . . 2.50
2 thru 6 . . . . @2.50
Summer Fun Spec #1 . . . . 2.50

MIGHTY MITES
Eternity, 1986
1 I:X-Mites. 2.50
2 & 3 . . . . @2.50

MIGHTY MOUSE
ADVENTURE MAGAZINE
Spotlight, 1987
1 . . . . 5.00

MIGHTY TINY
Antarctic
1 . . . . 2.25
2 thru 4 . . . . @2.25
5 . . . . 2.50
Mouse Marines Collection rep. 7.50

MIKE HOFFMAN: ISLAND OF THE TIKI GODDESS
Basement, 2007
Spec. 3.00

MIKE HOFFMAN'S LOST WORLDS OF FANTASY AND SCI-FI
Antimater/Hoffman Int., 2003
1 . . . . 3.00
2 thru 10 . . . . @3.00
1a thru 10a special edition . . . . . @9.00

MIKE HOFFMAN'S MONSTERS AND MAIDENS
Antimater/Hoffman International, 2003
1 . . . . 3.50
2 . . . . 3.00

MIKE HOFFMAN'S TIGRESS
Black Daze, 2000
1 by Mike Hoffman 3.00
Antimater/Hoffman Int., 2003
Spec. Cover Gallery Spec. 9.00

MILK & CHEESE
Slave Labor, 1991–97
1 EDo, Milk Products gone bad . . 45.00
1a 2nd thru 7th printing. 4.00
2 . . . . 27.00
2a 2nd thru 4th printing. 4.00
3 . . . . 20.00
3a 2nd thru 4th printing. 4.00
4 . . . . 12.00
4a 2nd & 3rd printing 4.00
5 . . . . 12.00
5a 2nd & 3rd printing 4.00
6 . . . . 7.00
6a 2nd printing 3.00
7 . . . . 6.00
Other #1 . . . . 2.75
Third #1 . . . . 2.75
Fourth #1 . . . . 2.75
First #2 . . . . 2.75
Six Six Six #1 . . . . 2.75
Six Six Six 2nd printing, EDo. 2.75
Latest Thing 3.00

MILLENNIUM 2.5: THE BUCK ROGERS SAGA
ACG Comics, 2000
1 by Dick Calkin 3.00
2 thru 4 . . . . @3.00

MILTON CANIFF'S TERRY & THE PIRATES
ACG Comics, 1999
1 by Milton Caniff 3.00
2 . . . . 3.00
3 . . . . 3.00
4 . . . . 3.00

MINESHAFT
Fantagraphics Books, 2005
1 . . . . 5.00
16 . . . . 5.00
17 . . . . 6.00
18 thru 20 . . . . @7.00

MINIMUM WAGE
Fantagraphics, 1995
Vol. 1, new printing 11.00
Vol. 2, 1995
1 thru 4 . . . . @3.00
5 by Bob Fingerman 3.00
6 . . . . 3.00
7 . . . . 3.00
8 . . . . 3.00
9 Artsy Fartsy 3.00
10 . . . . 3.00

MIRACLE GIRLS
Tokyopop Press, 2000
1 . . . . 3.00
2 . . . . 3.00
3 thru 23 . . . . @3.00

MIRACLE SQUAD BLOOD & DUST
Apple, 1989
1 thru 3 . . . . @2.50

MISPLACED
Devil's Due Publishing, 2004
1 by Joshua Blaylock 3.00
2 . . . . 3.00
3 . . . . 3.00

MISTER BLANK
Amaze Ink, 1997
0 by Chris Hicks 2.25
0a 2nd printing 2.25
1 F:Sam Smith 3.00
2 thru 14 . . . . @3.00

MISTER X
Vortex, Vol 2, 1989–90
1 thru 11 . . . . @2.25

MITES
Continuum
1 . . . . 2.50
1a 2.25
2 thru 4 . . . . @2.25

MOBILE POLICE PATLABOR
Viz Communications, 1997
1 (of 12) by Masami Yuki 3.00
PART TWO, 1998
1 by Masami Yuki 3.00
2 thru 6 . . . . @3.00

MOBILE SUIT GUNDAM 0079
Viz Communications, 1999
1 (of 8) by Kazhisa Kondo 3.00
2 thru 7 . . . . @3.00
PART TWO, 1999
1 (of 5) 3.00
2 thru 5 . . . . @3.00

MOBILE SUIT GUNDAM WING: BLIND TARGET
Viz Communications, 2001
1 thru 4 . . . . @3.00

MOBILE SUIT GUNDAM WING: EPISODE ZERO
Viz Communications, 2001
1 thru 8 . . . . @3.00

MOBILE SUIT GUNDAM WING: GROUND ZERO
Viz Communications, 2000
1 (of 4) by Reku Fuyynagi 3.00
2 thru 4 . . . . @3.00

MODERN PULP
Special Studio
1 Rep.from January Midnight 2.75

MOEBIUS COMICS
Caliber, 1996
1 Moe 3.00
2 Moe 3.00
3 Moe 3.00
4 Moe,MP 3.00
5 Moe,SL 3.00
6 Moe 3.00

MOGOBI DESERT RATS
Midnight Comics, 1991
1 I&O:Desert Rats `Waste of the World' 2.25

MONNGA
Daikaiyu Enterprises, 1995
1 & 2 Titanic Omega 4.00

MONOGRAPHS
Coppervale, 1997
1 by James Owen 3.00
2 Bob Phantom 3.00
3 Sidekick Wanted—Benefits Available 3.00
4 thru 6 . . . . 3.00

Monster Boy #1
© *Slave Labor Graphics*

MONSTER BOY
Slave Labor, 1997
1 by Bob Supina 3.00
2 . . . . 3.00
3 . . . . 3.00
4 . . . . 3.00

MONSTER POSSE
Malibu Adventure, 1992
1 I:Monster Posse. 2.50
2 I:P.O.N.E,Wack Mack Dwac's sister,D-Vicious 2.50
3 . . . . 2.50

MONSTERS ATTACK
Globe
1 GM,JSe	2.25
2 GC	2.25
3 ATh,GC	2.25

MONSTERS FROM OUTER SPACE
Adventure, 1992
1	2.50
2 thru 3	@2.50

MONSTER HIGH
Sirius Entertainment, 2001
1 (of 3) by Aaron Bordner	3.00
2	3.00
3	3.00

MOONSTONE MONSTERS
Moonstone Books, 1999
1-shot Werewolves	3.00
1-shot Mummies	3.00
1-shot Sea Creatures	3.00
1-shot Vampire Vixens	3.00
1-shot Ghosts	3.00
1-shot Witches	3.00
1-shot Demons	3.00
1-shot Zombies	3.00

MOONSTONE NOIR
Moonstone 2002
GN Boston Blackie,	5.50
GN The Hat Squad	5.50
GN Jack Hagee, Private Eye	5.50
GN The Mysterious Traveler	5.50
GN The Lone Wolf, Vol. #1	5.00
GN Johnny Dollar	5.00
GN Mysterious Traveler Returns	5.00
GN Bulldog Drummond	5.00

MORBID ANGEL: DESPERATE ANGELS
London Night, 1998
0 EHr, & Jude Millien	3.00
0A Powell(c)	5.00
0B Powell(c)	5.00

MORBID ANGEL: PENANCE
London Night Studios, 1995
1 I:Brandon Watts	4.00

MORBID ANGEL: TO HELL AND BACK
London Night, 1996
1 (of 3) EHr,	4.00
2 and 3	@3.00

MORE THAN MORTAL: A LEGEND REBORN
Avatar Press, 2006
Spec.	2.50
Spec. Wraparound (c)	3.00
Spec. variant (c)	3.00
Spec. Premium (c)	10.00
Spec. Ruby Red Con Foil (c)	5.00
Spec. Heroic (c)	6.00

MORNING GLORY
Radio Comix, 1998
1 by Loran Gayton & Michael Vega	3.00
2 thru 6	@3.00

MORTAL COIL
Mermaid
1 thru 3	@2.25
4 F:Red-Line,Gift	2.25
5 Pin-Up Issue	2.25

MORTOL COILS
Red Eye Press, 2003
1	2.50
2	3.50
3	2.50

MORTAR MAN
Marshall Comics, 1993
1 I:Mortar Man	2.25
2 thru 3	@2.25

MOSAIC
Oktober Black Press
1 F:Halo,Daeva	2.25
2 "Gun Metal Gray"	2.50
3	2.50
4 Elf(c)	2.50
5 Wisps	2.50

MOSAIC
Sirius, 1999
1 by Kyle Hotz	3.00
2 thru 5 conclusion	@3.00

MOUNTAIN WORLD
Newcomers Press, 1995
1 I:Jeremiah Rainshadow	3.00

MR. BEAT ADVENTURES
Moordam Comics, 1997
1	3.00
1 deluxe	5.00
Spec. House of Burning Jazz Love	3.00
Spec. deluxe	5.00
Two-Fisted Atomic Action Super Spec.	3.00
Two-Fisted Atomic Action Super Spec., deluxe	10.00
Two-Fisted Atomic Action Super Spec., mega deluxe	20.00
Spec. Mr. Beat: Superstar	3.00
Spec. Mr. Beat: Superstar, deluxe	10.00
Ann.#1 Babes and Bongos	3.00

MR. FIXITT
Apple, 1989
1 and 2	@2.50

MR. KEEN: TRACER OF LOST PERSONS
Moonstone, 2003
1 (of 3)	3.00
2	3.00
3	3.00

MR. MOTO
Moonstone, 2003
1 (of 3) Welcome Back, Mr. Moto	3.00
2 thru 3	@3.00

MR. MYSTIC
Eclipse
1 Will Eisner	2.50

MR. NIGHTMARE'S WONDERFUL WORLD
Moonstone, 1995
1 thru 3 Dreams So Real, pt.1–pt.3	@3.00

MS. CHRIST
Draculina Publishing, 1995
1 I:Ms. Christ	3.00

Ms. Tree #21
© Renegade

MS. TREE
Aardvark–Vanaheim, 1984
1-10 see Other Pub. (color)
11 thru 18	@2.50

Renegade, 1985
19 thru 49	@2.50
50	4.50
1 3-D Classic	3.00

MULTIPLE WARHEADS
Onipress, 2007
1	6.00
2	3.00

MUMMY, THE
Monster Comics
1 A:Dr.Clarke,Prof.Belmore	2.25
2 Mummy's Curse	2.25
3 A:Carloph	2.25
4 V:Carloph, conc.	2.25

MUMMY'S CURSE
Aircel, 1990
1 thru 4 B.Blair	@2.25

MUNSTERS, THE
TV Comics, 1998
1 photo (c)	3.00
1a variant (c)	8.00
2 Beverly Owen(c)	3.00
2 Pat Priest (c)	3.00
2 Pat Priest (c) signed	15.00
3	3.00
3a Celebrity autograph edition	19.00
4	3.00
4a variant photo (c)	3.00
4b variant (c) celebrity autograph edition	19.00
5 Herman photo (c)	3.00
5 Grandpa photo (c)	3.00
Spec. Comic Con edition	10.00
Celebrity Autograph Edition: Butch Patrick	23.00
Spec.#1 Herman/Grandpa (c)	3.00
Spec.#1a Grandpa (c)	3.00
Halloween Spec. Munsters 1313	3.00
Golden Age Adventure Spec.A(c)	3.00
Golden Age Adventure Spec.B(c)	3.00

MUNSTERS CLASSICS
TV Comics
0 The Fregosi Emerald 3.00
0 variant (c) 8.00

MURCIELAGA: SHE-BAT
Hero Graphics, 1993
1 Daerick Gross reps 2.25
2 Reps. contd 3.00

MURDER
Renegade, 1986
1 SD 2.50
2 Cl(c) 2.50
3 SD 2.50

[2nd series]
1 . . . . 2.50

MURDER CAN BE FUN
Slave Labor, 1996
1 thru 6 . . . . @3.00
2 2nd printing 3.00
7 . . . . 3.00
8 . . . . 3.00
9 Seedy Side of Sex 3.00
10 We Love Sports 3.00
11 . . . . 3.00
12 Amusement Park Terror 3.00

MURDER ME DEAD
El Capitan Books, 2000
1 (of 8) by David Lapham 3.00
2 . . . . 3.00
3 thru 8 . . . . @3.00
9 64-pg 5.00

MUTANT, TEXAS: TALES OF SHERIFF IDA RED
Oni Press, 2002
1 (of 4) by Paul Dini & J. Bone 3.00
2 thru 4 . . . . @3.00

MUTANT ZONE
Aircel, 1991
1 Future story 2.50
2 F.B.I. Drone Exterminators 2.50
3 conclusion 2.50

MY INNER BIMBO
Oni Press, 2006
1 (of 5) 3.00
2 thru 4 . . . . @3.00

MYRIAD
Approbation Comics, 2005
1 (of 6) 3.00
2 thru 6 . . . . @3.00

MYSTERY MAN
Slave Labor Graphics, 1988
1 thru 5 . . . . @2.50

MYTH ADVENTURES
Warp Graphics, 1984
1 Mag size 2.50
2 thru 4 . . . . @2.50
5 Comic size 2.50
6 thru 11 . . . . @2.50
12 . . . . 2.50

MYTH CONCEPTIONS
Apple, 1987
1 . . . . 2.50
2 thru 8 . . . . @2.50

The Mystery Man #1
© *Slave Labor Graphics*

MYTHOGRAPHY
Bardic Press, 1966
1 F:Poison Elves 6.00
2 fantasy stories 6.00
3 fantasy stories, inc. Elfquest 6.00
4 . . . . 5.00
5 72-pg 5.00
6 F:Anubis Squadron 72pg 5.00
7 80-pg 5.00
8 72-pg 5.00

MYTHOS
Wonder Comix, 1987
1 . . . . 2.50
2 . . . . 2.50

NANTUCKET BROWN ROASTERS
House of Usher, 2003
1 (of 2) 2.00
2 . . . . 2.00
GN Second Law of
  Thermodynamics 7.50
1-shot The Lady of Shadows 2.50
GN The Third Twin 5.00

NAT TURNER
Kyle Baker Publishing, 2005
1 . . . . 3.00
2 . . . . 3.00
3 . . . . 3.00
4 . . . . 3.00

NATURE OF THE BEAST
Caliber
1 'The Beast' 3.00
2 . . . . 3.00
3 . . . . 3.00

NAUGHTY BITS
Fantagraphics, 1991–2004
1 by Roberta Gregory 5.00
2 thru 10 F:Bitchy Bitch . . . . @4.00
11 thru 20 . . . . @3.50
21 I:Bitchy Butch 3.00
22 Adult-erated 3.00
23 O:Bitchy Butch 3.00
24 thru 39 . . . . @3.00
40 . . . . 3.50

NAUSICAA OF THE VALLEY OF WIND
Viz Select, 1988
Book One 4.50
Book Two 5.50
Book Three 4.00
Book Four 3.00
Book Five 2.50
Book Six 3.00
Book Seven 3.00
[Part 2] 1989
#1 thru #4 . . . . @3.00
[Part 3] 1993
#1 thru #3 . . . . @3.00

NAUTILUS
Shanda Fantasy Arts, 1999
1 (of 6) by Mike Curtis &
  Louis Frank 3.00
2 thru 6 . . . . @3.00

NAZRAT
Imperial, 1986
1 . . . . 2.50
2 thru 6 . . . . @2.25

NECROSCOPE
Caliber, 1997
1 Brian Lumley adapt 3.00
1 signed 3.00
2 . . . . 3.00
3 . . . . 3.00
4 . . . . 3.00

NEGATIVE BURN
Caliber, 1993
1 I:Matrix 7, Flaming Carrot 5.00
2 . . . . 3.50
3 Bone preview 12.00
4 thru 12 various stories . . . . @4.00
13 Strangers in Paradise 11.00
14 thru 18 various stories . . . . . . @4.00
19 Flaming Carrot 5.00
20 In the Park 4.00
21 Trollords 4.00
22 Father the Dryad 4.00
23 I:The Creep 4.00
24 The Factor 4.00
25 The Factor 4.00
26 Very Vicki 4.00
27 Nancy Kate 4.00
28 Favorite Song 4.00
29 thru 33 . . . . 4.00
34 Kaos Moon 6.00
35 thru 38 . . . . @4.00
39 'Iron Empires,' pt. 4 . . . . 4.00
40 'Suzi Romaine' 4.00
41 'Iron Empires,' cont. 4.00
42 . . . . 4.00
43 'Iron Empires,' concl. 4.00
44 'Skeleton Key' 4.00
45 'Divine Winds' 4.00
46 'A Bullet For Me' 4.00
47 . . . . 4.00
48 special 80-pg. issue 5.00
49 special 80-pg. issue 5.00
50 96-pg., final issue 7.00

NEIL THE HORSE
Aardvark–Vanaheim, 1983
1 Art:Arn Sara, satire 5.00
1a 2nd printing 2.50
2 . . . . 3.00
3 . . . . 4.00
4 . . . . 3.00
5 Video Warriors 2.50
6 Video Warriors 2.50

7 Video Warriors 2.50
8 Outer Space 2.50
9 Canine the Barbarian 2.50
10 Canine the Barbarian 2.50

Renegade, 1985

11 Fred Astair 2.50
12 . . . . 2.50
13 . . . . 2.50
14 Special 3.00
15 . . . . 2.50

NEMESIS THE WARLOCK
Fleetway, 1989

1 thru 16 . . . . @2.50

Neon Genesis Evangelion, Book Six #4
© *Viz Communications*

NEON GENESIS EVANGELION
Viz Communication, 1997

1 (of 6) by Gainax & Yoshiyuki
Sadamoto 3.25
1 special collectors edition 3.00
2 thru 6 . . . . @3.00
2 thru 6 special collectors ed. . . . @3.00

BOOK TWO, 1998

1 (of 5) by Yoshiyuki Sadamoto . . . 3.00
1 special collectors edition 3.00
2 thru 5 . . . . @3.00
2 thru 6 special collectors ed. . . . @3.00

BOOK THREE, 1998

1 thru 6 by Yoshiyuki Sadamoto . @3.00
1a thru 6a Collectors edition . . . . @3.00

BOOK FOUR, 1999

1 thru 7 by Yoshiyuki Sadamato . @3.00
1a thru 7a special collectors ed. . @3.00

BOOK FIVE, 2000

1 . . . . 3.00
1a collectors ed. 3.00
2 thru 7 . . . . @3.00
2a thru 7a deluxe . . . . @3.00

BOOK SIX, 2001

1 thru 4 . . . . @3.50
1a thru 4a coll. ed. . . . . @3.50

BOOK SEVEN

1 (of 7) 3.50
2 thru 5 . . . . @3.00
6 . . . . 3.50
2a thru 5a collector's edition . . . . @3.00
6a collector's edition . . . . @3.50

NERVOUS REX
Blackthorne, 1985

1 . . . . 3.00

1a 2nd printing 2.50
2 . . . . 3.00
3 . . . . 3.00
4 . . . . 2.50
5 thru 10 . . . . @2.50
GraphicNovel 3.50

NEW ADVENTURES OF TERRY & THE PIRATES
ACG Comics, 1998

1 by Bros. Hildebrandt 3.00
2 thru 7 . . . . @3.00

NEWCOMERS ILLUSTRATED
Newcomers Publishing

1 thru 5 various artists. . . . . @3.00
6 Science Fiction 3.00
7 thru 8 . . . . @3.00
9 Shocking Machines 3.00
10 . . . . 3.00
11 Hitman. 3.00
12 final issue 3.00

NEW ERADICATORS

Vol 2 #1 NewBeginnings 2.25
Vol 2 #2 NewBeginnings 2.25
Vol 2 #3 NewFriends 2.25

NEW FRONTIERS

1 CS(c) 3.00
1a 2nd Printing 2.25

NEW FRONTIERS
Evolution

1 A:Action Master, Green Ghost . . . 2.25
2 . . . . 2.25

NEW HERO COMICS
Pierce

1 and 2 . . . . @2.25

NEW HORIZONS
Shanda Fantasy Arts, 1997

1 . . . . 5.00
2 thru 5 . . . . @4.50
6 thru 15 . . . . @5.00

NEW HUMANS
Pied Piper, 1987

1 and 2 . . . . @2.50

NEW HUMANS
Eternity, 1987

1 . . . . 2.50
2 thru 15 . . . . @2.50
Ann. #1. 3.00

NEW HUMANS

1 Shattered Earth Chronicles 2.50

NEW LOVE
Fantagraphics, 1996

1 GHe, Love & Rockets tie-in 3.00
2 thru 3 GHe . . . . @3.00
4 thru 6 GHe . . . . @3.00

NEW PULP ADVENTURES SPECIAL
Dunewadd Comics

1 I:Kawala 2.50

NEW REALITY

1 thru 6 . . . . @2.25

NEWSTRALIA
Innovation, 1989
(Prev. Color)

4 . . . . 2.50
5 . . . . 2.50

NEW TALES OF OLD PALOMAR
Fantagraphics Books 2006

1 GHe 7.95
2 . . . . 8.00
3 . . . . 8.00

NEW TRIUMPH
Matrix Graphics, 1985

1 F:Northguard 3.00
1a 2nd printing 2.50
2 thru 4 . . . . @2.50

NEW VAMPIRE MIYU
Ironcat, 1997

1 by Narumi Kakinouchi 3.00
2 thru 6 . . . . @3.00
7 The Past Lies Beyond a Door,
finale 3.00

VOL. 2, 1998

1 by Narumi Kakinouchi 3.00
2 thru 6 . . . . @3.00

VOL. 3, 1998

1 . . . . 3.00
2 thru 7 . . . . @3.00

VOL. 4, 1999

1 by Narumi Kakinouchi 3.00
2 thru 6 . . . . @3.00

VOL. 5

1 . . . . 3.00
2 thru 7 . . . . @3.00

NEW WORLD DISORDER
Millennium, 1995

1 I:King Skin Gang 3.00

NEW WORLD ORDER
Blazer Studios, 1993

1 . . . . 2.50
2 thru 8 . . . . @2.50

NEW YORK CITY OUTLAWS
Outlaw

1 . . . . 2.50
2 thru 5 . . . . @2.50

NEW YORK, YEAR ZERO
Eclipse, 1988

1 thru 4 . . . . @2.50

NEXT EXIT
Amaze Ink, SLG, 2004

1 by Christy Kijewski. 3.00
2 thru 6 . . . . @3.00
7 thru 11 . . . . @3.00

NEXUS
Capital, 1981

1 SR,I:Nexus,large size 18.00
2 SR,Mag size 12.00
3 SR,Mag size 10.00

NIGHT
Amaze Ink, 1995

0 V:The Prince 2.25

NIGHT ANGEL
Substance Comics, 1995
1 I:Night Angel 3.00

NIGHT CRY
CFD Productions, 1995
1 Evil Ernie & Razor story 8.00
1 signed 9.00
2 . . . . 6.00
3 . . . . 5.00
4 . . . . 4.00
4a platinum (c) 6.00
5 . . . . 4.00
6 . . . . 2.75
6a signed 8.00

NIGHT LIFE
Caliber
1 thru 7 . . . . @2.25

NIGHTMARES & FAIRY TALES
Amaze Ink/SLG, 2002
1 . . . . 3.00
2 thru 5 . . . . @3.00
6 thru 14 . . . . @3.00
15 thru 20 . . . . @3.00
21 . . . . 3.50

NIGHT MASTER
Silver Wolf, 1987
1 Vigil 5.50
2 Vigil 2.50
3 . . . . 2.50

NIGHT OF THE LIVING DEAD
Fantaco
0 prelude 2.25
1 based on cult classic movie 5.00
2 Movie adapt,continued 5.00
3 Movie adapt,conclusion 5.00
5 . . . . 6.00

NIGHT'S CHILDREN
Fantaco
1 . . . . 3.50
2 . . . . 3.50
3 . . . . 3.50
4 . . . . 3.50

NIGHT'S CHILDREN
Millennium, 1995
1 The Ripper, Klaus Wulfe 4.00
Spec. High Noon (1996) 3.00
Spec. The Churchyard (1997) 3.25

NIGHT'S CHILDREN: THE VAMPIRE
Millennium, 1995
1 F:Klaus Wulfe 3.00
2 F:Klaus Wulfe 3.00

NIGHT STREETS
Arrow, 1986
1 . . . . 2.50
2 thru 4 . . . . @2.50

NIGHTVISION
London Night, 1996
1 DQ,KHt, All About Eve 3.00
1 signed 13.00
1a erotica edition 10.00

Nightvision #3
© Rebel Studios

Rebel Studios, 1997
3 Love Bleeding Pictures 2.25
4 Winter 3.00

NIGHT WARRIORS: DARKSTALKERS' REVENGE
Viz Communications, 1998
1 (of 6) by Run Ishida 3.00
2 . . . . 3.25
3 thru 6 . . . . @3.00

NIGHTWOLF: THE PRICE
Devil's Due Publishing, 2006
0 . . . . 1.00
1 thru 3 . . . . @3.00
4 . . . . 3.50
5 . . . . 3.00

NIGHT ZERO
Fleetway
1 thru 4 . . . . @2.25

NIKKI BLADE
High Impact, 1997
0 . . . . 3.00
0a deluxe adult cover 10.00
0b gold edition variant cover 15.00
Spec.#0 Nikki Blade: Forever Nikki
    (1997) MIB(c) 3.00
    Deluxe RCI(c) 10.00
ABC Comics, 1998
Spec. Nikki Blade: Blades of Death
    (1998) by RCI & Clayton Henry . 3.00
    Puzzle variant A cover 6.00
    Puzzle variant B cover 6.00
    Puzzle variant C cover 6.00
Spec. Nikki Blade: Revenge 3.00

NIMROD, THE
Fantagraphics, 1998
1 by Lewis Trondheim 3.00
2 thru 4 . . . . @3.00
5 . . . . 4.00
6 . . . . 3.50
7 . . . . 4.00

NINJA
Eternity
1 . . . . 3.00

2 thru 5 . . . . @2.25
6 thru 13 . . . . @2.25

NINJA ELITE
Adventure, 1987
1 thru 5 . . . . @2.50
6 thru 8 . . . . @2.50

NINJA FUNNIES
Eternity
1 and 2 . . . . @2.25
3 thru 5 . . . . @2.25

NINJA HIGH SCHOOL
Antarctic, 1987
1 . . . . 15.00
2 thru 4 . . . . @11.00
Eternity, 1988
5 thru 22 . . . . @4.00
23 Zardon Assassin 3.00
24 . . . . 3.00
25 Return of the Zetramen 3.00
26 Stanley the Demon 3.00
27 Return of the Zetramen 3.00
28 Threat of the super computer . . . 3.00
29 V:Super Computer 3.00
30 I:Akaru 3.00
31 Jeremy V:Akaru 3.00
32 thru 34 V:Giant Monsters Pt.1
    thru Pt. 3 . . . . @3.00
35 thru 43 . . . . @3.00
44 Combat Cheerleaders 2.75
45 Cheerleader Competition 2.75
46 Monsters From Space 2.75
47 . . . . 2.75
48 F:Jeremy Feeple 2.75
49 thru 51 . . . . 3.00
52 thru 57 Time Warp, pt.4–pt.8 . @3.00
58 Zardon ambassador, BU:BDn . . . 3.00
59 Akaru overwhelmed 3.00
60 to the Himalayas 3.00
61 ancient Himalayan temple 3.00
62 Hillbilly girl 3.00
63 F:Tetsuo Rivalsan 3.00
64 Jeremy Feeple: Saboteur? 3.00
65 Quagmire Trial of the Century . 3.00
66 . . . . 3.00
67 F:Eolata 3.00
68 F:Akaru & Asrial 3.00
69 Guri-Guri Island 3.00
70 Mad Bomber in Space 2.50
71 traitor in secret police 3.00
72 . . . . 2.50
73 . . . . 2.50
74 Girl Scouts 2.50
Special #1 . . . . 3.00
Special #2 . . . . 3.00
Special #3 . . . . 3.00
Special #3 1/2 . . . . 2.50
Ann. 1989 . . . . 3.00
Ann.#3 . . . . 4.00
Yearbook 1994 . . . . 4.00
Yearbook 1995 . . . . 4.00
Yearbook 1996 . . . . 4.00
Yearbook 1997, cover A 4.00
Yearbook 1997, cover B 4.00
Yearbook 1998, cover A 3.00
Yearbook 1998, cover B 3.00
Spec. Girls of Ninja High School
    (1997) 4.00
Spec. Girls of Ninja High School
    1998 cover A 3.00
    1998 cover B 3.00
Spec. 1999 . . . . 3.00
Spotlight #4 Rod Espinosa 3.00
Summer Spec.#1 . . . . 3.00
Antarctic Press, 2000
Swimsuit Spec. 2000 . . . . 4.50
Swimsuit Spec. 2001 . . . . 4.50

All comics prices listed are for *Near Mint* condition.

Antarctic, 2006

145 thru 155 . . . . @3.00
Yearbook 2007 . . . . 4.50

NINJA HIGH
SCHOOL GIRLS
Antarctic Press

0 . . . . 2.75
1 and 2 rep . . . . @2.75
3 thru 5 rep . . . . @4.00
Yearbook 4.00

NINJA HIGH SCHOOL
PERFECT MEMORY
Antarctic Press, 1993

1 thru 2, 96pg . . . . @5.00

NINJA HIGH SCHOOL
SMALL BODIES
Antarctic Press

1 "Monopolize" 2.50
2 Omegadon Cannon 2.75
3 Omegadon Cannon 2.75
3a deluxe 4.50
4 Omegadon Cannon 2.75
5 Wrong Order 2.75
6 Chicken Rage 3.00
7 . . . . 3.00

NIRA X: CYBERANGEL
Entity Comics, 1996

1 . . . . 5.00
1a deluxe 8.00
2 BMs 4.00
3 and 4 BMs . . . . @3.00
4a with PC Game 8.00
Ann.#1 BMs flip-cover 2.75

2nd Mini Series, 1995

1 . . . . 4.00
1a 2nd printing 2.50
2 thru 4 . . . . @2.50

3rd Mini Series, 1995–96

1 . . . . 2.50
1a Gold(c) 5.00
2 . . . . 2.50
3 . . . . 3.00

Regular Series

1 . . . . 2.75
1a with game 7.00
2 thru 4 . . . . @2.75
4a with game 7.00
Spec. Nira X:Headwave, encore
   special toy edition 2.50
Encore special toy edition,
   signed & numbered 13.00
Spec. Nira X:Memoirs (1997) BMs . 2.75
   Deluxe 3.50

NIRA X/HELLINA:
HEAVEN & HELL
Entity Comics

1 San Diego Con edition, BMs 5.00
1a foil 3.00

NIRA X: EXODUS
Avatar, 1997

0 (of 2) BMs 3.00
0a Leather cover 15.00
0b signed 9.00
1 (of 2) 3.00
1a leather cover 15.00
1b signed 9.00
2 . . . . 3.00
Spec. Shoot First 3.00
Spec. Summer Splash 5.00

NIRA X: HISTORY
Avatar Press, 1999

1 (of 2) by Bill Maus 3.50
2 . . . . 3.50

NIRA X: SOUL SKURGE
Entity, 1996

1 (of 3) BMs, A:Vortex 2.75
2 BMs, ... 2.75
3 . . . . 2.75

NITRO-GEN
Arcade Comics, 2005

Preview, limited 7.00
1 . . . . 4.00
1a signed ed. 10.00
1b resketch ed. 25.00

NOBODY
Oni Press, 1998

1 (of 4) 3.00
2 thru 4 . . . . @3.00

NODWICK
Henchman Publishing, 2000

1 by Aaron Williams 3.00
2 & 3 . . . . @3.00

Dork Storm, 2000

1 by Aaron Williams 3.00
2 thru 5 . . . . @3.00
6 thru 11 . . . . @3.00
12 thru 30 . . . . @3.00
31 thru 35 . . . . 3.00
36 . . . . 3.00

NO GUTS, NO GLORY
Fantaco

1-shot, K.Eastman's 1st solo
   work since TMNT 3.00

NOMADS OF ANTIQUITY
1 thru 6 . . . . @2.25

NO NEED FOR TENCHI
Viz Comics
PART ONE

1 thru 7 (of 7) . . . . @3.00

PART TWO, 1996

1 thru 7 by Hitoshi Okuda . . . . . @3.00

PART THREE, 1997

1 (of 6) by Hitoshi Okuda 3.00
2 . . . . 3.00
3 thru 6 . . . . @3.00

PART FOUR, 1997

1 (of 6) by Hitoshi Okuda 3.00
2 thru 6 . . . . @3.00

PART FIVE, 1998

1 (of 6) 3.00
2 thru 6 . . . . @3.00

PART SIX, 1998

1 (of 6) 3.00
2 thru 6 . . . . @3.00

PART SEVEN, 1999

1 (of 6) 3.00
2 thru 6 . . . . @3.00

PART EIGHT, 1999

1 (of 5) by Hitoshi Okuda 3.25
2 thru 5 . . . . @3.00

PART NINE

1 (of 6) by Hitoshi Okuda 3.00
2 thru 6 . . . . @3.00

PART TEN, 2000

1 (of 7) 3.00
2 thru 7 . . . . @3.00

No Need For Tenchi Part 3 #1
© *Viz Communications*

PART ELEVEN, 2001

1 . . . . 3.50
2 thru 4 . . . . @3.50

PART TWELVE, 2001

1 . . . . 3.50
2 thru 4 (of 6) . . . . @3.50
5 thru 6 . . . . @3.00

NORM, THE
The Norm Comics, 2003

1 . . . . 5.00
2 thru 8 . . . . @5.00
9 thru 11 . . . . @3.00
1-shot The 12 Steps to Marriage . . . 5.00

NORMAL MAN
Aardvark–Vanaheim, 1984

1 . . . . 4.00
2 thru 9 . . . . @3.00

Renegade

10 thru 19 . . . . @2.50

NOSFERATU:
PLAGUE OF TERROR
Millennium

1 I:Orlock 2.50
2 19th Century India,A:Sir W.
   Longsword 2.50
3 WWI/WWII to Viet Nam 2.50
4 O:Orlock,V:Longsword,conc. . . . 2.50

NOTHING BETTER
Dementian Comics, 2005

1 by Tyler Page 3.00
2 thru 4 . . . . @3.00

NOVA GIRLS
MN Design, 1998

1 The Immortality Quest, pt.1 . . . . 2.25
1a JJu (c) 3.00
1b photo (c) 4.00
1 variant Starship Discover #0(c) . . 4.00
1 variant Phazer #0 cover. 4.00
2 The Immortality Quest, pt.2 . . . . 2.25
2a deluxe 3.00
3 The Immortality Quest, pt.3 . . . . 2.25
3a deluxe 3.00
Space 34–24–34 Gold Seal 10th
   Anniv. Edition. 75.00

NOWHERE
Drawn & Quarterly Oct., 1996
1 by Debbie Drechsler 3.75
2 . . . . 3.75
3 . . . . 3.75
4 . . . . 3.75
5 . . . . 3.75

NOWHERESVILLE
Caliber, 1996
1 thru 3 by MRc . . . . @3.00
Spec. The History of Cool 3.00

NUCLEAR WAR
New England Comics, 2000
1 by Ron Ledwell 3.50
2 . . . . 3.50
3 . . . . 3.50
4 . . . . 3.50

NYOKA
THE JUNGLE GIRL
AC Comics
3   . . . . 2.25
4   . . . . 2.25
5   . . . . 2.50

OAK
Fat Cat March, 1997
1 by M.F. Mangione & Al Diaz 2.75
2 thru 5 . . . . @2.75
4 . . . . 2.75
6 . . . . 2.75

OCTOBRIANA
Revolution Comics
0 16pg. 2.00
1 `The Octobriana Files,'pt.1 . . . . . 3.00
2 `The Octobriana Files,'pt.2 . . . . . 3.00
3 `The Octobriana Files,'pt.3 . . . . . 3.00
4 `The Octobriana Files,'pt.4 . . . . . 3.00
5 `The Octobriana Files,'pt.5 . . . . . 3.00
Alchemy Texts, 2001
Spec. 30th Anniv. Spec. 3.00

ODDBALLZ
NBM Books, 2002
1 by Trondheim & Larcenet 3.00
2 thru 4 . . . . @3.00
5 thru 8 . . . . @3.00

ODDBALLZ:
VENETIAN BLIND
NBM Books, 2003
1 . . . . 3.00
2 . . . . 3.00

ODD JOB
Amaze Ink/SLG, 2000
1 by Ian Smith & Tyson Smith 3.00
2 thru 8 . . . . @3.00

OFFERINGS
Cry For Dawn
1 Sword & Sorcery stories 7.00
2 and 3 . . . . @6.00

OFFICIAL BUZ SAWYER
Pioneer, 1988
1   . . . . 2.50
2   . . . . 2.50
3   . . . . 2.50
4   . . . . 2.50
5   . . . . 2.50
6   . . . . 2.50

OFFICIAL HOW TO
DRAW G.I. JOE
Blackthorne, 1987
1 thru 5 . . . . @2.50

OFFICIAL HOW TO
DRAW ROBOTECH
Blackthorne, 1987
1 thru 11 . . . . @2.50
12 . . . . 3.00
13 thru 16 . . . . @2.50

OFFICIAL HOW TO
DRAW TRANSFORMERS
Blackthorne, 1987
1 thru 7 . . . . @2.50

OFFICIAL
JOHNNY HAZARD
Pioneer, 1988
1 thru 3 . . . . @2.50
4 . . . . 2.50
5 . . . . 2.50

OFFICIAL JUNGLE JIM
Pioneer, 1988
1 thru 5 AR,rep. . . . . @2.50
6 AR,rep. 2.50
7 thru 10 AR,rep. . . . . @2.50
11 thru 20 AR,rep. . . . . @2.50
Ann.#1 . . . . 2.50
Giant Size 4.00

OFFICIAL MANDRAKE
Pioneer, 1988
1 thru 5 . . . . @2.50
6 . . . . 2.50
7 thru 10 . . . . @2.50
11 . . . . 3.00
12 . . . . 2.50
13 thru 17 . . . . @2.50
Ann. #1 . . . . 4.00
King Size #1 . . . . 4.00
Giant Size #1 . . . . 4.00

OFFICIAL MODESTY
BLAISE
Pioneer, 1988
1 thru 4 . . . . @2.50
5 . . . . 2.50
6 thru 14 . . . . @2.50
Ann. #1 . . . . 4.00
King Size #1 . . . . 4.00

OFFICIAL
PRINCE VALIANT
Pioneer, 1988
1 Hal Foster,rep. 2.50
2 Hal Foster,rep. 2.50
3 Hal Foster,rep. 2.50
4 Hal Foster,rep. 2.50
5 Hal Foster,rep. 2.50
6 Hal Foster,rep. 2.50
7 . . . . 2.50
8 thru 14 . . . . @2.50
15 thru 24 . . . . @2.50
Ann. #1 . . . . 4.00
King Size #1 . . . . 4.00

OFFICIAL RIP KIRBY
Pioneer, 1988
1 thru 3 AR . . . . @2.50
4 AR 2.50
5 and 6 AR . . . . @2.50

Official Secret Agent #4
© *Pioneer*

OFFICIAL SECRET AGENT
Pioneer, 1988
1 thru 5 AW rep . . . . @2.50
6 AW 2.50
7 thru 9 AW . . . . @2.50

OF MIND AND SOUL
Rage Comics, 1997
0 . . . . 3.00
1 . . . . 2.50
2 . . . . 2.50
3 . . . . 2.50
Spec. Standing on a Beach 2.50
Spec. Soul'd Out 3.00
Spec. A Day in Hell 3.00
Spec. 1-shot 2.50

OHM'S LAW
Imperial Comics
1 thru 2 . . . . @2.25
3 V:Men in Black 2.25
4 A:Damonstriek 2.25
5 F:Tryst 2.25

OH MY GOTH!
Sirius/Dog Star, 1998
1 by Voltaire 3.00
2 thru 4 . . . . @3.00

OH MY GOTH:
HUMANS SUCK!
Sirius Entertainment, 2000
1 (of 3) 3.00
1 deluxe 5.00
2 and 3 . . . . @3.00

OJO
Oni Press, 2004
1 (of 5) 3.00
2 thru 5 . . . . @3.00

OKTOBERFEST
Now & Then
1 (1976) Dave Sim 20.00

OMEGA
North Star
1 1st pr by Rebel,rare 50.00
1a Vigil(Yellow Cov.) 15.00
2 . . . . 2.25

B & W PUB.

OMEGA ELITE
Blackthorne
1 .... 2.25
2 .... 2.25

OMEN
North Star, 1987
1 .... 8.00
1a 2nd printing 2.50
2 thru 4 .... @3.50

OMICRON
Pyramid, 1987
1 and 2 .... @2.50
3 .... 2.50

OMNI MEN
Blackthorne, 1989
1 & 2 .... @2.50

ONE-POUND GOSPEL
Viz Communications, 1996
1 .... 3.50
2 .... 3.50
3 & 4 .... @3.00

ROUND TWO, 1997
1 .... 3.00
2 thru 8 by Rumiko Takahashi .. @3.00

PART 7
1 (of 13) by Rumiko Takahashi 3.00

ONE SHOT WESTERN
Calibur
1-shot F:Savage Sisters, Tornpath
    Outlaw 2.50

1000 DEATHS OF
BARON VON DONUT
Arsenic Lullaby Publishing 2005
1 .... 3.00
2 .... 3.00
3 .... 3.00

ONI DOUBLE FEATURE
Oni Press, 1997
1 F:Jay & Silent Bob 10.00
1a 2nd printing 3.00
2 F:Car Crash on the 405 ...... 3.50
3 F:Troy Nixey 3.50
4 F:A River in Egypt 3.50
5 F:Fan Girl From Hell 4.00
6 inc. NGa Only the End of the
    World, pt.1 .... 3.00
7 inc. NGa Only the End of the
    World, pt.2 .... 3.00
8 inc. NGa Only the End of the
    World, pt.3 .... 3.00
9 thru 10 .... @3.00
11 Usagi Yojimbo 3.50
12 Bluntman & Chronic 7.00
13 .... 3.00

ONIGAMI
Antarctic Press, 1998
1 (of 3) by Michael Lacombe, sequel
    to Winter Jade storyline from
    Warrior Nun: Black and White. . 3.00
2 .... 3.00
3 concl. 3.00

OPEN SEASON
Renegade, 1987
1 .... 2.50
2 thru 7 .... @2.50

OPPOSITE FORCES
Funny Pages Press, 2002
1 by Tom Bancroft 3.00
1a Convention Exclusive (c) 3.00
2 .... 3.00
3 .... 3.00
4 .... 3.00

OPTIC NERVE
Adrian Tomine, 1990
1 thru 5, mini-comic 10.00
6 .... 7.00
7 .... 5.00
8 .... 3.00
9 .... 4.00

OPTIC NERVE
Drawn & Quarterly, 1995
1 Summer Job 9.00
1a 2nd printing 6.00
2 .... 5.00
3 and 4 .... @5.00
5 thru 11 .... @4.00

ORACLE PRESENTS
Oracle, 1986
1 thru 4 .... @2.50

ORBIT
Eclipse, 1990
1 and 2 .... @5.00
3 .... 5.00

OR ELSE
Drawn & Quarterly, 2004
1 .... 3.50
2 thru 3 .... @4.00
4 .... 6.00

ORIGINAL TOM CORBETT
Eternity, 1990
1 thru 10 rep. newspaper strips . @3.00

ORIGINS OF REID
FLEMING, WORLD'S
TOUGHEST MILKMAN
Deep Sea Comics, 1998
1 by David Boswell 3.00

ORLAK: FLESH & STEEL
Caliber
1 1991 A.D. 2.50

ORLAK REDUX
Caliber, 1991
1 rep. Caliber Presents, 64-pg.. . 4.00

OUTLAW OVERDRIVE
Blue Comet Press
1 Red Edition I:Deathrow 3.00
1a Black Edition 3.00
1b Blue Edition 3.00

OZ
Imperial Comics, 1996
1 Land of Oz Gone Mad 8.00
2 Land of Oz Gone Mad 7.00
3 Land of Oz Gone Mad 6.00
4 Tin Woodsmen 6.00
5 F:Pumkinhead 6.00
6 Emerald City 6.00
7 V:Bane Wolves 4.00
8 V:Nome Hordes 4.00
9 Freedom Fighters Vs. Heroes .. 4.00
10 thru 15 .... @4.00

16 .... 3.50
Spec.#1 .... 6.00
Spec. Scarecrow #1 .... 3.00
Spec. Lion #1. .... 3.00
Spec. Tin Man #1. .... 3.00
Spec. Freedom Fighters #1 ...... 3.00

Caliber `New Worlds'
17 by Ralph Griffith, Stuart Kerr &
    Tim Holtrop 3.50
18 thru 20 .... @3.00
21 `Witches War' pt.1 (of 5) 3.00
22 .... 3.00

Oz, Romance in Rags 1
© Caliber

OZ: ROMANCE IN RAGS
Caliber, 1996
1 thru 3 Bill Bryan .... @3.00

OZ SQUAD
Patchwork Press, 1992
1 .... 4.00
2 thru 8 .... @3.00

OZ: STRAW
AND SORCERY
Caliber `New Worlds', 1997
1 thru 3 .... @3.00

PAKKINS' LAND
Caliber Tapestry, 1996
1 .... 6.00
1a signed edition. 3.00
1a second edition, new cover..... 3.00
2 .... 4.00
2a second edition, new cover..... 4.00
3 .... 4.00
3 2nd edition, new cover. 3.00
4 thru 6 .... @3.00
GN Book One: Paul's Adventure . . 10.00

PAKKINS' LAND:
FORGOTTEN DREAMS
Caliber, 1998
1 by Gary & Rhoda Shipman 3.00
2 thru 5 .... @3.00

PAKKINS' LAND:
QUEST FOR KINGS
Caliber, 1997
1G by Gary & Rhoda Shipman,
    Shipman(c) 3.00

1J by Gary & Rhoda Shipman,
JSi(c) 3.00
2 . . . . 3.00
3 Rahsha's city 3.00
4 . . . . 3.00
5 . . . . 3.00

PALANTINE
Gryphon Rampant, 1995
1 thru 5 V:Master of Basilisk 2.50

PALEO TALES:
LATE CRETACEOUS
Zeromayo Studios, 2001
1 thru 6 . . . . 3.00

Empty Sky, 2003
7 . . . . 3.00
8 . . . . 3.00

PALOOKA-VILLE
Drawn & Quarterly
1 third printing 3.00
1 10th Anniv. Ed. 3.75
10 by Seth 3.75
11 Clyde Fans, pt.2 . . . . 3.75
12 Clyde Fans, pt.3 . . . . 3.75
13 Clyde Fans 3.75
14 thru 15 . . . . @3.75
16 thru 18 . . . . @4.75

PANDA KHAN
1 thru 4 . . . . @2.25

PANDEMONIUM
Curtis Comics, 2002
Vol. 1 Manga
1 by Jaeongtae Lee 3.00
2 thru 5 . . . . @3.00
Vol. 2
1 . . . . 3.00

PANDORA
Brainstorm, 1996
1 (of 2) 3.00

PANDORA
Avatar Press, 1997
0 . . . . 3.00
1 signed 10.00
2 (of 2) 3.00
2 deluxe 9.00
X-over Pandora/Ranzor:Devil Inside
(1998) signed 10.00
Haley (c) 5.00
X-over Pandora/Razor (1999) 3.50
Leather cover, signed 12.00
Expanded Edition 5.00
X-over Pandora/Shotgun Mary:
Demon Nation (1998) 3.00
Deluxe 5.00
Leather 15.00
Royal Blue edition 40.00
X-over Pandora/Widow (1997) 4.00
Leather cover 15.00
Spec. Arachnophobia 3.50
Spec. Pandora Special (1997) 3.00
Leather cover 15.00
Avatar convention (c) ed. 15.00
Spec. Pandora Pin-up (1997) 3.00
Signed 15.00
Spec. Nudes (1997) 3.50
GN Love and War (2003) 6.00

PANDORA'S CHEST
Avatar Press, 1999
1 (of 3) 2.75

PANDORA:
DEMONOGRAPHY
Avatar Press, 1997
1 . . . . 3.00
2 (of 3) 3.00
3 (of 3) 3.00

PANDORA
DEVILS ADVOCATE
Avatar Press, 1999
1 (of 3) 3.50
1a Previews exclusive foil (c) 11.00
2 . . . . 3.50
3 . . . . 3.50

PANDORA:
PANDEMONIUM
Avatar Press, 1997
1 Pandora goes to Hell 3.00
1 leather cover 25.00
1 signed 10.00
2 (of 3) 3.00

PANTHEON
Lone Star Press, 1998
1 (of 12) 3.00
2 Welcome to the Machine 3.00
3 V:Death Boy 3.00
4 F:Tangeroa 3.00
5 Under Pressure 3.00
6 All-villain issue 3.00
7 thru 9 . . . . @3.00
10 thru 12 . . . . @3.00
13 . . . . 5.00
Spec. Ancient History (1999) 3.50

PANZER: 1946
Antarctic Press, 2004
1 . . . . 6.00
2 . . . . 6.00
3 . . . . 6.00
4 . . . . 6.00
5 . . . . 6.00

PAPER CUTS
1 E Starzer-1982 . . . . 12.00
2 and 3 . . . . @2.50

PARIS
Amaze Ink/SLG, 2005
1 . . . . 3.00
2 thru 4 . . . . @3.00

PARTICLE DREAMS
Fantagraphics, 1986
1 . . . . 3.00
2 thru 6 . . . . @2.50

PARTNERS IN
PANDEMONIUM
Caliber
1 Hell on Earth 2.50
2 Sheldon & Murphy are mortal . . . 2.50
3 A:Abra Cadaver 2.50

PARTS OF A HOLE
Caliber, 1991
1 Short Stories 2.50

PARTS UNKNOWN
Eclipse, 1992
1 I:Spurr,V:Aliens 2.50
2 Aliens on Earth cont. 2.50

Parts Unknown #1
© Eclipse

PARTS UNKNOWN:
DARK INTENTIONS
Knight Press, 1995
0 . . . . 3.00
1 I:Prelude to limited Series 3.00
2 V:Luggnar 3.00
3 V:Luggnar 3.00
4 . . . . 3.00
1-shot, Handbook, The Roswell
Agenda 3.00
Super-Ann. #1 . . . . 4.00

PATRICK THE WOLF BOY
Blindwolf Studios, 2000
1 by Art Baltazar & Franco 3.00
Halloween Special 3.00
Next Halloween Special 3.00
Valentine's Day Special 3.00
Christmas Spec 3.00
Mother's Day Special 3.00
Summer Spec. 3.00
Superhero Spec.(2002) 3.00
Sci-Fi Special (2002) 3.00
Another Halloween Special (2002) . 3.00
Spec. This Year's Halloween Spec. . 3.00
Spec. Grimm Reaper Super Spec. . 3.00
Spec. Wedding Special 3.00
Spec. After School Special 3.00
Spec. Rock-n-Roll spec. 3.00
Spec. Father's Day spec. 3.00
Spec. Happy Birthday 3.00

PATTY CAKE
Caliber Tapestry, 1996
1 by Scott Roberts 3.00
2 . . . . 3.00
3 . . . . 3.00
4 . . . . 3.00
Christmas special. 4.00

PATTY-CAKE & FRIENDS
Slave Labor, 1997
1 by Scott Roberts 3.00
2 thru 15 . . . . @3.00
Halloween Spec. 4.00
VOL. 2, 2000
1 by Scott Roberts, 48-pg. 5.00
2 thru 4 48-pg. . . . . @5.00
5 thru 15 . . . . @5.00

PAULA PERIL
Atlantis Studios 2006

1	3.00
2 Case of the Haunted Museum	3.00
3	3.00

Paul The Samurai #3
© New England Comics

PAUL THE SAMURAI
New England Comics, 1991

1 thru 3	@2.75
Bonanza #2 100pg.	5.00
GN Collected	9.00

PENDULUM
Adventure, 1993

1 Big Hand,Little Hand	2.50
2 The Immortality Formula	2.50
3	2.50

PENNY CENTURY
Fantagraphics, 1997

1 by Jaime Hernandez	3.00
2 thru 7	@3.00

PENTACLE:
THE SIGN OF THE FIVE
Eternity, 1991

1	2.25
2 Det.Sandler,H.Smitts	2.25
3 Det.Sandler becomes New Warlock	2.25
4 5 warlocks Vs. Kaji	2.50

PETE THE P.O.'D
POSTAL WORKER
Sharkbait Press, 1998

1 by Marcus Pierce & Pete Garcia, Route 666	3.00
2 prison mail	3.00
3 To Aliens with Love	3.00
4 Special Delivery to Conad the Alien	3.00
5 England Vacation	3.00
6 Benedict Postman	3.00
7 Postman on Elm Street	3.00
8 Postman on Elm Street	3.00
9 Pete Meets Jerry Ringer	3.00
10 Y2K Express	3.00
11 Postal Wars	3.00
12	3.00

X-mas Spec.#1	3.50
Spec. War Journal	3.00

PHANTOM

1 thru 3	@6.00
4 and 5	@7.00

PHANTOM OF FEAR CITY
Claypool, 1994–95

1 thru 12	2.50

PHANTOM OF
THE OPERA
Eternity

1	2.25

PHASE ONE
Victory, 1986

1	3.00
2	2.50
3 thru 5	@2.50

PHIGMENTS
Amazing, 1987

1	5.00
2	2.50
3	2.50

PHONEY PAGES
Renegade

1 and 2	@2.50

PINEAPPLE ARMY
Viz Communications, 1988

1 thru 10	@2.50

PINK FLOYD EXPERIENCE
Revolutionary, 1991

1 based on rock group	2.50
2 Dark Side of the Moon	2.50
3 Dark Side of the Moon, Wish you were here	2.50
4 The Wall	2.50
5 A Momentary lapse of reason	2.50

PIRATE CLUB
Amaze Ink/SLG, 2004

1	3.00
2 thru 4	@3.00
5 thru 7	@3.00
8 thru 10	@3.00

PIRATE CORPS!
Eternity, 1987

6 and 7	@2.50
Spec. #1	2.50

PIRATES VS. NINJAS
Antarctic Press, 2007

1 (of 3)	3.50
2 thru 4	@3.50

PIRANHA! IS LOOSE
Special Studio

1 Drug Runners,F:Piranha	3.00
2 Expedition into Terror	3.00

PIXY JUNKET
Viz, 1993

1 thru 6	@2.75

P.J. WARLOCK
Eclipse, 1986

1 thru 3	@2.50

PLANET COMICS
Blackthorne, 1988
(Prev. Color)

4 and 5	@2.50

PLANET COMICS
A-List Comics, 1997

1 by L.Hampton & R.Leonardo	2.50
2 rep. from 1940	3.00
3	3.00
4 thru 6	@3.00

PLANET COMICS
ACG Comics, 2000

1 WW, rep.	7.00
2 64-pg.	6.00

PLANET OF THE APES
Adventure Comics, 1990

1 WD,collect.ed.	6.00
1 2 covers	4.00
1a 2nd printing	2.50
1b 3rd printing	2.25
2	3.00
3	3.00
4	3.00
5 D:Alexander?	3.00
6 Welcome to Ape City	3.00
7	3.00
8 Christmas Story	2.75
9 Swamp Ape Village	2.75
10 Swamp Apes in Forbidden City	2.75
11 Ape War continues	2.75
12 W:Alexander & Coure	2.75
13 Planet of Apes/Alien Nation/ Ape City x-over	2.75
14 Countdown to Zero Pt.1	2.75
15 Countdown to Zero Pt.2	2.75
16 Countdown to Zero Pt.3	2.75
17 Countdown to Zero Pt.4	2.75
18 Ape City (after Ape Nation mini-series)	2.75
19 1991 `Conquest..' tie-in	2.75
20 Return of the Ape Riders	2.75
21 The Terror Beneath,Pt.1	2.75
22 The Terror Beneath,Pt.2	2.75
23 The Terror Beneath,Pt.3	2.75
Ann #1,`Day on Planet o/t Apes'	3.50
Lim.Ed. #1	5.00

PLANET OF THE APES:
BLOOD OF THE APES
Adventure Comics, 1991

1 A:Tonus the Butcher	3.00
2 Valia/Taylorite Connection	2.75
3 Ape Army in Phis	2.75
4	2.75

PLANET OF THE APES:
FORBIDDEN ZONE
Adventure

1 Battle for the Planet of the Apes & Planet of the Apes tie-in	2.75
2 A:Julus	2.75

PLANET OF THE APES:
SINS OF THE FATHER
Adventure Comics, 1992

1 Conquest Tie-in	2.75

PLANET OF THE APES
URCHAKS' FOLLY
Adventure Comics, 1991

1	3.00
2 thru 4	@2.75

B & W PUB.

PLANET 29
Caliber
1 A Future Snarl Tale 2.50
2 A:Biff,Squakman 2.50

PLANET-X
Eternity, 1991
1 three horror stories 2.50

PLAN 9 FROM
OUTER SPACE
Eternity, 1991
1 . . . . 2.50
2 and 3 . . . . @2.25

PLASTIC LITTLE
CPM Comics, 1997
1 (of 5) Manga, by Satoshi
  Urushihara R:Captain Tita 3.00
2 F:Joshua Balboa 3.00
3 . . . . 3.00
4 . . . . 3.00
5 concl. 3.00

PLASTRON CAFE
Mirage, 1992
1 RV,inc.North by Downeast 2.25
2 thru 4 . . . . @2.25

POE
Cheese Comics, 1996
1 by Jason Asala, reoffer 3.00
2 . . . . 3.00
3 'The System of Doctor Tarr and
  Professor Fether' 3.00
4 thru 6 . . . . @3.00

Sirius/Dog Star
VOL 2, 1997
1 by Jason Asala 3.00
2 House of Usher, pt.1 (of 4) 3.00
3 House of Usher, pt.2 . . . . 3.00
4 House of Usher, pt.3 . . . . 3.00
5 House of Usher, pt.4 . . . . 3.00
6 . . . . 3.00
7 . . . . 3.00
8 Small Town 3.00
9 Small Town, pt.2 . . . . 3.00
10 Small Town, pt.3 . . . . 3.00
11 Gold & Lead, pt.1 . . . . 3.00
12 Gold and Lead, pt.2 . . . . 3.00
13 F:Pluto the cat. 3.00
14 A:Mad Meg Mayflower 3.00
15 Airship 3.00
16 path of next demon 3.00
17 22 one-page stories 3.00
18 Airship 3.00
19 thru 24 Balloon Hoax . . . . @3.00

POINT BLANK
Acme/Eclipse, 1989
1 . . . . 3.00
2 thru 5 . . . . @3.00

POISON ELVES
Mulehide Graphics, 1993–95
Previously: I, Lusipher
8 DHa(c&a) 12.00
9 DHa 10.00
10 DHa 10.00
11 DHa, comic size 10.00
12 DHa 10.00
13 DHa 13.00
14 and 15 DHa . . . . @13.00
15a 2nd printing 6.00
16 and 17 DHa . . . . @7.00
17a 2nd printing 6.00

Poison Elves #11
© *Sirius*

18 DHa 7.00
19 DHa 7.00
20 DHa 7.00

2nd Series, Sirius, 1995–2007
1 F:Lusipher 5.00
2 V:Assassins Guild 4.00
3 Sanctuary, pt.3 . . . . 4.00
4 Sanctuary, pt.4 . . . . 4.00
5 Sanctuary, pt.5 . . . . 4.00
6 I:Lester Gran 4.00
7 thru 24 . . . . @4.00
25 DHa 3.00
26 DHa 3.00
27 DHa, ... 3.00
28 DHa,F:Lusiphur 3.00
29 DHa, ... 3.00
30 DHa,F:Vido 3.00
31 DHa 3.00
32 DHa, Cassandra is dead 3.00
33 DHa, temporary truce 3.00
34 DHa, Lusiphur's feminine side . . 3.00
35 DHa, Purple Marauder
  reappears 3.00
36 DHa, Lusiphur tracked down . . . 3.00
37 DHa, questionable help 3.00
38 DHa 3.00
39 DHa 3.00
40 DHa, Sanctuary, concl 3.00
41 DHa, on to Amrahly'nn 3.00
42 DHa, Just in Town
  for the Night,pt.1 . . . . 3.00
43 DHa, Town for the Night, pt.2 . . 3.00
44 DHa, Town for the Night, pt.3 . . 3.00
45 DHa, Petunia 3.00
46 DHa, High Price of
  Unemployment 2.50
47 The Fairy and the Imp 2.50
48 South for the Winter,pt.1 . . . . . . 2.50
49 South for the Winter,pt.2 . . . . . . 2.50
50 South for the Winter,pt.3 . . . . . . 3.00
51 South for the Winter,pt.4 . . . . . . 3.00
52 South for the Winter,pt.5 . . . . . . 3.00
53 South for the Winter,pt.6 . . . . . . 3.00
54 South for the Winter,pt.7 . . . . . . 3.00
55 thru 60 . . . . @3.00
61 by The Fillbach Brothers 3.00
62 thru 68 . . . . @3.00
69 thru 82 . . . . @3.00
Spec. Poison Elves Companion . . . 3.50
Sketchbook 3.00
Sketchbook, limited 13.00

POISON ELVES:
DOMINION
Sirius Entertainment, 2005
1 . . . . 3.50
1a limited, sign, numbered 12.00
2 . . . . 3.50
3 thru 6 . . . . @3.50

POISON ELVES:
HYENA
Sirius Entertainment, 2004
1 (of 4) 3.00
2 thru 4 . . . . @3.00

POISON ELVES:
LOST TALES
Sirius Entertainment, 2006
1 . . . . 3.00
2 thru 12 . . . . @3.00

POISON ELVES:
LUSIPHER & LIRILITH
Sirius Entertainment, 2001
1 (of 4) by Drew Hayes 3.00
1a limited ed. 9.00
2 . . . . 3.00
2a delux 9.00
3 . . . . 3.00
3a limited 6.50
4 . . . . 3.00
4a limited 6.50

POISON ELVES:
PARINTACHIN
Sirius Entertainment, 2001
1 (of 3) 3.00
2 . . . . 3.00
3 . . . . 3.00

POISON ELVES:
VENTURES
Sirius Entertainment, 2005
1 Cassandra 3.50
2 Lynn 3.50
3 Purple Marauder 3.50
4 Jace 3.50
5 Fleece 3.50
6 Chowmba 3.50

POIZON: DEMON HUNTER
London Night, 1998
1 . . . . 3.00
2 . . . . 3.00
3 . . . . 3.00
4 double sized finale 3.00

POKEMON ADVENTURES
Viz Communications, 1999
1 (of 5) Mysterious Mew 6.00
2 Wanted: Pikachu 6.00
3 The Snorlax Stop 6.00
4 . . . . 6.00
5 The Ghastly Ghosts 6.00
PART TWO, 2000
1 (of 6) Team Rocket Returns 3.00
2 The Hunt for Eevee 3.00
3 The Nidoking Safari 3.00
4 Mission: Magmar 3.00
5 The Dangerous Dragonite 3.00
6 The Mythical Moltres 3.00
PART THREE, 2000
1 . . . . 3.00
2 thru 7 . . . . @3.00

PART FOUR, 2001
Spec. 5.00
PART FIVE, 2001
1 . . . . 5.00
2 thru 5 . . . . @5.00
PART SIX
1 (of 4) 5.00
2 thru 4 . . . . @5.00
PART SEVEN
1 (of 5) 5.00
2 thru 5 . . . . @5.00

POKEMON: ELECTRIC
PIKACHU BOOGALOO
Viz Communications, 1999
1 (of 4) by Toshihiro Ono, 48-pg. . . 3.50
2 . . . . 3.00
3 . . . . 3.00
4 finale 3.00

POKEMON:
THE ELECTRIC
TALE OF PIKACHU
Viz Communications, 1998
1 (of 4) by Toshihiro Ono 10.00
1a 2nd printing 4.00
2 . . . . 7.00
2a 2nd printing 4.00
3 . . . . 4.00
4 . . . . 4.00
GN The Electric Tale of Pikachu . . 13.00

POKEMON: PIKACHU
SHOCKS BACK
Viz Communications, 1999
1 (of 4) by Toshihiro Ono 3.25
2 thru 4 . . . . @3.25

POKEMON:
SURF'S UP PIKACHU
Viz Communications, 1999
1 (of 4) 3.00
2 thru 3 . . . . @3.00
4 . . . . 3.50

POKEMON TALES
Viz Communications, 2001
Prev. Color
17 Mewtwos Watching You 5.00
18 Magnemites Mission 5.00
19 Don't Laugh Charizard 5.00
20 Onix Underground 5.00
Gold and Silver Board Books
Vol. 1 Chikorita 5.50
Vol. 2 Cyndaquil 5.50
Vol. 3 Totodile 5.50
Vol. 4 Muddy Pichi 5.50
Vol. 5 Wobuffet Watches Clouds . . . 5.50
Vol. 6 Swinub's Nose 5.50
Vol. 7 Wake Up Lugia 5.50
Vol. 8 Look Out Hondour 5.50
Vol. 9 Corsola's Brave New World . . 5.50

POKEWOMON: GOTTA
SHAG 'EM ALL!
Blatant Comics, 1999
1 by Mike Rosenzweig 3.00

POLLY AND THE PIRATES
Oni Press, 2005
1 by Ted Naifeh 3.00
2 . . . . 3.00
3 thru 6 . . . . @3.00

POOT
Fantagraphics, 1997
1 by Walt Holcombe 3.00
2 Swollen Holler, pt.2 . . . . 3.00
3 sex issue 3.00
4 final issue, 40-pg. 4.00

POPCORN
Discovery, 1993
1 . . . . 4.00

POP PARODY
Studio Chikara, 1999
Big Fat Sci-Fi Spec.:Stawars 3.00
Pokymon–World Domination 3.00
Dixxi Chix vs. Spice Galz 3.00
The Blair Snitch Project 4.00

PORTIA PRINZ
OF THE GLAMAZONS
Eclipse, 1986
1 thru 6 . . . . @2.50

POST BROTHERS
Rip Off Press
15 thru 18 . . . . @2.50
19 and 20 . . . . @2.50

POWER COMICS
Power Comics, 1977
1 Smart-Early Aardvark 15.00
1a 2nd printing 7.00
2 I:Cobalt Blue 10.00
3 and 4 . . . . @8.00
5 . . . . 8.00

POWER COMICS
Eclipse, 1988
1 BB,DGb,Powerbolt 2.50
2 BB,DGb 2.50
3 BB,DGb 2.50

PPV
Antarctic Press, 2002
1 by Tom Root & Jerzy Drozd 3.00
2 thru 3 . . . . @3.00

PREMIERE
Diversity Comics, 1995
1 F:Kolmec The Savage 2.75

PRETEEN DIRTY GENE
KUNG FU KANGAROOS
Blackthorne, 1986
1 and 2 . . . . @2.50

PREY
Monster Comics
1 I:Prey,A:Andrina 2.25
2 V:Andrina 2.25
3 conclusion 2.25

PRICE, THE
1 Dreadstar mag. size 20.00

PRIMITIVES
Spartive Studios, 1995
1 thru 3 On the Moon . . . . @2.50

PRIME CUTS
Fantagraphics
1 adult 3.50
2 thru 6 . . . . @3.50
7 thru 12 . . . . @4.00

PRIMER
Comico, 1982
1 . . . . 10.00
2 MW,I:Grendel 100.00
3 . . . . 9.00
4 . . . . 8.00
5 SK(1st work),I:Maxx 30.00
6 IN,Evangeline 14.00

Prime Slime Tales #2
© Mirage

PRIME SLIME TALES
Mirage, 1986
1 . . . . 5.00
2 . . . . 2.50
3 thru 6 . . . . @2.50

PRINCE VALIANT
1 thru 4 . . . . @5.00
Spec #1 . . . . 7.00

PRINCE VALIANT
MONTHLY
Pioneer
1 thru 6 . . . . @4.00
6 . . . . 5.00
7 . . . . 5.00
8 . . . . 5.00
9 . . . . 7.00

PRINCESS PRINCE
CPM Manga, 2000
1 . . . . 3.00
1a Leah Hernandez (c) 3.00
2 thru 14 . . . . @3.00
15 . . . . 3.00
16 . . . . 3.00

PRIVATE BEACH
Amaze Ink/SLG, 2001
1 by David Hahn 3.00
2 . . . . 3.00
3 . . . . 3.00
4 . . . . 3.00
5 thru 8 . . . . @3.00

PRIVATE EYES
Eternity, 1988
1 Saint rep 2.50
2 . . . . 2.50
3 . . . . 2.50
4 . . . . 2.50
5 . . . . 2.50

PROJECT ARMS
Viz Communications, 2002
1 by Ryoji Minagawa 3.25
2 thru 6 . . . . @3.25

PROTHEUS
Caliber, 1986
1 . . . . 2.50
2 . . . . 2.50

PS238
Dork Storm Press, 2002
1 . . . . 3.00
2 thru 5 . . . . @3.00
6 thru 14 . . . . @3.00
15 thru 19 . . . . @3.00
20 thru 28 . . . . @3.00

PSI–JUDGE ANDERSON
Fleetway, 1989
1 thru 15 . . . . @2.50

PULP FICTION
A-List Comics, 1997
1 thru 2 rep. of golden age . . . . @2.50
3 . . . . 3.00
4 . . . . 3.00
5 . . . . 3.00
6 . . . . 3.00
7 . . . . 3.00
Spec. Art of Pulp Fiction 3.00

Puma Blues #6
© Aardvark-Vanaheim

PUMA BLUES
Aardvark–Vanaheim, 1986
1 10,000 printed 4.00
1a 2nd printing 2.50
2 . . . . 3.00
3 thru 19 . . . . @2.50
20 Special 2.50
Mirage
21 thru 24 . . . . @2.50
25 . . . . 2.50
26 thru 28 . . . . @2.50

PURITY
Dakuwaka Productions 2006
1 . . . . 3.00
2 thru 4 . . . . @3.00

PVP
Dork Storm Press, 2001
1 by Scott Kurtz 3.00
2 . . . . 3.00
3 . . . . 3.00
4 . . . . 3.00
5 thru 8 . . . . @3.00
Collected ed. #1 Hat Trick 3.00

QUACK!
Star Reach, 1976
1 Duckaneer 11.00
1a 2nd printing 4.00
2 Newton the Rabbit Wonder 8.00
3 Dave Sim,The Beavers 8.00
4 Dave Sim 8.00
5 Dave Sim 8.00
6 . . . . 8.00

QUAGMIRE USA
Antarctic Press, 2004
1 . . . . 3.00
2 thru 6 . . . . @3.00

QUANTUM MECHANICS
Avatar, 1999
1 (of 2) by Barry Gregory &
   Jacen Burrows 3.50
1a wraparound cover 4.00
2 conclusion 3.50
2a wraparound cover 4.00

QUANTUM: ROCK OF AGES
Dreamchilde Press, 2003
1 (of 12) 3.00
2 thru 4 . . . . @3.00

QUEEN & COUNTRY
Oni Press, 2001
1 by Greg Rucka & Steve Rolston 12.00
2 . . . . 10.00
3 thru 5 . . . . @5.00
6 thru 24 . . . . @3.00
25 . . . . 6.00
26 thru 28 . . . . @3.00
29 thru 32 . . . . @3.00

QUEEN & COUNTRY: DECLASSIFIED
Oni Press, 2002
1 (of 3) 3.00
2 thru 3 . . . . @3.00
Vol. 2
1 . . . . 3.00
2 thru 3 . . . . @3.00
Vol. 3
1 (of 3) 3.00
2 . . . . 3.00

QUEST FOR DREAMS LOST
Literacy Vol. of Chicago, 1987
1-shot inc. TMNTurtles 2.50

QUEST PRESENTS
Quest, 1983
1 JD 2.50
2 JD 2.50
3 JD 2.50

QUICKEN FORBIDDEN
Cryptic Press, 1998
1 . . . . 3.00

2 . . . . 3.00
3 . . . . 3.00
4 . . . . 3.00
5 . . . . 3.00
6 Trial Separation,pt.1 . . . . 3.00
7 Trial Separation,pt.2 . . . . 3.00
8 Trial Separation, concl. 3.00
9 Anxiety Disorder, pt.1 . . . . 3.00
10 Anxiety Disorder, pt.2 . . . . 3.00
11 thru 13 . . . . @3.00

RABID MONKEY
D.B.I. Comics, 1997
1 thru 4 by Joel Steudler . . . . @2.25
5 thru 7 . . . . @2.25
8 thru 13 . . . . @2.50
#1–#5 Autographed pack 12.00
Dreamriders Workshop, 1998
Vol. 2
1 . . . . 3.00

RADICAL DREAMER
Mark's Giant Economy Sized Comics, 1995–96
1 thru 3 F:Max Wrighter . . . . @3.00
4 is Max the Devil? 3.00
VOL 2, 1998
1 (of 6) by Mark Wheatley, sci-fi . . . 3.00

RAGMOP
Planet Lucy Press, 1995
See Image also
1 by Rob Walton, 3rd. printing 3.00
2 thru 8 reoffer . . . . @2.75
8 thru 10 . . . . @2.75
VOL 2, 1997
3 by Rob Walton 3.00
4 O-ring saga, pt. 2 (of 3) 3.00

RAGNAROK
Tokyopop Press, 2002
1 (of 4) by Myung Jin Lee 3.00
2 thru 4 . . . . @3.00

RAGNAROK GUY
Sun Comics, 1992
1 I:Ragnarok Guy,Honey 2.50
2 The Melder Foundation 2.50
3 Guy/Honey mission contd 2.50
4 I:Big Gossage 2.50

RAIJIN COMICS
Gutsoon! Entertainment, 2002
1 manga 5.00
2 thru 36 . . . . @5.00
37 thru 44 . . . . @6.00
45 . . . . 9.00
46 . . . . 6.00

RAIKA
Sun Comics
1 thru 12 . . . . @2.50

RAISING HELL
ABC Comics, 1997
1 . . . . 3.00
1a gold series, 2 extra pages 3.00
2 RCI,F:China & Jazz 3.00
3 conclusion, A:Wild Things 3.00
3 Baby Cheeks edition 9.00
3 Baby Cheeks Gold Edition 12.00

RALPH SNART
Now, 1986
1 . . . . 5.00

B & W PUB.

2 . . . . 4.00
3 . . . . 4.00

[Volume 2] 1986
1 . . . . 3.00
2 thru 8 . . . . @2.50
Trade Paperback 3.00

RAMBO
Blackthorne, 1988
1 thru 5 . . . . @2.50

RAMBO III
Blackthorne
1 . . . . 2.50

RAMM
Megaton Comics, 1987
1 and 2 . . . . @2.50

RANMA 1/2
Viz, 1993
Parts 1 & 2, see color
PART 3, 1993–94
1 thru 13 . . . . @3.00
PART 4, 1995
1 thru 11 . . . . @3.00
PART 5, 1996
1 thru 9 . . . . @3.00
10 thru 12 . . . . @3.00
PART 6, 1996
1 thru 8 (of 14) . . . . @3.00
9 thru 14 . . . . @3.00
PART 7, 1998
1 (of 14) 3.00
2 thru 14 . . . . @3.00
PART 8, 1999
1 (of 13) thru 5 . . . . @3.00
6 thru 13 . . . . @3.00
PART 9, 2000
1 (of 11) 3.00
2 thru 11 . . . . @3.00
PART 10, 2001
1 (of 11) 3.00
2 thru 8 . . . . @3.00
9 thru 11 . . . . @3.00
PART 11, 2002
1 (of 11) 3.00
2 thru 11 . . . . 3.00
Part 12 (March, 2003)
1 . . . . 3.00

RAPHAEL
Mirage, 1985
1 TMNT 17.50
1a 2nd printing 7.50

RAPTUS
High Impact
1 . . . . 3.00
1 2nd printing, new cover 3.00
2 . . . . 3.00
3 . . . . 3.00

RAPTUS:
DEAD OF NIGHT
High Impact
1 . . . . 3.00
2 . . . . 3.00
3 . . . . 3.00

RAT FINK
World of Fandom
1 . . . . 2.50

Raphael #1
© Mirage

2 . . . . 2.50
3 . . . . 2.50

RAVAGER
Kosmic Comic, 1997
0 Ashcan 2.25
1 The First Coming 3.55
2 . . . . 3.55
3 . . . . 3.55
4 by Kirk Patrick & Babak
  Homayoun 3.55
5 . . . . 3.55
6 by Kirk Patrick & Romel Cruz . 3.55

RAVEN
Ariel Press, 2003
1 . . . . 2.25
2 thru 6 . . . . @2.25
7 thru 10 . . . . @2.00

RAVEN CHRONICLES
Caliber Press, 1995
1 . . . . 3.00
1a Special Edition 6.00
2 Landing Zone 3.00
3 The Rain People 3.00
4 The Healer 3.00
5 thru 9 . . . . @3.00
Caliber `New Worlds'
10 by Scott Andrews, Laurence
  Campbell & Tim Perkins 3.00
11 `The Ghost of Alanzo Mann' . . 3.00
12 `The Compensators' flip book
  with Boston Bombers #1 . . . . . 3.00
13 48pg, bagged with back issue . . 4.00
14 . . . . 3.00
15 . . . . 3.00
16 inc. Black Mist 3.00
Spec. Heart of the Dragon . . . 3.00
GN 192pg rep. 17.00

RAVENING, THE
Avatar Press, 1997
0 Trevlin Utz (c) 4.00
0 Matt Martin (c) 4.00
0 Matt Haley (c) 4.00
0 leather cover 20.00
0 signed 12.00
1 . . . . 3.00
1 leather cover 20.00
1 Avatar con cover edition . . . 12.00
2 (of 2) 3.00
Spec. Secrets of the Ravening . . . 2.75

RAW CITY
Dramenon Studios
1 I:Dya,Gino 3.00
2 V:Crucifier 3.00
3 The Siren's Past 3.00

RAW MEDIA MAGS.
Rebel
1 TV,SK,short stories 5.00

RAZOR
London Night, 1992
6 signed 20.00
10 signed 15.00
GN Let Us Prey, rep. of Razor/Wild
  Child, 80pg. 5.00
X-over Razor/Embrace: The
  Spawning (1997) 3.00
  Carmen Electra photo (c) 3.00
  Carmen Electra photo
  embossed (c), signed 19.00
Spec. Razor: Switchblade
  Symphony, Tour Book, limited
  black leather 15.00

RAZOR ANALOG BURN
London Night Studios, 1999
1 by Lee Duhig 2.50
2 . . . . 2.50

RAZOR: ARCHIVES
London Night, 1997
1 EHr, rep #1–#4 . . . . 5.00
1a signed 12.00
2 EHr, rep #5–#8 . . . . 5.00
3 EHr, rep #9–#15 . . . . 5.00
4 EHr, rep #16–#17 . . . . 5.00

RAZOR:
BLEEDING HEART
Avatar Press, 2001
1 Fillion (c) 3.50
1a Martin (c) 3.50
1b Wraparound (c) 5.00
1c Adult (c) 6.00
1d Worship (c) 6.00

RAZOR/DARK ANGEL:
THE FINAL NAIL
Boneyard/London Night
1 X-over (Boneyard Press) 4.00
2 X-over concl.(London Night) . . . 3.00

RAZOR:
THE DARKEST NIGHT
London Night, 1998
1 . . . . 5.00
1a white velvet 20.00
2 velvet edition 10.00
EH! Productions, 1999
1 . . . . 5.00
1a Velvet Edition, signed 25.00
2 . . . . 5.00
3 . . . . 5.00
3a Fan ed.. . . . . 6.00

RAZOR: THE FURIES
Avatar, 2000
1 48-pg. 5.00
1a Previews Exclusive 5.00

RAZOR: GOTHIC
London Night, 1998
1 (of 4) by EHr and Scott Wilson . . 3.00
1 leather 12.00

---

2 EHr 3.00
2a Graphic/violent cover......... 6.00
2b Gothic/leather cover......... 15.00

EH! Productions

3 .... 3.00
3a Elite Fan ed. 5.00
4 .... 3.00
4a Elite Fan ed. 5.00
Spec. Gotherotica 5.00

RAZOR: TILL I BLEED DAYLIGHT
Avatar, 2000

1 (of 2) Tim Vigil (c) 3.50
1a wraparound (c). 4.00
1b Vampire Razor (c) 5.00
1c adult (c) 6.00
1d prism foil 13.00
1e expanded edition 5.00
2 .... 3.50
2a wraparound (c). 4.00
2b adult (c) 6.00
2c expanded edition, 56-pg...... 5.00

RAZOR: TORTURE
London Night, 1995

0 chromium signed 4.00
1 platinum signed 3.00

RAZOR UNCUT
London Night Studios, 1995
Prev. RAZOR (Ind. Color)

13 .... 3.00
14 V:Child Killer 3.00
15 Questions About Father 3.00
16 Nicole's Life,pt.1 .... 3.00
17 Nicole's Life,pt.2 .... 3.00
18 .... 3.00
19 thru 21 Kiss from a Rose ... @3.00
22 thru 24 .... @3.00
25 mild cover I:Knyfe........... 3.00
25b signed 13.00
26 .... 3.00
27 A:Sade, pt.1 .... 3.00
28 A:Sade, pt.2 .... 3.00
29 .... 3.00
30 .... 3.00
31 `Strength by Numbers' 3.00
32 double sized 3.50
33 `Let Us Prey,' pt.2........... 3.00
34 `Let Us Prey,' pt.4 (of 4) 3.00
35 Let the battle begin.......... 3.00
36 all-out war for Queen City..... 3.00
37 `After the Fall' pt.1 .... 3.00
38 `After the Fall,' pt.2 .... 3.00
39 `Money For Hire' 3.00
40 `Father's Bane,' pt.1 .... 3.00
41 `Father's Bane,' pt.2 .... 3.00
42 `Father's Bane,' pt.3 .... 3.00
43 `Father's Bane,' pt.4 .... 3.00
44 Razor finds abandoned child ... 3.00
45 An American Tragedy, pt.1 (of 5) 3.00
45a commemmorative edition, EHr . 5.00
46 An American Tragedy, pt.2 ..... 3.00
47 An American Tragedy, pt.3 ..... 3.00
48 An American Tragedy, pt.4 ..... 3.00
49 An American Tragedy, pt.5 ..... 3.00
50 back in Asylum, Tony Daniel (c) . 3.00
50a Michael Bair (c). 5.00
50b Stephen Sandoval 5.00
50c Blood Red Velvet EHr (c) 25.00
Spec. Deep Cuts (1997) 5th Anniv.
  rep. #6,#13–#15, 80 pg 5.00

EH! Productions, 1999

51 .... 3.00

RAZORGUTS
Monster Comics, 1992

1 thru 4 .... 2.25

RAZOR'S EDGE
London Night, 1999

0 Razor/Stryke (c) 5.00
0b Night Vixen (c)............ 5.00
1 .... 5.00
1a Arizona (c) 5.00
2 Razorblaze (c)............... 5.00
2a Battle Girl (c) 6.00
2b Nightvixen (c). 5.00
3 .... 5.00
3a Nightvixen (c). 5.00
4 .... 5.00
4a (c) 5.00
5 .... 5.00
5a Stryke (c) 5.00

EH! Productions, 1999

6 48-pg. 5.00
7 thru 9 .... @5.00

REACTOMAN
B-Movie Comics

1 .... 2.25
1a signed,numbered............ 2.75
2 thru 4 .... @2.25
collection 5.00

REAGAN'S RAIDERS
Solson

1 thru 6 .... @2.50

The Realm #18
© Caliber Press

REALM
Arrow, 1986

1 Fantasy 6.00
2 .... 4.00
3 .... 3.00
4 TV,Deadworld 21.00
5 I:L.Kazan 2.50
6 thru 13 .... @2.50

Caliber Press, 1990

14 thru 18 .... @2.50
19 .... 2.50

REAL STUFF
Fantagraphic, 1990

1 .... 2.50
2 .... 2.50
3 thru 12 .... 2.50

REAPER
Newcomers Publishing

1 V:The Chinde............... 3.00
2 .... 3.00
3 conclusion 3.00

REBELLION
Daikaiyu Enterprises, 1995

1 I:Rebellion 2.50

RED DIARY
Caliber, 1998

1 (of 4) F:Marilyn, JFK, Hoover,
  CIA. 4.00
1a deluxe 7.00
2 .... 4.00
3 (of 4) 4.00
1 signed). 4.00
4 .... 4.00

RED FOX
Harrier, 1986

1 scarce 6.00
1a 2nd printing 2.50
2 rare 5.00
3 .... 3.00
4 I:White Fox. 3.00
5 I:Red Snail 2.50
6 .... 2.50
7 Wbolton 2.50
8 .... 2.50
9 Demosblurth 2.50

RED & STUMPY
Parody Press

1 Ren & Stimpy parody......... 3.00

REFLECTIONS
Fantagraphics Books 2006

1 .... 7.95
2 thru 3 .... @8.00

RE:GEX: BLACK & WHITE
Awesome Entertainment, 1999

1 RLe,JLb 3.00

REHD
Antarctic Press, 2003

0 .... 2.50
1 .... 3.00
2 thru 3 .... @3.00

REID FLEMING, WORLD'S TOUGHEST MILKMAN
Blackbird-Eclipse, 1986

1 David Boswell,I:Reid Fleming ... 5.00
1a 2nd printing 3.00
1b 3rd–5th printing .... @2.50

Volume 2, 1986

#1 Rogues to Riches Pt.1 .... 5.00
#2 Rogues to Riches Pt.2 (1987) . 3.00
#2a Later printings 2.50
#3 Rogues to Riches Pt.3 (1988) . 3.00
#3a Later printings 2.50
#4 Rogues to Riches Pt.4 (1989) . 3.00
#5 Rogues to Riches Pt.5 (1990) . 2.50

Deep-Sea Comics, 1987

3 `Rogue to Riches', pt.2,4th pr ... 3.00
4 `Rogue to Riches', pt.3,3rd pr .. 3.00
5 `Rogue to Riches', pt.4,2nd pr ... 3.00
6 `Rogue to Riches', pt.5,2nd pr ... 3.00
7 `Another Dawn,'Pt.1. .... 3.00
8 `Another Dawn,'Pt.2. .... 3.00
9 `Another Dawn,'Pt.3. .... 3.00
Spec#1 Origins (1998).......... 3.00

B & W PUB.

REIVERS
Enigma
1 thru 2 Ch'tocc in Space 3.00

RENEGADES OF JUSTICE
Blue Masque
1 I:Monarch,Bloodshadow 2.50
2 Madfire 2.50
3 Television Chronicles 2.50
4 R:Karen Styles 2.50

RENFIELD
Caliber, 1994
1 thru 3 . . . . @3.00
GN Conclusion of series 9.00

REPENTANCE
Advantage Graphics, 1995
1 I:Repentance 2.25

REPLACEMENT GOD
Amaze Ink, 1995
1 Child in The Land of Man 6.00
1a 2nd & 3rd printing 3.00
2 Eye of Knute 4.00
3 & 4 `Bravery' . . . . @3.50
5 thru 7 . . . . @3.00
8 Fairie, book one, concl. 3.00

REPLACEMENT GOD
& OTHER STORIES
Handicraft Guild, 1998
Previously published by Image
6 by Zander Cannon, 80pg 7.00

RETALIATOR
Eclipse
1 I&O:Retaliator 2.50
2 O:Retaliator cont. 2.50
3 thru 5 . . . . @2.50

RETIEF
Adventure, 1987–88
1 thru 6 Keith Laumer adapt. . . . @2.50
[Vol. 2], 1989–90
1 thru 6 . . . . @2.50
Spec.#1 Retief:Garbage Invasion . . 2.50
Spec.#1 Retief:The Giant Killer,
  V:Giant Dinosaur (1991) 2.50

Retief #6
© Adventure

Spec.#1 Grime & Punishment,
  Planet Slunch (1991). 2.50

RETIEF OF THE CDT
Adventure, 1990
1 Keith Laumer Novel Adapt. 2.25
2 thru 6 . . . . @2.25

RETIEF AND
THE WARLORDS
Adventure Comics
1 Keith Laumer Novel Adapt. 2.50
2 Haterakans 2.50
3 Retief Arrested for Treason 2.50
4 Final Battle (last issue) 2.50

RETIEF: DIPLOMATIC
IMMUNITY
Adventure Comics, 1991
1 Groaci Invasion 2.50
2 Groaci story cont. 2.50

RETRO-DEAD
Blazer Unlimited, 1995
1 Dimensional Rift. 3.00
2 by Dan Reed 3.00

RETROGRADE
Eternity
1 thru 4 . . . . @2.25

RETURN OF
HAPPY THE CLOWN
Caliber Press
1 & 2 V:Oni 3.00

RETURN OF LUM
URUSEI* YATSURA, THE
Viz Comics, 1994
1 thru 6 . . . . @3.00
PART TWO, 1995
1 thru 13 . . . . @3.00
PART THREE, 1996
1 thru 11 by Rumiko Takahashi. . @3.00
PART FOUR, 1997
1 thru 11 by Rumiko Takahashi. . @3.00

RETURN OF THE SKYMAN
Ace Comics, 1987
1 SD 2.50

REVOLVER
Renegade, 1985
1 SD 2.50
2 thru 12 . . . . @2.50
Ann. #1 . . . . 2.50

REVOLVING DOORS
Blackthorne, 1986
1 . . . . 2.50
2 & 3 . . . . @2.50
Graphic Novel 4.00

RHEINTOCHTER
Antarctic Press, 1998
1 by Y.Paquette & M.Lacombe 3.00
2 (of 2) concl. 3.00

RHUDIPRRT
PRINCE OF FUR
MU Press, 1990–91
1 thru 6 . . . . @2.25

7 thru 12 . . . . @3.00

RICHARD MATHESON'S
HELL HOUSE
IDW Publishing, 2004
1 48-pgs. 6.50
2 thru 4 . . . . @6.50

RICH JOHNSTON'S
HOLED UP
Avatar Press, 2004
1 . . . . 3.50
2 thru 3 . . . . @3.50
1a thru 3a homeland
  security (c)s . . . . @3.50

RICK RAYGUN
1 . . . . 2.25
2 thru 8 . . . . @2.25

RIO KID
Eternity
1 I:Rio Kid 2.50
2 V:Blow Torch Killer 2.50
3 . . . . 2.50

RIOT
Viz, 1995
1 F:Riot,Axel 2.75
2 & 3 . . . . 2.75
4 final issue 2.75

RIOT ACT TWO
Viz Comics, 1996
1 thru 7 . . . . @3.00

RIP IN TIME
Fantagor, 1986
1 RCo,Limited series 3.00
2 RCo 2.50
3 RCo 2.50
4 RCo 2.50
5 RCo,Last 2.50

RIVAL SCHOOLS
Udon Entertainment, 2006
1 . . . . 5.00
2 . . . . 5.00
3 . . . . 5.00
1a thru 3a variant (c) . . . . @5.00
1b Power cell (c) 12.50

ROACHMILL
Blackthorne, 1986
1 . . . . 5.00
2 . . . . 3.00
3 and 4 . . . . @3.00
See: Dark Horse

ROBERT E. HOWARD'S
Cross Plains Comics, 1999
1-shot Horror, 64-pg. 6.00
1-shot Black Stone 4.00

ROB HANES
ADVENTURES
WCG Comics, 2000
1 by Randy Renoldo 2.50
2 thru 3 . . . . @2.50
4 . . . . 2.75
5 thru 8 . . . . @3.00

ROBIN HOOD
Eternity, 1989
1 thru 4 . . . . @2.50

ROBO DEFENSE TEAM MECHA RIDER
Castle Comics
1 I:RDT Mecha Rider 3.00
2 Identity of Outlaw. 3.00

ROBOTECH
Eternity
1-shot Untold Stories 2.50
Academy Comics, 1995–96
0 Robotech Information 2.50
Spec. Robotech: Macross Tempest
  F:Roy Fokker, Tempest (1995) . 3.00
Spec. Robotech: Mech Angel,
  I:Mech Angel (1995) 3.00
Spec. Robotech: The Misfits, from
  Southern Cross transferred to
  Africa 3.00
Spec. #1 & #2 Robotech The Movie,
  Benny R. Powell & Chi . . . . . @3.00
Spec. Robotech Romance 3.00
Spec. Robotech: Sentinels Star Runners
  Carpenter's Journey (1996) . . . 3.00
GN The Threadbard Heart. 10.00
Antarctic Press, 1998
Ann. #1. . . . . 3.00
Spec.#1 Robotech: Escape (1998) . 3.00

ROBOTECH: ACADEMY BLUES
Academy Comics
0 Classroom Blues 3.50
1 F:Lisa. 3.00
2 Bomb at the Academy 3.00
3 Roy's Drinking Buddy 3.00

ROBOTECH: AFTERMATH
Academy Comics
1 thru 10 R:Bruce Lewis . . . . @3.00
11 Zentradi Traitor 3.00
12 and 13 . . . . @3.00

ROBOTECH: CLONE
Academy Comics
1 Dialect of Duality 3.00
2 V:Monte Yarrow 3.00
3 Ressurection 3.00
4 Ressurection 3.00
5 F:Bibi Ava. 3.00

ROBOTECH: COVERT OPS
Antarctic Press, 1998
1 (of 2) by Greg Lane 3.00
2 . . . . 3.00

ROBOTECH: INVID WAR
Eternity, 1993
1 No Man's Land 2.50
2 V:Defoliators 2.50
3 V:The Invid,Reflex Point 2.50
4 V:The Invid. 2.50
5 Moonbase Aluce II 2.50
6 Moonbase-Zentraedi plot. 2.50
7 Zentraedi plot contd. 2.50
8 A:Lancer. 2.50
9 A:Johnathan Wolfe. 2.50
10 . . . . 2.50
11 F:Rand 2.50
12 thru 15. 2.50

ROBOTECH: INVID WAR AFTERMATH
Eternity
1 thru 6 F:Rand. 2.75

ROBOTECH: MORDECAI
Academy Comics
1 . . . . 3.00
2 Annie meets her clone 3.00

Robotech Return to Macross #3
© Eternity

ROBOTECH: RETURN TO MACROSS
Eternity, 1993
1 thru 12 . . . . @2.50
Academy Comics
13 thru 17 Roy Fokker . . . . @2.75
18 F:The Faithful 2.75
19 F:Lisa 2.75
20 F:Lisa 2.75
21 V:Killer Robot 3.00
22 War of the Believers 3.00
23 War of the Believers,pt.2 . . . . . 3.00
24 War of the Believers,pt.3 . . . . . 3.00
25 War of the Believers,pt.4 . . . . . 3.00
26 thru 30 . . . . @3.00
31 What is the Federalist Plan?. . . . 3.00
32 thru 34 . . . . @3.00
35 Typhoon threatens Macross
  Island. 3.00
36 . . . . 3.00
37 round up of Federalist Agents. . . 3.00

ROBOTECH: SENTINELS: RUBICON
Antarctic Press, 1998
1 (of 7) 3.00
2 Shadows of the Past 3.00

ROBOTECH II THE SENTINELS
Eternity, 1988
1 . . . . 3.00
2 & 3 . . . . @2.50
1a thru 3a 2nd printings . . . . @2.50
4 thru 16 . . . . @2.50
Book 2, 1990
1 thru 12 . . . . @2.25
13 thru 20. . . . . @2.25
Wedding Special #1 (1989) 2.25
Wedding Special #2. . . . . 2.25
Robotech II Handbook. 2.50
Book Three
1 thru 8 V:Invid 2.50

Book Four
Academy Comics, 1995
1 by Jason Waltrip 3.00
2 thru 4 F:Tesla . . . . @2.75
5 JWp,JWt,interior of Haydon IV . . 3.00
6 thru 8 . . . . @3.00
9 JWp,JWt,Breetai, Wolf & Vince
  return to Tirol 3.00
10 JWp,JWt,*Ark Angel* attacked by
  The Black Death Destroyers . . . 3.00
11 JWp,JWt,Tirol, Wolff, Vince &
  Breetai on trial for treason. 3.00
12 JWp,JWt,Dr. Lang exposes
  General Edwards' evil designs . 3.00
13 F:Tesla 2.75
14 V:Invid 2.75
15 . . . . 2.75
16 . . . . 2.75
17 V:Invid Mechas 2.75
18 F:"HIN" 3.00
19 V:Invid. 3.00
20 Final Aplp. Invid Regiss 3.00
21 Predator and Prey. 3.00
22 A Clockwork Planet. 3.00
Halloween Special JWp,JWt,. 3.00

ROBOTECH II: THE SENTINELS: CYBERPIRATES
Eternity, 1991
1 The Hard Wired Coffin. 2.25
2 thru 4 . . . . @2.25

ROBOTECH II: THE SENTINELS: THE MALCONTENT UPRISING
Eternity
1 thru 12 . . . . @2.25

ROBOTECH: VERMILION
Antarctic Press, 1997
1 (of 4) by Duc Tran 3.00
2 Why did Hiro die? 3.00
3 . . . . 3.00
4 . . . . 3.00

ROBOTECH: WARRIORS
Academy Comics, 1995
1 F:Breetai 3.00
2 F:Mirya 3.00
3 F:Mirya 3.00
GN The Terror Maker. 10.00

ROBOTECH: WINGS OF GIBRALTAR
Antarctic Press, 1998
1 (of 2) by Lee Duhig 3.00
2 . . . . 3.00

ROBO WARRIORS
CFW
1 thru 11 . . . . @2.25
Becomes:

KUNG FU WARRIORS

ROCK 'N' ROLL COMICS
Revolutionary, 1989
1 Guns & Roses 10.00
1a 2nd printing 3.50
1b 3rd printing. 3.00
1c 4th-7th printing. 3.00
2 Metalica 11.00
2a 2nd printing 3.00

All comics prices listed are for *Near Mint* condition.

2b 3rd-5th printing 3.00
3 Bon Jovi 9.00
4 Motley Crue 5.00
5 Def Leppard 5.00
6 Rolling Stones 8.00
6a 2nd-4th printing 3.00
7 The Who 5.00
7a 2nd-3rd printing 3.00
9 Kiss 15.00
9a 2nd-3rd Printing 5.00
10 Warrant/Whitesnake 6.00
10a 2nd Printing. 3.00
11 Aerosmith 5.00
12 New Kids on Block 5.00
12a 2nd Printing. 2.25
13 LedZeppelin 6.00
14 Sex Pistols 5.00
See Independent Color

ROCKET RANGERS
Adventure, 1992
1 . . . . 3.00
2 . . . . 3.00
3 . . . . 3.00

ROCKIN' ROLLIN' MINER ANTS
Fate Comics, 1992
1 As seen in TMNT #40 . . . . 2.25
1a Gold Variant copy 7.50
2 Elephant Hunting, A:Scorn,
   Blister 2.25
3 V:Scorn, Inc.,K.Eastman Ant
   pin-up. 2.25
4 Animal Experiments,V:Loboto . . . 2.25

ROLLING STONES: THE SIXTIES
Personality
1 Regular Version 3.00
1a Deluxe Version,w/cards 7.00

ROOTER
Custom Comics of America, 1996–97
1 Sweatin' Bullets 3.00
2 Big Bad Beaver 3.00
3 The Big Izzy 3.00
4 Da Voodoo Blues 3.00
5 . . . . 3.00
6 Blues Power. 3.00
Ann. #1, 120pg. 15.00
VOL 2, 1998
1 by Kelly Campbell 3.00
2 . . . . 3.00
3 Hot Rocks Mojo 3.00

ROSE
Hero Graphics, 1993
1 From The Champions 3.50
2 A:Huntsman 3.50
3 thru 5 . . . . @3.00

ROSE AND GUNN
London Night, 1996
1 . . . . 3.00
1b signed 9.00
2 . . . . 3.00
3 . . . . 3.00

ROSE AND GUNN: RECKONING
London Night
1 (of 2) 3.00

Rose 'N' Gunn, Creator's Choice #1
© Bishop Press

ROSE 'N' GUNN
Bishop Press, 1995
1 Deadly Duo 5.00
2 V:Marilyn Monroe. 3.00
3 Presidential Affairs 3.00
4 Without Each Other 3.00
5 V:Red 3.00
6 & 7 . . . . @3.00
Creator's Choice Rep. #1 . . . . 3.00
Creator's Choice Rep. #2 . . . . 3.00
Creator's Choice Rep. #3 . . . . 3.00

ROVERS
Eternity
1 thru 7 . . . . @2.25

RUBES REVIVED
Fish Warp
1 thru 3 . . . . @2.25

RUK BUD WEBSTER
Fish Warp
1 . . . . 2.25
2 thru 3 . . . . @2.25

RUMBLE PAK
Eigomanga, 2004
1 . . . . 5.00
2 thru 5 . . . . @5.00
Devil's Due Publishing 2005
1 Manga 6.00
2 thru 3 . . . . @6.00

RUNNERS: BAD GOODS
Serve Man Press, 2003
1 . . . . 3.00
2 thru 5 . . . . @3.00

SADE
Bishop Press, 1995
0 B:Adventures of Sade 3.00
1 . . . . 3.00
1a variant 6.00
2 . . . . 3.00

SADE SPECIAL
Bishop Press
1 V:Razor 5.00
1a signed 7.00

SADE
London Night, 1996
1 . . . . 3.00
2 thru 5 . . . . @3.00

SADE/ROSE AND GUNN
London Night, 1996
1 Confederate Mist 3.00

SADE: TESTAMENTS OF PAIN
London Night, 1997
1 (of 2) 3.00

SAGA OF THE MAN-ELF
Trident, 1989
1 thru 5 . . . . @2.25

SAGE
Fantaco, 1995
1 O:Sage. 5.00

SAILOR MOON
Mixx Entertainment, 1998
1 by Naoko Tekeuchi 20.00
2 thru 5 . . . . @12.00
6 thru 11 . . . . @5.00
12 thru 20 . . . . @5.00
Scout Guide: Sailor Mars: Fire . . . 13.00
Scout Guide: Sailor Venus: Love. . 13.00
Scout Guide: Sailor Jupiter:
   Thunder. 13.00
Novel A Scout is Born 5.00
Novel The Power of Love 5.00
Novel 3: Mercury Rising. 5.00
Tokyopop.Com, 2000
21 thru 25 . . . . @3.00
26 thru 35 . . . . @3.00

SAINT
Kick Ass Comics
1 & 2 V:Cerran 2.50

SAINT GERMAINE
Caliber `Core', 1997
0 O:St. Germaine 4.00
1 VcL, two immortals, St. Germain
   cover 3.00
1 Lilith cover 3.00
2 VcL. 3.00
3 VcL. 3.00
3a signed 3.00
4 VcL. 3.00
5 The Kilroy Mandate, VcL(c). . . . 3.00
5a Meyer (c) 3.00
6 Kilroy Mandate. 3.00
8 Ghost Dance 3.00
8 The Man in the Iron Mask 3.00
10 The Tragedy of Falstaff. 3.00
11 by Gary Reed & James Lyle . . . 3.00
GN Shadows Fall, rep. #1–#4 . . . 15.00
Spec. Casanova's Lament, 48-pg.. . 4.00
Spec. Restoration, VcL 4.00

SAINT GERMAINE: PRIOR ECHOES
Caliber `Core', 1998
1 (of 4) by Gary Reed. 3.00
2 . . . . 3.00
3 . . . . 3.00

SAINT TAIL
Tokyopop Press, 2000
1 . . . . 3.00
2 thru 13 . . . . @3.00

14 thru 16 . . . . @3.00
17 thru 20 . . . . @3.00

SAMURAI (1st series)
1 . . . . 50.00
2 . . . . 25.00
3 . . . . 25.00
4 . . . . 25.00
5 . . . . 25.00

SAMURAI
Aircel, 1985
1 rare 6.00
1a 2nd printing 3.00
1b 3rd printing 2.50
2 . . . . 5.00
2a 2nd printing 2.50
3 . . . . 3.00
4 . . . . 3.00
5 thru 12 . . . . @2.50
13 DK (1st art) 4.00
14 thru 16 DK . . . . @4.00
17 thru 23 . . . . @2.50

[3rd series], 1988
#1 thru 3 . . . . @2.50
#4 thru 7 . . . . @2.50
Compilation Book 5.00

SAMURAI
Warp Graphics, 1997
1 by Barry Blair & Colin Chan 3.00
2 . . . . 3.00
3 . . . . 3.00
4 . . . . 3.00

SAMURAI FUNNIES
Solson
1 thru 3 . . . . @2.25

SAMURAI PENGUIN
Solson, 1986
1 . . . . 3.00
2 I:Dr.Radium 2.50
3 . . . . 2.50
4 . . . . 2.50
5 FC 2.50
6 color 2.50
7 . . . . 2.50
8 . . . . 2.50
9 . . . . 2.50

SAMURAI 7
Gauntlet Comics
1 I: Samurai 7 . . . . 2.50

SAMURAI, SON OF DEATH
Eclipse
1 . . . . 4.00
1a 2nd printing 4.00

SANCTUARY
Viz Communications, 1993
1 World of Yakuza 5.00
2 thru 4 . . . . @5.00
5 thru 9 . . . . @5.00

[Part Two], 1994
1 thru 9 . . . . @5.00

[Part Three], 1994–95
1 thru 8 . . . . @3.50

[Part Four], 1995–96
1 thru 7 . . . . @3.50

[Part Five], 1996
7 thru 13 by Sho Fumimura &
  Ryoichi Ikegami . . . . @3.50

SANCTUARY
Fantagraphics Books 2006
1 (of 6) 4.00
2 thru 3 . . . . @4.00

SANTA CLAWS
Eternity
1 `Deck the Mall with Blood
  and Corpses' 3.00

SAPPHIRE
Ariel Press, 1996
1 by Vince Danks 3.00
6 thru 9 . . . . @3.00

SAVAGE HENRY
Vortex, 1987
1 . . . . 2.50
2 thru 13 . . . . @2.50

Rip Off Press, 1991
14 thru 15 . . . . @2.25
16 thru 24 . . . . @2.50

SAVAGE HENRY: POWERCHORDS
Aeon, 2004
1 (of 3) 3.00
2 and 3 . . . . @3.00
Spec. Puppet Trap 3.00

SAVAGE PLANET
Basement Comics, 2002
1 by Dan Parson & Kevin Rasel . . . 3.00
1a special edition 8.95
2 . . . . 3.00
2a special edition 8.95
3 . . . . 3.25
3a special edition 8.95

SAVAGE PLANET: SECRETS OF THE EMPIRE
Basement Comics, 2007
1-shot 3.50

SCARLET IN GASLIGHT
Eternity, 1988
1 A:SherlockHolmes 4.00
2 . . . . 3.00
3 & 4 . . . . @2.50

SCARLET SCORPION/ DARKSIDE
AC Comics, 1995
1 & 2 Flipbooks 3.50

SCARLET THUNDER
Amaze Ink, 1995
1 . . . . 2.50
2 thru 3 . . . . @2.50

SCARY GODMOTHER
Sirius Entertainment, 2001
1 by Jill Thompson 3.00
2 thru 6 concl. . . . . @3.00

SCARY GODMOTHER: BLOODY VALENTINE
Sirius Entertainment, 1998
1 . . . . 4.00
1a signed and numbered 9.00
Holiday Spooktacular 3.00

SCARY GODMOTHER: WILD ABOUT HARRY
Sirius Entertainment, 2000
1 (of 3) by Jill Thompson 3.00
2 . . . . 3.00
3 concl. 3.00

Science Fair #1
© Antarctic Press

SCIENCE FAIR
Antarctic Press, 2005
1 (of 8) 3.00
2 thru 4 . . . . @3.00

SCIMIDAR
Eternity
1 . . . . 4.00
1a 2nd Printing 2.50
2 and 3 . . . . @3.00
4 HotCover 3.50
4A MildCover 3.00

SCOOTER GIRL
Oni Press, 2003
1 (of 6) 3.00
2 thru 6 . . . . @3.00

SCORN
SCC Entertainment, 1996
Lingerie Spec. 3.00
Lingerie Spec. deluxe 10.00
Super Spec.#1 rep. Deadly
  Rebellion, Headwave, Fabric
  of the Mind 5.00
X-over Scorn/Ardy: Alien Influence
  (1997) by Rob Potchak & Timothy
  Johnson 4.00
  Bill Maus (c) 4.00
  Deluxe gold 10.00
X-over Scorn/Dracula: The Vampire's
  Blood (1997) 4.00
  Dracula cover 4.00
  Scorn cover 4.00
Spec.#1A Scorn; Dead or Alive
  (1997) Mike Morales(c) 4.00
  Andrea Seri(c) 4.00
Spec.# Scorn:Deadly Rebellion 4.00
  Birthday Suit cover 10.00
  Celebrity photo cover 10.00
Spec.#1 Scorb: Fractured (1997)
  Fear cover 4.00
  Rage cover 4.00
Spec: Scorn: Heatwave (1997) by
  Chris Crosby & Mike Morales . . 4.00

All comics prices listed are for *Near Mint* condition.

Spec. Scorn: Hostage 4.00
Spec. Scorn: Naked Truth (1997) . . 4.00

SCRATCH
Outside, 1986
1 . . . . 3.00
2 thru 4 . . . . @2.50

SCREAMING ANGELS
Antarctic Press, 2004
1 (of 3) 3.50
2 thru 3 . . . . @3.50

SCREWTOOTH
Amaze Ink/SLG2006
1 by Black Olive 3.00
2 . . . . 3.00
3 . . . . 3.00

SCRIMIDAR
CFD Productions, 1995
1 I:Bloody Mary. 2.75

Scud: Disposable Assassin #3
© Fireman Press

SCUD:
DISPOSABLE ASSASSIN
Fireman Press, 1994
1 I:Scud. 8.00
1a 3rd printing. 3.50
2 . . . . 6.00
3 . . . . 5.00
4 thru 6 F:Scud . . . . @5.00
7 Lupine Thoughts 4.00
8 Scud Looks for His Arm. 4.00
9 Scud Looks for His Arm. 4.00
10 thru 16 by Rob Schrab . . . . . @3.00
17 . . . . 3.00
18 . . . . 3.00
19 . . . . 3.00
20 Horse series, concl. 3.00

SCUD: TALES FROM
THE VENDING MACHINE
Fireman Press, 1998
1 . . . . 2.50
2 . . . . 2.50
3 . . . . 2.50
4 . . . . 2.50
5 . . . . 2.50

SEAMONSTERS
& SUPERHEROES
Amaze Ink/SLG, 2003
1 (of 3) 3.00
2 thru 8 . . . . @3.00

SEARCHERS
Caliber `New Worlds', 1996
1A Red cover, signed 3.00
1B Blue cover, signed. 3.00
3 . . . . 3.00
4 . . . . 3.00
5 flip book with Boston Bombers . . 3.00

SEARCHERS:
APOSTLE OF MERCY
Caliber, 1997
1 (of 2) 4.00
2 . . . . 4.00
Vol 2?
1 . . . . 3.00
2 . . . . 3.00
3 (of 3) 48pg 4.00

SECRET FILES
Angel Entertainment, 1996
0 gold edition 6.00
0 commemorative edition 3.00
1 . . . . 3.00
1 spooky silver foil edition. 5.00
2 . . . . 3.00
2 deluxe 5.00
Spec. Secret Files vs. Vampire Girls:
  The Vampire Effece (1997) . . 3.00
Pin-up Book Secret Files: Erotic
  Experiments (1997) 3.00
Spec.#1 Secret Files: F.B.I.
  Conspiracy (1997)F:Sabrina
  & Susanna Sorenson 3.00

SECRET FILES:
THE STRANGE CASE
Angel Entertainment, 1996
0 by David Campitti & Al Rio 3.00
1 by David Campiti & Al Rio 3.00

SECRET MESSAGES
NBM Books, 2001
1 Abductions, pt.1 . . . . 3.00
2 Abductions, pt.2 . . . . 3.00
3 Abductions, pt.3 . . . . 3.00
4 Abductions, pt.4 . . . . 3.00
5 Abductions, pt.5 . . . . 3.00

SECTION 8
Noir Press, 1995
1 Anthology series 2.50
2 thru 6 . . . . @2.50
7 `Retribution,' pt.1 . . . . 2.50
8 `Retribution,' pt.2 . . . . 2.50
9 . . . . 2.50
10 `Chance' 2.50

SEEKER
Caliber `Core', 1998
1M by Gary Reed & Chris
  Massarotto, Meadows(c). 3.00
1W David Williams(c) 3.00
1a variant Greg Louden (c). 3.00
1 premium, signed 10.00
2 . . . . 3.00
3 . . . . 3.00
4 . . . . 3.00
5 Gestalt vs. LeAnn Heywood . . . 3.00
Spec. Dawn of Armageddon,
  x-over, 48-pg. 4.00

SEMI-AUTO ANGEL:
SECOND HEAVEN
Alias Enterprises, 2006
1 (of 6) 3.50
2 . . . . 3.50

SENTINEL
Harrier, 1986
1 . . . . 2.50
2 thru 4 . . . . @2.50

SERAPHIN
Newcomers Press, 1995
1 I:Roy Torres 3.00

SERENITY ROSE
Amaze Ink/SLG, 2003
1 . . . . 3.00
2 thru 6 . . . . @3.00

7 GUYS OF JUSTICE, THE
False Idol Studios, 2000
1 Jerque Imperitive,pt.1 . . . . 2.25
2 Jerque Imperitive,pt.2 . . . . 2.25
3 Jerque Imperitive,pt.3 . . . . 2.25
4 thru 11 . . . . @2.25
12 thru 16 . . . . @2.25

777: THE WRATH
Avatar Press, 1998
1 (of 3) by David Quinn & Tim Vigil 3.00
1a wraparound cover 3.50
1c leather cover 6.00
1d royal blue foil logo 60.00
1e signed 15.00
1f foil platinum edition. 17.00
2 . . . . 3.00
3 concl. 3.00

SEVENTH SYSTEM, THE
Sirius Entertainment, 1997
1 (of 6) by Roel. 3.00
2 thru 6 . . . . @3.00

SFA SPOTLIGHT
Shanda Fantasy Arts, 1999
4 Tales of the Morphing Period. . . . 4.50
5 Zebra, by Carl Gafford 4.50
6 Women in Fur 1999 . . . . 5.00
7 Tales From Supermegatopia 5.00
8 Women in Fur 2000 . . . . 5.00
9 Knight & Mouse 5.00
10 Atomic Mouse 5.00
11 Plush Beauties 5.00
12 Courageous Man Adventures . . . 5.00
13 Women in Fur 2001 . . . . 5.00
14 Fission Chicken 5.00
15 Women in Fur 2002 . . . . 5.00
16 Star Quack 5.00

SF SHORT STORIES
Webb Graphics, 1991
1 & 2 . . . . @2.50

SHADES OF BLUE
AMP Comics, 2001
1 . . . . 2.50
2 thru 4 . . . . @2.50
5 Silence, pt.3 . . . . 2.50
6 F:Heidi, Marcus 2.50
7 Winter, pt.1 . . . . 3.00
8 Winter, pt.2. . . . . 3.00
9 Winter, pt.3. . . . . 3.00
10 . . . . 3.00
Digital Webbing, 2003
1 thru 5 . . . . @3.00

SHADES OF GRAY COMICS AND STORIES
Caliber Tapestry, 1996
1 . . . . 3.00
2 . . . . 3.00
3 . . . . 3.00
4 . . . . 3.00
Super Summer Spec. rep. 4.00

SHADOW CROSS
Darkside Comics, 1995
1 I:Shadow Cross 5.00
2 thru 7 . . . . @2.50

SHADOWGEAR
Antarctic Press, 1999
1 by Locke 3.00
2 . . . . 3.00
3 conclusion 3.00

SHADOWALKER
Aircel
1 thru 4 . . . . @2.25

SHADOW SLASHER
Pocket Change Comics, 1994
1 I:Shadow Slasher. 2.50
2 V:Riplash 2.50
3 F:Matt Baker 2.50
4 Evolution 2.50
5 F:Riplash 2.50
6 Next Victim. 2.50
7 What Can Kill Him 2.50
8 . . . . 2.50
9 final issue. 2.50

SHANDA [THE PANDA]
Mu, 1992
1 . . . . 2.50
Antarctic Press, 1993
1 thru 11 . . . . @2.75
12 thru 14. . . . . @3.00
Med Systems
15 and 16 . . . . @2.25
Vision Comics, 1996
17 by Mike Curtis & Michelle Light . 2.25
18 'Rocky Horror Picture Show' . . . 2.25
19 'Shine on Me, Cajun Moon' 2.50
20 falling in love. 2.50
22 Bright Eyes 3.00
Shanda Fantasy, 1999
23 Sweet Young Things 3.00
24 graduation night 3.00
25 48-pg. 5.00
26 thru 30. . . . . @3.00
31 thru 33. . . . . @3.00
34 48-pg. 5.00
35 thru 44 . . . . @5.00
45 Homeless 5.00
46 Dogfight. 5.00

SHANGHAIED
Eternity
1 & 2 . . . . @2.25
3 & 4 . . . . @2.25

SHARDS
Acension Comics, 1994
1 I:Silver, Raptor, RIpple. 2.50
2 F:Anomoly 2.50

SHATTERED EARTH
Eternity, 1988–89
1 thru 9 . . . . @2.25

SHATTERPOINT
Eternity, 1990
1 thru 4 Broid miniseries . . . . @2.25

SHEBA
Vol. 2, Sirius Dogstar, 1997
1 by Walter S. Crane IV 2.50
2 thru 4 . . . . @2.50
Sick Mind Press
5 thru 7 . . . . @3.00
Vol 3, Shanda Fantasy Arts, 2001
1 by Walter Crane IV 5.00
2 thru 4 . . . . @5.00

SHE-CAT
AC Comics, 1989
1 thru 4 . . . . @2.50

SHE-DEVILS ON WHEELS
Aircel, 1992
1 thru 3 by Bill Marimon 3.00

SHERLOCK HOLMES
Eternity, 1988
1 thru 22 . . . . @2.25

SHERLOCK HOLMES
Caliber/Tome Press, 1997
1-shot Dr. Jekyll and Mr. Holmes by
Steve Jones & Seppo Makinen . 3.00
1-shot Return of the Devil 4.00
1-shot Return of the Devil, signed. . 4.00

SHERLOCK HOLMES CASEBOOK
Eternity
1 and 2 . . . . @2.25

SHERLOCK HOLMES: CHRONICLES OF CRIME AND MYSTERY
Northstar
1 'The Speckled Band' 2.25

SHERLOCK HOLMES: HOUND OF THE BASKERVILLES
Caliber/Tome Press, 1997
1 (of 3) by Martin Powell & PO. . . . 3.00

SHERLOCK HOLMES: MARK OF THE BEAST
Caliber/Tome Press, 1997
1 (of 3) by Martin Powell
& Seppo Makinen 3.00
2 . . . . 3.00
GN 13.00

SHERLOCK HOLMES MYSTERIES
Moonstone, 1997
1-shot by Joe Gentile & Richard
Gulick. 3.00
1-shot Sherlock Holmes and the
Clown Prince of London (2001). 3.00

SHERLOCK HOLMES OF THE '30's
Eternity
1 thru 7 strip rep.. . . . . @3.00

SHERLOCK HOLMES READER
Caliber 'Tome Press', 1998
1 Curse of the Beast. 4.00
2 The Loch Ness Horror 4.00
3 The Loch Ness Horror 4.00
4 The Loch Ness Horror 4.00
5 . . . . 4.00

Sherlock Holmes, Return of the Devil #2
© Adventure

SHERLOCK HOLMES: RETURN OF THE DEVIL
Adventure, 1992
1 V:Moriarty. 2.50
2 V:Moriarty. 2.50

SHERLOCK JUNIOR
Eternity
1 Rep.NewspaperStrips 2.25
2 Rep.NewspaperStrips 2.25
3 Rep.NewspaperStrips 2.25

SHI
Crusade, 1999
0 rough cut edition 5.00
0 ashcan, signed. 9.00
Spec.#1 Black,White & Red. 3.00
Spec. San Diego (Con) Art of War
Tour Book 1998. . . . . 9.00
Spec. Lim. Ed. Shi/Daredevil
Banzai 14.00
Spec.#1 Kaidan, macabre 3.00
Spec.#1 Kaidan, signed & numb. . 20.00
Spec. Shi/First Wave, Voices
of the Dead x-over (2001) 3.00
Spec. Shi/FirstWave,variant BiT(c) . 3.00
Spec. Shi/FirstWave,signed 10.00
Spec. First Wave/Shi, Voices of
the Dead, pt.2 x-over (2001) . . . 3.00
Spec. FirstWave/Shi,variant BiT(c) . 3.00
Coll. Ed. Heaven & Earth,
Yin & Yang,96-pg. 6.00
Year of the Dragon preview book . . 3.00
Year of the Dragon tour book 5.00
Year of the Dragon tour Wizard. . . . 5.00
Year of the Dragon tour San Diego . 5.00
Umadoshi Tour Book, 2002 . . . . . . 5.00
Umadoshi, Tour Book, sketch (c). . . 5.00
Umadoshi, Tour Book, Pittsburgh . . 5.00
Tour Book, Art of War, remarked . . 20.00
Tour Bok Year of the Dragon,

remarked 20.00
Tour Book, Year of the Serpent
remarked 20.00
Avatar Press, 2005/
Avatar Fan Club
Shi: Poisoned Paradise preview . . . 6.00
Shi: Pandora's Box preview 6.00

SHI: THE ILLUSTRATED WARRIOR
Crusade Entertainment, 2002
1 (of 7) BiT 3.00
2 BiT thru 7 . . . . @3.00

SHI: SEMPO
Avatar, 2003
1/2 Prism Foil Edition 10.00
1/2 Royal Blue Edition 60.00
1/2 Prism Foil (c) 10.00
Preview edition. 2.25
Preview variant (c). 6.00
Preview wraparound (c). 6.00
Preview prism foil (c) 13.00
1 . . . . 3.50
1a variant (c). 3.50
2 . . . . 3.50
2a variant (c). 3.50
2b wraparound (c). 4.00

SHIP OF FOOLS
Caliber, 1996
1 signed edition. 3.00
2 'Dante's Compass' 3.00
3 The Great Escape begins 3.00
4 MiA 3.00
5 MiA 3.00
Spec. #1, Bon Voyage, Go to Hell,
Mama Hades 4.00
continued: See Image Comics

SHOCK THE MONKEY
Millennium
1 & 2 Entering the Psychotic Mind . 4.00

SHONEN JUMP
Viz Communications, 2002
1 thru 8 . . . . @5.00
Vol. 2
1 thru 12 . . . . @5.00
Vol. 3
1 thru 10 . . . . @5.00
35 thru 49 . . . . @5.00

SHOUJO
Antarctic Press, 2003
1 . . . . 6.00
2 thru 4 . . . . @6.00

SHRED
CFW
1 thru 10 . . . . @2.25

SHRIEK
Fantaco
1 . . . . 5.00
2 . . . . 5.00
3 . . . . 8.00

SHURIKEN
Victory, 1986
1 Reggi Byers 5.00
1a 2nd printing 2.50
2 . . . . 3.00
3 . . . . 2.50
4 . . . . 2.50
5 thru 13 . . . . @2.50

Shuriken #6
© Victory

Graphic Nov. Reggie Byers 8.00

SHURIKEN
Eternity, 1991
1 Shuriken vs. Slate 2.50
2 Neutralizer, Meguomo 2.50
3 R:Slate. 2.50
4 Morgan's Bodyguard Serrate. . . . 2.50
5 Slate as Shuriken & Megumo . . . 2.50
6 Hunt for Bionauts, final issue. . . . 2.50

SHURIKEN: COLD STEEL
Eternity, 1989
1 . . . . 2.50
2 . . . . 2.50
3 thru 6 . . . . @2.50

SHURIKEN TEAM-UP
ETernity, 1989
1 thru 3 . . . . @2.50

SIEGEL & SHUSTER
Eclipse, 1984
1 . . . . 2.50
2 . . . . 2.50

SILBUSTER
Antarctic Press, 1994
1 thru 10 . . . . @3.50
11 I:Kizuki Sister 3.50
12 thru 14 . . . . @3.50
15 . . . . 4.00
16 thru 19 . . . . @3.50

SILENT INVASION
Renegade, 1986
1 . . . . 4.00
2 thru 12, final issue . . . . @3.00
Combined Ed. #1 & #2 . . . . 17.00

SILENT INVASION
Caliber
4 Red Shadows, pt.1 . . . . 3.00
5 Red Shadows, pt.2 . . . . 3.00

SILENT INVASION: ABDUCTIONS
Caliber, 1998
1 by Larry Hancock & Michael
Cherkos. 3.00

SILENT MOBIUS
Viz Communications
Part 1 thru Part 4: See Color
Part 5 INTO THE LABYRINTH, 1999
1 (of 6) by Kia Asamiya 3.00
2 thru 4 . . . . @3.00
5 & 6 . . . . @3.25
Part 6 KARMA, 1999
1 (of 7) by Kia Asamiya 3.25
2 thru 7 . . . . @3.25
Part 7 CATASTROPHE, 2000
1 (of 6) by Kia Asamiya 3.00
2 thru 6 . . . . @3.00
Part 8 LOVE & CHAOS, 2000
1 thru 7 . . . . @3.00
Part 9 ADVENTURERS, 2001
1 thru 6 (of 6) . . . . @3.00
Part 10 TURNABOUT, 2002
1 (of 6) by Kia Asamiya 3.00
2 thru 6 . . . . @3.00
Part 11 BLOOD, 2002
1 (of 5) by Kia Asamiya 3.00
2 thru 5 . . . . @3.00
Part 12 HELL, 2003
1 thru 3 . . . . @3.00

SILENT RAPTURE
Brainstorm, 1996
1 Jacob Grimm vs. Six Devils
of Twilight. 3.00
1a Vicious variant edition 5.00
Avatar Press, 1997
2 by Jude Millien 3.00
2a deluxe (c). 9.00

SILLY DADDY
Joe Chiappetta, 1995
1 . . . . 3.50
2 thru 5 . . . . 3.00
6 thru 10 . . . . @2.75
11 thru 18 . . . . @2.75

SILVER STORM
Aircel, 1990
1 thru 4 . . . . @2.25

SIMON/KIRBY READER
1 . . . . 2.50

SINBAD
Adventure, 1989
1 . . . . 2.50
2 . . . . 2.50
3 . . . . 2.50
4 . . . . 2.50

SINBAD: HOUSE OF GOD
Adventure Comics, 1991
1 Caliph's Wife Kidnapped 2.50
2 Magical Genie 2.50
3 Escape From Madhi 2.50
4 A:Genie 2.50

SINNAMON
Catfish Comics, 1995
1 remastered. 2.75
1a remastered deluxe 3.75
6 thru 8 . . . . @2.75
Mythic Comics
9 'Ashes to Ashes—The Pyre-Anna
Saga,' pt.2 . . . . 2.75
10 'Twas Beauty Bashed
The Beast'. 2.75
11 . . . . 2.75

12 M.G.Delaney (c) 2.75
12 Poliwko (c) 2.75
Archives #1 . . . . 2.75

SISTER ARMAGEDDON
Dramenon Studios
1 & 2 Nun with a Gun . . . . @2.50
3 Mother Superior 2.50
4 V:Apoligon 3.00

SKELETON KEY
Amaze Ink, 1995
1 1 I:Skeleton Key 4.00
1 2nd printing 3.00
2 F:Tansin 3.00
3 V:Japanese Burglar 3.00
4 V:Closet Monster 3.00
5 thru 10 . . . . @3.00
11 . . . . 3.00
12 . . . . 3.00
14 by Andi Watson 3.00
15 `The Celestial Calendar' 3.00
16 thru 30 . . . . @3.00
Spec. 5.00
Spec.Skeleton Key/Sugar Kat 3.00
VOL 2
1 (of 4) 3.00
2 . . . . 3.00
3 . . . . 3.00
4 conclusion 3.00

SKIN 13
Entity/Parody, 1995
1/2a Grungie/Spider-Man 2.50
1/2b Heavy Metal 2.50
1/2c Gen-Et Jackson 2.50

SKULL MAN
Tokyopop Press, 2000
1 (of 5) 3.00
2 thru 5 . . . . @3.00

SKUNK, THE
Entity Comics, 1997
#Uno 2.75
5 BMs 2.75
6 BMs 2.75
Collection #1 rep. #1–#3 . . . . 5.00
Collection #1a signed & numbered 10.00
Collection #2 rep. #4–#6 . . . . 5.00

SKUNK/FOODANG
FOODANG/SKUNK
Entity Comics
Spec. 1 BMs, BMs(c) 2.75
Spec. 1a BMs, Mike Duggan(c) 2.75

SKYNN & BONES:
DEADLY ANGELS
Brainstorm, 1996
1 . . . . 3.00

SKYNN & BONES:
FLESH FOR FANTASY
Brainstorm, 1997
1 erotic missions 3.00
2 erotic missions 3.00
Spec. #1 Dare to Bare 3.00

SLACK
Legacy Comics
1 Slacker Anthology 2.50
2 Loser 2.50

SLACKER COMICS
Slave Labor, 1994
1 thru 15 by Doug Slack . . . . @3.00
16 . . . . 3.00
17 . . . . 3.00
18 . . . . 3.00
19 . . . . 3.00

SLAUGHTERHOUSE
Caliber
1 Bizarre medical Operations 3.00
2 House of Death 3.00
3 House of Death 3.00
4 Dead Killer vs. Mosaic 3.00

Slaughterman #1
© Comico

SLAUGHTERMAN
Comico, 1983
1 . . . . 2.50
2 . . . . 2.50

SLAYERS
CPM Manga, 1998
1 by Hajime Kanzaka & Rui
    Araizumi 3.00
2 thru 6 . . . . @3.00
Spec. #1 F:Lina Inverse 3.00
Spec. #2 thru #6 . . . . @3.00

SLAYERS: SUPER–
EXPLOSIVE DEMON
STORY
CPM Manga, 2001
1 by H. Kanzaka & S. Yoshinaka . . 3.00
2 thru 6 . . . . @3.00

SMILE
Tokyopop Press, 2000
Vol. 3
1 magazine 3.00
2 thru 12 magazine . . . . @5.00
Vol. 4
1 magazine 5.00
2 thru 4 . . . . @5.00
5 thru 6 . . . . @6.00
7 . . . . 5.00

SMITH BROWN JONES
Kiwi Studios, 1997
1 thru 5 . . . . @3.00

SMITH BROWN JONES:
ALIEN ACCOUNTANT
Slave Labor, 1998
1 by Jon Hastings 3.00
2 thru 4 . . . . @3.00
Spec.#1 Halloween Special 3.00
Spec. Convention Mayhem 6.00

SNOWMAN
Hall of Heroes, 1996
1 . . . . 12.00
1a variant (c). 15.00
1 3rd printing 2.75
1 San Diego Con. ed. 5.00
2 . . . . 8.00
2a 2nd printing 2.75
2b variant (c). 9.00
3 . . . . 6.00
3a variant (c). 7.00

SNOWMAN
Avatar Press, 1997
0 by Matt Martin, O:Snowman 3.00
0a Frozen Fear extra-bloody 5.00
0b Leather cover 20.00
0c signed 9.00
Spec.#1 Snowman 1944 . . . . 4.00
Spec.#1 Snowman 1944, deluxe . . . 5.00
Spec.#1 Snowman 1944, signed . . 9.00
1-shot Flurries, Glynn (c). 5.00
1-shotA Flurries, Snowman (c) 5.00

SNOWMAN:
DEAD & DYING
Avatar Press, 1997
1 (of 3) by Matt Martin 3.00
1 deluxe 5.00
1 signed 9.00
2 . . . . 3.00
2 deluxe 5.00
3 by Matt Martin 3.00
3 Frozen Fear 5.00
3 White Velvet 25.00

SNOWMAN:
HORROR SHOW
Avatar Press, 1998
1 by Matt Martin 3.00
1a Frozen Fear (c) 5.00
1b Leather cover. 20.00
1 deluxe 5.00

SNOWMAN: 1994
Entity, 1996
1 flip cover #0, by Matt Martin,
    O:Snowman. 3.00
1 signed, numbered 7.00
3 . . . . 2.75
3 deluxe, variant, foil cover. 3.50
4 . . . . 2.75
4 deluxe, variant, foil cover. 3.50

SNOWMAN2
Avatar Press, 1997
1 (of 2) Snowman vs. Snowman . . 3.00
1a Face-off cover 5.00
1b Leather cover. 20.00
1c Royal Blue edition 35.00
2 concl. 3.00
2a Sudden Death variant cover . . . 5.00

SOB: SPECIAL
OPERATIONS BRANCH
Promethean Studios, 1994
1 I:SOB 2.50

SOCKETEER
Kardia
Rocketeer parody 2.25

SOLD OUT
Fantaco, 1986
1 & 2 . . . . @2.50

SOLO EX-MUTANTS
Eternity
1 thru 6 . . . . @2.50

Something Different #2
© Wooga Central

SOMETHING DIFFERENT
Wooga Central, 1991
1 Tears of God 2.50
2 1601 . . . . 2.50

SONAMBULO: SLEEP OF THE JUST
Ninth Circle Studios, 1999
1 (of 3) by Rafael Navarro 3.00
2 . . . . 3.00
3 (of 3) 3.00
Spec. Strange Tales (2000) 4.00
Spec. Ghost of a Chance (2002) . . . 5.00
Spec. Mexican Stand-off (2004) 3.00

SONG OF THE CID
Calibre/Tome
1 Story of El Cid 3.00
2 Story of El Cid concl. 3.00

SONG OF THE SIRENS
Millennium
Earth 3.00
Earth, signed print edition 7.00
Fire 3.00
Fire, signed print edition 9.00
Wind 3.00
Wind collectors edition 5.00
Wind with trading card 5.00
Secrets, Lies, & Videotape Pin-Up
   Special 3.00
Secrets, Lies, & Videotape Pin-Up
   Special, foil logo 6.00
Secrets, Lies, & Videotape Pin-Up
   Special, deluxe 10.00

SOUL
Samson Comics
1 . . . . 2.50
2 thru 3 F:Sabbeth . . . . @2.50

SOULFIRE
Aircel
1 mini-series 2.25
2 . . . . 2.25
3 . . . . 2.25

SOULSEARCHERS AND CO.
Claypool, 1993–2007
1 thru 10 Peter David(s) . . . . . . @5.00
11 thru 20 . . . . @3.00
21 thru 24 . . . . @3.00
25 ACo&SL(c) 2.50
26 O:Soulsearchers, pt.1 . . . . 2.50
27 O:Soulsearchers, pt.2 . . . . 2.50
28 O:Soulsearchers, pt.3 . . . . 2.50
29 O:Soulsearchers, pt.4 . . . . 2.50
30 thru 74 . . . . @2.50
75 thru 82 . . . . @2.50

SOUTHERN KNIGHTS
Guild, 1983
1 See Crusaders
2 . . . . 7.00
3 and 4 . . . . @5.00
5 thru 7 . . . . @4.00
Fictioneer, 1985
8 thru 11 . . . . @3.00
12 thru 33 . . . . @3.00
34 . . . . 3.00
35 The Morrigan Wars Pt.#2 . . . . . 3.50
36 Morrigan Wars Pt.#5 . . . . 3.50
37 Hell in a Handbasket 3.00
Ann. #1 . . . . 2.50
DreadHalloweenSpec #1 . . . . 2.50
Primer #1 . . . . 2.50

SOUTHERN SQUADRON
Aircel, 1990
1 . . . . 2.25
2 thru 4 . . . . @2.25
Eternity
1 I:SQUAD 2.50
2 . . . . 2.25
3 . . . . 2.25
4 . . . . 2.25

SOUTHERN SQUADRON FREEDOM OF INFO. ACT.
Aircel, 1992
1 F.F.#1 Parody/Tribute cov. 2.50
2 A:Waitangi Rangers 2.50
3 . . . . 2.50

SPACE ARK
Apple, 1986
1 & 2 see color
3 . . . . 2.50
4 . . . . 2.50
5 . . . . 2.50

SPACE BEAVER
Ten-Buck Comics, 1986
1 . . . . 2.50
2 . . . . 2.50
3 O&I:Stinger 2.50
4 A:Stinger 2.50
5 . . . . 2.50
6 O:Rodent 2.50
7 thru 12 . . . . @2.50

SPACED
Anthony Smith Publ., 1988
1 I:Zip; 800 printed 30.00
2 . . . . 20.00
3 I:Dark Teddy 15.00
4 . . . . 15.00
5 and 6 . . . . @5.00
7 and 8 . . . . @2.50
Eclipse
9 . . . . 2.50
10 . . . . 2.50
11 thru 13 . . . . @2.50

SPACE PATROL
Adventure, 1992
1 thru 3 . . . . 2.50

SPACE USAGI
Mirage Studios, 1992
1 Stan Sakai,Future Usagi 3.00
2 Stan Sakai,Future Usagi 3.00
3 Stan Sakai,Future Usagi 3.00

SPACE WOLF
Antarctic Press
1 From Albedo,by Dan Flahive 2.50

SPANDEX TIGHTS
Lost Cause Prod.
Vol. 1, 1994
1 thru 6 . . . . @2.50
Vol. 2, 1997
1 . . . . 2.50
2 prelude to Space Opera 3.00
6 . . . . 3.00
Spec. Vs. Mighty Awful Sour
   Rangers, signed 3.00

SPANDEX TIGHTS PRESENTS: SPACE OPERA
Lost Cause Productions, 1997
Part 1 by Bryan J.L. Glass & Bob
   Dix, parody 3.00
Part 1, signed, Star Wars parody . . . 3.00
Part 2 `Star Bored,' pt.2 . . . . 3.00
Part 3 . . . . 3.00

SPANDEX TIGHTS PRESENTS: THE GIRLS OF '95
Lost Cause Productions
1 The Good, Bad and Deadly,
   signed (1997) 4.00

SPANDEX TIGHTS PRESENTS: WIN A DREAM DATE WITH SPANDEX-GIRL
Lost Cause Productions
1 (of 3) (1998) 3.00
2 . . . . 3.00
3 . . . . 3.00

SPANDEX TIGHTS: THE LOST ISSUES
Lost Cause Productions
1 (of 4) 3.00
2 . . . . 3.00
3 . . . . 3.00
4 concl. 3.00

SPANK THE MONKEY
Arrow Comics, 1999
1 by Randy Zimmerman 3.00
2 thru 6 . . . . @3.00
Skip Month Spec.#1 . . . . 3.00

SPANK THE MONKEY ON THE COMIC MARKET
Arrow Comics, 2000
1 (of 3) by Randy Zimmerman 3.25
2 and 3 . . . . @3.25

SPARKPLUG
Hero Graphics
1 From League of Champions 3.00

SPARKPLUG SPECIAL
Heroic Publishing
1 V:Overman 2.50

SPARROW
Millennium, 1995
1 I:Sparrow 3.00
2 . . . . 3.00
3 Valley of Fire 2.50

SPEED RACER CLASSICS
Now, 1998
1 . . . . 3.00
1a 2nd Printing 2.25

SPENCER SPOOK
A.C.E. Comics
1 thru 8 . . . . @2.25

SPICY TALES
Eternity, 1998
1 thru 20 . . . . @2.25
Special #2 . . . . 2.25

SPIDER KISS
1 Harlan Ellison 4.00

SPINELESS MAN
Parody Press, 1992
1 Spider-Man 2099 spoof 2.50

SPIRIT, THE
Kitchen Sink, 1986
Note: #1 to #11 are in color
12 thru 86 WE,rep (1986–92) . . . @3.00
GN The Spirit Casebook 17.00
TPB Vol.2 All About P'Gell 19.00
GN The Spirit Jam, 50 artists in
48-pg. (1998) 6.00

SPIRIT, THE: THE ORIGIN YEARS
Kitchen Sink, 1997
1 F:The Origin of the Spirit 3.00
2 F:The Black Queen's Army 3.00
3 F:Palyachi,The Killer Clown 3.00
4 F:The Return of the Orang 3.00
5 WE 3.00
6 WE,Kiss of Death 3.00
7 F:The Kidnapping of Ebony 3.00
8 F:Christmas Spirit of 1940 . . . . . 3.00
9 WE 3.00
10 F:The Substitute Spirits 3.00

SPIRITS
Mindwalker, 1995
1 thru 3 Silver City 3.00
4 Caleb Escapes Zeus 3.00

Spittin' Image #1
© *Eclipse*

SPITTIN' IMAGE
Eclipse, 1992
1 Marvel & Image parody 2.50

SQUEE
Slave Labor, 1997
1 by Jhonen Vasquez 5.00
1a 2nd printing 3.00
2 . . . . 3.00
3 . . . . 3.00
4 . . . . 3.00

STAIN
Fathom Press, 1998
1 Byler (c) 3.00
1a Vigil (c) 3.00
1b limited edition 8.00
2 . . . . 3.00
2a Vigil (c) 3.00
3 . . . . 3.00
3a Vigil (c) 3.00
4 . . . . 3.00
4a Vigil (c) 3.00
5 King cover 3.00
5a Ang cover 3.00
6 . . . . 3.00
7 . . . . 3.00

STAINLESS STEEL ARMIDILLO
Antarctic Press, 1995
1 I:Saisni, Tania Badan 3.00
2 V:Mirage 3.00
3 V:Mirage 3.00
4 Spirit of Gaia 3.00
5 V:Giant 3.00
6 finale 3.00

STAR BLEECH THE GENERATION GAP
Parody Press
1 Parody 4.00

STARCHILD
Taliesin Press, 1992–97
0 . . . . 12.00
1 . . . . 18.00
1a 2nd printing 4.00
2 . . . . 15.00
2a 2nd printing 4.00
3 . . . . 8.00

4 . . . . 6.00
5 thru 13 . . . . @5.00
14 . . . . 3.00
Coppervale
TPB Coll. Ed. Awakenings, rep.
  #1–#12 . . . . 5.00
Essential Starchild, Book 3 . . . . . . 7.00
Essential Starchild, Book 4 . . . . . . 7.00
Essential Starchild, Book 5 . . . . . . 7.00

STARCHILD: CROSSROADS
Coppervale, 1995
1 . . . . 3.00
2 thru 4, reoffer, by James Owen @3.00
Conoisseurs Edition 100.00

STARGATE: ATLANTIS
Avatar Press/ Pulsar Press, 2005
Preview 2.50
Preview photo (c) 3.00
Preview painted (c) 3.00
Preview Ready to Serve (c) 6.00
Preview Weir painted (c) 6.00
Preview Chicago Gold Seal (c) 5.00
Preview Look to the Future (c) 6.00
Preview Royal blue foil (c) 75.00
Preview Royal Prism (c) 13.00

STARGATE: THE NEW ADVENTURES COLLECTION
Entity, 1997
1 rep. Underworld; One Nation
  Under Ra 6.00
1a photo cover 5.00

STARGATE: ONE NATION UNDER RA
Entity, 1997
1 . . . . 3.00
1a deluxe 3.50

STARGATE: REBELLION
Entity, 1997
1 (of 3) from novel, sequel to movi 13.00
1 deluxe 3.50
2 . . . . 3.00
2 deluxe 3.50
3 (of 3) 3.00
3 foil cover 3.50
GN rep. 80-pg. 8.00
GN photo (c) 8.00

STARGATE: UNDERWORLD
Entity, 1997
1 . . . . 3.00
1a deluxe 3.50

STAR HAWKS
ACG Comics, 2000
1 by Ron Goulart & Gil Kane 3.00
2 . . . . 3.00
3 . . . . 3.00

STARK: FUTURE
Aircel, 1986
1 . . . . 2.50
2 thru 5 . . . . @2.50
6 thru 14 . . . . @2.50

STARLIGHT AGENCY
Antarctic Press, 1991
1 I:Starlight Agency	2.25
2 Anderson Kidnapped	2.25
3	2.25

STAR RANGERS
Adventure, 1987
1 thru 3	@3.00
4	2.50

BOOK II
1	2.50
2	2.50

STAR REACH
Taliesin Press, 1974
1 HC,I:CodyStarbuck	15.00
2 DG,JSn,NA(c)	6.00
3 FB	6.00
4 HC,HC(c)	6.00
5 JSon,HC(c)	6.00
6 GD,Elric	6.00
7 DS	6.00
8 CR,KSy	6.00
9 KSy	6.00
10 KSy	6.00
11 GD	6.00
12 MN,SL	10.00
13 SL,KSy	10.00
14	10.00
15	10.00
16 thru 18	@9.00

STAR WESTERN
ACG Comics, 2000
1	6.00
2 John Wayne	6.00
3 Clint Eastwood	6.00
4 Clayton Moore	6.00
5 F:Tonto	6.00
6 F:Fess Parker	6.00
7 F:Masked Riders of the Plains	6.00
8 James Arness-Matt Dillon(c)	6.00
9 Sam Elliott photo (c)	6.00
10 Chuck "Rifleman" Connors	6.00
11 John Hart	6.00
12 Davy Crockett, Daniel Boone	6.00
13 Gabby Hayes	6.00

STATIC
1 SD	2.25
2 SD	2.25
3 SD	2.25

STEALTH FORCE
Malibu, 1987
1 thru 7	@2.50

Eternity, 1988
8	2.50

STEALTH SQUAD
Petra Comics, 1993
0 O:Stealth Squad	2.50
1 I:Stealth Squad	2.50
2 I:New Member	2.50

Volume II
1 F:Solar Blade	2.50
2 American Ranger Vs.Jericho	2.50

STEELE DESTINES
Nightscapes
1 & 2 I:One Eyed Stranger	3.00
3 Kidnapped by Aliens	3.00

STEVE CANYON
Kitchen Sink
1 thru 14 by Doug Allen	@5.00

Steve Canyon #12
© Kitchen Sink

3-D Spec. #1 (1986)	6.00

STEVE DITKO'S STRANGE AVENGING TALES
Fantagraphics, 1997
1 SD	3.00
2 SD	3.00

STEVE GRANT'S MORTAL SOULS
Avatar Press, 2002
1	3.50
2	3.50
3	3.50
1a thru 3a wraparound (c)s	@4.00

STEVE GRANT'S MY FLESH IS COOL
Avatar Press, 2003
1	3.50
2	3.50
3	3.50
1a thru 3a wraparound (c)s	@3.50

STEVEN
Kitchen Sink
1	4.00
1a 2ndPrinting	3.00
2	4.00
3	3.00
4 and 5	@3.50

STICKBOY
Revolutionary
1	2.25
2 thru 5	@2.50

STIG'S INFERNO
Vortex, 1985
1	5.00
2	3.50
3	3.00
4	3.00
5	2.50

Eclipse
6	2.50
7	2.50

STINZ
Fantagraphics, 1989
1	4.00
2	4.00
3	4.00
4	4.00

[2nd series]
Brave New Words, 1990
1 thru 3	2.50

STITCH
Slave Labor, 1999
1 (of 4) by Tom Kovac	3.00
2	3.00
3	3.00
4 conclusion	3.00

STORMBRINGER
Taliesin Press
1 thru 3	@2.50

STORMWATCHER
Eclipse, 1989
1 thru 4	@2.50

STRANGE BEHAVIOR
Twilite Tone Press
1 LSn,MBr,Short Stories	3.00

STRANGE BREW
Aardvark–Vanaheim
1	5.00

STRANGEHAVEN
Abiogenesis Press, 1995
1 Surrealistic Comic	3.00
2 Secret Brotherhood	3.00
3 thru 10 by Gary S. Millidge	@3.00
11 thru 18	@3.00

STRANGE HEROES
Lone Star Press, 2000
1	3.00
2	3.00
3	3.00
4	3.00
5 thru 7	@3.00

STRANGE SPORTS STORIES
Adventure, 1992
1 w/2 card strip	2.50
2 The Pick-Up Game,w/cards	2.50
3 Spinning Wheels,w/cards	2.50
4 thru 6 w/cards	@2.50

STRANGE WEATHER LATELY
Metaphrog, 1997
1	3.50
2 thru 4	@3.50
5 thru 10	@3.00

STRANGERS IN PARADISE
Antarctic Press, 1993–94
1 by Terry Moore,I:Katchoo	65.00
1a 2nd printing	10.00
1b 3rd printing	5.00
2	45.00
3	35.00

Abstract Studio, 1994
1 TMr, Gold Logo edition	15.00
1a 2nd printing	6.00
2 and 3, Gold Logo edition	@9.00
4	6.00
5 R:Mrs. Parker	6.00
6	5.00
7 Darcey Uses Francine	5.00

Strangers in Paradise #11
© *Abstract Studio*

8 thru 13 TMr . . . . @4.00

VOL. 2
1 TMr, Gold Logo edition, I
   Dream of You. 3.00
2 thru 13 gold logo . . . . @3.00

VOL III, 1997
1 thru 8 See Image
9 TMr,Detective Walsh returns 4.00
10 . . . . 4.00
11 . . . . 3.00
12 . . . . 3.00
13 High School, pt.1 (of 3). 3.00
14 High School, pt.2 . . . . 9.00
15 High School, pt.3 . . . . 3.00
16A Francine/Katchoo Princess
   Warrior (c) 22.00
16B Tambi Princess Warrior (c). . . 25.00
17 . . . . 3.00
18 Francine & Datchoo 3.00
19 Lifesize nude of Francine 3.00
20 Night at the Opera 3.00
21 All not well in paradise 3.00
22 The Big Rift. 3.00
23 Katchoo moves out. 3.00
24 steamy affairs 3.00
25 All Beach, All the Time 3.00
26 . . . . 3.00
27 at odds with the Big Six 3.00
28 thru 35. . . . . @3.00
36 Katchoo vs. Veronica 3.00
37 return to Tennessee 3.00
38 from rags to ritches. 3.00
39 Good news and bad news 3.00
40 Engaged to right brother?. 3.00
41 Expelled from college 3.00
42 Slumber Party. 3.00
43 Tropic Of Desire 3.00
44 Marooned 3.00
45 Francine and Katchoo. 3.00
46 Molly & Poo, Borderline Lover . . 3.00
47 Francine pregnant. 3.00
48 Casey's Story 3.00
49 Molly & Poo. 3.00
50 Celebrate #50 . . . . 3.00
51 . . . . 3.00
52 Francine & Katchoo 3.00
53 My Maiden Voyage 3.00
54 Girl Trouble, pt.1 . . . . 3.00
55 Girl Trouble, pt.2 . . . . 3.00
56 Girl Trouble, pt.3 . . . . 3.00
57 Blue Bird of Happiness 3.00
58 thru 77. . . . . @3.00
78 thru 90 . . . . @3.00
90a & 90b variant (c)s . . . . @3.00
Spec. Sourcebook 3.00
Spec. #93268 Songs & Lyrics 2.75

STRANGELOVE
Entity Comics, 1995
1 I:Strangelove 2.50
2 V:Hyper Bullies 2.50
3 I:Bogie 2.50

STRANGEWAYS
Speakeasy Comics, 2005
1 . . . . 2.50
2 thru 4 . . . . @2.50

STRANGE WORLDS
Eternity
1 . . . . 4.00
2 thru 4 . . . . @4.00

STRATA
Renegade, 1986
1 . . . . 3.00
2 . . . . 2.50
3 . . . . 2.50
4 thru 6 . . . . @2.50

STRAW MEN
All American, 1989
1 thru 5 . . . . @2.50
6 thru 8 . . . . @2.50

STRAY BULLETS
El Capitan, 1995
1 . . . . 11.00
1a 2nd & 3rd printing 4.00
2 . . . . 7.00
2a 2nd printing 3.50
3 . . . . 6.00
4 . . . . 6.00
5 Dysfunctional Family 4.00
6 F:Amy Racecar 4.00
7 Virginias Freedom 4.00
8 DL,`Lucky to Have Her' 3.00
9 DL,`26 Guys Named Nick' 3.00
10 DL,`Here Comes the Circus'. . . . 3.00
11 DL,`How to Cheer Up Your
   Best Friend' 3.00
12 DL, People Will be Hurt 3.00
13 DL `Selling Candy' 3.00
14 DL,The Killers arrive,48pg 3.50
15 Sex and Violence 3.00
16 . . . . 3.00
17 While Ricky Fish Was Sleeping . 3.00
18 Sex and Violence, pt.2 . . . . 3.00
19 Young and sexy 3.00
20 Motel 3.00
21 . . . . 3.00
22 40-pg. 3.50
23 thru 30. . . . . @3.50
31 thru 34. . . . . @3.00
35 thru 40. . . . . @3.50
41 . . . . 3.50

STREET ANGEL
Amaze Ink/SLG, 2004
1 . . . . 3.00
2 thru 5 . . . . @3.00

STREET FIGHTER
Ocean Comics, 1986
1 . . . . 2.50
2 thru 4 limited series . . . . @2.50

STREET FIGHTER II
Udon Entertainment, 2005
0 Manga 2.00
1 . . . . 4.00
2 thru 5 . . . . @3.00
2a thru 6a variant (c)s . . . . @3.00
1b thru 6b power foil (c)s . . . . @12.50

STREET HEROES 2005
Eternity, 1989
1 . . . . 2.50
2 thru 3 . . . . @2.50

STREET MUSIC
Fantagraphics
1 . . . . 2.75
2 . . . . 2.75
3 . . . . 3.00
4 . . . . 3.00
5 . . . . 2.50
6 . . . . 4.00

STREET POET RAY
Fantagraphics, 1989
1 . . . . 2.50
2 . . . . 2.50
3 . . . . 3.00
4 . . . . 3.00

STREET WOLF
Blackthorne, 1986
1 limited series 2.50
2 . . . . 2.50
3 . . . . 2.50
Graphic Novel 7.00

STRIKER: SECRET OF THE BERSERKER
Viz Communications
1 & 2 V:The Berserker . . . . @2.75
3 F:Yu and Maia 2.75

STRIKER: THE ARMORED WARRIOR
Viz Communications, 1992
1 Overture. 2.75
2 V:Child Esper. 2.75
3 Professor taken hostage 2.75

STRONGHOLD
Devil's Due Publishing, 2006
1 (of 3) PhH 5.00
2 thru 3 . . . . @5.00

STUDENTS OF THE UNUSUAL
3 Boys Productions, 2004
1 . . . . 3.00
2 . . . . 3.00
3 thru 6 . . . . @3.50

STUPID, STUPID RAT TAILS:THE ADVENTURES OF BIG JOHNSON BONE
Cartoon Books, 1999
1 I:Big Johnson Bone,FrontierHero 3.00
2 . . . . 3.00

STYGMATA
Entity, 1994
0 . . . . 3.00
1 V:The Rodent. 3.00
2 thru 3 . . . . @3.00
Yearbook #1 (1995) 3.00

SUBCULTURE
Ape Entertainment, 2007
1 (of 4) 3.50
2 thru 4 . . . . @3.50

SUBTLE VIOLENTS
CFD Productions, 1991
1 Linsner (c&a) 10.00
1a San Diego Con 40.00

SUDDEN GRAVITY
Caliber, 1998
1 by Greg Ruth 3.00
2 . . . . 3.00
3 . . . . 3.00
4 . . . . 3.00
5 story arc concl. 3.00
Spec. Panopticon, 64-page 5.00

SUGAR BUZZ
Slave Labor, 1998
1 by I.Carney & W. Phoenix 3.00
2 . . . . 3.00
3 . . . . 3.00
4 . . . . 3.00
5 . . . . 3.00
6 F:Ultra Spacers 3.00
7 I:Precious & Percival 3.00
8 thru 10 . . . . @3.00

SUGAR RAY FINHEAD
Wolf Press, 1992
1 I&O Sugar Ray Finhead 2.50
2 I:Bessie & Big-Foot Benny the
   Pit Bull Man 3.00
3 thru 7 Mardi Gras . . . . @3.00
9 & 10 . . . . @3.00

Sultry Teenage Super-Foxes #1
© Solson

SULTRY TEENAGE SUPER-FOXES
Solson, 1987
1 thru 4 RB,Woj . . . . @2.50

SUPER HERO HAPPY HOUR
Geekpunk, 2003
1 . . . . 3.00
2 thru 5 . . . . @3.00

SUPERMODELS IN THE RAINFOREST
Sirius, 1998
1 (of 3) 3.00
2 and 3 . . . . @3.00

SUPERSWINE
Caliber
1 Parody, I:Superswine 2.50

SURVIVALIST CHRONICLES
Survival Art
1 . . . . 6.50
2 . . . . 6.50
3 I:Bessie & Big Foot Benny 2.25

SURROGATE SAVIOR
Hot Brazer Comic Pub.
1 I:Ralph 2.50
2 Baggage 2.50

SWAN
Little Idylls, 1995
1 thru 3 Ghost of Lord Kaaren . . @3.00
4 V:Slake 3.00

SWEET CHILDE BATTLE BOOK
Advantage Graphics, 1995
1 I:Tasha Radcliffe 2.50

SWEET CHILDE: LOST CONFESSIONS
Anarchy Bridgeworks, 1997
1 F:Tasha Radcliffe 3.00

SWEET LUCY
Brainstorm Comics
1 with 4 cards 2.50
2 . . . . 2.50

SWERVE
Amaze Ink, 1995
1 thru 3 by Kyle Hunter . . . . @2.25

SWIFTSURE
Harrier Comics, 1985
1 . . . . 2.50
2 . . . . 2.50
3 thru 8 . . . . @2.50
9 . . . . 9.00
9a 2nd printing 2.50
10 . . . . 2.50
11 . . . . 2.50

SWITCH B.L.A.Z.E. MANGA
London Night, 1999
0 . . . . 3.50
? Con special 5.00
? Con special, Japanese (c) 6.00
1 . . . . 3.50
1a Elite fan ed. 6.00
1b Anime cell ed. 20.00

SWORD OF VALOR
A Plus Comics
1 JAp,rep.Thane of Bagarth 2.50
2 JAp/MK rep 2.50
3 & 4 . . . . @2.50

SWORDS AND SCIENCE
Pyramid
1 thru 3 . . . . @2.25

SWORDS OF CEREBUS
Aardvark–Vanaheim
1 rep. Cerebus 1-4 . . . . 15.00

1a reprint editions 10.00
2 rep. Cerebus 5-8 . . . . 12.00
2a reprint editions 8.00
3 rep. Cerebus 9-12 . . . . 12.00
3a reprint editions 8.00
4 rep. Cerebus 13-16 . . . . 12.00
4a reprint editions 8.00
5 rep. Cerebus 17-20 . . . . 12.00
5a reprint editions 8.00
6 rep. Cerebus 21-25 . . . . 12.00
6a reprint editions 8.00

SWORDS OF SHAR-PAI
Caliber, 1991
1 Mutant Ninja Dog 2.50
2 Shar-Pei 2.50
3 Final issue 2.50

SWORDS OF VALORS: ROBIN HOOD
A Plus Comics
1 rep. of Charlton comics 2.50
2 thru 4 . . . . @2.50

SYSTEM SEVEN
Arrow, 1987
1 . . . . 2.50
2 thru 4 . . . . @2.50

TAKEN UNDER COMPENDIUM
Caliber
1 rep. Cal Presents #19-#22 . . . . . 3.00

TALES FROM THE ANIVERSE
Arrow
1 7,400 printed 9.00
2 . . . . 4.00
3 10,000 printed 2.50
4 . . . . 2.50

[2nd series]
Massive Comics Group
1 . . . . 2.25
2 thru 3 . . . . @2.25

TALES FROM THE BOG
Aberation Press, 1995
1 thru 4 by Marcus Lusk . . . . @3.00
1a thru 4a Director's cut . . . . @4.00
5 thru 7 . . . . @4.00
8 . . . . 3.00

TALES FROM THE EDGE
Vanguard, 1993
5 . . . . 3.00
5a signed 6.00
6 . . . . 3.00
7 . . . . 3.00
7a signed 6.00
8 . . . . 3.00
8a signed 6.00
9 . . . . 3.00
10 . . . . 3.00
10a signed 6.00
11 F:Sacred Monkeys 3.00
12 spec.F:Steranko 4.00
12a signed, limited 15.00
13 F:Steranko 3.00
14 . . . . 3.00
15 Sienkiewicz special 4.00
Spec. Nightstand Chillers Benefit
    Edition 5.00
Spec. Nightstand Chillers, signed . 10.00
Spec. Sienkiewicz Special 10.00

TALES FROM THE HEART
Entropy, 1988–94
1 thru 5 . . . . @2.50
6 . . . . 2.50
7 . . . . 2.50

TALES OF LEONARDO
Mirage Studios, 2006
1 (of 4) Blind Sight 3.25
2 thru 4 Blind Sight . . . . @3.25

TALES OF RAPHAEL: BAD MOON RISING
Mirage Studios, 2007
1 (of 4) 3.25
2 thru 4 . . . . @3.25

TALES OF THE BEANWORLD
Eclipse, 1985
1 . . . . 10.00
2 . . . . 4.00
3 . . . . 2.50
4 I:Beanish 2.50
5 thru 20 . . . . @2.50
21 . . . . 3.00

TALES OF THE FEHNRIK
Antarctic Press, 1995
1 I:Lady Zeista 3.00

TALES OF THE JACKALOPE
Blackthorne, 1986
1 . . . . 4.00
2 . . . . 3.00
3 and 4 . . . . @2.50
5 thru 9 . . . . @2.50

TALES OF THE NINJA WARRIORS
CFW
1 thru 14 . . . . @2.25
15 thru 19 . . . . @2.25

TALES OF THE PLAGUE
Eclipse
1 RCo 4.00

TALES OF THE SUNRUNNERS
Sirius, 1986
Vol. 2
1 thru 3 . . . . @2.50
Christmas Spec. 2.50

TALES OF THE TEENAGE MUTANT NINJA TURTLES
Mirage, 1987
1 . . . . 8.00
1B 2nd printing 3.00
2 . . . . 8.00
3 . . . . 5.00
4 . . . . 5.00
5 . . . . 5.00
6 thru 9 . . . . @4.00

Mirage Studios, 2004
1 . . . . 3.00
2 thru 9 . . . . @3.00
10 thru 16 . . . . @3.25
17 thru 29 . . . . @3.25
30 thru 40 . . . . @3.25

TALES TOO TERRIBLE TO TELL
New England Comics, 1991
1 . . . . 3.50
2 thru 6 Pre-code horror stories . @3.50

TALL TAILS
Vision Comics, 1998
1 Earth Shaking 3.00
1a Anime Blast cover 3.00
1b Spell Warrior cover 3.00
1c signed 5.00
2 Fire Quest, Pt.1 . . . . 3.00
3 Fire Quest, Pt.2 . . . . 3.00
4 Pain and Compromises,pt.1 . . . . 3.00
5 . . . . 3.00
6 Trail Blazing, pt.1 . . . . 3.00
7 Trail Blazing, pt.2 . . . . 3.00
8 When It Almost Happened. 3.00
GN Vol. 1 . . . . 9.00

TANTALIZING STORIES
Tundra, 1992
1 F:Frank & Montgomery Wart 2.25
2 Frank & Mont.stories cont. 2.25

TAOLAND
Sunitek
1 V:The Crocodile Warlord 2.25
2 & 3 I:New Enemy . . . . @3.25

TASK FORCE ALPHA
Academy Comics
1 I:Task Force Alpha 3.50

TEAM NIPPON
Aircel
1 . . . . 2.25
2 thru 7 by Barry Blair . . . . @2.25

TECHNOPHILIA
Brainstorm Comics
1 with 4 cards 2.50

TEENAGE MUTANT NINJA TURTLES*
Mirage Studios, 1981
*Counterfeits Exist - Beware
1 I:Turtles 275.00
1a 2nd printing 25.00
1b 3rd printing 20.00
1c 4th printing 12.00
1d 5th printing 4.00
2 . . . . 75.00
2a 2nd printing 12.00
2b 3rd printing 4.00
3 . . . . 55.00
3a 2nd printing 3.50
3b Special printing,rare 50.00
4 . . . . 40.00
4a 2nd printing 3.50
5 A:Fugitoid 20.00
5a 2nd printing 3.50
6 A:Fugitoid 15.00
6a 2nd printing 2.50
7 A:Fugitoid 8.00
7a 2nd printing 2.50
8 A:Cerebus 9.00
9 . . . . 8.00
10 V:Shredder 8.00
11 A:Casey Jones 6.00
12 thru 18 . . . . @6.00
19 Return to NY 4.00
20 Return to NY 4.00
21 Return to NY,D:Shredder 4.00
22 thru 32 . . . . @4.00

Teenage Mutant Ninja Turtles #38
© Mirage Studios

33 color, Corben 3.50
34 Toytle Anxiety 3.50
35 Souls Withering. 3.50
36 Souls Wake. 3.50
37 Twilight of the Rings 3.50
38 Spaced Out Pt.1, A:President
   Bush 3.50
39 Spaced Out Pt.2 . . . . 3.50
40 Spaced Out concl.,I:Rockin'
   Rollin' Miner Ants (B.U. story) . . 2.50
41 Turtle Dreams issue 2.50
42 Juliets Revenge 2.50
43 Halls of Lost Legends. 2.50
44 V:Ninjas. 2.50
45 A:Leatherhead. 2.50
46 V:Samurai Dinosaur 2.50
47 Space Usagi 2.50
48 Shades of Grey Part 1 . . . . 2.50
49 Shades of Grey Part 2 . . . . 2.50
50 Eastman/Laird,new direction,
   inc.TM,EL,WS pin-ups. 3.00
51 City at War #2. . . . . 2.50
52 City at War #3. . . . . 2.50
53 City at War #4. . . . . 2.50
54 City at War #5. . . . . 2.50
55 thru 65 . . . . @2.50
1990 Movie adaptation 6.50
Spec. The Haunted Pizza 2.50

Volume 2
1 . . . . 2.75
2 thru 8 . . . . @2.75
9 V:Baxter Bot. 2.75
10 Mr. Braunze 2.75
11 F:Raphael 2.75
12 V:DARPA. 2.75
13 J:Triceraton 2.75

Vol. 4, 2001
1 PLa & Jim Lawson. 3.00
2 thru 24 PLa . . . . @3.00
24 thru 30 . . . . @3.00

TEENAGE MUTANT NINJA TURTLES: THE MOVIE PREQUEL
Mirage Studios, 2007
1 Raphael 3.25
2 Michelangelo 3.25
3 DOnatello. 3.25
4 April 3.25
5 Leonardo 3.25

B & W PUB.

TEENAGE MUTANT NINJA TURTLES: THE MOVIE ADAPTATION
Mirage Studios, 2007
1-shot 5.00

TMNT TRAINING MANUAL
1 .... 5.00
2 thru 5 .... @3.00

TEMPEST COMICS PRESENTS
Academy Comics
1 I:Steeple, Nemesis. 2.50

TEMPORARY
Origin Comics, 2005
1 Cubes and Ladders 4.00
2 The Real Me 4.00
3 The Real Me 3.00
4 A Dirt Nap 3.00
5 Twilight. 3.00

10TH MUSE/ DEMONSLAYER
Avatar Press, 2002
Preview, 16-pg. 2.25
1 MMy(c). 3.50
1a Matt Martin (c) 3.50
1b SSh(c) 3.50
1c Karl Waller (c) 3.50
1d wraparound (c). 3.50
1e Red Leather (c) 20.00
1f prism foil edition 11.00
1g Aftermath (c) 6.00
1h Art Nouveau (c) 6.00
1/2 MMy bikini (c) 6.00
1/2 Conflict edition 6.00
1/2 Catfight (c) 6.00

TERROR ON THE PLANET OF THE APES
Adventure Comics, 1991
1 MP,collectors edition 2.50
2 MP, the Forbidden Zone 2.50
3 .... 2.50

TERRY AND THE PIRATES
ACG Comics, 1998
1 by Georges Wunder, Charlton
   reprint 3.00
2 .... 3.00
3 .... 3.00

TERRY & THE PIRATES
Tony Raiola, 2001
Feature Comics #6, 1938 reprint... 8.00
Feature Comics #2 1937 reprint ... 8.00
Feature Comics #28 1938 reprint ... 8.00
Raven Evermore 1941 reprint 8.00

TERRY MOORE'S PARADISE, TOO
Abstract Studio, 2000
1 .... 3.00
2 .... 3.00
3 .... 3.00
4 .... 3.00
5 thru 14 .... @3.00

TEX BENSON
Metro Comics
1 thru 4 .... @2.25

39 SCREAMS
Thunder Baas
1 thru 6 .... @2.25

THEY WERE 11
Viz
1 Galactic University............ 2.75
2 The Accident 2.75
3 Virus. 2.75
4 V:Virus 2.75

THIEVES AND KINGS
I Box, 1994–97
1 F:Ruebel The Intrepid 7.00
1a 2nd printing 2.50
2 .... 6.00
2a 2nd printing 2.50
3 .... 5.00
3a 2nd printing 2.50
4 .... 4.00
5 .... 4.00
6 V:Shadow Lady 4.00
7 V:Shadow Lady 3.00
8 thru 18 by Mark Oakley ...... @3.00
19 thru 24 .... @2.50
25 thru 36 .... @2.50
37 thru 39 .... @2.50
40 thru 47 .... @3.00
48 thru 49 .... @3.50

THIRD DEGREE
NBM Books, 2002
1 by Cris Rowley & Justin Norman. 3.00
2 thru 4 .... @3.00

THIRTEEN STEPS
Desperado Pub., 2007
1 .... 4.00
2 thru 4 .... @4.00

THORR SUERD OR SWORD OF THOR
Vincent
1 .... 3.00
1a 2nd printing 2.25
2 .... 2.25
3 .... 2.25

THOSE ANNOYING POST BROS.
1 thru 18 see Color
Becomes:

POST BROTHERS
Rip Off, 1991–94
19 thru 38 .... @2.25
Becomes:

THOSE ANNOYING POST BROS.
Vortex, 1994
39 thru 45 .... @2.50
46 thru 56 .... @3.00
57 Russ working on chaos wave... 3.00
58 Fearsome chaos wave 3.00
59 Recondite Silicates 3.00
60 .... 3.00
61 Assassinate JFK's ghost....... 3.00
62 Post Digestion 64pg.......... 6.00
63 .... 6.00
GN Distrub the Neighbors 10.00
Ann. #3 Before the Flood, 56pg.... 5.00

THREAT
Fantagraphics, 1985
1 .... 5.00
2 .... 3.00

3 and 4 .... @2.50
5 thru 10 .... @2.50

3 X 3 EYES
Innovation
1 Labyrinth of the Demons
   Eye,Pt.1 .... 2.25
2 Demons Eye, Pt.2 .... 2.25
3 Demons Eye, Pt.3 .... 2.25
4 Demons Eye, Pt.4 .... 2.25
5 Demons Eye, concl........... 2.25

THREE GEEKS, THE
3 Finger Prints, 1997
1 by Rich Koslowski, Going
   to the Con, pt.1 .... 8.00
2 Going to the Con, pt.2......... 6.00
3 Going to the Con, pt.3 (of 3) 3.00
4 .... 4.00
5 five more geeks 2.50
6 F:Allen 2.50
7 .... 2.50
8 48-pg...................... 4.00
9 24-pg...................... 2.50
10 Happy Birthday Allen 2.50
10a variant cover............. 3.50
11 Happy Birthday Allen, pt.2 ..... 2.50

THREE ROCKETEERS
Eclipse
1 JK,AW,rep................... 2.25
2 JK,AW,rep................... 2.25

THREE STRIKES
Oni Press, 2003
1 (of 5) 3.00
2 thru 5 .... @3.00

Threshold #1
© *Avatar*

THRESHOLD
Sleeping Giant, 1996
1 .... 2.50
2 .... 2.50

[2nd Series], 1997
1 .... 2.50
2 .... 2.50
3 .... 2.50

Avatar Press, 1998
1 Snowman cover.............. 4.50
1a Tales of the Cyberangels cover. 4.50
1b Furies cover............... 4.50
1c Fuzzie Dice cover 4.50
2 Snowman cover.............. 5.00

3 Ravening (c) 5.00
4 Donna Mia (c) 5.00
5 Black Reign (c) 5.00
6 Luna cover 5.00
7 Darkness in Collision,
  Cavewoman(c) 5.00
8 Vigil/Cuda (c) 5.00
9 August (c). 5.00
2a thru 9a variant (c)s . . . . @5.00
10 Calico (c) 5.00
11 Scythe (c) 5.00
12 Snowman (c). 5.00
13 Snowman (c). 5.00
14 Kaos Moon (c) 5.00
15 Luna (c). 5.00
16 Scythe (c) 5.00
17 Cimmerian (c). 5.00
18 Nightvision (c) 5.00
19 Pandora (c). 5.00
20 Kaos Moon (c) 5.00
21 Jungle Girl (c) 5.00
22 . . . . 5.00
23 Ravening (c) 5.00
24 Faust: Singha's Talons 5.00
25 Dark Blue (c). 5.00
26 Dark Blue (c). 5.00
27 Dark blue (c) 5.00
28 Dark blue (c) 5.00
29 Dark Blue (c). 5.00
30 Dark Blue (c). 5.00
10a thru 30a variant (c)s . . . . . . @5.00
31 Luna (c). 5.00
32 Ravening (c) 5.00
33 Pandora (c). 5.00
34 Pandora (c). 5.00
35 Pandora (c). 5.00
36 Pandora (c). 5.00
37 Pandora (c). 5.00
38 Pandora (c). 5.00
39 Razor (c). 5.00
40 Lookers (c) 5.00
41 Razor (c). 5.00
42 Razor (c). 5.00
43 Razor (c). 5.00
43 Razor (c). 5.00
45 Demonslayer (c) 5.00
46 Demonslayer (c) 5.00
47 Pandora (c). 5.00
31a thru 47a variant (c)s . . . . . . @5.00
48 Pandora (c). 5.00
49 Pandora (c). 5.00
48a thru 49a connecting (c). 6.00
50 64-pg. 9.00
50 connecting (c)s 9.00
50a variant (c)s . . . . @9.00
51 . . . . 5.00
51b Pandora Western edition 6.00
52 . . . . 5.00
51a and 52a variant (c)s . . . . . . @5.00
53 . . . . 5.00
53a wraparound (c) 5.00
53b Talented Twosome (c) 6.00
54 . . . . 5.00
54a variant (c) 5.00
54b School Days (c) 6.00
Pin-Ups Mythic Sirens (2007) 5.00
Pin-Ups Mythic Sirensvariant (c)s @5.00

THRESHOLD OF REALITY
Maintech, 1986
1 5,000 printed 2.50
2 thru 4 . . . . @2.50

THUNDERBIRD
Newcomers Publishing
1 & 2 2 Stories . . . . @3.00
3 . . . . 3.00
4 I:Mercer 3.00
5 R:Raven. 3.00
6 & 7 . . . . @3.00
8 final issue. 3.50

Ann.#1 The Great Escape 3.50

THUNDER BUNNY
Mirage, 1985
1 O:Thunder Bunny 2.50
2 VO:Dr.Fog 2.50
3 I:GoldenMan 2.50
4 V:Keeper 2.50
5 I:Moon Mess 2.50
6 V:Mr.Endall. 2.50
7 VI:Dr.Fog 2.50
8 . . . . 2.50
9 VS:Gen. Agents 2.50
10 thru 12 . . . . @2.50

THUNDER MACE
Rak, 1986
1 Proto type-blue & red very
  rare:1,000 printed 15.00
1a four color cover 3.00
2 thru 5 . . . . @2.50
6 . . . . 2.50
7 . . . . 2.50
Graphic Novel, rep.1-4. . . . . 5.00

Tick #6
© New England Comics

TICK
New England Comics, 1988
1 BEd 45.00
1a 2nd printing 10.00
1b 3rd printing. 8.00
1c 4th printing 5.00
2 BEd 50.00
2a 2nd printing 10.00
2b 3rd printing 4.00
2c 4th printing 2.50
3 BEd 10.00
3a 2nd printing 3.00
4 BEd 8.00
4a 2nd printing 3.00
5 BEd 8.00
6 BEd 7.00
7 BEd,A:Chairface Chippendale. . . 7.00
8 BEd 6.00
8a Spec.No Logo edition 12.00
9 BEd,A:Chainsaw Vigilante,
  Red Eye. 5.00
10 BEd 5.00
11 thru 12 BEd . . . . @4.00
9 thru 12, new printings . . . . @3.00
Spec. Ed. #1, I:Tick 25.00
Spec. Ed. #2, 2nd App. Tick 20.00
Spec. #1 Reprise edition 6.00
The Tick Big Yule Log Special 1998 3.50

The Tick Big Yule Log Special 1999 3.50
Tick's Big Yule Log Special 2001. . . 3.50
Big Giant Summer Special #1, The
  Sidekicks are Revolting. 3.50
Big Summer Annual #1 . . . . 3.50
Tick's Big Red-N-Green X-mas . . . 4.00
TPB Tick Bonanza #3 . . . . 5.00
TPB Tick Bonanza #4 . . . . 5.00
Spec.#1 Back to School. 3.50
Big Halloween Special #1 . . . . 3.50
Massive Summer Double Spectacle
  Photo-Cover set of 2 . . . . 8.00
13 Pseudo-Tick, not by Edlund . . . 3.50
Big Year 2000 Spectacle 3.50
Big Romantic Adventure #1, 2nd ed. 3.50
Big Tax Time Terror #1. . . . . 3.50
Big Mother's Day Spec. #1 . . . . . . 3.50
Big Halloween Special 2000 . . . . . 3.50
Big Father's Day Special 3.50
Big Cruise Ship Vacation Spec.#1 . 3.50
Massive Summer Double Spec.#1 . 3.50
Massive Summer Double Spec.#2 . 3.50

TICK AND ARTHUR, THE
New England Comics, 1999
1 by Sean Wang & Mike Baker . . . 3.50
2 Return of the Thorn,pt.2 . . . . 3.50
3 Return of the Thorn,pt.3 . . . . 3.50
4 Tick & Arthur meet Flea & Doyle . 3.50
5 Flea & Doyle superheroes. 3.50
6 Chainsaw Vigilantes 3.50
TPB Bonanza #1 rep. #1–#3 . . . . . 5.50
TPB Bonanza #2 rep. #4–#6 . . . . . 5.50

TICK, THE:
BIG BLUE DESTINY
New England Comics, 1997
1 by Eli Stone, Keen edition 3.00
1 Wicked Keen edition 5.00
2A cover A. 3.00
3B cover B 3.00
3 . . . . 3.50
4 . . . . 3.50
5 The Chrysalis Crisis. 3.50

TICK CIRCUS MAXIMUS
New England Comics, 2000
1 (of 4) by Sean Wang 3.50
2 . . . . 3.50
3 . . . . 3.50
4 concl. 3.50
Spec.#1 Circus Maximus
  Redux (2001). 3.50

TICK: GIANT CIRCUS
OF THE MIGHTY
New England Press, 1992
1 A-O. 3.00
2 P-Z. 3.00
3 . . . . 3.00

TICK, THE: GOLDEN AGE
New England Comics, 2002
1 Entertaining cover 5.00
1a Classic cover 5.00
2 extremely creepy cover 5.00
2a Ferociously heroic cover 5.00
3 Bleeding Heart (c) 5.00
3a Criminally Maniacal (c) 5.00

TICK, THE:
HEROES OF THE CITY
New England Comics, 1999
1 three stories. 3.50
2 . . . . 3.50
3 . . . . 3.50
4 . . . . 3.50

All comics prices listed are for *Near Mint* condition.

5	3.50
6	3.50
TPB Bonanza #1 rep. #1–#3	5.50
TPB Bonanza #2 rep. #4–#6	5.50

TICK: KARMA TORNADO
New England Press, 1993

1	4.00
1 2nd printing	3.00
2	3.50
2 2nd printing	3.00
3 thru 9	@3.50
3 thru 9 2nd printings	@3.00
TPB #1 second edition	14.00
TPB Bonanza Edition, Vol.2	5.00
TPB Bonanza Edition, Vol.3	5.00

TICK, THE: LUNY BIN
New England Comics, 1998

1 (of 3) by Eli Stone, Back to the Luny Bin	3.50
2 To the Rescue	3.50
3 Six Eyes in Tears	3.50
Preview Special, 32pg	2.50
TPB Luny Bin Trilogy 120-pg.	5.00

TICK'S BACK, THE
New England Comics, 1997

0 by Eli Stone, V:Toy DeForce	3.00

TIGERS OF THE LUFTWAFTE
Antarctic Press, 2001

1 48-pg.	6.00
2 48-pg.	6.00
3 48-pg.	6.00
4 Wild Angels, 48-pg.	6.00
5 Black Devil, 48-pg.	6.00
6 Black Devil, pt.2	6.00
7 April Fools phoney issue	6.00
8 Fighter General	6.00
9 Adolf Galland	6.00
10 final issue	6.00

TIGERS OF TERRA
Mind-Visions, 1992

1 6,000 printed	4.50
1a Signed & Num.	14.00
2	2.50
2a Signed & Num.	11.00
5 thru 7	@3.50
8 thru 10	@3.75

Antarctic, 1993

11 and 12	@4.00

[Vol. 2], 1993

0 thru 14	@2.75
15 Totenkopf Police,pt.2	2.75
16 Battleship Arizona,pt.3	2.75
17 thru 22	@3.00
23 'Trouble with Tigers' pt.3	3.00
24 48pg 10th Anniv.	4.00
25 'Battle for Terra' pt.1	3.00

TIGER-X
Eternity, 1988

Special #1	2.50
Spec. #1a 2nd printing	2.50
1 thru 3	@2.50

Book II, 1989

1 thru 4	@2.50

TIGRESS
Hero Graphics, 1992

1 Tigress vs. Flare	4.00
2	3.00
3 A:Lady Arcane	3.00
4 inc. B.U. Mudpie	4.00

5	4.00
6	4.00

TIGRESS
Basement Comics, 1998

1 by Budd Root and Mike Hoffman	3.00
2 concl.	3.00
1-shot Mike Hoffman special	9.00
1-shot green foil edition	12.50
1-shot gold foil edition	12.50

TIGRESS TALES
Amryl Entertainment, 2001

1 by Mike Hoffman	3.00
2 Slave Planet	3.00

Basement Comics, 2001

1a spec. edition	9.00
2 Special Edition	9.00
2 Blue foil (c)	10.00
3a Special ed.	9.00
3b special edition, purple foil	10.00
4	3.00
4a Special ed.	9.00
4b special edition, gold foil	10.00
5	3.00
5a Special ed.	9.00
Pin-Up book (2001)	3.50
Pin-Up Book, special edition	9.00

TIGRESS: THE HIDDEN LANDS
Basement Comics, 2002

1 by Mike Hoffman	3.50

TIME DRIFTERS
Innovation, 1990

1	2.25
2	2.25
3	2.25

TIME GATES
Double Edge

1 SF series,The Egg #1	2.25
2 The Egg #2	2.25
3 Spirit of the Dragon #1	2.25
4 Spirit of the Dragon #2	2.25
4a Var.cover	2.25

TIME JUMP WAR
Apple

1 thru 3	@2.25

TIME MACHINE
Eternity, 1990

1 thru 3 H.G. Wells adapt.	@2.50

TIME TRAVELER AI
CPM Manga, 1999

1 by Ai Ijima & Takeshi Takebayashi	3.00
2 thru 13	@3.00
14 thru 21	@3.00

TIME WARRIORS
Fantasy General, 1986

1 rep.Alpha Track #1	2.50
1a Bi-Weekly	2.50
2	2.50
3	2.50

TIM VIGIL'S WEBWITCH
Avatar Press, 2002

Preview, 16-pg.	2.25
Preview, Temptress (c)	6.00
Preview, Serenity (c)	6.00
Preview, prism foil exclusive(c)	13.00

Preview Cave of Evil edition	6.00
1 (of 3) Finch(c)	3.50
2 Vigil(c)	3.50
3 Adrian (c)	3.50
1a thru 3a variant(c)	@3.50
1b thru 3b wraparound (c)s	@4.00
Webwitch Companion	5.00
Webwitch Companion Waller (c)	5.00
Webwitch Companion Martin (c)	5.00

TITANESS
Draculina Publishing, 1995

1 I:Titaness,Tomboy	3.00

TO BE ANNOUNCED
Strawberry Jam, 1986

1 thru 6	@2.50

Tomb Tales #4
© Cryptic Entertainment

TOMB TALES
Cryptic Entertainment, 1997

1	3.00
2	3.00
3	3.00
4 A Rare Gem	3.00
5	3.00
6 The Flame Game	3.00
7 Invasion of the Shoddy Snatchers	3.00

TOM CORBETT SPACE CADET
Eternity, 1990

1	2.25
2	2.25
3	2.25
4	2.25

TOM CORBETT II
Eternity, 1990

1	2.25
2	2.25
3	2.25
4	2.25

TOMMI GUNN: KILLERS LUST
London Night, 1997

1	3.00
1 photo cover	6.00
Ann. #1	3.00

TOM MIX HOLIDAY ALBUM
Amazing Comics
1 .... 3.50

TOM MIX WESTERN
AC Comics, 1988
1 .... 2.50
2 .... 2.50

TOMMY & THE MONSTERS
New Comics
1 thru 3 .... @2.25

TOMMY ROCKET AND THE GOOBER PATROL
Top Hat Comics April, 1997
1 .... 1.99
2 .... 1.99
3 .... 2.00
4 .... 3.00
5 .... 3.00
6 conclusion 2.00

TOMORROW MAN
Antarctic, 1993
1 R:Tomorrow Man 3.00
Spec.#1 48-pg............... 4.00

TOMORROW MAN
Antarctic Press, 2000
1 Requiem for Nepton,pt.1 ... 5.00
2 Requiem for Nepton,pt.2 ... 3.00
3 Requiem for Nepton,pt.3 ... 3.00

TONY DIGEROLAMO'S JERSEY DEVIL
South Jersey Rebellion
1 by Tony DiGerolamo 3.00
2 .... 3.00
3 .... 2.25
4 .... 3.00
5 Robin Hood of the Pines,pt.1 ... 2.25
6 Robin Hood of the Pines,pt.2 ... 3.00

TONY DIGEROLAMO'S THE TRAVELERS
Kenzer & Company, 2000
1 thru 3 .... @2.25
7 .... 3.00
8 Vlad Tepes in Romania 3.00
9 Arcimedes & Time Machine..... 3.00
10 Strange storm 3.00
11 Wrath of the Imprechaun 3.00
12 thru 20................... @3.00
Wingnut Comics, 2003
21 thru 25.................. @3.00

TONY DIGEROLAMO'S THE FIX
South Jersey Rebellion, 2001
1 (of 4) 2.50
2 thru 4 .... @2.50

TOO MUCH COFFEE MAN
Adhesive Comics, 1994
1 F:Too Much Coffee Man 14.00
1a 2nd printing 4.00
2 Wheeler (s&a) 8.00
3 Wheeler (s&a) 6.00
4 In love 6.00
5 thru 7 .... @4.00

Too Much Coffee Man #3
© Adhesive Comics

8 thru 10 .... @3.00
Mag. #11 64-pg............... 5.00
Mag. #12 .... 5.00
Mag. #13 thru #22 .... @5.00

TOO MUCH HOPELESS SAVAGES
Oni Press, 2003
1 (of 4) 3.00
2 thru 3 .... @3.00

TORG
Adventure
1 Based on Role Playing Game ... 2.50
2 thru 3 Based on Game....... @2.50

TOR JOHNSON: HOLLYWOOD STAR
Monster Comics
1 Biographical story 2.50

TORRID AFFAIRS
Eternity, 1988
1 .... 2.50
2 .... 2.50
3 thru 5, 60-pg. .... @3.00

TOTALLY ALIEN
Trigon
1 .... 12.00
2 .... 9.00
3 .... 8.00

TOUCH OF DEATH
Brain Scan Studios, 2003
0 .... 2.50
1 thru 3 .... @2.50

TOUGH GUYS AND WILD WOMEN
Eternity, 1989
1 .... 2.50
2 .... 2.50

TOUPYDOOPS
Lobrau Productions 2006
1 by Kevin McShane........... 3.50
2 thru 4 .... @3.50
5 thru 6 .... @3.50

TOZZER 2
Ablaze Media, 2004
1 (of 5) 3.00
2 thru 5 .... @3.00

TRACKER
Blackthorne, 1988
1 .... 2.50
2 thru 4 .... @2.50

TRAILER PARK OF TERROR
Imperium Comics, 2003
1 .... 3.00
2 thru 8 .... @3.00
5a variant (c)................ 3.00
Spec. Halloween Special 4.00
Spec. Halloween Special #2 ...... 4.00

TRANSFORMERS, THE: MOVIE PREQUEL
IDW, 2007
1 B&W....................... 4.00

TRANSIT
Vortex, 1987
1 .... 2.50
2 thru 6 .... @2.50

TRICKSTER KING MONKEY
Eastern
1 thru 5 .... @2.25

TRIDENT
Trident, 1989
1 thru 7 .... @3.50
8 .... 4.50

TRIUMVERATE
Mermaid Productions
1 I:Trimverate 2.25
2 & 3 Team captured.......... @2.25
4 V:Ord,Ael 2.25

TROLLORDS
Tru Studios, 1986
1 1st printing................ 5.00
1a 2nd printing 2.50
2 .... 3.00
3 .... 2.50
4 thru 15 .... @2.50
#1 special................... 2.50

TROLLORDS
Apple Comics, 1989–90
1 thru 6 .... @2.50

TROLLORDS
Caliber Tapestry, 1996
1 and 2 .... @3.00

TROLLORDS: DEATH & KISSES
Apple Comics, 1989
1 .... 2.50
2 thru 5 .... @2.50

TROUBLE EXPRESS
Radio Comix, 1998
1 by Will Allison............. 3.00
2 thru 4 .... @3.00

All comics prices listed are for *Near Mint* condition.

TROUBLE SHOOTERS
Nightwolf, 1995
1 I:Trouble Shooters 2.50
2 V:Ifrit,Djin,Ghul. 2.50
3 V:Morgath 2.50

TROUBLE WITH GIRLS
Eternity, 1989–91
1 . . . . 3.00
2 thru 14 . . . . @2.50
15 thru 21 . . . . @2.50
22 Lester's Origin 2.50
Ann. #1 . . . . 3.00
Graphic Novel 8.00
Graphic Novel #2 . . . . 8.00
Xmas special `World of Girls' 3.00
NEW SERIES
1 thru 4 see color
5 thru 11 . . . . @2.25

TROUBLE WITH TIGERS
Antarctic Press, 1992
1 Ninja High School/Tigers x-over . 2.25
2 . . . . 2.25

TRUE CRIME
Eclipse
1 thru 2 . . . . @3.00

TRUE STORY,
SWEAR TO GOD
Clib's Boy Comics, 2001
5 thru 6 . . . . @3.00
7 thru 15 . . . . @3.00
16 thru 17 . . . . @3.00

TRUFAN ADVENTURES
THEATRE
Paragraphics, 1986
1 . . . . 7.00
2 3-D issue 5.00

TUPELO
Amaze Ink/SLG, 2003
1 . . . . 3.00
2 thru 4 . . . . @3.00

TURTLE SOUP
Mirage, 1985
1 A:TMNTurtles. 6.00

TURTLES TEACH KARATE
Solson
1 . . . . 4.00
2 . . . . 3.50

TV WESTERN
AC Comics, 2001
1 F:Jock Mahoney, Range Rider . . 6.00
Becomes:

WESTERN MOVIE HERO
AC Comics, 2001
2 F:Monte Hale 6.00
3 F:John Wayne 6.00
4 F:Rex Allen 7.00

TWILIGHT AVENGER
Eternity, 1988
1 thru 18 . . . . @2.50
Miracle Studios
Spec. Twilight Avenger Super
    Summer Special 2.75

Twilight Avenger #5
© Eternity

TWILIGHT-X:
INTERLUDE
Antarctic Press, 1992
1 . . . . 2.50
2 thru 3 by Joseph Wright . . . . . . @2.50
Vol. 2, 1993
1 thru 5 . . . . @2.50

TWILIGHT-X QUARTERLY
Antarctic Press, 1994
1 thru 3 by Joseph Wright. . . . . @3.00
4 Celebration 3.00

TWILIGHT X: STORM
Antarctic Press, 2003
1 . . . . 3.50
2 thru 6 . . . . @3.50
7 thru 8 . . . . @3.00

TWIST
Kitchen Sink, 1988
1 . . . . 2.50
2 and 3 . . . . @2.50

TWISTED TANTRUMS OF
THE PURPLE SNIT
Blackthorne, 1986
1 . . . . 2.50
2 . . . . 2.50

2001 NIGHTS
Viz, 1990–91
1 by Yukinobu Hoshino 5.00
2 . . . . 4.00
3 thru 5 . . . . @3.75
6 thru 10 . . . . @4.25

TYRANNY REX
Fleetway
GN reps. from 2000A.D. 8.00

ULTIMATE STRIKE
London Night, 1996
1 . . . . 2.25
1 holochrome edition 12.00
2 . . . . 2.25
3 thru 5 . . . . @2.25
6 sequel to Strike #0 . . . . 2.25

7 by Kevin Hill, `Strike: Year
    One' concl.. . . . . 2.25
8 Year One, ... 2.25
9 Year One, cont. 2.25
10 thru 12 . . . . @2.25

ULTRA KLUTZ
Onward Comics, 1986
1 . . . . 2.50
2 thru 18 . . . . @2.25
19 thru 24 . . . . @2.25
25 thru 30 . . . . @2.25
31 . . . . 3.00

UNCANNY MAN-FROG
Mad Dog
1 and 2 . . . . @2.25

UNCENSORED MOUSE
Eternity, 1989
1 Mickey Mouse 10.00
2 Mickey Mouse 11.00

UNFORGIVEN, THE
Trinity Comics Ministries
Mission of Tranquility
1 thru 6 V:Dormian Grath . . . . . . @2.25
7 I:Faith. 2.25

UNICORN ISLE
Genesis West, 1986
1 . . . . 2.50
2 . . . . 2.50
3 . . . . 2.50
Apple, 1987
4 thru 6 . . . . @2.50

UNLEASHED
Caliber Press
1 F:Carson Davis 3.00
2 V:North Harbor Crime 3.00

UNSUPERVISED
EXISTENCE
Fantagraphics
1 . . . . 2.25
2 and 3 . . . . @2.50

UNTOLD TALES OF
EVIL ERNIE
Chaos! Comics, 2000
Pieces of Me #1 . . . . 3.50
Black Death premium #1 . . . . 13.00
Evil Ernie:chromium #1 . . . . 16.00
Relentless 1 BnP (2002) 5.00
Relentless 1a premium ed. 10.00
Relentless 1b Super premium ed. 20.00
Relentless 1c signed ed. 15.00
Relentless, Script 5.00
Relentless Script, premium ed. . . . 20.00

UNTOUCHABLES
1 . . . . 2.25
2 thru 20 . . . . @2.25

UNTOUCHABLES
Caliber, 1997
1K by Joe Pruett & John Kissee,
    MK(c). 3.00
1S Showman (c). 3.00
2 . . . . 3.00
3 MK (c) 3.00
4 MK (c) 3.00
Spec. High Society Killer (1998) . . 4.00

UPTIGHT
Fantagraphics Books 2006
1	2.50
2	2.50
2	2.50

URSA MINORS
Amaze Ink/SLG, 2006
1	3.00
2 thru 3	@3.00
4	3.00

Usagi Yojimbo #20
© Fantagraphics

USAGI YOJIMBO
Fantagraphics, 1987
1 SS	10.00
1a 2nd printing	5.00
2 SS,Samurai	8.00
3 SS,Samurai,A:Croakers	6.00
4 SS	5.00
5 SS	5.00
6 SS	5.00
7 SS	5.00
8 SS,A Mother's Love	5.00
8a 2nd printing	3.00
9 SS	5.00
10 SS,A:Turtles	5.00
10a 2nd printing	3.00
11 thru 18 SS	@4.00
19 SS,Frost & Fire,A:Nelson Groundthumper	4.00
20 thru 21 SS	@4.00
22 SS,A:Panda Khan	4.00
23 SS,V:Ninja Bats	4.00
24 SS	4.00
25 SS,A:Lionheart	4.00
26 SS,Gambling	4.00
27 SS	4.00
28 thru 31 SS,Circles pt.1–4	@4.00
32	4.00
33 SS,Ritual Murder	4.00
34 thru 37	@4.00
Spec.#1 SS,SummerSpec, C:Groo	45.00

Radio Comix
Vol. 1 The Art of Usagi Yojimbo	4.00

UTOPIATES, THE
Bloodfire Studios 2006
1 (of 4)	3.00
2 thru 4	@3.00

VAGABOND
Viz Communications, 2001
1 (of 8) by Takehiko Inoue	5.00
2 thru 16	@5.00

VAISTRON
Amaze Ink/SLG, 2005
1	3.00
2 thru 5	@3.00

VALENTINE
Red Eye Press, 1997
1 by Dan Cooney	3.00
2 thru 6 Cinderella Undercover	@3.00
7 thru 8 Red Rain	@3.50
9 Gun for Hire	3.50
10	3.00
11 thru 13	@3.50
1-shot Valentine (2005)	3.00

VALENTINO
Renegade, 1985
1	2.50
2 and 3	@2.50

VAMPEROTICA
Brainstorm Comics, 1994
1 I:Luxura	8.00
1a 2nd & 3rd printing	3.00
2	6.00
2 2nd printing	3.00
3	4.00
4 I:Blood Hunter	4.00
5 Deadshot	4.00
6 Deadshot	4.00
7 Baptism	4.00
8 Pains,Peepers	4.00
9 thru 11	@4.00
12 thru 16	@3.00
17 thru 22 see: color	
20 signed	5.00
23	3.00
23 encore edition	3.00
24	3.00
25	3.00
26	3.00
27	3.00
28 A:China & Jazz	3.00
29 mild cover	3.00
30 Legends of Luxura x-over, concl.	3.00
31 V:Red Militia	3.00
32	3.00
33 by Kirk Lindo	3.00
34 V:Pontius Vanthor	3.00
34a luxury edition	5.00
35	3.00
36 I:Countess Vladimira	3.00
36a photo cover edition	4.00
37	3.00
37a statue cover	4.00
38	3.00
39 Death From Above, pt.1	3.00
40 Death From Above, pt.2	3.00
41	3.00
42 Hostile Seduction	3.00
43 Harvest	3.00
44 F:Luxura	3.00
45 The Kindred Kill	3.00
45b photo cover	4.00
46 Murder Most Foul	3.00
47 Camelot	3.00
48 Reflections Over Blood	3.00
49 Love's Story	3.00
50 final issue, 48-pg.	5.00
50b commemorative edition, Julie Strain photo (c)	7.00
50c commem. signed	10.00
Commemorative Edition	3.00
Lingerie Special #1	3.00

Spec. Lingerie, encore edition	3.00
Spec. Lingerie, deluxe	4.00
Spec. Swimsuit, encore edition	3.00
Gallery #1	5.00
Gallery #2	5.00
Bondage Spec. #1	3.00
Bondage Spec. #1, manga	4.00
Ann. #1 Encore	3.00
Spec.#2 Dare to Bare	3.00
Spec.#4 Encore Edition, new(c)	3.00
Spec.#5 Encore Edition	3.00
Spec.#1 Vamperotica Presents: Countess Vladimira (1998)	3.00
Vamperotica Collector Vol. 1	4.00
Pin-Up #1 (2000)	3.00
Spec. Blood of Japan	3.00
1-shot Blond Goddess (2003)	3.00
1-shot Dark Fantasy	3.00
1-shot Bondage Gallery	3.00
Spec. #1 Voluptuous Vamps (2004)	3.00
GN Blood of the Impaler	8.00
GN Deadly Vixens	8.00
GN Drop Dead Dangerous	8.00
GN Vamperotica Maximum Excitement (2001)	8.00
GN Vamperotica Slave to Love (2000)	8.00
GN Dark Ages, series rep.	8.00

VAMPEROTICA: BLOND GODDESS
Vamperotica, 2003
1-shot Blond Goddess	3.00
1-shot Dark Fantasy	3.00
1-shot Bondage Gallery	3.00

VAMPEROTICA: DARK FICTION
Vamperotica Ent., 2001
1 F:Vampress Luxura	3.00
1a adult (c)	4.00
1b premium edition	5.00
2	3.00
3	3.00
4	3.00

VAMPEROTICA: DIVIDE & CONQUER
Brainstorm, 1999
1 V:The Juicious Edicts	3.00
1b Commemorative #1	5.00
1c Commemorative #1 deluxe	7.00
2 conclusion	3.00

VAMPEROTICA ILLUSTRATED
Brainstorm
1 F:Vampress Luxura	3.00
1b premium ed.	5.00
1c premium signed	6.00
2	3.00
3	3.00
4	3.00
5	3.00
6	3.00

VAMPEROTICA LUST FOR LUXURA
Vamperotica, 2002
1 by Kirk Lindo	3.00
1a premium edition	5.00
2	3.00
3	3.00
1c Sketch cover edition	4.00
3a photo(c)	5.00

All comics prices listed are for *Near Mint* condition.

VAMPEROTICA MANGA
Brainstorm, 1998
1 . . . . 3.00
2 . . . . 3.00

VAMPEROTICA'S PIN-UP ILLUSTRATED
Vamperotica, 2004
1 . . . . 5.00
2 thru 3 . . . . @5.00

VAMPEROTICA TALES
Brainstorm, 1998
1 . . . . 3.00
2 thru 5 . . . . @3.00

VAMPEROTICA: TALES FROM THE BLOODVAULT
Vamperotica Ent., 2000
Mag. #1 . . . . 5.00
Mag. #1b premium ed. 7.00

VAMPEROTICA: VOLUPTUOUS VAMPS
Vamperotica, 2004
1 . . . . 3.00

VAMPEROTICA: WHEN DARKNESS FALLS
Vamperotica Ent., 2002
1 . . . . 3.00
1b premium edition 5.00
2 . . . . 3.00
3 . . . . 3.00

VAMPFIRE
Brainstorm, 1996
1 . . . . 3.00
1b commemorative photo cover . . 10.00
2 . . . . 3.00
2b signed 5.00
2d Remastered 3.00
2e signed 10.00
2f deluxe with litho 20.00
3 remastered 4.00
3a signed 10.00
3b deluxe 20.00
Pin-Up Spec. 3.00
Pin-Up Spec. deluxe 4.00
Tour Book #1 . . . . 3.00

VAMPFIRE: EROTIC ECHO
Brainstorm, 1997
1 by Fauve 3.00
1b photo cover 3.00
2 . . . . 3.00
2b photo cover 3.00

VAMPFIRE: NECROMANTIQUE
Brainstorm, 1997
1 by Holly Golightly 3.00
1b luxury edition, virgin cover 5.00
1c luxury edition, signed 15.00
1d regular, signed 8.00
2 by Fauve 3.00

VAMPIRE BITES
Brainstorm, 1995
1 . . . . 3.00
2 . . . . 3.00

VAMPIRE CONFESSIONS
Brainstorm, 1998
1 . . . . 3.00

VAMPIRE DAHLIA, THE
Ironcat, 2001
1 (of 6) by Narumi Kakinouchi 3.00
2 thru 6 . . . . @3.00

VAMPIRE GIRLS: CALIFORNIA 1969
Angel Entertainment, 1996
1 blood red foil deluxe edition 6.00
2 . . . . 3.00
2 deluxe 6.00

VAMPIRE GIRLS: NEW YORK 1979
Angel Entertainment, 1996
0 . . . . 3.00
0 gold edition 8.00
1 . . . . 3.00

VAMPIRE GIRLS: BUBBLEGUM & BLOOD
Angel Entertainment, 1996
1 . . . . 3.00
1 deluxe edition 6.00
2 . . . . 3.00
2 deluxe edition 6.00

VAMPIRE GIRLS EROTIQUE
Angel Entertainment, 1996
1 . . . . 3.00
2 . . . . 3.00
3 . . . . 3.00
4 . . . . 3.00
5 . . . . 3.00
6 . . . . 3.00
7 Bloodsucker cover 3.00
Spec. Gravedigger (1996) by
   Alexandra Scott & Bill Wylie . . . 3.00
Spec. Paris 1968 (1997) by
   Alexandra Scott & Dean Burnett 3.00
Spec. Titanic 1912 (1998) by
   Alexandra Scott & Dean Burnett 3.00

VAMPIRE GIRLS EROTIQUE: GRAVEDIGGER
Angel Entertainment, 1996
1 by Alexandra Scott & Bill Wylie . . 3.00

VAMPIRE GIRLS VS. ANGEL GIRL
Angel Entertainment, 1997
1 . . . . 3.00

VAMPIRELLA
Harris
1 DC,SL,Summer Nights,48pg. . . . 4.00
Pantha Ashcan, 16-pg. 6.00
Dangerous Games Preview Ashcan 6.00
Hell on Earth, Leather Ashcan . . . 15.00
Hell on Earth, Leather Ashcan,
   signed 30.00
30th Ann. Spec. Julie
   Strain photo (c) 10.00
Painkiller Jane preview Ashcan 6.00
Spec.#1 Vampirella vs. Hemorrhage,
   Limited Preview Ashcan 5.00
Vampirella/Lady Death Ashcan
   16-pg., Rematch 6.00
Vampirella/Lady Death Ashcan
   16-pg., Finale 6.00
Vampirella/Lady Death Ashcan
   16-pg., Revenge, platinum . . . 20.00
Vampirella 2999 A.D.
   Manga Ashcan 8.00
Vampirella 2999 A.D. Manga
   Ashcan, leather edition 15.00
Vampirella 3000 A.D.
   Manga Ashcan 8.00
Vampirella 3000 A.D.Manga
   Ashcan, leather edition 15.00

VAMPIRELLA
Harris Comics, 2002
#1 magazine reprint from 1969 . . . 30.00
#1 royal blue foil (c) 60.00
#1 platinum foil (c) 20.00

VAMPIRELLA
Anarchy/Harris Comics, 2004
Spec. Vol. 1 Black & White
   Collection 5.00
Spec. Halloween Special #1 . . . . 10.00
Spec. Halloween Special #1 JJu
   virgin (c) 19.00
Spec. 2006 Halloween Special 3.00
Spec. 2006 Halloween limited
   B&W (c)s . . . . @20.00
Spec. Intimate Visions 4.00
Spec. Intimate Visions Joe Jusko #1 4.00
Spec. Intimate Visions #1 virgin (c) 15.00
Spec. #1 Quarterly Spring 2007 . . . 5.00
Spec. #1 variant (c) 5.00

*Vampirella Silver Anniversary #4
(Good Girl cover) © Harris*

VAMPIRELLA
Silver Anniversary Collection
Harris, 1996
0 Vampirella of Darkulon, EM 3.00
1 good girl edition 2.50
1a bad girl edition 2.50
2 good girl edition 2.50
2a bad girl edition 2.50
3 good girl edition 2.50
3a bad girl edition 2.50
4 Silkie(c) 2.50
4a MBc(c) 2.50

VAMPIRELLA COMICS MAGAZINE
Harris Comics, 2003
1 . . . . 4.00

1a photo (c). 10.00
1b Frankenstein Mobster (c). 10.00
1c JP(c). 10.00
2 thru 9 . . . . @4.00
2a thru 9a photo (c)s. . . . . @10.00

VAMPIRELLA:
MORNING IN AMERICA
Harris/Dark Horse, 1991–92
Book 1 thru 4 . . . . @7.00
Book 2 thru 4 . . . . @5.00

VAMPIRELLA NOVELLA
Anarchy/Harris Comics, 2004
1 Deadly Sins 4.00
1a limited 10.00

VAMPIRELLA RETRO
Harris, 1998
1 (of 3) rep. Warren stories. 2.50
2 (of 3) rep. Warren stories. 2.50
3 (of 3) rep. Warren stories. 2.50

VAMPIRELLA:
LEGENDARY TALES
Harris Comics, 2000
1 . . . . 3.00
1a deluxe 10.00
1b Julie Strain photo (c) 10.00
2 . . . . 3.00
2a variant (c). 10.00
2b Julie Strain photo (c) 10.00

VAMPIRELLA:
REVELATIONS
Anarchy/Harris Comics, 2005
Prototype ed. 5.00
0 16-page 9.00
0a variant JJu virgin (c) 9.00
1 . . . . 3.00
1a variant (c). 3.00
1b & c variant virgin (c)s 12.00
2 . . . . 3.00
2a variant (c) 3.00
2b & c variant virgin (c)s. 12.00
3 . . . . 3.00
3a variant (c) 3.00
3b & c variant virgin (c)s. 9.00
Book 2
1 prototype edition 5.00
1 prototype limited edition 15.00

VAMPIRE MIYU
Antarctica Press, 1996
1 I:Vampire Princess Miyu 3.00
2 thru 5 . . . . @4.00
6 48pg. 5.00

VAMPIRE PRINCESS MIYU
Ironcat, 2000
1 by Narumi Kakinouchi 3.00
2 thru 4 . . . . @3.00

VAMPIRE PRINCESS YUI
Ironcat, 2000
Vol. 1
1 . . . . 3.00
2 thru 6 . . . . @3.00
Vol. 2
1 . . . . 3.00
2 thru 6 . . . . @3.00

VAMPIRE YUI
Ironcat, 2000
Vol. 3
1 . . . . 3.00
2 thru 4 . . . . @3.00
5 thru 6 . . . . @3.00
Vol. 4 (2002)
1 thru 7 . . . . @3.00
Vol. 5
1 . . . . 3.00
2 thru 7 . . . . @3.00

VAMPIRE'S TATTOO
London Night, 1997
1 (of 2) by Art Wetherell 3.00
2 . . . . 3.00
3 . . . . 3.00

VAMPIRE VERSES, THE
CFD Productions, 1995
1 thru 3 . . . . @3.00

VAMPIRE ZONE, THE
Brainstorm, 1998
1 . . . . 3.00

VAMPORNRELLA
Forbidden, 1997
1 parody 3.00

Vampyres #1
© *Eternity*

VAMPYRES
Eternity, 1988
1 thru 4 . . . . @2.25

VAPOR LOCH
Sky Comics, 1994
1 . . . . 2.50

VENGEANCE OF
DREADWOLF
Lightning Comics
1 O:Dreadwolf. 2.75

VENGEANCE OF
THE AZTECS
Caliber, 1993
1 . . . . 2.50
2 . . . . 2.50

VERDICT
Eternity, 1988
1 thru 4 . . . . @2.50

VEROTIKA
Verotika, 1995–97
1 Magical Times 10.00
2 . . . . 7.00
3 . . . . 5.00
4 thru 6 . . . . @4.00
7 thru 15 . . . . @3.00

VERY VICKY
Meet Danny Ocean, 1993
1 . . . . 3.50
1a 2nd printing 3.00
2 thru 8 . . . . @2.50
Spec. Calling All Hillbillies 2.50

VIC & BLOOD
Renegade, 1987
1 and 2 RCo,Ellison . . . . @2.50

VICKY VALENTINE
Renegade, 1985
1 thru 4 . . . . @2.50

VICTIM
Silver Wolf, 1987
1 & 2 . . . . @2.50

VICTIMS
Eternity, 1988
1 thru 5 . . . . @2.50

VIDEO
Lost in the Dark Press, 2004
1 . . . . 3.00
2 thru 4 . . . . @3.00
5 thru 6 . . . . @3.00

VIDEO CLASSICS
Eternity
1 Mighty Mouse 3.50
2 Mighty Mouse 3.50

VIETNAM JOURNAL
Apple Comics, 1987
1 . . . . 5.00
1a 2nd printing 3.00
2 . . . . 3.00
3 thru 5 . . . . @3.00
6 thru 13 . . . . @3.00
14 thru 16 . . . . @3.00

VIGIL
Duality Press, 1997
Baby Steps. 3.00
Dirt, by A.Laudermilk & M.Iverson . . 3.00
Slash and Burn, Bloodline story . . . 3.00
The Vegas Shuffle, Bloodline story . 3.00
Desertion 3.00
Outreach 3.00
Penetration. 3.00
Daddy's Little Girl, final issue 3.00

VIGIL: DESERT FOXES
Millennium, 1995
1 & 2 F:Grace Kimble . . . . @4.00

VIGIL: ERUPTION
Millennium, 1996
1 (of 2) vampire hunters 4.00
2 (of 2) 4.00

VIGIL: FALL FROM GRACE
Innovation, 1992
1 `State of Grace' 2.75
2 The Graceland Hunt 2.50

VIGIL: SCATTER SHOTS
Duality Press, 1997
1 by A.Laudermilk & M.Iverson. . . . 4.00
2 . . . . 4.00

VINSON WATSON'S RAGE
Trinity Visuals
1 I:Rena Helen 3.00

VINSON WATSON'S SWEET CHILDE
Advantage Graphics
Vol. 2
1 F:Spyder 2.25

VIRGIN: SLUMBER
Entity, 1997
1 BMs 2.75
1 deluxe 3.50

VIRGIN: SURROUNDED
Entity, 1997
1 BMs 2.75
1 deluxe 3.50

VIRGIN: TILL DEATH DO US PART
Entity, 1997
1 BMs 2.75
1 deluxe 3.50

VISIONS
Vision Publication, 1979–83
1 I:Flaming Carrot. 60.00
2 Flaming Carrot. 35.00
3 Flaming Carrot. 20.00
4 Flaming Carrot. 25.00

VISUAL ASSAULT OMNIBUS
Visual Assault Comics, 1995
1 thru 4 O:Dimensioner. . . . . . . @3.00

VIXEN
Meteor Comics
1 & 2 Battle of the Vixens . . . . . . @3.00

VORTEX
Hall of Heroes, 1993
1 . . . . 12.00
1a commemorative 5.00
2 . . . . 8.00
3 thru 5 . . . . @3.50
6 V:The Reverend. 3.00

VORTEX SPECIAL: CYBERSIN
Avatar Press, 1997
1 by Matt Martin & Bil Maus 3.00
1b velvet cover 12.00
1c signed 8.00
1d Snowman spec. (c) 5.00

VORTEX: DR. KILBOURN
Entity, 1997
1 by Matt Martin 3.00

1a deluxe 3.50

VORTEX: INTO THE DARK
Entity, 1997
1 . . . . 3.00
1 deluxe 3.50

VOX
Apple, 1989
1 JBy(c). 2.50
2 and 3 . . . . @2.50
4 and 5 . . . . @2.50

WABBIT WAMPAGE
Amazing Comics, 1987
1 . . . . 2.50

WAFFEN SS
New England Comics, 2000
1 by Ron Ledwell 3.50
2 thru 7 . . . . @3.50

WAITING PLACE, THE
Slave Labor, 1997
5 . . . . 3.00
6 . . . . 3.00
Vol. 2, 2000
1 . . . . 3.00
2 . . . . 3.00
3 A Sporting Chance. 3.00
4 I Care. 3.00
5 The Road Home 3.00
6 . . . . 3.00
7 . . . . 3.00
8 Under a Frozen Sky. 3.00
9 Intrusions, pt.1 . . . . 3.00
10 Intrusions, pt.2 . . . . 3.00
11 Intrusions, pt.3 . . . . 3.00

WALKING DEAD
Aircel
1 . . . . 2.25
2 thru 4 . . . . @2.25
Zombie Spec. 1 . . . . 2.25

WALK THROUGH OCTOBER
Caliber
1 I:Mr. Balloon. 3.00
2 . . . . 3.00
3 All Hallow's Eve 3.00

WALT THE WILDCAT
Motion Comics, 1995
1 I:Walt the Wildcat. 2.50

WANDERING STAR
Pen & Ink, 1993
1 I:Casandra Andrews 10.00
1a 2nd & 3rd printing 3.00
2 . . . . 7.00
3 . . . . 5.00
4 . . . . 4.00
5 . . . . 4.00
6 thru 11 . . . . @3.00
Sirius, 1995–97
12 thru 20 TWo . . . . @2.50
21 TWo, final issue 2.50

WANDERLUST
Antarctic Press, 2000
1 (of 3) by Bryant Shiu 2.50
2 . . . . 2.50
3 conclusion 2.50

Wandering Star #17
© Sirius

WARCAT
Alliance Comics
1 thru 7 A:Ebonia . . . . @2.50

WARD: A BULLET SERIES
Liar Comics
1 Foresight,pt.1. . . . . 2.50
2 Foresight,pt.2. . . . . 2.50
3 Foresight,pt.3. . . . . 2.50

WARLOCK 5
Aircel, 1986
1 . . . . 6.00
2 . . . . 5.00
3 . . . . 6.00
4 . . . . 5.00
5 . . . . 5.00
6 thru 11 . . . . @4.00
12 . . . . 3.50
13 . . . . 3.50
14 thru 16 . . . . @3.00
17 . . . . 3.00
18 . . . . 3.00
19 thru 22 . . . . @3.00
Book 2 #1 thru #7. . . . . @3.00

WARLOCK 5
Sirius, 1997
1 (of 4) by Barry Blair & Colin Chan 2.50
2 . . . . 2.50
3 . . . . 2.50
4 finale 2.50

WARLOCKS
Aircel, 1988
1 thru 3 . . . . @2.50
4 thru 12 . . . . @2.50
Spec #1 Rep. 2.50

WARMAGEDDON ILLUSTRATED
Digital Webbing, 2005
1 . . . . 6.00
2 . . . . 6.00

WAR OF THE WORLDS
Eternity
1 TV tie-in 2.50
2 . . . . 2.50
3 thru 6 . . . . @2.50

War of the Worlds #4
© Caliber

WAR OF THE WORLDS, THE
Caliber `New Worlds', 1996
1 from H.G. Wells	3.00
1a signed	3.00
2 war for Kansas City	3.00
3 Haven & The Hellweed	3.00
4	3.00
5	3.00

WAR OF THE WORLDS: THE MEMPHIS FRONT
Arrow Comics, 1998
1 (of 5) by Randy Zimmerman & Richard Gulick	3.00
2 thru 5	@3.00
Spec.#1 signed & numbered	3.00

WARREN ELLIS' APPARAT
Avatar Press, 2004
Preview	2.00

WARREN ELLIS' ATMOSPHERICS
Avatar Press, 2002
GN	6.00

WARREN ELLIS' BAD WORLD
Avatar Press, 2001
1 (of 3)	3.50
2	3.50
3	3.50
1a thru 3a wraparound (c).	@4.00

WARREN ELLIS'
Avatar Press, 2004–05
1-shot Angel Stomp Future	3.50
1-shot Frank Ironwine	3.50
1-shot Quit City	3.50
1-shot Simon Spector	3.50

WARREN ELLIS' SCARS
Avatar Press, 2002
1 (of 6)	3.50
2 thru 6	@3.50
1a–6a wraparound (c).	4.00

WARREN ELLIS' STRANGE KILLINGS
Avatar Press, 2002
1 (of 3) WEI.	3.50
1a wraparound (c).	4.00
2	3.50
2a wraparound (c).	4.00
3	3.50
3a wraparound (c).	3.50

WARREN ELLIS' STRANGE KILLINGS: THE BODY ORCHARD
Avatar Press, 2002
1 (of 6) WEI.	3.50
2 thru 6 WEI	@3.50
1a thru 6a wraparound (c).	@4.00

WARREN ELLIS' STRANGE KILLINGS: NECROMANCER
Avatar Press, 2004
1	3.50
2 thru 6	@3.50
1a thru 6a wraparound (c)s.	@3.50

WARREN ELLIS' STRANGE KILLINGS: STRONG MEDICINE
Avatar Press, 2003
1	3.50
2 thru 3	@3.50
1a thru 3a wraparound (c).	@4.00

WARREN ELLIS' STRANGE KISS
Avatar Press, 1999
1	3.00
1a	4.00
1b signed	25.00
2	2.25
2a wraparound (c).	4.00
3	3.00
3a wraparound (c).	4.00

WARREN ELLIS' STRANGER KISSES
Avatar Press, 2000
1 (of 3)	3.00
1a leather signed	20.00
2	3.00
3	3.00
1a thru 3a wraparound (c).	@4.00

WARRIOR NUN AREALA: BOOKS OF PERIL
Antarctic Press, 2001
1 (of 4)	3.00
2 The Book of Sharate	3.00
3 Book of Xitan	3.00
4 Devil's Deal	3.00
5 Scepter of the Crescent Moon.	3.00
6 Scepter of the Crescent Moon.	3.00
7 Scepter of the Crescent Moon.	3.00
8 The Good Son, pt.1	3.00
9 The Good Son, pt.2	3.00
10 The Good Son, pt.3	3.00
11 Dissension, pt.1	3.00
12 Dissension, pt.2	3.00
13 Dissension, pt.3	3.00
14 Curse of Looming Plague,pt.1	3.50
15 Curse of Looming Plague,pt.2	3.50
16 Curse of Looming Plague,pt.3	3.50

17 Soul Reaper	3.50
18 Soul Reaper, pt.2	3.50
19 Soul Reaper, pt.3	3.50
20 thru 22	@3.50
Spec. Swimsuit Special (2002)	4.00

WARRIOR NUN AREALA: DANGEROUS GAME
Antarctic Press, 2001
1 (of 3)	3.00
2	3.00
3	3.00

WARRIOR NUN AREALA: GHOSTS OF THE PAST
Antarctic Press, 2001
1 (of 4)	3.00
2 thru 4	@3.00

WARRIOR NUN AREALA/RAZOR: DARK PROPHECY
London Night, 1999
1 16-pg.	2.50
2 16-pg.	2.50

Antarctic Press
3	2.50
4	2.50

WARRIOR NUN AREALA: THE MANGA
Antarctic Press, 2000
1-shot	3.00

WARRIOR NUN BRIGANTIA
Antarctic Press, 2000
1 V:Fata Morgana	3.00
2 Sister Anna	3.00
3	3.00

WARRIOR NUN: BLACK AND WHITE
Antarctic Press, 1997
1	3.00
2	3.00
3	3.00
4 Winter Jade, pt.1 F:Ninja Nun	3.00
5 Winter Jade, pt.2	3.00
6 Winter Jade, pt.3	3.00
7	3.00
8	3.00
9 Return of the Redeemers	3.00
10 Return of Lillith	3.00
11 The Redeemers, cont.	3.00
12 The Redeemers, cont.	3.00
13 I:Sister Trinity	3.00
14 Redeemers saga again.	3.00
15 F:Sister Trinity.	3.00
16 F:Sister Trinity.	3.00
17 Showdown	3.00
18 Reaction	3.00
19 Carnivale.	3.00
20 Twilight Earth	3.00
21 Lost Souls of Blue Moon Mountain	2.50
Spec. Warrior Nun Areala/Razor: Revenge	3.00
Spec.A Revenge, deluxe	6.00

WARRIORS
1	2.50
2 thru 7	@2.25

All comics prices listed are for *Near Mint* condition.

WARZONE
Entity, 1995
1 I:Bella & Supra 3.00
2 F:Bladeback, Alloy, Granite 3.00
3 F:Bladeback 3.00

WASTELAND
Oni Press, 2006
1 . . . . 15.00
2 . . . . 11.00
3 . . . . 7.00
4 . . . . 7.00
5 thru 13 . . . . @3.00

WEAPONS FILE
Antarctic Press, 2005
1 photo reference 5.00
2 photo reference 5.00
3 Manga 5.00

WEASEL
Fantagraphics, 1999
1 by Dave Cooper, 48-page 5.00
2 . . . . 5.00
3 . . . . 5.00
5 . . . . 5.00
6 . . . . 13.00
6a signed 19.95

WEATHER WOMAN
CPM Manga, 2000
1 signed & limited 15.00
4 thru 8 . . . . @3.00

WEBWITCH
Avatar Press, 1997
0 by Raff Ienco 3.00
1 (of 2) signed 9.00
1 (of 2) 3.00
2 (of 2) 3.00
Boxed Set, all rare editions 35.00

WEBWITCH:
PRELUDE TO WAR
Avatar Press, 1998
1 by Raff Jenco 3.00
1b Leather cover 25.00

WEBWITCH: WAR
Avatar Press, 1998
1 (of 2) by Bill Maus 3.00
1b Leather cover 25.00
2 conclusion 3.00

WEIRDFALL
Antarctic Press, 1995
1 I:Weirdfall 2.75
2 O:Weirdfall 2.75
3 . . . . 2.75

WEIRD SPACE
ACG Comics, 2000
1 rep. collection 3.00
2 pre-code sci-fi, BW 3.00
3 . . . . 3.00
4 . . . . 3.00
5 . . . . 3.00

WEIRDSVILLE
Blindwolf Studios, 1997
1 . . . . 3.50
1 2nd printing 3.00
2 . . . . 3.50
2 2nd printing 3.00
3 . . . . 3.50
3 2nd printing 3.00

4 . . . . 3.50
5 . . . . 3.00
6 The Usual Weirdoes, concl 3.00
7 . . . . 3.00
8 An American Werewolf in
   Weirdsville, pt.1 (of 2) 3.00
9 An American Werewolf in
   Weirdsville, pt.2 . . . . 3.00
10 . . . . 3.00

WEIRDSVILLE/CRYBABY:
HEY YOU TWO
Blindwolf Studios, 1999
1 . . . . 3.00

WEREWOLF
Blackthorne, 1988–89
1 TV tie-in 2.50
2 thru 7 . . . . @2.50

WESTERN TALES
OF TERROR
**Hoarse and Buggy Productions,
2004**
1 . . . . 3.50
2 thru 5 . . . . @3.50

WHAT IS THE FACE?
A.C.E. Comics, 1986
1 SD/FMc,I:New Face 2.50
2 SD/FMc 2.50
3 SD 2.50

WHISPERS & SHADOWS
Oasis
1 8 1/2 x 11 . . . . 2.50
1a Regular size 2.50
2 8 1/2 x 11 . . . . 2.50
3 8 1/2 x 11 . . . . 2.50
4 thru 9 . . . . @2.50

WHITE DEVIL
Eternity, 1991
1 thru 6 adult . . . . @2.50

WHITE ORCHID, THE
Atlantis
1 (of 6) 3.00
2 . . . . 3.00
3 . . . . 3.00

Whiteout #3
© Oni Press

4 . . . . 3.50
5 'Death Trap,' pt.1 . . . . 3.00
6 The Price of Vengeance 3.50

WHITEOUT
Oni Press, 1998
1 (of 4) by Greg Rucka &
   Steve Leiber 3.00
2 . . . . 3.00
3 . . . . 3.00
4 conclusion 3.00

WHITEOUT: MELT
Oni Press, 1999
1 (of 4) by Greg Rucka
   & Steve Lieber 3.00
2 . . . . 3.00
3 . . . . 3.00
4 concl 3.00

WHITE RAVEN
Visionary Publications
1 Government Intrigue 3.00
2 . . . . 3.00
3 Mystery Man Gets Wheels 3.00
4 Facility 3.00
5 V:Douglas 3.00
6 . . . . 3.00
7 . . . . 3.00

WHITLEY STRIEBER'S
BEYOND COMMUNION
Caliber, 1997
1 UFO Odyssey 3.00
1 signed 3.00
1 special edition, signed
   by Strieber 7.00
1a 2nd printing 3.00
2 . . . . 3.00
3 . . . . 3.00
4 . . . . 3.00

WICKED
Millennium, 1994
1 thru 4 . . . . @2.50

WICKED:
THE RECKONING
Millennium
1 R:Wicked 3.00
2 F:Rachel Blackstone 3.00

WIDOW
Ground Zero, 1996
Cinegraphic Spec.#1: Daughter
   of Darkness 4.00

WIDOW/LUXURA:
BLOOD LUST
Ground Zero, 1996
Alpha x-over, pt.1 . . . . 3.50
see Luxura/Widow for pt. 2

WIDOW:
BOUND BY BLOOD
Ground Zero, 1996
1 thru 5 by Mike Wolfer . . . . @3.50

WIDOW: PROGENY
Ground Zero, 1997
1 by Mike Wolfer & Karl Moline . . . 3.00
2 (of 3) 3.00
3 concl 3.00

WIDOW
Avatar Press, 1997
0 by Mike Wolfer............... 4.00
0b Black leather cover 25.00
0 signed 10.00

Widow The Origin #1
© Avatar Press

WIDOW: THE ORIGIN
Avatar Press, 1997
1 (of 3) by Mike Wolfer........ 4.00
1a leather cover 25.00
2 (of 3) 3.00

WILD, THE
1 ....2.25
2 thru 7 ....@2.25

WILDFLOWER
Sirius/Dog Star, 1998
1 by Billy Martinez 2.50
2 thru 6 ....@2.50

WILDFLOWER: DARK EUPHORIA
Neko Press, 2004
1 ....3.00
2 ....3.00
1a thru 2a variant (c)s......... @4.00

WILDFLOWER: THE LOST YESTERDAYS
Neko Press, 2003
1 ....3.00

WILDFLOWER: TRIBAL SCREAMS
Neko Press, 2002
1 Martinez (c) 3.00
1a Dark One (c) 5.00
2 thru 4 ....@3.00
Spec. Wildflower Y2K, 16-pg. 10.00

WILDFLOWER: TWO TALES
Neko Press, 2003
1-shot signed & numbered....... 3.00

WILD FRONTIER
Shanda Fantasy Arts, 2000
1 (of 2) 3.00
2 concl. 3.00
3 ....3.00

WILD KNIGHTS
Eternity, 1988
1 ....2.50
2 thru 10 ....@2.50
Shattered Earth Chron. #1..... 2.50

WILDLIFE
Antarctic, 1993
1 ....2.75
2 thru 12 ....@2.75

WILDMAN
Miller
1 and 2 ....@2.25
3 thru 6 ....@2.25

WILD THINGZ
ABC Comics, 1998
0 RCI & Armando Huerta 3.00
0a painted cover.............. 6.00
0b Fan edition................. 6.00
0c Summer edition 6.00
0d Leather cover, original art ... 40.00
1 (of 2) RCI 3.00
1b Leather cover.............. 22.00
1c virgin cover................. 3.00
1d gold cover................. 6.00
1e Platinum cover............. 6.00

WILLOW
Angel Entertainment, 1996
0 commemorative edition 3.00
1 ....3.00
1 black magic foil edition 6.00
2 ....3.00
2 gold edition 8.00
2 nude platinum cover 15.00

WIND BLADE
1 Elford 1st Blair.............. 40.00

WINGS
A-List Comics, 1997
1 rep. of golden age 2.50
2 ....3.00
3 ....3.00
4 ....3.00
5 ....3.00

WINDRAVEN
Hero Graphics/Blue Comet
1 The Healing,(see Rough Raiders) 3.00

WITCH
Amaze Ink/SLG, 2001
1 by Lorna Miller.............. 3.00
2 ....3.00
3 thru 4 ....@3.00

WIZARD OF TIME
David House, 1986
1 ....2.50
1a 2nd printing(blue)........... 2.50
2 and 3 ....@2.50

WIZARDS OF THE LAST RESORT
Blackthorne, 1987
1 ....2.50

WOLFF & BYRD, COUNSELORS OF THE MACABRE
Exhibit A, 1994
1 ....6.00
1a new printing............... 3.00
2 thru 4 ....@3.50
5 thru 11 ....@2.50
12 thru 16 BLs ....@2.50
17 thru 23...................@2.50
Spec.#1 Greatest Writs (1997) BLs . 3.00
Spec. #1 Secretary Mavis (1998) .. 3.00
Spec. #2 Secretary Mavis (1999) .. 3.00
Becomes:

SUPERNATURAL LAW
Exhibit A Press, 2000
24 ....2.50
25 The end of 1999 .... 2.50
26 Black Market Souls........... 2.50
27 Creatures of the Night,
   with lawyers................ 2.50
28 While the City Doesn't Sleep ... 2.50
29 thru 31 ....@2.50
32 ....3.00
33 thru 35...................@2.50
36 thru 40...................@3.00
Spec. #101 10th anniversary 3.50
1-shot First Amendment......... 3.50
Spec. Wolf & Byrd #1 new printing . 3.00
Spec. #1 With a Silver Bullet...... 3.50
Spec. #1 At the Box Office........ 3.50
Spec. Wolff & Byrd The Movie..... 3.50

WORDSMITH
Renegade, 1985
1 ....3.00
2 thru 6 ....@2.50
7 thru 12 ....@2.50
Series 2, Caliber, 1996
1 thru 6 ....@3.00

WORLD HARDBALL LEAGUE
Titus Press, 1994
1 F:Big Bat 3.00
2 F:Big Bat 3.00
3 Mount Evrest 3.00
4 Juan Hernandez 3.00

WORLD OF WOOD
Eclipse, 1986
1 thru 4 see color
5 Flying Saucers............... 2.50

WORLDS OF FANTASY
Newcomers Publishing, 1995
1 The Jenn Chronicles 3.00

WORLDS OF H.P. LOVECRAFT
Caliber Tome Press, 1997
1-shot The Alchemist 3.00
1-shot The Tomb............... 3.00
1-shot The Lurking Fear......... 3.00
1-shot Beyond the Walls of Sleep . 3.00

WORLD WAR 2
New England Comics, 2001
3 Eastern Front, pt.2........... 3.50
4 Falaise Pocket............... 3.50
5 D-Day..................... 3.50
6 Tarawa.................... 3.50
7 Afrika Korps 3.50
8 Midway.................... 3.50

All comics prices listed are for *Near Mint* condition.

WORLD WAR 2: STALINGRAD
New England Comics, 2000
1 by Ron Ledwell 3.50
2 . . . . 3.50

WORLDWATCH
Austen Comics, 2004
1 . . . . 3.00
2 thru 7 . . . . @3.00

WRETCH, THE
Caliber, 1996
1 PhH 3.00
2 PhH 3.00

Amaze Ink, 1997
3 PhH 3.00
4 PhH 3.00
5 PhH & Jim Woodyard 3.00
6 PhH & Bruce McCorkindale 3.00
7 PhH 3.00

WU WEI
Animus, 1995
1 `Debaser'. 2.50
2 Blind Whisper. 2.50
3 . . . . 2.50
4 . . . . 2.50
5 `Testament' pt.5 . . . . 2.50
6 by Oscar Stern. 2.50
7 Explicador 3.00
8 Dead Skin 3.00
9 Apotheosis or Bang You're Dead. 3.00

WW2
New England Comics, 2003
1-shot Snipers 4.00
1-shot War in the Air 4.00
1-shot Mercenaries 4.00
1-shot U-Boats. 4.00
1-shot Hitler's Special Forces 4.00
1-shot Last Ditch Stand at Berlin . . 4.00
1-shot Hitler's Paratroopers
    The Assult on Crete. 4.00
1-shot Tobruk. 4.00
1-shot Rommel. 4.00
1-shot Waffen Storm Troops 4.00
1-shot Flying Tigers 4.00

WW2: PRESENTS KAMAKAZI
New England Comics, 2007
1 . . . . 4.00

WYATT EARP: DODGE CITY
Moonstone, 2005
1 CDi 3.00
2 thru 3 CDi. . . . . @3.00

WYRD: THE RELUCTANT WARRIOR
Amaze Ink, 1999
1 (of 6) JSn 3.00
2 . . . . 3.00
3 Telemarketing Horrors 3.00
4 Maxi-Man 3.00
5 . . . . 3.00
6 . . . . 3.00

XANADU
Thoughts & Images, 1988
1 thru 5 . . . . @2.50

XENON
Eclipse, 1987
1 . . . . 3.00
2 thru 23 . . . . @2.50

XENO'S ARROW
Cup O' Tea Studios, 1999
1 by Greg Beettam 2.50
2 thru 10 . . . . @2.50

Radio Comix, 2001
Book 2
1 (of 6) 3.00
2 and 3 . . . . @3.00
4 and 5 . . . . @3.00

Xenozoic Tales #3
© Kitchen Sink

XENOZOIC TALES
Kitchen Sink, 1986
1 by Mark Schultz 9.00
1a Reprint 2.50
2 . . . . 5.00
2a Reprint 2.50
3 . . . . 6.00
4 . . . . 5.00
5 thru 7 . . . . @5.00
8 thru 13 . . . . @5.00
14 MSh. 5.00

X-BABES VS. JUSTICE BABES
Personality
1 Spoof/parody 3.00

X-CONS
Parody Press
1 X-Men satire,flip cover 2.50

X-FARCE
Eclipse, 1992
One-Shot X-Force parody 3.00

X-FLIES BUG HUNT
Twist and Shout, 1997
1 Vampires 3.00
2 Monsters 3.00
3 Aliens 3.00
4 The Truth 3.00
Conspiracy 3.00
Spec. #1 Flies in Black 3.00

XIOLA
Zion Comics
1 thru 3 F:Kantasia . . . . @2.25
4 Visitor. 2.25

XMEN
1 Parody 2.25

X-1999
Viz Communications
1 I:Kamir Shiro 2.75
2 thru 5 F:Princess Hitane . . . . @2.75
6 Battle for X-1999 . . . . 2.75

X-THIEVES
1 . . . . 3.00
2 . . . . 2.25
3 . . . . 2.25

YAHOO
Fantagraphics, 1988
1 thru 4 . . . . @2.50

YAKUZA
Eternity, 1987
1 thru 5 . . . . @2.50

YAWN
Parody Press
1 Spawn parody 2.50
Enigma
1 Spawn parody rep.? 2.75

YELLOW CABALLERO
Viz Communications, 2001
1 thru 4 Pikachu's New Partner . @3.00

YETS
Airwave Comics, 2003
1 . . . . 3.50
2 . . . . 3.50
3 . . . . 3.50

YOU & ME
Ironcat, 2002
Volume 1
1 . . . . 3.00
2 thru 5 . . . . @3.00
6 . . . . 3.00
Volume 2
1 . . . . 3.00

YOUNG DRACULA: PRAYER OF THE VAMPIRE
Boneyard Press, 1997
1 (of 5) sequel to Young Dracula:
    Diary of a Vampire. 3.00
2 Empire of Madness, pt.2 . . . . . . 3.00
3 Children of Madness 3.00
4 Madness Prime 3.00
5 V:Cartiphilus. 4.00

YOUNG MASTERS
New Comics, 1987
1 thru 10 . . . . @2.50

YUGGOTH CREATURES
Avatar Press, 2004
1 . . . . 4.00
2 thru 3 . . . . @4.00
1a thru 3a wraparound (c). . . . . @4.00
1b thru 3b connecting (c) 6.00

Z

Keystone Graphics, 1994
1 . . . . 2.75
2 House of Windsor-YakonaraI. . . . 2.75
3 House of Windsor-YakonaraII . . . 2.75

ZACHERLEY'S
MIDNIGHT TERRORS
Chanting Monks Press, 2004
1 . . . . 4.00
2 . . . . 4.00
3 . . . . 4.00
4 . . . . 4.00

ZED
Gagne International, 2001
1 by Michel Gagne 3.00
2 . . . . 3.00
3 . . . . 3.50
4 . . . . 3.00
5 Resurrection 3.00
6 In the Shadow of Maxuss 3.00
7 thru 8 . . . . @3.50

ZELL THE
SWORDDANCER
Thoughts & Images, 1986
1 Steve Gallacci 5.50
2 and 3 . . . . @2.50

ZEN BOUNTY HUNTER
SSSComics.Com, 2005
1 . . . . 3.00
2 thru 3 . . . . @3.00

ZEN ILLUSTRATED
NOVELLA
Entity
1 thru 4 R:Bruce Lewis . . . . @3.00
5 Immortal Combat 3.00
6 Bubble Economy 3.00
7 Zen City 3.00
8 V:Assassins 3.00

ZEN, INTER-
GALACTIC NINJA
Zen, 1987
1 . . . . 15.00
2 . . . . 9.00
3 thru 9 . . . . @6.00
X-mas Spec #1,V:Black Hole Bob . . 3.00

[2nd Series]
1 `Down to Earth' 3.00
2 RA, A:Jeremy Baker 3.00
2a polybagged, limited 5.00
3 thru 5 . . . . @3.00

[3rd Series]
0 . . . . 3.00
1 thru 3 A:Niro . . . . @3.00
Sourcebook #1 . . . . 3.50

ZEN:
THE NEW ADVENTURES
Zen Comics, 1997
1 SSt & Joel Orbeta 2.50
2 . . . . 3.00
3 . . . . 3.00
4 . . . . 3.00

Zen Intergalactic Ninja: Starquest #3
© Entity

ZEN INTERGALACTIC
NINJA: STARQUEST
Entity
1 thru 6 V:Nolan the Destroyer . . @3.00
7 V:Dimensional 3.00
8 thru 9 I:New Team . . . . @3.00
10 In Deep Space 3.00
11 Dimensional Terrorists 3.00

ZEN INTERGALACTIC
NINJA VS. MICHEAL
JACK-ZEN
Entity
1 Cameos Galore 3.00

ZENISMS WIT
AND WISDOMS
Entity
1 R:Bruce Lewis 3.00

ZEN: MISTRESS
OF CHAOS
1 . . . . 3.00

ZENITH: PHASE II
Fleetway
1 GMo(s),SY,Rep.2000 AD 2.25

ZERO ZERO
Fantagraphics, 1995
1 thru 7 . . . . @5.00
8 . . . . 6.00
9 thru 15 . . . . @5.00
16 . . . . 6.00
17 thru 22 . . . . @5.00
23 F:`Tired' 5.00
24 F:Smilin' Ed 4.00
25 . . . . 4.00
26 final issue, 56-pg. 5.00
27 really final 64-pg. 5.00

ZETRAMAN
Antarctic, 1991
1 thru 3 . . . . @2.25

[Vol. 2], 1992
1 and 2 . . . . @2.75

ZETRAMAN: REVIVAL
Antarctic Press, 1993
1 thru 3 . . . . @2.75

ZILLION
Eternity, 1993
1 . . . . 2.50
2 thru 4 . . . . @2.50

ZOLASTRAYA AND
THE BARD
Twilight Twins, 1987
1 thru 5 . . . . @2.50

ZOMBIE COMMANDOS
FROM HELL
Boneyard Press, 2002
1 . . . . 3.00
1a soundtrack edition 6.00
2 thru 3 . . . . @3.00
2a thru 3a soundtrack edition . . . @6.00
4 . . . . 3.00

ZOMBIE-SAMA
Narwain Publishing, 2006
1-shot BTi 5.00
1-shot variant (c) 5.00
1-shot special ed. 13.00

ZOMBIE HIGHWAY
Digital Webbing, 2004
1 . . . . 4.00
2 thru 3 . . . . @4.00

ZOMBIE WAR: EARTH
MUST BE DESTROYED
Fantaco, 1993
1 thru 3 Kevin Eastman . . . . @4.00

ZONE CONTINUUM
Caliber
1 Master of the Waves 3.00
2 . . . . 3.00

ZOOT!
Fantagraphics, 1993
1 . . . . 2.50
2 thru 5 . . . . @2.50

ZOT!
Eclipse, 1987
(#1-#10 See: Color)
11 New Series 3.00
12 thru 15 . . . . @3.00
16 A:De-Evolutionaries 3.00
17 thru 36 . . . . @3.00

ZU
Mu Press, 1995
1 thru 11 . . . . @3.00
12 `The Monkey Tales' 3.00
13 . . . . 3.00
14 . . . . 3.00
15 `Curse of the Re-Possessed' . . . 3.00
16 thru 19 . . . . 3.00
20 final issue 3.00

B & W PUB.

All comics prices listed are for *Near Mint* condition.

Classics Illustrated

Classics Illus.

[Issued As Classic Comics]

001-THE THREE MUSKETEERS
By Alexandre Dumas

10/41 (——) MKd(a&c),
   Original,10¢ (c) Price 7,500.00
05/43 (10) MKd(a&c),
   No(c)Price; rep 500.00
11/43 (15) MKd(a&c),Long
   Island Independent Ed; 300.00
6/44 (18/20) MKd(a&c),
   Sunrise Times Edition;rep . . . 200.00
7/44 (21) MKd(a&c),Richmond
   Courier Edition;rep 175.00
6/46 (28) MKd(a&c);rep 150.00
4/47 (36) MKd(a&c),
   New CILogo;rep 75.00
6/49 (60) MKd(a&c),CI Logo;rep . . 50.00
10/49 (64) MKd(a&c),CI Logo;rep . 50.00
12/50 (78) MKd(a&c),15¢(c)
   Price; CI Logo;rep 30.00
03/52 (93) MKd(a&c),
   CI Logo;rep 30.00
11/53 (114) CI Logo;rep 25.00
09/56 (134) MKd(a&c),New
   P(c),CI Logo,64 pgs;rep 30.00
03/58 (143) MKd(a&c),P(c),
   CI Logo,64 pgs;rep 25.00
05/59 (150) GE&RC New Art,
   P(c),CILogo;rep 30.00
03/61 (149) GE&RC,P(c),
   CI Logo;rep 18.00
62-63 (167) GE&RC,P(c),
   CI Logo;rep 18.00
04/64 (167) GE&RC,P(c),
   CI Logo;rep 18.00
01/65 (167) GE&RC,P(c),
   CI Logo;rep 18.00
03/66 (167) GE&RC,P(c),
   CI Logo;rep 18.00
11/67 (166) GE&RC,P(c),
   CI Logo;rep 18.00
Sp/69 (166) GE&RC,P(c),25¢(c)
   Price,CILogo, Rigid(c);rep 18.00
Sp/71 (169) GE&RC,P(c),
   CI Logo,Rigid(c);rep 18.00

002-IVANHOE
By Sir Walter Scott

1941 (——) EA,MKd(c),Original . 3,500.00
05/43 (1) EA,MKd(c),word "Presents"
   Removed From(c);rep 400.00
11/43 (15) EA,MKd(c),Long Island
   Independent Edition;rep 250.00
06/44 (18/20) EA,MKd(c),Sunrise
   Times Edition;rep 200.00
07/44 (21) EA,MKd(c),Richmond
   Courier Edition;rep 175.00
06/46 (28) EA,MKd(c),rep 150.00
07/47 (36) EA,MKd(c),New
   CI Logo; rep 100.00
06/49 (60) EA,MKd(c),CI Logo;rep 50.00
10/49 (64) EA,MKd(c),CI Logo;rep 40.00
12/50 (78) EA,MKd(c),15¢(c)
   Price; CI Logo;rep 30.00
11/51 (89) EA,MKd(c),CI Logo;rep 25.00
04/53 (106) EA,MKd(c),CI
   Logo;rep 20.00
07/54 (121) EA,MKd(c),CI
   Logo;rep 30.00

01/57 (136) NN New Art,New
   P(c),CI Logo;rep 30.00
01/58 (142) NN,P(c),CI Logo;rep . . 18.00
11/59 (153) NN,P(c),CI Logo;rep . . 18.00
03/61 (149) NN,P(c),CI Logo;rep . . 18.00
62/63 (167) NN,P(c),CI Logo;rep . . 15.00
05/64 (167) NN,P(c),CI Logo;rep . . 15.00
01/65 (167) NN,P(c),CI Logo;rep . . 15.00
03/66 (167) NN,P(c),CI Logo;rep . . 15.00
09/67 (166) NN,P(c),CI Logo;rep . . 15.00
1968 (166) NN,P(c),CI Logo;rep . . 15.00
Wr/69 (169) NN,P(c),CI
   Logo Rigid(c);rep 15.00
Wr/71 (169) NN,P(c),CI
   Logo,Rigid(c);rep 15.00

003-THE COUNT OF MONTE CRISTO
By Alexandre Dumas

03/42 (——) ASm(a&c),Orig. 2,200.00
05/43 (10) ASm(a&c);rep 400.00
11/43 (15) ASm(a&c),Long Island
   Independent Edition;rep 250.00
06/44 (18/20) ASm(a&c),
   Sunrise Times Edition;rep . . . 225.00
06/44 (20) ASm(a&c),Sunrise
   Times Edition;rep. 200.00
07/44 (21) ASm(a&c),Richmond
   Courier Edition;rep 175.00
06/46 (28) ASm(a&c);rep 150.00
04/47 (36) ASm(a&c),New
   CI Logo; rep 100.00
06/49 (60) ASm(a&c),CI
   Logo;rep 60.00
08/49 (62) ASm(a&c),CI
   Logo;rep 75.00
05/50 (71) ASm(a&c),CI
   Logo;rep 50.00
09/51 (87) ASm(a&c),15¢(c)
   Price, CI Logo;rep 30.00
11/53 (113) ASm(a&c),
   CI Logo;rep 25.00
11/56 (——) LC New Art,New
   P(c), CI Logo;rep 25.00
03/58 (135) LC,P(c),CI Logo;rep . . 30.00
11/59 (153) LC,P(c),CI Logo;rep . . 18.00
03/61 (161) LC,P(c),CI Logo;rep . . 18.00
62/63 (167) LC,P(c),CI Logo;rep . . 15.00
07/64 (167) LC,P(c),CI Logo;rep . . 15.00
07/65 (167) LC,P(c),CI Logo;rep . . 15.00
07/66 (167) LC,P(c),CI Logo;rep . . 15.00
1968 (166) LC,P(c),25¢(c)
   Price, CI Logo;rep 15.00
Wn/69 (169) LC,P(c),CI Logo,
   Rigid(c);rep 15.00

004-THE LAST OF THE MOHICANS
By James Fenimore Cooper

08/42 (——) RR(a&c),Original . . 1,800.00
06/43 (12) RR(a&c),Price
   Balloon Deleted;rep 400.00
11/43 (15) RR(a&c),Long Island
   Independent Edition;rep 250.00
06/44 (20) RR(a&c),Long Island
   Independent Edition;rep 225.00
07/44 (21) RR(a&c),Queens
   Home News Edition;rep. 200.00
06/46 (28) RR(a&c);rep 150.00
04/47 (36) RR(a&c),New
   CI Logo; rep 100.00
06/49 (60) RR(a&c),CI Logo;rep . . 50.00
10/49 (64) RR(a&c),CI Logo;rep . . 35.00

12/50 (78) RR(a&c),15¢(c)
   Price,CI Logo rep 35.00
11/51 (89) RR(a&c),CI Logo;rep . . 30.00
03/54 (117) RR(a&c),CI Logo;rep . 28.00
11/56 (135) RR,New P(c),
   CI Logo; rep. 28.00
11/57 (141) RR,P(c),CI Logo;rep . . 30.00
05/59 (150) JSe&StA New Art;
   P(c), CI Logo;rep 35.00
03/61 (161) JSe&StA,P(c),CI
   Logo; rep 15.00
62/63 (167) JSe&StA,P(c),CI
   Logo; rep 15.00
06/64 (167) JSe&StA,P(c),CI
   Logo; rep 15.00
08/65 (167) JSe&StA,P(c),CI
   Logo; rep 15.00
08/66 (167) JSe&StA,P(c),CI
   Logo; rep 15.00
1967 (166) JSe&StA,P(c),25¢(c)
   Price, CI Logo;rep 15.00
Sp/69 (169) JSe&StA,P(c),CI
   Logo, Rigid(c);rep 15.00

005-MOBY DICK
By Herman Melville

09/42 (——) LZ(a&c),Original . . . 2,300.00
05/43 (10) LZ(a&c),Conray Products
   Edition, No(c)Price;rep 450.00
11/43 (15) LZ(a&c),Long Island
   Independent Edition;rep 275.00
06/44 (18/20) LZ(a&c),Sunrise
   Times Edition;rep 250.00
07/44 (20) LZ(a&c),Sunrise
   Times Edition;rep. 225.00
07/44 (21) LZ(a&c),Sunrise
   Times Edition;rep 200.00
06/46 (28) LZ(a&c);rep 150.00
04/47 (36) LZ(a&c),New CI
   Logo;rep 100.00
06/49 (60) LZ(a&c),CI Logo;rep. . . 50.00
08/49 (62) LZ(a&c),CI Logo;rep. . . 55.00
05/50 (71) LZ(a&c),CI Logo;rep. . . 40.00
09/51 (87) LZ(a&c),15¢(c)
   Price, CI Logo;rep 30.00
04/54 (118) LZ(a&c),CI Logo;rep . . 25.00
03/56 (131) NN New Art,New
   P(c), CI Logo;rep 35.00
05/57 (138) NN,P(c),CI Logo;rep. . 18.00

CC #5, Moby Dick
© Gilberton Publications

All comics prices listed are for *Near Mint* condition.

01/59 **(148)** NN,P(c),CI Logo;rep . . 18.00
09/60 **(158)** NN,P(c),CI Logo;rep . . 18.00
62/63 **(167)** NN,P(c),CI Logo;rep . . 18.00
06/64 **(167)** NN,P(c),CI Logo;rep . . 18.00
07/65 **(167)** NN,P(c),CI Logo;rep . . 18.00
03/66 **(167)** NN,P(c),CI Logo;rep . . 18.00
09/67 **(166)** NN,P(c),CI Logo;rep . . 18.00
Wn/69 **(166)** NN,P(c),25¢(c) Price,
CI Logo, Rigid(c);rep 25.00
Wn/71 **(169)** NN,P(c),CI Logo;rep . 20.00

006-A TALE OF TWO CITIES
By Charles Dickens

11/42 **(——)** StM(a&c),Original . . 2,000.00
09/43 **(14)** StM(a&c),No(c)
Price; rep 400.00
03/44 **(18)** StM(a&c),Long Island
Independent Edition;rep 275.00
06/44 **(20)** StM(a&c),Sunrise
Times Edition;rep. 235.00
06/46 **(28)** StM(a&c),rep 150.00
09/48 **(51)** StM(a&c),New CI
Logo; rep 75.00
10/49 **(64)** StM(a&c),CI
Logo;rep 40.00
12/50 **(78)** StM(a&c),15¢(c)
Price, CI Logo; rep 30.00
11/51 **(89)** StM(a&c),CI Logo;rep. . 30.00
03/54 **(117)** StM(a&c),CI
Logo;rep 25.00
05/56 **(132)** JO New Art,New
P(c), CI Logo;rep 35.00
09/57 **(140)** JO,P(c),CI Logo;rep . . 15.00
11/57 **(147)** JO,P(c),CI Logo;rep . . 15.00
09/59 **(152)** JO,P(c),CI Logo;rep . 250.00
11/59 **(153)** JO,P(c),CI Logo;rep . . 18.00
03/61 **(161)** JO,P(c),CI Logo;rep . . 18.00
62/63 **(167)** JO,P(c),CI Logo;rep . . 15.00
06/64 **(167)** JO,P(c),CI Logo;rep . . 15.00
08/65 **(167)** JO,P(c),CI Logo;rep . . 15.00
05/67 **(166)** JO,P(c),CI Logo;rep . . 15.00
Fl/68 **(166)** JO,NN New P(c),
25¢(c)Price,CI Logo;rep 25.00
Sr/70 **(169)** JO,NN P(c),CI
Logo, Rigid(c);rep 20.00

007-ROBIN HOOD
By Howard Pyle

12/42 **(——)** LZ(a&c),Original . . . 1,400.00
06/43 **(12)** LZ(a&c),P.D.C.
on(c) Deleted;rep. 350.00
03/44 **(18)** LZ(a&c),Long Island
Independent Edition;rep 225.00

CI #7, Robin Hood
© Gilberton Publications

06/44 **(20)** LZ(a&c),Nassau
Bulletin Edition;rep 250.00
10/44 **(22)** LZ(a&c),Queens
City Times Edition;rep 225.00
06/46 **(28)** LZ(a&c),rep 150.00
09/48 **(51)** LZ(a&c),New CI
Logo;rep 75.00
06/49 **(60)** LZ(a&c),CI Logo;rep. . . 35.00
10/49 **(64)** LZ(a&c),CI Logo;rep. . . 32.00
12/50 **(78)** LZ(a&c),CI Logo;rep. . . 32.00
07/52 **(97)** LZ(a&c),CI Logo;rep. . . 35.00
03/53 **(106)** LZ(a&c),CI Logo;rep. . 30.00
07/54 **(121)** LZ(a&c),CI Logo;rep. . 30.00
11/55 **(129)** LZ,New P(c),
CI Logo;rep 35.00
01/57 **(136)** JkS New Art,P(c);rep . 30.00
03/58 **(143)** JkS,P(c),CI Logo;rep . 18.00
11/59 **(153)** JkS,P(c),CI Logo;rep . 15.00
10/61 **(164)** JkS,P(c),CI Logo;rep . 15.00
62/63 **(167)** JkS,P(c),CI Logo;rep . 15.00
06/64 **(167)** JkS,P(c),CI Logo;rep . 20.00
05/65 **(167)** JkS,P(c),CI Logo;rep . 15.00
07/66 **(167)** JkS,P(c),CI Logo;rep . 15.00
12/67 **(166)** JkS,P(c),CI Logo;rep . 20.00
Sr/69 **(169)** JkS,P(c),CI
Logo, Rigid(c);rep 15.00

008-ARABIAN KNIGHTS
By Antoine Galland

03/43 **(——)** LCh(a&c),Original . . 2,200.00
09/43 **(14)** LCh(a&c);rep 750.00
01/44 **(17)** LCh(a&c),Long Island
Independent Edition;rep 750.00
06/44 **(20)** LCh(a&c),Nassau
Bulletin Edition,64 pgs;rep. . . 600.00
06/46 **(28)** LCh(a&c),rep 400.00
09/48 **(51)** LCh(a&c),New CI
Logo; rep 400.00
10/49 **(64)** LCh(a&c),CI
Logo;rep 300.00
12/50 **(78)** LCh(a&c),CI
Logo;rep 250.00
10/61 **(164)** ChB New Art,P(c),
CI Logo;rep 225.00

009-LES MISERABLES
By Victor Hugo

03/43 **(——)** RLv(a&c),Original . . 1,300.00
09/43 **(14)** RLv(a&c);rep 400.00
03/44 **(18)** RLv(a&c),Nassau
Bulletin Edition;rep 275.00
06/44 **(20)** RLv(a&c),Richmond
Courier Edition;rep 250.00
06/46 **(28)** RLv(a&c);rep 200.00
09/48 **(51)** RLv(a&c),New CI
Logo; rep 100.00
05/50 **(71)** RLv(a&c),CI
Logo;rep 75.00
09/51 **(87)** RLv(a&c),CI Logo,
15¢(c)Price;rep 60.00
03/61 **(161)** NN New Art,GMc
New P(c), CI Logo;rep. 60.00
09/63 **(167)** NN,GMc P(c),CI
Logo; rep 35.00
12/65 **(167)** NN,GMc P(c),CI
Logo; rep 35.00
1968 **(166)** NN,GMc P(c),25¢(c)
Price, CI Logo;rep 35.00

010-ROBINSON CRUSOE
By Daniel Defoe

04/43 **(——)** StM(a&c),Original . . 1,100.00
09/43 **(14)** StM(a&c),rep 400.00
03/44 **(18)** StM(a&c),Nassau Bulletin
Ed.,'Bill of Rights'Pge.64;rep. 300.00
06/44 **(20)** StM(a&c),Queens
Home News Edition;rep. 250.00
??/45 **(23)** StM(a&c);rep 150.00
06/46 **(28)** StM(a&c),rep 150.00
09/48 **(51)** StM(a&c),New CI
Logo; rep 75.00

10/49 **(64)** StM(a&c),CI Logo;rep. . 50.00
12/50 **(78)** StM(a&c),15¢(c)
Price, CI Logo;rep 35.00
07/52 **(97)** StM(a&c),CI Logo;rep. . 32.00
12/53 **(114)** StM(a&c),CI
Logo;rep 30.00
01/56 **(130)** StM,New P(c),CI
Logo; rep 32.00
09/57 **(140)** SmC New Art,P(c),
CI Logo; rep 32.00
11/59 **(153)** SmC,P(c),CI Logo;rep 16.00
10/61 **(164)** SmC,P(c),CI Logo;rep 16.00
62/63 **(167)** SmC,P(c),CI Logo;rep 18.00
07/64 **(167)** SmC,P(c),CI Logo;rep 20.00
05/65 **(167)** SmC,P(c),CI Logo;rep 16.00
06/66 **(167)** SmC,P(c),CI Logo;rep 18.00
Fl/68 **(166)** SmC,P(c),CI Logo,
25¢(c)Price;rep 18.00
1968 **(166)** SmC,P(c),CI Logo,No
Twin Circle Ad;rep 16.00
Sr/70 **(169)** SmC,P(c),CI Logo,
Rigid(c);rep 16.00

CI#11, Don Quixote
© Gilberton Publications

011-DON QUIXOTE
By Miguel de Cervantes Saavedra

05/43 **(——)** LZ(a&c),Original . . . 1,300.00
03/44 **(18)** LZ(a&c),Nassau
Bulletin Edition;rep 350.00
07/44 **(21)** LZ(a&c),Queens
Home News Edition;rep. 250.00
06/46 **(28)** LZ(a&c),rep 150.00
08/53 **(110)** LZ,TO New P(c),New
CI Logo;rep 50.00
05/60 **(156)** LZ,TO P(c),Pages
Reduced to 48,CI Logo;rep. . . 30.00
1962 **(165)** LZ,TO P(c),CI Logo;rep 20.00
01/64 **(167)** LZ,TO P(c),CI
Logo;rep 20.00
11/65 **(167)** LZ,TO P(c),CI
Logo;rep 20.00
1968 **(166)** LZ,TO P(c),CI Logo,
25¢(c)Price;rep 40.00

012-RIP VAN WINKLE & THE HEADLESS HORSEMAN
By Washington Irving

06/43 **(——)** RLv(a&c),Original. 1,300.00
11/43 **(15)** RLv(a&c),Long Island
Independent Edition;rep 350.00
06/44 **(20)** RLv(a&c),Long Island
Independent Edition;rep 250.00

Classics Illus.

10/44 **(22)** RLv(a&c),Queens
City Times Edition;rep 225.00
06/46 **(28)** RLv(a&c);rep 150.00
06/49 **(60)** RLv(a&c),New CI
Logo;rep 75.00
08/49 **(62)** RLv(a&c),CI
Logo;rep 45.00
05/50 **(71)** RLv(a&c),CI
Logo;rep 35.00
11/51 **(89)** RLv(a&c),15¢(c)
Price, CI Logo;rep 30.00
04/54 **(118)** RLv(a&c),CI
Logo;rep 32.00
05/56 **(132)** RLv,New P(c),
CI Logo; rep 35.00
05/59 **(150)** NN New Art;P(c),
CI Logo; rep 35.00
09/60 **(158)** NN,P(c),CI Logo;rep . . 20.00
62/63 **(167)** NN,P(c),CI Logo;rep. . 20.00
12/63 **(167)** NN,P(c),CI Logo;rep. . 20.00
04/65 **(167)** NN,P(c),CI Logo;rep. . 22.00
04/66 **(167)** NN,P(c),CI Logo;rep. . 20.00
1969 **(166)** NN,P(c),CI Logo,
25¢(c)Price,Rigid(c);rep. 26.00
Sr/70 **(169)** NN,P(c),CI Logo,
Rigid(c);rep 25.00

013-DR. JEKYLL
AND MR. HYDE
By Robert Louis Stevenson

08/43 **(—)** AdH(a&c),Original . . 2,000.00
11/43 **(15)** AdH(a&c),Long Island
Independent Edition;rep 500.00
06/44 **(20)** AdH(a&c),Long Island
Independent Edition;rep 275.00
06/46 **(28)** AdH,HcK New(c)
Price; rep 225.00
06/49 **(60)** AdH,HcK New(c),New CI
Logo,Pgs.reduced to 48;rep . . 75.00
08/49 **(62)** AdH,HcK(c),CI
Logo;rep 45.00
05/50 **(71)** AdH,HcK(c),CI
Logo;rep 40.00
09/51 **(87)** AdH,HcK(c),Erroneous
Return of Original Date,
CI Logo;rep 40.00
10/53 **(112)** LC New Art,New
P(c), CI Logo;rep 40.00
11/59 **(153)** LC,P(c),CI Logo;rep . . 20.00
03/61 **(161)** LC,P(c),CI Logo;rep . . 20.00
62/63 **(167)** LC,P(c),CI Logo;rep . . 20.00
08/64 **(167)** LC,P(c),CI Logo;rep . . 20.00
11/65 **(167)** LC,P(c),CI Logo;rep . . 20.00
1968 **(166)** LC,P(c),CI Logo,
25¢(c)Price;rep 22.00
Wr/69 **(169)** LC,P(c),CI Logo,
Rigid(c);rep 20.00

014-WESTWARD HO!
By Charles Kingsley

09/43 **(—)** ASm(a&c),Orig. . . . 3,000.00
11/43 **(15)** ASm(a&c),Long Island
Independent Edition;rep 750.00
07/44 **(21)** ASm(a&c);rep 650.00
06/46 **(28)** ASm(a&c),No(c)
Price; rep 500.00
11/48 **(53)** ASm(a&c),Pages reduced
to 48, New CI Logo;rep 450.00

015-UNCLE TOM'S CABIN
By Harriet Beecher Stowe

11/43 **(—)** RLv(a&c),Original . . 1,000.00
11/43 **(15)** RLv(a&c),Blank
Price Circle, Long Island
Independent Ed.;rep 350.00
07/44 **(21)** RLv(a&c),Nassau
Bulletin Edition;rep 250.00
06/46 **(28)** RLv(a&c),No(c)
Price; rep 200.00

CC #15 Uncle Tom's Cabin
© Gilberton Publications

11/48 **(53)** RLv(a&c),Pages Reduced
to 48, New CI Logo;rep 75.00
05/50 **(71)** RLv(a&c),CI Logo;rep. . 45.00
11/51 **(89)** RLv(a&c),15¢(c)
Price, CI Logo;rep 45.00
03/54 **(117)** RLv,New P(c),CI
Logo, Lettering Changes;rep. . 32.00
09/55 **(128)** RLv,P(c),"Picture
Progress"Promotion,CI
Logo 22.00
03/57 **(137)** RLv,P(c),CI Logo;rep . 15.00
09/58 **(146)** RLv,P(c),CI Logo;rep . 15.00
01/60 **(154)** RLv,P(c),CI Logo;rep . 15.00
03/61 **(161)** RLv,P(c),CI Logo;rep . 17.00
62/63 **(167)** RLv,P(c),CI Logo;rep . 15.00
06/64 **(167)** RLv,P(c),CI Logo;rep . 15.00
05/65 **(167)** RLv,P(c),CI Logo;rep . 15.00
05/67 **(166)** RLv,P(c),CI Logo;rep . 15.00
Wr/69 **(166)** RLv,P(c),CI
Logo, Rigid(c);rep 26.00
Sr/70 **(169)** RLv,P(c),CI
Logo, Rigid(c);rep 25.00

016-GULLIVER'S TRAVELS
By Johnathan Swift

12/43 **(—)** LCh(a&c),Original. 1,200.00
06/44 **(18/20)** LCh(a&c),Queen's
Home News Edition,No(c)Price;
rep 300.00
10/44 **(22)** LCh(a&c),Queen's
Home News Editon;rep 225.00
06/46 **(28)** LCh(a&c);rep 150.00
06/49 **(60)** LCh(a&c),Pgs. Reduced
To 48, New CI Logo;rep 75.00
08/49 **(62)** LCh(a&c),CI Logo;rep . 45.00
10/49 **(64)** LCh(a&c),CI Logo;rep . 45.00
12/50 **(78)** LCh(a&c),15¢(c)
Price, CI Logo;rep 35.00
11/51 **(89)** LCh(a&c),CI Logo;rep. . 30.00
03/60 **(155)** LCh,New P(c),CI
Logo; rep 35.00
1962 **(165)** LCh,P(c),CI Logo;rep . 20.00
05/64 **(167)** LCh,P(c),CI Logo;rep . 20.00
11/65 **(167)** LCh,P(c),CI Logo;rep . 20.00
1968 **(166)** LCh,P(c),CI Logo,
25¢(c)Price;rep 20.00
Wr/69 **(169)** LCh,P(c),CI
Logo, Rigid(c);rep 20.00

017-THE DEERSLAYER
By James Fenimore Cooper

01/44 **(—)** LZ(a&c),Original . . 1,000.00
03/44 **(18)** LZ(a&c),No(c)Price;
rep 350.00

10/44 **(22)** LZ(a&c),Queen's
City Times Edition;rep 200.00
06/46 **(28)** LZ(a&c);rep 150.00
06/49 **(60)** LZ(a&c),Pgs. Reduced
to 48,New CI Logo;rep 75.00
10/49 **(64)** LZ(a&c),CI Logo;rep. . 35.00
07/51 **(85)** LZ(a&c),15¢(c)
Price, CI Logo;rep 30.00
04/54 **(118)** LZ(a&c),CI Logo;rep. . 28.00
05/56 **(132)** LZ(a&c),CI Logo;rep. . 25.00
11/66 **(167)** LZ(a&c),CI Logo;rep. . 25.00
1968 **(166)** LZ,StA New P(c),CI
Logo, 25¢(c)Price;rep 35.00
Sg/71 **(169)** LZ,StA P(c),CI Logo,
Rigid(c), Letters From Parents
and Educators;rep 25.00

018-THE HUNCHBACK
OF NOTRE DAME
By Victor Hugo

03/44 **(—)** ASm(a&c),Original
Gilberton Edition 1,200.00
03/44 **(—)** ASm(a&c),Original
Island Publications Edition . 1,000.00
06/44 **(18/20)** ASm(a&c),Queens
Home News Edition;rep 350.00
10/44 **(22)** ASm(a&c),Queens
City Times Edition;rep 250.00
06/46 **(28)** ASm(a&c);rep 225.00
06/49 **(60)** ASm,HcK New(c)8 Pgs.
Deleted, New CI Logo;rep . . . 75.00
08/49 **(62)** ASm,HcK(c),CI
Logo;rep 40.00
12/50 **(78)** ASm,HcK(c),15¢(c)
Price; CI Logo;rep 35.00
11/51 **(89)** ASm,HcK(c),CI
Logo;rep 32.00
04/54 **(118)** ASm,HcK(c),CI
Logo;rep 35.00
09/57 **(140)** ASm,New P(c),CI
Logo; 32.00
09/58 **(146)** ASm,P(c),CI Logo;rep 32.00
09/60 **(158)** GE&RC New Art,GMc
New P(c),CI Logo;rep 20.00
1962 **(165)** GE&RC,GMc P(c),CI
Logo; rep 20.00
09/63 **(167)** GE&RC,GMc P(c),CI
Logo; rep 20.00
10/64 **(167)** GE&RC,GMc P(c),CI
Logo; rep 20.00
04/66 **(167)** GE&RC,GMc P(c),CI
Logo; rep 20.00
1968 **(166)** GE&RC,GMc P(c),CI
Logo, 25¢(c)Price;rep 20.00
Sr/70 **(169)** GE&RC,GMc P(c),CI
Logo, Rigid(c);rep 20.00

019-HUCKLEBERRY FINN
By Mark Twain

04/44 **(—)** LZ(a&c),Original
Gilberton Edition 800.00
04/44 **(—)** LZ(a&c),Original Island
Publications Company Ed. . . 850.00
03/44 **(18)** LZ(a&c),Nassau
Bulletin Editon;rep 350.00
10/44 **(22)** LZ(a&c),Queens City
Times Edition;rep. 250.00
06/46 **(28)** LZ(a&c);rep 200.00
06/49 **(60)** LZ(a&c),New CI Logo,
Pgs.Reduced to 48;rep 75.00
08/49 **(62)** LZ(a&c),CI Logo;rep. . . 40.00
12/50 **(78)** LZ(a&c),CI Logo;rep. . . 35.00
11/51 **(89)** LZ(a&c),CI Logo;rep. . . 30.00
03/54 **(117)** LZ(a&c),CI Logo;rep. . 30.00
03/56 **(131)** FrG New Art,New
P(c), CI Logo;rep 30.00
09/57 **(140)** FrG,P(c),CI Logo;rep . 20.00
05/59 **(150)** FrG,P(c),CI Logo;rep . 20.00
09/60 **(158)** FrG,P(c),CI Logo;rep . 20.00
1962 **(165)** FrG,P(c),CI Logo;rep . 20.00
62/63 **(167)** FrG,P(c),CI Logo;rep . 20.00

06/64 **(167)** FrG,P(c),CI Logo;rep . 20.00
06/65 **(167)** FrG,P(c),CI Logo;rep . 20.00
10/65 **(167)** FrG,P(c),CI Logo;rep . 20.00
09/67 **(166)** FrG,P(c),CI Logo;rep . 20.00
Wr/69 **(166)** FrG,P(c),CI Logo,
25¢(c)Price, Rigid(c);rep 20.00
Sr/70 **(169)** FrG,P(c),CI Logo,
Rigid(c);rep 20.00

020-THE CORSICAN BROTHERS
By Alexandre Dumas

06/44 **(—)** ASm(a&c),Original
Gilberton Edition 650.00
06/44 **(—)** ASm(a&c),Original
Courier Edition. 550.00
06/44 **(—)** ASm(a&c),Original Long
Island Independent Edition . . 550.00
10/44 **(22)** ASm(a&c),Queens
City Times Edition;rep 275.00
06/46 **(28)** ASm(a&c);rep 250.00
06/49 **(60)** ASm(a&c),No(c)Price,
New CI Logo,Pgs. Reduced
to 48;rep 225.00
08/49 **(62)** ASm(a&c),CI
Logo;rep 175.00
12/50 **(78)** ASm(a&c),15¢(c)
Price, CI Logo;rep 165.00
07/52 **(97)** ASm(a&c),CI
Logo;rep 150.00

CC #21, Famous Mysteries
Arthur's Court © Gilberton Publications

021-FAMOUS MYSTERIES
By Sir Arthur Conan Doyle
Guy de Maupassant
& Edgar Allan Poe

07/44 **(—)** AdH,LZ,ASm(a&c),
Original Gilberton Edition . . 1,400.00
07/44 **(—)** AdH,LZ,ASm(a&c),
Original Island Publications
Edition; No Date or Indicia 1,450.00
07/44 **(—)** AdH,LZ,ASm(a&c),
Original Richmond Courier
Edition. 1,200.00
10/44 **(22)** AdH,LZ,ASm(a&c),
Nassau Bulletin Edition;rep . . 500.00
09/46 **(30)** AdH,LZ,ASm(a&c);
rep 350.00
08/49 **(62)** AdH,LZ,ASm(a&c),
New CI Logo;rep 300.00
04/50 **(70)** AdH,LZ,ASm(a&c),
CI Logo;rep 275.00
07/51 **(85)** AdH,LZ,ASm(a&c),
15¢(c) Price,CI Logo;rep 250.00
12/53 **(114)** ASm,AdH,LZ,New
P(c), CI Logo;rep 250.00

022-THE PATHFINDER
By James Fenimore Cooper

10/44 **(—)** LZ(a&c),Original
Gilberton Edition 650.00
10/44 **(—)** LZ(a&c),Original
Island Publications Edition; . 500.00
10/44 **(—)** LZ(a&c),Original
Queens County Times Edition 450.00
09/46 **(30)** LZ(a&c),No(c)
Price;rep 200.00
06/49 **(60)** LZ(a&c),New CI Logo,
Pgs.Reduced To 48;rep 50.00
08/49 **(62)** LZ(a&c),CI Logo;rep . . 45.00
04/50 **(70)** LZ(a&c),CI Logo;rep. . . 35.00
07/51 **(85)** LZ(a&c),15¢(c)
Price, CI Logo;rep 32.00
04/54 **(118)** LZ(a&c),CI Logo;rep . . 30.00
05/56 **(132)** LZ(a&c),CI Logo;rep . . 30.00
09/58 **(146)** LZ(a&c),CI Logo;rep . . 35.00
11/63 **(167)** LZ,NN New P(c),CI
Logo;rep 30.00
12/65 **(167)** LZ,NN P(c),CI
Logo;rep 30.00
08/67 **(166)** LZ,NN P(c),CI
Logo;rep 30.00

023-OLIVER TWIST
By Charles Dickens
(First Classic produced by the Iger shop)

07/45 **(—)** AdH(a&c),Original . . . 700.00
09/46 **(30)** AdH(a&c),Price
Circle is Blank;rep 450.00
06/49 **(60)** AdH(a&c),Pgs. Reduced
To 48, New CI Logo;rep 50.00
08/49 **(62)** AdH(a&c),CI
Logo;rep 45.00
05/50 **(71)** AdH(a&c),CI
Logo;rep 35.00
07/51 **(85)** AdH(a&c),15¢(c)
Price CI Logo;rep 32.00
04/52 **(94)** AdH(a&c),CI
Logo;rep 32.00
04/54 **(118)** AdH(a&c),CI
Logo;rep 30.00
01/57 **(136)** AdH,New P(c),CI
Logo; rep 30.00
05/59 **(150)** AdH,P(c),CI Logo;rep . 25.00
1961 **(164)** AdH,P(c),CI Logo;rep . 25.00
10/61 **(164)** GE&RC New Art,P(c),
CI Logo;rep 35.00
62/63 **(167)** GE&RC,P(c),CI
Logo; rep 15.00
08/64 **(167)** GE&RC,P(c),CI
Logo; rep 15.00
12/65 **(167)** GE&RC,P(c),
CI Logo;rep 15.00
1968 **(166)** GE&RC,P(c),CI
Logo, 25¢(c)Price;rep 15.00
Wr/69 **(169)** GE&RC,P(c),CI
Logo, Rigid(c);rep 15.00

024-A CONNECTICUT YANKEE IN KING ARTHUR'S COURT
By Mark Twain

09/45 **(—)** JH(a&c),Original 550.00
09/46 **(30)** JH(a&c),Price Circle
Blank;rep 200.00
06/49 **(60)** JH(a&c),8 Pages
Deleted,New CI Logo;rep 50.00
08/49 **(62)** JH(a&c),CI Logo;rep. . . 45.00
05/50 **(71)** JH(a&c),CI Logo;rep . . . 35.00
09/51 **(87)** JH(a&c),15¢(c) Price
CI Logo;rep 30.00
07/54 **(121)** JH(a&c),CI Logo;rep. . . 30.00
09/57 **(140)** JkS New Art,New
P(c),CI Logo; rep. 35.00
11/59 **(153)** JkS,P(c),CI Logo . 18.00

1961 **(164)** JkS,P(c),CI Logo;rep . 15.00
62/63 **(167)** JkS,P(c),CI Logo;rep . 15.00
07/64 **(167)** JkS,P(c),CI Logo;rep . 15.00
06/66 **(167)** JkS,P(c),CI Logo;rep . 15.00
1968 **(166)** JkS,P(c),CI logo,
25¢(c)Price;rep 15.00
Sg/71 **(169)** JkS,P(c),CI Logo,
Rigid(c);rep 15.00

025-TWO YEARS BEFORE THE MAST
By Richard Henry Dana Jr.

10/45 **(—)** RWb,DvH,Original; . . 600.00
09/46 **(30)** RWb,DvH,Price Circle
Blank;rep 200.00
06/49 **(60)** RWb, DvH,8 Pages
Deleted,New CI Logo;rep 50.00
08/49 **(62)** RWb,DvH,CI Logo;rep . 45.00
05/50 **(71)** RWb,DvH,CI Logo;rep . 35.00
07/51 **(85)** RWb,DvH,15¢(c) Price
CI Logo;rep 30.00
12/53 **(114)** RWb,DvH,CI Logo;rep 28.00
05/60 **(156)** RWb,DvH,New P(c),
CI Logo, 3 Pgs. Replaced
By Fillers;rep 32.00
12/63 **(167)** RWb,DvH,P(c),CI
Logo; rep 15.00
12/65 **(167)** RWb,DvH,P(c),CI
Logo; rep 15.00
09/67 **(166)** RWb,DvH,P(c),CI
Logo; rep 15.00
Wr/69 **(169)** RWb,DvH,P(c),25¢(c)
Price, CI Logo,Rigid(c);rep . . . 15.00

026-FRANKENSTEIN
By Mary Wollstonecraft Shelley

12/45 **(—)** RWb&ABr(a&c),
Original. 1,450.00
09/46 **(30)** RWb&ABr(a&c),
Price Circle Blank;rep 400.00
06/49 **(60)** RWb&ABr(a&c),
New CI Logo;rep 175.00
08/49 **(62)** RWb&ABr(a&c),
CI Logo;rep 165.00
05/50 **(71)** RWb&ABr(a&c),
CI Logo;rep 75.00
04/51 **(82)** RWb&ABr(a&c),
15¢(c) Price,CI Logo;rep 65.00
03/54 **(117)** RWb&ABr(a&c),
CI Logo;rep 30.00
09/58 **(146)** RWb&ABr,NS
New P(c), CI Logo; rep 35.00
11/59 **(153)** RWb&ABr,NS
P(c),CI Logo; rep 50.00
01/61 **(160)** RWb&ABr,NS
P(c),CI Logo; rep 16.00
165 **(1962)** RWb&ABr,NS P(c),
CI Logo; rep. 16.00
62/63 **(167)** RWb&ABr,NS P(c),
CI Logo; rep. 15.00
06/64 **(167)** RWb&ABr, P(c),
CI Logo; rep 15.00
06/65 **(167)** RWb&ABr,NS P(c),
CI Logo; rep. 15.00
10/65 **(167)** RWb&ABr,NS P(c),
CI Logo; rep. 15.00
09/67 **(166)** RWb&ABr,NS P(c),
CI Logo; rep. 15.00
Fl/69 **(169)** RWb&ABr,NS P(c),25¢(c)
Price,CI Logo,Rigid(c);rep 15.00
Sg/71 **(169)** RWb&ABr,NS P(c),
CI Logo, Rigid(c);rep 15.00

027-THE ADVENTURES MARCO POLO
By Marco Polo & Donn Byrne

04/46 **(—)** HFl(a&c);Original . . . 550.00
09/46 **(30)** HFl(a&c);rep 200.00

Classics Illus.

04/50 **(70)** HFI(a&c),8 Pages Deleted,
   No(c) Price,New CI Logo;rep . 45.00
09/51 **(87)** HFI(a&c),15¢(c)
   Price,CI Logo;rep 30.00
03/54 **(117)** HFI(a&c),CILogo;rep. . 25.00
01/60 **(154)** HFI,New P(c),CI
   Logo;rep 25.00
1962 **(165)** HFI,P(c),CI Logo;rep . . 15.00
04/64 **(167)** HFI,P(c),CI Logo;rep . 15.00
06/66 **(167)** HFI,P(c),CI Logo;rep . 15.00
Sg/69 **(169)** HFI,P(c),CI Logo,
   25¢(c)Price,Rigid(c);rep. 15.00

028-MICHAEL STROGOFF
By Jules Verne
06/46 **(—)** AdH(a&c),Original . . . 550.00
09/48 **(51)** AdH(a&c),8 Pages
   Deleted,New CI Logo;rep . . . 200.00
01/54 **(115)** AdH,New P(c),CI
   Logo; rep 45.00
03/60 **(155)** AdH,P(c),CI Logo;rep. 20.00
11/63 **(167)** AdH,P(c),CI Logo;rep. 20.00
07/66 **(167)** AdH,P(c),CI Logo;rep. 20.00
Sr/69 **(169)**AdH,NN,NewP(c),25¢(c)
   Price, CI Logo,Rigid(c);rep . . 30.00

029-THE PRINCE
AND THE PAUPER
By Mark Twain
07/46 **(—)** AdH(a&c),Original . . . 850.00
06/49 **(60)** AdH,New HcK(c),New CI
   Logo,8 Pages Deleted;rep. . . 100.00
08/49 **(62)** AdH,HcK(c),CILogo;rep 50.00
05/50 **(71)** AdH,HcK(c),CILogo;rep 35.00
03/52 **(93)** AdH,HcK(c),CILogo;rep 32.00
12/53 **(114)** AdH,HcK(c),CI
   Logo;rep 30.00
09/55 **(128)** AdH,New P(c),CI
   Logo; rep 30.00
05/57 **(138)** AdH,P(c),CI Logo;rep. 18.00
05/59 **(150)** AdH,P(c),CI Logo;rep. 18.00
1961 **(164)** AdH,P(c),CI Logo;rep . 18.00
62/63 **(167)** AdH,P(c),CI Logo;rep. 18.00
07/64 **(167)** AdH,P(c),CI Logo;rep. 18.00
11/65 **(167)** AdH,P(c),CI Logo;rep. 18.00
1968 **(166)** AdH,P(c),CI Logo,
   25¢(c)Price;rep 18.00
Sr/70 **(169)** AdH,P(c),CI Logo,
   Rigid(c);rep 18.00

030-THE MOONSTONE
By William Wilkie Collins
09/46 **(—)** DRi(a&c),Original. . . . 550.00
06/49 **(60)** DRi(a&c),8 Pages
   Deleted,New CI Logo;rep . . . 100.00
04/50 **(70)** DRi(a&c),CI Logo;rep. . 65.00
03/60 **(155)** DRi,LbC New P(c),
   CI Logo;rep 90.00
1962 **(165)** DRi,LbC P(c),CI Logo;
   rep 35.00
01/64 **(167)** DRi,LbC P(c),CI Logo;
   rep 28.00
09/65 **(167)** DRi,LbC P(c),CI Logo;
   rep 20.00
1968 **(166)** DRi,LbC P(c),CI Logo,
   25¢(c)Price;rep 18.00

031-THE BLACK ARROW
By Robert Louis Stevenson
10/46 **(—)** AdH(a&c),Original . . . 500.00
09/48 **(51)** AdH(a&c),8 Pages
   Deleted,New CI Logo;rep 75.00
10/49 **(64)** AdH(a&c),CI
   Logo;rep 35.00
09/51 **(87)** AdH(a&c),15¢(c)
   Price;CI Logo;rep 30.00
06/53 **(108)** AdH(a&c),CI
   Logo;rep 28.00
03/55 **(125)** AdH(a&c),CI
   Logo;rep 27.00

CLASSICS Illustrated THE BLACK ARROW By Robert Louis Stevenson

Featuring Stories by the World's Greatest Authors

No. 31 25¢

CI #31, The Black Arrow
© Gilberton Publications

03/56 **(131)** AdH,New P(c),CI
   Logo; rep 22.00
09/57 **(140)** AdH,P(c),CI Logo;rep. 20.00
01/59 **(148)** AdH,P(c),CI Logo;rep. 20.00
03/61 **(161)** AdH,P(c),CI Logo;rep. 20.00
62/63 **(167)** AdH,P(c),CI Logo;rep. 20.00
07/64 **(167)** AdH,P(c),CI logo;rep . 20.00
11/65 **(167)** AdH,P(c),CI Logo;rep . 20.00
1968 **(166)** AdH,P(c),CI Logo,
   25¢(c)Price;rep 20.00

032-LORNA DOONE
By Richard Doddridge
Blackmore
12/46 **(—)** MB(a&c),Original. . . . 550.00
10/49 **(53/64)** MB(a&c),8 Pages
   Deleted,New CI Logo;rep . . . 150.00
07/51 **(85)** MB(a&c),15¢(c)
   Price, CI Logo;rep 65.00
04/54 **(118)** MB(a&c),CI Logo;rep . 35.00
05/57 **(138)** MB,New P(c); Old(c)
   Becomes New Splash Pge.,CI
   Logo;rep 35.00
05/59 **(150)** MB,P(c),CI Logo;rep. . 20.00
1962 **(165)** MB,P(c),CI Logo;rep . . 20.00
01/64 **(167)** MB,P(c),CI Logo;rep. . 22.00
11/65 **(167)** MB,P(c),CI Logo;rep. . 22.00
1968 **(166)** MB,New P(c),
   CI Logo;rep 35.00

033-THE ADVENTURES
OF SHERLOCK HOLMES
By Sir Arthur Conan Doyle
01/47 **(—)** LZ,HcK(c),Original . 1,800.00
11/48 **(53)** LZ,HcK(c),"A Study in Scarlet"
   Deleted,New CI Logo;rep . . . 700.00
05/50 **(71)** LZ,HcK(c),CI Logo;rep 500.00
11/51 **(89)** LZ,HcK(c),15¢(c)
   Price,CI Logo;rep 400.00

034-MYSTERIOUS ISLAND
By Jules Verne
Last Classic Comic
02/47 **(—)** RWb&DvH,Original . . 600.00
06/49 **(60)** RWb&DvH,8 Pages.
   Deleted,New CI Logo;rep 65.00
08/49 **(62)** RWb&DvH,CI Logo;rep 45.00
05/50 **(71)** RWb&DvH,CI Logo;rep 65.00
12/50 **(78)** RWb&DvH,15¢(c) Price,
   CI Logo;rep 35.00
02/52 **(92)** RWb&DvH,CI Logo;rep 35.00
03/54 **(117)** RWb&DvH,CI Logo;
   rep 35.00

09/57 **(140)** RWb&DvH,New P(c),
   CI Logo;rep 35.00
05/60 **(156)** RWb&DvH,P(c),CI
   Logo;rep 20.00
10/63 **(167)** RWb&DvH,P(c),CI
   Logo;rep 20.00
05/64 **(167)** RWb&DvH,P(c),CI
   Logo;rep 20.00
06/66 **(167)** RWb&DvH,P(c),CI
   logo;rep 20.00
1968 **(166)** RWb&DvH,P(c),CI Logo,
   25¢(c)Price;rep 20.00

CLASSICS ILLUSTRATED
Gilberton 1947-60s

035-LAST DAYS
OF POMPEII
By Lord Edward Bulwer Lytton
First Classics Illustrated
03/47 **(—)** HcK(a&c),Original . . . 600.00
03/61 **(161)** JK,New P(c),
   15¢(c)Price;rep 65.00
01/64 **(167)** JK,P(c);rep 30.00
07/66 **(167)** JK,P(c);rep 30.00
Sg/70 **(169)** JK,P(c),25¢(c)
   Price, Rigid(c);rep 30.00

036-TYPEE
By Herman Melville
04/47 **(—)** EzW(a&c),Original. . . 350.00
10/49 **(64)** EzW(a&c),No(c)price,
   8 pages deleted;rep. 90.00
03/60 **(155)** EzW,GMc New
   P(c);rep 35.00
09/63 **(167)** EzW,GMc P(c);rep . . 25.00
07/65 **(167)** EzW,GMc P(c);rep . . 25.00
Sr/69 **(169)** EzW,GMc P(c),25¢(c)
   Price, Rigid(c);rep 25.00

037-THE PIONEERS
By James Fenimore Cooper
05/47 **(37)** RP(a&c),Original 300.00
08/49 **(62)** RP(a&c),8 Pages
   Deleted;rep 45.00
04/50 **(70)** RP(a&c);rep. 35.00
02/52 **(92)** RP(a&c),15¢(c)price;
   rep 35.00
04/54 **(118)** RP(a&c);rep 30.00
03/56 **(131)** RP(a&c);rep 30.00
05/56 **(132)** RP(a&c);rep 30.00
11/59 **(153)** RP(a&c);rep 25.00
05/64 **(167)** RP(a&c);rep 25.00
06/66 **(167)** RP(a&c);rep 25.00
1968 **(166)** RP,TO New P(c),
   25¢(c)Price;rep 35.00

038-ADVENTURES
OF CELLINI
By Benvenuto Cellini
06/47 **(—)** AgF(a&c),Original . . . 400.00
1961 **(164)** NN New Art,New P(c);
   rep 35.00
12/63 **(167)** NN,P(c);rep 25.00
07/66 **(167)** NN,P(c);rep 25.00
Sg/70 **(169)** NN,P(c),25¢(c)
   Price, Rigid(c);rep 28.00

039-JANE EYRE
By Charlotte Bronte
07/47 **(—)** HyG(a&c),Original . . . 400.00
06/49 **(60)** HyG(a&c),No(c)Price,
   8 pages deleted;rep 50.00
08/49 **(62)** HyG(a&c);rep 45.00
05/50 **(71)** HyG(a&c);rep 35.00
02/52 **(92)** HyG(a&c),15¢(c)
   Price; rep 32.00
04/54 **(118)** HyG(a&c);rep 32.00

Classics Illus.

01/58 **(142)** HyG,New P(c). . . . 32.00
01/60 **(154)** HyG,P(c);rep. 32.00
1962 **(165)** HjK New Art,P(c);rep . . 32.00
12/63 **(167)** HjK,P(c);rep 32.00
04/65 **(167)** HjK,P(c);rep 32.00
08/66 **(167)** HjK,P(c);rep 32.00
1968 **(166)** HjK,NN New P(c);rep . 75.00

040-MYSTERIES

**(The Pit & the Pendulum,
The Adventures of Hans Pfall,
Fall of the House of Usher)
By Edgar Allan Poe**
08/47 **(—)** AgF,HyG,HcK(a&c),
Original 1,000.00
08/49 **(62)** AgF,HyG,HcK(a&c),
8 Pages deleted;rep 350.00
09/50 **(75)** AgF,HyG,
HcK(a&c);rep 300.00
02/52 **(92)** AgF,HyG,HcK(a&c)
15¢(c) Price;rep 250.00

041-TWENTY YEARS AFTER

By Alexandre Dumas
09/47 **(—)** RBu(a&c),Original . . . 600.00
08/49 **(62)** RBu,HcK New(c),No(c)
Price, 8 Pages Deleted;rep . . . 65.00
12/50 **(78)** RBu,HcK(c),15¢(c)
Price; rep 45.00
05/60 **(156)** RBu,DgR New P(c);
rep 35.00
12/63 **(167)** RBu,DgR P(c);rep . . . 50.00
11/66 **(167)** RBu,DgR P(c);rep 50.00
Sg/70 **(169)** RBu,DgR P(c),25¢(c)
Price, Rigid(c);rep 50.00

042-SWISS FAMILY ROBINSON

By Johann Wyss
10/47 **(42)** HcK(a&c),Original. . . . 300.00
08/49 **(62)** HcK(a&c),No(c)price,
8 Pages Deleted,Not Every Issue
Has 'Gift Box' Ad;rep 75.00
09/50 **(75)** HcK(a&c);rep 35.00
03/52 **(93)** HcK(a&c);rep 32.00
03/54 **(117)** HcK(a&c);rep 30.00
03/56 **(131)** HcK,New P(c);rep. . . . 28.00
03/57 **(137)** HcK,P(c);rep. 28.00
11/57 **(141)** HcK,P(c);rep. 28.00
09/59 **(152)** NN New art,P(c);rep. . 28.00
09/60 **(158)** NN,P(c);rep. 25.00
12/63 **(165)** NN,P(c);rep 30.00
12/63 **(167)** NN,P(c);rep 15.00
04/65 **(167)** NN,P(c);rep 15.00
05/66 **(167)** NN,P(c);rep 15.00
11/67 **(166)** NN,P(c);rep 15.00
Sg/69 **(169)** NN,P(c);rep 15.00

043-GREAT EXPECTATIONS

By Charles Dickens
11/47 **(—)** HcK(a&c),Original . . 1,400.00
08/49 **(62)** HcK(a&c),No(c)price;
8 pages deleted;rep. 900.00

044-MYSTERIES OF PARIS

By Eugene Sue
12/47 **(44)** HcK(a&c),Original . . 1,000.00
08/47 **(62)** HcK(a&c),No(c)Price,
8 Pages Deleted,Not Every Issue
Has'Gift Box'Ad;rep 400.00
12/50 **(78)** HcK(a&c),15¢(c)
Price; rep 350.00

*Cl #44, Mysteries of Paris
© Gilberton Publications*

045-TOM BROWN'S SCHOOL DAYS

By Thomas Hughes
01/48 **(44)** HFl(a&c),Original,
1st 48 Pge. Issue 250.00
10/49 **(64)** HFl(a&c),No(c)
Price;rep 60.00
03/61 **(161)** JTg New Art,GMc
New P(c) 30.00
02/64 **(167)** JTg,GMc P(c);rep. . . . 20.00
08/66 **(167)** JTg,GMc P(c);rep. . . . 20.00
1968 **(166)** JTg,GMc P(c),
25¢(c)Price;rep 20.00

046-KIDNAPPED

By Robert Louis Stevenson
04/48 **(47)** RWb(a&c),Original . . . 250.00
08/49 **(62)** RWb(a&c),Red Circle
Either Blank or With 10¢;rep . 100.00
12/50 **(78)** RWb(a&c),15¢(c)
Price; rep. 35.00
09/51 **(87)** RWb(a&c);rep. 32.00
04/54 **(118)** RWb(a&c);rep. 30.00
03/56 **(131)** RWb,New P(c);rep . . . 30.00
09/57 **(140)** RWb,P(c);rep 18.00
05/59 **(150)** RWb,P(c);rep 18.00
05/60 **(156)** RWb,P(c);rep 18.00
1961 **(164)** RWb,P(c),Reduced Pge.
Wdth;rep 18.00
62/63 **(167)** RWb,P(c);rep 18.00
03/64 **(167)** RWb,P(c);rep 18.00
06/65 **(167)** RWb,P(c);rep 18.00
12/65 **(167)** RWb,P(c);rep 18.00
09/67 **(167)** RWb,P(c);rep 18.00
Wr/69 **(166)** RWb,P(c),25¢(c)
Price, Rigid(c);rep 18.00
Sr/70 **(169)** RWb,P(c),Rigid(c);rep. 18.00

047-TWENTY THOUSAND LEAGUES UNDER THE SEA

By Jules Verne
05/58 **(47)** HcK(a&c),Original . . . 250.00
10/49 **(64)** HcK(a&c),No(c)
Price; rep 45.00
12/50 **(78)** HcK(a&c),15¢(c)
Price; rep. 35.00
04/52 **(94)** HcK(a&c);rep 35.00
04/54 **(118)** HcK(a&c);rep 30.00
09/55 **(128)** HcK,New P(c);rep. . . . 30.00
07/56 **(133)** HcK,P(c);rep 25.00
09/57 **(140)** HcK,P(c);rep. 18.00
01/59 **(148)** HcK,P(c);rep. 18.00

05/60 **(156)** HcK,P(c);rep 18.00
62/63 **(165)** HcK,P(c);rep. 18.00
05/48 **(167)** HcK,P(c);rep. 18.00
03/64 **(167)** HcK,P(c);rep. 18.00
08/65 **(167)** HcK,P(c);rep. 18.00
10/66 **(167)** HcK,P(c);rep. 18.00
1968 **(166)** HcK,NN New P(c),
25¢(c)Price;rep 25.00
Sg/70 **(169)** HcK,NN P(c),
Rigid(c);rep 25.00

048-DAVID COPPERFIELD

By Charles Dickens
06/48 **(47)** HcK(a&c),Original . . . 250.00
10/49 **(64)** HcK(a&c),Price Circle
Replaced By Image of Boy
Reading;rep 45.00
09/51 **(87)** HcK(a&c),15¢(c)
Price; rep 35.00
07/54 **(121)** HcK,New P(c);rep. . . . 30.00
10/56 **(130)** HcK,P(c);rep 18.00
09/57 **(140)** HcK,P(c);rep. 18.00
01/59 **(148)** HcK,P(c);rep. 18.00
05/60 **(156)** HcK,P(c);rep. 18.00
62/63 **(167)** HcK,P(c);rep. 18.00
04/64 **(167)** HcK,P(c);rep. 18.00
06/65 **(167)** HcK,P(c);rep. 18.00
05/67 **(166)** HcK,P(c);rep. 18.00
R/67 **(166)** HcK,P(c);rep 25.00
Sg/69 **(166)** HcK,P(c),25¢(c)
Price, Rigid(c);rep 18.00
Wr/69 **(169)** HcK,P(c),Rigid(c);rep. 18.00

049-ALICE IN WONDERLAND

By Lewis Carroll
07/48 **(47)** AB(a&c),Original. 275.00
10/49 **(64)** AB(a&c),No(c)Price;
rep 75.00
07/51 **(85)** AB(a&c),15¢(c)Price;
rep 50.00
03/60 **(155)** AB,New P(c);rep. 50.00
1962 **(165)** AB,P(c);rep 35.00
03/64 **(167)** AB,P(c);rep. 30.00
06/66 **(167)** AB,P(c);rep. 30.00
Fl/68 **(165)** AB,TO New P(c),25¢(c)
Price, New Soft(c);rep 50.00
Fl/68 **(166)** AB,P(c),Both Soft &
Rigid(c)s;rep 100.00

050-ADVENTURES OF TOM SAWYER

By Mark Twain
08/48 **(51)** ARu(a&c),Original . . . 250.00
09/48 **(51)** ARu(a&c),Original. . . . 300.00
10/49 **(64)** ARu(a&c),No(c)
Price; rep 35.00
12/50 **(78)** ARu(a&c),15¢(c)
Price; rep. 30.00
04/52 **(94)** ARu(a&c);rep 30.00
12/53 **(114)** ARu(a&c);rep 30.00
03/54 **(117)** ARu(a&c);rep 25.00
05/56 **(132)** ARu(a&c);rep 25.00
09/57 **(140)** ARu,New P(c);rep. . . . 22.00
05/59 **(150)** ARu,P(c);rep 25.00
10/61 **(164)** New Art,P(c);rep. 15.00
62/63 **(167)** P(c);rep. 15.00
01/65 **(167)** P(c);rep. 15.00
05/66 **(167)** P(c);rep. 15.00
12/67 **(166)** P(c);rep. 15.00
Fl/69 **(169)** P(c),25¢(c) Price,
Rigid(c);rep 15.00
Wr/71 **(169)** P(c);rep 15.00

Classics Illus.

All comics prices listed are for *Near Mint* condition.

051-THE SPY
By James Fenimore Cooper
09/48 **(51)** AdH(a&c),Original,
  Maroon(c) 225.00
09/48 **(51)** AdH(a&c),Original,
  Violet(c) 200.00
11/51 **(89)** AdH(a&c),15¢(c)
  Price; rep 35.00
07/54 **(121)** AdH(a&c);rep 30.00
07/57 **(139)** AdH,New P(c);rep. . . . 30.00
05/60 **(156)** AdH,P(c);rep 18.00
11/63 **(167)** AdH,P(c);rep. 18.00
07/66 **(167)** AdH,P(c);rep. 18.00
Wr/69 **(166)** AdH,P(c),25¢(c)Price,
  Both Soft & Rigid(c)s;rep. . . . 35.00

052-THE HOUSE OF
SEVEN GABLES
By Nathaniel Hawthorne
10/48 **(53)** HyG(a&c),Original . . . 200.00
11/51 **(89)** HyG(a&c),15¢(c)
  Price; rep 35.00
07/54 **(121)** HyG(a&c);rep 30.00
01/58 **(142)** GWb New Art,New
  P(c); rep. 35.00
05/60 **(156)** GWb,P(c);rep 18.00
1962 **(165)** GWb,P(c);rep 18.00
05/64 **(167)** GWb,P(c);rep 18.00
03/66 **(167)** GWb,P(c);rep 18.00
1968 **(166)** GWb,P(c),25¢(c)
  Price; rep. 18.00
Sg/70 **(169)** GWb,P(c),Rigid(c);rep 18.00

053-A CHRISTMAS
CAROL
By Charles Dickens
11/48 **(53)** HcK(a&c),Original. . . . 275.00

054-MAN IN THE
IRON MASK
By Alexandre Dumas
12/48 **(55)** AgF,HcK(c),Original . . 200.00
03/52 **(93)** AgF,HcK(c),15¢(c)
  Price; rep 45.00
09/53 **(111)** AgF,HcK(c);rep 60.00
01/58 **(142)** KBa New Art,New
  P(c); rep. 35.00
01/60 **(154)** KBa,P(c);rep. 18.00
1962 **(165)** KBa,P(c);rep 18.00
05/64 **(167)** KBa,P(c);rep. 18.00
04/66 **(167)** KBa,P(c);rep. 18.00

CI #54 The Man in the Iron Mask
© Gilberton Publications

Wr/69 **(166)** KBa,P(c),25¢(c)
  Price, Rigid(c);rep 18.00

055-SILAS MARINER
By George Eliot
01/49 **(55)** AdH,HcK(c),Original . . 200.00
09/50 **(75)** AdH,HcK(c),Price Circle
  Blank,'Coming next'Ad(not
  usually in reps.);rep. 45.00
07/52 **(97)** AdH,HcK(c);rep 32.00
07/54 **(121)** AdH, New P(c);rep. . . . 30.00
01/56 **(130)** AdH,P(c);rep 18.00
09/57 **(140)** AdH,P(c);rep 18.00
01/60 **(154)** AdH,P(c);rep 18.00
1962 **(165)** AdH,P(c);rep 18.00
05/64 **(167)** AdH,P(c);rep 18.00
06/65 **(167)** AdH,P(c);rep 18.00
05/67 **(166)** AdH,P(c);rep 18.00
Wr/69 **(166)** AdH,P(c),25¢(c) Price,
  Rigid(c);rep,Soft & Stiff 35.00

056-THE TOILERS
OF THE SEA
By Victor Hugo
02/49 **(55)** AgF(a&c),Original 350.00
01/62 **(165)** AT New Art,New
  P(c); rep. 60.00
03/64 **(167)** AT,P(c);rep. 35.00
10/66 **(167)** AT,P(c);rep. 35.00

057-THE SONG OF
HIAWATHA
By Henry Wadsworth
Longfellow
03/49 **(55)** AB(a&c),Original. 200.00
09/50 **(75)** AB(a&c),No(c)price,'
  Coming Next'Ad(not usually
  found in reps.);rep 50.00
04/52 **(94)** AB(a&c),15¢(c)
  Price;rep 35.00
04/54 **(118)** AB(a&c);rep 32.00
09/56 **(134)** AB,New P(c);rep 30.00
07/57 **(139)** AB,P(c);rep. 18.00
01/60 **(154)** AB,P(c);rep 18.00
62/63 **(167)** AB,P(c),Erroneosly
  Has Original Date;rep 18.00
09/64 **(167)** AB,P(c);rep. 18.00
10/65 **(167)** AB,P(c);rep. 18.00
Fl/68 **(166)** AB,P(c),25¢(c)Price;
  rep 18.00

058-THE PRAIRIE
By James Fenimore Cooper
04/49 **(60)** RP(a&c),Original 200.00
08/49 **(62)** RP(a&c);rep 75.00
12/50 **(78)** RP(a&c),15¢(c) Price
  In Double Circle;rep. 35.00
12/53 **(114)** RP(a&c);rep 30.00
03/56 **(131)** RP(a&c);rep 30.00
05/56 **(132)** RP(a&c);rep 30.00
09/58 **(146)** RP,New P(c);rep 30.00
03/60 **(155)** RP,P(c);rep 20.00
05/64 **(167)** RP,P(c);rep 18.00
04/66 **(167)** RP,P(c);rep 18.00
Sr/69 **(169)** RP,P(c),25¢(c)
  Price; Rigid(c);rep 18.00

059-WUTHERING HEIGHTS
By Emily Bronte
05/49 **(60)** HcK(a&c),Original. . . . 225.00
07/51 **(85)** HcK(a&c),15¢(c)
  Price; rep 50.00
05/60 **(156)** HcK,GB New P(c);rep 35.00
01/64 **(167)** HcK,GB P(c);rep. 25.00
10/66 **(167)** HcK,GB P(c);rep. 25.00
Sr/69 **(169)** HcK,GBP(c),25¢(c)
  Price, Rigid(c);rep 22.00

060-BLACK BEAUTY
By Anna Sewell
06/49 **(62)** AgF(a&c),Original 200.00
08/49 **(62)** AgF(a&c);rep 250.00
07/51 **(85)** AgF(a&c),15¢(c) Price;
  rep 40.00
09/60 **(158)** LbC&NN&StA New
  Art, LbC New P(c);rep 35.00
02/64 **(167)** LbC&NN&StA,LbC
  P(c); rep. 30.00
03/66 **(167)** LbC&NN&StA,LbC
  P(c); rep. 30.00
03/66 **(167)** LbC&NN&StA,LbC
  P(c), 'Open Book'Blank;rep. . . 30.00
1968 **(166)** LbC&NN&StA,AIM New
  P(c) 25¢(c)Price;rep 75.00

061-THE WOMAN
IN WHITE
By William Wilke Collins
07/49 **(62)** AB(a&c),Original,
  Maroon & Violet(c)s. 200.00
05/60 **(156)** AB,DgR New P(c);rep 40.00
01/64 **(167)** AB,DgR P(c);rep. 30.00
1968 **(166)** AB,DgR P(c),
  25¢(c)Price;rep 30.00

062-WESTERN STORIES
(The Luck of Roaring Camp &
The Outcasts of Poker Flat)
By Bret Harte
08/49 **(62)** HcK(a&c),Original. . . . 200.00
11/51 **(89)** HcK(a&c),15¢(c)
  Price; rep. 40.00
07/54 **(121)** HcK(a&c);rep 32.00
03/57 **(137)** HcK,New P(c);rep. . . . 30.00
09/59 **(152)** HcK,P(c);rep. 20.00
10/63 **(167)** HcK,P(c);rep. 20.00
06/64 **(167)** HcK,P(c);rep. 18.00
11/66 **(167)** HcK,P(c);rep. 18.00
1968 **(166)** HcK,TO New P(c),
  25¢ Price;rep. 30.00

063-THE MAN WITHOUT
A COUNTRY
By Edward Everett Hale
09/49 **(62)** HcK(a&c),Original. . . . 200.00
12/50 **(78)** HcK(a&c),15¢(c)Price
  In Double Circles;rep. 40.00
05/60 **(156)** HcK,GMc New P(c);
  rep 35.00
01/62 **(165)** AT New Art,GMc P(c),
  Added Text Pages;rep. 32.00
03/64 **(167)** AT,GMc P(c);rep 18.00
08/66 **(167)** AT,GMc P(c);rep 18.00
Sr/69 **(169)** AT,GMc P(c),25¢(c)
  Price, Rigid(c);rep 18.00

064-TREASURE ISLAND
By Robert Louis Stevenson
10/49 **(62)** AB(a&c),Original. 200.00
04/51 **(82)** AB(a&c),15¢(c)
  Price;rep 40.00
03/54 **(117)** AB(a&c);rep 32.00
03/56 **(131)** AB,New P(c);rep 30.00
05/57 **(138)** AB,P(c);rep 18.00
09/58 **(146)** AB,P(c);rep 18.00
09/60 **(158)** AB,P(c);rep 18.00
1962 **(165)** AB,P(c);rep 18.00
62/63 **(167)** AB,P(c);rep 18.00
06/64 **(167)** AB,P(c);rep 18.00
12/65 **(167)** AB,P(c);rep 22.00
10/67 **(166)** AB,P(c);rep 18.00
10/67 **(166)** AB,P(c),GRIT Ad
  Stapled In Book;rep 100.00
Sg/69 **(169)** AB,P(c),25¢(c)
  Price, Rigid(c);rep 18.00

065-BENJAMIN FRANKLIN
By Benjamin Franklin
11/49 **(64)** AB,RtH,GS(Iger Shop),
 HcK(c),Original 200.00
03/56 **(131)** AB,RtH,GS(Iger Shop),
 New P(c) ;rep 35.00
01/60 **(154)** AB,RtH,GS(Iger Shop),
 P(c);rep 20.00
02/64 **(167)** AB,RtH,GS(Iger Shop),
 P(c);rep 18.00
04/66 **(167)** AB,RtH,GS(Iger Shop),
 P(c);rep 18.00
Fl/69 **(169)** AB,RtH,GS(Iger Shop),
 P(c), 25¢(c)Price,Rigid(c);rep . 20.00

066-THE CLOISTER AND THE HEARTH
By Charles Reade
12/49 **(67)** HcK(a&c),Original. . . . 400.00

067-THE SCOTTISH CHIEFS
By Jane Porter
01/50 **(67)** AB(a&c),Original 200.00
07/51 **(85)** AB(a&c),15¢(c)
 Price;rep 40.00
04/54 **(118)** AB(a&c);rep 35.00
01/57 **(136)** AB,New P(c);rep. 32.00
01/60 **(154)** AB,P(c);rep. 20.00
11/63 **(167)** AB,P(c);rep. 25.00
08/65 **(167)** AB,P(c);rep. 20.00

068-JULIUS CEASAR
By William Shakespeare
02/50 **(70)** HcK(a&c),Original. . . . 200.00
07/51 **(85)** HcK(a&c),15¢(c)
 Price; rep 40.00
06/53 **(108)** HcK(a&c);rep 32.00
05/60 **(156)** HcK,LbC New P(c);rep 35.00
1962 **(165)** GE&RC New Art,
 LbC P(c);rep 35.00
02/64 **(167)** GE&RC,LbC P(c);rep . 18.00
10/65 **(167)** GE&RC,LbC P(c);Tarzan
 Books Inside(c) 18.00
1967 **(166)** GE&RC,LbC P(c);rep . 18.00
Wr/69 **(169)** GE&RC,LbC P(c),
 Rigid(c);rep 18.00

069-AROUND THE WORLD IN 80 DAYS
By Jules Verne
03/50 **(70)** HcK(a&c),Original. . . . 200.00
09/51 **(87)** HcK(a&c),15¢(c)
 Price; rep. 45.00
03/55 **(125)** HcK(a&c);rep 32.00
01/57 **(136)** HcK,New P(c);rep. . . . 32.00
09/58 **(146)** HcK,P(c);rep. 20.00
09/59 **(152)** HcK,P(c);rep. 20.00
1961 **(164)** HcK,P(c);rep. 20.00
62/63 **(167)** HcK,P(c);rep. 18.00
07/64 **(167)** HcK,P(c);rep. 18.00
11/65 **(167)** HcK,P(c);rep. 18.00
07/67 **(166)** HcK,P(c);rep. 18.00
Sg/69 **(169)** HcK,P(c),25¢(c)
 Price, Rigid(c);rep 18.00

070-THE PILOT
By James Fenimore Cooper
04/50 **(71)** AB(a&c),Original. 175.00
10/50 **(75)** AB(a&c),15¢(c)
 Price;rep. 45.00
02/52 **(92)** AB(a&c);rep 32.00
03/55 **(125)** AB(a&c);rep 35.00
05/60 **(156)** AB,GMc New P(c);rep 30.00
02/64 **(167)** AB,GMc P(c);rep 30.00
05/66 **(167)** AB,GMc P(c);rep 28.00

071-THE MAN WHO LAUGHS
By Victor Hugo
05/50 **(71)** AB(a&c),Original. 250.00
01/62 **(165)** NN,NN New P(c);rep 125.00
04/64 **(167)** NN,NN P(c);rep 100.00

072-THE OREGON TRAIL
By Francis Parkman
06/50 **(73)** HcK(a&c),Original. . . . 150.00
11/51 **(89)** HcK(a&c),15¢(c)
 Price; rep. 40.00
07/54 **(121)** HcK(a&c);rep 32.00
03/56 **(131)** HcK,New P(c);rep. . . . 30.00
09/57 **(140)** HcK,P(c);rep. 20.00
05/59 **(150)** HcK,P(c);rep. 18.00
01/61 **(164)** HcK,P(c);rep. 18.00
62/63 **(167)** HcK,P(c);rep. 18.00
08/64 **(167)** HcK,P(c);rep. 18.00
10/65 **(167)** HcK,P(c);rep. 18.00
1968 **(166)** HcK,P(c),25¢(c)Price;
 rep 18.00

073-THE BLACK TULIP
By Alexandre Dumas
07/50 **(75)** AB(a&c),Original. 550.00

074-MR. MIDSHIPMAN EASY
By Captain Frederick Marryat
08/50 **(75)** BbL,Original 500.00

CI #75, The Lady of the Lake
© Gilberton Publications

075-THE LADY OF THE LAKE
By Sir Walter Scott
09/50 **(75)** HcK(a&c),Original. . . . 150.00
07/51 **(85)** HcK(a&c),15¢(c)
 Price; rep 40.00
04/54 **(118)** HcK(a&c);rep 35.00
07/57 **(139)** HcK,New P(c);rep. . . . 35.00
01/60 **(154)** HcK,P(c);rep. 18.00
1962 **(165)** HcK,P(c);rep 18.00
04/64 **(167)** HcK,P(c);rep. 18.00
05/66 **(167)** HcK,P(c);rep. 18.00
Sg/69 **(169)** HcK,P(c),25¢(c)
 Price, Rigid(c);rep 18.00

076-THE PRISONER OF ZENDA
By Anthony Hope Hawkins
10/50 **(75)** HcK(a&c),Original. . . . 150.00
07/51 **(85)** HcK(a&c),15¢(c) Price;
 rep 40.00
09/53 **(111)** HcK(a&c),rep 35.00
09/55 **(128)** HcK,New P(c);rep. . . . 35.00
09/59 **(152)** HcK,P(c);rep. 20.00
1962 **(165)** HcK,P(c);rep. 18.00
04/64 **(167)** HcK,P(c);rep. 18.00
09/66 **(167)** HcK,P(c);rep. 18.00
Fl/69 **(169)** HcK,P(c),25¢(c) Price,
 Rigid(c);rep 18.00

077-THE ILLIAD
By Homer
11/50 **(78)** AB(a&c),Original 175.00
09/51 **(87)** AB(a&c),15¢(c)
 Price;rep 40.00
07/54 **(121)** AB(a&c);rep 35.00
07/57 **(139)** AB,New P(c);rep. 35.00
05/59 **(150)** AB,P(c);rep. 20.00
1962 **(165)** AB,P(c);rep 18.00
10/63 **(167)** AB,P(c);rep. 18.00
07/64 **(167)** AB,P(c);rep. 18.00
05/66 **(167)** AB,P(c);rep. 18.00
1968 **(166)** AB,P(c),25¢(c)
 Price;rep 18.00

078-JOAN OF ARC
By Frederick Shiller
12/50 **(78)** HcK(a&c),Original. . . . 150.00
09/51 **(87)** HcK(a&c),15¢(c)
 Price; rep. 40.00
11/53 **(113)** HcK(a&c);rep 35.00
09/55 **(128)** HcK,New P(c);rep. . . . 35.00
09/57 **(140)** HcK,P(c);rep. 20.00
05/59 **(150)** HcK,P(c);rep. 20.00
11/60 **(159)** HcK,P(c);rep. 18.00
62/63 **(167)** HcK,P(c);rep. 18.00
12/63 **(167)** HcK,P(c);rep. 18.00
06/65 **(167)** HcK,P(c);rep. 18.00
06/67 **(166)** HcK,P(c);rep. 18.00
Wr/69 **(166)** HcK,TO New P(c),
 25¢(c)Price, Rigid(c);rep 35.00

079-CYRANO DE BERGERAC
By Edmond Rostand
01/51 **(78)** AB(a&c),Original,Movie
 Promo Inside Front(c) 175.00
07/51 **(85)** AB(a&c),15¢(c)
 Price;rep 40.00
04/54 **(118)** AB(a&c);rep 35.00
07/56 **(133)** AB,New P(c);rep. 35.00
05/60 **(156)** AB,P(c);rep 30.00
08/64 **(167)** AB,P(c);rep. 30.00

080-WHITE FANG
**By Jack London
(Last Line Drawn (c)**
02/51 **(79)** AB(a&c),Original. 175.00
09/51 **(87)** AB(a&c);rep 40.00
03/55 **(125)** AB(a&c);rep 35.00
05/56 **(132)** AB,New P(c);rep. 35.00
09/57 **(140)** AB,P(c);rep 20.00
11/59 **(153)** AB,P(c);rep 20.00
62/63 **(167)** AB,P(c);rep. 18.00
09/64 **(167)** AB,P(c);rep. 18.00
07/65 **(167)** AB,P(c);rep. 18.00
06/67 **(166)** AB,P(c);rep. 18.00
Fl/69 **(169)** AB,P(c),25¢(c)
 Price, Rigid(c);rep 18.00

Classics Illus.

All comics prices listed are for *Near Mint* condition.

081-THE ODYSSEY
By Homer
(P(c)s From Now on)
03/51 **(82)** HyG,AB P(c),Original . 175.00
08/64 **(167)** HyG,AB P(c);rep 30.00
10/66 **(167)** HyG,AB P(c);rep 30.00
Sg/69 **(169)** HyG,TyT New P(c),
Rigid(c);rep 35.00

082-THE MASTER OF BALLANTRAE
By Robert Louis Stevenson
04/51 **(82)** LDr,AB P(c),Original . . 150.00
08/64 **(167)** LDr,AB P(c);rep 30.00
Fl/68 **(166)** LDr,Syk New P(c),
Rigid(c);rep 35.00

083-THE JUNGLE BOOK
By Rudyard Kipling
05/51 **(85)** WmB&AB,AB P(c),
Original 150.00
08/53 **(110)** WmB&AB,AB P(c);rep 20.00
03/55 **(125)** WmB&AB,AB P(c);rep 20.00
05/58 **(134)** WmB&AB,AB P(c);rep 20.00
01/58 **(142)** WmB&AB,AB P(c);rep 20.00
05/59 **(150)** WmB&AB,AB P(c);rep 18.00
11/60 **(159)** WmB&AB,AB P(c);rep 18.00
62/63 **(167)** WmB&AB,AB P(c);rep 18.00
03/65 **(167)** WmB&AB,AB P(c);rep 18.00
11/65 **(167)** WmB&AB,AB P(c);rep 18.00
05/66 **(167)** WmB&AB,AB P(c);rep 18.00
1968 **(166)** NN Art,NN New P(c),
Rigid(c);rep 35.00

084-THE GOLD BUG & OTHER STORIES
(Inc. The Telltale Heart & The Cask of Amontillado)
By Edgar Allan Poe
06/51 **(85)** AB,RP,JLv,AB P(c),
Original 200.00
07/64 **(167)** AB,RP,JLv,AB
P(c);rep 125.00

085-THE SEA WOLF
By Jack London
08/51 **(85)** AB,AB P(c),Original . . 150.00
07/54 **(121)** AB,AB P(c);rep 20.00
05/56 **(132)** AB,AB P(c);rep 20.00
11/57 **(141)** AB,AB P(c);rep 20.00
03/61 **(161)** AB,AB P(c);rep 18.00
02/64 **(167)** AB,AB P(c);rep 18.00
11/65 **(167)** AB,AB P(c);rep 18.00
Fl/69 **(169)** AB,AB P(c),25¢(c)
Price, Rigid(c);rep 18.00

086-UNDER TWO FLAGS
By Oiuda
08/51 **(87)** MDb,AB P(c),Original . 125.00
03/54 **(117)** MDb,AB P(c);rep 25.00
07/57 **(139)** MDb,AB P(c);rep 20.00
09/60 **(158)** MDb,AB P(c);rep 20.00
02/64 **(167)** MDb,AB P(c);rep 18.00
08/66 **(167)** MDb,AB P(c);rep 18.00
Sr/69 **(169)** MDb,AB P(c),25¢(c)
Price, Rigid(c);rep 18.00

087-A MIDSUMMER NIGHTS DREAM
By William Shakespeare
09/51 **(87)** AB,AB P(c),Original . . 125.00
03/61 **(161)** AB,AB P(c);rep 20.00
04/64 **(167)** AB,AB P(c);rep 18.00
05/66 **(167)** AB,AB P(c);rep 18.00
Sr/69 **(169)** AB,AB P(c),25¢(c)
Price; rep 18.00

088-MEN OF IRON
By Howard Pyle
10/51 **(89)** HD,LDr,GS,Original . . 125.00
01/60 **(154)** HD,LDr,GS,P(c);rep . . 20.00
01/64 **(167)** HD,LDr,GS,P(c);rep . . 18.00
1968 **(166)** HD,LDr,GS,P(c),
25¢(c)Price;rep 18.00

089-CRIME AND PUNISHMENT
By Fedor Dostoevsky
11/51 **(89)** RP,AB P(c),Original . . 125.00
09/59 **(152)** RP,AB P(c);rep 25.00
04/64 **(167)** RP,AB P(c);rep 18.00
05/66 **(167)** RP,AB P(c);rep 18.00
Fl/69 **(169)** RP,AB P(c),25¢(c)
Price, Rigid(c);rep 18.00

090-GREEN MANSIONS
By William Henry Hudson
12/51 **(89)** AB,AB P(c),Original . . 125.00
01/59 **(148)** AB,New LbC P(c);rep . 30.00
1962 **(165)** AB,LbC P(c);rep 18.00
04/64 **(167)** AB,LbC P(c);rep 18.00
09/66 **(167)** AB,LbC P(c);rep 18.00
Sr/69 **(169)** AB,LbC P(c),25¢(c)
Price, Rigid(c);rep 18.00

091-THE CALL OF THE WILD
By Jack London
01/52 **(92)** MDb,P(c),Original 125.00
10/53 **(112)** MDb,P(c);rep 20.00
03/55 **(125)** MDb,P(c),'PictureProgress'
Onn. Back(c);rep 20.00
09/56 **(134)** MDb,P(c);rep 20.00
03/58 **(143)** MDb,P(c);rep 18.00
1962 **(165)** MDb,P(c);rep 18.00
1962 **(167)** MDb,P(c);rep 18.00
04/65 **(167)** MDb,P(c);rep 18.00
03/66 **(167)** MDb,P(c);rep 18.00
03/66 **(167)** MDb,P(c),Record
Edition;rep 18.00
11/67 **(166)** MDb,P(c);rep 18.00
Sg/70 **(169)** MDb,P(c),25¢(c)
Price, Rigid(c);rep 18.00

092-THE COURTSHIP OF MILES STANDISH
By Henry Wadsworth Longfellow
02/52 **(92)** AB,AB P(c),Original . . 100.00
1962 **(165)** AB,AB P(c);rep 20.00
03/64 **(167)** AB,AB P(c);rep 20.00
05/67 **(166)** AB,AB P(c);rep 20.00
Wr/69 **(169)** AB,AB P(c),25¢(c)
Price, Rigid(c);rep 20.00

093-PUDD'NHEAD WILSON
By Mark Twain
03/52 **(94)** HcK,HcK P(c),Original 125.00
1962 **(165)** HcK,GMc New P(c);rep 25.00
03/64 **(167)** HcK,GMc P(c);rep . . . 20.00
1968 **(166)** HcK,GMc P(c),25¢(c)
Price, Soft(c);rep 20.00

094-DAVID BALFOUR
By Robert Louis Stevenson
04/52 **(94)** RP,P(c),Original 125.00
05/64 **(167)** RP,P(c);rep 25.00
1968 **(166)** RP,P(c),25¢(c)Price;rep 25.00

095-ALL QUIET ON THE WESTERN FRONT
By Erich Maria Remarque
05/52 **(96)** MDb,P(c),Original 200.00
05/52 **(99)** MDb,P(c),Original 85.00
10/64 **(167)** MDb,P(c);rep 35.00
11/66 **(167)** MDb,P(c);rep 35.00

CI #96, Daniel Boone
© *Gilberton Publications*

096-DANIEL BOONE
By John Bakeless
06/52 **(97)** AB,P(c),Original 100.00
03/54 **(117)** AB,P(c);rep 20.00
09/55 **(128)** AB,P(c);rep 20.00
05/56 **(132)** AB,P(c);rep 20.00
—— **(134)** AB,P(c),'Story of
Jesus'on Back(c);rep 20.00
09/60 **(158)** AB,P(c);rep 20.00
01/64 **(167)** AB,P(c);rep 18.00
05/65 **(167)** AB,P(c);rep 18.00
11/66 **(167)** AB,P(c);rep 18.00
Wr/69 **(166)** AB,P(c),25¢(c)
Price, Rigid(c);rep 25.00

097-KING SOLOMON'S MINES
By H. Rider Haggard
07/52 **(96)** HcK,P(c),Original 100.00
04/54 **(117)** HcK,P(c);rep 20.00
03/56 **(131)** HcK,P(c);rep 20.00
09/51 **(141)** HcK,P(c);rep 20.00
09/60 **(158)** HcK,P(c);rep 18.00
02/64 **(167)** HcK,P(c);rep 18.00
09/65 **(167)** HcK,P(c);rep 18.00
Sr/69 **(169)** HcK,P(c),25¢(c)
Price; Rigid(c);rep 20.00

098-THE RED BADGE OF COURAGE
By Stephen Crane
08/52 **(98)** MDb,GS,P(c),Original. 100.00
04/54 **(118)** MDb,GS,P(c);rep 20.00
05/56 **(132)** MDb,GS,P(c);rep 20.00
01/58 **(142)** MDb,GS,P(c);rep 20.00
09/59 **(152)** MDb,GS,P(c);rep 20.00
03/61 **(161)** MDb,GS,P(c);rep 20.00
62/63 **(167)** MDb,GS,P(c),Erronously
Has Original Date;rep 20.00
09/64 **(167)** MDb,GS,P(c);rep 20.00
10/65 **(167)** MDb,GS,P(c);rep 20.00
1968 **(166)** MDb,GS,P(c),25¢(c)
Price, Rigid(c);rep 30.00

Classics Illus.

099-HAMLET

By William Shakespeare
09/52 **(98)** AB,P(c),Original 125.00
07/54 **(121)** AB,P(c);rep 20.00
11/57 **(141)** AB,P(c);rep 20.00
09/60 **(158)** AB,P(c);rep 18.00
62/63 **(167)** AB,P(c),Erroneously
   Has Original Date;rep 18.00
07/65 **(167)** AB,P(c);rep 18.00
04/67 **(166)** AB,P(c);rep 18.00
Sg/69 **(169)** AB,EdM New P(c),
   25¢(c)Price, Rigid(c);rep 30.00

100-MUTINY ON
THE BOUNTY

By Charrles Nordhoff
10/52 **(100)** MsW,HcK P(c),Orig . . 100.00
03/54 **(117)** MsW,HcK P(c);rep . . . 20.00
05/56 **(132)** MsW,HcK P(c);rep . . . 20.00
01/58 **(142)** MsW,HcK P(c);rep . . . 20.00
03/60 **(155)** MsW,HcK P(c);rep . . . 18.00
62/63 **(167)** MsW,HcK P(c),Erroneously
   Has Original Date;rep 18.00
05/64 **(167)** MsW,HcK P(c);rep . . . 18.00
03/66 **(167)** MsW,HcK P(c),N#
   or Price;rep 20.00
Sg/70 **(169)** MsW,HcK P(c),
   Rigid(c); rep 18.00

101-WILLIAM TELL

By Frederick Schiller
11/52 **(101)** MDb,HcK P(c),Orig . . 100.00
04/54 **(118)** MDb,HcK P(c);rep . . . 20.00
11/57 **(141)** MDb,HcK P(c);rep . . . 20.00
09/60 **(158)** MDb,HcK P(c);rep . . . 18.00
62/63 **(167)** MDb,HcK P(c),Erroneously
   Has Original Date;rep 18.00
11/64 **(167)** MDb,HcK P(c);rep . . . 18.00
04/67 **(166)** MDb,HcK P(c);rep . . . 18.00
Wr/69 **(169)** MDb,HcK P(c)25¢(c)
   Price, Rigid(c);rep 18.00

102-THE WHITE
COMPANY

By Sir Arthur Conan Doyle
12/52 **(101)** AB,P(c),Original 150.00
1962 **(165)** AB,P(c);rep 40.00
04/64 **(167)** AB,P(c);rep 40.00

103-MEN AGAINST
THE SEA

By Charles Nordhoff
01/53 **(104)** RP,HcK P(c),Original 125.00
12/53 **(114)** RP,HcK P(c);rep 30.00
03/56 **(131)** RP,New P(c);rep 35.00
03/59 **(149)** RP,P(c);rep 30.00
09/60 **(158)** RP,P(c);rep 30.00
03/64 **(167)** RP,P(c);rep 25.00

104-BRING 'EM BACK
ALIVE

By Frank Buck & Edward
Anthony
02/53 **(105)** HcK,HcK P(c)Original 100.00
04/54 **(118)** HcK,HcK P(c);rep 20.00
07/56 **(133)** HcK,HcK P(c);rep 20.00
05/59 **(150)** HcK,HcK P(c);rep 18.00
09/60 **(158)** HcK,HcK P(c);rep 18.00
10/63 **(167)** HcK,HcK P(c);rep 18.00
09/65 **(167)** HcK,HcK P(c);rep 18.00
Wr/69 **(169)** HcK,HcK P(c),25¢(c)
   Price, Rigid(c);rep 18.00

CI #105, From the Earth to the Moon
© Gilberton Publications

105-FROM THE EARTH
TO THE MOON

By Jules Verne
03/53 **(106)** AB,P(c),Original 100.00
04/54 **(118)** AB,P(c);rep 20.00
03/56 **(132)** AB,P(c);rep 20.00
11/57 **(141)** AB,P(c);rep 20.00
09/58 **(146)** AB,P(c);rep 20.00
05/60 **(156)** AB,P(c);rep 20.00
62/63 **(167)** AB,P(c),Erroneously
   Has Original Date;rep 18.00
05/64 **(167)** AB,P(c);rep 18.00
05/65 **(167)** AB,P(c);rep 18.00
10/67 **(166)** AB,P(c);rep 18.00
Sr/69 **(169)** AB,P(c),25¢(c)
   Price, Rigid(c);rep 18.00
Sg/71 **(169)** AB,P(c);rep 18.00

106-BUFFALO BILL

By William F. Cody
04/53 **(107)** MDb,P(c),Original . . . 100.00
04/54 **(118)** MDb,P(c);rep 20.00
03/56 **(132)** MDb,P(c);rep 20.00
01/58 **(142)** MDb,P(c);rep 20.00
03/61 **(161)** MDb,P(c);rep 18.00
03/64 **(167)** MDb,P(c);rep 18.00
07/67 **(166)** MDb,P(c);rep 18.00
Fl/69 **(169)** MDb,P(c),Rigid(c);rep . 18.00

107-KING OF THE
KHYBER RIFLES

By Talbot Mundy
05/53 **(108)** SMz,P(c),Original . . . 100.00
04/54 **(118)** SMz,P(c);rep 20.00
09/58 **(146)** SMz,P(c);rep 20.00
09/60 **(158)** SMz,P(c);rep 18.00
62/63 **(167)** SMz,P(c),Erroeously
   Has Original Date;rep 18.00
62/63 **(167)** SMz,P(c);rep 18.00
10/66 **(167)** SMz,P(c);rep 18.00

108-KNIGHTS OF THE
ROUND TABLE

By Howard Pyle?
06/53 **(108)** AB,P(c),Original 125.00
06/53 **(109)** AB,P(c),Original 70.00
03/54 **(117)** AB,P(c);rep 20.00
11/59 **(153)** AB,P(c);rep 18.00
1962 **(165)** AB,P(c);rep 18.00
04/64 **(167)** AB,P(c);rep 18.00
04/67 **(166)** AB,P(c);rep 18.00

109-PITCAIRN'S ISLAND

By Charles Nordhoff
07/53 **(110)** RP,P(c),Original 125.00
1962 **(165)** RP,P(c);rep 20.00
03/64 **(167)** RP,P(c);rep 20.00
06/67 **(166)** RP,P(c);rep 20.00

110-A STUDY IN
SCARLET

By Sir Arthur Conan Doyle
08/53 **(111)** SMz,P(c),Original . . . 200.00
1962 **(165)** SMz,P(c);rep 150.00

111-THE TALISMAN

By Sir Walter Scott
09/53 **(112)** HcK,HcK P(c),Orig . . . 125.00
1962 **(165)** HcK,HcK P(c);rep 20.00
05/64 **(167)** HcK,HcK P(c);rep 20.00
Fl/68 **(166)** HcK,HcK P(c),
   25¢(c)Price;rep 20.00

112-ADVENTURES OF
KIT CARSON

By John S. C. Abbott
10/53 **(113)** RP,P(c),Original 125.00
11/55 **(129)** RP,P(c);rep 20.00
11/57 **(141)** RP,P(c);rep 20.00
09/59 **(152)** RP,P(c);rep 18.00
03/61 **(161)** RP,P(c);rep 18.00
62/63 **(167)** RP,P(c);rep 18.00
02/65 **(167)** RP,P(c);rep 18.00
05/66 **(167)** RP,P(c);rep 18.00
Wr/69 **(166)** RP,EdM New P(c),
   25¢(c)Price, Rigid(c);rep 25.00

113-THE FORTY-FIVE
GUARDSMEN

By Alexandre Dumas
11/53 **(114)** MDb,P(c),Original . . . 150.00
07/67 **(166)** MDb,P(c);rep 50.00

114-THE RED ROVER

By James Fenimore Cooper
12/53 **(115)** PrC,JP P(c),Original . 150.00
07/67 **(166)** PrC,JP P(c);rep 50.00

115-HOW I FOUND
LIVINGSTONE

By Sir Henry Stanley
01/54 **(116)** SF&ST,P(c),Original . 200.00
01/67 **(167)** SF&ST,P(c);rep 60.00

116-THE BOTTLE IMP

By Robert Louis Stevenson
02/54 **(117)** LC,P(c),Original 200.00
01/67 **(167)** LC,P(c);rep 60.00

117-CAPTAINS
COURAGEOUS

By Rudyard Kipling
03/54 **(118)** PrC,P(c),Original . . . 200.00
02/67 **(167)** PrC,P(c);rep 32.00
Fl/69 **(169)** PrC,P(c),25¢(c)
   Price, Rigid(c);rep 30.00

118-ROB ROY

By Sir Walter Scott
04/54 **(119)** RP,WIP,P(c),Original . 200.00
02/67 **(167)** RP,WIP,P(c);rep 60.00

Classics Illus.

119-SOLDERS OF FORTUNE

By Richard Harding Davis
05/54 **(120)** KS,P(c),Original 150.00
03/67 **(166)** KS,P(c);rep 32.00
Sg/70 **(169)** KS,P(c),25¢(c)
Price, Rigid(c);rep 30.00

120-THE HURRICANE

By Charles Nordhoff
1954 **(121)** LC,LC P(c),Original . . 150.00
03/67 **(166)** LC,LC P(c);rep 45.00

121-WILD BILL HICKOK

Author Unknown
07/54 **(122)** MI,ST,P(c),Original . . 110.00
05/56 **(132)** MI,ST,P(c);rep 20.00
11/57 **(141)** MI,ST,P(c);rep 20.00
01/60 **(154)** MI,ST,P(c);rep 20.00
62/63 **(167)** MI,ST,P(c);rep 18.00
08/64 **(167)** MI,ST,P(c);rep 18.00
04/67 **(166)** MI,ST,P(c);rep 18.00
Wr/69 **(169)** MI,ST,P(c),Rigid
(c);rep 18.00

122-THE MUTINEERS

By Charles Boardman Hawes
09/54 **(123)** PrC,P(c),Original . . . 125.00
01/57 **(136)** PrC,P(c);rep 20.00
09/58 **(146)** PrC,P(c);rep 20.00
09/60 **(158)** PrC,P(c);rep 18.00
11/63 **(167)** PrC,P(c);rep 18.00
03/65 **(167)** PrC,P(c);rep 18.00
08/67 **(166)** PrC,P(c);rep 18.00

123-FANG AND CLAW

By Frank Buck
11/54 **(124)** LnS,P(c),Original . . . 125.00
07/56 **(133)** LnS,P(c);rep 20.00
03/58 **(143)** LnS,P(c);rep 20.00
01/60 **(154)** LnS,P(c);rep 18.00
62/63 **(167)** LnS,P(c),Erroneously
Has Original Date;rep 18.00
09/65 **(169)** LnS,P(c);rep 18.00

124-THE WAR OF THE WORLDS

By H. G. Wells
01/55 **(125)** LC,LC P(c),Original . 200.00
03/56 **(131)** LC,LC P(c);rep 20.00
11/57 **(141)** LC,LC P(c);rep 20.00
01/59 **(148)** LC,LC P(c);rep 20.00
05/60 **(156)** LC,LC P(c);rep 25.00
1962 **(165)** LC,LC P(c);rep 20.00
62/63 **(167)** LC,LC P(c);rep 20.00
11/64 **(167)** LC,LC P(c);rep 20.00
11/65 **(167)** LC,LC P(c);rep 20.00
1968 **(166)** LC,LC P(c),25¢(c)
Price;rep 20.00
Sr/70 **(169)** LC,LC P(c),Rigid
(c);rep 20.00

125-THE OX BOW INCIDENT

By Walter Van Tilberg Clark
03/55 **(——)** NN,P(c),Original 125.00
03/58 **(143)** NN,P(c);rep 20.00
09/59 **(152)** NN,P(c);rep 20.00
03/61 **(149)** NN,P(c);rep 20.00
62/63 **(167)** NN,P(c);rep 18.00
11/64 **(167)** NN,P(c);rep 18.00
04/67 **(166)** NN,P(c);rep 18.00
r/69 **(169)** NN,P(c),25¢(c)
Price, Rigid(c);rep 18.00

126-THE DOWNFALL

By Emile Zola
05/55 **(——)** LC,LC P(c),Original,'
Picture Progress'Replaces
Reorder List. 125.00
08/64 **(167)** LC,LC P(c);rep 30.00
1968 **(166)** LC,LC P(c),25¢(c)
Price;rep 30.00

127-THE KING OF THE MOUNTAINS

By Edmond About
07/55 **(128)** NN,P(c),Original 150.00
06/64 **(167)** NN,P(c);rep 22.00
Fl/68 **(166)** NN,P(c),25¢(c)
Price;rep 22.00

128-MACBETH

By William Shakespeare
09/55 **(128)** AB,P(c),Original 125.00
03/58 **(143)** AB,P(c);rep 20.00
09/60 **(158)** AB,P(c);rep 20.00
62/63 **(167)** AB,P(c);rep 18.00
06/64 **(167)** AB,P(c);rep 18.00
04/67 **(166)** AB,P(c);rep 18.00
1968 **(166)** AB,P(c),25¢(c)
Price;rep 18.00
Sg/70 **(169)** AB,P(c),Rigid(c);rep . . 18.00

129-DAVY CROCKETT

Author Unknown
11/55 **(129)** LC,P(c),Original 200.00
09/66 **(167)** LC,P(c);rep 125.00

CI #130, Caesar's Conquests
© *Gilberton Publications*

130-CAESAR'S CONQUESTS

By Julius Caesar
01/56 **(130)** JO,P(c),Original 125.00
01/58 **(142)** JO,P(c);rep 20.00
09/59 **(152)** JO,P(c);rep 20.00
03/61 **(149)** JO,P(c);rep 20.00
62/63 **(167)** JO,P(c);rep 18.00
10/64 **(167)** JO,P(c);rep 18.00
04/66 **(167)** JO,P(c);rep 18.00

131-THE COVERED WAGON

By Emerson Hough
03/56 **(131)** NN,P(c),Original 125.00
03/58 **(143)** NN,P(c);rep 20.00

09/59 **(152)** NN,P(c);rep 20.00
09/60 **(158)** NN,P(c);rep 20.00
62/63 **(167)** NN,P(c);rep 18.00
11/64 **(167)** NN,P(c);rep 18.00
04/66 **(167)** NN,P(c);rep 18.00
Wr/69 **(169)** NN,P(c),25¢(c)
Price, Rigid(c);rep 18.00

132-THE DARK FRIGATE

By Charles Boardman Hawes
05/56 **(132)** EW&RWb,P(c),Orig. . 125.00
05/59 **(150)** EW&RWb,P(c);rep . . . 20.00
01/64 **(167)** EW&RWb,P(c);rep . . . 20.00
05/67 **(166)** EW&RWb,P(c);rep . . . 20.00

133-THE TIME MACHINE

By H. G. Wells
07/56 **(132)** LC,P(c),Original 175.00
01/58 **(142)** LC,P(c);rep 20.00
09/59 **(152)** LC,P(c);rep 20.00
09/60 **(158)** LC,P(c);rep 20.00
62/63 **(167)** LC,P(c);rep 20.00
06/64 **(167)** LC,P(c);rep 25.00
03/66 **(167)** LC,P(c);rep 20.00
03/66 **(167)** LC,P(c),N# Or Price;
rep 20.00
12/67 **(166)** LC,P(c);rep 20.00
Wr/71 **(169)** LC,P(c),25¢(c)
Price, Rigid(c);rep 20.00

134-ROMEO AND JULIET

By William Shakespeare
09/56 **(134)** GE,P(c),Original 125.00
03/61 **(161)** GE,P(c);rep 20.00
09/63 **(167)** GE,P(c);rep 18.00
05/65 **(167)** GE,P(c);rep 18.00
06/67 **(166)** GE,P(c);rep 18.00
Wr/69 **(166)** GE,EdM New P(c),
25¢(c)Price, Rigid(c);rep 32.00

135-WATERLOO

By Emile Erckmann & Alexandre Chatrian
11/56 **(135)** Grl,AB P(c),Original . 125.00
11/59 **(153)** Grl,AB P(c);rep 20.00
62/63 **(167)** Grl,AB P(c);rep 18.00
09/64 **(167)** Grl,AB P(c);rep 18.00
1968 **(166)** Grl,AB P(c),25¢(c)
Price; rep 18.00

136-LORD JIM

By Joseph Conrad
01/57 **(136)** GE,P(c),Original 150.00
62/63 **(165)** GE,P(c);rep 18.00
03/64 **(167)** GE,P(c);rep 18.00
09/66 **(167)** GE,P(c);rep 18.00
Sr/69 **(169)** GE,P(c),25¢(c)
Price, Rigid(c);rep 18.00

137-THE LITTLE SAVAGE

By Captain Frederick Marryat
03/57 **(136)** GE,P(c),Original 125.00
01/59 **(148)** GE,P(c);rep 20.00
05/60 **(156)** GE,P(c);rep 20.00
62/63 **(167)** GE,P(c);rep 18.00
10/64 **(167)** GE,P(c);rep 18.00
08/67 **(166)** GE,P(c);rep 18.00
Sg/70 **(169)** GE,P(c),25¢(c)
Price, Rigid(c);rep 18.00

138-A JOURNEY TO THE CENTER OF THE EARTH

By Jules Verne
05/57 **(136)** NN,P(c),Original 175.00
09/58 **(146)** NN,P(c);rep 20.00
05/60 **(156)** NN,P(c);rep 20.00

09/60 **(158)** NN,P(c);rep 20.00
62/63 **(167)** NN,P(c);rep 18.00
06/64 **(167)** NN,P(c);rep 20.00
04/66 **(167)** NN,P(c);rep 20.00
1968 **(166)** NN,P(c),25¢(c)
   Price;rep 18.00

139-IN THE REIGN OF TERROR
By George Alfred Henty
07/57 **(139)** GE,P(c),Original 125.00
01/60 **(154)** GE,P(c);rep 20.00
62/63 **(167)** GE,P(c),Erroneously
   Has Original Date;rep 18.00
07/64 **(167)** GE,P(c);rep 20.00
1968 **(166)** GE,P(c),25¢(c)
   Price;rep 18.00

140-ON JUNGLE TRAILS
By Frank Buck
09/57 **(140)** NN,P(c),Original 125.00
05/59 **(150)** NN,P(c);rep 20.00
01/61 **(160)** NN,P(c);rep 20.00
09/63 **(167)** NN,P(c);rep 18.00
09/65 **(167)** NN,P(c);rep 18.00

141-CASTLE DANGEROUS
By Sir Walter Scott
11/57 **(141)** StC,P(c),Original 150.00
09/59 **(152)** STC,P(c);rep 20.00
62/63 **(167)** StC,P(c);rep 18.00
07/67 **(166)** StC,P(c);rep 18.00

142-ABRAHAM LINCOLN
By Benjamin Thomas
01/58 **(142)** NN,P(c),Original 150.00
01/60 **(154)** NN,P(c);rep 20.00
09/60 **(158)** NN,P(c);rep 20.00
10/63 **(167)** NN,P(c);rep 18.00
07/65 **(167)** NN,P(c);rep 18.00
11/67 **(166)** NN,P(c);rep. 18.00
Fl/69 **(169)** NN,P(c),25¢(c) Price,
   Rigid(c);rep 18.00

143-KIM
By Rudyard Kipling
03/58 **(143)** JO,P(c)Original 125.00
62/63 **(165)** JO,P(c);rep 18.00
11/63 **(167)** JO,P(c);rep 18.00
08/65 **(167)** JO,P(c);rep 18.00
Wr/69 **(169)** JO,P(c),25¢(c) Price,
   Rigid(c);rep 18.00

144-THE FIRST MEN IN THE MOON
By H. G. Wells
05/58 **(143)** GWb,AW,AT,RKr,
   GMC P(c), Original 175.00
11/59 **(153)** GWb,AW,AT,RKr,
   GMC, P(c); rep 20.00
03/61 **(161)** GWb,AW,AT,RKr,
   GMC, P(c); rep 18.00
62/63 **(167)** GWb,AW,AT,RKr,
   GMC, P(c); rep 18.00
12/65 **(167)** GWb,AW,AT,RKr,
   GMC, P(c); rep 18.00
Fl/68 **(166)** GWb,AW,AT,RKr,GMC
   P(c),25¢(c) Price,Rigid(c);rep . 18.00
Wr/69 **(169)** GWb,AW,AT,RKr,GMC
   P(c), Rigid(c);rep 28.00

145-THE CRISIS
by Winston Churchill
07/58 **(143)** GE,P(c),Original 125.00
05/60 **(156)** GE,P(c);rep 20.00
10/63 **(167)** GE,P(c);rep 18.00

03/65 **(167)** GE,P(c);rep 18.00
1968 **(166)** GE,P(c),25¢(c)
   Price;rep 18.00

146-WITH FIRE AND SWORD
By Henryk Sienkiewicz
09/58 **(143)** GWb,P(c),Original . . 125.00
05/60 **(156)** GWb,P(c);rep 25.00
11/63 **(167)** GWb,P(c);rep 20.00
03/65 **(167)** GWb,P(c);rep 20.00

147-BEN-HUR
By Lew Wallace
11/58 **(147)** JO,P(c),Original 125.00
11/59 **(153)** JO,P(c);rep 65.00
09/60 **(158)** JO,P(c);rep 20.00
62/63 **(167)** JO,P(c),Has the
   Original Date;rep 20.00
——— **(167)** JO,P(c);rep 18.00
02/65 **(167)** JO,P(c);rep 18.00
09/66 **(167)** JO,P(c);rep 18.00
Fl/68 **(166)** JO,P(c),25¢(c)Price,
   Both Rigid & Soft (c)s;rep 50.00

148-THE BUCKANEER
By Lyle Saxon
01/59 **(148)** GE&RJ,NS P(c),orig. 125.00
——— **(568)** GE&RJ,NS P(c),Juniors
   List Only;rep 20.00
62/63 **(167)** GE&RJ,NS P(c);rep . 20.00
09/65 **(167)** GE&RJ,NS P(c);rep . . 20.00
Sr/69 **(169)** GE&RJ,NS P(c),25¢(c)
   Price, Rigid(c);rep 20.00

149-OFF ON A COMET
By Jules Verne
03/59 **(149)** GMc,P(c),Original. . . 125.00
03/60 **(155)** GMc,P(c);rep 20.00
03/61 **(149)** GMc,P(c);rep 20.00
12/63 **(167)** GMc,P(c);rep 18.00
02/65 **(167)** GMc,P(c);rep 18.00
10/66 **(167)** GMc,P(c);rep 18.00
Fl/68 **(166)** GMc,EdM New P(c),
   25¢(c)Price;rep 30.00

150-THE VIRGINIAN
By Owen Winster
05/59 **(150)** NN,DrG P(c),Original 175.00
1961 **(164)** NN,DrG P(c);rep 30.00
62/63 **(167)** NN,DrG P(c);rep. 35.00
12/65 **(167)** NN,DrG P(c);rep. 30.00

151-WON BY THE SWORD
By George Alfred Henty
07/59 **(150)** JTg,P(c),Original . . . 125.00
1961 **(164)** JTg,P(c);rep. 25.00
10/63 **(167)** JTg,P(c);rep 25.00
1963 **(167)** JTg,P(c);rep 25.00
07/67 **(166)** JTg,P(c);rep 25.00

152-WILD ANIMALS I HAVE KNOWN
By Ernest Thompson Seton
09/59 **(152)** LbC,LbC P(c),Orig. . . 150.00
03/61 **(149)** LbC,LbC P(c),P(c);rep 20.00
09/63 **(167)** LbC,LbC P(c);rep 18.00
08/65 **(167)** LbC,LbC P(c);rep 18.00
fl/69 **(169)** LbC,LbC P(c),25¢(c)
   Price, Rigid(c);rep 18.00

153-THE INVISIBLE MAN
By H. G. Wells
11/59 **(153)** NN,GB P(c),Original . 150.00
03/61 **(149)** NN,GB P(c);rep 20.00

62/63 **(167)** NN,GB P(c);rep 18.00
02/65 **(167)** NN,GB P(c);rep 18.00
09/66 **(167)** NN,GB P(c);rep 18.00
Wr/69 **(166)** NN,GB P(c),25¢(c)
   Price, Rigid(c);rep 18.00
Sg/71 **(169)** NN,GB P(c),Rigid(c),
   Words Spelling'Invisible Man'
   Are' Solid'Not'Invisible';rep . . . 18.00

154-THE CONSPIRACY OF PONTIAC
By Francis Parkman
01/60 **(154)** GMc,GMc P(c),
   Original 125.00
11/63 **(167)** GMc,GMc P(c);rep . . . 30.00
07/64 **(167)** GMc,GMc P(c);rep . . . 30.00
12/67 **(166)** GMc,GMc P(c);rep . . . 30.00

155-THE LION OF THE NORTH
By George Alfred Henty
03/60 **(154)** NN,GMc P(c),Orig. . . 125.00
01/64 **(167)** NN,GMc P(c);rep 25.00
1967 **(166)** NN,GMc P(c),25¢(c)
   Price; rep. 20.00

CI #156, The Conquest of Mexico
© Gilberton Publications

156-THE CONQUEST OF MEXICO
By Bernal Diaz Del Castillo
05/60 **(156)** BPr,BPr P(c),Original 125.00
01/64 **(167)** BPr,BPr P(c);rep. 20.00
08/67 **(166)** BPr,BPr P(c);rep. 20.00
Sg/70 **(169)** BPr,BPr P(c),25¢(c)
   Price; Rigid(c);rep 18.00

157-LIVES OF THE HUNTED
By Ernest Thompson Seton
07/60 **(156)** NN,LbC P(c),Original 150.00
02/64 **(167)** NN,LbC P(c);rep. 28.00
10/67 **(166)** NN,LbC P(c);rep. 28.00

158-THE CONSPIRATORS
By Alexandre Dumas
09/60 **(156)** GMc,GMc P(c),
   Original 150.00
07/64 **(167)** GMc,GMc P(c);rep . . . 28.00
10/67 **(166)** GMc,GMc P(c);rep . . . 28.00

159-THE OCTOPUS
By Frank Norris
11/60 **(159)** GM&GE,LbC P(c),
Original 150.00
02/64 **(167)** GM&GE,LbC P(c);rep. 28.00
166 **(1967)** GM&GE,LbC P(c),25¢(c)
Price;rep 28.00

160-THE FOOD OF THE GODS
By H.G. Wells
01/61 **(159)** TyT,GMc P(c),Orig. . . 150.00
01/61 **(160)** TyT,GMc P(c),Original;
Same Except For the HRN# . . 60.00
01/64 **(167)** TyT,GMc P(c);rep 28.00
06/67 **(166)** TyT,GMc P(c);rep 28.00

161-CLEOPATRA
By H. Rider Haggard
03/61 **(159)** NN,Pch P(c),Original 125.00
01/64 **(167)** NN,Pch P(c);rep 30.00
08/67 **(166)** NN,Pch P(c);rep 30.00

162-ROBUR THE CONQUEROR
By Jules Verne
05/61 **(162)** GM&DPn,CJ P(c),
Original 125.00
07/64 **(167)** GM&DPn,CJ P(c);rep. 28.00
08/67 **(166)** GM&DPn,CJ P(c);rep. 28.00

163-MASTER OF THE WORLD
By Jules Verne
07/61 **(163)** GM,P(c),Original. . . . 125.00
01/65 **(167)** GM,P(c);rep 28.00
1968 **(166)** GM,P(c),25¢(c)
Price;rep 28.00

164-THE COSSACK CHIEF
By Nicolai Gogol
1961 **(164)** SyM,P(c),Original 125.00
04/65 **(167)** SyM,P(c);rep 28.00
FI/68 **(166)** SyM,P(c),25¢(c)
Price;rep 28.00

165-THE QUEEN'S NECKLACE
by Alexandre Dumas
01/62 **(164)** GM,P(c),Original. . . . 125.00

CI Jr. #513, Pinocchio
© Print Mint

04/65 **(167)** GM,P(c);rep 28.00
FI/68 **(166)** GM,P(c),25¢(c)
Price;rep 28.00

166-TIGERS AND TRAITORS
By Jules Verne
05/62 **(165)** NN,P(c),Original 175.00
02/64 **(167)** NN,P(c);rep 40.00
11/66 **(167)** NN,P(c);rep. 40.00

167-FAUST
By Johann Wolfgang von Goethe
08/62 **(165)** NN,NN P(c),Original . 250.00
02/64 **(167)** NN,NN P(c);rep 100.00
06/67 **(166)** NN,NN P(c);rep 100.00

168-IN FREEDOM'S CAUSE
By George Alfred Henty
Wr/69 **(169)** GE&RC,P(c),
Original, Rigid (c). 275.00

169-NEGRO AMERICANS THE EARLY YEARS
AUTHOR UNKNOWN
Sg/69 **(166)** NN,NN P(c),
Original, Rigid(c) 300.00
Sg/69 **(169)** NN,NN P(c),
Rigid; rep 125.00

CLASSICS ILLUSTRATED GIANTS
An Illustrated Library of Great
Adventure Stories -(reps. of
Issues 6,7,8,10) 2,200.00
An Illustrated Library of Exciting
Mystery Stories -(reps. of
Issues 30,21,40,13) 2,400.00
An Illustrated Library of Great
Indian Stories -(reps. of
Issues 4,17,22,37) 2,200.00

CLASSICS ILLUSTRATED JUNIOR
Oct., 1953–Spring., 1971
501-Snow White and the
Seven Dwarfs 150.00
502-The Ugly Duckling 100.00
503-Cinderella 75.00
504-The Pied Piper 75.00
505-The Sleeping Beauty 75.00
506-The Three Little Pigs 75.00
507-Jack and the Beanstalk 75.00
508-Goldilocks & the Three Bears. 75.00
509-Beauty and the Beast 75.00
510-Little Red Riding Hood 75.00
511-Puss-N-Boots 75.00
512-Rumpelstiltskin 75.00
513-Pinocchio 75.00
514-The Steadfast Tin Soldier . . . 100.00
515-Johnny Appleseed 75.00
516-Aladdin and His Lamp 75.00
517-The Emperor's New Clothes . . 75.00
518-The Golden Goose 75.00
519-Paul Bunyan 75.00
520-Thumbelina 75.00
521-King of the Golden River 75.00
522-The Nightingale. 75.00
523-The Gallant Tailor 75.00
524-The Wild Swans 75.00
525-The Little Mermaid 75.00
526-The Frog Prince 75.00
527-The Golden-Haired Giant 75.00
528-The Penny Prince 75.00
529-The Magic Servants 75.00

530-The Golden Bird 75.00
531-Rapunzel. 75.00
532-The Dancing Princesses. 75.00
533-The Magic Fountain 75.00
534-The Golden Touch 75.00
535-The Wizard of Oz 100.00
536-The Chimney Sweep 75.00
537-The Three Fairies 75.00
538-Silly Hans 75.00
539-The Enchanted Fish 75.00
540-The Tinder-Box 75.00
541-Snow White and Rose Red . . 75.00
542-The Donkey's Tail 75.00
543-The House in the Woods 75.00
544-The Golden Fleece 75.00
545-The Glass Mountain 75.00
546-The Elves and the Shoemaker 75.00
547-The Wishing Table 75.00
548-The Magic Pitcher 75.00
549-Simple Kate 75.00
550-The Singing Donkey 75.00
551-The Queen Bee 75.00
552-The Three Little Dwarfs 75.00
553-King Thrushbeard 75.00
554-The Enchanted Deer 75.00
555-The Three Golden Apples. . . . 75.00
556-The Elf Mound 75.00
557-Silly Willy. 75.00
558-The Magic Dish,LbC(c). 75.00
559-The Japanese Lantern,LbC(c) 90.00
560-The Doll Princess,LbC(c) 90.00
561-Hans Humdrum,LbC(c) 75.00
562-The Enchanted Pony,LbC(c) . 90.00
563-The Wishing Well,LbC(c) 75.00
564-The Salt Mountain,LbC(c). . . . 75.00
565-The Silly Princess,LbC(c) 75.00
566-Clumsy Hans,LbC(c). 75.00
567-The Bearskin Soldier,LbC(c). . 75.00
568-The Happy Hedgehog,LbC(c). 75.00
569-The Three Giants 75.00
570-The Pearl Princess 75.00
571-How Fire Came to the Indians 75.00
572-The Drummer Boy 75.00
573-The Crystal Ball 75.00
574-Brightboots 75.00
575-The Fearless Prince 75.00
576-The Princess Who Saw
Everything 90.00
577-The Runaway Dumpling 100.00

CLASSICS ILLLUSTRATED SPECIAL ISSUE
Dec., 1955–July, 1962
N# United Nations 425.00
129-The Story of Jesus,Jesus on
mountain(c) 150.00
129a-Three Camels(c). 150.00
129b-Mountain(c),HRN to 161 . 125.00
129c-Mountain(c) (1968) 100.00
132A-The Story of America 125.00
135A-The Ten Commandments. . 125.00
138A-Adventures in Science 125.00
138Aa-HRN to 149 . . . . 100.00
138Ab-rep.,12/61 . . . . 100.00
141A-GE,The Rough Rider 125.00
144A-RC,GE,Blazing the Trails . . 125.00
147A-RC,GE,Crossing the
Rockies 125.00
150A-Grl,Royal Canadian Police. 125.00
153A-GE,Men, Guns, & Cattle. . . 125.00
156A-GE,GM,The Atomic Age . . . 125.00
159A-GE,GM,Rockets, Jets and
Missiles 125.00
162A-RC,GE,War Between
the States 200.00
165A-RC/GE,JK,Grl,To the Stars. 125.00
166A-RC/GE,JK,Grl,World War II 150.00
167A-RC/GE,JK,Prehistoric
World 150.00
167Aa-HRN to 167. . . . . 110.00

UNDERGROUND

ADVENTURES OF FAT FREDDY'S CAT, THE
Rip Off Press, Feb., 1977
1 . . . . 20.00
2 . . . . 12.00
3 . . . . 15.00
4 . . . . 10.00
5 & 6 . . . . @10.00

AMAZING DOPE TALES
Greg Shaw
1 Untrimmed black and white pages,
  out of order;artist unknown . . 110.00
2 Trimmed and proper pages 95.00

AMERICAN SPLENDOR
Harvey Pekar, May, 1976
1 B:Harvey Pekar Stories,
  HP,RCr,GDu,GBu 25.00
2 HP,RCr,GDu,GBu 10.00
3 HP,RCr,GDu,GBu 10.00
4 HP,RCr,GDu,GBu 8.00
5 HP,RCr,GDu,GBu 8.00
6 HP,RCr,GDu,GBu 7.00
7 HP,GSh,GDu,GBu 5.00
8 HP,GSh,GDu,GBu 3.00
9 and 10 HP,GSh,GDu,GBu . . . . @3.00
11 . . . . 3.00
12 . . . . 4.50
13 thru 19 . . . . @4.00
20 E:Harvey Pekar Stories 4.00

ANTHOLOGY OF SLOW DEATH
Wingnut Press/Last Gasp
1 140 pgs, RCr,RCo, GiS, DSh,
  Harlan Ellison VB,RTu 37.00

APEX TREASURY OF UNDERGROUND COMICS, THE
Links Books Inc., Oct., 1974
1 . . . . 40.00

APEX TREASURY OF UNDERGROUND COMICS –BEST OF BIJOU FUNNIES
Quick Fox, 1981
1 Paperback,comix,various artists 21.00

ARCADE THE COMICS REVUE
Print Mint Inc. Spring, 1975
1 ASp,BG,RCr,SRo,SCW 25.00
2 ASp,BG,RCr,SRo 15.00
3 ASp,BG,RCr,RW,SCW 10.00
4 ASp,BG,RCr,WBu,RW,SCW . . . 10.00
5 thru 7 ASp,BG,SRo,RW,SCW . @7.50

BABYFAT
Comix World/Clay Geerdes, 1978
1 B:8pg news parodies, one page
  comix by various artists 4.50
2 thru 9 same . . . . @3.00
10 thru 26 same . . . . @2.00

Arcade The Comics Revue #4
© Print Mint

BATTLE OF THE TITANS
University of Illinois SF Society, 1972
1 Sci-Fi;VB,JGa 50.00

BEST BUY COMICS
Last Gasp Eco-Funnies
1 Rep Whole Earth Review;RCr . . . 3.50
1-shot R. Crumb reprints (2004) . . . 2.50

BEST OF BIJOU FUNNIES, THE
Links Books Inc., 1975
1 164 pgs,paperback 250.00

BEST OF RIP-OFF PRESS
Rip Off Press Inc., 1973
1 132 pgs paperback,SCW,
  RCr,SRo,RW 25.00
2 100 pgs,GS,FT 27.50
3 100 pgs,FS 15.00
4 132 pgs,GiS,DSh 16.00

BIG ASS
Rip Off Press, 1969–71
1 28 pgs,RCr. 80.00
2 RCr 50.00

BIJOU FUNNIES
Bijou Publishing Empire, 1968
1 B:JLy,editor;RCr,GS SW 300.00
2 RCr,GS,SW 125.00
3 RCr,SWi,JsG 80.00
4 SWi,JsG 45.00
5 SWi,JsG 50.00
6 E:JLy,editor,SWi,RCr,JsG 40.00
7 and 8 . . . . @40.00

BINKY BROWN MEETS THE HOLY VIRGIN MARY
Last Gasp Eco-Funnies, March, 1972
N# Autobiography about Growing up
  w/a Catholic Neurosis,JsG . . . 25.00

2nd Printing:only text in
  bottom left panel 12.00
TPB Sampler (2004) 16.95

BIZARRE SEX
Kitchen Sink Komix, May, 1972
1 B:DKi,editor,various artists 30.00
2 . . . . 25.00
3 . . . . 20.00
4 thru 6 . . . . @15.00
7 . . . . 10.00
8 . . . . 10.00
9 Omaha the Cat Dancer,RW 25.00
10 inc.Omaha the Cat Dancer,RW 20.00

BLACK LAUGHTER
Black Laughter Pub. Co, Nov,. 1972
1 James Dixon art 64.00

BLOOD FROM A STONE (GUIDE TO TAX REFORM)
New York Public Interest Research Group Inc., 1977
1 Tax reform proposals 15.00

BOBBY LONDON RETROSPECTIVE AND ART PORTFOLIO
Cartoonist Representatives
1 . . . . 20.00

BOBMAN AND TEDDY
Parrallax Comic Books Inc., 1966
1 RFK & Ted Kennedy's struggle to
  control Democratic party 55.00

BODE'S CARTOON CONCERT
Dell, Sept., 1973
1 132 pgs; VB 27.50

BOGEYMAN COMICS
San Fransisco Comic Book Co., 1969
1 Horror,RHa. 65.00
2 Horror,RHa. 50.00
The Company & Sons
3 . . . . 35.00

BUFFALO RAG/THE DEAD CONCERT COMIX
Kenny Laramey, Dec., 1973
1 Alice in Wonderland parody 60.00

CAPTAIN GUTS
The Print Mint,1969
1 Super patriotV:Counter
  culture 30.00
2 V:Black Panthers 20.00
3 V:Dope Smugglers 20.00

CAPTAIN STICKY
Captain Sticky, 1974–75
1 Super lawyer V:SocialInjustice . 20.00

All comics prices listed are for *Near Mint* condition.

CARTOON HISTORY OF THE UNIVERSE
Rip Off Press, Sept., 1978
1 Evolution of Everything;
   B:Larry Gonick 12.00
2 Sticks and Stones 8.00
3 River Realms-Sumer & Egypt .. 8.00
4 Part of the Old Testament 5.00
5 Brains and Bronze 5.00
6 Who are these Athenians 5.00

CASCADE COMIX MONTHLY
Everyman Studios, March, 1978
1 Interviews,articles about
   comix & comix artists 8.00
2 and 3 same .... @8.00
4 thru 11 .... @4.00
12 thru 23................. @3.00

CHECKERED DEMON
Last Gasp, July, 1977
1 SCW 15.00
2 SCW 8.50
3 SCW 6.50

CHEECH WIZARD
Office of Student Publications, Syracuse U, 1967
n/n VB................... 150.00

Cherry Poptart #1
© Last Gasp

CHERRY POPTART
Last Gasp, 1982–85
1 by Larry Welz.............. 10.00
2............................ 7.00
Becomes:
CHERRY
3 .... 5.00
4 .... 5.00
5 .... 5.00
6 thru 13 .... @4.00
Kitchen Sink
14 .... 4.00
15 .... 4.00
TPB Cherry Collection #1 .... 15.00
TPB Cherry Collection #2 .... 15.00
TPB Cherry Collection #3 .... 13.00
Cherry's Jubilee #1 thru #4 ..... @3.00

CHICAGO MIRROR
Jay Lynch/Mirror Publishing Empire, Autumn, 1967
1 B:Bijou Funnies 50.00
2 same 40.00
3 same 125.00

COCAINE COMIX
Last Gas, Inc., 1976–82
1 .... 15.00
2 thru 4 .... @10.00
2005
1 .... 3.00
2 .... 3.00

COLLECTED CHEECH WIZARD, THE
Company & Sons, 1972
n/n VB 60.00
Print Mint, 1976
n/n VB 15.00

COLLECTED TRASHMAN #1, THE
Fat City & The Red Mountain Tribe Productions
n/n SRo.................... 32.50

COMICS & COMIX
Oct., 1975
1 .... 15.00

COMIX BOOK
Magazine Management Co. Oct., 1974
1 Compilation for newsstand
   distribution 20.00
2 and 3 .... @10.00
Kitchen Sink Enterprises
4 .... 20.00
5 .... 10.00

COMIX COLLECTOR, THE
Archival Press Inc., Dec., 1979
1 Fanzine 6.00
2 & 3 Fanzine .... @5.00

COMMIES FROM MARS
Kitchen Sink, March, 1973
1 TB 40.00
Last Gasp
2 thru 5 TB .... @15.00

COMPLETE FRITZ THE CAT
Belier Press 1978
n/n RCr,SRo,DSh............. 65.00

CONSPIRACY CAPERS
The Conspiracy, 1969
1 Benefit Legal Defense of the
   Chicago-8 .... 100.00

DAN O'NEIL'S COMICS & STORIES
Company & Sons, Vol.1
1 B:Dan O'Neill.............. 50.00
2 & 3 .... @30.00
1971 Vol. 2
1 .... 6.50
2 and E:Dan O'Neill .... @4.50

DAS KAMPF
Vaughn Bode, May, 1963
N# 100 Loose pgs. 750.00
2nd Printing 52pgs.-produced by
   W.Bachner & Bagginer,1977 .. 25.00

DEADBONE EROTICA
Bantam Books Inc., April, 1971
n/n 132 pgs VB.............. 50.00

DEADCENTER CLEAVAGE
April, 1971
1 14 pgs 50.00

DEATH RATTLE
Kitchen Sink, June, 1972
1 RCo,TB 25.00
2 TB 20.00
3 TB 16.00

DESPAIR
The Print Mint, 1969
1 RCr 50.00

DIRTY DUCK BOOK, THE
Company & Sons, March, 1972
1 Bobby London 30.00

DISNEY RAPES THE 1st AMENDMENT
Dan O'Neil, 1974
1 Benefit Air Pirates V:Disney
   Law suit; Dan O'Neill 15.00

DR. ATOMIC
Last Gasp Eco-Funnies, Sept., 1972
1 B:Larry S. Todd 15.00
2 and 3 .... @12.00
4 .... 10.00
5 E:Larry S. Todd 8.00
6 .... 6.00

DR. ATOMIC'S MARIJUANA MULTIPLIER
Kistone Press, 1974
1 How to grow great pot 10.00

DOPE COMIX
Kitchen Sink, Feb., 1978
1 Drugs comix;various artists 10.00
2 same 8.00
3 & 4 LSD issue .... @6.00
5 Omaha the Cat Dancer, RW ... 10.00

DOPIN DAN
Last Gasp Eco-Funnies, April, 1972
1 TR 15.00
2 and 3 TR .... @10.00
4 Todays Army,TR............ 9.00

DORI STORIES
Last Gasp, 2004
TPB Dori Deda collection........ 20.00

DRAWINGS BY S. CLAY WILSON
San Francisco Graphics
1 28 pgs 200.00

DYING DOLPHIN
The Print Mint ,1970
n/n 20.00

EBON
**San Francisco Comic
Book Company**
1 Comix version; RCr 30.00
1 Tabloid version 20.00

EL PERFECTO COMICS
The Print Mint, 1973
N# Benefit Timothy Leary 30.00
2nd Printing-1975 . . . . 4.00

ETERNAL TRUTH
Sunday Funnies Comic Corp
1 Christian Comix 25.00

EVERMUCH WAVE
Atlantis Distributors
1 Nunzio the Narc; Adventures
    of God 60.00

E.Z. WOLF'S
ASTRAL OUTHOUSE
Last Gasp, 2005
1-shot 3.00

FABULOUS FURRY
FREAK BROTHERS, THE
COLLECTED ADVENTURES OF
Rip Off Press, #1 Feb., 1971
1 GiS 90.00
FURTHER ADVENTURES OF
Rip Off Press, #2
1 GiS,DSh 60.00
A YEAR PASSES LIKE
NOTHING WITH
Rip Off Press #3
1 GiS 25.00
BROTHER CAN YOU
SPARE $.75 FOR
Rip Off Press #4
1 GiS,DSh 20.00
FABULOUS FURRY
FREAK BROTHERS, THE
Rip Off Press #5
1 GiS,DSh 15.00
SIX SNAPPY SOCKERS
FROM THE ARCHIVES OF
Rip Off Press #6
1 GiS 10.00

FANTAGOR
1970
1 (Corben), fanzine 125.00
Last Gasp
1a 22.00
2 & 3 . . . . @25.00
4 . . . . 35.00

FEDS 'N' HEADS
Gilbert Shelton/Print Mint, 1968
N# I:Fabulous Furry Freak Bros.;
    Has no `Print Mint' Address
    24 pgs. 400.00
2nd printing, 28 pgs. 60.00
3rd printing, May, 1969 . . . . 50.00
4th printing, Says `Forth
    Printing' 25.00

5th-12th printings . . . . @10.00
13th printing 7.00
14th printing 6.00

FELCH
Keith Green
1 RW,SCW,RCr 45.00

FEVER PITCH
**Kitchen Sink Enterprises,
July, 1976**
1 RCo 25.00
Jabberwocky Graphix
2 250 signed & numbered 20.00
3 400 signed & numbered 18.00
4 . . . . 10.00

50'S FUNNIES
Kitchen Sink Enterprises, 1980
1 Larry Shell, editor,various
    artists 10.00

FLAMING CARROT
**Kilian Barracks Free Press,
1981**
1 Bob Budden,various artists 15.00

FLASH THEATRE
Oogle Productions, 1970
1 44 pgs 50.00

FLESHAPOIDS FROM
EARTH
Popular Culture, Dec., 1974
1 36 pgs 40.00

THE COMPLETE FOO!
Bijou Publishing, Sept., 1980
1 RCr, Charles Crumb, r:Crumb
    brothers fanzines 50.00

FRITZ BUGS OUT
Ballentine Books, 1972
n/n RCr 70.00

FRITZ THE CAT
Ballentine Books, 1969
n/n RCr 125.00

FRITZ THE NO-GOOD
Ballentine Books, 1972
n/n RCr 60.00

FRITZ: SECRET AGENT
FOR THE CIA
Ballentine Books, 1972
n/n RCr 60.00

FUNNY AMINALS
**Apex Novelties/Don Donahue,
1972**
1 RCr 65.00

GAY COMIX
Kitchen Sink Sept., 1981
1 36 pgs 8.00
2 36 pgs 6.00

GEN OF HIROSHIMA
**Educomics/Leonard Rifas,
Jan., 1980**
1 Antiwar comix by Hiroshima
    survivor Keiji Nakawaza 10.00

---

2 same 8.00

GHOST MOTHER COMICS
John "Mad" Peck, 1969
1 SCw,JsG 55.00

GIMMEABREAK COMIX
Rhuta Press, Feb., 1971
2 48 pgs, #0 & #1 were advertised,but .
    may not have been printed 125.00

GIRLS & BOYS
Lynda J. Barry, 1980
1 B:12 pgs with every other page
    blank, all Barry art 12.00
2 thru 10 same . . . . @8.00
11 thru 20 same . . . . @6.00
20 thru 25 same . . . . @5.00

GOD NOSE
**Jack Jackson/
Rip Off Press, 1964**
N# 42 pgs. 135.00
2nd printing,Pinkish(c);44p 60.00
3rd printing,Blue Border(c) 30.00
4th printing,Red Border(c) 15.00

GOTHIC BLIMP
WORKS LTD.
**East Village Other/
Peter Leggieri, 1969**
1 VB,Editor,various artists 200.00
2 same 145.00
3 KDe,editor 135.00
4 KDe,editor 130.00
5 thru 7 KDe,editor . . . . @125.00
8 various artists 185.00

GREASER COMICS
Half-Ass Press, Sept., 1971
1 28 pgs, George DiCaprio 25.00
Rip Off Press, July, 1972
2 George DiCaprio 15.00

GRIM WIT
Last Gasp, 1972
1 RCo 40.00
2 RCo 30.00

Grim Wit #2
© *Last Gasp*

All comics prices listed are for *Near Mint* condition.

HAROLD HEAD, THE COLLECTED ADVENTURES OF
Georgia Straight, 1972
1 .... 50.00
2 .... 20.00

HARRY CHESS THAT MAN FROM A.U.N.T.I.E.
The Uncensored Adventures, Trojan Book Service, 1966
N# 1st Comix By & For Gay
   Community 150.00

HEAR THE SOUND OF MY FEET WALKING....
Glide Urban Center, 1969
1 Dan O'Neill, 128 pgs. 70.00

HISTORY OF UNDERGROUND COMIX
Straight Arrow Books, 1974
1 Book by Mark James Estren about
   Underground Comix 40.00

HOMEGROWN FUNNIES
Kitchen Sink, 1971
1 RCr 60.00

HONKYTONK SUE, THE QUEEN OF COUNTRY SWING
Bob Boze Bell, 1979
1 BBB 17.00
2 & 3 BBB .... @12.00

IKE LIVES
Warm Neck Funnies, 1973
1 20 pgs,Mark Fisher 15.00

Image of the Beast #1 (1979)
© Last Gasp

IMAGE OF THE BEAST
Last Gast, 1973
1 Phillip Jose Farmer adapt...... 16.00
1 rep. 1979 .... 10.00

INSECT FEAR
Last Gasp, 1970
1 SRo,GiS,RHa,JsG 75.00
Print Mint, 1970–72
2 .... 30.00
3 .... 20.00

IT AIN'T ME BABE
Last Gasp Eco-Funnies, 1970
n/n First all women comix
   Womens Liberation theme ... 40.00

JAPANESE MONSTER
Carol Lay, July, 1979
1 8pgs, Carol Lay 10.00

JESUS LOVES YOU
Zondervan Books/Craig Yoe, 1972
1 Christian, RCr 35.00

THE NEW ADVENTURES OF JESUS
Rip Off Press, Nov., 1971
1 44 pgs, FSt 50.00

JIZ
Apex Novelty, 1969
1 36 pgs; RCr, SRo, VMo, SCW; hand
   trimmed and unevenly stapled 60.00

JUNKWAFFEL
The Print Mint, 1971
1 VB 35.00
2 and 3 VB .... @30.00
4 VB,JJ 25.00

KANNED KORN KOMIX
Canned Heat Fan Club, 1969
1 20pgs................... 25.00

KAPTAIN AMERIKA KOMIX
Brief Candle Comix, March 1970
1 anti U.S. involvement in Laos... 35.00

KING BEE
Apex/Don Donahue & Kerry Clark, 1969
1 RCr,SCW................ 140.00

KURTZMAN COMIX
Kitchen Sink, Sept., 1976
1 HK,RCr,GiS,DKi,WE 30.00

LAUGH IN THE DARK
Last Gasp
n/n KDe,RHa,SRo,SCW 20.00

LENNY OF LAVEDO
Sunbury Productions/Print Mint, 1965
N# Green(c);1st Joel Beck-a ... 550.00
2nd printing, Orange(c)....... 400.00
3rd printing, White(c) 200.00

THE MACHINES
Office of Student Publications Syracuse University, 1967
1 VB 135.00

THE MAN
Office of Student Publications Syracuse University, 1966
1 VB 165.00

MAGGOTZINE
Charles Schneider, May, 1981
1 Various Artists,conceptual
   maggot stuff 10.00

MANTICORE
Joe Kubert School of Cartooning & Graphic Arts Inc., Autumn, 1976
1 Fanzine,various artists........ 10.00

MEAN BITCH THRILLS
The Print Mint, 1971
1 SRO..................... 15.00

MICKEY RAT
Los Angeles Comic Book Co., May, 1972
1 Robert Armstrong........... 35.00
2 same 35.00
3 same 15.00

MR. NATURAL
San Fransisco Comic Book Co., August, 1970
1 RCr 130.00
2 RCr 70.00
Kitchen Sink
3 RCr, (B&W) 35.00

MOM'S HOMEMADE COMICS
Kitchen Sink, June, 1969
1 DKi, RCr................ 130.00
The Print Mint
2 DKi.................... 40.00
Kitchen Sink Enterprises
3 DKi,RCr 30.00

MONDAY FUNNIES, THE
Monday Funnies, 1977
1 8pgs,various artists 8.00
2 16pgs,various artists 10.00
3 16pgs,various artists 8.00
4 16pgs,various artists 7.00

MONDAY FUNNIES, THE
Passtime Publ., July–Aug., 1980
1 thru 8 Marc L.Reed .... @8.00

MOONCHILD COMICS
Nicola Cuti, 1968
0 Nicola Cuti................ 35.00
2 Nicola Cuti................ 35.00
3 Nicola Cuti................ 35.00

MOONDOG
The Print Mint, March, 1970
1 All George Metzer 25.00
2 same 18.00
3 and 4 same .... @12.00

MORE ADVENTURES OF FAT FREDDY'S CAT
Rip Off Press, Jan., 1981
1 GiS..................... 14.00

MOTOR CITY COMICS
Rip Off Press, April, 1969
1 RCr 180.00
2 RCr 140.00

MOUSE LIBERATION FRONT
COMMUNIQUE #2, August, 1979
1 SRo, SCW, VMo,DKi; Disney's sues
   Dan O'Neil's Air Pirates 15.00

NARD 'N' PAT, JAYZEY LYNCH'S
Cartoonists Cooperative Press, March, 1974
1 Jay Lynch. 18.00
2 Jay Lynch. 12.00
Kitchen Sink Press, 1972
3   . . . . 17.00

NEVERWHERE
Ariel Inc., Feb., 1978
1 RCo 25.00

NICKEL LIBRARY
Gary Arlington
1 1 pg heavy stock colored
   paper, Reed Crandall 5.00
2 Kim Deitch 2.50
3 Harrison Cady 2.50
4 Frank Frazetta 4.00
5 Will Eisner 4.00
6 Justin Green 2.50
7 C.C. Beck 4.00
8 Wally Wood 4.00
9 Winsor McCay 2.50
10 Jim Osborne 2.50
11 Don Towlley. 2.50
12 Frank Frazetta 4.00
13 Will Eisner. 4.00
14 Bill Griffith 2.50
15 George Herriman 2.50
16 Cliff Sterrett. 2.50
17 George Herriman 2.50
18 Rory Hayes & Simon Deitch 2.50
19 Disney Studios 2.50
20 Alex Toth 2.50
21 Will Eisner. 2.50
22 Jack Davis 3.00
23 Alex Toth 2.50
24 Michele Brand. 2.50
25 Roger Brand 2.50
26 Arnold Roth 2.50
27 Murphy Anderson 2.50
28 Wally Wood. 3.00
29 Jack Kirby 4.00
30 Harvey Kurtzman 3.00
31 Jay Kinney 2.50
32 Bill Plimpton 2.50
33   . . . . 2.50
34 Charles Dallas 2.50
35 thru 39. . . . . @2.50
40 Bill Edwards 2.50
41 Larry S. Todd 2.50
42 Charles Dallas 2.50
43 Jim Osborne 2.50
43 1/2 Larry S. Todd 2.50
44 Jack Jackson 2.50
45 Rick Griffin 2.50
46 Justin Green 2.50
47 and 48 Larry S. Todd. . . . . @2.50
49 Charles Dallas 2.50
50 Robert Crumb 4.00
51 Wally Wood. 4.00
52 Charles Dallas 4.00
53 and 54 Larry S. Todd. . . . . @2.50
55 Charles Dallas 2.50

No Ducks #1
© Last Gasp

56 Jim Chase 2.50
57 Charles Dallas 2.50
58 Larry S. Todd 2.50
59 Dave Geiser 2.50
60 Charles Dallas 2.50

NO DUCKS
Last Gasp, 1977–79
1 . . . . 15.00
2 . . . . 12.00
2005
2 . . . . 2.95

ODD WORLD OF RICHARD CORBEN
Warren Publishing, 1977
1 84pgs paperback 20.00

O.K. COMICS
Kitchen Sink, June, 1972
1 and 2 Bruce Walthers . . . . . . @15.00

O.K. COMICS
O.K. Comic Company, 1972
1 Tabloid with comix, articles,
   reviews, nudie cuties photos . . 30.00

Omaha the Cat Dancer #20
© Reed Waller

2 thru 18 . . . . @20.00

OMAHA THE CAT DANCER
Steel Dragon Press, 1984
1 RW,F:Omaha, Shelly, Chuck . . . 15.00
Kitchen Sink, 1986
1 RW. 10.00
2 RW 8.00
3 thru 5 . . . . @7.00
6 thru 10 . . . . @6.00
11 thru 20 . . . . @5.00
Spec.#0, 25th Anniv. Classic . . . 15.00
Images of Omaha, RW benefit . . . 8.00
Images No. 2 . . . . 7.00
TPB Collected Omaha #1, rep. . . . 15.00
TPB Collected Omaha #2, rep. . . . 13.00
TPB Collected Omaha #3, rep. . . . 13.00
TPB Collected Omaha #4, rep. . . . 13.00
TPB Collected Omaha #5, rep. . . . 13.00
Vol. 2, Fantagraphics, 1994
1 . . . . 6.00
2 . . . . 6.00

ORACLE COMIX
Thru Black Holes Comix Productions, Oct., 1980
1 and 2 Michael Roden . . . . @6.00

PENGUINS IN BONDAGE
Sorcerer Studio/ Wayne Gibson, July, 1981
1 8pgs,Wayne Gibson 5.00

PHANTOM LADY
Randy Crawford, June, 1978
1 Sex funnies 6.00

PHUCKED UP FUNNIES
Suny Binghamton, 1969
1 ASp;insert bound in yearbook . 400.00

PINK FLOYD, THE
October, 1974
1 sold at concerts 35.00

PLASTIC MAN
Randy Crawford, May, 1977
1 Sex funnies,RandyCrawford . . . 12.00

PORK
Co-op Press, May, 1974
1 SCW 15.00

PORTFOLIO OF UNDERGROUND ART
Schanes & Schanes, 1980
1 SRo,SCW,VMo,RW and many others
   13 loose sheets in folder, 32pg
   book, 1200 signed & numb. . . 75.00

POWERMAN AND POWER MOWER SAFETY
Frank Burgmeir, Co. Outdoor Power Equipment
1 VB; educational comic about power
   mower safety 185.00

PROMETHIAN ENTERPRISES
Promethian Enterprises Memorial Day, 1969
1 B:Jim Vadeboncuor editor 75.00

2 same 60.00
3 thru 5 . . . . @25.00

PURE ART QUARTERLY
John A. Adams, July, 1976
1 16pgs, All John A.Adams 12.00
2 thru 5 same . . . . @12.00
6 thru 10 same . . . . @10.00
11 thru 14 same . . . . @8.00

PURE TRANCE
Last Gasp, 2005
GN 20.00

QUAGMIRE COMICS
Kitchen Sink, Summer, 1970
1 DKi,Peter Poplaski 15.00

RAW
Raw Books, 1980
1 36pgs,10pgs insert 300.00
2 36pgs,20pgs insert 185.00
3 52pgs,16pgs insert 155.00
4 44pgs,32pgs insert,Flexi
disk record 125.00

R. CRUMB'S COMICS
AND STORIES
Rip Off Press, 1969
1 RCr 125.00

RAWARARAWAR
Rip Off Press, 1969
1 GSh 65.00

RED SONJA & CONAN
"HOT AND DRY"
Randy Crawford, May, 1977
1 Sex funnies,Randy Crawford . . . 10.00

REID FLEMING
WORLD'S TOUGHEST
MILKMAN
David E. Boswell, Dec., 1980
1 . . . . 7.00

RIP OFF COMIX
Rip Off Press, April, 1977
1 GiS,FSt,JsG,DSh 20.00
2 thru 5 GiS,FSt . . . . @12.00
6 thru 10 . . . . @6.00

ROWLF
Rip Off Press, July, 1971
1 RCo 55.00

RUBBER DUCK TALES
The Print Mint, March, 1971
1 Michael J Becker 22.00
2 Michael J Becker 17.00

SACRED & PROFANE
Last Gasp, Inc., 2005
1-shot 5.00

S. CLAY WILSON
TWENTY DRAWINGS
Abington Book
Shop Inc., 1967
N# (a),Cowboy(c) 500.00
(b),Pirate(c) 475.00
(c),Motorcyclist(c) 475.00
(d),Demon(c) 475.00
(e),Deluxe with all 4
variations on same(c) with
Gold Embossed Lettering . 675.00

SAN FRANCISCO
COMIC BOOK
San Francisco Comic
Book Co., Jan.-Feb., 1970
1 . . . . 120.00
2 . . . . 25.00
3 . . . . 20.00
4 . . . . 15.00
5 . . . . 15.00
6 . . . . 15.00

SAVAGE HUMOR
The Print Mint, 1973
1 . . . . 12.00

SAY WHAT?
Loring Park Shelter
Community Cartooning
Workshop, April, 1979
1 B:Charles T. Smith,editor,
various artists 12.00
2 thru 6 same . . . . @10.00

SCARYGIRL
Last Gasp Inc., 2005
GN 15.00

SCHIZOPHRENIA,
CHEECH WIZARD
Last Gasp Eco-Funnies, 1973
1 VB 30.00

SEX AND AFFECTION
C.P. Family Publishers, 1974
1 Sex Education for Children 10.00

Schizophrenia, Cheech Wizard #1
© Last Gasp Eco-Funnies

Skull Comics #6
© Last Gasp Funnies

SHORT ORDER COMIX
Head Press/Family Fun, 1973
1 50 cents,36pgs 12.00
2 75 cents,44pgs 8.00
Last Gasp, Inc., 2005
1-shot 3.00

SKULL COMICS
Rip Off Press
1 Horror,RHa 50.00
Last Gasp, 1970
2 GiS,DSh,RCo 30.00
3 SRo,DSh,RCo 20.00
4 DSh,Lovecraft issue 20.00
5 SRo,RCo,Lovecraft issue 20.00
6 RCo,Herman Hesse 20.00

SLOW DEATH FUNNIES
Last Gasp, 1970–92
1 Ecological Awarness & Red
Border on (c) 50.00
2nd-4th Printings White
Border(c) 12.00
Becomes:

SLOW DEATH
2 Silver(c);1st edition' 34 pgs . . . 100.00
2b Non Silver(c);Says 1st
Edition, 34 pgs 20.00
2nd Amorphia Ad on pg 34 . . . . . 8.00
3rd Yellow Skull on (c) 8.00
4th 'Mind Candy For the Masses'
Ad on pg. 34 . . . . 7.00
5th $1.00(c) price 5.00
3 thru 5 . . . . @12.00
6 thru 11 . . . . @6.00

SMILE
Kitchen Sink, Summer, 1970
1 Jim Mitchell 15.00
2 Jim Mitchell 12.00
3 Jim Mitchell 11.00

SNARF
Kitchen Sink, Feb., 1972
1 DKi,editor,various artists 27.00
2 thru 5 same . . . . @15.00
6 thru 9 same . . . . @6.50
1987–90
10 thru 15 . . . . @5.00

SNATCH COMICS
Apex Novelties, 1968
1 RCr,SCW 320.00
2 RCr,SCW 160.00
3 RCr,SCW,RW. 80.00

SNATCH SAMPLER
Keith Green, 1979
n/n RCr,SCw,RW,RHa 35.00

SPACE INVADERS COMICS, DON CHIN'S
Comix World/Clay Geerdes, April, 1972
1 8pgs 10.00

SPASM!
Last Gasp Eco-Funnies, April, 1973
1 JJ 15.00

STONED PICTURE PARADE
San Francisco Comic Book Co., 1975
1 RCr,SRo,SCW,WE 25.00

SUBVERT COMICS
Rip Off Press, Nov., 1970
1 SRo 25.00
2 SRo 20.00
3 SRo 15.00

TALES OF SEX & DEATH
Print Mint, 1971
1 JsG,KDe.RHa,SRo 35.00
2 JsG,KDe.RHa,SRo. 20.00

THRILLING MURDER COMICS
San Francisco Comic Book Co., 1971
1 SCW,KDe,RCr,SRo,Jim
   Arlington,editor 32.00

2 (TWO)
Keith Green, Feb., 1975
1 SCW 12.00

VAMPIRELLA
Randy Crawford, June, 1978
1 Sex Funnies. 8.00

VAUGHN BODE THE PORTFOLIO
Northern Comfort Com., 1976
1 VB,16pgs 125.00

VAUGHN BODE PORTFOLIO #1
Vaughn Bode Productions, 1978
1 VB,10 pgs 35.00

VAUGHN BODE'S CHEECH WIZARD, THE COLLECTED ADVENTURES OF THE CARTOON MESSIAH
Northern Comfort Com., 1976
1 VB,88pgs 55.00

VAUGHN BODE'S DEADBONE, THE FIRST TESTAMENT OF CHEECH WIZARD
Northern Comfort Com., 1975
1 VB 65.00

VIETNAM
N# 20pgs. Role of Blacks in
   the War,TG Lewis 125.00

Weirdo #1 © Last Gasp

WEIRDO
Last Gasp Eco-Funnies, 1981–93
1 thru 3 RCr . . . . @12.00
4 thru 10 . . . . @7.50
11 thru 28 . . . . @5.00

WEIRDO, THE
Rodney Schroeter, Oct., 1977
1 B:Rodney Schroezer,1pg. 7.00
2 88pgs. 7.00
3 44pgs 7.00

WIMMEN'S COMIX
Last Gasp Eco-Funnies, 1972–85
1 All women artists&comix 15.00
2 thru 3 same . . . . @12.00
4 thru 10 same . . . . @8.00

WONDER WART-HOG AND THE NURDS OF NOVEMBER
Rip Off Press, Sept., 1980
1 GiS 20.00

WONDER WART-HOG, CAPTAIN CRUD & OTHER SUPER STUFF
Fawcett Publications, 1967
1 GiS,VB 25.00

YELLOW DOG
The Print Mint, May, 1968
1 4pgs,RCr 45.00
2 and 3 8pgs,RCr . . . . @30.00
4 8pgs,RCr,SCW 30.00
5 8pgs,RCr,SCW,KDe 30.00
6 thru 12 . . . . @25.00
13/14 52pgs RCr,Jay Lynch. 12.00
15 Don Scheneker,editor 65.00
16. . . . . 55.00
17 thru 24. . . . . @15.00

YOUNG AND LUSTLESS
San Francisco Comic Book Co., 1972
1 BG 20.00

YOUNG LUST
Company & Sons, Oct., 1970
1 BG,ASp 30.00
Print Mint
2 BG 15.00
3 BG,JsG,RCr,ASp 15.00
4 KDe,BG,SRo 12.00
Last Gasp
5 BG,SRo 9.00
6 SRo,KDe 8.00
7 and 8 . . . . @5.00

YOW
Last Gasp, April, 1978
1 BG 7.00
2 BG 6.00
Becomes:

ZIPPY
3 BG 6.50

ZAP COMIX
Apex Novelties, Oct., 1967
0 RCr 360.00
1 RCr 350.00
2 RCr,SCW 135.00
3 RCr,SCW,VMo,SRo 60.00
4 VMo,RW,RCr,SCW.SRo,GiS . . 60.00
5 RW,GiS,RCr,SCW,SRo 50.00
6 RW,GiS,RCr,SCW,SRo 30.00
7 RW,GiS,RCr,SCW,SRo 20.00
8 RW,GiS,RCr,SCW,SRo 15.00
9 RW,GiS,RCr,SCW,SRo 20.00
Last Gasp
10 thru 14 . . . . @10.00

ZIPPY: NATION OF PINHEADS
Last Gasp, Inc., 2005
GN 6.00

ZIPPY: YOW!
Last Gasp, Inc., 2004
1-shot from comic strip 2.50
3 . . . . 3.50

All comics prices listed are for *Near Mint* condition.

Index

CVA GRADING GUIDE

Grading comics is an objective art. This grading guide outlines the many conditions you should look for when purchasing comics, from the highest grade and top condition to the lowest collectible grade and condition. Your own comics will fall into one of these categories. A more complete description and our comments on comics grades can be found inside. We would like to point out, however, that no reader or advertiser is required to follow this or any other standard. All prices in Comics Values Annual are for comics in Near Mint condition. Happy collecting!

Mint: Perfect, pristine, devoid of any trace of wear or printing or handling flaws. Covers must be fully lustrous with sharply pointed corners. No color fading. Must be well centered. Many "rack" comics are not "Mint" even when new.

Near Mint: Almost perfect with virtually no wear. No significant printing flaws. Covers must be essentially lustrous with sharp corners. Spine is as tight as new. In older comics, minimal color fading is acceptable, as is slight aging of the paper. Most price guides, including CVA, quote prices in this grade.

Very Fine: Well preserved, still pleasing in appearance. Small signs of wear, most particularly around the staples. Most luster is readily visible. Corners may no longer be sharp, but are not rounded. Typical of a comic read only a few times and then properly stored.

Fine: Clean, presentable, with noticeable signs of wear. Some white may show through enamel around staples, and moderate rounding of corners. No tape or writing damage. Book still lies flat.

Very Good: A well worn reading copy with some minor damage such as creasing, small tears or cover flaking. Some discoloration may be evident, with obvious wear around the staples. Little luster remains, and some rolling of the spine may be seen when comic is laid flat on the table.

Good: A fully intact comic with very heavy wear. Tears, cover creases and flaking, and rolled spine will all be evident. No tape repairs present. Only very scarce or valuable issues are collected in this state.

The adjoining price table shows the prices for the other collectible grades which correspond to any "near mint" price given in this book.

Mint	Near Mint	Very Fine	Fine	Very Good
$6,000	$5,000	$3,500	$2,000	$1,000
4,800	4,000	2,800	1,600	800
3,600	3,000	2,100	1,200	600
2,400	2,000	1,400	800	400
1,800	1,500	1,050	600	300
1,200	1,000	700	400	200
1,080	900	630	360	180
960	800	560	320	160
900	750	525	300	150
840	700	490	280	140
780	650	455	260	130
720	600	420	240	120
660	550	385	220	110
600	500	350	200	100
570	475	332	190	95
540	450	315	180	90
510	425	297	170	85
480	400	280	160	80
450	375	262	150	75
420	350	245	140	70
390	325	227	130	65
360	300	210	120	60
330	275	192	110	55
300	250	175	100	50
270	225	157	90	45
240	200	140	80	40
210	175	122	70	35
180	150	105	60	30
150	125	87	50	25
120	100	70	40	20
114	95	66	38	19
108	90	63	36	18
102	85	59	32	17
96	80	56	32	16
90	75	52	30	15
84	70	49	28	14
78	65	45	26	13
72	60	42	24	12
66	55	38	22	11
60	50	35	2	10
54	45	31	18	9
48	40	28	16	8
42	35	24	14	7
36	30	21	12	6
30	25	17	10	5
24	20	14	8	4
22	18	12	7	4
21	17	11	7	4
18	15	10	6	3
17	14	9	5	3
16	13	9	5	3
15	12	8	5	2
14	11	7	4	2
12	10	7	4	2
11	9	6	4	2
10	8	5	3	1
9	7	5	3	1
7	6	4	3	1
6	5	4	2	1
5	4	3	2	0
4	3	2	1	0
3	2	2	0	0
2	1	0	0	0